HOW TO USE THIS ENCYCLOPEDIA

This encyclopedia has two distinct parts: (a) the first three volumes that contain the subject matter of psychology in alphabetical order and (b) the fourth volume that contains biographies, a bibliography, a name index, a subject index, and appendixes.

If you are looking for a particular topic, the first place to look in would be one of the first three volumes. If what you are looking for is not found, then you should examine the subject index. If the topic is mentioned in the encyclopedia, you will be directed to a specific volume or volumes and particular pages where the topic is discussed.

If you are looking for information about any person, then go to the first part of the fourth volume where biographies are found. However, should you not find a biography of that person, there are two other places where person information can be found. The first is the bibliography. There you may find some of that person's publications listed. The other place to look would be in the name index and from there you will be directed to the volume(s) and page(s) on which that person is mentioned.

An important additional source for locating information is the cross references at the end of almost every entry. For example, at the end of the entry *respiratory disorders,* a list of related entries is found at the end of the entry. Examining these entries you may find the information you are looking for. Each of these entries in turn will have cross references to other related items.

Every attempt has been made to make finding information as easy as possible. The bibliography, the name and subject indexes and the spines of the four volumes have been designed to make locating the proper volumes and pages convenient for users.

ENCYCLOPEDIA OF PSYCHOLOGY

(SECOND EDITION)

ENCYCLOPEDIA OF PSYCHOLOGY

SECOND EDITION

Volume 4

RAYMOND J. CORSINI, Editor

A Wiley-Interscience Publication

JOHN WILEY & SONS

New York   •   Chichester   •   Brisbane   •   Toronto   •   Singapore

This text is printed on acid-free paper.

This publication is designed to provide accurate and authoritative
information in regard to the subject matter covered. It is sold
with the understanding that the publisher is not engaged in
rendering professional services. If legal, accounting, medical,
psychological, or any other expert assistance is required, the
services of a competent professional person should be sought.
ADAPTED FROM A DECLARATION OF PRINCIPLES OF A JOINT COMMITTEE OF
THE AMERICAN BAR ASSOCIATION AND PUBLISHERS.

Library of Congress Cataloging in Publication Data:

Encyclopedia of psychology / Raymond J. Corsini, editor ; consulting
    editors, Anne Anastasi . . . [et al.] ; associate editors, Mary Allen
    . . . [et al.] ; foreign editors, Ruben Ardila . . . [et al.] ;
    biography editor, Robert Lundin ; foreign editor, Neal Pinckney ;
    managing editor, Kristine Altweis. –– 2nd ed.
        p.   cm.
    "A Wiley-Interscience publication."
    Includes bibliographical references.
    ISBN 0–471–55819–2 (hard : set : alk. paper)
    1. Psychology—Encyclopedias. I. Corsini, Raymond J.
    BF31. E52   1994   93–22638
    150′ .3—dc20

BF
31
.E52
1994
vol.4

Printed in the United States of America
10 9 8 7 6 5 4 3 2 1

ENCYCLOPEDIA OF PSYCHOLOGY

(SECOND EDITION)

BIOGRAPHIES

ABELES, NORMAN (1928–   )

Abeles received the B.A. in psychology from New York University and the M.A. and Ph.D. (1958) from the University of Texas. After the Master's, he served in the U.S. Army as a clinical psychology specialist in the United States, France, and Germany. His first academic appointment was at the Michigan State University Counseling Center in 1957. In 1959, he was appointed an assistant professor at the Counseling Center and the department of psychology. He served as Fulbright professor at the University of Utrecht in the Netherlands in 1968, the year he became a full professor at Michigan State University. He became director of the Psychological Clinic at Michigan State University in 1978 and codirector of the clinical psychology program in 1981. He founded the clinical neuropsychology laboratory in the psychology department in 1982.

Among his primary contributions have been his publications, journal editing, and training of graduate students. He was founding editor of the *Academic Psychology Bulletin* and editor of *Professional Psychology: Research and Practice*. Abeles views as his major contribution the development of one of the largest psychotherapy tape libraries in the United States for research by his graduate students and himself. He also is active in research in aging and neuropsychology.

Abeles is listed in *Who's Who in America* and has served as president of the Michigan Psychological Association. He also has served as president of the Division of Clinical Psychology and the Division of Psychotherapy of the American Psychological Association. In addition, he has been the recording secretary of the association and chair of its Policy and Planning Board and its Education and Training Board. He also has served on its Publication and Communications Board and its Council of Representatives. He is a diplomate of the American Board of Professional Psychology and a member of the National Academy of Practice in Psychology.

ABRAHAM, KARL (1877–1925)

Abraham took the M.D. degree at the University of Freiburg and secured a position at the Berlin Municipal Mental Hospital. His hospital work continued for about seven years, and he then entered private psychiatric practice in Berlin. He was the founder of the Berlin Psychoanalytic Society, which was important in extending Freud's influence.

Abraham made numerous contributions to psychoanalytic theory. He proposed the view that biology dictates a specific sequence in developing the aims of the libido, and he contributed to the theory of stages of psychosexual development. He further proposed that adult personality can be understood in terms of fixation at a particular stage of psychosexual development. He studied the manic-depressive psychosis and distinguished two types, one which could be given a psychodynamic interpretation, and a second which is basically biological and not subject to psychological explanation.

Abraham was a member of Freud's inner circle and one of Freud's closest collaborators. Ernest Jones described him as the most normal member of the group with distinguishing traits of "steadfastness, common sense, shrewdness, and a perfect self-control."

Volumes of Abraham's collected essays have been published posthumously.

P. E. LICHTENSTEIN

ACH, NARZISS (1871–1946)

Ach took both the M.D. and Ph.D. at Würzburg. He was also associated with Göttingen and Königsberg. He was an assistant of Carl Stumpf and studied with G. E. Müller and Otto Külpe. A prominent member of the Wurzburg School, Ach is given credit for three basic notions.

1. *Systematic experimental introspection.* This method was systematic in that it limited the introspection of the subject to either the *fore* period (warning signal until the actual stimulus) or the *mid* period (stimulus proper and its effects). The *after* period was the time during which the introspection occurred. The method was experimental in that precise apparati such as the Hipp chronoscope were used.
2. *Determining tendency.* Ach was able to show that there were unconscious influences on the behavior of the subjects, including instructions of the experimenter. Talking about addition just prior to the presentation of two numbers, for example, would tend to produce the sum of the numbers as the initial reaction of the subject. The research in this area lent support to the notion of imageless thought as the subject had no special image in mind from the conversation.
3. *Awareness.* This is a conscious, imageless attitude of the subject. Thus one can be conscious of the possibility that the alarm clock will ring without experiencing the actual sensation.

Ach stated that determining tendencies must be known by means *other than* introspection. This led researchers away from the exclusive use of introspection as a research method.

C. S. PEYSER

ADLER, ALFRED (1870–1937)

Adler founded the school of Individual Psychology, a theory of personality and psychopathology, and a method of psychotherapy. Based on the concepts of the unity, goal striving, and active participation of the individual, it is a humanistic value psychology rather than a mechanistic drive psychology. It stresses cognitive rather than unconscious processes. Adler accepted being called "father of the inferiority complex."

Adler graduated from the Vienna medical school in 1895 and became a general practitioner. He soon wrote some articles on public health issues, in line with his early interest in the social democratic movement. In 1902 he was invited by Freud with three others for weekly discussions of problems of neurosis. From these meetings the Vienna Psychoanalytic Society developed, of which Adler became president in 1910.

In 1911 Adler resigned from the society to form the Society for Free Psychoanalytic Research, soon afterward renamed the Society of Individual Psychology. He objected primarily to what became known as Freud's metapsychology, then essentially limited to the mechanistic concepts of libido and repression. Adler sought a conception of neurosis "only in psychological terms, or terms of cultural psychology." In this quest he had published in 1907 his *Study of organ inferiority and its psychical compensation,* broadening the biological foundation from sex to the entire organism; in 1908 a paper on the *aggression drive,* a drive to prevail, replacing sex as the primary drive; and in 1910 a paper on *inferiority feeling* and *masculine protest* as overcompensation, replacing the concept of drive altogether with one of value. Masculine protest in its original sense was shortly afterward replaced by *striving for power,* for *superiority.* Adler saw the individual in its unity and goal orientation operating as if according to a self-created life plan, later called *life-style.*

Drives, feelings, emotions, memory, the unconscious, all processes are subordinated to the life style.

In 1912 Adler presented his new psychology in *The neurotic constitution*. It contained most of his main concepts, except *social interest*. He introduced this last concept in 1918. It became, with striving for overcoming and inferiority feelings, Adler's most important concept—the criterion for mental health. In cases of psychopathology, which Adler called failures in life, the aptitude for social interest has not been adequately developed. Such persons are striving on the socially useless side for personal power over others, as against the healthy, socially useful striving for overcoming general difficulties. The psychotherapist raises the patient's self-esteem through encouragement, demonstrates the patient's mistakes to the patient, and strengthens his or her social interest. The therapist works for a cognitive reorganization and more socially useful behavior. Particularly, early recollections and birth-order position, but also dreams, are used to give the patient an understanding of his life style.

During the 1920s Adler became largely interested in prevention. This included child-guidance training of teachers at the Vienna Pedagogical Institute, where Adler had his first academic appointment; the establishment of numerous child-guidance centers in public schools; and adult education courses that resulted in his popular book, *Understanding human nature*.

From 1926 on Adler visited the United States regularly, lecturing to a wide range of audiences. He was a successful speaker, attracting up to 2000 listeners. In 1932 he became professor of medical psychology at Long Island Medical College. In 1934 he settled permanently in New York City.

In 1897 he had married Raissa Timofejevna Epstein, a radical student from a highly privileged Jewish family in Moscow, who later worked at times with her husband. They had four children, three girls and a boy, of whom the second child, Alexandra, and the third, Kurt, became Adlerian psychiatrists. He died of a heart attack on May 28, 1937, in Aberdeen, Scotland.

Regarding Adler's work there is a paradox: his concepts have been generally validated and have entered most personality theories, including psychoanalysis in particular, yet this has remained largely unrecognized. However, the Adlerian tradition is being continued by the North American Society of Adlerian Psychology, which publishes both a newsletter and the quarterly *Individual psychology,* holds regular meetings, and sponsors workshops. There are Adlerjan training institutes as well as scores of local organizations, family education centers, and study groups, for which the groundwork was done largely by Rudolf Dreikurs (1897–1972). Abroad, Adlerian societies exist in numerous countries, the largest being in West Germany, which publishes the quarterly *Zeitschrift für Individualpsychologie.* An International Association of Individual Psychology holds congresses every three years. Affiliated with it is the International Committee for Adlerian Summer Schools and Institutes, which conducts a yearly two-week institute in various countries.

H. L. ANSBACHER

ADORNO, THEODOR (1903–1969)

Adorno was educated at the University of Frankfurt. His writings include contributions to the fields of philosophy, psychology, and the sociology of music. When the Nazis came to power in Germany he left for England and then went to the United States, where he worked at the now defunct New York Institute of Social Research from 1938 to 1941. Thereafter he was director of the Princeton Raduc Research Project until 1948. He then became codirector of the Research Project on Social Discrimination at the University of California at Berkeley.

He wrote *Introduction to the sociology of music,* in which he interpreted the dance form of jitterbugging as a deliberately induced outer frenzy attempting to counteract the inner frenzy that many young people felt during periods of adjustment. After World War II he returned to Germany, where he wrote a controversial treatise analyzing the compositions of Richard Wagner and suggesting that they were the origin of Hitlerism.

In 1950, with others he wrote his best-known book in psychology, *The authoritarian personality.* In it he suggested that authoritarianism was the core around which the personality organizations of some people were built. He described this personality as having great concern for authority, both in its own exercise and in its deference to superior authority.

In his philosophical thinking, he was much influenced by the writings of Hegel and Marx. His book in collaboration with Max Hockheimer, *Dialectic of enlightenment,* was published in an English translation posthumously in 1979.

R. W. LUNDIN

AINSWORTH, MARY D. SALTER (1913–   )

Ainsworth received the B.A., M.A., and Ph.D. (1939) from the University of Toronto. She was appointed assistant professor at University of Toronto (1946), professor at Johns Hopkins University (1963), commonwealth professor at University of Virginia (1975), and professor emeritus from 1984. Ainsworth devoted a lifetime to researching infant–mother relationships and introduced a 20-min controlled laboratory technique called the "strange situation."

At London's Tavistock Clinic, under John Bowlby's direction, she investigated the effects on personality of infant–mother separation (1950). This was the beginning of a 40-yr productive scholarly association with Bowlby, establishing a new field of scientific study by means of Bowlby's ethological theories of attachment, separation, and loss and by Ainsworth's empirical longitudinal studies from home visits and the strange situation technique.

Ainsworth wrote numerous scientific articles and books. She also extended her research into attachment beyond infancy by examining other affectional bonds throughout the life cycle. Ainsworth was cited as one of the outstanding *Models of achievement . . . of eminent women in psychology* (O'Connell & Russo, 1983) and received APA's award for Distinguished Scientific Contribution (1989), award for Distinguished Professional Contributions to Knowledge (1987), and was elected a fellow of the American Academy of Arts and Sciences (1992).

S. S. BROWN

AKITA, MUNEHIRA (1930–   )

Akita, a major contributor to the study of human color perception, received the B.A. (1953) and M.A. (1955) from Kyoto University, where he became an instructor and began research on human sensory mechanisms in the laboratory of Koji Sato during 1955–1958. In 1958 he went to America on a Fulbright scholarship to study further visual psychophysics and work with Mathew Alpern at the University of Michigan. Pursuing graduate work at Columbia, he came under the tutelage of Clarence H. Graham and, aided by Yun Hsia, wrote a Ph.D. dissertation dealing primarily with hue contrast in 1962. After this training in America, he has worked for the Kyoto Institute of Technology as professor of psychology since 1963. In 1981–1982 he took an official leave abroad and was visiting professor at the University of Michigan Medical School (sponsored by M. Alpern) and visiting scholar at the University of Freiburg's Neurologische Universitäts-Klinik in West Germany (sponsored by R. Jung, L. Spillmann, and the DAAD).

He has concentrated on research of color psychology in its various fields, from basic to applied. He has published more than 70 research reports, written in either Japanese or English, that appeared in professional journals and proceedings, including several chapters. He is a member of the Japanese Psychological Association and many other organizations.

ALBEE, GEORGE W. (1921–   )

Albee is best known for his fervent opposition to the "medical model" explanation of psychopathology, and his advocacy of primary prevention rather than one-to-one therapy. He graduated with honors in psychology from Bethany College in 1943, and entered the U.S. Air Force. He did graduate study after the war at the University of Pittsburgh, followed by two years full-time clinical research at Western Psychiatric Institute and Clinic. He then went to Washington as assistant executive secretary of the APA; spent 1953–1954 in Finland as a Fulbright professor; then for 16 years was at Western Reserve University (1954–1970), where he served three terms as chair and as director of the Clinical Training Program. He served as president of the Ohio Psychological Association (1963), where his presidential address, entitled "A Declaration of Independence for Psychology," argued for establishing psychological centers and professional schools of psychology. He took time out in 1958–1959 to work as a director of the Task Force on Manpower of the Joint Commission on Mental Health Illness and Health, an effort that resulted in *Mental health manpower trends,* a book that helped shape the nation's planning for community mental health centers. Active over the years on many committees and boards of the APA, he was elected president of APA (1969–70) and stirred controversy with his address, "The Uncertain Future of Clinical Psychology." In 1971 he moved to Vermont, where with colleagues he established the Vermont Conference on Primary Prevention and, with Justin M. Joffe, became general editor of a series of books on primary prevention. He has testified frequently in federal courts against involuntary incarceration and treatment, and against the use of I.Q. tests with minorities. In 1975 he received the Distinguished Professional Contribution Award of the APA, and in 1981 the Award for Distinguished Contributions to Community Psychology.

ALBERTUS MAGNUS (1193–1280) (Albert the Great)

One of the greatest scholastic theologians, philosophers, and scientists of his time, Albertus Magnus was born in Swabia. He joined the Dominican Order at Padua in 1223 and then went to the University of Paris. There, he graduated from the theological faculty. In 1931 he was canonized as a saint by the Roman Catholic Church.

His writings embraced the entire knowledge of the time in theology, philosophy, and natural sciences. He alone of all medieval scholars made commentaries of all of Aristotle's writings on natural science. These exercised great influence until modern times. He was unique for his time for having made available the works of Aristotle (embellished by the Arabs) on the natural sciences.

In the history of science he deserves a preeminent place for his observations on nature. He is of particular interest in the history of psychology for his ideas of the localization of certain psychological traits in the brain. He suggested that feeling was located in the anterior ventricle, memory in the posterior ventricle, and thinking in many parts of the brain.

R. W. LUNDIN

ALCOCK, JAMES E. (1942–   )

Alcock received the honors B.Sc. in physics from McGill University and the Ph.D. (1972) in psychology from McMaster University. Follow-ing the bachelor's degree, Alcock worked as a systems engineer for IBM. Following the doctorate, Alcock was appointed to York University in Toronto, Canada, where he became professor of psychology. His major academic interest was in social psychology, but following a clinical internship in 1974, he combined his university duties with a private practice in clinical psychology. He is a fellow of the Canadian Psychological Association and has served as chair of its Social Psychology section. He also has served as a member and chair of the Ontario Board of Examiners in Psychology, as a member of the Council of the Canadian Register of Health Service Providers in Psychology, and as a member of the Joint Designation Committee of the National Register/American Association of State Psychology Boards.

Alcock's main research interest has been in the area of belief and credulity, and he has written extensively about the psychology of anomalous experience and the methodological shortcomings of parapsychological research. He is author of *Parapsychology: Science or magic?* and *Science and supernature: A critical appraisal of parapsychology,* and he is coauthor of *A textbook of social psychology,* the only social psychology textbook written specifically for Canadian students.

ALLEN, MARY J. (1946–   )

Allen received the B.A. in psychology, the M.A. in statistics and the Ph.D. in psychology (1973) from the University of California at Berkeley and has been at California State University at Bakersfield since 1972, and served as department chair from 1986 to 1992.

She coauthored *Introduction to measurement theory,* has contributed sections to several other books, has published more than a dozen journal articles, and has presented over 40 papers at national and regional meetings. Her scholarship interests mainly concern measurement, the psychology of gender, and social issues. Her major teaching responsibilities are in statistics, research methods, and psychometric theory.

She has served on the Council of University Representatives to the Western Psychological Association since 1986 and was on the Steering Committee of the Council of Undergraduate Psychology Programs from 1990 to 1992.

ALLPORT, FLOYD HENRY (1890–1978)

Allport was the third of four boys, his youngest brother being Gordon W. Allport, also a famous psychologist. He received the Ph.D. from Harvard in 1919 and then taught at the University of North Carolina and at Syracuse University until his retirement in 1957. He received the Distinguished Scientific Contribution Award from the American Psychological Association and the Gold Medal Award from the American Psychological Foundation.

Allport is considered to be the father of experimental social psychology. His first book, *Social psychology,* was based heavily on experimental and research studies. In both his theories and research he set a direction in social psychology which was followed by psychologists in that area for several decades. His behavioristic approach was in direct conflict with the instinct theories of William McDougall, whose social psychology was also popular at the time. In his book, Allport discussed such topics as group experimentation, personality assessment, and the applications of psychology to many fields. His studies also led the way for the examination of social behavior in field settings outside the laboratory in religion, politics, industry, and the community.

One of his most famous contributions to social psychology was the J curve hypotheses of conforming behavior, in which the institutional norm and the personality norm did not necessarily conform. He led the way for studies of attitude development, an area which was to become extremely popular. He attacked group fictions such as the "group mind" and the fallacy which endowed entire groups with their own personality and attributes. In *Theories of perception and the concept of structure*, Allport reviewed theories of perception and put forth his own theory of structure, which held that social structure had no anatomical or physical basis, but consisted of cycles of events that return upon themselves to complete and maintain the cycle.

R. W. LUNDIN

ALLPORT, GORDON WILLARD (1897–1967)

Allport gained the bachelor's and doctoral degrees at Harvard University. The Ph.D. thesis foreshadowed his life's work, since it dealt with the psychology of personality, and its assessment. For two years he traveled and studied in Turkey, Germany, and England. Returning as an instructor at Harvard, he was appointed assistant professor of psychology at Dartmouth College in 1937. He came back to Harvard in 1930 and stayed there till his retirement, serving for several years as chairman of the Psychology Department. He was president of the American Psychological Association in 1939 and received numerous honorary doctorates. His outstanding position in the psychology of personality attracted many students to Harvard, who now hold posts of distinction in American and other universities.

He regarded personality as the natural subject matter of psychology and believed that other standard topics, such as human learning, could not be adequately studied without taking into account the self or ego who wanted to learn. His approach was eclectic, drawing on a wide variety of sources: McDougall's theory of motives, experimental and social psychology, psychometric studies of personality traits, German *verstehende* psychology, as well as psychodynamic theories. However, he was strongly opposed to Freudian views of the unconscious; his position was much closer to that of Alfred Adler. He rejected any reductionist theory that attributed human behavior to innate instincts, childhood conditioning, or repressed complexes. Personality is an organized whole, not a bundle of habits and fixations. It is present now, and it looks to the future rather than the past. Thus in his book *Becoming* (1955) he argued that the self can make choices and to some extent influence the development of its own personality. A fundamental part in personality growth is played by what Allport called the functional autonomy of motives—that is, the emergence of new motivational systems. For example, a son may take up medicine because his father is a doctor; but gradually his interests develop, and medicine becomes a goal in its own right, independent of the initial drive.

Allport was not given to extreme views. He avoided writing dogmatically or provocatively and preferred courtesy to controversy. He could aptly be called one of the first humanists in psychology, but he did not allow his humanitarian sentiments to interfere with scientific integrity and logical thinking in his writings. He realized, however, that there is a fundamental contradiction between the scientific and intuitive views of man. These he referred to as the nomothetic and idiographic standpoints. The nomothetist tries to arrive at general laws which apply to all human kind, and his procedures are based on accurate measurements of behavior. Inevitably this involves fragmentation of the individual into measurable variables. But the idiographic view sees each particular individual as a unique whole and relies largely on intuitive understanding. Allport believed that the two should be combined. Nomothetic characteristics can be measured, for example, by personality questionnaires which measure extraversion, dominance, anxiety, etc. But idiographic description must be based on case study data, or inferred from personal documents such as diaries or imaginative writing. But he rejected the usefulness of projective techniques for understanding normal people, as distinct from neurotics. He himself did devise certain tests of personality traits, attitudes, and values, but saw little point in factorial studies of personality.

Allport's personality theory put him at odds with the vast majority of American psychologists, who had been indoctrinated by behaviorist empiricism. Nevertheless, they did respect his viewpoint. He dealt with the bewildering complexity of personality by positing personality traits as the basic units or components. A trait is a generalized type of behavior which characterizes each individual and distinguishes that person from others. It is a real and causal neuropsychic structure, not merely "biosocial"—that is, deriving from the impressions of people who observe the individual. This concept has been attacked by later writers who point out the frequent inconsistency, rather than the generality, of people's behavior in different situations. Unfortunately, he did not live long enough to answer such critics as Walter Mischel who regard personal behavior as determined more by the situation than by internal traits. But he did allow for the uniqueness of each individual personality by distinguishing common traits—variables which occur in different strengths in all persons—from unique traits or personal dispositions peculiar to the particular person.

While Allport's main work was the development of a comprehensive theory of personality, he had wide-ranging interests, including eidetic imagery, religion, social attitudes, rumor, and radio. The book which probably has the greatest practical and social value is his analysis of *The nature of prejudice* (1954). His major book is *Pattern and growth in personality*.

It is appropriate to close with the citation he received when awarded the Gold Medal of the American Psychological Foundation in 1963: "To Gordon Willard Allport, outstanding teacher and scholar, He has brought warmth, wit, humanistic knowledge, and rigorous enquiry to the study of human individuality and social process."

P. E. VERNON

ALMEIDA, EDUARDO (1937–   )

Almeida, a Mexican social psychologist, received his education in France, Mexico, and the United States. After obtaining the Ph.D. from Cornell University in 1976, he engaged in a broad range of research activities linked by a conducting thread: *The concern for making Social Psychology an active contributor to human development*. Almeida's work has focused on four research areas: education, politics, women's status, and rural development. He holds that cognitive development will play a major role in all of them.

He conducted a program for the development of competence in school children from Mexico City (*Educación y realidad socioeconómica*, p. 181). A similar program is under way in two small towns (*Investigaciones en educación*, p. 74). In 1979 he developed an instrument for studying public opinion toward the political system for the National System of Evaluation.

Under the auspices of the International Union of Psychological Science, with M. E. Sánchez he coordinated the cross-cultural project entitled *Psychological factors affecting change in women's roles and status*. The research was carried out in Mexico, Tunisia, France, and the United States. The topic, according to Almeida, relates to the core cultural problem of psychological development in Mexico for both males and females.

In 1973 Almeida's wife, a sociologist, initiated a rural development program in a Nahuat village. With an interdisciplinary team, the Almeidas now live there and participate in the creation of a community which intends to look for new ways to face economic, cultural, and ecological problems.

AMES, LOUISE B. (1908–   )

Ames received the B.A. from the University of Maine, the M.A. and Ph.D. (1937) from Yale. She has received honorary doctorates from both Yale and the University of Wisconsin. After receiving her Ph.D. she served as research associate with Arnold Gesell at the Yale Clinic of Child Development. In 1950 she became cofounder and director of the Gesell Institute of Child Development. With Frances L. Ilg she wrote a daily syndicated newspaper column on child behavior (1952–1955).

She wrote *Youth: the years from ten to sixteen* (1956) and *Infant and child in the culture of today* (1974) with Arnold Gesell and Frances Ilg; *School readiness* with Frances Ilg; and *Stop school failures* with Clyde Gillespie and J. W. Streff.

For many years her coauthored books have been standard references for psychologists and parents in observing the developmental processes, since they present developmental schedules for biological growth and behavior. In keeping with the Gesell tradition she has stressed maturational growth processes over environmental influences, without dismissing environmental influences entirely. These reports have been the result of much research in child development. Among her many other researches, Ames has studied the sense of time in children and children's responses on the Rorschach Inkblot Test and how they may relate to personality and development.

ANASTASI, ANNE (1908–   )

Anastasi is most closely associated with the development of differential psychology. She received the B.A. from Barnard and the Ph.D. from Columbia, the latter at age 21. Although her long-standing plan had been to specialize in mathematics, a course using Pillsbury's *Essentials of psychology* as the text aroused her interest in this field. Then a course with Harry L. Hollingworth and an article by Charles Spearman clinched matters, the latter convincing her that psychology and mathematics could be combined. Her Columbia professors included Henry E. Garrett (her dissertation advisor), Albert T. Poffenberger, Carl J. Warden, and Robert S. Woodworth as well as visiting professors Richard M. Elliott and Clark L. Hull. Through her husband, John P. Foley, Jr., who had majored in psychology at Indiana University, she was exposed to the ideas of J. Robert Kantor. To all these influences she attributes her generalist orientation and her firm commitment to psychology as an objective science.

Anastasi taught at Barnard, Queens College (CUNY), and Fordham University. Her major books include *Differential psychology, Fields of applied psychology,* and *Psychological testing.* Her research centered chiefly on factor analysis and traits, problems of test construction, and the interpretation of test scores with special reference to the role of cultural factors in individual and group differences. Active in association affairs throughout her professional life, Anastasi was president of the American Psychological Association in 1972, the first woman to be elected to this office in 50 years. The holder of several honorary degrees, she received many awards including the APA Distinguished Scientific Award for the Application of Psychology (1981), the American Psychological Foundation Gold Medal (1984), and the National Medal of Science from the president of the United States (1987).

ANGELL, FRANK (1857–1939)

Angell received the Ph.D. degree in psychology under Wilhelm Wundt at Leipzig. He established a psychological laboratory at Cornell, but left after one year to establish a laboratory at the new Stanford University, where he remained until his retirement.

Angell's research centered upon psychophysics and his important papers dealt with auditory sensation. He is best remembered, however, as an outstanding teacher, particularly in the field of general psychology.

From 1895 to 1925 Angell served as an editor of the *American Journal of Psychology*.

P. E. LICHTENSTEIN

ANGELL, JAMES ROLAND (1867–1949)

Angell is best known as one of the founders of the functionalist school of psychology at the University of Chicago in the first quarter of the twentieth century. He had studied with John Dewey at the University of Michigan, before Dewey came to Chicago as an early participant in the functionalist movement. Angell received the M.A. under William James at Harvard. He never received the Ph.D. degree, although in the course of his career he was granted 23 honorary doctorates.

By the time Angell came to the University of Chicago, the grains of functionalism had been sown. He was appointed chairman of the Psychology Department, a position he held for 25 years until he left to become president of Yale. By the time Angell left Chicago, functionalism had become an extremely popular school of psychology.

In 1903 Angell published his first views on functional psychology in an article in the *Philosophical Review* attacking structuralism. The following year he published *Psychology: An introductory study of the structure and functions of human consciousness.* Extremely popular, the book went into a fourth edition by 1908. The book was somewhat eclectic, bringing together what was known about psychology at the time, but it did have a strong functionalist flavor. The introduction stated, "Mind seems to be the master device by means of which the adaptive operations of organic life may be made most perfect."

Angell's clearest exposition of the functionalist position was in his presidential address to the American Psychological Association in 1906, in which he stated the following points characterizing what functional psychology was all about.

1. Functional psychology is the study of mental operations as opposed to contents. The task of the functional psychologist is to discover how a mental process worked.

2. Functional psychology should be considered a study of the functional utilities of consciousness. The adaptation of mental functions to environmental demands enables an organism to survive.

3. Functional psychology is concerned with the entire psychophysical relationship between the organs of the body and the environment. There is a constant interaction between mind and body.

R. W. LUNDIN

ANGYAL, ANDRAS (1902–1960)

Angyal received the doctorate in psychology from the University of Vienna and his medical degree from the University of Turin. Thereafter he came to the United States and for many years was a psychiatrist at Worcester State Hospital in Massachusetts, and then was in private practice in Boston. During part of his stay at Worcester he was director of research and carried out investigations of schizophrenic hallucinations in relation to kinesthesis and to hypnagogic states.

Angyal developed a theory of personality which he set forth in *Foundations for a science of personality.* He described two basic patterns of motivation in man: striving toward mastery, or autonomy, and striving toward love, or homonomy. Personality is a system governed by autonomy and homonomy, while connections between parts of the system are functions of the superordinate system of which they are parts. Health is one system and neurosis is another. Therapy is a process of restoring the health system to a dominant position.

Angyal's personality theory was holistic or organismic. In certain fundamental respects it was close to the thinking of Kurt Goldstein, Abraham Maslow, and P. Lecky. Perhaps because Angyal's theory was developed within a clinical setting, it exerted less influence on academic psychology than might otherwise have been the case. Angyal extended his theoretical position in *Neurosis and treatment: A holistic theory* (1965).

P. E. LICHTENSTEIN

ANSBACHER, HEINZ L. (1904–   )

Ansbacher is primarily known as the interpreter of the work of Alfred Adler. With his wife Rowena Ripin Ansbacher, he has coedited three volumes of Adler's writings (Adler, 1956, 1964, 1978).

Ansbacher came to the United States in 1924 and settled in New York. His first contact with psychology was evening lectures by Adler at Columbia University in 1930. Eventually he became friendly with Adler, through him met his future wife (who had studied with Adler), and decided to make psychology his life work. He obtained the Ph.D. at Columbia University in 1937 under Robert S. Woodworth. His dissertation dealt with the influence of social factors on perception. Other important personal influences were Max Wertheimer and Kurt Goldstein.

Ansbacher's first position in psychology was as assistant editor of the *Psychological Abstracts* under Walter S. Hunter at Brown University. This was followed by work as survey officer with the Office of War Information overseas, and teaching positions at Brooklyn College and Duke University. In 1946 he went to the University of Vermont. He was a Fulbright lecturer at the University of Kiel in Germany (1954–1955), then edited the *Journal of Individual Psychology* (1957–1973). He has served as president of the North American Society of Adlerian Psychology and of the Division of Philosophical Psychology of the American Psychological Association.

Ansbacher considers his most important single contributions to be his clarification of Adler's concepts of life style (1967) and especially of social interest (1978). He sees Adler as the first to have abandoned the metapsychology which Freud developed during the time of their association (1974). His position is that psychoanalysis, as it increasingly turns away from metapsychology, rediscovers positions taken originally by Adler. A representative bibliography of Ansbacher is appended to his autobiography *Psychology: A way of living*.

ANZIEU, DIDIER (1923–   )

Anzieu obtained his early education in Paris, getting his qualification in philosophy and psychology and has *doctorat ès lettres et sciences humaines* (1957) at the Sorbonne. At first he taught philosophy. Then he became an assistant instructor in psychology at the Sorbonne (1951–1954), and later professor of psychology at Strasbourg (1954–1964). In 1964 he founded the Department of Psychology and the laboratory of clinical psychology at the newly created University of Paris-X-Nanterre. Under the penname of Epistemon, he wrote a work about what happened there in May–June 1968. He is a psychoanalyst and has been vice president of the French Psychoanalytical Association and president of the French Group Psychotherapy Society. At the Dunod publishing firm he is the manager of the series "Psychismes" (18 volumes published) and comanager of the series "Inconscient et Culture" (20 volumes published).

Anzieu's major contributions include *Les méthodes projectives, La dyna mique des groupes restreints* (with J. Y. Martin), *Le groupe et l'inconscient, L'auto-analyse de Freud et la découverte de la psychanalyse* (2 vol.), *Le psychodrame analytique chez l'enfant et l'adolescent,*

and *Le corps de l'oeuvre: Essais psychanalytiques sur le travail créateur*. The main psychological concepts he has elaborated are those of "group delusion," "skin ego," "paradoxical transference," and "creative psychological work."

ARAGON, ENRIQUE O. (1880–1942)

Aragon was a Mexican physician. As a senior in the preparatory school he took the first course ever given in Mexico City on experimental psychology. Starting from the notes taken there, he wrote the first book of general psychology by a Mexican author, with the title *La psicología* (1902). In 1904, he graduated as a physician and in 1906 entered and won a contest for the university chair of psychology. From 1906 until his death, he taught courses in psychology both at the preparatory level (a blend between senior high and junior college) and in what became the facultad de filosofía y letras (FFL) at the Universidad Nacional de México. With the apparatus brought from Leipzig, he founded the first laboratory of experimental psychology in 1906.

In 1932, at the FFL, he organized the sección de psicología, the first embryonic department of psychology in Mexico. In the 1920s, he taught psicología especial to the cadets of the Colegio Militar. He became a member of the National Academy of Medicine and other scientific bodies. In the journal of the academy, *La Gaceta Medica de Mexico*, he published most of the research he conducted at his laboratory. He wrote two books: *Mis 31 años de académico* and *Historia del alma*.

P. VALDERRAMA-ITURBE

ARDILA, RUBEN (1942–   )

Ardila is a Colombian psychologist who has specialized in experimental psychology, psychophysiology, and history of psychology. He has served as a bridge between Latin American psychology and psychology in other parts of the world through his books, journal articles, and the editing of the *Revista Latinoamericana de Psicología* (*Latin American Journal of Psychology*), which he founded.

Ardila received his degree of psychologist at the National University of Colombia in 1964, and his Ph.D. in experimental psychology from the University of Nebraska in 1970. He has worked as chairman of the Psychology Department of the National University of Colombia, and was founder and first chairman of the Psychology Department of the University of the Andes, and director of the Psychology Graduate Program at the University of St. Thomas. As a visiting professor in Puerto Rico, Argentina, the Federal Republic of Germany, the United States, and other countries, he has helped make Latin American psychology better known.

His books include: *Psychology of learning, Contemporary psychology, Physiological psychology, Psychology in Colombia, Psychological investigations, The profession of psychologist, The origins of human behavior, Walden three, Behavior therapy, Psychology in Latin America*, and *Psychology and human nature*. Originally published in Spanish, some of his writings have been translated into other languages.

Ardila has been president of the Colombian Federation of Psychology, of the Interamerican Society of Psychology, and of the Latin American Association for the Analysis and Modification of Behavior that he founded in 1975.

Ardila introduced the experimental analysis of behavior and its applications into his country and other Latin American nations. In doing research on early learning and early experience, he explored some of the developmental parameters that explain psychological changes in infancy, in both animals and children. His work on patterns of child rearing has demonstrated the influence of cultural and social factors on psychological development.

ARDREY, ROBERT (1908–   )

A leading popularizer of ethological psychology, Ardrey published a number of books on the subject, including *African genesis, The territorial imperative, The social contract,* and *The hunting hypothesis.* He has also contributed articles to *Psychology Today.* Ardrey received the Ph.B. from the University of Chicago in 1930 and is listed in *Who's Who in America.* His view on ethology is succinctly presented in *The territorial imperative,* where he wrote that ethology "brings into focus a single aspect of human behavior which I believe to be characteristic of our species as a whole, to be shaped but not determined by environment and experience, and to be a consequence not of human choice but of evolutionary development" (p. ix).

ARGYRIS, CHRIS (1923–   )

Argyris received the Ph.D. in Organizational Behavior from Cornell University in 1951. The first focus of his work was on unintended counterproductive consequences of the management theories used to design and implement formal pyramidal structures, production technology, control systems, and human control systems such as pay and benefits.

He then turned his attention to intervention, in order to reduce organizational problems. His strategy is to begin at the top level and work down only as genuine changes are implemented. The genuineness of the change is exemplified when the upper levels of the organization not only alter their actions but also become the change agents for the level below them.

His early work in intervention focused on experiential learning. His later efforts have focused on reasoning and learning at the individual and organizational levels. This focus has been combined with an action science research emphasis. The objectives of action science are to provide disconfirmable propositions about (1) the world as it is; (2) the world as it might be; (3) how to move from (1) to (2) in such a way that (4) people and organizations learn to change not only their actions but their underlying values and policies.

Some of his major works are *Integrating the individual and the organization, Intervention theory and method,* and, with D. A. Schön, *Organizational learning: A theory of action perspective.*

ARISTOTLE (384–322 B.C.)

Aristotle was a student in Plato's *Academy in Athens.* Later, he tutored Alexander the Great at Philip of Macedonia's court. Aristotle's early writings reflected his schooling in the theory of ideas at the Academy, whereas his later works are a chronicle of the gradual development of his own philosophical position.

Aristotle created a new science of logic, the art and method of correct thinking. His methods made two important contributions. First, his thinking was more analytical than Plato's, although there was no dominant insight such as the theory of ideas. Instead, Aristotle used his concepts—form, matter, substance, cause, potentiality, actuality, substratum—as *tools* for problem solving. Second, he evolved a technique for surveying all previous and possible answers to a question. By classifying an infinite number of solutions to the problem, it is possible to formulate an efficient method that reveals the characteristics of any good answer to the problem. The incorrect solutions can then be eliminated by comparing them to an equivalent answer that can be shown to be unacceptable. The *self-evident principles* are those universal truths that no properly disciplined mind can deny.

In Aristotelian thought, knowledge is expanded to include two classifications: theoretical science and practical science. Theoretical science, as in Plato's definition, represents what is necessarily and always true; practical science represents what is merely true in many cases and of value for practical action, but need not be true if human beings desire to make some change. Informed opinion is, therefore, a kind of practical knowledge.

As a teacher and philosopher, Aristotle's subject matter and writings were voluminous. The library of his titles is often divided into works of logic, science, aesthetics, and philosophy.

N. A. HAYNIE

ARONSON, ELLIOT (1932–   )

Aronson is an experimental social psychologist best known for his innovative applications of the experimental method toward the solution of contemporary social problems.

A Stanford Ph.D., he has taught at Harvard, Minnesota, Texas, and the University of California. As an undergraduate he was inspired by his teacher Abraham Maslow, who convinced him that psychologists could make important contributions to human welfare. As a graduate student he was most influenced by Jean Festinger, who aroused an excitement about basic research, especially laboratory experiments.

In the early 1970s the turmoil and violence surrounding school desegregation launched him into an eight-year program of action research and field experimentation in public school classrooms. As part of this program, he invented a structured technique of interdependent learning ("jigsaw") which produced a reduction in prejudice among schoolchildren, as well as an increase in self-esteem and an improvement in classroom performance. For this research program, Aronson was honored with both APA's Distinguished Research in Social Psychology Award (1980) and the Gordon Allport Prize in Intergroup Relations (1981).

The American Psychological Foundation presented him with its Distinguished Teaching Award (1980) and its National Media Award (1973) for *The social animal.* With Gardner Lindzey, he has edited the monumental *Handbook of social psychology.*

ASCH, SOLOMON (1907–   )

Asch received the Ph.D. from Columbia University in 1932. He taught at the New School for Social Research in New York City and at Rutgers University. He was a close friend and colleague of Max Wertheimer, one of the founders of the Gestalt school of psychology. In 1952 he wrote a text, *Social psychology,* much in keeping with the tenets of Gestalt psychology.

He is best known for a series of experiments (1956) on the effects of group pressure on a single individual. In these experiments the situation was so contrived that all members of a group were in collusion except one. For example, subjects were asked to compare the length of lines as longer or shorter. Those in collusion purposely made incorrect judgments, so the single naive subject was caught between what he or she wanted to report and what was reported by the other members of the group. The general tendency was for the single subject to go along with the reports of his peers, despite the fact that his or her own sensory discriminations indicated otherwise. With an increase in the size of the majority group, the pressure toward conformity was strengthened. Conformity did not occur for all subjects. Some maintained their independence in what they judged to be correct, going against the consensus of the majority.

ATKINSON, JOHN W. (1923–   )

Atkinson is known for his study of achievement motivation and a reconstruction of the theory of motivation accomplished in collaboration with David Birch in *The dynamics of action* (1970). After service as an air force pilot in World War II, he received the B.A. from Wesleyan University and the Ph.D. in 1950 from the University of Michigan, where he has served ever since, becoming professor of psychology in 1960.

An early collaboration with David C. McClelland and others, *The achievement motive,* was followed by edited monographs reporting the development of his research program at Michigan: *Motives in fantasy, action, and society; A theory of achievement motivation* (with Norman T. Feather); and *Motivation and achievement* (with Joel O. Raynor). *An introduction to motivation* (1964) identified important historical transitions in conceptual analysis of motivation and was among the first to emphasize ''expectations'' as much as ''drive.'' Later revised with Birch, it contrasted the traditional analysis of motivation in terms of discrete goal-directed episodes, and their new viewpoint emphasizing temporal continuity in both the stream of behavior and its underlying motivational structure. By means of computer simulations based on the new motivational principles (instead of classical test theory), Atkinson resolved two puzzles in the study of personality: (1) the validity of thematic apperceptive measurement of a motive does not depend on its reliability (i.e., internal consistency) and (2) stable individual differences in personality (e.g., motives) may be expressed in systematically variable—that is, *inconsistent*—behavior. These and other recent advances appear in *Motivation, thought, and action* (with Julius Kuhl). See also *Personality, motivation, and action: Selected papers* (1983).

Atkinson was a Social Research Council faculty research fellow (1952–1955), a fellow at the Center for Advanced Study in the Behavioral Sciences (1955–1956), and a John Simon Guggenheim fellow (1960–1961). He was elected fellow of the American Academy of Arts and Sciences (1975) and received the Distinguished Scientific Contribution Award of the American Psychological Association (1979) and an honorary degree from Ruhr-Universität Bochum in 1980.

ATKINSON, RICHARD C. (1929–   )

After obtaining the Ph.B. from the University of Chicago, Atkinson continued studies at Indiana University, where he received the Ph.D. in 1955. His long association with Stanford University began in 1956 after service in the U.S. Army.

Atkinson's research in psychology and cognitive science has been concerned with problems of memory and cognition. He transformed intuitive ideas about the nature of human memory into an explicit theory that was formulated in mathematical terms. This theory was the basis for a great deal of modern research on memory and has played an important role in specifying correlates between brain structures and psychological phenomena and in explaining the effects of drugs on memory. His research led him to an interest in the more applied problems of learning in the classroom. He developed one of the first computer-controlled systems for instruction, which served as a prototype for the commercial development of computer-assisted instruction. An important application of his work has been the teaching of reading under computer control to primary-school children.

He left active research in psychology when he was appointed deputy director of the National Science Foundation in 1975 by President Ford and director in 1977 by President Carter. Since 1980, he has served as chancellor of the University of California, San Diego.

AUBERT, HERMAN (1826–1892)

Aubert was one of the mid-19th-century physiological psychologists along with Volkmann, Helmholtz, and Hering. He was professor of physiology at Breslau (Poland) and then at Rostok from 1862 to 1892. He is primarily known for his work on physiological optics, visual space perception, and color sensitivity. He determined that Weber's law as applied to visual space perception is a function of the light intensity.

He also worked with other senses, including touch and bodily orientation. He was one of the first editors of the prestigious *Zeitschrift fur Psychologie.*

R. W. LUNDIN

AUGUSTINE OF HIPPO (354–430)

St. Augustine (Aurelius Augustinus) was a philosopher and theologian whose ideas and achievements profoundly influenced Western culture and left an indelible mark particularly on the Christian world. His thought is still widely studied, not merely as a historical phenomenon, but as a relevant source for understanding the human condition of the past and present. Augustine was born in Tagaste (in what is now Tunisia) of a pagan father and devout Christian mother. After his studies, Augustine chose the career of a teacher of rhetoric and taught at Tagaste, Carthage, and Rome, and eventually received a post in Milan. By his own account he lived a life of sin and had a mistress who bore him a son. At 33 he experienced conversion, changed his life, received baptism, and returned to Tagaste, where he led a life devoted to prayer and study. After four years he became a priest and, in 396, bishop of Hippo (now Annaba in Algeria), where he remained to the end of his life, intensively active as churchman, preacher, and writer. He left over 120 works.

Soon after his conversion, Augustine wrote in his *Soliloquies* (1948, p. 350): ''I desire to know God and the soul [and] absolutely nothing more.'' He pursued this goal faithfully the rest of his life. Augustine's psychology was influenced by his Christian beliefs and the philosophy of Neoplatonism which, as he tells us, taught him to conceive the reality of spiritual being. This latter realization was a key experience for Augustine: besides reinforcing his religious attitude, it increased his interest in spiritual reality, the soul, and in the psychological problems. The soul, Augustine held, is endowed with three main faculties—memory, understanding, and will, known as the Augustinian ''psychological triad,'' of which will was the most important. Although Augustine has not left any systematic treatise of psychology, an extensive body of psychological material can be found in many of his writings. In fact, the starting point of all Augustine's philosophical and theological deliberations is psychological, because his deepest spiritual yearning was to find truth and happiness. This yearning is particularly evident in Augustine's *Confessions,* a classic of perennial appeal, written when the author was 44 and already bishop of Hippo.

Augustine's path to the knowledge of God and truth was through the analysis of his inner being, his soul. Augustine believed that all aspects of being are reflected in the soul as in a mirror. Consequently, the key to the knowledge of objective reality can be found only in the soul, or more concretely, in one's consciousness. With this conviction, Augustine embarked on a thorough, meticulous, unbiased analysis of his inner experiences, thoughts, feelings, emotions, and memories. Through this painstaking and penetrating self-analysis and self-examination—so well exemplified in his *Confessions*—Augustine brought forth a rich treasury of observations on human nature and the workings of the human mind. At the same time, his masterful self-observation became the prototype of the introspection and phenomenology of modern psychology. Prominent among the psychological problems discussed and analyzed by Augustine are memory and its phenomena, feelings, will, and their meaning in human life. His knowledge of the complexity of human nature helped Augustine in his dealings with people and especially in his numerous sermons. In them, he was careful to consider the mentality and intellectual level of his audiences and to adapt his sermons to them. He knew how to capture the attention of his listeners, how to move, amuse, and convince them.

Because of his intense preoccupation with psychological problems, human nature, and existence, and his contributions to the understanding of man, Augustine occupies a prominent place in the history of psychology. Many eminent psychologists and historians have recognized Augustine's significance and have paid tribute to him. He has been called the "first modern psychologist," "the most eminent empirical psychologist of antiquity," and "the first psychologist of motivation." D. B. Klein in his *History of scientific psychology* reviews in some detail Augustine's contributions to psychology in nine different areas. Among the contributions Klein lists are Augustine's distinctions between concepts and percepts, between sensory and ideational perception, and between language symbols and their referents. Klein also points out that Augustine formulated some of the basic issues of the psychology of time perception and anticipated the concept of space-time continuum. Robert B. MacLeod (1975) in his essay on the five classic doctrines of man (relativistic, materialistic, idealistic, technological, and religious) credits Augustine's writings, notably *Confessions* and *City of God*, with the "best expression of the religious doctrine of man."

H. MISIAK

AUSTAD, CAROL DONNA SHAW (1946–   )

Austad received the B.A. in psychology from Carleton University in Ottawa, Canada, and the M.A. from Stephen F. Austin State University in Nacogdoches, Texas. She received the Ph.D. in clinical psychology from the University of North Texas in 1982 and completed a doctoral and a postdoctoral internship at Connecticut Valley Hospital in Middletown.

In 1982, she became a staff psychologist at Hall-Brooke Hospital in Westport, Connecticut, and began a part-time private practice. From 1983 to 1987 she worked full-time at Community Health Care Plan (CHCP) a staff model health maintenance organization in New Haven, Connecticut. In 1987, she joined the faculty of Central Connecticut State University where she took a full-time, tenure-track position. In 1989, she returned to CHCP, while working at the university, to conduct research on the practice of psychotherapy in the managed care setting.

In addition to teaching and practicing psychotherapy, Austad published numerous articles and made multiple professional presentations. She defines her major contribution as her publications, which discuss psychotherapy models and practice habits that are consistent with the demands of a changing American health care system. Her book, coedited with William Berman, *Psychotherapy in managed health care: The optimal use of time and resources* describes models devised and conducted by grass-roots psychotherapists in managed health care settings.

AVENERIUS, RICHARD (1843–1896)

Avenerius was professor of philosophy at the University of Zurich from 1877 to 1896. It is reported his students found him a difficult and uninspiring teacher. He worked at the same time as Ernest Mach but apparently was unaware of Mach's work. Like Mach he set out to develop a theory of science.

He began with the hypothesis that there was a system he called C on which consciousness depended. This system appeared to be synonymous with the central nervous system but apparently went beyond it. C was considered to be essential for the mind. He wrote about R values (stimuli) and E values (experience), the latter depending entirely on System C. The system constantly changed between anabolism and catabolism. He also wrote about vital series that were dependent and independent of the system.

The significance of this concept in the history of psychology has to do with its influence on Titchener who used the word *dependent* to refer to the experience dependent on the experiencing individual, which is what psychology studies, and *independent* to refer to the physical outside world.

R. W LUNDIN

AZUMA, HIROSHI (1926–   )

Azuma's work centers around cognitive development of children, concept learning, and methods of instruction. In recent years he has been working on a U.S.–Japanese comparison of the relationships between mother's and teacher's teaching styles and future cognitive development of the child. His position is that teaching, which in itself is a part of the formative function of a culture, is effective only in interaction with broader cultural context.

He received his first degree from the University of Tokyo, majoring in experimental and general psychology. After serving as an instructor of psychology and educational psychology for a few years at the University of Tokyo, he did his graduate study under the Fulbright program at the University of Illinois and received a Ph.D. in 1960, majoring in educational psychology. His dissertation, written under the direction of Lee J. Cronbach, was an attempt to analyze the process of learning a complex artificial concept. He subsequently served as an associate professor and the chairman of the Department of Child Study at the Japanese Women's University, then in 1964 joined the faculty of education at the University of Tokyo, where he now is a professor of education.

Since Azuma was one of the first post-World War II Japanese psychologists to receive a doctorate overseas, and since the University of Tokyo was a strategic center of academic communication in Japan, he had to act as a facilitator of international communication and cooperation for Japanese psychologists. Involved in this role were positions such as general secretary of the Organization Committee for the 1972 International Congress of Psychology, and member of the executive committee of the International Union of Psychological Science.

Under joint authorship with Keiko Kashiwagi and Robert D. Hess, Azuma published a book in Japanese on the influence of maternal attitude and styles upon the cognitive development of the child. An English version of the report of the same study is forthcoming.

BACH, GEORGE R. (1914–1986)

Bach completed his higher education at the University of Iowa, where he studied with Kurt Lewin. He is primarily known for his work in group and family therapy, and his espousal of his theoretical system of creative aggression. He is the author of nine books including *Intensive group psychotherapy* and a popular best seller, the *Intimate enemy*, coauthored with Peter Wyden. Bach taught at many universities and presented many institutes and workshops throughout the world.

BACON, FRANCIS (SIR) (1561–1636)

Bacon's lineage was that of a ranking family. He was an attorney, a Member of Parliament and Lord Keeper of the Great Seal. He studied at Trinity College, Cambridge. In 1620 he published his most celebrated book, *Novum organism*.

His writings fall into three classes: professional, literary, and philosophical. It is in his psychology (then considered philosophy) that his influence has been most marked. His writings preceded John Lock's *Essay concerning human understanding* but had a strong influence on it. In Bacon's *Novum organism* he wrote, "Man who is the server and interpreter of nature can act and understand no further than he can observe either in the operation or contemplation of the method and order of nature." It is suggested by scholars that through the practical tendency of his philosophy and through John Locke, Bacon was the father of British empiricism. Bacon proposed that the value of understanding is assessed in terms of the potential benefit to the human race. If a project can do an individual little or no good in his or her daily affairs of life, then the presumption is that it is worthless.

In an earlier work, *The advancement of learning,* Bacon's empiricism is more limited. In it he stated that what we today would call human psychology bears the stamp of heriditary influences. Bacon stated that in science there were two kinds of experiments, (1) those that shed light and (2) those that would bear fruit. Both were necessary for scientific inquiry.

He was the first of a series of philosphers (mostly British) to call a halt to medieval speculation and superstition. He can be paraphrased as saying, "Open your eyes and look at the world as it is."

R. W. LUNDIN

BADDELEY, ALAN (1934–   )

Baddeley was educated at University College, London, where he graduated in Psychology in 1956. He spent the following year at Princeton where he obtained an M.A. before returning to Britain where he was employed by the Medical Research Council at the Applied Psychology Unit Cambridge from 1958 to 1967. During this time he completed a Ph.D. at Cambridge and carried out research, primarily in the area of human memory. Results included the demonstration that long-term memory tends to rely heavily on meaning in contrast to short-term memory, which relies more heavily on sound or speech coding. Other research concerned performance under stress and in particular the open-sea performance of deep sea divers. In 1967 he moved to the University of Sussex, and in 1972 became Professor of Psychology at Stirling University in Scotland. Work at this time involved elaborating the unitary concept of short-term memory into that of working memory, an alliance subsistence controlled by a limited capacity central executive system. In 1974 he returned to the Applied Psychology Unit Cambridge as Director. Books published include *The psychology of memory,* and a more popular overview of human memory, *Your memory: A user's guide.* Honors include the President's Award of the British Psychological Society, 1981, and Presidency of the Experimental Psychology Society, 1983.

BAIN, ALEXANDER (1818–1903)

Bain was a Scotsman and spent his entire life in Aberdeen. Although he devoted most of his efforts to psychology, the chair he held at the University of Aberdeen beginning in 1860 was actually in logic. His two most important works were *The senses and the intellect* (1855) and *The emotions and the will* (1859). These books have been considered by many to be the first real books on psychology.

Along with Herbert Spencer, Bain was the last in the line of British associationists which began with John Locke over a century earlier and continued into the nineteenth century with David Hartley, James Mill, and John Stuart Mill. Like a number of his predecessors, Bain stressed two basic laws of association, similarity and contiguity. In the latter instance, for example, sensations and feelings come together in close succession in such a way that, when one of them is brought to mind, the other will most likely occur.

Like no other psychologist before him, Bain brought together in his works all that was known about psychology up to his time. He was interested in every mode of experience and analysis of its contents. He also wrote on learning (habit), memory, and retention.

He has been considered the first modern physiological psychologist. He drew on the vast literature of nineteenth-century physiology of the nervous system. He discussed the sense organs and how they worked.

He wrote on the reflex and recounted what was known about the brain and how it worked. In all of this he attempted to relate the mental events of experience and their physiological correlates.

In 1876 Bain founded *Mind,* the first psychological journal in any country, though it had more of a philosophical bent than subsequent journals to be founded in Germany and America. He appointed one of his pupils, Croom Robertson, to be its first editor. In this journal Bain published many of his most important papers.

Bain brought associationism to a point where it was not merely a verbal description, but could be demonstrated in the experimental studies of Pavlov, Wundt, and Thorndike.

R. W. LUNDIN

BAIRD, JOHN WALLACE (1873–1919)

John Wallace Baird was a native of Ontario, Canada, and received his undergraduate education at the University of Toronto. After postgraduate study at Leipzig he took the Ph.D. degree in psychology under Edward Titchener at Cornell.

At one time Baird was regarded as Titchener's most representative follower. He was, however, strongly influenced by the work of Oswald Külpe and others of the Würzburg school on the higher mental processes. As director of the psychological laboratory of Clark University, he made systematic experimental introspection of the higher mental processes the central topic.

Baird's most significant experimental study dealt with the role of accommodation and convergence in depth perception. He concluded that convergence provided more important cues than accommodation. Baird served as executive editor of the *American Journal of Psychology* and as cooperating editor of several other journals.

P. E. LICHTENSTEIN

BAKAN, DAVID (1921–   )

Bakan obtained his early education in New York City. He then attended Brooklyn College (B.A.), and Ohio State University (Ph.D., 1948). After holding positions at the University of Chicago, Harvard University, the University of Missouri, and Ohio State University, he became a professor of psychology at York University in Toronto in 1968, and has remained there ever since. He was a Terry lecturer at Yale in 1976, and has been president of three divisions of the American Psychological Association: History of Psychology, Philosophical Psychology, and Humanistic Psychology.

Bakan's writings range over the history and theory of psychology, research method, psychology of religion, education, pain, and social commentary. His books include *Sigmund Freud and the mystical tradition; The duality of human existance; Disease; Pain and sacrifice; On method: Toward a reconstruction of psychological investigation; Slaughter of the innocents: A study of the battered child phenomenon;* and *And they took themselves wives: On the emergence of patriarchy in Western civilization.*

BAKARE, CHRISTOPHER G. M. (1935–   )

Bakare received his early education there in various locations where his father worked as an Anglican clergyman. He received his university education at Ibadan University in Nigeria and at Oxford University in England, and received the Ph.D. in psychology from Columbia University in New York in 1969. At Columbia's Teachers' College he studied under Arthur Jerslid, Robert Thorndike, Morton Deutsch, Donald Super, and Samuel Ball.

Since graduating from Columbia, Bakare has worked at Ibadan University, where he is currently professor of psychology. In that university he has served as head of the Department of Guidance and Counseling and as dean of the prestigious Faculty of Education. He was editor of the *Nigerian Journal of Psychology* and now edits the *African Journal of Psychology*. He is past president of the Nigerian Psychological Society and was a foundation member and executive committee member of the International Association for Cross-Cultural Psychology.

In his research Bakare is basically interested in how psychology can foster the adjustment of various African peoples to the modern technological world. Thus in his method of *metaperceptual congruence*, he has devised a statistical technique for identifying the "kernel of truth" in interethnic stereotypes as contribution to an understanding of the interethnic conflicts which now plague the continent's development. He has constructed and validated for African subjects a number of psychometric tests, and more recently has formulated a theory of the *cumulative cognitive deficit syndrome* in African children and has produced a number of cognitive stimulation materials for correcting such deficits.

Among Bakare's published tests are the Vocational Interest Inventory and the Academic Need Achievement Test. His published cognitive stimulation materials include the Visual perception workbooks, and the *Picture arrangement kit*.

BALDWIN, JAMES MARK (1861–1934)

Known as a founding father of both developmental psychology and symbolic interactionism, Baldwin was educated at Salem Collegiate Institution, and received his doctorate from Princeton in 1888. At Princeton, he was a student of the Scottish philosopher James McCosh.

Grounded in the "mental philosophy" tradition, Baldwin first held a chair in philosophy at Lake Forest College. Moving on to chairs in logic and metaphysics at Toronto and in psychology at Princeton, he emerged from that tradition and developed a thoroughgoing Darwinian genetic psychology. His chief goal was to explain the adaptive correspondence of thought to things, which he argued came about through the formation and transformation of habits by interacting processes of assimilation and imitation. He maintained a functional view of mind as sensorimotor process, and stressed the importance of intentional action as the instrument of selection in mental development.

During this period, he combined Darwinian and Lamarckian concepts to develop a sophisticated hypothesis of organic selection, accounting for the directedness of evolution. This idea came to be known as the "Baldwin effect."

At the turn of the century Baldwin applied the model of intentional action to the social, moral, and religious spheres. Cycles of reciprocal interpersonal suggestion and imitation were conceived as a mechanism by which self and other underwent simultaneous social development. He linked this psychological model to an account of social progress through "social selection" and the conservation and transmission of adaptive values.

Between 1903 and 1915 Baldwin turned to the construction of a "genetic logic," the forerunner of what is now known as genetic or evolutionary epistemology. He brought Hegelian idealism into the empirical domain with this ambitious theory that explained psychological development in terms of successive, qualitatively different structures of consciousness. Children passed from "prelogical" sense and memory to a "quasi-logical" level in which fantasy gave way to concepts of mind, body, and self, and thence to a "logical" stage of rational judgment, an "extralogical" level of morality, and finally a "hyperlogical" aesthetic consciousness.

In 1908 Baldwin suffered severe embarrassment in a scandal which precipitated his resignation from all academic positions and his voluntary exile to Mexico, where he was a consultant on social development to President Diaz, and to Paris, where he became an active correspondent concerning the threat of war. Despite the premature termination of his academic career, his pioneering conceptual work has lasting importance for evolutionary theory, developmental psychology, and social psychology.

J. M. BROUGHTON

BALTES, PAUL B. (1939–   )

Baltes is a developmental psychologist and gerontologist best known for his work on life-span developmental theory, longitudinal methodology, and intellectual development during adulthood and old age. After receiving the Ph.D. in psychology from the University of Saarbrucken, Germany, in 1967, he spent the next 12 yr in academic appointments at West Virginia University, Pennsylvania State University, and Stanford University. In 1980 he returned to Germany to become codirector of the Berlin Max Planck Institute for Human Development and Education.

Baltes emphasized that individuals continue to maintain a capacity for change across the entire lifespan. This is illustrated in research with his colleagues (M. Baltes, R. Kliegel, J. Smith, and S. Willis) on the plasticity of intelligence in aging persons. Another major theme of life-span developmental theory is the interplay between distinct sources of change that codefine the rate and directionality of human development: age-graded, history-graded, and nonnormative factors. Such an approach engenders interdisciplinary collaboration and underscores the role of social change in psychological development.

Baltes's publications include several books on life-span developmental psychology (Baltes & Schaie, 1973; Baltes & Eckensberger, 1979; Goulet & Baltes, 1970) and developmental and longitudinal methodology (Baltes, Reese, & Nesselroade, 1977; Nesselroade & Baltes, 1979) as well as *Successful aging* (with M. M. Baltes).

BANDURA, ALBERT (1925–   )

A proponent of social cognitive theory, Bandura received the B.A. from the University of British Columbia. After completing the doctorate at the University of Iowa in 1952, Bandura joined the faculty at Stanford University, where he has since remained to pursue his scientific career.

Social cognitive theory explains human functioning in terms of triadic reciprocal causation between cognitive and other personal determinants, behavior, and environmental influences. Bandura assigns a central role to cognitive, vicarious, self-regulative, and self-reflective processes in human mastery and adaptation. Recognizing that virtually all learning phenomena resulting from direct experience can occur by means of vicarious influence, Bandura assigns modeling a prominent role in the acquisition and regulation of thought, affect, and action. Another major focus of Bandura's conceptual analysis is the extraordinary symbolizing capacity of humans. By drawing on their symbolic capabilities, people can construct internal models of their environment and courses of action, solve problems cognitively, engage in foresightful action, gain new knowledge by reflective thought, and communicate with others at any distance in time and space. A further distinctive feature of social cognitive theory that Bandura singles out for special attention is self-regulatory processes. Through internal standards and self-reactive influences, people make causal contributions to their own motivation and actions. The capability for self-reflection concerning one's functioning and personal efficacy to exercise control over one's performances and environment is another human attribute that is featured prominently in social cognitive theory. As a major mechanism of personal agency, self-beliefs of efficacy influence the choices people make, their thought patterns, level of motivation and perseverance in the face of difficulties, and their vulnerability to stress and depression.

His publications include *Social learning and personality development* (with R. H. Walters), *Adolescent aggression* (with R. H. Walters), *Principles of behavior modification*, *Psychological modeling*, *Conflicting theories* (as editor), *Aggression: A social learning analysis*, and *Social learning theory*. *Social foundations of thought and action: A social cognitive theory* provides the conceptual framework and analyzes the vast body of knowledge bearing on this theory.

BARBER, THEODORE X. (1927–   )

After earning undergraduate majors in several areas (philosophy, biology, physiology, and psychology), Barber pursued graduate studies in psychology at American University and was awarded the Ph.D. degree in 1956. His dissertation was on hypnosis. He continued investigating hypnosis during the next three years (1956–1959) at the Laboratory of Social Relations at Harvard University as a postdoctoral research fellow sponsored by the National Institute of Mental Health.

From 1959 to 1978 Barber researched hypnosis at the Medfield (Massachusetts) State Hospital, and reported his findings in *Hypnosis: A scientific approach*, and *LSD, marihuana, yoga and hypnosis*.

Barber's experimental studies led to the book *Pitfalls in human research: Ten pivotal points*, and to edited books such as *Advances in altered states of consciousness and human potentialities*, *Biofeedback and self-control* and *Biofeedback and behavioral medicine*.

After moving to Cushing Hospital in Framingham, Massachusetts, in 1978, Barber continued studies in clinical hypnosis, hypnosuggestive therapy, and the development of a theory of mind-body interrelationships.

BARKER, ROGER G. (1903–1990)

Barker was educated in public schools of the Middle West and at Stanford University (Ph.D., 1934), where he was greatly influenced by Lewis M. Terman, Calvin P. Stone, and Walter R. Miles. A two-year postdoctoral fellowship at the University of Iowa with Kurt Lewin was of crucial importance to him.

The Midwest Psychological Field Station of the University of Kansas was established in Oskaloosa, Kansas, by Barker and H. F. Wright in 1947; it operated for 25 years as a pioneering center for research in environmental psychology (Barker & Wright, 1966, 1971; Barker & Schoggen, 1973). The goals of the Station were to discover and describe the environments the town provided its children (in its streets, dentists' offices, stores, vacant lots, churches, scout troop, etc.); to describe how these environments treated children; to record the amounts and characteristics of children's behavior within the various environments; and to investigate the relationships between environment and behavior within the town.

Scientific work in psychology at that time was limited almost entirely to laboratory, clinical, testing, and interview situations where investigators create the environments their studies require; consequently, few methods, concepts, and theories were available for dealing with investigator-free environments and behavior. In the beginning, therefore, the work of the Station was largely devoted to developing nondestructive methods of investigating and analyzing behavior *in situ;* among these were specimen records, behavior episodes, environmental force units, and behavior settings. Through these and other methods, studies were made of individuals, institutions, and communities, as for example the environments and behavior of normal and disabled children during entire days; the occurrence of frustration among children; and the environments of small and large schools and of an American and an English town, and the behavioral consequences.

BARTLETT, FREDERIC C. (1886–1979)

Bartlett, the leading British psychologist of his time, did much to further experimental psychology in the United Kingdom. After graduating in philosophy in the University of London, he moved to Cambridge with the initial intention of studying anthropology under W. H. R. Rivers. However, World War I intervened and, on the advice of Charles S. Myers, Bartlett turned to experimental psychology and virtually took charge of the Cambridge Psychological Laboratory when Myers left Cambridge for war service. After the war, Bartlett succeeded Myers as director of the laboratory and in 1931 was appointed the first professor of experimental psychology in the university. He held this post until his retirement in 1952, but remained active for some years thereafter as an honorary consultant to the Applied Psychology Unit which he himself had built up during and after World War II.

Bartlett's psychological standpoint was strongly empirical, with a distinct bias toward applied interests. His intellectual approach was greatly influenced by three Cambridge teachers: James Ward, a philosopher with a background in physiology; W. H. R. Rivers, who began in physiology and medicine but is best known for his later works in ethnology; and C. S. Myers, who likewise qualified in medicine but whose subsequent career was devoted wholly to psychology. Myers provided Bartlett with his first real introduction to experimental psychology and invited him to assist in the revision of his *Textbook of experimental psychology* (Myers, 1925/1909), which was for many years the standard British source.

Although an accomplished teacher, Bartlett is best remembered for his outstanding achievement in directing research. His own early work fell largely within the traditional sphere of human experimental psychology and is best represented by his celebrated book, *Remembering,* based upon a successful fellowship dissertation submitted many years earlier to St. John's College, Cambridge. This book represented both a clean break with the Ebbinghaus tradition and an attempt to study memory in circumstances akin to those of everyday life.

Bartlett's studies led him to stress the constructive rather than reproductive aspects of recall and to repudiate the classical "trace" theory, which he considered wholly inappropriate to the realities of memory. In its place, he proposed an admittedly vague theory of "schemata" adapted from Henry Head's 1920 work on sensation and the cerebral cortex. Unfortunately, this theory proved too speculative to gain wide acceptance, though it led many people to think rather differently about the nature and dynamics of memory (Oldfield & Zangwill, 1943; Zangwill, 1972).

During and after World War II, Bartlett turned his department almost exclusively to wartime activities. A wide variety of practical problems, for the most part relating to training methods, fatigue, and human performance, were referred to the department, and its considerable success depended on Bartlett's exceptional psychological acumen together with the ingenuity and skill of his research workers, in particular a young man of outstanding originality, Kenneth Craik.

As a result of his wartime experience, Bartlett became increasingly preoccupied with the need to base experimental psychology upon the solution of practical problems, being convinced that advances in basic psychological theory would come only through such an approach (Bartlett, 1948). Although this standpoint had its critics, Bartlett's good sense and authority did much to narrow the gap between fundamental and applied psychology and to endow psychological experiments with more realistic flavor.

Bartlett was a fellow of the Royal Society of London and a foreign associate of the U.S. National Academy of Sciences. He was the recipient of many honors, including honorary degrees from the universities of Athens, Edinburgh, London, Louvain, Oxford, Princeton, and Padua.

O. L. ZANGWILL

BARTLEY, S. HOWARD (1910–1988)
Bartley graduated from Greenville College in Illinois and then received the A.M. degree and Ph.D. (1931) from the University of Kansas. Henry Helson introduced him to the study of vision, which resulted in his first book, *Vision: A study of its basis,* published in 1941. After the Ph.D. he went to study ophthalmology at Washington University (St. Louis) School of Medicine. He then went to the Dartmouth Eye Institute, Michigan State University, and finally after his retirement from Michigan to Memphis State University in Tennessee where he was distinguished professor of psychology. He remained there until his death. Besides vision he wrote, researched, and published in the fields of fatigue and perception.

R. W. LUNDIN

BASOV, MIKHAIL YAKOVIEVICH (1892–1931)
In the first years of Soviet psychology the prevailing attitude was extremely mechanistic, as expressed in the work of Vladimir Bekhterev. Basov was one of the Soviet psychologists of the Moscow school who opposed this tendency.

His concerns were in the areas of child psychology, personality development, and general psychology. He felt that heredity and environment both contributed to human growth and development, their roles changing from one phase of development to another. The role of environment was extremely important and consistent with the goals of Soviet education. In stressing environment, he felt that the potentialities of knowledge were unlimited. Whatever limitations existed were to be found in the social environment.

In the development of human personality, Basov believed activity to be extremely important. As a result of this conviction he developed methods for the psychological observation of preschool children and schoolchildren which were reported in his book, *Methods of psychological observation* in 1923. In it he stressed the objectivity of observation and reacted against subjectivism in the interpretation of infant and child behavior.

R. W. LUNDIN

BATESON, GREGORY (1904–1980)
Bateson studied at the University of Geneva, and received the B.A. and M.A. from Cambridge. He conducted anthropological research with the Baining and the Sulka of the Gazelle Peninsula and with the Iatmul of New Guinea. He served at various times with the American Museum of Natural History, the Museum of Modern Art, and the O.S.S. He also was a visiting professor or lecturer at Harvard University, the New School for Social Research, the University of Hawaii, and the Langley Porter Clinic. In 1950 he joined the Veterans Administration Hospital in Palo Alto, California, as ethnologist.

Bateson was at one time married to Margaret Mead, with whom he coauthored *Naven* (1928), a picture of the culture of a New Guinea tribe. He is also the author of *Steps to an ecology of mind* (1972) and *Mind and nature: A necessary unity* (1979).

P. E. LICHTENSTEIN

BATESON, WILLIAM (1861–1926)
Bateson, educated at Rugby and Cambridge, was one of the most eminent zoologists of his time. He is best known for his contributions to the establishment of the Mendelian concept of heredity and variations. Bateson named the new science "genetics" and extended his efforts in the early part of his career to a study of chromosomes and genes, although not much was known at the time about these carriers of heredity. He experimented on hybridization in an effort to seek exact knowledge of the transmission of inherited characteristics from parents to immediate offspring.

After Gregory Mendel's initial work (1866) in breeding experiments with peas, little further attention had been paid to genetics. Bateson rediscovered Mendel's findings and reinterpreted them in the light of more recent findings.

As a spokesman for the new sciences of genetics, he founded the *Journal of Genetics* in 1910. Since he could not find any visible correlation between every chromosome and the consequent bodily feature, he devised a vibratory theory of inheritance founded on force and motion. This never received much favor among his colleagues.

For Bateson, the basic problem of genetics was to find the source of the undeniable evolutionary changes. He believed that in variation he could find the answer. He hoped an explanation for variation would be found in his vibratory theory of heredity. A public battle followed between Bateson and the biometric school led by Karl Pearson, the statistician. Bateson emphasized the imprecision of statistical analyses and decried the biometrician's defense of natural selection. He believed the best answers would be found to explain evolutionary discontinuities in a straightforward Mendelism.

Bateson applied his genetic views to his conception of human society, where an intellectual elite was struggling against a rising middle class that would lead to an equalization of all men to mediocrity. For Bateson, Darwin's theory of natural selection was unacceptable.

R. W. LUNDIN

BAYÉS, RAMÓN (1930–)
Bayés, after qualifying in electrical engineering, worked in this professional sector for a number of years. Later, he graduated in psychology at Barcelona University, where he received the Ph.D.

Bayés has worked on a wide variety of subjects, although always with a deep concern for functional analysis and basic methodology. He is author of the first Spanish book on behavioral pharmacology (1977) and was one of the first in Spain to be actively interested in health psychology, behavioral medicine, and psychoneuroimmunology.

Since 1974 he was attached to the faculty of psychology of the Autonomous University of Barcelona, where he became a full professor. He has maintained close contact with Latin American psychologists, has carried out interdisciplinary work and in his publications, and has defended the possibility of finding a solution to the crisis that psychology faces, without abandoning the strict framework of a natural science. His more recent books and papers deal with topics such as AIDS, cancer, and palliative care.

BAYLEY, NANCY (1899–)
A pioneer in longitudinal multidisciplinary research, Bayley was born to a family that homesteaded in the Northwest in the mid-1800s. Trained as a psychologist at the University of Washington (B.S., M.S., and the State University of Iowa (Ph.D., 1926), she also acquired expertise on physical growth at Iowa and through later study and collaboration with outstanding anatomists and physicians.

Among Bayley's seminal studies are longitudinal research on much of the life span; techniques for measuring behavioral, motor, and physical development; and assessment of interactions between behavioral and biological development. She was one of the first to consider the life span as a frame of reference for research; to report change as well as stability in I.Q., and the maintenance of I.Q. in adulthood; to study the influence of maternal behavior on offspring; and to examine associations of behavior with body build and with rate of physical maturing.

Bayley began her career at the University of Wyoming. In 1928 she joined the Institute of Child Welfare at the University of California, Berkeley. There she founded the Berkeley Growth Study and developed scales for assessing early mental and motor development. The revised Bayley Scales of Infant Development are used worldwide by scientists and professionals from a number of disciplines; they are the most carefully standardized instruments available for this age range.

From 1954 to 1964 Bayley was chief of the Section on Early Development, Laboratory of Psychology, National Institute of Mental Health. She returned to Berkeley in 1964 and retired in 1968. Among her many honors are presidencies of the Society for Research in Child Development, of the Western Psychological Association, and of the Division on Developmental Psychology and the Division on Adult Development and Aging of the American Psychological Association; the Gold Medal Award of the American Psychological Foundation; the APA Distinguished Scientific Contribution Award; the G. Stanley Hall Award for Distinguished Contributions to Developmental Psychology; and the American Education Research Association Award.

BEACH, FRANK A. (1911–1988)

Known for his work in human and animal sexual behavior, Beach (with Clellan S. Ford) published his findings in *Patterns of sexual behavior*. In it sex is reviewed in its cultural and evolutionary perspective.

After receiving the bachelor's and master's degrees from Kansas State Teachers College of Emporia, Beach went on to earn the Ph.D. from the University of Chicago in 1940. He served as research assistant to K. S. Lashley of Harvard's Department of Psychology (1935–1936). The next decade (1936–1946) he spent as assistant curator and curator of museums at various locations. He came to public attention as professor of psychology at Yale, a tenure that lasted from 1946 to 1958. Since 1958 he has been at the University of California, Berkeley.

BEEBE-CENTER, JOHN G. (1897–1958)

Beebe-Center received the Ph.D. in psychology at Harvard University, where he remained as a lifetime lecturer in psychology. His early work on affectivity led to the development of the concept of adaptation level. His major work was *The psychology of pleasantness and unpleasantness* (1932).

Beebe-Center was one of a very small number of investigators of hedonic tone, although it is quite apparent—particularly in the case of odor or taste—that sensory reactions very frequently involve strong and immediate feeling qualities of pleasantness or unpleasantness. Having studied the feeling value of odors, Beebe-Center was led to investigate taste. As a result of his studies of taste thresholds and the scaling of taste values, he developed a psychological scale of taste named the *gust scale*.

P. E. LICHTENSTEIN

BEERS, CLIFFORD W. (1876–1943)

Beers graduated from Yale University. While still a young man he developed a manic-depressive psychosis and for three years was a patient in several state and private mental hospitals. Following his recovery he wrote a popular and influential book, *A mind that found itself*, which described the inadequate and often inhumane treatment of patients in our mental hospitals. The book evoked a positive response on the part of many leading citizens, which led Beers to organize the first Society

for Mental Hygiene in Connecticut in 1908. In 1909 he assisted in the formation of the National Committee for Mental Hygiene and became the acknowledged leader of the mental hygiene movement. His work was instrumental in educating the public and promoting the establishment of clinics aimed at prevention as well as treatment of mental illness.

In 1930 Beers promoted the First International Congress of Mental Hygiene. He also founded the International Committee for Mental Hygiene. Beers' lifelong efforts were rewarded by the existence at the time of his death of a powerful mental hygiene movement which he had brought into being, sustained, and strengthened.

P. E. LICHTENSTEIN

BÉKÉSY, GEORG VON (1899–1972)

Born György von Békésy, von Békésy studied initially at the University of Berne. He received the Ph.D. from Budapest in 1923. His first university appointment was at Budapest in 1932. He moved to the Royal Caroline Institute in Stockholm in 1946. In 1949 he joined S. S. Stevens at Harvard University as senior research fellow in psychophysics. From 1966 until his death he was professor of sensory sciences at the University of Hawaii.

Although his research included the visual, tactile, and gustatory senses, von Békésy is best known for his work in audition. Fascinated with sound from the time he heard high-pitched gypsy music as a boy, he first worked as an engineer in the research laboratory of the Hungarian telephone system. There he was asked to determine the smallest sound range a new cable must transmit while retaining the intelligibility of voices. Von Békésy not only devised many new tools or micromanipulators for his own research, but designed the Békésy audiometer for measuring loss of hearing.

The scholarly approach to his work was demonstrated in his 1948 article on the history of hearing research in which von Békésy distinguishes five major periods of work. Clarity and precision of writing is illustrated in his 1957 *Scientific American* article on the ear.

Von Békésy devised many new techniques. To discern the workings of the inner ear, he replaced the cochlear fluid of cadavers with saline containing fine aluminum and coal particles. With the aid of a microscope and both stroboscopic and steady light, he was able to see the movement of the basilar membrane. He also glued tiny mirrors on the eardrum to measure its vibration.

Von Békésy reported that the stapedius muscle reacts to loud sounds by changing the way the stapes strikes the cochlea, thus preventing ear damage. He also showed that Hermann von Helmholtz's "piano theory" of hearing was incorrect, because the basilar membrane fibers are not free to resonate like the strings of a piano with the sustaining pedal depressed. Rather, the fibers are connected, as if a sheet of rubber or light cloth were laid across the piano strings.

In 1961 von Békésy received the Nobel Prize in medicine and physiology for "discoveries concerning the physical mechanisms of stimulation within the cochlea." His research career is described by part of the Nobel citation: "There is hardly any problem concerning the physical mechanics of acoustic stimulation to which von Bekesy has not added clarity and understanding" (*New York Times*, Oct. 20, 1961).

C. S. PEYSER

BÉKHTEREV, VLADIMIR MIKHAÏLOVÏCH (1857–1927)

Békhterev received the M.D. from St. Petersburg in 1881, studied with Charcot and duBois-Reymond, spent a year with Wundt, and then returned to found the first two experimental psychology laboratories in Russia—in 1886 at Kazan, and in 1895 at St. Petersburg, where he spent most of his career.

He also rounded the first journal anywhere with "experimental psychology" in the title—the *Review of Psychiatry, Neuropathology, and Experimental Psychology,* 1896—and, in 1907, a psychoneurological institute with special departments for mental cases, alcoholics, epileptics, and neurosurgery.

Békhterev is best known for his work on associated reflexes (usually referred to by Ivan Pavlov's term "conditioned reflexes"). Working about the same time as Pavlov, Békhterev gave breadth to the area. Whereas Pavlov dealt primarily with glandular secretions, Békhterev conditioned motor withdrawal responses: the paw of a dog, the hand of a man. He also used such reflexes as the sudden application of cold to the skin, which produces a breath-catching reflex. Békhterev conceived of the associated reflex as the basis for all behavior, and worked with speech as a complex reflex. John B. Watson drew on the 1913 German/French translation of Békhterev's book for the 1915 American Psychological Association presidential address, at a time when he had only a few translated articles of Pavlov. Despite Békhterev's more extensive methodology, Pavlov was more comprehensive and had a more stimulating conceptualization, so that today we have Pavlovian conditioning. Also, for political reasons, V. I. Lenin supported Pavlov over Békhterev.

Whereas Pavlov was primarily a neurologist who disdained psychology, Békhterev was far more behavioral and interested in pedagogical problems, including child rearing. For example, he emphasized that music should be present from the child's first days for aesthetic training to occur. He studied reaction time, the span of attention, and the point in development when the vestibular reflexes first appear (on the fifteenth day in humans). In neuroanatomy and medicine labels bearing his name are still used, as for instance Békhterev's disease.

C. S. PEYSER

BELL, SIR CHARLES (1774–1842)
Bell became one of the most eminent physiologists, surgeons, and lecturers of his time. He was widely known not only in Great Britain but in France as well. He held chairs as professor of physiology, anatomy, and surgery in the College of Surgeons at the University of London, and in 1835 accepted a chair as professor of surgery at the University of Edinburgh.

In his own time his discoveries in physiology were considered by many to be the most important since Harvey's discovery of the circulation of the blood. He is best known for his discovery that the sensory fibers of a mixed nerve enter the spinal cord at the dorsal root, whereas the motor fibers of the same nerve leave the cord by a ventral root. The differentiation of the sensory and motor nerve functions had been known by Galen, but subsequently this knowledge had been lost sight of by later physiologists, who held that the nerves function indiscriminately in carrying both sensory and motor impulses. Bell's work, *Idea of a new anatomy of the brain,* was published privately as a monograph of only 100 copies around 1811. It later appeared in a larger work.

Working quite independently in France, François Magendie came to the same discovery and published his work seven years later. A controversy arose as to the priority of the discovery. The discovery is now known as the Bell-Magendie law.

R. W. LUNDIN

BENEDICT, RUTH F. (1887–1948)
Benedict was raised by her mother in her grandparents' strict Baptist farm home after the death of her father. It was a troubled childhood in a troubled family. In addition to poverty and restrictive fundamentalism, she became partially deaf in childhood, and her mother never overcame her grief over the death of her husband. By her own description, Benedict lived in two psychological worlds as a child, one of beauty and death, represented by her father, and the other of anguish and tears, as seen in her mother's outbursts. She appears to have been in conflict over her being a woman, and her role relative to men, throughout most of her life.

Benedict abandoned her Baptist faith while an undergraduate at Vassar, where she received the B.A. She married very unhappily—apparently, following a temporary decision to resolve her conflicts by becoming a traditional wife and mother. While still married she earned a Ph.D. in anthropology under Franz Boas at Columbia. Completing her degree in 1923, she worked as Boas's assistant and during this time helped inspire Margaret Mead to a career in anthropology.

Despite her brilliant accomplishments, Benedict was held on temporary appointment for a number of years at Columbia. Full psychological recovery occurred when she finally separated from her husband and was appointed an assistant professor in 1931. Earlier she had served as editor of the *Journal of American Folklore,* and later became president of the American Anthropological Association. After Boas died in 1942 and until her own death, she was the leading, if not the least controversial, anthropologist in America. Appointment as a full professor was delayed until months before her death in 1948.

Most of Benedict's research dealt with the origins of American Indian cultures. She saw in each culture an assemblage of elements from many other cultures. Like Mead, she was often controversial, making unfavorable comparisons between Western culture and the cultures she found among the Indians of the American Southwest. Under the inspiration of Edward Sapir and Mead, she later turned to describing Indian cultures as personalities, using Nietzschean psychological types. She saw the cultural personality as deriving from the influence of the culture on the individual during his or her development, not from any sort of genetic determinism. This work is of particular importance to psychology in that it suggests a culturally determined definition of normality.

Benedict's major publications include *Psychological types in the cultures of the Southwest,* in which she compares two Indian tribes, and her very important *Patterns of culture.* As part of her wartime work she also wrote *The Chrysanthemum and the sword: Patterns of Japanese culture* (1946), a still-useful explanation of Japanese culture for Westerners. Also of interest are her early work, *Tales of the Cochiti Indians,* and her two-volume *Zuni mythology.*

T. KEITH-LUCAS

BENJAMIN, LUDY T., JR. (1945–   )
Benjamin studied at the University of Texas (Austin), Auburn University, and Texas Christian University (Ph.D., 1971). He served on the faculty of Nebraska Wesleyan University (1970–1978) before moving to Washington, D.C., as director of educational affairs for the American Psychological Association (APA). In 1980 he joined the faculty of Texas A&M University where he became professor of psychology and director of undergraduate studies.

Initially trained in visual perception, since 1975 Benjamin's research interests centered on the history of American psychology. His program of research focuses on the metamorphosis of psychology, marking its transition from philosophical discourse to laboratory science. He has published on the founding of the early laboratories (Nebraska) and the early psychology organizations (Eastern Psychological Association, Midwestern Psychological Association, Psychological Round Table), on the applications of psychology to education (child study, teaching machines) and industry (advertising), on the popularization of psychology, and on the public image of American psychology. He is the author of more than a dozen books, including *A history of psychology in notes and news, Harry Kirke Wolfe: Pioneer in psychology,* and *A history of psychology in letters.*

Benjamin is a member of the Board of Advisors for the Archives of the History of American Psychology at the University of Akron and is associate editor for the *American Psychologist.* He served as president of two APA divisions: history of psychology and teaching of psychology. In 1936, he received the Distinguished Teaching Award from the American Psychological Foundation.

BENTHAM, JEREMY (1748–1832)

An eminent English philosopher and jurist, Bentham's *Principles of morals and legislation* was published in 1789. In this work he defined his principle of utility, pleasure, good, and happiness. He felt that the object of legislation must be "the general happiness of the greatest number" measured by "the sum total of human happiness."

Thus he was one of the main proponents of the motivational theory known as hedonism, which lasted well into the twentieth century. Human activity arose out of a desire to seek pleasure and avoid pain. Actually, the principle went back to the Greek writings of Aristoppos and Epicurus. According to Bentham, all action arose out of self-interest.

His philosophy of utility and hedonism influenced later British writers such as John Stuart Mill and Herbert Spencer. Many Christian theologians relied on the promises of the pleasures of heaven and the avoidance of pain in hell. Likewise, Sigmund Freud in his early writings wrote of the pleasure principle as a striving force of the unconscious id. Twentieth-century learning theorists such as Edward Thorndike stated in his *Law of effect* that actions which led to satisfying consequences were "stamped in." More modern statements can be found in the principle of reinforcement stated in the learning theories of B. F. Skinner and Clark Hull.

R. W. Lundin

BENTON, ARTHUR L. (1909–   )

Benton was educated at Oberlin College (B.A., M.A.,) and Columbia University (Ph.D., 1935). His early training was in experimental psychology, but a graduate assistantship at the New York State Psychiatric Institute (1933–1935) directed his interest toward clinical psychology. Experience with brain-injured patients at the San Diego Naval Hospital during World War II focused that interest specifically on clinical neuropsychology. After World War II, he became associate professor of psychology at the University of Louisville School of Medicine (1946–1948), then professor of psychology and director of the Graduate Training Program in Clinical Psychology at the University of Iowa (1948–1958). In 1958 he became professor of neurology and psychology at Iowa and established a neuropsychological laboratory in the Department of Neurology of the University of Iowa Hospitals. He retired in 1978, but continued to be active in research.

Benton's teaching and research covered a variety of aspects of clinical neuropsychology including hemispheric cerebral dominance, brain injury in childhood, aphasia, perceptual disabilities, and the development of diagnostic tests. His laboratory attracted many students and became internationally known for its contributions, which included over 200 research papers and a number of monographs authored by Benton and his coworkers.

Benton served as president of the American Orthopsychiatric Association (1964–1965), president of the International Neuropsychological Society (1970–1972), and secretary general of the Research Group on Aphasia of the World Federation of Neurology (1972–1978). He received the Distinguished Professional Contribution Award of the American Psychological Association in 1978, and the Outstanding Scientific

Achievement Award of the International Neuropsychological Society in 1981. Upon his retirement, the laboratory which he had established was designated the Benton Laboratory of Neuropsychology of the University of Iowa Hospitals.

BENUSSI, VITTORIO (1878–1927)

Benussi spent his most productive years at the University of Graz in Austria between 1902 and the outbreak of World War I in 1914. He became a follower of the Act school of psychology, which had been started by Franz Brentano in opposition to the psychology of content fostered by Wilhelm Wundt. However, Benussi was more of an experimentalist and less of a systematic psychologist. His experiments on space perception resulted in the conclusion that perception could be interpreted as a mental act. He also experimented on the perception of time, weight, and touch, and on optical illusions.

Although a psychologist of the Act school, he fostered the idea of an element of form-quality in perception. His influence was also apparent in Gestalt psychology, which arose in Germany around 1913 and at once launched the study of apparent visual movement. The original phi phenomenon, already identified, was the movement of one straight line to another, when the two were presented successively with a time difference of about $\frac{1}{15}$ of a second; one line appeared to move to the next. Benussi identified another kind of apparent movement known as "bow movement," where the movement did not follow a straight line from the first to the second presentation of the stimulus. When an obstructing stimulus was presented between the first and second, the apparent movement curved around the obstruction, taking the form of a bow.

R. W. Lundin

BERKELEY, GEORGE (1685–1753)

Berkeley spent 13 years as a student and teacher at Trinity College in Dublin. He went to England in 1713 and for the next 15 years lived in England and on the continent. In 1728 he went to America, but returned to Ireland when funding for his missionary efforts in the New World failed. He was Bishop of Cloyne for the last 20 years of his life.

Berkeley's teachings were in opposition to the world view of Descartes, Newtonian physics, and John Locke, which Berkeley identified as materialism with little room for man and spiritual values. Locke took the position that the mind can have no knowledge of anything except in experience through sensory perception. Berkeley accepted this doctrine that the origin and test of all knowledge lies in experience, but whereas for Locke the result of such thought was a knowledge of the external world of matter, for Berkeley it was a knowledge of ideas. God takes the place of matter as the cause of sense perception and as the ultimate explanation for an orderly world.

The sum of Berkeley's philosophy is stated: "to be is to be perceived." Three principles were involved in the philosophy: (1) what we perceive is real, (2) what we perceive are ideas, and (3) the ability to have ideas presupposes the mind as the idea maker, so that mind becomes the sole substance of reality. All is contained as part of God's essence and being.

Berkeley had identified the major beliefs of his system by age 23. By age 28 he had published three volumes of philosophy stating his position: the most systematic of them being *a treatise concerning the principles of human knowledge* (1710). In his later years Berkeley's philosophy changed toward a Platonic idealism described in his last book, *Siris: A chain of philosophical reflections.* His philosophy was brought to America when Samuel Johnson described it in his *Elementa philosophica*, the first American textbook of philosophy, published by Benjamin Franklin in 1752.

N. A. HAYNIE

BERLYNE, DANIEL E. (1924–1976)

Berlyne received the B.A. from Cambridge, the M.A. and Ph.D. (1953) from Yale. He taught at St. Andrews University and the University of Aberdeen in Scotland, the University of California at Berkeley, and the University of Toronto from 1962 until his death. His most important books include *Conflict, arousal and curiosity, Structure and direction in thinking,* and *Aesthetics and psychobiology.* His main contributions to psychology were in the areas of motivation and arousal, thinking and psychological aesthetics, and especially visual art. Throughout his career he was an active experimenter and theoretian in these areas.

According to his theory, structures involved in arousal or de-arousal involve substances in the blood such as hormones, the sense organs and sensory nerves to the reticular formation in the brain, and fibers that convey excitations to centers in the brain stem from the cerebral cortex. The kinds of factors that raise arousal include changes in the nervous system such as alterations between sleep and waking, and seasonal variations. Arousal is raised during states of high drive and emotion, as well as during intellectual effort and muscular activity. Of particular concern to Berlyne is aesthetic arousal, which can be raised through properties of stimulus patterns such as novelty, the capacity to provoke surprise, complexity, ambiguity, and puzzling. He also wrote about *arousal potential,* referring to the strength of stimulus patterns, and the degree to which they can alert the organism or counter conflicting stimuli.

In investigating novelty in sensory experience, Berlyne found that it declines gradually with the repetition of the stimulus and with the time between presentations. What is reported to be most novel is a function of how much a stimulus differs from what has just been experienced.

In investigating the relationship between play and art, he noted that frequently both are pleasurable because the immediate internal effects on the nervous system are rewarding. The difference between the two is that play is frivolous and unproductive, while art is revered and credited as human accomplishment. Further, the pleasure of play is transitory, while that of art may be permanent.

R. W. LUNDIN

BERNARD, CLAUDE (1813–1878)

France's greatest physiologist, Bernard, returned frequently to Rhone throughout his celebrated life. His early education was that of the village; it inclined him to literature, not science, despite an apprenticeship to a local apothecary. He went to Paris to seek his career, began a medical career in order to support himself, and soon blossomed as a physiologist.

Bernard completed the M.D. under François Magendie in 1843. While Magendie's assistant, he began his work in digestion and neurophysiology. He failed to gain an academic appointment in 1844, but then married into a wealthy family and continued work on his own. He finally gained an appointment, again under Magendie, in 1847 at the Collége de France, and inherited Magendie's chair in 1852. Bernard was the first vice-president of the Société de Biologie in 1848 and completed a doctorate in science at the Sorbonne in 1853. A full professor at the Collége de France in 1855, he went on to become the first holder of the chair in experimental physiology at the Sorbonne. He took a chair in general physiology and established a modern laboratory at the Museum of Natural History in 1868. His later life was filled with honors, culminating in the first state funeral ever given to a scientist in France.

Bernard studied two major areas of physiology—digestion and neural activity—with the underlying goal of finding general principles common to all animals rather than isolated processes. In retrospect, both are of importance to psychology. His massive and inspired work on carbohydrate digestion and sugar balance in the blood is of interest, partly because it guided Ivan Pavlov into his work on digestion and on to conditioned reflexes first observed in the digestive process. It also contributed to our understanding of homeostasis. His neural work included demonstration of the neural control of sugar production, demonstration of the role of the vagus nerve, and the discovery of vasoconstricting and dilating neurons. Of most importance to psychology is his concept of antagonistic innervation, by which organs may respond to both stimulation and inhibition, or to a balance between the two, rather than only to stimulation. This concept, extended to neural centers, is important to our present understanding of control of the body by the central nervous system, and is in its own right important to homeostasis.

T. KEITH-LUCAS

BERNE, ERIC L. (1910–1970)

Berne received the M.D. from McGill University in 1935. After a psychiatric residency at Yale, he was on the staff of Mount Zion Hospital in New York and undertook training at the New York Psychoanalytic Institute. After almost 10 years of affiliation with the San Francisco Psychoanalytic Institute, he parted company "on friendly terms" with the Freudian movement and five years later published his *Transactional analysis in psychotherapy* (1961). Most of his time was devoted to private clinical practice. Although intended for a professional audience, his book *Games people play* (1964) became a best seller.

Transactional analysis (TA) is a system of group therapy that takes its name from analyzing interactions between individuals in terms of three ego states in each of us: the child (feelings and desires up to age 6), the parent (parental values and rules), and the adult (an approach to the world based upon previous observations of what occurs). Transactions that are parallel (my child to your parent and vice versa) can last almost indefinitely, but a response that is not parallel usually ends the conversation (my child to your parent, answered by your adult to my adult). Berne denied the obvious parallel with Freud's id, superego, and ego, claiming that his triad were all ego functions.

Underlying everything is the script theory (similar to Adler's lifestyle): early in life each person fashions a life script that he carries out, usually unknowingly. One of four life positions is assumed, combinations of I'm (not) O.K. and you're (not) O.K. To play out the life script and also obtain stroking (time and attention of others), one engages in games. A maladaptive individual might play "kick me" with the payoff of depression and confirmation that "I'm not O.K., you're O.K."

Group therapy, for Berne, should be maintained on the adult-to-adult level. He was known for having one group observe a second group session and then join them to make comments and observations; the positions were then reversed. The tone of Berne's approach is perhaps best summed up in the conditions required of an alcoholic before being accepted for therapy: the alcoholic must give up alcohol and take Antabuse regularly as proof of sincerity. The elimination of alcohol consumption, however, is *not* the cure: cure occurs only when the individual has restructured sufficiently so as to resume social drinking without the alcoholic life script.

The *Transactional Analysis Journal* founded by Berne continues, as does the International Transactional Analysis Association which certifies expertise in TA.

C. S. PEYSER

BERNHEIM, HIPPOLYTE (1840–1919)

Bernheim was a well-known neurologist who practiced medicine in Nancy, France. He was converted to the use of hypnosis by A. A.

Liébeault when the latter "cured" a patient suffering from sciatica after Bernheim had failed (1882). Eventually, both Bernheim and Liébeault followed Braid's theory that hypnosis was really nothing more than suggestion. He published several papers on the subject in 1884. Together, Bernheim and Liébeault founded a clinic which became known as the Nancy School. This developed in opposition to a school founded in Paris by Jean M. Charcot, who held that hypnosis was really a hysterical symptom which had its foundation in a weak nervous system.

Bernheim and Liébeault were convinced that hypnosis as a therapeutic device could be used on persons who were not hysterical. However, the fact that hypnosis was successful gave Bernheim some qualms, since he realized that the will of man was not always free. This meant that when a person was put under hypnosis, new attitudes and beliefs, when suggested, could be accepted uncritically by the patient, who would behave accordingly.

The clinic at Nancy became a rival with Charcot's in Paris. Although the two schools seemed theoretically far apart, both used hypnosis primarily to treat neurotic patients.

R. W. LUNDIN

BERNSHTEIN, NIKOLAI (1896–1966)

Starting his career in the 1920s in the Institute of Work in Moscow, where he studied human body movements, Bernshtein gradually developed an antimechanistic psychophysiological theory that emphasized the *active* rather than the *reactive* nature of human behavior. In 1935, a decade before the "discovery" of cybernetics by Norbert Wiener, Bernshtein suggested the concept of a feedback mechanism for the interpretation of voluntary movements. Years of research resulted in the publication of *O postroenii dvizhenij* (The formation of movements, 1947), which presented a comprehensive analysis of the development of voluntary movements and acquisition of sensory-motor skills.

Bernshtein uncompromisingly discouraged attempts to make conditional reflexes the basis for the study of human behavior. He thoroughly examined the methodological premises of the Pavlovian doctrine and qualified it as out-of-date. His challenge to the Pavlovian School was enhanced by the practicality of his ideas, which were successfully implemented in the design of prosthetic appliances, in sports psychology, and in the training of Soviet astronauts. In the late 1940s he was harshly criticized by Pavlovians and prevented from publishing.

A full recognition came to him only in the 1960s. His works of that period centered on a study of probabilistic mechanisms of the anticipation of events and formation of the "image of the future." This "image," which is a psychological rather than a physiological concept, determines the strategy of behavior and exercises an executive control over elementary behavioral acts.

A. KOZULIN

BERNSTEIN, JULIUS (1839–1917)

Bernstein received the M.D. degree from the University of Berlin in 1862. During the course of his career he was a professor at the University of Heidelberg, the University of Berlin, and the University of Halle, the latter from 1872 to 1917.

By measuring the polarization of nerves, he showed that the nerve impulse is a "wave of negativity." In 1902 he helped to establish the membrane theory of conduction when the wave of negativity became the "wave of depolarization."

In 1871 he stated the projection theory of nerve conduction that postulated a point-to-point correspondence between the receptors stimulated and the ganglion cells in the brain center on which stimulation

from the receptors is projected. This theory went a long way toward explaining binocular vision, blind areas in brain injury, the pnenomena of cutaneous two-point threshold, the error of localization, and other brain phenomena. Since his time there has been little improvement on Bernstein's idea. He also was the author of several books on neurophysiology and electrobiology.

R. W. LUNDIN

BERRIDGE, KENT C. (1957–   )

Berridge received the B.S. with honors in psychology from the University of California at Davis, and the M.A. and Ph.D. (1983) in psychology from the University of Pennsylvania. Following this, he spent 2 yr as a postdoctoral research fellow at Dalhousie University in Nova Scotia, Canada.

Berridge was appointed assistant professor of psychology at the University of Michigan in 1985. He was promoted to associate professor in 1990.

Berridge's research and teaching has concerned primarily physiological and comparative psychology. His research interests have ranged from basic motivation and emotion, in which he has focused on brain mechanisms of pleasure and of appetite, to the neural substrates of instinctive behavioral patterns, to the causation of movement and thought disorders. Research honors have included an early career award from the American Psychological Association and a James McKeen Cattell Foundation award. Teaching honors include an award from the University of Michigan, and a Master Lecturer award from the Michigan Psychological Association.

BERTALANFFY, LUDWIG VON (1901–1972)

Bertalanffy is generally regarded as the father of general systems theory. He began his career in the 1930s as a professor of biology at the University of Vienna. In 1948 he emigrated to Canada, where he was a professor of biology at the University of Ottawa until 1955, at which time he moved to the United States, where he worked at Mt. Sinai Hospital in Los Angeles (1955–1959) and at the Menninger Foundation (1959–1961). He returned to Canada in 1961, accepting an appointment at the University of Alberta's Center for Advanced Study in Theoretical Psychology and its Department of Zoology. He remained in Alberta until retirement in 1969, at which time he went to the State University of Buffalo, remaining there until his death in 1972.

His major works include *General systems theory, Modern theories of development* and *Problems of life* .

J. R. ROYCE

BESSEL, FREDRICH WILHELM (1784–1846)

As a German scientist, Bessel was trained in astronomy. In 1804 he calculated the orbit of Halley's comet from observations made in 1607 by Thomas Harriot. He then became the chief astronomer at Königberg observatory, a new structure constructed under his supervision. Every student of the history of psychology knows that Maskelyne had dismissed D. Kinnebrook for his inaccuracy in reporting the movement of stars across the meridian of a telescope because Kinnebrook's observations were too slow. This suggested to Bissel that there was a personal error in observation, i.e., there tended to be individual differences in people's reports. By making numerous observations with a variety of individuals, Bissel was able to develop the "personal equation" and note the fact of its individual variability.

In further study he found for himself that his error was less when using a clock beating every half-second. This allowed astronomers to establish their own "personal equation" and to correct for them. These studies were the beginnings of the realization that individual differences existed in all forms of behavior.

R. W. LUNDIN

BETTELHEIM, BRUNO (1903–1990)

Bettelheim received the Ph.D. at the University of Vienna, the same year the Nazis invaded Austria. He was not able to escape from Austria and was sent to prison and then the concentration camps of Buchenwald and Dachau. He eventually came to the United States and began a long association with the University of Chicago. For 34 yr he directed the university's Orthogenic School, a residential treatment center for children with emotional problems. He was particularly concerned with autistic and psychotic children. Here he was able to gather data for his theories, which tended to be psychoanalytic in opposition to the more biological approaches to childhood psychoses. He is well known for the case of "Joey, the Mechanical Boy." In it he proposed that the boy's autistic behavior was the result of parental aloofness and neglect.

He authored many books, including *Dialogues with mothers, Children of the dream, The uses of Enchantment: The meaning and importance of fairy tales,* and *Love is not enough.* His last book, *Good enough parents,* was published in 1982. From these titles one can discern his interest in children and parenting.

R. W. LUNDIN

BEVAN, WILLIAM (1922–   )

Bevan received the A.B. degree from Franklin and Marshall College with honors in psychology and the M.A. degree from Duke University. He entered the U.S. Navy in 1944. He was awarded the Ph.D. in psychology by Duke University in 1948. He then joined the faculty of Emory University in the fall of 1948 where he remained until 1959. During 1952 to 1953, he was a Fulbright scholar at the University of Oslo, Norway. In 1959, he moved to Kansas State University as chairman of the psychology department. After 3 yr as chairman, he became Dean of Arts and Science and later was made Vice President for Academic Affairs. Following a year as a fellow at the Center for Advanced Study in the Behavioral Sciences, he moved to Johns Hopkins University as vice president and provost, in 1966, and professor of psychology. In 1970 on leave from Hopkins, he accepted an appointment as executive officer of the American Association for the Advancement of Science and publisher of *Science* magazine. In 1974 he was appointed the William Preston Few Professor of psychology at Duke University, an appointment he held until retirement. He was the founding director of the Duke Round Table on Science and Public Affairs. He served as provost of Duke University from 1979 to 1982. He then became director of the Health Program at the John D. and Catherine T. MacArthur Foundation until he retired in September 1991.

Bevan is the author of some 180 papers and invited chapters in psychology, and edited with Harry Helson, *Contemporary approaches to psychology.* He is a member of Phi Beta Kappa, Sigma Xi, the Institute of Medicine of the National Academy of Sciences, and the Society of Experimental Psychologists. He holds honorary doctoral degrees from Duke University, Emory University, Florida Atlantic University, Franklin and Marshall College, Kansas State University, the University of Maryland, and Southern Illinois University. In 1989, he received the APA award for Contributions to Psychology in the Public Interest and, in 1991, the APF Gold Medal Award for Life Contribution by a Psychologist in the Public Interest.

BICHAT, MARIE-FRANCOIS XAVIER (1771–1802)

Bichat studied anatomy and surgery at Lyon, France. The disturbances of the French Revolution drove him to Paris in 1793. He is best known for developing a doctrine of tissue as the building blocks of anatomical organs. He discovered that tissues were integrated into organs: the nervous system, muscles, stomach, and brain. He showed that every part of the human body was composed of a few types of tissue and thus founded the science of histology.

In his studies of tissue, Bichat came in contact with neuropathology and thus with psychopathology, viewing mental disease in terms of abnormalities of anatomical factors and histological structures. With these discoveries "physiological psychology" was beginning to take shape.

R. W. LUNDIN

BIESHEUVEL, SIMON (1908–   )

Biesheuvel's parents moved to Belgium, then back to Holland, then to Brazil and back to Belgium again, settling eventually in South Africa in 1922. He attended school in all these countries, obtained the M.A. in psychology at the University of Cape Town and the Ph.D. at Edinburgh University in 1933 under James Drever. He was a lecturer in psychology at the Universities of Stellenbosch and the Witwatersrand in South Africa, and served in the South African Air Force for five years as officer commanding the Aptitude Test Section and consultant on the psychological care of air crews. Demobilized, he was appointed the first director of the newly formed National Institute for Personnel Research. After 17 years in this post, he joined the S. A. Breweries Group as personnel director. In 1973 he was appointed director of the Graduate School of Business Administration of the University of the Witwatersrand. He was named emeritus professor and an honorable research fellow on retirement.

His major research interests have included cross-cultural psychology, individual differences, and personnel psychology. His first book, *African intelligence* (1943), broke new ground in linking the nature-nurture controversy on individual differences with the cross-cultural study of group differences. Among his more significant contributions are the following: *Objectives and methods of African psychological research; Race, culture and personality; The development of personality in African cultures;* "African culture patterns and the learning of abilities and skills"; *Methods for the measurement of psychological performance;* a chapter on South Africa in *Psychology around the world to-day;* "The development of psychomotor skills: Cross-cultural and occupational implications".

BIJOU, SIDNEY W. (1908–   )

Bijou received the B.S. from the University of Florida, the M.S. in psychology from Columbia University, and the Ph.D. (1941) in psychology from the University of Iowa. He pursued postdoctoral study (1961) at Harvard University on a NIMH Senior Fellowship.

He was a research psychologist at the Wayne County Training School, Northville, Michigan, for 2 yr. In 1946, he was appointed assistant professor of psychology and director of clinical training at Indiana University. From 1948 he was director of the Institute of Child Development and associate professor (then professor) of psychology at the University of Washington. In 1965 he was appointed director of the Child Research Laboratory and professor of psychology at the Institute of Research in Exceptional Children at the University of Illinois, Champaign-Urbana. In 1975 he became professor emeritus of the University of Illinois and adjunct professor of psychology and special education and rehabilitation at the University of Arizona.

Bijou was founding editor of the *Journal of Experimental Child Psychology* and authored or coauthored more than 130 journal articles. Furthermore, he edited, authored, and coauthored 13 books. He wrote *Child development: The basic stage of early childhood* and coauthored (with Donald M. Baer) *Behavior analysis of child development* and *Child development: The basic stage of infancy*.

Bijou was president of the APA Division of Child Development as well as the Association of Behavior Analysis. Honors received include the G. Stanley Hall Award in Developmental Psychology (APA), the Edgar Doll Award in Mental Retardation (APA), the Don Hake Memorial Award in Basic and Applied Behavior Analysis (APA), and research awards from the American Association on Mental Deficiency, the American Academy of Mental Retardation, and the National Association of Retarded Citizens.

Bijou's achievements include his research and writings on the application of behavior principles to the development of normal and handicapped children, lecturing on a Fulbright-Hayes Fellowship in a number of foreign countries.

computed, regardless of his actual chronological age. Three degrees of mental retardation were identified: idiot (lowest), imbecile, and moron.

The last of Binet's revisions appeared in 1911, the year of his death. He added new tests, and discarded old ones which he thought depended too much on school information. He also designated a given number of tests for a particular year, so mental age could be expressed in months. If there were six tests at a particular age level, each test passed could be given a score of two months at that level. Thus all the tests passed, regardless of the years at which they were passed, could be added together to give a total mental age.

Binet never developed the concept of the I.Q. or intelligence quotient. This was developed by a German psychologist, William Stern. MA (mental age) divided by the actual chronological age (CA) times 100 equaled the I.Q.

$$\frac{MA}{CA} \times 100 = I.Q.$$

R. W. LUNDIN

BINET, ALFRED (1857–1911)

Binet took his first degree in law at Paris. While in Paris he became acquainted with Jean Charcot and studied hypnosis under him. His interests changed to the natural sciences, in which he received his second degree. He became particularly interested in the higher mental processes of humans.

Binet also became interested in abnormal psychology and wrote *The alterations of personality* and *Suggestability*. In addition, he became concerned about the thinking processes in children and drew much of his data by studying his daughters. He gave them problems to solve and asked them to report to him the steps they went through in the process. All this led to his concept of "intelligence." He became aware that considerable individual differences existed in children. He realized that there were those who were slow, whom he identified as "feeble-minded." He was sharply critical of the medical profession for considering mental deficiency a disease.

He was aware of the work of Ebbinghaus on memory and forgetting, as well as the research on sensory, perceptual, and motor measures which included reaction time, sensory acuity, and the span of attention. In association with Victor Henri he discovered that there were different kinds of memory: visual memory, memory for numbers, musical memory, and memory for sentences. Together they developed tests to measure these different types of memory.

All these studies set the stage for the development of a scale of intelligence. In 1904 the Minister of Public Instruction appointed a committee to recommend what should be done about the education of subnormal children in the schools of Paris. The decision to place them in special schools depended on the development of some means of identifying them. Binet was called upon to develop a test which became the first scale for the measurement of intelligence. In 1905 this test appeared as a result of the collaboration of Binet and Theodore Simon. The scale consisted of a series of tasks of increasing difficulty. In 1908 the test was revised and the individual tasks were arranged, not only according to difficulty, but also according to the age at which the average child could complete them.

In the "tryouts" of the tests these tasks were arranged and rearranged so as to be appropriate for various age levels. If a test was too easy at the eight-year level, for example, then it was placed at an earlier level, say at seven years. The general rule was that if 60–90% of the children passed it at a given level, that level was appropriate for the test. Thus the mentally retarded child who performed appreciably below the norm for his age was considered a deviant from the norm and could be identified. In this way the *mental age* of a child could be

BINGHAM, WALTER V. (1880–1952)

A pioneer in applied psychology, Bingham got his start in experimental psychology, receiving the Ph.D. at the University of Chicago under James R. Angell. He held teaching positions at Teacher's College of Columbia University, Dartmouth University, and Carnegie Institute of Technology. In 1924 he became director of the Personnel Research Federation, where for many years he carried on independent research and served as a consultant in industrial psychology.

During World War I Bingham served as executive secretary of the committee on classification of personnel in the U.S. Army, and later in the war served as lieutenant colonel in the Personnel Branch of the Army General Staff. He was one of a small group that developed intelligence testing for the Army, and with Walter Dill Scott worked on the classification of Army personnel. One of the founders of the Psychological Corporation in 1921, he served as director throughout his life.

From 1940 to 1947 Bingham was chief psychologist of the Adjutant General's Office of the War Department, serving as consultant or adviser to the Surgeon General, the Army General Staff, and the Secretary of Defense.

Bingham carried out editorial responsibilities for several journals and was the author of many books. His *Aptitudes and aptitude testing* (1937/1942) is a classic in the field.

P. E. LICHTENSTEIN

BINSWANGER, LUDWIG (1881–1966)

Binswanger took his medical degree at the University of Zurich in 1907. He first applied existential ideas to treating disordered personalities in what he called "existential analysis." This therapy had as its aim the reconstruction of the inner world of experience for those mentally disturbed.

Like other existential psychologists, Binswanger rejected positivism, determinism, and materialism. In his view, we are completely responsible for our own existence, free to decide what we can and cannot do. Being in the world is the whole of our existence. We cannot live apart from the world or exist in a world apart from ourselves. It is possible, however, for us to go beyond the world, often in a transcendental way. This means that we can realize the full possibilities of our existence. Our aim in being is an authentic existence. When we allow others to dominate us or yield to environmental forces, our existence becomes inauthentic.

Binswanger wrote of many modes of existence. In a singular mode one lives only for oneself. A dual mode can be achieved by two people in love. A mode of anonymity refers to a person who gets lost in a crowd.

Becoming is also important for human development. This means becoming something more than what one is at the moment. As existence changes, there is always the possibility of becoming something more or better. A person who refuses to become will remain static. From a psychiatric point of view, people who develop neurotic or psychotic tendencies have refused to grow or become.

R. W. LUNDIN

BLAKE, ROBERT R. (1918–   )

A pioneer in applying behavioral science research on management and organization development, Blake received the Ph.D. in 1947 from the University of Texas, where he later served as professor of psychology. A Fulbright scholar in 1949–1950, Blake subsequently became a lecturer at the University of Reading in England, an honorary clinical psychologist at the Tavistock Clinic in London, and a lecturer and research associate at Harvard University.

Blake is probably best known for his work in the area of leadership. In 1964 he and Jane Srygley Mouton coauthored *The managerial Grid*. The Grid provides a research-based conceptual framework for comparing various leadership styles and determining their effectiveness in generating productivity, creativity, motivation, and satisfaction. Blake also guided the first organization development effort in one of the largest factories of a major American corporation, introducing a process designed to enable organizations to escape the constraints of history by viewing sound alternatives to outmoded traditions, precedents, and past practices.

Blake has also studied and provided insight into group and intergroup dynamics, concentrating particularly on the organizational impact of group norms and the resolution of intergroup conflict. His 36 books as well as numerous articles have contributed to understanding human effectiveness in organizational settings.

BLAU, THEODORE H. (1928–   )

Blau received the B.A., M.A., and doctorate from Pennsylvania State University under Robert Bernreuter, Bruce V. Moore, and William U. Synder. Blau began his career in psychology as an intern at the Elmira Penitentiary, under the influence and tutelage of Raymond J. Corsini. He followed his postdoctoral training with entry into independent practice in 1953. This was a fairly unacceptable venture for well-trained psychologists in those days, but Blau demonstrated that the community is ready and anxious to welcome well-trained professional psychologists. His first book, *Private practice in clinical psychology* was made a part of the traditional Appleton-Century-Crofts Century Series in Psychology in 1959.

Blau has always represented independent clinical practice within the structure of the American Psychological Association. Serving twice as chair of the Board of Professional Affairs, he served over 20 years on the APA Counsel of Representatives, representing divisions of Clinical Psychology, Consulting Psychology, and Psychotherapy as well as the Division of Childhood and Youth. In 1977 Blau served as the 85th president of the American Psychological Association, the first independent practitioner so honored.

Blau's research work is focused on the nature and effects of mixed cerebral dominance. Author of the Torque Test, Blau proposed a neuropsychological/social influence theory of schizophrenia first published in 1977. In more recent years Blau has devoted his attention to psychology and the law; his most recent work is *The psychologist as expert witness*.

Blau has served extensively as consultant (U.S. Army Combat Arms, U.S. Army Traddoc, the State Department, U.S. Army INSCOM, the Surgeon General of the U.S. Army, the Surgeon General of the United States Air Force, the Riot Prosecution Office of the State of New Mexico, the U.S. Navy Scientists In The Sea Project, and the State of Florida HRS Human Rights Advocacy Committee). As national consultant to the Surgeon General of the U.S. Air Force, Blau held the equivalent rank of brigadier general.

BLEULER, EUGEN (1857–1939)

Paul Eugen Bleuler spent most of his career in Zurich at the psychiatric hospital of the university. He received his M.D. from Bern and studied briefly with Charcot at Salpêtrière. He encouraged his assistant Jung to apply Freud's theories to the hospital patients. Piaget was another colleague. Some consider his writings to anticipate the existential movement, with a direct link through his student Binswanger.

Bleuler's classic 1908 paper *Dementia praecox* was based on 647 cases observed over an eight-year period. He proposed the name schizophrenia because the dementia was not uniform but occurred only at certain times in relation to certain types of questions. His 1911 *Dementia praecox: Or the group of schizophrenias* continued his careful analysis, emphasizing that the disorder was not due to brain damage with its inevitable deterioration, but rather that the prognosis was related to the extent of the symptoms. Carefully distinguishing between primary and adjunctive symptoms, he introduced concepts such as neologism, word salad, and negative speech into the descriptive vocabulary. Bleuler added the category of simple schizophrenia to Kraepelin's three (hebephrenic, paranoid, catatonic). His 1916 *Textbook of psychiatry* had added two additional fundamental concepts to the analysis of schizophrenia: autism, meaning loss of contact with reality, and ambivalence, designating the concurrent existence, at the intellectual, emotional, or volitional level, of mutually exclusive contradictions.

An excellent practicing psychiatrist, Bleuler postulated that underlying schizophrenia was a loosening of association. He also identified neurasthenia as a preschizophrenic symptom rather than a disorder in its own right, and similarly identified hypochondriasis as a mask for severe mental illness—usually schizophrenia, some types of depression, or early organic psychosis.

C. S. PEYSER

BLONSKII, PAVEL (1884–1941)

Blonskii, who was one of the founding fathers of Soviet psychology, started before the Revolution as a promising young philosopher. He received the Ph.D. in 1913 from Moscow University, where he studied philosophy and psychology under G. Chelpanov. Immediately after the Revolution he broke ranks with the pre-Revolutionary academic establishment and held a number of administrative positions in public education. In 1920 he published *Reforma Nauki* (The reform of science), an impassioned critique of "bourgeois" philosophy, psychology, and education. In his positive program Blonskii espoused biological reductionism and technocratic sociocentrism. "Psychology as a behavioral science is a biological science. . . . The human being is a homo *technicus* and homo *socialis*" (*The reform of science*, p. 31).

The educational psychology of Blonskii mostly echoed the ideas of John Dewey. Blonskii saw the necessity of replacing the scholastic methods of instruction by those responding to the reality of industrialized society. He suggested making industrial work the cornerstone of the new education. The new school should also be child-oriented, democratic, and concerned with concrete problems of everyday life. Blonskii's educational progressivism hardly fit the reality of Soviet life. He confessed later that he wrote *Trudovaja Shkola* (*Die Arbeitschule*, the working school), as if the classless society of the future were already a reality. Blonskii's other initiatives such as mental testing became victims of the state decree of 1936 abolishing any kind of psychological testing in the U.S.S.R.

A. KOZULIN

BOAS, FRANZ (1858–1942)

During 1877–1881 Boas studied at Heidelberg, Bonn, and Kiel. He taught at Clark University (1882–1892), then in 1899 was appointed professor of anthropology at Columbia University, and served as curator of New York City's Museum of Natural History (1901–1905).

He is considered one of the most eminent anthropologists of the late nineteenth and early twentieth centuries. At the time Boas was beginning his studies, anthropology was a new area of investigation, but Boas had an earnest desire to make it a rigorous and exact science. He expected its data to be quantitative.

In many of his investigations Boas noted that parallel development in widely separated areas could occur, and that such might owe their similarities to the operation of identical psychological processes. In investigating language development he noted that some phonetic, morphological, and classification features must owe their similarities to similar psychological causes.

He was a prime contributor to the emergence of the culture concept, stressing the weight of social traditions as molding forces in human behavior. Along with his interest in the language of primitive peoples, he also considered folklore to be of great importance, observing that nothing seemed to travel as rapidly as fanciful tales. He noted obvious connections between the mythology of northeast Asia and that of the peoples of the northeast coastal areas of North America. Myths also provided a useful tool for investigating the language and understanding the psychology of a particular group of people. Art was the third medium that Boas used to demonstrate that human behavior is highly variable and has complex and historic social and psychological roots.

Physical anthropology was the fourth way of demonstrating the scientific nature of anthropological measurement. Boas studied almost 18,000 immigrants to New York. This study indicated that physical variations could change with the environment.

Boas was largely responsible for the conduct of the Jesup North Pacific Expedition of 1897–1900. This sought answers to cultural relations linking Siberian and Northwest coastal peoples of North America. He was also the first to initiate growth studies in North America and the first to chart standardized heights and weights of American children according to chronological age. He also pointed out the close correlation between physical and mental development.

R. W. LUNDIN

BODER, DAVID PABLO (1886–1961)

Boder studied with Wilhelm Wundt and then with Vladimir Bekhterev; he graduated from the Psycho-Neurological Institute at St. Petersburg in 1917. After the Russian Revolution, Boder traveled to Mexico where he was in charge of psychological research in penal institutions. His interest in intelligence testing led him to publish the first adaptation of the Stanford-Binet scale for Mexico.

Boder arrived in the United States in 1926 and began teaching at Lewis Institute in Chicago and working toward the Ph.D. in psychology from Northwestern University (1934). While at Lewis, he realized a long-standing dream with the establishment of a psychological museum

in 1937. It was the first museum in the United States devoted to the science of psychology, and it included displays, interactive exhibits, and live lectures and demonstrations, many of them conducted by Boder. His desire was to portray psychology as a science concerned with benefiting humankind.

The museum was never well funded and never successful. It closed in 1957, although Boder had largely withdrawn from its functioning by 1946, when he went to Europe to interview concentration camp survivors. The wire-spool recorder had been recently invented and Boder carried one with him to Europe for his interviews, an action that places him among the forefront of oral historians. Eight of his interviews were published in his book, *I did not interview the dead.* He continued his oral history work with interviews of survivors of the Kansas City flood of 1951. That work was the beginning of a research program to investigate the psychology of disaster sufferers. He was involved with that work at UCLA when he died in 1961.

LUDY T. BENJAMIN

BOLLES, ROBERT C. (1928–   )

Bolles was an undergraduate at Stanford and did graduate work at the University of California, Berkeley, getting the Ph.D. there in 1956. He has taught at Princeton and Hollins College, but returned to the West in 1966 to teach at University of Washington.

Bolles' early research ranged over different areas of animal motivation, eating, drinking, exploration, general activity, and circadian cycles. He then focused on avoidance behavior. In attempting to account for why animals learn some avoidance responses much more easily than others, he developed the concept of species-specific defense reactions, suggesting a more naturalistic alternative to the conventional two-factor theory of avoidance learning. During the 1970s his research moved toward classical conditioning paradigms, and his thinking moved increasingly in a naturalistic, evolutionary direction. He has also become increasingly cognitive in outlook, preferring an expectancy view of animal behavior to the traditional S-R reinforcement orientation. This outlook is reflected in his *Learning theory*.

Bolles tends to regard his view of animal behavior as functionalistic, insisting that laboratory results on learning and conditioning be understood and interpreted in the broader context of how animals solve their problems in nature. Motivation of behavior should be understood in terms of how motivational systems help animals solve their biological problems, rather than in mechanistic or physiological terms.

BONNET, CHARLES (1720–1793)

Bonnet was a Swiss naturalist and philosopher. In 1745 he was admitted as a fellow in the Royal Society. In his researches on the anatomy of plants, he suggested they possessed the same powers of sensation and discrimination as animals.

With failing eyesight he turned to study philosophy and psychology. In 1754 he published his *Essay on psychology.* In it, he expanded his views on the physiology of mental activity.

In general, Bonnet followed the ideas of Etienne Condillac, with some differences. Both had used the analogy of the statue. Condillac had avoided physiology but Bonnet wrote of nervous fluids and agitation of the nerve fibers. Historians of psychology suggest he anticipated the doctrine of the "specific energies of nerves." Bonnet suggested that every sense is probably limited to different fibers.

His other difference with Condillac had to do with the activity of the soul. Condillac had suggested the idea of the *tabula rasa*, taken up by John Locke. Bonnet considered the soul to be more active and not merely the recipient of experience. In both cases, they anticipated the ideas of French materialism and British empiricism.

R. W. LUNDIN

BORGATTA, EDGAR F. (1924–   )

Borgatta is a social psychologist active in both sociology and psychology. After World War II he moved from natural sciences to complete the Ph.D. in sociology at New York University with extensive training in psychology, economics (statistics), and mathematics.

Having contact with J. L. Moreno, his early research focused on role-playing techniques and sociometric analysis. At Harvard his research focused on the formal properties of small groups and the structure of interaction processes, as well as scaling and statistical analysis, introducing analytic procedures from other disciplines. He continued to pursue these interests subsequently at New York University, Russell Sage Foundation, and Cornell University. He also developed a number of tests.

During the 1960s, as Brittingham professor at the University of Wisconsin, he concentrated on the study of values (including student movements), factorial ecology of cities, and evaluation research. During this period, with David Fanshel he also developed rating procedures for evaluating child behavior. After accepting a distinguished professorship at Queens College (CUNY), he focused particularly on methodology in research, working at the CUNY Graduate School during the 1970s.

Borgatta has published on a wide variety of topics. He initiated the Sociological Methodology book series for the American Sociological Association, edited journals such as *Group Psychotherapy and Sociometry,* and was founding coeditor of the journals *Sociological Methods and Research* and *Research on Aging.* In addition, he has written, edited, or collaborated on numerous works, including *Small groups* (with Hare & Bales), *Sociological theory, Social psychology, Handbook of personality theory and research,* and *Aging and society.*

BORING, EDWARD G. (1886–1968)

Boring studied psychology at Cornell University under E. B. Titchener, and received the doctorate in 1914. He went to Clark University in 1919, but moved to Harvard in 1922 and remained there for the rest of his career as a general experimental psychologist. He influenced many generations of students through his teaching of the introductory course in psychology at Harvard.

Although Boring accomplished some classical research on his own, most of his publications were theoretical. He served as editor of *American Journal of Psychology* from 1920 until his death, writing many papers and editorials. Boring is most famous for his histories of psychology. His *History of experimental psychology* was first published in 1929; the 1950 edition, a widely accepted classic, is still considered by many to be the outstanding history. The book's theme brought together the individual creative scientist and the *Zeitgeist* or spirit of the times, and explained how the interaction of the two influenced the direction of psychology.

One of Boring's early books, *The physical dimensions of consciousness,* defined the basic terms of psychology such as sensation, consciousness, and body-mind dualism. He theorized that the body-mind split was not necessary for psychology. In effect, Boring began to move away from Titchener's dualism toward monism, the belief that there is basically only one kind of reality.

Because of his long and distinguished career at Harvard, and his service to psychology in general through its organizations and institutions, Boring was popularly referred to as "Mr. Psychology."

N. A. HAYNIE

BOSS, MEDARD (1903–   )

Boss received his M.D. at the University of Zurich in 1928. As a psychiatrist he has spent most of his career at that university as professor of psychotherapy. He was the first president of the International Society for Medical Psychotherapy. Much influenced by the writings of Martin Heidegger, he has taken a strong existential approach to psychology and psychotherapy. Although trained in traditional psychoanalysis, he has cast off the complex mental apparatus of Freud and Jung.

Like his Swiss colleague, Ludwig Binswanger, Boss has stressed man's freedom, denying all inferences to causality. His interpretation of being-in-the-world refers to man's possibilities for relating what he has encountered to his own existence. When man abandons his freedom, psychological difficulties are bound to occur. Existence is not a static state but a constant process of becoming.

As a psychiatrist he is very much concerned with existential therapy and dream analysis. His two important books, *The analysis of dreams* and *Psychoanalysis and daseinsanalysis,* reflect his views. He points out that dreams are simply another mode of being-in-the-world. They have their own special meaning, or they may duplicate the modes of existence of waking life. In his analysis of 823 dreams of a patient in therapy, he noted that changes in the content of the dreams paralleled improved changes in his waking experiences. The advantage of dream analysis is that it can bring to light events which the dreamer is not aware of in the waking state.

BOWDITCH, HENRY PICKERING (1840–1911)

Bowditch received the M.D. from Harvard University in 1866 and opened the first American physiological laboratory there in 1871. Although primarily a physiologist, he collaborated with William James and G. Stanley Hall. At that time, James was into physiology. Bowditch directed Hall's doctoral dissertation on the muscular sense. Later, Bowditch and Hall published a paper on apparent motion in which the waterfall illusion machine was described and used in psychology for the first time. Bowditch also was the first to demonstrate the all-or-nothing law of nerve impulse transmission in heart muscles fibers. The principle that nerves cannot be fatigued is referred to as Bowditch's law.

R. W. LUNDIN

BOWER, GORDON HOWARD (1932–   )

Bower received the B.A. from Western Reserve University and the Ph.D. from Yale (1959), where he was exposed to Clark Hull's behavior theory and studied under Neal E. Miller and Frank Logan. He then went to Stanford University, where he has remained ever since. In 1979 he received the Distinguished Scientific Contribution award from the American Psychological Association.

Bower's early research involved operant conditioning with lower animals. His interests then turned to problems in human learning, including mathematical models of learning. He developed the "one-element" or "all-or-none" model, which he used to describe hypothesis-testing behavior in conceptual learning. This research and theorizing resulted in a book, *Attention to learning* (1968), in collaboration with Thomas Trabasso. Bower's work on how memorizing could be improved through mnemonics, imagery, organizing strategies, and propositional learning were set forth in *Human association memory,* written with John Anderson. He also coauthored *Theories of learning* with Ernest R. Hilgard.

Besides his contributions to human learning and cognitive psychology, Bower has also been interested in hypnosis, emotions, and subconscious influences on behavior. In his research he has found that hypnotically induced emotional states are helpful in understanding the recall of memories acquired while in that mood.

BOWLBY, JOHN (1907–   )

Bowlby is known for work on the ill effects on personality development of maternal deprivation, and for formulating attachment theory as a way of conceptualizing a child's tie to the mother. The son of a London surgeon, he read medicine and psychology at Cambridge, completed his medical training in London (1933), and at once specialized in child psychiatry and psychoanalysis. After five years as an Army psychiatrist, he joined the Tavistock Clinic and Tavistock Institute of Human Relations, where he worked full time (1946–1972) as a clinician, teacher, and researcher in child and family psychiatry. His Tavistock association has continued.

Believing that the influence of children's real experiences with their parents had been greatly underestimated in accounting for personality disorders and neuroses, he selected the responses of very young children to brief or long separations from parents as a focus for research. His early publications include "Forty-four juvenile thieves" and *Maternal care and mental health*, the latter contributing to radical changes in the care of children in hospitals and institutions.

In 1951, dissatisfied with existing psychological and psychoanalytic theorizing as ways of understanding children's social and emotional development, he began developing a new conceptual framework drawing on ethology, control theory and, later, cognitive psychology, as well as psychoanalysis. Preliminary papers appeared in 1958–1963, followed by the trilogy, *Attachment and loss* (1973, 1980). Influential colleagues have been Robert A. Hinde and Mary D. S. Ainsworth.

BRADLEY, FRANCIS HERBERT (1846–1924)

Bradley was educated at University College, Oxford. His influence on psychology is found basically in his philosophy. He emphasized the importance for individuals to find themselves first as a whole and then bring themselves into line with the world of completely harmonized experience with an infinite coherent unity.

He was, indeed, the last of the Scottish School of psychology set forth by Thomas Brown and Sir William Hamilton. His main book was *Principles of logic* published in 1883. His ethical, logical, and metaphysical writings exercised their influence on psychology in opposition to the British associationists such as the Mills and Bain. He maintained that the main fact of reality is experience which is an indessuble unity with the perceived. Nature is an appearance within reality and an imperfect manifestation of the absolute spirit (mind).

He was admitted to the Order of Merit in the same year in which he died.

R. W. LUNDIN

BRAID, JAMES (ca. 1795–1860)

Braid is generally credited to be the discoverer of hypnosis, although the phenomenon had been known and practiced earlier by Mesmer, Elliotson, and Esdale. Following the denunciation of Anton Mesmer's practice of "animal magnetism" as a fraud in the late eighteenth century in Paris, this technique was considered disreputable by the medical profession.

Braid was a British surgeon who witnessed demonstrations of mesmerism (animal magnetism) in 1841. At first he was skeptical of what he observed, but eventually he became convinced that this was a genuine phenomenon which needed to be explained. He described the mesmeric trance as a "nervous sleep" and invented the term "neuryponology." In time, the first part of the term was dropped and the word "hypnotism" remained. Mesmer had contended that his powers to cure resided in magnetic powers which came from outer planetary forces. Braid obviously did not accept this notion, and as a member of the medical profession felt that there had to be some physiological cause residing in the subject. He found that he could induce this "nervous sleep" by having a subject fixate on some visual object placed above the line of vision.

He thus concluded that the mesmeric phenomenon was caused by paralyzing the levator muscles of the eyelids through their continued action in the protracted state.

Braid later realized that the factor of suggestion was of primary importance. His real significance for psychology is that he took the phenomenon out of the realm of mystical explanation and put it on a physical basis.

R. W. LUNDIN

BRAY, CHARLES, W. II (1904–1982)

Bray grew up in Youngstown, Ohio. He received the B.A., M.A., and Ph.D. degrees from Princeton University. He was appointed instructor in psychology at Princeton rising through the ranks to full professor in 1945. Most of his research was carried out in collaboration with E. G. Wever with whom he published 36 articles on hearing. These papers reported electrical potentials in the cochlea and auditory nerve in response to sounds. This important work initiated the field of auditory electrophysiology, and in recognition of it the Warren Medal was awarded jointly to Wever and Bray.

After 1950, Bray was involved in defense activities. He became a research director with the U.S. Air Force Human Resources Research Center and later in defense work contracted through the Smithsonian Institution. Here he applied psychological principles to the selection and training of Air Force personnel. In recognition of his success in this effort he was awarded the Presidential Certificate of Merit.

P. E. LICHTENSTEIN

BRENMAN-GIBSON, MARGARET (1918–   )

Best known for her work on altered states of consciousness and their uses in psychoanalytic psychotherapy, Brenman-Gibson has extended this interest to the creative state in writers. She received the M.A. from Columbia University, where she studied with Gardner Murphy, Otto Klineberg, Franz Boas, Ruth Benedict, Ralph Linton, and Margaret Mead.

While serving as the Menninger Clinic's first psychology intern under their first staff psychologist, David Rapaport, she received the Ph.D. from the University of Kansas. At the same time, she became the first nonmedical American to receive full psychoanalytic training at the Topeka Psychoanalytic Institute and was appointed director of the Department of Psychology at the Menninger Foundation.

At the Austen Riggs Center in Stockbridge, Massachusetts, where she was much influenced by the work of Erik Erikson, she has served as senior consultant in research and education. She engaged also in the private practice of psychoanalysis and psychotherapy and was a clinical professor at the Harvard University School of Medicine.

Commissioned with Merton Gill to find practical means for dealing with the traumatic war neuroses of World War II, she engaged in an investigation of hypnosis and related states, culminating in *Hypnotherapy*. She also published *Clifford Odets: American playwright, a psychosocial study*.

BRENTANO, FRANZ (1838–1917)

Brentano studied in Berlin, Munich, and Tubingen; he received his degree in philosophy in 1864. Between 1864 and 1874 Brentano served as an ordained priest at Würzburg, writing and lecturing on Aristotle. After resigning from this professorship and the Church over the doctrine of papal infallibility, he spent his time writing his most famous book, *Psychology from an empirical standpoint*. In 1874 the book was published and he was appointed professor of philosophy at the University of Vienna, where he taught for 20 years. Sigmund Freud, Christian von Ehrenfels, and Carl Stumpf were among his students. Brentano retired in 1894 to study and write.

In opposition to Wilhelm Wundt's book on physiological psychology, Brentano's *Psychology from an empirical standpoint* proclaimed that the primary method of psychology was observation and not experimentation. Whereas his contemporary Wundt was establishing psychology as a science by the experimental method of studying conscious processes and structure, Brentano's primary method was observation of the experience as an activity—the act of seeing color as differentiated from the sensory content of color.

Act Psychology, studying the mental activity, the act of experiencing, was differentiated from Wundt's study of the mental content. Act Psychology was more empirical than experimental, although it demanded careful observation of individual experience and included data from experimentation as well.

Brentano was an intellectual precursor of Gestalt psychology and humanistic psychology (D. Schultz, 1981/1975). His student Stumpf was influenced to accept a less rigorous form of introspection as a method of study and to proclaim phenomena as the primary data to be studied. Phenomenology was the examination of unbiased experience just as it occurs, without breaking the experience into elements. A student of Stumpf's, Edmund Husserl, later developed the philosophy of phenomenology, a precursor of other forms of psychology, including Gestalt psychology.

N. A. HAYNIE

BRETT, GEORGE S. (1879–1944)

Brett received the M.A. at Oxford. He is primarily known for his monumental three-volume work, *A history of psychology*. The first volume was published in 1912 and the two subsequent ones in 1921, by which time he was professor of philosophy at the University of Toronto. This was the first work of its kind and served as an impetus for many successors. In the three volumes Brett traced psychology from its earliest beginnings in ancient Greece through Plato and Aristotle, the Church Fathers, modern philosophy and experimental psychology down to the early twentieth century. In 1953, the work was revised and abridged into one volume by R. S. Peters.

Passages and interpretations from Brett's *History* were often quoted later by such historians of psychology as Gardner Murphy, Erwin Esper, and J. R. Kantor. The former two regarded Brett's interpretations as having much insight, though Kantor's *Scientific evolution of psychology* took exception. For example, Kantor wrote that Brett had misinterpreted Plato's psychology by making Plato less naturalistic and more spiritual than he really was.

R. W. LUNDIN

BREUER, JOSEPH (1842–1905)

As a successful physician in Vienna, Breuer is best known for his association with Sigmund Freud in the early years of the psychoanalytic movement. Prior to his first encounters with Freud, Breuer had been treating a young woman known as Anna O. (Her real name was Bertha Poppenheim.) She manifested a variety of hysterical symptoms including paralyses, anesthesias, and a phobia. Along with hypnosis, Breuer had been using the "talking out" method in treating her symptoms. He discovered that, if placed under hypnosis and encouraged to talk out her feelings and recall her past experiences, she felt better after being removed from the hypnotic state.

In 1886 Freud and Breuer became acquainted. It was a difficult time for Freud as he had recently married and was in dire financial straits. The elder Breuer was helpful to Freud and lent him money. They discussed some of his cases and in particular, Anna O. Freud became increasingly interested in Breuer's methods and began using them on his own patients. In 1895 they collaborated on *Studies in hysteria*, with Breuer as the senior author.

Their association cooled and Freud abandoned the use of hypnosis in favor of free association or the "talking out" method. Freud had found that hypnosis often did not work and the patients' symptoms returned. Freud and Breuer also differed in their attitude toward transference, the strong emotional attachment that the patient developed toward the analyst. Sometimes there was a countertransference as well in which the analyst developed attachments for patients. All this disturbed Breuer greatly, but Freud found that transference was a necessary aspect of successful analysis. On the basis of these differences the two men ended their association and Freud continued to develop his own psychoanalytic theory and therapy.

R. W. LUNDIN

BREZNITZ, SHLOMO (1936–   )

Breznitz discovered and documented the phenomenon of "incubation of threat," whereby fear of danger grows with anticipation. Breznitz received the Ph.D. in 1965 from the Hebrew University in Jerusalem, where he joined the faculty. In 1974 he moved to the University of Haifa, where he served as the academic head until 1979, when he established the R. D. Wolfe Centre for Study of Psychological Stress, of which he is the director. His research combines systematic laboratory work with field studies and research of primarily theoretical nature.

Following his work on "incubation of threat," Breznitz investigated the effects of false alarms on fear and protective behavior, leading to *Cry wolf: The psychology of false alarms*. His interest in coping with major stress led him to work on the mechanism of denial, which he summarized in *Denial of stress*. He views Israel as a natural laboratory of stress research, as discussed in *Stress in Israel*. The long-range effects of living in a highly stressful environment, and their implications to the theories of adjustment, are one of his primary interests. Considering the stress of modern life and the adaptation challenges for humankind in the near future to be of primary importance, he established the Mankind 2000 forum devoted to the multidisciplinary analysis of these issues.

BRIDGMAN, PERCY W. (1882–1961)

Educated at Harvard, Bridgman spent his entire career there as a physicist. His research in high pressure physics brought him a Nobel Prize in 1946. His writings were extensive, some covering technical areas while others dealt with methodological problems or broad philosophical issues.

In 1927 Bridgman wrote *The logic of modern physics*, which has had considerable impact on psychology. Seeking to clarify the nature of physical concepts, he introduced the notion of operational definition: a concept is to be defined in terms of the operations by which it is observed. Thus length (of a table) and distance (to the sun) are different concepts, because the operations used to measure them are different.

Because of the controversy in psychology over unobservables, the concept of operational definition looked promising as a way out. Sensations, for example, could be defined by the operations used to measure them. Operationism was popularized in psychology, particularly through the efforts of S. S. Stevens and Edwin Boring.

Bridgman did not accept all the applications of operationism made by psychologists. In *The way things are*, he discussed some of the peculiar problems of psychology. While accepting behaviorism up to a point, he emphasized that the operations by which one knows that one has a toothache, or that one's neighbor has a toothache, are so different as to introduce a sharp dichotomy. This dichotomy is one of the most insistent characteristics of the world and cannot be neglected in attempting to understand the person.

Bridgman's operational definition, which began as an attempt to clarify the nature of scientific concepts, came to be seen by him in radically subjective terms, since scientific operations rest ultimately upon private operations or consciousness.

P. E. LICHTENSTEIN

BRISLIN, RICHARD W. (1945–   )

Brislin received the B.A. degree in English and American literature from the University of Guam. He received the M.S. and the Ph.D. (1969) in psychology from the Pennsylvania State University, where he concentrated in the areas of cross-cultural, social, and industrial psychology.

After fulfilling a military obligation, he became a research associate at the Culture Learning Institute (later the Institute of Culture and Communication) at the East-West Center in Honolulu, Hawaii where he directed programs for international educators, cross-cultural researchers, specialists involved in formal programs that encourage intercultural interaction, and professors who wanted to integrate cross-cultural and intercultural research into their course offerings. He also taught courses at the University of Hawaii, Georgetown University of British Columbia, and Arizona State University.

His books include *Cross-cultural research methods, Cross-cultural encounters: Face-to-face interaction, Intercultural interactions: A practial guide, The art of getting things done: A practical guide to the use of power*, and *Understanding culture's influence on behavior.* He was coeditor of the *Handbook of cross-cultural psychology* (with H. Triandis) and the *Handbook of intercultural training.*

Brislin wrote the chapter on cross-cultural research for the 1983 *Annual Review of Psychology* and the G. Stanley Hall lecture (for the American Psychological Association in 1988) on issues in human diversity.

BROADBENT, DONALD E. (1926–   )

Primarily an occupational or "human factors" psychologist, Broadbent is probably best known for an early advocacy of information-processing models for human beings. His first book, *Perception and communication,* was described in an APA citation as "the first systematic treatment of the organism as an information-processing system, with a specific structure that could be investigated by experiment."

Broadbent was schooled at Winchester College and at Pembroke College, Cambridge, with the original aim of working in physical science. While in the Royal Air Force, however, he decided that the problems of human interaction with technical systems were of greater interest and importance than those systems alone, and so he took up psychology on returning to Cambridge. He was a pupil of Sir Frederic Bartlett, and on graduating joined the staff of the Applied Psychology Unit in Cambridge, where he worked for twenty-five years.

As director of the unit, Broadbent worked with his staff on a wide variety of problems, from the design of postal zip codes to the difficulties of shift work. Prevailing academic theories in psychology proved little suited to the handling of the data which emerged from these studies, because it was clear that human work involved internal processes mediating between stimulus and response. Hence Broadbent's espousal of

theorizing in terms of information, and the need to consider the selective functions that cause some stimuli to have much larger effects than others ("attention"). This approach is now widely approved in human experimental psychology, and indeed in other specializations as well.

His later work led to *Decision and stress.* His more general and philosophical works are *Behaviour* and *In defence of empirical psychology.* In the 1970s Broadbent moved to Oxford to concentrate on his research.

BROCA, PAUL (1824–1880)

Broca became one of the most eminent physicians and surgeons of his time. He is best known to us today for a specific discovery regarding the localization of the speech area in the brain. Prior to Broca's discovery, the doctrine of Pierre Florens had maintained that the brain functioned in a unitary manner.

Broca's discovery came about in a rather unique way. In a hospital for mentally disturbed patients outside Paris known as Bicêtre, there resided a man whose only defect was an inability to speak. He could communicate by signs and otherwise appeared to be mentally normal. In 1861 the patient was put under Broca's care; Broca examined him but found no defects in his vocal apparatus. Five days later the patient died, and Broca immediately performed an autopsy. He found a lesion in the third frontal convolusion of the left cerebral hemisphere. He presented his finding to the French Society of Anthropology.

This area of the brain became known as "Broca's area" and for some time was specified as the speech area of the brain. This was the first real challenge to Florens' doctrine of the unity of brain function. Later research indicated that speech is too complicated a mechanism to be confined to one specific area of the brain.

Broca's name is also closely associated with the modern development of physical anthropology. His research involved the study of craniology, for which he developed techniques and methods. He also studied the comparative morphology of the brain, as well as the topology of the brain and skull.

R. W. LUNDIN

BROWN, ROGER W. (1925–   )

A pioneer psycholinguist and well-known social psychologist, in 1952 Brown received a Ph.D. in psychology from the University of Michigan. Feeling a little daunted by the ancient and difficult problems of experimental psychology, he chanced upon the discipline of linguistics and envisioned bringing linguistic knowledge into psychology.

In 1952 Brown was appointed instructor in social psychology at Harvard. From Jerome Bruner's Cognition Project, in conjunction with linguistics, Brown acquired the conceptual tools that led to his first book, *Words and things.* From Gordon Allport, Brown got a teaching assignment in introductory social psychology, which led to his *Social psychology.*

Brown went to M.I.T. in 1957. Returning to Harvard five years later, he began the longitudinal study of the development of language in three children called Adam, Eve, and Sarah. The major product of this research was *A first language,* a work that helped to make developmental psycholinguistics a major research field. Brown's other books include *Psycholinguistics* and, with Richard Herrnstein, *Psychology.* In 1971, Brown received the Distinguished Scientific Contribution Award of the American Psychological Association; in 1972, he was elected to the National Academy of Sciences; in 1974, Harvard appointed him John Lindsley Professor of Psychology in Memory of William James.

BROWN, THOMAS (1778–1820)
Brown was brought up in Edinburgh, studied in London, and took his medical degree at the University of Edinburgh.

He was the third of a triumvirate which has become known as the "Scottish school" in the history of psychology, his predecessors being Thomas Reid and Douglas Stewart. This school arose as a revolt against British associationism, which was becoming increasingly popular at the time. The followers of the Scottish school believed strongly in the unity of the mind or soul. They objected to the idea set forth by the British empiricists that the mind was made up only of experiences. For the Scottish school, the mind had certain powers or functions; when the soul operated, it operated as a whole.

In his most important book, *Lectures on the philosophy of the human mind,* Brown held to the unitary nature of the soul, but felt he needed something else to explain how it went about its business. Thus he set forth what he called the primary and secondary laws of suggestion. In so doing, he was really bringing the Scottish school back to associationism by substituting "suggestion" for "association." The primary laws were contiguity, resemblance (similarity), and contrast—exactly the same as those Aristotle had set forth one thousand years before. The primary laws were based on the relations of objects or feelings to each other. The secondary laws accounted for the modification of situations or conditions which bore on the primary, by accounting for variation. They included duration (length of the original sensations), liveliness, recency, frequency of presentation, degrees of coexistence with other suggestions, constitutional influences, and prior habits. Thus Brown's psychology was a transition from the psychology of Reid and Stewart back to associationism.

Brown did not doubt the existence of the real world, as had George Berkeley and David Hume. To Aristotle's five senses he added the muscle sense (called kinesthetic or proprioceptive): one could learn about a rose by means of the senses of vision and smell, but by reaching out for it—which involved the muscle sense—one could not doubt the existence of that real object. The suggestions of the other senses, when added to the muscular sense, turned out to be an extension of the concept of association. The addition of this muscle sense gave the entire perception one of unity.

R. W. LUNDIN

BROWN-SÉQUARD, CHARLES-EDOUARD (1817–1894)
Brown-Séquard was educated at the University of Paris, where he received the M.D. degree. His thesis on the spinal cord established his reputation in neurophysiology. He traced the origin of sympathetic fibers in the spinal cord. More important, he demonstrated the crossing over of sensory fibers in the spinal cord and the effects of spinal cord lesions. He produced convulsions of an epileptiform character by means of experimental lesions in animals. He is best known, however, for the Brown-Séquard syndrome, characterized by lesion of one lateral half of the spinal cord, causing paralysis on one side and anesthesia on the other.

Brown-Séquard taught briefly at the Virginia Medical College and then at Paris, where he founded and edited the *Journal de Physiologie de l'Homme et des Animaux.* Later he served as physician at the National Hospital for the Paralyzed and Epileptic in London, and as professor of physiology and pathology of the nervous system at Harvard. He practiced medicine and taught in several countries. Eventually he returned to Paris to succeed to Claude Bernard's professorship at the Collège de France.

Late in his career Brown-Séquard published the results of experiments indicating that testicular injections induce sexual desire and that such extracts can be used for rejuvenation. As one result of his studies of the endocrine glands, a successful treatment was developed for myxedema. In 1889, with Vulpian and Charcot, Brown-Séquard founded and edited the *Archives de Physiologie.*

P. E. LICHTENSTEIN

BROŽEK, JOSEF (1913–)
In his infancy and early childhood Brožek lived in Russian-occupied Poland and Siberia. Through Vladivostok, Singapore, Hong Kong, and Trieste he returned to his birthplace at age seven. He obtained the Ph.D. in psychology in 1937 from the Charles University in Prague. He became briefly a vocational counselor, then an industrial psychologist. As an international exchange student he worked in 1939–1940 at the University of Pennsylvania with Morris Viteles. In 1940–1941 he explored individual differences with D. G. Paterson and student counseling with J. G. Darley, then in 1941 joined the Laboratory of Physiological Hygiene at the University of Minnesota, which led to collaborative volumes on *The biology of human starvation* (1950). Nutrition was a theme covered in two symposia that Brožek organized: *Symposium on nutrition and behavior* and *Behavioral effects of energy and protein deficits* (1979). He coedited a volume on *Performance capacity* and reviewed Soviet work on nutrition and behavior.

From 1959 to 1979 Brožek was on the faculty of Lehigh University, where his concerns were mostly with the history of psychology, resulting in a number of books and monographs: *Origins of psychometry* with M. S. Sibinga (1970); *Psychology in the U.S.S.R.* with D. I. Slobin; *Psychology in Czechoslovakia; R. I. Watson's selected papers on the history of psychology* with R. B. Evans; *Historiography of modern psychology* with L. J. Pongratz; and the collaborative *Explorations in the history of psychology in the United States.*

For many years Brožek covered Russian and other Slavic publications in the journal *Contemporary Psychology.* In the 1980s he served on boards of the *Journal of the History of the Behavioral Sciences, Archiv für Psychologie, Storia e Critica della Psicologia,* and *Revista de Historia de la Psicologia.* His autobiography appeared in 1974.

BRUCH, HILDE (1904–)
Bruch graduated from the University of Freiburg in Germany in 1928 with an M.D. degree. She trained in physiology at the University of Kiel and in pediatrics at Leipzig. She left Germany in 1933 and after one year in London came to the United States. She began her studies of childhood obesity while working at the Babies Hospital in New York. This work led her to seek psychiatric training at the Phipps Clinic of Johns Hopkins Hospital, and psychoanalytic training at the Washington–Baltimore Institute. Returning to New York, she practiced psychoanalysis until 1964 and worked as psychotherapeutic supervisor at the New York State Psychiatric Institute. Continuing to be interested in obesity, she became involved in the study of anorexia nervosa and the relationship of eating disorders to schizophrenic development. In 1964 she went to Houston as professor of psychiatry at Baylor College of Medicine.

Bruch has published more than 250 papers in scientific and professional journals, and six books, of which *Eating disorders, Learning psychotherapy* and *The golden cage: The enigma of anorexia nervosa.* In 1981 Bruch was given the American Psychiatric Association's Founders Award as well as the Agnes Purcell McGavin Award. The American Medical Association has honored her with the Joseph B. Goldberger Award in Clinical Nutrition.

BRUNSWIK, EGON (1903–1955)

Brunswik first studied engineering but then took the Ph.D. in 1927 under Karl Bühler at Vienna. He is credited with the establishment of the first psychology laboratory in Turkey while serving as a visiting lecturer at Ankara in 1931–1932. In 1935 he moved to the University of California at Berkeley at Tolman's invitation.

In a monograph in 1934 Brunswik set out the essential ideas for his probabilistic functionalism, although *The conceptual framework of psychology* is a more complete and integrated exposition of his ideas. An organism learns to use the proximal cues about it to the degree that these cues predict the distal situation; since we rarely have adequate information about our world (except in very special, limited circumstances), we perceive according to probability: the most frequent previous experience under the current conditions will ordinarily be expected. To understand perception, then, the researcher simply needs to take an "ecological survey"—a natural environment study of the way things are in the everyday world. In the case of both humans and animals, Brunswick emphasized studying the properties of the organism's environment as well as the organism itself. His probability notions make him the intellectual forerunnner of W. K. Estes.

Because of his work on shape and size constancy, Brunswik has been considered by some to be a Gestalt psychologist—something he vehemently denied. No doubt the prominent figures of the Gestalt movement would be rather uneasy with his notion that the laws of perceptual organization are learned.

C. S. PEYSER

BUBER, MARTIN (1878–1965)

Buber, a distinguished scholar in religion and sociology, was little known to American psychologists until existentialism was brought to their attention in the 1950s and 1960s. Buber's most important book in the existentialist tradition—hence most important to psychologists—was his *I and thou*.

Buber was a professor of religion at Frankfort for many years, until his defiance of Hitler forced his migration to Palestine in 1936. He taught the sociology of culture there, and as the state of Israel developed, became the first chairman of the Department of Sociology at the Hebrew University of Jerusalem.

As an intellectual leader among the Jews, he edited *Die Welt*, the Zionist weekly, from 1901 on, and later *Der Jude*, the journal of the German-speaking intellectuals. For a time he also edited *Gemeinschaft*, which published the writings of distinguished German sociologists. He wrote numerous books, including a translation of the Bible and studies of Jewish mysticism.

It is not easy to place him intellectually, because he reflected German sociology, Jewish religious and secular history, utopianism, and religious existentialism. He is often called the representative of Jewish existentialism, on a par with Paul Tillich and Reinhold Niebuhr, both Protestants, and Jacques Maritain, a Roman Catholic. While each of these remained faithful to the religious tradition in which he was brought up, there was much that was congenial among them in their philosophical and psychological views.

Because it was Buber's existentialism that made him relevant to psychology, his contribution to existentialism needs to be placed in context. The term "existentialist" refers to a distinction between *existence* and *essence*, with a preference expressed for existence. Existence emphasizes being over nonbeing. Nonbeing essences are scientific attributes such as physical size and weight or, in scientific psychology, such part functions as reflexes and drives.

The language of existentialism is somewhat alien to the uninitiated, as for example statements such as "the artist and his art are one," a reference to the faulty distinction that others commonly make between subject and object. This is indicated also by the expression "being-in-the-world," presenting being as not strictly subjective. Three modes of the world are distinguished by the following German words: *Umwelt* (the world around), referring to the natural environment; *Mitwelt* (with-world), the world of relations with other persons; and *Eigenwelt* (own world), the self's relation to itself. Buber's most important contribution to existentialism was his analysis of the *Mitwelt* in his I-thou relationship (1970/1958). He explained our relationship to God, as well as to other people, in the belief that a person alone is not human. In common with Soren Kierkegaard, who is taken as the modern representative of the existential tradition of earlier times, Buber accepts the great importance of dialogue in establishing humanity's place, as distinct from falling back on general principles such as those of Hegel, which Kierkegaard had taken pains to refute.

E. R. HILGARD

BUGELSKI, B. R. (1913–   )

Bugelski grew up in Buffalo, New York, where he took the B.A. and M.A. at the University of Buffalo. He earned the Ph.D. at Yale (1938). After teaching at Antioch (1937–1939) and the University of Toledo (1939–1943), he served with the Navy at Pensacola, where he started the Naval Aviation Safety Program. After World War II he began a long career at the University of Buffalo that lasted until he retired as distinguished professor emeritus in 1978. In 1970 he became president of the Eastern Psychological Association.

Bugelski combined a strong behaviorist orientation with an interest in practical problems, devoting himself largely to studies of learning in animals and humans. An underlying theme in his writings is the unresolved debate between Hull and Tolman: is a human only a verbalizing rat, or is a rat only a nonverbalizing human?

Bugelski describes himself as a "surface scratcher" who prefers to discover new problems rather than explore a limited area deeply. In his "surface scratching" Bugelski, with Neal Miller, described the Negative Goal Gradient (avoidance); simultaneously with B. F. Skinner, in 1938 he proposed subgoal reinforcement (secondary reinforcement). In 1962 he explored the total time hypothesis (number of trials × trial time = a constant). In the late 1960s he turned to the study of imagery, starting with mnemonics but turning quickly toward more theoretical issues in imagery, which he has tried to describe behavioristically as conditioned neural responses. Bugelski has shown a concern with everyday life issues, as seen in his *Handbook of practical psychology*, a joint effort with a clinical colleague, Anthony Graziano. His *Psychology of learning applied to teaching* is intended to help teachers make sense out of what they are doing.

BÜHLER, CHARLOTTE B. (1893–1974)

Bühler received the Ph.D. at Munich in 1918. Along with her husband she worked at the Dresden Institute of Technology and became the first woman lecturer there in 1920. In 1923 she came to the United States on a Rockefeller exchange fellowship to study with Edward Thorndike at Columbia University. After returning to Vienna, she and her husband, Karl Bühler, founded a psychological institute where she was the head of the Child Psychology Department. Her work in child psychology is said to have had a strong influence on the American child psychologist, Arnold Gesell. When the Nazis came to power in Germany, she and her husband went to Oslo and later, in 1940, to the United States.

In the United States her psychological interests turned to the new movement of humanistic psychology. Along with Abraham Maslow, Carl Rogers, and Viktor Frankl, she participated in the founding of the Association for Humanistic Psychology in 1964. Thus she became strongly identified with what Maslow called the "third force" in American psychology (the others being behaviorism and psychoanalysis). She served as president of this organization in 1965–1966. As a member of the "third force" she contributed two books to its cause; *The course of human life* and, in collaboration with Melanie Allen, *Introduction to humanistic psychology*.

R. W. LUNDIN

BÜHLER, KARL (1879–1963)

Bühler received the M.D. in 1903 from Freiburg im Breisgau with a dissertation on physiological color vision theory under von Kries, and the Ph.D. in 1904 from Strasbourg with a dissertation on Henry Home under Bäumker. He studied with Erdmann, Stumpf, and Külpe, and taught at Würzburg, Bonn, Munich, Dresden, Vienna, and several American colleges. His students at Vienna included Egon Brunswick, Konrad Lorenz, Edward Tolman, and Neal Miller. With Dürr, he was responsible for the posthumous editions of the works of Ebbinghaus.

Bühler is primarily remembered for a controversy with Wundt over proper experimental methods. Bühler proposed the *Ausfragemethode* in which a passage is read to the subject, and the subject is asked one of six types of questions about the material (always answerable by *yes* or *no*). The time to respond is measured, followed by a lengthy introspection by the subject that is prompted by follow-up questions from the experimenter. Wundt severely criticized this extension and refinement of introspective methodology.

A member of the Würzburg School, Bühler published in the areas of the psychology of thought and perception. He also wrote extensively in developmental psychology. He considered Freud's emphasis on the pleasure of satisfaction to be but one-third complete: he added the pleasure of functioning and the pleasure of creating. Seemingly obsessed with triads, he spoke of three equally valid, complementary aspects of behavior, each with its own methodology: experiential (introspection), behavioral (observation of others), and cultural-achievement (humanistic analysis). Speech functions were related to the triad: expression (by someone) to the experiential, appeal (to someone) to the behavioral, and representation (of something) to the cultural-achievement aspect.

C. S. PEYSER

BUJAS, ZORAN (1910–   )

Bujas studied psychology at the universities of Zagreb and Paris. After doing research at the Laboratory for the Psychophysiology of Senses headed by Henri Piéron in Paris, Bujas started his professional career in Zagreb as a consulting psychologist in vocational guidance. From 1938 to 1981 he was professor of experimental and physiological psychology at Zagreb University. After retirement he engaged in research at the Laboratory for Sensory Psychophysiology of the Academy of Sciences and Arts in Zagreb.

The main fields of his research interest were sensory psychophysiology, psychometrics, and work psychophysiology. In sensory psychophysiology he was primarily concerned with studies of taste and the problems of psychophysical scaling. In psychometrics he worked on the construction of achievement and cognitive tests, trying to bring test situations nearer to real situations in which these functions show themselves. In work psychophysiology he investigated manifestations of fatigue, various forms of rest, and effects of motivation on work output and energy expenditure.

In his research he was primarily interested in methodological problems and approaches in investigation. He was the editor of *Acta Instituti Psychologici Universitatis Zagrabiensis*.

BUROS, OSCAR K. (1905–1978)

After attending the State Normal School in Superior, Buros transferred to the University of Minnesota, from which he received the B.S. He received the M.A. from Teachen College of Columbia University. After several years as a high school history teacher and principal, he continued his professional career as a member of the faculty of Rutgers. He was the founder of the Buros Institute of Mental Measurements.

Buros published his first bibliography of research on psychological testing in 1935. After the third bibliography, he adopted the current format of the *Mental measurements yearbook* (MMYB). Essentially all commercially available psychological, educational, and vocational tests published in English are included. The instruments are described in moderate detail: purpose, administration time, age of those tested, alternate forms, publisher. A complete bibliography of journal articles and books dealing with each instrument is included. For the major tests a detailed critique is presented. Many of the critiques are original to MMYB, with some excerpted from professional journals. The eighth MMYB was completed and published posthumously in 1978 by Luella Buros, his wife and long-time editorial collaborator.

Buros also published the major bibliographic work *Tests in print,* as well as a dozen bibliographic indexes in areas such as reading, English, and personality.

C. S. PEYSER

BURT, CYRIL L. (1883–1971)

Burt was a leading British psychologist, especially in the areas of child development and statistics. Born the son of a doctor, he soon showed his talents in mathematics and classics. At Oxford University he was influenced by William McDougall to take up psychology. After studying under Külpe at Würzburg, he became a lecturer at Liverpool University in Charles Sherrington's Department of Physiology in 1909. In 1913 he was appointed by the London County Council as educational psychologist—probably the first psychologist anywhere to be so employed. In 1919 he joined Charles Myers' National Institute of Industrial Psychology, and in 1924 became professor of education at the University of London. In 1931 he succeeded Charles Spearman as professor and head of the Psychology Department at University College, London, where he remained until his retirement in 1950.

At Oxford and Liverpool he developed his interests in child guidance and delinquency, and also in mental tests and their statistical properties. The years with the London County Council were extremely prolific. He devised a large battery of achievement tests for 5–15-year-olds, as well as group intelligence tests, and compared the ability levels of various London boroughs with their vital statistics and delinquency rates (*Mental and scholastic tests,* 1921). He translated and standardized the Binet-Simon intelligence scale, and later adapted the Stanford-Binet scale for use in the United Kingdom. In statistics he developed techniques of factor analysis, including the formula for centroid analysis later used by Thurstone. While accepting the importance of "g" (the general intelligence factor), he broke away from Spearman by demonstrating the existence of other so-called group factors in particular kinds of tests such as sensory discrimination, verbal, and number.

He pioneered the development of child guidance clinics in England, arguing that these should be led by psychologists rather than psychiatrists, since children's problems are a psychological, not a medical, matter. He tested and amassed information on large numbers of delinquents and on backward or retarded, and emotionally maladjusted, children. These culminated in his best known books, *The young delinquent* and *The backward child*. They involved statistical comparisons of large groups of problem children with normal controls for isolating the main environmental and other factors underlying their symptoms.

He combined these with detailed case studies of individuals, based on the application of clinical insight. At the National Institute of Industrial Psychology he developed a system of vocational guidance which is still widely used. This included intelligence tests, educational records supplied by the schools, and interviews with the candidates and their parents. Here too he insisted that the psychologist's expertise is essential, requiring a thorough knowledge of occupations and their requisite qualifications, abilities, and personality characteristics.

Burt's interests ranged widely, including studies of personality, educational and vocational selection, examinations, psychology of aesthetics, mental telepathy, typography of books, and body-mind issues. His very numerous publications were not only fluent and lucid, but remarkable for their scholarship and erudite knowledge of history and culture. During World War II he gave unlimited help to psychologists involved in personnel work for the Armed Forces. He was in constant demand as a book reviewer, committee member, and/or consultant (e.g., to government commissions on educational matters). In 1946 he was knighted for his services to education and psychology—the first psychologist to be so honored.

His major interest, especially after retirement, was the application of R. A. Fisher's methods of analysis of variance to analyzing the factors involved in polygenic inheritance of intelligence. He claimed to have tested the intelligence of 53 pairs of identical twins reared apart, thus providing crucial data for demonstrating a large hereditary component. But many psychologists, particularly in the United States, doubted the validity of his work.

Although Burt gave immense amounts of help to students and others seeking advice all around the world, he could not brook any opposition to his views, and often showed paranoiac tendencies in his relations with colleagues and critics. This was especially apparent in the 21 years after his retirement, when he suffered much bad health. Most of his contemporaries had died, and his marriage had broken up. Shortly after his death, critics pointed out that many of his published correlations (e.g., between twins) had to be erroneous. A lengthy investigation undertaken by L. S. Hearnshaw was published in 1979. This provided irrefutable evidence that much of this work was fraudulent: many of the twin pairs never existed; to prove his views right, he had invented them. The tragic aspect is that such faking was unnecessary: most of his conclusions have been confirmed by other, more scrupulous, psychologists. It is not known how much of his earlier publications may likewise be flawed. Nevertheless, the value of Burt's influence on the development of psychology in Britain cannot be denied.

P. E. VERNON

NOTE ON CYRIL BURT: With reference to the final paragraph of this biography tha some of Burt's data on twins and other kinships were fraudulent has been brought into question recently by two independent investigations of the Burt scandal (Fletcher, 1991; Joynson, 1989), both summarized by Jensen (1992). The evidence in these two books cannot be ignored in making an assessment of Burt's contributions and his reputation.

Both authors conclude that the charges of fraud cannot be substantiated: some of the charges asserted by L. S. Hearnshaw (1979) are proved to be simply wrong and others are shown to be based only on conjecture and surmise. It remains undeniable that some of Burt's published studies on the inheritance of mental ability are flawed by unsystematic numerical errors in some of his tables (mainly in his articles published between his ages of 75 and 88) and, judged by the editorial standards present-day journals, by unduly sketchy reporting of methodological and statistical details.

BURTT, HAROLD E. (1890–1991)

Burtt's major contribution was, perhaps, the administration of the large Department of Psychology at the Ohio State University for 20 years. The program included practically all the aspects of psychology current at the time. He provided opportunity for teaching and research in these areas and maintained morale among the varied personnel. Prior to the chairmanship, he taught for 20 years at the same institution.

He graduated from Dartmouth (summa cum laude and salutatory level), then earned the Ph.D. at Harvard in 1915 under the direction of Hugo Muensterberg who at that time was one of few psychologists interested in the applied aspects of the science.

During World War I Burtt served on a committee that developed the first aptitude tests for airplane pilots and presently was commissioned a captain in the Air Force to set up testing units at Air Force ground schools. This project was terminated by the Armistice. He then worked at a Canadian tire factory developing aptitude tests, until he went to Ohio State.

He did some of the early research on blood pressure and breathing as diagnostic of deception, which was partly instrumental in the development of the "lie detector."

After retiring in 1960, he turned his interests to ornithology and banded 130,000 birds for the Wildlife Service. This led to publications in ornithology journals.

His publications in psychology include the textbooks: *Psychology and industrial efficiency, Psychology of advertising, Legal psychology,* and *Applied psychology,* and one text for the general reader, *Psychology of birds.*

CABANIS, GEORGE S. (1757–1808)

A pupil of E. B. Condillac and John Locke, Cabanis was an important participant in the eighteenth-century movement of French materialism. Early in his life his father, somewhat disenchanted with his son, sent him off to Paris to make his way in the world. There Cabanis studied medicine and read the classics.

Today he is considered one of the earliest physiological psychologists. In 1795 he wrote an essay on the problem—popular at the time—of whether or not victims of the guillotine suffered pain after decapitation. In this essay he examined the relationship between the mind and the body. For him mental events were functions of the whole organism and not simply the mind. This notion also involved a study of reflex action and the formulation of a concept which, described as a "series of levels," is still important to physiological psychology today. The spinal level was the simplest in a hierarchy; it carried out reflex acts. At a higher level semiconscious or semi-integrated activities occurred, and at the highest level were thought and volition. He believed there could be no mental processes unless the brain was involved. Those functions which did not involve the brain were merely mechanical. Going back to the original question of whether or not a person suffered pain following decapitation by the guillotine, Cabanis concluded that victims felt no pain after the guillotine: movements in the body after decapitation were mere reflexes of the lowest level.

Another contribution was his genetic approach to the nervous system, based on the fact that more complex mental activity is a function of a more complex structure of the nervous system. Finally, he suggested a social psychology derived from the fact that biological observations have clear implications for social behavior: only human organisms with the most complex nervous systems are capable of dealing with ethics.

R. W. LUNDIN

CALKINS, MARY (1863–1930)

Calkins was awarded the Ph.D. in psychology by Harvard University, where she worked under William James. When Hugo Munsterberg came to Harvard she worked for three years in his laboratory. At Wellesley College she established a psychological laboratory which she directed for 10 years. During this period she invented the method of paired associates for the study of memory.

As Calkins' interests shifted toward philosophy, she became increasingly dissatisfied with the Wundt-Titchener experimental tradition. She supported a self psychology which recognized the self as an integrating agent in the conscious life. As an introspectionist she appealed to the direct experience of the person. Her revised textbook, *A first book in psychology* (1909), presents her mature position. Calkins argued that the various schools of psychology might unite in a personalistic psychology.

Calkins served as president of the American Psychological Association and has been ranked in the second ten of psychologists starred in the first edition of *American men of science.*

P. E. LICHTENSTEIN

CAMPBELL, ANGUS (1910–1980)

Campbell grew up in Portland, Oregon, and received the M.A. degree at the University of Oregon and the Ph.D. from Stanford University in 1936. He first taught at Northwestern University. After serving in the armed forces during World War II, he accepted a position at the University of Michigan. There he became director of the Survey Research Center and the Institute for Social Research.

He is well known for his research on voting behavior, which began in 1948, the year in which the polls incorrectly predicted a victory by Thomas E. Dewey over Harry S. Truman. He also studied racial attitudes in 15 major urban areas, resulting in a two-volume work, one on attitudes of whites toward blacks and the other on attitudes of blacks toward whites. This work served as a beginning for other research on racial attitudes.

Campbell also developed a comprehensive set of measures on the quality of American life which resulted in a book coedited with Philip Converse, *The human meaning of social change.* Each author attempted to set out concepts and measures for specific areas of life: work, leisure, family, and the like. In 1976, along with Converse and Willard Rodgers, Campbell published *The quality of american life.* His last book, *The sense of wellbeing in America,* also reported his research on social change.

R. W. LUNDIN

CAMPBELL, DONALD T. (1916–   )

Campbell got the B.A., and the Ph.D. at the University of California at Berkely in 1947. He was a psychology faculty member at Ohio State University (1947–1950), at the University of Chicago, (1950–1953), and at Northwestern University (1953–1979). He was on the social science faculty at the Maxwell School, Syracuse University (1979–1982), and on the social relations faculty at Lehigh University (1982 to date). While defining himself from the beginning as a social psychologist, he retained a persisting interest in a general theory of behavior that was indebted to E. C. Tolman's purposive behaviorism; to Egon Brunswik's distal behaviorism and perceptual constancies; to the phenomenological social psychologies of Mustapha Sherif, Solomon Asch, David Kretch & Richard Crutchfield; and to cybernetics, resulting in a "phenomenological behaviorism" in which learned views of the world or tendencies to perceive are translated as equivalent to learned response tendencies. Research on social attitudes and intergroup stereotypes came out of this perspective.

He is best known for his methodological writings, of which Campbell and Fiske, "Convergent and discriminant validation by the multitrait-multimethod matrix," and Campbell and Stanley, *Experimental and quasi-experimental designs for research,* are the best known.

These methodological interests combined with his perceptual, learning, and evolutionary interests to produce a naturalistic, evolutionary, and sociological epistemology and theory of science (see Campbell, "Evolutionary epistemology"). A bibliography and brief research autobiography are included in M. B. Brewer & B. E. Collins, *Scientific inquiry and the social sciences: A volume in honor of Donald T. Campbell.*

Among his many honors are presidency of the American Psychological Association (1975) and membership in the National Academy of Sciences (1973).

CANNON, WALTER B. (1871–1945)

Cannon attended Harvard University, and studied medicine. After his graduation in 1900, he took a position there, lecturing, consulting, and doing research. He remained at Harvard 42 years.

In his study of endocrinology and physiology, Cannon made several discoveries that have been significant for psychologists. Cannon's research on emotion and its effect on digestive processes was especially important. Further exploration in this area led him to discoveries of other adaptive changes in the physiology of the body under emotion, stress, and tissue need which he reported in *Bodily changes in pain, hunger, fear, and rage.*

A critique of William James' theory of emotion was presented in this book. The *James-Lange theory* held that physical response preceded the appearance of emotion, that if bodily changes such as increased heart rate or muscle tension did not occur, there would be no emotion. Cannon's substitute theory, now known as the *Cannon-Bard theory of emotion,* held that emotion was an emergency reaction which caused the body to react with the resources needed to cope with the emergency. Cannon identified the hypothalamus as the control center in emotional behavior, and the adrenal gland as the mobilizer of energy resources of the body under stress.

Cannon studied the effects of traumatic shocks during World War I and published them in "Traumatic Shock". He discovered a hormone that stimulates heart activity and named it *sympathin.* Other discoveries of the autonomic nervous system followed which resulted in Cannon's formulation of the concept of *homeostasis:* the tendency for the body to maintain a steady internal state, a constancy of bodily environment, and to attempt to restore equilibrium if constancy is disturbed. This concept has strongly influenced psychology as well as other disciplines.

N. A. HAYNIE

CANTRIL, HADLEY (1906–   )

Cantril received the B.S. from Dartmouth and the Ph.D. from Harvard. He taught at Harvard, Columbia, and Princeton universities and has been associated with the International Institute for Social Research and UNESCO. His contributions to social psychology and personality include areas of social perception, public opinion polling, attitude measurement and value theory.

His book written in conjunction with Gordon Allport, *The psychology of radio* (1935), was the first on that subject. In 1940 he reported his analysis of interviews with people who had listened to a radio broadcast by Orson Wells which simulated in a dramatic way a presumed invasion from Mars. This broadcast caused a panic in certain parts of the eastern United States. He found that those who expressed the greatest fears of a real invasion tended to share personality characteristics.

In another investigation using 600 subjects, he found that in many cases personality characteristics could be judged by merely hearing different individuals read from a prepared manuscript. The judgments derived from merely hearing the voice alone were better than chance.

Under the auspices of UNESCO, through questionnaires Cantril investigated the attitudes that people from various nations had toward each other. For example, the British, Australians, French, German, and Italians tended to judge the Russian people as cruel, domineering, and hard-working, whereas the same groups judged Americans to be practical and progressive.

CAPRARA, GIAN VITTORIO (1944–   )

Caprara was raised in Milan where he received a degree in political science and a specialization diploma in psychology at the Catholic University. From 1973 he taught at the University of Rome, "La Sapienza." Caprara's early training in social psychology was soon directed toward personality psychology with an interactionist orientation. Early research focused on aggression and, subsequently, developed into the study of psychosocial risk with special attention on the processes that predispose and lead to problem behavior.

Research on aggression developed into a bidimensional model that plots the various forms of aggression in a space defined by two main dimensions: negative affect and interpersonal orientation (self versus other centered). Caprara's theory on risk processes hypothesized that the role of aggregation of marginal deviations may lead to amplification of deviance via contrast effect, to rejection, and to further margination.

Caprara served as president of the European Association of Personality. His publications include *Personality and aggression, Personality and individual differences,* and *Modern personality psychology,* which provides critical reviews and new directions.

CARLI, RENZO (1937–   )

Carli received a degree in medicine from the University of Padua, then continued his studies in psychology at the Catholic University of Milan. Currently, he is full professor of dynamic psychology at the University of Rome.

Carli is best known for his study of social organization and institutions. In his initial work on social perception, Carli's interest was focused on interpersonal relations in small groups. Research in this field led him to formulate an original model of analysis of sociometric behavior, based on application of the signal detection theory to social relations. This model is outlined in *Gruppo e istituzione a scuola* (Group and institution in school).

Practice and research in social psychology and psychoanalysis led him to the formulation of an interpretative theory of social interaction, analyzed as collective reproduction of primitive models of family relations within social organizations. In this way Carli developed a pragmatic model of psychosocial intervention based on the analysis of institutional transfer. This theory is discussed in *Psicosociologia delle organizzazione e delle istituzione* (Psychosociology of organizations and institutions) and *Esperienze di psicosociologia* (Experience of psychosociology). Carli is currently editor of *Psicologia Clinica.*

CARMICHAEL, LEONARD (1898–1973)

Carmichael is best remembered in psychology for a relatively small part of his diverse career, his editing and partial writing of the *Manual of child psychology.* Its successor, Paul Mussen's *Carmichael's manual of child psychology,* is a standard reference in the field.

Carmichael's academic career included the B.S. and the Sc.D. from Tufts University, the Ph.D. (1924) from Harvard University, a professorship at Brown University, the deanship of the College of Arts and Sciences at the University of Rochester, and the presidency of Tufts University (1938—1952). He then became the seventh secretary of the Smithsonian Institution, and in 1964 retired to an active position at the National Geographic Society.

In collaboration with Herbert H. Jasper, Carmichael was the first person in the United States to record electroencephalograms. This work led to the recording of eye muscle movements and in turn to research in fatigue in reading.

T. KEITH-LUCAS

CARR, HARVEY A. (1878–1954)

Carr studied in the local schools and attended De Pauw University. He received the M.A. from Colorado, and the Ph.D. from the University of Chicago in 1904. He later became head of the Psychology Department at Chicago, following James Angell.

With Carr, functionalism as a school of psychology reached its full fruition. The best statement of Carr's position is found in *Psychology: A study of mental activity* (1925).

Like other functionalists before him such as John Dewey and James Angell, Carr stressed the adaptation of an organism to its environment. Thus the core of his system is to be found in his discussion of the *adaptive act.* The adaptive act has three aspects: (1) a motivating stimulus which arouses an organism to activity; (2) a sensory stimulus which is an object toward which activity is directed—an incentive or goal; and (3) the response that alters the situation so as to satisfy the motivating stimulus. The response should continue until the motivating stimulus is satisfied by reaching the goal, which brings the adaptive act to a close. The adaptive act is a function of the whole situation involving all the adjustments an organism makes to its environment.

In explaining learning, Carr relied on the laws of association. Learning occurred through the laws of similarity and contiguity. The functional strength of a learned act depends on how frequently a particular association occurs. Emotions he defined as organic adjustments. For example, in anger there was an increase in body energy which allowed a person to overcome that which was in its way.

Although functionalism has been absorbed into the mainstream of psychology, certain aspects of Carr's psychology remain. (1) Psychology should be practical and utilitarian, applying itself to problems of everyday living. (2) Adaptation or adjustment to one's environment is a prerequisite for good mental health. Maladaptive acts lead to problems whose causes must be discovered and resolved.

R. W. LUNDIN

CARROLL, JOHN B. (1916–   )

Carroll received the B.A. in classical languages at Wesleyan University and the Ph.D. (1941) in psychology at the University of Minnesota, where he was a student of B. F. Skinner, although his doctoral dissertation on the factor analysis of verbal abilities was done partly under the direction of L. L. Thurstone. His teaching career, started at Mount Holyoke College and Indiana University, was interrupted by war service as an aviation psychologist in the U.S. Naval Reserve and as a civilian in the Department of the Army. His major positions have been as an educational psychologist at the Harvard Graduate School of Education (1949–1966), as a research psychologist at Educational Testing Service (1966–1974), and as a professor of psychology and psychometrics at the University of North Carolina at Chapel Hill (since 1974).

Influenced by his early acquaintance with B. L. Whorf, he was one of the first psychologists to recognize the contributions of linguistics, as pointed out in his *The study of language.* He edited the writings of Whorf in *Language, thought, and reality.* He developed a series of foreign-language aptitude tests that have been widely used in language-training programs in government and elsewhere. In education, he is best known for his "model of school learning" that formed the basis for mastery learning principles. He has made contributions to psychometric theory and factor analysis and has surveyed and reanalyzed factor-analytic studies of cognitive abilities. His honors include the APA's E. L. Thorndike Award for Distinguished Contributions to Education (1970) and the ETS Award for Distinguished Service to Measurement (1980).

CARTWRIGHT, DORWIN (1915–   )

A leading exponent of field theory in social psychology, Cartwright was persuaded to become a psychologist by Wolfgang Köhler, with whom he studied at Swarthmore College. Upon completing his doctorate at Harvard in 1940, he accepted a postdoctoral fellowship to work with Kurt Lewin at the University of Iowa. In 1942 he joined Rensis Likert to conduct research relating to the national war effort. His studies on the motives for the purchase of war bonds constituted some of the earliest research using a social psychological approach in the analysis of economic behavior.

Following the war, Cartwright helped Lewin found the Research Center for Group Dynamics at Massachusetts Institute of Technology; upon Lewin's death in 1947, he became director of the Center. In 1948 the Center moved to the University of Michigan and became part of the newly formed Institute for Social Research. Cartwright remained at Michigan until his retirement in 1978.

Cartwright is widely recognized as an authority on Lewin's work. He edited a major collection of Lewin's papers, published several analyses of field theory, and extended the Lewinian approach to such topics as social power, decision making, and social networks. He is perhaps most widely known as the author, with A. Zander, of the basic text on group dynamics (1953). In 1977 he received the Kurt Lewin Award of the Society for the Psychological Study of Social Issues.

CASTAÑO ASMITIA, DARVELIO A. (1939–   )

Castaño Asmitia received the master's and the Ph.D. in psychology from the Universidad Nacional Autónoma de México, and studied social psychology of groups at Columbia University in New York.

He has specialized in social psychology of organizations and organizational development. He is the founder of the Department of Industrial Psychology at the Universidad Nacional, and has been a professor there since 1971. He was vice-president of the Asociación Mexicana de Capacitación de Personal in 1976, and served as director of human resources in the National Council of Science and Technology of Mexico in 1978–1981.

His publications include *Desarrollo social y organizacional* and *Problemas de Importación tecnológica psicolaboral en los paises en desarrollo*. As of 1981 he was director of the Faculty of Psychology at the Universidad Nacional.

CATANIA, CHARLES (1936–   )

Catania took Fred S. Keller's introductory psychology course at Columbia College. He received the B.A. and M.A. in psychology from Columbia College and the Ph.D. (1961) from Harvard University, where he was an NSF fellow. As a postdoctoral research fellow, he ran B. F. Skinner's pigeon laboratory until 1962 and then took a position as behavioral pharmacologist at Smith Kline and French.

In 1964, he began teaching at New York University. He became professor and department chair in 1969. In 1973, he moved to the University of Maryland, Baltimore County, where he remained except for a 1-yr Fulbright senior research fellowship at the University College of North Wales (1986–1987).

Catania has written more than 100 articles and book chapters on topics in the experimental analysis of behavior, including learning, reinforcement schedules, and verbal behavior. One is a *Current contents*

citation classic, and his works have been translated into several languages. His text *Learning* had three editions (1992). *The selection of behavior* was coedited with Stevan Harnad. With E. Shimoff and B. A. Matthews, he coauthored the introductory course computer programs *Psychology on a disk* and *Sociology on a disk*.

He has been editor (1966–1969) and review editor (1969–1976; 1983–1991) of the *Journal of the experimental analysis of behavior* and associate editor for *Behavioral and brain sciences* (1980–   ) and has held grants from NSF and NIH. He has held a James McKeen Cattell Sabbatical Award, is a fellow and former president (1976–1979) of Division 25 of the American Psychological Association, and served as president of the Association for Behavior Analysis (1982–1983).

CATTELL, JAMES M. (1860–1944)

Cattell attended Lafayette College for his undergraduate work. He traveled to Europe and studied at Göttingen and then in Leipzig under Wilhelm Wundt. He received a fellowship to return to Johns Hopkins in 1882 and study philosophy. G. Stanley Hall began his lecture there in psychology; Cattell attended the course and began research on mental activities. He returned to Wundt in 1883 to study individual differences, which was characterized as a typically American project by the Germans. Cattell received his degree in 1886 in psychology.

Cattell lectured at Bryn Mawr and at the University of Pennsylvania. He went to England to lecture at Cambridge University, where he met Sir Francis Galton, who shared Cattell's interest in individual differences. From Sir Francis he learned measurement and statistics, and then became the first psychologist to teach and emphasize statistical analysis of experimental results. In 1888 Cattell was appointed professor of psychology at the University of Pennsylvania, the first psychology professorship in the world.

In 1891 Cattell went to Columbia University as professor of psychology and head of the department, where he remained for 26 years. During these years, more doctorates in psychology were awarded by Columbia than by any other graduate school in the United States. Cattell's students were encouraged and, indeed, required to do independent research and to work on their own. Many of them became prominent in the field.

As the years passed, Cattell's personal and professional independence strained his relationship with the administration at Columbia. During World War I he was dismissed on the grounds of being disloyal to his country. Cattell sued for libel and won, but he was not reinstated in his professorship.

In 1921 Cattell organized the Psychological Corporation to provide applied psychological services to industry, the professional community, and the public. As a spokesman and editor, he was an active supporter of psychological organizations and societies.

The theme of all of Cattell's research was mental tests and individual differences, a feature of American as opposed to German psychology. His mental tests were different from later intelligence tests, for he measured elementary bodily or sensory-motor responses. Correlations between his tests and the students' academic performance was low. Although tests of this kind were not valid predictors of intellectual ability (Alfred Binet developed a test of higher mental abilities that *was* an effective measure of intelligence), Cattell's influence was strong, particularly through his student, E. L. Thorndike. Columbia University was the center of the testing movement; Cattell's work contributed to the practical and applied psychology that was uniquely American, and functional.

N. A. HAYNIE

CATTELL, RAYMOND B. (1905–   )

Cattell received his education at Kings College, London, where he received the B.S. in 1924 and the Ph.D. in 1929, and came under the influence of Charles Spearman, the founder of factor analysis. Cattell lectured at University College in Exeter, England, from 1928 to 1931. The following year he undertook the directorship of the City Psychological Clinic in Leicester, England. In 1937 he left for the United States, spending a year at the Teachers College of Columbia University, and three more years at Clark University. The war years were spent at Harvard as a lecturer in psychology. His long tenure at the University of Illinois began in 1944.

Cattell derived his distinction in psychology from multivariate factor analysis. His books are generally based on factor analysis, and his theory of personality is a factor analytic or statistical approach to personality. His work in factor analysis culminated in the voluminous *Handbook of multivariate experimental psychology*. His many books on personality are written from the factor analytic orientation, including *Description and measurement of personality; An introduction to personality study; Personality; A systematic theoretical and factual study; Personality and motivation: Structure and measurement; Personality and social psychology; The scientific analysis of personality; Personality and learning theory: A systems theory of maturation and structures learning;* and *Personality and learning theory: The structure of personality in its environment.*

Cattell bases his findings on the inductive-hypothetico-deductive method, defining personality as "that which enables us to predict what [the individual] will do in a given situation" (*An introduction to personality study*, p. 21).

CHA, JAE-HO (1934–   )

Cha grew up in Yochu and Seoul, Korea. After receiving the bachelor's degree from Seoul National University, he went on to do graduate studies at Seoul National, the University of Arizona, and the University of California at Los Angeles, receiving the Ph.D. under Harold H. Kelley in 1971.

He was responsible for identifying a class of social perceptual phenomena, including dissonance effect and perceptual constancies that he named the *discounting effect* because he thought that a kind of cognitive discounting underlay all the phenomena subsumed under the name. Kelley later elevated the process of discounting to a principle: the discounting principle in attribution. The principle is akin to Cha's monopoly principle, which states that "when there is a prominent and sufficient cause for the focal behavior, the background information is not scanned by the observer for other causes." Cha also was the first to point out that effect constancy is a necessary condition for occurrence of a dissonance effect.

Since his return to Korea in 1972, Cha has been a faculty member of the Department of Psychology at Seoul National University. He has been actively involved with the Korean Psychological Association, serving as president of the Division of Social Psychology and president-elect of the Association (1983–1984). His latest research includes the nature of stranger and separation anxieties and object attachment. His publications include *Experimental designs in psychology and education* and *A study on boy preference and family planning in Korea*.

CHAPANIS, ALPHONSE (1917–   )

Sometimes called the father of human factors (as it is called in America), or ergonomics (as it is called throughout most of the rest of the world), Chapanis received the bachelor's degree from the University of Connecticut, and the M.A. and the Ph.D. from Yale.

Trained as an experimental psychologist, Chapanis put his science to practical use when he joined the Aero Medical Laboratory at Wright-Patterson Air Force Base in Dayton, Ohio, in 1942 as a civilian and, in the following year, as an officer. The first psychologist to be employed in that laboratory, Chapanis acquired his taste for applied work while wrestling with the difficult problems encountered by the men who had to fly and fight in the advanced military aircraft of that era. In 1946, Chapanis joined the Johns Hopkins University, where he remained until 1982, except for two leaves of absence; one in 1953–1954, when he was a member of the technical staff at Bell Laboratories, and the other in 1960–1961, when he was liaison scientist in the Office of Naval Research's branch office at the U.S. Embassy in London. Retired from teaching in 1982, he became president of his own consulting corporation.

Strict adherence to practical empiricism is characteristic of Chapanis's work. Disinclined to trust theories, hypotheses, hunches, or logic, he always demands empirical proof. Although he frequently uses precise experimental methods in his work, he is acutely aware of the limitations of this method of inquiry and readily uses other methods of investigation when appropriate. His insistence on empirical proof is demonstrated in his work as a consultant to industry and as a witness in law cases involving human factors issues.

CHARCOT, JEAN-MARTIN (1825–1893)

Charcot was appointed professor of pathological anatomy at the University of Paris in 1860. Two years later he was appointed senior physician at Salpêtrière, a hospital for mental patients in Paris.

He is best known for his studies on hypnosis and hysteria. An eminent physician of his time, his theory of hypnosis was in direct conflict with that developed shortly before by A. A. Liébeault and Hippolyte Bernheim at Nancy. They had placed emphasis on the suggestion of sleep to induce the hypnotic state. As the leader of what became known as the Paris School, Charcot believed that hypnosis was a condition peculiar to hysterical patients and a useful method for investigating hysterical predispositions. Further, he believed that there was a neurological predisposition for hysteria, while Liébeault and Beruheim felt that hypnosis was merely a special case of normal suggestibility.

Sigmund Freud had heard of Charcot's work and his use of hypnosis. In 1885 Freud went to Paris to hear Charcot's lectures and witness his hypnotic demonstrations. By this time Charcot had found hypnosis an excellent treatment for hysteria: in treating a patient with a hysterical paralysis, he would utter the phrase "ça passe" (it's going away) and presumably it did.

At one of Charcot's lectures which Freud attended, a member of the audience had asked about a difficulty he did not understand. As the story goes, Charcot replied, "This has to do with the sexual zone—always, always, always!" Whether or not this incident had any effect on Freud's theory of psychosexuality is debatable.

R. W. LUNDIN

CHAVEZ, EZEQUIEL A. (1868–1946)

Chavez, a Mexican lawyer, was considered by James Mark Baldwin, the pioneer of Mexican psychology. In 1896, Chavez promoted an educational reform, which permitted in 1897, his teaching of the first course ever in Mexico, in psychology. In 1901 he published his essay on the distinctive traits of sensibility as a factor of the Mexican character (*Ensayo sobre los rasgos distintivos de la sensibilidad como factor del caracter Mexicano*), which inaugerates the study of the Mexican national identity with an approach and conceptualization in agreement with the scientific psychology of his time.

Chavez translated, in 1904, E. B. Titchener's *A primer of psychology*, which served as textbook for the course he had introduced for the National Prepatory School (a junior college). In 1907, he organized the Society for Psychological Studies, the first in Latin America. He participated actively in the creation of the new National University of

Mexico, and invited Baldwin to dictate its inaugural course. He became president of the university and brought in scholars such as Peirre Janet, George Dumas, Franz Boas, and Andre Seigfried.

In 1928 Chavez published his book *Ensayo de psicologia de la adolescencia,* in which he proposed the idea of the famous inferiority feeling of Mexicans. He also taught courses in educational and adolescent psychology. In 1939, he was a participant in the creation of a curriculum leading to a masters degree in psychology. This was the first psychology program in Latin America. He wrote a psychological essay on Sor Juana Ines de la Cruz.

P. VALDERRAMA-ITURBE

CHELPANOV, GEORGII IVANOVICH (1862–1936)

Chelpanov studied at Leipzig under Wilhelm Wundt and brought Wundt's psychology of content back to Russia, where he became the chief exponent of Wundt's and Edward Titchener's psychology in pre-revolutionary Russia. In 1912 he founded the Moscow Psychological Institute; he was replaced as director by Konstantin Kornilow in 1924. In 1917 he founded the *Russian Psychological Review;* although it ceased publication shortly after the Revolution, through it Chalpanov became the chief founder of experimental psychology in Russia.

For Chelpanov, psychological activity was one of the expressions of the soul. The brain was the seat of the soul through which psychology could be expressed. The brain could not function without a soul which directed it. The soul was distinct from matter, but through proper experimental techniques it could be studied and understood. As an exponent of Wundt's experimental psychology he wrote the first experimental text in Russian, *Introduction to experimental psychology.* In the postrevolutionary period, Chelpanov's Western psychology was abandoned because it was too pure and idealistic, and inconsistent with Marxist dialectical materialism. However, the institute that Chelpanov founded continued to play an important role in the later development of Soviet psychology.

R. W. LUNDIN

CHEN, LI (1902–   )

Chen took his first degree in science at Shanghai University. In the early 1930s, he studied at University College at London and obtained the Ph.D. under the supervision of Charles Spearman. He worked at the National Institute of Industrial Psychology, London, and later, at the Institute of Psychology, Berlin. In 1935, Chen went back to China as a senior researcher at Institute of Psychology, Academia Sinica, and became professor at Qinhua University and later Zhejiang University. He then became the president of Hangzhou University and past vice president of the Chinese Psychological Society. For more than 60 yr, Chen has taught and done research in psychology, especially industrial psychology, and has made contributions to the development of modern Chinese psychology. His book *Essentials of industrial psychology* was the first industrial psychology book in China. Based on his doctoral dissertation, his article "Periodicity in oscillation" demonstrated the use of a smoothing curve to eliminate fatigue and adaptation and was considered a new perspective in this area. His study on the differentiation and integration of the g factor, published in the *Journal of Genetic Psychology,* was recognized as a landmark in understanding intellectual development. After the founding of the People's Republic of China, Chen published many books and more than 100 articles, including "Prospectus of industrial psychology" and "Psychology of industrial management." He has worked in diverse areas such as children's physical growth, feedback in technical training, programmed instruction, cogni-

tive development, test theory, and organizational reform. His work on attribution theory, group dynamics, managerial decision making, human–computer interaction, and macro ergonomics in the 1980s has affected the development of social, organizational, and engineering psychology in China.

Z. M. WANG

CHILAND, COLETTE, (1928–   )

Chiland was first trained in philosophy, and later in medicine, psychiatry, and psychology, at the University of Paris. She became an assistant to Jean Piaget for three years of his teaching at the University of Paris (1957–1960), and since then has herself been teaching there. She has the M.D. and the Ph.D.

Presently professor of clinical psychology at the René Descartes University in Paris, she is also a psychiatrist at the Alfred Binet Center (Mental Health Association of the 13th Arrondissement of Paris), and a training analyst at the Paris Psychoanalytic Society. She became vice president of the International Association of Child and Adolescent Psychiatry and Allied Professions in 1974, and is now president of this association. She has written or edited several books in French and English. Her book *L'enfant de six ans et son avenir* (The six-year-old and his future) was translated into Italian.

Her interest is focused on longitudinal development research, sex differences in psychopathology, and female sexuality.

CHILD, IRVIN L. (1915–   )

After study at U.C.L.A., graduate study at Yale, and two years teaching at Harvard, Child has spent the rest of his professional career at Yale University. The most constant theme in his work is the interaction between individual and society. His dissertation (1943/1970) analyzed the impact of differing cultural norms and of social position on the personality of second-generation Italian-Americans. Later, an interest in socialization was expressed in analysis of child-training practices of traditional societies. He did a number of holocultural studies: correlational research in which the unit of observation is a culture, not a person (J. W. M. Whiting & I. L. Child, 1953; Bacon, Child, & Barry, 1963). These studies provide empirical test of the universality of specific processes of learning and psychodynamics. Interaction between psychological and social processes characterized also his extensive research on psychological esthetics (Child, 1981).

Some of his research findings argued for the importance of physique as an important interactive influence on personality, at a time when psychologists tended to deny its importance. On doing some research on extrasensory perception and psychokinesis (Child, 1976) and becoming acquainted with the research of others, he was more impressed by the evidence for previously unrecognized phenomena than by theories suggesting the phenomena are impossible. Trust in observation is one strand in the humanistic emphasis which, according to Child, needs further integration with psychologists' traditional emphasis on rigorous research method (Child, 1973).

CHLEWIŃSKI, ZDZISŁAW (1929–   )

Chlewiński studied psychology and in 1963 received the Ph.D. in psychology at the Catholic University Of Lublin, and the title of *docent* in 1972. He conducted research in the United States at Stanford University, Utah State University, Michigan University, and the Catholic University of America, and also in England at Oxford University. He began his research in the domain of attitudes and their relationships with personality traits.

His major field of research is information processing, concept identification, transfer, learning, problem solving, and individual and group decision making with special emphasis on the structure of the group, the phenomenon of polarization, cognitive conservatism and radicalism in individual and group decisions, and aspiration and decision in task-and-achievement situations.

Chlewiński continues to research and lecture at the Catholic University in Lublin, where his professional career began. His publications include *Attitudes and personality traits, Selected problems of the psychology of religion,* and over 100 research papers.

CHOMSKY, A. NOAM (1928–   )

Chomsky is a controversial figure in psycholinguistics and probably the foremost theorist in the field. For his achievements he has received numerous honorary doctorates. Chomsky was educated at the University of Pennsylvania, where he received the B.A., M.A., and Ph.D. (1955). From the time he received the Ph.D., he has been on the faculty of Massachusetts Institute of Technology, although he has offered courses and lectured throughout the world, including Oxford and Berkeley.

Chomsky's books include *Syntactic structures, Current issues in linguistic theory, Aspects of the theory of syntax, Cartesian linguistics, Topics in the theory of generative grammar, The sound pattern of English* (with Morris Halle), *Language and the mind, Studies on semoantics in generative grammar, Reflections on language,* and *Language and responsibility.*

Chomsky views the understanding of language as genetically determined and developing comparably to other bodily organs. Because the human brain is preprogrammed by a "language acquisition device," humans generate sentences the grammar of which is universal. Chomsky argues that humans have an innate capacity for grasping language. Learning a language is both species-specific and species-uniform: only humans have the capacity for language acquisition, and all languages share a common underlying logical structure. Thus the logic (or logical syntax) of all languages is the same. Terming the logical structure *deep structure,* Chomsky holds that it is not learned. The language that human beings must learn is a *surface structure*—phonetic sounds or the sentence as uttered. Chomsky's psycholinguistics is labeled *generative transformational grammar,* a system that integrates both surface and deep structure.

Chomsky's psycholinguistics is diametrically opposed to B. F. Skinner's verbal learning theory.

CLAPARÈDE, EDOUARD (1873–1940)

Claparède is considered the founder of child psychology in Switzerland. He was encouraged by his cousin, Theodor Flournoy, who had studied psychology under Wundt at Leipzig, to enter the field of psychology. He received his medical degree at the University of Geneva in 1897 and then went to Paris, where he became a close friend of Alfred Binet.

Claparède's interest in child psychology emerged in his book, *Experimental pedagogy and the psychology of the child* (1911). From his early days, Claparède stressed the biological rather than the metaphysical basis for psychology. He defined experimental pedagogy as the study of the circumstances favorable to the development of the child and the means for educating the child properly. The book stressed the developmental processes in children and had a profound impact on the later thinking of Jean Piaget in the use of experimental techniques to study children.

Claparède's general approach tended to be functionalistic, studying the psychological phenomena in terms of their usefulness in meeting an individual's needs. According to this position, the child's mental processes came into play when needs were present. When placed in an environment that aroused those needs, useful mental activity would result. Accordingly, Claparède stressed the adaptive value of behavior, the significance of physical constitution in mental aptitudes and the role of heredity and environment as they participated in the educational process.

To improve teacher training and advance the psychological study of children, he established the J. J. Rousseau Institute in 1912. This institute became well known for the development of progressive methods in teaching.

R. W. LUNDIN

CLARK, KENNETH B. (1914–   )

Clark was brought to New York City by his mother when he was four. He attended schools in Harlem and graduated from George Washington High School in 1931. He received the B.S. and M.A. from Howard University, and the Ph.D. in psychology from Columbia University in 1940.

As a social psychologist, Clark worked with the lawyers in the series of cases on equality of educational opportunity which led to the historic 1964 *Brown v. Board of Education of Topeka, Kansas* decision. His studies on the effect of segregation on the personality development of children were cited by the U.S. sSupreme Court in footnote 11 of the decision.

In 1946 Clark and his wife, Dr. Mamie Phipps Clark, founded the interracial Northside Center for Child Development for the treatment of children with personality and learning problems. In 1964 he became founder and director of Harlem Youth Opportunities Unlimited (HARYOU), a prototype community development program which sought to increase the participation of low-income groups in decisions on education, housing, employment and training, and economic development.

A member of the faculty at City College of the City University of New York from 1942 to 1975, he was named Distinguished Professor of Psychology in 1971. He has been a member of the New York Board of Regents since 1966.

A member of Phi Beta Kappa and Sigma Xi, Clark has been president of the American Psychological Association (1970), of the Society for Psychological Studies of Social Issues (1959), and of the Metropolitan Applied Research Center (1967–1975). Since 1975 he has been president of Clark, Phipps, Clark & Harris, Inc., a human relations consulting firm.

CLARK, KENNETH E. (1914–   )

Clark is the president of the Center for Creative Leadership in Greensboro, North Carolina. He is also a professor of psychology at the University of Rochester and dean emeritus of the College of Arts and Science of the University of Rochester. He received the B.S. from Ohio State University, the M.A., and the Ph.D. in 1940. Appointed dean of the College of Arts and Science at the University of Rochester in 1963, he served until 1980, after serving as dean of the College of Arts and Sciences at the University of Colorado from 1961 to 1963.

Clark is a member of the American Association for the Advancement of Science; the American and Midwestern Psychological Associations; Psi Chi; Phi Delta Kappa; and Phi Beta Kappa. He served on the Army Science Board, the Board of Overseers for the Center for Naval Analysis, and the Panel on Behavior Sciences. He is also a consultant for various foundations and corporations.

Clark is the author of *America's psychologists; Vocational interests of non-professional men;* and *The graduate student as teacher* (with

Vincent Nowlis and Miriam Rock). He has also been published in various periodicals. He served as editor of the *Journal of Applied Psychology* from 1961 to 1970.

COAN, RICHARD W. (1928–   )

Coan received the B.A. and the M.A. from the University of California (Berkeley) and the Ph.D. from the University of Southern California. As a graduate student, he taught at Los Angeles City College and completed clinical internships at the Metropolitan State Hospital and as part of the facility of the California Youth Authority. In 1955, he joined the faculty of the University of Illinois and began research on child personality in collaboration with Raymond B. Cattell. In 1957, he moved to the University of Arizona, where he served on the psychology teaching faculty until 1990.

Coan's work reflects an abiding interest in personality theory, the psychology of science, and the study of myths and symbols, and his publications have contributed to an understanding of alternative goals of personality development and the psychological roots of theoretical orientation.

Three of Coan's books deal with various aspects of personality development: *The optimal personality; Hero, artist, sage or saint?;* and *The psychology of adjustment. Psychologists: Personal and theoretical pathways* is concerned with patterns and determinants of theoretical orientation in psychology. A subsequent work is *Human consciousness and its evolution: A multidimensional view.* In addition, he has authored several personality inventories and published papers on theoretical concepts, research methodology, openness to experience, the experience of control, and masculinity–femininity.

COHEN, RUDOLF J. (1932–   )

After training as a teacher for elementary schools in the postwar years, Cohen studied psychology at the University of Munich. Most lectures were then strongly influenced by phenomenology and concerned the area now called "nonverbal communication." Having obtained the Vordiplom degree, Cohen continued his studies at the University of Hamburg, where C. Bondy and later P. R. Hofstätter excited their students with the latest developments in social psychology, statistics, and psychological testing. Fascinated by the writings of Paul Meehl and David Rapaport, Cohen underwent an orthodox training in psychoanalysis. He took part in several diagnostic projects and conducted a series of experiments on person perception and the processing of apparently conflicting information. He received the Ph.D. in 1961, and the *Habilitation* in 1968. His main study from this period was later translated into English as *Patterns of personality judgment.*

In 1968 Cohen accepted a position at the Max Planck Institute for Psychiatry in Munich. He became interested in behavior modification and in the potentialities of experimental psychology and psychophysiology to elucidate regularities in the deviant behavior of schizophrenic and brain-damaged patients. A year later he was offered a chair in psychology at the University of Konstanz, which gave him a unique access to a research ward and a psychophysiological laboratory in the Psychiatric State Hospital. Apart from studies in the treatment of female alcoholics, his team has been mostly concerned with the social behavior and with psychophysiological correlates (especially event-related potentials) of information processing in chronic schizophrenics. Furthermore, Cohen is intensively engaged in experimental research on cognitive processes in aphasic patients. In the winter of 1979–1980 he was appointed Theodor Heuss Guest Professor at the New School for Social Research in New York.

COMBE, GEORGE (1788–1858)

Combe, along with Gall and Spurzheim, was one of the leading phrenologists of his time. He started out as an opponent of phrenology but got converted by Spurzheim and took up the cause from about 1817 until his death.

He was a prolific writer and lecturer. His *Essays on phrenology* was published in 1819. He was a Scotsman by birth but went to Canada and the United States to spread the word. He was a strong contender for a chair in logic at the University of Edinbergh but the position was given to Sir William Hamilton. Through his efforts the "new" science also spread to England. In 1820, he helped to found the Phrenological society, which in 1823 began to publish the *Phrenological Journal.*

His most popular work was *The constitution of man,* published in 1828. In 1848 he was invited to Germany to give a series of lectures on phrenology at the University of Heidelberg.

R. W. LUNDIN

COMTE, AUGUSTE (1798–1857)

Comte, along with Julien de la Mettrie and Pierre Cabanis, belonged to a movement roughly identified as French materialism. Passing beyond the materialists' view of considering man as a machine, Comte founded another movement called positivism. According to Comte, only objective and observable knowledge could be valid. He completely rejected introspection, which stressed the inner analysis of conscious experiences. Private knowledge could not be valid.

In the evolution of thought, Comte believed man had passed through three stages, from the theological through the metaphysical to the positivistic, which is the basis for scientific thought. He considered the current psychology of his time, which stressed subjective analysis and looking into the contents of one's consciousness, to be the last phase of theology.

His writings also had a strong impact on the social theories of the time. He believed that man must be emancipated from idealism in favor of direct experience. Society must be considered dynamic rather than static. The aim of the study of society—sociology—is to remove social phenomenon from the sphere of the theological and metaphysical, so as to subject them to the study of those same scientific laws found in the natural sciences.

Comte's ideas had a strong influence on modern behaviorism. Some have considered him the first behaviorist.

R. W. LUNDIN

CONDILLAC, ETIENNE BONNOT DE (1715–1780)

Condillac, in his early years in Paris, became acquainted with Diderot and his followers. Later he developed a friendship with Rousseau which lasted many years.

As a French intellectual and philosopher, Condillac with great success introduced the empiricism of John Locke to France. He reacted against Descartes' theory of innate ideas and Leibnitz's theory of the monad. Condillac's first work, published in 1746, was an *Essay on the origin of human knowledge.* This was a presentation of Locke's views that all knowledge came from experience. Condillac's most important work, *Treatise on sensations,* was published in 1754. In it he asked his readers to imagine a statue and what would follow if it were to experience sensations. He argued that the sum total of all human mental processes would follow, without any need to presuppose any laws of association. Variations in the quality of sensations would necessarily produce those acts of judgment and comparison which were necessary for human comprehension. The fact of having experiences was sufficient to explain judgments and knowledge. Mental functions did not need to be added to experiences, if the experiences carried out their own function. Thus Condillac did away with Locke's belief that the second function of the mind was reflection upon itself. For Condillac, the whole of mental life could be derived from sensations alone. Feelings of pleasantness or unpleasantness were inherent in the sensations themselves. His views were the ultimate in sensational empiricism.

For a while his views achieved great popularity, but inevitably their influence declined because they were too simple. Later critics explained that it could never be possible to reduce the mind to sensory experiences alone, and the idea of likening a human mind to mere sensations received by a statue lacked a certain human quality. However, Condillac's sensational empiricism had a strong impact on the movement of French materialism that was to follow. Furthermore, like Locke, he fostered the empirical attitude that is the basis for natural science.

R. W. LUNDIN

CONGER, JOHN (1921–   )

Conger received the B.A. from Amherst College, and the M.S. and Ph.D. (1949) from Yale. During World War II he served in the U.S. Navy. He has served as child psychologist at the Veterans Administration Hospital and is presently professor of psychology at the University of Colorado Medical School.

His main contributions to psychology have been in the fields of childhood and adolescence. His books include *Adolescence and youth: Psychological development in a changing world, Contemporary issues in adolescent development*, and with Paul Mussen and Jerome Kagan, *Child development and personality*.

His research studies in the field of adolescence have included numerous subjects: adolescent sexual patterns; peer relationships and parental influences; the social relationships of adolescents in crowds; cliques and individual friendships; identity formation; problems of alienation among minorities and the underprivileged; delinquency and its relation to social change; problems of adjustment involving physical and psychological disorders; the family and social change; and social change and adolescent vulnerability.

K. W. BACK

COOLEY, CHARLES HORTON (1864–1929)

As a sociologist, Cooley is best known to social psychologists through his conception of the self, the "looking-glass self."

He was the son of a prominent judge who was also the first dean of the University of Michigan Law School, and from whom he differed greatly in temperament, being naturally shy and retiring, and unsuited to administrative responsibility. For various reasons (his relation to his father may have been one), he took time to find his proper niche. Immediately upon graduating in engineering, he went to Washington, D.C., to prepare for graduate work in economics. He returned to Michigan and began graduate study in economics, in which field he became an instructor while still a graduate student, beginning in 1892. He received the Ph.D. in economics and sociology in 1894 and remained at the University of Michigan for the rest of his career. He achieved the status of full professor in 1907, and in 1918 was elected president of the American Sociological Society, which he had helped found in 1905.

Since Cooley did little quantitative work in the more modern tradition of measurement, he is sometimes classed as one of the last influential armchair sociologists, in the sense that William James was an armchair psychologist. Cooley had been influenced to enter sociology by reading Herbert Spencer, but he did not like Spencer's political and social views

and as a wide reader preferred Goethe. As more quantitative movements became popular, Cooley's views entered into a period of neglect, but he came to be quoted again after World War II for his views on the self, his emphasis on the significance of the primary group, and remarks on social process and institutional analysis.

His looking-glass concept states that we form an image of what others see in us as, quite literally, we see ourselves in a mirror. The idea traces back, as he clearly recognized, to the views of William James on the social self ("A man has as many selves as there are individuals who recognize him"), and to James Mark Baldwin, who had indicated that the self was developed as a product of social interaction.

Later interest in Cooley's work was prompted not only by revival of interest in the self, but by the extensive studies of reference-group behavior and the study of small groups.

E. R. HILGARD

COOMBS, CLYDE H. (1912–   )

Coombs obtained the B.A. and M.A. from the University of California (Berkeley), and the Ph.D. (1940) from the University of Chicago under L. L. Thurstone. He served as captain and major in World War II and received the Legion of Merit. He went to the University of Michigan in 1946, where he has remained ever since, except for numerous visiting professorships in the United States and abroad. He has a D.S.S. from the University of Leiden and is a member of the National Academy of Sciences.

Coombs' work has centered on choice behavior, with an interest in methodology. He integrated a system for relating methods of collecting data, called the "searchingness structure," and a system that related models for psychological scaling, into a theory of data. He developed a methodology for the analysis of preferential choice behavior called unfolding theory, which led to a general psychological theory of preference and hedonic tone using a mathematical theory of single-peaked functions derived from behavioral science principles. His experimental work on inconsistency of preference showed that it violated strong stochastic transitivity but satisfied a weaker form. This distinguished hedonic tone and its measurement from the measurement of sensation.

Coombs' experimental work on individual risky decision making led to the extension of conjoint measurement to tests of the general bilinear model using the $(2 \times 2) \times (2 \times 2)$ experimental design.

Coombs' research interests include empirical study of election data. Plurality as a social choice system was found to favor candidates who polarized the electorate. He also extended the theory of preference to the problem of conflict resolution. Two types of conflict between individuals are distinguished, and the theory of single-peaked functions clarifies the similarities and differences among such methods of conflict resolution as bargaining, negotiation, voting, the jury system, debate, and the use of peace commissions.

CORNELIUS, HANS (1863–1910)

Cornelius belonged to what is known in the 19th century as the Austrian school of psychology. Included among these Austrian universities were Vienna, Graz, Prague, and sometimes Munich. This was at a time when Brentano had set forth his act psychology and Wundt was involved with his elemental psychology of content.

Among other things, the Austrian school was concerned with what was the element or property of form quality of an experience. This notion eventually evolved into the Gestalt school in Germany.

Cornelius maintained that the form quality was an attribute of experience and must be perceived as a whole (not broken down into individual experiences as Wundt had suggested). Attention to any part of the whole form would destroy the whole experience.

R. W. LUNDIN

COUÉ, EMILE (1857–1926)

Coué first started his career as a chemist. He studied hypnotism and suggestion under Bernheim and Liébeault at Nancy. Like Bernheim he often treated many of his patients without charge. His practice of psychotherapy involved imagination as opposed to will. He claimed that, by means of autosuggestion, ideas that caused illness might be eliminated by being suggested away. He insisted that he was not himself a healer, but one who taught others how to heal themselves. His methods became widely popular in Great Britain and the United States during the early part of the twentieth century.

His famous statement, "Every day in every way I am becoming better and better," has become proverbial.

R. W. LUNDIN

CRAIK, FERGUS I. M. (1935–   )

Craik received the B.S.C. from the University of Edinburgh in 1960 and was then appointed to the scientific staff of the Medical Research Council's Unit for Research on Occupational Aspects of Aging at the University of Liverpool. He obtained the Ph.D. from that university in 1965. In the same year he was appointed lecturer in psychology at Birkbeck College, University of London, and remained there until 1971, when he moved to the University of Toronto as an associate professor (1971) and subsequently professor (1975). During 1982–1983 he was a fellow at the Center for Advanced Study in the Behavioral Sciences at Stanford University.

Craik's work has focused on problems of human memory, especially memory for linguistic material, and on adult age differences in memory. His earlier work was on short-term memory, and in 1972 he and Robert Lockhart proposed "levels of processing" view of the memory system. He has written some 80 articles and chapters and has co-edited five books. Craik has been on the editorial boards of several journals dealing with research in experimental psychology and was editor of the *Journal of Verbal Learning and Verbal Behavior* from 1980 to 1984. He is a fellow of CPA and APA and is a member of the Society of Experimental Psychologists. He was awarded a Guggenheim Fellowship (declined) in 1982 and held a Killam Research Fellowship in 1982–1984.

CRAIK, KENNETH J. W. (1914–1945)

Kenneth Craik was an Edinburgh graduate in philosophy who switched to experimental psychology and obtained the Ph.D. at the University of Cambridge. He was elected a Fellow of St. John's College, Cambridge, in 1940. He worked in the Cambridge Psychological Laboratory until his death in a traffic accident in 1945. Craik was a man of undisputed brilliance and his premature death was a loss of the first magnitude to psychology in the United Kingdom and further afield.

Craik's initial interests lay almost exclusively in vision; his early papers on visual adaptation and kindred problems formed the substance of both his Ph.D. thesis and his successful fellowship dissertation. Craik's experiments on differential brightness sensitivity, visual acuity, and subjective brightness convinced him that the adapting illumination "sets the eye" to a certain range of sensitivity and that, except at very dim levels of illumination, differential sensitivity is keenest at an illumination equal to that of the adapting illumination. This conception of the "range-setting" property of the eye aroused considerable interest

at the time, and the applied work which Craik undertook during World War II—much of it on behalf of the Royal Air Force—was mainly concerned with problems of visual adaptation (Zangwill, 1980).

The only study of any length which Craik lived to complete was a small volume entitled *The nature of explanation*, in which he put forward one of the earliest models of human thought based on the analogy of the digital computer. Although his argument was largely philosophical, it had wide influence on postwar experimental psychology.

Some years after Craik's death, a volume of his unpublished papers and manuscripts was published under the editorship of Stephen Sherwood. This owed much to the initiative of Warren McCulloch, who had a very high regard for Craik's originality and regarded him as a virtual cofounder of cybernetics. Had Craik completed the main theoretical study upon which he was engaged at the time of his death, it is probable that he would have produced a first-class contribution to psychological theory.

O. L. ZANGWILL

CRESPI, LEO P. (1916–   )

Armed with the B.A. summa cum laude from UCLA, Crespi began his career at Princeton University in comparative psychology with the Ph.D. thesis that posed a challenge to conventional motivation theory with what has come to be known as the "Crespi effect."

Crespi then shifted to social psychology, and after serving on the Princeton faculty left to direct the U.S. government's program of opinion surveying in postwar Germany. During his tenure abroad (1948–1954) he was elected president of the World Association of Public Opinion Research.

Crespi was invited back to Washington to direct the government's worldwide program of surveys for the U.S. Information Agency, and in 1962 received a Superior Service Award from then Director Edward R. Murrow for "making a unique and original contribution to the conduct of United States foreign information activities by his pioneering use of surveys."

One of Crespi's confidential government papers received possibly the widest attention of any public opinion survey in history, when it leaked out to become a central issue of U.S. prestige abroad in the 1960 Presidential campaign. The report was reproduced in its entirety in the *New York Times* (Oct. 27, 1960) and was deemed by some to have tipped an extremely close Presidential election to John F. Kennedy.

In later years Crespi assumed the role of an elder statesman as Senior Research Advisor in the Office of Research in the U.S. Information Agency, and reflected upon his experience in such papers as "The meaning and measurement of program effectiveness in the United States Information Agency."

CRISSEY, MARIE SKODAK (1910–   )

Crissey received the B.S. and the M.A. degrees at Ohio State University. She was a student of Henry H. Goddard and Sidney Pressey, among others, who stimulated her interest in mental development and school achievement. She became a fellow at the University of Budapest and received the Ph.D. from the University of Iowa in 1938.

Crissey administered the Child Guidance Center at Flint, Michigan (1938–1946), was director of school psychology and the special education program at Dearborn, Michigan (1949–1969), was a consultant to vocational rehabilitation services for the blind and handicapped, and had a private practice in psychology (1942–1982) with emphasis on parent–child relations, assessment, and guidance.

Her contributions can be divided into research and applied areas. The latter are primarily in schools and agencies, and include development of special education programs, compensatory programs for handicapped or deprived students, and educational and vocational guidance of high school students. Her research contributions include follow-up studies of mental development of adopted children and children receiving special educational programs, emphasizing effects of stimulation and appropriate experience on acceleration of learning skills. She found that children from deprived backgrounds showed delays, retardation, and associated social and vocational inadequacies. While not denying genetic differences, she highlighted the practicality and effectiveness of environmental and experimental enrichment. Her recent activities have focused on preserving archives of early studies in retardation, testing, and mental and general child development, with a view to reassessing these studies in the light of current knowledge and concepts.

CRONBACH, LEE J. (1916–   )

Cronbach received the B.A. from Fresno State College and the Ph.D. at the University of Chicago in 1940. He has taught at the universities of Chicago, Illinois, and Stanford. In 1957, he served as president of the American Psychological Association and, in 1974, received the Distinguished Scientific Contribution Award.

His most important books are *Essentials of psychological testing* and *Educational psychology*. In his research, he has been concerned with new approaches to the validation of psychological tests. His book on psychological testing emphasized general critical principles for test development and use. He chaired the 1951–1955 Committee on Test Standards of the American Psychological Association, to develop the original code for maintaining quality in tests of ability and personality.

In educational psychology Cronbach has stressed the relationship between classroom practices and basic psychological principles, particularly those of generalization and the transfer of training.

CUMMINGS, NICHOLAS A. (1924–   )

Cummings received the B.A. from the University of California at Berkeley, the M.A. from the Claremont Graduate School, and the Ph.D. (1958) from Adelphi University. Cummings's main contributions to professional psychology have been in the nature of innovations. He wrote the nation's first prepaid comprehensive psychotherapy insurance benefit; established a privately funded community mental health center, which became a model for the Kennedy C.M.H.C. Act; and established psychology's first professional school (California School of Professional Psychology), expanding it to four campuses. He founded American Biodyne, the nation's first mental health HMO. In research, he is the pioneer of the medical offset literature and a seminal contributor to empirically derived targeted, focused psychotherapy. His brief psychotherapy is known as "brief, intermittent therapy throughout the life cycle."

He is the author of more than 400 scientific papers, books, and book chapters. He has received numerous awards, including two honorary doctorates, and has served on the Mental Health Commission of two presidents (Kennedy and Carter). He served as president of the American Psychological Association 1979–1980.

DALLENBACH, KARL M. (1887–1971)

Dallenbach graduated from the University of Illinois and undertook graduate work in Psychology at the University of Pittsburgh. He completed his doctorate under Titchener at Cornell University. During these years he summered at Bonn University, where Oswald Külpe taught. In 1913 Dallenbach's career opened at the University of Oregon. Two years later he left for Ohio State University, before returning to Cornell.

Dallenbach supported Titchener's view that psychology, as the science of mind or consciousness, was to be investigated by methods of introspection or self-observation. To promote Titchener's views, Dallenbach purchased the *American Journal of Psychology* in 1920. Titchener became sole editor with Dallenbach as manager. In 1925, when relations between the two became strained, Titchener resigned, leaving Dallenbach as editor.

In addition to teaching, supervising research, and helping to build up a laboratory, Dallenbach published over a hundred articles. During World War I he and others administered psychological tests to Army personnel. In World War II he served as chairperson of the Emergency Research Committee of the War Department's National Research Council. In 1948, following a 30-year tenure at Cornell, he was appointed Distinguished Professor of Psychology at the University of Texas in Austin.

Dallenbach experimented on attention, seeking to support Titchener's view that attention is sensory or "attributive" clearness, rather than cognition (1930). Concerning the skin senses, he demonstrated that heat is experienced when neighboring warm and cold spots in the skin are simultaneously stimulated, the latter producing a "paradoxical cold." He also demonstrated pain adaptation in the skin.

He investigated "facial vision," the fact that the blind can detect obstacles without contacting them. Blindfolded seeing persons can also sense their presence and movement. The sense most involved proved to be hearing. In a minor study on the labyrinth sense, he found that many children like to be made dizzy by being whirled around.

With T. N. Jenkins, Dallenbach found that memorized lists of items are recalled better after intervals of sleep than after intervals of waking activity. These results proved that forgetting is not due to the mere lapse of time. Other studies showed that children learned relations of opposition and eause and effect with sudden insight, thus supporting Gestalt psychology.

In 1958 a volume of the *American Journal of Psychology* devoted a *Festschrift* to him. In 1966 the American Psychological Foundation awarded him its gold medal.

J. P. GUILFORD

DARLEY, JOHN GORDON (1910–1990)

After receiving the bachelor's degree at Wesleyan University in Middletown, Connecticut, Darley went to the University of Minnesota, completing the M.A. and the Ph.D. in 1937; his major adviser was the late Donald G. Paterson. From 1931 through 1934 he served as research assistant, editorial assistant, and psychological examiner in the Employment Stabilization Research Institute. From 1935 through 1938 he was director of the student personnel program of the university's General College. From 1938 through 1947 he was director of Student Counseling Bureau at Minnesota, except for a leave of absence for military service (1943–1946) with the National Defense Research Committee and the Navy Department. He served as associate dean of Minnesota's Graduate School from 1947 through 1959, when he became the executive officer of the American Psychological Association in Washington, D.C. Returning to Minnesota in 1962, he was chairman of the Psychology Department from 1963 to 1975. He retired in 1978, but continued work in psychology as a part-time consultant and editor.

Darley's publications have been in the areas of vocational interest measurement, student performance in higher education, student counseling, individual differences, social psychology, and psychometric theory. He is a member of Phi Beta Kappa and Sigma Xi. He has served on the editorial board of the *Annual Review of Psychology* (1948–1954), *Educational and Psychological Measurement* (1941–1954), and the *Journal of Educational Psychology* (1940–1948). He has been the editor of the

Journal of Applied Psychology (1955–1960), the *American Psychologist* (1959–1962), and the Journal Supplement Abstract Service's *Catalog of Selected Documents in Psychology,* now entitled *Psychological Documents* (1982 on). He is the recipient of the E. K. Strong Memorial Medal (1966), the research award of the American Personnel and Guidance Association (1953), the distinguished contribution award of Division 12 of the American Psychological Association (1958), and the outstanding contribution award of the Minnesota Psychological Association (1982). He was the first secretary–treasurer of the American Board of Examiners in Professional Psychology from 1947 through 1951.

DARWIN, CHARLES (1809–1882)

Erasmus Darwin, the grandfather of both Charles and Sir Francis Galton, anticipated evolutionary theory but did not reveal his beliefs for fear of the effect on his reputation. Charles' father, a wealthy physician, worried lest Charles disgrace the family. He was sent to Edinburgh to study medicine, then to Cambridge for theology, but spent his time with friends and his collections. Finally, one of his instructors got him appointed aboard the *H.M.S. Beagle* for a scientific voyage around the world (1831–1836). The voyage changed Darwin's life, he returned to England a committed and serious scientist whose one ambition was to promote the theory of evolution. However, he was extremely cautious about publicizing his findings. In 1842 a brief summary was begun and expanded into an essay, but Darwin shared his ideas only with Sir Charles Lyell, a geological evolutionist, and Joseph Hooker, a botanist. Finally in 1858, pressured by the creative insight of a young naturalist, Russell Wallace, and his friends, Darwin presented Wallace's paper and portions of his own book to a professional meeting (D. Schultz, 1981). Every copy of *On the origin of species by means of a natural selection* was sold on the first day of publication in 1859.

An exclusive man with an aloof, creative temperament, Darwin avoided the disputes over his theory. While the religionists were arguing that evolution was inconsistent with the Biblical account of creation, Darwin wrote other books for scientists and psychologists. *The descent of man and selection in relation to sex* reported evidence for human evolution from lower life forms, for similarities in animal and human mental processes, and for natural selection in evolution. "The importance of mental factors in the evolution of species was apparent in Darwin's theory, and he frequently cited conscious reactions in humans and animals. Because of this role accorded consciousness in evolutionary theory, psychology was compelled to accept an evolutionary point of view" (D. Schultz, 1981, p. 120).

Darwin's work influenced psychology in at least four ways: (1) it stressed the continuity of mental functioning between animals and humans; (2) it changed the subject matter of psychology to functions that consciousness might serve, rather than conscious content (structuralism's subject matter), and changed the goal of psychology to the study of the organism's adaptation to its environment; (3) it provided legitimate support for more eclectic methods of research and study that were not limited to experimental introspection; and (4) it placed increasing emphasis on individual differences with variation among members of the same species.

Darwin's work was an antecedent influence on the development of functionalism as a systematic, though diversified, position in psychology. Functionalists are interested in the applications of psychology to human adaptation and adjustment to the environment.

N. A. HAYNIE

DASHIELL, JOHN F. (1888–1975)

Dashiell received the B.A. from Evansville College, Indiana, and the Ph.D. from Columbia University under James M. Cattell in 1913. He spent the major portion of his academic career at the University of North Carolina at Chapel Hill from 1919 until his retirement in 1958. There, he founded the Department of Psychology and was the first Kenan Professor of Psychology. His major books include *Fundamentals of objective psychology* and a widely used introductory text, *Fundamentals of general psychology,* which went through several editions, the last in 1949. For many years he served as editor of *Psychological Monographs,* until 1947.

Dashiell was one of the early followers of the school of behaviorism founded by John Watson. Like Watson he fostered an entirely objective approach to psychology, denying any concepts of mind or mental activity, confining the subject matter of psychology solely to the study of behavior. One of the problems confronting early behaviorism was how to account for implicit behavior such as thinking. Typically, behaviorism had been an S-R (stimulus–response) psychology. In his attempt to resolve the problem, he suggested that responses could also serve as stimuli, and reactions inside the organism could operate as cues for other responses. According to his formulation, a stimulus set up some response inside the organism which eventually influenced and determined more overt behavior. This, then, was a mediating process. The issue still remains an important one for behavioristic psychology.

R. W. LUNDIN

DAWSON, JOSEPH G. (1918–   )

Perhaps Dawson's main contribution has been his conviction that schizophrenic individuals can be successfully treated by psychotherapeutic methods and, moreover, that such treatment can effectively occur in the client's community. Dawson graduated from the University of North Carolina, and received the Ph.D. from the University of Chicago in 1949. His early psychotherapeutic experiences with individuals of minimal prognosis was influenced by Carl Rogers and Frieda Fromm-Reichmann. Dawson headed clinical psychology programs at two hospitals, and the universities of North Carolina, Florida, and Louisiana. He became emeritus professor at LSU in 1979.

As a psychotherapist, Dawson believes that the living relationship with the individual provides the framework and emergence from psychosis or neurosis. He says, "It is the therapist's responsibility to create a relationship with the client or patient that allows alternatives to psychosis or neurosis. It is this interaction, involving both cognitive and emotional components, that mobilizes the client's energies and motivation to move toward a healthier, more productive life."

Publications include *Psychotherapy with schizophrenics* and more than a score of clinical and research articles that relfect his varied clinical practice. He coordinated research and practice in hypnosis. By request, he assessed the domestic peace corps program (VISTA). He worked for 20 yr with people in religious life, taught in a seminary, and conducted assessment and treatment of seminarians.

Dawson is a diplomate in clinical psychology (ABPP), a fellow in the Royal Society and professional groups, a reserve officer in USPHS, and a consultant to international organizations and universities.

DAY, ROSS H. (1927–   )

Day obtained the B.Sc. from the University of Western Australia and the Ph.D. from the University of Bristol in 1954, the latter for research on perception and human skill. He was first a lecturer and then a research fellow in the University of Bristol (1950–1955) and successively lecturer, senior lecturer, and reader at the University of Sydney (1955–1965). He was appointed to the foundation chair of psychology at Monash University in Victoria, Australia, in 1965.

Day's research interests are in the origins, processes, and principles of human perception. His research and publications encompass non-veridical perception—in particular, geometrical illusions and aftereffects, effects of optical transformation of visual input, visual perception in early infancy, and visual perception during the performance of skilled tasks. He has published extensively in all four areas. Day's main contributions have been concerned with the determinants and explanations of nonveridical perception and, with B. E. McKenzie, the occurrence in infancy of object constancies.

Day has served as president of the Australian Psychological Society (1966–1967) and as president of the Psychology Section of the Australian and New Zealand Association for the Advancement of Science (1968–1969). He is a Fellow of the Academy of the Social Sciences (Australia). In 1971–1972 he was awarded a Fulbright scholarship to the United States (Brown University) and, in 1971–1972 and 1977, British Commonwealth visiting professorships to the United Kingdom. Day's publications include some 130 papers and two books, *Human perception* and *Studies in Perception*, the latter with G. V. Stanley.

DEARBORN, WALTER F. (1878–1955)

A native of Massachusetts, Dearborn graduated from Wesleyan University and received the Ph.D. degree from Columbia. He also studied at Gottingen, Heidelberg, and Munich. He taught at Wisconsin and Chicago before going in 1912 to Harvard, where he spent the remainder of his career.

As an educational psychologist Dearborn was well known for his work on the psychology of reading and on intelligence and intelligence testing. He was the author of books on reading, intelligence, and the growth of schoolchildren, and a coauthor of books on the prediction of children's development and reading and visual fatigue.

P. E. LICHTENSTEIN

DEESE, JAMES E. (1921–   )

Deese has made contributions to psychology ranging from the physiological basis of learning to the production of language. Deese took a bachelor's degree at Chapman College (Orange, California), then did graduate study at Indiana University, where he worked with W. N. Kellogg on the possibilities of spinal conditioning. Though the main result of this work was to uncover artifacts in earlier research, subsequent investigation built upon the methods of Kellogg and Deese. In the mid-1950s Deese, working on contract from the U.S. Air Force, established the principle that vigilance depends upon the expected rate of signals. Turning to memory and language, he discovered the power of associations to make for structural relations in memory. This work naturally led to the use of associations to investigate the significance of subjective meaning in attitudes, beliefs, and social actions.

Deese has taken a firm methodological stand critical of the extension of the experimental method into social psychology and personality. Experimentation, he argues, is limited to variables that (1) are physical and (2) require little or no interpretation on the part of the experimental subjects for their effects.

Deese's professional career has been chiefly at two universities: Johns Hopkins from 1948 to 1972, and the University of Virginia since 1972, where he is Hugh Scott Hamilton Professor of Psychology.

DE GROOT, ADRIAAN D. (1914–   )

de Groot graduated in Psychology at the University of Amsterdam under the Hungarian-born professor Géza Révész. His early work on cognition, and in particular his thesis *Het denken van den schaker* (*Thought and choice in chess*), met with international acclaim. He is best known for his work as a methodologist and educational psychologist. Many of his publications (1966, 1971, 1972, 1980, 1982) contain research-based critical analyses of current problems in the Dutch educational system such as selection, evaluation, and strategies for innovation.

As a methodologist de Groot is known primarily as the author of *Methodologie*. De Groot's seemingly diverse scientific interests converge in his later methodological work, which is rooted in a concern for open-minded rationality and the responsibility of science.

DELABARRE, EDMUND B. (1863–1945)

Professor of Psychology at Brown University, Delabarre also made an important contribution to archaeology.

Delabarre attended Brown during 1882–1883, but graduated from Amherst College in 1886. After getting the M.A. at Harvard University and the Ph.D. at the University of Freiburg in Germany (1886), he returned to Brown, where he gained a chair in 1896. During 1896–1897 he directed the psychological laboratory at Harvard.

Delabarre was responsible for early work in visual perception, particularly in the perception of the orientation of lines. Yet he is perhaps better remembered for deciphering inscriptions found on Dighton Rock in the Taunton River in Massachusetts.

T. KEITH-LUCAS

DELEON, PATRICK H. (1943–   )

DeLeon received the B.A. from Amherst College and the M.A. and Ph.D. (1969) in clinical psychology from Purdue University. He received the M.P.H. (1973) from the University of Hawaii in health administration, and the J.D. (1980) from the Columbus School of Law, Catholic University. He is a diplomate in clinical and forensic psychology (ABPP).

Upon graduation, he worked as a training psychologist for the Peace Corps at the University of Hawaii, staffing two separate projects. He then worked in the state's division of mental health, on both an inpatient and outpatient basis for 3 yr, functioning as deputy director of a community mental health center.

In 1973, he began working for U.S. Senator Daniel K. Inouye and is currently chief-of-staff. He has been instrumental in significantly modifying the manner in which the federal government recognizes psychology and in educating psychology about the importance of the public policy–political process.

He is the author of nearly 100 journal articles and book chapters and has received national awards from range of health care disciplines. Active within the governance of the APA, he has served as president of several professional divisions and on the board of directors. He has received the presidential citation and Distinguished Contributions awards. He serves on various national advisory boards and is a member of the National Academies of Practice.

DENMARK, FLORENCE L. (1932–   )

Best known as a pioneer in the psychology of women and as a researcher on issues of public interest, Denmark received the B.A. from the University of Pennsylvania the first person to ever graduate there with honors in both history and psychology. She continued at the University of Pennsylvania, receiving the M.A. and the Ph.D. in 1958.

Shortly after earning her doctorate, Denmark relocated in the New York metropolitan area. She began as a lecturer in psychology at Queens College in 1958. In 1964 she joined the faculty at Hunter College as instructor. Denmark attained full professorship within a relatively short time. In addition to her research duties, she taught psychology on both the undergraduate and doctoral levels. In 1972 Denmark was appointed executive officer of the City University of New York Graduate School's doctoral program in psychology, serving in that capacity for seven years, until her election as the fifth woman president of the American Psychological Association.

Denmark has long been in the vanguard of work in the psychology of women and minority group achievement, and has served as a mentor and role model for many students in these areas. As director of a program for high-risk students at Hunter College and as president of Division 35 (Psychology of Women) of the American Psychological Association (among many other affiliations), Denmark found herself in a position to implement much of the knowledge and skill acquired over years of education and research. She was the first person to serve as both the president of the American Psychological Association and the national president of Psi Chi, the Honor Society in Psychology. In addition, Denmark was elected vice-president of the International Organization for the Study of Group Tensions, and served as chairperson for the Psychology Section of the New York Academy of Sciences.

In addition to a number of journal articles, Denmark's books include *Women: Dependent or independent variable?; Women: Volume I* (a professional research annual); *The psychology of women: Future directions in research; Psychology: The leading edge; Who discriminates against women?;* and *Women's choices, women's realities.*

DENNIS, WAYNE (1905–)

Dennis received the B.A. from Marietta College and the M.A. and Ph.D. (1930) from Clark University. He has taught at Clark University, the University of Virginia, the University of Pittsburgh, and Brooklyn College.

His contributions to psychology have been in developmental psychology and the history of psychology. In 1948 he edited *Readings in the history of psychology,* which included selections from original sources and in translation from the works of Aristotle down to writers of the twentieth century such as William James and Edward B. Titchener.

His contributions to developmental psychology have included many studies on the effects of heredity and environment, and cross-cultural studies of the American Indians and other groups. He is well known for his work with institutionalized children. For example, in examining studies of feral children, Dennis has suggested that their retardation may not result from lack of environmental stimulation; rather, they may have been abandoned because they were retarded. In his studies of the Hopi Indians he found that differences between sexes in a variety of different behaviors including drawing were due to cultural training. Further, he has observed that much of children's behavior differences has been the result of imposed values from different cultures.

DESCARTES, RENÉ (1596–1650)

Descartes ran away from his French Jesuit school at La Flèche when he was 16 and joined the army. After several years in military service, he settled in Paris and then in Holland to study mathematics. Descartes is renowned as the father of modern philosophy. He used his training in mathematical methodology to set forth his clear deductions from the analysis of self-evident principles; "out of his attempt grew some of the most persistent problems and basic distinctions of modern philosophy" (Edman & Schneider, 1941, p. 282).

The single feature of Descartes' philosophical writings that distinguishes them sharply from the works of Plato and Aristotle is Descartes' emphasis on the *individual* thinker: the question of what a particular man may know, rather than what *men* may know. Descartes, as a rationalist, defined knowledge as judgments or statements that can be said to be certain or indubitable, and denied that sense experience can lead to knowledge in this way. Empiricists, on the other hand, believe that sense experience is the source of knowledge.

Descartes began systematizing his philosophy with radical or absolute doubt and so acquired a new certainty: I cannot doubt that I am doubting. "I think, on this intuitive and certain truth he constructed his system. He gave new proofs for old beliefs, but in claiming to discover certainty for himself by precision of method, by self-examination, and by observation of the Bible, instead of by appeal to faith, schools, and tests, he formulated the principles of a secular philosophy of nature and of an unrestrained confidence in human reason."

Descartes published his *Discourse on method* in 1637. A few years later *Principia philosophia* and *Meditationes de prima philosophia* came out, but some early works were not published until after his death because he feared the Inquisition.

The Cartesian school of philosophy caught on quickly and influenced the thought of many intellectuals. It was the dominant system of philosophy until Hume and Kant, inspiring the ideas that served the Enlightenment.

N. A. HAYNIE

DEUTSCH, HELENE (1884–1982)

The leading female psychoanalyst to date, Deutsch was born Helene Rosenbach married another psychiatrist, Felix Deutsch, and distinguished herself in the psychoanalysis of women.

Graduating from the University of Vienna Medical School in 1912, Deutsch left for Munich to further her work in psychiatry, returning in 1913 to become a member of the University of Vienna's Psychiatric Department. Her deep involvement with psychoanalysis began in 1918, when she began analysis with Freud; she is believed to be his last pupil. At Freud's behest she left for Berlin to further her knowledge and training in psychoanalysis. In 1923 Freud appointed her director of the Training Institute of the Vienna Psychoanalytic Society.

After Hitler came to power, she left for the United States in 1935 and resided in the Boston area. She served as president and, for a quarter of a century, as an analyst of the Boston Psychoanalytic Society. In addition, she was a consultant to the Massachusetts General Hospital, honorary professor of psychiatry at Boston University, and author of several books, including *The psychology of women, Neuroses and character types;* and the *Psychoanalytic study of Dionysus and Apollo.* Her over 40 papers contributed to the "as if" character and pathological bereavement, as well as female sexuality.

W. S. SAHAKIAN

DEUTSCH, MORTON (1920–)

Deutsch was influenced by the intellectual atmosphere at the City College of New York in the 1930s, where psychoanalysis, Marxism, and Lewinian psychology were among the key ingredients. Initially drawn to clinical psychology, Deutsch went to the University of Pennsylvania for the M.A. and then served a clinical internship before entering the air force in 1941. World War II reoriented him toward social psychology, and he obtained the Ph.D. in 1948 at the Research Center for Group Dynamics at MIT, where he studied with Kurt Lewin. He is one of the people from Lewin's MIT Center who helped shape the development of modern social psychology. He has done research on cooperation and competition, interracial housing, informational and normative social influence, interpersonal conflict, and distributive justice. He was trained as a psychoanalyst at the Postgraduate Center for Mental Health and has practiced since 1957.

Deutsch has held positions at New York University, the Bell Telephone Laboratories, and Teachers College of Columbia University, where he is currently Thorndike Professor Emeritus of psychology and education. He has been president of the Society for the Psychological Study of Social Issues, the New York Psychological Association, the Eastern Psychological Association, and the International Society of Political Psychology. He has been awarded the AAAS sociopsychology prize, the Hovland Memorial Award, the Lewin Memorial Award, and the G. W. Allport prize. Among his books are *Interracial housing, Research methods in social relations, Preventing World War III: Some Proposals, The resolution of conflict, Applying social psychology,* and *Distributive justice.*

DEWEY, JOHN (1859–1952)

Dewey was an American philosopher, psychologist, and educator. He attended the University of Vermont, after which he taught high school and studied philosophy independently. He entered the graduate program at Johns Hopkins University and received his doctorate in philosophy in 1884. He taught at the University of Michigan and the University of Minnesota before going to the University of Chicago in 1894, the same year as James Rowland Angell. Dewey remained at Chicago for 10 years, and his influence and Angell's made the university a center for functional psychology. Dewey started an experimental or laboratory school at Chicago, a new approach to educational methods which made him both famous and controversial. When he left, the leadership of the functionalist school passed to Angell. From 1904 to 1930 Dewey was at Columbia University, working on applications of psychology to educational and philosophical problems.

Dewey's paper "The reflex arc concept in psychology" is usually credited with establishing functionalism as a defined school of psychology, rather than just an orientation or attitude. The paper contained the seeds of all the arguments against the use of the stimulus-response unit as the building block of behavior in psychological theory. In this paper Dewey attacked the molecular reductionism of elements in the reflex arc, with its distinction between stimulus and response. Dewey felt that behavior reduced to this basic sensory-motor description was not meaningful. He taught that behavior is continuous, not disjoined into stimuli and responses, and that sensory-motor behaviors continuously blend into one another.

Dewey understood the organism not as a passive receiver of stimuli but as an active perceiver. He believed that behavior should be studied in terms of its significant adaptation to the environment. The proper subject matter for psychology was the study of the total organism as it *functioned* in its environment. His functionalistic point of view was influenced by the theory of evolution and his own instrumentalistic philosophy, which held that ideas are plans for action arising in response to reality and its problems. The struggle of the human intellect is to activate conscious responses to bring about appropriate behavior that enables the organism to survive, to progress, to function. "Thus, functional psychology is the study of the organism in use" (D. Schultz, *History,* 1981, p. 163).

John Dewey wrote the first American textbook of psychology in 1886, called *Psychology,* which was popular until William James' *The principles of psychology* came out in 1890. But Dewey did not spend many years in psychology proper. After the 1896 paper, his interests turned to practical applications. In 1899, after retiring as president of the American Psychological Association, he became the leader of the progressive education movement. It is consistent with his functional

psychology and philosophy that he devoted most of his time to American education and its pragmatic development.

N. A. HAYNIE

DIAZ-GUERRERO, ROGELIO (1918–)

Roselio Diaz-Guerrero received the M.D. from the National University of Mexico, the M.A. in psychology from the State University of Iowa, which also gave him the Ph.D. in physiology and psychology in 1947. He is one of the pioneers of Latin American psychology. He was a founder of the Mexican Society of Psychology and of the Interamerican Society of Psychology, both in 1950. He was president of both societies and later vice-president of the International Union of Psychology. He is a member of the Executive Committee of the International Union of Scientific Psychology and president of the 23rd International Congress of Psychology (Mexico City, 1984). In 1974 he received the first prize for professional and scientific contributions from the Interamerican Society of Psychology.

Diaz-Guerrero is best known for his interest in culture and personality and in cross-cultural research. He has shown that cultural beliefs—what he calls the sociocultural premises—are related to both cognitive and personality development in Mexican culture. From 1948 to 1970 he practiced general psychotherapy as a psychiatrist. From 1959 on he has been fundamentally involved in teaching and research. Part of his research has been applied, but he has also contributed to theoretical and pure research. His work on the evaluation of Plaza Sesamo is well known, as are his cross-cultural studies with Wayne H. Holtzman and Robert F. Peck and with Charles E. Osgood, which have produced several books. His main interest is to prove that both normal and abnormal personality development is fundamentally a function of the culture in which the individual is born. His main contributions are to the knowledge and understanding of the psychology of the Mexican.

DICHTER, ERNEST (1907–1992)

Dichter, generally recognized as the father of motivational research, received his doctorate from the University of Vienna in 1934, having previously obtained the *licence ès lettres* in 1932. Even before emigrating to the United States in 1938, he sought to apply the behavioral sciences to economics, management, and advertising.

After coming to the United States, Dichter worked for an advertising agency as a psychologist. During World War II he was a propaganda specialist for the Columbia Broadcasting system. Later he founded Ernest Dichter Motivations, Inc., which maintained offices in Paris, Tokyo, Frankfurt, and Zurich as well as in New York. This organization had most of the major companies in the world as its clients, including practically everyone in the *Fortune* 500. His company specialized in finding answers to "Why?" questions which can not be answered directly but call for special techniques—many developed by his company—such as depth interviewing, psychodrama, and projective tests.

Dichter wrote over 15 books.

DILTHEY, WILHELM (1833–1911)

Dilthey received the doctorate at Berlin in 1864. After holding positions at Basel, Kiel, and Breslau, he returned to the faculty at Berlin. He is known as a philosopher with a keen historical focus.

Dilthey's importance in psychology is unclear. W. J. Wolman (1960, p. 42) lists him with Pavlov and Freud as one of the three "fathers" of contemporary psychology. On the other hand, neither E. G. Boring (1957) nor R. I. Watson (1968) make even passing reference to him in their histories. Even Wolman says that Dilthey was not as central to phenomenology/ field theory as Pavlov was to conditioning/behaviorism or Freud to psychoanalysis.

Dilthey's writings show the heavy influence of both Kant and nineteenth-century German romanticism. He distinguished between the understanding *(Verstehen)* of cultural science and the explanations of natural science. Just as mathematics was the method of the natural sciences, psychology was the method of the cultural sciences.

Dilthey rejected transcendentalism: the Platonic notion of ideal forms was anathema to him. Yet he was highly critical of the "easy" reductionism of behavior to physiological causes by the experimental psychologists of his day. For him the mind was a coherent unity, it could not be broken into components. Models were used in the natural sciences because the system was incoherent otherwise. But the psychologist was more fortunate; he had direct access to the mental processes. Thus the psychologist could *and must* stay at the descriptive level and generalize there.

According to Dilthey, man perceives his world meaningfully. We perceive a beautiful rose; we do not perceive a rose and then notice that it is beautiful. We perceive an angry man; we do not perceive a man and then notice that he is scowling and conclude that he is angry. Religion, myth, and art forms are all explicit examples of these meaningful perceptions that occur every day. Thus psychology is the most fundamental of all cultural sciences and the major tool for sociology, law, education, political science, economics, and so forth.

Dilthey was a philosophical psychologist; it remained for Eduard Spranger and the Gestalt movement to lend experimental support to his notions. He also markedly influenced philosophy through Martin Heidegger and sociology through Max Weber.

C. PEYSER

DOLLARD, JOHN (1900–1980)

Dollard received the Ph.D. in sociology at the University of Chicago in 1931 and then had a year's training in psychoanalysis in Berlin under Hans Sachs. In 1932 he joined the explorations of culture and personality being led by Yale anthropologist Edward Sapir. Dollard spent the rest of his career at Yale; he was a leading member of the Institute of Human Relations during its active years, and subsequently a professor in the Department of Psychology. His work is a notable example of the innovative value of bringing together in one mind central ideas and approaches of the usually separate social sciences.

Dollard's most influential books came during the period of his affiliation with the Institute of Human Relations. In *Criteria for the life history* he sought to define how life history study could best contribute to a unified understanding of human beings, and applied his analysis to a critique of well-known life histories that had been published by social scientists of diverse theoretical persuasions. In *Caste and class in a southern town,* his master work, he showed the relations between a social system and the psychodynamics of individuals in various positions within the system. He joined with various colleagues in other influential studies, notably *Frustration and aggression* (with Leonard Doob, Neal Miller, O. Hobart Mowrer, and Robert Sears), *Social learning and imitation* (with Neal Miller), and *Personality and psychotherapy* (also with Neal Miller).

Typifying the work of the Institute of Human Relations, these studies achieve a remarkable synthesis of psychoanalysis, experimental psychology of learning and motivation, sociological analysis of social structure, and anthropological awareness of cultural variation. Though some of their terminology is out of fashion, these books continue to be a direct source of understanding and an inspiration to the further development of psychology in integral relation to the other social sciences. In his later years, Dollard concentrated on teaching psychotherapy and on intensive study of the process of psychotherapy, bringing to this field the integrated viewpoint he had developed.

I. L. CHILD

DONDERS, FRANS C. (1818–1889)

Donders, a Dutch physiologist and opthalmologist, was responsible for introducing prismatic and cylindrical lenses for eyeglasses. He was also interested in color vision and suggested that color discrimination could be explained by color molecules decomposing while stimulating the fibers of the optic nerve.

Donders is most prominently known for his studies on reaction time. Prior to Donder's work, Friedrich W. Bessel, an astronomer at Königsberg at the beginning of the nineteenth century, became concerned with the accuracy of determining the time at which a star crossed the midline of a telescope. He had discovered that there were appreciable individual differences among observers, sometimes more than one second. The particular reaction time, as it differed from one astronomer to another, became known as the "personal equation."

By the time Donders began his studies, the chronoscope and chronograph had been invented, so it became possible to measure the personal equation to a thousandth of a second. The personal equation became the simple reaction time between the presentation of a single stimulus and the response. In 1868 Donders extended the study of the reaction time by using two or more stimuli which were to be responded to selectively. He found that the more complicated situation resulted in an increase in reaction time. For example, if a subject were asked to react to A out of a random presentation of A, B, C, and D (different colors), more mental activity had to be involved to account for the increase in time necessary to make the response. The amount of increase involved could be measured by subtracting the simple reaction time (one stimulus) from the discriminative time. Further studies and ramifications were later taken up by Wilhelm Wundt in his laboratory at Leipzig in the 1880s.

R. W. LUNDIN

DÖRNER, DIETRICH (1938–   )

Dörner is known for his work on thinking and problem solving. He grew up in Düsseldorf (West Germany). He began his studies at the University of Kiel in 1961 and took his degree in psychology in 1965. In 1969 he received the Ph.D. at Kiel and got the "venia legendi" (Habilitation) for psychology at the same university in 1972. His professional carreer began at Kiel. Later he was professor of psychology at Düsseldorf (1973–1974), and GieBen (1974—1979). Since 1979 he has been at the University of Bamberg as a professor of general psychology.

Since the beginning of his scientific carreer, Dörner's central interest has been the psychology of thinking and problem solving. His early work concerns concept formation and problem solving in mathematics. He was especially interested in the microanalysis of human information processing. His first book contains a theory about the realization of thinking processes in neural networks. Later his interest shifted to the role of thinking in the organization of action. Dörner has researched the way people solve difficult political and economical problems, using computer-simulated "realities" as a scenario.

Dörner's main interest is a system theory of the interaction of different psychic processes (thinking, emotion, motivation, learning, memory processes) in the organization of action.

DOWNEY, JUNE ETTA (1875–1932)

Downey graduated from the University of Wyoming in 1875 and received the M.A. and Ph.D. (1907) from the University of Chicago, where she studied under James Angell. Her dissertation was on handwriting analysis. She then returned to Wyoming where she became professor of philosophy and was the first woman department chair at a state university. She was a careful and productive researcher in the fields of aesthetics and imagery. Her interests turned to the field of personality and its assessment where she became best known. She was the first psychologist to study individual differences in temperament. She developed the Will Temperament Test, divided temperament traits into (1) mercurial, speedy, and hair–trigger; (2) dynamic, aggressive, and forceful; and (3) slow, deliberate, and inhibitive. She was not as well known for her experimental and field studies, probably because of the isolation of Laramie at that time. Often her contacts with fellow psychologists was through the mail. She served on the editorial boards of several psychological journals and was "starred" in the 1927 edition of *American Men of Science* as an outstanding scientist.

R. W. LUNDIN

DREIKURS, RUDOLF (1897–1972)

Dreikurs, a psychiatrist, educator, and counselor, began his medical studies in 1918. While still a student he met Alfred Adler, already a well-known psychiatrist. After beginning his own work, Dreikurs worked closely with Adler until Adler's departure from Austria. Both men advocated the importance of the interaction of social processes and mental health. They focused on the home and school, in the belief that the early years of life build permanent patterns and that proper training of children lays the foundation of healthy attitudes and goals. They trained parents and teachers and established child guidance clinics, in the conviction that preventive medicine begins when children experience positive human relationships and develop a sense of their own worth as contributing members of society.

Dreikurs was a leader in the development of social psychiatry in Vienna and the United States. In 1928 he pioneered group psychotherapy in his private practice, and until the end of his professional life he sought new ways of integrating group processes into psychotherapy. Rejecting the undemocratic trend developing in Austria, he left his native land in 1937. He first went to Brazil to lecture. While there, he founded the Adlerian Society of Rio de Janeiro. Later that year he went to Chicago and made that city his home. Following Adler's death in 1937, Dreikurs took on many leadership roles in Individual Psychology circles and founded the Adlerian journal in the United States. He helped found the American Society of Adlerian Psychology. He set up child guidance centers in Chicago, patterned after the ones that had been established by Adler in Vienna. He trained parent study group leaders and counselors in communities in the United States, Canada, and abroad.

In the 1940s Dreikurs developed "the double interview" in therapy, and in the 1950s contributed to the development of music therapy. A leader in the development of group psychotherapy, Dreikurs fostered the work of J. L. Moreno in the United States and used psychodrama as an adjunct in his private practice. A longtime vice-president of the American Humanist Association, he wrote on the interface of religion and mental health and was a delegate to the White House Conference on Children and Youth. He was deeply concerned with social values, above all with democratic living and social equality, which he viewed as the basis for social interest and mental health. Despite the painful ravages of terminal cancer, he actively taught and wrote until his death.

E. FERGUSON

DRENTH, PIETER J. D. (1935–   )

Drenth studied psychology at the Free University in Amsterdam, specializing in psychometrics and industrial psychology. In 1960 he received the Ph.D. and went to the United States for further study and experience. In 1962 he was offered a lectureship in psychodiagnostics at the Free University, Amsterdam. He became a strong advocate of a more objective, empirical approach in testing, in contrast to the strong emphasis on intuition and subjective test interpretation which prevailed in much of the psychodiagnostic practice in Europe at that time. He started a number of psychometric and test research projects and coauthored many intelligence and aptitude tests for the Netherlands.

Drenth published a monograph on testing, *De Psychologische Test* (1967), followed by *Inleiding in de test theorie* (1975). His test development expertise was solicited by a number of developing countries, which resulted in test development research projects in Indonesia, Surinam, and several African countries. Since 1967 Drenth has occupied a chair in work and organizational psychology at the Free University. Drenth has also edited two readers in industrial and organizational psychology (1970, 1973).

DUBOIS, PAUL-CHARLES (1848–1918)

Paul Dubois was educated at Geneva and Bern. After receiving the M.D. degree he became a lecturer of internal medicine at Bern and later professor of neuropathology. He founded the Swiss Archives for Neurology and Psychiatry and was a founder and president of the Swiss Society of Neurology.

Dubois created and defined the term "psychoneurosis." He conducted research on the nature and treatment of the neuroses in the course of which he worked with electrotherapy. His investigations led him to define persuasion as quite distinct from hypnosis and suggestion. He was the author of several books, some published in French and others in German. He may be considered the first psychotherapist in the modern tradition, in that he believed in "moral persuasion" in dealing with the mentally ill—that is, in simply talking with patients in an attempt to reason with them.

P. E. LICHTENSTEIN

DU BOIS-REYMOND, EMIL (1818–1896)

A German physiologist, du Bois-Reymond was a student of J. Müller at Berlin alongside his lifetime close friend Helmholtz. In many regards it is his intellectual stimulation of both Helmholtz and those who studied with him (Wundt, Békhterev, Sechenov, G. Stanley Hall) that constitutes du Bois-Reymond's contribution to psychology.

Du Bois-Reymond was known for his electrophysiology. With the development of new equipment and ideas by physicists such as Ohm and Faraday, he was able to use the galvanometer to measure the neural impulse. In 1848–1849 he published a two-volume work that postulated the polarization of animal tissue. Muscle and nerve, he argued, must be little more than charged molecules that have a positive charge at one face and a negative one opposite; these molecules must be oriented in the same direction much like a magnet. Although he was quite incorrect, his theory led Helmholtz to measure the velocity of the nerve impulse.

Following Müller's theory of specific nerve energies, du Bois-Reymond stated that the important anatomical fact is that the optic nerve connects to the occipital lobes and the auditory nerve to the temporal lobes. If one were able to cross-connect the optic and auditory nerves, the subject would see tones and hear colors.

Although they were students of Müller, du Bois-Reymond, Helmholtz, and Brücke made a pact that opposed vitalist notions. They agreed that no forces other than the common physical and chemical ones could be active within an organism. While thus following part of Müller's ideas, they also showed themselves open to new notions.

C. S. PEYSER

DUIJKER, HUBERT C. J. (1912–1983)

Duijker studied at the University of Amsterdam where, in 1948, he was appointed professor of psychology, and in 1950 became director of the Psychological Laboratory, in this latter function succeeding his teacher Géza Révész (1878–1955). One of Duijker's main interests is human communication. In this area as well as in others, he has argued for a problem-centered, interdisciplinary approach, and for the development of a conceptual system making such an approach feasible.

However, in his opinion traditional boundaries between disciplines usually are obstacles to understanding. He attempted to facilitate cooperation between the different areas of psychology, and has been an active member of several organizations founded for this purpose. In his national context this was the Netherlands Institute of Psychologists (N.I.P.), the Dutch equivalent of the American Psychological Association.

Duijker was long a member of the Executive Committee of the International Union of Scientific Psychology, and chairman of its Committee on Communication and Publication. With N. H. Frijda he published a trend report on national character and national stereotypes (1960). With E. H. Jacobson he edited the first two editions of the *International directory of psychologists*, and with Maria J. van Rijswijk, the *Trilingual psychological dictionary*.

DUMAS, GEORGES (1866–1946)

Dumas was a student of T. Ribot. He first studied philosophy but later shifted to abnormal psychology, and studied and obtained a degree in medicine. In 1897 he became the head of the psychological laboratory of the clinic for mental diseases in the faculty of medicine in Paris. In 1902 he also became a professor of experimental psychology in the faculty of letters at the Sorbonne, becoming a full professor in 1912. This double assignment in psychiatry and experimental psychology found its unity in an idea, borrowed from Ribot and also from Claude Bernard, that there was a continuity between the normal and the pathological. The same laws, biological and psychological, produced "normal" and "abnormal" effects.

In his research studies, especially on the emotions, Dumas strove to relate the conditions he observed to their physiological origins; practicing laboratory techniques, he utilized his understanding relative to nervous functioning. His research was explained in such works as *La tristesse et la joie* (1900) and *Le sourire et l'expression des émotions*. He edited the *Traité de Psychologie* and the *Nouveau Traité de Psychologie* (7 volumes). With Pierre Janet he found the *Journal de Psychologie Normale et Pathologique* in 1904. He had a profound influence in France and other countries, especially Latin America.

DUNBAR, HELEN F. (1902–1959)

Flanders Dunbar, as she preferred to be called, received the B.A. from Bryn Mawr and the M.A. and Ph.D. (1929) from Columbia University. While still at Columbia she enrolled at Yale Medical School and, after a visit to Vienna, returned to receive her M.D. in 1930.

During her distinguished career she held appointments in psychiatry at Presbyterian Hospital and the Vanderbilt Clinic in New York City. Her most important books dealing with psychosomatic disorders were *Psychosomatic diagnosis* and *Mind and body: Psychosomatic medicine*.

In 1938 she founded the medical journal *Psychosomatic Medicine*, and served as its editor until 1947.

As a pioneer in the studies of psychosomatic medicine, she demonstrated that psychosomatic disorders were emotional in origin, and related the specific type of disorder to personality characteristics. For example, the stomach-ulcer type was outwardly ambitious and tough, but underneath dependent and feminine. The high-blood-pressure type was on the surface friendly and calm, but unconsciously striving and aggressive. She also identified an accident-prone personality whose emotional disturbances found outlet in unconscious desires for self-injury. Later in her career she somewhat abandoned this specificity approach.

R. W. LUNDIN

DUNCKER, KARL (1903–1940)

Duncker studied with Max Wertheimer and Wolfgang Köhler at the University of Berlin before completing the M.A. degree at Clark University. He returned to Germany and, under the direction of Wertheimer and Köhler, received the Ph.D. from the University of Berlin in 1929. He remained as Köhler's assistant at the Psychological Institute in Berlin until 1934, when he was dismissed by the Nazi government. In 1936, Duncker emigrated to the UK, where he served as a research assistant to Frederic C. Bartlett at the Cambridge psychology laboratory. He returned to the United States and taught at Swarthmore College from the fall of 1938 until his death.

Duncker was a promising successor to the first generation of Gestalt psychologists. His publications cover a broad range of subjects, including problem solving, perception, motivation, systematic psychology, and philosophical issues. His master's thesis, published in the *Pedagogical Seminary*, contained several innovations, including the radiation problem (How can a ray beam be used to destroy only a stomach tumor without damaging the healthy tissue surrounding the diseased area?) and verbal protocols, a method that required the subject to think aloud while solving a problem, which became a major method for studying problem solving. Anders Ericsson and Herbert A. Simon published a book on it in 1984. In 1935, Duncker published the *Psychology of productive thought*, which reported a series of experiments on mathematical and practical problems; his discussion was divided into three main areas: the structure and dynamics of problem-solving processes; insight, learning, and simple solution finding; and the fixedness of thought. The latter concept, often referred to as functional fixedness, concerns the inability to find productive solutions for novel problems similar to familiar problems. Duncker's 1935 book was translated into English and published in *Psychological Monographs* in 1945.

Duncker's dissertation, published in 1929 in *Psychologische Forschung*, identified the phenomenon of induced motion, the tendency to perceive movement in an opposite direction when an object (including even the perceiver's own body) is stationary but an accompanying object in the perceptual field is in motion. His dissertation was cited in later theoretical work on the frame of reference and is widely regarded as a major contribution to the study of perception. Duncker also published articles on the perception of pain, the social modification of children's appetite, ethical relativity, the prevalence of behaviorism in American psychology, and a German–English dictionary of psychological terms.

Duncker's research is again receiving the attention of contemporary psychologists, particularly in the area of cognitive science.

D. B. KING

DUNLAP, KNIGHT (1875–1949)

Dunlap was an undergraduate at Berkeley, did graduate work at Harvard University primarily under Hugo Münsterberg, and spent the majority of his professional life at Johns Hopkins University.

Dunlap's contributions to psychology were primarily indirect: stimulation of others—notably John Watson, whom he steered away from introspection, consciousness, and sensation, and toward practicality, when Watson arrived at Johns Hopkins shortly after him—and through the gathering of materials. He was a founder and editor of *Psychobiology* (which later joined with the *Journal of Animal Behavior* to form the *Journal of Comparative Psychology,* which he also edited for many years), of *Comparative Psychology Monographs,* and of *Mental Measurements Monographs.* He also edited *Psychological Index* for two years.

An inventive researcher at a time of primitive apparatus, Dunlap was the prime developer of a synchronous-motor chronoscope later known as the Hopkins chronoscope. His published books ranged from social learning to psychobiology. A skeptic, when he heard Thorndike say that there were no practice effects in group intelligence tests, he immediately undertook a study that demonstrated the presence of the practice effect.

C. S. PEYSER

DUNNETTE, MARVIN D. (1926–   )

Dunnette received the B.Ch.E. degree, M.A., and Ph.D. (1954) from the University of Minnesota. He joined 3M Company as manager of employee relations research. At 3M, Dunnette developed procedures for selecting and appraising research scientists, sales personnel, and clerical employees. He left 3M in 1960 to become associate professor of psychology at the University of Minnesota.

He founded Personnel Decisions, Inc., a management consulting firm, in 1967 and served as its president until 1975, when he and two colleagues founded Personnel Decisions Research Institute (PDRI). The research institute does behavioral science research in areas related to improved and more productive use of human resources.

Dunnette has served as academic adviser to 56 students who have received the Ph.D. degrees in fields of industrial psychology, counseling psychology, and psychometrics. He has published many articles, technical reports, chapters, and books. Perhaps his best known book is the *Handbook of industrial and organizational psychology.* Other books include *Personnel selection and placement; Managerial behavior, performance, and effectiveness; Managerial motivation and compensation; Work and non-work in the year 2001;* and *Psychology applied to industry.* A second edition of *The handbook of industrial and organizational psychology* was published in four volumes.

Dunnette is a fellow of the American Psychological Association and holds the diplomate in industrial psychology granted by the American Board of Professional Psychology. He served as president of the American Psychological Association's Division of Industrial and Organizational Psychology during 1966–1967 and was the 1985 recipient of the division's award for Outstanding Scientific Contributions.

DUROJAIYE, MICHAEL O. A. (1943–   )

Durojaiye obtained the honors degree in psychology at Manchester, England, where he was trained as an educational psychologist. He worked as an educational psychologist for Lancashire County Council from 1964 to 1968, before going to the University of Ibadan, where he was a lecturer in psychology in the Department of Adult Education. He went on to Makerere University in Kampala in 1970 as senior lecturer, and in January 1972 became a professor of educational psychology. He went to Lagos in 1975 and was professor and dean of the Faculty of Education, and later deputy vice-chancellor and acting vice-chancellor of the University of Lagos in 1980.

His early research interest in England in 1966–1968 focused on race relations. For his Ph.D. in 1968 he studied educationally subnormal children. Subsequently in Nigeria he worked on functional literacy, ability of adult illiterates, and child-rearing practices. He continued his interest in child-rearing practices in Uganda. In both Nigeria and Uganda he played an active role in test development and educational improvement.

In 1973 Durojaiye edited *Psychological guidance of the school child,* in which he contributed most of the chapters. His textbook *A new introduction to educational psychology* related educational practices at home and at school to his research findings on human growth and development in African children.

Durojaiye revived the Nigerian Psychological Society and became its general secretary in 1969. He established a Department of Psychology at Makerere and became its first professor in 1973. With Marcel Ebode he began activities in 1975 in Yaounde to broaden the membership of the Association of African Psychologists to include all African psychologists. He worked with the late Michael Okonji to introduce cross-cultural psychology in Africa. He was president of the International Association for Cross-Cultural Psychology (1976–1978), and since 1976 has been a member of the executive committee of the International Union of Psychological Sciences. Currently he is a fellow of the British Psychological Society, a fellow of the Nigerian Psychology Society, a consulting editor for the *German Journal of Psychology,* and the first editor of the *Lagos Education Review.*

d'YDEWALLE, GERY (1946–   )

d'Ydewalle began his research career at the Laboratory of Experimental Psychology of the University of Louvain (Belgium), although his first studies were in philosophy. He worked under the supervision of J. R. Nuttin and received the Ph.D. in 1974. In 1980, he became Nuttin's successor, supervising a research group of about 20 people. First a deputy secretary-general (1974) and from 1978 the secretary-general of the Belgium Psychological Society, he has been instrumental in reshaping the society, stimulating communication among researchers and encouraging dissemination of research. In 1979, he was cofounder of the Federation of Belgian Psychologists.

d'Ydewalle was appointed editor (1979–1987) of the *International Journal of Psychology.* His editorial policy shifted the journal's focus from cross-cultural research to general issues in psychology as approached by different countries. In 1980, he was elected member of the Executive Committee of the International Union of Psychological Science and, from 1987, deputy secretary-general of the union. He was elected president of the XXV International Congress of Psychology in Brussels in 1992.

EBBINGHAUS, HERMANN (1850–1909)

Ebbinghaus studied at the universities of Bonn, Halle, and Berlin and received his degree in philosophy in 1873. He continued his study independently in Berlin, England, and France, where his interest shifted to science.

Ebbinghaus, the first psychologist to investigate learning and memory experimentally, invented the nonsense syllable which revolutionized the study of association and learning. After his appointment to an academic position at the University of Berlin, he continued his research on memory and published his findings in *Memory* in 1885. In 1894 he moved to Breslau where he worked until 1905 developing the sentence completion test, probably the first successful test of higher mental abilities.

Ebbinghaus' research methods were objective, experimental, and quantified through meticulous attention and recordings. His procedures have laid a foundation of data on the study of association and learning that has stood the test of time. The Ebbinghaus curve of retention or forgetting demonstrated that material is forgotten rapidly in the first few hours after learning, and more and more slowly with the passage of time. He founded the *Journal of Psychology and Physiology of the Sense Organs* in 1890. Ebbinghaus also published two successful textbooks, *The principles of psychology* and *A summary of psychology*, which appeared in several editions and revisions.

N. A. HAYNIE

ECCLES, JOHN C. (1903–   )

A Nobel prize winner, Eccles has distinguished himself in physiological psychology with his many psychobiological theories.

After obtaining the M.B. and B.S. degrees from Melbourne University, Eccles left for Oxford, where he earned the M.A. and D. Phil. degrees. The University of Cambridge bestowed a Sc.D. on him in 1960. The course of his career ran from the University of Cambridge, where he was a university lecturer from 1934 to 1937, to the State University of New York at Buffalo from 1968 on. In between he directed the Kancmatsu Memorial Institute of Pathology in Sydney, Australia (1937–1944), was professor of physiology at the University of Otago in New Zealand (1944–1951), and continued as professor of physiology at the Australian National University (1951–1966).

The specialty of neuroscience has moved rapidly in recent years, in no small part due to Eccles' efforts. In brain theory Eccles is an interactionist and personalist, viewing the mind and brain as separate and distinct entities. Eccles offered a "liaison between brain and mind hypothesis" to explain the interactive process. The essential quality that makes one human is self-awareness.

Eccles produced a number of books, including *Brain and conscious experience, The neurophysiological basis (mind, The understanding of the brain, Facing reality, The physiology of nerve cells,* and *The physiology of synapses.*

EHRENFELS, CHRISTIAN VON (1859–1932)

Ehrenfels, a native Austrian, was a student of Brentano at Vienna, received his doctorate in 1885 at Graz, taught at Vienna, and later was professor of philosophy at Prague, where Wertheimer attended his lectures.

Ehrenfels is remembered in psychology (which was but a small portion of his work) as a member of the Austrian school of act psychology and as an important forerunner of the Gestalt movement. Asch credits Ehrenfels and Wertheimer as the major influences on his use of the gestalt in social psychology.

In his 1890 paper Über Gestaltqualitaten, Ehrenfels developed Mach's notion of form-qualities. Ehrenfels noted that a melody is still the same when played with different notes (i.e., transposed to a different key), yet becomes a different motif if the notes are rearranged. This observation led to the notion of *transposability*, one criterion of a form-quality. He also noted the emergent quality of, for example, four lines that compose a square: the lines are now more than just four lines—a quality he labeled *supersummativity*. (Later the Gestalt workers insisted that the elements or parts disappear in the whole rather than being simply summated; for this reason Ehrenfels was not welcomed as a full member of the Gestalt movement.) Ehrenfels divided the form-qualities into two classes: temporal (musical melody, reddening, cooling) and nontemporal (spatial, tonal fusions, flavors, movement perception).

C. S. PEYSER

EISDORFER, CARL (1930–   )

Eisdorfer graduated from New York University, where he received the B.A., M.A., and Ph.D., and later he received the M.D. from Duke Medical School. He joined the Duke faculty becoming professor of psychiatry. In 1970, he was named director of the Duke University Center for Study of Aging and Human Development. He left Duke in 1972, going to the University of Washington as chair of psychiatry and behavioral science and founding director of the university's Institute on Aging. In 1980, he was senior scholar-in-residence at the Institute of Medicine of the National Academy of Sciences. In 1982, he went to the Montifiore Medical Center in New York as president and CEO and as professor in the departments of psychiatry and neurosciences at the Albert Einstein College of Medicine.

Eisdorfer has authored or edited more than 250 articles and 18 books. He was founding editor of the *Annual Review of Gerontology and Geriatrics.* He is a member of the Institute of numerous national and international awards for scholarly and clinical achievements, including awards from the American Psychological Association, the American Psychiatric Association, the Gerontological Society of America, the American Geriatrics Association, the American Society on Aging, and the American College of Physicians.

ELKIND, DAVID (1931–   )

As a student of both Piaget and dynamic psychology, Elkind is perhaps best known for his attempt to extend, integrate, and apply these psychologies to educational and social problems of children and youth. Elkind moved with his family to California when he was an adolescent, and he received both the B.A. and Ph.D. from U.C.L.A. His professional career began at Wheaton College in Norton, Massachusetts. Subsequently he taught at U.C.L.A., the University of Denver, and the University of Rochester. He is currently professor and chairman of the Eliot-Pearson Department of Child Study at Tufts University in Boston.

During a postdoctoral internship with David Rappaport at the Austen Riggs Center, Elkind was first introduced to the work of Jean Piaget, who became his mentor. Much of Elkind's research has been an attempt to replicate and extend Piaget's theory and research methods to new areas such as figure perception and religion. Elkind sees himself as an applied developmental psychologist who seeks to apply research and theory to practical problems, but to use practical experience to guide research and expand theory. He believes that psychology in general, and child psychology in particular, have attempted to become experimental too soon. A natural history stage of inquiry involving careful observation and categorization has preceded true progress in every science and cannot be bypassed in psychology.

His conceptions of the "imaginary audience," "the personal fable," "cognitive conceit," and "immaculate obesity"—all derived from clinical experience—are receiving research support. Such concepts reflect his view of the need to have a set of descriptive concepts which better enable us to take hold of the wide range of human behavior. Elkind's publications include: *Child development and education; A sympathetic understanding of the child; Children and adolescents; The child and society; The child's reality:' Three developmental themes;* and *The hurried child: Growing up too fast too soon.*

ELLIOTSON, JOHN (1791–1868)

Mesmerism had gone into disrepute with Anton Mesmer's failure to demonstrate to the Paris committee that he could really magnetize people and, as a result, relieve them of their ailments. Elliotson, an English physician and professor of medicine at University College, London, still believed in mesmerism. He had demonstrated to an editor of the prestigious journal, *Lancet,* that by putting a magnetized coin on a patient, the latter felt better. Elliotson practiced mesmerism at the university hospital with positive results. He used it in treating patients suffering from a variety of nervous disorders and also employed it as an anesthetic. Still, his colleagues refused to believe or even witness his demonstrations. In 1837 the council at the medical college passed a resolution forbidding the practice of mesmerism (animal magnetism) within the hospital or at the college, whereupon, Elliotson resigned from both. The practice of mesmerism fell further into disrepute when it became associated with phrenology. Elliotson believed that his hands had magnetic powers when placed on a particular part of the skull, so that the brain area beneath that spot would be brought into function. According to phrenology, the brain had very specialized functions related to bumps on the skull.

Another historical accident provoking disdain for mesmerism was the sudden rise of spiritualism in England. Although Elliotson rejected spiritualism, as such, there was a striking resemblance between the spiritualistic setting and Mesmer's earlier seances, where he had patients sit in a circle when he was practicing in Paris.

Despite all the opposition to mesmerism and its entanglements with suspect practices, mesmeric clinics continued to be established in London and other parts of England. These, of course, were condemned by the medical profession. It was left to James Braid, a physician from Manchester, to make mesmerism respectable. He suggested that the effects were due not to magnetic forces but to physiological causes—paralysis of the eyelids. It was he who substituted the term hypnotism for mesmerism.

R. W. LUNDIN

ELLIS, ALBERT (1913–   )

After first making contributions to psychoanalysis Ellis became thoroughly disillusioned and became one of its main opponents. He has been the only psychologist/psychoanalyst since Freud to found a major school of psychotherapy—rational-emotive therapy (RET)—and has become a foremost proponent of sexual liberation.

Ellis began to do research on sex, love, marriage, and family relations in 1939 at the age of 25, and within a couple of years read some 10,000 books and articles in the field. He serendipitously discovered that he could helpfully counsel people with sex and love problems. After obtaining the Ph.D. degree in clinical psychology from Columbia University in 1947, he undertook didactic and supervised psychoanalysis with Dr. Charles R. Hulbeck at the Karen Horney Institute. After practicing psychoanalysis from 1949 to 1953, Ellis rebelled against its dogma and inefficiency, experimented with several other methods, and at the beginning of 1955 started his own system of rational-emotive therapy (RET). RET was designed to weld hard-headed behaviorism with Ellis's long-term interest in philosophy—especially phenomenological, pragmatic, and humanistic philosophy. Although violently opposed at first by almost all other therapists, Ellis persisted in his talks and writings on RET and finally succeeded so well that he is generally recognized as the father of cognitive behavior therapy.

Even before he originated RET, Ellis pioneered in sex and marital therapy, and his active-directive methods paved the way for modern sex therapy. His prolific writings, culminating in the early 1960s when several of his books (such as *Sex without guilt*) sold millions of paperback copies, made him a prime influence in the modern "sex revolution."

ELLIS, HAVELOCK (1859–1939)

The English psychologist Henry Havelock Ellis was raised by his mother in a climate of Victorian asexuality. He credited this lack of information with spurring him to study the typical sexual behavior of humans.

Ellis' first work was the 1897 sexual inversion volume of his *Studies in the psychology of sex.* He concluded that homosexual behavior was congenital and a statistical anomaly, rather than a disease. He presented

some 80 cases of quite successful males who either accepted this feature of their personality or tried to minimize its effects; none had sought professional counseling. Two years later he published the volume on auto-erotism. Masturbation, he stated, did not inevitably lead to serious illness but rather was a legitimate source of mental relaxation. In adults, he observed, masturbation was more frequent in women.

In all his work he challenged the typical approach to sexual behavior in which the individual took as his reference point his own behavior and the behavior of friends and neighbors. Ellis stated that it was vital to remember that one was not necessarily like one's acquaintances, and that one's acquaintances were probably not as much alike as one might suppose. He objected to Freud's application of adult sexual terms to infants. Infants surely had an erotic life, but it certainly should not be conceptualized in language designed to apply to adult behavior. Unlike writers such as KrafftEbing and Freud, Ellis was interested in normal human sexuality, not in pathology. As such he was an important forerunner of both the surveys of Kinsey and the experimentation of Masters and Johnson.

Ellis described the essential characteristic of human coitus as the face-to-face position. When human coitus occurred in other positions, notably rear entry, it thereby took on some of the light/pursuit characteristics of animal coitus.

Ellis also wrote on such diverse topics as eugenics and manners. He reported on his own experiences with the hallucinogen mescal around the turn of the century. He wrote about the "literature of life," including such authors as Nietzsche, Casanova, Zola, and Huysmans. Life *is* an art, he said, but only some literature actually deals with the important questions of life.

C. S. PEYSER

ENDLER, NORMAN S. (1931–   )

Best known for his interactional model of personality and his studies on social conformity, Endler was born in Montreal and attended schools there, continuing at McGill University, where he received the B.A. (psychology and mathematics) and the M.A. (psychology). He continued his studies at the University of Illinois, where he received the Ph.D. in clinical psychology in 1958. Collaborating with J. M. Hunt, he focused on the joint effects of anxiety on persons and situations. Using a variance components technique, he found that behavior was determined primarily by persons through situation interactions, rather than by persons or situations *per se.*

Endler is primarily interested in personality theory and models, and has used the construct of anxiety to illustrate the various principles of an interactional psychology of personality. Together with David Magnusson of the University of Stockholm, he has developed an interaction model of personality. Endler's interaction model of anxiety postulates that both trait and state anxiety are multidimensional, and that interactions evoking state anxiety occur between persons and situations only when person factors and situational stress are congruent. Over 15 field and laboratory studies have validated this theory.

Endler is the author or coauthor of nine books and over 150 journal articles and professional monographs. He has been at York University since 1960, where he has been undergraduate coordinator (1964—1967), director of the graduate program (1968–1971), and chairman of the Psychology Department (1974–1979).

ENTWISTLE, NOEL J. (1936–   )

Entwistle has worked mainly in the fields of student learning and individual differences among college and university students. After working as a physics teacher, he moved into educational research and obtained the Ph.D. from Aberdeen University in 1967. Interest in pupils' difficulties at transfer from primary to secondary education led him into research on relationships between personality and school attainment, which he pursued after a move to Lancaster University in 1968.

At Lancaster, Entwistle carried out two five-year programs of research into student learning in higher education. Initially this involved the use of psychometric tests to predict degree performance from a combination of cognitive and noncognitive attributes of the individual. More recently his work has been concerned more with learning processes, and in particular the ways in which students interpret the explicit and implicit instructions about what and how lecturers expect them to learn.

Since his move to the Bell Chair of Education at Edinburgh University in 1978, Entwistle has developed an interest in learning styles and strategies in relation to personality. In *Styles of learning and teaching,* he explained the implications for both students and teachers of the wide differences in preferred styles of both learning and teaching. He concluded that "there can be no single 'right' way to study or 'best' way to teach." Findings from research on students may provide a rationale for study skills programs, as well as helping teachers to avoid extreme teaching styles which benefit only pupils with consonant learning styles.

Entwistle was editor of the *British Journal of Educational Research* (1975–1979), and has published four books on educational research, an educational psychology textbook, and *Degrees of excellence: The academic achievement game* (with John D. Wilson).

ERIKSON, ERIK H. (1902–   )

Erikson was psychoanalyzed by Anna Freud. After completing training at the Vienna Psychoanalytic Society in 1933, he left for Boston, became that city's first child psychoanalyst, and served as consultant to the Judge Baker Guidance Center and the Massachusetts General Hospital. In 1936 he did research at Yale's Institute for Human Relations and instruction at its medical school. In 1939, while associated with the Institute of Child Welfare at the University of California (Berkeley), he opened a private practice. Believing psychoanalysis should be an instrument for coping with the "vicissitudes of normal life," during the 1950s Erikson was on the Senior Staff of the Austen Riggs Center in Stockbridge, Massachusetts, where he treated youth with emotional problems. During the 1960s he served as professor of human relations at Harvard University until his retirement in 1970.

Erikson is known for his work in developmental psychology. He coined the term "identity crisis," and described the human life cycle as comprised of eight stages: (1) the oral-sensory stage; (2) the muscular-anal stage; (3) the locomotor-genital stage; (4) the latency period; (5) puberty or adolescence; (6) young adulthood; (7) adulthood; and (8) maturity and old age. Each stage has its accompanying psychosocial identity crisis, with its desired developmental outcome. For example, the desired outcome of the trust versus mistrust crisis of the oral-sensory stage is hope.

Erikson's books include two psychobiographies, *Young man Luther* and *Gandhi's truth,* which show how emotional conflicts can be utilized toward constructive social ends. He is best known, however, for his *Childhood and society,* in which human life cycles are described. In *Identity: Youth and crisis* he elaborates on the life stages of the individual and the identity crisis.

ESCALONA, SIBYLLE K. (1915–   )

Escalona emigrated to the United States in 1934 and studied at Cornell and the University of Iowa, where she received the B.A. and M.A.

degrees. She obtained the Ph.D. in psychology at Teachers College, Columbia University. Her primary interest was normal development in infancy and early childhood. She was among the first to undertake extensive systematic studies of normal infant behavior in naturalistic settings. *Prediction and outcome* (with G. Heider) and *The roots of individuality* document her conceptualization of the interactions between organismic characteristics and environmental conditions and events.

Working relationships with Kurt Lewin, David Rapaport, Jean Piaget, and Bärbel Inhelder among others were influential in generating a structural approach within her psychoanalytic framework. Escalona's first professional experience as psychologist assigned to a prison nursery led to a lasting involvement with the effects of socioeconomic factors upon development. She joined the Menninger Foundation in 1943, then became director of the Department of Research at Kansas University. Subsequently she was on the faculty of the Child Study Center at Yale and in 1956 became a professor at Albert Einstein College of Medicine, New York. She received Research Career and Research Scientist Awards from the National Institute of Mental Health and served on its study section.

ESDAILE, JAMES (1808–1859)

During the 1840s and earlier, British physicians had fought unsuccessfully for the use of mesmerism (hypnotism) as a therapeutic device in treating a variety of illnesses. At the same time Esdaile, a British surgeon, began practicing mesmerism in India, where, the British government was more open-minded. Having read of John Elliotson's work with mesmerism published in England, Esdaile used it to induce anesthesia before performing operations. At first his successful reports were ignored by the government, but in 1848 he was allowed to open a private hospital where he used mesmerism not only as an anesthesia but also to reduce postoperative shock. He reported performing 300 successful operations seemingly without pain, and attempted operations that other surgeons feared to undertake. In operations to remove scrotal tumors, he reported reducing mortality rates from 50% to 5%.

Because of the climate, in 1851 he left India for Scotland, where he continued to practice mesmerism until his death. However, neither in Great Britain nor in India could he get the medical journals to publish accounts of his successful work. He did publish his accounts privately. Meanwhile ether and chloroform were being introduced as anesthetic agents. However, Esdaile preferred mesmerism because of the unfortunate after-effects chemical agents had when used improperly; in some cases they were fatal.

R. W. LUNDIN

ESQUIROL, JEAN ÉTIENNE (1772–1840)

A successor to Philippe Pinel, who first started reforms in mental asylums in France about 1793 by allowing the chains to be cast off patients at La Bicêtre hospital in Paris, the French psychiatrist Esquirol instituted further humanitarian reforms and founded 10 new mental hospitals in various parts of France, each based on the humane and rational treatment developed by Pinel.

Esquirol was one of the first, if not the first, to apply statistical methods to clinical studies of the mentally ill. His book *Les Maladies Mentales* (*Mental Maladies*), begun in 1817, reported his results. Unlike his predecessors, he looked for psychological causes for mental diseases such as dissatisfaction in love, financial loss, or other kinds of failures. He also distinguished various kinds of depression from other forms of mental illness, and introduced the term "hallucination," giving it the clear-cut definition of today. Further, he defended criminals who were mentally ill. Prior to Esquirol's work, the physicians of the time had presumed some kind of physical or physiological causes for mental illness, but Esquirol was inclined toward more psychological interpretations.

R. W. LUNDIN

ESTES, WILLIAM K. (1919–   )

Estes earned the B.A. and Ph.D. (1943) from the University of Minnesota, where he studied under B. F. Skinner. Estes was considerably influenced, however, by the theories of C. L. Hull and especially E. R. Guthrie, and brought statistical (probability) theory to bear upon Guthrian learning theory. Estes's career began at the University of Indiana in 1946, where he remained until 1962, when he left for Stanford University. From Stanford he went to Rockefeller University, where he has been professor of psychology since 1968.

Known for his stimulus sampling theory, Estes developed a statistical theory of learning predicated on the principle of contiguity. Learning, complete in one trial, is a learned response, a conditioning which is a sample of all possible stimulus elements reaching the individual on subsequent trials.

Estes served as editor of the *Journal of Comparative and Physiological Psychology,* was a fellow of the Center for Advanced Study in Behavioral Sciences (1955–1956), and won the Warren Medal in 1963. His principal book (written with others) is *Modern learning theory.*

EVANS, RICHARD I. (1922–   )

Evans is best known as a pioneer in oral history, instruction via film and television, and human problem-oriented research (prejudice, juvenile delinquency, health) in social psychology. After completing with Milton Rokeach the first Ph.D. in psychology at Michigan State University (1950), he agreed to coordinate a new doctoral program in social psychology at the University of Houston. This program subsequently incorporated the first National Institutes of Health-supported research training program in health psychology, and currently focuses on research in the prevention of cardiovascular disease. His demonstration of how innoculation against peer pressure rather than focusing on fear arousal may deter adolescent smoking is a contribution to behavioral medicine and current public policy concerning smoking control.

His interest in instructional innovations led him in 1953 to become the first instructor of a university course on open-circuit public television. His book *Resistance to innovation in higher education* documented the resistance to replacing the classroom professor with didactic television lectures.

When a Ford Foundation grant allowed Evans to explore less didactic uses of media to enhance university courses, he persuaded C. G. Jung to participate in the first of a series of filmed dialogues and books. With support from the National Science Foundation, this oral history and instructional series of books and films includes major contributors to contemporary psychology (e.g., Gordon Allport, Erik Erikson, B. F. Skinner, Konrad Lorenz, Carl Rogers, Jean Piaget). Evans is currently a professor of psychology at the University of Houston.

EWALD, JULIUS RICHARD (1855–1921)

Ewald's academic life was spent at Strasbourg where he became professor of physiology. He was interested in the central nervous system and had a special interest in the physiology of receptor end organs. He developed the pressure–pattern theory of hearing, which challenged the resonance theory of Helmholtz. He served as an editor of the *Zeitscript fur Psychologie.*

P. E. LICHTENSTEIN

EYSENCK, HANS J. (1916–   )

Educated in Berlin, Eysenck left Germany in 1934 for political reasons (opposition to the Hitler regime) to study in Dijon, France, and Exeter, England, before enrolling in a psychology course at the University of London in 1935. He obtained the B.A. and the Ph.D. in 1940, and then joined the Maudsley Hospital and later the Institute of Psychiatry, which is part of the University of London. In the newly formed Institute he founded the Department of Psychology, becoming a professor at the University and psychologist to the Maudsley and Bethlem Royal Hospitals. He was given the task of starting clinical psychology as a profession in the United Kingdom, and his newly created department was the first to train clinical psychologists and to use the newly developed methods of behavior therapy.

Eysenck's main research has been in the areas of personality theory and measurement, intelligence, social attitudes and politics, behavioral genetics, and behavior therapy. He views psychology from a natural science approach, and is hostile to so-called humanistic, psychodynamic, and other literary and subjective approaches. He has published some 600 scientific papers in psychological, biological, genetic, and other journals, and has published some three dozen books. His autobiography has been published in *A history of psychology in autobiography,* and a book-length biography has been published by H. B. Gibson.

Eysenck's view of man, which has always governed his thinking and the direction of his research, is that of a biosocial organism whose actions are determined equally by biological (genetic, physiological, endocrine) factors and social (historical, economic, interactional) factors. He believes that a one-sided stress on either biological or social factors impedes the development of the science. This insistence on seeing man as a product of evolution, still bearing the traces of millions of years of development from earlier life forms, has not always been popular with social scientists more inclined to stress social factors, but is regarded by Eysenck as essential for a proper understanding of man.

FABRE, JEAN HENRI (1823–1915)

Fabre earned his Licence des Sciences at Montpellier, and his Doctorat és Sciences Naturelles at the University of Paris in 1854. His early studies were in mathematics and physics. Later he turned to the study of insects, for which he is best known in psychology.

In his ten-volume work, *Souvenirs entomologiques,* he described many aspects of insect behavior, including the relationship between the sex of the egg and the dimensions of the cell in the solitary bee, the behavior of dung beetles, and the paralyzing instinct of the solitary wasp. In general, he opposed Darwin's theory of evolution, being convinced that each animal species was created in a particular way not subject to change. Stressing the importance of instincts in insects, he opposed the notion that insects shared the human capacity to invent new solutions to problems. Instincts, being not acquired but inborn, served primarily to direct the insects' behavior.

R. W. LUNDIN

FARLEY, FRANK

Farley received the B.A. and M.A. from the University of Saskatchewan and the Ph.D. (1966) from the University of London. After completion of the Ph.D. he emigrated to the United States, joining the faculty of the University of Wisconsin at Madison, where he has remained since 1966.

His bibliography includes more than 175 items, including six books. The topics of the books range from the biological basis of personality to the foundations of aesthetics and the arts. His recent theory of Type T behavior and the Type T personality has received considerable attention inside and outside of the discipline. Type T refers to a basic personality dimension of risk taking and thrill seeking that is proposed to be a significant factor in a wide range of both positive and negative human behaviors and provides a psychological basis for human progress.

Farley has been elected president (1993) of the American Psychological Association (APA). Before that, he was president of APA's Division of Educational Psychology. He is also past president of the American Educational Research Association, among other organizations. He is a founder and was first secretary-treasurer of the Washington-based Federation of Behavioral, Psychological and Cognitive Sciences, an umbrella organization of 15 national scientific societies. Currently, he is a member of the U.S. National Committee of the International Union of Psychological Sciences, responsible for U.S. participation in the International Congress of Psychology held every 4 yr. Farley has received several honors, including the E.L. Thorndike Award for Distinguished Contributions of Psychology to Education.

FEATHER, NORMAN T. (1930–   )

An Australian psychologist, Norman Feather received the B.A. from the University of Sydney, the M.D. from the University of New England, and in 1960, the Ph.D. from the University of Michigan. In 1968 he was appointed to the Foundation Chair of Psychology at the Flinders University of South Australia in Adelaide, South Australia. He was president of the Australian Psychological Society in 1978–1979.

Feather has wide interests in psychology, but his most basic contributions concern human motivation and social psychology. His books and journal articles span the following topics: achievement motivation; the motivational analysis of choice, performance, and persistence; structural balance theory as applied to communication effects, causal attribution, and selective recall; information-seeking behavior; causal attributions in relation to a person's expectancies; the effects of discrepancies between information input and relatively stable abstract cognitive structures; self/other differences in causal attributions; sex roles and reactions to success and failure at occupations; masculinity and femininity; the psychology of human values; the correlates of conservatism; the analysis of national sentiment; the psychological impact of unemployment; and expectancy-value theory as a basic approach to the study of human motivation.

He has made theoretical contributions to expectancy-value theory, to the analysis of the effects of discrepancies between information input and cognitive structures, and to the study of human values and their relationship to attitudes and behavior.

With John W. Atkinson he edited *A theory of achievement motivation*. He is the author of *Values in education and society* and the editor of *Expectations and actions: Expectancy-value models in psychology*. He has also authored numerous journal articles.

FECHNER, GUSTAV THEODOR (1801–1887)

Fechner began his medical studies at the University of Leipzig in 1817. He remained there for the rest of his life, pursuing careers in physiology, physics and mathematics, psychophysics, and philosophy. He was appointed professor at Leipzig in 1833; however, because of severe ill health over a number of years, he was pensioned in 1844. He then recovered his health and every year thereafter made a serious contribution to his work.

Fechner is best remembered for his development of psychophysics, a study of the relationship between mind and the material world. "On the morning of October 22, 1850—an important date in the history of psychology—Fechner had an insight that the law of the connection between mind and body can be found in a statement of quantitative relation between mental sensation and material stimulus" (D. Schultz, 1981/1975, p. 52). The relationship between the two is stated in the equation: $S = K \log I$. As the stimulus intensity increases in geometrical series, the mental sensation increases in arithmetical series. In the early part of the century, Immanuel Kant had predicted that psychology could never become a science, because it would be impossible to experimentally measure psychological processes. Because of Fechner's work, for the first time scientists could measure the mind; by the mid-nineteenth century the methods of science were being applied to mental phenomena.

Fechner systematized three fundamental methods of psychophysics: (1) the method of average error, or calculating the mean to represent the best approximation of a large number of measures; (2) the method of constant stimuli, or finding the amount of difference in stimulation needed to identify that difference, which has been useful in measuring sensory thresholds and aptitudes; and (3) the method of limits, originally called the method of JND (just noticeable differences), for determining the thresholds of visual and temperature stimulations.

Although Ernst Weber's work on the method of just noticeable differences had preceded Fechner's, Fechner found a mathematical statement of the relationship between the mental and the physical worlds. He used and built upon Weber's work, with insights that revealed the implications and consequences of the work in application to psychology as an exact science. Later, Wilhelm Wundt would take these original and creative achievements and organize and integrate them into a "founding" of psychology.

Fechner published the *Elements of psychophysics* in 1860. It is considered one of the original contributions to the development of psychology as a science. Wundt, who developed psychophysics into experimental psychology, recognized the book's importance to his own work. Hermann Ebbinghaus, chancing upon a secondhand copy of the book in Paris about 1876, was inspired to apply the mathematical approach and method to his study of higher mental processes in the field of memory and learning.

N. A. HAYNIE

FERENCZI, SANDOR (1873–1933)

Ferenczi received the M.D. at Vienna in 1894. After service as a military physician, he entered the private practice of neurology and soon became a follower of Sigmund Freud. He visited Clark University with Freud in 1909, and founded the Hungarian Psychoanalytic Society in 1913. He became professor of psychoanalysis at the University of Budapest in 1919.

Ferenczi's major work was *Thalassa: A theory of genitality*. He also collaborated with Otto Rank in writing *The development of psychoanalysis*. He was interested in the relationship between biology and psychoanalysis, and extended the work of Freud during a very active career as a therapist. Ferenczi was a member of "the Committee," which served to maintain theoretical orthodoxy within the early psychoanalytic community. As such, he attacked Carl Jung's radical position.

T. KEITH-LUCAS

FERGUSON, GEORGE A. (1914–   )

Ferguson received the his early education in Nova Scotia. He graduated from Dalhousie University in Halifax with degrees in classics and education before proceeding to the University of Edinburgh. At Edinburgh he studied under Sir Godfrey Thomson and received the Ph.D. in psychology in 1940. His academic career began with an appointment as research associate to the Department of Educational Research at the University of Toronto, but was interrupted by service with the Canadian Army. After World War II and a short period as a consulting industrial psychologist, he joined the Department of Psychology at McGill University in 1947. Promoted to associate professor in 1948 and full professor in 1949, he spent the remainder of his academic career at McGill and served as chairman of the Department of Psychology for 12 years. He retired in 1981 and became emeritus professor of Psychology.

Ferguson is best known professionally for the text *Statistical analysis in psychology and education*. His published writings have also included contributions in psychometrics, human intelligence, and other areas. His work on transfer and human ability has aroused interest in the scientific community and has inspired empirical studies into the development of human abilities in different geographic environments.

Ferguson was one of the small number of Canadian psychologists who founded and developed the Canadian Psychological Association. He served as president of the Association in 1955. He was named Fellow of the Royal Society of Canada in 1962, was awarded the Canada Centennial Medal in 1967, was named honorary president of the Canadian Psychological Association, received an honorary doctorate from Memorial University of Newfoundland in 1975, and was awarded the Queen Elizabeth II Silver Jubilee Medal.

FERRIER, SIR DAVID (1843–1928)

Ferrier studied at Aberdeen University and Heidelberg before receiving degrees in medicine from Edinburgh. He became professor of medicine at King's College, London, and later professor of neuropathology. Ferrier was noted for his contributions regarding the localization of brain functions. He was the first to locate the visual center in the occipital lobes, and his work led to important advances in brain surgery. In 1876 Ferrier published *The functions of the brain* followed by *Cerebral localization* in 1878. An unusual honor was the establishment of the Ferrier Memorial Library by the Royal Society of Medicine.

P. E. LICHTENSTEIN

FERSTER, CHARLES B. (1922–1981)

Ferster received the B.S. from Rutgers University, and the Ph.D. in 1950 from Columbia, where he studied under such well-known behaviorists as Fred S. Keller and William N. Schoenfeld. He served as research scientist at Harvard University and the Indiana University School of Medicine. He then became professor of psychology at Georgetown University and finally at the American University in Washington, D.C., until his death.

Throughout his career he was dedicated to a behavioristic approach to psychology. His writings and research ranged from basic behavioral research to the applications of a behavioral approach to such areas as education and clinical psychology. With B. F. Skinner, Ferster published the results of a long research project in *Schedules of reinforcement* (1957). This work demonstrated the powerful control that various schedules of positive reinforcement could have over the behavior of lower animals such as the pigeon. With Mary C. Perrott he published *Behavior principles,* which involved the application of the principles of operant conditioning to various species of animals, including man. Other applications of operant conditioning principles involved the modification of the behavior of autistic children.

In the 1950s researchers in operant conditioning often had difficulty in getting their research published in the current journals of experimental psychology, because their methodology involved using small numbers of subjects rather than large groups. As a result, in 1958 Ferster was one editor of *The Journal of the Experimental Analysis of Behavior*. which was devoted to the publication of research using operant conditioning techniques. Following its founding, Ferster became the journal's first editor.

R. W. LUNDIN

FESTINGER, LEON (1919–1989)

Festinger received the bachelor's degree from the College of the City of New York. He then attended the State University of Iowa, receiving the M.A., and Ph.D. in 1942. There Festinger came under the influence of the Kurt Lewin's theories and developed them further, earning a reputation in social psychology.

Lewin's theories, oriented from Gestalt principles, include cognitive dissonance theory and social comparison theory. According to cognitive dissonance, people whose behavior is in discord with their thoughts will either structure their thoughts to comport with behavior, or vice versa. Because of psychological pressures toward uniformity, individuals compare their cognitions with others, seeking to convince others of their own position or abandoning their own thoughts for the views of the others. A person, for example, who feels hot in a room and wonders whether it is due to a fever or the room temperature, will inquire of others (provided there is no thermometer in the room). Thus social comparison drives us to convert others to our own opinions, or else yield to theirs.

Festinger's books include his classic *A theory of cognitive dissonance: Conflict, decision, and dissonance; Theory and experiment in social communications* (with others); *Research methods in the behavioral science* (with D. Katz); *Deterrents and reinforcement* (with D. H. Lawrence); *When prophecy fails* (with H. W. Riecken and S. Schachter); and *Social pressures in informal groups* (with S. Schachter and K. Back).

Before going to the New School for Social Research in 1968, Festinger was at the University of Rochester (1943–1945), M.I.T. (1945–1948), the University of Michigan (1951–1955), and Stanford University (1965–1968).

FICHTE, JOHANN GOTTLIEB (1762–1814)

Fichte was educated at the Universities of Jena and Leipzig. In 1793 he was appointed to the chair of philosophy at Jena. In 1795 he was appointed editor of the *Philosophisches Journal*

Along with Hegel and F. W. Schelling, Fichte was one of the successors to Kantian philosophy and psychology. Like Immanuel Kant, Fichte stressed the freedom of the human will in contrast to the determinism found in the physical sciences. Thus, for Fichte there could be no such thing as a scientific psychology. Psychology had to be a deductive, philosophical study which took as its subject matter the will and intentions of the self. The self affirmed its existence not through references to external objects, but through subjective reality. In its affirmation, the self focused its nature on the confirmation of the will. The will was free, but human existence imposed on it a sense which we call duty. To ignore duty would result in evil. The will's imposition on nature forms the foundation of a psychology of personality. There was a paradox between the freedom of the will and an otherwise deterministic world of nature. An understanding of the nature of the human mind involved an ability to reflect upon itself. In this we have the forerunner of Wilhelm Wundt's concept of introspection, as well as a freedom of self as expressed in contemporary humanistic and existential psychology. German philosophers of the post-Kantian era such as Fichte, Hegel, and

Schelling represent a rejection of a naturalistic approach to psychology in favor of a humanistic, subjective approach.

R. W. Lundin

FISCHER, HARDI (1922–   )

Fischer is known for his development of a psychologically based teaching method. He received his early education in Berne, Switzerland. After receiving his *Matura,* he studied mathematics and psychology at the University of Geneva, where he got a diploma, *licence,* and Ph.D. in psychology. His postdoctorate work involved statistical research in psychology and education. These endeavors resulted in *Les méthodes statistiques en psychologie et en pédagogie, Die modernen pädogogischen und psychologischen Forschungsmethoden,* and *Analyse psychologique du calcul scolaire et du facteur g en cinquième année primaire.*

Fischer is an experimental psychologist especially concerned with the relationships among visual perception, epistemology, and developmental psychology. His work in this area has been geared to applied didactics, as is evidenced by *Didactique de l'initiation mathématique à l'école primaire* (1957). Availing himself of the unique opportunities offered by his cosmopolitan country, Fischer ventured into ethnological work on the relations between the German and French subcultures at Switzerland *(Das Verhältnis zwischen Westschweizer und Deutschschweizer;* analytic work on the dynamics of group structure and performance *(Gruppenstruktur und Gruppenleistung;* development of a general theory of teaching *(Allgemeine Didaktik für Höhere Schulen;* and efforts in traffic psychology *(Leistungsmöglichkeiten von Kindern irn Strassenverkehr.*

Fischer's professional career began in Geneva as a school psychologist and university lecturer. In 1966 he was appointed professor of experimental psychology and teaching methodology at the Swiss Federal Institute of Technology in Zurich, teaching in the area of human cognition.

FISHER, RONALD A. (1890–1962)

Sir Ronald A. Fisher was educated at Cambridge. His early career was spent as a statistician at Rothamsted Experimental (agricultural research) Station in Hertfordshire. He was the second holder (after Pearson) of the Galton chair in eugenics and biometry at University College, London, and finished his career in the Balfour chair of genetics at Cambridge. Clearly the most creative statistician of modern times, Fisher gave psychology (1) the analysis of variance, (2) analysis techniques for small samples, (3) the concept of null hypothesis, and (4) the notion of significant/insignificant as a continuum rather than a dichotomy.

Fisher's work at Rothamsted led to his *Statistical methods for research workers* (1925), which presented for the first time precise inference based on small data samples and precise tests of statistical significance (theoretical chances of obtaining the same results if the study were repeated). He wrote extensively on the need to develop statistics which showed *sufficiency,* that is, which exhausted all information in the sample in arriving at the conclusion. He also developed the idea of the unbiased estimator—a measure that becomes more accurate as more observations are made.

Later at Rothamsted he turned to the more complex experimental situations, developing the notion of analysis of variance based on the classical least squares theory. For the first time it was possible to deal meaningfully with more than one manipulated variable at a time; his *Design of experiments* (1935) became the researcher's Bible. He later extended his work to multivariate procedures, permitting multiple outcome measures as well as multiple manipulations. With Yates (1938), he collected the statistical tables needed to perform the various inferential techniques.

C. S. Peyser

FLAMENT, CLAUDE (1930–   )

Flament studied mathematics, philosophy, law, and finally, psychology at the Sorbonne, where he got his *licence* and his first doctorate, then his state doctorate in 1971.

In 1954 he worked at the psychiatric hospital of Sainte-Anne, in Paris. From 1955 to 1961 he was a full-time researcher in experimental social psychology at the Laboratory of Experimental Psychology of the Sorbonne. From 1961 on, he has been teaching social psychology at the universities of Aix-en-Provence and Marseilles. Since 1979 he has been professor of mathematical psychosociology at the School of Advanced Studies in Social Sciences at Paris and Marseilles.

Flament was an invited professor at the universities of Michigan (1963), Geneva (1970), and Montreal (1972). He was president of the European Association for Experimental Social Psychology from 1972 to 1974. He has served on the editorial boards of the *Journal of Experimental Social Psychology, Social Networks, Mathematical Social Sciences,* and *Mathématiques et Sciences Humaines.*

In 1961 he published an elementary text on statistics, and in 1963, a work on graph theory as applied to social networks. His other publications are on varied topics: social influence, in-group behavior, structural balance cognitive theory, qualitative data analysis, and ordered set theory. He is seen as a psychologist by mathematicians and as a mathematician by psychologists and mathematicians.

FLAMMER, AUGUST (1938–   )

Flammer was trained as a high school teacher and psychologist in Paris, St. Gallen, Zurich, and Fribourg, and at Stanford and Wisconsin in the United States. He taught at the Teachers College in Fribourg and at the universities of. Basel, Bern, Fribourg, and Zurich. He was chairman of the Department of Psychology (1977–1982) and dean of the faculty of humanities (1983–1984) at Fribourg.

Flammer is a member of various organizations such as the Board of the Swiss National Psychological Association (1975–1982), the Board of the Swiss National Academy of Humanities (1979 on), and the National Research Council of the Swiss National Foundation (1981 on). Among his publications are *Individuelle Unterschiede im Lernen* and *Transfer und Korrelation.* With Walter Kintsch he edited *Discourse Processing.*

Flammer serves on the editorial board of several publications. His research centers on questional asking, selective memory, influence of titles, encoding, free discourse and perspective shifts between encoding and retrieval, and individual differences.

FLAVELL, JOHN H. (1928–   )

Best known for his research and writings on children's cognitive development, Flavell was educated in Boston and its environs. After receiving his bachelor's degree from Northeastern University, he became a graduate student in clinical psychology at Clark University, receiving the Ph.D. there in 1955. Although he continued to practice and teach in clinical psychology for several years, his research and scholarly activities became exclusively focused on cognitive development.

His major scientific accomplishments include the explication and popularization of Jean Piaget's work; some early and influential investigations of the development of communication and social cognition; pioneering developmental studies of children's spontaneous use of cognitive strategies and of their knowledge and cognition about cognition ("meta-cognition"); and theoretical papers on such developmental issues as the nature of cognitive-developmental stages and sequences.

Flavell's research style is to try to think of important cognitive competencies that others have not studied and then to investigate their development during childhood. He thinks of himself as a kind of developmental naturalist, always on the lookout for new and unexplored "developables."

Flavell taught first at the University of Rochester (1955–1965), next at the University of Minnesota (1965–1976), and from 1976 on at Stanford University. His publications include *The developmental psychology of Jean Piaget, The development of role-taking and communication skills in children,* and *Cognitive development.*

FLOURENS, PIERRE (1794–1867)

Marie Jean Pierre Flourens, a French neurophysiologist from Languedoc, received the M.D. from Montpellier before the age of 20. A protégé of the zoologist and paleontologist Cuvier, he spent most of his professional life in Paris on the faculty of the Collège de France. His historical publications include many concerning Cuvier.

His earliest work of note (1822–1824) confirmed what is today called the Bell-Magendie law, the separation of the nervous system into sensory and motor divisions. His later work, primarily with pigeons but also using other birds and rabbits, was known for its simple precision, as was his writing.

Flourens showed the very limited localization of function in the brain; his surgery was the earliest precise extirpation or ablation. He found that the quantity of cerebral tissue removed was more important than its location, although there was some local function (the cerebrum as a whole governed thought and volition; the cerebellum, locomotion). He precisely located the "vital node" of the medulla oblongata, which, when punctured, produces instant death by terminating respiration. His work, begun around 1824, led to *Phrenology examined,* which convincingly criticized the localization claims of Gall and Spurzheim and dealt their movement a major blow.

Flourens' other major contribution was in determining the function of the semicircular canals in the ear. As early as 1824 he was able to show that surgical lesions of one or more canals produced a lack of coordination in a pigeon; by 1830 he published definitive evidence that the canals were involved in "reflex orientation" rather than in hearing. J. Müller ignored his work, but Helmholtz accepted it as part of his resonance theory of hearing.

C. S. PEYSER

FLOURNOY, THÉODORE (1854–1920)

In Geneva Flournoy received his first degree in mathematics from the university. He then went to the universities of Freiburg and Strasbourg for the M.D. degree. In 1878 he went to Leipzig for a year to study with Wilhelm Wundt. Upon returning to Geneva, he was awarded a chair in physiological and experimental psychology at the university in 1891.

He was the initiator of scientific psychology in Switzerland and began the first psychological laboratory there in 1892. His research included studies on reaction time, imaging, sensation, and hypnosis. When the Sixth International Congress of Psychology met at Geneva in 1909, he served as its president. His cousin, Edouard Claparède, was one of his first students, and together in 1891 they founded the *Archives de Psychologie,* the first Swiss psychological journal. At Flournoy's death,

Claparède succeeded him in his chair in experimental psychology and took charge of the laboratory.

R. W. LUNDIN

FLÜGEL, JOHN CARL (1884–1955)

Flügel received the degree of D.Sc. from the University of London in 1908 and served at University College until 1955. His psychological interests centered in both academic psychology and psychoanalysis. His first book was *The psychoanalytic study of the family.* He published extensively, applying psychological concepts to broad general topics in such books as *Men and their motives; Man, morals, and society;* and *Population, psychology, and peace.*

Flügel's best-known work is *A hundred years of psychology: 1833–1933* (with D. J. West), a history of psychology written when few such were available, reflecting broad historical scholarship in psychology.

P. E. LICHTENSTEIN

FOPPA, KLAUS (1930–   )

Foppa studied at the University of Vienna, where he received the Ph.D. in psychology in 1954. He was granted a fellowship for 1955–1956, then went to the University of Würzburg, where he stayed until 1960. He returned to the University of Vienna, then became professor of psychology at the University of Bern in Switzerland in 1964.

In German-speaking countries Foppa is best known for his book on learning psychology (1965). A graduate textbook with extensive references to results of learning experiments and to different learning theories, the book may be considered an original theoretical contribution to the field. Contrary to other learning psychologists, Foppa stressed that organisms in their natural environments learn under permanently changing conditions. Since neither stimuli nor responses recur as identical units, learning cannot come about by mere strengthening of associative links between them. Instead, the organism must build up some kind of *situational concepts.* These concepts are exactly those aspects of the organism's interaction with its environment which it "believes" to be functional.

Foppa has worked mainly in the field of verbal communication, especially on the development of children's communicative skills. Above all he is interested in tracing the influence of adult partners' speaking characteristics on children's language behavior. With his students, he developed several methods for analyzing children's communicative skills and their knowledge about language.

FOREL, AUGUSTE-HENRI (1848–1931)

Forel of Switzerland spent most of his life in his native country of Switzerland. In 1866 he started his studies of medicine at the University of Zurich, but later went to Vienna to complete his studies in 1872. In 1879 he became professor of psychiatry at the University of Zurich. Here he concentrated on the treatment of alcoholics, working diligently for their rehabilitation to society. His approach stressed complete abstinence; he was gravely concerned with the adverse effects of alcohol on the working classes.

His studies of medicine concerned the anatomy of the human brain. He was the first to achieve biological preparations of human brain specimens. He studied the topography of various nerves in the brain and made such precise descriptions of the hypothalamus (a small organ inside the brain) that one of its regions was later named the campus Foreli in his honor.

Of particular interest to animal psychology was his study of insects. In 1893 he retired prematurely to devote himself to his first interest, the study of insects and in particular, ants. As an anatomist he studied their internal morphology. He then became engrossed with the psychology of these insects, particularly their social behavior. He was the first to describe parabiosis (the joining together of two animals for experimental research) in ants. He searched for new species, finding more than 3500 hitherto unknown insects. He also wrote the first book on the senses of insects.

R. W. LUNDIN

FOWLER, RAYMOND D. (1930–   )

Fowler received the B.A. and M.A. from the University of Alabama and the Ph.D. (1957) in clinical psychology from the Pennsylvania State University. He joined the faculty of the University of Alabama in 1956 and chaired the department of psychology from 1965 to 1983. He was chair of the psychology department at the University of Tennessee from 1987 to 1989, when he accepted his next position as chief executive officer of the American Psychological Association.

Fowler is recognized for his innovative work in computer interpretation of the MMPI; his system has been translated into most major European languages and is considered a prototype for other computer-based testing systems. He also is known for his work with substance abuse and criminal behavior and has been a consultant to the White House, the Department of Justice, the Rosalynn Carter Institute, and the Veterans Administration. He was a special consultant to the estate of the late Howard Hughes, Jr.

His publications include many articles, chapters, and books on personality assessment, corrections policies, and alcohol abuse. Fowler is a fellow of 12 divisions of the APA and served as the APA's 97th president in 1988. He has received numerous awards, including the Significant MMPI Contribution Award. He is listed in *Who's Who in America*.

FOX, RONALD E. (1936–   )

Fox received the A.B., M.A., and Ph.D. (1962) from the University of North Carolina at Chapel Hill. His clinical psychology internship was at the Palo Alto VA Medical Center in California (1962–1963). Upon completion of his internship, he was appointed assistant professor in the departments of psychiatry and psychology at the University of North Carolina where he worked on a psychotherapy outcome project with Hans Strupp. In 1968, Fox accepted a position as associate professor in the departments of psychiatry and psychology and director of internship training at the Ohio State University. While at Ohio State, Fox became involved with the professional school movement and led the effort to create a state-supported school in Ohio. When the Ohio legislature established the School of Professional Psychology at Wright State University in 1977, Fox was appointed as its first dean.

Fox has coauthored two books—*Patients view their psychotherapy* and *Abnormal psychology*—and has published book chapters and articles in scientific and professional journals. His major contributions include founding the Association of Psychology Internship Centers and the Wright State University School of Professional Psychology. He was the first psychologist appointed by the secretary of Health and Human Services to the National Advisory Committee on Health Professions Education. Fox has received awards for his professional contributions

from the APA Divisions of Clinical Psychology, Psychotherapy, and state associations. He is listed in *Who's Who in America*.

FRAISSE, PAUL (1911–   )

Fraisse is known for his contributions to time and rhythm psychology. An experimental psychologist, he got his initial training in Louvain under Albert Michotte, who oriented him toward the study of motor rhythms. In Paris, Fraisse collaborated with Henri Piéron (1937) and succeeded him as director of the Experimental Psychology Laboratory in 1952. There he effected research on diverse aspects of time, rhythm, and information processing. Additionally, he has devoted considerable effort to the training of young research workers who now occupy positions of responsibility in experimental psychology both in Paris and the provinces.

Fraisse has contributed to the development of institutions that recognize psychology as a science. He was subdirector and then director of the Institute of Psychology (1952–1969), and general secretary (1949–1959), then president (1962–1963), of the French Society of Psychology, of which he remains an active member. In 1952 he founded the French Language Association of Scientific Psychology, the members of which meet once every two years for conferences on a preestablished theme. Fraisse was a member of the Executive Committee of the International Union of Psychological Science (1960–1980), and president of the Union from 1966 to 1969. He organized and presided over the 21st International Congress of Psychology in Paris in 1976. A titular professor at the Sorbonne (1956–1979), Fraisse carried out a number of foreign missions in both Eastern and Western countries. He is doctor honoris causa of the University of Bonn, and professor extraordinary at the University of Rio de Janeiro.

Fraisse's nine-volume *Treatise on experimental psychology*, co-edited with Jean Piaget, has been partially or completely translated into nine languages. To facilitate the growth and promotion of psychology, since 1950 Fraisse has directed two series of psychological publications at the Presses Universitaires de France, where more than 150 titles have been published. Director of *L'Année Psychologique* since 1947, he also created the journal *French-Language Psychology* in 1980.

FRANK, JEROME D. (1909–   )

Frank, a professor emeritus of psychiatry at the Johns Hopkins University School of Medicine, entered Harvard, at 17 where he received the B.A., the Ph.D. in psychology, and an M.D. As a psychologist, he spent two years—one in Berlin and one at Cornell University—studying with Kurt Lewin, who deeply influenced his thinking.

After a medical internship at the New York Hospital he obtained his psychiatric training at the Johns Hopkins Hospital under Adolf Meyer and John C. Whitehorn, then spent three years with the U.S. Army Medical Corps in Australia, New Guinea, and the Philippines, and three years conducting a research project on group therapy for the U.S. Veterans Administration with Florence Powdermaker. He returned to Johns Hopkins in 1949, where he has remained.

Frank's major research has been on the factors shared by all methods of psychotherapy that contribute to their effectiveness. This research led to the formulation of the demoralization hypothesis, according to which patients come to psychotherapy suffering from demoralization as well as specific symptoms, so that the main healing power of all forms of psychotherapy lies in features that combat demoralization.

Having been in the Philippines when the atom bombs were dropped on Japan, he early became concerned with the horrendous implications of these weapons for the future of humanity. He has written and spoken extensively on the ever-more-menacing nuclear arms race. His views on psychotherapy have been summed up in *Persuasion and healing*, and on the nuclear arms race in *Sanity and survival in the nuclear age*, as well as in numerous articles in professional journals on both subjects.

FRANKENHAEUSER, MARIANNE (1925–   )

Best known for her research on human stress and coping as related to work and health, Marianne Frankenhaeuser was schooled in Finland. After receiving a diploma in psychology at the University of Oxford (1948), she received academic degrees at the universities of Helsinki (1951), Stockholm (1954), and Uppsala (1959). Her early research training included clinical and animal work in neuropsychology, psychopharmacology, and physiological psychology, after which she turned to the experimental study of human stress and coping processes. Her first major contribution (1959) was a monograph on time estimation as related to arousal level.

As a biobehavioral scientist with an interest in social issues, Frankenhaeuser has approached human stress and coping problems by combining methods and concepts from biomedical and biosocial sciences. She emphasizes the role of psychobiological research in social planning. She has examined health outcomes of occupational stress in the context of underload, overload, and lack of personal control related to highly mechanized and highly automated work processes. Another main line of her research concerns the comparison between male and female stress and coping patterns as related to sex differences in morbidity and mortality.

Frankenhaeuser's professional career began in Stockholm, where she continues her research and teaching as professor of psychology at the Medical School of the Karolinska Institute. Her publications include about 120 journals and review articles. Her international activities include visiting professorships at Stanford University and at Barnard College in New York City.

FRANKL, VIKTOR E. (1905–   )

Founder of logotherapy and *Existenzanalyse*, Frankl has seen his system designated as the Third Viennese School of Psychotherapy, the first two being Freud's and Adler's. In the mid-1920s, Frankl's earliest publications appeared: the first in Freud's *International Journal of Psychoanalysis* and the second in Adler's *International Journal of Individual Psychology*, the former by Freud's invitation and the latter by Adler's. Because of his unorthodox views, however, Frankl was expelled from Adler's Society of Individual Psychology. Frankl subsequently came under the influence of Oswald Schwarz and Rudolf Allers, both disenchanted Adlerians. The phenomenologist Max Scheler also influenced him.

Frankl's psychotherapy, designated logotherapy, is predicated on "man's search for meaning"; accordingly, Frankl has entitled the book for which he is best known, *Man's search for meaning*. The book opens with Frankl's three-year experience in Nazi concentration camps, including the notorious Auschwitz. The remainder of the book outlines the theory and practice of logotherapy, a psychiatry spawned from his concentration camp experience. His later works—*The will to meaning, The unconscious God, The unheard cry for meaning, Psychotherapy and existentialism,* and *The doctor and the soul*—elaborate and expand his logotherapy.

Frankl's university affiliations include the University of Vienna, where he received the M.D. and the Ph.D. in 1949; a distinguished professorship at the United States International University; and visiting professorships at Harvard, Stanford, Duquesne, and Southern Methodist universities. Over the years he has served as head of the Department of Neurology at the Poliklinik Hospital of Vienna.

FRANKLIN, BENJAMIN (1706–1790)

The great American patriot and one of the founding fathers is known in the history of psychology for four things. (1) His experiments with a kite in a thunderstorm helped in the verification of electricity, which eventually helped the understanding of the nature of the electrical potential of the nerve impulse. (2) While in France (1784) the king appointed him to a commission to investigate the "animal magnetism" claimed by Mesmer. Mesmer was accused of having a "secret" that he used in the treatment of his patients (hypnosis). The commission concluded that the cures were real but the maladies were imaginary. (3) In the psychology of sensation, he showed that the after image will be positive on the dark field of the closed eye and negative when the eyes are open and fixated on a white piece of paper. This demonstration came to be known as Franklin's experiment. (4) His publication *Poor Richard's almanac* contains some practical psychology such as "You can catch more flies with a teaspoon of honey than a gallon of vinegar."

R. W. LUNDIN

FRANZ, SHEPERD I. (1874–1933)

Franz received the Ph.D. under James McKeen Cattell at Columbia University in 1899. He held positions at Harvard Medical School, McLean Hospital (now St. Elizabeth's), later at the Government Hospital in Washington, D.C., and finally at the University of California at Los Angeles.

While at McLean Hospital he worked with Karl Lashley on problems of brain localization in lower animals as well as humans. His 1902 publication, "On the function of the cerebrum", drew great attention among psychologists and physiologists. He applied the relatively new method for surgically removing parts of animals' brains to study the effects of their removal on behavior. Using cats and monkeys as his subjects, he found that removing the frontal lobes of the animals' brains resulted in the loss of recently acquired habits but not of older ones. Furthermore, the lost habits could be relearned in the absence of the removed tissue.

He collaborated with Lashley on a paper entitled, "The retention of habits by the rats after destruction of the frontal portion of the cerebrum," which led to Lashley's formulation of the principles of equipotentiality and mass action. There followed many other research studies which indicated that the localization of functions in the brain were very inexact, and that loss of function due to the destruction of a particular part of the brain could be restored through relearning.

R. W. LUNDIN

FRENKEL-BRUNSWIK, ELSE (1908–1958)

A central contributor to the psychoanalytically oriented psychology of personality that emerged shortly after World War II, Else Frenkel-Brunswik is best known for her major part in *The authoritarian personality* and for her empirical delineation of the concept of intolerance of ambiguity. After earning the doctorate at the University of Vienna with Karl Bühler, she collaborated with Charlotte Bühler in her studies of personality in life-course perspective. In Vienna, she was educated in psychoanalysis (analyzed by Ernst Kris) and in logical positivism and the "unity of science" movement. She and her husband-to-be, Egon Brunswik—later a professor at the University of California, Berkeley, and a proponent of ecologically "representative design" in experimental psychology—were participants in the Vienna Circle led by Moritz Schlick and Rudolph Carnap that launched the movement. These involvements, and her experience as a Jew in Hitler's Europe, underlay the problems she addressed during her two productive decades in the United States.

After Austria's incorporation into Hitler's Germany in 1938, Else Frenkel joined Egon Brunswik and became a research psychologist at the Institute of Child Welfare (later, the Institute of Human Development) at Berkeley, any professorial appointment being excluded by the prevailing rules against "nepotism." Her arrival was well-timed, since the new self-conscious psychology of personality and the new profession of clinical psychology were looking to psychoanalysis for guiding ideas, and were under pressure to defend psychoanalysis from "operationism," the version of American behaviorism or positivism that was then fashionable—a reductionist position that drew heavily on the contributions of the Vienna Circle. Her command of both psychoanalysis and logical positivism enabled her to champion the scientific respectability of psychoanalytic constructions.

After publishing "Motivation and behavior," an important monograph showing how ratings of underlying drives could bring discrepant data from self-reports and ratings of social behavior into congruence, she joined forces with Nevitt Sanford and Daniel Levinson in designing and launching major psychological studies of anti-Semitism; the émigré scholar T. W. Adorno of the Frankfurt School joined the project a little later. (She was responsible for conducting and analyzing the clinical interviews of highly prejudiced and unprejudiced persons.) Their product, The authoritarian personality, brought the clinical insights of psychoanalysis and the empirical methods of American social psychology to bear on social character and ideology. The book was sharply criticized on methodological grounds, but remains a classic treatment of issues that are still important and not fully resolved.

After this major work, Frenkel-Brunswik conducted related research on prejudice in children, wrote on "intolerance of ambiguity" as a cognitive style of personality that had emerged saliently in her studies of prejudice.

M. B. SMITH

FREUD, ANNA (1895–1982)

Known particularly for being the daughter of Sigmund Freud, but also in her own right a specialist in children's psychoanalysis, Anna Freud championed the needs of children.

She graduated from Vienna's Cottage Lyzeum in 1912. After the Nazis took over Austria in 1938, she accompanied her father to London, where she became a practicing psychoanalyst.

Deeply interested in the growth of personality, Anna Freud invested 50 years applying her father's psychoanalytic theories to children. Her writings, including collected papers, fill seven volumes under the title The writings of Anna Freud. The books for which she is best known are The ego and mechanisms of defence and Psychoanalysis for teachers and parents. The former discusses essentially the nonsexual mechanisms of the mind. The ego, in dealing with repressed impulses, resorts to defense mechanisms.

Clark University in Massachusetts, which had given her father an honorary degree when Freud delivered a series of lectures there in 1909, also gave Anna Freud an honorary doctorate in 1950. Her father's alma mater, the University of Vienna, conferred on her an honorary M.D. in 1972.

W. S. SAHAKIAN

FREUD, SIGMUND (1856–1939)

Freud moved from Moravia to Vienna at age four, and lived there for nearly 80 years. He demonstrated an unusual intellectual ability early in life and was encouraged by his family. Freud graduated with distinction from the Gymnasium at age 17 and entered the University of Vienna to study medicine and scientific research. Because of his diversified interests in biology, physiology, and teaching, as well as medicine, Freud spent eight years at the University. Finally persuaded to take his medical examinations, he entered private practice as a clinical neurologist in 1881.

Freud's interest in what was to become psychoanalysis began and developed during his associations with Josef Breuer in 1884. From Breuer he learned about the "talking cure" and the use of hypnosis for hysterical neuroses. In 1885, Freud spent four and a half months in France studying hypnosis with Jean Charcot, from whom he heard about a sexual basis for patients' problems. The idea stayed in his mind, and by the mid-1890s Freud was convinced that the dominant difficulty in neurosis was inadequate sexual development.

In 1895 Breuer and Freud published Studies on hysteria, often noted as the formal beginning of psychoanalysis. In 1897 Freud undertook the task of self-analysis. He diagnosed his own neurotic difficulties as anxiety neuroses, which he claimed were caused by an accumulation of sexual tension. The method of self-analysis that Freud used was dream analysis. This was both a creative period of his life and a time of intense inner turmoil. The analysis continued for about two years and was reported in The interpretation of dreams, now considered Freud's major work.

By 1902 Freud had become interested in promoting psychoanalytic theory and practice. A small number of colleagues including Alfred Adler joined him in a weekly discussion group at his home. These early discussions on the problems of neurosis were important to the development of the different theoretical beliefs and applied techniques of the four pillars of depth psychology: Freud, Adler, Otto Rank, and Carl Jung. The group became known as the Vienna Psychological Society; later, Freud expanded his efforts to promote psychoanalysis and formed the Vienna Psychoanalytical Association. In 1905 Freud published Three essays on the theory of sexuality. In 1909 he was invited to America by G. Stanley Hall of Clark University; in this, his first international recognition, he was awarded an honorary doctorate.

As Adler, Jung, and Rank developed their own theories and style, the original psychoanalytic group was disrupted with conflict and disagreement. Adler left the group in 1911; Jung, in 1914. The height of Freud's fame was from 1919 to his death in 1939. In the 1920s Freud developed a personality theory and system for all human motivation that expanded his influence beyond a method of treatment for the disturbed.

Freud's method of treatment in psychoanalysis identified resistances as a form of protection from pain, and repression as the way of eliminating that pain from conscious awareness. Repression became the fundamental principle of psychoanalysis. Repressed material was uncovered through free association and dream analysis in a long, intensive course of therapy lasting months or years. Effective therapeutic work depended on the personal relationship developed between client and therapist, or transference. Freud believed that transference of the client's emotional attitudes from parent figures to the therapist was necessary for curing the neuroses.

The personality system of psychoanalysis dealt with the driving forces or energies that have been called "instincts" in English translation, but that could also be called "drives." The life instincts or urges for self-preservation and creative forces were called libido. The death instincts were energies directed either inward toward self-destruction, or outward in aggression and hatred. Freud divided psychic mental life of the personality into id, ego, and superego. The id, corresponding to the unconscious, included sexual and aggressive instincts, no value judgments, and energies directed toward immediate satisfaction and tension reduction; it obeyed the pleasure principle. The ego, commonly known as reason or rationality, mediated between the id and the external world, holding under control the pleasure-seeking demands of the id; it obeyed the reality principle. The superego—the conscience developed in early childhood—worked toward inhibiting the id completely, and toward actualizing the ego ideal to a state of perfection. Anxiety resulted whenever the ego became too overburdened with the triple impact of the psychic energies of the pleasure-seeking id, the need to manipulate reality for tension reduction, and the perfectionistic superego.

Freud's theories and methods have been criticized on several grounds: (1) unsystematic and uncontrolled data collection and interpretation; (2) overemphasis on biological forces, particularly sex, as the primary influence on personality development; and (3) a deterministic view of the influence of past behavior, with a denial of free will and the role of future goals, dreams, and hopes in personal growth.

D. Schultz has written on the contributions of psychoanalysis to the field of clinical psychology and psychiatry: "Certain Freudian concepts have gained wide acceptance and been assimilated into the mainstream of contemporary psychology. These include the role of unconscious motivation, the importance of childhood experiences in shaping adult behavior, and the operation of defense mechanisms. Interest in these areas has generated much research" (Schultz, 1981, pp. 338–39).

Psychoanalysis retains its particular identity today, not having been absorbed into the mainstream of general psychological thought. Freud was an originator, a pioneer in new techniques and understandings of human nature, a great contributor to the history of psychology.

N. A. HAYNIE

FREUDENBERGER, HERBERT J. (1926–   )

Freudenberger received the B.A. from Brooklyn College, the M.A. in psychology, and the Ph.D. (1956) in clinical psychology from New York University. He is a graduate in psychoanalysis and senior member of the National Psychological Association for Psychoanalysis, (1961).

He has been in independent practice since 1955. He has been a consultant in substance abuse and staff training to U.S. Air Force, Daytop Village, Covenant House, and Project Return. He was director of the St. Mark's Tree Clinic, founder and director of Hispanic Therapeutic Community, chief psychologist for the Industrial Home for the Blind and Queens College Speech and Hearing Center.

He coined the term *burnout* and wrote the first article on this topic in 1974. Freudenberger has published *Burnout: The high cost of achievement; Situational anxiety; Women's burnout: How to spot it, how to reverse it and how to prevent it;* and *The free clinic handbook.*

Freudenberger has been associate editor of *Psychotherapy, Theory and Research;* president of the APA's Division of Psychotherapy, and president of the APA's Division of Independent Practice, and twice president of the New York Society of Clinical Psychologists. He was also chair of the APA's Policy and Planning Board and the Board of Professional Affairs. He has received the following honors: the Presidential Citation; APA: Distinguished Psychologist Award; and the Psychologist of the Year Award. He is a fellow of the APA.

FRIJDA, NICO H. (1927–   )

Frijda is a full professor in experimental psychology at the University of Amsterdam. He studied psychology at that university, where he got the Ph.D. in 1956 on the recognition of emotional expression (*Recognition of emotion*). He worked initially as a clinical psychologist, then moved to social psychology and studied characteristics of overseas migrants and methods of cross-cultural research (*National character and national stereotypes,* with H. C. J. Duijker). Next, he turned his attention to cognitive processes and computer simulation "Simulation of human long-term memory": Together with A. D. de Groot, he edited *Otto Selz: His contribution to psychology.*

Frijda's main interests are the development of the general theory of emotion, and integrating the study of emotion in the information-processing framework (*Can computers feel?*), while still doing justice to phenomenological and clinical viewpoints (*The meaning of emotional expression*).

Frijda is one of the founders of the Netherlands Psychonomic Foundation (1968) and the Foundation of Scientific Research in Psychology (1981). He is a member of the Royal Dutch Academy of Sciences.

FRISCH, KARL VON (1886–1982)

Von Frisch received the doctorate in zoology in 1910 from the universities of Munich and Vienna. His dissertation was based on the color adaptation and light perception of minnows. In medical school his initial research involved pigments in the compound eyes of butterflies, beetles, and shrimp. Upon transferring to the Zoological Institute in Munich, he was assigned to study the behavior of solitary bees. After holding positions at the universities of Rostock, Breslau, and Graz, he spent most of his lengthy career at the University of Munich.

Von Frisch is best known for his study of communication in honey bees. His ingenious research procedures demonstrated two different "dances," depending on the distance of the source of nectar or pollen. He isolated the visual, olfactory, and gustatory cues involved in the communication, and demonstrated that honey bees navigate by using the sun for orientation. In 1959 he received the Kalinga Prize for popularization of science from UNESCO. He shared the 1973 Nobel Prize for Physiology or Medicine with Konrad Lorenz and Nikolaas Tinbergen.

C. S. PEYSER

FROEBEL, FRIEDRICH (1782–1852)

Froebel studied at Jena, Göttingen, and Berlin. He believed that the goal of education was to develop or unfold the innate potential of the individual. The child was assumed to be inherently good; all human evil arises from wrong education methods. The teacher should assist children to reach their potential and must be careful not to coerce or force them into a preconceived mold.

In the 1830s in Bern, Switzerland, and later in Germany, Froebel lectured and wrote on detailed methods of teaching elementary and younger children. He emphasized the role of the mother, publishing a book of songs and finger plays that would encourage natural development, and suggested the use of balls, blocks, clay modeling, paper cutting, free play, and work. In 1840 he coined the term *kindergarten* and provided its rationale.

Froebel himself was basically unpopular because of his imperious demeanor, but his ideas were spread by the Baroness von Marenholtz-Bülow, who became his supporter when he moved to Marienthal. When the Prussian government banned the kindergarten (1851–1860), the Baroness proselytized in England, France, Italy, Switzerland, Holland, Belgium, and eventually Germany. In 1870 she set up a kindergarten teacher training college in Dresden. Prior to this, in 1855, two sisters trained by Froebel founded the first American kindergarten in Wisconsin.

Intellectually, Froebel may be considered to be the link between his mentor Pestalozzi and his successor in education, Herbart.

C. S. PEYSER

FROMM, ERICH (1900–1980)

Fromm received the Ph.D. at Heidelberg in 1922. He later studied at the Berlin Psychoanalytic Institute. In 1934 he immigrated to the United

States. He has taught at many schools in North America, including the New School for Social Research, Columbia, Yale, Michigan State, and the National University of Mexico.

In his system of personality Fromm acknowledged man's biological past but stressed his social nature. In his first book, *Escape from freedom*—considered by many to be his best—Fromm departed from the standard Freudian theory in stressing the effect of social forces on personality. The main theme involved human loneliness. As we evolved from early times, we gained greater independence from nature and social institutions (such as the medieval Church), but in so doing became isolated and lonely. Freedom, then, became a condition from which to escape. There were two solutions: either to join with others in a spirit of love and social productivity, or to submit to authority and conform to society. The general theme of productive love permeates much of Fromm's writings.

In *The sane society* Fromm envisioned an ideal solution where there is equality for all, where each person has the opportunity of becoming purely human, and where individuals relate to one another in a loving way. In *Man for himself* he developed various personality or character types which emerged as we reacted to social influences and were related to the methods of escape from the basic problem of loneliness. He designated five, four of which were undesirable. The *receptive character* demands all that it can get and is willing to take but not give. The *hoarding character* sees the outside world as a threat, therefore tries to keep all that it has and not share. The *exploitative character* satisfies its desires through force and cunning. The *marketing character* considers itself a commodity that can be bought or sold. Finally, the *productive character* is the desirable one. Being productive means realizing one's potentialities and in so doing devotes itself to the welfare and well-being of all mankind.

R. W. LUNDIN

GAGNÉ, ROBERT M. (1916–   )

Currently a professor of educational research in the College of Education at Florida State University, Gagné received his undergraduate education at Yale University, and his doctoral degree in experimental psychology from Brown University in 1940. His college teaching career began at Connecticut College. During World War II he served as an aviation psychologist, developing tests of motor and perceptual functions in the classification of aircrews. After a few postwar years of academic life, he served for eight years as technical director of two Air Force laboratories researching learning and methods of technical training.

From 1958 to 1962 Gagné was professor of psychology at Princeton University, where he carried out a series of studies on the acquisition of knowledge, learning hierarchies, and mathematics learning. From 1962 to 1965 he was director of research of the American Institute for Research, supervising research programs on human performance, instructional methods, and design and evaluation of educational procedures. His writings during this period dealt particularly with methods of instruction, problem solving, and the conditions of learning. From 1966 to 1969 he was a professor of educational psychology at the University of California, Berkeley. He supervised the establishment of a regional educational laboratory, managed a program of graduate training in educational research, and continued his research on the learning of school subjects. At Florida State University he completed research on learning hierarchies related to school instruction, studies of research and development outcomes and their dissemination, and investigations of adult learning from television.

His publications include more than a hundred articles in scholarly journals on human learning and instruction. Major books are *Essentials of learning for instruction*, *The conditions of learning* (now in its third edition), and *Principles of instructional design*, coauthored with L. J. Briggs.

GALEN (ca. 130–200)

Galen studied anatomy in Alexandria, returned to Pergamon as surgeon to the gladiators, and went to Rome in 161 A.D. He became personal physician to Emperor Marcus Aurelius, as well as distinguishing himself as an anatomist. He codified the then extant knowledge of medicine, anatomy, and physiology.

The unimpeachable authority for centuries, Galen knew the broad features of the nervous system (he had the brain as the seat of the mind) and distinguished motor and sensory nerves (a notion soon lost until the nineteenth century). He personally identified the "labyrinth" of the ear as the central organ of hearing with its nerve connections, and described the pinna, external meatus, and drumskin. He also knew that part of the nerves of each eye connect to the left brain and part to the right brain. On the other hand, he felt that the crystalline (lens) of the eye was responsible for visual sensations; he was unaware of the retina.

Hippocrates had taken Empedocles' four elements and in a general fashion related the four corresponding humors to pathology. Although he too was primarily concerned with medically pathological personalities, Galen systematized the relationship of these humors into a general personality theory: blood: sanguine (warm-hearted, cheerful); black bile: melancholic (sad, fearful); yellow bile: choleric (fiery, quick to action); phlegm: phlegmatic (slow). Much later Alfred Adler related his four styles of life to Galen's four temperaments.

An anecdote is told about Galen demonstrating that a young female patient was in love with a particular dancer by measuring her pulse rate on four successive days. On the first and last day, that particular gentleman's name was mentioned, with other male dancers' names on the middle days. The increased pulse served as an early form of lie detector.

C. S. PEYSER

GALL, FRANZ JOSEF (1757–1828)

Gall was a German physician who believed a correlation existed between mental abilities and the formation of the skull. Because he held that skull formation determines personality and behavior, he was charged with fatalism and hence with subverting religion. Consequently he was forced to leave Vienna, where he had settled in 1785, after completing medical studies at Strasbourg and Vienna.

His lectures in phrenology began in 1796, but by 1802 the Austrian government prohibited them. In 1805 he left Austria for an extended lecture tour to Germany, Holland, Sweden, and Switzerland. His fame peaked in Paris, where he settled as a physician in 1807. With his associate J. G. Spurzheim, he delivered an account of their research to the Institute of France, but that august body (which included Philippe Pinel and other notables) repudiated their report.

In the history of psychology, Gall is credited with being a pioneer in brain mapping or brain localization. Brain localization became accepted in psychology in 1861, when Paul Broca found the speech center in the brain. Phrenology's basic premise, however, was invalidated when it was discovered that the skull and the brain's topography do not accord, because the skull's thickness varies. Gall did, however, correctly identify the brain's gray matter with neurons and its white matter with ganglia or connective tissue.

Six volumes of Gall's writings were published as *Works: On the functions of the brain and each of its parts*. With Spurzheim, he published *Researches on the nervous system*, and *Anatomy and physiology of the nervous system.* His medical practice and research continued until his death at Montrouge, a suburb of Paris.

W. S. SAHAKIAN

GALTON, FRANCIS (1822–1911)

The father of differential psychology and one of the foremost progenitors of psychometrics, Galton was born into a wealthy English family, a half-cousin of Charles Darwin. Galton was a prodigy who could read and write at the age of three, but a problem pupil in school. After attending medical school and earning a degree in mathematics at Cambridge at 21, Galton fell heir to a family fortune that allowed him freely to pursue his scientific interests the rest of his long life, without need to earn a living. Strictly speaking, he could be regarded as a lifelong amateur inventor and scientist, but because he was also an authentic genius he made seminal contributions in a variety of fields: exploration and geography (of Africa), meteorology, photography, classification of fingerprints, genetics, statistics, anthropometry, and psychometry. His prodigious achievements and prolific publications brought him worldwide recognition and many honors, including knighthood, being named a Fellow of the Royal Society, and gold medals awarded by various scientific bodies in England and Europe.

Galton's contributions to differential psychology reflected his conviction that all human characteristics, both physical and mental, could ultimately be described quantitatively. This he believed a necessary condition for achieving a science of humanity. His motto was, "When you can, count." To promote quantitative thinking in the biological sciences, Galton and his disciple Karl Pearson founded the journal *Biometrika,* which continues to the present day.

Galton's long-term investigations of heredity culminated in *Natural inheritance,* in which he anticipated the polygenic theory of inheritance of continuous characteristics later developed by Sir Ronald Fisher. But it was *Hereditary genius: An inquiry into its laws and consequences,* that became Galton's best-known work and the one most relevant to psychology. He was the first scientist clearly to formulate the nature-nurture question—that is, the relative contributions of heredity and environment to individual and group differences in human traits, abilities, and talents. He was also the first to note the methodological importance of monozygotic and dizygotic twins for estimating the relative effects of genetic and environmental factors in human variation.

As intelligence tests had not yet been invented, in *Hereditary genius* Galton studied the inheritance of general mental ability by looking at nearly 1000 men who had achieved intellectual eminence and tabulating the frequency of eminent men among all their relatives. He found that as the degree of genetic kinship decreased, the percentage of eminent relatives also decreased in a markedly stepwise fashion, as one should predict from Galton's model of genetic inheritance, which also explained similar effects for indisputably hereditary traits such as stature and fingerprints, which Galton also investigated. From this, Galton argued that mental ability is inherited in the same fashion, and to much the same degree, as many physical traits. Stature, for example, also displayed Galton's "law of filial regression": the offspring of a deviant parent are, on average, less deviant from the mean of the population than is the parent regarding the trait in question.

Galton invented a number of sensory and motor tests, described in *Inquiries into human faculty and its development,* and he tested thousands of the general public in his laboratory in the South Kensington Science Museum. He was the first clearly to put forth the idea of *general* ability and *specific* abilities later developed by Charles Spearman, and held that general ability was by far the more important influence on a person's life achievements. He viewed general ability as largely heredi-

tary, with its distribution in the population following the normal or Gaussian curve.

Galton's contributions to statistics and psychometrics include formulations of regression and correlation, the bivariate scatter diagram, multiple correlation, standardized or scale-free scores, percentile ranks, the use of the median and geometric mean as measures of central tendency, and rating scales.

Galton devoted his last years to championing eugenics, and wrote a Utopian novel, *Kantsaywhere* (unpublished), based on eugenic principles. In 1904 he founded and endowed the Galton Laboratory at the University of London, which, under the directorship of such luminaries as Karl Pearson and Sir Ronald Fisher, has been a leading center for research in genetics and statistics.

A. R. JENSEN

GALVANI, LUIGI (1737–1798)

Galvani studied medicine and philosophy and was named professor of anatomy at the University of Bologna. Through an accidental discovery, he was led to investigate electrical phenomena in the animal organism. His original discovery was that the thigh muscles of a dissected frog would contract when touched with a scalpel and that touching the nerve with two different metals could produce the same effect. This work was a stimulus for many further developments in the understanding of electrical phenomena. Galvani's importance in this field of investigation is reflected in such terms as *galvanism, galvanic battery,* and *galvanometer.*

P. E. LICHTENSTEIN

GARCIA, GUILLERMO DAVILA (1902–1968)

Garcia was a Mexican psychiatrist and neurologist whose fundamental research and teaching interest was in psychopathology. His dedication as a teacher, administrator, and advocate for the profession and science of psychology is legendary. Many generations of students and some of the most distinguished Mexican psychologists of today were his disciples.

Garcia obtained the M.D. from the National University of Mexico (UNAM) in 1925 with a dissertation on schizophrenia. From this date until 1951, he worked at the state asylum (*La Castaneda*), the penitentiary, the *Tribunal de Menores* (children's court), and at the Mexican Social Securities System (IMSS) in addition to running his own private practice. Garcia also promoted vocational and professional guidance programs.

From 1951 to 1957, Garcia was head of the department of psychology at UNAM where he had taught since 1947. He remained at UNAM until his death.

Garcia was one of the leaders of a group that invited Erich Fromm to Mexico. In 1951, with Werner Wolf, O. Robles, R. Falcon, and R. Diaz-Guerrero, Garcia founded the Interamerican Society of Psychology and the Mexican Society of Psychology. As a major leader in Mexican psychology in the 1950s, he began contacts with W. Holtzman, R. Peck, and P. Worchel at the University of Texas. With Cuban J. A. Bustamante and Peruvian C. A. Seguin, Garcia founded the first Latin American group of cross-cultural studies.

P. VALDERRAMA-ITURBE

GARCIA, JOHN (1917–   )

Garcia attended school in Santa Rosa, California. During his youth he was a farm worker, a mechanic, and a soldier. Under the G.I. Bill, he earned an M.A. in 1949 from the University of California, Berkeley, assisting E. C. Tolman. Later he returned to obtain a Ph.D. in 1965, working with D. Krech and B. F. Ritchie. As an experimental psychobiologist he served at the Naval Radiological Defense Laboratory (1951–1958), Long Beach State College and Veterans Administration Hospital (1959–1965), Harvard Medical School and Massachusetts General Hospital (1965–1968), the State University of New York at Stonybrook (1968–1972), and the University of Utah (1972–1973). In 1973 he joined the departments of Psychology and Psychiatry at the University of California at Los Angeles.

Garcia was known for his studies on X rays as perceptible and aversive stimuli, selective and adaptive learning mechanisms, and the modification of predatory behavior with conditioned taste aversions. He stressed the evolutionary origins of learning mechanisms and couched his explanations in ecological and neurological terms. He received the Howard Crosby Warren Medal from the Society of Experimental Psychologists, a Distinguished Science Award from the American Psychological Society, and an honorary membership from Phi Beta Kappa.

GARFIELD, SOL L. (1918–   )

Garfield received the B.S., M.A., and Ph.D. (1942) degrees from Northwestern University. After receiving the Ph.D. he entered the U.S. Army, served as a clinical psychologist, and attended the Officers Clinical Psychology School. Upon his discharge from the army, he served as chief psychologist at the VA hospital in Mendota, Wisconsin; chief psychologist at the VA Mental Hygiene Clinic in Milwaukee, Wisconsin; and as regional director of psychology training for the VA in Chicago. He also has directed doctoral training programs in clinical psychology at the University of Connecticut, Teachers College, Columbia University, and Washington University in St. Louis. For 6 yr he was professor and chief of medical Psychology at the Nebraska Psychiatric Institute, University of Nebraska College of Medicine.

Garfield has been interested primarily in the training of clinical psychologists and in research on psychotherapy. Among his 150 publications are several editions of a textbook on clinical psychology, three editions of the *Handbook of psychotherapy and behavior change* (with Allen Bergin), and books on eclectic psychotherapy and brief psychotherapy. He is a former president of the Division of Clinical Psychology of the APA and of the Society for Psychotherapy Research, and a former editor of the *Journal of Consulting and Clinical Psychology*. Garfield is a recipient of the Distinguished Professional contribution to Knowledge Award and the Distinguished Contribution to Clinical Psychology Award from the APA. Other awards include Distinguished Research Career Award of the Society for Psychotherapy Research and the Award for Outstanding Contributions to Clinical Training from the Council of University Directors of Clinical Psychology.

GEMELLI, AGOSTINO (1878–1959)

A Franciscan priest, physician, founder and lifetime rector of a university (Sacro Cuore in Milan), president of the Pontifical Academy of Sciences and other learned societies, founder and editor of several journals, and member of various Italian governmental agencies, Gemelli always considered himself foremost a psychologist. However, his earliest interest revolved around biology, physiology, and medicine. In 1896, at the age of 18, he entered the University of Pavia to study medicine. He received the doctorate in medicine, but remained at the university to continue research as assistant to the famous histologist Camillo Golgi. But his mind was also attracted to problems of sociology, philosophy, and religion, and after four years of study at various European universities, he completed a doctorate in philosophy at the University of Louvain (1911).

During these years of scientific peregrinations, Gemelli became acquainted with experimental psychology. The psychologist who gave Gemelli his initial training in experimental psychology was Wilhelm Wundt's student Friedrich Kiesow, at the University of Turin. Gemelli was to become one of the most eminent psychologists in the history of Italian psychology and a prolific writer not only in psychology but also in philosophy and religion. His distinction as a psychologist stems from his numerous contributions to experimental, applied, and theoretical psychology, and also from his energetic promotion of psychology as a profession. He initiated and stimulated new areas of research, as for example the study of perception and spoken language, and applications of psychology to industry, vocational selection, education, delinquency, and aeronautics.

Gemelli perhaps will be best remembered for giving Italian psychology a stronger sense of identity and respectability, as well as gaining wider acceptance for it in Italian society and its scientific community.

H. MISIAK

GENDLIN, EUGENE T. (1926–   )

Gendlin is known in psychology for "focusing" and "experiential psychotherapy," and in philosophy for his basic work on symbolization. He was educated in the United States and received the Ph.D. from the University of Chicago in 1958. He rejected the representational view according to which we say in words what is already there in preverbal experience. Instead, he stated that symbolizing is itself a further living and carries the experiencing process forward. Experience is always already "symbolized" in some way, as for example by events. To symbolize in words is a further experiencing process. In *Experiencing and the creation of meaning* different kinds of such carrying forward by symbolization are directly examined. A *theory of personality change* reformulates basic concepts of pathology, the body, and the unconscious, showing how articulating one's experience to another person carries experiencing forward through the blockages and lacks of personal problems. In a series of research studies on psychotherapy, Gendlin and coworkers found that in successful cases there was significantly more direct attention to *unclear*, directly sensed experience, which would then "shift" in a physically felt way and "open" into *new* steps of therapeutic movement. Gendlin concluded that direct attention to the unclear "edge," consciously and physically sensed, was crucial to success in any method of therapy.

In 1963 Gendlin founded *Psychotherapy: Theory, Research and Practice*, the journal of the Psychotherapy Division of the American Psychological Association. He was its editor until 1976. In 1970 he was awarded that Division's first Distinguished Professional Psychologist award for his research measure of successful therapy process.

Gendlin has continued to teach at the University of Chicago and to publish in psychology and philosophy, including "Experiential phenomenology," "Experiential explication and the problem of truth," *Focusing*, and *Experiencing scale manual*.

GERGEN, KENNETH J. (1934–   )

Gergen received the B.A. from Yale University and, after serving as an officer in the U.S. Navy, went on to receive the Ph.D. at Duke University. After completing his graduate training, Gergen took a position in the department of social relations at Harvard University. After teaching at Harvard for 5 yr, he became chairman of the department of psychology at Swarthmore College. While at Swarthmore, Gergen took leaves to carry out research at the Istutoto Nazionale de Psicologia in

Rome, Kyoto University in Japan, The Sorbonne in Paris, Heidleberg University in Germany, and the Netherlands Institute for Advanced Study in Wassenaar. He has also served as a senior research scientist at the Eastern Pennsylvania Psychiatric Institute and acted as an organizational consultant.

Gergen has published more than 200 articles in journals and chapters in books and has authored or edited 18 books, including *The psychology of behavior exchange,* and *Social psychology.* He has published research monographs (*Toward Transformation in Social Knowledge*), edited anthologies (*Historical social psychology* and *Texts of identity*), and a volume for the broader public (*The saturated self*). Gergen received fellowships from the Guggenheim Foundation, the Rockefeller Foundation, and the Fulbright Foundation. He also is the recipient of an Alexander Humboldt prize in the humanities and honorary degrees from Tilburg University and Saybrook Institute.

GERMAIN, JOSÉ (1897–   )

Germain is a key figure bridging the gap between the scientific psychology that was gaining a foothold in Spain in the early 1930s, and the post–Spanish Civil War generations of Spanish psychologists.

He completed his secondary education in Belgium and France before studying medicine at Madrid University, where one of his professors was S. Ramón y Cajal. On completion he went to Geneva to work with Edouard Claparède, and afterward to Berlin, where he made friends with Wolfgang Köhler. He then studied psychiatry in Paris with Georges Dumas and Pierre Janet. Returning to Spain, he came under the influence of José Ortega y Gasset. He worked for a number of years as a psychiatrist with R. Lafora, while at the same time cooperating actively with the Service of Professional Orientation of the Institute for the Reeducation of Invalids, where he promoted the study, adoption, and application of psychological tests. After attending the Fourth International Conference of Psychotechnique in Paris in 1927, he established regular contacts with Henri Pieron and Paul Fraisse. He moved to Cambridge in 1934 to work with F. C. Barlett.

The International Congress of Scientific Psychology was due to be held in Madrid in 1936, with E. Mira y López as president and Germain as secretary general. But with the outbreak of the Spanish Civil War, the Congress was held in Paris. Germain, together with Mira y López, chose exile. However, unlike the latter, Germain returned to Spain at the end of the Civil War, and on his initiative the *Revista de Psicología General y Aplicada* appeared in 1946. In 1948 he organized the Department of Experimental Psychology, attached to the Higher Board of Scientific Investigations. In 1952 he founded the Spanish Society of Psychology, of which he was president until 1973.

Germain's influence in the development of psychology in Spain in recent decades has been considerable; in 1981 the *Revista de Psicología General y Aplicada* devoted a special number to him, including contributions from H. J. Eysenck, P. Fraisse, P. Pichot, and D. E. Super, as well as some well-known Spanish psychologists.

GESELL, ARNOLD L. (1880–1961)

Gesell received the B. Phil. from the University of Wisconsin. He received the Ph.D. from Clark University in 1906. While at Clark he was heavily influenced toward the study of child development by G. Stanley Hall. His first position was at the Los Angeles State Normal School. He soon moved to Yale University as assistant professor of education. His early work focused on retarded children, but he soon broadened his approach to normal children as well. Gesell obtained the M.D. from Yale in 1915 and remained associated there for the remainder of his career. The clinic he founded is known as the Gesell Institute of Child Development.

Gesell put the study of child development on a sound methodological base with his system of observing and measuring behavior. He was the first to use photographic techniques and observation through a one-way mirror. He concentrated on the extensive study of a small number of children. Gesell's method was published in *The mental growth of the pre-school child.* He later extended his work to children aged 5–10 (1946) and to youth aged 10–16.

Gesell's *Infant and child in the culture of today,* coauthored with his colleague Frances Ilg, had great influence on child rearing practices in the 1940s and 1950s. Gesell took a strictly constitutional or physiological approach in which the cultural or learning factors played little part. As a result, he is more known for his methodological advances and inspiration to his students than for his theoretical explanations of development of behavior.

C. S. PEYSER

GIBB, CECIL A. (1913–   )

Gibb was born in Sydney, Australia, and obtained his early education there. He was a lecturer in psychology in the University of Sydney (1937–1942, 1946–1947, 1949–1950). Between 1942 and 1946 he was a foundation member of the Australian Army Psychology Service, where he was successively head of a psychology section, the psychologist member of the Officer Selection Board, and assistant to the director of psychological services (Australia). After the war he completed the Ph.D. at the University of Illinois (1949). In 1950 he went to Dartmouth College as coordinator of an interdisciplinary program in human relations. He returned to Australia in 1955 as foundation professor of psychology and head of the department at Canberra University College, which in 1960 amalgamated with the Australian National University. He retired in 1978 and became emeritus professor and visiting fellow in the Office for Research in Academic Method.

Gibb's major contributions have been to university administration and educational leadership. His publications have been in the areas of personality, leadership, and executive behavior. Gibb received two university medals for scholarship, was elected to Phi Beta Kappa, and was appointed an officer of the Order of the British Empire (1970) in recognition of his service to education. He was also elected to fellowships of the British Psychological Society (1951), the Academy of the Social Sciences in Australia (1956), and the American Psychological Association (1963). He was a member of the Australian UNESCO Advisory Committee (1960–1964) and a delegate to UNESCO in 1962. He has been a visiting research associate at various universities in the United States and Great Britain.

GIBSON, ELEANOR J. (1910–   )

Gibson graduated from Smith College in 1931, and received the Ph.D. from Yale University in 1938. In 1932 she was married to James J. Gibson, who steered her interests toward experimental psychology and especially toward perception. At Yale she worked with Clark Hull.

Gibson's research has embraced learning in humans and animals, studies of controlled rearing in animals, development of reading skill, and especially perceptual development in infants and young children. She views perceptual development as a process of differentiation, and perceptual learning as an active process of information pickup. The perceptual world is not constructed by add-on processes of association and inference; rather, the infant explores the array of stimulation, searching for invariants underlying the permanent properties of the world and the persisting features of the layout and objects in it. Much of this is revealed in events, as change (transformations over time) discloses invariant properties. What comes to be perceived are affordances for action of places, things, and events in the world. These ideas are expressed in *Principles of perceptual learning and development* and in papers such as "The concept of affordances in development: The renascence of functionalism."

Gibson is a member of the National Academy of Sciences, the American Academy of Arts and Sciences, the National Academy of Education, a fellow of AAAS, and an honorary member of the British Psychological Society. She received the Distinguished Scientific Contribution Award from the American Psychological Association and from the Society for Research in Child Development.

GIBSON, JAMES J. (1904–1979)

Gibson studied at Northwestern University and received the Ph.D. at Princeton, where he was strongly influenced by the "philosophical" behaviorist, Edwin B. Holt. His first teaching position was at Smith College, where he met Kurt Koffka, one of the leaders of Gestalt psychology. Although Gibson never became converted to Gestalt psychology, he and Koffka shared a common interest in the psychology of perception. After serving in the Air Force during World War II, Gibson returned to Smith, where he wrote one of his most important books, *The perception of the visual world* (1950). He then went to Cornell University, where he worked and taught for the rest of his career. In 1961 he received the Distinguished Scientific Contribution Award from the American Psychological Association.

Gibson is primarily known for his research and theories of perception. He became a leader of a new movement in that field by considering perception to be direct without any inferential steps, intervening variables, or associations. According to his theory, perception is the process of maintaining contact with the world. It is a direct function of stimulation, which he interpreted as the types and variables of physical energy to which the sense organs respond. The proposition that perception is a direct function of the environment was a radical departure from tradition. Gibson formulated the concept of "stimulus ecology," referring to the stimuli that surround a person. These include the optics of slanting and reflecting surfaces, and the gravitational forces we all experience in walking, sitting, and lying down. He believed in "invariance" of perception, whereby the environment provides an active organism with a continuous and stable flow of information to which it can respond.

In 1966 Gibson wrote *The senses considered as perceptual systems*. In it he stressed the importance of texture gradients of surfaces as an important property of perception. There is a continuous change in the visual field whereby regions closer to the observer appear coarser and more detailed, and those farther away, finer and less detailed.

R. W. LUNDIN

GILBRETH, FRANK B. (1868–1924)

Gilbreth first worked as a bricklayer and then as a contracting engineer in Boston and later New York. Based upon his own work experience, he analyzed bricklaying to determine the one best way of doing it. As a result, scaffolding was redesigned so it could easily be raised a short distance and keep the working height close to ideal. Bricks were sorted by a laborer and brought to the bricklayer in a convenient packet. The consistency of the mortar was carefully regulated. The materials were arranged so that a brick was picked up simultaneously with a trowel of mortar. Gilbreth published his recommendations in 1909; he was able to reduce the number of motions for laying a single brick from 18 to 4½, almost tripling output. In *Motion study* he extended the micromotion study to other construction work.

Gilbreth's work from the time of his 1904 marriage was done in full partnership with his wife, Lillian. Together they adapted the motion

picture camera to analyze movement, often using a blinking light bulb to indicate time. They labeled the fundamental unit of movement the therblig—a palindrome of "Gilbreth." Their work was collected in *Applied motion study*.

Time and motion principles were applied to family life, as reported by two of their children in *Cheaper by the dozen* (1948). Frank Gilbreth died when interest in their procedures was at its peak. Lillian Gilbreth continued the work for almost 50 years.

C. S. PEYSER

GILBRETH, LILLIAN E. (1878–1972)

Lillian Gilbreth (née Moller) took the B.Litt. degree at the University of California and received the Ph.D. from Brown in 1915. Her dissertation was the basis for *The psychology of management* (1914). She worked as a full partner with her husband Frank in Gilbreth, Inc., a consulting and engineering firm located first in Providence, Rhode Island, and later in Montclair, New Jersey. Three days after her husband's sudden death in 1924, Lillian fulfilled his speaking engagements at the London Power Conference and the World Congress of Scientific Management. She raised the eleven surviving children (aged 2 years to a sophomore in college at Frank's death) and extended and developed her and her husband's work.

To spend more time at home, Lillian Gilbreth applied motion study to household management, publishing her findings in 1927. She also offered seminars in general micromotion principles, especially one entitled "The One Best Way." Her experiences in child management were published in the *Living with our children*.

Lillian Gilbreth held faculty positions at Rutgers and, briefly, at Purdue, Bryn Mawr, and the Newark College of Engineering. In 1944 the Gantt Medal of the American Society of Mechanical Engineers was presented to Lillian and Frank Gilbreth for a lifetime of work. She continued to develop management and equipment efficiency procedures and lectured throughout the world. Even in her 90s, Lillian Gilbreth was a much-sought-after speaker and served on public commissions.

C. S. PEYSER

GLASSER, WILLIAM (1925–   )

Reared in Cleveland, Glasser remained there until age 28, attending nearby Case Western Reserve University. On receiving the M.D. there in 1953, he left for California. There he formulated "reality therapy" and went on to found the Institute for Reality Therapy in Los Angeles. His books *Mental health or mental illness?* and *Reality therapy* appeared in the 1960s. Defining reality therapy in the latter book, he states that persons are born with basic needs, the most primary being (1) the need to belong and to be loved, and (2) the need to gain self-worth and recognition. Reality therapy asks clients to examine and evaluate their behavior. With the therapist, behavioral changes are planned to maximize the fulfillment of needs.

Based in Los Angeles, Glasser conducts one-day seminars in the United States, Canada, and abroad. A branch of the Institute, the Educator Training Center, applies reality therapy for use in schools. This effort, which has trained over 100,000 educators, resulted in the publication, *Schools without failure*.

Glasser's lectures have found their way into *The identity society*, *Positive addiction*, *Both-win management*, and *Stations of the mind*. New directions of reality therapy are found in the last-mentioned work, aimed at helping people increase control over their lives.

GODDARD, HENRY H. (1866–1957)

An early student of the causes of mental retardation, Goddard argued for hereditary intelligence and was an early advocate of eugenics.

Goddard was professor of abnormal and clinical psychology at Ohio State University, and served for many years as director of the research laboratory at the training school at Vineland, New Jersey. He is best known for *The Kallikak family*, in which he traced two branches of a family, one of which was largely mentally deficient. In *Feeble-mindedness, its causes and consequences*, he classified cases of retardation by cause, finding between one-half and two-thirds to be hereditary. This conclusion led him to advocate preventing reproduction by individuals judged to be feebleminded.

Goddard also helped popularize the Binet test of intelligence in the United States and introduced the term "moron." His very simple theory of inherited intelligence finds little support today.

T. KEITH-LUCAS

GOETHE, JOHANN WOLFGANG VON (1749–1832)

Primarily a German poet and dramatist, Goethe influenced psychology in two rather different areas: color vision and the theories of Sigmund Freud.

Goethe mistrusted experimentation but had great faith in intuitive observation, particularly when done by himself. In 1810 he published a two-volume work of over 1400 pages: *Zur Farbenlehre* (Science of colors). The first portion of Volume 1 contains very detailed descriptions of many subjective visual phenomena: light and dark adaptation, after-images and the flight of colors, contrast effects (e.g., a given shade of blue looks different when surrounded by gray than when surrounded by red), and cases of color blindness. These descriptions are very accurate at the qualitative level and stimulated the work of Purkinje and J. Müller, who acknowledged their inspiration. The second volume contained a history of optics. The second portion of volume 1 contained an anti-Newton polemic as well as Goethe's theory of color vision. Although "theory" is perhaps too grand a term for Goethe's imprecise writings, his ideas of how the eye works did lead to Hering's opponent-process theory and suppressed Young's tricolor theory until the time of Helmholtz. Today we know that the Goethe/Hering position does not describe the retinal functioning, whereas the Young-Helmholtz theory does so in remarkable detail.

Freud's choice of medicine was heavily influenced both by Darwin and by a Goethe essay on Nature read at a popular lecture shortly before he left for school. In this essay Nature is a beautiful mother who permits her favorite children to explore her secrets. Freud and his wife, Martha, often quoted Goethe's poetry to each other, and there are many other evidences of Freud being quite familiar with his works. Many scholars see fundamental ideas of Goethe in Freud's theory of the libido (psychic energy) and elsewhere in Freud's work.

C. S. PEYSER

GOLDEN, CHARLES J. (1949–   )

Golden received the B.A. from Pomona College and the Ph.D. in clinical psychology from the University of Hawaii in 1975. He completed an internship in clinical psychology at Hawaii State Hospital, and established the neuropsychology laboratory at the University of South Dakota (1975–1978) and later at the University of Nebraska Medical Center (1978 on). His strongest interests are in the areas of psychological assessment, with a major emphasis on clinical neuropsychology.

He is probably best known for his work in the development of the Luria-Nebraska Neuropsychological Battery. This battery attempted to integrate the qualitative approach to psychological assessment advocated by Luria with the quantitative, standardized approaches devised by Halstead and Reitan. It also tried to provide a broad evaluation of neuropsychological skills in a general battery applicable to a wide range of patients, which could be administered in diverse settings with a minimum of equipment.

Golden is also known for his study of the neurological basis of psychiatric disorders. His work includes an integration of test results from neurological procedures such as computerized tomography and regional cerebral blood flow with psychological test results and behavior of the subject. This work has found a subgroup of psychiatric patients with organic dysfunction which can be hypothesized to be the cause of their disorders.

Golden's major publications include *Diagnosis and rehabilitation in clinical neuropsychology; Clinical interpretation of objective psychological Tests; Interpretation of the Halstead-Reitan Neuropsychological Battery: A casebook approach* (with others); and *Item interpretation of the Luria-Nebraska Neuropsychological Battery* (with others).

GOLDSTEIN, KURT (1878–1965)

Goldstein, a neuropsychiatrist, obtained the M.D. in 1903 at Breslau and became associated with the clinic at Königsburg. He was at the universities of Frankfurt-am-Main and Berlin before the rise of Nazism forced him to emigrate to Amsterdam and eventually to the United States. He initially worked at Columbia University and Montefiore Hospital, and later at Tufts Medical School and Brandeis.

With psychologist Martin Scheerer at Montefiore, he developed a set of five tests to measure the loss of abstract attitude in patients with organic brain disease. Involving various color and form sorting, the tests were designed to measure a number of activities: assuming and shifting a mental set, grasping the essentials of a whole, breaking the whole into its parts, abstracting common properties, and planning ahead. Goldstein had observed that brain-injured patients tended to persevere when pushed to perform tasks they could no longer do; this clinging to a "comfortable" solution warded off the panic and agitation they would otherwise feel. This panic was termed by Goldstein the *catastrophic reaction*. He had begun his work with brain-injured military patients from World War I.

Goldstein is also known for his organismic theory of personality, first published in German in 1934. The Gestalt influence from his 14 years at Frankfurt-am-Main was evident in his holistic emphasis. The individual was to be studied intensively and as a totality. Partial measures taken in isolation were useful only when placed in the broader context of the entire personality and the psychological environment in which the behavior occurred. The context was needed for physiological measures just as much as for the more psychological ones.

Goldstein said that each organism has specific potentials; because it has these potentials, it needs to realize them. This driving force toward self-realization is an expression of preference for the "good Gestalt": individuals strive to actualize themselves in the best possible way according to their potential. One can obtain an indication of the goal by observing what an individual prefers to do and what an individual is successful at doing. Goldstein thus anticipated the self-actualization notions of Abraham Maslow and Fritz Perls. Indeed, he was one of the founders of the Association for Humanistic Psychology.

C. S. PEYSER

GOODENOUGH, FLORENCE L. (1886–1959)

Goodenough received the Ph.D. from Stanford in 1924 and spent her career as a developmental psychologist at the University of Minnesota.

Although most widely known for the Draw-a-Man Test, she was also a historian of early psychological testing (*Mental Testing*, 1949) and an originator of sophisticated, naturalistic observation methods. She was the guiding force behind the now obsolete Minnesota Preschool Scales (1932).

The Draw-a-Man Test asks the child to draw a figure which is scored not for artistic ability but for the presence or absence of details: parts of the body, articles of clothing. D. B. Harris, after joint publication with Goodenough, published a revised and extended version in 1963 that is scored for 73 specific items. Although it had been hoped that the Draw-a-Man Test would be culture-fair, comparative studies have shown the scores to be related to the amount of indigenous art in the culture and to socioeconomic level.

Although Goodenough noted that abnormal (brain-damaged, emotionally disturbed) children make highly individualistic and unusual drawings, it remained for others to extend this testing notion to personality measurement (Buck's House-Tree-Person; Machover's Draw-a-Person). Subsequent research has indicated only very limited support for the adaptation of figure drawing as a projective personality technique.

C. S. PEYSER

GOSSET, WILLIAM S. (1876–1937)

An English statistician and pioneer in the development of modern statistical method, Gosset derived the statistic *t* (Student's t), widely used in tests of differences between means of small samples. He attended Winchester College and Oxford University, where he studied chemistry and mathematics. In 1899 Gosset joined Arthur Guinness and Sons, the brewers, in Dublin. A mass of statistical data was available bearing on the relations between brewing methods, the characteristics of raw materials (barley and hops), and the quality of the finished product. The importance of controlling the quality of barley ultimately led him to study the design of agricultural field trials and to write the first report on "The application of the law of error" (1904).

Gosset studied in the biometric laboratory of Karl Pearson at University College in London (1906–1907). Gosset's most notable contribution to statistical theory was "The probable error of a mean." This article stated that the distribution of the ratio of the mean to its standard error does not follow a normal curve, if the sample is small. Since the rules of the Guinness brewing company prohibited Gosset from publishing his research on the variability of the brewing process, Gosset had to publish his paper in 1908 under a pseudonym of "Student," causing the statistic to be known as Student's *t*. Between 1907 and 1937, Gosset published 22 statistical papers which were reissued in 1942 under the title of *"Student's"* collected papers.

M. LACROCE

GOUIN DÉCARIE, THÉRÉSE (1923–   )

Gouin Décarie received a clinical formation in Montreal, Boston, and Paris, and then got the Ph.D. from the University of Montreal in 1960, where she has been a full professor since 1965. In 1962 she worked with thalidomide children. Her first books (translated later into Italian) bear on child and adolescent development. She then studied Piaget's object concept in relation to affectivity and designed the first operational scale to assess cognitive development in infancy. Her book *L'intelligence et l'affectivité chez le jeune enfant* (Intelligence and affectivity in early childhood) was translated in English, Spanish, and Italian.

Since 1970, her main interest has been an ethological approach to infant socialization, about which she has published many articles and a book, *La réaction du jeune enfant à la personne étrangère*, which was translated into English.

Gouin Décarie is a member of the Canadian Society of Psychology, the Society for Research in Child Development, the Royal Society of Canada, and the Order of Canada. Her works have also been published under the name of Décarie.

GRAHAM, FRANCES (1918–   )

Graham, née Keesler, received the B.A. from the Pennsylvania State University and, as an advisee of Clark L. Hull and Donald G. Marquis, the Ph.D. from Yale University (1942). Except for 3 yr at Barnard College, she was associated with the Washington University School of Medicine until 1957 and the University of Wisconsin at Madison until 1986. In 1986, she joined the University of Delaware psychology faculty.

Graham has related physiological changes in autonomic and brain activity to perceptual–cognitive function, especially during early development. Contributions include the Graham-Kendall Memory-for-Designs Test; the St. Louis prospective study of perinatal anoxia; delineation of the nature of startle, orienting, and defense reflexes; and the design of a reflex probe technique that demonstrates selective attentional effects on sensory input. Her work has been published in a number of monographs and in psychology, medical, and interdisciplinary journals.

She was president of the Society for Psychophysiological Research (SPR), Society for Research in Child Development (SRCD), APA Division of Comparative and Physiological Psychology, and chair of the Psychology Section of the American Association for the Advancement of Science. She also served on the NIMH Board of Scientific Counselors and the President's Commission on Ethics in Medicine and Biomedical and Behavioral Research. Honors include distinguished scientific contribution awards from SPR, SRCD, and APA, the G. Stanley Hall medal from APA's Division on Developmental Psychology, and election to the National Academy of Sciences.

GRAHAM, STANLEY R. (1926–   )

Graham received the B.S. from CCNY, the M.A. and Ph.D. (1952) from New York University. In 1953, he was appointed fellow at the New York State Institute for Psychobiologic Studies; in 1954, associate research scientist; in 1955, senior research scientist and chair of the psychology department of the institute. During 1954–1956 he was adjunct associate professor of psychology at Yeshiva University and director of research at the Long Island Center.

From 1958 on, Graham was director of the Fifth Avenue Center for Counseling and Psychotherapy and director of training of the Greenwich Institute for Psychoanalytic Studies. Later, he became adjunct professor at Yeshiva University, adjunct professor in Nova University's postdoctoral program, and supervisor of psychotherapy at Rutgers and Yeshiva doctoral programs. He became the associate editor of *Psychotherapy: Theory, Research and Practice* and of the *Psychotherapy Bulletin*. He was past president of Divisions 29, 32, and 42 of the APA and spent three terms in the APA Council of Representatives. He is a member of Psi Chi, a fellow of Divisions 12, 13, 29, and 42 of the APA, a diplomate in clinical psychology, a fellow of the American Orthopsychiatric Association, and founder of the Federation of Mental Health Clinics in 1971.

Graham has been honored by the APA's Distinguished Psychologist Award in 1983 (Division of Independent Practice), and Distinguished Psychologist Award in 1985 (Division of Psychotherapy). He is a member of the National Academy of Practice.

Graham has twenty-nine publications in psychology and was a founding member of the Division of Psychotherapy of the APA, founder and first president of the Division of Independent Practice, founding member of the Committee on Professional Psychology (OPP), president of the APA in 1990, and chair of the Task Force on Post Doctoral Residency Training.

GRAUMANN, CARL F. (1923–   )

With a basic training in psychology and phenomenological philosophy, Graumann received his doctorate at the University of Cologne in 1952, then took up postdoctoral studies at Bonn. His early work in the field of phenomenological psychology brought him to Duquesne University, Pittsburgh, as a visiting professor in 1962. In 1963 he was appointed as full professor at the University of Heidelberg. He was Theodor Heuss professor at the Graduate Faculty of the New School for Social Research in New York (1973–1974), and associate director of the School for Advanced Studies in Social Sciences in Paris (1982–1983).

In his research Graumann maintained and elaborated a phenomenological orientation in psychology, as initiated by the Utrecht school in the 1950s. The fundamental evidence for any comprehensive psychological inquiry is the experience and action of *situated subjects,* which have to be accounted for in terms of the historical, social, ecological, and linguistic context of human experience. Any empirical manipulation, mathematical control, or theoretical account must remain retranslatable to the original evidence. Graumann's major research fields comprise the historicity of behavior, social perception and cognition, ecological parameters, and the social psychology of language.

Graumann has edited *Phänomenologisch-Psychologische Forschungen* (1960 on), the *German Handbook of Social Psychology* (1969–1972), *Zeitschrift für Sozialpsychologie* (1970 on), *Studien zur Sprachpsychologie* (1970 on), *Enzyklopädie der Psychologie* (1982 on), and the seven-volume *Kurt Lewin Werkausgabe* (1981 on). He directs the Heidelberg Archives for the History of Psychology.

GREENWALD, HAROLD (1910–   )

Greenwald is best known for his direct decision therapy and his study of prostitution, *The call girl.* After completing his bachelor's degree at the City College of New York, he spent many years in a wide variety of jobs before returning for advanced education. Trained as a psychoanalyst at the National Psychological Association for Psychoanalysis and already practicing as a psychoanalyst, he returned to graduate school at Columbia University in New York and received the Ph.D. in 1952.

Greenwald's main interests have been the dynamics underlying occupational choice, the study and application of humor to the therapeutic situation, and creating a synthesis of the various forms of psychotherapy practiced. Experienced in many modalities, he is a fellow of the American Psychological Association and of the American Group Psychotherapy Association, and a member of the Institute of Rational-Emotive Therapy, as well as a former president of the National Psychological Association. He has taught at several institutes and universities; has been a visiting professor at Bergen University in Norway, the New School for Social Research, and has served as president of the Professional School for Humanistic Studies in San Diego. Since 1987 he has been clinical Professor of Psychiatry, University of California, San Diego. His publications include *Great cases in Psychoanalysis, Active psychotherapy,* and *Direct decision therapy.*

GREGORY, RICHARD L. (1923–   )

Richard Gregory, the son of C. C. L. Gregory, who was director of the University of London Observatory, served in the R.A.F. in World War II, then read philosophy and psychology at Cambridge under Sir Frederick Bartlett. He remained at Cambridge as a faculty member and directed a research group on the special senses. With Jean G. Wallace, he studied a rare case of recovery from infant blindness which demonstrated cross-modal transfer from touch to vision.

When the U.S. Air Force funded a space simulator for predicting perceptual capabilities and illusions of astronauts, Gregory undertook studies on size constancy during motion. He also designed instruments, especially a telescope camera to minimize effects of atmospheric turbulence by selecting its own moments for sampling the image from an internal representation. This initiated Gregory's interest in artificial intelligence, which led him to leave Cambridge to help found the Department of Machine Intelligence and Perception at Edinburgh with Donald Michie and Christopher Longuet-Higgins. He went back to studies of perception in 1970 at the University of Bristol, and developed the notion that perceptions are predictive hypotheses, somewhat like hypotheses in science.

Gregory founded the international journal *Perception* in 1973. His books include *Recovery from early blindness; Eye and brain; The intelligent eye; Illusion in nature and art* (with Sir Ernst Gombrich); *Concepts and mechanisms of perception;* and *Mind in science.*

GRONER, RUDOLF (1942–   )

Educated in Glarus, Switzerland, Groner pursued higher education in Austria, receiving the Ph.D. from the University of Vienna in 1966. After two years at the University of Alberta in Edmonton, Canada, he returned to Switzerland to teach and do research at the University of Bern.

Groner's main work *Hypothesen in Denkprocess* is aimed at a "generalized hypothesis theory" of cognitive activity, based on a formalized model. In its most general form, a series of model variants are constructed by specifying assumptions (e.g., number of hypotheses simultaneously processed, amount of memory for previous hypotheses and input information, etc.) in a systematic and exhaustive way. Exact quantitative predictions have been derived for probability distributions of solution latencies, different kinds of errors, and eye paths (measuring the visual information pickup). In this way the model variants create an efficiency hierarchy of possible problem-solving behaviors.

Tracing information utilization by means of eye fixations has been followed up by Groner in several edited books where he also attempted to coordinate work in different areas. More recently, he extended his research to methods of heuristics.

GUILFORD, JOY PAUL (1897–1987)

J. P. Guilford received the B.A. and M.A. degrees from the University of Nebraska, the latter in 1919. His bachelor's work was interrupted by his army service in World War I. While a graduate student, he became familiar with Spearman's g factor in intelligence. While working for a brief time at the University of Nebraska's psychological clinic he became convinced that intelligence was not a monolithic global attribute but consisted of a number of different abilities.

Guilford received the Ph.D. from Cornell University in 1927. While there, he worked with such eminent psychologists as Titchener, Helson, Dallenbach and Koffka. After brief stays at the Universities of Kansas and Illinois, Guilford returned to Nebraska until 1940. He then went to the University of Southern California until his retirement in 1962. His work at California was interrupted by service during World War II.

During his lifetime, he was an unusually productive researcher and writer, publishing numerous research articles, psychological tests, and books. His areas of investigation included traditional psychophysics, the autokinetic phenomena, attention, eye movements, scaling effects, and the phi phenomenon. His best known book was *Psychometric methods,* used by students of psychology for decades. In a readable manner, the methods used by psychologists over the previous years were carefully explained.

In the middle 1930s Carl Jung's personality dimension of introversion–extraversion was widely discussed as one dimension of personality. Guilford demonstrated, using factoral analysis, that this was not a unitary factor but consisted of a complex composit of several personality attributes.

During his career, Guilford received many honors including president of the American Psychological Association (1949), the Distinguished Contribution Award (1964), and the Gold Medal Award from the American Psychological Foundation (1983).

R. W. LUNDIN

GUILLAUME, PAUL (1878–1962)
After studying philosophy, Guillaume played an important role in the development of scientific psychology in France. His works concentrated mostly on child psychology (*L'imitation chez l'enfant*) and on the study of anthropoids ("La psychologie des singes"). In the area of theory, he demonstrated a great interest in the ideas of Gestalt psychology (*La psychologie de la forme*). He wrote a work on the epistemology of scientific psychology which helped strengthen the foundations of this discipline (*Introduction à la psychologie*, 1942). In addition, relative to education he produced his first work on learning with a scientific orientation, a text which has had a long-lasting influence (*Manuel de psychologie*). A professor at the Sorbonne, in 1937—with the support of Henri Pieron and in collaboration with Paul Fraisse—he introduced into French university teaching practical exercises in experimental psychology. With I. Meyerson he directed *Le Journal de Psychologie Normale et Pathologuique*.

M. REUCHLIN

GULLIKSEN, HAROLD O. (1903–   )
Gulliksen was introduced to psychology by Edwin Guthrie at the University of Washington, where he earned the B.A. degree. When Gulliksen was an instructor in psychology at Ohio State University (1927–1929), L. L. Thurstone lectured there, and Gulliksen was impressed by his ingenious use of mathematics to solve psychological problems. Gulliksen transferred to the University of Chicago, where he continued his dissertation on learning and studied mathematical psychology, obtaining the Ph.D. in 1931. As an examiner in social sciences, he was part of a group developing objective tests for the college-level courses of the university. At the same time he was an assistant professor of psychology.

During World War II Gulliksen's experience in testing led to his appointment as director of a war research project for the National Defense Research Committee in Princeton, New Jersey. After the war Gulliksen became research advisor at the Educational Testing Service and a professor of psychology at Princeton University, where he supervised the ETS Psychometric Fellowship Program, leading to a Ph.D. at Princeton for an outstanding group.

Gulliksen's main publication is the *Theory of mental tests*, in addition to about a hundred articles and books, some in collaboration. He is a member of the principal psychological associations, and was one of the group that founded the Psychometric Society and its publication *Psychometrika*.

GUTHRIE, EDWIN R. (1886–1959)
Guthrie received the Ph.D. from the University of Pennsylvania in 1914. The remainder of his academic career was spent at the University of Washington, until his retirement in 1956. In 1958, the year before his death, he was awarded the Gold Medal from the American Psychological Foundation.

Like John Watson, Guthrie maintained that psychology should be the study of observable behavior which was measurable and subject to proper experimental procedures. His first book, written in collaboration with Stevenson Smith, was entitled, *General psychology in terms of behavior*. Very much in the tradition of behaviorism, Guthrie was a learning theorist. His other books include *The psychology of learning*, *The psychology of human conflict*, and in collaboration with A. L. Edwards, *Psychology: A first course in human behavior*.

Guthrie is considered one of the most important learning theorists of the twentieth century. His theory is extremely simple. He starts out with one basic law of learning; what is being noticed becomes a signal for what is being done. Thus learning is simply a matter of an S-R (stimulus–response) association by contiguity. Further, a subprinciple states that when an S-R connection occurs, it reaches its full strength on the first trial (one trial learning), and will remain so indefinitely unless some succeeding event occurs to replace or destroy it. He accounts for improvement with practice simply by adding more and more S-R connection to a given performance.

The loss of behavior either through extinction or forgetting is accounted for by *associative inhibition*, which means that an incompatible response has been learned which interferes with the previous one. Thus no new learning principle is needed. A new S-R connection occurs to replace the previous one. Forgetting is simply a matter of interference by succeeding associations.

Motivation and reward, according to Guthrie, are not essential to the learning process. In animal experimentation deprivation of food merely causes greater activity, thus allowing for the possibility of more new connections to be established. Reward is useful only because it allows the organism to move away from a situation so that previous learned associations will not be destroyed. Unlike other learning theorists such as B. F. Skinner or Clark Hull, who stressed the crucial role of reinforcement (reward) in the learning process, Guthrie maintained that learning occurs simply because S-R associations are established.

What many consider Guthrie's most important research in support of his theory was a study done with C. P. Horton using cats in a puzzle box. They demonstrated that extremely stereotyped responses were established when a cat entered a box, hit a pole, and then left the box via a door opposite the one of entry. They observed that the way in which the cat hit or bumped the pole on the first trial was the same way it would do so on succeeding trials. If differences occurred, the stimulus situation somehow had changed.

Guthrie has been praised for the simplicity of his theory, which does not require numerous postulates, principles, and intervening variables (as does Hull's) to explain the results. It is straightforward and sticks with the observable events. On the other hand, his opponents claim he has tried to explain too much on the basis of too few principles. Furthermore, those who stress the importance of reinforcement (reward) as crucial to learning wonder how Guthrie can set forth a theory where the overwhelming experimental evidence supports a concept of reward. They feel that Guthrie dodged the issue of reward.

R. W. LUNDIN

GUTTMAN, LOUIS H. (1916–   )
Guttman began his professional career at the University of Minnesota, from which he received the Ph.D. in 1942. After graduate school he was employed by Cornell University. While at Cornell, Guttman was also an expert consultant to the Secretary of War with the Research Branch, Information and Education Division, of the War Department in Washington, D.C. Leaving Cornell, Guttman became a visiting professor at Harvard University, a fellow at the Center for Advanced Study in Behavioral Science at Stanford University, and distinguished visiting professor at Michigan State and the University of Michigan, before moving to the Hebrew University in Israel. He became a professor of

psychology, sociology, and measurement at the Hebrew University, and science director of the Jerusalem and Israel Institute of Applied Social Research.

Guttman's positions relate to his major interest in psychometrics, nonparametric analysis, and social psychology. Over one hundred publications covering topics related to his interest bear Guttman's name and appear in scientific periodicals. His books include *Measurement and prediction* and *Visit to the doctors*.

In addition to belonging to professional psychological associations, Guttman became involved in community and social organizations which include the Association of Americans and Canadians in Israel, the Institute of Differing Civilizations, the Israeli Association for Research on Labor Relations, and the Committee on Job Evaluation and Public Committee on Salaries. Honors bestowed on Guttman include the Rothschild Prize for Social Research in 1963, the title of professor-at-large of Cornell University (1972–1976), and foreign honorable member of the American Academy of Arts and Science.

GUTTMANN, GISELHER (1934–   )

Guttmann's schooling was in the humanities. His academic studies were in psychology, zoology, and philosophy, including neuroanatomy, psychiatry, and psychotherapy. He had several years of applied and experimental clinical practice in neurophysiology and electroencephalography (Erlangen, Keidel, and Bente). His *The acoustic evoked potential as reflection of psychic processes* indicates his life-long occupation with brain–electric correlates of human behavior. His special interests include brain research, information processing, learning research, sports psychology, levels of activation, performance optimization, theory of science, epistemology, and photobiology. One line of research Guttmann pursues is unique: the brain trigger design (BTD) whereby a subject's brainwave activity is defined as the independent variable. His research has led to definitions of new concepts such as ergopsychometry (testing under load), the training champion, the teachable moment (empirically defined, optimal brain–electric state), and paradoxical sleep (hypnosis as defined by different brain–electric parameters). BTD methods are applicable toward optimizing performance in school, sports, traffic, the conference room, and on the stage.

Guttmann's philosophical interests center on ego-consciousness and Oriental epistemology (Zen). His works include *Basic neuropsychology, On the psychophysiology of consciousness;* and *I see, think, dream, die.* He has served as dean of two faculties of the University of Vienna, where he has held the chair for general and experimental psychology since succeeding Rohracher in 1973. Guttmann is the only psychologist member of the Austrian Academy of Sciences.

HAGA, JUN (1931–   )

Best known for his study of psychology of language and psychology of bilingualism, Haga was educated in both Seoul and Japan. After receiving the bachelor's degree from University of Tokyo, he studied at that university's graduate school, receiving his master's degree in educational psychology. He further studied education and language at Manchester University in England. A desire to understand meaning and the functions of language led him to review and integrate the areas concerned ("Aims and methods of psychology of language"), and to write papers on psychology of language, thinking, and development, culminating in *Child's development and learning* and *Psychology of bilingualism.*

Haga regards himself as an educational psychologist, seeking to incorporate the study of language into the theory and practice of teaching. He holds that meaning is conveyed by logical and emotive functions of language, including phonetic and colors symbolism and nonverbal signs. He emphasizes selective use of these mutually complementary

functions for effective communication (*Method of effective writing in Japanese*) and for language teaching (*Language development and teaching*).

His study expanded further into genetic epistemology, where he experimentally analyzed logical use of language, and into bilingual memory and development. In connection with the latter study, he showed that Japanese students learning foreign languages as second languages have different patterns of code switching from those who are bilingual.

Haga has taught at Hokkaido University of Education and Kobe University, and has lectured at many universities. In 1974 he moved to the Institute of Literature and Linguistics at Tsukuba University, where he continues to research and lecture on psychology of language, psycholinguistics ("Psycholinguistics and psychology of language"), and modern Japanese writing.

HALL, CALVIN S. (1909–1985)

Known for his investigations of dreams and books on personality theory, Hall decided to become a psychologist during his junior year at the University of Washington, while taking a course on psychological theories taught by Edwin Guthrie. Not permitted to enroll for his senior year because he refused to take required courses in military science, he transferred to the University of California at Berkeley. There his interest in theoretical psychology was nourished by Edward Tolman, and he was introduced to statistics and behavior genetics by Robert Tryon, who became his dissertation advisor.

For the next 15 years Hall's primary area of research was the inheritance of temperament in the rat. He obtained his first faculty appointment at the University of Oregon in the depths of the Great Depression. Three years later, in 1937, he became chairman of the department at Western Reserve University, where he remained for 20 years. He began to read Freud at 30, but his interest in dreams did not emerge until six years later when he began to collect dreams from college students.

After two years at Syracuse University, becoming weary of teaching, administration, and campus politics, Hall decided to devote the remainder of his life to writing and dream research. His writing has been about equally divided between books on psychological theories and books on dreams. His chief contributions to the study of dreams are the application of quantitative content analysis to large samples of dreams, and a cognitive theory of dreams and dream symbolism. He believes that chance played the greatest role in shaping his personal and professional life.

HALL, G. STANLEY (1844–1924)

If William James is honored as the initial hero of modern psychology in America, Hall, his student, deserves to be honored as the founder and promoter of organized psychology as a science and profession. He founded the American Psychological Association in 1892, was its first president, and in 1887 founded the first psychological journal in America, the *American Journal of Psychology*. He also founded other journals: the *Pedagogical Seminary* (later the *Journal of Genetic Psychology*) in 1894, the *Journal of Religious Psychology* in 1904, and the *Journal of Applied Psychology* in 1917.

After study at Williams College, a year at the Union Theological Seminary, then a year of study in Germany in which he moved toward physiology, Hall returned to America jobless. To pay off his debts, he tutored some children in New York for a year, taught English and foreign languages (among other duties) at Antioch College, then accepted an instructorship in English at Harvard University. While occupying that post, he found time to work in the physiological laboratory of Henry P. Bowditch and to study psychology with William James, and was granted the Ph.D. in psychology under their joint auspices in 1878. It was the first Ph.D. in psychology earned in America, and only the 18th

Ph.D. granted at Harvard in all fields of study. Setting off again for Europe, Hall became the first of a succession of American students to seek out Wilhelm Wundt at Leipzig, and was there when Wundt's laboratory was founded.

His American career as a university psychologist began with his professorship in psychology and pedagogics, a title won after his second year at the new Johns Hopkins University, where he had gone in 1882. During his few years at Hopkins he had a number of students who became distinguished psychologists, among them W. H. Burnham, J. M. Cattell, John Dewey, Joseph Jastrow, and E. C. Sanford, four of whom were later presidents of the American Psychological Association. The laboratory that Hall founded was second only to a demonstration laboratory that William James had arranged earlier at Harvard.

Hall became the president of Clark University, which opened its doors in 1889, and he served there until his death in 1924. In the last decade of the nineteenth century, through 1898, of the 54 Ph.D.s that were granted in psychology, 30 were students of Hall. He continued to turn out Ph.D.s—a total of 81 from his department during his active years there. Two of these also became presidents of the American Psychological Association, William L. Bryan and Lewis M. Terman. Other prominent students from the Clark days were Arnold Gesell, important in child development, and Henry H. Goddard, known for his studies of mental retardation.

Hall had his hand in on many aspects of child development and education, and was widely sought as an adviser for new innovations. A promoter of new views, he invited Sigmund Freud to come to Clark University for a series of lectures in 1909, giving Freud his first public academic recognition and his only honorary degree.

Hall remains important primarily for what he did for the child study movement, with its many consequences for education and developmental psychology. His theoretical emphasis was upon the doctrine of recapitulation as promoted by Haeckel: ontology recapitulates phylogeny. While the theory became discredited, it permitted Hall to call attention to adolescence as an important turning point in psychological growth. He thought of childhood essentially as an extention of embryological development. The long period of dependency and of assimilating knowledge and skills in maturing stages leads eventually to the flowering of independence at adolescence. Hall's two-volume *Adolescence* was influential in its day.

The focus on the child and the introduction of questionnaire methods, which soon led to a variety of tests other than merely intellectual ones, are more important contemporary residues from Hall's career than any basic theoretical ideas. His leadership and organizational and promotional skills were needed by the psychology of his day, and contemporary psychology is broader and more viable because of him.

E. R. HILGARD

HALL, MARSHALL (1790–1837)
Hall became an eminent practicing physician in London.

At the time of Hall's discoveries, there existed a confusion between voluntary and conscious movements as opposed to those which were involuntary and unconscious. In one experiment he severed a snake between the second and third vertebrae and found that, even in this decapitated animal, movements continued to occur in the presence of adequate stimulation. On the bases of this and other experiments, Hall undertook a classification of movements into four categories: (1) voluntary and conscious movements dependent on the brain; (2) respiratory, involuntary movements dependent on the medulla (upper part of the spinal cord); (3) involuntary movements dependent on muscular irritability; and (4) reflex, involuntary movements dependent on the spinal cord and independent of the brain.

Basically, he made a distinction between the voluntary and conscious activities which were dependent on the higher centers of the brain, and the involuntary and unconscious movements which were a function of lower centers and the spinal cord. These discoveries are relevant for contemporary psychology in making a separation between simple reflex acts which can be conditioned according to the method later developed by Ivan Pavlov, and the more complex, coordinated movements— referred to as "instrumental" or "operant" conditioning (learning)— which are emphasized in particular by B. F. Skinner in his studies of operant behavior.

R. W. LUNDIN

HAMILTON, WILLIAM (SIR) (1788–1836)
Hamilton was educated at Glasgow, Edinburgh, and Oxford. In 1832 he was appointed to the chair of civil history at the University of Edinburgh.

Hamilton stands as the culmination of the Scottish tradition in psychology, often referred to as the Scottish School. His thinking was strongly influenced by the earlier Scottish psychologist, Thomas Reid. His edition of Reid's works appeared in 1846. In revolt against the British associationists, Hamilton held that the first principle of psychology was the unity and activity of the human mind. He denied that the mind was made up of a series of merely associated experiences.

Hamilton fostered a "faculty psychology" which stressed not only the unitary function of the mind but the various faculties or powers of the mind to act in different ways. Some of these faculties included perception, memory, imagination, abstraction, and attention. Hamilton's interpretation of the power of memory is unique: he introduced the concept of "redintegration," whereby each impression brings back to consciousness the whole situation of which it had at one time been a part.

R. W. LUNDIN

HARA, KAZUO (1929–   )
Hara, after some teaching experience following graduation from Osaka Teachers' College, received the B.A. and M.A. from San José State College, and the Ph.D. from Stanford University in 1960. His professional career began at International Christian University (ICU) in Tokyo, where he has served in various administrative positions besides teaching. He has done research at the Animal Behavior Research Laboratory of Pennsylvania State University, the Perinatal Physiology Laboratory of the National Institutes of Health, and the Behavioral Genetics Research Institute of the University of Colorado at Boulder, as well as at ICU, his home institution.

Reflecting his earlier experiences with the handicapped and with cross-cultural living, he has been interested in two lines of research: physiological psychology and the measurement of social attitudes. The former led him to establish an animal model of agnosia by cortical and thalamic lesions, to discover modality-specific differential recovery processes from the deficits, and to provide a learning-set interpretation for the interocular transfer of visual discrimination in commissurectomized animals. From the latter, he disclosed a "reactional realism" in prejudicial attitudes of minority groups under extreme stress. Similar dynamism was also found among value orientations of deviant college students.

As an empiricist, Hara has attempted to integrate the above two lines into one scheme, biosociopsychology, by pursuing neuropharmacological bases of memory, behavioral traits, and the microgenesis of cognition. Hara has also translated many books by G. W. Allport, J. W. Brown, W. L. Dunn, J. A. Parkins, and others.

HARLOW, HARRY F. (1905–1981)

Harlow received the B.A. and Ph.D. (1930) from Stanford University. He spent the major portion of his academic career at the University of Wisconsin. In 1960 he received the Distinguished Scientific Contribution Award from the American Psychological Association, and for many years served as editor of the *Journal of Comparative and Physiological Psychology*.

Harlow was an experimental and comparative psychologist whose early work analyzed problem solving and discriminative learning in primates. His research led him to conclude that in the process the animals learned particular "sets" or ways of doing things. As a result of these studies he developed a "uniprocess learning theory" according to which learning involved the gradual suppression over learning trials of specific types of incorrect responses that reflected "error factors" such as stimulus preservation, response shifts, and positive preferences.

Along with I. E. Farber, Harlow described the behavior of prisoners of war during the Korean War. They noted a common syndrome which they called the DDD (debility, dependency, and dread). Debility was induced by severe starvation, disease, and fatigue; dependency, by solitary confinement and loss of leaders; dread, by fear of death, pain, or permanent deformity due to neglect and inadequate medical treatment.

Harlow is best known for his studies with infant monkeys raised with surrogate mothers. This series of studies extended over several years. Infant monkeys were separated from their mothers at birth and raised in isolation with artificial mothers (wire flames, and wire frames covered with terry cloth). As a result, they spent hours clinging to the terry cloth mother. At maturity they failed to develop normal sexual relationships, and those that did bear young became helpless and dangerous mothers. This extended social deprivation led to severe disruption of later social behavior. If the early isolation continued for as long as the first 12 months of life, there was a severe loss of both social and sexual behavior, nor could the deficits be completely remedied by later experience.

R. W. LUNDIN

HARTLEY, DAVID (1705–1765)

Hartley is considered the founder of British associationism. A contemporary of David Hume, the third of the British empiricists, he was educated at Cambridge and practiced medicine in London. As the father of British associationism, Hartley was followed by James Mill, Mill's son John Stuart Mill, Alexander Bain, and Herbert Spencer. Hartley's psychology is found in his *Observations on man, his frame, his duty and his expectations* (1749).

As a physician Hartley was greatly concerned with the relationship between the mind and the body. Impressed with Sir Isaac Newton's studies on motion and in particular with the law of the pendulum, Hartley carried the idea of motion into the mental world: when light struck the eye, the motion of particles of vibration changed from the ether waves to vibrations set up in the nervous system and brain. These smaller vibrations he called *vibratiuncles*. Hartley argued that when vibrations from light were cut off, vibrations in the brain continued but became weaker. Memories were simply the reactivation of the original vibrations.

Hartley proposed one law of association, that of contiguity—things occurring together in space or time. When two sensations reach the brain, they set up vibrations in such a way that they become connected. Later, when an idea correlates with one vibration, the other vibration will occur again. For example, when one series of vibrations (A, B, C, D) occurs in succession, they leave a trace of vibrations (a, b, c, d). The reoccurrence of the original A then reactivates the traces of b, c, and d.

Besides being the founder of associationism, Hartley is considered one of the earliest physiological psychologists, although René Descartes had given some earlier physiological explanations (albeit primitive) of how the nervous system worked. Hartley attempted to relate the mental (association of ideas) with the physical (brain vibrations). He concluded that the two ran parallel to each other: mental ideas and images were absolutely correlated with vibrations in the brain.

R. W. LUNDIN

HATFIELD, ELAINE C. (1937–   )

Hatfield received the B. A. from the University of Michigan and the Ph.D. (1963) from Stanford University. She taught at the universities of Minnesota (1963–1966), Rochester (1967–1968), Wisconsin (1968–1981), and Mannheim in Germany (1972). In 1981 she became head of the psychology department at the University of Hawaii.

Hatfield's main contribution is the application of rigorous scientific theorizing and research methodology to areas once thought to be taboo or impossible to investigate: love, emotion, and justice in interpersonal relationships.

In *A new look at love*, Hatfield proposed that passionate relations can be fueled not only by intensely positive but also by intensely negative experience. Both can contribute to a state of intense emotion and physiological–sexual response. In *Equity: Theory and research* (with Ellen Berscheid and G. W. Walster), she reviewed the evidence that considerations of justice are critically important in the workplace, in casual encounters, and intimate relations. In *Mirror, mirror: The importance of looks in everyday life* (with Susan Sprecher), she provided an encyclopedic review of what scientists know about the antecedents and consequences of physical appearance. In *Psychology of emotion* (with John Carlson) and *Love, sex, and intimacy: Their psychology, biology and history* (with Richard Rapson), she outlined what is known about intense emotion. Some of her early works were published under the name Elaine Walster.

HAYNES, STEPHEN N. (1944–   )

Haynes received the Ph.D. (1971) from the University of Colorado. He was an assistant and associate professor of psychology at the University of South Carolina from 1971 to 1976 and an associate professor in psychology at Southern Illinois University from 1976 to 1984. From 1984 to 1988 he was professor and director of clinical training at the Illinois Institute of Technology. In 1988, Haynes moved to the University of Hawaii as professor and director of the Clinical Studies Program.

Haynes has been on several editorial boards, received numerous grants and published widely in the areas of psychopathology, assessment, and psychophysiological disorders. He is the author of *Causal models in psychopathology*, *Behavioral assessment*, *Recent advances in behavioral assessment* (with Chrisman Wilson), *Psychosomatic disorders* (with Linda Gannon), and the *Southern Illinois epicurean* (with Linda Gannon).

HEALY, WILLIAM (1869–1963)

Healy came to the United States from the UK as a child. He received his undergraduate education at Harvard College and also studied at the Harvard Medical School. He earned the degree of M.D. at the University of Chicago and took postgraduate work in Vienna, Berlin, and London. He held appointments in several hospitals and taught at the Northwestern University Medical School. From 1909 to 1917 he served as director of the Juvenile Psychopathic Institute in Chicago and from 1917 to 1946 as director of the Judge Baker Guidance Center in Boston.

Healy was actively involved in psychology as well as psychiatry. He developed performance tests to supplement the Stanford-Binet Intelligence Scale of which the Healy Picture Completion test is perhaps the most widely known and used. Healy made significant contributions to our understanding of delinquency and criminality and pioneered in the establishment of guidance clinics for problem children and disadvantaged youths. He was the author or coauthor of 14 books and many articles ranging over such topics as psychoanalysis, crime and delinquency, mental testing, and mortality.

P. E. LICHTENSTEIN

HEARNSHAW, LESLIE S. (1907—   )

Hearnshaw is known as an industrial psychologist, historian of British psychology, and biographer of Cyril Burt. He was educated first at Oxford University in classics and philosophy, then at London University in psychology under Francis A. P. Aveling, a pupil of Albert Michotte. Upon graduating, Hearnshaw joined the staff of the National Institute of Industrial Psychology in London, rounded in 1921 by Charles S. Myers, and worked for five years as an industrial psychologist. In 1938 he was appointed a lecturer in psychology at the University of New Zealand. After the outbreak of World War II he founded and directed the Industrial Psychology Division of the New Zealand Department of Scientific and Industrial Research. In 1947 he returned to England to the newly created chair of psychology at the University of Liverpool, where he remained until his retirement in 1975. In Liverpool he built up the Department of Psychology, and also set up and directed a research establishment on the occupational aspects of aging financed by the Medical Research Council of Great Britain. He was assisted in this work for a time by Alastair Heron.

Hearnshaw, whose father was a well-known historian, had always been interested in the historical aspects of psychology, on which he began to concentrate in the mid-1950s. A short history (British psychology, 1840–1940 was published in 1964.

In 1971, on the death of Sir Cyril Burt, Hearnshaw was invited to write an official biography. It took him five years to read Burt's voluminous publications, correspondence, reports, notebooks, and memoranda, and by that time Burt's reputation had come under attack. Hearnshaw, though not a pupil of Burt's, was originally an admirer of his work; but the evidence, particularly from diaries and correspondence, forced him to accept the view that Burt's work on twins, as well as certain other work, was at least in part fraudulent.

Hearnshaw was president of the British Psychological Society in 1955–1956, and vice-president of the International Association of Applied Psychology from 1964 to 1974. During these years he also edited the Association's journal, The International Review of Applied Psychology.

HEBB, D. O. (1904–1985)

During his first appointment Hebb met the problem that determined the course of his later work. Some cases of large loss of brain tissue showed little effect on intelligence as measured by I.Q. tests or as seen in everyday life. How could one explain a high I.Q. with a damaged brain? The theory of cell assemblies was proposed as an answer, and this turned out to be relevant to other problems. Experiments confirmed the importance of early experience in the growth of mind and intelligence, and at maturity, the continued need of exposure to a normal sensory environment for mental health.

HEBB, DONALD OLDING (1904–1985)

Hebb graduated from Dalhousee University where he majored in English. He did postgraduate work at McGill University. He then worked with Karl Lashley at the University of Chicago. He received the Ph.D. from Harvard in 1936 and eventually returned to McGill where he was professor of psychology from 1947 to 1972. He is reported to have been a slow starter as far as psychology was concerned and did not develop a real interest in the subject until after receiving his bachelor's degree.

Hebb took a biological approach to psychology and became one of the first brain theorists of modern times. His first major work was The organization of behavior. He combined behavioral and neurophysiological approaches to psychology. His A textbook of psychology promoted his psychobiological position. The book was eventually translated into 11 languages. He believed the roots of psychology would be found in biology. In so doing, he felt that psychology could eventually be a real science. He did not take kindly to mentalistic attitudes that would take psychology into the realm of the mind and spirit.

R. W. LUNDIN

HECHT, SELIG (1892–1947)

Hecht came to the United States as a young child. His 1917 Ph.D. from Harvard was based on a dissertation in sensory physiology. After an initial position at the Creighton University College of Medicine, he became a national research fellow in physical chemistry and physiology at Harvard, Liverpool University, and the Zoological Station in Naples, Italy. The last 20 years of his career were spent as professor of biophysics at Columbia University. He was a member of the Army-Navy National Council on Vision.

In 1946 Hecht became the only nonnuclear physicist on the nine-member Emergency Committee of Atomic Scientists chaired by Albert Einstein. Consonant with the committee goal of acquainting the public with the problems of atomic energy, his book Explaining the atom did just that.

Hecht is primarily remembered in psychology for his research on the basic functioning of the eye. One early paper with R. E. Williams established the sensitivity curve to different wavelengths (colors) under low-illumination viewing with the rods. Hecht brought the extant literature together in his 1937 paper in a hypothetico-deductive theory of chemical breakdown and recombination in the rods and cones. Later, with Simon Shlaer and H. M. Pirenne, he showed that the smallest amount of light that can be detected under the most ideal of viewing conditions is very close to the physiological limit. Shortly after Hecht's death, the New York Times editorialized, "It is not too much to say that since the days of [Hermann yon] Helmholtz no biophysicist did more brilliant work in the field of vision than Hecht."

C. S. PEYSER

HECKHAUSEN, HEINZ (1926—   )

Heckhausen studied in Münster from 1947 till the mid-1950s under Wolfgang Metzger. Mainly influenced by Kurt Lewin and Henry A. Murray, he started his research career with the search for individual motive differences in goal setting. David McClelland's use of the TAT as a motive measure for need achievement and John Atkinson's risk-taking model were timely challenges. Heckhausen constructed TAT measures for the independent assessment of "hope of success" and "fear of failure." These measures became the base of the rapidly growing German achievement motivation research. In 1967 Heckhausen published The anatomy of achievement motivation, the first synopsis of the English- and German-language state of knowledge.

Since 1964 Heckhausen has held a chair at Ruhr University in Bochum, where he built up one of Germany's leading psychology departments. Bochum became a center of motivation research, attracting visiting professors from abroad and producing well-known researchers. Heckhausen integrated findings into elaborated motivation models, such as *motive as a self-reinforcing system* or the *extended motivation model* stressing the functional difference between action outcome and consequence, most often neglected in expectancy-value models. His present research concentrates on the early development of achievement-related acts and the expressive reactions to success and failure, partly pursued in longitudinal studies.

Heckhausen was a fellow of the Netherlands Institute of Advanced Study in 1971–1972 and in 1981 received an honorary doctoral degree from the University of Oslo. He was president of the German Society of Psychology in 1980–1982.

HEGEL, GEORGE FRIEDRICH (1770–1831)

Hegel received his theological degree at Tübingen. Along with G. Fichte, Hegel was an immediate successor to Immanuel Kant. These philosophers forged an idealistic psychology in the Kantian tradition. The foundations of nineteenth-century German idealism are to be found in the philosophical and logical works of Hegel. For him, psychology could never be objective. The phenomenological method of current existential and humanistic psychologies owes much to Hegel. It is thus clear that Hegel rejected the empiricism of Locke, Berkeley, and Hume. Hegel saw reason, not experience, as the first principle.

Hegel's psychology is best set forth in *The phenomenology of mind.* His psychology of mind involved stages of development. In his concepts of ego and antiego conflicts and the intent of a death wish, there is a clear anticipation of the ideas of Sigmund Freud.

In Hegel's psychology the mind was merely a stage in the development of the soul. As the soul developed and was able to distinguish objects in the external world from itself, it could be said to have consciousness and become mind. Consciousness likewise passed through stages: sensuous consciousness, perceptual consciousness, and intellect.

Modern notions of self-consciousness, self-actualization, consciousness raising, and self-concern are direct outgrowths of Hegel and neo-Hegelian idealism. Likewise, the cognitive development expressed in the writings of Jean Piaget shows a close relation to Hegel: Piaget's six stages of cognition fit neatly into Hegel's three stages of sensation, perception, and intellect. Piaget attempted to demonstrate experimentally the logical structure of thought as developed by Hegel.

R. W. LUNDIN

HEIDBREDER, EDNA (1890–1985)

Heidbreder received the B.A. degree from Knox College. The next several years were spent teaching history in high school. In 1924 she received the Ph.D. from Columbia and then taught at the University of Minnesota until 1934. While at Minnesota she collaborated with D. G. Patterson and others on the *Minnesota Mechanical Ability Tests.* She also became interested in the qualification of certain personality traits such as introversion and extraversion. After Minnesota, she went to Wellsley College. There she remained until her retirement in 1955. Subsequently, she taught several years at the Radcliff College Seminars.

Heidbreder is best known for her book *Seven psychologies* (1933). This was one of the first books to be written on theories and systems of psychology. It was taught to generations of students who followed. The work was concerned with the theories of Titchener (structuralism), functionalism, behaviorism, (Watson), Freud, and William James. One chapter was devoted to Robert Woodworth's dynamic psychology. She had studied under Woodworth while at Columbia. The book sold tens of thousands of copies because of its clarity of style and its fairness and unbiased approach to each system.

R. W. LUNDIN

HEIDEGGER, MARTIN (1889–1976)

A German philosopher, Heidegger is considered by many to be the center of existential philosophy of the twentieth century. Of particular concern for psychology, Heidegger is considered to be the bridge between existential philosophy and existential psychology.

The central focus of Heidegger's philosophy is that the individual is a being-in-the-world. Of all mammals, humans alone have the capacity to be conscious of their existence. They do not exist as a self in relation to the external world, nor as a body interacting with other things in the world. Humans exist by being-in-the-world, and the world has an existence because they are in it. Like Soren Kirkegaard, Heidegger considers humans to be in conflict. They contemplate the thought of inescapable death which results in the experience of anguish and dread. They have to accept that death is inevitable and that nothingness will follow. Our existence is neither of our own making nor our choice. Existence has been thrust upon us and will continue to be until our death.

Heidegger's philosophy has had a strong influence on contemporary existential psychology, particularly that of Ludwig Binswanger who has taken up his concept of being-in-the world as a basic tenet of existential psychology.

R. W. LUNDIN

HEIDER, FRITZ (1896–1988)

Heider received the doctorate from the University of Graz under the philosopher Alexius Meinong in 1920. During the next several years he worked on aptitude tests for apprentices for the provincial government of Styria, traveled extensively, and attended lectures by Max Wertheimer, Wolfgang Köhler, and Kurt Lewin at the University of Berlin. In 1927 he became assistant to William Stern at Hamburg.

In 1930 Heider went to Smith College in Northampton, Massachusetts, as a member of Kurt Koffka's Research Laboratory, with the primary task of carrying on research at the Clarke School for the Deaf in the same city. He remained there for 17 years, working on problems related to deafness, teaching at Smith College, and developing the ideas on which his book, *The psychology of interpersonal relations,* is based. In 1947 he went to the University of Kansas, where he taught graduate students and also had two years on Guggenheim fellowships to complete the book. He spent 1960–1961 at the University of Oslo as a Fulbright fellow and has been visiting professor at Stanford, Cornell, and Duke universities. Since his retirement from the University of Kansas in 1966 he has given papers in this country and abroad, and has continued work in the field of social psychology.

In 1959 Heider received the Lewin Memorial Award given by the Society for the Psychological Study of Social Issues, and in 1965, the Award for Distinguished Scientific Contributions from the American Psychological Association.

HELMHOLTZ, HERMANN VON (1821–1894)

Helmholtz was a German physicist. He received his medical degree in Berlin, then served seven years as an army surgeon. He studied mathematics and physics, and formulated the mathematical foundation for the law of conservation of energy. After leaving the army, Helmholtz held academic appointments over the next 30 years at Bonn, Heidelberg, and Berlin, first as a physiologist and then as a physicist.

Helmholtz published in several areas of science; of special interest to psychologists are his investigations of the speed of the neural impulse, vision, and audition. Before Helmholtz, the neural impulse was thought to be instantaneous—too fast to be measured. Helmholtz provided the first measurement of the rate of conduction with experiments using frogs; he was less successful with humans. Helmholtz demonstrated that conduction is not instantaneous, and suggested that thought and movement follow one another at a measurable interval. His research was used by other scientists in experiments on reaction time.

Helmholtz invented the ophthalmoscope in the course of his work on vision and optics. *Physiological optics* reported this work in three volumes. He extended the theory of color vision that had originated with Thomas Young in 1802; it became known as the Young-Helmholtz theory of color vision. His research on acoustical problems resulted in *On the sensations of tone*. Helmholtz's work in audition included perception of combined and individual tones, the nature of harmony and discord, and his resonance theory of hearing.

Although not a psychologist, Helmholtz contributed a great body of knowledge to sensory psychology. He influenced the experimental approach to psychological problems, and his work strongly supported the development of an empirical tradition, especially in perception and sensation.

N. A. HAYNIE

HELSON, HARRY (1898–   )

Helson distinguished himself chiefly by developing the adaptation-level theory. A 1921 graduate of Bowdoin College, Helson went on to Harvard, where he obtained the Ph.D. in experimental psychology in 1924. His career opened as instructor in psychology at Cornell University in 1924, and closed at the University of Massachusetts in 1971.

Helson published *Adaptation level theory: An experimental and systematic approach to behavior* in 1964. His theory holds that the quality and magnitude of a response is a function of the distance above or below level. A subjective point of equality, the adaptation level is that at which stimuli are neutral, that is, indifferent.

HENLE, MARY (1913–   )

Henle is a Gestalt psychologist, best known for her work in thinking and in the analysis of theories in psychology. She received the B.A. and M.A. degrees from Smith College, and the Ph.D. from Bryn Mawr College in 1939.

Henle's doctoral research combined the methods of Kurt Lewin with hypotheses derived from Gestalt psychology. Also drawing largely on the work of Lewin, with Donald W. MacKinnon she wrote what was probably the first laboratory manual for motivation and personality, *Experimental studies in psychodynamics*. Her work has been in the tradition of Gestalt psychology. She edited *Documents of Gestalt psychology* and *The selected papers of Wolfgang Köhler* and wrote numerous articles on the history of Gestalt psychology, trying to correct misunderstandings about this approach and developing Gestalt ideas.

Henle is concerned with the relation of logic to thinking. She has been cautious in her claims, though her findings point in the direction of the rationality of human thinking. In the analysis of theories, she has turned her attention to problems in the theories of Lewin, Freud, Gibson, Titchener, and other major approaches.

She held a post-doctoral position at Swarthmore College, then taught at the University of Delaware, Bryn Mawr College, and Sarah Lawrence College before coming to the New School for Social Research, where she is professor emeritus of psychology in the graduate faculty. She was twice a Guggenheim fellow and among other positions was a research fellow in cognitive studies at Harvard University and a visiting professor at Cornell University. She was president of the Eastern Psychological Association in 1981–1982 and has been president of Divisions 24 and 26 of the American Psychological Association.

HERBART, JOHANN FRIEDRICH (1776–1841)

Herbart studied with J. G. Fichte at Jena and then taught at Königsberg and Göttingen. A philosopher, psychologist, and mathematician, he proposed psychology to be a science based on experience, metaphysics, and mathematics. However, psychology was not to be experimental because Herbart could conceive of no way to experiment on the mind.

Herbart agreed with Kant on the nature of a unitary mind or soul, but also believed the mind could be a compound of smaller units. He thought of it as an *apperception mass* made up of psychic states that could cross the threshold of consciousness and enter into the apperception mass. Unconscious ideas existed in a sort of static state. These states had forces or intensities. If the forces were strong enough, they could overcome the counterforces already in the apperception mass and enter into consciousness. The interaction of psychic states in and out of consciousness amounted to "psychic dynamics."

The mathematics involved in all this amounted to a calculation of what could and could not enter consciousness. One had to calculate the amount of one force that was going to oppose another. It was also possible for two forces (ideas) to combine and suppress the ideas that were weaker. The amount of assistance provided by one idea to another enabling it to get back into consciousness could also be calculated. According to J. R. Kantor in *The scientific evolution of psychology*, the whole business of calculation was utterly fictitious. Nonetheless, Herbart brought to psychology the notion that it could be quantified. Even though Herbart denied that psychology could be experimental, the entire movement of quantification is critical to contemporary experimental psychology.

HERING, EWALD (1834–1918)

Hering enrolled at the University of Leipzig at the age of 19. He was a student of such famous men as E. H. Weber and Gustav Fechner, and was also much impressed with the work of Johannes Muller. Later he became professor of physiology at Leipzig and then at the Academy at Vienna.

During the 1860s Hering devoted himself to the study of visual space perception. With regard to visual perception he fostered the doctrine of nativism, the view that one can judge space and depth in an inherent way. This idea was later taken up by the Gestalt psychologists, but in Hering's time it was in opposition to the more empirical approach of Hermann Helmholtz.

In the 1870s Hering devoted himself to the development of a theory of color vision in opposition to that of Helmholtz. According to Hering's theory, the retina of the eye had different substances for responding to red-green, blue-yellow and black-white, each of which could be excited by either of the opposing reactions. There could be a dissimilation (catabolism) or an assimilation (anabolism). The dissimilative reaction responded to red, yellow, and white, while the assimilative one responded to the opposite dimensions of green, blue, or black. The theory also explained negative afterimages and color contrast which gave opposite reactions to the initial stimulation. For example, if one focuses on yellow, the negative afterimage will be blue, and so forth. Each color was believed to produce a chemical change in the various receptors in the eye. The afterimage was stimulated by the opposite reaction of the initial color presented. The theory also explained color blindness. Red and green color blindness tend to go together. For about 50 years Hering's theory was widely held as an alternative to that of Helmholtz.

Hering was also concerned with the temperature sense. E. H. Weber had previously believed that the changes in skin temperature (warm to cold) resulted from the rising or falling of the basic temperature of the skin. Hering proposed that it was not the rising or falling, but the relative temperature of the skin, that determined whether one considered a feeling to be warm or cold. He observed that if one hand were placed in warm water and the other in cold, then both placed in lukewarm water, the hand previously placed in the cold would appear warmer by contrast. Thus the skin of each hand had adapted itself to a given temperature.

R. W. LUNDIN

HERRMANN, THEO (1929–   )

Herrmann studied psychology and philosophy at the University of Mainz, where he received the Ph.D. in 1956 and held a postdoctoral position. Following his first appointment as professor at the Technische Universität Braunschweig, he taught at Marburg University and has been at the University of Mannheim since 1977.

Herrmann is best known for his work in cognitive psychology, psychology of language, and philosophy of psychological science. His books on these subjects are *Psychologie der kognitiven ordnung* (Psychology of cognitive structures), and the first monograph in the German language specifically devoted to the psychology of speech production, *Sprechen und Situation* (Speech and situation). His *pars pro toto* principle of speech production has gained considerable recognition. In *Psychologie als Problem* (Psychology as a problem), he put forth his general theoretical and methodological position, best described as a decided nomological orientation on the basis of neopragmatism. He reconstructed a history of psychology, utilizing a theory of research networks. Although cognitive psychology and the psychology of language are traditionally viewed as paradigms within the field of information processing, Herrmann has extended them to include aspects of a theory of "action in a situation."

In addition to his work in these main domains of interest, Herrmann is the author of A German textbook on the psychology of personality: *Lehrbuch der empirischen persönlichkeitsforschung* (Empirical personality research, 3rd ed.,). His research in this field culminated in the Marburg Model on the effects of child-rearing attitudes.

HERRNSTEIN, RICHARD J. (1930—   )

Herrnstein was educated at City College before leaving for graduate studies at Harvard, where he earned the Ph.D. in 1955. Leaving Harvard, Herrnstein served as a research psychologist at Walter Reed Army Medical Center in Washington, D.C., for a number of years. After spending another year as lecturer at the University of Maryland, he began his tenure at Harvard in 1958, where he served as director of the psychological laboratories and chaired the department.

Herrnstein's publications include *A sourcebook in the history of psychology* edited with E. G. Boring; *Laboratory experiments in psychology* with J. C. Stevens and G. S. Reynolds; and an introductory text on *Psychology* coauthored with R. Brown.

Herrnstein tends toward nativism, especially with respect to the factor of intelligence. Because of it, he has been a subject of contention. His interests, however, are basically in the field of experimental psychology.

HILGARD, ERNEST R. (1905–   )

Hilgard graduated with honors in chemical engineering at the University of Illinois, and received the Ph.D. (1930) in experimental psychology

from Yale with a dissertation on conditioned human eyelid responses under Raymond Dodge. He became a teaching assistant and remained at Yale as an instructor from 1929 to 1933, when he accepted an invitation from Lewis M. Terman to join the faculty at Stanford University, where, except for World War II, he spent the rest of his career, becoming an emeritus professor in 1969. He held a joint appointment between the School of Humanities and the School of Education, served as executive head of the department of psychology from 1942 to 1950, and was dean of the graduate division from 1951 to 1955.

His research interests before World War II were primarily in psychology of learning and motivation, and during the war years he turned to in social psychology in various agencies as a civilian in Washington. During 1957–1979, he headed a laboratory of hypnosis research within the department of psychology. In the meantime, he continued publishing and revising his more general books as well as publishing in the field of hypnosis. Later he turned to historical writing: his primary contribution to the field is *American psychology: A historical survey*.

Hilgard was elected president of the American Psychological Association and is a member of the National Academy of Sciences, the National Academy of Education, the American Academy of Arts and Sciences, and the American Philosophical Society. He received the Gold Medal Award from the American Psychological Foundation in recognition of his lifetime contributions to psychology.

HINDE, ROBERT A. (1923–   )

Trained as a biologist at Cambridge, Hinde earned the Ph.D. at Oxford under David Lack. There he also came under the influence of Tinbergen. In 1950 Hinde became curator of the Ornithological Field Station of the Sub-Department of Animal Behavior). Later Hinde was appointed Royal Society research professor and honorary director of a medical research council unit based at Madingley. His early work on bird behavior entails comparative studies of courtship behavior, analysis of motivational conflicts, and the study of habituation.

During the 1950s Hinde's work focused on relations between ethology and other disciplines, and mother–child relations. The former deals with behavioral endocrinology in the reproductive behavior of canaries. Hinde's theoretical interest in the relation between ethology and psychology led to *Animal behaviour: A synthesis of ethology and comparative psychology,* and to his editing *Constraints on learning* with J. Stevenson-Hinde. Other edited works include *Bird vocalizations* with G. Horn, and *Non-verbal communication.* Hinde's multidisciplinary interest in behavior culminated in *Ethology: Its nature and contacts with other sciences.*

In the 1950s studies of imprinting brought Hinde into contact with John Bowlby. Influenced by Bowlby's multidisciplinary seminars, toward the end of the 1950s Hinde established a rhesus monkey colony at Madingley to study the effects of short-term separation between infant and mother. To categorize the main dimensions of human interpersonal relationships, and show the relevance of his categories to the main theories of interpersonal dynamics, he wrote *Towards understanding relationships.* Later, Hinde researched the interplay of mother–child and peer–peer relationships, with special emphasis on the 3–6 age range.

HIPPOCRATES (ca.460–ca.377 B.C.)

Hippocrates of Cos, the father of medicine, is the name under which we know Greek medical thought of his period; he himself may have written little. Medical practice then focused on the use of symptoms to classify the illness. Hippocrates described the etiology in terms of the four body humors and prescribed purgatives, baths, vapors, or special diets to change the balance of the humors. Surgery was used for external trauma such as fractures of limbs. Hippocrates said it was impossible to treat any part of the body without taking account of the whole body.

Hippocrates took the four elements according to Empedocles—earth, air, fire, and water—and developed his theory of disease with four corresponding bodily humors: black bile, blood, yellow bile, and phlegm. Too much bile could cause overheating of the brain and thus fear or terror (the flushed face was partial evidence), while too much phlegm could cause overcooling and thus anxiety and grief. His book *On the sacred disease* concerned epilepsy; after stating that it was really no more sacred than any other disease, Hippocrates described it as hereditary and due to an imbalance of humors, particularly blood and phlegm. He also described severe phobias and the depression of postpartum psychosis.

Hippocrates had a primitive typology as well. He noted that the apoplecticus (the short, thickset individual) tended to have seizures, whereas the phthisicus (the slender, frail person) would have tuberculosis. Thus he anticipated the pyknic and asthenic types of Kretschmer and the work of Sheldon. It was Galen, however, who developed Hippocrates' vague notions of humors affecting behavior into a complete theory of temperament or personality.

HOBBES, THOMAS (1588–1679)

Educated at Oxford, Hobbes is considered the father of British empiricism and associationism. His psychology is set forth in two books, *Human nature* (1651) and *Leviathan* (1651).

Influenced by Galileo's concept of motion, Hobbes concluded that psychological (mental) activities were motions in the nervous system resulting from motions in the external world. Thinking, therefore, was nothing more than movement excited in the brain. In this way he also accounted for action and emotion. In stating that everything in nature was motion, Hobbes tried to deny the existence of a mind separate from the body. Antagonistic to any theological interpretation of mind or soul, he reduced consciousness—like other mental activity—to motions of atoms in the brain. However, he offered no explanation as to the coexistence of these brain movements and mental activity; it simply happened. As a contemporary of Rene Descartes, Hobbes rejected the former's conception of an interaction between body and mind (soul) via the pineal gland. In stating his thesis of the coexistence of motions and mental activity, Hobbes was still left with some concept of a mind. He also rejected Descartes' notion that some ideas in the mind were inherited. Some mental activity was the residual of previous sensory experiences; for example, images and memory were mere decay of the original sensations.

Hobbes touched on the notion of the association of ideas, but left the details to be worked out by the later empiricists and associationists. He referred to the associations as "trains of thought" and described them as being of two types: one unguided or rambling, and the second orderly, as when a person associated two ideas which were appropriately related.

Hobbes also wrote of the passions and desires, which, though also motions, arose from within parts of the body other than the brain. He made it clear that passions could influence reason. They seemed to direct thought, but in so doing could distort logical thinking. In the end, the passions determined conduct. In stating that we seek pleasure and avoid pain, Hobbes was anticipating a psychological hedonism to be elaborated later by Julien La Mettrie and Jeremy Bentham.

Hobbes' psychology was derived from his concern for political and social conduct. In the *Leviathan* he wrote that man had originally lived in a state of mutual warfare; only calculated selfishness had produced cooperation in the establishment of a state or government. Without government, life would be "poor, nasty, brutish and short." On the basis of self-interest and fear of destruction, humans established government to control themselves.

Historians agree that Hobbes had little influence on his successor, John Locke, who really established the empirical movement. They also agree that Hobbes' writings were vague, unclear, and often contradictory.

R.W. LUNDIN

HÖFFDING, HARALD (1843–1931)

A Danish philosopher and psychologist, Höffding spent most of his academic career at the University of Copenhagen. He was well acquainted with Fechner's psychophysical methods and Wundt's theories and experiments. He felt that the task of the experimental psychologist was to discover the conditions under which psychological phenomena were found and quantitatively to discover the degrees and shadows of each experience. This attitude, however, held only for the simple psychological phenomena. More complicated events such as thought depended on a qualitative analysis, so that experiments could not give complete answers to the nature of higher mental activity.

In his book *Psychology*, first published in Danish in 1882, Höffding set forth his doctrine of the various functions of the mind: memory, comprehension, grief, doubt, concentration on purpose, and a search for the means to carry out problems. Mental functions could best be understood by analysis and synthesis. Behind all this was the central fact of psychology: the will. In relating mental activity to bodily functions, in particular the nervous system, he followed Spinoza's solution of double aspectism: there were two different ways of looking at the same event.

Höffding also stressed the psychological-historical approach. Present events could be more fully understood by looking into the past. He applied this approach to studying the thinking of various religious leaders of the past. In so doing, he felt he could understand their emotions, imagination, and will, which expressed themselves in various religious conceptions.

He was elected president of the International Psychological Association in 1931, but died before taking office.

R.W. LUNDIN

HOLLINGWORTH, HARRY L. (1880–1956)

Hollingworth took the Ph.D. at Columbia under James M. Cattell. For many years he was head of the Department of Psychology at Barnard College. He was a prolific writer with some 25 books to his credit covering such fields as abnormal psychology, experimental psychology, applied psychology, vocational psychology, and educational psychology.

A central concept in Hollingworth's psychology is redintegration, a term he took from Sir William Hamilton, although the concept goes back to Christian Wolff. Redintegration is the reinstatement of a total experience in the form of memory upon the presentation of only a part of the previous experience. It may also mean the arousal of a response by only part of the stimulus combination which previously aroused it. Hollingworth employed redintegration as a general principle and saw it as the basis of an improved association psychology. He applied the principle to thinking, reasoning, judging, and neurotic behavior. In *Psychology: Its facts and principles* (1928) Hollingworth made the principle of redintegration the foundation of a systematic general psychology.

P.E. LICHTENSTEIN

HOLLINGWORTH, LETA S. (1886–1939)

Hollingworth received the Ph.D. in education at Columbia Teachers College, where she then taught for over 20 years. Her interests centered upon children and individual and group differences. Her early work on subnormal children was summarized in *The psychology of subnormal children* and *Special talents and defects*. She pointed out that children with serious problems may frequently be intellectually retarded; furthermore, they suffer emotionally and their emotional problems tend to increase during adolescence. Hollingworth's textbook *The psychology of the adolescent* was widely used.

Impressed by the fact that gifted children may also suffer from emotional problems, Hollingworth concentrated her attention in this area. She noted that very high intelligence may lead to isolation and consequently may disqualify the gifted for popular leadership. Hollingworth spoke eloquently for the gifted and wrote *Gifted children*.

Working at a time when there were few women psychologists, Hollingworth set for herself high standards of scholarship and fully earned the respect of her colleagues.

P.E. LICHTENSTEIN

HOLT, EDWIN B. (1873–1946)

One of the early behaviorists, Holt received the Ph.D. at Harvard in 1901 and remained there until 1917. After taking some time out for writing, he taught at Princeton from 1926 to 1936.

Holt felt strongly that psychology should study behavior, or what he called "the specific response relationship." However, unlike Watson's atomistic or "muscle twitch" psychology, Holt thought of a response system as involving a whole, or what Tolman later called "molar behavior." For example, rather than saying a man was walking step by step down the street, Holt would say he was walking to the grocery store. Thus there was a certain purpose in the behavior.

Holt was much concerned with psychological meaning. When one responded adequately to a thing, one got its meaning. When a response specified something, that constituted meaning. Our capacity to respond specifically to the world constituted knowledge. Thus Holt made his behaviorism into a cognitive psychology wherein the specific response relation was the essence of the event.

This notion also became the basic dynamic principle for Holt. He termed the dynamic principle "wish." In *The Freudian wish and its place in ethics* he said Freud had given psychology back its will. The wish as a specific response relation provided psychology with a notion of cause. Furthermore, the wish was to be regarded as a purpose. It was a cause of action wherein some mechanism of the body was set to carry out an act directed toward a goal.

Holt's psychology can be related to William McDougall's purposivism, Alfred Adler's teleology, and Edward Tolman's purposive behaviorism.

R.W. LUNDIN

HOLT, ROBERT R. (1917–   )

Holt graduated from Princeton and got the Ph.D. from Harvard in 1946 under H. A. Murray. After 2 yr in public opinion research, he went to the VA in Topeka to learn diagnostic testing and psychoanalytic theory from David Rapaport. He left there in 1953 as director of the psychological staff of the Menninger Foundation, then founded and directed for 16 yr the Research Center for Mental Health at New York University. During his final years there, he founded and directed a program on peace and global policy studies.

His first major research, in collaboration with Lester Luborsky, on the selection of psychiatrists, led to their book *Personality patterns of psychiatrists* and to the series of papers on clinical and statistical prediction for which Holt is perhaps best known. Arguing that the central

issue was the role of judgment in assessment, Holt strove to integrate the best in the two approaches, not to pit one against the other. A similar effort at synthesis and reconciliation marks his main works on psychodiagnosis, his revision of Rapaport's *Diagnostic psychological testing*, and his *Assessing personality*.

In the program of experimental research on the psychoanalytic theory of thinking he developed the *Manual for the scoring of manifestations of the primary process in Rorschach responses*, which is used as a means of measuring adaptive versus maladaptive regression. Holt's interests turned increasingly to Freudian theory and the understanding of it through biographical, historical, and philosophical analyses (*Freud reappraised*). He strove to purge Freud's ideas of their errors and fallacies, retaining the lasting insights and putting them into a larger systems–theoretical context. Other publications include *Motives and thought*, *New horizon for psychotherapy*, and *Methods in clinical psychology*.

HORAS, PLÁCIDO A. (1916–   )

Horas took his degree in philosophy at the University of Buenos Aires and the Ph.D. (honoris causa) at the University of San Luis. He organized psychology at the latter institution, and served as head of its Department of Psychology and as dean of the Faculty of Educational Sciences. Having founded the Institute for Psychopedagogical Research, he edited seven volumes of the Institute's *Annals*. In them he published material on his principal interest, educational psychology.

Horas has occupied various chairs of psychology at the National University of San Luis, where he offered courses on psychology in the Freudian and behavioral tradition. He regards himself as a doctrinarian generalist, one who endeavors to establish integrative bonds between discordant trends in contemporary psychology. He believes psychology should emanate from a biopsychological conception of human behavior, emphasizing its cognitive aspects.

A member of the editorial board of several specialized journals, Horas belongs to Argentinian and international scientific societies. As a visiting professor, Horas lectured in Argentinian and other universities. In 1965 and 1968 he served as president of the second and third Argentinian Psychological Conventions. He is presently involved in forensic psychology.

Horas' publications include "Freud and the development of psychoanalytic thought," "Deviated and delinquent youth," and "Duties and organization of a psychopedagogical laboratory."

HORNEY, KAREN D. (1885–1952)

Horney received the M.D. from the University of Berlin in 1915. Horney was originally trained in Freudian psychoanalysis at the Berlin Psychoanalytical Institute. However, she eventually broke from the standard Freudian orthodoxy over the issue of female sexuality. In *New ways in psychoanalysis* she strongly criticized Freud's libido theory, stating that his stress on the sexual instinct was completely out of proportion. In 1932 she emigrated to the United States, where she practiced her new form of analysis in Chicago and New York.

Although Horney kept many of the basic Freudian concepts (repression, resistance, transference, free association), like other social analysts (Alfred Adler, Erich Fromm, Harry Stack Sullivan) she stressed the importance of social and environmental conditions in molding the personality. In her first book, *The neurotic personality of our times* (1937), she stressed one of her most important concepts, *basic anxiety*. This feeling of the child resulted from "being isolated and helpless in a potentially hostile world," hence was not inherited but a product of our culture and upbringing. Such anxiety was a primary condition for later personality difficulties. Out of this feeling arose a basic drive for safety or security: to be secure meant to be free from anxiety. Unlike Freud, Horney believed anxiety to be a striving force.

Through interaction with society humans also acquired other needs. In *Our inner conflicts* (1945), Horney divided these needs into three groups: (1) to move toward people (approach, affection); (2) to move against people (power, exploitation); and (3) to move away from people (restriction of one's life, self-sufficiency). These three forces could obviously come in conflict with one another. The normal person resolved the conflict by integrating them, or the conflicts could be resolved or avoided if a child were raised amid love and respect, feeling wanted and secure, and being surrounded by trust. When a person took one orientation to the exclusion of others, three types of personality might emerge, depending on the orientation: (1) the compliant type (moving toward people), (2) the hostility type (moving against people), and (3) the detached type (moving away from people).

Another of Horney's basic concepts—also related to the conflicts—was the *idealized image*. In actuality, this image was fictitious and illusory. Here there was a discrepancy between a person's self-image and the person's real self. Through this self-deception, persons create an image of what they believe or feel they ought to be: a saint, a mastermind, or a Casanova. This image expresses the fact that the person cannot tolerate his or her real self.

R.W. LUNDIN

HORST, A. PAUL (1903–   )

Horst is probably best known for his work in the development of mathematical models for multivariate analysis and prediction techniques. He received the bachelor's degree from the University of California, Berkeley, and the Ph.D. from the University of Chicago in 1931.

He worked for more than 50 years in governmental, industrial, military, and educational institutions on the development and application of psychological measurement and prediction procedures. His major preoccupation during these years was the development of models and techniques to further the optimal utilization of human resources in social institutions. His goal was to solve complex human problems with rigorous mathematical and quantitative techniques, rather than with rhetoric and semantics.

His early work was with the Proctor and Gamble Company where, over a 12-year period, he served as supervisor of personnel selection research and later as manager of the Personnel Research Department. During World War II he was chief of air crew selection research for the Army Air Forces Training Command. From 1947 until his retirement in 1969, he was professor of psychology at the University of Washington; during a large part of this time, he was also executive director of the Division of Counseling and Testing Services at that institution. Under his direction the statewide differential grade prediction program was developed. After retirement, he continued his research.

With others, Horst organized the Psychometric Society and launched its journal, *Psychometrika*. He has held offices in the American Psychological Association and the Psychometric Society. His publications include upward of a hundred journal articles, technical reports, and chapters in books. In addition, he has published four books: *Matrix algebra for social scientists; Factor analysis of data matrices; Psychological measurement and prediction;* and *Personality: Measurement of dimensions.*

HOSHINO, AKIRA (1927–   )

Hoshino is best known for his study of "culture shock," a review and critical theory of sojourners' assimilation and adjustment to a new culture and reentry to their own culture after a long stay abroad.

After receiving the bachelor's degree from Tokyo University, Hoshino continued studies at the Nagoya National University School of Medicine, where he received training in clinical psychology and psychological anthropology from Tsuneo Muramatsu, Kaname Hori, George DeVos, and others. Hoshino went to the United States for graduate study at the University of Iowa and for research work at the University of Michigan as a Fulbright scholar. After returning to Japan, Hoshino began his professional career at the International Christian University in Tokyo, where he continues to research, lecture, and counsel.

His publications include "Cross-cultural study of socialization of children into compliance systems," and *"The ethnic heritage of the Italian-Americans in the United States and their community life."*

HOSKOVEC, JIŘÍ (1933–   )

Hoskovec is best known for his research in general and applied psychchology (perception, behavior, learning). He was educated at Palacký University, Olomouc; Comenius University, Bratislava; and Charles University, Prague (Ph.D., 1965). He is an independent scientist, teaching general psychology and history of psychology in the Department of Psychology at Charles University. In 1965 and 1971 he was affiliated with Lehigh University; in 1966, with Stanford University; and in 1968–1969, with the Verkehrspsychologisches Institut of Vienna.

Through journeys connected with study and instruction to the Far East (1967, 1981), Egypt (1975), and the U.S.S.R. (1957, 1967, 1976) he met psychologists from various countries. He is a member of the Czechoslovak Psychological Society, the Czech Medical Society, the Cheiron International Society for the History of Behavioral and Social Sciences, the International Society of Hypnosis, and the American Society of Clinical Hypnosis. He is coeditor of the *American Journal of Clinical Hypnosis;* the *Revista Latino-Americana de Hipnosis Clínica (Argentina); the Revista Brasileira de Hipnologia* and the *Medicina Psicosomática* (Mexico).

His publications include *Hypnosis and suggestion* and *Theory of hypnosis.*

HOVLAND, CARL I. (1912–1961)

Known for his research in the psychology of attitudes and the psychology of communication, Hovland earned his reputation at the Yale Communication and Attitude Change Program, an institute that he founded. The B.A. and M.A. were earned at Northwestern University; Yale conferred the Ph.D. upon him in 1936, the year he began his career at Yale as an instructor. During World War II Hovland served as chief psychologist and director of experimental studies in the office of the chief of staff of the War Department. His long tenure at Yale was interrupted at the height of his career by death from cancer.

While heading the Yale Studies in Attitude and Communication Program, Hovland with his associates published several important volumes, including *The order (presentation in persuasion, Attitude organization and change, Communication and persuasion, Experiments in mass communication,* and *Social judgment: Assimilation and contrast effects in communication and attitude change* (Sherif & Hovland, 1961). Hovland's research team is credited with a number of contributions to psychology, among them being (1) the sleeper effect, (2) communicator credibility, (3) the preferred value of stating a conclusion, and (4) valuable effects due to the order of presenting propaganda.

W. S. SAHAKIAN

HULL, CLARK L. (1884–1952)

Hull's most important contribution to psychology lies in his theory of learning, considered one of the most important learning theories of the twentieth century.

He received the Ph.D. in 1918 at the University of Wisconsin. Early in his career he was interested in the field of aptitude testing, an area he abandoned because he did not see much future in it. He then turned to the field of hypnosis and suggestibility. In 1929 he accepted an appointment as research professor at Yale University, a post he held until his retirement.

For most of his career Hull devoted himself to the development of a theory of learning along with experimental research to support it. In 1940, with a number of colleagues he published *A mathematico-deductive theory of rote learning.* This was considered a masterpiece in theory construction, but it was so complicated that most psychologists failed to understand it. In 1943 he published the first complete statement of his theory of learning, *Principles of behavior,* of which revisions followed in 1951 and 1952.

Hull's theory was basically an S-R (stimulus–response) theory and reflected some influences from the behavioristic ideas of John Watson. Hull was also influenced by Ivan Pavlov's work on the conditioned reflex, which he considered to be a simple form of learning on which more complex kinds of learning could be built.

Like B. F. Skinner, Hull stressed the importance of reinforcement, if learning was to take place. Reinforcement was successful because it resulted in the reduction of drives. Thus the concept of drives and their reduction became an important aspect of Hull's theory. He considered the environmental influences on the organism as well: these were the input, while the responses the organism made were the output.

The formulation of a hypothetico-deductive theory of learning involved a series of postulates which should eventually be tested by experimentation. The final formulation of the theory consisted of 18 postulates and 12 corollaries, stated in both mathematical and verbal forms. Hull's theory also includes intervening variables, constructs which are assumed but never really subject to experimental verification.

Hull's theory was systematic and generated a great deal of research. Hull insisted on well-controlled experiments and on the quantification of the resulting data.

R. W. LUNDIN

HUME, DAVID (1711–1776)

Hume studied at the university in Edinburgh. During his career he held a variety of posts: judge advocate, keeper of the Advocate's Library in Edinburgh, a staff member of the British embassy in Paris, and undersecretary of state in London. He never received a university appointment because his unorthodox religious views were unacceptable to university authorities in Scotland. His most important books for psychology were the *Treatise of human knowledge* and *An inquiry concerning human understanding* (1748), which was a condensed version of the *Treatise.*

As the third of the British empiricists, Hume conceded that all knowledge was experience, but rejected the belief of his predecessors John Locke and George Berkeley that there had to be human minds to receive these experiences. For Hume, all that existed were experiences. In his *Treatise* he wrote: "Mind is nothing but a bundle or collection of different perceptions unified by certain relations and suppos'd tho' falsely to be endowed with a perfect simplicity and identity." The belief that real objects existed was merely the result of our impressions (sensations), which tended to fit together. All Hume found was a flowing stream of impressions and ideas.

Like Locke and Berkeley, Hume was concerned with associations. He stated three principles of association: resemblance (similarity), contiguity (togetherness in space or time), and cause and effect. With regard to causality, Hume eventually realized that there was no way to understand that one thing caused another. Humans conceived this idea only because of association, so he ultimately reduced cause and effect to contiguity: one thing followed another. There were no experiences of

God. The idea that we existed as minds or personalities apart from experiences was an assumption that filled in the gaps when no impressions were known. The notion that our bodies actually existed was assumed only because impressions of the body came together.

Some philosophers and psychologists have considered Hume to be the supreme skeptic. Others have suggested that in doing away with the idea of a mind apart from experiences, Hume removed a dualism which had existed for centuries. However, in his subjectivism Hume was stressing the mental as opposed to the physical, which phenemonological psychology might appreciate but objective psychology would condemn.

R. W. LUNDIN

HUNT, J. McVICKER (1906–1991)

Although tagged an environmentalist, Hunt prefers to call himself an interactionist. The environmentalist label stems from his work *Intelligence and experience.* But Hunt is perhaps better known for the two-volume publication *Personality and behavior disorders* edited by him in 1944.

Hunt obtained the B.A. from the University of Nebraska before heading for Cornell University, where he was granted the Ph.D. in 1933. He spent a decade going from instructor to associate professor at Brown University (1936–1946), and a year or two at Teachers College of Columbia University and at New York University, before settling down at the University of Illinois, where he stayed from 1951 until his retirement in 1974. He was also affiliated with the Institute of Welfare Research of the Community Service Society in New York from 1944 to 1951. He was president of the American Psychological Association in 1952.

HUNT, THELMA (1903–1992)

Hunt has been most active in psychological testing, and secondarily in clinical psychology. Most of her life and psychological activities have been spent in the Washington, D.C., metropolitan area. She received the Ph.D. in psychology and the M.D. from George Washington University. She is a licensed psychologist and a licensed physician in the District of Columbia, and a diplomate in clinical psychology of the American Board of Professional Psychology.

Hunt considers her major career to have been academic. She taught full-time for 41 years at George Washington University, during 25 of which she headed the Psychology Department. During her academic career she wrote a textbook in psychological testing, and was coauthor of a textbook in abnormal psychology.

She has been active in organizations. In the American Psychological Association she was on the Council of Representatives for six years, was secretary of the Conference of State Psychological Associations, and conducted a Post-Doctoral Institute for the Clinical Division. She is an expresident of the District of Columbia Psychological Association. Since retirement from full-time academic work, she has been active in the International Personnel Management Association, over whose annual conference she recently presided. She is a member of their Advisory Committee on the Uniform Guidelines on Employee Selection.

Hunt is the author of a Social Intelligence Test, widely used in industrial selection and promotion, and of a series of Nursing Tests. Her research has been in the personnel psychology field, where she has developed tests to meet problems growing out of the Civil Rights Act and government regulatory and court measures relating to tests.

HUNTER, WALTER S. (1889–1953)

Hunter studied under the functionalists James Angell and Harvey Carr at the University of Chicago, receiving the Ph.D. there in 1912. After several academic appointments, he became head of the Psychology

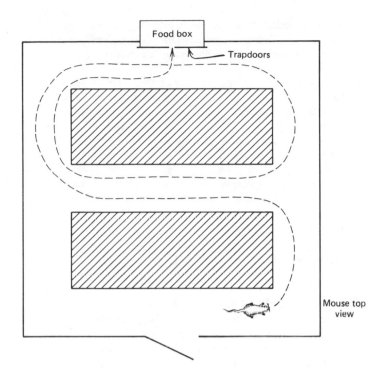

Figure 1. Hunter's figure 8 maze. Condition X: The mouse must take the path to be fed.

Department and director of the experimental laboratory at Brown University.

Like John Watson, Hunter abandoned the functionalists' ideas to join the new movement started by Watson called behaviorism. Like other behaviorists, Hunter deplored the use of any concepts which made reference to "mind" or "mental." Since the term "psychology" was derived from the Greek *psyche,* loosely defined as "soul," he suggested an alternative term for the new science, *anthroponomy.* "Anthro" meant man and "nomes" referred to the laws that govern human behavior. He believed that an objective, behavioristic approach to psychology should not continue with a subject matter imposed on it by philosophy. Despite much effort and argument, Hunter failed in his efforts and the term "psychology" remained.

As an experimental psychologist, Hunter invented the delayed reaction apparatus to study remembering in a variety of animal species. In this device, an animal first learned to discriminate between two doors, behind one of which there was food. The signal for the correct response was a light above the correct door. After the preliminary training, the light of the correct door was illuminated and then turned off. The animal was restrained for various periods of time, then released to see if it could make the correct response. If the choice was eventually correct, Hunter concluded that the animal had "remembered" the correct response. In many species, particularly dogs, he noted that during the period of delay before the animal was released, it would maintain a particular bodily posture which oriented it in the right direction.

He also developed a temporal maze (see Figure 1) which had no blind alleys but contained a continuous pathway in the shape of a rectangular 8 with eight square corners. The animals were required to travel around the pathways for a given number of times before food was given. He reported that they followed the pathway in a highly selective manner for the designated number of times before being rewarded. This did not appear to be trial-and-error learning.

R. W. LUNDIN

HUSSERL, EDMUND (1859–1938)

Husserl was the founder and most prominent exponent of a new philosophic movement, *phenomenology,* which found many followers, especially in Continental Europe, and greatly influenced both the philosophical and psychological thought of the twentieth century. When Husserl began his academic studies, his main interest lay in mathematics and the natural sciences. He studied in Leipzig, Berlin, and Vienna, where he received the Ph.D. in 1883. After serving briefly as an assistant in mathematics at the University of Berlin, he returned to Vienna to study philosophy under Franz Brentano.

Husserl's academic career began at the University of Halle in 1887, where he lectured for 14 years. Later he was professor at Göttingen and at Freiburg in Breisgau, where he died. He was active to the end in developing and improving his system. At the time of his death phenomenology had become a powerful movement, and Husserl had won recognition as one of the keenest intellects and most influential philosophers of the century. During his lifetime Husserl published six books, but left an enormous amount of manuscripts from which dozens of volumes have been published posthumously and still more are currently being prepared for publication. Husserl's first exposition of phenomenology appeared in a two-volume book *Logische Untersuchungen* (Logical Investigations), later revised and enlarged.

The point of departure of Husserl's phenomenology is two affirmations: (1) philosophical inquiry cannot begin with anything but with phenomena of consciousness, because they are the only givens accessible to us, the only material at our immediate disposal; (2) only phenomena of consciousness can reveal to us what things essentially are. Thus Husserl's phenomenology is principally a systematic and full exploration of consciousness. The phenomena of consciousness are numerous and manifold: things, persons, events, experiences, memories, feelings, moods, thoughts, images, fantasies, mental constructs, and the like. Phenomenology explores them through a method especially adapted for this purpose, known as the *phenomenological method.* This method became the keystone of Husserl's entire philosophical system. Through its use Husserl hoped to reform philosophy and to establish a rigorously scientific philosophy which could provide a firm basis for all other sciences.

The phenomenological method consists of examining whatever is found in consciousness—all the data or phenomena of consciousness. The basic prerequisite for the successful practice of the method is freeing oneself from any preconceptions or presuppositions. It is imperative that in the exploration of consciousness all biases, theories, beliefs, and habitual modes of thinking be suspended or "bracketed," that is, put between "brackets," as Husserl described it, using an expression familiar in algebra. The ultimate goal of the phenomenological method is to reach and grasp the essences of things appearing in consciousness.

Phenomenology has profoundly affected psychology, in both theory and practice, especially in Germany and Austria. Husserl's intent was to bridge the psychology of his day with phenomenology by developing a new and special psychological discipline which he called *phenomenological psychology*. Its goal was to study consciousness in its meaningful structure and function. Among the eminent psychologists influenced by Husserl's ideas were David Katz, August Messer, Karl Bühler, and Albert Michotte. European psychologists sympathetic to Husserl's conception of psychology, emigrating to the United States in the 1930s, introduced American psychologists to phenomenology and helped form the so-called Third Force in American psychology.

H. MISIAK

HUTT, MAX L. (1908–1985)

Hutt did his undergraduate work at the City College of New York, and his graduate training at both that school and Columbia University. He has been a college teacher of psychology, and of clinical psychology in particular. Beginning in 1928, when he taught courses in tests and measurements, psychodiagnosis, and scaling theory at the City College of New York, he has taught successively in the officers' course in clinical psychology for the Armed Forces during World War II, then at Columbia University, then at the University of Michigan; finally, after an interval of several years, he reentered teaching at the University of Detroit to help establish a doctoral program in clinical psychology. His early work, characteristic of the field of clinical psychology of that time, emphasized measurement and diagnosis. During his years at Michigan, he was director of the graduate program in clinical psychology and taught courses in psychotherapy, projective methods, and the relationships between diagnosis and therapy. Much of his time was spent in consultation with psychiatric hospitals and clinics, mental hygiene departments, school systems, and community clinics.

Hutt has authored or coauthored 17 books in psychology, including a general psychology text (*Psychology: the science of interpersonal behavior*) with Isaacson and Blum; an abnormal psychology text (*Patterns of abnormal psychology*) and a book on mental retardation (*The mentally retarded child*) with R. G. Gibby; a treatise on psychotherapy (*Psychosynthesis: Vital therapy*); and a clinical manual on the objective and projective uses of the Bender–Gestalt test (The *Hutt adaptation of the Bender–Gestalt test*). He is known best for his pioneering work in the use of perceptual-motoric phenomena for both diagnosis and psychotherapy, having published many research studies in this field. His approach to therapy is characterized by individual tailoring of the therapeutic method to the individual's unique personality and motivations. Role modeling is important in this approach. Hutt has also done significant work in developing training models and programs for clinical psychologists.

IKEDA, HIROSHI (1932–   )

Ikeda is best known as a psychometrician, a disseminator of test theory and practice in Japan. Ikeda received the bachelor's and master's degrees from the University of Tokyo, then continued studies at the University of Illinois as a Fulbright exchange student, receiving the Ph.D. in 1965.

As Ikeda felt that the most essential thing in psychological study is scientific data collection and measurement, and that Japanese psychology needs more systematic disciplines, he has devoted himself to promoting the scientific ideas of research, including computer application in psychology, statistical reasoning of data collection, multivariate analysis of educational data, and test construction under the psychometric theory.

Ikeda's professional career began at St. Paul's University in Tokyo in 1965. From 1979 to 1982 he was a professor of the Center for Research and Development of Educational Technology (CRADLE) of the Tokyo Institute of Technology, and is now doing research, lecturing, and counseling at St. Paul's (Rikkyo) University. As a visiting professor, he has lectured and consulted in statistical and psychometric methods at more than 10 universities and institutions, including the National Center for University Entrance Examinations and the National Center for Development of Broadcast Education. Ikeda is an author of more than 10 books on theory and methods of behavioral research and an editor of the *Japanese Journal of Behaviormetrics*, the *Japanese Journal of Psychology*, and the *Japanese Journal of Educational Psychology, as* well as other journals.

IRITANI, TOSHIO (1932–   )

Iritani is best known for his pioneer work in psycholinguistic research and theory in Japan, and as an integrator of various interdisciplinary fields which are mainly considered to be psychological. After receiving the bachelor's and master's degrees from Tokyo University of Education (now the University of Tsukuba), he continued his graduate studies at Clark University (where he got the Ph.D in 1962) and at Harvard University, MIT, and the University of Geneva.

In Japan, Iritani launched a new field of psycholinguistics, about which he published several books and many professional articles, the result of which is summarized in *An invitation to psycholinguistics*. In a second major thrust of publication, his *New social psychology* proposed a broad, integrative unification of social psychological phenomena in the areas of politics, economy, population, geography, and history. Later he published *A way of environmental psychology*, offering a psychologist's solution to the Japanese problems of environmental disruptions.

Iritani teaches and does research at Tokai University. He is formulating a model of universal human behavior based on the theory of causation of linguistic performance and human acquisition of knowledge by way of the description of environmental structures.

ITARD, JEAN MARIE-GASPARD (1775–1838)

Itard acquired a medical education through practice. He was a pioneer in the field of otology and author of a two-volume work on diseases of the ear. He was also a pioneer in the study of mental deficiency having attempted to train Victor the so-called wild boy of Averyron. While his efforts with Victor met with little success, he developed methods that proved useful in training retardates. For many years, Itard worked with deaf–mutes, and his studies provided a sound basis for modern methods of treating the deaf.

P. E. LICHTENSTEIN

IWAO, SUMIKO FURUYA (1935–   )

Iwao received the B.A. degree from Keio University in Tokyo, and the M.S. and Ph.D. (1962) from Yale University. She taught at Harvard Graduate School of Education, and has been a professor of social psychology at Keio University since 1963.

Her experiences as a foreign student led her to conduct cross-cultural studies of aesthetics; studies of the relationship between attitudes toward foreign countries and the amount of knowledge one has with respect to the country in question; and studies of foreign students in Japan and Japanese students in the United States.

Regarding the relationship between the knowledge about and attitude toward foreign people, Iwao's findings suggest that the level of knowledge plays a crucial role: if the amount of knowledge is small, one finds a linear positive relationship between knowledge and attitude, whereas if the amount of knowledge is large, the relationship is negative.

Iwao is best known for her comparative studies of the effects of U.S. and Japanese television violence upon children. According to her hypothesis, a description of pain and suffering resulting from violent acts are important as an inhibiting factor for young viewers, tending to keep those identifying with "good guys" from imitating the violent acts. If the violence is described as a means to an end without the resulting pain and suffering, it would facilitate learning the violent acts.

Iwao is a frequent contributor to mass media and has given lectures in the United States, Europe, and Australia. She serves on numerous government councils.

JAENSCH, ERICH R. (1883–1940)

Jaensch studied at Göttingen under G. E. Müller and Ebbinghaus. For most of his career he was at Marburg.

Jaensch showed his applied tendencies in his 1909 dissertation, in which his research showed that visual acuity was greater for near objects than for far objects. Two years later he published data on space or depth perception that indicated the perceived size of an object was not directly related to the size of the image on the retina.

A footnote to the understanding of how the ear operates is his *Duplicitätstheorie*, proposing that periodic vibration (tone) excites the cochlea, whereas aperiodic vibration (noise) excites some other organ, perhaps the vestibule. Intermediate sounds were said to excite both organs. Although now totally discredited, his analogy to the duplex nature of the retina was ingenious (he argued that noise is more primitive than tone, just as rods are more primitive than cones).

Jaensch is best known for his work on eidetic imagery, done in collaboration with his brother Walter. Originally thought to be a very strong visual afterimage of great clarity, eidetic images were commonly found among the young. From his research Jaensch proposed two biotypes: The B-type (later called "integrate") was a vivid memory image under voluntary control, and related to a hyperactive thyroid. The T-type (later called "disintegrative") was similar to an afterimage and not under voluntary control, and was related to underactivity of the parathyroid. The work of the Jaensch brothers was more important for the notion of relating the workings of personality to physiology than for the specific ideas.

C. S. PEYSER

JAHODA, MARIE (1907–   )

Jahoda received the D.Phil. (psychology) from the University of Vienna in 1933. From the beginning of her career she has concentrated on social psychological research outside the laboratory and on relevant methods, concepts, and theories. She directed a social research institute in Vienna (1933–1936), then lived in England (1937–1945) and the United States (1945–1958), and in 1958 returned to England.

Corresponding to this geographical mobility is the variety of topics she investigated. Two connecting threads are her efforts to prevent social psychology from splitting into a psychological and a sociological branch, and to engage in problem-centered rather than method-centered work. From her first book, *Marienthal* (with others), to her latest, *Employment and unemployment,* a dominant interest has been the study of the meaning of work in the twentieth century.

She regards her teaching—based on a broad conception of social psychology—first at New York University and then at Brunel University and the University of Sussex in England, as one of her most rewarding contributions to the field. She is a consultant to the Science Policy Research Unit at the University of Sussex.

Her books include *Research methods in human relations* (with Deutsch and Cook), *Current concepts of positive mental health, The education of technologists,* and *Freud and the dilemmas of psychology.*

JALOTA, SHYAM SWAROOP (1904–   )

Jalota is best known for his pioneering work for standardized tests of "general mental ability" in Hindi. He received his schooling at Phagwara (Kapurthala) and his college education at Lahore, then took postgraduate studies at Calcutta University. He has published experimental studies, but the hard realities of the paucity of laboratory equipment forced him toward extralaboratory fieldwork in the assessment of mental ability. Because of suspect age data, he has preferred the modal age-grade data for norms. He has stressed a background in the physical, biological, and social sciences for an adequate grasp of psychology.

Jalota and his research students in the universities at Banaras, Chandigarh, and Raipur have prepared verbal and nonverbal tests for all ages from the primary schools to college adults. He has helped in the study of social problems and has modified a number of statistical techniques.

Jalota has published a number of books for Indian students. Recently he formulated a covert hypothesis that "each human experience carries within it the active or latent seeds of contrary impulses." He holds that all social institutions are *ambivalent,* and that "when the authority of religious necessity for social regulation was weakened . . . then the prospects of biological and social utility were duly proclaimed as the unshakable bases for social regulations as well as of their sanctions" (*Patterns of social behaviour,* p. 145).

JAMES, WILLIAM (1842–1910)

An American philosopher and psychologist, James was educated in Europe, England, and America and who encouraged their intellectual independence. Frequent trips abroad made James a man of the world. Although he was supported and encouraged to pursue a scientific education, James suffered physical illnesses, indecision, and depression throughout his early years. Finally he earned his medical degree from Harvard in 1869 and took a teaching position there in 1872. In 1875–1876 James taught the first psychology course in an American university at Harvard. He was given funds for laboratory and demonstration equipment for the course in the same year that Wilhelm Wundt established his psychology laboratory in Leipzig: 1875.

After 12 years of work, in 1890 James published *The principles of psychology,* a major contribution to the field. Dissatisfied with his work, he decided that he had nothing else to offer psychology. He left the Harvard psychological laboratory and the course work to Hugo Munsterberg, and concentrated on philosophy for the remainder of his 20 years of life. In the 1890s James became America's leading philosopher.

James is considered America's greatest psychologist because of his brilliant clarity of scientific writing and his view of the human mind as functional, adaptive mental processes, in opposition to Wundt's structural analysis of consciousness into elements. The concept of functionalism in James's psychology became the central principle of American functional psychology: the study of living persons as they adapt to their environment.

James treated psychology as a natural, biological science. Mental processes he believed to be functional activities of living creatures attempting to adapt and maintain themselves in a world of nature. The function of consciousness was to guide persons toward adaptation for survival. James emphasized the nonrational aspects of human nature, in addition to the reasonable. He described mental life as always changing—a total experience that flows as a unit, a "stream of consciousness." His most famous theoretical contribution concerned emotions. He stated that the physical response of arousal preceded the appearance of emotion—that *because of* the bodily changes such as increased heart rate or muscle tension, the person experienced emotion. The example of this chain of events was "see the bear, run, and *then* feel afraid." A simultaneous discovery of this theory by the Danish physiologist Carl Lange led to its designation as the *James–Lange theory*.

James believed that mental and emotional activities should be studied as processes, and not as the static elements of consciousness being taught by the structural psychologists of that time. Because of the dynamic nature of his theories and views, James' psychology was named *functionalism*. With G. Stanley Hall and James M. Cattell, James anticipated the school of functional psychology at the University of Chicago under John Dewey and James Rowland Angell. James' *The principles of psychology* influenced thousands of students. He is one of the most important psychologists the United States has ever produced.

N. A. HAYNIE

JANET, PIERRE (1859–1947)

Janet received his doctor of letters from the University of Paris in 1889. Becoming a pupil of Jean Charcot, he worked in Charcot's neurological laboratory and clinic at Salpêtrière, the Parisian hospital for insane women. He took over as director of the laboratory from Charcot in 1890 and finished his degree in medicine while working there until 1894. Under Janet's direction the emphasis of the laboratory work changed from neurological to psychological. In 1895 Janet went to the Sorbonne, and from 1920 to 1936 he was at the Collège de France.

Janet was a systematic psychopathologist. Although he worked under Charcot, who was primarily a neurologist, Janet rejected the opinion that the hysteria of the patients at Salpêtrière was a physiological disorder. He classified hysteria as a mental disorder instead and his preferred treatment was hypnosis, which he used especially for the problems of memory impairment and fixed ideas. He developed a system of psychology and psychopathology which he called "psychologie de la conduite" (psychology of conduct or behavior). His chief effort at reporting this work was *The major symptoms of hysteria*.

A decrease in psychic energy was a central belief in Janet's explanation of mental disorders. He taught that a healthy personality was one that had a stable psychic energy level supporting an integrated system of ideas and emotions; in contrast, fluctuations in psychic energy and lowered mental tension caused insufficient energy to cope with problems, leading to neurosis. Hysteric patients had a weakness, characterized by exaggerated suggestibility, faulty memory, and fixed ideas. Hysterical personalities lacked integration: their mind could dissociate into conscious and unconscious processes, so that multiple personalities resulted. Janet believed that the fixed ideas of the hysteric narrowed conscious attention and forced unacceptable mental ideas into the unconscious realm, where they were converted into symbolic symptoms. This belief closely resembled Sigmund Freud's, and a controversy arose between the two about which of them first used the concept of the unconscious.

Janet wrote 15 other books and many articles. He published in the *Journal de la Psychologie*, which he founded with Georges Dumas in 1904, and of which Janet was editor until 1937.

N. A. HAYNIE

JANIS, IRVING LESTER (1918–1990)

Janis received the B.S. degree from the University of Chicago and the Ph.D. from Columbia University in 1948. During World War II he was a senior social scientist analyst with the Special War Policies Unit of the Department of State. In 1940 he joined the faculty of Yale University for a long tenure. He published *Air war and emotional stress* and *Communication and persuasion* in collaboration with Hovland and Kelley. Then followed *Personality and Persuasability* and *Victims of groupthink*.

According to the Janis–Feisrabend hypothesis, an argument is most effective when the pro side is advanced before the negative. In other experimental studies Janis demonstrated that a positive relationship exists between high persuasability and low self-esteem, also between persuasability and feelings of inadequacy. Finally, he demonstrated experimentally that hostile individuals are less susceptible to persuasion.

R. W. LUNDIN

JASPERS, KARL (1883–1969)

Germany, Jaspers received the M.D. degree at Heidelberg in 1909, and began his career as a psychiatrist. In *General psychopathology* (1913) he emphasized the need for a description of a patient's subjective experiences not only for proper diagnosis but for therapy as well. He came to hold a chair in philosophy at Heidelberg, then in 1949 became professor of philosophy at the University of Basel in Switzerland.

Jaspers and Martin Heidegger have been considered the leading figures in existential philosophy in the twentieth century. Jaspers' systematic philosophy was presented in his three-volume work *Philosophy*. In his existential approach, Jaspers distinguished three modes of being: being-there, being-oneself, and being-in-itself. Being-there referred to the objective, real world which we know through our observations. Being-oneself meant one's personal existence or an awareness of our self, our conflicts, desires, and expectations. Being-in-itself involved an ability to transcend the world and know other worlds.

In the existential tradition, Jaspers was concerned with major problems that humans must face: death, conflict, suffering, and anxiety. A person need not deal with these problems alone, but could communicate with others who also existed. This communication made existence possible. Further, from a philosophical point of view, communication among various systems of thought was also necessary, because no philosophical system in itself contained the entire truth.

R. W. LUNDIN

JASTROW, JOSEPH (1863–1944)

Jastrow came to the United States as a young man and received the Ph.D. at Johns Hopkins University in 1886. Historians consider this to be the first Ph.D. granted in psychology as such. While at Johns Hopkins, Jastrow was a colleague of G. Stanley Hall. In 1888 he went to the University of Wisconsin, where he established the first psychological laboratory. The remainder of his career was spent at Wisconsin until his retirement in 1927.

Jastrow's early work was in the field of psychophysics. An early paper published with C. S. Peirce described a new way to determine the difference limen (the point of just noticeable difference in discriminating a sensation). Previously, the difference limen had been defined as the point where judgments of correct responses were at the level of 50%, half right and half wrong. Jastrow argued that the point of 50% was mere chance, so the subject was really not able to make a proper discrimination. He suggested the criterion be raised to 75% correct—better than chance, but still a fine discrimination in which some error was made.

Jastrow is best known for his books which popularized psychology, including *The subconscious* and *The house that Freud built*. In *Fact and fable* he wrote on the occult, psychic research, mental telepathy, spiritualism, hypnosis, and dreams of the blind. Jastrow was at least in part a believer in psychic phenomena. In *The house that Freud built* he attacked Freudian theory, likening it to a house built of playing cards which could easily be demolished by appropriate arguments. Although Jastrow was not a behaviorist in any interpretation of the term, his book was one of the early attacks on Freudian theory and was followed by many from other authors in a more behavioristic tone.

R. W. LUNDIN

JENNINGS, HERBERT S. (1868–1947)

A particularly ingenious laboratory student of animal behavior, Jennings was responsible for overthrowing Jacques Loeb's simplistic local action tropism theory of behavior.

Jenning's diverse early academic career included a position as an assistant professor of botany and horticulture at Texas Agricultural and Mechanical College at age 21, without a bachelor's degree. Eventually he completed the Ph.D. at Harvard in 1896. He held a number of appointments, often in botany, before settling at Johns Hopkins University in zoology. He was the mentor of Karl Lashley.

Jenning's work was of particular importance to psychology in two areas. In the first, he used ingenious techniques, including a side-looking microscope, to demonstrate that the local action theory of tropisms was not valid. Tropism theory, one of the attempts to find a true "atom" of behavior, held that behavior is based on invariable reactions to external behavior. Loeb's local action theory had this reaction occurring between receptors and muscles in the area of the body exposed to the external stimulus; no central processes were involved.

Very simple reactions of this sort that Loeb found in metazoa were then extrapolated into an explanation for complex behavior in higher organisms. Jennings devastated this theory by demonstrating that even the simpler protozoa did not conform to Loeb's model. This work is described in his *Behavior of the lower organisms*.

Jennings also demonstrated mutations, the inheritance of mutations, and the fact that mutations were likely to involve very small changes in the organism. Charles Darwin, with no knowledge of genetics or mutation, was unable to describe the source of the variation necessary to his theory of natural selection, or its inheritance; he was forced to the unsupported hypothesis of pangenesis. Jennings' work filled this important gap.

T. KEITH-LUCAS

JENSEN, ARTHUR R. (1923–   )

An educational psychologist, Jensen was educated at the University of California, Berkeley, and at Teachers College of Columbia University. After completing a clinical internship at the University of Maryland's Psychiatric Institute and a two-year postdoctoral research fellowship at the University of London's Institute of Psychiatry under Hans J. Eysenck, in 1958 he joined the faculty of the University of California, Berkeley, as professor of educational psychology and research psychologist at the Institute of Human Learning.

After a decade of research on classical problems in verbal learning, particularly serial role learning, Jensen turned to the study of differential psychology, especially the nature and causes of individual, cultural, and racial group differences in scholastic performance. When he argued in "How Much Can We Boost IQ and Scholastic Achievement?" that genetic, as well as environmental and cultural, factors should be considered for understanding not only individual differences, but also social class and racial differences in intelligence and scholastic performance, there arose a storm of protest from many educators and social scientists. The hypothesis that both individual and racial differences in abilities

are in part a product of the evolutionary process and have a genetic basis came to be termed "jensenism"—often pejoratively. Although Jensen's research was at first misrepresented and denounced by the popular media and even by some social scientists, his research and voluminous writings in this field have since commanded the serious consideration of many scientists and educators. Jensen has explicated his position in this controversy in a series of books: *Genetics and education, Educability and group differences, Educational differences, Bias in mental testing* and *Straight talk about mental tests*.

JING, QICHENG (1926–   )

Jing received the B.Ed. and M.A. degrees at Fu Jen University, China. In 1950, he joined the Institute of Psychology of Chinese Academy of Sciences, later became the institute's deputy director and then became chairman of its Academic Committee. Jing was president of the Chinese Psychological Society. He was adjunct professor at Peking University, University of Illinois at Champaign–Urbana, and several other universities. He was a visiting scholar at University of Michigan; distinguished visitor to La Trobe University, Australia (1985); Henry Luce fellow at the University of Chicago; fellow at Center for Advanced Study in the Behavioral Sciences; and member of executive committee of International Union of Psychological Science.

Jing has published in the fields of systems of psychology, visual performance, visual perception, and color measurement. His studies in perception of size and distance are well known in China. His books *Colorimetry* and *Human vision* were the first books in visual science in China. He also has published studies of psychological development of Chinese only children. His other publications include *Theoretical foundation of structuralism of Wundt and Titchener, Introduction to psychology, Contemporary trends in the development of psychology, Concise encyclopedia of psychology,* and *Chinese encyclopedia· Psychology*.

Jing was one of the first psychologists to have visited the West from mainland China in three decades since the founding of the People's Republic of China in 1949. He devoted much effort in establishing exchanges between Chinese psychology and Western psychlogy, he arranged psychologists from Western countries to lecture in China, and Chinese students and psychologists to study and do research abroad.

JOHN, ERWIN R. (1924–   )

John received his degrees from the University of Chicago, the B.S. and the Ph.D. in 1954. John then became a research associate in physiology at the University of Rochester, where he eventually became director of the center for brain research. His present position as director of the brain research laboratory at New York Medical College began in 1964.

John is known for his material theory of memory. He hypothesized a statistical configuration theory of learning based on Lashley's conclusions. John argued for mass action rather than learning centers in the brain. Learning is explained by averaging neuronal activity distributed throughout the brain. Hence learning and memory are not localized functions in delimited centers of the brain.

JONES, MARY COVER (1896–1987)

Jones was an undergraduate at Vassar and received the Ph.D. from Columbia. Most of her career was spent at the Institute of Human Development of the University of California, Berkeley. Much of her later work on longitudinal studies of development was in collaboration with her husband, Harold E. Jones.

Her name is most prominent, however, as the first researcher to remove a fear in a child, the case of Peter. On a weekend trip to New York during her last semester at Vassar, she attended a lecture by

John Watson in which he discussed and showed movies of the fear conditioning of Little Albert. By the time Jones became a graduate student at Columbia, Watson had been expelled by Johns Hopkins for his sensationally publicized divorce and was working with the J. Walter Thompson Advertising Agency in New York. Since Jones had been a classmate and friend of his second wife, Rosalie Raynor Watson, Jones was able to obtain Watson's advice on most Saturday afternoons throughout the project. The therapeutic experiments were carried on in the children's home where, as it happened, Jones lived with her husband and daughter. The project ended with the article, "A laboratory study of fear."

Since a single case study was unacceptable as a dissertation, Jones extended Watson's studies of developmental activities to a larger and more representative sample. Her comparison of observations of 300 normal babies was accepted. In 1936, with Barbara Burks, she published an extended monograph on the topic.

JUDD, CHARLES H. (1873–1946)

Judd received his early education in that country. Upon coming to the United States, he entered Wesleyan University and graduated in 1894. He then went to Leipzig to receive the Ph.D. under Wilhelm Wundt two years later. He was one of the first generation of American psychologists to study under Wundt. In his *Autobiography* he wrote glowingly of Wundt, his teaching, and his laboratory. Upon his return to America, Judd translated Wundt's *Principles of psychology* into English. In 1907 he became director of the psychological laboratory at Yale, taking over from G. T. Ladd. Two years later he was appointed dean of the School of Education at the University of Chicago. There, as an educational and social psychologist he came under the influence of the Chicago school of functionalism. In his textbook *Psychology* (1907) he stressed motor activity (behavior), which he considered to have a biological basis.

In *Genetic psychology for teachers* Judd discussed how learning to read and write was a result of social inheritance. He studied the process of reading by photographing eye movements. In *Psychological analysis of the fundamentals of arithmetic* he described how number consciousness was very much a function of reasoning and other high mental processes.

His *Psychology of social institutions* stressed the thesis that collective intellectual efforts have brought into existence such things as tools, numbers, language, and government, which never could have been created by any single individual. The products of collective efforts became sufficient causes for new kinds of mental activity.

R. W. LUNDIN

JUNG, CARL (1875–1961)

Jung was a Swiss psychoanalyst and the founder of analytical psychology. Born and raised in Switzerland in an unhappy family, he learned early to depend upon his own inner resources for guidance and encouragement. He graduated in 1900 with a medical degree from the University of Basel. He was appointed to the University of Zurich psychiatric clinic to work under Eugen Bleuler, noted for his interest in schizophrenia. Jung also studied with Pierre Janet, the French clinical psychologist known for his work in hysteria and multiple personality. In 1905 Jung was a lecturer in psychiatry at the University of Basel, but after several years he resigned to concentrate on private practice, research, and writing. From 1932 to 1942 he was professor at the Federal Polytechnical University of Zurich. Illness forced his resignation; his last years were spent in writing and publishing books about analytic psychology.

Jung read Sigmund Freud's *The interpretation of dreams* in 1900 and met Freud in 1907. In 1909 he accompanied Freud to Clark University in America, at which they both delivered lectures. In 1911 Jung became president of the International Psychoanalytic Association with Freud's complete endorsement. However, Jung's interpretations and theories of psychoanalysis, the unconscious, and the libido differed from Freud's. After Jung published *Psychology of the unconscious,* dissent and disagreement grew between him and Freud, and in 1914 their relationship ended. Thereafter, Jung's theory and practice was known as analytical psychology.

In 1913 Jung suffered an inner turmoil that lasted for about three years. Like Freud, he used self-analysis through dream interpretations to resolve his emotional distress. It was a time of creativity and growth, leading to Jung's unique approach to personality theory. Jung came to appreciate the myths and symbols of humankind throughout the centuries. He made several field trips in the 1920s to study preliterate peoples in Africa and the southwestern United States, their myths, folkways, religions, and mores.

Jung's basic difference from Freud's psychoanalytic theory concerned the libido: Freud insisted upon its sexual energy, whereas Jung regarded it as a generalized life energy. A second difference was with Freud's deterministic view of the influences of childhood on the personality. Jung believed that personality can change later in life and is shaped by future goals and aspirations.

Jung's personality system included three levels of the *psyche,* or mind: (1) the conscious or *ego;* (2) the *personal unconscious:* forgotten and repressed experiences sometimes formed into complexes; and (3) the deeper *collective unconscious,* containing the cumulative experiences of previous generations, including animal heritage. The collective or transpersonal unconscious forms the basis of personality and is its most powerful influence. It is a storehouse of universal evolutionary and latent memory traces inherited from man's ancestral past.

The components of the collective unconscious Jung called *archetypes.* There are numerous archetypes including energy, the hero, the earth mother, death, birth and rebirth, unity, the child, God, and demon. Some archtypes are identified as separate systems with the personality: the *persona* or masked "public" personality; the *anima* and *animus* or bisexual characteristics; the *shadow* or animal-like part of human nature; and the *self* which, composed of all parts of the unconscious, strives for unity and equilibrium as expressed in the symbol of the circle, the mandala. The self attempts to achieve integration, self-actualization, and harmony of the personality.

Jung is probably best known for his descriptions of the orientations of the personality, *extraversion* and *introversion,* published in *Psychological types* (1921). He also identified four psychological functions: thinking and feeling, sensing and intuiting. Research has been generated about these dimensions of personality, although scientific psychology has ignored Jung's work.

Jung has been influential and inspirational to other disciplines, art, literature, film making, religion, anthropology, and history. He published prolifically, but many of his works did not appear in English until after 1965. Only a few days before his death, Jung finished his own chapter and the drafts of his disciples' chapters for *Man and his symbols,* a book that has popularized and explained Jung's use of dream analysis and his theories of universal symbolic representations of man's deeper nature.

N. A. HAYNIE

KAGAN, JEROME (1929–   )

Kagan received the B.S. from Rutgers University and a Ph.D. (1954) from Yale University. His first position was in the department of psychology at Ohio State University. Because of the Korean War, he was drafted into the army in the spring of 1955 and served until January 1957. In early 1957 he went to the Fels Research Institute in Yellow Springs, Ohio, as a senior psychologist to conduct the analyses of the data gathered on the longitudinal sample that was an essential part of the Fels program. The product of that work was published with Howard Moss in 1962 in *Birth to maturity*. After serving as chairman of the department of psychology at Fels, Kagan went to Harvard in 1964 as a professor of psychology and has remained there ever since.

Kagan's research has been on varied aspects of the development of children, including variation in the cognitive styles called reflectivity and impulsivity; the maturation of memory, self-awareness, and moral sense over the first 2 yr of life; the effect of day care on young infants; and the influence of temperament on children's behavior. He has authored many books and articles, including *Change and continuity in infancy, Infancy, The nature of the child,* and *Unstable ideas*. He has received distinguished scientist awards from the American Psychological Association and the Society for Research in Child Development, the Kenneth Craik Award from St. John's College, Cambridge University, the Wilbur Cross Medal from Yale University, and is a member of the Institute of Medicine of the National Academy of Sciences.

KAMIYA, JOE (1925–   )

A biofeedback specialist, Kamiya earned all his degrees from the University of California at Berkeley: the B.A., the M.A., and the Ph.D. in 1954. From 1951 to 1953 he served there as a research assistant then left for the University of Chicago, where he was a faculty member from 1951 to 1960. Raymond Corsini was his first Ph.D. candidate there.

Kamiya's career then began at the Langley–Porter Neuropsychiatric Institute of the University of California, where he specialized in trained, self-controlled psychophysiological states. He is one of the pioneers of biological control by feedback and has delved deep into sleep and dream research. His current research, which has earned him distinction, involves the psychophysiology of consciousness and heightened awareness; he directs a psychophysiology of consciousness laboratory. He is in the forefront of research in altered states of consciousness and transpersonal consciousness.

KANEKO, HIROSHI (1909–   )

Graduating from Tokyo University, Kaneko entered the Japanese Navy's Technical Research Institute in 1932, doing pioneering work in aptitude testing and training. By 1945 he had under his direction most of the men who would dominate postwar psychology and applied psychology in Japan.

With the Labor Party ministry of 1946–1948, Kaneko did social surveys on the new trade union movement, then became director of the National Personnel Authority's Efficiency Bureau (1948–1953). As professor at Hiroshima National University (1953–1959) and at Waseda University (1959–1971), he taught and guided graduate research in the new fields of social and industrial psychology, and spent 1955–1956 at the University of Michigan's Institute of Social Research as a Fulbright scholar. At Waseda's Institute of Industrial Productivity Research, he guided pure research and consultancy studies for numerous corporations, developing and disseminating the concepts and methods of modern industrial and management psychology.

In 1946 Kaneko and Minoru Makita founded the Public Opinion Association (Yoron-Kyōkai), Japan's first Gallup-type organization. In 1959 Kaneko initiated the Marketing Center, one of Japan's first scientific market survey organizations. From 1971 to 1979 he served as director of the newly established National Institute of Vocational Research, building an organization doing pioneer work in the increasingly im-

portant areas of worker retraining, rehabilitation, lifetime education, and research on aging.

Kaneko has had numerous publications. For many years he was a member of the executive boards of the Japanese Psychological Association and the Japan Association of Applied Psychology.

KANEKO, TAKAYOSHI (1928–   )

Kaneko is a professor at the University of Tsukuba in Tsukuba Science City, Japan. Primarily an experimental psychologist in vision, he was born and educated in Tokyo, receiving the B.A. He studied in the United States at the universities of Texas and Missouri, and from the latter received the M.A., the thesis being on photic driving of brain waves. He earned the Ph.D. in 1963 in Tokyo with research on psychophysics of colorimetry. Part of his theory is summarized in D. B. Judd's note in *Adaptation level theory* (M. H. Appley, 1971). Kaneko has been influenced by the late Torao Obonai, a leading Japanese psychologist.

Kaneko has translated into Japanese works such works as Gregory's *Intelligent eye*, Arbib's *Metaphorical brain*, Dondis' *A primer of visual literacy*, and Sokolov's *Perception and conditioned reflex* (Russian edition). He is on the editorial board of *Japanese Psychological Research* (an English-language journal) and the *Japanese Journal of Psychology*. He presently sits on the Executive Committee of the Japanese Psychological Association and also is a voting representative of Japan for the International Union of Psychological Science.

KANT, IMMANUEL (1724–1804)

Educated at Königsberg, Kant spent most of his career as a professor of philosophy there. One of the most influential philosophers of the eighteenth century, he dominated philosophy for generations thereafter. His *Critique of pure reason* (1781) and his *Anthroponomy* (1798) contain what implications his philosophy had for psychology.

Kant represented the viewpoint of the German rational philosophers. He had read the British empiricists—in particular David Hume—and agreed that known objects were phenomena of consciousness and not realities independent of the mind. He disagreed with the empiricist argument that knowledge amounted to nothing more than mere bundles of sensation. For Kant, knowledge was characterized by *a priori* principles. Consciousness of time and extension in space were real enough, but not the result of mere bodily sensations. The way humans perceived the world was already predetermined. Thus Kant advanced a nativistic conception of space perception.

Kant rejected the mind as mental substance. Mental processes could not be measured, since they had only the dimension of time and not space. Psychology could never be an experimental science. He did not reject a conception of mind as such, but considered it a means whereby concepts could be known. The mind ordered perceptual phenomena through innate principles. The mind was active and took the material from the world and ordered it into conceptual phenomena. "Apperception" was the term Kant used for the mind's perceiving, assimilating, and interpreting new experiences. This was all part of the nativism which stressed certain inborn ways of knowing and perceiving that which was true and not dependent only on sensations.

The presupposition that perceptions could not be broken down into divisible forms became a basic premise of Gestalt psychology of the twentieth century. Kant's nativism also was taken up by Gestalt psychologists in what they referred to as the "primitive organization of experience." This meant that we tend to perceive things in natural ways not dependent on previous experience or learning. This is related also to Noam Chomsky's linguistic theory. Other reflections of nativism in perception are found in the work of the animal ethologists, and in experiments with perception of infants which propose that certain perceptions of depth are innate.

R. W. LUNDIN

KANTOR, JACOB R. (1888–1984)

Kantor received the Ph.D. at the University of Chicago in 1917. After teaching at Chicago and the University of Minnesota, in 1920 he went to Indiana University, where he remained until his retirement in 1959.

Kantor proposed a systematic psychology called interbehaviorism. It shares with the behavioristic tradition a denial of mind or mental activity in favor of an objective approach. The first statement of his position appeared in his two-volume *Principles of psychology*. The subject matter of psychology consists of the interactions of an organism with stimulus objects. Both the responding organism and the stimulus object are of equal importance. These interactions constitute a series of behavior segments and are a function of the interbehavioral history of the organism, as well as setting factors which constitute the background against which the interactions take place. Furthermore, for interactions to take place there must be a medium of contact. For example, it would be impossible to perceive a visual object in the absence of light.

Kantor believed that psychology is a science with its own subject matter and should not be considered a branch of biology, although biological factors may participate in psychological interactions. In the framework of this paradigm, Kantor explains psychological activity such as feelings, emotion, reasoning, learning, memory, and various kinds of implicit behavior.

Besides the construction of his systematic psychology, Kantor was a historian of psychology. His two-volume *Scientific evolution of psychology* is one of the most carefully researched works in the field of the history of psychology. Kantor has also written in the areas of social psychology, physiological psychology, the philosophy of science, the logic of psychology, and linguistics.

KASLOW, FLORENCE W.

Kaslow received the A.B. from Temple University, the M.A. from Ohio State University, and the Ph.D. from Bryn Mawr College (1969). She is director of Florida Couples and Family Institute, West Palm Beach, Florida, and president of Kaslow Associates, P.A. She is a visiting professor of medical psychology in psychiatry at Duke University and of psychology at Florida Institute of Technology in Melbourne.

She was the recipient of the Family Psychologist of the Year Award from the Division of Family Psychology (#43) of American Psychological Association (1985), of APA's Distinguished Contribution to Applied Psychology Award (1989), and of American Association for Marriage and Family Therapy Award for Significant Contribution to the Field of Marital and Family Therapy (1991). Kaslow was elected to the National Academies of Practice as a Distinguished Psychologist in 1987, served as first president of the International Family Therapy Association (1987–1990), and as president of APA's Division of Family Psychology (1987).

She has authored or edited 12 books, more than 110 articles, and 30 book chapters. She is a former editor of *Journal of Marital and Family Therapy* and serves as an editorial board member of over a dozen American and foreign journals. Kaslow's work is eclectic in that she builds on a wide range of theoretical and substantive perspectives. This is the basis of her comprehensive diaclectic model, which incorporates individual, marital, and family therapies separately or sequentially, depending on what she believes constitutes the treatment of choice. Her major contributions have been in family, clinical, and forensic psychology; she holds diplomates in each of these specialties from ABPP.

Kaslow is listed in *Who's Who in America* and other biographical references. She guest lectures throughout the world.

KATONA, GEORGE (1901–1981)

Katona enrolled at the University of Budapest in 1918 to study law, but political upheavals caused him to move to Göttingen, Germany. There he studied psychology under Georg Elias Müller and received the Ph.D. in 1921. His subsequent work in a Frankfort bank led him to study of economics. He moved to Berlin where, in addition to writing for the *German Economist*, he studied Gestalt psychology and was the Berlin correspondent for the *Wall Street Journal*. Emigrating to the United States after 1933, Katona continued his work on behavioral economics, working for a time as an investment counselor. In 1942, he published *War without inflation*. He later joined Rensis Likert in conducting economic surveys for the Department of Agriculture. Following World War II he moved to the University of Michigan to help found the Survey Research Center, and served there as professor of both psychology and economics until he retired from teaching in 1972.

Katona's major contributions are his studies of consumer expectations and behavior found in such works as *Aspirations and affluence* (with B. Strumpel and E. Zahn), *A new economic era*, and *Essays on behavioral economics*.

B. OZAKI

KATZ, DAVID (1884–1953)

Inspired by Husserl's phenomenology, Katz was the first psychologist who systematically and effectively used both the experimental and the phenomenological methods in the investigation of perception and other psychological problems. He received the Ph.D. at Göttingen University in 1906 and remained there until 1919 as Georg E. Müller's assistant. He became a professor in Rostock, but left this post in 1933 and went to England, and later to Sweden when a professorship was offered him in Stockholm. Twice he was a visiting professor in the United States, in 1929 and 1950.

Katz made numerous original contributions to the understanding of touch, taste, proprioception, and particularly color perception. His explorations of the phenomenology of color perception, described in his highly successful book, *The world of colour*, revealed several new and diverse phenomena extending beyond the basic parameters of color, such as hue, brightness, and saturation. The same color, Katz discovered, can appear to the viewer in different modes such as surface or film color, or as bulky, shiny, transparent, or luminous. His findings demonstrated the influence of the total visual field on color perception. Katz also studied problems of child psychology, animal behavior, teaching, hunger, appetite, and drug effects.

The investigative approach used by Katz was adopted in some European psychological laboratories and stimulated much research. Katz's approach and theoretical views were close to those of the Gestalt school, whose appraisal Katz presented in his book *Gestalt psychology*. In its preface he declared that he did not agree with this school on all matters and did not believe that all psychological facts are in accord with the Gestalt viewpoint.

H. MISIAK

KEFIR, NIRA (1937–   )

Kefir received her undergraduate education from Bal Illan University and the Ph.D. from the Sorbonne in Paris.

Her major contribution is the concept of personality priorities, based on the notion that people's personalities are primarily functions of attempts to avoid "impasses" based on primitive early-life experiences occurring prior to stream-of-consciousness memory. Consequently, as one grows older one appears to be developing control over self and others, whereas in actuality one is symbolically escaping from fear of helplessness in terms of specific impasses, such as the fear of being ridiculed.

In 1970 Kefir became head of the sociotherapeutic clinic of the Alfred Adler Institute of Tel Aviv. She presented her theory for the first time in Israel in 1971. In 1973, together with the Israeli Ministry of Defense, she developed a community volunteer network to assist war-bereaved parents. She has developed a complex three-year system of psychotherapy and has published a system of typology (Kefir & Corsini). Kefir has also been active in teaching, demonstrating her impasse-priority therapy in Israel, Europe, and the United States.

KELLER, FRED S. (1899–   )

Keller received the B.S. from Tufts College, the M.A. and Ph.D. (1931) from Harvard University. He taught psychology at Colgate University from 1931 to 1938, and at Columbia University from 1938 to 1964, when he became professor emeritus. On leave from Columbia in 1961, he taught at the University of São Paulo, in Brazil. In 1964, he helped to organize the psychology department at the new University of Brasília. He spent the next 3 yr at Arizona State University, and in 1968, he went to Western Michigan University for 5 yr, which were interrupted by short appointments at Texas Christian University and Colorado State. From 1974 to 1976 he was at Georgetown University's Center for Personalized Instruction. In 1990 he became an adjunct research professor at the University of North Carolina in Chapel Hill.

His contributions to psychology include *Principles of psychology* (with W. N. Schoenfeld), *The definition of psychology, learning (reinforcement theory), Summers and sabbaticals, Pedagogue's progress,* and *The Keller plan handbook: PSI* (with J. G. Sherman). He has published approximately 80 papers on learning, training, or education.

His honors included the Certificate of Merit from President Truman in 1948; several honorary degrees (Long Island University, Colgate University, Western Michigan University, and the University of Brasília) and awards from various organizations in the United States and abroad (Brazil, Canada, China/Taiwan, Mexico, Peru, and Venezuela).

KELLEY, HAROLD H. (1921–   )

Kelley received the B.A. and M.A. in psychology from the University of California at Berkeley, and, after serving in the Aviation Psychology Program, completed the Ph.D. (1948) in group psychology at the Research Center for Group Dynamics, MIT. He then taught and conducted research at the University of Michigan (1948–1950), Yale University (1950–1955), the University of Minnesota (1955–1961), and finally, at the University of California at Los Angeles, from which he retired in 1991.

Kelley's major contributions, all in social psychology, have been to the theory of small groups (via a long collaboration with John Thibaut, beginning with *The social psychology of groups*, 1959), to attribution theory dealing with the perception of causes of behavior, and to the study of close relationships. He has served as president of the Division of Personality and Social Psychology of APA (1965), of the Western Psychological Association (1969), and of the International Society for the Study of Personal Relationships (1990). His awards include the Distinguished Scientific Contribution Award from the American Psychological Association (1971), the Distinguished Senior Scientist Award from the Society for Experimental Social Psychology (1981), and the

Kurt Lewin Memorial Award from the Society for the Psychological Study of Social Issues (1990). He is a member of the National Academy of Sciences and the American Academy of Arts and Sciences.

KELLOGG, WINTHROP N. (1898–1972)

Kellogg, after taking the A.B. at Indiana University, received the Ph.D. in 1929 from Columbia University with a thesis comparing the psychophysical methods. He served on the faculties of Columbia, Indiana, and Florida State universities and published several texts.

Kellogg's early work involved visual and auditory perception; at Indiana University he was director of the Conditioning Laboratory. He is better known for the study, done jointly with his wife Luella, published as *The ape and child.* When their son Donald was 10 months old, they obtained a $7\frac{1}{2}$-month-old female chimpanzee, Gua, who was raised as a sibling for nine months. Despite their attempt at equal treatment, the chimpanzee was initially superior, particularly in physical growth and sensory reactions. But Donald caught up with and surpassed Gua before the end of the study.

Later Kellogg undertook the study of porpoises (bottle-nosed dolphins), analyzing their emission of sound for echo-ranging, as well as the decoding of the information received for navigation and orientation. His research has implications for marine navigation and sonar.

C. S. PEYSER

KELLY, LOWELL E. (1905–1986)

Kelly received the B.S. degree from Purdue University, the M.A. from Colorado Northern University and the Ph.D. from Stanford. He researched and published in a wide variety of areas. He taught at the University of Hawaii (1930–1932) and at the University of Connecticut (1933–1939). In 1939 he went back to Purdue to establish its psychological clinic. He served on active duty in the navy from 1942 to 1946 and then went to the University of Michigan with primary responsibility for developing its program in clinical psychology. There he instituted a program to develop the validity of a wide range of assesment procedures for selecting students for the clinical program and, later, one for selecting medical students.

He instituted a longitudinal study of 300 engaged couples that lasted from 1939 to 1980. The investigation involved blood typing, anthropological measures, psychological tests, acquisition ratings, and a biographical questionnaire. One of the conclusions was that marital compatibility was only a small function of sex and social attributes.

Throughout his career he researched and wrote in other areas of psychology such as synesthesia, graphology, pharmacology, and apparent movement. He received the Gold Medal Award from the American Psychological Foundation in 1986.

R. W. LUNDIN

KELLY, GEORGE A. (1905–1967)

Kelly attended four different colleges (and spent an exchange year at Edinburgh), receiving the Ph.D. from the State University of Iowa in 1931. He spent most of his career building the clinical psychology program at Ohio State University with the assistance of Julian Rotter.

Kelly's theory of *personal constructs* is a broad, inclusive personality theory based upon the notion that each individual attempts to anticipate and control his or her environment. Behavior is conceptualized as a question. Will mother spank me if I have a piece of cake as a snack, or can I talk her into just a scolding? Is Jeff as nice as he seems, or does he have a mean streak? Only by experiencing the world, can individuals obtain answers which become their personal constructs, their view of the world.

Personal constructs specific to the individual and created by the individual can be exemplified by the following: A spanking is (1) to the parent, a corrective action that benefits the child; (2) to the child, an unfortunate part of a random world that must be tolerated; (3) to a social worker, a cruel and ineffective punishment; (4) to a preacher, an extension of divine judgment to a sinful earth. Each point of view, each personal construct, approximates truth. To understand the world, one must be able to understand the points of view of others. Set down in a formal postulate with 11 corollaries in his 1955 book, Kelly's theory is difficult to classify and contrast with other views. Sechrest (1977) describes it as having lots of second cousins, but no siblings.

Kelly always sought to develop a therapeutic technique, but had very little contact with severe pathology. Although known for his innovative fixed-role therapy (the client "tries on" a role much as one tries on new clothing at the store), Kelly used that technique only for a few selected clients. In his counseling, he was as flexible and varied in technique as was Carl Jung.

C. S. Peyser

KENDLER, HOWARD H. (1919–   )

Kendler obtained the B.A. from Brooklyn College and the M.A. and Ph.D. (1943) from the University of Iowa. He served in the U.S. Army during World War II as chief clinical psychologist at Walter Reed General Hospital. He was an assistnat professor at the University of Colorado 1946–1948. In 1951, he became professor of psychology and chairman of the department of psychology at the New York University College. He moved to the University of California at Santa Barabara in 1963, retiring as professor emeritus in 1989.

Kendler's major contributions have been in the analysis of the interaction between motivational and reward conditions in animal learning (the latent learning controversy); in the formulation and testing, with Tracy S. Kendler, of a comparative-developmental theory of discrimination and conceptual learning, involving both associative and mediational (cognitive) processes; and in a methodological–historical analyses of systematic approaches in psychology. Kendler has published three major books (*Basic psychology, psychology: A science in conflict,* and *Historical foundations of modern psychology*), more than 125 journal articles, and co-edited (with Janet T. Spence) a memorial volume to Kenneth W. Spence.

Kendler was elected to the Society of Experimental Psychology, was a fellow at the Center for Advanced Studies in the Behavioral Sciences (1969–1970), and honored as a distinguished graduate of the department of psychology of the University of Iowa. He was elected chairman of the Governing Board of the Psychonomic Society (1968–1969), president of the Western Psychological Association (1970–1971), and president of the Division of Experimental Psychology (1964–1965), and Division of General Psychology (1967–1968) of the American Psychological Association.

KEREKJARTO, MARGIT (1930–   )

Kerekjarto received her schooling in Hungary and Germany. Her postgraduate studies were undertaken in Hamburg. She worked at the Psychology Institute and Medical School before becoming director of the Department of Medical Psychology at the University of Hamburg in 1973.

Kerekjarto's major research work has been in neuropsychology (differential diagnosis of brain damage and studies of multiple sclerosis), psychopharmacology (comparison of the differential influences on the effects of drugs in patients, effects of tranquilizers and stimulants on depressives and nondepressives), test construction (the Hamburg depression scale and a symptom check list similar to the Cornell Medical Index), psychosomatic studies (particularly in bronchial asthma, allergies, immunology, and personality assessment), and psychooncology (evaluation of supportive psychotherapies with seriously ill patients). She also developed the first major curriculum work in medical psychology education for Germany.

She is a member of the International Collegium of Neuropsychopharmacology and president of the German Society for Medical Psychology. Her major publications include *Der Asthmatiker* (with A. Jores) and "The influence of experimenters on drug effects in normal subjects."

KIERKEGAARD, SOREN A. (1813–1855)

A major influence on Christian, non-Christian, and atheistic existentialists in Europe and North America in the twentieth century, Kierkegaard was little known outside Scandinavia prior to this century, because he wrote in Danish. Family circumstances afflicted him with depression characterized by morbid dejection and self-reproach, although he learned early to mask his melancholy from others. Engaged to be married, he broke it off sacrificially, fearing lest his inner conflicts destroy his fiancée.

Writing prolifically in his last 12 years of life, simultaneously publishing religious, philosophical, psychological texts and even books on humor, he presented consistent biographical issues as an existential thinker seeking to understand life by relating everything to—rather than abstracting principles from—one's own situation. His first book, *Either/or,* focused on the choice between freedom and bondage, a theme found throughout his writings. Insisting that both responsibility and determinism are intertwined in humans, he anticipated depth psychology, depersonalization, and the crisis of the will. For while the self includes many factors not willed or self-created, the self is still not a machine. He rejected the skepticism and detached spectatorship of determinism and dramatized the gross judgmentalism and hopeless despair fostered by moral and ethical responsibility as a universal goal. He understood the peculiar modern malaise of "spiritlessness": the self-alienation or estrangement in which authentic selfhood remains unrealized and seems unrealizable. The cure for this condition is a leap in trust; faith that a "new life" is possible through a gracious God. The new life or authentic selfhood is a journey of individuation and differentiation by a person away from a thoroughgoing identification with one's sociocultural milieu. The normative structure for this selfhood to be realized is embodied and disclosed in the central figure of Christianity, Jesus. In one's coming to selfhood, another can be midwife—that is, attend the birth—but the labor is finally one's own.

Anticipating Freud, Kierkegaard also wrote the first book devoted entirely to anxiety: *The concept of dread.*

W. Coleman

KIESOW, FEDERICO (1858–1940)

Kiesow took the doctor's degree in philosophy in 1894 in Leipzig under Wilhelm Wundt, and was the assistant first of Wundt, with whom he studied taste, and later of the great Italian physiologist, Angelo Mosso. Kiesow founded the Psychological Institute at Turin University in 1895 and brought Wundtian experimental psychology to Turin. He directed the Psychological Institute as professor in ordinary from 1906 to 1933. Under Kiesow, the Psychological Institute was known throughout the world as a center of psychological research.

Among the many areas researched by Kiesow are taste sensitivity, thermic and tactile points, geometric illusions, the Weber–Fechner Law, eidetic imagery, psychophysics, the specific function of the organs of sense, feelings and their concomitant phenomena, the conceptions of sense and sensation, reaction times, dreams, the conception of soul, and psychic causality. In addition to numerous publications in these experimental areas, Kiesow wrote philosophical papers on Socrates. Kiesow was Italy's most prominent experimental psychologist for many years. He was emeritus professor of the Royal University of Turin, and LL.D. honoris causa of Wittenberg College in Springfield, Ohio.

M. LaCROCE

KINSEY, ALFRED C. (1894–1956)

Kinsey received the B.S. from Bowdoin College. He received the Sc.D. in biology from Harvard in 1920. His entire career was spent in the zoology department of Indiana University.

Kinsey's first study was of the behavior of birds in the rain. He published several biology texts, including one on research methodology. By 1938 he was the leading authority on the gall wasps of Mexico and Central America. His research had important implications for evolutionary theory.

While teaching a course at Indiana on marriage problems in the 1930s, he turned to the study of sexual behavior because of the lack of adequate information. His initial interviews were with individuals living in the central United States. His work showed sufficient promise that both the National Research Council and the Rockefeller Foundation supported more extensive surveys of sexual behavior. The Institute for Sex Research, affiliated with Indiana University, was founded in 1947. The next year the results of the research on males was published, followed by *Sexual behavior in the human female* in 1953.

Authored by Kinsey and three colleagues, these works became popularly known as "the Kinsey reports." They provided the only quantified, thorough description of a large number of diverse human self-reports of sexual experience. Kinsey found a far wider variation in experience than anticipated. The data also put to rest many misconceptions about childhood sexuality, homosexuality, and the sexual arousal of females.

C. S. PEYSER

KLAGES, LUDWIG (1872–1956)

Klages is generally considered the originator of German characterology. The notion of characterology, typically European, stresses the structure of character known through human expression. For Klages, one type of human expression was to be found in hand movements and in particular, handwriting. He believed that an analysis of handwriting—often called graphology—was a basic method for personality analysis.

From a philosophical point of view, Klages believed that body and soul interacted and that the point of this interaction was the human personality. An individual personality was a system of dynamic relationships. The total individuality of a person was to be found in its expression, so in any action or movement the total individual was expressed. The particular type of movement that Klages selected and developed as a means of discovering the true nature of a person was handwriting, which provided a permanent and measurable record of movement. Each person's handwriting expressed the writer's uniqueness; through it, the nature of the personality could be discovered.

He described his psychology of handwriting in *The Problem of graphology,* and in *Handwriting and character,* which went through 26 editions (some of them unrevised new printings). As a result of his efforts, graphology has been a significant diagnostic tool particularly in Germany for discovering the nature of personality. However, because

of its highly subjective nature, it has remained suspect in the United States.

R. W. LUNDIN

KLINEBERG, OTTO (1899–1992)

Klineberg received the B.A. from McGill University and the Ph.D. from Columbia, where he taught from 1925 to 1962. He then went to the University of Paris, and in 1965 to the Ecole des Hautes Etudes, also in Paris.

During his long career he devoted his research and writings to various aspects of social psychology. While at Columbia he developed a strong interest in anthropology. In an early book, *Race differences* (1935), he described differences in various psychological characteristics such as intelligence, emotions, and personality in various races including the Chinese, American Indians, and American blacks. His general conclusion was that these differences are by and large culturally determined. In comparing differences in intelligence between blacks in the northern and southern United States, he attributed the general superiority of those in the North to better education.

His strong anthropological interests were also reflected in *Social psychology* (1940), which reported his own research and that of other social psychologists in discussions of behavioral differences among social classes, the sexes, and various ethnic origins. Once again he found strong cultural forces at work.

While in Paris he turned his interests to the psychology of international relations. His book *The human dimension in international relations* (1964) advocates programs for improving international cooperation.

KLOPFER, BRUNO (1900–1971)

Klopfer, during his youth, enjoyed sailing, mountain climbing, and skiing. His education was interrupted for a time by World War I. Later he returned to the University of Munich, where he received the Ph.D. at the age of 22; his dissertation was entitled "The psychology of inhibition."

Klopfer and his family spent 1933–1934 in Switzerland, then emigrated to the United States, where Klopfer taught at Columbia University for 13 years. During this time he established his first regular workshop in projective techniques in New York State. Later he added other workshops in California and other parts of the country. Joining the staff at UCLA, he remained there until his retirement in 1963.

Klopfer started dealing with Jungian psychology as an intellectual task and gradually it became his philosophy of life. His speciality in his later years was Jungian analysis and the teaching of Jungian theory and practice. This tended to replace the Rorschach as his primary interest.

He was editor of the *Journal of Personality Assessment* for 36 years and developed it from an obscure newsletter into a major professional organ. He himself was a prolific writer and a tremendous stimulant to his students and colleagues. His major work was *The Rorschach technique* first published in 1942 with Douglas Kelly and revised in 1962 with H. H. Davidson; it became the single most authoritative source on the Rorschach test. He received tributes from the Division of Clinical Psychology of the American Psychological Association, from the Society for Personality Assessment, and from the Analytical Psychology Club of New York.

W. G. KLOPFER

KLÜVER, HEINRICH (1897–   )

Klüver studied at the universities of Hamburg and Berlin. In 1923 he came to the United States and in 1924 he received the Ph.D. degree from Stanford University. He taught briefly at the University of Minnesota and then devoted his attention primarily to research. He held various appointments at the University of Chicago, eventually becoming a distinguished service professor of biological psychology.

Klüver developed the method of equivalent and nonequivalent stimuli for studying behavior and determined the role of the brain, particularly the striate cortex, in vision. He discovered the presence of free porphyrins in the central nervous system and a new technique (the Klüver–Barrera method) for staining nervous tissue. He also discovered and described the Klüver–Bucy syndrome, in which placidity is a typical feature of temporal lobe ablation. His writings covered the experimental investigation of eidetic imagery types, the effects of mescaline, and behavior mechanisms in monkeys.

Over many years Klüver served as associate editor of a number of journals in psychology, biology, and medicine. His research contributions led to a number of awards, including the Lashley award in neurobiology, the Hamilton award in psychopathology, and the gold medal award of the American Psychological Foundation.

KOCH, SIGMUND (1917–   )

Koch studied at New York University, the University of Iowa, and Duke University (Ph.D., 1942). Currently the university professor of psychology and philosophy at Boston University, he has held senior appointments at the University of Texas, Austin, and at Duke. He has also taught at University College, London (as a Fulbright professor), at Clark University, and at the University of North Carolina. In the mid-1960s he was director of the Ford Foundation Program in the Humanities and Arts, and in the early 1970s he served as academic vice-president of Boston University.

Koch's persisting interests have been in theoretical and philosophical foundations of psychology. Early on, he did theoretico-experimental work in learning and motivation. His later interests have been in the analysis of inquiry, the theory of value and of language, and the empirical study of art. His critical writings were influential in liberating psychology from the hegemony of behaviorism. He is also known for his view that psychology is not a coherent science, but rather a collectivity of discrete and often incommensurable *psychological studies*, many of which require methods more like those of the humanities than the natural sciences (1969a, 1971, 1981). Also significant are his *perceptual theory of definition*, offered as an antidote to the muddles of "operationism," and his early priority in repairing the neglect by motivational theory of *intrinsic motivation* via his concept of objective *value properties*.

Koch directed and edited the American Psychological Association/NSF-sponsored study of the status of psychology at mid-century which resulted in the six-volume study *Psychology: A study of a science*. With D. E. Leary he edited a second large study, *A century of psychology as science*. He has also been president of three divisions of the American Psychological Association: General Psychology, Philosophical Psychology (twice), and Psychology and the Arts.

KOFFKA, KURT (1886–1941)

Koffka, except for a year at Edinburgh, studied at Berlin's university. His 1908 Ph.D. under Carl Stumpf was based on a dissertation on rhythm. He assisted Otto Külpe at Würzburg and Friedrich Schumann at Frankfurt. When the Nazis came to power he left the faculty at Giessen, emigrated to the United States, and accepted a position at Smith College.

Koffka was Wertheimer's second subject for his classic 1912 paper on the Phi Phenomena (apparent movement, as in motion pictures). Along with Max Wertheimer and Wolfgang Köhler, Koffka was a founder of the Gestalt psychology movement; of the three, he was

particularly noted for his extensive publications. The Gestalt movement—a reaction against Wundt and (later) behaviorism—emphasized perceptual processes and the necessity for dealing with behavior in all its complexity, (an holistic, emergent approach) as opposed to attempts to analyze behavior by components.

Prior to becoming Wertheimer's assistant in 1911, Koffka had done research on imagery and thought. He was responsible for applying Gestalt principles to developmental psychology. For him, learning was the same as perceptual reorganization, particularly a goal-directed tendency to restore equilibrium of perceptions (*Prägnanz*).

The most comprehensive—albeit a difficult—exposition of the Gestalt approach is Koffka's *Principles of Gestalt psychology*. In his last years his research primarily concerned color vision and perceptual organization. His basic position on the nature/nurture question was a further development of Stern's convergence theory: psychological development is a collaboration of inner (hereditary) and outer (learned) conditions.

C. S. Peyser

KOHLBERG, LAWRENCE (1927–1987)

Kohlberg is best known for his research on the moral development in children. He received the B.A. degree and the Ph.D. from the University of Chicago in 1958. The following year, he went to Yale University and remained there until 1961. After several interim appointments he went to Harvard in 1967. His principal work was *Essays on moral development* (2 vols.).

Following the lines of Piaget, Kohlberg stated that children followed moral development in three stages: (1) in the preconditioned level children's moral development followed from external standards, (2) in the conventional level morality is basically one of the following correct rules, and (3) in the conventional level morality is basically one of the shared standards of rights and duties. Each of these levels comprised two stages of orientation. The first is characterized by obedience and punishment and naive eogism; the second by "good boy" and authority, and the third combined legalism and conscience. Like Piaget's theory, Kohlberg's is one of cognitive development. His results were the result of 20 yr of longitudinal study.

R. W. Lundin

KÖHLER, IVO (1915–   )

Köhler opted to become an experimental psychologist at the University of Innsbruck, where he was stimulated by Theodor Erismann, who advocated the empiricist point of view in psychology, and by Franziska Mayer-Hillebrand, who represented the nativistic view.

First as a student and again after World War II, Köhler plunged into the Helmholtz–Hering dispute on perception. The issue was whether perception should be considered as a learned performance or as an inborn ability. Discussions arising from wearing various kinds of goggles resulted in a series of crucial experiments. Wedge prisms initiated by Hermann Helmholtz and used again by James J. Gibson, were used. They were roof prisms comparable to half-glasses and other types of spectacles. In contrast to the precursors, the volunteers in Innsbruck extended the experimental period from a few weeks to months. The result was the "situational aftereffect": a "dependent" or "contingent" kind of sensory adaptation which takes into account a lot of marginal conditions of environmental stimuli (Köhler, 1962, 1964).

Retired since 1981, Köhler has been honored with the title of emeritus at the University of Innsbruck, where his scientific research and publications continue.

KÖHLER, WOLFGANG (1887–1967)

Köhler studied at Tübingen, Bonn, and Berlin. He received the Ph.D. under Carl Stumpf at Berlin in 1909 for a dissertation on psychoacoustics. During 1913–1920 he was director of the Prussian Academy of Sciences station at Tenerife in the Canary Islands. With the rise of Nazism, he left his position at Berlin for the United States, where he taught at Swarthmore and Dartmouth. He was president of the American Psychological Association in 1959.

Köhler was Wertheimer's first subject for his classic 1912 paper on the Phi Phenomena (apparent movement, as in motion pictures). Along with Wertheimer and Koffka, Köhler was a founder of the Gestalt psychology movement, of which he was particularly noted as the public spokesman.

The Gestalt movement was a reaction against Wundt and behaviorism. It emphasized perceptual processes and the necessity for dealing with behavior in all its emergent complexity, rather than attempting to analyze it by components.

Köhler's *The mentality of apes* (1917) established the applicability of the Gestalt to animal behavior. Based upon his work at Tenetife, the book focuses on insightful or "aha!" solutions to problems. Most of the problems were *Ümweg* or roundabout solutions. In the simplest case the desired object of food was placed on the other side of a fence at the end of an alley. If the ape conceptualized the Gestalt, it turned back down the alley, went around to the other side of the fence, and obtained the goal.

In another problem Köhler placed a banana outside a cage at a distance that could not be directly reached by arm. The chimpanzees invariably placed the stick beyond the fruit and knocked the fruit within reach. Although some required several trials to become proficient at the task, their intention or Gestalt was clear from the first successful attempt with the stick. Sultan, one of the brighter chimpanzees, has become known for his solving of the two- and three-stick problems. In these cases a single stick was not long enough to reach the fruit; rather, the smaller bamboo rod had to be inserted inside the larger hollow rod to create a longer stick. When the banana was within reach by a single stick, Sultan usually stopped using the extended stick. Other problems required tearing a branch off a small tree to obtain the stick, or piling boxes under fruit suspended from the ceiling.

Köhler also did work on relational or transposition learning at Tenerife. Chickens were taught to peck grain from the darker of two adjacent gray sheets. Then the sheets were changed, so that the lighter of the two was the same shade as the darker had been during training. The birds still pecked on the (even) darker gray, thus demonstrating that they had learned a relationship rather than a specific shade of gray.

Köhler also published important work on time error. In the United States he was primarily a defender of the principles of the Gestalt movement.

C. S. PEYSER

KONORSKI, JERZY (1903–1973)

Konorski, an internationally recognized Polish physiological psychologist, made numerous factual and theoretical contributions to the understanding of conditioned reflexes, their central neurophysiological mechanisms, and the integrative functions of the brain. He faithfully and indefatigably pursued his life's pervading goal, to learn "how the brain works," formulated when he was hardly 20 years of age. In 1928 he and his friend Stefan Miller, stimulated by Ivan Pavlov's work, conducted experiments which led them to discover a type of conditioned reflex which differed from the classical Pavlovian reflex. Later, this type became known, in the Skinnerian behavioral framework, as operant behavior.

In 1931 Konorski, invited by Pavlov, went to Leningrad and spent almost two years in Pavlov's laboratories. Upon his return to Warsaw, he worked in the Nencki Institute of Experimental Biology until 1939. After the war he again joined this institute, later became its director, and remained associated with it until his death. The scope of Konorski's research expanded to a wide area of brain–behavior relations, including associations, perceptions, skilled movements, behavioral effects of brain lesions, and others.

Although Konorski admired and was deeply grateful to Pavlov, he rejected his theory in favor of Charles Sherrington's ideas as a sounder basis for his own research and theories. During the Stalinist period, when Pavlov's theory became obligatory doctrine for all scientists in the communist countries, Konorski was sharply criticized, denounced, and ostracized. After 1955, when the political climate changed, Konorski gained even greater popularity and respect in Poland.

From 1957 on, Konorski made frequent visits to the United States, lectured there, received grants from the National Institutes of Health, and maintained a lively scientific exchange with American scientists. His most important book is *Integrative activity of the brain*.

H. MISIAK

KORCHIN, SHELDON JEROME (1921–1989)

Korchin received the B.A. from Brooklin College, the M.A. from Clark University, and the Ph.D. from Harvard in 1947. After several years at the VA Hospital in Philadelphia and Michael Reese Hospital in Chicago, he went to the University of California at Berkeley in 1963 and founded the psychological clinic there.

He served as clinical director until 1972 and again from 1984 to 1987. He published his best known book while at Berkeley, *Modern clinical psychology*. This book has been translated into both Japanese and Italian. The enduring theme of the book is that psychologists who want to eleviate suffering must consider the intrapsychic dynamics of the individual as well as the social context and values in which that individual plays his or her life. In recognition of his contribution to research and clinical training, he received the Distinguished contribution to Science and Profession of Psychology Award from Division 12 of the American Psychological Association in 1978.

R. W. LUNDIN

KORNADT, HANS-JOACHIM (1927–)

Kornadt is a graduate of the University of Marburg, where he received his diploma in psychology in 1952 and the Ph.D. in 1956. He was a research assistant at the universities of Marburg and Hamburg, before he started teaching at the University of Würzburg in 1957. Now professor of educational psychology of the University of the Saar at Saarbrücken, he was previously professor at the Teacher Training College of Saarbrücken (1964) and guest professor of the University of Bochum (1967).

Trained in general and experimental psychology, Kornadt moved into the fields of motivation, child development, and education. He has specialized in cross-cultural research, particularly concerning the development of aggression. He developed a motivation theory of aggression and aggression inhibition which is used as basis for deriving hypotheses about culture-specific phenomena. On several occasions he did research abroad in East Africa, Indonesia, and Japan.

From 1975 to 1981 Kornadt was a member of the Wissenschaftsrat (National Science Council), and chairman of its Scientific Commission. Since 1976 he has been chairman of the Council for University Entrance Tests of the Conference of Ministers of Education. In 1982 he was elected president of the Deutsche Gesellschaft für Psychologie (German Psychological Society).

KORNILOV, KONSTANTIN N. (1879–1957)

Kornilov was one of the most significant Soviet psychologists of the postrevolutionary period. He was a member of the Academy of Pedagogical Sciences and served as president from 1944 to 1950. Earlier he had been director of the Institute of Psychology.

In *A theory of human reaction from the psychological point of view*, Kornilov presented the basic aspects of his psychology. He developed the idea of a *reaction psychology*, rather than the simple reflexology proposed by V. M. Bekhterev. The reaction referred to *all* the response movements of an organism and not simply the reflex of a single organ. Reactions were considered *biosocial*. This involved all the phenomena of the living organism, from the simplest responses to the most complex forms of human behavior. He distinguished psychology from physiology, which dealt with simple human reactions but ignored social relations. He also attempted a synthesis between the subjective and objective aspects of psychology.

Kornilov was one of the earliest Soviet psychologists to build a psychology based on Marxist philosophy. His theory of the reaction has been considered an eclectic combination of Marxist principles, including mechanical and energy propositions. He stressed the application of the reaction to both biological and social phenomena. He believed that humans had as many instincts as animals, but that human instincts were masked by socially acquired reactions. As a result, he received much criticism. His opponents claimed that he failed to understand the inherited features of behavior.

R. W. LUNDIN

KOŠČO, JOZEF (1920–   )

Best known for his work on the history of psychology in connection with the development of philosophy and theoretical science, Koščo is the head of the Department of Biodromal and Counseling Psychology at Comenius University in Bratislava, Czechoslovakia, where he teaches counseling psychology and history of psychology.

Koščo characterizes in a new way the genesis and importance of psychological practice, so as to more adequately define applied psychology and develop and better understand psychology's professionalization and institutionalization. He developed and justified new, open classifications of metatheoretical and systems disciplines, special theoretical disciplines, and applied psychological disciplines.

On the basis of a critical analysis of Western and Marxist conceptions of life-span psychology, he developed the concept of "biodromal psychology." The biodromal approach explains personality as a unity of a dialectical interaction of phylogenetic, historic-social, and unique individual factors, emphasizing personality as a special evolutionary unity.

Koščo supervised the works of his collective in a project of integrated and biodromal models of counseling. He is author of more than 150 scientific studies published in Czechoslovakia and abroad.

KOVACS, ARTHUR L. (1931–   )

Kovacs received the B.A. in psychology from UCLA and the M.A. and Ph.D. from the University of Michigan in 1958. Upon completion of his graduate education, he entered independent practice as an associate at the Western Psychological Center in Sherman Oaks, California, leaving to enter solo practice in 1971. In 1970, Kovacs was chosen to be the founding campus dean of the California School of Professional Psychology at Los Angeles. He remained in that role until 1977 when he returned to private practice and was granted the role of founding dean emeritus and distinguished professor by the institution.

Kovacs has been active in the governance of the American Psychological Association, serving as a representative to council for six terms, with terms as president of its Divisions of Psychotherapy and of Independent Practice, and for 6 yr as a member of the Committee for the Advancement of Professional Practice. He is the recipient of Distinguished Professional Psychologist awards from APA's Divisions 29 and 42. The APA Board of Directors honored him in 1990 with a citation of merit for his long service to the association. He is a past editor (1974–1981) of the journal and he has written articles on psychotherapy and professional practice.

KOZULIN, ALEX (1949–   )

Kozulin earned the medical degree from the Moscow Pirogov Institute of Medicine in 1972 and the Ph.D. in psychology from the Moscow Institute of Psychology in 1978.

Dissatisfied with Pavlovian doctrine, in the early 1970s he joined a group of scholars who developed an alternative concept of the "psychophysiology of activity" originally suggested by N. Bernshtein. The probabilistic behavior of normal subjects and mental patients became the center of his experimental work.

A desire to understand the relationship between tacit philosophical premises and actual methodology of behavioral research led Kozulin to theoretical scholarship. He focused on comparison of the genetic psychology of J. Piaget with the "psychophysiology of activity" of N. Bernshtein. He saw both these theoretical systems as representing developmental structuralism. The historical analysis of the concepts of "structure" and "development" led him to study behaviorism, ethology, and so-called sociobiology in their relation to the methodological principles of atomism or structuralism.

In the late 1970s the focus of his work shifted toward the history of Soviet psychology, later expanded into *Psychology in utopia*, published in the United States. In 1979 Kozulin emigrated to the United States and continued his research in the history of psychology at Boston University Center for the Philosophy and History of Science.

KRAEPELIN, EMIL (1855–1926)

At the time Kraepelin entered the medical scene in the latter part of the nineteenth century, the classification of mental disorders was in a state of confusion. His interest in psychiatry began when he was still in medical school. For a time he was associated with Wilhelm Wundt at the University of Leipzig. At that time Wundt was concerned with the new psychology and was experimenting with sensory functions and the analysis of states of consciousness. It was against this background of scientific investigation that Kraepelin approached the problem of mental disorders. He believed that one should take a scientific approach to mental disorders since they were predetermined. It seemed to him that a person who was mentally disturbed might naturally recover or might not.

Through careful observation of many patients and statistical tabulation of symptoms, he came to the conclusion that there were two major mental disorders: dementia praecox and the manic-depressive psychosis. He further divided these disorders into various subtypes: dementia praecox could be subdivided into the hebephrenic, catatonic, and paranoid, while the manic-depressive psychosis had many more subdivisions, depending on the regularity or irregularity of the cycles of mania and depression. As a result, he became known as the "great classifier" of mental disorders.

In 1883 he published the first edition of his *Clinical psychiatry*; the ninth edition appeared in 1927, the year after his death. Kraepelin's classifications were the culmination of efforts of various psychiatrists both in France and Germany for over a generation. Through his efforts the study, diagnosis, and prognosis of outcome of mental disorders became a legitimate branch of medicine. By and large, Kraepelin considered the causes of these disorders to be predetermined and basically of a biological nature. Physiological factors and malfunctions of various body organs seemed to be the important factors, rather than the psychological causes proposed by many from the French schools and by Sigmund Freud.

R. W. LUNDIN

KRAFFT-EBING, RICHARD VON (1840–1902)

Krafft-Ebing held positions in psychiatry at the universities of Strasbourg, Graz, and Vienna. He published extensively on hypnosis, criminology, and sexual behavior. His basic psychiatry text was considered by many to be undistinguished, yet it is credited with influencing Carl Jung to choose psychiatry as a medical specialty.

In his early work Krafft-Ebing inoculated general paresis patients with syphilis. Since they did not contract the disease, they must have had it previously. In this fashion he demonstrated the link between syphilis and general paresis prior to the serological tests such as the Wassermann used today. At the Moscow International Congress of 1897 he made popular the phrase "civilization and syphilization."

Psychopathia sexualis is Krafft-Ebing's best-known work. First published in 1886, it went through a dozen editions and many translations. Krafft-Ebing took a purely constitutional approach. All sexual variations are based upon genetic defects, although masturbation can hasten or even produce disorders. True to the German ideas of the time, he considered anything other than marital coitus for the purpose of procreation a perversion. A male was expected to have orgasm during coitus, but not a female. Krafft-Ebing discussed sexual perversions ranging from lust murder to fetish and masturbation with equal condemnation. His writings influenced the work of Sigmund Freud.

C. S. PEYSER

KRASNER, LEONARD (1924–   )

Krasner attended the City College of New York. After three years in military service during World War II, he received the Ph.D. from Columbia University as a clinical psychologist.

Influenced by the experimental orientation of the faculty, particularly Fred Keller, Krasner's research efforts focused on the development of a behavioral approach in clinical psychology. Working with Leonard Ullmann, Krasner edited two volumes bringing together virtually all of the then extant research and applications in behavior modification: *Case studies in behavior modification* (1963) and *Research in behavior modification* (1965). Ullmann and Krasner then published the first text in abnormal psychology to offer a systematic behavioral model: *A psychological approach to abnormal psychology*. The two authors then further developed and broadened their behavioral/social learning model in *Behavior influence and personality: The social matrix of human action*.

Krasner has also published reports on studies in verbal conditioning, token economy, placebo effect, social responsibility, values, behavior therapy, clinical psychology, and other related areas. Later he broadened his behavioral approach in *Environmental design and human behavior: A psychology of the individual in society*, which describes the research, training, community, and school applications of himself and his colleagues and students.

KREITLER, HANS (1916–   )

Kreitler studied with Karl Bühler and Egon Brunswick in Vienna, and with Martin Buber and S. Bonaventura in Jerusalem, and after World War II received the Ph.D. from the Gestalt-oriented University of Graz in Austria. Imbued with the idea of cognitive supremacy, he dedicated most of his research to cognition and its behavioral implications. Together with his wife Shulamith, he developed a cognitive theory about the evocation and guidance of human behavior and a theory of the art experience. Based on the orientative impact of meanings and beliefs, the Kreitlers' theory of *cognitive orientation* describes the chain of events between sensory input and behavioral output, and provides the instruments for prediction and modification of molar behavior.

In *Psychology of the arts* Kreitler analyzed art perception as well as the established laws of the arts in terms of content variables, Gestalt laws, physiological findings, and depth-psychological processes. These analyses provide the building blocks for a theory of the experiential impacts of painting, sculpture, music, dance, and literature. The theory is used as a guide for art education and experimental aesthetics.

Since 1959 Kreitler has worked as lecturer and researcher at Tel Aviv University in Israel. In 1961 he founded and chaired the department of psychology at Tel Aviv University. He has also worked in research at the Educational Testing Service of Princeton, New Jersey, and has taught at Harvard and Yale universities. In 1977 the Johan Gutenberg University at Mainz awarded Kreitler an honorary doctorate for "extraordinary scientific contributions to cognitive psychology."

The Kreitlers' joint publications include *Cognitive orientation and behavior, Psychology of the Arts, Die Weltanschauliche Orientierung der Schizophrenen,* and *Die kognitive Orientierung des Kindes.*

KRETSCHMER, ERNST (1888–1964)

Kretschmer studied medicine at Munich under Kraepelin, from whom he took the notion of an organic basis for psychiatric disorders. His 1914 dissertation dealt with the manic-depressive. His career was spent on the faculty of Tübingen and Marburg.

Kretschmer is best known for his typology within the framework of constitutional psychology: body structure/physiology determines personality. Hippocrates had proposed two basic types, and Galen, four. Although about 20 psychologists in the nineteenth and early twentieth centuries had proposed three or four types, it is Kretschmer's expansion in *Physique and character* that is remembered. Hippocrates' short and thick type he called *pyknic,* noting that such individuals tend toward extraversion and manic-depressive disorders. The slender, frail type he labeled *asthenic* and described their proneness to introversion, disorganization, and schizophrenia (delusions). He added the broad and muscular *athletic* type and the *dysplastic* or "mixed" type. Sheldon later elaborated upon his system and put it on a far sounder empirical basis.

Kretschmer also published in child and adolescent psychopathology, developed new techniques of hypnosis and psychotherapy, and proposed laws that would permit the rehabilitation of the compulsive criminal.

C. S. PEYSER

KRISHNAN, B. (1917–1980)

Krishnan obtained his graduate and master's degrees with honors from the University of Mysore. He spent 1953–1955 at the University of Minnesota as a Fulbright Scholar, then became a professor of psychology at the University of Mysore in 1962. Krishnan's research interests were both in the traditional as well as unorthodox psychological issues. He impressed his students by his teaching and his human and personal relationships. He devoted much of his energy to making the Indian Psychological Association a truly national professional organization. He wrote several books in Kannad. His special interest was research in clinical, counseling, and Indian psychology.

From 1956 to 1977 he edited the *Psychological Studies* published by the Department of Psychology at Mysore University. He served as president of the Indian Psychological Association (1979), the section on Psychology and Educational Sciences of the Indian Science Congress (1973), and the Indian Academy of Applied Psychology (1967–1968). He was founder president of the Mysore Psychological Association (1963–1977), and founder secretary of the All India Vocational Educational Guidance Association. He retired as senior professor of psychology from Mysore University in 1977.

Krishnan provided a great deal of inspiration and enthusiasm to the younger generation of psychologists in India. He developed a strong interest in the psychology of consciousness and biopsychology in his later career.

KRUGLANSKI, ARIE W. (1938–   )

Known in particular for his work in *attribution theory* and *lay epistemology;* Kruglanski emigrated to Israel in 1950. Educated in Poland and Israel, Kruglanski went on to study psychology at the University of Toronto, where he received the bachelor's degree in 1966. Kruglanski carried out his graduate studies at UCLA, receiving the Ph.D. in 1968.

Interested initially in attribution theory and scientific methodology, Kruglanski combined these two perspectives in a model of lay epistemology, on which he published papers in the *Psychological Review,* the *Journal of Personality and Social Psychology,* and other scientific journals and books in both the United States and Europe. In this work Kruglanski set out to demonstrate how his general theory of the knowledge acquisition process provides a basis for integrating major heretofore disparate formulations in social psychology such as attribution theory, cognitive consistency theories, social comparison theory, and attitude-change theories. Kruglanski's theory stresses the essential similarity of process whereby lay and scientific knowers form their beliefs. This means both that lay beliefs are essentially logical and internally coherent, and that scientific beliefs are subject to bias and error.

Kruglanski has applied his epistemic theory to the problem of cognitive therapy. His approach maintains that what needs to change in the course of treatment are the *contents* of patients' dysfunctional ideas, rather than the *process* whereby they arrive at those ideas.

Throughout his professional career Kruglanski has been a member of the Department of Psychology at Tel Aviv University, where he continues to lecture and carry out research. His major publications include "The endogenous-exogenous partition in attribution theory," "The human subject in the psychology experiment; Fact and artifact," and "Lay epistemologic process and contents: Another look at attribution theory."

KUGELMASS, SOL (1926–   )

Kugelmass did his undergraduate work at George Washington University and received the Ph.D. in psychology at Columbia University in 1953. He worked on a number of research projects at the New York State Psychiatric Institute under Joseph Zubin in the first operations of the Biometric Unit of that institution.

Moving to Israel in 1954, he began working with patients at the Kfar Shaul Mental Hospital and participated in research on unilateral disequilibrium with Halperin at the University Department of Neurology. In 1956 he reopened the Department of Psychology at the Hebrew University of Jerusalem. During the formative years of the department he served as chairman, then became director of the Human Development Institute in 1968. He also served as the dean of the Faculty of Social Sciences from 1973 to 1976, and later as chief scientist of the Ministry of Education.

Kugelmass has attempted to exploit the opportunities for cross-cultural research in Israel to add to our knowledge of such areas as psychophysiology, perception, and moral judgment. Much of this research is reviewed in a chapter in volume 2 of (N. Warren's) *Studies in cross-cultural psychology.*

KÜLPE, OSWALD (1862–1915)

In 1881 Külpe went to the University of Leipzig to study history, but there he became acquainted with Wilhelm Wundt, who directed him into psychology. At that time psychology was a new way of thinking, separate from philosophy. In his studies with Wundt he became very excited about Wundt's new analysis of consciousness. This analysis was a kind of mental chemistry, analyzing the contents of consciousness into elements and compounds.

From 1886 to 1894 Külpe was an active participant in Wundt's laboratory. At this time he was totally sympathetic with Wundt's analysis and his method of introspection. In 1893 he published his *Grundriss der Psychologie* (Outline of psychology) and dedicated the work to Wundt.

The following year Külpe was appointed to a chair at the University of Würzburg. He established a laboratory there which at the time was second only to Wundt's. He began to believe that the analysis of consciousness involved more than what Wundt had suggested. For Wundt the method of introspection involved having an experience and describing it. Külpe became more concerned with "attitudes" and "higher mental processes," which were more complex. A subject could be required to perform some mental activity such as thinking and then examine how this came about. The analysis involved dividing the various experiences into fractions. Külpe concluded that thinking could occur in the absence of mental images or sensations and termed this "imageless thought." Thus a nonsensory component of consciousness could be identified.

The Würzburg school of "imageless thought" was established, and many psychologists of the time participated in experiments to demonstrate the new finding. Psychologists such as Karl Marbe, N. Ach, Henry Watt, and Karl Bühler became associated with this school.

R. W. LUNDIN

LADD, GEORGE TRUMBULL (1842–1920)

Although a theologian-philosopher by training, Ladd published many books of a psychological nature. He graduated from the Andover Theological Seminary in 1869 and spent the next 10 years in the active ministry of the church. He then became professor of mental and moral philosophy at Bowdoin College (1879–1881). There his thinking took a direction toward psychology. He became interested not only in mental activity or functions, but also in the relationships between the mind and the functioning of the nervous system.

From 1881 to 1905 Ladd was at Yale University, where he held the same title as at Bowdoin. Although he did have a kind of informal laboratory at Yale, he never became an experimental psychologist. His main concern was physiological psychology; he wrote one of the first texts on the subject. At that time research in the field was proceeding, but the subject matter was fragmented. His *Elements of physiological psychology* became a standard text and was widely read throughout the United States and England; it was revised by Robert S. Woodworth in 1911.

Ladd was also interested in general psychology. His book *Psychology, descriptive and explanatory* followed a position later to be taken up by the functionalist school at the University of Chicago. This position met with mixed reactions; some called it dreary. However, it was an important step in the direction of functional psychology.

As time passed, Ladd found that psychology was becoming more mechanistic, with greater emphasis on body and behavior and less on the mental side. His interests then turned again to philosophy.

Ladd believed that consciousness should operate to solve problems, though he granted that there is a biological side to the nervous system. The function of the mind is to adapt, and in adapting it must look to the future. Psychology should be practical: the mind must be useful in carrying out the activities of life.

R. W. LUNDIN

LADD-FRANKLIN, CHRISTINE (1847–1930)

Ladd-Franklin was an American psychologist and logician who studied at Johns Hopkins, Göttingen, and Berlin. For most of her career she was associated with Columbia University. She was an associate editor of Baldwin's *Dictionary of philosophy and psychology*. In philosophy she was known for her method that reduced all syllogisms to a single formula. Her experimental papers ranged from bioluminescence to an extension of the Purkinje Phenomenon to gray stimuli.

Ladd-Franklin is best known for her theory of color vision. She first became acquainted with sensory psychology in the laboratories of G. E. Müller and König. Her theory is based on that of F. C. Donders, but with a developmental or genetic focus. She attempted a reconciliation of Hermann Helmholtz's trichromatic theory and the tetrachromatic explanation of Donders.

Ladd-Franklin postulated that the white receptor is more basic to vision as it occurs under more conditions, notably very low illumination and at the extreme periphery of the visual field. She suggested that some white receptors developmentally split into blue receptors and some into yellow receptors; later some yellow receptors evolve into red and some into green receptors. A primary piece of evidence was the fact that blue and yellow can be seen farther from the center of vision than can red or green. However, Ladd-Franklin never was able to explain why the limits of the red and green fields were not identical, or why the blue and yellow visual limits were not the same. Although both the Ladd-Franklin and the Hering tetrachromatic theories had periods of popularity, the Young–Helmholtz trichromatic explanation of retinal color vision is most widely accepted today.

C. S. PEYSER

LAING, RONALD D. (1927–   )

The psychiatrist Laing attracted international attention with his books *The divided self* and *The politics of experience*, constituting one of the early discussions on the phenomenology of schizophrenia. According to Laing, schizophrenia is a no-win situation, a double bind that immobilizes the individual.

Laing attended the university at Glasgow, Scotland, receiving the M.D. in 1951. After spending several years as a British Army psychiatrist, he returned to Scotland for advanced training in psychiatry. In 1957 he left for London and the Tavistock Institute of Human Relations. In 1962 he directed the Langham Clinic, and in 1965 he cofounded Kingsley Hall, in London.

LAMARCK, JEAN-BAPTISTE DE MONET DE (1744–1829)

Lamarck started his career as a botanist by developing a new method for identifying plants, and made the first effort to formulate a natural method of classification for the vegetable kingdom. He recognized the importance of environmental influences, especially climate, for vegetable development. For these efforts he was elected to the Académie des Sciences in 1779. His most important institutional affiliation was with the Jardin du Roi, an important scientific center at the time.

As his interests turned to zoology, he became affiliated with the Musée d'Histoire Naturelle as professor of "insects and worms." In this field he developed a classification system for invertebrates.

Out of these zoological interests Lamarck developed the theory of evolution that he first presented in 1800 in a public lecture. In the statement of his theory he presumed four laws. The first concerned the natural tendency toward increasing organic complexities. The second dealt with why new organs evolve by indirect environmental influences. The third was the use–disuse principle, which accounted for changes in an organ as a result the acquisition of new habits or the disappearance of organs which were no longer useful. The last law dealt directly with the inheritance of acquired characteristics, which Lamarck thought to be necessary to explain cumulative changes and the emergence of new structures. At the time, this belief became so widely accepted that any proof of its validity seemed unnecessary.

Lamarck's theory went unchallenged for over 50 years, until Charles Darwin published his *Origin of species by means of natural selection* in 1859. Still, Lamarck's theory did not suddenly die out: it became the basis for Herbert Spencer's theory of the inheritance of associated ideas, which appeared late in the nineteenth century. In the late 1930s William McDougall attempted to prove Lamarck's theory in his experiments at Duke University by breeding successive generations of rats who had learned an escape problem. The work of Carl Jung reflected Lamarckian ideas in the theory of the archetypes which developed generation after generation in man's collective unconscious. However, most biologists and other natural scientists have abandoned Lamarck's theory in favor of Darwin's.

R. W. LUNDIN

LA METTRIE, JULIEN OFFROY DE (1709–1751)

La Mettrie became a leader of French materialism. He first studied theology, becoming a Jesuit priest and a follower of St. Augustine's doctrine of predestination. Later, however, convinced that he could earn a better living as a physician, he got a degree in medicine and took up practice in Rheims. In 1742 he was appointed physician to the guards of the Duc de Gramont.

During the seige of Freiburg, La Mettrie became ill with a high fever. During this illness, he presumably acquired the belief that thought was nothing more than the result of mechanical activity in the brain, since he realized that as he became physically weaker, his mental functions also failed. Thus for him no distinction could be made between thought and the soul. Like the body, the soul was mortal; humans were nothing more than machines. Descartes had thought of animals as machines, and of human bodily functions as acting in a mechanical way. However, La Mettrie went a step further, making the brain the seat of the mind.

In 1748 La Mettrie published *L'homme machine* (Man as machine), which gave him a place in the history of behaviorism. In his later years he developed the doctrine of hedonism, asserting that pleasure was the goal of life and that all motivation was selfish.

R. W. LUNDIN

LANDA, LEV N. (1927–   )

Landa received the Ph.D. from the Moscow Institute of Psychology in 1955 and his postdoctoral degree from the University of Leningrad in 1967. From 1963 to 1976 he was professor and director of a department at the Institute of General and Educational Psychology in Moscow.

Having emigrated to the West in 1976, in 1976–1979 he was visiting professor at universities in Europe and the United States. Currently he is with Teachers College of Columbia University. More than a third of his 102 published books and articles have been translated into 15 languages.

Landa developed the algorithmic-heuristic (algo-heuristic) theory and method of performance, learning, and instruction, labeled "Landamatics" in the United States. This theory deals with componental and systemic analysis of operations involved in the acquisition and application of knowledge and the formation of cognitive and psychomotor skills and abilities. As a method, Landamatics represents a system of specific techniques for the following purposes: (1) penetrating the unobservable mental processes that underlie expert performance, learning, and problem solving, of which experts themselves are unaware; (2) breaking these processes down into their relatively elementary component operations; (3) explicitly describing these operations (building descriptive operational models); (4) composing algorithmic and heuristic prescriptions (prescriptive models) of the described processes; (5) designing training methods, systems, and materials, including a new type of algorithm-based self-adaptive textbooks, aimed at specific development in students of general algo-heuristic processes (general methods of thinking); and (6) designing algorithmic computerizable methods for a troubleshooting diagnosis of psychological processes that makes possible remedial adaptive instruction. Landamatics is being applied in academia, industry, business, government, and the military; wherever used, it has permitted a significant increase in the efficiency of learning and instruction.

LANGE, CARL GEORG (1834–1900)

A Danish physician and psychologist, Lange was professor of pathological anatomy at the University of Copenhagen for most of his life.

Lange is best known for his theory of emotion, which he published in 1885, a year after a very similar theory had been set forth by the American philosopher and psychologist William James. The two men came to similar conclusions quite independently of each other, but while there were some differences, the similiarities were so great that the theory has long been identified as the James–Lange theory of emotions.

Lange distinguished emotion from passion, which James did not. For Lange, emotions included joy, sorrow, fear, and anger, while passions referred to love, hate, and admiration. Thus his theory applied only to the emotions. Also, his theory was more limited in formulation than that of James. But for both men the emotional experience *followed* the perception of internal physiological processes. An earlier theory, prevalent at the time, stated the reverse: the emotional experience *preceded* the physiological processes. For Lange, the emotion arose out of a perception of the activity of the circulatory system. James had related the emotion to a perception of visceral activity, as well as to body movement such as running from a feared object.

After reading Lange's paper on emotion, James republished his original theory with amplifications in his *Principles of psychology* (1890). In 1922 Knight Dunlap edited Lange's book *The emotions,* in which he gave credit to both James and Lange.

R. W. LUNDIN

LANGFELD, HERBERT SIDNEY (1879–1958)

Langfeld received his undergraduate education at Haverford College. He took the Ph.D. in psychology at Berlin under Carl Stumpf. Nearly all his professional life was spent at Princeton University, where he directed the psychological laboratory for many years. He served as editor of *Psychological Monographs* and the *Psychological Review.*

Early in his career Langfeld wrote *The aesthetic attitude* (1920), introducing the idea that the feeling aroused by a work of art is projected at once onto that work, which then seems to possess the quality of the feeling. Langfeld also emphasized the role played by the muscles in consciousness, holding that consciousness is not to be studied or understood in isolation. His experimental work covered several areas but had limited impact upon the discipline of psychology, perhaps because it did not lead to a general and distinct theoretical position.

Langfeld collaborated with Edwin Boring and H. P. Weld in editing two impressive and influential textbooks: *Psychology: A factual textbook* and *Foundations of psychology.* He also helped edit the National Research Council's *Psychology for the fighting man.*

For his generation, Langfeld was an acknowledged leader in psychology. He served as president of the American Psychological Association and as secretary general of the International Congress of Psychology.

P. E. LICHTENSTEIN

LASHLEY, KARL (1890–1958)

One of the early behaviorists in psychology in the United States, Lashley is best known for his work on localization of brain functions and his discoveries of how imprecise and generalized the functions of the brain can be. He was a student of John B. Watson at Johns Hopkins University, where he got the Ph.D. in 1915. He was on the staff of the universities of Minnesota (1917–1926), Chicago (1929–1935), Harvard (1935–1952), and the Yerkes Laboratory of Primate Biology.

His behavioristic interpretation of consciousness put him in general agreement with the ideas of John Watson. He had no use for the concept of consciousness or the method of introspection. Watson considered the brain a "mystery box," while Lashley was interested in digging—quite literally—into the brain to find out the nature of its functions.

As a result of his own research and that done with Shepard I. Franz, Lashley formulated two principles of brain functioning: mass action and equipotentiality. To illustrate the principle of *mass action,* Lashley taught cats to escape from a puzzle box, then removed various parts of the cortex of the animals' brains. After the cats had recovered from the operation, they were placed back in the box. He found that the cats could no longer perform the acquired task, but with further training they could relearn the task even in cases where both frontal lobes had been removed. On the basis of this experiment and many others, the principle of mass action indicated that learning was not dependent on specific neural connections in the brain but on the brain as a whole. The rate of relearning turned out to be a function of the total mass of brain tissue involved.

The principle of *equipotentiality* stated that each part of the brain was just as important as any other. If some parts of the brain were removed, other parts could carry on their functions. For example, when the visual area of rats' brains was removed, although they lost patterning, the rats could still discriminate differences in light intensity and could follow light.

Lashley's major publication was *Brain mechanisms and intelligence.*

R. W. LUNDIN

LAZARUS, ARNOLD A. (1932–   )

Educated in Johannesburg, South Africa, Lazarus did his academic studies at the University of the Witwatersrand and obtained the Ph.D. in clinical psychology in 1960, serving part of his internship in London at the Marlborough Day Hospital. While a full-time private practitioner in Johannesburg, he maintained an interest in clinical research. He gained recognition as a clinical innovator through an article on group therapy published in 1961 in the *Journal of Abnormal and Social Psychology*. Invited to spend a year teaching at Stanford University, he first came to the United States in 1963.

In 1958 Lazarus was the first to use the term "behavior therapy" and "behavior therapist" to describe certain objective treatment strategies. He has contributed papers, articles and chapters to the behavior therapy literature, and was elected president of the Association for Advancement of Behavior Therapy in 1968. Then professor of psychology at Temple University Medical School, he later went to Yale University (1970–1972) as director of clinical training. Since 1972 he has been a professor at Rutgers University, teaching at the Graduate School of Applied and Professional Psychology. His book *Behavior therapy and beyond* (1971) was the forerunner of his subsequent methods of multimodal therapy. *Multi-modal behavior therapy* (1976) was subsequently followed by *The practice of multimodal therapy* (1981).

LAZARUS, RICHARD S. (1922–)

Lazarus obtained the B.A. from the City College of New York. After military service in World War II, he returned to graduate school and obtained the Ph.D. (1948) from Pittsburgh, taught at Johns Hopkins and Clark universities, then went to the University of California at Berkeley in 1957. Lazarus's research career at Johns Hopkins and Clark centered on new look experiments on personality and perception, with a concern for individual differences. Among other research topics such as perceptual defense and studies of projective methods, he did research on autonomic discrimination without awareness (which he and McCleary called subception).

After forming the Berkeley Stress and Coping Project, he mounted efforts to generate a comprehensive theoretical framework for psychological stress and undertook programmatic research based on these formulations, pioneering the use of motion picture films to generate stress reactions naturalistically in the laboratory. Later he shifted to field research and a systems theoretical point of view. His efforts contributed to what has been called the cognitive revolution in psychology.

Lazarus has published more than 200 scientific articles and 17 monographs and textbooks in personality and clinical psychology. In 1966, his *Psychological stress and the coping process*, was published. With Susan Folkman, he published *Stress, appraisal, and coping*. He published *Emotion and adaptation*, which presents a cognitive–motivational–relational theory of the emotions.

He became professor emeritus at Berkeley in 1991.

LE BON, GUSTAVE (1841–1931)

A Frenchman by birth, Le Bon received his degree in medicine. His career involved three overlapping areas of intellectual endeavor: anthropology, natural science, and social psychology. His first studies were in developing measurement techniques for the physical characteristics of the various human races.

He then developed the doctrine of the hierarchy of races. To be considered a race or a subrace, in his sense, a group of people had to share the same sentiments and ways of thinking. The criteria he set up involved the degree of reasoning ability, power of attention, and mastery of instinctual needs. For example, comparing the mental characteristics of the Anglo-Saxons with those of the Latins, he found the Anglo-Saxons superior in every way.

He also developed another hierarchy which he called the hierarchy of sexes. According to this system animals, the insane, socialists, children, degenerates, and primitive people were considered inferior beings.

His most famous book, *The crowd*, was published in 1895. He believed that the behavior of people in a crowd differed essentially from human individual behavior. In a crowd there was a mutual unity of minds which could be expressed as intolerance, irresistible power, or irresponsibility. The action of crowds could be sudden and extreme; the intellectual processes were rudimentary and mechanical. This was one of the several "group mind" theories which flourished at the time. In a crowd situation the most rational of humans could behave as brutes. There developed a mental contagion which allowed the unconscious minds of the leader and the crowd to penetrate each other by a mysterious mechanism. Le Bon summed it up by saying that any individual conviction that is weak may be reinforced when it becomes collective.

R. W. LUNDIN

LEE, CHANG-HO (1936–)

Lee received the B.A. and M.A. degrees from Seoul National University and went to the University of Texas at Austin, receiving a Ph.D. under the supervision of Richard Mowsessian in 1974. Lee has been one of the main figures for identifying an Oriental model of counseling and psychotherapy. The emphasis in his model includes educative dialogue, integrational approach, tolerance training, assets reinforcement and enhancing social interest rather than empathy, analytical approach, catharsis, behavior modification, and self-introspection.

Since his return to the faculty of the department of psychology at Seoul National University in 1974, he has been actively involved with the national psychological associations and Asian–Oceanian psychological societies, serving as president of Korean Counselor's Association (1987–1989) and Korean Psychological Association (1992–1993). His publications include *Introduction to counseling psychology, Foundations of counseling interview*, and *Principles and practice of group counseling*.

LEEPER, ROBERT WARD (1904–1986)

Leeper received the B.A. from Allegheny College and planned to go on to theological seminary. For a while he worked at a variety of jobs to learn more about people. He went to Clark University receiving the M.A. and the Ph.D. in 1930. While at Clark, he studied with the behaviorist Walter Hunter, but he never really became attached to behaviorism's point of view. He taught briefly at the University of Arkansas, then received a Guggeheim Fellowship to study under Karl Lashley at the University of Chicago. He then taught at Cornell College in Iowa. While in Iowa, he became acquainted with Kurt Lewin and was attracted to his theoretical position. As a result he wrote a readable and understandable book on Lewin's psychology (for many, Lewin's original works were difficult to understand).

In 1937 he went to the University of Oregon where he remained for the rest of his career. Other books included *The psychology of personality* (with Peter Madison) and *Toward understanding human personality*.

R. W. LUNDIN

LEFCOURT, HERBERT (1936–)

Lefcourt obtained the B.A. from Antioch College, and the M.A. and Ph.D. (1963) from Ohio State University. He interned in clinical psychology at the U.S.P.H.S. Hospital in Lexington, Kentucky, for two years. Upon graduation he assumed a position on the faculty of the University of Waterloo in Ontario. He has been there ever since, having been clinical director twice during that time.

A full professor since 1971, Lefcourt has been a major contributor to research concerned with the personality construct known as locus of control, having helped create specific measures of the construct. Among his publications are *Locus of control: Current trends in theory and research* and *Research with the locus of control construct*, volumes 1, 2, and 3. A 1966 *Psychological Bulletin* article was cited as a citation classic in 1979.

He has served on the editorial boards of several journals and was an associate editor of Personality and Social Psychology Bulletin and an advisory editor of the *Journal of Personality and Social Psychology*. He is a fellow in the American and Canadian Psychological Associations and has been a member of the Personality-Cognition Study section of NIMH. His more recent research has focused upon locus of control, humor, and social support as moderators of stress.

LEIBNITZ, GOTTFRIED WILHELM (1646–1716)

Leibnitz studied at the universities of Leipzig and Jena. He received the doctorate at Mainz in 1666. He was one of the inventors of the calculus, as well as a philosopher, historian, scientist, and diplomat. Between 1676 and 1716 he served as librarian and privy councilor to the Duke of Brunswick. Only after his death did he become a real intellectual force in Europe, for only his *Theodicy* (1710) was published during his lifetime.

His unique contribution to the understanding of nature and the human mind was in his theory of the "monad," his term for the unit or individuality of all substances. He believed that the world consisted of an infinite number of monads which were points of force rather than substance. All monads acted independently of one another. They were created by God, the supreme monad in a pre-established harmony with other monads. Monads might appear to interact but did not influence one another in any way. Each monad had its own individual existence, so there was no causation among them. Both mind and body followed their own laws in perfect agreement. The destiny of all monads was pre-established by God. Leibnitz's parallelism was one solution to the mind–body problem which has concerned philosophers and psychologists for centuries. The implications of this psychophysical parallelism were to become clear in the psychologies of Wilhelm Wundt and Edward Titchener in the late nineteenth and early twentieth centuries. For these men and others, all mental events ran parallel to their physical correlates.

Also basic to Leibnitz's philosophy was his principle whereby states in nature were continuous; there were no gaps. There was a continuity of change which was almost indistinguishable. All monads had various degrees of clarity or consciousness, ranging from the relatively unclear and unconscious to the most conscious and perceptible. The degrees of consciousness were a relative matter. The lower degrees of consciousness (unconscious) Leibnitz called *petites perceptions* (little perceptions). When actualized, they became *apperceptions*. Thus the lowliest tree or stone had a slight degree of consciousness and the progression continued to the human mind and finally to God, who had the greatest degree of consciousness. Leibnitz was probably the first to develop a theory of degrees of consciousness, which was to become the cornerstone for Sigmund Freud's conception of the mental apparatus. Besides Freud, Alfred Adler, Carl Jung, and other adherents to psychoanalytical thinking have made use of degrees of consciousness and unconsciousness in their explanation of the human personality.

R. W. LUNDIN

LE NY, JEAN-FRANÇOIS (1924–   )

Le Ny studied philosophy and psychology at the Sorbonne. After five years as a psychologist in a counseling center, he entered the National Center of Scientific Research as a full-time scientist. In 1961 he received the newly created third-cycle doctorate, and in 1967 the state doctorate, both while working on psychology of learning. In 1961 he became a lecturer at the University of Lille; since 1968 he has been a professor at the University of Paris. His teaching concerns the fields of general, experimental, and cognitive psychology, as does his research work. He was the chairman of the program committee for the 19th International Congress of Psychology, held in Paris in 1976.

Le Ny has published *La généralisation du stimulus, Le conditionnement et l'apprentissage, Apprentissage et activités psychologiques*, and *La sémantique psychologique*. With Walter Kintsch he edited a book published in French as a special issue of the *Bulletin de Psychologie* under the title *Langage et compréhension* (Paris, 1982), and in English as *Language and comprehension*. His recent work is devoted to various theoretical and experimental problems regarding meaning, discourse comprehension, and computer-assisted cognitive instruction.

LEONTIEV, ALEKSEI (1903–   )

Leontiev studied at Moscow State University, where he received the Ed.D degree. There he became associated with Lev Vygotsky, who had developed a cultural-historical theory of higher human mental processes. Leontiev then went to the University of Moscow to teach psychology in 1924. When the 18th International Congress of Psychology met in Moscow in 1966, he served as its president.

Leontiev held to the cultural-historical theory, which attempted to use Marxist doctrine as a basis for human development. Besides accounting for human psychological processes, the theory held that when persons interact, psychological processes develop. He was particularly concerned with applying the theory to children and their development. The end product of development was cultural-historical, rather than hereditary. Thus Leontiev made a distinct separation between psychology and biology. In an article in *Soviet Psychology* edited by R. B. Winn, Leontiev argued that "the consciousness of man is social and historical in nature . . . it is determined by social existence and . . . changes qualitatively with changes in social and economic conditions." He did not consider the personality of an individual to be a natural process, but rather the product of behavior involved in social relations. In this process, education was critical. Thus training in Marxist tradition would result in an individual's adherence to Soviet principles.

LEPLAT, JACQUES (1921–   )

LePlat received the doctorate from the University of Paris in 1974. From 1966 on he has been the director of the Laboratory of Work Psychology at the Ecole des Hautes Etudes in Paris. He is the codirector and editor of *Le Travail Humain*, a French journal of work psychology, physiology, and ergonomics. He was a founding member of the French Language Ergonomics Society.

LePlat's major contributions in the field of work psychology deal with vigilance, control, cognitive processes, ergonomics, training, and safety. LePlat has published approximately 80 articles in French and international journals, as well as contributions to edited books. His major publications include *Attention et incertitude dans les travaux de surveillance et d'inspection* (1968); *La formation par l'apprentissage* (with C. Enard and A. Weill-Fassina, 1970); *Introduction à la psychologie du travail* (with X. Cuny, 1977); *Les accidents de travail* (with X. Cuny, 1979); and *La psychologie ergonomique* (1980).

LERNER, ARTHUR (1915–   )

Lerner obtained his formal schooling in Chicago and Los Angeles, earning degrees from Central YMCA College (now Roosevelt University), Northwestern University, and two doctorates from the University of Southern California. He is best known for the application of poetry to the therapy/counseling experience. He holds that "poetry in therapy is a tool and not a school" (*Poetry in the therapeutic experience*, p. xv).

An early interest in literature, particularly poetry, led him to believe that the greatest human achievement was language and that life was a "poetic unraveling," the theme of his books *Rhymed and unrhymed, Follow-up,* and *Starting points.* Lerner regards all literary genres as vital sources for understanding behavior; he holds that one's cognitive and unconscious understanding is shaped by the language, symbols, metaphors, and similes which influence one's growth and development.

His professional career includes work as a poet, psychotherapist, pioneer in poetry therapy, and professor of psychology at Los Angeles City College, where he helped train human services workers and taught courses in psychology and the humanities. He is director of poetry therapy at the Woodview-Calabasas Hospital in Calabasas, California; consultant in poetry therapy at the Van Nuys Psychiatric Hospital in Van Nuys, California; and founder and director of the Poetry Therapy Institute in Encino, California.

LEVELT, WILLEM J. M. (1938–   )

Levelt is the founder and director of the Max Planck Institute for Psycholinguistics in Nijmegen, The Netherlands. Levelt received the Ph.D. in experimental psychology from Leyden University in 1965. His initial research, at the Institute for Perception in Soesterberg, was in vision, audition, and mathematical psychology. *On binocular rivalry* is one of several publications from that period. While he was a research fellow at Harvard University's Center for Cognitive Studies in 1965–1966, his interests moved to psycholinguistics and linguistics.

After a visiting professorship at the University of Illinois, Levelt obtained the chair of experimental psychology at Groningen University, The Netherlands. There he continued work in perception, especially in dichoptic color vision and in dichotic loudness (binaural additivity of loudness), and began research in sentence perception, and the structure of linguistic intuitions such as grammaticality and syntactic relatedness. As a member of the Institute of Advanced Study at Princeton (1971–1972), he developed much of the latter research into his three-volume *Formal grammars in linguistics and psycholinguistics*.

Levelt has been editor or coeditor of several anthologies, among them *Studies in the perception of language*, and of several professional journals, including *Cognitive Psychology*.

LEWIN, KURT (1890–1947)

Lewin received the Ph.D. from the University of Berlin in 1914. Among his early associates were two of the Gestalt psychologists, Max Wertheimer and Wolfgang Kohler. Some psychologists consider Lewin's system to be an extension of the Gestalt movement.

Lewin considered his system to be a *topological and vectoral psychology*. He took the terms "topology" and "vector" from mathematics. Topology investigates the properties of space. But topology was not enough: he needed a concept of force or vector.

Lewin began his system of psychology with the concept of *life space*. This was a psychological field, the space in which a person moved. This constituted the totality of facts that determined the behavior of an individual at any one time. Behavior was a function of life space at any moment: $B = fL$. L was a psychological field and not necessarily a physical one. The life space included oneself and other people and objects as one perceived them.

The life space was divided into regions by boundaries. Each region might be considered a psychological fact. The boundaries had several dimensions such as nearness/remoteness. This could be illustrated by a college student wanting to be a physician: the region of setting up practice as a physician is quite remote from the present situation. Other regions which must be passed through might include graduating from college, entering medical school, graduation from medical school, internship, and finally setting up practice. Another dimension of boundaries was firmness/weakness. Some boundaries were easy to cross, while others, such as passing a qualifying examination could be firm and difficult.

When a person passed from one region to another, movement occurred which had direction. In such movement one followed a pathway. Here Lewin invented a kind of geometry which he called "hodological space." The characteristics of a given path varied according to the situation, and the direction depended on the properties of the entire field.

On the dynamic side, Lewin postulated a concept of tension. Tension occurred when needs arose. Needs could be either psychological or physiological.

Objects in the life space also had valences—plus or minus, depending on whether they were attractive or repulsive. Often a life space might contain several regions in which several valences existed at the same time. A conflict could occur between two objects both of which had a positive valence, or in a case where two objects were equally repulsive, but a person had to choose between the two. The vector or force constituted the push which directed a person toward or away from a goal. This force was correlated with the valence of the object.

In his later years Lewin directed his attention to problems of social psychology. A major research effort (Lewin, Lippitt, & White, 1939) related to various social climates and aggression. Lewin also developed the concept of group dynamics, an application to the group that he borrowed from his earlier individual psychology. Just as the person in his life space constituted the psychological field, so the group and its environment constituted the social field. The group was characterized by a dynamic interdependence of its members. One's status depended on one's region as it related to other regions (members of the group). The group was subject to cohesive and disruptive forces. Disruptive forces arose out of too strong barriers between members which hampered communication. The group constituted a field of forces and individuals were attracted or repelled, depending on the kinds of valences existing in the group.

R. W. LUNDIN

LIÉBEAULT, AMBROISE-AUGUSTE (1823–1904)

Liébeault spent most of his life as a quiet, hard-working country doctor in the provinces of France. While in medical school he had had some acquaintance with hypnosis. In 1864 he settled in the city of Nancy. Here he treated the peasants in a kindly way and became known to them as "le bon père" (the good father). He told his patients that if they wished to be treated with drugs they would have to pay, but if they allowed him to hypnotize them as a treatment for their symptoms, there would be no fee. He established a clinic which consisted of two rooms in a corner of his garden.

The work of Liébeault and that of James Braid, an English physician, marked a unique event in the history of psychology and medicine. Hypnosis was not only a new way of treating people with certain ailments, but it marked the beginnings of psychotherapy.

In 1882 Liébeault became acquainted with Hippolyte Bernheim, a well known physician of the time. Liébeault taught Bernheim the hypnotic technique and together they published a text on the subject. Treating patients with hypnosis, they became known as the Nancy School, in rivalry with another center in Paris, headed by Jean Charot, also using the hypnotic technique.

Liébeault and Bernheim used the method of suggesting sleep to induce the hypnotic trance. While under hypnosis the patients were presented with new attitudes and beliefs that they accepted without question. Thus they were told that they would be well and rid of their symptoms. It is clear now that many of the patients were suffering from hysterical symptoms such as functional blindness, deafness, and paralysis. In a number of cases the symptoms returned, so the hypnotic suggestions had only a transitory influence; but in other cases the cure seemed permanent.

By the turn of the century the Nancy School came under the influence of the "autosuggestion" proposed by Emile Coué, who advised his patients to tell themselves, "Every day in every way I am feeling better and better." Thus a distinction was made between the "Old Nancy School" of Liébeault and Bernheim, and the "New Nancy School" of Coué.

Interpretations as to the nature of hypnosis and hysteria differed between the Nancy School and the Paris School. Charcot in Paris regarded hypnosis as a pathological physiological state and related it to inadequate functioning of the nervous system, which manifested itself in the form of hysteria. Liébeault and Bernheim did not agree, feeling that there was nothing basically wrong with the nervous system of hysterics, and that the whole matter revolved around the matter of suggestion.

R. W. LUNDIN

LIENERT, GUSTAV A. (1920–   )

Lienert was educated in Czechoslovakia. Entering military service, he was wounded at Stalingrad, then later became a POW of U.S. forces in 1945. Discharged in 1946, he resumed medical training in Innsbruck and in 1950 got the M.D. degree in Vienna.

More than 20 years later Lienert was honored with a doctor of science degree by Colgate University, being commended as follows:

His study of psychology started as a hobby in 1947, and in 1952 he was awarded the Ph.D. at Vienna. He has taught at the universities of Marburg, Hamburg, Düsseldorf, and Erlangen-Nürnberg. In his native land, Dr. Lienert has helped reshape the scope and direction of German psychology during the last three decades. He is the author of an authoritative German language text on diagnostic methods and an internationally known three-volume work on nonparametric statistical methods. He was elected president of the International Biometric Society (German Region) in 1976. Last year colleagues and former students all over the world honored Dr. Lienert with a "Festschrift" to mark his 60th birthday. At the same occasion an international symposium on "Experimental Psychology in the Year 2000" was dedicated to him who "reestablished experimental animal research in German psychological institutes with Colgate's assistance."

Beyond being nicknamed "the nonparametric Lienert," he was also associated, with the age-regression hypothesis of intellectual deterioration under alcohol and LSD. He engaged in developing configural frequency analysis (CFA) as a method for classifying persons by dichotomous variables rather than by scores of hypothetical traits, favoring typological rather than dimensional personality theories. Heuristically proposed in 1968, CFA was presented as an inferential method (Krauth & Lienert, 1973) and has been promoted by subsequent papers, mainly in the English-language *Biometrical Journal*.

LIKERT, RENSIS (1903–1981)

Likert began college at the University of Michigan in engineering, but ended up getting the B.A. in sociology and economics. The Ph.D. was conferred by Columbia University in 1932; his landmark dissertation, "A technique for the measurement of attitudes," was published in *Archives of Psychology*. This dissertation was the basis for development of the Likert Scale, a standard tool of social scientists.

After a brief teaching stint at New York University, Likert worked for the Life Insurance Sales Research Bureau, where his findings from interviews and paper-and-pencil questionnaires resulted in the series *Morale and agency management* (with J. M. Willits), a comparative study of the 10 best and 10 mediocre insurance agencies. This study presaged his continuing interest and findings in organizational leadership.

In late 1939 Likert was hired by the Division of Program Surveys in the Bureau of Agricultural Economics, where he developed techniques for interviewing, coding, and sampling techniques fundamental to social science research today. His government work during World War II included Office of War Information studies concerning public attitudes, public experiences, and behavior. His collaboration with Iowa State University led to a method of sampling households which has become known as probability sampling. He and others conducted extensive studies concerning war bonds, alien nationals, and the effects of wartime bombing.

In 1946, with several of his cross-discipline colleagues from those government projects, he was invited to the University of Michigan to establish the Survey Research Center. With the addition of three more centers, it is now called the Institute for Social Research. Likert directed this institute until his retirement in 1970. During that time two of his major books, *New patterns of management* and *The human organization*, were published. Another book, *New ways of managing conflict*, coauthored with his wife Jane Gibson Likert, was published in 1976. These books—and more than 100 journal articles—presented his metatheoretical statement of participative management, and continued the refinement of conclusions which had begun with his insurance agency work and engaged Likert's attention throughout his life. Upon retiring from the university, he organized a consulting firm which bears his name—Rensis Likert Associates—in which he worked vigorously until his death in 1981, applying research findings in management and organizational areas.

LINDZEY, GARDNER (1920–   )

Lindzey received the B.A. from the Pennsylvania State University and the Ph.D. (1949) from Harvard. He was professor of psychology at Syracuse, Harvard, Minnesota, and Texas before becoming president and director of the Center for Advanced Study in the Behavioral Sciences (1975–1989). He was president of the American Psychological Association (1966–1967) and is a member of the American Academy of Arts and Sciences, the American Philosophical Society, the National Academy of Sciences and the Institute of Medicine.

He is perhaps best known for his contributions to the fields of personality, social psychology, and behavior genetics. Author or editor of more than 20 books and 100 technical articles his most widely cited books are *Theories of personality* (with C. S. Hall), three editions of the *Handbook of social psychology*, and four editions of the *History of psychology in autobiography*. *Theories of personality* was the first book of its kind, leading the way for many others and for courses designed after this landmark publication.

LIPPITT, RONALD O. (1914–1986)

Lippitt did his undergraduate work at Springfield College in Massachusetts and earned the M.A. and Ph.D. degrees at the State University of Iowa. There he became a close associate of Kurt Lewin. While at Iowa, along with Ralph White he performed the series of research studies on the effects of various kinds of leadership: democratic, authoritarian, and laissez-faire with boys' groups. These studies are now classics and still frequently quoted in a variety of psychology texts. They demonstrated how conditions may be changed to improve social relations in many settings.

After World War II he rejoined Lewin and his colleagues who had founded the Research Center for Group Dynamics at MIT. After Lewin's untimely death in 1947, the center moved to the University of Michigan where the name was changed to the Institute for Social Research (IST). During the next decades Lippitt directed his efforts toward planned change, writing a book on the subject. His professional life was devoted to social psychology and its applications.

R. W. LUNDIN

LIPPS, THEODOR (1851–1914)

Lipps was educated at Erlangen, Tübingen, Utrecht, and Bonn. He held university appointments at Bonn, Breslau, and Munich. In 1896 he rounded the Psychological Institute at Munich. In the same year he was the joint president with Carl Stumpf of the Third International Congress of Psychology.

Lipps published on a wide range of topics including literature (mostly tragedy), paleobotany, ethics, logic, optical illusions, wit and humor, hypnotism, and musical consonance/dissonance. A peripheral member of the Austrian School, Lipps considered psychology to be philosophy made scientific through the use of logic. (He considered logic to be a special branch of psychology.)

Lipps is remembered most for his empathy theory (*Einfühlung*) of esthetic enjoyment, published in his *Raurnaesthetik* (1897). The aesthetic feeling was grounded in four different types of projection of the observer into the perceived object: (1) general apperceptive empathy: the animation of the forms of common objects, such as seeing a line as movement; (2) empirical empathy: the humanizing of natural objects, as when one talks about a "babbling" brook; (3) mood empathy: putting feelings into colors or music, such as describing an object as "relaxed blue" or mentioning a "triumphant march", and (4) empathy for the sensible appearance of living beings: interpreting gestures and other behaviors of individuals as indicators of their inner lives. Through these four types of empathy, it was clear that beauty is a function both of the object and of the beholder.

C. S. PEYSER

LOCKE, JOHN (1632–1704)

Although Locke lived in the seventeenth century, his writings expressed more the spirit of the eighteenth. He was the first of the British empiricists and bridged the gap between the rational continental philosophers such as Descartes, Leibnitz, and Spinoza and a new attitude toward knowledge which was fostered in the empirical tradition to follow.

Locke was educated at Oxford, he dabbled in medicine but never received a degree in that subject. He spent most of his life in politics and minor government offices. At the age of 58 he published his most famous work, *An essay\concerning human understanding*. This was revised several times; the fourth edition (1670) was of particular importance because it first introduced Locke's notion of the association of ideas.

In the *Essay* Locke stated that all ideas came from experience. At birth the human mind could be considered analogous to a clean slate, a *tabula rasa*. Here he opposed Descartes, who considered some ideas inborn. For Locke the mind was basically passive and could do only two things. First, it could receive experiences from the outside world, which involved the act of sensing which was the primary source of knowledge. Second, the mind could reflect upon itself. It was through this process of reflection—what we today call introspection—that hu-

mans engaged in the process called thinking. Ideas could be simple or complex, as in merely sensing a color or combining a number of senses into a complex idea.

Ideas also had qualities, *primary and secondary*. The primary qualities were inseparable from the object, which include movement, extension, shape, solidarity. The secondary qualities resided in the mind as experiences of the real world like touch, taste, smell, vision, and hearing; they were known apart from the object.

Locke had no doubt about the existence of a real world (though his successors George Berkeley and David Hume questioned this). However, Locke realized he could never know that real world's substance. He argued that he could not experience the qualities of things without there being something behind them, but that something was "I know not what."

Locke was the first in a long tradition to write about the association of ideas. He exemplified the significance of association in his affirmation of the "man born blind and suddenly made to see." Such a man could not identify a cube by sight, if he had not experienced it also through the sense of touch: these two experiences had to be associated.

His great significance for psychology is that he started an empirical tradition. The fact that things exist as a basic reality is a presupposition of all science. Furthermore, the concept of association introduced by him is the basis for many current psychological theories.

R. W. LUNDIN

LOEB, JACQUES (1859–1924)

Loeb, a German zoologist and physiologist, spent most of his productive career in the United States at Bryn Mawr, the universities of Chicago and California, and the Rockefeller Institute.

He put forth his theory of the tropism as applied to animal behavior while still in Germany (1890). The following year he came to the United States. His theory represented a return to the mechanistic view set forth earlier by René Descartes, which stated that animals acted like machines. Loeb thought of a tropism as a physical-chemical action toward or away from objects, as had been found in plants. He generalized the conception to animals as an orientation of an organism in a field of forces. This orientation occurred through adjustive movements which equalized the innervation on the organism's two sides as cybernetic action.

As one of the early animal psychologists, Loeb influenced the thinking of John B. Watson, the founder of behaviorism, who studied under Loeb at the University of Chicago early in the twentieth century. Loeb believed that animals were so structured that they would react selectively to certain kinds of energy expended upon them. Although most of his examples involved fairly low forms of animals—jellyfish, starfish, and worms—theoretically, he extended his theory to higher forms. Like other animal psychologists of his time, he wanted to ascertain at what point on the evolutionary scale animals achieved consciousness. His criterion for consciousness was whether or not the animal was capable of "associative memory."

Although he was concerned with the concept of consciousness, Loeb's basic influence on psychology was as a forerunner of an objective, naturalistic psychology fostered by the behavioristic movement that followed.

R. W. LUNDIN

LOGAN, FRANK A. (1924–   )

Logan was named after his father, who had developed the gas-mask cannister used in both World Wars. After receiving the Ph.D. from the

University of Iowa in 1951, he continued his education as a postdoctoral fellow at the Institute of Human Relations of Yale University, where he became a member of the faculty and developed his major theoretical position, *micromolar theory*.

The essence of micromolar theory is that quantitative dimensions of a response (e.g., speed and amplitude) are defining properties and hence are part of what gets learned. In an extensive series of studies with rats (*Incentive*), Logan rejected the view that quantitative dimensions measure response strength. Later research with humans showed that performance speed and even learning to learn depend on practice speed.

Most of Logan's research was done within the context of stimulus-response incentive theory in the Hull-Spence tradition. He was one of the first to study the free behavior situation, in which an organism earns all its food or water by emitting operant behavior. Later Logan began to develop a "hybrid" learning theory, combining features of various existing theories into a single system. Among the unique aspects of his hybrid theory is the postulation of two kinds of learning processes, a cognitive-associative one for classical conditioning and a stimulus-response one for operant conditioning.

Logan was elected president of the Division of Experimental Psychology of American Psychological Association, where he has also served on the council and in various other capacities. He was chairman of the Psychology Department of the University of New Mexico, where he is currently a professor.

LORENZ, KONRAD (1903–1989)

Along with Tinbergen, Lorenz is generally considered one of the founders of ethology. He received the M.D. then the Ph.D. (1933), both from the University of Vienna. During this early period, he set up many of his hypothesis on animal behavior, such as imprinting, innate releasing mechanism, and fixed action patterns.

Lorenz's methods were not always conventional. He never did a formal experiment, and his descriptive observations were often anecdotal. He infuriated his more conventional colleagues by saying, "If I have one good example, I don't give a fig for statistics." By this he meant that if he had seen an animal do something striking, he did not need to see a lot of other animals do the same thing to confirm what he already knew. His doctrine of imprinting is still a focus of research interest after a half century. Lorenz loved animals and kept an enormous variety, including jackdows, geese, dogs, and fish.

He received the Nobel Prize in 1973 which he shared with Niko Tinbergen and Karl von Friwsch. One of his later theories has been subject to considerable debate, namely, that of innate aggression. According to Lorenz, aggression involves stored instinctive energy and needs to be discharged. Then follows a refactory phase to build up the energy that has been flushed much like the flushing and refilling of a toilet.

Lorenz authored many articles (only one with Tinbergen) and books. Some of his books are *King Soloman's ring: New light on animal ways, Evolution and modification of behavior, On aggression,* and *Civilized man's eight deadly sins.*

R. W. LUNDIN

LOTZE, HERMANN (1817–1881)

Lotze received both the M.D. and Ph.D. at Leipzig. He was apparently an impressive student under Weber, Volkmann, and Fechner, as he was immediately made *Dozent* in faculties of both philosophy and medicine. Most of his career was spent at Göttingen with such outstanding students as Carl Stumpf, G. E. Müller, and Franz Brentano.

Lotze's 1852 text, *Medicinische Psychologie,* is considered the first on physiological psychology. Actually, only the first part deals with the topic; the second deals with sensations, feeling, instinct, and space perception, and the third with behavior pathology and therapy.

In addition to this text, Lotze is known for his doctrine of local signs, typical of nineteenth-century thought, in which philosophical concepts rather than empirical data dominated the interpreted physiology of sense organs. How do we perceive space—tell where on our skin or in our field of vision the stimulation has occurred? Lotze's answer was that the locality encoded a sign in the neural transmission and that our mind put the information together; by noting which sensations were adjacent, we perceived the total space.

Lotze also wrote about sensory illusions such as color and afterimages. Later in his life, his writing turned more toward the philosophy of religion, logic, aesthetics, and metaphysics. But he was always known as a stimulating teacher at a time of vigorous intellectual development in psychology.

C. S. PEYSER

LUNDIN, ROBERT W. (1920–   )

Lundin received the B.A. from DePauw University and the M.A. and Ph.D. from Indiana University, where he studied with such eminent behaviorists as B. F. Skinner and J. R. Kantor. He taught at Denison University and Hamilton College, and became William R. Kenan Professor of Psychology and department chairman at The University of the South.

Lundin's first book, *An objective psychology of music* (1967/1953) reflected his interest in music as well as his behavioristic attitudes. He wrote it as a protest against the mentalistic approaches to the psychology of music presented by Carl Seashore and Max Schoen. He attempted to put the study of musical behavior on firm experimental and empirical grounds.

His book *Personality: An experimental approach* and its successor, *Personality: A behavioral analysis* were attempts to apply behavioral concepts to the field of personality. Many Freudian concepts were reinterpreted in the light of a behavioristic psychology. *Principles of psychopathology* presented abnormal behavior in the light of an experimental and behavioristic approach. *Theories and systems of psychology* deals with major schools and theories in the light of their positive contributions to psychology, as well as their difficulties and drawbacks.

LURIA, ALEXANDER R. (1902–   )

Luria graduated from the University of Kazan, U.S.S.R. He received the degrees of M.D., Ed.D., and D.Med. from the University of Moscow, where he later became a professor in the Department of Psychology and head of the Department of Neuropsychology.

Luria had a broad background in psychoneurology and carried out research on aphasia, the restoration of functions following brain trauma, speech, and higher cortical functions. He developed theories of language disorders and of the functions of the frontal lobe. He believed that mental functions are complex functional systems which cannot be localized in isolated cell groups or narrow regions of the cortex. Rather, the cell groups must be organized in systems of zones working in concert, each performing its role in the complex system.

Since many of his works have been available in English, Luria is well known in the United States. In the 1920s he studied human conflict, using hand movements and associative responses into which a conflict situation was introduced. This work was summarized in *The nature of human conflicts.*

MACCOBY, ELEANOR E. (1917–   )

Maccoby distinguished herself in the field of the psychology of sex differences. She received the B.A. from the University of Washington in 1939. She spent the World War II years in Washington, D.C., and then went to the University of Michigan for the M.A. and Ph.D. (1950). For the next 8 yr, she was a lecturer in social relations at Harvard, before joining the faculty at Stanford, as professor of psychology. Her books include *The psychology of sex differences* (with C. N. Jacklin) and two edited texts: *Readings on social psychology* (with others) and *The development of sex differences*.

MacCORQUODALE, KENNETH (1919–1986)

MacCorquodale received the B.A. at the University of Minnesota with the intention of pursuing a career in art. However, his interests turned to psychology, and he entered the Minnesota graduate school in that field. Among other distinguished professors, he studied with B. F. Skinner who had recently become an assistant professor there. He received the Ph.D. at Minnesota after returning from the military service in 1946. He remained a member of the Minnesota faculty until his retirement.

His career was intertwined with that of Paul Meehl in their combined work in the philosophy of science and learning theory, most notably that of E. C. Tolman. MacCorquodale and Meehl are well known for their joint article "On a distinction between hypothetical constructs and intervening variables." They also collaborated on Tolman's theory in Estes et al.'s *Modern learning theory*.

MacCorquodale published a retrospective review of Skinner's verbal behavior and a rebuttal to Chomsky's critical review of Skinner's book. Besides his scholarship, he was highly regarded as a teacher, receiving the Liberal Arts College's Distinguished Teaching Award.

R. W. LUNDIN

MACH, ERNST (1838–1916)

In 1864 Mach was appointed professor of mathematics at the University of Graz and three years later became professor of physics at Prague.

In his early years at Prague, Mach was concerned with the study of visual space perception, but was better known at that time for his work in the perception of rotation of movement. To explain how one perceives bodily rotation, he set forth the theory that the sense organs for this experience were to be found in the semicircular canals of the inner ear. This theory, with some modification, is still prevalent today.

Mach has also been identified as one of the early positivists who believed that sensations were the data of all science. All science is observational, and the primary data of observation are sensations. However, unlike Comte and other positivists, he did not deny the validity of introspection as a method. Thus he brought the data of physics and psychology very close together. In *The analysis of experience* he went beyond the mere analysis of simple sensory experience, adding a space–form dimension illustrated by a triangle or any other geometric figure: triangles can be large or small or of different colors, but they do not lose the dimension of triangularity. Likewise, he added the time–form dimension, as in a melody which can be played in a variety of different keys and still maintain the quality of that melody. Thus the space and time forms were independent of their elements. The implication of this concept of "form" was to be taken up later by the Gestalt psychologists.

R. W. LUNDIN

MacKINNON, DONALD WALLACE (1903–1987)

MacKinnon received the A.B. (summa cum laude) from Bowdin College in history. His graduate education was in psychology at Harvard University. (M.A. and Ph.D. in 1933). During this period, he also served as instructor in psychology at the universities of Maine and Harvard. He was the first American student to work with Kurt Lewin at the University of Berlin.

Between 1931 and 1933, MacKinnon joined the faculty at Bryn Mawr College, often teaching summers at Harvard. During World War II, he served in the Office of Strategic Services (OSS).

He joined the faculty at the University of California at Berkeley in 1947. There he was the first director of the Institute of Personality Assessment (1949–1970). During his career he was active in the fields of personality, assessment, and creativity. He brought together much of his research in the volume *In search of effectiveness: Identifying and development of creativity*.

MacKinnon was on the editorial boards of many psychological journals and served as president of the Division of Personality of the American Psychological Association.

R. W. LUNDIN

MACKINTOSH, NICHOLAS J. (1935–   )

Mackintosh was educated in Canada and England, receiving the B.A. in psychology and philosophy at Oxford, and the Ph.D., on animal discrimination learning, at Oxford in 1963. At Oxford he was taught, both as an undergraduate and as a graduate student, by N. S. Sutherland, with whom he collaborated in research and writing over the next 10 years.

Mackintosh held the following positions: university lecturer at Oxford from 1964 to 1967; Killam research professor at Dalhousie University until 1973; professor at the University of Sussex until 1981; professor and department head at the University of Cambridge from 1981 on; and visiting appointments at the universities of Pennsylvania (1965–1966) and Hawaii (1972–1973), and at Bryn Mawr College (1977).[2]

His early research was on discrimination learning and mechanisms of attention in animals. Extension to animals other than rats (birds, fish, octopus) produced some comparative psychology. This was followed by a return to research on basic mechanisms of simple associative learning in classical and instrumental conditioning. Comparative psychology and intelligence testing remain subsidiary interests.

Mackintosh is a member of the Experimental Psychology Society and the British Psychological Society. He was editor of the *Quarterly Journal of Experimental Psychology* (1977–1980), and of the Comparative and Physiological Section of that journal from 1981 on.

MADDI, SALVATORE R. (1933–   )

Maddi received the B.A. and the M.A. in psychology from Brooklyn College and the Ph.D. (1960) in clinical psychology from Harvard. Maddi was an instructor, at the University of Chicago and later became chair of undergraduate psychology (1966–1970), director of clinical psychology (1971–1973), and director of divisional masters program (1975–1978). In 1986, he went to the University of California at Irvine and served as director of its program in social ecology (1986–1989).

Maddi has authored many papers and books. He has specialized on hardiness, creativity, existential psychology, and personality theory and research. Among his books are *Personality theories: A comparative analysis* and *The hardy executive: Health under stress*. He has practiced existential psychotherapy and is the founder of the Hardiness Institute, a psychological consulting company providing planning, assessment, and training to organizations and individuals.

Maddi has been president of Divisions I (General Psychology) and 10 (Psychology and the Arts) of the American Psychological Association and a visiting professor at the Educational Testing Service (1963–1964),

Harvard University (1969–1970), and the University of Rome (1987–1988). He was a Fulbright scholar at the Escola Paulista de Medicina in Sao Paolo, Brazil (1984–1985).

MAGENDIE, FRANÇOIS (1783–1855)

The French physiologist Magendie discovered that sensory fibers of a mixed nerve enter the spinal cord at a posterior nerve root, and that the motor fibers of the same nerve leave the cord by an anterior root. Since in 1811, unknown to Magendie, the British anatomist Sir Charles Bell had published the same discovery privately, a controversy resulted as to the priority of the discovery. In a sense history solved the problem, in that the joint discovery is known as the Bell–Magendie law. This discovery of the distinction between sensory and motor nerves paved the way for the work of Marshall Hall on reflex functions and the reflex arc.

Magendie was also concerned with the relationship of sensations to the nervous system. He contended that the seat of sensations was in the spinal cord, and that the cerebrum (brain) perceived the sensations from the cord. This being the case, the cerebrum could reproduce the sensations, thus accounting for memory.

Magendie also observed that the number of convolutions in the brains of animals differed according to their place on the scale of animal development. The number of convolutions correlated with the degrees of "perfection or imperfection of the intellectual faculties." Therefore the greater the number of convolutions, the higher the intellect would be.

R. W. LUNDIN

MAIER, STEVEN (1942–   )

Maier obtained a B.S. in biology from New York University. He studied with Richard L. Solomon and Henry Gleitman at the University of Pennsylvania and received the Ph.D. degree in psychology from that institution in 1968. After teaching at the University of Illinois for 5 yr, he joined the faculty of the department at the University of Colorado at Boulder in 1973 and has remained there since.

Maier's graduate training in experimental psychology concentrated on the psychology of learning and motivation, with special emphasis on the nature of the effects of stress. This work, carried on at the beginning with Martin Seligman, led him and Seligman to develop a theory of learned helplessness that has been influential in both theoretical and applied areas of psychology and psychiatry. Often with students and colleagues as co-authors, Maier published more than 100 scientific papers. Among his honors are Career research development awards, a research scientist award from the National Institute of Mental Health, and numerous research grants from the National Science Foundation and the National Institute of Health as well as the editorship of a major journal in his field, *Learning and Motivation*.

M. WERTHEIMER

MAILLOUX, NOËL (1909–   )

Mailloux obtained his early education in Montreal, getting the B.A. at the University of Montreal (1930), and the Ph.D. (1934) and S.Th.L. (1938) at St. Thomas University in Rome. He was ordained a priest of the Dominican Order in 1937. He is now professor emeritus of psychology at the University of Montreal, where he founded the Department of Psychology in 1942, served as chairman (1942–1975, 1969–1973), and devoted his whole career to teaching and research (1942–1975). Currently, he is director of the Centre of Research on Human Relations and chief editor of *Contributions à l'Etude des Sciences de l'Homme*.

Mailloux is an ex-president and honorary fellow of the Canadian Psychological Association. He was president of the Canadian Society of Criminology and vice-president of the International Society of Criminology. He was a member of the Executive Board of the International Union of Psychological Science (1954–1977). He has published and edited six books and over 120 articles or monographs. Besides receiving several prizes and awards from scientific societies, he is a fellow of the Royal Society of Canada, an officer of the Order of Canada, and a member of the Accademia di Santa Chiara (Genoa).

MAIMONIDES, MOSES (1135–1204)

Maimonides is considered the greatest of the medieval Jewish philosophers and interpreters of Rabbinical literature. He was born in Córdoba, Spain. When Córdoba fell to the Almohades (1148), he fled to Morocco and then settled in Cairo, where he practiced medicine. His medical fame came from his writings and translations. He translated the *Canon* of Avicenna into Hebrew and some of the works of Hippocrates and Galen into Arabic. His original medical writings were on a variety of topics: asthma, reptile poisoning and its treatment, and hemorrhoids.

As a philosopher Maimonides attempted to reconcile Greek science as he had found it in Arabic sources and his own Jewish faith. This resulted in his *Guide to the perplexed*, written in Arabic between 1176 and 1191. While he felt that in the matter of creation one should follow the Scriptures, he followed Aristotle in stating that the existence of a Creator could not be proved. Yet the necessary existence of some reason for change and motion in the world could be philosophically demonstrated. In his description of the universe, he derived a series of descending intellects, similar to that of Plotinus. These came from God, who presided over the heavenly spheres, and terminated in the active intellect found in human thinking. He agreed with Aristotle that the intellects were pure form and made a sharp distinction between the matter of the heavenly spheres and things on earth.

He rejected a personal immortality. The capacity for individual thinking disappeared with the destruction of the body. Yet in earthly existence an individual might increase in understanding and knowledge, and so in this life attain peace and happiness and a kind of immortality in the here and now.

R. W. LUNDIN

MAKARENKO, ANTON SEMYONOVICH (1899–1939)

Makarenko's thinking has had a great impact on Russian personality theory and practice. His major work, *The road to life: An epic of education* (1933), has been cited by most Soviet writers on personality, education, and pedagogy. In 1920 he was assigned the task of rehabilitating children made homeless by the 1917 revolution. His work also involved the rehabilitation of thousands of young delinquents. Out of this work he developed a theory of personality development and character training which became the basis of Soviet personality research and educational practices.

His basic principle of personality development involved the development of socially desirable behavior in the collective, by the collective, and for the collective. The collective was the link between the individual and society. Each person had a definite place in the collective and an opportunity to demonstrate independence and self-reliance.

The aim of therapy was the reconstruction of the personality through social interaction, working and living in common. The therapist was a teacher of life to the patient. Makarenko emphasized the application of personality theory to educating the postrevolutionary Soviet people. Education should begin in infancy in the day nurseries, kindergartens, children's homes, and schools. A Soviet citizen should be physically, morally, and mentally healthy. There must be the greatest involvement of children in assuming responsibility on behalf of their family, community, and society in general.

R. W. LUNDIN

MALEBRANCHE, NICOLAS de (1638–1715)

A philosopher, physicist, and Catholic priest, Malebranche was educated in philosophy and theology at the Collège de la Marche and the Sorbonne. He studied the nature of light and color, the conditions of vision, and the foundations of infinitesmal calculus. He taught that nothing could be demonstrated except mathematics.

Malebranche was a Cartesian philosopher who differed with René Descartes on several issues, including the mind–body problem. Malebranche rejected Descartes' interactionism in favor of the doctrine of occasionalism. According to this view one event does not cause another but is simply an occasion for God, the cause of all things, to cause the second event to occur. Thus physical events cannot cause mental events, nor can mental events cause the body to act. Mental events have nothing to do with physical events, yet when a physical event occurs, God can cause a corresponding mental event. The doctrine of occasionalism can be regarded as an early version of what was later known as psychophysical parallelism.

While Malebranche did not believe that one can have true knowledge of the soul, he regarded introspection as affording the possibility of a science of mind. The mind can know only ideas, not bodies in the physical sense. When we speak of seeing bodies we are talking about intelligible extension, not physical extension. We cannot, in fact, demonstrate the existence of material objects but have only the proof of divine revelation. Here Malebranche anticipated the teachings of George Berkeley.

In addition to the faculty of understanding, Malebranche postulated the will. Because our volitions are usually followed by movements, we feel that we have the power to act upon the body. Yet it is God who acts—according to laws which connect mental events to brain events—and makes possible our acting in accordance with our volitions. Like Descartes, Malebranche made the brain the essential organ in mediating the mind–body relationship.

P. E. LICHTENSTEIN

MALMO, ROBERT BEVERLEY (1912–   )

Malmo spent his early years chiefly in the Middle West. He was a Phi Beta Kappa undergraduate at the University of Missouri, where he stayed on to get a master's degree in psychology with A.W. Melton, then obtained the Ph.D. in physiological psychology at Yale. Malmo took a clinical-psychology internship at the state hospital at Norwich, Connecticut, then spent three years as psychophysiologist at the National Institutes of Health, doing research on anoxia and related problems. In 1945 he went to McGill University, where he collaborated with W. G. Penfield on functions of the frontal and parietal lobes.

He and his wife codirected the neuropsychology laboratory of that university's Department of Psychiatry. *On emotions, needs, and our archaic brain* (1975) summarizes much of his work in psychophysiology.

Malmo, the author of more than 100 scientific articles, has received the Citation of Merit from the University of Missouri and an honorary degree (LL.D.) from the University of Manitoba. He is ex-president of La Société de Psychologie du Québec, the Canadian Psychological Association, and the Interamerican Society of Psychology.

MANDLER, GEORGE (1924–   )

Mandler was educated in the UK, New York University, University of Basel, and Yale University (Ph.D., 1953). He taught at Harvard University (1953–1960) and University of Toronto (1960–1965) before moving in 1965 to the University of California at San Diego, as founding chair of the psychology department. Since 1990, he has been a permanent visiting professor at University College, London.

Mandler's scientific contributions have been in organizational processes and the distinction between activation and elaboration in human memory, in discrepancy–evaluation theory in emotion and contribution to autonomic arousal, and in phenomenal and theoretical analyses of consciousness. His books include *The language of psychology* (with W. Kessen), *Thinking: From association to gestalt* (with J. M. Mandler), *Mind and emotion, mind and body: Psychology of emotion and stress,* and *Cognitive psychology: An essay in cognitive science.*

Mandler has been a fellow at the Center for Advanced Study in the Behavioral Sciences and a J. S. Guggenheim fellow. He received the APA's William James Award and a fellowship of the Society of Experimental Psychologists and the American Academy of Arts and Sciences. He has been president of the Divisions of Experimental Psychology and General Psychology of the American Psychological Association and was founding president of the Federation of Behavioral, Psychological, and Cognitive Sciences. He was editor of *Psychological Review* from 1970 to 1976.

MANN, LEON (1937–   )

Mann received the bachelor's and masters' degrees from the University of Melbourne. He then enrolled at Yale University, graduating with the Ph.D. in social psychology in 1965. While at Yale he was the first recipient of the Carl I. Hovland Memorial Fellowship. Mann then taught at the University of Melbourne (1965–1967), Harvard University (1968–1970), and the University of Sydney (1971–1972), before moving to Flinders University of South Australia, where he is professor of psychology. Mann has also held visiting professorships at the Hebrew University of Jerusalem and at Stanford University.

Mann's research interests include the study of decision making, social influence, and collective behavior. He is the author of *Social psychology* and coauthor with Irving Janis of *Decision making.* Mann was elected a fellow of the Australian Academy of the Social Sciences in 1975. He is on the editorial board of four international journals and, since 1981, has been editor of the *Australian Journal of Psychology.*

MARBE, KARL (1869–1953)

Marbe received the Ph.D. at Leipzig under Wilhelm Wundt. From there he went to Würzburg to join the school of "imageless thought" established by Otto Külpe. Actually, Marbe was one of the later members, for Külpe left Würzburg shortly after Marbe arrived.

Marbe is best known for his experimental study of judgment, completed in 1901. When a subject was asked to make a judgment such as telling which of two weights was heavier, the subject was usually correct if the differences were not too small. Marbe then asked the subject to introspect as to what went on in consciousness while making the judgment. The reply was that one could not really describe how the judgments came about. Marbe concluded that judgment was not a conscious process, since the subject told nothing in the introspections. Judgment had to be something more than mental content. He therefore related it to the subject's attitude or purpose, which was more like an act of the mind than the result of its contents. The conscious set was a new "imageless" element of the mind which would be useful in understanding the psychology of judgment.

R. W. LUNDIN

MARSELLA, ANTHONY J. (1940–   )

Marsella, known for his cross-cultural studies of psychopathology and psychotherapy, received the B.A. degree in psychology from Baldwin-Wallace College, and the Ph.D. (1968) degree in clinical psychology from the Pennsylvania State University. Following a Fulbright Research Scholarship to the Philippines and an appointment as a NIMH Culture and Mental Health Fellow, he joined the department of psychology at the University of Hawaii in 1970, achieving full professor in 1980. He also serves as director of the World Health Organization Psychiatric Research Center in Honolulu and as chief scientific adviser to the National Center for Post-Traumatic Stress of the Department of Veterans Affairs. He has been visiting professor in China, India, Korea, and the Philippines, and he has lectured at Columbia, Michigan, UCLA, Yale, and other major universities. Between 1986 and 1989, he served as vice president of academic affairs at the University of Hawaii. Marsella has published nine books and more than 90 book chapters, journal articles, and technical reports on such topics as cross-cultural studies of psychopathology, personality, cognition, sensory functioning, measurement, stress-coping, and psychotherapy and counseling. Some of his books include *Cultural conceptions of mental health and therapy, Cross-cultural counseling and psychotherapy, Culture and self: Asian and Western perspectives, Mental health services: The cross-cultural perspective,* and *The measurement of depression.*

MARSHALL, HENRY RUTGERS (1852–1927)

Marshall graduated from Columbia College in 1876. He studied architecture for 2 yr and began practicing that profession in 1878. Marshall held no degrees in psychology, nor did he hold any academic appointments in his career. Psychology and philosophy were his avocation, and in a 30-yr span he wrote seven books and more than 50 articles, most of those on the psychology of aesthetics.

Marshall's first book, was *Pain, pleasure, and aesthetics.* He opposed the view of pain and pleasure as based on sensory physiology and argued instead for a psychological interpretation as mental qualities. For Marshall, pain and pleasure were the bases for all aesthetic experiences and judgments.

Marshall's book *Consciousness* sought to define an introspective psychology of consciousness in terms of the interdependence of hedonism and aesthetics. The book attacked functional psychology and the growing interest in a study of objective behavior as evidence of movements to abandon psychology as the study of mental life. Such views cemented friendships with Edward B. Titchener and William James.

Marshall's published works established him as an international authority on aesthetics and led to his election, in 1907, as the 16th president of the American Psychological Association (APA). However, mentalism was losing favor in psychology, and Marshall showed no interest in altering his views. He lost interest in psychology (which was losing interest in him) and returned to his work in architecture. When he died in 1927, no American psychology journal published his obituary, a singular distinction among the early APA presidents.

L. T. BENJAMIN

MARVIT, ROBERT C. (1938–   )

Marvit is a graduate of Tufts and Harvard Universities with an M.D. degree and a M.S. degree in behavioral sciences. He served as lieutenant commander in the U.S. Public Health Service, performing multiple duties on behalf of the U.S. Department of Justice and the Immigration Service. He was special fellow at the Harvard Law School in 1969–1970, studying the interface of psychiatry and the law with Allan Dershowitz. He was a career development fellow with the National Institute of Mental Health from 1967 to 1970.

In residence in Hawaii since 1970, he has served as research coordinator for the Mental Health Division of the State of Hawaii as well as professor of public health at the University of Hawaii. He was instrumental in the revision and development of legislation relating to the insanity defense, informed consent, and civil commitment. He was the principal investigator for the legislatively mandated study on the criminally insane.

He has served on many local, state, and national committees in the area of forensic psychiatry. He is the author of multiple articles relating to litigation, traumatology, and the criminal justice system. He has served as the associate editor of the bulletin of the American Academy of Psychiatry and the Law for 10 yr. Marvit is in private practice of forensic psychiatry, specializing in evaluation and treatment of traumatically injured claimants/defendants.

MARX, KARL HEINRICH (1818–1883)

Marx studied law, history, and philosophy at Bonn, and received the Ph.D. at Jena in 1841. While in Paris he met the German socialist Friedrich Engels. In 1847 they published jointly the *Communist manifesto*, consisting of a history of the working class and a critical summary of existing socialist and communist literature. In 1864 the International Working Man's Association was founded in London; Marx became, at least in name, the head of its general council.

The starting point of Marx's socialism is the doctrine of class struggle. This provided the key to two of his most widely known doctrines: A materialist conception of history and the theory of surplus value. According to the latter, the worker was exploited by the extraction of his surplus value by the capitalist's exploitation of labor.

Marx was also exposed to the philosophy of G. W. F. Hegel and his dialectics. According to Hegel each idea, as it was affirmed as truth, brought with it the idea of its negation. The ideas did battle and out of their conflict a new and higher idea came to the forefront and conquered in turn—a process that could be stated as thesis–antithesis–synthesis. For the battle of ideas, Marx substituted a battle of economic forces. One set of economic forces brought a class to power and that class formed a State, but it could not rule without bringing an antagonistic class into play. The concept of the necessity for social and political change became the driving force behind socialism and communism.

Certain aspects of Marx's philosophy bore significance for sociology and psychology. In his materialism, Marx found individuals to be products of their society and the social forces imposed upon them. Because of a social structure imposed by the ruling class, individuals could not really be responsible for their misdeeds. These were the result of social evils imposed upon the working class, so that society as it existed was basically to blame.

Marx felt that the economic systems imposed by capitalism gave rise to class distinctions, and that these distinctions should be eliminated. He blamed individual differences on the material conditions surrounding a person and did not come to grips with the fact that other causes might be involved.

At a time of nineteenth-century conservatism in France and Great Britain, Marx was a radical, but he and his sympathizers were speaking directly to the people. This brought to light the aspects of a society that the proper Victorian intellectuals considered "vulgar." Not depending on rational solutions to human problems, the Marxists sought more radical support for what was best for the common people.

More directly, Marx's philosophy had a profound influence on dialectical materialism in the Soviet Union, starting with K. N. Kornilov's call for a psychology based on Marxist principles in 1923. Thus began a switch from a psychology based on reflexology to one resulting from a complex social environment. Humans were capable of changing their own circumstances.

As the Soviet government came into full power, it supported the work of Ivan Pavlov, which was not identical with Soviet policy but at least considered acceptable to Marxist doctrine. Here, then, was a shift back to a concern for the higher nervous centers (the brain), since Pavlov and later Soviet psychologists stressed the importance of the functioning of organized activity in the brain.

R. W. LUNDIN

MARX, MELVIN H. (1919–   )

Marx received his higher education at Washington University (Ph.D. in experimental psychology, 1943). He went from instructor to professor at the University of Missouri at Columbia. He became a research career awardee (National Institute of Mental Health) in 1964 and retired in 1984.

Among other appointments, Marx was a distinguished visiting professor at Monash University in Melbourne, Australia (1979) and at Western Carolina University in Cullowhee, North Carolina, (1991); visiting professor at Florida International University in Miami (1984) and Florida Institute of Technology in Melbourne (1990); and senior research scientist at Georgia State University in Atlanta (1985–1989).

During the first half or so of his research career, Marx focused on learning and motivation problems in animals, mainly rats (e.g., food hoarding, frustration, and experimental extinction). More recently, he has investigated problems of cognitive development in children (e.g., numerosity and especially judgment of event frequency as well as the role of inferences as biasing factors in memory).

Marx has written approximately 150 research reports in scientific journals and has authored or edited 14 books. He is probably best known for his books on systems and theories.

MASKELYNE, NEVIL (1732–1811)

Maskelyne was educated at Trinity College, Cambridge, UK. He served as a clergyman before becoming astronomer and director of the Greenwich Observatory in 1765. Maskelyne made many contributions to astronomical methods, founded the Nautical Almanac, and was the recipient of numerous honors including the Copley medal.

In 1796, Maskelyne dismissed his assistant, Kinnebrook, because he observed the times of stellar transits about eight-tenths of a second later than Maskelyne. Bessel, astronomer at Konigsberg, became aware of the incident, and in the 1820s, he studied the phenomenon that came to be known as the personal equation. The work of Bessel and other astronomers led in psychology to the investigation of reaction time.

P. E. LICHTENSTEIN

MASLOW, ABRAHAM H. (1908–1970)

Maslow studied with two of the leading Gestalt psychologists, Max Wertheimer and Kurt Koffka, at the New School for Social Research. From these men he got the idea for a holistic psychology. He took all three of his academic degrees from the University of Wisconsin, receiving the Ph.D. in 1934. Along with Carl Rogers, Rollo May, and Charlotte Buhler, Maslow was one of the founders of the American Association of Humanistic Psychology. His most important books, presenting his

humanistic position, include *Motivation and personality* and *Toward a psychology of being*.

Maslow considered his basic approach to psychology to fall within the broad range of humanistic psychology, which he characterized as the "Third Force" in American psychology, the other two being behaviorism and psychoanalysis. His main efforts were directed to the field of personality. He believed that psychology had dealt too much with human frailty and not enough with human strengths. In deploring the pessimism of so many psychologists—Freud, for example—Maslow looked to the more positive side of humanity. He believed human nature was essentially good. As personality unfolded through maturation, the creative powers manifested themselves ever more clearly. If humans were miserable or neurotic, it was the environment that made them so. Humans were not basically destructive or violent, but became so when their inner nature was twisted or frustrated.

Maslow proposed a theory of motivation which has become extremely popular in humanistic circles. Our basic needs or drives could be arranged in a hierarchy, often pictured as a pyramid. At the bottom were the basic physiological needs: hunger and thirst. Next were safety needs: security from attack, avoidance of pain, freedom from invasion of privacy. On top of these were the needs for love and belonging. Higher up were the needs for self-esteem: feeling good, pride, confidence. At the top of the hierarchy was the need for self-actualization, a basic driving force for self-fulfillment. This emphasis on self-actualization is shared by many humanistic psychologists.

To understand human nature, Maslow felt it was more profitable to study people who have realized their potentiality rather than those who were crippled (psychologically) or neurotic. He selected a group of people, some from history, whom he felt had reached a considerable degree of self-actualization—such persons as Abraham Lincoln, Thomas Jefferson, Albert Einstein, and Eleanor Roosevelt. In studying them he found certain distinguishing characteristics such as (1) a realistic orientation, (2) acceptance of themselves and others, (3) spontaneity of expression, (4) attitudes which were problem-centered rather than self-centered, (5) independence, (6) identification with humanity, (7) emotional depth, (8) democratic values, (9) a philosophic rather than a caustic sense of humor, (10) transcendence of the environment, and (11) creativity.

R. W. LUNDIN

MASSERMAN, JULES H. (1905–   )

Masserman, a prolific writer and professional leader in psychiatry and psychoanalysis, has contributed over 350 articles to journals and magazines related to his professional expertise, and observations on everyday life. He has published 12 textbooks, plus articles on history, philosophy, and music. Although Masserman continues to do research on comparative human and animal conduct, his personal objective is "to integrate and clarify the sciences and arts of human behavior."

Masserman came to the United States as a young boy and as an adult became a naturalized U.S. citizen. He received his professional education from Wayne State University where he received the M.B. in 1930 and the M.D. in 1931. Masserman obtained his certificate from the Chicago Psychoanalytic Institute in 1940.

Masserman's career took him to a number of prestigious institutions, but he remained committed to Northwestern University Medical School, where he was an educator, professor, and administrator of neurology and psychiatry for more than 25 years. Masserman received professor emeritus status from Northwestern in 1974.

An active member of many professional organizations, Masserman was elected president of the American Academy of Psychoanalysis, the American Society of Biological Psychiatry, the International Association for Social Psychiatry, the American Society for Group Psychotherapy and Psychodrama, and the American Association for Social Psychiatry. His leadership and scholarship were noted by the many honors awarded him, including the Sigmund Freud Award, the Taylor Manor Award, and the Lasker Award. His autobiography is entitled *A psychiatric odyssey.*

MATARAZZO, JOSEPH D. (1925–   )

Matarazzo received the Ph.D. in psychology from Northwestern University in 1952. He taught at the Washington University School of Medicine (1952–1955) and the Harvard Medical School (1955–1957), following which he established (and still continued to serve as chairman of) the first administratively autonomous department of medical psychology at the Oregon Health Sciences University.

Matarazzo has served as president of the Academy of Behavioral Medicine Research, the International Council of Psychologists, Western Psychological Association, and the American Association of State Psychology boards. In 1989, Matarazzo served as the 97th president of the American Psychological Association.

His publications include the fifth edition of *Wechsler's measurement and appraisal of adult intelligence,* co-author of a book on the interview and another on nonverbal communication, and editor-in-chief of *Behavioral health: A handbook of health enhancement and disease prevention.* His more than 200 publications are in three areas: (1) intellectual and neuropsychological functions, (2) nonverbal indices of empathy and related psychological processes, and (3) the role of lifestyle risk factors in health and illness.

He is a diplomate of the American Board of Professional Psychology and, as a full-time faculty member in a school of medicine, has been in the active and continuous clinical practice of psychology since 1952. Since 1975, he has been concurrently the national consultant in clinical psychology to the surgeons general of the U.S. Army, Navy, and Air Force.

MAY, ROLLO (1909–   )

May identifies himself as a humanist. His undergraduate studies were concluded at Oberlin College. From there he left for New York City and Union Theological Seminary, where he obtained a theological degree (B.D.). He received the Ph.D. from Columbia University *summa cum laude* in 1949.

From 1934 to 1944, May was student advisor and student counselor at Michigan State University and the College of the City of New York. His psychiatric experience dates from 1948, when he joined the faculty of the William Alanson White Institute of Psychiatry, Psychology, and Psychoanalysis. By 1955 he was also serving on the faculty of the New School for Social Research in New York City. As a visiting professor, May has lectured at Harvard, Princeton, Yale, and elsewhere.

May is known for his vanguard leadership in humanistic psychology. He is the most celebrated of the current American existentialist psychotherapists, articulating existential tenets of the "encounter," the "choice," "authenticity," "responsibility," "transcendence," "I-thou relationship," "presence," "moment of decision," "kairos," and other existential hypotheses. These and other theories are discussed in his books: *The meaning of anxiety; Man's search for himself; Psychology and the human dilemma; Love and will; Power and innocence; Existential psychology; Existence, My quest for beauty, and the cry for myth.*

McCLELLAND, DAVID C. (1917–   )

McClelland is known for his work in the field of motivation and especially in the area of the need for achievement. He received the B.A. degree from Wesleyan University and the M.A. from the University of Mis-

souri. Yale conferred a Ph.D. on him in 1941. For his accomplishments, he has received a number of honorary degrees. After serving as an instructor at Wesleyan from 1941 to 1946, McClelland left for Harvard, where he is emeritus professor in the department of psychology.

Conceiving an early interest in social motivation, McClelland developed a method of measuring human needs through content analysis of imaginative thought. He has researched extensively the role of the needs for achievement, power and affiliation in occupational success, economic and political development, health, and personal adjustment. Among McClelland's books are *Personality; The achievement motive* (with others), *The achieving society, Motivating economic achievement* (with D. Winter), *The drinking man* (with others), *Power: The inner experience,* and *Human motivation.*

McCONNELL, JAMES V. (1925–1990)

Founder, editor, and for 20 years (1959–1979) publisher of the *Worm Runner's Digest/Journal of Biological Psychology,* McConnell was one of the last students to take the doctorate (1956) with Karl M. Dallenbach at the University of Texas. He began his "memory transfer" research with planarian flatworms at Texas, but performed most of his work in the area of "memory transfer" at the University of Michigan, where he went in 1956. He became a full professor there in 1963.

After demonstrating that planarians could be trained in a variety of situations, McConnell began a "search for the engram" (to use Karl Lashley's phrase). When cut in half, head and tail segments of planarians rapidly replace all missing parts. In 1959 McConnell, Allan Jacobson, and Daniel Kimble showed that both regenerated heads and tails remember the training given the original (intact) planarian. In 1961 McConnell, Reeva Jacobson, and Barbara Humphries demonstrated that when untrained cannibal worms ingest trained planarians, the cannibals show some "transfer" of the training given the donors. In 1962 McConnell, Arthur Zelman, Larry Kabat, and Reeva Jacobson obtained a similar "transfer of training" by extracting RNA from trained planarians and injecting it into untrained worms. By 1981 the "memory transfer" effect had been replicated successfully more than 500 times in a variety of experimental animals. This research suggests that memories may be stored biochemically.

McConnell was a Fulbright scholar at the University of Oslo in Norway in 1954. The American Psychological Foundation gave him its Distinguished Teaching Award in 1976. The first edition of his introductory textbook, *Understanding human behavior,* was published in 1974.

McDOUGALL, WILLIAM (1871–1938)

McDougall received his medical training at Cambridge and London. He then taught at Oxford and University College, London, from 1904 to 1920, except for an interruption during World War I, when he served in the British Medical Corps. His observations on mental patients during this period led to his writing the *Outline of abnormal psychology.* In 1920 he was called to Harvard to fill a chair once occupied by William James. In 1927 he accepted an invitation to become chairman of the Psychology Department at Duke University, where he remained until his death.

McDougall was much concerned with social psychology. *An introduction to social psychology* (1908) set forth his theory of instincts to explain human behavior and, in particular, social behavior. McDougall antedated John Watson in defining psychology as the "science of conduct" (behavior). In this book he described an instinct as having three aspects: (1) a predisposition to notice certain stimuli; (2) a predisposition to make movements towards a goal; and (3) an emotional core which involved the energy that gave impetus to the activity, once a stimulus was presented to trigger an organism to action. McDougall's was a purposive psychology which was goal-directed. He called it "hormic" from the Greek *hormé,* meaning "urge."

In the first edition of *An introduction to social psychology,* McDougall postulated 12 basic instincts. By 1932 the number had grown to 17, including hunger, sex, curiosity, escape, pugnacity, gregariousness, self-assertion, and acquisition. In the 1930s, as the term "instinct" was growing out of fashion, McDougall changed the name to "propensity," but the concept was the same. Often two or more instincts could combine to account for other behavior. For example, a man's love for his wife could be a combination of the sex and maternal instincts, which he called sentiment.

In *Body and mind* McDougall presented his doctrine of "soul." He believed there was a bit of "soul" in everything, even inorganic matter. This doctrine never became very popular at a time when psychology was fighting vigorously to cast off any theological implications. In addition, McDougall was a firm believer in psychic phenomena. He welcomed the research on extrasensory perception by J. B. Rhine at Duke University. This involved mental telepathy, clairvoyance, and other psychic phenomena.

Among the unpopular causes that McDougall supported was the Lamarckian hypothesis that characteristics acquired by one generation could be passed on to their offsprings through the mechanisms of heredity. In one experiment—now generally discredited because of its lack of proper controls—he trained 23 generations of white rats to escape from a tank by one or two exits. If a rat attempted the wrong exit, it was given an electric shock. At the conclusion of the experiment those animals that had had the training, performed in a superior way, as compared with the rats which never had any training in previous generations. However, the experiment has never been replicated.

Although, as far as human behavior is concerned, instinct doctrine is not generally accepted today (except by the Freudians), McDougall's ideas have led to a revival of interest in instincts among animal ethologists in particular, as seen in the work of N. Tinbergen and K. Z. Lorenz. Furthermore, McDougall's idea of purposive or goal-directed behavior is still advocated by some contemporary psychologists.

R. W. LUNDIN

McGEOCH, JOHN A. (1897–1942)

McGeoch received the Ph.D. in psychology at the University of Chicago. He held teaching positions at Washington University, the University of Arkansas, the University of Missouri, and Wesleyan University, before going to the University of Iowa as head of the Psychology Department. He served as editor of the *Psychological Bulletin* and handled editorial responsibilities for the *American Journal of Psychology* and the *Journal of Psychology.*

Working within the functional tradition, McGeoch concentrated upon the experimental investigation of human learning. At a time when grand theories of learning were flourishing, McGeoch's rugged empiricism was refreshing. McGeoch saw learning situations as ranging through a continuum from Pavlovian conditioning to complex human problem solving. In addition to studies treating various aspects of association, he developed an interference theory of forgetting supported by a series of careful studies of retroactive inhibition.

While McGeoch was careful in keeping his theories close to experimental data, he had an interest in broad, theoretical issues. This interest was reflected in an important paper on the formal criteria for a systematic psychology. His text *The psychology of human learning* was the most comprehensive treatment of the subject for many years.

P. E. LICHTENSTEIN

McGRAW, MYRTLE B. (1899–1988)

McGraw received the B.A. from Ohio Wesleyan University and the M.A. degree and Ph.D. degrees from Columbia University Teachers College. In 1930, she became associate director of the Normal Child Development Study at Columbia Presbyterian Medical Center. During the following 12 yr, McGraw contributed greatly to our understanding of the capacities of babies.

McGraw's co-twin studies led to the publication of *Growth: A study of Johnny and Jimmy.* This pioneering study provided important data regarding development but was inconclusive in regard to inheritance because of the limited genetic technology of the times. In 1953, McGraw became professor of psychology at Briarcliff College where she remained until her retirement.

P. E. LICHTENSTEIN

McGUIRE, WILLIAM J. (1925–   )

McGuire's early psychological studies at Fordham University (M.A, 1950), and at the University of Louvain, included both philosophical and experimental topics. His thesis dealt with human learning issues. He moved into social psychology by taking a year's postdoctoral fellowship at the University of Minnesota with Leon Festinger (1954–1955), after which he returned to Yale (1955–1958) as a faculty member, working on attitude change topics such as order of presentation and personality effects on persuasibility. He then moved to Charles Osgood's Communication Research Institute at the University of Illinois (1958–1961), where he did a series of studies on immunization against persuasion which received the AAAS Annual Socio-Psychological Award in 1963.

At Columbia University (1961–1967) McGuire developed a general theory of personality–influenceability relations and developed a historical data archive for testing psychological theories. McGuire served as editor of the *Journal of Personality and Social Psychology,* did research on distinctiveness as a determinant of perceptual salience, and began a series of reviews of the current status and future directions of social psychology. He spent a year at the London School of Economics and then returned to Yale (1971), where he developed his contextualist philosophy of science.

McGuire has been a Guggenheim, Social Science Research Council, Center for Advanced Study in the Behavioral Sciences, and Fulbright fellow, as well as president of the Social and Personality Division of the American Psychological Association.

McKEACHIE, WILBERT J. (1921–   )

McKeachie got the Ph.D. at the University of Michigan and spent his entire career at that university, as professor of psychology and director of the Center for Research on Learning and Teaching. His primary activities have been college teaching, research on college teaching, and training college teachers.

McKeachie has written a number of books and articles, including *Teaching tips: A guidebook for the beginning college teacher* and "Student ratings of faculty: A reprise." Much of his research has been concerned with attribute-treatment interactions, particularly with respect to those teaching variables interacting with student motivation such as test anxiety.

He is ex-president of the American Psychological Association and the American Association of Higher Education; president of the American Psychological Foundation; and past chairman of the Committee on Teaching, Research, and Publication of the American Association of University Professors. He has been a member of various governmental advisory committees on mental health, behavioral and biological research, and graduate training. He holds honorary degrees from Northwestern University, Denison University, Eastern Michigan University, and the University of Cincinnati, and is a member of the National Academy of Education.

McNEMAR, QUINN (1900–1986)

At the time of his death, McNemar was professor emeritus at Sanford University, where he had served on the faculty for many years. After his retirement at age 65, he served as professor of psychology and education at the University of Texas at Austin. He received the B.A. from Juniata College in Pennsylvania and the Ph.D. at Stanford in 1932. There he served on its faculty, rising through the ranks to become professor.

His main area of interest in psychology was statistics, particularly factor analysis and the analysis of variance. Earlier, he had taught high-school mathematics. While at Stanford he was involved in the revision of the Stanford–Binet intelligence test. His best-known book is *Psychological statistics,* which went through four editions.

R. W. LUNDIN

McREYNOLDS, PAUL W. (1919–   )

McReynolds received the Ph.D. from Stanford in 1949, with concentrations in clinical and personality psychology. Before that he had earned the B.S. from Central Missouri State University and the M.A. from the University of Missouri. In 1976, he carried out advanced study at Cambridge University.

Following the doctorate, McReynolds was employed as a clinical psychologist at the Palo Alto VA Medical Center, and later he established and headed the Behavioral Research Laboratory there, carrying out research on anxiety and schizophrenia. During this period, he served as consulting associate professor at Stanford and during leave periods taught at the University of California at Berkeley and the University of Oregon. In 1959, he moved to the University of Nevada at Reno, where he established a doctoral program in clinical psychology and conducted research on assessment and personality. In 1987, he was selected as the outstanding researcher in the university and later in the same year became emeritus professor. Subsequently, under the impetus of his former students, an endowment was set up to provide an annual university lecture in his name.

McReynolds's research interests have been in personality, assessment, psychopathology, motivation, and the history of psychology. He founded and edited the book series *Advances in psychological assessment,* edited two books on the history of psychology, and is the author of numerous papers and reviews in the areas noted.

MEAD, GEORGE H. (1863–1931)

Mead was educated at Harvard, where he became acquainted with William James. He joined the Philosophy Department at the University of Chicago in the same year as John Dewey (1894) and remained there until his death.

At Chicago Mead came under the influence of the functionalist movement as well as that of early behaviorism. He has been called by some a social behaviorist. He is best known for his concept of the self and has become one of the most important of the self theorists of the twentieth century. His most important book, *Mind, self and society,* was a combination of notes taken by his students from his lectures and published posthumously in 1934. Mead himself never wrote books.

For Mead, the self was an object of awareness rather than a system of processes. At birth there is no self because a person cannot enter his own experiences directly. However, as a result of experiences received from the outside world, one learns to think of oneself as an object and develops attitudes and feelings about oneself; hence, the development of self-consciousness. Important to the development of the self is the social setting where social communication occurs. Mead believed that one becomes a "self" to the degree that one can take the attitudes of others and act toward oneself as others act.

Actually, as we develop we can acquire many selves, each of which represents a separate set of responses acquired from different social groups. For example, there can be a family self, a school self, or a self developed from other groups with which one interacts. Incorporated into the conception of the self is the "I" and the "me." The "me" is the social self or one of the social selves, developed through role taking. The "I" is the unique individual which has never existed as an object of consciousness.

Mead's concept of the self has some implications for current self theories to be found in contemporary humanistic psychology—in particular, for the person-centered theory of Carl Rogers.

R. W. LUNDIN

MEAD, MARGARET (1901–1978)

Mead received the B.A. from Barnard College, where she became acquainted with two famous anthropologists, Franz Boas and Ruth Benedict. She received the M.A. in psychology and the Ph.D. in anthropology (1929) from Columbia. She then became associated with the American Museum of Natural History from 1926 to 1959.

Mead was one of the foremost anthropologists of her time. She pioneered in research methods that helped to turn cultural anthropology into a major science. Her anthropological expeditions included trips to Samoa, New Guinea, Bali, and other parts of the South Pacific.

Her first book, *Coming of age in Samoa,* was a result of her study of female adolescents in that society. In it she pointed out that the storm and stress of adolescence found in America was rare in Samoa. She discovered no conflict or revolt among girls of that age group, for their status was determined by their age; as far as their rights and privileges were concerned, they progressed according to their age and nothing else. In *Sex and temperament in three primitive societies,* Mead studied three contrasting tribes in New Guinea. There she found sex roles and temperament to be a function of each particular culture. Males or females were aggressive or passive in terms of what the culture dictated. Likewise in *Male and female* (1949) she attributed the differences in behavior between the sexes to the kind of upbringing, particularly by the mother.

Throughout her career Mead promoted the importance of environmental influences, women's rights, and racial harmony.

R. W. LUNDIN

MEAZZINI, PAOLO A. (1942–   )

Meazzini is best known in Italy for being the cultural leader of behaviorism and behavior therapy. Meazzini started his academic and research career at the University of Trieste and Padua and finally moved to Rome, where he is full professor of clinical psychology. He was invited as a visiting professor to the University of Honolulu.

Although his earlier research interests were mainly focused on cognitive processes, afterwards Meazzini gradually moved to behaviorism and behavior therapy. He studied the philosophical background of behaviorism and its present-day connections with the philosophy of science, which helped give a firm theoretical and epistemological basis to the growing Italian behavior therapy and modification movement. He is involved in applied and theoretical research on behavioral applications to school settings and the management of developmental disabilities, while at the same time establishing close connections between basic research and behavioral applications.

Meazzini is editor-in-chief of the *Giornale Italiano di Analisi e Modificazione del Comportamento* (Italian Journal of Behavior Analysis and

Modification), and of *Psicologia e Scuola* (School Psychology) and *Handicap e Disabilità di Apprendimento* (Handicap and Learning Disabilities). His publications include *Apprendimento e memoria* (Learning and memory); *Apprendimento ed emozioni* (Learning and emotion); *Watson; Il comportamentismo : una storia culturale* (Behaviorism: A cultural history); *Handicappato : passi verso l'autonomia* (The handicapped school child: From self-sufficiency to cognition); and *Trattato teorico-pratico di terapia e modificazione del comportamento* (Handbook of behavior therapy and modification).

MEEHL, PAUL E. (1920–   )

Best known for his work on personality assessment, Meehl took the B.A. and Ph.D. degrees at the University of Minnesota, where he studied under Starke Hathaway, B. F. Skinner, Donald Paterson, William Heron, the philosopher Herbert Feigl, and statisticians Palmer Johnson, Dunham Jackson, and Alan Treloar. His early animal work with Kenneth MacCorquodale was on latent learning and efforts to improve formulation of Edward Tolman's cognitive theory. Meanwhile he was working on validation and interpretation of the MMPI, as well as on philosophical problems of psychology. He was a cofounder (1953) of the Minnesota Center for Philosophy of Science, and as a staff member has continued to publish in that area.

In 1954 Meehl's monograph *Clinical versus statististical prediction* aroused wide interest (and anxiety!) and is considered a minor classic. Meehl's orientation is a fusion of Freudian, cognitive, and Skinnerian concepts, plus a large residue of old-fashioned Allportian trait theory and "dustbowl empiricist psychometrics." He was considerably influenced by his Rado-oriented analyst and analytic supervisor Bernard C. Glueck, and has a theory of schizophrenia stemming partly from that influence. Since 1951 he has engaged in private therapeutic practice. He is a diplomate (clinical) of the American Board of Professional Psychology (board member, 1956–61) and a fellow of the Institute for Rational Emotive Therapy.

In recent years Meehl's interests have included behavior genetics, forensic psychology, and new taxometric methods. Meehl received the APA Distinguished Scientific Contributor Award, the Distinguished Scientific Award of Division 12, and the Klopfer Distinguished Contribution Prize, and served as president of the American Psychological Association (1962). He is a fellow of the American Academy of Art and Sciences, and in 1968 was created Regents' Professor of Psychology at Minnesota.

MEICHENBAUM, DONALD (1940–   )

Meichenbaum obtained his early education there, receiving the bachelor's degree at the City College of New York. He then went to the University of Illinois and received the Ph.D. in clinical psychology in 1966. Since 1966 he has been in the Department of Psychology of the University of Waterloo in Ontario, Canada.

Meichenbaum's major contributions are in pioneering a variety of cognitive-behavior modifications treatment procedures for both children and adults. *Cognitive-behavior modification: An integrative approach* summarizes this work. He has also authored several other books and articles. His other research areas include coping with stress and cognitive development.

MEILI, RICHARD (1900–   )

Meili studied in Berlin, where Wolfgang Köhler, Max Wertheimer, and Kurt Lewin introduced him to the theory of Gestalt psychology. In his doctoral thesis he demonstrated that the classification of objects presented simultaneously depended on the totality of impressions and followed analogously the principles of perception.

Invited by Edouard Claparède to head the J. J. Rousseau Institute, he devoted himself to psychological diagnoses, mostly of intelligence, which resulted in several psychological diagnostic manuals (Meili, 1936, 1951, 1978). After six years as head of an office of vocational guidance, he was appointed as a professor of psychology at the University of Berne.

Since the 1930s he has been preoccupied with definitions of intellectual factors. These he sees not as aptitudes but rather as independent conditions of individual differences. In his latest work (Meili, 1981), summarizing some 20 research studies, four fundamental factors were found to be constant from age six on. In his longitudinal researches, Meili (1959) attempted to ferret out the primary elements of various character traits. He did research studies (Meili, 1963) relative to environmental variables of intelligence, along with other studies on the correspondence between intelligence and scholastic achievement.

Meili was the editor-in-chief of the *Swiss Review of Psychology* from 1952 to 1980.

MEINONG, ALEXIUS RITTER VON HANDSCHUCHSHEIM (1853–1920)

Meinong studied under Franz Brentano at Vienna. A member of the Austrian School, he spent his entire career at Graz, where he founded the psychology laboratory in 1894. A philosopher as well as a psychologist, he published a theory of assumptions, a theory of evidence, a theory of objects, and a theory of value. He was also an editor of the important journal, *Zeitschrift für Psychologie*.

In his theory of objects, Meinong accepted Plato's notions of ideal objects that subsist and other objects that exist, but he added a third possibility: objects that are nonexisting but have objective characteristics. Thus we can speak of impossible-to-exist-or-subsist entities like round squares. One can make true statements about far more than the objects that exist. The law of contradiction, which would forbid a round square, applies only to existing objects. The character (*Sosein*) of objects is independent of being (*Sein*), except that contradictory *Sosein* preclude *Sein*. The statement "the mountain of which I am thinking is golden" is meaningful regardless of whether or not the mountain exists. This golden mountain cannot be contrasted with Mount Everest, however, as the object is incomplete. A statement such as "I wish that your wish would come true" also uses an incomplete object, as I do not know what you are wishing. Nonetheless, the statement is meaningful and is either true or false.

In his theory of value, Meinong took as his basis the psychology of humans. Our emotional reactions are not consistent, he noted, as we show more sorrow in the nonexistence of the good than pleasure in its existence, when considering a common good like our health. Similarly, our reactions to evil—displeasure in its existence, joy in its nonexistence—are often unbalanced. Meinong anticipated contemporary thought with his subdivisions of good and bad: [1] good that is meritorious, [2] good that is merely required, [3] bad that is excusable, and [4] bad that is inexcusable.

C. PEYSER

MELZACK, RONALD (1929–   )

Melzack was educated in Montreal and received the Ph.D. at McGill University in 1954. After carrying out research on pain at the University of Oregon Medical School (1954–1957), he spent a year as visiting lecturer at University College, London, followed by a year in physiological research at the University of Pisa in Italy. He was appointed to the faculty at the Massachusetts Institute of Technology in 1959, and in

1963 joined the faculty at McGill University, where he has remained ever since.

Melzack's doctoral research on the effects of early sensory experience on pain in dogs led to several studies on the neural mechanisms that underlie the modulation of pain signals by psychological processes. In 1965 he and Patrick D. Wall published the gate control theory of pain, which is now the most widely accepted theory of pain. He also published papers that led to the development of the McGill Pain Questionnaire for the measurement of subjective pain experience. In addition to more than 100 scientific papers, he published *The puzzle of pain*, and (with Patrick Wall) *The challenge of pain*. He edited *Pain measurement and assessment* and, with Patrick Wall, *Textbook of pain*.

MERCADO-DOMENECH, SERAFIN J. (1939–   )

Mercado-Domenech is known for his role in the development of Mexican psychology, and for his research in cognitive and environmental psychology. Born in Mexico City, he obtained his *licenciatura* (bachelor's) degree from the National Autonomous University of Mexico (UNAM), and did graduate work at the University of Texas at Austin, receiving the Ph.D. in educational psychology in 1971. His interests shifted from cognitive to environmental psychology, on which he has been doing research in Mexico.

Mercado-Domenech has worked on the effects of noise on cognitive processes, the development of a scale of habitability of buildings, and the concepts and attitudes that people have about automobiles. He helped develop academic programs in several universities of Mexico, including UNAM, the Metropolitan University, and Veracruz University. He was responsible for the introduction in Mexico of graduate programs in educational, experimental, and environmental psychology.

MERCIER, DÉSIRÉ (1851–1926)

A Belgian philosopher, educator, writer, and church leader, Mercier was ordained priest in 1874. He continued his studies and obtained doctorates of philosophy and theology. From 1882 on he was associated with the University of Louvain as a professor and administrator.

Mercier was the first among Catholic philosophers to recognize scientific psychology as an independent science and to introduce it into a Catholic university—Louvain—in 1891. As the director of the philosophical studies at Louvain, he chose Armand Thiéry to study psychology with Wilhelm Wundt and to establish a psychological laboratory at Louvain. He also encouraged Albert Michotte to study in Germany and later to direct the Louvain laboratory after Thiéry. In 1906 he left the university to become archbishop of Malines and primate of Belgium, and eventually a cardinal. He was recognized as one of the most influential spiritual leaders of Europe. During his visit to America in 1919, 17 universities bestowed honorary degrees on him.

Psychology and its development at Louvain was Mercier's lifelong concern. Among his writings, the book of greatest interest to psychologists is *Les origines de la psychologie contemporaine*, first published in 1897 and translated into English in 1918. It described the philosophical roots of both the philosophical and the scienitific psychology of the nineteenth century. It was not merely a history and critique of psychological ideas, but also an exposition of the philosophy of Thomas Aquinas and its relevance to psychology. A firm believer in the value of this philosophy—known in its modern form as Neothomistic philosophy—Mercier worked to reconcile it with modern science, and with psychology in particular. According to Mercier, psychology should not be estranged from philosophy. However, to be a *science vivante* (living science), it has to maintain close contact with biological sciences

and grow by absorbing the findings of animal, child, abnormal, social, and all other areas of psychological research.

H. MISIAK

MERLEAU-PONTY, MAURICE (1907–1961)

Merleau-Ponty studied at the Ecole Normale Supérieure in Paris. He held a variety of distinguished professorships at the University of Lyons, the Sorbonne, and the Collège de France. He is considered one of the most distinguished French philosophers of the first half of the twentieth century. Along with Jean-Paul Sartre, he was cofounder and coeditor of *Les Temps Modernes*, a significant journal of existential philosophy.

Even though his primary commitment was to philosophy, Merleau-Ponty frequently wrote on psychological subjects. Of particular interest for psychology where his books, *Structure du comportement* (The structures of behavior) and *La phénoménologie de la perception* (Phenomenology of perception). His primary concern was with an understanding of the relationship between human consciousness and nature. Nature referred to external events in their causal relationships. Consciousness, on the other hand, was not subject to causality. The appropriate method for studying consciousness was the phenomenology of perception. Through perception one could understand the essential feature, which was an interchange between consciousness and reality. Perception was the first human contact with the world.

Merleau-Ponty opposed any elemental or associationist approach to the study of consciousness, much like Gestalt psychology in Germany. Instead, one should explain the phenomenal field, which involved a focus on bodily being and then on the world as perceived. Bodily being involved the body image, the body in space and motion, the body as sexual being, and the body as expressed in gestures and speech. The perceptual side involved an analysis of the perceptual process. Like other existential philosophers and psychologists, he also stressed "being-for-itself" or "being-in-the world." This concept has been expressed in various ways, but for Merleau-Ponty it referred to the world as experienced or as perceived subjectively by any particular individual.

R. W. LUNDIN

MESCHIERI, LUIGI (1919–1985)

Meschieri received the M.D. from the University of Rome; 2 yr later, he completed a specialization in occupational medicine. In 1951, he received a specialization in psychology, which enabled him to teach this discipline at the university level. He was professor of psychology at the University of Urbino from 1959 and at the University of Rome from 1974 until his death. For a large portion of his active professional life, Meschieri was also associated with the Institute of Psychology of the Italian National Research Council, first as researcher and, from 1960 to 1968, as director of the institute.

Meschieri played a significant role in the development of postwar Italian psychology, both as an active member (and sometimes founder and president) of various scientific and professional associations and as a researcher in a number of applied fields. Most notable were his contributions to the psychology of individual differences, especially with respect to its psychometric aspects in social psychology and to problems in the training of social workers. He wrote various books, including *Introduction to differential and applied psychology, An introduction to psychology for social workers,* and *Problems of professional orientation.*

Meschieri's professional and scientific career was characterized by scientific rigor. The postwar reconstruction of the Italian economy and society posed many social problems and it was thought that psychology could provide some of the answers to these problems. Meschieri was very active and successful both organizationally and scientifically in mobilizing the scientific and methodological resources of the discipline for this purpose.

D. PARISI

MESMER, FRANZ ANTON (1734-1815)

Mesmer, despite the controversies about him as a person, is commonly recognized as the founding father of modern hypnosis. His own position he called animal magnetism, but even if that theory was misguided, he had evidence that *something* was happening in his encounters with his patients.

For his doctoral dissertation on the influence of the planets on human behavior (1766), he relied heavily upon a book by Isaac Newton's friend Richard Mead, who had published on the influence of the planets on human beings in 1704. Thus he was attempting to build upon the rock of Newtonian ideas to find some basis for understanding human illness and cures. Perhaps there were physiological tides that ebbed and flowed with the moon in the body, as ocean tides did around the world.

Mesmer's marriage to a wealthy widow in Vienna permitted him to live well while carrying on his practice. He was a patron of the arts, and one of Mozart's operas was performed for the first time in his private theater. He was also involved in the development of the glass harmonica, still used to this day. He had access to prominent people, and his ideas became popular for a time. He began experimenting with magnets, a practice that had entered medicine with Paracelsus (1493-1541) and been revived at intervals thereafter by Van Helmont and others. A local Jesuit astronomer, Maximilian Hell, had been fashioning magnets, and some of Mesmer's first cures were done with one of his magnets, starting in 1774. By 1775 he was well enough known to be called upon to defy a Catholic priest, Johann Gassner, who had been curing people by casting out demons. Mesmer showed that he could produce and cure the same symptoms by his method of animal magnetism, and won what was the only successful empirical contest of his career. However, he got into trouble in Vienna, and moved to Paris in 1778, where he attained the height of his success.

During the years of popularity he had a fashionable clientele of prominent citizens who would gather about his *baquet* in order to be cured of their troubles. The baquet consisted of a tank in which there were iron filings and other magnetized materials, and bottles of water magnetized by Mesmer, to which each of the seated patients was connected by means of an iron rod so as to share in the magnetic properties. As Mesmer moved from one to another in his fancy robe, one responsive patient after another would go into a crisis and be removed to a recovery room, where, on recovery, the person would be free of symptoms. The medical profession was skeptical throughout, and a Royal Commission—of which Benjamin Franklin, the American ambassador, was the nominal chairman—was established to investigate. Their negative verdict, along with other attacks, put an end to Mesmer's welcome in Paris; in 1784 he left for Switzerland. His disciples continued his practices, particularly under the Marquis de Puységur, and only after many years was animal magnetism given up in favor of hypnotism. Hypnotism did not become fully respectable medically in France until J. M. Charcot's presentation before the Academy of Sciences in 1882.

Mesmer returned to Paris briefly between 1798 and 1802, but then moved back to his childhood village in Switzerland, where he spent his last years in retirement.

The character of Mesmer was such as to leave an ambiguous impression: he was part showman, part serious scientist trying to make the best of the inadequate knowledge of psychological disease and its treatment at the time. His names lives on, however, in the term "mesmerism" (with a small "m"), still heard occasionally as a name for hypnosis.

E. R. HILGARD

MESSER, AUGUST (1867-1937)

Messer was educated at Giessen and Heidelberg and spent a summer with Külpe at Würzburg. Most of his academic life was spent at the University of Giessen. A philosopher by training, he had strong interests in psychology and epistemology and worked in the borderland between these two fields.

Impressed with the work of Oswald Külpe and sharing his interests, Messer carried out an experimental study of thought which became one of the important studies of the Würzburg School. German psychology had been divided into the content psychology of Wilhelm Wundt (experimental analysis of the content of consciousness, such as sensations and images) and the act psychology of Franz Brentano (empirical investigation of conscious or intentional acts, such as judging and believing). Külpe was moving toward a bipartite psychology of act and content, but it was Messer who made this position explicit in his *Psychologie*. Messer distinguished three kinds of intentional experiences or acts, taken in a broad sense: knowing, feeling, and willing; elements of both content and act entered into each. In the case of knowing, for example, the contents were sensations, images, temporal and spatial contents, and impressions, while the acts of knowing were perception, memory, and imagination.

P. E. LICHTENSTEIN

METELLI, FABIO (1907-   )

Metelli is best known for his studies on visual perception. He was schooled at the University of Padua, where he earned the doctoral degree in 1929 in classics. He then turned to psychology. His early interest lay in the study of personality, memory, and forensic and industrial psychology, but soon he concentrated on perceptual phenomena, especially perceptual illusions. He brought to light and analyzed the phenomenon of apparent rest, and for 15 years devoted himself to the study of the perception of transparency, developing a model with a set of equations describing the phenomenon. Another effect that he and his collaborators discovered is the illusory perception of a surface at the mouth of a hole. Metelli maintains that the study of perceptual illusions leads to the discovery of the laws of perception.

Metelli's professional career developed in Padua, where he worked at the psychological laboratory, became a lecturer in 1943 and a professor in 1950; he retired in 1982. He was president of the Italian Psychological Association from 1964 to 1966, and in 1973 was awarded the Golden Medal of the President of the Republic for achievements in education, culture, and art. He is a member of the Academy of Padua (founded by Galileo) and the Venetian Institute of Sciences and Arts, and a fellow of the American Psychological Association. His 50 publications include "The perception of transparency," "Zur Theorie der optischen Bewegungswahrnehmung," and "Repos apparent et phénoménes de totalisation cyclique."

MEYER, ADOLF (1866-1950)

Meyer attended medical school in Zurich. Unable to find a university position in Europe, he emigrated to the United States and took a position as pathologist at the state hospital in Kankakee, Illinois, in 1893. He later became professor of psychiatry at Cornell Medical College in New York City. In 1909 he was invited by G. Stanley Hall to participate in the celebration of the twentieth anniversary of the founding of Clark University, along with Freud and Jung. The remainder of his career was spent at the Phipps Clinic in Baltimore.

Meyer is best known for his theory of psychobiology, which emphasized the importance of a biographical study in understanding an individual's personality in all its aspects. He considered each person a biological unit that always functioned, whether alone or in a group. Because of the complexity of the human personality, the psychiatrist must study the individual from various aspects: medical, biographical, artistic, and educational. He stressed an objective approach to the understanding of a person based on biological, social, and psychological forces. Furthermore, the psychiatrist must study both normal and abnormal behavior from these various perspectives. Meyer opposed those theories of personality which made use of abstract and fictional constructs in favor of a common-sense approach.

In making a psychiatric diagnosis, argued Meyer, the physician must examine the patient's life history (biographical approach) and his present personality traits as well as his physical, neurological, and genetic conditions, in order to formulate a plan for therapy. Psychobiological therapy started with an evaluation of the person's assets and liabilities. This involved an examination of the life history. The psychiatrist started by examining a patient's "better self." The general aim of the entire therapy was to help a person, hampered by abnormal conditions, to make the best adjustment possible to life and change. Rather than stressing unconscious processes as Freud had done, Meyer felt that a person's problems should be approached at the conscious level. This involved a face-to-face contact to implement the psychiatrist's efforts to focus on the current situation and reactions to everyday difficulties, as well as the patient's long-term life adjustment. In the process of therapy the person was led to modify unhealthy adjustments. Meyer called this "habit training." It involved the use of guidance, suggestion and reeducation.

Meyer remained for 32 years at the Phipps Clinic, which became a world-renowned center for the training of psychiatrists. While at the clinic he became acquainted with John B. Watson, who was director of the psychological laboratory from 1913 to 1920, and 10 years later with W. Horsley Gantt, who established the Pavlovian laboratory there.

R. W. LUNDIN

MICHON, JOHN A. (1935–   )

Michon obtained a first degree in psychology from the University of Utrecht and the Ph.D. from the University of Leyden. Originally trained as a clinical and forensic psychologist, he opted for a career in experimental psychology when, in 1960, he became a research associate at the Institute for Perception-TNO in Soesterberg. There he specialized in human information processing, working on problems of mental load, visual and auditory search, and skill acquisition. In 1971 he was appointed professor of experimental psychology and traffic science at the University of Groningen.

Michon was one of the founders of the Netherlands Psychonomics Foundation (1968) and principal editor of the *Handbook der psychonomie* (1976; English edition 1979). He also founded the Traffic Research Center at the University of Groningen (1977), of which he is now chairman. He is a member of the Royal Netherlands Academy of Arts and Sciences.

Michon is known for his work on the role of time and timing in the organization of behavior (*Timing in temporal Tracking*, 1967; "The making of the present," 1978).

MICHOTTE, ALBERT E. (1881–1965)

Michotte was one of the most eminent representatives of phenomological psychology and an influential teacher and investigator in Europe. He studied at the University of Louvain, and worked for some time at the Leipzig and Würzburg laboratories. He owed his maturation as a psychologist to Oswald Külpe. In 1905 he started his teaching career at the University of Louvain, with which he was associated until his retirement in 1946. A skillful experimentalist, he devoted his best efforts to the Louvain laboratory, which he directed for 25 years.

Michotte's investigations comprised three periods: (1) studies of higher mental processes (memory, cognition, will) in the spirit of the Würzburg School; (2) research on perception, movement, rhythm, and learning; and after 1939, (3) his most original and fruitful work on the perception of causality, which resulted in the publication of his most significant book, *The perception of causality*, which attracted wide attention. In it the author demonstrated that perception of causality is not a secondary interpretation of experiences or other perceptions; rather, it constitutes a primary perception such as that of color, tone, or touch, and occurs spontaneously and invariably under certain conditions.

Because of his long teaching career, during which he trained and influenced students from many countries, and his active participation in psychological meetings and his numerous publications, Michotte was one of the best-known and respected psychologists in Europe.

H. MISIAK

MILES, WALTER R. (1885–1978)

Miles received the B.A. from Earlham College. During the following year, while teaching at Penn College in Oskaloosa, Iowa, he was recruited for graduate work at Iowa State by Carl Seashore. His dissertation involved the accuracy of the voice in simple pitch singing.

After a year of teaching at Wesleyan College, he was on the staff of the Carnegie Nutrition Laboratory in Boston for a number of years. He found that males on war ration diets had a decreased interest in sexual matters. His research for *Alcohol and human efficiency* also came from this period.

Missing the stimulation of working with students, he moved to Stanford to serve as the "laboratory man" under Terman. Noting that rats spent a lot of time smelling every inch of the alley maze, he obtained more rapid acquisition of learning with an elevated, narrow-path maze. Miles was involved in the validation and implementation of admissions testing for entrance to the University. Along with his colleagues, L. M. Terman, E. K. Strong, and S. Stone, he directed the longitudinal Stanford Later Maturity Study. Among his distinguished students at Stanford were Harry Harlow and Floyd Ruch.

Miles moved to the new Institute of Human Relations at Yale, where he continued his varied research interests. He was president of the American Psychological Association in 1931–1932 and shortly after became a member of the National Academy of Sciences. Alphonse Chapanis was his most distinguished student at Yale.

During World War II his research ingenuity and precision were again called upon to solve a practical problem. Fighter pilots had to always be prepared to fly, even at night. If they used any light in the "ready room," it would require at least 20 minutes of dark adaptation before they could see adequately. Miles, recalling that the cone system of vision was sensitive to wavelengths that rods were not, devised red goggles for the pilots to wear. Thus they were able to read and play cards in the red world of their ready room, yet were immediately prepared for night flying.

Upon reaching the mandatory age, Miles "retired" to the Turkish University in Istanbul, where he spent three years developing the experimental psychology faculty and facilities. He then once more "retired," this time as scientific director of the U.S. Naval Submarine Base Medical Research Laboratory at New London, Connecticut, where he supervised research on the health, motivation, and performance of men in limited work space. He was heavily involved in the research conducted under the name Sealab I. In 1962 he became the fifth psychologist to receive the Gold Medal of the American Psychological Foundation.

C. S. PEYSER

MILGRAM, STANLEY (1933–1984)

Milgram received the Ph.D. in social psychology from Harvard in 1960. Using an auditory judgment task rather than the visual judgment task of the original Solomon Asch studies, Milgram compared the conformity levels of Norwegians and Frenchmen and found Norwegians to be the more conforming.

His best-known studies were on the dynamics of obedience to authority. In these studies, a subject was commanded to give increasingly higher voltages of electric shock to a learner, every time the latter gave a wrong answer on a verbal-learning task. The learner was an actor who feigned increasingly intense suffering with increases in shock levels. Milgram found an unexpectedly high rate of obedience. Milgram conducted more than 20 variations of this basic experiment. A full report of his research program on obedience to authority is found in *Obedience to authority: An experimental view,* which has been translated into 11 languages.

From the beginning, the obedience studies were embroiled in controversy; praised by some, vilified by others. Much of the controversy had to do with the ethics of deceiving participants into believing that they may have harmed an innocent human being (e.g., Baumrind, 1964; Kelman, 1967; Milgram, 1964, 1977b). For an exploration of ethical issues raised by these experiments, see Miller (1986).

The obedience work became one of the best-known pieces of research in the social sciences. The 1963 report became a "Citation Classic" in 1981 (Milgram, 1981) and has been reprinted in dozens of anthologies.

Milgram went on to make a number of other original contributions. The following are brief summaries of the principal ones: in 1970 Milgram published the article "The experience of living in cities," in which he introduced the concept of overload as a way to understand urban–rural differences in social behavior. In 1965, Milgram and colleagues (Milgram, 1969; Milgram, Mann & Harter, 1965) introduced an unobtrusive way of measuring community attitudes and opinions. They scattered 400 "lost letters" throughout New Haven—on sidewalks, in phone booths, on car windshields. One hundred each were addressed to Friends of the Nazi Party, Friends of the Communist Party, Medical Research Associates, and a Mr. Walter Carnap. While a majority of the latter two were mailed, only a minority of the first two were. This technique is the most widely used nonreactive measure of attitudes.

In 1967, Milgram introduced a technique for studying the small-world phenomenon, the not-uncommon situation of meeting someone in, say, San Francisco who happens to know your first cousin in Toronto. In the small-world method, a sample of "starters" are each given a packet that needs to reach a designated stranger, the "target person," in another city, with the limitation that each person can send it to only someone he or she knows on a first-name basis. Milgram found that among completed chains it typically required only a small number of intermediaries—averages ranged from 4.4 to 5.9—for the mailing to reach the target. The technique is an important tool of social-network researchers (Kadushin, 1989).

An integrative review of the whole corpus of Milgram's work can be found in Blass (1992). An updated version of most of Milgram's published writings has been published (Sabini & Silver, 1992). A symposium exploring Milgram's contributions to social psychology was conducted at the annual convention of the American Psychological Association in Boston in 1990 (Blass, 1990).

MILL, JOHN STUART (1806–1873)

John Stuart Mill was educated primarily by his father. A child prodigy, he began learning Greek at the age of three and was reading Herodotus and Plato in the original at the age of eight.

Like his father, James Mill, he was primarily a social theorist and political economist. Both were leaders in the Utilitarian movement which dominated British philosophy during the first part of the nineteenth century. This was guided by the principle of utility set forth earlier by Jeremy Bentham. Also like his father, Mill was a leader in the nineteenth-century psychology of British associationism.

Mill's psychology is to be found in an expanded edition of his father's *Analysis of the phenomena of the human mind.* In this he reacted against his father's atomistic associationism, which had fostered a kind of "mental mechanics" whereby associations added together to form complex ideas. John Stuart Mill held that the mind was active, not passive: it was more than the mere addition of experiences. He believed that a combination of mental events resulted in something totally new which was not present in the original experiences—a notion that became identified as a "mental chemistry." Experiences lost their original identity in a fusion into new complex ideas. However, Mill did accept his father's idea of the association of ideas, but believed that in the combination of experiences there was a loss of specific parts. In implying that the whole (new idea) was something more than the sum of its parts, he was anticipating Wundt's notion of a "creative synthesis" as well as Gestalt psychology, which holds that perceptions come to us as a whole and can not be broken down by analysis.

In 1843 Mill's *Logic* was published. Here he explained logical induction and deduction, and methods of agreement, difference, concomitant variation, and residue. This work has become a classic in scientific method. However, the contents of the volume were broader than the title suggested. In it he argued for a science of human nature as well as a new science to be called ethology or the science of character.

R. W. LUNDIN

MILLER, GEORGE A. (1920–   )

Known for his work in cognitive psychology, especially cognitive learning theory, Miller obtained the B.A. and M.A. from the University of Alabama and the Ph.D. in experimental psychology at Harvard University in 1946. He served as a research fellow at Harvard's Psycho-Acoustic Laboratory during the latter half of the 1940s, and by 1958 became a professor of psychology. He left Harvard for his present position at Rockefeller University in 1968.

Miller's research in language and communication led to cognitive learning theory, which he, Eugene Galanter, and Karl Pribram published under the title *Plans and the structure of behavior.* The book develops the concept of "image," a view reminiscent of Tolman's cognitive map. As the total accumulation of one's learning, the image "is all the accumulated, organized knowledge that the organism has about itself and its world" (p. 17). Miller also wrote *Psychology: The study of mental life,* an elementary text that attempts to explain psychology by key topics in historical order.

MILLER, NEAL E. (1909–   )

Miller obtained the B.S. from the University of Washington, the M.A. from Stanford, and the Ph.D. from Yale in 1935. He was an SSRC fellow at the Vienna Psychoanalytic Institute in 1935–1936. At Yale, he was a member of the Institute of Human Relations (1936–1950), a professor of Psychology (1950–1952) and James Rowland Angell Professor of Psychology (1952–1966). At Rockefeller University he was professor and head of a laboratory of physiological psychology (1966–1980), then emeritus (1980 on).

Miller collaborated with John Dollard (1941) in experiments on learning of and by imitation and on how models acquire prestige. After an experimental analysis of conflict behavior, displacement, and fear-reduction as reinforcement, he collaborated with Dollard (1950) in a detailed theoretical analysis of how neuroses are learned, how repression interferes with thinking, and how these processes can be corrected by therapeutic learning. Next, with Delgado and Roberts (1954), Miller produced the first demonstration of trial-and-error learning motivated by electrical stimulation of the brain. He studied motivational effects of electrical and chemical brain stimulation. Then he investigated how instrumental learning may modify visceral responses, and the possible role of such learning in normal homeostasis, disease, and therapy (*Selected Papers*).

Among other honors, Miller was elected president of the APA, the Society for Neuroscience, the Academy of Behavioral Medicine Research, and the APA's Division of Health Psychology. He was elected to the National Academy of Sciences, the American Philosophical Society, and the American Academy of Arts and Sciences, and has served on the Life Sciences Panel of the President's Science Advisory Committee. He received the National Medal of Science, the APA Gold Medal Award, and honorary degrees from the universities of Pennsylvania, Michigan, and Uppsala, St. Lawrence University, and La Salle College.

MILNER, BRENDA L. (1918–   )

Brenda Milner, née Langford, attended Withington Girls' School and Newnham College, Cambridge. While at Cambridge, she studied experimental psychology under Oliver Zangwill, whom she credits with inspiring her interest in human brain function.

The outbreak of World War II found Milner at Newnham College, Cambridge, doing graduate work. As the work of the Cambridge Psychological Laboratory shifted to applied research in the war effort, Milner became involved in designing tests to be used in the selection of air crew members, and later in examining and evaluating different methods of radar display and control.

After her marriage in 1944 to Peter Milner she moved to Montreal and, because of her ability to speak French fluently, obtained a teaching position at the University of Montreal. Milner's influence was felt immediately by the newly formed Institut de Psychologie, where she taught comparative and experimental psychology in its formative years. While maintaining this position, she began Ph.D. studies at McGill University and obtained the Ph.D. in 1952.

Milner's doctoral thesis explored the intellectual effects of temporal lobe damage in humans, and was the beginning of a gradually expanding study of memory disorders. More recently, her work has explored the effect of brain lesions or injury on cerebral organizations. In 1971–1972 Milner returned to Cambridge for a year and earned the Sc.D. degree. Presently, she holds the position of professor of psychology in the Department of Neurology and Neurosurgery at McGill.

MINAMI, HIROSHI (1914–   )

A pioneer in the field of social psychology in Japan, Minami was educated in Tokyo and Kyoto. After receiving the bachelor's degree from Kyoto University, he continued his studies at Cornell University, where he received the Ph.D. in 1943. He remained at Cornell as a research fellow until 1945. Upon his return to Japan in 1946 Minami joined the faculty of Hitotsubashi University, of which he was made professor emeritus in 1978. Minami received the degree of Litt. D. from Kyoto University in 1962.

In 1952 Minami published *Introduction to social psychology*, the first systematic presentation of social psychology in Japan. His interest in the study of the Japanese national character led to the publication of *Psychology of the Japanese people*, which has been translated into English. In 1950 Minami founded the Institute of Social Psychology, where he does research on various aspects of postwar Japanese society such as mass communications, mass culture, and human relations. Minami has also applied his theory of psychohistory in the study of prewar Japan. His three-volume *Collected papers on social psychology* is a culmination of his research on the process of modernization and its sociopsychological impact on the Japanese people. Another work, *Science of human behavior*, was published in 1980.

Minami has served as president of the Japanese Society of Social Psychology, and as an officer of the International Society of Psychological Science and the International Association of Applied Psychology.

MIRA y LÓPEZ, EMILIO (1896–1964)

Mira y López studied medicine at Barcelona with Pi Sunyer, an important physiologist in the tradition of Claude Bernard and Ramon y Cajal. In 1919, he was elected director of the section of psychotecnics of the Institute for Vocational Guidance of Barcelona, created in 1917 and one of the first centers of applied psychology in the world. The institute organized two International Conferences of Psychotecnics in Barcelona, in 1922 and 1930. In 1931, Mira y López was elected the head of the Institute. In 1936, Mira y López was to have been president of the 12th International Congress of Psychology in Madrid, which was canceled because of the outbreak of the Spanish Civil War.

A prolific writer, Mira y López was probably the first Spanish-speaking psychologist to show an interest in behaviorism and one of the first to study the work of Sigmund Freud. His published writings include works on psychoanalysis, legal psychology, psychiatry, evolutive psychology, vocational guidance, and experimental psychology. His best-known contribution is a personality test, which is called myokinetic psychodiagnosis (MKP), presented to the Royal Society of Medicine, in 1939, and later published as a book in French, Spanish, English, and German. At the end of the Spanish Civil War, Mira y López went into exile and died in Brazil after living in several countries. In 1945, he founded and directed until his death, the Institute for Selection and Vocational Guidance of São Paulo in Brazil.

MISIAK, HENRYK (1911–1992)

Misiak was ordained a Roman Catholic priest and held various educational posts in his native country and, after the outbreak of World War II, in Hungary, France, and Great Britain. He studied psychology at the University of Glasgow in Scotland, then in 1944 came to the United States and continued his studies at Fordham University, where he received the Ph.D. in psychology. After postdoctoral studies in physiology, neuroanatomy, and endocrinology at Columbia University, his specialty became neuropsychology. His experimental research focused on the perception of intermittent light, particularly on various parameters and applications of critical flicker frequency (CFF). He and his collaborators demonstrated that CFF decreases with age, and that in old age CFF correlates with some measures of intellectual functioning. He published about 50 articles and presented dozens of reports at national and international meetings.

Another area of Misiak's teaching and research has been the history of psychology, especially the historical links between European and American psychologies. One problem he studied with Virginia S. Sexton was the impact of phenomenological and existential philosophies on American psychology (Misiak & Sexton, 1973). Misiak was author, coauthor, or editor of six books dealing with historical problems of psychology, including a textbook also with Sexton, *History of psychology: An overview*.

Misiak taught psychology at Fordham University from 1946 to 1980. During this period he was mentor or comentor of 70 master's and 22 doctoral dissertations. As a consulting psychologist at St. Barnabas Hospital in the Bronx, he participated in a series of studies on the psychological concomitants of various neurological disorders, particularly Parkinson's disease.

MISUMI, JYUJI (1924–   )

Misumi majored in psychology at Kyushu University and received the D.Litt. in 1969. Studying infant perception, he found visual size constancy in six-month-old babies. He became professor of group dynamics in 1955, when the chair of group dynamics was established at the Faculty of Education of Kyushu University. Since 1976 he has been professor of social psychology at the Faculty of Human Sciences of Osaka University. He founded the Japan Group Dynamics Association in 1949 and became its president.

Misumi is known for his research in experimental psychology concerning the leadership PM theory, and his studies on leadership behavior in various business and industrial organizations, local government organizations, schools, sports groups, and political groups, whose validity he verified by identifying group functions in terms of the PM dimensions. The PM theory aims at classifying leadership behavior by using combinations of the problem-solving or goal achievement-oriented functional dimension (P) and the group maintenance-oriented functional dimension (M). P stands for performance, and M for maintenance.

Misumi also carried out a PM-style sensitivity training program based on a number of empirical and experimental studies. He conducted action research on organizational development in Japanese industries by applying the concept and methodology of group dynamics. Among his main publications are *New patterns of leadership*, *Group dynamics*, and *The behavioral science of leadership*.

MITTENECKER, ERICH (1922–   )

Mittenecker started his academic career in 1947 in Vienna as an assistant of H. Rohracher. He spent 1950–1951 in the United States. He was appointed to a chair of applied psychology at the University of Vienna in 1961. From 1965 to 1968 he held a chair in Tübingen, Germany. From 1968 on he has been head of the Department of Psychology of the University of Graz.

His research spans several fields. In his lectures he attempts to integrate behaviorism and introspectionism, pure and applied research, and substance with methodology. In 1952 he published a book in German on experimental design. With W. Toman, in 1951 Mittenecker constructed the first German multidimensional personality and interest inventory. In a group of research papers he treated problems of "Perseveration and personality." *Information theory in psychology* appeared in 1973.

His research in applied psychology culminated in a book and a number of papers on the causes of accidents in traffic and industry. His former students include many distinguished researchers, among them G. Fischer, G. Guttmann, G. A. Lienert, and K. Pawlik.

MONTAGU, ASHLEY (1905–   )

An anthropologist and social biologist, Montagu has been mainly interested in the origin, evolution, and development of human behavior. He was a student of Charles Spearman, J. C. Flugel, Elliot Smith, Bronislaw Malinowski, Charles C. Seligman, Franz Boas, and Ruth Benedict. His work has been at the interface between the biological and the social influences in the development of human behavior.

Montagu's major contributions have been to show the following: (1) the importance of prenatal influences on the subsequent development

of the individual; (2) the reproductive development of the female, and the consequences of a genuine understanding of that process for the responsibilities of childbearing and child rearing; (3) the origin of the practice of rooming-in; (4) the importance of breastfeeding; (5) the superiority of home births; (6) the replacement of obstetricians by midwives; (7) the natural superiority of women; (8) love as the most important of all basic needs; (9) the biological and social bases of cooperation; (10) the fallacies of I.Q. testing; (11) humanity's most dangerous myth: the fallacy of "race"; (12) the importance of neoteny in the development of behaviorally healthy humans; (13) the discovery of physiological nescience of maternity among Australian aborigines, and the demonstration of the reality of physiological paternity among the aborigines; (14) sociogenic brain damage; (15) natural selection and the mental capacities of humankind; (16) natural selection and the origin and significance of weeping; (17) natural selection and the origin of laughter; (18) the natural history of swearing; (19) the origin of menstrual taboos; (20) the mind of the skin: touching; and (21) the nature of human aggression.

MONTESSORI, MARIA (1870–1952)

Following her graduation from medical school in Italy, Montessori attacked exploitation of child labor and championed the cause of working women. Her practice as a physician brought her into contact with retarded children. She helped establish and directed a state orthophrenic school in Rome. That school became her training grounds for learning about retarded children whom she taught to read and write. For 2 yrs, she studied the children, and *they* became Montessori's teachers. This experience had a profound influence on her, which resulted in a career change from medicine to education.

She returned subsequently to the university classroom to register formally for courses in psychology and philosophy. There she was able to transfer her training and knowledge of the retarded to "normal" children. She began to formulate her own theories of child growth and developed a philosophy of education. Montessori used her scientific background to create universal principles and special methods and materials for a new pedagogy. In 1909, she published the first book on the Montessori method, which became an instant success, translated into over 20 foreign languages. Other books followed: *The secret of childhood*, *What you should know about your child*, and *To educate the human potential*.

For more than 40 years, Montessori labored to impart her novel ideas through writing, lecturing, and teacher training. She was described as a lecturer par excellence. Demand for her lectures came not only from Italy but also from other European countries and the United States. She initiated a number of schools and trained as many as 5000 teachers from every part of the globe.

A Montessori society arose in Rome and others followed. The American Montessori Society was organized under the presidency of Alexander Graham Bell, but did not follow the European model. Montessori presided at eight international Montessori congresses.

Among her accolades were the French medal Legion d'Honneur, the Dutch Officer of the Order of Orange-Nassau, and an honorary doctorate from the University of Amsterdam. According to Montessori, "Work is necessary. It can be nothing less than a passion. A person is happy only in accomplishment."

S. S. BROWN

MORENO, JACOB L. (1892–1974)

Moreno received his M.D. in Vienna in 1917 and worked there until coming to the United States in the early 1930s. During his early years in the United States he developed a methodology for social psychology called sociometry and founded a journal by that name. He was also involved in prison reform.

Moreno is best known as the developer of psychodrama. This technique had its roots in the early 1920s in Vienna, where he was involved with the Theater of Spontaneity. He objected to the Freudian approach as being an artificial world of dreams and words occurring in offices. Instead, he emphasized acts or behaviors in natural surroundings, including role-training methods. In the several years before Moreno came to the United States, this became known as Impromptu Theater with publications in *Impromptu Magazine*. In the group setting it was important to have a genuine two-way cohesion that he called *tele*. More than simple transference and empathy, it involved cognitions, wishes, desires, choices, and behaviors. Moreno was a European pioneer in group psychotherapy.

In the United States Moreno developed the technique further and published *Psychodrama*. The technique involves time, reality, space, and warming up. As regards *time,* problems can occur in the past, the present, or the future. The past should be dealt with, but not overemphasized as in Freud. One needs to anticipate the future to be better prepared for it. The encounter itself occurs in the here-and-now; for purposes of the technique, all problems are transferred to the present. Although one can deal with actual *reality* or a limited portion of it, most often it is useful to deal with the "surplus" reality of role playing (including role reversal), auxiliary ego, or bodily contact (within ethical limits). As for *space,* psychodrama occurs in an action-centered stage, not in the limited, language-centered restrictions of a professional office. Just as athletes, singers, and engines require *warming up* for best performance, the first phase is the critical phase-in. The psychodrama then proceeds to the action phase and finally to the post-action sharing.

Various psychodrama techniques may be used. In *therapeutic soliloquy* the patient acts out feelings in the current situation. Since in reality the other characters could not observe these feelings, they do not react to this portion of the patient's behavior. In *multiple double* several others take the role of the patient, but at different periods in the patient's life. Perhaps one will play the patient of now, another the patient of five years ago, and still another the patient during a particular life crisis. In *mirror* the patient joins the group and observes someone else taking the patient's role.

Moreno claimed to obtain more catharsis or emotional reliving that at least partially solved the psychological problem with his psychodrama than Freud did by just talking with the client. For Moreno, action was the key to realism.

C. S. PEYSER

MORGAN, CONWAY LLOYD (1852–1936)

Morgan became professor of zoology and geology at University College, Bristol, in England in 1884 and was principal of the college from 1887 to 1908. He was one of the most distinguished zoologists and comparative psychologists of his time. His most famous book (Morgan, 1894) was on comparative psychology; it detailed the relationships between the animal mind and the human. He wrote other books on animal behavior which included descriptions of the behavior of animals in their natural environments as well as in the laboratory.

At the time, other animal psychologists such as George Romanes were inclined to endow animal behavior with human characteristics. This was an attempt to follow the Darwinian theory as far as the evolution of human behavior from lower forms. But Morgan found dangers in this anthropomorphic tendency, and in the third chapter of his book on comparative psychology set forth what is known as Lloyd Morgan's Canon. This was an attempt to apply the Law of Parsimony to an explanation of animal behavior. It states (Morgan, 1894): "In no case

may we interpret an action as the outcome of the exercise of a higher psychical faculty, if it can be interpreted as the outcome of the exercise of one which stands lower in the psychological scale."

The justification of the canon is to be found in the necessity for offering the simplest possible explanation. At the time when the proof of Darwin's evolutionary theory was upermost in the minds of biologists and psychologists, a demonstration of the canon was a definite advantage.

R. W. LUNDIN

MORITA, SHOMA (1874–1938)

Morita was a professor of psychiatry at the Tokoyo Jikeikai School of Medicine. At the time, Japanese psychiatry was very much dominated by theories of Emil Kraepelin which suggested that behavior disorders were caused by biological and constitutional disturbances. Morita took a new approach not only to the causes of disorders but the ways in which they should be treated. His important books include *Theory of nervosity and neurasthenia* and *Nature and theory of nervosity.*

His main contribution to psychiatry and psychology was the development of a new form of psychotherapy, generally known as Morita Therapy. Apparently he suffered from a variety of neurotic symptoms from the time of his adolescence, and is reported to have entered the field of psychiatry in an attempt to understand his own personality difficulties. He contended that neurotic disorders were not due to constitutional or body conditions but the result of intense attention paid to them by the patient. The more attention given, the more severe the symptoms became. Thus a vicious circle arose which Morita termed "to be caught." The most successful way of treating these symptoms was to gain insight. Morita's method combined psychotherapy and Zen Buddhism. To gain insight, the patient must be in harmony with the universe. One should not challenge nature but accept it and, in so doing, live in peace with it. According to Morita nature *was* the therapist and the task of the psychotherapist was merely to assist the patient in gaining insight. In the process of Morita therapy, the patient went through various stages, of which the first was bed rest. During this period, isolation might intensify the symptoms. In the next stages a diary was kept and the therapist's function was to comment on and interpret what was written. The last stage involved "taking things as they are": learning to be natural and comfortable with oneself.

R. W. LUNDIN

MOUNOUD, PIERRE (1940–   )

In the Swiss tradition, Pierre Mounoud is a developmental psychologist. Having participated in the research work of the Genevan school on mental image, memory, causality and learning, he received the Ph.D. in psychology from the University of Geneva in 1968. He subsequently graduated in neurophysiology at Marseilles. Nominated associate professor at Lausanne in 1973, he has been a professor at Geneva since 1975. An invited professor in various universities, he is frequently asked to lecture in Europe and the Americas.

Mounoud is known for his research on the acquisition of motor skills and on the development of practical intelligence, which he refuses to consider as different in nature from so-called conceptual intelligence. His critical positions on Piaget's theory are equally known. He has also carried out research on self-image recognition with children and teenagers.

Mounoud's conception of development is based on the idea that the child constructs representations in the sense of internal models or memories. In his view, the information-processing capacities are preformed, as are coding abilities. However, the representations constructed by the child (by means of different coding systems) depend directly on the situations the subject has happened to experience. At each stage (determined by the appearance of new coding abilities), representations are constructed by means of the same procedure. This procedure defines a developmental sequence which may be described in terms of successive revolutions.

MOUTON, JANE S. (1930–   )

Mouton has contributed to behavioral science, especially in the fields of management and organization development. She received the Ph.D. in psychology from the University of Texas in 1957, and for a while thereafter was an assistant professor in the University's Psychology Department.

Mouton was instrumental in refining the Managerial Grid, a theory of leadership effectiveness and management practice which identifies and compares basic approaches to integrating the two primary concerns of work: people and production. Mouton's research with Robert Blake has shown that individual and organizational effectiveness is enhanced by leadership which promotes participation, involvement, openness, inquiry, advocacy, candor, and critique.

A primary area of Mouton's exploration is synergogy, a learning model. Synergogy is student-centered learning which requires the exercise of self-responsibility. In the context of provided learning designs, students are active participants in a learning process which involves listening, explaining, evaluating, and interacting.

Mouton has coauthored more than 25 books and numerous articles which provide insights into how people can operate with maximum productivity, creativity, motivation, and satisfaction in today's complex organizational environments.

MOWRER, O. HOBART (1907–1982)

Mowrer first published a series of 19 papers concerning vestibulo-ocular reflexes and spatial orientation which, while not often cited in psychological literature, were well received in otology and sensory physiology. They also served, somewhat paradoxically, to gain him an appointment (1934–1940) at Yale's Institute of Human Relations. There he developed theoretical and research interests in the psychology of learning, language, psychopathology, certain cognitive processes, and interpersonal relations which importantly influenced his subsequent professional career.

During his tenure at the Harvard Graduate School of Education (1940-1948), Mowrer had a courtesy appointment in the Department of Psychology and was associated with Talcott Parsons, Clyde Kluckhohn, Gordon Allport, and Henry Murray in the establishment of the Department of Social Relations. During the latter part of this period he was editor of the *Harvard Educational Review* and was instrumental in the ultimate transfer of all editorial responsibility to a student board.

In 1948 Mowrer was appointed research professor of psychology at the University of Illinois, a position he held until his retirement in 1975. In 1953–1954 he was president of the American Psychological Association, and served on the editorial panel of several professional journals. His best-known and probably most enduring practical contribution is a means of treating nocturnal enuresis known as the bell-and-pad method. His more substantive contributions are in learning, language, and interpersonal psychology.

Mowrer's complete bibliography contains some 235 items, a dozen of which are books. His major publications include *Abnormal reactions or actions; Learning theory and personality dynamics;* Chapter 11 in the *History of psychology in autobiography; Learning theory and behavior; Leaves from many seasons; Selected papers;* and *Learning theory and symbolic processes.*

MÜLLER, GEORG ELIAS (1850–1904)

Müller entered the University of Leipzig in 1868 to study philosophy and history. There he became acquainted with Gustav Fechner and his studies in psychophysics. Müller's refinements of Fechner's psychophysical methods are classics. In 1881 Müller went to the University of Göttingen, where he remained for the next 40 years until retirement.

Besides his studies in psychophysics, Müller's career was devoted to the psychology of vision and memory. In his work on memory he followed the original work of Hermann Ebbinghaus. Along with one of his students, Adolf Jost, he discovered what he called Jost's Law, which stated that when two associations are of equal strength, a repetition strengthens the older one more than the recent.

Müller also improved on Ebbinghaus' method for the presentation of the stimuli in learning by devising a method for their uniform presentation. He placed them on a revolving drum (today called a memory drum) so that nonsense syllables, for example, could be presented at a constant rate or systematically varied. Another improvement on Ebbinghaus' procedures was the development of lists of nonsense syllables of equal difficulty. In studying memory, Müller also discovered the phenomenon called "retroactive inhibition." If, immediately after a learning period, the subject was confronted with a new task, recall of the originally learned material was appreciably less efficient than if recall of material was followed by a period of rest.

In his studies of vision, Müller followed Hering's theory of color vision, which involved the three reversible photochemical substances (black-white, red-green, and blue-yellow), but he considered the process to be chemical, rather than metabolic as Hering had thought. Müller also added his concept of "cortical gray" as the zero point from which color sensations diverge. He believed there was a constant gray aroused by the molecular action of the cerebral cortex of the brain.

R. W. LUNDIN

MÜLLER, JOHANNES (1801–1858)

In 1883 Müller became professor of physiology at the University of Berlin. He was one of the most important experimental physiologists of the nineteenth century. His *Handbook on the physiology of man* (1838) was one of the most scholarly texts of its time.

One of Müller's important early studies was on the reflex. Earlier, Sir Charles Bell had distinguished between the functions of the sensory and motor nerves. Using frogs as his subjects, Müller gave experimental support to this distinction. The reflex activity involved three aspects: (1) impulse from the sense organ to the dorsal root of the spinal cord; (2) connections in the cord; and (3) impulse going out via the ventral root to the muscle.

Müller is best known for his doctrine of the "specific energies of nerves," which he set forth in his *Handbook.* In summary, the doctrine states that, regardless of how it is stimulated, each sensory nerve will lead to one kind of sensation and no other. The importance of the sensation lies not in the stimulus itself, but in the nerve connected to the sense organ and in the brain center where the nerve terminates. For example, regardless of how we stimulate the eye—whether it be light waves, pressure of the thumb on the eyeball, or electricity—what we experience is a visual sensation. Müller probably realized—although it is not certain—that he was expanding on Kant's notion of the innateness of perception.

Although there are some who still support Müller's doctrine, most scientists consider it in error. Nerves simply do not have specific energies. The significance of this doctrine is that it served as a basis for later theories of vision and hearing to be set forth by Hermann Helmholtz and Ewald Hering.

R. W. LUNDIN

MUNDY-CASTLE, ALASTAIR C. (1923–   )

Mundy-Castle was schooled at Tonbridge and served as a flying instructor with the Royal Air Force before graduating in psychology at Cambridge University under Sir Frederic Bartlett. Most of his subsequent career has been spent in Africa, first in the South with Simon Biesheuvel, later in Ghana, and currently in Nigeria, where he is professor at the University of Lagos. There are two phases to his working life, the first as cross-cultural neuropsychologist, the second as developmental psychologist and architect of the now powerful Lagos Psychology Department. A bridge between these phases was provided by three years with Jerome Bruner at Harvard University.

Mundy-Castle's major first-phase contributions were the identification of individually characteristic labile and stable galvanic skin response patterns, the latter habituating to repetitive stimulation, the former not; and his pioneering studies of interrelationships among electrophysiological measures and indices of temperament, personality, perceptual-motor functioning, and intelligence. In this period he recognized the integral part played by culture in the making of persons.

His contributions in the second phase comprise the experimental delineation of culturally universal stages in the development of perception (with Anglin and Bundy) and of cooperative understanding (with Trevarthen). The latter invoke intersubjectivity and nonverbal interaction as a matrix for language development and acculturation.

MUNRO, DONALD (1940–   )

Munro studied engineering at Glasgow University, but gave it up to qualify in social work. After getting the B.A. and M.A. in psychology from Manchester University, he became a research fellow in the Human Development Research Unit of the new University of Zambia (founded by Alistair Heron, with Jan Deregowski and Robert Serpell). After four years there he moved to a lecturing post in the (then) University College of Rhodesia, became founding head of the Department of Psychology in 1974 and professor in 1977. The Ph.D. for London University was completed in 1973.

Munro's early research work in Zambia was concerned with the effects of home environment and parental stimulation on the intellectual development of children in the poorer Lusaka suburbs. However, a conviction which arose from that work was that the motivational factors were at least as important as cognitive ones, and that much of the good work on cognitive development being done in Africa was marred by ignoring the motivational constraints on responding. He has continued this theme. His studies for the Ph.D. (1968–1973) were on locus of control. He then moved to a concern with psychometric methods for assessing motivation, personality, and values. A new local test of occupational interests was produced with a student in 1975. This test has been used in part-time vocational guidance counseling, and an adaptation is being prepared for the Zimbabwe Ministry of Education.

Munro's current research activities include an in-depth interview study of the development of black civil servants and managers, and participation in the international Work Importance Study coordinated by Donald Super. He also has an interest in computers, and is working with one on behavior simulation programs to aid psychological decision making. He has published or given papers in these areas of interest.

MÜNSTERBERG, HUGO (1863–1916)

Münsterberg earned the Ph.D. under Wundt at Leipzig and a medical degree at Heidelberg. Like many of Wundt's students, he founded a psychology laboratory, at Freiburg. William James considered his 1888 dissertation "a little masterpiece" and invited him to Harvard as professor of psychology and director of the Psychology Laboratories. Münsterberg was a true *Deutscher Gelehrter*. In addition to writings in philosophy, psychotherapy, and educational psychology and his early experimentation in sensory psychology, he touched four main areas.

1. *Forensic psychologist.* As early as the 1890s, Münsterberg was writing and speaking about the relationship between blood pressure and the detection of veracity. He made newspaper headlines with comments on two celebrated murder cases. *On the witness stand* (1908) developed the notion of the "lie detector" and discussed the fallibility of eyewitness testimony, the dynamics of false confessions, and the effects of suggestibility upon witness, jury, and judge. Münsterberg also popularized Jung's notion of word association as a means of determining guilt. Later he did experimental work on the group dynamics of the jury.

2. *Economic psychologist.* Around 1910 Münsterberg suggested validating aptitude tests by success on the job. His greatest impact came with *Psychology and industrial efficiency* (1913), which organized his work into (1) the best possible man (personnel selection), (2) the best possible work (time and motion studies), and (3) the best possible effect (marketing and advertising).

3. *Aesthetic psychologist.* Although *Principles of art education* (1905) was widely read, Münsterberg is known for *The photoplay: A psychological study* (1916), which discussed the development of motion pictures and film criticism. In addition to general aesthetics, he presented the psychological impact of the flashback, the dissolve and the close-up.

4. *Social commentator.* In talks, newspaper and magazine articles, and books such as *Tomorrow* (1916), Münsterberg predicted the ultimate failure of world government and peace leagues (only the alliance of England, Germany, and America would bring peace); predicted that prohibition would create worse problems than those caused by alcohol abuse; exposed the fakery of popular mystics and occult figures; and generally applied psychology to everyday life. With Jastrow, he was responsible for the psychology exhibit at the 1893 World Fair in Chicago. Originally quite welcome at the White House of Presidents Theodore Roosevelt and Taft, Münsterberg was later denounced by both.

This exceedingly controversial man is one of the few to have held the presidency both of the American Psychological Association (1898) and the American Philosophical Association (1908). The first edition of J. M. Cattell's *American men of science* ranked him clearly below William James, but in a three-way tie for the second rank with Cattell and G. Stanley Hall. Appreciably below him were Titchener, Ladd, Dewey, Thorndike, Angell, and Woodworth.

Yet other contemporaries, particularly in the industrial psychology area, considered his work but a minimal contribution. Part of the animosity was no doubt due to his tendency to speak and write for the lay audience and public press; part, to his use of "armchair" speculation rather than observations; and part, to his failure to follow through on an apparently promising experimental psychology career. But surely some was due to his ardent German nationalism, proudly voiced at a time when the United States was preparing for war with Germany.

C. S. PEYSER

MURCHISON, CARL (1887–1961)

Murchison took the Ph.D. under Knight Dunlap at Johns Hopkins University. At Clark University he became noted as an author, editor, and publisher. Upon the death of G. Stanley Hall he assumed direction of the *Pedagogical Seminary* (later the *Journal of Genetic Psychology*) and under the Clark University Press he edited, managed, and controlled *Genetic Psychology Monographs, The Journal of General Psychology, The Journal of Social Psychology,* and *The Journal of Psychology.*

Under Murchison the Clark University Press published several important collections and handbooks: *Foundations of experimental psychology, A handbook of child psychology, A handbook of social psychology, Psychologies of 1925,* and *Psychologies of 1930.* The two-volume *Psychological register* was an extensive bibliographic work. Murchison also edited the first three volumes of *A history of psychology in autobiography,* published by the Clark University Press. After leaving Clark, Murchison established the Journal Press, where he continued to publish the journals previously published under the Clark University Press.

P. E. LICHTENSTEIN

MURPHY, GARDNER (1895–1979)

Murphy's formal schooling included the Hotchkiss School, Yale, Harvard, and Columbia (1919–1923). In 1926 he married Lois Barclay, who later became a psychologist known worldwide for her innovative work in child psychology; they collaborated on a number of books. Murphy held the Richard Hodgson Fellowship in Psychical Research at Harvard University (1922–1925); taught at Columbia (1920–1940) and at the City College of New York (1940–1952); was director of research at the Menninger Foundation (1952–1968); and after retirement was a visiting professor (emeritus) at George Washington University (until 1973).

Murphy formulated the biosocial approach to psychology that by the 1950s was recognized as one of the most vital and influential movements in the field. Though there has not been a formal "school" nor any significant identifiable group of disciples, in K. E. Clark's 1957 survey of American psychologists Murphy ranked second only to Sigmund Freud in frequency of listing as the individual most influential in leading the respondents into work in psychology. As a teacher, he was superb. Class after class of graduating seniors at the City College of New York voted him "best liked teacher."

Murphy was elegantly discriminating and creatively eclectic in organizing and reorganizing material from an extraordinarily wide range of sources to create an integrated, holistic, functional system. He believed firmly that the study of origins and evolution was important for the understanding of phenomena; that the separation of psychology from either the biological or the social sciences is arbitrary and likely to be harmful; that psychology studies the whole individual and would have to include both internal (subjective) and external (objective) phenomena; that behavioral studies are good and behavioristic beliefs are bad for science; that if the findings are suggestive and helpful in developing a comprehensive perspective, many primitive groping efforts must be encouraged, though they may be far from achieving the status of science at present. Though his biosocial eclectic approach necessarily overlapped with the presentations of others, Murphy's systematization included a number of core ideas that were essentially his. His discussions of biological facets of motivation include, for example, an unusual em-

phasis on sensory and activity needs; he saw curiosity as reflecting a brain drive. The following concepts represent major recurring emphases in his writings: (1) *autism:* cognitive processes tend to move in the direction of need satisfaction; (2) *canalization:* needs tend to become more specific in consequence of being satisfied in specific ways; (3) a *three-phase developmental theory:* all reality tends to move from an undifferentiated, homogeneous condition through a differentiated, heterogeneous reality to an integrated, structured reality; (4) *feedback:* information from outside provides a basis for reality testing and a mode of escape from autistic self-deception; and (5) *field theory:* the human personality is conceived as "a nodal region, an organized field within a larger field, a region of perceptual interaction, a reciprocity of outgoing and incoming energies" (Murphy, 1947).

The esteem in which Murphy was held by his colleagues in psychology is reflected, in part, by the professional honors accorded him. He was elected to the presidency of the American Psychological Association, the Eastern Psychological Association, the Southwestern Psychological Association, the Society for the Psychological Study of Social Issues, the London Society for Psychical Research, and the American Society for Psychical Research. He was awarded the Butler Medal by Columbia University in 1932, and the Gold Medal Award of the American Psychological Foundation in 1972. Honorary doctorates were given him by the City University of New York and the University of Hamburg, Germany. His publications included about 25 books and well over 100 articles.

E. L. HARTLEY

MURRAY, HENRY A. (1893–1988)

Murray received the B.A. degree from Harvard and later the M.A. and then the M.D. degree from Columbia University. He completed a residency in surgery at Columbia Presbyterian Hospital. During his residency, he had the unusual experience of helping to care for the future president of the United States, Franklin D. Roosevelt. Following this, he spent 4 yr at the Rockefeller Institute studying embryology. In 1927 he received the Ph.D. from Cambridge University in the UK. While there he became acquainted with the writings of Carl Jung whose work *Psychological types* had recently been translated into English.

This apparently contributed to a change in his interest from the biological sciences to psychology. Upon returning to the United States, he was invited to be Morton Prince's assistant at the newly formed psychological clinic at Harvard University. Over the objections of some, he succeeded Prince as its director. His interests began to turn more toward the Freudian approach to psychology. In 1928 he helped form the Boston Psychoanalytic Association and in 1933 he became a member of The American Psychoanalytic Association.

His interests continued in the direction of personality. By 1938, he embarked on the research published in *Explorations in personality.* In this work he developed his taxonomy of needs and presses to characterize people's directions in their lives and activities. Thus he developed a systematic and dynamic approach to personality. Out of these studies there developed the Thematic apperception test (TAT) a projective technique consisting of semivague pictures in which the subject was asked to tell a story about each. The responses were analyzed in terms of Murray's system. The test is still widely used as a clinical diagnostic tool.

During World War II, Murray served in the Army Medical Corps. After the war, he returned to Harvard, where he was instrumental in establishing the Harvard interdisciplinary department of social relations. His association with Clyde Kluckhohn resulted in the classic work *Personality in nature society and culture.*

In 1961 the American Psychological Association honored him with its Distinguished Contribution Award. He received in 1969 the Gold Medal Award of the American Psychological Foundation for lifelong significant contributions to psychology. Murray had hoped to foster a more comprehensive and systematic approach to personality as well as an analysis of the writings of Herman Melville, but failing health prevented the completion of these efforts. He died of pneumonia at the age of 95. He goes down in history as one of the most important personality theorists of this century.

R. W. LUNDIN

MUSSEN, PAUL HENRY (1922–   )

Mussen received the B.A. (1942) and M.A. (1943) from Stanford University, and the Ph.D. from Yale (1949). He has taught at the University of Wisconsin, Ohio State University, and the University of California at Berkeley.

He is best known for his research and writings in developmental psychology. His revision of *Carmichael's manual of child psychology* (1970) is a standard reference work in the field. He is the senior author of a widely used text, *Child development and personality,* in collaboration with John Conger and Jerome Kagan. This work traces in a longitudinal manner behavioral development from the prenatal period through adolescence. Another work, *Psychological development: A life-span approach* in collaboration with Conger, Kagan, and James Gewitz, stresses development from childhood through adolescence, early adulthood, the middle years, and old age.

Mussen's experimental research has involved the study of developmental processes in preschool children, generosity in children of nursery school age, and the impact of television cartoons on children's aggressive behavior.

MYASISHCHEV, VLADIMIR N. (1893–1973)

Myasishchev, a coworker of Vladimir Bekhterev, later renounced reflexology. Myasishchev was able to remain active in psychology despite the pressure to form an official Soviet psychology during the 1920s, and was still influential in Soviet personality theory in the 1960s.

Myasishchev's orientation within psychology was toward physiology and physiological explanations of behavior. His work in personality was important in uniting physiological psychology and clinical practice. He was particularly interested in the relationship between personality and underlying neural activity.

Myasishchev came into conflict with reflexology over the application of reflex concepts to complex human behavior. He objected first to explaining all of human behavior as the conditioning of reflexes, particularly including such examples as a change in behavior following instructions. He later suggested that conditioned reflexes might not be an adequate explanation of human motor behavior.

T. KEITH-LUCAS

MYERS, CHARLES S. (1873–1946)

Myers received the D.Sc. from Cambridge University in 1909. In the same year he succeeded William H.R. Rivers as director of the experimental psychology laboratory there. He also held the post of lecturer in experimental psychology during the same period (1909–1921). He was cofounder of the *British Journal of Psychology* and served as its editor from 1911 to 1924. Along with Rivers and William McDougall, he led the Cambridge Anthropological Expedition to the Torres Straits

in New Guinea and to Borneo. In 1923 he was elected president of the International Congress of Psychology held at Oxford.

While director of the Cambridge laboratory he published *A textbook of experimental psychology* (1909), the first text in experimental psychology to be printed in England. It went through several editions and was subsequently revised by Frederic Bartlett, who became Myers' successor as director of the Cambridge laboratory. In Myers' time this laboratory was where most British experimental psychologists received their training and where most experimental research in Britain was carried out. The areas of primary concern were sensation, perception, and the higher mental processes.

In 1921 Myers left Cambridge to become director of the National Institute for Industrial Psychology. Thus his interests turned to what was then a new area of psychology.

R. W. LUNDIN

MYERS, C. ROGER (1906–1985)

Myers obtained his education in Ontario, getting the Ph.D. from the University of Toronto in 1937. In 1929 he was appointed to the faculty of the Department of Psychology at the University of Toronto, where he became a full professor (1948), chairman of the Department of Psychology (1956–1968), and professor emeritus (1970).

During World War II Myers served as training advisor to the Royal Air Force at the Air Ministry in London. He was the first president of the Ontario Psychological Association (1947–1948), president of the Canadian Psychological Association (1950–1951), first chairman of the Ontario Board of Examiners in Psychology (1960–1965), president of the American Association of State Psychology Boards (1965–1966), and editor of the first *Manual on legal issues for members of state psychology boards.*

Myers frequently represented Canadian psychology both at home and abroad. He was the first Executive Officer of the Canadian Psychological Association (1971–1979). He was a member of the Advisory Group on Human Factors of the North Atlantic Treaty Organization (1963–1965). He took part in a conference on international exchange in psychology at La Napoule, France, in 1962, and was the author of the section on Canada of a book which grew out of this conference: *International opportunities for advanced training and research in psychology* (1966). He was a member of the Committee on International Relations of the American Psychological Association (1974–1977).

Myers was the author of a seminal article on the identification of scientific eminence in psychology (Myers, 1970), and coauthor of the first book on the history of psychology in Canada (Wright & Myers, 1982). He has been honored with the Canadian Centennial Medal (1967), the Queen Elizabeth Jubilee Medal (1977), and an LL.D. from the University of Manitoba (1970).

NANDY, ASHIS (1937–   )

Originally from Calcutta, Nandy has been educated—and, as he likes to add, "de-educated"—in a number of universities and disciplines. His formal training has been in sociology and clinical psychology; the Ph.D is in the latter area.

Nandy's main work has been in political psychology and psychology of science. In the first area he has used Freudian critical theory, non-Western psychologies, cultural anthropology, and political philosophy to focus on issues such as authoritarianism, femininity, violence, colonialism, creativity, utopias, and theories of oppression. His early work on Indian politics and culture from such a vantage point is in *At the edge of psychology.* In recent years Nandy has explored more directly the possibilities of a visionary or normative political psychology ("Oppression and human liberation," "Reconstructing childhood") and of alternative theories of oppression (*The intimate enemy*).

In psychology of science, Nandy's *Alternative science* is a study of two Indian pioneers of science who searched for indigenous meanings, not only in the context of science (e.g., in organization, funding, or professional culture), but also in the text (e.g., in methodological and normative assumptions of science and in forms of creativity). In later works Nandy has questioned the dominant culture of science and the universality, objectivity, and cumulativeness of modern science. The ground for such questioning is sought in an alternative critical psychology, partly rooted in nonmodern traditions ("Science, authoritarianism and culture," "Dialogue on the traditions of technology"). The framework has recently been applied to psychology itself ("Towards an alternative politics of psychology").

NEISSER, ULRIC (1928–   )

Neisser received the A.B. from Harvard, the M.A. from Swarthmore and the Ph.D. from Harvard in 1956. He taught at Brandeis University (1957–1964), at the University of Pennsylvania (1964–1967), and at Cornell (1967–1983) before moving to Emory University in 1983 where he was the Robert W. Woodruff Professor of psychology and director of the Emory Cognition Project. The author of more than 100 articles and book chapters on perception, attention, and memory, Neisser is best known for three books: *Cognitive psychology*, which helped to establish that field in 1967; *Cognition and reality*, which attempted to reorient it in 1976; and *Memory observed: Remembering in natural contexts*, which introduced the ecological approach to the study of memory in 1982. More recent books include *The school achievement of minority children, Concepts and conceptual development*, and *Remembering reconsidered* (with Eugene Winograd). Neisser has been a fellow of the Center for Advanced Study in the Behavioral Sciences, a Guggenheim Fellow, and a Sloan Fellow. He is a member of the National Academy of Sciences.

NETTER, PETRA (1937–   )

Netter obtained her training in psychology at the universities of Hamburg and Innsbruck, and her medical training at the universities of Hamburg and Mainz. She combined the two subjects in several research programs in the fields of psychosomatics, psychopharmacology, and psychophysiology. She obtained the Ph.D. in Psychology in 1963, and the M.D. in 1970, both at the University of Hamburg.

Netter's Ph.D. thesis was concerned with personality types and drug response; her M.D. thesis with the concept of masculinity/feminity and dimensions of bodily constitution. During her activities as a research fellow at the Department of Medical Statistics of the University of Mainz (1968–1975), she was concerned with the statistical evaluation of epidemiological studies investigating multidimensional relationships among psychological or medical factors of pregnancy and child development. She became professor of psychology at the University of Düsseldorf, teaching personality theory, psychosomatics, and methodology of clinical studies. Then, as professor of medical psychology at the University of Mainz, she initiated research activities in the field of sensory suggestibility in relation to pain tolerance and placebo response.

Since 1979 Netter has held a chair in psychology of individual differences at the University of Giessen, where her interests and activities are directed toward the following:

1. Relationships between somatic variables and emotions, performances, and personality traits.
2. Statistical identification of subtypes of essential hypertensives.
3. Interindividual differences in psychotropic drug response.
4. Investigations of placebo susceptibility and sensory suggestibility.

As president of the Society of Psychopharmacology of the German-speaking countries (AGNP) from 1979 to 1983, Netter encouraged research in and contributed to knowledge about personality and situational factors as predictors of interindividual variability in drug response, and monitored methodology in drug research and therapeutic investigations.

NEWCOMB, THEODORE M. (1903–1984)

Newcomb was among the first psychologists to identify himself with social psychology, a field scarcely known until the 1940s. Before that, there had been two social psychologies—one psychological and one sociological—and the twain rarely met. Newcomb's *Social psychology* (1950) took pains to show how intrapersonal (psychological) and interpersonal (sociological) events are interdependent, each being an essential aspect of the socialization process that influences the other.

Newcomb's research is typically longitudinal and carried out in the field rather than in the laboratory. His first well-known study (1943), involving changes in attitudes toward public affairs on the part of all students in Bennington College over a four-year period, showed that individuals' characteristics and their group memberships interacted to influence attitude change—both over four years or less in college and over 15 years after leaving college. A study (1961) of interpersonal attraction within 17-person groups of students, replicated in two successive years, supported Heider's theories of the relationship between perceived agreement with fellow members and liking (attraction) of individual fellowmembers.

Particularly during and after World War II, Newcomb was active in affairs of the American Psychological Association. He was president of the Society for the Psychological Study of Social Issues (1946), of the Division of Personality and Social Psychology (1950), and of the American Psychological Association (1955–1956). In 1981 he received the APA's annual gold medal award.

NIETZSCHE, FRIEDRICH WILHELM (1844–1900)

Nietzsche was a German philosopher of the last century whose ideas have had a powerful influence on the attitudes and philosophies of the twentieth century. He attended the University of Leipzig and received his doctorate in classical philology in 1869. He took an appointment at the University of Basel from 1869 to 1879 teaching classical philology. He spent much of his life in the mountains of Switzerland and in Italy for reasons of health.

Nietzsche felt a need to devise a completely new system of values to account for the advances in the scientific field, particularly in biology and psychology. The human-individual was now considered as a biological specimen, a member of the animal kingdom; the old idealism of humanity had lost its meaning. Charles Darwin had promoted the idea of life as a struggle for survival; Nietzsche redefined this life force as a creative, active surge. He taught that the human expression of this life force is the *will to power*, based on the biologic urge to excellence and equilibrium. The will to power was the motive force in the human evolutionary process (Edman & Schneider, 1941). Nietzsche was convinced that psychology should consider the will to power as the primary human motive.

Nietzsche influenced many important European writers, philosophers, and psychologists, Sigmund Freud among them. Freud's theories of the unconscious and of the instinctual nature of man were similar to Nietzsche's. Nietzsche taught that human motives are found in our instincts and drives, not in thoughts and reason; consciousness and conscious acts are done in service to untamed drives.

In another respect, Nietzsche foreshadowed the humanistic movement in psychology by criticizing the elemental approach of the experimental psychologists and by calling for "a psychology 'in the grand style' that would consider the entirety of a man's psyche" (Zuane, 1975, p. 196).

N. A. HAYNIE

NOIZET, GEORGES (1925–   )

Noizet obtained his university education at the Sorbonne. He passed the *Agrégation* in philosophy in 1948 and then did his higher doctoral thesis. He taught psychology at the University of Aix-Marseille I (1958–1979), where he founded and directed the laboratory of experimental psychology. In 1979 he was appointed as professor of psychology at the University René Descartes in Paris, where he is director of the laboratory of experimental psychology associated with the Centre National de la Recherche Scientifique. He was president of the Société Française de Psychologie (1973–1974) and is coeditor with Paul Fraisse of *L'Année Psychologique*.

Noizet's special field is psycholinguistics. His main work deals with (1) strategies in the comprehension of utterances, and (2) reading (*De la perception à la compréhension du langage*, 1980). He also published works on evaluative judgments (*Psychologie de l'évaluation scolaire*, 1978, with J.-P. Caverni).

NORMAN, DONALD A. (1935–   )

Norman received the B.S. degree from MIT, the M.S. degree from the University of Pennsylvania, both in electrical engineering, and the Ph.D. from the University of Pennsylvania in psychology. He was a faculty member at Harvard University, leaving to join the newly founded department of psychology at the University of California at San Diego. He served as chair of the psychology department from 1974 to 1978. In 1987 he helped establish the department of cognitive science and in July 1988, became its first chair. He was one of the founders of the Cognitive Science Society and has served that organization as chair, secretary-treasurer, and editor of its journal, *Cognitive Science*. He has been a fellow at the Center for Advanced Studies in the Behavioral Sciences. He serves on the editorial boards of several professional journals and book publishers and is a fellow of the American Academy of Arts & Sciences, the American Psychological Society and the American Association for the Advancement of Science.

The premise of Norman's research is that the unaided mind is limited in power, but that cognition, when distributed across people and objects, is powerful. Traditional studies of cognition focus on the unaided mind, yet people normally work with tools. Norman studies the design and functionality of these tools: cognitive artifacts.

Norman has published extensively in journals and books, and is the author or coauthor of 10 books, including *The design of everyday things*, *Notes of a technology watcher*, and *Things that make us smart*.

NÚÑEZ, RAFAEL (1921–   )

Núñez is best known for his research on Mexican personality characteristics and the utilization of the Minnesota Multiphasic Personality Inventory in Latin American countries. Núñez was schooled in Nicaragua. After receiving the bachelor's degree from the University of Dubuque in Iowa, he continued at the University of Houston and the National University of Mexico, receiving the Ph.D. from the latter in 1954. Afterward he studied psychoanalysis at the school of Medicine of the National

University of Mexico, directed by Erich Fromm. A desire to work with the underprivileged induced him to look for methods of understanding the psychological problems of the lower economic classes in Latin America.

Núñez regards himself a therapist and a professor, seeking to convey the thought that "clinical psychology is a profession that merits all respect and encouragement. It is important that we become aware of our problems in Latin America and of the necessity of more solid bases for our own future as professionals and as human beings." (*Memorias del Congreso de la SIP, México*, 1963). Núñez's practical expertise extends to psychotherapy. He holds that as therapists increase their understanding of their relationship with their patients and with people and use this understanding to relieve suffering, they will find few endeavors in life more deeply gratifying.

Núñez's professional career began in Mexico City, at the National University, where he continues to research, lecture, and counsel. His publications include *Aplicación del Inventario Multifásico de la Personalidad a la psicopatologia*.

NUTTIN, JOSEPH R. (1909–1988)

Nuttin was one of the first psychologists to formulate an integrated cognitive theory of human selective learning. He is also known for his theory of human motivation in terms of behavioral relations "required" for optimal functioning.

He studied philosophy and letters as well as psychology with Albert Michotte at Louvain and theology in Bruges. He received the Ph.D. (1941) from Louvain with an experimental thesis on the law of effect. Thereafter, he was appointed professor at the University of Louvain, a visiting professor at Kansas University, a fellow at the Center for Advanced Studies of Behavioral Sciences (at Stanford), and president (1972–1976) of the International Union of Psychological Science. He lectured in many universities in Europe and North and South America.

In Belgium, Nuttin promoted the first full psychology program within a separate department (Louvain, 1944). Many of his laboratory associates became university professors in different countries. He was awarded the quinquennial Solvay Prize for the Behavioral Sciences in 1975, and doctor honoris causa at the University of Coimbra (Portugal).

As early as 1941, Nuttin emphasized the informational aspect of reinforcement: reward informs subjects about the utility of a response in open-task experiments and retention is improved by incorporation of that response in the persisting interest system. More experimental evidence and theoretical framework were published in French (Nuttin, 1953), and 15 yr later were partially translated into English. A constant theme in Nuttin's work is motivation as cognitively processed into behavioral plans, projects, and tasks; thus a future time perspective is introduced in behavior, and its extension can be measured. As to his personality model, the individual and his or her world are conceived as one functional unit.

G. D'YDEWALLE

OKONJI, MICHAEL OGBOLU (1936–1975)

Okonji was educated in Nigeria, Ghana, and Scotland. He was awarded a first class honors degree by the University of Legon in Ghana, where he studied sociology (1964). After working in Nigeria for an oil company, he received a Commonwealth Scholarship and went to Strachtclyde University in Scotland for postgraduate work in developmental psychology under Gustav Jahoda. He received the Ph.D. degree in 1968 and taught at Makerere University Kampala, as a lecturer, until 1971. He next taught at the University of Zambia (1971–1973), before returning to Nigeria as a senior lecturer in psychology at the University of Lagos.

He was to be named an associate professor when he died suddenly, while playing tennis, in November 1975.

Okonji's first publication appeared in 1968. From then until his death, he maintained a steady stream of articles in international journals in the area of intellectual development, especially Piagetian studies. His last major research focused on child rearing, especially the relationship between the field-independence perspective of his friend H. Witkins and the intellectual perspective of Jean Piaget.

In international psychological circles, he was greatly admired for his scholarship and his contribution to the development of cross-cultural psychology and the study of behavioral development. He was an ardent advocate of childhood education.

M. O. A. DUROJAIYE

OLDS, JAMES (1922–1976)

Olds obtained his graduate degrees from Harvard University, the M.A. and the Ph.D. in 1952. His undergraduate degree was earned at Amherst College. During 1952–1953, he was a lecturer and research associate at the Laboratory of Social Relations at Harvard, and from 1953 to 1955, a postdoctoral fellow at McGill University. It was at McGill that he met Peter Milner, the psychologist who collaborated with him in his work on mapping pleasure centers in the brain. In 1957, Olds joined the University of Michigan, but left in 1969 to assume a post as professor at the California Institute of Technology. His premature death occurred on August 21, 1976.

In 1954, Olds and Milner were able, by chance, to produce pleasurable effects by electically stimulating the brain. This led them to assume a "reward mechanism" in the brain, which serves as a motivational apparatus. Their contentions, however, were the subject of constant debate, forcing them to make certain concessions. They reported their findings in a paper entitled "Positive reinforcement produced by electrical stimulation of septal area and other regions of rat brain."

W. S. SAHAKIAN

OSGOOD, CHARLES EGERTON (1916–)

Osgood received the A.B. degree from Dartmouth College and the Ph.D. degree from Yale in 1945. He then served as research associate for the U.S. Office of Scientific Research and Development, where he worked on the training of B-29 gunners. Following World War II, he joined the faculty of the University of Illinois and became professor of psychology and director of the Institute of Communication Research. In 1960 he received the Distinguished Scientific Contribution Award from the American Psychological Association. He was elected president of the American Psychological Association in 1963.

Osgood's experimental research has centered around the role of meaning within the context of learning theory. To do so, he developed the Semantic Differential Method, which has been applied to the analysis of attitudes, attitude change, personality structure, clinical diagnosis, vocational choice, consumer reactions to products and brands, and the role of meaning within different cultures. The technique was described in *The measurement of meaning*. The Semantic Differential consists of a quantitative procedure for measuring connotations of any given concept; it involves ratings and a variety of statistical techniques involving factorial analysis.

Many psychologists believe that Osgood's technique is a useful tool for exploring many of the higher mental processes in human beings. He published *Method and theory in experimental psychology* in 1953.

OTIS, ARTHUR SINTON (1886–1964)

Otis earned B.A, M.A., and Ph.D. (1920) degrees from Stanford, where he had originally enrolled to study civil engineering. After a brief academic appointment at Stanford, he spent the bulk of his career as an editor for the World Book Company.

While a graduate student under Lewis M. Terman, Otis developed the core of his famous group test for intelligence. Terman, who served on Robert M. Yerkes' committee for the psychological testing of recruits during World War I, was the route by which this test became a central part of the original Army Alpha, and the first mass screening of recruits for intelligence. The Otis Group Intelligence Scale incorporated, for the first time, completely objective scoring and multiple-choice items, the keys to group testing and administration by minimally trained personnel. As such, it was long used as a school screening test. Although it was revised, it fell into disrepute when it was found to be culturally sensitive.

Otis wrote a number of textbooks, largely on arithmetic and geometry. During World War II, he wrote texts on aeronautics, although he himself did not learn to fly until 1948. He was very active physically and mentally, with diverse interests even in retirement.

T. KEITH-LUCAS

OVERMIER, J. BRUCE (1938–)

Overmier took the A.B. degree in Chemistry at Kenyon College followed by the M.A. degree in psychology at Bowling Green State University. Upon completion of the Ph.D. degree in experimental psychology (University of Pennsylvania, 1965), he became assistant professor of psychology at the University of Minnesota where he has remained, having been appointed full professor in 1971. Overmier also holds appointments to the graduate faculties of neuroscience, psychoneuroimmunology, and cognitive science.

Overmier has held postdoctoral fellowship awards from the National Science Foundation, National Academy of Sciences, Fogarty Center, Fulbright-Hayes, James McKeen Cattell Foundation, and the Norwegian Marshall Fund. He was named scholar of the college at Minnesota in 1989. In 1990, he received a Sc.D. degree from Kenyon College.

Overmier has been president of the Midwestern Psychological Association (1987–1988), APA Division of Physiological and Comparative Psychology (1990–1991), and APA Division of Experimental Psychology (1992–1993).

He was editor of the journal *Learning and Motivation* from 1973 to 1976 and has served on several editorial boards and federal research advisory panels. He has authored more than 125 book chapters and research articles in his specialties of learning, memory, stress, and psychosomatic disorders and their neurobiological substrates. This research is carried out with a range of animal models and with human clients with specific neural dysfunctions.

PAILLARD, JACQUES (1920–)

Paillard took classical studies at Lycée Lakanal and then studied advanced mathematics at the Lycée St. Louis for two years. After obtaining a degree in mathematics and physics at the University of Paris, he completed postgraduate degrees in biology and psychophysiology and in psychology. He was a pupil of Henri Pieron and Alfred Fessard, under whose supervision he completed his doctoral research on proprioceptive regulation in human beings.

He was appointed, in 1947, a research worker at the National Center for Scientific Research and a lecturer in psychophysiology at the Sorbonne in 1955. In 1957, he was named an assistant professor of psychophysiology at the University Aix-Marseille and director of the Institute of Human Biometry in Marseilles. He became a full professor and assistant director of the Institute of Neurophysiology and Psychophysiology in 1961, and since 1969 has been director.

Paillard's main area of research is in proprioception and visuomotor coordination. He is on the editoral boards of several international journals, including *Brain Research, Behavioral Brain Research,* and *Physiology and Behavior.* He was president of the European Brain and Behaviour Society in 1971–1973.

PAIVIO, ALLAN (1925–   )

Paivio obtained his early education in Canada, and received the Ph.D. degree from McGill University in 1959. He worked as a research psychologist at Cornell University and was on the faculty of the University of New Brunswick before he moved to the University of Western Ontario in 1962, where he remained professor of psychology.

Paivio's major contributions have been in cognitive psychology. In his research, he has particularly sought to further the understanding of mental imagery and its role in memory, language, and thought. His research findings have led to the development of a dual coding theory, according to which performance on cognitive tasks is mediated by the cooperative activity of nonverbal and verbal symbolic systems.

His theoretical ideas and research findings have appeared in numerous journal articles and book chapters as well as in a widely cited book titled *Imagery and verbal processes.* He also is author of *Mental representation* and *Images of the mind* (1991). A past president of the Canadian Psychological Association, Paivio is a fellow of that association, the American Psychological Association, and the Royal Society of Canada. He was awarded a Queen's Silver Jubilee Medal in 1977 and was the 1982 recipient of the Canadian Psychological Association Award for Distinguished Contributions to Psychology as a Science.

PARAMESWARAN, E. G. (1935–   )

Parameswaran was educated in Madras. After obtaining the doctoral degree in psychology from the University of Madras, he joined in faculty of psychology at Madras University and later transferred to Osmania University to establish the Department of Psychology; there he became professor of psychology in 1969. He was a Canada Council Fellow at Queen's University, Kingston, Canada, and a visiting professor at the California State College, Los Angeles. Since then, he has held several academic and administrative positions at Osmania University. He is active in such national bodies as the National Council of Education Research and Training, the University Grants Commission, and the Indian Council of Social Science Research.

Parameswaran is known for his Indian approach to the study of personality—and is a pioneering researcher in the area of developmental psychology in India. His teaching experience and insight into experimental psychology have resulted in two books on experimental psychology. He advocates psychotherapy for the treatment of the mentally disturbed, and has been continuously engaged in research, counseling, and lecturing. He is involved in organizing and participating in training programs for employees of various organizations.

PAVLOV, IVAN PETROVICH (1849–1936)

Pavlov was the eldest of 11 children. He learned about hard work and responsibility at an early age. In 1860, Pavlov entered a theological seminary, but in 1870 he changed his mind and went to the University of St. Petersburg to study animal physiology. He received his degree in 1875, started medical training, studied in Germany, and returned to St. Petersburg to begin a long career in physiological research. He earned his doctorate in 1883 from the Military Medical Academy. In 1891, he was appointed director of the Department of Physiology at the

Institute of Experimental Medicine in St. Petersburg, and in 1897, he became a professor at the university. In 1904, his research work on the primary digestive glands was recognized with the Nobel prize.

Pavlov's research also concerned nerves of the heart and studies of the higher nerve centers of the brain. His methodology for the research, and his greatest scientific achievement was conditioning, a technique that significantly influenced the development of psychology. Pavlov's research became a model and standard for objectivity and precision. In his controlled experiments, he studied the formation of conditioned responses, reinforcement, extinction, spontaneous recovery, generalization, discrimination, and higher order conditioning (all applied concepts to learning and association in psychology). Pavlov's most important writings were *The work of the digestive glands* and *Conditioned reflexes.*

Pavlov's work was a cornerstone for the development of behaviorism, in which the conditioned reflex is so important. John B. Watson took the conditioned reflex as the basic unit of behavior and made it the building block of his program of behaviorism. The conditioned response was used during the 1920s, in the United States, as the foundation for learning theories, thus generating further research and theory.

N. A. HAYNIE

PAWLIK, KURT F. (1934–   )

Pawlik became a student of H. Hohracher at the University of Vienna. Following positions at the universities of Vienna, Graz, and Illinois, he was appointed professor of psychology and department director at the University of Hamburg, West Germany, in 1965.

His major research contributions relate to personality research, multivariate methodology, and the psychophysiology of learning. He has concentrated on the biological roots of individual differences and the environmental determinants of the covariance structure of such differences. He has developed a "trait-free theory of personality factors" in terms of interindividual difference covariations in developmental learning.

Pawlik has contributed to the understanding of subcortical mechanisms in long-term memory consolidation and retrieval as related to cerebral protein synthesis and catecholamine release.

His major works include *Personality factors in objective test devices, Dimensionen des Verhaltens, Diagnose der Diagnostik,* and *Multivariate Persönlichkeitsforschung.*

A former president and vice president of the Germany Society of Psychology, Pawlik has also furthered international exchange and communication in psychology.

PEARSON, KARL (1857–1936)

Called the founder of the science of statistics, Pearson made contributions of major importance to the development of the biological, behavioral, and social sciences. His application of mathematical and statistical methods to the study of biological problems, particularly evolution and genetics, ranks among the great achievements of science.

An exceptionally brilliant student, Pearson was graduated with honors in mathematics from Cambridge University, where he also studied physics, philosophy, religion, and law (he was admitted to the bar). His motto was the basic theme of his life: "We are ignorant; so let us work." While a professor of applied mathematics at the University of London, he published works on elasticity and on the philosophy of science, before coming under the influence of Sir Francis Galton, who helped to shape Pearson's subsequent career. Mainly as a result of reading Galton's *Natural inheritance* (1889), he became a devoted disciple and personal friend of the great man, and his career was set on the course that led to the development of statistical theory and methods suited to dealing with the problems posed by Galton's work on human variation, heredity, and eugenics. Inspired by Galton's ideas, Pearson stated that "real knowledge must take the place of energetic but untrained philanthropy in dictating the lines of feasible social reform." Galton's great influence on Pearson is attested to by the latter's devoting almost 20 years to writing a four-volume biography, *The life, letters, and labours of Francis Galton* (1914–1930). In 1904, Pearson was appointed the first director of the Galton Laboratory at the University of London, and was the first professor to occupy the Chair of Eugenics, which Galton had endowed with a gift of £45,000.

Pearson's many statistical contributions are now a standard part of the research methodology of the behavioral and social sciences. They include mathematical formulations of types of frequency distributions, measures of skewness and kurtosis, curve fitting, the standard deviation σ, the "chi-square" test, the contingency coefficient, the product-moment correlation coefficient r; biserial, multiple, tetrachoric, and nonlinear correlation, and derivation of the probable errors and sampling distributions of a variety of statistics, published in Pearson's *Tables for statisticians and biometricians* (1914). He also invented principal components analysis, a forerunner of factor analysis later developed by Charles Spearman. Few scientists have contributed a more useful and enduring legacy than did Pearson.

A. R. JENSEN

PECJAK, VID (1929–   )

Pecjak received the Ph.D. degree from the University of Ljubljana in 1966, pursued postdoctoral studies at the University of Edinburgh and University of Illinois (Urbana), and attended a summer workshop at Lehigh University in Bethlehem, Pa. Since 1966, he has been a professor of psychology at the University of Ljubljana, and as a visiting professor has taught at the University of Hawaii, the University of Illinois, and Monash University in Melbourne, Australia. Among the subjects he has taught are the history of psychology, personality, psychology of cognition, and developmental psychology.

At the beginning of his career Pecjak studied concepts and conceptual interrelations (net theory of concepts); later, upon spending six months working with C. E. Osgood, he became interested in psycholinguistics. One of his research interests is the study of symbols and their cultural dependence. He has found that some symbols are universal whereas others are unique to individual cultures. In recent years, he has been largely involved in the study of the history of psychology, resulting in *Psychology in making* (1982) which describes the development of psychology. Most recently, he produced *Great psychologists about psychology*, which includes interviews with 150 of the world's most famous psychologists. Another major publication was *Psychology of cognition*.

PEDERSEN, PAUL B. (1936–   )

Best known for his writings on cross-cultural counseling, Pedersen lectured at universities and conducted research in Indonesia, Malaysia, and Taiwan for six years, and was a counseling psychologist for foreign students at the University of Minnesota for eight years. From 1978 to 1981, he organized a National Institute of Mental Health training program through the East–West Center and the University of Hawaii for the development of interculturally skilled counselors. Later, Pedersen became chairman of counseling and guidance at Syracuse University.

Pedersen's education emphasized interdisciplinary area studies with special attention to core values as they are influenced by cultural perspectives. After receiving the B.A. degree in history–philosophy from the University of Minnesota, he earned masters' degrees in American studies (1959), religion (1962), and counseling psychology (1966). He then completed a Ph.D. degree at Claremont Graduate School, in Asian studies with an emphasis on counseling and student personnel psychology.

Pedersen has been most interested in training counselors and therapists to work with culturally different clients. The emphasis of training has been on intentionality, which includes an awareness of one's own cultural bias and the biases of others; complexity, which includes an awareness of age, gender, life-style, and socioeconomic differences in addition to national and ethnic differences in counseling; and balance, which includes the skill to match a wide range of counselor intervention styles appropriately to the client's cultural perspective.

He has written or edited 16 books, 35 chapters in books, 57 articles in journals, and 19 monographs. His books include *Counseling across cultures* and *Cross cultural counseling and psychotherapy*.

PEIRCE, CHARLES SANDERS (1839–1914)

Peirce received his first degree from Harvard University in 1859 and a second in chemistry, in 1863, from the Lawrence Scientific School. In 1879, he was appointed lecturer at Johns Hopkins University, where he remained until 1884. Shortly thereafter, he received an inheritance and retired to Milford, Pa., and lived there in relative isolation for the remainder of his life.

Peirce was a systematic philosopher and prolific writer. His writings covered many fields of philosophy: epistemology, scientific method, metaphysics, cosmology, and to a lesser degree ethics and logic. In a well-known article, "The architecture of theories," he held that the domain of knowledge could be so characterized that general assertions could be proved true of all knowledge and that all knowledge depended on logic that made such a characterization possible.

He is best known to psychology for his theory of pragmatism, which was to have a strong influence on William James, John Dewey, and other members of the functionalist school. In fact, James made pragmatism more popular than did Peirce. According to Peirce, pragmatism is a theory of meaning, not of truth. He considered it a principle of scientific definition whereby concepts could be made into observable events under the proper conditions. Thus concepts must be translated into "practical effects." He further stressed the utilitarian aspects of science and of all knowledge. What was significant lay in its relation to ends desired.

R. W. LUNDIN

PENFIELD, WILBER GRAVES (1891–1976)

Educated in the United States, Penfield moved to Canada in 1928 and became a Canadian citizen in 1934. After receiving a medical degree, he specialized in neurology and neurosurgery. His experience as a clinician and researcher at various institutions in America and Europe was extensive and varied. As a member of the faculty of McGill University in Montreal, Penfield founded the Montreal Neurological Institute, which he directed until his retirement in 1960. He remained active to the end of his life as a lecturer, consultant, and writer. He was editor, author, or coauthor of six books on the nervous system, and the author of a book of essays, a biography (of Alan Gregg), and two historical novels. His last book, *The mystery of the mind,* is a venture into a critical study of the mind–brain relationship.

Among Penfield's numerous contributions, the most outstanding were the development of neurosurgical treatment of certain forms of epilepsy; a better understanding of the functional organization of the human cerebral cortex; and the discovery that electric stimulation of certain parts of the cortex in human subjects can evoke vivid memories of past life experiences, a kind of "flashback" of earlier life events.

Penfield's theory of the mind–brain relationship, based on his experience as a neurosurgeon and brain investigator, is original and provocative. He refused to equate mind with the brain activity and did not preclude the possibility of the survival of the mind after brain's death. Penfield (1975, p. 89) once stated: "Whether the mind is truly a separate element or whether, in some way not yet apparent, it is an expression of neuronal action, the decision must wait for further scientific evidence." In a preceding paragraph, however, he wrote: "It is obvious that science can make no statement at present in regard to the question of man's existence after death, although every thoughtful man must ask that question."

H. MISIAK

PERLS, FREDRICK (FRITZ) (1893–1970)

Perls studied at the University of Freiburg, and received the M.D. degree at the University of Berlin. In 1926, he became an assistant to Kurt Goldstein at the Institute for Brain-Injured Soldiers. His association with Goldstein gave him the idea of the gestalt or "whole," which he later incorporated into his own method of psychotherapy. He studied with and was psychoanalyzed by well-known analysts William Reich, Karen Horney, and Otto Fenichel. When Hitler came to power, Perls left Germany for Holland in 1933. In 1946, he came to the United States, where he founded the New York Institute for Gestalt Therapy. His first book, Gestalt therapy, was published in conjunction with Ralph Hefferline and Paul Goodman. Other books included Gestalt therapy verbatim (1969) and his autobiography, In and out of the garbage pail, published in the same year.

His major contribution to psychology was the development of a new method of psychotherapy, which he named Gestalt therapy. It was both an outgrowth and a rejection of psychoanalysis. Perls accepted the psychoanalytic concept that behavior disorders are the result of unresolved conflicts arising from a person's past. These conflicts must be discovered and "worked through." On the other hand, he stressed the "here and now" in a more humanistic approach that emphasized responsibility, freedom, and an active attempt to "become." His therapy also made use of "acting out" as vividly as possible. This could involve screaming, kicking, yelling, and crying. In this way, the client could confront inner feelings, take responsibility, and learn to control them, and in this way unify these feelings and actions into a new whole (gestalt) and learn to live an open and honest life.

Perls' therapy stressed a rather authoritarian role on the part of the therapist. Feelings and candor were emphasized rather than reason. Those humanistic therapists who have preferred a gentler, more acquiescent role on the part of the therapist have criticized Perls' method as inappropriate for proper human growth.

R. W. LUNDIN

PETERSON, DONALD R. (1923–   )

Peterson received the B.S., M.A., and Ph.D. (1952) degrees from the University of Minnesota and accepted a position at the University of Illinois at Urbana-Champaign, following receipt of the doctorate. At Illinois, he taught a wide range of subjects from introductory psychology to graduate seminars in behavior disorders and clinical assessment. He became director of the Illinois Psychological Clinic in 1963 and director of clinical training in 1964. In the latter position, he organized the first doctor of psychology program in the country, admitting the first class of students in 1968. In 1975, he became the first dean of the Graduate School of Applied and professional Psychology at Rutgers University,

where he remained until and beyond his retirement in 1989. He is author, coauthor, and editor of several books, including The clinical study of social behavior, Close relationships, and Assessment for decision. His journal publications include research reports on personality structure, children's behavior disorders, and interpersonal relationships, but his articles on the education of professional psychologists are probably best known. In 1983, he received the APA award for distinguished contributions to professional psychology as a practice, and in 1989 the APA award for distinguished career contributions to education and training in psychology.

PFAFFMAN, CARL (1913–   )

Pfaffman graduated from Cambridge University as a Rhodes scholar, having studies first at Brown University and at Oxford.

His major interest was in physiology, especially in the area of taste. He received the Ph.D. degree in 1939. Following graduation, he returned to the United States and worked for the Johnson Foundation for Medical Physics under Detley Bronk, who later became president of Rockefeller University. During World War II, he participated in research on selection of naval air cadets. He then joined the faculty at Brown University, where he worked closely with Walter Hunter, chairman of the Psychology Department, and continued his research on taste and other chemical senses. Pfaffman later became interested in dynamic personality psychology and attempted to find basic relationships between the physiological and psychological aspects of organisms.

Pfaffman has published widely, with over 80 publications. Probably his best known works are his contribution on "Taste and smell" to Stevens' Handbook of experimental psychology and his article of the same title in the Encyclopedia Brittanica. He was the editor of Volume III in the series Oilaction and taste.

PFLÜGER, EDUARD FRIEDRICH WILHELM (1829–1910)

Pflüger received the M.D. degree under Johannes Müller at the University of Berlin. In 1859, he succeeded to the chair in physiology at Bonn previously held by Hermann von Helmholtz.

His early work in physiology was on electrotonus. This involved the basic laws regarding changes in sensitivity that take place in a section of nerve subjected to a direct current from a cathode and an anode, which, as a result of polarization, spread "extrapolarization." Other studies in physiology involved embryonal development of the ovary, the nerve endings in the salivary gland, and gas exchange in the blood and cells.

Of particular interest to psychology were his studies of the nervous system, which he attributed as the underlying force in the organism. In his studies, he became involved in the controversy over whether or not reflexes are conscious or unconscious. Marshall Hall, earlier, had stated that they were unconscious, but Pflüger maintained that since reflexes were controlled by the nervous system, they had to be conscious. He argued that as consciousness was a function of all nervous activity and one could not distinguish between the action of the brain and spinal cord, spinal reflexes must be regarded as conscious. He pointed out that reflexes are purposive and specifically useful to the organism.

R. W. LUNDIN

PHILLIPS, E. LAKIN (1915–   )

Phillips is a clinical/child psychologist, who also has worked in rehabilitation of handicapped children, and more extensively in individual psychotherapy from a behavioral viewpoint. He received the Ph.D. degree from the University of Minnesota.

Phillips' work is based on learning principles, especially conflict theory, as the conceptual basis for understanding psychopathology and psychotherapy. He sees the social environment as the setting in which one's most important far-reaching learning takes place, where personality development occurs and is maintained. A position often espoused is, "Change the environment and you change behavior." Phillips also has emphasized that if one understands a phenomenon, it can (in principle) be changed; that being able to control or change phenomena is the hallmark of knowledge. These positions constitute the conceptual basis for his interest in and work with handicapped children, in the study of social skills (as fundamental to understanding psychopathology and as the central issue in psychotherapy), and in the study and practice of short-term psychotherapy and behavior change.

Phillips founded and directed the School for Contemporary Education (a school for various handicapped children and adolescents), and was cofounder of the first experimental program in a public school in the United States for emotionally disturbed children. Recent interests extend the study of social skills to studying and evaluating societies and cultures in terms of the quality of life they promote.

PIAGET, JEAN (1896–1980)

Piaget published his first scientific paper at the age of 10, and received his doctorate in 1917, at the age of 21, from the University of Neuchatel, in his research studies on mollusks. After working in a psychology laboratory in Zurich, he went to Paris and to Geneva, where he studied the psychology of thought and was appointed professor of psychology in 1940. In 1952, he was named professor of child psychology at the Sorbonne in Paris. He was actively involved in UNESCO and in educational activities in Switzerland.

Piaget's major interest was in intellectual or cognitive behavior throughout childhood and adolescence. His field was genetic epistemology—the examination of the formation of knowledge itself, that is, of the cognitive relations between subject and objects. Piaget studied the relationships that are formed between the individual as knower and the world he or she endeavors to know.

The two most important concepts of genetic epistemology are *functional invariants* and *structures*. Functional invariants are cognitive processes that are inborn, universal, and independent of age: accommodation, assimilation, and organization. Structures are defined as intellectual processes that change with age. Piaget's structures are identified in the developmental stages of the period of sensorimotor intelligence, the period of preoperational thought, the period of concrete operations, and the period of formal operations.

The structure for the sensorimotor period (birth to 2 years of age) is circular reaction, a simple sensorimotor adaptive response to a specific stimulus, repeated a number of times. The principal structures of preoperational thought (ages 2 to 6 years) are egocentrism (sees only his or her own point of view), centration (attention to only one feature of a situation), and irreversibility (inability to reverse direction of thinking once started). During the period of concrete operations (ages 6 to 11 years), the main structural concept is grouping, a system of classification. It is a coherent and organized symbolic system of thinking with assimilation and accommodation in balance; intellectual adaptation takes place. In formal operations (ages 11 to 15), a lattice-group structure performs scientific reasoning with hypotheses, predictions, and the testing of these. It is a network of ideas in which everything is related to everything else. The balancing of cognitive growth patterns is called the equilibration process; it is the assimilation of new cognitive structures without destroying the existing structure (Nordby & Hall, 1974).

Piaget's early books were based on observations and experiments done with his two daughters. Four volumes appeared between 1926 and 1930 on thought processes and conceptualizations in children. In the 1950s, he published *The psychology of intelligence* and *The origins of intelligence in the child*.

N. A. HAYNIE

PIERON, HENRI (1881–1964)

Pieron played a decisive role in the development of French scientific psychology. In 1912, at the death of Alfred Binet, he became the director of the psychological laboratory at the Sorbonne in Paris, and in 1923, professor at the College of France. Pieron was the founder of the Institute of Psychology at the University of Paris (1921) and of the National Institute for the study of Work and Professional Orientation (*Institut National d' Etude du Travail professionelle*) (1928). He was instrumental in establishing the Applied School of Advanced Studies, (*Ecole Practique des Hautes Etudes)*, a laboratory for the psychobiology of infants, and a laboratory of applied psychology.

Pieron was a behavioral psychologist. From 1908 on, this to him was psychology. Behavior was for him the "activities of beings and their sensory-motor relations with the environment." The essential direction of his work was toward psychophysiology. During an early part of his career, his interests were in animal psychology (ants, crabs, etc.), and he studied, in these animals, the mechanisms of sleep. He also established the laws of mnemonic fixation in people. But it was the psychophysiology of sensations that constituted the center of his scientific work with the publication in 1955 of *La sensation, guide de vie*, (*Sensation, guide to Life*). He was also interested in differential psychology, in which he saw the scientific foundations of applied psychology, especially scholarly and professional applications. Among his many other publications were *Le probleme physiologique du sommeil (Physiological problems of sleep); Le cerveau et la pensée (The brain and thought); La Psychologie differentielle (Differential psychology); De l'actinie a l'homme (From the sea anenome to man)*.

M. REUCHLIN

PILLSBURY, WALTER BOWERS (1872–1960)

Pillsbury had his first contact with psychology in a course at the University of Nebraska under H. K. Wolfe—an early Wundt student known primarily for stimulating his students to psychological careers. Pillsbury then progressed to a dissertation under E. B. Titchener at Cornell; his research concerned the apperception of blurred and partial words under brief exposure. Another research effort involved measurement of the cutaneous and kinesthetic senses, such as how far a limb could be moved before being detected.

Most of Pillsbury's career was spent at the University of Michigan, and when the Psychology Department was created in 1929, he was its first chairman. He was a member of the 1910 American Psychological Association Committee on standardizing the procedure in experimental tests. He always carried a heavy teaching load (reported as 42 hours a week one term) and wrote extensively. His books included two on the psychology of language, an abnormal psychology text, and the social psychology of nationality. Both his one-semester and two-semester introductory texts saw three editions. His *Education as the psychologist sees it* questioned whether education involves the changing of behavior (teaching) or merely the selection of the more gifted pupils who would have succeeded even without the classroom experience.

Pillsbury is probably best known as a historian of psychology, and his 1929 work was considered important for detailing the growth of ·

psychology out of philosophy. In collaboration with Pennington, he published a voluminous handbook of general psychology.

C. S. PEYSER

PINEL, PHILIPPE (1745–1856)

At the beginning of the nineteenth century, France became the first country to initiate reforms involving more humane care for those people identified as insane. At that time, Pinel was one of the leading physicians in Paris. In 1792, he was appointed superintendent of the hospital, La Bicêtre. There the inmates were chained up in dungeons as if they were wild beasts, and frequently were put on display for those curious enough to pay a small fee to view them.

Pinel made a personal plea to the Revolutionary Commune to unchain some of the inmates and allow them to see the light of day. They were put under the care of physicians who shared his humane attitude, and were allowed to live in sunny rooms, and even to walk about on the grounds of the hospital. All of this was an "experiment." Pinel could have lost his head if it had been a failure, but in many cases the results were nothing short of miraculous. In his *Treatise on insanity,* Pinel described the behavior of the patients. One case was that of an English officer who had been chained for 40 years. When he tottered out, on legs weak from lack of use, into the sunny day, he exclaimed, "Oh, how beautiful!" Pinel also made a plea for more humane treatment of the insane, who, at that time, were regarded by many as wicked and possessed by demons. He set forth an alternative, naturalistic explanation, which related disturbed behavior to some possible malfunction of the brain.

Pinel was later transferred to the hospital called Salpêtière, where he instituted similar reforms with equal success. He was succeeded by Jean Esquirol, who continued such reforms throughout many parts of France.

R. W. LUNDIN

PINILLOS, JOSÉ L. (1919–   )

Considered one of the pioneers of Spanish modern psychology, the Bilbao-born Pinillos received the Ph.D. degree from Madrid University in 1949. After having studied psychology at Bonn and at Maudsley Hospital in London through 1954, he became professor of general psychology, at the Universidad Complutense de Madrid.

Pinillos considers himself primarily a generalist. In his search for an open model of scientific psychology, he is faithful to both the essentials of scientific method and the active, mental condition of human beings. He pursued this aim in his *Introduction to contemporary psychology* and *Principles of psychology.* His premise is that knowledge improves by articulating multiple points of view, rather than by adhering to a single paradigm. This is particularly true when paradigms are premature and one-side. Theoretical perspectivism and an expanded concept of method are the key ideas of his manuscript, *History and method of psychology. The human mind* is his most popular book.

In research, Pinillos is best known for his work on social attitudes and political stereotypes, and for his analysis of the *F*-scale. Earlier, he researched perception and personality. Other publications include *Psychopathology of urban life* and *Body-build and personality.*

R. BAYÉS

PIZZAMIGLIO, LUIGI (1937–   )

Pizzamiglio received the M.D. from the University of Milan in Italy and studied at the postgraduate School of Experimental Psychology at the Catholic University in Milan. Subsequently, he worked for a year at Ohio State University and was research associate for 10 yr in the department of psychology at the Catholic University in Rome. In 1975, Pizzamiglio was appointed full professor at the State University in Rome.

His primary interest is in the field of neuropsychology. Much of his early research contributed to introducing psycholinguistic models in the study of aphasia. Special emphasis was placed on various aspects of verbal comprehension. Since the 1970s, Pizzamiglio has been involved in studying hemispheric dominance for cognitive abilities.

Interest in the biology of individual differences in cognitive dimensions led Pizzamiglio into the area of behavior genetics. His most recent work was directed toward the neuropsychological study of emotions in normal subjects and in patients with cerebral pathology.

New research has been devoted to the problem of visual heminattention, approached both from the perspective of basic underlying mechanisms and rehabilitation.

Publications include *Neuropsychology of language, Perception, and emotions* and *Behavior genetics,* and the *Handbook of neuropsychology.*

PLATO (427–347 B.C.)

Plato was born to parents of old, aristocratic Athenian families. He had political ambitions but became disillusioned with politics and abandoned them after the forced suicide of Socrates. Plato left Athens, and traveled to Megara, Syracuse, and Tarentum, before returning to Athens. Here he founded the Academy, which continued until 529 A.D. Plato's influence on Western thought has been inestimable, extending to metaphysics, epistemology, ethics, politics, mathematics, and several branches of natural science.

Plato's psychological views were not presented in a systematic form but may be found scattered through the dialogues. As a philosopher, Plato valued above all the life of reason, which could put humans in touch with timeless essences, permanent and exact. These stood in sharp contrast to the temporary and imprecise appearances revealed by sense perception. Thus there is in Plato a dualism of things known through the senses and Ideas and Forms known through reason. It is the Ideas that are real, for they are absolute, permanent, and perfect. While reason is capable of grasping Ideas, and therefore of gaining true knowledge, the senses can yield only opinion at best.

If knowledge cannot be obtained through the senses, it must be intuited through a higher power, the mind or soul. Some passages in the dialogues make it appear that for Plato the soul was immaterial and immortal and totally different in principle from the body, but it is possible that he was simply using fable, myth, and metaphor to stress the point that the soul as the virtue and dignity of human beings (a Socratic view) was to be most highly esteemed. Greek doctrines of soul were generally naturalistic, but most classical scholars have regarded Plato as an exception, a Greek dualist who divided a human being into material body and immaterial soul. Plato did speak of the transmigration of souls and probably was influenced by Pythagorean and Orphic mystery views.

For Plato the body was a hindrance to the soul in the acquisition of knowledge, and sight and hearing were inaccurate witnesses. Plato, as a rationalist, appeared quite ready to abandon the body and the senses for the unimpeded activity of the soul capable of handling absolute being. Plato argued that all knowledge is recollection and that we have carried it with us from an earlier existence. In the *Meno,* Socrates questions an untutored slave boy in such a way as to demonstrate that the boy knows geometry even though he had been unaware that he possessed the knowledge. It seemed obvious that the knowledge must be attributed to acquaintance before birth. This is the essence of Plato's famous reminiscence doctrine.

Plato spoke of the soul as a unity, but he also described it as having three aspects: reason, located in the head; spirit or courage, located in the chest; and appetite, located in the abdomen. While Plato exalted reason, he was keenly aware of the irrational element in people that frequently gives rise to conflict. Reason is analogous to the charioteer who has trouble controlling an unruly and headstrong horse (appetite) but little difficulty with a fine, spirited animal (spirit). Reason must serve as a guide, producing harmony in the soul and leading appetite and spirit toward goals that reason alone understands.

Plato favored rational, deductive science over the empirical and inductive. Yet while he did not formulate a coherent or systematic psychology, he did develop, on the basis of astute observation, a variety of psychological descriptions and theories. These extended from the special senses, through imagination, memory, desire, sleep and dreams, feeling, and understanding to thinking and reasoning.

P. E. LICHTENSTEIN

PLOTINUS (204–270)

Born in Egypt of Roman parents, Plotinus lived and taught in Rome for 25 years. From his *Ennaedes* it is clear that he was acquainted with the writings of the Greek philosophers, in particular, Plato and Aristotle.

The school of thought that Plotinus represented is often called Neoplatonism, as Plotinus took Plato's concept of *pure form,* which represented the ultimate in perfection and harmony, and made it into a conception of soul. Even though Plotinus was not a Christian, his psychology presented a concept of soul similar in many ways to that of St. Augustine and other Church fathers who were to follow. In Plotinus we have one of the earliest statements of a spirit apart from the body. To understand the nature of the soul, the beginning was with the One (God). From this was derived, by a process of emanation or spilling over, the universal intelligence (nous) or world soul. The final emanation resulted in the souls or spirits as the highest features of human beings.

Plotinus described the soul as a unitary entity without parts or spatial dimensions. Being completely separate from the body, it was indestructible and thus immortal. Its relation to the body was one of collateral existence. It did not mix with the body but dwelled beside it, having an independent existence of its own.

Plotinus thus presented grades of being, with the soul superior to the body and the nous and the One superior to the soul.

Like Plato, Plotinus did not have great faith in the human senses, as they, in part, were mixed with the body. Remembering, thinking, and reasoning were activities of the soul alone. On the other hand, emotions and desires also involved the body, although Plotinus did not understand just how the body operated in these conditions. There is, however, according to some scholars, an implication of a soul-body interaction.

R. W. LUNDIN

PONZO, MARIO (1882–1960)

Ponzo was one of the pioneers of psychology in Italy. He began as assistant professor to F. Kiesow, one of Wundt's pupils, who initiated experimental psychology in Italy. Ponzo then became professor of psychology on the medical faculty in Rome. His 240 publications attest to his very broad field of interests.

A large part of Ponzo's research was in general and experimental psychology. Ponzo's first publications concerned the histology and psychophysiology of taste. Other studies dealt with tactile and thermic stimulus localization in different regions of the skin. He used the method of continuous variation of stimuli for the study of weight sensations. With great originality, Ponzo ran studies on breathing activity with pneumographic analysis. With this analysis, forms of mental activity determine modifications similar to those of exterior verbalization. Ponzo's scientific activity shows a clear relationship between his data on psychomotor activity and his psychology of action theory. Ponzo was critical of the atomistic thought of his times and considered single actions as starting points for the study and understanding of personality. His other scientific contributions include the psychology of work and education and the verification of young people's capacities.

His publications include *Rapporto fra alcune illusioni visive di contrasto angolare e l'apprezzamento di grandezza degli astri all'orizzonte* (Relationship between some visual illusions of angular contrast and the appraisal of the planets on the horizon), *Modificazioni del respiro durante la lettura mentale e loro significato* (Breathing's modifications during mental reading and their meaning), *Psicologia dell'azione e comprensione della personalita* (Psychology of action and understanding of personality).

E. PONZO

PORTEUS, STANLEY DAVID (1883–1972)

Porteus, after a decade as a school teacher in Victoria, studied at the Melbourne Educational Institute and the University of Melbourne. During this period, he was superintendent of special schools in Melbourne. In 1919, he became director of research of the Psychological Laboratory at the Training School at Vincland, N.J. He moved to the University of Hawaii in 1922, where he was professor of clinical psychology and director of the psychological and psychopathic clinic. From 1948 until his death, he held the titles *emeritus.*

In 1929, Porteus led an expedition to northwest Australia, and another expedition to the Kalahari Desert of South Africa in 1934. He published two books on Hawaii and two novels—one about early Australia and the other concerning Archibald Campbell's voyage around the world in the early nineteenth century.

Porteus began his best known work in psychology while at the Vineland Training School. In 1915, he published his Porteus Maze Test as a supplement to Henry H. Goddard's 1909 translation of Alfred Binet's intelligence tests. The printed mazes on which the proper path was drawn with a pencil were used in the diagnosis of mental retardation. In particular, they were designed to measure foresight and planning capacity. As soon as the subject made an error by entering a cul-de-sac or crossing a line, the maze was removed and a second trial given. The mazes were graded in difficulty from age 3 to adult. Since the mazes could be administered without verbal instructions and had no time limits, they were widely used in unusual circumstances. One adaptation was for cerebral-palsied children. The mazes were included in Grace Arthur's 1930 Point Scale of Performance Tests.

The technical quality of the Porteus Mazes restricts them to research use only. No information on consistency upon reexamination (reliability) is available and the comparison groups for the scores are inadequately described. Porteus himself stated that the utility or validation was far less than satisfactory.

In his other research, Porteus reported on cross-cultural abilities, particularly with African and Hawaiian groups. He also published articles on mental changes after psychosurgery, such as a bilateral prefrontal lobotomy.

C. S. PEYSER

POSTMAN, LEO JOSEPH (1918–   )

Known for his work in learning theory, especially the psychology of memory, Postman received his undergraduate degree from the College of the City of New York in 1943. He pursued graduate school at Harvard, obtaining the M.A. degree and the Ph.D. degree in 1946. In 1946, he began his career at Harvard University as an instructor, and by 1950 had transferred to the University of California at Berkeley.

PRATKANIS, ANTHONY R. (1957–   )

Pratkanis received the B.S. in psychology, sociology, and social work from Eastern Mennonite College and the M.A. and Ph.D. (1984) in social psychology from Ohio State University. After graduate school he taught in the Business School at Carnegie Mellon University, and then became associate professor of psychology at the University of California at Santa Cruz.

A frequent contributor to scientific journals, Pratkanis's research interest include persuasion, social influence, social cognition, and consumer behavior. Some of his research has demonstrated the conditions under which a sleeper effect (a delayed increase in persuasion) will occur, the ineffectiveness of subliminal persuasion, how phantoms (unavailable options) influence decision making, how the self influences information processing, the possible negative consequences of preferential selection, and the conditions under which attitudes influence learning and memory.

Pratkanis is coauthor (with Elliot Aronson) of *Age of propaganda: The everyday use and abuse of persuasion* and a coeditor (with Steven J. Breckler and Anthony G. Greenwald) of *Attitude structure and function*. He has worked for private and public organizations; his testimony on the ineffectiveness of subliminal persuasion at the trial of CBS Records/Judas Priest was instrumental in winning that case for the defense.

PRIBRAM, KARL H. (1919–   )

Receiving the M.D. degree from the University of Chicago during the Hutchins period, Pribram went on in 1948 to become certified in neurological surgery. Most of his subsequent career, however, was devoted to brain–behavior research, initially at the Yerkes Laboratories of Primate Biology when Karl Lashley was director, later at Yale University where Pribram taught neurophysiology and physiological psychology, and since the 1960s at Stanford University, where he is professor of neuroscience.

Pribram is the author or coauthor of *Plans and the structure of behavior* (with Miller and Galanter), *Freud's "project" reassessed* (with Gill), and *Languages of the brain*. As editor, he has published the *Biology of learning; Biology of memory* (with Broadbent); *Psychophysiology of the frontal lobes* (with Luria); *Central processing of sensory input;* two volumes on *The hippocampus* (with Isaacson); and four volumes on *Brain and behavior*.

Pribram has investigated mind–brain problems with a view to their philosophical implications, drawing upon laboratory data for support of his premises. Essays on these problems are compiled in a volume on *Mind in the world of objects*. Much of Pribram's time continues to be occupied as a "bench" scientist: gathering, analyzing, and reporting research. The results appear in four volumes: (1) on forebrain systems; (2) on the limbic forebrain; (3) on the frontal cortex; and (4) on the dorsolateral cerebral convexity.

Pribram chaired the American Psychological Association's Committee on International Affairs, and has served as president of the APA's Division of Physiological and Comparative Psychology, and as president of the Division of Theoretical and Philosophical Psychology.

PRINCE, MORTON (1854–1929)

Prince was one of the early American pioneers in the study of abnormal psychology. Shortly after receiving the M.D. degree, he became a fol-

lower of S. Weir-Mitchell, who had developed a "rest cure" for a disorder characterized by psychological weakness called neurasthenia. He then studied in Paris and became acquainted with the famous French physician, Pierre Janet, who had developed a theory of abnormal behavior in which certain symptoms were an expression of a *dissociation* or splitting off from the normal organization of the personality. Thus Prince became a member of the school of "dissociation" and applied the concept later to his study of the multiple personality. He also was attracted to Freud's idea of a dynamic psychology, according to which the bases of human conduct are to be found in drives or instincts.

In 1905, Prince founded the *Journal of Abnormal Psychology* and became its first editor. He encouraged the publication of clinical and experimental studies of abnormal behavior in this journal, and, in fact, admonished American psychologists of the time for ignoring that area of psychology. In 1927, he founded the Psychological Clinic at Harvard.

He is best known for *The dissociation of a personality,* in which he described the biography of a multiple personality. Sally Beauchamp had three distinct personalities, which alternated with each other. These he characterized as the saint, the devil, and the woman. Two of the personalities had no knowledge of the existence of the others, except from what they were told. Thus each of these had complete amnesia for the others, so each was dissociated from the others. The third had knowledge of the existence of the other two and thus existed in a *coconscious* manner (a term invented by Prince). The significance of the work lay in the fact that it was the first extensive record of a multiple personality and laid the foundation for further study of this unusual condition.

R. W. LUNDIN

PURKINJĚ, JAN EVANGELISTA (1787–1869)

Purkinjě, a Czech physiologist, worked at Prague and Breslau. Inspired by Goethe's color studies, he did extensive research in sensory psychology in the phenomenological tradition. He also published works on the history of medicine in Czechoslovakia, on Austrian nationalism, and on the bird egg previous to incubation.

The first volume of his major sensory research, in 1819, included work on dark adaptation, the flight of colors, the location and characteristics of the blind spot, a comparison of monocular and binocular vision, and afterimages (Bidwell's ghost). Another book, in 1823, reported his work on physiological optics and with the skin.

The second volume, which appeared in 1825 under a slightly different title, was dedicated to Goethe. Purkinjě described the change in color sensitivity as the stimulus moves from the center to the periphery of the visual field. He reported that all colors tended to change in hue as one moved outward, but that different colors changed at different places. This research anticipated Hermann Aubert's color-field mapping. Visual sensitivity was reported to decrease continuously from the center to the periphery, with all colors tending toward gray at the extreme. He coined the term *indirect vision* to label the phenomenon.

Also appearing in the 1825 volume were the first solid data that visual accommodation was the result of the change of the shape of the lens. Purkinjě measured the change in reflection of a flame from the cornea, from the anterior lens surface, and from the posterior lens surface when the subject was focusing on near and on far objects. The similar work of a later investigator is memorialized in the term *Sanson images,* occasionally called Purkinjě–Sanson images.

The well-known Purkinjě phenomenon was described in three paragraphs in the 1825 work. Clearly, to its author, it was just one of hundreds of research findings, but not so to sensory psychologists. He described how colors emerged from darkness at dawn: At first there is only black and gray, with red the blackest; then the blues appear; eventually the reds are seen. Von Kries postulated two separate visual systems in 1895 primarily based upon this "Purkinjě shift." But it was left to Selig Hecht firmly to establish the duplicity theory of rod and cone visual systems in the early twentieth century. One important piece of evidence he used was the Purkinjě phenomenon.

C. S. PEYSER

QUETELET, LAMBERT ADOLPHE JACQUES (1796–1874)

Quetelet was appointed a mathematics professor at the University of Ghent in 1815. In 1819, he received the doctorate from Ghent based on a dissertation in analytic geometry, and in that same year transferred to the faculty of the Athénée of Brussels. Later he founded the Brussels Royal Observatory, where he remained as astronomer.

Quetelet wrote poetry, collaborated on the writing of an opera, published in geometry, physics, astronomy, and criminology. His work that had the most impact on psychology was in probability and statistics.

Pierre de Laplace and Karl Gauss had developed the concept of the normal distribution of error and applied it to measurements of human physiology. Quetelet extended the notion, describing the distribution as being the true state rather than simply measurement error. Quetelet proposed the notion of the Average Man. The average is nature's ideal value. The normal distribution is an indication of how often nature errs in seeking this ideal. The error is reality rather than a problem in measurement. In the early 1830s, Quetelet published data showing that chest measurements of Scottish soldiers and the heights of French military draftees fell in a normal distribution. Sir Francis Galton later extended Quetelet's work to human mental characteristics.

Quetelet also had an impact on researchers in sociology. He suggested that the same procedures be used as are used in physics, with the researcher observing a large number of cases and taking an average.

C. S. PEYSER

RAIMY, VICTOR (1913–1987)

In a doctoral dissertation written at Ohio State University in 1943, Raimy proposed that changes in the self-concept could be used to chart the course of psychotherapy as well as general changes in personality. Educated at Antioch College, Raimy became impressed with the ubiquity and influence of the self-concept. In his theory, the self-concept was seen as a guide or map that persons consult when faced with choices.

Always employed in an academic setting (University of Pittsburgh, Ohio State University, and the University of Colorado), Raimy conducted psychotherapy with both college students and hospitalized mental patients while exploring cognitive phenomena related to the self-concept. In 1975, he published a book explaining therapy in terms of cognitive principles—*Misunderstandings of the self: Cognitive psychotherapy and the misconception hypothesis*. Misconceptions about the self were proposed as disturbing aspects of the self-concept that account for much maladjustment and neurosis. Two major misconceptions that impede treatment are *phrenophobia*, the belief that one is losing one's mind, and the *Special Person misconception*, the spoiled child's refusal to come to terms with reality.

In addition to his interest in therapy, Raimy also participated in the postwar frenzy to train psychologists. In 1950, he compiled and wrote *Training in clinical psychology; The report of the Boulder conference on graduate education in clinical psychology*, which still serves as a major guideline for university psychology departments.

In 1978, Raimy retired to Honolulu, to part-time private practice.

RAINA, MAHARAJ K. (1943–   )

Prior to joining the National Council of Educational Research and Training, New Delhi, to be engaged in conducting and guiding research and developmental work, Raina served as reader in the Division of Behavioral Science, Meerut University, Meerut. He began his professional career in Madhya Pradesh at Indore University. The Srinagar-born Raina was educated in Srinagar, Simla, Panjab, and Rajasthan. After receiving his bachelor's degree from Rajasthan University, he continued his studies at this university and received the Ph.D. degree in 1968. His deep interest in understanding creative and talented behavior in various groups led him to explore these areas. Papers based on such attempts have been published in India and elsewhere. Some of the work is summarized in his book *Creativity research: International perspective*.

Raina has been involved in research on the National Talent Search Scheme, a prestigious talent search program in India, out of which came the book *Studies on national talent search*, of which he is coauthor. He has concentrated on longitudinal studies of the talented and on studying the role of creativity in the talent search. He produced a report, *Research and development in talent: The role of creativity tests*, based on these findings.

Another issue that has interested Raina is the role of biochemical variables in various behaviors, which led him to compile a report on *Serum urate concentrations, intellectual style and personality*. Other papers relating to such attempts have been published in England, the United States, and India. He has also been interested in understanding the role of hemisphericity in different functions to relate it to education and other relevant aspects of life.

RAMON Y CAJAL, SANTIAGO (1832–1934)

Ramon y Cajal was forced by his father to study medicine instead of art, as he would have preferred. An uninspired student early in his career, he earned his first degree in medicine in 1873. After a short tour of service in the Spanish army and a case of malaria, he left the military and earned a doctorate in anatomy, in 1877. Ramon y Cajal held professorships in Valencia, Barcelona, and Madrid, and the chair in histology and pathology at Madrid from 1892 until his retirement in 1922. He shared the Nobel prize in medicine and physiology in 1906, and was elected a foreign member of the Royal Society in 1909.

A largely self-taught histologist, Ramon y Cajal made such important contributions to the understanding of the nervous system that he is called the father of present-day physiological psychology. His techniques for tracing neurons histologically, still a basic approach to physiological psychology, led him to demonstrate that the central nervous system is comprised of separate but communicating nerve cells. He described the basic structure and physiology of neurons, the direction of conduction of a neuron, and the means of regeneration of a severed cell. He also described the structure of the retina and provided a histological basis for cerebral localization of function.

Ramon y Cajal spent his entire career in Spain and insisted on publishing his research in Spanish. His publications were voluminous, but two stand out as central to his work. The first was his three-volume text on the nervous system (1899–1904); the other was his two-volume study of neural degeneration and regeneration (1913–1914).

T. KEITH-LUCAS

RANK, OTTO (1884–1939)

Of the distinguished followers of Sigmund Freud, Otto Rank was the first whose professional formation was from the outset in a psychoanalytic framework. Viennese, and a graduate of a technical school, he was oriented toward becoming a novelist and poet when, at the age of 20, he discovered Freud's writings and drew on them in formulating an essay on artistic creativity. This essay made a great impression on Freud, who welcomed Rank into his inner circle and encouraged his university education. The essay was eventually published as a book in 1907 and was followed by a series of books interpreting mythic and literary themes (the anomalous birth of heroes, the incest theme, the stories of Lohengrin and of Don Juan, the theme of the "double"). His activities in the psychoanalytic movement expanded during these years into an important role as editor and as secretary of the small central group of leaders. After his return from war duties, he began, about 1920, to work also as a psychoanalytic therapist in Vienna.

Experience with patients led Rank to theoretical developments embodied in *The trauma of birth*. The idea that birth is the prototype of later anxiety had previously been advanced by Freud, and Rank felt his own elaboration to be a constructive advance in psychoanalytic theory. Rank considered dual anxiety about the birth process and about fantasies of return to uterine life the explanation for much that had been ascribed to sexual conflicts, including the Oedipus complex, and this replacement focused more attention on the child's relation to its mother rather than its father. Both of these elements disturbed Freud, and other members of the inner circle of psychoanalysis even more. The controversy initiated by this book led to Rank's expulsion from the inner circle and, eventually, to his contrasting his own approach to that of psychoanalysis.

During this period of controversy, and in the following years of work largely in Paris and New York, Rank continued his clinical practice and writing, and increasingly engaged also in teaching. He developed a highly innovative version of what he at times called "psychoanalysis of the ego structure," best represented in English by the double volume *Will therapy* and *Truth and reality*. After these technical works on therapeutic technique and personality theory, Rank wrote four books that were broader in character, at once psychological and philosophical. One centered on the concept of soul (Rank, 1931), one on education, and one—posthumously published—on social psychology (Rank, 1941); the other (Rank, 1932) was a more mature treatment of the topic of his first essay, artistic creativity. These considered the implications of his theory for a psychological interpretation of human history, for various problems of modern life, and for the sources of creative potential both in the artist and in all persons.

Rank was unusual among psychoanalytic writers in the extent to which he drew on historical and anthropological sources. This orientation was established in his early work in "applied psychoanalysis"—that is, the application of psychoanalytic theory to the interpretation of art, myth, and human culture generally. In that period, he had no clinical experience of his own to draw on. The same orientation remained strong in his later career, even though he now also had a fund of clinical experience and had abandoned much of the psychoanalytic theory with which he had previously been working. This orientation gives distinctive value to his work, particularly since it seems to have been a source of much that is most original in it. At the same time, it tends to alienate the modern reader, because it revolves around an early and outmoded anthropology. Like his predecessors (including Freud), he was much concerned with when and how various features of culture originated; he assumed the reality of a single course of development from primitive to civilized, and often treated almost as fact conjectures about the unknowable distant past. The tolerant reader, however, will find a wealth of ideas that can be easily transplanted to a setting of modern scientific thought.

Rank's mature thought was based on rejecting the aim, shared by Freud and most of academic psychology, of mechanistic explanation of human behavior or experience with a cause–effect paradigm. He sought to develop an alternative scientific approach built on the person as a voluntary interpreter of meaning and initiator of action. For example,

his earlier conception of the birth trauma as source of anxiety was largely replaced by a conception of womb and birth ideas as apt symbols used by an individual to express conflicting thoughts of moving on to risky new possibilities or stagnating comfortably in familiar routines, expressed metaphorically (and at times literally) as fear of life versus fear of death. Rank was thus a forerunner of tendencies that only later became conspicuous in orthodox psychoanalysis and academic psychology, and became the basis of such major developments as humanistic psychology.

I. L. CHILD

RAO, K. RAMAKRISHNA (1932–   )

Rao is the director of the Institute for Parapsychology and the Foundation for Research on the Nature of Man founded by J. B. Rhine in Durham, North Carolina, and formerly professor of psychology and vice-chancellor at Andhra University, Visakhapatnam, India. His contributions to psychology, both theoretical and experimental, focus mainly on those aspects, such as psi, that receive little attention in conventional psychology.

Rao's theoretical writings, inspired by classic Indian thought, attempt to reconcile transcendental and empirical conceptions of consciousness and self. His experimental work is directed toward understanding the bidirectional nature of psi, focusing on its volitional and attentional aspects. Rao's interests in psychology include cross-cultural psychology, nocturnal dreaming, and meditation.

He is editor of the *Journal of Indian Psychology* and the *Journal of Parapsychology*. Author of many journal articles and four books, Rao, in his *Experimental parapsychology*, sets forth the philosophy and methods of contemporary parapsychology within the framework of laboratory research. He served thrice as president of the Parapsychological Association and is involved in the ongoing effort to make parapsychology a rigorous discipline within the boundaries of psychology.

Rao was elected twice as the president of the Indian Academy of Applied Psychology and was adviser on higher education to the government of Andhra Pradesh, India. As a member of several committees at the national and state levels, Rao had helped to shape some significant higher education policies in India, including the establishment of autonomous state councils of higher education.

RATH, RADHANATH (1920–   )

Known for his work in cognitive growth and educational problems of socially disadvantaged children, Rath received the M.A. degree from Patna and the Ph.D. degree from the London University, in 1948. After his early specialization in psychophysics, he turned to social psychology and produced *Psycho-social problems of social change*. While involved in the reorientation of primary school education and textbooks in Orissa, he carried on intensive research in the area of early education and published many papers and books, including *Cognitive abilities and school achievements of socially disadvantaged in primary schools*.

Rath is known as a popular writer on psychology, sociopolitical problems, and travel diaries on the United Kingdom, the United States, the U.S.S.R., and other countries. As a widely traveled scholar, he has presided at, and participated in, many national and international conferences and seminars. He was the organizing local secretary of the Indian Science Congress in 1962 and 1977, and chairman of the International Conference of Cross-Cultural Psychology in 1980. He has been a member of or a consultant to almost all the national centers in education and psychology.

Rath's professional career began in 1944 in Cuttack. He started the first undergraduate department of psychology in 1953 and a postgraduate department in 1958 at Utkal University. This department is the first advanced center in psychology in India. Rath has been awarded a National Fellowship, one of the most coveted academic awards in India.

RAVIV, AMIRAM (1939–   )

Raviv studied psychology at the Hebrew University of Jerusalem. He received the doctoral degree in psychology in 1974 from the Hebrew University and a graduate diploma in psychotherapy from the Tel-Aviv University Sackler School of Medicine in 1977.

From 1967 on, Raviv taught in the Department of Psychology at Tel-Aviv University. In 1978–1979, he was a visiting scholar in the Social Ecology Laboratory, School of Medicine, Stanford University.

For many years, Raviv directed and coordinated school psychological services in Israel. He served as the chief psychologist of Ministry of Education and as the professional supervisor of school psychological services of the Israeli educational system. He was a member of the Israel Psychological Association committee and of the Psychologists' Council, assisting the Minister of Health in the implementation of the Psychologists' Law. Raviv is a clinical and educational psychologist. His research areas include prosocial behavior, pupils' attribution of success and failure, social climate in various settings, and issues related to the role of school psychologists.

RAZRAN, GREGORY (1901–1973)

Razran came to the United States in 1920 and was naturalized in 1927. As an American psychologist and leading authority on Russian psychological research, he kept U.S. psychologists informed concerning developments in psychology in the Soviet Union. Razran was graduated from Columbia College in 1927, was a University Scholar there in 1929–1930, and received the Ph.D. degree in psychology in 1933 under R.S. Woodworth. He lectured on psychology at Columbia in 1930–1938 and was a research associate in 1938–1940.

In 1940, Razran joined the faculty at Queens College, where he was chairman of the Psychology Department from 1945 to 1966. He was a statistical consultant to the Office of Strategic Services during World War II and a Guggenheim Fellow in 1948–1949. He left Queens College in 1952 to help establish a psychology department at the Hebrew University in Jerusalem. Razran served as cochairman of the International Pavlovian Conference on Higher Nervous Activity in America (1961), as president of the division on General Psychology of the American Psychological Association, and as chairman of the Psychology Division of the New York Academy of Sciences.

Razran did extensive research in the area of classical conditioning and contributed more than 50 papers, 10 of which were concerned with the conditioned reflex as an index of meaning. Two years before his death, Razran wrote *Mind in evolution: An east–west synthesis* (1971), in which he integrated classical and instrumental conditioning and sign learning by relating the various types of learning to levels of evolutionary development.

M. LaCroce

REICH, WILHELM (1897–1957)

Reich's pursuits in various scientific realms constitute the body of work known as Orgonomy. Reich became a practicing analyst while still a medical undergraduate. He became interested in the outcome of analysis, particularly the bases for unsatisfactory results. He found that patients whose analyses were successful had all developed satisfactory genital functioning of a specific, and heretofore undescribed kind—a capacity he investigated and called *orgastic potency*.

Concurrently, in his analytic work, Reich began to attack resistances (in terms of behavioral traits). This new technique caused character structure to change, suggesting that not only were symptoms evidence of neurosis, but that character itself was neurotic. Reich called his new method *character analysis*. In successful analyses, Reich often elicited strong emotions, the expression of which he encouraged. After consistent, thorough release of affect, changes occurred in bodily attitudes, posture, and tonus. He became convinced that, concomitant with psychic character armor, there is a somatic muscular armor. This discovery led to an important innovation in technique, that of the possibility of attacking the neurosis somatically.

Reich parted from psychoanalysis as his pursuits led him into realms the analysts could not or would not follow. Emotions came to mean the manifestations of a tangible, demonstrable biological energy (*orgone*, as Reich called it, from "organism" and "orgasm")—the reality of the Freudian libido. Orgone therapy involves the therapeutic methodology evolved to bring the patient to a condition of health manifested by a state of orgastic potency. The function of the orgasm is to regulate the organism's energy, the further investigation of which became Reich's focus until his death.

A. Nelson

REID, THOMAS (1710–1796)

Reid, a Scottish clergyman, was graduated from the University of Aberdeen in 1726. After serving as librarian, he was appointed to a chair in philosophy. He then accepted a professorship in moral philosophy at the University of Glasgow.

Reid was the first member of the "Scottish School" of psychology. His successors were Douglas Stewart and Thomas Brown. They objected to the empiricism and associationism of the earlier British philosophers, and in particular, to David Hume, who had dismissed any concept of mind, stating that all we know are our experiences. In *Essays on the intellectual powers of the human mind*, Reid proposed that not only did people possess minds, but that any individual mind knew more than it possessed. He proposed what later became known as *faculty psychology*. In this theory, the mind is an organized unity with powers to perform various activities, including self-preservation, desire, self-esteem, pity, and gratitude, in addition to six intellectual powers—perception, judgment, memory, conception, moral taste, and will. Reid objected not only to Hume's laws of association, but also to his doubt concerning the existence of a real world. Reid said, "All mankind could not be wrong and go against the wisdom of the ages." As a strong Scottish Presbyterian, he held that people did receive experiences from real objects, and that God's wisdom added the pluses to turn sensations into an understanding of the world.

R. W. Lundin

REIK, THEODOR (1888–1969)

Reik received the Ph.D. degree at the University of Vienna in 1912. He became an early follower of Freud and was psychoanalyzed by Karl Abraham, an eminent psychoanalyst. Reik taught at the Berlin Psychoanalytical Institute and in 1938 came to the United States. His writings were intended for the intelligent lay person and were not specifically directed toward his professional colleagues.

He never received the M.D. degree but became one of the early lay analysts. Freud wrote *The question of lay analysis* in defense of Reik's ability to practice psychoanalysis in the absence of medical training.

In *The unknown murderer*, Reik wrote of the criminal's unconscious desire to confess the crime. Criminals, he said, unconsciously betray themselves by bringing about their own self-punishment through a purposive act. In another book, *Listening with the third ear,* he described the ability of a good analyst to make use of intuitions, sensitivity, and subliminal cues to interpret clinical observations in individual and group psychotherapy. Actually the idea was first introduced by Friedrich Nietzsche and later applied by Reik to therapeutic situations.

Although a believer in many basic psychoanalytical concepts, Reik disagreed with Freud over certain matters of love and sex. Reik believed that true romantic love has little to do with sex, that it is felt most strongly when the loved one is absent. Further, he took issue with Freud's notion of primary narcissism (self-love), which he felt did not exist. He pointed out that normal sexual relations occur simply as a means of relieving the tensions of the sex drive. In falling in love, in a romantic way, one sees one's better self in someone else. For example, we show our dissatisfaction with ourselves by finding in another the qualities we lack. Another possible way to resolve our own dissatisfactions is by ''falling in hate''—by having hostile feelings toward those who seem more satisfied with themselves than we are. Other possibilities include putting lesser demands on ourselves or doing something creative, which allows us to have a better opinion of ourselves.

Reik also wrote on primitive rituals, death rites, and religion as expressions of the fulfillment of unconscious desires.

R. W. LUNDIN

RESNICK, ROBERT J. (1940–   )

Resnick was born in Syracuse, New York, the middle child of working class parents. He graduated from Syracuse University with a Psychology major in 1962 where he was on the University Crew Team. He received his Ph.D. in Clinical Psychology from the University of Tennessee in 1968 after completing a Master's degree at Temple University in 1963. From 1963 to 1964, he worked at a Veteran's Administration Hospital. His sub-specialty within clinical psychology is child/adolescent. He was recruited to the Department of Psychiatry, Division of Clinical Psychology at the Medical College of Virginia/Virginia Commonwealth University. He is presently a Professor of Psychiatry and Pediatrics and Chair of the Division of Clinical Psychology.

Resnick's clinical and research interest are Attention Deficit Disorders in children and adolescents. Professionally, he has spend his career establishing the autonomous practice of psychology. He filed the landmark ''Virginia Blues'' litigation establishing the autonomous practice of psychology. He helped to write model on Medicaid legislation and has testified before Congress on National Health.

He has been active in the American Psychological Association as a member of the Committee on Professional Practice and as Chair of the Board of Professional Affairs. He chaired several task forces producing documents on hospital-based practice. He was among the earliest advocates of expanded psychopharmacological training and privileges. Resnick was a member of the Board of Directors of the American Psychological Association and the 1995 President. He is past-chair of the Association for the Advancement of Psychology, past president of Division 42, the Division of Independent Practice. He has received national awards for advocacy and the 1993 Division 12 awardee for Distinguished Professional Contributions. Dr. Resnick is a member of the National Academy of Practice and is a Diplomate in Clinical Psychology (ABPP).

REUCHLIN, MAURICE (1920–   )

Reuchlin began his research career in Paris under the direction of H. Pieron at the National Center of Scientific Research in 1947. He later became the director of the National Institute of Work and Professional Orientation (1963), then professor of psychology at the University of Caen (1966). He transferred to the Sorbonne in Paris in 1968.

Since 1964, Reuchlin also has directed the Laboratory of Differential Psychology of the School of Advanced Studies (third section); his specialty is differential psychology. He believes that one only should pose problems in the framework of the laws and models of experimental psychology to achieve precision in establishing its laws and models. He has modeled his research according to Piaget's theory. He attempts not to limit his research to the laboratory, but to extend it to psychopedagogical inquiries of samplings of high school students, notably with regard to their academic orientation. He has been concerned with the use of statistical methods in psychology and has taken the position that the choice of method and interpretations of the results cannot be based only on the formal criteria of statistics, but that the content of the data and the context of the research must be considered as well.

Reuchlin has published many works on such topics, including: *Histoire de la psychologie, (History of psychology), Les méthodes quantitatives en psychologie (Quantitative methods in psychology), Méthode d'analyse factorielle a l'usage des psychologues (The method of factor analysis in psychological usage), La psychologie différentielle, Differential psychology, Précis de statistique (Manual of statistics),* and *Psychologie (Psychology).*

REVUSKY, SAM (1933–   )

Revusky helped pioneer an approach to learning that emphasized innate associative predispositions. John Garcia found that animals selectively associate between tastes and sickness, tending to ignore cues not naturally connected with feeding. As a result, learned taste aversions could develop if a sickness followed long after ingestion. Revusky (1968) demonstrated that such learning could occur over delays of hours. Whereas others thought taste aversion learning was a unique type of learning, Revusky (1971, 1977) insisted that it followed the same basic principles as other types of learning, except that the role of selective association was unusually prominent. Presumably, association would readily occur over indefinitely long delays if principles of selective association could override this interference. Bow Tong Lett used this theory to devise a situation in which a reward delayed by as much as an hour would be effective in a T maze. This is unique in that a theory of animal learning was successfully used to predict a clearly counterintuitive result.

Boland, Mellor, and Revusky (1978) improved the chemical aversion treatment of alcoholism by applying the results of animal studies of learned taste aversions. Their six-month abstinence rate was 36% in patients so poor in their control of alcohol that their abstinence rate with a control treatment was 12%.

Revusky and his collaborators have written five papers (e.g., Revusky & Coombes, 1982) delineating the conditioning that occurs when a conditioned stimulus (CS) drng is injected prior to an unconditioned stimulus (US) drug. Cronholm and Revusky (1965) were responsible for the first multiple baseline design and its statistical analysis. Following some work of Douglas Anger, Revusky (1962) was responsible for the first mathematical model of an operant reinforcement schedule.

REYKOWSKI, JANUSZ (1929–   )

Reykowski is best known for developing a theory of intrinsic motivation to prosocial behavior. He graduated from the University of Warsaw in 1954, becoming a Ford Foundation Fellow in 1958/59, and receiving the Ph.D. in 1959.

Initially he studied reactions to psychological stress and determinants of tolerance for stress, conducting experiments in seminatural conditions. His study of prosocial behavior began in the late 1960s. He has argued that while in some cases a behavior oriented toward maintenance, protection, or enhancement of well being of External Social Object (ESO) is instrumental for self-interest, it can be motivated by intrinsic prosocial motives. Some of those motives stem from the fact that prosocial norms become incorporated into Ideal Self and prosocial behavior is a precondition of Self-Esteem. Prosocial motivation can arise, as well, as reaction to the situation of objects being in semantic connections with a psychological distance of those objects from the Self. Moreover, the well-developed cognitive representation of ESO can be a source of intrinsic prosocial motivation whenever there is a discrepancy between cognitive schemata of those objects and incoming information.

Reykowski, formerly a professor of psychology at the University of Warsaw, became Director of the Department of Psychology in the Polish Academy of Science in Warsaw in 1980. His publications include: "Motivation of prosocial behavior"; "Social motivation"; and with D. Bar-Tal, J. Karylowski, and J. Staub, *Development and Maintenance of Prosocial Behavior,* as well as many books in Polish.

RHINE, JOSEPH BANKS (1895–1980)

Rhine, considered the father of experimental parapsychology, spent over 50 years in active research that brought psychic research from closed séance rooms of mediums into open laboratories of scientists. Born into a farming family he was originally headed for a career in the ministry. But Rhine soon became disenchanted with religious studies because of their lack of objectivity, and turned to science, eventually earning the Ph.D. degree in plant physiology at the University of Chicago in 1925. In 1920, he married another botanist, Louisa Ella Weckesser, who remained his partner at home and work until his death.

Begun in 1927 under the sponsorship of William McDougall at Duke University, Rhine's work soon provided strong evidence for extrasensory perception (ESP), the ability to acquire information shielded from the senses. The results of his early studies were published in 1934 in his *Extrasensory perception,* a book "of such a scope and of such promise as to revolutionize psychical research and to make its title literally a household phrase" (Mauskopf & McVaugh, 1980). The book received worldwide attention and became the focus of controversy that was to continue for many years. In *Extrasensory perception after sixty years,* which he wrote in 1940 with a number of his colleagues, Rhine dealt meticulously with all of the objections raised against his and similar work. Rhine's research results also provided evidence for the existence of psychokinesis (PK), the ability to influence external systems shielded from normal energetic sources, and for the relative independence of ESP and PK from space–time constraints. Nontechnical and more popular accounts of his work and its implications are contained in his *New frontiers of the mind, The reach of the mind,* and *New world of the mind.*

For almost a half century, Rhine was the undisputed leader in the field of parapsychology. He gave it its concepts and methods, defined its scope, mapped out its territory, and provided the instrumentalities necessary for its professionalization, including the establishment of the *Journal of Parapsychology* and the founding of the Parapsychological Association. Yet he felt that his work was far from complete. In some of his unpublished notes, he briefly indicated what he considered to be the main challenge of parapsychology—the great elusiveness of the phenomena. "It has functions wide and lawful enough," he wrote. "Yet it evades most of the controlled applications all the known sensorimotor abilities permit."

Though he pursued psi research with total devotion, parapsychology for Rhine was not an end in itself. It was the implications of the existence of psi that fascinated him most. "Like many of the founders of parapsychology," he once said, "I am searching for light on man's nature with respect to the physical order. I had found it hard to hold on to a religious view that rested on the supernatural." The science of parapsychology, he hoped, would answer questions about "man's transcendent nature."

During all his professional life, Rhine waged a battle to gain academic acceptance for parapsychology, a battle that he did not quite win. But he stirred up a significant number of academics who are continuing the work.

K. R. RAO

RIBES-IÑESTA, EMILIO (1944–   )

Ribes-Iñesta was raised in Mexico, and obtained his professional degree in psychology in 1966 from the National Autonomous University of Mexico (UNAM). He continued his studies at the University of Toronto, where he obtained the M.A. degree in experimental psychology under D. E. Berlyne. One of those responsible for the introduction of experimental psychology into Mexico, Ribes-Iñesta contributed to the development of the first professional and graduate research programs on behavior modification and behavior analysis, both at the University of Veracruz at Xalapa (1968) and at the south (Villa Obregón) and north (Iztacala) campuses of UNAM. He was the first Spanish-speaking psychologist to write a book on behavior modification (*Técnicas de modificación de conducta: Su aplicación al retardo en el desarrollo),* and has conducted research both on animal behavior (temporal parameters of stimulation) and on human behavior (language development, human problem solving and concept formation, reading, imitation). Ribes-Iñesta has been deeply concerned with the design of behaviorally oriented training programs, relating basic science to technological applications. Also, as a result of the influence of J. R. Kantor's Interbehavioral Psychology, he has been elaborating on a field approach to behavior theory to include complex human activities in a behavioral framework stressing processes, ontogeny and phylogeny. He has introduced the concept of external mediation to describe behavioral field organization. His publications include *Behavior modification: Issues and extensions* (with Sidney W. Bijou); *Behavior modification: Applications to education* (with Fred S. Keller); *Analysis of delinquency and aggression* (with Albert Bandura); *Enseñanza, investigación y ejercicio de la psicología: Un modelo integral* (with Francisco López et al.); and *El conductismo: Reflexiones críticas.*

RIBOT, THEODULE (1839–1916)

Together with Alfred Binet and Pierre Janet, Ribot was one of the founders of modern French psychology. He taught at the Sorbonne (1885–1889) and at the College of France (1889–1896). The development of his psychology can be divided into three periods. In the early part of his career, he brought the psychology then popular in England and Germany to France. In his book *English psychology,* he stressed British associationism, and in the second book, *German psychology of to-day* (1879), he reported the work of the experimental psychologists that was gaining in popularity in that country. The French psychologists did not react positively to either.

In the second period, he devoted his efforts to studying abnormal behavior. This resulted in such books as *The diseases of memory* and *Diseases of the will.* He regarded these disorders as resulting from faulty brain functioning. His concern for abnormal psychology resulted from the belief that mental phenomena should be studied not only from the viewpoint of their normal "biological evolution" but also from that of their "morbid dissolution."

The third period was devoted to an emphasis on affective and emotional factors in psychological functioning. He also stressed motivational forces in personality development, which resulted in what we today would call a dynamic psychology. Although his chair at the College of

France was in experimental psychology, he was not an experimentalist and he based his findings on clinical observation.

Ribot believed strongly that psychology should not be limited to studying normal civilized adults, but should also encompass animals, children, and abnormal people. In 1875, he founded and edited the journal *Revue Philosophique,* which included a considerable number of articles devoted to psychology.

R. W. Lundin

RICHARD, J. F. (1932–   )

Richard received his first training in philosophy as a fellow at the Ecole Normale Supérieure in Paris. He moved to psychology through the influence of A. Ombredane and later of P. Fraisse. He served as assistant professor at the universities of Rennes and Nantes and is currently a professor at the University of Paris.

His first work was on learning, and he developed a two-step model of learning—attentional and associative. Individual and species differences in discrimination learning were explained by the relative values of the attentional and associative parameters. The learning approach was then applied to stimulus detection. Stochastic learning models were developed to explain the effects of set and previous experience in detection tasks.

Richard's further efforts were devoted to concept learning and hypothesis testing behavior. He described the genetic development of the decision rules underlying the evolution of strategies from the one-hypothesis-at-a-time strategy to the focusing strategy. The late development of experimental reasoning was explained by this evolution.

He is presently working on problem solving.

Simulation models are developed to explain how the representation of a problem is changed: Hypotheses are built and tested by using the results of previous action; new relations are then discovered, thus allowing new solution processes. This work is closely connected to artificial intelligence; applications are made to instructional psychology.

His books are *Utilisation de l'information dans l'apprentissage, Généralisation du signal et de la réponse, Attention et apprentissage,* and *L'attention.*

RICHTER, CURT PAUL (1894–1988)

Richter received the A.B. from Harvard University where he studied with E. B. Holt and Robert Yerkes. After two years in the army, he went to Johns Hopkins University, receiving the Ph.D. in 1921. At Johns Hopkins he worked under John B. Watson. When Watson left the university, Richter took over his laboratory.

The breadth of his early research included such areas as spontaneous behavior in the rats (his dissertation), biological clocks, galvanic skin response, and rhythms in both normal and abnormal humans. His studies of the biological clock are reported in his *Biological clocks in medicine and psychiatry.* His studies of nutrition and self-selection of diets in rats are classics in psychology. Most of his research was done at the medical school at Johns Hopkins, so he actually directed few doctoral dissertations in psychology. During World War II, he studied poison avoidance in wild rats.

Perhaps because of the wide breadth of his contributions he did not receive the recognition he deserved. He was an innovator but not a theorist. A major theme that went through much of his work was the adjustments of the whole organism through behavioral changes to the internal and external environments.

R. W. Lundin

RIVERS, WILLIAM HALSE (1864–1922)

Rivers received M.A. and M.D. degrees at St. Andrews, Scotland. He was appointed to the first lectureship at Cambridge in the experimental psychology and physiology of the senses. Having worked with Ewald Hering at Prague, Rivers continued research on vision. When an anthropological expedition to the Torres Straits of New Guinea was arranged, he went along with Charles S. Myers and William McDougall to make observations and psychological measurements of primitive people.

Rivers' interests turned more and more toward anthropology and he later traveled to South India and Melanesia, where he continued his observations of preliterate people. These studies were reported in *The Todas* and *The history of Melanesian society.*

In an experiment conducted with Henry Head, Rivers had a nerve in his arm severed to make observations of changes in sensitivity during the regeneration process. He became deeply interested in neurology and medical psychology during World War I. With Elliot Smith and T. H. Pear, he was the first to recognize "shell shock" as a distinct clinical entity.

In 1904, Rivers with Myers and Thomas W. Ward founded the *British Journal of Psychology* and served as coeditor with Ward until 1910. Late in life, he wrote at a hectic pace and several books resulted: *Instinct and the unconscious, Psychology and politics, Conflict and dream, Medicine, magic and religion,* and *Psychology and ethnology.*

P. E. Lichtenstein

ROBACK, ABRAHAM AARON (1890–1965)

Roback received his undergraduate education at McGill University in Canada and the Ph.D. degree in psychology from Harvard. Most of his life was spent in Cambridge, Massachusetts. Roback held brief teaching appointments at major universities but for many years he taught for the Massachusetts Department of University Extension. Primarily, however, Roback was a writer, author of several books and approximately 2000 articles. His major psychological contributions were *The psychology of character, Behaviorism and psychology, Behaviorism at Twenty-five,* and *History of American psychology.* Roback carried on extensive correspondence with many of the intellectual and political leaders of his day, and he was widely known as an interpreter of Jewish culture.

P. E. Lichtenstein

ROGERS, CARL RANSOM (1902–1987)

As Rogers pointed out, both hard work and a commitment to Protestant Christianity were equally stressed in his youth. Certainly, both are implicit in his theories. He received the B.A. degree from the University of Wisconsin and then attended the Union Theological Seminary in New York City. He received the Ph.D. in 1931 from Teacher's College of Columbia University. He began his career at the Institute for Child Guidance there and later accepted a position in the child study department of the Society for the Prevention of Cruelty to Children in Rochester, New York, where he soon became the director. In 1939 he accepted a post at the Rochester Guidance Center. The following year he moved to Ohio State University, where he began to develop a new system of psychotherapy known first as nondirective, then client-centered, and more recently, person-centered therapy. It began to gain attention with the publication of his first book, *Counseling and psychotherapy.* Some considered it to be an affront to Freudian psychoanalysis, because interpretations were not given. In 1945, he went to the University of Chicago serving as executive of their counseling center. After Chicago, he returned to his alma mater, Wisconsin, as professor. During the next decade he published *Client-centered therapy* and probably his most popular book, *On becoming a person.*

In the therapeutic process, the individual (designated as a client not a patient) enters with the therapist into a relationship in which the client becomes increasingly aware of his or her own feelings and experiences. In the process, the therapist reflects the feelings of the client. Their relationship becomes warm and friendly. The therapist may never make any critical or punishing statement.

Rogers also became renowned for helping to develop the prevailing trend of humanistic psychology, following in the footsteps of Abraham Maslow. The theory gradually envolved stressing the final inherent goal of self-actualization. In Rogers's therapy, the client, not the therapist decides each move. Everyone, of course, does not reach self-actualization. Furthermore, he believed the technique could be applied to other areas outside psychology such as pastoral counseling, teaching, and nursing. In his last fifteen years Rogers applied his methods to training policymakers, leaders, and groups in conflict.

His theories were very much at odds with the behaviorist B. F. Skinner. Rogers was concerned with inner feelings and experiences, whereas Skinner emphasized only external behavior. On several occasions the two engaged in friendly debates at various universities. Neither ever won, as the listener has the distinct impression that the two really were not communicating.

Even when Rogers was in his 80s, he was active at the Center for the Study of the Person at La Jolla, of which he had been a cofounder. His many distinctions included the presidency of the American Psychological Association and the Distinguished Contribution Award of the same organization.

R. W. LUNDIN

ROHRACHER, HUBERT (1907–1972)

Young Hubert felt his calling to science early. He had the good fortune of supportive parents and inspiring teachers. He defied federal law by pursuing two courses of study: law (". . . for pragmatic reasons") and psychlogy (under E. Becher and R. Pauli). He trained in law by day and experimented in Erismann's lab with Ivo Kohler (reversal glasses) by night. The contradictory nature of human personality became one of his tenets. In the days of thriving behaviorism, Rohracher remained convinced of the significance of nature's (genetic) contribution to psychological performance. Notice of Hans Berger's EEG-registrations from the intact scalp fascinated him. His pioneering psychophysiological EEG-studies demonstrated this approach's potential for understanding the relationship between psychological performance and its physiological expression. Rohracher rejected Freud's concept of the subconscious ("defies empirical examination") and insisted on the indispensility of introspection as conduit to conscious and subjective experience in psychology.

In 1943 he was awarded the chair in psychology (Vienna) vacated by the Karl Bühler. Rohracher offered Bühler the chair as soon as World War II ended; Bühler declined. Rohracher remained for 29 yr as a legendary teacher (his pupils today occupy chairs in all parts of the German-speaking world), and he remained a strictly empirical scientist until his death.

G. GUTTMAN

ROKEACH, MILTON (1918–1988)

What people believe, why they believe, and what difference it makes are the recurring themes that have preoccupied Rokeach in his research career. His earliest work in the late 1940s moved away from conceptualizations about rightist forms of authoritarianism and intolerance to more general formulations: the study of ideology and cognitive functioning, the organization and measurement of belief systems and ideological dogmatism, the effects of race versus belief as determinants of racial and

ethnic discrimination. These investigations were followed by detailed accounts of the closed belief systems of three paranoid schizophrenics claiming to be Christ, and by observations of the cognitive and behavioral effects of confrontations among them over the issue of identity.

A decade of continuing focus on belief systems led him back to the classical issue of social attitudes and their relation to behavior, the effects of attitude change on behavioral change, and theories of cognitive interaction. His work in the 1970s moved from a concern with the nature of attitudes to the nature of human values, their measurement, their distribution, and their changes within U.S. society, as well as their functional relation to attitudes and behavior, the conditions under which they will undergo change, and the effects of long-term value change on attitude and behavioral change. In demonstrating such long-term effects—in the laboratory, in the classroom, and, most recently, through television in the natural context—Rokeach has provided a theory of cognitive and behavioral change.

His work in the 1980s moved beyond earlier formulations of G. W. Allport to the view that there are really three central concepts in social psychology—the self, values, and attitudes—in that order of importance, and to the view that theories of cognitive change in social psychology must become reunified with theories of cognitive stability, thus overcoming the present compartmentalization of the fields of personality and social psychology.

ROMANES, GEORGE JOHN (1848–1894)

Romanes spent all but a few months of his life in Great Britain. Educated at Cambridge, he received such a large inheritance that the only academic position he ever held was a part-time one at the University of Edinburgh.

A personal friend of Darwin, Romanes set forth in his trilogy to provide evidence for the continuity of humans and animals. The first book, *Animal intelligence*, established the notion of comparative psychology (a term he coined). Unfortunately Romanes chose to use the anecdotal method, which he culled from both the scientific and popular literature. Despite his explicit and stringent rules for accepting vignettes, the method is considered inherently defective for serious work today. He was also severely criticized for his tendency to anthropomorphize, that is, to attribute human characteristics such as insight to animals. Since such a notion was his thesis to be proved, many considered that he begged the question. A year later, *Mental evolution in animals* and *Mental evolution in man* completed his argument for the continuity. Few found his evidence compelling. Romanes also published original research on ocean invertebrates, notably the jellyfish, starfish, and sea urchins.

One reaction to his work was Lloyd Morgan's canon of parsimony (1894), in which higher psychological faculties were not to be postulated if the behavior could be interpreted as a lower function. Despite the failure to accomplish his aims, Romanes did provide (some might say saddle) the field with its major divisions of reflex, instinct, and habit, and served to stimulate other researchers.

C. S. PEYSER

RORSCHACH, HERMANN (1884–1922)

Rorschach received his degree from Zürich in 1912 with a dissertation concerning hallucinations that was supervised by Bleuler. Except for a year on the staff of a sanitorium near Moscow, his career was spent in posts at Swiss mental hospitals. Heavily influenced by Freud, he was a promoter of psychoanalysis among Swiss psychiatrists.

In 1896, Binet and Henri had suggested the use of standardized inkblots to measure imagination. Rorschach was also familiar with

Jung's verbal free association testing technique. Putting these two notions together, he extended the inkblot technique to the measurement of the entire personality, but especially unconscious emotions.

Rorschach developed the 10 bilaterally symmetrical cards we know today from a very large number administered to a variety of psychiatric groups beginning in 1911. After supplementary testing with normals, retardates, and other special groups, he issued the first German edition in 1921. Intended for use from preschool to adult (although his data were mostly from adults), the test was scored primarily for the ratio of color to movement responses. His somewhat typological scoring system was based upon a combination of the observable and clinical insight or intuition.

With the development of a statistically based scoring system by Samuel Beck during the 1930s and by Bruno Klopfer in the early 1940s, the technique became popular in the United States. Both the Beck and Klopfer systems have declined in popularity, being replaced either by the Exner method of scoring the Rorschach or by the more empirically based Holtzman Inkblot Technique.

C. S. PEYSER

ROSENZWEIG, SAUL (1907–   )

Rosenzweig received all three of his academic degrees from Harvard University (B.A., M.A., and Ph.D. in 1932). His first research involved the investigation, through laboratory methods, of psychoanalytic concepts (e.g., repression). His first publication (1933), titled "The experimental situation as a psychological problem," anticipated the flurry of research in the 1950s on experimenter bias and related issues in experimental–social psychology. He was a research associate at the Harvard Psychological Clinic to 1934 and at the Worcester State Hospital, Massachusetts, to 1943. He was chief psychologist at the Western State Psychiatric Institute (Pittsburgh, 1943–1949) and chief psychologist at the Child Guidance Clinic of Washington University (St. Louis, 1949–1959). He has taught at Clark University, the University of Pittsburgh, and Washington University where he is professor emeritus in the departments of psychology and psychiatry.

Rosenzweig formulated a theory of aggression as related to frustration in 1937 and in 1948 devised the Rosenzweig Picture-Frustration (P-F) Study, now used worldwide. At the Worcester State Hospital he investigated schizophrenia with emphasis on personality dynamics and the role of sex hormones. At Washington University he developed his theory of *Idiodynamics*. He investigated the creative process and the history of psychodynamics. He was the founding president of the International Society for Research on Aggression; he also founded the Society of Professors Emeriti at Washington University. In 1972, he established the Foundation for Idiodynamics and the Creative Process, of which he is managing director.

Rosenzweig has published four books and 190 articles in the areas of experimental psychodynamics, psychodiagnosis, aggressive behavior, and creativity. His latest book is *Freud, Jung, and Hall, The king-maker: A historic expedition to America 1909, with Hall as host and William James as guest.*

ROT, NIKOLA (1910–   )

Rot was graduated from the University of Zagreb, Yugoslavia, in 1933. Although a constant companion, psychology was not, for a time, his basic occupation. He was a high school teacher until 1941. The next 10 years were spent as a soldier—first as a partisan during World War II, and then for several years as an officer in the Yugoslav Army.

From 1950 on, he lectured, mainly on social psychology, at the Department of Psychology at Belgrade University. For many years, he was the head of the department and director of the Institute of Psychology. He wrote on diverse psychological subjects. Three areas are central in his empirical research. The first is the study of the psychological characteristics of judgments. He established the existence of a sort of sensorial realism and he found great confidence and great resistance to pressure in judgments on perceptive evidence. The second area of his studies includes attitudes, stereotypes, and forms of national attachments. Different in both content and intensivity, national attachments appear as a broad and dynamic orientation. The third area of study concerns psychological problems connected to self-management, and the sociopolitical system in Yugoslavia. There exist convincing psychological reasons to set up self-management, but these are not sufficient conditions for its further development. A considerable amount of scientific study has been spent on his pedagogical activity and on the development of his conceptions, surveys in several areas of social psychology, including social learning and socialization, formation of attitudes and prejudices, person perception, communication as interaction, and psychological characteristics of groups and organizations. The theory of open system and ideas of Gestalt psychology seem to Rot an adequate base for relating materialistic research, even if those results differ from theoretical and methodological approaches.

ROTTER, JULIAN B. (1916–   )

Rotter received the B.A. from Brooklyn College, the M.A. from the University of Iowa, and the Ph.D. (1914) from Indiana University. He interned at Worcester State Hospital in 1938–1939. In 1941, Rotter went to Norwich State Hospital for 1 yr. Then he went into the army as a personnel consultant in the armored force and then as an aviation psychologist in the air force. He left the army in 1946 to teach at the Ohio State University, where he directed the clinical psychology training program from 1951 to 1959 and in 1962 to 1963. In 1963, he went to the University of Connecticut as director of Clinical Psychology Training Program, retiring in 1987.

Rotter has been a frequent instructor of APA- and NSF-sponsored postdoctoral courses and a visiting professor at the universities of Colorado, Minnesota, California, and Pennsylvania. He also served as a consultant for the Veterans Administration, Surgeon General's Office, and Peace Corps. He served in numerous positions in APA, including two terms on the Education and Training Board and the APA Council and as president of the Division of Social Personality and the Division of Clinical Psychology. He was president of the Eastern Psychological Association, and his honors include awards for Distinguished Contribution to the Science and Profession of Clinical Psychology, Distinguished Scientific Contribution (APA), and Award for Contributions to Clinical Psychology Training (Council of University Directors of Clinical Training). He has received an honorary D.Sci. degree from the Ohio State University. He is best known for his social learning theory and for several personality tests.

ROYCE, JOSEPH R. (1921–1989)

Royce received the Ph.D. degree from the University of Chicago in 1951, under L. L. Thurstone. He became the first head of the Department of Psychology at the University of Alberta, serving from 1960 to 1967, and founded the Center for Advanced Study in Theoretical Psychology, of which he has been the director since 1967. He is the author or editor of 10 books and over 100 articles in journals and books. Royce's major experimental research has focused on determining the gene correlates of factors of emotion. He has also contributed to a wide range of theoretical issues, the most significant being a book-length theory of individual differences (with Arnold Powell, *A theory of personality and individual differences: Factors, systems, and processes*). Other theoretical books include *Theoretical advances in behavior genetics, Toward unification in psychology,* and *The encapsulated man.* For more biographical details see "Royce, Joseph R. The life style of a theory oriented generalist in a time of empirical specialists," in T. S. Krawiec's *The psychologists,* vol. 3.

ROYCE, JOSIAH (1855–1916)

Royce pursued undergraduate work at the University of California, and studied at Leipzig and Göttingen prior to taking his doctorate at Johns Hopkins University. He taught English and logic at the University of California before joining the Department of Philosophy at Harvard, where he established himself as the foremost representative of idealistic philosophy in the United States.

Royce taught that truth could be proved, that an absolute mind exists, and that human beings as part of this mind can grasp truth. His writings ranged widely over such fields as logic, religion, ethics, psychology, and social issues. He defended a Christian world view but saw no conflict in the acceptance at the same time of modern science. He believed that life is a struggle between good and evil, and he stressed the importance of community in the fulfillment of the goals of the individual.

P. E. LICHTENSTEIN

RUBIN, EDGAR (1886–1951)

Rubin studied under Höffding in Copenhagen. Subsequently he was a student of G. E. Müller at Göttingen before returning to the University at Copenhagen for most of his career.

Rubin's earliest published work, in 1912, involved the phenomenon of paradoxical warmth, a phenomenon in which cool stimuli just below the temperature of the skin can produce a sensation of warmth. Rubin is best known for his dissertation, published in 1915 after three years of work in Müller's laboratory: the figure/ground distinction. When one looks at a situation, part of it stands out (the figure) and part of it recedes (the ground). This occurs both with everyday situations such as a house against the sky or these black words on the white page and with laboratory figures. Under some circumstances, figure and ground can reverse. Rubin is known for two of these illustrations—the vase/profile and the claw/three fingers. The phenomenon is independent of any retinal change and, according to Rubin, is determined by variables such as color(s), size, and conscious intent. Indeed, there is a figural aftereffect in that a person who has viewed such a figure tends always to see the same portion of the figure on each subsequent viewing.

The 1915 paper was in Danish and largely ignored. However, the Gestalt psychologists immediately adopted his work when it was published in German in 1921, particularly Köhler, who gave a neurological explanation for the figure/ground phenomenon. Rubin must be considered a major contributor to the Gestalt movement led by Wertheimer, Koffka, and Köhler.

C. S. PEYSER

RUBINSTEIN, SERGEI LEONIDOVICH (1889–1960)

Like L. S. Vygotsky, Rubinstein made a strong plea for Soviet psychology to become a psychology of consciousness. When he was a student of philosophy in Germany, Rubinstein became acquainted with Hegel's philosophy. In an early work, *Foundations of psychology* (1935), he formulated the general theory of a close relationship between consciousness and activity. This meant overcoming the view that consciousness was passive.

In 1943, he formulated the following principles of Soviet psychology: (1) the principle that the mind was a function of matter, but also a reflection of material reality; (2) the principle that the human psyche was a function of historical evolution and had a capacity to change; (3) the principle of the unity of consciousness and activity; and (4) the principle of the unity of theory and practice.

In 1953, Rubinstein undertook an extensive study of the process of problem solving at the Department of Psychology at Moscow University. He proposed two major methods for the study of problem solving. First was the subject's reformulation of the problem during the process. Underlying this method was the notion that thinking is a verbal process. The second method involved presenting the subject with cues or auxillary problems at different stages of solving the original problem.

His approach to thinking involved analysis and synthesis, abstraction, and generalization. Analysis was achieved by synthesis, that is, separation of the parts was dependent upon the characteristics of the whole. Finally, there were two levels of analysis and synthesis. The first was related to the sensory images of objects and the second to the verbal images.

R. W. LUNDIN

RUSSELL, ROGER W. (1914–   )

Emeritus Professor Russell has the distinction of having held senior positions in psychology on three continents and of representing three national psychological societies on such international bodies as the International Union of Psychological Science, which he served as secretary general and president. Such a peripatetic career would not have been predicted from his early life. He studied for the B.A. degree in biological sciences and the M.A. degree in psychology at Worcester's Clark University. His first move into the wider world, as Du Pont Research Fellow, led to the Ph.D. degree at the University of Virginia. Appointments at universities in Nebraska and Michigan preceded active service in the U.S. Army Air Corps. Tours of duty in Europe stimulated an interest in the European academic system, which led eventually to a period in the United Kingdom, first as Fulbright Advanced Research Fellow, and later as professor of psychology and head of the department at University College, London. Returning to the United States as executive officer of the American Psychological Association, he later became chairman of psychology at Indiana University and vice-chancellor at the University of California, Irvine. His work there led to his final appointment before retiring as vice-chancellor (executive head) of Flinders University in Australia.

From the start of his career, Russell has viewed behavior as one property of living organisms, interacting with other properties—biochemical, electrophysiological, and morphological. He was one of the first to search for neurochemical mechanisms underlying normal and abnormal behavior. The majority of his writings have reported progress at the frontiers of that search. They have provided the bases upon which he earned the University of London's D.Sc. degree and received honorary D.Sc. degrees from two other universities.

RUTHERFORD, WILLIAM (1839–1899)

Rutherford received his M.D. degree from the University of Edinburgh. After a position at King's College, London, he returned to Edinburgh as professor of physiology in 1874.

Rutherford is known for his 1880 textbook in physiology, as well as for research on the influence of the vagus nerve on circulation and the action of drugs on the secretion of bile. In psychology, he is known primarily for his "Telephone Theory" of hearing. The theory postulates that the organ of Corti vibrates as a whole in phase with the tympanic membrane (eardrum) and stapes. Thus the ear merely transmits the frequency of the incident sound onto the brain, where it is analyzed. His theory was the major competitor of Hermann von Helmholtz' place-resonance theory.

Two major criticisms have been made of Rutherford's theory. First, there is no evidence of nerve transmission at frequencies above approximately 1000 Hz (hertz) in mammals, yet many mammals hear frequencies of at least 20,000 Hz. Second, Rutherford had no explanation of how loudness is encoded. Nonetheless, it was an influential theory that today forms a part of the frequency–place theory of E. G. Wever.

C. S. PEYSER

SAHAKIAN, WILLIAM S. (1921–1986)

Sahakian received the B.A. from Northeastern University and the Ph.D. from Boston University in 1951. He developed a therapeutic technique that he identified as philosophical psychotherapy. Its aim was to change a person's values and attitudes. In this cognitive approach, the goal was a behavioral change and emotional control through altering a person's thinking processes. The technique is described in his books *Psychotherapy and counseling* and *Psychotherapy today*.

Sahakian identified another area of interest as infection theory. Accordingly, ideas are perpetuated through interpersonal relationships. This theory is elaborated in his book *History and systems of social psychology*. He was also well known for a number of other books: *History and systems of psychology* and the edited book *History of psychology*. Other areas of interest in psychology in which he wrote were the psychology of learning and personality. At the time of his death he was a lecturer, researcher and counselor at Suffolk University in Boston.

R. W. LUNDIN

SAKEL, MANFRED (1900–1957)

Sakel received the M.D. degree from the University of Vienna in 1925. After some years at the Vienna Hospital, he went to Berlin, and then returned to Vienna where, in 1936, he became associated with the Neuropsychiatric Clinic at the University of Vienna. With the rise of the Nazis during the 1930s, he migrated to the United States and continued his work in New York City.

He is primarily known for his discovery of the insulin coma treatment for schizophrenia. Insulin had been discovered in the 1920s. In the early 1930s, insulin was frequently used in small doses in treating a variety of mental disorders. Sakel's discovery came about quite by accident. One of his schizophrenic patients, who was hypersensitive to insulin, went into a coma. Following recovery from the coma, Sakel observed much improvement in the patient's behavior. He then tried using the treatment by gradually inducing a coma with increased doses of insulin and found equally satisfactory results. This discovery occurred in 1933. He reported overall improvement in 88% of his cases although the effectiveness of the treatment depended on the patient's age (better with young people) and prepsychotic stability. Chronic cases were less receptive to the treatment. He published a series of articles on the subject in the *Vienna Medical Journal* between 1934 and 1936.

He described his treatment as four phases, including (1) precoma relaxation, (2) coma, (3) recovery from coma, and (4) administration of milder doses as the patient became more lucid, until treatment was gradually terminated.

R. W. LUNDIN

SALTER, ANDREW (1914–   )

Salter planned to major in physics in college, but dropped out at the end of the first year. He returned two years later and majored in psychology,

graduating from New York University with the B.S. degree in 1937. Salter has been in private practice in New York City since 1941.

Salter's writings include "Three techniques of autohypnosis," which established autohypnosis as a viable therapeutic technique. John B. Watson said of Salter's *What is hypnosis?* (1944), "Very sound and excellent. I wish I had thought of this, but the fact is I didn't." This book showed that hypnosis is an aspect of conditioning, and also reported Salter's experiments in the military applications of autohypnosis.

Salter's *Conditioned reflex therapy* founded behavior therapy. The revolutionary character of the book was recognized upon its publication. *The New York Times* published simultaneous pro and con reviews, and Paul de Kruif, the most important medical writer of the time, said, "In the field of psychology, this work may well become a landmark of the order of Darwin's *Origin of species."*

His *Case against psychoanalysis* offended many in the psychiatric establishment. Rudolf Flesch called it "A masterpiece of inspired pamphleteering—in the best sense of the word."

SANFORD, EDMUND CLARK (1869–1924)

Sanford received the Ph.D. degree in psychology under G. Stanley Hall at Johns Hopkins University. When Hall left Johns Hopkins for Clark University, Sanford followed him. Although Hall established the first psychological laboratory at Clark, Sanford became its first director.

As an innovator of psychological apparatus, Sanford developed the vernier pendulum chronoscope, which for a time was a standard instrument for studying reaction time. Because of generally poor health, he did not publish very much, nor did he take part in the professional arguments that abounded in psychology at the time.

Sanford's main accomplishment for psychology was the publication of the first laboratory manual for the new experimental psychology. Entitled "Course for experimental psychology, Part I: Sensation and perception," it began to appear in the *American Journal of Psychology* in 1891. It was published in book form in 1898, three years before Edward Titchener published his manual for experimental psychology. It covered only experiments in sensation and perception. Sanford had intended a second part, but that was never completed. For a number of years, this manual served as a basic source for references, experiments, and appropriate classroom demonstrations in sensory psychology.

R. W. LUNDIN

SAPIR, EDWARD (1884–1939)

Sapir earned A.B., A.M., Ph.D. (1909), and Sc.D. (1929) degrees from Columbia University, and held appointments at the universities of California, Pennsylvania, and Chicago before founding the study of cultural anthropology at Yale University. He was a source of inspiration to Ruth Benedict, Margaret Mead, and many other cultural anthropologists of the day. He died at age 55 after only eight years at Yale.

Sapir's study of language in American Indian tribes led to his book *Language,* an early and major contribution to linguistic anthropology. Sapir took the position that understanding a language is central to understanding the culture that uses it.

T. KEITH-LUCAS

SATO, KOJI (1905–1971)

The contributions of Sato have been admired internationally as well as in Japan. Born in Yamagata, Japan, Sato was professor of psychology in the faculty of art and science in Kyoto University (1950–1961), professor in the faculty of education, and chairman of educational psychology. At Otemongakuin University, he served as professor in the faculty of literature.

The focus of Sato's most influential work was on five areas. For his thesis for the D.Litt degree, he wrote *Study of apprehension of relation* (1955), on the basis of an introspective analytic study of transient experience and developmental research of transposition. A second area investigated by Sato was pathological mentality, which he studied while at the Department of Psychiatry at Kyoto Imperial University (1929). Morale was a third area of study for Sato, and he introduced many theories concerning Yoki (cultivation of the spirit). He was interested in feeling and will and felt that it was difficult to solve the problem of Ki (psychovitality) by those functions. He wrote books and articles on the psychology of human life and on Zen psychology, which captured his interest in 1950. He investigated the teachings of Zen from psychological, medical, and philosophical perspectives, and used important truths he had found for the improvement of human nature. Sato's study and promotion of Zen culture made his name widely known internationally. He developed Zen as well as psychology in Japan and throughout the world.

Sato participated in initiating the 20th International Congress of Psychology in Tokyo. He also founded and edited the journal *Psychologia*, which describes how Oriental psychological theories and practices contribute to world psychology.

M. LaCroce

SCARR, SANDRA WOOD (1936–   )

Scarr was graduated from Vassar in 1958. After working for two years, she entered graduate school at Harvard. She overcame faculty pessimism about women and rebelled against the prevailing view that genetic differences were unrelated to human behavioral differences. In 1965, she received the Ph.D. degree from the Social Relations Department with a dissertation on genetic differences in children's motivation. She taught for six years at the Universities of Maryland and Pennsylvania. She explored genetic variability in human behaviors through twin, adoption, and intervention studies. *Race, social class, and individual differences in IQ* summarizes 15 years of research.

In 1971, Scarr moved to the University of Minnesota. In 1976–1977, she was a Fellow at the Center for Advanced Study in the Behavioral Sciences. And in 1977, she was appointed professor of psychology at Yale University.

She holds a middle ground between genetic and environmental determinists.

SCHACHTER, STANLEY (1922–   )

The social psychologist Schachter obtained the bachelors and masters degrees from Yale University before leaving for the University of Michigan to work for the Ph.D. degree, which he received in 1950. Most of Schachter's career was spent at Columbia University, where he has been a professor in the Psychology Department since 1960. Before that, he was a Fulbright professor at the University of Amsterdam in the early 1950s and later served for some years with the Organization of Comparative Social Research. For his accomplishments, the American Psychological Association bestowed on him its Distinguished Scientific Award in 1969.

Schachter developed a cognitive theory of emotion in which he established that people cannot discriminate one emotion from another unless they have some cognitive indication as to what their feelings relate. Schachter's is a psychobiological theory of emotion, claiming that physiological arousal is insufficient to induce emotion, as cognition also must be present.

Schachter's other research interests include obesity, smoking, stress, hunger, and the need for affiliation. This last subject was discussed in detail in *The psychology of affiliation*. Other subjects are found in his *Emotion, obesity and crime*.

SCHAIE, K. WARNER (1928–   )

Schaie received the B.A. in psychology from the University of California at Berkeley and the M.S. and Ph.D. (1956) from the University of Washington. He then was a postdoctoral fellow in medical psychology at Washington University. After completing the fellowship, he received his first academic appointment at the University of Nebraska at Lincoln. He then moved to West Virginia University, where he served as director of clinical training, director of the Human Resources Research Institute, and professor and chair of the psychology department. While at West Virginia, he developed the first formal life-span developmental psychology training program supported by NIH. He then moved to the University of Southern California as professor of psychology and director of the Gerontology Research Institute of the Andrus Gerontology Center.

He was appointed Evan Pugh Professor of human development and psychology and director of the Gerontology Center at the Pennsylvania State University.

Schaie's principal efforts are long-term longitudinal research on adult intellectual development and contributions to developmental research methodology. He is the author or editor of more than 20 books including *Adult development and aging* (with S. L. Willis) and the *Handbook of the psychology of aging* (with J. E. Birren), and of more than 150 research articles. Schaie is the recipient of the distinguished research contribution award of Division 20 of the American Psychological Association, the Kleemeier award for distinguished research of the Gerontological Society of America, and a merit award from the National Institute on Aging (NIH).

SCHOPENHAUER, ARTHUR (1788–1860)

Schopenhauer studied at Göttingen and Berlin, and received the Ph.D. degree at Jena. In an important book, *The world as will and idea*, Schopenhauer stated that scientific explanations could do no more than systematize and classify the mass of experiences that appears to be reality to the human mind. It was the task of the philosopher to discover the eventual reality, the real source of knowledge that resides in human beings. In the sense of will, reality was revealed. Will was force but more than force. The creed of naturalism, he said, was dangerous.

Schopenhauer stressed the redemption of the soul from its sensual bonds. According to him, human beings had an obligation to sensual things, but the final goal was to rise above the senses into the bosom of a peaceful Nirvana. Thus the phenomenal world of idea (representation) and the real world of will were in conflict. Basically the forces of the real world were irrational and unresponsive to reason. For example, the irrational forces of instincts, such as self-preservation and sex, dominated. The sex drive conflicted with the intellect. Sex was selfishness seeking its own satisfaction, while love, on the other hand, was concerned with others. Owing to an individual's instincts, a person was either in a state of need (want) or ennui (boredom).

Actually there was no final instinctual fulfillment, only a constant repetition, which Freud later called the "repetition compulsion," as one of the basic characteristics of all instincts. They arose and were fulfilled, but the satisfaction was only temporary, and the instinctual desire recurred. This failure to fulfill the instinctual desires was a basic human problem. When needs were not satisfied, suffering resulted. One way out of this conflict was sublimation. Here Schopenahuer anticipated Freud. When the relief of an irrational instinct forced the possibility of satisfaction through art, music, philosophy, or literature, sublimation was achieved. If sublimation could not be achieved, there was always the possibility of an ascetic life.

R. W. LUNDIN

SCHUMANN, FRIEDRICH (1863–1940)

While at the University of Berlin, Schumann was a student of and assistant to Carl Stumpf. There he performed a series of experiments that he felt tended to disprove the proposition of form-quality as a separate element of consciousness. The school of form-quality headed by Christian von Ehrenfels at Graz had insisted that a certain content of form-quality existed apart from other elements of consciousness. In his experiments, Schumann studied a great many visual forms and illusions without finding any necessity to appeal to the concept of form-quality. Instead, this could be accounted for by the laws of attention as well as eye movements.

Along with George E. Müller, he introduced the revolving drum (memory drum) for the uniform presentation of nonsense syllables in learning. An exposure slot made it possible for the subject to see one syllable in one unit of time. The time of presentation also could be systematically varied. Another improvement in the presentation of nonsense syllables for learning was the development of lists of syllables that were found in practice to be of equal difficulty. Furthermore, they demonstrated that the nature of the instructions to the subject could have a marked effect on how rapidly the subject learned.

Later, Schumann was appointed to a chair at Frankfurt (1910—1928). In Schumann's laboratory, Max Wertheimer brought to light the new Gestalt psychology in his study of apparent movement in 1912. However, Schumann would have no part of these studies, as they tended to reinstate the concept of the form-quality.

R. W. LUNDIN

SCOTT, WALTER DILL (1869–1955)

Scott, regarded as the founder of industrial psychology, was largely self-taught relative to his early education. As a farm boy, he studied in the fields at 10-min intervals while his horses rested from plowing. His undergraduate work was at Northwestern University. Later he became a student of Wilhelm Wundt. After earning the Ph.D. in psychology from the University of Leipzig in 1900, Scott returned to the United States to study laboratory techniques under Edward B. Titchener and to accept a faculty position at Northwestern University. He was hired to teach laboratory psychology, but without a laboratory. At Northwestern, he made his mark as an innovative teacher and a caring person.

Scott sought to transfer his psychological insights into the world of work. With the publication of *The theory and practice of advertising* followed by *The psychology of advertising* and other books, he introduced the business uses of psychology into advertising, selling, and consumer behavior. Thus he created a new field—industrial psychology, which has been combined into industrial–organizational psychology. He also was an advertising consultant and conducted market surveys. He eventually became head of a firm of business and industry consultants. In recognition of his contributions to the field of advertising, Scott was elected to the Advertising Hall of Fame.

In 1918, his colleagues chose him to be the president of the American Psychological Association. At the same time he was appointed as the world's first professor of applied psychology, and lectured at the Carnegie Institute of Technology where he established the Bureau of Salesmanship Research.

Scott contributed to military psychology by spearheading a system for classifying and promoting army personnel during World War I. His

efforts were rewarded with the Distinguished Service Medal in 1919. In the same year, Northwestern University recalled its notable alumnus to serve as president, and for nearly two decades Scott built the institution academically and structurally into one of America's leading universities.

S. S. BROWN

SCRIPTURE, EDWARD WHEELER (1864–1945)

Scripture was one of the pioneering American psychologists who took the Ph.D. degree under Wundt at Leipzig in the late nineteenth century at about the same time as other American psychologists such as C. H. Judd, E. B. Titchener, and G. S. Hall. His thesis, which he completed in 1891, involved the association of ideas, one of the popular areas of experimentation at the Leipzig laboratory.

He taught at Clark University and then was invited by G. T. Ladd to teach experimental psychology at Yale University. He was in charge of the laboratory there from the time of his arrival in 1892, but officially served as director from 1898 to 1903. In 1902, there was an upheaval in Yale's Psychology Department, and he was dismissed after a year's leave of absence.

In 1897, Scripture wrote *The new psychology*, which was basically a manual for experimental psychology. It presented pictures of apparatus and discussions of methods and measurement procedures. There was no theory. The "new" psychology referred to experiments on reaction time, psychophysics, and sensory processes. While at Yale, he started the publication of the *Studies from the Yale Psychological Laboratory*. Of the 45 studies published in 10 years, 23 were by Scripture alone or in collaboration with others.

After leaving Yale, Scripture went to Munich to receive a M.D. degree in 1906, and was a professor at Vienna from 1923 to 1933. He coined the term *armchair psychology* to describe those psychologies that state theories and speculations without experimental verification.

R. W. LUNDIN

SEARS, ROBERT R. (1908–1989)

Sears received the A.B. degree from Stanford University and the Ph.D. degree from Yale University in 1932. His initial interests in physiological psychology shifted to personality and motivation in his first appointment at the University of Illinois. During the next decade, he performed a number of verification studies on psychoanalytic concepts, culminating in the publication of his *Survey of objective studies of psychoanalytic concepts* (1943). At Yale, between 1936 and 1942, he participated in research and theory building in the Institute of Human Relations, and was a coauthor of *Frustration and aggression* (Dollard, et al.). This was the first major attempt to bring Freud's psychoanalytic theory and Hull's behavior theory together.

Sears turned to the developmental study of personality in 1942, when he became director of the Iowa Child Welfare Research Station. Working with preschool children, he and a research team (V. Nowlis, J. Whiting, P. S. Sears) investigated the child-rearing antecedents of dependency and aggression. A major finding was the influence of punishment as an inducer of aggression. At Iowa, also, the two Sears published the first research on the effects of father absence. In 1949, Sears established another laboratory at the Harvard Graduate School of Education, from which came the multiauthored *Patterns of child rearing*. He continued research on early childhood when he went to Stanford as department head in 1953, publishing *Identification and child rearing* in 1965, but much of his time was devoted to university administration after he became dean of the School of Humanities and Sciences in 1961. In later years, he has continued the Terman Gifted Children longitudinal research and has published psychobiographical papers on Mark Twain.

SEASHORE, CARL EMIL (1866–1949)

Seashore received the Ph.D. degree at Yale University in 1895, and subsequently worked in the Yale psychological laboratory under Edward Scripture. He then transferred to the University of Iowa, and for many years devoted his experimental efforts there to the study of the psychology of music. He is considered the leading pioneer in this area. In 1919, he published the first set of tests to measure various aspects of musical talent. Seashore's thesis was that musical talent consisted of many different capacities. His initial tests measured the ability to discriminate various aspects of tone, including pitch, loudness, time, rhythm, consonance, and tonal memory. In 1939, the tests were revised, in this battery, the test of consonance was dropped and one for timbre discrimination was added.

Seashore maintained that these talents or capacities were strictly inherited and were not necessarily related to each other, but the person who scored well on all in the ability to make fine discriminations in these areas would be in the best possible position to take up the study of a musical instrument. *The psychology of music* by Seashore remains a classic in the field. In it he related the various aspects of musical discriminations to the sound wave.

Besides attempting to predict musical success through his tests, he devised experimental techniques for measuring musical performance on the piano, violin, and voice. In his studies of the vibrato, using an apparatus he invented called the tonoscope, he measured the degree in fluctuation in the production of a musical sound. In the book *In search of beauty in music*, he set forth his theory of musical aesthetics. He believed that aesthetic experience is closely related to how a person reacts emotionally to the music heard.

R. W. LUNDIN

SECHENOV, IVAN MIKHAILOVICH (1829–1905)

The founder of Russian physiology, Sechenov was mentor to Ivan Pavlov and instrumental in bringing psychology and science together. He was born in the village that is now Sechenovo, and first became a military engineer before studying medicine, in which he completed his degree at Moscow University in 1856. He later studied in the laboratories of Johannes Müller and Hermann von Helmholtz.

In 1862, while working in the laboratory of Claude Bernard, Sechenov discovered the inhibition of spinal reflexes by the central nervous system. Although simple spinal reflexes could involve invariable connections between receptors and effectors via the spinal cord, he found that the reflexes were often modified by influences from the brain. This discovery, and his early work on feedback control of movement, led to his popular text *Reflexes of the brain*. Renewed interest in Sechenov's work led to the reprinting of that book in English in 1965.

Sechenov held that behavior and even consciousness were comprised of reflexes. He firmly believed that through physiological study of reflexes the major questions of psychology could be answered—that psychology, properly studied, was the domain of physiologists, not of philosophers. His belief in the reflex as the "atom" of behavior and in physiology as the means of studying psychology is obvious in the work of his students, Ivan Pavlov and Vladimir Bekhterev.

T. KEITH-LUCAS

SEGUIN, EDOUARD (1812–1880)

Seguin started his career as assistant to the eminent physician Jean Itard. In 1798, there had come to Itard's attention a wild boy found by some hunters in the forest of Aveyron. Itard had attempted to civilize the boy, but abandoned the project because he felt the boy was an idiot or an imbecile and that little could be done for him in the way of training. Seguin continued to work with the boy because he felt the gains made, even though slight, made the boy happier and better adjusted. He then devoted himself to the training of retarded children and was eventually put in charge of a school for the mentally retarded in 1837. The first institution of its kind, it served as a beginning for other training schools in France and the United States for the education of the mentally handicapped.

In 1848, Seguin migrated to the United States, where he originated sense and muscle training techniques whereby retarded children were given intensive exercise in sensory discriminations and in the development of muscle control. In 1866, he developed a test, now known as the Seguin Form Board. It was originally devised in conjunction with his program for training the mentally retarded. Basically the test consists of 10 pieces of wood of various geometric forms that are removed from their slots in the board by the examiner and stacked in a standard arrangement. The subject is instructed to put the blocks back in their spaces as quickly as possible. It is employed now as one of the subtests in the Arthur Point Scale of Performance Intelligence. The significance of Seguin's test is that it was the first to be used as some measure of intellectual functioning.

R. W. LUNDIN

SELIGMAN, MARTIN E. P. (1942–   )

Seligman's intellectual life began when he failed to make the eighth-grade basketball team in his home town of Albany, N.Y. Cut off thereby from everything of value to 13-year-olds, he began to read books, and Freud's *Introductory lectures* particularly impressed him. Over the years, his sense of what counted as valid insight was to change, but not his sense of what counted as an important question.

He took his undergraduate degree at Princeton University and then studied experimental psychology with Richard L. Solomon at the University of Pennsylvania. Working first with Bruce Overmier, and then with Steven Maier, Seligman took seriously the passivity of dogs pretreated with inescapable trauma. Maier and Seligman tested and found wanting conventional learning-theoretic explanations and ultimately proposed that animals could learn that outcomes were independent of their actions; that the animals were, in short, helpless.

After attaining the Ph.D. degree in 1967, Seligman taught at Cornell University until 1969 and returned to the University of Pennsylvania in 1970. In 1971, he rejoined the Psychology Department of the university after spending a year in clinical training in the Psychiatry Department. He was promoted to professor in 1976, and during this period he published *Helplessness: On depression, development, and death*.

In 1978, with Lyn Abramson and John Teasdale, he reformulated the helplessness model, claiming that attributions governed the expression of helplessness. He then found that individuals who have an attributional style that interprets the cause of bad events as internal, stable, and global are at risk for depression when bad events occur.

SELYE, HANS (1907–1982)

Selye has become internationally known as the father of the stress concept. He studied in Prague, Paris, and Rome, receiving both the M.D. and Ph.D. from the German University at Prague and then the D. Sci. from McGill University in Montreal, Canada. As a medical student he became aware of what he called the syndrome of "just being sick." This led to the development of his stress concept. The whole nature of stress that is so widely discussed today led him to realize that many degenerative diseases including coronary thrombosis, kidney failure, arthritis, peptic ulcer, hypertension, and possibly cancer can result from the uncontrollable handling of stress.

The mechanisms, of course, are biological. Fairly early in his career he identified the general adaptation syndrome (GAS) to refer to the various stressors in life and our general reaction to them. He identified three stages of GAS: (1) the alarm reaction, (2) resistance, and (3) exhaustion. What are commonly called psychosomatic symptoms occur and persist in the body's defense system as reactions to prolonged stress. These biological findings led Selye to investigate in more detail both the psychological and philosophical implications of stress. He believed in what he called altruistic egoism. This is interpreted as gaining the respect and goodwill of others.

He served as professor and director of the Institute of Experimental Medicine and Surgery at the University of Montreal and as president of the International Institute of Stress. He was the author of 18 books and hundreds of articles. His best-known books include *The psychology and pathology of exposure to stress, The stress of life, Selye's guide to stress research,* and *Stress without distress.*

R. W. LUNDIN

SERPELL, ROBERT (1944–   )

Serpell was educated at a French lycée, an English "public school," Singapore University, and Oxford University, before going to Zambia to join the newly established Human Development Research Unit (HDRU) in 1965. At Oxford, his training was centered on biological and experimental psychology under Sutherland and Mackintosh and on the linguistic approach to philosophy established by Wittgenstein and Austin. His active involvement in the student politics of race relations brought him into association with Tajfel, as well as the Anti-Apartheid Movement.

The first phase of his research (1966–1972) centered on the application of attention theory to various aspects of child development, notably perceptual errors on Western intelligence tests and second-language learning in Zambia, and basic literacy and numeracy for severely mentally handicapped children in England. During this period, he also collaborated with Deregowski on studies of pictorial perception, and obtained his doctorate from Sussex University (1969).

Subsequently his interests shifted toward the interface between socciocultural factors and behavior: the cultural definition of intelligence, situational code switching in speech, and community participation in health care and in special education. His introductory textbook, *Culture's influence on behaviour* (1976), is generally critical of grand theory in cross-cultural psychology, and leans toward cultural relativism. His articles have appeared in many journals and books.

The sometimes political flavor of Serpell's writing reflects his situation as a naturalized citizen of Zambia while its wide range arises from his work experience. At the University of Zambia, he was head of the Psychology Department from 1974 to 1977, and then director of the multidisciplinary Institute for African Studies (1977–1983). In both settings, he has consistently worked at bringing research to bear directly on public policy.

SEXTON, VIRGINIA STAUDT (1916–   )

Sexton received the B.A. degree from Hunter College in classics and the M.A. and Ph.D. (1946) degrees in psychology from Fordham University. In 1944, she began her college teaching career at Notre Dame College of Staten Island, where she remained until 1952. Following a Ford Foundation Fellowship spent in research on the evaluation of the somatotherapies in schizophrenia at the New York State Psychiatric Institute, she was appointed to the faculty of Hunter College of the City University of New York. She was named professor of psychology emerita in 1979. In that same year, she joined the faculty of psychology at St. John's University, Jamaica, N.Y.

Sexton's principal research interests are history of psychology, international psychology, and psychology of women. Among her publications are five books on the history of psychology published with Henryk Misiak: *Catholics in psychology; History of psychology: An overview; Historical perspectives in psychology; Phenomenological, existential and humanistic psychologies;* and *Psychology around the world.* For two years she served as associate editor of *Psychological Abstracts* (1961–1962). Sexton has been president of the American Catholic Psychological Association (1965); member and chair of the New York State Board of Psychology (1971–1978); vice-president of the New York Academy of Sciences (1979–1982); president of the International Council of Psychologists (1981–1982); president of the New York State Psychological Association (1982–1983); member of the Board of Directors of the Eastern Psychological Association (1977–1980); and member of the Board of Directors of the American Psychological Association since 1982.

SHAKOW, DAVID (1901–1982)

Shakow received the undergraduate and graduate degrees from Harvard University. He worked for several years as a psychologist in mental hospitals, including the McLean Hospital, Worcester State Hospital, and Boston Psychopathic Hospital. Next he became affiliated with the Worcester Child Guidance Clinic. In 1946, he became professor of psychology at the University of Illinois College of Medicine. He served as consultant to many commissions and committees and in 1967 became senior research psychologist with the National Institute of Mental Health.

Shakow was the recipient of many honors and awards for his contributions to clinical psychology. He was the coauthor of *The influence of Freud on American psychology (1963)* and author of *Clinical psychology as science and profession: A forty-year odyssey (1969).*

P. E. LICHTENSTEIN

SHEEHAN, PETER (1940–   )

Sheehan obtained his early tertiary education at the University of Sydney, where he received the Ph.D. degree in 1965. He has served on the faculties of the University of Pennsylvania, the City College of the City University of New York, and the University of New England, Armidale, Australia. Currently he is professor of psychology at the University of Queensland, a position he has held since 1973.

Sheehan is a Fellow of the Academy of the Social Sciences in Australia, the Australian Psychological Society, and the American Psychological Association. He is past president of the Australian Psychological Society and has been a member of the Australian Research Grants Committee since 1979.

Sheehan's major fields of research interest are mental imagery, hypnosis, and research methodology in the social sciences and he has published extensively in these fields. He is editor of *The function and nature of imagery,* and coauthor of *Methodologies of hypnosis* and *Hypnosis and experience.* He serves on the editorial boards of five major professional journals, is a past member of the Australian Vice-Chancellors' Committee's Inter-University Committee on Research, and a current member of the Australian Commonwealth Cinematograph Films Board of Review. He assumed the chairmanship of the Queen Elizabeth II Fellowship and Australian Research Grants Committee in 1983.

SHELDON, WILLIAM HERBERT (1899–1977)

A native of Warwick, R. I., Sheldon received the undergraduate degree from Brown University, the master's degree from the University of Colorado, and the Ph.D. degree (1925) and M.D. degree (1933) from the University of Chicago. The godson of William James, he developed his godfather's interests in classification. By the age of 12, he was a recognized numismatist and later wrote two important books on coin classification. He held positions at almost a dozen universities, most notably at Harvard where S. S. Stevens was a collaborator in the early 1940s. Some historians feel his life's work was laid out by William James' protege, Martin Peck, who said that Freud had done but half the job of emancipating human beings. What remained was the need for a classification scheme of the constitutional patterns underlying psychiatric patterns.

Sheldon developed an empirical basis for the structural theory of personality first suggested by Hippocrates and Galen. The most notable of some 20 eighteenth and twentieth century structural theorists was Kretschmer, partly because Sheldon refined what were essentially Kretschmer's three basic body types. A structural theory is quite simple: Body structure, and body structure alone, determines personality. A fat man is jolly; a skinny kid is a withdrawn bookworm; a "muscle man" is vigorously outgoing.

Sheldon's 1940 *Varieties of human physique* describes some 76 body types or somatotypes based on 4000 men (17 basic anthropometric measurements made from photographs). Each individual was rated from 1 (low) to 7 on each body type: endomorphy (generally hefty), mesomorphy (essentially muscular development), and ectomorphy (thin tissue development). Santa Claus would be 7–2–1; Wilt the Stilt, 1–1–7; and the average man, 4–4–4.

In 1942, Sheldon published *Varieties of temperament* corresponding to the somatotypes: endomorphy-visceratonia (sociable, relaxed, affectionate), mesomorphy-somatotonia (energetic, competitive), ectomorphy-cerebrotonia (restrained, inhibited). Critics have noted with disfavor that the original personality types were based on the data of only 33 male college students.

Although proper somatotyping is quite complex (see *Atlas of Men),* a rough index of body type can be obtained by dividing height in inches by the cube root of weight in pounds; endomorphs tend to be under 12, mesomorphs about 12½, and ectomorphs at least 14.

Body type and personality type correlate about 0.80 in Sheldon's work, however, such high correlations were not found by others. The problem, of course, is why not a perfect relationship if physique is the *sole* determining factor?

Sheldon's work has not gone unnoticed. Bill Wilson, a cofounder of Alcoholics Anonymous, credits Sheldon with providing the philosophical foundation of that organization.

SHERIF, MUZAFER (1906–1988)

Sherif received the B.A. degree from Izmir International College and the M.A. degree from Istambual University. He came to the United States in 1929, where he entered Harvard University and earned a second M.A. degree in 1932. He returned to Turkey where he began to work on norm formulation that eventually resulted in his doctoral dissertation. In 1935 he received the Ph.D. degree from Columbia University. He returned to Turkey for a second time but found himself in conflict with the Turkish government and some officials at Ankara University over certain of their pro-Nazi attitudes. He was imprisoned and put in solitary confinement, but he was eventually released through the efforts of the U.S. State Department and of a number of influential American psychologists with whom he had been associated at Columbia. He spent the next 2 yr at Princeton University, where he collaborated with Hadly Cantril on *The psychology of ego-involvement.*

His collaboration with Carl Hovland on the anchoring effects of social judgment resulted in the book *Social judgment, assimilation and contrast effects in communication and cultural change.* For the next 16 yr he taught at the University of Oklahoma, where he published his best-known works: *Intergroup conflict and cooperation* and the *Introduction to social psychology* (with Carolyn Wood). In 1966, he and Wood joined the faculty at the Pennsylvania State University: she in psychology and he in sociology.

In 1967 he received the APA's Distinguished Contribution Award and the first Cooley-Mead Award for contributions to social psychology from the American Sociological Association. His efforts mark him as one of the scientific pioneers in social psychology.

R. W. LUNDIN

SHERRINGTON, CHARLES SCOTT (1857–1952)

Sherrington received the M.D. degree at Cambridge, and taught and conducted research at Liverpool, London, and Oxford. He was Gifford lecturer at Edinburgh and received the Nobel prize in physiology and medicine. He was knighted in 1922.

While at Liverpool, Sherrington began investigations in sensory psychology. He published studies on color vision and flicker and wrote on the tactual and muscular senses. He introduced the terms *interoceptor,* *exteroceptor,* and *proprioceptor,* and demonstrated the existence of receptor cells essential to coordination in the muscles.

No work in neurophysiology has had greater influence than Sherrington's *The integrative action of the nervous system.* He introduced the concepts of neuron, synapse, and integrative action of the nervous system. In his work on the reflex, he studied it as a functional unit operating not in isolation, but under control of higher levels of neural activity. He placed great emphasis on the concept of integration and investigated its mechanisms. In so doing, he discovered reciprocal innervation and worked out many details of excitation and inhibition.

Sherrington's more speculative views found expression in *Man on his nature* (1940). He emphasized human consciousness and its origins in living substance. He remained a dualist in his psychology, never accepting any view that would reduce mind to brain function.

P. E. LICHTENSTEIN

SHEVENELL, RAYMOND HENRY (1908–   )

Shevenell was brought up in Dover, N.H. He became an Oblate of Mary Immaculate (O.M.I.) in 1929, and was ordained a Roman Catholic priest in 1934. He was educated at Dover, Sherbrooke, Harvard, and Ottawa (Ontario), receiving the Ph.D. degree in 1949, and subsequently the honorary degrees of D.Ed. (Sherbrooke, 1967) and D.Ps. (Moncton, N.B., 1976).

Shevenell was strongly influenced by Gordon Allport, Aristotle, and St. Thomas Aquinas. He pioneered in teaching psychology at the University of Ottawa, where he founded an institute in 1941. Appointed professor in 1944, he was named professor emeritus in 1979, and served as dean, in 1955–1973. Also a pioneer in professional psychology, he founded a guidance center in 1942, a child guidance clinic in 1953, and a psychological services center in 1965.

He is a member of the Canadian Psychological Association, the American Psychological Association, and the Ontario Psychological Association among others, as well as a registered psychologist in Ontario.

Shevenell has taught Thomistic psychology and Christian personalism. He also prepared French versions of American paper-and-pencil tests and wrote a bilingual textbook, *Recherches et theses (Research and theses).*

SHIRAI, TSUNE (1910–   )

A graduate of Tokyo Women's Christian College, Shirai received the bachelor's degree from Tokyo Bunrika University in 1946, where she had to repeat her undergraduate studies to qualify for the B.A. degree. Her previous college, as a woman's college, could not award degrees because of the sexual discrimination existing in the academic field prior to World War II. She received the Ph.D. degree from the latter school in 1954 and a Litt. D. degree from the former in 1961. She taught at her alma mater for 16 years until she retired in 1976.

As a developmental psychologist, Shirai has studied transposition problems with children and has found their transposition behavior conspicuously different from that of the animals that had previously served as subjects in that field. She is also interested in the problem of early experience and did considerable laboratory work with rats.

Since her retirement, Shirai has led a team of psychologists and television producers seeking to make educational TV programs for 2-years-olds. She is writing a series of 12 books entitled *Early childhood education in the world* on the basis of data acquired in interviews with specialists in the field and observations of educational facilities collected during her visits to 12 countries in 1982 and 1983.

SHNEIDMAN, EDWIN S. (1918–   )

Shneidman is a suicidologist and thanatologist. A professor of thanatology at the University of California at Los Angeles, he has degrees from UCLA (A.B. and M.A.) and the University of Southern California (M.S. and Ph.D.). He was codirector of the Los Angeles Suicide Prevention Center from 1955 to 1960, and from 1966 to 1969, he was chief of the National Institute of Mental Health Center for the Study of Suicide Prevention. He has been a public health service special research fellow and visiting professor at Harvard and a fellow at the Center for Advanced Study in the Behavioral Sciences at Stanford, has served as president of the divisions of Clinical and Public Service of the APA, as president of the Society for Projective Techniques, and was founder–president of the American Association of Suicidology.

From 1971 to 1981, Shneidman edited the journal *Suicide and Life-Threatening Behavior*. His edited books include *Thematic test analysis, Essays in self-destruction, On the nature of suicide, Death and the college student, Suicidology: Contemporary developments, Death: Current perspectives, Endeavors in psychology: Selections from the personology of Henry A. Murray,* and *Suicide thoughts and reflections.* He is coeditor of *Clues to suicide, The cry for help,* and *The psychology of suicide.* The author of the MAPS Test, *Deaths of man, Voices of Death,* and *Definition of suicide.* He has written more than 100 articles on death and suicide.

Shneidman's main lifelong professional interests have been suicidology and thanatology. He also has an abiding interest in logic and projective techniques.

SIEGEL, MAX (1918–1984)

Siegel's career has had three distinct aspects: as a teacher, as a therapist, and as an activist in psychological affairs. Upon graduation from New York University in 1951, he trained at the William Alanson White Institute of Psychoanalysis, and began his teaching career at the Brooklyn College of the City College of New York, where he became associate dean of students in charge of counseling services, and professor and head of the department of the graduate program in school psychology. For 15 years, he was clinical professor of psychology of the postdoctoral program in psychotherapy at Adelphi University.

Concerned with understanding the process of psychotherapy, Siegel concentrated on the group method. As an interpersonal psychologist and psychoanalyst, he has shown a strong humanistic, existential, and transpersonal bent. He published two books and more than 40 professional papers. However, he was probably best known for his strong activist positions relative to professional psychology, concerning himself with a wide variety of matters, including professional ethics.

Siegel was active in various psychological organizations, and was a member of the American Psychology Board of Social and Ethical Responsibility in Psychology. He was president of seven psychological associations. He was named Psychologist of the Year in New York in 1976 and has been the recipient of other honors, including election to the presidency of the American Psychological Association in 1983.

SIGUAN, MIGUEL (1918–   )

Siguan studied philosophy in Barcelona and, after the war, studied industrial psychology in London. Since 1953, he has been the principal proponent of the new industrial psychology in Spain (inspired by the work of Elton Mayo), and of the objectives of industrial democracy. He summarized his ideas on this subject in *Human problems of industrial work* In the decades of the 1950s and 1960s, Spain went through an accelerated industrial expansion that caused great social changes. Siguan, in further dedication to industrial psychology, directed various psychosocial investigations concerning these changes. For a book *(Del campo al suburbio, Madrid)* on the life of immigrants from the south of Spain living in the slums of Madrid, he received the national prize for literature.

In 1960, he was appointed head of the Department of Psychology at the University of Barcelona. From then on, without abandoning his social interests, he dedicated himself primarily to topics related to language. In the field of infant language, he has been one of the pioneers, attempting to explain the origins of verbal language as arising from nonverbal communication. Trilingual since childhood, Siguan's principal dedication has been toward the problems of bilingualism. His investigations concern the learning of two languages in early childhood, memory processes of the bilingual, and bilingualism and personality. Interested also in history, he has published a history of *Psychology in Catalonia* and various articles on contemporary psychology in Spain.

SIMON, HERBERT A. (1916—   )

Simon, with Allen Newell, has pioneered in creating information-processing psychology. He earned the B.A. and Ph.D. degrees at the University of Chicago, where he majored in political science and minored in economics. His doctoral research on decision making in organizations, later expanded into *Administrative behavior* (1947), brought him to psychology, and by the middle 1950s his major research interest lay in the psychology of problem solving.

Simon has been active in mathematical economics and organization theory, advancing the thesis that the economists' assumption of "economic man" claimed excessive powers for human mental processes and needed to be replaced by an empirically based theory of "bounded rationality." His research and its applications to economic decision making were recognized in 1978 by the award of the Nobel Prize in economics.

About 1954, Simon and Newell conceived of using computer programming languages to build theories of human symbolic behavior. Inventing (with J. C. Shaw) the first list-processing languages as tools for this task, they constructed and tested empirically a series of simulation programs, work subsequently synthesized in *Human problem solving.* Simon and his colleagues showed, in *Models of thought,* how a wide range of cognitive processes in problem solving and problem understanding, concept attainment, language behavior, and language learning can be explained in information-processing terms and modeled with computer programs.

To help institutionalize and diffuse these new scientific paradigms, Simon has played major administrative roles at Carnegie-Mellon University, and participated in the National Academy of Sciences, the National Research Council, and the President's Science Advisory Committee.

SINGER, GEORGE (1922–   )

Singer obtained his high school education in Vienna, Austria. He migrated to Sydney, Australia, in 1939, and graduated with a diploma in industrial chemistry from Sydney Technical College in 1945. He received the B.A. degree with honors in psychology, the M.A. degree with honors in psychology, and the Ph.D. degree in 1965, all from the University of Sydney.

Singer served in the chemical industry until 1948, in industrial management until 1960, as a lecturer and senior lecturer in psychology at the University of Sydney until 1967, and as associate professor of psychology at Macquarie University, Sydney, until 1971. In 1972, he became Foundation professor of psychology and Foundation dean of the School of Behavioural Sciences at La Trobe University, Melbourne.

His major contributions to psychological research are in perception, in the psychobiology of eating and drinking behaviour and drug intake behaviors, and the application of biochemical methods to the assessment of industrial stress and stress management programs. A major feature of Singer's research is the translation of findings from the laboratory into clinical and industrial settings.

Singer is the author of 10 books (five are social satire and five on psychology) and about 140 articles in international scientific journals. He was instrumental in the formation of the Australian Psychological Society in 1965 and was its president in 1975. He is a member of the International Commission on the Physiology of Food and Fluid Intake and of the International Organization of Psychophysiology. He has received many research awards and was a Senior Foreign Research Scientist at Syracuse University in Syracuse, N.Y., in 1974, sponsored by the National Science Foundation. He also was a visiting professor at the Medical School, New York University, in 1969–1970, at Syracuse University in 1973–1974, at Ben Gurion University, Israel, in 1979, and at Stockholm University and the Karolinska Institute in 1979–1980.

SINGH, SHEO DAN (1932–1979)

Singh received the master's degree from Aligarh Muslim University and the Ph.D. degree from the University of London in 1958. He served as professor and department head from 1959 to 1961 at Agra University, and was a reader in the Department of Psychology at Punjab University from 1961 to 1967. Earlier, during 1957–1958, he worked in the animal laboratory in the Royal Bethelem Hospital in England on the problem of emotionality in rats. In 1967, Singh joined Western Washington State College as a visiting professor. He was a visiting professor of primate research at the University of Wisconsin during 1967 and 1969. He then joined the Department of Psychology at the University of New Brunswick as associate professor, where he established a Primate Laboratory. In 1970, he became a consultant at the Regional Primate Research Center at Wisconsin University. He returned to India in that same year as professor of psychology and dean of the Division of Behavioral Science at Meerut University, and served there until his death.

Singh received most of his training in comparative and physiological psychology at the Institute of Psychiatry in London, and at the Primate Research Center and Department of Neuroanatomy and Physiology at the University of Wisconsin. He established India's first Primate Research Laboratory at Meerut, and for field studies, chose the Dehra Dun forests. His major area of interest was the impact of urban conditions on the development of social, emotional, and cognitive behavior and the brain chemistry of rhesus monkeys. He was deeply interested in studying the involvement of the frontal lobe in the social and sexual development of rhesus monkeys. Besides publishing in the area of primate behavior and behavioral pharmacology, Singh also published studies on cognitive and personality development. His paper on urban monkeys in *Scientific American* has become a classic.

In addition to his membership on many committees, Singh was a member of the Psychology Panel of the University Grants Commission, and was a National Professor. He was very anxious to improve the status of psychology in India. One of the few Indian psychologists to have achieved international fame, he was highly individualistic, courageous in his convictions, dedicated, and talented.

SINHA, DURGANAND (1922–   )

Sinha was educated at Patna University and at Cambridge University in England, obtaining the B.A. and M.A. degrees in philosophy from Patna University, and the M.Sc. degree (psychology) from Cambridge University in 1949, where he worked with Fredric C. Bartlett and D. Russell Davis. He taught at Patna University and the Indian Institute of Technology (Kharagpur) before joining Allahabad University in 1961, where he established the Department of Psychology. Since January 1982, he has been the director of the Institute of Social Studies, Patna. His early research contributions were in the area of remembering as it takes place in real-life situations, rumors, and measurement and correlates of anxiety. He has also contributed to industrial psychology, in particular, to psychological factors in absenteeism and job satisfaction.

During the past two decades, Sinha's main area of research has been psychological dimensions of socioeconomic development, deprivation and poverty, and cognitive style and cross-cultural psychology generally. Currently he is investigating the impact of certain sociocultural factors, especially family experience and life-style, on the development of psychological differentiation.

He has received many professional honors and has occupied high positions in various national and international associations, including the presidency of the International Association of Cross-Cultural Psychology (1980–1982) and the Indian Psychological Association (1978–1979).

SKINNER, BURHUS FREDRICK (1904–1990)

Skinner is judged by many as one of a half dozen most important psychologists of the 20th century. However, like anyone who takes a strong position, he had throughout his career many critics. He will be regarded as a great teacher, experimental psychologist, behavior theorist, and never-ending promoter of a strictly objectiver psychology.

Skinner received the A.B. from Hamilton College, where he majored in English and the classics. He received the M.A. and Ph.D. (1931) from Harvard University. After a period of postdoctoral research, he went to the University of Minnisota (1931–1943), Indiana University (1943–1948), and then returned to Harvard for the remainder of his teaching career.

During the 1930s his experimental research efforts were devoted to developing a set of learning principles using white rats as his subjects. When he went to Indiana, he began to use pigeons instead. His research with the rats resulted in the pbulication of his first book, *The behavior of organisms*. Perhaps his most important contribution to experimental psychology was the invention of the operant-conditioning chamber, commonly referred to as the Skinner box. In the original version with rats, the animals pressed a lever on the side of the cage to receive what Skinner called a reinforcement (usually a pellet of food). Later, Skinner and others adapted the apparatus for pigeons, monkeys, humans, and a variety of other organisms. This apparatus has been used for thousands of experiments to test various principles of learning. The rate of responding is measured by a cumulative recorder, also invented by Skinner.

As the period of the 1960s approached, Skinner became appalled by the inefficiency of American education, and he put his efforts to developing a teaching machine and programmed learning. In this process the subject is allowed to proceed at his or her own rate in very small steps until a body of knowledge has been mastered. Subjects are given immediate feedback as to the correctness of their answers. Over the years programmed learning never was adopted by most educators, perhaps because they were afraid that the machine would take over their jobs. However, it has been and is being used in business, industry, and other aspects of human endeavor.

Earlier in 1953, Skinner applied his ideas to human behavior, which resulted in the book *Science and human behavior*. Earlier, in 1948, he tried his hand at writing a novel (*Walden two*), a book that was used more in psychology classes than in English assignments. It presented a psychological utopia. In 1957 Skinner collaborated with Charles Ferster in a large research project that culminated in the publication of *Schedules of reinforcement*, which showed that reinforcements need not be delivered after every response but could be programmed as to time and ratio. In the same year, he published *Verbal behavior*, an analysis of language applying principles of learning developed in the laboratory to human speech. His book *Beyond freedom and dignity* hit the best-seller list, but it generally received poor reviews from the literary press. In it he dealt with social issues, freedom, dignity, value, and control. Basically, his reviewers, not being psychologists, probably did not understand what he was trying to say. In the late 1970s, he wrote a three-volume autobiography: *Particulars of my life, The shaping of a behaviorist*, and *A matter of consequences*. Up until the night before his death, he continued to write and lecture.

Skinner received many awards and honors, including APA's Distinguished Contribution Award, the National Medal of Science Award, and the Gold Medal Award from the American Psychological Foundation. Shortly before his death, he received a special award from the American Psychological Association for a lifetime of distinguished service to psychology, the first ever to be given.

Besides the establishment of a division of the American Psychological Association (Division 25) devoted to his brand of psychology, several journals are devoted to experiments and theorizing of his position, the most important being *The Journal of the Experimental Analysis of Behavior*. Like the founder of behaviorism, John B. Watson, Skinner's ideas have been controversial. He remained a radical behaviorist to the end. Those who are symphathetic to his position believe he did more to promote psychology as a science than anyone else of the time. He fostered a completely objective approach and opposed the mentalism of psychoanalysis, humanistic, and cognitive psychologies.

R. W. LUNDIN

SMALL, WILLARD STANTON (1870–1943)

Small received the Ph.D. degree in psychology from Clark University. He taught at Michigan State Normal College and Los Angeles State Normal School and held a variety of administrative positions in education. In 1923, he became dean of the College of Education at the University of Maryland. Small is known for his paper published in 1899 that described his study of the mental processes of the rat in solving a copy of the Hampton Court maze. He reported results supporting the work of Thorndike. The maze technique used by Small caught on and became the accepted procedure with the white rat as the preferred subject in studies of animal learning in the United States. Small emphasized that

he had developed a technique that permitted one to translate thinking into sensory and motor terms.

P. E. LICHTENSTEIN

SMITH, EDWARD E. (1940–   )

Smith received the B.A. in psychology from Brooklyn College and the Ph.D. from the University of Michigan. He then served as a public health service officer at St. Elizabeth's Hospital in Washington D.C. He began his acdemic career at the University of Wisconsin in 1968, moved to Stanford University in 1970, then to the BBN labs in Cambridge, Massachusetts, in 1979, and then (back) to the University of Michigan in 1986.

Smith has worked in the areas of perception, memory, and text processing, but his main contributions have been in categorization and reasoning. His most influential work on categorization includes a number of papers on semantic memory published in the 1970s, his 1981 book *Categories and concepts* (with Douglas Medin), and a number of papers on conceptual combination published in the 1980s. In addition to his scholarly publications, he has coauthored a number of textbooks, including *Introduction to psychology*.

Smith has been active in journal reviewing and professional organizations. He has been a consulting editor for 10 journals and was an editor of *Cognitive Science* (1981–1985). He was elected to the Governing Board of the Cognitive Science Society (1982–1987) and was chair of that organization in 1987. He was elected to the Governing Board of the Psychonomics Society (1987–1992) and to the Society of Experimental Psychologists in 1986, and was appointed to the Executive Committee of that society in 1990.

SMITH, M. BREWSTER (1919–   )

Educated at Reed, Stanford, and Harvard before World War II, Smith contributed to the psychology of opinions and attitudes, and more generally to the social psychology of personality. In various advisory roles to government and in organized psychology (he was president of the Society for the Psychological Study of Social Issues in 1958–1959 and of the American Psychological Association in 1978), he encouraged the application of psychology to social problems.

During World War II, he worked with Samuel Stouffer, Carl Hovland, and Arnold Rose in U.S. Army studies that laid a basis both for survey research and for the experimental study of persuasive communication. Upon returning to Harvard, he collaborated with Jerome Bruner and Robert White on *Opinions and personality*, a classic of functional attitude theory.

In a career of teaching and administration at Vassar, New York University, the University of California at Berkeley, the University of Chicago, and the University of California at Santa Cruz, he became increasingly committed to a view of human psychology as rooted in its historical and cultural context and requiring interpretive methods as well as those more characteristic of natural science. Empirically, he studied antisemitism and race prejudice, competence in Peace Corps volunteers, and moral judgment in the student activists of the 1960s. His later theoretical work sought to link the complementarities of scientific and humanistic psychology in a focus on selfhood or personality, carrying forward, as he saw it, the traditions of his teachers Gordon Allport and Henry Murray.

SOLOMON, RICHARD LESTER (1919–1992)

Solomon received all three of his academic degrees from Brown University (A.B., M.S., Ph.D., 1947). During World War II, he served as

Research Psychologist for the Office of Scientific Research and Development. He has taught at Brown and Harvard, and also at the University of Pennsylvania, where he was director of a research program involving the effects of Pavlovian conditioning on instrumental learned behavior. In 1966, he received the Distinguished Scientific Contribution Award from the American Psychological Association.

His research has involved many areas of experimental psychology, with both human and animal subjects. He has studied problems in sensory discrimination, word recognition thresholds, and Pavlovian and instrumental conditioning in lower animals. Of particular importance have been his many studies of traumatic avoidance learning in dogs. In these studies, he explored many parameters of the problem. For example, he found that the avoidance of electric shock can be quickly learned in a matter of a few trials, and once the behavior has been acquired, the animals will continue to avoid the shock for hundreds of trials when a buzzer is pressed as a warning signal.

SPEARMAN, CHARLES EDWARD (1863–1945)

Spearman came to psychology relatively late in life. As a youth, he entered a career in the military service, which he referred to many years later as "the mistake of my life . . . for these almost wasted years I have since mourned as bitterly as ever Tiberius did for his lost legions" (Spearman, 1930, p. 300). Having attained the rank of major, he retired from the British army at the age of 34, and thenceforth devoted himself completely to academic studies, except for a brief return to service during the Boer War. His first love, philosophy, along with his scientific and mathematical bent, led him to psychology, in which he earned the Ph.D. degree at Leipzig, under Wilhelm Wundt. After further study of psychology in Germany, under Kulpe and Müller, Spearman, at the age of 40 returned to London. There, on the recommendation of William McDougall, he was appointed reader in psychology at the University of London. Soon after, when McDougall moved to Oxford, Spearman succeeded him as professor of psychology at London; he held that chair for 25 years, and was succeeded by Sir Cyril Burt.

Spearman claimed Wundt and Galton as the major influences and inspiration for his psychological research. The importance of his own contributions to cognitive and differential psychology and psychometrics can hardly be exaggerated. His first important article on "General intelligence" (1904) is a landmark in the psychology of human abilities. He had discovered that individual differences on all tests of mental abilities, however diverse the knowledge and skills they call upon, are positively intercorrelated in representative samples of the general population. Spearman's predecessors had failed to make this important discovery, although they had tried, because they did not take into account the effect of measurement error (i.e., unreliability) on the correlation between tests. To solve this problem, Spearman invented the method for correcting the correlation coefficient for attenuation (i.e., weakening of the correlation because of unreliability of the correlated measurements). His discovery of consistently positive intercorrelations among diverse tests of mental abilities inspired his well-known two-factor theory: Every mental test measures a general ability, g, common to all tests, and a specific ability, s, peculiar to each test. Spearman developed a mathematical procedure, factor analysis, that permitted a rigorous test of the two-factor theory and, more important, made it possible to estimate precisely the correlation (or "factor loading") of each test in a battery of tests with the g factor. Spearman regarded g as the *sine qua non* of intelligence tests. He characterized the g factor as a capacity for grasping relationships ("the eduction of relations and correlates") and abstraction. Further empirical studies eventually forced Spearman to recognize that his two-factor theory was too simple and that other abilities ("group factors") besides g could be found in batteries of diverse tests. He conceived of g theoretically as the overall level of "mental energy" that a person could bring to bear in performing a cognitive task; other abilities were viewed as independent specialized "engines" for the performance of certain types of tasks. The theory is most fully explicated in Spearman's most famous work, *The abilities of man,* which ranks among the classics of psychology. But the development of factor analysis, aside from any theoretical interpretation of the factors themselves, is now generally recognized as Spearman's greatest contribution. His other enduring contributions to psychometric methodology are the correction of correlation for attenuation, the rank-order correlation coefficient, and the exact formulation of the relationship of test reliability to the length of the test (known as the Spearman-Brown prophesy formula).

Spearman himself valued his first book on the *Nature of intelligence* the most highly of all his efforts. It established him as the first major cognitive theorist. In it, he expressed his faith that: "Cognitive events do, like those of physics, admit throughout of being reduced to a small number of definitely formulatable principles in the sense of ultimate laws" (Spearman, 1923, p. 341). The three basic "noegenetic" laws of cognition propounded by Spearman concern the apprehension of experience and the education of relations and correlates. Although these principles are closely linked to Spearman's theory of intelligence, the most enduring aspect of his theory is the g factor in all cognitive tests. As g is a large source of individual differences that cannot be described in terms of any particular knowledge or skills required by the diverse tests that reflect g, its theoretical explanation continues to challenge present-day cognitive psychologists.

A. R. JENSEN

SPENCE, JANET TAYLOR (1923–   )

A consistent theme underlying the scholarly pursuits of Spence is motivation and how individual differences in motive strengths are related to behavior. Upon graduation from Oberlin College, she entered the clinical psychology program at Yale University and completed her doctoral studies at the University of Iowa in 1949. Interested in bringing clinical-personality phenomena into the laboratory for study and in integrating them into learning theory, Spence developed the well-known Manifest Anxiety Scale as a vehicle for testing her and Kenneth Spence's theory about the interactions between task characteristics and drive or arousal level in determining task performance, a theory that grew out of her doctoral dissertation and occupied her attention for a number of years while on the faculty at Northwestern University.

After joining the faculty at the University of Texas at Austin, her interest turned to an examination of trait and motivational differences between men and women. This work, some reported in *Masculinity and femininity,* (with Robert L. Helmreich), led to the development of several psychometric instruments, including a multidimensional measure of achievement motivation. Her most recent work has been concerned with the development and testing of a theoretical model that relates achievement motives in men and women to academic and vocational achievements. She was elected as president of the American Psychological Association in 1984.

SPENCE, KENNETH W. (1907–1967)

Over the course of his career, Spence gained eminence as a theorist, experimentalist, and methodologist, distinctions that resulted in his election to the National Academy of Sciences. He was raised in Montreal, Canada, and received the B.A. and M.A. degrees from McGill University. In 1933, he was awarded the Ph.D. degree by Yale University, where he did his dissertation with Robert Yerkes. After appointments at the Yale Laboratories of Primate Biology and the University of Virginia, he moved in 1938 to the University of Iowa, where he remained until 1964. At the time of his death, he was on the faculty at the University of Texas at Austin.

Spence's name was linked throughout his career to that of Clark L. Hull, since his theoretical and experimental contributions represented elaborations and extensions of Hull's general theory of learning and behavior. Although Spence's approach and theoretical views differed from Hull's in significant ways, such as his greater emphasis on motivational processes, both were committed to the development of an objective theory of behavior based on classical and instrumental conditioning.

In collaboration with the philosopher Gustav Bergmann, Spence sought in the philosophy of science and the tenets of logical empiricism the bases on which psychology could proceed as an objective, empirical science. His brand of pragmatic, methodological behaviorism has its roots in the early, rather than later, radical behaviorism of John B. Watson, or, more contemporaneously, of B. F. Skinner. Spence's methodological and metatheoretical interests led him to write several penetrating analyses of competing theories of behavior, in which he sought to discern the similarities as well as the more apparent differences.

His publications include *Behavior theory and conditioning,* a book outlining Hull–Spence theory that was based on the Silliman Lectures at Yale, delivered in 1955, and *Behavior theory and learning*

J. SPENCE

SPENCER, HERBERT (1820–1903)

Spencer was the son of a school master. Except for tutoring by his father, he was, for the most part, self-educated. His most important psychological work was the *Principles of psychology,* first published in 1855. In it, he considered associationism the most binding psychological principle. Along with his contemporary, Alexander Bain, he brought the whole movement of British associationism to an end. From a nonexperimental point of view, it could go no further. What was new in his book was his theory of evolutionary associationism. He began work on this theory in 1850, thus antedating Darwin by nine years. According to Spencer's theory, everything in the universe began as an expanding totality. As evolution progressed, a process of differentiation took place whereby recognizable distinct parts emerged. In humans, this resulted in the ability to comprehend more complex experiences. Along with this differentiation process, there was an integrating principle that brought things together. This was the principle of association.

Spencer applied J. B. P. Lamarck's evolutionary theory of inheritance of acquired characteristics to his own theory. He believed that when the same associations occurred over and over again in an individual, they could be passed onto that person's offspring. After many generations, these eventually would take on the form of instincts. With the publication of Charles Darwin's *Origin of species,* a different theory of evolution appeared with significant supporting data. Rather than oppose Darwin, Spencer joined forces in support of his theory of the survival of the fittest in a particular environment by means of natural selection. Darwin accepted Spencer, and called him "our philosopher."

As British associationism came to an end in the writings of Spencer and Bain, it remained for later individuals, such as Ivan Pavlov in Russia and E. L. Thorndike in the United States, to put its principles to the experimental test.

R. W. LUNDIN

SPERRY, ROGER WOLCOTT (1913–   )

Sperry won a Nobel prize (1981) for his split-brain experiments conducted at the California Institute of Technology. After receiving the B.S. and M.A. degrees from Oberlin College in Ohio, Sperry went on to the University of Chicago for the Ph.D. degree, awarded in 1941. As a Fellow at Harvard, he worked at the Yerkes Laboratories from 1941 to 1946. From 1946 to 1953, he was assistant professor of anatomy, and later associate professor of psychology, at the University of Chicago. His long tenure at the California Institute of Technology began in 1954. In addition to the Nobel prize, he has received the Warren Medal of the Society of Experimental Psychologists, the Distinguished Science Contribution award of the American Psychological Association, and the California Scientist of the Year award.

Sperry's finding, the split-brain phenomenon, has created considerable discussion among neuropsychologists, and has led to the dual personality theory.

SPINOZA, BENEDICT (BARUCH) (1632–1677)

Spinoza received his education under several rabbis and later a German tutor. He was excommunicated from the synagogue for unorthodox views, refused a chair of philosophy, and earned his living as a lens grinder. Spinoza published little but carried on extensive correspondence. His major work, *Ethics,* was published posthumously.

Spinoza's philosophy was extremely rationalistic and deductive. He identified the one true substance as God or nature, as much physical object as immaterial thought. He said that human beings, as a manifestation of God, reflect the psychophysical parallelism that prevails throughout the universe. People have two aspects, mind and body, which are basically one. This solution of the mind–body problem is known as double aspectism, and appeared to Spinoza to escape the difficulties of René Descartes' interactionism. Various modifications of this position have been, and still are, popular with psychologists.

Spinoza developed his psychological views in the context of his ethics. Psychology, and in fact all of the sciences, he believed, had one aim, which was to attain the highest possible human perfection. Given his deterministic outlook, he was inclined to seek out natural causes for human actions, appetites, and emotions. He discussed in detail the joys and pleasures of everyday living as well as the passive emotions, such as hatred and fear, that interfere with the life of reason. It was Spinoza's belief that people can live an ethical life when they have been liberated by a knowledge of nature. When people are ignorant, external nature determines their conduct, but when they have gained knowledge, they have also gained freedom to act in the light of necessity. Here Spinoza appears to have anticipated Sigmund Freud, although there is no evidence that Freud was influenced directly by Spinoza's writings.

In contrast to the cognitive emphasis in Descartes' psychology, Spinoza stressed the conative or drive element. He saw in human beings a self-preservative impulse manifested as desire when self-conscious, but otherwise as appetite.

P. E. LICHTENSTEIN

SPRANGER, EDUARD (1882–1963)

Spranger was a follower of the German philosopher/psychologist Wilhelm Dilithey, whose psychological concern was with the structure of the mind. For Spranger, the individual must be considered as a whole in relation to the environment. He called his approach *Strukturpsychologie* (psychology of structure). However, this was in contrast to Wilhelm Wundt's elementalistic psychology, which was concerned with the analysis of conscious experience into its elements. For Spranger, mental life consisted of unique structures, but he made no attempt to break each of these down into its elements.

In *Types of men* (1914), Spranger identified six types of people in terms of their life goals and values that operated apart from any biological drives or needs. These included (1) the theoretical or knowledge seeking, (2) the aesthetic, (3) the economic or practical, (4) the religious, (5) the social or "helping others," and (6) the political or managerial. These were "ideal" types, and any person could be a combination or blend of several. This became a leading type theory of personality based on motivational principles. Unlike the type theory of Carl Jung, Spranger's was based more on intuition and less on empirical observation. The theory later led to a personality test, devised by Gordon Allport and Philip E. Vernon published as *A study of values*.

R. W. LUNDIN

SPURZHEIM, JOHANN GASPAR (1776–1832)

Spurzheim, originally named Johann Christoph, was the pupil of Gall in Vienna and Paris and collaborated on the first two volumes of Gall's four-volume major work. After a dozen years, the two separated, with Spurzheim moving on to popularize their work in England and the United States. He published four major books in English, in addition to delivering innumerable lectures.

Spurzheim and Gall drew upon the faculty psychology of the Scottish School for the basic types of functionings or faculties of the mind, which they related to specific areas of the brain. Over- or underdevelopment of an area was correlated with the personality. Spurzheim adopted Forster's term *phrenology* (science of the mind) in 1815, the most common name for the theory today. Spurzheim revised the terminology and presented a new and more complete topography in his 1825 book, in which he identified 37 faculties of the mind, each related to a specific cortical location. His grouping of the faculties into mental, motive, and vital types anticipated Sheldon's somatotypes.

Phrenology was popular for almost a century with the general public and produced many charlatans who claimed to be able to change personality by developing a particular part of the brain or skull. Most researchers were highly critical of Spurzheim for his sloppy selection of subjects, for his correlational research, and for the apparent lack of correspondence between the contours of the brain (theoretical basis of phrenology) and the skull (actual site of measurement). Research by Flourens that demonstrated global rather than localized function of the cortex ended professional interest in the movement.

C. S. PEYSER

STAATS, ARTHUR W. (1924–   )

Staats began work on a comprehensive, unified theory of psychology while at the University of California at Los Angeles, taking the Ph.D. degree in general psychology and completing study of, and a Veterans Administration internship in, clinical psychology. He advanced from instructor to full professor at Arizona State University, where he introduced a program that became a center of behavioral psychology.

His theoretical and experimental analyses and his books served as a foundation for the development of behavior modification, with his contributions including the token reinforcer system (token economy) and the origination of conceptions of behavioral assessment, of parent–child interactions in child learning (including language development), of a learning theory of reading, of a behavioral taxonomy of abnormal behavior, and of a behavioral theory of personality as a cause. His first book, *Complex human behavior*, helped shape the form of behavioral psychology and social learning theory, and presented a unified learning theory that broadly treats the areas of human behavior. While at the University of California at Berkeley, the University of Wisconsin, and the University of Hawaii, Staats produced works such as (1) *Learning, language and cognition*, a beginning for the change in behavioral psychology and

social learning theory toward the contemporary rapprochement with cognitive phenomena and concepts; (2) *Child learning, intelligence, and personality: A behavioral interaction approach*, which introduced new concepts of intelligence as learned, of intelligence as composed of analyzable cognitive skills, and of personality–environment interaction (each a contemporary focus in psychology); and (3) *Social behaviorism*, which presents in methodology and substance the full unified theory that penetrates the major areas of psychology.

STEINER, RUDOLF (1861–1925)

An Austrian philosopher, scientist, and artist, Steiner received the Ph.D. in philosophy after which he was invited to Weimar to edit the scientific papers of Goethe for an edition of the author's complete works. While in Wiemar he wrote *The philosophy of freedom*, which he considered his most significant work.

Later, he moved to Berlin where he edited the *Magasin für Literatur* while lecturing at a worker's college. After 1902 he began lecturing at a worker's college. After 1902 he began lecturing to the Theosophical Society and published numerous books on his evolving philosophy, including *Theosophy* and *Occult science*. In 1913, he split with the Theosophists and founded the Anthroposophical Society. Eventually the organization established its headquarters near Basel in Switzerland at Dornach. There an extraordinary building (designed by Steiner), the Goetheanum, was erected to house a theater and society offices. Performances of Faust, the mystery dramas of Steiner, and eurythmy (a new art of movement pioneered by Steiner) were held in the wood structure.

After 1913, Steiner's prolific writing and lecturing (he wrote 60 books and most of his 6000 or so lectures have been published) as well as his practical activities spread into the most diverse directions. In Stuttgart, he founded the first Waldorf school, the first of what is now the largest nonsectarian private school system in the world. In 1921 a medical clinic was founded in Arleshiem, Switzerland. The field of anthroposophic medicine has since grown to include cancer clinics, psychiatric hospitals, pharmaceutical research and production, and allied cosmetics manufacture. A series of curative homes were begun for emotionally disturbed and developmentally disturbed children (and later communities for adults)—this impulse later gave birth to the Camphill schools and villages begun in the UK (where they now number more than 40) but since spread worldwide. Further endeavors inspired by Steiner included schools of nursing, massage, biodynamic organic agriculture, art and art therapy. As a foundation to this enormous array of contributions Steiner taught that the development of humankind's intellectual and spiritual faculties could lead to a "spiritual science" inspired by a supersensible realm but manifesting humankind's professional endeavors here on earth.

T. POPLAWSKI

STEKEL, WILHELM (1868–1940)

Stekel was one of the original group of psychoanalysts gathered around Sigmund Freud. He had received his medical training at the University of Vienna and studied under Richard Kraff-Ebing. Stekel, who had been analyzed by Freud, first suggested that the group constitute itself as "Psychological Wednesday Evenings" to read papers and participate in discussions. He was highly regarded by Freud and others of the group for his work on symbolism. He broke with Freud about a year after the Freud–Alfred Adler break, but difficulties had been developing for some time. Stekel had little interest in theory, was primarily a practitioner, and was closer in his thinking to Adler than to Freud. He was, however, even more avid than Freud in finding a sexual basis for psychological disorders.

It has been stated that Stekel psychoanalyzed over 10,000 people. Stekel stressed the teaching role of the analyst and saw the therapeutic relationship as an active partnership. He believed that the goals of the patient are important and that the patient should be led to distinguish between genuine and false goals. He placed less emphasis than Freud upon the necessity for the patient to understand the childhood background of any problems.

Stekel was a prolific writer whose works are of uneven quality. Many of them have not been translated into English. Of those available in English, the best known are *The homosexual neurosis, Sex and dreams, Frigidity in women in relation to their love life, Impotence in the male, Sexual abberations, Techniques of analytical psychotherapy, The interpretation of dreams,* and *Compulsion and doubt.* Stekel's autobiography was published in 1950.

P. E. LICHTENSTEIN

STEPHENSON, WILLIAM (1902–1989)

Stephenson was internationally known for his work on psychometrics and, in particular, for the development of the Q technique and factor analysis. Originally trained in physics, he received the Ph.D. from Durham University in 1926. He left Durham to study with Charles Spearman at University College, London. His first book was on educational psychology, *Teaching school children.*

In 1935, Stephenson became assistant director (later director) of Oxford's Institute of Experimental Psychology. There he first introduced what has become known as the Q methodology, and he contributed more than 120 publications on this topic: After World War II he emigrated to the United States and in 1948 joined the faculty of the University of Chicago, where he wrote his best known work, *The study of behavior, Q technique and its methodology.* He then went to the University of Missouri's School of Journalism to engage in advertising research. Upon his retirement, Stephenson was honored with a volume of essays titled, *Science, psychology and communication.* In 1985 the University of Missouri established the Stephenson Center for Communication Research. He continued to write and research in the fields of both psychology and physics.

R. W. LUNDIN

STERN, LEWIS WILLIAM (1871–1938)

Stern received the Ph.D. degree at Berlin in 1892 under Hermann Ebbinghaus. In 1897, after teaching at Berlin, he went to Breslau, and then in 1915 to the Colonial Institute at Hamburg, where he taught philosophy and psychology. In 1933, because of the rise of Nazism in Germany, he migrated to the United States. He assumed a position at Duke University, and remained there until his retirement.

While at Hamburg, Stern attempted to bridge the gap between experimental and human psychology. In his three-volume work *Person and thing,* published in 1906 and twice revised (1918 and 1924), he presented what he considered to be a synthesis, which he called a personalistic psychology. He attempted a reconciliation between the scientific and philosophical approaches to human beings. The individual person (personality) is a totality, a blending of the physical and mental, and this personalism, as he called it, is the science of the total human individual.

Stern distinguished three modalities in all life; biological (vital forces), experience (salience and embeddedness), and introception. This third modality was completely human, being developed as a result of social, cultural, moral, and religious values.

He made many other contributions to psychology. He was a pioneer in the study of individual differences, and was concerned with child psychology and with the applications of psychology to the law in his researches on the psychology of testimony.

He is also well known for his development of the concept of the I.Q. (intelligence quotient). Alfred Binet had constructed a series of tests to measure intelligence, applied particularly to young people. In the third edition just prior to his death (1911), Binet had developed the concept of the mental age, the age at which a child is functioning intellectually regardless of the child's actual chronological age. In 1912, Stern pointed out that by dividing the mental age by the chronological age, the I.Q. could be determined to indicate a child's *relative* standing in comparison with other children, at any particular chronological age.

R. W. LUNDIN

STEVENS, STANLEY SMITH (1906–1973)

Stevens took the Ph.D. degree in 1933 at Harvard University under Edwin Boring. He was a distinguished psychophysicist and early in his career he established the sensory attribute of tonal density. He also developed a method for equating tones on one attribute when they differed on a second attribute. In the field of auditory theory, Stevens accepted a modification of the resonance theory of Herman von Helmholtz, which involved traveling waves throughout the basilar membrane.

Stevens collaborated with Hallowell Davis on *Hearing* (1938), which summarized much of his research, as well as that of others. He also edited the *Handbook of experimental psychology* (1951).

Stevens had an abiding interest in problems of measurement and psychological scaling. He developed some new scaling methods and found that physical continua generally conform to a psychophysical power law rather than Gustav Fechner's logarithmic law. Quantitative sensory continua (intensity) were found to obey the power law while qualitative sensory continua such as hue or pitch may follow Fechner's law.

Shortly after the publication of Percy Bridgman's *The logic of modern physics,* Stevens, joined by other Harvard psychologists, began to explore the significance of operational thinking for psychology. He published several papers on operationism and did more than anyone else to bring operationism before the psychological profession and to establish what might be called operational behaviorism. His paper "Psychology and the science of science" exerted a powerful influence in this regard and revealed the close ties between operationism and logical positivism.

Stevens combined experimental ingenuity and expertise with broad methodological and philosophical interests. His interest in measurement led to collaboration with W. H. Sheldon on *The varieties of human physique* and *The varieties of temperament,* books that developed a method for classifying individuals into personality types on the basis of body build.

P. E. LICHTENSTEIN

STEVENSON, HAROLD W. (1924–   )

Stevenson received the B.A. at the University fo Colorado and the M.A. and Ph.D. (1951) in psychology at Stanford University. He was an instructor and assistant professor of psychology at Pomona College (1950–1953) and assistant and then associate professor of psychology at the University of Texas (1953–1959). He became professor of child psychology and director of the Institute of Child Development at the University of Minnesota in 1959. Since 1971, he has been at the University of Michigan, as professor of psychology, fellow at the Center for Human Growth, and director of the Michigan Program in Child Development and Social Policy.

Stevenson has been president of the Society for Research in Child Development, of the Division of Developmental Psychology of the

American Psychological Association, and of the International Society for the Study of Behavioral Development. He is a fellow of the American Academy of Arts and Sciences and has been a fellow at the Center for Advanced Study in the Behavioral Sciences. He has received a Guggenheim fellowship and the G. Stanley Hall Award of the Division of Developmental Psychology of the American Psychological Association.

Stevenson has been the editor or author of nearly a dozen books, and has written research articles and chapters in books. His primary areas of interest are in children's learning, cognitive development, cross-cultural studies of academic achievement, and social policy.

ŠTIKAR, JIŘÍ (1934–   )

Štikar is best known for his research in engineering psychology, accident analysis, and prevention. He was educated at Charles University, Prague, where he received the Ph.D. degree in 1966. On the staff of the Department of Psychology at Charles University he has taught engineering psychology, traffic psychology, and models of skill development.

Štikar's expertise extends also to applied psychological research, especially professional job analyses and problems of safety work. He is a member of the Czechoslovak Psychological Society and coeditor of the *Journal of Applied Industrial Psychology*.

His publications include *Psychology and physiology of driver* (with E. Bena and J. Hoskovec), and *Driver training and psychology* (with J. Hoskovec and J. Pour). These books, originally in Czech, were translated into Polish, and the first one also into Russian and Bulgarian.

STOUT, GEORGE FREDERICK (1860–1944)

Stout studied philosophy and psychology at Cambridge, primarily with James Ward. After briefly holding positions at St. John's College Cambridge, Aberdeen, Oxford, and the University of London, Stout spent over 30 years in Scotland at St. Andrews.

Stout is remembered as the disciple, interpreter, and popularizer of his mentor James Ward, through his systematic textbooks of act psychology. The professional sought his 1896 *Analytical psychology* while his 1899 *A manual of psychology* was the most widely used text in Britain for many years (a fifth edition was published in 1938). He also had great impact upon British psychology from his position as editor of *Mind* (1892–1920).

British psychology of the period included but two rival positions: Galton (evolution, individual differences focus) and Ward/Stout (philosophical speculative psychology). The holistic, qualitative focus on cognitions of Ward and Stout was in the tradition of the Scottish School and Kant. Unlike Galton, they had little impact on psychology in the United States.

Essentially an "armchair" psychologist, Stout was known for his acute analysis of cognitive and perceptual processes. He rejected the mental chemistry of J. S. Mill and criticized the Associationists for confusing the "presented whole" with the "sum of its presented components." Thus Stout anticipated the Gestalt rallying cry that "the whole is greater than the sum of its parts."

C. S. PEYSER

STRATTON, GEORGE MALCOLM (1865–1957)

Stratton was one of the first generation of American psychologists to study under Wilhelm Wundt at Leipzig, along with G. Stanley Hall, James Cattell, Charles Judd, and Frank Angell in the latter part of the nineteenth century. Upon his return to the United States, Stratton went to the University of California in 1896 and founded the psychological laboratory there.

He is best known for his classic experiment on reversed vision. Using himself as subject, he wore special lenses—which reversed the field of vision, up for down and right for left—during his waking hours for eight consecutive days. Although utterly confused and helpless at first, after three days he was able to make relatively automatic and skilled movements and to adjust to seeing an inverted world. By the end of the experiment, he had become so familiar with his new visual world that he felt that the world was right side up. He believed that he had demonstrated that the absolute localization of position on the retina of the eye was learned and that the body could reorient itself as to the context and place of visual excitation.

This study was first reported at the Third International Congress of Psychology at Munich in 1896 and published a year later in the *Psychological Review*. Furthermore, his demonstration served to support an empirical conception of visual perception in favor of a natavistic one as formulated by Immanuel Kant.

Other areas of psychology that concerned Stratton and on which he published included the history of psychology, emotions, and the psychology of religion.

R. W. LUNDIN

STREET, WARREN R. (1942–   )

Street received the B.A. degree in psychology from Occidental College and the M.A. and Ph.D. (1967) degrees in experimental psychology from Claremont Graduate School. In 1967, he joined the faculty at Central Washington University as professor of psychology. His teaching and research interests have been in social psychology, the history of psychology, computer methods, and behavior analysis.

Street established and updated a large collection of exact dates of noteworthy events in the history of psychology, with special attention to American psychology. This work has been supported by Central Washington University and the American Psychological Association and is the basis of the APA's *1992 centennial calendar* and similar publications appearing during the APA's centennial celebrations. Street was a founder of the William O. Douglas Honors College at Central Washington University and was its first director (1976–1986). In 1987, he received the university's first student-sponsored Outstanding Professor Award.

STRONG, EDWARD KELLOGG, JR. (1884–1963)

Strong received the Ph.D. degree under J. McK. Cattell and began his teaching career at the then Carnegie Institute of Technology. His publications included an introductory psychology text and a book on selling and advertising. He also published in the areas of industrial training and job analysis.

While at Carnegie, he participated in a seminar on the measurement of interests conducted by C. S. Yoakum. The Interest Blank developed was a series of items that were answered "like," "dislike," or "?—insufficient information to decide." Several years after moving to Stanford in 1923, he jointly supervised the doctoral dissertation of K. M. Cowdery. This dissertation involved the comparison of interests of doctors, engineers, and lawyers, and used a modification of the Carnegie Interest Blank. Cowdery found distinctive response patterns for each group. The patterns remained consistent on a new sample (cross-validation).

Strong extended Cowdery's work to 18 occupation groups, used larger samples, and in other ways improved the technical quality of the inventory. First published in 1927, the Strong Vocational Interest Blank, or SVIB, quickly became the instrument of choice for the empirically minded. The published instrument had 420 items; slightly more than 40% were retained from Cowder's version.

Later revisions included separate blanks for men (SVIB-M) and women (SVIB-W). The technically sophisticated 1974 revision by David P. Campbell of Minnesota is called the SCII or Strong-Campbell Interest Inventory. The single form for use by men and women offers 124 occupational scale comparisons as well as other measures. More than 1500 articles and books have been published concerning the instrument.

Strong spent most of his career in the measurement of vocational interests. His later publications dealt with the variation of interests over time, including a large group studied 18 years after completing college.

C. S. PEYSER

STRUPP, HANS H. (1921–   )

Strupp was best known as a psychotherapy researcher whose theoretical orientation is broadly psychoanalytic. After briefly attending the City College of New York, he continued his studies at George Washington University (B.A., M.A., Ph.D. degree, 1954). His clinical interests were markedly influenced by the Washington School of Psychiatry, from which he received the Certificate in Applied Psychiatry in 1952. Strupp's professional career began as a research psychologist for the U.S. Air Force (1949–1954), gradually shifting to clinical psychology, and, more particularly, to psychotherapy research. Following a research position at George Washington University (1955–1957), he accepted a professional appointment in the Departments of Psychiatry and Psychology at the University of North Carolina in Chapel Hill (1957–1966). Since 1966, he has been a faculty member in the Department of Psychology at Vanderbilt University, where, in 1976, he was awarded the title of Distinguished Professor.

Strupp came to see the nature of the psychotherapist's influence and the patient's susceptibility to that influence as one of the core problems in psychotherapy research. Research in this area is no longer the esoteric pursuit of a few people concerned with evaluating a particular treatment method. Instead it is concerned with how we become relatively autonomous adults who participate in creating our destiny.

Reliance on empirical data, systematic research, and conceptual clarification of basic issues is seen as the best hope for advancing knowledge in this increasingly important area. Strupp's research has been guided by a commitment to open and nondogmatic inquiry, and excellence in training and practice.

In addition to numerous journal articles, Strupp's publications include *Psychotherapists in action; Research in psychotherapy, vol II* (with L. Luborsky); *Changing frontiers in the science of psychotherapy* (with A. Bergin); *Psychotherapy: Clinical research, and theoretical issues; Patients view their psychotherapy* (with R. Fox and K. Lessler); and *Psychotherapy for better or worse* (with S. Hadley and B. Gomes-Schwartz).

STUMPF, CARL (1848–1946)

Stumpf entered the University of Würzberg. He had a strong interest in music, but in those days, universities did not grant degrees in that subject. At Würzberg, he became acquainted with Franz Brentano, who was to have a strong effect on his thinking on psychological matters. Stumpf then went to Gottingren, where he received his doctor's degree in philosophy under Lotze in 1865. In 1875, he began work on his *Tonpsychologie,* which was to be his most famous publication and the first work on the psychology of music. One of the most important aspects of this work was his theory of consonance and dissonance in music. According to that theory, tonal combinations judged most consonant

are those that tend to fuse together. The greater the degree of fusion (as in an octave), the greater is the consonance. Likewise in dissonance, when tones are played together, the degree to which they separate out and can be heard as single tones, the greater is the dissonance.

In 1894, Stumpf received an appointment to a chair at the University of Berlin and devoted his efforts to research on hearing, which also included hearing music. During this period, he completed his two-volume *Tonpsychologie* (1883–1890). A controversy arose between Stumpf and Wundt, which emerged in a series of publications devoted to the introspective method used in studying tones. The controversy revolved around the question of whether a trained introspectionist of the Wundtian variety or a trained musician (Stumpf) was more qualified to make tonal judgments. The problem was never resolved.

As a student and friend of Franz Brentano, Stumpf followed the act school of psychology, which arose in opposition to Wundt's psychology of content. For Stumpf and Brentano, the subject matter of psychology was the acts of the mind rather than merely its contents. Such acts of the mind included perceiving, conceiving, desiring, and willing.

R. W. LUNDIN

SULLIVAN, ARTHUR M. (1932–   )

Sullivan is known for his research on teaching and learning at the college and university level. Sullivan received all of his early education in one- and two-room schools. His university education was completed at Memorial University of Newfoundland, Dalhousie University, McGill University, and at Oxford, which he attended as a Rhodes Scholar.

Sullivan's entire professional career was spent at Memorial University of Newfoundland, where he established a one-man Department of Psychology in 1960. He chaired the department during its early growth and saw it become a major department in the university. In 1968, he became dean of Junior Studies, and in 1975, principal of the university's first two-year college. These positions gave him an opportunity to investigate teaching and learning at the remedial level as well as at the first- and second-year university level. He was able to measure the characteristics of teachers and of students who had been randomly assigned to small classes in various subject areas. His findings in this area have been replicated in U.S. and other Canadian universities. The teaching and remedial programs devised resulted in dramatic increases in academic success, especially of students from isolated rural communities.

Sullivan has long been involved with the professional life of his discipline and has served as president of the Association of Newfoundland Psychologists, the Atlantic Provinces Psychological Association, and the Canadian Psychologic Association. In 1968, he was appointed the founding editor of the *Canadian Journal of Behavioural Science.*

He became involved in labor-management cooperation and, through that, in studies of transportation. In 1977, he was appointed by the Federal Government of Canada as Chief Commissioner for the Commission of Inquiry into Newfoundland Transportation. This activity resulted in the two-volume report of the *Commission of inquiry into Newfoundland transportation* (1978).

Sullivan's most recent professional activity has been in the area of aging. He was instrumental in setting up the Newfoundland Association of Gerontology and in encouraging research in gerontology in Newfoundland.

SULLIVAN, HARRY STACK (1892–1949)

Distinguished for his *interpersonal theory of psychiatry,* Sullivan, a lifelong bachelor, defined psychiatry as the "study of interpersonal relations." Psychiatry, for him, was an adjunct of social psychology. A wholesome personality derives from healthy interpersonal relationships. Personality itself is defined in terms of interpersonal relationships.

Sullivan entered Cornell University at the age of 16. Problems arose in his second term, causing him to leave college for the workaday world. By 1915, he had earned sufficient funds to see him through medical school. However, his biographer, A. H. Chapman, writes that, because of his lack of a college education, "he could gain admittance to only a shabby, run-for-profit medical school in Chicago which in later years he described as a 'diploma mill' "(Chapman, 1976, p. 27). In some respects, this lack of a decent undergraduate and professional school education is to his credit, because his accomplishments were in spite of them. Furthermore, it allowed him to enter psychiatry free from preconceived notions regarding mental disorders. Instead he learned psychopathology from first-hand experience, when he began his career at important health centers in Washington, D.C., and Baltimore, Md. In Washington at St. Elizabeth's Hospital, Sullivan came under the influence of the distinguished psychiatrist, William Alanson White, and also became familiar with the social psychology and anthropology of Bronislaw Malinowski, Charles Cooley, G. H. Mead, and Edward Sapir. The social psychologist William McDougall and the British psychologist W. H. R. Rivers too had an influence on him.

The social character of psychiatry embedded itself in Sullivan's thinking. Not only is personality couched in interpersonal relations, he believed, but the patient-therapist interpersonal relationship is critical for successful therapy. As a participant observer, the therapist participates in patients' explorations of their problems. Anxiety, basic to virtually all emotional problems, is the incapacitating element that must be displaced with a sense of security, a sense of emotional ease.

As Sullivan's ideas solidified, they were recorded. With the exception of *Conceptions of modern psychiatry,* his books appeared posthumously: *The interpersonal theory of psychiatry; The psychiatric interview; Schizophrenia as a human process; The fusion of psychiatry and social science, and Personal psychopathology.* Except for *Personal psychopathology,* a 1921 account of experiences with patients, these later books, the product of lectures and seminars from 1943 to his death in 1949, best represent his thought.

Sullivan was professor of psychiatry and interim director of the Department of Psychiatry at Georgetown University Medical School for several months in 1939, but otherwise never held an academic position. Even his stay from 1923 to 1930 at the Sheppard and Enoch Pratt Hospital in Baltimore was in the capacity of staff psychiatrist. It was in Baltimore at Johns Hopkins that he met Adolf Meyer, a second great influence on his thinking. Sullivan's career came abruptly to a close when he died of a brain hemorrhage in a Paris hotel en route home from an executive meeting of the World Federation of Mental Health.

In addition to the ideas already mentioned, Sullivan is known for a variety of concepts: dynamisms, the self-system, parataxic distortion, the one-genus postulate, and his theory of personality development. Unlike many celebrities, Sullivan gained in fame posthumously.

W. S. SAHAKIAN

SUNDBERG, NORMAN D. (1922–   )

A clinical, community, and cross-cultural psychologist, Sundberg grew up in the ethnic patchwork of rural Nebraska and obtained his baccalaureate degree from the University of Nebraska in Lincoln. After military service in Germany, he received the Ph.D. degree in 1952 from the University of Minnesota, where he majored in clinical psychology and minored in neuropsychiatry; he then moved to the University of Oregon, where he remains. His doctoral dissertation on psychotherapists' "knowledge of others" initiated his lifelong search for understanding the development of usable knowledge for work with people. Later,

as dean of a new applied social science school, he evolved its motto "Knowledge for Action."

Sundberg's view of psychology emphasizes both the "horizontal" and the "vertical"—horizontal in the sense of knowledge across cultures, communities, and applied activities, and vertical in the sense of an appreciation of time, of the history and future of applied psychology and human services, and of life history, the life span. He has expressed these interests both in practical action and in research. He was the first director of the University of Oregon Guidance Clinic (later called the University Psychology Clinic), helped to establish gerontology programs at Oregon, and was the founding dean of the Wallace School of Community Service and Public Affairs at the same university and served as director of Clinical Psychology Training. His major publications are *Clinical psychology* (with Leona Tyler and Julian Taplin) and *Assessment of persons.*

SUPER, DONALD E. (1910–   )

Super is most often associated with career development theory and its applications. After contributing first to the applications of differential psychology to vocational guidance and personnel selection and classification, he shifted his attention to developmental approaches to vocational choice and development. With students and colleagues such as John Crites, Albert Thompson, and Jean Pierre Jordaan at Teachers College, Columbia University, and colleagues elsewhere, such as Henry Borow and David Tiedeman, he established the terms, and with them the field of vocational or career development, and wrote the first books and monographs using these concepts. Developmental tasks, life stages, and self-concepts have loomed large in his work.

A graduate of Oxford University and the recipient of the Ph.D. degree from Columbia and the D.Sc. degree from Lisbon, he has taught at Clark, Harvard, the University of California at Berkeley, the University of Paris (Sorbonne and René Descartes), Virginia Institute of Technology, Lisbon, Cambridge, and the University of Florida (Gainesville), while based primarily at Teachers College, Columbia University, and he maintains active ties with the last six universities. He is international coordinator of the Work Importance Study and professor emeritus of psychology and education at Columbia, where he was for some years chairman of the Department of Psychology and division director.

Super has served as president of the Division of Counseling Psychology of the American Psychological Association (APA), the American Personnel and Guidance Association, and the National Vocational Guidance Association, and is president of the International Association for Educational and Vocational Guidance and a member of the board of directors of the International Association for Applied Psychology. A Fellow of APA and of the British Psychological Society, and an Honorary Member of the Spanish Psychological Society, he consults with a variety of educational and industrial organizations, including IBM, AT&T, General Electric, UNESCO, and OECD.

SZASZ, THOMAS S. (1920–   )

Szasz is best known for his proposition that mental illness is a myth and for his uncompromising opposition to psychiatric coercions and excuses. He received his primary and secondary education in Budapest, migrating to the United States in 1938. He was graduated from the College of Medicine at the University of Cincinnati in 1944. Following his medical education, he was trained in psychiatry at the University of Chicago, and in psychoanalysis at the Chicago Institute for Psychoanalysis, where he became a member of the staff.

After a period of private practice in Chicago, Szasz was called to active duty with the United States Naval Reserve and was stationed at the Bethesda Naval Hospital. Following his discharge from the Navy in 1956, he joined the faculty of the State University of New York's Upstate Medical Center in Syracuse, as a professor of psychiatry.

In a series of articles and books, beginning in the mid-1950s, Szasz has argued that literal illnesses are bodily illnesses and that so-called mental illnesses are either bodily diseases with mental symptoms (such as organic psychoses) or metaphorical diseases (and hence not diseases at all). Partly on such epistemological grounds, and partly on moral and political grounds, Szasz has also opposed the use of psychiatry and psychology in a wide variety of legal situations, from civil commitment to the insanity defense. The two principle themes in his work are thus a philosophical analysis of the medicalization (psychiatrization) of life, creating what he has called the "Therapeutic State," and a libertarian critique of the moral and political consequences of that modern scientistic tendency.

SZEWCZUK, WLODZIMIERZ L. (1913–   )

After receiving the bachelor's degree from Jagellonian University in Cracow, Poland, Szewczuk continued his studies at the same university, receiving the Ph.D. degree in 1938. He regards himself as a generalist, seeking the general laws of the psychical functioning of human beings.

His essential attainments concern the problems of memorization, understanding, the psychological unity of education, and teaching. On the basis of thousands of experiments presented in *Psychology of memorization*, the theory of three necessary conditions for any memorization is elaborated: (1) an active attitude toward new data (stimulus material); (2) association with earlier experience; and (3) association with emotional reactions including biochemical components. His book *Experimental investigations on the understanding of sentences* discussed the theory of understanding as a phased process of constructive activation of earlier experience, cognitive and emotional, in relation to objects and products of human action. Of importance in this respect are the field of the reception of relations, and image logical and grammatical imagination. The establishment of psychophysiological mechanisms of teaching in *Psychological foundations of education* surmounted the traditional (from the time of Pestalozzi) dualism of teaching principles and indefinite-intuitive rules of education leading to universally uniform principles.

Szewczuk's professional career has covered these phases: 1954–1966, head of the Department of Psychology and, in 1967–1981, director of Institute of Psychology at Jagellonian University; 1970–1972, president of the Polish Psychological Association; 1974–1981, Committee of Psychological Sciences (member of presidium) of the Polish Academy of Sciences. His publications include *Les illusions optico-geometriques, Theory of gestalt and psychology of gestalt, Great dispute about psyche, and Psychological album.*

SZONDI, LIPOT (1893–1977)

Szondi received the M.D. degree at Budapest in 1919. He was an assistant in experimental psychology at Budapest until 1926, when he founded the State Laboratories for Research in Psychopathology in the Academy of Medicine of the University of Budapest. After fleeing Hungary in 1941, he finally settled in Zurich, where he was a practicing analyst and established his own institute.

Szondi developed *Schicksalanalyse,* or analysis of destiny and fate, a system of diagnosis and therapy. The focus is on repressed ancestral demands. Much in the fashion of Carl Jung, Szondi claimed that inhibition and failure to deal with the unconscious lead to psychological problems. He focused on the familial unconscious rather than the personal unconscious of Sigmund Freud or the collective unconscious of Jung. *Schicksalanalyse* postulates four major drives: sexual, startle, ego, and contact. Each drive has two factors; sexual, for example, is composed of the personal and collective amorousness and the need for sadomasochism.

In the Szondi test a client selects the 12 photographs most liked and the 12 most disliked from a total of 48. The test is taken once a day for six to 10 days. The photographs are composed of six sets of eight "pure personality types." In each set, for example, the bisexual represents the amorousness factor. One affirms the amorousness factor by "liking" the bisexual photographs; in so doing, a tendency toward personal love is displayed. The client who dislikes the bisexual pictures negates the factor and thereby expresses love of humanity. A liking for the pictures of sadistic murderers shows aggression whereas disliking them indicates passivity or submission.

The Szondi test is, at best, a research tool, with no clinical utility. Although those with psychological training can classify the pictures by disorder, evidence of internal consistency and predictability are totally lacking despite considerable research.

TAFT, RONALD (1920–   )

Taft was graduated from the University of Melbourne in 1939. He obtained the M.A. degree in psychology from Columbia University and the Ph.D. degree from the University of California, Berkeley, in 1951, having worked for seven years (1942–1950) as an industrial psychologist and consultant. After teaching at the University of Western Australia in Perth and the University of Melbourne, in 1968 he accepted the foundation chair of social psychology in the faculty of education at Monash University in Melbourne.

Taft's major contributions to psychology are clinical assessment processes, and the adaptation of immigrants and ethnic minorities. On the former topic, his work has concentrated on subjective processes in clinical judgment. He is joint author, with Sarbin and Bailey, of *Clinical inference and cognitive theory* and the author of *From stranger to citizen.*

Taft is a former editor of the *Australian Journal of Psychology* and chairman of the Australian Branch of the British Psychological Society. He is a Fellow of the Academy of Social Sciences in Australia and of the Australian Psychological Society, is on the Executive Committee of the International Union of Psychological Science and the International Association of Applied Psychology, and is vice-president of the International Association of Cross-Cultural Psychology.

TAKUMA, TAKETOSHI (1927–   )

Takuma is known for his continuing study on personality development. After receiving the B.A. from Tokyo University in Japan, he was awarded a scholarship by the Alexander von Humboldt Stiftung in West Germany. He continued his studies in personality theory at Munich University under Philipp Lersch, and in human genetics at Munster University under Otmar von Verschuer. On his return to Tokyo, he received the Litt.D. degree from his alma mater.

Takuma's main concern has been to clarify the complicated process of personality development. Believing that the comparative study of twins is an effective and reliable source for finding the determinants of development, he has done research on several hundred pairs of twins. Stratification theory (*Schichtentheorie*) is basic to Takuma's research. He also has strong interests in such subjects as the relationship between infants and mothers, sex differences, aging problems, culture, and personality.

In 1982, Takuma was invited to be a visiting professor at the Technological University of Munich and he presented several lectures on the Japanese people and culture. After teaching at Gakushuin University from 1956 to 1971, he has been a professor of psychology at Tokyo Metropolitan University since 1972.

Since 1979, he has been an executive board member of the Japanese Psychological Association as well as chief editor of both the *Japanese Journal of Psychology* and *Japanese Psychological Research*.

TANAKA, YASUMASA (1931–   )

Tanaka was educated at Tokyo's Gakushuin University, where he received the B.A. degree. He then attended the University of Illinois and earned M.A. and Ph.D. degrees. He later was awarded the Litt.D. degree in psychology, for his work on the psychology of human communications.

At the University of Illinois Institute of Communications Research, Tanaka was involved in a 12-nation cross-cultural research project on affective meaning. As a result of this project, his interest shifted from political science to cross-cultural psychology. At Gakushuin, he has participated in a number of cross-cultural research studies.

Tanaka is best known as a cross-cultural psychologist. He was one of the founders of the International Association for Cross-Cultural Psychology, and has served as associate editor of the *Journal of Cross-Cultural Psychology* and as editor of the *Cross-Cultural Social Psychology Newsletter*. He has published eight books and some 170 articles in Japanese, as well as 35 articles in English. He was a coauthor of the *Analysis of subjective culture* with H. C. Triandis, V. and G. Vassiliou, and A. V. Shanmugam.

TAPE, GOZE (1947–   )

Tape, after completing his secondary studies and obtaining the baccalaureate degree in 1967, studied psychology at Caen University in France. He received the B.S. degree and the master's degree in psychology at the University of Paris, he was awarded the Ph.D. degree in 1976 by an examining committee composed of Pierre Grèco, René Zazzo, and Denise Paulme.

Named to the position of assistant professor in 1973, and then associate professor in 1977, Tape taught psychology to Ivorian teachers-in-training. He has served as director of studies since 1977, and conducts research in the area of developmental psychology of the African child in relation to the educational practices of his environment. Tape is the author of several publications, including "Les activités de classifications et les opérations logiques chez l'enfant Ivoirien," "Le langage des amulettes en pays M'batto," "Mathématique et milieu en Afrique," and "Le profil du professeur de l'enseignement secondaire."

TAYLOR, FREDERICK WINSLOW (1856–1915)

Taylor passed the entrance examinations for Harvard with honors after a period at Phillips Exeter Academy. But poor eyesight forced him to work in a machine shop rather than matriculate. At the Midvale Steel Company, where he started at the age of 22, he progressed from ordinary laborer to general foreman of the plant in a three-year period. He obtained a mechanical engineering degree from Stevens Institute in 1882.

Moving to the Bethlehem Steel Works in 1898, Taylor studied the most efficient methods of shoveling iron ore and coal in the yard. He changed the method of shoveling, scheduled the rest periods, and prescribed different shovel sizes for different materials. He was able vastly to increase the quantity shoveled per person and markedly increased the hourly wage for each worker. As was true of his later work, both the workers and the company benefited. Despite the additional wages, tools to be provided by the company, and employees on the planning staff, the company saved more than $75,000 per year with Taylor's "scientific shoveling."

Taylor first came to general notice with his 1903 paper on shop management. He held almost 100 patents, including the Taylor–White

process of treating modern high-speed tools. He was particularly known for methods of cutting metal and setting concrete. Taylor's book *Principles of scientific management* opened the area of industrial efficiency. The book prescribed the time study with standardized tools and procedures organized by a planning department. Equipment was redesigned to be consonant with human abilities. Bonuses were paid workers as their portion of the savings.

C. S. PEYSER

TEPLOV, BORIS MIKHAILOVICH (1886–1965)

One of the leading postrevolutionary Soviet psychologists, Teplov served in the postrevolutionary army and during that time did some of his important research on sensory processes. He was later associated with the Institute of Psychology in Moscow and in 1945 became a member of the Soviet Academy of Pedagogical Sciences.

Teplov's early studies in the 1920s were concerned with visual processes and the interrelationship of the sensory modalities. While in the army, he was particularly interested in the means whereby objects perceived through vision could be camouflaged.

Somewhat later Teplov's interests turned to the study of musical aptitudes and individual differences in musical ability. His concern for individual differences dominated much of his later research. He studied individual differences in knowledge, skills, and habits, as well as differences in temperament and character, and developed short tests for their measurement. In his later research, he proposed to relate these differences to the properties of the nervous system, stressing the importance of involuntary reflexes in a manner first studied by Ivan Pavlov. To do this, Teplov and his colleagues used such measures as the galvanic skin response and the electroencephalogram (brain waves). He advanced the theory of various dimensional properties of the nervous system. In studying the dimension of strength–weakness, he concluded that weakness involves a low level of working ability but a high level of reactivity.

R. W. LUNDIN

TERMAN, LEWIS MADISON (1877–1956)

Terman studied at Clark University, and received his doctorate in 1905 under E. C. Sanford. In 1906, he held a position at Los Angeles State Normal School. From 1910 to 1943, he was at Stanford University; for 20 of those years, he served as head of the Psychology Department there.

Terman's major research contribution to American psychology was his work in intelligence testing and his evaluation of gifted persons. He translated and adapted the French Binet–Simon intelligence to American circumstances. He introduced William Stern's mental quotient to measure intelligence, multiplied it by 100, and called it the intelligence quotient, or I.Q. The test became known as the *Stanford–Binet Intelligence Scale* because Terman was at Stanford at this time (1916). The test was revised in 1937 and again in 1960. For a long time, the Stanford–Binet was the most widely used individual intelligence test in the English language.

During World War I, he served with other psychologists in the construction of the first group intelligence test. The Army Alpha and the nonverbal Army Beta were used to assign army recruits to training and duties in the military service.

Terman began a longitudinal study of gifted children in 1921 with a sample of 1500 California children who had intelligence test quotients of 140 or above. Five volumes were published, at intervals of several years, reporting the findings of this unusual study. The last volume of the *Genetic studies of genius* was published after Terman's death, and was entitled *The gifted group at mid-life*, written with M. H. Oden. Terman dispelled the old belief that gifted persons are eccentric, maladjusted, and sickly; he found instead that they are taller, healthier, and physically better developed than average people, and superior to them in leadership and social adaptability.

N. A. HAYNIE

THIBAUT, JOHN W. (1917–1986)

After undergraduate study in philosophy at the University of North Carolina, Thibaut continued with graduate work at North Carolina and Ohio State, with a major interest in epistemology and moral philosophy. During World War II, he served in the Aviation Psychology Program. After the war, he resumed graduate study at the Massachusetts Institute of Technology's Research Center for Group Dynamics, where he was influenced by Kurt Lewin, Leon Festinger, and fellow students, Ben Willerman and Harold Kelley. He received the Ph.D. degree in group psychology in 1949. Subsequently Thibaut joined the faculties of Boston University and Harvard, and finally returned to North Carolina in 1953.

Thibaut collaborated for many years with Harold Kelley. Together they contributed chapters on group problem solving to the 1954 and 1969 editions of the *Handbook of social psychology*. After a year together at the Center for Advanced Study in the Behavioral Sciences, they wrote *The social psychology of groups*, followed by *Interpersonal relations*. As part of a longstanding interest in processes of conflict resolution, Thibaut collaborated with Laurens Walker, professor of law, in writing *Procedural justice*. Later he worked closely with Chester Insko in developing research on the social evolution of group norms.

Thibaut was the founding editor (1965–1970) of the *Journal of Experimental Social Psychology*. He was elected a Fellow of the American Academy of Arts and Sciences in 1978.

THOMAS AQUINAS (1225–1274)

St. Thomas Aquinas was the most famous defender and teacher of Christian philosophy. His early education was at the Benedictine monastery of Monte Cassino and at the University of Naples. He studied at Cologne under Albertus Magnus, the first of a long line of distinguished Dominican teachen. In Paris, Albertus and Thomas continued teaching and writing. Aquinas's most celebrated book is the *Summa theologica*.

Two major themes may be drawn from St. Thomas's work. First, human nature culminates in reason, and reason is to know God. God is known through his power, acts, or will, but humans cannot necessarily know *why* or *how* God does all things. St. Thomas tried to prove that God is reasonable and therefore faith and reason, both God-given, can never conflict. Some things can be known by faith only, others by reason only, and still others by both revelation *and* rational proof.

Second, being and value are one; as humans seek truth, they are also seeking the final good in which human nature finds perfect happiness. St. Thomas followed Aristotelian thought, insisting that body and soul are in union. This union is the real being of the individual. The natural goal of human life is the perfection of this union, of the rational soul. The soul's faith and the body's reason must be united in fulfillment of truth and happiness.

N. A. HAYNIE

THOMPSON, RICHARD F. (1930–   )

Best known for his work on the neuronal substrates of behavioral plasticity and learning and memory, Thompson attended Reed College. He received the Ph.D. degree from the University of Wisconsin with W. J. Brogden in physiological psychology, and also studied with Harry Harlow and David Grant. He then spent a three-year postdoctoral with Clinton Woolsey in neurophysiology at the University of Wisconsin School of Medicine. Subsequently he held posts ranging from assistant professor to professor in psychiatry and medical psychology at the University of Oregon Medical School and later held professorships at the University of California, Irvine, and Harvard. In 1980, he moved to Stanford University, as Bing professor in human biology and professor of psychology.

Perhaps his best known work, on neural mechanisms of habituation and sensitization, was the result of a collaboration with W. Alden Spencer when they were both beginning their careers at the University of Oregon Medical School. They developed the now widely accepted defining criteria for habituation and evidence that the basic process was a form of synaptic depression that occurs presynaptically. This was later developed into a more general dual-process theory of habituation that stimulated much research in the area.

In the early 1970s, Thompson shifted his research effort to the "search for the engram"—the localization and analysis of the neuronal substrates of associative learning. Two critical systems have been identified to date, one involving the hippocampus and the other the cerebellum.

In addition to research, Thompson has written several texts, including *Foundations of physiological psychology*; *Introduction to physiological psychology*; *Psychology* with Harry F. Harlow and James McGaugh; and *Psychology* with Gardner Lindzey and Calvin Hall.

THOMSON, GODFREY H. (1881–1955)

Thomson was associated with the universities of Durham and Newcastle as student, lecturer, and eventually professor of education. He obtained his doctorate (in physics) at the University of Strasbourg in 1906. His early interest was in mathematics and its application to the measurement of sensation. But in 1914 he came across Spearman's work in factor analysis of human abilities, which he criticized strongly. His major book on *The factorial analysis of human ability* first appeared in 1937.

Thomson spent the year 1923–1924 at Columbia University, where he was considerably influenced by Edward L. Thorndike's psychological theories. Thus, instead of Spearman's notion of g (general intellectual ability) as a single mental energy, he regarded the mind as made up of a very large number of "bonds," similar to Thorndike's "connections." Any mental act would draw on a sample of bonds, while other acts would draw on some of the same, and some different. This would account for the positive correlations that are found between all cognitive abilities.

One of Thomson's main goals was to provide opportunities for a good education to all clever children, regardless of socioeconomic status or place of residence. In 1920, he produced the first group test of intelligence to be used in the selection of Northumbrian children for secondary schools. He became professor of education at the University of Edinburgh in 1925, and rounded the Moray House research unit, which constructed new intelligence, English, and arithmetic tests every year. At one time, more than a million copies of these tests were sold annually to education authorities in the United Kingdom. Thomson was very active in stimulating educational research in Scotland, and was mainly responsible for the two surveys of all 11-year-old Scottish children in 1933 and 1949. The results showed convincingly that the intelligence level of the population was not declining as had been expected because the lower classes were more prolific than the middle and upper classes. Thomson was also a brilliant teacher. His own views on education and psychology were published in books published in 1924 and 1929.

P. VERNON

THORNDIKE, EDWARD LEE (1874–1949)

Thorndike was an undergraduate at Wesleyan University, and then studied under William James at Harvard University where he began animal research in psychology. He moved to Columbia University and continued his work with dogs, cats, and chicks. He created puzzle boxes with which he studied animal intelligence, and his work was published in a monograph, "Animal intelligence." He received his doctorate in 1898.

Thorndike stayed at Columbia for all of his career; at James M. Cattell's suggestion, he applied animal research techniques to children. During his 50 years at Columbia, he did research and teaching in human learning, education, and mental testing, and published many books and monographs.

Thorndike taught that psychology should study behavior, not mental elements or conscious experience. He described *connectionism*—not associations between ideas, but connections between situations and responses. He said that the stimulus-response units are the elements of behavior, the building blocks from which more complex behaviors are constructed.

In 1898, Thorndike discovered the *law of effect,* which was similar to Pavlov's *law of reinforcement* reported four years later. Pavlov recognized Thorndike's work as preceding his, a simultaneous independent discovery, and complimented Thorndike's classical style of research and presentation for its "bold outlook" and accuracy. The law of effect was defined as the stamping in or out of a response tendency. Response tendencies that lead to success are stamped in after a number of trials—through "trial-and-error" learning. In the 1930s, in a study of the law of effect with humans, Thorndike found that rewarding the response was effective in stamping in or strengthening the behavior, but that punishment did not have a comparable negative effect of stamping out. Rather, prolonged disuse of the response led to a weakening of the behavior. These results were reported in his book *Human learning*.

Thorndike's research and theories of association or learning catapulted learning theory to its prominent place in American psychology.

N. A. HAYNIE

THURSTONE, LOUIS LEON (1887–1955)

Considered the foremost American leader in psychometrics, Thurstone spent his childhood in Sweden, and returned to the United States to earn a degree in electrical engineering at Cornell University in 1912. While still a student, he invented and patented a motion picture projector. It attracted the attention of Thomas A. Edison, who hired him as an assistant. Working in Edison's laboratory, Thurstone became interested in problems of acoustics, sensory psychology, and the objective measurement of sensation. This led him to graduate study in psychology at the University of Chicago, where he received the Ph.D. degree in 1917. After eight years at the Carnegie Institute of Technology, where he became professor and chairman of the Psychology Department, Thurstone returned to the University of Chicago, to serve as professor of psychology for 28 years. The last three years of his life were spent at the University of North Carolina as the first director of the Psychometric Laboratory, which now bears his name. He was president of the American Psychological Association in 1932; in 1936, he was one of the founders, and first president, of the Psychometric Society.

Thurstone made many contributions to measurement theory and its applications to psychophysics, cognitive abilities, attitudes, social judgment, and personality. Essentially he invented methods for devising interval and ratio scales for the measurement of psychological variables. He was the first to point out the psychometric inadequacies of Binet's concept of mental age (MA) as a scale for mental ability, and of the I.Q. when calculated as the ratio of MA to chronological age (CA). Mental age has the undesirable property that it can mean two quite different things: the average test score of children of a given age, or the average age of children obtaining a given score. There is no rational basis for choosing between these meanings of MA. Therefore, Thurstone argued that percentile ranks or standard scores should replace MA and I.Q., a practice that has been adopted by all modern tests. (Today most I.Q.'s are standard scores with a population mean of 100 and standard deviation of 15 or 16.) Thurstone also invented a ratio scale for the measurement of intelligence. He estimated the absolute zero of intelligence on the measurement scale by extrapolating the variance downward on the scale until it decreased to zero; zero intelligence thus was defined as the level of ability at which individual differences completely vanish.

Thurstone is best known for his contributions to factor analysis. The conceptual limitations and mathematical unwieldiness of Spearman's method of factor analysis when there are more than one factor made Thurstone's development of multiple factor analysis a boon to psychometrics and, at the time, was virtually essential for analyzing large correlation matrices that comprised a number of factors. Thurstone's multiple factor theory has endured, although, with the advent of electronic computers, his centroid method of factor extraction has been replaced by more exact, but computationally more difficult, methods such as principal component analysis and principal factor analysis.

By subjecting the matrix of intercorrelations among more than 50 diverse tests of mental abilities to a multiple factor analysis, Thurstone extracted a number of factors he labeled "primary mental abilities." He devised relatively "factor-pure" tests for each of these factors, such as verbal comprehension, reasoning, word fluency, number, spatial visualization, perceptual speed, and associative memory. Spearman's *g* (general ability) factor seemed to have disappeared in Thurstone's analysis, which for a time was a point of great contention between British and American psychometricians. The conflict was resolved when Thurstone showed that the primary mental abilities were themselves positively intercorrelated and that, when they are factor analyzed, Spearman's *g* is recovered as a second-order or superfactor. It has, in fact, proved impossible to construct factor-pure tests of Thurstone's primary mental abilities that do not also measure Spearman's *g*, and usually each test is more highly loaded on *g* than on the special factor it was specially devised to measure. Hence factor-pure tests, at best, measure *g* plus one primary ability.

Thurstone's most important contribution to factor analysis was the principle of "simple structure," a criterion for the rotation of the factor axes (or principal dimensions of the matrix) that results in a set of factors, each with very high loadings on a few tests and near-zero loadings on the rest—a condition that facilitates psychological interpretation of the factors. The principle of simple structure dominates modern computerized techniques of factor analysis, such as Kaiser's widely used varimax method.

A. R. JENSEN

TILLICH, PAUL (1886–1965)

Having received a theological and philosophical education, Tillich was ordained and served as an Army chaplain in World War I. He then taught theology and philosophy at Berlin, Marburg, Dresden, and Frankfurt. In 1933, he came to the United States and was appointed professor of systematic theology and philosophy of religion at Union Theological Seminary. From 1956 on, he held chairs at Harvard and the University of Chicago.

Tillich believed that religious questions arise out of human situations and therefore are practical and not primarily theoretical. He was strongly influenced by existentialism and this fact is reflected in a book dealing with the predicament of modern man, *The courage to be*. Here he discusses our existential anxiety arising inevitably as we confront death, meaninglessness, and guilt. People acquire the courage to be fully themselves through participation with others. Such participation, which involves acceptance by another, eventually leads a person to self-acceptance. Neurosis arises primarily from difficulties in human relationships resulting in alienation and withdrawal. The key to therapy is a genuine encounter with others in which helpful knowledge comes through participation.

Tillich's major work is *Systematic theology,* three volumes. A popular account of his position is given in *The dynamics of faith.* Although he was primarily a theologian, Tillich's work helped to bridge the gap separating modern psychology from religion and from existential philosophy.

P. E. LICHTENSTEIN

TINBERGEN, NIKOLAAS (1907–1988)

Tinbergen received the Ph.D. from the University of Leiden in 1932. He then left on a Dutch expedition to Greenland to study animals native to that region. He returned to Leiden and introduced a course in animal behavior there. By 1947, he had become a professor of animal zoology. In the same year he went to Oxford University to introduce a newly formed department of animal behavior. He first became acquainted with Konrad Lorenz in 1936. Together they studied the behavior of ducks following cardboard dummies. Their only joint published work was on the rolling behavior of greylag geese. Thus began the emergence of a new branch of biology and psychology: animal ethology.

Many of Tinbergen's works have become classics in both psychology and biology, including his work on courting behavior in sticklebacks, orienting behavior in wasps, and the behavior of grayling butterflies. His important books include *The study of instinct, The animal in its world,* and *Curious naturalists.*

Among his major accomplishments was the establishment of the study of adaptive significance. He showed that the function could be studied quantitatively under field conditions. Tinbergen believed that the study of ethology should be applied to human behavior as well as animals. This did not mean that animal behavior should be extrapolated to humans but that the same *methodology* could be applied. His last major study, in collaboration with his wife, was on early infantile autism. His Nobel Prize address was "Ethology and stress diseases." The prize money was used to help younger students study infantile autism. In his research, the always emphasized careful observation and clear formation of questions. The peak of recognition was reached when he received the Nobel Prize for Medicine, sharing it with Konrad Lorenz and Karl von Frisch. Other recognitions included the Distinguished Service Award of the American Psychological Association and his election as a fellow of the Royal Society (England).

R. W. LUNDIN

TITCHENER, EDWARD BRADFORD (1867–1927)

Titchener attended Malvern College and then Oxford University, where he studied philosophy, the classics, and physiology. He became interested in Wilhelm Wundt's new psychology and spent two years studying in Leipzig, receiving his degree in 1892. Titchener was a genuine disciple of his mentor Wundt and he kept his German temperament, both personally and professionally, throughout his life.

Titchener transplanted structuralism to U.S. soil from Wundt's laboratory in Leipzig. At the age of 25, he went to Cornell University, where he taught psychology and developed a laboratory of his own. He remained at Cornell for the rest of his life. Through his more than 50 doctoral students, Titchener's ideas were disseminated with systematic attention to research that reflected his thoughts and theories.

Titchener translated the works of Wundt, wrote over 200 articles, and had many books to his credit. The four volumes of *Experimental*

psychology, were widely used as laboratory manuals and speeded the growth of research in psychology. Through these volumes, Titchener influenced experimental psychology in the United States, including John B. Watson, the founder of behaviorism. *A textbook of psychology* was published in 1909.

The subject matter of structuralism was experience. Consciousness was defined as the sum total of experience at any given moment, and mind as the sum total of experience over a lifetime. Titchener felt that psychology should study the generalized human mind, not individual minds, and certainly not individual differences. Titchener's psychology was a pure science with no application to cures or reforms. The method of introspection was highly developed and formalized; the well-trained observers have been compared to impartial and detached human machines, objectively recording the characteristics of the object being observed.

Titchener taught that there are three elementary states of consciousness—sensations, images, and affective states. Sensations are the basic elements of perception; images are the elements of ideas; affections are the elements of emotion. Research on affection or feeling resulted in the rejection of Wundt's tridimensional theory, with support being found for one dimension only, pleasure-displeasure.

Toward the later years of his life, Titchener began to argue that psychology should not study elements but the dimensional attributes of mental life, which he listed as quality, intensity, protensity (duration), extensity, and attensity (clearness). He came to question the controlled method of introspection and to favor a more open, phenomenological approach.

N. A. HAYNIE

TOLMAN, EDWARD CHASE (1886–1959)

Tolman received his first degree, in engineering, from the Massachusetts Institute of Technology. However, he later changed to psychology, and was awarded the Ph.D. degree by Harvard in 1915. He taught at Northwestern University but spent most of his career at the University of California at Berkeley, where he established a rat laboratory.

In his early years, he was much impressed with John Watson's new behaviorism. However, he departed from the typical S-R (stimulus–response) psychology and began to develop a different concept, which he called "purposive behaviorism." Unlike the more traditional behaviorists, he placed great emphasis on cognition, emphasizing the importance of how individuals perceive the fields they are in.

Tolman is primarily known for his theory of learning. Many psychologists consider this theory a "cognitive field theory," although in his many experiments, primarily with the white rat, he always stressed behavior. He considered the behavioral event to be molar rather than molecular, which means that the event should be identified and described as a whole rather than reduced to a series of reflexes. Furthermore, he considered behavior to be purposive, indicating the importance of goal direction; the direction an organism takes depends on its perception of the goal and the totality of the situation along with expectations developed with regard to the situation.

Learning as such consists of the organism's moving along a path guided by various stimuli, both internal and external. One learns by signs, that is, what leads to what. What is learned is not a series of movements, but meanings. One learns a route to a goal and a "cognitive map" results that enables an organism to go from one point in the environment to another without depending on a set of bodily movements. Learning involves both expectancies and their confirmation. The importance of the goal is not to be thought of as a reward or reinforcement as in the learning theories of Thorndike, Hull, and Skinner, but merely as a confirmation of the expectancies.

Tolman is usually credited with introducing the concept of the "intervening variable" into psychology. Intervening variables involve inferred or unobservable factors that help in the explanation of the event but are not directly verifiable.

Finally, he believed that learning could occur in the absence of a goal. He identified this as "latent learning." Although not directly observable, learning could take place implicitly, and later, when a goal was introduced, the reality of the latent learning would become evident.

R. W. LUNDIN

TRENTINI, GIANCARLO G. (1928–)

Trentini has been a professor of psychology since 1975 at the faculty of arts and philosophy of the University of Venice. He graduated in medicine at the State University and he received postgraduate degree in psychology in 1959. He was licensed to teach psychology in 1963 and social psychology in 1966. Since 1969, he has been a professor of psychology and social psychology at the Catholic University of Milan.

Author or coauthor of some 90 scientific papers in the field of psychosocial knowledge, Trentini generally is concerned with the application of the psychosocial point of view to such problems as organization, work, school, consumer decision processes, and communication. In particular, his interest has been the study of the problems of groups, seen as an important matter of debate in psychology; of birth order, and of the particular functional roles of each position on the same order; of leadership and of power, authority, and freedom in intra- and interpersonal relationships; and of marketing research, from an epistemological point of view.

Another field of interest has been the methodological problem of the interview. He is editor of the *Manuale del colloquio e dell'intervista*, a handbook founded on the epistemology, methodology, technique, and deontology of the interview.

Trentini believes in and uses the psychodynamic approach, and is much more oriented toward the intensive-qualitative than the extensive-quantitative one approach.

TRIANDIS, HARRY C. (1926–)

Triandis received an engineering degree from McGill University, and a masters of commerce degree from the University of Toronto. During the latter studies, he became interested in psychology, which led to graduate work at Cornell University (Ph.D., 1958). He was assistant professor of psychology (1958–1961), associate professor (1961–1966), and full professor (1966) at the University of Illinois at Urbana-Champaign. He was (1968–1969) visiting scholar and professor at the Center for International Studies of Cornell University. He was named University of Illinois scholar in 1987.

His books include *Attitudes and attitude change, The analysis of subjective culture, Variations of black and white perceptions of the social environment, Interpersonal behavior,* and *Management of R & D organizations.* He was the general editor of the six-volume *Handbook of cross-cultural psychology.* He has published about 75 chapters in books and about 90 articles and monographs in journals.

He has been president of the Society for the Psychological Study of Social Issues, the Society for Personality and Social Psychology, the International Association of Cross Cultural Psychology, the Interamerican Society of Psychology (whose Award for Major Contributions to the Science and Profession of Psychology he received in 1983), and the International Association of Applied Psychology.

TRSTENJAK, ANTON (1906–)

Trstenjak is best known for his research on perceptual interactions, especially of colors, whereby he established highly significant negative correlations between a color's wavelength and its reaction time. After receiving the Ph.D. and D.D. degrees from the University of Innsbruck, Austria, he specialized in psychology in Milan, Italy, with Agostino Gemelli, and as a research assistant at the University of Montreal.

Trstenjak is considered as "one of the last encyclopedists among psychologists." He started with an original *Pastoral psychology,* regarded as the first of its kind in the world, and went on to the psychology of perception, including time and monotony, where he made a distinction between the objective monotony and subjective experience of boredom. He then proceeded to the psychology of work, basing it on viewpoints of the general system theory, and he continues with the psychology of scientific and artistic creativity, which is developing parallel with the intelligence, and has its root in the ability for symbolic thinking. He rejects the philosophic base of Szondi's Test (1956). He developed a special theory of personality, and through it has dealt with psychohygienic, economic psychological, and anthropological problems in his numerous books and articles.

Until his retirement, Trstenjak remained professor of psychology at the University of Ljubljana, Yugoslavia.

TSUJIOKA, BIEN (1925–)

Tsujioka is known for his personality testing and psychometric theory. He was educated in Kyoto. After receiving his bachelor's degree from Kyoto University, he continued his studies there and received the Ph.D. degree in 1962. His central concern was to develop a methodology of personality testing, especially via personality questionnaires through factor-analytic techniques.

Tsujioka constructed the Y-G Personality Inventory in 1957 in accordance with the principle of internal consistency and factor validity. He also cooperated with R. B. Cattell while a research associate at the University of Illinois. In addition to the use of factor validity in constructing questionnaire scales, he pointed out the importance of factor trueness and transferability. According to the principle of factor trueness, the directions of composites of item scores should coincide with those of the factor axes obtained in factor-analytic study. The latter principle claims that the correlations among the composite vectors should be constrained in oblique confirmatory factor analyses from different subject samples.

Tsujioka called these methods Patternmax and Factormax rotations—to maximize the pattern congruence or correlations of factor scores in the least-square-sense. He developed computer programs to establish pan-cultural or transcultural scales in psychology, as well as in sociology and anthropology. From this viewpoint, he developed the *Parent-child relation scales,* which involve constrained factor correlations and factor trueness among father–son, father–daughter, mother–son, and mother–daughter relationships.

TULVING, ENDEL (1927–)

Tulving was educated at the University of Heidelberg, the University of Toronto (B.A. degree), and Harvard University (Ph.D. degree, 1957). He has taught at the University of Toronto for most of his professional life, except for a brief interlude at Yale University (1970–1975).

Tulving is known for his experimental and theoretical contributions to the study of human memory. Among the empirical phenomena and theoretical concepts he introduced into the literature are subjective organization, availability and accessibility of information, retrieval cue, encoding specificity, recognition failure of recallable words, the reduction method for determining trace structure, the distinction between episodic and semantic memory, the Tulving–Wiseman function, and synergistic ecphory.

According to Tulving, recollection of an event occurs when appropriate retrieval information is combined with the informational aftereffects of the original perception of the event, the memory trace. The relation between the trace and the retrieval cue is one of interaction. Thus the memory trace can be thought of as a set of specifications as to the kinds of retrieval cues that are effective in actualizing the trace, while the observed effectiveness of retrieval cues provides evidence about informational properties of the trace. The interaction between the trace and the cue—or between encoding and retrieval, or between the past and the present—is the central process in remembering, and the most important object of psychological inquiry in the study of memory. Tulving's theoretical position is presented in *Elements of episodic memory*.

TURRÓ, RAMÓN (1854–1926)

As a student at the Faculty of Medicine of Barcelona, Turró undertook the forceful defense of the experimental method, personifying the spirit of Claude Bernard, against his professors who were representatives of the mentalistic views that prevailed in Spain in the latter part of the past century. In disagreement with the faculty, he left his studies of medicine. Turró was a creative self-made man, who carried out scientific research on important topics from outside the academic world. However, his need for academic recognition led him to obtain a degree in veterinarian medicine in 1893. In that same year, Turró presented a lecture at the Royal Academy of Medicine of Barcelona with the title "Immunity." In 1906, he was elected head of the Municipal Institute of Hygiene of Barcelona.

A great admirer of Ivan P. Pavlov (who, as it happened revealed the results of his research on conditioned reflexes in Madrid in 1903), Turró pursued some interesting experiments with newborn animals to determine how they learned their first specific responses as a basis for all later knowledge. Despite the fact that Pavlov's influence is obvious in all his work, Turrós standpoint on many subjects was truly original. Had he had followers, the psychological dimensions of his work would probably have had broad repercussions.

His works on learning based on hunger, published in French, German, Spanish, and Catalan, were appreciated by European psychophysiologists. Among his books was *The objective method*, in which Turró defended the advantages and rules of the scientific method.

R. Bayés

TUTUNDJIAN, HOUSEP M. (1918–   )

Tutundjian is known for his research on the history of psychology, in which he specialized in French and Armenian psychology. After graduating from the American University in Cairo in 1947, he pursued graduate studies in Moscow. He earned two doctoral degrees, one from Moscow State University in 1967, where he wrote a dissertation on the "History of French scientific psychology," and the Ph.D. degree from the Regional Pedagogical Institute, where his specialty was the psychology of sports.

Since 1971, he has been professor of psychology at Erevan State University in Soviet Armenia—where he founded a department in 1975, established a chair in 1976, and set up a laboratory of engineering psychology in 1978. In 1976, he organized a conference on the history of psychology, and in 1982, the First Soviet All-Union Conference on the History of Psychology.

Tutundjian's career has taken him to France, where he delivered a course of lectures at The Sorbonne, the University of Strasbourg, the Centre de Psychologie Historique in Paris, and other centers of psychol-

ogy. He chaired the Psychological Society of the U.S.S.R., and currently is psychology editor of the *Armenian Encyclopedia*.

Tutundjian's publications include *Contemporary problems of history and theory of psychology* and *Contemporary problems of history of psychology*. Among his other interests are the psychology of education, engineering psychology, and cognitive psychology.

TYLER, LEONA E. (1906–1993)

Tyler is best known for her textbooks *The psychology of human differences, The work of the counselor,* and *Tests and measurements,* and for the offices she has held in psychological associations, culminating in the presidency of the American Psychological Association in 1972–1973. She grew up in the Iron Range country of northern Minnesota and received the B.A. from the University of Minnesota, where she majored in English. The next 13 years were spent teaching, mainly English and mathematics, in junior high schools in Minnesota and Michigan. Her career as a psychologist did not really begin until she returned to the University of Minnesota in 1938 for graduate work in psychology. She was awarded the Ph.D. degree in 1941.

Tyler's thinking was a synthesis of ideas from three major sources. The first was her teaching specialty, individual differences. The second was practical counseling activity, which was an important part of her work for many years. The third was research on interest measurement, in which she was continuously involved from 1937 to the early 1960s. Out of this combination has emerged a philosophical-theoretical point of view expressed most clearly in her book *Individuality: Human possibilities and personal choice in the psychological development of men and women* and in *The concept of multiple possibilities in psychology*.

Tyler had been a member of the faculty of the University of Oregon since 1940, teaching a variety of courses and serving for six years as dean of the Graduate School. She retired from active duty in 1971.

ULLMANN, LEONARD P. (1930–   )

Best known for his work extending the behavioral approach to a general psychological theory, the New York City-born Ullmann received the B.A. degree from Lafayette College and the M.A. and Ph.D. (1955) degrees from Stanford University. Upon completing his internship at Palo Alto Veterans Administration Hospital, he became its coordinator of Psychiatric Evaluation Project until moving into academic work at the universities of Illinois (1963–1972), Hawaii (1972–1981), and Houston (1981–present).

Ullmann's procedure is to investigate human behavior with as little distortion due to cultural or theoretical preconceptions as possible. This has led him to an educational and sociopsychological position as opposed to traits, diseases, types, or unconscious processes. The creative acts of artists and scientists, and the change-worthy behavior of bureaucrats and people called schizophrenic, were all approached in the same way; namely, by asking what activities, under what conditions, led to what particular social designations. Among the major products of this orientation is a book on psychiatric hospitals called *Institution and outcome* and, with Leonard Krasner, *Case studies in behavior modification, Research in behavior modification, A psychological approach to abnormal behavior,* and *Behavior influence and personality*.

UNDERWOOD, BENTON J. (1915–   )

Underwood received the B.A. degree from Cornell College (Iowa) and the Ph.D. degree from the University of Iowa in 1942 where he studied under John A. McGeoch, a specialist in human learning. After serving in the U.S. Navy during World War II, he joined the faculty at Northwestern University, where he has remained. He is a member of the National Academy of Science.

His first book, *Experimental psychology,* has been a widely used undergraduate text in that area. It stresses methodology and design rather than content. His discussions on experimental design are applied to motivation, frustration, and various areas of learning and memory. He published *Psychological research,* and was coauthor of *Elementary statistics* with C. P. Duncan and Janet Taylor.

Over the years, his research efforts have been devoted to the field of human learning, and he is the author or coauthor (with Carl P. Duncan, Jack Richardson, and others) of more than 120 articles. Underwood has explored many facets of verbal learning processes, including problems of retroactive and proactive inhibition, distributed practice, and the role of meaningfulness in associative learning, as well as a variety of variables that contribute to the degree of remembering and forgetting following verbal learning.

UZNADZE, DMITRII NIKOLAYEVICH (1886–1950)

As a Soviet psychologist, Uznadze rounded the Georgian Institute of Psychology, now named for him. He is best known for his theory of "set" as an objective approach to the unconscious. Aware of Freud's theory of the unconscious and its contents, Uznadze developed a method for studying a complex of superthreshold influences that set upon a subject from the whole situation arising under the influence of the situation's "meaning" for the subject.

A model experiment will illustrate. For several trials, a subject is given two spheres of equal weight but of different volume, one to be held in each hand. Then the subject is given two spheres of equal weight and volume. Asked which sphere is larger, the subject in this "critical" trial answers that the larger sphere is in the hand that previously received the smaller sphere. What is the nature of this illusion? Underlying the weight illusion is, according to Uznadze, a particular "inner state" or a particular change in the functional condition of the central nervous system. Analysis of this "state" or functional disturbance made it possible to throw some light on its characteristic. The illusion appeared to be an extremely complex reflex action. Thus Uznadze used the word "set" for the unconscious change of the functional condition of the nervous system.

R. W. LUNDIN

VAIHINGER, HANS (1852–1933)

Vaihinger was on the faculty at Halle, Germany. He was a Kant scholar, and founded the journal *Kant Studien.*

Vaihinger is important to psychology because of his impact on Adler. Shortly after its 1911 publication, Adler came upon Vaihinger's book that set forth the philosophy of "as-if": Something can work as if true even though it is false and recognized as false. Adler incorporated the notion into his teleological *fictional goals.* For Vaihinger, the fictions are justified by their utility, but it is more than pragmatism. The individual is not simply skeptical but recognizes that the fiction is indeed false. False is almost too strong a term here, as something that is genuinely verifiable is not really a fiction at all but a hypothesis. The true fiction is false only in that it can never be verified (e.g., God and the orderly cosmos, human immortality, the virgin birth, the concept of the atom). Thus fictions can be seen either to deviate from reality or to be self-contradictory. Fictions are used provisionally—a fiction is a nonrational solution. Intuition and experience are "higher" faculties than reason. Accepting the fiction means that the contradiction and misery accompanying it fade away. Vaihinger had little patience with philosophers who tended to torture themselves with unanswerable questions. He felt that

true wisdom involved being content to live life on a very practical level. Truth is nothing more and nothing less than expedient fiction, and we must accept that fact.

Another central idea in Vaihinger's philosophy was that the categories supplied by the mind influence the perception of objects.

C. S. PEYSER

VAITL, DIETER (1940–   )

Vaitl is known for his behavioral approach to psychosomatic diseases, particularly cardiovascular disorders. After receiving his licentiate in philosophy in 1963 from the University Gregoriana in Rome, he began his studies in psychology at Freiburg University, from which he received his diploma in 1967. Until 1969, he worked as a clinical psychologist in the Psychosomatic Division of the Pediatric Department at Freiburg. After moving to the Department of Clinical Psychology at the University of Muenster, he expanded his psychosomatic research to psychophysiology and behavior therapy, and in 1971, he received the Ph.D. degree in psychology. From 1970 through 1976, he extended his practical expertise to basic research on self-control of cardiovascular functions and developed a biofeedback technique for patients with functional heart disorders. In 1976, he became chairman of the Department of Clinical Psychology at Giessen University, where he continues to lecture, counsel, and conduct research.

Vaitl regards himself as a behaviorist and psychophysiologist, seeking to understand the psychological aspects of somatic diseases and to apply psychological and psychophysiological knowledge (cardiac arrhythmia, essential hypertension). Using this approach, he is particularly interested in finding out if and to what extent human physiology provides sufficient plasticity to be modified by procedures derived from psychological principles. His publication *Essentielle hypertonie* summarizes his ideas about this interdisciplinary approach. Only when the heterogeneity and the specific psychobiological components of cardiovascular malfunctions are fairly well understood, can psychology be expected to make a valuable contribution to medical problems.

VALENSTEIN, ELLIOT S. (1923–   )

Valenstein completed the B.S. degree at the City College of New York and the M.A. and Ph.D. (1954) degrees from the University of Kansas, where he studied the interaction of genetic hormonal, and environmental factors influencing reproductive behavior in animals. In 1955, following a U.S. Public Health postdoctoral fellowship, Valenstein joined the staff of the Walter Reed Institute of Research where he became chief of the neuropsychology section. At Walter Reed, he completed anatomical studies on the limbic system in collaboration with Walle Nauta and brain–behavior studies on the physiology of motivation. In 1961, Valenstein spent 6 months in the Soviet Union on a National Academy of Science fellowship, following which he joined the staff of the Fels Research Institute (Yellow Springs, Ohio) as a senior scientist; he also was appointed professor at Antioch College. Following a leave as visiting professor at the University of California at Berkeley in 1970, Valenstein became professor of psychology and neuroscience at the University of Michigan.

Valenstein has written more than 150 experimental and theoretical articles and has authored four books, including *Brain control* and *Great and desperate cures.* Valenstein is a foreign member of the Academy of Science of Mexico. Among other honors are the Kenneth Craik Research Award from Cambridge University, the award for Outstanding Achievement in Psychology from CCNY, the award for Outstanding Achievement in Published Works, elected president of the Physiological and Comparative Division of APA, and member of Phi Beta Kappa and the Society of Experimental Psychologists.

VERNON, PHILIP E. (1905–1987)

Vernon received his bachelor's degree from Cambridge University, in natural sciences and psychology. His Ph.D. thesis at Cambridge was entitled *The psychology of musical appreciation*, and this led to several articles that also included theories of audition. However, two years of his graduate studies in the field of personality were spent in the United States, with Mark May at Yale and Gordon Allport at Harvard. He was appointed psychologist to the Child Guidance Clinic at the Maudsley Hospital, London, in 1933, and moved to Glasgow in 1935, where he subsequently became head of the Psychology Department. During World War II, he worked with the personnel selection departments of the British Army and Navy, on test constrnction and validation, factor analysis, and methods of training.

In 1949, Vernon became professor of educational psychology at the London University Institute of Education, where he published several books on seleetion, intelligence and achievement tests, factor analysis, and personality assessment. He migrated to Canada in 1968, as professor of educational psychology at the University of Calgary, Alberta. His main interest in the 1960s and 1970s was in the effects of environmental and cultural factors on intellectual development. Assisted by his wife, Dorothy, he carried out a series of comparative studies of abilities in different parts of the world, from Tanzania to the Arctic. They also contributed to the psychology of gifted children and creativity.

VERPLANCK, WILLIAM S. (1916–   )

Verplanck completed the B.S. and M.S. at the University of Virginia. He took the Ph.D. (1941) at Brown, going directly to the Naval Medical Research Laboratory at the Sub Base in New London, Connecticut. At the end of World War II, he joined the department at Indiana University, acting part-time as assistant department head to both B. F. Skinner and J. R. Kantor. In 1950, he began a 5-yr stint at Harvard, followed by 1 yr at Stanford, 1 yr of travel, 2 yr at Hunter College, and 4 yr at the University of Maryland. Verplanck then arrived at the University of Tennessee for a 10-yr term as head, where he remained until retirement in 1981.

During World War II, night vision and lookout training–evaluation gave Verplanck experience infield research. Work on psychophysical judgment followed; he showed that successive psychological judgments are not independent of one another, as theory dictated. Evaluation of Skinner's work led to pioneering research on operant conditioning of humans and on thinking—behaviors that lead observation into action. Verplanck also worked to introduce ethological method and thinking to American psychologists. His *Glossary of terms* facilitated communication between ethologists and behavior theorists. This in turn led to analysis of experimental research in terms of the decisions made in its design and in its execution. Since retiring he has been preparing a glossary/thesaurus of psychological terms aimed at clarifying the language of psychological theory and practice and embodying the current scientific status of psychology. He is listed in *Who's Who* and was the founder of the Psychonomic Society.

VITELES, MORRIS S. (1898–   )

Viteles is frequently described as the "grandfather of industrial psychology." He was not, in fact, the first in the field, as Hugo Münsterberg had already roughly outlined the objectives and scope of the area. Viteles was initially responsible for eliminating a prevalent misconception that equated industrial psychology with employment psychology. In *Indus-*

trial psychology, he structured the field as it largely remains today. His repeated emphasis on the need for a solid experimental basis for industrial applications helped to counter an ongoing conversion of industrial psychology into industrial psychotechnology.

Motivation and morale in industry, which, among other developments, recorded shifts in emphasis from selection-training to motivation-management-organization, is marked by preoccupation with industrial psychology as primarily science, rather than technology. It may be this, more than anything else, that led Haire to write, "It is hard to realize the critical role that Morris Viteles played in shaping and directing this growth of the area . . . that we work in a field which is the way it is because of the rigor and ingenuity of Morris Viteles in the early days." In many later publications, Viteles has frequently voiced deep criticism of experimental imperfections and of untested fads, frequently described as theories, that creep into, and in some areas, such as organizational, appear to dominate new developments.

Viteles received the A.B., A.M., and Ph.D. (1921) degrees from the University of Pennsylvania, followed by a year at the University of Paris and a year in the U.S.S.R. as a Social Science Council Research Fellow. He taught at the University of Pennsylvania for 50 years. During World War II, he was chairman of the National Research Council Committee on Aviation Psychology (1941–1951), and a member of the NDRC Committee on Applied Psychology. He was the first non-European to be elected president of the International Association of Applied Psychology (1958–1968). Publications include an autobiographical chapter in volume V of *A history of psychology in autobiography* and another in *The psychologists*, vol. II.

VIVES, JUAN LUIS (1492–1540)

Vives, a Spanish philosopher and Renaissance humanist, stands alone as a forerunner of modern psychology. Vives graduated from the University of Paris in 1512 and taught at the University of Louvain (1519) and at Oxford University (1523–1527).

No writer of the Renaissance period was as distinguished by his application of psychology to education as Vives, an advocate of education for women. A master of introspection and observation, Vives stressed the importance of understanding the human mind for philosophy, education, science, and politics. In 1538 he published a book on psychology entitled *De anima et vita libri tres*, which delineates the following points: Psychology should be used in education. Philosophical and psychological truths are to be discovered inductively rather than deductively, avoiding speculation. It is paramount to know the manifestations of the soul (what it is like) rather than the essence of the soul (what it is). For knowledge to be of value, it must be used. Vives was concerned with how the mind works and not with the essence of mind. His book was rooted in the functionalist school.

Vives covered three major areas in his book: (1) association of ideas, memory, and learning; (2) the rational soul and intelligence; and (3) emotions and passions. He stressed the manifold character of emotions and passions, temporal variations, interaction with temperament and habit patterns, and coloring of perception by emotions and their influence in creating a special world for that individual.

M. LaCroce

VYGOTSKY, LEV SEMYONOVICH (1896–1934)

Educated at Moscow State University, Vygotsky was one of the significant postrevolutionary Soviet psychologists. His first entrance into psychology was with a paper in which he made a strong plea for the inclusion of consciousness in the subject matter of psychology. He opposed the reflexology of Bekhterev, arguing that a study of mind was necessary, since it distinguished humans from lower animals. However, he rejected introspection as a method. In this sense, he was closer to behaviorism than to the psychologists who accepted introspection, not only as a legitimate method, but as the main method of psychology. A study of mind was necessary to distinguish human beings from the lower animals, he believed. Thus consciousness consisted of a relationship among the psychical functions and should be the major topic of Soviet psychology.

Perhaps Vygotsky is best known for his theory of signs. The genesis of signs was a process of internalizing the means of social communication. According to this theory, during the cultural development of a child, each higher psychical function passes through an external phase, since it originally had a social function. There are three phases in the process of internalization, which can be illustrated in the development of speech. In the first, words express the relationship of the child to objects. In the second, the relationship between words and things is used by the adult as a means of communication with the child. In the third, words become intrinsically meaningful to the child. Hence words as signs become a social tool that help people to control the "lower" mental functions. Finally, the concept of sign was assumed to provide a resolution between a biological and social conflict.

R. W. LUNDIN

WAGNER-JAUREGG, JULIUS (1857–1940)

A Viennese psychiatrist and neurologist, Wagner-Jauregg received the M.D. at the University of Vienna, where he worked until his appointment at Graz. In 1894, he returned to the University of Vienna and remained there until his retirement in 1928.

Wagner-Jauregg is best known for his discovery of a treatment for general paresis (syphilitic infection of the brain) that involved inducing malaria infection into his patients. For his discovery of the means for controlling what had been a fatal disease, and his use of it in treating paresis, he was awarded the Nobel prize in 1927. Like Sakel's discovery of the use of insulin coma treatment for schizophrenia, Wagner-Jauregg's discovery came about quite by accident. He observed that one of his patients who suffered from paresis showed considerable improvement after an attack of malaria. The effect of the high fever resulting from the disease was to arrest the brain damage that occurs with syphilis. He had learned from reading the ancient Greek philosopher Parmenides that the induction of fever could cure illnesses, and he proceeded systematically to treat other patients suffering from paresis.

Wagner-Jauregg published his classic paper on "The effects of malaria in progressive paralysis" in 1918. The procedure in treatment as described involved taking the blood from an individual during an attack of malaria and spreading it in small "scarifications" on the arm of the paretic. It was not until Alexander Flemming's discovery of penicillin that such diseases could be treated successfully without inducing infection. Wagner-Jauregg was able to use quinine to control the malaria while treating the paresis.

R. W. LUNDIN

WALKER, C. EUGENE (1939–   )

Walker received the B.S. from Geneva College, with special honors in psychology, and the M.S. and Ph.D. (1965) from Purdue University. While at Purdue, he was an NIMH fellow and a VA trainee in psychology. His M.S. and Ph.D. were in clinical psychology with minors in experimental psychology and sociology. He completed an internship (1963–1964) at Riley Children's Hospital and at the VA hospital, both in Indianapolis.

Walker's first teaching position was assistant professor (1964–1968) at Westmont College. From 1966 to 1968 he was chair of the Division of Education and Psychology at Westmont College. He became associate professor of psychology at Baylor University. In 1974, he moved to the University of Oklahoma Medical School as professor, director of training and pediatric psychology, and associate chief, mental health services, Children's Hospital of Oklahoma. At the University of Oklahoma, he received awards for excellence in classroom teaching (1984) and for sustained excellence in departmental educational endevors (1988). He is a fellow of the American Psychological Association and a past president of the Southwestern Psychological Association, the Oklahoma Psychological Association, and the Society of Pediatric Psychology. He received the award for Distinguished Contributions to the Profession of Psychology from the Oklahoma Psychological Association (1986).

Walker's main contributions have been in the area of writing and research on psychopathology, psychological testing, and behavioral treatment. Throughout his career he has been administratively responsible for educational training programs that have turned out large numbers of clinical psychologists and pediatric psychologists. He has produced more than 200 publications, including 15 books.

WALLON, HENRI (1879–1962)

Wallon, with his friend and colleague Henri Pieron, were the pioneers of scientific psychology in France. Graduated in philosophy in 1909, and obtaining the M.D. (his thesis was on delusions of persecution, *Délire de persécution*) he became well known in 1925 with his thesis *The disturbed child (L'enfant turbulent)*. That same year he established the Laboratory for Psychobiology for the Child. In 1939, with Henri Pieron, he created the Institute of Psychology of Paris and the National Institute for Professional Guidance. From 1937 to 1949, he was a professor at the College of France, the senior institution of higher learning in France.

Psychobiology was Wallon's specialty. He was a student of the neurologists Babinski and Nageotte, and psychobiology was the direction of all his work. During the 1920s, at the same time that Arnold Gesell was working in the United States, he insisted on the importance of biological maturation in contrast to the behaviorism of John B. Watson.

His theory of emotions was his chief contribution. Emotion he saw as a physiological fact with humoral and physiological aspects, but it also had a social portion serving basic adaptive functions. Emotions mediated between sensations and the social world. What characterized Wallon and distinguished him from his colleague Jean Piaget, with whom he was perpetually in dialog and controversy, was not only his field of study (behavior, emotions), but above all his dialectical approach. In his works on the origins of thought, as in his major book *The origins of character*, what he sought to analyze were the conflicts, tensions, and internal contradictions that are the driving forces of development through progress, problems, and crises.

R. ZAZZO

WANG, ZHONG-MING (1949–   )

Wang received the M.A. in organizational psychology from Hangzhou University in China in 1982. Since then, Wang has been on the faculty of the department of psychology at Hangzhou University. During 1984–1985, he studied in Sweden and obtained an M.A. in applied psychology from the Gothenborg University. Wang received the Ph.D. (1987) in industrial psychology under the supervision of Li Chen from Hangzhou University and became a professor in 1988.

He is the deputy director of the National Committee of Industrial Psychology of the Chinese Psychological Society and the executive committee member of the Chinese Ergonomics Society. He has been visiting scholar at Gothenburg University (Sweden), Tavistock Institute of Human Relations (UK), Murdoch University (Australia), and Gottingen University (Germany). In 1990, he taught as the Fulbright scholar-in-residence at Old Dominion University (United States).

Wang is the associate editor of the *Chinese Journal of Applied Psychology*, the executive editor of *Ergonomics* (UK) and is on the editorial board of *Human Relations, Current Psychological Research and Review, Leadership Quarterly*, and the *Journal of Managerial Psychology*. He has published several books, including *Work and personnel psychology* and *Research methods in psychology*, and more than 60 articles at home and abroad. He has been active in the areas of reward systems design, group attributional training, high-tech innovations, judgment and decision making, knowledge acquisition, human–computer interaction, organization development, and decision support systems. Wang has received the Chinese National Excellent University Young Teacher Award by the Fok Ying Tung Educational Foundation in China.

WARD, JAMES (1843–1924)

An English psychologist, considered by some to be the successor of Alexander Bain, Ward also owed a psychological debt to Franz Brentano and his Act psychology. He was educated at Cambridge and also studied at Berlin and Göttenham under Rudolf Lotze. His views on psychology were first published in the ninth edition of the *Encyclopaedia Britannica* in 1886. Somewhat later he wrote the book *Psychological principles*, published in 1918.

Ward's systematic position divided psychology into cognition, conation, and feeling. In dealing with the person (subject), cognition referred to nonvoluntary attending processes on the sensory continuum. Conation referred to voluntary attention that produced changes in motor activity. Feeling involved being pleased or in pain. All of this was on the side of the subject. On the side of the object, cognition referred to the presentation of sensory objects. Conation involved the presentation of motor objects or objects in motion. Feeling was not considered on the object side but was only the consequence of presenting sensory or motor objects.

Ward's psychology never experienced great popularity as many considered it too difficult to comprehend. A more effective presentation of the system was left to his successor, George F. Stout.

Even though Ward was considered by many to be more a philosopher than a psychologist, he was instrumental in establishing the first psychological laboratory at Cambridge. After various attempts and failures, in 1891 he was successful in getting enough funds (£50) to get the laboratory started. It was primarily devoted to experiments using Fechner's psychophysical methods.

R. W. LUNDIN

WARREN, HOWARD CROSBY (1867–1934)

Warren graduated from Princeton University and received his graduate training at Leipzig in the experimental tradition of Wilhelm Wundt. For 30 years he taught at Princeton, first as director of the Psychological Laboratory, and then as the first chairman of the independent Department of Psychology.

Warren is best known as a writer and editor. Having obtained the *Psychological Review, Psychological Index*, and *Psychological Monographs* from James Mark Baldwin, he established the Psychological Review Company. This company also controlled the *Psychological Bulletin* and the *Journal of Experimental Psychology*. Warren sold all of these journals to the American Psychological Association in 1922. He was a contributor to James Baldwin's *Dictionary of philosophy and psychology* and published a *Dictionary of psychology*, which was a standard work for many years.

In the textbook field, Warren contributed *Human psychology*, a general exposition of his views, and *A history of the association psychology*. His psychology was evolutionary and deterministic and stressed the introspective method. He accepted a double-aspect theory of the mind-body relationship and consequently emphasized the key role of the central nervous system in psychology. While he considered himself sympathetic to John Watson's behaviorism, Warren believed that overt behavior alone provides inadequate materials for research.

P. E. LICHTENSTEIN

WASHBURN, MARGARET FLOY (1871–1939)

Washburn received the A.B. degree from Vassar College and the Ph.D. degree under Edward B. Titchener at Cornell in 1894. She taught at Wells College and the University of Cincinnati, and in 1903 returned to Vassar, where she remained until her retirement in 1937. In 1925, she became one of the four coeditors of the *American Journal of Psychology*, after Titchener resigned as its editor. She was elected president of the American Psychological Association in 1921, and in 1931 was elected to the National Academy of Sciences, the second woman ever to be named to that prestigious group.

As an experimental psychologist, she published many of her research studies in the *Psychological studies of Vassar College*. These included work on individual differences, color vision in animals, and aesthetic preferences by students for colors and speech sounds. Her most important book, *The animal mind*, was first published in 1908. This was the first book by an American psychologist on animal psychology. It contained a wide survey of the literature on the behavior of animals and reflected her vast interest in animals and their behavior.

With her training in introspection under Titchener, she believed that conscious processes and overt behavior were two distinct phenomena, neither of which could be reduced to the other. But unlike Titchener and Wilhelm Wundt, who limited themselves to the study of conscious experience, Washburn stressed the importance of movements and behavior. In 1916, she presented her ideas on this matter in *Movement and mental images*. In a sense, she took a middle view between the structuralists, who studied only conscious experience, and the behaviorists, who limited psychology to behavior.

R. W. LUNDIN

WATSON, JOHN B. (1878–1958)

The founder of American Behaviorism, Watson was the first University of Chicago student to receive a degree in psychology. "With animals I was at home," he said, and so he devoted much of his life to animal psychology. Even his doctoral dissertation in 1903 was on *Animal education*. So impressed with it was Chicago's Henry Donaldson, that he lent Watson $350 to have it published.

By the 1920s, Watson had developed an interest in human subjects. Not long after his son John was born in 1904, he remarked: "A baby is more fun to the square inch than all the rats and frogs in creation." During this period, his range of friends extended from J. R. Angell and Harvey Carr to J. M. Baldwin and R. M. Yerkes.

Watson left Chicago in 1903 for a professorship at Johns Hopkins. During his Johns Hopkins tenure, behaviorism was born. He found its two tenets (psychology as an objective science, and psychology as the science of behavior) in W. B. Pillsbury's *Essentials of psychology*. His behaviorist manifesto "Psychology as a behaviorist views it" appeared in 1913, and its book-length elaboration, *Behavior: An introduction to comparative psychology*, the following year.

A career crisis occurred in 1920 with his abrupt dismissal from Johns Hopkins. He married Rosalie Rayner, a graduate student, and together they published two important papers on human conditioning and counterconditioning: "Conditioned emotional reactions" and "Studies in infant behavior." During this period, he wrote chapters for his *Psychology from the standpoint of a behaviorist,* and used some of his observations on children for it.

On leaving Johns Hopkins for the world of advertising, Watson's penchant for new ideas waned, despite the publication in the 1920s of *Behaviorism, The ways of behaviorism,* and some lesser known works. Chiefly known for his *radical behaviorism,* Watson boldly declared: "Give me a dozen healthy infants . . . and I'll guarantee to take any one at random and train him to become any type of specialist" (*Psychology from the standpoint of a behaviorist*). His enthusiasm failed to hold, for a mere four years later, he despairingly remarked: "I used to feel quite hopeful of reconditioning even adult personalities. . . . But . . . the zebra can as easily change his stripes as the adult his personality" (*The ways of behaviorism*). Nevertheless, when Watson died in 1958, behaviorism virtually dominated American psychology.

W. S. SAHAKIAN

WATT, HENRY JACKSON (1879–1925)

Watt was one of the members of the Würzburg School established by Otto Külpe at that university in Germany. The main efforts of the school were to study "imageless thought," that thinking could occur in the absence of any conscious experience of it. Established in the late nineteenth century, the school held a dominant position in German psychology for several decades.

Watt's main contribution involved the study of experience as it occurred in word associations. He divided his approach into four stages. The first was the preparation or instructions to the subject as to the nature of the task to be performed. The second involved the presentation of a single word by means of visual representation. The third involved the search for the appropriate word, and the fourth the actual verbal response. In each phase, he asked his subjects to introspect regarding what conscious processes were occurring. He concluded that the subjects were able to respond with an appropriate word in the absence of any conscious effort. The key to the problem was to be found in the instructions or task *(Aufgabe),* which brought about a set *(Einstellung)* in the minds of the subjects. He felt there was a determining tendency to react in the way the given instructions called for. These tendencies were not present in the consciousness during the actual reaction (searching for and saying the appropriate word). Thus the thought itself was imageless and could not be described introspectively. Regarding the conscious experience, subjects did their thinking before they knew what they were to think about. With the proper preparation, the thought ran off automatically without conscious content.

In 1906, Watt left Wurzburg and became a lecturer at Liverpool. A year later, he was appointed lecturer in psychology at Glasgow, where he turned his attention to the psychology of sound. It had already been accepted that certain dimensions of tone existed, such as pitch and loudness. Watt concluded that another dimension existed, that of volume—high pitches had little volume but loud tones in the lower register were judged to be very voluminous.

R. W. LUNDIN

WEBB, WILSE BERNARD (1920–   )

Webb received the B.A. from Louisiana State University in psychology and the M.A. and Ph.D. (1947) from the State University of Iowa. He served in the air force in World War II (1942–1946) and as assistant professor at the University of Tennessee (1947–1948) and at Washington University (1948–1953). From 1953 to 1958, he directed the Aviation Psychology Laboratory of the Naval School of Aviation Medicine (Pensacola) and became chair of the department of psychology at the University of Florida in 1959. He was appointed graduate research professor at Florida (1969) until his retirement in 1989. He served twice on the Board of Directors of the American Psychological Association and as president of the divisions of Teaching and of History of Psychology. He was president of the Southeastern Psychological Association and of the Southern Society for Philosophy and Psychology.

Webb is best known for the application of psychological research to sleep. Working with both animals and humans, he has written seven books and more than 200 articles. His research emphasizes the role of individual differences and biological rhythms as determinants of sleep deprivation and performance and the effects of aging. His theoretical writings emphasize the adaptive nature of sleep.

WEBER, ERNST HEINRICH (1795–1878)

Weber was one of the important physiologists of the nineteenth century. Shortly before 1820, he began to teach anatomy and physiology at the University of Leipzig, where he remained for the rest of his career.

Although a physiologist, many of his experiments have great psychological significance. His main research concern was in the field of sensory physiology. His early studies of the temperature sense led him to conclude that the feeling of warm or cold was not directly dependent on the temperature of the stimulus but on increases or decreases in the temperature of the skin.

Another area of investigation involved the sense of touch. He found that if two separate pinpoints were applied to a region on the skin, one would ordinarily report feeling two different points. If the distance between the two points were gradually reduced, a point would be reached at which one felt only one point even though two stimuli were still being presented. This has become known as the two-point threshold, or limen. If the distance were decreased further, a person still would report feeling only one point. A greater distance would be reported as two points. Weber further observed that the two-point threshold differed for different parts of the body. It was very small for the fingertips and much larger for the back of the body.

Most important were Weber's studies of the muscle sense. He was interested in finding how well a person could discriminate differences in the weights of objects by lifting one and comparing it with another. He found that one's ability to tell the difference between a standard and various comparison weights was not absolute. There was a threshold or points of "just noticeable difference" below which a comparison weight and the standard seemed the same. As the difference in the magnitude of the comparison weight and the standard became greater, the comparison weight was more easily detected as heavier. Likewise, as the comparison weight became increasingly lighter than the standard, a difference could be detected. Furthermore, if the comparison and standard weights were doubled in magnitude, the point of just noticeable difference would be twice that of the original. Thus the point of just noticeable difference bore a constant relationship to the standard. This relationship was set down in a formula by Gustav Fechner, who identified it as Weber's law, $\Delta I / I = k$, in which the ΔI is the point of just noticeable difference from the standard and the I is the standard weight.

R. W. LUNDIN

WECHSLER, DAVID (1896–1981)

Wechsler is one of the founders of modern clinical psychology and the author of the most widely used tests for assessing individual intelligence.

When David was 6 years old, his family migrated to New York City, where he completed the A.B. degree at the City College of New York in 1916. Clinical psychology as it is known today was not yet launched, let alone envisioned by the approximately 1000 predominately academic and experimental psychologists who were members of the American Psychological Association that year. Nevertheless a few psychologists had left academia and had ventured to work in child guidance, educational, and even psychiatric clinics. Thus young Wechsler was allowed to carry out a thesis for the M.A. degree (1917) at Columbia University under Robert S. Woodworth on a topic (retention in Korsakoff's psychosis) in the emerging field of experimental psychopathology.

Wechsler also sought out his own opportunities for other clinical experiences in psychology. For example, in 1917, while awaiting Army induction as the United States prepared to enter World War I, Wechsler gained his first applied experience working under E. G. Boring at an Army camp on Long Island. There Wechsler helped score the performances of several thousand recruits on the Army Alpha, a group-administered offshoot of the Stanford-Binet, which had been produced by a handful of U.S. psychologists. After formal induction a few months later, Wechsler was assigned by the Army to the psychology unit at Fort Logan in Texas. There his duties as a psychology technician consisted largely of testing reeruits needing individual assessment. This brief experience involved adult recruits who could not read English, or who had had no formal schooling, and others for whom the group-administered Army Alpha and Army Beta tests were less appropriate than was one-on-one assessment in which the examiner utilized both verbal (Stanford–Binet) and nonverbal (Yerkes and Army Performance Scales) tests of measured intelligence. The realization that written tests such as the Army Alpha yielded an inaccurate index of measured intelligence for these subgroups of adults who previously had functioned adequately as civilians, and the more realistic index of this sociooccupational adaptiveness provided for them by nonverbal tests, gave Wechsler two invaluable insights: First, the debates between Spearman and Thorndike and other academician-theorists on the nature of intelligence were based on a conception that was too narrow to fit the realities presented to a psychologist who examined people in situations in which real-life decisions based on such assessment were necessary. Second, the Stanford-Binet, while suitable for children, was not satisfactory for adults—the literate, as well as the foreign-born Americans who did not understand English.

Following his transfer to France, Wechsler was assigned, in 1919, as an Army student to the University of London, where he studied with Charles Spearman and Karl Pearson. Both men had a great influence on him—Spearman through his concept of general intelligence, which Wechsler later would find inadequate to encompass the "nonintellective" components of intelligence, and Pearson through his innovative correlational methods.

Soon after his Army discharge in England (August 1919), Wechsler won a fellowship to the University of Paris (1920–1922). There he studied with Henri Pieron and Louis Lapique, and also gathered data on the psychogalvanic response and emotion that became the basis for his 1925 Ph.D. dissertation at Columbia, again under the direction of Woodworth. While completing the Ph.D. degree, Wechsler worked as a psychologist in New York City's newly created Bureau of Child Guidance (1922–1924). Following his doctorate, he served as acting secretary of the Psychological Corporation (1925–1927), and then spent the next several years in private clinical practice (1927–1932). Wechsler became chief psychologist at Bellevue Psychiatric Hospital in 1932, with a concurrent faculty appointment at New York University College of Medicine (1933). He held both positions until 1967 and combined research with clinical work.

Beginning in 1934, Wechsler's creative efforts were largely directed to two of his most important contributions to psychology: (1) the development and standardization of the adult (and later preschool and children's) intelligence scales that bear his name; and (2) the substitution for Binet's Mental Age of a Deviation Quotient (so important in evaluating the intelligence level of adults) that related each person's raw intelligence test score to his or her own age group as a reference, rather than to a mental age and an upper age limit of 15 years for adults, as had been done by Binet, Terman, and others. The immediate spur to these two contributions was the need for a suitable instrument for testing the multilingual adult population referred to Wechsler for psychological examination at Bellevue. This effort culminated in a single battery called the *Bellevue-Wechsler Scale* (1939).

Wechsler continued using a comparable multitest battery (of 10 or 11 verbal and performance subtests) in the development of his 1942 *Army Wechsler (Bellevue-Wechsler II)*, *Wechsler Intelligence Scale for Children*, *Wechsler Adult Intelligence Scale*, *Wechsler Preschool and Primary Scale of Intelligence*, *Wechsler Intelligence Scale for Children*, and *Wechsler Intelligence Scale for Adults*. The development of his ideas about the nature of intelligence, which provided the framework for these Wechsler scales, can be found in the test manuals that accompany each scale, in *Wechsler's measurement and appraisal of adult intelligence: Fifth edition* by Joseph D. Matarazzo, and in the volume of his selected papers, with Allen J. Edwards' introduction.

J. D. MATARAZZO

WEDDING, DANNY (1949–   )

Wedding received the B.A. and M.S. from Illinois State University, and the Ph.D. (1979) from the University of Hawaii. He completed his clinical internship on neuropsychology service at the Hawaii State Hospital and followed this with a year of postdoctoral training in neuropsychology and behavioral medicine at the University of Mississippi Medical Center. After completing his postdoctoral training, Wedding taught in the departments of psychiatry and psychology at East Tennessee State University at Johnson City and in the department of psychiatry at Marshall University at Huntington, West Virginia.

Wedding was the first psychologist selected to participate in the Robert Wood Johnson Health Policy Fellowship program sponsored by the Institute of Medicine. He spend his fellowship year working for Senator Tom Daschle (D–SD). He subsequently received an American Psychological Association Science Policy Fellowship and spent a year working as a health policy adviser for the Government Operations Committee in the House of Representatives. In 1991, Wedding became the director of the Missouri Institute of Mental Health, a mental health policy and research center located in St. Louis associated with the School of Medicine at the University of Missouri at Columbia. His has published multiple books and articles, including *Current psychotherapies* (edited with Raymond J. Corsini) and *Behavior and medicine*.

WEINERT, F. E. (1930–   )

Weinert attended the Teacher's College in Bamberg, Czechoslavakia. After teaching for several years in primary and secondary schools, he studied psychology and educational sciences at the University of Erlangen, where he received the Ph.D. degree in 1958. Subsequently he was a research and teaching assistant at the University of Bonn and became a professor of psychology and head of the Department of Psychology at the University of Heidelberg in 1968.

Weinert's scientific interests are focused on problems concerning psychological development and the enhancement of human learning. Central to the empirical studies, he has been concerned with the relationships between intellectual development and learning in childhood, the role of metacognitive components in solving memory tasks for individuals in different age groups, and the analysis of inter- and intraindividual differences in learning and memory performance. In close relation to these developmental investigations are his studies concerning cognitive and motivational determinants of school achievement, of conditions and processes of the acquisition of knowledge, and of causes of students' failures in achievement situations. Thus, the research program starts from the theoretical assumption that there is no opposition between basic research in developmental psychology and applied research in educational psychology, but that these are two perspectives that promote each other. These studies are being continued in the Max-Planck Institute for Psychological Research, founded in 1981, of which Weinert is now the director. Topics of his publications include human learning, developmental psychology, educational psychology, and school psychology.

WERNER, HEINZ (1890–1964)

Werner received the Ph.D. in psychology from the University of Vienna. He held positions at the University of Munich, the Psychological Institute in Hamburg, and the University of Hamburg before coming to the United States. He taught at the University of Michigan, Harvard University, and Brooklyn College, and in 1949 he assumed the chair of the psychology department at Clark University. He remained at Clark until his retirement in 1960.

Werner was distinguished for his work in developmental psychology, which resulted in the publication of *The comparative psychology of mental development*. In it he held that development proceeds from the undifferentiated and unarticulated to the differentiated and articulated. Together with Wapner, he developed the sensory–tonic field theory of perception. The authors emphasized motor aspects of perception and introduced effective demonstrations that led perceptual research in new directions. Werner was a highly productive researcher and scholar publishing more than 100 papers. His last book, coauthored with Kaplan, was *Symbol formation*. After Werner's death, the institute for developmental psychology at Clark University was named the Heinz Werner Institute of Developmental Psychology.

P. E. LICHTENSTEIN

WERTHEIMER, MAX (1880–1943)

Wertheimer's father Wilhelm directed a private business college for many years; his mother was an accomplished amateur violinist. A competent violinist and pianist himself, Wertheimer was educated at a Catholic school in Prague, and studied at Charles University in Prague, first law and then philosophy and psychology. He was particularly impressed by the teachings of the philosopher-psychologist Christian von Ehrenfels, who in 1890 had published an important paper on form qualities. In 1902, Wertheimer transferred to the University of Berlin, where he studied primarily philosophy and psychology with a number of notable members of the faculty, especially Carl Stumpf. In 1904, he moved to the University of Würzburg, where he completed the Ph.D. degree in psychology the same year, under Oswald Külpe, with a dissertation on the use of the word-association method for the detection of criminal guilt.

During the next six years, Wertheimer worked at psychological and physiological institutes and clinics in Vienna, Berlin, Würzburg, and Prague, doing further experiments on the word-association technique and applying the methods of experimental psychology to clinical studies of aphasia. In the summer of 1910, while on the train to a vacation destination, he had an insight about the perception of apparent motion, disembarked at Frankfurt, bought a toy stroboscope, and began perceptual experiments in his hotel room. He soon moved his work to Friedrich

Schumann's psychological institute at the Frankfurt Academy (later the University of Frankfurt), where Wolfgang Köhler and Kurt Koffka, who served as his subjects in these experiments, joined him in elaborating the principles of what was to become the influential school of Gestalt psychology. All three saw the experiments on the "phi phenomenon" (perception of a particular form of motion in stimuli that are actually stationary) as refuting the then-prevalent theories of this kind of perception; the studies, published in the *Zeitshrift für Psychologie* in 1912, are generally considered to have launched the Gestalt School.

Wertheimer stayed at Frankfurt for some years, worked as a civilian during World War I on a military device for detecting the direction from which a sound is coming, and moved to the University of Berlin in 1922. In 1929, he accepted the chair in psychology at the University of Frankfurt, and early in 1933, wary of the growing Hitler menace, emigrated to Czechoslovakia and then to the United States. He taught at the New School for Social Research in New York from the fall of 1933 until his death in the fall of 1943.

Ehrenfels' form-quality doctrine had challenged the prevailing theories of perception. A whole percept is not just the sum total of its constituent elementary sensations, Ehrenfels argued, but this sum total plus one more element: the form quality (a square, for example, is four equal straight lines plus four right angles, *plus squareness*); the whole is not equal to, but more than, the sum of its parts. Wertheimer's Gestalt theory went much further than Ehrenfels' doctrine. He suggested that the whole is quite *different* from the sum of its parts—not just more, but *prior to* the parts. Most wholes are integrated systems, the subparts of which stand in complex relationships to each other; the parts are what they are *because* of their place, role, and function in the whole of which they are parts. In a genuine systemic whle (a Gestalt), change of one part can cause a major change in the whole and in many other parts.

This radical approach became a major school of psychology during the first half of the twentieth century, with Werthcimer, Köhler, and Koffka as its chief proponents. Many Gestalt ideas reappeared during the 1970s and 1980s, in the modern areas of information processing, problem solving, artificial intelligence, and other aspects of cognitive psychology. The approach also stayed viable in the psychology of personality and in social psychology.

Wertheimer's publications were sparse, but they were highly influential. Aside from the 1912 paper on the phenomenon, among the most significant were a fundamental contribution in 1923 that provided a Gestalt analysis of the principles of organization in perception; several papers in the 1930s and 1940s that applied a Gestalt approach to the analysis of the nature of freedom, democracy, and truth; and a posthumous book, *Productive thinking*. The book's Gestalt analyses of problem solving and of scientific thinking (including how Albert Einstein formulated the theory of relativity) continue to challenge contemporary cognitive psychologists.

M. WERTHEIMER

WERTHEIMER, MICHAEL (1927–   )

Wertheimer emigrated to the United States in 1933. After receiving the B.A. degree from Swarthmore College and the M.A. degree from The Johns Hopkins University, he obtained the Ph.D. degree in experimental psychology from Harvard University in 1952, and took an internship in clinical psychology at Worcester (Mass.) State Hospital.

He taught at Wesleyan University from 1952 to 1955, and went to the University of Colorado in 1955, where he has been professor of psychology since 1961. He has been a visiting professor at the University of Hawaii, Principal Research Scientist in Psychology at Rockland

(N.Y.) State Hospital, and Acting Administrative Officer for Educational Affairs of the American Psychological Association.

Within the American Psychological Association, he has been president of four divisions: 1 (general psychology), 2 (teaching of psychology), 24 (theoretical and philosophical psychology), and 26 (history of psychology). He has also been president of the Rocky Mountain Psychological Association.

Wertheimer's research career began in sensory and perceptual processes but soon broadened to include cognition, individual differences, psycholinguistics, person perception, and eventually the history of psychology. He has published over 100 articles and more than 15 books, including *A brief history of psychology, Fundamental issues in psychology, History of psychology: A guide to information sources,* and *Psychology and the problems of today.* Recent work includes biographical and theoretical articles on his father, Max Wertheimer, founder of the Gestalt school of psychology.

WHIPPLE, GUY MONTROSE (1876–1941)

An early leader in the testing movement in the United States, Whipple published his *Manual of mental and physical tests* in 1910. This was a compendium of available tests with descriptions of the tests, how they were to be administered, and bibliographies of studies done with the tests. Fifty-four tests were described. The early edition of Alfred Binet's test of intelligence was mentioned along with a number of manual measurements, including tests of tapping, aiming, tracing, and steadiness.

In 1915, he warned the American Psychological Association against charlatans and otherwise unqualified practitioners who were making their inroads into clinical psychology. As a result, the association set forth in 1921 proper procedures for qualified psychological examiners. However, not until the mid-nineteenth century were adequate regulations for professional psychologists effected.

In 1917, Whipple served on a committee to test U.S. servicemen in World War I. Other members of the committee who became prominent in the testing movement were Robert M. Yerkes (chairman), Louis M. Terman, Walter V. Bingham, and Henry Goddard.

R. W. LUNDIN

WHITE, ROBERT W. (1904–   )

With a Harvard M.A. degree in history, White began teaching at the University of Maine (1926–1928). He then changed to graduate work in psychology at Harvard and, after a teaching interlude at Rutgers (1930–1933), received the Ph.D. degree in 1937. He taught at Harvard from that date until his retirement in 1968, serving terms as director of the Psychological Clinic and chairman of the Department of Social Relations.

Always interested in undergraduate education, he became known to many students through *The abnormal personality, Lives in progress,* and *The enterprise of living.* His largest intellectual debt was to Henry A. Murray, with whom he worked for a number of years, and he became something of a specialist in the intensive study of lives, abnormal and normal. Such studies were the basis of *Opinions and personality,* written jointly with M. Brewster Smith and Jerome Bruner.

Not primarily a theorist, White made a timely contribution to theory in 1959 when he published "Motivation reconsidered: The concept of competence," soon followed by several other papers on competence. The central idea was hardly new: that among the motivating processes in animals and humans is an urge to explore and play, the biological significance of which is to gain competence in dealing with the environment. The resulting sense of competence or efficacy he believed to be a highly significant aspect of personality and its growth. At a time when psychologists talked mostly of drive reduction and instinct gratification, the concept of competence helped restore a balanced and biologically plausible outlook on motivation, and stimulated considerable research.

WHITE, WILLIAM ALANSON (1870–1937)

White received his medical degree from the Long Island Medical College. After a decade as physician at the Binghamton State Hospital in New York, he went to St. Elizabeth Hospital in Washington, D.C. As superintendent, he made St. Elizabeth's a leading center for psychiatric care and training and a model for the profession. He also served as professor of psychiatry at Georgetown Universtiy and George Washington University and as lecturer at the U.S. Naval and Army Medical School.

At the time White took charge at St. Elizabeth, physical restraint was commonly practiced in psychiatric institutions. He abolished the various forms of physical restraint that had been in use, substituting concerned and humane treatment. He was favorably disposed toward psychoanalysis and helped to spread psychoanalytic doctrine in the United States.

White was active in the mental hygiene movement and served as president of the First International Congress of Mental Hygiene. He emphasized the social basis of mental disorder and stressed the concept of the organism as a whole. His mental hygiene outlook with its psychoanalytic overtones is reflected in his *Principles of mental hygiene* and *Mental hygiene of childhood.* He edited (with Smith Ely Jelliffe) the *Nervous and mental diseases monograph series.* He was also a founder of the *Psychoanalytic Review.* Of his many books, the best known might include *Outlines of psychiatry, Diseases of the nervous system, Foundations of psychiatry,* and *Lectures in psychiatry: The major psychoses.*

White was regarded as the leader of the Washington school of psychiatry, which included Harry Stack Sullivan, Karen Horney, and Freida Fromm-Reichmann, among others.

P. E. LICHTENSTEIN

WICKENS, DELOS D. (1909–1988)

Wickens obtained the B.A. degree from Centre College of Kentucky, the M.A. degree in English literature from the University of North Carolina, and the Ph.D. degree in psychology from the latter in 1937. He held academic posts at Ohio State University (1937–1939), the University of Colorado (1939–1940), Oberlin College (1940–1941), the University of Wisconsin (1941–1946), and Ohio State University from 1946 until retiring in 1980. During the years 1943–1946, he served with the National Defense Research Committee on a project dealing with naval gunnery.

He has published over 100 experimental or theoretical articles in the technical journals in psychology, is a coauthor of two textbooks, and has contributed chapters to other books.

Wickens has held elected offices in a number of professional societies, including that of president of the Midwestern Psychology Association and of Divisions 1 and 3 of the APA.

Among Wickens' honors are the Distinguished Teaching Award from the APA, the Warren Medal from the Society of Experimental Psychology, a Distinguished Research Award from Ohio State University, and a Distinguished Alumni Award from the University of North Carolina's Psychology Department.

His research activities have been almost equally divided between work with human subjects and with animals—a distribution expressing a bias toward addressing a basic psychology process by the most promising means. He has done extensive work in classical conditioning with both humans and cats, and is probably best known for his work on memory with humans, and for introducing proactive and retroactive inhibition in the conditioned response, thus demonstrating a parallel between human verbal memory processes and the conditioned response.

WIGGINS, JACK G. (1926–   )

Wiggins attained the B.A. in psychology from the University of Oklahoma, the M.A. degree in psychology from Southern Methodist University, and the Ph.D. (1952) in clinical psychology from Purdue University. Wiggins's internship was at Elgin State Hospital in Elgin, Illinois. His contributions to the field and profession of psychology cover more than 40 yr of service. He has spearheaded a multitude of movements to help put psychologists on the political map.

Wiggins chaired the APA Committee on Health Insurance, which formulated and promoted state Freedom Choice Laws and mandated mental health benefits. He is responsible for including psychology at parity in the Vocational Rehabilitation Act of 1973, in the Federal Employees Benefit Program, and achieved parity with psychiatry in the U.S. Criminal Code.

Wiggins conceived the idea and names for the National Register and the Psychology Defense Fund. He established APA peer review standards and system, was a founder of CAPPS, negotiated the recognition of psychologists in CHAMPUS, and improved and expanded insurance coverage for APA members. He served as the centennial president of the American Psychological Association.

WILLIAMS, JOANNA P. (1935–   )

Williams received the A.B. from Brown University, the Ed.M. from Harvard, and the M.S. and Ph.D. (1961) from Yale. In 1956–1957, she was a Fulbright scholar at the University of Paris. She taught at the Graduate School of Education, University of Pennsylvania, from 1961 to 1971; in 1971, she went to Teachers College at Columbia University as professor of psychology and education.

Williams was editor of the *Journal of Educational Psychology* (1973–1978). She served as president of Division 15 (Educational Psychology) of the American Psychological Association (1977–1978) and as vice president of Division C (Learning and Instruction) of the American Educational Research Association (1974–1976). In 1983, the National Reading Conference gave her its Oscar Causey Award for Distinguished Research and Service.

She has done research on beginning reading instruction, with a focus on phonemic skills, and on reading comprehension (main idea and theme identification and critical reading). She developed and evaluated the ABDs of Reading, a remedial program that teaches phonemic segmentation and blending and decoding as well as instructional programs in reading comprehension specifically designed for learning-disabled students.

WILSON, EDWARD OSBORNE (1929–   )

Wilson rose to become the leading figure in sociobiology. An extension of ethology, sociobiology is occasionally called behavioral biology or psychobiology. Sociobiologists contend that interpersonal behavior results from an interaction of human genes with the environment.

After receiving the B.A. and M.A. degrees from the University of Alabama, Wilson turned to Harvard for the Ph.D. degree in 1955. Within three years, Wilson (even then a controversial figure) had become a full professor at Harvard, and later Baird professor of science. His sociobiology claims that the human body with its social behavior serves to perpetuate the genes. People exist for the sake of their genes. "The

organism is only DNA's way of making more DNA" (Wilson, 1975, p. 3).

Wilson's views are described in three major publications: *The insect societies, Sociobiology: The new synthesis,* and *On human nature.* The first book describes animal behavior; the other two treat human social psychology.

WITKIN, HERMAN A. (1916–1979)

Best known for his extensive studies of field dependence-independence, Witkin contributed greatly to the conceptualization of the relation between cognitive styles and personality. He was educated in New York City, and received the Ph.D. degree from New York University in 1939. He taught at Brooklyn College from 1940 to 1952, and was a professor in the Department of Psychiatry, Downstate Medical Center, State University of New York, from 1952 to 1971, after which he moved to the Educational Testing Service. At the time of his death, he was a distinguished research scientist at Educational Test Service. His many honors included an honorary doctor of social sciences degree from Tillburg University, presented in 1977 by Queen Juliana of the Netherlands.

Witkin's widely known research on cognitive styles started with his studies in the 1940s of individual differences in the perception of the upright in space. When visual and bodily cues are contradictory, and one has to judge whether an object is upright, some people are more determined by the visual cues (field-dependent people) while others depend more on bodily cues (field-independent people). Pursuing the meaning of such differences was the focus of Witkin's research. In time, he discovered that these differences in perception and cognition were expressions of pervasive aspects of human functioning in the domains of emotion, personality, and neuropsychological processes. People move, in general, from field dependence toward field independence as they mature. However, those who become most field independent are those raised in ways that foster personal autonomy and a secure sense of self. Witkin's research—involving a wide range of empirical and experimental approaches unified within a common theoretical framework—led him and his colleagues into an extraordinary variety of studies, including research on dreaming, cultural differences in socialization, intellectual processes, psychopathology, interpersonal relations (between teachers and students, therapists and patients, and parents and children), brain laterality, and chromosomal aberrations.

Witkin published many research papers and books, including *Personality through perception, Psychological differentiation, Cognitive styles in personal and cultural adaptation,* and *Cognitive styles: Essence and origins.*

S. J. KORCHIN

WITMER, LIGHTNER (1861–1956)

In 1896 Witmer established the first psychological clinic at the University of Pennsylvania. This event is universally recognized as marking the beginning of the science and profession of clinical psychology—although not yet by that name. In 1907, Witmer founded the journal *The Psychological Clinic,* and in the first issue he called for the establishment of a new helping profession, to be called clinical psychology.

Witmer received the B.A. from the University of Pennsylvania in 1888, and after teaching briefly at the Rugby Academy in Philadelphia, he enrolled for graduate work at Pennsylvania, where he became an assistant to James McKeen Cattell, the new professor of psychology. In 1891, Cattell moved to Columbia and Witmer left for Leipzig to study with Wilhelm Wundt. After earning the Ph.D., Witmer returned to head the psychology laboratory at Pennsylvania. For the first few years he immersed himself in experimental research but showed increasing interest in applied work with children, leading to his founding of the clinic. Under Witmer's leadership, the Psychological Clinic grew rapidly and was the model for other early clinics. In conjunction with the University of Pennsylvania's psychology department, which Witmer also headed for many years, it became a major training center for clinical psychologists. In his clinical work, Witmer emphasized direct remedial work and decried overemphasis on tests. Witmer retired in 1937 and died in 1956, after having seen the field he pioneered become a major profession.

P. McReynolds

WOLFE, HARRY KIRKE (1858–1918)

Wolfe received the B.A in philosophy from the University of Nebraska in 1880. He studied with Herman Ebbinghaus at Berlin University and then became the second American to receive the Ph.D. in psychology with Wilhelm Wundt at the University of Leipzig (1886), doing research on the memory for tones. In 1889, Wolfe founded the psychology laboratory at the University of Nebraska, perhaps the first to be devoted solely to undergraduate research.

Wolfe was a leader in the child study movement in the Midwest, helping to found the Nebraska Child Study Society, establishing teacher training programs, editing a child study journal, and conducting his own research program on perceptual processes in children. Wolfe was popular lecturer whose classes were oversubscribed. He added laboratories to all of his courses, believing strongly that such training was important for undergraduates. Wolfe sent so many of his undergraduate students on to graduate study and careers in psychology that two national surveys in the 1920s placed the University of Nebraska third among all universities where psychologists received their initial exposure to the discipline. Three of his undergraduate students eventually became presidents of the American Psychological Association: Walter Pillsbury, Madison Bentley, and Edwin Guthrie.

L. T. Benjamin

WOLFF, CHRISTIAN VON (1679–1754)

Wolff was one of the eminent German philosophers and mathematicians of his time. He studied at Jena and lectured at Leipzig until 1706. He then became a professor of philosophy at Halle. In general, his philosophy was modeled after that of Gotfried Leibnitz.

His psychology, which appeared in two books, *Empirical psychology* and *Rational psychology*, also reflected the ideas of Leibnitz. Wolff was more interested in the rational aspects of the soul (mind) than in the sensationalistic. Unlike the British empiricist John Locke, Wolff stressed an active mind rather than one made up of the mere elements of experience as Locke had suggested. For Wolff, the mind consisted of faculties or functions such as knowing, remembering, feeling, and willing. His faculty psychology led the way for the Scottish school of Thomas Reid and Thomas Brown, as well as other faculty psychologies that were to follow. Wolff's psychology also was to have a significant impact on that of Immanuel Kant.

In Wolff's psychology, rational and empirical aspects were interrelated. Rational psychology was deduced from metaphysics while empirical psychology was concerned with the human being, who was the composite of both body and soul. Rational psychology depended more on reason and empirical psychology more on experience. Although there was an interaction between the two, the soul was more the concern of rational psychology, and human beings (soul and matter) the concern of empirical psychology. Rational psychology gave clear and distinct ideas while empirical psychology could only yield vague ideas of things.

On the one side were the vague ideas from sensations and on the other the clear ideas of reason. In essence, mental activities operated in various degrees of clarity. Yet both stressed a unified soul with different "potencies of action" expressed as powers of the soul.

R. W. Lundin

WOLFGANG, MARVIN EUGENE (1924–   )

Wolfgang received the B.A. from Dickinson College and the M.A. and the Ph.D. (1955) from the University of Pennsylvania. From 1948 to 1952, he was instructor and assistant professor at Lebanon Valley College and, in 1952, became instructor of sociology at the University of Pennsylvania. He was chair of that department from 1968 to 1972 and professor of law and sociology in 1972.

Wolfgang is the director of the Sellin Center for Studies in Criminology and Criminal Law, was a visiting professor and fellow at Churchill College at Cambridge University (1968–1969), and chair of the Review Committee on Crime and Delinquency for the NIMH (1971–1973). He was research director for the National Committee on Causes and Prevention of Violence (1968–1969) and commissioner for the National Committee on Obscenity and Pornography (1968–1970).

Wolfgang is chair of the board of directors for the Thomas Skelton Harrison Foundation, was a recipient of a Fulbright Research Award (1957–1958), received the Research Award of the American Society of Criminology (1960), and was a Guggenheim fellow (1957–1958, 1968–1969). He is a member of the American Philosophical Society, the American Academy of Arts and Sciences, the International Society of Criminology, the American Academy of Political and Social Science (president), and the Pennsylvania Prison Society. He is the author of *Patterns in criminal homicide*, *The subculture of violence*, and *Delinquency in Puerto Rico*.

WOLMAN, BENJAMIN B. (1908–   )

Originator of the "interactional approach" to psychotherapy, Wolman received the Ph.D. degree from the University of Warsaw. As clinical professor in psychoanalysis and psychotherapy, he taught a generation of psychiatrists and psychologists. His 40 years in private practice and authorship of over 200 scientific papers and 18 books in psychology and related fields gave birth to the 12-volume *International encyclopedia of psychiatry, psychology, psychoanalysis, and neurology*. Many of his publications have been translated into over nine languages. Recipient of the Dartmouth Medal of the American Library Association and the Distinguished Contribution Award of the American Psychological Association, Wolman's experience culminated in the modification of the classic Freudian psychoanalytic technique.

Wolman's interactional psychotherapy "is based on the awareness that all people have problems and experience emotional difficulties. . . . All living organisms have a beginning and end of their life and . . . the only thing which is left between human thinking, dreaming and decision-making is what one can do as long as one is alive" (*Principles of interactional psychotherapy*).

As president of the International Organization for the Study of Group Tensions, Wolman organized and chaired the International Scientific Conference on Terror and Terrorism, which brought together governments from all around the world. His varied interests are shown by such diverse works as *Children's fears*, *Victims of success*, *Call no man normal*, *Psychoanalysis and Catholicism*, and *Handbook of parapsychology*.

WOLPE, JOSEPH (1915–   )

Wolpe received his medical qualifying degree from the University of Witwatersrand, South Africa, in 1939. After medical and surgical internships, he entered private practice until 1942, when he volunteered for the South African Medical Corps, serving until 1946. Thereafter, he went into psychiatric training and research.

The centerpoint of his research was experimental studies on the production and cure of neuroses in animals that showed these neuroses to be produced by learning and to be reversible by learning. Techniques for treating human neuroses were derived from these findings, and were reported in detail in his book *Psychotherapy by reciprocal inhibition,* written during a fellowship at the Center for Advanced Study in Behavioral Sciences at Stanford, Calif. Wolpe has written about 150 papers and three other books, *The Practice of behavior therapy, Theme and variations: A behavior therapy casebook,* and *Our useless fears.* He has also edited *The conditioning therapies,* in collaboration with Andrew Salter and L. J. Reyna, and *Behavior therapy for psychiatrists,* in collaboration with L. J. Reyna.

Wolpe was professor of psychiatry at the University of Virginia School of Medicine from 1960 to 1965. Since 1965, he has been professor of psychiatry and director of the Behavior Therapy Unit at Temple University Medical School and a senior research psychiatrist at Eastern Pennsylvania Psychiatric Institute in Philadelphia. In 1979, he received the American Psychological Association's Distinguished Scientific Award for the Applications of Psychology.

WOODWORTH, ROBERT SESSIONS (1869–1962)

An American psychologist, Woodworth received the A.B. degree from Amherst College, the M.A. degree from Harvard University, where he studied under William James, and the Ph.D. degree from Columbia University in 1899. Most of his academic career was spent at Columbia. He was well known for his introductory text *Psychology,* first published in 1921, which went through five editions. His *Experimental psychology,* first published in 1939, was a major handbook of research in that area. It was later revised in collaboration with Harold Schlosberg in 1954. He presented a systematic position in psychology in his book *Dynamic psychology,* published in 1918 and later revised as the *Dynamics of behavior* in 1958.

For Woodworth, the subject matter of psychology was both behavior and consciousness. He felt that the behaviorists of the time such as John Watson, who had rejected any idea of consciousness or mind, had left out part of a legitimate aspect of psychology. Consciousness was very much a part of what the psychologist should study and could be done through introspection. His was not a simple S–R (stimulus–response) psychology. Although psychological events had their causes in the stimulus environment, there was something more to be added, and that was the organism, itself. Therefore, the resulting behavior was a function of both the environmental stimuli and what went on inside the body (organism). Thus the paradigm S–O–R and not simply S–R was appropriate. This idea was later developed in a more sophisticated manner into what Tolman and others called the intervening variable.

Two other basic aspects of Woodworth's psychology were *mechanism* and *drive.* Mechanism referred to how a thing was done and drive referred to why it was done. For example, in the functioning of an automobile, the mechanism referred to those parts that made it run. The drive was the power applied. When these concepts were applied to psychology, an organism might behave in certain ways as when a cat, in its trial-and-error-behavior, attempted to escape from a puzzle box. This was mechanism, but for the activity to occur, the cat had to be hungry. The hunger that motivated the cat to action was the drive.

In the course of the behavioral history of an organism, it was possible for the mechanism to take on the function of drive. What started out as mere mechanism might also involve drive or become drive for other activities. Take, for example, a businessman who worked for a living (mechanism) to fulfill many of his bodily needs (drive) as well as those of his family. After he has acquired a considerable estate with all the money possible to fulfill his needs, he still continued to work for the joy of working or to see his bank account increase. In this instance, the mechanism of working had also taken on the function of its own drive.

R. W. LUNDIN

WRIGHT, LOGAN (1933–   )

Wright received the M.A. then the Ph.D. from Peabody College of Vanderbilt University. He completed a clinical child internship at the University of North Carolina. He later served as an NIMH Career Development Research Fellow and assistant professor at Purdue University. In 1966 Wright became head of the Division of Pediatric Psychology at the University of Oklahoma Medical School. He was elected first president of the Society for Pediatric Psychology. Write also has served as president of the Southwestern Psychological Association and of APA's Division of Clinical Psychology. He was APA's president in 1986.

Wright is the author of five books and more than 200 articles on medical and child psychology. His first book, *Parent power,* won the 1979 APA Media Award for books and monographs. He edited the *Encyclopedia of pediatric psychology.* Wright's APA Presidential Address on the Type A behavior pattern is considered a statement in that area.

In 1987, Wright chaired APA's task force, which failed in its efforts to reorganize the association. The following year, he became the American Psychological Society's first chief administrative officer. He then served as the executive officer for the American Association of Applied and Preventive Psychology and as professor in the psychology department at the University of Oklahoma at Norman.

WRIGHT, MARY J. (1915–   )

Wright obtained her education: the B.A. degree from the University of Western Ontario (1939) and the M.A. degree (1940) and the Ph.D. degree (1949) from the University of Toronto. During the World War II (1942–1944), she served in Birmingham, England, with the Canadian Children's Service, training teachers for wartime day nurseries. In 1946, she was appointed to the faculty of the Department of Psychology at the University of Western Ontario, where she later became a full professor (1962). She was chairman of the Department of Psychology (1960–1970), and was the first director of the department's Laboratory Preschool (1972–1980), which she founded to provide facilities for research and graduate training in early childhood education. She became professor emeritus in 1980.

Wright was president of the Ontario Psychological Association (1950–1951), the first woman president of the Canadian Psychological Association (1968–1969), the first woman chairperson of the Ontario Board of Examiners in Psychology (1973–1974), and chairperson of the Certification Board of the Ontario Nursery Education Association (1964–1966). She has represented psychology in Canada on committees and boards at both the national and international level, and served on the Committee on International Relations of the American Psychological Association (1977–1980). She also coedited the first book on the history of academic psychology to appear in Canada and has published papers and a major monograph on compensatory education in the preschool. Among Wright's honors are the Queen Elizabeth Jubilee Medal (1977), LL.D. degrees from Brock University (1980) and the University of Western Ontario (1982), a certificate of recognition from Psi Chi of the American Psychological Association (1980), and awards from the Ontario Psychological Association (1980), the Ontario Psychological

Foundation (1980), and the Association for Early Childhood Education, Ontario (1982).

WUNDT, WILHELM (1832–1920)

Wundt studied medicine at the University of Tubingen and at Heidelberg, then changed his major to physiology and earned his doctorate from Heidelberg in 1855. He remained there, teaching until 1874, and formulating his ideas about psychology. His books of 1858 and 1862, *Contributions to the theory of sensory perception,* formalized these ideas. He was appointed professor of philosophy in 1875 at Leipzig, where he worked for the next 45 years. Edward B. Titchener was Wundt's student and the proponent of his structural psychology in the United States.

Wundt created and developed the first school of psychological thought, *structuralism,* whose basic building block was sensation. He established a laboratory for experimental research and a journal called *Philosophical Studies,* and he wrote what has been claimed to be the most important book in the history of psychology, *Principles of physiological psychology.* His students were carefully instructed in his methodology of introspection or self-observation. Although structuralism is no longer a school of thought in contemporary psychology, Wundt's systematic efforts established psychology as a new and reeognized science in Germany in the nineteenth century.

Using the method of introspection, students and researchers investigated the subject matter of immediate experience through exacting attention to sensations and feelings. The goals of structuralism were to analyze conscious processes into basic elements, to discover how these elements are connected, and to establish the laws of these connections. The elements of immediate experience included sensations that were classified by modality, intensity, and duration, and feelings that were identified in a tridimensional theory of equilibrium between pleasure–displeasure, tension–relaxation, and excitement–depression. Wundt also introduced the idea of apperception, that the creative synthesis of these elements of experienee is an active process whereby something new arises. This synthesis has been called the *law of psychic resultants,* and it seems analogous to the Gestalt idea that the whole is more than the sum of its parts.

In the first part of the twentieth century, Wundt concerned himself with the various levels of mental development as expressed in language and myths, art forms, and social customs, including laws and morals. These higher mental processes were recorded in ten volumes of *Folk psychology,* and were differentiated from the simpler mental processes of sensation and perception. This work served to divide psychology into the experimental, using laboratory methods, and the social, using nonexperimental approaches of sociology and anthropology.

N. Haynie

YATES, AUBREY JAMES (1925–   )

Yates obtained his first degree at Liverpool University in 1951. He then completed a graduate diploma in clinical psychology at the Institute of Psychiatry in London, followed by the Ph.D. degree (1954). He was a lecturer at the institute from 1954 to 1957, until emigrating to Australia in 1957. In Australia, he eventually held a chair of psychology at the University of New England in New South Wales (1965–1967) until he was appointed to a chair of psychology at the University of Western Australia, Nedlands (Perth), in 1967.

Yates' major contributions have been in the area of experimental abnormal psychology, resulting in four books and numerous articles. In 1970, his book on *Behaviour therapy* critically evaluated the entire literature of that field; and in 1980, he completed a similar task with

respect to biofeedback in the book *Biofeedback and the modification of behaviour.* He has also made numerous experimental contributions to the abnormal psychology literature in areas as diverse as schizophrenia, stuttering, and tics. He is interested in the relationship between the discrimination and voluntary control of autonomic functions, and psychophysiology of stress in psychosomatic disorders.

Yates was head of the Department of Psychology at the University of Western Australia from 1967 to 1981, and president of the Australian Psychological Society from 1970 to 1971.

YELA, MARIANO (1921–   )

Yela received the master's and Ph.D. degrees from Madrid University with further study and research in Washington, D.C., Chicago, London, Louvain, and Freiburg. He has been an associate professor (philosophy) and, since 1957, a professor (general, experimental, mathematical psychology) at Madrid, and visiting professor of mathematical psychology at Louvain (1964–1974). He devoted much of his time to the promotion of psychology in Spain, where he was the founder or cofounder of most of the country's psychological institutions.

His research has concentrated on intelligence and perception. His theory of intelligence as one heterogeneous continuum of covariation (*The psychology of aptitudes, The structure of intelligence*) tries to integrate the factorial results since Spearman and the ontogenetic findings of Piaget's school. More specifically, he has worked on mechanical and verbal intelligence, and has studied perception through factorial, psychophysiological, and phenomenological-experimental approaches.

Yela's general theoretical view (*The structure of behavior*) conceives of psychology as a multiparadigmatic science centered on behavior considered as a physical activity with biological and/or biographical significance. He has published on personality, epistemology, and the history of psychology, and on applied topics such as *Psychology of work* and *Psychology of education,* and he is the author of about 100 psychological tests.

He has been an executive member of the International Unions of Psychology and of Philosophy and is consulting editor on many national and international journals. Among Yates' honors are the International Prize Francqui Chair, the Medal of Honor (Louvain), and the National Prizes of Philosophy and Psychology (Spain). He is a member of the Spanish Royal Academy of Moral and Political Sciences.

YERKES, ROBERT MEARNS (1876–1956)

Yerkes studied at Harvard University, and received the doctorate in psychology in 1902. He held positions at Harvard and the University of Minnesota before he settled at Yale University in 1924 and remained there for 20 years. Yerkes and E. L. Thorndike were pioneers in the experimental study of animal behavior, following the tradition of C. Lloyd Morgan and George Romanes, the founders of comparative psychology.

Yerkes began his animal studies in 1900 and took charge of comparative psychology at Harvard in 1902. His research included a wide range of animals. He invented an experimental maze to study animal learning and the evolution of intelligence through the animal species. Yerkes is associated with the first primate laboratory at Yale University, where he was the director from 1929 to 1941. The laboratory was later transferred to Orange Park, Fla., and is now the Yerkes Regional Primate Center of Emory University in Georgia.

Out of his work in comparative, or animal, behavior, Yerkes formulated methods and techniques to test intelligence, monochromatic light to study color vision, and multiple-choice tests to measure concept formation. From his experiments he formed a theory that is called the Yerkes-Dodson law. It states that there is an optimal level of arousal for tasks, and that moderate levels of motivation facilitate problem solving and change. If stress is too high, the individual may not process relevant cues for learning; if it is too low, irrelevant as well as relevant cues will be processed indiscriminately (Easterbrook, 1959).

Later Yerkes was interested also in human learning and developed a revision of the Stanford-Binet Intelligence Scale called the Point Scale. During World War I, Yerkes was chief of a group of psychologists who developed measures of abilities for assignments of army recruits to military positions and duties. These tests were the Army Alpha and the Army Beta, which were used to classify some 1.75 million men.

N. A. HAYNIE

YOUNG, PAUL THOMAS (1892–   )

Young received the A.B. degree from Occidental College and the Ph.D. degree, in 1918, from Cornell University, where he studied with Edward B. Titchener. Young is known for his studies in sound localization using a pseudophone in which the auditory inputs are right–left reversed. He found that auditory localization is significant, particularly when one cannot see the sounding object.

His book, *The motivation of behavior,* was published in 1936. The book brought together empirical studies in experimental psychology of motivation both in animals and in humans.

During the 1960s, his research efforts were directed toward studying food preferences in rats. He concluded that specific food preferences (appetites) resulted from internal motivation effects, as in the deficiency of certain nutritional elements, but that preference habits can be learned and can function separately from nutritional needs.

A second book, *Motivation and emotion,* was published in 1961. In this work, he stressed the fact that a human being is very much an emotional creature as well as a rational one.

YOUNG, THOMAS (1773–1829)

Young received a D.Physic degree from the University of Göttingen in 1796. Involved in medical practice in London, he was awarded the M.D. degree by Cambridge University in 1808.

As a physicist, Young was known for his wave theory of light and atmospheric refraction. He was an authority on the phenomena of ocean tides. In addition to a keen interest in music, he was a noted Egyptologist who contributed to the development of the hieroglyphic alphabet and was instrumental in the deciphering of the Rosetta stone.

As a result of his interest in vision, he became prominent in psychology. He described and measured visual astigmatism. By measuring the focal length of the eye, he demonstrated that the accommodation was attributable to the changing shape of the lens. In his research, he ruled out the cornea as the accommodation mechanism by attaching a glass lens to the cornea with wax.

In an 1801 paper, Young proposed that color vision was due to three different kinds of visual fibers. His theory, based upon Isaac Newton's demonstration of three primary colors, was expressed in four paragraphs incidental to a treatment of the physics of colored light. His theory was somewhat expanded in his 1807 lectures but remained essentially unknown until rediscovered and popularized by Hermann von Helmholtz starting in 1852. Young's work was the first exposition of what is today the generally accepted explanation of color vision, called the Young-Helmholtz theory.

C. S. PEYSER

ZAJONC, ROBERT B. (1923–   )

Zajonc received his elementary and secondary education in Lodz, Poland, before coming to the United States for graduate work in psychology

at the University of Michigan. After receiving the doctorate in social psychology from Michigan in 1955, Zajonc joined the university's Psychology Department, as full professor. In addition to his academic duties as teacher and researcher, Zajonc has also been associated with the Research Center for Group Dynamics since the early 1950s.

Zajonc has been recognized for his versatility and for the impact of his theoretical and empirical work in social psychology. He believes that there exists in social behavior fundamental factors that can be analyzed by experimental and mathematical methods, and throughout his career he has been involved in research inspired by a desire to understand those basic forms of behavior that are impervious to the influence of cultural differences.

Early research addressed the paradox of how thought and action could be enhanced or impaired by others, and has resulted in a body of research into the basics of group dynamics. More recently, Zajonc's interest has been drawn to the relationship between family structure and intellectual development, another area of social significance in need of rigorous study.

Zajonc has served on the editorial boards of numerous professional journals, and as advisor to various professional, national, and community organizations. He has held a Fulbright Fellowship and a postdoctoral fellowship at Oxford, and has been honored by several scientific and professional organizations.

ZANGWILL, OLIVER L. (1913–   )

A prominent British psychologist, Zangwill is a professor of experimental psychology at King's College, Cambridge (professorial fellow since 1955), and senior researcher at the Cambridge Psychological Laboratory. Although experimental psychology got off to a relatively slow start in Great Britain, the Cambridge Psychological Laboratory (the first of its kind in the country, established in 1897 by F. C. Bartlett) offered Zangwill an established support and direction for psychological research on memory and thought processes that emphasized the organizational pattern of cerebral processes. Numerous papers and studies on memory, amnesia, and aphasia in psychological and medical journals attest to Zangwill's leadership in these areas of psychology.

Zangwill's formal education was at University College, London, and King's College, Cambridge. He was a research student at the Cambridge Psychological Laboratory (1935–1940) and a psychologist at the Brain Injuries Unit, Edinburgh. Zangwill was also a visiting psychologist at the National Hospital for Nervous Diseases, London, and an honorary consulting psychologist to United Cambridge Hospitals. Prior to his position at Cambridge, he was senior lecturer in general psychology at Oxford (1948–1950) and also assistant director of Oxford's Institute of Experimental Psychology (1945–1952).

Professional activities include editing the *Quarterly Journal of Experimental Psychology* and serving as president of the British Experimental Psychology Society and the British Psychological Society. He is an honorary foreign member of Société Française de Neurologie. Among his publications are *An introduction to modern psychology, Cerebral dominance and its relation to psychological function, Current problems in animal behaviour,* and *Amnesia.*

ZAPOROZHETS, ALEXANDER (1905–1981)

Zaporozhets is best known for his concept of "perceptual action" and theory of voluntary actions. Zaporozhets' psychological career started in the 1920s at the Academy of Communist Education (Moscow). In 1931, he moved to Kharkov, where a group of students and followers of Lev Vygotsky organized the Center for Developmental Psychology affiliated with the Academy of Psychoneurology. Zaporozhets' research of that period centered on the role of active perception in the development of children's intelligence. He succeeded in elaborating a concept of perceptual action that bound together the problems of sensorimotor skills and of cognitive development. He proved that perceptual action has an affinity with external motor action; as does the latter, it helps to "construct" objects through their manipulation. Programs focusing on the perceptual training of children were developed on the basis of these studies.

After World War II, Zaporozhets returned to Moscow and was appointed head of the Laboratory of Psychology of Preschool Children at the Moscow Institute of Psychology. Later he became the first director of the Institute for Preschool Education, which he organized in 1960. Following the 1940s, Zaporozhets undertook a number of research projects in the psychology of voluntary movement and sensorimotor coordination. These studies resulted in a monograph *Razvitie proizvol'nykh dvizhenii (Development of voluntary movements)*.

For many years, Zaporozhets conducted a creative critical dialog with Piaget's school of genetical psychology; his own approach has many features in common with that of Piaget.

ZAZZO, RENÉ (1910–   )

Zazzo studied at the Sorbonne (1929–1933) under Henri Wallon and later at Yale University under Arnold Gesell. From Gesell he borrowed observation techniques, and from Wallon certain themes (e.g., twins, inverted images) as well as dialectical materialism as research methodology. Since 1940 he has pursued a double career as a clinician and as an experimentalist—as director of the Laboratory of Pathological Psychology (Henri Rousselle Hospital) and in the Laboratory of Psychobiology of Children (École Pratique des Hautes Etudes), founded by Henri Wallon. In 1950, Zazzo replaced Wallon, and received the Ph.D. degree in 1958 at the Sorbonne with his thesis, under Jean Piaget, *Twins: A couple and a unity*. From 1967 to his retirement in 1980, he was professor of child psychology at the University of Paris. He was twice elected (1955 and 1966) president of the French Society of Psychology.

The author of 10 books, his first was on the history of American psychology. He has worked on three themes: mental deficiency, twins, and inverted images. Zazzo was concerned with solving experimentally the question of how a child achieves a self-image and becomes a person. Observation of identical twins showed that the individuals are psychologically quite different despite the same heredity and environment, with each having an independent personality. They are not two copies of the same person but become a couple. Zazzo discovered the "couple effect," which constitutes a third factor in the genesis of personality along with heredity and environment. Via "inverted images" or "specular reactions," he found how one's visual self-identification is a process of objectifying the exterior of others and the material world. Paradoxically, children integrate their personal identities when they can locate themselves in the environment as individuals among others.

ZEĬGARNIK, BLIŪMA (1900–   )

Zeĭgarnik completed her dissertation under Kurt Lewin at Berlin in 1927. Her professional career was spent at Moscow University.

Zeĭgarnik is best known in the West for her dissertation, the first formal test of Lewin's theory that attainment of a goal or successful locomotion toward a positive valence relieves tension. She assumed that the assignment of a simple task produces tension. In her test, the tasks included clay figure modeling, solving simple puzzles, and laying blocks in a particular pattern. Subjects were interrupted in midtask on some tasks but permitted to finish other tasks. An hour later the inter-

rupted tasks were better recalled than those completed, thus lending support to Lewin's theory. The phenomenon has become known as the Zeĭgarnik effect.

In a country where behavior pathology is the almost exclusive domain of the psychiatrist, Zeĭgarnik is one of the very few clinical psychologists in the Western sense. Her area of research focused upon the psychoses, although she also published papers on the history of abnormal psychology in the U.S.S.R. Two of her books have been published in English, *Pathology of thinking* and *Experimental abnormal psychology*.

C. S. PEYSER

ZIMBARDO, PHILIP G. (1933–   )

The social psychologist Zimbardo obtained the B.A. degree from Brooklyn College of the City University of New York, and the M.S. and Ph.D. (1959) degrees, from Yale University. His career moved from Yale to New York University, and in 1968 to his current position as professor at Stanford University.

It is not his publication *The cognitive control of motivation* that called attention to Zimbardo as much as his experiments. Simulating prison conditions at Stanford, Zimbardo found inmates becoming deindividualized and losing time perspective. Furthermore, it was found that prison experience is emasculating, and promotes homosexuality, dependency, loss of control over one's life, and tendencies toward regression. The experiment was so successful that it had to be canceled prior to completion. Zimbardo discovered that when normally good people were designated as guards, they tended toward brutal, sadistic, dehumanizing behavior. The hypothesis is that when good people are placed in an evil situation, evil dominates them. He thus argues that society trains people to be cruel guards and emasculated prisoners.

ZUBIN, JOSEPH (1900–1990)

Zubin was born in Lithuania. After immigrating to the United States, he received the A.B. degree from Johns Hopkins University and the Ph.D. (1932) from Columbia University. His main writings and research in psychology were involved in classification and measurement in the area of mental illness. He was instrumental in developing techniques of observation and quantification of the behavior of mental patients. He evaluated many of the tests and therapies introduced in psychology since the 1930s. He was also instrumental in the construction of behavior models in psychopathology from the physiological, behavioral, developmental, genetic, and psychosocial perspectives.

He joined the research staff of the New York State Psychiatric Institute in 1936. There he established the Biometric Research Unit and became its first chief of psychiatric research. Approximately 30 yr later, Zubin became distinguished research professor of psychiatry at the University of Pittsburgh, where he established a laboratory devoted principally to the study of the vulnerability of patients to functional disorders and in searching for reliable physiological behavior and other markers of their vulnerability. While in New York, he also joined the faculty of Columbia University in 1930. In 1969 he retired to professor emeritus.

He was the author of more than 200 papers and chapters in various books devoted to psychopathology. He also edited and coedited 30 volumes of the *Proceedings of the American Psychopathological Association*. Among his many awards were honorary degrees from the University of Lund (Sweden) and the University of Rochester (New York).

R. W. LUNDIN

BIBLIOGRAPHY

All citations throughout the text are referenced in this single bibliography. This feature has several advantages: It saves space, permits closer examination of details, and provides convenience.

Originally some 20,000 references came in from the entry authors, and when duplicates were partialed out, 15,000 remained. One book, for example, was cited 34 times. With fewer references there is greater accuracy. Also, a single bibliography makes it easy to locate all items by any one author.

You will note that some references include a number of dates. The last date generally refers to the date of original publication; others refer to various editions. Thus at the end of Sigmund Freud's *A general introduction to psychoanalysis,* one will find these years: 1966/1938/ 1935/1920. This means that the book, originally issued in 1920, is cited in the various editions listed.

The editor would appreciate being notified of any discovered errors, discrepancies, or incompletions.

Aaker, D. A., & Day, G. S. (1974). *Consumerism: Search for the consumer interest.* New York: Free Press.

Aapro, M. S. (1991). 5-HT3 receptor antagonists—An overview of their present status and future potential in cancer therapy-induced emesis. *Drugs, 42,* 551–568.

Abate, M., & Berrien, F. K. (1967). Validation of stereotypes: Japanese versus American students. *Journal of Personality and Social Psychology, 7,* 435–438.

Abegg, L. (1952). *The mind of East Asia.* London, New York: Thames & Hudson.

Abel, E. L. (1984). *Fetal alcohol syndrome and fetal alcohol effects.* New York: Plenum.

Abel, E. L. (1989). *Behavioral teratogenesis and behavioral mutagenesis.* New York: Plenum.

Abel, E. L., & Sokol, R. J. (1987). Incidence of fetal alcohol syndrome and economic impact of FAS-related anomalies. *Drug and Alcohol Dependence, 19,* 51–70.

Abel, S. M. (1972). Duration discrimination of noise and tone bursts. *Journal of the Acoustical Society of America, 51,* 1219–1224.

Abel, T. M. (1962). The dreams of a Chinese patient. In W. Meuensterberger & S. Axelrod (Eds.), *The psychoanalytic study of society,* Vol. 11. New York: International Universities Press.

Abel, T. M., & Hsu, F. L. K. (1949). Chinese personality revealed by the Rorschach. *Rorschach Research Exchange, 13,* 285–301.

Abel, T. M., & Métraux, R. (1974). *Culture and psychotherapy.* New Haven, Conn.: College & University Press.

Abel, T. M., & Wilson, J. E. (1979). Spinal cord injured and family systems: A pilot study. In L. R. Wolberg, & M. L. Aronson (Eds.), *Group therapy.* New York: Stratton.

Abele, A. (1985). Thinking about thinking: Causal, evaluative and unalistic cognitions about social solutions. *European Journal of Social Psychology, 15,* 315–332.

Abeles, G. (1976). Researching the unresearchable: Experimentation on the double bind. In C. Sluzki & D. Ransom (Eds.), *Double bind: The foundation of the communicational approach to the family.* New York: Grune & Stratton.

Abeles, N., & Iscoe, I. (1954). Motivational differences between high and low scholarship students. *Journal of Educational Psychology, 45,* 215–223.

Abelson, H. I., Fishburne, P. M., & Cisin, I. (1977). *National survey of drug abuse: 1977,* Vol. 1. DHEW Publication O, (ADM) 78–618.

Abelson, R. P., Aronson, E., McGuire, W. J., Newcomb, T. M., Rosenberg, M. J., & Tannenbaum, P. H. (Eds.). (1968). *Theories of cognitive consistency: A sourcebook.* Chicago: Rand-McNally.

Aberle, D. F., Cohen, A. K., Davis, A. K., Levy, M. J., Jr., & Sutton, F. X. (1950). The functional prerequisites of a society. *Ethics, 50,* 100–111.

Ability testing: Uses, consequences, and controversies, Parts I and II. (1982). Washington, D.C.: National Academy Press.

Abiri, J. O. O. (1966). The educational attitudes of some Nigerian adolescent grammar school pupils. *West African Journal of Education, 10,* 118–121.

Abiola, E. T. (1965). The nature of intellectual development of Nigerian children. *Teacher Education, 6,* 37–57.

Abraham, K. (1927/1921). Contributions to the theory of the anal character. In *Selected papers on psychoanalysis.* London: Hogarth.

Abraham, K. (1927/1924). The influence of oral eroticism on character formation. In *Selected papers on psychoanalyses.* London: Hogarth.

Abraham, K. (1927). *Selected papers on psychoanalysis,* London: Hogarth.

Abraham, K. (1966). *On character and libido development: Six essays by Karl Abraham.* New York: Norton.

Abrahams, B., Feldman, S. S., & Nash, S. C. (1978). Sex role self-concept and sex role attitudes: Enduring personality characteristics or adaptations to changing life situations? *Developmental Psychology, 14,* 393–400.

Abrahamsen, A. A. (1977). *Child language: An interdisciplinary guide to theory and research.* Baltimore, Md.: University Park Press.

Abrahms, T. W. (1985). Activity-dependent presynaptic facilitation: An associative mechanism in Aplysia. *Cellular and Molecular Neurobiology, 5,* 123–145.

Abrahms, T. W., Karl, K. A., & Kandel, E. R. (1991). Biochemical studies of stimulus convergence during classical conditioning in aplysia: Dual regualtion of adenylate cyclase by Ca^{2+}/calmodulin and transmitter. *The Journal of Neuroscience, 11,* 2655–2665.

Abramovitch, H. (1988). An Israel account of a near-death experience: A case study in cultural dissonance. *Journal of Near-Death Studies, 6,* 175–184.

Abramovitch, R., Corter, C., & Lando, B. (1979). Sibling interaction in the home. *Child Development, 50,* 997–1003.

Abramson, E. E., & Stinson, S. G. (1977). Boredom and eating in obese and non-obese individuals. *Addictive Behaviors, 2,* 181–185.

Abromowitz, E. A. (1981). School psychology: A historical perspective. *School Psychology Review, 10(2),* 121–126.

Abrams, H. S., & Hollender, M. H. (1974). Factitious blood disease. *Southern Medical Journal 67,* 691–696.

Abrams, N. (1979). Definitions of mental illness and the insanity defense. *Journal of Psychiatry and Law, 7,* 441–456.

Abramson, L. Y., Garber, J., & Seligman, M. E. P. (1980). Learned helplessness in humans: An attributional analysis. In M. E. P. Seligman (Ed.), *Human helplessness.* New York: Academic Press.

Abramson, L. Y., & Seligman, M. E. P. (1977). Modeling psychopathology in the laboratory: History and rationale. In J. D. Maser & M. E. P. Seligman (Eds.), *Psychopathology: Experimental models.* San Francisco: Freeman.

Abramson, L. Y., Seligman, M. E. P., & Teasdale, J. D. (1978). Learned helplessness in humans: Critique and reformulation. *Journal of Abnormal Psychology, 87,* 49–74.

Abramson, P. (1977). *The political socialization of black Americans: A critical evaluation of research on efficacy and trust.* New York: Free Press.

Accident facts. (1979). Chicago: National Safety Council.

Ach, N. (1905). *Über die Willenstätigkeit und das Denken. Eine experimentelle Untersuchung mit einem Anhange: Über das Hippsche Chronoskop.* Göttingen, West Germany: Vandenhoeck & Ruprecht.

Ach, N. K. (1944). *Lehrbuch der Psychologie.* Vol. 3: *Praktische Psychologie.* Bamberg: Buchner.

Achenbach, T. M. (1978). Psychopathology of childhood: Research problems and issues. *Journal of Consulting and Clinical Psychology, 46,* 759–776.

Achenbach, T. M. (1978). *Research in developmental psychology: Concepts, strategies, methods.* New York: Free Press.

Achenbach, T. M., Conners, C. K., Quay, H. C., Verhulst, F. C., & Howell, C. T. (1989). Replication of empirically derived syndromes as a basis for taxonomy of child/adolescent psychopathology. *Journal of Abnormal Child Psychology, 17,* 299–323.

Achterberg, J., Collerain, I., & Craig, P. (1978). A possible relationship between cancer, mental retardation, and mental disorders. *Journal of Social Science and Medicine, 12,* 135–139.

Achterberg, J., & Lawlis, G. F. (1979). A canonical analysis of blood chemistry variables related to psychological measures of cancer patients. *Multivariate Experimental Clinical Research, 4,* 1–10.

Achterberg, J., & Lawlis, G. F. (1979). *Imagery of disease: A diagnostic tool for behavioral medicine.* Champaign, IL: Institute for Personality and Ability Testing.

Ackerknecht, E. (1955). *A short history of medicine.* New York: Ronald Press.

Ackerman, N. W. (1943). Group therapy from the point of view of the psychiatrist. *American Journal of Orthopsychiatry, 13,* 678–687.

Ackerman, N. W. (1958). *The psychodynamics of family life.* New York: Basic Books.

Ackerman, N. W. (1966). *Treating the troubled family.* New York: Basic Books.

Ackoff, R. L. (1956). The development of operations research as a science. *Operations Research, 4,* 265.

Acuna, H. (1979). *Environmental health risks.* Paper presented at the Conference on New Ways to Wellness, St. Louis University, St. Louis, Mo., March.

Adair, J. (1981). Canadian psychology as a profession and discipline. *Canadian Psychology, 22,* 163–172.

Adair, J. G. (1973). *The human subject: The social psychology of the psychological experiment.* Boston: Little, Brown.

Adams, B. (1968). *Kinship in an urban setting.* Chicago: Markham.

Adams, D. K. (1929). Experimental studies of adaptive behavior in cats. *Comparative Psychology Monographs, 6.*

Adams, G. R., & Munro, G. (1979). Portrait of the North American runaway: A critical review. *Journal of Youth and Adolescence, 8,* 359–373.

Adams, H. (1927). The good judge of personality. *Journal of Abnormal and Social Psychology, 22,* 172–181.

Adams, J., Kenney, T. J., & Canter, A. (1973). The efficacy of the Canter Background Interference Procedure in identifying children with cerebral dysfunction. *Journal of Consulting and Clinical Psychology, 40(3),* 489.

Adams, J. F. (1964). Adolescent personal problems as a function of age and sex. *Journal of Genetic Psychology, 104,* 207–214.

Adams, J. S. (1963). Toward an understanding of inequity. *Journal of Abnormal and Social Psychology, 67,* 422–436.

Adams, J. S. (1965). Inequity in social exchange. In L. Berkowitz (Ed.), *Advances in experimental social psychology,* Vol. 2. New York: Academic Press.

Adams, J. S., & Rosenbaam, W. B. (1962). The relationship of worker productivity to cognitive dissonance. *Journal of Applied Psychology, 46,* 161–164.

Adams, P. (1981). Statement before the Subcommittee on Science, Research, and Technology, U. S. House of Representatives. Hearings on ''The use of animals in medical research and testing,'' October 14.

Adams, R. L., & Phillips, B. N. (1972). Motivational and achievement differences among children of various ordinal birth positions. *Child Development, 43(1),* 155–164.

Adams, R. M., Kocsis, J. J., & Estes, R. E. (1974). Soft neurological signs in learning-disabled children and controls. *American Journal of Diseases of Children, 128,* 614–618.

Adams, R. M., & Victor, M. *Principles of neurology.* (1977). New York: McGraw-Hill.

Adams, R. R., Lerner, L., & Anderson, J. (1979). Children with learning problems: A developmental view for parents. *Journal of Learning Disabilities, 12,* 315–319.

Adams, S. (1962). The PICO project. In N. Johnston, L. Savitz, & M. E. Wolfgang (Eds.), *The sociology of punishment and correction.* New York: Wiley.

Adams, W. J. (1972). Utilizing the interpersonal relationship concept in marriage counselling. In H. Silverman (Ed.), *Marital therapy.* Springfield, Ill.: Thomas.

Adams-Webber, J. (1970). An analysis of the discriminant validity of several repertory grid indices. *British Journal of Psychology, 61,* 83–90.

Adams-Webber, J. (1979). *Personal construct theory: Concepts and applications.* New York: Wiley.

Adams-Webber, J. (1981). Fixed role therapy. In R. J. Corsini (Ed.), *Handbook of innovative psychotherapies.* New York: Wiley.

Adams-Webber, J., & Benjafield, J. (1976). The relationship between cognitive complexity and assimilative projection in terms of personal constructs. *Bulletin of the British Psychological Society, 29,* 219.

Adamson, R. E. (1952). Functional fixedness as related to problem solving: A repetition of three experiments. *Journal of Experimental Psychology, 44,* 288–291.

Adamson, W. C., & Adamson, K. K. (Eds.). (1979). *A handbook for specific learning disabilities*. New York: Gardner Press.

Adelman, H. S. (1978). Diagnostic classification of learning problems: Some data. American Journal of Orthopsychiatry, *48*, 717–726.

Adelmann, P. K., & Zajonc, R. B. (1989). Facial efference and the experience of emotion. *Annual Review of Psychology, 40,* 249–280.

Adelson, J. (1979). Adolescence and the generalization gap. *Psychology Today,* February, 33–37.

Adelson, J., & O'Neill, R. P. (1966). Growth of political ideas in adolescence: The sense of community. *Journal of Personality and Social Psychology, 4,* 295–306.

Ader, R. (1981). *Psychoneuroimmunology*. New York: Academic Press.

Ader, R., & Cohen, N. (1975). Behaviorally conditioned immunosuppression. *Psychosomatic Medicine,* 37, 333–340.

Ader, R., & Cohen, N. (1982). Behaviorally conditioned immunosuppression and murine systemic lupus erythematosus. *Science, 215,* 1534–1536.

Ader, R., & Cohen, N. (1981). Conditioned immunopharmacologic response. In R. Ader (Ed.), *Psychoneuroimmunology*. New York: Academic Press.

Ader, R. & Conklin, P. M. (1963). Handling of pregnant rats: Effects on emotionality of their offspring. *Science, 142,* 411–412.

Ader, R., Felten, D. L., & Cohen, N. (Eds.). (1981). *Psychoneuroimmunology* (2nd ed.). San Diego: Academic Press.

Ader, R., Felten, D. L., & Cohen, N. (Eds.). (1990). *Psychoneuroimmunology II*. Orlando, FL: Academic Press.

Adler, A. (1910). Über männliche Einstellung bei weiblichen Neurotiken. *Zentlichblatt Psychoanalyse, 1,* 174–178.

Adler, A. (1917). *Study of organ inferiority and its psychical compensation*. New York: Nervous and Mental Diseases.

Adler, A. (1922). Erziehungsberatungsstellen. In A. Adler & C. Furtmüller (Eds.), *Heilen und Bilden*. Munich: Bergmann.

Adler, A. (1928). Characteristics of the 1st, 2nd, and 3rd child. *Children, 14*(5).

Adler, A. (1928). Feelings and emotions from the standpoint of Individual Psychology. In M. Reymert (Ed.), *The Wittenberg Symposium*. Worcester, Mass.: Clark University Press.

Adler, A. (1929). *Problems of neurosis*. London: Routledge & Kegan.

Adler, A. (1937). Position in family constellation influences life style. *International Journal of Individual Psychology, 3*(3), 211–227.

Adler, A. (1939). *Social interest: A challenge to mankind*. New York: Putnam.

Adler, A. (1956). The onset of the neuroses. In H. L. Ansbacher & R. R. Ansbacher (Eds.), *The individual psychology of Alfred Adler*. New York: Basic Books.

Adler, A. (1957). *The education of children*. London: Allen & Unwin.

Adler, A. (1957/1927). *Understanding human nature*. Greenwich, Conn.: Fawcett.

Adler, A. (1959). Problems in psychotherapy. In K. A. Adler & D. Deutsch (Eds.), *Essays in individual psychology*. New York: Grove Press.

Adler, A. (1962/1931). *What life should mean to you*. New York: Capricorn Books.

Adler, A. (1963/1930). *The problem child*. New York: Capricorn Books.

Adler, A. (1964). *Problems of neurosis*. New York: Harper & Row.

Adler, A. (1964/1956). *The individual psychology of Alfred Adler: A systematic presentation in selections from his writings*. New York: Harper & Row.

Adler, A. (1969/1929). *The science of living*. New York: Anchor Books.

Adler, A. (1970). *Superiority and social interest, a collection of later writings*. Evanston, Ill.: Northwestern University Press.

Adler, A. (1971/1927). *Practice and theory of individual psychology*. New York: Humanities Press.

Adler, A. (1972/1964). Advantages and disadvantages of the inferiority feeling. In H. L. Ansbacher & R. R. Ansbacher (Eds.), *Superiority and social interest*. New York: Viking Press.

Adler, A. (1972/1964). The structure of neurosis. In H. L. Ansbacher & R. R. Ansbacher (Eds.), *Superiority and social interest*. New York: Viking Press.

Adler, A. (1974/1912). *The neurotic constitution*. New York: Arno Press.

Adler, A. (1980/1978). *Cooperation between the sexes: Writings on women, love and marriage, sexuality and its disorders*. H. L. Ansbacher, & R. R. Ansbacher (Eds.). New York: Aronson.

Adler, F. (1973). Socioeconomic factors influencing jury verdicts. *New York University Review of Law and Social Change, 3,* 1–10.

Adler, G. (1961). *The living symbol: A case study in the process of individuation*. New York: Pantheon.

Adler, K. A. (1961). Depression in the light of individual psychology. *Journal of Individual Psychology, 17,* 56–67.

Adler, K. A., & Deutsch, D. (1959). *Essays in individual psychology*. New York: Grove Press.

Adler, L. E., Sadja, L., & Wilets, G. (1980). Cimetidine toxicity manifested as paranoia and hallucinations. *American Journal of Psychiatry, 137,* 1112–1113.

Adler, L. L. (1982). Cross-cultural research and theory. In B. B. Wolman (Ed.) *Handbook of developmental psychology*. Englewood Cliffs, N.J.: Prentice-Hall.

Adler, N., & Coleman, D. (1969). Gambling and alcoholism: Symptom substitution and functional equivalents. *Quarterly Journal of Studies on Alcohol,30,* 733–736.

Adler, P. S. (1975). The transition experience: An alternative view of culture shock. *Journal of humanistic psychology, 15*(4), 13–23.

Adolph, E. F. (1939). Measurements of water drinking in dogs. *American Journal of Physiology, 125,* 75–86.

Adolph, E. F. (1941). The internal environment and behavior: Water content. *American Journal of Psychiatry, 97,* 1365–1373.

Adolph, E. F., Barker, J. P., & Hoy, P. A. (1954). Multiple factors in thirst. *American Journal of Physiology, 178,* 538–562.

Adorno, T. W. (1950). *The authoritarian personality*. New York: Harper.

Adorno, T. W. (1976). *Introduction to the sociology of music,* New York: Seabury Press.

Adorno, T. W., Frenkel-Brunswik, E., Levinson, D. J., & Sanford, R. N. (1950). *The authoritarian personality*. New York: Harper.

Aduan, R. P., Fauci, A. S., Dale, D. C., Herzberg, J. H, & Wolff, S. M. (1979). Factitious fever and self-induced infection. *Annals of Internal Medicine, 90,* 230–242.

Advertising Research Foundation. (1958). *The application of subliminal perception in advertising*. New York: Author.

Aebli, H. (1981/1980). *Denken: Das Ordnen des Tuns* Vol. I: *Kognitive Aspekte der Handlungstheorie* Vol. II: *Denkprozesse*. Stuttgart: Klett & Cotta.

AFL-CIO. (1961). *The worker's stake in mental health*. Washington, D.C.: AFL-CIO.

Age discrimination in employment act. In Vol. 29, *United States Code* §621, et seq., 81 Stat. 602, 1967 as amended 1978.

Ageton, S. S. (1983). *Sexual assault among adolescents.* Lexington, MA: Lexington Books.

Aging: Stability and change in the family (pp. 253–274). New York: Academic Press.

Aghajanian. G. K., & Bunney, B. S. (1973). Central dopaminergic neurons: Neurophysiological identification and responses to drugs. In E. Usdin & S. H. Snyder (Eds.), *Frontiers in catecholamine research.* New York: Pergamon Press.

Agras, S., & Jacob, R. (1979). Hypertension. In O. F. Pomerleau, & J. P. Brady (Eds.), *Behavioral medicine: Theory and practice.* Baltimore, Md.: Williams & Wilkins.

Agras, W. S. (1982). Behavioral medicine in the 1980s: Non-random connections. *Journal of Consulting Clinical Psychology, 50,* 797–803.

Aguado, O., & Zucker, D. (1978). *Gravity, the netherside of paradise.* South Laguna, Calif: School of the Form.

Agulera, D. C.,& Messick, J. M. (1974). *Crisis intervention: Theory and methodology.* St. Louis, Mo.: Mosby.

Ahern, F. M., Johnson, R. C., Wilson, J. R., McClearn, G. E., & Vandenberg, S. G. (1982). Family resemblances in personality. *Behavior Genetics, 12,* 261–280.

Ahlfeld, K. (1970). The Montessori revival: How far will it go? *Nation's Schools,* January.

Ahsen, A. (1965). *Eidetic psychotherapy: A short introduction.* Lahore, Pakistan: Nai Mat Booat.

Ahsen, A. (1968). *Basic concepts in eidetic psychotherapy.* New York: Brandon House.

Ahsen, A. (1977). *Psycheye: Self-analytic consciousness.* New York: Brandon House.

Aiken, L. R. (1982). *Psychological testing and assessment* (4th ed.). Boston: Allyn & Bacon.

Ainsworth, M. D., & Blehar, M. C. (1978). *Patterns of attachment: A psychological study of the strange situation.* Hillsdale, NJ: Lawrence Erlbaum.

Ainsworth, M. D. S. (1967). *Infancy in Uganda.* Baltimore, Md.: The Johns Hopkins Press.

Ainsworth, M. D. S. (1973). The development of infant-mother attachment. In B. Caldwell & H. Ricciuti (Eds.), *Review of child development research,* (Vol. 3). Chicago: University of Chicago Press.

Ainsworth, M. D. S., & Bell, S. M. (1969). Some contemporary patterns of mother-infant interaction in the feeding situation. In J. A. Ambrose (Ed.), *Stimulation in early infancy.* London: Academic Press.

Ainsworth, M. D. S., Blehar, M. C., Wayers, E., & Wall, S. (1974). *Patterns of attachment.* New York: Halstead Press.

Ainsworth, M. D. S., Salter, D., & Wittig, B. A. (1967). Attachment and exploratory behavior of one-year-olds in a strange situation. In B. M. Foss (Ed.), *Determinants of infant behavior,* Vol. 4. New York: Wiley.

Aizenberg, D., Schwatz, B., & Zemishlany, Z. (1991). Delusional parasitosis associated with phenelzine. *British Journal of Psychiatry, 159,* 716–717.

Akers, M. E. (1972). Prologue: The why of early childhood education. In I. J. Gordon (Ed.), *Early childhood education—The seventy-first yearbook of the National Society for the Study of Education.* Chicago: University of Chicago Press.

Akey, D. S. (Ed.). (1982). *Encyclopedia of associations* (16th ed.). Detroit, Mich.: Gale Research.

Akhilanand, S. (1965). *Hindu psychology,* London: Routledge & Kegan Paul.

Akishige, Y. (1973). *Psychological studies in Zen.* Tokyo: Zen Institute of Komazawa University.

Akiskal, H. (1979). A biobehavioral approach to depression. In R. Depue (Ed.), *The psychobiology of the depressive disorders.* New York: Academic Press.

Akiskal, H. S, Djenderedjian, A. H., Rosenthal, R. H., & Khani, M. K. (1977). Cyclothymic disorder. Validating criteria for inclusion in the bipolar affective group. *American Journal of Psychiatry, 134,* 1227.

Akiskal, H. S., & McKinney, W. T., Jr. (1975). Overview of recent research methods in depression: Integration of ten conceptual models into a comprehensive framework. *Archives of General Psychiatry, 32,* 285–305.

Akiskal, H. S., & W. T., Jr. (1973). Depressive disorders: Toward a unified hypothesis. *Science, 182,* 20–29.

Akita, M. (1969). Color theories. In R. Osaka (Ed.), *Sensation, lecture series in psychology,* Vol. 3. Tokyo: Tokyo University Press.

Akita, M. (1973). Experimental methods for the study of visual sensation. In T. Oyama (Ed.), *Experimentation 1, Research methods in psychology,* Vol. 2. Tokyo: Tokyo University Press.

Akita, M. (1982). Basic process of vision—The receptive field. In S. T. Akia (Ed.), *Perception I. Basic psychology today.* Vol. 2. Tokyo: Tokyo University Press.

Akita, M. (1982). Cognitive frame of reference. In S. Torii (Ed.), *Perception II, Basic psychology today.* Vol. 3. Tokyo: Tokyo University Press.

Albee, G. W. (1960). The manpower crisis in mental health. *American Journal of Public Health, 50,* 1895–1900.

Albee, G. W. (1961/1959). *Mental health manpower trends.* New York: Basic Books.

Albee, G. W. (1972). *Needed: A revolution in the treatment of the retarded.* In J. McV. Hunt (Ed.), *Human intelligence.* New Brunswick, N.J.: Transaction Books.

Albee, G. W. (1970). The uncertain future of clinical psychology. *American Psychologist, 25,* 1071–1080.

Albee, G. W. (1974). The sickness model of mental disorder means a double standard of care. In G. J. Williams & S. Gordon (Eds.), *Clinical child psychology.* New York: Behavioral Publications.

Albee, G. W. (1977). The Protestant ethic, sex, and psychotherapy. *American Psychologist, 32,* 150–161.

Albee, G. W. (1981). The prevention of sexism. *Professional Psychology, 12,* 20–28.

Albee, G. W. (1985). An intellectual autobiography. In D. P. Rogers (Ed.), *Foundations of psychology: Some personal views.* New York: Praeger.

Albee, G. W. (1986). Toward a just society: Lessons from observations on the primary prevention of psychopathology. *The American Psychologist, 41*(8), 891–897.

Albee, G. W. (1990). The answer is prevention. In P. Chance & T. G. Harris (Eds.), *The best of Psychology Today.* New York: McGraw-Hill.

Albee, G. W. (1990). The futility of psychotherapy. In D. Cohen (Ed.), Special issue. *Mind and Behavior, 11*(3–4), 369–384.

Albee, G. W. (1991). *A short history of the APA Ethics Code.* Paper presented at the APA Annual Convention, Symposium on Ethics.

Albee, G. W. (1991). Powerlessness, politics and prevention: A community mental health approach. In S. Staub & P. Green (Eds.), *In our hands: Psychology, peace and social responsibility, in a global age.* New York University Press.

Albee, G. W., Bond, L. A., & Monsey, T. V. (Eds.). (1992). *Improving children's lives: Global perspectives on prevention.* Newbury Park, CA: Sage.

Albee, G. W., & Joffe, J. M. (1981/1977). *The primary prevention of psychopathology: The issues.* Hanover, N.H.: University Press of New England.

Albemarle Paper Company v. Moody. (1975). 422 U.S. 405, OFEP1181.

Albert, D. A., Munson, R., & Resnik, M. D. (1988). *Reasoning in medicine: An introduction to clinical inference.* Baltimore, MD: Johns Hopkins University Press.

Albert, D. J., Dyson, E. M., & Walsh, M. L. (1987). Competitive behavior in male rats: Aggression and success enhanced by medial hypothalamic lesions as well as by testosterone implants. *Physiology & Behavior, 40,* 695–701.

Albert, D. J., Dyson, E. M., Walsh, M. L., & Wong, R. (1988). Defensive aggression and testosterone-dependent intermale social aggression are each elicited by food competition. *Physiology & Behavior, 43,* 21–28.

Albert, D. J., Walsh, M. L., Gorzalka, B. B., Mendelson, S., & Zalys, C. (1986). Intermale social aggression: Suppression by medial preoptic lesions. *Physiology & Behavior, 38,* 169–173.

Albert, M. L. (1979). Alexia. In K. M. Heilman & E. Valenstein (Eds.), *Clinical neuropsychology.* New York: Oxford University Press.

Albert, R. S. (1975). Toward a behavioral definition of genius. *American Psychologist, 30,* 140–151.

Albert, R. S. (1976). Toward a behavioral definition of genius. In W. Dennis and M. W. Dennis (Eds.), *The intellectually gifted: An overview.* New York: Grune & Stratton.

Albert, S. M. (1991). Cognition of caregiving tasks: Multidimensional scaling of the caregiver task domain. *The Gerontologist, 31,* 726–734.

Alberti, R. E., & Emmons, M. L. (1974). *Your perfect right: A guide to assertive behavior* (2nd ed.). San Luis Obispo, Calif.: Impact.

Alcock, J. (1979). *Animal behavior.* Sunderland, Mass.: Sinauer Associates.

Alcock, J. E. (1981). *Parapsychology: Science or magic?* New York: Pergamon Press.

Alcoholics Anonymous. (1973). *Came to believe.* New York: A.A. World Services.

Alcoholics Anonymous. (1976/1937). *Alcoholics anonymous.* New York: A.A. World Services.

Aldag, R. J., Barr, S. H., & Brief, A. P. (1981). Measurement of perceived task characteristics. *Psychological Bulletin, 90,* 415–431.

Aldag, R. J., & Brief, A. P. (1979). *Task design and employee motivation.* Glenview, Ill.: Scott, Foresman.

Alden, L. (1989). Short-term structured treatment for avoidant personality disorder. *Journal of Consulting and Clinical Psychology, 57,* 756–764.

Alden, L. (1992). Cognitive-interpersonal treatment of avoidant personality disorder. In L. Vandecreek (Ed.), *Innovations in clinical practice* (Vol. 11). Indiana, PA: Professional Resource Press.

Alden, L., & Cappe, R. (1981). Nonassertiveness: Skills deficit or selective self-evaluation. *Behavior Therapy, 12,* 107–114.

Alden, L., & Safran, J. (1978). Irrational beliefs and nonassertive behavior. *Cognitive Therapy and Research, 2,* 357–364.

Alderfer, C. P. (1969). An empirical test of a new theory of human needs. *Organizational Behavior and Human Performance, 4,* 142–175.

Aldrich, C. K., & Mendkoff, E. (1973). Relocation in the aged and disabled: A mortality study. In B. L. Neugarten (Ed.), *Middle age and aging: A reader in social psychology.* Chicago: University of Chicago Press.

Alessandra, A., & Wexler, P. (1979). *Nonmanipulative selling.* Reston, Va.: Reston.

Alexander, C. N. (1964). Concensus and mutual attraction in natural cliques: A study of adolescent drinkers. *American Journal of Sociology, 69,* 395–403.

Alexander, C. N. (1982). Ego development, personality, and behavioral change in inmates practicing the Transcendental Meditation technique or participating in other programs: A cross-sectional and longitudinal study (Doctoral dissertation, Harvard University). *Dissertation Abstracts International, 43*(2), 539B.

Alexander, C. N., Cranson, R., Boyer, R., & Orme-Johnson, D. W. (1987). Transcendental consciousness: A fourth state of consciousness beyond sleep, dreaming, and waking. *Sleep and dreams: A sourcebook* (pp. 282–315). New York: Garland.

Alexander, C. N., Davies, J. L., Dixon, C. A., Dillbeck, M. C., Druker, S. M., Oetzel, R. M., Muehlman, J. M., & Orrne-Johnson, D. W. (1990). Growth of higher states of consciousness: The Vedic psychology of human development. In C. N. Alexander & E. J. Langer (Eds.), *Higher stages of human development: Perspectives on adult growth* (pp. 286–340). New York: Oxford University Press.

Alexander, C. N., Langer, E., Newman, R., Chandler, H. M., & Davies, J. L. (1989). Transcendental Meditation, mindfulness and longevity: An experimental study with the elderly. *Journal of Personality and Social Psychology, 57,* 950–964.

Alexander, C. N., Langer, E., Chandler, H. M., Davies, J. C., & Newman, R. (1989). *Journal of Personality and Social Psychology, 41,* 1051–1063.

Alexander, C. N., Larimore, W. E., Dash, P., Titus, B., & Israelson, L. (1991). Distinguishing between Transcendental Meditation, sleep and other forms of rest according to electrophysiological criteria. In R. K. Wallace, D. W. Orme-Johnson, & M. C. Dillbeck (Eds.), *Scientific research on Maharishi's Transcendental Meditation and TM-Sidhi program: Collected papers* (Vol. 5, pp. 3015–3016). Fairfield, IA: Maharishi Intenational University Press.

Alexander, C. N., Rainforth, M. V., & Gelderloos, P. (1991). Transcendental Meditation, self-actualization, and psychological health: A conceptual overview and statistical metaanalysis. *Journal of Social Behavior and Personality, 6*(5), 189–247.

Alexander, C. N., Rainforth, M. V., Gerace, D., Beto, Z., & Boyer, R. (1993). The seven states of consciousness in Maharishi's Vedic psychology. In J. Gackenbach, H. Hunt, & C. N. Alexander (Eds.), *Higher states of consciousness: Theoretical and experimental perspectives.* New York: Plenum.

Alexander, C. N., & Sands, D. (1993). Meditation and relaxation. In F. N. McGill (Ed.), *McGill's survey of the social sciences: Psychology.* Pasadena, CA: Salem Press.

Alexander, C. N., Swanson, G. C., Rainforth, M. V., Carlisle, T. W., & Todd, C. C. (1992, November). *A prospective study on the Transcendental Meditation program in two occupational settings: Effects on stress-reduction, health, and employee development.* Paper presented at the American Psychological Association/National Institute for Occupational Safety and Health Conference, Washington, DC.

Alexander, F. (1959). In O. Strunk (Ed.), *Readings in the psychology of religion.* Nashville, Tenn.: Abingdon Press.

Alexander, F. (1963). The dynamics of psychotherapy in light of learning theory. *American Journal of Psychiatry, 120,* 440–448.

Alexander, F., & French, T. M. (1946). *Psychoanalytic psychotherapy: Principles and applications.* New York: Ronald Press.

Alexander, F., & Healy, W. (1935). *The roots Of crime*. New York: Knopf.

Alexander, F. G. (1950). *Psychosomatic medicine: Its principles and applications*. New York: Norton.

Alexander, F. G., & French, T. M. (1946). *Psychoanalytic therapy*. New York: Ronald Press.

Alexander, F. G., & French, T. M. (1948). *Studies in psychosomatic medicine*. New York: Ronald Press.

Alexander, F. G., & Selesnich, S. T. (1966). *The history of psychiatry*. New York: New American Library.

Alexander, F. M. (1932). *The use of the self*. New York: Dutton.

Alexander, H. (1976). *The initial interview in psychotherapy*. New York: Human Sciences Press.

Alexander, I. E. (1990). *Personology: Method and content in personality assessment and psychobiography*. Durham, NC: Duke University Press.

Alexander, R. D. (1975). The search for a general theory of behavior. *Behavioral Science, 20*, 77–100.

Alexander, R. D. (1979). *Darwinism and human affairs*. Seattle, Wash.: University of Washington Press.

Alexander, T. (1963). *Psychotherapy in our society*. Englewood Cliffs, N.J.: Prentice-Hall.

Alexander, T. (1972/1969). *Children and adolescents: A biocultural approach to psychological development*. New York: Aldine-Atherton.

Alexander, T. (1973). *Human development in an urban age*. Englewood Cliffs, N.J.: Prentice-Hall.

Alexander, T. (1982). The life course issues. *Academic Psychology Bulletin*.

Al-Issa, I., & Dennis, W. (1970). *Cross-cultural studies of behavior*. New York: Holt, Rinehart & Winston.

Alker, H. R., Jr., Hosticka, C., & Mitchell, M. (1976). Jury selection as a biased social process. *Law and Society Review, 11*, 9–41.

Alkon, D. L. (1989). Memory storage and neural systems. *Scientific American, 261*, 42–50.

Allan, S. W. (1958). Rehabilitation: A community challenge, New York: Wiley.

Allen, A. (1971). Life style. *The Counseling Psychologist, 3*, 25–29.

Allen, B. P., & Potkay, C. R. (1981). On the arbitrary distinction between states and traits. *Journal of Personality and Social Psychology, 41*, 916–928.

Allen, D. F., & Allen, V. S. (1979). *Ethical issues in mental retardation*. Nashville, Tenn.: Abingdon.

Allen, D. W., & Ryan, K. A. (1969). *Microteaching*. Reading, Mass.: Addison-Wesley.

Allen, H., Halperin, J., & Friend, R. (1985). Removal and diversion tactics and the control of auditory hallucinations. *Behaviour Research & Therapy, 23*, 601–605.

Allen, K. E. (1980). Mainstreaming: What have we learned? *Young Children, 35*, 54–63.

Allen, L., & Britt, P. W. (1983). Social class, mental health, and mental illness: The impact of resources and feedback. In R. D. Felner, L. A. Jason, J. N. Moritsugu, & S. S. Farber (Eds.), *Preventive psychology: Theory, research, and practice* (pp. 149–161). New York: Pergamon.

Allen, L. S., & Gorski, R. A. (1992, August). Sexual orientation and the size of the anterior commissure in the human brain. *Proceedings of the National Academy of Sciences, 89*, 7199–7202.

Allen, L. S., Hines, M., Shryne, J. E., & Gorski, R. A. (1989). Two sexually dimorphic cell groups in the human brain. *The Journal of Neuroscience, 9*(2) 497–506.

Allen, M. (1976). Twin studies of affective illness. *Archives of General Psychiatry, 33*, 1476–1478.

Allen, M., & Yen, W. (1979). *Introduction to measurement theory*. Monterey, Calif.: Brooks/Cole.

Allen, N. (1975). Chemical neurotoxins in industry and environment. In D. B. Tower (Ed.), *The nervous system*, Vol. 2: *The clinical neurosciences*. New York: Raven Press.

Allen, R. D. (1931). A group guidance curriculum in the senior high school. *Education, 2*, 189.

Allen, R. D., & Westbrook, W. H. (1979). *The handbook of animal welfare: Biomedical, psychological and ecological aspects of pet problems and control*. New York: Garland STPM Press.

Allen, T. W. (1971). The individual psychology of Alfred Adler: An item of history and a promise of a revolution. *The Counseling Psychologist, 111*(1), 3–25.

Allen, V. L. (1965). Situational factors in conformity. In L. Berkowitz (Ed.), *Advances in experimental social psychology*, Vol. 2. New York: Academic Press.

Allen, V. L. (1976). *Children as teachers*. New York: Academic Press.

Allen, V. L., & Bragg, B. W. (1969). *Ordinal position and conformity*. Washington, D.C.: Office of Education (DHEW) Bureau of Research. (ERIC Document Reproduction Service no. ED 035 960.)

Alley, G. R, Solomons, G., & Opitz, E. (1971). Minimal cerebral dysfunction as it relates to social class. *Journal of Learning Disabilities, 4*, 246—250.

Allison, A. C. (1954). Protection afforded by sickle-cell trait against subtertian malarial infection. *British Medical Journal, 1*, 290–294.

Allison, J., Blatt, S. J., & Zimet, C. N. (1967). *The interpretation of psychological tests*. New York: Harper & Row.

Allison, P. D. (1973). Sociological aspects of innovations: The case of parapsychology. Unpublished M. S. thesis, University of Wisconsin.

Allman, D. E. (1974). *An inquiry into the interrelationship of birth order, personality and innovativeness*. Ph.D. dissertation, Florida State University.

Allman, L., & Jaffe, K. (1978). *Abnormal psychology in the life cycle*. New York: Harper & Row.

Allon, N. (1975). The stigma of overweight in everyday life. In G. A. Bray (Ed.), *Obesity in perspective*, Vol. 2, Part 2 (DHEW Publication No. 75-708, National Institutes of Health). Washington, D.C.: U.S. Government Printing Office.

Alloy, L. B., & Ehrman, R. N. (1981). Instrumental to Pavlovian transfer: Learning about response-reinforcer contingencies affects subsequent learning about stimulus-reinforcer contingencies. *Learning and Motivation, 12*, 109–132.

Allport, D. A., Antonis, B., & Reynolds, P. (1972). On the division of attention: A disproof of the single-channel hypothesis. *Quarterly Journal of Experimental Psychology, 24*, 225–235.

Allport, F. H. (1920). The influence of the group upon association and thought. *Journal of Experimental Psychology, 3*, 159–182.

Allport, F. H. (1924). *Social psychology*. Boston: Houghton Mifflin.

Allport, F. H. (1934). The J-curve hypothesis of conforming behavior. *Journal of Social Psychology, 5*, 141–183.

Allport, F. H. (1955). *Theories of perception and the concept of structure*. New York: Wiley.

Allport, F. H., & Allport, G. W. (1921). Personality traits: Their classification and measurement. *Journal of Abnormal and Social Psychology, 16*, 6–40.

Allport, G. W. (1929). The study of personality by the intuitive method. *Journal of Abnormal and Social Psychology, 24*, 14–27.

Allport, G. W. (1937). *Personality: A psychological interpretation*. New York: Holt.

Allport, G. W. (1937). The functional autonomy of motives. *American Journal of Psychology, 50*, 141–156.

Allport, G. W. (1940). The psychologist's frame of reference. *Psychological Bulletin, 37*, 1–28.

Allport, G. W. (1942). *The use of personal documents in psychological science*. New York: Social Science Research Council.

Allport, G. W. (1950). *The nature of personality: Selected papers*. Cambridge, Mass.: Addison-Wesley.

Allport, G. W. (1953). The trend in motivational theory. *The American Journal of Orthopsychiatry, 23*, 107–119.

Allport, G. W. (1954). The nature of prejudice. Cambridge, Mass.: Addison-Wesley.

Allport, G. W. (1955). *Becoming: Basic considerations for a psychology of personality*. New Haven, Conn.: Yale University Press.

Allport, G. W. (1960). *Personality and social encounter*. Boston: Beacon Press.

Allport, G. W. (1960). The open system in personality theory. *Journal of Abnormal and Social Psychology, 61*, 301–310.

Allport, G. W. (1961). *Pattern and growth in personality*. New York: Holt, Rinchart & Winston.

Allport, G. W. (1962). *The individual and his religion*. New York: Macmillan.

Allport, G. W. (1966). Traits revisited. *American Psychologist, 21*, 1–10.

Allport, G. W. (1968). *The person in psychology: Selected essays*. Boston: Beacon Press.

Allport, G. W. (Ed.). (1965). *Letters from Jenny*. New York: Harcourt Brace Jovanovich.

Allport, G. W., & Odbert, H. S. (1936). Trait names. A psychological study. *Psychological Monographs, 47* (1, entire no. 211).

Allport, G. W., & Pettigrew, T. F. (1957). Cultural influence on the perception of movement: The trapezoidal illusion among Zulus. *Journal of Abnormal and Social Psychology, 55*, 104–113.

Allport, G. W., & Postman, L. J. (1945). The basic psychology of rumor. *Journal, New York Academy of Social Sciences, 8*, 61–81.

Allport, G. W., & Postman, L. J. (1947). *The psychology of rumor*. New York: Holt.

Allport, G. W., Vernon, P. E., & Lindzey, G. (1960/1931). *Study of values* (3rd ed.). Boston: Houghton Mifflin.

Allred, G. H. (1976). *How to strengthen your marriage and family*. Provo, Utah: Brigham Young University Press.

Allred, G. H., & Graft, T. T. (1979). The AIA, a mental map for communicators: A preliminary report. *Journal of Marital and Family Therapy, 5*, 33–42.

Allred, G. H., Harper, J. M., Wadham, R. A., & Wooley, B. H. (1981). Expanding the frontiers of interactional research. In E. E. Filsinger and R. A. Lewis (Eds.), *Assessing marriage*. Beverly Hills, Calif.: Sage Publications.

Almeida, E. (1978). Effects of parental involvement in teacher training. *International Journal of Psychology, 13*, 221–236.

Almeida, E. (1979). Efectos de la participación de los padres en el entrenamiento de maestros. In A. C. Cee (Ed.), *Educación y realidad socioeconómica*. México D.F.: Centro de Estudios Educativos.

Almeida, E. (1981). Investigación educativa y efectividad del maestro. In Pniie (Ed.), *Investigaciones en educación (2nd ed.)*. México D.F.: Conacyt.

Almeida, E., & Díaz-Guerrero, R. (1979). The National Institute for the Behavioural Sciences and public opinion. *International Review of Applied Psychology, 28*, 49–56.

Almeida, E., & Díaz-Guerrero, R., & Sánchez, M. E. (1980). *Un sistema para analizar la opinión pública acerca de la coyuntura nacional*. Final report presented to Sistema Nacional de Evaluación. México, D.F.: INCCA-PAC.

Almeida, E., & Sánchez, M. E. (1981). *Psychological factors affecting change in women's roles and status. A cross-cultural study*. Final report presented to the International Social Sciences Council of UNESCO. Paris.

Almond, R. (1974). *The healing community: Dynamics of the therapeutic millieu*. New York; Aronson.

Almy, T. P. (1978). The gastrointestinal tract in man under stress. In M. H. Sleisenger & J. S. Fordtran (Eds.), *Gastrointestinal disease* (Vol. 1, 2nd ed.). Philadelphia: Saunders.

Alpern, M. (1962). Part 1: Movements of the eyes. In H. Davson (Ed.), *The eye*. Vol. 3: *Muscular mechanisms*. New York: Academic Press.

Alperson, E. D. (1977). Experimental movement psychotherapy. *The American Journal of Dance, 1*, 8–12.

Alpert, J. L., Ballantyne, D., & Griffiths, D. (1981). Characteristics of consultants and consultees and success in mental health consultation. *Journal of School Psychology, 19*(4), 312–322.

Alpert, M., & Silvers, K. (1970). Perceptual characteristics distinguishing auditory hallucinations in schizophrenia and acute alcoholic psychoses. *American Journal of Psychiatry, 127*, 298–302.

Alpert, R., & Haber, R. N. (1960). Anxiety in academic achievement situations. *Journal of Abnormal and Social Psychology, 61*, 207–215.

Alsop, R. (1977). Hospital pays ante for gamblers trying to shake the habit. *The Wall Street Journal*, July 8, pp. 1, 13.

Altman, I. (1975). *The environment and social behavior*. Monterey, Calif. Brooks/Cole.

Altman, I. (1987). Community psychology 20 years later: Still another crisis in psychology? *American Journal of Community Psychology, 15*, 613–628.

Altman, K. (1973). *The relationship between social interest dimensions of early recollections and selected counselor variables*. Unpublished doctoral dissertation, University of South Carolina.

Altrocchi, J. (1972). Mental health consultation. In S. E. Golann & C. Eisdorfer (Eds.), *Handbook of community mental health*. New York: Appleton-Century-Crofts.

Altrocchi, J., Spielberger, C. D., & Eisdorfer, C. (1965). Mental health consultation with groups. *Community Mental Health Journal, 1*, 127–134.

Altus, W. (1966). Birth order and its sequence. *International Journal of Psychiatry, 3*, 23–31.

Altus, W. (1966). Birth order and its sequence. *Science, 151*, 44–49.

Alvarez, A. (1970). *The savage god*. New York: Random House.

Alvarez, G., & Ramirez, M. (1979). En busca del tiempo perdido. *Enseñanza e Investigacion en Psicologia, 5*, 386–391.

Alvin, J. (1978). *Music therapy for the autistic child*. London: Oxford University Press.

Amabile, T. M. (1983). *The social psychology of creativity*. New York: Springer-Verlag.

Ambron, S. R. (1977/1972). A review and analysis of infant and parent education programs. In M. C. Day & R. K. Parker (Eds.), *The preschool in action—Exploring early childhood programs* (2nd ed.). Boston: Allyn & Bacon.

Ambrosino, L. (1971). *Runaways*. Boston: Beacon Press.

American Board of Professional Psychology. (1980). *Directory of diplomates*, Washington, D.C.: American Board of Professional Psychology.

The American College Testing Program. (1973). *Technical report for the ACT Assessment Program,* Volume I. Iowa City, Iowa: American College Testing Program.

The American College Testing Program. (1982a). *Using the ACT assessment on campus.* Iowa City, Iowa: American College Testing Program.

The American College Testing Program. (1982b). *Using your ACT assessment results.* Iowa City, Iowa: American College Testing Program.

American Council on Education. (1980). *Accredited Institutions of Higher Education.* Washington, D.C.: American Council on Education.

American Heritage dictionary. (1969). W. Morris (Ed.). Boston: Houghton Mifflin.

American Managed Care and Review Association Newsletter. (1990). Vol. 22, pp. 6, 8.

American Marketing Association. (1974). *A basic bibliography on marketing research.* Chicago: American Marketing Association.

American Medical Association quality of life, Vols. 1–3. (1974). Acton, Mass.: Publishing Sciences Group.

American Psychiatric Association. (1974). *Clinical aspects of the violent individual.* Washington, DC: Author.

American Psychiatric Association. (1978). *Electroconvulsive therapy* (Task force report 14). Washington, D.C.: American Psychiatric Association.

American Psychiatric Association. (1980). *A psychiatric glossary* (5th ed.). Washington, DC: Author.

American Psychiatric Association. (1980). *Diagnostic and statistical manual of mental disorders* (DSM III). Washington, D.C.: American Psychiatric Association.

American Psychiatric Association. (1980). *Diagnostic and statistical manual of mental disorders* (3rd ed.). Washington, DC: Author.

American Psychiatric Association. (1987). *Diagnostic and statistical manual of mental disorders* (3rd ed., rev.). Washington DC: Author.

American Psychological Association. (1952). Division of Counseling Psychology, Committee on Counselor Training. Recommended standards for training counseling psychologists at the doctorate level. *American Psychologist, 7,* 175–181. Also in J. M. Whiteley (Ed.), *The history of counseling psychology.* Monterey, Calif.: Brooks/Cole, 1980.

American Psychological Association. (1952). Division of Counseling Psychology, Committee on Counselor Training. The practicum training of counseling psychologists. *American Psychologist, 7,* 182–188. Also in J. M. Whiteley (Ed.). *The history of counseling psychology.* Monterey, Calif.: Brooks/Cole, 1980.

American Psychological Association. (1956). Counseling psychology as a specialty: Report of the committee on definition, division of counseling psychology. *American Psychologist, 11,* 282–285.

American Psychological Association. (1956). Division of Counseling Psychology, Committee on Definition. Counseling psychology as a specialty. *American Psychologist, 11,* 282–285. In J. M. Whiteley (Ed.), *The history of counseling psychology.* Monterey, Calif.: Brooks/Cole, 1980.

American Psychological Association. (1965). *Preconference materials for the conference on the professional preparation of clinical psychologists.* Washington, D.C.: American Psychological Association.

American Psychological Association. (1966). *International opportunities for advanced training in research and psychology.* Washington, D.C.: American Psychological Association.

American Psychological Association. (1973). *Ethical principles in the conduct of research with human participants.* Washington, D.C.: American Psychological Association.

American Psychological Association, American Educational Research Association, and National Council on Measurement in Education. (1974). *Standards for educational and psychological tests.* Washington, D.C.: American Psychological Association.

American Psychological Association. (1974). *Standards for educational and psychological tests.* Washington, D.C.: American Psychological Association.

American Psychological Association. (1976). Task Force on Health Research. Contributions of psychology to health research. *American Psychologist, 31,* 263–274.

American Psychological Association. (1977). *Ethical standards of psychologists.* Washington, D.C.: American Psychological Association.

American Psychological Association. (1977). *Standards for providers of psychological services.* Washington, D.C.: American Psychological Association.

American Psychological Association. (1978). Report of the task force on the role of psychology in the criminal justice system. *American Psychologist, 33,* 1099–1113.

American Psychological Association. (1979, January 19–20). Council of Representatives minutes.

American Psychological Association. (1980). *Criteria for accreditation of doctoral programs and internships in professional psychology.* Washington, D.C.: American Psychological Association.

American Psychological Association. (1980). Division of Industrial and Organizational Psychology. *Principles for the validation and use of personnel selection procedures* (2nd ed.). Washington, D.C.: American Psychological Association.

American Psychological Association (Division 14). (1980). *Principles for the validation and use of personnel selection procedures* (2nd ed.), Washington, D.C.: American Psychological Association.

American Psychological Association. (1981). *Directory of the American Psychological Association.* Washington, D.C.: American Psychological Association.

American Psychological Association. (1981). Ethical principles of psychologists. *American Psychologist. 36,* 633–638.

American Psychological Association. (1981). Specialty guidelines for the delivery of services by counseling psychologists. *American Psychologist, 36,* 652–663.

American Psychological Association. (1982). *Division and state association membership.* Washington, D.C.: American Psychological Association.

American Psychological Association. (1985). *Standards for educational and psychological testing.* Washington, DC: Author.

American Psychological Association. (1986). *Graduate study in psychology and related fields.* Washington, DC: Author.

American Psychological Association. (1991). *Making APA work for you.* Washington, DC: Author.

American Psychological Association (1992). DOD prescription privileges training program continues. *Practitioner, 5,* 5.

American Psychological Association. (1992). The ethical principles of psychologists and code of conduct. *American Psychologist, 47,* 12.

American Psychological Society. (1992). The aging society. In The human capital initiative [Special Issue]. *APS Observer.*

American Psychologist. (1981). Special issue on Testing: Concepts, policy, practice and research, *American Psychologist, 36*(10).

Ames, A. (1951). Visual perception and the rotating trapezoidal window. *Psychological Monographs, 65* (entire no. 324).

Ames, A. (1961). Aniseikonic glasses. In F. P. Kilpatrick (Ed.), *Explorations in transactional psychology*. New York: New York University Press.

Ames, L. B. (1974). Calibration of aging. *Journal of Personality Assessment, 38*(6) 505–529.

Ames, L. B., Gillespie, C., Haines, J., & Ilg, F. L. (1979). *The Gesell Institute's child from one to six*. New York: Harper & Row.

Ames, L. B., Gillespie, C., & Streff, J. W. (1972). *Stop school failures*. New York: Harper & Row.

Ames, L. B., & Ilg, F. L. (1965). *School readiness*. New York: Harper.

Ames, L. B., Métranx, R. W., Rodell, J. L., & Walker, R. N. (1973). *Rorschach responses in old age*. New York: Brunner/Mazel.

Ames, L. B., Métraux, R. W., Rodeil, J. L., & Walker, R. N. (1974). *Child Rorschach responses*. New York: Brunner/Mazel.

Ames, L. B., Métraux, R. W., & Walker, R. N. (1971). *Adolescent Rorschach responses*. New York: Brunner/Mazel.

Amir, Y., & Ben-Ari, R. (1981). Psychology and society in Israel. *International Journal of Psychology, 16*, 239–247.

Amir, Y., Sharan, S., & Ben-Ari, R. *School integration: Cross cultural perspectives*. Hillsdale, N. J.: Erlbaum, in press.

Ammon, K. G. (1976). Germany: Psychiatry. In B. B. Wolman (Ed.), *International encyclopedia of psychiatry, psychology, psychoanalysis, and neurology*, Vol. 5. New York: Van Nostrand.

Amoore, J. D., Johnston, J. W., & Rubin, M. (1964). The stereochemical theory of olfaction. *Scientific American, 210*, 42–49.

Amoore, J. E. (1962). The stereochemical theory of olfaction, 2. Elucidation of the stereochemical properties of the olfactory receptor sites. *Proceedings of the Scientific Section of the Toilet Goode Association, 37*(Suppl.), 13–23.

Amoore, J. E. (1970). *Molecular basis of odor*. Springfield, IL: Thomas.

Amoore, J. E. (1982). Odor theory and odor classification. In E. T. Theimer (Ed.), *Fragrance chemistry—The science of the sense of smell* (pp. 27–76). New York: Academic Press.

Amoss, P. T., & Steven, H. (1981). *Other ways of growing old*, Stanford, Calif.: Stanford University Press.

Amsel, A. (1958). The role of frustrative nonreward in noncontinuous reward situations. *Psychological Bulletin, 55*, 102–119.

Amsel, A. (1962). Frustrative nonreward in partial reinforcement and discrimination learning; some recent history and a theoretical extension. *Psychological Review, 69*, 306–328.

Amsel, A. (1971). Positive induction, behavioral contrast, and generalization of inhibition in discrimination learning. In H. H. Kendler & J. T. Spence (Eds.), *Essays in neobehaviorism: A memorial volume to Kenneth W. Spence*. New York: Appleton-Century-Crofts.

Amsel, A., & Roussel, J. (1952). Motivational properties of frustration. I. Effect on a running response of the addition of frustration to the motivational complex. *Journal of Experimental Psychology, 43*, 363–368.

Amthauer, R. (1973/1953). *Der Intelligenz-Struktur-Test (IST)*. Göttingen, West Germany: Hogrefe.

Amundson, J. (1981). Will in the psychology of Otto Rank: A transpersonal perspective. *Journal of Transpersonal Psychology, 13, 113–124*.

Amundson, M., Hart, C., & Holmes, T. (1981). *Manual for the schedule of recent experience* (SRE). Seattle, Wash.: Department of Psychiatry and Behavioral Sciences, University of Washington School of Medicine.

Anand, B., Chinna, G., & Singh, B. (1961). Some aspects of electroencephalographic studies in yogis. *Electroencephalography and Clinical Neurophysiology, 13*, 452–456.

Anand, B. K., & Brobeck, J. R. (1951). Hypothalamic control of food intake in rats and cats. *Yale Journal of Biology and Medicine, 24*, 123–140.

Anand, B. K., & Brobeck, J. R. (1951). Localization of a feeding center in the hypothalmus of the rat. *Proceedings of the Society of Experimentation and Medicine, 77*, 323–324.

Anandalakshmy, S. (1980). Developmental processes. In U. Pareek (Ed.), *A survey of research in psychology*. Bombay: Popular Prakashan.

Ananiev, B. (1931). Onekotoryh voprosah Marxistsko-leninskoj rekonstrukcii psikhologii (Certain problems of the Marxist-Leninist reconstruction of psychology). *Psikhologija, 4*(3–4), 325–344.

Anastnsi, A. (1956). Intelligence and family size. *Psychological Bulletin, 53*, 187–209.

Anastasi, A. (1958). Heredity, environment, and the question "how"? *Psychological Review, 65*, 197–208.

Anastasi, A. (1958/1949/1937). *Differential psychology* (3rd ed.). New York: Macmillan, (translations: German, Italian, Portuguese, Spanish).

Anastasi, A. (Ed.). (1965). *Individual differences*. New York: Wiley.

Anastasi, A. (1961). L'etablissement de normes de comportement. *Revue de Psychologie Appliquée, 11*, 87–90.

Anastasi, A. (1967). Psychology, psychologists, and psychological testing. *American Psychologist, 22*, 297–306.

Anastasi, A. (1968). A inteligência: Sua natureza e origens. *Arquivos Brasileiros de Psicotécnica, 20*, 11–24.

Anastasi, A. (1970). On the formation of psychological traits. *American Psychologist, 25*, 899–910.

Anastasi, A. (1972). The cultivation of diversity. *American Psychologist, 27*, 1091–1099.

Anastasi, A. (1979/1964). *Fields of applied psychology* (2nd ed.). New York: McGraw-Hill (translations: Chinese, Dutch, German, Italian, Japanese, Portuguese, Spanish—Argentina and Spain editions).

Anastasi, A. (1981). Coaching, test sophistication, and developed abilities. *American Psychologist, 36*, 1086–1093.

Anastasi, A. (1981). Evolving concepts of test validation. *Annual Review of Psychology, 37*, 1–15.

Anastasi, A. (1981). Sex differences: Historical perspectives and methodological implications. *Developmental Review, 1*, 187–206.

Anastasi, A. (1982). *Psychological testing* (5th ed.). New York: Macmillan.

Anastasi, A. (1982/1976/1968/1961/1954). *Psychological testing* (5th ed.). New York: Macmillan, (translations: Italian, Portuguese, Russian, Spanish, Thai).

Anastasi, A. (1983). Evolving trait concepts. *American Psychologist, 38*, 175–184.

Anastasi, A. (1985). Reciprocal relations between cognitive and affective development—With implications for sex differences. In T. B. Sonderegger & R. A. Dienstbier (Eds.), *Psychology and Gender: Vol. 32. Nebraska Symposium on Motivation* (pp. 3–35). Lincoln: University of Nebraska Press.

Anastasi, A. (1985). Some emerging trends in psychological measurement. *Applied Psychological Measurement, 9*, 121–138.

Anastasi, A. (1986). Experiential structuring of psychological traits. *Developmental Review, 6,* 181–202.

Anastasi, A. (1988). Explorations in human intelligence: Some uncharted routes. *Applied Measurement in Education, 1*(3), 207–213.

Anastasi, A. (1988). *Psychological testing* (6th ed.). New York: Macmillan.

Anastasi, A. (Ed.). (1982). *Contributions to differential psychology: Selected papers.* New York: Praeger.

Anastasi, A., & Schaefer, C. E. (1969). Biographical correlates of artistic and literary creativity in adolescent girls. *Journal of Applied Psychology, 53,* 267–273.

Anastasiow, N. J. (1978). Strategies and models for early childhood intervention programs in integrated settings. In M. J. Guralnick (Ed.). *Early intervention and the integration of handicapped and nonhandicapped children.* Baltimore, Md.: University Park Press.

Anchin, J. C., & Kiesler, D. J. (1982). *Handbook of interpersonal psychotherapy.* New York: Pergamon.

Ancona, L. (1960). Agostino (Edoardo) Gemelli: 1878–1959. *American Journal of Psychology, 73,* 156–159.

Anderson, A., & Goolishian, H. A. (1988). Human systems as linguistic systems: Preliminary and evolving ideas about the implications for clinical theory. *Family Process, 27,* 371–393.

Anderson, B. F., Deane, D. H., Hammond, K. R., McClelland, G. H., & Shanteau, J. C. (1981). *Concepts in judgement and decision research: Definitions, sources, interrelations, comments.* New York: Praeger.

Andersen, E. B. (1980). *Discrete statistical models with social science applications.* Amsterdam: North-Holland.

Anderson, G., & Brown, R. I. (1984). Real and laboratory gambling, sensation seeking and arousal. *British Journal of Psychology, 75,* 401–410.

Anderson, H. H., & Anderson, G. L. (Eds.). (1951). *An introduction to projective techniques.* New York: Prentice-Hall.

Anderson, J., (1930). Pediatrics and child psychology. *JAMA, 95,* 1015–1018.

Anderson, J. A., & Rosenfeld, E. (Eds.). (1988). *Neurocomputing: Foundations of research.* Cambridge: MIT Press.

Anderson, J. R. (1976). *Language, memory, and thought.* Hillsdale, N.J.: Erlbaum.

Anderson, J. R. (1980). *Cognitive psychology and its implications.* San Francisco: Freeman.

Anderson, J. R. (1989). A theory of the origins of human knowledge. *Artificial Intelligence, 40,* 313–351.

Anderson, J. R. (Ed.). (1981). *Cognitive skills and their acquisition.* Hillsdale, N.J.: Erlbaum.

Anderson, J. R., & Bower, G. H. (1973). *Human associative memory.* Washington, D.C.: Winston.

Anderson, J. R., Dillon, J. L., & Hardaker, J. B. (1977). *Agricultural decision analysis.* Ames, Iowa: Iowa State University Press.

Anderson, N. H. (1965). Averaging versus adding as a stimulus-combination rule in impression formation. *Journal of Experimental Psychology, 70,* 394–400.

Anderson, N. H. (1961). Scales and statistics: Parametric and nonparametric. *Psychological Bulletin, 58,* 305–316.

Anderson, N. H. (1981). *Foundations of information integration theory.* New York: Academic Press.

Anderson, R., Manoogian, S. T., & Reznick, J. S. (1976). The undermining and enhancing of intrinsic motivation in preschool children. *Journal of Personality and Social Psychology, 34,* 915–922.

Anderson, V. V. (1929). *Psychiatry in industry,* New York: Harper.

Andersson, B. (1953). The effect of injections of hypertonic NaCl-solutions into different parts of the hypothalamus of goats. *Acta Physiologica Scandinavica, 28,* 188–201.

Andersson, B., & Kärrqvist, C. (1981). Ljuset och dess egenskaper (Light and its qualities). EKNA-rapport no. 8, *Institutionen för Praktisk Pedagogik, Göteborgs Universitet.*

Andreasen, N. (1987). The measurement of genetic aspects of depression. In A. J. Marsella, R. Hirschfeld, & M. Katz (Eds.), *The measurement of depression.* New York: Guilford Press.

Andreasen, N. C. (1987). Creativity and mental illness: Prevalence rates in writers and their first-degree relatives. *American Journal of Psychiatry, 144,* 1288–1292.

Andreassi, J. L. (1980). *Psychophysiology.* New York: Oxford University Press.

Andreev, B. F. (1960). *Sleep therapy in neuroses.* New York: Plenum.

Andrew, D. M., & Paterson, D. G. (1946). *Manual revised in 1946 for the Minnesota Vocational Test for Clerical Workers.* New York: Psychological Corporation.

Andrew, G., Walton, R. E., Hartwell, S. W., & Hutt, M. L. (1951). The Michigan picture test: The stimulus values of the cards. *Journal of Consulting Psychology, 15,* 51–54.

Andrew, R. J. (1965). The origins of facial expressions. *Scientific American, 213,* 88–94.

Andrews, K. R. (1966). *The effectiveness of university management development programs.* Boston: Harvard University, Graduate School of Business Administration.

Andrykowski, M. A. (1990). The role of anxiety in the development of anticipatory nausea in cancer chemotherapy: A review and synthesis. *Psychosomatic Medicine, 52,* 458–475.

Angell, J. R. (1903). The relation of structural and functional psychology to philosophy, *Philosophical Review, 12,* 243–71.

Angell, J. R. (1904). *Psychology: An introductory study of the structures and functions of human consciousness.* New York: Holt.

Angell, J. R. (1907). The province of functional psychology. *Psychological Review. 14,* 61–91.

Angle, H. V., Hay, L. R., Hay, W. M., & Ellinwood, E. H. (1977). Computer assisted behavioral assessment. In J. D. Cone & R. P. Hawkins (Eds.), *Behavioral Assessment: New directions in clinical psychology.* New York: Brunner/Mazel.

Angoff, W. H. (1971). Scales, norms, and equivalent scores. In R. L. Thorndike (Ed.), *Educational measurement* (2nd ed.). Washington, D.C.: American Council on Education.

Angoff, W. H. (Ed.). (1971). *The College Board Admissions Testing Program: A technical report on research and development activities relating to the Scholastic Aptitude Test and achievement tests.* New York: College Entrance Examination Board.

Angrist, B., & Sudilovsky, A. (1978). Central nervous system stimulants: Historical aspects and clinical effects. In L. L. Iversen, S. D. Iversen, & S. H. Snyder (Eds.), *Handbook of psychopharmacology,* Vol. 11. New York: Plenum.

Angyal, A. (1941). *Foundations for a science of personality.* New York: Commonwealth Foundation.

Angyal, A. (1965). *Neurosis and treatment: A holistic theory.* New York: Wiley.

Anisman, H. (1982). Vulnerability to depression. In R. M. Post and J. C. Ballenger (Eds.), *Neurobiology of mood disorders.* Baltimore, Md.: Williams & Wilkins.

Anisman, H., & Zacharko, R. M. (1982). Depression: The predisposing influence of stress. *Behavioral and Brain Sciences, 5,* 89–137.

Anita. (1979). Gamblers Anonymous. In D. Lester (Ed.), *Gambling today.* Springfield, Ill.: Thomas.

Annau, Z. (Ed.). (1986). *Neurobehavioral toxicology.* Baltimore, MD: Johns Hopkins University Press.

Annesley, F., Odhner, F, Madoff, E., & Chansky, N. (1970). Identifying the first grade underachiever. *Journal of Educational Research, 63,* 459–462.

Annett, J. (1969). *Feedback and human behavior.* Baltimore, Md.: Penguin Books.

Annett, M. (1973). Laterality of childhood hemiplegia and the growth of speech and intelligence. *Cortex, 9,* 4–33.

Annett, M. (1974). Handedness in the children of two left handed parents. *British Journal of Psychology, 65,* 129–131.

Annis H. M. (1979). The detoxication alternative to the handling of public inebriates: The Ontario experience. *Journal of Studies on Alcohol, 40,* 196–210.

Annis, H. M., & Liban, C. B. (1979). A follow-up of male halfway-house residents and matched nonresident controls. *Journal of Studies on Alcohol, 40,* 63–69.

Annis, L. F. (1978). *The child before birth.* Ithaca, N.Y.: Cornell University Press.

Annon, J. S. (1974). *The behavioral treatment of sexual problems.* Vol. 1: *Brief therapy.* Vol. 2: *Intensive therapy.* Honolulu: Enabling Systems. New York: Harper & Row.

Annon, J. S. (1975). *The behavioral treatment of sexual problems,* Vol. 2. Honolulu: Enabling Systems.

Anonymous. (1968). The Carl Jung, Bill W. letters. *Grapevine, 24*(8), 16–21.

Anonymous. (1970). The making of modern science: Biographical studies. *Journal of the American Academy of Arts and Sciences, Daedalus,* Fall.

Anonymous. (1976). *Alcoholics Anonymous* (3rd ed.). New York: Alcoholics Anonymous World Services.

Anonymous. (1977). Reading readability formulae. *Teaching of Psychology, 4,* 49–51.

Ansbacher, H. (1982). Alfred Adler's views on the unconscious. *Journal of Individual Psychology, 38*(1), 32–41.

Ansbacher, H., & Ansbacher, R. R (Eds.). (1956). *The individual psychology of Alfred Adler.* New York: Basic Books.

Ansbacher, H. L. (1959). The significance of the socio-economic status of the patients of Freud and Adler. *American Journal of Psychotherapy, 13,* 376—382.

Ansbacher, H. L. (1967). Life style: A historical and systematic review. *Journal of Individual Psychology, 23,* 191–212.

Ansbacher, H. L. (1974). Psychology: A way of living. In T. S. Krawiec (Ed.), *The Psychologists,* Vol. 2. New York: Oxford University Press.

Ansbacher, H. L. (1974). The first critique of Freud's metapsychology: An extension of George S. Klein's "Two theories or one?" *Bulletin of the Menninger Clinic, 38,* 78–84.

Ansbacher, H. L. (1978). The development of Adler's concept of social interest: A critical study. *Journal of Individual Psychology, 34,* 118–152.

Ansbacher, H. L. & Ansbacher, R. R. *Cooperation between the sexes.* (See Adler, A.)

Ansbacher, H. L., & Ausbacher, R. R. (Eds.). *Superiority and social interest.* (See Adler, A.)

Ansbacher, H. L., & Ausbacher, R. R. (Eds.). *The individual psychology of Alfred Adler.* (See Adler, A.)

Anschütz, G. (1953). *"Die Phantasie" in Psychologie Grundlage, Ergebnisse and Probleme der Forschung,* Hamburg: Meiner.

Anschuetz, N. (1979). Marketing psychology. *Professional Psychology, 10*(2), 154–160.

Anshutz, L., Camp, C., Markley, R., & Kramer, J. (1987). Remembering mnemonics: A three-year follow-up on the effects of mnemonics training in elderly adults. *Experimental Aging Research, 13,* 141–143.

Ansley, N., & Horvath, F. (1977). *Truth and science.* Linthicum Heights, Md.: American Polygraph Association.

Anspach, K. A. (1967). *The why of fashion.* Ames, Iowa: Iowa State University Press.

Anthony, E. J., & Chiland, C. (Eds.). (in press). *Children in turmoil: Tomorrow's parents.* New York: Wiley.

Anthony, J. (1974). Children at risk from divorce: A review. In J. Anthony & C. Koupernic (Eds.), *The child in his family: Children in psychiatric risk* New York: Wiley.

Anthony, S. (1940).*The child's discovery of death: A study in child psychology.* New York: Harcourt, Brace, & World.

Anthony, W. A. (1969). The effects of contact on individual's attitude toward disabled persons. *Rehabilitation Counseling Bulletin, 12,* 168–170.

Antonovsky, A. (1979). *Health, stress and coping.* San Francisco: Jossey-Bass.

Antze, P. (1976). The role of ideologies in peer psychotherapy organizations: some theoretical considerations and three case studies. *The Journal of Applied Behavioral Science, 12,* 323–346.

Anzieu, D. (1975–1976). *L'auto-analyse de Freud et la découverte de la psychanalyse.* Paris: Presses Universitaires de France.

Anzieu, D. (1978/1960). *Les méthodes projectives.* Paris: Presses Universitaires de France.

Anzieu, D. (1979). *Le psychodrame analytique chez l'enfant et l'adolescent.* Paris: Presses Universitaires de France.

Anzieu, D. (1981). *Le corps de l'oeuvre. Essais psychanalytiques sur le travail créateur.* Paris: Gallimard.

Anzieu, D. (1981/1975). *Le groupe et l'inconscient.* Paris: Dunod.

Anzieu, D., & Martin, J. Y. (1982/1968). *La dynamique des groupes restreints.* Paris: Presses Universitaires de France.

APA Task Force on Late Neurological Effects of Antipsychotic Drugs. (1980). Tardive dyskinesia: Summary of a Task Force Report of the APA. *American Journal of Psychiatry, 137,* 1163–1172.

Apfelbaum, E. (1974). On conflicts and bargaining. *Advances in Experimental Social Psychology, 7,* 103–156.

Appel, F. W., and Appel, E. M. (1959). Intracranial variation in the weight of the human brain. In J. E. Birren (Ed.), *Handbook of aging and the individual-psychological and biological aspects.* Chicago: University of Chicago Press.

Appel, K., & Haken, W. (1977). Every planar map is four colorable. Part I: Discharging. *Illinois Journal of Mathematics, 21,* 429–490.

Appel, K., & Haken, W. (1979). The four-color problem. In L. A. Steen (Ed.), *Mathematics today: Twelve informal essays* (pp. 153–180). New York: Springer-Verlag.

Appelbaum, P. S., & Roth, L. H. (1981). Clinical issues in the assessment of competency. *American Journal of Psychiatry, 138,* 1462–1467.

Appelbaum, S. A. (1976). The dangerous edge of insight. *Psychotherapy, 13,* 202–206.

192   BIBLIOGRAPHY

Appelbaum, S. A. (1978). Pathways to change in psychoanalytic therapy. *Bulletin of the Menninger Clinic, 42,* 239–251.

Appelbaum, S. A., & Siegal, R. S. (1965). Half-hidden influences on psychological testing practice. *Journal of Personality Assessment, 29,* 128–133.

Appenzeller, O. (1976). *Autonomic nervous system.* Amsterdam: North-Holland.

Appenzeller, O. (1981). What makes us run? *New England Journal of Medicine, 305,* 578–580.

Applewhite, P. B., and Gardner, F. T. (1971). Rapid leaf closure of *Mimosa* in response to light. *Nature, 233,* 279–280.

Appley, M. H. (Ed.). (1970). The place of psychology in the university. *American Psychologist, 25,* 387–468.

Appley, M. H. (Ed.). (1971). *Adaptation level theory.* New York: Academic Press.

Aram, J., & Piraino, T. (1978). The hierarchy of needs theory: An evaluation in Chile. *Interamerican Journal of Psychology, 12,* 179–188.

Aranda Lopez, J. (1965). El panorama actual de la psicologia industrial en Mexico. *Revista de la Sociedad Cientifica Universitaria de Psicologia, 23–24,* 6–8.

Araoz, D. L. (1985). *Hypnosis and sex therapy.* New York: Brunner/Mazel.

Araoz, D. L. (1985). *The new hypnosis.* New York: Brunner/Mazel.

Arbuckle, D. S. (1977). Counselor licensure: To be or not to be. *Personnel and Guidance Journal, 55,* 581–585.

Archer, E. J. (1960). Re-evaluation of the meaningfulness of all possible CVC trigrams. *Psychological Monographs, 74,* 497.

Archer, R. P., Maruish, M., Imhof, E. A., & Piotrowski, C. (1991). Psychological test usage with adolescent clients: 1990 survey findings. *Professional Psychology: Research and Practice, 22,* 247–252.

Archibald, W. P. (1974). Alternative explanations for self-fulfilling prophecy. *Psychological Bulletin, 81,* 74–84.

Arcuri, A. F. (1979). Illegal gambling. In D. Lester (Ed.), *Gambling today.* Springfield, Ill.: Thomas.

Ardell, D. (1979/1977). *High level wellness.* New York: Bantam Books.

Ardila, R. (1968). Psychology in Latin America. *American Psychologist, 23,* 567–574.

Ardila, R. (1969). Desarrollo de la psicologia Latinoamericana. *Revista Latinoamericana de Psicologia, 1,* 63–71.

Ardila, R. (1970). Applied psychology in Colombia. *International Review of Applied Psychology, 19,* 155–160.

Ardila, R. (1970). Ingenieros, psychologist. *Journal of the History of the Behavioral Sciences. 6,* 41–47.

Ardila, R. (1970). La psychologie latino-américaine. *Bulletin de Psychologie* (Paris), *23,* 410–415.

Ardila, R. (1970). Landmarks in the history of Latin American psychology. *Journal of the History of the Behavioral Sciences, 6,* 140–146.

Ardila, R. (1970). Psicología del aprendizaje. Mexico, D.F.: Siglo XXI.

Ardila, R. (1971). A contecimientos importantes en la historia de la psicologia Latinoamericana. *Revista Interamericana de Psicologia, 5,* 1–11.

Ardila, R. (1971). *Los pioneros de la psicologia.* Buenos Aires: Paidos.

Ardila, R. (1971). Professional problems of psychology in Latin America. *Interamerican Journal of Psychology, 5*(1–2), *53–57.*

Ardila, R. (1971). *Psicología contemporánea.* Buenos Aires: Paidos.

Ardila, R. (1973). *La psicología en Colombia, desarrollo histórico.* Mexico, D.F.: Trillas.

Ardila, R. (1973). *Manual de psicología fisiológica.* Mexico, D.F.: Trillas.

Ardila, R. (1975). Behavior therapy in Colombia. *Newsletter of the Association for the Advancement of Behavior Therapy, 2*(4), 5–6.

Ardila, R. (1975). La psicología como ciencia y como profesión en Colombia. *Acta Psiquiátrica y Psicológica de América Latina, 21,* 215–220.

Ardila, R. (1975). The First Latin American Conference on Training in Psychology. *International Journal of Psychology, 10,* 149–158.

Ardila, R. (1976). Educational psychology in Latin America. In C. D. Catterall (Ed.), *Psychology in the schools in international perspective,* Vol. 1. Columbus, Ohio: International School Psychology Steering Committee.

Ardila, R. (1976). Latin America. In V. S. Sexton & H. Misiak (Eds.), *Psychology around the world.* Monterey, Calif.: Brooks/Cole.

Ardila, R. (1976). Necesidades de psicólogos para Colombia. *Revista Latinoamericana de Psicología, 8,* 135–138.

Ardila, R. (1976). Tendencias en la psicología experimental colombiana. *Revista Latinoamericana de Psicología, 8,* 303–317.

Ardila, R. (1977). *Investigaciones psicológicas.* Bogota: Siglo XXI.

Ardila, R. (1977). La psicología profesional en Latinoamérica: roles cambiantes para una sociedad en proceso de transformación. *Enseñanza e Investigación en Psicologia, 3,* 5–20.

Ardila, R. (1978). Behavior modification in Latin America. In M. Hersen, R. M. Eisler, & P. M. Miller (Eds.), *Progress in behavior modification,* Vol. 6. New York: Academic Press.

Ardila, R. (1979). La psicología en Argentina: Pasado, presente y futuro. *Revista Latinoamericana de Psicología, 11,* 72–91.

Ardila, R. (1979). *Los orígenes del comportamiento humano.* Barcelona: Fontanella.

Ardila, R. (1979). Walden tres. Barcelona: CEAC.

Ardila, R. (1980). Historiography of Latin American psychology. In J. Brozek, & L. J. Pongratz (Eds.), *Historiography of modern psychology.* Toronto: Hogrefe.

Ardila, R. (1980). *Terapia del comportamiento.* Bilbao, Spain: Desclée de Brouwer.

Ardila, R. (1982). *El futuro de la psicología.* Barranquilla: Ediciones Pedagógicas Latinoamericanas.

Ardila, R. (1982). International developments in behavior therapy in Latin America. *Journal of Behavior Therapy and Experimental Psychiatry, 13*(1), 15–20.

Ardila, R. (1982). International psychology. *American Psychologist, 37,* 323–329.

Ardila, R. (1982). *La psicología en América Latina, pasado, presente y futuro.* Mexico, D.F.: Trillas.

Ardila, R. (1982). La terapia del comportamiento en América Latina. *Enseñanza e Investigación en Psicologia.*

Ardila, R. (1982). Psychology in Latin America today. *Annual Review of Psychology, 33,* 103–122.

Ardila, R. (in press). *Psicología y naturaleza humana.*

Ardila, R. (Ed.). (1974). *El análisis experimental del comportamiento, la contribución latinoamericana.* Mexico, D.F.: Trillas.

Ardila, R. (Ed.). (1978). *La profesión del psicólogo.* Mexico, D.F.: Trillas.

Ardila, R., & Finley, G. (1975). Psychology in Latin America: A bibliography. Special issue, *Interamerican Journal of Psychology, 9.*

Ardrey, R. (1961). *African genesis.* New York: Atheneum.

Ardrey, R. (1970). *The social contract.* New York: Atheneum.

Ardrey, R. (1976). *The hunting hypothesis*. New York: Atheneum.

Ardrey, R. (1980/1966). *The territorial imperative*. New York: Atheneum.

Arenberg, D., & Robertson-Tchabo, E. A. (1977). Learning and aging. In J. E. Birren & K. W. Schaie (Eds.), *Handbook of the psychology of aging*. New York: Van Nostrand Reinhold.

Argulewicz, E. N., Mealor, D. J., & Richmond, B. O. (1979). Creative abilities of learning disabled children. *Journal of Learning Disabilities, 12*, 21–24.

Argyle, M. (1969). *Social interaction*. London: Methuen.

Argyle, M. (1972). Non-verbal communication in human social interaction. In R. A. Hendi (Ed.), *Non-verbal communication*. Cambridge, England: Cambridge University Press.

Argyle, M. (1972). *The psychology of interpersonal behavior*. London: Penguin.

Argyle, M. (1976). Personality and social behavior. In R. Harré (Ed.), *Personality*. Oxford: Blackwell.

Argyle, M. (1981). The contribution of social interaction research to social skills training. In J. D. Wine & M. D. Syme (Eds.), *Social competence*. New York: Guilford.

Argyle, M., Furnham, A., & Graham, J. (1981). *Social situations*. London: Cambridge University Press.

Argyris, C. (1964). *Integrating the individual and the organization*. New York: Wiley.

Argyris, C. (1970). *Intervention theory and method*. Reading, Mass.: Addison-Wesley.

Argyris, C, & Schön, D. A. (1978). *Organizational learning: A theory of action perspective*. Reading, Mass.: Addison-Wesley.

Ariès, P. (1962). *Centuries of childhood: A social history of family life*. New York: Knopf.

Ariès, P. (1974). *Western attitudes toward death from the middle ages to the present*. Baltimore, Md.: Johns Hopkins.

Arieti, S. (1974). *Interpretation of schizophrenia* (2nd ed.). New York: Basic Books.

Arieti, S. (1976). *Creativity: The magic synthesis*. New York: Basic Books.

Arieti, S., & Lorraine, S. (1972). The therapeutic assistant in treating the psychotic. *International Journal of Psychiatry, 10*, 11–22.

Aristotle. (1910). *Physiognomica*. Oxford: Oxford University Press.

Aristotle. (1931). De memoria et reminiscentia, from the *Parva Naturalia*. In W. D. Ross (Ed.), *The works of Aristotle translated into English*. Oxford: Clarendon Press.

Aristotle. (1941). De anima (On the soul). In R. McKeon (Ed.), *The basic works of Aristotle*. New York: Random House.

Aristotle. (1941). De memoria et reminiscentia (On memory and reminiscence). In R. McKeon (Ed.), *The basic works of Aristotle*. New York: Random House.

Aristotle. (1952). *Physics*. In R. M. Hutchins (Ed.), *Great books of the western world*, Vol. 8. Chicago: Encyclopedia Britannica.

Aristotle. (1965/1951). *De Anima*, in the version of William of Moerbeke, and the *Commentary* of St. Thomas Aquinas. New Haven, Conn.: Yale University Press.

Aristotle. (1975). *From natural science, psychology, the Nichomachean ethics*. New York: Odyssey Press.

Arkes, H. R. (1981). Impediments to accurate clinical judgment and possible ways to minimize their impact. *Journal of Consulting and Clinical Psychology, 49*, 323–330.

Arkes, H. R., Christensen, C., Lai, C., & Blumer, C. (1987). Two methods of reducing overconfidence. *Organizational Behavior and Human Decision Processes, 39*, 133–144.

Arkes, H. R., Faust, D., Guilmette, T. J., & Hart, K. (1988). Eliminating the hindsight bias. *Journal of Applied Psychology, 73*, 305–307.

Arkes, H. R., & Harkness, A. R. (1980). The effect of making a diagnosis on subsequent recognition of symptoms. *Journal of Experimental Psychology: Human Learning and Memory, 6*, 568–575.

Arkin, A. M., Antrobus, J. S., & Ellman, S. J. (Eds.). (1978). *The mind in sleep*. Hillsdale, N.J.: Erlbaum.

Arkowitz, H. (1989). The role of theory in psychotherapy integration. *Journal of Integrative and Eclectic Psychotherapy, 8*, 191–215.

Arkowitz, H., Lichtenstein, E., McGovern, K. & Hines, P. (1975). The behavioral assessment of social competence in males. *Behavior Therapy, 6*, 3–13.

Armor, T. (1969). A note on the peak experience and a transpersonal psychology. *Journal of Transpersonal Psychology, 1*, 47–50.

Armstrong, D. M. (1961). *Perception and the physical world*. London: Routledge & Kegan Paul.

Armstrong, D. M. (1968). *A materialist theory of the mind*. London: Routledge.

Armstrong, D. M. (1980). *The nature of mind and other essays*. Ithaca, NY: Cornell University Press.

Arnheim, R. (1949). The Gestalt theory of expression. *Psychological Review, 56*, 156–171.

Arnheim, R. (1962). *The genesis of a painting: Picasso's Guernica*. Berkeley, Los Angeles: University of California Press.

Arnheim, R. (1969). *Visual thinking*. Berkeley, Los Angeles, London: University of California Press.

Arnheim, R. (1974/1966/1954). *Art and visual perception: A psychology of the creative eye*. Berkeley, Los Angeles: University of California Press.

Arnkoff, D. B., & Glass, C. R. (1989). Cognitive assessment in social anxiety and social phobia. *Clinical Psychology Review, 9*, 61–74.

Arnold, A. P., & Gorski, R. A. (1984). Gonadal steroid induction of structural sex differences in the central nervous system. *Annual Review of Neuroscience, 7*, 413–442.

Arnold, M. B. (1954). Feelings and emotions as dynamic factors in personality integration. In M. B. Arnold & J. A. Gasson (Eds.), *The human person*. New York: Ronald Press.

Arnold, M. B. (1960). *Emotion and personality*, (2 vols.). New York: Columbia University Press.

Arnold, W. (1975/1951). *Der Pauli-Test*. Munich: Barth.

Arnold, W. J. (Ed.). (1976). *Nebraska symposium on the conceptual foundations of theory and methods in psychology*. Lincoln, Neb.: University of Nebraska Press.

Aronfreed, J. (1968). *Conduct and conscience: The socialization of internalized control over behavior*. New York: Academic Press.

Aronfreed, J. (1970). The socialization of altruistic and sympathic behavior: Some theoretical and experimental analyses, In J. Macaulay & L. Berkowitz (Eds.), *Altruism and helping behavior* (pp. 103–126). New York: Academic Press.

Aronow, E., & Reznikoff, M. (1976). *Rorschach content interpretation*. New York: Gruene & Stratton.

Arons, M. (1981). *Graduate programs in humanistic-transpersonal psychology in North America* (3rd ed.). Carrollton: West Georgia College Psychology Department.

Aronson, E. (1980). Persuasion via self-justification: Large commitments for small rewards. In L. Festinger (Ed.). *Retrospections on social psychology*. New York: Oxford University Press.

Aronson, E. (1980/1972). Self-justification. In E. Aronson (Ed.), *The social animal* (3rd ed.). San Francisco: Freeman.

Aronson, E., (1980/1976/1972). *The social animal*. San Francisco: Freeman.

Aronson, E., Carlsmith, J. M., & Ellsworth, P. C. (1976). *Methods of research in social psychology*. Reading, Mass.: Addison-Wesley.

Aronson, E., & Linder, D. (1965). Gain and loss of esteem as determinants of interpersonal attractiveness. *Journal of Experimental Social Psychology, 1,* 156–71.

Aronson, E., & Lindzey, G. (1968). *Handbook of social psychology* (2nd ed.), Reading, Mass.: Addison-Wesley. Vol. I: *Theories,* 1968; Vol. II: *Research methods,* 1969; Vol. III: *The individual in a social context,* 1969; Vol. IV: *Group psychology and phenomena of interaction,* 1969; Vol. V. *Applied social psychology,* 1969.

Aronson, E., & Mills, J. (1959). Effect of severity of initiation on liking for a group. *Journal of Abnormal and Social Psychology, 59,* 177–181.

Aronson, E., & Pines, A. (1981). *Burnout: From life tedium to personal growth*. New York: Free Press.

Aronson, E., & Pratkanis, A. R. (Eds.). (1992). *Social psychology*. (Vols. 1–3). Cheltenham, UK: Elgar.

Aronson, E., Stephan, C., Sikes, J., Blaney, N., & Snapp, M. (1978). *The jigsaw classroom*. Beverly Hills, Calif.: Sage Publications.

Arreghini, E., Agonstini, C., Wilkinson, G. (1991). General practitioner referral to specialist psychiatric services: A comparison of practices in north- and south-Verona. *Psychological Medicine, 21*(2), 485–494.

Arrington, R. E. (1943). Time sampling in studies of social behavior: A critical review of technqiues and results with research suggestions. *Psychological Bulletin 40*(2), 81–124.

Arroba, T. (1978). Styles of decision-making and their use. *British Journal of Guidance and Counseling, 5,* 149–158.

Arthur, G. (1949). The Arthur adaptation of the Leiter International Performance Scale. *Journal of Clinical Psychology, 5,* 345–349.

Artola, A., & Singer, W. (1987). Long-term potentiation and NMDA receptors in rat visual cortex. *Nature, 330,* 649–652.

Arvey, R. D. (1979). *Fairness in selecting employees*. Reading, Mass.: Addison-Wesley.

Asayama, S. (1976). Sexual behavior in Japanese students: Comparisons for 1974, 1960, and 1952. *Archives of Sexual Behavior, 5*(5), 371–390.

Asbury, C. A. (1974). Selected factors infuencing over- and under-achievement in young school-age children. *Review of Educational Research, 44,* 409–428.

Asch, S. E. (1946). Forming impressions of personality. *Journal of Abnormal and Social Psychology, 41,* 258–290.

Asch, S. E. (1951). Effects of group pressure upon the modification and distortion of judgment. In H. Guetzkow (Ed.), *Groups, leadership, and men*. Pittsburgh, Pa.: Carnegie.

Asch, S. E. (1952). *Social psychology*. New York: Prentice-Hall.

Asch, S. E. (1955). Opinions and social pressure. *Scientific American, 193,* 31–35.

Asch, S. E. (1956). Studies of independence and conformity: I. A minority of one against a unanimous majority. *Psychological Monographs, 70* (9, entire No. 416), 1–70.

Ascher, E. J. (1935). The adequacy of current intelligence tests for testing Kentucky mountain children. *Journal of Genetic Psychology, 46,* 480–486.

Ascher, L. M., & Cautela, J. R. (1972). Covert negative reinforcement: An experimental test. *Journal of Behavior Therapy and Experimental Psychiatry, 3,* 1–5.

Ascher, L. M., & Cautela, J. R. (1974). An experimental study of covert extinction. *Journal of Behavior Therapy and Experimental Psychiatry, 5,* 233–238.

Aschoff, J. (Ed.). (1981). *Handbook of behavioral neurobiology*. Vol. 4: *Biological rhythms*. New York: Plenum.

Aserinsky, E., & Kleitman, N. (1953). Regularly occurring periods of eye motility and concomitant phenomena during sleep. *Science, 118,* 273–274.

Ash, P. (1947). Grade achievement of adolescent delinquents. *Journal of Applied Psychology, 31,* 323–328.

Ash, P. (1948). The reliability of job evaluation rankings. *Journal of Applied Psychology, 32,* 313–320.

Ash, P. (1948). The reliability of psychiatric diagnosis. *Journal of Abnormal and Social Psychology, 44,* 272–276.

Ash, P. (1949). The reliability of psychiatric diagnosis. *Journal of Abnormal and Social Psychology, 44,* 272–277.

Ash, P. (1952). The effect of anonymity on attitude scale reponse. *Journal of Abnormal and Social Psychology, 37,* 292–299.

Ash, P. (1964). Psychology in labor relations. *Personnel Psychology, 17,* 361–363.

Ash, P. (1966). A note on the judgement of speaker effectiveness. *Journal of Applied Psychology, 50,* 204–205.

Ash, P. (1970). Validation of an instrument to predict the likelihood of employee theft. In *Proceedings of the 78th Annual Convention of the American Psychological Association*. Washington, D.C.: American Psychological Association.

Ash, P. (1971). Screening employment applicants for attitudes toward theft. *Journal of Applied Psychology, 55,* 161–164.

Ash, P. (1973). Attitudes of work applicants toward theft. *Proceedings of the XVIIth International Congress of Applied Psychology*. Liege, Belgium: Editest.

Ash, P. (1974). Attitudes of convicted felons toward theft. *Criminal Justice and Behavior, 1* (1), 21–29.

Ash, P., & Kroeker, L. (1975). Personnel selection, classification, and placement: Testing and civil rights. *Annual Review of Psychology, 25,* 486–494.

Ashby, R. (1960/1952). *Design for a brain*. New York: Wiley.

Ashby, R. (1968). Regulation and control. From Ashby, R., *An introduction to cybernetics*, (1956). In W. Buckley (Ed.), *Modern systems research for the behavioral scientist*. Chicago: Aldine.

Ashcraft, M. H. (1989). *Human memory and cognition*. Glenview, IL: Scott, Foresman.

Asher, J. J., & Sciarrino, J. A. (1974). Realistic work sample tests: A review. *Personnel Psychology, 27* 519–533.

Asher, J. W. (1976). *Educational research and evaluation methods*. Boston: Little, Brown.

Asher, R. (1951). Munchausen's syndrome. *Lancet, 1,* 339–341.

Asher, R. (1972). *Talking sense*. Baltimore Md.: University Park Press.

Asher, S. R., & Gottman, J. M. (Eds.). (1981). *The development of children's friendships*. Cambridge, England: Cambridge University Press.

Asher, S. R., & Hummel, S. (1981). Children's social competence in peer relations: Sociometric and behavioral assessment. In J. D. Wine & M. D. Syme (Eds.), *Social competence*. New York: Guilford.

Ashley, W. R., Harper, R. S., & Runyon, D. L. (1951). The perceived size of coins in normal and hypnotically-induced economic states. *American Journal of Psychology, 64,* 564–572.

Ashton, N. (1979). Gamblers: Disturbed or healthy? In Lester, D. (Ed.), *Gambling today*. Springfield, Ill.: Thomas.

Aslin, R. N., & Smith, L. B. (1988). Perceptual development. *Annual Review of Psychology, 39,* 435–473.

Aspy, D. (1972). *Toward a technology for humanizing education*. Champaign, Ill.: Research Press.

Aspy, D., & Roebuck, F. M. (1975). From humane ideas to humane technology and back again, many times. *Education, 95,* 163–171.

Aspy, D., & Roebuck, F. M. (1976). *A lever long enough*. Washington, D.C.: National Consortium for Humanizing Education.

Asquith, P. (1991). Primate research groups in Japan: Orientation and East-West differences. In L. M. Fedigan & P. J. Asquith (Eds.), *The Monkeys of Arashiyama*. Albany: SUNY Press.

Assagioli, R. A. (1972/1965). *Psychosynthesis: A manual of principles and techniques.*New York: Hobbs-Dorman.

Asselin, C., Nelson, T., & Platt, J. (1976). *Teacher study leaders manual*. Chicago: Alfred Adler Institute.

Association for Research in Nervous and Mental Diseases. (1968). *The addictive states*. (Proceedings of the Association, 2 and 3, December 1966). New York; Baltimore, Md.: Williams & Wilkins.

Association of Sleep Disorders Centers. (1979). Diagnostic classification of sleep and arousal disorders. *Sleep, 2,* 1–137.

Atchley, R. C. (1975). Adjustment of loss of job at retirement. *International Journal of Aging and Human Development, 6,* 17–27.

Atchley, R. C. (1977). *The social forces in later life, an introduction to social gerontology* (2nd ed.). Belmont, Calif.: Wadsworth.

Atkinson, D. R., Maruyama, M., & Matsui, S. (1978). Effects of counselor race and counseling approach on Asian Americans' perceptions of counselor credibility and utility. *Journal of Counseling Psychology, 25,* 76–83.

Atkinson, D. R., Morton, G., & Sue, D. W. (1979). *Counseling American minorities: cross-cultural perspective*. Dubuque, Iowa: Brown.

Atkinson, D. R., Morton, G., & Sue, D. W. (1989). *Counseling American minorities*. (3rd ed.). Dubuque, IA: Brown.

Atkinson, J. W. (Ed.) (1958). *Motives in fantasy, action, and society: A method of assessment and study*. Princeton, N.J.: Van Nostrand.

Atkinson, J. W. (1978/1964). *An introduction to motivation*. New York: Van Nostrand.

Atkinson, J. W., & Birch, D. (1970). *The dynamics of action*. New York: Wiley.

Atkinson, J. W., & Birch, D. (1978/1964). *Introduction to motivation* (2nd ed.). New York: Van Nostrand.

Atkinson, J. W., & Feather N. T. (Eds.). (1966). *A theory of achievement motivation*. New York: Wiley.

Atkinson, J. W., & McClelland, D.C. (1948). The effect of different intensities of the hunger drive on thematic apperception. *Journal of Experimental Psychology, 38,* 643–658.

Atkinson, J. W., & Raynor, J. O. (Eds.) (1974). *Motivation and achievement*. Washington, D.C.: Winston.

Atkinson, R. C. (1975). Mnemotechnics in second-language learning. *American Psychologist, 30,* 821–828.

Atkinson, R. C. (Ed.). (1964). *Studies in mathematical psychology*. Stanford, Calif.: Stanford University Press.

Atkinson, R. C., Bower, G. H., & Crothers, E. J. (1965). *Introduction to mathematical learning theory*. New York: Wiley.

Atkinson, R. C., & Raugh, M. R. (1975). An application of the mnemonic keyword method to the acquisition of a Russian vocabulary. *Journal of Experminental Psychology: Human Learning and Memory, 104,* 126–133.

Atkinson, R. C. & Shiffrin, R. M. (1968). Human memory: A proposed system and its control processes. In K. W. Spence & J. T. Spence (Eds.), *The psychology of learning and motivation,* Vol. 2. New York: Academic Press.

Atkinson, R. C., & Wilson, H. A. (Eds.) (1969). *Computer assisted instruction*. New York: Academic Press.

Atkinson, R. F. (1978). *Knowledge and explanation in history: An introduction to the philosophy of history*. Ithaca, N.Y.: Cornell University Press.

Atkinson, R. L., Atkinson, R. C., & Hilgard, E. R. (1983). *Introduction to psychology*. New York: Harcourt Brace Jovanovich.

Atlas, R. (1982). Crime site selection for assaults in four Florida prisons. *Man-Environment Systems, 12,* 59–66.

Attarian, P. (1978). Early recollections: Predictors of vocational choice. *Journal of Individual Psychology, 34,* 56–61.

Atthowe, J. M., Jr., & Krasner, L. A. (1968). A preliminary report on the application of contingent reinforcement procedures (token economy) on a "chronic" ward. *Journal of Abnormal Psychology, 73,* 37–43.

Attkisson, C. C., et al. (Eds.). (1978). *Evaluation of human service programs*. New York: Academic Press.

Attneave, F. (1954). Some informational aspects of visual perception. *Psychological Review, 61,* 183–193.

Attneave, F., & Arnoult, M. D. (1956). The quantitative study of shape and pattern perception. *Psychological Bulletin, 53,* 452–471.

Atwater, E. (1979). *Psychology of adjustment: Personal growth in a changing world*. Englewood Cliffs, N.J.: Prentice-Hall.

Atwater, P. M. H. (1988). *Coming back to life: The after-effects of the near-death experience*. New York: Dodd, Mead.

Atwood, J. D., & Maltin, L. (1991). Putting Eastern philosophies into Western psychotherapies. *American Journal of Psychotherapy, 45*(3), 368–382.

Augustine, Saint. (1887). On the trinity. In F. Schaf (Ed.), *A select library of the Nicene and post Nicene fathers*, Vol. 3. Boston: Christian Literature.

Augustine, Saint. (1912,/397). *Confessions,* London: Heinemann.

Augustine, Saint. (1948). The soliloquies. In *The Fathers of the Church*, Vol. 1. New York: Cima

Augustine, Saint. (1950, 1952, 1954). City of God. In *The fathers of the church*, Vols. 8, 14, 24. New York: Fathers of the Church.

Augustine, Saint. (1953). Confessions. In *The fathers of the church*, Vol. 21. New York: Fathers of the Church.

Aurelius, Marcus. (1945). The meditations of Marcus Aurelius. In *Marcus Aurelius and his times*. New York: Black.

Aurobindo, Sri. (1970). *The life divine*. Pondicherry, India: Sri Aurobindo Ashram.

Austad, C. S., & Berman, W. (1991). Psychotherapy in managed health care: *The optimal use of time and resources*. Washington, DC: American Psychological Association.

Austin, G. R. (1976). *Early childhood education—An international perspective*. New York: Academic Press.

Austin, W., & Walster (Hatfield), E. (1974a). Participants' reactions to "equity with the world." *Journal of Experimental Social Psychology, 10,* 528–548.

Austin, W., & Walster (Hatfield), E. (1974b). Reactions to confirmations and disconfirmations of expectancies of equity and inequity. *Journal of Personality and Social Psychology, 30,* 208–216.

Austin, W. G., & Worchel, S. (1979). *The social psychology of intergroup relations*. Monterey, Calif: Brooks/Cole.

Australian Psychology Society by-laws. (1978). *Australian Psychologist, 13*, 88–101.

Ausbel, D. P. (1952). *Ego development and the personality disorders*. New York: Grune & Stratton.

Ausubel, D. P. (1969). Is there a discipline of educational psychology? *Psychology in the Schools, 4*, 232–244.

Ausubel, D. P., Novak, J. D., & Hanesian, H. (1978). *Educational psychology: A cognitive view* (2nd ed.). New York: Holt, Rinehart & Winston.

Avant, L. (1965). Vision in the Ganzfeld. *Psychological Bulletin, 64*, 245–258.

Averill, J. (1982). *Anger and aggression*. New York: Springer-Verlag.

Averill, J. R. (1980). A constructionist view of emotion. In R. Plutchik & H. Kellerman (Eds.), *Emotion: Theory, research and experience*. New York: Academic Press.

Avey, A. E. (1968). *Primary questions, historical answers*. Boston: Christopher Publishing House.

Avicenna. (1473). *Canon Medicinae Lib. I–V*. Strassburg: Rusch.

Avis, H. H. (1974). The neuropharmacology of aggression: A critical review. *Psychological Bulletin, 81*, 47–63.

Ax, A. F. (1953). Physiological differentiations between fear and anger in humans. *Psychosomatic Medicine, 15*, 433–442.

Axelson, J. A. (1985). *Counseling and development in a multicultural society*. Belmont, CA: Brooks Cole.

Axline, V. M. (1947). *Play therapy: The inner dynamics of childhood*. Boston: Houghton Mifflin.

Axline, V. M. (1964). *Dibs: In search of self*. New York: Houghton Mifflin.

Ayers, A. J. (1936). *Language, truth and logic*. London: Gollancz.

Ayers, A. J. (Ed.) (1959). *Logical positivism*. New York: Free Press.

Ayllon, T., & Azrin, N. H. (1965). The measurement and reinforcement of behavior of psychotics. *Journal of Experimental Analysis of Behavior, 8*, 357–383.

Ayllon, T., & Azrin, N. H. (1968). *The token economy*. New York: Appleton-Century-Crofts.

Ayllon, T. & Haughton, E. (1962). Control of the Behavior of Schizophrenic Patients by Food. *Journal of Experimental Analysis of Behavior, 5*, 343–352.

Ayllon, T., & Michael, J. (1959). The psychiatric nurse as a behavioral engineer. *Journal of Experimental Analysis of Behavior, 2*, 323–334.

Ayllon, T., & Rainwater, N. (1976). Behavioral alternatives to the drug control of hyperactive children in the classroom. *School Psychology Digest, 5*, 33–39.

Ayres, A. J. (1972). *Sensory integration and learning disorders*. Los Angeles: Western Psychological Services.

Ayres, A. J. (1975). Sensorimotor foundations of academic ability. In W. Cruickshank & D. Hallahan (Eds.), *Perceptual and learning disabilities in children*, Vol. 2. Syracuse, N.Y.: Syracuse University Press.

Azam, E. E. (1887). *Hypnotisme, double conscience et altération de la personalité*. Preface by J. M. Charcot. Paris; Ballière.

Azrin, N., & Foxx, R. (1974). *Toilet training in less than a day*. New York: Simon & Schuster.

Azrin, N. H. (1977). A strategy for applied research: Learning based but outcome oriented. *American Psychologist, 32*, 140–149.

Azrin, N. H., & Besalel, V. B. (1979). *Job Club counselors manual*. Baltimore, Md.: University Park Press.

Azrin, N. H. & Holz, W. C. (1961). Punishment during fixed-interval reinforcement. *Journal of the Experimental Analysis of Behavior, 4*, 343–347.

Azrin, N. H., & Holz, W. C. (1966). Punishment. In W. K. Honig (Ed.), *Operant behavior: Areas of research and application*. New York: Appleton-Century-Crofts.

Azrin, N. H., Hutchinson, R., & Hake, D. F. (1967). Attack, avoidance, and escape reactions to aversive shock. *Journal of the Experimental Analysis of Behavior, 10*, 131–148.

Baars, B. J. (1988). *A cognitive theory of consciousness*. New York: Cambridge University Press.

Babad, E. Y., & Salomon, G. (1978). Professional dilemmas of the psychologist in an organizational emergency. *American Psychologist, 33*, 840–846.

Babbage, C. (1832). *On the economy of machinery and manufacturers*. London: Knight.

Babbie, E. R. (1973). *Survey research methods*. Belmont, Calif.: Wadsworth.

Babikian, Y. (1971). An empirical investigation to determine the relative effectiveness of discovery, laboratory, and expository methods of teaching science concepts. *Journal of Research in Science Teaching, 8*, 201–209.

Babkin, B. P. (1938). Experimental neurosis in animals and their treatment with bromides. *Edinburgh Medical Journal, 45*, 605–619.

Bach, G. R. (1954). *Intensive group psychotherapy*. New York: Ronald Press.

Bach, G. R. (1966). The marathon group: Intense practice of intimate interaction. *Psychological Reports, 18*, 995–1002.

Bach, G. R., & Bernhard, Y. (1971). *The aggressive lab: The fair fight training manual*. Iowa: Kendail/Hunt.

Bach, G. R., & Goldberg, H. (1974). *Creative aggression*. Garden City, N.Y.: Doubleday.

Bach, G. R., & Wyden, P. (1965). *The intimate enemy: How to fight fair in love and marriage*. New York: Morrow.

Bach, S. (1977). On narcissistic fantasies. *International Review of Psycho-Analysis, 4*, 281–293.

Bachara, G. H., & Zaba, J. N. (1978). Learning disabilities and juvenile delinquency. *Journal of Learning Disabilities, 11*, 242–246.

Bachelder, B. L., & Denny, M. R. (1977). A theory of intelligence: I. Span and the complexity of stimulus control. *Intelligence, 1*, 127–150.

Bachelder, B. L., & Denny, M. R. (1977). A theory of intelligence: II. The role of span in a variety of intellectual tasks. *Intelligence, 1*, 237–256.

Bachman, J. G., Johnston, D., & O'Malley, P. M. (1981). Smoking, drinking and drug use among American high school students: Correlates and trends, 1975–1979. *American Journal of Public Health, 71*(1), 59.

Bachrach, L. L. (1980). Overview: Model programs for chronic mental patients. *American Journal of Psychiatry, 137*, 1023–1031.

Bachrach, W. H. (1982). Psychological elements in gastrointestinal disorders. In W. E. Fann, I. Karacan, A. D. Pokorny, & R. L. Williams (Eds.), *Phenomenology and treatment of psychophysiological disorders* (pp. 1–14). New York: Spectrum Books.

Back, K. (1973/1972). *Beyond words: The story of sensitivity training and the encounter movement*. New York: Russell Sage Foundation.

Back, K. W. (1965). Meaning of time in later life. *Journal of Genetic Psychology, 109*, 9–25.

Bacon, F. (1952). *Advancement of learning*. In R. M. Hutchins (Ed.), *Great books of the western world*, Vol. 30. Chicago: Encyclopedia Britannica.

Bacon, F. (1960). Novum organum (1620). In F. H. Anderson (Ed.), *The new organon and related writings*. New York: Liberal Arts Press.

Bacon, M. K. (1981). Cross-cultural perspectives on motivation for drinking. In R. H. Munroe, R. L. Munroe, & B. B. Whiting (Eds.), *Handbook of cross-cultural human development*. New York: Garland STPM Press.

Bacon, M. K., Child, I. L., & Barry, H. III. (1963). A cross-cultural study of correlates of crime. *Journal of Abnormal and Social Psychology, 66*, 291–300.

Badawi, K., Wallace, R. K., Orme-Johnson, D. W., & Rouzere, A. M. (1984). Electrophysiologic characteristics of respiratory suspension periods occurring during the practice of the Transcendental Meditation program. *Psychosomatic Medicine, 46*(3), 267–276.

Baddeley, A. (1982). *Your memory: A user's guide*. New York: Macmillan.

Baddeley, A. D. (1966). Short-term memory for word sequences as a function of acoustic, semantic and formal similarity. *Quarterly Journal of Experimental Psychology, 18*, 362–365.

Baddeley, A. D. (1976). *The psychology of memory*. New York: Basic Books.

Baddeley, A. D. (1982). *Your memory: A user's guide*. London: Sidgwick & Jackson.

Baddeley, A. D. (1986). *Working memory*. Oxford: Clarendon Press.

Baddeley, A. D. (1990). *Human memory: Theory and practice*. Boston: Allyn & Bacon.

Baddeley, A. D. (1990). *Human memory: Theory and practice*. Hillsdale, N.J. Hove: Erlbaum

Baddeley, A. D. (1992). Working memory. *Science, 255*, 556–559.

Baddeley, A. D., & Hitch, G. (1974). Working memory. In G. Bower (Ed.), *Recent advances in learning and motivation*, Vol. VIII. New York: Academic Press, 47–89.

Baddeley, A. D., & Lieberman, K. (1980). Spatial working memory. In R. Nickerson (Ed.), *Attention and performance* (pp. 521–539). Hillsdale, NJ: Erlbaum.

Baddeley, A. D., Logie, R., Nimmo-Smith, L., & Brereton, J. (1985). Components of fluent reading. *Journal of Memory and Language, 24*, 119–131.

Baddeley, A. D., Papagno, C., & Vallar, G. (1988). When long-term Teaming depends on short-term storage. *Journal of Memory and Language, 27*, 586–595.

Baddeley, A. D., & Warrington, E. (1970). Amnesia and the distinction between long- and short-term memory. *Journal of Verbal Learning and Verbal Behavior, 9*, 176–189.

Baechler, J. (1979). *Suicides*. New York: Basic Books. (Originally published under the title *Les suicides*, 1975.)

Baehr, M. E., & Williams, G. B. (1968). Prediction of sales success from factorially determined dimensions of personal background data. *Journal of Applied Psychology, 52*, 98–103.

Baer, J. A. (1991). *Women in American law: The struggle toward equality from the new deal to the present*. New York: Holmes & Moler.

Bahr, H. M. (1971). Birth order and failure: The evidence from skid row. *Quarterly Journal of Studies on Alcohol, 32*, 669–686.

Bahrick, H. P., Bahrick, P. O., & Wittlinger, R. P. (1975). Fifty years of memory for names and faces: A cross-sectional approach. *Journal of Experimental Psychology: General, 104*, 54–75.

Baier, K., & Rescher, N. (Eds.). (1969). *Values and future: The impact of technological change on American values*. New York: Free Press.

Bailey, D. B., Jr., & Harbin, G. L. (1980). Nondiscriminatory evaluation. *Exceptional Children, 46*, 590–596.

Bailey, J. M., & Pillard, R. C. (1991). A genetic study of male sexual orientation. *Archives of General Psychiatry, 48*, 1089–1096.

Bailey, K. G., Hartnett, J. J., & Glover, H. W. (1973). Modeling and personal space behavior in children. *Journal of Psychology, 85*, 143–150.

Bain, A. (1894/1859). *The emotions and the will*. London: Longman.

Bain, A. (1875). *Mental science*. New York: Appleton.

Bain, A. (1855). *The senses and the intellect*. London: Longman, Green.

Baird, J. C., & Noma, E. (1978). *Fundamentals of scaling and psychophysics*. New York: Wiley.

Baird, M., & Reiss, E. (1981). Aesthetic Realism. In R. J. Corsini (Ed.), *Handbook of innovative psychotherapies*. New York: J. Wiley.

Bakal, D. A. (1979). *Psychology and medicine: Psychobiological dimensions of health and illness*. New York: Springer.

Bakal, D. A., & Kaganov, J. A. (1977). Muscle contraction and migraine headache: Psychophysiologic comparison. *Headache, 17*, 208–214.

Bakan, D. (1966). Behaviorism and American urbanization. *Journal of the History of the Behavioral Sciences, 2*, 5–28.

Bakan, D. (1971/1968). *Disease, pain and sacrifice: Toward a psychology of suffering*. Boston: Beacon Press.

Bakan, D. (1966). *The duality of human existence*. Boston: Beacon Press.

Bakan, D. (1967). *On method: Toward a reconstruction of psychological investigation*. San Francisco: Jossey-Bass.

Bakan, D. (1958). *Sigmund Freud and the Jewish mystical tradition*. Princeton, N.J.: Van Nostrand.

Bakan, D. (1973/1971). *Slaughter of the innocents: A study of the battered child phenomenon*. Boston: Beacon Press.

Bakan, D. (1979). *And they took themselves wives: On the emergence of patriarchy in Western civilization*. New York, Toronto: Harper & Row.

Bakan, P. (1971). The eyes have it. *Psychology Today, 4*, 64–67, 96.

Bakare, C. G. M. (1972). Social class differences in the performance of Nigerian children on the Draw-a-Man test. In L. J. Cronbach & P. J. D. Drenth (Eds.), *Mental tests and cultural adaptation*. The Hague: Mouton.

Bakeman, R., & Brownlee, J. R. (1980). The strategic use of parallel play: A sequential analysis. *Child Development, 51*, 873–878.

Baker, E. (1981). An hypnotherapeutic approach to enhance object relatedness in psychotic patients. *The International Journal of Clinical and Experimental Hypnosis, 29*, 136–147.

Baker, E. F. (1967). *Man in the trap*. New York: Macmillan.

Baker, E. F. (1978). Orgone therapy. *Journal of Orgonomy, 12*(1,2), 41–54, 201–215.

Baker, F., & O'Brien, G. M. (1969). Birth order and fraternity affiliation. *Journal of Social Psychology, 78*(1), 41–43.

Baker, F. B. (1988). Computer technology in test construction and processing. In R. L. Linn (Ed.), *Educational measurement* (pp. 409–428) New York: Macmillan.

Baker, H., & Willis, U. (1978). School phobia: Classification and treatment. *British Journal of Psychiatry, 132*, 492–499.

Bakwin, R. M., & Bakwin, H. (1948). Accident proneness. *Journal of Pediatrics, 32*, 749–752.

Balaraman, S. (1981). Psychology in search of identity. *Journal of Higher Education, 7,* 117–121.

Balay, J., & Shevrin, H. (1988). The subliminal psychodynamic activation method: A critical review. *American Psychologist, 43,* 161–174.

Baldauf, R. J. (1975). Parental intervention. In H. R. Myklebust (Ed.), *Progress in learning disabilities.* New York: Grune & Stratton.

Baldwin, J. D., & Baldwin, J. I. (1981). *Behavior principles in everyday life.* Englewood Cliffs, N.J.: Prentice-Hall.

Baldwin, J. M. (1976/1902). *Development and evolution.* New York: A.M.S. Press.

Baldwin, J. M. (Ed.). (1901–1905). *Dictionary of philosophy and psychology.* 4 vols. New York: Macmillan. (Reprinted, Gloucester, Mass.: Smith, 1960.)

Baldwin, J. M. (1976/1889–1891). *Handbook of psychology* (2 vols.). New York: A.M.S. Press.

Baldwin, J. M. (1894). *Mental development in the child and in the race.* New York: Macmillan. (Reprinted, Fairfield, N.J.: Kelley, 1966.)

Baldwin, J. M. (1897). *Social and ethical interpretations in mental development: A study in social psychology.* New York: Macmillan. (Reprinted, New York: Arno Press, 1973.)

Baldwin, J. M. (1906–1911). *Thought and things* (3 vols.). London: Swan Sonnenschein. (Reprinted, New York: A.M.S. Press, 1976.)

Bales, R. F. (1950). *Interaction process analysis: A method for the study of small groups.* Reading, Mass.: Addison-Wesley.

Balinsky, B. (1941). An analysis of the mental factors of various age groups from nine to sixty. *Genetic Psychology Monographs, 23,* 191–234.

Balkan, L. (1970). *Les effets du bilinguisme français anglais sur les aptitudes intellectuelles.* Brussels: AIMAV.

Ball, R. S., Merrifield, P., & Statt, L. H. (1978). *The extended Merrill-Palmer scale, instruction manual.* Chicago: Stoelting.

Ball, S. (1981, December). Educational psychology as an academic chameleon: An historical survey of published research and some thoughts on the future. Presented at the University of Iowa.

Ball, S. A., & Zuckerman, M. (1992). Sensation seeking and selective attention. Focused and divided attention on a dichotic listening task. *Journal of Personality and Social Psychology, 63,* 825–831.

Ballenger, J. C., Post, R. M., Jimerson, D. C., Lake, C. R., Murphy, D. L., Zuckerman, M., & Cronin, C. (1983). Biochemical correlates of personality traits in normals: An exploratory study. *Personality and Individual Differences, 4,* 615–625.

Ball-Rokeach, S. (1973). From pervasive ambiguity to a definition of the situation. *Sociometry, 36,* 43–51.

Balis, G. U. (1974). The use of psychomimetic and related conscious-altering drugs. In Arietti, S. & Brody, E. B. (Eds.), *American handbook of psychiatry: Vol. 3. Adult clinical psychiatry* (2nd ed.). New York: Basic Books.

Balota, D. A., d'Arcais, G. B. F., & Rayner, K. (Eds.). (1990). *Comprehension processes in reading.* Hillsdale, NJ: Erlbaum.

Baltes, P., Sowarka, D., Kleigl, R. (1989). Cognitive training research on fluid intelligence in old age: What can older adults achieve by themselves? *Psychology and Aging, 4,* 217–222.

Baltes, P. B. (1968). Longitudinal and cross-sectional sequences in the study of age and generation effects. *Human Development, 11,* 145–171.

Baltes, P. B. (1987). Theoretical propositions of life-span developmental psychology: On the dynamics between growth and decline. *Developmental Psychology, 23,* 611–626.

Baltes, P. B., & Brim, O. G., Jr. (Eds.). (1978). *Life-span development and behavior,* (Vol. 1). New York: Academic Press.

Baltes, P. B., & Eckensberger, L. (Eds.). (1979). *Entwicklungs psychologie der Lebensspanne.* Stuttgart: Klett-Cotta.

Baltes, P. B., & Labouvie, G. V. (1973). Adult development of intellectual performance: Description, explanation and modification. In C. Eisdorfer & M. P. Lawton (Eds.), *The psychology of adult development and aging.* Washington, D.C.: American Psychological Association.

Baltes, P. B., Reese, H. W., & Lipsitt, L. P. (1980). Life-span developmental psychology. *Annual Review of Psychology, 31,* 65–110.

Baltes, P. B., Reese, H. W., & Nesselroade, J. R. (1977). *Lifespan developmental psychology: An introduction to research methods.* Monterey, Calif.: Brooks/Cole.

Baltes, P. B., Schaie, W. K. (1974). Aging and the IQ: The myth of the years. *Psychology 40,* 35–38.

Baltes, P. B., & Schaie, K. W. (1976). On the plasticity of intelligence in adulthood and old age: Where Horn and Donaldson fail. *American Psychologist, 31,* 720–725.

Baltes, P. B., & Schaie, K. W. (Eds.). *Life-span developmental psychology: Personality and socialization.* New York: Academic Press.

Baltes, P. B., & Willis, S. L. (1982). Enhancement (plasticity) of intellectual functioning in old age: Penn State's Adult Development and Enrichment Project (ADEPT). In F. Craik & S. Trehub (Eds.), *Aging and cognitive process* (pp. 353–389). New York: Plemum.

Baltes, P. B., & Willis, S. L. (1982). Plasticity and enhancement of intellectual functioning in old age: Penn State's Adult Development and Enrichment Project (ADEPT). In F. Craik & S. E. Trehub (Eds.), *Aging and cognitive processes.* New York: Plenum.

Ban, T. A. (1978). The treatment of depressed geriatric patients. *American Journal of Psychotherapy, 32,* 93–104.

Bandler, R., & Grinder, J. (1978). *The structure of magic* (2 vols.). Palo Alto, Calif.: Science & Behavior Books.

Bandler, R., & Grinder, J. (1979). *Frogs into princes.* Moab, Utah: Real People Press.

Bandura, A. (1961). Psychotherapy as a learning process. *Psychological Bulletin, 58,* 143–159.

Bandura, A. (1965). Influence of models reinforcement contingencies on the acquisition of imitative responses. *Journal of Personality and Social Psychology, 1,* 589–595.

Bandura, A. (1965). Vicarious processes: A case of no-trial learning. In L. Berkowitz (Ed.), *Advances in experimental social psychology,* Vol. 2. New York: Academic Press.

Bandura, A. (1968). A social learning interpretation of psychological dysfunctions. In P. London & D. Rosenhan (Eds.), *Foundations of abnormal psychology.* New York: Holt, Rinehart & Winston.

Bandura, A. (1968). Modelling approaches to the modification of phobic disorders. In R. Porter (Ed.), *The role of learning in psychotherapy.* London: Churchill.

Bandura, A. (1969). *Principles of behavior modification.* New York: Holt, Rinehart & Winston.

Bandura, A. (1969). Social-learning theory of identificatory processes. In A. D. Goslin (Ed.), *Handbook of socialization theory and research.* Chicago: Rand-McNally.

Bandura, A. (1971). Psychotherapy based upon modeling principles. In A. E. Bergin & S. L. Garfield (Eds.), *Handbook of psychotherapy and behavior change: An empirical analysis.* New York: Wiley.

Bandura, A. (1973). *Aggression: A social learning analysis.* Englewood Cliffs, N.J.: Prentice-Hall.

Bandura, A. (1974). Behavior therapy and models of man. *American Psychologist, 29,* 859–969.

Bandura, A. (1977). Self-efficacy: Toward a unifying theory of behavioral change. *Psychological Review, 84,* 191–215.

Bandura, A. (1977). *Social learning theory.* Englewood Cliffs, N.J.: Prentice-Hall.

Bandura, A. (1978). Learning and behavioral theories of aggression. In I. L. Kutash, S. B. Kutash, & L. B. Schlesinger (Eds.), *Violence: Perspectives on murder and aggression.* San Francisco: Jossey-Bass.

Bandura, A. (1978). The self-system in reciprocal determinism. *American Psychologist, 33,* 344–358.

Bandura, A. (1982). Self-efficacy mechanism in human agency. *American Psychologist, 37,* 122–147.

Bandura, A. (1982). The psychology of chance encounters and life paths. *American Psychologist, 37,* 747–755.

Bandura, A. (1982). Self-efficacy mechanism in human agency. *American Psychologist, 37,* 122–147.

Bandura, A. (1986). *Social foundations of thought and action: A social cognitive theory.* Englewood Cliffs, NJ: Prentice-Hall.

Bandura, A. (1989). Human agency in social cognitive theory. *American Psychologist, 44,* 1175–1184.

Bandura, A. (1991). Self-regulation of motivation through anticipatory and self-regulatory mechanisms. In R. A. Dienstbier (Ed.), *Perspectives on motivation: Nebraska symposium on motivation* (Vol. 38, pp. 69–164). Lincoln: University of Nebraska Press.

Bandura, A. (1992). Exercise of personal agency through the self-efficacy mechanism. In R. Schwarzer (Ed.), *Self-efficacy: Thought control of action.* Washington, DC: Hemisphere.

Bandura, A., Adams, N. E., & Beyer, J. (1977). Cognitive processes mediating behavioral change. *Journal of Personality and Social Psychology, 35,* 125–139.

Bandura, A., & Barab, P. (1973). Process governing disinhibitory effects through symbolic modeling. *Journal of Abnormal Psychology, 82,* 1–9.

Bandura, A., Blanchard, E. B., & Ritter, B. (1969). Relative efficacy of desensitization and modeling approaches for inducing behavioral, affective and attitudinal changes. *Journal of Personality and Social Psychology, 13,* 173–199.

Bandura, A. (Ed.). (1971). *Psychological modeling: Conflicting theories.* Chicago: Aldine-Atherton.

Bandura, A., & Jeffrey, R. W. (1937). Role of symbolic coding and rehearsal processes in observational learning. *Journal of Abnormal and Social Psychology, 26,* 122–130.

Bandura, A., Ross, D., & Ross, S. A. (1963). Imitation of film-mediated aggressive models. *Journal of Abnormal and Social Psychology, 66,* 3–11.

Bandura, A., & Walters, R. H. (1959). *Adolescent aggression.* New York: Ronald Press.

Bandura, A., & Walters, R. H. (1963). *Social learning and personality development.* New York: Holt, Rinehart & Winston.

Banham, K. M. (1950). The development of affectionate behavior in infancy. *Journal of Genetic Psychology, 76,* 283–289.

Banner, L. W. (1983). *American beauty.* Chicago: The University of Chicago Press.

Bannister, D. (1963). The genesis of schizophrenic thought disorder: A serial invalidation hypothesis. *British Journal of Psychiatry, 109,* 680–686.

Bannister, D. (1968). The myth of physiological psychology. *Bulletin of the British Psychological Society, 21,* 229–231.

Bannister, D. (Ed.). (1970). *Perspectives in personal construct theory.* New York: Academic Press.

Bannister, D. (Ed.). (1977). *New perspectives in personal construct theory.* New York: Academic Press.

Bannister, D., & Fransella, F. (1966). A grid test of schizophrenic thought disorder. *British Journal of Social and Clinical Psychology, 5,* 95–102.

Bannister, D., & Fransella, F. (1980). *Inquiring man: The psychology of personal constructs.* New York: Penguin.

Bannister, D., & Mair, J. M. M. (1968). *The evaluation of personal constructs.* New York: Academic Press.

Bannister, R. (1978/1973). *Brain's clinical neurology.* New York: Oxford University Press.

Banta, T. J., & Hetherington, M. (1963). Relations between needs of friends and fiancés. *Journal of Abnormal and Social Psychology, 66,* 401–404.

Barak, A., Carney, C. G., & Archibald, R. (1975). The relationship between vocational information seeking and educational and vocational decidedness. *Journal of Vocational Behavior, 7,* 149–159.

Barash, D. (1977). *Sociobiology and behavior.* New York: Elsevier/North Holland.

Barash, D. P. (1973). Social variety in the yellow-bellied marmot (*Marmota flaviventris*). *Animal Behavior, 21,* 579–584.

Barash, D. P. (1974). The social behavior of the hoary marmot (*Marmota caligata*). *Animal Behavior, 72,* 1–6.

Barbach, L. G. (1975). *For yourself.* New York: Doubleday.

Barbatsis, G., Wong, M., & Herek, G. M. (1983). A struggle for dominance: Relational communication patterns in television drama. *Communication Quarterly, 31*(2), 148–155.

Barber, T. X. (1962). Hypnotic age regression: A critical review. *Psychosomatic Medicine, 24,* 286–299.

Barber, T. X. (1969). *Hypnosis: A scientific approach.* New York: Van Nostrand Reinhold.

Barber, T. X. (1970). *LSD, marihuana, yoga and hypnosis.* Chicago: Aldine.

Barber, T. X. (1976). *Advances in altered states of consciousness and human potentialities.* New York: Psychological Dimensions.

Barber, T. X. (1976). *Pitfalls in human research: Ten pivotal points.* New York: Pergamon Press.

Barber, T. X., et al. (Eds.). (1970–1978). *Biofeedback and self-control: An Aldine annual on the regulation of bodily processes and consciousness.* Chicago: Aldine.

Barber, T. X., et al. (Eds.). (1981). *Biofeedback and behavioral medicine.* Hawthorne, N.Y.: Aldine.

Barber, T. X., & Calvervey, D. S. (1962). "Hypnotic behavior" as a function of task motivation. *Journal of Psychology, 54,* 363–389.

Barber, T. X., Dicara, L. B., Kamiya, J., Miller, N. E., Shapiro, D., & Stoyva, J. (Eds.). (1970). *Biofeedback and self-control.* Chicago: Aldine.

Barber, T. X., Spanos, N. P., & Chaves, J. F. (1974). *Hypnosis, imagination, and human potentialities.* Elmsford, N.Y.: Pergamon Press.

Barbizet, J. (1970). *Human memory and its pathology* (E. K. Jardine, Trans.). San Francisco: Freeman.

Barbrack, C. R., & Maher, C. A. (Eds.). (1980). Program planning, program evaluation and school psychology. *School Psychology Review, 9,* 197–198.

Barclay, A. M. (1969). The effect of hostility on physiological and fantasy responses. *Journal of Personality, 37,* 651–667.

Barclay, A. M. (1970). The effect of female aggressiveness on aggressive and sexual fantasies. *Journal of Projective Techniques, 34,* 19–26.

Barclay, A. M. (1971). Linking sexual and aggressive motives: Contributions of "irrelevant" arousals. *Journal of Personality, 39,* 481–492.

Bard, M. (1970). Training police as specialists in family crisis intervention. Washington, D.C.: National Institute of Law Enforcement and Criminal Justice, U.S. Government Printing Office.

Bard, M., Bordin, E. S., Goldstein, S. G., & Webb, W. B. (1970). Viewpoints on the new California School of Professional Psychology. *Professional Psychology, 1,* 253–264.

Bard, P. A. (1928). A diencephalic mechanism for the expression of rage with special reference to the sympathetic nervous system. *American Journal of Physiology, 84,* 490–515.

Bardon, J. I. (1976). The state of the art (and science) of school psychology. *American Psychologist, 31*(12) 785–796.

Barenboim, C. (1981). The development of person perception in childhood and adolescence: From behavioral comparisons to psychological constructs to psychological comparisons. *Child Development, 52,* 129–144.

Barker, A. J., Mathis, J. K., & Powers, C. (1953). Drawings characteristic of male homosexuals. *Journal of Clinical Psychology, 9,* 185–188.

Barker, J. A. (1990). *Future edge.* New York: William Morrow.

Barker, J. C., & Miller, M. (1968). Aversion therapy for compulsive gambling. *Journal of Nervous and Mental Disease, 146,* 285–302.

Barker, R. G. (1953). *Adjustment to handicap and illness.* New York: Social Science Research Council.

Barker, R. G. (1968). *Ecological psychology: Concepts and methods for studying the environment of human behavior.* Stanford, Calif.: Stanford University Press.

Barker, R. G. (Ed.). (1963). *The stream of behavior.* New York: Appleton-Century-Crofts.

Barker, R. G., et al. (1978). *Habitats, environments and human behavior: Studies in ecological psychology and eco-behavioral science from the Midwest Psychological Field Station, 1947–1972.* San Francisco: Jossey-Bass.

Barker, R., Dembo, T., & Lewin, K. (1941). Frustration and regression. In R. G. Barker, J. S. Kounin, & H. F. Wright (Eds.), *Child behavior and development.* New York: McGraw-Hill.

Barker, R. G., & Schoggen, P. (1973). *Qualities of community life: Methods of measuring environment and behavior applied to an American and an English town.* San Francisco: Jossey-Bass.

Barker, R. G., & Wright, H. F. (1971/1955). *Midwest and its children.* Evanston, Ill.: Row, Peterson.

Barker, R. G., & Wright, H. F. (1966/1951). *One boy's day.* Hamden, Conn.: Shoe-String Press.

Barker, S. (1978). *The Alexander technique.* New York: Bantam Books.

Barkley, R., Conners, C., Barkley, A., Gadow, K., Gittleman, R., Sprague, R., & Swanson, J. (1990). Task force report: The appropriate role of clinical child psychologists in the prescribing of psychoactive medications for children [Monograph]. *Journal of Clinical Child Psychology, 19*(Suppl.), 1–38.

Barkley, R. A. (1977). A review of stimulant drug research with hyperactive children. *Journal of Child Psychology and Psychiatry, 18,* 137–165.

Barkley, R. A. (1978). Recent Developments in research on hyperactive children. *Journal of Pediatric Psychology, 3,* 158–163.

Barkley, R. A., & Cunningham, C. E. (1978). Do stimulant drugs improve the academic performance of hyperkinetic children? *Clinical Pediatrics, 17,* 85–92.

Barlow, D. H. (1988). *Anxiety and its disorders.* New York: Guilford.

Barlow, D. H., Agras, W. S., Leitenberg, H., Callahan, E. J., & Moore, R. C. (1972). The contribution of therapeutic instructions to covert sensitization. *Behavior Research and Therapy, 10,* 411–415.

Barlow, D. H., & Hersen, M. (1984). *Single case experimental designs: Strategies for studying behavior change* (2nd ed.). New York: Pergamon.

Barlow, D. H., Leitenberg, H., & Agras, W. S. (1969). Experimental control of sexual deviation through manipulation of the noxious scene in covert sensitization. *Journal of Abnormal Psychology, 74,* 596–601.

Barlow, D. H., Reynolds, E. J., & Agras, W. S. (1973). Gender identity change in a transsexual. *Archives of General Psychiatry, 28,* 569–576.

Barlow, G. W., & Silverberg, J. (Eds.). (1980). *Sociobiology: Beyond nature/nurture?* Boulder, Colo.: Westview Press.

Barlow, W. (1973). *The Alexander technique.* New York: Knopf.

Barnes, G. E. (1979). The alcoholic personality: A reanalysis of the literature. *Journal of Studies on Alcohol, 40,* 571–634.

Barnett, S. A. (1981). *Modern ethology: The science of animal behavior.* New York: Oxford University Press.

Barnlund, D. C. (1959). A comparative study of individual, majority and group judgment. *Journal of Abnormal and Social Psychology, 58,* 55–60.

Barón, A., Jr. (1979). *The utilization of mental health services by Mexican-Americans: A critical analysis.* Palo Alto, Calif.: R & E Research Associates.

Barón, A., Jr. (Ed.). (1981). *Explorations in Chicano psychology.* New York: Praeger.

Barón, A., Jr., Klein, R. L., & Thurman, C. W. (1981). Student use of a university telephone counseling service: A three-year overview. *Crisis Intervention, 11,* 54–59.

Baron, R. A. (1974). The aggression-inhibiting influence of heightened sexual arousal. *Journal of Personality and Psychology, 30,* 318–322.

Baron, R. A. (1974b). Sexual arousal and physical aggression: The inhibiting influence of "cheesecake" and nudes. *Bulletin of the Psychonomic Society, 3,* 337–339.

Baron, R. A. (1977). *Human aggression.* New York: Plenum.

Baron, R. A., & Bell, P. (1973). Effects of heightened sexual arousal on physical aggression. *Proceedings of the 81st Annual Convention of the American Psychological Association, 8,* 171–172.

Baron, R. M., Graziano, W. G., & Stangor, C. (1991). *Social psychology.* Fort Worth, TX: Holt, Rinehart & Winston.

Baron-Cohen, S., Wyke, M. A., & Binnie, C. (1987). Hearing words and seeing colours: An experimental investigation of a case of synaesthesia. *Perception, 16,* 761–767.

Barr, E. DeY. (1934). A psychological analysis of fashion motivation. *Archives of Psychology, 171,* 100.

Barraclough, C. A., & Gorski, R. A. (1962). Studies on mating behavior in the androgen-sterilized female rat in relation to the hypothalamic regulation of sexual behavior. *Journal of Endocrinology, 25,* 175–182.

Barrera, M., Jr. (1981). Social support in the adjustment of pregnant adolescents: Assessment issues. In B. H. Gottlieb (Ed.), *Social networks and social support* (pp. 69–96). Beverly Hills: Sage.

Barrera, M., Jr. (1982). Distinctions between social support concepts, measures, and models. *American Journal of Community Psychology, 14,* 413–446.

Barrera, M., Jr., & Ainlay, S. L. (1983). The structure of social support: A conceptual and empirical analysis. *Journal of Community Psychology, 11,* 133–143.

Barrera, M., Jr., Sandler, I. N., & Ramsay, T. B. (1981). Preliminary development of a scale of social support: Studies on college students. *American Journal of Community Psychology, 9,* 435–447.

Barrera, M., & Maurer, D. (1981). The perception of facial expressions by the three month old. *Child Development, 52,* 203–206.

Barrera, M., & Maurer, D. (1981). Recognition of mother's photographed face by the three-month-old infant. *Child Development, 52,* 714–716.

Barrett, D. (1980). The first memory as a predictor of personality traits. *Journal of Individual Psychology, 36,* 136–149.

Barrett-Lennard, G. T. (1979). The client-centered system unfolding. In F. J. Turner (Ed.), *Social work treatment: Interlocking theoretical approaches* (2nd ed.). New York: Free Press.

Barrios, B. A. (1988). On the changing nature of behavioral assessment. In S. A. Bellack, & M. Hersen (Eds.), *Behavioral Assessment: A practical handbook* (3rd. ed., pp. 3–41).

Barron, F. (1953). An ego-strength scale which predicts response to psychotherapy. *Journal of Consulting Psychology, 17,* 327–333.

Barron, F. (1954). Personal soundness in university graduate students. *University of California Publications Personality Assessment and Research,* no. 1.

Barron, F. (1970). Heritability of factors in creative thinking and aesthetic judgment. *Acta Geneticae Medicae et Gemelogie, 19,* 204–208.

Barron, F. (1990). *Creativity and psychological health.* Buffalo, NY: Creative Education Foundation Press. (Original work published 1963)

Barron, F., & Harrington, D. M. (1981). Creativity, intelligence, and personality. *Annual Reviews of Psychology, 32,* 439–476.

Barron, J. (1989). Prescription rights: Pro and con. *Psychotherapy Bulletin, 24,* 22–24.

Barrow, J., & Hayashi, J. (1980). Shyness clinic: A social development program for adolescents and young adults. *Personal and Guidance Journal, 59*(1), 58–61.

Barry, A. (1979). A research project on successful single-parent families. *American Journal of Family Therapy, 7,* 65–73.

Barry, H. (1980). Description and uses of the Human Relations Area Files. In H. Triandis & J. Berry (Eds.), *Handbook of cross-cultural psychology,* Vol. 2. Boston: Allyn & Bacon.

Barry, H., Bacon, M. K., & Child, I. L. (1957). A cross-cultural survey of some sex differences in socialization. *Journal of Abnormal and Social Psychology, 55,* 327–332.

Barry, H., III, & Barry, H., Jr. (1967). Birth order, family size and schizophrenia. *Archives of General Psychiatry, 17,* 435–440.

Barry, H., III, & Blane, H. T. (1977). Birth positions of alcoholics. *Journal of Individual Psychology, 33,* 62–69.

Barry, H., III, & Paxson, L. M. (1971). Infancy and early childhood: Cross-cultural codes 2. *Ethnology, 10,* 466–493.

Barry, R. L., & Bradley, G. V. (Eds.). (1992). *Set no limits: A rebuttal to Daniel Callahan's proposal to limit health care for the elderly.* Baltimore: University of Illinois Press.

Barsalou, L. W. (1990). Access and inference in categorization. *Bulletin of the Psychonomic Society, 28,* 268–271.

Barsky, A. J. (1979). Patients who amplify bodily sensations. *Annals of Internal Medicine, 91,* 63–70.

Barsley, M. (1979). *Left handed people.* North Hollywood, Calif.: Wilshire Books.

Bart, P. (1971). The myth of a value-free psychotherapy. In W. Bell & J. Mav (Eds.), *Sociology and the future.* New York: Russell Sage Foundation.

Barta, P., Pearlson, G., Powers, R., & Richards, S. (1990). Auditory hallucinations and smaller superior temporal gyral volume in schizophrenia. *American Journal of Psychiatry, 147,* 1457–1462.

Bar-Tal, D. (1976). Prosocial behavior: *Theory and research.* New York: Halsted.

Bar-Tal, D. (1979). Interactions of teachers and pupils. In I. Frieze, D. Bar-Tal, & J. S. Carroll (Eds.), *New approaches to social problems: Applications of attribution theory.* San Francisco: Jossey-Bass.

Bar-Tal, D., Karylowski, J., Reykowski, J., & Staub, E. (Eds.). (1983). *Development and maintenance of prosocial behavior.* New York: Plenum.

Bartel, N., & Guskin, S. (1980). A handicap as a social phenomenon. In W. Cruickshank (Ed.), *Psychology of exceptional children and youth* (4th ed.). Englewood Cliffs, N.J.: Prentice-Hall.

Barth, F. (Ed.) (1969). *Ethnic groups and boundaries: The social organization of culture difference.* London: Allen & Unwin.

Barthes, R. (1967). *Writing degree zero.* London: Cape.

Barthol, R. P., & Ku, N. D. (1959). Regression under stress to first learned behavior. *Journal of Abnormal and Social Psychology, 59,* 134–136.

Bartlett, F. C. (1932). *Remembering: A study in experimental and social psychology.* Cambridge, England: Cambridge University Press

Bartlett, F. C. (1948). Challenge to experimental psychology. In *Proceedings and papers of the 12th International Congress of Psychology at Edinburgh, 1948.* Edinburgh: Oliver & Boyd.

Bartley, S. H. (1951). The psychophysiology of vision. In S. S. Stevens (Ed.), *Handbook of experimental psychology.* New York: Wiley.

Bartley, S. H. (1980). *Introduction to perception.* New York: Harper & Row.

Bartley, S. H., & Chute, E. (1947). *Fatigue and impairment in man.* New York: McGraw-Hill.

Barto, A. G. (1985). *Learning by statistical cooperation of self-interested neuronlike computing elements* (COINS Technical Report 85–11). Amherst: University of Massachusetts.

Bartol, C. R. (1975). Extraversion and neuroticism and nicotine, caffeine, and drug intake. *Psychological Reports, 36,* 1007–1010.

Bartollas, C. (1990). The Prison: Disorder Personalized. In Murphy & Dixion (Eds.), *Are prisons any better?* (pp. 11–22). Beverly Hills, CA: Sage.

Bartollas, C. (in press). Little girls grow up. In C. Culliver (Ed.), *Female criminality: The state of the art.* New York: Garland.

Barton, R. (1966). *Institutional neurosis* (2nd ed.). Bristol, England: Wright.

Bartoshuk, L. M. (1974). NaCl thresholds in man: Thresholds for water taste or NaCl taste? *Journal of Comparative and Physiological Psychology, 87,* 310–325.

Bartoshuk, L. M., Lee, C-H., & Scarpellino, R. (1972). Sweet taste of water induced by artichoke (*Cynara scolymus*). *Science, 178,* 988–990.

Bartrop, R., Penny, R., Forcier, L., & Jones, M. (in press). Grief, immunity, and morbidity. In S. L. Engleman (Ed.), *Confronting life-threatening illness: Mind-body approaches.* New York: Irvington.

Bartsch, J. R., & Dawson, J. G. (1979). Rorschach content analysis of the use of sexual imagery by Catholic seminarians. *Psychological Reports, 45,* 647–655.

Baruch, D., & Miller, H. (1951). The use of spontaneous drawings in group therapy. *American Journal of Psychotherapy, 5,* 45–58.

Baruth, L., & Eckstein, D. (1981). *Life style: Theory, practice, and research.* Dubuque, Iowa: Kendall/Hunt.

Baruth, L. G., & Manning, M. L. (1991). *Multicultural counseling and psychotherapy: A lifespan perspective.* New York: Macmillan.

Bash, K. W. (1955). *Lehrbuch der Psychopathologie, Grundlagen und Klinik.* Stuttgart: Thieme.

Bashir, Z. I., & Collingridge, G. L. (1992). Synaptic placticity: long term potentiation in the hippocampus. *Current Opinion in Neurobiology, 2*(3), 328–335.

Basmajian, J. V. (Ed.). (1979). *Biofeedback: Principles and practice for clinicians.* Baltimore, Md.: Williams & Wilkins.

Basov, M. Y. (1931). *Problems of general psychology,* Moscow: Gosizdat.

Basow, S. A. (1980). *Sex-role stereotypes: Traditions and alternatives.* Monterey, Calif.: Brooks/Cole.

Basowitz, H., Persky, H., Korchin, S. J., & Grinker, R. R. (1955). *Anxiety and stress.* New York: McGraw-Hill.

Bass, B. M. (1977). Utility of managerial self-planning on a simulated production task with replications in twelve countries. *Journal of Applied Psychology, 62,* 506–509.

Bass, B. M. (1980). Team productivity and individual member competence. *Small Group Behavior. 11,* 431–504.

Bass, B. M. (1981). *Stogdill's handbook of leadership* (rev.). New York: Free Press.

Bass, B. M. (1982). Individual capability, team response, and productivity. In E. A. Fleishman & M. D. Dunnette (Eds.), *Human performance and productivity,* Vol. I. Hillsdale, N.J.: Erlbaum.

Bass, B. M., & Barrett, G. V. (1981/1972). *People, work, and organizations.* Boston: Allyn & Bacon.

Bass, B. M., Gaier, E. L., & Farese, F. J. (1956). Metagnosiometry: The study of changing behavior in groups. Technical Report 6, Contract N7 O N R 35609, Louisiana State University, Baton Rouge.

Bass, B. M., & Ryterband, E. (1979). *Organizational psychology.* Boston: Allyn & Bacon.

Bass, B. M., & Valenzi, E. R. (1974). Contingent aspects of effective management styles. In J. G. Hunt & L. L. Larson (Eds.), *Contingent approaches to leadership.* Carbondale, Ill.: Southern Illinois University Press.

Bass, B. M., Valenzi, E. R., Farrow, D. L., & Solomon, R. L. (1975). Management styles associated with organizational, task, personal, and interpersonal contingencies. *Journal of Applied Psychology, 60,* 720–729.

Bassuk, E. L., & Gerson, S. (1978). Deinstitutionalization and mental health services. *Scientific American, 238,* 46–53.

Bastick, T. (1982). *Intuition: How we think and act.* Chichester, England: Wiley.

Bates, A. (1942). Parental roles in courtship. *Social Forces, 20,* 483–486.

Bates, J., Maslin, C., & Frankel, K. (1985). Attachment security, mother-child interaction, and temperament as predictors of behavior prob-

lem ratings at age three years. *Monographs of the Society for Research in Child Development, 50*(1–2), Serial No. 209), 167–193.

Bates, J. E., Bayles, K., Bennett, D. S., Ridge B., & Brown, M. M. (1991). Origins of externalizing behavior problems at eight years of age. In D. J. Pepler & K. H. Rubin (Eds.), *The development and treatment of childhood aggression* (pp. 93–120). Hillsdale, NJ: Erlbaum.

Bateson, B. (Ed.). (1928). *William Bateson: F. R. S. naturalist, his essays and addresses.* Cambridge, England: Cambridge University Press.

Bateson, G. (1958/1928). *Naven* (2nd ed.). Stanford, Calif.: Stanford University Press.

Bateson, G. (1972). *Steps to an ecology of mind.* New York: Ballantine Books.

Bateson, G. (1979). *Mind and nature.* New York: Dutton.

Bateson, G., Jackson, D., Haley, J., & Weakland, J. (1956). Towards a theory of schizophrenia. *Behavioral Science, 1,* 251–264.

Bateson, G., & Mead, M. (1962/1942). *Balinese character.* New York: New York Academy of Sciences.

Bateson, P. P. G., & Hinde, R. A. (Eds.). (1976). *Growing points in ethology.* Cambridge, England: Cambridge University Press.

Batson, C. D., & Marz, B. (1979). Dispositional bias in trained therapists, diagnoses: Does it exist? *Journal of Applied Social Psychology, 9,* 476–489.

Batson, C. D., O'Quin, K. & Pych, V. (1982). An attribution theory analysis of trained helpers' inferences about clients' needs. In T. A. Wills (Ed.), *Basic processes in helping relationships.* New York: Academic.

Batson, D., & Coke, J. (1981). Empathy: A source of altruistic motivation for helping. In *Altruism and helping behavior.* Hillsdale, N.J.: Erlbaum.

Battersby, W. S., Teuber, H. L., & Bender, M. B. (1953). Problem-solving behavior in men with frontal or occiptal brain injuries. *Journal of Psychology, 35,* 329–351.

Battin, M. P. (1982). *Ethical issues in suicide.* Englewood, N.J.: Prentice-Hall.

Battlegay, R., Muhleman, R., & Zehnder, R. (1975). Comparative investigations of the abuse of alcohol, drugs, and nicotine for a representative group of 4,082 men of age. *Comprehensive Psychiatry, 16*(3), 245–254.

Baudelaire, C. P. (1971). *Artificial paradise; on hashish and wine as a means of expanding individuality.* New York: Herder & Herder.

Baudry, M., & Davis, J. L. (Eds.). (1991). *Long-term potentiation: A debate of current issues.* Cambridge: MIT Press.

Bauer, M. (1985). Near death experiences and attitude change. *Anabiosis: The Journal of Near-Death Studies, 5*(1), 39–47.

Bauer, R. A. (1952). *The new man in Soviet psychology.* Cambridge, Mass.: Harvard University Press.

Bauer, R. A. (Ed.). (1966). *Social indicators.* Cambridge, Mass.: M.I.T. Press.

Baum, A., & Epstein, Y. M. (Eds.). (1978). *Human response to crowding.* Hillsdale, N.J.: Erlbaum.

Baum, A., Riess, M., & O'Hara, J. (1974). Architectural variants of reaction to spatial invasion. *Environment and Behavior, 6,* 91–100.

Baum, A., Singer, J. E., & Baum, C. S. (1981). Stress and the environment. *Journal of Social Issues, 37,* 4–35.

Baum, A., & Valins, S. (1977). *Architecture and social behavior: Psychological studies in social density.* Hillsdale, N.J.: Erlbaum.

Baum, M., & Page, M. (1991). Caregiving and multigenerational families. *The Gerontologist, 31*, 762–769.

Baum, W. M. (1973). Behaviorism and feedback control (letters to the editor). *Science, 181*, (1114).

Bauman, G. (1951). *The stability of the individual's mode of perception, and of perception-personality relationships.* Unpublished doctoral dissertation, New York University.

Baumeister, A., & Klosowski, R. (1965). An attempt to group toilet train severely retarded patients. *Mental Retardation, 3*, 24–26.

Baumgarten, F. (1928). *Die Berufseignungprüfungen. Theorie und Praxis.* Munich: Oldenburg.

Baumrind, D. (1964). Some thoughts on ethics of research: After reading Milgram's "Behavioral study of obedience." *American Psychologist, 19*, 421–423.

Baumrind, D. (1966). Effects of authoritative parental control on child behavior. *Child Development, 37*, 887–907.

Baumrind, D. (1971). Current patterns of parental authority. *Developmental Psychology Monographs,* (1, pt. 2), 1–103.

Baumrind, D. (1980). New directions in socialization research. *American Psychologist, 35*, 639–652.

Bavelas, A. (1951). Communication patterns in task-oriented groups. In D. Lerner & H. D. Laswell (Eds.), *The policy sciences.* Stanford, Calif.: Stanford University Press.

Bavelas, J. B. (1978). *Personality: Current theory and research.* Monterey, Calif.: Brooks/Cole.

Bavelas, J. B., Chan, A. S., & Guthrie, J. A. (1976). Reliability of traits measured by Kelly's repertory grid. *Canadian Journal of Behavioral Science, 8*, 23–38.

Baxley, G. B., Turner, P. F., & Greenwald, W. E. (1978). Hyperactive children's knowledge and attitudes concerning drug treatment. *Journal of Pediatric Psychology, 3*, 172–176.

Bayer, R. (1987). *Homosexuality and american psychiatry: The politics of diagnosis* (2nd ed.). Princeton, NJ: Princeton University Press.

Bayés, R. (1977). *Iniciación a la farmacología del comportamiento.* Barcelona: Fontanella.

Bayés, R. (1979). *Psicología y Medicina: Interacción, cooperación, conflicto.* Barcelona: Fontanella.

Bayés, R. (1980). *Una introducción al método científico en Psicología* (3rd ed.). Barcelona: Fontanella.

Bayés, R. (Ed.). (1977). *Chomsky o Skinner? La génesis del lenguaje.* Barcelona: Fontanella.

Bayh, B. (1973). *Runaway youth.* Washington, D.C.: U.S. Government Printing Office.

Bayley, N. (1933). Mental growth during the first three years: A developmental study of sixty-one children by repeated tests. *Genetic Psychology Monographs, 14*, 1–92.

Bayley, N. (1954). Some increasing parent–child similarities during the growth of children. *Journal of Educational Psychology, 45*, 1–21.

Bayley, N. (1969). *Manual for the Bayley scales of infant development.* New York: Psychological Corp.

Bazelon, D. L. (1969). Introduction. In D. S. Burris (Ed.), *The right to treatment: A symposium.* New York: Springer.

Bazelon, D. L. (1975). A jurist's view of psychiatry. *Journal of Psychiatry and Law, 3*, 175–190.

Beach, F. A. (1948). *Hormones and behavior.* New York: Hoeber.

Beach, F. A. (1956). Characteristics of masculine "sex drive." Nebraska symposium on motivation. *Lincoln, Neb.: University of Nebraska Press, 4*, 1–32.

Beach, F. A. (1970). Coital behavior in dogs. VI. Long-term effects of castration upon mating in the male. *Journal of Comparative and Physiological Psychology Monograph, 70*, 1–32.

Beach, F. A. (1976). *Human sexuality in four perspectives.* Baltimore, Md.: Johns Hopkins University Press.

Beach, F. A. (1975). Behavioral endocrinology: An emerging discipline. *American Scientist, 63*, 178–187.

Beach, F. A., & Jordan, L. (1956). Sexual exhaustion and recovery in the male rat. *Quarterly Journal of Experimental Psychology, 8*, 121–133.

Beahrs, J. O. (1971). The hynotic psychotherapy of Milton H. Erickson. *The American Journal of Clinical Hypnosis, 14*(2), 73–90.

Beahrs, J. O. (1982). *Unity and multiplicity: Multilevel consciousness of self in hypnosis, psychiatric disorder and mental health.* New York: Brunner/ Mazel.

Bear, J. (1988). *Bear's guide to earning non-traditional college degrees* (10th ed.). Berkeley, CA: Ten Speed Press.

Beardslee, D.C., & Wertheimer, M. (Eds.). (1958). *Readings in perception.* Princeton, N.J.: Van Nostrand.

Beatty, J. (1982). Task-evoked pupillary responses, processing load, and the structure of processing resources. *Psychological Bulletin, 91*, 276–292.

Beaudet, A. L., Scriver, C. R., Sly, W. S., Valle, D., Cooper, D. N., McKusick, V. A., & Schmidke, J. (1989). Genetics and biochemistry of variant human phenotypes. In C. R. Scriver, A. L. Beaudet, W. S. Sly, & D. Valle (Eds.), *The metabolic basis of inherited disease* (6th ed., pp. 3–163). New York: McGraw-Hill.

Beauvoir, S. de (1971). *The second sex* (H. M. Parshley, Trans.). New York: Vintage. (Original work published 1949)

Bebbington, P. (1978). The epidemiology of depressive disorder. *Culture, Medicine, and Psychiatry, 2*, 297–341.

Bech, K., & Hilden, T. (1975). The frequency of essential hypertension. *Acta Medica Scandinavica, 197*, 65–69.

Bechtel, W., & Abrahamsen, A. (1991). *Connectionism and the mind.* Cambridge, MA: Basil Blackwell.

Bechterev, V. (1933). *General principles of human reflexology.* London: Hutchinson.

Bechtold, M. L. (1964). Validation of the K D scale and checklist as predictors of delinquent proneness. *Journal of Experimental Education, 32*, 413–416.

Beck, A. (1964). Thinking and depression: Theory and therapy. *Archives of General Psychiatry, 10*, 561–571.

Beck, A. (1976/1974). *Cognitive therapy and the emotional disorders.* New York: International Universities Press.

Beck, A., Rush, A., Shaw, B., & Emery, G. (1979). *Cognitive therapy of depression.* New York: Guilford Press.

Beck, A. T. (1967). *Depression: Clinical, experimental, and theoretical aspects.* New York: Hoeber.

Beck, A. T. (1973). *The diagnosis and management of depression.* Philadelphia, Pa.: University of Pennsylvania Press.

Beck, A. T. (1974). Cognition, affect, and psychopathology. In H. London & R. E. Nisbett (Eds.), *Thought and feeling.* Chicago: Aldine.

Beck, A. T. (1975/1967). *Depression: Causes and treatment.* Philadelphia, Pa.: University of Pennsylvania Press.

Beck, A. T. (1976). *Cognitive therapy and the emotional disorders.* New York: International Universities Press.

Beck, A. T., Brown, C., & Steer, R. A. (1989). Prediction of eventual suicide in psychiatric impatients by clinical ratings of hopelessness. *Journal of Consulting and Clinical Psychology, 57*, 309–310.

Beck, A. T., & Freeman, A. (1990). *Cognitive therapy of personality disorders*. New York: Guildford.

Beck, A. T., & Rush, J. (1978). Cognitive therapy of depression and suicide. *American Journal of Psychotherapy, 32*, 252–269.

Beck, A. T., Ward, C. H., Mendelson, M., Mock, J., & Erbaugh, J. (1962). Reliability of psychiatric diagnosis. *American Journal of Psychiatry, 119*, 351–357.

Beck, A., & Weishaar, M. (1989a). Cognitive therapy. In A. Freeman, K. M. Simon, L. E. Beutler, & H. Arkowitz (Eds.), *Comprehension handbook of cognitive therapy*. New York: Plenum Press.

Beck, A., & Weishaar, M. (1989b). Cognitive therapy. In R. Corsini & D. Wedding (Eds.), *Current psychotherapies*. Itasca, NY: Peacock.

Beck, A. T., Weissman, A., Lester, D., & Trexler. L. (1974). The measurement of pessimism: The Hopelessness Scale. *Journal of Consulting and Clinical Psychology, 42*, 861–865.

Beck, C. (1971). *Moral education in the schools: Some practical suggestions*. Toronto: Institute for Studies in Education.

Beck, L., Langford, W. S., MacKay, M., & Sum, G. (1974). Childhood chemotherapy and later drug abuse and growth curve: A follow-up study of 30 adolescents. *The American Journal of Psychiatry, 132*, 436–438.

Beck, S. J. (1930). The Rorschach test and personality diagnosis. 1. The feebleminded. *American Journal of Psychiatry, 10*, 19–52.

Beck, S. J. (1945 & 1947). *Rorschach's test*, Vols. 1 and 2. New York: Grune & Stratton.

Becker, E. (1973). *Escape from evil*. New York: Free Press.

Becker, E. (1973). *The denial of death*. New York: Free Press.

Becker, G. (1964). The complementary-need hypothesis: Authoritarianism dominance and other Edwards personality preference schedule scores. *Journal of Personality, 32*, 45–56.

Becker, G. (1978). *The mad genius controversy*. Beverly Hills, Calif.: Sage Publications.

Becker, H. G. (1977). How young people find career entry jobs—A review of the literature. Technical Report no. 241, Center for Social Organization of Schools. Johns Hopkins University, Baltimore, Md.

Becker, H. S. (1963). *Outsiders: Studies in the sociology of deviance*. New York: Free Press.

Becker, H. S. (1982). *The sociology of art*. Los Angeles: University of California Press.

Becker, J. H. (1983). Englisch-sprachig publizieren. In O. Ewert, (Ed.), *Bericht über den 33. Kongress der Deutschen Gesellschaft für Psychologie in Mainz 1982*. Gottingen, West Germany: Hogrefe.

Becker, R. O. (1990). *Cross currents: The perils of electropollution, the promise of electromedicine*. Los Angeles: Tarcher.

Becker, W. C. (1973). Applications of behavioral principles in typical classrooms. In C. E. Thoresen, (Ed.), *Behavior modification in education. NSSE 72nd yearbook* Chicago: University of Chicago Press.

Beckhard, R. (1967). The confrontation meeting. *Harvard Business Review, 45*, 149–155.

Beckhard, R. (1969). *Organization development: Strategies and models*. Reading, Mass.: Addison-Wesley.

Beckhard, R., & Harris, R. T. (1977). *Organizational transitions: Managing complex change*. Reading, Mass.: Addison-Wesley.

Beckman, H., & Goodwin, F. K. (1975). Antidepressant response to tricyclics and urinary MHPG in unipolar patients. *Archives of General Psychiatry, 32*, 17–21.

Becknell, J., & McIsaach, R. W. (1963). Test marketing cookware coated with teflon. *Journal of Advertising Research*, September 2–8.

Becvar, R., & Becvar, D. (1982). *Systems theory and family therapy: A primer*. Washington DC: University Press of America.

Bednar, R. R., & Lawlis, G. F. (1971). Empirical research in group therapy. In A. E. Bergen & S. L. Garfield (Eds.), *Handbook of psychotherapy and behavior change*. New York: Wiley.

Beebe-Center, J. G. (1932). *The psychology of pleasantness and unpleasantness*. New York: Van Nostrand.

Beeby, C. E. (1930). An experimental investigation into the simultaneous constituents of an act of skill. *British Journal of Psychology, 20*, 336–353.

Beecher, H. K. (1959). *Measurement of subjective responses: Quantitative effects of drugs*. New York: Oxford University Press.

Beecher, H. K. (1961). Surgery as placebo. *Journal of the American Medical Association, 176*, 1102–1107.

Beecher, M., & Beecher, W. (1971). *The mark of Cain*. New York: Harper & Row.

Beecher, W., & Beecher, M. (1966). *Beyond success and failure*. New York: Julian Press.

Beecher, W., & Beecher, M. (1966). *Parents on the run*. New York: Agora Press.

Beehr, T. A., & Newman, J. E. (1978). Job stress, employee health, and organizational effectiveness: A facet analysis, model, and literature review. *Personnel Psychology, 31*, 665–699.

Beer, M. (1980). *Organizational change and development. A systems view*. Santa Monica, Calif.: Goodyear.

Beer, M., & Ruh, R. A. (1976). Employee growth through performance management. *Harvard Business Review, 54*, 59–66.

Beers, C. (1908; 1970/1935). *A mind that found itself, an autobiography*. New York: Longman, Green. 25th anniversary edition. New York: Doubleday Doran.

Begleiter, H., & Platz, A. (1969). Cortical evoked potentials to semantic stimuli, *Psychophysiology, 6*, 91–100.

Beidler, L. M. (1961). Biophysical approaches to taste. *American Science* (Winter) 421–431.

Beier, E. G. (1966). *The silent language of psychotherapy*. Chicago: Aldine.

Beigel, A., & Levenson, A. (Eds.). (1972). *The community mental health center*. New York: Basic Books.

Beishon, J., & Peters, G. (Eds.). (1972). *Systems behaviour*. New York: Open University Press/Harper & Row.

Beit-Hallahmi, B. (1972). Some psychosocial and cultural factors in the Arab-Israeli conflict: A review of the literature. *Journal of Conflict Resolution, 16*, 269–280.

Beit-Hallahmi, B., & Rabin, A. I. (1977). The Kibbutz as a social experiment and as a child-rearing laboratory. *American Psychologist, 32*, 532–541.

Békésy, G. von. (1957). The ear. *Scientific American, 197*(2), 66–78.

Békésy, G. von. (1960). *Experiments in hearing*. E. G. Weber (Ed.). New York: McGraw-Hill.

Bekesy, G. von. (1960). *Experiments in hearing*. New York: McGraw-Hill.

Békésy, G. von. (1967). *Sensory inhibition*. Princeton, N.J.: Princeton University Press.

Békésy, G. von, & Rosenblith, W. A. (1948). The early history of hearing—Observations and theories. *Journal of the Acoustical Society of America, 20,* 727–748.

Békhterev, V. M. (1932/1928). *General principles of human reflexology, an introduction to the objective study of personality.* New York: International Publishers.

Belasco, J. (1966). Broadening the approach to salesmen selection. *Personnel, 43,* 67–72.

Belbin, E. (1950). The influence of interpolated recall upon recognition. *Quarterly Journal of Experimental Psychology, 2,* 163–169.

Belfer, M. L., Krener, P. K., & Miller, F. B. (1988). AIDS in children and adolescents. *Journal of the American Academy of Child and Adolescent Psychiatry, 27,* 147–151.

Bell, A. B. (1970). Role models of young adulthood: Their relationship to occupational behaviors. *Vocational Guidance Quarterly, 18,* 280–284.

Bell, A. P., & Weinberg, M. S. (1978). *Homosexualities: A study of diversity among men and women.* New York: Simon & Schuster.

Bell, A. P., Weinberg, M. S., & Hammersmith, S. K. (1981). *Sexual preference.* Bloomington, Ind.: Indiana University Press.

Bell, A. P., Weinberg, M. S., & Keefer, S. (1981). *Sexual preference, its development in men and women.* Bloomington, Ind.: Indiana University Press.

Bell, C. (1811). *Idea of a new anatomy of the brain.* London: Strahan & Preston.

Bell, D. (1976). *The coming of post-industrial society.* New York: Basic Books.

Bell, D. S. (1965). Comparison of amphetamine psychosis and schizophrenia. *British Journal of Psychiatry, 111,* 701–707.

Bell, E. C. (1958). Nutritional deficiencies and emotional disturbances. *Journal of Psychology, 45,* 47–74.

Bell, H. M. (1938). *Youth tell their story.* Washington, D.C.: American Council on Education.

Bell, H. M. (1940). *Matching youth and jobs.* Washington, D.C.: American Council on Education.

Bell, J. E. (1948). *Projective techniques: A dynamic approach to the study of the personality.* New York: Longman, Green.

Bell, J. E. (1976). A theoretical framework for family group therapy. In P. J. Guerin (Ed.), *Family therapy: Theory and practice* (pp. 129–143). New York: Gardner Press.

Bell, R. O. (1960). Relations between behavior manifestations in the human neonate. *Child Development, 31,* 463–477.

Bell, R. Q. (1968). A reinterpretation of the direction of effects and studies of socialization. *Psychological Review, 75,* 81–95.

Bell, R. Q. (1979). Parent, child and reciprocal influences. *American Psychologist, 34,* 821–826.

Bell, W., & Freeman, W. E. (Eds.). (1974). *Ethnicity and nation-building: Comparative, international and historical perspectives.* Beverly Hills, Calif.: Sage Publications.

Bellack, A. S. (1979). A critical appraisal of strategies for assessing social skill. *Behavioral Assessment, 1,* 157–176.

Bellack, A. S., & Hersen, M. (1977). *Behavior modification: An introductory textbook.* Baltimore, Md.: Williams & Wilkins.

Bellack, A. S., & Hersen, M. (1988). *Behavioral analysis: A practical handbook* (3rd ed.). New York: Pergamon.

Bellack, A. S., & Hersen, M. (Eds.). (1979). *Research and practice in social skills training.* New York: Plenum.

Bellack, A. S., Hersen, M., & Kazdin, A. E. (Eds.). (1990). *International handbook of behavior modification and behavior therapy* (2nd ed.). New York: Plenum Press.

Bellak, R. N., & Glock, C. Y. (Eds.). (1976). *The new religious consciousness.* Berkeley, Calif.: University of California Press.

Bellak, L. (1975/1954). *The TAT, CAT and SAT in clinical use* (3rd ed.). New York: Grune & Stratton.

Bellak, L. (1979). Psychiatric aspects of minimal brain disfunction in adults: Their ego function assessment. In L. Bellak (Ed.), *Psychiatric aspects of minimal brain dysfunction in adults.* New York: Grune & Stratton.

Belli, R. F. (1989). Influences of misleading postevent information: Misinformation interference and acceptance. *Journal of Experimental Psychology: General, 118,* 72–85.

Bellows, R. (1961). *Psychology of personnel in business and industry* (3rd ed.). Englewood Cliffs, N.J.: Prentice-Hall.

Bellugi, U., Klima, E. S., & Siple, P. (1975). Remembering in signs. *Cognition, 3,* 93–125.

Belmont, L. (1977). Birth order, intellectual competence, and psychiatric status. *Journal of Individual Psychology, 33,* 97–104.

Belmont, L., Belmont, L., Wittes, J., & Stein, Z. (1978). Child spacing and birth order: Effect on intellectual ability in two-child families. *Science, 202,* 995–996.

Belsky, J. (1981). Early human experience: A family perspective. *Developmental Psychology, 17,* 3–23.

Belsky, J., & Steinberg, L. D. (1978). The effects of day care: A critical review. *Child Development, 49,* 929–949.

Beltman, B. D., Goldfried, M. R., & Norcross, J. C. (1989). The movement toward integrating the psychotherapies: An overview. *American Journal of Psychiatry, 146,* 138–147.

Bem, D. (1967). Self-perception: An alternative interpretation of cognitive dissonance phenomena. *Psychological Review, 74,* 183–200.

Bem, D. J. (1971). The concept of risk in the study of human behavior. In R. C. Carney (Ed.), *Risk-taking behavior.* Springfield, Ill.: Thomas.

Bem, D. J. (1972). Constructing cross-situational consistencies in behavior: Some thoughts on Alker's critique of Mischel. *Journal of Personality, 40,* 17–26.

Bem, D. J., & Allen, A. (1974). On predicting some of the people some of the time: The search for cross-situational consistencies in behavior. *Psychological Review, 81,* 506–520.

Bem, S. L. (1974). The measurement of psychological androgyny. *Journal of Consulting and Clinical Psychology, 42,* 155–162.

Bem, S. L. (1975). Sex role adaptability: One consequence of psychological androgyny. *Journal of Personality and Social Psychology, 31,* 634–643.

Bem, S. L. (1977). On the utility of alternative procedures for assessing psychological androgyny. *Journal of Consulting and Clinical Psychology, 45,* 196–205.

Bem, S. L. (1981). Gender schema theory: A cognitive account of sex typing. *Psychological Review, 88,* 354–364.

Bem, S. L., & Lenney, E. (1976). Sex typing and the avoidance of cross-sex behavior. *Journal of Personality and Social Psychology, 33,* 48–54.

Bem, S. L., Martyna, W., & Watson, C. (1976). Sex typing and androgyny: Further explorations of the expressive domain, *Journal of Personality and Social Psychology, 34,* 1016–1023.

Benbow, C. P., & Stanley, J. C. (1980). Sex differences in mathematical ability: Fact or artifact? *Science, 210,* 1262–1264.

Benbow, C. P., & Stanley, J. C. (1981). Mathematical ability: Is sex a factor? *Science, 212,* 118, 121.

Benbow, C. P., & Stanley, J. C. (in press). Consequences in high school and college of sex differences in mathematical reasoning ability: A longitudinal perspective. *American Educational Research Journal.*

Bender, B. (1976). Self-chosen victims: Scapegoating behavior sequential to battering. *Child Welfare, 17,* 417–422.

Bender, L. (1938). *A visual-motor Gestalt test and its clinical use.* Research Monograph (no. 3). New York: American Orthopsychiatric Association.

Bender, L. (1946). *Instructions for the use of the visual-motor Gestalt test.* New York: American Orthopsychiatric Association.

Bender, L. (1956). *Psychopathology of children with organic brain disorders.* Springfield, Ill.: Thomas.

Bender, L. (1956). Schizophrenia in childhood: Its recognition, description, and treatment. *American Journal of Opthopsychiatry, 26,* 499–506.

Bender, L. (1957). Specific reading disability as a developmental lag. *Bulletin of the Orton Society, 7,* 9–18.

Bendix, R., & Lipset, S. M. (1955). *Class, status, and power.* Glencoe, Ill.: Free Press.

Benedict, R. F. (1931). *Tales of the Cochiti Indians.* Washington: U.S. Government Printing Office.

Benedict, R. F. (1935). *Zuni mythology* (2 vols.). New York: Columbia University Press.

Benedict, R. F. (1946). *The chrysanthemum and the sword: Patterns of Japanese culture.* Boston: Houghton Mifflin.

Benedict, R. F. (1960/1946). *Patterns of culture.* New York: Mentor Books.

Bengtson, V., Cuellar, J., & Ragan, R. (1977). Stratum contrasts and similarities in attitudes toward death. *Journal of Gerontology, 32,* 76–88.

Benjafield, J., & Adams-Webber, J. (1976). The golden section hypothesis. *British Journal of Psychology, 67,* 11–15.

Benjamin, A. C. (1955). *Operationism.* Springfield, IL: Thomas.

Benjamin, F. S. (1955). Effect of pain on simultaneous perception of non-painful sensory stimulation. *Journal of Applied Physiology, 6,* 630–634.

Bejamin, H. (1966). *The transsexual phenomenon.* New York: Julian.

Benjamin, L. (1989). Is chronicity a function of the relationship between the person and the auditory hallucination? *Schizophrenia Bulletin, 15,* 291–310.

Benjamin, L. S. (1974). Structural analysis of social behavior. *Psychological Review, 81,* 392–425.

Benjamin, L. T., Jr. (1979). A century of science. *APA Monitor, 10(2),* 1, 3.

Benjamin, M., McKeachie, W. J., Lin, Y. G., & Holinger, D. P. (1981). Test anxiety: Deficits in information processing. *Journal of Educational Psychology, 73,* 816–824.

Benne, K. D. (1964). History of the T-Group in the laboratory setting. In L. P. Bradford, J. R. Gibb, & K. Benne (Eds.), *T-Group theory and laboratory method.* New York: Wiley.

Bennett, B. (1992). Personal communication.

Bennett, C. C., Anderson, L. S., Cooper, S., Hassol, L., Klein, D. C., & Rosenblum, G. (Eds.) (1966). *Community psychology: A report of the Boston conference on the education of psychologists for community mental health.* Boston: Boston University Press.

Bennett, D. (1980). The chronic psychiatric patient today. *Journal of the Royal Society of Medicine, 73,* 301–303.

Bennett, D., & Holmes, D. S. (1975). Influence of denial (situation redefinition) and projection on anxiety associated with threat to self-esteem. *Journal of Personality and Social Psychology, 32,* 915–921.

Bennett, G. K., Seashore, H. G., & Wesman, A. G. (1974). *Fifth edition manual for the Differential Aptitude Tests.* New York: Psychological Corporation.

Bennett, G. K., Seashore, H. G., & Wesman, A. G. (1977). *Counseling from profiles: second edition—A casebook for the DAT.* New York: Psychological Corp.

Bennett, M., & Rittledge, J. (1989). Self-disclosure in a clinical context by Asian and British psychiatric, out-patients. *British Journal of Clinical Psychology, 28(2),* 155–163.

Bennett, M. J. (1988). The greening of the HMO: Implications for prepaid psychiatry. *American Journal of Psychiatry, 145(12),* 1544–1548.

Bennett, R., & Eisdorfer, C. (1975). The institutional environment and behavior change. In S. Sherwood (Ed.), *Long-term care: A handbook for researchers, planners and providers.* New York: Spectrum.

Bennis, W. G. (1965). Theory and method in applying behavioral science to planned organizational change. *Journal of Applied Behavioral Science, 1(4):*337–360.

Benoit, M. (1981). Minimal brain dysfunction: The psychiatric examination. In R. Ochroch (Ed.), *Diagnosis and treatment of minimal brain dysfunction in children: A clinical approach.* New York: Human Sciences Press.

Benson, D. F. (1981). Alexia and the neuroanatomical basis of reading. In F. J. Pirozzolo & M. C. Wittrock (Eds.), *Neuropsychological and cognitive processes in reading.* New York: Academic Press.

Benson, H. (1975). *The relaxation response.* New York: Morrow.

Benson, H. (1978). *The mind/body effect.* New York: Simon & Schuster.

Benson, H., Marzetta, B. R., Rosner, V. A., & Klemchuck, H. M. (1974). Decreased blood pressure in pharmacologically treated hypertensive patients who regularly elicited the relaxation response. *Lancet, 7852,* 289–291.

Benson, J. S., & Kennelly, K. J. (1976). Learned helplessness: The result of uncontrollable reinforcements or uncontrollable aversive stimuli? *Journal of Personality and Social Psychology, 34,* 138–145.

Bentall, R. P., Kaney, S., & Dewey, M. E. (1991). Paranoia and social reasoning: An attribution theory analysis. *British Journal of Clinical Psychology, 30(1),* 13–23.

Bentham, J. (1830). In J. Bowruy (Ed.), *Works.* Edinburgh: Hait.

Bentham, J. (1914/1798). *Theory of legislation,* Oxford: Clarendon Press.

Bentler, P., Shearman, R., & Prince, C. (1970). Personality characteristics of male transvestites. *Journal of Clinical Psychology, 126,* 287–291.

Bentler, P. M. (1980). Multivariate analysis with latent variables: Causal modeling. *Annual Review of Psychology, 31,* 419–456.

Bentler, P. M. (1983). Some contributions to efficient statistics in structural models: Specification and estimation of moment structures. *Psychometrika, 48,* in press.

Bentler, P. M., & Huba, G. J. (1982). Symmetric and asymmetric rotations in canonical correlation analysis: New methods with drug variable examples. In N. Hirschberg & L. G. Humphreys (Eds.), *Multivariate applications in the social sciences.* Hillsdale, N.J.: Erlbaum.

Bentler, P. M., & Newcomb, M. D. (1978). Longitudinal study of marital success and failure. *Journal of Consulting and Clinical Psychology, 46,* 1053–1070.

Bentley, I. M. (1899). The memory image and its qualitative fidelity. *American Journal of Psychology, 1,* 1–48.

Benton, A. L. (1945). A visual retention test for clinical use. *Archives of Neurology and Psychiatry, 54,* 212–216.

Benton, A. L. (1950). A multiple choice type of the visual retention test. *Archives of Neurology and Psychiatry, 64,* 699–707.

Benton, A. L. (1959). *Right-left discrimination and finger localization: Development and pathology.* New York: Hoeber-Harper.

Benton, A. L. (1966). *Problemi di neuropsicologia.* Florence, Italy: Editrice Universitaria.

Benton, A. L. (1972). Abbreviated versions of the visual retention test. *The Journal of Psychology, 80,* 189–192.

Benton, A. L. (1974). *The revised visual retention test* (4th ed.). New York: Psychological Corporation.

Benton, A. L. (1975). Psychological tests for brain damage. In A. M. Freedman, H. I. Kaplan, & B. J. Sadock (Eds.), *Comprehensive textbook of psychiatry* (2nd ed.). Baltimore, Md.: Williams & Wilkins.

Benton, A. L. (Ed.). (1969). *Contributions to clinical neuropsychology.* Chicago: Aldine.

Benton, A. L., Hamsher, K., Varney, N. R., & Spreen, O. (1982). *Contributions to neuropsychological assessment.* New York: Oxford University Press.

Benton, A. L., & Joynt, R. J. (Eds.). (1970). *Behavioral change in cerebrovascular disease.* New York: Harper & Row.

Benton, A. L., Levin, H. S., & Van Allen, M. W. (1974). Geographic orientation in patients with unilateral brain disease. *Neurosychologia, 12,* 183–188.

Benton, A. L., & Pearl, D. (1978). *Dyslexia: An appraisal of current knowledge.* New York: Oxford University Press.

Benus, R. F., Bohus, B., Koolhaas, J. M., & van Oortmerssen, G. A. (1991). Heritabel veriation for aggression as a reflection of individual coping strategies. *Experientia, 47,* 1008–1019.

Benware, C., & Deci, E. L. (1984). The quality of learning with an active versus passive motivational set. *American Educational Research Journal,* in press.

Benyamini, K., & Klein, Z. (1970). The educational system and mental health. In A. Jarus, J. Marcus, J. Oren, & H. Rapaport (Eds.), *Children and families in Israel: Some mental health perspectives.* New York: Gordon & Breach.

Berdie, R. F. (1960). Validity of the Strong Vocational Interest Blank. In W. L. Layton (Ed.), *The Strong Vocational Interest Blank.* Minneapolis, Minn.: University of Minnesota Press.

Berelson, B. (1960). *Graduate education in the United States.* New York: McGraw-Hill.

Berenbaum, H., Snowhite, R., & Oltmans, T. F. (1987). Anhedonia and emotional responses to affect evoking stimuli. *Psychological Medicine, 17*(3), 677–684.

Berg, B. O. (1979). Neuromuscular disease. In F. C. Rose (Ed.), *Paediatric neurology.* Oxford: Blackwell.

Berg, I. A. (1967). *Response set in personality assessment.* Chicago: Aldine.

Berg, I. A. (1980). Some alternative roads for counseling psychology. In J. M. Whiteley (Ed.), *The history of counseling psychology.* Monterey, Calif: Brooks/Cole.

Berg, I. A., Pepinsky, H. B., & Shoben, E. J. (1980). The status of counseling psychology. In J. M. Whiteley (Ed.), *The history of counseling psychology.* Monterey, Calif.: Brooks/Cole.

Berg, I. K., & Miller, S. D. (1992). *Working with the problem drinker: A solution-focused approach.* New York: Norton.

Berg, R. C., & Landreth, G. L. (1979). *Group counseling; Fundamental concepts and procedures.* Muncie, Ind.: Accelerated Development.

Berger, A. (1929). Über das Elektroenzephalogramm des Menschen. *Archiv für Psychiatrie und Nervenkrankheiten, 87,* 527–571.

Berger, C. S. (1954). An experimental study of doodles. *Psychology Newsletter,* 138–141.

Berger, E. M. (1971). MMPI item differences between smoker and nonsmoker college freshmen males. *Journal of Consulting and Clinical Psychology, 36*(3), 446.

Berger, J., Cohen, B. P., & Zelditch, M., Jr. (1973). Status characteristics and social interaction. In R. J. Ofshe (Ed.), *Interpersonal behavior in small groups.* Englewood Cliffs, N.J.: Prentice-Hall.

Berger, M. (1977). The survivor syndrome: A problem of nosology and treatment. *American Journal of Psychotherapy, 31,* 238–251.

Berger, M. (1985). Temperament and individual differences. In M. Rutter & L. Hersov (Eds.), *Child and adolescent psychiatry: Modern approaches* (2nd ed., pp. 3–16). Oxford UK: Blackwell.

Berger, P., & Luckman, T. (1967). *The social construction of reality.* New York: Doubleday/Anchor.

Berger, S. (1962). Conditioning through vicarious instigation. *Psychological Review, 69,* 450–466.

Berger, S. (1987). *Bay area directory of graduate schools in counseling and psychology.* San Francisco: Author.

Berger, T. W., Alger, B. E., & Thompson, R. F. (1976). Neuronal substrate of classical conditioning in the hippocampus. *Science, 192,* 483–485.

Berghner, R. M. (1981). The overseer regime: A descriptive and practical study of the obsessive-compulsive personality style. *Advances in Descriptive Psychology, 1,* 245–271.

Berghorn, F. J., & Schafer, D. E. (1981). *The dynamics of aging.* Boulder, Colo.: Westview Press.

Bergin, A. E. (1966). Some implications of psychotherapy research for therapeutic practice. *Journal of Abnormal Psychology, 71,* 235–246.

Bergin, A. E. (1971). The evaluation of therapeutic outcomes. In A. E. Bergin & S. L. Garfield (Eds.), *Handbook of psychotherapy and behavior change: An empirical analysis.* New York: Wiley

Bergin, A. E. (1982). *Comment on converging themes in psychotherapy.* NY: Springer.

Bergin, A. E. (1983). Values and evaluating therapeutic change. In J. Helm & A. E. Bergin (Eds.), *Therapeutic behavior modification* (pp. 9–14). Berlin: VIEB Deutscher Verlag der Wissenschaten.

Bergin, A. E. (1985). Proposed values for guiding and evaluating counseling and psychotherapy. *Counseling and Values, 29,* 99–116.

Bergin, A. E., & Garfield, S. L. (Eds.). (1971). *Handbook of psychotherapy and behavior change.* New York: Wiley.

Bergin, A. E., & Lambert, M. J. (1978/1971). The evaluation of therapeutic outcomes. In S. L. Garfield & A. E. Bergin (Eds.), *Handbook of psychotherapy and behavior change.* New York: Wiley.

Bergin, A. E., & Strupp, H. H. (1972). *Changing frontiers in the science of psycho-therapy.* Chicago: Aldine-Atherton.

Bergin, A. E., & Suinn, R. M. (1975). Individual psychotherapy and behavior therapy. *Annual Review of Psychology, 26,* 509–556.

Bergler, E. (1970). *The psychology of gambling.* New York: International Universities Press.

Bergman, G., & Spence, K. W. (1941). Operationism and theory in psychology. *Psychological Review, 48,* 1–14.

Bergmann, G. (1954). *The metaphysics of logical positivism*. New York: Longman, Green.

Bergmann, G. (1956). The contribution of John B. Watson. *Psychological Review, 63*, 265–276.

Bergman, K. (1971). The neuroses of old age. In Recent developments in psychogeriatrics. *British Journal of Psychiatry*, Special Publication 6, 39–50.

Bergson, H. (1911). *Creative evolution*. New York: Holt.

Bergson, H. (1913). *Matter and memory* (N. M. Paul & W. S. Palmer, Trans.). New York: Macmillan.

Bergson, H. (1914/1901). *Dreams*. New York: Huebsch.

Berkeley, G. (1948/1910). Essay toward a new theory of vision (1709). In Luce, A. A., & Jessop, T. E. (Eds.), *The works of George Berkeley, Bishop of Cloyne*. Toronto: Nelson.

Berkeley, G. (1950/1710). *A treatise concerning the principles of human knowledge*. LaSalle, Ill.: Open Court.

Berkeley, G., Siris. (1901/1744). In A. C. Fraser (Ed.), *The works of George Berkeley*. Oxford: Clarendon Press.

Berkowitz, B., Ross-Townsend, A., & Kohberger, R. (1979). Hypnotic treatment of smoking: The single-treatment method revisited. *American Journal of Psychiatry, 136*(1), 83–85.

Berkowitz, L. (1959). Anti-semitism and the displacement of aggression. *Journal of Abnormal and Social Psychology, 59*, 182–188.

Berkowitz, L. (1962). *Aggression: A social psychological analysis*. New York: McGraw-Hill.

Berkowitz, L. (1969). The frustration-aggression hypothesis revisited. In L. Berkowitz (Ed.), *Roots of aggression: A reexamination of the frustration-aggression hypothesis* (pp. 1–28). New York: Atherton Press.

Berkowitz, L. (1972). Social norms, feeling, and other factors affecting helping behavior and altruism. In L. Berkowitz (Ed.), *Advances in experimental social psychology*, Vol. 6. New York: Academic Press.

Berkowitz, L. (1983). Aversively stimulated aggression: Some parallels and differences in research with humans and animals. *American Psychologist, 38*, 1135–1144.

Berkowitz, L. (1989). Frustration-aggression hypothesis: Examination and reformulation. *Psychological Bulletin, 106*, 59–73.

Berkowitz, L., & Daniels, L. R. (1963). Responsibility and dependency. *Journal of Abnormal and Social Psychology, 66*, 429–436.

Berkowitz, L., & Le Page, A. (1967). Weapons as aggression-eliciting stimuli. *Journal of Personality and Social Psychology, 25*, 202–207.

Berkowitz, W. R. (1970). Spectator responses at public war demonstrations. *Journal of Personality and Social Psychology, 14*, 305–311.

Berleant, A. (1970). *The aesthetic field: A phenomenology of aesthetic experience*. Springfield, Ill.: Thomas.

Berlin, I. (1958). *Two concepts of liberty*. Oxford: Clarendon Press.

Berlin, I. (1969). *Four essays on liberty*. Oxford: Oxford University Press.

Berlin, I. N. (1964). Learning mental health consultation: History and problems. *Mental Hygiene, 48*, 257–266.

Berlin, I. N. (1974). Minimal brain dysfunction: Management of family distress. *Journal of the American Medical Association, 9*, 1454–1456.

Berlin, I. N. (1981). Psychotherapy with MBD children and their parents. In R. Ochroch (Ed.), *The diagnosis and treatment of minimal brain dysfunction in children: A clinical approach*. New York: Human Sciences Press.

Berliner, B. (1958). Role of object relations in moral masochism. *Psychoanalytic Quarterly, 27*, 38–56.

Berlo, D. K. (1960). *The process of communication: An introduction to theory and practice*. New York: Holt, Rinehart & Winston.

Berlyne, D. E. (1955). The arousal and satiation of perceptual curiosity in the rat. *Journal of Comparative Psychology, 48*, 238–246.

Berlyne, D. E. (1960). *Conflict, arousal and curiosity*, New York: McGraw-Hill.

Berlyne, D. E. (1965). *Structure and direction in thinking*, New York: Wiley.

Berlyne, D. E. (1966). Curiosity and exploration. *Science, 153*, 25–33.

Berlyne, D. E. (1968). American and European psychology. *American Psychologist, 23*, 447–452.

Berlyne, D. E. (1969). La section d'or et la composition pictoriale occidentale et orientale. *Sciences de l'Art, 6*, 1–6.1

Berlyne, D. E. (1969). Laughter, humor, and play. In G. Lindzey & E. Aronson (Eds.), *Handbook of social psychology*, Vol. 3. Reading, Mass.: Addison-Wesley.

Berlyne, D. E. (1971). *Aesthetics and psychobiology*. New York: Appleton.

Berlyne, D. E. (1971). *Psychobiology and aesthetics*. New York: Appleton-Century-Crofts.

Berlyne, D. E. (1972). Humor and its kin. In J. Goldstein & P. McGhee (Eds.), *The psychology of humor*. New York: Academic Press.

Berlyne, D. E. (1974). *Studies in the new experimental aesthetics: Steps toward an objective psychology of aesthetic appreciation*. New York: Wiley.

Berlyn, D. E., Borsa, D. M., Hamacher, J. H., & Koenig, I. D. U. (1966). Paired-associate learning and the timing of arousal. *Journal of Experimental Psychology, 72*, 1–6.

Berman, A. (1979). Parenting learning-disabled children. *Journal of Clinical Child Psychology, 8*, 245–249.

Berman, E. (1981). Growing pains of professional clinical psychology: A report from Israel. *The Clinical Psychologist, 34*, 6–8.

Berman, J., & Sales, B. D. (1977). A critical evaluation of the systematic approach to jury selection. *Criminal Justice and Behavior, 4*, 219–240.

Berman, P. W. (1980). Are women more responsive than men to the young? A review of developmental and situational variables. *Psychological Bulletin, 88*, 668–695.

Berman, R. (1980). Advertising and social change. In *Twentieth century advertising and the economy of abundance*. Chicago: Advertising Age.

Bermant, G., & Davidson, J. M. (1974). *Biological bases of sexual behavior*. New York: Harper & Row.

Bernal, M. E., Pruett, H. L., Duryee, J. S., & Burns, B. J. (1968). Behavior modification and the brat syndrome. *Journal of Consulting and Clinical Psychology, 32*, 447–454.

Bernard, C. (1873). *Leçons sur le phénomène de la vie commune aux animaux et végétaux*, Vol. 1. Paris: Ballière.

Bernard, C. (1957/1865). *An introduction to the study of experimental medicine*. New York: Dover.

Bernard, H. S. (1981). Identity formation during late adolescence: A review of some empirical findings. *Adolescence, 16*, 349–358.

Bernard, J. (1972). *The future of marriage*. New York: Macmillan.

Bernard, J. M. (1979). Supervisor training: A discrimination model. *Counselor Education and Supervision, 19*, 60–68.

Bernard, J. M. (1981). Inservice training for clinical supervisors. *Professional Psychology, 12*, 740–748.

Bernard, J. W. (1986). Messiaen's synaesthesia: The correspondence between color and sound structure in his music. *Music Perception, 4*, 41–68.

Bernat, J. L., Culver, C. M., & Gert, B. (1982). Defining death in theory and practice. *The Hastings Center Report, 12*, 5–9.

Bernatowicz, A. I. (1958). Teleology in science teaching. *Science, 128*, 1402–1405.

Berndt, T. (1979). Developmental changes in conformity to peers and parents. *Developmental Psychology, 15*, 608–616.

Berne, E. (1949). The nature of intuition. *Psychiatric Quarterly, 23*, 203–226.

Berne, E. (1961). *Transactional analysis in psychotherapy; a systematic individual and social psychiatry.* New York: Grove Press.

Berne, E. (1964). *Games people play; The psychology of human relationships.* New York: Grove Press.

Berne, E. (1966). *Principles of group treatment.* New York: Oxford, University Press.

Berne, E. (1972). *What do you say after you say hello?* New York: Grove Press.

Bernhardt, K. S. (Ed.). (1961). *Training for research in psychology.* Toronto: University of Toronto Press.

Bernheim, H. (1947). *Suggestive therapeutics.* New York: London Book.

Bernheim, H. (1964). *Hypnosis and suggestability in psychotherapy: A treatise on the nature and use of hypnosis,* New Hyde Park, N.Y.: University Books.

Bernheim, H. (1980/1891). *New studies in hypnotism.* New York: International Universities Press.

Bernshtein, N. (1947). *O postroenii dvizhenij.* Moscow: Medgiz.

Bernshtein, N. (1966). *Ocherki po fiziologii dvizhenij i fiziologii aktivnosti.* Moscow: Meditsyna.

Bernshtein, N. (1967). *The coordination and regulation of movements.* Oxford: Pergamon Press.

Bernshtein, N. (1969). Methods for developing physiology as related to the problems of cybernetics. In M. Cole & I. Maltzman (Eds.), *A Handbook of contemporary Soviet psychology.* New York: Basic Books.

Bernstein, B. (1964). Elaborated and restricted codes: Their social origins and some consequences. *American Anthropologist, 66*, 55–69.

Bernstein, B. L., & Lecompte, C. (1976). An integrative competency-based counselor education model. *Counselor Education and Supervision, 16*, 26–36.

Bernstein, B. L., & Lecomte, C. (1981). Licensing in psychology: Alternate directions. *Journal of Professional Psychology, 12*, 200–208.

Bernstein, D., & Borkovec, T. (1973). *Progressive relaxation training, a manual for the helping professions.* Champaign, Ill.: Research Press.

Bernstein, E., & Putnam, F. W. (1986). Development, reliability and validity of a dissociation scale. *Journal of Nervous and Mental Disease, 174*, 727–735.

Bernstein, I. L. (1991). Aversion conditioning in response to cancer and cancer treatment. *Clinical Psychology Review, 11*, 185–191.

Bernstein, I. N., & Freeman, H. E. (1975). *Academic and entrepreneurial research: The consequences of diversity in federal evaluation studies.* New York: Russell Sage Foundation.

Bernstein, L., et al. (1974). *Interviewing: A guide for health professionals.* New York: Appleton Century.

Bernstein, P. (Ed.). (1979). *Eight theoretical approaches in dance-movement therapy.* Dubuque, Iowa: Kendall/Hunt.

Bernstein, S. R. (1980). What is advertising? *Twentieth century advertising and the economy of abundance.* Chicago: Advertising Age.

Berofsky, B. (Ed.). (1966). *Free will and determinism.* New York: Harper & Row.

Berrien, F. K. (1968). *General and social systems.* New Brunswick, N.J.: Rutgers University Press.

Berrill, K. T., & Herek, G. M. (1990). Primary and secondary victimization in antigay hate crimes: Official response and public policy. *Journal of Interpersonal Violence, 5*(3), 401–413. [Revised and reprinted: Herek & Berrill (Eds.), (1992). In *Hate crimes: Confronting violence against lesbians and gay men.* Newbury Park, CA: Sage]

Berruata-Clement, J. R., Schweinhart, L. J., Barnett, W. S., & Weikart, D. P. (1987). The effects of early educational intervention on crime and delinquency in adolescence and early adulthood. In J. D. Burchard & S. N. Burchard (Eds.), *Prevention of delinquent behavior* (pp. 220–240). Newbury Park, CA: Sage.

Berry, J. (1969). On cross-cultural comparability. *International Journal of Psychology, 4*, 119–128.

Berry, J. (1980). Introduction to methodology. In H. Triandis & J. Berry (Eds.), *Handbook of cross-cultural psychology,* Vol. 2. Boston: Allyn & Bacon.

Berry, J. W. (1966). Temne and Eskimo perceptual skills. *International Journal of Psychology, 1*, 207–229.

Berry, J. W. (1967). Independence and conformity in subsistence-level societies. *Journal of Personality and Social Psychology, 7*, 415–418.

Berscheid, E., Boye, D., & Darley, J. M. (1968). Effect of forced association upon voluntary choice to associate. *Journal of Personality and Social Psychology, 8*, 13–19.

Berscheid, E., & Hatfield (Walster), E. (1974). Physical attractiveness. In L. Berkowitz (Ed.), *Advances in experimental social psychology,* New York: Academic Press

Berscheid, E., & Walster, E. H. (1978/1969). *Interpersonal attraction* (2nd ed.). Reading, Mass.: Addison-Wesley.

Berscheid, E., & Walster, E. (1974). Physical attractiveness. In L. Berkowitz (Ed.), *Advances in experimental social psychology,* Vol. 7. New York: Academic Press.

Berscheid, E., & Walster (Hatfield), E. (1967). When does a harm-doer compensate a victim? *Journal of Personality and Social Psychology, 6*, 435–441.

Berscheid, E., Walster (Hatfield), E., & Barclay, A. (1969). Effect of time on tendency to compensate a victim. *Psychological Reports, 25*, 431–436.

Bersoff, D. N. (1981). Testing and the law. *American Psychologist, 36*, 1047–1056.

Bersoff, D. N., & Grieger, R. M. (1971). An interview model for the psychositutional assessment of children's behavior. *American Journal of Orthopsychiatry, 41*, 483–493.

Bertalanffy, L. von. (1933). *Modern theories of development.* London: Oxford University Press.

Bertalanffy, L. von. (1952). *Problems of life.* London: Watts.

Bertalanffy, L. von. (1955). General systems theory. *Main Currents in Modern Thought, 11*, 75–83.

Bertalanffy, L. von. (1967). *Robots, men and minds: Psychology in the modern world.* New York: Braziller.

Bertalanffy, L. von. (1968). *General systems theory.* New York: Braziller.

Bertalanffy, L. von. (1974). General systems theory and psychiatry. In S. Arieti (Ed.), *American handbook of psychiatry,* Vol. 1. New York: Basic Books.

Bertier, P., & Bouroche, J. M. (1975). *Analyse des données multidimensionnelles*. Paris: Presses Universitaires, France.

Bertin, M. A. (1974). *An overview of psychology in Latin America*. Department of the Navy, Office of Naval Research, Arlington, Va., ONR-35.

Berube, A. (1990). *Coming out under fire: The history of gay men and women in World War II*. New York: Free Press.

Berwick, P., & Oziel, L. J. (1973). The use of meditation as a behaviour technique. *Behaviour Therapy, 4*, 743–745.

Berzonsky, M. D. (1981). *Adolescent development*. New York: Macmillan.

Berzonsky, M. D., & Barclay, C. R. (1981). Formal reasoning and identity formation: A reconceptualization. In J. A. Meacham N. R. Santilli (Eds.), *Social development in youth: Structure and function*. Basel: Karger.

Besedovsky, H. O., & Sorkin, E. (1981). Immunologic-neuroendocrine circuits: Physiological approaches. In R. Ader (Ed.), *Psychoneuroimmunology*. New York: Academic Press.

Besedovsky, H. O., Sorkin, E., Felix, D., & Haas, H. (1977). Hypothalamic changes during the immune response. *European Journal of Immunology, 7*, 325–328.

Best, G. A. (1977). Mainstreaming characteristics of orthopedically handicapped children in California. *Rehabilitation Literature, 38*, 205–209.

Bettelheim, B. (1943). Individual and mass behavior in extreme situations. *Journal of Abnormal and Social Psychology, 38*, 417–452.

Bettelheim, B. (1950). *Love is not enough*. New York: Macmillan.

Bettelheim, B. (1960). *The informed heart*. New York: Macmillan.

Bettelheim, B. (1962). *Dialogues with mothers*. New York: Macmillan.

Bettelheim, B. (1967). *The empty fortress*. New York: Free Press.

Bettelheim, B. (1969). *The children of the dream*. New York: Macmillan.

Betts, G. H. (1909). The distribution and functions of mental imagery. *Teachers' College Columbia University Contributions to Education*, no. 26, 1–99.

Betz, N. E., & Hackett, G. (1986). Applications of self-efficacy theory to understanding career choice behavior. *Journal of Social and Clinical Psychology, 4*, 279–289.

Beulka, R. P. (1976). Setting the tone: The psychology-Judaism dialogue. *Journal of Psychology and Judaism, 1*, 3–13.

Beutler, L. E., Crago, M., & Arizmedi, T. G. (1986). Research on therapist variables in psychotherapy. In S. L. Garfield & A. E. Bergin (Eds.), *Handbook of psychotherapy and behavior change* (pp. 257–310). NY: Wiley.

Beven, R. B., Foder, J. A., & Garrett, M. (1968). A formal limitation of associationism. In T. R. Dixon & D. L. Horton (Eds.), *Verbal behavior and general behavior theory*. Englewood Cliffs, N.J.: Prentice-Hall.

Bewley, B. R., Bland, J. J., & Harris, R. (1974). Factors associated with the starting of cigarette smoking by primary school children. *British Journal of Preventive and Social Medicine, 28*(1), 37–44.

Bexton, W. H., Heron, W., & Scott, T. H. (1956). Effects of decreased variation in the sensory environment. *Canadian Journal of Psychology, 10*, 13–18.

Bhawuk, D. P. S. (1990). Cross-cultural orientation programs. In R. Brislin. (Ed.), *Applied cross-cultural psychology* (pp. 325–346). Newbury Park, CA: Sage.

Bhise, V. D., & Rinalducci, E. J. (1981). Special issues preface. *Human Factors, 23*, 385–386.

Biäsch, H., & Fischer, H. (1969/1939). *Testreihen zur Prüfung yon Schweizerkindern vom 14.-15. Schuljahr*. Bern: Huber.

Bick, W., Müller, P. J., Bauer, H., & Gieseke, O. (1977). *Multidimensional scaling and clustering techniques (theory and applications in the social sciences). A bibliography*. Cologne, West Germany: University of Cologne.

Bickersteth, P., & Das, J. (1981). Syllogistic reasoning among school children from Canada and Sierra Leone. *International Journal of Psychology, 16*, 1–11.

Bickerton, D. (1982). *Roots of language*. Ann Arbor, Mich.: Karoma.

Bickman, L. (1974). Social roles and uniforms: Clothes make the person. *Psychology Today, 7*(11), 48–57.

Biddle, B. J., & Thomas, E. J. (1966). *Role theory: Concepts and research*. New York: Wiley.

Biderman, A. D., & Zimmer, H. (1961). *The manipulations of human behavior*, New York: Wiley.

Bieber, E., et al. (1962). *Homosexuality: A psychoanalytic study*. New York: Basic Books.

Bierer, J. (1964). The Malborough experiment. In L. Bellack (Ed.), *Handbook of community psychiatry and community mental health*. New York: Grune & Stratton.

Bieri, J. (1955). Cognitive complexity-simplicity and predictive behavior. *Journal of Abnormal and Social Psychology, 51*, 263–268.

Bieri, J., Atkins, A. L., Briar, S., Leaman, R. L., Miller, H., & Tripodi, T. (1966). *Clinical and social judgment*. New York: Wiley.

Bierman, E. L., & Hazzard, W. R. (1973). Biology of aging. In D. Smith & E. Bierman (Eds.), *The biologic ages of man*. Philadelphia, Pa.: Saunders.

Bierman, K. L., Miller, C. L., & Stabb, S. D. (1987). Improving the social behavior and peer acceptance of rejected boys: Effects of social skills training with instructions and prohibitions. *Journal of Consulting and Clinical Psychology, 55*, 194–200.

Biesheuvel, S. (1943). *African intelligence*. Johannesburg: South African Institute of Race Relations.

Biesheuvel, S. (1952). Personnel selection tests for Africans. *South African Journal of Science, 49*, 3–12.

Biesheuvel, S. (1952). The occupational abilities of Africans. *Optima, 2*, 18–22.

Biesheuvel, S. (1955). Incentives and human relations in industry. *Industrial Review of Africa, 2*, 1–7.

Biesheuvel, S. (1958). Objectives and methods of African psychological research. *Journal of Social Psychology, 47* 161–168.

Biesheuvel, S. (1959). Further studies on the measurement of attitudes towards western ethical concepts. *Journal of the National Institute of Personnel Research, 7*, 141–155.

Biesheuvel, S. (1959). *Race, culture and personality*. Johannesburg: South African Institute of Race Relations.

Biesheuvel, S. (1959). *The development of personality in African cultures*. Lagos: Commission for Technical Cooperation in Africa, South of the Sahara.

Biesheuvel, S. (1969). *Methods for the measurement of psychological performance* (IBP Handbook no. 10). Oxford: Blackwell.

Biesheuvel, S. (1972). African culture patterns and the learning of abilities and skills. In S. H. Irvine & J. T. Sanders (Eds.), *Cultural adaptation within modern Africa*. New York: Columbia University Teachers College Press.

Biesheuvel, S. (1976). South Africa. In H. Misiak & V. S. Sexton (Eds.), *Psychology around the world today*. Monterey, Calif.: Brooks/Cole.

Biesheuvel, S. (1979). The development of psychomotor skills: Cross-cultural and occupational implications. *Journal of Cross-cultural Psychology, 10*(3), 271–294.

Bigelow, A. (1991). Blindness interfered with development of spatial knowledge. *Journal of Visual Implairment and Blindness, 85,* 113–117.

Biggs, J. B. (1978). Individual and group differences in study processes. *British Journal of Educational Psychology, 48,* 266–279.

Biggs, J. B. (1979). Individual differences in study processes and the quality of learning outcomes. *Higher Education, 8,* 381–394.

Biggs, J. B. (1982). The SOLO-taxonomy: An applied learning theory. Presented at the British Psychological Society's annual conference, April 1–5, York, England.

Biggs, J. B., & Coilis, K. F. (1982). *Evaluating the quality of learning. The SOLO-taxonomy.* New York: Academic Press.

Bijou, S. W., & Orlando, R. (1961). Rapid development of multiple-schedule performances with retarded children. *Journal of Experimental Analysis of Behavior, 4,* 7–16.

Bijou, S. W., & Ribes-Inesta, E. (1972). *Behavior modification: Issues and extensions.* New York: Academic Press.

Biles, D. (1971). Birth order and delinquency. *Australian Psychologist, 6,* 189–193.

Biller, H. B. (1968). A multiaspect investigation of masculine development in kindergarten age boys. *Genetic Psychology Monographs, 78,* 89–138.

Biller, H. B. (1969). Father absence, maternal encouragement and sex role development in kindergarten age boys. *Child Development, 40,* 539–546.

Biller, H. B.(1970). Father absence and the personality development of the male child. *Developmental Psychology, 2,* 181–201.

Billig, M. (1976). *Social psychology and intergroup relations.* London: Academic Press.

Billig, M. (1987). *Arguing and thinking: A rhetorical approach to social psychology.* Cambridge, UK: Cambridge University Press.

Billings, A. G., & Moos, R. H. (1981) The role of copying responses and social resources in attenuating the stress of life events. *Journal of Behavorial Medicine, 4,* 139–157.

Billings, A. G., & Moos, R. H. (1982). Social support and functioning among community and clinical groups: A panel model. *Journal of Behavorial Medicine, 5,* 295–311.

Billingslea, F. Y. (1946). The Bender Gestalt: An objective scoring method and validating data. *Journal of Clinical Psychology Monograph* (no. 1).

Bilmes, J., & Boggs, S. (1979). Language and communication: The foundations of culture. In A. Marsella, R. Tharp, & T. Ciborowski (Eds.), *Perspectives on cross-cultural psychology.* New York: Academic Press.

Bilotta, J., & Lindauer, M. S. (1980). Artistic and nonartistic backgrounds as determinants of the cognitive response to the arts. *Bulletin of the Psychonomic Society, 15,* 354–356.

Bilu, Y., Witztum, E., Vanderhart, O. (1990). Paradise regained: Miraculous healing: an Israeli psychiatric clinic. *Culture, Medicine and Psychiatry, 14* (1), 105–127.

Binder, J. L., & Smokler, I. (1980). Early memories: A technical aid to focusing in time-limited dynamic psychotherapy. *Psychotherapy: Theory, Research and Practice, 17,* 52–62.

Binder, V., Binder, A., & Rimland, B., (Eds.). (1976). *Modern therapies.* Englewood Cliffs, N.J.: Prentice-Hall.

Bindman, A. J. (1966). The clinical psychologist as a mental health consultant. In L. E. Abt & B. J. Reiss (Eds.), *Progress in clinical psychology.* New York: Grune & Stratton.

Bindrim, P. (1968). A report on a nude marathon: The effect of physical nudity upon the practice interaction in the marathon group. *Psychotherapy: Theory, Research, and Practice, 5,* 180–188.

Bindrim, P. (1972). Nudity a quick grab for intimacy in group therapy. In *Readings in psychology today* (2nd ed.). Del Mar, Calif.: CRM Books.

Bindrim, P. (1975). Outcome research and analysis of the nude marathon as an application of Reichian concepts to group therapy. Doctoral dissertation, International College, Los Angeles, Calif.

Bindrim, P. (1981). *Aqua-Energetics.* In R. J. Corsini (Ed.), *Handbook of innovative psychotherapies.* New York: Wiley.

Binet, A. (1986). *Psychology of prestidigitation* (Annual Report of the Board of Regents of the Smithsonian Institution, 555–571). Washington, DC: U. S. Government Printing Office.

Binet, A., & Henri, V. (1895). La psychologie individuelle. *Année psychologique, 2,* 411–463.

Binet, A., & Henri, V. (1908). La psychologie individuale. *Année psychologique, 4,* 1–14.

Binet, A., & Simon, T. (1905). Application des methodes nouvelles au diagnostic intellectual chez des enfants normal et anormaux d'hospice et d'école primitive. *Année psychologique, 11,* 245–336.

Binet, A., & Simon, T. (1905). Méthodes nouvelles pour le diagnostic du niveau intellectuel des anormaux. *L'Année Psychologique, 11,* 191–244.

Binet, A., & Simon, T. (1908). Le development de l'intelligence chez les infants. *Année psychologique, 14,* 1–90, 245–366.

Binet, A., & Simon, (1915). T. *A method of measuring the development of intelligence of young children.* Chicago: Medical Books.

Bingham, J., & Piotrowski, C. (1989). House arrest: A viable alternative for sex offenders? *Psychological Reports, 65,* 559–562.

Bingham, W. V. (1910). Educational psychology at the Boston meeting of the American Association for the Advancement of Science. *Journal of Educational Psychology, 1,* 159–167.

Bingham, W. V. (1942/1937). *Aptitudes and aptitude testing.* New York: Harper.

Bingham, W. V., & Moore, B. V. (1931). *How to interview.* New York: Harper.

Bingham, W. V. D. (1968/1952). Autobiography. In E. G. Boring (Ed.), A history of psychology in autobiography, Vol. IV. New York: Russell & Russell.

Bingol, N., Schuster, C., Fuchs, M., Iosub, S., Turner, G., Stone, R. K., & Gromisch, D. S. (1987). The influence of socioeconomic factors on the occurrence of fetal alcohol syndrome. *Advances in Alcohol and Substance Abuse, 6*(4), 105–118.

Binkin, M., & Bach, S. J. (1977). *Women and the military.* Washington, D.C.: Brookings Institution.

Binstock, R. H., & Post, S. G. (Eds.). (1991). *Too old for health care? Controversies in medicine, law, economics, and ethics.* Baltimore: Johns Hopkins University Press.

Binstock, R. H., & Shams, E. (Eds.) (1976). *Handbook of aging and the social sciences.* New York: Van Nostrand Reinhold.

Binswanger, L. (1953). *Grundformen und Erkenntnis menschlichen Daseins.* Zurich: Niehaus.

Binswanger, L. (1958). The existential analysis school of thought. In R. May, E. Angel, & H. F. Ellenberger (Eds.), *Existence.* New York: Basic Books.

Binswanger, L. (1963). *Being-in-the-world: Selected papers of Ludwig Binswanger* (J. Needleman, Trans.). New York: Basic Books, 1963.

Binswanger, L. (1973). *Being-in-the world: Selected papers of Ludwig Binswanger,* New York: Basic Books.

Bion, W. R. (1952). Group dynamics: A re-view. *International Journal of Psychoanalysis, 33,* 235–247.

Bion, W. R. (1961). *Experiences in groups, and other papers.* London: Tavistock Publications.

Bion, W. R. (1961). *Experiences in groups.* New York: Basic Books.

Birch, H. G. (1945). The relation of previous experience to insignificant problem-solving. *Journal of Comparative Psychology, 38,* 367–383.

Birch, H. G. (1956). Sources of order in the maternal behavior of animals. *American Journal of Orthopsychiatry, 26,* 279–284.

Birch, H. G. (Ed.). (1964). *Brain damage in children.* Baltimore, Md.: Williams & Wilkins.

Birchwood, M. (1986). Control of auditory hallucinations through occlusion of monaural auditory input. *British Journal of Psychiatry, 149,* 104–107.

Bird, C. (1933). Maturation and practice: Their effects on the feeding reaction of chickens. *Journal of Comparative Psychology, 16,* 343–363.

Birdwhistell, R. L. (1952). *Introduction to kinesics.* Louisville, Ky.: University of Louisville Press.

Birdwhistell, R. L. (1968). Kinesics. In D. Sills (Ed.), *International encyclopedia of the social sciences,* Vol. VIII. New York: Macmillan.

Birdwhistell, R. L. (1970). *Kinesics and context.* Philadelphia, Pa.: University of Pennsylvania Press.

Birk, L. (1973). (Ed.). *Biofeedback: Behavioral medicine.* New York: Grune & Stratton.

Birkhuff, G. D. (1933). *Aesthetic measure.* Cambridge, Mass.: Harvard University Press.

Birnbaum, M. (1960). The right to treatment. *American Bar Association Journal 46,* 499.

Birren, J. E., Kinney, D. K., Sehaie, K. W., & Woodruff, D. S. (1981). *Developmental psychology: A life-span approach.* Boston: Houghton Mifflin.

Birren, J. E., & Sehaie, K. W. (Eds.). (1977). *Handbook of the psychology of aging.* New York: Van Nostrand Reinhold.

Birren, J. E., & Schaie, K. W. (Eds.). (1990). *Handbook of the psychology of aging.* New York: Van Nostrand Reinhold. (Other editions published in 1977 and 1985).

Birren, J. E., & Sloane, R. B. (Eds.). (1980). *Handbook of mental health and aging.* Englewood Cliffs, N. J.: Prentice-Hall.

Birtchenell, J., & Mayhew, J. (1977). Toman's theory: Tested for mate selection and friendship formation. *Journal of Individual Psychology, 33*(1), 18–36.

Birth defects. White Plains, N.Y.: The National Foundation-March of Dimes.

Bischehof, N. (1966). Psychophysik der Raumwahrnehmung. In W. Metzger & H. Erkle (Eds.), *Handbuch der Psychologie,* Vol. I/I. Göttingen, West Germany.

Bischof, L. (1964). *Interpreting personality theories.* New York: Harper & Row.

Bishnay, N. R., Peterson, N., Tarrier, N. (1989). An uncontrolled study of cognitive therapy for morbid jealousy. *British Journal of Psychiatry, 154,* 386–389.

Bisiach, E., Rusconi, M. L., & Vallar, G. (1991). Remission of somatoparaphrenic delusion through vestibular stimulation. *Neuropsychologia, 29*(10), 1029–1031.

Bissell, J. S. (1973). The cognitive effects of preschool programs for disadvantaged children. In J. L. Frost (Ed.), *Revisiting early childhood education-readings.* New York: Holt, Rinehart & Winston.

Bistline, J. L., Jaremko, M. E., & Sobleman, S. (1980). The relative contributions of covert reinforcement and cognitive restructuring to test anxiety reduction. *Journal of Clinical Psychology, 36,* 723–728.

Bitterman, M. E. (1965). Phyletic differences in learning. *American Psychologist, 20,* 396–410.

Bitterman, M. E. (1975). The comparative analysis of learning. *Science, 188,* 699–709.

Bittner, E., & Messinger, S. L. (1980). *Criminology review yearbook,* Vol. II. Beverly Hills, Calif.: Sage Publications.

Bjork, R., & Druckman, D. (1991). How do you improve human performance? *American Psychological Society Observer, 4,* 13–15.

Blachor-Dixon, J. (1979). Preschool mainstreaming: Current state of the art. Presented at the 57th Annual International Council for Exceptional Children Convention, Dallas, April 22–27, ED 171087, EC 115296.

Black, B. L., Humphrey, J. H., & Niven, J. S. (1963). Inihibition of mantoux reaction by direct suggestion under hypnosis. *British Medical Journal, 6,* 1649–1652.

Black, D. (1970). Production of crime roles. *American Sociological Review, 35,* 733–748.

Black, D. (1971). The social organization of arrest. *Stanford Law Review, 23,* 1087–1111.

Black, D. (1972). The boundaries of legal sociology. *Yale Law Journal, 81,* 1086–1100.

Black, D. (1973). The mobilization of law. *Journal of Legal Studies, 2,* 125–149.

Black, D. (1976). *The behavior of law.* New York: Academic Press.

Black, D. (1979). A strategy of pure sociology. In S. G. McNall (Ed.), *Theoretical perspectives in sociology.* (pp. 149–168). New York: St. Martin's.

Black, D. (1979). Common sense in the sociology of law. *American Sociological Review, 44,* 18–27.

Black, D. (1980). *The manners and customs of the police,* New York: Academic Press.

Black, D. (1983). Crime as social control. *American Sociological Review, 48,* 34–45. [Enlarged: (1984). In D. Black (Ed.), Toward a general theory of social control: Vol. 2. Selected problems (pp. 1–27). Orlando, FL: Academic Press]

Black, D. (1984). Social control as a dependent variable. In D. Black (Ed.), *Toward a General Theory of Social Control: Vol. 1. Fundamentals* (pp. 1–36). Orlando, FL: Academic Press.

Black, D. (1985). *An interview with Donald Black on* The Behavior of Law. Helsinki: University of Helsinki Language Center.

Black, D. (1987). Compensation and the social structure of misfortune. *Law and Society Review, 21,* 563–584.

Black, D. (1989). *Sociological justice.* New York: Oxford University Press.

Black, D. (1990). The elementary forms of conflict management. In School of Justice Studies, Arizona State University (Ed.), *New Directions in the Study of Justice, Law, and Social Control* (pp. 43–69). New York: Plenum Press.

Black, D. (1992). Social control of the self. In *J. Virginia Review of Sociology: Vol. 1. Law and Conflict Management* Tucker (Ed.). (pp. 39–49). Greenwich: JAI Press

Black, D. (1993). *The social structure of right and wrong.* San Diego: Academic Press.

Black, D., & A. J. Reiss, Jr. (1970). Police control of juveniles. *American Sociological Review, 35,* 63–77.

Black, D., & Baumgartner, M. P. (1983). Toward a theory of the third party. In K. O. Boyum & L. Mather (Eds.), *Empirical theories about courts* (pp. 84–114). New York: Longman.

Black, D. (Ed.). (1984). *Toward a general theory of social control: Vol. 1, Fundamentals; Vol. 2, Selected Problems.* Orlando, FL: Academic Press.

Black, D., & M. Mileski. (1972). The social organization of homosexuality. *Urban Life and Culture, 1,* 187–202.

Black, D., & M. Mileski, (Eds.). (1973). *The social organization of law.* New York: Academic Press.

Black, F. (1974). The word explosion in learning disabilities: A notation of literature trends 1962–72. *Journal of Learning Disabilities, 7,* 323–325.

Black, F. (1976). Cognitive, academic, and behavioral findings in children with suspected and documented neurological dysfunction. *Journal of Learning Disabilities, 9,* 182–187.

Black, R. R., & Mouton, J. S. (1976). Strategies of consultation. In W. G. Bennis, K. O. Benne, R. Chin, & K. E. Corey (Eds.), *The planning of change* (pp. 48–68). New York: Holt, Rinehart, & Winston.

Blackburn, J., & Papalia, D. (1988). Modifiability of fluid intelligence: A comparison of two training approaches. *Journal of Gerontology, 43,* 87–89.

Blackford, R. C. & LaRue, A. (1989). Criteria for diagnosing age associated memory impairment: Proposed, improvements from the field. *Developmental Neuropsychology, 5,* 295–306.

Blackman, J. A. (1990). Update on AIDS, CMV, and herpes in young children: Health, developmental, and educational issues. In M. Wolraich & D. K. Routh (Eds.), *Advances in developmental and behavioral pediatrics* (Vol. 9, pp. 33–58). London: Kingsley.

Blackmore, S. (1980). The extent of selective reporting on ESP ganzfeld studies. *European Journal of Parapsychology, 3,* 213–219.

Blainey, G. N. (1966). *The tyranny of distance.* Melbourne, Australia: Sun Books.

Blair, G. M. (1941). The vocabulary of educational psychology. *Journal of Educational Psychology, 32,* 365–371.

Blair, G. M. (1949). The content of educational psychology. *Journal of Educational Psychology, 40,* 267–273.

Blake, R. R., & Dinnis, W. (1943). The development of stereotypes concerning the Negro. *Journal of Abnormal and Social Psychology, 38,* 525–531.

Blake, R. R., & Moaton, J. S. (1961). *Group dynamics: Key to decision making.* Houston, Tex.: Gull.

Blake, R. R., & Mouton, J. S. (1964). *The managerial grid.* Houston, Tex.: Gulf.

Blake, R. R., & Mouton, J. S. (1975). *Synergogy: An instrumented team learning approach.* Austin, Tex.: Scientific Methods.

Blake, R. R., & Mouton, J. S. (1975). *The grid for supervisory effectiveness.* Austin, Tex.: Scientific Methods.

Blake, R. R., & Mouton, J. S. (1976). *Consultation.* Reading, Mass.: Addison-Wesley, 1976.

Blake, R. R., & Mouton, J. S. (1978). *The new managerial grid.* Houston, Tex.: Gulf.

Blake, R. R., & Mouton, J. S. (1980). *Guideposts for effective salesmanship.* New York: Playboy Paperbacks.

Blake, R. R., & Ramsey, G. V. (1951). *Perception: An approach to personality.* New York: Ronald Press.

Blakely, C., & Davidson, W. S. (1981). Prevention of aggression. In A. P. Goldstein, E. G. Carr, W. S. Davidson & P. Wehr (Eds.), *In response to aggression.* New York: Pergamon Press.

Blakeslee, T. R. (1980). *The right brain.* Garden City, N.Y.: Anchor Press/Doubleday.

Blakey, G. R. (1979). State conducted lotteries: History, problems, and promises. *Journal of Social Issue, 35,* 62–86.

Blalock, H. M., Jr. (Ed.). (1985b). *Causal models in panel and experimental designs.* New York: Aldine.

Blalock, H. M., Jr. & Wilken, P. (1979). *Intergroup processes: A Micromacro perspective,* New York: Free Press.

Blanchard, E. B., & Young, L. D. (1974). Clinical applications of biofeedback training: A review of evidence. *Archives of General Psychology, 30,* 573–789.

Blanchard, E. G. (1982). Behavorial medicine: Past, present and future. *Journal of Consulting and Clinical Psychology, 50,* 795–796.

Blanchard, W. H. (1969). Psychodynamic aspects of the peak experience. *Psychoanalytic Review, 56,* 87–112.

Blanck, G., & Blanck, R. (1974). *Ego psychology: Theory and practice.* New York: Columbia University Press.

Blanck, G. & Blanck, R. (1979), *Ego Psychology: Theory and practice.* New York: Columbia University Press.

Blane, H. T. (1977). Psychotherapeutic approach. In B. Kissin & H. Begleiter (Eds.), *The biology of alcoholism.* Vol. 5, *Treatment and rehabilitation of the chronic alcoholic.* New York: Plenum.

Blane, H. T., & Barry, H., III. (1973). *Quarterly Journal of Studies on Alcohol, 34*(3, pt. A), 837–852.

Blaney, P. H. (1986). Affect and memory: A review. *Psychological Bulletin, 22,* 229–246.

Blank, L. (1964). Clinical psychology training, 1945–1962: Conferences and issues. In L. Blank & H. P. David (Eds.), *Sourcebook for training in clinical psychology.* New York: Springer.

Blanton, S. (1960). *The healing power of poetry.* New York: Crowell.

Blanz, F., & Ghiselli, E. E. (1972). The mixed standard scale: A new rating system. *Personnel Psychology, 25,* 185–199.

Blashfield, R. K., & Draguns, J. G. (1976). Evaluative criteria for psychiatric classification. *Journal of Abnormal Psychology, 85,* 140—150.

Blasi, A. (1980). Bridging moral cognition and moral action: A critical review of the literature. *Psychological Bulletin, 88,* 1–45.

Blasi, G. L. (1990). Social policy and social science research on homelessness. *Journal of Social Issues, 46,* 207–219.

Blasingame, M. C., Schneider, K. R., & Hawk, D. L. (1981). *Performance appraisal bibliography of recent publications: 1981 edition.* Greensboro, N. C.: Center for Creative Leadership, Special Report.

Blass, E. M., & Teicher, M. H. (1980). Suckling. *Science, 210,* 15–22.

Blass, T. (1977). On personality variables, situations, and social behavior. In T. Blass (Ed.), *Personality variables in social behavior.* Hillsdale, N.J.: Erlbaum.

Blass, T. (1991). Understanding behavior in the Milgram obedience experiment: The role of personality, situations and their interactions. *Journal of Personality and Social Psychology, 60,* 398–413.

Blass, T. (1992). The social psychology of Stanley Milgram. In M. P. Zanna (Ed.), *Advances in experimental social psychology* (Vol. 25, pp. 277–329). San Diego, CA: Academic Press.

Blass, T. (Chair). (1990, August 13). Perspectives on Stanley Milgram's contributions to social psychology. Symposium conducted at the annual meeting of the American Psychological Association, Boston.

Blaszczynski, A., McConoghy, N., & Frankova, A. (1990). Boredom proneness in pathological gambling, *Psychological Reports, 67,* 35–42.

Blatner, H. A. (1973). *Acting-in: Practical applications of psychodramatic methods.* New York: Springer.

Blau, P. M. (1964). *Exchange and power in social life.* New York: Wiley.

Blau, P. M., Gastad, J. W., Jessor, R., Parnes, H. S., & Wilcock, R. C. (1956). Occupational choice: A conceptual framework. *Industrial and Labor Relations Review, 9,* 531–543.

Blau, T. (1993). *Police psychology: Behavioral science services for law enforcement.* New York: Wiley.

Blau, T. H. (1950). Report on a method of predicting success in psychotherapy. *Journal Of Clinical Psychology, 6,* 403–406.

Blau, T. H. (1955). The sucking reflex: The effects of long feeding vs. short feeding on the behavior of a human infant. *Journal of Abnormal and Social Psychology, 51,* 123–126.

Blau, T. H. (1959). *Private practice in clinical psychology.* New York: Appleton-Century-Crofts.

Blau, T. H. (1972). The love effect. In H. Otto (Ed.), *Love today: A new exploration.* New York: Association Press.

Blau, T. H. (1977). Quality of life, social indicators and criteria of change. *Professional Psychology, 8*(4), 464–473.

Blau, T. H. (1977). The sinister child. *JSAS Journal of Selected Documents in Psychology, 7,* ms. no. 1595.

Blau, T. H. (1977). The Torque Test. Standardization manual. *Journal of Selected Documents in Psychology, 1,* ms. no. 1431.

Blau, T. H. (1977). Torque and schizophrenic vulnerability. *American Psychologist, 32*(12), 997–1005.

Blau, T. H. (1979). Diagnosis of disturbed children. *American Psychologist. 34,* 10.

Blau, T. H. (1979). Minimum competency testing: Psychological implications for students. In R. M. Jaeger & C. K. Tittle (Eds.), *Minimum competency achievement testing.* Berkeley, Calif.: McCutchan.

Blau, T. H. (1982). Roles and professional practice. In M. Hersen, A. E. Kazdin, & A. S. Bellack (Eds.), *The clinical psychology handbook.* Elmsford, N.Y.: Pergamon Press.

Blau, T. H., & Schaffer, R. E. (1960). The spiral aftereffect test (SAET) as a predictor of normal and abnormal electroencephalographic records in children. *Journal of Consulting Psychology, 24,* 35–43.

Blauner, R. (1964). *Alienation and freedom.* Chicago: University of Chicago Press.

Blechman, E. A. (1985). *Solving child behavior problems at home and at school.* Champaign, IL: Research Press.

Blehar, M. (1980). *Development of mental health in infancy.* Washington, D.C.: U.S. Government Printing Office, NIMH Science Monograph 3.

Blehar, M., & Rosenthal, N. (1989). Seasonal affective disorders and phototherapy. *Archives of General Psychiatry, 46,* 469–474.

Bleick, C. R., & Abrams, A. I. (1987). The Transcendental Meditation program and criminal recidivism in California. *Journal of Criminal Justice, 15*(3), 211–230.

Bleuler, E. (1912/1906). *Affectivity, suggestibility, paranoia.* Utica, N.Y.: State Hospitals Press.

Bleuler, E. (1924/1916). *Textbook of psychiatry.* New York: Macmillan.

Bleuler, E. (1932). *Naturgeschichte der Seek und ihres Bewusstwerdens.* Berlin: Springer.

Bleuler, E. (1950/1911). *Dementia praecox:* Or the group of schizophrenias. (J. Zinkin, Trans.). New York: International Universities Press.

Bleuler, M. (1954). *Endokrinologische Psychiatrie.* Stuttgart, West Germany: Thieme.

Blewett, D. B. (1954). Experimental study of the inheritance of intelligence. *Journal of Mental Science, 100,* 922–933.

Bliss, S. A. (1916). The significance of clothes. *American Journal of Psychology, 27,* 217–226.

Bliss, T. V. P., Douglas, R. M., Errington, M. L., & Lynch, M. A. (1986). Correlation between long-term potentiation and release of endogenous amino acids from dentate gyrus of anesthetized rats. *Journal of Physiology, 377,* 391–408.

Bliss, T. V. P., & Lomo, T. (1973). Long-lasting potentiation of synaptic transmission in the dentate area of anesthetized rabbit following stimulation of the perforant path. *Journal of Physiology, 232,* 331–356.

Bliss, W. D. (1970). Birth order of creative writers. *Journal of Individual Psychology, 26,* 200–202.

Bloch, D. (1974). Fantasy and the fear of infanticide. *Psychoanalytic Review, 61,* 5–31.

Bloch, G. J. (1980). *Mesmerism: A translation of the original medical and scientific writings of F. A. Mesmer, M. D.* Los Altos, Calif.: Kaufmann.

Bloch, I. (1908). *The sexual life of our time.* New York: Rebman.

Blocher, D. H. (1974/1966). *Developmental counseling* (2nd ed.). New York: Ronald Press.

Block, C. B. (1981). Black Americans and the cross-cultural counseling and psychotherapy experience. In A. J. Marsella, & P. B. Pederson (Eds.), *Cross-cultural counseling and psychotherapy.* New York: Pergamon Press.

Block, J. (1961). *The Q-sort method in personality assessment and psychiatric research.* Springfield, Ill.: Thomas.

Block, J. (1965). *The challenge of response sets.* New York: Appleton-Century-Crofts.

Block, J. (1981). Some enduring and consequential structures of personality. In A. I. Rabin (Ed.), *Further explorations in personality.* New York: Wiley.

Block, J. H. (1972). Generational continuity and discontinuity in the understanding of societal rejection. *Journal of Personality and Social Psychology, 22,* 333–345.

Block, J. H. (1973). Conceptions of sex role: Some cross-cultural and longitudinal perspectives. *American Psychologist, 28,* 512–526.

Block, J. H. (1976). Debatable conclusions about sex differences (Review of *The psychology of sex differences* by E. E. Maccoby & C. N. Jacklin). *Contemporary Psychology, 21,* 517–522.

Block, J. H. (1976). Issues, problems, and pitfalls in assessing sex differences: A critical review of the psychology of sex differences. *Merrill-Palmer Quarterly, 22,* 283–308.

Block, J. H. (1978). Another look at sex differentiation in the socialization behaviors of mothers and fathers. In J. Sherman & F. Denmark (Eds.), *Psychology of women: Future directions of research.* New York: Psychological Dimensions.

Block, J. H., & Burns, R. B. (1976). Mastery learning. *Review of Research in Education, 4,* 3–49.

Block, N. (Ed.). (1981). *Imagery.* Cambridge, Mass.: M.I.T. Press.

Block, R. (1981). Victim-offender dynamics in violent crime. In *Victims of crime, A review of research issues and methods.* Washington, DC: National Institute of Justice.

Blocker, H. (1969). Physiognomic perception. *Philosophy and Phenomenological Research, 29.* 377–390.

Blodgett, H. C. (1929). The effect of the introduction of reward upon the maze performance of rats. *University of California Publications in Psychology, 4,* 113–134.

Blomberg, M. (1989). AIDS: Analyzing a new dimension in rape victimization. *Justice Professional, 4,* 189–206.

Blomberg, M. (in press). Needle and syringe exchange programs: An examination of the empirical evidence. *Criminal Justice Journal.*

Blomberg, M. (in press). The transmission of FHV: Exploring some misconceptions related to criminal justice. *Criminal Justice Policy Review.*

Blondel, A., & Rey, J. (1911). Sur la perception des lumières breves à la limite de leur portée *Journal de Physiologie, 1,* 530–550.

Blonskii, P. (1920). *Reforma Nauki.* Moscow: Izdotdnarpros.

Blonskii, P. (1964). *Izbrannye Psikhologicheskie Proizvedenija.* Moscow: Prosveschenie.

Blonskii, P. (1973). *Die Arbeitsschule.* Paderborn: Schonigh.

Blonskii, P. (1979). *Izbrannye Pedagogicheskie i Psikhologicheskie Sochinenija.* Moscow: Pedagogika.

Blood, M. R. (1974). Spin-offs from behavior expectation scale procedures. *Journal of Applied Psychology, 59,* 513–515.

Blood, M. R., & Hulin, C. L. (1967). Alienation, environmental characteristics, and worker responses. *Journal of Applied Psychology, 51,* 284–290.

Bloom, B. L. (1975). *Community mental health: A general introduction.* Belmont, Calif.: Wadsworth.

Bloom, B. L. (1992). *Planned short-term psychotherapy,* Boston: Allyn & Bacon.

Bloom, B. L., Hodges, W. F., Kern, M. B., & McFaddin, S. C. (1985). A prevention program for the newly separated: Final evaluations. American Journal of Orthopsychiatry, 55, 9–26.

Bloom, B. S. (1974). Time and learning. *American Psychologist, 29,* 682–688.

Bloom, B. S. (1976). *Human characteristics and school learning.* New York: McGraw-Hill.

Bloom, B. S. (Ed.). (1956). *Taxonomy of educational objectives. Handbook 1: Cognitive domain.* New York: Lougman, Green.

Bloom, B. S., Hastings, J. T., & Madaus, G. F. (Eds.). (1971). *Handbook of formative and summative evaluation of student learning.* New York: McGraw-Hill.

Bloom, F. E. (1977). Neural mechanisms of benzodiazepine actions. *American Journal of Psychiatry, 134,* 669–672.

Bloom, H. (1973). *The anxiety of influence.* New York: Oxford University Press.

Bloom, H. (1976). *Poetry and repression.* New Haven, Conn.: Yale University Press.

Bloom, H, de Man, P., Derrida, J., Hartman, G., & Miller, J. H. (1979). *Deconstruction and criticism.* New York: Seabury.

Bloom, L. (1970). *Language development: Form and functions in emerging grammars.* Cambridge, Mass.: M.I.T. Press, Research Monograph 59.

Bloom, L., Houston, B. K., Holmes, D. S., & Burish, T. (1977). The effectiveness of attentional diversion and situation redefinition for reducing stress due to a nonambiguous threat. *Journal of Research in Personality, 11,* 83–94.

Bloom, L., & Mudd, S. (1991). Depth of processing approach to face recognition: A test of two theories. *Journal of Experimental Psychology: Learning, Memory, and Cognition, 17,* 556–565.

Bloom, M. V. (1980). *Adolescent parental separation.* New York: Gardner Press.

Bloombaum, M. (1968). The conditions underlying race riots as portrayed by multidimensional scalogram analysis: A reanalysis of Lieberson and Silverman's data. *American Sociological Review, 33,* 76–91.

Bloomfield, H. H., Cain, M. P., & Jaffe, D. T. (1975). *TM, discovering inner energy and overcoming stress.* New York: Delacorte Press.

Bloomfield, T. M. (1969). Behavioral contrast and the peak shift. In R. M. Gilbert & N. S. Sutherland (Eds.), *Animal discrimination learning.* London: Academic Press.

Blouin, B. A., Bornstein, R. A., & Trites, R. L. (1978). Teenage alcohol use among hyperactive children: A five year follow-up study. *Journal of Pediatric Psychology, 3,* 188–194.

Bloxom, B. (1968). Individual differences in multidimensional scaling. *Research Bulletin 68–45.* Princeton, N.J.: Educational Testing Service.

Blum, G. S. (1949). A study of the psychoanalytic theory of psychosexual development. *Genetic Psychology Monographs, 39,* 3–99.

Blum, G. S. (1950). *The Blacky pictures: A technique for the exploration of personality dynamics.* Ann Arbor, Mich.: Psychodynamic Instruments.

Blum, G. S. (1961). *A model of the mind.* New York: Wiley.

Blum, G. S. (1967). Hypnosis in psychodynamic research. In J. E. Gordon (Ed.), *Handbook of clinical and experimental hypnosis.* New York: Macmillan.

Blum, G. S. (1968). Assessment of psychodynamic variables by the Blacky pictures. In P. McReynolds (Ed.), *Advances in psychological assessment,* Vol. 1. Palo Alto, Calif.: Science & Behavior Books.

Blum, G. S. (1979). Hypnotic programming techniques in psychological experiments. In E. Fromm & R. E. Shor (Eds.), *Hypnosis: Developments in research and new perspectives.* New York: Aldine.

Blum, G. S., & Barbour, J. S. (1979). Selective inattention to anxiety-linked stimuli. *Journal of Experimental Psychology: General 108,* 182–224.

Blum, G. S., Graef, J. R., & Hauenstein, L. S. (1968). Overcoming interference in short-term memory through distinctive mental contexts. *Psychonomic Science, 11,* 73–74.

Blum, G. S., Graef, J. R., Hauenstein, L. S., & Passini, F. T. (1971). Distinctive mental contexts in long-term memory. *International Journal of Clinical and Experimental Hypnosis,* 117–133.

Blum, K., & Manzo, L. (Eds.). (1985). *Neurotoxicology.* New York: Marcel Dekker.

Blum, M. L. (1949). *Industrial psychology and its social foundations.* New York: Harper.

Blum, M. L., & Appel, V. (1961). Consumer versus management reaction in new package development. *Journal of Applied Psychology, 45,* 222–224.

Blumberg, E. S. (1979). *Criminal justice.* New York: New Viewpoints.

Blumberg, M. (1977). Treatment of the abused child and the child abuser. *American Journal of Psychotherapy, 31,* 204—215.

Blumberg, M. (1989). Issues and controversies with respect to the management of AIDS in corrections. *The Prison Journal, 69,* 1–13.

Blumberg, M. (1989). Transmission of the AIDS virus through criminal activity. *Criminal Law Bulletin, 25,* 454–465.

Blumberg, M. (1990). *AIDS: The impact on the criminal justice system.* Columbus, OH: Merrill.

Blumberg, M., & D. Langston. (1991). HIV testing in criminal justice settings. *Crime and Delinquency, 37,* 5–18.

Blumenthal, A. L. (1975). A reappraisal of Wilhelm Wundt. *American Psychologist*, 30, 1081–1088.

Blumenthal, A. L. (1977). *The process of cognition*. Englewood Cliffs, N.J.: Prentice-Hall.

Blumenthal, M. (1976) Violence in America: Still viewed by many as a necessary tool for social order, social change. *Institute for Social Research Newsletter*, 4, 2–23.

Blumer, H. (1969). *Symbolic interactionism: Perspective and method*. Englewood Cliffs, N.J.: Prentice-Hall.

Blumer, H. (1978). Social unrest and collective protest. In N. K. Denzin (Ed.), *Studies in symbolic interaction*, Vol. I. Greenwich, Conn.: JAI Press.

Blumrosen, R. G. (1979). Wage discrimination, job segregation, and Title VII of the Civil Rights Act of 1964. *University of Michigan Journal of Law Reform*, 12, 397–502.

Blumstein, P. W., & Schwartz, P. (1976). Bisexuality in men. *Urban Life*, 5(3), 339–358.

Blumstein, P. W., & Schwartz, P. (1977). Bisexuality: Some social psychological issues. *Journal of Social Issues, 33*(2), 30–45.

Blumstein, P. W., & Schwartz, P. (1983). *American couples*. New York: William Morrow.

Blumstein, A., Cohen, J. M., Roth, J. A., & Visher, C. A. (Eds.). (1986). *Criminal careers and "career criminals."* Washington, DC: National Academy of Sciences.

Blyth, D. A., Simmons, R. G., & Bush, D. The transition into early adolescence: A longitudinal comparison of youth in two educational contexts. *Sociology of Education*, in press.

Boadella, D. (1973). Wilhelm Reich: *The evolution of his work*. London: Vision Press.

Boakes, R. A. (1979). Interactions between Type I and Type II processes involving positive reinforcement. In A. Dickinson & R. A. Boakes (Eds.), *Mechanisms of Learning and motivation: A memorial volume to Jerey Konorski*. Hillsdale, N.J.: Erlbaum.

Baokes, R. A. (1984). *From Darwin to behaviorism*. Cambridge, UK: Cambridge University Press.

Boakes, R. A., & Halliday, M. S. (1972). *Inhibition & learning*. London: Academic Press.

Board of Professional Affairs Task Force Report. (1981). Psychologists' use of physical interventions. Washington, DC: American Psychological Association.

Boas, F. (1955/1927). *Primitive art*. New York: Dover.

Boaz, J. T. (1988). *Delivering mental health care: A guide for HMO*. Chicago: Pluribus Press.

Bobertag, O. (1914). *Ueber Intelligenzpruefungen nach der Methode von Binet und Simon*. Leipzig: Barth.

Bock, R. D., & Jones, L. V. (1968). *The measurement and prediction of judgment and choice*. San Francisco, Cambridge, London, Amsterdam: Holden-Day.

Bockar, J. A. (1981). *Primer for the non-medical psychotherapist*. New York: Spectrum.

Bocknek, G. (1980). *The young adult*. Monterey, Calif.: Brooks/Cole.

Bockoven, J. S. (1956). Moral treatment in American psychiatry. *Journal Of Nervous and Mental Disease*, 124, 167–183.

Bockoven, J. S. (1963). *Moral treatment in American psychiatry*. New York: Springer.

Boden, J. L. (1984). The hand test. In D. J. Keyser & R. C. Sweetland (Eds.), *Test critiques*. (Vol. 1, pp 315–321). Kansas City, MO: Test Corporation of America.

Boden, M. A. (1988). *Computer models of mind.*. Cambridge, UK: Cambridge University Press.

Boden, M. A. (1989). *Artificial intelligence in psychology: Interdisciplinary essays*. Cambridge: The MIT Press.

Boden, M. A. (Ed.). (1990). *The philosophy of artificial intelligence*. Oxford, UK: Oxford University Press.

Boder, E. (1957). Specfic reading disability as a developmental lag. *Bulletin of the Orton Society*, 7, 9–18.

Boder, E. (1971). Developmental dyslexia: Prevailing diagnostic concepts and a new diagnostic approach. In H. Myklebust (Ed.), *Progress in learning disabilities*. New York: Grune & Stratton.

Boder, E. (1973). Developmental dyslexia: A diagnostic approach based on three atypical reading-spelling patterns. *Developmental Medicine and Child Neurology*, 15, 663–687.

Bodman, P. L., Mincher, M., Williams, C., & Lindauer, M. S. (1979). What's in a name? Evaluations of literary names in context and in isolation. *Poetics*, 8, 491–496.

Boe, E. E., & Church, R. M. (1967). Permanent effects of punishment during extinction. *Journal of Comparative and Physiological Psychology*, 63, 486–492.

Boehm, V. R. (1968). Mr. Prejudice, Miss Sympathy and the authoritarian personality: An application of psychological measuring techniques to the problem of jury bias. *Wisconsin Law Review, 3*, 734–747.

Bogardus, E. S. (1928). *Immigration and race attitudes*. Boston: Heath.

Bogdan, R. & Taylor, S. J. (1975). *An introduction to qualitative research methods: A phenomenological approach to the social sciences*. New York: Wiley.

Bogden, H. E., & Taylor, E. K. (1950). The theory and classification of criterion bias. *Educational and Psychological Measurement, 10*, 159–186.

Boggiano, A. K., & Ruble, D. N. (1979). Competence and the overjustification effect: A developmental study. *Journal of Personality and Social Psychology*, 37, 1462–1468.

Bohm, E. (1972/1951). *Lehrbuch der Rorschach-Psychodiagnostik*. Bern: Huber.

Bohman, M., & yon Knorring A. L. (1979). Psychiatric Illness among adults adopted as infants. *Acta Psychiatrica Scandinavica, 60*, 106–112.

Bohr, N. (1937). Causality and complementarity. *Philosophy of Science, 4*, 289–298.

Bohr, N. (1958). *Atomic physics and human knowledge*. New York: Wiley.

Bohrnstedt, G. W., & Borgatta, E. F. (Eds.). (1981). *Social measurement*. Beverly Hills, Calif.: Sage Publications.

Boice, R. (1977). Surplusage. *Bulletin of the Psychonomics Society, 9*, 452–454.

Bok, D. C., & Dunlop, J. T. (1970). *Labor and the American community*. New York: Simon & Shuster.

Boland, F., Mellor, C. S., & Revusky, S. (1978). Chemical aversion treatment of alcoholism: Lithium as the aversive agent. *Behaviour Research and Therapy, 16*, 401–409.

Bolen, D. W., & Boyd, W. H. (1968). Gambling and the gambler. *Archives of General Psychiatry, 38*, 617–630.

Boll, T. J. (1974). Behavioral correlates of cerebral damage in children aged 9 through 14. In R. M. Reitan & L. A. Davison (Eds.), *Clinical neuropsychology: Current status and applications*. Washington, D.C.: Winston.

Boll, T. J. (1978). Diagnosing brain impairment. In B. B. Wolman (Ed.), *Clinical diagnosis of mental disorders*. New York: Plenum.

Bolles, R. (1978). *The three boxes of life*. Berkeley, Calif.: Ten Speed Press.

Bolles, R. C. (1970). Species-specific defense reactions and avoidance learning. *Psychological Review, 77*, 32–48.

Bolles, R. C. (1975). *Theory of motivation*. New York: Harper & Row.

Bolles, R. C. (1975) *Learning memory*. New York: Holt, Reinhart, & Winston.

Bolles, R. C. (1979). *Learning theory* (2nd ed.). New York: Holt, Rinehart & Winston.

Bolles, R. C, & Faneslow, M. S. (1982). Endorphins and behavior. *Annual Review of Psychology, 33*, 87–101.

Bolton, C. D. (1961). Mate selection as the development of a relationship. *Marriage and Family Living, 23*, 234–240.

Bolz, F, & Hershey, E. (1979). *Hostage cop*. New York: Rawson, Wade.

Bonaparte, M., Freud, A, & Kris, E. (Eds.). (1954). *The origins of psychoanalysis. Letters to William Fliess, Drafts and notes: 1887–1902, by Sigmund Freud* New York: Basic Books.

Bonarius, H, Holland, R., & Rosenberg, S. (Eds.). (1981). *Personal construct psychology: Recent advances in theory and practice*. London: Macmillan.

Bonarius, J. C. J. (1965). Research in the personal construct theory of George A. Kelly. In B. A. Maher (Ed.), *Progress in experimental personality research*, Vol. 2. New York: Academic Press.

Bonarius, J. C. J. (1977). The interaction model of communication. In A. W. Landfield (Ed.), *Nebraska Symposium on Motivation 1976: Personal construct psychology*. Lincoln, Neb.: University of Nebraska Press.

Bond, C. F., Jr. (1990) Lie detection across cultures. *Journal of Nonverbal Behavior, 14*, 189–204.

Bond, J., & Morgenroth D. (1974). Regional cerebral blood flow. *Journal of Neurosurgical Nursing, 6*, 137–141.

Bond, L, & Rosen, J. (Eds.). (1980). *Primary prevention of psychopathology: Competence and coping during adulthood*. Hanover, N.H.: University Press of New England.

Bond, N. W. (1984). *Animal models in psychopathology*. Sydney: Academic Press.

Bond, W. S. (1989). Delusions of parasitosis: A case report and management guidelines. *DICP, 23*(4), 304–306.

Bondy, C. (1956). *Social psychology in West Germany*. Washington, D.C.: Library of Congress.

Bondy, C. (Ed.). (1956). *Hamburg-Wechsler-Intelligenz-test für Erwachsene (HAWIE)*, Bern: Huber.

Boneau, C. A., Golann, S. E., & Johnson, M. M. (1970). Selection from *A career in psychology*. Washington, D.C.: American Psychological Association, pp. 3–12.

Bonett, D. G, & Bentler, P. M. (1983). Goodness-of-fit procedures for the evaluation and selection of log linear models. *Psychological Bulletin, 93*, 149–166.

Bongers, H. (1947). *The history and principles of vocabulary control, as it affects the teaching of foreign language in general and of English in particular*. Woerden, Netherlands: Wocopi.

Bonica, J. (Ed.). (1974). *Advances in Neurology*, Vol. 4. *International symposium on pain*. New York: Raven Press.

Bonica, J. J. (1953). *The management of pain*. Philadelphia, Pa.: Lee & Febiger.

Bonjean, C. M., Hill, R. J, & McLemore, S. D. (1967). *Sociological measurement: An inventory of scales and indices*. San Francisco: Chandler.

Bonnet, C. (1781–1783). Essai de psychologie. In *Oeuvres d'histoire naturelle et de philosophie*, Vol. 17.

Bonnet, C. (1970/1770). *Essai analytique sur les faculté de l'âme*. Geneva: Slatkine.

Bonnie, K. J. (1977). Commentary: Criminal responsibility in *Diagnosis and debate*. New York: Insight Communications.

Bonny, H., & Savary, L. M. (1973). *Music and your mind*. New York: Harper & Row.

Bons, P. M., & Fiedler, F. E. (1976). Changes in organizational leadership and the behavior of relationship- and task-motivated leaders. *Administrative Science Quarterly, 21*, 433–472.

Boole, G. (1854). *An invitation to the laws of thought*. New York: Macmillan.

Boone, J. A. (1954). *Kinship with all life*. New York: Harper & Row.

Boorstein, S. (Ed.). (1980). *Transpersonal psychotherapies*. Palo Alto, Calif.: Science and Behavior Books.

Booth, C. L. (1981). Contingent responsiveness and mutuality in mother-infant interaction: Birth-order and sex difference? Presented at the Society for Research in Child Development, Boston, April.

Bootzin, R. R., & Max, D. (1980). Learning and behavioral theories. In I. L. Kutash and L. B. Schlesinger (Eds.), *Handbook on stress and anxiety*. San Francisco: Jossey-Bass.

Bootzin, R. R., & Nicassio, P. M. (1978). Behavioral treatments for insomnia. In M. Hersen, R. M. Eisler, & P. M. Miller (Eds.) *Progress in behavior modification, (Vol. 6)*. New York: Academic Press.

Borbely, A. A. (1980). Sleep: Circadian rhythm versus recovery process. In M. Koukkow, D. Lermann, & J. Angst (Eds.), *Functional states of the brain: Their determinants* (151–161). Amsterdam: Elsevier.

Borden, G. A. (1971). *An introduction to human communication theory*. Dubuque, Iowa: William Brown.

Borden, J. G., & Harris, K. S. (1980). *Speech science primer: Physiology, acoustics, and perception of speech*. Baltimore, Md.: Williams & Wilkins.

Bordin, E. S. (1968). *Psychological counseling* (2nd ed.). New York: Meredith.

Bordin, E. S. (1979). Fusing work and play: A challenge to theory and research. *Academic Psychology Bulletin, 1*, 5–9.

Bordin, E. S. (1979). The generalizability of the psychoanalytic concept of the working alliance. *Psychotherapy, 15*, 252–260.

Bordin, E. S., Nachmann, B., & Segal, S. J. (1963). An articulated framework for vocational development. *Journal of Counseling Psychology, 10*, 107–117.

Borg, W. R. (1966). *Ability grouping in the public schools* (2nd ed.). Madison, Wis.: Dembar Educational Research Services.

Borgatta, E. F. (1956). Analysis of social interaction: Actual roleplaying and projective. *Journal of Abnormal and Social Psychology, 40*, 190–196.

Borgatta, E. F. (1961). Roleplaying specification, personality and performance. *Sociometry, 24*, 218–233.

Borgatta, E. F. (1964). The structure of personality characteristics. *Behavioral Science, 9*, 8–17.

Borgatta, E. F. (1969). *Social psychology*. Chicago: Rand-McNally.

Borgatta, E. F. (Ed.). (1969). *Sociological methodology*. San Francisco: Jossey-Bass.

Borgatta, E. F., & Lambert, W. (Eds.). (1968). *Handbook of personality theory and research*. Chicago: Rand-McNally.

Borgatta, E. F., & McClusky, N. J. (Eds.). (1980). *Aging and society*. Beverly Hills, Calif.: Sage Publications.

Borgatta, E. F., & Meyer, H. J. (Eds.). (1956). *Sociological theory*. New York: Knopf.

Boring, E. G. (1933). *The physical dimensions of consciousness*. New York: Century.

Boring, E. G. (1942). *Sensation and perception in the history of experimental psychology*. New York: Appleton-Century.

Boring, E. G. (1954). The nature and history of experimental control. *American Journal of Psychology, 67,* 573–589.

Boring, E. G. (1957/1950/1929). A history of experimental psychology (2nd ed.). New York: Appleton-Century-Crofts.

Boring, E. G. (1965). On the subjectivity of important historical dates: Leipzig, 1879. *Journal of the Behavioral Sciences, 1,* 5–9.

Boring, E. G., Karl M. Dallenbach. (1958). *American Journal of Psychology, 71,* 1–40.

Boring, E. G., Langfeld, H. S. & Weld, H. P. (1948). *Foundations of psychology*. New York: Wiley.

Boring, E. G., Langfeld, H. S., & Weld, H. P. (1935). *Psychology: A factual textbook*. New York: Wiley.

Boring, E. G., & Lindzey, G. (Eds.). (1967). *History of psychology in autobiography*. Vol. 5. New York: Appleton-Century-Crofts.

Borkovec, T. D., Stone, N. M., O'Brien, G. T., & Kaloupek, D. G. (1974). Evaluation of a clinically relevant target behavior for analog outcome research. *Behavior Therapy, 5,* 503–513.

Borland, D. M. (1975). An alternative model of the wheel theory. *The Family Coordinator, 24,* 289–292.

Borman, L. (Ed.). (1975). *Explorations in self-help and mutual aid*. Evanston, Ill.: Center for Urban Affairs, Northwestern University.

Bormans, M. (1968). Contribution à l'étude des mentalités sur la famille: Ce qu'en pensent les jeunes Sahariens. *Revue Occident Musulman, 5,* 15–39.

Borneman, E. (1976/1973). *The psychoanalysis of money*. New York: Urizen.

Bornstein, M., Bellack, A. S., & Hersen, M. (1980). Social skills training for highly aggressive children. *Behavior Modification, 4,* 173–186.

Bornstein, M., Bellack, A. S., & Hersen, M. (1980). Social skills training for highly aggressive children. Treatment in an inpatient psychiatric setting. *Behavior Modification, 4,* 173-186.

Bornstein, M. H. (1978). Chromatic vision in infancy. In H. W. Reese & L. P. Lipsitt (Eds.), *Advances in child development and behavior,* Vol. 12. New York: Academic Press.

Bornstein, M. H., & Kessen, W. (1979). *Psychological development from infancy: Image to intention*. Hillsdale, N.J.: Erlbaum.

Bornstein, M. H., Kessen, W., & Weiskopf, S. (1976). Color vision and hue categorization in young human infants. *Journal of Experimental Psychology: Human Perception and Performance, 2,* 115–129.

Bornstein, P. H., Anton, B., Harowski, K. J. Weltzein, R. T., McIntyre, T. J., & Hocker-Wilmot, J. (1981). Behavioral-communications treatment of marital discord: Positive behaviors. *Behavior Counseling Quarterly, 1,* 189–199.

Bornstein, R. F. (1990). Critical importance of stimulus unawareness for the production of subliminal psychodynamic activation effects: A meta-analytic Review. *Journal of Clinical Psychology, 46,* 201–210.

Bortner, R. W., & Hultsch, D. F. (1974). Personal time perspective in adulthood. *Developmental Psychology, 10,* 534–545.

Borton, T. (1970). *Reach, touch, and teach*. New York: McGraw-Hill.

Boruch, R. F., & Gomez, H. (1977). Sensitivity, bias, and theory in impact evaluations. *Professional Psychology, 8,* 411–434.

Boruch, R. F., McSweeney, A. J., & Soderstrom, J. (1978). Bibliography: Illustrative randomized field experiments. *Evaluation Quarterly, 2,* 655–695.

Borup, J. H., Gallego, D. T., & Hefferman, P. G. (1979). Relocation and its effect on mortality. *The Gerontologist, 19,* 135–140.

Bose, G. (Ed.). (1940). *The progress of science in India during the past twenty five years*. Calcutta: Indian Science Congress.

Bose, S., Das Gupta, S. K., & Lindgren, H. C. (1979). Achievement motivation of engineering and nonengineering students in India. *Journal of Social Psychology, 108,* 273–274.

Boss, M. (1958). The analysis of dreams, New York: Philosophical Library.

Boss, M. (1963). *A psychiatrist discovers India*. New York: Basic Books.

Boss, M. (1963). *Psychoanalysis and daseinsanalysis*. (L. B. Lefebre, Trans.). New York: Basic Books.

Boss, M. (1970/1963). *Psychoanalysis and daseinsanalysis*, New York: Basic Books.

Boss, M. (1977). "*I dreamt last night… ": A new approach to the revelations of dreaming—and its uses for psychotherapy*. New York: Gardner Press.

Bossard, J. (1956). *The large family system, an original study in the sociology of family behavior*. Philadelphia, Pa.: University of Pennsylvania Press.

Bossard, J. H. S., & Boll, E. S. (1966). *The sociology of child development* (4th ed.). New York: Harper & Row.

Bosse, R., & Rose, C. L. (1973). Age and interpersonal factors in smoking cessation. *Journal of Health and Social Behavior, 14,* 381–386.

Boston Lesbian Psychologies Collective (Eds.). (1989). *Lesbian psychologies: Explorations and challenges*. Urbana: University of Illinois Press.

Bostow, D. E., & Bailey, J. B. (1969). Modification of severe disruptive and aggressive behavior using brief time out and reinforcement procedures. *Journal of Applied Behavior Analysis, 2,* 31–37.

Boswell, D., & Litwin, W. (1992). Limited prescription privilege for psychologists: A 1-year follow-up. *Professional Psychology: Research and Practice, 23,* 108–113.

Boswell, J. (1980). *Christianity, social tolerance, and homosexuality*. Chicago: University of Chicago Press.

Boszormenyi-Nagy, I., & Spark, G. (1973). *Invisible loyalties*. New York: Harper & Row.

Bothwell, R. K., Deffenbacher, K. A. & Brigham, J. C. (1987). Correlation of eyewitness accuracy and confidence: Optimality hypothesis revisited. *Journal of Applied Psychology, 72,* 691–695.

Bottome, P. (1939). *Alfred Adler, apostle of freedom*. New York: Putnam.

Bottome, P. (1957). *Alfred Adler—A portrait from life*. New York: Vanguard Press.

Botwinick, J. (1984). *Aging and behavior*. New York: Springer.

Bouchard, T. J. (1977). Whatever happened to brainstorming? In S. Parnes, R. Noller, & J. A. Biondi (Eds.), *Guide to creative action*. New York: Scribner's.

Bouchard, T. J., Jr. (1968). Current conceptions of intelligence and their implications for assessment. In P. McReynolds (Ed.), *Advances in psychological assessment*, Vol. I. Palo Alto, Calif.: Science & Behavior Books.

Bouchard, T. J., Jr. (1976). Field research methods: Interviewing, questionnaires, participant observation, systematic observation, unobtrusive measures. In M. D. Dunnette (Ed.), *Handbook of industrial and organizational psychology*. Chicago: Rand-McNally.

Boudewyns, P. A., & Shipley, R. H. (1983). *Flooding and implosive therapy: Direct therapeutic exposure in clinical practice*. NY: Plenum Press.

Boudouris, J. (1971). Homicide and the family. *Journal of Marriage and the Family, 33,* 667–676.

Boudreau, L. (1972). TM and yoga as reciprocal inhibitors. *Journal of Behaviour Therapy and Experimental Psychiatry, 3,* 97–98.

Bouillaud, J. (1825). Recherches cliniques propres a demontrer que la perte de la parole corresponde la lesion des lobules anterieurs du cerveau et a confirmer l'opinion de M. Gall, sur le siège de l'organ du langage articule. *Archives Generale de Medecine (Paris), 8,* 25–45.

Boulding, K. (1956). *The image.* Ann Arbor, Mich.: University of Michigan Press.

Boulton, A. A., Baker, G. B., & Martin-Irverson, M. T. (Eds.). (1991). *Animal models in psychiatry.* Clifton, NJ: Humana Press.

Bourne, E. (1978). The state of research on ego identity: A review and appraisal. Part I. *Journal of Youth and Adolescence, 7,* 223–251.

Bourne, L. E., Dominowski, R. L., & Loftus, E. L. (1979). *Cognitive Processes.* Englewood Cliffs, N.J.: Prentice-Hall.

Bouroche, J. M. (1977). *Analyse des données en marketing.* Paris: Masson.

Bousfield, A. K., & Bousfield, W. A. (1966). Measurement of clustering and of sequential constancies in repeated free recall. *Psychological Reports, 19,* 935.

Bousfield, W. A. (1953). The occurrence of clustering in the recall of randomly arranged associates. *Journal of General Psychology, 49,* 229–240.

Bouthilet, L. (1948). The measurement of intuitive thinking. Unpublished Ph.D. thesis, University of Chicago.

Bouwsma, W. J. (1976). Christian adulthood. In Adulthood, *Daedalus, 105,* 77–92.

Bovet, P. (1917). *L'instinct combatif.* Neuchâtel, Switzerland: Delachaux et Niestlé.

Bovet, P. (1925). *Le sentiment religieux et la psychologie de l'enfant.* Neuchâtel, Switzerland: Delachaux et Niestlé, 1925.

Bowden, C. L., Schoenfeld, L. S., & Adams, L. (1980). Mental health attitudes and treatment expectations as treatment variables. *Journal of clinical Psychology, 36,* 653–657.

Bowen, M. (1971). The use of family theory in clinical practice. In J. Haley (Ed.), *Changing families.* New York: Grune & Stratton.

Bowen, M. (1978). *Family therapy in clinical practice.* New York: Aronson.

Bower, D. W., & Christopherson, V. A. (1977). University student habitation: A regional comparison of selected attitudes and behavior. *Journal of Marriage and the Family, 2,* 447–453.

Bower, G. H. (1970). Analysis of a mnemonic device. *American Scientist, 58,* 496–510.

Bower, G. H. (1972). Mental imagery and associative learning. In L. Gregg (Ed.), *Cognition in learning and memory.* New York: Wiley.

Bower, G. H. (1972). Mental imagery and associative learning. In L. W. Gregg (Ed.), *Cognition in learning and memory* pp. 51–58). New York: Wiley.

Bower, G. H. (1975). Cognitive psychology: An introduction. In W. K. Estes (Ed.), *Handbook of learning and cognitive processes,* Vol. 1. *Introduction to concepts and issues.* Hillsdale, N. J.: Erlbaum.

Bower, G. H. (1981). Mood and memory. *American Psychologist, 36,* 129–148.

Bower, G. H., & Anderson, J. (1973). *Human associative memory.* Washington, D.C.: Winston.

Bower, G. H., Clark, M. C., Lesgold, A. M., & Winzenz, D. (1969). Hierarchical retrieval schemes in recall of categorical word lists. *Journal of Verbal Learning and Verbal Behavior, 8,* 323–343.

Bower, G. H., & Hilgard, E. R. (1981). *Theories of learning* (5th ed.). Englewood Cliffs, N.J.: Prentice-Hall.

Bower, G. H., & Mayer, J. D. (1985). Failure to replicate mood-dependent retrieval. *Bulletin of the Psychonomic Society, 23,* 39–42.

Bower, G. H., & Trabasso, W. T. (1968). *Attention to learning.* New York: Wiley.

Bower, R. T., & DeGasparis, P. (1978). *Ethics in social research: Protecting the interests of human subjects.* New York: Praeger.

Bower, T. G. R. (1966). The visual world of infants. *Scientific American, 215,* 85–92.

Bower, T. G. R. (1979). *Human development.* San Francisco: Freeman.

Bower, T. G. R. (1982/1974). *Development in infancy.* San Francisco: Freeman.

Bower, T. G. R., Broughton, J. M, & Moore, M. K. (1970). Infant responses to approaching objects: An indicator of response to distal variables. *Perception and Psychophysics, 9, 193–196.*

Bowerman, C. E., & Day, B. R. (1956). A test of the theory of complementarity needs as applied to couples during courtship. *American Sociological Review, 21,* 602–605.

Bowerman, C. E., & Irish, D. P. (1962). Some relationships of stepchildren to their parents. *Marriage and Family Living. 24,* 113–121.

Bowers, D. G. (1969). Work organizations as dynamic systems. *ONR Technical Report,* September.

Bowers, D. G. (1975). Hierarchy, function and the generalizability of leadership practices. In J. Hunt & L. Larson (Eds.), *Leadership frontiers.* Kent, Ohio: Kent State University.

Bowers, D. G., & Franklin, J. L. (1977). *Survey-guided development I: Data-based organizational change.* San Diego, Calif.: University Associates.

Bowers, D. G. & Seashore, S. E. (1966). Predicting organizational effectiveness with a four-factor theory of leadership. *Administrative Science Quarterly, 11,* 238–263.

Bowers, K. S. (1973). Situationism in psychology: An analysis and a critique. *Psychological Review, 80,* 307–336.

Bowers, M. B. (1977). Psychoses precipitated by psychotomimetic drugs: A followup study. *Archives of General Psychiatry, 34,* 832–835.

Bowlby, J. (1944). Forty-four juvenile thieves: their characters and home life. *International Journal of Psychoanalysis, 25,* 19–52, 107–127.

Bowlby, J. (1953). Some pathological processes set in train by early mother-child separation. *Journal of Mental Science, 99,* 265–267.

Bowlby, J. (1954/1951). *Maternal care and mental health.* Geneva: World Health Organization.

Bowlby, J. (1958). The nature of the child's tie to his mother. *International Journal of Psycho-Analysis, 39,* 350–373.

Bowlby, J. (1960). Separation anxiety. *International Journal of Psychoanalysis, 41,* 89–113.

Bowlby, J. (1961). Process of mourning. *International Journal of Psychoanalysis, 42,* 317–334.

Bowlby, J. (1965). *Child care and the growth of love.* Baltimore, Md.: Penguin Books.

Bowlby, J. (1973). *Attachment and loss.* Vol. 2: *Separation: Anxiety and anger.* London: Hogarth Press. New York: Basic Books.

Bowlby, J. (1973). *Separation and loss.* New York: Basic Books.

Bowlby, J. (1977). The making and breaking of affectional bonds. *Journal of Psychiatry, 130,* 201–210.

Bowlby, J. (1979). *The making and breaking of affectional bonds.* London: Tavistock Publications. New York: Methuen.

220   BIBLIOGRAPHY

Bowlby, J. (1980). *Attachment and loss*. Vol. 3. *Loss: Sadness and depression*. London: Hogarth Press. New York: Basic Books.

Bowlby, J. (1982/1969). *Attachment and loss*. Vol. 1: *Attachment* London: Hogarth Press. New York: Basic Books.

Bowler, P. J. (1983). *The eclipse of Darwinism*. Baltimore: Johns Hopkins University Press.

Box, G. E. P., Hunter, W. G., & Hunter, J. S. 1978). *Statistics for experimenters: An introduction to design, data analysis, and model building*. New York: Wiley.

Box, G. E. P., & Jenkins, G. M. (1970). *Time-series analysis: Forecasting and control*. San Francisco: Holden-Day.

Box, G. E. P., & Taio, G. C. (1965). A change in level of a nonstationary time series. *Biometrika, 52,* 181–192.

Box, G. E. P., & Taio, G. C. (1975). Intervention analysis with applications to economic and environmental problems. *Journal of the American Statistical Association, 70,* 70–79.

Box, G. E. P., & Taio, G. C. (1976). Comparison of forecast and actuality. *Applied Statistics, 25,* 195–200.

Boyanowky, E., & Griffith, C. (1982). Instigators or inhibitors of aggressive arousal in police-citizen interaction. *Journal of Applied Social Contact, 12,* 398–407.

Boyce, W. D., & Jensen, L. C. (1978). *Moral reasoning: A psychological-philosophical integration*. Lincoln, Neb.: University of Nebraska Press.

Boyd, J. (1978). *Counselor supervision*. Muncie, Ind.: Accelerated Development.

Boyd, J., & Weissman, M. (1982). Epidemiology. In R. Paykel (Ed.), *Handbook of affective disorders*. New York: Guilford Press.

Boyer, L. B. (1979). *Childhood and folklore: A psychoanalytic study of Apache personality*. New York: Library of Anthropology.

Boyle, A. J. (1980). 'Found experiments' in accident research: Report of a study of accident rates and implications for future research. *Journal of Occupational Psychology, 53,* 53–64.

Boyle, C. M. (1968). Some factors affecting the smoking habits of a group of teenagers. *Lancet, 2*(581), 1287–1289.

Boynton, R. M. (1971). Color vision. In J. Kling & L. Riggs (Eds.), *Woodworth and Schlosberg's experimental psychology* (3rd ed.). New York: Holt, Rinehart & Winston.

Brackbill, Y. (1958). Extinction of the smiling response in infants as a function of reinforcement schedule. *Child Development, 29,* 115–124.

Bracken, H. von. (1925). *Persöanlichkeitserfassung aufgrund von Persoenlichkeitsbeschreibung. Önär Beiträge I.* Langensalza: Beltz.

Bracken, H. von & David, H. P. (Eds.). (1957). *Perspectives in personality theory*. London: Tavistock Publications.

Bradburn, N. M. (1969). *The structure of psychological well-being*. Chicago: Aldne.

Bradburn, N. M., Sudman, S., et al. (1980). *Improving interview method and questionnaire design*. San Francisco: Jossey-Bass.

Braddick, O. J., Campbell, F. W., & Atkinson, J. (1978). Channels in vision: Basic aspects. In R. Held, H. W. Leibowitz, and H. L. Teuber (Eds.), *Handbook of sensory physiology*, Vol. 8. Heidelberg: Springer.

Braden, V. (1977). *Tennis for the future*. Boston: Little, Brown.

Bradford, L. P., Gibb, J. R., & Benne, K. D. (1964). *T-group theory and laboratory method: Innovation in re-education*. New York: Wiley.

Bradley, C. (1937). The behavior of children receiving Benzedrine. *American Journal of Psychiatry, 94,* 577–585.

Bradley, G. (1978). Self-serving biases in the attribution process: A reexamination of the fact or fiction question. *Journal of Personality and Social Psychology 36,* 56–71.

Bradley, R. H., Caldwell, B. M., & Elardo, R. (1977). Home environment, social status, and mental test performance. *Journal of Educational Psychology, 69,* 697–701.

Bradshaw, J. (1972). The concept of social need. *New Society, 30,* 640–643.

Brady, J. P., Davison, G. C., Dewald, P. A., Egan, G., Fadiman, J., Frank, J. D., Gill, M. M., Hoffman, I., Kempler, W., Lazarus, A. A., Raimy, V., Rotter, J. B., & Strupp, H. H. (1980). Some views on effective principles of psychotherapy. *Cognitive Therapy and Research, 4,* 269–306.

Brady, J. V. (1958). Ulcers in "executive monkeys." *Scientific American, 199,* 95–103.

Brady, J. V., & Mauta, W. J. H. (1953). Subcortical mechanisms in emotional behavior, affective changes following septal forebrain lesions in the albino rat. *Journal of Comparative and Physiological Psychology, 46,* 339–346.

Brady, J. V., Porter, R. W., Conrad, D. G., & Mason, J. W. (1958). Avoidance behavior and the development of gastroduodenal ulcers. *Journal of the Experimental Analysis of Behavior, 1,* 69–72.

Braginsky, B. M. & Braginsky, D. D. (1967). Schizophrenic Patients in the Psychiatric Interview: An Experimental Study of Their Effectiveness at Manipulation. *Journal of Consulting Psychology, 3,* 543–547.

Brahms, S. J. & Davis, M. D. (1976). A game-theory approach to jury selection. *Trial 12,* 47–49.

Braid, J. (1899/1843) Neurhypnology, or the rationale of nervous sleep considered in relation with animal magnetism. London: Redway.

Brain, P. F., & Benton, D. (Eds.). (1981). *Multidisciplinary approaches to aggression research*. New York: Elsevier.

Bramel, D. & Friend, R. (1981). Hawthorne, the myth of the docile worker, and class bias in psychology. *American Psychologist, 36,* 867–878.

Brammer, L. M., & Shostrom, E. L. (1978). *Therapeutic psychology*. Englewood Cliffs, N.J.: Prentice-Hall.

Bramwell, S. T., Masuda, M., Wagner, N. N., & Holmes, T. H. (1980). Psychosocial factors in athletic injuries. In R. Suinn (Ed.), *Psychology in sports*. Minneapolis, Minn.: Burges.

Brandt, A. (1980). Face reading: The persistence of physiognomy. *Psychology Today, 14,* 90–96.

Brandt, R. M. (1972). *Studying behavior in natural settings*. New York: Holt, Rhinehart, & Winston.

Brannon, R. (1978). Measuring attitudes toward women (and otherwise): A methodological critique. In J. Sherman & F. Denmark (Eds.), *The psychology of women: Future directions of research*. New York: Psychological Dimensions.

Brannon, R. (1981). Current methodological issues in paper-and-pencil measuring instruments. *Psychology of Women Quarterly, 5,* 618–627.

Bransford, J. D. (1979). *Human cognition; learning, understanding, and remembering*. Belmont, Calif.: Wadsworth.

Branson, R., Raynor, G., Cox, J., Furman, J., King, F, & Hannum, W. (1975). *Interservice procedures for instructional systems development* (Executive summary and Phases I-V), Fort Benning, Ga.: Interservice Committee for Instructional Systems Development, (available through the Defense Technical Information Center, Alexandria, Va., report no. AD019486–90).

Branstrom, M. (1979). Preferred perceptual mode and biofeedback training. Unpublished doctoral dissertation, Pacific Graduate School of Psychology.

Brasel, J. A. (1974). Cellular changes in intrauterine malnutrition. In M. Winick (Ed.), *Nutrition and fetal development*. New York: Wiley.

Brauchli, B. (1981). *Zur Nosologie in der Psychiatrie. Methodische Ansätze empirischer Forschung: Theorie und Methodenstudien zur Clusteranalyse*. Stuttgart: Ferdinand Enke.

Braun, B. (1988). The BASK model of dissociation: Part 2. Treatment. *Dissociation, 1*,(2), 16–23.

Braun, B. (1989). Comments. *Ritual child abuse: A professional overview* [Videotape]. Uria, CA: Cavalcade Productions.

Braun, C. (1976). Teacher expectation: Sociopsychological dynamics. *Review of Educational Research, 46*, 185–213.

Braverman, H. (1974). *Labor and monopoly capital*. New York: Monthly Review.

Braverman, L. (Ed.). (1988). *Women, feminism and family therapy*. New York: Haworth Press.

Bravo, M., Canino, C. J., Rubio-Stipec, M., Woodbury-Farina, M. (1991). A cross-cultural adaptation of a psychiatric epidemiologic instrument: the diagnostic interview schedule's adaptation in Peurto Rico. *Culture, Medicine, and Psychiatry, 15*(1), 1–18.

Bray, D. W. (1982). The assessment center and the study of lives. *American Psychologist, 37*, 180–189.

Bray, D. W., Campbell, R. J., & Grant, D. L. (1974). *Formative years in business: A long term AT&T study of managerial lives*. New York: Wiley.

Bray, D. W., Campbell, R. J., & Grant, D. L. (1974). The assessment center in the measurement of potential business management. *Psychological Monographs, 80* (17, entire no. 625).

Bray, G. A. (1976). *The obese patient*. Philadelphia, Pa.: Saunders.

Bray, R. M., & Gigeroff, A. (1977). *Exhibitionism: Facts, fictions, and solutions*. Toronto: Grenville Press.

Bray, R. M., & Kerr, N. L. (1979). Use of the simulation in the study of jury behavior: Some methodological considerations. *Law and Human Behavior, 3*, 107–119.

Breasted, J. H. (1930). *The Edwin Smith Surgical Papyrus*. Chicago: University of Chicago Press.

Brebner, J., & Drever, J. (1973). Psychology in Europe, Australia, and Canada. In M. Marx & W. Hillix (Eds.), *Systems and theories in psychology* (2nd ed.). New York: McGraw-Hill.

Brecher, E. M. (1972). (and the editors of *Consumer Reports*). *Licit and illicit drugs*. Boston: Little, Brown.

Brecher, E. M. (1975). History of human sexual research and study. In A. M. Freedman, H. I. Kaplan, & B. J. Sadock (Eds.), *Comprehensive textbook of psychiatry*, Vol. 2. Baltimore, Md.: Williams & Wilkins.

Breckler, S. J., Pratkanis, A. R., & McCann, D. (1991). The representation of self in multidimensional cognitive space. *British Journal of Social Psychology, 29*, 97–112.

Breed, W. (1963). Occupational mobility and suicide among white males. *American Sociological Review, 28*, 179–188.

Breer, W. (1987). *The adolescent molester*. Springfield, IL: Thomas.

Breggin, P. (1991). *Toxic psychiatry*. New York: St. Martin's Press.

Bregman, J. D., Dykens, E., Watson, M., Ort, S. I., & Leckman, J. F. (1987). Fragile-X syndrome: variability of phenotypic expression. *Journal of the American Academy of Child and Adolescent Psychiatry, 26*, 463–471.

Brehm, J. W. (1966). *A theory of psychological reactance*. New York: Academic Press.

Brehm, J. W., & Mann, M. (1975). Effect of importance of freedom and attraction to group members on influence produced by group pressure. *Journal of Personality and Social Psychology, 31*, 816–824.

Brehm, J. W., Stires, L. K., Sensenig, J., & Shaban, J. (1966). The attractiveness of an eliminated choice alternative. *Journal of Experimental Social Psychology, 2*, 301–313.

Brehm, S. S., & Brehm, J. W. (1981). *Psychological reactance: A theory of freedom and control*. New York: Academic Press.

Brehm, S. S., & Smith (1986). Social psychological approaches to behavior therapy and behavior change. In S. L. Garfield & A. E. Bergin (Eds.), *Handbook of psychotherapy and behavior change* (3rd ed, pp. 69–115).

Brehm, S. S., & Weinraub, M. (1977). Physical barriers and psychological reactance: 2-year-olds' responses to threats to freedom. *Journal of Personality and Social Psychology, 35*, 830–836.

Brehmer, B. (1980). In one word: Not from experience. *Acta Psychologica, 45*, 223–241.

Breland, H. M. (1972). Birth order and intelligence. Doctoral dissertation, State University of New York at Buffalo, 1972. *Dissertation Abstracts International 33*, 1536–A–1820A (University Microfilms no. 72–27238).

Breland, K., & Breland, M. (1961). The misbehavior of organisms. *American Pscyhologist, 16*, 681–684.

Brengelmann, J. C. (1975). Therapy of dependencies and addictions: Tobacco, food, alcohol and drugs. *Analisis y Modificacion de Conducta, 1*, 105–127.

Brenman, M., & Gill, M. M. (1971/1947). *Hypnotherapy*. New York: International Universities Press.

Brenman-Gibson, M. (1976). Notes on the study of the creative process. In M. M. Gill and P. S. Holzman (Eds.), *Psychology versus metapsychology*. New York: International Universities Press.

Brenman-Gibson, M. (1978). The war on human suffering, a psychoanalyst's research odyssey. In S. Smith (Ed.), *The human mind revisited, essays in honor of Karl Menninger*. New York: International Universities Press.

Brenman-Gibson, M. (1981). *Clifford Odets: American playwright, a psychosocial study*, Vol. I. New York: Atheneum.

Brenman-Gibson, M. (1983). *Beyond the child's play: A psychosocial view of creativity, psychotherapy and survival*. New York: Guilford Press.

Brennan, J. F. (1982). *History and systems of psychology*. Englewood Cliffs, N.J.: Prentice-Hall.

Brennan, R., Mednik, S., & Kandel, E. (1991). Congenital determinants of violent and property offending. In D. J. Pepler & K. H. Rubin (Eds.), *The development and treatment of childhood aggression* (pp. 81–92). Hillsdale, NJ: Erlbaum.

Brenner, C. (1959). The masochistic character. *Journal of the American Psychoanalytic Association, 7*, 197–226.

Brenner, C. (1974/1973). *An elementary textbook of psychoanalysis* (rev. ed.). New York: Anchor Books.

Brenner, D. (1982). *The effective psychotherapist*. New York: Pergamon Press.

Brenner, M. H. (1977). Personal stability and economic security. *Social Policy, 8*, 2–6.

Brenner, P. (1981). *Life is a shared creation*. Marina del Rey, Calif.: Devorss.

Brentano, F. (1874). *Psychologie vom empirischen Standpunkte.* Leipzig: Dunker & Humblot.

Brentano, F. (1895). *Meine letzten Wünsche für Österreich.* Stuttgart: Cotta.

Brentano, F. (1973). *Psychology from an empirical standpoint.* (A. C. Rancurello, Trans.). New York: Humanities Press. (Original work published 1874).

Brentano, F. (1973/1874). *Psychology from an empirical standpoint.* New York: Humanities Press.

Brentar, J., & McNamara, J. (1991a). The right to prescribe medication: Considerations for professional psychology. *Professional Psychology: Research and Practice, 22,* 179–187.

Brentar, J., & McNamara, J. (1991b). Prescription privileges for psychology: The next step in its evolution as a profession. *Professional Psychology: Research and Practice, 22,* 194–195.

Breslau, N., Davis, G. C., Andreski, D., & Peterson, E. (1991). Traumatic events and post-traumatic stress disorder in an urban population of young adults. *Archives of General Psychiatry, 48,* 216–222.

Breslin, F. D. (1974). *The adolescent and learning.* New York: Collegium.

Bressler, D. (1980). Chinese health and holistic medicine. In A. Hastings, J. Fadiman, & J. Gordon (Eds.), *Health for the whole person.* Boulder, Colo.: Westview.

Brett, G. S. (1921). *A history of psychology.* (3 vols.). London: Allen & Unwin.

Breuer, J., & Freud, S. (1957/1895). *Studies on hysteria.* New York: Basic Books.

Brewer, J. M. (1942/1940). *History of vocational guidance.* New York: Harper & Row.

Brewer, M. B. (1968). Determinants of social distance among East-African tribal groups. *Journal of Personality and Social Psychology, 10,* 279–289.

Brewer, M. B. (1979). In-group bias in the minimal intergroup situation: A cognitive-motivational analysis. *Psychological Bulletin, 86,* 307–324.

Brewer, M. B., & Campbell, D. T. (1976). *Ethnocentrism and intergroup attitudes: East African evidence.* New York: Halsted Press/Sage Publications.

Brewer, M. B., & Collins, B. E. (1981). *Scientific inquiry and the social sciences: A volume in honor of Donald T. Campbell.* San Francisco: Jossey-Bass.

Brewer, W. F. (1974). There is no convincing evidence for operant or classical conditioning in adult humans. In W. B. Weimer & D. S. Palermo (Eds.), *Cognition and the symbolic processes.* Hillsdale, N.J.: Erlbaum.

Breznitz, S. (1967). Incubation of threat: Duration of anticipation and false alarm as determinants of fear reaction to an unavoidable frightening event. *Journal of Experimental Research in Personality, 2,* 173–180.

Breznitz, S. (1983). *Cry wolf: The psychology of false alarms.* Hillsdale, N.J.: Erlbaum.

Breznitz, S. (1983). *Stress in Israel.* New York: Van Nostrand Reinhold.

Breznitz, S. (in press). *Denial of stress.* New York: International Universities Press.

Breznitz, S, & Goldberger, L. (1983). *Handbook of stress.* New York: Free Press.

Brick, H. J., & Swinth, R. L. (1980). A process model of group decision making in a multi-disciplinary health care agency. *Journal of Pediatric Psychology, 5*(3), 305–321.

Brickman, P., Coates, D, & Janoff-Bulman, R. (1978). Lottery winners and accident victims: Is happiness relative? *Journal of Personality and Social Psychology, 36,* 917–927.

Bridge, T. P., & Wyatt, R. J. (1980). Paraphrenia: Paranoid states of late life. I. European research. II. American research. *Journal of the American Geriatrics Society, 28,* 193–200, 201–205.

Bridgeman, D. L., & Marlowe, D. (1979). Jury decision making: An empirical study based on actual felony trials. *Journal of Applied Psychology, 64,* 91–98.

Bridger, H. (1976). The changing role of pets in society. *Journal of Small Animal Practice, 17*(1), 1–8.

Bridges, K. M. B. (1932). Emotional development in early infancy. *Child Development, 3,* 324–341.

Bridges, K. M. B. (1933). A study of social development in early infancy. *Child Development, 4,* 36–49.

Bridges, W. (1980). *Transitions: Making sense of life's changes.* Reading, Mass.: Addison-Wesley.

Bridgman, D. S. (1939). Success in college and business. *Personnel Journal, 9,* 1–19.

Bridgman, P. W. (1927). *The logic of modern physics.* New York: Macmillan.

Bridgman, P. W. (1952). *The nature of some of our physical concepts.* New York: Philosophical Library.

Bridgman, P. W. (1956). Probability, logic, and ESP. *Science, 123,* 15–17.

Bridgman, P. W. (1959). *The way things are.* Cambridge, Mass.: Harvard University Press.

Brief, A. P, & Aldag, R. J. (1981). The "self" in work organizations: A conceptual review. *Academy of Management Review, 6,* 75–88.

Brief, A. P., Schular, R. S., & Van Sell, M. (1981). *Managing job stress.* Boston: Little, Brown.

Briggs, S. R. (1992). *Shyness, social phobia, and avoidant personality disorder.* Manuscript submitted for publication.

Brigham, C. C. (1923). *A study of American intelligence.* Princeton, N.J.: Princeton University Press.

Brigham, J. (1990). Target person distinctiveness and attractiveness as moderator variables in the confidence-accuracy relationship in eyewitness identifications. *Basic and Applied Social Psychology, 11,* 101–115.

Brigham, J. C. (1971). Ethnic stereotypes. *Psychological Bulletin, 76,* 15–38.

Brigham, J. C. (1986) The influence of race on face recognition. In H. D. Ellis, M. A. Jeeves, F. Newcombe, & A. Young (Eds.), *Aspects of face processing* (pp.170–177). Dordrecht, The Netherlands: Martinus Nijhoff.

Brigham, J. C., & Cairns, D. L. (1988). The effect of mugshot inspections on eyewitness identification accuracy. *Journal of Applied Social Psychology, 18,* 1394–1410.

Brigham, J. C., Ready, D., & Spier, S. (1990). Standards for evaluating the fairness of photograph lineups. *Basic and Applied Social Psychology, 11,* 149–163.

Brigham, J. C., & Wolfskiel, M. P. (1983). Opinions of attorneys and law enforcement personnel on the accuracy of eyewitness identification. *Law and Human Behavior, 7,* 337–349.

Brighouse, G. (1939). A study of aesthetic apperception. *Psychological Monographs, 51* (5, entire no. 231.).

Bright, R. (1973). *Music in geriatric care.* New York: St. Martins Press.

Brill, A. A. (Ed.). (1938). *The basic writings of Sigmund Freud.* New York: Random House.

Brim, O. G., Jr. (1966). Socialization through the life cycle. In O. G. Brim, Jr., & S. Wheeler (Eds.), *Socialization after childhood: Two essays.* New York: Wiley.

Brim, O. G., Jr., Crutchfield, R. S., & Holtzman, W. H. (1966). *Intelligence: Perspectives 1965, the Terman-Otis Memorial Lectures.* New York: Harcourt Brace Jovanovich.

Brim, O. G., Jr., & Kagan, J. (Eds.). (1980). *Constancy and change in human development.* Cambridge, Mass.: Harvard University Press.

Brim, O. G., Jr., & Ryff, C. D. (1980). On the properties of life events. In P. B. Baltes & O. G. Brim, Jr. (Eds.), *Life-span development and behavior,* (Vol. 3). New York: Academic Press.

Bringmann, W. G., Balance, E. D. G., & Evans, R. B. (1975). Wilhelm Wundt 1832-1920: A brief bibliographical sketch. *Journal of the History of the Behavioral Sciences, 11,* 287-297.

Bringmann, W. G., & Tweney, R. D. (Eds.) (1980). *Wundt studies: A centennial collection.* Toronto: Hogrefe.

Bringmann, W. G., & Ungerer, G. A. (1980). The foundation of the Institute for Experimental Psychology at Leipzig University. *Psychological Research, 42,* 5-18.

Brinich P. (1980). Some potential effects of adoption on self and object representations. *The Psychoanalytic Study of the Child, 35,* 107-133.

Brion, S., Mikol, J., & Psimaras, A. (1973). Recent findings in Pick's disease. In H. M. Zimmerman (Ed.), *Progress in neuropathology,* Vol. 2. New York: Grune & Stratton.

Briscoe, M. E. (1970). Attribution of responsibility and assignment of sanctions for violations of positive and negative norms. Doctoral dissertation, University of Florida, Gainesville.

Brislin, R. (1976). Comparative research methodology: Cross-cultural studies. *International Journal of Psychology, 1,* 215-229.

Brislin, R. (1980). Translation and content analysis of oral and written materials. In H. Triandis & J. Berry (Eds.), *Handbook of cross-cultural psychology, Vol. 2.* Boston: Allyn & Bacon.

Brislin, R. (1981). *Cross-cultural encounters: Face-to-face interaction.* Elmsford, N. Y.: Pergamon Press.

Brislin, R. (1989). Intercultural communication training. In M. Asante & W. Gudykunst (Eds.), *Handbook of international and intercultural communication* (pp. 441-457). Newbury Park, CA: Sage.

Brislin, R. (1991). *The art of getting things done: A practical guide to the use of power.* New York: Praeger.

Brislin, R. (Ed.). (1976b). *Translation: Applications and research.* New York: Gardner Press/Wiley/Halsted.

Brislin, R., Cushner, K., Cherrie, C., & Yong, M. (1986). *Intercultural interactions: A practical guide.* Newbury Park, CA: Sage.

Brislin, R., Lonner, W., & Thorndike, R. (1973). *Cross-cultural research methods.* New York: Wiley.

Britt, S. H. (1970). *The spenders.* New York: McGraw-Hill.

Brittain, C. V. (1963). Adolescent choices and parent-peer cross pressures. *American Sociological Review, 28,* 385-391.

Broadbent, D. E. (1958). *Perception and communication.* London: Pergamon Press.

Broadbent, D. E. (1961). *Behaviour.* London: Eyre & Spottiswood.

Broadbent, D. E. (1971). *Decision and stress.* New York: Academic Press.

Broadbent, D. E. (1973). *In defense of empirical psychology.* London: Methuen.

Broadbent, D. E. (1979). Human performance and noise. In C. M. Harris (Ed.) *Handbood of noise control.* New York: McGraw-Hill.

Brobeck, J. R. (1947-1948). Food intake as a mechanism of temperature regulation. *Yale Journal of Biology and Medicine, 20,* 545-552.

Brobeck, J. R, Tepperman, J., & Long, C. N. H. (1943). Experimental hypothalamic hyperphagia in the albino rat. *Yale Journal of Biology and Medicine, 15,* 831-853.

Broberg, M. (1980). Veterans Administration policy with regard to elderly veterans and their wives. *The Gerontologist, 20* (pt. II), 72.

Broca, P. (1861). Remarques sur le siege de la faculte du langage articule; suivies d'une observation d'aphemie (perte de la parole). *Bulletins de la Socidte Antomigue, 6,* 330-357, 398-407.

Broca, P. (1865). Sur la siege de la faculte du langage articule. *Bulletins de la Societe d'Anthropologie (Paris), 6,* 337-393.

Broca, P. (1861). Remarques sur le siège de la faculté de langage articulé suivi d'une observation aphémie, *Bulletin Societé d'Anatomie* (2nd series), *6,* 330-357.

Broca, P. (1878). Anatomie comparée des circonvolutions cérébrales, Le grand lobe limbique et la scissure limbique dans la série des mammifères. *Review of Anthropology, 1,* 385-498.

Brock, T. C., & Becker, L. (1966). Debriefing and susceptability to subsequent experimental manipulations. *Journal of Experimental Social Psychology, 2,* 314-323.

Brock, T. C., & Buss, A. H. (1962). Dissonance, aggression and evaluation of pain. *Journal of Abnormal and Social Psychology, 65,* 197-202.

Brock, T. C., & Buss, A. H. (1964). Effects of justification for aggression in communication with the victim on post-aggression dissonance. *Journal of Abnormal and Social Psychology, 68,* 403—412.

Brockman, J. & Darcy, C. (1978). Correlates of attitudinal social distance toward the mentally ill: A review and re-survey. *Social Psychiatry, 13,* 69-77.

Brodal, A. (1981). *Neurological anatomy in relation to clinical medicine* (3rd ed.). New York: Oxford University Press.

Brodal, A. (1981/1969). *Neurological anatomy in relation to clinical medicine.* New York: Oxford University Press.

Brodigan, D. L., & Peterson, G. B. (1976). Two-choice discrimination performance of pigeons as a function of reward expectancy, prechoice delay, and domesticity. *Animal Learning and Behavior, 4,* 121-124.

Brodsky, S. L. (1977). The mental health professional on the witness stand: A survival guide. In B. D. Sales (Ed.), *Psychology in the legal process.* New York: Spectrum.

Brody, G. H., & Forehand, R. (1986). Maternal perceptions of child maladjustment as a function of the combined influence of child behavior and maternal depression. *Journal of Consulting and Clinical Psychology, 54,* 237-240.

Brody, H. (1955). Organization of the cerebral cortex. A study of aging in the human cerebral cortex. *Journal of Comparative Neurology, 102,* 511-556.

Brody, H. (1977). *Placebos and the philosophy of medicine: Clinical, conceptual, and ethical issues.* Chicago: University of Chicago Press.

Brody, H. (1980). *Neuroanatomy and neuropathology of aging.* In E. W. Busse, & D. G. Blazer (Eds.), *Handbook of geriatric psychiatry.* New York: Van Nostrand Reinhold.

Brody, N. (1980). Social motivation. *Annual Review of Psychology, 31,* 143-168.

Brody, N. (1992) *Intelligence* (2nd ed.). San Diego: Academic Press.

Broeder, D. W. (1959). The University of Chicago jury project. *Nebraska Law Review, 38,* 744-760.

Broeder, D. W. (1965). Occupational expertise and bias as affecting jury behavior: A preliminary look. *New York University Law Review, 40,* 1079–1100.

Broeder, D. W. (1965). Plaintiffs family status as affecting jury behavior: Some tentative insights. *Journal of Public Law, 14,* 131–143.

Broeder, D. W. (1965). Previous jury trial service affecting juror behavior. *Insurance Counselors Journal.*

Brogan, D. W. (1944). *The American character.* New York: Knopf.

Brogden, W. J. (1939). Sensory pre-conditioning *Journal of Experimental Psychology, 25,* 323–332.

Brogden, W. J. (1949). Acquisition and extinction of a conditioned avoidance response in dogs. *Journal of Comparative and Physiological Psychology, 42,* 296–302.

Bromley, D. B. (1977). Natural language and the development of the self. In H. E. Howe, Jr. (Ed.), *Nebraska Symposium on Motivation,* Vol. 25. Lincoln, Neb.: University of Nebraska Press.

Bronfenbrenner, U. (1959). Socialization and social class through time and space. In E. E. Maccoby, T. M. Newcomb, & E. L. Hartley, (Eds.), *Readings in social psychology* (3rd ed.). New York: Holt, Rinehart & Winston.

Bronfenbrenner, U. (1960). Freudian theories of identification and their derivatives. *Child Development, 31,* 15–40.

Bronfenbrenner, U. (1974). *A report on longitudinal evaluations of preschool programs.* Vol. II: *Is early intervention effective?* DHEW Publication No. (OHD) 75–25.

Bronfenbrenner, U. (1976). Reality and research in the ecology of human development. *Journal Supplement Abstract Service,* American Psychological Association, ms. no. 1333.

Bronfenbrenner, U. (1979). *The ecology of human development.* Cambridge, MA: Harvard University Press.

Bronfenbrenner, U. (1982/1979). *The ecology of human development.* Cambridge, Mass.: Harvard University Press.

Bronfenbrenner, U., Harding, J. & Gallwey, M. (1958). The measurement of skill in social perception. In D. McClelland, A. Baldwin, U. Bronfenbrenner, & F. Strodtbeck. *Talent and society.* Princeton, N.J.: Van Nostrand.

Bronowski, J. (1956). *Science and human values.* New York: Harper & Row.

Bronowski, J. (1973). *Ascent of man.* Boston: Little, Brown.

Bronson, W. C. (1959). Dimensions of ego and infantile identification. *Journal of Personality, 27,* 532–545.

Bronstein, P. M., Levine, M. J., & Marcus, M. (1975). A rat's first bite: The nongenetic cross-generational transfer of information. *Journal of Comparative and Physiological Psychology, 89,* 295–298.

Brook, R., Kamberg, C. J., & Mayer-Oakes, A. (1989). *Appropriateness of acute medical care for the elderly: Analysis of the literature* (R3717). Santa Monica, CA: Rand.

Brooke, M. H. (1977). *A clinician's view of neuromuscular diseases.* Baltimore, Md.: Williams & Wilkins.

Brookhart, J. M., & Dey, F. L. (1941). Reduction of sexual behavior in male guinea pigs by hypothalamic lesions. *American Journal of Physiology, 133,* 551–554.

Brookhart, J. M., Dey, F. L., & Ranson, S. W. (1940). Failure of ovarian hormones to cause mating reactions in spayed guinea pigs with hypothalamic lesions. *Proceedings of the Society of Experimental Biologists, 44,* 61–64.

Brookover, W. B, Thomas, S, & Paterson, A. (1964). Self concept of ability and school achievement. *Sociology and Education, 37,* 271–279.

Brooks, A., (1973). *Law, psychiatry and the mental health system.* Boston: Little, Brown.

Brooks, C. (1974). *Sensory awareness.* New York: Viking Press.

Brooks, C. M, & Cranefield, P. F. (Eds.). (1959). *The historical development of physiological thought.* New York: Hafner.

Brooks, G. P, & Johnson, R. W. (1980). Contributions to the history of psychology, XXIV. Johann Caspar Lavater's "Essays on physiognomy." *Psychological Reports, 46,* 3–20

Brooks, J. S., & Scarano, T. (1985). Transcendental Meditation in the treatment of the post-Vietnam adjustment. *Journal of Counseling and Development, 64,* 212–215.

Brooks, L. (1968). Spatial and verbal components of the act of recall. *Canadian Journal of Psychology, 22,* 349–368.

Brooks, R. A. (1991). Intelligence without representation. *Artificial Intelligence, 47,* 139–159.

Brookshire, K. H. (1970). Comparative psychology of learning. In M. H. Marx (Ed.), *Learning: Interactions.* New York: Macmillan.

Brophy, J. (1981). Teacher praise: A functional analysis. *Review of Educational Research, 51,* 5–32.

Brophy, J. E, & Good, T. L. (1974). *Teacher-student relationships: Causes and consequences.* New York: Holt.

Brotemarkle, R. A. (1931). *Studies in honor of Lightner Witmer.* Philadelphia, Pa.: University of Pennsylvania Press.

Brotemarkle, R. A. (1947). Clinical psychology, 1896–1946. *Journal of Consulting Psychology, 11,* 1–4.

Broughton, J. M. (1980). Genetic metaphysics: The developmental psychology of mind-body concepts. In R. W. Rieber (Ed.), *Body and mind.* New York: Academic Press.

Broverman, I. K., Broverman, D. M, Clarkson, F. E, Rosenkrantz, P, & Voget, S. R. (1970). Sex-role stereotypes and clinical judgments of mental health. *Journal of Consulting Psychology, 34,* 1–7.

Broverman, I. K., Vogel, S. R., Broverman, D. M., Clarkson, F. E., & Rosenkrantz, P. S. (1972). Sex-role stereotypes: A current appraisal. *Journal of Social Issues, 28,* 59–78.

Broverman, I. L., Broverman, D. M., Clarkson, R., Rosencrantz, P., & Vogel, S. (1970). Sex role stereotypes and clinical judgements of mental health. *Journal of Consulting and Clinical Psychology, 34,* 1,1–7.

Brown, A. L. (1975). The development of memory: Knowing, knowing about knowing, and knowing how to know. In H. W. Reese (Ed.), *Advances in child development,* Vol. 10. New York. Academic Press

Brown, A. L. (1978). Knowing when, where, and how to remember: A problem of metacognition. In R. Glaser (Ed.), *Advances in instructional psychology,* Vol. 1. Hillsdale, N.J.: Erlbaum.

Brown, B., & Grotberg, E. H. (1980). *Head Start: A successful experiment.* Washington, D. C.: Administration for Children, Youth and Families, OHD, DHHS.

Brown, B. S., Wienckowski, L. A., & Bivens, L. W. (1973). Psychosurgery: Perspective on a current issue *(U. S. Department of Health, Education and Welfare release).* Washington, D. C.: U. S. Government Printing Office.

Brown, B. W. (1972). Statistics, scientific method, and smoking. In J. M. Tanur (Ed.), *Statistics: a guide to the unknown.* San Francisco: Holden-Day.

Brown, C. W., & Ghiselli, E. E. (1955). *Scientific method in psychology.* New York: McGraw-Hill.

Brown, D. (1956). Sex-role preference in young children. *Psychological Monographs, 70,* no. 421.

Brown, D. (1977). A model for the levels of concentrative meditation. *International Journal of Clinical Hypnosis 25*, 236–273.

Brown, D. (1979). Learning disabilities: The need for cross disciplinary research. *Journal of Clinical Child Psychology, 8*, 144–145.

Brown, D. T., & Minke, K. (1982). *Directory of school psychology training programs in the United States*. Washington, D.C.: National Association of School Psychologists.

Brown, E., Deffenbacher, K., & Sturgill, W. (1977). Memory for faces and the circumstances of encounter. *Journal of Applied Psychology, 62*, 311–318.

Brown, E., & Sechrest, L. (1980). Experiments in cross-cultural research. In H. Triandis & J. Berry (Eds.), *Handbook of cross-cultural psychology*, Vol. 2. Boston: Allyn & Bacon.

Brown, F. M., & Graeber, R. C. (Eds.). (1982). *Rhythmic aspects of behavior*. Hillsdale, N.J.: Erlbaum.

Brown, G. (1971). *Human teaching for human learning* New York: Viking Press

Brown, G. I. (1975). *The live classroom: Innovation through confluent education and Gestalt*. New York: Viking Press.

Brown, G. W. (1979). The social etiology of depression: London studies. In R. A. Depue (Ed.), *The psychobiology of the depressive disorders*. New York: Academic Press.

Brown, G. W., & Harris, T. W. (1978). *Social origins of depression*. New York: Free Press.

Brown, J. A. C. (1963). *Techniques of persuasion*. Harmondsworth, England: Penguin.

Brown, J. S. (1948). Gradients of approach and avoidance responses and their relation to level of motivation. *Journal of Comparative and Physiological Psychology, 41*, 450–465.

Brown, J. S. (1969). Factors effecting self-punitive locomotor behavior. In B. A. Campbell & R. M. Church (Eds.), *Punishment and aversive behavior*. New York: Appleton-Century-Crofts.

Brown, L. (1990). The meaning of a multicultural perspective for theory-building in feminist therapy. *Women and Therapy, 14*, 1–21.

Brown, L., & Brodsky, A. (1992). The future of feminist therapy. *Psychotherapy, 29*(1), 51–57.

Brown, M. (1973). The new body psychotherapies. *Psychotherapy: Theory, Research, and Practice, 10*(2), 98–116.

Brown, M. (1979). *Left handed: Right handed*. North Pomfret, Vt.: David & Charles.

Brown, N. O. (1959). *Life against death*. Middletown, Conn.: Wesleyan University Press.

Brown, P., & Elliott, R. (1965). Control of aggression in a nursery school class. *Journal of Experimental Child Psychology, 2*, 103–107.

Brown, P. K., & Wald, G. (1964). Visual pigments in single rods and cones of the human retina. *Science, 144*, 45–52.

Brown, P. K., & Wald, G. (1965). Visual pigments in human and monkey retinas. *Nature, 200*, 37–39.

Brown, P. L., & Jenkins, H. M. (1967). Conditioned inhibition and excitation in operant discrimination learning. *Journal of Experimental Psychology, 75*, 255–266.

Brown, R. (1978). *Stress and the art of biofeedback*. New York: Bantam Books.

Brown, R., & McNeill, D. (1966). The "tip of the tongue" phenomenon. *Journal of Verbal Learning and Verbal Behavior, 5*, 325–337.

Brown, R. E. (1979). Mammalian social odors: A critical review. *Advances in the Study of Behavior, 10*, 103–162.

Brown, R. T. (1980). A closer examination of the Education for all Handicapped Children Act: A guide for the 1980s. *Psychology in the Schools, 17*, 355–360.

Brown, R. T. (1986). Etiology and development of exceptionality. In R. T. Brown & C. R. Reynolds (Eds.), *Psychological perspectives on childhood exceptionality: A handbook* (pp. 181–229). New York: Wiley.

Brown, R. T. (1986). Fetal alcohol syndrome. In C. R. Reynolds & L. Mann (Eds.). *Encyclopedia of special education* (pp. 660–664). New York: Wiley.

Brown, R. W. (1954). Mass phenomena. In G. Lindzey (Ed.), *Handbook of social psychology*, Vol. 2. Reading, Mass.: Addison-Wesley.

Brown, R. W. (1958). A stimulus-response analysis of language and meaning. In P. Henle (Ed.), *Language, thought, and culture*. Ann Arbor, Mich., University of Michigan Press.

Brown, R. W. (1958). *Words and things*. New York: Free Press.

Brown, R. W. (1965). *Social psychology*. New York: Free Press.

Brown, R. W. (1970). *Psycholinguistics; selected papers*. New York: Free Press.

Brown, R. W. (1973). *A first language: The early stages*. Cambridge, Mass.: Harvard University Press.

Brown, R. W., et al. (1962). *New directions in psychology*. New York: Holt, Rinehart & Winston.

Brown, R. W., Black, A. H., & Horowitz, A. E. (1955). Phonetics symbolism in natural languages. *Journal of Abnormal and Social Psychology, 50*, 388–393.

Brown, R. W., & Herrnstein, R. (1974). *Psychology*. Boston: Little, Brown, 1974.

Brown, R. W., & McNeill, D. (1966). The "tip of the tongue" phenomenon. *Journal of Verbal Learning Behavior, 5*, 325–337.

Brown, T. (1820). *Lectures on the philosophy of the human mind*, Edinburgh: Tait.

Brown, T. S., & Wallace, P. M. (1980). *Physiological psychology*. New York: Academic Press.

Brown, W. F. (1965). Student-to-student counseling for academic adjustment. *Personnel and Guidance Journal 43*, 811–817.

Brown, W. F. (1974). *Student's guides to effective study*. San Marcos, Tex.: Effective Study Materials.

Brown, W. F. (1975). *Effective study test*. San Marcos, Tex.: Effective Study Materials.

Brown, W. F. (1977). *Student-to-student counseling*. Austin, Tex.: University of Texas Press.

Brown, W. F. (1978). *Study skills surveys*. San Marcos, Tex.: Effective Study Materials.

Brown, W. F. (1981). *Student-to-student counseling: Comparison of successful and unsuccessful disseminations*. San Marcos, Tex.: Effective Study Materials.

Brown, W. F., Gadzella, B. M., & Forristall, D. Z. (1982). *Computer-assisted study skills improvement program*. San Marcos, Tex.: Effective Study Materials.

Brown, W. F., & Holtzman, W. H. (1953). *Survey of study habits and attitudes*. New York: Psychological Corp.

Brown, W. F., & Holtzman, W. H. (1956). Use of the survey of study habits and attitudes for counseling students. *Personnel and Guidance Journal, 35*, 214—218.

Brown, W. F., & Holtman, W. H. (1967). *Survey of study habits and attitudes: Forms C and H*. New York: Psychological Corp.

Brown, W. F., & Holtzman, W. H. (1972). *A guide to college survival*. Englewood Cliffs, N.J.: Prentice-Hall.

Brown, W. F., Wehe, N. O., & Hislam, W. L. (1971). Effectiveness of student-to-student counseling on the academic achievement of potential college dropouts. *Journal of Educational Psychology, 62,* 285–289.

Brown, W. H., & Sharp, L. W. (1910). The closing response in *Dionaea. Botanical Gazette, 49,* 290–302.

Brown, W. T. (1990). Invited editorial: The fragile X: Progress toward solving the puzzle. *American Journal of Human Genetics, 47,* 175–180.

Brown, W. T., Jenkins, E. C., Krawczum, M. S., Wisniewski, K., Rudelli, R., Cohen, I. R., Fisch, G., Wolf-Schein, E., Miezejewski, C., & Dobkin, C. (1986). The fragile X syndrome. In H. M. Wisniewski & D. A. Snider (Eds.), Mental retardation: Research, education, and technology transfer [Special Issue]. *Annals of the New York Academy of Sciences, 447.*

Browne, M. W. (1982). Covariance structures. In D. M. Hawkins (Ed.), *Topics in applied multivariate analysis.* Cambridge, England: Cambridge University Press.

Brownell, K. D. (1984). Behavorial medicine. In G. T. Wilson, C. M. Franks, K. D. Brownell, & P. C. Kendall (Eds.), *Annual review of behavior therapy: Vol. 9. Theory and practice* (pp. 180–210). New York: Guilford Press.

Brownell, K. D., Hayes, S. C., & Barlow, D. H. (1977). Patterns of appropriate and deviant sexual arousal: The behavioral treatment of multiple sexual deviation. *Journal of Consulting and Clinical Psychology, 45,* 1144–1155.

Brownmiller, S. (1975). Against our Will: Men, women, and rape. New York: Bantam.

Broyler, C. R., Thorndike, E. L., & Woolyard, E. (1927). A second study of mental discipline in high school subjects. *Journal of Educational Psychology, 18,* 377–404.

Brožek, J. (1970). Research on diet and behavior. *Journal of the American Dietetic Association, 57,* 321–325.

Brožek, J. (1972). Quantitative explorations in the history of psychology in Yugoslavia: Translations. *Psychological Reports, 31,* 397–398.

Brožek, J. (1973). Marcus Marulus (1450–1524), author of *Psichologia:* Early references and the dating. *Proceedings 81st Annual Convention,* APA, 21–22.

Brožek, J. (1974). The American adventure. In T. S. Krawiec (Ed.), *The psychologists,* Vol. 2. New York: Oxford University Press.

Brožek, J. (1977). *Psychology in Czechoslovakia: Background, bibliographies, current topics, and perspectives for the future.* Cologne, West Germany: Bundesinstitut für Ostwissenschaftliche und internationale Studien, Bericht no. 15.

Brožek, J. (1978). Nutrition, malnutrition, and behavior. *Annual Review of Psychology, 29,* 151–171.

Brožek, J. (1979). *Behavioral effects of energy and protein deficits.* Washington, D.C.: NIH Publication no. 79–1906.

Brožek, J. (1982). Malnutrition and human behavior. In *Present knowledge of nutrition.* New York: Nutrition Foundation.

Brožek, J., & Evans, R. B. (Eds.). (1977). *R. I. Watson's selected papers on the history of psychology.* Hanover, N.H.: University Press of New England.

Brožek, J., & Pongratz, L. G. (1980). *Historiography of modern psychology.* Toronto: Hogrefe.

Brožek, J., & Sibinga, M. S. (1970). *Origins of psychometry.* Niewkoop, Netherland: De Graaf.

Brožek, J., & Slobin, D. I. (Eds.). (1972). *Psychology in the USSR: An historical perspective.* White Plains, N.Y.: International Arts & Sciences Press.

Bruch, H. (1948). Psychological aspects of obesity. *Bulletin of the New York Academy of Medicine 24,* 73–86.

Bruch, H. (1957). *The importance of overweight.* New York: Norton.

Bruch, H. (1974). Interpersonal theory: Harry Stack Sullivan. In A. Burton (Ed.), *Operational theories of personality.* New York: Brunner/Mazel.

Bruch, H. (1974). *Learning psychotherapy.* Cambridge, Mass.: Harvard University Press.

Bruch, H. (1978). *The golden cage: The enigma of anorexia nervosa.* Boston: Harvard University Press.

Bruch, H. (1979/1973). *Eating disorders: Obesity, anorexia nervosa, and the person within.* New York: Basic Books.

Bruch, M. A. (1981). A task analysis of assertive behavior revisited: Replication and extension. *Behavior Therapy, 12,* 217–230.

Brunell, L. F., & Young, W. T. (Eds.). (1982). *Multimodal handbook for a mental hospital.* New York: Springer.

Bruner, J. (1992). Another look at New Look 1. *American Psychologist, 47,* 780–783.

Bruner, J. S. (1957). On perceptual readiness. *Psychological Review, 64,* 123–152.

Bruner, J. S. (1961). The act of discovery. *Harvard Educational Review, 31,* 21–32.

Bruner, J. S. (1961). *The process of education.* Cambridge, Mass.: Harvard University Press.

Bruner, J. S. (1962). *On knowing: Essays for the left hand.* Cambridge, Mass.: Harvard University Press.

Bruner, J. S. (1964). The course of cognitive thought. *American Psychologist 19,* 1–15.

Bruner, J. S. (1966). *Toward a theory of instruction.* Cambridge, Mass.: Harvard University Press.

Bruner, J. S. (1968). *Processes of cognitive growth: Infancy.* Worcester, Mass.: Clark University Press.

Bruner, J. S. (1972). The nature and uses of immaturity. *American Psychologist, 27,* 1–22.

Bruner, J. S. (1973). *The relevance of education* (rev. ed.). New York: Norton.

Bruner, J. S. (1975). From communication to language—A psychological perspective. *Cognition, 3,* 255–287.

Bruner, J. S. (1977). Early social interaction and language acquisition. In H. R. Schaffer (Ed.), *Studies in mother-infant interaction.* London: Academic Press.

Bruner, J. S., et al. (1966). *Studies in cognitive growth.* New York: Wiley,.

Bruner, J. S., & Goodman, C. C. (1947). Value and need as organizing factors in perception. *Journal of Abnormal and Social Psychology, 42,* 33–44.

Bruner, J. S., Goodnow, J. J., & Austin, G. A. (1956). *A study of thinking.* New York: Wiley.

Bruner, J. S., Jolly, A., & Sylva, K. (Eds.). (1976). *Play—Its role in development and evolution.* New York: Basic Books.

Bruner, J. S., Olver, R. R., Greenfield, P. M., et al. (1966). *Studies in cognitive growth: A collaboration at the center for cognitive studies.* New York: Wiley.

Bruner, J. S., & Postman, L. (1947). Emotional selectivity in perception and reaction. *Journal of Personality, 16,* 69–77.

Brunnell, P. A. (1992). Rubella (German measles). In J. B. Wyngaarden, L. H. Smith, Jr., & J. C. Bennett (Eds.), *Cecil textbook of medicine* (19th ed., pp. 1827–1829). Philadelphia: Saunders.

Brunner, J. S., & Postman, L. (1949). On the perception of incongruity: A paradigm. *Journal of Personality, 18,* 206–223.

Bruner, G. A., et al. (1966). *User determined attributes of ideal transportation systems: An empirical study.* College Park, Md.: University of Maryland.

Bruno, F. J. (1974). *Psychology: A life-centered approach.* Santa Barbara, Calif.: Hamilton.

Bruns, B. P. (1973). *Compulsive gambler.* New York: Stuart.

Brunson, B. I., & Matthews, K. A. (1981). The type A coronary-prone behavior pattern and reactions to uncontrollable stress: An analysis of performance strategies, affect, and attributions during failure. *Journal of Personality and Social Psychology 40,* 906–918.

Brunswick, E. (1952). *The conceptual framework of psychology.* Chicago: University of Chicago Press.

Brunswick, E. (1947). *Systematic and representative design of psychological experiments, with results in physical and social perception.* Berkeley, Calif.: University of California Press.

Brunswik, E. (1939). Probability as a determiner of rat behavior. *Journal of Experimental Psychology, 25,* 175–197.

Brunswik, E. (1939). The conceptual focus of some psychological systems. *Journal of Unified Science, 8,* 36–49.

Brunswik, E. (1952). The conceptual framework of psychology. *International Encyclopedia of Unified Science, 1* (entire no. 10).

Brunswik, E. (1956a). Historical and thematic relations of psychology to other sciences. *Scientific Monthly, 83,* 151–161.

Brunswik, E. (1956b). *Perception and the representative design of psychological experiments.* Berkeley, Calif.: University of California Press.

Brunton, T. L. (1883). On the nature of inhibition, and the action of drugs upon it. *Nature, 27,* 419–487.

Brush, F. R. (1971). *Aversive conditioning and learning.* New York: Academic press.

Brussel, J. A. (1967). *The layman's guide to psychiatry* (2nd ed.). New York: Barnes & Noble.

Brutten, M., Richardson, S., & Mangel, C. (1973). *Something's wrong with my child —A parent's book about children with learning disabilities.* New York: Harcourt Brace Jovanovich.

Bryan, T. H. (1974). An observational analysis of classroom behaviors of children with learning difficulties. *Journal of Learning Disabilities, 7,* 35–43.

Bryan, T. H. (1978). Social relationships and verbal interactions of learning disabled children. *Journal of Learning Disabilities, 11,* 107–115.

Bryan, T. H., Donahue, M., & Pearl, R. (1981). Learning disabled children's communicative competence on referential communication tasks. *Journal of Pediatric Psychology, 6,* 383–393.

Bryan, T. H., & Pearl, R. (1979). Self concepts and locus of control of learning disabled children. *Journal of Clinical Child Psychology, 8,* 223–226.

Bryden, M. P. (1965). Tachistoscopic recognition, handedness, and cerebral dominance. *Neuropsychologia, 3,* 1–8.

Bryden, M. P. (1979). Evidence for sex-related differences in cerebral organization. In M. A. Wittig & A. C. Petersen (Eds.), *Sex-related differences in cognitive functioning: Developmental issues.* New York: Academic Press.

Bryne, D., & Wong, T. (1962). Racial prejudice, interpersonal attraction, and assumed dissimilarity of attitudes. *Journal of Abnormal and Social Psychology, 65,* 246–253.

Bryngelson, B. (1933). Left-handedness and stuttering. *Journal of Heredity, 24,* 387–390.

Bryson, R. B., Bryson, J. B., Licht, M. H., & Licht, B. G. (1976). The professional pair: Husband and wife psychologists. *American Psychologist 31,* 10–16.

Buber, M. (1949). *The prophetic faith.* New York: Macmillan.

Buber, M. (1952). *The eclipse of God: Studies in the relations between religion and philosophy.* New York: Harper.

Buber, M. (1956). *The writings of Martin Buber.* Cleveland, Ohio: World.

Buber, M. (1957). Distance and relation. *Psychiatry, 20,* 97–104.

Buber, M. (1963). *Israel and the world: Essays in a time of crisis.* New York: Shoeken.

Buber, M. (1965). *The knowledge of man.* New York: Harper.

Buber, M. (1970/1958). *I and thou.* New York: Scribner.

Buch, J., Basavaraju, N. E., Charatan, F. B., & Kamen, S. (1976). Preventive medicine in a long-term care institution. *Geriatrics 31,* 99–104, 108.

Buchanan, B. G., & Feigenbaum, E. A. (1978). Dendral and metadendral: Their application dimension. *Artificial Intelligence, 11,* 5–24.

Buchanan, W., & Cantril, H. (1953). *How nations see each other.* Urbana, Ill.: University of Illinois Press.

Buchsbaum, R. (1938). *Animals without backbones.* Chicago: University of Chicago Press.

Buck, J. N. (1948). The H-T-P technique: A qualitative and quantitative scoring manual, part one. *Journal of Clinical Psychology, 4,* 397–405.

Buck, J. N. (1949). The H-T-P technique: A qualitative and quantitative scoring manual, part two. *Journal of Clinical Psychology, 5,* 37–76.

Buck, J. N. (1948). The H-T-P test. *Journal of Clinical Psychology, 4,* 151–158.

Buck, P. H. (1938). *Vikings of the sunrise.* Philadelphia, Pa.: Lippincott.

Buck, R. W., & Parke, R. D. (1972). Behavioral and physiological response to the presence of a friendly or neutral person in two types of stressful situations. *Journal of Personality and Social Psychology, 24,* 143–153.

Buckley, R. E. (1977). Nutrition, metabolism, brain functions and learning. *Academic Therapy, 12,* 321–326.

Buckley, W. (1967). *Sociology and modern systems theory.* Englewood Cliffs, N.J.: Prentice-Hall.

Buckley, W. (1968). *Modern systems research for the behavioral scientist.* Chicago: Aldine.

Buckner, H. (1970). The transvestic career path. *Psychiatry, 33,* 381–389.

Buckout, R. (1980). Eyewitness identification and psychology in the courtroom. In G. Cooke (Ed.), *The role of the forensic psychologist* (pp. 175–188). Springfield, IL: Thomas.

Budd, L. S. (1976). Problems, disclosure, and commitment of cohabitating and married couples. Unpublished doctoral dissertation, University of Minnesota.

Buder, G. (1989). Issues in the application of cognitive and behavioral strategies to the treatment of social phobia. *Clinical Psychology Review, 9,* 91–106.

Budman, S. H., & Gurman, A. S. (1988). *Theory and practice of brief psychotherapy.* New York: Guilford.

Budman, S., & Wertlieb, D. (Eds.). (1979). Psychologists in health care settings. *Professional Psychology, 10,* 397–644 (special issue).

228 BIBLIOGRAPHY

Budoff, M., & Gottlieb, J. (1976). Special-class EMR children main-streamed: A study of an aptitude (learning potential) X treatment interaction. *American Journal of Mental Deficiency, 81*, 1–11.

Budzynski, T. H. (1976). Biofeedback and the twilight states of consciousness. In G. E. Schwartz, & D. Shapiro (Eds.), *Consciousness and self-regulation: Advances in Research*, Vol. 1. New York: Plenum.

Budzynski, T. H. (1978). Biofeedback in the treatment of muscle-contraction headache. *Biofeedback and Self Regulation, 3*, 409–434.

Budzynski, T. H., Stoyva, J. M., Adler, C. S., & Mullaney, D. J. (1973). EMG biofeedback and tension headache: A controlled study. *Psychosomatic Medicine 35*, 484–496.

Bugelski, B. R. (1938). Extinction with and without sub-goal reinforcement. *Journal of Comparative Psychology, 26*, 121–133.

Bugelski, B. R. (1962). Presentation time, total time, and mediation in paired associate learning. *Journal of Experimental Psychology, 63*, 409–412.

Bugelski, B. R. (1970). Words and things and images. *American Psychologist, 25*, 1002–1012.

Bagelski, B. R. (1971). *The psychology of learning applied to teaching* (2nd ed.). Indianapolis, Ind.: Bobbs-Merrill.

Bugelski, B. R. (1974). Imagery and affect in motor skills. In W. C. Schwank (Ed.), *The winning edge*. Washington, D.C.: American Alliance for Health, Physical Education and Recreation.

Bugelski, B. R. (1974). Images as mediators in one-trial paired-associate learning, III. Sequential functions in serial lists. *Journal of Experimental Psychology, 103*, 298–303.

Bugelski, B. R. (1977). Imagery and verbal behavior. *Journal of Mental Imagery, 1*, 39–52.

Bugelski, B. R. (1979). *The principles of learning and memory*. New York: Praeger.

Bugelski, B. R., & Alampay, D. (1961). The role of frequency in developing peceptual sets. *Canadian Journal of Psychology, 15*, 205–211.

Bugelski, B. R., & Graziano, A. M. (1980). *The handbook of practical psychology*. Englewood Cliffs, N.J.: Prentice-Hall.

Bugelski, B. R., Kidd, E., & Segmen, J. (1968). Image as a mediator in one-trial paired-associate learning. *Journal of Experimental Psychology, 76*, 69–73.

Bugelski, B. R., & Miller, N. E. (1938). A spatial gradient in the strength of avoidance responses. *Journal of Experimental Psychology, 23*, 494–505.

Bugental, J. F. T. (1961). *The search for authenticity*. New York: Holt, Rinehart & Winston.

Bugental, J. F. T. (1963). Humanistic psychology: A new break-through. *American Psychologist, 18*, 563–567.

Bühler, C. (1930). *The first year of life*. New York: Day.

Bühler, C. (1933). *Der menschliche Lebenslauf als psychologisches Problem*. Leipzig: Hirzel.

Bühler, C. & Allen, M. (1972). *Introduction to humanistic psychology*. Monterey, Calif.: Brooks/Cole.

Bühler, C., & Hetzer, H. (1932). *Kleinkindertests*. Leipzig: Barth.

Bühler, C., & Massarik, F. (Eds.). (1968). *The course of human life: A study of goals in the humanistic perspective*. New York: Springer.

Bühler, K. (1907). Tatsachen und Probleme zu einer Psychologie der Denkvorgänge. I. Über Gedanken. *Archiv für die Gesamte Psychologie, 9*, 297–365.

Bühler, K. (1913). *Die Gestaltwahrnehmungen*. Stuttgart: Spemann.

Bühler, K. (1918). *Die geistige Entwicklung des Kindes*. Jena: Fischer.

Bühler, K. (1927). *Die Krise der Psychologie*. Jena, Germany: Fischer.

Bühler, K. (1930/1928). *The mental development of the child: A summary of modern psychological theory*. London: Paul Trench, Trubner.

Bühler, K. (1960). *Das Gestaltprinzip im Leben der Menschen und Tiere*. Bern: Huber.

Bujas, Z. (1953). *L'adaptation gustative et son mécanisme*. Zagreb, Yugoslavia: AIPUZ.

Bujas, Z. (1968). *Psychophysiological studies of some aspects of fatigue and rest*. Zagreb, Yugoslavia: Arh. Hig. Rada.

Bujas, Z. (1968). *Psychophysiology of work*, Zagreb, Yugoslavia: Izd. Jug. Akad.

Bujas, Z. (1971). Electrical taste. In L. M. Beidler, (Ed.), *Handbook of sensory physiology*. Berlin: Springer.

Bujas, Z. (1980). Reaction time as a tentative measure of taste intensity. In *Olfaction and Taste VII*. London: IRL.

Bujas, Z. (1981). *Introduction to methods of experimental psychology*. Zagreb, Yugoslavia: Školska Knjiga.

Bujas, Z., & Ostojčić, A. (1942). *Intelligence and its measurement*, Zagreb, Yugoslavia: Albrecht.

Bulka, R. P., Fabry, J. B., & Sahakian, W. S. (Eds.). (1979). *Logotherapy in action*. New York: Aronson.

Bull, J. A. & Overmier, J. B. (1968). The additive and subtractive properties of excitation and inhibition. *Journal of Comparative and Physiological Psychology. 66*, 511–514.

Bull, R., & Rumsey, N. (1988). *The social psychology of facial appearance*. New York: Springer-Verlag.

Bull, W. D. (1960). The validity of behavioral rating scale items for the assessment of individual creativity. *Journal of Applied Psychology, 44*, 407–412.

Bullard, D. M. (1953). Preface to the second edition. In H. S. Sullivan (Ed.), *Conceptions of modern psychiatry*. New York: Norton.

Bullinger, A. (1973). Comparaison, mesure et transitivité. *Archives de Psychologie*, Monographie 1.

Bulloch, K. (1985). Neuroanatomy of lymphoid tissue: A review. In R. Guillemin & M. Cohn (Eds.), *Neural modulation of immunity* (pp. 111–141). New York: Raven.

Bulloch, K., & Moore, R. Y. (1981). Innervation of the thymus gland by brainstem and spinal cord in mouse and rat. *American Journal of Anatomy, 161*, 157–166.

Bullough, E. (1957). *Aesthetics: Lectures and essays*. Stanford, Calif: Stanford University Press.

Bullough, V. L. (1981). Age at menarche: A misunderstanding. *Science, 213*, 365–366.

Bulman, R. J., & Wortman, C. B. (1977). Attributions of blame and coping in the "real world": Severe accident victims react to their lot. *Journal of Personality and Social Psychology, 35*, 351–363.

Bumpass, L., & Westoff, C. F. (1970). The "perfect contraceptive" population. *Science, 169*, 1177–1182.

Bundy, R. P., & Mundy-Castle, A. C. (1982). Looking strategies in Nigerian infants: A cross-cultural study. In V. Curran (Ed.), *The developing child: A Nigerian perspective*. London: Routledge & Kegan Paul.

Bunge, M. (1962). *Intuition and science*. Englewood Cliffs, N.J.: Prentice-Hall.

Bunney, W. E., Van Kammen, D. P., Post, R. M., & Garland, B. L. (1979). A possible role for dopamine in schizophrenia and manic-depressive illness (a review of evidence). In E. Usdin, I. J. Kopin, & J. Barchas (Eds.), *Catecholamines: Basic and clinical frontiers*. New York: Pergamon Press.

Burack, J. A., Hodapp, R. M., & Zigler, E. (1988). Issues in the classification of mental retardation: Differentiating among organic etiologies. *Journal Child Psychology and Psychiatry, 29,* 765–779.

Buranelli, V. (1975). *The wizard from Vienna, Franz Anton Mesmer: A biography of the 18th century doctor who laid the foundation for modern psychiatry.* New York: Coward, McCann & Geoghagen.

Burck, E. (1947). Low-pressure selling. *Harvard Business Review, 25,* 227–242.

Burden, R. (1979). The proper study of educational psychology: A reply to David Hargreaves. *Association of Educational Psychologists Journal 4*(10), 47–50.

Bureau of National Affairs. (1981). *The comparable worth issue.* Washington, D,C.: Bureau of National Affairs.

Burg, C., Quinn, P. O., & Rapaport, J. L. (1978). Clinical evaluation of one-year-old infants: Possible prediction of risk for the "hyperactive syndrome." *Journal of Pediatric Psychology, 3,* 164–167.

Burgemeister, B. B., Blum, L. H., & Lorge, I. (1971). *Manual for the Columbia mental maturity scale.* New York: Psychological Corp.

Burgess, A., & Holmstrom, L. (1976). Coping behavior of the rape victim. *American Journal of Psychiatry, 133*(4), 413—417.

Burgess, P., & Nystul, M. S. (1977). The single parent family: A review of the literature. *Australian Child and Family Welfare, 8,* 19–26.

Burgess, R. L., & Conger, R. D. (1978). Family interaction in abusive, neglectful and normal families. *Child Development, 49,* 1163–1173.

Burgoon, J. K., & Saine, T. (1978). *The unspoken dialogue: An introduction to nonverbal communication.* Boston: Houghton Mifflin.

Burisch, M. (1984). Approaches to personality inventory contruction, *American Psychologist, 39,* 214–227.

Burk, R. D. (1967). The nature of disability. *Journal of Rehabilitation, 33,* 10–14.

Burka, J. B., & Yuen, L. M. (1982). Mind games procrastinators play *Psychology Today, 16,* 32–37, 44.

Burke, A., Heuer, F., & Reisberg, D. (1992). Remembering emotional events. *Memory & Cognition, 20,* 277–290.

Burke, W. (1978). *The cutting edge: Current theory and practice in organization development.* La Jolla, Calif.: University Associates.

Burke, W. W. (1982). *Organization development: Principles and practices.* Boston: Little, Brown.

Burks, H. M., Jr., & Stefflre, B. (1979). *Theories of counseling* (3rd ed.). New York: McGraw-Hill.

Burnam, M. A., Pennebaker, J. W., & Glass, D. C. (1975). Time consciousness, achievement striving and the type A coronary-prone behavior pattern. *Journal of Abnormal Psychology, 84,* 76–79.

Burnham, J. C. (1968). On the origins of behaviorism. *Journal of the History of the Behavioral Sciences, 4,* 143–151.

Burnham, W. H. (1888). Memory, historically and experimentally considered. *American Journal of Psychology, 2,* 39–90.

Burnham, W. H. (1924). *The normal mind.* New York: Appleton.

Burns, A., Jacoby, R., & Levy, R. (1990). Psychiatric phenomena in Alzheimer's disease: II. Disorders of perception. *British Journal of Psychiatry, 157,* 76–81.

Burns, B. D. (1958). *The mammalian cerebral cortex.* London: Arnold.

Burns, J. E. (1990). Contemporary models of consciousness: Part I. *Journal of mind and behavior, 11,* 153–172.

Burns, S., DeLeon, P., Chemtob, C., Welch, B., & Samuels, R. (1988). Psychotropic medications: A new technique for psychology? *Psychotherapy, 25,* 508–515.

Burns, T., & Stalker, G. M. (1961). *The management of innovation.* London: Tavistock Publications.

Buros, O. K. (1949). *Mental measurements yearbook.* Highland Park, N.J.: Gryphon Press.

Buros, O. K. (1968). The story behind the mental measurements yearbooks. *Measurement and Evaluation in Guidance, 1*(2), 86–95.

Buros, O. K. (Ed.). (1935). *Educational psychological and personality tests of 1933 and 1934.* New Brunswick, N.J.: Rutgers School of Education.

Buros, O. K. (Ed.). (1974). *Tests in print; a comprehensive bibliography of tests for use in education, psychology, and industry* (2nd ed.). Highland Park, N.J.: Gryphon Press.

Buros, O. K. (Ed.). (1978). *The eighth mental measurements yearbook.* Highland Park, N.J.: Gryphon Press.

Burrell, A. P. (1951). Facilitating learning through emphasis on meetings children's basic emotional needs. *Journal of Educational Sociology, 24,* 381–393.

Burris, D. S. (1969). *The right to treatment: A symposium.* New York: Springer.

Burrow, T. (1927). The group method of analysis. *Psychoanalytic Review, 19,* 268–280.

Burrow, T. (1927). *The social basis of consciousness.* New York: Harcourt, Brace.

Burrow, T. (1937). *The biology of human conflict.* New York: Macmillan.

Burrow, T. (1953). *Science and man's behavior.* New York: Philosophical Library.

Burrow, T. (1958). *A search for man's sanity: Selected letters.* New York: Oxford University Press.

Burrows, G. D., & Dennerstein, L. (Eds.). (1980). *Handbook of hypnosis and psychosomatic medicine.* New York: Elsevier/North-Holland.

Burstein, H. (1971). *Attribute sampling: Tables and explanations.* New York: McGraw-Hill.

Burt, C. (1921). *Mental and scholastic tests.* London: King.

Burt, C. (1949). The structure of the mind: A review of the results of factor analysis. *British Journal of Educational Psychology, 19,* 100–111, 176–199.

Burt, C. (1958). The inheritance of mental ability. *American Psychologist, 13,* 1–15.

Burt, C. (1961). Intelligence and social mobility. *British Journal of Statistical Psychology, 14,* 3–24.

Burt, C. (1962). Francis Galton and his contributions to psychology. *British Journal of Statistical Psychology, 15,* 1–49.

Burt, C. (1972). The inheritance of general intelligence. *American Psychologist, 27,* 175–190.

Burt, C. L. (1925). *The young delinquent.* London: University of London Press,

Burt, C. L. (1937). *The backward child.* London: University of London Press.

Burt, C. L. (1940). *The factors of the mind.* London: University of London Press.

Burt, C. L. (1966). The genetic determination of differences in intelligence: A study of monozygotic twins reared together and apart. *British Journal of Psychology, 57,* 137–153.

Burton, B. T. (1976). *Human Nutrition.* New York: McGraw-Hill.

Burton, R. V. (1963). The generality of honesty reconsidered. *Psychological Review,70,* 481–499

Burton, R. V. (1976). Honesty and dishonesty. In T. Lickona (Ed.), *Moral development and behavior.* New York: Holt, Rinehart & Winston.

Burtt, H. E. (1929). Psychology and industrial efficiency. New York: Harper.

Burtt, H. E. (1931). Legal psychology. New York: Prentice-Hall.

Burtt, H. E. (1938). Psychology of advertising. Boston: Houghton Mifflin.

Burtt, H. E. (1941). An experimental study of early childhood memory. *Journal of Genetic Psychology, 58,* 435–439.

Burtt, H. E. (1942). Principles of employment psychology. New York: Harper.

Burtt, H. E. (1957). Applied psychology. New York: Prentice-Hall.

Burtt, H. E. (1967). Psychology of birds. New York: Macmillan.

Busby, L. J. (1975). Sex-role research on the mass media. *Journal of Communication,* Autumn 107–131.

Busemann, A. (1948). *Stil und Charakter.* Meisenheim: Hain.

Bush, N. E. (1983). The near death experience in children: Shades of the prison-house reopening. *Anabiosis: The Journal of Near-Death Studies, 3,* 177–193.

Bush, R. (1980). *A parent's guide to child therapy.* New York: Delacorte.

Bush, R. R., Luce, R. D., & Rose, R. M. (1964). Learning models for psychophysics. In R. C. Atkinson (Ed.), *Studies in mathematical psychology.* Stanford, Calif.: Stanford University Press.

Bush, R. R., & Mosteller, F. (1955). *Stochastic models for learning* New York: Wiley.

Buskirk, E. (1978). Cold stress: A selective review. In L. Folinsbee, J. Wagner, J. Borgia, B. Drinkwater, J. Gliner, & J. Bedi (Eds.), *Environmental stress: Individual human adaptation.* New York: Academic Press.

Buss, A. H. (1961). The psychology of aggression. New York: Wiley.

Buss, A. H., & Lang, P. J. (1965). Psychological deficity in schizophrenia. I. Affect, reinforcement and concept attainment. *Journal of Abnormal Psychology, 70,* 2–24.

Buss, A. H., & Plomin, (1975). *R. A temperament theory of personality development.* New York: Wiley.

Buss, A. R. (1975). The emerging field of the sociology of psychological knowledge. *American Psychologist, 30,* 988–1002.

Buss, A. R. (1976). Buss replies. *American Psychologist 31,* 312.

Buss, A. R. (1976). Galton and sex differences: An historical note. *Journal of the History of the Behavioral Sciences, 12,* 283–285.

Buss, A. R. (1978). The structure of psychological revolutions, *Journal of the History of the Behavioral Sciences, 14,* 57–64.

Buss, A. R. (1979). *A dialectical psychology.* New York: Irvington.

Buss, A. R. (1979–1980). Methodological issues in life-span developmental psychology from a dialectical perspective. *Journal of Aging and Human Development, 10,* 121–163.

Busse, E. W., & Blazer, D. G. (Eds.). (1980). *Handbook of geriatric psychiatry.* New York: Van Nostrand Reinhold.

Butcher, J. N., & Koss, M. P. (1978). Research on brief and crisis-oriented therapies. In S. L. Garfield & A. E. Bergin (Eds.), *Handbook of psychotherapy and behavior change: An empirical analysis* (2nd ed., pp. 725–767). New York: Wiley.

Butcher, J. N., & Owen, P. L. (1978). Objective personality inventories. In B. B. Wolman (Ed.), *Clinical diagnosis of mental disorders.* New York: Plenum.

Butcher, J. W., & Koss, M. P. (1978). Research on brief and crisis oriented psychotherapies. In S. L. Garfield & A. E. Bergin (Eds.), *Handbook of psychotherapy and behavior change* (2nd ed.). New York: Wiley.

Butler, J. M., Rice, L. N., & Wagstaff, A. K. (1963). *Quantitative naturalistic research: An introduction to naturalistic observation and investigation.* Englewood Cliffs, Prentice-Hall.

Butler, M. (1985). Guidelines for feminist therapy. In L. B. Rosewater & L. E. Walker (Eds.), *Handbook of feminist therapy: Women's issues.* New York: Springer.

Butler, M., Retzlaff, P., & Vanderploeg, R. (1991). Neuropsychological test usage. *Professional Psychology: Research and Practice, 22,* 510–512.

Butler, R. A. (1953). Discrimination learning by rhesus monkeys to visual-exploration motivation. *Journal of Comparative and Physiological Psychology, 46,* 95–98.

Butler, R. A., & Harlow, H. F. (1954). Persistence of visual exploration in monkeys. *Journal of Comparative and Physiological Psychology, 47,* 258–263.

Butler, R. N. *Why survive? Being old in America.* New York: Harper & Row.

Butt, D. S. (1976). *Psychology of sport.* New York: Van Nostrand Reinhold, 1976.

Butters, N., & Cermak, L. S. (1980). *Alcoholic Korsakoff's syndrome.* New York: Academic Press.

Buxton, C. E. (1956). *College teaching: A psychologist's view.* New York: Harcourt Brace.

Bychowski, G. (1968). Permanent character changes as an after-effect of persecution. In H. Krystal (Ed.), *Massive psychic trauma.* New York: International Universities Press.

Byham, W. C., & Spitzer, M. C. (1971). *The law and personnel testing.* New York: American Management Association.

Byrne, A., & Yatham, L. N. (1989). Pimozide in pathological jealousy. *British Journal of Psychiatry, 155,* 249–251.

Byrne, D. (1961). Interpersonal attraction and attitude similarity. *Journal of Abnormal and Social Psychology, 62,* 713–715.

Byrne, D. (1961). The repression-sensitization scale: Rationale reliability, and validity. *Journal of Personality, 29,* 334–349.

Byrne, D. (1971). *The attraction paradigm.* New York: Academic Press.

Byrne, D., & Blaylock, B. (1963). Similarity and assumed similarity of attitudes between husbands and wives. *Journal of Abnormal and Social Psychology, 67,* 636–640.

Byrne, J. H. Gingich, K. J., & Baxter, D. A. (1989). Computational capabilities of single neurons: Relationship to simple forms of associative and nonassociative learning in aplasia. In R. D. Hawkins & G. H. Bower (Eds.), *Computational models of learning in simple neural systems* (pp. 31–63). San Diego, CA: Academic Press.

Byrnes, F. (1966). Role shock: An occupational hazard of American technical assistants abroad. *Annals of the American Academy of Political and Social Science, 368,* 95–108.

Bytheway, W. R. (1981). The variation with age of age differences in marriage. *Journal of Marriage and Family, 43,* 923–927.

Cabanis, P. J. G. (1799). *Rapports du physique et du moral de l'homme.* Paris: Sorbonne.

Cacioppo, J. T., Klein, D. J., Berntson, G. G., & Hatfield, E. (in press). The psychophysiology of emotion, In M. Lewis & J. Haviland (Eds.), *The handbook of emotions.* New York: Guilford.

Cacioppo, J. T., & Petty, R. E. (Eds.). (1983). *Social psychophysiology: A sourcebook.* New York: Guilford Press.

Cacioppo, J. T., & Petty, R. E. (in press). Social psychophysiology. In L. Stegagno (Ed.), *Psychophysiology.* Turin, Italy: Boringhieri.

Cacioppo, J. T., Uchino, B. N., Crites, S. L., Snyder, M. A., Smith, G., Berntson, G. G., & Lang, P. (in press). The relationship between facial expressiveness and sympathetic activation in emotion: A critical review with emphasis on modeling underlying mechanisms and individual differences. *Journal of Personality and Social Psychology*.

Cadoret, R. J., & Pratt, J. G. (1950). The consistent missing effect in ESP. *Journal of Parapsychology, 14*, 244–256.

Cadwallader, T. C., Cadwallader, J. V., & Semrau, L. (1974). Examination of the interpretation that the principles of neural control and brain localization were recognized. Presented at the meeting of the History of Science Society, Norwalk, Conn.

Cagan, R. H. (1973). Chemostimulatory protein, a new type of stimulus. *Science, 18*, 32–35.

Cain, A. C. (Ed.). (1972). *Survivors of suicide*. Springfield, Ill.: Thomas.

Caine, E. D. (1981). Pseudodementia. *Archives of General Psychiatry, 38*, 1359–1364.

Caine, E. D. (1981). Pseudodementia: Current concepts and future directions. *Archives of General Psychiatry, 38*, 1359–1364.

Cairns, R. B. (1972). Attachment and dependency: A psychobiological and social learning synthesis. In J. L. Gewirtz (Ed.), *Attachment and dependency*. Washington, D.C.: Winston.

Cairns, R. B. (1979). *Social development: The origins and plasticity of interchanges*. San Francisco: Freeman.

Cairns, R. B., Cairns, B. D., & Neckerman, H. J. (1989). Early school dropout: Configurations and determinants. *Child Development, 60*, 1437–1452.

Calder, B. J., & Staw, B. M. (1975). Self-perception of intrinsic and extrinsic motivation. *Journal of Personality and Social Psychology, 31*, 599–605.

Calder, N. (1970). *The mind of man*. New York: Viking Press.

Calhoun, A. W. (1945). *A social history of the American family*. New York: Barnes & Noble.

Calhoun, D. (1981). *Sports, culture, and personality*. West Point, N.Y.: Leisure Press.

Calhoun, J. B. (1962). Population density and social pathology. *Scientific American, 206*, 139–148.

Calhoun, K. S., & Matherne, P. (1975). The effects of varying schedules of timeout on aggressive behavior of a retarded girl. *Journal of Behavior Therapy and Experimental Psychiatry, 6*, 139–143.

Calkins, M. W. (1901). *An introduction to psychology*. New York: Macmillan.

Calkins, M. W. (1909). *A first book in psychology*. New York: Macmillan.

Calkins, M. W. (1915). The self in scientific psychology. *American Journal of Psychology, 26*, 495–524.

Callahan, D. (1987). *Setting limits: Medical goals in an aging society*. New York: Simon & Schuster.

Callahan-Levy, C. M., & Messe, L. A. (1979). Sex differences in the allocation of pay. *Journal of Personality and Social Psychology, 37*, 433–446.

Callan, M. F., & Yeager, D. C. (1991). *Containing the health care cost spiral*. New York, McGraw-Hill.

Callaway, E., Tueting, P., & Koslow, S. H. (Eds.). (1978). *Event related brain potentials in man*. New York: Academic Press.

Caldwell, B. M. (1964). The effects of infant care. In M. L. Hoffman & L. W. Hoffman (Eds.), *Review of development research*, Vol. 1. New York: Russell Sage Foundation.

Caldwell, B. M. (1972). What does research teach us about day care: For children under three? *Children Today, 1*, 6–11.

Cameron, C. (1973). A theory of fatigue. *Ergomatics, 16*, 633–648.

Cameron, N. (1959). Paranoid conditions and paranoia. In S. Arieti (Ed.), *American handbook of psychiatry* (pp. 508–539). New York: Basic Books.

Cameron, O. G., Thyer, B. A., Nesse, R. M., & Curtis, G. C. (1986). Symptom profiles of patients with DSM-III anxiety disorders. *American Journal of Psychiatry, 141*, 572–575.

Camp, B. W., & Bash, M. A. S. (1985). *"Think aloud": Increasing social and cognitive skills. A problem solving program for children*. Champaign, IL: Research Press.

Campbell, A. (1981). *The Sense of well-being in America*. New York: McGraw-Hill.

Campbell, A., & Converse, P. E. (Eds.). (1972). *The human meaning of social change*. New York: Russell Sage Foundation.

Campbell, A., Converse, P. E., Miller, W. E., & Stokes, D. (1960). *The American voter*. New York: Wiley.

Campbell, A., Converse, P. E., & Rodgers, W. L. (1976). *The quality of American life*. New York: Russel Sage Foundation.

Campbell, B. (1960). The factor of safety in the nervous system. *Bulletin of the Los Angeles Neurological Society, 25*, 109–117.

Campbell, B. A., & Teghtsoonian, R. (1958). Electrical and behavioral effects of different types of shock stimuli on the rat. *Journal of Comparative and Physiological Psychology, 51*, 185–192.

Campbell, D. D. (1975). On the conflict between biological and social evolution and between psychology and moral tradition. *American Psychologist, 30*, 1103–1126.

Campbell, D. P. (1966). The stability of vocational interests within occupations over long time spans. *Personnel and Guidance Journal, 44*, 1012–1019.

Campbell, D. P. (1968). The Strong Vocational Interest Blank: 1927–1967. In P. McReynolds (Ed.), *Advances in psychological assessment* (Vol. 1, pp. 105–130). Palo Alto, CA: Science and Behavior Books.

Campbell, D. P. (1971). *Handbook for the Strong Vocational Interest Blank*. Stanford, Calif.: Stanford University Press.

Campbell, D. P., & Hansen, J. C. (1981). *Manual for the SVIB-SCII Strong-Campbell Interest Inventory* (3rd ed.). Stanford, Calif.: Stanford University Press.

Campbell, D. R. (1965). Ethnocentrism and other altruistic motives. In D. Levine (Ed.), *Nebraska Symposium on Motivation*. Lincoln, Neb.: University of Nebraska Press.

Campbell, D. T. (1960). Blind variation and relative retention in creative thought as in other knowledge processes. *Psychological Review, 67*, 380–400.

Campbell, D. T. (1963). Social attitudes and other acquired behavioral dispositions. In S. Koch (Ed.), *Psychology: A study of a science*, Vol. 6. New York: McGraw-Hill.

Campbell, D. T. (1969). Reform as experiments. *American Psychologist, 24*, 409–428.

Campbell, D. T. (1970). Natural selection as an epistemological model. In R. Narroll & R. Cohen (Eds.), *A handbook of method in cultural anthropology*. New York: Natural History Press.

Campbell, D. T. (1974). Evolutionary epistemology. In P. A. Schlipp (Ed.), *The philosophy of Karl Popper* (Vol. 14, pp. 413–463). LaSalle, IL: Open Court.

Campbell, D. T., & Fiske, D. W. (1959). Convergent and discriminant validation by the multitrait-multimethod matrix. *Psychological Bulletin, 56*, 81–105.

Campbell, D. T., & Stanley, J. (1963). Experimental and quasi-experimental designs for research. In N. L. Gage (Ed.), *Handbook of research on teaching*. Chicago: Rand-McNally.

Campbell, D. T., & Stanley, J. C. (1966). *Experimental and quasi-experimental designs for research.* Chicago: Rand-McNally.

Campbell, D. T., & Stanley, J. C. (1967). *Experimental and quasi-experimental designs for research.* Chicago: Rand McNally.

Campbell, E. Q. (Ed.). (1972). *Racial tensions and national identity.* Nashville, Tenn.: Vanderbilt University Press.

Campbell, F. (1976). Gambling: A positive view. In W. R. Eadington (Ed.), *Gambling and society.* Springfield, Ill.: Thomas.

Campbell, J. (1964). *The masks of God: Occidental mythology.* New York: Viking Press.

Campbell, J. P. (1971). Personnel training and development. *Annual Review of Psychology, 22,* 565–602.

Campbell, J. P. (1976). Psychometric theory. In M. D. Dunnette (Ed.), *Handbook of industrial and organizational psychology.* Chicago: Rand-McNally.

Campbell, J. P., & Dunnette, M. D. (1968). Effectiveness of T-group experiences in managerial training and development. *Psychological Bulletin, 70,* 73–104.

Campbell, J. P., Dunnette, M., Lawler, E. E., III, & Weick, K. E., Jr. (1970). *Managerial behavior, performance, and effectiveness.* New York: McGraw-Hill.

Campbell, R. E., & Cellini, J. V. (1981). A diagnostic taxonomy of adult career problems. *Journal of Vocational Behavior, 19,* 175–190.

Campbell, S. B. (1976). Hyperactivity: Course and treatment. In A. Davids (Ed.), *Child personality and psychopathology: Current topics,* Vol. 3. New York: Wiley.

Campbell, S. B., Breaux, A. M., Ewing, L. J., & Szumowski, E. K. (1986). Correlates and predictors of hyperactivity and aggression: A longitudinal study of parent-referred problem preschoolers. *Journal of Abnormal Child Psychology, 14,* 217–234.

Campos, J., & Aguado, L. (1977). La investigación psicológica en España. *Cuadernos de Psicología, 3,* 16–27.

Campos, J. J., Langer, A., & Krowitz, A. (1970). Cardiac responses on the visual cliff in prelocomotor human infants. *Science, 170,* 196–197.

Canadian Government Commission of Inquiry. (1970). *The non-medical use of drugs: Interim report of the Canadian Government Commission of Inquiry.* Ottawa: Penguin Books.

Cancro, R. (1971). *Intelligence: Genetic and environmental influences.* New York: Grune & Stratton.

Cannon, M. S. (1973). *Alcoholism halfway houses: General characteristics* (DHEW Pub. no. HMS–73–9005). Washington, D.C.: U.S. National Institute of Mental Health, Survey and Report Section.

Cannon, W. B. (1927). The James-Lange theory of emotions: Critical examination and an alternative theory. *American Journal of Psychology, 39,* 106–124.

Cannon, W. B. (1929/1915). *Bodily changes in pain, hunger, fear, and rage; an account of recent researches into the functions of emotional excitement.* New York: Appleton.

Cannon, W. B. (1934). Hunger and thirst. In C. Murchison (Ed.), *Handbook of general experimental psychology.* Worcester, Mass.: Clarke University Press.

Cannon, W. B. (1935). Stresses and strains of homeostasis. *American Journal of Medical Science, 189,* 1–14.

Cannon, W. B. (1935). Traumatic shock. *Journal of the American Medical Association, 105,* 1353–1354.

Cannon, W. B. (1942). Voodoo death. *American Anthropologist, 44,* 169–181.

Cannon, W. B. (1960/1932). *The wisdom of the body.* New York: Norton.

Cannon, W. B. (1973/1925). Some general features of endocrine influence on metabolism. In L. L. Langley (Ed.), *Homeostasis.* Stroudsburg, Pa.: Dowden, Hutchinson, & Ross.

Cannon, W. B. (1973/1926). Physiological regulation of normal states: Some tentative postulates concerning biological homeostasis. In L. L. Langley (Ed.), *Homeostasis.* Stroudsburg, Pa.: Dowden, Hutchinson, & Ross.

Cannon, W. B. (1973/1929). Organization for physiological homeostasis. In L. L. Langley (Ed.), *Homeostasis.* Stroudsburg, Pa.: Dowden, Hutchinson, & Ross.

Cannon, W. B., & Washburne, A. L. (1912). An explanation of hunger. *American Journal of Physiology, 29,* 444–454.

Canter, A. (1966). A background interference procedure to increase the sensitivity of the Bender Gestalt Test to organic brain disorders. *Journal of Consulting Psychology, 30,* 91–97.

Canter, A., Cluff, L. E., & Imboden, J. B. (1972). Hypersensitive reactions to immunization inoculations and antecedent psychological vulnerability. *Journal of Psychosomatic Research, 16,* 99–101.

Canter, M. B., & Freudenberger, H. J. (1990). Fee scheduling and monitoring. In E. Margenau (Ed.), *The encyclopedia handbook of private practice.* New York: Gardner Press.

Cantilli, E. J. (1974). *Programming environmental improvements in public transportation.* Lexington, Mass.: Heath.

Cantor, J. H. (1965). Transfer of stimulus pretraining to motor paired-associate and discrimination learning tasks. In L. P. Lipsitt, & C. C. Spiker (Eds.), *Advances in child development and behavior,* Vol. 2. New York: Academic Press.

Cantor, N. (1982). ''Everyday'' versus normative models of clinical and social judgment. In G. Weary & H. L. Mirels (Eds.), *Integrations of clinical and social psychology.* New York: Oxford University Press.

Cantor, N., & Mischel, W. (1979). Prototypicality and personality: Effects on free recall and personality impressions. *Journal of Research in Personality, 13,* 187–205.

Cantor, N., Smith, E. E., French, R., & Mezzich, J. (1980). Psychiatric diagnosis as prototype categorization. *Journal of Abnormal Psychology, 89,* 181–193.

Cantrell, V. L., & Prinz, R. J. (1985). Multiple perspectives of rejected, neglected, and accepted children: Relationship between sociometric status and behavioral characteristics. *Journal of Consulting and Clinical Psychology, 53,* 884–889.

Cantril, H. (1953). *How nations see each other.* Urbana, Ill.: University of Illinois Press.

Cantril, H. (1965). *The pattern of human concerns.* New Brunswick, N.J.: Rutgers University Press.

Cantril, H. (1966/1940). *The invasion from Mars.* New York: Harper & Row.

Cantril, H., & Allport, G. W. (1935). *The psychology of radio.* New York: Harper.

Cantril, H., & Hunt, W. A. (1932). Emotional effects produced by the injection of adrenalin. *American Journal of Psychology, 44,* 300–307.

Cantwell, D. P. (1977). Psychopharmacologic treatment of the minimal brain dysfunction syndrome. In J. M. Weiner (Ed.), *Psychopharmacology in childhood and adolescence.* New York: Basic Books.

Capaldi, E. J. (1974). Partial reward either following or preceding consistent reward: A case of reinforcement level. *Journal of Experimental Psychology, 102,* 954–962.

Capes, M. (Ed.). (1960). Communication or conflict: Conferences, their structure, dynamics and planning. London: Tavistock.

Caplan, A. (1978). *The sociobiology debate: Readings on ethical and scientific issues.* New York: Harper & Row.

Caplan, D., & England, F. (1980). The Alexander technique. In R. Herink (Ed.), *The psycotherapy handbook.* New York: Meridian.

Caplan, G. (1961). *An approach to community mental health.* New York: Grune & Stratton.

Caplan, G. (1963). Types of mental health consultation. *American Journal of Orthopsychiatry, 33,* 470–481.

Caplan, G. (1970). *The theory and practice of mental health consultation.* New York: Basic Books.

Caplan, G. (1974). *Support systems and community mental health: Lectures on concept development.* New York: Behavioral Publications.

Caplan, G. (1974/1964). *Principles of preventative psychiatry.* New York: Basic Books.

Caplan, G., & Killilea, M. (Eds.). (1976). *Support systems and mutual help.* New York: Grune & Stratton.

Caplan, N., & Nelson, S. D. (1973). On being useful: The nature and consequences of psychological research on social problems. *American Psychologist, 28,* 199–211.

Caplan, R. B. (1969). *Psychiatry and the community in nineteenth century America.* New York: Basic Books.

Caplan, R. D., Cobb, S., French, J. R., Van Harrison, R. D., & Pinneau, S. R. (1975). *Job demands and worker health: Main effects and occupational differences.* Washington, D.C.: U.S. Government Printing Office.

Cappella, J. N., & Green, J. O. (1984). The effects of distance and individual differences in arousability on nonverbal involvement: A test of discrepancy arousal theory. *Journal of Nonverbal Behavior, 8,* 259–286.

Capra, F. (1977/1976). *The tao of physics.* New York: Bantam Books.

Capra, F. (1982). *The turning point.* New York: Simon & Schuster.

Card, J. J., et al. (1975). *Development of an ROTC/Army career-commitment model.* Palo Alto, Calif.: American Institute for Research.

Carder, B., & Berkowitz, K. (1970). Rats' preference for earned in comparison with free food. *Science, 167,* 1273–1274.

Cardinet, J., & Rousson, M. (1967; 1968). Etude factorielle de tests d'aptitudes scolaires. *Revue Suisse de Psychologie, 26,* 256–270, 362–380; *27,* 40–66.

Carek, D. J. (1972). *Principles of child psychotherapy.* Springfield, Ill.: Thomas.

Carew, T. J., Castelucci, V. F., & Kandel, E. R. (1971). Analysis of dishabituation and sensitization of gill withdrawal reflex in *Aplysis californica. International Journal of Neuroscience, 2* 79–98.

Carew, T. J., Hawkins, R. D., & Kandel, E. R. (1983). Differential classical conditioning of a defensive withdrawl reflex in *Aplysis californica. Science, 219,* 397–400.

Carey, J. E., & Goss, A. E. (1957). The role of mediating verbal responses in the conceptual sorting behavior of children. *Journal of Genetic Psychology, 90,* 69–74.

Carey, M. P., & Burish, T. G. (1988). Etiology and treatment of the psychological side effects associated with cancer chemotherapy: A critical review and discussion. *Psychological Bulletin, 104,* 307–325.

Carich, M. S. (1990a). The basics of hypnosis and trancework. *Individual Psychology, 46*(4), 401–410.

Carkhuff, R. R. (1969). *Helping and human relations: A primer for lay and professional helpers.* Vol. 1: *Selection and training.* New York: Holt, Rinehart, & Winston.

Carkhuff, R. R. (1969). *Helping and human relations: A primer for lay and professional helpers.* Vol. 2. *Practice and research.* New York: Holt, Rinehart & Winston.

Carkhuff, R. R. (1971). *The development of human resources: Education, psychology and social change.* New York: Holt, Rinehart & Winston.

Carlberg, C., & Kavale, K. (1980). The efficiency of special versus regular class placement for exceptional children: A meta-analysis. *Journal of Special Education, 14,* 295–309.

Carli, R. (1980). *Gruppo e istituzione a scuola.* Turin, Italy: Boringhieri.

Carli, R. (1981). *Aggiornamento degli insegnanti: Una proposta di intervento psicosociale.* Florence, Italy: La Nuova Italia.

Carli, R., & Ambrosiano, L. (Eds.). (1982). *Esperienze di psicosociologia.* Milan, Italy: Angeli.

Carli, R., & Paniccia, R. M. (1981). *Psicosociologia delle organizzazioni e delle istituzioni.* Bologna, Italy: Il Mulino.

Carlsmith, J. M., & Gross, A. E. (1969). Some effects of guilt on compliance. *Journal of Personality and Social Psychology, 11,* 232–239.

Carlson, C. L., Lahey, B. B., & Neeper, R. (1984). Peer assessment of the social behavior of accepted, rejected, and neglected children. *Journal of Abnormal Child Psychology, 12,* 189–198.

Carlson, E. R. (1956). Attitude change and attitude structure. *Journal of Abnormal and Social Psychology. 52,* 256–261.

Carlson, G. A., & Cantwell, D. P. (1980). A survey of depressive symptoms, syndrome and disorder in a child psychiatric population. *Journal of Child Psychology and Child Psychiatry, 21,* 19–25.

Carlson, J., & Davis, D. (1971). Cultural values and the risky shift: A cross-cultural test in Uganda and the United States. *Journal of Personality and Social Psychology, 20,* 392–399.

Carlson, J. G., & Hatfield, E. (1991). Psychology of emotion. New York: Harcourt, Brace, Jovanovich.

Carlson, J. S., Cook, S. W., & Strombert, E. L. (1936). Sex difference in conversations. *Journal of Applied Psychology, 20,* 727–735.

Carlson, N. R. (1977). *Physiology of behavior.* Boston: Allyn & Bacon.

Carlton, P. I. (1963). Cholinergic mechanisms in the control of behavior by the brain. *Psychological Review, 70,* 19–39.

Carman, J., & Wyatt, R. (1979). Calcium: Bivalent cation in the bivalent psychoses. *Biological Psychiatry, 14,* 295–336.

Carmichael, L. (1927). A further study of the development of behavior in vertebrates experimentally removed from the influence of external stimulation. *Psychological Review, 34,* 34–47.

Carmichael, L. (1954/1946). *Manual of child psychology.* New York: Wiley.

Carmichael, L. (1970). Onset and early development of behavior. In P. H. Mussen (Ed.), *Carmichael's manual of child psychology,* Vol. I. New York: Wiley.

Carmichael, L., Hogan, H. P., & Walter, A. A. (1932). An experimental study of the effect of language on the reproduction of visually perceived form. *Journal of Experimental Psychology, 15,* 73–86.

Carnap, R., & Morris, C. (Eds.). (1948). *International encyclopedia of unified science.* Chicago: University of Chicago Press.

Carnegie, D. (1936). *How to win friends and influence people.* New York: Simon & Schuster.

Carney, M. W. P. (1980). Artefactual illness to attract medical attention. *British Journal of Psychiatry, 136,* 542–547.

Carney, M. W. P., & Brozovic, M. (1978). Self-inflicted bleeding and bruising. *Lancet, 1,* 924—925.

Carney, R. E. (1978). Reactions of planarians after cannibalization of planarians exposed to four stimulus combinations. *Journal of Biological Psychology, 20,* 44–49.

Carothers, J. C. (1972). *The mind of man in Africa.* London: Stacey.

Carpenter, C. R. (1964). *Naturalistic behavior of nonhuman primates.* University Park: Pennsylvania State University Press.

Carpenter, J. C. (1976). Single case study change in a schizophrenic adolescent as a result of a series of rage-reduction treatments. *Journal of Nervous and Mental Disease, 162,* 58–63.

Carpenter, M. B. (1978). *Core text of neuroanatomy.* Baltimore, Md.: Williams & Wilkins.

Carpenter, M. B., & Sutin, J. (1983). *Human neuroanatomy.* Baltimore: William & Wilkins.

Carpenter, P., Just, M., & Shell, P. (1990). What one intelligence test measures: A theoretical account of the processing in the Raven Progressive Matrices Test. *Psychological Review, 97,* 404–431.

Carpenter, P. A., & Eisenberg, P. (1978). Mental rotation and the frame of reference in blind and sighted individuals. *Perception and Psychophysics, 23,* 117–124.

Carpenter, R. H. S. (1977). *Movements of the eyes.* London: Pion.

Carpenter, W. T. (1976). Current diagnostic concepts in schizophrenia. *American Journal of Psychiatry, 133,* 172–177.

Carpintero, H. (1976). *Historia de la psicología.* Madrid: Universidad Nacional de Educación a Distancia.

Carpintero, H. (1980). La psicología española: Pasado, presente, futuro. *Revista de Historia de la Psicología, 1,* 33–58.

Carpintero, H. (1981). Wundt y la psicología en España. *Revista de Historia de la Psicología, 2,* 37–55.

Carr, D. B., Bullen, B. A., Skrinar, G. A., Arnold, M. A., Rosenblatt, M., Bettins, I. Z., Martin, J. B., & McArthur, J. (1981). Physical conditioning facilitates the exercise-induced secretion of beta-endorphin and beta-lipotropin in women. *New England Journal of Medicine, 305,* 560–563.

Carr, H. A. (1925). *Psychology: A study of mental activity.* New York: Longman, Green.

Carr, H. A. (1930). Functionalism. In C. Murchison (Ed.), *Psychologies of 1930.* Worcester, Mass.: Clark University Press.

Carr, H. A. (1931). The laws of association, *Psychological Review, 38,* 212–228.

Carrington, P. (1977). *Freedom in meditation.* New York: Anchor/ Doubleday.

Carroll, J. B. (1962). The prediction of success in intensive foreign language training. In R. Glaser (Ed.), *Training research and education.* Pittsburgh, Pa.: University of Pittsburgh Press.

Carroll, J. B. (1963). A model of school learning. *Teachers College Record, 64,* 723–733.

Carroll, J. B. (1964). Words, meanings, and concepts. *Harvard Educational Review, 34,* 178–202.

Carroll, J. B. (1967). On sampling from a lognormal model of word-frequency distributions. In H. Kučera & W. N. Francis (Eds.), *Computational analysis of present-day American English.* Providence, R.I.: Brown University Press.

Carroll, J. B. (1970). An alternative to Juilland's usage coefficient for lexical frequencies, and a proposal for a standard frequency index (SFI). *Computer Studies in the Humanities and Verbal Behavior, 3,* 61–65.

Carroll, J. B. (1971). Measurement properties of subjective estimates of word frequency. *Journal of Verbal Learning and Verbal Behavior, 10,* 722–729.

Carroll, J. B. (1973). The aptitude-achievement distinction: The case of foreign language aptitude and proficiency. In D. R. Green (Ed.), *The aptitude- achievement distinction.* Monterey, Calif.: CTB/ McGraw-Hill.

Carroll, J. B. (1976). Psychometric tests as cognition tasks: A new "structure of intellect." In L. Resnick (Ed.), *The nature of intelligence.* Hillsdale, N.J.: Erlbaum.

Carroll, J. B. (1981). Twenty-five years of research on foreign language aptitude. In K. C. Diller (Ed.), *Individual differences and universals in language learning aptitude.* Rowley, Mass.: Newbury House.

Carroll, J. B. (1983). The "model of school learning": Progress of an idea. In C. Fisher & D. Berliner (Eds.), *Perspectives on instructional time.* New York: Longman.

Carroll, J. B., Davies, P., & Richman, B. (1971). *The American Heritage word frequency book.* Boston: Houghton Mifflin.

Carroll, J. B., & Maxwell, S. E. (1979). Individual differences in cognitive abilities. *Annual Review of Psychology,* 603–640.

Carroll, J. B., & Sapon, S. M. (1967/1959). *Modern language aptitude test—Elementary, manual.* New York: Psychological Corp.

Carroll, J. B., & White, M. N. (1973). Word frequency and age of acquisition as determiners of picture-naming latency. *Quarterly Journal of Experimental Psychology, 25,* 85–95.

Carroll, J. D. (1971). An overview of multidimensional scaling methods emphasizing recently developed models for handling individual differences. In C. W. King, & D. Tigert (Eds.), *Attitude research reaches new heights.* Chicago: American Marketing Association.

Carroll, J. D. (1980). Models and methods for multidimensional analysis of preferential choice (or other dominance) data. In E. D. Lantermann, & H. Feger (Eds.), *Similarity and choice.* Bern, Stuttgart, Vienna: Huber.

Carroll, J. D., & Arabie, P. (1980). Multidimensional scaling. *Annual Review of Psychology, 31,* 607–649.

Carroll, J. D, & Chang, J. J. (1970). Analysis of individual differences in multidimensional scaling via an N-way generalization of Eckart-Young decomposition. *Psychometrika, 35,* 283–319.

Carroll, J. D., & Pruzansky, S. (1980). Discrete and hybrid scaling models. In E. D. Lantermann & H. Feger (Eds.), *Similarity and choice.* Bern, Stuttgart, Vienna: Huber.

Carroll, J. D., & Wish, M. (1974). Models and methods for three-way multidimensional scaling. In D. H. Krantz, R. C. Atkinson, R. D. Luce, & P. Suppes (Eds.), *Contemporary developments in mathematical psychology,* Vol. II. San Francisco: Freeman.

Carruthers, M. (1976). Modification of the noradrenaline related effects of smoking by beta-blockade. *Psychological Medicine, 6,* 251–256.

Carruthers, M. (1981). Field studies: Emotion and beta-blockade. In M. J. Christie & P. G. Mellett (Eds.), *Foundations of psychosomatics.* New York: Wiley.

Carson, R. C. (1969). *Interaction concepts of personality.* Chicago: Aldine.

Carson, T. P., & Carson, R. C. (1984). The affective disorders. In H. E. Adams & P. B. Sutker (Eds.), *Comprehensive handbook of psychopathology.* New York: Plenum.

Carstairs, G. M. (1961). Cross-cultural psychiatric interviewing. In B. Kaplan (Ed.), *Studying personality cross-culturally.* Evanston, Ill.: Row, Peterson.

Carter, E. A., & McGoldrick, M. (Eds.). (1980). *The family life cycle: A framework for family therapy*, New York: Gardner Press.

Carter, E. N., & Reynolds, J. N. (1976). Imitation in the treatment of a hyperactive child. *Psychotherapy: Theory, research, and practice, 13*, 160–161.

Carter, L. F., & Schooker, K. Y. (1949). Value, need, and other factors in perception. *Psychological Review, 56*, 200–207.

Carterette, E. C., & Friedman, M. P. (Eds.). (1974). *Handbook of perception*, (2 vols.). New York: Academic Press.

Carterette, E. C., & Friedman, M. P. (Eds.). (1978). *Handbook of perception*. Vol. IV: *Hearing*. New York: Academic Press.

Cartledge, G., & Milburn, J. F. (Eds.). (1980). *Teaching social skills to children*. New York: Pergamon Press.

Carton, S., Jouvent, R., Bungener, C., & Wildloecher, D. (1992). Sensation seeking and depressive mood. *Personality and Individual Differences, 7*, 843–849.

Cartwright, D. (1949). Some principles of mass persuasion. *Human Relations, 2*, 253–267.

Cartwright, D. (1959). Lewinian theory as a contemporary systematic framework. In S. Koch (Ed.), *Psychology: A study of a science*, Vol. 2. New York: McGraw-Hill.

Cartwright, D. (1959). *Studies in social power*. Ann Arbor, Mich.: Institute of Social Research.

Cartwright, D. (Ed.). (1951). *Field theory in social science*. New York: Harper.

Cartwright, D., & Lestinger, L. (1943). A quantitative theory of decision. *Psychological Review, 50*, 595–621.

Cartwright, D., & Zander, A. (1968/1953). *Group dynamics: Research and theory*. New York: Harper & Row.

Cartwright, R., Samelson, C. F., Weber, S., Gordon, L., Krusnow, R., Paul, L., & Stephenson, K. (1980). A mechanical treatment for obstructive sleep apnea: The tongue retaining device (TRD). In M. H. Chase, D. F. Kripke & P. L. Walter (Eds.), *Sleep research*, Vol. 9. Los Angeles: BIS/BRS.

Carver, C. S., & Scheier, M. F. (1981). *Attention and self-regulation: A control theory approach to human behavior*. New York: Springer-Verlag.

Carver, C. S., & Scheier, M. F. (1982). Control theory: A useful conceptual framework for personality—social, clinical, and health psychology. *Psychological Bulletin, 92*(1), 111–135.

Casa, J. M., Beemsterboer, P., & Clark, G. T. (1982). A comparison of stress reduction behavioral counseling and contingent nocturnal EMG feedback for the treatment of bruxism. *Behavior Research and Therapy, 20*(1), 9–15.

Casas, J. M. (1984). Policy training and research in counseling psychology: The racial/ethnic minority perspective. In S. Brown & R. Lent (Eds.), *Handbook of counseling psychology* (pp. 785–831). New York: Wiley.

Cascio, W. F. (1982). *Applied psychology in personnel management* (2nd ed.). Reston, Va.: Reston.

Cascio, W. F., & Bernardin, H. J. (1981). Implications of performance appraisal litigation for personnel decisions. *Personnel Psychology, 34*, 211–226.

Casey, D. E. (1978). Managing tardive dyskinesia. *Journal of Clinical Psychiatry, 39*, 748–753.

Casey, E. S. (1976). *Imagining: A phenomenological study*. Bloomington, Ind.: Indiana University Press.

Cash, H. C., & Crissy, W. J. E. (1965). *The psychology of selling*. New York: Personal Development Associates.

Cashdan, S. (1982). Interactional psychotherapy: Using the relationship. In J. Anchin & D. Kiesler (Eds.), *Handbook of interpersonal psychotherapy*. New York: Pergamon Press.

Casino, E. (1983). Integrating consultants into cross-cultural programs. In D. Landis & R. Brislin (Eds.), *Handbook of intercultural training*, Vol. 2. Elmsford, N.Y.: Pergamon Press.

Casler, L. (1961). Maternal deprivation: A critical review of the literature. *Monographs of the Society for Research in Child Development, 26*(80), serial no. 2.

Cason, H. (1930). Common annoyances: A psychological study of everyday aversions and irritations. *Psychological Monographs*, no. 182.

Casper, R., Eckert, E., Halmi, K., Solomon, G., & Davis, J. (1980). Bulimia: Its incidence and clinical importance in patients with anorexia nervosa. *Archives of General Psychiatry, 37*, 1030–1035.

Cass, E. L., & Zimmer, F. G. (Eds.). (1975). *Man and work in society*. New York: Van Nostrand Reinhold.

Cassedy, J. H. (1969). *Demography in early America: Beginnings of the statistical mind, 1600–1800*. Cambridge, Mass.: Harvard University Press.

Cassel, J. (1975). Social science in epidemiology: Psychosocial processes and "stress" theoretical formulation. In E. Struening & M. Guttentag (Eds.), *Handbook of evaluation research*. Beverly Hills, Calif.: Sage Publications.

Cassell, E. J. (1991). *The nature of suffering and the goals of medicine*. New York: Oxford University Press.

Cassirer, E. (1950). *The problem of knowledge*. New Haven, Conn.: Yale University Press.

Cassirer, E. (1953–1955, 1957). *Philosophy of symbolic forms*, Vols. I, II, III, New Haven, Conn.: Yale University Press.

Cassirer, E. (1970/1956). *An essay on man*. Toronto: Bantam Books.

Castaño, D. A., & Sanchez Bedoya, G. (1978). Problemas de la importacion tecnologico-psicolaboral en los paises en desarrollo. *Revista Latinoamericana de Psicologia, 10*, 71–82.

Catania, A. C. (1987). Some Darwinian lessons for behavior analysis. A review of Peter J. Bowler's The eclipse of Darwinism. *Journal of the Experimental Analysis of Behavior, 47*, 249–257.

Catania, A. C. (1992). *Learning* (3rd ed.). Englewood Cliffs, NJ: Prentice-Hall.

Catania, A. C., & Harnad, S. (Eds.). (1988). *The selection of behavior*. New York: Cambridge University Press.

Catlin, N., Croake, J. W., & Keller, J. F. (1978). Commitment and relationship factors in consensual cohabitation. *International Journal of Sociology of the Family, 3*, 185–193.

Caton, R. (1875). The electric currents of the brain. *The British Medical Journal, 2*, 278.

Cattell, J. McK. (1890) Mental tests and measurements. *Mind, 15*, 373–381.

Cattell, J. McK. (1903). *American men of science*. New York: Science Press.

Cattell, J. McK. (1903). A statistical study of eminent men. *Popular Science Monthly, 62*, 359–377.

Cattell, R. (1937). Measurement versus intuition in applied psychology. *Character and Personality, 6*, 114–131.

Cattell, R. B. (1935). On the measurement of perseveration. *British Journal of Educational Psychology, 5*, 76–92.

Cattell, R. B. (1940). A culture-free intelligence test. *Journal of Educational Psychology, 31*, 161–179.

Cattell, R. B. (1946). *Description and measurement of personality*. New York: Harcourt.

Cattell, R. B. (1950). *An introduction to personality study*. London, New York: Hutchinson's University Library.

Cattell, R. B. (1950). *Personality: A systematic theoretic and factual study*. New York: McGraw-Hill.

Cattell, R. B. (1957). *Personality and motivation: Structure and measurement*. New York: World.

Cattell, R. B. (1957/1949). *Culture fair intelligence tests*. Champaign, Ill.: Institute for Personality and Ability Testing.

Cattell, R. B. (1963). Theory of fluid and crystallized intelligence: A critical experiment. *Journal of Educational Psychology, 54*, 1–22.

Cattell, R. B. (1964). *Personality and social psychology*. San Diego, Calif.: Knapp.

Cattell, R. B. (1965). *The scientific analysis of personality*. Baltimore, Md.: Penguin Books.

Cattell, R. B. (1966). *Handbook of multivariate experimental psychology*. New York: Rand-McNally.

Cattell, R. B. (1971). *Abilities: Their structure, growth and action*. Boston: Houghton Mifflin.

Cattell, R. B. (1973). *Personality and mood by questionnaire*. San Francisco: Jossey-Bass.

Cattell, R. B. (1979–1980). *Personality and learning theory* (2 vols.). New York: Springer.

Cattell, R. B., & Dreger, R. M. (Eds.). (1977). *Handbook of modern personality; theory*. Washington, D.C.: Hemisphere.

Cattell, R. B., & Eber, H. W. (1967). *Handbook of the sixteen personality factor questionnaire*. Champaign, Ill.: Institute for Personality and Ability Testing.

Cattell, R. B., Eber, H. W., & Tatsuoka, M. M. (1978). *Handbook for the Sixteen Personality Factor Questionnaire (16PF)*. Champaign, Ill.: Institute for Personality and Ability Testing.

Cattell, R. B., & Kline, P. (1977). *The scientific analysis of personality and motivation*. New York: Academic Press.

Cautela, J. (1971). Covert conditioning. In A. Jacobs, & L. Sachs (Eds.). *The psychology of private events: Perspectives on covert response systems*. New York: Academic Press.

Cautela, J. R. (1966). Treatment of compulsive behavior by covert sensitization. *Psychological Record, 16*, 33–41.

Cautela, J. R. (1967). Covert sensitization. *Psychological Record, 20*, 459–468.

Cautela, J. R. (1970). Covert negative reinforcement, *Journal of Behavior Therapy and Experimental Psychiatry, 1*, 273–278.

Cautela, J. R. (1970). Covert reinforcement. *Behavior Therapy, 1*, 33–50.

Cautela, J. R. (1971). Covert extinction. *Behavior Therapy, 2*, 192–200.

Cautela, J. R. (1972). *Covert sensitization scenes: A compilation of typical scenes used in the application of covert sensitization to a variety of maladaptive behaviors*. Unpublished manuscript, Boston College.

Cautela, J. R. (1973). Covert processes and behavior modification. *Journal of Nervous and Mental Disease, 1*, 157.

Cautela, J. R. (1976). Covert response cost. *Psychotherapy: Therapy, Research and Practice, 13*, 397–404.

Cautela, J. R. (1976). The present status of covert modeling. *Journal of Behavior Therapy and Experimental Psychiatry, 7*, 323–326.

Cautela, J. R. (1977). Covert conditioning: Assumptions and procedures. *Journal of Mental Imagery, 1*, 53–64.

Cautela, J. R., & Baron, M. G. (1977). Covert conditioning: A theoretical analysis. *Behavior Modification, 1*, 351–368.

Cautela, J. R., & Bennett, A. K. (1981). Covert conditioning. In R. J. Corsini (Ed.), *Handbook of innovative psychotherapies*. New York: Wiley.

Cautela, J. R., Flannery, R. B., Jr., & Hanley, S. (1974). Covert modeling: An experimental test. *Behavior Therapy, 5*, 494–502.

Cautela, J. R., & Groden, J. (1978). *Relaxation: A comprehensive manual for adults, children, and children with special needs*. Champaign, Ill.: Research Press.

Caution urged in use of Armed Forces Battery. (1978, February 16). *APGA Guidepost, 1*, 10.

Cavallaro, S. A., & Porter, R. H. (1980). Peer references of at-risk and normally developing children in a preschool mainstream classroom. *American Journal of Mental Deficiency, 84*, 357–366.

Cavanaugh, K. L. (1987). Time series analysis of U.S. and Canadian inflation and unemployment: A test of a field-theoretic hypothesis. In *Proceedings of the American Statistical Association, Business and Economics Statistics Section* (pp. 799–804). Alexandria, VA: American Statistical Association.

Cavanaugh, K. L., & King, K. D. (1988). Simultaneous transfer function analysis of Okun's misery index: Improvements in the economic quality of life through Maharishi's Vedic science and technology. In *Proceedings of the American Statistical Association, Business and Economics Statistics Section* (pp. 491–496). Alexandria, VA: American Statistical Association.

Cavanaugh, K. L., King, K. D., & Ertuna, C. (1989). A multiple-input transfer function model of Okun's misery index: An empirical test of the Maharishi effect. In *Proceedings of the American Statistical Association, Business and Economics Statistics Section* (pp. 565–570). Alexandria, VA: American Statistical Association.

Cavanaugh, R. M. (1983). Encopresis in children and adolescents. *American Family Physician, 27*, 107–109.

Cayward, T. (1974). A quadriplegic young man looks at treatment. *Journal of Rehabilitation, 49*, 22–25.

Ceci, S. J., Toglia, M. P., & Ross, D. F. (1987). *Children's eyewitness memory*. New York: Springer-Verlag.

Celsus, A. A. C. (1478). *De medicina*. Florence, Italy: Nicolaus (Laurentius).

Center of Advanced Study in Psychology. (1982). *Profile report*.

Centers, R. (1949). *The psychology of social classes*. Princeton, N.J.: Princeton University Press.

Cerletti, U. (1950). Old and new information about electroshock. *American Journal of Psychiatry, 107*, 87–94.

Cermak, L. S., & Craik, F. I. M. (1979). *Levels of processing in human memory*. Hillsdale, N.J.: Erlbaum.

Cernoch, J. M., & Porter, R. (1985). Recognition of maternal axillary odors by infants. *Child Development, 56*, 1593–1598.

Cesana, T. (1978). *Fra Agostino Gemelli: Dalla nascita alia professione religiosa, 1878–1904*. Milan, Italy: Edit. Biblioteca Francescana.

Cevallos, M. A. (1953). La psicologia en Mexico en los ultimos cincuenta años. In Universidad Naciona Autonoma de Mexico (Ed.), *Memoria del Congreso Cientifico Mexicano*, Ciencias de la Educacion, Psicologia-Filosofia, (Vol. 15, pp. 563–569), Mexico, D.F.

Cha, J. H. (1971). Clarity of the focal stimulus cue and the mediation of two opposing social perceptual effects. Doctoral dissertation, University of California at Los Angeles.

Cha, J. H. (1976). [History and present status of Korean psychology and possible directions for interdisciplinary research among social sciences.] *Social Science Journal, 1*, 61–100. (In Korean)

Cha, J. H. (1978). Korean psychology: A study of a science and profession. *Social Science Journal, 5*, 142–184.

Cha, J. H. (1987). Korean psychology. In G. H. Blowers & M. Turtle (Eds.), *Psychology moving East: The status of Western psychology in Asia and Oceana* (pp. 163–182). London: Sydney University Press.

Cha, J. H. (1990). The landmarks in the history of Korean psychology. In Korean Psychological Association (Ed.), *The guide for the Korean psychological association* (pp.1–28). Seoul: Editor. (In Korean)

Cha, J. H. (1992). The current status of Korean psychology. *Japanese Journal of Psychology, 62*, 383–390. (In Japanese)

Cha, J. H., Chug, B. M., & Lee, S. J. (1975). *A study of boy preference and family planning in Korea.* Seoul: Korean Institute for Research in Behavioral Science.

Chadwick, P. D., & Lowe, C. F. (1990). Measurement and modification of delusional beliefs. *Journal of Consulting and Clinical Psychology, 58*(2), 225–232.

Chafetz, M. E. (1975). Alcoholism and alcoholic psychoses. In A. M. Freedman, H. I. Kaplan, & B. J. Sadock (Eds.), *Comprehensive textbook of psychiatry,* Vol. 2. Baltimore, Md.: Williams & Wilkins.

Chaffin, J. D. (1974). Will the real "mainstreaming" program please stand up! (or . . . should Dunn have done it?). *Focus on Exceptional Children, 6*(5).

Chaiken, S. (1980). Heuristic versus systematic information processing and the use of source versus message cues in persuasion. *Journal of Personality and Social Psychology, 39*, 752–766.

Chaiklin, H. (Ed.). (1975). *Marian Chace: Her papers.* Columbus, Md.: American Dance Therapy Association.

Chaiklin, S. (1975). Dance therapy. In *American handbook of psychiatry.* New York: Basic Books.

Chaimowitz, G., & Moscovitch, A. (1991). Patient assaults on psychiatric Canadian Journal of Weapons and eye contact as residents: The Canadian experience. *Psychiatry, 36*, 107–111.

Chally Group. (1978). *How to select a sales force that sells.* Dayton, Ohio: Chally Group.

Chalfant, J., & Scheffelin, M. A. (1969). *Central processing dysfunctions in children: A review of research. NINDS Monograph no. 9.* Washington, D.C.: U.S. Government Printing Office.

Chamberlain, H. D. (1928). The inheritance of left-handedness. *Journal of Heredity, 19*, 557–559.

Chamberlain, N. W., Cullen, D. E., & Lewin, D. (1980). *The labor sector.* New York: McGraw-Hill.

Chambers, D., & Reisberg, D. (1985). Can mental images be ambiguous? *Experimental Psychology: Human Perception and Performance, 11*, 317–328.

Chamorro, A., Sacco, R., Ciecierski, K., & Binder, J. (1990). Visual hemineglect & hemihallucinations in a patient with a subcortical infarction. *Neurology, 40*, 1463–1464.

Champion, R. A. (1969). *Learning and activation.* New York: Wiley.

Champion, R., & Parish, W. (1972). Atopic dermatitis. In F. Ebling, A. Rook, & D. Wilkinson (Eds.), *Textbook of dermatology* (2nd ed.). Oxford: Blackwell.

Chandler, A. R. (1934). *Beauty and human nature.* New York: Appleton-Century-Crofts.

Chandler, C. (1970). *Every man's book of superstition,* Oxford: Maudsay.

Chandler, H. M. (1991). Transcendental Meditation and awakening wisdom: A 10-year longitudinal study of self development. *Dissertation Abstracts International, 51*, 5048B.

Chandler, H. N. (1981). Teaching LD students in the public schools: A return to the closet. *Journal of Learning Disabilities, 14*, 482–485, 547–549.

Chanowitz, B., & Langer, E. (1980). Knowing more (or less) than you can show: Understanding control through the mindlessness-mindfulness distinction. In M. E. P. Seligman (Ed.), *Human helplessness.* New York: Academic Press.

Chanowitz, B., & Langer, E. (in press). Knowing more (or less) than you can show: Understanding control through the mindlessness/mindful distinction. In M. E. P. Selicjman & J. Garber (Eds.), *Human helplessness.* New York: Academic Press. (Original work published 1980)

Chapanis, A. (1959). *Research techniques in human engineering.* Baltimore, Md.: Johns Hopkins University Press.

Chapanis, A. (1961). Men, machines and models. *American Psychologist, 16*, 113–131.

Chapanis, A. (1965). *Man-machine engineering.* Belmont, Calif.: Wadsworth.

Chapanis, A. (1965). Words, words, words. *Human Factors, 7*, 1–17.

Chapanis, A. (1971). Prelude to 2001: Explorations in human communication. *American Psychologist, 26*, 949–961.

Chapanis, A. (1976). Engineering psychology. In M. D. Dunnette (Ed.), *Handbook of industrial and organizational psychology.* Chicago: Rand-McNally.

Chapanis, A. (1976). Ergonomics in a world of new values. *Ergonomics, 19*, 252–268.

Chapanis, A. (Ed.). (1975). *Ethnic variables in human factors engineering.* Baltimore, Md.: Johns Hopkins University Press.

Chapanis, A., Garner, W. R., & Morgan, C. T. (1949). *Applied experimental psychology: Human factors in engineering design.* New York: Wiley.

Chapin, F. S. (1947). *Experimental designs in sociological research.* New York: Harper.

Chaplin, J. (1988). *Feminist counseling in action.* Newbury Park, CA: Sage.

Chaplin, J. P., & Krawiec, T. S. (1970). *Systems and theories of psychology.* New York: Holt, Rinehart & Winston.

Chapman, A., & Foot, H. (Eds.). (1976). *Humour and laughter: Theory, research and applications.* London: Wiley.

Chapman, A., & Foot, H. (Eds.). (1977). *It's a funny thing, humour.* Oxford: Pergamon Press.

Chapman, A. J., & Jones, D. M. (Eds.). (1980). *Models of man.* Leicester, England: British Psychological Society.

Chapman, L., & Chapman, J. (1967). Genesis of popular but erroneous psychodiagnostic observations. *Journal of Abnormal Psychology, 72*, 193–204.

Chapman, L. F., & Wolff, H. (1959). The cerebral hemispheres and highest integrative functions of man. *Archives of Neurology, 1*, 357–424.

Chapman, L. J., & Chapman, J. P. (1967). Genesis of popular but erroneous psychodiagnostic observations. *Journal of Abnormal Psychology, 72*, 193–204.

Chapman, L. J., Chapman, J. P., & Rawlin, M. L. (1976). Scales for physical and social anhedonia. *Journal of Abnormal Psychology, 85*, 374–382.

Chapman, M. (1977). Father absence, stepfathers, and the cognitive performance of college students. *Child Development, 48*, 1144–1158.

Chappell, N. L. (1990). *The aging of the Canadian population*. Ottawa: Minister of Supply and Services.

Chappell, N. L. (1991). Caregiving research and more caregiving research. What good is it? *The Gerontologist, 31*, 567–569.

Chapple, E. (1949). The interaction chronograph: Its evolution and present application. *Personnel, 25*, 295–307.

Chapple, E. D., & Coon, C. S. (1942). *Principles of anthropology*. New York: Holt.

Charache, S., Lubin, B., & Reid, C. D. (1989). *Management and therapy of sickle cell disease* (NIH Publication No. 89–2117). Washington, DC: National Institutes of Health.

Charcot, J. M. (1889). *Clinical lectures on the diseases of the nervous system*. London: New Syndenham Society.

Charcot, J. M. (1890). *Complete works*. Vol. IX: *Metalothérapie et hypnotisme*. Paris: Fourneville & Brissand.

Charmez, K. C. (1980). The social construction of self-pity in the chronically ill. In N. K. Denzin (Ed.), *Studies in symbolic interaction*, Vol. 3. Greenwich, Conn.: JAI Press.

Chase, H. P. (1976). Undernutrition and growth and development of the human brain. In J. D. Lloyd-Still (Ed.), *Malnutrition and intellectual development*. Littleton, Mass.: Publishing Sciences Group.

Chase, M. H. (Ed.). (1972). *The sleeping brain*. Los Angeles: BIS/BRS.

Chase, M. H., Kripke, D. F., & Walter, P. L. (Eds.). (1972–1981). *Sleep research*, Vol. 1–10. Los Angeles: Brain Information Service, Brain Research Institute.

Chase, T. N., Wexler, N. S., & Barbeau, A. (Eds.). (1979). *Advances in neurology*. Vol. 23: *Huntington's disease*. New York: Raven Press.

Chase, W. G., & Ericsson, K. A. (1982). Skill and working memory. In G. H. Bower (Ed.), *The psychology of learning and motivation*. New York: Academic Press.

Chassan, J. B. (1979). *Research design in clinical psychology and psychiatry* (2nd ed.). New York: Irvington.

Chatwin, B. (1987). *The songlines*. New York: Penguin Books.

Chauncey, H. (Ed.). (1969). *Soviet preschool education*. New York: Holt, Rinehart & Winston.

Chavez, A., & Martinez, C. (1979). Behavioral effects of undernutrition and food supplementation. In J. Brožek (Ed.), *Behavioral effects of energy and protein deficits*. Washington, D.C.: NIH Publication no. 79–1906.

Chavez, E. A. (1901). Ensayo sobre los rasgos distintivos de la sensibilidad como factor del caracter mexicano. *Revista Positiva, 1*, 81–90.

Chavez, E. A. (1956/1928). *Ensayo de la psicologia de la adolescencia*. Mexico, D.F.: Editorial Jus.

Cheek, D. B., & LeCron, L. M. (1968). *Clinical hypnotherapy*. New York: Grune & Stratton.

Cheesman, J., & Merikle, P. M. (1985). Word recognition and consciousness. In D. Besner, T. G. Waller, & G. E. MacKinnon (Eds.), *Reading research: Advances in theory and practice* (Vol. 5, pp. 311–352). New York: Academic Press.

Chein, I. (1972). *The science of behavior and the image of man*. New York: Basic Books.

Chelpanov, G. I. (1924). *Psychology and Marxism*. Moscow: Russki-Lpizbnik.

Chelpanov, G. I. (1925). *Psychology in Russia and America*. Moscow: Dunnov.

Chelune, G. J., Tucker, D. M., & O'Neill, C. P. (1982). Organic disturbances. In L. Goodstein & J. Calhoun (Eds.), *Abnormal psychology*. Boston: Addison-Wesley.

Chemers, M. M., Rice, R. W., Sundstrom, E., & Butler, W. (1975). Leader esteem for the least preferred coworker score, training, and effectiveness: An experimental examination. *Journal of Personality and Social Psychology, 31*, 401–409.

Chen, D. R. (1980). 30 years of physiological psychology in China. *Acta Psychologica Sinica, 12*, 22–29.

Chen, L. (1935). *Essentials of industrial psychology*. Beijing, China: Chinese Business Press.

Chen, L. (1944). The correction formula for matching tests. *The Journal of Educational Psychology, 35*(9), 565–566.

Chen, L. (1948). A factor study of a test battery at different education levels. *The Journal of Genetic Psychology, 73*, 187–199.

Chen, L. (1983). *Prospectus of industrial psychology*. Zhejiang, China: People's Press.

Chen, L. (1988). *Psychology of industrial management*. Shanghai, China: People's Press.

Cheng, D. (1975). *Philosophical aspects of the mind-body problem*. Honolulu: University of Hawaii Press.

Cherniss, C. (1980). *Staff burnout: Job stress in human services*. Beverly Hills, Calif.: Sage Publications.

Chernoff, G. F. (1977). The fetal alcohol syndrome in mice: an animal model. *Teratology, 15*, 223–230.

Chernoff, G. F. (1980). The fetal alcohol syndrome in mice: maternal variables. *Teratology, 22*, 71–75.

Chernoff, P. A., & Schaffer, W. G. (1972). Defending the mentally ill: Ethical quicksand. *American Criminal Law Review, 10*, 505–531.

Cherry, E. C. (1953). Some experiments on the recognition of speech, with one and with two ears. *Journal of the Acoustical Society of America, 25*, 975–979.

Cherry, F., & Deaux, K. (1978). Fear of success versus fear of gender-inappropriate behavior. *Sex Roles, 4*, 97–101.

Chertok, L. (1977). Experimental psychosomatic medicine. Blisters. *Annals of Medical Psychology (Paris), 2*, 1–13.

Cherulnik, P. D., & Citrin, M. M. (1974). Individual difference in psychological reactance: The interaction between locus of control and mode of elimination of freedom. *Journal of Personality and Social Psychology, 29*, 398–404.

Chesler, P. (1972). *Women and madness*. Garden City, NY: Doubleday and New York: Avon Books.

Chess, S. (1971). Genesis of behaviour disorders. In J. G. Howells (Ed.), *Modern perspectives in international child psychiatry*. New York: Brunner/Mazel.

Chess, S., Clark, K. B., & Thomas, A. (1953). The importance of cultural evaluation in psychiatric diagnosis and treatment. *Psychiatric Quarterly, 27*, 102–114.

Chess, S., & Thomas, A. (1973). Temperament in the normal infant. In J. C. Westman (Ed.), *Individual differences in children*. New York: Wiley.

Chess, S., & Thomas, A. (1977). Temperamental individuality from childhood to adolescence. *Journal of Child Psychiatry, 16*, 218–226.

Chess, S., Thomas, A., & Birch, G. H. (1965). *Your child is a person*. New York: Viking (Compass Books).

Chessick, R. (1977). *Great ideas in psychotherapy*. New York: Aronson.

Chevalier-Skolnikoff, S. (1981). The Clever Hans phenomenon, cuing, and ape signing: A Piagetian analysis of methods for instructing animals. In T. A. Sebeok & R. Rosenthal (Eds.), *The Clever Hans phenomenon: Communication with horses, whales, apes, and people.* New York: New York Academy of Sciences.

Chew, P. (1976). *The inner world of the middle-aged man.* New York: Macmillan.

Cheyne, A. (1991). Bad seeds and vile weeks: Metaphors of determinism. In D. J. Pepler & K. H. Rubin (Eds.), *The development and treatment of childhood aggression* (pp. 121–136). Hillsdale, NJ: Erlbaum.

Chiba, A. (1978). *Developmental structure of intelligence.* Tokyo: International Office of Intelligence Education.

Chiland, C. (1982/1971). *L'enfant de six ans et son avenir.* Paris: Presses Universitaires de France.

Chiland, C. (1983). *L'entretien clinique.* Paris: Presses Universitaires de France.

Child, I. L. (1943, 1970). *Italian or American? The second generation in conflict.* New Haven, Conn.: Yale University Press, New York: Russell & Russell.

Child, I. L. (1950). The relation of somatotype to self ratings on Sheldon's temperament traits. *Journal of Personality, 18,* 440–453.

Child, I. L. (1973). *Humanistic psychology and the research tradition: Their several virtues.* New York: Wiley.

Child, I. L. (1976). Parapsychology and the rest of psychology: A mutual challenge. In G. R. Schmeidler (Ed.), *Parapsychology: Its relation to physics, biology, psychology, and psychiatry.* Metuchen, N.J.: Scarecrow Press.

Child, I. L. (1978). Aesthetic theories. In E. C. Carterette & M. P. Friedman (Eds.), *Handbook of perception,* Vol. X. New York: Academic Press.

Child, I. L. (1981). Bases of transcultural agreement in response to art. In H. I. Day (Ed.), *Advances in intrinsic motivation and aesthetics.* New York: Plenum.

Child I., & Waterhouse, I. (1952). Frustration and the quality of performance: I. A critique of the Barker, Dembo, and Lewin experiment. *Psychological Review, 59,* 351–362.

Childers, P. R., & Matusiak, I. (1972). Social-emotional maturity correlates of achievement and adjustment in kindergarten and first grade. *Psychology in the Schools, 9,* 396–403.

Chiles, A., Miller, M. L., & Cox, G. B. (1980). Depression in an adolescent delinquent population. *Archives of General Psychiatry, 37,* 1179–1184.

Chiles, J. A. (1974). A practical therapeutic use of the telephone. *American Journal of Psychiatry, 131,* 9.

Chin, R., & Benne, K. D. (1976). General strategies for effecting changes in human systems. In W. G. Bennis, K. D. Benne, R. Chin, & K. E. Corey (Eds.), *The planning of change* (pp. 22–45). New York: Holt, Rinehart, & Winston.

Ching, C. C. (1980). Psychology in the People's Republic of China. *American Psychologist, 35,* 1084–1089.

Ching, C. C., & Jiao, S. L. (1981). Sensory and perceptual studies in the People's Republic of China. *Psychologia, 24,* 133–145.

Chiriboga, D. (1978). Life events and metamodels: A life span study. Presented at the meeting of the Gerontological Society, Dallas, Tex., November.

Chiszar, D. A., & Spear, N. E. (1969). Stimulus change, reversal learning and retention in the rat. *Journal of Comparative and Physiological Psychology, 69,* 190–195.

Chiu, S., McFarlane, A. H., & Dobson, N. (1990). The treatment of monodelusional psychosis associated with depression. *British Journal of Psychiatry, 156,* 112–115.

Chlewinski, Z. (1976). Poland, In V. S. Sexton and H. Misiak (Eds.), *Psychology around the world.* Monterey, Calif.: Brooks/Cole.

Chlewinski, Z. (1983). *Postawy i cechy osobowości (Attitudes and personality traits).* Lublin, Poland: Towarzystwo Naukowe KUL.

Chlewinski, Z. (1983). *Psychologia religii (Selected problems of the psychology of religion).* Lublin, Poland: Towarzystwo Naukowe KUL.

Choate, R. B. (1980). The politics of change. In E. L. Palmer & A. Dorr (Eds.), *Children and the faces of television: Teaching, violence, selling.* New York: Academic Press.

Chodoff, P. (1970). The German concentration camp as a psychological stress. *Archives of General Psychiatry, 22,* 78–87.

Chodoff, P. (1982). Assessment of psychotherapy. *Archives of General Psychiatry, 39,* 1097–1103.

Chodorow, N. (1978). *The reproduction of mothering: Psychoanalysis and the sociology of gender.* Berkeley, Calif.: University of California Press.

Chodorow, N. J. (1989). *Feminism and psychoanalytic theory.* New Haven, CT: Yale University Press.

Chomsky, N. (1957). *Syntactic structures.* The Hague: Mouton.

Chomsky, N. (1959). A review of Skinner's Verbal behavior *Language, 35,* 26–58.

Chomsky, N. (1964). *Current issues in linguistic theory.* The Hague: Mouton.

Chomsky, N. (1965). *Aspects of the theory of syntax.* Cambridge, Mass.: M.I.T. Press.

Chomsky, N. (1966). *Cartesian linguistics.* New York: Harper & Row.

Chomsky, N. (1966). *Topics in the theory of generative grammar.* The Hague: Mouton.

Chomsky, N. (1968). *Language and the mind.* New York: Harcourt, Brace & World.

Chomsky, N. (1972). *Studies on semantics in generative grammar.* The Hague: Mouton.

Chomsky, N. (1975). *Reflections on language.* New York: Pantheon.

Chomsky, N. (1976). After decoding: what? *Language Arts, 53,* 288–296, 314.

Chomsky, N. (1978). Language and unconscious knowledge. In J. H. Smith (Ed.), *Psychiatry and the humanities,* Vol. 3. *Psychoanalysis and language.* New Haven, Conn.: Yale University Press.

Chomsky, N. (1979). *Language and responsibility.* New York: Pantheon.

Chomsky, N. (1980). *Rules and representations.* New York: Columbia University Press.

Chomsky, N. (1986). *Knowledge of language: Its nature origin and use.* New York: Praeger.

Chomsky, N., & Halle, M. (1968). *The sound pattern of English.* New York: Harper & Row.

Chonko, L., & Enis, B. (1980). *Selling and sales management in bibliography.* Chicago: American Marketing Association.

Choron, J. (1972). *Suicide.* New York: Scribners.

Chorover, S. L., & Schiller, P. H. (1965). Short-term retrograde amnesia in rats. *Journal of Comparative and Physiological Psychology, 59,* 73–78.

Chow, S., Elmore, P., & Ertle, V. (1970). *Early childhood education, PREP Report No. 37.* Washington, D.C.: DHEW Publication no. (OE)73-26724.

Chow, S. H. L., & Elmore, P. (n.d.) *Resource manual and program descriptions.* San Francisco: Far West Laboratory for Educational Research and Development, Early Childhood Information Unit.

Chown, S. M. (1959). Rigidity—A flexible concept. *Psychological Bulletin, 56*, 195–223.

Choynowski, M. (1958). Psychology in Poland: Past and present. *The Polish Review, 3*, 86–103.

Christal, R. E., & Weissmuller, J. J. (1976). *New Comprehensive Occupational Data Analysis Programs (CODAP) for analyzing task factor information* (AFHRL Interim Professional Paper no. TR-76-3). Lackland Air Force Base, Tex.: Air Force Human Resources Laboratory.

Christen, A. G., & Cooper, K. H. (1979). Strategic withdrawal from cigarette smoking. *CA-A Cancer Journal for Clinicians, 29*(2), 96–107.

Christensen, A. L. (1975). *Luria's neuropsychological investigation.* New York: Spectrum.

Christensen, J. M. (1971). The emerging role of engineering psychology. In W. C. Howell & I. L. Goldstein (Eds.), *Engineering psychology. Current perspectives in research.* New York: Appleton-Century-Crofts.

Christian, W. P., Schaeffer, R. W., & King, G. D. (1977). *Schedule-induced behavior.* Montreal: Eden.

Christianson, S.-Å. (1992). Emotional stress and eyewitness memory; A critical review. *Psychological Bulletin, 112*, 284–309.

Christie, M. J., & Mellett, P. G. (Eds.). (1981). *Foundations of psychosomatics.* New York: Wiley.

Christie, R., & Garcia, J. (1951). Subcultural variation in authoritarian personality. *Journal of Abnormal Social Psychology, 46*, 457.

Christie, R., & Jahoda, M. (Eds.). (1954). *Studies in the scope and method of "The authoritarian personality"* New York: Free Press.

Christopher, M. (1970). *ESP, seers and psychics.* New York: Crowell.

Christy, N. P. (Ed.). (1971). *The human adrenal cortex.* New York: Harper & Row.

Chrzanowska, D., & Zdanska, B. M. (1974). Psychomotor development of twins in the first six months of life. *Acta Geneticae Medicae et Gemellologiae* (Bologna), *22*(suppl.), 129–131.

Chumlea, E. C. (1982). Physical growth in adolescence. In B. B. Wolman (Ed.), *Handbook of developmental psychology.* Englewood Cliffs, N.J.: Prentice-Hall.

Chung, C. Y. (1990). Psychotherapist and expansion of awareness. *Psychotherapy Psychosomatics, 53*(1–4), 28–32.

Church, A. (1982). Sojourner adjustment. *Psychological Bulletin, 91*, 540–572.

Churchill, R., & Crandall, V. T. (1955). The reliability and validity of the Rotter incomplete sentences test. *Journal of Consulting Psychology, 19*, 345–350.

Churchman, C. W., & Ackoff, R. L. (1950). Purposive behavior and cybernetics. *Social Forces, 29*(1), 32–39.

Chusid, J. G. (1979/1970). *Correlative neuroanatomy and functional neurology.* Los Altos, Calif.: Lange.

Cialdini, R. (1988). *Influence: Science and practice* (2nd ed.). Glenview, IL: Scott, Foresman.

Ciba Foundation. (1979). *Brain and mind: Ciba Foundation Symposium 69.* Amsterdam, Oxford, New York: Excerpta Medica.

Cicirelli, V. G. (1976a). Family structure and interactions: Sibling effects on socialization. In M. F. McMillan & S. Henao (Eds.), *Child psychiatry: Treatment and research.* New York: Brunner/Mazel.

Cicirelli, V. G. (1976b). Siblings teaching siblings. In V. L. Allen (Ed.), *Children as teachers: Theory and research on tutoring.* New York: Academic Press.

Cicirelli, V. G. (1978). Effect of sibling presence on mother–child interaction. *Developmental Psychology, 14*(3), 315–316.

Citizen Participation. (1982). *3* (3: Special issue: Self-help in America).

Citrin, J., McClosky, H., Shanks, M., & Sniderman, P. (1975). Personal and political sources of political alienation. *British Journal of Political Science, 5*, 1–31.

Civil Rights Act, (1964). Public Law 88-352, in Vol. 42, *United States Code*, 200e, Stat. 253.

Civil Rights Act of July 2, 1964, P.L. 88-352, 42 U.S.C., 1964 Ed., effective July 2, 1965, as amended March 2, 1972, P.L. 92-261, 86 Stat. 103, Equal Employment Opportunities Act of 1972.

Claghorn, J. L. (1976). *Successful psychotherapy.* New York: Brunner/Mazel.

Claiborn, W. L. (1982). The problem of professional incompetence. *Journal of Professional Psychology, 13*, 153–158.

Clanton, B., & Smith, L. G. (Eds.). (1977). *Jealousy.* Englewood Cliffs, N.J.: Prentice-Hall.

Claparède, E. (1903). *L'association des idées.* Paris: Dion.

Claparède, E. (1905). *Esquisse d'une théorie biologique du sommeil.* Geneva: Kündig.

Claparède, E. (1905). *Psychologie de l'enfant et pédagogie expérimentale.* Geneva: Kündig. Posthumous edition with an autobiography of the author. Neuchâtel, Switzerland: Delachaux & Niestlé, 1946.

Claparède, E. (1911). *Experimental pedagogy and the psychology of the child.* London: Longman.

Chaparède, E. (1928). Théorie biologique du sommeil et de l'hystérie. Opinions et critiques. *Archives de Psychologie, 21*, 113–174.

Claparède, E. (1931–1968). *L'éducation fonctionnelle.* Neuchâtel, Switzerland: Delachaux & Niestlé.

Claparède, E. (1934). *La genèse de l'hypothèse.* Bern: Kündig.

Claparède, E. (1940/1925). *Comment diagnostiquer les aptitudes chez les écoliers.* Paris: Flammarion.

Claridge, G. S., Canter, S., & Hume, W. I. (1973). *Personality differences and biological variations: A study of twins.* Oxford: Pergamon Press.

Clark, D.C. (1971). Teaching concepts in the classroom: A set of prescriptions derived from experimental research. *Journal of Educational Psychology Monograph, 62*, 253–278.

Clark, D. M., Salkovskis, P. M., & Chalkley, A. J. (1985). Respiratory control as a treatment for panic attacks. *Journal of Behavior Therapy and Experimental Psychiatry, 16*, 23–30.

Clarke, E., & O'Malley, C. D. (1968). *The human brain and spinal cord.* Berkeley, Calif.: University of California Press.

Clark, H. H., & Clark, E. V. (1977). *Psychology and language: An introduction to psycholinguistics.* New York: Harcourt Brace Jovanovich.

Clark, J. (1977). The effects of religious cults on the health and welfare of their converts. *Proceedings and debates of the 95th Congress, first session. 123*, (181) Congressional Record—Extension of Remarks, November 4, E6894, E6896.

Clark, J. C., & Jackson, J. A. (1983). *Hypnosis and behavior therapy.* New York: Springer.

Clark, K. B. (1954). Desegregation: An appraisal of the evidence: The role of social scientist. *Journal of Social Issues, 9*, 2–8.

Clark, K. B. (1963/1955). *Prejudice and your child.* Boston: Beacon Press.

Clark, K. B. (1965). *Dark ghetto: Dilemmas of social power.* New York: Harper & Row.

Clark, K. B. (1967). Implications of Adlerian theory for an understanding of civil rights problems and action. *Journal of Individual Psychology, 23,* 181–190.

Clark, K. B. (1974). *The American Revolution: Democratic politics and popular education.* Washington, D.C.: American Enterprise.

Clark, K. B. (1974). *Pathos of power.* New York: Harper & Row.

Clark, K. B. (1980). Empathy, a neglected topic in psychological research. *American Psychologist, 35,* 187–190.

Clark, K. B., & Hopkins, J. (1969). *Relevant war against poverty.* New York: Harper & Row.

Clark, K. B., & MARC staff. (1972). *A possible reality: A design for the attainment of high academic achievement for inner-city students.* New York: Emerson Hall.

Clark, K. E. (1957). *America's psychologists: A survey of a growing profession.* Washington, D.C.: American Psychological Association.

Clark, K. E. (1961). *The vocational interests of nonprofessional men.* Minneapolis, Minn.: University of Minnesota Press.

Clark, K. E., Nowlis, V., & Rock, M. (1968). *The graduate student as teacher.* Washington, D.C.: American Council on Education.

Clark, L. D., Hughes, R., & Nakashima, E. N. (1970). Behavioral effects of marijuana: Experimental studies. *Archives of General Psychiatry, 23,* 193–198.

Clark, R. G. (1975). *Manter and Gatz's essentials of clinical neuroanatomy and neurophysiology.* Philadelphia, Pa.: Davis.

Clark, W. E. (1966). Buddha and Buddhism. In *Encyclopedia Americana,* Vol. IV.

Clark, W. H. (1958). *The psychology of religion.* New York: Macmillan.

Clarke, A. C. (1952). An examination of the operation of residential propinquity as a factor in mate selection. *American Sociological Review, 17,* 17–22.

Clarke, A. M., & Clarke, A. D. B. (1976). *Early experience: Myth and evidence.* New York: Free Press.

Clarke, E., & Dewhurst, K. (1972). *An illustrated history of brain function.* Berkeley: University of California Press.

Clarke, E., & O'Malley, C. D. (1968). *The human brain and spinal cord.* Berkeley, Los Angeles: University of California Press.

Clarke, R. B., & Campbell, D. T. (1955). A demonstration of bias in estimates of Negro ability. *Journal of Abnormal and Social Psychology 51,* 585–588.

Clarke, W. V., & Hasler, K. R. (1967). Differentiation of criminals and non-criminals with a self-concept measure. *Psychological Reports, 20,* 623–632.

Clarren, S. K., & Smith, D. W. (1978). The fetal alcohol syndrome. *New England Journal of Medicine, 298,* 1063–1067.

Clatworthy, N. (1975). Couples in quasi-marriage. In N. Glazer-Malbin (Ed.), *Old family/new family: Interpersonal relationships.* New York: Van Nostrand.

Clay, P. L. (1987). *At risk of loss: The endangered future of low-income rental housing resources.* Washinton, DC: National Reinvestment Corp.

Clayton, R. R., & Voss, H. L. (1977). Shacking up: Cohabitation in the 1970s. *Journal of Marriage and the Family, 39,* 273–284.

Cleary, P. D. (1987). Gender differences in stress-related disorders. In R. C. Barnett, L. Biener, & G. K. Baruch (Eds.), *Gender and stress* (pp. 39–62). New York: The Free Press.

Cleary, R., & Hay, R. A., Jr. (1980). *Applied time series analysis for the social sciences.* Beverly Hills, Calif.: Sage Publications.

Cleary, T., & Cleary, J. C. (1978). *The blue cliff record.* Boulder, Colo.: Prajna Press.

Cleary, T. A., Humphreys, L. G., Kendrick, S. A., & Wesman, A. (1975). Educational uses of tests with disadvantaged students. *American Psychologist, 30,* 15–41.

Clebsch, W. A., & Jaekle, C. R. (1964). *Pastoral care in historical perspective.* Englewood Cliffs, N.J.: Prentice-Hall.

Cleckley, H. (1976/1941). *The mask of sanity.* St. Louis, Mo.: Mosby.

Clee, M. A., & Wicklund, R. A. (1980). Consumer behavior and psychological reactance. *Journal of Consumer Research, 6,* 389–405.

Clegg, H. (1976). *Trade unionism under collective bargaining.* Oxford: Basic/Blackwell.

Clemans, W. C. (1971). Test administration. In R. L. Thorndike (Ed.), *Educational measurement.* Washington, D.C.: American Council on Education.

Clements, S. D. (1966). Minimal brain dysfunction in children: terminology and identification. Institute of Neurological Diseases, Monograph no. 3, Public Health Service Publications, no. 1415. Washington, D.C.: U.S. Government Printing Office.

Clements, S. D., & Barnes, S. M. (1978). The three R's and central processing training. *Academic Therapy, 13,* 535–547.

Cleveland, P. (1981). Comparison of covert conditioning, relaxation training, biofeedback and placebo as treatments for myofascial pain (or TMJ) dysfunction syndrome. Unpublished doctoral dissertation, Boston College.

Cleveland, W. W. (1991). Redoing the health care quilt: Patches or whole cloth? In *Caring for the uninsured and underinsured: A compendium from the specialty journals of the American Medical Association.* Chicago: American Medical Association.

Cliff, N. (1959). Adverbs as multipliers. *Psychological Review, 66,* 27–44.

Cliff, N. (1973). Scaling. *Annual Review of Psychology. 24,* 473–506.

Cliff, N., Bradley, P., & Girard, R. (1973). The investigation of cognitive models for inventory response. *Multivariate Behavioral Research, 8,* 407–425.

Clifford, G. J. (1978). Words for schools: The applications in education of the vocabulary researches of Edward L. Thorndike. In P. Suppes (Ed.), *Impact of research on education: Some case studies.* Washington, D.C.: National Academy of Education.

Clignet, M. R. (1964). Education et aspirations professionelles. *Tiers Monde, 5,* 61–82.

Cline, F. W. (1978). Z therapy may aid non-psychotic, anti-social children. *Clinical Psychiatry News, 5,* 50.

Cline, J. (1977). Validation of Adlerian life style analysis in vocational assessment. Unpublished dissertation, Georgia State University.

Cline, J., Riordan, R., & Kern, R. (1978). An investigation of the interjudge agreement on a subject's vocational choice and life style type. In L. Baruth & D. Eckstein (Eds.), *Life style: Theory, practice, and research.* Dubuque, Iowa: Kendall/Hunt.

Cline, V. (1955). Ability to judge personality assessed with a stress interview and sound-film technique. *Journal of Abnormal and Social Psychology, 50,* 183–187.

Clinebell, H. J., Jr. (1965). *Basic types of pastoral counseling.* Nashville, Tenn.: Abingdon.

Cloninger, C. R., Reich, T., & Guze, S. B. (1978). Genetic-environmental interactions and antisocial behavior. In R. Hare & D. Schalling (Eds.), *Psychopathic behavior: Approaches to research.* New York: Wiley.

Clopton, W. (1973). Personality and career change. *Industrial Gerontology, 17,* 9–17.

Clore, G. L., & Byrne, D. (1974). A reinforcement-affect model of attraction. In T. L. Huston (Ed.), *Foundation of interpersonal attraction.* New York: Academic Press.

Cloward, R. (1967). Studies in tutoring. *Journal of Experimental Education, 36,* 14–25.

Cloward, R., & Ohlin, L. (1959). Illegitimate means, anomie, and deviant behavior. *American Sociological Review, 24,* 164–177.

Clum, G. A. (1989). Psychological interventions vs. drugs in the treatment of panic. *Behavior Therapy, 20,* 429–457.

Clutton, B., & Harvey, P. (1978). *Readings in sociobiology.* San Francisco: Freeman.

Coan, R. (1972). The changing personality. In R. Dreger (Ed.), *Multivariate personality research.* Baton Rouge, La.: Claitors.

Coan, R. W. (1974). *The optimal personality.* New York: Columbia University Press.

Coan, R. W. (1977). *Hero, artist, sage, or saint.* New York: Columbia University Press.

Coates, J. J., & Thoresen, C. E. (1981). Treating sleep disorders: Few answers, some suggestions, and many questions. In S. M. Turner, K. S. Calhoun, & H. E. Adams (Eds.), *Handbook of clinical behavior therapy.* New York: Wiley.

Coates, T., Thoresen, C. T. (1978). What to use instead of sleeping pills. *Journal of the American Medical Association, 240,* 2311–2314.

Cobb, S. (1976). Social support as a moderator of life stress. *Psychosomatic Medicine, 38,* 300–314.

Cobliner, W. G. (1950). Feminine fashion as an aspect of group psychology. *Journal of Social Psychology, 31,* 283–289.

Coch, L., & French, J. (1948). Overcoming resistance to change. *Human Relations, 1,* 512–532.

Cochran, A. A. (1966, March, April). Mind, matter, and quanta. *Main currents in Modern Thought,* 79–88.

Cochran, W. G. (1977). *Sampling techniques.* (3rd ed.). New York: Wiley.

Cochran, W. G., & Cox, G. M. (1957). *Experimental designs* (2nd ed.). New York: Wiley.

Cockerhand, W. (1981). *Sociology of mental disorder.* Englewood Cliffs, N.J.: Prentice-Hall.

Cocozza, J. J., Hartstone, E., & Braff, J. (1981). Mental health treatment of violent juveniles: An assessment of need. *Crime and Delinquency, 27,* 487–496.

Cocozza, J. J., & Steadman, H. (1974). Some refinements in the measurement and prediction of dangerous behavior. *American Journal of Psychiatry,* 1012–1020.

Coe, W. C. (1972). A behavioral approach to disrupted family interactions. *Psychotherapy: Theory, Research, and Practice, 9,* 80–85.

Coenders, C., Kerbusch, S. M. L., Vossen, J. M. H., & Cools, A. R. (1992). Problem-solving behavior in apomorphone-susceptible and insusceptible rats. *Pysiology and Behavior, 52,* 321–326.

Cofer, C. N. (Ed.). (1976). *The structure of human memory.* San Francisco: Freeman.

Coffman, T. L., & Harris, M. C. (1978, May 18). *Transition shock and the de-institutionalization of the mentally retarded citizen.* Paper presented at the 102nd annual meeting of the American Association on Mental Deficiency, Denver.

Cohen, A., & Margolis, B. (1973). Initial psychological research related to Occupational Safety and Health Act of 1970. *American Psychologist, 28,* 600–606.

Cohen, B. H., Lilienfeld, A. M., & Sigler, T. (1963). Some epidemiological aspects of mongolism: A review. *American Journal of Public Health, 53*(2), 223–236.

Cohen, D. (1979). *J. B. Watson, the founder of behaviourism: A biography.* London: Routledge & Kegan Paul.

Cohen, D., & Wilkie, F. (1979). Sex-related differences in cognition among the elderly. In M. A. Wittig & A. C. Petersen (Eds.), *Sex-related differences in cognitive functioning: Developmental issues.* New York: Academic Press.

Cohen, F., & Lazarus, R. S. (1973). Active coping processes, coping dispositions, and recovery from surgery. *Psychosomatic Medicine, 35,* 375–389.

Cohen, F., & Lazarus, R. S. (1979). Coping with the stresses of illness. In G. C. Stone, F. Cohen, & N. E. Adler (Eds.), *Health psychology: A handbook,* San Francisco: Jossey-Bass.

Cohen, G. D. (1977, February 28). Mental health and the elderly. Unpublished issue paper, National Institute of Mental Health.

Cohen, H. (1980). *You can negotiate anything.* Secaucus, N.J.: Stuart.

Cohen, H. L., & Filipzak, T. (1971). *A new learning environment.* San Francisco: Jossey-Bass.

Cohen, I. S. (1989, December). Memorandum. Office of Educational Affairs.

Cohen, J. (1968). Multiple regression as a general data-analytic system. *Psychological Bulletin, 70,* 426–443.

Cohen, J. (1977). *Statistical power analysis in the behavioral sciences* (rev. ed.). New York: Academic Press.

Cohen, J., & Cohen, P. (1975). *Applied multiple regression/correlation analysis for the behavioral sciences.* Hillsdale, N.J.: Erlbaum.

Cohen, J., & Cohen, P. (1983). *Applied multiple regression/correlation analysis for the behavioral sciences* (2nd ed.). Hillsdale, NJ: Erlbaum.

Cohen, L. B. (1979). Our developing knowledge of infant perception and cognition. *American Psychologist, 34,* 894–899.

Cohen, L. B., DeLoache, J. S., & Strauss, M. S. (1979). Infant visual perception. In J. D. Osofsky (Ed.), *Handbook of infant development.* New York: Wiley.

Cohen, L. P., Claiborn, W. L., & Specter, G. A. (Eds.). (1982). *Crisis intervention.* New York: Human Sciences Press.

Cohen, M., Seghorn, T., & Calmas, W. (1969). Sociometric study of the sex offender. *Journal of Abnormal Psychology, 74,* 249–255.

Cohen, M. M. (1981). Visual-proprioceptive interactions. In R. D. Walk & H. L. Pick, Jr. (Eds.), *Intersensory perception and sensory integration.* New York: Plenum.

Cohen, S. (1978). Environmental load and the allocation of attention. In A. Baum, J. E. Singer, & S. Valins (Eds.), *Advances in Environmental Psychology,* Vol. 1. Hillsdale, N. J.: Erlbaum.

Cohen, S. (1980). Aftereffects of stress on human performance and social behavior: A review of research and theory. *Psychological Bulletin, 88,* 82–108.

Cohen, S. (1991). Social supports and physical health: Symptoms, health behaviors, and infectious disease. In E. M. Cummings, A. L. Greene, & K. H. Harraker (Eds.), *Life-span developmental psychology: Perspectives on stress and coping* (pp. 213–234). Hillsdale, NJ: Erlbaum.

Cohen, S. (1992). Stress, social support and disorder. In H. O. F. Veiel & U. Baumann (Eds.), *The meaning and measurement of social support* (pp. 109–124). New York: Hemisphere Press.

Cohen, S., Evans, G. W., Krantz, D. S., & Stokols, D. (1980). Physiological, motivational and cognitive effects of aircraft noise on children: Moving from the laboratory to the field. *American Psychologist, 35*, 231–243.

Cohen, S., Glass, D. C., & Singer, J. E. (1973). Apartment noise, auditory discrimination, and reading ability in children. *Journal of Experimental Social Psychology, 9*, 407–422.

Cohen, S., & Hoberman, H. M. (1983). Positive events and social supports as buffers of life change stress. *Journal of Applied Social Psychology, 13*, 99–125.

Cohen, S., Krantz, D., Stokols, D., & Evans, G. (1982). *Behavior, health, and environmental stress*. New York: Plenum.

Cohen, S., & McKay, G. (1984). Social support, stress, and the buffering hypothesis: A theoretical analysis. In A. Baum, S. E. Taylor, & J. E. Singer (Eds.), *Handbook of psychology and health: Vol. 4. Social psychological aspects of health* (pp. 253–267). Hillsdale, NJ: Erlbaum.

Cohen, S., & Weinstein, N. (1981). Nonauditory effects of noise on behavior and health. *Journal of Social Issues, 37*(1), 36–70.

Cohen, S., & Wills, T. A. (1985). Stress, social support, and the buffering hypothesis. *Psychological Bulletin, 98*, 310–357.

Cohen, S. E. (1980). Advertising regulation: Changing, growing area. In *Twentieth century advertising and the economy (abundance.* Chicago: Advertising Age.

Colarusso, C. A., & Nemroff, R. A. (1981). *Adult development: A new dimension in psychodynamic theory*. New York: Plenum.

Colby, A. (1978). Evolution of a moral-developmental theory. In W. Damon (Ed.), *New directions in child development: Moral development*. San Francisco: Jossey-Bass.

Colby, A. (1979). *Measurement of moral judgment: A manual and its results*. New York: Cambridge University Press

Colby, A., Kohlberg, L., et al. (1982). A longitudinal study of moral judgment. *Monographs of the Society for Research in Child Development*.

Colby, C. Z., Lanzetta, J. T., & Kleck, R. E. (1977). Effects of the expression of pain on autonomic and pain tolerance responses to subject-controlled pain. *Psychophysiology, 14*(6), 537–540.

Colby, K. M. (1975). *Artificial paranoia: A computer simulation of paranoid processes*. New York: Pergamon Press.

Colby, K. M., & McGuire, M. T. (1981, November). Signs and symptoms. Zeroing in on a better classification of neuroses. *The Sciences*, 21–23.

Cole, B., & Oettinger, M. (1978). *Reluctant regulators*. Reading, Mass.: Addison-Wesley.

Cole, J. D., Helding, M., & Underwood, M. (1988). Aggression and peer rejection in childhood. In B. B. Lahey & A. E. Kazdin (Eds.), *Advances in clinical child psychology* (Vol. 11, pp. 125–158). New York: Plenum Press.

Cole, M. (1975). An ethnographic psychology of cognition. In R. Brislin, S. Bochner, & W. Lonner (Eds.), *Cross-cultural perspectives on learning*. Beverly Hills, Calif.: Sage Publications

Cole, M., Gay, J., Glick, J., & Sharp, D. (1971). *The cultural context of learning and thinking*. New York: Basic Books.

Cole, M., & Maltzman, I. (Eds.). (1969). A *handbook of contemporary Soviet psychology*. New York: Basic Books.

Cole, M., & Means, B. (1981). *Comparative studies of how people think*. Cambridge, Mass.: Harvard University Press.

Cole, M., & Scribner, S. (1974). *Culture and thought: A psychological introduction*. New York: Wiley

Cole, N. S. (1981). Bias in testing. *American Psychologist, 36*, 1067–1077.

Coleman, J. (1975). *The mathematics of collective action*. London: Heinemann.

Coleman, J. (1979). *Contemporary psychology and effective behavior*. Glenview, Ill.: Scott, Foresman.

Coleman, J., Butcher, J., & Carson, R. (1984). *Abnormal psychology and modern life* (7th ed.). Glenview, IL: Scott, Foresman.

Coleman, J. C., Butcher, J. N., & Carson, R. C. (1980). *Abnormal psychology and modern life*. Oakland, N. J.: Scott, Foresman.

Coletta, N. (1980). Ponape: Cross-cultural contact, formal schooling, and foreign dominance. In M. Hamnett & R. Brislin (Eds.), *Research in culture learning: Language and conceptual studies*. Honolulu: University Press of Hawaii.

Colker, J. (1981). *Psychodrama and "the Willhite"* Dubuque, Iowa: Kendall/Hunt.

Colker, J., & Funk, E. (1981). Psychodrama and "the Willhite" In L. Baruth & D. Eckstein (Eds.), *Life style: Theory, practice and research* (2nd ed.). Dubuque, Iowa: Kendall/Hunt.

Collard, J. (1981). The MBD child: The art of definitive history-taking for diagnostic classification. In R. Ochroch (Ed.), *The diagnosis and treatment of minimal brain dysfunction in children: A clinical approach*. New York: Human Sciences Press.

College Entrance Examination Board. (1981). *An SAT: Test and technical data for the Scholastic Aptitude Test administered in April 1981*. New York: College Entrance Examination Board.

College Entrance Examination Board. (1981). *Five SATs*. New York: College Entrance Examination Board.

College Entrance Examination Board. (1982). *Admissions testing program guide for high schools and colleges, 1982–83*. New York: College Entrance Examination Board.

Colletti, L. F. (1979). Relationship between pregnancy and birth complications and the later development of learning disabilities. *Journal of Learning Disabilities, 12*, 769–863.

Collier, R. O., & Hummel, T. J. (1977). *Experimental design and interpretation*. Berkeley, Calif.: McCutchan.

Colligan, R. C. (1974). Psychometric deficits related to perinatal stress. *Journal of Learning Disabilities, 7*, 155–161.

Collins, A. H. (1973). *The human services: An introduction*. Indianapolis, New York: Bobbs-Merrill.

Collins, B. E. (1974). Four components of the Rotter Internal-External Scale: Belief in a difficult world, a just world, a predictable world, and a politically responsive world. *Journal of Personality and Social Psychology, 29*, 381–391.

Collins, B. E. & Guetzkow, H. (1964). *A social psychology of group processes for decision-making*. New York: Wiley.

Collins, C., Stommel, M., King, S., & Given, C. W. (1991). Assessment of the attitudes of family caregivers toward community services. *The Gerontologist, 31*, 756–761.

Collins, G. R. (1977). *The rebuilding of psychology: An integration of psychology and Christianity*. Wheaton, Ill.: Tyndale.

Collins, G. R. (1980). *Christian counseling: A comprehensive guide*. Waco, Tex.: Word.

Collins, G. R. (Ed.). (1980). *Helping people grow: Practical approaches to Christian counseling*. Santa Ana, Calif.: Vision House.

Collins, H. M., & Pinch, T. J. (1979). The construction of the paranormal: Nothing unscientific is happening. In R. Wallis (Ed.), *On the margins of science: The social construction of rejected knowledge*.

(*Sociological review Monograph 27*). Keele, England: University of Keele.

Collins, R. L. (1968). On the inheritance of handedness. I: Laterality in inbred mice. *Journal of Heredity, 59,* 9–12.

Collins, R. L. (1969). On the inheritance of handedness. II. Selection for sinistrality in mice. *Journal of Heredity, 60,* 117–119.

Collis, K. F. (1975). *A study of concrete and formal operations in school mathematics: A Piagetian viewpoint.* Melbourne, Australia: Australian Council for Educational Research.

Collison, M. N-K. (1990a, January 17). Apparent rise in students' cheating has college officials worried. *Chronical of Higher Education,* A33–A34.

Collison, M. N-K. (1990b, October 24). Survey at Rutgers suggests that cheating may be on the rise in large universities. *Chronicle of Higher Education,* A31–A32.

Colotla, V. A., & Gallegos, X. (1978). La psicologia en Mexico. In R. Ardila (Ed.) *La profesion del psicologo.* Mexico D. F.: Editorial Trillas.

Colquhoun, W. P. (Ed.). (1971). *Biological rhythms and human performance.* London: Academic Press.

Colquhoun, W. P., Folkard, S., Knauth, P., & Rutenfranz, J. (1975). *Experimental studies of shiftwork* Opladen, West Germany: Westdeutscher Verlag.

Colvin, R. W., & Zaffiro, E. M. (1974). *Preschool education: A handbook for the training of early childhood educators.* New York: Springer.

Comalli, P. E., Jr. (1960). Studies in physiognomic perception: VI. Differential effects of directional dynamics of pictured objects in real and apparent motion in artists and chemists. *Journal of Psychology, 49,* 99–109.

Comarr, A. E., & Gunderson, B. B. (1975). Sexual function in traumatic paraplegia and quadriplegia. *American Journal of Nursing, 75,* 205–255.

Comas-Diaz, L., & Jacobsen, F. M. (1987). Ethnocultural identification in psychotherapy. *Psychiatry, 50*(3), 232–241.

Comas-Diaz, L., Padilla, A. M. (1990). Countertransference in working with victims of political repression. *American Journal of Orthopsychiatry, 60*(1), 125–134.

Combs, A. W. (1962). *Perceiving, behaving, becoming: A new focus for education.* Washington, D. C.: Association for Supervision and Curriculum Development.

Combs, A. W., & Snygg, D. (1959). *Individual behavior: A perceptual approach to behavior (rev. ed.).* New York: Harper.

Combs, M. L, & Slaby, D. A. (1977). Social skills training with children. In B. Lahey & A. Kazdin (Eds.), *Advances in clinical child psychology,* New York: Plenum.

Comfort, A. (1972). *Joy of sex.* New York: Crown.

Comfort, A. (1976). *A good age.* New York: Crown.

Comings, D. E. (1980, April). Genetics of Tourette syndrome. *Tourette Syndrome Association Newsletter,* 10.

Commission on the Review of the National Policy Toward Gambling. (1976). *Gambling in America.* Washington, D.C.: U.S. Government Printing Office.

Committee on Counselor Training, Division of Counseling and Guidance, American Psychological Association. (1952). Recommended standards for training counseling psychologists at the doctorate level. *American Psychologist, 7,* 175–181.

Committee on National Statistics. (1990). Effect of school desegregation on the academic achievement of black children. In K. W. Wachter & M. L. Straf (Eds.), *The future of meta-analysis* (pp. 53–119). New York: Russell Sage Foundation.

Committee on Nomenclature and Statistics of the American Psychiatric Association. (1980). *Diagnostic and statistical manual: Mental disorders (DSM III).* Washington, D.C.: American Psychiatric Association.

Committee on Veterans' Affairs. (1979). *Medal of honor recipients, 1863–1979.* Washington, D.C.: U.S. Government Printing Office.

Commons, J. R., et al. (1936). *History of labor in the United States.* New York: Macmillan.

Commonwealth v. Drew, 397 Mass. 65, 78–80, 489 N.E.D. 1233 (1986).

Compayré, G. (1887/1879). Lectures on pedagogy, theoretical and practical. Boston: Heath.

Compernolle, T., Hoogduin, K., & Joele, L. (1979). Diagnosis and treatment of the hyperventilation syndrome. *Psychosomatics, 20,* 612–625.

Compton, A. (1980). Psychoanalytic theories. In I. L. Kutash & L. B. Schlesinger (Eds.), *Handbook on stress and anxiety.* San Francisco: Jossey-Bass.

Comrey, A. L. (1962). A study of 35 personality dimensions. *Educational and Psychological Measurement, 22,* 543–552.

Comrey, A. L. (1970). *Comrey personality scales.* San Diego, Calif.: Educational & Industrial Testing Service.

Comrey, A. L. (1970). *Manual for the Comrey personality scales.* San Diego, Calif.: Educational & Industrial Testing Service.

Comrey, A. L. (1971). *A first course in factor analysis.* New York: Academic Press.

Comrey, A. L., Backer, T. E., & Glaser, E. M. (1973). *A sourcebook for mental health measures.* Los Angeles: Human Interaction Research Institute.

Comrey, A. L., & Duffy, K. E. (1968). Cattell and Eysenck factor scores related to Comrey personality factors. *Multivariate Behavioral Research, 3,* 379–392.

Comrey, A. L., Jamison, K, & King, N. (1968). Integration of two personality factor systems. *Multivariate Behavioral Research, 3,* 147–160.

Comrey, A. L., & Newmeyer, J. (1965). Measurement of radicalism-conservatism. *Journal of Social Psychology, 67,* 357–369.

Comte, A. (1896/1853). *The positive philosophy.* London: Bell.

Condillac, E. B. (1930/1754). *Tratie des sensations.* Los Angeles: University of Southern California.

Condillac, E. B. (1974). *Essay on origin of human knowledge.* New York: AMS Press.

Condon, W. S. (1969). Linguistic-kinesic research and dance therapy. *Proceedings. Third Annual Conference of the American Dance Therapy Association, 1968.* Baltimore, Md.: ADTA.

Condon, W. S., & Ogston, W. D. (1967). A segmentation of behavior. *Journal of Psychiatric Research, 5,* 221–235.

Condon, W. S., & Sander, L. W. (1974). Neonate movement is synchronized with adult speech: Interactional participation and language acquisition. *Science, 183,* 99–101.

Condry, J., & Condry, S. (1976). Sex differences: A study in the eye of the beholder. *Child Development, 47,* 812–819.

Cone, J. D. (1988). Psychometric considerations and the multiple models of behavioral assessment. In A. S. Bellack, & M. Hersen (Eds.),

Behavioral assessment: A practical handbook (3rd ed., pp. 42–66). New York: Pergamon.

Conger, J. J. (1977). *Adolescence and youth: Psychological development in a changing world* (2nd ed.). New York: Harper & Row.

Conger, J. J. (1981). Freedom and commitment: Families, youth, and social change. *American Psychologist, 36,* 1475–1484.

Conger, J. J. (Ed.). (1977/1975). *Contemporary issues in adolescent development.* New York: Harper & Row.

Congressional Budget Office (CBO). (1992, October). *Economic implications of rising health costs.* Washington, DC: U.S. Government Printing Office.

Congressional Record, October 10, 1978, H-12179.

Conn, L. K., & Crowne, D. P. (1963). Instigation to aggression, emotional arousal, and defensive emulation. *Journal of Personality, 32,* 163–179.

Connelly, D. (1975). *Traditional acupuncture, the law of the five elements.* Columbia, Md.: Center for Traditional Acupuncture.

Conners, C. K. (1963). Birth order and needs for affiliation. *Journal of Personality, 31,* 408–416.

Connolly, K. J., & Pharoah, P. O. D. (1981). Behavior sequelae of fetal iodine deficiency. In A. E. Harper & G. K. Davis (Eds.), *Nutrition in health and disease and international development: Symposia from the XII International Congress of Nutrition.* New York: Liss.

Conoley, J. C., & Kramer, J. J. (1989). *The tenth mental measurements yearbook.* Lincoln: University of Nebraska Press.

Conrad, E., & Maul, T. (1981). *Introduction to experimental psychology.* New York: Wiley.

Conrad, K. (1941). *Der Konstitutionstyp als genetisches Problem; Versuche einer genetischen Konstitutionslehre.* Berlin: Springer.

Conrad, L., Trismen, D., & Miller, R. (Eds.). (1977). *GRE technical manual.* Princeton, N.J.: Educational Testing Service.

Conrad, R. (1964). Acoustic confusions in immediate memory. *British Journal of Psychology 55,* 75–84.

Conroy, G. C. (1990). *Primate evolution.* New York: Norton.

Conroy, R. T. W., & Mills, J. N. (1970). *Human circadian rhythms.* London: Churchill.

Consensus Conference. (1987). Newborn screening for sickle cell disease and other hemoglobinopathies. *JAMA, 258,* 1205–1209.

Constantine, L. C., & Martinson, F. M. (Eds.). (1981). *Children and sex.* Boston: Little, Brown.

Constantinidis, J., Richard, J., & Tissot, R. (1974). Pick's disease: Histological and clinical correlations. *European Neurology, 11,* 208–217.

Constantinople, A. (1969). An Eriksonian measure of personality development in college students. *Developmental Psychology, 1,* 357–372.

Constantinople, A. (1973). Masculinity–femininity: An exception to a famous dictum? *Psychological Bulletin, 80,* 389–407.

Conte, H., Weiner, M., & Plutchik, R. (1982). Measuring death anxiety: Conceptual, psychometric, and factor analytic aspects. *Journal of Personality and Social Psychology, 43,* 775–785.

Contract Research Corporation Education and Human Development. *Mainstreaming preschoolers series.* Washington, D.C.: U.S. Department of Health, Education, and Welfare, Office of Human Development Services, Administration for Children, Youth and Families, Head Start Bureau, n.d.

Converse, P. (1975). Public opinion and voting behavior. In F. Greenstein & N. Polsby (Eds.), *Handbook of political science,* Vol. 4. Reading, Mass.: Addison-Wesley.

Conway, F., & Siegelman, J. (1978). *Snapping.* New York: Lippincott.

Conyne, R., & Rogers, R. (1977). Psychotherapy as ecological problem-solving. *Psychotherapy: Theory, Research and Practice, 14,* 298–305.

Conyne, R. K., & Clack, R. J. (1981). *Environmental assessment and design: A new tool for the applied behavioral scientist.* New York: Praeger.

Cook, E., Christie, M. J., Gartshore, S., Stern, R. M., & Venables, P. H. (1981). After the executive monkey. In M. J. Christie & P. G. Mellett (Eds.), *Foundations of psychosomatics* (pp. 245–258). Chichester: Wiley.

Cook, J., & Bowles, R. (Eds.). (1980). *Child abuse: Commission and ommission.* Scarborough, Ont.: Butterworth.

Cook, K., Emerson, R., Gillmore, M., & Yamagishi, T. (1983). The distribution of power in exchange networks. *American Journal of Sociology, 89,* 275–305.

Cook, M. (1979). *Perceiving others: The psychology of interpersonal perception.* London: Methuen.

Cook, M., & Wilson, G. (1979). *Love and attraction: An international conference.* Oxford: Pergamon Press.

Cook, T., & Leviton, L. (1980). Reviewing the literature: A comparison of traditional methods with meta-analysis. *Journal of Personality, 48,* 449–472.

Cook, T. D., & Campbell, D. T. (1979/1966). *Quasi-experimentation: Design and analysis issues for field settings.* Chicago: Rand-McNally.

Cook, T. D., & Campbell, D. T. (1979). *Quasi-experimentation: Design and analysis issues for field settings.* Boston: Houghton Mifflin.

Cook, T. D., & Flay, B. R. (1978). The persistence of experimentally induced attitude change. In L. Berkowitz (Ed.), *Advances in experimental social psychology* (Vol. 11, pp. 1–57). New York: Academic Press.

Cook, Thomas D., & Campbell, D. T. (1979). *Quasi experimentation* Chicago: Rand McNally.

Cooke, G. (1969). The court study unit: Patient characteristics and differences between patients judged competent and incompetent. *Journal of Clinical Psychology, 25,* 140–143.

Cooke, G. (1980). *The role of the forensic psychologist.* Springfield, Ill.: Thomas.

Cooke, S., & Slack, N. (1984). Making management decisions. London: Prentice-Hall International.

Cooley, C. H. (1927). *Life and the student.* New York: Knopf.

Cooley, C. H. (1956/1902). *Human nature and the social order.* Glencoe, Ill.: Free Press.

Cooley, C. H. (1966/1918). *Social process.* Carbondale, Ill. Southern Illinois University Press.

Cooley, C. H. (1969/1930). *Sociological theory and social research, being the selected papers of Charles H. Cooley.* New York: Kelly.

Cooley, W. W., & Lohnes, P. R. (1971). *Multivariate data analysis.* New York: Wiley.

Cooley, W. W., & Lohnes, P. R. (1976). *Evaluation research in education.* New York: Irvington.

Coombs, C. H. (1950). Psychological scaling without a unit of measurement. *Psychological Review, 57,* 148–158.

Coombs, C. H. (1958). On the use of inconsistency of preferences in psychological measurement. *Journal of Experimental Psychology, 55,* 1–7.

Coombs, C. H. (1975). Portfolio theory and the measurement of risk. In M. F. Kaplan & S. Schwartz (Eds.), *Human judgment and decision processes*. New York: Academic Press.

Coombs, C. H. (1976/1964). A *theory of data*. New York: Wiley.

Coombs, G. H. (1983). *Psychology and mathematics*. Ann Arbor, Mich.: University of Michigan Press.

Coombs, C. H., & Avrunin, G. S. (1977). Single-peaked functions and the theory of preference. *Psychological Review, 84*, 216–230.

Coombs, C. H., Coombs, L. C., & McClelland, G. H. (1975). Preference scales for number and sex of children. *Population Studies, 29*, 273–298.

Coombs, C. H., Dawes, R. M., & Tversky, A. (1969/1970/1981). *Mathematical psychology, an elementary introduction*. Englewood Cliffs, N.J., Prentice-Hall.

Coombs, C. H., & Keith-Smith, J. E. (1973). On the detection of structure in attitudes and developmental processes. *Psychological Review, 80*, 337–351.

Coombs, R. H. (1962). Reinforcement of values in the premarital home as a factor in mate selection. *Marriage and Family Living, 24*, 155–157.

Coombs, R. H., & Kenkel, W. F. (1966). Sex differences in dating aspirations and satisfaction with computer-selected partners. *Journal of Marriage and the Family, 28*, 62–66.

Coons, P. M. (1988). Psychophysiological aspects of multiple personality disorder. *Dissociation, 1*, 47–53.

Coop, R. H., & Sigel, I. E. (1971). Cognitive style: Implications for learning and instruction. *Psychology in the Schools, 8*, 152–161.

Cooper, C. L., & Payne, P. (Eds.). (1980). *Current concerns in occupational stress*. New York: Wiley.

Cooper, E. (1991). A critique of six measures for assessing creativity. *Journal of Creative Behavior, 25*, 194–205.

Cooper, E., & Jahoda, M. (1947). The evasion of propaganda: How prejudiced people respond to anti-prejudice propaganda. *Journal of Psychology, 23*, 15–25.

Cooper, H. M. (1979). Pygmalion grows up: A model for teacher expectation communication and performance influence. *Review of Educational Research, 49*, 389–410.

Cooper, H. M. (1979). Statistically combining independent studies: A meta-analysis of sex differences in conformity research. *Journal of Personality and Social Psychology, 37*, 131–146.

Cooper, H. M. (1982). Scientific guidelines for conducting integrative research reviews. *Review of Educational Research, 52*, 291–302.

Cooper, J. R., Bloom, F. E., & Roth, R. H. (1978/1970). *The biochemical basis of neuropharmacology*. New York: Oxford University Press.

Cooper, L. A., & Shepard, R. N. (1973). Chronometric studies of the rotation of mental images. In W. G. Chase (Ed.), *Visual information processing*. New York: Academic Press.

Cooper, M. (1957). *Pica*. Springfield, Ill.: Thomas.

Cooper, R. M., & Zubeck, J. T. (1958). Effects of enriched and restricted early environments on the learning ability of bright and dull rats. *Canadian Journal of Psychology, 12*, 159–164.

Cooper, W. H. (1961). Usability of American tests with African students. *West African Journal of Education, 5*, 86–91.

Coopersmith, S. (1967). *The antecedents of self-esteem*. San Francisco: Freeman.

Coover, J. E. (1927). Metapsychics and the incredulity of psychologist In C. Murchison (Ed.), *The case for and against psychic belief*. Worcester, Mass.: Clark University Press.

Coover, J. E. (1975/1917). *Experiments in psychical research*. New York: Arno Press.

Copi, I. M. (1982/1953). *Introduction to logic* (6th edition). New York: Macmillan.

Coppen, A. (1967). The biochemistry of affective disorders. *British Journal of Psychiatry, 113*, 1237–1264.

Coppen, A. (1971). Biogenic amines and affective disorders. In B. T. Ho & W. M. McIssac (Eds.), *Brain chemistry and mental disease*. New York: Plenum.

Corballis, M. C. (1983). *Human laterality*. New York: Academic Press.

Corcoran, K. J. (1981). Experiential empathy: A theory of a level experience. *Journal of Humanistic Psychology, 21*, 29–38.

Coren, S. (1969). Brightness contrast as a function of figure-ground relations. *Journal of Experimental Psychology, 80*, 517–524.

Coren, S. (1992). *The left-hander syndrome: The causes and consequences of left-handedness*. New York: Free Press.

Coren, S., & Girgus, J. S. (1978). *Seeing is deceiving: The psychology of visual illusions*. Hillsdale, N. J.: Erlbaum.

Coren, S., Porac, C., & Duncan, P. (1981). Lateral behaviors preference in preschool children and young adults. *Child Development, 52*, 443–450.

Coren, S., Porac, C., & Ward, L. M. (1979). *Sensation and perception*. New York: Academic Press.

Coren, S., & Ward, L. M. (1989). *Sensation and perception* (3rd ed.). San Diego: Harcourt, Brace, Jovanovich.

Corey, C. H. (1977). Relative utility of computerized versus paper-and-pencil tests for predicting job performance. *Applied Psychological Measurement, 1*, 551–554.

Corey, G. (1982/1977). *Theory and practice of counseling and psychotherapy* (2nd ed.). Monterey, Calif.: Brooks/Cole.

Corey, G. (1983). *I never knew I had a choice*. Monterey, Calif.: Brooks/Cole.

Corey, G., & Corey, M. S. (1977). *Groups: Process and practice*. Monterey, Calif.: Brooks/Cole.

Corey, G., Corey, M., & Callanan, P. (1979). *Professional and ethical issues in counseling and psychotherapy*. Monterey, Calif.: Brooks/Cole.

Corey, S. M. (1953). *Action research to improve school practices*. New York: Bureau of Publications, Teachers College, Columbia University.

Coriat, I. H. (1943). The psychoanalytic conception of stuttering. *The Nervous Child 2*, 167–171.

Corkin, S. (1980). A prospective study of cingulotomy. In E. Valenstein (Ed.), *The psychosurgery debate*. San Francisco: Freeman.

Cormack, A. M. (1980). Early two-dimensional reconstruction (CT scanning) and recent topics stemming from it. *Journal of Computer Assisted Tomography, 4*, 658–464.

Cormack, R. W. & Strand, A. L. (1970). *T. A. survey*. Oak Brook, Ill.: Government Personnel Consultants.

Corman, B. R. (1957). Action research: A teaching or a research method? *Review of Educational Research, 27*, 544–547.

Cornell, W. B. (1917). *Psychology vs psychiatry in diagnosing feeblemindedness*. New York State Journal of Medicine, 17, 485–486.

Corner, G. W. (Ed.). (1948). *The autobiography of Benjamin Rush*. Princeton, N.J.: Princeton University Press.

Corning, W. C., Dyal, J. A., & Willows, A. O. D. (Eds.). (1973). *Invertebrate learning* (3 vols.). New York: Plenum.

Cornoldi, C., & Fattori, L. C. (1976). Age spacing in firstborns and symbiotic dependence. *Journal of Personality and Social Psychology, 33*(4), 431–434.

Corriere, R. J., & Hart, J. T. (1979). *Psychological fitness.* New York: Harcourt Brace Jovanovich.

Corrigan, J. D., Dell, D. M., Lewis, K. N., & Schmidt, L. D. (1980). Counseling as a social influence process. *Journal of Counseling Psychology, 27,* 395–441.

Corsellis, J. A. (1962). *Mental illness and the aging brain.* Maudsley Monographs, no. 9. London: Oxford University Press.

Corsini R. J. (1951). Fields of psychology. *American Psychologist, 6,* 177–179.

Corsini R. J. (1951). *The immediate test.* Orange, Calif.: Sheridan Psychological Services.

Corsini R. J. (1956). Multiple predictors of marital happiness. *Marriage and Family Living, 17,* 240–242.

Corsini, R. J. (1956). Understanding and similarity in marriage. *Journal of Abnormal and Social Psychology,52,* 327–332.

Corsini, R. J. (1957). *Methods of group psychotherapy.* New York: McGraw-Hill.

Corsini, R. J. (1957). *The Chicago Q sort.* Chicago: Psychometric Affiliates.

Corsini R. J. (1977). Individual education. *Journal of Individual Psychology, 33,* 295–349.

Corsini, R. J. (1977). A medley of current personality theories. In R. J. Corsini (Ed.), *Current personality theories* (pp. 399–431). Itasca, IL: Peacock.

Corsini R. J. (1981). Individual education. In E. Ignas & R. J. Corsini (Eds.), *Alternative educational systems.* Itasca, Ill.: Peacock.

Corsini, R. J. (1991). *Five therapists and one client.* Itasca, Il.: Peacock.

Corsini R. J. (Ed.). (1981). *Handbook of innovative psychotherapies.* New York: Wiley.

Corsini, R. J. (Ed.). (1984/1979/1973). *Current psychotherapies* (3rd ed.). Itasca, Ill.: Peacock.

Corsini, R. J., & Marsella, A. J. (Eds.). (1983). *Personality theory, research and assessment.* Itasca, Ill.: Peacock.

Corsini, R. J., & Painter, G. (1975). *The practical parent.* New York: Harper & Row.

Corsini, R. J., & Putzey, L. J. (1956). *Bibliography of group psychotherapy.* Beacon, N.Y.: Beacon Press.

Corsini, R. J., & Rosenberg, B. (1955). Mechanisms of group psychotherapy. *Journal of Abnormal and Social Psychology, 51,* 406–411.

Corsini, R. J., & Wedding, D. (Eds.). (1989). *Current psychotherapies.* Itasca, IL: Peacock.

Corso, J. F. (1957). Absolute judgments of musical tonality. *Journal of the Acoustical Society of America, 29,* 138–144.

Corso, J. F. (1963). A theoretico-historical review of the threshold concept. *Psychological Bulletin, 60,* 356–370.

Corso, J. F. (1967). *The experimental psychology of sensory behavior.* New York: Holt, Rinehart & Winston.

Corso, J. F. (1971). Adaptation-level theory and psychophysical scaling. In M. H. Appley (Ed.), *Adaptation-level theory. A symposium.* New York: Academic Press.

Corso, J. F. (1981). *Aging sensory systems and perception.* New York: Praeger.

Corso, J. F., Wright, H. N., & Valerio, M. (1976). Temporal summation function in presbycusis and noise exposure. *Journal of Gerontology, 31,* 58–63.

Corteen, R. S., & Wood, B. (1972). Autonomic responses to shock associated words. *Journal of Experimental Psychology, 94,* 308–313.

Cortés, J. B., & Gatti, F. M. (1965). Physique and self-description of temperament. *Journal of Consulting Psychology, 29,* 432–439.

Coser, L. A. (1956). *The functions of social conflict.* Glencoe, Ill.: Free Press.

Coser, L. A. (1977). Charles Horton Cooley, 1864–1929. In *Masters of sociological thought.* New York: Harcourt Brace Jovanovich.

Costa, E., & Garattini, S. (1970). *Amphetamine and related compounds.* New York: Raven Press.

Costa, P. T., Jr., & McCrae, R. R. (1980). Still stable after all these years: Personality as a key issue in adulthood and old age. In P. B. Baites & O. G. Brim, Jr. (Eds.), *Life-Span development and behavior,* Vol. 3. New York: Academic Press.

Costanzo, P. R. (1970). Conformity development as a function of self-blame. *Journal of Personality and Social Psychology 14,* 366–374.

Costello, C. G., & Comrey, A. L. (1967a). Two scales to measure achievement motivation. *Journal of Psychology, 66,* 231–235.

Costello, C. G., & Comrey, A. L. (1967b). Scales for measuring depression and anxiety. *Journal of Psychology, 66,* 303–313.

Costello, E. J. (1990). Child psychiatric epidemiology: Implications for clinical research and practice. In B. B. Lahey & A. E. Kazdin (Eds.), *Advances in clinical child psychology* (Vol. 13, pp. 53–90). New York: Plenum.

Cott, A. (1973). Medical orthodoxy and orthomolecular psychiatry. *Psychiatric Opinion, 10,* 12–15.

Cott, A. (1981). Orthomolecular treatment of children with learning disabilities. In R. Ochroch (Ed.), *The diagnosis and treatment of minimal brain dysfunction in children: A clinical approach.* New York: Human Sciences Press.

Cott, H. B. (1940). *Adaptive coloration in animals.* London: Methuen.

Cottingham, H. F., & Swanson, C. D. (1976). Recent licensure developments: Implications for counselor education. *Counselor Education and Supervision, 16,* 84–97.

Cottler, L. B., Robins, L. N., Grant, B. F., Blaine, J., Towle, L. H., Wittchen, H. U., & Sartorious, N. (1991). The CIDI core substance abuse and dependence questions: Cross-cultural and nosological issues. *British Journal of Psychiatry, 152,* 653–658.

Cotton, J. W. (1975). *Par for the Corps: A review of the literature on selection, training, and performance of Peace Corps Volunteers.* ERIC Document Reproduction Service, Document ED 110 672.

Cotton, P. G., & Macht, L. B. (1980). Assessing the acute inpatient psychiatric needs of the state hospital patients. *American Journal of Psychiatry, 137,* 480–482.

Cottrell, L. S., Jr. (1942). The adjustment of the individual to his age and sex roles. *American Sociological Review, 7,* 617–620.

Couch, A., & Keniston, K. Y. (1960). Yeasayers and naysayers: Agreeing response set as a personality variable. *Journal of Abnormal and Social Psychology, 60,* 151–174.

Coué, E. (1912). La maitrise de soi-même par l'autosuggestion consciente. Conférence fait par M. Coué à Chaumont.

Coué, E. (1922). *Self mastery through conscious suggestion.* London: Allen & Unwin.

Coué, E. (1922). *The practice of autosuggestion.* New York: Doubleday.

Council for the National Register of Health Service Providers in Psychology. (1981). *National Register of Health Service Providers in Psychology.* Washington, D.C.: Council for the National Register.

Council, J. R., & Greyson, B. (1985, August). *Near-death experiences and the "fantasy-prone personality": Preliminary findings*. Paper presented at the annual convention of the American Psychological Association, Los Angeles.

Council of Counseling Psychology Training Programs. (1982, February). *Manuel of policies and procedures*.

Cousins, N. (1957, October 5). Smudging the subconscious. *Saturday Review*, p. 20.

Cousins, N. (1976). Anatomy of an illness. *New England Journal of Medicine, 295*, 1458–1463.

Cousins, N. (1979). *Anatomy of an illness, as perceived by the patient.* New York: Norton.

Cousins, N. (1981). *The anatomy of an illness.* New York: Cancer Book House.

Coutu, W. (1951). Roleplaying vs. roletaking. *American Sociological Review, 16*, 180–187.

Covarrubias de Levy, A. C. (1970). La realidad del psicologo mexicano. Estudio del mercado de trabajo de la psicologia en la industria y en escuelas del Distrito Federal. *Journal de Psicologia, 4*, 3–8.

Covner, B. J. (1942). Studies in phonographic recordings of verbal material. I and II. *Journal of Consulting Psychology, 6*, 105–113, 149–153.

Covner, B. J. (1944). Studies in phonographic recording of verbal material: III. The completeness and accuracy of counseling interview reports. *Journal of General Psychology, 30*, 181–203.

Covner, B. J. (1944). Studies in phonographic recordings of verbal material. IV. Written reports of interviews. *Journal of Applied Psychology, 28*, 89–98.

Cowan, P. A. (1978). *Piaget with feeling.* New York: Holt, Rinehart & Winston.

Cowen, E. (1980). The wooing of primary prevention. *American Journal of Community Psychology, 8*(3), 258–284.

Cowen, E. L. (1973). Social and community interventions. *Annual Review of Psychology, 24*, 423–472.

Cowen, E. L. (in press). Help is where you find it: Four informal helping groups. *American Psychologist*.

Cowen, E. L., Gardner, E. A., & Zax, M. (1967). *Emergent approaches to mental health problems.* New York: Appleton-Century-Crofts.

Cowen, E. L., Trost, M. A., Lorion, R. P., Dorr, D., Izzo, L. D., & Isaacson, R. V. (1975). *New ways in school mental health: Early detection and prevention of school rnaladaption.* New York: Human Sciences Press.

Cowie, J., Cowie, V., & Slater, E. (1968). *Delinquency in girls.* New York: Humanities Press.

Cowles, J. T. (1937). Food tokens for incentives for learning by chimpanzees. *Comparative Psychology Monographs, 14*(71).

Cox, D. R. (1958). Planning of experiments, New York: Wiley.

Cox, R. D. (1970). *Youth into maturity.* New York: Mental Health Materials Center.

Cox, T. (1978). *Stress.* Baltimore, Md.: University Park Press.

Cox, W. M. (1977). Some changes in articles published in the Journal of Applied Psychology during a twenty-year period. *Journal of Applied Psychology, 62*, 241–244.

Cox, W. M. (Ed.). (1987). *Treatment and prevention of alcohol problems.* New York: Academic.

Coxon, A. P. M. (1982). *The user's guide to multidimensional scaling* Exeter, New Hampshire: Heinemann Educational Books.

Coyne, J. (1989, March–April). Change the channel. *The Family Therapy Networker*, 40–41.

Coyne, J. C., & Bolger, N. (1990). Doing without social support as an explanatory concept. *Journal of Social and Clinical Psychology, 9*, 148–158.

Craig, J. B., & Powell, B. L. (1987). Review: The management of nausea and vomiting in clinical oncology. *The American Journal of the Medical Sciences, 293*, 34–44.

Craig, T. (Ed.). (1976). *The humanistic and mental health aspects of sports, exercise and recreation.* Chicago: American Medical Association.

Craig, T. J., & Behar, R. (1980). Trends in the prescription of psychotropic drugs (1970–1977) in a State hospital (Rockland, N. Y.). *Comprehensive Psychiatry, 21*, 336–345.

Craighead, W. E., Kazdin, A. E., & Mahoney, M. J. (1981). *Behavior modification: Issues, principles and applications* (2nd ed.). Dallas: Houghton Mifflin.

Craik, F., & Lockhart, R. S. (1972). Levels of processing: A framework for memory research. *Journal of Verbal Learning and Verbal Behavior, 11*, 671–684.

Craik, F. I. M. (1977). Age differences in human memory. In J. E. Birren & K. W. Schaie (Eds.), *Handbook of the psychology of aging.* New York: Van Nostrand Reinhold.

Craik, F. I. M. (1979). Human memory. In M. R. Rosenszweig & L. W. Porter (Eds.), *Annual review of psychology*, Vol. 30. Palo Alto, Calif.: Annual Reviews.

Craik, K. J. W. (1943). *The nature of explanation.* Cambridge, England: Cambridge University Press.

Craik, K. J. W. (1966). *The nature of psychology: A selection of papers, essays and other writings by the late K. J. W. Craik*, S. L. Sherwood (Ed.). Cambridge, England: Cambridge University Press.

Cranach, M. von, Foppa, K., Lepenies, W., & Ploog, D. (Eds.). (1979). *Human ethology.* Cambridge, England: Cambridge University Press. Paris: Maison des sciences de l'Homme.

Cranach, M. von, Kalbermatten, U., Indermühle, K., & Gugler, B. (1980). *Zielgerichtetes Handeln.* Bern: Huber.

Crandall, R., Harrison, A. A., & Zajonc, R. B. (1976). *The permanence of positive and negative effects of stimulus exposure: A sleeper effect.* Unpublished manuscript, University of Michigan.

Crandall, V. C., Katkowsky, W., & Crandall, V. J. (1965). Children's beliefs in their own control of reinforcement in intellectual-academic achievement situations. *Chief Development, 36*, 91–109.

Cranson, R. W., Orme-Johnson, D. W., Gackenbach, J., Dillbeck, M. C., Jones, C. H., & Alexander, C. N. (1991). Transcendental Meditation and improved performance on intelligence-related measures: A longitudinal study. *Personality and Individual Differences, 12*(10), 1105–1116.

Crasilneck, H. B., & Hall, J. A. (1968). The use of hypnosis in controlling cigarette smoking. *Southern Medical Journal 61*, 999–1002.

Crasilneck, H. B., & Hall, J. A. (1975). *Clinical hypnosis: Principles and applications.* New York: Grune & Stratton.

Cratty, B. J. (1967). *Movement behavior and motor learning.* Philadelphia, Pa.: Lea & Febiger

Cravens, H. (1978). *The triumph of evolution: American scientists and the heredity environment controversy 1900–1941.* Philadelphia, Pa.: University of Pennsylvania Press.

Creak, M., Cameron, K., Cowie, V., Ini, S., MacKeith, R., Mitchell, G., O'Gorman, G., Orford, F., Rogers, W., Shapiro, A., Stove, F., Stroh, G., & Yudkin, S. (1961). Schizophrenia syndrome in childhood. *British Journal of Medicine, 2*, 889–890.

Cremer, J. (1973). Effects of a two week Z-process treatment program with hyperkinetic children. Master's thesis, California State University, Long Beach.

Crespi, L. P. (1942). Quantitative variation of incentive and performance in the white rat. *American Journal of Psychology, 55*, 467–517.

Crespi, L. P. (1944). Amount of reinforcement and level of performance. *Psychological Review, 51*, 341–357.

Crespi, L. P. (1974, July). The meaning and measurement of program effectiveness in U.S.I.A. In *The 27th Report, United States Advisory Commission on Information*, pp. 65–102.

Crews, D. (Ed.). (1987). *Psychobiology of reproductive behavior: An evolutionary Perspective*. Englewood Cliffs, NJ: Prentice-Hall.

Criddle, W. (1975). Guidelines for challenging irrational beliefs. *Rational Living, 9*(1), 8–13.

Crider, A. (1983). The promise of social psychophysiology. In J. T. Cacioppo & R. E. Petty (Eds.), *Social psychophysiology: A sourcebook*. New York: Guilford Press.

Crider, A. B., Schwartz, G. E., & Shnidman, S. (1969). On the criteria for instrumental autonomic conditioning: A reply to Katkin and Murray. *Psychological Bulletin, 71*, 455–461.

Crijns, A. G. J. (1962). African intelligence: A critical survey of cross cultural research in Africa south of the Sahara. *Journal of Social Psychology, 57*, 283–301.

Crijns, A. G. J. (1966). African basic personality structure: A critical review of bibliographical sources and of principal findings. *Gawein, 14*, 239–248.

Crissey, M. S. (1983). School psychology reminiscences of earlier times. *Journal of School Psychology, 21*, 163–177.

Crissey, M. S., Scholl, G., & Bauman, M. K. (1959). *A study of the vocational success of groups of the visually handicapped*. Ann Arbor, Mich.: University of Michigan School of Education.

Crissy, W. J. E., Cunningham, W., & Cunningham, I. (1977). *Selling: The personal force in marketing*. New York: Wiley.

Critchley, M. (1939). *The language of gesture*. London: Arnold.

Critchley, M. (1975). *Silent language*. London: Butterworth.

Critchley, M., & Critchley, E. A. (1978). *Dyslexia defined*. London: Heinemann.

Critelli, J. W., & Waid, L. R. (1980). Physical attractiveness, romantic love, and equity restoration in dating relationships. *Journal of Personality Assessment 44*, 624–629.

Crites, J. O. (1969). *Vocational psychology*. New York: McGraw-Hill.

Crites, J. O. (1978). *The career maturity inventory*. Monterey, Calif.: CTB/McGraw-Hill.

Crites, J. O. (1981). *Career counseling*. New York: Wiley.

Croake, J. W. (1969a). Fears of children. *Human Development, 12*, 239–247.

Croake, J. W. (1969b). Dissonance theory and fear retention. *Psychology, 6*, 19–23.

Croake, J. W. (1967). Fears of adolescence. *Journal of Adolescence, 2*, 459–468.

Croake, J. W., & Catlin, N. (1975, Spring). Adlerian theory and fears. *International Journal of Sociology of the Family*.

Croake, J. W., & Glover, K. E. (1977). A history and evaluation of parent education. *Family Coordinator, 26*, 151–158.

Croake, J. W., & Hinkle, D. E. (1976). Methodological problems in the study of fears. *Journal of Psychology, 93*, 197–202.

Croake, J. W., & Kelly, D. F. (1978). Application of Adlerian theory to school phobia. *The Individual Psychologist, 4*, 73–81.

Croake, J. W., & Knox, F. (1971a). A reinvestigation of fear retention and dissonance. *Psychology, 6*, 51–54.

Croake, J. W., & Knox, F. (1971b). A second look at adolescent fears. *Journal of Adolescence, 6*, 223–227.

Croake, J. W., & Knox, F. (1973). The changing nature of children's fears. *Child Study Journal, 3*, 91–105.

Croake, J. W., Protinsky, H. O., & Catlin, N. (1977). *Adolescence: Developmentally*. Bremerton, Wash.: Eco Printing.

Croake, J. W., & Singh, A. (1982). Adult fears. Unpublished manuscript, University of Washington.

Crocetti, G. M., Spiro, H. R., Lemkau, P. V., & Siassi, I. (1972). Multiple models and mental illnesses: A rejoinder to failure of a moral enterprise: Attitudes of the public toward mental illness, by T. R. Sarbin & J. C. Mancuso. *Journal of Consulting and Clinical Psychology, 39*(1), 1–5.

Crocker, E. C. (1945). *Flavor*. New York: McGraw-Hill.

Crocker, J. (1981). Judgment of covariation by social perceivers. *Psychological Bulletin, 90*, 272–292.

Crockett, W. H. (1965). Cognitive complexity and impression formation. In B. A. Maher (Ed.), *Progress in experimental personality research*, Vol. 2. New York: Academic Press.

Crockett, W. H. (1982). The organization of construct systems. In J. C. Mancuso & J. Adams-Webber (Eds.), *The construing person*. New York: Praeger.

Crockett, W. H., & Meisel, P. (1974). Construct connectedness, strength of disconfirmation and impression change. *Journal of Personality, 42*, 290–299.

Cronbach, L. (1955). Processes affecting scores on "understanding of others" and "assumed similarity." *Psychological Bulletin, 52*, 177–193.

Cronbach, L. J. (1946). Response sets and test validity. *Educational and Psychological Measurement, 6*, 475–494.

Cronbach, L. J. (1950). Further evidence on response sets and test design. *Educational and Psychological Measurement, 10*, 3–31.

Cronbach, L. J. (1957). The two disciplines of scientific psychology. *American Psychologist, 12*, 671–684.

Cronbach, L. J. (1971). Test validation. In R. L. Thorndike (Ed.), *Educational measurement* (2nd ed.) Washington, D. C.: American Council on Education.

Cronbach, L. J. (1975). Beyond the two disciplines of scientific psychology. *American Psychologist, 30*, 116–127.

Cronbach, L. J. (1975). Five decades of public controversy over mental testing. *American Psychologist, 30*, 1–14.

Cronbach, L. J. (1973/1954). *Educational psychology*, New York: Harcourt, Brace.

Cronbach, L. J. (1983/1960). *Essentials of psychological testing*. New York: Harper & Row.

Cronbach, L. J., et al. (1980). *Toward reform of program evaluation*. San Francisco: Jossey-Bass.

Cronbach, L. J., & Drenth, P. J. D. (Eds.). (1972). *Mental tests and cultural adaptation*. The Hague: Mouton.

Cronbach, L. J., & Gleser, G. C. (1965/1953). *Psychological tests and personnel decisions* (2nd ed.). Urbana, Ill.: University of Illinois Press.

Cronbach, L. J., Gleser, C. C., Nanda, N., & Rajaratnam, N. (1972). *The dependability of behavioral measurements*. New York: Wiley.

Cronbach, L. J., & Snow, R. E. (1977). *Aptitudes and instructional methods: A handbook for research on interactions*. New York: Irvington.

Cronholm, J. N., & Revusky, S. (1965). A sensitive rank test for comparing the effects of two treatments on a single group. *Psychometrika, 30*, 459–467.

Cronin, C., & Zuckerman, M. (1992). Sensation seeking and bipolar affective disorder. *Journal of Nonverbal Behavior, 8,* 259–286.

Crook, T., Bartus, R. T., Ferris, S. H., Whitehouse, P., Cohen, G. D. & Gershon, S. (1986). Age-associated memory impairment: Proposed diagnostic criteria and measures of clinical change. Report of a National Institute of Mental Health work group. *Developmental Neuropsychology, 2,* 261–276.

Crook, T., & Cohen, G. D. (Eds.). (1981). *Physicians' handbook on psychotherapeutic drug use in the aged.* New Canaan, Conn.: Powley.

Crooks, L. A. (1977). The selection and development of assessment center techniques. In J. L. Moses & W. C. Byham (Eds.), *Applying the assessment center method.* New York: Pergamon Press.

Cropley, A. L., & Weckowicz, T. E. (1966). The dimensionality of clinical depression. *Australian Journal of Psychology, 18,* 18–25.

Crosby, F. J., & Herek, G. M. (1986). Male sympathy with the situation of women: Does personal experience make a difference? *Journal of Social Issues, 42*(2), 55–66.

Crossman, S. M., & Adams, G. R. (1980). Divorce, single parenting, and child development. *The Journal of Psychology, 106,* 205–217.

Crow, J. F., & Kimura, (1970). *M. An introduction to population genetics theory.* New York: Harper & Row.

Crow, W. B. (1973/1968). *A history of magic, witchcraft and occultism.* London: Abacus.

Crowder, R. G. (1976). *Principles of learning and memory.* Hillsdale, N.J.: Erlbaum.

Crowe, R. R., Noyes, R., Pauls, D. L., & Slymen, D. J. (1983). A family study of panic disorder. *Archives of General Psychiatry, 40,* 1065–1069.

Crowne, D. P., & Marlowe, D. (1960). A new scale of social desirability independent of psychopathology. *Journal of Consulting Psychology, 24,* 349–354.

Crozier, R. (1979). Shyness as anxious self-preoccupation. *Psychological Reports, 44,* 959–962.

Cruickshank, W. (Ed.). (1980). *Psychology of exceptional children and youth* (4th ed.). Englewood Cliffs, N.J.: Prentice-Hall.

Cruickshank, W. M. (1979). Learning disabilities: Perceptual or other? *ACLD Newsletter, 125,* 7–10.

Cruickshank, W. M. (1981). A new perspective in teacher education: The oeducator. *Journal of Learning Disabilities, 94,* 337–367.

Cruickshank, W. M., & Hallahan, D. P. (Eds.). (1975). *Perceptual and learning disabilities in children* (2 vols.). Syracuse, N. Y.: Syracuse University Press.

Crumbaugh, J. C. (1968). Cross-validation of the Purpose-in-Life Test based on Frankl's concept. *Journal of Individual Psychology, 24,* 74–81.

Crumbaugh, J. C., & Maholik, L. T. (1964). An experimental study in existentialism: The psychometric approach to Frankl's concept of noogenic neurosis. *Journal of Clinical Psychology, 20,* 200–207.

Crusco, A. H., & Wetzel, C. G. (1984). The midas touch: The effects of interpersonal touch on restaurant tipping. *Personality and Social Psychology Bulletin, 10,* 512–517.

Crutchfield, R. S. (1955). Conformity and character. *American Psychologist, 10,* 191–198.

Cruz Hernández, M. (1981). El doctor José Germain y la psicología en los años cuarenta. *Revista de Psicología General y Aplicada, 36,* 1059–1063.

Csank, J. Z., & Zweig, J. P. (1980). Relative mortality of chronically ill geriatric patients with organic brain syndrome damage, before and after relocation. *Journal of the American Geriatric Society, 28,* 76–83.

Csikszentmihalyi, M. (1975). *Beyond boredom and anxiety.* San Francisco: Jossey-Bass.

Csikszentmihalyi, M. (1990). *Flow: The psychology of optimal experience.* New York: Harper & Row.

Csikszentmihalyi, M., & Csikszentmihalyi, I. S. (1988). *Optimal experience: Psychological studies of flow in consciousness.* Cambridge, UK: Cambridge University Press.

Cui, G., & Van Den Berg, S. (1991). Testing the construct validity of intercultural effectiveness. *International Journal of Intercultural Relations, 15,* 227–241.

Cullen, J. H. (Ed.). (1974). *Experimental behaviour.* Dublin: Halsted Press.

Cummings, N., & VandenBos, G. (1979). The general practice of psychology. *Professional Psychology, 10,* 430–440.

Cummings, N. A. (1977). The anatomy of psychotherapy under national health insurance. *American Psychologist, 32,* 711–718.

Cummings, N. A. (1979). Mental health and national health insurance: A case history of the struggle for professional autonomy. In C. A. Kiesler, N. A. Cummings, & G. R. VandenBos (Eds.), *Psychology and national health insurance: A sourcebook.* Washington, D.C.: American Psychological Association.

Cummings, N. A. (1986). The dismantling of our health system: Strategies for the survival of psychological practice. *American Psychologist, 41,* 426–431.

Cummings, N. A. (1988). Emergence of the mental health complex: Adaptive and maladaptive responses. *Professional Psychology: Research and Practice, 19,* 308–315.

Cummings, N. A. (1988). The emergence of the mental health complex. *Professional Psychology, 19*(3), 323–335.

Cummings, N. A. (1991). Brief intermittent therapy throughout the life cycle. In C. S. Austad & W. H. Berman (Eds.), *Psychotherapy in managed health care: The optimal use of time and resources* (pp. 35–45). Washington, DC: The American Psychological Association.

Cummings, N. A. (1991). The somatizing patient. In C. S. Austad & W. H. Berman (Eds.), *Psychotherapy in managed health care: The optimal use of time and resources* (pp. 234–247). Washington, DC: The American Psychological Association.

Cummings, N. A., Dorken, H., Pallak, M. S., & Henke, C. (1990). *The impact of psychological intervention on health care utilization and costs.* San Francisco: Biodyne Institute.

Cummings, N. A., & Duhl, L. D. (1989). The new delivery system. In L. Duhl & N. A. Cummings (Eds.), *The future of mental health services: Coping with crises* (pp. 85–99). New York: Springer.

Cummings, N. A., & Folette, W. (1968). Psychiatric services and medical utilization in a prepaid health plan setting—Part II. *Medical Care, 6,* 31–41.

Cummings, N. A., & VandenBos, G. R. (1982). Relations with other professions. In C. E. Walker (Ed.), *Handbook of clinical psychology.* New York: Dow-Jones Irwin.

Cunningham, A. J. (1978). *Understanding immunology.* New York: Academic Press.

Cunningham, C. (1974). The trial of the Gainesville Eight: The legal lessons of a political trial. *Criminal Law Bulletin, 10,* 215–227.

Cunningham, M. D., & Murphy, P. J. (1981). The effects of bilateral EEG biofeedback on verbal, visual-spatial and creative skills in learning disabled male adolescents. *Journal of Learning Disabilities, 14,* 204–208.

Cunningham, M. R., Barbee, A. P., & Pike, C. L. (1990). What do women went? Facialmetric assessment of multiple motives in the perception of male facial physical attractiveness. *Journal of Personality and Social Psychology, 59*, 61–72.

Cunningham, W., & Owens, W. (1983). The Iowa State study of the adult development of intellectual abilities. In K. W. Schaie (Ed.), *Longitudinal studies of adult Psychological development* (pp. 20–39). New York: Guilford.

Cunningham, W. R. (1987). Intellectual abilities and age. In K. W. Schaie (Ed.), *Annual review of gerontology and geriatrics* (Vol. 7, pp. 117–134). New York: Springer.

Curfs, L. M. G., Wiegers, A. M., & Fryns, F. P. (1990). Fragile-X syndrome: A review. *Brain dysfunction, 3*, 1–8.

Curiel, J. L. (1962). *El psicologo.* Mexico, D.F.: Libreria Porrua y Hnos.

Curran, J. P. (1975). Convergence toward a single sexual standard? *Social Behavior and Personality, 3*, 189–195.

Curran, J. P. (1975). Social skills training and systematic desensitization in reducing dating anxiety. *Behaviour Research and Therapy, 13*, 65–68.

Curran, J. P. (1979). Social skills: Methodological issues and further directions. In A. S. Bellack & M. Hersen (Eds.), *Research and practice in social skills training.* New York: Plenum.

Curran, J. P.,& Gilbert, F. J. (1975). A test of the relative effectiveness of a systematic desensitization program and an interpersonal skill training program with date anxious subjects. *Behavior Therapy, 6*, 510–521.

Curran, J. P., & Mariotto, M. J. (1980). A conceptual structure for the assessment of social skills. In M. Hersen, R. M. Eisler, & P. M. Miller (Eds.), *Progress in behavior modification,* Vol. 10. New York: Academic Press.

Curran, J. P., Wessberg, H. W., Farrell, A. D., Monti, P. M., Corriveau, D. P, & Coyne, N. A. (1982). Social skills and social anxiety: Are different laboratories measuring the same constructs? *Journal of Consulting and Clinical Psychology, 50*, 396–406.

Curtis, G., Nesse, R., Buxton, M., Wright, J., & Lippman, D. (1976). Flooding in vivo as a research tool and treatment method for phobias: A preliminary report. *Comprehensive Psychiatry, 17*, 153–160.

Cushing, H. (1928). *Consecratio medici and other papers.* Boston: Little, Brown.

Cushner, K. (1989). Assessing the impact of a culture-general assimilator. *International Journal of Intercultural Relations, 13*, 125–146.

Custer, R. L. (1982). On overview of compulsive gambling. In P. A. Carone, S. F. Yolles, S. N. Kieffer, & L. W. Krinsky (Eds.), *Addictive disorders update.* New York: Human Sciences Press.

Cutler, B. L., Fisher, R. P., & Chicvara, C. L. (1989). Eyewitness identification from live versus videotaped lineups. *Forensic Reports, 2*, 93–106.

Cutler, B. L., & Penrod, S. D. (1988). Improving the reliability of eyewitness identification: Lineup construction and presentation. *Journal of Applied Psychology, 73*, 281–290.

Cutler, B. L. & Penrod, S. D. (1989). Forensically relevant moderators of the relation between eyewitness identification accuracy and confidence. *Journal of Applied Psychology, 74*, 650–652.

Cutler, B. L., Penrod, S. D., & Stuve, T. E. (1988). Juror decision making in eyewitness identification cases. *Law and Human Behavior, 12*, 41–55.

Cutrona, C. E. (1990). Stress and social support: In search of optimal matching. *Journal of Social and Clinical Psychology, 9*, 148–158.

Cutrona, C. E., & Russell, D. W. (1990). Type of social support and specific stress: Toward a theory of optimal matching. In I. G. Sarason, B. R. Sarason, & G. R. Pierce (Eds.), *Social support: An interactional view* (pp. 319–366). New York: Wiley.

Cutting, J. E., & Proffitt, D. R. (1981). Gait perception as an example of how we may perceive events. In R. D. Walk & H. L. Pick, Jr. (Eds.), *Intersensory perception and sensory integration.* New York: Plenum.

Cutts, N. E. (Ed.). (1955). *School psychologists at mid-century.* Washington, D.C.: American Psychological Association.

Dacey, J. S. (1989). *Fundamentals of creative thinking.* Lexington, MA: Heath.

Dahlgren. L. O., & Marton, F. (1978). Students' conceptions of subject matter: An aspect of learning and teaching in higher education. *Studies in Higher Education, 3*, 25–35.

Dahlström, A., & Fuxe, K. (1964). Evidence for the existence of monamine-containing neurons in the central nervous system. *Acta Physiologia Scandanavia, 62* (suppl. 232), 1–55.

Dahlstrom, A., & Fuxe, K. (1964). A method for the demonstration of monoamince-containing nerve fibres in the central nervous system. *Acta Physiologica Scandinavia, 60*, 293–294.

Dahlstrom, W. G. (1985). The development of psychological testing. In G. A. Kimble & K. Schlesinger (Eds.), *Topics in the history of psychology* (Vol. 2, pp. 63–113). Hillsdale, NJ: Erlbaum.

Dahlstrom, W. G., Welsh, G. S., & Dahlstrom, L. E. (1972). *An MMPI handbook.* Vol. I: *Clinical interpretation.* Minneapolis, Minn.: University of Minnesota Press.

Dahlstrom, W. G., Welsh, G. S., & Dahlstrom, L. E. (1975). *An MMPI handbook.* Vol. II: *Research developments and applications,* Minneapolis, Minn.: University of Minnesota Press.

Daily, C. A. (1952). The effects of premature conclusion upon the acquisition of understanding of a person. *Journal of Psychology, 33*, 133–152.

Dainoff, M. J., Happ, A., & Crane, P. (1981). Visual fatigue and occupational stress in VDT operators. *Human Factors, 23*, 421–438.

D'Albas, A. (1957). *Death of a navy: Japanese naval action in World War II.* New York: Devin-Adair.

Dale, E., & Chall, J. S. (1948). A formula for predicting readability: Instructions. *Educational Research Bulletin, 27*, 37–54.

Dale, E., & O'Rourke, J. (1976). *The living word vocabulary: The words we know, a national inventory.* Chicago: Field Enterprises.

Dale, J. H., Jr. (1973). *The significance of sibling position and the frequency of participation by adults in group counseling activities.* Tallahassee, Fla.: Florida State University. (ERIC Document Reproduction Service No. ED 078289).

Dale, P. S. (1976/1972). *Language development: Structure and function* (2nd ed.). New York: Holt.

Dallenbach, J. W., & Dallenbach, K. M. (1943). The effects of bitter adaptation on sensitivity to the other taste qualities. *American Journal of Psychology, 56*, 21–31.

Dallenbach, K. M. (1930). Attention. *Psychological Bulletin, 27*, 497–513.

Dallenbach, K. M. (1939). Pain: History and present status. *American Journal of Psychology, 52*, 311–347.

Dallenbach, K. M. (1946). The Emergency Research Committee in Psychology, National Research Council. *American Journal of Psychology, 59*, 496–482.

Dallenbach, K. M. (1967). Karl M. Dallenbach. In E. G. Boring & G. Lindzey (Eds.), *History of psychology in autobiography.* New York: Appleton-Century-Crofts.

Dalton, J. E., Maier, R. A., & Posavac, E. J. (1977). A self-fulfilling prophecy in a competitive psychomotor task. *Journal of Research on Personality, 11,* 487—495.

Daly, M. (1973). *Beyond God the father.* Boston: Beacon Press.

Daly, M. (1979). Why don't male mammals lactate? *Journal of Theoretical Biology, 78,* 325–345.

Daly, M., & Wilson, M. (1978). *Sex, evolution, and behavior.* North Scituate, Mass.: Duxbury.

D'Amato, M. R. (1970). *Experimental psychology: Methodology, psychophysics, and learning.* New York: McGraw-Hill.

Dambauer, J. (Ed.). (1973,1979). *Bibliographie der deutschsprachigen psychologischen Literatur,* Vol. 2: 1972; Vol. 9: 1979. Frankfurt am Main: V Klostermann.

Damiani, J. T., Flowers, F. P., & Pierce, D. K. (1990). *Journal of the American Academy of Dermatology, 22*(2), 312–313.

Damon, A. (1973). Smoking attitudes and practices in seven preliterate societies. In W. L. Dunn (Ed.), *Smoking behavior: Motives and incentives.* Washington, D.C.: Winston.

Damon, W. (1981). Patterns of change in children's reasoning: A two-year longitudinal study. *Child Development, 51,* 1010–1017.

Damrad-Frye, R., & Laird, J. D. (1989). The experience of boredom: The role of self-perception of attention. *Journal of Personality and Social Psychology, 57,* 315–320.

Dan, A. J. (1979). The menstrual cycle and sex-related differences in cognitive variability. In M. A. Wittig & A. C. Petersen (Eds.), *Sex-related differences in cognitive functioning: Developmental issues.* New York: Academic Press.

Dana, R. H., & Graham, E. D. (1976). Feedback of client-related information in clinical practice. *Journal of Personality Assessment, 40,* 464–469.

D'Andrade, R. G. (1966). Sex differences in cultural institutions. In E. E. Maccoby (Ed.), *The development of sex differences.* Stanford, Calif.: Stanford University Press.

Daneman, M., & Carpenter, P. (1980). Individual differences in working memory and reading. *Journal of Verbal Learning and Verbal Behavior, 19,* 450–466.

Daniels, H. W., & Otis, J. L. (1950). A method for analyzing employment interviews. *Personnel Psychology, 3,* 425–444.

Daniels, J. C. (1961). Effects of streaming in the primary school. II: A comparison of streamed and unstreamed schools. *British Journal of Educational Psychology, 31,* 119–127.

Daniels, L. M. (1976). *Business information sources.* Berkeley, Calif.: University of California Press.

Daniels, P. (1981). Dream vs. drift in women's careers. In B. Forisha & B. H. Goldman (Eds.), *Outsiders on the inside.* Englewood Cliffs, N.J.: Prentice-Hall.

Danish, S. J., & Hauer, A. L. (1973). *Helping skills: A basic training program,* (Vols. 1, 2). New York: Human Sciences Press.

Danzig, F. (1962, September 17). Subliminal advertising—Today it's just historic flashback for researcher Vicary. *Advertising Age.*

Danziger, K. (1980). On the threshold of the new psychology: Situating Wundt and James. In W. Bringmann & R. Tweney (Eds.), *Wundt Studies/ Wundt Studien.* Göttingen, West Germany: Hogrefe.

Darley, J. G. (1964). The substantive bases of counseling psychology. In A. S. Thompson & D. E. Super (Eds.), *The professional preparation of counseling psychologists, Report of the 1964 Greyston Conference.* New York: Bureau of Publications, Teachers College, Columbia University.

Darley, J. G., & Hagenah, T. (1955). *Vocational interest measurement.* Minneapolis, Minn.: University of Minnesota Press.

Darley, J. G., Paterson, D. G., & Peterson, I. E. (1933). *Occupational testing and the public employment service.* Bulletin of the Employment Stabilization Research Institute, Additional Publication no. 19. Minneapolis, Minn.: University of Minnesota Press.

Darley, J. M., & Latane, B. (1970). *The unresponsive bystander: Why doesn't he help?* New York: Appleton-Century-Crofts.

Darlington, C. D. (1954). Heredity and environment. Proceedings of the IX International Congress of Genetics. *Caryologia,* 370–381.

Darlington, R. B. (1990). *Regression and linear models.* New York: McGrawHill.

Darwin, C. (1859). *On the origin of species.* London: John Murray.

Darwin, C. (1859, 1860). *On the origin of species by means of natural selection.* London: Murray, New York: Appleton.

Darwin, C. (1868). *The variation of plants and animals under domestication* (2 vols.). London: Murray.

Darwin, C. (1871). *The descent of man and selection in relation to sex.* London: Murray.

Darwin, C. (1952). *The origin of species by means of natural selection and The descent of man and selection in relation to sex* (Great Books of the Western World: 49, Darwin). Chicago: Encyclopedia Britannica. (Original work published 1859 and 1871)

Darwin, C. (1965). *The expression of the emotions in man and animals.* Chicago: University of Chicago Press. (Original work published 1872)

Darwin, C. (1965/1872). *The expression of the emotions in man and animals.* Chicago: University of Chicago Press.

Darwin, C. A. (1877). A biographical sketch of an infant. *Merid, 2,* 285–294.

Das, N. N., & Gastant, H. (1957). Variations de l'activite electrique du cerveau, du coeur et des muscles squilettiques au cours de la meditation et de l'extas yogigue. In *Conditionnement et reactivite en electroencephalographie.* Paris: Masson.

Das, S. (1969). Some psychological problems of quadriplegics. *Medical Journal of Australia, 2,* 562–564.

Dasen, P., & Heron, A. (1981). Cross-cultural tests of Piaget's theory. In H. Triandis & A. Heron (Eds.), *Handbook of cross-cultural psychology,* Vol. 4. Boston: Allyn & Bacon.

Dasen, P., Inhelder, B., Lavallée, M., & Retschitzki, J. J. (1978). *Naissance de l'intelligence chez l'enfant Baoulé de Côte d'Ivoire.* Bern: Huber.

Dasen, P., Lavallée, M., & Retschitzki, J. (1979). Training conservation of quantity (liquids) in West African (Baoule) children. *International Journal of Psychology, 14,* 57–68.

Dashiell, J. F. (1928). *Fundamentals of objective psychology,* Boston: Houghton Mifflin.

Dashiell, J. F. (1930). Direction orientation in maze running by the white rat. *Comparative Psychological Monographs, 7*(32), 72.

Dashiell, J. F. (1949). *Fundamentals of general psychology,* Boston: Houghton Mifflin.

Datan, N., & Ginsberg, L. H. (Eds.). (1975). *Life-span developmental psychology: Normative life crises.* New York: Academic Press.

Datan, N., & Reese, H. W. (1977). *Life-span developmental psychology: Dialectical perspectives on experimental research.* New York: Academic Press.

D'Augelli, A. R., Vallance, T. R., Danish, S. J., Young, C. E. & Gerdes, J. L. (1981). The community helpers project: A description of a prevention strategy for rural communities. *American Journal of Community Psychology, 1,* 209–224.

Davey, G. (Ed.). (1983). *Applications of conditioning theory.* London: Methuen.

David, H. P. (1964). *International resources in clinical psychology.* New York: McGraw-Hill.

Davids, A. (1956). Comparison of three methods of personality assessment: Direct, indirect and projective. *Journal of Personality, 24,* 328–338.

Davids, A. (Ed.). (1973). *Issues in abnormal child psychology.* Monterey, Calif.: Brooks/Cole.

Davidson, A., Jaccard, J., Triandis, H. C., Morales, M., & Diaz-Guerrero, R. (1976). Cross-cultural model testing: Toward a solution of the emic-etic dilemma. *International Journal of Psychology, 11,* 1–13.

Davidson, G. W. (1978). *The hospice: Development and administration.* New York: Hemisphere.

Davidson, J. (1964). Cognitive familiarity and dissonance reduction. In L. Festinger (Ed.), *Conflict, decision, and dissonance.* Stanford, Calif.: Stanford University Press.

Davidson, J. R. T., & Foa, E. B. (Eds.). (1993). *Posttraumatic stress disorder: DSM-IV and beyond.* Washington, DC: American Psychiatric Press.

Davidson, M., McInnes, R., & Parnel, R. (1957). The distribution of personality traits in seven year old children. *British Journal of Educational Psychology, 27,* 48–61.

Davidson, M. A. (1977). The scientific/applied debate in psychology: A contribution. *Bulletin of the British Psychological Society, 30,* 273–278.

Davidson, R., & Schwartz, G. E. (1976). The psychobiology of relaxation and related states: A multi-process theory. In D. I. Mostofsky (Ed.), *Behavior control and modification of physiological activity.* Englewood Cliffs, N.J.: Prentice-Hall.

Davidson, T. (1978). *Conjugal crime: Understanding and changing the wifebeating problem.* New York: Hawthorn.

Davies, D. L. (1976). Definitional issues in alcoholism. In R. E. Tarter & A. A. Sugarman (Eds.), *Alcoholism: Interdisciplinary approaches to an enduring problem.* Reading, Mass.: Addison-Wesley.

Davies, G., & Drinkwater, J. (Eds.). (1988). *The child witness: Do the courts abuse children?* (Issues in Criminological and Legal Psychology No. 13). Leicester, UK: The British Psychological Association.

Davies, J. B. (1978). *The psychology of music.* Stanford, Calif.: Stanford University Press.

Davies, J. D. (1955). *Phrenology—Fad and science.* New Haven, Conn.: Yale University Press.

Davies, J. L. (1988). Alleviating political violence through enhancing coherence in collective consciousness: Impact assessment analyses of the Lebanon war. *Dissertation Abstracts International, 49*(8), 23 8 1 A.

Davies, J. L., & Alexander, C. N. (1989). Alleviating political violence through enhancing coherence in collective consciousness: Impact assessment analyses of the Lebanon War. In *Proceedings of the American Political Science Association.* Atlanta.

Davies, K. E. (Ed.). (1990). *The fragile-X syndrome.* Oxford, UK: Oxford University Press.

Davies, M. (1992). The role of the amygdala in conditioned fear. In J. Aggleton (Ed.), *The amygdala.* New York: Wiley.

Davies, M. F. (1987). Reduction of hindsight bias by restoration of foresight perspective: Effectiveness of foresight-encoding and hind-

sight-retrieval strategies. *Organizational Behavior and Human Decision Processes, 40,* 50–68.

Davies, N. B., & Houston, A. I. (1984). Territory economics. In J. R. Krebs & N. B. Davies (Eds.), *Behavioural ecology: An evolutionary approach* (pp. 148–169). Sunderland, MA: Sinauer.

Davis, B. D. (1975). Social determinism and behavioral genetics. *Science, 189,* 1049.

Davis, C. M. (1928). Self-selection of diet by newly weaned children. *American Journal of Diseases of Children, 36,* 651–679.

Davis, E. C. (1967). *The quality of work life.* Dubuque, Iowa: Brown.

Davis, G. E., & Leitenberg, H. (1987). Adolescent sex offenders. *Psychological Bulletin, 101,* 417–427.

Davis, G. S. (1990). A managed health care primer. In D. A. Hastings, W. L. Krasner, J. L. Michael, & N. D. Rosenlier (Eds.), *The insiders guide to managed care* (pp. 13–35). Washington, DC: The National Lawyers Association.

Davis, H., & Hurwitz, H. M. B. (Eds.). (1977). *Operant-Pavlovian interactions.* Hillsdale, N. J.: Erlbaum.

Davis, H., & Silverman, S. R. (Eds.). (1960). *Hearing and deafness* (rev. ed.). New York: Holt, Rinehart & Winston.

Davis, J. (1969). Individual-group problem solving, subject preference, and problem type. *Journal of Personality and Social Psychology, 13,* 362–374.

Davis, J. (1978). Reliability and validity issues of Adlerian life style analysis. Unpublished dissertation, Georgia State University.

Davis, J., & Restle, R. (1963). The analysis of problems and a prediction of group problem solving. *Journal of Abnormal and Social Psychology, 66,* 103–116.

Davis, J. M. (1958). A reinterpretation of the Barker, Dembo, and Lewin study of frustration and regression. *Child Development, 29,* 503–506.

Davis, J. M. (1975). Overview: Maintenance therapy in schizophrenia. 1. Schizophrenia. *American Journal of Psychiatry, 132,* 1237–1245.

Davis, J. M. (1980). Antipsychotic drugs. In H. I. Kaplan, A. M. Freedman, & B. J. Sadock, (Eds.), *Comprehensive textbook of psychiatry III.* Baltimore, Md.: Williams & Wilkins.

Davis, K. (1977). Sexual behavior. In R. K. Merton & R. Nisbet, (Eds.), *Contemporary social problems.* New York: Harcourt Brace Jovanovich.

Davis, K., Anderson, G. F., Rowland, D., & Steinberg, E. P. (1990). *Health care cost containment.* Baltimore: Johns Hopkins.

Davis, K., Frederick, W. C., & Blomstrom, R. L. (1980). *Business and society: Concepts and policy issues.* New York: McGraw-Hill.

Davis, K., & Moore, W. E. (1945). Some principles of stratification. *American Sociological Review, 10,* 242–249.

Davis, K. E., & Jones, E. E. (1960). Changes in interpersonal perception as a means of reducing cognitive dissonance. *Journal of Abnormal and Social Psychology, 60,* 402–410.

Davis, L. E., & Cherns, A. B. (Eds.). (1975). *The quality of working life.* New York: Free Press.

Davis, L. E., & Taylor, J. C. (1972). *The design of jobs.* London: Penguin Books.

Davis, M. (1970). Movement characteristics of hospitalized psychiatric patients. *Proceedings of the Fifth Annual Conference of the American Dance Therapy Association,* 25–45.

Davis, M. (1975). *Anthropological perspectives of movement.* New York: Arno Press.

Davis, M. (1975). *Towards understanding the intrinsic in body movement.* New York: Arno Press.

Davis, P., & Hersh, R. (1981). *The mathematical experience*. Boston: Birkhauser.

Davis, R. (1961). The fitness of names to drawings. A cross cultural study in Tanganika. *British Journal of Psychology, 52*, 259–268.

Davis, R., & Lenat, D. (1980). *Knowledge-based systems in artificial intelligence*. New York: McGraw-Hill.

Davis, R. C., Buchwald, A. M., & Frankmann, R. W. (1955). Autonomic and muscular responses, and their relation to simple stimuli. *Psychological Monographs, 69*, 1–71.

Davis, S. A., & Dawson, J. G. (1980). Hypnotherapy for weight control. *Psychological Reports, 46*, 311–314.

Davis, S. A., Dawson, J. G., & Seay, B. (1978). Prediction of hypnotic susceptibility from imaginative involvement. *American Journal of Clinical Hypnosis, 20*(3), 194–198.

Davis-Eells test of general intelligence. (1953). New York: Harcourt Brace Jovanovich.

Davison, G. C. (1968). Systematic desensitization as a counter conditioning process. *Journal of Abnormal Psychology, 73*, 91–99.

Davison, G. C., & Neale, J. M. (1978). *Abnormal psychology*. New York: Wiley.

Davison, K., Brierly, H., & Smith, C. (1971). A male monozygotic twinship discordant for homosexuality. *British Journal of Psychiatry, 118*, 675–682.

Davison, M. L., Robbins, S., & Swanson, D. B. (1978). Stage structure in objective moral judgments. *Developmental Psychology, 14*, 137–146.

Davitz, J. R. (1964). *The communication of emotional meaning*. New York: McGraw-Hill.

Dawes, R. M. (1972). *Fundamentals of attitude measurement*. New York: Wiley.

Dawes, R. M. (1979). The robust beauty of improper linear models in decision making. *American Psychologist, 34*, 571–582.

Dawes, R. M. (1980). Social dilemmas. *Annual Review of Psychology, 30*, 169–193.

Dawes, R. M., Faust, D., & Meehl, P. E. (1989). Clinical versus actuarial judgment. *Science, 243*, 1668–1674.

Dawkins, R. (1976). *The selfish gene*. New York: Oxford University Press.

Dawkins, R. (1986). *The blind watchmaker*. New York: Norton.

Dawkins, R., & Krebs, J. R. (1978). Animal signals: Information or manipulation? In J. R. Krebs & N. B. Davies (Eds.), *Behavioral ecology: An evolutionary approach*. Sunderland, Mass.: Sinauer.

Dawson, J. G., Dellis, N. P., & Stone, H. K. (Eds.). (1961). *Psychotherapy with schizophrenics*. Baton Rouge, La.: Louisiana State University Press.

Dawson, J. L. M. (1967). Traditional versus western attitudes in West Africa: the construction, validation and application of a measuring device. *British Journal of Social and Clinical Psychology, 6*, 81–96.

Dawson, J. L. M. (1975). Socio-economic differences in size-judgments of discs and coins by Chinese primary VI children in Hong Kong. *Perceptual and Motor Skills, 41*, 107–110.

Dawson, N. V., Arkes, H. R., Siciliano, C., Blinkhorn, R., Lakshmanan, M., & Petrelli, M. (1988). Hindsight bias: An impediment to accurate probability estimation in clinicopathologic conferences. *Medical Decision Making, 8*, 259–264.

Day, D. (1979). *The adoption of black children*, Lexington, Mass.: Lexington.

Day, H. I. (1971). The measurement of specific curiosity. In H. I. Day, D. E. Berlyne, & D. E. Hunt (Eds.), *Intrinsic motivation: A new direction in education*. Toronto: Holt, Rinehart & Winston.

Day, H. I. (1979). Why people play. *Loisir et Société, 2*(1), 129–147.

Day, H. I. (1981). *Advances in intrinsic motivation and aesthetics*. New York: Plenum.

Day, H. I. (1981). Play: A ludic behavior. In H. I. Day (Ed.), *Advances in intrinsic motivation and aesthetics*. New York: Plenum.

Day, J. L. (1974). *Platonic essences utilized as models for Maslow's peak experiences*. Unpublished doctoral dissertation, U.S. International University.

Day, M., & Manschreck, T. C. (1988). Delusionial (paranoid) disorders. In A. M. Nicholi, Jr. (Ed.), *The new Harvard guide to psychiatry* (pp. 296–308). Cambridge, MA: Belknap.

Day, M. C. (1977/1972). A comparative analysis of center-based preschool programs. In M. C. Day & R. K. Parker (Eds.), *The preschool in action—Exploring early childhood programs*. Boston: Allyn & Bacon.

Day, M. C., & Parker, R. K. (Eds.). (1977). *The preschool in action—Exploring early childhood programs* (2nd ed.). Boston: Allyn & Bacon.

Day, M. E. (1964). An eye movement phenomenon relating to attention, thought and anxiety. *Perceptual and Motor Skills, 19*, 443–446.

Day, R. H. (1969). *Human perception*. Sydney, Australia: Wiley.

Day, R. H., & Stanley, G. V. (1977). *Studies in perception*. Perth, Australia: University of Western Australia Press.

Dean, R. S., Schwartz, N. H., & Smith, L. S. (1981). Lateral preference patterns as a determinator of learning difficulties. *Journal of Consulting and Clinical Psychology, 49*, 227–235.

Dean, S. R. (1971). Self-help group psychotherapy: Mental patients rediscover will power. *International Journal of Social Psychiatry, 17*, 72–78.

Dean, S., & Beersma D. (1984). Circadian gating of human sleep-wake cycles. In M. Moore-Ede & C. Czeisler (Eds.), *Mathematical models of circadian sleep-wake cycle* (pp. 129–158). New York: Raven.

Dean, S., Beersma D., & Borbely, A. A. (1984). Timing of human sleep: Recovery process gated by a circadian pacemaker. *American Journal of Physiology, 246*, R161–178.

Deans' projects—Proceedings of 1975 conference—mainstreaming: Origins and implications. *Minnesota Education, 1976, 2*(2).

Dearborn, G., & Van N. (1918–1919). The psychology of clothing. *Psychological Review Monographs, 26*, 1–72.

Dearborn, W. F., & Rothney, J. W. (1963). *Predicting the child's development*. Cambridge, MA: Sci-Art.

Deaton, A., & Muellbauer, J. (1980). *Economics and consumer behavior*. New York: Cambridge University Press.

Deaux, K. (1976). *The behavior of women and men*. Monterey, Calif.: Brooks/Cole.

Deaux, K., & Major, B. (1977). Sex-related patterns in the unit of perception. *Personality and Social Psychology Bulletin, 3*, 297–300.

de Boer, T. (1975). The descriptive method of Franz Brentano: Its two functions and their significance for phenomenology. In L. McAlister (Ed.), *The philosophy of Brentano*. Atlantic Highlands, N.J.: Princeton University Press.

de Boer, T. (1978/1966). *The development of Husserl's thought*. The Hague: Nijhoff.

DeBord, J. B. (1989). Paradoxical interventions: A review of the recent literature. *Journal of Counseling and Development, 61*, 394–398.

Debus, A. G. (1966). *The English Paracelsians*. New York: Watts.

Decarie, T. (1965). *Intelligence and affectivity in early childhood*. New York: International Universities Press.

Decarie, T. (1971/1953). *Le développement psychologique de l'enfant*. Montreal: Fides.

Decarie, T. (1971/1955). *De l'adolescence á la maturité*. Montreal: Fides.

DeCasper, A. J., & Spence, M. J. (1986). Prenatal maternal speech influences newborns' perception of speech sounds. *Infant Behavior and Development, 9*, 133–150.

DeCecco, J. P. (1987). Homosexuality's brief recovery: Pertaining sex research. *The Journal of Sex Research, 23*(1), 106–129.

de Charms, R. (1968). *Personal causation: The internal affective determinants of behavior*. New York: Academic Press.

de Charms, R. (1976). *Enhancing motivation: Change in the classroom*. New York: Irvington.

de Charms, R. (1979). Personal causation and perceived control. In L. Perlmuter & R. Monty (Eds.), *Choice and perceived control*. Hillsdale, N. J.: Erlbaum.

de Charms, R., & Muir, M. S. (1978). Motivation: Social approaches. *Annual Review of Psychology, 29*, 91–113.

DeChenne, T. K. (1988). Boredom as a clinical issue. *Psychotherapy, 25*, 71–81.

Deci, E. L. (1971). Effects of externally mediated rewards on intrinsic motivation. *Journal of Personality and Social Psychology, 18*, 105–115.

Deci, E. L. (1975). Intrinsic motivation. New York: Plenum.

Deci, E. L. (1980). *The psychology of self-determination*. Lexington, Mass.: Heath.

Deci, E. L., & Ryan, R. M. (1980). The empirical exploration of intrinsic motivational processes. In L. Berkowitz (Ed.), *Advances in experimental social psychology*, Vol. 13. New York: Academic Press.

Deci, E. L., & Ryan, R. M. (1984). *Intrinsic motivation and human behavior*. New York: Plenum.

Deeg, M. E., & Paterson, G. G. (1947). Change in the social status of occupations. *Occupation, 25*, 205–208.

Deese, J. (1959). Influence of interitem associative strength upon immediate free recall. *Psychology Reports, 5*, 305–312.

Defee, J. F., Jr., & Himelstein, P. (1969). Children's fear in a dental situation as a function of birth order. *Journal of Genetic Psychology, 115*, 253–255.

Deffenbacher, K. A. (1980). Eyewitness accuracy and confidence: Can we infer anything about their relationship. *Law and Human Behavior, 4*, 243–260.

Deffenbacher, K. A. (1983). The influence of arousal on reliability of testimony. In S. M. A. Lloyd-Bostock & B. R. Clifford (Eds.), *Evaluating witness evidence* (pp. 235–251). Chichester, UK: Wiley.

Deffenbacher, K. A., & Loftus, E. F. (1982). Do jurors share a common understanding concerning eyewitness behavior? *Law and Human Behavior, 6*, 15–30.

De Fries, J. C., Corley, R. P., Johnson, R. C., Vandenberg, S. G., & Wilson, J. R. (1982). Sex-by-generation and ethnic group-by-generation interactions in the Hawaii Family Study of Cognition. *Behavior Genetics, 12*, 223–230.

De Fries, J. C., Vandenberg, S. C., & McClearn, G. E. (1976). Genetics of specific cognitive abilities. *Annual Review of Genetics, 10*, 179–207.

Degler, C. N. (1991). *In search of human nature: The decline and revival of Darwinism in American social thought*. New York: Oxford University Press.

De Greene, K. B. (1970). *Systems psychology*. New York: McGraw-Hill.

De Groot, A. D. (1966/1949). *Saint Nicholas. A psychoanalytic study of his history and myth*. Amsterdam, Berlin, New York: Mouton.

De Groot, A. D. (1969/1966). *Fünfen und Sechsen. Zensurengebung: System oder Zufall?* Weinheim, Berlin: Verlag Julius Beltz.

De Groot, A. D. (1969/1961). *Methodology. Foundations of inference and research in the behavioral sciences*. Amsterdam, Berlin, New York: Mouton.

De Groot, A. D. (1971). *Standpunt. Over onderwijs, democratie en wetenschap*. Amsterdam, Berlin, New York: Mouton.

De Groot, A. D. (1972). *Selectie voor en door het hoger onderwijs. COWO rapport 3*. The Hague: Staatsuitgeverij.

De Groot, A. D. (1978/1946). *Thought and choice in chess*. Amsterdam, Berlin, New York: Mouton.

De Groot, A. D. (1981). Intelligence theory after Selz. In N. H. Frijda, & A. D. De Groot (Eds.), *Otto Selz. His contribution to psychology*. Amsterdam, Berlin, New York: Mouton.

De Groot, A. D. (1982). *Academie en Forum. Over hoger onderwijs en wetenschap*. Amsterdam, Meppel: Boom.

De Groot, A. D., & Traas, J. C. (1980). *Onderwijs van binnen en van buiten*. Deventer, Netherlands: Van Loghum Slaterus.

Deikman, A. J. (1977). Comments on the GAP report on mysticism. *Journal of Nervous and Mental Disease, 165*(5), 217.

Deissler, K. (1985). Beyond paradox and counterparadox. In G. Weeks (Ed.), *Promoting change through paradoxical therapy* (pp. 60–99). Homewood, IL: Dow Jones-Irwin.

Dejerine, J. (1891). Sur un cas de cecite verbal avec graphie suivi d'autopsie. *Memories de la Societé de Biologie, 3*, 197–201.

De Kraai, M. B., & Sales, B. D. (1981). *Privileged communication of psychologists*. Lincoln, Neb.: De Kraai & Sales.

Delacato, K. H. (1970). *A new start for the old with reading problems*. New York: Van Reese Press.

De Lacey, P. (1970). A cross-cultural study of classificatory ability in Australia. *Journal of Cross-Cultural Psychology, 1*, 293–304.

Delahunt, J., & Curran, J. P. (1976). Effectiveness of negative practice and self-control techniques in the reduction of smoking behavior. *Journal of Consulting and Clinical Psychology, 44*, 1002–1007.

DeLeon, P. (1988). Public policy and public service. *American Psychologist, 43*, 309–315.

DeLeon, P. (1990). The medication debate: Hawaii's legislature acts. *Register Report*, 9–11.

DeLeon, P. (1992a). National health insurance—Alive and doing well. *Register Report, 18*, 4–6.

DeLeon, P. (1992b). Prescription privileges: Our educational systems become involved. *The Independent Practitioner, 12*, 27–29.

DeLeon, P., Folen, R., Jennings, F., Willis, D., & Wright, R. (1991). The case for prescription privileges: A logical evolution of professional practice. *Journal of Clinical Child Psychology, 3*, 254–267.

DeLeon, P., Fox, R., & Graham, S. (1991). Prescription privileges: Psychology's next frontier? *American Psychologist, 46*, 384–393.

DeLeon, P., Fox, R., & Graham, S. (1993). Prescription privileges: Psychology's next frontier? In J. A. Mindell (Ed.), *Issues in clinical psychology* (pp. 63–73). Dubuque: Brown. (Original work published 1991)

DeLeon, P. H. (1986). Increasing the societal contribution of organized psychology. *American Psychologist, 43*, 466–474.

DeLeon, P. H. (1989). New Roles for "old" psychologists. *The Clinical Psychologist, 42*(1), 8–11.

DeLeon, P. H., Frohboese, R., & Meyers, J. C. (1984). Psychologist on Capitol Hill: A unique use of the skills of the scientist/practitioner. *Professional Psychology: Research and Practise, 15,* 697–705.

DeLeon, P. H., VandenBos, G. R., & Kraut, A. G. (1984). Federal legislation recognizing psychology. *American Pscyhologist, 39,* 933–946.

De Levita, D. J. (1965). *The concept of identity.* The Hague: Mouton.

Delgado, J. M. R., Roberts, W. W., & Miller, N. E. (1954). Learning motivated by electrical stimulation of the brain. *American Journal of Physiology, 179,* 587–593.

de Lint, J., Blane, H. T., & Berry, H., III. (1974). Birth order and alcoholism. *Quarterly Journal of Studies on Alcohol 35,* 292–295.

Dell, P. F. (1981). Some irreverent thoughts on paradox. *Family Process, 20,* 37–41.

Dellis, N. P., & Stone, H. K. (1960). *The training of psychotherapists.* Baton Rouge, La.: Louisiana State University Press.

De Long, A. R. (1972). What have we learned from psychoactive drug research on hyperactives? *American Journal of Diseases of Children, 123,* 177–180.

Delprato, D. J., & Denny, M. R. (1970). Passive avoidance as a function of the duration of nonshock confinement. *Learning and Motivation, 1,* 44–45.

Deltito, J. A., & Perugi, G. (1986). A case of social phobia with avoidant personality disorder treated with MAOI. *Comprehensive Psychiatry, 27,* 255–258.

Delworth, U. (1974). Paraprofessionals as guerillas. Recommendations for system change. *Personnel and Guidance Journal, 53,* 335–338.

Delworth, U., & Brown, W. F. (1977). The paraprofessional as a member of the college guidance team. *Paraprofessionals today. Vol. I: Education.* New York: Human Sciences Press.

De Mause, L. (1974). The evolution of children. In L. de Mause (Ed.), *The history of childhood.* New York: Psychohistory Press.

De Mause, L. (Ed.). (1974). *The history of childhood.* New York: Psychohistory Press.

Dembroski, T. M., MacDougall, J. M., Herd, J. A., & Shields, J. L. (1979). Effects of challenge on pressor and heart responses in Type A and B subjects. *Journal of Applied Social Psychology, 9,* 209–228.

Dembroski, T. M., MacDougall, J. M., & Lushene, R. (1979). Interpersonal interaction and cardiovascular response in Type A subjects and coronary patients. *Journal of Human Stress, 5,* 28–36.

Dembroski, T. M., Weiss, S. M., Shields, J. L., Haynes, S. G., & Feinleib, M. (Eds.). (1978). Coronary-prone behavior. New York: Springer-Verlag.

Dement, W. C., & Kleitman, N. (1957). Cyclical variations in EEG during sleep and their relation to eye movements, bodily motility and dreaming. *Electroencephalography and Clinical Neurophysiology, 9,* 673–690.

Dement, W. C., & Kleitman, N. (1957). The relation of eye movements during sleep to dream activity; An objective method for the study of dreaming. *Journal of Experimental Psychology, 53,* 339.

D'Emilio, J. (1983). *Sexual politics, sexual communities: The making of a homosexual minority in the United States, 1940–1970.* Chicago: University of Chicago Press.

Deming, W. E. (1966). *Some theory of sampling.* New York: Dover.

De Morsier, G. (1969). Studies of hallucinations. *Journal de Psychologie Normale et Pathologigue, 66,* 421–452.

Dempsey, J., & Tomlinson, B. (1980). Learning centers and instructional curricular reform. In *New directions for college learning assistance.* San Francisco: Jossey-Bass.

Dence, M. (1980). Toward defining the role of CAI: A review. *Educational Technology, 20,* 50–54.

Denckla, M. B. (1972). Clinical syndromes in learning disabilities: The case for "splitting" vs. "lumping." *Journal of Learning Disabilities, 5,* 401–406.

Denckla, M. B. (1977/1964). The neurological basis of reading disability. In F. G. Roswell & G. Natchez (Eds.), *Reading disability: A human approach to learning* (3rd ed.) New York: Basic Books.

DeNelsky, G. (1991). Prescription privileges for psychologists: The case against. *Professional Psychology: Research and Practice, 22,* 188–193.

Dengrove, E. (Ed.). (1976). *Hypnosis and behavior therapy.* Springfield, Ill.: Thomas.

Denham, C., & Lieherman, A. (Eds.). (1980). *Time to learn: A review of the Beginning Teacher Evaluation Study.* Washington, D. C.: National Institute of Education.

Denham, S. A., & Almeida, M. C. (1987). Children's social problem-solving skills, behavioral adjustment, and interventions: A meta-analysis evaluating theory and practice. *Journal of Applied Developmental Psychology, 8,* 391–409.

Denis, M. (1980). Intuitive learning among adults. Unpublished Ph. D. dissertation, University of Toronto. *Dissertation Abstracts International, 40,* 4846.

Denmark, F. L. (Ed.). (1974). *Who discriminates against women: Sage contemporary social science issues.* Beverly Hills, Calif.: Sage Publications.

Denmark, F. L. (Ed.). (1976). *Woman: Volume I (A professional research annual).* New York: Psychological Dimensions.

Denmark, F. L. (Ed.). (1980). Psychology: The leading edge. *Annals of the New York Academy of Sciences.*

Denmark, F., & Unger, R. (Eds.). (1975). *Women: Dependent or independent variable?* New York: Psychological Dimensions.

Dennett, D. C. (1978). *Brainstorms.* Montgomery, Vt.: Bradford Books.

Denney, N. W. (1979). Problem solving in later adulthood: Intervention research. In P. B. Baltes & O. G. Brim, Jr. (Eds.), *Life-span development and behavior* (Vol. 2, pp. 38–67). New York: Academic Press.

Dennis, W. (1940). The effect of cradling practice upon the onset of walking in Hopi children. *Journal of Genetic Psychology, 56,* 77–86.

Dennis, W. (1960). Causes of retardation among institutional children: Iran. *Journal of Genetic Psychology, 96,* 47–59.

Dennis, W. (1966). Creative productivity between ages of 20 to 80 years. *Journal of Gerontology, 21,* 1–8.

Dennis, W. (1973). *Children of the Creche.* New York: Appleton-Century-Crofts.

Dennis, W. (Ed.) (1948). *Readings in the history of psychology.* New York: Appleton-Century-Crofts.

Dennis, W., & Boring, E. G. (1952). The founding of the APA. *American Psychologist, 7,* 95–97.

Denny, M. R. (1958). The "Kamin effect" in avoidance conditioning [Abstract]. *American Psychologist, 13,* 419.

Denny, M. R. (1980). *Comparative psychology: An evolutionary analysis of animal behavior.* New York: Wiley.

Denny, M. R. (1991). Relaxation/relief: The effect of removing, postponing or terminating aversive stimuli. In M. R. Denny (Ed.), *Fear, avoidance and phobias: A fundamental analysis* (pp. 199–229). Hillsdale, NJ: Erlbaum.

Denny, M. S. (1977). *Human spatial learning: The effect of movement patterns on kinesthetic and visual representations of a kinestheti-*

cally experienced spatial layout. Unpublished doctoral dissertation, Michigan State University.

Denzin, N. K. (1970). *The research act*. Chicago: Aldine.

Denzin, N. K. (1974). The methodological implications of symbolic interactionism for the study of deviance. *The British Journal of Sociology, 25*, 269–282.

Denzin, N. K. (1977). *Childhood socialization*. San Francisco: Jossey-Bass.

Denzin, N. K. (1978). *The research act*. New York: McGraw-Hill.

Denzin, N. K. (1983). Triangulation. In T. Husen & T. N. Postlethwaite (Eds.), *International encyclopedia of education: Research and studies*. Oxford: Pergamon Press.

Department of the Air Force. (1974). *Handbook for designers of instructional systems* (AFP 50–58, Vols. I-V). Washington, D.C.: Headquarters, U.S. Air Force.

Department of the Army. (1975). *Interservice procedures for instructional systems development* (TRADOC Pam 350–30, Executive Summary and Phases I-V). Fort Monroe, Va.: Training & Doctrination Command.

Department of Health, Education, and Welfare. (1977). Protection of human subjects. Use of psychosurgery in practice and research: Report and recommendations for public comment. *Federal Register*, May 23, no. 99, 26318–26332.

Department of Health and Social Security. (1975). Cmnd 6233. London: Her Majesty's Printing Office.

Department of the Navy. (1978). *Instructional systems development* (A-110, Vols. I-II). Memphis, Tenn.: Commander, Education & Training (CNTT).

Department of Justice. (1978).*Criminal victimization in the United States*, Washington, DC: U.S. Government Printing Office.

DePauw, K. W. (1990). Three thousand days of pregnancy. A case of monosymptomatic delusional pseudocyesis responding to pimozide. *British Journal of Psychiatry, 157*, 924–928.

Depue, R., & Iacono, W. (1988). Neurobehavioral aspects of affective disorders. *Annual Review of Psychology, 40*, 457–492.

Depue, R. A. (Ed.). (1979). *The psychobiology of the depressive disorders*. New York: Academic Press.

Deregowski, J. B. (1968). Pictorial recognition in subjects from a relatively picture-less environment. *African Social Research, 5*, 356–364.

Deregowski, J. B. (1971). Responses mediating pictorial recognition. *Journal of Social Psychology, 84*, 27–34.

Deregowski, J. B. (1972). The role of symmetry in pattern reproduction by Zambian children. *Journal of Cross Cultural Psychology, 3*, 303–307.

Derenzi, E., & Piercy, M. (1969). The fourteenth international symposium of Neuropsychology. *Neuropsychologia, 7*, 583–585.

De Rita, L. (1954). Controllo sociometrico di vicinati in una località lucana. *Bollettino di Psicologia Applicata*, no. 4–5.

De Rita, L. (1954). *I vicinati a Grassano. Aspetti di psicologia comunitaria*. Atti della Commissione Parlamentare di inchiesta sulla miseria e sui mezzi per combatterla, vol. XIV.

De Rita, L. (1955). *Il vicinato come gruppo*. Centro Sociale, no. 1.

De Rita, L. (1964). *I contadini e la televisione*. Bologna, Italy: Mulino.

Derlega, V. J. (1978). Social psychology in Poland. *Personality and Social Psychology Bulletin, 4*, 631–637.

Derlega, V. J., & Chaikin, A. L. (1977). Privacy and self-disclosure in social relationships. *Journal of Social Issues, 33*, 102–119.

Derlega, V. J., & Grzelak, J. (Eds.). (1981). *Cooperation and helping behavior: Theories and research*. New York: Academic Press.

Dermer, M., & Thiel, D. L. (1975). When beauty may fail. *Journal of Personality and Social Psychology, 31*, 1168–1176.

De Ropp, R. S. (1968). *The master game*. New York: Delacorte Press.

Derrida, J. (1976). *Of grammatology*. Baltimore: Johns Hopkins University Press.

Derrida, J. (1976/1967). *Of grammatology*. New York: Norton.

Derry, P. A., & Stone, G. L. (1979). Effects of cognitive-adjunct treatments on assertiveness. *Cognitive Therapy and Research, 3*, 213–221.

Desai, M. M. (1939). *Surprise: A historical and experimental study*. *The British Journal of Psychology: Monograph Supplements*. Cambridge, England: Cambridge University Press.

De Santillana, G. (1961). *The origins of scientific thought*. New York: Mentor.

De Saussure, F. (1959). *Course in general linguistics*. New York: Philosophical Library.

Descartes, R. (1649). *Les passions de l'âme*. Paris: Le Gras.

Descartes, R. (1955/1911). Discourse on the method of rightly conducting the reason (1637). In E. S. Haldane & G. R. T. Ross (Eds.), *The philosophical works of Descartes*, Vol. 1. New York: Dover.

Descartes, R. (1955/1911). The passions of the soul (1649). In E. S. Haldane & G. R. T. Ross (Eds.), *The philosophical works of Descartes*, Vol. 1. New York: Dover.

Descartes, R. (1960/1637). *Discourse on method, and meditations*. Indianapolis, Ind.: Bobbs-Merrill.

Descartes, R. (1961). The passions of the soul. In L. Blair (Ed.), *The essential works of Descartes*. New York: Bantam. (Original work published 1650)

De Schill, S. (1974). *The challenge for group psychotherapy*. New York: International Universities Press.

de Shazer, S. (1985). *Keys to solution in brief therapy*. New York: Penguin.

de Shazer, S. (1991). *Putting differences to work*. New York: Norton (1958).

Deshler, D., Lowrey, N., & Alley, G. (1979). Programming alternatives for LD adolescents: A nationwide survey. *Academic Therapy, 14*.

Desiderato, O., MacKinnon, J. R., & Hissom, H. (1974). Development of gastric ulcers in rats following stress termination. *Journal of Comparative and Physiological Psychology, 87*, 208–214.

De Silva, H. R. (1967). Age and highway accidents. In K. Soddy & M. C. Kidson (Eds.), *Men in middle life*. London: Tavistock Press.

De Silva, W. A. (1972). The formation of historical concepts through contextual ones. *Educational Review, 24*, 174—182.

Desmond, A. J. (1979). *The ape's reflexion*. New York: Dial Press.

Desoille, R. (1965). *The directed daydream*. New York: Psychosynthesis Research Foundation.

Desor, J. A. (1972). Toward a psychological theory of crowding. *Journal of Personality and Social Psychology, 21*, 79–83.

Despine, A. (père). (1840). *De l'emploi du magnétisme animal et des eaux minérales dans le traitement des maladies nerveuses, suivi d'une observation trés curieuse de guarison de névropathie*. Paris: Germer, Baillière.

Dess, N. K., & Overmier, J. B. (1989). Generalized teamed irrelevance: Preactive effects on Pavlovian conditioning of dogs. *Learning and Motivation, 20*, 1–14.

Dessoir, M. (1893). The psychology of legerdemain. *The Open Court, 7,* 3599–3602, 3608–3611, 3616–3619, 3626–3627, 3633–3634.

De Tocqueville, A. (1958/1933). *Democracy in America.* New York: Vintage Books.

Deutseh, A. (1949). *The mentally ill in America: A history of their care and treatment from colonial times* (2nd ed.). New York: Columbia University Press.

Deutsch, C. P. (1973). Social class and child development. In B. M. Caldwell & H. N. Ricciuti (Eds.), *Review of child development research,* Vol. 3. Chicago: University of Chicago Press.

Deutsch, D. (1975). Musical illusions. *Scientific American, 233*(4), 92–104.

Deutsch, D. (1978). The psychology of music. In E. C. Carterette & M. P. Friedman (Eds.), *Handbook of perception,* Vol. X. New York: Academic Press,.

Deutsch, F. (1947). Analysis of postural behavior. *Psychoanalytic Quarterly, 16,* 195–213.

Deutsch, F. (1949). Thus speaks the body: An analysis of postural behavior. *Transactions of the New York Academy of Sciences, 12,* 58–62.

Deutsch, F. (1975). Birth order effects on measures of social activities for lower-class preschoolers. *Journal of Genetic Psychology, 127,* 325–326.

Deutsch, F. (1982). *Child services: On behalf of children.* Monterey, Calif.:Brooks/Cole.

Deutsch, F. (1982). Toward knowledge about children's views of life events. *Journal of Genetic Psychology.*

Deutsch, H. (1945). *The psychology of women.* New York: Grune, Vol. 1, 1944; Vol. 2.

Deutsch, H. (1965). *Neuroses and character types.* New York: International Universities Press.

Deutsch, H. (1969). *Psychoanalytic study of Dionysus and Apollo: Two variants of the son–mother relationship.* New York: International Universities Press.

Deutseh, J. A., & Deutsch, D. (1963). Attention: Some theoretical considerations. *Psychological Review, 70,* 80–90.

Deutsch, K. (1968). Toward a cybernetic model of man and society, from K. W. Deutsch, "Some notes on research on the role models in the natural and social sciences," *Synthese, 1,* (1948–1949). Reprinted in W. Buckley (Ed.), *Modern systems theory for the behavioral scientist.* Chicago: Aldine.

Deutsch, M. (1950). A theory of cooperation and competition. *Human Relations, 2,* 129–152.

Deutseh, M. (1954). Field theory in social psychology. In G. Lindzey (Ed.), *Handbook of social psychology.* Cambridge, Mass.: Addison-Wesley Press.

Deutsch, M. (1962). Cooperation and trust: Some theoretical notes. In M. R. Jones (Ed.), *Nebraska Symposium on Motivation,* Lincoln, Neb.: University of Nebraska Press.

Deutsch, M. (1973). *The resolution of conflict.* New Haven, Conn.: Yale University Press.

Deutsch, M., & Collins, M. (1951). *Interracial housing.* Minneapolis, Minn.: University of Minnesota Press.

Deutsch, M., & Gerard, H. B. (1955). A study of normative and informational social influences upon individual judgment. *Journal of Abnormal and Social Psychology, 51,* 629–636.

Deutsch, M., & Hornstein, H. A. (Eds.) (1975). *Applying social psychology.* Hillsdale, N. J.: Erlbaum.

Deutsch, M., & Krauss, R. M. (1960). The effect of threat upon interpersonal bargaining. *Journal of Abnormal and Social Psychology, 61,* 181–189.

Deutsch, M., & Krauss, R. M. (1962). *Series research in social psychology.* Washington, D. C.: National Institute of Social and Behavioral Sciences.

Deutsch, M., & Krauss, R. M. (1965). *Theories of social psychology.* New York: Basic Books.

Deutsch, M. P., & Brown, B. (1964). Social influences in Negro–White intelligence differences. *Journal of Social Issues, 20,* 24–35.

DeValois, R. L., & DeValois, K. K. (1975). Neural coding of color. In E. Carterette & M. Friedman (Eds.), *Handbook of perception.* Vol. V: *Seeing.* New York: Academic Press.

Devereux, G. (1969/1951). Reality and dream. In *Psychotherapy of a Plains Indian.* New York: Doubleday.

De Villiers, J. G., & de Villiers, P. A. (1978). *Language acquisition.* Cambridge, Mass.: Harvard University Press.

Devine, S., & Sakheim, D. (1992). *Out of darkness.* New York: Lexington.

Devore, I. (1973). Primate behavior. In M. Argyle (Ed.), *Social encounters: Readings in social interaction.* Chicago: Aldine.

De Vos, G. A. (1973). *Socialization for achievement.* Berkeley, Calif.: University of California Press.

De Vries, D. L., Edwards, K. J., & Slavin, R. E. (1978). Biracial learning teams and race relations in the classroom: Four field experiments using teams-games-tournament. *Journal of Educational Psychology, 70,* 356–362.

De Vries, D. L., Morrison, A. M., Shullman, S. L., & Gerlach, M. L. (1980). *Performance appraisal on the line.* Greensboro, N.C.: Center for Creative Leadership, Technical Report no. 16.

Dewey, E. A. (1978). *Basic application of Adlerian psychology.* Coral Springs, Fla.: CMTI Press.

Dewey, J. (1886). *Psychology.* New York: Harper.

Dewey, J.(1896). The reflex arc concept in psychology. *Psychological Review, 3,* 357–370.

Dewey, R., & Gould, J. (Eds.). (1970). *Freedom: Its history, nature and varieties.* New York: Macmillan.

Dewsbury, D. A. (1972). Patterns of copulatory behavior in male mammals. *Quarterly Review of Biology, 47,* 1–33.

Dewsbury, D. A. (1975). Diversity and adaptation in rodent copulatory behavior. *Science, 190,* 947–954.

Dewsbury, D. A. (1978). *Comparative animal behavior.* New York: McGraw-Hill.

Dewsbury, D. A. (1981). *Mammalian sexual behavior: Foundations for contemporary research.* Stroudsburg, Pa.: Hutchinson Ross.

Dexton, W. H., Heron, W., & Scott, T. H. (1954). Effects of decreased variation in the sensory environment. *Canadian Journal of Psychology, 8,* 70–76.

Dhanaraj, V., & Singh, M. (1976). Effect of yoga relaxation and transcendental meditation on metabolic rate. In D. Orme-Johnson, L. Donash, & J. Farrow (Eds.), *Scientific research on the transcendental meditation program, collected papers.* Livingston Manor, N. Y.: MIU Press.

d'Heurle, A. (1979). Play and the development of the person. *The Elementary School Journal, 79,* 225–234.

Diagnostic and statistical manual of mental disorders (DSM III). (1980). Washington, D.C.: American Psychiatric Association.

Diamond, E. E. (Ed.). (1975). *Issues of sex bias and sex fairness in career interest measurement.* Washington, D.C.: National Institute of Education.

Diamond, G. W. (1989). Developmental problems in children with HIV infection. *Mental Retardation, 27,* 213–217.

Diamond, G. W., Gurdin, P., Wiznia, A. A., Belman, A. L., Rubinstein, A., & Cohen, H. J. (1990). Effects of congenital HIV infection on neurodevelopmental status of babies in foster care. *Developmental Medicine and Child Neurology, 32,* 999–1005.

Diamond, J., & Zeisel, T. W. (1974). A courtroom experiment on jury selection and decision-making. *Personality and Social Psychology Bulletin, 1,* 276–284.

Diamond, M. (1965). A critical evaluation of the ontogeny of human sexual behavior. *Quarterly Review of Biology, 40,* 147–175.

Diamond, M. (1982). Sexual identity, monozygotic twins reared in discordant sex roles and a BBC follow-up. *Archives of Sexual Behavior, 11*(2), 181–185.

Diamond, M. (1990). Selected cross-generational sexual behavior in traditional Hawaii: A sexological ethnography. In J. Feierman (Ed.), *Pedophilia: Biological dimensions* (pp. 422–443). New York: Springer-Verlag.

Diamond, M. (1992). *Sex watching: Looking into the world of sexual behavior.* London: Prion.

Diamond, M. (1993a). Genetic considerations in the development of sexual orientation. In M. Haug, R. E. Whalen, C. Aron, & K. L. Olsen (Eds.), *The development of sex differences and similarities in behavior.* Dordrecht/Boston/London: Kluwer Academic Publishers.

Diamond, M., & Karlen, A. (1980). *Sexual decisions.* Boston: Little, Brown.

Diamond, M. L. (1960). *Martin Buber: Jewish existentialist.* New York: Oxford University Press.

Diamond, S., Balvin, R. S., & Diamond, F. R. (1963). *Inhibition and Choice.* New York: Harper & Row.

Diamond, S. (Ed.). (1974). *The roots of psychology: A sourcebook in the history of ideas.* New York: Basic Books.

Diamond, S., Diamond-Falk, J., & Deveno, T. (1978). Biofeedback in the treatment of vascular headache. *Biofeedback and Self-Regulation, 3,* 385–408.

Diaz-Guerrero, R. (1964). A research proposal submitted to the Foundations' Fund for Research in Psychiatry. *Anuario de Psicologia,* III, 100–109, Universidad Nacional Autonoma de Mexico.

Diaz-Guerrero, R. (1966). Mexico. In S. Ross, I. Alexander, H. Basowitz, M. Werber, & P. O. Nicholas (Eds.), *International opportunities for advanced training and research in psychology.* Washington, D.C.: American Psychological Association.

Diaz-Guerrero, R. (1969). La enseñanza de la investigacion psicologica en Latinoamerica. Un paradigma. *Revista Latinoamericana de Psicologia, 3,* 5–36.

Diaz-Guerrero, R. (1974). El psicologo mexicano, ayer, hoy y mañana. *Memorias del Primer Congreso Mexicano de Psicologia.* Mexico, D. F.: Imprenta Universitaria, Universidad Nacional Autonoma de Mexico.

Diaz-Guerrero, R. (1976). Mexico. In V. S. Sexton & H. Misiak (Eds.), *Psychology around the world.* Monterey, Calif.: Brooks/Cole.

Diaz-Guerrero, R. (1979). Mexico. In B. B. Wolman (Ed.), *International directory of psychology.* New York, London: Plenum.

Diaz-Guerrero, R. (1981). Momentos culminantes de la historia de la psicologia en Mexico. *Revista de Historia de la Psicologia* (Spain), 2, 125–142.

Diaz-Guerrero, R. (1981). The National Institute for the Behavioral Sciences and Public Opinion of Mexico. *Spanish Language Psychology, 1,* 347–356.

Diaz-Guerrero, R. (1984). Psychology in mexico. *Annual Reviews of Psychology, 35,* 83–112.

Diaz-Guerrero, R. (1989). Una etnopsicologia mexicana. *Ciencia v Desarrollo, 15*(86), 69–85.

Diaz-Guerrero, R. (1991, February) *Mexican ethnopsychology: Pictures in an exhibition.* Lecture presented at the 20th annual meeting of the Society for Cross Cultural Research, Isla Verde, Puerto Rico.

Diaz-Guerrero, R., & Diaz-Loving, R. (1990). Interpretation in cross-cultural personality assessment. In C. R. Reynolds & R. W. Kamphaus (Eds.), *Handbook of psychological and educational assessment of children: Personality, behavior, and context* (pp. 491–523). New York: Guilford.

Diaz-Guerrero, R., & Diaz-Loving R. (1990). *La etnopsicologia Mexicana. El centro de la corriente.* Revista de pivulgacion y culture psicologica, Universidad Nacaional Autonoma de Mexico.

Dichter, E. (1958). The use of symbolism in commercial communication, *Quarterly Psychological Research Reports for Business,* June.

Dichter, E. (1962). The world customer. *Harvard Business Review,* July–August.

Dichter, E. (1964). *Handbook of consumer motivations.* New York: McGraw-Hill.

Dichter, E. (1965). Discovering the "inner Jones:' *Harvard Business Review,* May–June.

Dichter, E. It ain't necessarily so. *Advertising Age.*

Dichter, E. (1976). *Total self knowledge.* New York: Stein & Day.

Dichter, E. (1978). Interpretive versus descriptive research. *Research in Marketing,* Vol. I.

Dicken, C. (1978). Sex roles, smoking and smoking cessation. *Journal of Health and Social Behavior, 19,* 324–334.

Dickenson, W. A., & Truax, C. B. (1966). Group counseling with college underachievers. *Personnel and Guidance Journal, 45,* 243–247.

Dickerson, M. G. (1979). FI schedules and persistence at gambling in the U.K. betting office. *Journal of Applied Behavior Analysis, 12,* 315–323.

Dickey, W. (1980). Incompetency and the nondangerous mentally ill client. *Criminal Law Bulletin, 16,* 22–40.

Dickinson, A. (1980). *Contemporary animal learning theory.* Cambridge, England: Cambridge University Press.

Dickinson, A., Hall, G., & Mackintosh, N. J. (1976). Surprise and the attenuation of blocking. *Journal of Experimental Psychology: Animal Behavior Processes, 2,* 313–322.

Dickinson, A., & Pearce, J. (1977). Inhibitory interactions between appetitive and aversive stimuli. *Psychological Bulletin, 84,* 690–711.

Dickinson, J. (1977). *A behavioral analysis of sport.* Princeton, N.J.: Princeton Books.

Dickinson, R. L. (1933). *Human sex anatomy.* Baltimore, Md.: Williams & Wilkins.

Dickinson, T. L., & Zellinger, P. M. (1980). A comparison of the behaviorally anchored rating and mixed standard scale formats. *Journal of Applied Psychology, 65,* 147–154.

Dicks, H. V. (1967). *Marital tensions.* London: Routledge & Kegan Paul.

Dictionary of occupational titles. (1977/1965). Washington, D.C.: U.S. Department of Labor.

Didlbeck, M. C. (1990). Test of a field theory of consciousness and social change: Time series analysis of participation in the TM-Sidhi program and reduction of violent death in the U.S. *Social Indicators Research, 22,* 399–418.

Diederich, P. B, French, J. W., & Carlton, S. T. (1961). *Factors in judgments of writing ability.* Educational Testing Service Research Bulletin, RB 61–15; Princeton, N.J.: Educational Testing Service.

Diehman, T. E. (1979). Gambling: A social problem? *Journal of Social Issues, 35,* 36–42.

Diener, E. (1980). Deindividuation: The absence of self-awareness and self-regulation in group members. In P. B. Paulus (Ed.), *Psychology of group influence.* Hillsdale, N. J.: Erlbaum.

Diener, E., & Crandall, R. (1978). *Ethics in social and behavioral research.* Chicago: University of Chicago Press.

Dies, R. R., & Hess, A. K. (1971). An experimental investigation of cohesiveness in marathon and conventional group psychotherapy. *Journal of Abnormal Psychology, 77,* 258–262.

Dieterly, D., & Schneider, B. (1974). The effect of organizational environment on perceived power and climate: A laboratory study. *Organizational Behavior and Human Performance, 11,* 316–337.

Dietze, D. A. (1955). The facilitating effect of words on discrimination and generalization. *Journal of Experimental Psychology, 50,* 255–260.

Digman, J. M. (1959). Growth of a motor skill as a function of distribution of practice. *Journal of Experimental Psychology, 57,* 310–316.

DiLalla, L. F., & Gottesman, I. I. (1991). Biological and genetic contributors to violence—Widom's untold tale. *Psychological Bulletin, 109,* 125–129.

DiLeo, J. H. (1983). *Interpreting children's drawings.* New York: Brunner/Mazel.

Dillbeck, M. C., & Abrams, A. I. (1987). The application of the Transcendental Meditation pregam to correction. *International Journal of Comparative and Applied Criminal Justice, 11*(1), 111–132.

Dillbeck, M. C., & Alexander, C. N. (1989). Higher states of consciousness: Maharishi Mahesh Yogi's Vedic psychology of human development. *The Journal of Mind and Behavior, 10*(4), 307–334.

Dillbeck, M. C., Banus, C. B., Polanzi, C., & Landrith, G. S. III. (1988). Test of a field model of consciousness and social change: The Transcendental Meditation and TM-Sidhi program and decreased urban crime. *The Journal of Mind and Behavior, 9*(4), 457–486.

Dillbeck, M. C., Cavanaugh, K. L., Glenn, T., Orme-Johnson, D. W., & Mittlefehldt, V. (1987). Consciousness as a field: The Transcendental Meditation and TM-Sidhi pregam and changes in social indicators. *The Journal of Mind and Behavior, 8*(1), 67104.

Dillbeck, M. C., Landrith, G. III, & Orine-Johnson, D. W. (1981). The Transcendental Meditation pregam and crime rate change in a sample of forty-eight cities. *Journal of Crime and Justice, 4,* 25–45.

Dillbeck, M. C., & Orme-Johnson, D. W. (1987). Physiological differences between Transcendental Meditation and rest. *American Psychologist, 42,* 879–881.

Dillbeck, M. C., Orme-Johnson, D. W., & Wallace, R. K. (1981). Frontal EEG coherence, H-reflex recovery, concept teaming, and the TM-Sidhi program. *International Journal of Neuroscience, 15,* 151–157.

Diller, K. C. (Ed.). (1981). *Individual differences and universals in language learning aptitude.* Rowley, Mass.: Newbury House.

Dillman, D. (1978). *Mail and telephone surveys: The total design method.* New York: Wiley.

Dillon, H. J. (1949). *Early school leavers: A major educational problem.* New York: National Child Labor Committee.

Dillon, J. L., & Scandizzo, P. L. (1978). Risk attitudes of subsistence farmers in northeast Brazil: A sampling approach. *American Journal of Agricultural Economics, 60,* 425–435.

Dillon, K. M., Minchoff, B., & Baker, K. H. (1985–1986). Positive emotional states and enhancement of the immune system. *International Journal of Psychiatry in Medicine, 15,* 13–17.

Dillon, R. F., & Schmeck, R. R. (Eds.). (1982). *Individual differences in cognition.* New York: Academic Press.

Dilthey, W. (1883). *Einleitung in die Geisteswissenschaften: Versuch einer Grundlegung für das Studium der Gesellschaft und der Geschichte. Erster Band.* Leipzig: Duncker & Humblot.

Dilthey, W. (1914–1977). *Gesammelte Schriften (18 vols.).* Stuttgart: Teubner, Gottingen: Vandenhoeck & Ruprecht.

Dilthey, W. (1954). *The essence of philosophy.* Chapel Hill, N.C.: University of North Carolina Press.

Dilthey, W. (1958/1924). *Die geistige Welt; Einleitung in die Philosophie des Lebens.* Stuttgart: Teubner.

Dilthey, W. (1977/1894). Ideas concerning a descriptive and analytic psychology. In R. M. Zaner & K. I. Heiges (Eds.), *Descriptive psychology and historical understanding.* The Hague: Nijhoff.

Dilts, A. B., Grinder, J., Bandier, R., DeLozier, J., & Cameron-Bandler, L. (1979). *Neuro-linquistic programming I.* Cupertino, CA: Meta.

Dilts, R. B., Grinder, J., Bandier, R., DeLozier, J., & Cameron-Bandler, L. (1979). *Neuro-linguistic programming I.* Cupertino, Calif.: Meta.

DiMascio, A., & Goldberg, H. L. (1981/1976). *Emotional disorders: An outline guide to diagnosis and pharmacological treatment* (3rd ed.). Oradell, N.J.: Medical Economics.

Dimberg, U. (1982). Facial reactions to facial expressions. *Psychophysiology, 19,* 643–647.

Dimond, R. E., Havens, R. A., & Jones, A. C. (1978). A conceptual framework for the practice of prescriptive eclecticisn in psychotherapy. *American Psychologist, 33*(3), 239–248.

Dimond, S. J. (1978). *Introducing neuropsychology.* Springfield, Ill.: Thomas.

DiNardo, P. A., Barlow, D. H. Cerny, J., Vermilyea, B. B., Vermilyea, J. A., Himadi, W., & Waddell, M. T. (1985). *Anxiety Disorders Interview Schedule—Revised (ADIS-R).* Albany: State University of New York, Phobia and Anxiety Disorders Clinic.

DiNardo, P. A., O'Brien, G. T., Barlow, D. H., Waddell, M. T., & Blanchard, E. B. (1983). Reliability of DSM-III anxiety disorder categories using a new structured interview. *Archives of General Psychiatry, 40,* 1070–1074.

Diner, J. (1979). *Physical and mental suffering of experimental animals.* Washington, D.C.: Animal Welfare Institute.

Dinkmeyer, D., & Losoncy, L. (1980). *The encouragement book.* Englewood Cliffs, N.J.: Prentice-Hall.

Dinkmeyer, D., & McKay, G. (1973). *Raising a responsible child.* New York: Simon & Shuster.

Dinkmeyer, D., & Mackay, G. (1976). *Systematic training for effective parenting.* Circle Pines, Minn.: American Guidance Services.

Dinkmeyer, D. C., Pew, W. L., & Dinkmeyer, D. C, Jr. (1979). *Adlerian counseling and psychotherapy.* Monterey, Calif.: Brooks/Cole.

Dinnerstein, D. (1976). *The mermaid and the minotaur.* New York: Harper & Row.

Dinsmoor, J. A. (1954). Punishment: I. The avoidance hypothesis. *Psychological Review, 61,* 34–46.

Dinsmoor, J. A. (1955). Punishment: II. An interpretation of empirical findings. *Psychological Review, 62,* 96–105.

Dinsmoor, J. A. (1966). Operant conditioning. In J. B. Sidowski (Ed.), *Experimental methods and instrumentation in psychology.* New York: McGraw-Hill.

Dion, K., Berscheid, E., & Walster (Hatfield), E. (1972). What is beautiful is good. *Journal of Personality and Social Psychology, 24,* 285–290.

Dion, K. E., Berscheid, E., & Hatfield, E. (1972). What is beautiful is good. *Journal of Personality and Social Psychology, 24*, 285–290.

Dion, K. K. (1973). Physical attractiveness and evaluation of children's transgressions. *Journal of Personality and Social Psychology, 24.*

Dion, K. L., & Dion, K. K. (1976). The Honi phenomenon revisited: Factors underlying the resistance to perceptual distortion of one's partner. *Journal of Personality and Social Psychology, 33*, 170–177.

Di Pasquale, G. W., Moule, A. D., & Flewelling, R. W. (1980). The birthdate effect. *Journal of Learning Disabilities, 13*, 4–8.

Disaster Relief Act of 1974, Public Law 93–288, Rules and Regulations. *Federal Register,* November 26, 1976.

Discrimination in public employment: Summary of recent and pending cases. (July 1972). New York: National Employment Law Project.

Dishion, T. J., & Loeber, R. (1985). Adolescent marijuana and alcohol use: The role of parents and peers revisited. *American Journal of Drug and Alcohol Abuse, 11*, 11–26.

Division of Psychotherapy, APA. (1982). *Psychotherapy and psychologists.* River Edge, N.J.: APA.

Dixon, D. N., & Glover, J. A. (1983). *Problem solving counseling.* Elmsford, N.Y.: Pergamon Press.

Dixon, B. W., Streiff, E. J., & Brunwasser, A. H. (1991). Pilot study of a household survey to determine HIV seroprevalence. *Morbidity and Mortality Weekly Report, 40*(1), 1–5.

Dixon, N. (1981). *Preconscious processing.* New York: Wiley.

Dixon, N. F. (1971). *Subliminal perception: The nature of a controversy.* London: McGraw-Hill.

Dixon, N. F. (1981). *Preconscious processing.* Chichester, England: Wiley.

Doane, G. G. (1977). *Hostage negotiator's manual.* Dublin, Calif.: Police Press.

Dobbins, C. (1968). *American Council on Education: Leadership and chronology.* Washington, D.C.: American Council on Education.

Doberman, M. B., Vicinus, M., & Chauncey, G., Jr. (1989). *Hidden from history. Reclaiming the gay and lesbian past.* New York: New American Library.

Dobzhansky, T. (1960). *The biological basis of freedom.* New York: Columbia University Press.

Dobzhansky, T. (1962). *Mankind evolving: The evolution of the human species.* New Haven, Conn.: Yale University Press.

Dobzhansky, T. (1970). *The genetics of the evolutionary process.* New York: Columbia University Press.

Dobzhansky, T. (1973). *Genetic diversity and human equality.* New York: Basic Books.

Dobzhansky, T., Ayala, R. J., Stebbins, G. L., & Valintine, J. W. (1977). *Evolution.* San Francisco: Freeman.

Doctor, R. F. (1988). *Transvestites and transexuals.* New York: Plenum Press.

Dodds, E. R. (1971). Supernormal phenomena in classical antiquity. *Proceedings of the Society for Psychical Research, 55*, 189–237.

Dodge, D., & Martin, W. (1970). *Social stress and chronic illness mortality patterns in industrial society.* Notre Dame, Ind.: University of Notre Dame Press.

Dodge, K. A. (1985). Attributional bias in aggressive children. In R. C. Kendal (Ed.), *Advances in cognitive-behavioral research and therapy* (Vol. 4, pp. 73–110). Orlando, FL: Academic Press.

Dodge, K. A. (1986). A social information processing model of social competence in children. In M. Perimutter (Ed.), *Minnesota symposium on child psychology* (Vol. 18 pp. 77–125). Hillsdale, NJ: Erlbaum.

Dodge, K., & Cole, J. D. (1987). Social-information-processing factors in reactive and proactive aggression in children's peer groups. *Journal of Personality and Social Psychology, 53*, 1146–1157.

Dodge, K. A., & Frame, C. L. (1982). Social cognitive biases and deficits in aggressive boys. *Child Development, 53*, 620–635.

Dodge, P. R., Prensky, A. L., & Feigin, R. D. (1975). *Nutrition and the developing nervous system.* St. Louis, Mo.: Mosby.

Doehring, D. G., Trites, R. L., Patel, P. G., & Fiedorowicz, C. A. M. (1981). *Reading disabilities: The interaction of reading, language, and neuropsychological deficits.* New York: Academic Press.

Dohrenwend, B., & Dohrenwend, B. (Eds.). (1974). *Stressful life events: Their nature and effects.* New York: Wiley.

Dohrenwend, B. P., & Crandall, D. L. (1970). Psychiatric symptoms in community, clinic and mental hospital groups. *American Journal of Psychiatry, 126*, 1611–1621.

Dohrenwend, B. P., Dohrenwend, B. S., Schwartz-Gould, M., Linke, B., Neugebauer, R., & Wunsch-Hitzig, R. (1980). *Mental illness in the United States: Epidemiological estimates.* New York: Praeger.

Dohrenwend, B. P., Oksenberg, L., Shout, P. E., Dohrenwend, B. S, & Cook, D. (1979). What brief psychiatric screening scales measure. In National Center for Health Services Research, *Health Survey Research Methods: Third Biennial Research Conference.* Washington, D.C.: U.S. Department of Health and Human Services, DHHS Publication no. (PHS)81-3268, pp. 188–198.

Dohrenwend, B. S. (1978). Social stress and community psychology. *American Journal of Community Psychology, 6*, 1–14.

Doi, T. (1973/1971). *The anatomy of dependence.* New York: Kodanasha International.

Doig, B. (1991, June). Comments made at meetings held at the Australian Council for Educational Research Limited.

Doll, E. A. (1953). *Measurement of social competence: A manual for the Vineland Social Maturity Scale.* Circle Pines, Minn.: American Guidance Service.

Dollard, J. (1935). *Criteria for the life history.* New Haven, Conn.: Yale University Press.

Dollard, J. (1937). *Caste and class in a southern town.* New Haven, Conn.: Yale University Press.

Dollard, J., Doob, L. W., Miller, N. E., Mowrer, O. H., & Sears, R. R. (1939). *Frustration and aggression.* New Haven, Conn.: Yale University Press.

Dollard, J., & Miller, N. E. (1950). *Personality and psychotherapy: An analysis in terms of learning, thinking, and culture.* New York: McGraw-Hill.

Dollinger, S. J., & Thefen, M. H. (1978). Overjustification and children's intrinsic motivation: Comparative effects of four rewards. *Journal of personality and Social Psychology, 36*, 1259–1269.

Dolliver, R. H., Irvin, J. A., & Bigley, S. E. (1972). Twelve-year follow-up of the Strong Vocational Interest Blank. *Journal Of Counseling Psychology, 19*, 212–217.

Domingo, P. (1970). *Turró, hombre de ciencia mediterráneo.* Barcelona, Spain: Pòrtio, 1970.

Domino, G. (1989). Synesthesia and creativity in fine arts students: An empirical look. *Creativity Research Journal, 2*, 17–29.

Don, N. S. (1977–1978). The transformation of conscious experience and its EEG correlates. *Journal of Altered States of Consciousness, 3*(2), 147168.

Donahoe, J. W., Crowley, M. A., Millard, W. J., & Stickney, K. A. (1982). A unified principle of reinforcement: Some implications for matching. In M. L. Commons, R. J. Herrnstein, & H. Rachlin

(Eds.), *Quantitative analyses of behavior. 2: Matching and maximizing accounts.* New York: Ballinger.

Donahoe, J. W., & Palmer, D. C. (1993). *Learning and complex behavior.* Boston: Allyn & Bacon.

Donahoe, J. W., & Wessells, M. G. (1980). *Learning, language, and memory.* New York: Harper & Row.

Donaldson, J. (1980). Changing attitudes toward handicapped persons: A review and analysis of research. *Exceptional Child, 46,* 504–514.

Donchin, E. (1981). Surprise! . . . surprise? *Psychophysiology, 18,* 493–513.

Donchin, E., & Isreal, J. B. (1979). Event-related potentials and psychological theory. In H. H. Kornhuber & L. Deeke (Eds.), *Proceedings of the 5th International Symposium on Electrical Potentials Related to Motivation, Motor and Sensory Processes of the Brain.*

Donchin, E, McCarthy, G., Kutas, M., & Ritter, W. (1981). Event-related brain potentials in the study of consciousness. In R. J. Davidson, G. E. Schwartz, & D. Shapiro (Eds.), *Consciousness and self regulation, Vol. 3.* New York: Plenum.

Donders, F. C. (1868). Die Schelligkeit psychischer processe. *Archives of Anatomy and Psychology* 657–681.

Donegan, N. H., Gluck, M. A., & Thompson, R. F. (1989). Integrating behavioral and biological models of classical conditioning. In R. D. Hawkins & G. H. Bower (Eds.), *Computational models of learning in simple neural systems* (pp. 109–156). San Diego, CA: Academic Press.

Donnelly, D. (1979). Augustine of Hippo: Psychologist-saint. *Spiritual Life,* Spring *25,* 13–26.

Donnerstein, E., Donnerstein, M., & Evans, R. (1975). Erotic stimuli and aggression: Facilitation or inhibition. *Journal of Personality and Social Psychology, 32,* 237–244.

Donofrio, A. F. (1977). Grade repetition: Therapy of choice. *Journal of Learning Disabilities, 10,* 346–351.

Donovan, J. M. (1975). Identity status and interpersonal style. *Journal of Youth and Adolescence, 4,* 37–55.

Donovan, W. A., Leavitt, L. A., & Bailing, J. D. (1978). Maternal physiological response to infant signals. *Psychopsio, 15,* 68–74.

Doob, L. E. (1971). *Patterning of time.* New Haven, Conn.: Yale University Press,.

Doob, L. W. (1965). Psychology. In R. Lystad (Ed.), *The African World.* London: Pall Mall Press.

Dooley, D. (1985). Causal inference in the study of social support. In S. Cohen & S. L. Syme (Eds.), *Social support and health* (pp. 109–125). Orlando, FL: Academic Press.

Dooley, D., Catalano, R., & Serxner, S. (1987). Economic development and community mental health. In L. A. Jason, R. E. Hess, R. D. Felner, & J. N. Moritsugu (Eds.), *Prevention: Toward a multidisciplinary approach* (pp. 91–115). New York: Haworth.

Dorcos, R. M., & Jones, M. H. (1950). *Handbook of employee selection.* New York: McGraw-Hill.

Dorian, B., & Garfinkel, P. E. (1987). Stress, immunity, and illness—a review. *Biological Medicine, 17,* 393–407.

Doris, J. (Ed.). (1991). *The suggestibility of children's recollections: Implications for eyewitness testimony.* Arlington, VA: American Psychological Association.

Dorken, H. (1990). Malpractice claims experience of psychologists: Policy issues, cost comparisons with psychiatrists and prescription privilege implications. *Professional Psychology: Research and Practice, 21,* 150–152.

Dörken, H., et al. (Eds.). (1976). *The professional psychologist today: New developmenu in law, health insurance, and health practice.* San Francisco: Jossey-Bass.

Dörner, D. (1972). Illegal thinking. In A. Elithorn & D. Jones (Eds.), *Artificial and human intelligence.* Amsterdam: Elsevier.

Dörner, D. (1974). *Die kognitive Organisation beim Problemlösen.* Bern: Huber.

Dörner, D. (1976). *Problemlösen als Informationsverarbeitung.* Stuttgart: Kohlhammer.

Dörner, D. (1978). Self reflection and problem solving. In F. Klix (Ed.), *Human and artificial intelligence.* Berlin: Deutscher Verlag der Wissenschaften.

Dörner, D. (1980). On the difficulties people have in dealing with complexity. *Simulation and Games, 11,* 87–106.

Dörner, D. (1980). The construction and use of memory structures in controlling very complex systems. In F. Klix & J. Holmann (Eds.), *Cognition and memory.* Berlin: Deutscher Verlag der Wissenschaften.

Dörner, D. (1982). The ecological conditions of thinking. In D. R. Griffin (Ed.), *Animal mind—Human mind.* Berlin: Springer.

Dörner, D. (1982). Cognitive processes and the organization of action. In W. Hacker et al. (Eds.), *Cognitive and motivational aspects of action.* Berlin: Deutscher Verlag der Wissenschaften.

Dörner, D. (1983). Heuristics and cognition in complex systems. In R. Groner, M. Groner, & W. F. Bischof (Eds.), *Methods of heuristics.* Hillsdale, N.J.: Erlbaum.

Dörner, D., Kreuzig, H. W., Reither, F., & Stäudel, T. (1982). *Lohhausen: Vom Umgang mit Komplexität.* Bern: Huber.

Dor-Shav, N. K. (1977). Physiognomic form perception: Mature or immature? *Perceptual and Motor Skills, 44,* 475–478.

Dostoyevsky, F. (1971). *The gambler.* New York: Penguin Books.

Doty, D. W. (1975). Role playing and incentives in the modification of the social interaction of chronic psychiatric patients. *Journal of Consulting and Clinical Psychology, 43,* 676–682.

Doty, S. A. (1979). Runaway behavior and perceived resource availability in adolescent females. Dissertation, University of Texas at Austin.

Douglas, J. D. (1967). *The social meanings of suicide.* Princeton, N.J.: Princeton University Press.

Douglas, M. (1970). *Natural symbols.* London: Barrie & Rockliff.

Douglas, M. (1975). *Implicit meanings: Essays in anthropology.* London: Routledge & Kegan Paul.

Douglas, R. J. (1966). Cues for spontaneous alteration. *Journal of Comparative and Physiological Psychology, 62,* 171–183.

Douglas, V. I. (1975). Are drugs enough? To treat or train the hyperactive child. In R. Gittelman-Klein (Ed.), *Recent advances in child psychopharmacology.* New York: Human Sciences Press.

Douglas, V. I., Barr, R. G., O'Neill, M. E., & Britton, B. G. (1986). Short term effects of methylphenidate on the cognitive, learning and academic performance of children with attention deficit disorder in the laboratory and the classroom. *Journal of Child Psychology and Psychiatry, 27,* 191–211.

Douglas, V. I. (Chair). (1971). *The future of Canadian psychology.* Canadian Psychological Association. April.

Douty, H. I. (1963). Influence of clothing on perception of persons. *Journal of Home Economics, 55,* 197–202.

Douvan, E., & Adelson, J. (1966). *The adolescent experience.* New York: Wiley.

Douvan, E., & Adelson, J. (1958). The psychodynamics of social mobility in adolescent boys. *Journal of Abnormal and Social Psychology*, 56, 31–44.

Dowd, E. T. (1983). *Leisure counseling: Concepts and applications.* Springfield, Ill.: Thomas.

Dowd, E. T., & Milne, C. R. (1986). Paradoxical interventions in counseling psychology. *The Counseling Psychologist*, 14, 237–282.

Dowling, W. J. (1982). Melodic information processing and its development. In D. Deutsch (Ed.), *The psychology of music.* New York: Academic Press.

Down, J. L. (1866). Observations on an ethnic classification of idiots. *London Hospital Reports.*

Downey, J, & Low, N. (1982). *The child with disabling illness. Principles of rehabilitation.* New York: Raven Press.

Downie, N. M., & Heath, R. W. (1974). *Basic statistical methods* (4th ed.). New York: Harper & Row.

Downing, L. N. (1975). *Counseling theories and techniques: Summarized and critiqued.* Chicago: Nelson-Hall.

Downs, C. W., Smeyak, G. P., & Martin, E. (1980). *Professional interviewing.* New York: Harper & Row.

Downs, G. W., & Mohr, L. B. (1976). Conceptual issues in the study of innovation. *Administrative Science Quarterly*, 21, 200–214.

Downs, R. M., & Stea, D. (1973). *Image and environment.* Chicago: Aldine.

Dowrick, P. W., et al. (1991). *Practical guide to using video in the behavioral sciences.* New York: Wiley.

Doyere, V., & Laroche, S. (1992). Linear relationship between the maintenance of hippocampal long-term potentiation and retention of an associative memory. *Hippocampus*, 2(1), 39–48.

Doyle, A., Connolly, J., & Rivest, L. (1980). The effect of playmate familiarity on the social interactions of young children. *Child Development*, 51, 217–223.

Doyle, M. A., & Biagglo, M. K. (1981). Expression of anger as a function of assertiveness and sex. *Journal of Clinical Psychology*, 37, 154–157.

Draguns, J. (1981). Cross-cultural counseling and psychotherapy: History, issues current status. In A. J. Marsella & P. B. Pedersen (Eds.), *Cross cultural counseling and psychotherapy* (pp. 3–27). New York: Pergamon.

Draguns, J. (1989). Dilemmas and choices in cross-cultural counseling: The universal versus the culturally distinctive, in P. Pedersen, J. Draguns, W. Lonner, & J. Tremble (Eds.), *Counseling across cultures* (3rd ed.). Honolulu: University of Hawaii Press.

Draguns, J. G. (1980). Psychological disorders of clinical severity. In H. C. Triandis & J. G. Draguns (Eds.), *Handbook of cross cultural psychology*, Vol. VI, *Psychopathology.* Boston: Allyn & Bacon.

Draguns, J. G. (1981). Cross-cultural counseling and psychotherapy: History, issues and current status. In A. Marsella & P. Pedersen (Eds.), *Cross-cultural counseling and psychotherapy.* Elmsford, N.Y.: Pergamon Press.

Drake, R. M. (1957). *Musical aptitude tests* (rev. ed.). Chicago: Science Research Associates.

Drake, W. E. (1968). Clinical and pathological findings in a child with a developmental learning disability. *Journal of Learning Disabilities*, 1, 486–502.

Drapkin, I., & Viano, E. (Eds.). (1974). *Victimology.* Lexington, Mass.: Heath.

Dreese, M. (1949). Present and future plans of college guidance centers operating under VA contracts as related to pre-VA status of center. *American Psychologist*, 7, 297.

Dreher, R. E. (1947). The relationship between verbal reports and galvanic skin responses to music. Unpublished doctoral dissertation, Indiana University.

Dreikurs, R. (1946). *The challenge of marriage.* New York: Duell, Sloan, & Pearce.

Dreikurs, R. (1947). The four goals of children's misbehavior. *Nervous Child*, 6, 3–11.

Dreikurs, R. (1950). Guilt feelings as an excuse. *Individual Psychology Bulletin*, 8, 12–21.

Dreikurs, R. (1954). The psychological interview in medicine. *American Journal of Individual Psychology*, 10, 99–122.

Dreikurs, R. (1955/1950). *Fundamentals of Adlerian Psychology.* Chicago: Alfred Adler Institute.

Dreikurs, R. (1957). Group psychotherapy from the point of view of Adlerian psychology. *International Journal of Group Psychotherapy*, 7, 363–375.

Dreikurs, R. (1958/1948). *The challenge of parenthood.* New York: Duell, Sloan, & Pearce.

Dreikurs, R. (1960). *Group psychotherapy and group approaches: Collected papers.* Chicago: Alfred Adler Institute.

Dreikurs, R. (1962). *Prevention and correction of juvenile delinquency.* Chicago: Alfred Adler Institute.

Dreikurs, R. (1967). *Psychodynamics, psychotherapy, and counseling: Collected papers.* Chicago: Alfred Adler Institute.

Dreikurs, R. (1967). The function of emotions. In R. Dreikurs (Ed.), *Psychodynamics, psychotherapy, and counseling.* Chicago: Alfred Adler Institute.

Dreikurs, R. (1968/1957). *Psychology in the classroom.* New York: Harper & Row .

Dreikurs, R. (1972). Family counseling: A demonstration. *Journal of Individual Psychology*, 28, 202–222.

Dreikurs, R. (1972). *The challenge of child training: A parents' guide.* New York: Hawthorn/Elsevier-Dutton.

Dreikurs, R. (1981/1971). *Social equality: The challenge of today.* Chicago: Alfred Adler Institute.

Dreikurs, R., Corsini, R. J., Lowe, R., & Sonstegard, M. (1959). *Adlerian family counseling.* Eugene, Oreg.: University of Oregon Press.

Dreikurs, R., & Dinkmeyer, D. (1963). *Encouraging children to learn: The encouragement process.* Englewood Cliffs, N.J.: Prentice-Hall.

Dreikurs, R., Gould, S., & Corsini, R. J. (1974). *Family council: The Dreikurs technique for putting an end to the war between parents and children.* Chicago: Regnery.

Dreikurs, R., & Grey, L. (1968). *Logical consequences: A new approach to discipline.* New York: Meredith.

Dreikurs, R., Grunwald, B., & Pepper, F. (1981/1971). *Maintaining sanity in the classroom: Illustrated teaching techniques.* New York: Harper & Row.

Dreikurs, R., & Mosak, H. H. (1967). The tasks of life. II. The fourth task. *Individual Psychologist*, 4, 51–56.

Dreikurs, R., & Soltz, V. (1967/1964). *Children: The challenge.* New York: Duell, Sloan, & Pearce.

Drenth, P. J. D. (1975). *Inleiding in de testtheorie.* Deventer, Netherlands: Van Loghum Slaterus.

Drenth, P. J. D., et al. (1981). *Industrial democracy in Europe*, Vol. I, *Industrial relations in Europe*, Vol. II. Oxford: Oxford University Press.

Drenth, P. J. D. (1981). Research and education in industrial and organizational psychology in the Netherlands: An overview. *Bulletin de la Commission Internationale des Tests*, 15, 3–22.

Drenth, P. J. D., Thierry, H., Willems, P. J., & de Wolff, C. (Eds.). (1980–1982). *Handboek Arbeids—en Organisatiepsychologie (Handbook of industrial and organizational psychology).* Deventer, Netherlands: Van Loghum Slatems.

Drew, C. J. (1980). *Introduction to designing and conducting research.* St. Louis, Mo.: Mosby.

Drickamer, L. C., & Vessey, S. H. (1982). *Animal behavior: Concepts, processes and methods.* Boston: Grant Press.

Driesch, H. (1980). *The science and philosophy of the organism* (2 vols.). London: Black.

Driscoll, R. E. & Eckstein, D. G. (1982). Empirical studies of the relationship between birth order and personality. In D. Eckstein et al. (Eds.), *Life style what it is and how to do it.* Dubuque, Iowa: Kendall/Hunt.

Driscoll, R. E., & Eckstein, D. G. (1982). Life style questionnaire. In J. Pfieffer & L. Goodstein (Eds.), *1982 Annual handbook for facilitators, trainers and consultants.* San Diego, Calif.: University Associates.

Droppelt, J. E., & Wallace, W. L. (1955). Standardization of the Wechsler Adult Intelligence Scale for older persons. *Journal of Abnormal and Social Psychology, 51,* 312–330.

Droz, R. L. (1965). Contribution à l'étude des dévaluations et sousestimations d'existants visuels en présentation tachistoscopique bréve. *Archives de Psychologie.*

Drucker, P. (1967). How to double your sales. *Nation's Business 55,* 81–83.

Druckman, D., & Bjork, R. A. (Eds.). (1991). *In the mind's eye: Enhancing human performance.* Washington, DC: National Academy Press.

Druckman, D. (Ed.) (1977). *Negotiations: Social psychological perspectives.* Beverly Hills, Calif.: Sage Publications.

Drugs and Therapeutics Bulletin, (1975). Drugs for dementia. *Drugs and Therapeutics Bulletin, 13,* 85–87.

Dryden, W., & Scott, M. (Eds.). (1990). *An introduction to cognitive-behaviour therapy: Theory and applications.* Loughton, UK: Gale Centre.

D'Souza, D. (1991). *Illiberal education: The politics of race and sex on campus.* New York: Free Press.

Duberman, L. (1973). Step-kin relationships. *Journal of Marriage and Family, 35,* 282–292.

Dubey, D. R. (1976). Organic factors in hyperkinesis: A critical evaluation. *American Journal of Orthopsychiatry, 46,* 353–366.

Dublin, L. I. (1963). *Suicide: A sociological and statistical study.* New York: Ronald Press.

Dublin, L. I. (1969). Suicide prevention. In E. S. Shneidman (Ed.), *On the nature of suicide.* San Francisco: Jossey-Bass.

Du Bois, P. (1909/1904). *The psychic treatment of nervous disorders.* New York: Funk & Wagnalls.

Du Bois, P. H. (1947). The classification program. AAF aviation psychology program. Research Report.

Du Bois, P. H. (1970). *A history of psychological testing.* Boston: Allyn & Bacon.

Du Bois-Reymond, E. H. (1852). *On animal electricity.* London: Churchill.

DuBois, N. F. (1987, April). *Training students to become autonomous learners.* Paper presented at American Educational Research Association, Washington, DC.

DuBois-Reymond, E. H. (1848). *Untersuchungen über thierische Elektrizität* (2 vols.). Berlin: Reimer.

Dubonowsky, W. (1980, February). *Pain cues as maintainers of human violence.* Paper Presented at the Symposium on Dangerousness Prediction. Honolulu.

Dubos, R. (1959). *Mirage of health.* New York: Harper & Row.

Dubos, R. (1968). *Man, medicine, and environment.* New York: Praeger.

Ducanis, A. J., & Golin, A. K. (1979). *The interdisciplinary health care team: A handbook.* Germantown, Md.: Aspen Systems.

Duck, S. (Ed.). (1990). *Personal relationships and social support.* London: Sage.

Duck, S. W. (1973). *Personal constructs and personal relationships.* New York: Wiley.

Duck, S. W. (Ed.). (1977). *Theory and practice in interpersonal attraction.* London: Academic Press.

Duck, S. W. (Ed.). (1982). *Personal relationships.* Vol. 4: *Dissolving personal relationships.* New York: Academic Press.

Duck, S., & Gilmour, R. (Eds.). (1980). *Personal relationships.* Vol. 1: *Studying personal relationships.* London: Academic Press.

Duck, S., & Gilmour, R. (Eds.). (1981). *Personal relationships.* London: Academic Press.

Duckworth, G. S., Kedward, H. B., & Bailey, W. F. (1979). Prognosis of mental illness in old age: A four-year follow-up study. *Canadian Journal of Psychiatry, 24,* 674–682.

Dudai, Y. (1989). *The neurobiology of memory.* Oxford, UK: Oxford University Press.

Dueker, H. (1943). Psychopharmakologische Untersuchungen über die Wirkung von Keimdrüsenhormonen auf die geistige Leistungsfähigkeit. *Archiv für Experimentelle Pathologie und Pharmakologie, 202,* 262–313.

Duerksen, G. L. (1980). Music therapy. In R. Herink (Ed.), *The psychotherapy handbook.* New York: Meridian Books.

Duffey, J. B., Salivia J., Tucker, J., & Ysseldyke, J. (1981). Nonbiased assessment: A need for operationalism. *Exceptional Children, 47,* 427–434.

Duffy, E. (1934). Emotion: An example of the need for reorientation in psychology. *Psychological Review, 41,* 184—198.

Dugdale, R. L., (1877). *The Jukes: A study in crime, pauperism, disease and heredity.* New York: Putnam.

Duggan, D. (1981). Dance therapy. In R. J. Corsini (Ed.), *Handbook of innovative psychotherapies.* New York: Wiley.

Dubera, P. (1954). *The aim and structure of physical theory.* Princeton, N.J.: Princeton University Press.

Duhl, L. J., & Cummings, N. A. (1987). *The future of mental health services: Coping with crisis.* New York: Springer.

Duhl, L., & Cummings, N. A. (Eds.). (1989). *The future of mental health services: Coping with crises.* New York: Springer.

Duijker, H. C. J. (1980). *Psychopolis. Een essay over de beoefening der psychologie.* Deventer, Netherlands: Van Loghum Slaterus.

Duijker, H. C. J., Dudink, A. C., & Vroon, P. A. (1981/1958). *Leerboek der psychologie.* Groningen, Netherlands: Wolters-Noordhoff.

Duijker, H. C. J., & Frijda, N. H. (1960). *National character and national stereotypes. A trend report.* Amsterdam: North Holland.

Duijker, H. C. J., & Jacobson, E. H. (Eds.). (1966). *International directory of psychologists.* Assen, Netherlands: Van Gorcum.

Duijker, H. C. J., & van Rijswiojk, M. J. (1975). *Trilingual psychological dictionary,* Vol. 1: *English-French-German.* Vol. 2: *Français-Allemand-Anglais.* Vol. 3: *Deutsch-Englisch-Französisch.* Bern, Stuttgart, Vienna: Huber.

Duke, D. L. (1978). How administrators view the crisis in school discipline. *Phi Delta Kappan, 59*(5), 325–330.

Duke, M. P., & Nowicki, S., Jr. (1982). A social learning theory analysis of interactional theory concepts and a multidimensional model of human interaction constellations. In J. Anchin & D. Kiesler (Eds.), *Handbook of interpersonal psychotherapy.* New York: Pergamon Press.

Dulit, E. (1972). Adolescent thinking à la Piaget: The formal stage. *Journal of Youth and Adolescence, 1,* 281–301.

Dumas, G. (1900). *La tristesse et la joie.* Paris: Alcan.

Dumas, G. (1906). *Le sourire et l'expression des émotions.* Paris: Alcan.

Dumas, G. (Ed.). (1923). *Traité de psychologie.* Paris: Alcan.

Dumas, G. (Ed.). (1931). *Nouveau traité de psychologie.* Paris: Alcan.

Dumas, J. E. (1986). Indirect influence of maternal social contacts on mother-child interactions: A setting event analysis. *Journal of Abnormal Child Psychology, 14,* 205–216.

Dumas, J. E. (1989). Treating antisocial behavior in children: Child and family approaches. *Clinical Psychology Review, 9,* 197–222.

Dumas, J. E., & Gibson, J. A. (1990). Behavioral correlates of maternal depressive symptomatology in conduct-disorder children: II. Systemic effects involving fathers and siblings. *Journal of Consulting and Clinical Psychology, 58,* 877–881.

Dumas, J. E., Gibson, J. A., & Albin, J. B. (1989). Behavioral correlates of maternal depressive symptomatology in conduct-disorder children. *Journal of Consulting and Clinical Psychology, 57,* 516–521.

Dumas, J. E., & Wahler, R. G. (1983). Predictors of treatment outcome in parent training: Mother insularity and socioeconomic disadvantage. *Behavioral Assessment, 5,* 301–313.

Dumas, J. E., & Wahler, R. G. (1985). Indiscriminate mothering as a contextual factor in aggressive-oppositional child behavior: "Damned if you do damned if you don't." *Journal of Abnormal Child Psychology, 18,* 1–17.

Dumoulin, H. (1963/1959). *A history of Zen.* Boston: Beacon Press.

Dumoulin, H., & Sasaki, R. F. (1953). *The development of Chinese Zen.* New York: First Zen Institute of America.

Dunbar, F. (1947). *Mind and body: Psychosomatic medicine.* New York: Random House, 1947.

Dunbar, H. F. (1943). *Psychosomatic diagnosis.* New York: Hoeber.

Dunbar, H. F. (1944). Susceptibility to accidents. *Medical Clinics of North America, 28,* 653.

Dunbar, J. (1980). Adhering to medical advice: A review, *International Journal of Mental Health, 9,* 70–87.

Duncan, J. (1980). The demonstration of capacity limitation. *Cognitive Psychology, 12,* 75–96.

Duncan, M. H. (1979). Attention deficit disorder (ADD) 1980: Unnecessary mistakes in diagnosis and treatment of learning and behavior problems of the MBD/hyperkinetic syndrome. *Journal of Clinical Child Psychology, 8,* 180–182.

Duncan, O. D. (1973). *Introduction to structural equation models.* New York: Academic Press.

Duncan-Johnson, C. C., & Donchin, E. (1977). On quantifying surprise: The variation of event-related potentials with subjective probability. *Psychophysiology, 14,* 456–467.

Duncker, K. (1945). On problem-solving. *Psychological Monographs, 58*(5).

Dunham, J. L., Guilford, J. P., & Hoepfner, R. (1968). Multivariate approaches to discovering the intellectual components of concept learning. *Psychological Review, 75,* 206–221.

Dunham, P. (1977). The nature of reinforcing stimuli. In W. K. Honig & J. E. R. Staddon (Eds.), *Handbook of operant behavior.* Englewood Cliffs, N.J.: Prentice-Hall.

Dunham, P. J. (1971). Punishment: Method and theory. *Psychological Review, 78,* 58–70.

Dunham, R. B, & Smith, F. J. (1979). *Organizational surveys.* Glenview, Ill.: Scott, Foresman.

Dunlap, K. (1914). *An outline of psychobiology.* Baltimore: Johns Hopkins Press.

Dunlap, K. (1922). *The elements of scientific psychology.* St. Louis, Mo.: Mosby.

Dunlap, K. (1928). The development and function of clothing. *Journal of General Psychology, 1,* 64–78.

Dunlap, K. (1930). Autobiography. In C. Murchison (Ed.), *A history of psychology in autobiography,* Vol. 2. Worcester, Mass.: Clark University Press.

Dunlap, K. (1930). Repetition in the breaking of habits. *Science Monthly, 30,* 66–70.

Dunlap, K. (1932). *Habits: Their making and unmaking.* New York: Liveright.

Dunlap, K. (1946). *Religion: Its functions in human life.* New York: McGraw-Hill.

Dunn, B. R., Mathews, S. R., & Bieger, G. R. (1982). Deviation from hierarchical structure in recall: Is there an "optimal" structure? *Journal of Experimental Child Psychology, 34,* 371–386.

Dunn, B. R., & Reddix, M. D. (1991). Modal processing style differences in the recall of expository text and poetry. *Learning and Individual Differences, 3*(4), 265–293.

Dunn, J., & Kendrick, C. (1981). Social behavior of young siblings in the family context: Difference between same sex and different sex dyads. *Child Development, 52,* 1265–1273.

Dunn, J., Kendrick, C., & MacNamee, R. (1981). The reaction of first-born children to the birth of a sibling: Mothers' reports. *Journal of Child Psychology and Psychiatry, 22,* 1–18.

Dunn, L. M., & Dunn, L. M. (1981). *Peabody picture vocabulary test—revised: Manual for forms L and M.* Circle Pines, Minn.: American Guidance Service.

Dunn, S., Bliss, J., & Siipola, E. (1958). Effects of impulsivity, introversion, and individual values upon association under free conditions. *Journal of Personality, 26,* 61–76.

Dunn, S. W. (1969). *Advertising: Its role in modern marketing.* New York: Holt, Rinehart & Winston.

Dunnette, H. D., Hough, L. K. (Eds.). (1990). *Handbook of industrial and organizational psychology* (2nd ed.). Palo Alto, CA: Consulting Psychologists Press.

Dunnette, M. D. (1976). Aptitudes, abilities, and skills. In M. D. Dunnette (Ed.), *Handbook of industrial and organizational psychology.* Chicago: Rand-McNally.

Dunnette, M. D. (Ed.). (1976). *Handbook of industrial and organizational psychology.* Chicago: Rand-McNally.

Dunnette, M. D., Arvey, R. D., & Banas, P. A. (1973). Why do they leave? *Personnel, 50,* 25–39.

Dunnette, M. D., & Borman, W. C. (1979). Personnel selection and classification systems. In M. R. Rosenzweig & L. W. Porter (Eds.), *Annual Review of Psychology, 30,* 477–525.

Dunnette, M. D., & Campbell, J. P. (1968). Laboratory education: Impact on people and organizations. *Industrial Relations, 8,* 145.

Dunnette, M. D., & Fleishman, E. A. (1981). *Human performance and productivity.* Vol. 1: *Human capability assessment.* Hillsdale, N.J.: Erlbaum.

Dunnette, M. D., & Kirchner, W. (1960). Psychological test differences between industrial salesmen and retail salesmen. *Journal of Applied Psychology, 44,* 121–125.

Dunning, D., Griffin, D. W., Milojkovic, J. D., & Ross, L. (1990). The overconfidence effect in social prediction. *Journal of Personality and Social Psychology, 58,* 568–581.

Dunsted, M. (1970). Fetal growth and mental ability. *Developmental Medicine and Child Neurology (London), 12*(2), 222–224.

DuPaul, G. J., Rapport, M. D., & Perriello, L. M. (1991). Teacher ratings of academic skills: The development of the Academic Performance Rating Scale. *School Psychology Review, 20,* 284–300.

Dupont, J.-B. (1954). *La sélection des conducteurs de véhicules.* Neuchâtel, Switzerland: Delachaux & Niestlé.

Dupont, J.-B., Gondre, F., Berthoud, S., & Descombes, J.-P. (1979). *La psychologie des intérêts.* Paris: Presses Universitaires de France.

Dupont, R. J., Goldstein, A., O'Donnelly, J., & Brown, B. (Eds.). (1979). *Handbook on drug abuse.* Rockville, Md.: National Institute on Drug Abuse.

Durkheim, E. (1912). *The elementary forms of the religious life.* London: Allen & Unwin.

Durkheim, E. (1966/1897). *Suicide: A study in sociology.* Glencoe, Ill.: Free Press.

Durlak, J. A. (1983). Social problem-solving as a prevention strategy. In R. D. Felner, L. A. Jason, J. N. Moritsugu, & S. S. Farber (Eds.), *Preventive psychology: Theory, research, and practice* (pp. 31–48). New York: Pergamon.

Durlak, J. A., Fuhrman, T., & Lampman, C. (1991). Effectiveness of cognitive-behavior therapy for maladapting children: A meta-analysis. *Psychological Bulletin, 110,* 204–214.

Durojaiye, M. O. A. (1970). Psycho-cultural constraints on formal education of the African child. Presented at Universities of East Africa Social Sciences Conference, Dar es Salaam.

Durojaiye, M. O. A. (1976). *A new introduction to educational psychology.* London: Evans.

Durr, R. A., (1970). *Poetic vision and the psychedelic experience,* Syracuse, N.Y.: Syracuse University Press.

Dusay, J. M., & Dosay, K. M. (1979). Transactional analysis. In R. J. Corsini (Ed.), *Current psychotherapies.* Itasca, Ill.: Peacock.

Dusek, J. B. (1975). Do teachers bias children's learning? *Review of Educational Research, 45,* 661–684.

Dush, D. M., Hirt, M. L., & Schroeder, H. E. (1989). Self-statement modification in the treatment of child behavior disorders: A meta-analysis. *Psychological Bulletin, 106,* 97–106.

Dutta, R., Schulenberg, J. E., & Lair, T. J. (1986, April). The effects of job characteristics on cognitive abilities and intellectual flexibility. Paper presented at the annual meeting of the Eastern psychological Association, New York.

Dutton, D., & Aron, A. (1974). Some evidence for heightened sexual attraction under conditions of high anxiety. *Journal of Personality and Social Psychology, 30,* 510–517.

Dutton-Douglas, M. A., & Walker, L. E. A. (Eds.). (1988). *Feminist psychotherapies: Integration of therapeutic and feminist systems.* New Jersey: Ablex.

Duvall, E. M. (1971). *Family development.* Philadelphia, Pa.: Lippincott.

Duvall, S., & Maloney, M. P. (1978). A comparison of the WAIS and Leiter International Performance Scale in a large urban community mental health setting. *Psychological Reports, 43,* 235–238.

Dvorkin, L. (1980). Evaluation of cognitive remediation programs. *The Gerontologist, 20,* pt. II, 95.

Dweck, C. S. (1975). The role of expectations and attributions in the alleviation of learned helplessness. *Journal of Personality and Social Psychology, 31,* 674–685.

Dweck, C. S., & Reppucci, N. D. (1973). Learned helplessness and reinforcement responsibility in children. *Journal of Personality and Social Psychology, 25,* 109–116.

Dworkin, R. H., Burke, B. W., Maher, B. A., & Gottesman, I. I. (1977). Genetic influences on the organization and development of personality. *Developmental Psychology, 13,* 164–165.

Dworkin, R. H., Burke, B. W., Maher, B. A., & Gottesman, I. I. (1976). A longitudinal study of the genetics of personality. *Journal of Personality and Social Psychology, 34,* 510–518.

Dwyer, C. A. (1976). Test content in mathematics and science: The consideration of sex. Presented at the annual meeting of the American Educational Research Association, San Francisco.

Dwyer, E., & Hargie, O. (1980). Microteaching in special education. *Special Education: Forward Trends, 7,* 17–19.

Dwyer, J., & Mayer, J. (1968/1969). Psychological effects of variations in physical appearance during adolescence. *Adolescence, 3,* 353–380.

Dwyer, J. H. (1983). *Statistical models for the social and behavioral sciences.* New York: Oxford University Press.

d'Ydewalle, G. (Ed.). *International Journal of Psychology.* Amsterdam: North-Holland.

d'Ydewalle, G. (1979). Performing versus observing "right" and "wrong" responses in incidental and intentional learning. *American Journal of Psychology, 92,* 427–436.

d'Ydewalle, G. Test expectancies in free recall and recognition. *Journal of General Psychology, 105,* 173–195.

d'Ydewalle, G., Degryse, M., & De Corte, E. (1981). Expected time of test and the acquisition of knowledge. *British Journal of Educational Psychology, 51,* 23–31.

d'Ydewalle, G., & Eelen, P. (1975). Repetition and recall of "right" and "wrong" responses in incidental and intentional learning. *Journal of Experimental Psychology: Human Learning and Memory, 104,* 429–441.

d'Ydewalle, G., & Lens, W. (Eds.). (1981). *Cognition in human motivation and learning: Festschrift J. R. Nuttin.* Louvain, Belgium: Leuven University Press.

d'Ydewalle, G., & Rosselle, H. (1978). Test expectations in text learning. In M. M. Gruneberg, P. E. Morris, & R. N. Sykes (Eds.), *Practical aspects of memory.* New York: Academic Press.

Dye, T. (1979). *Who's running America? The Carter years* (2nd ed.). Englewood Cliffs, N.J.: Prentice-Hall.

Dye, T., & Zeigler, H. (1978). *The irony of democracy: An uncommon introduction to American politics.* North Scituate, Mass.: Duxbury.

Dyer, F. C. (1991). Bees acquire route-based memories but not cognitive maps in a familiar landscape. *Animal Behavior, 42,* 239–246.

Dyer, J. A. T., & Kreitman, N. (1984). Hopelessness, depression and suicidal intent in parasuicide. *British Journal of Psychiatry, 144,* 127–133.

Dyer, W. E. *Teambuilding: Issues and alternatives.* Reading, Mass.: Addison-Wesley.

Dykens, E., & Leckman, J. (1990). Developmental issues in fragile X syndrome. In R. M. Hodapp, J. A. Burack, & E. Zigler (Eds.), *Issues in the developmental approach to mental retardation* (pp. 226–245). Cambridge, UK: Cambridge University Press.

Dymond, R. (1949). A scale for measurement of empathetic ability. *Journal of Consulting Psychology,14,* 127–133.

Dynes, W. R. (Ed.). (1985). *Homolexis: A historical and cultural lexicon of homosexuality.* New York: Gay Academic Union.

Dyson-Hudson, R., & Smith, E. A. (1978). Human territoriality: An ecological reassessment. *American Anthropologist, 80,* 21–41.

Dywan, J., & Bowers, K. (1983). The use of hypnosis to enhance recall. *Science, 222,* 184–185.

D'Zurilla, T., & Goldfried, M. (1971). Problem solving and behavior modification. *Journal of Abnormal Psychology, 78,* 107–126.

Eadinton, W. R. (Ed.) (1976). *Gambling and society.* Springfield, Ill.: Thomas.

Eagan, C. J. (1963). Introduction and terminology: Habituation and peripheral tissue adaptations. *Federation Proceedings, 22,* 930–933.

Eagley, A. H., Ashmore, R. D., Makhijani, M. G., & Kennedy, L. C. (1991). *What is beautiful is good, but . . . : A meta-analytic review of research on the physical attractiveness stereotype.* Unpublished manuscript, West Lafayette, IN: Purdue University.

Eagly, A. H. (1978). Sex differences in influenceability. *Psychological Bulletin, 85,* 86—116.

Eagly, A. H., & Carli, L. L. (1981). Sex of researchers and sex-typed communications as determinants of sex differences in influenceability: A metaanalysis of social influence studies. *Psychological Bulletin, 90,* 1–20..

Earles, T. *Adlerian Life Style and clinical depression in mothers of emotionally disturbed children.* Dissertation in progress, Georgia State University.

Eash, M. J. (1961). Grouping: What have we learned? *Educational Leadership 18,* 429–439.

Easterbrook, J. A. (1959). The effect of emotion on cue utilization and the organization of behavior. *Psychological Review, 66,* 183–201.

Easton, S. C. (1975). *Man and the world in the light of anthroposophy,* Spring Valley, NY: Anthroposophic Press.

Eastwood, M. R., & Ross, H. E. (1974). The reliability of the psychiatric amnesis. *British Journal of Psychiatry,124,* 357–358.

Eaton, W. O., & Von Bargen, D. (1981). Asynchronous development of gender understanding in preschool children. *Child Development, 52,* 1020–1027.

Eaves, L., & Eysenck, H. (1975). The nature of extraversion: A genetical analysis. *Journal of Personality and Social Psychology, 32,* 102–112.

Ebbinghaus, H. (1885). *Über das Gedächtnis.* Leipzig: Duncker.

Ebbinghaus, H. (1902). *The principles of psychology.* Leipzig: Veit.

Ebbinghaus, H. (1908). *A summary of psychology.* Leipzig: Veit.

Ebbinghaus, H. (1964/1885). *Memory: A contribution to experimental psychology.* New York: Dover.

Ebbinghaus, H. (1985) *Memory: A contribution to experimental psychology.* New York: Dover (Original work published 1964)

Ebel, R. L. (1982). Three radical proposals for strengthening education. *Phi Delta Kappan, 63,* 375–378.

Ebersole, E. (1974). *A teacher's guide to programmed tutoring in reading.* Los Angeles: Pepperdine University Press.

Eccles, J. (1953). *The neurophysiological basis of mind.* Oxford: Clarendon.

Eccles, J. (1957). *The physiology of nerve cells.* Baltimore, Md.: Johns Hopkins.

Eccles, J. (1964). *The physiology of synapses.* Göttingen, West Germany: Springer.

Eccles, J. (1966) *Brain and conscious experience.* Heidelberg: Springer.

Eccles, J. (1973). Preface. In E. P. Polten, *Critique of the psychophysical identity theory.* The Hague: Mouton.

Eccles, J. (1977). *The understanding of the brain.* New York:McGraw-Hill.

Eccles, J. C. (1977). The human person in its two-way relationship to the brain. In J. D. Morris, W. G. Roll, & R. L. Morris (Eds.), *Research in parapsychology 1976* (pp. 251–262). Metuchen, NJ: Scarecrow.

Eckberg, D. L. (1979). *Intelligence and race.* New York: Praeger.

Eckenrode, J., & Wethington, E. (1990). The process and outcome of mobilizing social support. In S. Duck (Ed.), *Personal relationships and social support* (pp. 83–103). Newbury Park, CA: Sage.

Eckerman, C. O., Whatley, J. L., & Kutz, S. L. (1975). Growth of social play with peers during the second year of life. *Developmental Psychology, 11,* 42–49.

Eckert, E., Bouchard, T., Bohlen, J., & Heston, L. (1986). Homosexuality in monozygotic twins reared apart. *British Journal of Psychiatry, 148,* 421–425.

Eckert, P. (1982). Peer groups in the high school. Presented at the Spencer Grant Foundation Colloquia, Ann Arbor, Mich. January.

Eckhardt, W. (1965). War propaganda, welfare values, and political ideologies. *Journal of Conflict Resolution, 9,* 345–358.

Eckhoff, E., Gauslaa, J., & Baldwin, A. L. (1961). Parental behavior toward boys and girls of preschool age. *Acta Psychologica* (Amsterdam), *18*(2), 85–99.

Eckman, P., Friesen, W., & Ellsworth, P. (1972). *Emotion in the human face.* New York: Pergamon Press.

Eckstein, D. G. (1981). An Adlerian primer. In J. E. Jones & J. W. Pfeiffer (Eds.), *The 1981 annual handbook for group facilitators.* San Diego, Calif.: University Associates.

Eckstein, D. G. (1978). Leadership, popularity and birth order in women. *Journal of Individual Psychology, 34*(1), 63–66.

Eckstein, D. G., Baruth, L., & Mahrer, D. (1978). *Life style: What is it?* Dubuque, Iowa: Kendall/Hunt.

Eckstein, D. G., & Driscoll, R. (1982). An introduction to life style assessment. In J. Pfeiffer & L. Goodstein (Eds.), *Annual handbook for facilitators, trainers and consultants.* San Diego, Calif.: University Associates.

Eckstein, D. G., et al. (1982/1981). *Life style: What it is and how to do it.* Dubuque, Iowa: Kendall/Hunt.

Eddy, E. M., & Partridge, W. L. (Eds.) (1978). *Applied anthropology in America.* New York: Columbia University Press.

Edelman, R. (1970). Effects of progressive relaxation on autonomic processes. *Journal of Clinical Psychology, 26,* 421–425.

Edelson, K., & Oreto, R. C. (1970). *The Children's House parent-teacher guide to Montessori.* New York: Capricorn Books.

Edelson, M. (1975). *Language and interpretation in psychoanalysis.* New Haven, Conn.: Yale University Press.

Edelstein, B. A., & Michelson, L. (Ed.). (1986). *Handbook of prevention.* New York: Plenum.

Edelstein, M. G. (1981). *Trauma, trance and transformation: A clinical guide to hypnotherapy.* New York: Brunner/Mazel.

Eden, A. (1975). Fat-proof your child. *Reader's Digest,* December.

Eden, D. (1975). Intrinsic and extrinsic rewards and motives. *Journal of Applied Social Psychology, 5,* 348–361.

Edgerton, R. B. (1971). *The individual in cultural adaptation.* Berkeley, Calif.: University of California Press.

Edgington, E. S. (1972). An additive method for combining probability values from independent experiments. *Journal of Psychology, 80,* 351–361.

Edinger, E. F. (1972). *Ego and archetype.* New York: Putnam.

Edman, I., & Schneider, H. W. (Eds.). (1941). *Landmarks for beginners in philosophy.* New York: Holt, Rinehart & Winston.

Edmonston, W. E. (1960). An experimental investigation of hypnotic age regression. *American Journal of Clinical Hypnosis, 3,* 127–138.

Edmonston, W. E. (1981). *Hypnosis and relaxation.* New York: Wiley.

Edmands, E. P. (1978). *Early retirement: Expectations of middle-aged workers and reports of early retirees.* Lubbock, Tex.: Texas Tech University.

Edmunds, F. (1975). *Rudolf Steiner's gift to education.* London: Steiner Press.

Edney, J. J. (1974). Human territoriality. *Psychological Bulletin, 81,* 959–975.

Educational Testing Service. (1962). *Hidden figures test.* Princeton, N.J.: Educational Testing Service.

Edwards, A. J. (1971). *Individual mental testing: Part 1. History and theories.* San Francisco: Intext Educational.

Edwards, A. L. (1957). *Techniques of attitude scale construction.* New York: Appleton-Century-Crofts.

Edwards, A. L. (1957). *The social desirability variable in personality assessment and research.* New York: Dryden Press.

Edwards, A. L. (1957). *The social desirability variable in personality assessment and research.* New York: Holt, Rinehart & Winston.

Edwards, A. L. (1959). *Manual for the Edwards Personal Preference Schedule* (rev. ed.) New York: Psychological Corp..

Edwards, A. L. (1966). Relationship between probability of endorsement and social desirability scale values for a set of 2,824 personality statements. *Journal of Applied Psychology, 50,* 238–239.

Edwards, A. L. (1970). *The measurement of personality traits by scales and inventories.* New York: Holt, Rinehart & Winston.

Edwards, A. L., & Abbott, R. D. (1973). Measurement of personality traits: Theory and techniques. *Annual Review of Psychology, 24,* 241–278.

Edwards, H. B. (1974). A developmental study of the acquisition of some moral concepts in children aged 7 to 15. *Educational Research, 16,* 83–93.

Edwards, W. (1954). The theory of decision making. *Psychological Bulletin, 51,* 380–417.

Edwards, W. (1961). Behavioral decision theory. *Annual Review of Psychology, 12,* 473–98.

Edwards, W. (1968). Conservatism in human information processing. In B. Kleinmuntz (Ed.), *Formal representation of human judgment.* New York: Wiley.

Edwards, W., Guttentag, M., & Snapper, K. (1975). A decision-theoretic approach to evaluation research. In M. Guttentag & E. L. Struening (Eds.), *Handbook of evaluation research,* Vol. 1. Beverly Hills, Calif.: Sage Publications.

Efron, D. (1972). Gesture, face, and culture. Atlantic Highlands, N.J.: Humanities Press.

Efrussi, P. (1923). *Uspehi psikhologii v Rossii (The advancement of Russian psychology).* Petrograd.

Egan, G. (1975). *Exercises in helping skills.* Monterey, Calif.: Brooks/Cole.

Egan, G. (1982/1975). The skilled helper. Monterey, Calif.: Brooks/Cole.

Egan, G., & Cowan, M. A. (1980). *Moving into adulthood.* Monterey, Calif.: Brooks/Cole.

Egan, J. R., Jackson, L., & Eanes, R. H. (1951). Study of neuropsychiatric rejectees. *Journal of the American Medical Association, 145,* 466–469.

Egdahl, R. H., Walsh, D. C., & Goldbeck, W. (Eds.) (1980). *Mental wellness programs for employees.* New York: Springer-Verlag.

Ege, K. (1979). *An evident need of our times: Goals of education at the close of the century.* Hillsdale, N.Y.: Adonis Press.

Egeland, B. & Sroufe, L. A. (1981). Attachment and early maltreatment. *Child Development, 52,* 44–52.

Egeland, J. Gerhard, D., Pauls, D., Sussex, J., Kidd, K., Allen, C., Hostetter, A., & Housman, D. (1987). Bipolar affective disorders linked to DNA markers on chromosome 11. *Nature, 325,* 783–787.

Eggers, C. (1978). Course and prognosis of childhood schizophrenia. *Journal of Autism and Childhood Schizophrenia, 8,* 21–36.

Ehrenfeld, D. (1978). *The arrogance of humanism.* New York: Oxford University Press.

Ehrenfels, C. von. (1890). Über Gestaltqualitäten. *Vierteljahrschrift der wissenschaftlichen Philosophie, 14,* 249–292.

Ehrenfels, C. von. (1937). On Gestalt-qualities. *Psychological Review, 44,* 521–524.

Ehrenfreund, D. (1952). A study of the transposition gradient. *Journal of Experimental Psychology, 43,* 81–87.

Ehrenreich, B., & Ehrenreich, J. (1974). Health care and social control. *Social Policy, 5,* 26–40.

Ehrenstein, W. (1935). *Grundlegung einer ganzheitspsychologischen Typenlehre.* Berlin: Juncker & Duennhaupt.

Ehrenzweig, A. (1953). *The psychoanalysis of artistic vision and hearing.* New York: Julian Press.

Ehrhardt, A., Meyer-Bahlburg, H. F. L., Rosen, L. R., Feldman, J. F., Veridiano, N. P., Elkin, E. J., & McEwen, B. S. (1989). The development of gender-related behavior in females following prenatal exposure of diethylstilbestrol (DES). *Hormones and Behavior, 23,* 526–541.

Ehrhardt, H. B. An overview of cognitive style. Unpublished manuscript, Mountain View College, Dallas, Tex.

Ehrlich, M. I. (1980). Adolescents in transition: A look at transitional treatment center. *Journal of Community Psychology, 8,* 323–331.

Ehrlich, P. R., & Feldman, S. S. (1977). *The race bomb: Skin color, prejudice, and intelligence.* New York: Quadrangle.

Eibl-Eibesfeldt, I. (1963). Angeborenes und Erworbenes im Verhalten einiger Säuger. *Zeitschrift für Tierpsychologie, 20,* 705–754.

Eibl-Eibesfeldt, I. (1971). *Love and hate: The natural history of behavior patterns.* New York: Holt, Rinehart & Winston.

Eibl-Eibesfeldt, I. (1971). *Love and hate.* New York: Holt, Rinehart, & Winston.

Eibl-Eibesfeldt, I. (1975). *Ethology: The biology of behavior.* New York: Holt, Rinehart & Winston.

Eibl-Eibesfeldt, I. (1971). Transcultural patterns of ritualized contact behavior. In A. H. Esser (Ed.), *Behavior and environment: The use of space by animals and men.* New York: Plenum.

Eich, E., & Hyman, R. (1991). Subliminal self-help. In D. Druckman & R. A. Bjork (Eds.), *In the mind's eye: Enhancing human performance* (pp. 107–119). Washington, DC: National Academy Press.

Eich, J. E. (1980). The cue-dependent nature of state-dependent retrieval. *Memory and Cognition, 8,* 157–173.

Eichelman, B. S., & Thoa, N. B. (1973). The aggressive monoamines. *Biological Psychiatry, 6, 143–164.*

Eiduson, B. T. (1962). *Scientists: Their psychological world.* New York: Basic Books.

Eifermann, R. R. (1971). *Determinents of children's game styles.* Jerusalem: Israel Academy of Sciences & Humanities.

Eigen, M., & Winkler, R. (1975). *Das spiel. Naturgesetze steuern den Zufall.* Munich: Piper.

Eimas, P. D., & Tartter, V. C. (1979). On the development of speech perception: Mechanisms and analogies. In H. W. Reese & L. P. Lipsitt (Eds.), *Advances in child development and behavior,* Vol. 13. New York: Academic Press.

Einhorn, H., & Hogarth, R. M. (1981). Behavioral decision theory: Processes of judgment and choice. *Annual Review of Psychology, 32, 53–88.*

Einhorn, H. J. (1988). Diagnosis and causality in clinical and statistical prediction. In D. C. Turk & P. Salovey (Eds.), *Reasoning, inference, and judgment in clinical Psychology* (pp. 51–70). New York: The Free Press.

Einhorn, H. J., & Hogarth, R. M. (1978). Confidence in judgment: Persistence in the illusion of validity. *Psychological Review, 85, 395–416.*

Einstein, A. (1933). *The method of theoretical physics.* Oxford, UK: Oxford University Press.

Einstein, A. (1959). Space-time. In *Encyclopedia Britannica.*

Eisenberg, L. (1972). Psychiatric implications of brain damage in children. In S. I. Harrison & J. F. McDermott (Eds.), *Childhood psychopathology.* New York: International Universities Press.

Eisenberg, N., & Strayer, J. (1987). *Empathy and its development.* New York: Cambridge University Press.

Eisenberg S. & Patterson, L. E. (1979). *Helping clients with special concerns.* Chicago; Rand-McNally.

Eisenberg-Berg, N. (Ed.). (1982). *Development of prosocial behavior.* New York: Academic Press.

Eisenbid, R. J. (1967). Masochism revisited. *Psychoanalytic Review, 54, 561–582.*

Eisenman, R., & Cherry, H. O. (1970). Creativity, authoritarianism, and birth order. *Journal of Social Psychology, 80, 233–235.*

Eisenman, R., & Schussel, N. (1970). Creativity, birth order and preference for symmetry. *Journal of Consulting Clinical Psychology, 34, 275–280.*

Eisenstadt, J. M. (1978). Parental loss and genius. *American Psychologist, 33, 211–223.*

Eisert, D. C., & Kahle, L. R. (1982). Self-evaluation and social comparison of physical and role change during adolescence: A longitudinal analysis. *Child Development, 53, 90–104.*

Eisler, R. M., & Frederiksen, L. W. (1980). *Perfecting social skills.* New York: Plenum.

Eisler, R. M., Frederiksen, L. W., & Peterson, G. L. (1978). The relationship of cognitive variables to the expression of assertiveness. *Behavior Therapy, 9, 419–427.*

Eisler, R. M., Hersen, M., Miller, P. M., & Blanchard, E. B. (1975). Situational determinants of assertive behaviors. *Journal of Consulting and Clinical Psychology, 43, 330–340.*

Ekehammar, B. (1974). Interactionism in personality from a historical perspective. *Psychological Bulletin, 81, 1026–1048.*

Ekman, G. (1961). Methodological note on scales of sensory intensity. *Scandinavian Journal of Psychology, 2, 185–190.*

Ekman, G. (1964). Is the power law a special case of Fechner's law? *Perceptual and Motor Skills, 19, 730.*

Ekman, P. (1965). Differential communication of affect by head and body cues. *Journal Social Psychology, 2, 726–335.*

Ekman, P. (1971). Universal and cultural differences in facial expression of emotion. In T. K. Cole (Ed.), *Nebraska Symposium on Motivation.* Lincoln, Neb.: University of Nebraska Press.

Ekman, P. (1972) Universal and cultural differences in facial expressions. In J. Cole (Ed.), *Nebraska Symposium on Motivation.* (Vol. 19, pp. 207–282). Lincoln: University of Nebraska Press.

Ekman, P. (1980). *The face of man: Expressions of universal emotions in a New Guinea village.* New York: Garland.

Ekman, P., & Friesen, W. V. (1971). Constants across cultures in the face and emotion. *Journal of Personality and Social Psychology, 17, 124–129.*

Ekman, P., & Friesen, W. V. (1975). *Unmasking the face.* Englewood Cliffs, N.J.: Prentice-Hall.

Ekman, P., Friesen, W. V., & Ellsworth, P. (1972). *Emotion in the human face.* Elmsford, N.Y.: Pergamon Press.

Ekman, P., & Oster, H. (1979). Facial expressions of emotion. *Annual Review of Psychology, 30, 527–554.*

Ekman, P., & O'Sullivan, M. (1991) Facial expression: Methods, means and moues. In R. S. Feldman & B. Rimer (Eds.), *Fundamentals of nonverbal behavior.* (pp. 163–199) Cambridge, UK: Cambridge University Press.

Ekstein, R., & Wallerstein, R. (1972/1959). *The teaching and learning of psychotherapy.* New York: Basic Books.

Ekstrand, B. R., Wallace, W. P., & Underwood, B. J. (1966). A frequency theory of verbal-discrimination learning. *Psychological Review, 73, 566–78.*

Ekstrom, R. B., French, J. W., Harman, H., & Derman, D. (1976). *Kit of factor-referenced cognitive tests* (rev. ed.). Princeton, NJ: Educational Testing Service.

El Abd, H. A. (1971). The intellect of East African students. *Multivariate Behavioral Research, 5, 423–433.*

Elashoff, D., & Snow, R. E. (Eds.). (1971). *Pygmalion reconsidered.* Worthington, Ohio: Jones.

Elashoff, J. D., & Elashoff, R. M. (1978). Effects of errors in statistical assumptions. In W. H. Kruskal & J. M. Tanur (Eds.), *International encyclopedia of statistics,* Vol. 1. New York: Free Press.

Elder, G. H., Jr. (1962). Structural variations in the child-rearing relationship. *Sociometry, 25, 241–262.*

Elder, G. H., Jr. (1963). Parental power legitimation and its effect on the adolescent. *Sociometry, 26, 50–65.*

Elder, G. H., Jr. (1968). Adolescent socialization and development. In E. F. Borgatta & W. W. Lambert (Eds.), *Handbook of personality theory and research.* Chicago: Rand-McNally.

Elder, G. H., Jr. (1974). *Children of the great depression.* Chicago: University of Chicago Press.

Elder, J. P., Edelstein, B. A., & Narick M. M. (1979). Modifying aggressive behavior with social skills training. *Behavior Modification, 3, 161–178.*

Elderton, E. M. & Pearson, K. (1910). A first study of the effect influence of parental alcoholism on the physique and ability of the offspring. *Eugenics Laboratory Memoir, 10, 1–46.*

Eleftheriou, B. E., Bailey, D. W., & Denenberg, V. H. (1974). Genetic analysis of fighting behavior in mice. *Physiology and Behavior, 13, 773–777.*

Eleftheriou, B. E., & Sprott, R. L. (Eds.). (1975). *Hormonal correlates of behavior* (2 vols.). New York: Plenum.

Eliade, M. (1964). *Shamanism: Archaic techniques of ecstasy.* Princeton, N.J.: Princeton University Press.

Eliade, M. (1975/1958). *Rites and symbols of initiation: The mysteries of birth and rebirth.* New York: Harper & Row.

Elitz, S. (1963). *Housing for the aged and disabled in Sweden.* Stockholm: Swedish Institute for Cultural Relations with Foreign Countries.

Elizur, D. (1980). *Job evaluation: A systematic approach.* Westmead, England: Gower.

Elkin, I., Shea, T., Watkins, J. T., Imber, S. D., Stotsky, S. M., Collins, J. F., Glass, D. R., Pilkonis, P. A., Leber, W. R., Docherty, J. P., Fiester, S. J., & Parloff, M. B. (1989) National Institute of Mental Health Treatment of Depression Collaborative Research Program. General effectiveness of treatments. *Archives of General Psychiatry, 46,* 971–982.

Elkind, D. (1971). *A sympathetic understanding of the child six to sixteen.* Boston: Allyn & Bacon.

Elkind, D. (1974). *Children and adolescents.* New York: Oxford University Press.

Elkind, D. (1978). Understanding the young adolescent. *Adolescence, 13,* 127–134.

Elkind, D. (1979). Growing up faster. *Psychology Today,* February 38–43.

Elkind, D. (1981). Child development and early childhood education: Where do we stand today? *Young Children, 36,* 2–9.

Elkind, D., & Flavell, J. H. (Eds.). (1969). *Studies in child development: Essays in honor of Jean Piaget.* New York: Oxford University Press.

Elkind, D., & Weiner, I. (1978). *Development of the child.* New York: Wiley.

Elkourie, F., & Elkourie, E. A. (1973). *How arbitration works.* New York: West.

Ellenberger, H. F. (1968). Impressions psychiatriques d'un séjour á Dakar. *Psychopathologie Africaine, 4,* 469–480.

Ellenberger, H. F. (1970). Alfred Adler and individual psychology. In *The discovery of the unconscious.* New York: Basic Books.

Ellenberger, H. F. (1970). *The discovery of the unconscious: The history and evolution of dynamic psychiatry.* New York: Basic Books.

Ellinwood, E. H. (1974). Behavioral and EEG changes in the amphetamine model of psychosis. In E. Usdin (Ed.). *Neuropsychopharmacology of monoamines and their regulatory enzymes.* New York: Raven Press.

Elliot, J. (1971). The nude marathon in a conversation with Paul Bindrim. In L. Blank, G. B. Gottsegen, & M. G. Gottsegen (Eds.), *Confrontation.* New York: Macmillan.

Elliotson, J. (1843). *Numerous cases of surgical operations without pain in the mesmeric state.* Philadelphia, Pa.: Lea & Blanchard.

Elliott, A. (1973). Student tutoring benefits everyone. *Phi Delta Kappan, 54,* 535–538.

Elliott, C. H., & Denny, D. R. (1978). A multiple component treatment approach to smoking reduction. *Journal of Consulting and Clinical Psychology, 46*(6), 1330–1339.

Elliott, D. L. (1973). Early childhood education: A perspective. In J. L. Frost (Ed.), *Revisiting early childhood education—Readings.* New York: Holt, Rinehart & Winston.

Elliott, D. S., & Ageton, S. S. (1980). Reconciling race and class differences in self-reported and official estimates of delinquency. *American Sociological Review, 45,* 95–110.

Elliott, D. S., Huizings, D., & Ageton, S. S. (1985). *Explaining delinquency and drug use.* Beverly Hills, CA: Sage.

Elliott, D. S., & Voss, H. L. (1974). *Delinquency and dropout.* Lexington, Mass.: Heath.

Ellis, A. (1950). An introduction to the principles of scientific psychoanalysis. *Genetic Psychology Monographs, 41,* 147–212.

Ellis, A. (1953). Is the vaginal orgasm a myth? In A. P. Pillay & A. Ellis (Eds.), *Sex, society and the individual.* Bombay: International Journal of Sexology Press.

Ellis, A. (1958). Rational psychotherapy. *The Journal of General Psychology, 59,* 35–49.

Ellis, A. (1961/1954). *The American sexual tragedy.* New York: Stuart/Grove Press.

Ellis, A. (1962). *Reason and emotion in psychotherapy.* New York: Stuart.

Ellis, A. (1963). *Sex and the single man.* New York: Stuart/Dell Books.

Ellis, A. (1965/1958). *Sex without guilt.* New York: Stuart. Hollywood, Calif.: Wilshire Books.

Ellis, A. (1965/1960). *The art and science of love.* New York: Stuart/Bantam Books.

Ellis, A. (1971). *Growth through reason.* Palo Alto Calif.: Science & Behavior Books, 1971. Hollywood, Calif.: Wilshire Books.

Ellis, A. (1971). Reason and emotion in the individual psychology of Alfred Adler. *Journal of Individual Psychology, 27,* 50–64.

Ellis, A. (1972). *Executive leadership: A rational approach.* New York: Institute for Rational Living.

Ellis, A. (1972). *How to master your fear of flying.* New York: Institute for Rational Living.

Ellis, A. (1973). *Humanistic psychotherapy: A rational approach.* New York: Julian Press.

Ellis, A. (1973). Rational emotive behavior therapy. In R. J. Corsini (Ed.), *Current psychotherapies.* Itasca, IL: Peacock.

Ellis, A. (1975). The rational-emotive approach to sex therapy. *Counseling Psychologist, 5*(1), 14–22. (Reprinted, New York: Institute for Rational Living, 1975.)

Ellis, A. (1975/1957). *How to live with a "neurotic."* New York: Crown.

Ellis, A. (1976). *Sex and the liberated man.* Secaucus, N.J.: Stuart.

Ellis, A. (1978). Fun as psychotherapy. In A. Ellis & R. Grieger (Eds.), *Handbook of rational-emotive therapy.* New York: Springer.

Ellis, A. (1979). *The intelligent woman's guide to dating and mating.* Secaucus, N.J.: Stuart.

Ellis, A. (1979/1973). Rational-emotive therapy. In R. J. Corsini (Ed.), *Current psychotherapies.* Itasca, Ill.: Peacock.

Ellis, A. (1980). The treatment of erectile dysfunction. In S. R. Leiblum & L. A. Pervin (Eds.), *Principles and practice of sex therapy.* New York: Guilford Press.

Ellis, A. (1983). *Rational-emotive therapy and cognitive behavior therapy.* New York: Springer.

Ellis, A. (1986). *Handbook of rational-emotive therapy.* New York: Springer.

Ellis, A. (1989). The history of cognition in psychotherapy. In A. Freeman, K. M. Simon, L. E. Beutler, & H. Arkowitz (Eds.), *Comprehensive handbook of cognitive therapy.* New York: Plenum Press.

Ellis, A., & Abarbanel, A. (Eds.). (1973/1960). *Encyclopedia of sexual behavior.* New York: Hawthorn.

Ellis, A., & Abrahms, E. (1978). *Brief psychotherapy in medical and health practice.* New York: Springer.

Ellis, A. (Ed.) (1954). *Sex life of the American woman and the Kinsey report.* New York: Greenberg.

Ellis, A., & Grieger, R. (Eds.). (1977). *Handbook of rational-emotive therapy.* New York: Springer.

Ellis, A., & Harper, R. A. (1975/1961). *A new guide to rational living.* Englewood Cliffs, N.J.: Prentice-Hall. Hollywood, Calif.: Wilshire Books.

Ellis, A., & Sagarin, E. (1965). *Nymphomania: A study of the oversexed woman.* New York: McFadden-Bartell.

Ellis, A., & Whiteley, J. M. (Eds.). (1979). *Theoretical and empirical foundations of rational-emotive therapy.* Monterey, Calif,: Brooks/Cole.

Ellis, A., Wolfe, J. L., & Moseley, S. (1966). *How to raise an emotionally healthy, happy child.* Hollywood, Calif.: Wilshire Books.

Ellis, H. (1894). *Man and woman: A study of human secondary sexual characters.* London: Scott.

Ellis, H. (1898). Auto-erotism: a psychological study. *Alienist and Neurologist. 19,* 260–299.

Ellis, H. (1911). *The world of dreams.* London: Constable.

Ellis, H. (1931). *More essays of love and virtue.* New York: Doubleday, Doran.

Ellis, H. (1936/1897). *Studies in the psychology of sex* (4 vols.). New York: Random House.

Ellis, H. (1939). *My life.* Boston: Houghton Mifflin.

Ellis, H. (1954). *Psychology of sex.* New York: Emerson.

Ellis, H. C., & Ashbrook, P. W. (1989). The "state" of mood and memory research: A selective review. *Journal of Social Behavior and Personality, 4,* 1–21.

Ellis, H. C., Bennett, T. L., Daniel, T. C., & Rickert, E. J. (1979). *Psychology of learning and memory.* Monterey, Calif.: Brooks/Cole.

Ellis, H. C., & Hunt, R. R. (1989). *Fundamentals of human memory and cognition* (4th ed.). Dubuque, IA: Brown.

Ellis, M. J. (1973). *Why people play.* Englewood Cliffs, N.J.: Prentice-Hall.

Ellis, M. J., & Scholtz, G. J. L. (1978). *Activity and play of children.* Englewood Cliffs, N.J.: Prentice-Hall.

Ellis, N. R. (1963). Toilet training and the severely defective patient: An S-R reinforcement analysis. *American Journal of Mental Deficiency, 68,* 48–103.

Ellis, N. R. (1990). Is memory for spatial location automatically encoded? *Memory and Cognition, 18,* 584–592.

Ellis, W. D. (Ed.) (1939). *A source book of Gestalt psychology.* New York: Harcourt, Brace.

Ellison, J. (1978). *Life's second half: The pleasures of aging.* Old Greenwich, Conn.: Devin-Adair.

Elmore, E. (1979). Economic aspects of gambling. In D. Lester (Ed.), *Gambling today.* Springfield, Ill.: Thomas.

Elmore, R. F. (1983). Social policymaking as strategic intervention. In E. Seidman (Ed.), *Handbook of social intervention* (pp. 212–236). Beverly Hills, CA: Sage.

Elms, A. (1972). *Social psychology and social relevance.* Boston: Little, Brown.

Elms, A. C., & Milgram, S. (1966). Personality characteristics associated with obedience and defiance toward authoritative command. *Journal of Experimental Research in Personality, 1,* 282–289.

Elster, J. (Ed.). (1986). *Rational choice.* Oxford, UK: Blackwell.

Emde, R. N., Gaensbauer, T. J., & Harmon, R. J. (1976). *Emotional expression in infancy: A biobehavioral study.* New York: International Universities Press.

Emerson, R. (1962) Power-dependency relations. *American Sociological Review, 27,* 31–41.

Emerson, V. F. (1972). Can belief systems influence neurophysiology? Some implications of research on meditation. *Newsletter Review, 5.*

Emery, F. (1969). *System thinking.* Hammondsworth, England: Penguin Books.

Emery, F. E., & Trist, E. L. (1960). Socio-technical systems. In C. W. Churchman M Verhulst (Eds.), *Management sciences, models, and techniques,* Vol. 2. London: Pergamon Press.

Emery, G., Hollon, S. D., & Bedrosian, R. C. (Eds.). (1981). *New directions in cognitive therapy: A casebook:* New York: Guilford Press.

Emmelkamp, P. M. G. (1982). *Phobic and obsessive-compulsive disorders: Theory, research and practice.* New York: Plenum Press.

Emmelkamp, P. M. G. (1986). Behavior therapy with adults. In S. L. Garfield & A. E. Bergin (Eds.), *Handbook of pschotherapy and behavior change.* (3rd cd., pp. 385–442). New York: Wiley.

Emmerich, W., & Shepard, K. (1982). Development of sex-differentiated preferences during late childhood and adolescence. *Developmental Psychology, 18,* 406–417.

Employee Polygraph Protection Act of 1988, Public Law 100-347, 29 U. S. C. 2001 (1988).

Ender, N. (1979). Where the stars are: The 25 most cited psychologists in Canada. *Canadian Psychology Review, 20*(1), 12–21.

Endicott, C. (1980). Ad growth mirrors rise in world living standard. In *Twentieth century advertising and the economy of abundance.* Chicago: Advertising Age.

Endicott, J., & Spitzer, R. L. (1978). A diagnostic interview. *Archives of General Psychiatry, 35,* 837–844.

Endler, N. S. (1982). *Holiday of darkness. A psychologist's personal journey out of his depression.* New York: Wiley.

Endler, N. S. (1982). Interactionism comes of age. In M. P. Zanna, E. T. Higgins, & C. P. Herman (Eds.), *Consistency in social behavior: The Ontario Symposium,* (Vol. 2). Hillsdale, N.J.: Erlbaum.

Endler, N. S. (1983). Interactionism: A personality model, but not yet a theory. In M. M. Page & R. Dienstbier (Eds.). *Nebraska Symposium on Motivation, 1982: Personality—Current theory and research.* Lincoln, Neb.: University of Nebraska Press.

Endlet, N. S., Boulter, L. R., & Osser, H., (Eds.). (1976). *Contemporary issues in developmental psychology.* New York: Holt, Rinehart & Winston.

Endler, N. S., & Magnusson, D. (Eds.). (1976a). *Interactional psychology and personality.* Washington, D.C.: Hemisphere.

Endler, N. S., & Magnusson, D. (Eds.). (1976b). Toward an interactional psychology of personality. *Psychological Bulletin, 83,* 956–974.

Engel, G. L. (1977). The need for a new medical model: A challenge for biomedicine. *Science, 196,* 129–136.

Engel, J. F., Kollat, D. T., & Blackwell, R. D. (1973). *Consumer behavior.* Hinsdale, Ill.: Dryden Press.

Engelberg, S. (1980). Open systems consultation: Some lessons learned from case experience. *Professional Psychology, 11*(6), 972–979.

Engelman, K., & Braunwald, E. (1977). *Hypertension and the shock syndrome.* In G. W. Thorn, R. D. Adams, E. Braunwald, K. J. Isselbacher, & R. G. Petersdorf (Eds.), *Harrison's principles of internal medicine.* New York: McGraw-Hill.

Engelman, S. R. (Ed.). (in press). *Confronting life-threatening illnesses: Mind-body approaches.* New York: Irvington.

Engels, W., & Wittkower, E. (1980). Skin disorders. In H. Kaplan, A. Freedman, & B. Saddock (Eds.), *Comprehensive textbook of psychiatry,* Vol. 2. Baltimore, Md.: Williams & Wilkins.

Engelsmann, F. (1977). The psychologist's role in psychosomatics. *Psychosomatics, 18,* 47–52.

Englander, M. E. (1976). Educational psychology and teacher education. *Phi Delta Kappan, 57,* 440–442.

Engle, M. (1959). The stability of the self concept in adolescence. *Journal of Abnormal and Social Psychology, 58,* 211–215.

English, H., & English, A. (1974). *A comprehensive dictionary of psychological and psychoanalytical terms: A guide to usage.* New York: McKay.

English, H. B. (1961). *Dynamics of child development.* New York: Holt, Rinehart & Winston.

English, H. B., & English, A. C. (1958). *A comprehensive dictionary of psychological and psychoanalytical terms: A guide to usage,* New York: McKay.

English, H. B., & Raimy, V. (1941). *Studying the individual school child.* New York: Holt.

Enloe, C. H. (1973). *Ethnic conflict and political development.* Boston: Little, Brown.

Enna, S. J., Samorajski, T., & Beer, B. (Eds.). (1981). *Brain neurotransmitters and receptors in aging and age-related disorders.* New York: Raven Press.

Ennis, B., & Emery, R. (1978). *The Rights of mental patients.* New York: Avon.

Ennis, B. J. (1972). *Prisoners and psychiatry.* New York: Avon.

Ennis, B. J., & Emery, R. D. (1973). *The rights of mental patients.* New York: Avon.

Ennis, B. J., & Litwack, T. R. (1974). Psychiatry and the presumption of expertise: Flipping coins in the courtroom. *California Law Review, 62,* 693–752.

Enright, G., & Kerstiens, G. (1980). The learning center: Toward an expanded role. In *New directions for college learning assistance.* San Francisco: Jossey-Bass.

Enroth, R. (1977). *Youth, brainwashing and the extremist cults.* Grand Rapids, Mich.: Zondervan.

Enthoven, A., & Kronick, R. (1990a). A consumer-choice health plan for the 1990s: Universal health insurance in a system designed to promote quality. *New England Journal of Medicine, 320*(1), 29–37.

Enthoven, A., & Kronick, R. (1990b). A consumer-choice health plan for the 1990s: Part 2. *New England Journal of Medicine, 320*(2), 94–101.

Entwistle, N. J. (1979). Stages, levels, styles or strategies: Dilemmas in the description of thinking. *Educational Review, 31,* 123–132.

Entwistle, N. J. (1981). *Styles of learning and teaching.* New York: Wiley.

Entwistle, N. J. (1982). *Learning from the student's perspective.* Leicester, England: British Psychological Society.

Entwistle, N. J., & Morison, S. (1983). Personality and cognitive style in studying. In N. J. Entwistle & P. Ramsden (Eds.). *Student learning: Approach and context.* London: Croom Helm.

Entwistle, N. J., & Ramsden, P. (1983). *Understanding student learning.* London: Croom Helm.

Entwistle, N. J., & Wilson, J. D. (1977). *Degrees of excellence: The academic achievement game.* London: Hodder & Stoughton.

Epictetus. (1890). *The works of Epictetus.* Boston: Little, Brown.

Eppley, K., Abrams, A., & Shear, J. (1989). The differential effects of relaxation techniques on trait anxiety: A metaanalysis. *Journal of Clinical Psychology, 45*(6), 957–974.

Epstein, H. T. (1978). Growth spurts during brain development: Implications for educational policy and practice. In J. S. Chard & A. F. Mirsky (Eds.), *Education and the brain.* Chicago: University of Chicago Press.

Epstein, M. A., Markowitz, R. L., Gallo, D. M., Holmes, J. W., & Gryboski, J. D. (1987). Munchausen syndrome by proxy: Considerations in diagnosis and confirmation by video surveillance. *Pediatrics, 80,* 220–224.

Epstein, R., Kirshnit, C. E., Lanza, R. P., & Rubin, L. C. (1984). "Insight" in the pigeon: Antecedents and determinants of an intelligent performance. *Nature, 308,* 61–62.

Epstein, S. (1973). The self-concept revisited or a theory of a theory. *American Psychologist, 28,* 404–416.

Epstein, S. (1984). The stability of behavior across time and situations. In R. A. Zucker, J. Aronoff, & A. I. Rabin (Eds.), *Personality and the prediction of behavior.* New York: Academic Press.

Epstein, W. (Ed.). (1977). *Stability and constancy in visual perception.* New York: Wiley.

Epting, F. R. (1984). *Personal construct counseling and psychotherapy.* New York: Wiley.

Epting, F., & Amerikaner, M. (1980). Optimal functioning: A personal construct approach. In A. W. Landfield & L. M. Leitner (Eds.), *Personal construct psychology: Psychotherapy and personality.* New York: Wiley.

Equal Employment Opportunity Commission, Civil Service Commission, Department of Justice and Department of Labor. Adoption by four agencies of uniform guidelines on employee selection procedures (1978). *Federal Register,* August 25, 1978, *43,* 38290–38315.

Equal Pay Act, In Vol. 29 *United States Code,* par. 209(d)(1).

Erdelyi, M. H. (1974). A new look at the new look: Perceptual defense and vigilance. *Psychological Review, 81,* 1–25.

Erdelyi, M. H. (1992). Psychodynamics and the unconscious. *American Psychologist, 47,* 784–787.

Erelemeyer-Kimling, L. & Jarvik, L. F. (1963). Genetics and intelligence: A review. *Science. 142,* 1477–1478.

Erickson, C. (1976). *The medieval vision.* New York: Oxford University Press.

Erickson, K. T. (1962). Notes on the sociology of deviance. *Social Problems, 9,* 308.

Erickson, M. H., Hershman, S, & Secter, I. I. (1961). *The practical application of medical and dental hypnosis.* New York: Julian Press.

Erickson, M. H., & Rossi, E. L. (1979). *Hypnotherapy: An exploratory case book.* New York: Irvington.

Erickson, M. H., & Rossi, E. L., (1981). *Experiencing hypnosis.* New York: Irvington.

Erickson, M. H., Rossi, E. L., & Rossi, S. I. (1976). *Hypnotic realities: The induction of clinical hypnosis and forms of indirect suggestion.* New York: Irvington.

Erickson, R., & Hyerstay, B. (1980). Historical perspectives on the treatment of the mentally ill. In M. S. Gibbs, J. R. Lackenmeier, & J. Sigal (Eds.), *Community psychology: Theoretical and empirical approaches.* New York: Gardner Press.

Ericsson, K. A., Chase, W. G., & Faloon, S. (1980). Acquisition of a memory skill. *Science, 208,* 1181–1182.

Ericsson, K. A., & Simon, H. A. (1980). Verbal reports as data. *Psychological Review, 87,* 215–251.

Ericsson, K. A., & Simon, H. A. (1984). Protocol analysis: Verbal reports as data. Cambridge: The MIT press.

Eriksen, C., & Pierce, J. (1968). Defense mechanisms. In E. Borgatta & W. Lambert (Eds.), *Handbook of personality theory and research.* Chicago: Rand-McNally.

Eriksen, C. W. (1956). Subception: Fact of artifact? *Psychological Review, 63,* 74–80.

Eriksen, C. W. (1960). Discrimination and learning without awareness: A methodological survey and evaluation. *Psychological Review, 67,* 279–300.

Erikson, E. (Ed.). (1978). *Adulthood,* New York: Norton.

Erikson, E. E. (1975). *Life history and the historical movement.* New York: Norton.

Erikson, E. H. (1945). Childhood and tradition in two American Indian tribes. In *Psychoanalytic study of the child,* Vol. 1. Universities Press.

Erikson, E. H. (1959). Identity and the life cycles. In *Psychological issues,* 1–1. New York: International Universities Press.

Erikson, E. H. (1963). Psychosocial crises in the life-cycle. Adapted from *Childhood and society.* New York: Norton.

Erikson, E. H. (1963/1950). *Childhood and society.* New York: Norton.

Erikson, E. H. (1964). Human strength and the cycle of generations. In *Insight and Responsibility.* New York: Norton.

Erikson, E. H. (1964). *Insight and responsibility.* New York: Norton.

Erikson, E. H. (1968). *Identity: Youth and crisis.* New York: Norton.

Erikson, E. H. (1969). *Gandhi's truth: On the origins of militant nonviolence.* New York: Norton.

Erikson, E. H. (1972). Autobiographic notes on the identity crisis. In G. Holton, (Ed.), *The 20th century sciences.* New York: Norton.

Erikson, E. H. (1977). *Toys and reasons.* New York: Norton.

Erikson, E. H. (1978/1958). *Young man Luther.* New York: Norton.

Erikson, E. H. (1980). *Identity and the life cycle.* New York: Norton.

Erikson, E. H. (1980). On the generational cycle: An address. *International Journal of Psychoanalysis, 2,* 213–223.

Erikson, E. H. (1982). *Configurations in children's play.* New York: Norton.

Erikson, E. H. (1982). *The life cycle completed.* New York: Norton.

Erikson, R., Luttbeg, N., & Tedin, K. (1980). *American public opinion: Its origins, content, and impact* (2nd ed.). New York: Wiley.

Erlenmeyer-Kimling, L., & Jarvik, L. F. (1963). Genetics and intelligence: A review. *Science, 142,* 1477–1479.

Ermarth, M. (1978). *Wilhelm Dilthey: The critique of historical reason,* Chicago: University of Chicago Press.

Ernhart, C. B., Sokol, R. J., Ager, J. W., Morrow-Tlucak, M., & Martier, S. (1989). Alcohol-related birth defects: Assessing the risk. *Annals of the New York Academy of Sciences, 592,* 159–172.

Erwin, E. (1978). *Behavior therapy: Scientific, philosophical and moral foundations.* New York: Cambridge University Press.

Escalona, S. (1954). The influence of topological and vector psychology upon current research in child development: An addendum. In L. Carmichael (Ed.), *Manual of child psychology.* New York: Wiley.

Escalona, S. K. (1953). Emotional development during the first year of life. *Transactions of the Josiah Macy, Jr., Foundation Conference on Infancy and Early Childhood,* 11–91.

Escalona, S. K. (1968) *The roots of individuality: Normal patterns of development in infancy.* Chicago: Aldine.

Escalona, S. K. (1973). Basic modes of social interaction: Their emergence during the first two years of life. *Merrill-Palmer Quarterly, 19*(3), 204–232.

Escalona, S. K. (1982). Babies at double hazard: Early development of infants at biologic and social risk. *Pediatrics, 70,* 670.

Escalona, S. K., & Bergman, P. (1949). Unusual sensitivities in very young children. *The Psychoanalytic Study of the Child, 3–4,* 333–352.

Escalona, S. K., & Corman, H. H. (1969). Stages of sensorimotor development: A replication study. *Merrill-Palmer Quarterly, 15*(4), 351–369.

Escalona, S. K., & Heider, G. (1959). *Prediction and outcome: A study of child development.* New York: Basic Books.

Escher, M. C. (1971). *The graphic work of M. C. Escher.* New York: Ballantine Books.

Esdaile, J. (1957/1847). *Hypnosis in medicine and surgery.* New York: Julian Press.

Esman, A. H. (1979). Some reflections on boredom. *Journal of the American Psychoanalytic Association, 27,* 432–439.

Espinoza, R., & Newman, Y. (1979). *Step-parenting.* DHEW Publication N(ADM) 78–579. Washington, D.C.: U.S. Government Printing Office.

Esquirol, J. E. D. (1845/1838). *Mental maladies.* Philadelphia, Pa.: Lea & Blanchard.

Essman, W. B. (1973). Nicotine-related neurochemical changes: Some implications for motivational mechanisms and differences. In W. L. Dunn (Ed.), *Smoking behavior: Motives and incentives.* Washington, D.C.: Winston.

Estabrook, A. H. (1916). *The Jukes in 1915.* Washington, D.C.: Carnegie Institute.

Estabrooks, G. H. (1927). *A contribution to experimental telepathy.* Boston: Boston Society for Psychical Research.

Estes, W. K. (1950). Toward a statistical theory of learning. *Psychological Review, 57,* 94—107.

Estes, W. K. (1959). Component and pattern models with Markovian interpretations. In R. R. Bush & W. K. Estes (Eds.), *Studies in mathematical learning theory.* Stanford, Calif.: Stanford University Press.

Estes, W. K. (1959). The statistical approach to learning theory. In S. Koch (Ed.), *Psychology: A study of a science,* (Vol. 2, pp. 380–391). New York: McGraw-Hill.

Estes, W. K. (1960). Learning theory and the new mental chemistry. *Psychological Review, 67,* 207–233.

Estes, W. K. (1981). Cognitive processes in reinforcement and choice. In G. d'Ydewalle & W. Lens (Eds.), *Cognition in human motivation and learning.* Louvain, Belgium: Leuven University Press.

Estes, W. K. (1988). Toward a framework for combining connectionist and symbol-processing models. *Journal of Memory and Language, 27,* 196–212.

Estes, W. K. (Ed.). (1975–1977). *Handbook of learning and cognitive processes.* Vol. 1–6. Hillsdale, N.J.: Erlbaum.

Estes, W. K., Koch, S., MacCorquodale, K., Meeht, P. E., Mueller, C. G., Jr., Schoenfeld, W. N., & Verplanck, W. S. (1954). *Modern learning theory.* New York: Appleton-Century-Crofts.

Estes, W. K., & Skinner, B. F. (1941). Some quantitative properties of anxiety. *Journal of Experimental Psychology, 29,* 390–400.

Ethical issues in research with animals. Symposium at the 88th annual meeting of the American Psychological Association, Montreal, Que., Canada, September 5, 1980.

ETS in fact, 1982. Princeton, N.J.: Educational Testing Service, 1982.

ETS publications, 1982. Princeton, N.J.: Educational Testing Service, 1982.

ETS. *Test use and validity: A response to charges in the Nader/Nairn report on ETS*. Princeton, N.J.: Educational Testing Service, 1980.

Etzioni, A. (1960). *The active Society*. New York: Free Press.

Etzioni, A. (1967). The Kennedy experiment. *The Western Political Quarterly, 20*, 361–380.

Eurich, A. C. (Ed.). (1981). *Major transitions in the human cycle*. Lexington, Mass.: Lexington.

Evans, C. (1967). An attempt at group therapy as a cure for the smoking habit. *Medical Journal of Australia, 2*(15), 702–705.

Evans, D. R., Gemeinhardt, M., Austin, G., Shatford, L., & Bolla, P. *Human adjustment: Skills*. Monterey, Calif.: Brooks/Cole, in press.

Evans, D. R., Hearn, M. T., Uhlemann, M. R., & Ivey, A. E. (1979). *Essential interviewing*. Monterey, Calif.: Brooks/Cole.

Evans, E. (1975/1971). *Contemporary influences in early childhood education* (2nd ed.). New York: Holt, Rinehart & Winston.

Evans, F. B. (1959). Psychological and objective factors in the prediction of brand choice: Ford vs. Chevrolet. *Journal of Business*, 340–369.

Evans, F. J. (1981). The placebo response in pain control. *Psychopharmacology Bulletin, 17*, 72–76.

Evans, I. M., & Smith, P. A. (1970). *Psychology for a changing world*. New York: Wiley.

Evans, J. R. (1980). *Consumerism in the United States: An inter-industry analysis*. New York: Praeger.

Evans, R. B. (1972). Karl Dallenbach: 1887–1971. *American Journal of Psychology, 85*, 463–476.

Evans, R. B., Sexton, V. S., & Cadwallader, T. C. (1992). *100 years of the American Psychological Association: A historical Perspective*. Washington, DC: American Psychological Association.

Evans, R. I. (1952). Personal values as factors in antisemitism. *Journal of Abnormal and Social Psychology, 47*(4), 749–756.

Evans, R. I. (1955). A theoretical examination of individual differences among high and low scorers of the F scale. *American Psychologist, 10*, 169.

Evans, R. I. (1955). An evaluation of the effectiveness of instruction and audience reaction to programming on an educational television station. *Journal of Applied Psychology, 39*(4), 277–279.

Evans, R. I. (1955). The planning and implementation of a psychology series on a non-commercial educational television station. *American Psychologist, 10*, 602–605.

Evans, R. I. (1961). A psychological investigation of a group of demographic, personality and behavioral variables as they relate to viewing educational television. *Journal of Applied Psychology, 45*, 25–29.

Evans, R. I. (1975). *Konrad Lorenz: The man and his ideas*. New York: Harcourt Brace Jovanovich.

Evans, R. I. (1976). Smoking in children: Developing a social psychological strategy of deterrence. *Preventive Medicine, 5*, 122–127.

Evans, R. I. (1976). *The making of psychology: Discussions with creative contributors*. New York: Random House/Knopf.

Evans, R. I. (1980). A new applied challenge to social psychologists: Behavioral medicine. In L. Bickman (Ed.), *Applied social psychology annual*, Vol. 1. Beverly Hills, Calif.: Sage Publications.

Evans, R. I. (1980). *The making of social psychology*. New York: Gardner Press.

Evans, R. I. (1981). *Dialogue with B. F. Skinner*. New York: Praeger.

Evans, R. I. (1981). *Dialogue with Carl Rogers*. New York: Praeger.

Evans, R. I. (1981). *Dialogue with C. G. Jung*. New York: Praeger.

Evans, R. I. (1981). *Dialogue with Erich Fromm*. New York: Praeger.

Evans, R. I. (1981). *Dialogue with Gordon Allport*. New York: Praeger.

Evans, R. I. (1981). *Dialogue with Jean Piaget*. New York: Praeger.

Evans, R. I. (1981). *Dialogue with R. D. Laing*. New York: Praeger.

Evans, R. I. (1981). *Psychology and Arthur Miller*. New York: Praeger.

Evans, R. I. (1981/1967). *Dialogue with Erik Erikson*. New York: Praeger.

Evans, R. I., & Borgatta, E. F. (1970). An experiment in smoking dissuasion among university freshmen: A followup. *Journal of Health and Social Behavior, 11*, 30–36.

Evans, R. I., Hansen, W., & Mittelmark, M. (1977). Increasing validity of self reports of behavior in a smoking in children investigation. *Journal of Applied Psychology, 62*, 521–523.

Evans, R. I., Henderson, A. H., Hill,, P. C., & Raines, B. E. (1979). Current psychological, social, and educational programs in control and prevention of smoking: A critical methodological review. In A. M. Gotto & R. Paoletti (Eds.), *Atherosclerosis reviews*, Vol. 6. New York: Raven Press.

Evans, R. I., Henderson, A. H., Hill, P. C., & Raines, B. E. (1979). Smoking in children and adolescents: Psychosocial determinants and prevention strategies. Chapter 17 in U.S. Public Health Services: *Smoking and health: A report of the Surgeon General*. Washington, D.C.: U.S. Department of Health, Education and Welfare.

Evans, R. I., & Leppman, P. K. (1970). *Resistance to innovation in higher education: A social psychological exploration focused on television and the establishment*. San Francisco: Jossey-Bass.

Evans, R. I., & Rozelle, R. M. (1973). *Social psychology in life*. Boston: Allyn & Bacon.

Evans, R. I., Rozelle, R. M., Lasater, T. M., & Allen, B. P. (1970). Fear arousal, persuasion and actual vs. implied behavioral change: New perspective utilizing a real-life dental hygiene program. *Journal of Personality and Social Psychology, 16*, 220–227.

Evans, R. I., Rozelle, R. M., Maxwell, S. E., Raines, B. E., Dill, C. A., Guthrie, T. J., Henderson, A. H., & Hill, P. C. (1981). Social modeling films to deter smoking in adolescents: Results of a three year field investigation. *Journal of Applied Psychology, 66*(4), 399–414.

Evans, R. I., Rozelle, R. M., Mittelmark, M. B., Hansen, W. B., Bane, A. L., & Havis, J. G. (1978). Deterring the onset of smoking in children: Knowledge of immediate physiological effects and coping with peer pressure, media pressure and parent modeling. *Journal of Applied Social Psychology, 8*(2), 126–135.

Evans, R. I., Wieland, B. A., & Moore, C. W. (1961). An examination of the differential effects on viewers of experience in taking telecourses on attitudes toward instruction by television and the social psychological impact of a controversial educational television program. *Journal of Applied Psychology, 45*, 326–329.

Evans, S. L., Reinhart, J. B., & Succop, R. A. (1972). Failure to thrive: A study of forty-five children and their families. *American Academy of Child Psychiatry Journal, 11*, 440–457.

Evans, T., & Denny, M. R. (1978). Emotionality of pictures and the retention of related and unrelated phrases. *Bulletin of the Psychonomic Society, 11*, 149–152.

Evans, W. (1912). *The great doctrines of the Bible*. Chicago: Moody Press.

Evans-Wentz, W. Y. (Ed.). (1973). *Tibetan Yoga and secret doctrines*. New York: Oxford University Press.

Everett, E. C. C. (1892). *Fichte's science of knowledge*, Chicago: Grigg.

Everitt, B. (1974). *Cluster analysis*. London: Heinemann.

Everly, G. S., & Rosenfeld, R. (1981). *The nature and treatment of the stress response*. New York: Plenum.

Everstine, L., Everstine, D. S., Heyman, G. M., True, R. H., Frey, D. H., Johnson, H. G. J., & Seiden, R. W. (1980). Privacy and confidentiality in psychotherapy. *American Psychologist, 35*, 838.

Everts, J. (1988). The marae-based Hui: Intensive induction to cross-cultural counselling, a New Zealand experiment. *International Journal for the Advancement of Counselling, 11*, 97–104.

Ewen, R. B. (1980). *An introduction to theories of personality*. New York: Academic Press.

Exner, J. E. (1980). Diagnosis versus description in competency issues. In F. Wright, C. Bahn, & R. W. Rieber (Eds.), *Forensic psychology and psychiatry*. New York: New York Academy of Sciences.

Exner, J. E. (1974). *The Rorschach: A comprehensive system*. New York: Wiley/ Interscience.

Exner, J. E. (1978). *The Rorschach: A comprehensive system*. Vol. 2: *Current research and advanced interpretations*. New York: Wiley/ Interscience.

Exner, J. E., Jr. (1974). *The Rorschach: A comprehensive system* (Vol. 1) New York: Wiley.

Exner, J. E., Jr., & Sutton-Smith, B. (1971). Birth order, and hierarchical versus innovative role requirements. Unpublished manuscript, Long Island University.

Eyberg, S., & Boggs, S. R. (1989). Parent training for oppositional-defiant preschoolers. In C. E. Schaefer & J. M. Briesmeister (Eds.), *Handbook of parent training: Parents as co-therapists for children's behavior problems* (pp. 105–132). New York: Wiley.

Eysenck, H. J. (1939). Primary mental abilities. *British Journal of Educational Psychology, 9, 270–275.*

Eysenck, H. J. (1941). The empirical determination of an aesthetic formula. *Psychological Review, 48*, 83–92.

Eysenck, H. J. (1947). *Dimensions of personality*. London: Routledge & Kegan Paul.

Eysenck, H. J. (1947). Types of personality. *Journal of Mental Sciences, 90*, 851–861.

Eysenck, H. J. (1952). The effects of psychotherapy: An evaluation. *Journal of Consulting Psychology, 16*, 319–324.

Eysenck, H. J. (1952). *The scientific study of personality*. London: Routledge & Kegan Paul.

Eysenck, H. J. (1953). *Uses and abuses of psychology*. Baltimore, Md.: Penguin Books.

Eysenck, H. J. (1954). *The psychology of politics*. London: Routledge & Kegan Paul.

Eysenck, H. J. (1955). A dynamic theory of anxiety and hysteria. *Journal of Mental Science, 101*, 28–51.

Eysenck, H. J. (1957). Characterology, stratification theory, and psychoanalysis. In H. P. David & H. von Bracken (Eds.), *Perspectives in personality theory*. London: Tavistock.

Eysenck, H. J. (1958). *Sense and nonsense in psychology* (rev. ed.). Baltimore, Md.: Pelica.

Eysenck, H. J. (1959). *Das 'Maudsley Personality Inventory' MPI*. Göttingen, West Germany: Hogrefe.

Eysenck, H. J. (1959). Learning theory and behaviour therapy. *Journal of Mental Science, 195*, 61–75.

Eysenck, H. J. (1961). The effects of psychotherapy. In H. J. Eysenck (Ed.), *Handbook of abnormal psychology*. (pp. 697–725). New York: Basic Books.

Eysenck, H. J. (1964). The nature of behaviour therapy. In H. J. Eysenck (Ed.), *Experiments in behaviour therapy*. Oxford: Pergamon Press.

Eysenck, H. J. (1966). *The effects of psychotherapy*. New York: International Science.

Eysenck, H. J. (1967). Personality and extrasensory perception. *Journal of the Society for Psychical Research, 44*, 55–71.

Eysenck, H. J. (1967). *The biological basis of personality*. Springfield, Ill.: Thomas.

Eysenck, H. J. (1970). *The structure of human personality*. London: Methuen.

Eysenck, H. J. (1971). Factors determining aesthetic preference for geometrical designs and devices. *British Journal of Aesthetics, 11*, 154–166.

Eysenck, H. J. (1971). *The IQ argument: Race, intelligence, and Education*. New York: Library Press.

Eysenck, H. J. (1972). Traits. In H. J. Eysenck, W. Arnold, & R. Meili (Eds.), *Encyclopedia of psychology*, Vol. 3. New York: Herder & Herder.

Eysenck, H. J. (1973). *Eysenck on extraversion*. New York: Wiley.

Eysenck, H. J. (1973). Personality and maintenance of the smoking habit. In W. L. Dunn (Ed.), *Smoking behavior: Motives and incentives*. Washington, D.C.: Winston.

Eysenck, H. J. (1973). *Race, intelligence, and education*. London: Smith.

Eysenck, H. J. (1973). *The inequality of man*. London: Smith.

Eysenck, H. J. (1973). *The measurement of intelligence*. Lancaster, England: Medical & Technical.

Eysenck, H. J. (1976). Ideology run wild. *American Psychologist, 31*, 311–312.

Eysenck, H. J. (1977). Personality and factor analysis. A reply to Guilford. *Psychological Bulletin, 84*, 405–411.

Eysenck, H. J. (1979). Behavior therapy and the philosophers. *Behaviour Research and Therapy, 17*, 511–514.

Eysenck, H. J. (1980). A comment on the Traxel-Lienert discussion regarding publication in English by German psychologists. *Psychologische Beiträge, 22*, 372–376.

Eysenck, H. J. (1980). Hans Jürgen Eysenck. In G. Lindzey (Ed.), *A history of psychology in autobiography*, Vol. 7. San Francisco: Freeman.

Eysenck, H. J. (1982). The psychophysiology of intelligence. In C. D. Spielberger, & J. N. Butcher (Eds.), *Advances in personality assessment*, Vol. 1. Hillsdale, N.J.: Erlbaum.

Eysenck, H. J. (Ed.). (1960). *Behaviour therapy and the neuroses*. New York: Pergamon Press.

Eysenck, H. J. (Ed.). (1964). *Experiments in behavior therapy: Readings in modern methods of mental disorders derived from learning theory*. Oxford: Pergamon Press.

Eysenck, H. J. (Ed.). (1981). *A model for personality*. Berlin, Heidelberg, New York: Springer.

Eysenck, H. J. (Ed.). (1982). *A model for intelligence*. Berlin: Springer-Verlag.

Eysenck, H. J., & Eysenck, S. B. G. (1969). *Personality structure and measurement*. London: Routledge & Kegan Paul.

Eysenck, H. J., & Fuller, D. (1979). *The structure and measurement of intelligence*. Berlin, Heidelberg, New York: Springer.

Eysenck, H. J., & Iwawaki, S. (1971). Cultural relativity in aesthetic judgments: An empirical study. *Perceptual and Motor Skills, 32*, 817–818.

Eysenck, H. J., & Kamin, L. (1981). *The intelligence controversy.* New York: Wiley.

Eysenck, H. J., Wakefield, J. A., Jr., & Friedman, A. F. (1983). Diagnosis and clinical assessment: The DSM-III. *Annual Review of Psychology, 34,* 167–193.

Eysenck, M. W. (1982). *Attention and arousal: Cognition and performance.* Berlin: Springer Verlag.

Eysenck, M. W., & Eysenck, H. J. (1980). Mischel and the concept of personality. *British Journal of Psychology, 71,* 191–204.

Ezekiel, M., & Fox, K. A. (1959). *Methods of correlation and regression analysis.* New York: Wiley.

Ezriel, H. (1950). A psychoanalytic approach to group treatment. *British Journal of Medical Psychology, 23,* 59–74.

Fabisch, W. (1980). Psychiatric aspects of dermatitis artefacta. *British Journal of Dermatology, 102,* 29–34.

Fabrikant, B., Barron, J., & Krasner, J. D. (1977). *To enjoy is to live.* Chicago: Nelson-Hall.

Factor, M. (1954). A woman's psychological reaction to attempted rape. *Psychoanalytic Quarterly, 23,* 243–244.

Facultad de Psicologia. (1979). *Organizacion academica 1979–1980.* Secretaria de la Rectoria, Direccion General de Orientacion Vocacional. Mexico D.F.: Universidad Nacional Autonoma de Mexico.

Faderman, L. (1991). *Odd girls and twilight lovers: A history of lesbian life in twentieth century American.* New York: Columbia University Press.

Fagan, M. J., & Shepherd, I. L. (1970). *Gestalt therapy now.* Palo Alto, Calif.: Science & Behavior Books.

Fagot, B. I. (1978). The influence of sex of child on parental reactions to toddler children. *Child Development, 49,* 459–465.

Fahrenberg, J. (1967). *Psychophysiologische Persönlichkeitsforschung.* Göttingen: Hogrefe.

Fairchild, T. N., & Henson, F. O. (1976). *Mainstreaming exceptional children.* Austin, Tex.: Learning Concepts.

Fairweather, G. W., Sanders, D. H., & Tornatzky, L. G. (1974). *Creating change in mental health organizations.* New York: Pergamon Press.

Fairweather, G. W., & Tornatzky, L. G. (1977). *Experimental methods for social policy research.* Oxford: Pergamon Press.

Falbo, T. (1977). The only child: A review. *Journal of Individual Psychology, 33,* 47–61.

Falbo, T. (1981). *The consequences of being and having an only child on intelligence, interpersonal orientation, attitudes, and time use* (National Technical Information Service Report no. NICHD/CPR/ SBSB/82–3 submitted to the U.S. Department of Commerce). Austin, Tex.: University of Texas.

Falconer, D. S. (1960). *An introduction to quantitative genetics.* New York: Ronald Press.

Falk, J. S. (1973). *Linguistics and language.* Lexington, Mass.: Xerox.

Fallon, D. (1977). *The German university.* Boulder, Colo.: Colorado Associated University Press.

Fallows, J. (1981). *National defense.* New York: Random House.

Falls, J. B. (1988). Does song deter territorial intrusion in white-throated sparrows *(Zonotrichia albicollis)? Canadian Journal of Zoology, 66,* 206–211.

Faludi, S. (1991). *Backlash: The undeclared war against American women.* New York: Crown.

Fancher, R. E. (1973). *Psychoanalytic psychology: The development of Freud's thought.* New York: Norton.

Fancher, R. E. (1979). *Pioneers of psychology.* New York: Norton.

Fang, G., & Liu, F. (1981a). The development of children's cognition of velocity of moving objects (I). *Acta Psychologica Sinica, 13,* 21–29.

Fang, G., & Liu, F. (1981b). The development of children's cognition of velocity of moving objects (II). *Acta Psychologica Sinica, 13,* 273–279.

Fann, W. E., Smith, R. C., Davis, J. M., & Domino, E. F. (1980). *Tardive dyskinesia.* Jamaica, N.Y.: Spectrum.

Fantino, E., & Logan, C. A. (1979). *The experimental analysis of behavior: A biological perspective.* San Francisco: Freeman.

Fantuzzo, J. W., DePaola, L. M., Lambert, L., Martino, T., Anderson, G., & Sutton, S. (1991). Effects of interparental violence on the psychological adjustment and competencies of young children. *Journal of Consulting and Clinical Psychology, 59,* 258–265.

Fantz, R. L. (1961). The origin of form perception. *Scientific American, 204*(5), 66–72.

Fantz, R. L. (1963). Pattern Vision in Newborn Infants. *Science, 140,* 296–297.

Fantz, R. L., & Nevis, S. (1967). Pattern preferences and perceptual-cognitive development in early infancy. *Merrill-Palmer Quarterly, 13,* 77–108.

Farber, S. L. (1981). *Identical twins reared apart: A reanalysis.* New York: Basic Books.

Farberow, N. L. (1980). Indirect self-destructive behavior in diabetics and Buerger's disease patients. In N. L. Farberow (Ed.), *The many faces of suicide: Indirect self-destructive behavior.* New York: McGraw-Hill.

Farberow, N. L. (Ed.). (1961). Part II—The therapeutic response to the cry for help. In N. L. Farberow & E. S. Shneidman (Eds.), *The cry for help.* New York: McGraw-Hill.

Farberow, N. L. (Ed.). (1972/1969). *Bibliography on suicide and suicide prevention, 1897–1970.* Washington, D.C.: U.S. Department of Health, Education and Welfare (HSM) 72–9080.

Farberow, N. L. (Ed.). (1980). *The many faces of suicide.* New York: McGraw-Hill.

Farberow, N. L., & Shneidman, E. S. (Eds.). (1961). *The cry for help.* New York: McGraw-Hill.

Farley, F. H. (1978). Note on creativity and scholastic achievement of women as a function of birth order and family size. *Perceptual and Motor Skills, 47*(1), 13–14.

Farley, F. H., & Davis, S. A. (1977). Arousal, personality, assortative mating in marriage. *Journal of Sex and Marital Therapy, 3,* 122–127.

Farley, F. H., & Weinstock, C. A. (1980). Experimental aesthetics: Children's complexity preference in original art and photoreproductions. *Bulletin of the Psychonomic Society, 15,* 194–196.

Farmer, R., & Sundberg, N. D. (1986). Boredom proneness—The development and correlates of a new scale. *Journal of Personality Assessment, 50,* 4–17.

Farmer, R. H. (1978). Alcoholism. In R. M. Goldenson, J. R. Dunham, & C. S. Dunham (Eds.), *Disability and rehabilitation handbook.* New York: McGraw-Hill.

Farnsworth, P. R. (1969). *The social psychology of music* (2nd ed.). Iowa City, Iowa: State University of Iowa Press.

Farquhar, W. W., & Payne, D. A. (1964). A classification and comparison of techniques used in selecting under- and overachievers. *Personnel and Guidance Journal. 42,* 874–884.

Farr, C. H. (1922). The psychology of plants. *Atlantic Monthly, 130,* 775–783.

Farr, J. N., Jenkins, J. J., & Patterson, D. G. (1951). Simplification of Flesch Reading Ease Formula. *Journal of Applied Psychology, 35*, 333–337.

Farrell, M. P., & Rosenberg, S. D. (1981). *Men at midlife.* Boston: Auburn House.

Farrelley, F., & Brandsma, J. (1974). *Provocative therapy.* Cupertino, Calif.: Meta.

Farrington, D. P. (1991). Long-term prediction of offending and other life outcomes. In H. Wegener, F. Losel & J. Haisch (Eds.), *Criminal behavior and the justice system: Psychological perspectives* (pp. 26–39). New York: Springer-Verlag.

Farrington, D. R. (1983). Offending from 10 to 25 years of age. In K. T. Van Dusen & S. A. Mednick (Eds.), *Antisocial and prosocial behavior* (pp. 17–38). Boston: Kluwer-Nijhoff.

Farrington, D. R. (1989). Long-term prediction of offending and other life outcomes. In H. Wegener, F. Losel, & J. Haisch (Eds.), *Criminal behavior and the justice system: Psychological perspectives* (pp. 26–39). New York: Springer-Verlag.

Farrington, D. R., & West, D. J. (1981). The Cambridge study in delinquent development (United Kingdom). In S. A. Mednick & A. E. Baert (Eds.), *Prospective longitudinal research: An empirical basis for the primary prevention of psychosocial disorders.* New York: Oxford University Press.

Farris, H. E. (1967). Classical conditioning of courting behavior in the Japanese quail, *Coturnix coturnix japonica. Journal of the Experimental Analysis of Behavior, 10*, 213–217.

Farrow, J. T., & Hebert, J. R. (1982). Breath suspension during the Transcendental Meditation technique *Psychosomatic Medicine, 44*(2), 133–153.

Farson, R. (1978). The technology of humanism. *Journal of Humanistic Psychology, 18*, 5–35

Farwell, L. A. (1990). Personal communication.

Farwell, L. A., & Donchin, E. (1986). The "Brain detector": P300 in the detection of deception [Abstract]. *Psychophysiology, 23*(4), 434.

Farwell, L. A., & Donchin, E. (1989). Detection of guilty knowledge with ERPs [Abstract]. *Supplement to Psychophysiology, 26*(4A).

Farwell, L. A., & Donchin, E. (1988). Event-related potentials in interrogative polygraphy: Analysis using bootstrapping [Abstract]. *Psychophysiology, 25*(4), 445.

Fauconnet, P. (1920). *La responsibilite, étude de sociologie.* Paris: Alcan.

Faunce, P. S. (1985). A feminist philosophy of treatment. In L. B. Rosewater & L. E. A. Walker (Eds.), *Handbook on feminist therapy: Women's issues in psychotherapy.* New York: Springer.

Faust, D., Guilmette, T. J., Hart, K., Arkes, H. R., Fishburne, F. J., & Daves, L. (1988). Neuropsychologists: training, experience, and judgment accuracy. *Archives of Clinical Neuropsychology, 3*, 145–163.

Faust, D., & Ziskin, J. (1988). The expert witness in psychology and psychiatry. *Science, 241*, 31–35.

Faust, W. (1959). Group versus individual problem solving. *Journal of Abnormal and Social Psychology, 59*, 68–72.

Fawcett, J., Maas, J. W., & Dokirmenjiam, H. (1972). Depression and MHPG excretion. Response to dextroamphetamine and tricyclic antidepressants. *Archives of General Psychiatry. 26*, 246–251.

Fawcett, S. B., Seekins, T., Whang, P. L., Muiu, C., & Suarez de Balacazar, Y. (1984). Creating and using social technologies for community empowerment. In J. Rappaport, C. Swift & R. Hess (Eds.), *Studies in empowerment: Steps toward understanding and action* (pp. 145–171).

Fay, R. E., Turner, C. F., Klassen, A. D., & Gagnon, J. H. (1989). Prevalance and patterns of same-gender sexual contact among men. *Science, 243*, 343–348.

Fazio, R. H., Zanna, M. P., & Cooper, J. (1977). Dissonance and self-perception: An integrative view of each theory's proper domain of application. *Journal of Experimental Social Psychology, 13*, 464–479.

Feather, N. T. (1962). Cigarette smoking and lung cancer: A study of cognitive dissonance. *Australian Journal of Psychology, 14*, 55–64.

Feather, N. T. (1975). *Values in Education and society.* New York: Free Press.

Feather, N. T. (1982). *Expectations and actions: Expectancy-value models in psychology.* Hillsdale, N.J.: Erlbaum.

Featherman, D. L. (1971). A research note: A social structure model for the socioeconomic career, *American Journal of Sociology, 77*, 293–304.

Featherman, D. L. (1973). Comments on models for the socioeconomic career. *American Sociological Review, 38*, 785–791.

Fechner, G. T. (1897). *Vorschule der Aesthetik* Leipzig: Breithopf & Haertel.

Fechner, G. T. (1960). Elements of psychophysics. New York: Holt, Rinehart & Winston. (Original work published in 1860)

Fechner, G. T. (1966;1860). *Elements of psychophysics,* Vol. I. D. H. Howes & E. G. Boring (Eds.), New York: Holt, Rinehart & Winston. German edition.

Feder, B., & Ronall, R. (Eds.). (1980). *Beyond the hot seat: Gestalt approaches to group.* New York: Brunner/Mazel.

Feder, E., & Feder, B. (1981). *Expressive arts therapies.* Englewood Cliffs, N.J.: Prentice-Hall.

Federal Register, December 29, 1977, 42,(250).

Federal Trade Commission staff report on television advertising to children. *Advertising Age,* February 27, 1978, 73–77.

Federman, D. D. (1967). *Abnormal sexual development: A genetic and endocrine approach to differential diagnosis.* Philadelphia: Saunders.

Federn, P. (1952). *Ego psychology and the psychoses.* New York: Basic Books.

Fedler, F. (1978). *An introduction to the mass media.* New York: Harcourt Brace Jovanovich.

Feger, H., & Westhoff, K. (1976). Germany: Psychology. In B. B. Wolman (Ed.), *International encyclopedia of psychiatry, psychology, psychoanalysis, and neurology,* Vol. 5. New York: Van Nostrand.

Fehr, L., & Stamps, L. (1979). Guilt and shyness: A profile of social discomfort. *Journal of Personality Assessment, 43*(5), 481–484.

Feifel, H. (1977/1959). *New meanings of death.* New York: McGraw-Hill.

Feifel, H., & Nagy, V. T. (1980). Death orientation and life-threatening behavior. *Journal of Abnormal Psychology, 89*, 38–45.

Feifel, H., & Nagy, V. T. (1981). Another look at fear of death. *Journal of Consulting and Clinical Psychology, 49*, 278–286.

Feifel, H., & Schwartz, A. D. (1953). Group psychotherapy with acutely disturbed psychotic patients. *Journal of Consulting Psychology, 17*, 113–121.

Feigenberg, L. (1980). *Terminal care: Friendship contracts with dying cancer patients.* New York: Brunner/Mazel.

Feighner, J. P., Robins, E., Guze, S. B., Woodruff, R. A., Winokur, G., & Munoz, R. (1972). Diagnostic criteria for use in psychiatric research. *Archives of General Psychiatry, 26*, 57–63.

Feigl, H. (1953). The mind-body problem in the development of logical empiricism. In H. Feigl & M. Brodbeck (Eds.), *Readings in the philosophy of science*. New York: Appleton-Century-Crofts.

Fein, G. G. (1981). Pretend play in childhood: An integrative review. *Child Development, 52,* 1095–1118.

Fein, G. G., & Clarke-Stewart, A. (1973). *Day care in context.* New York: Wiley/Interscience.

Feinberg, M. R., Feinberg, G., & Tarrant, J. J. (1978). *Leavetaking.* New York: Simon & Schuster.

Feinberg, W., & Rapcsak, S. (1989). "Peduncular hallucinosis" following paramedian thalamic infarction, *Neurology, 39* 1535–1536.

Feingold, B. F. (1974). *Why your child is hyperactive.* New York: Random House.

Feinman, S. (1981). Why is cross-sex role behavior more approved for girls than for boys? A status characteristic approach. *Sex Roles, 7,* 289–300.

Feiring, C., & Lewis, M. (1978). The child as a member of the family system. *Behavioral Science, 23,* 225–233.

Feldenkrais, M. (1972). *Awareness through movement.* New York: Harper & Row.

Feldhusen, J. (1977). Issues in teaching undergraduate educational psychology courses. In D. J. Treffinger, J. K. Davis, & R. E. Ripple (Eds.), *Handbook on teaching educational psychology*. New York: Academic Press.

Feldman, B. (1969). *Prediction of first grade reading achievement from selected structure-of-intellect factors*. Doctoral dissertation, University of Southern California.

Feldman, D. (1980). *Beyond universals in cognitive development*. Norwood, N.J.: Ablex.

Feldman, G. C. (1976). *The only child as a separate entity*. Ph.D. dissertation, University of New Mexico.

Feldman, J. A. (Ed.). (1985). Special issue on connectionist models and their applications. *Cognitive Science, 9,* 1–169.

Feldman, K. V. (1974). *Instructional factors relating to children's principle learning* (Technical Report no. 309). Madison, Wis.: Wisconsin Research and Development Center for Cognitive Learning.

Feldman, K. V., & Klausmeier, H. J. (1974). Effects of two kinds of definition on the concept attainment of fourth and eighth graders. *Journal of Educational Research, 67,* 219–223.

Feldman, M. P. (1977). *Criminal behavior: A psychological analysis*. New York: Wiley.

Feldman, R., Jenkins, L., & Popoola, O. (1979). Detection of deception in adults and children via facial expressions. *Child Development, 50,* 350–355.

Feldman, R. S., & Rimé, B. (Eds.). (1991) *Fundamentals of nonverbal behavior*. Cambridge, UK: Cambridge University Press.

Feldman, S. (1990). Varicella (chickenpox). In R. L. Summitt (Ed.), *Comprehensive pediatrics*, (pp. 878–881). St. Louis, MO: Mosby.

Feldman, S. (Ed.). (1992). *Managed mental health services*. Springfield, IL: Thomas.

Feldman, S. S., Biringen, Z. C., & Nash, S. C. (1981). Fluctuations of sex-related self-attributions as a function of stage of family life cycle. *Developmental psychology, 17,* 24–35.

Feldstein, S., & Jaffe, J. (1962). Vocabulary diversity of schizophrenics and normals. *Journal Of Speech and Hearing Research, 5,* 76–78.

Felgi, H. (1967). *The "mental" and the "physical."* Minneapolis: University of Minnesota Press.

Felner, R., Stolberg, A., & Cowen, E. (1975). Crises events and school mental health referral patterns of young children. *Journal of Counsulting and Clinical Psychology, 43,* 305–310.

Felner, R. D., Ginter, M., & Primavera, J. (1982). Primary prevention during school transitions: Social support and environmental structure. *American Journal of Community Psychology, 10,* 277–290.

Felner, R. D., Jason, L. A., Moritsugu, J. N., & Farber, S. S. (1983). *Preventive psychology: Theory, research and practice*. New York: Pergamon.

Felthous, A. R. (1979). Competency to waive counsel: A step beyond competency to stand trial. *Journal of Psychiatry and Law, 7,* 471–478.

Fenichel, O. (1945). *The psychoanalytic theory of neurosis*. New York: Norton.

Fenichel, O. (1951). On the psychology of boredom. In D. Rappaport (Ed.), *Organization and pathology of thought* (pp. 349–361). New York: Columbia University Press.

Fennema, E., & Sherman, J. (1977). Sex-related differences in mathematics achievement, spatial visualization, and sociocultural factors. *American Educational Research Journal, 14,* 51–71.

Fensterheim, H., & Baer, J. (1975). *Don't say yes when you want to say no.* New York: Dell.

Fenstermaker, D. (1991, February). *An innovative abreactive process for dissociative disorders: Eye movement desensitization and reprocessing* (EMDR). Paper presented at the meeting of the California Psychological Association conference, San Diego.

Fenstermacher, G. D. (1982). Three nonradical proposals for strengthening Ebel's argument. *Phi Delta Kappan, 63,* 379–380.

Fenton, G., & McRae, D. (1989). Musical hallucinations in a deaf elderly woman. *British Journal of Psychiatry, 155,* 401–403.

Ferenczi, S. (1916). *Contributions to psychoanalysis*. Boston: Badger.

Ferenczi, S. (1916). *Stages in the development of the sense of reality*. Boston: Badger.

Ferenczi, S. (1921). Psycho-analytic observations on tic. *International Journal of Psycho-Analysis, 2,* 1–30.

Ferenczi, S. (1926). *Further contributions to the theory and technique of psychoanalysis*. London: Institute of Psychoanalysis.

Ferenczi, S., (1938). *Thalassa: A theory of genitality. The Psychoanalytic Quarterly.*

Ferenczi, S. (1950–1955). *Selected papers* (3 vols.). New York: Basic Books.

Ferenczi, S. (1950/1913). Stages in the development of the sense of reality. In S. Ferenczi (Ed.), *Sex in psychoanalysis*, Vol. 1. New York: Basic Books.

Ferenczi, S., & Rank, O., (1925). *The development of psychoanalysis.* New York; Washington, D.C.: Nervous and Mental Disease.

Ferguson, E. D. (1958). The effect of sibling competition and alliance on level of aspiration, expectation, and performance. *Journal of Abnormal and Social Psychology, 56,* 213–222.

Ferguson, E. D. (1964). The use of early recollections for assessing life style and diagnosing psychopathology. *Journal of Projective Techniques and Personality Assessment, 28,* 403–412.

Ferguson, E. D. (1981). Anxiety and performance: Each affects the other one. Presented at the meeting of the American Psychological Association, Los Angeles, August.

Ferguson, E. D. (1982/1976). *Motivation: An experimental approach*. Melbourne, Fla.: Krieger.

Ferguson, G. A. (1949). On the theory of test discrimination. *Psychometrika, 14,* 61–68.

Ferguson, G. A. (1948/1941). *The reliability of mental tests*. London: University of London Press.

Ferguson, G. A. (1981). *Statistical analysis in psychology and education* (5th ed.). New York: McGraw-Hill.

Ferguson, L. W. (1961). The development of industrial psychology. In B. von Haller Gilmer (Ed.), *Industrial psychology*. New York: McGraw-Hill.

Ferguson, M. (1979). Special issue: Prigogine's science of becoming. *Brain/Mind Bulletin, 4,*(13).

Ferguson, M. (1980). *The Aquarian conspiracy: Personal and social transformations in the 1980s*. Los Angeles: Tarcher.

Fernald, G. M. (1943). *Remedial techniques in basic school subjects*. New York: McGraw-Hill.

Fernald, G. M., & Keller, H. (1921). The effect of kinesthetic factors in development of word recognition in the case of nonreaders. *Journal of Educational Research, 4,* 357–377.

Fernandez, J. (1978). Passage to community: Encounter groups in evolutionary perspective. In K. W. Back (Ed.), *In search of community: Encounter groups and social change*. Boulder, Colo.: Westview Press.

Ferraz, M. (1869). *De la psychologie de Saint Augustin* (2nd ed.). Paris: Thorin.

Ferrier, D. (1876). *The functions of the brain*. London: Smith, Elder.

Ferster, C. B. (1961). Positive reinforcement and behavioral deficits of autistic children. *32,* 437–456.

Ferster, C. B. (1973). A functional analysis of depression. *American Psychologist, 28,* 857–870.

Ferster, C. B., Nurnberger, J. I., & Levitt, E. B. (1962). The control of eating. *Journal of Mathetics, 1,* 87–109.

Ferster, C. B., & Perrott, M. C. (1973/1968). *Behavior principles*. New York: Appleton-Century-Crofts.

Ferster, C. B., & Skinner, B. F. (1957). *Schedules of reinforcement*. New York: Appleton-Century-Crofts.

Feshbach, S. (1970). Aggression. In P. H. Mussen (Ed.), *Carmichael's manual of child psychology*, Vol. 2. New York. Wiley.

Feshback, N. & Roe, K. (1968). Empathy in six- and seven-year-olds. *Child Development, 39,* 133–145.

Festinger, L. (1950). Informal social communication. *Psychological Review, 57,* 271–282.

Festinger, L. (1954). A theory of social comparison processes. *Human Relations, 7,* 117–140.

Festinger, L. (1957). *A theory of cognitive dissonance*. Stanford, Calif.: Stanford University Press.

Festinger, L. (1961). The psychological effects of insufficient rewards. *American Psychologist, 16,* 1–11.

Festinger, L. (1964). *Conflict, decision, and dissonance*. Stanford, Calif.: Stanford University Press.

Festinger, L., & Carlsmith, J. M. (1959). Cognitive consequences of forced compliance. *Journal of Abnormal and Social Psychology, 58,* 203–210.

Festinger, L. (Ed.). (1980). *Retrospectives in social psychology*. New York: Oxford University Press.

Festinger, L., et al. (1950). *Theory and experiment in social communications*. Ann Arbor, Mich.: Institute of Social Research.

Festinger, L, & Katz, D. (Eds.). (1953). *Research methods in the behavioral sciences*. New York: Dryden.

Festinger, L., & Lawrence, D. H. (1962). *Deterrents and reinforcement: The psychology of insufficient reward*. Stanford, Calif.: Stanford University Press.

Festinger, L. Pepitone, A., & Newcomb, T. (1952). Some consequences of deindividuation in a group. *Journal of Abnormal and Social Psychology, 47,* 382–389.

Festinger, L., Riecken, H. W., & Schachter, S. (1956). *When prophecy fails*, Minneapolis, Minn.: University of Minnesota Press.

Festinger, L., Schachter, S., & Back, K. (1950). *Social pressures in informal groups: A study of human factors in housing*. New York: Harper.

Festinger, L. J. (1955). Social psychology and group processes. In C. P. Stone & Q. McNemar (Eds.), *Annual review of psychology* (Vol 6, pp. 187–216). Stanford, CA: Annual Reviews.

Feuchtersleben, E. von (1976/1847). *Principles of medical psychology*. Vienna: Gerold.

Feuerstein, R. (1979). *The dynamic assessment of retarded performers*. Baltimore, Md.: University Park Press.

Feuerstein, R., Rand, Y., Hoffman, M. B., & Miller, R. (1980). *Instrumental enrichment: An intervention program for cognitive modifiability*. Baltimore, Md.: University Park Press.

Feyerabend, P. K. (1976). *Against method*. New York: Humanities Press.

Ficher, I. V., Zuckerman, M., & Neeb M. (1981). Marital compatibility in sensation seeking trait as a factor in marital adjustment. *Journal of Sex and Marital Therapy, 7,* 60–69.

Fick, M. L. (1929). Intelligence test results of poor white, native (Zulu), coloured and Indian schoolchildren and the educational and social implications. *South African Journal of Science, 26,* 904–920.

Fiedler, D., & Beach, L. R. (1978). On the decision to be assertive. *Journal of Consulting and Clinical Psychology, 46,* 537–546.

Fiedler, F. E. (1950). A comparison of therapeutic relationships in psychoanalytic, nondirective and Adlerian therapies. *Journal of Consulting Psychology, 14,* 436–445.

Fiedler, F. E. (1954). Assumed similarity measures as predictors of team effectiveness. *Journal of Abnormal and Social Psychology, 49,* 381–388.

Fiedler, F. E. (1964). A contingency model of leadership effectiveness. In L. Berkowitz (Ed.), *Advances in experimental social psychology*. New York: Academic Press.

Fiedler, F. E. (1967). *A theory of leadership effectiveness*. New York: McGraw-Hill.

Fiedler, F. E. (1971). *Leadership*, Morristown, Pa.: General Learning Press.

Fiedler, F. E. (1978). The contingency model and the dynamics of the leadership process. In L. Berkowitz (Ed.), *Advances in experimental social psychology*, New York: Academic Press.

Fiedler, F. E., & Chemers, M. N. (1974). *Leadership and effective management*. Glenview, IL: Scott, Foresman.

Fiedler, F. E., Chemers, M. M. & Mahar, L. (1976). *Improving leadership effectiveness: The leader match concept*. New York: Wiley.

Fiedler, F. E., & Mahar, L., (1979). The effectiveness of contingency model training: Validation of Leader Match. *Personnel Psychology, 32,* 45–62.

Fiedler, F. E., Potter, E. H., III, Zais, M. M., & Knowlton, W. A., Jr., (1979). Organizational stress and the use and misuse of managerial intelligence and experience. *Journal Of Applied Psychology, 64*(6) 635–647.

Fiefel, H., & Nagy, V. (1981). Another look at fear of death. *Journal of Consulting and Clinical Psychology, 49,* 278–286.

Field, G. D., & Test, M. A. (1975). Group assertive training for severely disturbed patients. *Journal of Behavior Therapy and Experimental Psychiatry, 6,* 129–134.

Field, J. V. (1973). Effects of parent's and child's age and sex upon children's perceptions of parental behavior. *Dissertation Abstracts International, 33,* 4486B-4578B (University Microfilms no. 73-834).

Field, M. J., & Lohr, K. N. (Eds.). (1990). *Clinical practice guidelines: Directions for a new program*. Washington, DC: National Academy Press.

Field, T. (1978). Interaction patterns of primary versus secondary caretaking fathers. *Developmental Psychology, 14*, 183–185.

Field, T. M., Sostek, A. M., Vietze, P., & Leiderman, P. H. (Eds.). (1981). *Culture and early interactions*. Hillsdale, N.J.: Erlbaum.

Fielding, J. F. (1977). The irritable bowel syndrome: An historical review. *Journal of the Irish College of Physicians and Surgeons, 6*, 133.

Fielding W. J. (1927). *Sex and the love life*. New York: Blue Ribbon Books.

Fields, R. (1981). *How the swans came to the lake: A narrative history of Buddhism in America*. Boulder, Colo.: Shambhala.

Fields, S. (1979). Mental health and the melting pot. *Innovations, 6*(2), 2–3.

Fiester, S., & Siipola, E. (1972). Effects of time pressure on the management of aggression in TAT stories. *Journal of Personality Assessment, 36*, 230–240.

Fieve, R. R. (1977). The revolution defined: It is pharmacologic. *Psychiatric Annals, 7*(10), 10–18.

Fieve, R. R., Rosenthal, D., & Brill, H. (1975). *Genetic research in psychiatry*. Baltimore, Md.: Johns Hopkins University Press.

Filer, R. N. (1952). The clinician's personality and his case reports. *American Psychologist, 7*, 336.

Filsinger, E. E., & Anderson, C. A. (1982). Social class and self-esteem in late adolescence: Dissonant context or self-efficacy? *Developmental Psychology, 18*, 380–384.

Filsinger, E. E., & Lewis, R. A. (Eds.). (1981). *Assessing marriage: New behavioral approaches*. Beverly Hills, Calif.: Sage Publications.

Filskov, S. B., & Boll, T. J. (Eds.). (1981). *Handbook of clinical neuropsychology*. New York: Wiley Interscience.

Filskov, S. B., & Goldstein, S. G. (1974). Diagnostic validity of the Halstead–Reitan neuropsychological battery. *Journal of Consulting and Clinical Psychology, 42*(3), 382–388.

Filstead, W. J. (Ed.). (1970). *Qualitative methodology. Firsthand involvement with the social world*. Chicago: Markham.

Findlay, S., & Brownlee, S. (1990, July 2). The delicate dance of body and mind. *U.S. News & World Report*, p. 54.

Findley, M. J., & Cooper, H. M. (1983). Locus of control and academic achievement: A literature review. *Journal of Personality and Social Psychology, 44*, 419–427.

Findley, W., & Bryan, M. (1975). *The pros and cons of ability grouping*. Bloomington, Ind.: Phi Delta Kappa Educational Foundation.

Fine, B. S., & Yanoff, M. (1972). *Ocular histology*. New York: Harper & Row.

Fine, L. J. (1979). Psychodrama. In R. J. Corsini (Ed.), *Current psychotherapies* (2nd ed.). Itasca, Ill.: Peacock.

Fine, M. J. (1980). *Handbook on parent education*. New York: Academic Press.

Fine, M. J., Grantham, V. L., & Wright, J. G. (1979). Personal variables that facilitate or impede consultation. *Psychology in the Schools, 16*(4), 533–539.

Fine, S. A., & Wiley, W. W. (1971). An introduction to functional job analysis: Methods for manpower analysis (Monograph no. 4). Kalamazoo, Mich.: Upjohn Institute for Employment Research.

Finer, M. (Chair.) (1974). *Report of the committee on one parent families*. London: Her Majesty's Stationery Office.

Fingarette, H. (1972). *The meaning of criminal insanity*. Berkeley, Calif.: University of California Press.

Finger, F. W. (1982). Circadian rhythms: Implications for psychology. *New Zealand Psychologist, 11*, 1–12.

Finger, S., & Stein, D. G. (1982). *Brain damage and recovery: Research and clinical perspectives*. New York: Academic Press.

Fink, H. K. (1940). Hereditary epistaxis in man. *Journal of Heredity, 31*, 319–322.

Fink, H. K. (1954). *Long journey*. New York: Julian Press.

Fink, H. K. (1961). Compulsive gambling. *Acta Psychotherapeutics, 9*, 251–261.

Finke, R. A. (1979). The functional equivalence of mental images and errors of movement. *Cognitive Psychology, 11*, 235–264.

Finke, R. A. (1980). Levels of equivalence in imagery and perception. *Psychological Review, 87*, 113–132.

Finke, R. A. (1989). *Principles of mental imagery*. Cambridge: MIT Press.

Finke, R. A., & Schmidt, M. (1977). Orientation-specific color after effects following imagination. *Journal of Experimental Psychology: Human Perception and Performance, 3*, 599–606.

Finkel, N. J. (1976). *Mental illness and health: Its legacy, tensions, and changes*. New York: Macmillan.

Finkel, N. J. (1980). *Therapy and ethics: The courtship of law and psychology*. New York: Grune & Stratton.

Finkelhor, D. (1979). *Sexually victimized children*. New York: Free Press.

Finkelhor, D. (1980). Sex among siblings: A survey of prevalence, variety and effects. *Archives of Sexual Behavior, 9*, 171–194.

Finkelhor, D., Williams, L., & Burns, N. (1988). *Sexual abuse in day care: A national study*. Durham, NC: University of New Hampshire Press.

Finkelhor, D., & Yilo, K. (1986). *License to rape: Sexual abuse of wives*. New York: The Free Press.

Finlayson, D. S., & Loughran, J. L. (1978). Pupils' perceptions in high and low delinquency schools. *Educational Research, 18*, 138–145.

Finlayson, M. A. J., Johnson, K. A., & Reitan, R. M. (1977). Relationship of education to neuropsychological measures in brain damaged and nonbrain damaged adults. *Journal of Consulting and Clinical Psychology, 45*, 536–542.

Finn, J. D. (1980). Sex differences in educational outcomes: A cross-national study. *Sex Roles, 6*, 9–26.

Firestone, P., Poitras-Wright, H., & Douglas, H. (1978). The effect of caffeine on hyperactive children. *Journal of Learning Disabilities, 11*, 133–141.

Firestone, S. (1970). *The dialectic of sex*. New York: Morrow.

Fisch, R., & Minkmar, H. (1983). Die künftige Entvicklung des Berufsmarktes für Diplom-Psychologen. *Psychologische Rundschau, 34*.

Fisch, R., Weakland, J. H., & Segal, L. (1982). *The tactics of chance*. San Francisco: Jossey-Bass.

Fischer, E. H., Wells, C. F., & Cohen, S. L. (1968). Birth order and expressed interest in becoming a college professor. *Journal of Counseling Psychology, 15*(2), 111–116.

Fischer, H. (1957). *Die modernen pädagogischen und psychologischen Forschungsmethoden*. Göttingen: Hogrefe.

Fischer, H. (1961). *Einführung in die Schulpsychologie*. Munster, Westfalen: Aschendorff.

Fischer, H. (1971/1962). *Gruppenstruktur und Gruppenleistung*. Bern: Huber.

Fischer, H. (1981). *Allgemeine Didaktik für Höhere Schulen*. Zürich: Verlag der Fachvereine.

Fischer, J. (1973). Is casework effective? A review. *Social Work, 18*, 5–20.

Fischer, J. (1978). *Effective casework practice: An eclectic approach*. New York: McGraw-Hill.

Fischer, J. (1981). The social work revolution. *Social Work, 26*, 199–207.

Fischer, M. (1974). Development and validity of a computerized method for diagnoses of functional psychoses (DIAX). *Acta Psychiatrica Scandinavica, 50*, 243–288.

Fischhoff, B. (1975). Hindsight/foresight: The effect of outcome knowledge on judgment under uncertainty. *Journal of Experimental Psychology: Human Perception and Performance, 1*, 288–299.

Fischhoff, B. Debiasing. (1982). In D. Kahneman, P. Slovic, & A. Tversky (Eds.), *Judgment under uncertainity: Heuristics and biases*. New York: Cambridge University Press.

Fischhoff, B., & Slovic, P. (1980). A little learning . . . : Confidence in multicue judgment tasks. In R. Nickerson (Ed.), *Attention and performance, VIII*. Hillsdale, N.J.: Erlbaum.

Fish, S. (1980). *Is there a text in this class? The authority of interpretive communities*. Cambridge, MA: Harvard University Press.

Fishbein, H. (1982). The identified patient and stage of family development. *Journal of Marital and Family Therapy, 8*, 57–61.

Fishbein, M. (1940). *Modern home medical advisor*. Chicago: American Medical Association.

Fishbein, M. (1959). *Illustrated medical and health encyclopedia*. New York: Stuttman, pp. 1492–1501.

Fishbein, M., & Ajzen, I. (1975). *Belief, attitude, intention, and behavior*. Reading, Mass.: Addison-Wesley.

Fishbourne, P. M., Abelson, H. I., & Cisin, I. (1979). *National survey on drug abuse: Main findings, 1979*. Rockville, Md.: National Institute on Drug Abuse.

Fisher, B. A. (1978). *Perspectives on human communication*. New York: Macmillan.

Fisher, C., Magoun, H. W., & Ranson, S. W. (1938). Dystocia in diabetes insipidus. *American Journal of Obstetrics and Gynecology, 36*, 1–9.

Fisher, D. F., Monty, R. A., & Senders, J. W. (Eds.). (1981). *Eye movements: Cognition and visual perception*. Hillsdale, N.J.: Erlbaum.

Fisher, G. H. (1964). Spatial location by the blind. *American Journal of Psychology, 77*, 2–14.

Fisher, J. E., & Carstensen, L. L. (1990). Behavior management of the dementias. *Clinical Psychology Review, 10*, 611–619.

Fisher, L., Anderson, A., & Jones, J. E. (1981). Types of paradoxical intervention and indications/contraindications for use in clinical practice. *Family Process, 20*, 25–36.

Fisher, M. A., & Zeaman, D. (1970). Growth and decline of retardate intelligence. In N. R. Ellis (Ed.), *International review of research in mental retardation*, Vol. 4, New York; Academic Press.

Fisher, R. A. (1918). The correlations between relatives on the supposition of Mendelian inheritance. *Transactions of the Royal Society, Edinburgh, 52*, 399–433.

Fisher, R. A. (1925). *Statistical methods for research workers*. Edinburgh: Oliver & Boyd.

Fisher, R. A. (1933). The concepts of inverse probability and fiducial probability referring to unknown parameters. *Proceedings of the Royal Society of London*, Series A, *139*, 343–348.

Fisher, R. A. (1934–35). The fiducial argument in statistical inference. *Annals of Eugenics, VI*, 391–398.

Fisher, R. A. (1948). Combining independent tests of significance. *American Statistician, 2*(5), 30.

Fisher, R. A. (1959). *Statistical methods and scientific inference*. New York: Hafner.

Fisher, R. A. (1966/1935). *Design of experiments*. Edinburgh: Oliver & Boyd. New York: Hafner.

Fisher, R. A. (1973/1925). *Statistical methods for research workers*. New York: Hafner.

Fisher, R. A., & Yates, F. (1938). *Statistical tables for biological agricultural and medical research*. London: Oliver & Boyd.

Fisher, R. P., Geiselman, R. E., & Amador, M. (1989). Field test of the cognitive interview: Enhancing the recollection of the actual victims and witnesses of crime. *Journal of Applied Psychology, 74*, 722–727.

Fisher, R. P., Geiselman, R. E., Raymond, D. S., & Jurkevich, L. M. (1987). Enhancing enhanced eyewitness memory: Refining the cognitive interview. *Journal of Police Science & Administration, 15*, 291–297.

Fisher, S. (1973). *The female orgasm*. New York: Basic Books.

Fisher, S., & Cleveland, S. (1968). *Body image and personality*. New York: Dover.

Fisher, S., & Fisher, R. (1981). *Pretend the world is funny and forever: A psychological analysis of comedians, clowns, and actors*. Hillsdale, N.J.: Erlbaum.

Fishman, C. G. (1965). Need for approval and the expression of aggression under varying conditions of frustration. *Journal of Personality and Social Psychology, 2*, 809–816.

Fishman, D. B., & Franks, C. M. (1992). Evolution and differentiation within behavior therapy: A theoretical and epistemological review. In D. K. Freedheim (Ed.), *History of psychotherapies: A century of change* (pp. 159–196) Washington, DC: American Psychological Association.

Fisk, A. A. (1981). *A new look at senility: Its causes, diagnosis, treatment and management*. Springfield, Ill.: Thomas.

Fisk, A. D., & Schneider, W. (1981). Control and automatic processing during tasks requiring sustained attention: A new approach to vigilance. *Human Factors, 23*, 737–750.

Fisk, J. L., & Rourke, B. P. (1979). Identification of subgroups of learning-disabled children at three age levels: A neuropsychological, multivariate approach. *Journal of Clinical Neuropsychology, 1*, 289–310.

Fiske, S. T., & Taylor, S. E. (in press). *Social cognition*. Reading, Mass.: Addison-Wesley.

Fitts, P. M. (1951). Engineering psychology and equipment design. In S. S. Stevens (Ed.), *Handbook of experimental psychology*. New York: Wiley.

Fitts, P. M. (1963). Engineering psychology. In S. Koch (Ed.), *Psychology: A study of a science*, (Vol. 5) *The process areas, the person, and some applied fields: Their place in psychology and in science*. New York: McGraw-Hill.

Fitts, P. M., & Posner, M. I. (1967). *Human performance*. Belmont, Calif.: Brooks/Cole.

Fitzgerald, F. (1973). *Fire in the lake*. New York: Random House.

Fitzgerald, J. F., Peszke, M. A., & Goodwin, R. C. (1978). Competency evaluations in Connecticut. *Hospital and Community Psychiatry, 29*, 450–453.

Fitzsimons, J. T. (1961). Drinking by rats depleted of body fluid without increase in osmotic pressure. *Journal of Physiology* (London), *159*, 297–309.

Fix, A. J., & Haffke, E. A. (1976). *Basic psychological therapies: Comparative effectiveness.* New York: Human Sciences Press.

Fivush, R. (1992). Developmental perspectives on autobiographical recall. In G. Goodman & B. L. Bottoms (Eds.), *Understanding and improving children's testimony.* New York: Guilford Press.

Fixsen, D. L., Wolf, M. M., & Phillips, E. L. (1973). Achievement place: A teaching family model of community based group homes for youth in trouble. In Hammerlynch et al. (Eds.), *Behavior modification.* Champaign, Ill.: Research Press.

Flaccus, L. W. (1906). Remarks on the psychology of clothes. *Pedagogical Seminary, 13,* 61–83.

Flammer, A. (1970). *Transfer und Korrelation.* Basel: Beltz.

Flammer, A. (1975). *Individuelle Unterschiede im Lernen.* Basel: Beltz.

Flammer, A., & Kintsch, W. (1982). *Discourse processing* Amsterdam: North-Holland.

Flanagan, J. C. (1949). Critical requirements: A new approach to employee evaluation. *Personnel Psychology, 2,* 419–425.

Flanagan, J. C. (1954). The critical incident technique. *Psychological Bulletin, 51,* 327–358.

Flanagan, J. C. (1977). Planning career goals based on data from Project Talent. *Vocational Guidance Quarterly, 25,* 270–273.

Flanagan, J. C. (1978). A research approach to improving our quality of life. *American Psychologist, 33,* 138–147.

Flanagan, J. C. (Ed.). (1948). *The aviation psychology program in the Army Air Forces: Report no. 1.* Washington, D.C.: U.S. Government Printing Office.

Flanagan, J. C., & Burns, R. K. (1955). The employee performance record: A new appraisal and development tool. *Harvard Business Review, 33*(5), 95–102.

Flanagan, J. C., Dailey, J., Shaycroft, M., Gorham, W., Orr, D., & Goldberg, I. (1962). *Design for a study of American youth.* Boston: Houghton Mifflin.

Flanagan, J. C., Tiedeman, D., Willis, M., & McLaughlin, D. (1973). *The career data book.* Palo Alto, Calif.: American Institutes for Research.

Flannigan, K. P., & Whishaw, I. Q. (1977). The effects of some pharmacological agents on the durations of immobility shown by rabbits placed in various postures. *Bulletin of the Psychonomic Society, 10,* 499–502.

Flannagan, R. (1960). Tobacco. In *World book encyclopedia* (T). Chicago: Field Enterprises Educational Corp.

Flavell, J. H. (1963). *The developmental psychology of Jean Piaget.* Princeton, N.J.: Van Nostrand.

Flavell, J. H. (1977). *Cognitive development.* Englewood Cliffs, N.J.: Prentice-Hall.

Flavell, J. H. (1979). Metacognition and cognitive monitoring. *American Psychologist, 34,* 906–911.

Flavell, J. H. (1982). Monitoring social-cognitive enterprises: Something else that may develop in the area of social cognition. In J. H. Flavell & Ross (Eds.), *Social cognitive development: Frontiers and possible futures.* New York: Cambridge University Press.

Flavell, J. H., (et al.) (1968). *The development of role-taking and communication skills in children.* New York: Wiley.

Flavell, J. H., & Markman, E. M. (Eds.). (in press). *Handbook of child psychology: Cognitive development,* Vol. 3. New York: Wiley.

Flavell, J. H., & Ross, L. (Eds.). (1981). *Social cognitive development: Frontiers and possible futures:* New York: Cambridge University Press.

Flechsig, P. E. (1895). Weitere Mittheilungen Jiber die Sinnes—und Associationscentren des menschlichen Gehirns. *Neurologisches Centralblatt, 14,* 1118–1124, 1177–1179.

Fleck, J. R., & Carter, J. D. (Eds.). (1981). *Psychology and Christianity: Integrative readings.* Nashville, Tenn.: Abingdon.

Fleet, M. L., Brigham, J. C., & Bothwell, R. K. (1987). The confidence-accuracy relationship: The effects of confidence assessment and choosing. *Journal of Applied Social Psychology, 17,* 171–187.

Fleishman, E. A. (1957). A leader behavior description for industry. In R. M. Stogdill and A. E. Coons (Eds.), *Leader behavior: Its description and measurement.* Columbus, Ohio: Bureau of Business Research, Ohio State University.

Fleishman, E. A. (1967). The perceived menthol intensity of different brands of menthol cigarettes. In E. A. Fleishman (Ed.), *Studies in personnel and industrial psychology.* Homewood, Ill.: Dorsey Press.

Fleishman, E. A., & Hempel, W. C., Jr. (1955). The relation between abilities and improvement with practice in a visual discrimination reaction task. *Journal of Experimental Psychology, 49,* 301–312.

Fleischman, M. J. (1981). A replication of Patterson's "Intervention for boys with conduct problems." *Journal of Consulting and Clinical Psychology, 49,* 342–351.

Fleming, D. (1967). Attitude: The history of a concept. *Perspectives in American history, 1,* 287–365.

Flesch, R. (1948). A new readability yardstick. *Journal of Applied Psychology, 32,* 221–233.

Flesch, R. (1951). *How to test readability.* New York: Harper.

Flesch, R. (1974). *The art of readable writing* (rev. ed.). New York: Harper & Row.

Fletcher, R. (1948). *Instinct in man.* Aberdeen, Scotland: University Press.

Fletcher, R. (1991). *Science, ideology & the media.* New Brunswick, NJ: Transaction.

Flexser, A. J., & Tulving, E. (1978). Retrieval independence in recognition and recall. *Psychological Review, 85,* 153–171.

Flinch, C. E., & Hayflick, L. (Eds.). (1977). *Handbook of the biology of aging.* New York: Van Nostrand Reinhold.

Flood, N. B., Overmier, J. B., & Savage, G. E. (1976). Teleost telencephalon and teaming: An interpretive review of data and hypotheses. *Physiology and Behavior, 16,* 783–796.

Flourens, P. (1830). Expériences sur les canaux semi-circulaires de l'oreille, dans les oiseaux. Lues à l'Académie royale des sciences le 11 août 1828. In *Mémoires de l'Académie royale des sciences de l'Institut de France.* Paris: Académie Royale.

Flourens, P. (1845). *Phrenology examined.* Philadelphia: Hogan & Thompson.

Flournoy, T. (1900). *Des Indes á la planète Mars: Étude sur un cas de somnambulisme avec glossolalie.* Paris: Alcan.

Flournoy, T. (1911). *Esprit et médiums: Mélanges de métapsychique et de psychologie.* Geneva: Kündig.

Flowers, J. W. (1979). The differential effects of simple advice, alternatives, and instructions in psychotherapy. *International Journal of Group Psychotherapy, 29,* 305–316.

Flugel, J. C. (1945). *Man, morals and society.* New York: International Universities Press.

Flugel, J. C. (1947). *Men and their motives.* New York: International Universities Press.

Flugel, J. C. (1950/1921). *The psycho-analytic study of the family*. London: Hogarth Press Institute of Psycho-analysis.

Flugel, J. C. (1975/1930). *The psychology of clothes*. New York: AMS Press.

Flugel, J. C., & West, D. J. (1964). *A hundred years of psychology: 1833–1933*. New York: Basic Books.

Flynn, C. P. (1986). *After the beyond: Human transformation and the near-death experience*. Englewood Cliffs, NJ: Prentice-Hall.

Flynn, J. R. (1980). *Race, IQ and Jensen*. London: Routledge & Kegan Paul.

Flynn, T. M., & Storandt, M. (1990). Supplemental group discussions in memory training for older adults. *Psychology and Aging, 5*, 178–198.

Foa, E. B., Zinbarg, R., & Rothbaum, B. O. (1992). Uncontrollability and unpredictability of post-traumatic stress disorder: An animal model. *Psychological Bulletin, 112*, 218–238.

Foa, U. (1971). Interpersonal and economic resources. *Science, 171*, 345–351.

Foa, U. G., & Foa, E. B. (1974). *Societal structures of the mind*. Springfield, Ill.: Thomas.

Foa, V. (1985). Neurotoxicity of elemental mercury: Occupational aspects. In K. Blum & L. Manzo (Eds.), *Neurotoxicology* (pp. 323–343). New York: Marcel Dekker.

Fobes, J. L., & King, J. E. Measuring primate learning abilities. In J. Fobes & J. King (Eds.), *Primate behavior*. New York: Academic Press.

Fobes, J. L., & King, J. E. Vision: The dominant primate modality. In J. Fobes & J. King (Eds.), *Primate behavior*. New York: Academic Press.

Focillon, H. (1948). *Life of forms in art*. New York: Wittenborn Schultz.

Fodor, J. (1968). *Psychological explanation*. New York: Random House.

Fodor, J. A. (1975). *The language of thought*. New York: Crowell.

Fodor, J. A. & Pylyshyn, Z. W. (1988). Connectionism and cognitive architecture: A critical analysis, *Cognition, 28*, 3–71.

Fogarty, T. (1978). On emptiness and closeness. In E. Pendagast (Ed.), *The family*. New Rochelle, N.Y.: Center for Family Learning.

Folen, R. A. (1978). *Peer counselor-consultant training: Changing attitudes and interpersonal behavior in the school setting*. Unpublished doctoral dissertation, University of Hawaii.

Foley, V. (1974). *An introduction to family therapy*. New York: Grune & Stratton.

Foley, V. (1975). Family therapy with black, disadvantaged families: Some observations on roles, communication and techniques. *Journal of Marriage and Family Counseling, 1*, 29–38.

Foley, V. (1979). Family therapy. In R. J. Corsini (Ed.), *Current psychotherapies*, (2nd ed.). Itasca, Ill.: Peacock.

Folkins, C. H. (1970). Temporal factors and the cognitive mediators of stress reaction. *Journal of Personality and Social Psychology, 14*, 173–184.

Folkman, S., & Lazarus, R. S. (1980). An analysis of coping in a middle-aged community sample. *Journal of Health and Social Behavior, 21*, 219–239.

Fondi, M., Hay, J., Kincaid, M. B., & O'Connell, K. (1977). *Feminist therapy: A working definition*. Unpublished manuscript; University of Pennsylvania.

Fontaine, C. (1963). Notes sur une expérience d'application de tests au Mali (1962–1963). *Revue de Psychologie Appliquée, 13*, 235–246.

Fontaine, G., & Dorch, E. (1980). Problems and benefits of close intercultural relationships. *International Journal of Intercultural Relations, 4*, 329–337.

Fontana, A. F., Hughes, L. A., Marcus, J. L., & Dowds, B. N. (1979). Subjective evaluation of life events. *Journal of Consulting and Clinical Psychology, 47*, 906–911.

Fontana, V. J. (1973). *Somewhere a child is crying*. New York: Macmillan.

Foppa, K. (1975). *Apprendimento e comportamento*. Rome: Armando.

Foppa, K. (1975/1965). *Lernen, Gedächtnis, Verhalten*. Cologne, West Germany: Kiepenheuer & Witsch.

Foppa, K. (1976). Comparative implications of learning psychology. In M. von Cranach (Ed.), *Methods of inference from animal to human behaviour*. Chicago: Aldine: The Hague: Mouton.

Foppa, K. (1981). Über die Angemessenheit psychologischer Betrachtungsweisen. In K.-H. Wewetzer (Ed.), *Experiment-Test-Befragung*. Darmstadt, West Germany: Wissenschaftliche Buchgesellschaft.

Foppa, K., & Groner, R. (Eds.). (1981). *Kognitive Strukturen und ihre Entwicklung*. Bern: Huber.

Foppa, K., & Käsermann, M.-L. (1981). Das kindliche Wissen über Sprache: Überlegungen zu einem ungelösten Problem. In K. Foppa, & R. Groner (Eds.), *Kognitive Strukturen und ihre Entwicklung*. Bern: Huber.

Forbes, T. W. (Ed.). (1972). *Human factors in highway traffic safety research*. New York: Wiley/Interscience.

Ford, C., & Beach, F. A. (1951). *Patterns of sexual behavior*. New York: Harper & Row.

Ford, D. II. (1962). Group and individual counseling in modifying behavior. *Personnel and Guidance Journal, 40*, 770–773.

Ford, D. H., & Urban, H. B. (1963). Existential analysis or *Daseinanalyse*. Chapter 12 in *Systems of psychotherapy: A comparative study*. New York: Wiley.

Ford, J. D. (1979). Research on training counselors and clinicians. *Review of Educational Research, 49*(1), 87–130.

Ford, N. J. (1981). Recent approaches to the study and teaching of "effective learning" in higher education. *Review of Educational Research, 51*, 345–377.

Fordyce, W. E. (1976). *Behavioral methods for chronic pain and illness*. St. Louis, Mo.: Mosby.

Fordyce, W. E., Fowler, R. S., Lehmann, J. F., DeLateur, B., Sand, P. L., & Trieschmann, R. B. (1973). Operant conditioning in the treatment of chronic pain. *Archives of Physical Medicine and Rehabilitation, 54*, 399–408.

Fordyce, W. E., & Steger, J. C. (1979). Chronic pain. In O. F. Pomerleau & J. P. Brady (Eds.), *Behavioral Medicine*. Baltimore, Md. Williams & Wilkins.

Forehand, R., & McMahon, R. J. (1981). *Helping the noncompliant child: A clinician's guide to parent training*. New York: Guilford Press.

Forehand, R., Wells, K. C., & Griest, D. L. (1980). An examination of the social validity of a parent training program. *Behavior Therapy, 11*, 488–502.

Forel, A. H. (1891). *Les formidices*, Paris: Imprimière.

Forel, A. H. (1908). *The senses of insects*. London: Mathuen.

Forer, B. R. (1949). The fallacy of personal validation: A classroom demonstration of gullibility. *Journal of Abnormal and Social Psychology, 44*, 118–123.

Forer, L. K. (1976). *The birth order factor*. New York: McKay.

Forer, L. K. (1977). Bibliography of birth order literature in the 70's. *Journal of Individual Psychology, 33*(1), 122–141.

Forer, R. B. (1950). A structured sentence completion test. *Journal of Projective Techniques, 14*, 15–29.

Forest, J., & Sicz, G. (1981). Pseudo-self-actualization. *Journal of Humanistic Psychology. 21*, 77–83.

Foreyt, J. P., Goodrick, G. K., & Gotto, A. M. (1981). Limitations of behavioral treatment of obesity: Review and analysis. *Journal of Behavioral Medicine, 4*, 159–174.

Forgas, J. E. (Ed.). (1981). *Social cognition: Perspectives on everyday understanding*. New York: Academic Press.

Forgatch, M. S. (1991). The clinical science vortex: A developing theory of antisocial behavior. In D. J. Pepler & K. H. Rubin (Eds.), *The development and treatment of childhood aggression* (pp.93–120). Hillsdale, NJ: Erlbaum.

Forisha, B. (1978). *Sex roles and personal awareness*. Morristown, N.J.: General Learning Press.

Forisha, B. (1981). The inside and the outsider. In B. Forisha & B. Goldman (Eds.), *Outsiders on the inside*. Englewood Cliffs, N.J.: Prentice-Hall.

Forisha, B. (1982). *Power of love*. Englewood Cliffs, N.J.: Prentice-Hall.

Forisha, B. (1983). *Organizational synchrony*. Englewood Cliffs, N.J.: Prentice-Hall.

Forisha, B., & Goldman, B. (1981). *Outsiders on the inside*. Englewood Cliffs, N.J.: Prentice-Hall.

Form, W. H., & Miller, D. C. (1949). Occupational career patterns as a sociological instrument. *American Journal of Sociology, 54*, 317–329.

Forman, S. G., & O'Malley, P. L. (1984). A legislative field experience for psychology graduate students. *Professional Psychology: Research and Practice, 15*, 324–332.

Fornari, F. (1974). *The psychoanalysis of war*. New York: Anchor Books.

Forness, S. R. (1979). Clinical criteria for mainstreaming mildly handicapped children. *Psychology in the Schools, 16*, 508–514.

Forrest, D. W. (1974). *Francis Gaiton: The life and work of a Victorian genius*. New York: Taplinger.

Forristall, D. Z. (1982). *Student-to-student study skills instruction in the learning assistance center*. San Marcos, Tex.: Effective Study Materials.

Fortes, M., & Mayer, D. Y. (1966). Psychosis and social change among the Tallensi of northern Ghana. *Cahiers d'Etudes Africaines, 6*, 5–40.

Fortune, R. (1932). *Sorcerers of Dobu*. New York: Dutton.

Fosberg, I. A. (1938). Roschach reactions under varied instructions. *Rorschach Research Exchange, 3*, 12–31.

Foscarinis, M. (1991). The politics of homelessness. *American Psychologist, 46*, 1232–1238.

Fosco, F., & Geer, J. H. (1971). Effects of gaining control over aversive stimuli after differing amounts of no control. *Psychological Reports, 29*, 1153–1154.

Foshay, A. W., & Beilin, L. A. (1969). Curriculum. In R. L. Ebel (Ed.), *Encyclopedia of educational research*. New York: Macmillan.

Foster, J. W., & Archer, S. J. (1979). Birth order and intelligence: An immunological interpretation. *Perceptual and Motor Skills, 48*(1), 79–93.

Foster, L. M. (1980). State confidentiality laws: The Illinois act as model for new legislation in other states. *American Journal of Orthopsychiatry. 50*, 659–665.

Foster, M. (1901). *Lectures on the history of physiology during the sixteenth, seventeenth and eighteenth centuries*. Cambridge, England: University Press.

Foster, P. J. (1965). *Education and social change in Ghana*. London: Routledge & Kegan Paul.

Foster, P. J. (1968). Some remarks on education and unemployment in Africa. *Manpower and Unemployment Research in Africa, 1*, 19–20.

Foucault, M. (1973). *Madness and civilization: A history of insanity in the age of reason*. New York: Vintage Books.

Foucault, M. (1979). *Discipline and punish: The birth of the prison*. New York: Random House.

Foucault, M. (1980). *The history of sexuality* (Vol. 1). New York: Random House.

Foulkes, D. (1978). *A grammar of dreams*. New York: Basic Books.

Foulkes, D. (1981). *Children's dreams: Longitudinal studies*. New York: Wiley.

Foulkes, S. H., & Anthony, E. J. (1948). *Group psychotherapy: The psychoanalytic approach*. London: Heinemann.

Fournies, F. (1978). *Coaching for improved work performance*. New York: Van Nostrand Reinhold.

Fouts, R. S. (1973). Acquisition and testing of gestural signs in four young chimpanzees. *Science, 180*, 978–980.

Fowler, C. A., Wolford, G., Slade, R., & Tassinary, L. (1981). Lexical access with and without awareness. *Journal of Experimental Psychology: General, 110*, 341–362.

Fowler, F. D. (1980). Air traffic control problems: A pilot's view. *Human Factors, 22*, 645–653.

Fowler, H. (1965). *Curiosity and exploratory behavior*. New York: Macmillan.

Fowler, H. (1978). Cognitive associations as evident in the blocking effects of response-contingent CSs. In S. H. Hulse, H. Fowler, & W. K. Honig (Eds.), *Cognitive processes in animal behavior*. Hillsdale, N.J.: Erlbaum.

Fowler, R. D. (1980). The role of the psychologists in class action suits. In G. Cooke (Ed.), *The role of the forensic psychologist*. Springfield, Ill.: Thomas.

Fowler, R. D., & Brodsky, S. L. (1978). Development of a correctional–clinical psychology program. *Professional Psychology, 9*, 440–447.

Fowler, S. A. (1978). Ecological considerations in the education and integration of young handicapped children. Presented at Council for Exceptional Children Symposium, Kansas City, Mo.

Fowler, W. L. (1957). A comparative analysis of pupil performance on conventional and culture-controlled mental tests. In *14th Yearbook, National Council on Measurements Used in Education*.

Fowler, W. R., & Merricks, D. L. (1978). Crisis in Chattanooga: The men from M.A.R.S. *Emotional First Aid: A Journal of Crisis Intervention, 5*, 25–30.

Fox, A. (1979). *If I'm the better player why can't I win?* New York: Tennis Magazine Publications.

Fox, B. H. (1978). Premorbid psychological factors as related to cancer incidence. *Journal of Behavioral Medicine, 1*, 45–133.

Fox, D. J. (1969). *The research process in education*. New York: Holt, Rinehart & Winston.

Fox, J. (1980). Making decisions under the influence of memory. *Psychological Review, 87*, 190–211.

Fox, L. H. (1981). Identification of the academically gifted. *American Psychologist, 36*, 1103–1111.

Fox, L. H., Tobin, D., & Brody, L. (1979). Sex-role socialization and achievement in mathematics. In M. A. Wittig & A. C. Petersen (Eds.), *Sex-related differences in cognitive functioning: Developmental issues*. New York: Academic Press.

Fox, M. (1980). *Returning to Eden: Animal rights and human responsibility*. New York: Viking.

Fox, R. (1988) Prescription privileges: The implication for the practice of psychology. *Psychotherapy, 25*, 501–507.

Fox, R. (1989). Some practical and legal objections to prescription privileges for psychologists. *Psychotherapy in Private Practice, 6*, 23–39.

Fox, R. E. (1976). Family therapy. In I. B. Weiner (Ed.), *Clinical methods in psychology*. New York: Wiley.

Fox, R., Schwelitz, F., & Barclay, A. (in press). A proposed curriculum for psychopharmacology training for psychologists. *Professional Psychology: Research and Practice*.

Foxall, G. R. (1979). Farmers' tractor purchase decisions: A study of interpersonal communication in industrial buying behavior. *European Journal of Marketing, 13*, 299–308.

Fozard, J. L. (1981). Special issue preface. *Human Factors, 23*, 3—6.

Fracchia, J., Sheppard, C., & Merlis, S. (1974). Early cigarette smoking and drug use: Some comments, data and thoughts. *Psychological Reports, 34*, 371–374.

Fraiberg, S. (1959/1968). *The magic years: Understanding and handling the problems of early childhood*. New York: Scribner.

Fraisse, P. (in press). The adaptation of the child to time. In W. J. Friedman (Ed.), *The developmental psychology of time*. New York: Academic Press.

Fraisse, P. (1956). *Les structures rythmiques: Etude psychologique*. Louvain, Belgium: Presses Universitaires.

Fraisse, P. (1963). *The psychology of time*. New York: Harper & Row.

Fraisse, P. (1974). *Manuel pratique de psychologie experimentale* (4th ed.) Paris: Presses Universitaires de France.

Fraisse, P. (1974). *Psychologie du rhythme*. Paris: Presses Universitaires de France.

Fraisse, P. (1978). Time and rhythm perception. In E. Carterette & M. P. Friedman (Eds.), *Handbook of perception*, Vol. 8. New York: Academic Press.

Fraisse, P. (1979/1966). *La psychologie expérimentale*. Paris: Presses Universitaires de France.

Fraisse, P. (1980). Elements of chronopsychology. *Le Travail Humain, 43*, 353–372.

Fraisse, P. (1981). Cognition of time in human activity. In G. d'Ydewalle & W. Lens (Eds.), *Cognitions of human motivation and learning*. Hillsdale, N.J.: Erlbaum.

Fraisse, P. (1981). Multisensory aspects of rhythm in intersensory perception and sensory integration. In D. Walk & H. Pick (Eds.), *Perception and experience*, Vol. 2. New York: Plenum.

Fraisse, P. (Ed.). (in press). *La psychologie de demain*. Paris: Presses Universitaires de France.

Fraisse, P. (in press). Rhythm and tempo. In D. Deutch (Ed.), *Psychology of music*. New York: Academic Press.

Fraisse, P., & Piaget, J. (Eds.). (1963–1966). *Traite dé psychologie expérimentale*. (9 vols). Paris: Presses Universitaires de France.

Framo, J. (1970). Symptoms from a family transactional viewpoint. In N. Ackerman, J. Lieb, & J. Pearce (Eds.), *Family therapy in transition*. Boston: Little, Brown.

Framo, J. (1981). Family of origin as a therapeutic resource for adults in marital and Family therapy: You can and should go home again. In R. Green & J. Framo (Eds.), *Family therapy major contributions*. New York: International Universities Press.

France, C. J. (1975). The gambling impulse. In J. Halliday & P. Fuller (Eds.), *The psychology of gambling*. New York: Harper & Row.

Frances, A., & Munro, A. (1989). Treating a woman who believes she has bugs under her skin. *Hospital Community Psychiatry, 40*(11), 1113–1114.

Franchina, J. J., Kash, J. S., Reeder, J. R., & Sheets, C. T. (1978). Effects of exteroceptive feedback and safe-box confinement durations on escape behavior in rats. *Animal Learning and Behavior, 6*, 423–428.

Franco, S., & Andrews, B. (1977). Reduction of cerebral palsy by neonatal intensive care. *Pediatric Clinics of North America, 24*, 639.

Frank, A. R. (1973). Breaking down learning tasks: A sequence approach. *Teaching Exceptional Children, 6*, 16–19.

Frank, J. D. (1941). Recent studies of the level of aspiration. *Psychological Bulletin, 38*, 218–226.

Frank, J. D. (1967). *Sanity and survival: Psychological aspects of war and peace*. New York: Random House.

Frank, J. D. (1968). The role of hope in psychotherapy. *International Journal of Psychiatry, 5*, 383–395.

Frank, J. D. (1973). *Persuasion and healing*. Baltimore: Johns Hopkins University Press. (Original work published 1961)

Frank, J. D. (1973/1961). *Persuasion and healing* (2d ed.). Baltimore, Md.: Johns Hopkins University Press.

Frank, J. D. (1974). Psychotherapy: The restoration of morale. *American Journal of Psychiatry, 131*, 271–274.

Frank, J. D. (1975). An overview of psychotherapy. In G. Usdin (Ed.). *395*.

Frank, J. D. (1975). An overview of psychotherapy. In G. Usdin (Ed.). *Overview of the psychotherapies*. New York: Brunner/Mazel.

Frank, J. D. (1976). Restoration of morale and behavior change. In A. Burton (Ed)., *What makes behavior change possible?* New York: Brunner/Mazel.

Frank, J. D. (1977). Nature and functions of belief systems: Humanism and transcendental religion. *American Psychologist, 32*, 555–559.

Frank, J. D. (1978). *Psychotherapy and the human predicament*. New York: Schocken Books.

Frank, J. D. (1979). Thirty years of group psychotherapy. *International Journal of Group Psychotherapy, 29*, 439–452.

Frank, J. D. (1982). Therapeutic components shared by all psychotherapies. In J. H. Harvey & M. M. Parks (Eds.), *The master lecture series: Vol. 1: Psychotheraphy research and behavior change* (pp. 9–37). Washington, DC: American Psychological Association.

Frank, J. D. (1982). Therapeutic components shared by all psychotherapies. Master lecture, American Psychological Association, Los Angeles, August 24, 1981. Washington, D.C.: American Psychological Association.

Frank, J. D., et al. (1978). *Effective ingredients of successful psychotherapy*. New York: Brunner/Mazel.

Frank, L. (1939). Time perspectives. *Journal of Social Philosophy, 4*, 239–312.

Frank, L. K. (1939). Projective methods for the study of personality. *Journal of Psychology, 8*, 389–413.

Frank, L. K. (1948). *Projectire methods*. Springfield, Ill.: Thomas.

Frank, L. K. (1957). Research for what? *Journal of Social Issues*, Suppl., series no. 10, 5–22.

Frank. M. L. (1976). Why people gamble: A behavioral perspective. In D. Lester (Ed.), *Gambling today*. Springfield, Ill.: Thomas.

Frankel, A. S. (1970). Treatment of a multisymptomatic phobic by a self-directed, self-reinforced imagery technique: A case study. *Journal of Abnormal Psychology, 76*, 496–499.

Frankel, F. H. (1978). Hypnosis and altered states of consciousness in treatment of patients with medical disorders. In T. B. Karasu, R. I. Steinmuller (Eds.), *Psychotherapeutics in medicine*. New York: Grune & Stratton.

Frankel, F. H. (1976). *Hypnosis: Trance as a coping mechanism*. New York: Plenum.

Franken, R. E., Gibson, F. J., & Mohan, P. (1990). Sensation seeking and disclosure to close and casual friends. *Personality and Individual Differences, 11*, 829–832.

Frankenhaeuser, M. (1959). *Estimation of time: an experimental study*. Stockholm: Almqvist & Wiksell.

Frankenhaeuser, M. (1975). Experimental approaches to the study of catecholamines and emotion. In L. Levi (Ed.), *Emotions: Their parameters and measurement*. New York: Raven Press.

Frankenhaeuser, M. (1976). The role of peripheral catecholamines in adaptation to understimulation and overstimulation. In G. Serban (Ed.), *Psychopathology of human adaptation*. New York: Plenum.

Frankenhaeuser, M. (1978). Coping with job stress: A psychobiological approach. Reports from the Department of Psychology, University of Stockholm (532).

Frankenhaeuser, M. (1979). Psychoneuroendocrine approaches to the study of emotion as related to stress and coping. In H. E. Howe & R. A. Dienstbier (Eds.), *Nebraska Symposium on Motivation 1978*. Lincoln, Neb.: University of Nebraska Press.

Frankenhaeuser, M. (1980). Psychobiological aspects of life stress. In S. Levine & H. Ursin (Eds.), *Coping and health*. New York: Plenum.

Frankenhaeuser, M. (1980). Psychoneuroendocrine approaches to the study of stressful person-environment transactions. In H. Selye (Ed.), *Selye's guide to stress research*, Vol. I. New York: Van Nostrand Reinhold.

Frankenhaeuser, M. (1981). Coping with stress at work. *International Journal of Health Services, 11*, 491–510.

Frankenhaeuser, M. (1982). The sympathetic-adrenal and pituitary-adrenal response to challenge: Comparison between the sexes. In T. M. Dembroski, T. H. Schmidt, & G. Blumchen (Eds.), *Biobehavioral bases of coronary heart disease*. Basel, New York: Karger.

Frankenhaeuser, M., & Gardell, B. (1976). Underload and overload in working life: Outline of a multidisciplinary approach. *Journal of Human Stress, 2*, 35–46.

Frankenhaeuser, M., Lundberg, V., & Forsman, L. (1980). Note on arousing Type A persons by depriving them of work. *Journal of Psychosomatic Research, 24*, 45–47.

Frankenhaeuser, M., Myrsten, A. L., Post, B., & Johansson, G. (1970). Behavioral and physiological effects of cigarette smoking in a monotonous situation. *Reports from the Psychological Laboratories, University of Stockholm, 301*, 7.

Frankl, V. (1951). *Logos und Existenz*. Vienna: Amandus.

Frankl, V. (1960). Paradoxical intention: A logotherapeutic technique. *American Journal of Psychotherapy, 14*, 520–535.

Frankl, V. (1965). *The doctor and the soul*. (2nd ed., R. Winston & C. Winston, Trans.). New York: Knopf.

Frankl, V. (1966). Self-transcendence as a human phenomenon. *Journal of Humanistic Psychology*, Fall, 97–106.

Frankl, V. E. (1959). *From deathcamp to existentialism*. Boston: Beacon Press.

Frankl, V. E. (1960). Paradoxical intention: A logotherapeutic technique. *American Journal of Psychotherapy, 14*, 520–535.

Frankl, V. E. (1972). The feeling of meaninglessness: A challenge to psychotherapy. *American Journal of Psychoanalysis, 32*, 85–89.

Frankl, V. E. (1977/1955). *The doctor and the soul: From psychotherapy to logotherapy*. New York: Knopf.

Frankl, V. E. (1978). *The unconscious God: Psychotherapy and theology*. New York: Simon & Schuster.

Frankl, V. E. (1978/1967). *Psychotherapy and existentialism*. New York: Simon & Schuster.

Frankl, V. E. (1979). *The unheard cry for meaning: Psychotherapy and humanism*. New York: Touchstone.

Frankl, V. E. (1980/1962). *Man's search for meaning: An introduction to logotherapy*. New York: Simon & Schuster.

Frankl, V. E. (1981). *The will to meaning: Foundations and applications of logotherapy*. New York: New American Library.

Frankl, V. E. (1991). Paradoxical intention. In G. E. Weeks (Ed.), *Promoting change through paradoxical therapy* (pp. 99–110). New York: Brunner/Mazel.

Franklin, B. (1956). Letter to Joseph Priestly. In *The Benjamin Franklin sampler*. New York: Fawcett.

Franks, C. M. (1981). 2081: Will we be many or one—or none? *Behavioural Psychotherapy, 9*, 287–290.

Franks, C. M. (1983). On conceptual and technical integrity in psychoanalysis and behavior therapy, two fundamentally incompatible systems. In H. Arkowitz & S. B. Messer (Eds.), *Psychoanalytic and behavior therapy: Are they compatible?* New York: Plenum.

Franks, C. M. (1993). Basic concepts and models: Behavioral model. In V. B. Van Hassett & M. Hersen (Eds.), *Advanced abnormal psychology*. New York: Plenum Press.

Franks, C. M. (Ed.). (1969). *Behavior therapy*. New York: McGraw-Hill.

Franks, C. M., & Barbrack, C. R. (1983). Behavior therapy with adults: An integrative perspective. In M. Hersen, A. E. Kazdin, & A. S. Bellack (Eds.), *The clinical psychology handbook*, New York: Pergamon Press.

Franks, C. M., & Rosenbaum, M. (1983). Behavior therapy: Overview and personal reflections. In M. Rosenbaum, C. M. Franks, & Y. Jaffe (Eds.), *Perspectives on behavior therapy in the eighties* (pp. 3–16). New York: Springer.

Franks, C. M., & Wilson, G. T. (Eds.). (1973). *Annual review of behavior therapy: Theory and practice* (Vol. 1). New York: Brunner/Mazel.

Franks, C. M., & Wilson, G. T. (1975). Ethical and related issues in behavior therapy. In C. M. Franks & G. T. Wilson (Eds.), *Annual review of behavior therapy: Theory and practice*, Vol. 3. New York: Brunner/ Mazel.

Franks, J. (1963). *Persuasion and healing*. New York: Schocken Books.

Franks, J. (Ed.). *Behavior therapy: Appraisal and status* (pp. 495–523). New York, McGraw-Hill.

Fransella, F. (1968). Self concepts and the stutterer. *British Journal of Psychiatry, 114*, 1531–1535.

Fransella, F. (1972). *Personal change and reconstruction*. New York: Academic Press.

Fransella, F. (1978). *Personal construct psychology 1977*. New York: Academic Press.

Fransella, F., & Bannister, D. (1977). *A manual for repertory grid technique*. New York: Academic Press.

Fransson, A. (1977). On qualitative differences in learning. IV—Effects of motivation and test anxiety on process and outcome. *British Journal (Educational Psychology, 47,* 244–257.

Franz, S. I. (1915). Variations in the distribution of the motor centers, *Psychological Monographs, 19,* 147–160.

Franz, S. I. (1932). Autobiography. In C. Murchison (Ed.), *A history of psychology in autobiography,* Vol. 2. Worcester, Mass.: Clark University Press.

Franz, S. I. (1933). *Persons one and three: A study in multiple personalities.* New York: McGraw-Hill.

Fraser, D. A. S. (1958). *Statistics: An introduction.* New York: Wiley.

Fraser, R. M., & Glass, I. B. (1978). Recovery from ECT in elderly patients. *British Journal of Psychiatry, 133,* 524–528.

Fraser, R. M., & Glass, I. B. (1980). Unilateral and bilateral ECT in elderly patients. *Acta Psychiatrica Scandinavia, 62,* 13–31.

Frazer, A., & Winokur, A. (Eds.). (1977). *The biological bases of psychiatric disorders.* New York, London: Spectrum.

Frazer, J. (1963/1890). *The golden bough* (13 vols.). London: Macmillan.

Frazer, J. G. (1911). *Taboo and the perils of the soul.* London: Macmillian.

Frazer, M. (1984). *Self therapy for stutters.* Memphis: Speech Foundation of America.

Frazer, M. (1988). *Self therapy for stutterers* (5th ed.). Memphis: Speech Foundation of America.

Frederick, C. (1978). *Dangerous behavior: A problem in law and mental health* (NIMH, DHEW Publication No. (ADM) 78-563). Washington, DC: U.S. Government Printing Office.

Frederick, C. J. (1955). *An investigation of learning theory and reinforcement as related to stuttering behavior.* Doctoral dissertation, University of California at Los Angeles.

Frederick, C. J. (1977). Current thinking about crisis and psychological intervention in United States disasters. *Mass Emergencies, 2,* 43–50.

Frederick, C. J. (1980). The suicide prone depressive: The widening circle. In *Depression in the '80s. Lederle Laboratory/New York University Symposium. Science and Medicine.* New York.

Frederick, C. J. (1982). Learning theory and stuttering behavior. Unpublished manuscript.

Frederick, J. T. (1978). Jury behavior: A psychologist examines jury selection. *Ohio Northern University Law Review, 5,* 571–585.

Frederick, O. I. (1941). Curriculum development. In W. S. Monroe (Ed.), *Encyclopedia of educational research.* New York: Macmillan.

Fredericks, C. (1981/1976). *Psycho-nutrition,* New York: Grosset & Dunlap.

Frederiksen, N., Jensen, O., & Beaton, A. E. (1972). *Prediction of organizational behavior.* Elmsford, N.Y.: Pergamon Press.

Freedheim, D. K. (Ed.). (1992). *History of psychotherapy: A century of change.* Washington, DC: American Psychological Association.

Freedman, A. M., Kaplan, H. I., & Sadock, B. J. (1976). *Modern synopsis of psychiatry* (2nd ed.). Baltimore, Md.: Williams & Wilkins.

Freedman, A. M., Kaplan, H. I., & Sadock, (Eds.). (1975). *Comprehensive textbook of psychiatry,* Vols. I, II. Baltimore, Md.: Williams & Wilkins.

Freedman, A. M., Kaplan, H. I., & Sadock, B. J. (Eds.). (1980). *Comprehensive textbook of psychiatry,* Vol. III. Baltimore, Md.: Williams & Wilkins.

Freedman, D. G., & Freedman, N. A. (1969). Behavioral differences between Chinese-American and European-American newborns. *Nature, 224,* 1227.

Freedman, D. G., & Keller, B. (1963). Inheritance of behavior in infants. *Science, 140,* 196.

Freedman, J. L. (1975). *Crowding and behavior.* San Francisco: Freeman.

Freedman, J. L. (1982). *Introductory psychology* (2nd ed.). Reading, Mass.: Addison-Wesley.

Freedman, J. L., & Fraser, S. C. (1966). Compliance without pressure: The foot-in-the-door technique. *Journal of Personality and Social Psychology, 4,* 195–202.

Freedman, J. L., Wallington, S. A., & Bless, E. (1967). Compliance without pressure: The effect of guilt. *Journal of Personality and Social Psychology, 7,* 117–124.

Freedman, R., & Coombs, L. (1966). Child spacing and family economic position. *American Sociological Review, 31,* 631–648.

Freeman, A., Simon, K., Beutler, L., & Arkowitz, M. (Eds.). (1989). *Comprehensive handbook of cognitive therapy.* New York: Plenum Press.

Freeman, D. (1983). *Margaret Mead and Samoa: The making and unmaking of an anthropological myth.* Cambridge, Mass.: Harvard University Press.

Freiberg, P. (1992). Civil Rights Act is signed: Interpretation will be next arena for debate. *APA Monitor, 23*(1), 1.

Freibergs, V., & Tulving, E. (1961). The effect of practice on utilization of information from positive and negative instances in concept identification. *Canadian Journal of Psychology, 15,* 101–106.

Freidman, R. (1970). A rage-reduction diagnostic technique with young children. *Child Psychiatry and Human Development, 1,* 112–125.

Freidman, R., Dreizen, K., Harris, L., Schoer, P., & Shulman, P. (1978). *Parent power: a holding technique in the treatment of omnipotent children. International Journal of Family Counseling, 6,* 66–73.

French, J. D. (1957). The reticular formation. *Scientific American, 196*(5), 54–60.

French, J. L. (1979). Intelligence: Its measurement and its relevance for education. *Professional Psychology, 10,* 753–759.

French, J. R. P. (1944). Retraining an autocratic leader. *Journal of Abnormal and Social Psychology, 39,* 224–237.

French, J. R. P. (1973). Person role fit. *Occupational Mental Health, 3,* 15–20.

French, J. R. P., & Caplan, R. D. (1970). Psychosocial factors in coronary heart disease. *Industrial Medicine and Surgery, 39,* 31–45.

French, J. R. P., & Caplan, R. D. (1973). Organizational stress and individual strain. In A. J. Marrow (Ed.), *The failure of success.* New York: American Management Association.

French, J. R. P., & Raven, B. H. (1959). The basis of social power. In D. Cartwright (Ed.), *Studies in social power.* Ann Arbor, Mich.: University of Michigan Press.

French, J. W. (1953). *The description of personality measurement in terms of rotated factors.* Princeton, N.J.: Educational Testing Service.

French, T. M. (1952). *The integration of behavior,* Vols. I, II. Chicago: University of Chicago Press.

French, W. L., & Bell, C. H. (1973). *Organization development: Behavioral science intervention for organization improvement.* Englewood Cliffs, N.J.: Prentice-Hall.

Frenkel-Brunswik, E. (1942). Motivation and behavior. *Genetic Psychology Monographs, 26,* 121–265.

Frenkel-Brunswik, E. (1949). Intolerance of ambiguity as an emotional and perceptual personality variable. *Journal of Personality, 18,* 108–143.

Frenkel-Brunswik, E. (1963). Adjustments and orientation in the course of the life span. In R. G. Kuhlen & G. G. Thompson (Eds.), *Psychological studies in human development.* New York: Appleton-Century-Crofts.

Frenkel-Brunswik, E. (1974). Else Frenkel-Brunswik: Selected papers. In N. Heiman & J. Grant (Eds.), *Psychological Issues, 8,* Monograph 31.

Frenkel-Brunswik, E., Levinson, D. J., & Sanford, R. N. (1947). The antidemocratic personality. In T. M. Newcomb & E. L. Hartley (Eds.), *Readings in social psychology.* New York: Holt.

Fretz, B. R. (1981). Evaluating the effectiveness of career interventions. *Journal of Counseling Psychology Monograph, 28,* 77–90.

Fretz, B. R. (Ed.). (1977). Professional identity. *The Counseling Psychologist, 1,* 8–94.

Freud, A. (1946). *The psycho-analytic treatment of children.* London: Imago.

Freud, A. (1946/1937). *The ego and mechanisms of defense.* New York: International Universities Press.

Freud, A. (1947). *Psychoanalysis for teachers and parents.* New York: Emerson Books.

Freud, A. (1969). Adolescence as a developmental disturbance. In Kaplan, G., & Lebovici, S. (Eds.), *Adolescence: Psychological perspectives.* New York: Basic Books.

Freud, A. (1974). *The writings of Anna Freud* (7 vols.). New York: International Universities Press.

Freud, A., & Burlingham, D. (1944). *Infants without families: The case for and against residential nurseries.* New York: International Universities Press.

Freud, S. (1915). The unconscious. In J. Strachey (Ed.), *Standard edition of the complete psychological works of Sigmund Freud* (Vol. 14). London: Hogerth.

Freud, S. (1924). A short account of psycho-analysis. In *The standard edition of the complete psychological works of Sigmund Freud,* Vol. 19. London: Hogarth Press.

Freud, S. (1927). *The future of an illusion.* Garden City, N.Y.: Doubleday.

Freud, S. (1933). The psychology of women. In *New introductory lectures on psychoanalysis.* New York: Norton.

Freud, S. (1934). Psychoanalytic notes upon an autobiographical account of a case of paranoia (dementia paranoides). In *Collected papers,* Vol. 3. London: Hogarth Press.

Freud, S. (1934). Repression. In *Collected Papers,* Vol. 4. London: Hogarth Press.

Freud, S. (1934/1925/1908). Character and anal eroticism. In *Collected papers.* London: Hogarth Press.

Freud, S. (1936). *The problem of anxiety.* New York: Norton.

Freud, S. (1938). Symptomatic and chance actions. In A. A. Brill (Ed.), *The basic writings of Sigmund Freud.* New York: Random House.

Freud, S. (1938/1930). Three contributions to the theory of sex. In A. A. Brill (Ed.), *The basic writings of Sigmund Freud.* New York: Modern Library.

Freud, S. (1950). A special type of object-choice. In *Collected Papers,* Vol. 4. London: Hogarth Press.

Freud, S. (1950). Extracts from the Fliess letters. In *The standard edition of the complete psychological works of Sigmund Freud,* Vol. 1. London: Hogarth Press.

Freud, S. (1950). Infantile genital organization, 1923. In *Collected Papers,* Vol. II. London: Hogarth Press.

Freud, S. (1950). Medusa's head. In *Collected Papers,* Vol. V. London: Hogarth Press.

Freud, S. (1950). Mourning and melancholia. In *Collected Papers,* Vol 4. London: Hogarth Press.

Freud, S. (1950/1925). The passing of the oedipus complex. In *Collected papers,* Vol. 2. London: Hogarth Press.

Freud, S. (1953). Analysis of a phobia in a five-year-old boy. In *The standard edition of the complete psychological works of Sigmund Freud,* Vol. 10. London: Hogarth Press.

Freud, S. (1953). Early studies on the psychial [sic] mechanism of hysterical phenomena. In *The standard edition of the complete psychological works of Sigmund Freud,* Vol. 2. London: Hogarth Press.

Freud, S. (1953) Fragment of an analysis of a case of hysteria. In J. Strachey (Ed.), *The standard edition of the complete psychological works of Sigmund Freud* (Vol. 7). London: Hogarth. (Original work published 1905)

Freud, S. (1953). Working through. In *The standard edition of the complete psychological works of Sigmund Freud,* Vol. 12. London: Hogarth Press.

Freud, S. (1953/1905). Three essays on the theory of sexuality. In *The standard edition of the complete psychological works of Sigmund Freud,* Vol. 7. London: Hogarth Press.

Freud, S. (1953/1906). The transformation of puberty. In *The standard edition of the complete psychological works of Sigmund Freud,* Vol. 7. London: Hogarth Press.

Freud, S. (1953/1920). Beyond the pleasure principle. In *The standard edition of the complete psychological works of Sigmund Freud,* Vol. 19. London: Hogarth Press.

Freud, S. (1953/1934). Instincts and their vicissitudes. In *Collected papers,* Vol. 4. London: Hogarth Press.

Freud, S. (1953–1964). *The standard edition of the complete psychological works of Sigmund Freud* (24 vols.). London: Hogarth Press.

Freud, S. (1953–1966). Analysis terminable and interminable. In *The standard edition of the complete psychological works of Sigmund Freud,* Vol. 23. London: Hogarth Press.

Freud, S. (1956/1928). Humor. In *Collected papers,* Vol. 5. London: Hogarth Press.

Freud, S. (1957). The antithetical meaning of primal words (1910). In *The standard edition of the complete psychological works of Sigmund Freud,* Vol. 11. London: Hogarth Press.

Freud, S. (1957/1912). Totem and taboo and other works. In *The standard edition of the complete psychological works of Sigmund Freud,* Vol. 13. London: Hogarth Press.

Freud, S. (1957/1914). On narcissism: An introduction. In *The standard edition of the complete psychological works of Sigmund Freud,* Vol. 14. London: Hogarth Press.

Freud, S. (1957/1914). On the history of the psychoanalytic movement. In *The standard edition of the complete psychological works of Sigmund Freud,* Vol. 14. London: Hogarth Press.

Freud, S. (1958). *On creativity and the unconscious.* New York: Harper.

Freud, S. (1959/1907). The collected papers of Sigmund Freud. New York: Basic Books.

Freud, S. (1959/1925). Inhibitions, symptoms and anxiety. In *The standard edition of the complete psychological works of Sigmund Freud,* Vol. 20. London: Hogarth Press.

Freud, S. (1960/1921). *Group psychology and the analysis of the ego.* New York: Bantam Books.

Freud, S. (1961/1924). The economic problem in masochism. In *The standard edition of the complete psychological works of Sigmund Freud*, Vol. 19. London: Hogarth Press.

Freud, S. (1961/1925). Some psychical consequences of the anatomical distinction between the sexes. In *The standard edition of the complete psychological works of Sigmund Freud*, Vol. 19. London: Hogarth Press.

Freud, S. (1962). On the grounds for detaching a particular syndrome from neurasthenia under the description anxiety neurosis. In *The standard edition of the complete psychological works of Sigmund Freud*, Vol. 3. London: Hogarth Press.

Freud, S. (1962). Psycho-analytic notes on an autobiographical account of a case of paranoia (dementia paranoides). In J. Strachey (Trans. and Ed.), *The standard edition of the complete works of Sigmund Freud* (Vol. 12, pp. 3–82). London: Hogarth Press.

Freud, S. (1962/1923). *The ego and the id.* New York: Norton.

Freud, S. (1962/1930). *Civilization and its discontents.* New York: Norton.

Freud, S. (1963). Some points in a comparative study of organic hysterical paralyses. In M. Meyer (Ed.), *Freud: Early psychoanalytic writings.* New York: Collier Brooks. (Original work published 1893)

Freud, S. (1964). A case of hysteria. In *The standard edition of the complete psychological works of Sigmund Freud.* London: Hogarth Press.

Freud S. (1964). New introductory lectures in psychoanalysis. In J. Strachey (Ed.), *The standard edition of the complete psychological works of Sigmund Freud.* (pp. 7–184). London: Hogarth (Original work published 1933)

Freud, S. (1964). *The complete psychological works of Sigmund Freud,* Vols. 1–24. London: Hogarth Press.

Freud, S. (1964/1894). The neuropsychoses of defense. In *The standard edition of the complete psychological works of Sigmund Freud*, Vol. 3. London: Hogarth Press.

Freud, S. (1964/1911). Formulations regarding the two principles of mental functioning. In *The standard edition of the complete psychological works of Sigmund Freud.* Vol. 12. London: Hogarth Press.

Freud, S. (1964/1914). The history of the psychoanalytic movement. In *The standard edition of the complete psychological works of Sigmund Freud.* Vol. 14.

Freud, S. (1966/1885). Project for a scientific psychology. In *The standard edition of the complete psychological works of Sigmund Freud*, Vol. 1. London: Hogarth Press.

Freud, S. (1966/1933). *The complete introductory lectures on psychoanalysis.* New York: Norton.

Freud, S. (1968/1900). The interpretation of dreams. In *The standard edition of the complete psychological works of Sigmund Freud.* Vols. 4, 5. London: Hogarth Press.

Freud, S. (1968/1901). The psychopathology of everyday life. In *The standard edition of the complete psychological works of Sigmund Freud*, Vol. 6. London: Hogarth Press.

Freud, S. (1968/1905). Jokes and their relation to the unconscious. In *The standard edition of the complete psychological works of Sigmund Freud.* Vol 8. London: Hogarth Press.

Freud, S. (1968/1908). Creative writers and day-dreams. In *The standard edition of the complete psychological works of Sigmund Freud*, Vol. 9. London: Hogarth Press.

Freud, S. (1968/1916). Introductory lectures on psychoanalysis. In *The standard edition of the complete psychological works of Sigmund Freud*, Vols. 15, 16. London: Hogarth Press.

Freud, S. (1968/1919). The "uncanny" In *The standard edition of the complete psychological works of Sigmund Freud*, Vol. 17. London: Hogarth Press.

Freud, S. (1968/1928). Dostoevsky and parricide. In *The standard edition of the complete psychological works of Sigmund Freud*, Vol. 21. London: Hogarth Press.

Freud, S. (1969/1938/1935/1920). *A general introduction to psychoanalysis.* New York: Pocket Books.

Freud, S. (1969/1940). *An outline of psychoanalysis* (rev. ed.). New York: Norton.

Freud, S. (1973). The libido theory. In *The standard edition of the complete psychological works of Sigmund Freud* Vol. 18. London: Hogarth Press.

Freud, S. (1973/1933). New introductory lectures on psychoanalysis. In *The standard edition of the complete psychological works of Sigmund Freud*, Vol. 22. London: Hogarth Press.

Freud, S. (1974/1920). The psychogenesis of a case of female homosexuality. In *The standard edition of the complete psychological works of Sigmund Freud*, Vol. 18. London: Hogarth Press.

Freud, S. (1974/1924). The dissolution of the Oedipus complex. In *The standard edition of the complete psychological works of Sigmund Freud*, Vol. 19. London: Hogarth Press.

Freud, S. (1974/1931). Female sexuality. In *The standard edition of the complete psychological works of Sigmund Freud*, Vol. 21. London: Hogarth Press.

Freud, S. (1975). Dostoevsky and parricide. In J. Halliday & P. Fuller (Eds.), *The psychology of gambling.* New York: Harper & Row.

Freud, S., & Breuer, J. (1953/1892). On the psychical mechanism of hysterical phenomena. In *Collected papers*, Vol. 1. London: Hogarth Press.

Freud, S., & Breuer, J. (1953/1895). Studies on hysteria. In *The standard edition of the complete psychological works of Sigmund Freud*, Vol. 2. London: Hogarth Press.

Freudenberger, H. J. (1974). Staff burn-out. *Journal of Social Issues, 30,* 159–165.

Freudenberger, H. J. (1990). Therapists as men and men as therapists. *Psychotherapy, 27*(3), 340–343.

Freudenberger, H. J., Freedheim, D. K., & Kurtz, T. S. (1989). Treatment of individuals in family business. *Psychotherapy, 26*(1), 47–54.

Freund, K., Langevin, R., Zajac, Y., Steiner, B., & Zajac, A. (1974). The transsexual syndrome in homosexual males. *Journal of Nervous and Mental Diseases, 158,* 145–153.

Frey, F. (1970). Cross-cultural survey research in political science. In R. Holt & J. Turner (Eds.), *The methodology of comparative research.* New York: Free Press.

Frey, S., Hirsbrunner, H. P., Florin, A., Daw, W., & Crawford, R. (1982). Unified approach to the investigation of nonverbal and verbal behavior in communication research. In S. Moscovici & W. Dois (Eds.), *Current issues in European social psychology.* Cambridge, England: Cambridge University Press.

Frey-Rohn, L. (1990). *From Freud to Jung: Comparative study of the psychology of the unconscious.* Boston: Shambhala. (Original work published 1974)

Freyd, M. (1923). Measurement in vocational selection: An outline of research procedure. *Journal of Personnel Research, 2,* 268–284, 377–385.

Frich, C. E., & Hayflick, L. (Eds.). (1977). *Handbook of the biology of aging.* New York: Van Nostrand Reinhold.

Frick, R. J., Kamphaus, R. W., Lahey, B. B., Loeber, R., Christ, M. A. G., Hart, E., & Tannenbaum, L. E. (1991). Academic underachievement and the disruptive behavior disorders. *Journal of Consulting and Clinical Psychology, 59,* 289–294.

Frick, R. W. (1988). Issues of representation and limited capacity in the auditory short-term store. *British Journal of Psychology, 79,* 213–240.

Fried, E. (1976). The impact of nonverbal communication of facial affect on children's learning. Dissertation, Rutgers University.

Friedan, B. (1963). *The feminine mystique.* New York: Norton.

Friedberg, L. (1975). Early recollections of homosexuals as indicators of their life styles. *Journal of Individual Psychology, 30,* 196–204.

Friedhoff, A. J., & Hekimian, L. (1980). A report on a study of rapid onset of action in a new psychotherapeutic agent. In *Depression in the '80s. Lederle Laboratory/New York University Symposium. Science and Medicine.* New York.

Friedlander, F. (1968). A comparative study of consulting processes and group development. *Journal of Applied Behavioral Science, 4,* 377–399.

Friedman, G. D. (1987). *Primer of epidemiology* (3rd ed.). New York: McGraw-Hill.

Friedman, J. H., Jackson, B. J., & Nogas, C. (1978). Birth order and age at marriage in females. *Psychological Reports, 42,* 1193–1194.

Friedman, M., Byers, S. O., Diamant, J., & Rosenman, R. H. (1975). Plasma catecholamine response for coronary prone subjects (Type A) to a specific challenge. *Metabolism, 24,* 205–210.

Friedman, M., & Rosenman, R. H. (1959). Association of specific overt behavior pattern with blood and cardiovascular findings. *Journal of the American Medical Association, 169,* 1286–1296.

Friedman, M., & Rosenman, R. H. (1974). *Type A behavior and your heart.* New York: Fawcett Crest.

Friedman, M. I., & Stricker, E. M. (1976). The physiological psychology of hunger: A physiological perspective. *Physiological Review, 83,* 409–431.

Friedman, M. J. (1991). Biological approaches to the diagnosis and treatment of post-traumatic stress disorder. *Journal of Traumatic Stress, 4,* 67–91.

Friedman, M. S. (1955). *Martin Buber: The life of dialogue.* Chicago: University of Chicago Press.

Friedman, N. (1976). From the experiential in therapy to experiential psychotherapy: A history. *Psychotherapy: Theory, Research and Practice, 13,* 236–243.

Friedman, P. (Ed.). (1967). *On suicide.* New York: International Universities Press.

Friedman, P. R. (1975). Legal regulation of applied behavior analysis in mental institutions and prisons. *Arizona Law Revue, 17,* 39–104.

Friedman, R., & Katz, M. (1974). *The psychology of depression.* Washington, D.C.: Winston.

Friedman, R. C., Wollesen, F., & Tendler, R. (1976). Psychological development and blood levels of sex steriods in male identical twins of divergent sexual orientation. *Journal of Nervous and Mental Diseases, 163,* 282–288.

Friedmann, E., & Havighurst, R. J. (1954). *The meaning of work and retirement.* Chicago: University of Chicago Press.

Fries, J. F. (1980). Aging, natural death, and the compression of morbidity. *New England Journal of Medicine, 303,* 130–135.

Friesen, J. (1991). *Uncovering the mystery of MPD: Its shocking origins . . . its surprising cure.* San Bernardino, CA: Here's Life Publishers.

Friesen, J. (1992a). *More than survivors: Conversations with multiple-personality clients.* San Bernardino, CA: Here's Life Publishers.

Friesen, J. (1992b). Ego-dystonic or ego-alien: Alternate personality or evil spirit? *Journal of Psychology and Theology, 20*(3), 197–200.

Frijda, N. H. (1968). Expressive behavior. In D. L. Sills (Ed.), *International encyclopedia of the social sciences,* Vol. 5. New York: Macmillan.

Frijda, N. H., (1968). Recognition of emotion. In L. Berkowitz (Ed.), *Advances in experimental social psychology,* Vol. 4. New York: Academic Press.

Frijda, N. H. (1972). Simulation of human long-term memory. *Psychological Bulletin, 77,* 1–31.

Frijda, N. H. (1980). The meaning of emotional expression. In *Révész Berichten.* Amsterdam: Psychological Laboratory, University of Amsterdam.

Frijda, N. H., & De Groot, A. D. (Eds.). (1981). *Otto Selz. His contribution to psychology.* Amsterdam, Berlin, New York: Mouton.

Frijda, N. H., & Jahoda, G. (1966). On the scope and methods of cross-cultural research. *International Journal of Psychology, 1,* 109–127.

Frisch, K. Von. (1950). *Bees: Their vision, chemical senses, and language.* Ithaca, N.Y.: Cornell University Press.

Frisch, K. von. (1923). *Über die Sprache der Bienen.* Jena, East Germany: Fischer.

Frisch, K. von. (1954/1927). *The dancing bees: An account of the life and senses of the honey bee.* London: Methuen.

Frisch, K. von. (1967). *The dance language and orientation of bees.* Cambridge, Mass.: Harvard University Press.

Fritsch, G., & Hitzig, E. (1870). Uber die elektrische Erregbarkeit des Grosshirns. *Archiv fur Anatomic und Physiologie,* 300–332.

Fritz, M., Wolfensburger, W., & Knowlton, M. (1971). *An apartment living plan to promote integration and normalization of mentally retarded adults.* Downsview, Ont.: Candian Association for the Retarded.

Frodi, A., Macaulay, J., & Thome, P. R. (1977). Are women always less aggressive than men? A review of the experimental literature. *Psychological Bulletin, 84,* 634–660.

Froebel, F. (1885/1826). *The education of man.* New York: Lovell.

Froebel, F. (1895/1840). *Friedrich Froebel's pedagogics of the kindergarten, or his ideas concerning the play and playthings of the child.* New York: Appleton.

Froelich, R. E., & Bishop, F. M. (1977). *Clinical interviewing skills.* St. Louis, Mo.: Mosby.

Fromm, E. (1939). Selfishness and self-love. *Psychiatry, 2,* 507–523.

Fromm, E. (1947). *Man for himself: An inquiry into the psychology of ethics.* New York: Holt, Rinehart & Winston.

Fromm, E. (1950). *Psychoanalysis and religion.* New Haven, Conn.: Yale University Press.

Fromm, E. (1955/1950). *The sane society.* New York: Holt, Rinehart & Winston.

Fromm, E. (1956). *The art of loving.* New York: Harper.

Fromm, E. (1957/1951). *The forgotten language: An introduction to the understanding of dreams, fairy tales, and myths.* New York: Grove Press.

Fromm, E. (1959). Psychoanalysis and Zen Buddhism. *Psychologia 2.*

Fromm, E. (1960). Psychoanalysis and Zen Buddhism. In D. T. Suzuki, E. Fromm, & R. DeMartino (Eds.), *Zen Buddhism and psychoanalysis.* New York: Grove Press.

Fromm, E. (1961). *Marx's concept of man.* New York: Ungar.

Fromm, E. (1961). *May man prevail?* New York: Doubleday/Anchor.

Fromm, E. (1962). *Beyond the chains of illusion: My encounter with Marx and Freud.* New York: Simon & Schuster.

Fromm, E. (1964). *The heart of man: Its genius for good and evil.* New York: Harper & Row.

Fromm, E. (1964). *The present human condition.* New York: Holt, Rinehart & Winston.

Fromm, E. (1965/1941). *Escape from freedom.* New York: Avon Books.

Fromm, E. (1970). *The crisis of psychoanalysis.* New York: Holt, Rinehart & Winston.

Fromm, E. (1973). *The anatomy of human destructiveness.* New York: Holt, Rinehart & Winston.

Fromm, E. (1975). Self-hypnosis. *Psychotherapy: Theory, Research, and Practice, 12,* 295–301.

Fromm, E. (1976). *To have or to be?* New York; Harper & Row.

Fromm, E. (1980). *Greatness and limitations in Freud's thought.* New York: Harper & Row.

Fromm, E., & Shor, R. E. (Eds.). (1979). *Hypnosis: Developments in research and new perspectives.* New York: Aldine.

Fromm, E., & Xirau, R. (1968). *The nature of man.* New York: Macmillan.

Frost, P. J., et al. (1991). *Reframina organizational culture.* Newbury Park, CA: Sage.

Frost, R., & Holmes, D. S. (1979). Effects of displacing aggression by annoyed and nonannoyed subjects. *Journal of Research in Personality, 13,* 221–233.

Frostig, M. (1972). Visual perception, integrative functions and academic learning. *Journal of Learning Disabilities, 5,* 1–15.

Frostig, M. & Maslow, P. (1979). Neuropsychological contribution to education. *Journal of Learning Disabilities, 12,* 538–552.

Frude, N. (1981). *Psychological approaches to child abuse.* Toloma, N.J.: Rowman & Littlefield.

Fry, E. (1968). A readability formula that saves time. *Journal of Reading, 11,* 513–516, 575–578.

Fry, E. (1977). Fry's readability graph: Clarifications, validity, and extension to level 17. *Journal of Reading, 21,* 242–252.

Fry, E. B. (1963). *Teaching machines and programmed instruction.* New York: McGraw-Hill.

Fryns, J. P. (1990). X-linked mental retardation and the fragile X syndrome: A clinical approach. In K. E. Davies (Ed.) *The fragile-X syndrome* (pp.1–39). Oxford,UK: Oxford University Press.

Fudenberg, H. H., Stites, D. P., Caldwell, J. L., & Wells, J. V. (1980). *Basic and clinical immunology.* Los Altos, Calif.: Large.

Fudin, R. (1986). Subliminal psychodynamic activation: Mommy and I are not yet one. *Perceptual and Motor Skills, 63,* 1159–1179.

Fulker, D. W. (1981). The genetic and environmental architecture of psychoticism, extraversion and neuroticism. In H. Eysenck (Ed.), *A model for personality.* New York: Springer-Verlag.

Fulker, D. W., Eysenck, S. B. G., & Zuckerman, M. (1980). A genetic and environmental analysis of sensation seeking. *Journal of Research in Personality, 14,* 261–281.

Fullan, M., & Pomfret, A. (1977). Research on curriculum and instruction implementation. *Review of Educational Research, 47,* 335–397.

Fuller, H. J. (1934). Plant behavior. *Journal of General Psychology, 11,* 379–394.

Fuller, J. L. (1967). Experiential deprivation and later behavior. *Science, 158,* 1645–1652.

Fuller, J. L., & Thompson, W. R. (1960). *Behavior genetics.* New York: Wiley.

Fuller, J. L., & Thompson, W. R. (1978). *Foundations of behavior genetics.* St. Louis, Mo.: Mosby.

Fuller, P. (1975). Gambling: A secular "religion" for the obsessional neurotic. In J. Halliday & P. Fuller (Eds.), *The psychology of gambling.* New York: Harper & Row.

Fuller, P. (1978). Attention and the EEG alpha-rhythm in learning disabled children. *Journal of Learning Disabilities, 11,* 303–312.

Fuller, R. K., & Roth, H. P. (1979). Disulfiram for the treatment of alcoholism: An evaluation in 128 men. *Annals of Internal Medicine, 90,* 901–904.

Fullmer, D., & Bernard, H. (1968). *Family consultation.* Boston: Houghton Mifflin.

Fullmer, D. W. (1978). *Counseling: Group theory and system* (2nd ed.). Cranston, R. I.: Carroll Press.

Fulton, R. (1977). *Death, grief and bereavement: A bibliography, 1845–1975.* New York: Arno Press.

Fundamentals of co-counseling manuals. (1963). Seattle, Wash.: Rational Island.

Funkenstein, D. H. (1955). The physiology of fear and anger. *Scientific American, 192,* 74–80.

Furman, W., & Buhrmester, D. (1985). Children's perceptions of the personal relationships in their social networks. *Developmental Psychology, 21,* 1016–1024.

Furnham, A. (1988). The adjustment of sojourners, in Y. Y. Kim, & W. B. Gudykunst (Eds.), *Cross-cultural adaptation: Current approaches.* Newbury Park, CA: Sage.

Furnham, A., & Bochner, S. (1986). *Culture Shock: Psychological reactions to unfamiliar environments.* London: Methuen.

Furtmüller, C. (1979). Alfred Adler: A biographical essay. In A. Adler, *Superiority and social interest.* New York: Norton.

Fuster, J. M. (1980). *The prefrontal cortex.* New York: Raven Press.

Fyfe, J. F., & Blumberg, M. (1985). Response to Griswold: A more valid test of the justifiability of police actions. *American Journal of Police, 4,* 110–132.

Gabbard, G. O., & Twemlow, S. W. (1984). *With the eyes of the mind: An empirical analysis of out-of-body states.* New York: Praeger.

Gable, A., & Page, C. V. (1980). The use of artificial intelligence techniques in computer-assisted instruction: An overview. *International Journal of Man-Machine Studies, 12,* 259–282.

Gabriel, M. & Moore, J. W. (Eds.). (1990). *Learning and computational neuroscience: Foundations of adaptive networks.* Cambridge: MIT Press.

Gacek, R. R., & Schukaecht, H. F. (1969). Pathology of presbycusis. *International Audiology, 8,* 199–209.

Gackenback, J., Hunt, H., & Alexander, C. N. (Eds.). (1993). *Higher states of consciousness: Theoretical and experiential perspectives.* New York: Plennum.

Gadamer, H. G. (1976). *Philosophical hermeneutics.* Los Angeles, Calif.: University of California Press.

Gaddes, W. H. (1980). *Learning disabilities and brain function: A neuropsychological approach.* New York: Springer-Verlag.

Gadlin, H., & Engle, G. (1975). Through the one-way mirror. *American Psychologist, 30,* 1003–1009.

Gadzella, B. M. (1980). A comparison of CAI and class instruction approaches on study skills. ERIC Document Reproduction Service No. ED 188–599.

Gadzella, B. M. (1982). Computer-assisted instruction on study skills. *Journal of Experimental Education, 50,* 122–126.

Gael, S. (1977). Development of job Task inventories and their use in job analysis research. Ms. 1445. *Catalog of Selected Documents in Psychology, 7*(I), 2.

Gaeth, G. J., & Shanteau, J. (1981). *Training expert decision makers to ignore irrelevant information: A comparison of lecture and interactive training procedures.* Technical Report 81–1, Department of Psychology, Kansas State University.

Gaffney, L. R., & McFall, R. M. (1981). A comparison of social skills in delinquent and nondelinquent adolescent girls using a behavioral role-playing inventory. *Journal of Consulting and Clinical Psychology, 49,* 959–967.

Gagné, E. D., & Bell, M. S. (1981). The use of cognitive psychology in the development and evaluation of textbooks. *Educational Psychologist, 16,* 83–100.

Gagné, R. M. (1962). The acquisition of knowledge. *Psychological Review, 69,* 355–365.

Gagné, R. M. (1965/1970/1977). *The conditions of learning.* New York: Holt, Rinehart & Winston.

Gagné, R. M. (1972). Domains of learning. *Interchanges, 3,* 1–8.

Gagné, R. M. (1974). *Essentials of learning for instruction.* Hinsdale, Ill.: Dryden Press.

Gagné, R. M. (1977). Analysis of objectives. In L. J. Briggs (Ed.), *Instructional design.* Englewood Cliffs, N.J.: Educational Technology.

Gagné, R. M, & Briggs, L. J. (1974/1979). *Principles of instructional design.* New York: Holt, Rinehart & Winston.

Gagné, R. M. (Ed.). (1963). *Psychological principles in system development.* New York: Holt, Rinehart & Winston.

Gagné, R. M. (Ed.). (1967). *Learning and individual differences.* Columbus, Ohio: Merrill.

Gagné, R. M., & Fleishman, E. A. (1959). *Psychology and human performance.* New York: Holt, Rinehart & Winston.

Gagnon, J. (1977). *Human sexualities.* Glenville, Ill.: Scott, Foresman.

Gagon, J. H., & Simon, W. (1973). *Sexual conduct: The social origins of human sexuality.* Chicago: Adeline.

Galaburda, A. M., & Kemper, T. L. (1979). Cytoarchitectonic abnormalities in developmental dyslexia: A case study. *Annals of Neurology, 6,* 94–100.

Galaburda, A. M., LeMay, M., Kemper, T. L., & Geschwind, N. (1978). Right–left asymmetries in the brain. *Science, 199,* 852–856.

Galassi, J. P., DeLo, J. S., Galassi, M. D., & Bastien, S. (1974). The college self-expression scale: A measure of a assertiveness. *Behavior Therapy, 6,* 550–561.

Galbraith, J. K. (1958). *The affluent society.* Boston: Houghton Mifflin.

Galen, (1956). *On anatomical procedures.* London: Oxford University Press.

Galindo, E. (1988). La psicologia Mexicana a traves de sus obras, 1959–1987. *Revista Mexicans de Psicologia 5*(2), 183–202.

Gall, F. J. (1835). *Works: On the functions of the brain and each of its parts.* Boston: Marsh, Capen & Lyon.

Gall, F. J., & Spurzheim, J. G. (1809). *Researches on the nervous system.* Paris: Schoell & Nicolle.

Gall, F. J., & Spurzheim, J. G. (1810–1819). *Anatomy and physiology of the nervous system.* Paris: Schoell.

Gall, F. J., with Spurzheim, J. (1810–1819). *Anatomie et Physiologie du Systeme Nerveux en General, et du Cerveau en Particulier* (4 vols.). Paris: Schoell.

Gallagher, R. P. (1991). *National survey of counseling center directors.* Pittsburgh, PA: The University of Pittsburgh.

Gallatin, J. E. (1975). *Adolescence and individuality.* New York: Harper.

Gallegos, X., (1980). James M. Baldwin's visits to Mexico. *American Psychologist, 35,* 772–773.

Gallistel, C. (1981). Bell, Magendie, and the proposals to restrict the use of animals in neurobehavioral research. *American Psychologist, 36,* 4, 357–360.

Gallistel, C. R. (1990). Representations in animal cognition: An introduction. *Cognition, 37,* 1–22.

Gallup, G. (1972). *The sophisticated poll watcher's guide.* Princeton, N.J.: Princeton Opinion Press.

Gallup, G. G., Jr. (1970). Chimpanzees: Self-recognition. *Science, 167,* 86–87.

Gallup, G. G., Jr. (1977). Self-recognition in primates: A comparative approach to the bidirectional properties of consciousness. *American Psychologist, 32,* 329–338.

Gallup, G. G., Jr. (1977). Tonic immobility: The role of fear and predation. *The Psychological Record, 1,* 41–46.

Gallup, G. G., Jr. (1979). Self-awareness in primates. *American Scientist, 67,* 417–421.

Gallup, G. G., Jr. (1982). Self-awareness and the emergence of mind in primates. *American Journal of Primatology, 2,* 238–248.

Gallup, G. G., Jr. (1985). Do minds exist in species other than our own? *Neuroscience & Biobehavioral Reviews, 9,* 631–641.

Gallup, G. G., Jr., McClure, M. K., Hill, S. D., & Bundy, R. A. (1971). Capacity for self-recognition in differentially reared chimpanzees. *The Psychological Record, 21,* 69–74.

Gallup, G. H. (1978). The tenth annual Gallup Poll on education. *Phi Delta Kappan, 60*(2), 33–45.

Gallup, G., Jr., & Proctor, W. (1982). *Adventures in immortality: A look beyond the threshold of death.* New York: McGraw-Hill.

Gallup Poll. (1992, April 27). *USA Today,* p. 1B.

Gallwey, T. (1974). *The inner game of tennis.* New York: Random House.

Gallwey, T. (1979). *The inner game of golf.* New York: Random House.

Galton, F. (1872). Statistical Inquiries Into the Efficacy of Prayer. *The Fortnightly Review, 12,* 125–135.

Galton, F. (1874). *English men of science: Their nature and nurture.* London: Macmillan.

Galton, F. (1879–1980). Psychometric experiments. *Brain, 2,* 149–162.

Galton, F. (1883). *Inquiries into human faculty and its development.* London: Macmillan.

Galton, F. (1888). Co-relations and their measurements, chiefly from anthropometric data. *Proceedings of the Royal Society, 45,* 135–140.

Galton, F. (1907/1883). *Inquiries into human faculty and its development.* London: Macmillan.

Galton, F. (1961). Classification of men according to their natural gifts. In J. J. Jenkins & D. G. Paterson (Eds.), *Studies in individual differences.* New York: Appleton-Century-Crofts.

Galton, F. (1962/1869). *Hereditary genius: An inquiry into its laws and consequences.* London: Collins.

Galton, F. (1973/1889). *Natural inheritance.* New York: AMS Press.

Galton, F. (1974/1908). *Memories of my life.* New York: AMS Press.

Galton, L. (1973). *The silent disease: Hypertension.* New York: Crown.

Gambaro, S., & Rabin, A. (1969). Diastolic blood pressure response following direct and displaced aggression after anger arousal in high- and low-guilt subjects. *Journal of Personality and Social Psychology, 12,* 87–94.

Gamble, K. R. (1972). The Holtzman Inkblot Technique: A review. *Psychological Bulletin, 77,* 172–194.

Gamblers Anonymous. (1977). *Gamblers Anonymous.* Los Angeles: Gamblers Anonymous.

Gambrill, E. D. (1978). *Behavior modification: Handbook of assessment, intervention, and evaluation.* San Francisco: Jossey-Bass.

Gambrill, E. D., & Richey, C. A. (1975). An assertion inventory for use in assessment and research. *Behavior Therapy, 6,* 550–561.

Gampopa. (1971). *The jewel ornament of liberation.* Boulder, Colo.: Shambhala Press.

Ganaway, G. (1989). Historical truth versus narrative truth: Clarifying the role of exogenous trauma in the etiology of multiple personality and its variants. *Dissociation, 21*(4), 205–220.

Ganaway, G. (1990, November). *A psychodynamic look at alternative explanations for satanic ritual abuse in MPD patients.* Paper presented at Seventh International Conference on Multiple Personality/Dissociative States, Chicago.

Ganaway, G. (1992). Some additional questions: A response to Shaffer & Cozolino, to Gould and Cozolino and to Friesen. *Journal of Psychology and Theology, 20*(3), 201–205.

Gandelman, R. (1983). Gonadal hormones and sensory function. *Neuroscience and Biobehavioral Reviews, 7,* 1–17.

Ganikos, M. L. (Ed.). (1979). *Counseling the aged: A training syllabus for educators.* Washington, D.C.: American Personnel and Guidance Association.

Gans, H. J. (1962). *The urban villagers.* New York: Macmillan.

Gantt, L., & Schmal, M. S. (1974). *Art therapy—A bibliography, January 1940–June 1973.* Bethesda, Md.: National Institute of Mental Health.

Garb, H. N. (1989). Clinical judgment, clinical training, and professional experience. *Psychological Bulletin, 105,* 387–396.

Garbarino, J. (1982). *Children and families in the social environment.* New York: Aldine.

Garbarino, J., & Stocking, S. H. (1980). *Protecting children from abuse and neglect: Developing and maintaining effective support systems for families.* San Francisco: Jossey-Bass.

Garber, J., Miller, S., & Abramson, L. Y. (1980). On the distinction between anxiety and depression: Perceived control, certainty, and probability of goal attainment. In M. E. P. Seligman (Ed.), *Human helplessness.* New York: Academic Press.

Garber, J., & Seligman, M. E. P. (1980). *Human helplessness: Theory and applications.* New York: Academic Press.

Garcia, J., Rusiniak, K. W., & Brett, L. P. (1977). Conditioned food illness aversion in wild animals: *Caveant canonici.* In H. Davis & H. M. B. Hurwitz (Eds.), *Operant–Pavlovian interactions.* Hillsdale, N.J.: Erlbaum.

Garcia, L. T., & Griffitt, W. (1978). Impact of testimonial evidence as a function of witness characteristics. *Bulletin of the Psychonomic Society, II,* 37–40.

Gardiner, J. K. (1981). On female identity and writing by women. *Critical Inquiry, 8,* 347–361.

Gardiner, P. C., & Edwards, W. (1975). Public values: Multiattribute-utility measurement for social decision making. In M. F. Kaplan & S. Schwartz (Eds.), *Human judgment and decision processes.* New York: Academic Press.

Gardner, W. L. (1970). *Psychology: A story of a search.* Belmont, Calif.: Brooks/Cole.

Gardner, A. (1987). *An artificial intelligence approach to legal reasoning.* Cambridge: The MIT Press.

Gardner, B. T., & Gardner, R. A. (1971). Two-way communications with an infant chimpanzee. In A. M. Schirer & F. Stollnitz (Eds.), *Behavior of nonhuman primates,* Vol. 4. New York: Academic Press.

Gardner, B. T., & Gardner, R. A. (1980). Two comparative psychologists look at language acquisition. In K. E. Nelson (Ed.), *Children's language,* Vol. 2. New York: Gardner Press.

Gardner, E. (1975/1963). *Fundamentals of neurology.* Philadelphia, London: Saunders.

Gardner, G. G., & Olness, K. (1981). *Hypnosis and hypnotherapy with children.* New York: Grune & Stratton.

Gardner, H. (1973). *The arts and human development.* New York: Wiley.

Gardner, H. (1975). *The shattered mind.* New York: Knopf.

Gardner, H. (1981). *The quest for mind: Piaget, Lévi-Strauss, and the structuralist movement,* (2nd ed.). Chicago: University of Chicago Press.

Gardner, H. (1982). *Art, mind, and brain: A cognitive approach to creativity.* New York: Basic Books.

Gardner, H. (1982). *Developmental psychology.* Boston: Little, Brown.

Gardner, J. G. (1968). *No easy task.* New York: Harper & Row.

Gardner, J. W. (1961). *Excellence: Can we be equal and excellent too?* New York: Harper & Row.

Gardner, M. (1981). *Science: good, bad and bogus.* Buffalo, N.Y.: Prometheus Books.

Gardner, P. (1975). Scales and statistics. *Review of Educational Research, 45,* 43–57.

Gardner, R. A. (1979). *The objective diagnosis of minimal brain dysfunction.* Cresskill, N.J.: Creative Therapeutics.

Gardner, R. A., Gardner, A. K., Caemmerer, A., & Browman, M. (1979). An instrument for measuring hyperactivity and other signs of MBD. *Journal of Clinical Child Psychology, 8,* 173–179.

Gardner, R. A., & Gardner, B. T. (1969). Teaching sign language to a chimpanzee. *Science, 165,* 664–672.

Gardner, R. C., & Kalin, R. (1981). *A Canadian social psychology of ethnic relations.* Toronto: Methuen.

Gardner, R. C., & Lambert, W. E. (1972). *Attitudes and motivation in second-language learning.* Rowley, Mass.: Newbury House.

Gardos, G., & Cole, J. E. (1980). Overview: Public health issues in tardive dyskinesia. *American Journal of Psychiatry, 137,* 776–781.

Garfield, S. (1974). *Clinical psychology.* Chicago: Aldine.

Garfield, S. L. (1957). *Introductory clinical psychology.* New York: Macmillan.

Garfield, S. L. (1978). Research on client variables in psychotherapy. In S. L. Garfield & A. E. Bergin (Eds.), *Handbook of psychotherapy and behavior change: An empirical analysis.* New York: Wiley.

Garfield, S. L. (1978). Research problems in clinical diagnosis. *Journal of Consulting and Clinical Psychology, 46,* 596–607.

Garfield, S. L. (1980). *Psychotherapy: An eclectic approach.* New York: Wiley.

Garfield, S. L. (1981). Psychotherapy: A 40-year appraisal. *American Psychologist, 36,* 174–183.

Garfield, S. L. (1989). *The practice of brief psychotherapy.* Elmsford, NY: Pergamon.

Garfield, S. L., & Bergin, A. E. (1978/1971). *Handbook of psychotherapy and behavior change: An empirical analysis* (2nd ed.). New York: Wiley.

Garfield, S. L., & Bergin, A. E. (1986). Introduction and historical overview. In S. L. Garfield & A. E. Bergin (Eds.), *Handbook of psychotherapy and behavior change* (3rd ed., pp. 3–22).

Garfield, S. L., & Kurtz, R. (1976). Clinical psychologists in the 1970's. *American Psychologist, 31,* 1–9.

Garfinkel, H. (1967). *Studies in ethnomethodology.* Englewood Cliffs, N.J.: Prentice-Hall.

Garfunkel, P., Maldofsky, H., & Garner, D. (1980). The heterogeneity of anorexia nervosa: Bulimia as a distinct subgroup. *Archives of General Psychiatry, 37*(9), 1036–1040.

Gargiulo, R. M., & Kuna, D. (1979). Arousal level and hyperkinesis: Implications for biofeedback. *Journal of Learning Disabilities, 12,* 137–138.

Garling, T., Book, A., Lindberg, E., & Arce, C. (1990). Is elevation encoded in cognitive maps? *Journal of Personality and Social Psychology, 13,* 145–152.

Garn, S. M. (1971/1961). *Human races* (3rd ed.). Springfield, Ill.: Thomas.

Garner, W. R. (1974). *The processing of information and structure.* Englewood Cliffs, N.J.: Prentice-Hall.

Garnets, L., Herek, G. M., & Levy, B. (1990). Violence and victimization of lesbians and gay men: Mental health consequences. *Journal of Interpersonal Violence, 5*(3), 366–383.

Garrett, A. (1949). Historical survey of the evolution of casework, *Journal of Social Casework, 30,* 219–229.

Garrett, C. S., Ein, P. L., & Tremaine, L. (1977). The development of gender stereotyping of adult occupations in elementary school children. *Child Development, 48,* 507–512.

Garrity, T. (pseud., "J.") (1971). *The sensuous woman.* Secaucus, N.J.: Stuart.

Gartner, A. (1971). *Paraprofessionals and their performance.* New York: Praeger.

Gartner, A., & Riessman, F. (1977). *Self-help in the human services.* San Francisco: Jossey-Bass.

Garvey, C., & Hogan, R. (1973). Social speech and social interaction: Egocentrism revisited. *Child Development, 44,* 562–568.

Garvey, C. R. (1929). List of American psychological laboratories. *Psychological Bulletin, 26,* 652–660.

Garvey, W. P., & Hegrenes, J. R. (1966). Desensitization technique in the treatment of school phobia. *American Journal of Orthopsychiatry, 36,* 147–152.

Garwood, S. G., Alberto, P., Du Bose, R. F., Hare, B. A., Hare, J. M., Kauffman, J., Kodera, T. I., Langley, M. B., & Page, D. A. (1979). *Educating young handicapped children—A developmental approach.* Germantown, Md.: Aspen Systems.

Garza Garcia, F. (1953). La psicologia industrial en Mexico. In Universidad Nacional Autonoma de Mexico (Ed.) *Memoria del Congreso Cientifico Mexicano Ciencias de la educacion, psicologiafilosofia,* (Vol. 15.), Mexico, D.F.: UNAM.

Gaston, L. (1990). The concept of the alliance and its role in psychotherapy: Theoretical and empirical considerations. *Psychotherapy, 27,* 143–153.

Gatchel, R. I., & Proctor, J. D. (1976). Physiological correlates of learned helplessness in man. *Journal of Abnormal Psychology, 85,* 27–34.

Gatchel, R. J., & Price, K. P. (Eds.). (1979). *Clinical applications of biofeedback: Appraisal and status.* New York: Pergamon Press.

Gates, A. I. (1917). Recitation as a factor in memorizing. *Archives of Psychology, 6*(40).

Gates, A. I. (1930). *Psychology for students of education* (rev. ed.). New York: Macmillan.

Gates, M. (1991, May 14). It's healthy to always be honest (Wait, we lied!). *Honolulu Star-Bulletin.*

Gathercole, S., & Baddeley, A. D. (1989). Evaluation of the role of phonological STM in the development of vocabulary in children: A longitudinal study. *Journal of Memory and Language, 28,* 200–213.

Gathercole, S., & Baddeley, A. D. (1990). The role of phonological memory in vocabulary acquisition: A study of young children learning arbitrary names of toys. *British Journal of Psychology, 81,* 439–454.

Gaughan, L. D., & La Rue, L. H. (1978). The right of a mental patient to refuse antipsychotic drugs in an institution. *Law and Psychology Review, 4,* 43–85.

Gauron, E. G., & Dickinson, J. K. (1966). Diagnostic decision-making in psychiatry: 1. Information usage. *Archives of General Psychiatry, 14,* 225–232.

Gay, P. (1988). *Freud: A life of our time.* New York: Norton.

Gaylord, C., Orme-Johnson, D., & Travis, F. (1989). The effects of the Transcendental Meditation technique and progressive muscle relaxation on EEG coherence, stress reactivity, and mental health in black adults. *International Journal of Neuroscience 46,* 77–86.

Gazda, G. M. (1981). Multiple impact training. In R. J. Corsini (Ed.), *Handbook of innovative psychotherapies.* New York: Wiley.

Gazda, G. M., Childers, W. C., Maynie, N. A. & Walters, R. P. (1982). *Interpersonal development: A handbook for health professionals.* Rockville, Md.: Aspen Systems.

Gazda, G. M. (Ed.). (1968). *Innovations to group psychotherapy.* Springfield, Ill.: Charles C Thomas.

Gazda, G. M. (Ed.). (1975/1968). *Basic approaches to group psychotherapy and group counseling.* Springfield, Ill.: Charles C Thomas.

Gazzaniga, M. S. (1970). *The bisected brain.* New York: Appleton-Century-Crofts.

Gazzaniga, M. S., & Hillyard, S. A. (1971). Language and speech capacity of the right hemisphere. *Neuropsychologia, 9,* 273–280.

Gazzaniga, M. S., Steen, D., & Volpe, B. T. (1979). *Functional neuroscience.* New York: Harper & Row.

Geber, M., & Dean, R. A. F. (1957). Gesell tests on African children. *Pediatrics, 20,* 1055–1065.

Geber, M., & Dean, R. F. A. (1957). The state of development of newborn African children. *Lancet, 272,* 1216–1219.

Gebhard, J. W. (1961). Hypnotic age regression: A review. *American Journal of Clinical Hypnosis, 3,* 139–168.

Gebhard, P. H. (1969). Fetishism and sadomasochism. *Science and Psychoanalysis, 15,* 71–80.

Gebhard, P. H., Gagnon, J., Pomeroy, W., & Christenson, C. (1965). *Sex offenders: An analysis of types.* New York: Harper & Row.

Geen, R., & Berkowitz, L. (1967). Some conditions facilitating the occurrence of aggression after the observation of violence. *Journal of Personality, 35,* 666–676.

Geen, R. G., & Gange, J. J. (1977). Drive theory of social facilitation: Twelve years of research and theory. *Psychological Bulletin, 84,* 1267–1288.

Geertz, C. (1973). *The interpretation of cultures: Selected essays.* New York: Basic Books.

Geertz, C. (1973). Thick description: Toward an interpretive theory of culture. In *The interpretation of cultures*. New York: Basic Books.

Geffen, N. (1966). Rumination in man. *American Journal of Digestive Diseases, 11*, 963.

Gehlen, A. (1940). *Der Mensch, seine Nation und seine Stellung in der Welt*. Berlin: Junker & Duennhaupt.

Geiselman, R. E. (1984). Enhancement of eyewitness memory: An empirical evaluation of the cognitive interview. *Journal of Police Science and Administration, 12*, 74–80.

Geiselman, R. E., & Machlovitz, H. (1987). Hypnosis memory recall: Implications for forensic use. *American Journal of Forensic Psychology, 5*, 37–47.

Geiselman, R. E., & Padilla, J. (1988). Cognitive interviewing with child witnesses. *Journal of Police Science & Administration, 16*, 236–242.

Geiselman, R. E., Saywitz, K. & Bornstein, G. (1991, April). *Enhancing children's eyewitness memory: A test of the cognitive interview with children*. Paper presented at the annual meetings of the Society for Research on Child Development, Seattle.

Geisinger, K. F. (1982). Marking systems. In H. E. Mitzel (Ed.), *Encyclopedia of educational research* Vol. 3, (5th ed.). New York: Macmillan/Free Press.

Geiwitz, P. J. (1966). Structure of boredom. *Journal of Personality and Social Psychology, 3*, 592–600.

Geldard, F. A. (1972/1953). *The human senses*. New York: Wiley.

Geldard, F. A. (1975). *Sensory saltation*. Hillsdale, N.J.: Erlbaum.

Gelderloos, P., Hermans, H. I. M., Ahlstrom, H. H., & Jacoby, R. (1990). Transcendence and psychological health: Studies with long-term participants of the Transcendental Meditation-Sidhi program. *Journal of Psychology, 124*(2), 177–197.

Gelderloos, P., Walton, K. G., Orme-Johnson, Ei. W., & Alexander, C. N. (1991). Effectiveness of the Transcendental Meditation program in preventing and treating substance misuse: A review. *International Journal of the Addictions, 26*, 293–325.

Gelles, R. (1976). Abused wives: Why do they stay? *Journal of Marriage and the Family, 38*, 659–668.

Gelles, R. J., & Straus, M. A. (1979). Determinants of violence in the family: Toward a theoretical integration. In W. R. Burr, R. Hill, F. I. Nye, & I. L. Reiss (Eds.), *Contemporary theories about the family*. New York: Free Press.

Gellhorn, E. (Ed.). (1968). *Biological foundations of emotion*. Glenview, Ill.: Scott, Foresman.

Gelpi, B. C., Harstock, C. M., Novak, C. C., & Strober, M. H. (Eds.). (1986). *Women and poverty*. Chicago: University of Chicago Press.

Gelso, C. J. (1979). Research in counseling: Methodology and professional issues. *The Counseling Psychologist, 8*, 7–67.

Gemelli, A. (1952). Autobiography. In E. G. Boring et al. (Eds.), *History of psychology in autobiography*, Vol. 4. Worcester, Mass.: Clark University Press.

Gendlin, E. (1979). Experimental explication and the problem of truth. In R. C. Solomon (Ed.), *Phenomenology and existentialism*. Washington D.C.: Universities Press of America.

Gendlin, E. T. (1964). A theory of personality change. In P. Worchel & D. Byrne (Eds.), *Personality change*. New York: Wiley.

Gendlin, E. T. (1967). Focusing ability in psychotherapy, personality and creativity. In J. Shlien (Ed.), *Research in psychotherapy*, Vol. 3. Washington D.C.: American Psychological Association.

Gendlin, E. T. (1968). The experiential response. In E. Hammet (Ed.), *Use of interpretation in treatment*. New York: Grune & Stratton.

Gendlin, E. T. (1969). Focusing. *Psychotherapy: Theory, Research, and Practice, 6*, 4–15.

Gendlin, E. T. (1970/1962). *Experiencing and the creation of meaning*. New York: Free Press.

Gendlin, E. T. (1973). Experiential phenomenology. In M. Natanson (Ed.), *Phenomenology and the social sciences*. Evanston Ill.: Northwestern University Press.

Gendlin, E. T. (1974). Client-centered and experiential psychotherapy. In D. A. Wexler and L. N. Rice (Eds.), *Innovations in client-centered therapy*. New York: Wiley.

Gendlin, E. T. (1979/1973). Experiential psychotherapy. In R. J. Corsini (Ed.), *Current psychotherapies*. Itasca, Ill.: Peacock.

Gendlin, E. T. (1981/1978). *Focusing*. New York: Everest House.

Gendlin, E. T., Beebe, J., Cassues, J., Klein, M., & Oberlander, M. (1968). Focusing ability in psychotherapy, personality and creativity. *Research in Psychotherapy, 3*, 217–241.

Gendre, F. (1970). *L'orientation professionnelle à l'ère des ordinateurs*. Neuchâtel, Switzerland: Delachaux & Niestlé.

General Accounting Office. (1978). *Better services at reduced costs through an improved "Personal Care" program recommended for veterans*. Washington, D.C.: U.S. Government Printing Office.

Gennep, A. van. (1909). *The rites of passage*. London: Routledge.

George, D. H. (1980). *Blake and Freud*. Ithaca, N.Y.: Cornell University Press.

George, F. H. (1953). Formalization of language systems for behavior theory. *Psychological Review, 60*, 232–240.

George, J. M., Scott, D. S., Turner, S. P., & Gregg, J. M. (1980). The effects of psychological factors and physical trauma on recovery from oral surgery. *Journal of Behavioral Medicine, 3*, 291–310.

Gerbasi, K. C., Zuckerman, M., & Reis, H. T. (1977). Justice needs a new blindfold: A review of mock jury research. *Psychological Bulletin, 84*, 323–345.

Gergen, K. (1991). *The saturated self*. New York: Basic Books.

Gergen, K. J. (1973). Social psychology as history. *Journal of Personality and Social Psychology, 26*, 309–320.

Gergen, K. J. (1982). *Toward transformation in social knowledge*. New York: Springer-Verlag.

Gergen, K. J. (in press). *Toward transformation in social psychology*. New York: Springer-Verlag.

Gergen, K. J., & Gergen, M. M. (1988). Narrative and the self as relationship. In L. Berkowitz (Ed.), *Advances in experimental social psychology* (Vol. 21). New York: Academic Press.

Gergen, K. J., Greenberg, M. S., & Willis, R. H. (Eds.). (1980). *Social exchange: Advances in theory and research*. New York: Plenum.

Germain, C. (1970). Casework and science: A historical encounter. In W. Roberts & H. Nee (Eds.), *Theories of social casework*. Chicago: University of Chicago Press.

Germain, C. B., & Gitterman, A. (1980). *The life model of social work practice*. New York: Columbia University Press.

Germain, J. (1980). José Germain: Autobiografía (I). *Revista de Historia de la Psicología, 1*, 5–32.

Germain, J. (1980). José Germain: Autobiografía (II). *Revista de Historia de la Psicología, 1*, 139–169.

Gershon, E. S. (1973). The search for genetic markers in affective disorders. In M. A. Lipton, A. Dimascio, & K. D. Killam (Eds.), *Psychopharmacology: A generation of progress*. New York: Raven Press.

Gershon, M., & Biller, H. B. (1977). *The other helpers*. Lexington, Mass.: Lexington Books.

Gershon, S., & Shopsin, B. (Eds.). (1973). *Lithium: Its role in psychiatric treatment*. New York: Plenum.

Gerson, M., & Barsky, M. (1976). The new family therapist: A glossary of terms. *American Journal of Family Therapy, 4*(1), 15–30.

Gerstein, D. R., & Harwood, H. J. (Eds.). (1990). *Treating drug problems: Vol 1. A study of the evolution, effectiveness and financing of public and private drug treatment systems* (Committee for the Substance Abuse Coverage Study Division of Health Care Services, Institute of Medicine). Washington, DC: National Academy Press.

Geschwind, N. (1965). Disconnexion syndromes in animals and man. *Brain, 88*, 23–194.

Geschwind, N. (1970). The organization of language and the brain. *Science, 27*, 940–945.

Geschwind, N. (1972). Language in the brain. *Scientific American, 226*, 76–86.

Geschwind, N. (1974). *Selected papers on language and the brain*. Boston: Reidel.

Geschwind, N., & Levitsky, W. (1968). Human brain: Left-right asymmetries in temporal speech region. *Science, 161*, 168–187.

Gesell, A. (1925). *The mental growth of the pre-school child; a psychological outline of normal development from birth to the sixth year, including a system of developmental diagnosis*. New York: Macmillan.

Gesell, A. (1928). *Infancy and human growth*. New York: Macmillan.

Gesell, A. (1940). The stability of mental-growth careers. In *Intelligence: its nature and nurture*. Bloomington, Ill.: Public School Publishing.

Gesell, A. (1942). The documentation of infant behavior in relation to cultural anthropology. In *Proceedings of the 8th American Scientific Congress, Anthropological sciences*, Vol. 2. Washington, D.C.: Department of State.

Gesell, A. (1950). Infant vision. *Scientific American, 182*, 20–22.

Gesell, A., & Amatruda, C. (1947/1941). *Developmental diagnoses: Normal and abnormal child development* (2nd ed.). New York: Haeber.

Gesell, A., Halverson, H. M., Thompson, H., Ilg, F., Castner, B., Ames, L., & Amatruda, C. (1940). *The first five years of life*. New York: Harper.

Gesell, A., & Ilg, F. L. (1942). *Infant and child in the culture of today*. New York: Harper.

Gesell, A., & Ilg, F. L. (1946). *The child from five to ten*. New York: Harper.

Gesell, A., Ilg, F. L., & Ames, L. B. (1956). *Youth: The years from ten to sixteen*. New York: Harper.

Gesell, A., Ilg, F. L., & Ames, L. B. (1974). *Infant and child in the culture of today*. New York: Harper & Row.

Gesell, A., & Thompson, H. (1934). *Infant behavior: Its genesis and growth*. New York: McGraw-Hill.

Gesell, A., & Thompson, H. (1941). Twins T & C from infancy to adolescence: A biogenetic study of individual differences by the method of co-twin control, *Genetic Psychology Monographs, 24*(1), 3–121.

Geston, E. L., & Jason, L. A. (1987). Social and community intervention. *Annual Review of Psychology, 38*, 427–460.

Gettinger, M., & White, M. A. (1979). Which is the stronger correlate of school learning? Time to learn or measured intelligence? *Journal of Educational Psychology, 71*, 405–412.

Getzels, J. W. (1968). Pre-school education. In J. L. Frost (Ed.), *Early childhood education rediscovered—readings*. New York: Holt, Rinehart & Winston.

Getzels, J. W., & Csikszentmihali, M. (1976). *The creative vision: A longitudinal study of problem solving in art*. New York: Wiley.

Getzels, J. W. and Jackson, P. W. (1960). 5C Occupational choice and cognitive functioning career aspirations of highly intelligent and highly creative adolescents. *Journal of Abnormal and Social Psychology, 65*, 413–419.

Getzels, J. W., & Jackson, P. W. (1961). Family environment and cognitive style: A study of the sources of highly intelligent and of highly creative adolescents. *American Sociological Review, 26*.

Gewertz, D. B. (1983). *Sepik River societies: A Historical ethnology of the Chambi and their neighbors*. New Haven, Conn.: Yale University Press.

Gewirtz, J. L. (1972). Attachment, dependence, and a distinction in terms of stimulus control. In J. L. Gewirtz (ed.), *Attachment and dependency*. Washington, D.C.; Winston.

Gewirtz, J. L., & Baer, D. M. (1958). Deprivation and satiation of social reinforcers as drive conditions. *Journal of Abnormal and Social Psychology, 57*, 165–172.

Ghiselin, M. T. (1981). Categories, life, and thinking. *The Behavioral and Brain Sciences, 4*, 269–313.

Ghiselli, E. E. (1966). The validity of a personnel interview. *Personnel Psychology, 19*, 389–394.

Ghiselli, E. E. (1973). The validity of aptitude tests in personnel selection. *Personnel Psychology, 26*, 461–477.

Ghiselli, E. E., & Barthol, R. P. (1953). The validity of personality in the selection of employees. *Journal of Applied Psychology, 37*, 18–20.

Ghiselli, E. E., & Brown, C. W. (1955). *Personnel and industrial psychology*. New York: McGraw-Hill.

Ghiselli, E. E., Campbell, J. P., & Zedeck, S. (1981). *Measurement theory for the behavioral sciences*. San Francisco: Freeman.

Giambra, L. M. (1977). Adult daydreaming across the life-span: A replication, further analyses, and tentative normas based upon retrospective reports. *International Journal of Aging and Human Development, 8*, 197–228.

Giarratano, J., & Riley, G. (1989). *Expert systems: Principles and programs*. Boston: PWS-KENT Publishing.

Gibb, J. R. (1964). The T-group as a climate for trust formation. In L. F. Bradford, J. R. Gibb, & K. D. Benne (Eds.), *T-group theory and laboratory method*. New York: Wiley.

Gibbard, G. S., Hartman, J. J., & Mann, R. D. (1978). *Analysis of groups*. San Francisco: Jossey-Bass.

Gibbons, D. C., & Jones, J. F. (1975). *The study of deviance: Perspectives and problems*. Englewood Cliffs, N.J.: Prentice-Hall.

Gibbs, G., Morgan, A., & Taylor, E. (1982). A review of the research of Ference Marton and the Göteborg Group: A phenomenological research perspective of learning. *Higher Education, 11*, 123–145.

Gibbs, J. (1968). Crime, punishment, and deterrence. *Southwestern Social Science Quarterly, 48*, 515–530.

Gibbs, J. P., & Martin, W. T. (1964). *Status integration and suicide: A sociological study*. Eugene, Oreg.: University of Oregon Press.

Gibson, C. (1889). *The characteristics of genius. A popular essay*. London: Scott.

Gibson, E. J. (1969). *Principles of perceptual learning and development*. New York: Appleton-Century-Crofts.

Gibson, E. J. (1970). The development of perception as an active process. *American Scientist, 58*, 98–107.

Gibson, E. J. (1982). The concept of affordances in development: The renascence of functionalism. In A. W. Collins (Ed.), *The concept* of development. *Minnesota Symposium on Child Development*, Vol. 15. Hillsdale, N.J.: Erlbaum.

Gibson, E. J. (1987). Introductory essay: What does infant perception tell us about theories of perception? *Journal of Experimental Psychology: Human Perception and Performances, 13*, 515–523.

Gibson, E. J., & Levin, H. (1975). *The psychology of reading*. Cambridge, Mass.: M.I.T. Press.

Gibson, E. J., & Spelke, E. (1980). The development of perception. In P. H. Mussen (Ed.), *Carmichael's handbook of child psychology*, Vol. 3 (4th ed.). New York: Wiley.

Gibson, E. J., & Walk, R. D. (1960). The "visual cliff." *Scientific American, 202*, 64–71.

Gibson, H. B. (1981). *Hans Eysenck: The man and his work*. London: Owen.

Gibson, J., Olum, P., & Rosenblatt, F. (1955). Parallax and perspective during aircraft landings. *American Journal of Psychology, 68*, 372–385.

Gibson, J. J. (1929). The reproduction of visually perceived forms. *Journal of Experimental Psychology, 12*, 1–39.

Gibson, J. J. (1950). *The perception of the visual world*. Boston: Houghton Mifflin.

Gibson, J. J. (1954). A theory of pictorial perception. *Audio-Visual Communication Review, 1*, 3–23.

Gibson, J. J. (1960). Pictures, perspective and perception. *Daedalus, 89*, 216–227.

Gibson, J. J. (1966). *The senses considered as perceptual systems*. Boston: Houghton Mifflin.

Gibson, J. J. (1971). The information available in pictures. *Leonardo, 4*, 27–35.

Gibson, J. J. (1972). Outline of a theory of direct visual perception. In J. R. Royce & W. W. Rozeboom (Eds.), *The psychology of knowing*. London: Gordon & Breach.

Gibson, J. J. (1975). Pickford and the failure of experimental aesthetics. *Leonardo, 8*, 319–321.

Gibson, J. J. (1979). *The ecological approach to visual perception*. Boston: Houghton Mifflin.

Gibson, J. J., & Gibson, E. J. (1955). Perceptual learning: Differentiation or enrichment? *Psychological Review, 62*, 32–44.

Gibson, J. T. (1978). *Growing up: A study of children*. Reading, Mass.: Addison-Wesley.

Gidro-Frank, L., & Bowersbuch, M. K. (1948). A study of the plantar response in hypnotic age regression. *Journal of Nervous and Mental Disorders, 107*, 443–458.

Giedion, E. (1967). *Space, time and architecture: The growth of a new tradition*. Cambridge, Mass.: Harvard University Press.

Giel, R., Dijk, S. & van Weerden-Dijkstra, J. R. (1978). Mortality in the long-stay population of all Dutch mental hospitals. *Acta Psychiatrica Scandinavia, 57*, 361–368.

Giel, R., & Van Luijk, J. M. (1969–1970). Psychiatric morbidity in a rural village in South-Western Ethiopia. *International Journal of Social Psychiatry, 16*, 63–71.

Giffin, K. (1967). The contribution of studies of source credibility to a theory of interpersonal trust in the communication process. *Psychological Bulletin, 68*, 104–121.

Gifford, R., & Price, J. (1979). Personal space in nursery school children. *Canadian Journal of Behavioral Science, 11*, 318–326.

Gifi, A. (1981). *Nonlinear multivariate analysis*. Leiden, Netherlands: University of Leiden.

Gigli, I., & Baer, R. (1979). Atopic dermatitis. In T. Fitzpatrick, A. Eisen, W. Klaus, I. Freedberg, & F. Austen (Eds.), *Dermatology in general medicine* (2nd ed.). New York: McGraw-Hill.

Gil, D. G. (1970). *Violence against children*. Cambridge, Mass.: Harvard University Press.

Gil, K. M. (1984). Coping with invasive medical procedures: A descriptive model. *Clinical Psychology Review, 4*, 339–362.

Gil, K. M. (1989). Coping with sickle cell disease pain. *Annals of Behavioral Medicine, 11*, 49–57.

Gil, K. M. (1992). Psychologic aspects of acute pain. In R. S. Sinatra, A. H. Hord, B. Ginsberg, & L. Preble (Eds.) *Acute pain: Mechanisms and Management*. St. Louis: Mosby Year Book.

Gil, K. M., Abrams, M. R., Phillips, G., & Williams, D. A. (1992). Sickle cell disease pain: 2. Predicting health care use and activity level at 9-month follow-up. *Journal of Consulting and Clinical Psychology, 60*.

Gil, K. M., Abrams, M. R., Phillips, G., & Keefe, F. J. (1989). Sickle cell disease pain: Relation of coping strategies to adjustment. *Journal of Consulting and Clinical Psychology, 57*, 725–731.

Gil, K. M., Williams, D. A., Thompson, R. J., & Kinney, T. R. (1991). Sickle cell disease in children and adolescents: The relation of child and parent pain coping strategies to adjustment. *Journal of Pediatric Psychology, 16*, 643–663.

Gilbert, G. M. (1942). Sex differences in musical aptitude and training. *Journal of Genetic Psychology, 26*, 19–33.

Gilbert, J., & Lombardi, D. (1967). Personality characteristics of male narcotic addicts. *Journal of Consulting Psychology, 31*, 536–538.

Gilbert, J. G. (1941). Memory loss in senesenche. *Journal of Abnormal and Social Psychology, 36*, 73–86.

Gilbert, L. A. (1980). Feminist therapy. In A. M. Brodsky & R. T. Hare-Mustin (Eds.), *Women and psychotherapy*. New York: Guilford.

Gilbert, R. (Ed.). (n.d.). *Edited transcript, AHP theory conference, Tucson, Arizona, April 4–6, 1975*. San Francisco, Association for Humanistic Psychology.

Gilbertson, S. (1971). Television attitudes and cognitive dissonance phenomena in Ghana, M.Sc. thesis, University of Bristol.

Gilbreth, F. B. (1909). *Bricklaying system*. New York: Clark.

Gilbreth, F. B. (1911). *Motion study, a method for increasing efficiency*. New York: Van Nostrand.

Gilbreth, F. B., & Gilbreth, L. E. (1916). *Fatigue study*. New York: Sturgis & Walton.

Gilbreth, F. B., & Gilbreth, L. E. (1917). *Applied motion study; a collection of papers on the efficient method to industrial preparedness*. New York: Sturgis & Walton.

Gilbreth, F. M., Jr., & Carey, E. G. (1948). *Cheaper by the dozen*. New York: Crowell.

Gilbreth, L. E. (1914). *The psychology of management; The function of the mind in determining, teaching and installing methods of least waste*. New York: Sturges & Walton.

Gilbreth, L. E. (1927). *The home-maker and her job*. New York: Appleton.

Gilbreth, L. E. (1928). *Living with our children*. New York: Norton.

Gilgen, A. R. (1982). *American psychology since World War II: A profile of the discipline*. Westport, CT: Greenwood Press.

Gilinsky, A. S. (1969). The brain and the mind of a man. A review of *Integrative activity of the brain* by J. Konorski. *Contemporary Psychology, 14*, 224; 226–228.

Gill, M. M., & Brenman, M. (1959). *Hypnosis and related states*. New York: International Universities Press.

Gillam, B. (1971). A depth processing theory of the Poggendorff illusion. *Perception and Psychophysics. 10*, 211–216.

Gillan, D. J. (1981). Reasoning in the chimpanzee: II. Transitive inference. *Journal of Experimental Psychology: Animal Behavior Processes. 7*, 150–164.

Gillan, D. J., Premack, D., & Woodruff, G. (1981). Reasoning in the chimpanzee: I. Analogical reasoning. *Journal of Experimental Psychology: Animal Behavior Processes, 7*, 1–17.

Gillespie, R. (1991). *A History of the Hawthorne experiment*. New York: Cambridge University Press.

Gillespie, W. H. (1963). Some regressive phenomena in old age. *British Journal of Medical Psychology, 3*, 203–209.

Gillig, P. M., & Greenwald, A. G. (1974). Is it time to lay the sleeper effect to rest? *Journal of Personality and Social Psychology, 29*, 132–139.

Gilligan, C. (1982). In a *different voice*. Cambridge, MA: Harvard University Press.

Gillingham, A. & Stillman, B. W. (1966). *Remedial training for children with specific difficulty in reading, spelling, and penmanship* (7th ed.). Cambridge, Mass.: Educators Publishing Service.

Gilman, A. (1937). The relation between blood osmotic pressure, fluid distribution and voluntary water intake. *American Journal of Physiology, 120*, 323–328.

Gilman, A. G., Goodman, L. S., & Gilman, A. (Eds.). (1980/1941). *Goodman and Gilman's the pharmacological basis of therapeutics* (6th ed.). New York: Macmillan.

Gilman, E. B. (1978). *The curious perspective. Literary and pictorial wit in the Seventeenth Century*. New Haven, Conn.: Yale University Press.

Gilman, L., & Paperte, F. (1952). Music as psychotherapeutic agent. In E. A. Gutheil (Ed.), *Music and your emotions*. New York: Liveright.

Gilman, S., & Newman, S. W. (1992). *Manter and Gatz's essentials of clinical neuroanatomy and neurophysiology* (8th ed.). Philadelphia: Davis.

Gilmer, B. von H. (1961). *Industrial psychology*. New York: McGraw-Hill.

Gilmore, S. K. (1973). *The counselor-in-training*. New York: Appleton-Century-Crofts.

Giner de los Ríos, F. (1874). *Lecciones sumarias de psicología*. Madrid: Imp. J. Noguera.

Ginott, H. (1969/1956). *Between parent and child*. New York: Macmillan.

Ginzberg, E. (1970). The development of a developmental theory of occupational choice. In W. H. Van Hoose & J. F. Pietrofesa (Eds.), *Counseling and guidance in the twentieth century*. Boston: Houghton Mifflin.

Ginzberg, E., et al. (1951). *Occupational choice*. New York: Columbia University Press.

Giorgi, A. (1968). Existential phenomenology and the psychology of the human person. *Review of Existential Psychology and Psychiatry, 8*, 102–116.

Giorgi, A. (1970). *Psychology as a human science*. New York: Harper & Row.

Giorgi, A. (1974). The metapsychology of Merleau-Ponty as a possible basis for unity in psychology. *Journal of Phenomenological Psychology, 5*, 53–74.

Giovannoni, J. M., & Billingsley, A. (1970). Child neglect among the poor: A study of parental adequacy in families of three ethnic groups. *Child Welfare, 49*, 196–204.

Girden, E. (1962). A review of psychokinesis (PK). *Psychological Bulletin, 59*, 353–388.

Gittelman-Klein, R., Klein, D. F., Abikoff, H., Katz, S., Gloisten, A. C., & Kates, W. (1976). Relative efficacy of methylphenidate and behavior modification in hyperkinetic children: An interim report. *Journal of Abnormal Child Psychology, 4*, 361–379.

Gitter, A. G., & Mostofsky, D. I. (1973). The social indicator: An index of the quality of life. *Social Biology, 20*, 289–227.

Gitter, L. (1967). The promise of Montessori for special education. *The Journal of Special Education, 2*, 5–13.

Glaister, B. (1985). A case of auditory hallucinations treated by satiation. *Behaviour Research and Therapy, 23*, 213–215.

Glanzer, M., & Cunitz, A. R. (1966). Two storage mechanisms in free recall. *Journal of Verbal Learning and Verbal Behavior, 5*, 351–360.

Glaser, B. G., & Strauss, A. L. (1965). *Awareness of dying*. Chicago: Aldine.

Glaser, B. G., & Strauss, A. L. (1967). Awareness contexts and social interaction. *American Sociological Review, 29*, 669–679.

Glaser, B. G., & A. L. Strauss. (1967). *The discovery of grounded theory*. New York: Aldine.

Glaser, B. G., & Strauss, A. L. (1971). *Status passage: A formal theory*. Chicago: Aldine.

Glaser, D. E. (1975). *Strategic criminal justice planning*. Washington, D.C.: U.S. Government Printing Office.

Glaser, R. (1963). Instructional technology and the measurement of educational outcomes. *American Psychologist, 18*, 519–522.

Glaser, R., & Bond, L. (Eds.). (1981). Testing: Concepts, policy, practice, and research. *American Psychologist* (special issue), *36*, 995–1189.

Glaser, R., & Resnick, L. B. (1972). Instructional psychology. *Annual Review of Psychology, 23*, 207–276.

Glasgow, R. E. (1978). Effects of a self-control manual, rapid smoking and amount of therapist contact on smoking reduction. *Journal of Consulting and Clinical Psychology, 46*, 1439–1447.

Glass, C. R., & Arnkoff, D. B. (1989). Behavioral assessment of social anxiety and social phobia. *Clinical Psychology Review, 9*, 75–90.

Glass, D. C. (1964). Changes in liking as a means of reducing cognitive discrepancies between self-esteem and aggression. *Journal of Personality, 32*, 520–549.

Glass, D. C. (1977). *Behavior patterns, stress, and coronary disease*. Hillsdale, N.J.: Erlbaum.

Glass, D. C. (1977). Stress, behavior patterns, and coronary disease. *American Scientist, 65*, 178–187.

Glass, D. C., & Carver, C. S. (1980). Helplessness and the coronary-prone personality. In M. E. P. Seligman (Ed.), *Human helplessness*. New York: Academic Press.

Glass, D. C., Neulinger, J., & Brim, O. G., Jr. (1974). Birth order, verbal intelligence and educational aspiration. *Child Development, 45*, 807–811.

Glass, D. C., & Singer, J. E. (1972). *Urban stress: Experiments on noise and social stressors*. New York: Academic Press.

Glass, D. C., Snyder, M. L., & Hollis, J. (1974). Time urgency and the Type A coronary-prone behavior pattern. *Journal of Applied Social Psychology, 4*, 125–140.

Glass, G. (1976). Primary, secondary, and meta-analysis of research. *Educational Researcher, 5*, 351–379.

Glass, G. V., & Ellett, F. S. (1980). Evaluation research. *Annual Review of Psychology, 31,* 211–228.

Glass, G. V., McGaw, B., & Smith, M. L. (1981). *Meta-analysis in social research.* Beverly Hills, Calif.: Sage Publications.

Glass, G. V., & Stanley, J. C. (1970). *Statistical methods in education and psychology.* Englewood Cliffs, N.J.: Prentice-Hall.

Glass, G. V., Wilson, V. L. & Gottman, J. M. (1975). *Design and analysis of time-series experiments.* Boulder, Colo.: Associated University Press.

Glass, T. A. (1972). *The Gestalt approach to group therapy.* Presented at the 80th annual convention of the American Psychological Association, Honolulu, September.

Glasser, W. (1961). *Mental health or mental illness.* New York: Harper.

Glasser, W. (1965). *Reality therapy: A new approach to psychiatry.* New York: Harper & Row.

Glasser, W. (1969). *Schools without failure.* New York: Harper & Row.

Glasser, W. (1972). *The identity society.* New York: Harper & Row.

Glasser, W. (1976). *Positive addiction.* New York: Harper & Row.

Glasser, W. (1980). *Both-win management.* New York: Harper & Row.

Glasser, W. (1981). *Stations of the mind.* New York: Harper & Row.

Glatt, M. (1966). Who is vulnerable? *Mental Health, 28,* 26–28.

Glazer, N., & Moynihan, D. P. (1975). *Ethnicity.* Cambridge, Mass.: Harvard University Press.

Gleitman, H. (1981). *Psychology.* New York: Norton.

Glenn, C. M. (1980). Ethical issues in the practice of child psychotherapy. *Professional Psychology, 11,* 613–773.

Glenn, N. D. (1982). Interreligious marriage in the United States: Patterns and recent trends. *Journal of Marriage and the Family, 44,* 555–556.

Glezor, D. (1981). Current contributions for psychiatry in rape cases. *Psychlogie Medicale,* 1981, *13,* 1583–1585.

Glezos, S. P. (1991, January–February). NIMH demonstrations to test prevention of youth suicide and conduct problems. *ADAMHA News,* p. 15.

Glick, P., Gottesman, D., & Jolton, J. (1989). The fault is not in the stars: Susceptibility of skeptics and believers in astrology to the Barnum effect. *Personality and Social Psychology Bulletin, 15,* 572–5E33.

Glick, P. G., & Norton, A. J. (1977). Marrying, divorcing, and living together in the U.S. today. *Population Bulletin, 32,* 1–39.

Glick, P. G., & Spanier, G. B. (1980). Married and unmarried cohabitation in the United States. *Journal of Marriage and the Family, 42,* 19–30.

Glick, P. G., & Spanier, G. B. (1981). Cohabitation in the United States. In P. J. Stein (Ed.), *Single life: Unmarried adults in social context.* New York: St. Martin's Press.

Glickman, A. S., Hahn, C. P., Fleishman, E. A., & Baxter, B. (1969). *Top management development and succession: An exploratory study.* New York: Macmillan.

Glickman, S. E. (1961). Preservative neural processes and consolidation of the memory trace. *Psychological Bulletin, 58,* 218–233.

Gliedman, J., & Roth, W. (1980). *The unexpected minority: Handicapped children in America.* New York: Harcourt Brace Jovanovich.

Globus, G. (1980). On I: The conceptual foundations of responsibility. *American Journal of Psychiatry,* 147. 4, 417–422.

Globus, G., & Globus, M. (in press). The man of knowledge. In R. Walsh & D. H. Shapiro (Eds.), *Beyond health and normality: Toward a vision of exceptional psychological health.* New York: Van Nostrand.

Globus, G. G., Maxwell, G., & Savodnik, I. (Eds.). (1976). *Consciousness and the brain: A scientific and philosophical inquiry.* New York: Plenum.

Glor, B. A. K., & Barko, W. F. (1982). Sociotechnical systems using an industrial tested technology to design quality assurance standards in health care systems. *Military Medicine, 147,* 313–317.

Gluck, M. A. (1991). Stimulus generalization and representation in adaptive network models of category learning. *Psychological Science, 2,* 50–55.

Gluck, M. A., & Bower, G. H. (1988). Evaluating an adaptive network model of human learning. *Journal of Memory and Language, 27,* 166–195.

Glueck, B. C., & Stroebel, C. F. (1975). Biofeedback and meditation in the treatment of psychiatric illness. *Comprehensive Psychiatry, 16*(4), 303–321.

Glueck, S., & Glueck, E. (1950). *Unraveling juvenile delinquency.* Cambridge, MA: Harvard University Press.

Glueck, S., & Glueck, E. (1951). *Unravelling juvenile delinquency.* Cambridge, Mass.: Harvard University Press.

Glueck, S., & Glueck, E. (1974). *Of delinquency and crime: A panorama of years of search and research.* Springfield, Ill.: Thomas.

Glueck, S., & Glueck, E. T. (1968). *Delinquents and non-delinquents in perspective.* Cambridge, Mass.: Harvard University Press.

Gluckman, M. L. (1972). Psychiatric observations on obesity. *Advances in Psychosomatic Medicine, 7,* 194–216.

Gobeil, O. (1973). El susto: A descriptive analysis. *The International Journal of Social Psychiatry, 19,* 38.

Goble, F. (1970). *The third force.* New York: Grossman.

Goddard, G. V. (1964). Functions of the amygdala. *Psychological Bulletin, 62,* 89–109.

Goddard, H. H. (1912). *The Kallikak family; a study in the heredity of feeblemindedness.* New York: Macmillan.

Goddard, H. H. (1914). *Feeble-mindedness; its causes and consequences.* New York: Macmillan.

Godden, E. R., & Baddeley, A. D. (1975). Context-dependent memory in two natural environments: On land and under water. *British Journal of Psychology, 66,* 325–331.

Gödel, K. (1931). Über formal unentscheidbare Sätze der principia Mathematica und verwandter Systeme I. *Monatshefte für Mathematik und Physik, 38,* 173–198.

Godkewitsch, M. (1976). Thematic and collative properties of written jokes and their contribution to funniness. *Canadian Journal of Behavioral Science, 8,* 88–97.

Godlovitch, S., Godlovitch, R., & Harris, J. (Eds.). (1972). *Animals, Men and morals.* New York: Taplinger.

Goethe, J. W. von. (1810). *Zur Farbenlehre* (2 vols.). Tübingen, West Germany: Cotta.

Goffman, E. (1959). *The presentation of self in everyday life.* New York: Doubleday.

Goffman, E. (1961). *Asylums.* New York: Doubleday.

Goffman, E. (1961). *Encounters.* Indianapolis, Ind.: Bobbs Merrill.

Goffman, E. (1963). *Stigma: Notes on the management of spoiled identity.* Englewood, N.J.: Prentice-Hall.

Goffman, E. (1971). *Relations in public.* New York: Basic Books.

Goffman, E. (1974). *Frame analysis.* New York: Harper & Row.

Goffman, E. (1980). *Forms of talk.* Philadelphia, Pa.: University of Pennsylvania Press.

Golan, N. (1978). *Treatment in crisis situations.* New York: Free Press.

Golann, S. E., & Eisdorfer, C. (Eds.). (1972). *Handbook of community mental health.* New York: Appleton-Century-Crofts.

Golann, S. E., & Fremouw, W. J. (Eds.). (1976). *The right to treatment for mental patients.* New York: Irvington.

Gold, P. W., Goodwin, P. K., & Chrousos, C. P. (1988). Clinical and biochemical manifestations of depression (Part II). *New England Journal of Medicine, 319,* 413–420.

Gold, R. F. (1978). Constitutional growth delay and learning problems. *Journal of Learning Disabilities, 11,* 427–429.

Goldberg, G. (1973). The psychological, physiological and hypnotic approach to bruxism in the treatment of periodontal disease. *Journal of the American Society of Psychosomatic Dentistry and Medicine, 20*(3), 75–91.

Goldberg, H. (1976). *The hazards of being male.* New York: Nash.

Goldberg, L. R. (1971). A historical survey of personality scales and inventories. In P. McReynolds (Ed.), *Advances in psychological assessment* (Vol. 2, pp. 293–336). Palo Alto, CA: Science and Behavior Books.

Goldberg, L. R. (1982). From ace to zombie: Some explorations in the language of personality. In C. D. Speilberger & J. N. Butcher (Eds.), *Advances in personality assessment,* Vol. 1. Hillsdale, N.J.: Erlbaum.

Goldberg, P. A. (1965). A review of sentence completion methods in personality assessment. *Journal of Projective Techniques and Personality Assessment, 29,* 12–45.

Goldberg, P. A. (1968, April). Are women prejudiced against women? *Transaction,* 28–30.

Goldberg, P. A. (1974). Prejudice toward women: Some personality correlates. *International Journal of Group Tensions, 4,* 53–63.

Goldberger, A. S. (1973). Structural equation models: An overview. In A. S. Goldberger & O. D. Duncan (Eds.), *Structural equation models in the social sciences.* New York: Seminar.

Golde, P. (Ed.). (1970). *Women in the field: Anthropological experiences.* Chicago: Addison-Wesley.

Golden, C. J. (1976). The role of the psychologist in the training of the neurologically impaired. *Professional Psychology, 7,* 579–584.

Golden, C. J. (1977). The validity of the Halstead–Reitan neuropsychological battery in a mixed psychiatric and neurological population. *Journal of Consulting and Clinical Psychology, 45,* 1043–1051.

Golden, C. J. (1979). *Clinical interpretation of objective psychological tests.* New York: Grune & Stratton.

Golden, C. J. (1980). Organic brain syndromes. In R. H. Woody (Ed.), *Encyclopedia of clinical assessment,* Vol. 1. San Francisco: Jossey-Bass.

Golden, C. J. (1981/1978). *Diagnosis and rehabilitation in clinical neuropsychology.* Springfield, Ill.: Thomas.

Golden, C. J., Hammeke, T. A., & Purisch, A. D. (1978). Diagnostic validity of a standardized neuropsychological battery derived from Luria's neuropsychological tests. *Journal of Consulting and Clinical Psychology, 46,* 1258–1265.

Golden, C. J., Hammeke, T. A., & Purisch, A. D. (1980). *The Luria–Nebraska neuropsychological battery: A manual for clinical and experimental uses.* Los Angeles: Western Psychological Services.

Golden, C. J., Hammeke, T. A., Purisch, A. D., Berg, R. A., Moses, J. A., Jr., Newlin, D. B., Wilkening, G. N., & Puente, A. E. (1982). *Item interpretation of the Luria–Nebraska neuropsychological battery.* Lincoln, Neb.: University of Nebraska Press.

Golden, C. J., Kane, R., Sweet, J., Moses, J. A., Cardellino, J. P., Templeton, R., Vicente, P., & Graber, B. (1981). Relationship of the Halstead-Reitan Neuropsychological Battery to the Luria-Nebraska Neuropsychological Battery. *Journal of Consulting and Clinical Psychology, 49,* 410–417.

Golden, C. J., MacInnes, W. D., Ariel, R. N., Ruedrich, S. L., Chu, C. C., Coffman, J. A., Graber, B., & Bloch, S. (1982). Cross-validation of the ability of the Luria-Nebraska Neuropsychological Battery to differentiate chronic schizophrenics with and without ventricular enlargement. *Journal of Consulting and Clinical Psychology, 50,* 87–95.

Golden, C. J., & Moses, J. A., Jr. (1982). *Casebook for the Luria–Nebraska Neuropsychological Battery.* New York: Grune & Stratton.

Golden, C. J., & Moses, J. A., Jr. (1982). *Neuropsychological effects of neurological disorders.* New York: Grune & Stratton.

Golden, C. J., Moses, J. A., Fishburne, F. J., Engrem, E., Lewis, G. P., Wisniewski, A. M., Conley, F. K., Berg, R. A., & Graber, B. (1981). Cross-validation of the Luria-Nebraska Neuropsychological Battery for the presence, lateralization, and localization of brain damage. *Journal of Consulting and Clinical Psychology, 49,* 491–507.

Golden, C. J., Moses, J. A., Zelazowski, M. A., Graber, B., Zatz, L. M., Horvath, T. B., & Berber, P. A. (1980). Cerebral ventricular size and neuropsychological impairment in young chronic schizophrenics. *Archives of General Psychiatry, 37,* 619–623.

Golden, C. J., Osmon, D. C., Moses, J. A., Jr., & Berg, R. A. (1981). *Interpretation of the Halstead–Reitan Neuropsychological Battery: A casebook approach.* New York: Grune & Stratton.

Golden, C. J., & Schlutter, L. C. (1978). The interaction of age and diagnosis in neuropsychological test results. *International Journal of Neuroscience.*

Goldenberg, H. (1973). *Contemporary clinical psychology.* Monterey, Calif: Brooks/Cole.

Goldenberg, H. (1977). *Abnormal psychology: A social community approach.* Monterey, Calif.: Brooks/Cole.

Goldfarb, A. I. (1969). The psychodynamics of dependency and the search for aid. In R. Kalish (Ed.), *The dependencies of old people.* Ann Arbor, Mich.: University of Michigan Occasional Papers.

Goldfarb, W. (1943). The effects of early institutional care on adolescent personalities. *Journal of Experimental Education, 12,* 106–129.

Goldfarb, W. (1955). Emotional and intellectual consequences of psychological deprivation in infancy: A revaluation. In P. H. Hock & J. Zubin (Eds.), *Psychopathology of childhood.* New York: Grune & Stratton.

Goldfarb, W. (1970). Child psychosis. In P. H. Mussen (Ed.), *Carmichael's manual of child psychology,* Vol. 2 (3d ed.). New York: Wiley.

Goldfried, M. (1971). Systematic desensitization as training in self-control. *Journal of Consulting and Clinical Psychology, 37,* 228–234.

Goldfried, M. (1980). Some views on effective principles of psychotherapy. *Cognitive Therapy and Research, 4,* 271–306.

Goldfried, M. (1980). Toward the delineation of therapeutic principles. *American Psychologist, 35,* 991–999.

Goldfried, M. R. (1980). Toward the delineation of therapeutic change principles. *American Psychologist, 35,* 991–999.

Goldfried, M. R., & Davison, G. C. (1975). *G. C. Clinical behavior therapy.* New York: Holt, Rinehart & Winston.

Goldfried, M. R., Decentecio, E. T., & Weinberg, L. (1974). Systematic rational restructuring as a self-control technique. *Behavior Therapy, 5*, 247–254.

Goldfried, M. R. (Ed.). (1982). *Converging themes in psychotherapy.* New York: Springer.

Goldfried, M. R., et al. (1971). *Rorschach handbook of clinical and research applications.* Englewood Cliffs, N.J.: Prentice-Hall.

Goldfried, M. R. & Newman, C. (1986). Psychotherapy integration: An historical perspective. In J. C. Norcross (Ed.), *Handbook of eclectic psychotherapy.* (pp. 25–61). New York: Brunner/Mazel.

Goldiamond, I. (1965). Self-control procedures in general behavior problems. *Psychological Reports, 17*, 851–868.

Goldln, C. (1990). *Understanding the gender gap: An economic history of American women.* New York: Oxford University Press.

Goldman, J., Maitland, K. A., & Norton, P. L. (1975). Psychological aspects of jury performance. *Journal of Psychiatry and Law, 3*, 367–380.

Goldman, R. D., & Slaughter, R. E. (1976). Why college grade point is difficult to predict. *Journal of Educational Psychology, 68*, 1–14.

Goldofski, O. B. (1904). The psychology of testimony. *Vyestnik Prava*, nos. 16–18, 185.

Goldsmith, H. H., & Gottesmann, I. I. (1981). The origins of variation in behavioral style: A longitudinal study of temperament in young twins. *Child Development, 52*, 91–103.

Goldsmith, J. B., & McFall, R. M. (1975). Development and evaluation of an interpersonal skill-training program for psychiatric inpatients. *Journal of Abnormal Psychology, 84*, 51–58.

Goldsmith, S. (1981). *Health care management.* London: Aspen Systems.

Goldstein, A. M. (1980). The "uncooperative" patient: Self-destructive behavior in hemodialysis patients. In N. L. Farberow (Ed.), *The many faces of suicide: Indirect self-destructive behavior.* New York: McGraw-Hill.

Goldstein, A. P. (1962). *Therapist–patient expectancies in psychotherapy.* New York: Pergamon Press.

Goldstein, A. P. (1981). *Psychological skills training.* New York: Pergamon Press.

Goldstein, A. P., Carr, E. G., Davidson, W. S., & Wehr, P. (1981). *In response to aggression.* New York: Pergamon Press.

Goldstein, A. P., et al. (1978/1971). *Psychotherapy and the psychology of behavior change.* New York: Wiley.

Goldstein, A. P., Monti, P. J., Sardino, T. J., & Green, D. J. (1979). *Police crisis intervention.* New York: Pergamon Press.

Goldstein, A. P., & Rosenbaum, A. (1982). *Aggress-less.* Englewood Cliffs, N.J.: Prentice-Hall.

Goldstein, A. P., Sprafkin, R. P., & Gershaw, N. J. (1976). *Skill training for community living.* New York: Pergamon Press.

Goldstein, A. P., Sprafkin, R. P., Gershaw, N. J., & Klein, P. (1980). *Skillstreaming the adolescent.* Champaign, Ill.: Research Press.

Goldstein, A. S. (1967). *The insanity defense.* New Haven, Conn.: Yale University Press.

Goldstein, H. (1973). *Social work practice: A unitary approach.* Columbia, S.C.: University of South Carolina Press.

Goldstein, H. (1979). *The design and analysis of longitudinal studies: Their role in the measurement of change.* New York: Academic Press.

Goldstein, I. L. (1974). *Training: Program development and evaluation.* Monterey, Calif.: Brooks/Cole.

Goldstein, I. L. (1980). Personnel development and training. *Annual Review of Psychology, 31*.

Goldstein, I. L. (1980). Training in work organizations. *Annual Review of Psychology, 31*, 229–272.

Goldstein, J. (1976). *The experience of insight.* Santa Cruz, Calif.: Unity Press.

Goldstein, J., & McGhee, P. (Eds.). *The psychology of humor: Theoretical perspectives and empirical issues.* New York: Academic Press.

Goldstein, J., Suls, J., & Anthony, S. (1972). Enjoyment of specific types of humor content: Motivation or salience? In J. Goldstein & P. McGhee (Eds.), *The psychology of humor.* New York: Academic Press.

Goldstein, K. (1927). Die Lokalisation in der Grosshirnrinde (Localization in the cortex). In A. Bethe (Ed.), *Handbuch der Normalen und Pathologischen Physiologie (Handbook of normal and pathological physiology).* Berlin: Springer.

Goldstein, K. (1947). *Language and language disturbances; aphasic symptom complexes and their significance for medicine and theory of language.* New York: Grune & Stratton.

Goldstein, K. (1947). *Human nature in the light of psychopathology.* Cambridge, Mass.: Harvard University Press.

Goldstein, K. (1959/1934). *The organism. A holistic approach to biology derived from pathological data in man.* New York: American Book.

Goldstein, K. (1967). Autobiography. In E. G. Boring & G. Lindzcy (Eds.), A *history of psychology in autobiography*, Vol. 5. New York: Appleton-Century-Crofts.

Goldstein, K., & Scheerer, M. (1941). Abstract and concrete behavior: An experimental study with special tests. *Psychological Monographs, 53* (2, entire no. 239).

Goldstein, K. M., & Blackman, S. (1977). Assessment of cognitive style. In P. McReynolds (Ed.), *Advances in psychological assessment*, Vol. 4. San Francisco: Jossey Bass.

Goldstein, R. (1974). Brain research and violent behavior. *Archives of Neurology, 30*, 1–18.

Goldstein, R. (1974). Brain research and violent behavior. *Neurology, 30*, 1–18.

Goleman, D. (1971). Meditation as meta-therapy: Hypotheses toward a proposed fifth state of consciousness. *Journal of Transpersonal Psychology, 3*, 1–25.

Goleman, D. (1974). Perspectives on psychology, reality, and the study of consciousness. *Journal of Transpersonal Psychology 6*, 73–85.

Goleman, D. (1977). *The varieties of the meditative experience.* New York: Dutton.

Goleman, D. (1980, February). 1,528 little geniuses and how they grew. *Psychology Today, 13*, 28–53.

Goleman, D. (1981). The new competency tests. *Psychology Today, 15*, 35–46.

Goleman, D., & Davidson, R. (Eds.). (1979). *Consciousness: Brain, states of awareness and mysticism.* New York: Harper & Row.

Goleman, D. (Ed.). (1992). *Mind-body.* New York: Consumer Reports.

Goleman, D., & Epstein, M. (1983). Meditation and wellbeing. In R. Walsh and D. H. Shapiro (Eds.), *Beyond health and normality: Toward a vision of exceptional psychological health.* New York: Van Nostrand.

Goleman, D., & Schwartz, G. E. (1976). Meditation as an intervention in stress reactivity. *Journal of Consulting and Clinical Psychology, 44*, 456–466.

Golightly, C., & Reinehr, R. (1972). Fantasy production of quadriplegic males. A preliminary investigation. *American Correctic Therapy Journal, 26*, 47–49.

Golledge, R. G., & Rayner, J. N. (Eds.). (1980). *Multidimensional analysis of large data sets.* Minneapolis, Minn.: University of Minnesota Press.

Gollob, H. F. (1968). Rejoinder to Tucker's "Comments on confounding sources of variation in factor analytic techniques." *Psychological Bulletin, 70,* 355–360.

Gollwitzer, P. M., & Kinney, R. F. (1989). Effects of deliberative vs. instrumental mindsets on the illusion of control. *Journal of Personality and Social Psychology, 56,* 531–542.

Gologor, E. (1977). Group polarization in a non-risk taking culture. *Journal of Cross-Cultural Psychology, 8,* 331–346.

Golub, A. M., Masiarz, F. R., Villars, T., & McConnell, J. V. (1970). "Behavior induction" or "memory transfer?" *Science, 169,* 1342.

Gombrich, E. H. (1960). On physiognomic perception. *Daedalus,* (Winter), 228–242.

Gombrich, E. H. (1960). *The story of art.* Greenwich, Conn.: Phaidon P.

Gombrich, E. H. (1961). *Art and illusion: A study in the psychology of pictorial representation.* Princeton, N.J.: Princeton University Press.

Gombrich, E. H. (1972). The mask and the face: The perception of physiognomic likeness in life and art. In E. H. Gombrich, J. Hochberg, & M. Black (Eds.), *Art, perception, and reality.* Baltimore, Md.: Johns Hopkins.

Gombrich, E. H., Hochberg, J., & Black, M. (1972). *Art, perception, and reality.* Baltimore, Md.: Johns Hopkins.

Gomes-Schwartz, B., Hadley, S. W., & Strupp, H. H. (1978). Individual psychotherapy and behavior therapy. *Annual Review of Psychology, 29,* 435–471.

Gonsiorek, J. C. (1980). What health care professionals need to know about lesbians and gay men. In J. M, et al. (Eds.), *Psychological factors in health care.* Lexington, MA: Heath.

Gonsiorek, J. C., & Weinrich, J. D. (Eds.). *Homosexuality: Research findings for public policy.* Newbury Park, CA: Sage.

Gonzalez, J. C., Routh, D. K., Saab, P. G., Armstrong, F. D., Shifman, L., Guerra, E., & Fawcett, N. (1989). Effects of parent presence on children's reactions to injections: Behavioral, psychological and subjective aspects. *Journal of Pediatric Psychology, 14,* 449–462.

Gonzalez, R. C., & Champlin, G. (1974). Positive behavioral contrast, negative simultaneous contrast and their relation to frustration in pigeons. *Journal of Comparative and Physiological Psychology, 87,* 173–187.

Good, T. L., & Brophy, J. E. (1977). *Educational psychology: A realistic approach.* New York: Holt, Rinehart & Winston.

Good, T. L., & Brophy, J. E. (1978). *Looking in classrooms* (2nd ed.). New York: Harper & Row.

Goodall, J. (1986). *The chimpanzees of Gombe: Patterns of behavior.* Cambridge, UK: Belknap Press.

Goodchilds, J. (1972). On being witty: Causes, correlates, and consequences. In J. Goldstein & P. McGhee (Eds.), *The psychology of humor.* New York: Academic Press.

Goode, W. J. (1960). A theory of role strain. *American Sociological Review, 25,* 483–496.

Goode, W. J. (1963). *World revolution and family patterns.* New York: Free Press.

Goodenough, D. R., Gandini, F., Olkin, I., Pizzamiglio, L., Thayer, D., & Witkin, H. A. (1977). A study of X chromosome linkage with field dependence and spatial visualization. *Behavior Genetics, 7,* 373–387.

Goodenough, F. L. (1926). *Measurement of intelligence by drawings.* Yonkers, N.Y.: World Book.

Goodenough, F. L. (1928). The relation of the intelligence of preschool children to the occupation of their fathers. *American Journal of Psychology, 40,* 284–294.

Goodenough, F. L. (1932). Expression of the emotions in a blind-deaf child. *Journal of Abnormal and Social Psychology, 27,* 328–333.

Goodenough, F. L. (1934). *Developmental psychology; An introduction to the study of human behavior.* New York: Appleton-Century.

Goodenough, F. L. (1949). *Mental testing: Its history, principles, and applications.* New York: Rinehart.

Goodenough, F. L., & Harris, D. B. (1950). Studies in the psychology of children's drawings: II. 1928–1949. *Psychological Bulletin, 47,* 369–433.

Goodenough, W. (1980). Ethnographic field techniques. In H. Triandis & J. Berry (Eds.), *Handbook of cross-cultural psychology,* Vol. 2. Boston: Allyn & Bacon.

Goodglass, H. (1980). Disorders of naming following brain damage. *American Scientist, 68,* 647–655.

Goodglass, H., & Kaplan, E. (1972). *The assessment of aphasia and related disorders.* Philadelphia, Pa.: Lea & Febiger.

Goodglass, H., & Kaplan, E. (1979). Assessment of cognitive deficit in the brain-injured patient. In M. S. Gazzaniga (Ed.), *Handbook of behavioral neurobiology.* New York: Plenum.

Goodglass, H., & Kaplan, E. (1979). Assessment of cognitive deficit in the brain-injured patient. In M. S. Gazzaniga (Ed.), *Handbook of behavioral neurobiology* (Vol. 2, pp. 3–22). New York: Plenum.

Goodman, G., & Bottoms, B. L. (Eds.). (1992). *Understanding and improving children's testimony.* New York: Guilford Press.

Goodman, K. S., & Goodman, Y. M. (1977). Learning about psycholinguistic processes by analyzing oral reading. *Harvard Educational Review, 47,* 317–333.

Goodman, L., & Miller, H. (1980). Mainstreaming: How teachers can make it work. *Journal of Research and Development in Education, 13,* 46–57.

Goodman, L. M. (1981). *Death and the creative life: Conversations with prominent artists and scientists.* New York: Springer.

Goodman, L. S., & Gilman, A. (1974/1941). *The pharmacological basis of therapeutics* (4th ed.). New York: Macmillan.

Goodman, N. (1968). *Languages of art: An approach to a theory of symbols.* Indianapolis, Ind.: Bobbs-Merrill.

Goodman, R. M., Smith, W. S., & Migeon, C. J. (1967). Sex chromosome abnormalities. *Nature, 216,* 942–943.

Goodrich, T. J., Rampage, C., Ellman, B., & Halstead, K. (1988). *Feminist family therapy: A casebook.* New York: Norton.

Goodstadt, B. E., & Hjelle, L. A. (1973). Power to the powerless: Locus of control and the use of power. *Journal of Personality and Social Psychology, 27,* 190–196.

Goodstein, L. D. (1971). Management development and organization development: A critical difference in focus. *Business Quarterly, 36*(4), 30–37.

Goodstein, L. D., & Reinecker, V. M. (1974). Factors affecting self-disclosure: A review of the literature. In B. A. Maher (Ed.), *Progress in experimental personality research,* Vol. 7. New York: Academic Press.

Goodstein, L. D., & Sandler, I. (1978). Using psychology to promote human welfare. *American Psychologist, 33,* 882–892.

Goodwin, D. W. (1980). The genetics of alcoholism. *Substance and Alcohol Actions/Misuse, 1,* 101–117.

Goodwin, D. W., & Guze, S. B. (1979). *Psychiatric diagnosis.* New York: Oxford University Press.

Goodwin, F., & Potter, W. (1979). Catecholamines. In E. Usdin, I. Kopen, & J. Barchas (Eds.), *Catecholamines: Basic and clinical frontiers.* New York: Pergamon Press.

Goodwin, J. (1990, November). *Sadistic sexual abuse: Illustration from Marquis de Sade.* Paper delivered at Seventh International Conference on Multiple Personality/Dissociative States, Chicago.

Goodwin, J. (1992, November). *Pre-conference workshop: Sadistic ritual abuse issues in the 1990's.* Comments made at the Ninth International Conference on Multiple Personality Dissociative States, Chicago.

Goodwin, W. L., & Driscoll, L. A. (1980). *Handbook for measurement and evaluation in early childhood education.* San Francisco: Jossey-Bass.

Goodyear, R. K. (Producer). *Psychotherapy supervision by major theorists.* Videotape featuring Eckstein, Ellis, Hackney, Kagan, Polster, and Rogers. Available through the Instructional Media Center, Kansas State University, Manhattan, Kans.

Gooran, L. Fliers, E., & Courtney, K. (1990). Biological determinants of sexual orientation. In J. Bankroft (Ed.), *Annual review of sex research* (pp. 175–196). Lake Mills, IA: The Society for the Scientific Study of Sex.

Goorney, A. B. (1968). Treatment of a compulsive horse race gambler by aversion therapy. *British Journal of Psychiatry, 114,* 329–333.

Goran, M. J. (1992). Managed mental health and group insurance. In S. Feldman (Ed.), *Managed mental health services* (pp. 27–43). Springfield, IL: Thomas.

Gordon, B. L. (1949). *Medicine throughout antiquity.* Philadelphia, Pa.: Davis.

Gordon, C., & Gergen, K. (1978). *Self and social interaction.* New York: Wiley.

Gordon, D. A., Forehand, R., & Picklesimer, D. K. (1978). The effects of dextroamphetamine on hyperactive children using multiple outcome measures. *Journal of Clinical and Child Psychiatry, 7,* 125–128.

Gordon, E. (1965). *Musical aptitude profile,* New York: Houghton Mifflin.

Gordon, H. (1923). Mental and scholastic tests among retarded children. London: Board of Education Pamphlet no. 44.

Gordon, I. J. (1972). An instructional theory approach to the analysis of selected early childhood programs. In I. J. Gordon (Ed.), *Early childhood education—the seventy-first yearbook of the National Society for the Study of Education.* Chicago: University of Chicago Press.

Gordon, J. (1980). The paradigm of holistic medicine, In A. Hastings, J. Fadiman, and J. Gordon (Eds.), *Health for the whole person.* Boulder, Colo.: Westview.

Gordon, M. (1978). Was Waller ever right? The rating and dating complex reconsidered. *Journal of Marriage and the Family, 43,* 67–76.

Gordon, R. (1972). A very private world. In P. Sheehan (Ed.), *The function and nature of imagery.* New York: Academic Press.

Gordon, R. (1972). *Your healing hands.* Marina del Rey, Calif.: DeVorss.

Gordon, R. (1978). Pilot study of the efficacy of mainstreaming—Integrating handicapped children. New York University Medical Center, Institute of Rehabilitative Medicine, Rehabilitation Monograph no. 58.

Gordon, T. (1970). *Parent effectiveness training.* New York: Wyden.

Gordon, T. (1975). *T.E.T.: Teacher effectiveness training.* New York: Wyden.

Gore, S. (1978). The effect of social support in moderating the health consequences of unemployment. *Journal of Health and Social Behavior, 19,* 157–165.

Gorer, G. (1955). *Exploring English character.* New York: Criterion Books.

Gorer, G. (1964/1948). *The American people: A study in national character* (rev. ed.). New York: Norton.

Gorer, G., & Rickman, J. (1962/1949). *The people of Great Russia: A psychological study.* New York: Norton.

Gorlitz, D. (Ed.). (1980). *Perspectives in attribution and theory.* Cambridge, Mass.: Ballinger.

Gorman, B. S., & Wessman, A. E. (1974). The relationship of cognitive styles and moods. *Journal of Clinical Psychology, 30,* 18–25.

Gorman, C. D., Clover, W. H., & Doherty, M. E. (1978). Can we learn anything about interviewing real people from "interviews" of paper people? Two studies of the external validity of a paradigm. *Organizational Behavior and Human Performance, 22,* 165–192.

Gormezano, I., Scheiderman, N., Deaux, E. B., & Fuentes, I. (1962). Nictitating membrane: Classical conditioning and extinction in the albino rabbit. *Science, 138,* 33–34.

Gorry, T. H., & Ober, S. E. (1970). Stimulus characteristics of learning over long delays in monkeys. Presented at meeting of the Psychonomic Society, San Antonio, Tex.

Gorski, R. A., Gordon, J. H., Shryne, J. E., & Southam, A. M. (1978). Evidence for a morphological sex difference within the medial preoptic area of the rat brain. *Brain Research, 148,* 333–346.

Gorsuch, R. L. (1974). *Factor analysis.* Philadelphia, Pa.: Saunders.

Goshen, C. E. (1967). *Documentary history of psychiatry.* New York: Philosophical Library.

Goss, A. E., & Moylan, M. C. (1958). Conceptual block-sorting as a function of type and degree of mastery of discriminative verbal responses. *Journal of Genetic Psychology, 93,* 191–198.

Goss, A. E., & Nodine, C. F. (1965). *Paired-associates learning.* New York: Academic Press.

Gosset, W. S. (1942). In E. S. Pearson & J. Wishart (Eds.), *"Student's" collected papers.* London: Cambridge University Press.

Gotestam, K., & Melin, L. (1974). Covert extinction of amphetamine addiction. *Behavior Therapy, 5,* 90–92.

Goth, A. (1978). *Medical pharmacology.* St. Louis, Mo.: Mosby.

Gottesman, I. I. (1963). Heritability of personality: A demonstration. *Psychological Monographs, 77,* (entre no. 572).

Gottesman, I. I. (1965). Genetic variance in adaptive personality traits. Presented at the Annual Meeting of the American Psychological Association, Division of Developmental Psychology.

Gottesman, I. I. (1966). Genetic variance in adaptive personality traits. *Journal of Child Psychology and Psychiatry, 7,* 199–208.

Gottesman, I. I., & Shields, J. (1966). Contributions of twin studies to perspectives on schizophrenia. In B. A. Maher (Ed.), *Progress in experimental personality research,* Vol. 3. New York: Academic Press.

Gottlieb, B. (1981). *Social networks and social support.* Beverly Hills, Calif.: Sage Publications.

Gottlieb, B. H. (1983). *Social support strategies: Guidelines for mental health practice.* Beverly Hills, CA: Sage.

Gottlieb, B. H. (1992). Quandaries in translating support concepts to intervention. In H. O. F. Veiel & U. Baumann (Eds.), *The meaning* and measurement of social support (pp. 293–309). New York: Hemisphere.

Gottlieb, B. H. (Ed.). (1981). *Social networks and social support.* Beverly Hills, CA: Sage.

Gottlieb, B. H., & Todd, D. M. (1979). Characterizing and promoting social support in natural settings. In R. F. Munoz, L. R. Snowden, & J. G. Kelly (Eds.), *Social and psychological research in community settings.* San Francisco: Jossey-Bass.

Gottman, J., & Leiblum, S. (1974). *How to do psychotherapy and how to evaluate it.* New York: Holt, Rinehart & Winston.

Gottman, J., Markman, H., & Notarius, C. (1977). The topography of marital conflict: A sequential analysis of verbal and nonverbal behavior. *Journal of Marriage and the Family, 39,* 461–478.

Gottman, J., Notarius, C., Markman, H., Bank, S., Yoppi, B., & Rubin, M. E. (1976). Behavior exchange theory and marital decision making. *Journal of Personality and Social Psychology, 34,* 14–23.

Gottman, J. M. (1979). *Marital interaction: Experimental investigations.* New York: Academic Press.

Gottman, J. M. (1981). *Time-series analysis: A comprehensive introduction for social scientists.* Cambridge, England: Cambridge University Press.

Gottman, J. M., & Glass, G. V. (1978). Analysis of interrupted time-series experiments. In T. R. Kratochwill (Ed.), *Single-subject research: Strategies for evaluating change.* New York: Academic Press.

Gotts, E. E. (1973). Head Start research, development, and evaluation. In J. L. Frost (Ed.), *Revisiting early childhood education—readings.* New York: Holt, Rinehart & Winston.

Gotts, E. E. (1981). The training of intelligence as a component of early interventions: Past, present, and future. *Journal of Special Education, 15,* 257–268.

Gottschaldt, K. (1926; 1929). Über den Einfluss der Erfahrung auf die Wahrnehmung von Figuren. *Psychologische Forschung, 8,* 114–260; *11,* 1–87.

Gottschaldt, K. (1942). *Die Methodik der Persönlichkeitsforschung in der Erbpsychologie.* Leipzig: Barth.

Gottschaldt, K., Lersch, P., Sander, F., & Thomae, H. (Eds.). (1957–1978). *Handbuch der Psychologie* (12 vols.). Göttingen, West Germany: Hogrefe.

Gottschalk, L. A. (1978). Psychosomatic medicine today: An overview. *Psychosomatics, 19,* 89–93.

Gottschalk, L. A., & Davidson, R. S. (1971). Sensitivity groups, encounter groups, training groups, marathon groups, and the laboratory movement. In H. I. Kaplan & B. J. Sadock (Eds.), *Comprehensive group psychotherapy.* Baltimore, Md.: Williams & Wilkins.

Gough, H. C. (1957). *Manual, California Psychological Inventory,* Palo Alto, CA: Consulting Psychologists.

Gough, H. G. (1952). Identifying psychological femininity. *Educational and Psychological Measurement, 12,* 427–439.

Gough, H. G. (1962). Clinical versus statistical prediction in psychology. In L. Postman (Ed.), *Psychology in the making.* New York: Knopf.

Gough, H. G. (1964). A cross-cultural study of achievement motivation. *Journal of Applied Psychology, 48,* 191–196.

Gough, H. G. (1965). Cross-cultural validation of a measure of asocial behavior. *Psychological Reports, 17,* 379–387.

Gough, H. G. (1965). *The adjective check list.* Palo Alto, Calif.: Consulting Psychologists Press.

Gough, H. G., & Peterson, D. R. (1952). The identification and measurement of pre-dispositional factors in crime and delinquency. *Journal of Consulting Psychology, 16,* 207–212.

Gould, A. (1968). *The founders of psychical research.* New York: Schocken Books.

Gould, C. (1989). Comments. In *Ritualistic child abuse: A professional overview* [Videotape]. Uria, CA: Cavalcade Productions.

Gould, C. (1992). Diagnosis and treatment of ritually abused children. In *Out of darkness.* New York: Lexington Books.

Gould, C. & Cozolino, L. (1992). Ritual abuse, multiplicity, and mind-control. *Journal of Psychology and Theology, 20*(3), 194–196.

Gould, J. L. (1974). Genetics and molecular ethology. *Zeitschrift für Tierpsychologie, 36,* 267–292.

Gould, J. L. (1976). The dance-language controversy. *Quarterly Review of Biology, 51,* 211–244.

Gould, J. L. (1976). The honey bee dance—Language controversy. *Quarterly Review of Biology, 51,* 211–244.

Gould, J. L. (1982). *Ethology: The mechanisms and evolution of behavior.* New York: Norton.

Gould, R. L. (1978). *Transformations: Growth and change in adult life.* New York: Simon & Schuster.

Gould, S. J. (1977). *Ontogeny and phylogeny.* Cambridge, MA: Harvard University Press.

Gould, S. J. (1981). *The mismeasure of man.* New York: Norton.

Gould, S. J., & Lewontin, R. C. (1979). The spandrels of San Marco and the Panglossian paradigm: A critique of the adaptationist programme. *Proceedings of the Royal Society of London B, 205,* 581–598.

Goulding, M. M., & Goulding, R. L. (1979). *Changing lives through redecision therapy.* New York: Brunner/Mazel.

Goulet, L. R., & Baltes, P. B. (Eds.). (1970). *Life-span developmental psychology: Research and theory.* New York: Academic Press.

Gouvier, W. D., Uddo-Crane, M., & Brown, L. M. (1988). Base rates of post-concussional symptoms. *Archives of Neuropsychology, 3,* 273–278.

Gove, W. R. (1972, September). Relationships between sex roles, marital status, and mental illness. *Social Forces,* 34–44.

Gove, W. R. (1980). *The labeling of deviance* (2nd ed.). Beverly Hills, Calif.: Sage Publications.

Gove, W., & Tudor, J. (1973). Adult sex roles and mental illness. *American Journal of Sociology, 78*(4), 812–835.

Govinda, L. A. (1969). *Foundations of Tibetan mysticism.* New York: Weiser.

Grace, W. J., & Graham, D. T. (1952). Relationship of specific attitudes and emotions to certain bodily diseases. *Psychosomatic Medicine, 14,* 243–251.

Grady, J. S. (1979). Statistics in employment decisions. *Labor Law Journal, 30,* 748–753.

Graen, G., & Cashman, J. F. (1976). A role-making model of leadership in formal organizations: A developmental approach. In J. G. Hunt & L. L. Larsen (Eds.), *Leadership frontiers.* Kent, Ohio: Kent State University Press.

Graesser, A. C., & Bower, G. H. (1990). *Inferences and text comprehension.* The psychology of learning and motivation (Vol. 25). New York: Academic.

Graham, C. A., & McGrew, W. C. (1980). Menstrual synchrony in female undergraduates living on a coeducational campus. *Psychoneuroendocrinology, 5,* 245–252.

Graham, C. H. (Ed.). (1965). *Vision and visual perception.* New York: Wiley.

Graham, D. T. (1971). Psychophysiology and medicine. *Psychophysiology, 8,* 121–131.

Graham, F. K., & Clifton, R. K. (1966). Heart rate change as a component of the orienting response. *Psychological Bulletin, 65*, 305.

Graham, J. A., & Kligman, A. M. (1985). *The psychology of cosmetic treatments.* New York: Praeger.

Graham, J. R. (1978/1977). *The MMPI: A practical guide.* New York: Oxford.

Graham, N. (1981). Psychophysics of spatial-frequency channels. In M. Kubovy and J. Pomerantz (Eds.), *Perceptual organization.* Hillsdale, N.J.: Erlbaum.

Graham, P., Rutter, M., & George, S. (1973). Temperamental characteristics as predictors of behavior disorders in children. *American Journal of Orthopsychiatry, 43*, 328–339.

Graham, R. B. (1990). *Physiological psychology.* Belmont, CA: Wadsworth.

Graham, S., Hudson, F., Burdg, N. B., & Carpenter, D. (1980). Educational personnel's perceptions of mainstreaming and resource room effectiveness. *Psychology in the Schools, 17*, 128–134.

Graham, S. R. (1980, March). A suggestion for the development of a national residency training program in professional psychology. *The Psychotherapy Bulletin, 15*(1), 4.

Graham, S. R. (1981, August). Practicing license without a medicine. *The Independent Practitioner, 1*(1), 1.

Graham, S. R. (1982, August). The new face of psychology. *The Independent Practitioner, 2*(2), 1.

Grandjean, E. (1980). *Fitting the task to the man.* (3rd ed.). London: Taylor & Francis.

Grant, D. L. (1980). Issues in personnel selection. *Professional Psychology, 11*, 369–384.

Grant, D. L., & Bray, D. W. (1969). Contributions of the interview to assessment of management potential. *Journal of Applied Psychology, 53*, 24–34.

Grant, I., & Adams, K. M. (Eds.). (1986). *Neuropsychological assessment of neuropsychiatric disorders.* New York: Oxford University Press.

Grant, M. (1962). *Myths of the Greeks and Romans.* New York: New American Library.

Grater, M. (1968). Effects of knowledge of characteristics of self-actualization and faking of a self-actualized response on Shostrom's Personal Orientation Inventory. Unpublished master's thesis, University of Toledo, Toledo, Ohio.

Graubard, S. R. (Ed.). (1990). *The artificial intelligence debate.* Cambridge: MIT Press.

Graumann, C. F. (1960). *Grundlagen einer Phänomenologie und Psychologie der Perspektivität.* Berlin: De Gruyter.

Graumann, C. F. (1969). *Motivation.* (Einführung in die Psychologie, Vol. 1.) Frankfurt: Akademische Verlagsgesellschaft. Bern: Huber.

Graumann, C. F. (1969). Sozialpsychologie: Ort, Gegenstand und Aufgabe. In C. F. Graumann (Ed.) *Sozialpsychologie,* Vol. 1. Göttingen, West Germany: Hogrefe.

Graumann, C. F. (1972). Interaktion und Kommunikation. In C. F. Graumann (Ed.), Sozialpsychologie, Vol. 2. Göttingen, West Germany: Hogrefe.

Graumann, C. F. (Ed.). (1978). *Ökologische Perspektiven in der Psychologie.* Bern: Huber.

Graumann, C. F. (Ed.). (1981 ff). *Kurt Lewin Werkausgabe (7 vols.).* Bern: Huber. Stuttgart: Klett-Cotta.

Graumann, C. F., Herrmann, T., Hoermann, H., Irle, M., Thomae, H., & Weinert, F. E. (Eds.). (1982). *Enzyklopaedie der Psychologie* (88 vols. in 22 series). Göttingen, Germany: Hogrefe.

Graves, P. L. (1979). Cross-cultural comparisons of mothers and their undernourished infants in Asia. In J. Brožek (Ed.), *Behavioral effects of energy and protein deficits.* Washington, D.C.: NIH Publication no. 79–1906.

Grawe, K. (1976). *Differentielle Psychotherapie,* Bern: Huber.

Gray, J. A. (1971). *Psychology of fear and stress.* New York: McGraw-Hill.

Gray, J. L., & Starke, F. A. (1979). *Organizational behavior: Concepts and applications.* Columbus, Ohio: Merrill.

Graymer, L., & Thompson, F. (1982). *Reforming social regulation: Alternative public policy strategies.* Beverly Hills, CA: Sage.

Graziano, A. M., DeGiovanni, I. S., & Garcia, K. A. (1979). Behavioral treatment of children's fears: A review. *Psychological Bulletin, 86*, 804–830.

Greaves, G. (1989, October). *A cognitive behavioral approach to the treatment of MPD ritually abused satanic cult survivors.* Paper presented at Sixth International Conference on Multiple Personality/Dissociative States. Chicago.

Greden, J. (1980). Caffeine and tobacco dependence. In *Comprehensive textbook of psychiatry,* Vol. 2 (3rd ed.) Baltimore, Md.: Williams & Wilkins.

Gredler, G. R. (1978). A look at some important factors in assessing readiness for school. *Journal of Learning Disabilities, 11*, 284–290.

Greeley, A. M., & McCready, W. C. (1975). Are we a nation of mystics? *New York Times Magazine,* January 26.

Green, A. W. (1941). The 'cult of personality' and sexual relations. *Psychiatry, 4*, 343–348.

Green, B., & Hall, J. A. (1984). Quantative methods for literature review. *Review of Psychology, 35*, 37–53.

Green, D. M. (1976). *An introduction to hearing.* Hillsdale, N.J.: Erlbaum.

Green, D. M., & Swets, J. A. (1966). *Signal detection theory and psychophysics.* New York: Wiley.

Green, D. R. (1975). What does it mean to say a test is biased? *Education and Urban Society, 8*, 33–52.

Green, E. E., & Green, A. M. (1977). *Beyond biofeedback.* New York: Delacorte.

Green, E. E., & Green, A. M., & Walters, E. P., (1970). Voluntary control of internal states: Psychological and physiological. *Journal of Transpersonal Psychology, 2*, 1–26.

Green, K. A. (1979). *The positive parenting program* (rev. ed). Chicago: YMCA Family Communications Skill Center.

Green, L. S. (1977). Hyperendemic goiter, cretinism and social organization in Highland Ecuador. In L. S. Green (Ed.), *Malnutrition, behavior, and social organization.* New York: Academic Press.

Green, P. E., & Carmone, F. J. (1970). *Multidimensional scaling, and related techniques in marketing analysis.* Boston: Allyn & Bacon.

Green, P. E., & Carroll, J. D. (1976). *Mathematical tools for applied multivariate analysis.* New York: Academic Press.

Green, P. E., & Rao, V. R. (1972). *Applied multidimensional scaling.* New York, Chicago, San Francisco, Atlanta, Dallas, Montreal, Toronto, London, Sydney: Holt, Rinehart & Winston.

Green, R. (1974). *Sexual identity conflict in children and adults.* New York: Basic Books.

Green, R., & Money, J. (1969). *Transsexualism and sex reassignment.* Baltimore, Md.: Johns Hopkins University Press.

Green, R., & Mooney, J. (1969). *Transsexualism and sex reassignment.* Baltimore: Johns Hopkins University Press.

Green, R., & Stoller, R. J. (1971). Two monozygotic (identical) twin pairs discordant for homosexuality. *Archives of Sexual Behavior, 1*(4), 321–327.

Green, S. B., Burkhart, B. R., & Harrison, W. H. (1979). Personality correlates of self-report, role-playing, and in vivo measures of assertiveness. *Journal of Consulting and Clinical Psychology, 47,* 16–24.

Green, S. G., & Mitchell, T. R. (1979). Attributional processes of leaders in leader–member interactions. *Organizational Behavior and Human Performance, 23,* 429–458.

Greenauer, M., & Lindauer, M. S. (1981). Physiognomic perception of positive and negative stimuli among five-year old children. *ERIC Resources in Education,* PS 012 417 ED 206 416.

Greenbaum, C. W., & Kugelmass, S. (1980). Human development and socialization in cross-cultural perspective: Issues arising from research in Israel. In N. Warren (Ed.), *Studies in cross-cultural psychology,* Vol. 2. London: Academic Press.

Greenbaum, C. W., Rogovsky, I., & Shalit, B. (1977). The military psychologist during war-time: A model based on action research and crisis intervention. *Journal of Applied Behavioral Science, 13,* 7–21.

Greenberg, I. A. (Ed.). (1974). *Psychodrama: theory and therapy.* New York: Behavioral Publications.

Greenberger, E., & Steinberg, L. (1986). *When teenagers work: The psychological and social costs of adolescent employment.* New York: Basic Books.

Greenblatt, M., Solomon, M. H., Evans, A. S., & Brooks, G. W. (Eds.). (1965). *Drug and social therapy in chronic schizophrenia.* Springfield, Ill.: C. Thomas.

Greene, D., & Lepper, M. R. (1974). Intrinsic motivation: How to turn play into work. *Psychology Today,* September, *54,* 49–52.

Greene, D., Sternberg, B., & Lepper, M. R. (1976). Overjustification in a token economy. *Journal of Personality and Social Psychology, 34,* 1219–1234.

Greene, H. W., & Burghardt, G. M. (1978). Behavior and phylogeny: Constriction in ancient and modern snakes. *Science, 200,* 74–77.

Greene, R. L. (1984). Incidental learning of event frequency, *Memory and Cognition, 12,* 90–95.

Greene, R. L., & Clark, J. R. (1968). Birth order and college attendance in a cross-cultural setting. *Journal of Social Psychology, 75,* 289–290.

Greene, R. L., & Clark, J. R. (1970). Adler's theory of birth order. *Psychological Reports, 26,* 387–390.

Greening, T. C. (Ed.). (1971). *Existential humanistic psychology.* Belmont, Calif.: Brooks/Cole.

Greenson, R. (1968). *The technique and practice of psychoanalysis,* Vol. 1. New York: International Universities Press.

Greenson, R. R. (1975). On gambling. In J. Halliday & P. Fuller (Eds.), *The psychology of gambling.* New York: Harper & Row.

Greenspan, M. (1983). *A new approach to women and therapy.* New York: McGraw-Hill.

Greenspan, S. I., & Pollock, G. H. (Eds.). (1981). *The course of life.* Vol. III: *Adulthood and the aging process.* Adelphi, Md.: U.S. Department of Health and Human Services, National Institute of Mental Health.

Greenstone, J., & Leviton, S. (1981). *Crisis intervention directory.* New York: Facts on File.

Greenstone, J. L., & Leviton, S. C. (1979). *Stress reduction: Personal energy management.* Tulsa, Okla.: Affective House.

Greenstone, J. L., & Leviton, S. C. (1979). *The crisis intervener's handbook,* Vol. I. Dallas, Tex.: Crisis Management Workshops.

Greenstone, J. L., & Leviton, S. C. (1980). *The crisis intervener's handbook, Vol. II.* Dallas, Tex.: Rothschild.

Greenstone, J. L., & Leviton, S. C. (1982). *Crisis intervention: A handbook for interveners.* Dubuque, Iowa: Kendall-Hunt.

Greenwald, A. G. (1982). Self and memory. In G. H. Bower (Ed.), *Psychology of learning and motivation,* Vol. 15. New York: Academic Press.

Greenwald, A. G. (1992). New look 3: Unconscious cognition reclaimed. *American Psychologist, 47,* 766–779.

Greenwald A. G., Brock, T. C., & Ostrom, T. M. (Eds.). (1968). *Psychological foundations of attitudes.* New York: Academic Press.

Greenwald, A. G., & Pratkanis, A. R. (1984). The self. In R. S. Wyer & T. K. Srull (Eds.), *The handbook of social cognition* (Vol. 3, pp. 129–178). Hillsdale, NJ: Erlbaum.

Greenwald, A. G., & Pratkanis, A. R. (1988). On the use of "theory" and the usefulness of theory. *Psychological Review, 95,* 575–579.

Greenwald, A. G., Pratkanis, A. R., Leippe, M. R., & Baumgardner, M. H. (1986). Under what conditions does theory obstruct research progress? *Psychological Review, 93,* 216–229.

Greenwald, A. G., Spangenberg, E. R., Pratkanis, A. R., & Eskenazi, J. (1991). Double-blind tests of subliminal self-help audiotapes. *Psychological Science, 2,* 119–122.

Greenwald, H. (1958). *The call girl: A social and psychoanalytic study.* New York: Ballantine Books.

Greenwald, H. (1973). *Direct decision therapy.* San Diego, Calif.: Edits.

Greenwald, H. (1973/1967). *Active psychotherapy.* New York: Aronson.

Greenwald, H. (1976/1959). *Great cases in psychoanalysis.* New York: Aronson.

Greer, G. (1979). *The obstacle race: The fortunes of women painters and their work.* New York: Farrar, Straus & Giroux.

Gregg, A., et al. (1947). *The place of psychology in an ideal university.* Cambridge, Mass.: Harvard University Press.

Gregg, L. W., & Simon, H. A. (1967). Process models and stochastic theories of simple concept formation. *Journal of Mathematical Psychology, 4,* 246–276.

Gregory, P. M. (1947). An economic interpretation of women's fashions. *Southern Economic Journal, 14,* 148–162.

Gregory, R. L. (1970). *The intelligent eye.* New York: McGraw-Hill.

Gregory, R. L. (1974). *Concepts and mechanisms of perception.* London: Duckworth.

Gregory, R. L. (1978). *The psychology of seeing* (3rd ed.). New York: McGraw-Hill.

Gregory, R. L. (1978/1966). *Eye and brain: The psychology of seeing.* New York: McGraw-Hill.

Gregory, R. L. (1981). *Mind in science: A history of explanations in psychology and physics.* Cambridge, England: Cambridge University Press.

Gregory, R. L., & Gombrich, E. (Eds.). (1973). *Illusion in nature and art.* London: Duckworth.

Gregory, R. L., & Wallace, J. G. (1963). Recovery from early blindness: A case study. *Experimental Psychology Society monograph, no. 2.* Cambridge, England: Heffers.

Gregory, W. E. (1957). *The orthodoxy of the authoritarian personality. Journal of Social Psychology, 45,* 229.

Gregory, W. L., Chartier, G. M., & Wright, M. H. (1979). Learned helplessness and learned effectiveness: Effects of explicit response cues on individuals differing in personal control expectancies. *Journal of Personality and Social Psychology, 37,* 1982–1992.

Greifer, E. (1963). *Principles of poetry therapy.* New York: Poetry Therapy Center.

Greist, J. H., Eischens, R., Klein, M., & Faris, J. (1979). Antidepressant running. *Psychiatric Annals, 9,* 23–25, 28–29, 32–33.

Greist, J. H., Gustafson, D., Stauss, R., Rowse, G., Laughren, T., & Childs, J. (1974). Suicide risk prediction: A new approach. *Life Threatening Behavior, 4,* 212–223.

Greist, J. H., Klein, M., Eischens, R., Faris, J., Gurman, A. S., & Morgan, W. (1979). Running as treatment for depression. *Comprehensive Psychiatry, 20,* 41–54.

Grencavage L. M., & Norcross, J. C. (1990). What are the commonalities among the therapeutic factors? *Professional Psychology: Research and Practice, 21,* 372–378.

Gresham, F. M. (1985). Utility of cognitive-behavioral procedures for social skills training with children: A critical review. *Journal of Abnormal Child Psychology, 13,* 411–423.

Gresham, W. L. (1969). Fortune tellers never starve. *Esquire,* November 1949, *32*(5). Reprinted in N. H. Pronko (Ed.), *Panorama of psychology.* Belmont, Calif.: Brooks/Cole.

Grether, C. B. (1975). Engineering psychology. In B. L. Margolis & W. H. Kroes (Eds.), *The human side of accident prevention.* Springfield, Ill.: C. Thomas.

Grether, W. F. (1968). Engineering psychology in the United States. *American Psychologist, 23,* 743–751.

Greven, P. J., Jr. (Ed.). (1973). *Child rearing concepts, 1928–1861: Historical sources.* Itasca, Ill.: Peacock.

Grey, M. (1985). *Return from death: An exploration of the near-death experience.* London: Arkana.

Greyson, B. (1982, May). *Organic brain dysfunction and near-death experience.* Paper presented at the annual meeting of the American Psychiatric Association, Toronto, Ontario.

Greyson, B. (1983a). The near-death experience scale: Construction, reliability, and validity. *Journal of Nervous and Mental Disease, 171,* 369–375.

Greyson, B. (1983b). The psychodynamics of near-death experiences. *Journal of Nervous and Mental Disease, 171,* 376–381.

Greyson, B. (1983c). Near-death experiences and personal values. *American Journal of Psychiatry, 140,* 618–620.

Greyson, B. (1985). A typology of near-death experiences. *American Journal of Psychiatry, 142,* 967–969.

Greyson, B. (1991). Near death experiences precipitated by suicide attempt: Lack of influence of psychopathology, religion and expectations. *Journal of Near-Death Studies, 9,* 183–188.

Greyson, B., & Flynn, C. P. (1984). *The near-death experience: Problems, prospects, perspectives.* Springfield, IL: Thomas.

Greyson, B., & Stevenson, I. (1980). The phenomenology of near-death experiences. *American Journal of Psychiatry, 137,* 1193–1196.

Griesel, R. D. (Ed.). (1980). *Malnutrition in Southern Africa.* Pretoria: University of South Africa.

Griesinger, W. (1867/1845). *Mental pathology and therapeutics.* London: New Syndenham Society.

Griffen, D. R. (1958). *Listening in the dark: The acoustic orientation of bats and men.* New Haven, Conn.: Yale University Press.

Griffin, D. R. (1981/1976). *The question of animal awareness: Evolutionary continuity of mental experience.* New York: Rockefeller University Press.

Griffin, J. (1978). Practical considerations of bibliotherapy. In A. Lerner (Ed.), *Poetry in the therapeutic experience.* Elmsford, N.Y.: Pergamon Press.

Griffith, E. R., & Trieschmann, R. B. (1975). Sexual functioning in women with spinal cord injury. *Archives of Physical and Medical Rehabilitation, 56,* 18–21.

Griffith, J. D., Cavanaugh, J. H., Held, J., & Oates, J. A. (1970). Experimental psychosis induced by the administration of d-amphetamine. In E. Costa & S. Garattini (Eds.), *Amphetamines and related compounds.* New York: Raven Press.

Griffitts, C. H. (1927). Individual differences in imagery. *Psychological Monographs, 37,* (172).

Grigg, C. M. (1965). *Graduate education.* New York: Center for Applied Research in Education.

Griggs v Duke Power Company. (1971). 1 Fair Employment Practices 175, Bureau of National Affairs, Washington, D.C..

Griggs v. Duke Power Company. (1971). 401 U.S. 424, 3FEP175.

Grikscheit, G., Cash, H., & Crissy, W. J. E. (1981). *Handbook of selling.* New York: Wiley.

Grimes, J. (1981). Shaping the future of school psychology. *School Psychology Review, 10*(2), 206–231.

Grimshaw, A. (1981). Talk and social control. In M. Rosenberg & R. Turner (Eds.), *Social psychology.* New York: Basic Books.

Grimson, E. W., & Patil, R. S. (Eds.). (1987). *AI in the nineteen eighties and beyond: An MIT survey.* Cambridge: MIT Press.

Grinberg, L., Sor, D., & Tabak Debianchedi, E. (1977). Groups. *Introduction to the work of Bion* (pp. 1–21). New York: Jason Aronson.

Grinder, R. E. (1967). *A history of genetic psychology: The first science of human development.* New York: Wiley.

Grinder, R. E. (1967). The growth of educational psychology as reflected in the history of Division 15. *Educational Psychologist, 4,* 12–35.

Grindley, G. C. (1932). The formation of a simple habit in guinea pigs. *British Journal of Psychology, 23,* 127–147.

Grinker, R., Miller, J., Sabshin, M., Nunn, R., & Nunally, J. (1961). *The phenomenology of depression.* New York: Hoeber

Grinker, R., Miller, J., Sabshin, M., Nunn, R., & Nunnally, J. (1961). *The phenomena of depressions.* New York: Hoeber.

Grinker, R. R. (1953). *Psychosomatic research.* New York: Norton.

Grinspoon, L., & Bakalar, J. (1980). Drug dependence: Non-narcotic agents. In H. I. Kaplan, A. M. Freedman, & B. J. Saddock, (Eds.), *Comprehensive textbook of psychiatry,* Vol. 2 (3rd ed.). Baltimore, Md.: Williams & Wilkins.

Grinspoon, L., & Bakalar, J. B. (1981). Marihuana, In J. H. Lowinson & P. Ruiz (Eds.), *Substance abuse: Clinical problems and perspectives.* Baltimore, Md.: Williams & Wilkins.

Grisso, T. (1981). *Juveniles' waiver of rights: Legal and psychological competence.* New York: Plenum.

Grof, S. (1975). *Realms of the Human unconscious: Observations from LSD research.* New York: Viking Press.

Grof, S. (1980). *LSD psychotherapy.* Pomona, Calif.: Hunter House.

Grof, S. (1980). Realms of the human unconscious: Observations from LSD research. In R. Walsh & F. Vaughan (Eds.), *Beyond ego: Transpersonal dimensions in psychology.* Los Angeles: Tarcher.

Grof, S., & Grof, J. H. (1977). *The human encounter with death.* New York: Dutton.

Groner, R. (1972). Cue utilization and memory structure in logical thinking. In J. R. Royce & W. W. Rozeboom (Eds.), *The psychology of knowing.* New York: Gordon & Breach.

Groner, R. (1978). *Hypothesen im Denkprozess. Grundlagen einer verallgemeinerten Theorie auf der Basis elementarer Informationsverarbeitung.* Bern: Huber.

Groner, R., & Fraisse, P. (Eds.). (1983). *Cognition and eye movements.* Amsterdam: North Holland.

Groner, R., & Groner, M. (1983). Towards a hypothetico-deductive theory of cognitive activity. In R. Groner & P. Fraisse, (Eds.), *Cognition and eye movements.* Berlin: Deutscher Verlag der Wissenschaften. Amsterdam: North Holland.

Groner, M., Groner, R., & Bischof, W. F. (1983). Approaches to heuristics: A historical review. In R. Groner, M. Groner, & W. F. Bischof (Eds.), *Methods of heuristics.* Hillsdale, N.J.: Erlbaum.

Groner, R., Keller, B., & Menz, C. (1980). Formal precision, where and what for, or: The ape climbs the tree. In R. H. Kluwe & H. Spada (Eds.), *Developmental models of thinking.* New York: Academic Press.

Groner, R., Menz, C., Fisher, D. F., & Monty, R. A. (Eds.). (1983). *Eye movements and psychological function: International views.* Hillsdale, N.J.: Erlbaum.

Groner, R., & Spada, H. (1977). Some Markovian models for structural learning. In H. Spada & W. F. Kempf (Eds.), *Structural models of thinking and learning.* Bern: Huber.

Groos, K. (1898). *The play of animals.* New York: Appleton.

Gross, M. (1979). *The psychological society.* New York: Simon & Schuster.

Gross, N., Mason, W. S., & McEachern, A. W. (1957). *Explorations in role analysis.* New York: Wiley.

Grossman, H. J. (1977/1973). *Manual on terminology and classification in mental retardation: 1977 revision. American Association on Mental Deficiency.* Baltimore, Md.: Garamond/Pridemark Press.

Grossman, M. I., & Cummings, G. M., (1947). The effect of insulin on food intake after vagotomy and sympathectomy. *American Journal of Physiology, 149,* 100–119.

Grossman, S. R. (1975). Role of the hypothalamus in the regulation of food and water intake. *Psychological Review, 82,* 200–224.

Grossman, S. R. (1983). Contemporary problems concerning our understanding of brain mechanisms that regulate food intake and body weight. In S. R. Stunkard & E. Stellar (Eds.), *Psychobiology of eating and its disorders.* New York: Raven.

Grosso, M. (1985). *Flight of mind: A psychological study of the out-of-body experience.* Metuchen, NJ: Scarecrow.

Grotevant, H. D., Scarr, S., & Weinberg, R. A. (1977). Patterns of interest similarity in adoptive and biological families. *Journal of Personality and Social Psychology, 35,* 667–676.

Groth-Marnat, G. (1990). *Handbook of psychological assessment* (2nd ed.). New York: Wiley.

Groves, P. M., & Thompson, R. F. (1970). Habituation: A dual-process theory. *Psychological Review, 77,* 419–450.

Gruber, B. L., Hall, N. R., Hersh, S. P., & Dubois, P. (1988). Immune system and psychological changes in metastatic cancer patients using ritualized relaxation and guided imagery: A pilot study. *Scandinavian Journal of Behavior Therapy, 17,* 25–46.

Gruber, H., & Voneche, J. (1977). *The essential Piaget.* New York: Basic Books.

Gruber, H. E. (1974). *Darwin on man: A psychological study of scientific creativity* together with *Darwin's early and unpublished notebooks.* New York: Dutton.

Gruber, H. E. (1980). Darwin on man, mind, and materialism. In R. W. Rieber (Ed.), *Body and mind.* New York: Academic Press.

Gruber, H. E., Terrell, G., & Wertheimer, M. (Eds.). (1962). *Contemporary approaches to creative thinking.* New York: Atherton.

Gruder, C. L., Cook, T. D., Hennigan, K. M., Flay, B. R., Alessis, C., & Halamaj, J. (1978). Empirical tests of the absolute sleeper effect predicted from the discounting cue hypothesis. *Journal of Personality and Social Psychology, 36,* 1061–1074.

Grueneich, R. (1982). Issues in the developmental study of how children use intention and consequence information to make moral evaluations. *Child Development, 53,* 29–43.

Grumet, G. W. (1979). Telephone therapy: A review and case report. *American Journal of Orthopsychiatry, 49,* 4.

Grumet, G. W. (1979). Telephone therapy: A review and case report. *American Journal of Orthopsychiatry, 49,* 574–584.

Grünbaum, A. (1973). Can we ascertain the falsity of a scientific hypothesis? In R. S. Cohen & M. W. Wartofsky (Eds.), *Philosophical problems of space and time.* Boston studies in the philosophy of science, vol. XII. Boston, Dordrecht: Reidel.

Grünbaum, A. (1976). The Duhemian argument. *Philosophy of Science,* 27 1960. Reprinted in S. G. Harding (Ed.), *Can theories be refuted?* Boston, Dordrecht: Reidel.

Grunebaum, H. (Ed.). (1970). *The practice of community mental health.* Boston: Little, Brown.

Grüsser, O. J., & Grüsser-Cornehls, U. (1973). Neuronal mechanisms of visual movement perception and some psychophysical and behavioral correlations. In R. Jung (Ed.), *Handbook of sensory physiology.* Vol. 7 (3a); *Central processing of information.* Heidelberg: Springer.

Guandolo, V. L. (1985). Munchausen syndrome by proxy: An outpatient challenge. *Pediatrics, 75,* 526–530.

Guba, E. G., & Lincoln, Y. S. (1981). *Effective evaluation.* San Francisco: Jossey-Bass.

Gubernick, D. J., & Klopfer, P. H. (Eds.). (1981). *Parental care in mammals.* New York: Plenum.

Gubser, A. (1968). *Monotonie im Industriebetrieb.* Bern: Huber.

Gudykunst, W., Hammer, M., & Wiseman, R. (1977). An analysis of an integrated approach to cross-cultural training. *International Journal of Intercultural Relations, 1*(2), 99–110.

Guerin, F. (Ed.). (1976). *Family therapy.* New York: Gardner Press.

Guerney, F. (1979). Play therapy with learning disabled children. *Journal of Clinical Child Psychology, 8,* 242–244.

Guerney, L. F. (1976). Filial therapy program. In D. Olson (Ed.), *Treating relationships.* Lake Mills, Iowa: Graphic.

Guertin, W. H., et al. (1971). Research with the Wechsler-Bellevue scales for adults: 1965–1970. *The Psychological Record, 21,* 239–289.

Guetzkow, H., Forehand, G. A., & James, B. J. (1962). An evaluation of educational influence on administrative judgement. *Administrative Science Quarterly, 6,* 483–500.

Guha, D., & Pradhan, S. N. (1976). Effects of nicotine on EEG and evoked potentials and their interactions with autonomic drugs. *Neuropharmacology, 15*(4), 225–232.

Guha, D., & Pradhan, S. N. (1974). Conditioning of gastric secretion of epinephrine in rats. *Proceedings of the Society for Experimental Biology and Medicine, 147,* 817–819.

Guide to the use of the Graduate Record Examinations (1981). Princeton, N.J.: Educational Testing Service.

Guidelines for the re-evaluation counseling communities. (1979). Seattle, Wash.: Rational Island.

Guilford, J. P. (1932). A generalized psychophysical law. *Psychological Review, 39*, 73–85.

Guilford, J. P. (1950). Creativity. *American Psychologist, 14*, 469–479.

Guilford, J. P. (1954/1936). *Psychometric methods*. New York, Toronto, London: McGraw-Hill.

Guilford, J. P. (1956). The structure of intellect. *Psychological Bulletin, 53*, 267–293.

Guilford, J. P. (1959). *Personality*. New York: McGraw-Hill.

Guilford, J. P. (1959). Three faces of intellect. *American Psychologist, 14*,469–479.

Guilford, J. P. (1966). Intelligence: 1965 model. *American Psychologist, 21*, 20–26.

Guilford, J. P. (1967). *The nature of human intelligence*. New York: McGraw-Hill.

Guilford, J. P. (1969). Intellectual aspects of decision making. In A. F. Welford & J. E. Birren (Eds.), *Interdisciplinary topics in gerentology*, Vol. 4. Basel: Karger.

Guilford, J. P. (1975). Factors and factors of personality. *Psychological Bulletin, 82*, 803–814.

Guilford, J. P. (1977). *Way beyond the IQ: Guide to improving intelligence and creativity*. Buffalo, N.Y.: Creative Education Foundation.

Guilford, J. P. (1977). Will the real factor of extraversion-introversion please stand up? A reply to Eysenck. *Psychological Bulletin, 84*, 412–416.

Guilford, J. P. (1977a). Development of intelligence: A multivariate view. In J. C. Uzgiris & F. Weitzmann (Eds.), *The structuring of experience*. New York: Plenum.

Guilford, J. P. (1978/1942). *Fundamental statistics in psychology and education*. New York: McGraw Hill.

Guilford, J. P. (1979). *Cognitive psychology with a frame of reference*. San Diego, Calif.: EDITS.

Guilford, J. P. (1980). Cognitive styles: What are they? *Educational and Psychological Measurements, 40*, 715–735.

Guilford, J. P. (1980b). La intelligencia desde el punto de vista del procesamiento de la informacion. *Intersciencia, 5*, 285–292.

Guilford, J. P. (1981). Higher-order SI abilities. *Multivariate Behavioral Research, 16*, 411–435.

Guilford, J. P. (1982). Cognitive psychology's ambiguities: Some suggested remedies. *Psychological Review, 89*, 48–59.

Guilford, J. P., Christensen, P. R., Bond, N. A., Jr., & Sutton, M. A. (1954). A factor analysis study of human interests. *Psychological Monographs, 68*(4, entire no. 375).

Guilford, J. P., & Fruchter, B. (1977). *Fundamental statistics in psychology and education*. New York: McGraw-Hill.

Guilford, J. P., & Guilford, R. B. (1934). An analysis of the factors in a typical test of introversion-extraversion. *Journal of Abnormal and Social Psychology, 28*, 377–399.

Guilford, J. P., & Hoepfner, R. (1971). *The analysis of intelligence*. New York: McGraw-Hill.

Guilford, J. P., & Tenopyr, M. L. (1968). Implications of the structure-of-intellect model for high school and college students. In W. B. Michael (Ed.), *Teaching for creative endeavor*. Bloomington, Ind.: Indiana University Press.

Guillaume, P. (1925). *L' imitation chez l'enfant*. Paris: Alcan.

Guillaume, P. (1932). *Manuel de psychologie*. Paris: Alcan.

Guillaume, P. (1937). *La psychologie de la forme*. Paris: Flammarion.

Guillaume, P. (1942). *Introduction à la psychologie*. Paris: Vrin.

Guillaume, P. (1942). La psychologie des singes. In G. Dumas (Ed.), *Nouveau traité de psychologie*. Paris: Presses Universitaires de France.

Guilleminault, C., Passouant, P., & Dement, W. C. (1976). *Narcolepsy*. New York: Spectrum.

Guion, R. M. (1965). *Personnel testing*. New York: McGraw-Hill.

Guion, R. M. (1976). Recruiting, selection, and placement. In M. D. Dunnette, (Ed.), *Handbook of industrial and organizational psychology*. Chicago: Rand-McNally.

Guiora, A., Bolin, R., Dutton, C., & Meer, B. (1965). Intuition: a preliminary statement. *Psychiatric Quarterly Supplement, 39* (part 1), 110–122.

Guiraud, P. (1954). *Bibliographie critique de la statistique linguistique*. Utrecht, Netherlands: Editions Spectrum.

Gulick, W. L. (1971). *Hearing: Physiology and psychophysics*. New York: Oxford University Press.

Gulliksen, H. (1927). The influence of occupation upon the perception of time. *Journal of Experimental Psychology, 10*, 52–59.

Gulliksen, H. (1932). A new form of tachistoscope. *Journal of General Psychology, 6*, 223–226.

Gulliksen, H. (1932). Transfer of response in human subjects. *Journal of Experimental Psychology, 15*, 496–516.

Gulliksen, H. (1934). A rational equation of the learning curve based on Thorndike's law of effect. *Journal of Genetic Psychology, 11*, 395–434.

Gulliksen, H. (1936). The content reliability of a test. *Psychometrika, 1*, 189–194.

Gulliksen, H. (1936). The relationship between degree of original learning and degree of transfer. *Psychometrika, 1*, 37–43.

Gulliksen, H. (1942). An analysis of learning data which distinguishes between initial preference and learning ability. *Psychometrika, 7*, 171–194.

Gulliksen, H. (1950). Intrinsic validity. *American Psychologist, 5*, 511–517.

Gulliksen, H. (1950). *Theory of mental tests*. New York: Wiley.

Gulliksen, H. (1953). A generalization of Thurstone's learning function. *Psychometrika, 18*, 297–307.

Gulliksen, H. (1953). Learning. *Encyclopedia Britannica, 13*, 839–845.

Gulliksen, H. (1953). Memory. *Encyclopedia Britannica, 15*, 233–235.

Gulliksen, H. (1956). A tribute to L. L. Thurstone. *Psychometrika, 21*, 309–312.

Gulliksen, H. (1956). Measurement of subjective values. *Psychometrika, 21*, 229–244.

Gulliksen, H. (1959). Mathematical solutions for psychological problems. *American Scientist, 47*, 178–201.

Gulliksen, H. (1964). *Contributor, structure of individual differences in optimality judgments*. New York: Wiley.

Gulliksen, H. (1968). Louis Leon Thurstone, experimental and mathematical psychologist. *American Psychologist, 23*, 786–802.

Gulliksen, H. (1974). Looking back and ahead in psychometrics, *American Psychologist, 29*, 251–261.

Gulliksen, H. (1975). Characteristic roots and vectors indicating agreement of data with different scaling laws. *Sankhya: The Indian Journal of Statistics, 37*, 363–384.

Gulliksen, H. (1977; 1979). Application of psychological scaling methods, I, II, III, LV. *Indian Psychological Research Journal, 2*, 11–21; *3*, 1–10.

Gulliksen, H., & Frederiksen, N. (1964). *Contributions to mathematical psychology*. New York: Holt, Rinehart & Winston.

Gulliksen, H., & Gulliksen, D. (1972). Attitudes of different groups toward work, aims, goals and activities. In *Multivariate behavioral research*, Austin, Tex.: Society of Multivariate Experimental Psychology.

Gulliksen, H., & Messick, S. (1960). *Psychological scaling, theory and applications*. New York: Wiley.

Gulliksen, H., & Tucker, L. R. (1961). A general procedure for obtaining paired comparisons from multiple rank orders. *Psychometrika, 26,* 173–183.

Gulliksen, H., & Tukey, J. W. (1958). Reliability for the law of comparative judgment. *Psychometrika, 23,* 95–110.

Gulliksen, H., & Voneida, T. (1975). An attempt to obtain replicate learning curves in the split-brain cat. *Physiological Psychology, 3,* 77–85.

Gulliksen, H., & Wilks, S. S. (1950). Regression tests for several samples. *Psychometrika, 15,* 91–114.

Gulliksen, H., & Wolfe, D. L. (1938). A theory of learning and transfer: I, and II. *Psychometrika, 3,* 127–149, 225–251.

Gumbukco, P. (1968). The efficacy of a psychiatric halfway house: A three-year study of a therapeutic residence. *Sociological Quarterly, 9,* 374–386.

Gunderson, E. K. E. (1965). Body size, self-evaluation and military effectiveness. *Journal of Personality Social Psychology, 2,* 902–906,

Gunderson, E. K. E. (1976). Health and adjustment of men at sea. In N. L. Goldman & D. R. Segal (Eds.), *The social psychology of military service*. Beverly Hills, Calif.: Sage Publications.

Gundu Rao, H. V. (1958). Some experiments on a Yogi in controlled states. *Pratibha, Journal of the All India Institute for Mental Health, 1,* 99–106.

Gunning, R. (1952). *The technique of clear writing*. New York: McGraw-Hill.

Gupta, G. C. (1980). Cognitive processes. In U. Pareek (Ed.), *A survey of research in psychology*. Bombay: Popular Prakashan.

Gur, R. E. (1975). Conjugate lateral eye movements as an index of hemispheric activation. *Journal of Personality and Social Psychology, 31,* 751–757.

Guralnick, M. J. (1978). *Early intervention and the integration of handicapped and nonhandicapped children*. Baltimore, Md.: University Park Press.

Gurian, J. (1970). The importance of dependency in Native American-White contact. *American Indian Quarterly,* Spring, 51–70.

Gurian, J., & Gurian, J. (1983). *The dependency tendency: Returning to each other in modern America*. Washington, D.C.: University Press of America.

Gurin, G., Veroff, J., & Feld, S. (1960). *Americans view their mental health*. New York: Basic Books.

Gurk, M. D., & Wicas, E. A. (1979). Generic models of counseling supervision: Counseling/instruction dichotomy and consultation metamodel. *Personnel and Guidance Journal, 57,* 402–408.

Gurman, A., & Rice, D. (Eds.). (1975). *Couples in conflict*. New York: Aronson.

Gurman, A. S., & Kniskern, D. P. (1978/1971). Research on marital and family therapy: Progress, perspective, and prospect. In S. L. Garfield & A. E. Bergin (Eds.), *Handbook of psychotherapy and behavior change*. New York: Wiley.

Gurney, E. (1888). Recent experiments in hypnotism. *Proceedings of the Society for Psychical Research, 5,* 3–17.

Gurney, E., Myers, F. W. H., & Podmore, F. (1975). Phantasms of the living. In E. M. Sidgwick (Ed.), *Phantasms of the living: Cases of telepathy printed in the Journal of the Society for Psychical Research during thirty-five years*. New York: Arno Press.

Gusdorf, G. (1967). *Les origines des sciences humaines*. Paris: Pagot.

Gusdorf, G. (1974). *Introduction aux sciences humaines*. Paris: Editions Ophys.

Gushurst, R. (1971). Technique, utility and validity of life style analysis. *The Counseling Psychologist 3*(1), 30–40.

Gustavson, A. R., Dawson, M. E., & Bonnet, D. G. (1987). Androstenol, a putative human phermone, affects human (*Homo sapiens*) male choice performance. *Journal of Comparative Psychology, 101,* 210–212.

Gustavson, C. R., Garcia, J., Hankins, W. G. & Rusiniak, K. W. (1974). Coyote Predation Control by Aversive Conditioning. *Science, 184,* 581–583.

Gustafson, G. E., Green, J. A., & West, M. J. (1979). The infant's changing role in mother–infant games: The growth of social skills. *Infant Behavior and Development, 2,* 301–308.

Gustafson, H. W. (1977). Job performance evaluation as a tool to evaluate training. *Improving Human Performance Quarterly, 5,* 133–152.

Gutheil, E. A. (1952). *Music and your emotions*. New York: Liveright.

Gutheil, T. G. (1980). Editorial: In search of true freedom: Drug refusal, involuntary medication, and "rotting with your rights:" *American Journal of Psychiatry, 137,* 327–328.

Guthrie, E. R. (1935). *The psychology of learning*. New York: Harper & Row.

Guthrie, E. R. (1938). *The psychology of human conflict*. New York, London: Harper.

Guthrie, E. R. (1944). Personality in terms of associative learning. In J. M. Hunt, (Ed.), *Personality and the behavior disorders*, Vol. 1. New York: Ronald Press.

Guthrie, E. R. (1952/1935). *The psychology of learning*. New York: Harper.

Guthrie, E. R., & Edwards, A. L. (1949). *Psychology: A first course in human behavior,* New York: Harper.

Guthrie, E. R., & Horton, C. P. (1946). *Cats in a puzzle box*. New York: Holt.

Guthrie, G. (1975). A behavioral analysis of culture learning. In R. Brislin, S. Bochner & W. Lonner (Eds.), *Cross-cultural perspectives on learning*. New York: Wiley.

Guthrie, G. (1977). Problems of measurement in cross-cultural research. In L. Loeb-Adler (Ed.), Issues in cross-cultural research. *Annals of the New York Academy of Sciences, 285,* 131–140.

Guthrie, G. M. (1963). Structure of abilities in a non-Western culture. *Journal of Educational Psychology, 54,* 94–103.

Guthrie, J. T., Seifert, M., & Kline, L. W. (1978). Clues from research on programs for poor readers. In S. J. Samuels, (Ed.), *What research has to say about reading instruction*. Newark, Dela.: International Reading Association.

Gutierres, S. E., & Reich, J. W. (1981). A developmental perspective on runaway behavior; its relationship to child abuse. *Child Welfare, 60,* 89–94.

Gutkin, T. B. (1981). Relative frequency of consultee lack of knowledge, skills, confidence, and objectivity in school settings. *Journal of School Psychology, 19*(1), 57–61.

Gutkin, T. B., & Curtis, M. (1982). School-based consultation: Theory and techniques. In C. R. Reynolds & T. B. Gutkin (Eds.), *The handbook of school psychology,* New York: Wiley.

Gutman, J. (1972). The attorney-conducted *voir dire* of jurors: A constitutional right. *Brooklyn Law Review, 39,* 290–304.

Guttentag, M., & Struening, E. L. (Eds.). (1975). *Handbook of evaluation research,* Vols. 1, 2. Beverly Hills, Calif.: Sage Publications.

Guttman, E. S. (1970). Effects of short-term psychiatric treatment for boys in two California Youth Authority institutions. In D.C. Gibbons (Ed.), *Delinquent behavior.* Englewood Cliffs, N.J.: Prentice-Hall.

Guttman, L. (1941). The quantification of a class of attributes: A theory and method of scale construction. In P. Horst et al. (Eds.), *The prediction of personal adjustment.* New York: Social Science Research Council.

Guttman, L. (1944). A basis for scaling qualitative data. *American Sociological Review, 2,* 139–150.

Guttman, L. (1947). Suggestions for further research in scale and intensity analysis of attitudes and opinions. *International Journal of Opinion and Attitude Research, 1,* 30–35.

Guttman, L. (1947). The Cornell technique for scale and intensity analysis. *Educational and Psychological Measurement, 7,* 247–280.

Guttman, L. (1949). The basis for scalogram analysis. In S. A. Stouffer et al. (Eds.), *Studies in social psychology in World War II.* Vol. 4: *Measurement and Prediction.* Princeton, N.J.: Princeton University Press.

Guttman, L. (1968). A general nonmetric technique for finding the smallest coordinate space for a configuration of points. *Psychometrika, 33,* 465–506.

Guttman, L., Mann, K. J., et al. (1970). *Visits to the doctors.* Jerusalem: Academic Press.

Guttman, L., Stouffer, S. A., et al. (1950). *Measurement and prediction.* Princeton, N.J.: Princeton University Press.

Guttman, L., & Suchman, E. A. (1947). Intensity and a zero point for attitude analysis. *American Sociological Review, 12,* 57–67.

Guttman, N. (1963). Laws of behavior and facts of perception. In S. Koch (Ed.), *Psychology: A study of a science,* Vol. 5. New York: McGraw-Hill.

Guttman, N., & Kalish, H. I. (1956). Discriminability and stimulus generalization. *Journal of Experimental Psychology, 51,* 79–88.

Guttmann, G. (1971). Die psychologische Bedeutung akustisch evozierten Potentials. *Zeitschrift der Nervenarzt, 42,* 193–197.

Guttmann, G. (1974/1972). *Einführung in die Neuropsidologie.* Bern: Huber.

Guttmann, G. (1976). *Introduccion a la neuropsicologia.* Freiburg, West Germany: Herder.

Guttmann, G. (1977). Neuropsychologie des lernens. In G. Nissen (Ed.), *Intelligenz, Lernen und Lernstörungen: Theorie, Praxis und Therapie.* Berlin: Springer.

Guttmann, G. (1982). Ergopsychometry: Testing under physical or psychological load. *The German Journal of Psychology, 6.*

Guttmann, G. (1982). *Lehrbuch der Neuropsychologie.* Bern: Huber.

Guttmann, G., & Bauer, H. (1982). Learning and information processing in dependence on contical DC-potentials. In Sinz & Rosenzweig (Eds.), *Psychophysiology 1980.* Fischer & Elsevier.

Guy, W., Gross, M., & Dennis, H. (1967). An alternative to double blind procedure. *American Journal of Psychiatry, 123,* 1505–1012.

Guyton, A. C. (1977). *Basic human physiology.* Philadelphia, Pa.: Saunders.

Guze, S. (1976). *Criminality and psychiatric disorders.* Oxford University Press.

Guze, S. B., Tuason, V. B., Stewart, M. A., & Pickens, B. (1963). The drinking history: A comparison of reports by subjects and their relatives. *Quarterly Journal of Studies of Alcohol, 24,* 249–260.

Haan, N. (1963). Proposed model of ego functioning: Coping and defense mechanisms in relationship to IQ change. *Psychological Monographs, 77,* (8, entire no. 571).

Haan, N. (1977). Coping and defending. New York: Academic Press.

Haan, N., Smith, M. B., & Block, J. (1968). The moral reasoning of young adults: Political-social behavior, family background and personality correlates. *Journal of Personality and Social Psychology, 10,* 183–201.

Haase, G., & Reinmuth, O. (1976). Probing the perplexities of MS. *Patient Care, 32.*

Haase, G. R. (1977). Diseases presenting as dementia. In C. E. Wells (Ed.), *Dementia.* Philadelphia, Pa.: Davis.

Haber, P. (1980). The Veterans Administration experience in extended care settings: Issues impacting clinical and program management. *The Gerontologist, 20* (pt. II), 250.

Haber, R. N. (1959). Public attitudes regarding subliminal advertising. *Public Opinion Quarterly, 23,* 291–293.

Haber, R. N. (1969). Eidetic images. *Scientific American, 220,* 36–55.

Haber, R. N. (1979). Twenty years of haunting eidetic imagery: Where is the ghost? *The Behavioral and Brain Sciences, 2,* 583–630.

Haber, R. N., & Hershenson, M. (1980). *The psychology of visual perception* (2nd ed.). New York: Holt, Rinehart & Winston.

Häberlin, P. (1921). *Der Gegenstand der Psychologie.* Berlin: Springer.

Haberman, M. C., Chapman, J. P., & Rawlin, M. L. (1976). Scales for physical and social anhedonia. *Journal of Abnormal Psychology, 85,* 374–382.

Habermas, J. (1971). *Knowledge and human interests.* Boston: Beacon Press.

Hacker, F. J. (1976). *Crusaders, criminals, crazies.* New York: Norton.

Hackett, T. P., & Cassem, N. H. (1975). Psychological management of the myocardial infarction patient. *Journal of Human Stress, 1,* 25–38.

Hackett, T. P., Cassem, N. H., & Wishnie, H. A. (1968). The coronary-care unit: An appraisal of its psychologic hazards. *New England Journal of Medicine, 279,* 1365–1370.

Hackman, J., & Morris, C. (1975). Group tasks, group interaction and group performance effectiveness: A review and proposed integration. In L. Berkowitz (Ed.), *Advances in experimental social psychology,* Vol. 8. New York: Academic Press.

Hackman, J. R., & Lawler, E. E., III. (1971). Employee reactions to job characteristics. *Journal of Applied Psychology Monographs, 55,* 259–286.

Hackman, J. R., & Oldham, G. R. (1975). Development of the job diagnostic survey. *Journal of Applied Psychology, 60,* 159–170.

Hackman, J. R., & Oldham, G. R. (1980). *Work redesign.* Reading, MA: Addison-Wiley.

Hackney, H. (1978). The evolution of empathy. *Personnel and Guidance Journal, 57,* 35–38.

Hadas, M. (1965). Self-control: The Greek paradigm. In S. Z. Klausner (Ed.), *The quest for self-control.* New York: Free Press.

Hadden, J., & Borgatta, E. (1965). *American cities: Their social characteristics.* Chicago: Rand McNally.

Hafner, R. J., & Marks, I. M. (1976). Exposure in vivo in agoraphobics: Contributions of diazepam, group exposure, and anxiety evocation, *Psychological Medicine, 6,* 71–88.

Haga, J. (1957). Aims and methods of psychology of language. In K. Hatano & K. Sawada (Eds.), *Psychology of language today.* Tokyo: Maki-Shoten.

Haga, J. (1974). *Child's development and learning.* Tokyo: Meiji-Tosho.

Haga, J. (1978). Psycholinguistics and psychology of language. *Mathematical Linguistics, 11,* 236–252.

Haga, J. (1979). *Psychology of bilingualism.* Tokyo: Asakura-Shoten.

Haga, J. (Ed.). (1982). *Language development and teaching.* Tokyo: Kaseikyoikusha.

Haga, J., & Hayashi, S. (1978). *Method of effective writing in Japanese.* Tokyo: Shuei-Shuppan.

Hagedorn, H. J., Beck, K. J., et al. (1976). *A working manual of simple program evaluation techniques for community mental health centers.* Washington, D.C.: National Institute of Mental Health.

Hagelin, J. S. (1989). Restructuring physics from its foundation in light of Maharishi's Vedic science. *Modern Science and Vedic Science, 3,* 3–72.

Hagen, M. A. (Ed.). (1980). *The perception of pictures* (2 vols.). New York: Academic Press.

Hagen, M. A., & Jones, R. K. (1978). Cultural effects on pictorial perception: How many words is one picture really worth? In R. D. Walk & H. L. Pick, Jr. (Eds.), *Perception and experience.* New York: Plenum.

Hagen, R. L., Foreyt, J. P., & Durham, T. W. (1976). The dropout problem: Reducing attrition in obesity research. *Behavior Therapy, 7,* 463–471.

Hagerman, R. (1990). Behaviour and treatment of the fragile X syndrome. In K. E. Davies (Ed.), *The fragile-X syndrome* (pp. 66–75). Oxford, UK: Oxford University Press.

Haggard, H. W., & Jellinek, E. M. (1942.). *Alcohol explored.* Garden City, NY: Doubleday.

Haggard, E. A., & Isaacs, F. S. (1966). Micromomentary facial expressions as indicators of ego mechanisms in psychotherapy. In L. A. Gottschalk & A. H. Auerback (Eds.), *Methods of research in psychotherapy* (pp. 154–165). New York: Appleton-Century-Crofts.

Haggerty, M. E., Terman, L. M., Thorndike, E. L., Whipple, G. M., & Yerkes, R. M. (1929). *National intelligence tests.* New York: Psychological Corporation. (Originally published by World Book, Yonkers, N.Y.)

Haggerty, R. J., Roghmann, K. J., & Pless, I. B. (1975). *Child health and the community.* New York: Wiley.

Haglund, E., & Stevens, V. L. (1980). *A resource guide for mainstreaming.* Springfield, Ill.: Thomas.

Hahn, M. E. (1955). Counseling psychology. *American Psychologist, 10,* 279–282.

Hailman, J. P. (1967). The ontogeny of an instinct. *Behavior Supplements, 15,* 1–159.

Haimowitz, L. (1979). A social system's approach to the study of failure-to-thrive in infants. The role of family interactions. Unpublished dissertation, University of Denver.

Haire, M. (1950). Projective techniques in marketing research. *Journal of Marketing,* April, 649–656.

Hakstian, A. R., & Cattell, R. B. (1976). *Comprehensive ability battery.* Champaign, Ill.: Institute for Personality and Ability Testing.

Hakstian, A. R., & Cattell, R. B. (1978). Higher-stratum ability structures on a basis of twenty primary abilities. *Journal of Educational Psychology, 70,* 657–669.

Halas, E. S., Burger, P. A., & Sandstead, H. H. (1980). Food motivation of rehabilitated malnourished rats: Implications for learning studies. *Animal Learning and Behavior, 8,* 152–158.

Hale, J. A., & Hunter, M. M. (1988). *From HMO movement to managed care industry.* Minneapolis: Interstudy.

Haley, J. (1963). *Strategies of psychotherapy.* New York: Grune & Stratton.

Haley, J., (1970–1971). Family therapy. *International Journal of Psychiatry, 8,* 233–242.

Haley, J. (1973). *Uncommon therapy.* New York: Norton.

Haley, J. (1973). *Uncommon therapy: The psychiatric techniques of Milton H. Erickson, MD.* NY: Norton.

Haley, J. (1976). *Problem-solving therapy.* San Francisco: Jossey-Bass.

Haley, J. (Ed.). (1967). *Advanced techniques of hypnosis and therapy: Selected papers of Milton H. Erickson, M.D.* New York: Grune & Stratton.

Haley, J., & Hoffman, L. (1967). *Techniques of family therapy.* New York: Basic Books.

Hall, C. S. (1934). Emotional behavior in the rat. I. Defecation and urination as measures of individual differences in emotionality. *Journal of Comparative Psychology 18,* 385–403.

Hall, C. S. (1954). *A primer of Freudian psychology.* Cleveland, Ohio: World.

Hall, C. S. (1966/1953). *The meaning of dreams.* New York: McGraw-Hill.

Hall, C. S., & Lindzey, G. (1970). Lewin's field theory. In C. S. Hall & G. Lindzey (Eds.), *Theories of personality.* New York; Wiley.

Hall, C. S., & Lindzey, G. (1970). *Theories of personality* (2nd ed.). New York: Wiley.

Hall, C. S., & Lindzey, G. (Eds.). (1978/1957). *Theories of personality* (3rd ed.). New York: Wiley.

Hall, C. S., & Nordby, V. J. (1972). *The individual and his dreams.* New York: New American Library.

Hall, C. S., & Nordby, V. J. (1973). *A primer of Jungian psychology.* New York: New American Library.

Hall, C. S., & Van de Castle, R. L. (1966). *The content analysis of dreams.* New York: Appleton-Century-Crofts.

Hall, D., & Lerner, P. (1980). Career development in work organizations. *Professional Psychology, 11,* 428–435.

Hall, E. (1977). *Beyond culture.* Garden City, N.Y.: Anchor Books.

Hall, E. J. (1966). *The hidden dimension.* New York: Doubleday.

Hall, E. T. (1959). *The silent language.* Garden City, NY: Doubleday.

Hall, E. T. (1963). A system of notation of proxemic behavior. *American Anthropologist, 65,* 1003–10026.

Hall, E. T. (1966). *The hidden dimension.* Garden City, NY: Doubleday.

Hall, E. T. (1974). Prosemics. In S. Weitz (Ed.), *Nonverbal communication: Readings with Commentary.* New York: Oxford University Press.

Hall, G. S. (1883). Contents of children's minds. *Princeton Review, 11,* 249–272.

Hall, G. S. (1893–1894). On the history of American college textbooks. *American Antiquarian Society, 9,* 160–161.

Hall, G. S. (1904). *Adolescence: Its psychology and its relations to physiology, anthropology, sociology, sex, crime, religion, and education,* Vol. 1. Englewood Cliffs, N.J.: Prentice-Hall.

Hall, G. S. (1915). Thanatophobia and immortality. *American Journal of Psychology, 26,* 550–613.

Hall, G. S. (1917). *Jesus, the Christ, in the light of psychology.* New York: Doubleday, Page.

Hall, G. S. (1922). *Senescence: The last half of life.* New York: Appleton.

Hall, G. S. (1923). *Life and confessions of a psychologist.* New York: Appleton.

Hall, G. S., & Pearce, J. M. (1979). Latent inhibition of a CS during CS-US pairings. *Journal of Experimental Psychology: Animal Behavior Processes, 5*, 31–42.

Hall, H. V. (1982). Dangerousness prediction and the maligned forensic professional: Suggestions for estimating true basal violence. *Criminal Justice and Behavior, 9*, 3–12.

Hall, H. V. (1984). Predicting dangerousness for the courts. *American Journal of Forensic Psychology, 4*, 5–25.

Hall, H. V. (1985). Cognitive and volitional capacity assessment: A proposed decision tree. *American Journal of Forensic Psychology, 3*, 3–17.

Hall, H. V. (1986). The forensic distortion analysis: A proposed decision tree and report format. *American Journal of Forensic Psychology, 4*, 31–59.

Hall, H. V. (1987). *Violence prediction: Guidelines for the forensic practitioner.* Springfield, IL: Thomas.

Hall, H. V. (1990). *Truth or lies: Guidelines for detecting malingering and deception.* Paper presented at the Psychological Consultants and Forest Institute of Professional Psychology Workshop, East-West Center, University of Hawaii, Honolulu.

Hall, H. V., Catlin, E., Boissevain, A., & Westgate, J. (1984). Dangerous myths about predicting dangerousness. *American Journal of Forensic Psychology, 2*, 173–193.

Hall, H. V., & Hall, F. L. (1987). Post-traumatic stress disorder as a legal defense in criminal trials. *American Journal of Forensic Psychology, 5*, 45–53.

Hall, H. V., & McNinch, D. (1988). Linking crime-specific behavior to neuropsychological impairment. *International Journal of Clinical Neuropsychology, 10*, 113–122.

Hall, H. V. & Pritchard, D. (in press). *The forensic distortion analysis (FDA): Detecting malingering and deception.* Orlando: Deutsch.

Hall, H. V., & Shooter, E. (1989). Explicit alternative testing for feigned memory deficits. *Forensic Reports, 2*, 277–286.

Hall, H. V., Shooter, E., Craine, J., & Paulsen, S. (1991). Explicit alternative testing for claimed visual recall deficits: A trilogy of studies. *Forensic Reports, 4*, 259–279.

Hall, J. (1976). Subjective measures of quality of life in Britain: 1971 to 1975—Some developments and trends. In *Social trends no. 7.* London: Her Majesty's Stationery Office.

Hall, J. A. (1979). Gender, gender roles, and nonverbal communication skills. In R. Rosenthal (Ed.), *Skill in nonverbal communication: Individual differences.* Cambridge, MA: Oelgeschlager, Gunn, & Hain.

Hall, J. A. (1980). Gender differences in nonverbal communication skills. *New Directions for Methodology of Social and Behavioral Science, 5*, 63–77.

Hall, J. F. (1976). *Classical conditioning and instrumental conditioning.* Philadelphia, Pa.: Lippincott.

Hall, M. (1833). On the reflex action of the medulla oblongata and medulla spinalis. *Philosophical Transactions of the Royal Society, 123*, 635–665.

Hall, M. C. (1978). *The responsive parenting program.* Lawrence, Kans.: H. & H. Enterprises.

Hall, N. R., & Goldstein, A. L. (1981). Neurotransmitters and the immune system. In R. Ader (Ed.), *Psychoneuroimmunology.* New York: Academic Press.

Hall, R. C. W. (1980). *Psychiatric presentations of medical illness, somatopsychic disorders.* New York, London: Spectrum.

Hall, R. C. W., Gardner, E. R., Stickney, S. K., LeCann, A. F., & Popkin, M. K. (1980). Physical illness manifesting as psychiatric

disease II. Analysis of a state hospital inpatient population. *Archives of General Psychiatry, 37*, 989–995.

Hall, R. H. (1959). *Occupations and the social structure.* Englewood Cliffs, N.J.: Prentice-Hall.

Hall, S. R. (1921). *The advertising handbook: A reference work covering the principles and practice of advertising.* New York: McGraw-Hill.

Hall-Quest, A. L. (1915). Present tendencies in educational psychology. *Journal of Educational Psychology, 6*, 601–614.

Hallam, R. N. (1969–1970). Piaget and the teaching of history. *Educational Research, 12*, 3–12.

Hallaq, J. H. (1977). Scaling and factor analyzing peak experiences. *Journal of Clinical Psychology, 33*, 77–82.

Halleck, S. L. (1980). *Law in the practice of psychiatry: A handbook for clinicians.* New York: Plenum.

Haller, M. H. (1979). The changing structure of American gambling in the twentieth century. *Journal of Social Issues, 35*, 87–114.

Hallgren, B. (1950). Specific dyslexia. *Acta Psychiatrica Neurologica,* suppl. 65.

Halliday, J. L. (1945). The significance of the concept of psychosomatic affection. *Psychosomatic Medicine, 7*, 240.

Hallpike, C. R. (1976). Is there a primitive mentality? *Man, 11*, 253–270.

Halmi, K. (1980). Anorexia nervosa. In H. Kaplan, A. Freedman, & B. Saddock (Eds.), *Comprehensive textbook of psychiatry,* Vol. 2. Baltimore, Md.: Williams & Wilkins.

Halpern, A. L. (1977). The insanity defense: A judicial anachronism, *Psychiatric Annals,* no. 8.

Halpern, J. (1978). Raising the mandatory retirement age: Its effect on the employment of older workers. *New England Economic Review,* May/June.

Halpin, A. W., & Croft, D. (1963). *The organizational climate of schools.* Chicago: University of Chicago Press.

Halpin, A. W., & Winer, B. J. (1957). A factorial study of the leader behavior descriptions. In R. M. Stogdill & A. E. Coons (Eds.), *Leader behavior: Its description and measurement.* Columbus, Ohio: Bureau of Business Research, Ohio State University.

Halsell, G. (1976). *Los viejos—Secrets of long life from the Sacred Valley.* Emmaus, Pa.: Rodale Press.

Halstead, L. S. (1976). Team care in chronic illness: A review of the literature of the past twenty-five years. *Archives of Physical Medicine and Rehabilitation, 57*, 507–511.

Halstead, W. C. (1947). *Brain and intelligence.* Chicago: University of Chicago Press.

Hamachek, D. E. (1971). *Encounters with the self.* New York: Holt, Rinehart & Winston.

Hamberger, K., & Lohr, J. M. (1980). Rational restructuring for anger control: A quasi-experimental case study *Cognitive Therapy and Research, 4*, 99–102.

Hamberger, K. L., & Lohr, J. M. (1984). *Stress and stress management: Research and applications.* New York: Springer.

Hamburg, D. A., Elliott, G. R., & Parron, D. L. (1982). *Health and behavior. Frontiers of research in the biobehavioral sciences.* Washington, D.C.: National Academy Press.

Hamilton, D. L. (Ed.). (1981). *Cognitive processes in stereotyping and intergroup behavior.* Hillsdale, N.J.: Erlbaum.

Hamilton, G. (1951/1940). *Theory and practice of social casework* (rev. ed.). New York: Columbia University Press.

Hamilton, J. A. (1983a). Development of interest and enjoyment in adolescence: I. Attentional capacities, *Journal of Youth and Adolescence, 12*, 355–362.

Hamilton, J. A. (1983b). Development of interest and enjoyment in adolescence: II. Boredom and psychopathology. *Journal of Youth and Adolescence, 12,* 363–372.

Hamilton, J. A., Haier, R. J., & Buchsbaum, M. S. (1984). Intrinsic enjoyment and boredom coping scales: Validation with personality, evoked potential and attention measures. *Personality and Individual Differences, 5,* 183–193.

Hamilton, J. L. (1979). Assessment in mental retardation toward instructional relevance. In R. B. Kearsley & I. E. Sigel (Eds.) *Infants at risk—Assessment of cognitive functioning.* Hillsdale, N.J.: Erlbaum.

Hamilton, M., & Reid, H. (Eds.). (1980). *A hospice handbook:* Grand Rapids, Mich.: Eerdmans.

Hamilton, W. (1859–1860). *Lectures on metaphysics,* London: Blackwood.

Hamilton, W. D. (1964). The genetical theory of social behavior: I and II. *Journal of Theoretical Biology, 7,* 1–52.

Hamlyn, D. W. (1957). *The psychology of perception.* London: Routledge & Paul.

Hammeke, T. A., Golden, C. J., & Purisch, A. D. (1978). A standardized, short and comprehensive neuropsychological test battery based on the Luria neuropsychological evaluation. *International Journal of Neuroscience, 8,* 135–141.

Hammen, C. L., Jacobs, M., Mayol, A., & Cochran, S. D. (1980). Dysfunctional cognitions and the effectiveness of skills and cognitive-behavioral assertion training. *Journal of Consulting and Clinical Psychology, 48,* 685–695.

Hammer, M. (1989). Intercultural communication competence. In M. Asante & W. Gudykunst (Eds.), *Handbook of international & intercultural communication* (pp. 247–260). Newbury Park, CA: Sage.

Hammer, M. (1992). Intercultural communication skills. *Communique 21*(1), 6–15.

Hammersley, (1992). *What's wrong with ethnography?* New York: Routledge.

Hammill, D. D., & Larsen, S. C. (1978). The effectiveness of psycholinguistic training: A reaffirmation of position. *Exceptional Children, 44,* 402–412.

Hammill, D. D., Leigh, J. E., McNutt, G., & Larsen, S. C. (1981). A new definition of learning disabilities. *Learning Disability Quarterly, 4,* 336–342.

Hammond, D. C. (1982). *Handbook of hypnotic suggestions and metaphors.* New York: Norton.

Hammond, K. R. (1972). Inductive learning. In J. F. Royce & W. W. Rozeboom (Eds.), *The psychology of knowing.* New York: Gordon & Breach.

Hammond, K. R., & Allen, J. J. (1953). *Writing clinical reports.* New York: Prentice-Hall.

Hampden-Turner, C. (1981). Maps of the mind: Charts and concepts of the mind and its labyrinths. New York: Macmillan.

Hanan, M. (1973). Motivation's flip side turns out to be education. *Sales and Marketing Management, 111,* 21–23.

Hanan, M., Cribbin, J., & Heiser, H. (1973). *Consultative selling* (rev. ed.). New York: AMACOM.

Handel, M. I. (1977, September). The Yom Kippur War and the inevitability of surprise. *International Studies Quarterly, 21,*(3), 461–502.

Handel, M. I. (1982, March). Intelligence and deception. *The Journal of Strategic Studies, 5,* 122–154.

Handler, L. (1988). Monkey see, monkey do: The prescription-writing controversy. *The Clinical Psychologist, 41,* 44–48.

Handy, E. S. C. (1927). *Polynesian religion.* Honolulu, B. P. Bishop Museum.

Haney, R. E. (1969). Classical conditioning of a plant: *Mimosa pudica. Journal of Biological Psychology, 11,* 5–12.

Hanfmann, E., & Getzels, J. W. (1953). Studies of the sentence completion test. *Journal of Projective Techniques, 17,* 280–294.

Hanley, C. (1951). Physique and reputation of junior high school boys. *Child Development, 22,* 247–260.

Hannan, M. T., Tuma, H. B., & Groenvald, L. P. (1977). Income and marital events: Evidence from an income maintenance experiment. *American Journal of Sociology, 82,* 1186–1211.

Hänni, R., & Hunkeler, R. (1980). Von der Entwicklung der kindlichen Erzählsprache. *Schweizerische Zeitschrift für Psychologie, 39,* 16–32.

Hannigan, M. C. (1954). An experience in group bibliotherapy. *American Library Association Bulletin, 48,* 148–150.

Hannum, J., Thoresen, C. E., & Hubbard, D. (1974). A behavioral study of self-esteem with elementary teachers. In M. J. Mahoney & C. E. Thoresen (Eds.), *Self-control: Power to the person.* Monterey, Calif.: Brooks/Cole.

Hans, V. P. (1981). Evaluating the jury: The uses of research in policy formation. In R. Roesch & R. R. Corrado (Eds.), *Evaluation and criminal justice policy.* Beverly Hills, Calif.: Sage Publications.

Hans, V. P., & Doob, A. N. (1976). Section 12 of the Canada Evidence Act and the deliberations of simulated jurors. *Criminal Law Quarterly, 11,* 235–253.

Hansel, C. E. M. (1980). *ESP and parapsychology: A critical reevaluation.* Buffalo, N.Y.: Prometheus Books.

Hansen, D. J., St. Lawrence, J. S., & Christoff, K. A. (1989). Group conversational-skills training with impatient children and adolescents. *Behavior Modification, 13,* 4–31.

Hansen, J., Pound, R., & Petro, C. (1976). Review of research on practicum supervision. *Counselor Education and Supervision, 16,* 107–116.

Hansen, M. H., Hurwitz, W. N., & Madow, W. G. (1953). *Sampling survey methods and theory.* Vol. I: *Methods and applications.* Vol. II: *Theory.* New York: Wiley.

Hanson, H. M. (1959). Effects of discrimination training on stimulus generalization. *Journal of Experimental Psychology, 58,* 321–334.

Hanson, J. W., Jones, K. L., & Smith, D. W. (1976). Fetal alcohol syndrome. *Journal of the American Medical Association, 235,* 1458–1460.

Hanson, P. G. (1982). *Learning through groups: A trainer's basic guide.* San Diego, Calif.: University Associates.

Hanusa, B. H., & Schulz, R. (1977). Attributional mediators of learned helplessness. *Journal of Personality and Social Psychology, 35,* 602–611.

Hara, K. (1961). A study of certain attitudes and their personality correlates among Japanese-Americans. *Educational Studies, 8,* 163–211.

Hara, K. (1973). Biological bases of psychology. In T. Oyama & T. Takuma (Eds.), *Outline of psychology.* Tokyo: Shinyo-sha. (In Japanese.)

Hara, K. (1979). Coordinates and missions of environmental psychology. In M. Mochizuki & T. Oyama (Eds.), *Environmental psychology.* Tokyo: Asakura-shoten. (In Japanese.)

Hara, K. (1981). Functional integration of the cerebral hemispheres. In T. Hirano (Ed.), *Modern basic psychology,* Vol. 12. Tokyo: Tokyo University Press. (In Japanese.)

Hara, K. (1982). Cerebral dominancy: Meanings of functional asymmetry. In *Psychology (no. 27)*. Tokyo; Science-sha. (In Japanese.)

Harary, F., Norman, R. Z., & Cartwright, D. (1965). *Structural models: An introduction to the theory of directed graphs*. New York: Wiley.

Harasymiw, S. J., & Horne, M. D. (1975). Integration of handicapped children: Its effect on teacher attitudes. *Education, 96*, 153–158.

Haratani, T., & Henmi, T. (1990a). Effects of Transcendental Meditation on mental health of industrial workers. *Japanese Journal of Industrial Health, 37*(10), 729.

Haratani, T., & Henmi, T. (1990b). Effects of Transcendental Meditation on mental health of industrial workers. *Japanese Journal of Industrial Health, 32*, 177.

Haraway, D. (1989). *Primate visions: gender, race, and nature in the world of modern science*. New York: Routledge.

Hardaway, R. (1990). Subliminally activated symbiotic fantasies: Facts and artifacts. *Psychological Bulletin, 107*, 177–195.

Hardeman, M. A. (1978). A dialogue with Abraham Maslow. *Journal of Humanistic Psychology, 19*, 23–28.

Hardiman, G. W., & Zernich, T. (1977). Preferences for the visual arts: A review of recent studies. *Perceptual and Motor Skills, 44*, 455–463.

Harding, S. G. (Ed.). (1976). *Can theories by refuted?* Boston, Dordrecht: Riedel.

Hardy-Brown, K., Plomin, R., Greenhalgh, J., & Jax, K. (1980). Selective placement of adopted children: Prevalence and effects. *Journal of Child Psychology and Psychiatry and Allied Disciplines, 21*, 143–151.

Hardyck, J. A., & Braden, M. (1962). Prophecy fails again: A report of a failure to replicate. *Journal of Abnormal and Social Psychology, 65*, 136–141.

Hare, A. P. (1976). *Handbook of small group research*, 2nd Edition. New York: Free Press.

Hare, A. P., Bales, R. F., & Borgatta, E. F. (Eds.). (1965). *Small groups: Studies in social interaction* (rev. ed.). New York: Knopf.

Hare, E. H., & Price, J. S. (1969). Birth order and family size: Bias caused by changes in birth rate. *British Journal of Psychiatry, 115*(523), 647–657.

Hare, R. D. (1970). *Psychopathy: Theory and research*. New York: Wiley.

Hare, R. D., & Schalling, D. (Eds.). (1978). *Psychopathic behavior: Approaches to research*. New York: Wiley.

Hare-Mustin, R. T. (1975). Treatment of temper tantrums by a paradoxical intervention. *Family Process, 14*, 481–485.

Hare-Mustin, R. T., & Marecek, J. (1990). On making a difference. In R. T. Hare-Mustin & J. Marecek (Eds.), Making a difference. (pp. 1–21). New Haven, CT: Yale University Press.

Hargreaves, D. (1978). The proper study of educational psychology. *Association of Educational Psychologists Journal, 4*(9), 3–8.

Haring, N. G., & Phillips, E. L. (1962). *Educating emotionally disturbed children*. New York: McGraw-Hill.

Harkness, S. (1980). The cultural context of child development. *New Directions for Child Development, 8*, 7–13.

Harlow, C. W. (1991, January). *Female victims of violent crime* (NCJ-126826). Rockville, MD: U.S. Department of Justice.

Harlow, H. F. (1949). The formation of learning sets. *Psychological Review, 56*, 51–65.

Harlow, H. F. (1953). Motivation as a factor in the acquisition of new responses. In *Nebraska Symposium on Motivation*. Lincoln, Neb.: University of Nebraska Press.

Harlow, H. F. (1958). The evolution of learning. In A. Roe & G. G. Simpson (Eds.), *Behavior and evolution*. New Haven, Conn.: Yale University Press.

Harlow, H. F. (1958). The nature of love. *American Psychologist, 13*, 673–685.

Harlow, H. F. (1958). The nature of love, *American Psychologist, 17*, 673–685.

Harlow, H. F. (1971). *Learning to love*. New York: Ballantine Books.

Harlow, H. F., & Harlow, M. K. (1962). Social deprivation in monkeys. *Scientific American, 207*, 137–146.

Harlow, H. F., & Harlow, M. K. (1962). The effect of rearing conditions on behavior. *Bulletin of the Menninger Clinic, 26*, 213–224.

Harlow, H. F., & Harlow, M. K. (1966). Learning to love. *American Scientist, 54*, 244–272.

Harlow, H. F., & Harlow, M. K. (1967). The young monkeys. *Psychology Today, 1*(5) 40–47.

Harlow, H. F., Harlow, M. K., & Suomi, S. J. (1971). From thought to therapy: Lessons from a primate laboratory. *American Scientist, 59*, 538–649.

Harlow, H. F., & McClearn, G. E. (1954). Object discrimination learned by monkeys on the basis of manipulation motives. *Journal of Comparative Physiological Psychology, 47*, 73–76.

Harlow, H. F., & Suomi, S. J. (1960). The nature of love-simplified. In M. Haimowitz & H. Haimowitz, (Eds.), *Human development*. New York: Crowell.

Harlow, H. F., & Zimmerman, R. R. (1959). Affectional responses in the infant monkey. *Science, 130*, 431–432.

Harman, H. H. (1976/1960). *Modern factor analysis*. Chicago: University of Chicago Press.

Harman, H. H., Ekstrom, R. B., & French, J. W. (1976). *Kit of factor reference tests*. Princeton, N.J.: Educational Testing Service.

Harmon, L. W., Birk, J. M., Fitzgerald, L. E., & Tanney, M. F. (Eds.). (1978). *Counseling women*. Monterey, Calif.: Brooks/Cole.

Harms, E. (1938). The psychology of clothes. *American Journal of Sociology, 44*, 239–250.

Harner, M. J. (Ed.). (1973). *Hallucinogens and shamanism*. London: Oxford University Press.

Harper, A. E., & Davis, G. K. (Eds.). (1981). *Nutrition in health and disease and international development*. New York: Liss.

Harper, J. M., Scoresby, A. L., & Boyce, D. W. (1977). The logical levels of complementary, symmetrical, and parallel interaction classes in family dyads, *Family Process, 16*, 199–210.

Harper, R. (1959). *Psychoanalysis and psychotherapy*. Englewood Cliffs, N.J.: Prentice-Hall.

Harper, R. A. (1975). *The new psychotherapies*. Englewood Cliffs, N.J.: Prentice Hall.

Harper, R. G., Wiens, A. N., & Matarazzo, J. D. (1978). *Nonverbal communication: The state of the art*. New York: Wiley.

Harper, R. S. (1950). The first psychological laboratory. *Isis, 41*, 158–161.

Harper, R. S. (1949). The laboratory of William James. *Harvard Alumni Bulletin, 52*, 169–173.

Harré, R. (1979). *Social being*. Oxford: Blackwell.

Harre, R. (1986). The social construction of emotions. Oxford, UK: Blackwell.

Harré, R. (Ed.). (1976). *Personality*. Oxford: Blackwell.

Harré, R., & Secord, P. (1972). *The explanation of social behavior*. Oxford: Blackwell.

Harrell, D. E. (1976). *All things are possible: The healing and charismatic revivals in modern America*. Bloomington, Ind.: University of Indiana Press.

Harren, V. A. (1976). Preliminary manual for interpretation of the Assessment of Career Decision-making (form B). Unpublished manuscript, Southern Illinois University.

Harren, V. A. (1979). *A career decision-making model*. Presented at the Convention of the American Personnel and Guidance Association, April.

Harris, A. J. (1968). Five decades of remedial reading. In J. A. Figurel (Ed.), *Forging ahead in reading. Conference Proceedings*. Newark, Dela.: International Reading Association.

Harris, A. J. (1977). Ten years of progress in remedial reading. *Journal of Reading, 21,* 29–35.

Harris, A. J. (1980). Current issues in the diagnosis and treatment of reading disabilities. In C. M. McCullough (Ed.), *Inchworm, Inchworm: persistent problems in reading education*. Newark, Del.: International Reading Association.

Harris, A. J. (1981). What is new in remedial reading? *The Reading Teacher, 34,* 405–410.

Harris, A. J. (in press). How many kinds of reading disability are there? *Journal of Learning Disabilities*.

Harris, A. J., & Sipay, E. R. (1980/1940). *How to increase reading ability* (7th ed.). New York: Longman.

Harris, B. (1979). Whatever happened to little Albert? *American Psychologist, 34,* 151–160.

Harris, C. S. (1965). Perceptual adaptation to inverted, reversed and displaced vision. *Psychological Review, 72,* 419–444.

Harris, C. W. (1963). *Problems in measuring change*. Madison, Wis., Milwaukee, London: University of Wisconsin Press.

Harris, D. H., & Chaney, F. B. (1969). *Human factors in quality assurance*. New York: Wiley.

Harris, H. (1979). A handbook for aqua-energetics. Master's thesis, California State University, Northridge.

Harris, H., Lipman, A., & Slater, R. (1977). Architectural design: The spatial location and interactions of old people. *Gerontology, 23,* 390–400.

Harris, H., & Zangwill, O. L. (1973). The writings of Sir Frederic Bartlett, C.B.E., F.R.S.: An annotated handlist. *British Journal of Psychology,* 493–510.

Harris, J. A. et. al. (1930). *The measurement of man*. Minneapolis, Minn.: University of Minnesota Press.

Harris, M. (1968). *The rise of anthropological theory: A history of theories of culture*. New York: Crowell.

Harris, M. (1979). *Cultural materialism: The struggle for a science of culture*. New York. Vintage Press.

Harris, M. J., & Rosenthal, R. (1985). Mediation of interpersonal expectancy effects: 31 meta-analyses. *Psychological Bulletin, 97,* 363–386.

Harris, M. L., & Harris, C. W. (1973). *A structure of concept attainment abilities* (Wisconsin Monograph Series). Madison, Wis.: Wisconsin Research and Development Center for Cognitive Learning.

Harris, R. J. (1976). Handling negative inputs: On the plausible equity formulae. *Journal of Experimental and Social Psychology, 12,* 194–209.

Harris, S. (1971). Influence of subject and experimenter sex in psychological research. *Journal of Consulting and Clinical Psychology, 37,* 291–294.

Harris, T. L., & Hodges, R. E. (Eds.). (1981). *A dictionary of reading and related terms*. Newark, Dela.: International Reading Association.

Harris, T. O. (1992). Some reflections on the process of social support and nature of unsupportive behaviors. In H. O. F. Veiel & U. Baumann (Eds.), *The meaning and measurement of social support* (pp. 171–190). New York: Hemisphere.

Harrison, G., (1975). *How to organize an intergrade tutoring program in an elementary school*. Provo, Utah: Brigham Young University Press.

Harrison, J. E. (1912). *Themis: A study of social origins of Greek religion*. Cambridge, England: Cambridge University Press.

Harrison, J. F. (Ed.). (1977). *The management of sales training. National Society of Sales Training Executives*. Reading, Mass.: Addison-Wesley.

Harrison, N. (1979). *Understanding behavioral research*. Belmont, CA: Wadsworth.

Harrison, R. P., (1974). *Beyond words: An introduction to nonverbal communication*. Englewood Cliffs, N.J.: Prentice-Hall.

Harrower, M. (1972). *The therapy of poetry*. Springfield, Ill.: Thomas.

Hart, G. M. (1982). *The process of clinical supervision*. Baltimore, Md.: University Park Press.

Hart, J. L. (1982). *Exercising your personality, the psychological fitness approach to school psychology*. Anaheim, Calif.: California Association of School Psychologists and Psychometrists, March.

Hart, J. T. (1983). *Modern eclectic therapy*. New York: Plenum.

Hart, J. T. (1984). *The sales professional's survival kit*. Los Angeles: Sales Press.

Hart, J. T. (1981). The significance of William James' ideas for modern psychotherapy. *Journal of Contemporary Psychotherapy, 12,* 88–102.

Hart, J. T. M. (Eds.). (1970). *New directions in client-centered therapy*. Boston: Houghton Mifflin.

Hart, V. (1978). *Distrust and democracy: Political distrust in Britain and America*. New York: Cambridge University Press.

Hart, V. (1981). *Mainstreaming children with special needs*. New York: Longman.

Hart, Z., Rennick, P. M., Klinge, V., & Swartz, M. L. (1974). A pediatric neurologist's contribution to evaluations of school underachievers. *American Journal of Diseases of Children, 128,* 319–323.

Hartley, D. (1749). *Observations on man, his frame, his duty and his expectations*. London: Johnson.

Hartley, E. L., & Perelman, M. A. (1963). Deprivation and the canalization of responses to food. *Psychological Reports, 13,* 647–650.

Hartley, E. L., & Shames, C. (1959). Man and dog: A psychological analysis. In *Ninth Gaines veterinary sumposium*.

Hartline, H. K. (1949). Inhibition of activity of visual receptors by illuminating nearby retinal elements in the *Limulus* eye. *Federation Proceedings, 8,* 69.

Hartline, H. K., & Ratliff, F. (1957). Inhibitory interaction of receptor units in the eye of *limulus*. *Journal of General Physiology, 40,* 357–376.

Hartman, G. H. (Ed.). (1978). *Psychoanalysis and the question of the text*. Baltimore: Johns Hopkins Press.

Hartman, J. J. (1979). Small group methods of personal change. *Annual Review of Psychology, 30,* 453–476.

Hartmann, G. W. (1949). Clothing: A personal problem and social issue. *Journal of Home Economics, 41,* 295–298.

Hartmann, H. (1964/1958/1939). *Ego psychology and the problem of adaptation*. New York: International Universities Press.

Hartmann, H. (1964). *Essays on ego psychology: Selected problems in psychoanalytic theory*. New York: International Universities Press.

Hartmann, N. (1940). *Aufbau der realen Welt*. Berlin: De Gruyter.

Hartog, J., Audy, J. R., & Cohen, Y. A. (Eds.). (1980). *The anatomy of loneliness*. New York: International Universities Press.

Hartshorne, H., & May, M. A. (1928–1930). *Studies in the nature of character*. Vol. I: *Studies in deceit*. Vol. II: *Studies in self-control*. Vol. III: *Studies in the organization of character*. New York: Macmillian.

Hartup, W. W. (1978). Children and their friends. In H. McGurk (Ed.), *Issues in childhood social development*. London: Methuen.

Hartup, W. W. (1982). The peer system. In P. Mussen & E. Hetherington (Eds.), *Carmichael's manual of child psychology*, Vol. 4. New York: Wiley.

Hartwell, S. W., Hutt, M. L., Andrew, G., & Walton, R. E. (1951). The Michigan picture test: Diagnostic and therapeutic possibilities of a new projective test in child guidance. *American Journal of Orthopsychiatry, 21,* 124–137.

Harvey, J. (1976). Attribution of freedom. In J. Harvey, J. Ickes, & R. Kidd (Eds.), *New directions in attribution research*, Vol. I. Hillsdale, N.J.: Erlbaum.

Harvey, J., Harris, B., & Barnes, R. (1975). Actor-observer differences in the perceptions of responsibility and freedom. *Journal of Personality and Social Psychology, 32,* 22–28.

Harvey, J. A., & Hunt, H. F. (1965). Effect of septal lesions on thirst in the rat as indicated by water consumption and operant responding for water reward. *Journal of Comparative Physiological Psychology, 59,* 49.

Harvey, O. J., Kelley, H. H., & Shapiro, M. M. (1957). Reactions to unfavorable evaluations of the self made by other persons. *Journal of personality, 25,* 393–411.

Harwood, A. C. (1958). *Recovery of man in childhood*. London: Hodder & Stoughton.

Hasher, L., & Zacks, R. T. (1979). Automatic and effortful processes in memory. *Journal of Experimental Psychology; General, 108,* 356–388.

Hasher, L., & Zacks, R. T. (1984). Automatic processing of fundamental information: The case of frequency of occurrence. *American Psychologist, 39,* 1372–1388.

Hassenstein, B. (1971). *Information and control in the living organism*. London: Chapman & Hall.

Hassett, J. (1978). *A primer of psychophysiology*. San Francisco: Freeman.

Hastie, R. (1984). Causes and effects of causal attribution Journal of Personality and Social Psychology, 46, 44–56.

Hastie, R., Ostrom, T. M., Hamilton, D. L., Ebbesen, E., Wyer, R. S., & Carlston, D. (Eds.). (1980). *Person memory: The cognitive basis of social perception*. Hillsdale, N.J.: Erlbaum.

Hastings, A. C., Fadiman, J., & Gordon, J. S. (1980). *Health for the whole person*. Boulder, Colo.: Westview.

Hastings, D. A. (1990). Legal and regulatory issues in managed mental health care. In D. A. Hastings, W. L. Krasner, J. L. Michael, & N. D. Rosenber (Eds.), *The insiders guide to managed care*. Washington, DC: National Lawyers Association.

Hatcher, C., Brooks, B. S., et al. (1977). *Innovations in counseling psychology*. San Francisco: Jossey-Bass.

Hatfield, E. (1984). *Beauty*. Reading, Mass.: Addison-Wesley.

Hatfield, E., Cacioppo, J., & Rapson, R. L. (1993). *Emotional contagion*. Madison, WI: Brown.

Hatfield, E., & Rapson, R. L. (1992). Love and attachment processes. In M. Lewis & J. Haviland (Eds.), *The handbook of emotions*. New York: Guilford.

Hatfield, E., & Rapson, R. L. (1992). *Love, sex, and intimacy*. New York: Harper Collins.

Hatfield, E., & Sprecher, S. (1986). *Mirror, mirror—The importance of looks in everyday life*. New York: SUNY Press.

Hatfield, E., Traupmann, J., Sprecher, S., Utne, M., & Hay, J. (1982). Equity and intimate relations: Recent research. Unpublished manuscript.

Hatfield, E., Utne, M. K., & Traupmann, H. (1979). Equity theory and intimate relationships. In R. L. Burgess & T. L. Huston (Eds.), *Social exchange in developing relationships*. New York: Academic Press.

Hatfield, E., & Waister, G. W. (1978). *A new look at love*. Lanham, ND: University Press of America.

Hatfield, E., Waister, G. W., & Berscheid, E. (1978). *Equity: Theory and research*. Boston: Allyn & Bacon.

Hatfield, E., & Walster, G. W. (1981). *A new look at love*. Reading, Mass.: Addison-Wesley.

Hatfield, E., Walster, G. W., & Piliavin, J. (1978). Equity theory and helping relationships. In L. Wispe (Ed.), *Altruism, sympathy, and helping*. New York: Academic Press.

Hathaway, S. (1955). Clinical intuition and inferential accuracy. *Journal of Personality, 24,* 223–250.

Hathaway, S. R., & McKinley, J. C. (1943). *The Minnesota Multiphasic Personality Inventory*. New York: Psychological Corp.

Hathaway, S. R., & Meehl, P. E. (1951). *An atlas for the clinical use of the MMPI*. Minneapolis, Minn.: University of Minnesota Press.

Hathaway, S. R., & Monachesi, E. D. (Eds.). (1953). *Analyzing and predicting delinquency with the MMPI*. Minneapolis, Minn.: University of Minnesota Press.

Hatterer, L. J. (1971). *Changing homosexuality in the male*. New York: McGraw-Hill.

Hatterer, L. J. (1980). *The pleasure addicts: The addictive process—food, sex, drugs, alcohol, work and more*. San Diego, Calif.: Barnes.

Hatton, C. L., Valente, S. M., & Rink, A. (1977). *Suicide: Assessment and intervention*. New York: Appleton-Century-Crofts.

Hatton, D. C., Woodruff, M. L., & Meyer, M. E. (1975). Cholinergic modulation of tonic immobility in the rabbit (*Oryctolagus cuniculus*). *Journal of Comparative and Physiological Psychology, 89,* 1053–1060.

Haugeland, J. (1986). *Artificial intelligence: The very idea*. Cambridge: MIT Press.

Hauser, A. (1951). *The social history of art*. London: Routledge.

Hauser, A. (1963). *Facteurs humaines affectant la productivité des travailleurs industriels du Cap-Vert*. Dakar: Institut de Science Economique Appliquée.

Havenaar, J. M. (1990). Psychotherapy: healing by culture. *Psychotherapy Psychosomatics, 53*(1–4), 46–49.

Haveus, L. L. (1976). *Participant observation*. New York: Aronson, 1976.

Havighurst, R. J. *Developmental tasks and education* (3d ed.). New York: Longman.

Havighurst, R. J. (1953). *Human development and education.* New York: Longman Green.

Havighurst, R. J. (1957). The leisure activities of the middle-aged. *American Journal of Sociology, 63,* 152–162.

Havighurst, R. J. (1964). Youth in exploration and man emergent. In H. Borow (Ed.), *Man in a world at work.* Boston: Houghton Mifflin.

Havighurst, R. J. (1973). History of developmental psychology: Socialization and personality development through the lifespan. In P. B. Baites & K. W. Schaie (Eds.), *Life-span developmental psychology.* New York: Academic Press.

Havighurst, R. J. (1982). The world of work. In B. B. Wolman (Ed.), *Handbook of developmental psychology.* Englewood Cliffs, N.J.: Prentice-Hall.

Havighurst, R. J., & Breese, F. H. (1947). Relation between ability and social status in a Midwestern community. III. Primary mental abilities. *Journal of Educational Psychology, 38,* 241–247.

Haviland, J. M., & Lelwica, M. (1987). The induced affect response: 10-week-old infants' responses to three emotion expressions. *Developmental Psychology, 23,* 97–104.

Hawke, S., & Knox, D. (1978). The one-child family: A new life-style. *The Family Coordinator, 27*(3), 215–219.

Hawkins, D., & Pauling, L. (1973). *Orthmolecular psychiatry—Treatment of schizophrenia.* San Francisco: Freeman.

Hawkins, J. D., Von Cleve, E., & Catalano, R. F. (1991). Reducing early childhood aggression: Results of a primary prevention program. *Journal of American Academy of Child and Adolescent Psychiatry, 30,* 208–217.

Hawkins, R. D. (1991). Cell biological studies of conditioning in Aplysia. In J. Madden IV (Ed.), *Neurobiology of learning, emotion and affect* (pp. 3–28). New York: Raven.

Hawkins, R. D., & Bower, G. H. (Eds.). (1989). *Computational models of learning in simple neural systems.* San Diego, CA: Academic.

Hawkins, R. D., Carew, T. J., & Kandel, E. R. (1983). Effects of interstimulus interval and contingency on classical conditioning in Apylsia. *Socionomic Neuroscience Abstracts, 9,* 168.

Hawkins, R. D., Clark, G. A., & Kandel, E. R. (1988). Cell biological studies of learning in simple vertebrate and invertebrate systems. In F. Plum & V. Mountcastle (Eds.), *Handbook of physiological—The nervous system V* (pp. 25–83). Bethesda, MD: American Physiological Society.

Hawkins, R. P. (1986). Selection of target behaviors. In R. O. Nelson & S. C. Hayes (Eds.), *Conceptual foundations of behavioral assessment* (pp. 331–385). New York: Guilford.

Hay, D. F. (1977). Following their companions as a form of exploration for human infants. *Child Development, 48,* 1624–1632.

Hay, D. F., & Ross, H. S. (1982). The social nature of early conflict. *Child Development, 53,* 105–113.

Hay, J. C. (1966). Optical motions and space perception: An extension of Gibson's analysis. *Psychological Review, 73,* 550–565.

Hayduk, L. A. (1978). Personal space: An evaluative and orienting overview. *Psychological Bulletin, 85,* 117–134.

Hayeck, F. A. (1961). The nonsequitur of the ''dependence effect:'' *Southern Economic Journal, 27,* 346–348.

Hayes, C. (1951). *The ape in our house.* New York: Harper.

Hayes, J. R. (1976). It's the thought that counts: New approaches to educational theory. In D. Klahr (Ed.), *Cognition and instruction.* Hillsdale, N.J.: Erlbaum.

Hayes, K. J., & Hayes, C. (1951). The intellectual development of a home-raised chimpanzee. *Proceedings of the American Philosophical Society. 95,* 105–109.

Hayes, K. J., & Hayes, C. (1952). Imitation in a home-raised chimpanzee. *Journal of Comparative and Physiological Psychology, 45,* 450–459.

Hayes, S. C., Brownell, K. D., & Barlow, D. H. (1978). The use of self-administered covert sensitization in the treatment of exhibitionism and sadism. *Behavior Therapy, 9,* 283–289.

Haygood, R. C., & Bourne, L. E. (1965). Attribute and rule learning aspects of conceptual behavior. *Psychological Review, 72,* 179–195.

Haylett, C. H., & Rapoport, L. (1964). Mental health consultation. In L. Bellak (Ed.), *Handbook of community psychiatry and community mental health.* New York: Grune & Stratton.

Haynes, S., Wilson, C., Jaffe, P., & Britton, B. (1979). Biofeedback treatment of atopic dermatitis: Controlled case studies of eight cases. *Biofeedback and Self-regulation, 4*(3), 195–209.

Haynes, S. N. (1988). Casual models and the assessment-treatment relationship in behavior therapy. *Journal of Psychopathology and Behavioral Assessment, 10,* 171–183.

Haynes, S. N. (1992). *Models of causality in psychopathology: Toward dynamic, synthetic, and nonlinear models of behavior disorders.* New York: Macmillan.

Haynes, S. N., & O'Brien, W. H. (1988). The Gordian knot of DSM-III-R use: Integrating principles of behavior classification and complex causal models. *Behavioral Assessment, 10,* 95–105.

Haynes, S. N., & O'Brien, W. H. (1990) Functional analysis in behavior therapy. *Clinical Psychology Review, 10,* 649–668.

Haynes, S. N., & Wilson, C. C. (1979). *Behavioral assessment.* San Francisco: Jossey-Bass.

Haynie, N. A. (1982). Sensory modality checklist. In G. M. Gazda, W. C. Childers, & R. P. Walters (Eds.). *Interpersonal communications: A handbook for health professionals.* Rockville, Md.: Aspen Systems.

Hays, W. L. (1958). An approach to the study of trait implication and trait similarity. In R. Tagiuri & L. Petrullo (Eds.), *Person perception and interpersonal behavior.* Stanford, Calif.: Stanford University Press.

Hays, W. L. (1981/1973). *Statistics for the social sciences* (2nd ed.). New York: Holt, Rinehart & Winston.

Hayslip, B. (1989a). Alternative mechanisms for improvements in fluid ability performance among aged adults. *Psychology and Aging, 4,* 122–124.

Hayslip, B. (1989b). Fluid ability training: A past with a future? *Educational Gerontology, 16,* 573–596.

Hayslip, B., & Kennelly, K. (1985). Cognitive and noncognitive factors affecting learning among older adults. In D. B. Lumsden (Ed.), *The older adult as learner* (pp. 73–98). New York: Hemisphere.

Hayslip, B., Luhr, D., & Beyerlein, M. (1991). Levels of death anxiety in terminally ill men: A Pilot study. *Omega, 24,* 13–19.

Hayslip, B., & Stewart-Bussey, D. (1986). Locus of control—levels of death anxiety relationships. *Omega, 17,* 41–50.

Hayslip, B., & Walling, M. (1985–1986). Impact of hospice volunteer training on death anxiety and locus of control. *Omega, 16,* 243–254.

Head, H. (1920). *Studies in neurology II.* London: Oxford University Press/Hodder & Stoughton.

Head, H. (1926). *Aphasia and kindred disorders of speech.* Cambridge, England: Cambridge University Press.

Health resources statistics 1976–1977. U.S. Department of Health, Education, and Welfare, Public Health Services. Office of Health Research, Statistics, and Technology. National Center for Health Statistics.

Hearn, J. (1980). *The soldier and the monk: An evaluation of Western values*. Unpublished doctoral dissertation, Wright Institute, Los Angeles.

Hearnshaw, L. S. (1964). *A short history of British psychology, 1840–1940*. London: Methuen.

Hearnshaw, L. S. (1966). *The comparative psychology of mental development*. (36th L. T. Hobhouse Memorial Trust Lecture). London: Athlone Press.

Hearnshaw, L. S. (1978). Review of Nixon and Taft, 1977. *Australian Journal of Psychology, 30,* 104–105.

Hearnshaw, L. S. (1981/1979). *Cyril Burt: Psychologist*. New York: Vintage Books.

Hearnshaw, L. S. & Winterbourn, R. (1945). *Human welfare and industrial efficiency*. Wellington, New Zealand: Read.

Hearst, E. (1969). Excitation, inhibition, and discrimination learning. In N.J. Mackintosh & W. K. Honig (Eds.), *Fundamental issues in associative learning*. Halifax, N.S.: Dalhousie University Press.

Hearst, E. (1979). *The first century of experimental psychology*. Hillsdale, N.J.: Erlbaum.

Heath, A. (1976). *Rational choice and social exchange: A critique of exchange theory*. Cambridge, England: Cambridge University Press.

Heath, D. (1977). *Maturity and competence: A transcultural view*. New York: Gardner Press/Wiley.

Heath, D. (1983). The maturing person. In R. Walsh & D. H. Shapiro (Eds.), *Beyond health and normality: Toward a vision of extreme psychological health*. New York: Van Nostrand Reinholt.

Heath, D. H. (1965). *Explorations of maturity; Studies of mature and immature college men*. New York: Appleton-Century-Crofts.

Heath, D. H. (1977). *Maturity and competence: A trans-cultural view*. New York: Gardner Press.

Heath, R. (1964). *The reasonable adventurer*. Pittsburgh, Pa.: University of Pittsburgh Press.

Heathers, G. (1969). Grouping. In R. L. Ebel (Ed.), *Encyclopedia of educational research*. New York: Macmillan.

Heaton, R. K. (1976). The validity of neuropsychological evaluations in psychiatric settings. *Clinical Psychologist, 6,* 10–11.

Heaton, R. K., Baade, L. E, & Johnson, K. L. (1978). Neuropsychological test results associated with psychiatric disorders in adults. *Psychological Bulletin, 85,* 141–162.

Heaton, R. K., & Crowley, T. J. (1981). Effects of psychiatric disorders and their treatments on neuropsychologic test results. In S. B. Filskov & T. J. Boll (Eds.), *Handbook of clinical neuropsychology*. New York: Wiley.

Hebb, D. (1946). Emotion in man and animal: an analysis of the intuitive processes of recognition. *Psychological Review, 53,* 88–106.

Hebb, D. O. (1942). The effect of early and late brain injury upon test scores and the nature of normal adult intelligence. *Proceedings of the American Philosophical Society, 85,* 275–292.

Hebb, D. O. (1946). On the nature of fear. *Psychological Review, 53,* 259–276.

Hebb, D. O. (1947). *Organization of behavior*. New York: Wiley.

Hebb, D. O. (1948). Report on experimental, physiological and comparative psychology. In E. A. Bott (Ed.), Research planning in the Canadian Psychological Association. *Canadian Journal of Psychology, 1,* 13–14.

Hebb, D. O. (1949). *The organization of behavior*. New York: Wiley.

Hebb, D. O. (1951). The role of neurological ideas in psychology. *Journal of Personality, 20,* 39–55.

Hebb, D. O. (1961). Distinctive features of learning in the higher animal. In J. F. Delafresnay (Ed.), *Brain mechanisms and learning*. London, New York: Oxford University Press.

Hebb, D. O. (1966). *A textbook of psychology* (2nd ed.). Philadelphia: Saunders.

Hebb, D. O. (1972). *Textbook of psychology*. (3rd ed.). Philadelphia, Pa.: Saunders.

Hebb, D. O. (1980). *Essay on mind*. Hillsdale, N.J.: Erlbaum.

Hébert, J.-P. (1977). *Race et intelligence*. Paris: Copernic.

Hécaen, H., & Albert, M. L. (1978). *Human neuropsychology*. New York: Wiley.

Hécaen, H., & de Ajuriaguerra, J. (1964). *Lefthandedness: Manual superiority and cerebral dominance*. New York: Grune & Stratton.

Hecht, S. (1937). Rods, cones, and the chemical basis of vision. *Physiological Review, 17,* 239–290.

Hecht, S. (1947). *Explaining the atom*. New York: Viking Press.

Hecht, S., Shlaer, S., & Pirenne, M. H. (1942). Energy, quanta, and vision. *Journal of General Physiology, 25,* 819–840.

Hecht, S., & Williams, R. E. (1923). The visibility of monochromatic radiation and the absorption spectrum of visual purple. *Journal of General Physiology, 5,* 1–33.

Heckelman, R. G. (1966). Using the neurological impress remedial technique. *Academic Therapy Quarterly, 1,* 235–239.

Heckhausen, H. (1963). *Hoffnung und Furcht in der Leistungsmotivation*. Meisenheim: Hain.

Heckhausen, H. (1967). *The anatomy of achievement motivation*. New York: Academic Press.

Heckhausen, H. (1968). Achievement motivation research: Current problems and some contributions toward a general theory of motivation. In W. J. Arnold, (Ed.), *Nebraska Symposium on Motivation* Lincoln, Neb.: University of Nebraska Press.

Heckhausen, H. (1977). Achievement motivation and its constructs: A cognitive model. *Motivation and Emotion, 1,* 283–329.

Heckhausen, H. (1980). *Motivation und Handeln*. Berlin: Springer.

Heckhausen, H. (1982). The development of achievement motivation. In W. W. Hartup (Ed.), *Review of child development research*, Vol. 6. Chicago: University of Chicago Press.

Heckhausen, H. (1983). Zur Lage der Psychologie. In O. Ewert (Ed.), *Bericht über den 33. Kongress der Deutschen Gesellschaft für Psychologie in Mainz 1982*. Gottingen, West Germany: Hogrefe.

Hedvig, E. B. (1963). Stability of early recollections and thematic apperception stories. *Journal of Individual Psychology, 19,* 49–54.

Hedvig, E. B. (1965). Childhood and early recollections as basis for diagnosis. *Journal of Individual Psychology, 21,* 187–188.

Heelas, P., & Locke, A. (1981). *Indigenous Psychologies: the anthropology of the self*. London: Academic.

Hegel, G. W. F. (1910). *The phenomenonogy of mind*. New York: Allen & Unwin.

Heiby, E., & Greene, J. (1990, July). *Issue of psychologists prescribing psychotropic medications*. Paper presented at the Hawaii Psychological Association Meeting, Honolulu.

Heidbreder, E. (1924). An experimental study of thinking. *Archives of Psychology, 11,* 1–65.

Heidbreder, E. (1926). Meaning of introversion and extroversion. *Journal of Abnormal and Social Psychology, 21,* 120–134.

Heidbreder, E. (1927). The normal inferiority complex. *Journal of Abnormal and Social Psychology, 22,* 243–258.

Heidbreder, E. (1933). *Seven psychologies.* New York: Appleton-Century.

Heidbreder, E. (1945). The attainment of concepts, a psychological interpretation. *Transactions of the New York Academy of Sciences, 7,* 171–188.

Heidbreder, E. (1945). Toward a dynamic psychology of cognition. *Psychological Review, 52,* 1–22.

Heidbreder, E. (1969). Studying human thinking. In D. L. Krantz (Ed.), *Schools of psychology: A symposium.* New York: Appleton-Century-Crofts.

Heidbreder, E. M. (1972). Factors in retirement adjustment: White collar/blue collar experience. *Industrial Gerontology, 12,* 69–79.

Heidegger, M. (1962/1927). *Being and time,* New York: Harper.

Heidegger, M. (1982). *The basic problems of phenomenology.* Bloomington, Ind.: Indiana University Press.

Heider, F. (1936). Attitudes and cognitive organization. *Journal of Psychology, 21,* 107–112.

Heider, F. (1944). Social perception and phenomenal causality. *Psychological Review, 51,* 358–374.

Heider, F. (1958). *The psychology of interpersonal relations.* New York: Wiley.

Heider, F. (1959). On Lewin's method and theory. *Journal of Social Issues,* suppl. 13, 1–13..

Heider, F. (1959). On perception and event structure, and the psychological environment: Selected papers. *Psychological Issues, I*(3), 1–123.

Heider, F. (1970). Gestalt theory: Early history and reminiscences. *Journal of the History of the Behavioral Sciences, 6,* 131–139.

Heider, F. (1980). On balance and attribution. In D. Görlitz (Ed.), *Perspectives on attribution research and theory: The Bielefeld Symposium,* Cambridge, Mass.: Ballinger.

Heider, F., & Simmel, M. (1944). Experimental study of apparent behavior. *American Journal of Psychology, 57,* 243–259.

Heilbrun, A. (1990). The measurement of criminal dangerousness as a personality construct: Further validation of a research index. *Journal of Personality Assessment, 54,* 141–148.

Heilbrun, A., Diller, R., Fleming, R., & Slade, L. (1986). Strategies of disattention and auditory hallucinations in schizophrenics. *Journal of Nervous Mental Diseases, 174,* 265–273.

Heilman, J. D. (1933). Sex differences in intellectual ability. *Journal of Educational Psychology, 24,* 47–42.

Heilman, K. M., & Valenstein, E. (Eds.). (1979). *Clinical neuropsychology.* New York: Oxford University Press.

Heilman, K. M., & Valenstein, E. (Eds.). (1985). *Clinical neuropsychology* (2nd ed.). New York: Oxford University Press.

Heim, A. (1979). Quoted in J. Diner, *The physical and mental suffering of experimental animals.* Washington, D.C.: Animal Welfare Institute.

Heim, N. (1981). Sexual behavior of castrated sex offenders. *Archives of Sexual Behavior, 10,* 11–19.

Heiman, M. (1965). Psychoanalytic observations on the relationship of pet and man. *Veterinary Medicine/Small Animal Clinician, 60*(7), 713–718.

Heiman, N., & Grant, J. (Eds.). (1974). Else Frenkel-Brunswik: Selected papers. *Psychological Issues, 8,* Monograph 31.

Heimberg, R. G. (1989). Cognitive and behavioral treatments for social phobia: A critical analysis. *Clinical Psychology Review, 9,* 107–128.

Heimberg, R. G., Dodge, C. S., & Becker, R. E. (1987). Social phobia. In L. Michelson & M. Ascher (Eds.), *Cognitive behavioral assessment and treatment of anxiety disorders.* New York: Plenum Press.

Heimberg, R. G., Dodge, C. S., Hope, D. A., Kennedy, C. R., Zollo, L. J., & Becker, R. E. (1990). Cognitive behavioral group treatment for social phobia: Comparison with a credible placebo control. *Cognitive Therapy and Research, 11,* 1–23.

Heine, P. J. (1971). *Personality in social theory.* Chicago: Aldine.

Heine, R. W. (1953). A comparison of patients' reports of psychotherapytic experience with psychoanalytic, nondirective, and Adlerian therapists. *American Journal of Psychotherapy, 7,* 16–23.

Heineken, E. (1979). Zur Lage der Psychologie in Lateinamerika. *Psychologische Rundschau, 30,* 257–268.

Heinroth, O. (1910). Beiträge zur Biologie, nahmentlich Ethologie und Phsyiologie der Anatiden. In H. Schalow (Ed.), *Verhandlungen des 5. Internationalen Ornithologischen Kongresses in Berlin,* 589–702.

Heise, D. R. (1975). *Analysis.* New York: Wiley.

Heiss, J. (1981). Social roles. In M. Rosenberg, & R. H. Turner (Eds.), *Social psychology.* New York: Basic Books.

Heiss, J. S., & Gordon, M. (1964). Need patterns and the mutual satisfaction of dating and engaged couples. *Journal of Marriage and the Family, 26,* 337–339.

Heiss, R. (1949/1943). *Die Lehre vom Charakter.* Berlin: Springer.

Heiss, R., & Hiltmann, H. (1951). *Der Farbpyramidentest nach Max Pfister.* Bern: Huber.

Held, R., Leibowitz, H. W., & Teuber, H.-L. (Eds.). (1978). *Handbook of sensory physiology.* Vol. 8: *Perception.* Berlin: Springer.

Heller, F. A., & Wilpert, B. (1981). *Competence and power in managerial decision making.* Chichester, UK: Wiley.

Heller, K. (1979). The effects of social support: Prevention and treatment implications. In A. P. Goldstein & F. H. Kanfer (Eds.), *Maximizing treatment gains: Transfer enhancement in psychotherapy.* New York: Academic.

Heller, K. (1989). The return to community. *American Journal of Community Psychology, 17,* 1–15.

Heller, K. (1990). Social and community intervention. *Annual Review of Psychology, 41,* 141–168.

Heller, K., & Monahart, J. (1977). *Psychology and community change.* Homewood, Ill.: Dorsey Press.

Heller, K., Price, R. H., Reinharz, S., Riger, S., & Wandersman, A. (1984). *Psychology and community change: Challenges of the Future* (2nd ed.). Homewood, IL: Dorsey.

Heller, K., & Swindle, R. W. (1983). Social networks, perceived support, and coping with stress. In R. D. Felner, L. A. Jason, J. N. Moritsugu, & S. S. Farber (Eds.), *Preventive psychology: Theory, research, and practice* (pp. 87–103). New York: Pergamon.

Heller, K., Thompson, M. G., Trueba, P. E., Hogg, J. R., & Vlachos-Weber, I. (1991). Peer support telephone dyads for elderly women: Was this the wrong intervention? *American Journal of Community Psychology, 19,* 53–74.

Heller, R. (1973). *Edvard Munch: The scream.* New York: Viking.

Hellman, D., & Blackman, N. (1966). Enuresis, fire-setting, and cruelty to animals: A triad predictive of adult crime. *American Journal of Psychiatry, 122,* 1431–1435.

Hellpach, W. (1949/1942). *Deutsche Physiognomik.* Berlin: De Gruyter.

Hellpach, W. (1949/1946). *Klinische Psychologie.* Stuttgart: Thieme.

Helm, C. D. (1964). A multidimensional ratio scaling analysis of perceived color relations. *Journal of the Optical Society of America, 54,* 256–262.

Helm, C. D., & Tucker, L. R. (1962). Individual differences in the structure of color perception. *American Journal of Psychology, 75,* 437–444.

Helmholtz, H. L. F. von. (1856). *Handbuch der Physiologischen Optik.* Leipzig: Voss.

Helmholtz, H. L. F. von. (1863). *Lehre yon den Tonempfindungen als Grundlage für die Theorie der Musik.* Leipzig: Voss.

Helmholtz, H. L. F. von. (1924–25/1860–1866). In J. P. C. Southall (Ed.), *Treatise on physiological optics,* Vols. II, III. Rochester, N.Y.: Optical Society of America.

Helmholtz, H. L. F. von. (1954/1870). *On the sensations of tone as a physiological basis for the theory of music.* New York: Dover.

Helmholtz, H. L. von. (1856–1866). *Physiological optics* (3 vols.). Leipzig: Voss.

Helmholtz, H. L. von. (1873/1869). *The mechanisms of the ossicles of the ear.* New York: Woods.

Helmholz, H. V. (1948). On the rate of transmission of the nervous impulse. In W. Dennis (Ed.), *Readings in the history of psychology.* New York: Appleton-Century-Crofts. (Original work published in 1850).

Helson, H. (1964). *Adaptation level theory: An experimental and systematic approach to behavior.* New York: Harper.

Helson, H. (1969). Why did their precursors fail and the Gestalt psychologists succeed? *American Psychologist,* November.

Helzer, J. E., & Robins, L. N. (1980). Letter. *Archives of General Psychiatry, 38,* 1300–1301.

Helzer, J. E., Robins, L. N., Croughan, J. L., & Welner, A. (1981). Renard diagnostic interview. *Archives of General Psychiatry, 38,* 393–398.

Hempel, C. (1965). *Aspects of scientific explanation.* New York: Free Press.

Hemsley, G. D., & Doob, A. N. (1978). The effect of looking behavior on perceptions of a communictors' credibility. *Journal of Applied Social Psychology, 8,* 136–144.

Hendersen, R. W. (1978). Forgetting of conditioned fear inhibition. *Learning and Motivation, 9,* 16–30.

Henderson, N. D. (1982). Human behavior genetics. In M. R. Rosenzwieg & L. W. Porter (Eds.), *Annual review of psychology.* Palo Alto, Calif.: Annual Reviews.

Henderson, S., Byrne, D. G., Duncan-Jones, P., Scott, R., & Adcock, S. (1980). Social relationships, adversity and neurosis: A study of associations in a general population sample. *British Journal of Psychiatry, 136,* 574–583.

Hendin, H. (1965). *Suicide and Scandinavia.* Garden City, N.Y.: Doubleday.

Hendin, H. (1975). *The age of sensation.* New York: Norton.

Heneman, H. G., Schwab, D. P., Fossum, J. A., & Dyer, L. (1980). *Personnel/ human resource management.* Homewood, Ill.: Irwin.

Heninger, G., Charney, D., & Menkes, D. (1983). Receptor sensitivity and the mechanisms of action of anti-depressant treatment. In P. Clayton & J. Barrett, (Eds.), *Treatment of depression: Old controversies and new approaches.* New York: Raven.

Heninger, O. E. (1981). Poetry therapy. In S. Arieti (Ed.), *American handbook of psychiatry* (2nd ed.). New York: Basic Books.

Henker, F. O. (1982). Conflicting definitions of the term "psychosomatic:' *Psychosomatics, 23,* 8–11.

Henle, M. (1957). Some problems of eclecticism. *Psychological Review, 64,* 296–305.

Henle, M. (1978). One man against the Nazis—Wolfgang Köhler. *American Psychologist, 14,* 233–237.

Henle, M. (1984). Isomorphism: Setting the record straight. *Psychological Research, 46,* 317–327.

Henle, M. (Ed.). (1961). *Documents of Gestalt psychology.* Berkeley, Calif.: University of California Press.

Henle, M. (Ed.). (1971). *The selected papers of Wolfgang Köhler.* New York: Liveright.

Henle, M. (Ed.). (1976). *Vision and artifact.* New York: Springer.

Henle, M., Jaynes, J., & Sullivan, J. J. (1973). *Historical conceptions of psychology.* New York: Springer.

Henley, N. M. (1977). *Body politics.* Englewood Cliffs, N.J.: Prentice-Hall.

Henmon, V. A. C., Bohan, J. E., & Brigham, C. C. (1929). *Prognosis tests in the modern foreign languages.* New York: Macmillan.

Henn, F. A., Bardwell, R., & Jenkins, R. L. (1980). Juvenile delinquents revisited; adult criminal activity. *Archives of General Psychiatry, 37,* 1160–1163.

Hennessey, B. A., & Amabile, T. M.)1988. The conditions of creativity. In R. J. Sternberg (Ed.), *The nature of creativity,* (pp. 11–38). Cambridge, UK: Cambridge University Press.

Hennigan, K. M., Cook, T. D., & Gruder, C. L. (1982). Cognitive tuning set, source credibility, and attitude change. *Journal of Personality and Social Psychology, 42,* 412–425.

Henning, A. (1916). *Der Geruch.* Leipzig: Barth.

Henning, H. (1916). Duie Qualitatenreihe des Geschmacks. *Zeitschrift fuer Psychologie, 74,* 203–219.

Henning, H. (1924). *Der Geruch* (2nd. ed.) Leipzig: Engelmann.

Hennings, D. C., & Grant, B. M. (1973). *Content and craft: Written expression in the elementary school.* Englewood Cliffs, N.J.: Prentice-Hall.

Henriques, J., et al. (1984). *Changing the subject.* London: Methuen.

Henry, A. F., & Short, J. E., Jr. (1954). *Suicide and homicide.* Glencoe, Ill.: Free Press.

Henry, N. B. (1947). *The forty-sixth yearbook of the National Society for the Study of Education. Part II: Early childhood education.* Chicago: University of Chicago Press.

Henry, P. (1975). Manage your sales force as a system. *Harvard Business Review, 55,* 85–95.

Henry, W. E. (1949). The business executive: The psychodynamics of a social role. *American Journal of Sociology, 54,* 286–291.

Henry, W. E., Sims, J., & Spray, L. (1971). *The fifth profession: Becoming a psychotherapist.* San Francisco: Jossey-Bass.

Henrysson, S. (1971). Gathering, analyzing, and using data on test items. In R. L. Thorndike (Ed.), *Educational measurement* (2nd ed.). Washington, D.C.: American Council on Education.

Henslin, J. M. (1967). Craps and Magic! *American Journal of Sociology, 73,* 316–330.

Hepburn, J. R. (1980). The objective reality of evidence and the utility of systematic jury selection. *Law and Human Behavior, 4,* 89–101.

Heppner, P. (1978). A review of the problem-solving literature and its relationship to the counseling process. *Counseling Psychology, 25,* 366–375.

Herbart, J. F. (1824; 1925). *Psychologie als Wissenschaft.* Königsberg: Unzer, Vol. 1; Vol. 2.

Herbart, J. F. (1891/1816). *A textbook of psychology: An attempt to found the science of psychology on experience, metaphysics and mathematics.* New York: Appleton.

Herberman, R., & Ortaldo, J. R. (1981). Natural killer cells: The role in defenses against disease. *Science, 214,* 24–30.

Herbert, M. J., & Jaynes, W. E. (1961). Performance decrement in vehicle driving. *Journal of Engineering Psychology, 14,* 9–38.

Herdt, G. (Ed.). (1984). *Ritualized homosexuality in Melanesia*. Berkeley: University of California Press.

Hereford, C. F. (1966). Current status of psychology in Latin America. *Latin American Research Review, 1,* 97–108.

Herek, C. M. (1987). Can functions be measured? A new perspective on the functional approach to attitudes. *Social Psychology Quarterly, 50*(4), 285–303.

Herek, C. M. (1988). Heterosexuals' attitudes toward lesbians and gay men: Correlates and gender differences. *Journal of Sex Research, 25*(4), 451–477.

Herek, C. M. (1990). The context of anti-gay violence: Notes on cultural and psychological heterosexism. *Journal of Interpersonal Violence, 5*(3), 316–333.

Herek, G. M. (1982). Unisexual ideology and erotic hegemony. *National Women's Anthropology Newsletter, 6*(1), 17–21.

Herek, G. M. (1984a). Attitudes toward lesbians and gay men: A factor-analytic study. *Journal of Homosexuality, 10*(1–2), 39–51.

Herek, G. M. (1984b). Beyond "homophobia": A social psychological perspective on attitudes toward lesbians and gay men. *Journal of Homosexuality, 10*(1–2), 1–21.

Herek, G. M. (1986a). On heterosexual masculinity: Some psychical consequences of the social construction of gender and sexuality. *American Behavioral Scientist, 29*(5), 563–577.

Herek, G. M. (1986b). The instrumentality of attitudes: Toward a neo-functional theory. *Journal of Social Issues, 42*(2), 99–114.

Herek, G. M. (1986c). The social psychology of homophobia: Toward a practical theory. *Review of Law and Social Change, 14*(4), 923–934.

Herek, G. M. (1987). Religion and prejudice: A comparison of racial and sexual attitudes. *Personality and Social Psychology Bulletin, 13,*(1), 56–65.

Herek, G. M. (1989a). Gay people and government security clearances: A social science perspective. *American Psychologist, 45*(9), 1035–1042.

Herek, G. M. (1989b). Sexual orientation. In H. Tierney (Ed.), *Women's studies encyclopedia* (Vol. 1, pp. 344–346). New York: Greenwood.

Herek, G. M. (1990a). Homophobia. In W. R. Dynes (Ed.). *Encyclopedia of Homosexuality* (pp. 552–555). New York: Garland.

Herek, G. M. (1990b). Illness, stigma, and AIDS. In P. Costa & G. R. VandenBos (Eds.), *Psychological aspects of serious illness.* (pp. 103–150). Washington, DC: American Psychological Association.

Herek, G. M. (1991a). Myths about sexual orientation: A lawyer's guide to social science research. *Law and sexuality, 1,* 133–172.

Herek, G. M. (1991b). Stigma, prejudice, and violence against lesbians and gay men. In J. Gonsiorek & J. Weinrich (Eds.), *Homosexuality: Research implications for public policy* (pp. 60–80). Newbury Park, CA: Sage.

Herek, G. M. (1992a). Psychological heterosexism and antigay violence: The social psychology of bigotry and bashing. In C. M. Herek, & K. T. Berrill (Eds.), *Hate crimes: Confronting violence against lesbians and gay men*. Newbury Park, CA: Sage.

Herek, G. M. (1992b). The San Francisco response: Community united against violence. In G. M. Herek, & K. T. Berrill (Eds.), *Hate crimes: Confronting violence against lesbians and gay men*. Newbury Park, CA: Sage.

Herek, G. M. (in press). Documenting prejudice on campus: The Yale sexual Orientation Survey. *Journal of Homosexuality.*

Herek, G. M., Janis, I. L., & Huth, P. (1989). The quality of U.S. decision making during the Cuban missile crisis: Major errors in Welch's reassessment. *Journal of Conflict Resolution, 33*(3), 446–459.

Herek, G. M., & Berrill, K. (1990a). Documenting the victimization of lesbians and gay men: Methodological issues. *Journal of Interpersonal Violence, 5*(3), 301–315.

Herek, G. M., & Berrill, K. (1990b). Victimization, mental health, and heterosexism: Setting an agenda for research. *Journal of Interpersonal Violence, 5*(3), 414–423.

Herek, G. M., & Berrill, K. (Eds.). (1990c). Violence against lesbians and gay men: Issues for research, practice, and policy [Special Issue]. *Journal of Interpersonal Violence, 5*(3).

Herek, G. M., & Berrill, K. (Eds.). (1992). *Hate crimes: Confronting violence against lesbians and gay men*. Newbury Park, CA: Sage.

Herek, G. M., & Glunt, E. K. (1988). An epidemic of stigma: Public reactions to AIDS. *American Psychologist, 43*(11), 886–891.

Herek, G. M., & Glunt, E. K. (1991). AIDS-related attitudes in the United States: A preliminary conceptualization. *Journal of Sex Research, 28*(1), 99–123.

Herek, G. M., & Glunt, E. K. (in press). Public reactions to AIDS in the United States. In J. B. Pryor & G. D. Reeder (Eds.), *The social psychology of HIV infection*. Hillsdale, NJ: Erlbaum.

Herek, G. M., Janis, I. L., & Huth, P. (1987). Decision-making during international crises: Is quality of process related to outcome? *Journal of Conflict Resolution, 31,*(2), 203–226.

Herek, G. M., Kimmel, D. C., Amaro, H., & Melton, G. B. (1991). Avoiding heterosexist bias in psychological research. *American Psychologist, 44*(9), 957–963.

Hering, E. (1890). Beitrage zur Lehre vom Simultankontrast. *Zeitschrift für Psychologie, 1,* 18–28.

Hering, E. (1878). *Zur Lehre vom Lichtsinn*. Vienna: Gerolds.

Hering, E. (1964/1878). *Outlines of a theory of the light sense*. Cambridge, Mass.: Harvard University Press.

Herink, R. (1980). *The psychotherapy handbook*. New York: New American Library, 1980.

Herman, B. P. (1980). *A multidisciplinary handbook of epilepsy*. Springfield, Ill.: Thomas.

Herink, R. (Ed.). (1980). *The Psychotherapy handbook. The A to Z guide to more than 250 different therapies in use today*. New York: New American Library.

Herman, J. L. (1992). *Trauma and recovery*. New York: Basic Books.

Herman, R. D. (1976). *Gamblers and gambling*. Lexington, Mass.: Heath.

Herman, S. M., & Korenich, M. (1977). *Authentic management: A Gestalt orientation to organizations and their development*. Reading, Mass.: Addison-Wesley.

Hernández, C. A., Haug, M. J., & Wagner, N. N. (1976). *Chicanos: Social and psychological perspectives*. St. Louis, Mo.: Mosby.

Hernandez Luna, J. (1950). Primeros estudios sobre el mexicano en nuestro siglo. *Fifosofia y Letras, 20,* 327–353.

Hernandez, O. A. (1953). Las ideas sociales, politicas y juridicas del constituyente de 1917 en materia educativa. In Universidad Nacional Autonoma de Mexico (Ed.), *Memoria del Congreso Cientifico Mexicano*, Vol. 15. Mexico, D. F.: Ciencias de la Educacion, Psicologia-Filosofia.

Hernandez-Peon, R. (1961). Reticular mechanisms of sensory control. In W. A. Rosenblith (Ed.), *Sensory communication*. Cambridge, Mass.: Massachusetts Institute of Technology.

Hernandez-Peon, R., Scherrer, H., & Jouvet, M. (1956). Modification of electric activity in the cochlear nucleus during "attention" in unanesthetized cats. *Science, 123,* 331–332.

Heron, W. (1957). Perception as a function of retinal locus and attention. *American Journal of Psychology, 70,* 3848.

Heron, W. (1961). Cognitive and psychological effects of perceptual isolation. In P. Solomon (Ed.), *Sensory deprivation.* Cambridge, Mass.: Harvard University Press.

Heron, W., Doane, B. K., & Scott, T. H. (1956). Visual disturbances after prolonged perceptual isolation. *Canadian Journal of Psychology, 10,* 1318.

Herrigel, E. (1960). *Zen in the art of archery.* New York: Grove Press.

Herrman, L., & Hogben, L. (1932). The intellectual resemblance of twins. *Proceedings of the Royal Society of Edinburgh, 53,* 105–129.

Herrmann, D. J. (1987). Task appropriateness of mnemonic techniques. *Perceptual and Motor Skills, 64,*171–178.

Herrmann, L. (1976). *Lehrbuch der empirischen Persönlichkeitsforschung* (3rd ed.). Göttingen: West Germany: Hogrefe.

Herrmann, R. (1978). The philosophy of psychological science in the Federal Republic of Germany. *German Journal of Psychology, 2,* 320–334.

Hermann, R. O. (1973). Consumerism: Its goals, organization, and future. In B. B. Murray (Ed.), *Consumerism: The eternal triangle—business, government, and consumers.* Pacific Palisades, Calif.: Goodyear.

Herrmann, T. (1965). *Psychologie der kognitiven Ordnung.* Berlin: De Gruyter.

Herrmann, T. (1972). *Psychologie des elterlichen Erziehungsstils.* Bern: Huber, 1972. Stuttgart: Klett.

Herrmann, T. (1976). *Die Psychologie und ihre Forschungsprogramme.* Göttingen, West Germany: Hogrefe.

Herrmann, T. (1976). *Psychologie der Objektbenennung.* Bern: Huber.

Herrmann, T. (1979). *Psychologie als Problem.* Stuttgart: Klett-Cotta.

Herrmann, T. (1983/1982). *Sprechen und Situation (Speech and situation).* Heidelberg, New York: Springer.

Herrnstein, R. J. (1961). Relative and absolute strength of response as a function of frequency of reinforcement. *Journal of the Experimental Analysis of Behavior, 4,* 267–272.

Herrnstein, R. J. (1969). Method and theory in the study of avoidance. *Psychological Review, 76,* 49–69.

Herrnstein, R. J. (1970). On the law of effect. *Journal of the Experimental Analysis of Behavior, 13,* 243–266.

Herrnstein, R. J. (1971). I. Q. *The Atlantic Monthly, 228* (3), 43–64.

Herrnstein, R. J. (1973). *IQ in the meritocracy.* Boston: Atlantic Monthly Press.

Herrnstein, R. J. (1973). *I. Q. in the meritocracy.* Boston: Little, Brown.

Herrnstein, R. J. On the law of effect. *Journal of the Experimental Analysis of Behavior 13,* 243–266.

Herrnstein, R. J., & Boring, E. G. (1965). *A sourcebook in the history of psychology.* Cambridge, Mass.: Harvard University Press.

Herrnstein, R. J., & Brown, R. (1975). *Psychology.* Boston: Little, Brown.

Hersen, M., & Barlow, D. H. (1976). *Single-case experimental designs: Strategies for studying behavioral change.* New York: Pergamon Press.

Hersen, M., & Bellack, A. A. (1977). Assessment of social skills. In A. R. Ciminero, K. S. Calhoun, H. E. Adams (Eds.), *Handbook of behavioral assessment.* New York: Wiley.

Hersen, M., & Bellack, A. S. (Eds.). (1976). *Behavioral assessment: A practical handbook.* New York: Pergamon Press.

Hersey, P., & Blanchard, K. H. (1982). *Management of organizational behavior* (4th ed.). Englewood Cliffs, N.J.: Prentice-Hall.

Hershov, L., & Berg, I. (Eds.). (1980). *Out of school: Modern perspectives in truancy and school refusal.* New York: Wiley.

Herskovits, M. (1948). *Man and his work.* New York: Knopf.

Hersov, L. A. (1960). Refusal to go to school. *Journal of Child Psychology and Psychiatry, 1,* 137–145.

Hertzog, C., & Nesselroade, J. R. (1987). Beyond autoregressive models: Some implications of the trait-state distinction for the structural modeling of developmental change. *Child Development, 58,* 93–109.

Herzberg, A. (1945). *Active psychotherapy.* New York: Grune & Stratton.

Herzberg, F. (1966). *Work and the nature of man.* Cleveland, Ohio: World.

Herzberg, F. (1968). One more time: How do you motivate employees? *Harvard Business Review, 46,* 53–62.

Herzberg, F., Mausner, B., & Snyderman, B. (1959). *The motivation to work.* New York: Wiley.

Herzog, D. B. (1982). Bulimia: The secretive syndrome. *Psychosomatics, 23,* 481–484.

Heskin, K. (1980). *Northern Ireland: A psychological analysis.* New York: Columbia University Press.

Hess, A. K. (1980). *Handbook of psychotherapy supervision.* New York: Wiley.

Hess, A. K. (Ed.). (1980). *Psychotherapy supervision: Theory, research and practice.* New York: Wiley.

Hess, A. K., & Hess, K. A. (1982). Psychotherapy supervision: A survey of internship training practices. Manuscript submitted for publication.

Hess, A. K., & Hess, K. A. (1982). Research in supervision. Presented at the Southeastern Psychological Association Convention, New Orleans, La., March.

Hess, E. H. (1956). Space perception in the chick. *Scientific American, 195,* 71–80.

Hess, E. H. (1959). Imprinting: An effect of early experience. *Science. 130,* 133–141.

Hess, E. H. (1970). Ethology and developmental psychology. In P. H. Mussen (Ed.), *Carmichael's manual of child psychology,* Vol. 1 (3rd ed.). New York: Wiley.

Hess, E. H., & Polt, J. M. (1960). Pupil size as related to interest value of visual stimuli. *Science, 132,* 349–350.

Hess, R., Shipman, V., Brophy, J. E., & Bear, R. M. (1968). *The cognitive environment of urban preschool children.* Chicago: Graduate School of Education, University of Chicago.

Hess, W. R. (1962). *Psychologie in biologischer Sicht.* Stuttgart: Thieme.

Heston, L. L. (1966). Psychiatric disorders in foster home reared children of schizophrenic mothers. *British Journal of Psychiatry, 112,* 819–825.

Heston, L. L. (1970). The genetics of schizophrenia and schizoid disease. *Science, 167,* 249–256.

Heston, L. L., & Shields, J. (1986)/ Homosexuality in twins: A family study and a registry study. *Archives of General Psychiatry, 18,* 149–160.

Herb, C. D. (1976). Simultaneous and backward fear conditioning as a function of number of CS-UCS pairings. *Journal of Experimental Psychology: Animal Behavior Processes, 2,* 117–129.

Hetherington, A. N., & Ranson, S. W. (1942). The spontaneous activity and food intake of rats with hypothalamic lesions. *American Journal of Physiology, 136* 609–617.

Hetherington, B. M. (1972). Effects of father absence on personality development in adolescent daughters. *Developmental Psychology, 7,* 313–386.

Hetherington, B. M., Cox, M., & Cox, R. (1977). The aftermath of divorce. In J. H. Stevens, Jr., & M. Matthews (Eds.), *Mother-child, father-child relations.* Washington, D.C.: National Association for the Education of Young Children.

Hetherington, D. M., Cox, M., & Cox, R. (1975). Beyond father absence: Conceptualization of effects of divorce. Presented at the meeting of the Society for Research in Child Development, Denver, Colo. April.

Hetherington, D. M., Cox, M., & Cox, R. (1978). Family interaction and the social, emotional, and cognitive development of children following divorce. Presented at the Symposium on the Family: Setting Priorities, sponsored by the Institute for Pediatric Service of Johnson and Johnson, Washington, D.C., May.

Hetherington, E. M. (1975). The effects of familial variables on sex typing, on parent-child similarity, and on imitation in children. In P. Mussen, J. Conger, & J. Kagan (Eds.), *Basic and contemporary issues in developmental psychology.* New York: Harper & Row.

Hetherington, E. M., Cox, M., & Cox, R. (1979). Play and social interaction in children following divorce. *Journal of Social Issues, 35,* 26–49.

Hetherington, M., & Duer, J. (1972). The effects of father absence on child development. In W. W. Hartup (Ed.), *The young child: Review of research.* Vol. 2. Washington, D.C.: National Association for the Education of Young Children.

Heuer, F., Fischman, D., & Reisberg, D. (1986). Why does vivid imagery hurt colour memory? *Canadian Journal of Psychology, 40,* 161–175.

Heuer, F., & Reisberg, D. (in press). Emotion, arousal and memory for detail. In S. A. Christianson (Ed.), *Handbook of emotion and memory.* Hillsdale, NJ: Erlbaum.

Hevner, K. (1937). The affective value of pitch and tempo in music. *American Journal of Psychology, 49,* 621–630.

Hevner, K. (1936). The experimental study of the elements of expression in music. *American Journal of Psychology, 48,* 246–268.

Hevner, K. (1935). Expression in music: A discussion of experimental studies and theories. *Psychological Review, 49,* 621–630.

Hewes, G. W. (1955). World distribution of postural habits. *American Anthropologist, 57,* 231–244.

Hewett, F. M. (1968). *The emotionally disturbed child in the classroom.* Boston: Allyn & Bacon.

Heyns, R. W., Veroff, J., & Atkinson, J. W. (1958). A scoring manual for the afiliation motive. In J. W. Atkinson (Ed.), *Motives in fantasy, action, and society.* Princeton, N.J.: Van Nostrand.

Hibbard, W. S., & Worring, R. W. (1981). *Forensic hypnosis: The practical application of hypnosis in criminal investigation.* Springfield, Ill.: Thomas.

Hick, W. E. (1952). On the rate of gain of information. *Quarterly Journal of Experimental Psychology, 4,* 11–26.

Hickey, J. E., & Scharf, P. L. (1980). *Toward a just correctional system.* San Francisco: Jossey-Bass.

Hicks, H. G., & Gullett, C. R. (1975). *Organizations: Theory and behavior.* New York: McGraw-Hill.

Hicks, R. (1990a). Police pursuit of satanic crime, part 1. *Skeptical Inquirer, 14,* 276–286.

Hicks, R. (1990b). Police pursuit of satanic crime, part 2. *Skeptical Inquirer, 14,* 378–389.

Hicks, R. (1991). *In pursuit of satan: The police and the occult.* New York: Prometheus Books.

Hicks, R. E. (1966). Occupational prestige and its factors. *African Social Research, 1,* 41–58.

Hicks, R. E. (1969). The relationship of sex to occupational prestige in an African country. *Personnel and Guidance Journal, 47,* 665–668.

Higgins, E. T., Herman, C. P., & Zanna, M. P. (Eds.). (1981). *Social cognition: The Ontario symposium,* Vol. 1. Hillsdale, N.J.: Erlbaum.

Hilden, A. H. (1958). Q-sort correlation: Stability and random choice of statements. *Journal of Consulting Psychology, 22,* 45–50.

Hildum, D. C., & Brown, R. W. (1956). Verbal reinforcement and interviewer bias. *Journal of Abnormal and Social Psychology, 53,* 108–111.

Hilgard, E. (1980). Imagery and imagination in American Psychology. Presented at the fourth American Conference on Mental Imagery, San Francisco.

Hilgard, E. R. (1937). The relationship between the conditioned response and conventional learning experiments. *Psychological Bulletin, 34,* 61–102.

Hilgard, E. R. (1949). Human motives and the concept of the self. *American Psychologist, 4,* 374–382.

Hilgard, E. R. (1953). *Introduction to psychology.* New York: Harcourt, Brace.

Hilgard, E. R. (1965). *Hypnotic susceptibility.* New York: Harcourt, Brace & World.

Hilgard, E. R. (1968). *The experience of hypnosis.* New York: Harcourt, Brace, Jovanovich.

Hilgard, E. R. (1977). *Divided consciousness: Multiple controls in human thought and action.* New York: Wiley.

Hilgard, E. R. (1980). Consciousness in contemporary psychology. In M. R. Rosenszweig & L. W. Porter (Eds.), *Annual review of psychology, 1980,* Vol. 31. Palo Alto, Calif.: Annual Reviews.

Hilgard, E. R. (1986). *Divided consciousness: Multiple controls in human thought and action.* New York: Wiley.

Hilgard, E. R. (1987). *Psychology in America: A historical survey.* San Diego, CA: Harcourt, Brace, Jovanovich.

Hilgard, E. R. (1988). A review of B. F. Skinner's *The behavior of organisms. Journal of Experimental Analysis of Behavior, 50,* 283–286.

Hilgard, E. R. (1988). Milton Erickson as playwright and director. *International Journal of Clinical and Experimental Hypnosis, 36,* 128–139.

Hilgard, E. R. (1992). A theoretical focus: Divided consciousness and dissociation. *Consciousness and Cognition, 1,* 16–31.

Hilgard, E. R., & Atkinson, R. C. (1967). *Introduction to psychology* (4th ed.). New York: Harcourt, Brace & World.

Hilgard, E. R., Atkinson, R. C., & Atkinson, R. L. (1979). *Introduction to psychology* (7th ed.). New York: Harcourt, Brace, Jovanovich.

Hilgard, E. R., & Bower, G. H. (1975). *Theories of learning* (4th ed.). New York: Appleton-Century-Crofts.

Hilgard, E. R. (Ed.). (1978). *American psychology in historical perspective: Addresses of the presidents of the American Psychological Association, 1892–1977.* Washington, D.C.: American Psychological Association.

Hilgard, E. R. (Ed.). (1988). *Fifty years of psychology: Essays in honor of Floyd Ruch.* Glenview, IL: Scott, Foresmall.

Hilgard, E. R., & Hilgard, J. R. (1975). *Hypnosis in the relief of pain.* Los Altos, Calif.: Kaufmann.

Hilgard, E. R., Leary, D. E., & McGuide, G. R. A. (1991). The history of psychology: A survey and critical assessment. *Annual Review of Psychology, 42,* 79–107.

Hilgard, E. R., & Loftus, E. F. (1979). Effective interrogation of the eyewitness. *International Journal of Clinical and Experimental Hypnosis, 27,* 342–357.

Hilgard, E. R., & Marquis, D. G. (1940). *Conditioning and learning.* New York: Appleton-Century-Crofts.

Hilgard, J. R. (1979). Imaginative and sensory-affective involvements in everyday life and in hypnosis. In E. Fromm & R. E. Shor (Eds.), *Hypnosis: Developments in research and new perspectives.* New York: Aldine.

Hill, A. L. (1978). Savants: Mentally retarded individuals with special skills. In N. Ellis (Ed.), *International reviews of research in mental retardation,* Vol. 9. New York: Academic Press.

Hill, C. T., Rubin, Z., & Peplau, A. (1976). Breakups before marriage: The end of 103 affairs. *Journal of Social Issues, 32,* 147–167.

Hill, E. F. (1972). *The Holtzman inkblot technique.* San Francisco: Jossey-Bass.

Hill, G. (1982). Group versus individual performance: Are *N* + 1 heads better than one? *Psychological Bulletin, 91,* 510–539.

Hill, J. E. (1973). *The educational sciences.* Bloomfield Hills, Mich.: Oakland Community College Press.

Hill, J. P. (1978). Secondary schools, socialization, and social development during adolescence. Prepared for the National Institute of Education, U.S. Department of Health, Education, and Welfare.

Hill, J. P. (1980). The family. In M. Johnston (Ed.), *Toward adolescence: The middle school years. The seventy-ninth yearbook of the National Society for the Study of Education.* Chicago: University of Chicago Press.

Hill, K. A. (1987). Meta-analysis of paradoxical interventions. *Psychotherapy, 24,* 266–270.

Hill, R. (1949). *Families under stress: Adjustment to the crisis of war, separation and reunion,* New York: Harper.

Hill, R., & Mattessich, P. (1980). Family development theory and life-span development. In P. B. Baltes & O. G. Brim, Jr. (Eds.), *Life-span development and behavior,* Vol. 3. New York: Academic Press.

Hill, S., & Goodwin, J. (1989). Satanism: Similiarities between patient accounts and pre-inquisition historical sources. *Dissociation, 2*(1), 39–44.

Hill, T. & Lewicki, P. (1991). Personality and the unconscious. In V. Derlega & W. Jones (Eds.), *Introduction to contemporary research in personality* (pp. 208–229). New York: Nelson Hall.

Hill, T., Lewicki, P., Czyzewski, M. (1992). Nonconscious acquisition of information. *American psychologist, 47,* 796–801.

Hill, T., Lewicki, P., Czyzewski, M., & Boss, A. (1989). Self-perpetuating development of encoding biases in person perception. *Journal of Personality and Social Psychology, 57,* 373–387.

Hille, S. J., et al. (1967). *Studying transportation systems from the consumer viewpoint: Some recommendations.* College Park, Md.: University of Maryland.

Hillenbrand, E. D. (1970). Father absence in military families. *Dissertation Abstracts International, 31,* 6902B–7054B (University Microfilm no. 27074).

Hillier, F., & Lieberman, G. (1967). *Introduction to operations research.* San Francisco: Holden-Day.

Hilix, W. A., & Marx, M. H. (Eds.). (1974). *Systems and theories in psychology: A reader.* St. Paul, Minn.: West.

Hillix, W. A., & Marx, M. H. (1987). Response strengthening by information and effect in human learning. *Journal of Experimental Psychology, 60,* 97–102.

Hilton, D. D. (1971). Access and attitudes to smoking (letter). *British Medical Journal, 2*(757), 337.

Hinchcliffe, R. (1962). Aging and sensory thresholds. *Journal of Gerontology, 17,* 1, 50.

Hinde, R. A. (1970/1966). *Animal behaviour: A synthesis of ethology and comparative psychology.* New York: McGraw-Hill.

Hinde, R. A. (1979). *Towards understanding relationships.* London: Academic Press.

Hinde, R. A. (1982). *Ethology: Its nature and contacts with other sciences.* London: Fontana Open Books.

Hinde, R. A. (Ed.). (1972). *Non-verbal communication.* Cambridge, England: Cambridge University Press.

Hinde, R. A. & Horn, G. (Eds.). (1969). *Bird vocalizations.* Cambridge, England: Cambridge University Press.

Hinde, R. A., & Spencer-Booth, Y. (1971). Effects of brief separation from mother on rhesus monkeys. *Science, 173,* 111–118.

Hinde, R. A., & Steyenson-Hinde, J. S. (Eds.). (1973). *Constraints on learning.* London: Academic Press.

Hines, L. (1981). Nondiscriminatory testing: The state of the art. *Peabody Journal of Education,* 119–124.

Hines, M. (1993). Hormonal and neural correlates of sex-type cognitive development in human beings. In M. Haug, R. E. Whalen, C. Aron, & K. Olsen, (Eds.), *The development of sex differences and similarities in behavior.* Dordrecht/Kluwer Academic Publishers.

Hines, M., Chiu, L., McAdams, L. A., & Bentler, P. (1992). Cognition and the corpus callosum: Verbal fluency, visuospatial ability and language lateralization related to midsagittal surface areas of callosal subregions. *Behavioral Neurosciences, 106*(1), 3–14.

Hines, P. M., & Hare-Mustin, R. T. (1978). Ethical concerns in family therapy. *Professional Psychology, 9,* 165–171.

Hinkle, D. E., Wiersma, W., & Jurs, S. G. (1988). *Applied statistics for the behavioral sciences* (2nd ed.) Boston: Houghton Mifflin.

Hinrichs, J. R. (1971). Employees going and coming: The exit interview. *Personnel, 48,* 30–35.

Hinrichs, J. R. (1975). Measurement of reasons for resignation of professionals: Questionnaire versus company and consultant exit interviews. *Journal of Applied Psychology, 60,* 530–532.

Hinshaw, S. R. (1992). Externalizing behavior problems and academic underachievement in childhood and adolescence: Causal relationships and underlying mechanisms. *Psychological Bulletin, 111,* 127–155.

Hinshelwood, R. D. (1968). Schizophrenic birth order: The last but one position. *Nature, 220*(5166), 490.

Hinsie, L. E., & Campbell, R. A. (1975). *Psychiatric dictionary* (4th ed.). New York: Oxford University Press.

Hinson, J. M., & Staddon, J. E. R. (1983). Hill-climbing by pigeons. *Journal of the Experimental Analysis of Behavior, 39,* 25–48.

Hinson, R. E., & Siegel, S. (1986). Pavlovian inhibitory conditioning and tolerance to pentobarbital-induced hypothermia in rats. *Journal of Experimental Psychology: Animal Behavior Processes, 12,* 363–370.

Hinterkopf, E. (1981). *Clarifying and training advanced empathy using focusing and the experiential response.* Unpublished manuscript.

Hinton, H. E. (1973). Natural deception. In R. L. Gregory & E. H. Gombrich (Eds.), *Illusion in nature and art.* New York: Scribner's.

Hintzman, D. L. (1976). Repetition and memory. In G. H. Bower (Ed.), *The psychology of learning and motivation* (Vol. 10, pp. 47–93). New York: Academic.

Hirai, T. (1968). *Zen meditation therapy.* Tokyo: Japan Publications.

Hiriartborde, E., & Fraisse P. (1968). *Les aptitudes rythmiques.* Paris: CNRS.

Hiroto, D. S. (1974). Locus of control and learned helplessness. *Journal of Experimental Psychology, 102,* 187–193.

Hiroto, D. S., and Seligman, M. E. P. (1975). Generality of learned helplessness in man. *Journal of Personality and Social Psychology, 31,* 311–327.

Hirsch, B. J. (1979). Psychological dimensions of social networks: A multimethod analysis. *American Journal of Community Psychology, 7,* 263–277.

Hirsch, B. J. (1980). Natural support systems and coping with major life changes. *American Journal of Community Psychology, 8,* 159–172.

Hirsch, J. (1962). Individual differences in behavior and their genetic bases. In E. L. Bliss (Ed.), *Roots of behavior.* New York: Hoeber-Harper.

Hirsch, J. (1970). Behavior-genetic analysis and its biosocial consequences. *Seminars in Psychiatry, 2,* 89–105.

Hirsch, J. C. (1989). Intracellular analysis of synaptic placticity in the prefrontal cortex: An in vitro study in the rat. *Journal of Physiology, 411,* 11.

Hirst, W. (1988). *The making of cognitive science: Essays in honor of George Miller.* New York: Cambridge University Press.

Hisamatsu, S. (1974). *Zen and the fine arts.* Tokyo: Kodansha International.

Hitchcock, J. L., Munroe, R. L., & Munroe, R. H. (1976). Coins and countries: The value-size hypothesis. *Journal of Social Psychology, 100,* 307–308.

Hite, S. (1976). *The Hite report.* New York: Dell.

Hixon, T. J., Shriberg, L. D., & Saxman, J. H. (Eds.). (1980). *Introduction to communication disorders.* Englewood Cliffs, N.J.: Prentice-Hall.

Hjelle, L. (1974). Transcendental meditation and psychological health. *Perceptual and Motor Skills, 39,* 623–628.

Hjelle, L., & Ziegler, D. (1981). *Personality theories: Basic assumptions, research, and applications* (2nd ed.). New York: McGraw-Hill.

Hobart, C. W. (1958). The incidence of romanticism during courtship. *Social Forces, 36,* 362–367.

Hobbes, T. (1655). *DE Corpore.*

Hobbes, T. (1839/1651). *Human nature* (1651). In W. Molesworth (Ed.), *Hobbes' English works. Cambridge, England: Cambridge University Press.*

Hobbes, T. (1904/1651). *Leviathan.* Cambridge, England: Cambridge University Press.

Hobbs, J. R., & Moore, R. (Eds.). (1985). *Formal theories of the commonsense World.* Norwood, NJ: Ablex.

Hobfoll, S. E. (1988). *The ecology of stress.* Washington, DC: Hemisphere.

Hobfoll, S. E. (Ed.). (1990). Social support [Special issue]. *Journal of Social and Personal Relationships, 7*(4).

Hobfoll, S. E., & Jackson, A. P. (1991). Conservation of resources in community intervention. *American Journal of Community Psychology, 19,* 111–121.

Hobfoll, S. E., & Vaux, A. (in press). Social support: Social resources and social context. In Goldenberger & S. Brenitz (Eds.), *Handbook of stress* (2nd ed.). New York: Wiley.

Hoch, E. L., Ross, A. O., & Winder, C. L. (Eds.). (1966). *Professional preparation of clinical psychologists.* Washington, D.C.: American Psychological Association.

Hoch, E. M. (1990). Experiences with psychotherapy training in India. *Psychotheraphy Psychosomatics, 53*(1–4), 1–204.

Hoch, P. H., & Polatin, P. (1949). Pseudoneurotic form of schizophrenia. *Psychiatric Quarterly, 23,* 248–276.

Hochberg, J. E. (1966). Nativism and empiricism in perception. In L. Postman (Ed.), *Psychology in the making.* New York: Knopf.

Hochberg, J. E. (1970). In the mind's eye. In R. N. Haber (Ed.), *Contemporary theory and research in visual perception.* New York: Appleton-Century-Crofts.

Hochberg, J. E. (1971). Perception II. Space and movement. In J. W. Kling & L. A. Riggs (Eds.) *Woodworth and Schlosberg's experimental psychology.* New York: Holt, Rinehart, & Winston.

Hochberg, J. E. (1972). The representation of things and people. In E. H. Gombrich, J. Hochberg, & M. Black (Eds.), *Art, perception and reality.* Baltimore, Md.: Johns Hopkins.

Hochberg, J. E. (1978). *Perception* (2nd ed.) Englewood Cliffs, N.J.: Prentice-Hall.

Hochberg, J. E. (1979). Sensation and perception. In E. Hearst (Ed.), *The first century of experimental psychology.* Hillsdale, N.J.: Erlbaum.

Hochberg, J. E. (1981a). Levels of perceptual organization. In M. Kubovy & J. Pomerantz (Eds.), *Perceptual organization.* Hillsdale, N.J.: Erlbaum.

Hochberg, J. E. (1981b). On cognition in perception: Perceptual coupling and unconscious inference. *Cognition, 10,* 127–134.

Hochberg, J. E., & Beck, J. (1954). Apparent spatial arrangement and perceived brightness. *Journal of Experimental Psychology, 47* 263–266.

Hochberg, J. E., & Brooks, V. (1978). The perception of motion pictures. In E. C. Carterette & M. Friedman (Eds.), *Handbook of perception,* Vol. 10. New York: Academic Press.

Hochberg, J. E., & Galper, R. E. (1974). Attribution of intention as a function of physiognomy. *Memory and Cognition, 2,* 39–42.

Hochberg, J. E., & McAlister, E. (1953). A quantitative approach to figural "goodness," *Journal of Experimental Psychology, 46,* 361–364.

Hockheimer, M., & Adorno, T. W. (1979). *Dialectic of enlightenment,* New York: Herder & Herder.

Hodapp, A. F., & Lavoie, J. C. (1975). Imitation by second borns in adult sibling dyads. *Readings in Education, 7.*

Hodge, R. W., Siegel, P. M., & Rossi, P. H. (1964). Occupational prestige in the United States, 1925–63. *American Journal of Sociology, 70,* 286–302.

Hodges, H. A. (1952). *The philosophy of Wilhelm Dilthey,* London: Routledge & Kegan Paul.

Hodges, W., & Cooper, M. (1981). Head Start and follow through: Influences on intellectual development. *Journal of Special Education, 15,* 221–238.

Hodos, W., & Campbell, C. B. G. (1969). *Scala Naturae:* Why there is no theory in comparative psychology. *Psychological Review, 4,* 337–350.

Hodson, F. R., Kendall, D. G., & Tautu, P. (Eds.). (1971). *Mathematics in the archaeological and historical sciences*. Edinburgh: Edinburgh University.

Hoebel, E. A. (1954). *The law of primitive man: A study of comparative legal dynamics*. Cambridge, Mass.: Harvard University Press.

Hoehn-Saric, R. (1978). Emotional arousal, attitude change, and psychotherapy. In J. D. Frank, R. Hoehn-Saric, S. D. Imber, B. L. Liberman, & A. R. Stone (Eds.), *Effective ingredients of successful psychotherapy*. New York: Brunner/Mazel.

Hofer, M. A. (1981). *The roots of human behavior: An introduction to the psychobiology or early development*. San Francisco: Freeman.

Höffding, H. (1887). *Psychologie in Umrissen auf Grundlage der Erfahrung*, Leipzig: Reisland.

Höffding, H. (1891/1887). *Outline of psychology*, London: Macmillan.

Höffding, H. (1924–1930). *A history of modern philosophy* (2 vols). London: Macmillan.

Hoffer, A. (1962). *Niacin therapy in psychiatry*. Springfield, Ill.: Thomas.

Hoffer, A., & Osmond, H. (1966). *How to live with schizophrenia*. New Hyde Park, N.Y.: University Books.

Hoffman, H. S., & Ratner, A. M. (1973). A reinforcement model of imprinting: Implications for socialization of monkeys and man. *Psychological Review, 6*, 527–544.

Hoffman, J. A., & Teyber, E. D. (1979). Some relationships between sibling age spacing and personality. *Merrill-Palmer Quarterly, 25*(1), 77–80.

Hoffman, L. (1976). Breaking the homeostatic cycle. In P. Guerin (Ed.), *Family therapy*. New York: Gardner Press.

Hoffman, L. (1981). *Foundations of family therapy*. New York: Basic Books.

Hoffman, L. (1981). *Foundations of family therapy*. New York: Basic Books.

Hoffman, L. W. (1977). Changes in family roles, socialization, and sex differences. *American Psychologist, 32*, 644–657.

Hoffman, L. W. (1991). The influence of family environment on personality: Accounting for sibling differences. *Psychological Bulletin, 110*, 187–103.

Hoffman, M. (1977). Empathy, its development and prosocial implications. *Nebraska Symposium on Motivation, 25*, 169–211.

Hoffman, M. L. (1970). Moral development. In P. H. Mussen (Ed.), *Carmichael's manual of child psychology*, Vol. II (3rd ed.). New York: Wiley.

Hoffman, M. L. (1980). Moral development in adolescence. In J. Adelson (Ed.), *Handbook of adolescent psychology*. New York: Wiley.

Hoffman, M. L., & Saltzstein, H. D. (1967). Parent discipline and the child's moral development. *Journal of Personality and Social Psychology, 5*, 45–57.

Hofstadter, R. (1944). *Social Darwinism in American thought, 1860–1915*. Philadelphia, Pa.: University of Pennsylvania Press.

Hofstätter, P. R. (1948). *Einführung in die Tiefenpsychologie*. Vienna: Braumueller.

Hofstätter, P. R. (1953). *Einführung in die quantitativen Methoden der Psychologie*. Munich: Barth.

Hofstätter, P. R. (1956). *Sozialpsychologie*. Berlin: De Gruyter.

Hofstätter, P. R.(1971/1957). *Gruppendynamik*. Reinbek: Rowohlt.

Hofstätter, P. R. (1983/1957). *Das Fischer-Lexikon Psychologie*. Frankfurt am Main: Fischer Taschenbuch-Verlag.

Hofstede, G. (1980). *Culture's consequences: International differences in work-related values*. Beverly Hills, Calif.: Sage Publications.

Hogan, A. E., & Quay, H. C. (1984). Cognition in child and adolescent behavior disorders. In B. B. Lehey & A. E. Kazdin (Eds.), *Advances in clinical child psychology*. New York: Plenum.

Hogan, D. B. (1979). *The regulation of psychotherapists*. Vol. 1: A study in the philosophy and practice of professional regulation. Cambridge, Mass.: Ballinger.

Hogan, D. P. (1978). The variable order of events in the life course. *American Sociological Review, 43*, 573–586.

Hogan, R., DeSato, C. B., & Solano, C. (1977). Traits, tests and personality research. *American psychologist, 32*, 255–264.

Hogarth, R. M. (1980). *Judgment and choice: The psychology of decisions*. New York: Wiley.

Hogben, L. (1957). *Statistical theory*. London: Norton.

Hogg, J. (Ed.). (1969). *Psychology and the visual arts*. Harmondsworth, England: Penguin Books.

Hoiberg, A. (Ed.). (1978). Women as new "manpower:" Special issue of *Armed Forces and Society, 4*, 555–736.

Hokanson, J., Burgess, M., & Cohen, M. (1963). Effects of displaced aggression on systolic blood pressure. *Journal of Abnormal and Social Psychology, 67*, 214–218.

Hokanson, J. E., & Burgess, M. (1962). The effects of three types of aggression on vascular processes. *Journal of Abnormal and Social Psychology, 64*, 446–449.

Holahan, C. J., & Moos, K. H. (1985). Life stress and health: Personality, coping and family support in stress resistance. *Journal of Personality and Social Psychology, 49*, 738–747.

Holahan, C. K., & Holahan, C. J. (1987a). Self-efficacy, social support, and depression in aging: A longitudinal analysis. *Journal of Gerontology, 42*, 65–68.

Holden, R. R., & Jackson, D. N. (1979). Item subtlety and face validity in personality assessment. *Journal of Consulting and Clinical Psychology, 47*, 459–468.

Holden, R. R., & Jackson, D. N. (1985). Disguise and the structured self-report assessment of psychopathology: I. An analogue investigation. *Journal of Consulting and Clinical Psychology, 53*, 211–222.

Hölder, O. (1901). Die Axiome der Quantität und die Lehre vom Mass. *Berichte über die Verhandlungen der Küoniglich-sächsischen Akademie der Wissenschaften, Mathematisch-physische Classe, 53*, 1–64.

Holender, D. (1986). Semantic activation without conscious identification in dichotic listening, parafoveal vision, and visual masking: A survey and appraisal. *Behavior and Brain Sciences, 9*, 1–66.

Holland, C. J., & Kobasigawa, A. (1980). Observational learning: Bandura. In G. M. Gazda & R. J. Corsini (Eds.), *Theories of learning: A comparative approach*. Itasca, Ill.: Peacock.

Holland, J. (1981). *Too long a sacrifice: Life and death in Northern Ireland since 1969*. New York: Dodd Mead.

Holland, J. L. (1966). *The psychology of vocational choice*. Waltham, Mass.: Blaisdell.

Holland, J. L. (1970–1973). *The self-directed search*. Palo Alto, Calif.: Consulting Psychologists Press.

Holland, J. L. (1973). *Making vocational choices: A theory of careers*. Englewood Cliffs, N.J.: Prentice-Hall.

Holland, J. L. (1979). *Professional manual for the self-directed search*. Palo Alto, Calif.: Consulting Psychologists Press.

Holland, J. L., Daiger, D. C., & Power, P. G. (1980). Some diagnostic scales for research in decision-making and personality: Identity, information and barriers. *Journal of Personality and Social Psychology, 40*, 1191–1200.

Holland, J. L., & Holland, J. E. (1977). Vocational indecision: More evidence and speculation. *Journal of Counseling Psychology, 24,* 404–414.

Holland, J. L., Magoon, T. M., & Spokane, A. R. (1981). Counseling psychology: Career interventions, research and theory. *Annual Review of Psychology, 32,* 279–305.

Holland, N. M. (1968). *The dynamics of literary response.* New York: Oxford University Press.

Holland, N. N. (1966). *Psychoanalysis and Shakespeare.* New York: McGraw-Hill.

Holland, N. N. (1973). *Poems in persons: An introduction to the psychoanalysis of literature.* New York: Norton.

Holland, P. W. (1986). Statistics and causal inference. *Journal of the American Statistical Association, 81,* 945–960.

Holland, T., Holt, N., & Beckett, G. (1982). Prediction of violent versus nonviolent recidivism from prior violent and nonviolent criminality. *Journal of Abnormal Psychology, 3,* 17–182.

Hollander, E. P. (1958). Conformity, status and idiosyncrasy credit. *Psychological Review, 65,* 117–127.

Hollander, E. P., & Willis, R. H. (1967). Some current issues in the psychology of conformity and nonconformity. *Psychological Bulletin, 68,* 62–76.

Hollander, M., & Woffe, D. A. (1973). *Nonparametric statistical methods.* New York: Wiley.

Hollandsworth, J. G., & Wall, K. E. (1977). Sex differences in assertive behavior: An empirical investigation. *Journal of Counseling Psychology, 24,* 217–222.

Holley, W. H., Feild, H. S., & Barnett, N. H. (1976). Analyzing performance appraisal systems: An empirical study. *Personnel Journal 55,* 457–459, 463.

Hollin, C. R. (1990). Social skills training with delinquents: A look at the evidence and some recommendations for practice. *British Journal of Social Work, 20,* 483–493.

Hollingshead, A. B., & Redlich, F. C. (1958). *Social class and mental illness.* New York: Wiley.

Hollingworth, H. L. (1930). *Abnormal psychology.* New York: Ronald Press.

Hollingworth, H. L. (1928). *Psychology: Its facts and principles.* New York: Appleton.

Hollingworth, H. L. (1922). *Judging human character.* New York: Appleton.

Hollingworth, L. S. (1975). *Children above 180 I.Q.: Standford-Binet: Origin and development.* New York: Arno Press.

Hollingworth, L. S. (1926). *Gifted children.* New York: Macmillan.

Hollingworth, L. S. (1947/1928). *The psychology of the adolescent.* New York: Staples.

Hollingworth, L. S. (1920). *The psychology of subnormal children.* New York: Macmillan.

Hollingworth, L. S. (1923). *Special talents and defects.* New York: Macmillan.

Hollis, F., & Woods, M. E. (1981/1964). *Casework: A psychosocial therapy* (3rd ed.). New York: Random House.

Hollis, J. W., & Wantz, R. A. (1980). *Counselor preparation 1980.* Muncie, Ind.: Accelerated Development.

Hollis, K. L., & Ovemiier, J. B. (1978). The function of the teleost telencephalon in behavior: A reinforcement mediator. In D. I. Mostofsky (Ed.), *The behavior of fish and other aquatic animals.* (pp. 137–195) New York: Academic.

Hollister, L. E. (1980). Pharmacologic considerations in the treatment regimen. In *Depression in the '80s. Lederie Laboratory/New York University Symposium. Science and Medicine.* New York.

Hollon, S. D., DeRubeis, R. J., & Seligman, M. E. P. (1992). Cognitive therapy and the prevention of depression. *Applied and Preventive Psychology, 1,* 89–95.

Holman, C. W., & Muschenheim, C. (1972). *Bronchopulmonary diseases and related disorders.* New York: Harper & Row.

Holmberg, M. C. (1980). The development of social interchange patterns from 12 to 42 months. *Child Development, 51,* 448–456.

Holmes, D. (1984). Meditation and somatic arousal: A review of the experimental evidence. *American Psychologist, 39,* 1–10.

Holmes, D. S. (1968). Dimensions of projection. *Psychological Bulletin, 69,* 248–268.

Holmes, D. S. (1971). Compensation for ego threat: Two experiments. *Journal of Personality and Social Psychology, 18,* 217–220.

Holmes, D. S. (1972). Aggression, displacement, and guilt. *Journal of Personality and Social Psychology, 22,* 296–301.

Holmes, D. S. (1974). Investigations of repression: Differential recall of material experimental or naturally associated with ego threat. *Psychological Bulletin, 81,* 632—653.

Holmes, D. S. (1978). Projection as a defense mechanism. *Psychological Bulletin, 85,* 677–688.

Holmes, D. S. (1981). Existence of classical projection and the stress-reducing function of attributive projection: A reply to Sherwood. *Psychological Bulletin, 90,* 460–466.

Holmes, D. S., & Houston, B. K. (1974). Effectiveness of situational redefinition and affective isolation for reducing stress. *Journal of Personality and Social Psychology, 29,* 212–218.

Holmes, D. S., & Schallow, J. R. (1969). Reduced recall after ego threat: Repression of response competition? *Journal of Personality and Social Psychology, 13,* 145–152.

Holmes, E. W. (1992). Other disorders of purine metabolism. In J. B. Wyngaarden, L. H. Smith, Jr., & J. C. Bennett (Eds.), *Cecil textbook of medicine* (19th ed., pp. 1115–1116). Philadelphia: Saunders.

Holmes, F. L. (1980). Hans Krebs and the discovery of the ornithine cycle. *Federation Proceedings, 39,* 216–225.

Holmes, T. (1981). *The schedule of recent experience.* Seattle, Wash., Department of Psychiatry and Behavioral Sciences, University of Washington School of Medicine.

Holmes, T. H., & Masuda, M. (1974). Life changes and illness susceptibility. In B. S. Dohrenwend & B. P. Dohrenwend (Eds.), *Stressful life events: Their nature and effects.* New York: Wiley.

Holmes, T. H., & Rahe, R. H. (1967). The social readjustment rating scale. *Journal of Psychosomatic Research, 11,* 213–218.

Holmes, V. F. (1989). Treatment of monosymptomatic hypochondriacal psychosis with pimozide in an AIDS patient. *American Journal of Psychiatry, 146*(4), 554–555.

Holroyd, J. (1976). Psychotherapy and women's liberation. *Counseling Psychologist, 6,* 22–28.

Holroyd, K. A. (1979). Stress, coping, and the treatment of stress-related illnesses. In J. R. MacNamara (Ed.), *Behavioral approaches to medicine: Application and analysis.* New York: Plenum.

Holsopple, J., & Miale, F. R. (1954). *Sentence completion: A projective method for the study of personality.* Springfield, Ill.: Thomas.

Holsopple, J., & Phelan, J. G. (1954). The skills of clinicions in analysis of projective tests. *Journal of Clinical Psychology, 10,* 307–320.

Holsopple, J. G., & Phelan, J. G. (1954). The skills of clinicians in analysis of projective tests. *Journal of Clinical Psychology, 10,* 307–320.

Hostti, O. (1968). Content analysis. In G. Lindzey & E. Aronson (Eds.), *Handbook of social psychology*, Vol. 2 (2nd ed.). Reading, Mass.: Addison-Wesley.

Holt, A. G. (1965). *Handwriting in psychological interpretations.* Springfield, Ill.: Thomas.

Holt, E. B. (1914). *The Freudian wish and its place in ethics.* New York: Macmillan.

Holt, H. (1979). The case of Father M—A segment of an existential analysis. *Journal of Existentialism, 6,* 369–395. Reprinted in Wedding, D. & Corsini, R. J. (Eds.), *Great cases in psychotherapy.* Itasca, IL: Peacock.

Holt, J. (1967). *How children learn.* New York: Dell.

Holt, R. R. (1964). Imagery: The return of the ostracized. *American Psychologist, 19,* 254–264.

Holt, R. R. (1969). *Assessing personality.* New York: Harcourt Brace Jovanovich, 1971. Also in 1. L. Janis, G. F. Mahl, J. Kagan, & R. R. Holt, *Personality: dynamics, development, and assessment* (part 4). New York: Harcourt, Brace & World.

Holt, R. R. (1970). *Manual for the scoring of manifestations of the primary process in Rorschach responses.* New York: Research Center for Mental Health.

Holt, R. R. (1970). Yet another look at clinical and statistical prediction: Or, is clinical psychology worthwhile? *American Psychologist, 25,* 337–349.

Holt, R. R. (1978). *Methods in clinical psychology.* Vol. 1: *Projective assessment.* Vol. 2: *Prediction and research.* New York: Plenum.

Holt, R. R. (1980). Loevinger's measure of ego development: Reliability and national norms for male and female short forms. *Journal of Personality and Social Psychology, 39,* 909–920.

Holt, R. R. *The transformation of psychoanalysis* (2 vols.). New York: Guilford, in preparation.

Holt, R. R. (Ed.). (1967). Motives and thought: Psychoanalytic essays in memory of David Rapaport. *Psychological Issues, 5,* (2/3, entire nos. 18/19).

Holt, R. R. (Ed.). (1968). Revised edition of *Diagnostic psychological testing* by D. Rapaport, M. M. Gill, & R. Schafer. New York: International Universities Press.

Holt, R. R. (Ed.). (1971). *New horizon for psychotherapy: Autonomy as a profession.* New York: International Universities Press.

Holt, R. R., & Luborsky, L. (1958). *Personality patterns of psychiatrists. A study of methods for selecting residents* (2 vols.). New York: Basic Books.

Holton, G. (1978). *The scientific imagination: Case studies.* Cambridge, England: Cambridge University Press.

Holton, R. (1980). How advertising achieved respectability among economists—Well, almost. In *Twentieth century advertising and the economy of abundance.* Chicago: Advertising Age.

Holtzman, W. H. (1961/1958). *Holtzman inkblot technique: Administration and scoring guide.* New York: Psychological Corp.

Holtzman, W. H. (1965). A brief description of the Holtzman inkblot test. In B. I. Murstein (Ed.), *Handbook of projective techniques.* New York: Basic Books.

Holtzman, W. H. (1966). Inkblot perception and personality: The meaning of inkblot variables. In E. I. Megargee (Ed.), *Research in clinical assessment.* New York: Harper & Row.

Holtzman, W. H. (1968). Holtzman inkblot technique. In A. I. Rabin (Ed.), *Projectire techniques in personality assessment.* New York: Springer.

Holtzman, W. H. (1970). Los seminarios internacionales de Texas. Un experimento continuo de intercambio transcultural en psicologia. *Revista Interamericana de Psicologia, 4,* 279–282.

Holtzman, W. H. (1975). New developments in Holtzman inkblot technique. In P. McReynolds (Ed.), *Advances in psychological assessment,* Vol. 3. San Francisco: Jossey-Bass.

Holtzman, W. H., & Brown, W. F. (1968). Evaluating the study habits and attitudes of high school students. *Journal of Educational Psychology, 59,* 404–409.

Holtzman, W. H., Diaz-Guerrero, R., & Swartz, J. (1975). *Personality development in two cultures.* Austin, Tex.: University of Texas Press.

Holtzman, W. H., Iscoe, I., & Ned, J. W. (1964). Final report—Mexican Psychology Students Seminar, January 5–25, 1964. Austin, Tex.: University of Texas Press.

Holtzman, W. H., Thorpe, J. S., Swartz, J. D., & Herron, E. W. (1961). *Inkblot perception and personality: Holtzman inkblot technique.* Austin, Tex.: University of Texas Press.

Holway, A. H., & Boring, E. G. (1941). Determinants of apparent visual size with distance variant. *American Journal of Psychology, 54,* 21–37.

Holzberg, J. D. (1963). The companion program: Implementing the manpower recommendations of the Joint Commission on Mental Illness and Health. *American Psychologist, 18,* 224—226.

Holzkamp, K. (1964). *Theorie und Experiment in der Psychologie. Eine grundla-genkritische Untersuchung.* Berlin: De Gruyter.

Hölzl, R. & Whitehead, W. E. (Eds.). (1983). *Psychophysiology of the gastrointestinal tract: Experimental and clinical applications.* New York: Plenum.

Holzman, P. S., Proctor, L. R., Levy, D. L., et al. (1974). Eye-tracking dysfunction in schizophrenic patients and their relatives. *Archives of General Psychiatry, 31,* 143–151.

Homans, G. C. (1974/1961). *Social behavior: Its elementary forms.* New York: Harcourt, Brace & World.

Homby, P. (Ed.). (1927). *Bilingualism. Psychological, social and educational implications.* New York: Academic Press.

Homme, L. (1965). Perspectives in psychology: XXIV. Control of coverants, the operants of the mind. *Psychological Record, 15,* 501–511.

Honig, W. K. (Ed.). (1966). *Operant behavior: Areas of research and application.* New York: Appleton-Century-Crofts.

Honig, W. K., & Staddon, J. E. R. (Eds.). (1977). *Handbook of operant behavior.* Englewood Cliffs, N.J.: Prentice-Hall.

Honig, W. K., & Stewart, K. E. (1988). Pigeons can discriminate locations presented in pictures. *Journal of Experimental Analysis of Behavior, 50,* 541–551.

Honigfeld, G., & Howard, A. (1973). *Psychiatric drugs: A desk reference.* New York. Academic Press.

Honigmann, J. J. (Ed.). (1973). *Handbook of social and cultural anthropology.* Chicago: Rand-McNally.

Honore, T. (1978). *Sex law in England.* London: Archon Books.

Honorton, C. (1977). Psi and internal attention states. In B. B. Wolman (Ed.), *Handbook of parapsychology.* New York: Van Nostrand Reinhold.

Honorton, C., & Harper, S. (1974). Psi-mediated imagery and ideation in an experimental procedure for regulating perceptual input. *Journal of the American Society for Psychical Research, 68,* 156–168.

Honzik, M. P. (1957). Developmental studies of parent-child resemblance in intelligence. *Child Development, 28,* 215–228.

330 BIBLIOGRAPHY

Honzik, M. P., Macfarlane, J. W., & Allen, L. (1948). The stability of mental test performance between two and eighteen years. *Journal of Experimental Education, 17,* 309–324.

Hood, A. B. (1963). A study of the relationship between physique and personality variables measured by the MMPI. *Journal of Personality, 31,* 97–107.

Hook, R. H. (1979). *Fantasy and symbol formation.* New York, London: Academic Press.

Hook, S. (1962). *From Hegel to Marx.* Ann Arbor, Mich.: University of Michigan Press.

Hooker, E. (1957). The adjustment of the male overt homosexual. *Journal of Projective Techniques, 21,* 18–31.

Hoon, P. W., Wincze, J. P., & Hoon, E. F. (1977). A test of reciprocal inhibition: Are anxiety and sexual arousal in women mutually inhibitory? *Journal of Abnormal Psychology, 86, 1,* 65–74.

Hooper, F., Fitzgerald, J., & Papalia, D. (1971). Piagetian theory and the aging process: Extensions and speculations. *Aging and Human Development, 2,* 3–20.

Hooper, K. (1978). Perceptual aspects of architecture. In E. C. Carterette & M. P. Friedman (Eds.), *Handbook of perceptions,* Vol. 1. New York: Academic Press.

Hoopes, M. H., & Harper, J. M. (1981). Ordinal positions, family systems, and family therapy, In M. R. Textor (Ed.), *Theorie und praxis der familien-therapie.* Wurzburg, West Germany: Paderborn.

Hoorweg, J. C. (1974). Africa (south of the Sahara): Review of psychological literature. In V. S. Sexton & H. Misiak (Eds.), *Psychology around the world today.* Monterey, Calif.: Brooks/Cole.

Hoover, J. G., & Maher, C. A. (Eds.). (1978). School psychology and program evaluation. *Journal of School Psychology, 16.*

Hopkins, C. D. (1980). Evolution of electric communication channels of mormyrids. *Behavioral Ecology and Sociobiology, 7,* 1–13.

Hoppock, R. (1935). *Job satisfaction.* New York: Harper.

Hoppock, R. (1975). Reminiscences and comments on job satisfaction. *Vocational Guidance Quarterly, 24,* 107–115.

Hoppock, R. (1976). *Occupational information* (4th ed.). New York: McGraw-Hill.

Hops, M., Biglan, A., Sherman, L., Arthur, J., Friedman, L., & Osteen, V. (1987). Home observations of family interactions of depressed women. *Journal of Consulting and Clinical Psychology, 55,* 341–346.

Hopwood, J. H., Wei, K.-T., H, & Yellin, A. M. (1981). A computerized method for generating the Rorschach's structural summary from the sequence of scores. *Journal of Personality Assessment, 45,* 116–120.

Horabin, I. S., & Lewis, B. N., (1977). Fifteen years of ordinary-language algorithms. *Improving Human Performance Quarterly, 6* (2–3).

Horan, C. B. (1969). Multidimensional scaling: Combining observations when individuals have different perceptual structures. *Psychometrika, 34,* 139–165.

Horan, J. J. (1979). *Counseling for effective decision-making.* North Scituate, Mass.: Duxbury Press.

Horenstein, D., Houston, D. K., & Holmes, D. S. (1973). Clients', therapists', and judges' evaluations of psychotherapy. *Journal of Counseling Psychology, 20,* 149–153.

Höermann, H. (1977/1967). *Psychologie der Sprache.* Berlin: Springer.

Horn, G., & Hinde, R. A. (Eds.). (1970). *Short-term changes in neural activity and behaviour.* Cambridge, England: Cambridge University Press.

Horn, J. L. (1963). Equations representing combinations of components in scoring psychological variables. *Acta Psychologica, 21,* 184–217.

Horn, J. L. (1978). Human ability systems. In P. B. Baites (Ed.), *Life-span development and behavior,* Vol 1, New York: Academic Press.

Horn, J. L. (1978). Human ability systems. In P. B. Baites (Ed.), *Life-span development and behavior* (Vol. 1, pp. 211–256). New York: Academic Press.

Horn, J. L. (1985). Remodeling old models of intelligence. In B. B. Wolman (Ed.), *Handbook of intelligence: Theories, methods, and applications* (pp. 267–300). New York: Wiley-Interscience.

Horn, J. L., & Cattell, R. B. (1966). Refinement and test of the theory of fluid and crystallized intelligence. *Journal of Educational Psychology, 57,* 253–270.

Horn, J. L., & Donaldson, G. (1976). On the myth of intellectual decline in adulthood. *American Psychologist, 31,* 701–719.

Horn, J. M., Plomin, R., & Rosenman, R. (1976). Heritability of personality traits in adult male twins. *Behavior Genetics, 6,* 17–30.

Horn, W. (1962). *Leistungs-Pruef-System (L-P-S).* Göttingen, West Germany: Hogrefe.

Hornblum, J. N., & Overton, W. F. (1976). Area and volume conservation among the elderly: Assessment and training. *Developmental Psychology, 12,* 68–74.

Horne, A. M., & Ohlsen, M. M. (1982). *Family counseling and therapy,* Itasca, Ill.: Peacock.

Horne, M. D. (1979). Attitudes and mainstreaming: A literature review for school psychologists. *Psychology in the Schools, 16,* 61–67.

Horner, M. S. (1972). Toward an understanding of achievement-related conflicts in women. *Journal of Social Issues, 28,* 147–172.

Horner, M. S. (1973). A psychological barrier to achievement in women. The motive to avoid success. In D. C. McClelland & R. S. Steele (Eds.), *Human motivation: A book of readings.* Morristown, N.J.: General Learning Press.

Horney, K. (1967). *Feminine psychology.* New York: Norton.

Horney, K. (1950). *Neurosis and human growth: The struggle toward self-realization.* New York: Norton.

Horney, K. (1937). *The neurotic personality of our times.* New York: Norton.

Horney, K. (1935). The problem of feminine masochism. *The Psychoanalytic Review, 22,* 241–257.

Horney, K. (1940/1939). *New ways in psychoanalysis.* New York: Norton.

Horney, K. (1945). *Our inner conflicts: A constructive theory of neurosis.* New York: Norton.

Horowitz, E. L., & Horowitz, R. E. (1938). Development of social attitudes in children *Sociomentery, 1,* 301–338.

Horowitz, F. D. (Ed.) (1978). *Early developmental diagnosis: Predictors and precautions.* Boulder, Colo.: Westview Press.

Horowitz, I., & Willging, T. (1984). *The psychology of law.* Boston: Little, Brown.

Horowitz, M. (1976). *Stress response syndromes.* New York: Aronson.

Horowitz, M. J. (1970). *Image formation and cognition.* New York: Appleton-Century-Crofts.

Horowitz, R., & Murphy, L. B. (1938). Projective methods in the psychological study of children. *Journal of Experimental Education, 7,* 133–140.

Horst, A. P. (1932). A method for determining the absolute affective value of a series of stimulus situations. *Journal of Educational Psychology, 23,* 418–440.

Horst, A. P. (1963). *Matrix algebra for social scientists.* New York: Holt, Rinehart & Winston.

Horst, A. P. (1965). *Factor analysis of data matrices.* New York: Holt, Rinehart & Winston.

Horst, A. P. (1966). *Psychological measurement and prediction.* Belmont, Calif.: Wadsworth.

Horst, A. P. (1968). *Personality: Measurement of dimensions.* San Francisco: Jossey-Bass.

Horton, A. M., Jr., Wedding, D., & Phay, A. (1981). Current perspectives on assessment and therapy for the brain-damaged individual. In C. J. Golden, S. A. Alcaparras, F. D. Strider, & B. Graber (Eds.), *Applied techniques in behavioral medicine.* New York: Grune & Stratton.

Horton, D. L., & Mills, C. B. (1984). Human learning and memory. *Annual Review of Psychology, 35,* 361–394.

Horvath, P., & Zuckerman, M. (1993). Sensation seeking, risk appraisal and riskly behavior. *Personality and Individual Differences, 14,* 41–52.

Horvath, S. (1978). Summary. In L. Folinsbee, J. Wagner, J. Borgia, B. Drinkwater, J. Gliner, & J. Bedi (Eds.), *Environmental stress: Individual human adaptation.* New York: Academic Press.

Horwitz, L. (1976). *Clinical prediction in psychotherapy.* New York: Aronson.

Horwitz, L. (1976). New perspectives for psychoanalytic psychotherapy. *Bulletin of the Menninger Clinic, 40,* 263–271.

Hosch, H. M. (1980). A comparison of three studies of the influence of expert testimony on jurors. *Law and Human Behavior, 4,* 297–302.

Hoshino, A. (1968). Changing social structure and attitudes in the urbanization process. *The Journal of Social Science, 7,* 349–362.

Hoshino, A. (1969). National findings: Japanese data. In R. Hess et al. (Eds.), *Final report: Authority, rules and aggression—A cross national study of the socialization of children into compliance systems, Part I.,* Chicago: University of Chicago.

Hoshino, A. (1973). *An attempt to analyze Japanese invective lexemes by means of semantic differential.* JSPS Bulletin, report of Japan-U.S., Joint research project on cross-cultural equivalence of language, International House of Japan (in Japanese).

Hoshino, A. (1978). The ethnic heritage of the Italian-Americans in the United States and their community life. In T. Ayabe (Ed.), *Ethnicity and cultural pluralism in the U.S.A.* Kyushu, Japan: Research Institute of Comparative Education and Culture, Kyushu University Faculty of Education.

Hoshino, A. (1979). Cross-cultural study of socialization, In A. Kikuchi & K. Saito (Eds.), *Theory of socialization.* Tokyo: Yuhikaku (in Japanese).

Hoshino, A. (1979). Current major trends in psychology in Japan, *Psychologia, 22*(1), 1–20.

Hoshino, A. (1982). An elaboration of the "culture shock" phenomenon: Adjustment problems of Japanese youth returning from overseas, In R. C. Nann (Ed.), *Uprooting and surviving.* Toyko: Reidel.

Hoshino, A. (1983). Culture shock. In S. Nagano & A. Yoda (Eds.), *Men in culture: Invitation to developmental psychology,* Vol. 7. Tokyo: Shinyosha (in Japanese).

Hoskovec, J. (1970). *Hypnosis and suggestion.* (3rd ed.). Prague: Academia (in Czech).

Hoskovec, J. (1970). *Theory of hypnosis.* (in Czech) Prague: Charles University Press.

Hoskovec, J., & Diamant, J. (1966). Clinical psychology in Czechoslovakia. In B. F. Riess (Ed.), *Progress in clinical psychology.* New York: Grune & Stratton.

Hoskovec, J., & Štikar, J. (1977). *Models and skills.* Prague: Charles University Press (in Czech).

Hoskovec, J., & Štikar, J. (1977). *Theory of accidents and methods of psychological prevention.* Prague: Charles University Press (in Czech).

Houck, R. L., & Dawson, J. G. (1978). Comparative study of persisters and leavers in seminary training. *Psychological Reports, 42,* 1131–1137.

Hounsell, D. J. (1979). Learning to learn: Research and development in student learning. *Higher Education, 8,* 453–469.

Hounsfield, B. N. (1980). Computed medical imaging. *Journal of Radiology, 61,* 459–468.

House, J., & Mason, W. (1975). Political alienation in America, 1952–1968. *American Sociological Review, 40,* 123–147.

House, J. S. (1981). *Work stress and social support.* Reading, MA: Addison-Wesley.

House, J. S., & Kahn, R. L. (1985). Measures and concepts of social support. In S. Cohen & S. L. Syme (Eds.), *Social support and health* (pp. 83–108). Orlando: Academic.

House, R. J. (1971). A path-goal theory of leader-effectiveness. *Administrative Science Quarterly, 16,* 321–338.

House, R. J., & Dessler, G. (1974). The path-goal theory of leadership: Some post hoc and a priori tests. In J. Hunt & L. Larson (Eds.), *Contingency approaches to leadership.* Carbondale, Ill.: Southern Illinois University Press.

Houston, B. K. (1969). Regression under stress to early learned behavior. *Proceedings of the 77th Annual Convention of the American Psychological Convention,* 459–460.

Houston, B. K. (1971). Trait and situational denial and performance under stress. *Journal of Personality and Social Psychology, 18,* 289–293.

Houston, B. K. (1973). Viability of coping strategies, denial, and response to stress. *Journal of Personality 41,* 50–58.

Houston, B. K. (1977). Dispositional anxiety and the effectiveness of cognitive coping strategies in stressful laboratory and classroom situations. In C. D. Spielberger & I. G. Sarason (Eds.), *Stress and anxiety,* Vol. 1. Washington, D.C.: Hemisphere.

Houston, B. K., & Hodges, W. F. (1970). Situational denial and performance under stress. *Journal of Personality and Social Psychology, 16,* 726–730.

Houston, B. K., & Holmes, D. S. (1974). Effectiveness of avoidant thinking and reappraisal in coping with threat involving temporal uncertainty. *Journal of Personality and Social Psychology, 30,* 382–388.

Houstoun, R. A. (1932). New observations on the Weber-Fechner law. *Report of the Joint Discussion on Vision,* 167–181.

Houts, P. L. (1977). *The myth of measurability.* New York: Hart.

Houtz, J. C., Moore, J. W., & Davis, J. K. (1973). Effects of different types of positive and negative instances in learning "nondimensioned" concepts. *Journal of Educational Psychology, 64,* 206–211.

Hoyland, C. I. et al. (1957). *The order of presentation in persuasion.* New Haven, Conn.: Yale University Press.

Hovland, C. I., & Janis, I. L. (1959). *Personality and persuasibility.* New Haven, Conn.: Yale University Press.

Hovland, C. I, Janis, I. L., & Kelley, H. H. (1953). *Communication and persuasion: Psychological studies of opinion change.* New Haven, Conn.: Yale University Press.

Hovland, C. I., Lumsdaine, A. A., & Sheffield, F. D. (1949). *Experiments in mass communication.* Princeton, N.J.: Princeton University Press.

Hovland, C. I., & Weiss, W. (1951). The influence of source credibility on communication effectiveness. *Public Opinion Quarterly, 15,* 635–650.

Howard, A. (1974). *Ain't no big thing.* Honolulu: University Press of Hawaii.

Howard, G. S. (1991). Culture tales. A narrative approach to thinking, cross-cultural, psychology, and psychotherapy. *American Psychologist, 46*(3), 187–197.

Howard, I. P, & Templeton, W. B. (1966). *Human spatial orientation.* New York: Wiley.

Howard, J. (1784). *The state of the prisons in England and Wales* (3rd ed.). Warrington, England: Eyres.

Howard, K. I., Kopta, S. M., Krause, M. S., & Ortinsky, D. E. (1986). The dose-effect relationship in psychothcrapy. *American Psychologist, 41,* 159–164.

Howarth, E. (1980). Birth order, family structure and personality variables. *Journal of Personality Assessment, 44,* 299–301.

Howe, M. G., & Madgett, M. E. (1975). Mental health problems associated with the only child. *Canadian Psychiatric Association Journal 20,* 189–194.

Howe, M. J. A. (1982). Biographical evidence and the development of outstanding individuals. *American Psychologist, 37,* 1071–1081.

Howell, L. (1978). Epilepsy. In R. M. Goldenson, J. R. Dunham, & C. S. Dunham (Eds.), *Disability and rehabilitation handbook.* New York: McGraw-Hill.

Howell, W. C., & Goldstein, I. L. (Eds.) (1971). *Engineering psychology. Current perspectives in research.* New York: Appleton-Century-Crofts.

Howells, G. W. (1968). The successful salesman: A personality analysis. *British Journal of Marketing, 2,* 13–23.

Howes, D. H. (1957). On the relation between the intelligibility and frequency of occurrence of English words. *Journal of the Acoustical Society of America, 29,* 296–305.

Howes, D. H. (1957). On the relation between the probability of a word as an association and in general linguistic usage. *Journal of Abnormal and Social Psychology, 54,* 75–85.

Howes, D. H. (1962). An approach to the quantitative analysis of word blindness. In J. Money (Ed.), *Reading disability: Progress and research needs in dyslexia.* Baltimore, Md.: Johns Hopkins Press.

Howes, D. H. (1964). Application of the word-frequency concept to aphasia. In A. V. S. de Reuck & M. O'Connor (Eds.), *Ciba Foundation symposium on disorders of language.* London: Churchill.

Howes, D. H. (1966). A word count of spoken English. *Journal of Verbal Learning and Verbal Behavior, 5,* 572—606.

Howes, D. H., & Solomon, R. (1950). A note on McGinnies' "Emotionality and perceptual defence." *Psychological Review, 57,* 229–234.

Hoyer, W. J, & Plude, D. J. (1980). Attentional and perceptual processes in the study of cognitive aging. In L. W. Poon (Ed.), *Aging in the 1980s.* Washington, D.C.: American Psychological Association.

Hoyle, N. (Ed.) (1978). *Physical education/sports index.* New York: Marathon Press.

Hoyos, C. G. (1961). *Denkschrift zur Lage der Psychologie.* Wiesbaden, West Germany: Steiner.

Hoyt, C. A. (1981). *Witchcraft.* Carbondale, Ill.: Southern Illinois Press.

Hsee, C., Hatfield, E., Carlson, J. G., & Chemtob, C. (1990). The effect of power on susceptibility to emotional contagion. *Cognition and Emotion, 4,* 327–340.

Hsiao, J., Bartko, J., Potter, W. (1989). Diagnosing diagnoses: Receiver operating characteristic methods and psychiatry. *Archives of General Psychiatry, 46,* 664–667.

Hsu, L. K. (1980). Outcome of anorexia nervosa: A review of literature (1954 to 1978): *Archives of General Psychiatry, 37*(9), 1041–1046.

Hsu, L. K. (Ed.) (1972). *Psychological anthropology, new edition.* Cambridge, Mass.: Schenkman.

Hsu, L. T., Ching C. C., & Over, R. (1980). Recent developments in psychology within the People's Republic of China. *International Journal of Psychology, 15,* 131–144.

Huarte de San Juan, J. (1575). *Examen de ingenios para las ciencias. Donde se muestra la diferencia de habilidades que hay en los hombres y el género de letras que a cada uno responde en particular.* Baeza: Juan Bautista de Montoya.

Hubbard, J. I. (1975). *The biological basis of mental activity.* Reading, Mass.: Addison-Wesley.

Hubbard, J. R., Kalimi, M. Y., & Witorsch, R. J. (1986). *Review of endocrinology and reproduction.* Richmond, VA: Renaissance Press.

Hubbard, L. R. (1950). *Dianetics: The modern science of mental health, a handbook of dianetic therapy.* New York: Hermitage House.

Hubbard, R. L., Marsden, M. E., Rachal, J. V., Harwood, H. J., Cavanaugh, E. R., & Ginzburg, H. M. (1989). *Drug, abuse treatment. A national study of effectiveness.* Chapel Hill: The University of North Carolina Press.

Hubel, D. H., & Wiesel, T. N. (1963). Receptive fields of cells in striate cortex of very young, visually inexperienced kittens. *Journal of Neurophysiology, 26,* 994–1002.

Hubel, D. H., & Wiesel, T. N. (1965). Receptive fields and functional architecture in two nonstriate visual areas (18 and 19) of the cat. *Journal of Neurophysiology, 28,* 229–289.

Huber, G. P. (1980). *Managerial decision making.* Glenview, Ill.: Scott, Foresman.

Huchingsan, R. D. (1981). *New horizons for human factors in design.* New York: McGraw-Hill.

Huck, J. R. (1977). The research base. In J. L. Moses & W. C. Byham (Eds.), *Applying the assessment center method.* New York: Pergamon Press.

Huck, S. W., & Gleason, E. M. (1974). Using monetary inducements to increase response rates from mailed surveys: A replication of previous research. *Journal of Applied Psychology, 59,* 222–225.

Hudson, R. (1981). Some issues on which linguists can agree. *Journal of Linguistics, 17,* 333–343.

Hudson, W. (1960). Pictorial depth perception in sub-cultural groups in Africa. *Journal of Social Psychology, 52,* 183–208.

Hudson, W. (1967). The study of the problem of pictorial perception among unacculturated groups. *International Journal of Psychology, 2,* 90–107.

Huesmann, L. R., Eron, L. D., Lefkowitz, M. M., & Walder, L. O. (1984). Stability of aggression over time and generations. *Developmental Psychology, 20,* 1120–1134.

Huggins, W., & Entwisle, D. R. (1974). *Iconic communication.* Baltimore, Md.: Johns Hopkins.

Hughes, H. D. (1917). An interesting corn seed experiment. *The Iowa Agriculturalist, 17,* 424–425.

Hughes, J., Smith, T. W., Kosterlitz, H. W., Fothergill, L. A., Morgan, B. A., & Morris, H. R. (1975). Identification of two related pentapeptides from the brain with potent opiate agonist activity. *Nature, 258,* 577–579.

Hughes, J. R. (1980). Epilepsy: A medical overview. In B. P. Herman (Ed.), *A multidisciplinary handbook of epilepsy.* Springfield, Ill.: Thomas.

Hughes, K. R., & Zubek, J. P. (1956). Effect of glutamic acid on the learning ability of bright and dull rats: I. Administration during infancy. *Canadian Journal of Psychology, 10,* 132–138.

Hugo, J. J. (1969). *St. Augustine on nature, sex, and marriage.* Chicago: Scepter.

Huitema, B. E. (in press). The myth of autocorrelation in applied behavioral experiments. In Poling, A., Fuqua, R. W., and Ulrich, R. E. (Eds.), *The control of human behavior.* Vol. 4: *Issues in applied behavior analysis research methodology.* Glenview, Ill.: Scott, Foresman.

Hulin, C. L., & Blood, M. R. (1968). Job enlargement, individual differences, and worker responses. *Psychological Bulletin, 69,* 41–55.

Hull, C. L. (1920). Quantitative aspects of the evolution of concepts. *Psychological Monographs, 28*(8).

Hull, C. L. (1925). *Aptitude testing,* Yonkers, N.Y.: World.

Hull, C. L. (1929). A functional interpretation of the conditioned reflex. *Psychological Review, 36,* 498–511.

Hull, C. L. (1931). Goal attraction and directing ideas conceived as habit phenomena. *Psychological Review, 38,* 487–506.

Hull, C. L. (1933). *Hypnosis and suggestability,* New York: Appleton-Century.

Hull, C. L. (1943). *Principles of behavior.* New York: Appleton-Century-Crofts.

Hull, C. L. (1952). *A behavior system: An introduction to behavior theory concerning the individual organism.* New Haven, Conn.: Yale University Press.

Hull, C. L., Hovland, C. I. & Ross, R. T. (1940). *Mathematicodeductive theory of rote learning.* New Haven, Conn.: Yale University Press.

Hull, R. E. (1973). Selecting an approach to individualized education. *Phi Delta Kappan, 4,* 169–173.

Hultsch, D. F., & Dixon, R. (1990). Learning and memory in aging. In J. Birren & K. Schaie, (Eds.), *Handbook of the psychology of aging* (pp. 258–274). New York: Academic.

Hultsch, D. F., & Deutsch, F. (1981). *Adult development and aging: A life-span perspective.* New York: McGraw-Hill.

Hultsch, D. F., & Plemons, J. K. (1979). Life events and life-span development. In P. B. Baltes & O. G. Brim, Jr. (Eds.), *Life-span development and behavior,* Vol. 2. New York: Academic Press.

Humanist manifesto II. (1973). *The Humanist, 33,* 4–9

Hume, D. (1949). *An enquiry concerning human understanding* Chicago: Open Court Publishers. (Original work published 1748).

Hume, D. (1963/1748). *An enquiry concerning human understanding.* La Salle, Ill.: Open Court.

Hume, D. In E. A. Selby-Briggs (Ed.). (1896/1739). *Treatise of human knowledge,* Oxford: Clarendon Press.

Humphrey, B. M. (1946). Success in ESP as related to form of response drawings. I. Clairvoyance experiments. *Journal of Parapsychology, 10,* 78–106.

Humphrey, B. M. (1946). Success in ESP as related to form of response drawings. II. GESP experiments. *Journal of Parapsychology, 10,* 181–196.

Humphrey, G. (1922). The conditioned reflex and the elementary social reaction. *Journal of abnormal and Social Psychology, 17,* 113–119.

Humphrey, N. K. (1973). The illusion of beauty. *Perception, 2,* 429–430.

Humphreys, G. W. (1981). Direct vs. indirect tests of the information available from masked displays: What visual masking does and does not prevent. *British Journal of Psychology, 72,* 323–330.

Humphreys, L. G. (1939). The effect of random alternation of reinforcement on the acquisition and extinction of conditioned eyelid reactions. *Journal of Experimental Psychology, 25,* 141–158.

Humphreys, L. G. (1979). The construct of general intelligence. *Intelligence,* 105–120.

Hundeide, K. (1977). *Piaget i kritisk lys (Piaget in a critical light).* Trondheim, Norway: Cappelens.

Hundert, J. (1982). Some considerations of planning the integration of handicapped children into the mainstream. *Journal of Learning Disabilities, 15,* 73–80.

Hundleby, J. D., Pawlik, K., & Cattell, R. B. (1965). *Personality factors in objective test devices.* San Diego, Calif.: Knapp.

Hunt, E. (1976). Varieties of cognitive power. In L. B. Resnick (Ed.), *The nature of intelligence.* Hillsdale, N.J.: Erlbaum.

Hunt, E., & Love, T. (1972). How good can memory be? In A. W. Melton and E. Martin (Eds.), *Coding processes in human memory.* Washington, D.C.: Winston.

Hunt, E. B. (1978). Mechanisms of verbal ability. *Psychological Review, 85,* 109–130.

Hunt, J. (Ed.) (1972). *Human intelligence.* New Brunswick, N.J.: Transaction Books.

Hunt, J. M. (1941). The effects of infant feeding frustration upon adult hoarding in the albino rat. *Journal of Abnormal and Social Psychology, 36,* 338–360.

Hunt, J. M. (1961). *Intelligence and experience.* New York: Ronald Press.

Hunt, J. M. (1965). Intrinsic motivation and its role in psychological development. In D. Levine (Ed.), *Nebraska symposium on motivation,* Vol. 13. Lincoln, Neb.: University of Nebraska Press.

Hunt, J. M. (1979). Psychological development: Early experience. *Review of Psychology, 30,* 103–143.

Hunt, J. M. (1980). *Early development and experience. 1976 Heinz Werner Lecture Series,* Vol. 10.

Hunt, J. M. (Ed.) (1944). *Personality and behavior disorders* (2 vols.). New York: Ronald Press.

Hunt, L. A. (1959). A developmental study of factors related to children's clothing preferences. *Monographs of the Society for Research in Child Development, 24*(1).

Hunt, M. (1974). *Sexual behavior in the 1970's.* Chicago: Playboy Press.

Hunt, M. (1977). *Gay: What you should know about homosexuality.* New York: Farrar, Straus, & Giroux.

Hunt, M., & Hunt, B. (1977). *The divorce experience.* New York: McGraw-Hill.

Hunt, W. A. (1951). An investigation of naval neuropsychiatric screening procedures. In H. Guetzkow (Ed.), *Groups, leadership, and men.* Pittsburgh, Pa.: Carnegie Press.

Hunt, W. A. (1955). A rationale for psychiatric selection. *American Psychologist, 10,* 199–204.

Hunt, W. A. (1980). History and classification. In A. E. Kazdin, A. S. Bellack, & M. Herson (Eds.), *New perspectives in abnormal psychology.* New York: Oxford University Press.

Hunter J. (1786). *A treatise on the venereal disease.* London: Author.

Hunter, J. E., & Schmidt, F. L. (1981). Fitting people into jobs: The impact of personnel selection on national productivity. In M. D. Dunnette & E. A. Fleishman (Eds.), *Human performance and productivity.* Vol. 1: *Human capability assessment.* Hillsdale, N.J.: Erlbaum.

Hunter, J. E., Schmidt, F. L., & Hunter, R. (1979). Differential validity of employment tests by race: A comprehensive review and analysis. *Psychological Bulletin, 86,* 721–735.

Hunter, J. E., Schmidt, F. L., & Jackson, G. B. (1982). *Meta-analysis: Cumulating research findings across studies.* Beverly Hills, CA: Sage.

Hunter, R. Earl, C. J., & Thornicroft, S. (1964). An apparently irreversible syndrome of abnormal movements following phenothiazine medication. *Proceedings of the Royal Society of Medicine, 57,* 758–762.

Hunter, W. S. (1926). Psychology and anthroponomy. In C. Murchison (Ed.), *Psychologies of 1925,* Worcester, Mass.: Clark University Press.

Hunter, W. S. (1928). *Human behavior.* Chicago: University of Chicago Press.

Hunter, W. S. (1928). The behavior of raccoons in a double alternation temporal maze. *Journal of Genetic Psychology, 35,* 374–388.

Hunter, W. S. (1930). Anthroponomy and psychology. In C. Murchison (Ed.), *Psychologies of 1930,* Worcester, Mass.: Clark University Press.

Hunter, W. S. (1935). Conditioning and extinction in the rat. *British Journal of Psychology, 6,* 135–148.

Hunter, W. S., & Bartlett, S. C. (1948). Double alternation in young children. *Journal of Experimental Psychology, 38,* 558–567.

Hunter, W. S., & Nagge, J. W. (1931). The white rat and the double alternation temporal maze. *Journal of Genetic Psychology, 39,* 303–319.

Hunter College, Women's Studies Collective. (in preparation). *Women's choices, women's realities.* New York: Oxford University Press.

Huntington, E. (1945). *Mainsprings of civilization.* New York: Wiley.

Huntington, G. (1872). On chorea. *Medical and Surgical Reporter, 26,* 317–321.

Hurlock, E. B. (1929). Motivation in fashion. *Archives of Psychology,* no. 111.

Hurlock, E. B. (1929). *The psychology of dress.* New York: Ronald Press.

Hurlock, E. B. (1980/1953). *Developmental psychology: A life-span approach* (5th ed.). New York: McGraw-Hill.

Hurtig, A. L., Koepke, D., & Park, K. B. (1989). Relation between severity of chronic illness and adjustment in children and adolescents with sickle cell disease. *Journal of Pediatric Psychology, 14,* 117–132.

Hurvich, L. M. (1972). Color vision deficiencies. In D. Jameson & L. Hurvich (Eds.), *Handbook of sensory physiology,* Vol. 7/4. Berlin: Springer-Verlag.

Hurvich, L. M., & Jameson, D. (1974). Opponent-processes as a model of neural organization. *American Psychologist, 29,* 88–102.

Hurvitz, N. (1974). Peer self-help psychotherapy groups: Psychotherapy without psychotherapists. In T. M. Roman & H. M. Trice (Eds.), *The sociology of psychotherapy.* New York: Aronson.

Husbaud, R. W. (1957). What do college grades predict? *Fortune,* June, 157–158.

Huse, E. F., & Cummings, T. G. (1985). *Organization development and change.* St. Paul: West.

Husserl, E. (1900–1901/1890). *Logische Untersuchungen* (2 vols.). Halle, East Germany: Niemeyer.

Husserl, E. (1913). *Ideen zu einer reinen Phänomenologie und phänomenologischen Philosophie.* Halle, East Germany: Niemeyer.

Husserl, E. (1962/1925). *Phänomenologische Psychologie.* In *Husserliana: Gesammelte Werke,* Vol. 9. The Hague: Nijhoff.

Husserl, E. (1964). *The idea of phenomenology.* The Hague: Martinis Nijhoff.

Husserl, E. (1977/1962). *Phenomenological psychology* The Hague: Nijhoff.

Hustig, H., Tran, D., Hafner, & Miller, R. (1990). The effect of headphone music on persistent auditory hallucinations. *Behavioral Psychotherapy, 18,* 273–281.

Huston, T. L. (Ed.) (1974). *Foundations of interpersonal attraction.* New York: Academic Press.

Huston, T. L., & Levinger, G. (1978). Interpersonal attraction and relationships. In M. R. Rosenzweig & L. W. Porter (Eds.), *Annual Review of Psychology, 29,* 115–56.

Hutchin, R. M. (Ed.) (1952). *Writings of Hippocrates.* In *Great books of the Western world,* Vol. 10. Chicago: Encyclopaedia Britannica.

Huth, W. (1978). Psychische Störungen bei Adoptivkindern—Eine Übersicht über den Stand der klinischen Forschung *Zeitschrift für klinische Psychologie und Psychotherapie, 26,* 256–270.

Hutt, C. (1981). Toward a taxonomy and conceptual model of play. In H. I. Day (Ed.), *Advances in intrinsic motivation and aesthetics.* New York: Plenum.

Hutt, M. L. (1930). A simplified scoring method for the Kohs block-designs test. *American Journal of Psychology, 42,* 450–452.

Hutt, M. L. (1932). The Kohs block-designs test: A revision for clinical practice. *Journal of Applied Psychology, 16,* 298–307.

Hutt, M. L. (1947). A clinical study of "consecutive" and "adaptive" testing with the revised Stanford-Binet. *Journal of Consulting Psychology, 11,* 93–103.

Hutt, M. L. (1948). What did the clinical psychologist learn from the war? *New York Academy of Science, 49,* 907–912.

Hutt, M. L. (1949). Projective techniques in guidance. In W. T. Donahue, C. H. Coombs, & R. M. W. Travers (Eds.), *The measurement of student adjustment and achievement.* Ann Arbor, Mich.: University of Michigan.

Hutt, M. L. (1951). Bender Gestalt drawings. In E. S. Shneidman, W. Joel, & K. S. Little (Eds.), *Thematic test analysis.* New York: Grune & Stratton.

Hutt, M. L. (1953). Problems of supervision and training in clinical psychology. Round Table, 1952. *American Journal of Orthopsychiatry, 23,* 328–331.

Hutt, M. L. (1956). Actuarial and clinical approaches to psychodiagnosis. *Psychological Reports, 2,* 413–419.

Hutt, M. L. (1958). The psychodiagnostic test battery: General considerations. In D. Brower & L. E. Abt (Eds.), *Progress in clinical psychology,* Vol. II. New York: Grune & Stratton.

Hutt, M. L. (1960). Diagnosis. In G. W. Harris (Ed.), *Encyclopedia of educational research.* New York: Macmillan, 1960.

Hutt, M. L. (1960/1953). The revised Bender-Gestalt visual-motor test. In A. C. Carr et al. (Eds.), *The prediction of overt behavior through the use of projective techniques.* Springfield, Ill.: Thomas.

Hutt, M. L. (1963). Bender Gestalt test. In D. Rosenthal (Ed.), *The Genain quadruplets: A study of heredity and environment in schizophrenia.* New York: Basic Books.

Hutt, M. L. (1965). The Hutt adaptation of the Bender-Gestalt test. In M. Kornrich (Ed.), *Psychological test modifications.* Springfield, Ill.: C Thomas.

Hutt, M. L. (1968). Psychopathology, assessment, and psychotherapy. In A. I. Rabin (Ed.), *Projective techniques in personality assessment.* New York: Springer.

Hutt, M. L. (1968). The projective use of the Bender-Gestalt test. In A. I. Rabin *(Ed.), Projective techniques in personality assessment.* New York: Springer.

Hutt, M. L. (1976). The significance of perceptual adience-abience in child development. In D. V. Siva Sankar (Ed.), *Mental health in children.* Westbury, N.Y.: PJD Publications.

Hutt, M. L. (1977). *Psychosynthesis: vital therapy*. Oceanside, N.Y.: Dabor.

Hutt, M. L. (1977/1960). *The Hutt adaptation of the Bender Gestalt test* (3rd ed.). New York: Grune & Stratton.

Hutt, M. L. (1978). The Hutt adaptation of the Bender-Gestalt test: Diagnostic and therapeutic implications. In B. B. Wolman (Ed.), *Clinical Diagnosis of mental disorders: A handbook*. New York: Plenum.

Hutt, M. L. (1980). Adience-abience. In R. H. Woody (Ed.), *Encyclopedia of clinical assessment*, Vol. II. San Francisco: Jossey-Bass.

Hutt, M. L. (1980). *Manual: The Michigan picture test—revised*. New York: Grune & Stratton.

Hutt, M. L. (1980). Microdiagnosis and misuse of scores and standards. *Psychological Reports, 50,* 239–255.

Hutt, M. L., & Gibby, R. G. (1957). *Patterns of abnormal behavior.* Boston: Allyn & Bacon.

Hutt, M. L., & Gibby, R. G. (1959). *The child: Development and adjustment.* Boston: Allyn & Bacon.

Hutt, M. L., & Gibby, R. G. (1970). *An atlas for the Hutt adaptation of the Bender-Gestalt test.* New York: Grune & Stratton.

Hutt, M. L., & Gibby, R. G. (1979/1958). *The mentally retarded child: Development, education and training.* Boston: Allyn & Bacon.

Hutt, M. L., Isaacson, R. L, & Blum, M. L. (1966). *Psychology: The science of interpersonal behavior.* New York: Harper & Row.

Hutt, M. L., & Milton, E. O. (1947). An analysis of duties performed by clinical psychologists in the U.S. Army. *American Psychologist, 2,* 150–155.

Hutt, M. L., & Shor, J. (1965). Rationale for routine Rorschach "testing-the-limits." In M. Kornrich (Ed.), *Psychological test modifications.* Springfield, Ill.: C. Thomas.

Hutt, S. J., & Hutt, C. (1970). *Direct observation and measurement of behavior.* Springfield, IL: Thomas.

Hutton, J. T. (1980). Dementia: Results of evaluation and treatment. *The Gerontologist, 20,* 130.

Huxley, A. L. (1944). *The perennial philosophy.* New York: Harper & Row.

Huxley, A. L., (1954/1970). *The doors of perception and heaven and hell,* Middlesex, England: Penguin Books.

Hyde, J. S. (1981). How large are cognitive gender differences? A meta-analysis using ω^2 and *d. American Psychologist, 36,* 892–901.

Hyde, J. S., Rosenberg, B. G., & Behrman, J. Tomboyism. (1977). *Psychology of Women Quarterly, 2,* 73–75.

Hyland, M. (1981). *Introduction to theoretical psychology.* Baltimore, Md.: University Park Press.

Hyman, D. S. (1989). The wireless phone and confidentiality. *The California Psychologist, 23*(4), 26.

Hyman, R. (1964). *The nature of psychological inquiry.* Englewood Cliffs, N.J.: Prentice-Hall.

Hyman, R. (1975). *Industrial relations: A Marxist perspective.* London: Macmillan.

Hyman, R. (1981). Cold reading: How to convince strangers that you know all about them. In K. Frazier (Ed.), *Paranormal borderlands of science.* Buffalo, NY: Prometheus Books.

Hyman, R. (1981). Further comments on Schmidt's PK experiments. *Skeptical Inquirer, 5*(3), 34–40.

Hyman, R. (1989). The psychology of deception. *Annual Review of Psychology, 40,* 133–154.

Hymes, J. L. (1968). *Early childhood education.* Washington, D.C.: National Association for the Education of Young Children.

Hynd, G. W., & Cohen, M. (1983). *Dyslexia: Neuropsychological theory, research and clinical differentiation.* New York: Grune & Stratton.

Hynd, G. W., Pirozzolo, F. J., & Maletta, G. (1982). Progressive supranuclear palsy. *International Journal of Neuroscience, 6,* 87–98.

Hynes, A. M. (1981). Some observations on process in biblio-poetry therapy. *The Arts in Psychotherapy, 8,* 237–241.

Iacono, C. U. (1975). Judgmental and statistical prediction: A coalition. Ph.D. dissertation, University of Columbia-Missouri.

Iberg, J. R. (1982). Focusing states rather than traits: A suggested level of abstraction for person perception in psychotherapy. Submitted for publication.

Iberg, J. R. (1981). A suggestion to focusing teachers: Teach-listen-teach. *Focusing Folio, 1,* 1–8.

Iberg J. R. (1981). Focusing. In R. J. Corsini (Ed.), *Handbook of innovative psychotherapies.* New York: Wiley.

Ichamura, J. (1966). Ten year follow-up study of the early prediction of juvenile delinquency by means of the Rorschach test. *Japanese Psychological Research, 8,* 151–160.

Ignas, E. (1980). A parents handbook for Individual Education. Chicago: Human Resources Center, University of Chicago.

Ignas, E., & Corsini, R. J. (1981). *Alternative educational systems.* Itasca, Ill.: Peacock.

Ikard, F. F., & Tomkins, S. (1973). The experience of affect as a determinant of smoking behavior: A series of validity studies. *Journal of Abnormal Psychology, 81,* 172–181.

Ikeda, H. (1971). *Computer analysis of statistical research.* Tokyo; Toyo-Keizai-Shinposha.

Ikeda, H. (1971). *Research methods in behavioral sciences.* Tokyo; Tokyo-Daigaku-Shuppankai (University of Tokyo Press).

Ikeda, H (1973) Test theory. In the *Methods of psychological research series.* Tokyo: Tokyo-Daigaku-Shuppankai (University of Tokyo Press).

Ikeda, H. (1976). *Fundamentals of statistical methods.* Tokyo: Shinyosha.

Ikeda, H. (1978). *How can we understand one's ability by test.* Tokyo: Nihon-Keizai-Shinbunsha.

Ikeda, H. (1980). *A modern test construction.* Tokyo: Daiichi-Hoki-Shuppan.

Ikeda, H. (1982). *Test and measurement.* Tokyo; Daiichi-Hoki-Shuppan.

Ilardi, R., & May, W. (1968). A reliability study of Shostrom's Personal Orientation Inventory, *Journal of Humanistic Psychology, 8,* 68–73.

Ilg, F. L., & Ames, L. B. (1955). *Child behavior: From birth to ten.* New York: Harper & Row.

Ilg, F. L., Ames, L. B., Haines, J., & Gillespie, C. (1978/1964). *School readiness.* New York: Harper & Row.

Ilgen, D. R., & Feldman, J. M. (1983). Performance appraisal: A process approach. In L. L. Cummings & B. M. Staw (Eds.), *Research in organizational behavior.* Vol. 5. Greenwich, Conn.: JAI Press.

Imada, M. (1958). *Gendai no shinrigaku (Modern psychology).* Tokyo: Iwanami.

Imperato-McGinley, J., Geurrero, L., & Gautier, T. (1974). Steroid 5α-reductase deficiency in man: An inherited form of pseudohermaphroditism. *Science, 186,* 1213–1215.

Imperato-McGinley, J., & Peterson, R. E. (1976). Male pseudohermaphroditism: The complexities of male phenotypic development. *American Journal of Medicine, 61,* 251–272.

Imperato-McGinley, J. & Peterson, R. E., Gautier, T. & Sturia, E. (1979). Androgen and evolution of male-gender identity among male pseudohermaphrodites with 5a-reductase deficiency. *New England Journal of Medicine, 300,* 1233–1237.

Ingham, R. (1984). *Stuttering and behavior therapy.* San Diego: College-Hill Press.

Ingham, S. (1948). Cerebral localization of psychological processes occurring during a two minute period. *Journal of Nervous and Mental Disease, 107,* 399–391.

Inglehart, R. (1977). *The silent revolution.* Princeton, N.J.: Princeton University Press.

Inglis, B. (1977). *Natural and supernatural.* London: Hodder & Stoughton.

Ingram, J. A. (1984–1985). Differential diagnosis: The schizophrenic disorders and the hallucinogens. *Psychiatric Forum, 13,* 47–56.

Inhelder, B., & Piaget, J. (1955). *De la logique de l'enfant à la logique de l'adolescent.* Paris: Presses Universitaires de France.

Inhelder, B., & Piaget, J. (1958). *The growth of logical thinking: From childhood to adolescence.* New York: Basic Books.

Inhelder, B., Sinclair, H., & Bovet, M. (1974). *Apprentissage et structures de la connaissance.* Paris: Presses Universitaires de France.

Inkeles, A., Hannfann, E., & Beier, H. (1961). Modal personality and adjustment to the Soviet socio-political system. In B. Kaplan (Ed.), *Studying personality cross-culturally.* Evanston, Ill.: Row, Peterson.

Innes, I. R., & Nickerson, M. (1971). Drugs acting on postganglionic nerve endings and structures innervated by them (sympathomimetic drugs). In L. S. Goodman and A. Gilman (Eds.), *The pharmacological basis of therapeutics.* New York: Macmillan.

Insel, P., & Moos, R. H. (1974). Psychological environments: Expanding the scope of human ecology. *American Psychologist, 29,* 179–188.

Insel, P. M., & Lindgren, H. C. (1978). *Too close for comfort.* Englewood Cliffs, N.J.: Prentice-Hall.

Insko, C. A., Arkoff, A., & Insko, V. M. (1965). Effects of high and low fear-arousing communications upon opinions toward smoking. *Journal of Experimental Social Psychology, 1,* 256–266.

Institute for Behavioral Research in Creativity. (1968). *Alpha biographical inventory.* Greensboro, NC: Prediction.

International classification of diseases (8th rev.), (1968). Vols. 1, 2. Public Health Service Publication 1693, Washington, D.C.: U.S. Government Printing Office.

International studies of values in politics. (1971). In *Values and the active community: A cross-national study of the influence of local leadership.* New York: Free Press.

International Study Project. (1972). *Abraham H. Maslow: A memorial volume.* Belmont, Calif.: Wadsworth.

Interventions to manage Alzheimer's disease symptoms. (1992, February 21). *NIH Guide for Grants and Contracts, 21,* 2–2.

Ions, E. (1977). *Against behavioralism.* Oxford: Blackwell.

Ireland, P., Sapira, J. D., & Templeton, B. (1979). Munchausen's syndrome: An unusual case. *American Journal of Psychotherapy, 33,* 616–621.

Ireton, H., Thwing, E., & Currier, S. K. (1974). Minnesota Child Development Inventory—Identification of children with developmental disorders. *Pediatric Psychology, 3,* 15–19.

Irion, A. L. (1948). The relation of "set" to retention. *Psychological Review, 55,* 336–341.

Iritani, T. (1963). Recent development of Piaget's system. *Japanese Journal of Psychology, 34* (5), 28–38.

Iritani, T. (1969). *New social psychology* (4th ed.). Tokyo: Tokai University Press.

Iritani, T. (1972). Psychology rounded on Japanese wisdom. *Contemporary Psychology, 17* (7), 397–399.

Iritani, T. (1974). *A way of environmental psychology* (6th ed.). Tokyo: Japanese Broadcasting Corp..

Iritani, T. (1979). *Value of children: A cross-national study,* Vol. 6. Honolulu: East-West Center Press.

Iritani, T. (1980). The role of congnition and communication in the process of formation and organization of dialogues (invited lecture). In *Proceedings of the 22nd International Congress of Psychology.* Leipzig.

Iritani, T. (1981). *Discourse processes: Its mechanism and deployment.* Tokyo: Chūōkōron-sha.

Iritani, T. (1983). *An invitation to psycholinguistics.* Tokyo: Taishūkan.

Irle, M. (1979). Zur Lage der Psychologie. In L. H. Eckensberger (Ed.). *Bericht über den 31. Kongress der Deutschen Gesellschaft für Psychologie in Mannheim 1978.* Göttingen, West Germany: Hogrefe.

Ironson, G. H., & Subkoviak, M. J. (1979). A comparison of several methods of assessing item bias. *Journal of Educational Measurement, 16,* 209–225.

Irvine, S., & Carroll, W. (1980). Testing and assessment across cultures: Issues in methodology and theory. In H. Triandis & J. Berry (Eds.), *Handbook of cross-cultural psychology,* Vol. 2. Boston: Allyn & Bacon.

Irvine, S. H. (1965). Adapting tests to the cultural setting: A comment. *Occupational Psychology, 39,* 13–23.

Irvine, S. H. (1966). Towards a rationale for testing attainments and abilities in Africa. *British Journal of Educational Psychology, 36,* 24–32.

Irvine, S. H. (1969). Factor analysis of African abilities and attainments: Constructs across cultures. *Psychological Bulletin, 71,* 20–32.

Irvine, S. H. (1969). The dimensions of vocational preference and prestige in an African elite group. In *World yearbook of education.* London: Evans.

Irwin, M., Belendiuk, K., McCloskey, K., & Friedman, D., (1981). Tryptophan metabolism in children with attentional deficit disorder. *American Journal of Psychiatry, 138,* 1082–1085.

Irwin, M., Klein, R., Engle, P., Yarbrough, C., & Nerlove, S. (1977). The problem of establishing validity in cross-cultural measurements. In L. Loeb-Adler (Ed.), Issues in cross-cultural research. *Annals of the New York Academy of Sciences, 286,* 308–325.

Isaac, S., & Michael, W. B. (1974/1971). *Handbook in research and evaluation.* San Diego, Calif.: Knapp.

Isaacs, H. R. (1975). Idols of the tribe, group identity and political change. New York: Harper & Row.

Isaacs, W., Thomas, J., & Goldiamond, I. (1960). Application of operant conditioning to reinstate verbal behavior in psychotics. *Journal of Speech and Hearing Disorders, 25,* 8–12.

Isaacson, R. L. (1974). *The limbic system.* New York: Plenum.

Isaacson, R. L. (Ed.) (1964). *Basic readings in neuropsychology.* New York; Evanston, Ill.; London: Harper & Row.

Isaacson, R. L., & M. L. (1971/1965). *Psychology: The science of behavior.* New York: Harper & Row.

Isaacson, R. L., & Pribram, K. H. (Eds.) (1975–1976). *The hippocampus,* Vols. I & II. New York: Plenum.

Iscoe, I. (1972). Mental health in the Americas. Special issue of the *Interamerican Journal of Psychology, 6,* 1–2.

Iscoe, I., Bloom, B., & Spielberger, C. D. (Eds.) (1977). *Community psychology in transition*. Washington, D.C.: Hemisphere.

Isen, A. M., & Hastorf, A. H. (1982). Some perspectives on cognitive social psychology. In A. Hastoff & A. Isen (Eds.), *Cognitive social psychology*. New York: Elsevier/North-Holland.

Isen, A. M., & Levin, P. F. (1972). Effect of feeling good on helping: Cookies and kindness. *Journal of Personality and Social Psychology, 21*, 384–388.

Ishida, R. (1969). Naikan analysis. *Psychologia, 12*, 81–92.

Ismail, A. A. A., Harkness, R. A., Kirkham, K. E., Loraine, J. A., Whatmore, P. B., & Brittain, R. P. (1968). Effect of abnormal sex-chromosome complements on urinary testosterone levels. *Lancet, 1*, 220.

Iso-Ahola, S. E. (1980). *Social psychological perspectives on leisure and recreation*. Springfield, Ill.: C Thomas.

Iso-Ahola, S. E. (1980). *The social psychology of leisure and recreation*. Dubuque, Iowa: Brown.

Israeli, N. (1936). *Abnormal personality and time*. New York: Science Press.

Ittleson, W. H. (1968/1955). *The Ames demonstrations in perception*. New York: Hafner.

Ivanov-Smolensky, A. G. (1927). On methods of examining conditioned food reflexes in children and in mental disorders. *Brain, 50*, 138–141.

Iversen, L. L., Iversen, S. D., & Snyder, S. H. (1978). *Handbook of psychopharmacology*. New York: Plenum.

Iversen, S. D. (1977). Brain dopamine systems and behavior. In L. L. Iversen, S. D. Iversen, & S. H. Snyder (Eds.). *Handbook of psychopharmacology*, Vol. 8. New York: Plenum.

Ivey, A. E. (1979). Counseling psychology: The most broadly-based applied psychological specialty. *Counseling Psychologist, 8*, 3–6.

Ivey, A. E. (1980). Counseling psychology, the psyche-educator model, and the future. *The Counseling Psychologist, 1976, 6(3)*, 72–75. (Also in J. M. Whiteley, (Ed.), *The history of counseling psychology*. Monterey, Calif.: Brooks/Cole.

Ivey, A. E., & Authier, J. (1978). *Microcounseling: Innovations in interviewing, counseling, psychotherapy, and psychoeducation*. Springfield, Ill.: Thomas.

Ivy, T. T., & Boone, L. (1976). A behavioral science approach to effective sales presentations. *Journal of the Academy of Marketing Science, 4*, 456–466.

Iwao, S. (1967). A social psychological study of esthetics. In K. Yoneyama (Ed.), *Japanese society and modernization*. Tokyo: Keio Press.

Iwao, S. (1977). Foreign students' image of Japan: A comparative study of the images of Japan of occidental and oriental foreign students. *The Japanese Annals of Social Psychology, 18*, 129–147.

Iwao, S. (1979). *Jyoseigaku kotohajime (Invitation to women's studies)*. Tokyo: Kodansha.

Iwao, S. (1982). *Onna no chic*. Tokyo: Sanshusha.

Iwata, B. A., & Bailey, J. S. (1974). Reward versus cost token systems: An analysis of the effects on students and teacher. *Journal of Applied Behaviors Analysis, 7*, 567–576.

Izard, C. E. (1977). *Human emotions*. New York: Plenum.

Jack, L. (1934). *An experimental study of ascendant behavior in preschool children*. Iowa City, Iowa: University of Iowa Studies in Child Welfare.

Jackins, H. (1962). *Fundamentals of co-counseling*. Seattle, Wash.: Rational Islands.

Jackins, H. (1973). *The human situation*. Seattle, Wash.: Rational Island.

Jackins, H. (1978). *The human side of human beings* (2nd ed.). Seattle, Wash.: Rational Island.

Jackins, H. (1978). *The upward trend*. Seattle, Wash.: Rational Island.

Jacklin, E. G. (1978). Review of research on nonmarital cohabitation in the United States. In B. I. Murstein (Ed.), *Exploring intimate lifestyles*. New York: Springer.

Jacks, B., & Keller, M. E. (1978). A humanistic approach to the adolescent with learning disability: An educational, psychological, and vocational model. *Adolescence, 13*, 59–68.

Jackson, D. D. (1957). The question of family homeostasis. *The Psychiatric Quarterly Supplement, 31*, Part 1, 79–90.

Jackson, D. D. (Ed.) (1968). *Communication, family and marriage*, Vols. 1, 2. Palo Alto, Calif.: Science & Behavior Books.

Jackson, D. N. (1974). *Personality research form manual*. New York: Research Psychologists.

Jackson, D. N. (1976). *Jackson personality inventory*. Goshen, N.Y.: Research Psychologists Press.

Jackson, D. N. (1984). *Personality research form manual* (3rd ed.). Port Huron, MI: Research Psychologists Press.

Jackson, D. N., & Messick, S. (1968). Content and style in personality assessment. *Psychological Bulletin, 55*, 243–252.

Jackson, D. N., & Paunonen, S. V. (1980). Personality structure and assessment. *Annual Review of Psychology, 31*, 503–551.

Jackson, D. W., & Alday, R. J. (1974). Managing the sales force by objectives. *MSU Business Topics, 22*, 53–59.

Jackson, E. E. (1962). Status inconsistency and symptoms of stress. *American Sociological Review, 37*, 469–480.

Jackson, M., & Sechrest, L. (1962). Early recollections in four neurotic diagnostic categories. *Journal of Individual Psychology, 18*, 52–56.

Jackson, P. W. (1968). *Life in classrooms*. New York: Holt, Rinehart & Winston.

Jacobs, J. (1886). Review of The psychology of reasoning by A. Binet. *Mind, 11*, 414–419.

Jacobs, J. (1887). Experiments in prehension. *Mind, 12*, 75–79.

Jacobs, M. A. (1972). The addictive personality: Prediction of success in a smoking withdrawal program. *Psychosomatic Medicine, 34(1)*, 30–38.

Jacobs, P. A., Brunton, M., Melville, M. M., Brittain, R. P., & McClemont, W. F. (1965). Aggressive behavior, mental subnormality and the XYY male. *Nature, 208*, 1351–1352.

Jacobs, P. A., Price, W. H., Richmond, S., & Ratcliffe, R. A. W. (1971). Chromosome surveys in penal institutions and approved schools. *Journal of Medical Genetics, 8*.

Jacobsen, P. B., Manne, S. L., Rapkin, B., & Redd, W. H. (1990). Analysis of child and parent behavior during painful medical procedures. *Health Psychology, 9*, 559–576.

Jacobson, A. L., Horowitz, S. D., & Fried, C. (1967). Classical conditioning, pseudoconditioning, or sensitization in the planarian. *Journal of Comparative and Physiological Psychology, 64*, 73–79.

Jacobson, E. (1932). The electrophysiology of mental activities. *American Journal of Psychology, 44*, 677–694.

Jacobson, E. (1934). *You must relax*. New York: McGraw-Hill.

Jacobson, E. (1964). *Anxiety and tension control*. Philadelphia, Pa.: Lippincott.

Jacobson, E. (1971). The two methods of tension control and certain basic techniques in anxiety tension control. In J. Kamiya, T. Barber,

L. V. DiCara, N. E. Miller, D. Shapiro, & J. Stoyva, (Eds.), *Biofeedback and self-regulation*. Chicago: Aldine-Atherton.

Jacobson, E. (1974/1929). *Progressive relaxation*. Chicago: University of Chicago Press.

Jacobson, E. & Reineft, G. (Eds.) (1980). *International directory of psychologists* (3rd ed.). Amsterdam: North-Holland.

Jacobson, G. F. (1963). Crisis theory and treatment strategy: Some socio-cultural and psychodynamic considerations. *Journal of Nervous and Mental Disease, 141*, 209–218.

Jacobson, J. L. (1981). The role of inanimate objects in early peer interaction. *Child Development, 52*, 618–626.

Jacobson, J. Z. (1951). *Scott of Northwestern*. Chicago: Louis Mariano.

Jacobson, L., & Rosenthal, R. (1968). *Pygmalion in the classroom*. New York: Holt, Rinehart & Winston.

Jacobson, N. S. (1978). Problem solving and contingency contracting in the treatment of marital discord. *Journal of Consulting and Clinical Psychology, 45*, 92–100.

Jacobson, N. S., & Margolin, G. (1979). *Marital therapy: Strategies based on social learning and behavioral exchange principles*. New York: Brunner/Mazel.

Jacobson, N. S., & Martin, B. (1976). Behavioral marriage therapy: Current status. *Psychological Bulletin, 83*, 540–556.

Jacoby, J. (1975). Consumer psychology as a social psychological sphere of action. *American Psychologist, 30*, 977–987.

Jacoby, J. (1976). Consumer and industrial psychology. In M. D. Dunnett (Ed.), *Handbook of industrial and organizational psychology*. New York: Rand-McNally.

Jacoby, L. (1983). Remembering the data: Analyzing interactive processes in reading. *Journal of Verbal Learning and Verbal Behavior, 22*, 485–508.

Jacoby, L. L., Lindsay, D. S., & Toth, J. P. (1992). Unconscious influences revealed: Attention, awareness, and control. *American Psychologist, 47*, 802–809.

Jacques, J. M., & Chason, K. J. (1979). Cohabitation: Its impact on marital success. *The Family Coordinator, 28*, 35–39.

Jaensch, E. R. (1927). *Eidetic imagery and typological methods of investigation; their importance for the psychology of childhood, the theory of education, general psychology, and the psychophysiology of human personality*. London: Paul, Trench, Trubner.

Jaensch, E. R. (1929). *Grundformen menschlichen Seins*. Berlin: Elsner.

Jaensch, E. R. (1938). *Der Gegentypus*, Leipzig: Barth.

Jaensch, W. (1926). Psychophysische Konstitutionstypen. In K. Birnbaum (Ed.), *Wörterbuch der Medizinischen Psychologie*. Leipzig: Thieme.

Jaffe, J. H., & Jarvik, M. E. (1978). Tobacco use and tobacco use disorder. In M. A. Lipton, A. Di Mascio, & K. F. Killam (Eds.), *Psychopharmacology: A generation of progress*. New York: Raven Press.

Jaffe, S. (1903). Ein psychologisches experiment im kriminalistischen seminar der universität Berlin. *Beiträge zur Psychologie der Aussage, mit besonderer Berücksichtigung der Rechtspflege, Pädogogik, Psychiatrie und Geschichts-forschung, I*, 79.

Jaffee, Y., Malamuth, N., Feinbold, J., & Feshbach, S. (1974). Sexual arousal and behavioral aggression. *Journal of Personality and Social Psychology, 39*, 759–764.

Jaggar, A. M., & Rothenberg, P. S. (Eds.). (1984). *Feminist frameworks: Alternative theoretical accounts of the relations between women and men* (2nd ed.). New York: McGraw-Hill.

Jagim, R. D., Wittman, W. D., & Noll, J. O. (1978). Mental health professionals: Attitudes toward confidentiality, privilege, and third-party disclosure. *Professional Psychology, 9*, 458–466.

Jahoda, G. (1956). Assessment of abstract behaviour in a non-western culture. *Journal of Abnormal and Social Psychology, 53*, 237–243.

Jahoda, G. (1959). Nationality preferences and national stereotypes in Ghana before independence. *Journal of Social Psychology, 50*, 165–174.

Jahoda, G. (1961). *White man*. London: Oxford University Press.

Jahoda, G. (1961/1962). Aspects of Westernisation: A study of adult-class attitudes in Ghana: I. *British Journal of Sociology, 12*, 375–386; II, *13*, 43–56.

Jahoda, G. (1968). Scientific training and the persistence of traditional beliefs among West African university students. *Nature, 220*, 1356.

Jahoda, G. (1969a). Cross-cultural use of the perceptual maze test. *British Journal of Educational Psychology, 39*, 82–86.

Jahoda, G. (1969b). *The psychology of superstition*. London: Lane.

Jahoda, G. (1970). Supernatural beliefs and changing cognitive structures among Ghanaian university students. *Journal of Cross-Cultural Psychology, 1*, 115–130.

Jahoda, G. (1971). Retinal pigmentation, illusion susceptibility and space perception. *International Journal of Psychology, 6*, 159–208.

Jahoda, G., Deregowski, J. B., Ampene, B. & Williams, N. (1977). Pictorial recognition as an unlearned ability. In G. E. Butterworth (Ed.), *The child's representation of the world*. London: Plenum.

Jahoda, M. (1958). *Current concepts of positive mental health: A report to the Staff Director, Jack R. Ewalt*. New York: Basic Books.

Jahoda, M. (1963). *The education of technologists*. London: Tavistock.

Jahoda, M. (1977). *Freud and the dilemmas of psychology*. London: Hogarth.

Jahoda, M. (1982). *Employment and unemployment—A social & psychological analysis*. Cambridge, England: Cambridge University Press.

Jahoda, M., Deutsch, M. & Cook, S. W. (1951). *Research methods in social relations*. New York: Holt, Rinehart & Winston.

Jahoda, M., Lazarsfeld, P. F., & Zeisel, H. (1971/1933). *Marienthal*. Chicago: Aldine.

Jakobovits, L. A., & Miron, M. S. (Eds.) (1967). *Readings in the psychology of language*. Englewood Cliffs, N.J.: Prentice-Hall.

Jakulic, S., Todorovic, V., Mihailovic, N., & Simic, T. (1971). Correlation between birth order and schizophrenia. *Socijalna Psihijatrija*, 183–187.

Jalota, S. (1945). *Psychology of the political deadlock in India*. Lahore, India: Minerva.

Jalota, S. (1950). *Scientific personnel selection procedure: A study*. Banaras, India: Hind Art Press.

Jalota, S. (1951). *Educational psychology: Modification of man*. Banaras, India: Hind Art Press.

Jalota, S. (1970). *Introduction to psychology* (6th ed.). Bombay: Oxford University Press.

Jalota, S. (1974). *Essentials of psychology* (2nd ed.). New Delhi: Oxford/IBH.

Jalota, S. (1982). *Patterns of social behaviour: Some Indian traditions*. Chandigarh, India: Mohindra Capital.

Jalota, S. (1983). *Experiments in psychology: A student's guide*. Chandigarh, India: Mohindra Capital.

James, L. R., Mulaik, S. A., & Brett, J. M. (1982). *Causal analysis: assumptions, models, and data*. Beverly Hills, CA: Sage.

James, M., & Jongeward, D. (1971). *Born to win*. Reading, Mass.: Addison-Wesley.

James, R. M. (1959). Status and competence of jurors. *American Journal of Sociology, 64*, 563–570.

James, V., Diehl, B., & Wirsche, P. J. (1981). Teaching sign to great apes in a zoo environment. Presented at the meeting of the American Psychological Association, Los Angeles, August.

James, W. (1890). *The principles of psychology*. New York: Henry Holt.

James, W. (1892). *Psychology: Briefer course*. New York: H Holt.

James, W. (1895). *Science 2*, 626.

James, W. (1899). *Talks to teachers on psychology: And to students on some of life's ideals*. New York: Holt.

James, W. (1900). *Psychology: Briefer course*. New York: Henry Holt. (Original work published 1892)

James, W. (1907). *Pragmatism: A new name for some old ways of thinking*. New York: Longman Green.

James, W. (1907). The cnergies of men. *Philosophical Review*, January.

James, W. (1909). The final impressions of a psychical researcher. *American Magazine*, October.

James W. (1914). *The varieties of religious experience: A study in human nature*. New York: Longmans, Green. (Original work published 1902)

James, W. (1947). *Essays in radical empiricism*. New York: Longmans, Green. (Original work published 1912)

James, W. (1950/1894). *The principles of psychology*. New York: Dover.

James, W. (1958/1935/1929/1907). *The varieties of religious experience*. New York: New American Library.

James, W. T. (1953). Social facilitation of eating behavior in puppies after satiation. *Journal of Comparative and Physiological Psychology, 46*, 427–428.

Jamison, D., Suppes, P., & Wells, S. (1974). The effectiveness of alternative instructional media: A survey. *Review of Educational Research, 44*, 1–69.

Jampala, V., Sierles, F., & Taylor, M. (1988). The use of DSM-III in the United States: A case of not going by the book. *Comparative Psychiatry, 29*, 39–47.

Jancin, B. (1989, June). Says psychologists will win prescribing privileges fight. *Clinical Psychiatry News*, p. 1.

Jandy, E. C. (1942). *Charles Horton Cooley: His life and his social theory*. New York: Dryden.

Janet, P. (1894). *L'état mental des hysteriques*. Paris: Rueff.

Janet, P. (1901). *The mental state of hystericals: A study of mental stigmata and mental Accidents*. New York: Putnam.

Janet, P. (1903). *Les obsessions et la psychasthénie*. Paris: Alcan.

Janet, P. (1924). *Principles of psychotherapy*. New York: Macmillan.

Janet, P. (1965/1892). *The major symptoms of hysteria: fifteen lectures given in the medical school of Harvard University* (2nd ed.). New York: Hafner.

Janis, I. L. (1951). *Air war and emotional stress*. Westport, Conn.: Greenwood.

Janis, I. L. (1958). *Psychological stress: Psychoanalytic and behavioral studies of surgical patients*. New York: Wiley.

Janis, I. L. (1974). *Psychological stress*. New York: Academic Press.

Janis, I. L. (1977). *Decision making: A psychological analysis of conflict, choice, and commitment*. New York: Free Press.

Janis, I. L. (Ed.) (1982). *Counseling on personal decisions*. New Haven, Conn.: Yale University Press.

Janis, I. L., et al. (1959). *Personality and persuasibility*. New Haven, Conn.: Yale University Press.

Janis, I., & Mann, L. (1977). *Decision making: A psychological analysis of conflict choice and commitment*. New York: Free Press.

Janis, I. L., & Feshbach, S. (1953). Effects of fear-arousing communications. *Journal of Abnormal and Social Psychology. 48*, 78–92.

Janis, I. L., & King, B. T. (1954). The influence of role playing on opinion change. *Journal of Abnormal and Social Psychology, 49*, 211–218.

Janis, I. L., Mahl, G. F., Kagan, J., & Holt, R. R. (1969). *Personality: Dynamics, development, and assessment*. New York: Harcourt.

Janis, J. (1972). *Victims of groupthink: A psychological study of foreign decisions and fiascos*. Boston: Houghton Mifflin.

Janisse, M. J. (1981). A decade review. *Canadian Psychology, 22*(1) 3–99; *22*(2), 113–172.

Janke, W. (Hg.). (1982). *Beiträge zur Methodik in der differentiellen, diagnostischen und klinischen Psychologie*. Festschrift zum 60. Geburtstag von G. A. Lienert. Meisenheim: Hain.

Janov, A. (1970). *The primal scream*. New York: Vintage Books.

Janov, A., & Holden, E. M. (1976). *Primal man*. New York: Holden.

Jansen, K. L. R. (1990). Neuroscience and the near-death experience: Role for the NMDA-PCP receptor, the sigma receptor and the endopsychosins. *Medical Hypotheses, 31*, 25–29.

Jansen, M., & Barron, J. (1988). Introduction and overview: Psychologists' use of physical interventions. *Psychotherapy, 25*(4), 487–491.

Janus, S. S., Bess, B. E., Cadden, J. J., & Greenwald, H. (1980). Training police officers to distinguish mental illness. *American Journal of Psychiatry, 137*(2), 228–229.

Jarrad, L. E. (1986). Selective hippocampal lesions and behavior: Implications for current research and theorizing. In R. L. Isaacson & K. H. Pribram (Eds.), *The hippocampus* (pp. 93–126). New York: Plenum.

Jarvik, L. F., Kallman, F. J., & Falek, A. (1962). Intellectual changes in aged twins. *Journal of Gerontology, 17*, 289–294.

Jarvik, L. F., Klodin, V., & Matsuyama, S. S. (1973). Human aggression and the extra Y chromosome. *American Psychologist, 28*, 674–682.

Jarvik, M. E., Cullen, J. W., Gritz, E. R., Vogt, T. M., & West, L. J. (Eds.) (1977). *Research on smoking behavior*. NIDA Research Monograph 17. Washington, D.C.: Superintendent of Documents.

Jaspers, K. (1960). *Philosophy* (3 vols.). Chicago: University of Chicago Press.

Jaspers, K. (1963). *General psychopathology*, Chicago: University of Chicago Press.

Jaspers, K. (1965/1913). *Allgemeine psychopathology*. Berlin, Heidelberg, New York: Springer.

Jastrow, J. (1900). *Fact and fable in psychology*. Cambridge, MA: Riverside.

Jastrow, J. (1906). *The subconscious*, Boston: Houghton Mifflin.

Jastrow, J. (1932). *The house that Freud built*. New York: Greenburg.

Jawa, S. (1973). Birth order and its related changes in anxiety among adolescents. *Indian Journal of Applied Psychology Among Adolescents* (Madras), *10*, 6–11.

Jay, M. (1973). *The dialectical imagination*. London: Heinemann.

Jay, S. M., Elliott, C. H., Ozolins, M., Olson, R. A., & Pruitt, S. D. (1985). Behavioral management of children's distress during painful medical procedures. *Behaviour Research and Therapy, 23*, 513–520.

Jayaratne, S., & Levy, R. L. (1979). *Empirical clinical practice*. New York: Columbia University Press.

Jaynes, J. (1969). The historical origins of "ethology" and "comparative psychology." *Animal Behavior, 17,* 601–606.

Jecker, J., & Landy, D. (1969). Liking a person as a function of doing him a favor. *Human Relations, 22.* 371–378.

Jeffrey, D. A. (1943). A living environment for the physically disabled. *Rehabilitation Literature, 4,* 98–103.

Jelliffe, D. B., & Jelliffe, E. F. P. (1978). *Human milk in the modern world: Psychological nutritional and economic significance.* New York: Oxford University Press.

Jelliffe, S. E. & White, W. A. (1929). *Diseases of the nervous system.* Philadelphia, Pa.: Lea & Febiger.

Jellinek, A. (1949). Spontaneous imagery: A new psychotherapeutic approach. *American Journal of Psychotherapy, 3,* 372–391.

Jellinek, E. M. (1960). *The disease concept of alcoholism.* New Haven, Conn.: Hillhouse.

Jencks, C., Smith, M., Acland, H., Bane, M. J., Cohen, D., Gintis, H., Heyns, B., & Michelson, S. (1972). *Inequality: A reassessment of the effect of family and schooling in America.* New York: Basic Books.

Jendrek, M. P. (1989). Faculty reactions to academic dishonesty. *Journal of College Student Development, 30,* 401–406.

Jenkins, C. D., Roseman, R. H., & Friedman, M. (1967). Development of an objective psychological test for the determination of the coronary-prone behavior pattern in employed men. *Journal of Chronic Diseases, 20,* 371–379.

Jenkins, C. D., Zyzanski, S. J., & Roseman, R. H. (1971). Progress toward validation of a computer-scored test for the Type A coronary-prone behavior pattern. *Psychosomatic Medicine. 33,* 193–202.

Jenkins, H. M., & Harrison, R. H. (1962). Generalization gradients of inhibition following auditory discrimination learning. *Journal of the Experimental Analysis of Behavior, 5,* 435–441.

Jenkins, J. G. (1948). Nominating technique as a way of evaluating air group morale. *Journal of Aviation Medicine, 19,* 12–19.

Jenkins, J. G., & Dallenbach, K. M. (1924). Obliviscence during sleep and waking. *American Journal of Psychology, 35,* 605–612.

Jenkins, R. L. (1960). The psychopathic or antisocial personality. *Journal of Nervous and Mental Disease, 131,* 318–334.

Jenkins, R. L. (1971). The runaway reaction. *American Journal of Psychiatry,128,* 168–173.

Jenkins, W. O., Pascal, G. R., & Walker, R. W., Jr. (1958). Deprivation and generalization. *Journal of Experimental Psychology, 56,* 274–277.

Jennings, F. (1988). *Psychologists and prescription privileges.* Unpublished manuscript.

Jennings, H. H. (1950). *Leadership and isolation.* New York: Longman, Green.

Jennings, H. S. (1906). *Behavior of the lower organisms.* New York: Columbia University Press.

Jennings, H. S. (1935). *Genetic variations in relation to evolution.* Princeton, N.J.: Princeton University Press.

Jensen, A. R. (1969). How much can we boost IQ and scholastic achievement? *Harvard Educational Review, 39,* 1–123.

Jensen, A. R. (1969). *Understanding readiness.* Urbana, Ill.: ERIC Clearinghouse on Early Childhood Education.

Jensen, A. R. (1973). *Educability and group differences* New York: Harper & Row.

Jensen, A. R. (1973). *Educational differences.* London: Methuen.

Jensen, A. R. (1973). *Genetics and education.* London: Methuen. New York: Harper & Row.

Jensen, A. R. (1974). What is the question? What is the evidence? (Autobiography). In T. S. Krawiec (Ed.), *The psychologists,* Vol. 2. New York: Oxford University Press.

Jensen, A. R. (1977). Cumulative deficit in IQ of blacks in the rural South. *Developmental Psychology, 13,* 184–196.

Jensen, A. R. (1978). Genetic and behavioral effects of nonrandom mating. In R. T. Osborne, C. E. Noble, & N. Weyl (Eds.), *Human variation: Biopsychology of age, race, and sex.* New York: Academic Press.

Jensen, A. R. (1980). *Bias in mental testing.* New York: Free Press.

Jensen, A. R. (1980). Chronomatric analysis of intelligence. *Journal of Social and Biological Structures, 3,* 103–122.

Jensen, A. R. (1981). *Straight talk about mental tests.* New York: Free Press.

Jensen, A. R. (1985). Methodological and statistical techniques for the chronometric study of mental abilities. In C. R. Reynolds & V. L. Willson (Eds.), *Methodological and statistical advances in the study of individual differences.* New York: Plenum.

Jensen, A. R. (1992). Scientific fraud or false accusations? The case of Cyril Burt. In D. J. Miller & M. Hersen (Eds.), *Research fraud in the behavioral and biomedical sciences.* New York: Wiley.

Jensen, A. R. (1992). Understanding *q* in terms of information processing. *Educational Psychology Review, 4.*

Jensen, J. P., & Bergin, A. E. (1988). Mental health values of professional therapists: A national interdisciplinary survey. *Professional Psychology, 19,* 290–297.

Jensen, J. P., Bergin, A. E., & Greaves, D. W. (1990). The meaning of eclecticism: New survey and analysis of components. *Professional Psychology: Research and Practice, 21,* 124–130.

Jepsen, D. A. (1974). Vocational decision-making strategy types. *Vocational Guidance Quarterly, 23,* 17–23.

Jerger, S., & Jerger, J. (1981). *Auditory disorders: A manual for clinical evaluation.* Boston: Little, Brown.

Jerison, H. J. (1976). Paleneurology and the evolution of mind. *Scientific American, 234*(1), 90–101.

Jerome, J. (1980). *The sweet spot in time.* New York: Summit Books.

Jersild, A. T., & Holmes, F. B. (1933). A study of children's fears. *Journal of Experimental Education, 2,* 109–123.

Jersild, A. T., & Holmes, F. B. (1935). Children's fears. *Child Development Monographs,* no. 20.

Jessor, S., & Jessor, R. Transition from virginity to nonvirginity among youth: A social-psychological study over time. *Developmental Psychology, 11,* 474–485.

Jeste, D. U., Wagner, R. L., Weinberger, D. R., Rieth, K. G., & Wyatt, R. J. (1980). Evaluation of CT scans in tardive dyskinesia. *American Journal of Psychiatry, 137,* 247–248.

Jevning, R., Wilson, A. F., & Smith, W. R. (1978). The Transcendental Meditation technique, adrenocortical activity, and implications for stress. *Experientia, 34,* 618–619.

Jevons, W. S. (1958/1877). *The principles of science.* New York: Dover.

Jiménez Burillo, F. (1976). Psicología social en España. Notas para una historia de las ciencias sociales. *Revista de Psicología General y Aplicada, 31,* 235–283.

Jing, Q. (1958). Theoretical foundation of structuraUss of Wundt and Titchener. Beijing, People's Republic of China: Science Publishers.

Jing, Q. (1990). *Contemporary trends in the development of psychology.* Beijing, People's Republic of China: Peoples Publisher.

Jing, Q. (Ed.). (1991). *Concise encyclopedia of psychology.* Changsha, People's Republic of China: Hunan Educational.

Jing, Q., Jiao, S., & Ji, G. (1986). *Human vision.* Beijing, People's Republic of China: Science Publishers.

Jing, Q., Jiao, S., Yu, B., & Hu, W. (1979). *Colorimetry.* Beijing, People's Republic of China: Science Publishers.

Jing, Q., & Lin, Z. (Eds.). (1986). *Introduction to psychology.* Beijing, People's Republic of China: Science Publishers.

Jinks, P. C. (1964). An investigation into the effect of date of birth on subsequent school performance. *Educational Research, 6,* 220–225.

Jirgensen, P. (1989). Course and outcome in delusional psychoses. A 4-year re-follow-up. *Psychopathology, 22*(5), 233–238.

Joad, C. E. M. (1950). *A critique of logical positivism.* London: Gollancz.

Joffe, J. M., & Albee, G. W. (1981). *Prevention through political action and social change. The primary prevention of psychopathology, Vol. V.* Hanover, N.H.: University Press of New England.

Johannesson, R. (1973). Some problems in the measurement of organizational climate. *Organizational Behavior and Human Performance, 10,* 118–145.

Johansson, G. (1978). Visual event perception. In R. Held, H. W. Leibowitz, & H.-L. Teuber (Eds.), *Handbook of sensory physiology,* Vol. VIII: *Perception.* Berlin: Springer-Verlag.

John, E. R. (1967). *Mechanisms of memory.* New York: Academic Press.

John, E. R. (1972). Switchboard versus statistical theories of learning and memory. *Science, 177,* 850–864.

Johnson, A. B., & Cartwright, C. A. (1979). The roles of information and experience in improving teachers' knowledge and attitudes about mainstreaming. *Journal of Special Education, 13,* 453–462.

Johnson, C. H. (1980). Reality orientation in the nursing home: A test of effectiveness. *The Gerontologist, 20* (Part II), 132.

Johnson, C. W., Snibbe, J. R., & Evans, L. A. (1975). *Basic psychopathology: A programmed text.* New York: Spectrum.

Johnson, D. (1977). *The protean body: A Rolfer's view of human flexibility.* New York: Harper & Row.

Johnson, D. J., & Myklebust, H. R. (1967). *Learning disabilities: Educational principles and practices.* New York: Grune & Stratton.

Johnson, D. L., & Walker, T. (1985). *The primary prevention of behavior problems in Mexican-American children.* Paper presented at the Social Research Child Development meeting, Toronto.

Johnson, D. M. (1945). The "phantom anesthetist" of Mattoon: A field study of mass hysteria. *Journal of Abnormal and Social Psychology, 40,* 175–186.

Johnson, D. W. (1973). *Contemporary social psychology.* Philadelphia: Lippincott.

Johnson, D. W. (1979). *Educational psychology.* Englewood Cliffs, N.J.: Prentice-Hall.

Johnson, D. W. (1980). Constructive peer relationships, social development, and cooperative learning experiences: Implications for the prevention of drug abuse. *Journal of Drug Education, 10,* 7–24.

Johnson, D. W. (1980). Group processes: Influences of student-student interaction on school outcomes. In J. McMillan (Ed.), *The social psychology of school learning.* New York: Academic Press.

Johnson, D. W., & Johnson, F. P. (1982/1975). *Joining together: Group theory and group skills* (2nd ed.), Englewood Cliffs, N.J.: Prentice-Hall.

Johnson, D. W., & Johnson, R. T. (1974). Instructional goal structure: Cooperative, competitive, or individualistic? *Review of Educational Research, 44,* 213–240.

Johnson, D. W., & Johnson, R. T. (1975). *Learning together and alone: Cooperation, competition, and individualization.* Englewood Cliffs, N.J.: Prentice-Hall.

Johnson, D. W., & Johnson, R. T. (1978). Cooperative, competitive and individualistic learning. *Journal of Research and Development in Education, 12,* 3–15.

Johnson, D. W., & Johnson, R. T. (1982). Healthy peer relationships: A necessity not a luxury. In P. Roy (Ed.), *Structuring cooperative learning: The 1982 handbook:* Minneapolis, Minn.: Interaction Book.

Johnson, D. W., Johnson, R. T., & Maruyama, G. (1982). Interdependence and interpersonal attraction among heterogeneous and homogeneous individuals: A theoretical formulation and a meta-analysis of the research. Submitted for publication.

Johnson, D. W., Maruyama, G., Johnson, R. T., Nelson, D., & Skon, L. (1981). Effects of cooperative, competitive, and individualistic goal structures on achievement: A meta-analysis. *Psychological Bulletin, 89,* 47–62.

Johnson, G. O., Lavely, C. D., & Kline, R. (1975). Self-concept of educable mentally retarded in two educational settings. *Journal of Developmental Disabilities, 1,* 1–4.

Johnson, H. B. (1974). *Executive life-styles.* New York: Crowell.

Johnson, J. E. (1976). Relations of divergent thinking and intelligence test scores with social and nonsocial make-believe play of preschool children. *Child Development, 47,* 1200–1203.

Johnson, L., Backman, J., & O'Malley, P. M. (1980). The use of marijuana by high school seniors. Unpublished manuscript, University of Michigan Institute for Social Research, Ann Arbor.

Johnson, L. R. (Ed.) (1981). *Physiology of the gastrointestinal tract.* New York: Raven Press.

Johnson, M. (1967). Definitions and models in curriculum theory. *Educational theory, 17,* 127–140.

Johnson, M., & Wertheimer, M. (Eds.) (1979). *Psychology teacher's resource book: First course.* Washington, D.C.: American Psychological Association.

Johnson, M. K., & Hasher, L. (1987). Human learning and memory. *Annual Review of Psychology, 38,* 631–668.

Johnson, M. S. & Kress, R. A. (1965). *Informal reading inventories.* Newark, Dela.: International Reading Association.

Johnson, N. S., & Peck, R. (1978). Sibship composition and the adolescent runaway phenomenon. *Journal of Youth and Adolescence, 7*(3), 301–305.

Johnson, R. (1992). *Aspects of stuttering.* Unpublished manuscript, University of California at Los Angeles.

Johnson, R., & Carter, M. M. (1980). Flight of the young: Why children run away from their homes. *Adolescence, 15,* 483–489.

Johnson, R. C., Cole, R. E., & Ahern, F. M. (1981a). Genetic interpretation of racial/ethnic differences in lactose absorption and tolerance: A review. *Human Biology, 53,* 1–13.

Johnson, R. C., Cole, R. E., Ahern, F. M., Schwitters, S. Y., Ahem, E. H., Huang, Y. H., Johnson, R. M., & Park, J. Y. (1980). Reported lactose tolerance of members of various racial/ethnic groups in Hawaii and Asia. *Behavior Genetics, 10,* 377–385.

Johnson, R. C., Schwitters, S. Y., Cole, R. E., Ahern, F. M., & Au, K. A. (1981b). A family study of lactose tolerance. *Behavior Genetics, 11,* 369–372.

Johnson, R. N. (1972). *Aggression in man and animals.* Philadelphia, Pa.: Saunders.

Johnson, S. (1969). *Elementa philosophica.* New York: Kraus.

Johnson, S. B. (1979). Children's fears in the classroom setting. *School Psychology Digest, 8,* 382–386.

Johnson, S. M., & Bolstad, O. D. (1973). Methodological issues in naturalistic observations: Some problems and solutions for field research. In L. A. Hamerlynck, L. C. Handy, & E. J. Mash (Eds.), *Behavior change: Methodology, concepts, and practice.* Champaign, IL: Research Press.

Johnson, T. E., Antonucci, T. C., Fulmer, T., & Horowitz, A. (1991). Health challenges of an aging society. *The Gerontologist, 31,* 320–321.

Johnson, W. (1944). The Indians have no word for it. *I. Quarterly Journal of Speech, 30,* 330–337.

Johnson-Laird, P. N. (1988). *The computer and the Mind.* Cambridge, MA: Harvard University Press.

Johnston, A. W. & Briggs, E. (1968). Team performance as a function of team arrangement and work load. *Journal of Applied Psychology, 52,* 89–94.

Johnston, I. R. (1972). Visual judgments in locomotion. Doctoral dissertation, University of Melbourne, Australia.

Johnston, J. M., & Pennypacker, H. S. (1979). *Strategies and tactics of human behavioral research.* New York: Houghton Mifflin.

Johnston, T. D. (1981). Contrasting approaches to a theory of learning. *The Behavioral and Brain Sciences, 4,* 125–173.

Johnston, W. (1976). *Silent music: The science of meditation.* San Francisco: Harper & Row.

Joint Commission on Accreditation of Hospitals. (1974). *Accreditation Manual for Alcoholism Programs.* Chicago: JCAH.

Joint Commission on Accreditation of Hospitals. (1981). *Consolidated standards manual for child, adolescent, and adult psychiatric, alcoholism, and drug abuse facilities.* Chicago: JCAH.

Joint Commission on Mental Health and Illness. (1961). *Action for mental health.* New York: Basic Books.

Joliffe, N. (1952). *Reduce and stay reduced.* New York: Simon & Schuster.

Jones, A., & McGill, D. (1967). The homeostatic character of information drive in humans. *Journal of Experimental Research in Personality, 2,* 25–31.

Jones, B. P., & Butters, N. (1983). Neuropsychological assessment. In M. Hersen, A. Kazdin, & A. Bellack (Eds.), *The clinical psychology handbook.* New York: Pergamon Press.

Jones, D. (1991). Ritualism and child sexual abuse. *Child Abuse and Neglect, 15,* 163–170.

Jones, E. (1957/1953). *The life and work of Sigmund Freud* (3 vols.). New York: Basic Books.

Jones, E. (1981). Rebirthing. In R. J. Corsini (Ed.), *Handbook of innovative psychotherapies.* New York: Wiley.

Jones, E. E., & Davis, K. E. (1965). From acts to dispositions: The attribution process in person perception. In L. Berkowitz (Ed.), *Advances in experimental social psychology,* Vol. 2. New York: Academic press.

Jones, E. E., & Korchin, S. J. (Eds.). (1982). *Minority mental health.* New York: Praeger.

Jones, E. E., & Nisbett, R. E. (1972). The actor and the observer: Divergent perceptions of the causes of behavior. In E. E. Jones, D. E. Kanouse, H. H. Kelley, R. E. Nisbett, S. Valins, & B. W. Weiner (Eds.), *Attribution: Perceiving the causes of behavior* (pp. 79–94). Morristown, NJ: General Learning.

Jones, F. (1976). *Body awareness in action: A study of the Alexander technique.* New York: Schocken Books.

Jones, H. E., & Conrad, H. S. (1933). The growth and decline of intelligence: A study of a homogenous group between the ages of ten and sixty. *Genetic Psychology Monographs, 13,* 223–298.

Jones, H. E., & Conrad, H. S. (1933). The growth and decline of intelligence. *Genetic Psychology Monographs, 13*(3).

Jones, H. E., & Jones, M. C. (1928). A study of fear. *Childhood Education, 5,* 136–143.

Jones, J. J., & Terris, W. (1990). Integrity testing for personnel selection: An overview. *Forensic Reports, 4,* 117–140.

Jones, J. M., Levine, I. S., & Rosenberg A. A. (Eds.). (1991). Homelessness [Special issue]. *American Psychologist, 46*(11).

Jones, J. W. (Ed.). (1981). *The burnout syndrome: Current research, theory, interventions.* Park Ridge, Ill.: London House Press.

Jones, K., & Vischi, T. (1979). Impact of alcohol, drug abuse, and mental health treatment on medical care utilization. *Medical Care,* December 17(suppl.).

Jones, K. L., & Smith, D. W. (1973). Recognition of fetal alcohol syndrome in early infancy. *Lancet, 2,* 999–1001.

Jones, K. L., Smith, D. W., Ulleland, C. N., & Streissguth, A. P. (1973). Pattern of malformation in offspring of chronic alcoholic mothers. *Lancet, 1,* 1267–1271.

Jones, K. R., & Vischi, T. R. (1979). Impact of alcohol, drug abuse and mental health treatment on medical care utilization: A review of the research literature. *Medical Care, 17*(Suppl.), 1–82.

Jones, L. V. (1971). The nature of measurement. In R. L. Thorndike (Ed.), *Educational measurement* (2nd ed.). Washington, D.C.: American Council on Education.

Jones, L. V., & Wepman, J. M. (1966). *A spoken word count.* Chicago: Language Research Associates.

Jones, M. (1968). *Beyond the therapeutic community: Social learning and social psychiatry.* New Haven, Conn.: Yale University Press.

Jones, M. (1980). Desirable features of a therapeutic community in a prison. In H. Toch (Ed.), *Therapeutic communities in corrections.* New York: Praeger.

Jones, M., McGee, R., & Grant, J. (1952). *Social psychiatry.* London: Tavistock.

Jones, M. C. (1924). A laboratory study of fear: The case of Peter. *Pedagogical Seminary, 31,* 308–316.

Jones, M. C. (1924). Elimination of children's fears. *Journal of Experimental Psychology, 7,* 325–341.

Jones, M. C. (1933). Emotional development. In C. Murchison (Ed.), *A handbook of child psychology* (2nd ed.). Worcester, Mass.: Clark University Press.

Jones, M. C. (1965). Psychological correlates of somatic development. *Child Development, 36,* 899–911.

Jones, M. C. & Bayley, N. (1950). Physical maturing among boys as related to behavior. *Journal of Educational Psychology, 41,* 129–148.

Jones, M. C., & Burks, B. S. (1936). *Personality development in childhood, a survey of problems, methods and experimental findings.* Washington, D.C.: National Research Council.

Jones, M. E. (1975). A 1924 pioneer looks at behavior therapy. *Journal of Behavior Therapy and Experimental Psychiatry, 6,* 181–187.

Jones, R. A. (1977). *Self-fulfilling prophecies.* Hillsdale, N.J.: Erlbaum.

Jones, R. H., Crowell, D. H., & Kapuniai, L. E. (1969). Change detection model for serially correlated data. *Psychological Bulletin, 71,* 352–358.

Jones, W. H., Chernovetz, M. E. O'C., & Hansson, R. O. (1978). The enigma of androgyny: Differential implications for males and females? *Journal of Consulting and Clinical Psychology, 46,* 298–313.

Jonides, J., Kahn, R., & Rozin, P. (1975). Imagery instructions improve memory in blind subjects. *Bulletin of the Psychonomic Society, 5,* 424–426.

Jonker, F., & Jonker-Bakker, I. (1991). Experiences with ritualistic child sexual abuse: A case study from the Netherlands. *Child Abuse and Neglect, 15,* 191–196.

Jonker, F., & Jonker-Bakker, I. (1992). Safe behind the screen of "mass hysteria": A closing rejoinder to Benjamin Rossen. *Journal of Psychology and Theology, 20*(3), 267–270.

Jordaan, J. P., & Heyde, M. B. (1979). *Vocational maturity in the high-school years.* New York: Teachers College Press.

Jordaan, J. P., Myers, R. A., Layton, W. L., & Morgan, H. H. (1968; 1980). *The counseling psychologist.* New York: Teachers College Press. (Also in J. M. Whiteley (Ed.), *The history of counseling psychology.* Monterey, Calif.: Brooks/Cole.)

Jordan, C., & Tharp, R. (1979). Culture and education. In A. Marsella, R. Tharp, & T. Ciborowski (Eds.), *Perspectives on cross-cultural psychology.* New York: Academic Press.

Jordan, H. A. (1969). Voluntary intragastric feeding: Oral and gastric contributions to food intake and hunger in man. *Journal of Comparative and Physiological Psychology, 68,* 498–506.

Jordan, J. B., Hayden, A. H., Karnes, M. B., & Wood, M. M. (Eds.). (1977). *Early childhood education for exceptional children—A handbook of ideas and exemplary practices.* Reston, Va.: Council for Exceptional Children.

Jores, A., & Kerekjarto, M. (1966). *Der Asthmatiker.* Bern: Huber Verlag.

Joseph, R. (1956). *A letter to the man who killed my dog.* New York: Fell.

Joshi, M. C. (1965). Psychological researches in India. In S. D. Kapoor (Ed.), *Psychological researches in India: A commemoration volume.* Banaras, India: Jalota Commemoration Volume Committee.

Joslin, E. P. (1957). Diabetes. In M. Fishbein (Ed.), *Illustrated medical and health encyclopedia.* New York: Stuttman.

Josselson, R. L. (1973). Psychodynamic aspects of identity formation in college women. *Journal of Youth and Adolescence, 2,* 3–52.

Jost, A. (1953). Problems of fetal endocrinology: The gonadal and hypophysical hormones. *Recent Progress in Hormone Research, 8,* 379–418.

Jou, T. H. (1981). *The tao of tai-chi.* Rutland, Vt.: Tuttle.

Jourard, S. M. (1968). *Disclosing man to himself.* New York: Van Nostrand Reinhold.

Jourad, S. M. (1968/1963). *Personal adjustment: An approach through the study of healthy personality.* New York: Macmillan.

Jourard, S. M. (1971). *Self-disclosure: An experimental analysis of the transparent self.* New York: Wiley.

Jourard, S. M. (1971/1964). *The transparent self.* New York: Van Nostrand Reinhold.

Jourard, S. M., & Landsman, T. (1980/1974). *Healthy personality: An approach from the viewpoint of humanistic psychology.* New York: Macmillan.

Jouriles, E. N., Murphy, C. M., & O'Leary, K. D. (1989). Interspousal aggression, marital discord, and child problems. *Journal of Consulting and Clinical Psychology, 57,* 453–455.

Journal of Applied Behavioral Science, (1976), *12* (No. 3: Special issue: Selfhelp groups).

Joyce J. (1959/1939). *Finnegan's wake.* New York: Viking.

Joyce, J. (1961/1922). *Ulysses.* New York: Vintage Books.

Joyce, J. (1969/1916). *A portrait of the artist as a young man.* New York: Viking.

Joynson, R. B. (1989) *The Burt affair.* New York: Routledge.

Joynt, R. J., & Benton, A. L. (1964). The memoir of Marc Dax on aphasia. *Neurology, 14,* 851–854.

Joynt, R. L., & Shoulson, I. (1979). Dementia. In K. M. Heilman & E. Valenstein (Eds.), *Clinical neuropsychology.* New York: Oxford University Press.

Judd, C. H. (1907). *Psychology,* New York: Ginn.

Judd, C. H. (1908). The relation of special training to general intelligence. *Educational Review, 36,* 28–42.

Judd, C. H. (1909/1903). *Genetic psychology for teachers,* New York: Appleton.

Judd, C. H. (1915). *Psychology of high school subjects.* Boston: Ginn.

Judd, C. H. (1926). *Psychology of social institutions.* New York: Macmillan.

Judd, C. H. (1927). *Psychological analysis of the fundamentals of arithmetic,* Chicago: University of Chicago.

Judd, C. H. (1927). *Psychology of secondary education.* Boston: Ginn.

Judd, C. H. (1930). Autobiography. In C. Murchison (Ed.), *History of psychology in autobiography,* Vol. 2. Worcester, Mass.: Clark University Press.

Judd, C. H. (1939). *Educational psychology.* Boston: Houghton Mifflin.

Julesz, B. (1971). *Foundations of cyclopean perception.* Chicago: University of Chicago Press.

Julian, J. (1973). *Social problems.* Englewood Cliffs, NJ: Prentice-Hall.

Julien, R. M. (1981/1975). *A primer of drug action* (3rd ed.). San Francisco: Freeman.

Jung, C. G. (1909/1906). *Diagnostische Assoziationsstudien.* Leipzig: Barth.

Jung, C. G. (1912). *The psychology of the unconscious.* Leipzig: Deuticke.

Jung, C. G. (1918). *Studies in word association.* London: Heinemann.

Jung, C. G. (1928). *Contributions to analytical psychology.* (C. F. and H. G. Baynes transl.) New York: Harcourt Brace. London: Kegan Paul.

Jung, C. G. (1940). *The integration of the personality.* London: Routledge & Kegan Paul.

Jung, C. G. (1953). Anima and animus. In *Two essays on analytical psychology: Collected works of C. G. Jung,* Vol. 7. New York: Bollinger Foundation.

Jung, C. G. (1953). *Modern man in search of a soul.* New York: Harcourt, Brace.

Jung, C. G. (1953/1928). The relations between the ego and the unconscious. In *Collected works,* Vol. 7. Princeton, N.J.: Princeton University Press.

Jung, C. G. (1953–1965). *The collected works of C. G. Jung,* Vols. 1–19. Princeton, N.J.: Princeton University Press. London: Routledge & Kegan Paul.

Jung, C. G. (1954). On the nature of psyche. In H. Read et al. (Eds.), R. F. C. Hull (Trans.), *Collected works of C. G. Jung* (Vol. 8). Princeton, NJ: Princeton University Press. (Original work published 1919)

Jung, C. G. (1954). The development of the personality. In *Collected works,* Vol. 17. London: Routledge & Kegan Paul.

Jung, C. G. (1954). *The practice of psychotherapy.* New York: Pantheon.

Jung, C. G. (1957). *The undiscovered self*. Boston: Little, Brown.

Jung, C. G. (1958). The philosophical and the psychological approach to life. Self-knowledge. In R. F. C. Hull (Trans.), *The undiscovered self* (pp. 83–118). New York: New American Library.

Jung, C. G. (1960). The structure and dynamics of the psyche. In *Collected Works*, Vol. 8. Princeton, N.J.: Princeton University Press.

Jung, C. G. (1963/1961). *Memories, dreams, reflections*. New York: Pantheon.

Jung, C. G. (1966). *The spirit in man, art, and literature*. Princeton, N.J.: Princeton University Press.

Jung, C. G. (1968). *Analytical psychology: Its theory and practice*. New York: Random House.

Jung, C. G. (1968/1959). *Aion: Researches into the phenomenology of the self. The collected works of C. G. Jung*, Vol. 9, P. II. Princeton, N.J.: Princeton University Press.

Jung, C. G. (1969). The stages of life. In *The collected works: structure and dynamics of the psyche*. Vol. 8. New York: Pantheon.

Jung, C. G. (1969/1959/1934). *The archetypes and the collective unconscious. The collected works of C. G. Jung*. Vol. 9, Pt. I. Princeton, N.J.: Princeton University Press.

Jung, C. G. (1969/1960). A review of the complex theory. In *The collected works of C. G. Jung. Vol. 8: The structure and dynamics of the psyche*. Princeton, N.J.: Princeton University Press.

Jung, C. G. (1971). *Psychological types*. In *The collected works of C. G. Jung* (Vol. 6, Bollinger Series 20). Princeton, NJ: Princeton University Press.

Jung, C. G. (1972/1917–1928). *Two essays on analytical psychology*. Princeton, N.J.: Princeton University Press.

Jung, C. G. (1973). In G. Adler, (Ed.), *Letters*. Princeton, N.J.: Princeton University Press.

Jung, C. G. (1976/1921). *Psychological types*. Princeton, N.J.: Princeton University Press.

Jung, C. G. (1978). *Psychology and the east*. Princeton, N.J.: Princeton University Press.

Jung, C. G. (Ed.). (1968/1964). *Man and his symbols*. New York: Dell.

Jung, C. G., & Pauli, W. (1955). *The interpretation of nature and the psyche: Synchronicity and the influence of archetypal ideas on the scientific theories of Kepler*. New York: Pantheon.

Jurd, M. F. (1978). Concrete and formal operational thinking in history. In J. Keats, K. Collis, & G. Halford (Eds.). *Cognitive development*. Chichester, England: Wiley.

Justice, B., and Duncan, D. (1976). Running away: An epidemic problem of adolescence. *Adolescence, 43*, 365–371.

Justice, B., & Justice, R. (1982). Clinical approaches to family violence: I. Etiology of physical abuse of children and dynamics of coercive treatment. *Family Therapy Collections, 3*, 1–20.

Justice, B., Justice, R., & Kraft, J. (1974). Early warning signs of violence: *American Journal of Psychiatry, 131*, 457–459.

Justice, B., Justice, R., & Kraft, J. (1974). Early warning signs of violence: Is a triad enough? *American Journal of Psychiatry, 131*, 457–459.

Kadushin, A. (1974). *Child welfare services*. New York: Macmillan.

Kadushin, A. (1976). *Supervision in social work*. New York: Columbia University Press.

Kadushin, A., & Martin, J. (1981). *Child abuse: An interactional event*. New York: Columbia University Press.

Kadushin, C. (1989). The small world method and other innovations in experimental social psychology. In M. Kochen (Ed.), *The small world* (pp. xxiii–xxvi). Norwood, NJ: Ablex.

Kafka, G. (1914). *Einführung in die Tierpsychologie auf experimenteller und ethologischer Grundlage*. Leipzig: Barth.

Kagan, J., (1965). The new marriage: Pediatrics and psychology. *American Journal of Diseases of Children, 110*, 272–278.

Kagan, J. (1966). A developmental approach to conceptual growth. In H. J. Klausmeier & C. W. Harris (Eds.), *Analyses of concept learning*. New York: Academic Press.

Kagan, J. (1969). Inadequate evidence and illogical conclusions. *Harvard Education Review, 39*, 274–277.

Kagan, J. (1970). The determinants of attention in the infant. *American Scientist, 58*, 298–306.

Kagan, J. (1971). *Change and continuity in infancy*. New York: Wiley.

Kagan, J. (1976). Emergent themes in human development. *American Scientist, 64*, 186–196.

Kagan, J. (1976). Resilience and continuity in psychological development. In A. M. Clarke & A. D. B. Clarke (Eds.), *Early experience: Myth and evidence*. New York: Free Press.

Kagan, J. (1978). *The growth of the child*. New York: Norton.

Kagan, J. (1981). Fearfulness in first years need not cause concern. *American Academy of Pediatrics News Bulletin, 4*, 1–3.

Kagan, J. (1981). *The second year*. Cambridge, Mass.: Harvard University Press.

Kagan, J., Kearsley, R., & Zelaso, P. R. (1978). *Infancy: Its place in human development*. Cambridge, Mass.: Harvard University Press.

Kagan, J., & Moss, H. A. (1962). *Birth to maturity*. New York: Wiley.

Kagan, J., Moss, H. A., & Sigel, I. E. (1963). The psychological significance of styles of conceptualization. In J. F. Wright & J. Kagan (Eds.), *Basic cognitive processes in children. Monograph of the Society for Research in Child Development, 28*, 73–112.

Kagan, J., Reznick, S., & Snidman, N. (1988). Biological bases of childhood shyness. *Science, 240*, 167–171.

Kagan, N. (1975). Influencing human interaction—Eleven years with IPR. *Canadian Counselor, 9(2)*, 74–97.

Kagan, N., Fretz, B. R., Tanney, M. F., Harmon, L. W., & Myers, R. A. (Eds.). (1982). Counseling psychology—The next decade. *The Counseling Psychologist*.

Kahaner, L. (1988). *Cults that kill*. New York: Warner Books.

Kahle, L. & Sales, D. (1980). Due process of law and the attitudes of professionals toward involuntary civil commitment. In P. Lipsett & B. Sales (Eds.), *New directions in psychological research*. New York: Van Nostrand Reinhold.

Kahn, A., Clark, T., & Oyebode, F. (1988). Unilateral auditory hallucinations. *British Journal of Psychiatry, 152*, 297–298.

Kahn, A., & McGaughey, T. A. (1977). Distance and liking: When moving close produces increased liking. *Sociometry, 40*, 138–144.

Kahn, E. (1985). Heinz Kohut and Carl Rogers: A timely comparison. American *Psychologist, 40(8)*, 893–904.

Kahn, H. (1965). *On escalation: Metaphors and scenarios*. New York: Praeger.

Kahn, J., & Nursten, J. (1968). *Unwillingly to school*. (2nd ed.). New York: Pergamon Press.

Kahn, M. (1970). Non-verbal communication and marital satisfaction. *Family Process, 9*, 449–456.

Kahn, M., Baker, B., & Weiss, J. (1968). Treatment of insomnia by relaxation training. *Journal of Abnormal Psychology, 73*, 556–558.

Kahn, M. W. (1981). *Basic methods for mental health practitioners*. Cambridge, Mass.: Winthrop.

Kahn, R. L. (1975). In search of the Hawthorne effect. In E. L. Cass & F. G. Zimmer (Eds.), *Man and work in society*. New York: Van Nostrand Reinhold.

Kahneman, D. (1973). *Attention and effort*. Englewood Cliffs, N.J.: Prentice-Hall.

Kahneman, D., Slovic, P., & Tversky, A. (Eds.). (1982). *Judgment under uncertainty: Heuristics and biases*. Cambridge, England: Cambridge University Press.

Kahneman, D., Slovic, P., Tversky, A. (Eds.). (1982). Judgment under uncertainty: Heuristics and biases. Cambridge, MA: Cambridge University Press.

Kahneman, D., & Tversky, A. (1973). On the psychology of prediction. *Psychological Review, 80*, 237–251.

Kaimowitz v. Michigan Department of Mental Health. Civil No. 73–19434–AW 42 U.S.L.W. 2063 (Mich. Cir. Ct. 1973).

Kaiser, L. L. (1978). *A study of the Adlerian life style in relation to psychiatric diagnosis*. Unpublished dissertation, Georgia State University.

Kakar, S. (1978). *The inner world: A psychoanalytic study of childhood and society in India*. Delhi: Oxford University Press.

Kakar, S. (Ed.) (1979). *Identity and adulthood*. Delhi: Oxford University Press.

Kalat, J. (1992). *Biological psychology*. Belmont, CA: Wadsworth.

Kalat, J. W. (1981). *Biological psychology*. Belmont, Calif.: Wadsworth.

Kalat, J. W., & Rozin, P. (1973). "Learned safety" as a mechanism in long-delay taste aversion learning in rats. *Journal of Comparative and Physiological Psychology, 83*, 198–207.

Kales, A., Bixler, E. O., & Kales, J. D. (1974). Role of the sleep research and treatment facility: Diagnosis, treatment and education. In E. D. Weitzman (Ed.), *Advances in sleep research*, Vol. 1. New York: Spectrum.

Kales, A., & Tan, T. L. (1969). Sleep alterations associated with medical illness. In A. Kales (Ed.), *Sleep: physiology and pathology*. Philadelphia, Pa.: Lippincott.

Kalinoswky, L. B. (1975). The convulsive therapies. In A. M. Freedman, H. I. Kaplan, & B. J. Sadock (Eds.), *Comprehensive textbook of psychiatry*, Vol. 2. Baltimore, Md.: Williams & Wilkins.

Kalinowsky, L. B. (1980). The discoveries of somatic treatments in psychiatry: Facts and myths. *Comprehensive Psychiatry, 21*, 428–435.

Kalish, H. I. (1981). *From behavioral science to behavior modification*. New York: McGraw-Hill.

Kalish, R. (1985). The social context of death and dying. In R. Binstock & E. Shanas (Eds.), *Handbook of aging and the social sciences* (pp. 483–503). New York: Van Nostrand Reinhold.

Kalish, R., & Reynolds, D. (1976). *Death and ethnicity: A psychocultural study*. Los Angeles: University of Southern California Press.

Kalish, R. A. (1976). Death and dying in a social context. In R. H. Binstock & E. Shanas (Eds.), *Handbook of aging and the social sciences*. New York: Van Nostrand Reinhold.

Kallen, D. J. (1980). Les adolescents décident de leur sexualité. In M. Amdewachter, (Ed.), *Cahiers de bioéthique 3: Médicine et adolescence*. Québec: Les Presses de L'Université Laval.

Kallick-Kaufman, M., & Reuter, P. (1979). Introduction. *Journal of Social Issues, 35*, 1–6.

Kallmann, F. J. (1952a). Twin and sibship study of overt male homosexuality. *Journal of Human Genetics, 4*, 283–298.

Kallmann, F. J. (1952b). Comparative twin study on the genetic aspects of male homosexuality. *Journal of Nervous Mental Disease, 115*, 283–298.

Kallmann, F. J. (1963). Genetic aspects of sex determination and sexual maturation potentials in man. In G. Winokur (Ed.), *Determinants of human sexual behavior*. Springfield, IL: Thomas.

Kallmann, F. J., & Saunder, G. (1949). Twin studies on senescence. *American Journal of Psychiatry, 106*, 29–36.

Kalnins, I. V., & Bruner, J. S. (1973). The coordination of visual observation and instrumental behavior in early infancy. *Perception, 2*, 307–314.

Kalven, H., & Zeisel, H. (1966). *The American jury*. Boston: Little, Brown.

Kalyuzhnyi, V. V. (1968). The treatment of tobacco smoking with the aid of lobelin and the influence of lobelin on autonomic and vascular reactions. *Zhurnal Nevropatologii i Psikhiatrii, 68*(12), 1864–1870.

Kamil, A., & Roitblat, H. L. (1985). The ecology of foraging behavior: Implications for animal learning and memory. In M. R. Rosenzweig & L. W. Porter (Eds.), *Animal review of psychology*.

Kamil, A. C. (1987). *Foraging behavior*. New York: Plenum Press.

Kamin, L. J. (1957). The retention of an incompletely learned avoidance response. *Journal of Comparative and Physiological Psychology, 50*, 457–460.

Kamin, L. J. (1968). "Attention-like" processes in classical conditioning. In M. R. Jones (Ed.), *Miami symposium on the prediction of behavior*. Miami, Fla.: University of Miami Press.

Kamin, L. J. (1969). Predictability, surprise, attention and conditioning. In B. Campbell & R. Church (Eds.), *Punishment and aversive behavior*. New York: Appleton-Century-Crofts.

Kamin, L. J. (1974). *The science and politics of I.Q.* Hillsdale, N.J.: Erlbaum.

Kaminer, Y., & Hreczny, B. (1991). Lysergic acid diethylamide-induced chronic visual disturbances in an adolescent. *Journal of Nervous and Mental Diseases, 179*, 173–174.

Kamiya, J. (1968). Conscious control of brain waves. *Psychology Today, 1*, 57–60

Kamiya, J. (1969). Operant control of the EEG alpha rhythm and some of its reported effects on consciousness. In C. Tart (Ed.), *Altered states of consciousness*. New York: Wiley.

Kamiya, J., Barber, T., Dicara, L. B., Miller, N. E., Shapiro, D., & Stoyva, J. (1971). *Biofeedback and self-control*. Chicago: Aldine.

Kamiya, J., & Nowlis, D. (1970). The control of electroencephalographic alpha rhythms through auditory feedback and the associated mental activity. *Psychophysiology, 6*, 476–483.

Kammann, R. (1966). Verbal complexity and preferences in poetry. *Journal of Verbal Learning and Verbal Behavior, 5*, 536–540.

Kandel, E. R. (1979). Cellular insights into behavior and learning. *Harvey Lectures, 73*, 19–92.

Kandel, E. R. (1979). Small systems of neurons. *Scientific American, 241*, 66–85.

Kandel, E. R. (1991). Cellular mechanisms of learning and the biological basis of individuality. In E. R. Kandel, J. H. Schwartz, & T. H. Jessell (Eds.), *Principles of neural science* (pp. 1009–1031). New York: Elsevier.

Kandel, E. R., & Schwartz, J. H. (1981). *Principles of neural science*. New York: Elsevier North Holland.

Kandel, E. R., Schwartz, J. H., & Jessell, T. M. (1991). *Principles of neural science* (3rd ed.) New York: Elsevier.

Kandel, E. R., & Tauc, L. (1965). Mechanism of heterosynaptic facilitation in the giant cell of the abdominal ganglion of *Aplysia depilans*. *Journal of Physiology, 181,* 28–47.

Kane, A. (1988, February 1). When you're homeless in Boston. *The Boston Globe,* p. 17.

Kaneko H. (1943). Aptitude and training for the different branches: In *National defense psychology. Contemporary psychology series,* Vol. 7 *(Kakushuheika no tekisei to kunren, Kokubo-shinrigaku, Gendai-shinrigaku-sōsho* 7). Tokyo: Kawade Shobō.

Kaneko, H. (1963). *Introduction to management psychology* (Keiei-shinrigaku Nyumon), Tokyo: Diamond.

Kaneko, H. (1982). *Education and training in the company (Kigyōnai no kyōikukunren,* Tokyo: Japan Institute of Labor.

Kaneko, H. (Ed.). (1968). *Motivation management* (Kinrō-iyoku). Tokyo: Dainihon Shobō.

Kaneko, H., Yoshikawa, E., Inage, N., Kinoshita, S., & Tasaki, J. (1978). *Human Relations in the Workplace* (Shokuba no ningen-kankei). Tokyo: Japan Productivity Center.

Kaneko, T. (1968). *Science of color—Its psychophysics.* Tokyo: Misuzu Shobo, (in Japanese).

Kaneko, T., & Kosaki, T. (1977). *Essentials of modern psychology.* Tokyo: Nihon-Bunka-Kagaku-sha, (in Japanese).

Kanfer, F. (1979). Personal control, social control, and altruism: Can society survive the age of individualism? *American Psychologist, 34,* 231–239.

Kanfer, F. H. (1965). Issues and ethics in behavior manipulation. *Psychological Reports, 16,* 187–196.

Kanfer, F. H., & Grimm, L. G. (1980). Managing clinical change. *Behavior Modification, 4,* 419–444.

Kanfer, F. H., & Phillips, J. S. (1970). *Learning foundations of behavior therapy.* New York: Wiley.

Kanfer, F. H., & Saslow, G. (1969). Behavioral diagnosis. In C. Franks (Ed.), *Behavior therapy: Appraisal and status.* New York: McGraw-Hill.

Kanfer, R. (1990). Motivation theory and industrial and organizational psychology. In M. D. Dunnette & L. N. Hough (Eds.). (Vol. 1, pp. 75–170).

Kanin, E. J., Davidson, K. D., & Scheck, S. R. (1970). A research note on male-female differentials in the experience of heterosexual love. *The Journal of Sex Research, 6,* 64–72.

Kanner, A., Coyne, J., Schaefer, C., & Lazarus, R. (1981). Comparison of two modes of stress measurement: Daily hassles and uplifts versus major life events, *Journal of Behavioral Medicine, 4,* 1–39.

Kanner, A., Kafry, D., & Pines, A. (1978). Conspicuous in its absence: The lack of positive conditions as a source of stress, *Journal of Human Stress, 4,* 33–39.

Kanner, L. (1943). Autistic disturbances of affective contact. *Nervous Child, 2,* 217–250.

Kanner, L. (1972). *Child psychiatry* (4th ed.). Springfield, Ill.: Thomas.

Kanner, L. A. (1964). *A history of the care and study of the mentally retarded.* Springfield, Ill.: Thomas.

Kant, I. (1970). *Metaphysical foundations of natural science* (J. Ellington, Trans.). Indianapolis: Bobbs-Merrill. (Original work published 1786).

Kant, I. (1929/1781). *Critique of pure reason.* New York: St. Martin's Press.

Kant, I. (1974/1798). *Anthroponomy.* The Hague: Nijhoff.

Kanter, H. L. (1970). Birth order, background factors, and teacher referral for emotional disturbance. Doctoral dissertation, University of Texas at Austin.

Kanter, R. M. (1972). *Commitment and community.* Cambridge, Mass.: Harvard University Press.

Kanter, R. M. (1978). The changing shape of work: Psychological trends in America. Presented at the Plenary Session of the National Conference on Higher Education, Chicago.

Kanthamani, B. K., & Rao, K. R. (1972). Personality characteristics of ESP subjects. III. Extraversion and ESP. *Journal of Parapsychology, 36,* 190–212.

Kanthamani, H., & Kelly, E. F. (1974). Awareness of success in an exceptional subject. *Journal of Parapsychology, 38,* 355–382.

Kantor, J. R. (1926; 1924). *Principles of psychology.* New York: Knopf, Vol. 1, Vol. 2.

Kantor, J. R. (1929). *An outline of social psychology.* Chicago: Follett.

Kantor, J. R. (1947). *Problems of physiological psychology.* Chicago: Principia Press.

Kantor, J. R. (1958). *Interbehavioral psychology.* Bloomington, Ind.: Principia Press.

Kantor, J. R. (1969). *The scientific evolution of psychology,* Vol. 2. Chicago: Principia Press.

Kantor, J. R. (1977). *Psychological linguistics,* Chicago: Principia Press.

Kantor, J. R., & Smith, N. W. (1975). *The science of psychology: An interbehavioral survey.* Chicago: Principia Press.

Kantorowitz, D. A., Walters, J., & Pelder, K. (1978). Positive versus negative self-monitoring in the self-control of smoking. *Journal of Consulting and Clinical Psychology, 46*(5), 1148–1150.

Kantowitz, B. H. (1982). Interfacing human information processing and engineering psychology. In W. C. Howell & E. A. Fleishman (Eds.), *Human performance and productivity: Information processing and decision making,* Vol. 2. Hillsdale, N.J.: Erlbaum.

Kantowitz, B. H. (Ed.). (1974). *Human information processing.* Hillsdale, N.J.: Erlbaum.

Kantowitz, B. H., & Knight, J. L. (1976). Testing tapping timesharing. II: Auditory secondary tasks. *Acta Psychologica, 40,* 343–362.

Kantowitz, B. H., & Roediger, H. L. (1978). *Experimental psychology.* Chicago: Rand-McNally.

Kanuha, V. (1990). The need for an integrated analysis of oppression in feminist therapy ethics. In H. Lerman & N. Porter (Eds.), *Feminist ethics in psychotherapy.* New York: Springer.

Kanungo, R. (1979). The Concepts of alienation and involvement revisited. *Psychological Bulletin, 86,* 119–138.

Kanungo, R. N. (1982). *Work alienation.* New York: Praeger.

Kaplan, A. (1964). *The conduct of inquiry: Methodology for behavioral science.* San Francisco: Chandler.

Kaplan, A., & Surrey, J. (1984). The relational self in women: Developmental theory and public policy. In L. E. Walker (Ed.), *Women and mental health policy.* Beverly Hills, CA: Sage

Kaplan, A. G. (1979). Psychological androgyny: Further considerations. *Psychology of Women Quarterly, 3*(3).

Kaplan, A. G., & Sedney, M. A. (1980). *Psychology and sex roles: An androgynous perspective.* Boston: Little, Brown.

Kaplan, H. B. (1970). Self-derogation and childhood family structure. *Journal of Nervous and Mental Diseases, 151,* 13–23.

Kaplan, H. B., & Bloom, S. W. (1960). The use of sociological and social-psychological concepts in physiological research: A review of selected experimental studies. *Journal of Nervous and Mental Diseases, 131*, 128–134.

Kaplan, H. I., & Sadock, B. J. (1991). *Synopsis of psychiatry* (6th Ed.). Baltimore: Williams & Wilkins.

Kaplan, H. I., & Sadock, B. J. (Eds.). (1971). *Comprehensive group psychotherapy.* Baltimore, Md.: Williams & Wilkins.

Kaplan, H. I., & Sadock, B. J. (Eds.). (1985). *Modern synopsis of comprehensive textbook of psychiatry* (4th ed.). Baltimore: Wiliams & Wilkins.

Kaplan, H. R. (1975). How *do* workers view their work in America? *Vocational Guidance Quarterly, 24*, 165–168.

Kaplan, H. S. (1974). *The new sex therapy.* New York: Brunner/Mazel.

Kaplan, H. S. (1979). *Disorders of sexual desire.* New York: Brunner/Mazel.

Kaplan, R. M. (1982). Nader's raid on the testing industry. *American Psychologist, 37*, 15–22.

Kaplan, S. R. (1974). Therapy groups and training groups: Similarities and differences. In G. Gibbard, J. Hartman, & R. Mann (Eds.), *Analysis of groups* (pp. 94–126). San Francisco: Jossey-Bass.

Kaplan, S. R., & Roman, R. (1973). *The organization and delivery of mental health services in the ghetto: The Lincoln Hospital experience.* New York: Praeger.

Kapleau, P. (1965). *The three pillars of Zen: Teaching, practice and enlightenment.* Boston: Beacon Press.

Karasu, T. B. (1979). Toward unification of psychotherapies: A complementary model. *American Journal of Psychotherapy, 23*, 555–563.

Karasu, T. B. (1986). The psychotherapies: Benefits and limitations. *American Journal of Psychotherapy, 40*(3), 324–339.

Karasu, T. B. (1986). The specificity versus nonspecificity dilemma: Toward identifying therapeutic change agents. *The American Journal of Psychiatry, 143*, 687–695.

Kardiner, A. (1946/1939). *The individual and his society.* New York: Columbia University Press.

Kardiner, A. (1959/1945). *The psychological frontiers of society.* New York: Columbia University Press.

Karlen, A. (1971). *Sexuality and homosexuality: A new view.* New York: Norton.

Karl-Marx-Universitaet Leipzig (Ed.). (1980). *Wilhelm Wundt—Programmatisches Erbe. Wissenschaftsentwicklung und Gegenwart. Wissenschaftliche Beitraege der Karl-Marx-Universität Leipzig, Reihe Psychologie.* (Redaction: W. Meichsner & A. Metge.) Leipzig: Know.

Karl Pearson's early statistical papers (1894–1916). Cambridge, Mass.: Cambridge University Press, 1948.

Karnes, F. A., & Collins, E. C. (1980). *Handbook of instructional resources and references for teaching the gifted.* Boston: Allyn & Bacon.

Karnes, M. B., & Lee, R. C. Mainstreaming in the preschool. Urbana, Ill.: ERIC Clearhouse on Early Childhood Education, ED 152419, n.d.

Karnes, M. B., Teska, J. A., Stoneburner, R. L., Lee, R. C., & Appelbaum, L. (1981). Short-term and long-term effects of five preschool approaches to preventing mental retardation. In P. Mittler (Ed.), *Frontiers of knowledge in mental retardation,* Vol. I. Baltimore, Md.: University Park Press.

Karniol, R., & Ross, M. (1976). The development of causal attributions in social perception. *Journal of Personality and Social Psychology, 34*, 455–464.

Karp, J. M., & Sigel, I. (1965). Psychoeducational appraisal of disadvantaged children. *Review of Educational Research, 35*, 401–412.

Karpf, F. B. (1953). *The psychology and psychotherapy of Otto Rank.* New York: Philosophical Library.

Karpicke, J., & Hearst, E. (1975). Inhibitory control and errorless discrimination learning. *Journal of the Experimental Analysis of Behavior, 23*, 159–166.

Karpman, B. (1948). The myth of the psychopathic personality. *American Journal of Psychiatry, 104*, 523–534.

Kasamatsu, A., et al. (1957). The EEG of 'Zen' and 'Yoga' practitioners. *Electroencephalography and Clinical Neurophysiology, 9*, 51–52.

Kaschak, E. (1981). Feminist psychotherapy: The first decade. In S. Cox (Ed.), *Female psychology: The emerging self* (2nd ed.). New York: St. Martin's Press.

Kaschak, E. (1988). Limits and boundaries: Toward a complex psychology of women. *Women and Therapy, 7*(4), 109–123.

Käsermann, M.-L. (1980). *Spracherwerb und Interaktion.* Bern: Huber.

Käsermann, M-L., & Foppa, K. (1981). Some determinants of self correction: An interaction study of Swiss-German. In W. Deutsch (Ed.), *The child's construction of language.* New York: Academic Press.

Kashani, J. H., et al. (1981). Current perspectives on childhood depression: An overview. *American Journal of Psychiatry, 138*(2), 143–153.

Kaslow, F. W. (1977). *Supervision consultation, and staff training in the helping professions.* San Francisco: Jossey-Bass.

Kaslow, F. W. (1980). Dilemma in adult correctional settings: To treat or not to treat and if so, how? In G. Cooke (Ed.), *The role of the forensic psychologist.* Springfield, Ill.: Thomas.

Kaslow, F. W., & Abrams, J. C. (1979). Differential diagnosis and treatment of the learning disabled child and his/her family. *Journal of Pediatric Psychology, 4*, 253–264.

Kasper, S., Wehr, T., Bartko, J., Gaist, P., & Rosenthal, N. (1989). Epidemiological findings of seasonal changes in mood and behavior. *Archives of General Psychiatry, 46*, 823–833.

Kasschau, R. A. (1969). Semantic satiation as a function of duration of repetition and initial meaning intensity. *Journal of Verbal Learning and Verbal Behavior, 8*, 36–42.

Kasschau, R. A., & Wertheimer, M. (1974). *Teaching psychology in secondary schools.* Washington, D.C.: American Psychological Association.

Kassin, S., Ellsworth, P., & Smith, V. (1989). The "general acceptance" of psychological research on eyewitness testimony: A survey of the experts. *American Psychologist, 44*, 1089–1098.

Kassin, S. M. (1985). Eyewitness identification: Retrospective self-awareness and the accuracy-confidence correlation. *Journal of Personality and Social Psychology, 49*, 878–893.

Kastenbaum, R. (1964). The structure and function of time perspective. *Journal of Psychological Researches* (India), *8*, 1–11.

Kastenbaum, R. (1977). Death and development through the life span. In H. Feifel (Ed.), *New meanings of death.* New York: McGraw-Hill.

Kastenbaum, R. (1978). Death, dying and bereavement in old age: New developments and their possible implications for psychosocial care. *Aged Care and Services Review, 1*, 1–10.

Kastenbaum, R. (1978). Gerontology's search for understanding. *The Gerontologist, 18*, 54–63.

Kastenbaum, R. (1985). Dying and death: A life-span approach. In J. Birren & K. Schaie (Eds.), *Handbook of the psychology of aging* (pp. 619–643). New York: Van Nostrand Reinhold.

Kastenbaum, R. (in press). Time course and time perspective in later life. In C. Eisdorfer (Ed.), *Annual review of gerontology & geriatrics,* Vol. 3. New York: Springer.

Kastenbaum, R., & Aisenberg, R. (1972). *The psychology of death.* New York: Springer.

Kastenbaum, R., & Aisenberg, R. (1976). *Psychology of death.* New York: Springer.

Kastenbaum, R., & Costa, P. T. (1977). Psychological perspectives on death. *Annual Review of Psychology, 28,* 225–249.

Kaszniak, A. W., Poon, L. W., & Riege, W. (1986). Assessing memory deficits: An information-processing approach. In L. W. Poon (Ed.), *Clinical memory assessment of older adults* (pp. 168–188). Washington, DC: American Psychological Association.

Katchadourian, H. A. (1977). *The biology of adolescence.* San Francisco: Freeman.

Katchen, M., & Sakheim, D. (1992). Satanic beliefs and practices. In *Out of Darkness.* New York: Lexington Books.

Katkin, E. S., & Murray, N. E. (1968). Instrumental conditioning of autonomically mediated behavior: Theoretical and methodological issues. *Psychological Bulletin, 70,* 52–68.

Katona, G. (1960). *The powerful consumer.* Hightstown, N.J.: McGraw-Hill.

Katona, G. (1980). *Essays on behavioral economics.* Ann Arbor, Mich.: University of Michigan Press.

Katona, G., & Strumpel, B. (1978). *A new economic era.* New York: Elsevier.

Katona, G., Strumpel, B., & Zahn, E. (1971). *Aspirations and affluence.* New York: McGraw-Hill.

Katz, A. H., & Bender, E. I. (1976). *The strength in us: Self-help groups in the modern world.* New York: Franklin-Watts.

Katz, B. (1952). The nerve impulse. *Scientific American,* November 61.

Katz, D. (1911). *Die Erscheinungsweisen der Farben und ihre Beeinflussung durch die individuelle Erfahrung.* Leipzig: Barth.

Katz, D. (1925). *Der Aufbau der Tastwelt.* Leipzig: Barth.

Katz, D. (1935/1930). *The world of colour.* London: Kegan Paul, Trench, Trubner.

Katz, D. (1950). *Gestalt psychology: Its nature and significance.* New York: Ronald Press.

Katz, D. (1952). Autobiography. In E. G. Boring et al. (Eds.), *A history of psychology in autobiography,* Vol. 4. Worcester, Mass.: Clark University Press.

Katz, D., & Kahn, R. L. (1966). *The social psychology of organizations.* New York: Wiley.

Katz, D., & Katz, R. (Eds.). (1972/1957). *Kleines Handbuch der Psychologie* Basel: Schwabe.

Katz, D., McCoby, N., Gurin, G., & Floor, L. (1951). *Productivity, supervision, and morale among railroad workers.* Ann Arbor, Mich.: Survey Research Center, University of Michigan.

Katz, D., McCoby, N., & Morse, N. C. (1950). *Productive supervision and morale in an office situation.* Ann Arbor, Mich.: Survey Center for Social Research, University of Michigan.

Katz, E., & Lazarsfeld, P. F. (1955). *Personal influence: The part played by people in the flow of mass communications.* Glencoe, Ill.: Free Press.

Katz, I., Glass, D. D., & Cohen, S. (1973). Ambivalence, guilt, and the scapegoating of minority group victims. *Journal of Experimental Social Psychology, 9,* 423–436.

Katz, J. (1972). *Experimentation with human beings.* New York: Russell Sage Foundation.

Katz, J. (Ed.). (1972). *Handbook of clinical audiology.* Baltimore, Md.: Williams & Wilkins.

Katz, J. L., Weiner, H., Gallagher, T. G., & Hellman, L. (1970). Stress, distress, and ego defenses. *Archives of General Psychiatry, 23,* 131–142.

Katz, L., Epps, E. G., & Axelson, L. J. (1964). Effect upon Negro digit-symbol performance of anticipated comparison with whites and with other Negroes. *Journal of Abnormal and Social Psychology, 69,* 77–83.

Katz, M. M. (1976). Behavioral change in the chronicity pattern of dementia in the institutionalized geriatric resident. *Journal of the American Geriatric Society, 24,* 522–528.

Katz, N. W., & Crawford, C. L. (1978). A little trance and a little skill. Presented at the meeting of the Society for Clinical and Experimental Hypnosis. Chapel Hill, N.C., October.

Katz, P. A. (1979). The development of female identity, *Sex Roles: A Journal of Research, 5,* 155–178.

Katz, S. E. (1976). *The effect of each of four instructional treatments on the learning of principles by children* (Technical Report no. 381). Madison, Wis.: Wisconsin Research and Development Center for Cognitive Learning.

Katzell, A., & Guzzo, R. A. (1983). Psychological approaches to productivity improvement. *American Psychologist, 38,* 468–472.

Kaufman, A. S. (1979). *Intelligence testing with the WISC-R.* New York: Wiley/Interscience.

Kaufman, A. S. (1981). The WISC-R and learning disabilities assessment: State of the art. *Journal of Learning Disabilities, 14,* 520–526.

Kaufman, A. S. (1990). Age and IQ across the adult lifespan. In A. S. Kaufman (Ed.), *Assessing adolescent and adult intelligence* (pp. 181–232). Boston: Allyn & Bacon.

Kaufmann, J. H. (1983). On the definitions and functions of dominance and territoriality. *Biological Reviews, 58,* 1–20.

Kaufman, K. F., & O'Leary, K. D. (1972). Reward, cost, and self-evaluation procedures for disruptive adolescents in a psychiatric hospital school. *Journal of Applied Behavior Analysis, 5,* 293–310.

Kaufman, L. (1974). *Sight and mind: An introduction to visual perception.* New York: Oxford University Press.

Kaufman, M. (1991). Post-Tarasoff legal developments and the mental health literature. *Bulletin of the Menninger Clinic, 55,* 308–322.

Kaufman, P. (1979). Family therapy with adolescent substance abusers. In E. Kaufman & P. Kaufman (Eds.). *Family therapy of drug and alcohol abuse.* New York: Gardner Press.

Kaufman, R., Delange, W., & Selfridge, B. (1977). A system approach to psychotherapy. *Psychotherapy: Theory, Research and Practice, 14,* 286–292.

Kaufmann-Hayoz, R., Kaufmann, F., & Lang, A. (1978). Der Einfluss von Reiz und Zustand auf den Wahrnehmungsprozess bei Säuglingen. *Schweizerische Zeitschrift für Psychologie, 37,* 1–21.

Kausler, D. F. (1990). Motivation, human aging, and cognitive performance. In J. Birren & K. Schaie (Eds.), *Handbook of the psychology of aging* (pp. 172–183). New York: Academic.

Kausler, D. H. (1974). *Psychology of verbal learning and memory.* New York: Academic Press.

Kausler, D. H. (1991). *Experimental psychology cognition and human aging* (2nd ed.). New York: Springer-Verlag.

Kauss, D. R. (1980). *Peak performance.* Englewood Cliffs, N.J.: Prentice-Hall.

Kavanagh, D. J., & Wilson, P. H. (1989). Prediction of outcome with a group version of cognitive therapy for depression. *Behaviour Research and Therapy, 27,* 333–347.

Kavanagh, T. E. (1979). A systems approach to school-community prevention education. Presented at the Annual Convention of the American Psychological Association, New York, N.Y.

Kay, G. G. (1990). Casting stones at integrity testing, not at integrity tests. *Forensic Reports, 4,*163–169.

Kaye, B. (1962). *Bringing up children in Ghana.* London: Allen & Unwin.

Kaye, G. (1990). A community organizer's perspective on citizen participation research and the researcher-practitioner relationship. *American Journal of Community Psychology, 18,* 151–158.

Kayton, L., & Borge, G. F. (1967). Birth order and the obsessive-compulsive character. *Archives of General Psychiatry, 17*(6), 751–754.

Kazdin, A. (1978). Behavior therapy: Evolution and expansion. *The Counseling Psychologist. 7,* 34–37.

Kazdin, A. E. (1975). Characteristics and trends in applied behavior analysis. *Journal of Applied Behavior Analysis, 8,* 332.

Kazdin, A. E. (1977). Research issues in covert conditioning. *Cognitive Therapy and Research, 1,* 45–58.

Kazdin, A. E. (1978). Covert modeling: The therapeutic application of imagined rehearsal. In J. L. Singer & K. S. Pope (Eds), (1978). *The power of human imagination.* New York: Plenum.

Kazdin, A. E. (1978). *History of behavior modification: Experimental foundations of contemporary research.* Baltimore, Md.: University Park Press.

Kazdin, A. E. (1980). *Research design in clinical psychology.* New York: Harper & Row.

Kazdin, A. E. (1982). History of behavior modification. In A. S. Bellack, M. S. Hersen, & A. E. Kazdin (Eds.), *International handbook of behavior modification and therapy* (pp. 3–32). New York: Plenum.

Kazdin, A. E. (1982). *Single-case research designs: Methods for clinical and applied settings.* New York: Oxford University Press.

Kazdin, A. E. (1982). Symptom substitution, generalization and response covariation: Implications for psychotherapy outcome. *Psychological Bulletin, 91,* 349–365.

Kazdin, A. E. (1985). *Treatment of antisocial behavior in children and adolescents.* Homewood, IL. Dorsey.

Kazdin, A. E. (1986). Comparative outcome studies of psychotherapy: Methodological issues and strategies. *Journal of Consulting and Clinical Psychology, 54,* 95–105

Kazdin, A. E. (1987). Treatment of antisocial behavior in children: Current status and future directions. *Psychological Bulletin, 102,* 187–203.

Kazdin, A. E. (1990). Psychotherapy for children and adolescents. *Annual Review of Psychology, 41,* 21–54.

Kazdin, A. E., Bass, D., Siegel, T., & Thomas, C. (1989). Cognitive-behavioral therapy and relationship therapy in the treatment of children referred for antisocial behavior. *Journal of Consulting and Clinical Psychology, 57,* 522–535.

Kazdin, A. E., Esveldt-Dawson, K., French, N. H., & Unis, A. S. (1987). Problem-solving skills training and relationship therapy in the treatment of antisocial child behavior. *Journal of Consulting and Clinical Psychology, 55,* 76–85.

Kazdin, A. E., & Smith, G. A. (1979). Covert conditioning: A review and evaluation. *Advances in Behavior Research and Therapy, 2,* 57–98.

Kazdin, A. E., & Wilson, G. T. (1978). *Evaluation of behavior therapy.* Cambridge, Mass.: Ballinger.

Kealey, D. (1988). *Explaining and predicting cross-cultural adjustment and effectiveness: A study of Canadian technical advisors overseas.* Unpublished doctoral dissertation, Queens University, Kingston, Ontario, Canada.

Keane, S. P., & Conger, J. C. (1981). The implications of communication development for social skills training. *Journal of Pediatric Psychology, 6,* 369–381.

Keane, T. M., Wolfe, J., & Taylor, K. I. (1987). Post-traumatic stress disorder: Evidence for diagnostic validity and methods of psychological assessment. *Journal of Clinical Psychology, 43,* 32–43.

Kearsley, R. B., & Siegel, I. E. (1979). *Infant at risk: Assessment of cognitive functioning.* Hillsdale, N.J.: Erlbaum.

Keats, C., & Davis, K. (1970). The dynamics of sexual behavior of college students. *Journal of Marriage and the Family, 32,* 390–399.

Keats, D. M. (1976). Psychologists in education. *Australian Psychologist, 11,* 33–42.

Keefe, F. J., Brown, G. K., Wallston, K. A., & Caldwell, D. S. (1989). Coping with rheumatoid arthritis pain: Catastrophizing as a maladaptive strategy. *Pain, 37,* 51–56.

Keefe, F. J., Caldwell, D. S., Queen, K. T., Gil, K. M., Martinez, S., Crisson, J. E., Ogden, W., & Nunley J. (1987). Pain coping strategies in osteoarthritis patients. *Journal of Consulting and Clinical Psychology, 55,* 208–212.

Keefe, F. J., Caldwell, D. S., Williams, D. A., Gil, K. M., Mitchell, D., Robertson, C., Martinez, S., Nunley, J., Beckham, J., & Helms, M. (1990). Pain coping skills training in the management of osteoarthritic knee pain: A comparative study. *Behavior Therapy, 21,* 49–62.

Keehn, J. D. (Ed.). (1979). *Psychopathology in animals.* New York: Academic.

Keehn, J. D., & Prothro, E. T. (1956). National preferences of university students from 23 nations. *Journal of Psychology, 42,* 283–294.

Keen, E. (1975). *A primer in phenomenological psychology.* New York: Holt, Rinehart & Winston.

Keenan, J. M., & Moore, R. E. (1979). Memory for images of concealed objects: A reexamination of Neisser and Kerr. *Journal of Experimental Psychology: Human Learning and Memory, 5,* 374–385.

Keenan, V., Kerr, W., & Sherman, W. (1951). Psychological climate and accidents in an automobile plant. *Journal of Applied Psychology, 35,* 108–111.

Keeney, B. P. (1983). *Aesthetic of change.* New York: Guilford.

Keeney, B. P., & Ross, J. M. (1983). Cybernetics of brief family therapy. *Journal of Marital and Family Therapy, 9*(4), 375–382.

Keeney, B. P., & Thomas, F. (1986). Cybernetic foundations of family therapy. In F. P. Peircy & D. H. Sprenkle (Eds.), *Family therapy sourcebook* (pp. 262–287).

Keeney, R. L., & Raiffa, H. (1976). *Decisions with multiple objectives: Preferences and value tradeoffs.* New York: Wiley.

Kefir, N. (1981). Impasse/priority therapy. In R. J. Corsini (Ed.), *Handbook of innovative psychotherapies.* New York: Wiley.

Kefir, N., & Corsini, R. J. (1974). Dispositional sets: A contribution to typology. *Journal of Individual Psychology, 30,* 163–178.

Kegel, A. (1952). Stress incontinence and genital relaxation. *Ciba Clinical Symposia,* February-March *4,* 35–41.

Kehnan, H. C. (1967). Human use of human subjects: The problem of deception in social psychological experiments. *Psychological Bulletin, 67,* 1–11.

Kehoe, E. J. (1988). A layered network model of associative learning: Learning-to-learn and configuration. *Psychological Review, 95,* 411–433.

Kehoe, E. J. (1989). Connectionist models of conditioning: A tutorial. *Journal of the Experimental Analysis of Behavior, 52,* 427–440.

Keilhacker, M. (1940). Sprechweise und Persönlichkeit. *Zeitschrift für Angewandte Psychologie, 59,* 215–241.

Keith-Spiegel, P. (1972). Early conceptions of humor: Varieties and issues. In J. H. Goldstein & P. E. McGhee (Eds.), *The psychology of humor: Theoretical perspectives and empirical issues.* New York: Academic Press.

Kell, B. L., & Mueller, W. J. (1966). *Impact and change: A study of counseling relationships.* New York: Appleton-Century-Crofts.

Kellam, S. G., Branch, J. D., Argalwal, K. C., & Ensminger, M. E. (1975). *Mental health and going to school.* Chicago: University of Chicago Press.

Keller, F. S. (1968). "Good-bye, teacher . . ." *Journal of Applied Behavior Analysis, 1,* 79–89.

Keller, F. S. (1977). *Summers and sabbaticals.* Champaign, Ill.: Research Press.

Keller, F. S., & Ribes-Inesta, E. (1974). *Behavior modification: Applications to education.* New York: Academic Press.

Keller, M. (1976). Problems with alcohol: An historical perspective. In W. J. Filstead, J. J. Rossi, & M. Keller, (Eds.), *Alcohol and alcohol problems: New thinking and new directions.* Cambridge, Mass.: Ballinger.

Keller, S. E., Weiss, J. M., Schleifer, S. J., Miller, N. E., & Stein, M. (1981). Suppression of immunity by stress: Effect of a graded series of stressors on lymphocyte stimulation in the rat. *Science, 213,* 1397–1400.

Keller, W. (1954). *Psychologie und Philosophie des Willens.* Basel: Reinhardt.

Kellerman, H. (1981). *Sleep disorders.* New York: Brunner/Mazel.

Kelley, D. B. (1988). Sexually dimorphic behaviors. *Annual Review of Neuroscience, 11,* 225–251.

Kelley, H., & Thibaut, J. (1978). *Interpersonal relations: A theory of interdependence,* New York: Wiley.

Kelley, H., & Thibaut, J. (1969). Group problem solving. In G. Lindzey & A. Aronson (Eds.), *Handbook of social psychology* (2nd ed.). Reading, Mass.: Addison-Wesley.

Kelley, H. H. (1950). The warm-cold variable in first impressions of persons. *Journal of personality, 18,* 431–439.

Kelley, H. H. (1967). Attribution theory in social psychology. In D. Levine (Ed.), *Nebraska Symposium on Motivation.* Lincoln, Neb.: University of Nebraska Press.

Kelley, H. H. (1968). Interpersonal accommodation. *American Psychologist, 23,* 399–410.

Kelley, H. H. (1972). Causal schemata and the attribution process. In E. E. Jones, D. E. Kanouse, H. H. Kelley, R. E. Nisbett, S. Valins, & B. Weiner (Eds.), *Attribution: Perceiving the causes of behavior.* New York: General Learning Press.

Kelley, H. H. (1973). The process of causal attribution. *American Psychologist, 28,* 107–128.

Kelley, H. H. (1979). *Personal relationships: Their structures and processes.* Hillsdale, N.J.: Erlbaum.

Kelley, H. H., & Thibaut, J. W. (1978). *Interpersonal relations: A theory of interdependence.* New York: Wiley.

Kellogg, W. N. (1961). *Porpoises and sonar.* Chicago: University of Chicago Press.

Kellogg, W. N. (1968). Communication and language in the home-raised chimpanzee. *Science, 162,* 423–438.

Kellogg, W. N., & Kellogg, L. A. (1933). *The ape and child; A study of environmental influence upon early behavior.* New York: McGraw-Hill.

Kelly, C. (1976). *Crime in the United States: Uniform crime reports.* Washington, DC: U.S. Government Printing Office.

Kelly, E. L. (1947). Clinical psychology. In *Current trends in psychology.* Pittsburgh, Pa.: University of Pittsburgh Press.

Kelly, E. L. (1954). An evaluation of the interview as a selection technique. In *Proceedings of the 1953 Invitational Conference on Testing Problems.* Princeton, N.J.: Educational Testing Service.

Kelly, E. L. (1954). Theory and technique of assessment. In *Annual review of psychology.* Stanford, Calif.: Annual Review.

Kelly, E. L. (1955). Consistency of the adult personality, *American Psychologist, 10,* 659–681.

Kelly, E. L. (1963; 1966). Alternate criteria in medical education and their correlates. In *Proceedings of the Invitational Conference on Testing Problems.* Princeton, N.J.: Educational Testing Service. Reprinted in A. Anastasi (Ed.), *Testing in the professions: Testing problems in perspective.* Washington, D.C.: American Council of Education.

Kelly, E. L. (1967). *Assessment of human characteristics.* Belmont, Calif.: Brooks/Cole.

Kelly, E. L., & Fiske, D. W. (1969). *The prediction of performance in clinical psychology.* Ann Arbor, Mich.: University of Michigan Press, 1951. Reprinted, New York: Greenwood Press.

Kelly, E. L., & Goldberg, L. R. (1959). Correlates of later performance and specialization in psychology. *Psychological Monographs, 73, (entire no. 482).*

Kelly, G. (1964). The language of hypothesis: Man's psychological instrument. *Journal of Individual Psychology, 20,* 137–152.

Kelly, G. A. (1936). State supported child guidance clinic for Kansas school children. *Kansas Teacher 43,* 6–7.

Kelly, G. A. (1955). *The psychology of personal constructs.* New York: Norton.

Kelly, G. A. (1969). In B. A. Maher (Ed.), *Clinical psychology and personality: The selected papers of George Kelly.* New York: Wiley.

Kelly, G. A. (1973). Fixed role therapy. In R. M. Jurjevich (Ed.), *Direct psychotherapy: 28 American originals.* Coral Gables, Fla.: University of Miami Press.

Kelly, G. A. (1980). A psychology of the optimal man. In A. W. Landfield & L. M. Leitner (Eds.), *Personal construct psychology: Psychotherapy and personality.* New York: Wiley.

Kelly, J. A. (1982). *Social-skills training.* New York: Springer.

Kelly, J. A., & Worell, J. (1977). New formulations of sex roles and androgyny: A critical review. *Journal of Consulting and Clinical Psychology, 45,* 1101–1115.

Kelly, J. B., & Wallerstein, J. S. (1976). The effects of parental divorce: Experiences of the child in early latency. *American Journal of Orthopsychiatry, 46,* 20–32.

Kelly, J. P., & Van Essen, D. C. (1974). Cell structure and function in the visual cortex of the cat. *Journal of Physiology, 238,* 515–547.

Kelly, L. G. (1968). *Description and measurement of bilingualism.* Presented at International Seminar on Bilingualism. Toronto: Moncton.

Kelly, O. E. (1975). *Make today count.* New York: Delacorte.

Kelly, P. H. (1977). Drug-induced motor behavior. In L. L. Iversen, S. D. Iversen, & S. H. Snyder. *Handbook of psychopharmacology,* Vol. 8. New York: Plenum.

Kelly, S. (1989). Stress responses of children to sexual abuse and ritualistic abuse in day care centers. *Journal of Interpersonal Violence, 4*(4), 502–513.

Kelly, T. A. (1990). The role of values in psychotherapy: A critical review of process and outcome effects. *Clinical Psychology Review, 10,* 171–186.

Kelman, H. (1973). Violence without moral restraint. *Journal of Social Issues, 29,* 25–61.

Kelman, H. C. (1958). Compliance, identification, and internalization. *Journal of Conflict Resolution, 2,* 51–60.

Kelman, H. C. (1963). The role of the group in the induction of therapeutic change. *International Journal of Group Psychotherapy, 13,* 339–432.

Kelman, H. C. (Ed.). (1965). *International behavior: A social psychological analysis.* New York: Holt.

Kelsey, M. T. (1974). *Gods, dreams, and revelations.* Minneapolis: Augsburg.

Kelso, J., & Stewart, M. A. (1986). Factors which predict the persistence of aggressive conduct disorder. *Journal of Child Psychology and Psychiatry, 27,* 77–86.

Kelsoe, J., Ginns, E., Egeland, J., Gerhard, D., Goldstein, A., Bale, S., Pauls, D., Long, R., Kidd, K., Conte, G., Housman, D., & Paul, S. (1989). Re-evaluation of the linkage relationship between chromosome 11p loci and the gene for bipolar affective disorder in the Old Order Amish. *Nature, 342,* 238–243.

Kempe, C. H. & Helfer, R. E. (Eds.). (1980). *The battered child* (3rd ed.). Chicago: University of Chicago Press.

Kempe, C. H., Silverman, B. F., Steele, B. F., Droegemueller, W., & Silver, H. K. (1962). The battered child syndrome. *Journal of the American Medical Association. 181,* 17–24.

Kempe, R. S., & Kempe, C. H. (1978). *Child abuse.* Cambridge, Mass.: Harvard University Press.

Kemper, T. D. (1978). *A social interactional theory of emotions.* New York: Wiley.

Kempler, W. (1973). Gestalt therapy. In R. J. Corsini (Ed.), *Current psychotherapies.* Itasca, Ill.: Peacock.

Kempler, W. (1974). *Principles of Gestalt family therapy.* Costa Mesa, Calif.: Kempler Institute.

Kempler, W. (1981). *Experiential psychotherapy within families.* New York: Brunner/Mazel.

Kemsley, F. F. (1950). Weight and height of a population in 1932. *American Eugenics, 15,* 161–183.

Kendall, M. G. (1955). *Rank correlation methods* (2nd ed.). New York: Hafner.

Kendall, P. C. (1977). On the efficacious use of verbal self-instruction procedures with children. *Cognitive Therapy and Research, 1,* 331–341.

Kendall, P. C. (1982). Cognitive processes and procedures in behavior therapy. In C. M. Franks, G. T. Wilson, P. C. Kendall, & K. D. Brownell (Eds.), *Annual review of behavior therapy: Theory and practice,* Vol. 8. New York: Guilford Press.

Kendall, P. C., & Hollon, S. D. (Eds.). (1979). *Cognitive behavioral interventions: Theory, research, and procedures.* New York: Academic Press.

Kendall, R. C., & Braswell, L. (1985). *Cognitive-behavioral therapy for impulsive children.* New York: Guilford.

Kendler, H. H. (1981). *Psychology: A science in conflict.* New York: Oxford University Press.

Kendler, H. H., Glasman, L. D., & Ward, J. W. (1972). Verbal-labeling and cuetraining in reversal-shift behavior. *Journal of Experimental Child Psychology, 13,* 195–209.

Kendler, H. H., & Kendler, T. S. (1970/1963). *Basic psychology.* New York: Appleton-Century-Crofts.

Kendler, H. H., & Kendler, T. S. (1962). Vertical and horizontal processes in problem solving. *Psychological Review, 69,* 1–16.

Kenrick, D. T., & Braver, S. L. (1982). Personality: Idiographic *and* nomothetic! A rejoinder. *Psychological Review, 89,* 182–186.

Kenrick, D. T., & Cialdini, R. B. (1977). Romantic attraction: Misattribution vs. reinforcement explanations. *Journal of personality and Social Psychology, 35,* 381–391.

Keniston, K. (1975). Prologue: Youth as a stage of life. In R. J. Havighurst, P. H. Dreyer, & K. J. Rehage (Eds.), *Youth: The 1974 yearbook of the National Society for the Study of Education.* Chicago: University of Chicago Press.

Kennedy, F. (1898). On the experimental investigation of memory. *Psychological Review, 5,* 477–554.

Kennedy, G. C. (1953). The role of depot fat in the hypothalamic control of food intake in the rat. *Proceedings of the Royal Society* (London), Series B, *140,* 578–592.

Kennedy, J. F. (1963). Message from the President of the United States relating to mental illness and mental retardation. Presented before 88th Congress, First Session, February 5. Washington, D.C.: House of Representatives, Document no. 58.

Kenny, D. I. (1955). The contingency of humor appreciation on the stimulus-confirmation of joke-ending expectations. *Journal of Abnormal and Social Psychology, 51,* 644–648.

Kent, G., & Gibbons, R. (1987). Self-efficacy and the control of anxious cognitions. *Journal of Behavior Therapy and Experimental Psychiatry, 18,* 33–40.

Kent, G. H., & Rosanoff, A. J. (1910). A study of association in insanity. *American Journal of Insanity, 67,* 37–96, 317–390.

Kent, M. W., & Rolf, J. E. (Eds.). (1979). *Primary prevention of psychopathology: Promoting social competence in children,* (Vol. 4). Hanover, N.H.: University Press of New England.

Keogh, C. B. (1975). *GROW: The program of growth to maturity* (abridged ed.). Sidney, Australia: GROW Publications.

Keogh, C. B. (1977). *GROW: Australia's mental health movement and the start of a world mental health community.* Sidney, Australia: GROW Publications.

Keogh, C. B. (1979). *GROW: Group organizers' and sponsors' manual.* Sidney, Australia: GROW Publications.

Keogh, C. B. (Ed.). (1975). *Readings for mental health.* Sidney, Australia: GROW Publications.

Kephart, N. C. (1960). *The slow learner in the classroom.* Columbus, Ohio: Merrill.

Kephart, W. (1967). Some correlates of romantic love. *Journal of Marriage and the Family, 29,* 470–479.

Kephart, W. M. (1961). *The family, society, and the individual.* Boston: Houghton Mifflin.

Keppel, G. (1982). *Design and analysis* (2nd ed.). Englewood Cliffs, N.J.: Prentice-Hall.

Kerckhoff, A. C. (1973/1970). A theory of hysterical contagion. In T. Shibutani (Ed.), *Human nature and collective behavior.* New Brunswick, N.J.: Transaction Books.

Kerckhoff, A. C., & Back, K. W. (1968). *The June Bug: A study of hysterical contagion.* New York: Appleton-Century-Crofts.

Kerckhoff, A. C., & Davis, K. E. (1962). Value consensus and need complementarity in mate selection. *American Sociological Review, 27*, 295–303.

Kerekjarto, M. (1968). The influence of experimenters on drug effects in normal subjects. In K. Rickels (Ed.), *Nonspecific factors in drug therapy*. Springfield, Ill.: Thomas.

Kerekjarto, M. (1974). *Medizinische Psychologie.* New York: Springer Verlag.

Kerekjarto, M. (1981). Zur Entstehung des Faches "Medizinische Psychologie" in der BRD und ihre Beziehung zur Psychosomatik. *Therapiewoche, 31*, 928–934.

Kerekjarto, M. (1982). Considerations for the impact of medical therapy on quality of life. In M. Baum, R. Kay, & H. Scheurlen (Eds.), *Clinical trials in early breast cancer*. Basel, Boston, Stuttgart: Birkhauser Verlag.

Kerlinger, F. (1972). The structure and content of social attitude referents: A preliminary study. *Educational and Psychological Measurement, 32*, 613–630.

Kerlinger, F. N. (1973). *Foundations of behavioral research* (2nd ed.). New York: Holt, Rinehart & Winston.

Kerlinger, F. N. (1986). *Foundations of behavioral research* (3rd ed). New York: Holt, Rinehart, and Winston.

Kernberg, O. F. (1968). The therapy of patients with borderline personality organization. *International Journal of Psychoanalysis, 49*, 600–619.

Kernberg, O. F. (1975). *Borderline conditions and pathological narcissism.* New York: Aronson.

Kernberg, O. F. et al. (1972). Psychotherapy and psychoanalysis: Final report of the Menninger Foundation's Psychotherapy Research Project. *Bulletin of the Menninger Clinic, 36* (1, 2).

Kerr, M. (1981). Family systems theory and therapy. In A. Gurman & D. Kniskern (Eds.), *Handbook of family therapy*. New York: Brunner/Mazel.

Kerr, N. H. (1983). The role of vision in "visual imagery" experiments: Evidence from the congenitally blind. *Journal of Experimental Psychology: General, 112*, 265–277.

Kerr, N. H., & Neisser, U. (1983). Mental images of concealed objects: New evidence. *Journal of Experimental Psychology: Learning, Memory, and Cognition, 9*, 212–221.

Kerr, N. L. (1981). Effects of prior juror experience on juror behavior. *Basic and Applied Social Psychology, 2*, 175–193.

Kerr, S. (1977). Substitutes for leadership: Their meaning and measurement. *Organizational Behavior and Human Performance, 8*, 135–143.

Kersh, B. Y. (1962). The motivating effect of learning by directed discovery. *Journal of Educational Psychology, 53*, 65–71.

Kershaw, D., & Fair, J. (1976). *The New Jersey income maintenance experiment.* New York: Seminar Press.

Kessel, E. L. (1955). The mating activities of balloon flies. *Systematic Zoology, 4*, 97–104.

Kessen, W. (1979). The American child and other cultural inventions. *American Psychologist, 34*, 815–820.

Kessler, R. C., & McLeod, J. D. (1985). Social support and mental health in community samples. In S. Cohen & S. L. Syme (Eds.), *Social support and health* (pp. 219–240). Orlando: Academic.

Kessler, R. C., Price, R. H., & Wortman, C. B. (1985). Social factors in psychopathology: Stress, social support, and coping processes. *Annual Review of Psychology, 36*, 531–572.

Kessler, S. (1975). *The American way of divorce: Prescriptions for change.* Chicago: Nelson-Hall.

Kessler, S., & Moos, R. (1970). The XYY karyotype and criminality: A review. *Journal of Psychiatric Research, 7*, 153–170.

Ketterer, R. F. (1981). *Consultation and education in mental health* Beverly Hills, CA: Sage.

Kety, S. (1972). Toward hypotheses for a biochemical component in the vulnerability to schizophrenia. *Seminars in Psychiatry, 4*, 233–258.

Kety, S. (1976). Genetic aspects of schizophrenia. *Psychiatric Annals, 6*, 11–32.

Kety, S., Rosenthal, D., Wender, P., Schulsinger, F., & Jacobsen, B. (1978). The biologic and adoptive families of adopted individuals who became schizophrenic: Prevalence of mental illness and other characteristics. In L. C. Wynne, R. L. Cromwell, & S. Matthysse (Eds.), *The nature of schizophrenia: New approaches to research and treatment.* New York: Wiley.

Kety, S., & Schmidt, C. (1948). The nitrous oxide method for the quantitative determination of cerebral blood flow in man: Theory, procedure, and normal values. *Journal of Clinical Investigation, 27*, 476.

Kety, S. S. (1979). Disorders of the human brain. In *The brain.* San Francisco: Freeman.

Keutzer, C. S. (1982). Archetypes, synchronicity, and the theory of formative causation. *Journal of Analytic Psychology, 27*, 255–262.

Kevane, E. (1964). *Augustine the educator.* Westminster, Md.: Newman Press.

Kevles, D. J. (1985). *In the name of eugenics: Genetics and the uses of human heredity.* New York: Knopf.

Key, W. B. (1973). *Subliminal seduction.* Englewood Cliffs, NJ: Signet.

Key, W. B. (1976). *Media sexploitation.* Englewood Cliffs, NJ: Signet.

Key, W. B. (1980). *The clam-plate orgy.* Englewood Cliffs, NJ: Signet.

Keyes, K. (1975/1972). *Handbook to higher consciousness.* St. Mary, Ky.: Cornucopia Institute.

Keys, A., Brožek, J., Henschel, A., Mickelsen, O., & Taylor, H. L. (1950). *The biology of human starvation.* Minneapolis, Minn.: University of Minnesota Press.

Keys, C. B., & Frank, S. (1987). Community psychology and the study of organizations: A reciprocal relationship. *American Journal of Community Psychology, 15*, 239–251.

Khajavi, F., Broskowski, A., & Mermis, W. (1972). Team consultation to complex organizations. Some emerging issues for mental health workers. *Hospital and Community Psychiatry. 23*(8), 235–239.

Khanna, R., & Khanna, N. (1991). Delusions of substitution and diabetes mellitus. *International Journal of Psychiatry, 21*(1), 105–112.

Khatena, J., & Torrance, E. P. (1976). *Khatena-Torrance Creative Perception Inventory.* Chicago: Stoelting.

Kidd, G. A. (1971). *The employment of psychologists in Australia.* Sydney, Australia: Sydney University Appointments Board.

Kidd, J. M. (1982). *Self and occupational concepts in occupational preferences and entry into work.* Unpublished doctoral dissertation, National Institute for Careers Education and Counselling and the Hatfield Polytechnic, Hertford and Hatfield, England.

Kidder, L. H. (1981). *Research methods in social relations* (4th ed.). New York: Holt, Rinehart & Winston.

Kidder, L. H., & Stewart, V. M. (1975). *The psychology of intergroup relations.* New York: McGraw-Hill.

Kidwell, J. S. (1978). Adolescents' perceptions of parental affect: An investigation of only-children vs. first-borns and the effect of spacing. *Journal of Population, 1*(2), 148–166.

Kiecolt-Glaser, J. K., Fisher, L. D., Ogrocki, P., Stout, J. C., Speecher, C. E., & Glaser, R. (1987). Marital quality, marital disruption, and immune function. *Psychosomatic Medicine, 49*, 13–34.

Kiecolt-Glaser, J. K., Glaser, R., Williger, D., Stout, J., Messick, G., Sheppard, S., Ricker, D., Romisher, S. C., Briner, W., Bonnell, G., & Donnerberg, R. (1985). Psychosocial enhancement of immunocompetence in a geriatric population. *Health Psychology, 4,* 25–41.

Kiefhaber, A., & Goldbeck, W. B. (1979). *Employee mental wellness programs: A WBGH survey.* Washington, D. C.: Washington Business Group on Health.

Kiell, N. (1965). *Psychiatry and psychology in the visual arts and aesthetics, a bibliography.* Madison, Wis.: University of Wisconsin Press.

Kientzle, M. J. (1949). Properties of learning curves under varied distributions of practice. *Journal of Experimental Psychology, 36,* 187–211.

Kierkegaard, S. (1954). *Fear and trembling and the sickness unto death* (W. Lowrie, Trans.). Garden City, NY: Doubleday.

Kierkegaard, S. (1959). *Either-or.* (D. Stevenson & L. Stevenson, Trans.). Garden City, NY: Doubleday.

Kierkegaard, S. A. (1944). *The concept of dread* (2 vols.). Princeton, N.J.: Princeton University Press.

Kierkegaard, S. A. (1957/1944). *Either/or* (2nd ed.). Princeton, N.J.: Princeton University Press.

Kiesler, C. A. (1991). Homelessness and public policy priorities. *American Psychologist, 46,* 1245–1252.

Kiesler, C. A. (1993). Mental health policy and the psychiatric impatient care of children. *Applied and Preventative Psychology, 2,* 91–99.

Kiesler, C. A., & Pallak, M. S. (1976). Arousal properties of dissonance manipulations. *Psychological Bulletin, 83,* 1014—1025.

Kiesler, D. J. (1966). Some myths of psychotherapy research and the search for a paradigm. *Psychological Bulletin, 65,* 110–136.

Kiesler, D. J. (1973). *The process of psychotherapy.* Chicago: Aldine.

Kiesow, F. (1928). *The feeling-tone of sensation.* Worcester, Mass.: Clark University Press.

Kiesow, F. (1930). Autobiography. In *History of psychology in autobiography.* Worcester, Mass.: Clark University Press.

Kiesow, F., & Gemelli, A. (Eds.). (1920). *Archivio Italiano di Psicologia,* July *1*(1).

Kietz, G. (1948). *Der Ausdrucksgehalt des menschlichen Ganges.* Leipzig: Barth.

Kiev, A. (1968). *Curandismo: Mexican-American folk psychiatry.* New York: Free Press.

Kiev, A. (1972). *Transcultural psychiatry.* New York: Free Press.

Kiev, A. (1974). *Somatic manifestations of depressive disorders.* Princeton, N.J.: Excerpta Medica.

Kiev, A. (1976). Crisis intervention and suicide prevention. In E. S. Shneidman (Ed.), *Suicidology: Contemporary developments.* New York: Grune & Stratton.

Kifer, R. E., Lewis, M. A., Green, D. R., & Phillips, E. L. (1974). Training predelinquent youths and their parents to negotiate conflict situations. *Journal of Applied Behavior Analysis, 7,* 357–364.

Kilbey, M. M., & Asghar, K. (Eds.). (1992). *Methodological issues in epidemiological, prevention, and treatment research on drug-exposed women and their children* (Research Monograph 117). Rockville, MD: National Institute on Drug Abuse.

Kilbride, P., & Kilbride, J. (1974). Socio-cultural factors and the early manifestations of sociability among Baganda infants. *Ethos, 2,* 296–314.

Kilbride, P. L., Robbins, M. C., & Freeman, R. B. (1968). Pictorial depth perception and education among Baganda schoolchildren. *Perceptual and Motor Skills, 26,* 1116–1118.

Kilbridge, M. D. (1960). Reduced costs through job enrichment: A case. *The Journal of Business, 33,* 357–362.

Killilea, M. (1976). Mutual help organizations: Interpretations in the literature. In C. Caplan & M. Killilea (Eds.), *Support systems and mutual help: Multidisciplinary explorations.* New York: Grune & Stratton.

Kilmer, J. (1913). Trees. *Poetry: A Magazine of Verse,* August.

Kilpatrick, F. P. (Ed.). *Explorations in transactional psychology.* New York: New York University Press.

Kim, H. K., & Cha, J. H. (1966). *Experimental designs in psychology and education.* Seoul, Korea: Paeyongsa.

Kim, R. S., Poling, J., & Ascher, L. M. (1991). An introduction to research on the clinical efficacy of paradoxical intention. In G. E. Weeks (Ed.), *Promoting change through paradoxical therapy* (pp. 216–251). New York: Brunner/Mazel.

Kimble, G. A. (1953). Psychology as a science. *The Scientific Monthly, 77,* 156–160.

Kimble, G. A. (1956). *Principles of general psychology.* New York: Ronald Press.

Kimble, G. A. (1961). *Hilgard and Marquis' conditioning and learning.* New York: Appleton-Century-Crofts.

Kimble, G. A. (1967). *Foundations of conditioning and learning.* New York: Appleton-Century-Crofts.

Kimble, G. A., Garmezy, N., & Zigler, E. (1980). *Principles of general psychology.* New York: Wiley.

Kimmel, D. C. (1980). *Adulthood and aging* (2nd ed.). New York: Wiley.

Kimmel, D. C., Price, K. F., & Walker, J. W. (1978). Retirement choice and retirement satisfaction. *Journal of Gerontology. 33*(4), 575–585.

Kimmel, H. D. (1981). The relevance of experimental studies to clinical applications of biofeedback. *Biofeedback and Self-Regulation, 6,* 263–271.

Kimmel, H. D., & Kimmel, E. (1970). An instrumental conditioning method for the treatment of enuresis. *Journal of Behavior Therapy and Experimenta Psychiatry, 1,* 121–123.

Kimmel, H. D., van Olst, E. H., & Orlebeke, J. F. (Eds.). (1979). *The orienting reflex in humans.* Hillsdale, N.J.: Erlbaum.

Kimmel, M. S. (1987). Rethinking "masculinity": New directions in research. In M. S. Klmmel (Ed.), *Changing men: New directions in research on men and masculinity* (pp. 9–26). Newbury Park, CA: Sage.

Kimura, D. (1961). Cerebral dominance and the perception of verbal stimuli. *Canadian Journal of Psychology, 15,* 166–171.

Kimura, D. (1979). Neuromotor mechanisms in the evolution of human communication. In H. D. Steklis & M. J. Raleigh (Eds.), *Neurobiology of social communication in primates. New York: Academic Press.*

Kimura, D. (1979). The asymmetry of aesthetic preference and effects of exposure to aesthetic stimuli: Social emotional, and cognitive factors. In B. A. Maher (Ed.), *Progress in experimental personality research,* Vol. 9. New York: Academic Press.

Kimura, D. (1981). Neural mechanisms in manual signing. *Sign Language Studies, 33,* 291–312.

Kimura, D. (1982). Left-hemisphere control of oral and brachial movements and their relation to communication. *Philosophical Transactions of the Royal Society, 298,* 135–149.

Kimura, D. (in press). Sex differences in cerebral organization for speech and praxic functions. *Canadian Journal of Psychology.*

Kimura, D., & Durnford, M. (1974). Normal studies on the function of the right hemisphere in vision. In S. J. Dimond & J. G. Beaumont

(Eds.), *Hemisphere function in the human brain*. London: Elek, P.

Kinecni, V. J. (1979). Determinants of aesthetic preference and effects of exposure to aesthetic stimuli: Social, emotional, and cognitive factors. In B. A. Maher (Ed.), *Progress in experimental personality research*, Vol. 9. New York: Academic Press.

King C. W., & Tigert, D. (1971). *Attitude research reaches new heights*. Chicago: American Marketing Association.

King, G. F., Armitage, S. G, & Tilton, J. R. (1960). A therapeutic approach to schizophrenics of extreme pathology: An operant-interpersonal method. *Journal of Abnormal and Social Psychology, 61*, 276–286.

King, H. F. (1967). In K. Soddy & M. C. Kidson, Men in middle life. London: Tavistock Press.

King, K. J. (1971). Education and ethnicity in the Rift Valley: Maasai, Kipsigis and Kikuyu in the school system. Institute for Development Studies, Staff Paper no 113, Nairobi.

King, L. S. (1982). *Medical thinking: A historical preface*. Princeton, NJ: Princeton University Press.

King, N. J. (1980). The therapeutic utility of abbreviated progressive relaxation: A critical review with implications for clinical progress. In M. Hersen & A. Bellack (Eds.), *Progress in behavior modification*. New York: Academic Press.

King, S. H., & Henry, A. F. (1955). Aggression and cardiovascular reactions related to parental control over behavior. *Journal of Abnormal and Social Psychology, 50*, 206–210.

Kingsbury, S. (1992a). Some effects of prescribing privileges. *American Psychologist, 47*, 426–427.

Kingsbury, S. (1992b). Some effects of prescribing privileges. *Professional Psychology: Research and Practice, 23*, 3–5.

Kingslinger, H. S. (1966). Application of projective techniques in personnel psychology since 1940. *Psychology Bulletin, 66*, 134—149.

Kinsbourne, M. (1973). Criteria for diagnosis: Minimal brain dysfunction as neurodevelopmental lag. *Annals of the New York Academy of Sciences, 265*, 268–273.

Kinsbourne, M. (1981). Single-channel theory. In D. Holding (Ed.), *Human skills*. New York: Wiley.

Kinsbourne, M. (1982). Hemispheric specialization and the growth of human understanding. *American Psychologist, 37*, 411–420.

Kinsbourne, M. (1989). The laboratory stimulant medication assessment in the light of models of attention deficit disorder. In L. M. Bloomingdale & J. Swanson, (Eds.), *Attention deficit disorder: Current concepts and emerging trends in attentional and behavioral disorders of childhood* (pp. 113–123). New York: Pergamon.

Kinsbourne, M., & Caplan, P. J. (1979). *Children's learning and attention problems*. Boston: Little, Brown.

Kinsbourne, M., & Hiscock, M. (1978). Cerebral lateralization and cognitive development. In J. S. Chall (Ed.), *Education and the brain*. Part 2 of *77th Yearbook of the National Society for the Study of Education*. Chicago: University of Chicago Press.

Kinsbourne, M., & Swanson, J. M. (1979). Models of hyperactivity: Implications for diagnosis and treatment. In R. L. Trites (Ed.), *Hyperactivity in children: Etiology, measurement, and treatment implications* (pp. 1–20). Baltimore: University Park Press.

Kinscherff, R., & Barnum, R. (1992). Child forensic evaluation and claims of ritual abuse or satanic cult activity: A critical analysis. In *Out of Darkness*. New York: Lexington Books.

Kinsey, A. C., Pomeroy, W. B., & Martin, C. E. (1948). *Sexual behavior in the human male*. Philadelphia, Pa.: Saunders.

Kinsey, A. C., Pomeroy, W. B., Martin, C. E., & Gebhard, P. H. (1953). *Sexual behavior in the human female*. Philadelphia, Pa.: Saunders.

Kintsch, W. (1974). *The representation of meaning in memory*. Hillsdale, NJ: Erlbaum.

Kinzel, A. (1970). Body-buffer zones in violent prisoners. *American Journal of Psychiatry, 127*, 59–64.

Kipnis, D. (1976). *The powerholders*. Chicago: University of Chicago Press.

Kirchhoff, R. (1957). *Allgemeine Eindruckslehre*. Göttingen, West Germany: Hogrefe.

Kiresuk, T., & Sherman, R. (1968). Goal attainment scaling: A general method of evaluating comprehensive community mental health programs. *Community Mental Health Journal 4*, 443–445.

Kirk, R. E. (1968). *Experimental design: Procedures for the behavioral sciences*. Belmont, Calif.: Brooks/Cole.

Kirk, R. E. (Ed.) (1972). *Statistical issues: A reader for the behavioral sciences*. Monterey, Calif.: Brooks/Cole.

Kirk, S. A. (1977). Specific learning disabilities. *Journal of Clinical Child Psychology*, 23–26.

Kirkpatrick, C. (1936). The construction of a belief pattern scale for measuring attitudes toward feminism. *Journal of Social Psychology, 7*, 421–437.

Kirkpatrick, C. A. (1959). *Advertising: Mass communication in marketing*. Boston: Houghton Mifflin.

Kirsch, I. (1985). Response expectancy as a determinant of experience and behavior. *American Psychologist, 40*, 1189–1202.

Kirschenbaum, H. (1975). Recent research in values education. In J. Cholvat (Ed.), *Values education: Theory/practice/problems/prospects*. Waterloo, Ont.: Wilfrid Laurier University Press.

Kirschner, N. (1976). Generalization of behaviorally oriented assertive training. *The Psychological Record, 26*, 117–125.

Kirsh, D. (1991). Foundations of AI: The big issues. *Artificial Intelligence, 47*, 3–30.

Kirwan, J. R., Chaput de Saintonge, D. M., Joyce, C. R. B., & Currey, H. L. F. (1983). Clinical judgment in rheumatoid arthritis: II. Judging "current disease activity" in clinical practice. *Annals of Rheumatic Diseases, 42*, 648–651.

Kish, G. B. (1970). Reduced cognitive innovation and stimulous-seeking in chronic schizophrenics. *Journal or Clinical Psychology, 26*, 170–174.

Kish, G. B., & Donnenwerth, M. (1972). Sex differences in the correlates of stimulus seeking. *Journal of Consulting and Clinical Psychology, 38*, 42–49.

Kish, L. (1965). *Survey sampling*. New York: Wiley.

Kitchell, M., Okimoto, J., Barnes, J., Veith, R., & Raskind, M. (1980). Depression in the geriatric medical inpatient. *The Gerontologist, 20*, (pt. II), 140.

Kitson, G. C., & Sussman, M. B. (1982). Marital complaints, demographic characteristics, and symptoms of mental distress in divorce. *Journal of Marriage and the Family, 44*, 87–102.

Kitson, T. M. (1977). The disulfiram-ethanol reaction: A review. *Journal of Studies on Alcohol 38*, 96–113.

Kittrie, N. N. (1971). *The right to be different: Deviance and enforced therapy*. Baltimore, Md.: Johns Hopkins University Press.

Klaczynski, P. A., & Cummings, E. M. (1989). Responding to anger in aggressive and nonaggressive boys: A research note. *Journal of Child Psychology and Psychiatry, 30*, 309–314.

Klages, L. (1910). *Die Principien der Charakterologie*. Leipzig: Barth.

Klages, L. (1916). *Handschrift und Charakter*. Leipzig: Barth.

Klages, L. (1929–1932). *Der Geist als Widersacher der Seele* (3 vols.). Leipzig: Barth.

Klapp, D. E. (1972). *Currents of unrest*. New York: Holt, Rinehart & Winston.

Klapp, O. (1978). *Opening and closing*. Cambridge, England: Cambridge University Press.

Klass, E. T. (1981). A cognitive analysis of guilt over assertion. *Cognitive Therapy and Research, 5*, 283–297.

Klatzky, R. L. (1980). *Human memory; structure and processes* (2d ed.). San Francisco: Freeman.

Klaus, M. H., Leger, T. & Trause, M. (Eds.). (1975). *Maternal attachment and mothering disorders: A round table*. Johnson & Johnson.

Klausmeier, H. J. (1976). Conceptual development during the school years. In J. R. Levin & V. L. Allen (Eds.), *Cognitive learning in children: Theories and strategies*. New York: Academic Press.

Klausmeier, H. J. (1979). Organization of cognitive abilities based on CLD theory. In H. J. Klausmeier et al. (Eds.), *Cognitive learning and development: Information-processing and Piagetian perspectives*. Cambridge, Mass.: Ballinger.

Klausmeier, H. J. (1979). The CLD perspective in retrospect. In H. J. Klausmeier et al. (Eds.), *Cognitive learning and development: Information-processing and Piagetian perspectives*. Cambridge, Mass.: Ballinger.

Klausmeier, II. J. (1980). *Learning and teaching process concepts: A strategy for testing applications of theory*. New York: Academic Press.

Klausmeier, H. J., & Allen, P. S. (1978). *Cognitive development of children and youth: A longitudinal study*. New York: Academic Press.

Klausmeier, H. J., & Feldman, K. V. (1975). Effects of a definition and a varying number of examples and nonexamples on concept attainment. *Journal of Educational Psychology, 67*, 174–178.

Klausmeier, H. J., Ghatala, E. S., & Frayer, D. A. (1974). *Conceptual learning and development: A cognitive view*. New York: Academic Press.

Klausmeier, H. J., & Meinke, D. L. (1968). Concept attainment as a function of instructions concerning the stimulus material, a strategy, and a principle for securing information. *Journal of Educational Psychology, 59*, 215–222.

Klausmeier, H. J., & Ripple, R. E. (1971). *Learning and human abilities*. New York: Harper & Row.

Klausner, S. Z. (1965). *The quest for self-control*. New York: Free Press.

Klauss, R., & Bass, B. M. (1982). *Interpersonal communication styles in organizations*. New York: Academic Press.

Klavetter, R. E., & Mogar, R. E. (1967). Peak experiences: Investigation of their relationship to psychedelic therapy and self-actualization. *Journal of Humanistic Psychology, 7*, 171–177.

Klavetter, R. E., & Mogar, R. E. (1967). Stability and internal consistency of a measure of self-actualization, *Psychological Reports, 21*, 422–424.

Klawans, H. L. (1978). Levodopa-induced psychosis. *Psychiatric Annals, 8*, 19–29.

Klawans, H. L., Goetz, C. G., Paulson, G. W., & Barbeau, A. (1980). Levodopa and presymptomatic detection of Huntington's disease—Eight-year follow-up. *New England Journal of Medicine, 302*, 1090.

Klawans, H. L., Goetz, C. L., & Perlik, S. (1980). Tardive dyskinesia: Review and update. *American Journal of Psychiatry, 137*, 900–908.

Klawans, H. L., Jr., Paulson, C. G., Riegel, S. P., & Barbeau, A. (1972). Use of L-dopa in the detection of presymptomatic Huntington's chorea. *New England Journal of Medicine, 286*, 1332.

Kleck, R. E., Vaughan, R. C., Cartwright-Smith, J., Vaughan, K. B., Colby, C. Z., & Lanzetta, J. T. (1976). Effects of being observed on expressive, subjective, and physiological responses to painful stimuli. *Journal of Personality and Social Psychology, 34*, 1211–1218.

Klein, D. B. (1970). *A history of scientific psychology: Its origins and philosophical backgrounds*. New York: Basic Books.

Klein, D.C., & Seligman, M. E. P. (1976). Reversal of performance deficits and perceptual deficits in learned helplessness and depression. *Journal of Abnormal Psychology, 85*, 11–26.

Klein, D. F., & Gittelman-Klein, R. (Eds.) (1976). *Progress in psychiatric drug treatment.*, Vol. 2. New York: Brunner/Mazel.

Klein, G. (1958). Cognitive control and motivation. In G. Lindzey (Ed.), *Assessment of human motives*. New York: Rinehart.

Klein, G. S. (1968). Psychoanalysis: Ego psychology. In *International encyclopedia of social sciences*. New York: Macmillan.

Klein, G. S. (1976). *Psychoanalytic theory: An exploration of essentials*. New York: International Universities Press.

Klein, M. (1932). *The psychoanalysis of children*. London: Hogarth Press.

Klein, M. (1952). On the theory of anxiety and guilt (1948). In J. Riviere (Ed.), *Developments in psychoanalysis*. London: Hogarth Press.

Klein, M. (1976). Feminist concepts of therapy outcome. *Psychotherapy Theory, Research and Practice, 13*, (1), 89–95.

Klein, M., Mathiew, P., Kiesler, D., & Gendlin, E. (1970). *The Experiencing scale: A research and training manual*. Madison, Wis.: University of Wisconsin, Bureau of Audio-visual Instruction.

Klein, S. B. (1972). Adrenal-pituitary influence in reactivation of avoidance memory in the rat after intermediate intervals. *Journal of Comparative and Physiological Psychology, 79*, 341–349.

Klein, S. B., & Spear, N. E. (1970). Forgetting by the rat after intermediate intervals ("Kamin effect") as retrieval failure. *Journal of Comparative and Physiological Psychology, 71*, 165–170.

Klein, Z., & Eshel, Y. (1980). *Integrating Jerusalem schools*. New York: Academic Press.

Kleiner, K. A., & Banks, M. S. (1987). Stimulus energy does not account for 2-month-olds' face preferences. *Journal of Experimental Psychology: Human Perception and Performance, 13*, 594–600.

Kleinke, C. L. (1975). *First impressions: The psychology of encountering others*. Englewood Cliffs, N.J.: Prentice-Hall (Spectrum).

Kleinke, C. L. (1978). *Self-perception*. San Francisco: Freeman.

Kleinman, A., & Good, B. (Eds.). (1986). *Culture and depression*. Berkeley: University of California Press.

Kleinmuntz, B. (1972). *Computer in personality assessment*. Morristown, N.J. : General Learning Press.

Kleinsmith, L. J. & Kaplan, S. (1963). Paired-associate learning as a function of arousal and interpolated interval. *Journal of Experimental Psychology, 65*, 190–193.

Kleist, K. (1933). *Gehirnpathologie (Pathology of the brain)*. Leipzig: Barth.

Kleitman, N. (1963). *Sleep and wakefulness* (2nd ed.). Chicago: University of Chicago Press.

Klemer, R. H., & Smith, R. M. (1975). *Klemer's marriage and family relationships* (2nd ed.) New York: Harper & Row.

Klemm, O. (1914). *Geschichte der Psychologie*. Leipzig: Teubner.

Klemm, W. R. (1971). Neurophysiologic studies of the immobility reflex ("animal hypnosis"). In S. Ehrenpreis & O. C. Solnitzky (Eds.), *Neurosciences research*, Vol. 4. New York: Academic Press.

Kligerman, C. (1957). A psychoanalytic study of the *Confessions* of St. Augustine. *Journal of the American Psychoanalytic Association, 5*, 469–484.

Kline, M. V. (1958). *Freud and hypnosis*. New York: Julian Press/Institute for Research in Hypnosis Publication Society.

Kline, P. (1972). *Fact and fantasy in Freudian theory*. London: Methuen.

Klineberg, O. (1935). *Race differences*, New York: Harper.

Klineberg, O. (1938). Emotional expression in Chinese literature. *Journal of Abnormal and Social Psychology, 33*, 517–520.

Klineberg, O. (1954/1940). *Social psychology*, New York: Holt, Rinehart & Winston.

Klineberg, O. (1964). *The human dimension in international relations*, New York: Holt Rinehart & Winston.

Klineberg, O., & Zavalloni, M. (1969). *Nationalism and tribalism among African students. A study of social identity*. Paris: Mouton.

Kling, J. W., & Riggs, L. A. (Eds.), (1971). *Woodworth and Schlosberg's experimental psychology*, New York: Holt, Rinehart & Winston.

Klingberg, F. L. (1941). Studies in measurement of the relations between sovereign states. *Psychometrika, 6*, 335–352.

Klinger, E. (1978). Models of normal conscious flow. In K. S. Pope & J. L. Singer (Eds.), *The stream of consciousness: Scientific investigations into the flow of human experience*. New York: Plenum.

Klinger, E. (1980). Therapy and the flow of thought. In J. E. Shorr, G. E. Sobel, P. Robin, & J. A. Connella (Eds.), *Imagery: Its many dimensions and applications*. New York: Plenum.

Klintworth, G. K. (1962). A pair of male monozygotic twins discordant for homosexuality. *Journal of Nervous and Mental Disease, 135*, 113–125.

Klir, G. (1969). An approach to general systems theory. New York: Van Nostrand Reinhold.

Klopf, A. H. (1988). A neuronal model of classical conditioning. *Psychobiology, 16*, 85–125.

Klopfer, B. (1922). *The psychology of inhibition*. Unpublished doctoral dissertation, University of Munich.

Klopfer, B. & Davidson, H. H. (1962/1942). *The Rorschach technique: An introductory manual*. New York: Harcourt, Brace & World.

Klopfer, B. et al. (1954). *Developments in the Rorschach technique*, Vols. I, II, III. New York: Harcourt, Brace & World.

Klopfer, P. H. (1971). Mother love: What turns it on? *American Scientist, 59*, 404–407.

Klopfer, P. H. (1974). *An introduction to animal behavior: Ethology's first century*. Englewood Cliffs, N.J.: Prentice-Hall.

Klopfer, W. G. (1960). *The psychological report*. New York: Grune & Stratton.

Klopfer, W. G. (1973). The short history of projective techniques. *Journal of the History of the Behavioral Sciences, 9*(1), 60–65.

Klopfer, W. G., & Taulbee, E. S. (1976). Projective tests. *Annual Review of Psychology, 27*, 543–569.

Klosterhalfen, S., & Klosterhalfen, W. (1985). Conditioned taste aversion and traditional learning. *Psychological Research, 47*, 71–94.

Kluckhohn, C. (1952). *Culture: A critical review of concept and definitions*. Cambridge, Mass.: Harvard University Press.

Kluckhohn, C. & Murray, H. A., (1949). Personality under social catastrophe, *Personality in nature society*, New York: Knopf.

Kluft, R. (1989). Reflections on allegations of ritual abuse. *Dissociation, 2*(4).

Klugman, S. F. (1956). Retention of affectively toned verbal material by normals and neurotics. *Journal of Abnormal and Social Psychology, 53*, 321–327.

Klump, C. S. (1974). *The Stanton pre-employment survey*. Chicago: Stanton Analysis Center.

Klüver, H. (1928). *Mescal: The divine plant and its psychological effects*. London: Kegan Paul.

Klüver, H. (1933). *Behavior mechanisms in monkeys*. Chicago: University of Chicago Press.

Kluver, H., & Bucy, P. C. (1937). "Psychic blindness" and other symptoms following bilateral temporal lobectomy in rhesus monkeys. *American Journal of Physiology, 119*, 352–353.

Knapp, L. (1978). *Non-verbal communication in human interaction*. New York: Holt, Rinehart & Winston.

Knapp, P. H. (1948). Emotional aspects of hearing loss. *Psychosomatic Medicine, 10*, 203–222.

Knapp, P. H., & Nemetz, S. J. (1960). Acute bronchial asthma: Concomitant depression with excitement and varied antecedent patterns in 406 attacks. *Psychosomatic Medicine, 22*, 42.

Knapp, T. J. (1976). A functional analysis of gambling behavior. In W. R. Eadington (Ed.), *Gambling and society*. Springfield, Ill.: Thomas.

Knaus, W. A., Wagner, D. P., & Portnoi, V. A., (1982). Intensive treatment for the elderly. *Journal of the American Medical Association, 247*(23), 3185–3186.

Knecht v. *Gillman*, 488 F.2d 1136 (8th Cir. 1973).

Knight, R. P. (1953). Borderline states. Bulletin of the Menninger Clinic, *17*, 1–12.

Knights, R. M., & Bakker, D. (1976). *The neuropsychology of learning disorders*. Baltimore, Md.: University Park Press.

Knitzer, J. (1980). Advocacy and community psychology. In M. S. Gibbs, J. R. Lachenmeyer, & J. Sigal (Eds.), *Community psychology: Theoretical and empirical approaches* (pp. 293–309). New York: Gardner.

Knobloch, H. & Pasamanick, B. (Eds.) (1974). *Gesell and Amatruda's developmental diagnosis: The evaluation and management of normal and abnormal neuropsychologic development in infancy and early childhood* (3rd ed.). New York: Harper & Row.

Knowles, E. S. (1976). Searching for motivations in risk-taking and gambling. In W. R. Eadington (Ed.), *Gambling and society*. Springfield, Ill.: Thomas.

Knowles, J. H. (1977). Responsibility in the individual. *Daedalus, 106*, 57–80.

Knowles, J. H. (1977). The responsibility of the individual. In J. H. Knowles (Ed.), *Doing better and feeling worse: Health in the United States*. New York: Norton.

Knowles, M. (1978/1973). *The adult learner: A neglected species* (2nd ed.). Houston, Tex.: Gulf.

Knowlton, B. J., Ramus, S. J., & Squire, L. R. (1992). Intact artificial grammar learning in amnesia: Dissociation of classification learning and explicit memory for specific instances. *Psychological Science, 3*, 172–179.

Knox, A. B. (1977). *Adult development and learning*. San Francisco: Jossey-Bass.

Ko, Y., & Sun, L. (1965). Ordinal position and the behavior of visiting the child guidance clinic. *Acta Psychologia Taiwanica*, 1016–1062.

Ko, Y-H. (1973). Birth order and psychological needs. *Acta Psychologca Taiwanica* (Taipei), *15*, 68–80.

Kobasa, S. C. (1979). Stressful life events, personality, and health: An inquiry into hardiness. *Journal of Personality and Social Psychology, 37*, 1–11.

Kobasa, S. C. (1982). Commitment and coping in stress resistance among lawyers. *Journal of Personality and Social Psychology, 42*, 707–717.

Kobasa, S. C., & Maddi, S. R. (1977). Existential personality theory. In R. J. Corsini (Ed.), *Current personality theories*. Itasca, Ill.: Peacock.

Kobasa, S. C., Maddi, S. R., & Courington, S. (1981). Personality and constitution as mediators of the stress-illness relationship. *Journal of Personality and Social Psychology, 42*, 168–177.

Kobasa, S. C., Maddi, S. R., & Puccetti, M. (1982). Personality and exercise as buffers in the stress-illness relationship. *Journal of Behavioral Medicine, 4*, 391–404.

Kobasa, S. C., Maddi, S. R., Puccetti, M., & Zola, M. (1986). Relative effectiveness of hardiness exercise and social support as resources against illness. *Journal of Psychosomatic Research, 29*, 525–533.

Kobenhavn. The history of psychology in Denmark. In K. B. Madsen (Ed.), *Encyclopedia of psychology* (2nd ed., pp. 350–356). Copenhagen.

Koch, H. L. (1966). Some physical characteristics of twins and matched singletons. In H. Koch (Ed.), *Twins and twin relationships*. Chicago: University of Chicago Press.

Koch, J. L. A. (1891). *Die psychopathischen Minderwertigkeiten*. Ravensburg, West Germany: Maier.

Koch, S. (1956). Behavior as "intrinsically" regulated: Work notes towards a pretheory of phenomena called "motivational." In M. R. Jones (Ed.), *Current theory and research in motivation*, Vol. 4. Lincoln, Neb.: University of Nebraska Press.

Koch, S. (1959). Epilogue. In S. Koch (Ed.), *Psychology: A study of a science*, Vol. 3. New York: McGraw-Hill.

Koch, S. (1961). Psychological science versus the science-humanism antinomy: Intimations of a significant science of man. *American Psychologist, 16*, 629–639.

Koch, S. (1964). Psychology and emerging conceptions of knowledge as unitary. In T. W. Wann (Ed.), *Behaviorism and phenomenology: Contrasting bases for modern psychology*. Chicago: University of Chicago Press.

Koch, S. (1964). Psychology and emerging conceptions of knowledge. In *Behaviorism and phenomenology* (pp. 1–41). Chicago: University of Chicago Press.

Koch, S. (1969a). Psychology cannot be a coherent science. *Psychology Today*, March, *14*, 64, 66–68.

Koch, S. (1969b). Value properties: Their significance for psychology, axiology, and science. In M. Grene (Ed.), *The anatomy of knowledge*. London: Routledge & Kegan Paul.

Koch, S. (1971). Reflections on the state of psychology. *Social Research, 37*, 669–709.

Koch, S. (1971). The image of man implicit in encounter group theory. *Journal of Humanistic Psychology, 11*(2), 109–128.

Koch, S. (1973). Theory and experiment in psychology. *Social Research, 40*, 691–707.

Koch, S. (1976). Language communities, search cells, and the psychological studies. In W. J. Arnold (Ed.), *Nebraska Symposium on Motivation*, Vol. 23. Lincoln, Neb.: University of Nebraska Press.

Koch, S. (1981). The nature and limits of psychological knowledge: Lessons of a century *qua* science. *American Psychologist, 36*, 257–269.

Koch, S., Clark L. Hull. (1954). Section 1 of *Modern learning theory*. New York: Appleton-Century-Crofts.

Koch, S. (Ed.). (1959–1963). *Psychology: A study of a science* (6 vols.). New York: McGraw-Hill.

Koch, S., & Leary, D. E. (1985). *A century of psychology as science*. New York: McGraw-Hill.

Koch, S., & Leary, D. E. (Eds.) (1983). *A century of psychology as science: Retrospections and assessments*. New York: McGraw-Hill.

Koch, W. R., & Dodd, B. C. (1989). An investigation of procedures for computerized adaptive testing using partial credit scoring. *Applied Measurement in Education, 2*, 335–357.

Koch, W. R., Dodd, B. G., & Fitzpatrick, S. J. (1990). Computerized adaptive measurement of attitudes. *Measurement and Evaluation in Counseling and Development, 23*, 20–30.

Kochan, T. A. (1980). *Collective bargaining and industrial relations*. Homewood, Ill.: Irwin.

Kockelmans, J. J. (1967). *Edmund Husserl's phenomenological psychology: A historicocritical study*. Pittsburgh, Pa.: Duquesne University Press.

Koehler, D. (1992). Explanation, imagination, and confidence in judgment. *Psychological Bulletin, 110*, 499–519.

Koenig, K. (1981). *The Camphill movement*, Whitby, UK: Camphill.

Koestler, A. (1964). *The act of creation*. New York: Macmillan.

Koff, D. R. (1967). Education and employment perspective of Kenya primary pupils. In J. R. Sheffield (Ed.), *Education, employment and rural development*. Nairobi. East African Publishing House.

Koff, J. (in press). Current psychiatric practice in China. *The Journal of Training and Practice in Professional Psychology*.

Koffer, K. B., Coulson, G., & Hammond, L. (1976). Verbal conditioning without awareness using a highly discriminable, monetary reinforcer. *Psychological Reports, 39*, 11–14.

Koffka, K. (1912). *Zur Analyse der Vorstellungen und ihrer Gesetze*. Leipzig: Quelle & Meyer.

Koffka, K. (1924/1921). *The growth of the mind: An introduction to child-psychology*. London: Paul, Trench, Trubner.

Koffka, K. (1925/1921). *Die Grundlagen der psychischen Entwicklung*. Osterwieck: Zickfeld.

Koffka, K. (1935). *Principles of gestalt psychology*. New York: Harcourt, Brace.

Koffka, K. (1963/1935). *Principles of Gestalt psychology*. New York: Harcourt, Brace & World.

Kogan, J. (Ed.) (1980). *Gestalt therapy resources* (3rd ed.). Berkeley, Calif.: Transformations Press.

Kogan, N. (1971). Educational implications of cognitive styles. In G. Lesser (Ed.), *Psychological and educational practice*. Glenview, Ill.: Scott, Foresman.

Kogan, N., & Wallach, M. (1964). *Risk taking: A study in cognition and personality*. New York: Holt.

Kohl, H. (1967). *36 children*. New York: Signet Books/New American Library.

Kohl, H. (1969). *The open classroom*. New York: Vintage Books/Random House.

Kohlberg, L. (1958). The development of modes of moral thinking and choice in the years ten to sixteen. Unpublished doctoral dissertation, University of Chicago.

Kohlberg, L. (1964). Development of moral character and moral ideal-ogy. In M. L. Hoffman & L. W. Hoffman (Eds.), *Review of child development research*, Vol. 1. New York: Russell Sage Foundation.

Kohlberg, L. (1966). A cognitive-developmental analysis of children's sex-role concepts and attitudes. In E. E. Maccoby (Ed.), *The development of sex differences*. Stanford, Calif.: Stanford University Press.

Kohlberg, L. (1968). Early education—A cognitive-developmental view. *Child Development, 39*(4), 1013–1062.

Kohlberg, L. (1968). Moral development. In *International encyclopedia of the social sciences*. New York: Crowell, Collier/Macmillan.

Kohlberg, L. (1968). The child as moral philosopher, *Psychology Today, 7*, 25–30.

Kohlberg, L. (1969). Stage and sequence: The cognitive-developmental approach to socialization. In D. A. Goslin (Ed.). *Handbook of socialization theory and research*. Chicago: Rand-McNally.

Kohlberg, L. (1969). *Stages in development of moral thought and action*. New York: Holt.

Kohlberg, L. (1971). Stages of moral development as a basis for moral education. In C. M. Beck, B. S. Crittenden, & E. V. Sullivan (Eds.), *Moral education: Interdisciplinary approaches*. Toronto: University of Toronto Press.

Kohlberg, L. (1973). Continuities in childhood and adult moral development revisited. In P. B. Baites & K. Warner Schaie (Eds.), *Life-span developmental psychology: Personality and socialization*. New York: Academic Press.

Kohlberg. L. (1976). Moral stages and moralization: The cognitive-developmental approach. In T. Lickona (Ed.), *Moral development and behavior*. New York: Holt, Rinehart, & Winston.

Kohlberg, L. (1978). Revisions in the theory and practice of moral development. In W. Damon (Ed.), *New directions for child development: Moral development*. San Francisco: Jossey-Bass.

Kohlberg, L. (1981). *Essays on moral development*. Vol. 1. *The philosophy of moral development: Moral stages and the idea of justice*. San Francisco: Harper & Row.

Kohlberg, L. (1981). *The philosophy of moral development*. San Francisco: Harper & Row.

Kohlberg, L. (1981). Vol. I: *Essays on moral development. The philosophy of moral development: Moral stages and the idea of justice*. New York: Harper & Row.

Kohlberg, L., & Gilligan, C. (1971). The adolescent as a philosopher. *Daedalus, 100*, 1051–1086.

Kohlberg, L. A. (1969). A cognitive-developmental approach to socialization. In D. Goslin (Ed.), *Handbook of socialization*. Chicago: Rand-McNally.

Köhler, I. (1964). *The formation and transformation of the perceptual world*. New York: International Universities Press.

Köhler, J. (1962). Experiments with goggles. *Scientific American, 206*, 62–72.

Köhler, W. (1920). *Die physischen Gestalten in Ruhe und im stationären Zustand*. Braunschweig: Vieweg.

Köhler, W. (1925). *The mentality of apes*. London: Routledge & Kegan Paul.

Köhler, W. (1927). *Intelligenzprüfungen an Anthropoiden*. Berlin: Abhandlungen der Kocniglich Prüssischen Akademie der Wissenschaften, 1917. Reprinted, Berlin: Springer.

Köhler, W. (1929). *Gestalt psychology*. New York: Liveright.

Köhler, W. (1938). *The place of value in a world of facts*. New York: Liveright.

Köhler, W. (1939). Simple structural functions in the chimpanzee and the chicken. In W. D. Ellis (Ed.), *A source book of Gestalt psychology*. New York: Harcourt Brace.

Köhler, W. (1940). *Dynamics in psychology*. New York: Liveright.

Köhler, W. (1944). Max Wertheimer 1880–1943. *The Psychologial Review, 51*, 143–146.

Köhler, W. (1947/1938/1929). *Gestalt psychology*. New York: Liveright.

Köhler, W. (1959). Gestalt psychology today. *American Psychologist, 14*, 727–734.

Köhler, W. (1969). *The task of Gestalt psychology*. Princeton, N.J.: Princeton University Press.

Köhler, W. (1971). Psychological remarks on some questions of anthropology. In W. Köhler, *The selected papers*. New York: Liveright.

Köhler, W. (1971). *The selected papers*. New York: Liveright.

Köhler, W. (1976/1917). *The mentality of apes*. New York: Liveright.

Köhler, W., & Wallach, H. (1944). Figural after-effects: An investigation of visual processes. *Proceedings of the American Philosophical Society, 88*, 269–357.

Kohler, W. & Wallach, H. (1944). Figural after-effects. *Proceedings of the American Philosophical Society, 88*, 269–357.

Kohn, M. L. (1969). *Class and conformity*. Homewood, Ill.: Dorsey Press.

Kohn, M. L., & Schooler, C. (1973). Occupational experience and psychological functioning: An assessment of reciprocal effects. *American Sociological Review, 38*, 97–118.

Kohn, M. L., & Schooler, C. (1978). The reciprocal effects of substantive complexity of work and intellectual flexibility: A longitudinal assessment. *American Journal of Sociology, 84*, 24–52.

Kohnken, G., & Maass, A. (1988). Eyewitness testimony: False alarms on biased instruction? *Journal of Applied Psychology, 73*, 363–370.

Kohonen, T. (1977). *Associative memory: A system-theoretical approach*. Berlin: Springer-Verlag.

Kohonen, T. (1989). *Self-organization and associative memory* (3rd ed.). Berlin: Springer-Verlag.

Kohs, S. C. (1920). The block-design tests. *Journal of Experimental Psychology, 3*, 357–376.

Kohs, S. C. (1923). *Intelligence measurement: A psychological and statistical study based upon the block design tests*. New York: Macmillan.

Kohut, H. (1971). *The analysis of the self*. New York: International Universities Press.

Kohut, H. (1977). *The restoration of the self*. New York: International Universities Press.

Kohut, S., & Range, D. (1979). *Classroom discipline*. Washington, D.C.: National Education Association.

Kokkinidis, L., & Anisman, H. (1980). Amphetamine models of paranoid schizophrenia: An overview and elaboration of animal experimentation. *Psychological Bulletin, 88*, 551–579.

Kolb, B., & Whishaw, I. Q. (1980). *Fundamentals of human neuropsychology*. San Francisco: Freeman.

Kolb, B., & Whishaw, I. Q. (1980). *Human neuropsychology*. San Francisco: Freeman.

Kolb, B., & Wishaw, I. Q. (1990). *Human neuropsychology* (3rd ed.). New York: Freeman.

Kolb, L. C. (1977). *Modern clinical psychiatry* (9th ed.). Philadelphia, Pa.: Saunders.

Koller, P. S., & Kaplan, R. M. (1978). A two-process theory of learned helplessness. *Journal of Personality and Social Psychology, 36*, 1177–1183.

Kolodny, R. C., Masters, W. H., & Johnson, V. E. (1979). *Textbook of sexual medicine*. Boston: Little, Brown.

Komaki, J., Collins, R. L., & Thoene, T. J. F. (1980). Behavioral measurement in business, industry, and government. *Behavioral Assessment, 2*, 103–123.

Komisaruk, B. R. (1967). Effects of local brain implants of progesterone on reproductive behavior in ring doves. *Journal of Comparative and Physiological Psychology, 64*, 219–224.

Kompara, D. R. (1980). Difficulties in the socialization process of stepparenting. *Family Relations, 29*, 69–73.

Konecni, V., & Doob, A. (1972). Catharsis through displacement of aggression. *Journal of Personality and Social Psychology, 23*, 379–387.

Konig, R. (1973). *A la mode: On the social psychology of fashion*. New York: Seabury Press.

Konorski, J. (1948). *Conditioned reflexes and neuron organization*. Cambridge, England: University of Cambridge Press.

Konorski, J. (1970/1967). *Integrative activity of the brain: An interdisciplinary approach*. Chicago: University of Chicago Press.

Konorski, J. (1974). Autobiography. In G. Lindzey (Ed.), *A history of psychology in autobiography*. Englewood Cliffs, N.J.: Prentice-Hall.

Konotey-Ahulu, F. L. D. (1974). The sickle cell diseases: Clinical manifestations including the "sickle crisis." *Archives of Internal Medicine, 133*, 611–619.

Koocher, G. (1979). Credentialing in psychology. Close encounters with competence? *American Psychologist, 34*, 696–702.

Koopmans, H. S. (1981). The role of the gastrointestinal tract in the satiation of hunger. In L. A. Chioffi, W. R. T. James, & T. B. Van Italie (Eds.), *The body weight regulatory system: Normal and disturbed mechanisms*. New York: Raven Press.

Kopp, C. B. (1989). Regulation of distress and negative emotions: A developmental view. *Developmental Psychology, 25*, 343–354.

Kopp, C. B., & Krakow, J. B. (Eds.) (1982). *The child, development in a social context*. Reading, Mass.: Addison-Wesley.

Kopp, R. (1982). On clarifying basic Adlerian concepts: A response to Maddi. *Individual Psychology: The Journal of Adlerian Theory Research and Practice, 38*, 80–89.

Kopp, S. B. (1971). *Guru: Metaphors from a psychotherapist*. Palo Alto, Calif.: Science & Behavior Books.

Kopp, S. B. (1972). *If you meet the Buddha on the road, kill him*. New York: Bantam.

Koppe, S. (1983). *Psykologiens udvikling og formidling i Denmark i perioden 1850–1980* [The development and dissemination of psychology in Denmark in the period 1850–1980]. Copenhagen.

Koppitz, E. M. (1963). *The Bender Gestalt test for young children*. New York: Grune & Stratton.

Koppitz, E. M. (1975). *The Bender-Gestalt test for young children: Research and application, 1963–1973*. New York: Grune & Stratton.

Kora, T., & Ohara, K. (1973). Morita therapy. *Psychology Today*, October, 63–68.

Korchin, S. J. (1976). *Modern clinical psychology*. New York: Basic Books.

Korchin, S. J., & Cowan, P. A. (1982). Ethical perspectives in clinical research. In P. C. Kendall & J. C. Butcher (Eds.), *Handbook of research methods in clinical psychology*. New York: Wiley.

Korchin, S. J., & Schuldberg, D. (1981). The future of clinical assessment. *American Psychologist, 36*, 1147–1158.

Korman, A. K. (1966). "Consideration," "initiating Structure" and organizational criteria. *Personnel Psychology, 18*, 349–360.

Korman, M. (1974). National conference on levels and patterns of professional training in psychology: The major themes. *American Psychologist, 29*, 441–449.

Korman, M. (Ed.). (1976). *Levels and patterns of professional training in psychology*. Washington, D.C.: American Psychological Association.

Kornadt, H.-J. (1966). Einflüsse der Erziehung auf die Aggressivitäts-Genese In: To Herrmann (Ed.), *Psychologie der Erziehungsstile*. Göttingen, West Germany: Hogrefe.

Kornadt, H.-J. (1974). Toward a motivation theory of aggression and aggression inhibition. In J. de Wit & W. W. Hartup (Eds.), *Determinants and origins of aggressive behavior*. The Hague, Paris: Mouton.

Kornadt, H.-J. (1975). *Lehrziele, Schulleistung und Leistungsbeurteilung*. Düsseldorf: Schwann.

Kornadt, H.-J. (1979). Psychological procedures as decision basis for admission to higher education. In W. Mitter (Ed.), *Hochschulzugang in Europa*. Weinheim: Beltz.

Kornadt, H.-J. (1982). *Aggressionsmotiv und Aggressionshemmung* (2 vols.). Bern: Huber.

Kornadt, H.-J. (Ed.). (1981). *Aggression und Frustration als psychologisches Problem*, Vol. 1. Darmstadt, West Germany: Wissenschaftliche Buchgesellschaft.

Kornadt, H.-J., Eckensberger, L., & Emminghaus, W. B. (1980). Cross-cultural research on motivation and its contribution to a general theory of motivation. In H. C. Triandis & W. Lonner (Eds.), *Handbook of cross-cultural psychology*, Vol. 2. Boston: Allyn & Bacon.

Kornadt, H.-J., Koebnick, H.-J., & Paul, S. (1968). *Situation und Entwicklungsprobleme des Schulsystems in Kenia*, Vol. 1. Stuttgart: Klett.

Kornadt, H.-J., & Voigt, E. (1970). *Situation und Entwicklungsprobleme des Schulsystems in Kenia*, Vol. 2. Stuttgart: Klett.

Kornadt, H.-J., & Zumkley, H. (1964). Thematische Apperzeptionsverfahren. In R. Heiss (Ed.), *Psychologische Diagnostik, Handbuch der Psychologie* Vol. 6. Göttingen, West Germany: Hogrefe.

Kornfield, J. (1977). *Living Buddhist masters*. Santa Cruz, Calif.: University Press.

Kornhauser, W. (1959). *The politics of mass society*. New York: Free Press.

Kornheiser, A. S. (1976). Adaptation to laterally displaced vision. A review. *Psychological Bulletin, 83*, 783–816.

Kornilov, K. N. (1921). *A theory of human reaction from the psychological point of view*, Moscow: Gosudarstevennce.

Kornilov, K. N. (1930). Psychology in the light of dialectical materialism. In C. Murchison (Ed.), *Psychologies of 1930*, Worcester, Mass.: Clark University Press.

Korones, S. B. (1990). The newborn: perinatal pediatrics. In R. L. Summitt (Ed.), *Comprehensive pediatrics* (pp. 262–372). St. Louis: Mosby.

Kortlandt, A. (1965). How do chimpanzees use weapons when fighting leopards? *Yearbook of the American Philosophical Society*, 327–332.

Koscielska, M. (1975). Clinical child psychology in Poland. *Journal of Clinical Child Psychology, 4*, 57–60.

Koščo, J. (1964). *The history of psychology*. I: *Historical introduction into the study of psychology*. Bratislava, Czechoslovakia: SAV.

Koščo, J. (1974). System and classification of psychological sciences. In Pardel, Koščo (Eds.), *Object and system of psychological sciences.* Bratislava, Czechoslovakia: SPN.

Koščo, J. (1980). The starting points, perspectives and problems of coordinated and integrated alternative of the system of guidance and counseling. *Jednotna škola, 32,* 524–541.

Koščo, J. (1983). *Development of psychological thinking and psychological science in Slovakia 1.* Bratislava, Czechoslovakia: RUK.

Koščo, J., et al. (1980). *Theory and praxis of counselling psychology.* Bratishva, Czechoslovakia: SPN.

Koslow, S., & Gaist, B. (1987). The measurement of neurotransmitters in depression. In A. J. Marsella, R. Hirschfeld, & M. Katz (Eds.), *The measurement of depression.* New York: Guilford.

Kosman, M. E., & Unna, K. R. (1968). Effects of chronic administration of amphetamine and other stimulants on behavior. *Clinical and Pharmacological Therapeutics, 9,* 246–254.

Koss, M. P., & Butcher, J. N. (1986). Research on brief psychotherapy. In S. L. Garfield & A. E. Bergin (Eds.), *Handbook of psychotherapy and behavior change* (3rd ed., pp. 627–670). New York: Wiley.

Koss, M. T., & Harvey, M. R. (1991). *The rape victim.* Newbury Park, CA: Sage.

Kossakowski, A. (1980). Psychology in the German Democratic Republic. *American Psychologist, 18,* 30–54.

Kosslyn, S. (1980). *Image and mind.* Cambridge, Mass.: Harvard University Press.

Kosslyn, S. M. (1976). Can imagery be distinguished from other forms of internal representation? Evidence from studies of information retrieval times. *Memory and Cognition, 4,* 291–297.

Kosslyn, S. M. (1983). *Ghosts in the mind's machine.* New York: Norton.

Kosslyn, S. M., Ball, T. M., & Reiser, B. J. (1978). Visual images preserve metric spatial information: Evidence from studies of image scanning. *Journal of Experimental Psychology: Human Perception and Performance, 4,* 1–20.

Kosslyn, S. M., Brunn, J., Cave, K., & Wallach, R. (1985). Individual differences in mental imagery ability: A computational analysis. *Cognition, 18,* 195–243.

Kosslyn, S. M., Pick, H. L., & Fairello, G. R. (1974). Cognitive maps in children and men. *Child Development, 45,* 707–716.

Kostrubala, T. (1977). *The joy of running.* New York: Pocket Books.

Kosugu, Y., & Tanaka, M. (1976). Parental deprivation, birth order and alcoholism. *Journal of Studies on Alcohol, 37,* 779.

Kotelchuck, M. (1976). The infant's relationship to the father: Experimental evidence. In M. Lamb (Ed.), *The role of the father in child development.* New York: Wiley.

Kotter, J. (1982). What effective general managers really do. *Harvard Business Review, 60*(6), 157–167.

Kotter, J. P. (1978). *Organizational dynamics: Diagnosis and intervention.* Reading, Mass.: Addison-Wesley.

Kovač, D. (1981). Psychology in Czechoslovakia: 1976–1980. *Studia Psychologica, 23,* 171–182.

Kovacs, A. (1988). Shall we take drugs? Just say no. *Psychotherapy Bulletin, 23,* 8–11.

Kovacs, M., & Beck, A. T. (1979). Cognitive-affective processes in depression. In C. E. Izard (Ed.), *Emotions in personality and psychopathology.* New York: Plenum.

Koziol, J. A., & Perlman, M. D. (1978). Combining independent chi-squared tests. *Journal of the American Statistical Association, 1978, 73,* 753–763.

Kozłowski, L. T., Herman, C. P., & Frecker, R. C. (1980). What researchers make of what cigarette smokers say: Filtering smokers' hot air. *Lancet,* March, 699–700.

Kozol, H., Boucher, R., & Garofalo, R. (1972). The diagnosis and treatment of dangerousness. *Crime and Delinquency, 18,* 371–392.

Kozol, J. (1967). *Death at an early age.* New York: Bantam Books.

Kozulin, A. (1977). Dva podkhoda k biologicheskomu analizu povedenija (Biological analysis of behavior: Two approaches). *Voprosy Psikhologii,* no. 2, 49–61.

Kozulin, A. (1977). Sistemnyj pokhod v izuchenii detskoj psikhiki (Systems-theory approach in child psychology). In I. Blauberg et al. (Eds.), *Sistemnye issledivanija (Systems research).* Moscow: Nauka.

Kozulin, A. (1982). Pavel Blonsky and Russian progressivism: The early years. *Studies in Soviet Thought, 24,* 11–21.

Kozulin, A. (1983). *Psychology in Utopia: The essays in the history of Soviet psychology.* Cambridge, Mass.: M.I.T. Press.

Kozulin, A., & Rootman, E. (1975). Reflection of information analysis of stimuli and motor preparedness in different components of sensory evoked potentials. *Agressologie, 16,* 131–135.

Kozuma, H. (1977). Summary of research on Individual Education. *Journal of Individual Psychology, 33,* 371–379.

Kraepelin, E. (1892). *Über die Beeinflussung einfacher psychischer Vorgaenge.* Jena, East Germany: Fischer.

Kraepelin, E. (1904/1899). *Psychiatrie. Ein Lehrbuch für Studierende und Aerzte. Achte, vollstandig umgearbeitete Auflage. II. Band. Klinische Psychiatrie.* Leipzig: J. Barth.

Kraepelin, E. (1907/1883). *Clinical psychiatry.* New York: Macmillan.

Krafft-Ebing, R. von. (1889). *Eine experimentelle Studie auf dem Gebiete des Hypnotismus.* Stuttgart.

Krafft-Ebing, R. von. (1904/1879–1850). *Textbook of insanity, based on clinical observations for practitioners and students of medicine.* Philadelphia, Pa.: Davis.

Krafft-Ebing, R. von. (1922/1892). *Psychopathia sexualis.* Brooklyn, N.Y.: Physician's & Surgeon's.

Kramer, E. (1958). *Art therapy in the children's community.* Springfield, Ill.: Thomas.

Kramer, E. (1971). *Art therapy with children.* New York: Schocken Books.

Kramer, H., & Sprenger, J. (1951). *Malleus maleficarum.* London: Pushkin Press.

Krantz, D. H., Atkinson, R. C., Lace, R. D., & Suppes, P. C. (1974). *Contemporary developments in mathematical psychology. Vol. 2: Measurement psychophysics, and neural information processing.* San Francisco: Freeman.

Krantz, D. H., Luce, R. D., & Tversky, A. (1971). *Foundations of measurement. I. Additive and polynomial representations.* New York: Academic Press.

Krashen, S. D. (1977). The left hemisphere. In M. C. Wittrock (Ed.), *The human brain.* Englewood Cliffs, N.J.: Prentice-Hall.

Krasner, L. (1958). Studies of the conditioning of verbal behavior. *Psychological Bulletin, 55,* 148–170.

Krasner, L. (1962). The therapist as a social reinforcement machine. In H. H. Strupp & L. Luborsky (Eds.), *Research in psychotherapy,* Vol. 2. Washington, D.C.: American Psychological Association.

Krasner, L. (1965). The behavioral scientists and social responsibility: No place to hide. *Journal of Social Issues, 21,* 9–30.

Krasner, L. (1969). Behavior modification—Values and training: The perspective of a psychologist. In C. M. Franks (Ed.), *Behavior therapy: Appraisal and status.* New York: McGraw-Hill.

Krasner, L. (1971). Behavior therapy. *Annual Review of Psychology, 22,* 483–532.

Krasner, L. (1982). Behavior therapy: On roots, contexts, and growth. In G. T. Wilson & C. M. Franks (Eds.), *Contemporary behavior therapy* (pp. 11–62). New York: Guilford.

Krasner, L. (1990). History and behavior modification. In A. S. Bellack, M. S. Hersen, & A. E. Kazdin (Eds.), *International handbook of behavior modification and therapy* (2nd ed., pp. 3–25). New York: Plenum.

Krasner, L. (Ed.) (1980). *Environmental design and human behavior: A psychology of the individual in society.* Elmsford, N.Y.: Pergamon Press.

Krasner, L., & Ullmann, L. P. (1965). *Research in behavior modification.* New York: Holt, Rinehart & Winston.

Krasner, L., & Houts, A. (1984). A study of the "value" systems of behavioral scientists. *American Psychologist, 39,* 850.

Krasner, L., & Ullmann, L. P. (1973). *Behavior influence and personality: The social matrix of human action.* New York: Holt, Rinehart & Winston.

Krathwohl, D. R., Bloom, B. S., & Masia, B. B. (1964). *Taxonomy of educational objectives. Handbook II: Affective domain.* New York: McKay.

Kratochwill, T. R., Alper, S., & Cancelli, A. A. (1980). Nondiscriminatory assessment: perspectives in psychology and special education. In L. Mann & D. A. Sabatino (Eds.), *The fourth review of special education.* New York: Grune & Stratton.

Kratochwill, T. R. (Ed.). (1978). *Single-subject research: Strategies for evaluating change.* New York: Academic Press.

Kraus, F. (1919, 1926). *Allgemeine und spezielle Pathologie der Person.* Leipzig: Thieme, Vol. 1; Vol. 2.

Krauskopf, C. E., Thorenson, W. W., & McAleer, C. A. (1973). Counseling psychology: The who, what, and where of our profession. *Journal of Counseling Psychology, 20,* 2370–2374.

Krauth, J., & Lienert, G. A. (1973). *Die Konfigurationsfrequenzanalyse und ihre Anwendungen in Psychologie und Medizin.* Freiburg, West Germany: Alber.

Krebs, J. R., & Davies, N. B. (1981). *An introduction to behavioral ecology.* Sunderland, Mass.: Sinauer.

Krebs, L. L. (1982). Summary of research on an Individual Education (IE) school. *Individual Psychology, 38,* 245–252.

Krech, D. (1932). "Hypotheses" in rats. *Psychological Review, 39,* 516–532.

Krech, D. (1962). Cortical localization of function. In L. Postman (Ed.), *Psychology in the making.* New York: Knopf.

Krech, D., Crutchfield, R. S., & Ballaehey, E. L. (1962). *Individual in society: A textbook of social psychology.* New York: McGraw-Hill.

Krech, D., Crutchfield, R. S, et al. (1969/1958). *Elements of psychology.* New York: Knopf.

Kreezer, G., & Dallenbach, K. M. (1927). Learning the relation of opposition. *American Journal of Psychology, 41,* 418—431.

Kreitler, H., & Kreitler, S. (1965). *Die Weltanschauliche Orientierung der Schizophrenen.* Munich, Basel: Reinhardt Verlag.

Kreitler, H., & Kreitler, S. (1967). *Die kognitive Orientierung des Kindes.* Munich, Basel: Reinhardt Verlag.

Kreitler, H., & Kreitler, S. (1972). *Psychology of the arts.* Durham, N.C.: Duke University.

Kreitler, H., & Kreitler, S. (1976). *Cognitive orientation and behavior.* New York: Springer.

Kreitler, H., & Kreitler, S. (1982). The theory of cognitive orientation: Widening the scope of behavior prediction. In B. A. Maher & W. B. Maher (Eds.), *Progress in experimental personality research,* Vol. 11. New York: Academic Press.

Kren, G. M., & Rappoport, L. H. (Eds.) (1976). *Varieties of psychohistory.* New York: Springer.

Krener, P., & Adelman, R. (1988). Parent salvage and parent sabotage in the care of chronically ill children. *American Journal of Diseases of Children, 142,* 945–951.

Krener, P., & Miller, F. S. (1989). Psychiatric response to HIV spectrum disease in children and adolescents. *Journal of the American Academy of Child and Adolescent Psychiatry, 28,* 596–605.

Kretschmer, E. (1918). *Der sensitive Beziehungswahn.* Berlin: Springer.

Kretschmer, E. (1925). *Physique and character.* London: Kegan Paul.

Kretschmer, E. (1925/1922). *Physique and character; An investigation of the nature of constitution and of the theory of temperament.* London: Paul, Trench, Trubner.

Kretschmer, E. (1926). *Hysteria.* New York: Nervous and Mental Disease.

Kretschmer, E. (1934/1922). *A text-book of medical psychology.* London: Oxford University Press.

Kreuger, W. C. F. (1929). The effect of overlearning on retention. *Journal of Experimental Psychology, 12,* 71–78.

Krieckhaus, E. E., & Wolf, G. (1968). Acquisition of sodium by rats: Interaction of innate mechanisms and latent learning. *Journal of Comparative and Physiological Psychology, 65,* 197–201.

Krieger, D. T., & Hughes, J. C. (Eds.) (1980). *Neuroendocrinology.* Sunderland, Mass.: Sinauer.

Kris, E. (1964/1952). *Psychoanalytic explorations in art.* New York: Schocken Books.

Krishnan, B. (1961). A review of contributions of Indian psychologists. In T. K. N. Menon (Ed.), *Recent trends in psychology.* Bombay: Orient Longmans.

Kritchevsky, S. E., Prescott, E., & Walling, L. (1969). *Planning environments for young children: Physical space.* Washington, D.C.: National Association for the Education of Young Children.

Kroeber, A. (1919). On the principle of order in civilization as exemplified by changes of fashion. *American Anthropologist, 21,* 235–263.

Kroeber, A., & Kluckhohn, C. (1952). Culture. *Papers of the Peabody Museum, 47,* no. 1.

Kroger, W. S. (1977). *Clinical and experimental hypnosis* (2d ed.). Philadelphia, Pa.: Lippincott.

Kron, L., Katz, J., Gorzynski, G., & Weiner, H. (1978). Hyperactivity in anorexia nervosa: A fundamental clinical feature. *Comprehensive Psychiatry, 19,* 433–440.

Kroodsma, D. E. (1984). Songs of the alder flycatcher (*Empidonax alnorum*) and willow flycatcher (*Empidonax trailii*) are innate. *The Auk, 101,* 13–34.

Krouse, J. H., & Krouse, H. J. (1981). Toward a multimodel theory of academic underachievement. *Educational Psychologist, 16,* 151–164.

Krout, M. H. (1935). Autistic gestures: an experimental study in symbolic movement. *Psychological Monographs, 46,* 1–126 (entire no. 208).

Krstić, K. Marko Marulić— (1964). The author of the term "psychology," *Acta Instituti Psychologic Universitatis Zagrabiensis, 35,* 7–15.

Krueger, F. (1928). *Das Wesen der Gefuehle.* Leipzig: Akademische Verlagsgesellschaft.

Krueger, F. (1939). *Otto Klemm und das Psychologische Institut der Universitaet Leipzig. Deutsche Seelenforschung in den letzten 3 Jahrzehnten.* Leipzig: Barth.

Krueger, F. (1948). *Die Lehre vom Ganzen.* Bern: Huber.

Kruger, D. (1981). *An introduction to phenomenological psychology.* Pittsburgh, Pa.: Duquesne University Press.

Kruglanski, A. W. (1975). The endogenous-exogenous partition in attribution theory. *Psychological Review, 82,* 387–406.

Kruglanski, A. W. (1975). The human subject in the psychology experiment: Fact and artifact. In L. Berkowitz (Ed.), *Advances in experimental social psychology,* Vol. 8. New York: Academic Press.

Kruglanski, A. W. (1976). On the paradigmatic objections to experimental psychology. *American Psychologist,* 655–663.

Kruglanski, A. W. (1979). Causal explanation, teleological explanation: On radical particularism in attribution theory. *Journal of Personality and Social Psychology, 37* 1447–1457.

Kruglanski, A. W. (1980). Lay epistemologic process and contents: Another look at attribution theory. *Psychological Review, 87,* 70–87.

Kruglanski, A. W. (1981). The epistemic approach in cognitive therapy. *International Journal of Psychology, 16,* 275–297.

Krugman, H. E. (1943). Affective response to music as a function of familiarity. *Journal of Abnormal and Social Psychology, 38,* 388–392.

Krugman, H. E. (1982). Repetition revisited: Application of the three exposure theory to corporate advertising. Presented at the 13th Attitude Research Conference of the American Marketing Association, February.

Krugman, H. E., & Hartley, E. L. (1960). The learning of tastes. *Public Opinion Quarterly, 24,* 621–631.

Krumboltz, J. D. (1966). *Revolution in counseling.* New York: Houghton Mifflin.

Krumboltz, J. D., Becker-Haven, J. F, & Burnett, K. F. (1979). Counseling psychology. *Annual Review of Psychology, 30,* 555–602.

Kruse, J. M., Overmier, J. B., Konz, W. A., & Rokke, E. (1983). Pavlovian CSs effects upon instrumental choice behavior are reinforcer specific. *Learning and Motivation, 14,* 165–181.

Kruskal, H. (1957). Historical notes on the Wilcoxon unpaired two sample test. *Journal of the American Statistical Association, 52,* 356–360.

Kruskal, J. B. (1964). Multidimensional scaling by optimizing goodness of fit to a nonmetric hypothesis. *Psychometrika, 29,* 1–27.

Kruskal, J. B. (1964b). Nonmetric multidimensional scaling: A numerical method. *Psychometrika, 29,* 115–129.

Kruskal, J. B., & Wish, M. (1978). *Multidimensional scaling.* Beverly Hills, Calif.: Sage Publications.

Krutetskii, V. A. (1976). *The psychology of mathematical abilities in schoolchildren.* J. Kilpatrick, I. Wirszup (Eds.). Chicago: University of Chicago Press.

Krutezki, W. A. (1974). Die Entwicklung Leninscher Ideen in der sowjetischen Psychologie der Fähigheiten. In W. A. Krutezki (Ed.), *Lenins philosophisches Erbe und Ergebnisse der sowjetischen Psychologie.* Berlin: Deutscher Verlag der Wissenschaften.

Kryder, C., & Strickland, S. P. (Eds.) (1977). *Americans and drug abuse: Report from the Aspen Conference.* New York: Aspen Institute for Humanistic Studies.

Krystal, H. (1968). The problem of the survivor. In H. Krystal (Ed.), *Massive psychic trauma.* New York: International Universities Press.

Krystal, H., & Niederland, W. G. (1968). Clinical observations on the survivor syndrome. In H. Krystal (Ed.), *Massive psychic trauma.* New York: International Universities Press.

Kuang, P. Z., Luo, S. D., & Liu, S. X. (1980). Thirty years of physiological psychology in China. *Acta Psychologica Sinica, 12,* 144–151.

Kübler-Ross, E. (1969). *On death and dying.* New York: Macmillan.

Kübler-Ross, E. (1974). *On death and dying.* New York: Macmillan.

Kubler-Ross, E. (1975). *Death: The final stage of growth.* Englewood Cliffs, N.J.: Prentice-Hall.

Kublin, H. (1966). Zen Buddhism. *Encyclopedia Americana, 29.*

Kubovy, M., & Pomerantz, J. R. (1981). *Perceptual organization.* Hillsdale, N.J.: Erlbaum.

Kučera, H., & Francis, W. N. (1967). *Computational analysis of present-day American English.* Providence, R.I.: Brown University Press.

Kuchera, M. (1987). The effectiveness of meditation techniques to reduce blood pressure levels: A metaanalysis. *Dissertation Abstracts International, 47,* 11-B) 4639.

Kuder, F. (1966). *Occupational Interest Survey.* Chicago: Science Research Associates.

Kuder, F. (1977). *Activity interests and occupational choice.* Chicago: Science Research Associates.

Kuder, F., & Diamond, E. E. (1979/1966). *General manual, Occupational Interest Survey* (2nd ed.). Chicago: Science Research Associates.

Kuder, G. F. (1939). The stability of preference items. *Journal of Social Psychology, 10,* 41–50.

Kuder, G. F. (1979). *Kuder Occupational Interest Survey, revised: General manual.* Chicago: Science Research Associates.

Kuehnle, J., & Spitzer, R. (1981). DSM-III classification of substance use disorders. In J. H. Lowinson & P. Ruiz (Eds.), *Substance abuse: Clinical problems and perspectives.* Baltimore, Md.: Williams & Wilkins.

Kuenzli, A. E. (Ed.) (1959). *The phenomenological problem.* New York: Harper.

Kuffler, S. W. (1953). Discharge patterns and functional organization of mammalian retina. *Journal of Neurophysiology, 16,* 37–68.

Kugelmass, S. (1976). Israel. In V. S. Sexton & H. Misiak (Eds.), *Psychology around the world.* Bakersfield, Calif.: Brooks.

Kuhlen, R. G. (1964). Developmental changes in motivation during the adult years. In J. E. Birren (Ed.), *Relations of development and aging.* Springfield, Ill.: Thomas.

Kuhlstrom, J. F., Barnhardt, T. M., & Tataryn, D. J. (1992). The psychological unconscious: Found, lost, and regained. *American Psychologist, 47,* 788–791.

Kuhn, T. S. (1961). The function of measurement in modern physical science. *Isis, 52,* 161–193.

Kuhn, T. S. (1970). *The structure of scientific revolution.* Chicago: University of Chicago Press.

Kuhn, T. S. (1970/1962). *The structure of scientific revolutions.* Chicago: University of Chicago Press.

Kuhn, T. S. (1977). Objectivity, value judgment, and theory choice. In T. S. Kuhn (Ed.), *The essential tension: Selected studies in scientific tradition and change.* Chicago: University of Chicago Press.

Kulic, J. A. (1973). *Undergraduate education in psychology.* Washington, D.C.: American Psychological Association.

Kulick, A. R., Pope, H. G., Jr., Keck, P. E., Jr., (1990). Lycanthropy and self-indentification. *Journal of Nervous and Mental Disease, 178*(2), 134–137.

Kulka, R. A., Schlenger, W. E., Fairbank, J. A., Hough, R. L., Jordon, B. K., Marmar, C. R., & Weiss, D. S. (1990). *Trauma and the Vietnam War generation.* New York: Brunner/Mazel.

Kulkarni, D., & Simon, H. A. (1988). The processes of scientific discovery: The strategy of experimentation. *Cognitive Science, 12,* 139–175.

Külpe, O. (1893). *Grundriss der Psychologie.* Leipzig: Engelmann.

Kulys, R., & Tobin, S. S. (1980). Interpreting the lack of future concerns among the elderly. *International Journal of Aging and Human Development, 11,* 111–126.

Kung, C., Chang, S-Y., Satow, Y, van Houten, J., & Hansma, H. (1975). Genetic dissection of behavior in *Paramecium. Science, 188,* 898–904.

Kunin, T. (1955). The construction of a new type of attitude measure. *Personnel Psychology, 8,* 65–78.

Kunst-Wilson, W. R., & Zajonc, R. B. (1980). Affective discrimination of stimuli that cannot be recognized. *Science, 207,* 557–558.

Kunz, H. (1946). *Die Anthropologische Bedeutung der Phantasie,* Vols. I & II. Basel: Verlag für Recht Gesellschaft.

Kupersmidt, J. B., & Cole, J. D. (1990). Preadolescent peer status, aggression, and school adjustment as predictors of externalizing problems in adolescence. *Child Development, 61,* 1350–1362.

Kurke, M. I. (1980). Forensic psychology: A threat and a response. *Professional Psychology, 11,* 72–77.

Kurke, M. I. (1990). Dishonesty, corruption, and white-collar crime: Predicting honesty and integrity in the workplace. *Forensic Reports, 4,* 149–162.

Kurcz, I. (1980). Psychology in Poland. *Australian Psychologist, 15,* 33–40.

Kurpius, D. J., Baker, R. D., & Thomas, I. D. (Eds.) (1977). *Supervision of applied training.* Westport, Conn.: Greenwood Press.

Kurtines, W., & Greif, E. B. (1974). The development of moral thought: Review and evaluation of Kohlberg's approach. *Psychological Bulletin, 81,* 453–470.

Kushler, M., & Daivdson, W. S. (1981). Community and organizational level change. In A. P. Goldstein, E. G. Carr, W. S. Davidson, & P. Wehr (Eds.), *In response to aggression.* New York: Pergamon Press.

Kushner, M. G., & Beitman, B. D. (1990). Panic attacks without fear: An overview. *Behavioral Research and Therapy, 28,* 469–479.

Kusyszyn, I. (1976). How gambling saved me from a misspent sabbatical. In W. R. Eadington (Ed.), *Gambling and society.* Springfield, Ill.: Thomas.

Kutash, I. L. (1978). Treating the victim of aggression. In I. L. Kutash, S. B. Kutash, & L. B. Schlesinger (Eds.), *Violence: Perspectives on murder and aggression.* San Francisco: Jossey-Bass.

Kutash, I. L. (1980). Prevention and equilibrium-disequilibrium theory. In I. L. Kutash & L. B. Schlesinger, (Eds.), *Handbook on stress and anxiety.* San Francisco: Jossey-Bass.

Kutash, I. L., Kutash, S. B., & Schlesinger, L. B. (Eds.) (1978). *Violence: Perspectives on murder and aggression.* San Francisco: Jossey-Bass.

Kutash, L., Schlesinger, L. B., et al. (Eds.) (1980). *Handbook on stress and anxiety.* San Francisco: Jossey-Bass.

Kutz, I., Borysenko, J., Come, S., & Benson, H. (1980). Paradoxical emetic response to antiemetic treatment in cancer patients. *New England Journal of Medicine, 303,* 1480.

Kvale, S. (Ed.). (1992). *Psychology and postmodernism.* London: Sage.

Kvaraceus, W. C. (1966). *Anxious youth: Dynamics of delinquency.* Columbus, Ohio: Merrill.

Kvols-Riedler, B., & K. (1981). *Pictorial mini life style: A method for democratic group psychotherapy.* Dubuque, Iowa: Kendall/Hunt.

Kyllonen, P. C., & Cristal, R. E. (1990). Reasoning ability is (little more than) working-memory capacity? *Intelligence, 14,* 389–433.

La Barba, R. C. (1981). *Foundations of developmental psychology.* New York: Academic Press.

La Barre, W. (1947). The cultural bases for emotions and gestures. *Journal of Personality, 16,* 49–68.

Laben, J. K., Kashgarian, M., Nessa, D. B., & Spencer, L. D. (1977). Reform from the inside: Mental health center evaluations of competency to stand trial. *Journal of Community Psychology, 5,* 52–62.

La Berge, D., & Samuels, S. J. (1974). Toward a theory of automatic information processing in reading. *Cognitive Psychology, 6,* 293–323.

Laboratory of Comparative Human Cognition. (1979). What's cultural about crosscultural psychology? *Annual Review of Psychology, 30,* 145–172.

Labov, W. (1970). The logic of non-standard English. In F. Williams (Ed.), *Language and poverty.* Chicago: Markham.

Lacan, J. (1968). *The language of the self: The function of languages in psychoanalysis.* New York: Delta.

Lacan, J. (1977/1966). *Ecrits: A selection.* New York: Norton.

Lacey, D. W. (in press). Industrial counseling psychologists—The professional road not taken. *The Counseling Psychologist.*

Lacey, J. I. (1956). The evaluation of autonomic responses; toward a general solution. *Annals of the New York Academy of Sciences, 67,* 123–163.

Lacey, J. I. (1959). Psychophysiological approaches to the evaluation of psychotherapeutic process and outcome. In E. A. Rubinstein & M. B. Parloff (Eds.), *Research in psychotherapy.* Washington, D.C.: American Psychological Association.

Lacey, J. I., & Dallenbach, K. M. (1939). Acquisition by children of the cause–effect relationship *American Journal of Psychology, 52,* 103–110.

Lacey, J. I., Kagan, J., Lacey, B. C., & Moss, H. A. (1963). The visceral level: Situational determinants and behavioral correlates of autonomic response patterns. In P. H. Knapp (Ed.), *Expression of the emotions in man.* New York: International Universities Press.

Lachenmeyer, J. R. (1980). Mental health consultation and programmatic change. In M. S. Gibbs, J. R. Lachenmeyer, & J. Sigal (Eds.), *Community psychology: Theoretical and empirical approaches* (pp. 267–292). New York: Gardner.

Lachman, R., Lachman, J. L., & Butterfield, E. C. (1979). *Cognitive psychology and information processing: An introduction.* Hillsdale, N.J.: Erlbaum.

Ladd, E. (1972). *Ideology in America: Change and response in a city, a suburb, and a small town.* New York: Norton.

Ladd, G. S., Price, J. M., & Hart, C. H. (1990). Preschooler's behavioral orientations and patterns of peer control: Predictive of peer status? In S. R. Asher & J. D. Cole (Eds.), *Peer rejection childhood* (pp. 90–115). Cambridge, UK: Cambridge University Press.

Ladd, G. T. (1887). *Elements of physiological psychology,* New York: Scribner.

Ladd, G. T. (1894). *Psychology: Descriptive and explanatory.* New York: Scribner.

Ladd, J. (1952). Expert testimony. *Vanderbilt Law Review, 5,* 414, 419.

Ladd-Franklin, C. (1929). *Colour and colour theories.* London: Paul, Trench, Trubner.

Lader, M, & Mathews, A. (1970). Comparison of methods of relaxation using physiological measures. *Behavior Research and Therapy, 8,* 331–337.

Laderman, C. (1988). Wayward winds: Malay archetypes, and theory of personality in the context of shamanism. *Social Sicence and Medicine, 27*(8), 799–810.

Lafarga, J. (1975). ¿Por que programas de grado en psicologia en Mexico? *Enseñanza e Investigacion en Psicologia, 1,* 77–84.

La Fare, L. (1972). Humor judgments as a function of reference groups and identification classes. In J. Goldstein & P. McGhee (Eds.), *The psychology of humor.* New York: Academic Press.

Laffal, J. (1955). Response faults in word association as a function of response entropy. *The Journal of Abnormal and Social Psychology, 50,* 265–270.

La Follette, W. R. (1975). Is satisfaction redundant with organizational climate? *Organizational Behavior and Human Performance, 13,* 257–278.

Laforge, R., & Suczek, R. (1955). The interpersonal dimension of personality: III. An interpersonal check list. *Journal of Personality, 24,* 94–112.

La Greca, A. M., & Mesibov, G. B. (1979). Social skills intervention with learning disabled children: Selecting skills and implementing training. *Journal of Clinical Child Psychology, 8,* 234–241.

Lah, M. I., & Rotter, J. B. (1981). Changing college student norms on the Rotter Incomplete Sentences Blank. *Journal of Consulting and Clinical Psychology, 49,* 985.

Laidlaw, T. A., Malmo, C., et al. (1990). *Healing voices: Feminist approaches to therapy with women.* San Francisco: Jossey-Bass.

Laing, R. D. (1967). *The politics of experience.* New York: Pantheon.

Laing, R. D. (1969). *The divided self: A study of sanity and madness.* New York: Pantheon.

Laing, R. D. (1970). *The self and others* (2nd ed.). New York: Pantheon.

Laing, R. D. (1971). *The politics of the family, and other essays.* New York: Pantheon.

Lair, J. (1975). *I ain't well—but I sure am better—Mutual need therapy.* New York: Doubleday.

Laird, D. (1935). *What makes people buy.* New York: McGraw-Hill.

Laird, J. D., & Brosler, C. (1992). The process of emotional feeling: A self-perception theory. In M. Clark (Ed.), *Review of personality and social psychology.*

Lakatos, I. (1970). Falsification and the methodology of scientific research programmes. In I. Lakatos and A. Musgrage (Eds.), *Criticism and the growth of knowledge.* London: Cambridge University Press.

Lakatos, I., & Musgrave, A. (Eds.), (1970). *Criticism and the growth of knowledge.* London: Cambridge University Press.

Lake, D. A., & Bryden, M. P. (1976). Handedness and sex differences in hemispheric asymmetry. *Brain and Language, 3,* 266–282.

Lake, D. G., Miles, M. B., & Earle, R. B. (1973). *Measuring human behavior: Tools for the assessment of social functioning.* New York: Teachers College Press.

Lakin, M. (1957). Personality factors in mothers of excessively crying (colicky) infants. *Monographs of the Society for Research in Child Development, 22,* 64.

Lakin, M. (Ed.). (1979). What's happened to the small group? *Journal of Applied Behavioral Science, 15,* no. 3 (entire issue).

Lakoff, R. (1975). *Language and woman's place.* New York: Harper Colophon Books.

Lalonde, M. (1974). *A new perspective on the health care of Canadians: A working document.* Ottawa, Ontario: Government of Canada.

Lalonde, M. (1978/1974). *A new perspective on the health of Canadians.* Ottawa: Minister of Supply and Services.

Lamarck, J. B. (1914/1809). *Zoological philosophy: An exposition with regard to the natural history of animals.* London: Macmillan.

Lamb, H. R., Sorkin, A. P., & Zusman, J. (1981). Legislating social control of the mentally ill in California. *American Journal of Psychiatry, 138,* 334.

Lamb, M. E. (1975). Physiological mechanisms in the control of maternal behavior in rats: A review. *Psychological Bulletin, 82,* 104—119.

Lamb, M. E. (1976). Interactions between two-year-olds and their mothers and fathers. *Psychological Reports, 38,* 447–450.

Lamb, M. E. (1977). Father–infant and mother–infant interaction in the first year of life. *Child Development, 48,* 167–181.

Lamb, M. E. (1978). Interactions between eighteen-month-olds and their preschool-aged siblings. *Child Development, 49,* 51–59.

Lamb, M. E. (1978). The development of sibling relationships in infancy: A short-term longitudinal study. *Child Development, 49,* 1189–1196.

Lamb, M. E. (Ed.). (1976). *The role of the father in child development.* New York: Wiley.

Lamb, M. E., Frodi, A. M., Hwang, P., Frodi, M., & Steinberg, J. (in press). Attitudes and behavior of traditional and nontraditional parents in Sweden. In R. Emde & R. Harmon (Eds.), *Attachment and affiliative systems: Neurobiological and psychobiological aspects.* New York: Plenum.

Lamb, M. E., & Sherrod, L. R. (Eds.) (1981). *Infant social cognition.* Hillsdale, N.J.: Erlbaum.

Lambert, M. J. (1981). The implications of psychotherapy outcome research of cross-cultural psychotherapy. In A. Marsella & P. Pedersen (Eds.), *Cross-cultural counseling and psychotherapy: Foundations, evaluation, and ethnocultural considerations.* New York: Pergamon Press.

Lambert, M. J. (1986). Implications of psychotherapy outcome research for eclectic psychotherapy. In J. C. Norcross (Ed.), *Handbook of eclectic psychotherapy* (pp. 436–462). New York: Brunner/Mazel.

Lambert, M. J. (1991). Introduction to psychotherapy research. In L. Beuler, & M. Crago, (Eds.), *Psychotherapy research* (pp. 1–11). Washington, DC: American Psychological Association.

Lambert, M. J. & Bergin, A. E. (1992). Achievements and stations of psychotherapy research. In D. K. Freedheim (Ed.), *History of psychotherapy, A century of change* (pp. 360–390). Washington, DC: American Psychological Association.

Lambert, M. J., Shapiro, D. A. & Bergin, A. E., (1986). The effectiveness of psychotherapy. In S. L. Garfield & A. E. Bergin (Eds.), *Handbook of psychotherapy and behavior change* (3rd ed., pp. 157–211). New York: Wiley.

Lambert, N., Sandoval, J., & Sassone, D. (1978). Prevalence of hyperactivity in elementary school children as a function of system definers. *American Journal of Orthopsychiatry, 48,* 446–476.

Lambert, N. M., Wilcox, M. R., & Gleason, W. P. (1974). *The educationally retarded child.* New York: Grune & Stratton.

Lambert, W. E. (1978). Some cognitive and sociocultural consequences of being bilingual. In J. E. Alatis (Ed.), *International dimensions of bilingual education.* Washington, D.C.: Georgetown University Press.

Lambert, W. E., & Klineberg, O. (1967). *Children's views of foreign peoples.* New York: Appleton-Century-Crofts.

Lambert, W. E., & Tucker, G. R. (1972). *Bilingual education of children. The Saint Lambert experiment.* Neubury: Rowley.

Lamendella, J. T. (1979). Neurolinguistics. *Annual Review of Anthropology, 8,* 373–391.

La Mettrie, J. O. (1912). *Natural history of the soul.* LaSalle, Ill.: Open Court.

La Mettrie, J. O. (1961/1748). *Man as machine*. LaSalle, Ill.: Open Court.

Landa, L. N. (1974/1966). *Algorithmization in learning and instruction*, Englewood Cliffs, N.J.: Educational Technology Publications.

Landa, L. N. (1975). Some problems in algorithmization and heuristics in instruction. *Instructional Science, 4*, (2).

Landa, L. N. (1976). The ability to think—How can it be taught? In *Soviet education*, Vol. 18. White Plains, N.Y.: International Arts & Science Press.

Landa, L. N. (1978). Some problems in algo-heuristic theory of thinking, learning and instruction. In J. Scandura & C. Brainerd (Eds.), *Structural/process models of complex human behavior*. Alphen aan den Rijn: Sijthoff & Noordhoff.

Landa, L. N. (1979). Psychological troubleshooting diagnostics as a basis for deeper adaptive instruction. In G. T. Page & O. A. Whirlock (Eds.), *Educational technology twenty years on. Aspects of educational technology XIII*. London, New York: Kegan Page/ Nichols.

Landa, L. N. (1981). The contrastive algo-heuristic theory and method of teaching foreign languages. In E. Hopkins and R. Grotjahn (Eds.), *Studies in language teaching and language acquisition. Quantitative linguistics*, Vol. 9. Bochum, West Germany: Studienverlag Dr. N. Brockmeyer.

Landa, L. N. (1983/1976). *Instructional regulation and control: Cybernetics, algorithmization and heuristics in education*. Englewood Cliffs, N.J.: Educational Technology Publications.

Landauer, T. K., & Streeter, L. A. (1973). Structural differences between common and rare words: Failure of equivalence assumptions for theories of word recognition. *Journal of Verbal Learning and Verbal Behavior, 12*, 119–131.

Landfield, A. W. (1971). *Personal construct systems in psychotherapy* Chicago: Rand-McNally.

Landfield, A. W. (Ed.) (1977). *Nebraska symposium on motivation 1976: Personal construct psychology*. Lincoln, Neb.: University of Nebraska Press.

Landfield, A. W., & Leitner, L. M. (Eds.) (1980). *Personal construct psychology: Psychotherapy and personality*. New York: Wiley.

Landis, C., & Hunt, W. A. (1932). Adrenalin and emotion. *Psychological Review, 39*, 467–485.

Landis, C, & Hunt, W. A. (1939). *The startle pattern*. New York: Farrar.

Landis, D., & Brislin, R. (Eds.). (1983). *Handbook of intercultural training* (3 vols.). Elmsford, NY: Pergamon.

Landman, J. T., & Dawes, R. M. (1982). Psychotherapy outcome. Smith and Glass' conclusions stand up under scrutiny. *American Psychologist, 37*, 504–516.

Landman, W. D., & Sheldon, T. (1950). An investigation of nondirective group therapy with students in academic difficulty. *Journal of Consulting Psychology, 14*, 210–214.

Lando, H. A., & McCullough, J. (1978). Clinical application of a broad-spectrum behavioral approach to chronic smokers. *Journal of Consulting and Clinical Psychology, 46*, 1583–1585.

Landsman, T. (1974). The humanizer. *American Journal of Orthopsychiatry, 44*, 345–352.

Landy, E., & Dahlke, A. (1981). Twenty-four hour therapy. In R. J. Corsini (Ed.), *Handbook of innovative psychotherapies*. New York: Wiley.

Landy, E. E., & Dahlke, A. E. (1981). Twenty-four hour therapy. In R. J. Corsini, (Ed.), *Handbook of innovative psychotherapies*. New York: Wiley.

Landy, E. E. (1967). Sex differences in some aspects of smoking behavior. *Psychological Reports, 20*, 575–580.

Landy, E. E. (1968). *Mixed male-female nude group interaction as an effective method of personal growth*. Norman: Human Interaction Programs, University of Oklahoma.

Landy, E. E. (1970). Attitude and attitude change towards interaction as a function of participation vs. observation. *Compariative Group Studies, 1*, 128–155.

Landy, E. E. (1971). *The underground dictionary*. New York: Simon & Schuster.

Landy, E. E., Gordon, R. I., Heavin, S. L., & Hood, W. R. (1968). *A critical analysis of transaction*. Norman, OK: Institute of Group Relations.

Landy, F. J. (1976). The validity of the interview in police officer selection. *Journal of Applied Psychology, 61*, 193–198.

Landy, F. J., & Farr, J. L. (1980). Performance rating. *Psychological Bulletin, 87*, 72–107.

Lane, D. (1981). Attention. In W. C. Howell & E. A. Fleishman (Eds.), *Human performance and productivity*. Vol. 2. Hillsdale, N.J.: Erlbaum.

Lane, R. (1962). *Political ideology: Why the American common man believes what he does*. New York: Free Press.

Lane, R. (1969). *Political thinking and consciousness: The private life of the political mind*. Chicago: Markham.

Lane, R. (1972). *Political man*. New York: Free Press.

Laney, A. R. (1949). Occupational implications of the Jungian personality function types as identified by the Briggs-Myers type indicator. Unpublished master's thesis, George Washington University.

Lang, A. (1901). *Magic and religion*. New York: Longman, Green.

Lang, A. (1964). *Uber zwei Teilsysteme der Persönlichkeit*. Bern: Huber.

Lang, A. (1966). *Rorschach-Bibliographie 1931–1964*. Bern: Huber.

Lang, A. (1967). Über Wahrnehmungsverhalten beim 8–10 wöchigen Säugling. *Psychologische Forschung, 30*, 357–399.

Lang, P. J., & Buss, A. H. (1965). Psychological deficit in schizophrenia. II. Interference and activation. *Journal of Abnormal Psychology, 70*, 77–106.

Lang, P. J., & Melamed, B. B. (1969). Case report: Avoidance conditioning therapy of an infant with chronic ruminative vomiting. *Journal of Abnormal Psychology, 74*, 1–8.

Lange, A. J., & Jakubowski, P. (1980/1976). *Responsible assertive behavior: Cognitive/behavioral procedures for trainers*. Champaign, Ill.: Research Press.

Lange, C. G. (1922). The emotions. In K. Dunlap (Ed.), *Psychology classics*, Vol. 1. Baltimore, Md.: Williams & Wilkins.

Lange, C. G. (1922/1885). The emotions: A psychophysiological study. In W. James & C. G. Lange, *The emotions*. Baltimore, Md.: Williams & Wilkins.

Langely, P., & Zytkow, J. (1989). Data-driven approaches to empirical discovery. *Artificial Intelligence, 40*, 283–312.

Langer, E. (1975). The illusion of control. *Journal of Personality and Social Psychology, 32*, 311–328.

Langer, E. (in press). Playing the middle against both ends: The usefulness of adult cognitive activity as a model for cognitive activity in childhood and old age. In S. Yussen (Ed.), *The development of reflection.*New York: Academic Press.

Langer, E., Blank, A., & Chanowitz, B. (1978). The mindlessness of ostensibly thoughtful action: The role of placebic information in interpersonal interaction. *Journal of Personality and Social Psychology, 36*, 635–642.

Langer, E., & Imber, A. (1980). The role of mindlessness and the perception of deviance. *Journal of Personality and Social Psychology, 39,* 360–367.

Langer, E., & Imber, L. (1979). When practice makes imperfect: Debilitating effects of overlearning. *Journal of Personality and Social Psychology, 37,* 2014–2025.

Langer, E., Janis, I., & Wolfer, J. (1975). Reduction of psychological stress in surgical patients. *Journal of Experimental Social Psychology, 11,* 155–165.

Langer, E., Joss, J., Hatem, M., & Howell, M. (1989). Conditional teaching and mindful learning: the role of uncertainty in education, *Creative Research Journal, 2,* 139–150.

Langer, E., & Newman, H. (1979). The role of mindless in a typical social psychological experiment. *Personality and Social Psychology Bulletin, 5,* 295–298.

Langer, E., Perlmuter, L., Chanowitz, B., & Rubin, R. (1988). Two new applications of the mindlessness theory: Aging and alcoholism. *Journal of Aging Studies, 2,* 229–299.

Langer, E., & Piper, A. (1987). The prevention of mindlessness, *Journal of Personality and Social Psychology, 1987, 53,* 280–287.

Langer, E., & Rodin, J. (1976). The effects of choice and enhanced personal responsibility for the aged. *Journal of Personality and Social Psychology, 34,* 191–198.

Langer, E., & Weinman, C. (1981). When thinking disrupts intellectual performance: Mindfulness on an overlearned task. *Personality and Social Psychology Bulletin, 7,* 240–243.

Langer, E. J. (1977). The psychology of chance. *Journal for the Theory of Social Behavior, 7,* 185–207.

Langer, E. J., & Rodin, J. (1976). The effects of choice and enhanced personal responsibility for the aged: A field experiment in an institutional setting. *Journal of Personality and Social Psychology, 34,* 191–198.

Langer, S. (1967). *Mind,* Vol. I. Baltimore, Md.: Johns Hopkins University Press.

Langer, S. (1972). *Mind,* Vol. II. Baltimore, Md.: Johns Hopkins University Press.

Langer, S. K. (1967/1948). *Philosophy in a new key.* Cambridge, Mass.: Harvard University Press.

Langfeld, H. S. (1920). *The aesthetic attitude.* New York: Harcourt, Brace & Howe.

Langhorne, J. E., & Loney, J. (1979). A fourfold model for subgrouping the hyperkinetic/MBD syndrome. *Child Psychiatry and Human Development, 9,* 153–159.

Langley, C. W. (1971). Differentiation and integration of systems of personal constructs. *Journal of Personality, 39,* 10–25.

Langley, L. L. (Ed.) (1972). *Homeostasis: Origins of the concept.* Stroudsburg, Pa.: Dowden, Hutchinson & Ross.

Langley, P., Simon, H. A., Bradshaw, G. L., & Zytkow, J. (1987). *Scientific discovery: Computational explorations of the creative processes.* Cambridge: MIT Press.

Langlois, J. H., & Roggman, L. A. (1990). Attractive faces are only average. *Psychological Science, 1,* 115–121.

Langner, T. S., Gersten, J. C., & Eisenberg, J. B. (1977). The epidemiology of mental disorder in children: Implications for community psychiatry. In G. Serban & B. Astrachan (Eds.), *New trends of psychiatry in the community* (pp. 69–109). Cambridge, MA: Bollinger.

Langs, R. J. (1965). Earliest memories and personality. *Archives of General Psychiatry, 12,* 379–390.

Langs, R. J., Rothenberg, M. B., Fishmen, J. R., & Reiser, M. F. (1960). Method for clinical and theoretical study of earliest memory. *Archives of General Psychiatry, 3,* 523–534.

Lanning, K. (1989, October). Satanic, occult, ritualistic crime: A law enforcement perspective. *The Police Chief,* pp. 62–83.

Lanning, K. (1991). Ritual abuse: A law enforcement view or perspective. *Child Abuse and Neglect, 15,* 171–173.

Lanning, K. (1992). A law enforcement perspective on allegations of ritual abuse. In *Out of Darkness.* New York: Lexington Books.

Lansing, J. B., & Heyns, R. W. (1959). Need affiliation and frequency of four types of communication. *Journal of Abnormal and Social Psychology, 58,* 365–372.

Lansky, M., Bley, C., McVey, G., & Brotman, B. (1978). Multiple family groups as aftercare. *International Journal of Group Psychotherapy, 28,* 211–244.

Lanyon, R. I., & Goodstein, L. D. (1971). *Personality assessment.* New York: Wiley.

Lanzetta, J. T., Biernat, J. J., & Kleck, R. E. (1962). Self-focused attention, facial behavior, autonomic arousal and the experience of emotion. *Motivation and Emotion, 6,* 49–63.

Lanzetta, J. T., Cartwright-Smith, J., & Kleek, R. E. (1976). Effects of nonverbal dissimulation on emotional experience and autonomic arousal. *Journal of Personality and Social Psychology, 33*(3), 354–370.

Lanzetta, J. T., & Kleck, R. E. (1970). Encoding and decoding of nonverbal affects in humans. *Journal of Personality and Social Psychology, 16,* 12–19.

Lapidus, I. M. (1976). Adulthood in Islam: Religious maturity in the Islamic tradition. In Adulthood. *Daedalus,* 93–108.

Laponce, J. (1981). *Left and right: The topography of political perceptions.* Toronto: University of Toronto.

Laqueur, P. (1973). Multiple family therapy: Questions and answers. In D. Bloch (Ed.), *Techniques of family therapy, a primer.* New York: Grune & Stratton.

Laqueur, P., Laburt, H., & Morong, E. (1971). Multiple family therapy: Further developments. In J. Haley (Ed.), *Changing families.* New York: Grune & Stratton.

Larkin, J. H., Reif, F., Carbonell, J., & Gugliotta, A. (1988). FERMI: A flexible expert reasoner with multi-domain inferencing. *Cognitive Science, 12,* 101–138.

Laroche, S., Doyere, V., & Del-Negro, C. R. (1991). What role for long-term potentiation in learning and the maintenance of memories. In M. Baudry & J. L. Davies (Eds.), *Long-term potentiation: A debate of current issues.* (pp. 301–316). Cambridge: MIT Press.

Larrabee, G. J., & Crook, T. H. (1989). Dimensions of everyday memory in age associated memory impairment. *Psychological Assessment, 1,* 92–97.

Larrivee, B., & Cook, L. (1979). Mainstreaming: A study of the variables affecting teacher attitude. *Journal of Special Education, 13,* 315–324.

Larsen, S. C. (1975). The influence of teacher expectations on the school performance of exceptional children. *Focus on Exceptional Children, 6,* 1–14.

Larson, C. C. (1982). Animal research: Striking a balance. *APA Monitor, 13, 1,* 12–13.

Larson, D. (1980). Therapeutic schools, styles, and schoolism: A national survey. *Journal of Humanistic Psychology, 20,* 1–20.

Larson, L. E. (1972). The influence of parents and peers during adolescence: The situation hypothesis revisited. *Journal of Marriage and the Family, 34,* 67–74.

Larson, P. S., & Silvette, H. (1975). *Tobacco: Experimental and clinical studies*. Supplement III. Baltimore, Md.: Williams & Wilkins.

Larson, R. W. (1989–1990). Emotions and the creative process: Anxiety, boredom, and enjoyment as predictors of creative writing. *Imagination, Cognition and Persnality, 9*, 275–292.

LaRue, A. (1982). Memory loss and aging. *Psychiatric Clinics of North America, 5*, 89–103.

LaRue, A., Dessonville, C., & Jarvik, L. F. (1985). Aging and mental disorders. In J. Birren, & K. W. Schaie, (Eds.), *Handbook of the psychology of aging*. New York: Van Nostrand Reinhold.

Lasch, C. (1979). *The culture of narcissism: American life in an age of diminishing expectations*. New York: Norton.

Lashley, K. S. (1950). In search of the engram. *Symposia of the Society for Experimental Biology, 4*, 454–482.

Lashley, K. S. (1964/1929). *Brain mechanisms and intelligence*. Chicago: University of Chicago.

Lashley, K. S., & Chow, K. L., & Semmes, J. (1951). An examiniation of the electrical field theory of cerebral integration. *Psychological Review, 58*, 123–136.

Lashley, K. S., & Wade, M. (1946). The Pavlovian theory of generalization. *Psychological Review, 53*, 72–87.

Lasko, J. K. (1954). Parent behavior toward first and second children. *Genetic Psychology Monographs, 49*, 96–137.

Lass, N.J., McReynolds, L. V., Northern, J. L., & Yoder, D. E. (Eds.) (1982). *Speech, language, and hearing* Vol. 1: *Normal processes*. Philadelphia, Ala.: Saunders.

Lassen, N. A., Ingvar, D. H., & Skinhoj, E. (1978). Brain function and blood flow. *Scientific American, 239*, 62–71.

Lasswell, H., & Kaplan A. (1950). *Power and society: A framework for political inquiry*. New Haven, Conn: Yale University Press.

Lasswell, H. D. (1927). *Propaganda technique in the World War*. New York: Knopf.

Lasswell, H. D. (1946). Describing the contents of communications. In B. L. Smith, H. D. Lasswell, & R. D. Casey (Eds.), *Propaganda, communication, and public opinion*. Princeton, N.J.: Princeton University Press.

Lasswell, H. D. (1948). The structure and function of communication in society. In L. Bryson (Ed.), *The communication of ideas*. New York: Institute for Religious and Social Studies.

Last, J. M. (Ed.). (1988). *A dictionary of epidemiology* (2nd ed.). New York: Oxford University Press.

Laszlo, E. (1971). *Introduction to systems philosophy*. New York: Gordon & Breach.

Laszlo, E. (1980). *The systems of the world*. New York: Braziller.

Latané, B., & Darley, J. M. (1970). *The unresponsive bystander: Why doesn't he help?* New York: Appleton-Century-Crofts.

Latane, B., & Darley, J. M. (1960). Group Inhibition of Bystander Intervention in Emergencies. *Journal of Personality and Social Psychology, 10*, 215–221.

Latham, G. P., & Locke, E. A. (1979). Goal setting—A motivational tool that works. *Organization Dynamics*, Autumn, 68–80.

Latham, G. P., & Wexley, K. N. (1981). *Increasing productivity through performance appraisal*. Reading, Mass: Addison-Wesley.

Latimer, P. (1983). *Functional gastrointestinal disorders; A behavioral medicine approach*. New York: Springer.

Latour, B. (1987). *Science in action*. Cambridge, MA: Harvard University Press.

Lattanner, B., & Hayslip, B. (1984–1985). Occupation-related differences in levels of death anxiety. *Omega, 15*, 53–66.

Lauer, A. R. (1960). *The psychology of driving. Factors of traffic enforcement*. Springfield, Ill.: Thomas.

Laufer, M. W, & Shetty, T. (1980). Attention deficit disorders. In H. Kaplan, A. Freedman, & B. Sadock (Eds.), *Comprehensive textbook of psychiatry*, Vol. 3. Baltimore, Md.: William & Wilkins.

Laughlin, P., & Adamopoulous, J. (1980). Social combination processes and individual learning for six-person cooperative groups on an intellectual task. *Journal of Personality and Social Psychology, 38*, 941–947.

Laughlin, P., & Bitz, D. (1975). Individual versus dyadic performance on a disjunctive task as a function of initial ability level. *Journal of Personality and Social Psychology, 31*, 487–496.

Laurent, H. (1968). Research on the identification of management potential. In J. A. Myers (Ed.), *Predicting managerial success*. Ann Arbor, Mich.: Foundation for Research on Human Behavior.

Laurillard, D. (1979). The processes of student learning. *Higher Education, 8*, 395–409.

Lavater, J. C. (1968). *Physiognomische Fragmente zur Beförderung der Menschenkenntnisse und Menschenliebe*. Leipzig, Winterthur: Weidmanns Erben, 1775–1778. Zürich: Orel Füssli.

Laver, J. (1949). *Style in costume*. London: Oxford University Press.

Lawler, E. E. (1981). *Pay and organization development*, Reading, Mass: Addison-Wesley.

Lawler, E. E., Hall, D. T., & Oldham, G. R. (1974). Organizational climate. *Organizational Behavior and Human Performance, 11*, 139–155.

Lawlor, E. F. (1992). What kind of medicine? *The Gerontologist, 32*, 131–133.

Lawrence, D. A., & DeRivera, J. (1954). Evidence for relational transposition. *Journal of Comparative and Physiological Psychology, 47*, 463–472.

Lawrence, D. H., & Festinger, L. (1962). *Deterrents and reinforcement*. Stanford, Calif.: Stanford University Press.

Lawrence, P. R., & Lorseh, J. W. (1969). *Developing organizations: Diagnosis and action*. Reading, Mass.: Addison-Wesley.

Lawrence, P. R., & Seiler, J. A. (1965). *Organizational behavior and administration*. Irwin-Dorsey.

Laws, J. L. (1975). The psychology of tokenism: An analysis. *Sex Roles, 1*, 51–67.

Laws, J. L. (1978). Work motivation and work behavior of women: New perspectives. In J. Sherman & F. Denmark (Eds.), *The psychology of women; New directions of research*. New York: Psychological Dimensions.

Laws, J. L. (1979). *The second x*. New York: Elsevier.

Lawson, A. E., & Wollman, W. T. (1975). Encouraging the transition from concrete to abstract cognitive functioning: An experiment. Unpublished manuscript, University of California, Berkeley.

Lawton, G. (1947). *Aging successfully*. New York: Columbia University Press.

Lawton, J. T. (1982). *Introduction to child development*. Dubuque, Iowa: Brown.

Lazar, A. L., Gensley, J. T., & Orpet, R. E. (1971). Changing attitudes of young mentally gifted children toward handicapped persons. *Exceptional Children, 37*, 600–602.

Lazar, I., Hubbel, V. R., Murray, H., Rosche, M., & Royce, J. (1977). The persistence of preschool effects: A long-term follow-up of 14 infant and preschool experiments. Final Report, Grant no. 18–76-07843, U.S. Department of Health, Education and Welfare.

Lazarsfeld, P. (1929). *Statistisches Praktikum für Psychologen und Lehrer.* Jena, East Germany: Fischer.

Lazarsfeld, P. (1931). *Jugend und Beruf* Jena, East Germany: Fischer.

Lazarus, A. A. (1958). New methods in psychotherapy: A case study. *South African Medical Journal 33,* 660–664.

Lazarus, A. A. (1961). Group therapy of phobic disorders by systematic desensitization. *Journal of Abnormal and Social Psychology, 63,* 505–510.

Lazarus, A. A. (1963). The treatment of chronic frigidity by systematic desensitization. *Journal of Nervous and Mental Disease, 136,* 272–278.

Lazarus, R. S. (1966). *Psychological stress and the coping process.* New York: McGraw-Hill.

Lazarus, A. A. (1968). Behavior therapy in groups. In G. M. Gazda (Ed.), *Basic approaches to psychotherapy and group counseling.* Springfield, Ill.: Thomas.

Lazarus, A. A. (1968). The content of behavior therapy training. Presented at the meeting of the Association for the Advancement of the Behavioral Therapies, San Francisco, Calif..

Lazarus, A. A. (1971). *Behavior therapy and beyond.* New York: McGraw-Hill.

Lazarus, A. A. (1973). On assertive behavior: A brief note. *Behavior Therapy, 4,* 697–699.

Lazarus, A. A. (1976). *Multi-modal behavior therapy.* New York: Springer.

Lazarus, A. A. (1976). Psychiatric problems precipitated by transcendental meditation. *Psychological Reports, 39,* 601–602.

Lazarus, A. A. (1977). Has behavior therapy outlived its usefulness? *American Psychologist, 32*(7), 550–553.

Lazarus, A. A. (1981). *Multimodal therapy.* New York: Guilford Press.

Lazarus, A. A. (1981). *The practice of multimodal therapy.* New York: McGraw-Hill.

Lazarus, A. A. (1983). Multimodal therapy. In R. J. Corsini (Ed.), *Current psychotherapies.* Itasca, Ill.: Peacock.

Lazarus, R. S. (1966). *Psychological stress and the coping process.* New York: McGraw-Hill.

Lazarus, R. S. (1968). Emotions and adaptation: Conceptual and empirical relations. In W. J. Arnold (Ed.), *Nebraska Symposium on Motivation.* Lincoln, Neb.: University of Nebraska Press.

Lazarus, R. S. (1980). The stress and coping paradigm. In L. A. Bond & J. C. Rosen (Eds.), *Competence and coping during adulthood.* Hanover, N.H.: University Press of New England.

Lazarus, R. S. (1981). The stress and coping paradigm. In C. Eisdorfer, D. Cohen, A. Kleinman, & P. Maxim (Eds.), *Theoretical bases for psychopathology.* New York: Spectrum.

Lazarus, R. S. (1983). The costs and benefits of denial. In S. Breznitz (Ed.), *The denial of stress.* New York: International Universities Press.

Lazarus, R. S., Averill, J. R., & Oldton, E. M., Jr. (1970). Towards a cognitive theory of emotion. In M. B. Arnold (Ed.), *Feelings and emotions.* New York: Academic Press.

Lazarus, R. S., DeLongis, A., Folkman, S., & Gruen, R. (1985). Stress and adaptational outcomes: The problem of confounded measures. *American Psychologist, 40,* 770–779.

Lazarus, R. S., & Folkman, S. (1984). *Stress, appraisal, and coping.* New York: Springer.

Lazarus, R. S, Kanner, A. D., & Folkman, S. (1980). Emotions: A cognitive phenomenological analysis. In R. Plutchik & H. Kellerman (Eds.), *Theories of emotion.* New York: Academic Press.

Lazarus, R. S., & Launier, R. (1978). Stress-related transactions between person and environment. In L. A. Pervin & M. Lewis (Eds.), *Perspectives in interactional psychology.* New York: Plenum.

Lazarus, R. S., & McCleary, R. A. (1951). Autonomic discrimination without awareness: Study of subception. *Psychological Review, 58,* 113–122.

Lazzati, G. (Ed.) (1979). *Agostino Gemelli.* Milan, Italy: Vita e Pensiero.

Lazslo, J. (Ed.). (1983). *Antiemetics and cancer chemotherapy.* Baltimore: Williams & Wilkins.

Leach, E. R. (1968). Ritual. In D. L. Sills (Ed.), *International encyclopedia of the social sciences,* Vol. 13. New York: Macmillan Free Press.

Leach, E. R. (1982). *Social anthropology.* New York: Oxford University Press.

Leach, P. J. (1967). A critical study of the literature concerning rigidity. *British Journal of Social and Clinical Psychology, 6,* 11–22.

Leahey, T. H. (1980). *A history of psychology: Main currents in psychological thought.* Englewood Cliffs, N.J.: Prentice-Hall.

Leahey, T. H. (1980). The myth of operationism. *Journal of Mind and Behavior, 1,* 127–143.

Leahey, T. H., & Leahey, G. (1982). *Psychology's occult doubles: Psychology and the problem of pseudoscience.* Chicago: Nelson-Hall.

Leary, T. (1957). *Interpersonal diagnosis of personality.* New York: Ronald Press.

Leary, T. (1968). *The politics of ecstasy,* New York: Putnam.

Leavitt, E. (1978). *Animals and their legal rights.* Washington, D.C.: Animal Welfare Institute.

Leavitt, H. (1951). Some effects of certain communication patterns on group performance. *Journal of Abnormal and Social Psychology, 46,* 38–50.

LeBlanc, M., & Frechette, M. (1989). *Male criminal activity from childhood through youth.* New York: Springer-Verlag.

Le Bon, G. (1896). *The crowd. A study of the popular mind.* London: Benn.

Le Bon, G. (1903). *The crowd.* London: Unwin.

Leboyer, F. (1975). *Birth without violence.* New York: Knopf.

Lebra, T. S. (1976). *Japanese patterns of behavior.* Honolulu: University Press of Hawaii.

Lebra, T. S., & Lebra, W. P. (Eds.). (1974). *Japanese culture and behavior.* Honolulu: University Press of Hawaii.

Lebra, W. P. (Ed.). (1976). *Culture-bound syndromes, ethnopsychiatry, and alternative therapies.* Honolulu: University Press of Hawaii.

Lecky, P. (1969/1945). *Self-consistency: A theory of personality.* Garden City, N.Y.: Doubleday/Anchor.

Ledbetter, D. H., & Basen, J. A. (1982). Failure to demonstrate self-recognition in gorillas. *American Journal of Primatology, 2,* 307–310.

Leddick, G. R., & Bernard, J. M. (1980). The history of supervision: A critical review. *Counselor Education and Supervision, 19,* 186–196.

Leddick, G. R., & Stone, S. C. (1982). A nationwide survey of supervision practices. In preparation for publication.

Lederer, W. J., & Jackson, D. D. (1968). *Mirages of marriage.* New York: Norton.

Lederman, J. (1969). *Anger and the rocking chair: Gestalt awareness with children.* New York: McGraw-Hill.

Ledingham, J. E., & Schwartzman, A. E. (1984). A 3-year follow-up of aggressive and withdrawn behavior in childhood: Preliminary findings. *Journal of Abnormal Child Psychology, 12,* 157–168.

LeDoux, J. E. (1988). Emotion. In F. Plum & V. Mountcastle (Eds.), *Handbook of physiology. The nervous system V: Higher Functions* (pp. 419–459). Bethesda, MD: American Physiological Society.

Ledwidge, B. (1978). Cognitive behavior modification: A step in the wrong direction. *Psychological Bulletin, 85,* 353–375.

Ledwidge, B. (1979). A distinction worth preserving. *Behavioural Analysis and Modification, 3,* 161–164.

Lee, A. M.,& Lee, E. B. (1939). *The fine art of propaganda: A study of Father Coughlin's speeches.* New York: Harcourt, Brace.

Lee, C. C., & Richardson, B. L. (1991). *Multicultural issues in counseling: New approaches to diversity.* Alexandria, VA: American Association for Counseling and Development.

Lee, E. S. (1951). Negro intelligence and selective migration. *American Sociological Review, 16,* 227–233.

Lee, J. A. (1977). *The colors of love.* New York: Bantam.

Lee, J. M. (Admiral) Personal communication, May 1981.

Lee, R. (1992, Spring). United we stand: Residency in Massachusetts. *National Psychology Advisory Association Communicator,* pp. 1, 4.

Lee, S. G. (1958). Social influences in Zulu dreaming. *Journal of Social Psychology, 47,* 265–283.

Lee, S. G. (1972). Review of the Lüscher color test. In O. K. Buros (Ed.), *The seventh mental measurements yearbook.* Highland Park, N.J.: Gryphon Press.

Lee, T., & Seeman, P. (1980). Elevation of brain neuroleptic/dopamine receptors in schizophrenia. *American Journal of Psychiatry, 137,* 191–197.

Leeds, M., & Murphy, G. (1980). *The paranormal and the normal.* Metuchen, N.J.: Scarecrow Press.

Leedy, J. J. (Ed.). (1969). *Poetry therapy.* Philadelphia, Pa.: Lippincott.

Leedy, J. J. (Ed.). (1973). *Poetry the healer.* Philadelphia, Pa.: Lippincott.

Leeman, F. (1975). *Anamorfosen.* Amsterdam: Landshoff.

Leeper, R. W. (1943). *Lewin's topological and vectoral psychology,* Eugene, Ore.: University of Oregon Press.

Leeper, R. W. (1953). Learning and the fields of perception, motivation and personality. In S. Koch (Ed.), *Psychology: A study of a science,* Vol. 5. New York: McGraw-Hill.

Leeper, R. W. (1963). Theoretical methodology in the psychology of personality. In M. H. Marx (Ed.), *Theories in contemporary psychology,* New York: Macmillan.

Leeper, R. W. (1970). Cognitive learning theory. In M. H. Marx (Ed.), *Learning theories.* New York: Macmillan.

Leeper, S. H., Dales, R. J., Skipper, D. S., & Witherspoon, R. L. (1968). *Good schools for young children—A guide for working with three-, four-, and five-year-old children.* New York: Macmillan.

Lefcourt, H. M. (1966). Internal versus external control of reinforcement: A review. *Psychological Bulletin, 65,* 206–220.

Lefcourt, H. M. (1972). Recent developments in the study of locus of control. In B. A. Maher (Ed.), *Progress in experimental personality research,* Vol. 6. New York: Academic Press.

Lefcourt, H. M. (1979). Locus of control and coping with life's events. In F. Staub (Ed.), *Personality.* Englewood Cliffs, N.J.: Prentice-Hall.

Lefcourt, H. M. (1980). Personality and locus of control. In M. E. P. Seligman (Ed.), *Human helplessness.* New York: Academic Press.

Lefcourt, H. M. (1982/1976). *Locus of control: Current trends in theory and research.* Hillsdale, N.J.: Erlbaum.

Lefcourt, H. M. (1981; 1983). *Research with the locus of control construct.* New York: Academic Press, Vol. 1; Vol. 2.

Leff, G. (1976). *The dissolution of the medieval outlook.* New York: Harper & Row.

Lefkowitz, J., & Katz, M. (1969). Validity of exit interviews. *Personnel Psychology, 22,* 445–455.

Lefkowitz, M., Eron, L., Walder, L., & Heusmann, L. (1977). *Growing up to be violent.* New York: Pergamon Press.

Legallois, J. J. C. (1812). *Experiences sue le principe de la vie, notamment sur celui des movemens du coeur, et sur le siege de ce principe.* Paris: Hautel.

Lehman, H. C. (1953). *Age and achievement.* Princeton, N.J.: Princeton University Press.

Lehman, P. E. (1972). The medical model of treatment: Historical development of an archaic standard. *Crime and Delinquency, 17,* 204–212.

Lehman, R. E. (1978). Brief hypnotherapy of neurodermatitis: A case with four year followup. *American Journal of Clinical Hypnosis,* (July), *21*(1), 48–51.

Lehrman, D. S. (1953). A critique of Konrad Lorenz's theory of instinctive behavior. *Quarterly Review of Biology, 28,* 337–363.

Lehman, D. S. (1964). The reproductive behavior of ring doves. *Scientific American, 211*(5), 48–54.

Leibnitz, G. W. (1898/1714). *Monadology.* Oxford: Oxford University Press.

Leibnitz, G. W. (1934). *Philosophical writings,* London: Dent.

Leibnitz, G. W. (1952/1710). *Theodicy.* New Haven, Conn.: Yale University Press.

Leibowitz, Z. B., & Schlossberg, N. K. (1981). Training managers for their role in a career development system. *Training and Development Journal,* July, 72–79.

Leiderman, P. H., & Shapiro, D. (Eds.). (1964). *Psychobiological approaches to social behavior.* Stanford, Calif.: Stanford University Press.

Leiderman, P. H., Tulkin, S. R., & Rosenfeld, A. (1977). *Culture and infancy: Variations in the human experience.* New York: Academic Press.

Leiderman, P. H., Tulkin, S. R., & Rosenfeld, A. (1977). Overview of cultural influences in infancy. In P. H. Leiderman, S. R. Tulkin, & A. Rosenfeld (Eds.), *Culture and infancy: Variations in the human experience.* New York: Academic Press.

Leifer, R. (1964). The psychiatrist and tests of criminal responsibility. *American Psychologist, 19,* 825–830.

Leigh, H., & Reiser, M. (1977). Major trends in psychosomatic medicine. *Annals of Internal Medicine, 87,* 233–239.

Leighton, A. H. (1969). A comparative study of psychiatric disorder in Nigeria and rural North America. In S. C. Plog, & R. B. Edgerton (Eds.), *Changing perspectives in mental illness.* New York: Holt, Rinehart & Winston.

Leijonhielm, C. (1967). *Colours, forms and art.* Stockholm: Almquist & Wiksell.

Leinhardt, G., Zigmond, N., & Cooley, W. (1981). Reading instruction and its effects. *American Educational Research Journal, 18,* 343–362.

Leitenberg, H., Agras, W. S., Barlow, D. H., & Oliveau, D. C. (1969). Contribution of selective positive reinforcement and therapeutic instructions to systematic desensitization therapy. *Journal of Abnormal Psychology, 74,* 382–387.

Leiter, R. G. (1959/1969). Part I of the manual for the 1948 revision of the Leiter International Performance Scale: Evidence of the reliability and validity of the Leiter tests. *Psychological Service Center Journal, 11*, 1–72.

Leland, H., Shelhaas, J., Nihira, K., & Foster, R. (1967). Adaptive behavior: A new dimension in the classification of the mentally retarded. *Mental Retardation Abstracts, 4*, 359–387.

LeMagnen, J. (1981). The metabolic basis of dual periodicity of feeding in rats. *Behavioral Brain Sciences, 4*, 561–607.

Lemkau, J. P. (1978). Personality and background characteristics of women in asextypical occupations. *Dissertation Abstracts International 39*, 957B-1124B (University Microfilms no. 78–13268).

Lemon, N. (1973). *Attitudes and their measurement*. New York: Wiley.

Lenat, D. (1977). On automated scientific theory formation: A case study using the AM program. In J. E. Hayes, D. Michie, & L. Mikulich (Eds.), *Machine intelligence 9*. New York: Halstead.

Lenat, D., & Brown, J. S. (1984). Why AM and EURISKO appear to work. *Artificial Intelligence, 23*, 269–274.

Lenat, D., & Feigenbaum, E. (1991). On the thresholds of knowledge. Artificial Intelligence, 47, 185–250.

Lenin, V. I. (1973). *Materialism and empirio-criticism: Critical comments on a reactionary philosophy*. Moscow: Progress Publishers.

Lenin, W. I. (1965). Ein liberaler Professor Über die Gleicheit. In W. I. Lenin (Ed.), *Werke*, Vol. 20. Berlin: Deutscher Verlag der Wissenschaften.

Lenny, E. (1977). Women's self-confidence in achievement settings. *Psychological Bulletin, 84*, 1–13.

Lenski, G. E. (1966). *Power and privilege: A theory of social stratification*. New York: McGraw-Hill.

Lent, R. W., & Hackett, G. (1987). Career self-efficacy: Empirical status and future directions. *Journal of Vocational Behavior, 30*, 347–382.

Le Ny, J-F. (1979). *Apprentissage et activities psychologiques*. Paris: Presses Universitaires de France.

Le Ny, J-F. (1979). *La semantique psychologique*. Paris: Presses Universitaires de France.

Le Ny, J-F. (1980/1961). *Le conditionnement et l'apprentissage*. Paris: Presses Universitaires de France.

Le Ny, J-F, & Kintsch, W. (Eds.). (1982). *Language and comprehension*. Amsterdam: North-Holland.

Leon, M. (1974). Maternal pheromone. *Physiology and Behavior, 13*, 441–453.

León, R, & Brožek, J. (1980). Historiography of psychology in Spain: Bibliography with comment. In J. Brožec & L. J. Pongratz (Eds.), *Historiography of modern psychology*. Toronto: Hogrefe.

Leonard, G. (1968). *Education and ecstasy*. New York: Delta Books.

Leonard, G. (1974). *The ultimate athlete*. New York: Avon.

Leon Portilla, M. (1979). *La filosofia nahuatl*. New Mexico, D. F.: Direccion General de Publicaciones, UNAM.

Leontiev, A. (1961). The present tasks of Soviet psychology. In R. B. Winn (Ed.), *Soviet psychology*, New York: Philosophical Library.

Leopold, W. F. (1939–1949). *Speech development of a bilingual child*. Evanston, Ill.: Northwestern University Press.

Le Plat, J. (1968). *Attention et incertitude dans les travaux de surveillance et d'inspection*. Paris: Dunod.

Le Plat, J. (1980). *La psychologie ergonomique*. Paris: PUF.

Le Plat, J, & Cuny, X. (1979). *Les accidents du travail*. Paris: PUF.

Le Plat, J., & Cuny, X. (1977). *Introduction à la psychologie du travail*. Paris: PUF.

Le Plat, J., Enard, C., & Weill-Fassina, A. (1970). *La formation par l'apprentissage*. Paris: PUF.

Lepper, M. R, & Greene, D. (1976). On understanding "overjustification": A reply to Reiss and Sushinsky. *Journal of Personality and Social Psychology, 33*, 25–35.

Lepper, M. R., & Greene, D. (Eds.). (1978). *The hidden costs of reward*. Hillsdale, N.J.: Erlbaum.

Lepper, M. R., Greene, D., & Nisbett, R. E. (1973). Undermining children's intrinsic interest with extrinsic reward: A test of the "overjustification" hypothesis. *Journal of Personality and Social Psychology, 28*, 129–137.

Lerman, H. (1976). What happens in feminist therapy? In S. Cox (Ed.), *Female psychology: The emerging self*. Chicago: Science Research Associates.

Lerman, H. (1986). *A mote in Freud's eye: From psychoanalysis to the psychology of women*. New York: Springer.

Lerner, A. (1965). *Rhymed and unrhymed*. Los Angeles: Swordsman.

Lerner, A. (1967). *Follow-up*. Los Angeles: Swordsman.

Lerner, A. (1970). *Psychoanalytically oriented criticism of three American poets: Poe, Whitman, and Aiken*. Cranbury, N.J.: Associated Universities Press.

Lerner, A. (1971). *Starting points*. Los Angeles: Swordsman.

Lerner, A. (1981). Poetry therapy. In R. J. Corsini (Ed.), *Handbook of innovative psychotherapies*. New York: Wiley.

Lerner, A. (1982). Poetry therapy in the group experience. In L. E. Abt & I. R. Stuart (Eds.), *The newer therapies: A sourcebook*. New York: Van Nostrand Reinhold.

Lerner, A. (Ed.). (1978). *Poetry in the therapeutic experience*. New York: Pergamon Press.

Lerner, D. (1958). *The passing of traditional society*. Glencoe, Ill.: Free Press.

Lerner, I. M., & Libby, W. J. (1976/1968). *Heredity, evolution, and society* (2nd ed.). San Francisco: Freeman.

Lerner, J., Mardell-Czudnowski, C., & Goldenberg, D. (1981). *Special education for the early childhood years*. Englewood Cliffs, N.J.: Prentice-Hall.

Lerner, M. J., & Lerner, S. C. (Eds.) (1981). *The justice motive in social behavior: Adapting to times of scarcity and change*. New York: Plenum.

Lerner, M. J., & Matthews, G. (1967). Reactions to suffering of others under conditions of indirect responsibility. *Journal of Personality and Social Psychology, 5*, 319–325.

Lerner, M. J., & Simmons, C. S. (1966). Observer's reaction to the "innocent victim": Compassion or rejection? *Journal of Personality and Social Psychology, 4*, 203–210.

Lerner, M. J., Somers, D. G., Reid, D., Chiriboga, D., & Tierney, M. (1991). Adult children as caregivers: Egocentric biases in judgments of sibling contributions. *The Gerontologist, 31*, 746–755.

Lerner, R. M., & Busch-Rossnagel, N. A. (Eds.) (1981). *Individuals as producers of their development: A life-span perspective*. New York: Academic Press.

Le Roy Ladurie, E. (1978). *Montaillou: The promised land of error*. New York: Braziller.

Lersch, P. (1942). *Der Aufbau des Charakters*. Leipzig: Barth.

Lersch, P. (1961/1932). *Gesicht und Seele*. Munich: Reinhardt.

Lersch, P. (1962/1938). *Aufbau der Person*. Munich: Barth.

Lesch, M., & Nyhan, W. L. (1964). A familial disorder of uric acid metabolism and central nervous system function. *American Journal of Medicine, 36,* 561–570.

Lesgold, A. M., & Perfetti, C. A. (1981). *Interactive processes in reading.* Hillsdale, N.J.: Erlbaum.

Le Shan, L. (1966). Emotional life-history pattern associated with neoplastic disease. *Annals of the New York Academy of Sciences, 125,* 780–793.

Le Shan, L. (1969). Psychotherapy and the dying patient. In L. Pearson (Ed.), *Death and dying: Current issues in the treatment of the dying person.* Cleveland, Ohio: The Press of Case Western Reserve University.

Le Shan, L. (1974). *How to meditate.* Boston: Little, Brown.

Leshner, A. I. (1978). *An introduction to behavioral endocrinology.* New York: Oxford University Press.

Lesieur, H. R. (1977). *The chase.* New York: Doubleday.

Lesieur, H. R. (1979). The compulsive gambler's spiral of options and involvement. *Psychiatry, 42*(1), 79–87.

Lesser, G. S. (1974). *Children and television: Lessons from Sesame Street.* New York: Random House.

Lesser, G. S., Fifer, G., & Clark, D. H. (1965). Mental abilities of children from different social-class and cultural groups. *Monographs of the Society for Research in Child Development, 30,*(4).

Lesser, M. (1980). *Nutrition and vitamin therapy.* New York: Bantam.

Lesser, S. O. (1957). *Fiction and the unconscious.* Boston: Beacon.

Lester, D. (1974). Effects of suicide prevention centers on suicide rates in the U.S. *Health Service Reports, 89,* 37–39.

Lester, D. (1975). *Unusual sexual behavior: The standard deviations.* Springfield, Ill.: Thomas.

Lester, D. (1979). Modern psychological theories of punishment and their implications for penology and corrections. *Corrective and Social Psychiatry and Journal of Behavioral Technology, Methods and Therapy, 25*(3), 81–85.

Lester, D. (1979). The treatment of compulsive gamblers. In D. Lester (Ed.), *Gambling today.* Springfield, Ill.: Thomas.

Lester, D. (1980). Choice of gambling activity and belief in locus of control. *Psychological Reports, 47,* 22.

Lester, D., & Brockopp, G. (Eds.). (1973). *Telephone therapy and crisis intervention.* Springfield, Ill.: Thomas.

Lester, D., & Brockopp, G. W. (Eds.). (1973). *Crisis intervention by telephone.* Springfield, Ill. Thomas.

Lettvin, J. Y, Maturana, H. R, McCulloch, W. S., & Pitts, W. H. (1959). What the frog's eye tells the frog's brain. *Institute of Radio Engineers Proceedings, 47,* 1940–1951.

Leuba, J. H. (1925). *The psychology of religious mysticism.* London: Kegan Paul, Trench, Trubner.

Leuner, H. C. (1969). Guided affective imagery (GAI): A method of intensive psychotherapy. *American Journal of Psychotherapy, 23* 4—22.

Leung, E. H. L., & Rheingold, H. L. (1981). Development of pointing as a social gesture. *Development Psychology, 17,* 215–220.

LeVay, S. (1991). A difference in hypothalmic structure between heterosexual and homosexual men. *Science, 253,* 1034–1037.

Leve, C., & Pratkanis, A. R. (1990, April). *Where is the forewarning sleeper effect?* Los Angeles: Western Psychological Association.

Levelt, W. J. M. (1968). *On binocular rivalry.* The Hague: Mouton.

Levelt, W. J. M. (1974). *Formal grammars in linguistics and psycholinguistics.* The Hague: Mouton.

Levelt, W. J. M. (1981). The speaker's linearization problem. *Philosophical Transactions of the Royal Society* (London), Series B, *295,* 305–315.

Levelt, W. J. M., & Flores d'Arcais, G. B. (1978). *Studies in the perception of language.* Chichester, England: Wiley.

Levelt, W. J. M., Riemersma, J. B., & Bunt, A. A. (1972). Binaural additivity of loudness. *British Journal of Mathematical and Statistical Psychology, 25,* 51–68.

Levenson, H. (1972). Distinctions within the concept of internal-external control: Development of a new scale. *Proceedings of the 80th Annual Convention of the American Psychological Association.*

Leventhal, G. S., & Bergman, J. T. (1969). Self-depriving behavior as a response to unprofitable inequity. *Journal of Experimental Social Psychology, 5,* 153–171.

Leventhal, H., & Avis, N. (1976). Pleasure, addiction, and habit: Factors in verbal report or factors in smoking behavior? *Journal of Abnormal Psychology, 85*(5), 478–488.

Leveton, E. (1977). *Psychodrama for the timid clinic.* New York: Springer.

Left, L. (1971). *Society, stress and disease—The psychosocial environment and psychosomatic disease,* Vol. I. New York: Oxford University Press.

Levi, L. (1979). *Psychosocial factors in preventive medicine.* Washington, D.C.: U.S. Department of Health Education and Welfare, DHEW (PHS) Publication no. 79–55071A.

Levick, M. (1981). Art therapy. In R. J. Corsini (Ed.), *Handbook of innovative psychotherapies.* New York: Wiley.

Levin, A. P., Schneier, F. R., & Liebowitz, M. R. (1989). Social phobia: Biology and pharmacology. *Clinical Psychology Review, 9,* 129–140.

Levin, H., & Sears, R. R. (1956). Aggression in doll play. *Child Development, 27,* 135–153.

Levin, H. M. (1975). Cost-effectiveness analysis in evaluation research. In M. Guttentag & E. L. Struening (Eds.), *Handbook of evaluation research,* Vol. 2. Beverly Hills, Calif.: Sage Publications.

Levin, H. S., Benton, A. L., & Grossman, R. G. (1982). *Neurobehavioral consequences of closed head injury.* New York: Oxford University Press.

Levin, J. (1963). *Three-mode factor analysis.* Technical Report, Department of Psychology, University of Illinois.

Levin, J. (1965). Three-mode factor analysis. *Psychological Bulletin, 64,* 442–452.

Levin, J. R. (1981). The mnemonic '80s: Keywords in the classroom. *Educational Psychologist, 16,* 65–82.

Levin, M. (1953). Reflex action in the highest cerebral centers: A tribute to Hughlings Jackson. *Journal of Nervous and Mental Disease, 118,* 481–493.

Levin, M. E. (1979). *Metaphysics and the mind body problem.* Oxford: Clarendon Press.

Levine, A. (1973). *Culture, behavior, and personality.* New York: Aldine.

Levine, D. (1980). An exploratory assessment of APA internships with legal/forensic experiences. *Professional Psychology, 11,* 64–71.

Levine, D. S., & Levin, S. J. (Ed.). (1992). *Motivation, emotion, and goal direction in neural networks.* Hillside, NJ: Erlbaum.

Levine, E. L., Ash, R. A., & Bennett, N. (1980). Exploratory comparative study of four job analysis methods. *Journal of Applied Psychology, 65,* 524–535.

Levine, J., & Butler, J. (1932). Lecture versus group discussion in changing behavior. *Journal of Applied Psychology, 36,* 29–33.

Levine, J. M., & Murphy, G. (1943). The learning and forgetting of controversial material. *Journal of Abnormal and Social Psychology, 38,* 507–517.

Levine, M. (1976). The academic achievement test: Its historical context and social functions. *American Psychologist, 31,* 228–238.

Levine, M. (1988). An analysis of mutual assistance. *American Journal of Community Psychology, 16,* 167–183.

Levine, M., & Perkins, D. V. (1987). *Principles of community psychology.* New York: Oxford University Press.

Levine, M. A. (1966). Hypothesis behavior by humans during discrimination learning. *Journal of Experimental Psychology, 71,* 331–338.

Levine, M. A. (1975). *A cognitive theory of learning.* Hillsdale, N.J.: Erlbaum.

Levine, M. D., & Bakow, H. (1976). Children with encopresis: A study of treatment outcome. *Pediatrics, 58,* 845–852.

Levine, R. A. (1961). Africa. In F. L. K. Hsu (Ed.), *Psychological anthropology.* Homewood, Ill.: Dorsey Press.

Levine, R. A. (1966). *Dreams and deeds: Achievement motivation in Nigeria.* Chicago: University of Chicago Press.

Levine, R. A. (1970). Cross-cultural study in child psychology. In P. H. Mussen (Ed.), *Carmichael's manual of child psychology,* Vol. 2 (3rd ed.). New York: Wiley.

Levine, R. A., & Campbell, D. T. (1972). *Ethnocentrism: Theories of conflict, ethnic attitudes and group behavior.* New York: Wiley.

Levine, S., Coe, C., & Wiener, S. G. (1989). Psychoneuroendocrinology of stress: A psychobiological perspective. In F. R. Brush & S. Levine (Eds.), *Psychneuroendocrinology* (pp. 314–378). San Diego: Academic Press.

Levine, S. (Ed.). (1972). *Hormones and behavior.* New York: Academic Press.

Levine, S. Stress and behavior, *Scientific American, 224,* 26–31.

Levine, S., & Mullins, R. F. (1966). Hormonal influences on brain organization in infant rats. *Science, 152,* 1585–1592.

Levine, S., & Ursin, H. (1980). *Coping and health.* New York: Plenum.

Levinger, G. (1965). Marital cohesiveness and dissolution: An integrative review. *Journal of Marriage and the Family, 27,* 19–28.

Levinger, G. (1974). Physical abuse among applicants for divorce. In S. K. Steinmetz & M. A. Straus (Eds.), *Violence in the family.* New York: Dodd, Mead.

Levinger, G., & Breedlove, J. (1966). Interpersonal attraction and agreement: A study of marriage partners. *Journal of Personality and Social Psychology, 3,* 367–372.

Levinger, G., Senn, D. J., & Jorgensen, B. W. (1970). Progress toward permanence in courtship: A test of the Kerckhoff-Davis hypotheses. *Sociometry, 33,* 427–443.

Levinger, G., & Sonnheim, M. (1965). Complementarity in marital adjustment: Reconsidering Toman's family constellation hypothesis. *Journal of Individual Psychology, 21,* 137–145.

Levinger, L., & Ochroch, R. (1981). Psychodiagnostic evaluation of children with minimal brain dysfunction. In R. Ochroch (Ed.), *Diagnosis and treatment of children with minimal brain dysfunction: A clinical approach.* New York: Human Sciences Press.

Levinson, B. M. (1965). Pet psychotherapy: Use of household pets in the treatment of behavior disorder in childhood. *Psychological Reports, 17,* 695–698.

Levinson, B. M. (1966). The dog as a "co-therapist." *Practicing Veterinarian, 5,* 132–138.

Levinson, B. M. (1968). Interpersonal relationships between pet and human being. In M. W. Fox (Ed.), *Abnormal behavior in animals.* Philadelphia, Pa.: Saunders.

Levinson, B. M. (1969). Pets and old age. *Mental Hygiene, 53,* 364–368.

Levinson, B. M. (1970). Pets, child development, and mental illness. *Journal of American Veterinary Medical Association, 157*(11), 1759–1766.

Levinson, B. M. (1972). *Pets and human development.* Springfield, Ill.: Thomas.

Levinson, B. M. (1974). Psychology of pet ownership. *Proceedings of the National Conference on the Ecology of the Surplus Dog and Cat Problem,* 24–25.

Levinson, D. J., Darrow, C. N., Klein, E. B., Levinson, M. H., & McKee, B. (1978). *The seasons of a man's life.* New York: Knopf.

Levinson, H. (1963). *Men, management and mental health.* Cambridge, Mass.: Harvard University Press.

Levinson, H. (1964). *Emotional health in the world of work.* New York: Harper & Row.

Levinson, H. (1972). *Organizational diagnosis.* Cambridge, Mass.: Harvard University Press.

Levinson, H. (1980). Criteria for choosing chief executives. *Harvard Business Review, 58,* 113–120.

Levinson, H. N. (1980). *A solution to the riddle dyslexia.* New York: Springer-Verlag.

Lévi-Strauss, C. (1963). *Structural anthropology.* New York: Basic Books.

Lévi-Strauss, C. (1963). *Totemism.* Boston: Beacon.

Lévi-Strauss, C. (1966/1962). *The savage mind.* Chicago: University of Chicago Press.

Lévi-Strauss, C. (1967). The sorcerer and his magic. In C. Lévi-Strauss (Ed.), *Structural anthropology.* Garden City, N. Y.: Anchor Books.

Levi-Strauss, C. (1969). The elementary structures of kinship. Boston: Beacon. (Original work published 1949).

Lévi-Strauss, C. (1969). *The elementary structure of kinship.* Boston: Beacon Press.

Lévi-Strauss, C. (1969). *The raw and the cooked,* New York: Harper & Row.

Levitan, A. A. (1991). Hypnosis in the 1990s—and beyond. *American Journal of Clinical Hypnosis, 33,* 141–149.

Leviton, D. (1969). The need for education on death and suicide. *Journal of School Health, 39,* 270–274.

Levitsky, A., & Simkin, J. S. (1972). *Gestalt therapy.* In L. N. Solomon & B. Verzon (Eds.), *New perspectives on encounter groups.* San Francisco: Jossey-Bass.

Levitt, E. E. (1971). Sadomasochism. *Sexual Behavior, 1*(9), 69–80.

Levitt, E. E. (1973). Nymphomania. *Sexual Behavior, 3*(3), 13–17.

Levitt, E. E. (1980). *Primer on the Rorschach technique.* Springfield, Ill.: Thomas.

Levitt, E. E., & Chapman, R. W. (1979). Hypnosis as a research method. In E. Fromm & R. E. Shor (Eds.), *Hypnosis: Developments in research and new perspectives.* New York: Aldine.

Levitt, E. E., & Lubin, B. (1975). *Depression: Concepts, controversies, and some new facts.* New York: Springer.

Levy, D. (1937). Studies in sibling rivalry. In *American Orthopsychiatric Research Monographs no. 2.* New York: American Orthopsychiatric Association.

Levy, E., Allen, A., Caton, W., & Holmes, E. (1970). An attempt to condition the sensitive plant: *Mimosa pudica. Journal of Biological Psychology, 12,* 86–87.

Levy, J. (1978). *Play behavior*. New York: Wiley.

Levy, J. (1983). Developing intercultural competence in bilingual teacher training programs. In D. Landis & R. Brislin (Eds.), *Handbook of intercultural training*, Vol. 3. Elmsford, N.Y.: Pergamon Press.

Levy, L. H. (1976). Self-help groups: Types and psychological processes. *Journal of Applied Behavioral Science, 12,* 310–322.

Levy, S. M. (Ed.) (1982). *Biological mediators of behavior and disease: Neoplasia*. New York: Elsevier Biomedical.

Lévy-Bruhl, L. (1923). *Primitive mentality*. London: Allen & Unwin.

Lévy-Bruhl, L. (1926). *How natives think*. London: Allen & Unwin.

Lévy-Bruhl, L. (1975). *The notebooks on primitive mentality*. Oxford: Blackwell.

Levy-Leboyer, C. (Ed.) *International review of applied psychology*. London: Sage Publications.

Lewicki, P. (1986). Processing information about covariations that cannot be articulated. *Journal of Experimental Psychology: Learning, Memory and Cognition, 12,* 135–146.

Lewicki, P., Hill, T., & Bizot, E. (1988). Acquisition of procedural knowledge about a pattern of stimuli that cannot be articulated. *Cognitive Psychology, 20,* 24–37.

Lewicki, P., Hill, T., & Sasaki, I. (1989). Self-perpetuating development of encoding biases. *Journal of Experimental Psychology: General, 118,* 323–337.

Lewin, B. (1961). The psychoanalysis of elation. New York: *Psychoanalytic Quarterly*.

Lewin, K. (1922). Das Problem der Willensmessung und das Grundgesetz der Assoziation. *Psychologische Forschung, 1,* I, 191–302; *2,* II, 65–140.

Lewin, K. (1926). *Vorsatz, Wille und Bedürfnis*. Berlin, Springer.

Lewin, K. (1935). *A dynamic theory of personality*. New York: McGraw-Hill.

Lewin, K. (1936). *Principles of topological and vectoral psychology*, New York: McGraw-Hill.

Lewin, K. (1938). *The conceptual representation and measurement of psychological forces, contributions to psychological theory*. Durham, N.C.: Duke University Press.

Lewin, K. (1947). Group decision and change. In T. M. Newcomb & E. L. Hartley (Eds.), *Readings in social psychology* (pp. 330–334). New York: Holt.

Lewin, K. (1947). Group decision and social change. In T. Newcomb & E. Hartley (Eds.), *Readings in social psychology*. New York: Holt.

Lewin, K. (1948). *Resolving social conflicts*. New York: Harper.

Lewin, K. (1951). *Field theory in social science*. New York: Harper.

Lewin, K. (1951). Formalization and progress in psychology. In D. Cartwright (Ed.), *Field theory in social science*. New York: Harper.

Lewin, K. (1951). Intention, will, and need. In D. Rapaport (Ed.), *Organization and pathology of thought*. New York: Columbia University Press.

Lewin, K. (1952). Field theory and learning. In D. Cartwright (Ed.), *Field theory in social science: Selected theoretical papers by Kurt Lewin*. London: Tavistock Publications.

Lewin, K. (1954). Behavior and development as a function of the total situation. In L. Carmichael (Ed.), *Manual of child psychology (2nd ed.)*. New York: Wiley.

Lewin, K. & Lippitt, R. (1938). An experimental approach to the study of autocracy and democracy. *Sociometry, 1,* 292–300.

Lewin, K., Lippitt, R., & White, R. K. (1939). Patterns of aggressive behavior in experimentally created social climates. *Journal of Social Psychology, 10,* 271–299.

Lewinsohn, P. (1974). A behavioral approach to depression. In R. Friedman & M. Kaz (Eds.), *The psychology of depression*. Washington, DC: Winston-Wiley.

Lewinsohn, P. (1974). A behavioral approach to depression. In R. Friedman & M. Katz (Eds.), *The psychology of depression*. Washington, D.C.: Winston.

Lewinsohn, P., & Rohde, P. (1987). Psychological measurement of depression. In A. J. Marsena, R. Hirschfeld, M. Katz (Eds.), *The measurement of depression*. New York: Guilford.

Lewinsohn, P. M., & Libet, J. (1972). Pleasant events, activity schedules, and depressions. *Journal of Abnormal Psychology, 79,* 291–295.

Lewinsohn, P. M., Mischel, W., Chaplin, W., & Barton, R. (1980). Social competence and depression: The role of illusory self-perceptions. *Journal of Abnormal Psychology, 89,* 203–212.

Lewis, A. (1970). Paranoia and paranoid: A historical perspective. *Psychological Medicine, 1,* 2–12.

Lewis, A. (1970). *Preschool breakthrough: What works in early childhood education*. Washington, D.C.: National School Public Relations Association.

Lewis, A. (1974). Psychopathic personality: A most elusive category. *Psychological Medicine, 4,* 133–140.

Lewis, D. O, et al. (1979). Violent juvenile delinquents: psychiatric, neurological, psychological and abuse factors, *Journal of the American Academy of Child Psychiatry, 18,* 307–319.

Lewis, M. (1972). Introduction. *Human Development, 15,* 75–76.

Lewis, M., & Brooks, J. (1975). Infants' social perception: A constructivist view. In L. Cohen & S. Salapatek (Eds.), *Infant perception: From sensation to cognition*. Vol. 2: *Perception of space, speech, and sound*. New York: Academic Press.

Lewis, M., & Brooks-Gunn, J. (1979). *Social cognition and the acquisition of self*. New York: Plenum.

Lewis, M., & Rosenblum, L. (Eds.). (1978). *The development of affect*. New York: Plenum.

Lewis, M., & Weinraub, M. (1976). The father's role in the child's social network. In M. E. Lamb (Ed.), *The role of the father in child development*. New York: Wiley.

Lewis, O. (1966). *La Vida: A Puerto Rican family in the context of poverty—San Juan and New York*. New York: Random House.

Lewis, R. L., & Spanier, G. B. (1979). Theorizing about the quality and stability of marriage. In W. R. Burr, R. Hill, F. I. Nye, & I. L. Reiss (Eds.), *Contemporary theories about the family: Research-based theories*, Vol. I. New York: Free Press.

Lewkowicz, D. J., & Turkewitz, G. (1981). Intersensory interaction in newborns: Modification of visual preferences following exposure to sound. *Child Development, 52,* 827–832.

Lewontin, R. C. (1972). The apportionment of human diversity. In T. Dobzhansky, M. K. Hecht, & W. C. Steere (Eds.), *Evolutionary biology*, Vol. 6. New York: Appleton-Century-Crofts.

Ley, D., & Cybriwski, R. (1974). Urban graffiti as territorial markers. *Annals of the Association of American Geographers, 64,* 491–505.

Lezak, M. D. (1983). **Neuropsychological assessment** (2nd ed.). New York: Oxford University Press.

Lezak, M. D. (1983/1976). *Neuropsychological assessment*. New York: Oxford University Press.

Li, J. Z., He, B. Y., & Ma, M. Z. (1962). Experiments on the selection of flash light signal frequencies. *Acta Psychologica Sinica, 7,* 305–313.

Li, X. T., Xu, S. L., & Kuang, P. Z. (1980). 30 years of Chinese medical psychology. *Acta Psychologica Sinica, 12,* 135–143.

Liberman, A. M. (1982). On finding that speech is special. *American Psychologist, 37*, 148–167.

Liberman, A. M., Cooper, F. S., Shankweiler, D. P., & Studdert-Kennedy, M. (1967). Perception of the speech code. *Psychological Review, 74*, 431–461.

Liberman, A. M., & Studdert-Kennedy, M. (1978). Phonetic perception. In R. Held, H. W. Leibowitz, & H.-L. Teuber (Eds.), *Handbook of sensory physiology*. Vol. 8: *Perception*. Berlin: Springer-Verlag.

Liberman, B. L. (1978). The role of mastery in psychotherapy: Maintenance of improvement and prescriptive change. In J. D. Frank, R. Hoehn-Saric, S. D. Imber, B. L. Liberman, & A. R. Stone (Eds.), *Effective ingredients of successful psychotherapy*. New York: Brunner/Mazel.

Lieberman, M. G. (1957). Childhood memories as a projective technique. *Journal of Projective Techniques, 1*, 32–36.

Liberman, R. P., King, L. W., DeRisi, W. J., & McCann, M. (1975). *Personal effectiveness*. Champaign, Ill.: Research Press.

Liberman, R. P., & Smith, V. (1972). A multiple baseline study of systematic desensitization in a patient with multiple phobias. *Behavior Therapy, 3*, 597–603.

Libet, J. M. & Lewinsohn, P. M. (1973). The concept of social skills with special reference to the behavior of depressed persons. *Journal of Consulting and Clinical Psychology, 40*, 304–312.

Libo, M. (1966). Multiple functions for psychologists in community consultation. *American Psychologist, 21*:530–534.

Libow, J. A., & Schreier, H. A. (1986). Three forms of factitious illness in children: When is it Munchausen syndrome by proxy? *American Journal of Orthopsychiatry, 56*, 602–611.

Lichtenstein, E. (1980). *Psychotherapy*. Monterey, Calif.: Brooks/Cole.

Lichtenstein, E., & Rodrigues, M. P. (1977). Long-term effects of rapid smoking treatment for dependent cigarette smokers. *Addictive Behaviors, 2*, 109–112.

Lichtenstein, H. (1977). *The dilemma of human identity*. New York: Aronson.

Lichtenstein, S., Fischhoff, B., & Phillips, L. D. (1982). Calibration of probabilities: The state of the art to 1980. In D. Kahneman, P. Slovic, & A. Tversky (Eds.), *Judgment under uncertainty: Heuristics and biases*. New York: Cambridge University Press.

Licklider, J. C. R. (1951). Basic correlates of the auditory stimulus. In S. S. Stevens (Ed.), *Handbook of experimental psychology*. New York: Wiley.

Licklider, J. C. R., & Miller, G. A. (1951). The perception of speech. In S. S. Stevens (Ed.), *Handbook of experimental psychology*. New York: Wiley.

Lickona, T. (Ed.). (1976). *Moral development and behavior*. New York: Holt, Rinehart & Winston.

Lida, C. W., & Walker, A. L. (1980). *Heroin, deviance and morality*. Beverly Hills, Calif.: Sage Publications.

Liddell, H. S. (1956). *Emotional hazards in animals and man*. Springfield, IL: Thomas.

Lidoff, J. (1980). Another sleeping beauty: Narcissism in *The house of mirth*. *American Quarterly, 32*, 519–539.

Lidz, C. S. (1980). Assessment for development and implementation of the individual education program. *School Psychology Review, 9*, 207.

Lidz, C. S. (1981). *Improving assessment of schoolchildren*. San Francisco: Jossey-Bass.

Lidz, T. (1958). Schizophrenia and the family. *Psychiatry, 21*, 21–27.

Liebeault, A. (1866). *Du sommeil et des états analogues, considérés surtout au point de vue de l'action du moral sur le physique*. Paris: Masson.

Lieberman, D. A. (1979). Behaviorism and the mind: A (limited) call for a return to Introspection. *American Psychologist, 34*, 319–333.

Lieberman, J. N. (1977). *Playfulness. Its relationship to imagination and creativity*. New York: Academic Press.

Lieberman, M., & Gardner, J. (1976). Institutional alternatives to psychotherapy: A study of growth centers. *Archives of General Psychiatry, 33*, 157–162.

Lieberman, M. A. (1976). Change induction in small groups. In M. R. Rosenzweig & L. W. Porter (Eds.), *Annual Review of Psychology 27*.

Lieberman, M. A., & Borman, L. D. (1976). *Self-help* and social research. *The Journal of Applied Behavioral Science 12*, 455–463.

Lieberman, M. A. & Borman, L. D. (1979). *Self-help groups for coping with crisis: Origins, members, processes, and impact*. San Francisco: Jossey-Bass.

Lieberman, M. A., & Glidewell, J. C. (Eds.). (1978). The helping process. Special issue: *American Journal of Community Psychology, 6*(5).

Lieberman, M. A., Yalom, I. D., & Miles, M. B. (1973). *Encounter groups: First facts*. New York: Basic Books.

Liebert, R. M., & Baron, R. A. (1972). Some immediate effects of televised violence on children's behavior. *Developmental Psychology, 6*.

Liebert, R. M., & Wicks-Nelson, R. (1981). *Developmental psychology*. Englewood Cliffs, N.J.: Prentice-Hall.

Liebow, E. (1967). *Tally's corner: A study of Negro streetcorner men*. Boston: Little, Brown.

Liederman, P. H., Talkin, S. R., & Rosenfeld, A. (Eds.). (1977). *Culture and infancy: Variations in the human experience*. New York: Academic Press.

Lief, H. I. (1974). Sexual functions in men and their disturbances. In S. Arieti *(Ed.)*, *American handbook of psychiatry*, Vol. 1. New York: Basic Books.

Lienert, G. A. (1964). *Belastung und Regression. Versuch einer Theorie der systematischen Beeinträchtigung der intellektuellen Leistungsfähigkeit. Psychologia Universalis*, Vol. 7. Meisenheim: Hain.

Lienert, G. A. (1969). Die Konfigurationsfrequenzanalyse als Klassifikationsmethode in der klinischen Psychologie. In M. Irle (Ed.), *Bericht über den 26. Kongress der Deutschen Gesellschaft für Psychologie in Tübingen 1968*. Göttingen, Toronto: Hogrefe.

Lienert, G. A. (1969/1961). *Testaufbau und Testanalyse*. Weinheim: Beltz.

Lienert, G. A. (1973–1978/1962). *Verteilungsfreie Methoden in der Biostatistik* (3 vols.). Meisenheim: Hain.

Lienert, G. A. (1977). Über Werner Traxel: Internationalität oder Provinzialismus. Zur Frage: Sollten Psychologen in Englisch publizieren? *Psychologische Beiträge, 19*, 487–492.

Lienert, G. A. (1978). *Verteilungsfreie Methoden in der Biostatistik*. Meisenheim, Glan: Hain Verlag, Vol. 1, 1973; Tables, 1975; Vol. 2.

Lienert, G. A. (in press). *Subject variables in perceptional experimentation: A new paradigm of their control* Hillsdale, N.J.: Erlbaum.

Lifton, R. J. (1969). *Thought reform and the psychology of totalism*. New York: Norton.

Lifton, R. J. (1979). *The broken connection*. New York: Simon & Schuster.

Lifton, R. J., & Falk, R. (1982). *Indefensible weapons.* New York: Basic Books.

Lifton, W. M. (1972). *Groups: Facilitating individual growth and societal change.* New York: Wiley.

Light, D., Jr., & Laufer, R. S. (1975). College youth: Psychohistory and prospects. In R. J. Havighurst & P. H. Dreyers (Eds.), *Youth/74th yearbook for the study of education.* Chicago: University of Chicago Press.

Lightcap, J., Kurland, J. & Burgess, R. (1982). Child abuse. *Ethnology and Sociobiology, 3,* 61–67.

Likert, R. (1932). A technique for the measurement of attitudes. *Archives of Psychology, 140,* 1–55.

Likert, R. (1948). Public opinion polls. *Scientific American, 179*(6).

Likert, R. (1953). Motivation: The core of management. *American Management Association Personnel Series,* no. 155, 3–21.

Likert, R. (1958). Measuring organizational performance. *Harvard Business Review, 36*(2), 51–52.

Likert, R. (1960). The dual function of statistics. *Journal of the American Statistical Association, 5*(289), 1–7.

Likert, R. (1961). *New patterns of management.* New York: McGraw-Hill.

Likert, R. (1967). *The human organization: Its management and value.* New York: McGraw-Hill.

Likert, R. (1969). Organizational theory and human resource accounting. *American Psychologist, 24*(6), 585–592.

Likert, R. (1971). Human resource accounting: A human organizational measurement approach. *Financial Analysts Journal 27*(1), 75–84.

Likert, R. (1973, May/June). Human resource accounting: Building and assessing productive organizations. *Personnel,* 8–24.

Likert, R. (1975). Improving cost performance with cross-functional teams. *The Conference Board Record, 12*(9), 51–59.

Likert, R. (1977). *Past and future perspectives on System 4.* Ann Arbor, Mich.: Rensis Likert.

Likert, R., & Likert, J. G. (1976). *New ways of managing conflict.* New York: McGraw-Hill.

Likert, R., & Likert, J. G. (1980, April). New resources for improving school administration. *NAASP Bulletin, 64*(435).

Likert, R., & Murphy, G. (1938). *Public opinion and the individual.* New York: Harper.

Likert, R., & Willits, J. M. (1940–1941). *Morale and agency management* (4 vols.). Hartford, Conn.: Life Insurance Agency Management Association.

Lilly, J. (1977). *The deep self.* New York: Warner Books.

Lilly, J. C. (1973). *The center of the cyclone.* New York: Bantam Books.

Limber, J. (1977). Language in child and chimp? *American Psychologist, 32,* 280–295.

Lin, N. (1973). *The study of human communication.* New York: Bobbs-Merrill.

Lin, N. (1986a). Conceptualizing social support. In N. Lin, A. Dean, & W. Ensel (Eds.), *Social support, life events, and depression* (pp. 17–48). Orlando: Academic.

Lin, N. (1986b). Modeling the effects of social support. In N. Lin, A. Dean, & W. Ensel (Eds.), *Social support, life events, and depression* (pp. 173–212). Orlando: Academic.

Lin, N., Dean, A., & Ensel, W. (1986). *Social support, life events, and depression.* Orlando: Academic.

Lin, Z. X., & Fang, Z. (1980). Thirty years development in Chinese experimental psychology. *Acta Psychologica Sinica, 12,* 9–15.

Lincoln, Y., & Guba, E. (1985). *Naturalistic inquiry.* Beverley Hills, CA: Sage.

Lindauer, M. (1962). Ethology. *Annual Review of Psychology, 13,* 35–70.

Lindauer, M. S. (1970). Psychological aspects of form perception in abstract art. *Science de l'art, 7,* 19–24.

Lindauer, M. S. (1973). Toward a liberalization of experimental aesthetics. *Journal of Aesthetics and Art Criticism, 31,* 459–465.

Lindauer, M. S. (1977). Imagery from the point of view of psychological aesthetics, the arts, and creativity. *Journal of Mental Imagery, 1,* 343–362.

Lindauer, M. S. (1978). Psychology as a humanistic science. *Psychocultural Review, 2,* 139–145.

Lindauer, M. S. (in press). Imagery and the arts. In A. A. Sheikh (Ed.), *Imagery: Current theory, research, and application.* New York: Wiley.

Lindauer, M. S. (in press). Psychological aesthetics, aesthetic perception, and the aesthetic person. In D. O'Hare (Ed.), *Psychology and the arts.* Sussex, England: Harvester.

Lindauer, M. S. (in press). Psychology and literature. In M. H. Bornstein (Ed.), *Psychology and its allied disciplines.* Hillsdale, N.J.: Erlbaum.

Lindberg A. A. (1933). The formation of negatively conditioned reflexes by coincidence in time with the process of differential inhibition. *Journal of General Psychology, 8,* 392–419.

Lindeman, J, E. (1981). *Psychological and behavioral aspects of physical disability.* New York: Plenum.

Lindeman, R. H., Merenda, P. F., & Gold, R. Z. (1980). *Introduction to bivariate and multivariate analysis.* Glenview, Ill.: Scott, Foresman.

Lindemann, E. (1944). Symptomatology and management of acute grief. *American Journal of Psychiatry, 101,* 141–148.

Linden, K. W., & Linden, J. D. (1968). *Modern mental measurement: A historical perspective.* Boston: Houghton Mifflin.

Lindesmith, A. R. (1968). *Addiction and opiates.* Chicago: Aldine.

Lindgren, H. C. (1967). *Educational psychology in the classroom* (3rd ed.). New York: Wiley.

Lindgren, H. C. (1976). Measuring need to achieve by NachNaff scale—A forced-choice questionnaire. *Psychological Reports, 39,* 907–910.

Lindgren, H. C. (1980). *Great expectations: The psychology of money.* Los Altos, Calif.: Kaufmann.

Lindgren, H. C., & Byrne, D. (1971). *Psychology* (3rd ed.). New York: Wiley.

Lindgren, H. C., & Tebcherani, A. (1971). Arab and American auto and heterostereotypes: A cross-cultural study of empathy. *Journal of Cross-cultural Psychology, 2,* 173–180.

Lindner, R. M. (1950). The psychodynamics of gambling. *Annals of the American Academy of Political and Social Science, 268,* 93–107.

Lindsay, D. S. (1990). Misleading suggestions can impair eyewitnesses' ability to remember event details. *Journal of Experimental Psychology: Learning, Memory and Cognition, 16,* 1077–1983.

Lindsay, P. H., & Norman, D. A. (1977/1972). *Human information processing.* New York: Academic Press.

Lindsay, R. C., Lea, J. A., & Fulford, J. A. (1991). Sequential lineup presentation: Technique matters. *Journal of Applied Psychology, 76,* 741–745.

Lindsay, R. C., Wallbridge, H., & Drennan, D. (1987). Do the clothes make the man? An exploration of the effect of lineup attire on eyewitness identification accuracy. *Canadian Journal of Behavioural Science, 19*, 463–478.

Lindsay, R. C., & Wells, G. L. (1985). Improving eyewitness identifications from lineups: Simultaneous versus sequential lineup presentation. *Journal of Applied Psychology, 70*, 556–564.

Lindsay, R. C. L., Lea, J. A., Nosworthy, G., Fulford, J., Hector, J., LeVan, V. & Seabrook, C. (1991). Biased lineups: Sequential presentation reduces the problem. *Journal of Applied Psychology, 76*, 796–802.

Lindskold, S. (1978). Trust development, the GRIT proposal and the effects of conciliatory acts on conflict and cooperation. *Psychological Bulletin, 85*, 772–793.

Lindsley, D. B. (1940). Bilateral differences in brain potentials from two cerebral hemispheres in relation to laterality and stuttering. *Journal of Experimental Psychology, 26*, 211–225.

Lindsley, D. B. (1951). Emotion. In S. S. Stevens (Ed.), *Handbook of experimental psychology*. New York: Wiley.

Lindsley, D. B. (1982). Neural mechanisms of arousal, attention and information processing. In J. Orbach (Ed.), *Neuropsychology after Lashley*. Hillsdale, N.J.: Erlbaum.

Lindsley, O. R. (1963). Direct measurement and functional definition of vocal hallucinatory symptoms. *Journal of Mental and Nervous Disease, 136*, 293–297.

Lindsley, O. R., Skinner, B. F., & Solomon, H. C. (1953). *Studies in behavior therapy* (Status Report 1). Waltham, Mass.: Metropolitan State Hospital.

Lindzey, G. (1950). An experimental examination of the scapegoat theory of prejudice. *Journal of Abnormal and Social Psychology, 45*, 296–309.

Lindzey, G. (1952). Thematic Apperception Test: Interpretative assumptions and related empirical evidence. *Psychological Bulletin, 49*, 1–25.

Lindzey, G. (1961). *Projective techniques and cross-cultural research*. New York: Appleton-Century-Crofts.

Lindzey, G. (1965). Seer versus sign. *Journal of Experimental Research in Personality, 1*, 17–26.

Lindzey, G. (1967). Some remarks concerning incest, the incest taboo, and psychoanalytic theory. *American Psychologist, 22*, 1051–1059.

Lindzey, G. (1974). *History of psychology in autobiography*, Vol. 6. Cambridge, Mass.: Harvard University Press.

Lindzey, G. (Ed.). (1980). *History of psychology in autobiography*, Vol. 7. San Francisco: Freeman.

Lindzey, G., & Byrne, D. (1968). Measurement of social choice and interpersonal attractiveness. In G. Lindzey, & E. Aronson, (Eds.), *The handbook of social psychology*. Vol. II: *Research methods*. Reading, Mass.: Addison-Wesley.

Lindzey, G., Hall, C., & Thompson, R. F. (1975). *Psychology*. New York: Worth.

Lingoes, J. C. (1966). An IBM-7090 program for Guttman-Lingoes multidimensional scalogram analysis-l. *Behavioral Science, 11*, 76–78.

Lingoes, J. C. (Ed.). (1977). *Geometric representations of relational data: Readings in multidimensional scaling*. Ann Arbor, Mich.: Mathesis.

Linn, M. W., Klett, C. J., & Caffey, E. M., Jr. (1980). Foster home characteristics and psychiatric patient outcome. *Archives of General Psychiatry, 37*, 129–132.

Linn, R. L. (1978). Single-group validity, differential validity, and differential prediction. *Journal of Applied Psychology, 63*, 507–512.

Linstone, H., & Turoff, M. (1975). Introduction. In H. Linstone & M. Turoff (Eds.), *The Delphi method: Techniques and applications*. Reading, Mass.: Addison-Wesley.

Linwick, D., Overmier, J. B., Peterson, G. B., & Martens, M. (1988). The interactions of memories and expectancies as mediators at choice behavior. *American Journal of Psychology, 101*, 313–334.

Lipman, R. S. (1978). Stimulant medication and growth in hyperkinetic children. *Psychopharmacology Bulletin, 4*, 61–62.

Lipman, R. S., Di Mascio, A., Reatig, N., & Kirson, T. (1978). Psychotropic drugs and mentally retarded children. In M. A. Lipton, A. Di Mascio, & K. F. Killam (Eds.), *Psychopharmacology: A generation of progress*. New York: Raven Press.

Lipovechaja, N. G., Kantonistova, N. C., & Chamaganova, T. G. (1978). The role of heredity and environment in the determination of intellectual functions. *Medicinskie Problemy Formirovanija Livcnosti*, 48–59.

Lipowski, Z. J. (1968). Review of consultation psychiatry in psychosomatic medicine. III: Theoretical issues. *Psychosomatic Medicine, 30*, 395–422.

Lipowski, Z. J. (1977). Psychosomatic medicine in the seventies: An overview. *American Journal of Psychiatry, 134*, 233–244.

Lipowski, Z. J., Lipsitt, D. R., & Whybrow, P. C. (Eds.). (1977). *Psychosomatic medicine: Current trends and clinical applications*. New York: Oxford University Press.

Lippitt, G. L. (1982/1969). *Organization renewal*. Englewood Cliffs, N.J.: Prentice-Hall.

Lippitt, P., Eiseman, J., & Lippitt, R. (1969). *Cross age helping program: Orientation, training, and related materials*. Ann Arbor, Mich.: University of Michigan, Center for Research and Utilization of Scientific Knowledge, Institute for Social Research.

Lippitt, R. (1940). An experimental study of authoritarian and democratic group atmospheres. Studies in topological and vector psychology. *University of Iowa Studies in Child Welfare, 16*, 45–195.

Lippitt, R. (1940). An experimental study of three social climates. Ph.D. thesis, University of Iowa.

Lippitt, R., & White, R. K. (1943). The social climate of children's groups. In R. G. Barker, J. S. Kounin, & H. F. Wright, (EDs.), *Child behavior and development*. New York: McGraw-Hill.

Lippitt, R., & White, R. K. (1952). An experimental study of leadership and group life. In G. E. Swanson, T. M. Newcomb, & E. L. Hartley (Eds.), *Readings in social psychology*. New York: Holt.

Lippman, H. (1956). *Treatment of the child in emotional conflict*. McGraw-Hill.

Lippmann, W. (1922). *Public opinion*. New York: Harcourt Brace.

Lipps, T. (1897). *Raumästhetik und geometrisch-optische Täuschungen*. Leipzig: Barth.

Lipps, T. (1898). *Komik und Humor. Eine psychologisch-ästhetische Untersuchung*. Hamburg: Voss.

Lipps, T. (1926/1905). *Psychological studies*. Baltimore, Md.: Williams & Wilkins.

Lipset, S. (1960). *Political man: The social bases of politics*. New York: Doubleday.

Lipsitt, L. P. (1982). Infancy and life-span development. *Human Development, 25*, 41–48.

Lipsitt, L. P. (Ed.). (1976). *Developmental psychobiology: The significance of infancy*. Hillsdale, N.J.: Erlbaum.

Lipsitt, P. D., & Lelos, D. (1981). Decision makers in law and psychiatry and the involuntary civil committment process. *Community Mental Health Journal, 17*, 114.

Lipsitt, P. D., & Sales, B. D. (1980). *New directions in psychological research*. New York: Van Nostrand.

Lipstein, B., & McGuire, W. J. (1978). *Evaluating advertising: A bibliography of the communications process*. New York: Advertising Research Foundation.

Lipton, D., Martinson, R., & Wilks, J. (1975). *The effectiveness of correctional treatment: A survey of treatment evaluation studies*. New York: Praeger.

Lishman, W. A. (1978). *Organic psychiatry*. Oxford: Blackwell.

Litman, G. K. (1976). Behavioral modification techniques in the treatment of alcoholism: A review and critique. In R. J. Gibbins, Y. Israel, H. Kalant, R. E. Popham, W. Schmit, R. & G. Smart, (Eds.), *Research advances in alcohol and drug problems*, Vol. 3. New York: Wiley.

Litman, R. E. (1967). Sigmund Freud on suicide. In E. S. Shneidman (Ed.), *Essays in self-destruction*. New York: Science House.

Litman, R. E., & Wold, C. (1976). 1. Beyond crisis intervention. In E. S. Shneidman (Ed.), *Suicidology: Contemporary developments*. New York: Grune & Stratton.

Little, B. B., Snell, L. M., Rosenfeld, C. R., Gilstrap, L. C. III, & Gant, N. F. (1990). Failure to recognize fetal alcohol syndrome in newborn infants. *American Journal of Diseases in Children, 144*, 1142–1146.

Little, J. C. (1979). Neurotic illness in fitness fanatics. *Psychiatric Annals, 9*, 49–51.

Little, P., & Zuckerman, M. (1986). Sensation seeking and music preferences. *Personality and Individual Differences, 4*, 575–578.

Little, R. (1964). Buddy relations and combat performance. In M. Janowitz (Ed.), *The new military*. New York: Russell Sage Foundation.

Littman, R. A., & Rosen, E. (1950). Molar and molecular. *Psychological Review, 57*, 58–65.

Littrell, J. M., Lee-Borden, N., & Lorenz, J. (1979). A developmental framework for counseling supervision. *Counselor Education and Supervision, 19*, 129–136.

Litwin, G., & Stringer, R. (1968). *Motivation and organizational climate*. Cambridge, Mass.: Harvard University Press.

Liu, F. (1981). The current developmental psychology in China. *Acta Psychologica Sinica, 13*, 117–123.

Liu, F. (1982). Developmental psychology in China. *Acta Psychologica Sinica, 14*, 1–10.

Livermore, J. M., Malmquist, C. P., & Meehl, P. H. (1968). On the justifications for civil commitment. *University of Pennsylvania Law Review, 117*, 75–96.

Livernash, E. R. (Ed.). (1980). *Comparable worth: Issues and alternatives*. Washington, D.C.: Equal Employment Advisory Council.

Livingston, J. (1974). *Compulsive gamblers*. New York: Harper & Row.

Livington, J. S. (1969). Pygmalion in management. *Harvard Business Review, 47*, 94–102.

Lloyd, B. B. (1971). The intellectual development of Yoruba children: A re-examination. *Journal of Cross-Cultural Psychology, 2*, 29–38.

Lloyd, B. B. (1977). The intellectual development of Yoruba children. Additional evidence and a seredipitous finding. *Journal of Cross-Cultural Psychology, 8*, 3–16.

Lloyd, J. E. (1966). Studies on the flash communication system in *Photinus* fireflies. *Publications of the Museum of Zoology, University of Michigan, 130*, 1–95.

Lloyd, L., & Chang, H. F. (1979). The usefulness of distinguishing between a defensive and a nondefensive external locus of control. *Journal of Research on Personality, 13*, 316–325.

Lloyd-Bostock, S., & Clifford, B., eds. (1983). *Evaluating witness evidence: Recent psychological research and new perspectives*. New York: Wiley.

Loades, H. R., & Rich, S. G. (1917). Binet tests on South African natives—Zulus. *Journal of Genetic Psychology, 24*, 373–383.

Lobsien, M. (1904). Veber psychologie der aussage. *Zeitschrifi fur Pädagogische Psychologie, 6*, 161.

Lochman, J. E. (1987). Self and peer perceptions and attributional biases of aggressive boys. *Journal of Consulting and Clinical Psychology, 55*, 404–410.

Lockard, R. B. (1971). Reflexions on the fall of comparative psychology: Is there a message for us all? *American Psychologist, 26*, 168–179.

Locke, E. A. (1968). Toward a theory of task motivation and incentives. *Organizational Behavior and Human Performance, 3*, 157–189.

Locke, E. A. (1976). The nature and causes of job satisfaction. In M. D. Dunnette (Ed.), *Handbook of industrial and organizational psychology*. Chicago: Rand McNally.

Locke, E. A. (1978). The ubiquity of the techniques of goal setting in theories and approaches to employee motivation. *Academy of Management Review, 3*, 594–601.

Locke, E. A. & Bryan, J. F. (1966). Cognitive aspects of psychomotor performance goals on level of performance. *Journal of Applied Psychology, 50*, 286–291.

Locke, E. A., & Latham, G. P. (1990). *A theory of goal setting and task performance*. Englewood Cliffs, NJ: Prentice-Hall.

Locke, E. A., & Lathas, G. P. (1984). *Goal-setting: A motivational technique that works*. Englewood Cliffs, NJ: Prentice-Hall.

Locke, E. A., & Schweiger, D. M. (1979). Participation in decision-making: One more look. In B. M. Staw (Ed.), *Research in organizational behavior*, Vol. 1. Greenwich, Conn.: JAI Press.

Locke, E. A., Shaw, K. N., Saari, L. M., & Latham, G. P. (1982). Goal setting and task performance: 1969–1980. *Psychological Bulletin, 90*, 125–152.

Locke, J. (1934/1693). *Some thoughts concerning education*. Cambridge, England: Cambridge University Press.

Locke, J. (1965/1690). *An essay concerning human understanding*. London: Dent.

Locke, J. (1984). *An essay concerning human understanding*. edited (A. C. Fraser, Ed., 2 vols.). London: Oxford University Press.

Locke, T. P., & Shontz, F. C. (1983). Personality correlates of the near-death experience: A preliminary study. *Journal of the American Society for Psychical Research, 77*, 311–318.

Lockman, R. F. (1964). An empirical description of the subfields of psychology. *American Psychologist, 19*, 645–653.

Lockwood, G. (1981). Rational-emotive therapy and extremist-religious cults. *Rational Living, 16*, 13–18.

Loeb, J. (1908). *Forced movements, tropisms and animal conduct*, Philadelphia, Pa.: Lippincott.

Loeb, J. (1912). *The mechanistic conception of life: Biological essays*. Chicago: University of Chicago Press.

Loeber, R. (1982). The stability of antisocial and delinquent child behavior: A review. *Child Development, 53*, 1431–1446.

Loeber, R. (1988a). The natural histories of juvenile conduct problems, substance use, and delinquency: Evidence for developmental progressions. In B. B. Lahey & A. E. Kazdin (Eds.), *Advances in clinical child psychology* (Vol. 11, pp. 73–124). New York: Plenum.

Loeber, R. (1988b). Behavioral precursors and accelerators of delinquency. In W. Buikhuisen & S. A. Mednick (Eds.), *Explaining crime* (pp. 51–67). Leiden: Brill.

Loeber, R. (1990). Development and risk factors of juvenile antisocial behavior and delinquency, *Clinical Psychology Review, 10,* 1–41.

Loeber, R., Lahey, B. B., & Thomas, C. (1991). Diagnostic conundrum of oppositional defiant disorder and conduct disorder. *Journal of Abnormal Psychology, 100,* 379–390.

Loeber, R., & Schmaling, K. B. (1985). Empirical evidence for overt and covert patterns of antisocial conduct problems: A meta-analysis. *Journal of Abnormal Child Psychology, 13,* 337–352.

Loeber, R., & Stouthamer-Loeber, M. (1987). Prediction. In H. C. Quay (Ed.), *Handbook of Juvenile delinquency* (pp. 325–382). New York: Wiley.

Loeber, R., Tremblay, R. E., Gagnon, C., & Charlebois, P. (1989). Continuity and desistance in disruptive boys' early fighting at school. *Development and Psychopathology, 1,* 39–50.

Loehlin, J. C. (1982). Are personality traits differentially heritable? *Behavior Genetics, 12,* 417–428.

Loehlin, J. C. (1992). *Genes and environment in personality development.* Newbury Park, CA: Sage.

Loehlin, J. C., Lindzey, G., & Spuhler, J. N. (1975). *Race differences in intelligence.* San Francisco: Freeman.

Loehlin, J. C., & Nichols, R. C. (1976). *Heredity, environment, and personality.* Austin, Tex.: University of Texas Press.

Loening-Raucke, V. (1990). Modulation of abnormal defecation dynamics by biofeedback treatment in chronically constipated children with encopresis. *The Journal of Pediatrics, 116,* 214–222.

Loesch, L. C., & Wheeler, P. T. (1982). *Principles of leisure counseling.* Minneapolis, Minn.: Educational Media.

Loevinger, J. (1976). *Ego development: Conceptions and theories.* San Francisco: Jossey-Bass.

Loevinger, J., & Wessler, R. (1970). *Ego development.* San Francisco: Jossey-Bass.

Loevinger, J., Wessler, R., & Redmore, C. (1970). *Measuring ego development.* Vols. 1, 2. San Francisco: Jossey-Bass.

Loewald, H. W. (1960). On the therapeutic action of psycho-analysis. *International Journal of Psycho-Analysis, 41,* 16–33.

Lofquist, L. H., & Dawis, R. V. (1969). *Adjustment to work: A psychological view of man's problems in a work-oriented society.* New York: Appleton-Century-Crofts.

Loftus, B., & Klinger, M. R. (1992). Is the unconscious smart or dumb? *American Psychologist, 47,* 761–765.

Loftus, E. (1986). Ten years in the life of an expert witness. *Law and Human Behavior, 10,* 241–262.

Loftus, E., & Monahan, J. (1980). Trial by data: Psychological research as legal evidence. *American Psychologist, 35,* 270–283.

Loftus, E., & Palmer, J. C. (1974). Reconstruction of automobile destruction: An example of the interaction between language and memory. *Journal of Verbal Learning and Verbal Behavior. 13,* 585–589.

Loftus, E. F. (1974). Reconstructing memory: The incredible eyewitness. *Psychology Today, 8,* 116–119.

Loftus, E. F. (1979). *Eyewitness testimony.* Cambridge, Mass.: Harvard University Press.

Loftus, E. F., & Hoffman, H. G. (1989). Misinformation and memory: The creation of new memories. *Journal of Experimental Psychology: General, 118,* 100–104.

Loftus, E. F., & Zanni, G. (1975). Eyewitness testimony: the influence of the wording of a question. *Bulletin of the Psychonomic Society, 5,* 86–88.

Logan, F. A. (1956). A micromolar approach to behavior theory. *Psychological Review, 63,* 63–73.

Logan, F. A. (1960). *Incentive.* New Haven, Conn.: Yale University Press.

Logan, F. A. (1964). The free behavior situation. In M. R. Jones (Ed.), *Nebraska Symposium on Motivation.* Lincoln, Neb.: University of Nebraska Press.

Logan, F. A. (1966). Transfer of discrimination. *Journal of Experimental Psychology, 71,* 616–618.

Logan, F. A. (1971). Essentials of a theory of discrimination learning. In H. H. Kendler & J. T. Kendler (Eds.), *Essays in neobehaviorism: A memorial volume to Kenneth W. Spence.* New York: Appleton-Century-Crofts.

Logan, F. A. (1979). Hybrid theory of operant conditioning. *Psychological Review, 86,* 507–541.

Logan, F. A., & Ferraro, D. P. (1978). *Systematic analyses of learning and motivation.* New York: Wiley.

Logan, F. A., & Gordon, W. C. (1981). *Fundamentals of learning and motivation.* Dubuque, Iowa: Brown.

Logan, F. A., & Wager, A. R. (1965). *Reward and punishment.* Boston: Allyn & Bacon.

Logue, A. W., & Smith, M. E. (1986). Predictors of food preference in adult humans. *Appetite, 7,* 109–125.

LoLordo, V. M., & Fairless, J. L. (1985). Pavlovian conditioned inhibition: The literature since 1969. In R. R. Miller & N. E. Spear (Eds.), *Information Processing in Animal: Conditioned Inhibition* (pp. 1–49). Hillsdale, NJ: Erlbaum.

Lomax, A., Bartenieff, I., & Paulay, F. (1968). Dance style and culture. In A. Lomax (Ed.), *Folk song style and culture,* Washington, D.C.: American Association for the Advancement of Science, Publication no. 88.

Lombardi, D. (1969). Therapeutic community and drug addiction-moralistic considerations. Unpublished paper, Seton Hall University, South Orange, N.J.

Lombardi, D. (1969). The special language of the addict. *Pastoral Psychology, 20,* 51–52.

Lombardi, D. (1971). Self-reliance and social cooperation. *Journal of Drug Education, 1,* 279–284.

Lombardi, D. (1972). Some psychological aspects of drug abuse. Unpublished paper, Seton Hall University, South Orange, N.J.

Lombardi, D. (1975). *Search for significance.* Chicago: Nelson-Hall.

Lombardi, D., & Angers, W. P. (1967). First memories of drug addicts. *Individual Psychologist, 5,* 7–13.

Lombardi, D., & Isele, F. W. (1967). The young drug addict. *NJEA Review,* February, 28–29.

Lombardi, D., O'Brien, B. J., & Isele, F. W. (1968). Differential responses of addicts and nonaddicts on the MMPI. *Journal of Projective Techniques and Personality Assessment, 32,* 479–482.

London, M., & Bray, D. W. (1980). Ethical issues in testing and evaluation for personnel decisions. *American Psychologist, 35,* 890–901.

London, P. (1964). *The modes and morals of psychotherapy.* New York: Holt, Rinehart & Winston.

London, P. (1986). *The mode and morals of psychotherapy* (2nd ed.). New York: Norton.

Loney, J., Prinz, R. J., Mishalow, J., & Joad, J. (1978). Hyperkinetic/aggressive boys in treatment: Predictions of clinical response to methylphenidate. *American Journal of Psychiatry, 135,* 1487–1491.

Long, S. (1975). Personality and systemic rejection: A study of white and black adolescents. *Youth and Society, 7,* 99–129.

Long, S. (1976). Perceived relative deprivation and political orientation: A study of white and black adolescents. *Journal of Political and Military Sociology, 5,* 99–115.

Long, S. (1976). Political alienation among black and white adolescents: A test of the social deprivation and political reality models. *American Politics Quarterly, 4,* 267–304.

Long, S. (1977). Explaining systemic failure: A two-dimensional analysis. *Psychological Reports, 41,* 23–28.

Long, S. (1978). Personality and political alienation among white and black youth: A test of the social deprivation model. *Journal of Politics, 40,* 433–457.

Long, S. (1978). Political alienation: reality and reactance. *Journal of Social Psychology, 104,* 115–121.

Long, S. (1978). Political hopelessness: a new dimension of systemic disaffection, *Journal of Social Psychology, 105,* 205–211.

Long, S. (1979). Psychological sources of adolescent systemic rejection. *International Journal of Political Education, 2,* 247–272.

Long, S. (1980). Personality and political revenge: psychopolitical adaptation among black and white youth. *Journal of Black Studies, 11,* 77–104.

Long, S. (1980). Urban adolescents and the political system: Dimensions of disaffection. *Theory and Research in Social Education, 8,* 31–43.

Long, S. (1981). A psychopolitical theory of systemic disaffection. *Micropolitics, 1,* 395–420.

Long, S. (1982). Irrational political beliefs: A theory of systemic rejection. *International Journal of Political Education, 5,* 1–14.

Long, S. (forthcoming). Political reactance and political reality: A theory of political alienation. *International Journal of Political Education.*

Long, S. (forthcoming). Psychopolitical orientations of white and black youth: A test of five models. *Journal of Black Studies.*

Longabaugh, R. (1980). The systematic observation of behavior in naturalistic settings. In H. Triandis & J. Berry (Eds.), *Handbook of cross-cultural psychology,* vol. 2. Boston: Allyn & Bacon.

Longergan, W. G. (1957). Roleplaying in an industrial conflict. *Group Psychotherapy, 10,* 105–110.

Longstaff, H. P. (1948). Fakability of the Strong and Kuder. *Journal of Applied Psychology, 32,* 360–369.

Lonner, W., & Ibrahim, F. A. (1989). Assessment in cross-cultural counseling. In P. Pedersen, J. Draguns, W. Lonner, & J. Trimble (Eds.), *Counseling across cultures.* (3rd ed.). Honolulu: University of Hawaii Press.

Loomis, A. I., Harvey, E. N, & Hobart, G. A., III. (1937). Cerebral states during sleep, as studied by human brain potentials. *Journal of Experimental Psychology, 21,* 127–144.

Loosli-Usteri, M. (1938). *Le diagnostic individuel chez l'enfant au moyen du Test de Rorschach.* Paris: Hartmann.

Lopez, O. L., Becker, J. T., Brenner, R. P., Rosen, J., Bajulaiye, O. I., & Reynods, C. F. (1991). Alzheimer's disease with delusions and hallucinations. *Neurology, 41*(6), 901–912.

LoPiccolo, J., & Lobitz, W. C. (1978). The role of masturbation in the treatment of orgasmic dysfunction. In J. LoPiccolo & L. LoPiccolo (Eds.), *Handbook of sex therapy.* New York: Plenum.

Lo Piccolo, J., & Lo Piccolo, L. (Eds.). (1978). *Handbook of sex therapy.* New York: Plenum.

Loram, C. J. (1917). *The education of the South African native.* London: Longman Green.

Lorayne, H., & Lucas, J. (1974). *The memory book.* New York: Ballantine.

Lord, C. G., & Velicer, W. F. (1975). Effects of sex, birth order, target's relationship and target's sex on self-disclosure by college students. *Psychology Reports, 37*(3), 1167–1170.

Lord, F. M. (1971). Robbins-Monro procedures for tailored testing. *Educational and Psychological Measurement, 31,* 3–31.

Lord, F. M. (1980). *Applications of item response theory to practical testing problems.* Hillsdale, N.J.: Erlbaum.

Lorenz, K. (1942–1943). Die angeborenen Förmen moglicher Erfahrung. *Zeitschrift für Tierpsychologie, 5,* 235–409.

Lorenz, K. Z. (1937). The companion in the bird's world. *Auk, 54,* 245–273.

Lorenz, K. Z. (1941). Vergleichende bewegungsstudien an anatinen. *Journal fur Ornithologie Supplement, 79,* 194–294.

Lorenz, K. Z. (1941). Vergleichende Bewegungsstudien an Anatinen. *Supplement, Journal of Ornithology, 89,* 194–294.

Lorenz, K. Z. (1949). *King Solomon's ring: New light on animal ways.* New York: Crowell.

Lorenz, K. Z. (1950). *Man meets dog.* London: Methuen.

Lorenz, K. Z. (1950). The comparative method in studying innate behavior patterns. In *Symposium of the Society for Experimental Biology,* Vol. IV: *Physiological mechanisms in animal behavior.* London, New York: Cambridge University Press.

Lorenz, K. Z. (1965). *Evolution and modification of behavior.* Chicago: University of Chicago Press.

Lorenz, K. Z. (1966). *On aggression.* New York: Harcourt Brace Jovanovich.

Lorenz, K. Z. (1970). The establishment of the instinct concept. In K. Lorenz, *Studies in animal and human behavior,* Vol. I. London: Methuen.

Lorenz, K. Z. (1970–1971). *Studies on animal behavior.* Cambridge, Mass.: Harvard University Press

Lorenz, K. Z. (1973). *Civilized man's eight deadly sins.* New York: Harcourt Brace Jovanovich.

Lorenz, K. Z., & Tinbergen, N. (1938). Taxis und Instinkthandlung in der Eirollbewegung der Graugans. *Zeitschrift Für Tierpsychologie, 2,* 1–29.

Lorge, I. (1930). Influence of regularly interpolated time intervals on subsequent learning. *Teachers College Contributions to Education,* no. 438.

Lorge, I. (1951). The fundamental nature of measurement. In E. F. Lindquist (Ed.), *Educational measurement.* Washington, D.C.: American Council on Education.

Lorge, I. (1959). *The Lorge formula for estimating difficulty of reading material.* New York: Bureau of Publications, Teachers College, Columbia University.

Lorge, L, & Hollingworth, L. S. (1936). Adult status of highly intelligent children. *Journal of Genetic Psychology, 49,* 215–226.

Lorr, M. (Ed.). (1966). *Explorations in typing psychosis.* Oxford: Pergamon Press.

Losancy, L., (1977). *Turning people on: How to be an encouraging person.* Englewood Cliffs, N.J.: Prentice-Hall.

Lotze, H. (1852). *Medicinische Psychologie; oder, Physiologie der Seele.* Leipzig: Weidmann.

Lotze, H. (1884/1879). *Metaphysic, in three books, ontology, cosmology, and psychology.* Oxford: Clarendon Press.

Lotze, H. (1885/1864). *Microcosmus: An essay concerning man and his relation to the world.* Edinburgh: Clark.

Lou, H. C. (1990). Methylphenidate reversible hypoperfusion of striatal regions in ADHD. In K. Conners, & M. Kinsbourne (Eds.), *Atten-*

tion deficit hyperactivity disorder: ADHD; clinical experimental and demographic issues (pp. 137–148). Munich: MMV Medizin Verlag.

Louisell, D. W. (1955). The psychologist in today's legal world. *Minnesota Law Review, 39,* 235–272.

Loutitt, C. M. (1936). *Clinical psychology.* New York: Harpers.

Loutitt, C. M. (1939). The nature of clinical psychology. *Psychological Bulletin, 36,* 361–387.

Lovaas, O. I., Litrownik, A., & Mann, R. (1971). Response latencies to auditory stimuli in autistic children engaged in self-stimulatory behavior. *Behavior Research and Therapy, 2,* 39–49.

Lovallo, W. R., & Pishkin, V. (1980). Performance of type A (coronary-prone) men during and after exposure to uncontrollable noise and task failure. *Journal of Personality and Social Psychology, 38,* 963–971.

Lovell, K. (1971). *The growth of understanding in mathematics: Kindergarten through grade three.* New York: Holt, Rinehart & Winston.

Lovelock, J. (1979). *Gala: A new look at life on earth.* New York: Oxford University Press.

Lovin, B. C., & Casstevens, E. R. (1971). *Coaching, learning and action.* New York: American Management Association.

Low, A. A. (1952). *Mental health through will-training.* Boston: Christopher.

Lowen, A. (1958). *The language of the body.* New York: Collier.

Lowen, A. (1967). *The betrayal of the body.* New York: Macmillan.

Lowen, A. (1975). *Bioenergetics.* New York: Coward, McCann & Geoghegan.

Lowenstein, S., Weissberg, M., & Terry, D. (1990). Alcohol intoxication, injuries and dangerous behaviors—And the revolving emergency department doors. *Journal of Trauma, 30,* 1252–1258.

Lowenthal, M. F., Thurnher, M., & Chiriboga, D. (1975). *Four stages of life: A comparative study of women and men facing transitions.* San Francisco: Jossey-Bass.

Lowery, L. G., & Smith, G. (1933). *The institute for child guidance.* New York: Commonwealth Fund.

Lowinson, J. H., & Ruiz, P. (Eds.). (1981). *Substance abuse: Clinical problems and perspectives.* Baltimore, Md.: Williams & Wilkins.

Lowney, E. (1975). Contact dermatitis. In S. Moshella, D. Pillsbury, & H. Hurley (Eds.), *Dermatology.* Philadelphia, Pa.: Saunders.

Lowry, R. J. (1973). *A. H. Maslow: An intellectual portrait.* Monterey, Calif.: Brooks/Cole.

Lubin, A. (1953). Review of the Szondi test. In O. K. Buros (Ed.), *The fourth mental measurements yearbook.* Highland Park, N.J.: Gryphon Press.

Luborsky, L. (1984). *Principles of psychoanalytic psychotherapy: A manual for supportive expressive treatment.* New York: Basic Books.

Luborsky, L., Auerbach, A. H., Chandler, M., Cohen, J., & Bachrach, H. M. (1971). Factors influencing the outcome of psychotherapy. *Psychological Bulletin, 75,* 145–185.

Luborsky, L., Barber, J. P., & Crits-Christoph, P. (1990). Theory-based research for understanding the process of dynamic psychotherapy. *Journal of Consulting and Clinical Psychology, 58,* 281–287.

Luborsky, L., Docherty, J. P., & Penick, S. (1973). Onset conditions for psychosomatic symptoms: A comparative review of immediate observations with retrospective research. *Psychosomatic Medicine, 35,* 187–204.

Luborsky, L., Singer, B., & Luborsky, L. (1975). Comparative studies of psychotherapies. *Archives of General Psychiatry, 32,* 995–1008.

Luborsky, L., Singer, B., & Luborsky, S. (1975). Comparative studies of psychotherapies: Is it true that "Everyone has won and all must have prizes"? *Archives of General Psychiatry, 32,* 995–1008.

Lubs, H. A. (1969). A marker X chromosome. *American Journal of Human Genetics, 21,* 231–244.

Lucas, R. W., Mullin, P. J., Luna, C. C., & McInroy, D. C. (1977). Psychiatrists and a computer as interrogators of patients with alcohol-related illnesses: A comparison. *British Journal of Psychiatry, 131,* 160–167.

Luce, G. G. (1978/1970). *Biological rhythms in psychiatry and medicine* [DHEW Publication No. (ADM)78–247]. *Washington, D.C.: U.S. Government Printing Office.*

Luce, G. G., & Segal, J. (1966). *Sleep.* New York: Coward-McCann.

Luce, R. D. (1959). *Individual choice behavior.* New York: Wiley.

Luce, R. D. (1986). *Response times: Their role in inferring elementary mental organization.* New York: Oxford University Press.

Luce, R. D., Bush, R. R., & Galanter, E. (1963). *Handbook of mathematical psychology,* Vol. 1. New York, London, Sydney: Wiley.

Luce, R. D., Bush, R. R., & Galanter, E. (Eds.). (1963). *Readings in mathematical psychology I.* New York: Wiley.

Luce, R. D., & Raiffa, H. (1957). *Games and decisions: Introduction and critical survey.* New York: Wiley.

Luchins, A. S. (1942). Mechanization in problem solving—The effect of *Einstellung. Psychological Monographs, 54,* entire no. 248.

Luchins, A. S., & Luchins, E. H. (1970). *Wertheimer's seminars revisited. Problem solving and thinking,* Vol. III, Albany, N.Y.: State University of New York at Albany.

Luckey, J. W., & Berman, J. J. (1979). Effects of a new commitment law on involuntary admissions and service utilization patterns. *Law and Human Behavior, 3,* 149–162.

Luckhardt, A. B., & Carlson, A. J. (1915). Contributions to the physiology of the stomach. XVII. On the chemical control of the gastric hunger contractions. *American Journal of Physiology, 36,* 37–46.

Ludeman, K. (1981). The sexuality of the older person: Review of the literature. *The Gerontologist, 21*(2), 203–209.

Lueckert, H.-R. (1957). *Stanford Intelligenz-Test.* Göttingen, West Germany: Hogrefe.

Lüer, G. (Ed.). (1983). *Bericht über den 23. Kongress der Deutschen Gesellschaft für Psychologie in Mainz, 1982, Band 1 u. 2.* Göttingen, West Germany: Hogrefe.

Luft, J. (1961). The Johari window: A graphic model of awareness in interpersonal behavior. *Human Relations Training News, 5*(1), 6–7.

Luginbuhl, J. E. R., & Crowe, D. H. (1975). Causal attributions for success and failure. *Journal of Personality and Social Psychology, 31,* 86–93.

Lugo, J. O. (1984). *Human development: A life-span to psychological, biological, and sociological development* (3rd ed.). Monterey, Calif.: Brooks/Cole.

Lugo, J. O., & Hershey, G. L. (1981). *Living psychology* (3rd ed.). New York: Macmillan.

Luk, C. (1960). *Ch'an and Zen teaching.* (1st, 2nd, 3rd series). London: Rider.

Lukomnik, M. (1940). An experiment to test the canalization hypothesis. Unpublished master's thesis, Columbia University.

Lumsden, C. J., & Wilson, E. O. (1981). *Genes, mind and culture: The coevolutionary process.* Cambridge, Mass.: Harvard University Press.

Lund, F. H., & Anastasi, A. (1920). An interpretation of aesthetic experience. *American Journal of Psychology, 28,* 434–448.

Lund, R. D. (1978). *Development and plasticity of the brain*. New York: Oxford University Press.

Lundberg, G. A. (1926). Case work and the statistical method. *Social Forces, 5*, 60–63.

Lundin, R. W. (1961). *Personality: An experimental approach*, New York: Macmillan.

Lundin, R. W. (1965). *Principles of psychopathology*, Columbus, Ohio: Merril.

Lundin, R. W. (1967/1953). *An objective psychology of music*, New York: Ronald Press.

Lundin, R. W. (1974/1969). *Personality: A behavioral analysis*. New York: Macmillan.

Lundin, R. W. (1979/1972). *Theories and systems of psychology*, Lexington, Mass.: Heath.

Lunneborg, P. W. (1971). Birth order and sex of sibling effect on intellectual abilities. *Journal of Consulting and Clinical Psychology, 37*(3), 445.

Luria, A. (1981). *The language of clothes*. New York: Random House.

Luria, A. R. (1960/1932). *The nature of human conflicts*. New York: Basic Books.

Luria, A. R. (1966/1962). *Higher cortical functions in man*. New York: Basic Books.

Luria, A. R. (1968). *The Mind of a mnemonist*. Chicago: Regnery.

Luria, A. R. (1968). *The mind of a mnemonist*. New York: Basic Books.

Luria, A. R. (1973). *The working brain*. New York: Basic Books.

Luria, A. R. (1976). *Cognitive development: Its cultural and social foundations*. Cambridge, Mass.: Harvard University Press.

Luria, A. R. (1978). The human brain and conscious activity. In G. E. Schwartz & D: Shapiro (Eds.), *Consciousness and self-regulation: Advances in research and theory* (Vol. 2). New York: Plenum.

Luria, A. R. (1979). *The making of mind. A personal account of Soviet psychology*. Cambridge, Mass.: Harvard University Press.

Luria, A. R., & Majovski, L. V. (1977). Basic approaches used in American and Soviet clinical psychology. *American Psychologist, 32*, 959–968.

Lüscher, M. (1949). *Die Psychologie der Farben*. Basel: Test-Verlag.

Lushene, R. E., O'Neil, H. F., & Dunn, T. (1974). Equivalent validity of a completely computerized MMPI. *Journal of Personality Assessment, 38*, 353.

Lutey, C. (1977). *Individual intelligence testing, a manual and sourcebook*. Greeley, Colo.: Lutey.

Luthe, W. (1963). Autogenic training: Method, research, and application in medicine. *American Journal of Psychotherapy, 17*, 174–195.

Luthe, W. (1969). *Autogenic therapy*, New York: Grune & Stratton.

Lutz, K. (1988). *Unnatural emotions*. Chicago: University of Chicago Press.

Luus, C. E., & Wells, G. L. (1991). Eyewitness identification and the selection of distractors for lineups. *Law & Human Behavior, 15*, 43–57.

Lybeck, L. (1979). A research approach to science education at Göteborg. *European Journal of Science Education, 1*, 119–124.

Lykken, D. (1992, July 30). Personal Communication.

Lykken, D. T. (1957). A study of anxiety in the sociopathic personality. *Journal of Abnormal and Social Psychology, 55*, 6–10.

Lykken, D. T. (1972). Range correction applied to heart rate and to GSR data. *Psychophysiology, 9*, 373–379.

Lykken, D. T. (1981). *A tremor in the blood: Uses and abuses of the lie detector*. New York: McGraw-Hill.

Lykken, D. T., & Venables, P. H. (1971). Direct measurement of skin conductance: A proposal for standardization. *Psychophysiology, 8*, 656–672.

Lynch, J. J. (1977). *The broken heart: The medical consequences of loneliness*. New York: Basic Books.

Lynch, S. (1968). *Intense human experience: Its relationship to openness and self concept*. Unpublished doctoral dissertation, University of Florida.

Lynn, D. B. (1959). A note on sex differences in the development of masculine and feminine identification. *Psychological Review, 66*, 126–135.

Lynn, R. (1977). The intelligence of the Japanese. *Bulletin of the British Psychological Society, 30*, 69–72.

Lynn, R., Gluckin, N., & Kripke, B. (1978). *Learning disabilities: The state of the field 1978*. New York: Social Science Research Council.

Lyon, J., & Sales, R. J. (Eds.). (1966). *Psycholinguistic papers*. Edinburgh: University of Edinburgh.

Lyons, A. (1988). *Satan wants you: The cult of devil worship in America*. New York: Mysterious Books.

Lyons, A. S., & Petrucelli, R. J. (1978). *Medicine: An illustrated history*. New York: Abrams.

Lyotard, J. F. (1984). *The postmodern condition: A report on knowledge*. Manchester, UK: Manchester University Press.

Maas, J. W. (1975). Biogenic amines and depression. Biochemical and pharmacological separation of two types of depression. *Archives of General Psychiatry, 32*, 1357–1361.

Macaulay, L., & Berkowitz, L. (Eds.). (1970). *Altruism and helping behavior*. New York: Academic Press.

MacCallum, G. (1967). Negative and positive freedom. *Philosophical Review, 76*, 312–334.

Maccoby, E. E. (1980). *Social development: Psychological growth and the parent–child relationship*. New York: Harcourt Brace Jovanovich.

Maccoby, E. E. (Ed.). (1966). *The development of sex differences*. Stanford, Calif.: Stanford University Press.

Maccoby, E. E., & Jacklin, C. N. (1974). *The psychology of sex differences*. Stanford, Calif.: Stanford University Press.

Maccoby, E. E., & Jacklin, C. N. (1980). Sex differences in aggression: A rejoinder and reprise. *Child Development, 51*, 964–980.

Maccoby, E. E., Newcomb, T. M., & Hartley, E. L. (Eds.) (1958). *Readings in social psychology* (3rd ed.). New York: Holt.

Maccoby, M. (1981). *The leader*. New York: Simon & Shuster.

MacCorquodale, K., & Meehl, P. E. (1954). Edward C. Tolman. In W. K. Estes, S. Koch, K. MacCorquodale, P. E. Meehl, C. G. Mueller, W. N. Schoenfeld, & W. S. Verplanck (Eds.), *Modern learning theory*. New York: Appleton-Century-Crofts.

MacDonald, A. (1944–1945). *Selection Of African personnel. Report on the work of the Selection of Personnel, Technical and Research Unit, M.E.F.* London: Ministry of Defence.

MacDonald, A. P. (1971). Birth order and personality. *Journal of Consulting and Clinical Psychology, 36*(2), 171–176.

MacDonald, A. P., Jr. (1967). Birth order effects in marriage and parenthood: Affiliation and socialization. *Journal of Marriage and the Family, 29*(4), 656–661.

Mace, D. R. (1972). *Getting ready for marriage*. Nashville, Tenn.: Abington Press.

MacGinitie, W. M. (1969). Language development. In R. L. Ebel (Ed.), *Encyclopedia of educational research*. New York: Macmillan.

Mach, E. (1959/1914/1886). *The analysis of sensations and the relation of the physical to the psychical.* New York: Dover.

Mach, E. (1902). *The analysis of experience.* Jena, East Germany: Fisher.

Mach, E. (1907). *The science of mechanics.* Chicago: Open Court.

Machotka, P. (1974). *The nude: Perception and personality.* San Francisco: Halstead Press.

MacKay, C. (1932/1841). *Extraordinary popular delusions and the madness of crowds.* New York: Noonday Press.

MacKay, D. M. (1963). Psychophysics of perceived intensity: A theoretical basis for Fechner's and Stevens' law. *Science, 139,* 1213–1216.

Mackenzie, B. (1977). Three stages in the history of parapsychology. Presented at the Quadrennial Congress on History of Science, Edinburgh.

Mackenzie, B. D. (1972). Behaviorism and positivism. *Journal of the History of the Behavioral Sciences, 14,* 222–231.

Mackey, T. W. (1980). Jury selection: Developing the third eye. *Trial, 16,* 22–25.

MacKinnon, D. W. (1961). *The personality correlates of creativity: A study of American architects.* Berkeley, Calif.: Institute of Personality Assessment and Research.

MacKinnon, D. W. (1963). Creativity and images of the self. In R. W. White (Ed.), *The study of lives: Essays in honor of Henry A. Murray.* New York: Atherton.

MacKinnon, D. W. (1964). The creativity of architects. In C. Taylor (Ed.), *Widening horizons in creativity.* New York, Wiley.

MacKinnon, D. W. (1965). Personality and the realization of creative potential. *American Psychologist, 20,* 273–281.

MacKinnon, D. W., & Henle, M. (1948). *Experimental studies in psychodynamics: A laboratory manual.* Cambridge, Mass.: Harvard University Press.

MacKinnon, R. A., & Michels, R. (1971). *The psychiatric interview in clinical practice.* Philadelphia, Pa.: Saunders.

Mackintosh, N. J. (1965). Selective attention in animal discrimination learning. *Psychological Bulletin, 64,* 124–150.

Mackintosh, N. J. (1974). *The psychology of animal learning.* New York: Academic Press.

Mackintosh, N. J. (1975). A theory of attention: Variations in the associability of stimuli with reinforcement. *Psychological Review, 82,* 276–298.

Mackintosh, N. J. (1975). Blocking of conditioned suppression: Role of the first compound trial. *Journal of Experimental Psychology: Animal Behavior Processes, 1,* 335–345.

Mackintosh, N. J. (1983). *Conditioning and associative learning,* Oxford: Oxford University Press.

Maclean, D., & Reichlin, S. (1981). Neuroendocrinology and the immune process. In R. Ader (Ed.), *Psychoneuroimmunology.* New York: Academic Press.

Maclennan, B. W. (1975). Some problems in consultation. In F. V. Mannino, B. W. Maclennan, & M. F. Shore (Eds.), *The practice of mental health consultation.* New York: Gardner Press.

Maclennan, B. W., Quinn, R., & Schroeder, D. (1975). The scope of community mental health consultation. In F. V. Mannino, B. W. Maclennan, & M. F. Shore (Eds.), *The practice of mental health consultation.* New York: Gardner Press.

MacLeod, R. B. (1947). The phenomenological approach to social psychology. *Psychological Review,54,* 193–210.

MacLeod, R. B. (1951). The place of phenomenological analysis in social psychological theory. In J. H. Rohrer & M. Sherif (Eds.), *Social psychology at the crossroads.* New York: Harper.

MacLeod, R. B. (1969). *William James: Unfinished business.* Washington, D.C.: American Psychological Association.

MacLeod, R. B. (1975). *The persistent problems of psychology.* Pittsburgh, Pa.: Duquesne University Press.

MacMillan, D. L. (1973). *Behavior modification in education.* New York: Macmillan.

MacNeil, M. K., & Sherif, M. (1976). Norm change over subject generations as a function of arbitrariness of prescribed norms. *Journal of Personality and Social Psychology, 34,* 762–773.

Mactutus, C. F., McCutcheon, K. & Ricclo, D. C. (1980). Body temperature cues as contextual stimuli: Modulation of hypothermia-induced retrograde amnesia. *Physiology and Behavior, 25,* 875–883.

Macy, D. J, & Carter, J. L. (1978). Comparison of a mainstream and self-contained special education program. *Journal of Special Education, 12*(37), 303–313.

Madames, C. (1980). Protection, paradox, and pretending. *Family Process, 19,* 73–85.

Madden, R., Gardner, E. F., Rudman, H. C., Karlsen, B., & Merwin, J. (1975). *Stanford achievement test, manual, Part V: Technical data report.* New York: Harcourt Brace Jovanovich.

Maddi, R. (1967). The existential neurosis. *Journal of Abnormal Psychology, 72,* 311–325.

Maddi, S. R. (1967). The existential neurosis. *Journal of Abnormal Psychology, 72,* 311–325.

Maddi, S. R. (1970). The search for meaning. In M. Page (Ed.), *Nebraska symposium on motivation.* Lincoln: University of Nebraska Press.

Maddi, S. R. (1976/1968). *Personality theories: A comparative analysis* (3rd ed.). Homewood, Ill.: Dorsey Press.

Maddi, S. R. (1984). Personology for the 1980s. In R. A. Zucker, J. Aronoff & A. I. Rabin (Eds.), *Personality and the prediction of behavior.* New York: Academic Press.

Maddi, S. R. (1987). Hardiness training at Illinois Bell Telephone. In J. P. Opaty (Ed.), *Health promotion evaluation.* Stevens Point, WI: National Wellness Institute.

Maddi, S. R. (1988). On the problem of accepting facticity and pursuing possibility. In S. B. Messer, L. A. Sass, & R. J. Woolfolk (Eds.), *Hermeneutics and psychological theory: Interpretive perspectives on personality, psychotherapy and psychopathology.* New Brunswick, NJ: Rutgers University Press.

Maddi, S. R. (1988). *Personality theories: A comparative analysis.* Chicago, IL: Dorsey. (Original work published 1968).

Maddi, S. R. (1990). Issues and interventions in stress mastery. In H. S. Friedman (Ed.), *Personality and disease.* New York: Wiley.

Maddi, S. R., Hoover, M., & Kobasa, S. C. (1982). Alienation and exploratory behavior. *Journal of Personality and Social Psychology, 42,* 884–890.

Maddi, S. R., & Kobasa, S. C. (1984). *The hardy executive: health under stress.* Homewood, IL: Dow Jones-Irwin.

Maddi, S. R., Kobasa, S. C., & Hoover, M. (1979). An alienation test. *Journal of Humanistic Psychology, 19,* 73–76.

Maddock, J. M., Daley, D., & Moss, H. B. (1988). A practical approach to needs assessment for chemical dependency programs. *Journal of Substance Abuse Treatment, 5,* 105–111.

Maddux, J. E., & Rogers, R. W. (1980). Effects of source expertise, physical attractiveness, and supporting arguments on persuasion: A case of brains over beauty. *Journal of Personality and Social Psychology, 39,* 235–244.

Madison, P. (1961). *Freud's concept of repression and defense, its theoretical and observational language.* Minneapolis, Minn.: University of Minnesota Press.

Madsen, K. B. (1980). Psykologiens historie i Danmark [The history of psychology in Denmark]. In K. B. Madsen (Ed.), *Psykologisk leksikon* (2 udg) [Encyclopedia of psychology (2nd ed.)] (pp. 350–356). Copenhagen.

Maehr, M. L. (1974). *Sociocultural origins of achievement.* Monterey, Calif.: Brooks/Cole.

Maehr, M. L., & Nicholls, J. G. (1980). Culture and achievement motivation: A second look. In N. Warren (Ed.), *Studies in cross-cultural psychology,* Vol. 3. New York: Academic Press.

Magaro, P. A. (1981). The paranoid and the schizophrenic: The case for distinct cognitive style. *Schizophrenia Bulletin, 7,* 632–631.

Mager, R., & Pipe, P. (1970). *Analyzing performance problems.* Belmont, Calif.: Fearon.

Magnan, V. (1886). *Leçons cliniques sur les maladies mentales.* Paris: Battaille.

Magnusson, D. (1966). *Test theory.* Reading, Mass.: Addison-Wesley.

Magnusson, D., & Endler, N. S. (Eds.). (1977). *Personality at the crossroads: Current issues in interactional psychology.* Hillsdale, N.J.: Erlbaum.

Magoun, F. A. (1935). Scholarship and distinction. *Technology Review, M.I.T., 37,* 5–19.

Magreb, P. R. (1978). *Psychological management of pediatric problems* (Vols. 1 & 2). Baltimore: University Park Press.

Maharishi Mahesh Yogi. (1966). *The science of being and art of living.* Los Angeles: International SRM.

Maharishi Mahesh Yogi. (1969). *On the Bhagavad-Gita: A new translation and commentary.* Harmondsworth, UK: Penguin.

Maharishi Mahesh Yogi. (1972). *The science of creative intelligence: Knowledge and experience* (Lessons 1–33) [Course syllabus]. Los Angeles: Maharishi International University Press.

Maharishi Mahesh Yogi. (1978). *Enlightenment and invincibility.* Rheinweiler, Germany: Maharishi European Research University Press.

Maharishi Mahesh Yogi. (1986). *Life supported by natural law.* Washington, DC: Age of Enlightenment Press.

Mahler, M. S. (1965). On early infantile psychosis. The symbiotic and autistic syndromes. *Journal of the American Academy of Psychiatry, 4,* 554–568.

Mahler, M. S. (1968). *On human symbiosis and the vicissitudes of individuation,* Vol. 1; *Infantile psychosis.* New York: International Universities Press.

Mahler, M. S., Pine, F., & Bergman, A. (1975). *The psychological birth of the human infant: Symbiosis and individuation.* New York: Basic Books.

Mahoney, M. J. (1977b). Personal science: A cognitive learning therapy. In A. Ellis & R. Grieger (Eds.). *Handbook of rational-emotive therapy.* New York: Springer.

Mahoney, M. J. (1974). *Cognition and behavior modification.* Cambridge, MA: Ballinger.

Mahoney, M. J. (1977). Reflections on the cognitive-learning trend in psychotherapy. *American Psychologist, 32,* 5–13.

Mahoney, M. J. (1978). Experimental methods and outcome evaluations. *Journal of Clinical and Consulting Psychology, 46,* 660–672.

Mahoney, M. J. (1980). Psychotherapy and the structure of personal revolutions. In M. J. Mahoney (Ed.), *Psychotherapy process: Current issues and future directions.* New York: Plenum.

Mahoney, M. J., & Arnkoff, D. B. (1978). Cognitive and self-control therapies. In S. L. Garfield & A. E. Bergin (Eds.), *Handbook of psychotherapy and behavior change: An empirical analysis* (2nd ed.). New York: Wiley.

Mahoney, M. J., & Arnkoff, D. B. (1979). Self-management. In O. F. Pomerleau & J. P. Brady (Eds.), *Behavioral medicine: Theory and practice,* Baltimore, Md.: Williams & Wilkins.

Mahoney, M. J., & Bandura, A. (1972). Self-reinforcement in pigeons. *Learning motivation, 3,* 293–303.

Mahoney, M. J., & Thoresen, C. T. (1974). *Self-control: Power to the person.* Monterey, Calif.: Brooks/Cole.

Mahoney, M. J., Thoresen, C. E., & Danher, B. G. (1972). Covert behavior modification: An experimental analogue. *Journal of Behavior Therapy and Experimental Psychiatry, 3,* 7–14.

Mahoney, T. A., Jerdee, T. H., & Carroll, S. I. (1965). The job(s) of management. *Industrial Relations, 4,* 97–110.

Maier, E. L., & McAfee, R. B. (1979). *Cases in selling.* New York: McGraw-Hill.

Maier, H. W. (1965). *Three theories of child development.* New York: Harper & Row.

Maier, N. R. F. (1929). Reasonin in white rats. In S. H. Hulse, H. Fowler, & W. K. Honig (Eds.), *Cognitive processes in animal behavior.* Hillsdale, NJ: Erlbaum.

Maier, N. R. F., Glasser, N. M., & Klee, J. B. (1940). Studies of abnormal behavior in the rat. The development of behavior fixations through frustration. *Journal of Experimental Psychology, 26,* 521–546.

Maier, N. R. F. (1949). *Frustration: The study of behavior without a goal.* New York: McGraw-Hill.

Maier, S. F., & Seligman, M. E. P. (1976). Learned helplessness: Theory and evidence. *Behaviour Research and Therapy, 14,* 7–17.

Maier, S. F., Seligman, M. E. P., & Solomon, R. L. (1969). Pavlovian fear conditioning and learned helplessness. In B. A. Campbell and R. M. Church (Eds.), *Punishment.* Appleton-Century-Crofts.

Mailer, N. (1979). *The executioner's song.* Boston: Little, Brown.

Maimonides, M. (1881). *The guide to the perplexed.* New York: Hebrew Publishing.

Mainess, D. R. (1978). Bodies and selves: Notes on a fundamental dilemma in demography. In N. K. Denzin (Ed.), *Studies in symbolic interaction,* Vol. I. Greenwich, Conn.: JAI Press.

Mainzer, W. (1966). Accident prevention in the cowshed. *British Journal of Industrial Medicine, 23,* 24.

Maisel, E. (Ed.). (1969). *The resurrection of the body: The writings of F. Matthias Alexander.* New York: University Books.

Maistriaux, R. (1960). Les methodes actives en terre d'Afrique. *Problèmes Sociaux Congolais, 49,* 7–56.

Major, L. F., Lerner, P., Ballenger, J. C., Brown, G. L., Goodwin, F. K., & Lovenberg, W. (1979). Dopamine-β-hydroxylase in the cerebrospinal fluid: Relationship to disulfiram-induced psychosis. *Biological Psychiatry, 14,* 337–344.

Majorski, L., & Oettinger, L. (1979). Neuropsychological and treatment aspects of learning and behavior disorders in children. *Behavioral Disorders, 5,* 30–40.

Majumdar, A. K., & Roy, A. B. (1962). Latent personality content of juvenile delinquents. *Journal of Psychological Research* (Madras), 6, 4–8.

Makarenko, A. S. (1951/1933). *The road to life: An epic of education,* (2 vols.). Moscow: Foreign Language Publishing House.

Makarenko, A. S. (1967/1937). *The collective family,* Garden City, N.Y.: Doubleday.

Makens, J. C. (1965). Effect of brand preference upon consumers' perceived taste of turkey meat. *Journal of Applied Psychology, 49,* 261–263.

Makhlouf-Norris, F., & Norris, H. (1972). The obsessive compulsive syndrome as a neurotic device for the reduction of self-uncertainty. *British Journal of Psychiatry, 121,* 277–288.

Makkreel, R. A. (1975). *Dilthey: Philosopher of human studies.* Princeton, N.J.: Princeton University Press.

Makous, W. L. (1966). Cutaneous color sensitivity: Explanation and demonstration. *Psychological Review, 73,* 280–294.

Malebranche, N. de (1923/1688). *Dialogues on metaphysics.* New York: Macmillan.

Maletta, G., & Pirozzolo, F. J. (1980). *The aging nervous system.* New York: Praeger.

Malgady, R. G., Rogler, L. H., & Costaritirio, G. (1990). Culturally sensitive psychotherapy for Peurto Rican children and adolescents: A program of treatment outcome research. *Journal of Consulting and Clinical Psychology, 58*(6), 704–712.

Malin, D. H. (1976). *The frontier of brief psychotherapy.* New York: Plenum.

Malin, D. H., Golub, A. M., & McConnell, J. V. (1971). The effect of an RNA-rich extract on acquisition of a one-way avoidance response in rats. *Nature, 233,* 211–212.

Malinowski, B. (1927). *Sex and repression in savage society.* New York: Harcourt, Brace, & Co.

Malinowski, B. (1948/1939). *Magic, science, and religion: Essays.* Glencoe, Ill.: Free Press.

Malinowski, B. (1953). *Argonauts of the western Pacific: An account of native enterprise and adventure in the archipelagoes of Melanesian New Guinea.* New York: Dutton.

Malinowski, B. (1962/1913). *Sex, culture and myth.* New York: Harcourt.

Mallart, J. (1981). Memories de un aspirante a psicólogo (autobiografia). *Revista de Historia de la Psicologia, 2,* 91–123.

Malmo, H. P., & Malmo, R. B. (1982). On movement-related forebrain and midbrain multiple unit activity in rats. II: Some constraints on movement. *Electroencephalography and Clinical Neurophysiology, 53,* 104–114.

Malmo, R. B. (1942). Interference factors in delayed response in monkeys after removal of frontal lobes. *Journal of Neurophysiology, 5,* 295–308.

Malmo, R. B. (1959). Activation: A neuropsychological dimension. *Psychological Review, 66,* 367–386.

Malmo, R. B. (1967). Physiological concomitants of emotion. In A. M. Freedman & H. I. Kaplan (Eds.), *Comprehensive textbook of psychiatry.* Baltimore, Md.: Williams & Wilkins.

Malmo, R. B. (1975). *On emotions, needs, and our archaic brain.* New York: Holt, Rinehart & Winston.

Malmo, R. B., & Malmo, H. P. (1979). Responses of lateral preoptic neurons in the rat to hypertonic sucrose and NaCl. *Electroencephalography and Clinical Neurophysiology, 46,* 401–408.

Malo, D. (1951). *Hawaiian antiquities.* Honolulu: Bernice P. Bishop Museum.

Maloney, M. P., & Ward, M. P. (1976). *Psychological assessment: A conceptual approach.* New York: Oxford University Press.

Maloney, M. P., & Ward, M. P. (1979). *Mental retardation and modern society.* New York: Oxford University Press.

Malony, N. H. (Ed.). (1977). *Current perspectives in the psychology of religion.* Grand Rapids, Mich.: Eerdmans.

Malpass, R. S., & Devine, P. G. (1980). Realism and eyewitness identification research. *Law and Human Behavior, 4,* 347–358.

Malpass, R. S., & Devine, P. G. (1981). Eyewitness identification: Lineup instructions and the absence of the offender. *Journal of Applied Psychology, 66,* 482–489.

Malraux, A. (1953). *The voices of silence.* Garden City, N.Y.: Doubleday.

Maltz, M. (1960). *Psycho-cybernetics: A new way to get more living out of life.* Englewood Cliffs, N.J.: Prentice-Hall.

Maltzaman, I., & Morrisett, L., Jr. (1953). Different strengths of set in the solution of anagrams. *Journal of Experimental Psychology, 45,* 351–354.

Malzberg, B. (1950). Some statistical aspects of mongolism. *American Journal of Mental Deficiency, 54,* 27–37.

Manaceine, M. (1899/1897). *Sleep: Its physiology, pathology, hygiene and psychology.* New York: Scribners.

Manaster, G. J., & Corsini, R. J. (1982). *Individual psychology.* Itasca, Ill.: Peacock.

Manaster, G. J., & Perryman, T. B. (1974). Early recollections and occupational choice. *Journal of Individual Psychology, 30,* 232–237.

Mancuso, J. C., & Adams-Webber, J. (Eds.). (1982). *The construing person.* New York: Praeger.

Mandel, N., & Shrauger, J. (1980). The effects of self-evaluative statements on heterosexual approach in shy and nonshy males. *Cognitive Therapy and Research, 4*(4), 369–381.

Mandelbrot, B. (1961). On the theory of word frequencies and on related Markovian models of discourse. In R. Jakobson (Ed.), *Structure of language in its mathematical aspect.* Providence, R.I.: American Mathematical Society.

Mandler, G. (1975). *Mind and emotions.* New York: Wiley.

Mandler, J. M., & Johnson, N. S. (1977). Remembrance of things parsed: Story structure and recall. *Cognitive Psychology, 9,* 111–151.

Mangold, K. M. (1965). Comparison of delinquents and non-delinquents on the IES test. *Perceptual and Motor Skills, 22,* 317–318.

Mann, F. C., & Hoffman, L. R. (1964). *Automation and the workers: A study of social change in power plants.* New York: Holt.

Mann, G. V. (1974). The influence of obesity in health. *New England Journal of Medicine, 291,* 178–185, 226–232.

Mann, J. (1974). *Time-limited psychotherapy.* Cambridge, Mass.: Harvard University Press.

Mann, J., & Goldman, R. (1982). *A casebook in time-limited psychotherapy.* New York: McGraw-Hill.

Mann, J. H., & Mann, C. H. (1959). The effect of role playing experience on role playing ability. *Sociometry, 22,* 64–74.

Mann, L. (1969). *Social psychology.* New York: Wiley.

Mann, R. D. (1959). A review of relationships between personality and performance in small groups. *Psychological Bulletin, 56,* 241–270.

Mannheim, K. (1936). *Ideology and utopia.* New York: Harcourt, Brace & World.

Mannino, F. V. (1972). Task accomplishment and consultation outcome. *Community Mental Health Journal 8*(2), 102–108.

Mannino, F. V., Maclennan, B. W., & Shore, M. F. (Eds.). (1975). *The practice of mental health consultation.* New York: Gardner Press.

Mannino, F. V., & Robinson, S. A. (1975). A reference guide to the consultation literature. In F. V. Mannino, B. W. Maclennan, & M. F. Shore (Eds.), *The practice of mental health consultation.* New York: Gardner Press.

Mannino, F. V., & Shore, M. F. (1972). Research in mental health consultation. In S. E. Golann & C. Eisdorfer (Eds.), *Handbook of community mental health.* New York: Appleton-Century-Crofts.

Mannoni, O. (1964). *Prospero and Caliban: The psychology of colonization*. New York: Methuen.

Manry, W. E. (1974). Alcoholism, obesity, nicotine, etc. *Journal of the Florida Medical Association, 61*(7), 57.

Mansfield, E. (1968). *Industrial research and technological innovation: An econometric analysis*. New York: Norton.

Manzo, L., Blum, K., & Sabbioni, E. (1985). Neurotoxicity of selected metals. In K. Blum & L. Manzo (Eds.), *Neurotoxicology* (pp. 385–404). New York: Marcel Dekker.

Mao, T. T. (1965). On contradiction. In *Selected works of Mao Tze-tung* Vol. 1. Beijing: Foreign Languages Press.

Mao, Tze-tung. (1937). *On practice*. New York: International Publishers.

Maracek, J. (1976). Powerlessness and women's psychological disorders. *Voices, 12*(3), 50–66.

Marano, L. (in press). Windigo psychosis: The anatomy of an emicetic confusion. *Current Anthropology*.

Marantz, S. A., & Mansfield, A. F. (1977). Maternal employment and the development of sex-role stereotyping in five- to eleven-year-old girls. *Child Development, 48,* 668–673.

Marbe, K. (1901). *Experimentell psychologische Untersuchungen über das Urteil, eine Einleitung in die Logik*. Leipzig: Engelmann.

Marbe, K. (1926). *Praktische Psychologie der Unfälle und Betriebsschaden*. Munich: Oldenberg.

Marcel, A. J. (1978). Unconscious reading. *Visible Language, 12,* 391–404.

Marcel, A. J. (1980). Conscious and preconscious recognition of polysemous words: Locating the selective effects of prior verbal context. In R. S. Nickerson (Ed.), *Attention and performance VIII*. Hillsdale, N.J.: Erlbaum.

Marcel, A. J. (1983). Conscious and unconscious perception: Experiments on visual masking and word recognition. *Cognitive Psychology, 15,* 197–237.

March, J. G., & Simon, H. A. (1958). *Organizations*. New York: Wiley.

Marcia, J. E. (1964). *Determination and construct validity of ego identity status*. Unpublished doctoral dissertation, Ohio State University.

Marcia, J. E. (1966). Development and validation of ego-identity status. *Journal of Personality and Social Psychology, 3,* 551–558.

Marcia, J. E. (1967). Ego identity status: Relationship to change in self-esteem, 'general maladjustment,' and authoritarianism, *Journal of Personality, 1,* 118–134.

Marcia, J. E. (1980). Identity in adolescence. In J. Adelson (Ed.), *Handbook of adolescent psychology*. New York: Wiley.

Marcia, J. E., Rubin, B. M., & Efran, J. S. (1969). Systematic desensitization: Expectancy change or counterconditioning? *Journal of Abnormal Psychology, 74,* 382–387.

Marcus Aurelius. (1890). *The thoughts of the emperor Marcus Aurelius*. Boston: Little, Brown.

Marcus, J. (Ed.). (1972). *Growing up in groups: The Russian day care center and the Israeli kibbutz*. New York: Gordon & Breach.

Marcuse, H. (1955). *Eros and civilization*. New York: Vintage Books.

Mardia, K. V., Kent, J. T., & Bibby, J. M. (1979). *Multivariate analysis*. London: Academic Press.

Marecek, J., & Hare-Mustin, R. T. (1991). A short history of the future: Feminism and clinical psychology. *Psychology of Women Quarterly, 15,* 521–536.

Marecek, J., & Kravetz, D. (1977). Women and mental health: A review of feminist change efforts. *Psychiatry, 40,* 323–329.

Marenholtz-Bülow, B. M. (1877). *Reminiscences of Friedrich Froebel*. Boston: Lee & Shepard.

Marett, R. R. (1929). *The threshold of religion*. London: Methuen.

Margetts, E. L. (1950). The early history of the word psychosomatic. *Canadian Medical Association Journal, 63,* 402–404.

Margolis, B. L., & Kroes, W. H. (Eds.). (1975). *The human side of accident prevention*. Springfield, Ill.: Thomas.

Margolis, H. J. (1991). *Inhibitory control theory: A mind/body theory of sensory signaling and accommodation*. Green Valley Lake, CA: Silogram.

Marholin, D., II, & McInnis, E. T. (1978). Treating children in group settings: Techniques for individualizing behavioral programs. In D. Marholin, II (Ed.), *Child behavior therapy*. New York: Gardner Press.

Mariani, G. (1975). Peremptory challenge—divining rod for a sympathetic jury. *Catholic Lawyer, 21,* 56–81.

Marín, G. (Ed.). (1975). *La psicología social en Latino américa*. Mexico, D.F.: Trillas.

Maris, R. (1981). *Pathways to suicide*. Baltimore, Md.: Johns Hopkins University Press.

Marjoribanks, K., & Walberg, H. (1975). Ordinal position, family environment, and mental abilities. *Journal of Social Psychology, 95,* 77–84.

Mark, J. C. (1953). The attitudes of mothers of male schizophrenics toward child behavior. *Journal of Abnormal and Social Psychology, 48,* 185–189.

Mark, V. H. & Ervin, F. R. (Eds.). (1970). *Violence and the brain,* New York: Harper & Row.

Marketing, 1981, bibliography of cases, (1981). Vol. 5. Boston: Harvard Business School.

Markin, R. J. (1969). *The psychology of consumer behavior*. Englewood Cliffs, N.J.: Prentice-Hall.

Markle, S. M., & Tiemann, P. W. (1969). *Really understanding concepts*. Champaign, Ill.: Stipes.

Markman, H. J. (1979). The application of a behavioral model of marriage in predicting relationships satisfaction of couples planning marriage. *Journal of Consulting and Clinical Psychology, 4,* 743–749.

Markman, H. J, Notarius, C. I., Stephen, T., & Smith, R. J. (1981). Behavioral observation systems for couples: The current status. In E. E. Filsinger & R. A. Lewis (Eds.), *Assessing marriage: New behavioral approaches*. Beverly Hills, Calif.: Sage Publications.

Markov, A. A. (1954). *A theory of algorithms*. USSR: National Academy of Sciences.

Marks, D. (1983). Mental imagery and consciousness: A theoretical review. In A. Sheikh (Ed.), *Imagery: Current theory, research and application*. New York: Wiley.

Marks, D., & Kammann, R. (1980). *The psychology of the psychic*. Buffalo, N.Y.: Prometheus Books.

Marks, D. F. (1973). Visual imagery differences in the recall of pictures, *British Journal of Psychology, 64,* 17–24.

Marks, D. F. (1977). Imagery and consciousness: A theoretical review from an individual differences perspective. *Journal of Mental Imagery, 2,* 275–290.

Marks, I. M. (1978). *Living with fear: Understanding and coping with anxiety*. New York: McGraw-Hill.

Marks, I. M., & Mathews, A. M. (1979). Brief standard self-rating for phobic patients. *Behaviour Research and Therapy, 17,* 263–267.

Marks, J. (1978). *The benzodiazepines: Use, overuse, misuse, abuse.* Lancaster, England: MTP.

Marks, L. (1978). *The unity of the senses: Interrelations among the modalities.* New York: Academic Press.

Marks, L., Hammeal, R. J., & Bomstein, M. H. (1987). Perceiving similarity and comprehending metaphor. *Monographs of the Society for Research in Child Development, 52,* 1–92.

Marks, L. E. (1974). *Sensory processes: The new psychophysics* New York: Academic Press.

Marks, L. E. (1978). *The unity of the senses.* New York: Academic Press.

Marland, S. P. (1971). *Education of the gifted and talented.* Washington, D.C.: U.S. Office of Education.

Marler, P. (1970). A comparative approach to vocal learning: Song development in white-crowned sparrows. *Journal of Comparative and Physiological Psychology Monograph, 71*(2), 1–25.

Marler, P. (1972). The drive to survive. In National Geographic Society, *The marvels of animal behavior.* Washington, D.C.: National Geographic Society.

Marm, S. A., & Cree, W. (1976). 'New' long-stay psychiatric patients: A national sample survey of fifteen mental hospitals in England and Wales 1972/ 3. *Psychological Medicine, 6,* 603–616.

Marmor, G. S., & Zabeck, L. A. (1976). Mental rotation by the blind: Does mental rotation depend on visual imagery? *Journal of Experimental Psychology: Human Perception and Performance, 2,* 515–521.

Marmor, J. (1975). Homosexuality and sexual orientation disturbances. In A. M. Freedman, H. I. Kaplan, & B. J. Sadock (Eds.), *Comprehensive textbook of psychiatry—II* (2nd ed.). Baltimore, Md.: Williams & Wilkins.

Marmor, J. (1980). Historical roots. In H. Davenloo (Ed.), *Short-term dynamic psychotherapy,* Vol. 1. New York: Aronson.

Marmor, J. (1980). *Homosexual behavior: A modern reappraisal.* New York: Basic Books.

Marquis, S. M., & Phelps, C. E. (1985, July). *Demand for supplementary health insurance* (Pub. No. R-3285-HHS). Santa Monica, CA: Rand.

Marris, P. (1974). *Loss and change.* New York: Pantheon.

Marrow, A. J. (1969). *The practical theorist: The life and work of Kurt Lewin.* New York; Basic Books.

Marsden, P. V. (1982). Brokerage behavior in restricted exchange networks. In P. V. Marsden & N. Lin (Eds.), *Social structure and network analysis* (pp. 201–218). Beverly Hills, CA: Sage.

Marsella, A., Hirshfeld, R., & Katz, M. (Eds.). (1987). *The measurement of depression.* New York: Guilford.

Marsella, A., & Westermeyer. (in press). Cultural aspects of treatment: Conceptual, methodological and clinical issues and directions. In N. Sartorius, G. DeGuolanis, A. German, & L. Eisenberg (Eds.), *Cure, relief and comfort for the mentally ill.* Berne, Switzerland: Huber & Hogrefe.

Marsella, A. J. (1980). Depressive experience and disorder across cultures. In H. Triandis & J. Draguns (Eds.), *Handbook of cross-cultural psychology. Vol 6: Psychopathology.* Boston: Allyn & Bacon.

Marsella, A. J. (1982). Culture and mental health: an overview. In A. J. Marsella & G. White (Eds.), *Cultural conceptions of mental health and therapy.* Boston: Reidel.

Marsella, A. J., Freidman, M. J., & Spain, E. H. (in press). Ethnocultural aspects of PTSD: an overview of issues, research, and directions. In J. M. Oldham, A. Tasman, & M. Riba (Eds.), *American Psychiatric Press Review of Psychiatry, 12.*

Marsella, A. J., Kinzie, D., & Gordon, P. (1973). Ethnic variations in the expression of depression. *Journal of Cross-Cultural Psychology, 4,* 435–458.

Marsella, A. J., & Pederson, P. B. (1981). *Cross-cultural counseling and psychotherapy.* Elmsford, N.Y.: Pergamon Press.

Marsella, A. J., Sartorius, N., Jablensky, A., & Fenton, F. (1986). Depression across cultures. In A. Kleinman & B. Good, (Eds.), *Culture and depression.* Berkeley: University of California Press.

Marsella, A. J., Tharp, R, & Ciborowski, T. (Eds.). (1979). *Perspectives in cross-cultural psychology.* New York: Academic Press.

Marsella, A. J., & White, G. (Eds.). (1982). *Cultural conceptions of mental health and therapy.* New York: Reidel.

Marshall, W. E., Gauthier, J., & Gordon, A. (1979). The current status of flooding therapy. In M. Hersen, R. M. Eisler, & P. M. Miller (Eds.), *Progress in behavior modification,* Vol. 7. New York: Academic Press.

Martell, D. (1991, October). *The homeless mentally ill and violent crime: Prevalence estimates for New York City.* Paper presented at the Fourth Annual New York State Office of Mental Health, New York.

Martens, R. (1977). *Sports competition anxiety test.* Champaign, Ill.: Human Kinetics.

Martens, R. (1975). *Social psychology and physical activity.* New York: Harper & Row.

Martin, C., & Nagao, D. (1989). Some effects of computerized interviewing on job applicant responses. *Journal of Applied Psychology, 74,* 1.

Martin, D., & Lyon, P. (1972). *Lesbian woman.* New York: Bantam.

Martin, F. N. (1981). *Introduction to audiology* (2nd ed.). Englewood Cliffs, N.J.: Prentice-Hall.

Martin, F. N. (Ed.). (1981). *Medical audiology: Disorders of hearing.* Englewood Cliffs, N.J.: Prentice-Hall.

Martin, I., & Venables, P. H. (Eds.). (1980). *Techniques in psychophysiology.* New York: Wiley.

Martin, J. P., & Bell, J. (1943). A pedigree of mental defect showing sex-linkage. *Journal of Neurology, Neurosurgery, and Psychiatry, 6,* 154–157.

Martin, P. A. (1976). *A marital therapy manual.* New York: Brunner/ Mazel.

Martin, P. R. (Ed.). (1991). *Handbook of behavior therapy and psychological science: An integrative approach.* Elmsford, NY: Pergamon.

Martin, R. P. & Curtis, M. (1981). Consultants' perceptions of causality for success and failure of consultation. *Professional Psychology, 12*(6), 670–676.

Martindale, C. (1975). *Romantic progression: The psychology of literary history.* New York: Halstead (Wiley).

Martindale, C. (1978). Preface: Psychological contributions to poetics. *Poetics, 7,* 121–133.

Martindale, C. (1978). Sit with statisticians and commit a social science: Interdisciplinary aspects of poetics. *Poetics, 7,* 273–282.

Martindale, C. (1991). *Cognitive psychology: A neural-network approach.* Pacific Grove, CA: Brooks/Cole.

Martineau, H. (1853). *Comte's positive philosophy (2 vols.).* London: Chapman.

Martineau, W. (1972). A model of the social functions of humor. In J. Goldstein & P. McGhee (Eds.), *The psychology of humor.* New York: Academic Press.

Martínez, J. L. (Ed.). (1977). *Chicano psychology*. New York: Academic Press.

Martinez-Taboas, A. (1990). Controlled outcome research with paradoxical interventions: A review for clinicians. *Psychotherapy, 27,* 468–474.

Marton, F. (1984). Approaches to learning. In F. Marton, N. Entwistle, & D. Hounsell (Eds.), *The experience of learning.*

Marton, F. (1970). *Structural dynamics of learning.* Stockholm: Almqvist & Wiksell.

Marton, F. (1975–1976). On non-verbatim learning I–IV. *Scandinavian Journal of Psychology.*

Marton, F. (1981). Phenomenography: Describing conceptions of the world around us. *Instructional Science, 10,* 177–200.

Marton, F., et al. (1977). *Inlärning och omvarldsuppfattning (The learner and his world).* Stockholm: AWE/GEBERS.

Marton, F., & Dahlgren, L. O. (1976). On non-verbatim learning: III. The outcome space of some basic concepts in economics. *Scandinavian Journal of Psychology, 17,* 49–55.

Marton, F., Entwistle, N. J. & Hounsell, D. J. (Eds.). (1984). *The experience of learning.*

Marton, F., & Säljö, R. (1976). On qualitative differences in learning. I—Outcome and process. *British Journal of Educational Psychology, 46,* 4–11.

Marton, F., & Svensson, L. (1979). Conceptions of research in student learning. *Higher Education, 8,* 471–486.

Marton, F., & Wenestam, C. G. (1978). Qualitative differences in the understanding and retention of the main points in some texts based on the principle–example structure. In H. M. Gruneberg, P. E. Morris, & R. N. Sykes (Eds.), *Practical aspects of memory.* London: Academic Press.

Martuza, V. R. (1977). *Applying norm referenced and criterion referenced measurement in education.* Boston: Allyn & Bacon, 1977.

Marwell, G., Schmitt, D. R., & Shotola, R. (1970). Sex differences in a cooperative task. *Behavioral Science, 15,* 184–186.

Marx, J. L. (1980). Ape-language controversy flares up. *Science, 207,* 1330–1333.

Marx, K. (1925–1926/1867–1879). *Capital: A critique of political economy* (3 vols.). Chicago: Kerr.

Marx, K., & Engels, F. (1854/1848). *Communist manifesto.* New York: Washington Square Press.

Marx, M. (1951). Psychological theory: Contemporary readings. Intervening variable or hypothetical construct? In M. Marx (Ed.), *Psychological Reviews* (Vol. 589, pp. 235–247). New York: Macmillan.

Marx, M. (1966). The activation of habits. *Psychological Reports 19,* 527–550.

Marx, M. (1982). Habit activation in human learning. In G. d'Ydewalle (Ed.), *Cognition and memory: Essays in honor of J. Nuttin.* Hillsdale, NJ: Erlbaum.

Marx, M. (Ed.). (1951). *Psychological theory.* New York: Macmillan.

Marx, M., & Goodson, F. (Eds.). (1976). *Theories in contemporary psychology* (2nd ed.). New York: Macmillan.

Marx, M. H. (1951). A stimulus-response analysis of the hoarding habit in the rat. *Psychological Review, 5,* 80–93.

Marx, M. H. (1951). Intervening variable or hypothetical construct. *Psychological Review, 58,* 235–247.

Marx, M. H. (1956). Some relations between frustration and drive. In M. R. Jones (Ed.), *Nebraska symposium on motivation* (Vol. 4). Lincoln: University of Nebraska Press.

Marx, M. H. (1956). Spread of effect: A critical review. *General Psychology Monographs, 53,* 119–186.

Marx, M. H. (1970). Theory construction and evaluation. In M. H. Marx (Ed.), *Learning: Theories.* New York: Macmillan.

Marx, M. H. (1976). *Introduction to psychology: Problems, procedures, principles.* New York: Macmillan.

Marx, M. H. (1976a). Formal theory. In M. H. Marx & F. E. Goodson (Eds.), *Theories in contemporary psychology,* (2nd ed.). New York: Macmillan.

Marx, M. H. (1976b). Theorizing. In M. H. Marx & F. E. Goodson (Eds.), *Theories in contemporary psychology* (2nd ed.). New York: Macmillan.

Marx, M. H. (1986). More retrospective reports on frequency judgments: Shift from multiple traces to strength factor with age. *Bulletin of the Psychonomic Society, 24,* 183–185.

Marx, M. H. (1991). Development of inferences over elementary-school grades: I. Recall and association of implicit words. *Bulletin of the Psychonomic Society, 29,* 460–462.

Marx, M. H. (1992). Development of inferences over the elementary-school grades: III. Verbatim and forward-consequence inferential errors made by regular and gifted students. *Bulletin of the Psychonomic Society, 30.*

Marx, M. H. (Ed.). (1963). *Theories in contemporary psychology.* New York: Macmillan.

Marx, M. H. (Ed.). (1969). *Learning: Processes.* New York: Macmillan.

Marx, M. H. (Ed.). (1970). *Learning interactions.* New York: Macmillan.

Marx, M. H. (Ed.). (1970). *Learning: Theories.* New York: Macmillan.

Marx, M. H., & Bunch, M. E. (1951). New gradients of error reinforcement in multiple-choice human learning. *Journal of Experimental Psychology, 11,* 93–104.

Marx, M. H., & Ekunch, M. E. (Eds.). (1977). *Fundamentals and applications of learning.* New York: Macmillan.

Marx, M. H., & Goodson, F. E. (Eds.). (1976). *Theories in contemporary psychology.* New York: Macmillan.

Marx, M. H., & Hillix, W. A. (1979/1973/1963). *Systems and theories in psychology* (3rd ed.). New York: McGraw-Hill.

Marx, M. H., & Tombaugh, T. N. (1976). *Motivation: Psychological principles and educational implications.* San Francisco: Chandler.

Marx, M. H., & Van Spanckeren, W. J. (1952). Control of the audiogenic seizure by the rat. *Journal of Comparative and Physiological Psychology, 45,* 170–179.

Marx, M. with Hillix W. A. (1960). Response strengthening by information and effect in human learning. *Journal of Experimental Psychology, 60,* 97–102.

Marx, M., with Hillix, W. A. (1987). *Systems and theories in psychology.* New York: McGraw-Hill. (Original work published 1963)

Maser, J., & Seligman, M. E. P. (Eds.). (1977). *Psychopathology: Experimental models.* San Francisco: Freeman.

Maser, J. D., & Gallup, G. G., . Jr. (1977). Tonic immobility and related phenomena: A partially annotated, tricentennial bibliography, 1636–1976. *Psychological Record, 1,* 177–217.

Maser, J. D., & Seligman, M. E. P. (Eds.). (1977). *Psychopathology: Experimental models.* San Francisco: Freeman.

Mash, E. J., & Terdal, L. G. (Eds.). (1976). *Behavior-therapy assessment: Diagnosis, design and evaluation.* New York: Springer.

Maslach, C. (1976). Burned-out. *Human Behavior, 5,* 16–22.

Masling, J. (1960). The influence of situational and interpersonal variables in projective testing. *Psychological Bulletin, 57,* 65–85.

Masling, J., Weiss, L., & Rothschild, B. (1968). Relationships of oral imagery to yielding behavior and birth order. *Journal of Consulting and Clinical Psychology, 32*, 89–91.

Maslow, A. H. (1943). A theory of human motivation. *Psychological Review. 50*, 370–396.

Maslow, A. H. (1944). Unpublished lecture at Brooklyn College.

Maslow, A. H. (1954). *Motivation and personality.* New York: Harper & Brothers.

Maslow, A. H. (1956). *Main currents in modern thought,* Vol. 13. No. 2, November.

Maslow, A. H. (1959). Cognition of being in the peak experiences. *Journal of Genetic Psychology, 94*, 43–66.

Maslow, A. H. (1965). *Eupsychian management: A journal.* Homewood, Ill.: Irwin.

Maslow, A. H. (1966/1956). *Psychology of science.* New York: Harper & Row.

Maslow, A. H. (1967, Fall). A theory of metamotivation: The biological rooting of the value-life. *Journal of Humanistic Psychology,* 93–127.

Maslow, A. H. (1968/1962). *Toward a psychology of being.* New York: Van Nostrand Reinhold.

Maslow, A. H. (1969). The farther reaches of human nature. *Journal of Transpersonal Psychology, 1*, 1–9.

Maslow, A. H. (1970/1954). *Motivation and personality (2nd ed.).* New York: Harper & Row.

Maslow, A. H. (1971). *The farther reaches of human nature.* New York: Viking.

Maslow, A. H. (1976/1970). *Religions, values, and peak experiences.* New York: Penguin Books.

Mason, J. S. (1974). Adolescent judgment as evidenced in response to poetry. *Educational Review, 26*, 124–139.

Mason, J. W. (1968). Organization of psychoendocrine mechanisms. *Psychosomatic Medicine, 30*, 565–808.

Mason, J. W. (1972). Organization of psychoendocrine mechanisms: A review and reconsideration of research. In N. S. Greenfield & R. A. Sternbach (Eds.), *Handbook of psychophysiology.* New York: Holt, Rinehart & Winston.

Mason, J. W. (1975). A historical view of the stress field. *Journal of Human Stress, 1*(2), 22–36.

Mason, K. (Ed.). (1974). *Focus on dance VII: Dance therapy.* Washington, D.C.: American Alliance for Health, Physical Education and Recreation.

Mason, L., Alexander, C. N., Travis, F., & Gackenbach, J. (1990). EEG correlates of consciousness during sleep. *Lucidity Letter, 9*(2), 85–87.

Mason, S. T., Sanberg, P. R., & Fibiger, H. C. (1978). Kainic acid lesions of the striatum dissociate amphetamine and apomorphine stereotypy: Similarities to Huntington's chorea. *Science, 201*, 352–355.

Massad, C. M. (1981). Sex role identity and adjustment during adolescence. *Child Development, 52*, 1290–1298.

Massaro, D. W. (1988). Some criticisms of connectionist models of human performance. *Journal of Memory and Language, 27*, 213–234.

Massaro, D. W. (1989). *Experimental psychology: An information processing approach.* San Diego: Harcourt, Brace, Jovanovich.

Masserman, J. (1971). *A psychiatric odyssey.* New York: Science House.

Masserman, J. H. (1943). *Behavior and neurosis: An experimental psychoanalytic approach to psychobiologic principles.* Chicago: University of Chicago Press.

Masserman, J. H. (1946). *Principles of dynamic psychiatry.* Philadelphia, Pa.: Saunders.

Masserman, J. M., & Pechtel, C. (1953). Neurosis in monkeys; A preliminary report of experimental observations. *New York Academy of Science Annals, 56*, 253–265.

Masters, W. H., & Johnson, V. E., (1966). *Human sexual response.* Boston: Little, Brown.

Masters, W. H., & Johnson, V. E. (1970). *Human sexual inadequacy.* Boston: Little, Brown.

Masters, W. H., & Johnson, V. E. (1979). *Homosexuality in perspective.* Boston: Little, Brown.

Masters, W. H., Johnson, V. E., & Kolodny, R. C. (1982). *Human sexuality.* Boston: Little, Brown.

Masterson, J., Dunworth, R., & Williams, N. (1988). Extreme illness exaggeration in pediatric patients: A variant of Munchausen's by proxy? *American Journal of Orthopsychiatry, 58*, 188–195.

Masterson, J. F. (1976). *Psychotherapy of the borderline adult—developmental approach.* New York: Brunner/Mazel.

Masunaga, S., & Ohashi, W. (1977). *Shiatsu.* Tokyo: Japan Publications.

Masur, H. (1992). Toxoplasmosis. In J. B. Wyngaarden, L. H. Smith, Jr., & J. C. Bennett (Eds.), *Cecil textbook of medicine* (19th ed., pp. 1987–1991). Philadelphia; Saunders.

Matarazzo, J., Lubin, B., & Nathan, R. G. (1978). Psychologists membership on the medical staffs of university teaching hospitals. *American Psychologist, 33*, 23–39.

Matarazzo, J. D. (1972). *Wechsler's measurement and appraisal of adult intelligence* (5th ed.). Baltimore: Williams & Wilkins.

Matarazzo, J. D. (1972/1939). *Wechsler's measurement and appraisal of adult intelligence* (5th ed.). Baltimore, Md.: Williams & Wilkins.

Matarazzo, J. D. (1978). The interview: Its reliability and validity in psychiatric diagnosis. In B. B. Wolman (Ed.), *Clinical diagnosis of mental disorders: A handbook.* New York: Plenum.

Matarazzo, J. D. (1980). Behavioral health and behavioral medicine: Frontiers for a new health psychology. *American Psychologist, 35*, 807–817.

Matarazzo, J. D. (1980). Psychological assessment of intelligence. In *Comprehensive textbook of psychiatry/III.* Baltimore, Md.; London: Williams & Wilkins.

Matarazzo, J. D. (1982). Behavioral health's challenge to academic, scientific, and professional psychology. *American Psychologist, 37*, 1–14.

Matarazzo, J. D. (1983). The reliability of psychiatric and psychological diagnosis. *Clinical Psychology Review, 3*, 103–145.

Matarazzo, J. D. (1990). Psychological assessment versus psychological testing: Validation from Binet to the school, clinic, and courtroom. *American Psychologist, 45*, 999–1017.

Matarazzo, J. D., Meier, et al. (Eds.). (in press). *ABPP conference on accreditation of postdoctoral programs in professional psychology.* The University of Minnesota.

Matarazzo, J. D., & Saslow, G. (1960). Psychological and related characteristics of smokers and non-smokers. *Psychological Bulletin, 57*(6), 493–513.

Matarazzo, R. G. (1978). Research on the training and learning of psychotherapeutic skills. In S. L. Garfield & A. E. Bergin (Eds.), *Handbook of psychotherapy and behavior change: An empirical analysis.* New York: Wiley.

Matheny, A. P. (1980). Visual-perceptual exploration and accident liability in children. *Journal of Pediatric Psychology, 5*, 343–351.

Matheny, A. P., et al, (1981). Behavioral contrasts in twinships; Stability and patterns of differences in childhood. *Child Development, 52*, 579–588.

Matheny, A. P., & Dolan, A. B. (1980). A twin study of personality and temperament during middle childhood. *Journal of Research in Personality, 14,* 224–234.

Matheny, K., & Cupp, P. (1983, September). Control, desirability and anticipation as modulating variables between life change illness. *Journal of Human Stress.*

Matheny, K., Curlette, W., Aycock, D., Pugh, J., & Taylor, H. *Coping resources inventory.* Test construction underway in Department of Counseling and Psychological Services, Georgia State University.

Mather, K., & Jinks, G. L. (1971). *Biometrical genetics.* London: Chapman & Hall.

Mather, W. G., Kit, B. V., Block, G. A., & Herman, M. F. (1970). *Man, his job and the environment: An annotated bibliography* (National Bureau of Standards Special Publication no. 29). Washington, D.C.: National Bureau of Standards.

Mathews, C. O. (1977). A review of behavioral theories of depression and a self-regulation model for depression. *Psychotherapy: Theory, Research, and Practice, 14*(1), 79–86.

Matin, L. (1972). Eye movements and perceived visual direction. In D. Jameson & L. M. Hurvich (Eds.) *Handbook of sensory physiology.* Vol. 7 (4): *Visual psychophysics.* Heidelberg: Springer.

Matlin, M. W. (1983). *Cognition.* New York: Holt, Rinehart & Winston.

Maton, K. I. (1989). Community settings as buffers of life stress? Highly supportive churches, mutual help groups, and senior centers. *American Journal of Community Psychology, 17,* 203–232.

Maton, K. I. (1989). Towards an ecological understanding of mutual-help groups: The social ecology of "fit." *American Journal of Community Psychology, 17,* 729–754.

Matterson, J., Dunworth, R., & Williams N. (1988). Extreme illness exaggeration in pediatric patients: A variant of Munchausen's by proxy? *American Journal of Orthopsychiatry, 58,* 188–195.

Mattessini, F. (1962). Bibliografia su Padre Agostino Gemelli (1959–1961). *Studi Francescani, 59,* 84–92.

Matthews, C. G. (1974). Applications of neuropsychological test methods to mentally retarded subjects. In R. M. Reitan & L. A. Davison (Eds.), *Clinical neuropsychology: Current status and applications.* Washington, D.C.: Winston.

Matthews, J. (1978). The farm worker. In W. T. Singleton (Ed.), *The analysis of practical skills.* Baltimore, Md.: University Park Press.

Matthews, K. A. (1982). Psychological perspectives on the type A behavior pattern. *Psychological Bulletin, 91,* 293–323.

Matthews, K. A., & Brunson, B. I. (1979). Allocation of attention and the type A coronary-prone behavior pattern. *Journal of Personality and Social Psychology, 37,* 2081–2090.

Matthies, W. J. T. (1977). Behavioral models of depression in monkeys. In I. Hanin & E. Usdin (Eds.), *Animal models in psychiatry and neurology* (pp. 17–26). Oxford, UK: Pergamon.

Mattis, S. (1978). Dyslexia syndromes: A working hypothesis that works. In A. L. Benton & D. Pearl (Eds.), *Dyslexia: An appraisal of current knowledge.* New York: Oxford University Press.

Mattis, S. (1981). Dyslexia syndromes in children: Toward the development of syndrome-specific treatment programs. In F. J. Pirozzolo & M. C. Wittrock (Eds.), *Neuropsychological and cognitive processes in reading.* New York: Academic Press.

Matza, D. (1964). *Delinquency and drift.* New York: Wiley.

Maudsley, H. (1898). *Responsibility in mental disease.* New York: Appleton.

Mauer, D. (1974). *The American confidence man.* Springfield, IL: Thomas.

Maury, A. (1861). *Le sommeil et les rêves.* Paris: Didier.

Mauskopf, S. M., & McVaugh, M. R. (1980). *The elusive science: Origins of experimental psychical research.* Baltimore, Md.: Johns Hopkins University Press.

Mausner, J. S., & Kramer, S. (1985). *Mausner & Bahn's epidemiology: An introductory text* (2nd ed.). Philadelphia: Saunders.

Mauss, M. (1954). *The gift: Forms and functions of exchange in archaic societies.* Glencoe, IL: Free press.

Maxwell, M. (1979). *Improving student learning skills.* San Francisco: Jossey-Bass.

Maxwell, M. (1991). *The sociobiological imagination.* Albany: SUNY Press.

May, C. R., & Campbell, R. (1981). Readiness for learning: Assumptions and realities. *Theory Into Practice, 20,* 130–134.

May, P. R. A. (1968). *Treatment of schizophrenia: A temperature study of five treatment methods.* New York: Science House.

May, R. (1953). *Man's search for himself.* New York: Norton.

May, R. (1958). *Existence.* New York: Basic Books.

May, R. (1964). On the phenomenological bases of psychotherapy. *Review of Existential Psychology and Psychiatry, 4,* 22–36.

May, R. (1969). *Love and will.* New York: Norton.

May, R. (1972). *Power and innocence.* New York: Norton.

May, R. (1975). *The courage to create.* New York: Norton.

May, R. (1976). *The courage to create.* New Haven, Conn.: Yale University Press.

May, R. (1979/1950). *The meaning of anxiety.* New York: Ronald Press.

May, R. (1980). *Psychology and the human dilemma.* New York: Norton.

May, R. (1980). *Sex and fantasy* New York, London: Norton.

May, R., Angel, E., & Ellenberger, H. F. (Eds.). (1967/1958). *Existence: A new dimension in psychiatry and psychology.* New York: Touchstone Books.

May, R. (Ed.). (1981/1969/1961). *Existential psychology* New York: Random House.

May, W., & Belsky, J. (1992). Response to "Prescription privileges: Psychology's next frontier?" or the Siren call: Should psychologists medicate. *American Psychologist, 47,* 427.

Mayer, A. (1900). Variations de la tension osmotique du sang chez les animaux privés de liquides. *Comptes Rendus des Séances de la Société de Biologie et de ses Filiales 52,* 153–155.

Mayer, C. A. (1974). *Understanding young children: The handicapped child in the normal preschool class.* Urbana, Ill.: Publications Office/IREC; College of Education/University of Illinois, Catalog no. 114.

Mayer, J. (1953). Glucostatic mechanisms of regulation of food intake. *New England Journal of Medicine, 249,* 13–16.

Mayer, J. (1955). Regulation of energy intake and the body weight. The glucostatic theory and the lipostatic hypothesis. *Annals of the New York Academy of Sciences, 63,* 15–43.

Mayer, J., & Harris, T. G. (1970, January). Affluence: The fifth horseman of the apocalypse. *Psychology Today,* 43.

Mayer, N. (1978). *The male mid-life crisis.* New York: Signet.

Mayman, M. (1968). Early memories and character structure. *Journal of Projective Techniques and Personality Assessment, 32,* 303–316.

Maynard Smith, J. (1976). Evolution and the theory of games. *American Scientist, 64,* 41–45.

Maynard Smith, J. (1974). The theory of games and the evolution of animal conflicts. *Journal of Theoretical Biology, 47,* 209–221.

Mayo, C. & Henley, N. M. (Eds.). (1981). *Gender and nonverbal behavior.* New York: Springer-Verlag.

Mayo, E. (1960/1933). *The human problems of an industrial civilization.* New York: Macmillan.

Mayo, E. (1945). *The social problems of an industrial civilization.* Cambridge, Mass.: Harvard University, Graduate School of Business Administration.

Mayo, E. (1972/1952). *The psychology of Pierre Janet.* Westport, Conn.: Greenwood Press.

Mayo, P. (1976). Sex differences and psychopathology. In B. Lloyd & J. Archer (Eds.), *Exploring sex differences.* New York: Academic Press.

Mayr, E. (1963). *Animal species and evolution.* Cambridge, MA: Harvard University Press.

Mayr, E. (1982). *The growth of biological thought.* Cambridge, MA: Harvard University Press.

Mays, V. M., Albee, G. W., & Schneider, S. (Eds.). (1989). *Psychological approaches to the prevention of AIDS.* Newbury Park, CA: Sage.

McAdams, D. P. (1985). *Power, intimacy, and the life story: Personological inquiries into identity.* Homewood, IL: Dorsey.

McAdams, D. P., & Ochberg, R. L. (Eds.). (1988). *Psychobiography and life narratives.* Durham, NC: Duke University Press.

McAdoo, H. (1978). Factors related to stability in upwardly mobile black families. *Journal of Marriage and the Family, 40,* 762–778.

McAllister, W. R., & McAllister, D. E. (1971). Behavioral measurement of conditioned fear. In F. R. Brush (Ed.), *Aversive conditioning and learning* (pp. 105–179). New York: Academic Press.

McAllister, W. R., & McAllister, D. E. (1988). Reconditioning of extinguished fear after a one-year delay. *Bulletin of the Psychonomic Society.*

McArthur, C. (1956). Personalities of first and second children. *Psychiatry, 19,* 47–54.

McArthur, C., Waldron, E., & Dickinson, J. (1958). The psychology of smoking. *Journal of Abnormal and Social Psychology, 56,* 267–275.

McArthur, C. C. (1968). Comment on studies of clinical versus statistical prediction. *Journal of Counseling Psychology, 15,* 172–173.

McBrien, R. P. (1980). *Catholicism.* Minneapolis, Minn.: Winston Press.

McCall, R. B. (1970). *Fundamental statistics for psychology.* New York: Harcourt.

McCallum, R., Rusbult, C. E, Hong, G. K., Walden, T. A, & Schopler, J. (1979). Effects of resource availability and importance of behavior on the experience of crowding. *Journal of Personality and Social Psychology, 37,* 1304–1313.

McCann, S. C., Mueller, C. W., Hays, P. A., Shceuer, A. D., & Marsella, A. J. (1990). Scales for physical and social anhedonia, *Journal of Abnormal Psychology, 85,* 374–382.

McCarter, R. E., Schiffman, H. M., & Tomkins, S. S. (1961). Early recollections as predictors of the Tomkins–Horn picture arrangement test performance. *Journal of Individual Psychology, 17,* 177–180.

McCarthy, D. (1954). Language development in children. In L. Carmichael (Ed.), *Manual of child psychology.* New York: Wiley.

McCarthy, J. J. (1967). Sales managers: Managers of sales? Or managers of salesmen? *Sales and Marketing Management, 98,* 69–76.

McCarty, D., Argeriou, M., Huebner, R., & Lubran, B. (1991). Alcoholism, drug abuse, and the homeless. *American Psychologist, 46,* 1139–1148.

McCary, J. L. (1973/1967). *Human sexuality.* New York: Van Nostrand.

McCasland, S. V. (1951). *By the finger of God.* New York: Macmillan.

McCaulley, M. H. (1981). Jung's theory of psychological types and the Myers–Briggs type indicator. In P. McReynolds (Ed.), *Advances in psychological assessment,* Vol. 5. San Francisco: Jossey-Bass.

McCay, C. M. (1935). The effect of retarded growth upon the length of life span and upon the ultimate body size. *Journal of Nutrition, 10,* 63–79.

McChesney, K. Y. (1990). Family homelessness: A systemic problem. *Journal of Social Issues, 46,* 191–205.

McClain, P. (1982). Black female homicide offenders and victims: Are they from the same population? *Death Education, 6,* 265–278.

McClelland, D. (1970). The two faces of power. *International Affairs, 24*(1), 29–47.

McClelland, D. (1975). *Power: The inner experience.* New York: Irvington.

McClelland, D. (1982, May). Understanding psychological man. *Psychology Today*

McClelland, D. C. (1951). *Personality.* New York: Holt, Rinehart, & Winston.

McClelland, D. C. (1958). Risk taking in children with high and low need for achievement. In J. W. Atkinson (Ed.), *Motives in fantasy, action, and society.* New York: Van Nostrand.

McClelland, D. C. (1961). *The achieving society.* Princeton, N.J.: Van Nostrand.

McClelland, D. C. (1965). Need achievement and entrepreneurship: A longitudinal study. *Journal of Personality and Social Psychology, 1,* 389–392.

McClelland, D. C. (1973). Testing for competence rather than for "intelligence." *American Psychologist, 28,* 1–14.

McClelland, D. C. (1973). The two faces of power. In D. C. McClelland & R. S. Steele (Eds.), *Human motivation: A book of reading.* Morristown, N.J.: General Learning Press.

McClelland, D. C. (1975). Love and power: The psychological signals of war. *Psychology Today, 8*(8), 44–48.

McClelland, D. C. (1975). *Power: The inner experience.* New York: Irvington.

McClelland, D. C. (1981). Child rearing versus ideology and social structure as factors in personality development. In R. H. Munroe, R. L. Munroe, & B. B. Whiting (Eds.), *Handbook of cross-cultural human development.* New York: Garland STPM Press.

McClelland, D. C. (1981). Is personality consistent? In A. I. Rabin, J. Aronoff, A. M. Barclay, & R. A. Zucker (Eds.), *Further explorations in personality.* New York: Wiley.

McClelland, D. C., & Atkinson, J. W. (1948). The projective expression of needs. 1. The effect of different intensities of the hunger drive on perception. *Journal of Psychology, 25,* 205–222.

McClelland, D. C., Atkinson, J. W., Clark, R. A., & Lowell, E. G. (1976/1953). *The achievement motive.* New York: Irvington.

McClelland, D. C., Atkinson, J. W., Clark, R. A., & Lowell, E. L. (1953). *The achievement motive.* New York: Appleton-Century-Crofts.

McClelland, D. C., Davis, W. N., & Kalin, R. (1972). *The drinking man.* New York: Free Press.

McClelland, D. C., & Winter, D. G. (1971/1969). *Motivating economic achievement.* New York: Free Press.

McClelland, J. L., & Rumelhart, D. E. (1985). Distributed memory and the representation of general and specific information. *Journal of Experimental Psychology: General, 114.* 159–188.

McClelland, J. L., Rumelhart, D. E., & the PDP Research Group, (Eds.). (1986). *Parallel distributed Processing explorations in the* *microstructure of cognition 2: Psychological and biological models.* Cambridge: MIT Press/Bradford Books.

McClintock, C. G., & S. P. McNeel. (1966). Reward and score feedback as determinants of cooperative and competitive game behavior. *Journal of Personality and Social Psychology, 4*(6), 606–613.

McCloskey, M., & Egeth, H. (1983). Eyewitness identification: What can a psychologist tell a jury? *American Psychologist, 38,* 550–563.

McCloskey, M. (1992). Networks and theories: The place of connectionism in cognitive science. *Psychological Science, 2,* 387–395.

McClosky, H. (1958). Conservatism and personality. *American Political Science Review, 52,* 27–45.

McCloy, C. H. (1940). A preliminary study of factors of motor educability. *Research Quarterly, 11,* 28–39.

McClure, R. F. (1969). Birth order and school related attitudes. *Psychological Reports, 25*(2), 657–658.

McCluskey, N. J., & Borgatta, E. F. (Eds.). (1981). *Aging and retirement: Prospects, planning and policy.* Beverly Hills, Calif.: Sage Publications.

McCollum, I. N. (1971). Psychological thrillers: Psychology books students read when given freedom of choice. *American Psychologist, 26,* 921–927.

McConaghy, M. J. (1979). Gender permanence and the genital basis of gender: Stages in the development of constancy of gender identity. *Child Development, 50,* 1223–1226.

McConahay, J. B., Mullin, C. J., & Frederick, J. (1977). The uses of social science in trials with political and racial overtones: The trial of Joan Little. *Law and Contemporary Problems, 41,* 205–229.

McConkie, M. L. (1979). A clarification of the goal setting and appraisal processes in MBO. *Academy of Management Review, 4,* 29–40.

McConnell, J. V. (1962). Memory transfer through cannibalism in planarians. *Journal of Neuropsychiatry, 3,* 542–548.

McConnell, J. V. (1978). Confessions of a textbook writer. *American Psychologist, 33,* 159–169.

McConnell, J. V. (1980). *Understanding human behavior* (3rd ed.) New York: Holt, Rinehart & Winston.

McConnell, J. V. (Ed.). (1965). *The worm re-turns: The best from the Worm Runner's Digest.* Englewood Cliffs, N.J.: Prentice-Hall.

McConnell, J. V., Cutler, R. I., & McNeil, E. B. (1958). Subliminal stimulation: An overview. *American Psychologist, 13,* 229–242.

McCord, J. (1979). Some child rearing antecedents to criminal behavior in adult men. *Journal of Personality and Social Psychology, 37,* 1477–1486.

McCord, J. (1991a). Family relationships, juvenile delinquency, and adult criminality. *Criminology, 29,* 397–417.

McCord, J. (1991b). The cycle of crime and socialization practices. *The Journal of Criminal Law & Criminology, 82,* 211–228.

McCormick, E. J. (1976/1957). *Human factors in engineering and design.* New York: McGraw-Hill.

McCormick, E. J. (1976). Job and task analysis. In M. D. Dunnette (Ed.), *Handbook of industrial and organizational psychology.* Chicago: Rand-McNally.

McCormick, E. J. (1979). *Job analysis: Methods and applications.* New York: Amacom.

McCormick, E. J., & Ilgen, D. R. (1980). *Industrial psychology* (7th ed.). Englewood Cliffs, N.J.: Prentice-Hall.

McCormick, E. J., & Ilgen, D. R. (1985). *Industrial and organizational psychology* (8th ed.). Englewood Cliffs, NJ: Prentice-Hall.

McCormick, E. J., & Sanders, M. S. (1981). *Human factors in engineering and design* (5th ed.). New York: Wiley.

McCormick, E. J., & Tiffin, J. (1974/1942). *Industrial psychology.* Englewood Cliffs, N.J.: Prentice-Hall.

McCormick, K., & Baer, D. J. (1975). Birth order, sex of sibling as factors in extraversion and neuroticism in two-child families. *Psychological Reports, 37*(1), 259–261.

McCrae, R., Bartone, P., & Costa, P. (1976). Age, anxiety, and self reported health. *Aging and Human Development, 7,* 49–58.

McCranie, E. J., & Crasilneck, H. B. (1955). The conditioned reflex in hypnotic age regression. *Journal of Clinical and Experimental Psychopathology, 16,* 120–123.

McCranie, E. J., Crasilneck, H. B., & Teter, H. R. (1955). The electroencephalogram in hypnotic age regression. *Psychiatric Quarterly, 29,* 85–88.

McCubbin, H. I., Joy, C. B., Cabule, A. E., Comeau, J. K., Patterson, J. M., & Needle, R. H. (1980, November). Family stress and coping: A decade review. *Journal of Marriage and the Family.*

McCulloch, W. S., & Pitts, W. (1943). A logical calculus of the ideas immanent in nervous activity. *Bulletin of Mathematical Biophysics, 9,* 115–133.

McCurdy, H. G. (1957). The childhood pattern of genius. *Journal of the Elisha Mitchell Scientific Society, 73,* 448–462.

McDaniel, E. (1978). Hysterical neurosis. In G. Ballis, L. Wurmser, E. McDaniel, & R. Grenell (Eds.), *Clinical psychopathology.* Boston: Butterworth.

McDavid, J. W., & Harari, H. (1968). *Social psychology: Individuals, groups, societies.* New York: Harper & Row.

McDermott, J. J. (Ed.). (1977). *The writings of William James.* Chicago: University of Chicago Press.

McDermott, R. A. (1984). *The essential steiner.* San Francisco: Harper & Row.

McDougall, K. D., & McDougall, W. (1931). Insight and foresight in various animals—monkey, raccoon, rat and wasp. *Journal of Comparative Psychology, 2,* 237–274.

McDougall, W. (1901). On the seat of psychological processes. *Brain, 24,* 577–630.

McDougall, W. (1905). *Physiological psychology.* London: Dent.

McDougall, W. (1911). *Body and mind: A history and defense of animism.* London: Methuen.

McDougall, W. (1920). Motives in light of recent discussion. *Mind.*

McDougall, W. (1923). *Outline of psychology.* New York: Scribner's.

McDougall, W. (1923). Purposive or mechanical psychology? *Psychological Review, 30,* 273–288.

McDougall, W. (1926). *Outline of abnormal psychology.* New York: Scribner's.

McDougall, W. (1926/1908). *An introduction to social psychology.* Boston: Luce.

McDougall, W. (1927). *Character and the conduct of life.* London: Methuen.

McDougall, W. (1930). The hormic psychology. In *Psychologies of 1930.* Worcester, Mass.: Clark University Press.

McDougall, W. (1932). *Energies of men: A study of the fundamental dynamics of psychology.* London: Methuen.

McDougall, W. (1938). Further report on a Lamarckian experiment, Pts. I–IV. *British Journal of Psychology, 28,* 231–245.

McDowell, C. F. (1981). Leisure: Consciousness, well-being, and counseling. In E. T. Dowd (Ed.), Leisure counseling. *The Counseling Psychologist, 9,* 3–32.

McEwen, B. S., Luine, V. N., & Fishcette, C. T. (1988). Developmental actions of hormones: From receptors to function. In S. S. Easter,

Jr., K. F. Barald, & B. M. Carlson (Eds.), *From message to mind: Directions in developmental neurobiology* (pp. 272–287). Sunderland, MA: Sinauer.

McFall, R. M., & Lillesand, D. B. (1971). Behavior rehearsal with modeling and coaching in assertion training. *Journal of Abnormal Psychology, 77,* 313–323.

McFarland, D. (1971). *Feedback mechanisms in animal behavior.* New York: Academic Press.

McFarland, R. A. (1932). The psychological effects of oxygen deprivation (anoxemia) on human behavior. *Archives of Psychology, 145,* 1–35.

McFie, J. (1975). *Assessment of organic intellectual impairment.* New York: Academic Press.

McGarry, A. L. (1969). Demonstration and research in competency for trial and mental illness: Review and preview. *Boston University Law Review, 49,* 50–60.

McGarry A. L., et al. (1973). *Competency to stand trial and mental illness.* Washington, D.C.: U.S. Government Printing Office.

McGaugh, J. L. (1966). Time-dependent processes in memory storage. *Science, 153,* 1351–1358.

McGaugh, J. L. (1983). Hormonal influences on memory. *Annual Review of Psychology, 34,* 297–323.

McGaugh, J. L., & Petrinovich, L. F. (1965). Effects of drugs on learning and memory. *International Review of Neurobiology, 8,* 139–196.

McGavack, T. H. (1967). In K. Soddy & M. C. Kidson (Eds.), *Cross-cultural studies in mental health.* London: Tavistock.

McGaw, W. H., Farson, R. E., & Rogers, C. R. (1968). *Journey into self* (film). Berkeley, Calif.: University of California Extension Media Center.

McGaw, W. H., McGaw, A. P., Rice, C. P., & Rogers, C. R. (1973). *The steel shutter* (film). La Jolla, Calif.: Center for Studies of the Person.

McGee, R., Williams, S., & Silva, P. A. (1984). Background characteristics of aggressive, hyperactive, and aggressive-hyperactive boys. *Journal of the American Academy of Child Psychiatry, 23,* 280–284.

McGee, V. E. (1966). The multidimensional analysis of "elastic" distances. *British Journal of Mathematical and Statistical Psychology, 19,* 181–196.

McGehee, W., & Owen, E. B. (1940). Authorized and unauthorized rest pauses in clerical work. *Journal of Applied Psychology, 24,* 604–614.

McGeoch, J. A. (1930). The influence of associative value upon the difficulty of nonsense-syllable lists. *Journal of Genetic Psychology, 37,* 421–426.

McGeoch, J. A. (1942). *The psychology of human learning: An introduction.* New York: Van Rees Press.

McGeoch, J. A. (1942). *The psychology of human learning.* New York: David McKay.

McGeoch, J. A., & McDonald, W. T. (1931). Meaningful relation and retroactive inhibition. *American Journal of Psychology, 43,* 579–588.

McGhee, P. (1972). On the cognitive origins of incongruity humor: Fantasy assimilation versus reality assimilation. In J. Goldstein & P. McGhee (Eds.), *The psychology of humor.* New York: Academic Press.

McGhee, P. E. (1979). *Humor: Origins and development.* San Francisco: Freeman.

McGill, M. E. (1980). *The 40 to 60 year old male.* New York: Simon & Schuster.

McGinnies, E. (1949). Emotionality and perceptual defence. *Psychological Review, 56,* 244–251.

McGoldrick, M., & Pearce, J. (1981). Family therapy with Irish-Americans. *Family Process, 20,* 223–244.

McGovern, J. R. (1968). The American woman's pre-World War I freedom in manners and morals. *Journal of American History, 55,* 315–333.

McGranahan, D. V. (1946). A comparison of social attitudes among American and German youth. *Journal of Abnormal and Social Psychology, 41,* 245–257.

McGrath, J. (1970). *Social and psychological factors in stress.* New York: Holt, Rinehart & Winston.

McGrath, J. E., & Kravitz, D. (1982). Group research. *Annual Review of Psychology, 33,* 195–230.

McGrath, P. A. (1990). *Pain in children.* New York: Guilford.

McGraw, M. B. (1931). A comparative study of a group of southern white and Negro infants. *Genetic Psychology Monograph, 10,* 1–105.

McGregor, D. (1960). *The human side of enterprise,* New York: McGraw-Hill.

McGuigan, F. J. (1978). *Cognitive psychopharmacology.* Hillsdale, N.J.: Erlbaum.

McGuigan, F. J. (1979). *Psychophysiological measurement of covert behavior.* Hillsdale, N.J.: Erlbaum.

McGuigan, F. J. (1981). *Calm down: A guide for stress and tension control.* Englewood Cliffs, N.J.: Prentice-Hall.

McGuinness, D. (1976). Sex differences in the organization of perception and cognition. In B. Lloyd & J. Archer (Eds.), *Exploring sex differences.* New York: Academic Press.

McGuire, F. L. (1976). Personality factors in highway accidents. *Human Factors, 18,* 433–442.

McGuire, T. L., & Feldman, K. W. (1989). Psychologic morbidity of children subjected to Munchausen syndrome by proxy. *Pediatrics, 83,* 289–292.

McGuire, W. J. (1960). A syllogistic analysis of cognitive relationships. In M. J. Rosenberg, C. I. Hovland, W. J. McGuire, R. P. Abelson, & J. W. Brehm (Eds.), *Attitude organization and change: An analysis of consistency among attitude components* (pp. 65–111). New Haven, CT: Yale University Press.

McGuire, W. J. (1964). Inducing resistance to persuasion: Some contemporary approaches. In L. Berkowitz (Ed.), *Advances in experimental social psychology.* New York: Academic Press.

McGuire, W. J. (1968). Personality and susceptibility to social influence. In E. F. Borgatta & W. W. Lambert (Eds.), *Handbook of personality theory and research.* Chicago: Rand-McNally.

McGuire, W. J. (1969). Attitude and attitude change. In G. Lindzey & E. Aronson (Eds.), *Handbook of social psychology.* Reading, Mass.: Addison-Wesley.

McGuire, W. J. (1969). The nature of attitudes and attitude change. In G. Lindzey & E. Aronson (Eds.), *The handbook of social psychology* Vol. 3. (2nd ed.), Reading, Mass.: Addison-Wesley.

McGuire, W. J. (1973). The yin and yang of progress in social psychology: Seven koan. *Journal of Personality and Social Psychology, 26,* 446–456.

McGuire, W. J. (1980). The probilogical model of cognitive structure and attitude change. In R. Petty, T. Ostrom, & T. Brock (Eds.), *Cognitive responses in persuasion.* Hillsdale, N.J.: Erlbaum.

McGuire, W. J. (1982). Social psychology's second century. In S. Koch & M. D. Leary (Eds.), *A century of psychology as science.* New York: McGraw-Hill (in press).

McGurk, H., & Lewis, M. (1972). Birth order: A phenomenon in search of an explanation. *Developmental Psychology, 7, 366.*

McGurk, H., & MacDonald, J. (1976). Hearing lips and seeing voices. *Nature, 264,* 746–748.

McHenry, L. C., Jr. (1969). *Garrison's history of neurology.* Springfield, IL: Thomas.

McHugh, M. C., Koeske, R. D., & Frieze, I. H., (1981). *Guidelines for nonsexist research.* Report of the Task Force of Division 35 of APA, December.

McIntire, R. W., & White, J. (1975). Behavior modification. In B. L. Margolis & W. H. Kroes (Eds.), *The human side of accident prevention.* Springfield, Ill.: Thomas.

McKay, G., (1976). *The basics of encouragement.* Coral Springs, Fla.: CMII Press.

McKay, S., & Golden, C. J. (1979). Empirical derivation of experimental scales for localizing brain lesions using the Luria Nebraska Neuropsychological Battery. *Clinical Neuropsychology, 1,*(4) 19–23.

McKeachie, W. J. (1951). Anxiety in the college classroom. *Journal of Educational Research, 45,* 135–160.

McKeachie, W. J. (1958). Students, groups, and teaching methods. *American Psychologist, 13,* 580–584.

McKeachie, W. J. (1961). Motivation, teaching methods and college learning. In M. R. Jones (Ed.), *Nebraska Symposium on Motivation, 1961.* Lincoln, Neb.: University of Nebraska Press.

McKeachie, W. J. (1972). A tale of a teacher (an autobiography). In T. W. Krawiec *(Ed.), The psychologists.* New York: Oxford University Press.

McKeachie, W. J. (1974). Instructional psychology. *Annual Review of Psychology, 25,* 161–193.

McKeachie, W. J. (1978). *Teaching tips: A guidebook for the beginning college teacher.* Boston: Heath.

McKeachie, W. J. (1979). Student ratings of faculty: A reprise. *Academe, 65,* 384–397.

McKeachie, W. J. (1980). *Learning, cognition, and college teaching. New directions for teaching and learning, no. 2.* San Francisco: Jossey-Bass.

McKeachie, W. J., & Doyle, C. (1966). *Psychology.* Reading, Mass.: Addison-Wesley.

McKeachie, W. J., Lin, Y-G., Daugherty, M., Moffett, M. M., Neigler, C., Nork, J., Walz, M., & Baldwin, R. (1980). Using student ratings and consultation to improve instruction. *British Journal of Educational Psychology, 50,* 168–174.

McKeachie, W. J., & Milholland, J. E. (1961). *Undergraduate curricula in psychology.* Chicago: Scott, Foresman.

McKeachie, W. J., Pollie, D., & Spiesman, J. (1955). Relieving anxiety in classroom examinations. *Journal of Abnormal and Social Psychology, 50,* 93–98.

McKeag, A. J. (1910). The use of illustrative experiments in classes in education. *Journal of Educational Psychology, 1,* 467–472.

McKegney, F. P., Runge, C., Bernstein, R., & Willmuth, R. (1981). Severe psychiatric disorder in dialysis—Transplant patients. In N. Levy (Ed.), *Psychological factors in hemodialysis and transplantation,* New York, London: Plenum.

McKenna, W., & Kessler, S. J. (1977). Experimenter design as a source of sex bias in social psychology. *Sex Roles, 3,* 117–128.

McKeown, T. (1970). Prenatal and early postnatal influences on measured intelligence. *British Medical Journal* (London), 5714, 63–67.

McKillip, J. (1987). *Need analysis: Tools for human services and education.* Beverly Hills, CA: Sage.

McKinney, W. T. (1974). Animal models in psychiatry. *Perspectives in Biology and Medicine, 17,* 529–541.

McKinney, W. T. (1988). *Models of mental disorders: A new comparative psychiatry.* New York: Plenum Press.

McKnight, P. C. (1980). Microteaching: Development from 1968–1978. *British Journal of Teacher Education,* 214–227.

McKusick, V. A. (1964). *Human genetics.* Englewood Cliffs, N.J.: Prentice-Hall.

McKusick, V. A. (1990). *Mendelian inheritance in man* (9th ed). Baltimore: Johns Hopkins University Press.

McLaughlin, B. (1978). *Second-language acquisition in childhood.* Hillsdale, N.J.: Erlbaum.

McLaughlin, G. H. (1969). SMOG Grading—A new readability formula. *Journal of Reading, 12,* 639–646.

McLean, A. A. (1974). Mental health programs in industry. In S. Arieti (Ed.), *American handbook of psychiatry,* Vol. II. New York: Basic Books.

McLean, E. K., & Tarnopolsky, A. (1977). Noise, discomfort and mental health: A review of the socio-medical implications of disturbance by noise. *Psychological Medicine, 7,* 19–62.

McLeish, J. (1975). *Soviet psychology: History theory, content.* London: Methuen.

McLemore, C. W., & Benjamin, L. S. (1979). Whatever happened to interpersonal diagnosis? A psychosocial alternative to DSM-III. *American Psychologist, 34,* 17–34.

McLemore, C. W., & Hart, P. P. (1982). Relational psychotherapy: The clinical facilitation of intimacy. In J. Anchin & D. Kiesler (Eds.), *Handbook of interpersonal psychotherapy.* New York: Pergamon Press.

McLoyd, V. C. (1990). The impact of economic hardship on black families and children: Psychological distress, parenting, and socioemotional development. *Child Development, 61,* 311–346.

McLuhan, M. (1962). *The Gutenberg galaxy.* Toronto: University of Toronto Press.

McLuhan, M. (1964). *Understanding media: The extension of man.* New York: McGraw-Hill.

McLuhan, M., & Flore, Q. (1967). *The medium is the massage.* New York: Random House.

McMahon, C. E. (1973). Images as motives and motivators: A historical perspective. *American Journal of Psychology, 86,* 465–490.

McMullin, P. E., & Giles, T. R. (1981). *Cognitive-behavior therapy: A restructuring approach.* New York: Grune & Stratton.

McMullin, R. E. (1986). *Handbook of cognitive therapy techniques.* New York: Norton.

McMurrain, T., (1977). *Intervention in human crisis: A guide for helping families in crisis.* Atlanta, Ga.: Humanics Press.

McNamara, J. R., & Barclay, A. G. (Eds.) (1982). *Critical issues, developments, and trends in professional psychology.* New York: Praeger.

McNamara, P., & Durso, R. (1991). Reversible pathological jealousy (Othello syndrome) associated with amantadine. *Journal of Geriatric Psychiatry and Neurology, 4*(3), 157–159.

McNammee, S., & Gergen, K. J. (Eds.). (1992). *Therapy construction.* London: Sage.

McNaughton, B. L., Douglas, P. M., & Goddard, G. V. (1978). Synaptic enhancement in fascia dentata: Cooperativity among coactive afferents. *Brain Research, 157,* 277–293.

McNeil, D. R. (1973). Estimating an author's vocabulary. *Journal of the American Statistical Association, 68,* 92–96.

McNeill, D. (1970). *The acquisition of language: The study of developmental psycholinguistics*. New York: Harper & Row.

McNeill, D. A. (1966). Developmental psycholinguistics. In F. Smith & G. A. Miller (Eds.), *The genesis of language: A psycholinguistic approach*. Cambridge, Mass.: M.I.T. Press.

McNemar, Q. (1942). *The revision of the Stanford Binet scale*. Boston: Houghton Mifflin.

McNemar, Q. (1946). Opinion-attitude methodology. *Psychological Bulletin, 43,* 289–374.

McNemar, Q. (1947). Sampling error of the difference between correlated proportions or percentages. *Psychometrika, 12,* 153–157.

McNemar, Q. (1964). Lost: Our intelligence? Why? *American Psychologist, 19,* 871–882.

McNemar, Q. (1969/1949). *Psychological statistics*. New York: Wiley.

McPhail, P., Ungoed-Thomas, J. R. & Chapman, H. (1975). *Learning to care: Rationale and method of the lifeline program*. Niles, Ill.: Argus Communications.

McPhail, S. M., & Dickinson, T. L. (1977). MSS: A program for scoring mixed standard scales. *Applied Psychological Measurement, 1,* 402.

McQueen, A. J. (1965). Aspirations and problems of Nigerian school leavers. *Inter-African Labour Research Bulletin, 12,* 35–42.

McReynolds, P. (1975). Historical antecedents of personality assessment. In P. McReynolds (Eds.), *Advances in psychological assessment* (Vol. 3, pp. 447–532). San Francisco: Jossey-Bass.

McReynolds, P. (1986). History of assessment in clinical and educational settings. In R. O. Nelson & S. C. Hayes (Eds.), *Conceptual foundations of behavioral assessment* (pp. 42–80). New York: Guilford.

McReynolds, P., & Ludwig, K. (1984). Christian Tomasius and the origin of psychological rating scales. *Isis, 75,* 546–553.

McVaugh, M., & Mauskopf, S. H. (1976). J. B. Rhine's extra-sensory perception and its background in psychical research. *Isis, 67,* 161–189.

Mead, D. E. (1981). Reciprocity counseling: Practice and research. *Journal of Marriage and Family Therapy, 7,* 189–200.

Mead, G. H. (1913). The social self. *Journal of Philosophy, Psychology and Scientific Method, 10,* 374–380.

Mead, G. H. (1924/1925). The genesis of the self and social control, *International Journal of Ethics, 35,* 251–277.

Mead, G. H. (1934). *Mind, self, and society: From the standpoint of a social behaviorist:* Chicago: University of Chicago Press.

Mead, M. (1939). *From the South Seas (studies of adolescence and sex in primitive societies)*. New York: Morrow.

Mead, M. (1949). *Male and female: A study of the sexes in a changing world,* New York: Morrow.

Mead, M. (1959). As quoted in National Film Board of Canada (producer). *For families* (film). New York: McGraw-Hill Films.

Mead, M. (1961/1928). *Coming of age in Samoa*. New York: Dell.

Mead, M. (1961/1930). *Growing up in New Guinea*. New York: Dell.

Mead, M. (1969/1935). *Sex and temperament in three primitive societies*. New York: Dell.

Meador, A. E., & Ollendick, T. H. (1984). Cognitive behavior therapy with children: An evaluation of its efficacy and clinical utility. *Child and Family Behavior Therapy, 6,* 25–44.

Meadow, K. P. (1980). *Deafness and child development*. Berkeley, Calif.: University of California Press.

Meadow, R. (1977). Munchausen syndrome by proxy: The hinterland of child abuse. *Lancet, 2,* 342–345.

Meadows, A. W., (1959). **Lovibond, S. H., & John, R. D.** The establishment of psychophysical standards in the sorting of fruit. *Occupational Psychology, 33,* 217.

Meaney, M. J. (1988). The sexual differentiation of social play. *Trends in Neurosciences, 11,* 54–58.

Meares, A. (1961). A system of medical hypnosis. Philadelphia, Pa.: Saunders.

Mearig, J. S. (1981). The role of tests in assessing intellectual functioning of children with special needs. *Peabody Journal of Education, 58,* 108–117.

Mecacci L. (1979). *Brain and history: The relationship between neurophysiology and psychology in Soviet research*. New York: Brunner/Mazel.

Mechanic, D. (1972). Social psychologic factors affecting the presentation of bodily complaints. *New England Journal of Medicine, 286,* 1132–1140.

Mechanic, D. (1979). *Future issues in health care*. London: Collier Macmillan.

Mechanic, D. (1980). *Mental health and social policy*. Englewood Cliffs, N.J.: Prentice-Hall.

Mechanic, D. (1991). Sources of countervailing power in medicine. *Journal of Health Politics, Policy and Law, 16*(3), 485–498.

Meddis, R. (1971). *The sleep instinct*. London: Routledge & Kegan Paul.

Medin, D. L., Roberts, W. A., & Davis, R. T. (1976). *Processes of animal memory*. Hillsdale, N.J.: Erlbaum.

Medin, D. L., & Ross, B. H. (1992). *Cognitive psychology*. New York: Harcourt Brace Jovanovich.

Medina, G. S. (1965). Psychotrial: A new type of group therapy. *Corrective Psychiatry and Journal of Social Therapy, 11,* 157–162.

Mednick, M. T., & Urbanski, L. L. (1991). The origins and activities of APA's division of the psychology of women. *Psychology of Women Quarterly, 15,* 651–663.

Mednick, M. T. S., Tangri, S. S.,& Hoffman, L. W. (Eds.). (1975). *Women and achievement: Social and motivational analysis*. Washington, D.C.: Hemisphere.

Mednick, S., & Christiansen, K. (1977). *Biosocial bases of criminal behavior*. New York: Gardner Press.

Meehl, P. (1966). The complete autocerebroscopist: A thought experiment on Professor Feigl's mind/body identity thesis. In P. K. Feyerabend & G. Maxwell (Ed.), *Mind, matter, and method*. Minneapolis: University of Minnesota Press.

Meehl, P. E. (1950). On the circularity of the law of effect. *Psychological Bulletin, 47,* 52–57.

Meehl, P. E. (1954). *Clinical versus statistical procedures: A theoretical analysis and review of the evidence,* Minneapolis, Minn.: University of Minnesota Press.

Meehl, P. E. (1954). *Clinical versus statistical prediction*. Minneapolis, Minn.: University of Minnesota Press.

Meehl, P. E. (1956). Wanted—a good cookbook. *American Psychologist, 11,* 263–272.

Meehl, P. E. (1960). The cognitive activity of the clinician. *American Psychologist, 15,* 19–27.

Meehl, P. E. (1962). Schizotaxia, schizotypy, schizophrenia. *American Psychologist, 17,* 827–838.

Meehl, P. E. (1973). Psychodiagnosis: *Selected papers*. Minneapolis, Minn.: University of Minnesota Press.

Meehl, P. E. (1978). Theoretical risks and tabular asterisks: Sir Karl, Sir Ronald, and the slow progress of soft psychology. *Journal of Consulting and Clinical Psychology, 46,* 806–834.

Meehl, P. E. (in press). Subjectivity in psychoanalytic inference: The nagging persistence of Wilhelm Fliess's Achensee question. In J. Earman (Ed.), *Testing scientific theories, Minnesota studies in the philosophy of science,* vol. X. Minneapolis, Minn.: University of Minnesota Press.

Meehl, P. E., & Golden, R. R. (1978). Testing a single dominant gene theory without an accepted criterion variable. *Annals of Human Genetics* (London), 41, 507–514.

Meehl, P. E., & Golden, R. R. (1982). Taxometric methods. In P. Kendall & J. Butcher (Eds.), *Handbook of research methods in clinical psychology.* New York: Wiley.

Meehl, P. E., Livermore, J. M., & Malmquist, C. P. (1968). On the justifications for civil commitment. *University of Pennsylvania Law Review, 117,* 75–96.

Meehl, P. E., & Rosen, A. (1955). Antecedent probability and the efficiency of psychometric signs, patterns, or cutting scores. *Psychological Bulletin, 52,* 194–216.

Meeker, M. (1969). *The structure of intellect: Its interpretation and uses.* Columbus: OH: Merrill.

Meeker, M. N. (1969). *The structure of intellect model: Its interpretations and uses.* Columbus, Ohio: Merrill.

Meerloo, J. (1970). Pervasiveness of terms and concepts. (Tribute to Alfred Adler on his 100th birthday). *Journal of Individual Psychology, 26,* 14.

Megargee, E. (1970). The prediction of violence with psychological tests. In C. Spielberger (Ed.), *Current topics in clinical and community psychology.* New York: Academic.

Megargee, E. (1976). The prediction of dangerous behavior. *Criminal Justice and Behavior, 3,* 3–21.

Mehlman, B. (1952). The reliability of psychiatric diagnosis. *Journal of Abnormal and Social Psychology, 47,* 577–578.

Mehrabian, A. (1976). Questionnaire measures of affiliative tendency and sensitivity to rejection. *Psychological Reports, 38,* 199–209.

Mehrabian, A., & Ksionzky, S. (1974). *A theory of affiliation.* Lexington, Mass.: Heath.

Mehrabian, A., & Ross, M. (1979). Illness, accidents, and alcohol use as functions of the arousing quality and pleasantness of life changes. *Psychological Reports, 45,* 31–43.

Mehrabian, A., & Russell, J. A. (1974). *An approach to environmental psychology.* Cambridge, Mass.: M.I.T. Press.

Mehrens, W. A., & Lehmann, I. J. (1980). *Standardized tests in education* (3rd ed.). New York: Holt, Rinehart & Winston.

Meichenbaum, D. (1975). A self-instructional approach to stress management: A proposal for stress inoculation training. In I. Sarason & C. Spielberger (Eds.), *Stress and anxiety,* Vol. 2. New York: Wiley.

Meichenbaum, D. (1976). Toward a cognitive theory of self-control. In G. E. Schwartz & D. Shapiro (Eds.), *Consciousness and self-regulation: Advances in research,* Vol 1. New York: Plenum.

Meichenbaum, D. (1977). *Cognitive behavior modification: An integrative approach.* New York: Plenum.

Meichenbaum, D. (1980). Stability of personality: Change and psychotherapy. In E. Staub (Ed.), *Personality: Basic aspects and current research.* Englewood Cliffs, N.J.: Prentice-Hall.

Meichenbaum, D. (1989). *Cognitive behavior modification: An integrative approach* (2nd ed.). New York: Plemum.

Meichenbaum, D., & Jaremko, M. (1983). *Stress prevention and reduction.* New York: Plenum.

Meichenbaum, D. H., & Goodman, J. (1971). Training impulsive children to talk to themselves: A means of developing self-control, *Journal of Abnormal Psychology, 77,* 115–126.

Meier, D., & Bell, W. (1959). Anomia and differential access to the achievement of life goals. *American Sociological Review, 24,* 189–202.

Meier, E. B. (1964). Child neglect. In N. E. Cohen (Ed.), *Social work and social problems.* New York: National Association of Social Workers.

Meierhofer, M., & Keller, W. (1966). *Frustration im frühen Kindesalter.* Bern: Huber.

Meili, G., & Meili, R. (1972). *Grundlagen individueller Persönlichkeitsunterschiede.* Bern: Huber.

Meili, R. (1936). *Psychologische Diagnostik Eine Einführung Jür Psychologen und Erzieher.* Munich: Reinhardt.

Meili, R. (1946). L'analyse de l'intelligence. *Archives de Psychologie, 31,* 1–64.

Meili, R. (1957). *Anfänge der Charakterentwicklung und Ergebnisse einer Längsschnittuntersuchung. Beiträge zur genetischen Charakterologie.* 1. Bern: Huber.

Meili, R. (1959). Longitudinal study of personality development. In L. Jessner & E. Pavenstedt (Eds.), *Dynamic psychopathology in childhood.* New York: Grune & Stratton.

Meili, R. (1963). La structure de la personalité. In *Traité de psychologie expérimentale,* Vol. V Paris: Presses Universitaire de France.

Meili, R. (1965/1951). *Lehrbuch der psychologischen Diagnostik* Bern: Huber.

Meili, R. (1981). *Struktur der Intelligenz. Faktorenanalytische und denkpsychologische Untersuchungen.* Bern: Huber.

Meili, R., & Rohracher, H. (1972/1963). *Lehrbuch der experimentellen psychologie, Kap. I. Das psychologische Experiment, Kap. 5: Denken.* Bern: Huber.

Meili, R., & Steingruber, H. R. (1978). *Lehrbuch der psychologischen Diagnostik.* Bern: Huber.

Meili-Dworetzki, G. (1956). The development of perception in the Rorschach. In B. Klopfer (Ed.), *Rorschach technique.* Yonkers, N.Y.: World.

Meili-Dworetzki, G. (1982). *Spielarten des Menschenbildes. Ein Vergleich der Menschenzeichnungen japanischer und schweizerischer Kinder.* Bern: Huber.

Meili-Dworetzki, G., & Meili, R. (1972). *Grundlagen individueller Persönlichkeitsunterschiede. Ergebnisse eine Längsschnittuntrsuchung mit zwei Grup- pen yon der Geburt bis zum 8. und 16. Lebensjahr.* Bern: Huber.

Meinong, A. (1894). *Psychologisch-ethische untersuchungen zur werththeorie.* Graz, Austria: Leuschner & Lubensky.

Meinong, A. (1896). *Über die Bedeutung des Weber'schen Gesetzes; Beiträge zur Psychologie des Vergleichens und Messens.* Hamburg: Voss.

Meinong, A. (1914). *Abhandlungen zur psychologie.* Leipzig: Barth.

Meisels, S. J. (1977). *First steps in mainstreaming—Some questions and answers.* Boston: Massachusetts Department of Mental Health Media Resource Center.

Meisgeier, C. (1976). A review of critical issues underlying mainstreaming. In L. Mann & D. A. Sabatino (Eds.), *The third review of special education.* New York: Grune & Stratton.

Meissner, W. W. (1980). Theories of personality and psychopathology Classical psychoanalysis. In H. Kaplan, A. Freedman, & B. Sadock (Eds.), *Comprehensive textbook of psychiatry,* Vol. 1 (3rd ed.). Baltimore, Md.: Williams & Wilkins.

Meister, D. (1971). *Human factors: Theory and practice.* New York: Wiley.

Melamed, B. G., & Siegel, L. J. (1980). *Behavioral medicine. Practical applications in health care*. New York: Springer.

Melara, R. D. (1989a). Dimensional interaction between color and pitch. *Journal of Experimental Psychology: Human Perception and Performance, 15*, 69–79.

Melara, R. D. (1989b). Similarity relations among synesthetic stimuli and their attributes. *Journal of Experimental Psychology: Human Perception and Performance, 15*, 212–231.

Melara, R. D., & O'Brien, T. P. (1987). Interaction between synesthetically corresponding dimensions. *Journal of Experimental Psychology: General, 116*, 323–336.

Mellgren, R. L., & Ost, J. W. P. (1969). Transfer of Pavlovian differential conditioning to an operant discrimination. *Journal of Comparative and Physiological Psychology, 67*, 390–394.

Melton, A. W. (1963). Implications of short-term memory for a general theory of memory. *Journal of Verbal Learning and Verbal Behavior, 2*, 485–488.

Melton, A. W., & Martin, E. (Eds.). (1972). *Coding processes in human memory*. Washington, D.C.: Winston.

Melton, G. B. (1981). Children's competency to testify. *Law and Human Behavior, 5*, 73–85.

Meltzer, H. (1930). Individual differences in forgetting pleasant and unpleasant experiences. *Journal of Educational Psychology, 21*, 399–409.

Meltzer, H. (1965). Attitudes of workers before and after age 40. *Geriatrics, 20*, 425–432.

Meltzoff, J., & Kornreich, M. (1970). *Research in psychotherapy*. Chicago: Aldine.

Meltzoff, J., & Kornreich, M. (1970). *Research in psychotherapy*. New York: Atherton.

Meltzov, A. (1977). Imitation of facial and manual gestures by human neonates. *Science, 198*, 75–78.

Melzack, R. (1973). *The puzzle of pain*. New York: Basic Books.

Melzack, R. (1983). *Pain measurement and assessment*. New York: Raven Press.

Melzack, R., & Jeans, M. E. (1974, March). Acupuncture analgesia: A psychophysiological explanation. *Minnesota Medicine*, 161–166.

Melzack, R., & Scott, T. H. (1957). The effects of early experience on the response to pain. *Journal of Comparative and Physiological Psychology, 50*, 155–161.

Melzack, R., & Wall, P. (1982). *The challenge of pain*. New York: Basic Books.

Melzack, R., & Wall, P. D. (1965). Pain mechanism: A new theory. *Science, 150*, 971–981.

Menaker, E. (1953). Masochism—A defense reaction of the ego. *Psychoanalytic Quarterly, 22*, 205–220.

Menaker, E. (1973). Social matrix: Mother and child. *Psychoanalytic Review, 60*, 45–58.

Menaker, E. (1982). *Otto Rank: A rediscovered legacy*. New York: Columbia University Press.

Mencher, J. P. (1965). The Nayars of South Malabar. In M. F. Nimkoff (Ed.), *Comparative family systems*. Boston: Houghton Mifflin.

Mendel, W. M. The natural history of schizophrenia, in preparation.

Mendel, W. M. (1964). The phenomenon of interpretation. *American Journal of Psychoanalysis, 24*, 184–189.

Mendel, W. M. (1970). Tandem treatment, *Voices, 5*, 110–113.

Mendel, W. M. (1975). Precision in the diagnosis of schizophrenia. *Psychiatria Fennica*, 107–114.

Mendel, W. M.: (1975). *Supportive care: Theory and technique*. Los Angeles: Mara Books.

Mendel, W. M. (1976). *Schizophrenia: the experience and its treatment*. San Francisco: Jossey-Bass.

Mendel, W. M. (1977). A psychotherapy technique with planned interruption. In J. H. Masserman (Ed.), *Current psychiatric therapies*, Vol. 17. New York: Grune & Stratton.

Mendel, W. M., & Goren, S. (1981). *Mainstreaming*. In R. J. Corsini *Handbook of innovative psychotherapies*. New York: Wiley.

Mendelsohn, B. (1963). The origin of the doctrine of victimology. *Excerpta Criminologica, 3*, 239–244.

Mendelsohn, B. (1956). The victimology. *Études Internationales de Psycho-Sociologie Criminelle*, no. 11.

Mendelsohn, E. M., & Silverman, L. H. (1982). Effects of stimulating psychodynamically relevant unconscious fantasies on schizophrenic psychopathology. *Schizophrenia Bulletin, 8*, 532–547.

Mendelson, M. (1974). *Psychoanalytic concepts of depression*. Flushing, N.Y.: Spectrum.

Meneses, E. (1976). Veinticinco años de enseñanza de la psicologia en la Universidad Iberoamericana 1950–1975. *Enseñanza e Investigacion en Psicologia, 2*, 122–127.

Menne, J. W. (1981). Competency based assessment and the profession of psychology. *Journal of Professional Practice in Psychology, 2*, 17–28.

Menninger, K. (1938). *Man against himself*. New York: Harcourt, Brace.

Menninger, K. (1940). Character disorders. In J. F. Brown (Ed.), *The psychodynamics of abnormal behavior*. New York: McGraw-Hill.

Menninger, K. (1961). Reading as therapy. *American Library Association Bulletin, 55*, 316–319.

Menninger, K. (1964/1958). *Theory of psychoanalytic technique*. New York: Harper Torchbook.

Menninger, K. (1968). *The crime of punishment*. New York: Viking.

Menninger, K., Mayman, M., & Pruyser, P. (1963). *The vital balance*. New York: Viking.

Menninger, W. C. (1937). Bibliotherapy. *Bulletin of the Menninger Clinic, 1*, 263–274.

Menninger, W. C., & Levinson, H. (1957). *Human understanding in industry*. Chicago: Science Research Associates.

Mensh, I. N. (1959). Psychiatric diagnosis in the institutionalized aged. *Geriatrics, 14*, 511–517.

Mensh, I. N. (1979). Acute, reversible psychological reactions. In O. J. Kaplan *(Ed.)*, *Psychopathlogy of aging*. New York: Academic Press.

Mensh, I. N. (1979). Schizophrenia. In O. J. Kaplan (Ed.), *Psychopathology of aging*. New York: Academic Press.

Menta, M. (1972). Psycho-educational project utilizing Z-process therapy. Master's thesis, San Jose State University.

Menyuk, P. (1969). *Sentences children use*. Cambridge, Mass.: M.I.T. Press.

Menzel, E. W. (1972). Spontaneous invention of ladders in a group of young chimpanzees, *Folia Primatologia, 17*, 87–106.

Menzel, E. W. (1978). Cognitive mapping. In S. H. Hulse, H. Fowler, & W. K. Honig (Eds.), *Cognitive processes in animal behavior*. Hillsdale, NJ: Erlbaum.

Menzies, R. (1937). Conditioned vasomotor responses in human subjects. *Journal of Psychology, 4*, 75–120.

Menzies, R. J., Webster, C. D., Butler, B. T., & Turner, R. E. (1980). Outcome of forensic psychiatric assessment: A study of remands in six Canadian cities. *Criminal Justice and Behavior, 7*, 471–480.

Mercado, S. (1976). La lectura de los estudiantes de psicologia de la UNAM. *Revista de Educacion Superior de la Anuies, 20,* 24–33.

Mercado, S. (1978). *Procesamiento humano de informacion Mexico.* Mexico, D. F.: Trillas.

Mercado, S. (in press). Programa para un analisis teorico de psicologia ecologica

Mercer, J. R. (1976). Pluralistic diagnosis in the evaluation of black and Chicano children: A procedure for taking sociocultural variables into account. In C. A. Hernandez, M. J. Haug, & N. N. Wagner (Eds.), *Chicanos: Social and psychological perspectives.* St. Louis, Mo.: Mosby.

Mercer, J. R. (1977). *SOMPA, System of Multicultural Pluralistic Assessment.* New York: Psychological Corp.

Mercer, J. R. (1978). *System of Multiculture Puralistic Assessment* (SOMPA): Technical manual. New York: Psychological Corp.

Mercier, D. (1902/1900). *The relation of experimental psychology to philosophy.* New York: Benziger.

Mercier, D. (1923/1892). *Cours de philosophie* (11th ed.). (2 vols). Vol. 2: *Psychologie.* Paris: Alcan.

Mercier, D. (1925/1897). *The origins of contemporary psychology* (2nd ed.). New York: Kennedy.

Meredith, K. E., & Kligman, E. W. (1991). Indicators of perceived quality of life among healthy older adults. *The Gerontologist, 31,* 358–359.

Merikle, P., & Cheesman, J. (1986). Consciousness is a "subjective" state. *The Behavioral and Brain Sciences, 9,* 42.

Merikle, P. M. (1982). Unconscious perception revisited. *Perception and Psychophysics, 31,* 298–301.

Merikle, P. M. (1992). Perception without awareness: Critical Issues. *American Psychologist, 47,* 792–795.

Merleau-Ponty, M. (1963/1943). *The structure of behavior.* Boston: Beacon Press.

Merleau-Ponty, M. (1965/1943). *Phenomenology of perception,* New York: Humanities Press.

Merleau-Ponty, M. (1973). *The prose of the world.* Evanston, Ill.: Northwestern University Press.

Merluzzi, T. V., & Boltwood, M. D. (1989). Cognitive assessment. In A. Freeman, K. M. Simon, L. E. Beutler, & H. Arkowitz (Eds.), *Comprehensive handbook of cognitive therapy.* New York: Plenum.

Merrifield, P. R., Guilford, J. P., Christensen, P. R., & Frick, J. W. (1962). The role of intellectual factors in problem solving. *Psychological Monographs, 76, 10,* (entire no. 529).

Merrill, M. D., & Tennyson, R. D. (1977). *Concept teaching: An instructional design guide.* Englewood Cliffs, N.J.: Educational Technology.

Merrill, M. D., & Tennyson, R. D. (1978). Concept classification and classification errors as a function of relationships between examples and nonexamples. *Improving Human Performance, 7,* 351–364.

Merrill, P. F., (1977). Algorithmic organization in teaching and learning: Literature and research in the U.S.A. *Improving Human Performance: A Research Quarterly, 6*(2–3), 93–112.

Mersch, P. P. A., Emmelkamp, P. M. G., & Lips, C. (1991). Social phobia: Individual response patterns and the long-term effects of behavioral and cognitive interventions. A follow-up study. *Behaviour Research and Therapy, 29,* 357–362.

Mersch, P. P. A., Emmelkamp, P. M. G., Bogels, S. M., & van der Sleen, J. (1989). Social phobia: Individual; response patterns and the effects of behavioral and cognitive interventions. *Behaviour Research and Therapy, 27,* 421–434.

Merton, R. (1948). The self-fulfilling prophecy. *Antioch Review, 8,* 193–210.

Merton, R. K. (1957). The role set: Problems in sociological theory. *British Journal of Sociology, 8,* 106–120.

Merton, R. K. (1957/1949). *Social theory and social structure* (rev. ed.). New York: Free Press.

Mertz, W. H. (1975). A comparison of clinical prediction with several different methods of statistical prediction. Ph.D. dissertation, Bowling Green University.

Merz, F. (1960). Amerikanische und deutsche Psychologie. *Psychologie und Praxis, 4,* 78–91.

Meskinoff, A. M., Rainer, J. D., Kolb, L. C., & Carr, A. C. (1963). Intrafamilial determinants of divergent sexual behavior in twins. *American Journal of Psychology, 119,* 732–738.

Mesmer, F. A. (1766). *De planetarum inflexu* Vienna. Ghelem.

Mesmer, F. A. (1799). *Memoir.* New York: Eden Press. (First published in France.)

Mesmer, F. A. (1948). *Mesmerism: A translation of the original medical and scientific writings of F. A. Mesmer, M.D.* London: McDonald.

Messer, S. B. (1986). Behavioral and psychoanalytic perspectives at therapeutic choice points. *American Psychologist, 41*(11), 1261–1272.

Messer, S. B., Sass, L. A., & Woolfolk, R. L. (Eds.). (1988). *Hermeneutics and psychological theory.* New Brunswick, NJ: Rutgers University Press.

Messer, S. B., & Winokur, M. (1980). Some limits to the integration of psychoanalytic and behavior therapy. *American Psychologist, 35,* 818–827.

Messick, D. M., & W. B. Thorngate. (1967). Relative gain maximization in experimental games. *Journal of Experimental Social Psychology, 3*(1), 85–101.

Messick, S. (1980). Test validity and the ethics of assessment. *American Psychologist, 35,* 1012–1027.

Messick, S. (1981). Evidence and ethics in the evaluation of tests. *Educational Researcher, 10,* 9–19.

Metelli, F. (1950). *Ricerche sperimentali sul lavoro di cernita delle lane.* Padua, Italy.

Metelli, F. (1951). *Introduzione alla caratte rologia moderna.* Padua, Italy.

Metelli, F. (1967). *Analisi fattoriale.* Florence, Italy.

Metelli, F. (April 1974). The perception of transparency. *Scientific American, 230,* 90–98.

Metelli, F. (1974). Achromatic color conditions on the perception of transparency. In R. R. McLeod & H. L. Pick (Eds.), *Perception, essays in honor of James Gibson.* Ithaca, N.Y.: Cornell University Press.

Metelli, F. (1975). A contribution to the theory of motion perception. In *Studies in perception, Festschrift for F. Metelli.* Milan, Florence.

Metelli, F. (1976/1977). Some conditions regarding localization and mode of appearance of achromatic colors. *Atti dell'Accade mia di Padova* (Proceedings of the Academy of Padua).

Metropolitan Life Insurance Company. (1960). Frequency of overweight and underweight. *Statistical Bulletin, 41,* 4–7.

Mettler, F. A. (Ed.). (1949). *Selective partial ablation of the frontal cortex. A correlative study of its effects on human psychotic subjects.* New York: Hoeber.

Mettler, F. A. (Ed.). (1952). *Psychosurgical problems* (Columbia Greystone Associates, Second Group). New York: Blakiston.

Metzger, W. (1953/1948). *Gesetze des Sehens.* Frankfurt/Am Main: Kramer.

Meumann, E. (1907/1908). *Vorlesungen zur Einführung in die Experimentelle Pädagogik.* Leipzig: Englemann.

Meyer, A. (1906). The relation of emotional and intellectual functions in paranoia and obsessions. *Psychological Bulletin, 3*, 255–279.

Meyer, A. (1919). *Contributions to medical and biological research,* Vol. II. New York: Hoeber.

Meyer, A. (1948/1952). *Collected papers of Adolf Meyer,* Baltimore, Md.: Johns Hopkins University Press.

Meyer, A. (1957). *Psychobiology: A science of man.* Springfield, Ill.: Thomas.

Meyer, A. E. (Ed.) (1981). The Hamburg short psychotherapy comparison experiment. *Psychotherapy and Psychosomatics, 35*, 77–212.

Meyer, A. S., Friedman, L. N., & Lazarsfeld, P. F. (1973). Motivational conflicts engendered by the on-going discussion of cigarette smoking. In W. L. Dunn (Ed.), *Smoking behavior: Motives and incentives.* Washington, D.C.: Winston.

Meyer, B. J. F. (1975). *The organization of prose and its effects on memory.* Amsterdam, The Netherlands: North-Holland.

Meyer, D. E. Schvaneveldt, R. W., & Ruddy, M. G. (1974). Functions of graphemic and phonemic codes in visual word recognition. *Memory and Cognition, 2*, 309–321.

Meyer, H. H., Kay, E., & French, J. R. P., Jr. (1964). Split roles in performance appraisal. *Harvard Business Review, 43*, 124–129.

Meyer, W. U., Bachmann, M., Biermann, U., Hempelmann, M., Plöger, F. O., & Spiller, H. (1979). The informational value of evaluative behavior: Influences of praise and blame on perceptions of ability. *Journal of Educational Psychology, 71*, 259–268.

Meyers, C. E., Orpet, R. E., Sitka, E. G. & Watt, C. A. (1964). Four ability factor hypotheses at three preliterate levels in normal and retarded children. *Monographs of the Society for Research in Child Development, 29.*

Mezzich, J. E., & Solomon, H. (1980). *Taxonomy and behavioral science.* New York: Academic Press.

Miale, F. R., & Selzer, M. (1975). *The Nuremburg mind.* New York: Quadrangle/New York Times.

Michael, R. P. (Ed.) (1968). *Endocrinology and human behaviour.* London: Oxford University Press.

Michel, D. E. (1976). *Music therapy.* Springfield, Ill.: Thomas.

Michelson, L., Sugai, D., Wood, R., & Kazdin, A. E. (1983). *Social skills assessment and training with children: An empirically-based handbook.* New York: Plenum.

Michelson, L., & Wood, R. (1980). Behavioral assessment and training of children's social skills. In M. Hersen & A. Bellack (Eds.), *Progress in behavior modification.* New York: Academic Press.

Michener, H. A., & Suchner, R. (1972). The tactical use of social power. In J. Tedeschi (Ed.), *The social influence process.* Chicago: Aldine.

The Michigan picture test (manual). Chicago: Science Research Associates, (1953).

Michon, J. A., (1967). *Timing in temporal tracking.* Assen, Netherlands: Van Gorcum.

Michon, J. A., (1978). The making of the present. In J. Requin (Ed.), *Attention and performance VII.* Hillsdale, N.J.: Erlbaum.

Michon, J. A., (1980). Psychology: Aid or guide for travel-demand analysis? In J. B. Polak & J. B. van der Kamp (Eds.), *Changes in the field of transport studies.* The Hague: Nijhoff.

Michon, J. A., Eijkman, E. G. J., & De Jerk, L. F. W. (Eds.). (1976). *Handboek der Psychonomie.* Deventer, Netherlands: Van Loghum Slatruss.

Michon, J. A., Eijkman, E. G. J., & De Klerk, L. F. W. (Eds.). (1979). *Handbook of psychonomics.* Amsterdam: North Holland.

Michotte, A. E. (1952). Autobiography. In E. G. Boring et al. (Eds.), *A history of psychology in autobiography,* Vol. 4. Worcester, Mass.: Clark University Press.

Michotte, A. E. (1954). In H. Misiak, & V. M. Staudt, *Catholics in psychology: A historical survey.* New York: McGraw-Hill.

Michotte, A. E. (1963). *The perception of causality.* New York: Basic Books.

Michotte, A. E., et al. (1962). *Causalité, permanence et réalitéphéno-ménales.* Louvain, Belguim: Publications Universitaires.

Middlebrooks, M., & Whitley, R. J. (1992). In J. B. Wyngaarden, L. H. Smith, Jr., & J. C. Bcnnctt (Eds.), *Cecil textbook of medicine* (19th ed., pp. 1831–1835). Philadelphia: Saunders.

Middleton, J. (Ed.) (1967). *Magic, witchcraft, and curing.* Garden City, N.Y.: Natural History Press.

Miezitis, S. (1973). The Montessori method: Some recent research. In J. L. Frost (Ed.). *Revisiting early childhood education—reading.* New York: Holt, Rinehart & Winston.

Mikula, G. (1980). *Justice and social interaction: Experimental and theoretical contributions from psychological research.* New York: Springer-Verlag.

Milazzo-Sayre, L. (April-July 1975, March 1979). Admission rates by the highest level of education attained-State and county mental hospitals. *Mental Health Statistical Note,* no. 151, DHEW Publication no. (ADM) 79–158.

Milazzo-Sayre, L. (1971–1975, 1978). State trends in resident patients—State and county mental hospital inpatient services. *Mental Health Statistical Note,* no. 150, DHEW Publication no. (ADM) 78–158, June.

Miles, C. C., & Miles, W. R. (1932). The correlation of intelligence scores and chronological age from early to later maturity. *American Journal of Psychology, 44*, 44–78.

Miles, H. L. (1980). Acquisition of gestural signs by an infant orang-utan *(Pongo pygmaeus)* (abstract). *American Journal of Physical Anthropology, 52*, 256–257.

Miles, M. (1965). Changes during and following laboratory training: A clinical experimental study. *Journal of Applied Behavior Science, 1*, 215–242.

Miles, W. R. (1924). *Alcohol and human efficiency; Experiments with moderate quantities and dilute solutions of ethyl alcohol on human subjects.* Washington, D.C.: Carnegie Institution.

Miles, W. R. (1943). Red goggles for producing dark adaptation. *Federation Proceedings of the American Society of experimental Biology, 2*, 109–115.

Miles, W. R. (1967). Autobiography. In E. G. Boring & G. Lindzey (Eds.), *A history of psychology in autobiography,* Vol. 5. New York: Appleton-Century-Crofts.

Miles, W. R. (Ed.) (1936). *Psychological studies of human variability.* Princeton, N.J.: Psychological Review.

Miley, C. H. (1969). Birth order research 1963–1967: Bibliography and index. *Journal of Individual Psychology, 25*, 64—70.

Milgram, N. A. (1978). Psychological stress and adjustment in time of war and peace: The Israeli experience as presented in two conferences. *Israel Annals of Psychiatry and Related Disciplines, 16*, 327–338.

Milgram, S. (1960). *Conformity in Norway and France: An experimental study of national characteristics.* Doctoral dissertation, Harvard University.

Milgram, S. (1961). Nationality and conformity. *Scientific American,* 45–51.

Milgram, S. (1963). Behavioral study of obedience. *Journal of Abnormal and Social Psychology, 67,* 371–378.

Milgram, S. (1964). Issues in the study of obedience: A reply to Baumrind. *American Psychologist, 19,* 848–852.

Milgram, S. (1965). Liberating effects of group pressure. *Journal of Personality and Social Psychology, 1,* 127–134.

Milgram, S. (1965). Some conditions of obedience to authority. *Human Relations, 18,* 57–76.

Milgram, S. (1967, May). The small-world problem. *Psychology Today,* pp. 60–67.

Milgram, S. (1969, June). The lost-letter technique. *Psychology Today,* pp. 30–33, 66, 68.

Milgram, S. (1970). The experience of living in cities. *Science, 167,* 1461–1468.

Milgram, S. (1974). Obedience to authority: *An experimental view.* New York: Harper & Row.

Milgram, S. (1977). *The individual in a social world.* Reading, Mass.: Addison-Wesley.

Milgram, S. (1977a). *The individual in a social world: Essays and experiments.* Reading, MA: Addison-Wesley.

Milgram, S. (1977b). Subject reaction: The neglected factor in the ethics of experimentation. *Hastings Center Report, 7,* 19–23.

Milgram, S. (1981). This week's citation classic: Milgram, S., "Behavioral study of obedience." *Current Contents, Social and Behavioral Sciences,* 18.

Milgram, S., Mann, L., & Harter, S. (1965). The lost-letter technique: A tool of social research. *Public Opinion Quarterly, 29,* 437–438.

Milgram, S., & Shotland, R. (1973). *Television and antisocial behavior.* New York: Academic Press.

Milgram, S., & Toch, H. (1969). Collective behavior: Crowds and social movements. In G. Lindzey & E. Aronson (Eds.), *The handbook of social psychology,* Vol. 4. Reading, Mass.: Addison-Wesley.

Milkman, H. B. & Sederer, H. B. (Eds.). (1990). *Treatment choices for alcoholism and substance abuse.* New York: Lexington.

Mill, J. (1967/1829). *Analysis of the phenomena of the human mind.* New York: Kelley.

Mill, J. S. (1865). *An examination of Sir William Hamilton's philosophy.* London.

Mill, J. S. (1874). *A system of logic.* (8th ed.). New York: Harper.

Mill, J. S. (1924/1873). *Autobiography.* New York: Columbia University Press.

Mill, J. S., (1947/1859). *On liberty.* Northbrook, Ill.: AHM.

Mill, J. S. (1973/1843). A system of logic ratiocinative and inductive. In J. M. Robson *(Ed.), Collected works of John Stuart Mill, Vol. VII.* Toronto: University of Toronto Press.

Mill, J. S. (1980). *A system of logic* New York: Harper & Row. (Work also published 1869, 1872, 1900)

Millar, S. (1981). Cross-modal and intersensory perception and the blind. In R. D. Walk & H. L. Pick, Jr. (Eds.), *Intersensory perception and sensory integration.* New York: Plenum.

Miller, A. (1974). Political issues and trust in government: 1964—1970. *American Political Science Review, 68,* 951–972.

Miller, A. D. (1969). Amount of information and stimulus valence as determinants of cognitive complexity. *Journal of Personality, 37,* 141–157.

Miller, A. G. (1976). Constraint and target effects in the attribution of attitudes. *Journal of Experimental Social Psychology, 12,* 325–339.

Miller, A. G. (1986). *The obedience experiments: A case study of controversy social science.* New York: Praeger.

Miller, B., & McFall, S. (1991). Stability and change in the informal task support of frail older persons. *The Gerontologist, 31,* 735–745.

Miller, B. E., & Holt, G. L. (1977). Memory transfer in rats by injection of brain and liver RNA. *Journal of Biological Psychology, 19,* 4–9.

Miller, D. C., & Form, W. H. (1964/1951). *Industrial sociology.* New York: Harper & Row.

Miller, D. E., & Swanson, G. E. (1958). *The changing American parent.* New York: Wiley.

Miller, E. (1977). *Abnormal aging: The psychology of senile and presenile dementia.* New York: Wiley.

Miller, E. L. (1965). Ability and social adjustment at midlife of people earlier judged mentally deficient. *Genetic Psychology Monograph, 36,* 925–942.

Miller, G. (1962). *Psychology: The science of mental life.* New York: Harper & Row.

Miller, G. A. (1951). *Language and communication.* New York: McGraw-Hill.

Miller, G. A. (1951). Speech and language. In S. S. Stevens (Ed.), *Handbook of experimental psychology.* New York: Wiley.

Miller, G. A. (1956). The magical number seven plus or minus two: Some limits on our capacity for processing information. *Psychological Review, 63,* 81–97.

Miller, G. A. (1977). *Spontaneous apprentices: Children and language.* New York: Seabury Press.

Miller, G. A. (1990). Review of Shallice, T., *From neuropsychology to mental structure. Quarterly Review of Biology.* 65, 115.

Miller, G. A. (1991). *The science of words.* New York: Scientific American Library.

Miller, G. A. (Ed.). (1964). *Mathematics and psychology.* New York: Wiley.

Miller, G. A. (Ed.) (1973). *Communication, language, and meaning: Psychological perspectives.* New York: Basic Books.

Miller, G. A. (Ed.). (1973). *Communication, language and meaning.* New York: Basic Books.

Miller, G. A. & Buckbout, R. (1973). *Psychology: The science of mental life* (2nd ed.). New York: Harper & Row.

Miller, G. A., Galanter, E., & Pribram, K. (1960). *Plans and the structure of behavior.* New York: Holt.

Miller, G. A., Galanter, E., & Pribram, K. H. (1960). *Plans and the structure of behavior.* New York: Holt, Rinehart & Winston.

Miller, G. A., & Isard, S. (1963). Some perceptual consequences of linguistic rules. *Journal of Verbal Learning and Verbal Behavior, 2,* 212–228.

Miller, G. A., & Johnson-Laird, P. N. (1976). *Language and perception.* Cambridge, Mass.: Harvard University Press.

Miller, G. A., & Licklider, J. C. R. (1950). The intelligibility of interrupted speech. *Journal of the Acoustical Society of America, 43,* 66–69.

Miller, G. A. & McNeill, D. (1969). Psycholinguistics. In G. Lindzey & E. Aronson (Eds,), *The handbook of social psychology,* Vol. 3. Reading, Mass.: Addison-Wesley.

Miller, G. A., Newman, E. B., & Friedman, E. A. (1958). Length-frequency statistics for written English. *Information and Control, 1,* 370–389.

Miller, G. E., & Prinz, R. J. (1990). Enhancement of social learning family interventions for childhood conduct disorder. *Psychological Bulletin, 108,* 291–307.

Miller, J., Slomczynski, K., & Schoenberg, R. (1981). Assessing comparability of measurement in cross-national research: Authoritarianism—conservatism in different sociocultural settings. *Social Psychology Quarterly, 44,* 178–191.

Miller, J. B. (1976). *Toward a new psychology of women.* Boston: Beacon Press.

Miller, J. D., & Cisin, I. H. (1980). *Highlights from the national survey on drug abuse: 1979.* DHHS Publication no. (ADM) 80–1032. Washington, D.C. U.S. Government Printing Office.

Miller, J. G. (1939). Discrimination without awareness. *American Journal of Psychology, 52,* 563–578.

Miller, J. G. (1978). *Living systems.* New York: McGraw-Hill.

Miller, J. G. (1984). Culture and the development of everyday causal explanation. *Journal of Personality and Social Psychology, 46,* 961–978.

Miller, J. R. (1980). Problems of single parent families. *Journal of New York State Nurses Association, 11,* 5–8.

Miller, K. A., Kohn, M. L., & Schooler, C. (1985). Educational self direction and the cognitive functioning of students. *Social Forces, 63,* 923–944.

Miller, L. B. (1979). Development of curriculum models in Head Start. In E. Zigler & J. Valentine (Eds.), *Project Head Start—A legacy of the war on poverty.* New York: Free Press.

Miller, L. B., & Dyer, J. L. (1975). Four preschool programs: Their dimensions and effects. *Monograph of the Society for Research in Child Development, 40* (5–6).

Miller, L. J., & Hutt, M. L. (1975). Psychopathology scale of the Hutt adaptation of the Bender-Gestalt test: Reliability. *Journal of Personality Assessment, 39,* 129–131.

Miller, L. P. (Ed.) (1974). *The testing of black students: A symposium.* Englewood Cliffs, N.J.: Prentice-Hall.

Miller, M. E., & Barker, J. D. (1968). Aversion therapy for compulsive gambling. *Nursing Mirror, 18,* 21–25.

Miller, M. J., Small, I. F., Milstein, V., Malloy, F., & Stout, J. R. (1981). Electrode placement and cognitive change with ECT: Male and female response. *American Journal of Psychiatry, 138,* 384–386.

Miller, N. (May 1982). Understanding psychological man. *Psychology Today.*

Miller, N., & Campbell, D. T. (1959). Recency and primacy in persuasion as a function of the timing of speeches and measurement. *Journal of Abnormal and Social Psychology, 59,* 1–9.

Miller, N. E. (1937). Analysis of the form of conflict reaction. *Psychological Bulletin, 34,* 720.

Miller, N. E. (1941). The frustration-aggression hypothesis. *Psychological Review, 48,* 337–342.

Miller, N. E. (1944). Experimental studies of conflict behavior. In J. McV. Hunt *(Ed.), Personality and behavior disorders.* New York: Ronald Press.

Miller, N. E. (1948). Studies of fear as an acquirable drive: 1. Fear as motivation and fear-reduction as reinforcement in the learning of new responses. *Journal of Experimental Psychology, 38,* 89–101.

Miller, N. E. (1948). Theory and experiment relating psychoanalytic displacement to stimulus-response generalization. *Journal of Abnormal and Social Psychology, 43,* 155–178.

Miller, N. E. (1951). Comment on theoretical models illustrated by the development of a theory of conflict. *Journal of Personality, 20,* 82–100.

Miller, N. E. (1957). Experiments on motivation; studies combining psychological, physiological, and pharmacological techniques. *Science, 126,* 1271–1278.

Miller, N. E. (1958). Central stimulation and other new approaches to motivation and reward. *American Psychologist, 18,* 100–108.

Miller, N. E. (1959). Liberalization of basic S-R concepts: Extensions to conflict behavior, motivation and social learning. In S. Koch (Ed.), *Psychology: A study of a science,* Vol. 2. New York: McGraw-Hill.

Miller, N. E. (1969). Learning of visceral and glandular responses, 163, 434–453.

Miller, N. E. (1971). *Selected papers on conflict, displacement, learned drives and theory.* Chicago: Aldine.

Miller, N. E. (1978). Biofeedback and visceral learning. *Annual Review of Psychology, 29,* 373–404.

Miller, N. E. (1983). Behavioral medicine: Symbiosis between laboratory and clinic. *Annual Review of Psychology, 34,* 1–31.

Miller, N. E. (1985). The value of behavioral research on animals. *American Psychologist, 40,* 423–440.

Miller, N. E., & Bailey, C. J. (1950). Decreased "hunger" but increased food intake resulting from hypothalamic lesions. *Science, 112,* 256–259.

Miller, N. E., & Banuazizi, A. (1968). Instrumental learning by curarized rats of a specific vicceral response, intestinal or cardiac. *Journal of Comparative and Physiological Psychology, 65,* 1–7.

Miller, N. E., & Brucker, B. S. (1979). A learned visceral response apparently independent of skeletal ones in patients paralyzed by spinal lesions. In N. Birnbaume & H. D. Kimmel (Eds.), *Biofeedback and self-regulation.* Hillsdale, N.J.: Erlbaum.

Miller, N. E., & Bugelski, R. (1948). Minor studies in aggression: II. The influence of frustration by the in-group on attitudes toward out-groups. *Journal of Psychology, 25,* 437–442.

Miller, N. E., & Dollard, J. (1941). *Social learning and imitation.* New Haven, Conn.: Yale University Press.

Miller, N. E., & Kesson, M. L. (1952). Reward effects of food via stomach fistula compared with those of food via mouth. *Journal of Comparative and Physiological Psychology, 45,* 555–564.

Miller, P. M. (1976). *Behavioral treatment of alcoholism.* New York: Pergamon Press.

Miller, P. Y., & Simon, W. (1980). *The development of sexuality in adolescence.* In J. Adelson (Ed.), *Handbook of adolescent psychology.* New York: Wiley.

Miller, R. E., Banks, J. H., & Ogawa, N. (1963). Role of facial expression in "cooperative-avoidance conditioning" in monkeys. *Journal of Abnormal and Social Psychology, 67,* 24–30.

Miller, R. R., & Springer, A. D. (1973). Amnesia, consolidation, and retrieval. *Psychological Review, 80,* 69–79.

Miller, S., & Konorski, J. (1928). Sur une forme particuliere des réflexes conditionnels. *Social Biology* (Paris) 99, 1155–1157.

Miller, S., & Nardini, K. M. (1977). Individual differences in the perception of crowding. *Environmental Psychology and Nonverbal Behavior, 2,* 2–13.

Miller, S., Nunnally, E. W., & Wackman, D. (1976). Minnesota Couples Communication Program (MCCP): Premarital and marital groups. In D. Olson (Ed.), *Treating relationships,* Lake Mills, Iowa: Graphic.

Miller, S. M. (1980). When is a little information a dangerous thing: Coping with stressful events by monitoring vs. blunting. In S. Levine & H. Ursin (Eds.), *Coping and health.* New York: Plenum.

Miller, S. M. (1980). Why having control reduces stress: If I can stop the roller coaster, I don't want to get off. In M. E. P. Seligman (Ed.), *Human helplessness*. New York: Academic Press.

Miller, W. B. (1973). The telephone in outpatient psychotherapy. *American Journal of psychotherapy, 27*.

Miller, W. R., Rosellini, R. A., & Seligman, M. E. P. (1977). Learned helplessness and depression. In J. D. Maser & M. E. P. Seligman (Eds.), *Psychopathology: Experimental models* (pp. 104–139). San Francisco: Freeman.

Miller, W. R., Seligman, M. E. P., & Karlander, H. M. (1975). Learned helplessness, depression, and anxiety. *Journal of Nervous and Mental Disease, 161*, 347–357.

Miller, W. S. (1960). *Miller analogies test*. New York: Psychological Corp.

Millman, H. L. (1974). Psychoneurological learning and behavior problems: The importance of treatment considerations. *Journal of Clinical Child Psychology, 3*, 26–30.

Millman, J., & Westman, R. S. (1989). Computer-assisted writing of achievement test items: Toward a future technology. *Journal of Educational Measurement, 26*, 177–190.

Millon, T. (1969). *Modern psychopathology*. Philadelphia, Pa.: Saunders.

Millon, T. (1969). *Modern psychopathology: A biosocial approach to maladaptive learning and functioning*. Philadelphia: Saunders.

Millon, T. (1969). Paranoid personality: Independent and ambivalent borderline patterns. In T. Millon (Ed.), *Modern psychopathology* (pp. 326–337). Philadelphia: Saunders.

Millon, T. (1977). *Millon clinical multiaxial inventory manual*. Minneapolis, Minn.: National Computer Systems.

Millon, T. (1981). *Disorders of personality: DSM-III, Axis II*. New York: Wiley-Interscience.

Millon, T. (1991). Avoidant personality disorder: A brief review of issues and data. *Journal of Personality Disorders, 5*, 353–362.

Millon, T., Green, C. J., & Meagher, R. B. (1979). *Millon behavioral health inventory manual*. Minneapolis, Minn.: NCS Interpretive Scoring Systems.

Mills, C. A. (1942). *Climate makes the man*. New York: Harper.

Mills, C. J., & Bohannon, W. E. (1980). Character structure and jury behavior: Conceptual and applied implications. *Journal of Personality and Social Psychology, 38*, 662–667.

Mills, D. H. (1987). *Revision of the ethical principles of psychologists: APA task force's second annual progress report*. Paper presented at the APA annual meetings.

Mills, D. H. (1987, June). *Report of the Ethics Committee: 1986. American Psychologist*.

Milman, D. H. (1981). When thin is not beautiful: Anorexia nervosa. *Resident and Staff Physician*, 47–54.

Milner, B. (1974). Sparing of language function after early unilateral brain damage. *Neurosciences Research Program Bulletin, 12*, 213–217.

Milner, J. S. (1974, September). Effects of food deprivation and competition on interspecies aggression in the rat. Presented at the meeting of the American Psychological Association, New Orleans, La.

Milner-Brown, H., & Penn, R. (1979). Pathophysiological mechanisms in cerebral palsy. *Journal of Neurological Neurosurgical Psychiatry, 42*, 606.

Milsum, J. (1980). Lifestyle changes for the whole person: Stimulation through health hazard appraisal. In P. Davidson & S. Davidson (Eds.), *Behavioral medicine: Changing health lifestyles*. New York: Brunner/Mazel.

Milton, T., & Milton, R. (1974). *Abnormal behavior and personality: A biosocial learning approach*. Philadelphia, Pa.: Saunders.

Minami, H. (1958). *Shakai-shinrigaku nyūmon (Introduction to social-psychology)*. Tokyo: Iwanami.

Minami, H. (1964–1980). *Shakai shinri ronshū, I, II, III (Collected papers on social psychology, I, II, III)*. Tokyo: Keisō Shobō.

Minami, H. (1972). *Psychology of the Japanese people*. Toronto: University of Toronto Press, 1953.

Minami, H. (1979). *Taikei shakai shinrigaku (The system of social psychology)*, Tokyo: Kōbunsha.

Minami, H. (1980). *Ningen kōdō gaku (Science of human behavior)*. Tokyo: Iwanami.

Minami, H., & Dallenbach, K. M. (1946). The effect of activity upon learning and retention in the cockroach. *American Journal of Psychology, 59*, 1–58.

Minckler, J. (Ed.). (1972). *Introduction to neuroscience*. St. Louis, Mo.: Mosby.

Mindel, C. H. (1979). Multigenerational family households: Recent trends and implications for the future. *The Gerontologist, 19*(5), 456–463.

Mindess, H., & Turek, J. (1979). *The study of humor*. Los Angeles: Antioch.

Mineka, S., & Zinbarg, R. (1992). Animal models of psychopathology. In C. E. Walker (Ed.), *Clinical psychology: Historical and research foundations* (pp. 51–86). New York: Plenum.

Miner, J. B. (1977). Motivational potential for upgrading among minority and female managers. *Journal of Applied Psychology, 62*, 691–697.

Miner, M. G., & Miner, J. B. (1978). *Employee selection within the law*. Washington, D.C.: Bureau of National Affairs.

Minium, W. E. (1978). *Statistical reasoning in psychology and education*. New York: Wiley.

Minnigerode, F. A., & Lee, J. A. (1978). Young adults' perceptions of social sex roles across the life span. *Sex Roles: A Journal of Research, 4*, 563–569.

Minsky, M. (1986). *Society of mind*. New York: Simon & Schuster.

Minsky, M. L. (1967). *Computation: Finite and infinite machines*. Englewood Cliffs, N.J.: Prentice-Hall.

Minter, R. E., & Mandel, M. R. (1979). The treatment of psychiatric major depressive disorder with drugs and electroconvulsive therapy. *Journal of Nervous and Mental Disease, 167*, 726–733.

Minton, H. L. (1988). *Lewis M. Terman: Pioneer in psychological testing*. New York: New York University Press.

Minton, H. L., & Schneider, F. W. (1980). *Differential psychology*. Monterey, Calif.: Brooks/Cole.

Minturn, L., & Lambert, W. W. (1964). *Mothers of six cultures: Antecedents of child rearing*. New York: Wiley.

Mintz, E. E. (1971). *Marathon groups: Reality and symbol*. New York: Appleton-Century-Crofts.

Mintz, E. E. (1971). Therapy techniques and encounter techniques. *American Journal of Psychotherapy, 25*, 104–109.

Mintzberg, H. (1973). *The nature of managerial work*. New York: Harper & Row.

Minuchin, P. (1977). *The middle years of childhood*. Monterey, Calif.: Brooks/Cole.

Minuchin, S. (1974). *Families and family therapy*. Cambridge, Mass.: Harvard University Press.

Minuchin, S., Montalvo, B., Guerney, B., Rosman, B., & Schumer, F. (1967). *Families of the slums*. New York: Basic Books.

Minuchin, S., Rosman, B. L., & Barker, L., (1978). *Psychosomatic families: Anorexia nervosa in context*. Cambridge, Mass.: Harvard University Press.

Mirels, H. L. (1970). Dimensions of internal versus external control. *Journal of Consulting and Clinical Psychology, 34*, 226–228.

Mirkin, M. P. (Ed.). (1990). *The Social and political contexts of family therapy*. Boston: Allyn & Bacon.

Miron, M. S., & Goldstein, A. P. (1979). *Hostage*. New York: Pergamon Press.

Mischel, T. (Ed.). (1971). *Cognitive development and epistemology*. New York: Academic Press.

Mischel, W. (1966). A social-learning view of sex differences in behavior. In E. E. Maccoby (Ed.), *The development of sex differences*. Stanford, Calif.: Stanford University Press.

Mischel, W. (1968). *Personality and assessment*. New York: Wiley.

Mischel, W. (1970). Sex-typing and socialization. In P. H. Mussen (Ed.), *Carmichael's manual of child psychology*. New York: Wiley.

Mischel, W. (1973). Toward a cognitive social learning reconceptualization of personality. *Psychological Review, 80*, 252–283.

Mischel, W. (1974). Processes in delay of gratification. In L. Berkowitz (Ed.), *Advances in experimental social psychology*, Vol. 7. New York: Academic Press.

Mischel, W. (1976). *Introduction to personality* (2nd ed.). New York: Holt, Rinehart & Winston.

Mischel, W. (1977). On the future of personality measurement. *American Psychologist, 32*, 246–254.

Mischel, W., & Ebbesen, E. B. (1970). Attention in delay of gratification. *Journal of Personality and Social Psychology, 16*, 329–337.

Mischel, W., Ebbesen, E. B., & Zeiss, A. R. (1973). Selective attention to the self: Situational and dispositional determinants. *Journal of Personality and Social Psychology, 27*, 129–142.

Mischel, W., Ebbesen, E. B., & Zeiss, A. R. (1976). Determinants of selective memory about the self. *Journal of Consulting and Clinical Psychology, 44*, 92–103.

Mischel, W., & Mischel, H. N. (1976). A cognitive social learning approach to morality and self-regulation. In T. Lickona (Ed.), *Moral development and behavior: Theory, research, and social issues*. New York: Holt, Rinehart & Winston.

Mischel, W., & Peake, P. K. (1982). Beyond déja vu in the search for cross-situational consistency. *Psychological Review,89*, 730–755.

Mishima, Y. (1977). *The way of the samurai* New York: Basic Books.

Mishkin, M. (1978). Memory in monkeys severely impaired by combined but not be separate removal of amygdala and hippocampus. *Nature, 273*, 297–298.

Mishra, S. P., Ferguson, B. A., & King, P. V. (1985). Research with the Wechsler Digit Span subtest: Implications for assessment. *School Psychology Review, 14*, 37–47.

Misiak, H. (1961). *The philosophical roots of scientific psychology*. New York: Fordham University Press.

Misiak, H. (1980). Leipzig and Louvain University in Belgium. *Psychological Research, 42*, 49–56.

Misiak, H., & Sexton, V. S. (1966). *History of psychology: An overview*. New York: Grune & Stratton.

Misiak, H., & Sexton, V. S. (1973). *Phenomenological, existential, and humanistic psychologies: A historical survey*. New York: Grune & Stratton.

Misiak, H., & Staudt, V. M. (1954). *Catholics in psychology: A historical survey*. New York: McGraw-Hill.

Miskolczy-Fodor, R. (1959). Relation between loudness and duration of tonal pulses. I. Response of normal ears to pure tones longer than click-pitch threshold. *Journal of the Accoustical Society of America, 31*, 1128–1134.

Mistretta, C. M. (1981). Neurophysiological and anatomical aspects of taste development. In R. N. Aslin, J. R. Alberts, & M. P. Petersen (Eds.), *Development of perception* (Vol. 1, pp. 433–455). New York: Academic.

Misumi, J. (Ed.). (1972). *Social psychology in Japan*. Tokyo: Japanese Society of Social Psychology.

Misumi, J., Nakano, S., & Okamura, N. A cross-cultural study of the effect of democratic, authoritarian and laissez-faire atmosphere in Japanese children (II). Unpublished paper in Japanese.

Misumi, J., Nakano, S., & Ueno, Y. (1958). A cross-cultural study of the effect of democratic, authoritarian and laissez-faire atmosphere in Japanese children (I). *Research Bulletin of the Faculty of Education, Kyushu University, 5*, 41–59.

Mitchell, A. M., Jones, G. B., & Krumboltz, J. D. (1979). *Social learning and career decision making*. Cranston, R. I.: Carroll Press.

Mitchell, C. (1989). Successful treatment of chronic delusional parasitosis. *British Journal of Psychiatry, 155*, 556–567.

Mitchell, J., Pyle, R., & Eckert, E. (1981). Frequency and duration of binge-eating episodes in patients with bulimia. *American Journal of Psychiatry, 138*(6), 835–836.

Mitchell, J. V. (1985). *Nineth mental measurement yearbook*. Lincoln: University of Nebraska Press.

Mitchell, M. D. (1976). The transition meeting: A technique when changing managers. *Harvard Business Review, 54*(3), 13–16, 182–186.

Mitchell, R. E., & Trickett, E. J. (1980). Social networks as mediators of social support: An analysis of the effects and determinants of social networks. *Community Mental Health Journal, 16*, 27–44.

Mitchell, R. W. (1986). A framework for discussing deception. In R. W. Mitchell & N. S. Thompson (Eds.), *Deception: Perspective on human and nonhuman deceit* (pp. 3–40). Albany: SUNY.

Mitchell, S., & Rosa, P. (1981). Boyhood behavior problems as precursors of criminality: A fifteen year follow-up study. *Journal of Child Psychology and Psychiatry, 22*, 19–33.

Mitchell, T. R. (1970). The construct validity of three dimensions of leadership research. *Journal of Social Psychology, 80*, 89–94.

Mitchell, T. R. (1982). Motivation: New directions for theory, research, and practice. *Academy of Management Review, 7*, 80–88.

Mitra, S. C. (1955). Progress of psychology in India. *Indian Journal of Psychology,30*, 1–21.

Mitra, S. K. (Ed.). (1972). *a survey of research in psychology*. Bombay: Popular Prakashan.

Mittenecker, E. (1971/1952). *Planung und Auswertung von Experimenten*. Vienna: Deuticke.

Mitter, W. (Ed.). (1979). *The use of tests and interviews for admission to higher education*. Slough, England: NFER.

Miura, I., & Sasaki, R. F. (1965). *The Zen Koan: Its history and use in Rinzai Zen*. New York: Harcourt, Brace & World.

Miyagi, O. (1952). *Shinrigaku nyūmon (Introduction to psychology)*. Tokyo: Iwanami.

Mizuhara, T. (1950). Management of group activities and motivation. *Journal of Child Study and Mental Hygiene, 1*(3), 37–41.

Moczydlowski, K. (1980). Predictors of success in a correctional halfway house for youthful and adult offenders. *Corrective and Social Psy-*

chiatry and Journal of Behavior Technology, Method and Therapy, 26, 59–72.

Moede, W. (1920). *Experimentelle Massenpsychologie*. Leipzig: Hirzel.

Mohler, H., & Okada, T. (1977). Benzodiazepine receptor: Demonstration in the central nervous system. *Science, 198*, 849–851.

Mohr, J., Turner, R., & Jerry, M. (1964). *Pedophilia and exhibitionism*. Toronto: University of Toronto Press.

Moine, D. J. (1981). *A psycholinguistic study of the patterns of persuasion used by successful salespeople*. Unpublished doctoral dissertation, University of Oregon.

Molfese, D. L., Freeman, R. B., Jr., & Palermo, D. S. (1975). The ontogeny of the brain lateralization for speech and nonspeech stimuli. *Brain and Language, 2*, 356–368.

Moline, R. A., & Phillips, P. (1980). Freedom and control in the inpatient setting—A search for new directions. *Comprehensive Psychiatry, 21*, 101–110.

Molisch, H. (1929). Nervous impulse in *Mimosa pudica. Nature, 123*, 562–563.

Mollinger, R. N. (1980). Antithesis and the obsessive compulsive. *The Psychoanalytic Review, 4*, 456–477.

Molnar, J. M., Rath, W. R., & Klein, T. P. (1990). Constantly compromised: The impact of homelessness on children. *Journal of Social Issues, 46*, 109–124.

Molnos, A. (1970). *Attitudes towards family planning in East Africa*. Munich: Weltforum Verlag.

Moltz, H. (1963). Imprinting: An epigenetic approach. *Psychological Review, 70*, 123–138.

Monahan, J. (1973). Abolish the insanity defense?: Not yet. *Rutgers Law Review, 26*, 719–740.

Monahan, J. (1980). The role of research in changing the legal system. In R. H. Price & P. E. Politser (Eds.), *The role of research in changing the legal system*. New York: Academic Press.

Monahan, J. (1981). *Predicting violent behavior: An assessment of clinical technique*. Beverly Hills, Calif.: Sage Publications.

Monahan, J. (Ed.). (1976). *Community mental health and the criminal justice system*. New York: Pergamon Press.

Monahan, J. (1981). *The clinical prediction of violent behavior* (DHHS Publication No. ADM 81–92). Washington, DC: National Institute of Mental Health.

Monahan, J. (Ed.). (1980). *Who is the client?: The ethics of psychological intervention in the criminal justice system*. Washington, D.C.: American Psychological Association.

Monahan, J. (Ed.). (1981). *The clinical prediction of violent behavior*. Washington, D.C.: National Institute of Mental Health.

Monahan, J., & Loftus, E. F. (1982). The psychology of law. *Annual Review of Psychology, 33*, 441–475.

Monat, A., & Lazarus, R. S. (1977). *Stress and coping: An anthology*. New York: Columbia University Press.

Money, J., & Ehrhardt, A. (1972). *Man and woman, boy and girl: The differentiation and dimorphism of gender identity from conception to maturity*. Baltimore, Md.: Johns Hopkins University Press.

Money, J., & Ehrhart, A. A. (1972). *Man and woman, boy and girl*. Baltimore: Johns Hopkins University Press.

Moniz, E. (1936). *Tentatives opératoires dans le traitement de certaines psychoses*. Paris: Masson.

Monjan, A. A. (1981). Stress and immunologic competence: Studies in animals. In R. Ader (Ed.), *Psychoneuroimmunology*. New York: Academic Press.

Monroe, M. E. (Ed.). (1971). *Reading guidance and bibliotherapy in public, hospital and institution libraries*. Madison, Wis.: University of Wisconsin Library School.

Monroe, S. M. (1982). Life events assessment: Current practices, emerging trends. *Clinical Psychology Review, 2*, 435–453.

Monroe, S. M. (1988). The social environment and psychopathology. *Journal of Social and Personal Relationships, 5*, 347–366.

Monroe, S. M., & Simons, A. D. (1991). Diathesis-stress theories in the context of life stress research: Implications for depressive disorders. *Psychological Bulletin, 110*, 406–425.

Monroe, W. S. (1907). *History of the Pestalozzian movement in the United States*. Syracuse, N.Y.: Bardeen.

Monson, T. C., Keel, R., Stephens, D., & Genung, V. (1982). Trait attributions: Relative validity, covariation with behavior, and the prospect of future interaction. *Journal of Personality and Social Psychology, 42*, 1014–1024.

Montagu, A. (1944). Some factors in family cohesion. *Psychiatry, 7*, 349–352.

Montagu, A. (1945). Intelligence of northern Negroes and southern whites in the first World War. *American Journal of Psychology, 58*, 161–188.

Montagu, A. (1949). The origin and nature of social life and the biological basis of cooperation. *Journal of Social Psychology, 29*, 267–283.

Montagu, A. (1953). *The natural superiority of women*. New York: Macmillan.

Montagu, A. (1955). *The direction of human development*. New York: Harper.

Montagu, A. (1962). *Prenatal influences*. Springfield, IL: Thomas.

Montagu, A. (1965). *Life before birth*. New York: Signet.

Montagu, A. (1966). *On being human* (2nd ed.). New York: Hawthorn Books.

Montagu, A. (1974). *Coming into being among the Australian aborigines* (2nd ed.). Boston, & London: Routledge.

Montagu, A. (Ed.). (1974). *Culture and human development*. Englewood Cliffs, N.J.: Prentice-Hall.

Montagu, A. (1974). *Man's most dangerous myth: The fallacy of race* (5th ed.). New York: Oxford University Press.

Montagu, A. (1975). *Race and IQ*. New York: Oxford University Press.

Montagu, A. (1978). *The nature of human aggression*. New York: Oxford University Press.

Montagu, A. (1978). *Touching: The human significance of the skin* (2nd ed.). New York: Harper & Row.

Montagu, A. (1979). *The elephant man: A study in human dignity* (2nd ed.). New York: Dutton.

Montagu, A. (1980). *The reproductive development of the female* (3rd ed.). Littleton, Mass.: PSG.

Montagu, A. (1981). *Growing young*. New York: McGraw-Hill.

Montagu, M. F. A. (1950). Constitutional and prenatal factors in infant and child health. In M. J. Senn (Ed.), *Symposium on the healthy personality*. New York: Josiah Macy, Jr. Foundation.

Montessori, M. (1939). *The secret of childhood*. New York: Stokes. (Original work published 1936).

Montessori, M. (1948). *What you should know about your child*. Colombo, Ceylon: Bennet.

Montessori, M. (1949). *The absorbent mind*. Madras, India: Theosophical Publishing House.

Montessori, M. (1950). *To educate the human potential*. Madras, India: Kalakshetra.

Montessorri, M. (1964). *Dr. Montessori's own handbook*. Cambridge, Mass.: Bentley.

Montessorri, M. (1964). *The Montessori method*. New York: Schocken Books.

Montessorri, M. (1976). *Education for human development; understanding Montessori*. New York: Schocken Books.

Montiel-Marquez, M., Colotia-Espinosa, V., & Escalante-Davila, E. (1989). El posgrado y la investigacion en psicologia en Mexico. In J. Urbina-Soria (Ed.), *El psicologo, formacion, ejercicio profesional, prospective*. Mexico City: UNAM.

Montgomery, D. (1979). *Workers' control in America*. London: Cambridge University Press.

Montgomery, R. L., Hinkle, S. W., & Enzie, R. F. (1976). Arbitrary norms and social change in high and low authoritarian societies. *Journal of Personality and Social Psychology, 33,* 698–708.

Montross, D. H., & Shinkman, C. J. (1981). *Career development in the 1980s*. Springfield, Ill.: Thomas.

Moody, R. A., Jr., (1975). *Life after life*. Atlanta, Ga.: Mockingbird Books.

Mooney, R. L., & Gordon, L. V. (1950). *Mooney problem check list*. New York: Psychological Corp.

Mooney, T., Cole, T., & Chilgren, R. (1975). *Sexual options for paraplegics and quadriplegics*. Boston: Little, Brown.

Moore, B. C. J. (1977). *Introduction to the psychology of hearing*. Baltimore, Md.: University Park Press.

Moore, D. L., & Hutchinson, J. W. (1985). The influence of affective reactions to advertising: Direct and indirect mechanisms of attitude change. In L. F. Alwitt & A. A. Mitchell (Eds.), *Psychological processes and advertising effects* (pp. 65–87). Hillsdale, NJ: Erlbaum.

Moore, G. E. (1922). *Principia ethica*. Cambridge, UK: Cambridge University Press.

Moore, J., & Newell, A. (1974). How can Merlin understand? In L. W. Gregg (Ed.), *Knowledge and cognition*. New York: Wiley.

Moore, M. (1982). Endorphins and exercise: A puzzling relationship. *The Physician and Sports Medicine, 10*(2), 111–114.

Moore, M. E., Stunkard, A., & Srole, L. (1962). Obesity, social class, and mental illness. *Journal of the American Medical Association, 181,* 962–966.

Moore, M. L., & Dutton, P. (1978). Training needs analysis: Review and critique. *Academy of Management Review, 3,* 532–545.

Moore, N. V., Evertson, C. M., & Brophy, J. E. (1974). Solitary play: Some functional reconsiderations. *Developmental Psychology, 10*(6), 830–834.

Moore, O. K., & Lewis, D. J. (1953). Purpose and learning theory. *Psychological Review, 60,* 149–156.

Moore, R. (1981). *Compulsion: The true story of an addictive gambler*. New York: Doubleday.

Moore, R. L. (1977). *In search of white crows*. New York: Oxford University Press.

Moore, S. F., & Cole, G. (1978). Cognitive self-mediation training with hyperkinetic children. *Bulletin of the Psychonomic Society, 12,* 18–20.

Moore, S. G. (1977). The effects of Head Start programs with different curricula and teaching strategies. *Young Children, 32,* 54–61.

Moore, T. E. (1982). Subliminal advertising: What you see is what you get. *Journal of Marketing, 46,* 38–47.

Moore, T. E. (1988). The case against subliminal manipulation. *Psychology and Marketing, 5,* 297–316.

Moore, T. E. (1992). Subliminal perception: Facts and fallacies. *Skeptical Inquirer, 16,* 273–281.

Moos, R. (1987). *The social climate scales*. Palo Alto, CA: Consulting Psychologists.

Moos, R. H. (1973). Conceptualizations of human environments. *American Psychologist, 28,* 652–665.

Moos, R. H. (1977). *Coping with physical illness*. New York: Plenum.

Moos, R. H. (1979). Improving social settings by social climate measurement and feedback. In R. Munoz, L. Snowden, & J. Kelly (Eds.), *Social and psychological research in community settings*. San Francisco: Jossey-Bass.

Morales Bedoya, A., Remolina Suarez, A., & Espinosa de Restrepo, H. (1975). A study on drug dependence done in a school population of Medellin. *Cuadernos Cientificos CEMEF, 3,* 25–61.

Moran, E. (1970). Clinical and social aspects of risk-taking. *Proceedings of the Royal Society of Medicine, 63,* 41–44.

Moran, E. (1970). Varieties of pathological gambling. *British Journal of Psychiatry 116,* 593–597.

Moran, E. (1975). Pathological gambling. *British Journal of Psychology,* (Special Publication no. 9), 416–428.

Moran, L. J., Mefferd, R. B., Jr., & Kimble, J. P., Jr. (1964). Idiodynamic sets in word association. *Psychological Monographs, 78* (2, entire no. 579).

Morant, G. (Ed.) (1939). *A bibliography of the statistical and other writings of Karl Pearson*. Cambridge, England: Cambridge University Press.

Moray, N. (1959). Attention in dichotic listening: Affective cues and the influence of instructions. *Quarterly Journal of Experimental Psychology, 11,* 56–60.

Morely, J. E., Kay, N. E., Solomon, G. F., & Plotnikoff, N. P. (1987). Neuropeptides: Conductors of the immune orchestra. *Life Sciences, 41,* 527–544.

Moreno, J. L. (1932). *Plan and technique of developing a prison into a socialized community*. New York: National Committee on Prisons and Prison Labor.

Moreno, J. L. (1940). Mental catharsis and the psychodrama. *Sociometry, 3,* 209–244.

Moreno, J. L. (1944). A case of paranoia treated through psychodrama. *Sociometry, 7,* 312–327.

Moreno, J. L. (1944). *Psychodramatic treatment of performance neurosis*. New York: Beacon House.

Moreno, J. L. (1947/1924). *The theatre of spontaneity*. New York: Beacon House.

Moreno, J. L. (1953/1934). *Who shall survive?* New York: Beacon House, .

Moreno, J. L. (1957). *The first book on group psychotherapy* (3rd ed.). Beacon, N.Y.: Beacon House.

Moreno, J. L. (1959). *Psychodrama* (2 vols.). Beacon, NY: Beacon House. (Original work published 1946)

Moreno, J. L. (1959/1946). *Psychodrama* (2 vols.). Beacon, N.Y.: Beacon House.

Moreno, J. L., & Zeleny, L. D. (1958). Role theory and sociodrama. In J. S. Roucek (Ed.), *Contemporary sociology*. New York: Philosophical Library.

Morgan, C. D., & Murray, H. A. (1935). A method for investigating fantasies: The Thematic Apperception Test. *Archives of Neurology and Psychiatry, 34,* 289–306.

Morgan, C. L. (1890/1891). *Animal life and intelligence*. London: Arnold.

Morgan, C. L. (1899). *Introduction to comparative psychology* (2nd ed.). London: Scott.

Morgan, C. L. (1904/1894). *An introduction to comparative psychology*. London: Scott.

Morgan, C. T., Cook, J. S., Chapanis, A., & Lund, M. W. (Eds.). (1963). *Human engineering guide to equipment design*. New York: McGraw-Hill.

Morgan, C. T., & King, R. A. (1966). *Introduction to psychology*. New York: McGraw-Hill.

Morgan, H. W. (1980). *Drugs in America, a social history 1800–1980*. Syracuse, N.Y.: Syracuse University Press.

Morgan, M. (1981). The overjustification effect: A developmental test of self perception interpretations. *Journal of Personality and Social Psychology, 40*, 809–821.

Morgan, S. R. (1979). The learning disabilities population: Why more boys than girls? An area for research. *Journal of Clinical Child Psychology, 8*, 211–213.

Morgane, P. J. (1970). Raul Hernandez Peon (1924–1968). *Physiology and Behavior, 5*, 379–388.

Morgon, B. S. (1981). A contribution to the debate on homogamy, propinquity, and segregation. *Journal of Marriage and the Family, 43*, 909–921.

Moriss, R. K., Rovner, B. W., Folstein, M. F., German, P. S. (1990). Delusions in newly admitted residents of nursing homes. *American Journal of Psychiatry, 147*(3), 299–302.

Morita, S. (1956). *Nature and theory of nervosity*, Tokyo: Hakuyosha.

Morita, S. (1921). *Theory of nervosity and neurasthenia*, Tokyo: Nibon Seishiningskuki.

Mormino, S. C. (1974). Exploring racial prejudices on voir dire. *Boston University Law Review, 54*, 393–424.

Morris, C. (1946). *Signs, language and behavior*. New York: Prentice-Hall.

Morris, C. G. (Ed.) (1982). Undergraduate psychology education in the next decade. *Teaching of Psychology, 9*, 3–64.

Morris, D. (1967). *The naked ape*. New York: McGraw-Hill.

Morris, D. (1981/1977). *Manwatching: A field guide to human behavior*. New York: Abrams.

Morris, D., Collett, P., Marsh, P., & O'Shaughnessy, M., (1979). *Gestures: Their origins and distribution*. New York: Stein & Day.

Morris, D., Collet, P., March, P., & O'Shaughnessy, M. (1980) *Gestures: Their origins and distribution*. New York: Stein & Day.

Morris, D., Soroker, E., & Burruss, G. (1954). Follow-up studies of shy, withdrawn children. I. Evaluation of later adjustment. *American Journal of Orthopsychiatry, 24*, 743–754.

Morris, I. (1975). *The nobility of failure: Tragic heroes in the history of Japan*. New York: Holt, Rinehart & Winston.

Morris, N. (1968). Psychiatry and the dangerous criminal. *Southern California Law Review, 41*, 514–547.

Morris, R. G. M. (1981). Spatial localization does not require the presence of local cues. *Learning and Motivation, 12*, 239–260.

Morris, R. G. M. (Ed.). (1989). *Parallel distributed processing: Implications for psychology and neurobiology*. Oxford, UK: Clarendon Press.

Morris, R. G. M., Anderson, E., Lynch, G. S., & Baudry, M. (1986). Selective impairment of learning and blockade of long-term potentiation by an N-methy-d-aspartate receptor antagonist, AP5. *Nature, 319*, 774–776.

Morris, R. G. M., Garrud, R., Rawlins, J. N. P., & O'Keefe, J. (1982). Place-navigation impaired in rats with hippocampal lesions. *Nature, 297*, 681–683.

Morris, W. N., Miller, R. S., & Spangenberg, S. (1977). The effects of dissenter position and task difficulty on conformity and response conflict. *Journal of personality, 45*, 251–266.

Morrison, D. F. (1976). *Multivariate statistical methods*. New York: McGraw-Hill.

Morrison, J. K., & Teta, D. C. (1980). Reducing students' fear of mental illness by means of seminar–induced belief change. *Journal of Clinical Psychology, 36*(1), 275–276.

Morriss, M., Gould, R., & Matthews, P. (1964). Toward prevention of child abuse. *Children, 11*, 55–60.

Morrow, A. (1948). Industrial psychology pays off in this plant. *Modern Industry, 16*, 67.

Morrow, G. R., & Dobkin, P. L. (1988). Anticipatory nausea and vomiting in cancer patients undergoing chemotherapy treatment: Prevalence, etiology, and behavioral interventions. *Clinical Psychology Review, 8*, 517–556.

Morrow, G. R., Lindke, J., & Black, P. M. (1991). Anticipatory nausea development in cancer patients—Replication and extension of a learning model. *British Journal of Psychology, 82*, 61–72.

Morse, J. J., & Lorsch, J. W. (1970). Beyond theory Y. *Harvard Business Review, 48*, 61–68.

Morse, J. J., & Wagner, F. R. (1978). Measuring the process of managerial effectiveness. *Academic Management Journal, 21*, 23–35.

Morse, M., Castillo, Pl., Venecia, D., Milstein, J., & Tyler, D. C. (1986). Childhood near-death experiences. *American Journal of Diseases of Children, 140*, 1110–1114.

Morse, M. L., Venecia, D., & Milstein, J. (1989). Near-death experiences: A neurophysiological explanatory model. *Journal of Near-Death Studies, 8*, 45–53.

Morse, S. J., & Watson, R. I., Jr. (Eds.) (1977). *Psychotherapies*. New York: Holt, Rinehart & Winston.

Morse, W. H. (1966). Intermittent reinforcement. In W. K. Honig (Ed.), *Operant behavior: Areas of research and application* (pp. 52–108). Englewood Cliffs, NJ: Prentice-Hall.

Morselli, G. E. (1953). personalita alternante e patologia affectiva. *Archivo de Psicologia, Neurologia e Psichitria, 14*, 579–589.

Morton, G. M. (1926). Psychology of dress. *Journal of Home Economics, 18*, 584–586.

Morton, L. T. (1970). *A medical bibliography. An annotated checklist of texts illustrating the history of medicine*. Philadelphia, Pa.: Lippincott.

Moruzzi, G., & Magoun, H. W. (1949). Brain stem reticular formation and activation of the EEG. *Electroencephalography and Clinical Neurophysiology, 1*, 455–473.

Mosak, H. (1977). *On purpose: Collected papers*. Chicago: Alfred Adler Institute.

Mosak, H. H. (1955). Language and the interpretation of "sexual" symbolism. *Journal of Consulting Psychology, 19*, 108.

Mosak, H. H. (1958). Early recollections as a projective technique. *Journal of Projective Techniques, 22*, 302–311.

Mosak, H. H. (1969). Early recollections: Evaluation of some recent research. *Journal of Individual Psychology, 25*, 56–63.

Mosak, H. H. (1971). Lifestyle. In A. G. Nikelly (Ed.), *Techniques for behavior change*. Springfield, Ill.: Thomas.

Mosak, H. H. (1973). *Alfred Adler: His influence on psychology today*. Park Ridge, Ill.: Noyes Press.

Mosak, H. H. (1979). Adlerian psychotherapy. In R. J. Corsini (Ed.), *Current psychotherapies*. Itasca, Ill.: Peacock.

Mosak, H. H., & Dreikurs, R. (1967). The life tasks. III. The fifth task. *Individual Psychologist, 5*, 16–22.

Mosak, H. H., & Dreikurs, R. (1973). Adlerian psychotherapy, In R. J. Corsini (Ed.), *Current psychotherapies*. Itasca, Ill.: Peacock.

Mosak, H. H., & Schneider, S. (1977). Masculine protest, penis envy, women's liberation and sexual equality. *Journal of Individual Psychology, 33,* 193–201.

Mosak, H. H., & Shulman, B. H. (1963). *Individual psychotherapy: A syllabus.* Chicago: Alfred Adler Institute.

Moser, C. A. (1965). An exploratory-descriptive study of a self-defined S/M (sadomasochistic) sample. Unpublished doctoral dissertation, Institute for the Advanced Study of Human Sexuality, 1979.

Moser, U. *Psychologie der Partnerwahl.* Bern: Huber.

Moser, U., Zeppelin, I. von, & Schneider, W. (1970). Computer simulation of a model of neurotic defense processes. *Behavioral Science,* 194–202.

Moses, H. A., & Pattenon, C. H. (1971). *Readings in rehabilitation counseling.* Champaign, Ill.: Stipes.

Moses, J. L., & Byham, W. C. (1977). *Applying the assessment center method.* New York: Pergamon Press.

Mosher, L. B., & Meltzer, H. Y. (1980). Drugs and psychosocial treatment: Editors' introduction. *Schizophrenia Bulletin, 6*(1), 8–9.

Mosher, R., & Sprinthall, N. Psychological education in the secondary schools. *American Psychologist, 25,* 911–916.

Moskin, J. R. (1973). *The case for advertising.* New York: American Association of Advertising Agencies.

Moskitis, R. L. (1976). The constitutional need for discovery of pre-voir dire juror studies. *Southern California Law Review, 49,* 597–634.

Moskowitz, D. S., Schwartzman, A. E., & Ledingham, J. E. (1985). Stability of change in aggression and withdrawal in middle childhood and early adolescence. *Journal of Abnormal Psychology, 94,* 30–41.

Moskowitz, J. A. (April 1980). *Lithium and Lady Luck. New York State Journal of Medicine,* 785–788.

Moskowitz, M. J. (1977). Hugo Münsterberg: A study in the history of applied psychology. *American Psychologist, 32,* 824–842.

Moss, A. A. (1952). *Hypnodontics: Hypnosis in dentistry.* Brooklyn, N. Y.: Dental Items of Interest.

Moss, F. A. (1924). Study of animal drives. *Journal of Experimental Psychology,* 165–185.

Mosteller, F. (1978). Nonsampling errors. In W. H. Kruskal, & J. M. Tanur (Eds.), *International encyclopedia of statistics,* Vol. 1. New York: Free Press.

Mosteller, F. M., & Bush, R. R. (1954). Selected quantitative techniques. In Lindzey, G. (Ed.), *Handbook of social psychology* (Vol. 1). Cambridge, MA: Addison-Wesley.

Motoike, P., Steuer, J., Gerner, R., Rosen, R., & Jarvik, L. (1980). Depression and bodily concerns in the elderly. *The Gerontologist, 20,* pt. II, 168.

Moulton, J., Robinson, G. M., & Elias, C. (1978). Sex bias in language use: Neutral pronouns that aren't. *American Psychologist, 33,* 1032–1036.

Mounoud, P. (1968). Construction et utilisation d'instruments chez l'enfant de 4 a 8 ans: Intériorisation des schémes d'action et types de régulation. *Revue Suisse de Psychologie, 27,* 200–208.

Mounoud, P. (1970). *Structuration de l'instrument chez l'enfant.* Neuchatel, Paris: Delachaux & Niestlé.

Mounoud, P. (1971/1972). Développement des systémes de représentation et de traitement. *Bulletin de Psychologie, 25,* 5–7, 261–272.

Mounoud, P. (1976). Les révolutions psychologiques de l'enfant. *Archives de Psychologie, 44,* 103–114.

Mounoud, P. (1978). Gedächtnis und Intelligenz. In G. Steiner (Ed.), *Piaget und die Folgen. Die Psychologie des 20 Jahrhunderts,* Vol. 7, Zürich: Kindler Vetlag.

Mounoud, P., & Hauert, C.-A. (1982). Development of sensorimotor organization in children: Grasping and lifting objects. In G. E. Forman (Ed.), *Action and thought: From sensorimotor schemes to symbolic operations.* New York: Academic Press.

Mounoud, P., & Vinter, A. (1981). Representation and sensorimotor development. In G. Butterworth (Ed.), *Infancy and epistemology: An evaluation of Piaget's theory.* Brighton, England: Harvester Press.

Mounoud, P., & Vinter, A. (Eds.) (1981). *La reconnaissance de son image chez l'enfant et l'animal.* Neuchâtel, Paris: Delachaux & Niestlé.

Mouret Polo, E, & Ribes-Iñesta, E. (1977). Panoramica de la enseñanza de la psicologia en Mexico. *Enseñanza Investigacion en Psicologia, 3,* 6–20.

Moustakas, C. (1972). *The touch of loneliness.* Englewood Cliffs, N.J.: Prentice-Hall (Spectrum).

Moustgaard, I. K., & Petersen, A. F. (Eds.). (1986). *Udviklingslinier i dansk psykologi fra Alfred lehmann til i dag* [Developments in Danish psychology from Alfred Lehman until now]. Copenhagen.

Mowrer, O. H. (1940). An experimental analogue of "regression" with incidental observations of "reaction formation:' *Journal ofAbnormal and Social Psychology, 35,* 56–87.

Mowrer, O. H. (1947). On the dual nature of learning: A re-interpretation of "conditioning" and "problem solving:' *Harvard Educational Review, 17,* 102–148.

Mowrer, O. H. (1950). *Learning theory and personality dynamics.* New York: Ronald Press.

Mowrer, O. H. (1953). *Psychotherapy: Theory and research.* New York: Ronald Press.

Mowrer, O. H. (1954). Ego psychology, cybernetics and learning theory. In D. Adams, (Ed.), *Learning theory and clinical research.* New York: Wiley.

Mowrer, O. H. (1960). *Learning theory and behavior.* New York: Wiley.

Mowrer, O. H. (1960). *Learning theory and symbolic processes.* New York: Wiley.

Mowrer, O. H. (1961). *The crisis in psychiatry and religion.* Princeton, N. J.: Van Nostrand.

Mowrer, O. H. (1961). *The new group therapy.* Princeton, N.J.: Van Nostrand Reinhold.

Mowrer, O. H. (1966). Abnormal reactions or actions: An autobiographical answer. In J. A. Vernon (Ed.), *Introduction to psychology: A self-selection textbook.* Dubuque, Iowa: Brown.

Mowrer, O. H. (1968). New evidence concerning the nature of psychopathology. In M. Feldman (Ed.), *Studies in psychotherapy and behavior change.* Buffalo, N.Y.: University of Buffalo Press.

Mowrer, O. H. (1972). Integrity groups: Basic principles and procedures. *The Counseling Psychologist, 3,* 7–33.

Mowrer, O. H. (1974). Chapter 11. In *The history of psychology in autobiography,* Vol. VI. Englewood Cliffs, N.J.: Prentice-Hall.

Mowrer, O. H. (1976). How does the mind work?: Memorial address in honor of Jerzy Konorski. *American Psychologist, 31,* 843–857.

Mowrer, O. H. (1976). The present state of behaviorism. *Education, 97,* 4–23.

Mowrer, O. H. (1982). *Leaves from many seasons—Selected papers* (1930–1980). New York: Praeger.

Mowrer, O. H., & Mowrer, W. M. (1938). Enuresis: A method for its study and treatment. *American Journal of Orthopsychiatry, 8,* 436–459.

Mowrer, O. H., & Vattano, A. J. (1976). Integrity groups: A context for growth in honesty, responsibility and involvement. *Journal of Applied Behavioral Science, 12,* 419–431.

Mowrer, O. H., Vattano, A. J. Baxley, G., & Mowrer, M. (1975). *Integrity groups: The loss and recovery of community.* Urbana, Ill.: Integrity Groups.

Moyer, K. E. (1968). Kinds of aggression and their physiological basis. *Communications in Behavioral Biology, 2A,* 65–87.

Moyer, K. E. (1974). *The psychobiology of aggression.* New York: Harper & Row.

Moyer, K. E. (Ed.) (1976). *Physiology of aggression.* New York: Raven Press.

Moynihan, D. P. (1992). *Congressional Record,* S.1227.

Mozell, M. M. (1970). Evidence for a chromatographic model of olfaction. *Journal of General Physiology, 56,* 46–63.

Muchinsky, P. M. (1979). Some changes in the characteristics of articles published in the *Journal of Applied Psychology* over the past 20 years. *Journal of Applied Psychology, 64,* 455–459.

Mudd, E. H. (1951). *The practice of marriage counseling.* New York: Association Press.

Mugny, G., & Perez, J. A. (1991). *The social psychology of minority influence.* New York: Cambridge University Press.

Mueller, C. W., & Parcel, T. L. (1981). Measures of socioeconomic status: Alternatives and recommendations. *Child Development, 52,* 13–20.

Mueller, E. & Brenner, J. (1977). The origins of social skills and interaction among playgroup toddlers. *Child Development, 48,* 854–861.

Mueller, E., & Vandell, D. (1979). Infant-infant interaction. In J. D. Usotsky (Ed.), *Handbook of infant development.* New York: Wiley.

Mueller, W. J., & Kell, B. L. (1972). *Coping with conflict: Supervising counselors and psychotherapists.* New York: Appleton-Century-Crofts, 1972.

Muirhead, R. J. (1982). *Aspects of multivariate statistical theory.* New York: Wiley.

Mukherjee, B. N. (1980). Psychological theory and research methods. In U. Pareek (Ed.), *A survey of research in psychology.* Bombay: Popular Prakashan.

Mukherjee, K. (1965). Personality of criminals: A Rorschach study. *Council of Social and Psychological Research Bulletin* (Calcutta), no. 5, 15–18.

Mukherjee, S., et al. (1983). Misdiagnosis of schizophrenia in bipolar patients: A multiethnic comparison. *American Journal of Psychiatry, 140,* 1571–1574.

Mulhern, S. (1990, November). *Training courses and seminars on satanic ritual abuse: A critical review.* Paper presented at the Seventh International Conference on Multiple Personality/Dissociative States, Chicago.

Mulhern, S. (1992). Ritual abuse: Defining a syndrome versus defending a belief. *Journal of Psychology and Theology, 20*(3), 230–232.

Mulholland, T. (1962). The electro-encephalogram as an experimental tool in the study of internal attention gradients. *Transactions of the New York Academy of Sciences, 24,* 664–669.

Mulkey, Y. J. (1977a). *Character education and the teacher.* San Antonio, Tex.: American Institute for Character Education.

Mulkey, Y. J. (1977b). *Teacher training for character education.* San Antonio, Tex.: American Institute for Character Education.

Mullally, L. (1977). Educational cognitive style: Implications for instruction. *Theory into Practice, 16,* 238–242.

Mullan, H. (1978). The extended session in analytic group therapy. In H. Mullan & M. Rosenbaum (Eds.), *Group psychotherapy: Theory and practice (2nd ed.).* New York: Free Press.

Mullen, E. J. (1978). The construction of personal models for effective practice: A method for utilizing research findings to guide social interventions. *Journal of Social Service Research, 20,* 45–63.

Müller, G. E. (1878). *Zur Grundlegung der Psychophysik.* Berlin: Grüben.

Müller, G. E. (1911/1917). *Zur Analyse der Gedächtnistätigkeit und des Vorstellungsverlaufi.* Leipzig: Barth.

Müller, G. E. & Schumann, F. (1893). Experimentelle beiträge zur Untersuchung des Gedächtnisses, *Zeitschrift zur Psychologie, 6,* 81–190, 257–339.

Müller, J. (1833–1840). *Handbuch der Physiologie des Menschen* (2 vols.). Coblenz.

Müller, J. (1842, 1833–1840). *Elements of physiology,* London: Taylor & Walton.

Müller, J. (1848). *The physiology of senses, voice and muscular motion, with the mental faculties.* London.

Müller, P. (1958). *Le CAT (Children Apperception Test). Recherches sur le dynamisme enfantin.* Bern: Huber.

Müller, P. (1969). *The tasks of childhood.* New York: McGraw-Hill.

Muller, P., & Seeman, P. (1979). Presynaptic subsensitivity as a possible basis for sensitization by long-term dopamine mimetics. *European Journal of Pharmacology, 55,* 149–157.

Mullis, F. (1983). Factor analysis of the Wheeler-Kern-Curlette life style personality inventory. Dissertation in progress, Georgia State University.

Mumford, E., Schlesinger, H., & J. (1981). Reducing medical costs through mental health treatment. In A. Broskowski, E. Marks, & S. Budman (Eds.), *Linking health and mental health.* Beverly Hills, Calif.: Sage Publications.

Munari, A. (1973). Perception de densités stochastiques. Un essai de généralisation du modèle probabiliste des mécanismes perceptifs proposé par Jean Piaget. *Archives de Psychologie, 72,* 1–205.

Mundy-Castle, A. C. (1958). Electrophysiological correlates of intelligence. *Journal of Personality, 26,* 184–199.

Mundy-Castle, A. C. (1962). Central excitability in the aged. In H. T. Blumenthal *(Ed.), Medical and clinical aspects of aging.* New York: Columbia University Press.

Mundy-Castle, A. C. (1966). Pictorial depth perception in Ghanaian children. *International Journal of Psychology, 1,* 290–300.

Mundy-Castle, A. C. (1970). Epilepsy and the electroencephalogram in Ghana. *African Journal of Medical Science, 1,* 221–236.

Mundy-Castle, A. C. (1975). Cross-cultural electroencephalographic studies. In J. W. Prescott, M. S. Read, & D. B. Coursin (Eds.), *Brain function and malnutrition.* New York: Wiley.

Mundy-Castle, A. C. (1975). Social and technological intelligence in Western and non-Western cultures. In S. Pilowsky (Ed.), *Cultures in collision.* Adelaide, Australia: Australian National Association of Mental Health.

Mundy-Castle, A. C. (1980). Perception and communication in infancy: A cross–cultural study. In D. Olson (Ed.), *The social foundations of language and thought.* New York: Norton.

Mundy-Castle, A. C. (1982). Are western psychological concepts valid in Africa? A Nigerian review. In S. H. Irvine & J. W. Berry (Eds.), *Human assessment and cultural factors.* New York: Plenum.

Mundy-Castle, A. C., & Anglin, J. (1974). Looking strategies in infants. In J. L. Stone, H. T. Smith, & L. P. Murphy (Eds.), *The competent infant*. New York: Basic Books.

Mundy-Castle, A. C., & Nelson, G. K. (1960). Intelligence, personality and brain rhythms. *Nature, 185,* 484–485.

Mundy-Castle, A. C., & Nelson, G. K. (1962). A neuropsychological study of the Kenysna forest workers. *Psychologia Africana, 9,* 240–272.

Munkelt, P. (1965). Persönlichkeitsmerkmale (psychische Stabilität resp. Labilität und Geschlecht) als Bedingungsfaktoren der psychotropen Arzneimittelwirkung. *Psychologische Beiträge, 8,* 98–183.

Munn, N. L. (1940). The effect of knowledge of the situation upon judgment of emotion from facial expressions. *Journal of Abnormal and Social Psychology, 35,* 324–338.

Muñoz, R. F., Snowden, L. R., & Kelley, J. G. (Eds.) (1979). *Social and psychological research in community settings*. San Francisco: Jossey-Bass.

Muñoz Sabaté, L., Bayés, R., & Munné, F. (1980). *Introducción a la psicología jurídica*. Mexico, D.F.: Trillas.

Muñoz Sabaté, L., Bayés, R., & Munné, F. (1981). *Comportamento, diritto e societá. Contributi della scuola di Barcellona*. Milan, Italy: Giuffrè.

Munro, A. (1982). Paranoia revisited. *British Journal of Psychiatry, 141,* 344–349.

Munro, T. (1956). *Toward science in aesthetics*. New York: Liberal Arts.

Munro, T. (1964). Recent developments in aesthetics in America. *Journal of Aesthetics and Art Criticism, 23,* 251–260.

Munro, T., & Pepper, S. C. (1978). Aesthetics. In *Encyclopedia Britannica*, Vol. 1 (15th ed.). Chicago: Encyclopedia Britannica.

Munroe, R. L. (1955). Schools of psychoanalytic thought New York: Holt, Rinehart & Winston.

Munroe, R. L., Munro, R. H., & Whiting, B. B. (Eds.) (1981). *Handbook of cross-cultural human development*. New York: Garland.

Munsell book of color. (1942). Baltimore, Md.: Munsell Color.

Munsinger, H. (1975). The adopted child's I.Q.: A critical review. *Psychological Bulletin, 82,* 623–654.

Münsterberg, H. (1905). *Principles of art education*. New York: Prang.

Münsterberg, H. (1908). *On the witness stand; essays on psychology and crime*. New York: McClure.

Münsterberg, H. (1913). *Psychology and industrial efficiency*. Boston: Houghton Mifflin.

Münsterberg, H. (1914). *Grundzüge der Psychotechnik* Leipzig: Barth.

Münsterberg, H. (1970/1916). *The photoplay: A psychological study*. New York: Dover.

Murakami, H. (1952). *Ljō-shinrigaku* (Abnormal psychology). Tokyo: Iwanami.

Murase, T. (1974). Naikan therapy. In T. Lebra & W. Lebra (Eds.), *Japanese culture and behavior*. Honolulu: University Press of Hawaii.

Murayama, M. (1977). Hetereogenetics: An epistemological restructuring of biological and social sciences. *Acta Boiotheretica, 26,* 120–137.

Murchison, C. (1925). *Psychologies of 1925*. Worcester, Mass.: Clark University Press.

Murchison, C. (1929). *The psychological register*. Worcester, Mass.: Clark University Press.

Murchison, C. (1930). *Psychologies of 1930*. Worcester, Mass.: Clark University Press.

Murchison, C. (1931). *A handbook of child psychology*. Worcester, Mass.: Clark University Press.

Murchison, C. (1935). *A handbook of social psychology*. Worcester, Mass.: Clark University Press.

Murchison, C. (Ed.) (1929). *Foundations of experimental psychology*. Worcester, Mass.: Clark University Press.

Murdock, B. B. (1974). *Human memory; theory and data*. Hillsdale, N.J. : Erlbaum.

Murdock, G. P. (1945). The common denominator of cultures. In R. Linton (Ed.), *The science of man in the world crisis*. New York: Columbia University Press.

Murdock, G. P. (1949). *Social structure*. New York: Macmillan.

Murphy, A. H., & Winkler, R. L. (1977). Can weather forecasters formulate reliable probability forecasts of precipitation and temperature? *National Weather Digest, 2,* 2–9.

Murphy, D. L., Campbell, I., & Costa, J. L. (1978). Current status of the indoleamine hypothesis of the affective disorders. In M. A. Lipton, A. Di Mascio, & K. F. Killam (Eds.), *Psychopharmacology:A generation of progress*. New York: Raven Press.

Murphy, G. (1947). *Personality: A biosocial approach to origins and structure*. New York: Harper.

Murphy, G. (1951). *Introduction to psychology*. New York: Harper.

Murphy, G. (1967). Gardner Murphy. In E. G. Boring & G. Lindzey (Eds.), *A history of psychology in autobiography*, Vol. 5. New York: Appleton-Century-Crofts.

Murphy, G., & Ballou, R. O. (1969/1960). *William James on psychical research*. New York: Viking Press.

Murphy, G. & Kovach, J. K. (1972/1949). *Historical introduction to modern psychology*. (3rd ed.). New York: Harcourt Brace Jovanovich.

Murphy, G., & Leeds, M. (1975). *Outgrowing self-deception*. New York: Basic Books.

Murphy, G., & Likert, R. (1938). *Public opinion and the individual* New York: Harper.

Murphy, G., & Murphy, L. B. (Eds.) *Asian psychology*. New York: Basic Books.

Murphy, G., Murphy, L. B., & Newcomb, T. M. (1937). *Experimental social psychology*. New York: Harper.

Murphy, H. B. M. (1972). History and the evolution of syndromes: The striking case of *Latah* and *Amok*. In M. Hammer, K. Salzinger, & S. Sutton (Eds.), *Psychopathology: Contributions from the biological behavioral, and social sciences*. New York: Wiley.

Murphy, H. B. M. (1976). Notes for a theory of *latah*. In W. Lebra (Ed.), *Culturebound syndromes, ethnopsychiatry, and alternate therapies*. Honolulu: University Press of Hawaii.

Murphy, J. G. (1979). Therapy and the problem of autonomous consent. *International Journal of Law and Psychiatry, 2,* 415–430.

Murphy, L. B. (1937). *Social behavior and child personality: An exploratory study of some roots of sympathy*. New York: Columbia University Press.

Murphy, L. B., et al. (1962). *The widening world of childhood: Paths toward mastery*. New York: Basic Books.

Murphy, L. B., & Moriarty, A. E. (1976). *Vulnerability, coping, and growth*. New Haven, Conn.: Yale University Press.

Murphy, M. (January 5, 1976). Profile by C. Tomkins. *The New Yorker Magazine*.

Murphy, M., & White, R. (1978). *The psychic side of sports*. Reading, Mass.: Addison-Wesley.

Murray, E. A., & Mishkin, M. (1985). Amygdalectomy impairs crossmodal association in monkeys. *Science, 228*, 604–606.

Murray, E. J. & Jacobson, L. I. (1971). The nature of learning in traditional and behavioral psychotherapy. In A. E. Bergin & S. L. Garfield (Eds.), *Handbook of psychotherapy and behavior change: An empirical analysis*. New York: Wiley.

Murray, E. J. & Jacobson, L. I. (1978). Cognition and learning in traditional and behavioral therapy. In S. L. Garfield & A. E. Bergin (Eds.), *Handbook of psychotherapy and behavior change: An empirical analysis* (2nd ed.). New York: Wiley.

Murray, H. A. (1933). The effect of fear upon estimates of the maliciousness of other personalities. *Journal of Social Psychology, 4*, 310–329.

Murray, H. A. (1938). *Explorations in personality: A clinical and experimental study of fifty men of college age*. New York: Oxford.

Murray, H. A. (1943). *Thematic Apperception Test manual*. Cambridge, Mass.: Harvard University Press.

Murray, H. A. (1951). Foreword. In E. S. Shneidman (Ed.), *Thematic test analysis*. New York: Grune & Stratton.

Murray, H. A. (1951). Uses of the Thematic Apperception Test. *The American Journal of Psychiatry, 10*, 577–581.

Murray, H. A. (1955). Types of human needs. In D. C. McLelland (Ed.), *Studies in motivation*. New York: Appleton-Century-Crofts.

Murray, H. A. (1959). Preparations for the scaffold of a comprehensive system. In S. Koch (Ed.), *Psychology: A study of a science* (Vol. 3, pp. 7–54). New York: McGraw-Hill.

Murray, H. A. (1960). Historical trends in personality research. In H. P. David & J. C. Brengelmann (Eds.), *Perspectives in personality research*. New York: Springer.

Murray, H. A. (1962/1938). *Explorations in personality, a clinical and experimental study of fifty men of college age*. New York: Oxford University Press.

Murray, H. A. (1981). *Endeavors in psychology: Selections from the personology of Henry A. Murray*. (E. S. Shneidman (Ed.). New York: Harper.

Murray, H. A. (1981). This I believe (1954). In E. S. Shneidman (Ed.), *Endeavors in psychology: Selections from the personology of Henry A. Murray*. New York: Harper & Row.

Murray, H. A., et al. (1938). *Explorations in personality*. New York: Oxford University Press.

Murray, H. A., & Kluckhohn, C. (1953). Outline of a conception of personality. In C. Kluckhohn, H. A. Murray, & D. Schneider (Eds.), *Personality in nature, society, and culture* (pp. 3–52). New York: Knopf.

Murray, J. E. (1992). Human organ transplantation: Background and consequences. *Science, 256*, 1411–1416.

Murray, J. R., Powers, E. A., & Havighurst, R. J. (1971). Personal and situational factors producing flexible careers. *The Gerontologist, 11*, 4–12.

Murray, M. E. (1978). Psychological evaluation of specific learning disorders. *Bulletin of the Orton Society, 28*, 142–159.

Murray, M. E. (1979). Minimal brain dysfunction and borderline personality adjustment. *American Journal of Psychotherapy, 33*, 39–41.

Murrell, K. F. H. (1969). *Ergonomics: Man and his working environment*. London: Chapman & Hall.

Murrell, S. A. (1974). Relationships of ordinal positions and family size to psychosocial measures of delinquent *Journal of Abnormal Child Psychology, 2*(1), 39–46.

Murrell, S. A., & Norris, F. (1983). Quality of life as the criterion for need assessment and community psychology. *Journal of Community Psychology, 11*, 88–97.

Mursell, J. L. (1937). *The psychology of music*. New York: Norton.

Murstein, B. I. (1961). A complementary need hypothesis in newlyweds and middle-aged married couples. *Journal of Abnormal and Social Psychology, 63*, 194–197.

Murstein, B. I. (1961). Assumptions, adaptation-level and projective techniques. *Perceptual and Motor Skills, 12*, 107–125.

Murstein, B. I. (1965). *Theory and research in projective techniques (emphasizing the TAT)*. New York: Wiley.

Murstein, B. I. (1967). The relationship of mental health to marital choice and courtship progress: *Journal of Marriage and the Family, 29*, 447–451.

Murstein, B. I. (1972). Physical attractiveness and marital choice. *Journal of Personality and Social Psychology, 22*, 8–12.

Murstein, B. I. (1976). *Who will marry whom? Theories and research in marital choice*. New York: Springer.

Murstein, B. I. (1980). Mate selection in 1970. *Journal of Marriage and the Family, 42*, 777–795.

Murthy, H. N. (1980). Counseling and therapy. In U. Pareek (Ed.), *A survey of research in psychology*. Bombay: Popular Prakashan.

Muslin, H. & Epstein, L. J. (1980). Preliminary remarks on the rationale for psychotherapy for the aged. *Comprehensive Psychiatry, 21*, 112.

Mussen, P., & Eisenberg-Berg, N. (1977). *Roots of caring, sharing, and helping: The development of prosocial behavior in children*. San Francisco: Freeman.

Mussen, P., & Rutherford, E. (1961). Effects of aggressive cartoons on children's aggressive play. *Journal of Abnormal and Social Psychology, 62*, 461–464.

Mussen, P. H. (1970). *Carmichael's manual of child psychology* (3rd ed.). New York: Wiley.

Mussen, P. H. (Ed.) (1960). *Handbook of research methods in child development*. New York: Wiley.

Mussen, P. H. Some personality and social factors related to changes in children's attitudes toward Negroes. *Journal of Abnormal and Social Psychology, 45*, 423–441.

Mussen, P. H., Conger, J, & Kagan, J. (1979). *Child development and personality* (5th ed.). New York: Harper & Row.

Mussen, P. H., Conger, J., & Kagan, J. (1979). *Psychological development: A life-span approach*. New York: Harper & Row.

Mussen, P. H., & Jones, M. C. (1957). Self-conceptions, motivations, and interpersonal attitudes of late and early-maturing boys. *Child Development, 28*, 243–256.

Mussen, P. H., & Jones, M. C. (1958). The behavior-inferred motivations of late and early-maturing boys. *Child Development, 29*, 61–67.

Musso, J. R., & Granero, M. (1973). An ESP drawing experiment with a highscoring subject. *Journal of Parapsychology, 37*, 13–36.

Muzekari, L. H. (1972). Birth order and social behavior among chronic schizophrenics. *Journal of Clinical Psychology, 28*(4), 483–485.

Myart v. Motorola. (April-June 1964). Hearings before the Illinois Fair Employment practices Commission.

Myasishchev, V. N. (1960). *Personality and neurosis*. Leningrad.

Myers, A. (1980). *Experimental psychology*. New York: Van Nostrand.

Myers, C. R. (1970). Journal citations and scientific eminence in contemporary psychology. *American Psychologist, 25,* 1041–1048.

Myers, C. R. (1976). Psychology in Canada. In V. S. Sexton & H. Misak (Eds.), *Psychology around the world.* Monterey, Calif.: Brooks/Cole.

Myers, C. S. (1929/1909). *A text-book of experimental psychology,* London: Arnold.

Myers, C. S. (1930). Autobiography. In C. Murchison (Ed.), A *history of psychology in autobiography,* Vol. 3. Worcester, Mass.: Clark University Press.

Myers, F. (1903). *Human personality and its survival of bodily death* (2 vols.). London: Longman, Green.

Myers, F. W. H. (1915). *Human personality* (2 vols). New York: Longmans, Green. (Original work published 1903)

Myers, I. (1962). *The Myers-Briggs type indicator manual and test.* Palo Alto, Calif.: Consulting Psychologists Press.

Myers, J. K., Bean, K. L., & Pepper, M. P. (1968). *A decade later: A follow-up of social class and mental illness.* New York: Wiley.

Myers, J. L. (1979). *Fundamentals of experimental design.* Boston: Allyn & Bacon.

Myers, R. A. (1971). Research on educational and vocational counseling. In A. E. Bergin & S. L. Garfield (Eds.), *Handbook of psychotherapy and behavior change: An empirical analysis.* New York: Wiley.

Myers, R. E., & Sperry, R. W. (1958). Interhemispheric communication through the corpus callosum. Mnemonic carry-over between the hemispheres. *Archives of Neurology and Psychiatry, 80,* 298–303.

Myers, T. B., & Myers, P. B. (1980). *Gifts differing.* Palo Alto, CA: Consulting Psychologists.

Myklebust, H. (Ed.) (1968). *Progress in learning disabilities,* Vol. I. New York: Grune & Stratton.

Myrberg, A. A., Jr., & Thresher, R. E. (1974). Interspecific aggression and its relevance to the concept of territoriality in reef fishes. *American Zoologist, 14,* 81–96.

Myrsten, A. L., Post, B., Frankenhaeuser, M., & Johansson, G. (1972). Changes in behavioral and physiological activation induced by cigarette smoking in habitual smokers. *Psychopharmacologia, 27*(4), 305–312.

Nachman, M. (1962). Taste preferences for sodium salts by adrenalectomized rats. *Journal of Comparative and Physiological Psychology, 55,* 1124–1129.

Nadel, L., & Willner, J. (1980). Context and conditioning: A place for space. *Physiological Psychology, 8,* 218–228.

Nadelman, L. (1974). Sex identity in American children: Memory, knowledge, and preference tests. *Developmental Psychology, 10,* 43–47.

Nader, R. (1965). *Unsafe at any speed: The designed-in dangers of the American automobile.* New York: Grossman.

Nagel, E. (1961). *The structure of science.* London: Routledge & Kegan Paul.

Nagel, E. (1961). *The structure of science: Problems in the logic of scientific explanation.* New York: Harcourt, Brace & World.

Nagle, R. J., & Thwaite, B. C. (1979). Modeling effects on impulsivity with learning disabled children. *Journal of Learning Disabilities, 12,* 331–336.

Nagy, T. (1986). *Ethics and the provision of telephone consultation services by psychologists.* Paper presented at the APA annual meetings.

Nagy, T. (1992, Winter). Benefits and hazards of teletherapy. *Stanford Medicine.*

Nagy, T. F. (1987). *Revision of the Ethical Principles of Psychologists: Subcommittee progress report.* Paper presented at the APA annual meetings.

Nagy, T. F. (1988). *Revision of the Ethical Principles of Psychologists: APA task force's second annual progress report.* Paper presented at the APA annual meetings.

Nagy, T. F. (1989). *Revision of the Ethical Principles of Psychologists: APA task force's progress report—Three years later and ready for review.* Paper presented at the APA annual meetings.

Nahas, Q. G., & Paton, W. D. M. (Eds.) (1979). *Marihuana: Biological effects: Analysis, metabolism cellular responses, reproduction and brain.* Oxford: Pergamon Press.

Nairn, A., et al. (1980). *The reign of ETS: The corporation that makes up minds.* Washington, D.C.: Nader.

Nakajima, K. (1991). Visual hallucinations with anterior cerebral artery occlusion. *No to Shinkei (Brain and Nerves), 43,* 71–76.

Nakamura, H. (1964). In P. Wiener (Ed.), *Ways of thinking of Eastern peoples: India-China-Tibet-Japan.* Honolulu: East-West Center Press.

Nakane, C. (1972). *Japanese society.* Berkeley, Calif.: University of California Press.

Nakashima, T. (1909). Contribution to the study of affective processes. *American Journal of Psychology, 20,* 157–193.

Namikoshi, T. (1969). *Shiatsu,* Tokyo: Japan Publications.

Nandy, A. (1974). The non-paradigmatic crisis of Indian psychology: Reflections on a recipient culture of science. *Indian Journal of Psychology, 49,* 1–20.

Nandy, A. (1978). Oppression and human liberation: Towards a third world utopia. *Alternatives, 4,* 165–180.

Nandy, A. (1980). *At the edge of psychology: Essays in politics and culture.* New Delhi: Oxford University Press.

Nandy, A. (1981). *Alternative science: Creativity and authenticity in two Indian scientists.* New Delhi: Allied Publishers.

Nandy, A. (1981). Dialogue on the traditions of technology. *Development, 3/4,* 98–106.

Nandy, A. (1981). Science, authoritarian and culture: On the scope and limits of isolation outside the clinic. M. N. Roy memorial lecture 1980. *Seminar, 261,* 25–33.

Nandy, A. (1982). Reconstructing childhood: A critique of the ideology of adulthood. Lecture at International Conference on Human Values, Tsukuba University, 1981. Abridged in *Resurgence, 92,* 20–22.

Nandy, A. (1983). *The intimate enemy: Loss and recovery of self under colonialism.* New Delhi: Oxford University Press.

Nandy, A. (in press). Towards an alternative politics of psychology. *International Social Science Journal.*

Nandy, A., & Kakar, S. (1980). Culture and personality. In U. Pareek (Ed.), *A survey of research in psychology.* Bombay: Popular Prakashan.

Nandy, K., & Sherwin, I. (Eds.) (1977). *The aging brain and senile dementia.* New York: Plenum.

Naor, M., & Milgram, R. M. (1980). Two preservice strategies for preparing regular class teachers for mainstreaming. *Exceptional Children, 47,* 126–129.

Napier, J. (1980). *Hands.* New York: Pantheon.

Naranjo, C. (1973). *The techniques of Gestalt therapy.* Berkeley, Calif.: SAT Press.

Naranjo, C., & Ornstein, R. (1971). *On the psychology of meditation.* New York: Viking Press.

Naroll, R., & Cohen, R. (1973/1970). *A handbook of method in cultural anthropology.* New York: Columbia University Press.

Naroll, R., Michik, G., & Naroll, F. (1980). Holocultural research methods. In H. Triandis & J. Berry (Eds.), *Handbook of cross-cultural psychology,* Vol. 2. Boston: Allyn & Bacon.

Nash, E. M., Jessner, J., & Abse, D. W. (Eds.) (1964). *Marriage counseling in medical practice.* Hagerstown, Md.: Harper & Row.

Nash, J. R. (1976). *Hustlers and con men.* New York: Evans.

Nash, R. (1976). *Teacher expectations and pupil learning* London: Routledge & Kegan Paul.

Nash, R. J. (1976). Clinical research on psychotropic drugs and hyperactivity in children. *School Psychology Digest, 5,* 22–23.

Nash, S. C. (1975). The relationship among sex-role stereotyping, sex-role preference, and the sex difference in spatial visualization. *Sex Roles, 1,* 15–32.

Natansoa, M. (Ed.) (1973). *Phenomenology and the social sciences,* Vol. 1. Evanston, Ill.: Northwestern University Press.

Nathan, P., (1969). *The nervous system.* New York: Lippincott.

National Academy of Aging. (1992, March). *Gerontology News.* Washington, DC: Gerontological Society of America.

National Adolescent Perpetrator Network.(1988). Preliminary report from the rational task force on juvenile sexual offending. *Juvenile and Family Court Journal, 39*(2), 1–64.

National Advisory Committee on Dyslexia and Related Disorders. (1969). *Reading disorders in the United States.* Washington, D.C.: U.S. Government Printing Office.

National Assessment of Educational Progress. (1981). *Three national assessments of reading: Changes in performance, 197–80.* Denver, Colo.: Education Commission of the States.

National Association of Social Workers. (1980). *Code of ethics.* Washington, D.C.: National Association of Social Workers.

National Center, Educational Media and Materials for the Handicapped. (1978). *Mainstreaming handicapped children: toward a comprehensive bibliography.* Columbus, Ohio: Ohio State University Press.

National Center for Health Statistics. (1975). *National health survey: Blood pressure of persons 18–74 years, United States, 1971/1972* (U.S. Department of Health, Education, and Welfare, Series II. Publication no. 150). Washington, D.C.: U.S. Government Printing Office.

National Center for Health Statistics. (1975). *Self-reported health behavior and attitude of youth 12–17, United States.* Washington, D.C.: US Government Printing Office.

National Easter Seal Society for Crippled Children and Adults. (1976). *Housing and handicapped persons: A resource guide of available publications from 1970 forward.* Chicago: The Society.

National Education Association. (1976, October). *Survey. Today's education.*

National Education Association. (1979). *NEA handbook.* Washington, D.C.: National Education Association.

National Institute on Alcohol Abuse and Alcoholism. (1971). In M. Keller & S. S. Rosenberg (Eds.), *Alcohol and health.* First Special Report to the U.S. Congress on Alcohol and Health from the Secretary of Health, Education, and Welfare, December. DHEW Pub. No. (HSM) 72–9099. Washington, D.C.: U.S. Government Printing Office.

National Institute on Alcohol Abuse and Alcoholism. (1987). *Program strategies for preventing fetal alcohol syndrome and alcohol-related birth defects.* Rockville, MD: National Institute on Alcohol Abuse and Alcoholism.

National Institute of Education. (1978). *The safe school study report to the Congress.* Washington, D.C.: Department of Health, Education and Welfare.

National Institute of Justice. (1985). *National survey of crime severity* (WCJ-96017), Washington, DC: U.S. Department of Justice.

National Institute of Mental Health, U. S. Department of Health, Education and Welfare. (1970). Mental Health Publication no. 5027. Washington, D.C.: U.S. Government Printing Office.

National Research Council. (1991). *In the mind's eye: Enhancing human performances.* Washington, DC: National Academy.

National Society for the Study of Education. (1928). *Twenty-seventh yearbook. Nature and nurture.* Bloomington, Ill.: Public School Publishing.

National Society for the Study of Education. (1940). *Thirty-ninth yearbook. Intelligence: Its nature and nurture.* Bloomington, Ill.: Public School Publishing.

Natsoulas, T. (1978). Consciousness. *American Psychologist, 10,* 906–914.

Naumburg, M. (1947). *Studies of free art expression in behavior of children as a means of diagnosis and therapy.* New York: Coolidge Foundation.

Naumburg, M. (1953). *Psychoneurotic art.* New York: Grune & Stratton.

Nauta, W. J. H., & Domesick, V. B. (1981). Neural associations of the limbic system. In A. L. Beckman (Ed.), *The neural basis of behavior.* Jamaica, N.Y.: Spectrum.

Navon, D, & Gopher, D. (1979). On the economy of the human processing system. *Psychological Review, 86,* 214–255.

Ndetei, D., & Vadher, A. (1984). A comparative cross-cultural study of the frequencies of hallucinations in schizophrenics. *Acta Psychiatrics Scandinavica, 70,* 545–549.

Neale, J. M., & Oltmanns, T. F. (1980). *Schizophrenia.* New York: Wiley.

Neaman, J. S. (1975/1973). Suggestion of the devil: The origins of madness New York: Doubleday.

Nebes, R. D. (1974). Hemispheric specialization in commisurotomized man. *Psychological Bulletin, 81,* 1–14.

Needleman, J. (Ed.) (1963). *Being-in-the-world. Selected papers of Ludwig Binswanger.* New York: Basic Books.

Needleman, J., & Lewis, D. (Eds.) (1976). *On the way to self-knowledge.* New York: Knopf.

Neff, W. S. (1968). *Work and human behavior.* New York: Atherton Press.

Neher, A. (1980). *The psychology of transcendence.* Englewood Cliffs, N. J.: Prentice-Hall.

Neill, A. S. (1964). *Summerhill: A radical approach to child rearing.* New York: Hart.

Neill, A. S. (1954). *The free child.* Toronto Longman.

Neiman, L. J., & Hughes, J. W. (1951). The problem of the concept role—A resurvey of the literature. *Social Forces, 30,* 141–149.

Neimark, E. D., & Estes, W. K. (1967). *Stimulus sampling theory.* San Francisco: Holden-Day.

Neimeyer, R. (1989). Death anxiety. In H. Wass, F. Berardo, & R. Neimeyer (Eds.), *Dying: Facing the facts* (pp. 97–136). Washington, DC: Hemisphere.

Neisser, U. (1967). *Cognitive psychology.* New York: Appleton-Century-Crofts.

Neisser, U. (1982). Memory: What are the important questions. In U. Neisser (Ed.), *Memory observed: Remembering in natural contexts.* San Francisco: Freeman.

Neisser, U., & Harsch, N. (1990, February). *Phantom flashbulbs: False recollections of hearing the news about* Challenger. Paper presented at the Conference on Affect and Flashbulb Memories, Emory University.

Neisser, U., & Kerr, N. H. (1973). Spatial and mnemonic properties of visual images. *Cognitive Psychology, 5,* 138–150.

Neitzel, M. T. (1979). *Crime and its modification.* New York: Pergamon Press.

Neki, J. S. (1976). An examination of the cultural relativism of dependence as a dynamic of social and therapeutic relationships, I. *British Journal of Medical Psychology, 49,* 1–10.

Neki, J. S. (1976). An examination of the cultural relativism of dependence as a dynamic of social and therapeutic relationships, II. *British Journal of Medical Psychology, 49,* 11–22.

Nell, W. M. (1977). Teaching and practice of psychology in Australia in this first phase. In M. Nixon, & R. Taft (Eds.), *Psychology in Australia: Achievements and prospects.* Rushcutters Bay, Australia: Pergamon Press.

Nelsen, J. (1981). *Positive discipline (class meetings).* Fair Oaks, Calif.: Adlerian Consulting and Counseling Center.

Nelson, E. A., & Dannefer, D. (1992). Aged heterogeneity: Fact or fiction? The fate of diversity in gerontological research. *The Gerontologist, 32,* 17–23.

Nelson, J. (1987). The history and spirit of the HMO movement. *HMO Practice, 2*(1), 75–86.

Nelson, J. A. (1981). The impact of incest: Factors in self-evaluation. In L. L. Constantine & F. M. Martinson (Eds.) *Children and sex.* Boston: Little, Brown.

Nelson, K. (1974). Concept, word, and sentence: Interrelations in acquisition and development. *Psychological Review, 81,* 267–285.

Nelson, R. O., & Hayes, S. C. (1986). The nature of behavioral assessment. In R. O. Nelson & S. C. Hayes (Eds.), *Conceptual foundations of behavioral assessment.* (pp.3–41). New York: Guilford.

Nelson, S. A. (1981). Factors influencing young children's use of motives and outcomes as moral criteria. *Child Development, 51,* 823–829.

Nelson, S. E. (1939). The role of heredity in stuttering. *Journal of pediatrics, 14,* 642–654.

Nemeroff, C., Krishnan, R. D., Leder, R., Beam, C., & Dunnick, N. (1992). Adrenal gland enlargement in major depression: A computed tomographic study. *Archives of General Psychiatry, 49,* 384–387.

Nemeroff, C. B., & Loosen, P. T. (1987). *Clinical Psychoneuroendocrinology.* New York: Guilford.

Nesbitt, P. D. (1973). Smoking, physiological arousal, and emotional response. *Journal of Personality and Social Psychology, 25*(1), 137–144.

Nesselroade, J. R., & Baites, P. B. (Eds.) (1979). *Longitudinal research in the study of behavior and development.* New York: Academic Press.

Netter, F. H. (1977/1974). *The CIBA collection of medical illustrations.* Vol. I: *The nervous system.* Rochester, N.Y.: Case-Hoyt.

Netter, P. (1980). Suggestibilität und Medikamentenwirkung. *Medizinische Psychologie, 6,* 195–213.

Netter, P. (1982). Medizinische Grundlagen für die Schwerpunktausbildung Klinische Psychologie. In W. Minsel, & R. Scheller (Eds.), *Brennpunkte der Klinischen Psychologie,* Vol. III. *Psychologie und Medizin.* Munich: Kösel.

Netter, P. (1983). Somatic factors as predictors of psychotropic drug response. In W. Janke (Ed.), *Response variability to psychotropic drugs.* Oxford: Pergamon Press.

Netter, P., & Neuhäuser, S. (Novermber 1978, 1982). Überlegungen, Wege und Beispiele zur Identikation von Untertypen der essentiellen Hypertonie In D. Vaitl (Ed.), *Psychologisch-Medizinische Aspekte der essentiellen Hypertonie, Forschungskonferenz Hannover,* Berlin: Springer.

Netter, P., & Rammsayer, T. (1991). Reactivity to dopaminergic drugs and aggression related personality traits. *Personality and Individual Differences, 12,* 1009–1017.

Netter, P., & Wermuth, N. (1975). Psychosomatic complaints as related to contraceptive practice and frequency of intercourse. In H. Hirsch (Ed.), *Proceedings of the IVth International Congress of Psychosomatic Obstetrics and Gynecology in Tel Aviv 1974.* Basel: Karger.

Netter-Mankelt, P., Mau, G., & König, B. (1972). The dimension of neuroticism as a modifying factor in the association between biological conditions and nausea in pregnancy. *Journal of Psychosomatic Research, 16,* 395–404.

Neugarten, B. L. (1968). *Middle age and aging.* Chicago: University of Chicago Press.

Neugarten, B. L. (February 1980). Must everything be midlife crisis? *Prime Time.*

Neugarten, B. L., et al. (Eds.) (1964). *Personality in middle and later life.* Chicago: University of Chicago Press.

Neugarten, B. L., & Datan, N. (1973). Sociological perspectives on the life cycle. In P. B. Baites & K. Warner Schaie (Eds.), *Life-span development psychology and socialization.* New York: Academic Press.

Neugarten, B. L., & Gumann, D. L. (1968). Age-sex roles and personality in middle age. In B. Neugarten, (Ed.), *Middle age and aging.* Chicago: University of Chicago Press.

Neugarten, B. L., & Hagestad, G. O. (1976). Age and the life course. In R. H. Binstock & E. Shanas (Eds.), *Handbook of aging and the social sciences.* New York: Van Nostrand Reinhold.

Neugarten, B. L. & Moore, J. W. (1968). The changing age-status system. In B. Neugarten (Ed.), *Middle age and aging.* Chicago: University of Chicago Press.

Neugebauer, R. (1979). Medieval and early modern theories of mental illness. *Archives of General Psychiatry, 36,* 477–483.

Neulinger, J. (1981). *The psychology of leisure.* Springfield, Ill.: Thomas.

Neumann, E. (1955). *The origins and history (consciousness.* New York: Pantheon.

Neumann, J. von, & Morgenstern, O. (1947). *Theory of games and economic behavior.* Princeton, N.J.: Princeton University Press.

Neuringer, C. (1968). A variety of thematic methods. In A. I. Rabin (Ed.), *Projective techniques in personality assessment.* New York: Springer.

New, P. J., & Scott, W. R. (1974). *Computed tomography of the brain and orbit.* Baltimore, Md.: Williams & Wilkins.

Newby, H. A. (1979). *Audiology* (4th ed.). Englewood Cliffs, N.J.: Prentice-Hall.

Newberry, B. H., Gorden, T. L., & Meehan, S. M. (1991). Animal studies of stress and cancer. In C. L. Cooper & M. Watson (Eds.), *Cancer and stress* (pp.27–43). Chichester, UK: Wiley.

Newberry, E. (1954). Current interpretation and significance of Lloyd Morgan's canon. *Psychological Bulletin, 51,* 70–74.

Newcomb, M. D., & McGee, L. (1991). The influence of sensation seeking on general and specific problem behaviors from adolescence to young adulthood. *Journal of Personality and Social Psychology, 61*, 614–628.

Newcomb, P. R. (1979). Cohabitation in America: An assessment of consequences. *Journal of Marriage and the Family, 41*, 597–603.

Newcomb, T. M. (1943). *Personality and social change.* New York: Dryden.

Newcomb, T. M. (1950). *Social psychology.* New York: Dryden.

Newcomb, T. M. (1956). The prediction of interpersonal attraction. *American Psychologist 11*, 575–586.

Newcomb, T. M. (1961). *The acquaintance process.* New York: Holt, Rinehart & Winston.

Newcombe, N. (1980). Beyond nature and nurture. *Contemporary Psychology, 25*, 807–808.

Newell, A. (1973). Production systems: Models of control structures. In W. G. Chase (Ed.), *Visual information processing.* New York: Academic Press.

Newell, A. (1980). Physical symbol system. *Cognitive Science, 4*, 135–184.

Newell, A. (1990). *Unified theories of cognition.* Cambridge, MA: Harvard University Press.

Newell, A., Shaw, J. C., & Simon, H. A. (1958). Elements on a theory of human problem solving. *Psychological Review, 65*, 151–166.

Newell, A., & Simon, H. A. (1956). The logic theory machine. *IRE Transactions on Information Theory, IT-2*(3), 61–79.

Newell, A, & Simon, H. A. (1972). *Human problem solving* Englewood Cliffs, N.J.: Prentice-Hall.

Newell, A., & Simon, H. A. (1976). Computer science as empirical inquiry: Symbols and search. *Communications of the ACM, 19*, 113–126.

New Grolier multimedia encyclopedia, the (1992) Danbury: Grolier Electronic.

Newhouse, R. C. (1974). Reinforcement-responsibility differences in birth order, grade level, and sex of children in grades 4, 5, and 6. *Psychological Reports, 34*(3, 1), 699–705.

Newland, T. E. (1977). Tested "intelligence" in children. *School Psychology Monograph, 3*(3), 1–44.

Newman, E. B. (1939). Forgetting of meaningful material during sleep and waking. *American Journal of Psychology, 52*, 65–71.

Newman, F., & Oliver, D. (1970). *Clarifying public issues: An approach to teaching social studies.* Boston: Little, Brown.

Newman, G., & Nichols, C. R. (1974). Sexual activities and attitudes in older persons. In N. N. Wagner (Ed.), *Perspectives on human sexuality: Psychological social and cultural research findings.* New York: Behavioral Publications.

Newman, H. H., Freeman, F. N., & Holzinger, K. J. (1937). *Twins.* Chicago: University of Chicago Press.

Newman, J. P. (1989). Aging and depression. *Psychology and Aging, 4*, 150–165.

Newman, J. W. (1957). *Motivation research and marketing management.* Boston: Harvard University, Graduate School of Business Administration, Division of Research.

Newman, N. (1974). Creating community homes. In C. Cherington & G. Dybwad (Eds.), *New neighbors: The retarded citizen in quest of a home.* Washington, D.C.: U.S. Government Printing Office.

Newmann, E., & Blauton, R. (1970). The early history of electrodermal research. *Psychophysiology, 6*, 453–475.

Newsweek, (December 14, 1981). Special report: Troubled teenagers. 40–43.

New York Branch of the Orton Dyslexia Society. (1982). Background facts on dyslexia. *Newsletter, 5*, 8.

New York Times, October 20, 1961, p. 14, col. 3.

Nezlek, J., & Brehm, J. W. (1974). Hostility as a function of the opportunity to counteraggress. *Journal of Personality, 43*, 421–423.

Nichols, H. (1890). *The psychology of time.* New York: Holt.

Nichols, M. P. (1974). Outcome of brief cathartic psychotherapy. *Journal of Consulting and Clinical Psychology, 42*, 403–410.

Nichols, M. P., & Zax, M. (1977). *Catharsis in psychotherapy.* New York: Gardner Press.

Nicolaidis, S., & Even, P. (1985). Physiological determinant of hunger, satiation, and satiety. *American Journal of Clinical Nutrition, 42*, 1083–1092.

Nicolaidis, S., & Rowland, N. (1977). Intravenous self-feeding: long-term regulation of energy balance in rats. *Science, 195*, 589–591.

The nicotine habit. (1968). *Lancet, I*(542), 579–580.

Nideffer, R., & Sharpe, R. (1978). *A.C.T.: Attention control training.* New York: Wyden.

Nidich, S. I., Nidich, R. J., & Rainforth, M. V. (1986). School effectiveness: Achievement gains at Maharishi School of the Age of Enlightenment, *Education, 107*(1), 49–54.

Nie, N., Verba, S., & Petrocik, J. (1976). *The changing American voter.* Cambridge, Mass.. Harvard University Press.

Nield, J. B. (1976). A study of birth order and family constellation among high school and delinquent students (Doctoral dissertation, Idaho State University, 1976). *Dissertation Abstracts International, 37*, 3527A–3650A (University Microfilms no. 76—29252).

Nielsen, J., & Christensen, A.-L. (1974). Thirty-five males with double Y chromosome. *Psychological Medicine, 4*, 28–37.

Nielson, J. M. (1946). *Agnosia, apraxia, aphasia.* New York: Hoeber.

Nierenberg, G. I. (1968). *Art of negotiating.* New York. Cornerstone Library.

Nietzel, M. T., & Fisher, S. G. (1981). Effectiveness of professional and paraprofessional helpers: A comment on Durlak. *Psychological Bulletin, 89*, 555–565.

Nietzel, M. T., Winett, R. A., McDonald, M. L, & Davidson, W. S. (1977). *Behavioral approaches to community psychology.* Elmsford, N.Y.: Pergamon Press.

Nietzsche, F. (1931/1895). *The Antichrist.* New York: Knopf.

Nietzsche, F. (1935/1887). *Beyond good and evil.* Chicago: Regency.

Nietzsehe, F. W. (1956). *The birth of tragedy and the genealogy of morals.* Garden City, N.Y.: Doubleday.

Nilsson, N. J. (1991). Logic and artificial intelligence. *Artificial Intelligence, 47*, 31–56.

Nikelly, A. G. (1971). Fundamental concepts of maladjustment. In A. G. Nikelly *(Ed.), Techniques for behavior change: Applications of Adlerian theory.* Springfield, Ill.: Thomas.

Nikelly, A. G. (Ed.). (1971). *Techniques for behavior change.* Springfield, Ill.: Thomas.

Nisan, M., & Kohlberg, L. (1982). Universality and variation in moral judgment: A longitudinal and cross-cultural study in Turkey. *Child Development, 53*, 865–876.

Nisbet, A. R. (1975). *Twilight of authority.* New York: Oxford University Press.

Nisbett, R., & Ross, L. (1980). *Human inference: Strategies and shortcomings of social judgment.* Englewood Cliffs, N.J.: Prentice-Hall.

Nisbett, R. E. (1968). Determinants of food intake in obesity. *Science, 159*, 1254–1255.

Nisbett, R. E., & Wilson, T. D. (1977). Telling more than we can know: Verbal reports on mental processes. *Psychological Review, 84,* 231–259.

Nishisato, S. (1978). *Multidimensional scaling: A historical sketch and bibliography.* Toronto: Ontario Institute for Studies in Education.

Nitobe, I. (1977/1969). *Bushido: The soul of Japan.* Rutland, Vt.; Tokyo: Tuttle Books.

Nixon, M., & Taft, R. (Eds.) (1977). *Psychology in Australia: Achievements and prospects.* Rushcutters Bay, Australia: Pergamon Press (Australia).

Nizer, L. (1946). The art of the jury trial. *Cornell Law Quarterly,* 59–62.

Nobbs, K. L. G. (1973). Mental disorders in the elderly. In K. K. Hazell, K. L. G. Nobbs, W. A. Hurt, & W. E. Anderson (Eds.), *Social and medical problems of the elderly* (3rd ed.). London: Hutchinson.

Noble, C. E. (1961). Measurements of association value (a) rated associations (a) and scaled meaningfulness (m) for the 2100 CVC combinations of the English alphabet. *Psychological Reports, 8,* 487–521.

Nobel, G. K. (1939). The role of dominance in the life of birds. *Auk, 56,* 263–273.

Noël, J. (1926). Le psychologue et le logicien. *Revue Néo-Scolastique de Philosophie, 28,* 125–152.

Nogen, A. (1976). Medical treatment for spasticity in children with cerebral palsy. *Child's Brain, 2,* 304.

Noizet, G. (1980). *De la perception a la comprehension du langage.* Paris: Presses Universitaires de France.

Noizet, G., & Caverni, J-P. (1978). *Psychologie de l'évaluation scolaire.* Paris: Presses Universitaires de France.

Nolan, J. D. (1968). Self-control procedures in the modification of smoking behavior. *Journal of Consulting Clinical Psychology, 32*(1), 92–93.

Nolan, J. D. (1974). Freedom and dignity: A "functional" analysis. *American Psychologist, 3,* 157–160.

Noll, R. (1990). *Bizarre diseases of the mind.* New York: Berkeley.

Nora, J. J., & Fraser, F. C. (1989). *Medical genetics* (3rd. ed.). Philadelphia: Lea & Febiger.

Norback, C., & Norback, P. (1979). *The New American Library guide to athletics sports, and recreation.* New York: New American Library.

NORC. *General social surveys, 1972—80.* Chicago: NORC.

Norcross, J. C. (Ed.) (1986). *Handbook of eclectic psychotherapy.* New York: Brunner/Mazel.

Norcross, J. C., & Goldfried, M. R. (Eds.). (in press). *Handbook of psychotherapy integration.* New York: Basic Books.

Norcross, J. C., & Prochaska, J. O. (1982). A national survey of clinical psychologists: Affiliation and orientations. *The Clinical Psychologist, 35,* 1–6.

Nordby, V. J., & Hall, C. S. (1974). *A guide to psychologists and their concepts.* San Francisco: Freeman.

Norman, D. A. (1977). *Memory and attention: An introduction to human information processing* (2nd ed.). New York: Wiley.

Norman, D. A. (1982). *Human learning and memory.* San Francisco: Freeman.

Norman, D. A. (1991). Approaches to the study of intelligence. *Artificial Intelligence, 47,* 327–346.

Norman, D. A. (Ed.). (1970). *Models of human memory.* New York: Academic Press.

Norman, D. A. (Ed.) (1981). *Perspectives on cognitive science: The La Jolla conference.* Norwood, N.J.: Ablex, 1981. Hillsdale, N.J.: Erlbaum.

Norman, D. A., & Rumelhart, D. E. (1975). *Explorations in cognition.* San Francisco: Freeman.

Norman, D. A., & Schank, R. (1982). *Memory and cognitive science: A dialogue.* Hillsdale, N.J.: Erlbaum.

Norman, R. M. G., & Watson, L. D. (1976). Extraversion and reactions to cognitive inconsistency. *Journal of Research in Personality, 10,* 446–456.

Norman, W. T. (1967). *2800 personality trait descriptors: Normative operating characteristics for a university population.* Ann Arbor, Mich.: Department of Psychology, University of Michigan.

Northrup, E. (1957). *Science looks at smoking.* New York: Coward-McCann.

Norton, C. R., Harrison, B., Hauch, J., & Rhodes, L. (1985). Characteristics of people with infrequent panic attacks. *Journal of Abnormal Psychology, 64,* 226–322.

Norvell, M., & Guy, R. (1977). A comparison of adopted and non-adopted adolescents. *Adolescence, 12,* 443–448.

Nosworthy, G. J., & Lindsay, R. C. (1990). Does nominal lineup size matter? *Journal of Applied Psychology, 75,* 358–361.

Notman, M., & Nadelson, C. (1976). The rape victim: Psychodynamic considerations. *American Journal of Psychiatry, 133,* 408–412.

Notz, W. W. Work motivation and the negative effects of extrinsic rewards: A review with implications for theory and practice. *American Psychologist, 30,* 884–891.

Novaco, R. W. (1977). Stress inoculation: A cognitive therapy for anger and its application to a case of depression. *Journal of Consulting and Clinical Psychology, 45,* 600–608.

Novak, J. D., & Gowin, D. B. (1984). *Learning how to learn.* New York: Cambridge University Press.

Novick, M. R. (1981). Federal guidelines and professional standards. *American Psychologist, 36,* 1035–1046.

Novick, M. R., & Ellis, D. D. (1977). Equal opportunity in educational and employment selection. *American Psychologist, 32,* 306–320.

Noyes, R., Jr. (1972). The experience of dying. *Psychiatry, 35,* 174–178.

Noyes, R., Jr. (1980). Attitude change following near-death experience. *Psychiatry, 43,* 234–242.

Nsereko-Gyagenda, T. (1970). *An investigation of eleven mental abilities in Uganda children.* Thesis, Makerere University.

Nuehring, E. M. (1979). Stigma and state hospital patients. *American Journal of Orthopsychiatry, 49*(4), 626–633.

Núñez, R. (1954). *El sicodiagnóstico de Rorschach aplicado a niños.* Mexico, D.F.: Editorial Diana (edición agotada).

Núñez, R. (1962). *Problemas psicosociales de la prolesion de la psicologia clinica en Mexico.* Mexico, D.F.: Núñez.

Núñez, R. (1967). *Adaptación del Minnesota Multiphasic Personality Inventory al Español.* Mexico: D.F.: El Manual Moderno.

Núñez, R. (1969). *Investigación sobre las caracteristicas del Mexicano.* Memorias del Undécimo Congreso de la Sociedad Interamericana de Psicologia. Montevideo.

Núñez, R. (1979). *Aplicación del inventario multifasico de la personalidad a la psicopatología* (2nd ed.). Mexico, D.F.: El Manual Moderno.

Núñez, R. (in press). *Estudio normativo del MMPI en cuatro clases socioeconómicas con adultos de la ciudad de Mexico.*

Núñez, R., Kolb, R., & Velezquez Huerta, A. (in press). *El MMPI, manual en Español de Starke R. Hathaway, revisado y aumentado.* Mexico, D.F.: El Manual Moderno.

Nunnally, J. (1978/1967). *Psychometric theory.* New York: McGraw-Hill.

Nunney, D. H. (1964). Trends in the content of educational psychology. *Journal of Teacher Education, 15*, 372–377.

Nunney, D. N., & Hill, J. E. (February, 1972). Personalized educational programs. *Audiovisual Instruction*, 10–15.

Nurnberger, J., & Gershon, E. (1982). Genetics. In E. Paykel (Ed.), *Handbook of affective disorders*. New York: Guilford Press.

Nurnberger, J. I., Jr., Hamovit, J., Hibbs, E. D., Pellegrini, D., Guroff, J. J., Maxwell, M. E., Smith, A., & Gershon, E. S. (1988). A high-risk study of primary affective disorder: Selection of subjects, initial assessment, and 1-to-2 year follow-up. In D. L. Dunner, E. S. Gershon, & J. E. Barrett (Eds.), *Relatives at risk for mental disorder* New York: Raven Press.

Nuttin, J. (1961). *Psychology in Belgium*. Louvain, Belgium: Leuven University Press.

Nuttin, J. R. (1941). *De wet van bet effekt (The law of effect)*. Unpublished doctoral thesis, Louvain University.

Nuttin, J. R. (1941). *The law of effect and the role of tasks in the learning process*. Unpublished doctoral dissertation, Louvain University.

Nuttin, J. R. (1953). *Tâche, réussite et échec: Théorie de la conduite humaine*. Louvain, Belgium: University Press.

Nuttin, J. R. (1965). *La structure de la personnali*. Paris: Presses Universitaries de France.

Nuttin, J. R. (1976). Motivation and reward in human learning. In W. K. Estes (Ed.), *Handbook of learning and cognitive processes*, Vol. 3. Hillsdale, N.J.: Erlbaum.

Nuttin, J. R. (1980). *Motivation et perspectives d'avenir*. Louvain, Belgium: Presses Universitaries.

Nuttin, J. R. (1980). *Théorie de la motivation humaine*. Paris: Presses Universitaries de France.

Nuttin, J. R. (1984). *Motivation, planning and action*. Hillsdale, N.J.: Erlbaum.

Nuttin, J. R., & Greenwald, A. G. (1968). *Reward and punishment in human learning: Elements of a behavior theory*. New York: Academic Press.

Nye, F. I. (1976). *Role structure and analysis of the family*. Beverly Hills, Calif.: Sage Publications.

Nye, S. (1980). Patient confidentiality and privacy: The federal initiative. *American Journal of Orthopsychiatry, 50*, 649–658.

Nystul, M. S., & Garde, M. (1977). A comparison of the self-concepts of transcendental meditators and non-meditators. *Psychological Reports, 41*, 303–306.

Nystul, M. S., & Garde, M. (1979). The self-concepts of regular transcendental meditators, dropout meditators, and nonmeditators. *The Journal of Psychology, 103*, 15–18.

Oakland, J. A., Freed, F., Lovekin, A., Davis, J. P., Jr., & Camilleri, R. (1978). A critique of Shostrom's Personal Orientation Inventory. *Journal of Humanistic Psychology, 18*, 76–85.

Oakland, T. (1974/1975). Assessment, education, and minority-group children. *Academic Therapy, 10*, 133–140.

Oakland, T. (Ed.) (1977). *Psychological and educational assessment of minority children*. New York: Brunner/Mazel.

Oakland, T., & Laosa, L. M. (1977). Professional, legislative, and judicial influences on psychoeducational assessment practices in schools. In T. Oakland (Ed.), *Psychological and educational assessment of minority children*. New York: Brunner/Mazel.

Oaklander, V. (1978). *Windows to our children*. Moab, Utah: Real People Press.

Oberg, K. (1960). Culture shock: Adjustment to new cultural environments. *Practical Anthropology, 7*, 177–182.

Oberlander, M., Jenkin, N., Houlihan, K., & Jackson, J. (1970). Family size and birth order as determinants of scholastic aptitude and achievement in a sample of eighth graders. *Journal of Consulting and Clinical Psychology, 37*, 19–21.

Obermann, C. E. (1965). *A history of vocational rehabilitation in America*. Minneapolis, Minn.: Denison.

Oberndorf, C. P. (1953). *A history of psychoanalysis in America*. New York: Harper & Row.

O'Brien, W. H. & Haynes, S. N. (in press). Behavioral assessment in the psychiatric setting. In A. S. Bellack & M. Hersen (Eds.), *Handbook of behavior therapy in the psychiatric setting. New York: Plenum*.

Obudho, C. E. (1979). *Human nonverbal behavior: An annotated bibliography*. London: Greenwood Press.

Ochroch, R. (1981). A review of the minimal brain dysfunction syndrome. In R. Ochroch, (Ed.), *The diagnosis and treatment of minimal brain dysfunction in children: A clinical approach*. New York: Human Sciences Press.

Ochse, R. (1991). Why there were relatively few eminent women creators. *Journal of Creative Behavior, 25*, 334–342.

Ochsner, A., & Damrau, F. (1970). Control of cigarette habit by psychological aversive conditioning: Clinical evaluation in 53 smokers. *Journal of the American Geriatric Society, 18(5)*, 365–369.

O'Connell, A. N., & Russ, N. F. (1991). Women' heritage in psychology: Past and present. *Psychology of Women Quarterly, 15*, 495–504.

O'Connell, A. N., & Russ, N. F. (Eds.). (1983). *Models of achievement: Reflections of eminent women in psychology*. New York: Columbia University Press.

O'Connell, D., & Alexander, C. N. (Eds.). (1993). *Transcendental Meditation and Maharishi Ayur-Ved in the treatment and prevention of drug abuse*. New York: Haworth.

O'Connell, D. N., Shor, R. E., & Orne, M. T. (1970). Hypnotic age regression: An empirical and methodological analysis. *Journal of Abnormal Psychology Monograph, 76* (3, Pt. 2).

O'Connell, W. (1981). Natural high therapy. In R. J. Corsini (Ed.), *Handbook of innovative psychotherapies*. New York: Wiley.

O'Connor, N., & Hermelin, B. (1981). Coding strategies of normal and handicapped children. In R. D. Walk & H. L. Pick, Jr. (Eds.), *Intersensory perception and sensory integration*. New York: Plenum.

O'Connor v. *Donaldson*, (1975). 422 U. S. 563.

O'Connor, W. (1921). *The concept of the soul according to Saint Augustine*. Washington, D.C.: Catholic University of America.

O'Dell, T. J., Hawkins, R. D., Kandel, E. R., & Arancio, O. (1991). Tests of the roles of two diffusible substances in long-term potentiation: Evidence for nitric oxide as a possible long-early retrograde messanger. *Proceedings of the National Academy of Sciences, 88*, 11285–11289.

Oden, M. H. (1968). The fulfillment of promise: Forty-year follow-up of the Terman gifted group. *Genetic Psychology Monographs, 77*, 3–93.

O'Donnell, R., & Bradfield, R. (Eds.) (1976). *Mainstreaming: Controversy and consensus*. San Rafael, Calif.: Academic Therapy Publications.

Oesterreich, T. K. (1974/1921). *Possession and exorcism: Among primitive races in antiquity, the middle ages, and modern times*. New York: Causeway Books.

Offer, D., & Offer, J. (1974). Normal adolescent males: The high school and college years. *Journal of the American College Health Association, 22*, 209–215.

Office of Federal Contract Compliance Programs, Vol. 29, (1975). United States Code, Par. 701 (Supp V).

Office of Federal Contract Compliance, Executive Order 11246, 1965.

Offir, C. W. (1982). *Human sexuality*. New York: Harcourt Brace Jovanovich.

Offord, D. R. (1989). Conduct disorder: Risk factors and prevention. In *Prevention of mental disorders, alcohol, and other drug use in children and adolescents* (pp.273–308). Rockville, MD: U.S. Department of Health and Human Services.

Offord, D. R., Aider, R. J., & Boyle, M. H. (1986). Prevalence and sociodemographic correlates of conduct disorder. *American Journal of Social Psychiatry, 6,* 272–278.

Offord, D. R., Boyle, M. C., & Racine, Y. A. (1991). The epidemiology of antisocial behavior in childhood and adolescence. In D. J. Pepler & K. H. Rubin (Eds.), *The development and treatment of childhood aggression.* (pp.31–54). Hillsdale, NJ: Erlbaum.

Offord, D. R., Hershey, M. D., Aponte, J. F., & Cross, L. A. (1969). Presenting symptomatology of adopted children. *Archives of General Psychiatry, 20,* 110–116.

Ogden, E. J. D., & Del Horne, D. J. (1974). Birth order and delinquency: Findings from a youth training center. *Australian and New Zealand Journal of Criminology (Melbourne), 7*(3), 179–183.

Ogden, R. M. (1951). Oswald Külpe and the Würzburg School. *American Journal of Psychology, 64,* 4—19.

Ogilvie, B., & Tutko, T. (1966). *Problem athletes*. London: Pelham Books.

O'Halloran, J. P., Jevning, R. A., Wilson, A. F., Skowsky, R., & Alexander, C. N. (1985). Hormonal control in a state of decreased activation: Potentiation of arginine vasopressin secretion. *Physiology and Behavior, 35,* 591–595.

O'Hanlon, J. F. (1981). Boredom: Practical consequences and a theory. *Acta Psychologica, 49,* 53–82.

Ohlsen, M. M. (1977). *Group counseling*. New York: Holt, Rinehart & Winston.

Ohlsen, M. M. (1979). *Marriage counseling in groups*. Champaign, Ill.: Research Press.

O'Keefe, D. J., & Sypher, H. E. (1981). Cognitive complexity measures and the relationship of cognitive complexity to communication. *Human Communications Research, 8,* 72–92.

O'Keefe, J., & Nadel, L. (1978). *The hippocampus as a cognitive map*. Oxford, UK: Clarendon.

Okonji, O. M. (1971a). A cross cultural study of the effects of familiarity on classificatory behaviour. *Journal of Cross-Cultural Psychology, 2,* 39–49.

Okonji, O. M. (1971c). Culture and children's understanding of geometry. *International Journal of Psychology, 6,* 121–128.

Okonji, O. M. (1972). The development of logical thinking in pre-school Zambian children: Classification. Human Development Research Unit, Report no 23, University of Zambia.

Okonji, O. M. (1969a). Differential effects of rural and urban upbringing on the development of cognitive styles. *International Journal of Psychology, 4,* 293–305.

Okonji, O. M. (1970). The effect of special training on the classificatory behaviour of some Nigerian Ibo children. *British Journal of Educational Psychology, 40,* 21–26.

Okonji, O. M. (1969b). A grass-root approach to "revolution by education" in Africa. *Mawazo, 2,* 11–16.

Okonji, O. M. (1971b). Independence training and the development of cognitive style in Uganda. Presented at Universities of East Africa Social Sciences Conference, Kampala.

Okonji, O. M. (1974). Socio-economic background, race and audio-visual integration in children. In J. L. M. Dawson & W. Lonner (Eds). *Readings in cross-cultural psychology: Proceedings of the Inaugural Meeting of the International Association for Cross Cultural Psychology*. Hong Kong: University of Hong Kong Press.

Okorodudu, C. (1967). Achievement training and achievement motivation among the Kpelle in Liberia: A study of household structure antecedents. *Dissertation Abstracts, 29,* 1527–1529.

Olbrisch, M. (1977). Psychotherapeutic interventions in physical health. *American Psychologist, 32,* 761–777.

Oldendorf, W. H. (1980). *The quest for an image of brain*. New York: Raven Press.

Oldendorf, W. H., & Zabielski, W. (1982). The world divided: Your brain's split universe. *Science Digest, 3,* 56–59.

Oldfield, R. C., & Zangwill, O. L. (1942). Head's concept of the schema and its application in contemporary British psychology: Part III. Bartlett's theory of memory. *British Journal of Psychology, 33,* 113–129.

Olds, J. (1956). Pleasure centers in the brain. *Scientific American, 195,* 105–116.

Olds, J. (1958). Self-stimulation of the brain: Its use to study local effects of hunger, sex, and drugs. *Science, 127,* 315–324.

Olds, J., & Milner, P. (1954). Positive reinforcement produced by electrical stimulation of rat septal area and other regions of rat brain. *Journal of Comparative and Physiological Psychology, 47,* 419–427.

O'Leary, A. (1990). Stress, emotion, and human immune function. *Psychological Bulletin, 108,* 363–382.

O'Leary, K. D., Becker, W. C., Evans, M. B., & Saudargas, A. R. (1969). A token reinforcement program in a public school: A replication and systematic analysis. *Journal of Applied Behavior Analysis, 2,* 3–13.

O'Leary, K. D., & Drabman, R. (1971). Token reinforcement programs in the classroom: A review. *Psychological Bulletin, 75,* 379–398.

O'Leary, K. D., & O'Leary, S. G. (1972). *Classroom management: The successful use of behavior modification*. New York: Pergamon Press.

O'Leary, K. D., & Turkewitz, H. (1981). A comparative outcome study of behavioral marital therapy and communication therapy. *Journal of Marital and Family Therapy, 7,* 159–169.

O'Leary, K. D., & Wilson, G. T. (1975). *Behavior therapy*. Englewood Cliffs, N.J.: Prentice-Hall, 1975.

O'Leary, S. G., & Pelham, W. E. (1978). Behavior therapy and withdrawal of stimulant medication in hyperactive children. *Pediatrics, 61,* 211–217.

O'Leary, V. E. (1974). Some attitudinal barriers to occupational aspirations in women. *Psychological Bulletin, 81,* 809–826.

O'Leary, V. E., Unger, R. K., & Wallston, B. S. *Women, gender, and social psychology*. Hillsdale, N.J.: Erlbaum, in press.

Olin, H. (1976). Psychotherapy of the chronically suicidal patient. *American Journal of Psychotherapy, 30,* 570–575.

Oliven, J. F. (1965). *Sexual hygiene and pathology: A manual for the physician and the professions* (2nd ed.). Philadelphia, Pa.: Lippincott.

Oliver, J. (1973). *Climate and man's environment: An introduction to applied climatology*. New York: Wiley.

Olsen, M. (1965). Political assimilation, social opportunities, and political alienation. Unpublished doctoral dissertation, University of Michigan.

Olshansky, S. (1965). Stigma: Its meaning and some of its problems for vocational rehabilitation. *Rehabilitation Literature, 26,* 71–74.

Olson, D. H. (1970). Marital and family therapy: Integrative review and critique. *Journal of Marriage and Family Counseling, 32,* 501–538.

Olson, D. H. (Ed.). (1976). *Treating relationships.* Lake Mills, Iowa: Graphic.

Olson, D. H., & Sprenkle, D. H. (1976). Emerging trends in treating relationships. *Journal of Marriage and Family Counseling,* 317–329.

Olson, H. A. (1979). *Early recollections: Their use in diagnosis and psychotherapy.* Springfield, Ill.: Thomas.

Olson, J. M., & Zanna, M. P. (1979). A new look at selective exposure. *Journal of Experimental Social Psychology, 15,* 1–15.

Olson, M. (1965). *The Logic of collective action: Public goods and the theory of groups,* Cambridge, MA: Harvard University Press.

Olson, R. P., Ganley, R., Devine, V. T., & Dorsey, G. C., Jr. (1981). Long-term effects of behavioral versus insight-oriented therapy with inpatient alcoholics. *Journal of Consulting and Clinical Psychology, 49,* 866–877.

Olson, T. D. (1973). Family constellation as related to personality and achievement. Ph. D. dissertation, Florida State University.

Olton, D. S. (1977). Spatial memory. *Scientific American, 236*(6), 82–98.

Olton, D. S., Becker, J. T., & Handelmann, G. (1979). Hippocampus, space, and memory. *The Behavioral Brain Sciences, 2,* 313–365.

Olwens, D. (1969). Prediction of aggression. Scandinavian Test Corporation. Reported in E. R. Hilgard et al *Introduction to psychology* (7th ed.). New York: Harcourt Brace Jovanovich, 1979.

Olwens, D. (1977). A critical analysis of the "modern" interactionist position. In D. Magnusson & N. S. Endler (Eds.), *Personality at the crossroads: Current issues in interactional psychology.* Hillsdale, N.J.: Erlbaum.

Olweus, D. (1979). Stability of aggressive reaction patterns in males: A review. *Psychological Bulletin, 86,* 852–875.

Ombredane, A. (1951). Principes pour une étude psychologique des noirs du Congo Beige. *Année Psychologique, 30,* 521–547.

Ombredane, A. (1954). L'exploration de la mentalité des noirs congolais au moyen d'une épreuve projective. Le Congo TAT. *Mémoires de l'Institut Royal Colonial Beige. Section des Sciences Morales et Politiques, 37,* 1–243.

Ombredane, A. (1956). Etude psychologique des noirs Asalampasu. I. Le comportement intéllectuel dans l'épreuve du matrix-couleur. *Memoires de l'Academie Royale des Sciences Coloniales. Ire Classe, 6,* fasc. 3.

Ombredane, A., Bertelson, P., & Beniest-Noirot, E. (1958). Speed and accuracy of performance of an African native population and of Belgian children on a paper and pencil perceptual test. *Journal of Social Psychology, 47,* 327–337.

Ombredane, A., & Robaye, F. (1953). Le problème de l'épuration des résultats des tests d'intelligence étudiés sur le matrix-couleur. Comparaison des techniques de reduplication et d'explication. *Bulletin du Centre d'Etudes et Recherches Psychotechniques, 32,* 3–17.

Ombredane, A., Robaye, F., & Plumail, H. (1956). Résultats d'une application répétée du matrix-couleur à une population de noirs congolais. *Bulletin du Centre d'Etudes et Recherches Psychotechniques, 6,* 149–160.

Ombredane, A., Robaye, F., & Robaye, E. (1957). Etude psychotechnique des Baluba. Application expérimentale du test d'intelligence matrix 38 à 485 noirs Baluba. *Mémoires de l'Academie Royale des Sciences Coloniales, Ire Classe, 6,* fasc. 5.

Ombredane, A., Robaye, F., & Robaye, E. (1958). Etude psychologique des noirs Asalampasu. II. Analyse du comportement dans le test des relations spatiales de Minnesota. *Mémoires de l'Academie Royale des Sciences Coloniales, Ire Classe, 6,* fasc. 6.

Omer, H. (1981). Paradoxical treatments: A unified concept. *Psychotherapy: Theory, Research, and Practice, 18,* 320–324.

O'Neill, P. (1989). Responsible to whom? Responsible for what? Some ethical issues in community intervention. *American Journal of Community Psychology, 17,* 323–342.

O'Neill, W. M. (1958). Basic issues in perceptual theory. *Psychological Review, 65,* 348–361.

Ono, H. (1969). Apparent distance as a function of familiar size. *Journal of Experimental Psychology, 79,* 109–115.

O'Piper, A., & Langer, E. (1984). Aging and mindful control. In M. Baltes (Ed.), *Aging and control.* Hillsdale, NJ: Erbaum.

Opjordsmoen, S., & Retterstol, N. (1991). Delusional disorder: The predictive validity of the concept. *Acta Psychiatry, 84*(3), 250–254.

Oppenheim, F. (1961). *Dimensions of freedom.* New York: St. Martins Press.

Orano, P. (1902). *Psicologia sociale.* Bari, Italy: Laterza.

Orbach, J. (Ed.). (1982). *Neuropsychology after Lashley.* Hillsdale, N.J. Erlbaum.

Orbach, S. (1978). Social dimensions in compulsive eating in women. *Psychotherapy: Theory, Research, and Practice, 15,* 186–189.

Orem, R. C. (1971). *Learning to see—Seeing to learn.* Johnstown, Pa.: Fax.

Orendi, B. (1979). Die Arbeitssituation von Lokomotivführern. *Schweizerische Zeitschrift für Psychologie, 38,* 228–238.

Organization of Economic Cooperation and Development. (1976). *Measuring social well-being.* Paris: OECD.

Orgler, H. (1965/1967). *Alfred Adler: The man and his work.* New York: Capricorn.

Orlansky, H. (1949). Infant care and personality. *Psychological Review, 46,* 1–48.

Orley, J. (1970). *Culture and mental illness.* Nairobi: East African Publishing House.

Orlinsky, D., & Howard, K. (1978). The relation of process to outcome in psychotherapy. In S. L. Garfield & A. E. Bergin (Eds.), *Handbook of psychotherapy and behavior change: An empirical analysis* (2nd ed.). New York: Wiley.

Orlinsky, D. E., & Howard, K. I. (1986). Process and outcome in psychotherapy. In S. L. Garfield & A. E. Bergin (Eds.), *Handbook of psychotherapy and behavior change* (3rd ed., pp. 283–330). New York: Wiley.

Orlinsky, D. E., & Howard, K. I. (1987). A generic model of psychotherapy. *Journal of Integrative and Eclectic Psychotherapy, 6,* 6–26.

Orlofsky, J. L., Marcia, J. E., & Lesser, I. M. (1973). Ego identity status and the intimacy versus isolation crisis in young adulthood. *Journal of Personality and Social Psychology, 27,* 211–219.

Orme-Johnson, D. W. (1973). Autonomic stability and Transcendental Meditation. *Psychosomatic Medicine, 35,* 341–349.

Orme-Johnson, D. W. (1987). Medical care utilization and the Transcendental Meditation *program. Psychosomatic Medicine, 49,* 493–507.

Orme-Johnson, D. W. (1988). The cosmic psyche—An introduction to Maharishi's Vedic psychology: The fulfillment of modern psychology. *Modern Science and Vedic Science, 2,* 113–163.

Orme-Johnson, D. W., Alexander, C. N., & Davies, J. L. (1990). The effects of the Maharishi technology of the unified field: Reply to a methodological critique. *Journal of Conflict Resolution, 34,* 756–768.

Orme-Johnson, D. W., Alexander, C. N., Davies, J. L., Chandler, H. M., & Larimore, W. E. (1988). International peace project in the Middle East: The effects of the Maharishi technology of the unified field. *Journal of Conflict Resolution, 32,* 776–812.

Orme-Johnson, D. W., & Dillbeck, M. C. (1993). Higher states of collective consciousness. In J. Gackenbach, H. Hunt, & C. N. Alexander (Eds.), *Higher states of consciousness: Theoretical and experimental perspectives.* New York: Plenum.

Orme-Johnson, D. W., Dillbeck, M. C., Alexander, C. N., Chandler, H. M., & Cranson, R. W., (1989). *Time series impact assessment analysis of reduced international conflict and terrorism: effects of large assemblies of participants in the Transcendental Meditation and TM-Sidhi program.* Paper presented to the American Political Science Association, Atlanta.

Orme-Johnson, D. W., Dillbeck, M. C., Alexander, C. N., Gelderloos, P., Boyer, R. M., & Charleston, P. (in press). *The Vedic psychology of Maharishi Mahesh Yogi.* Fairfield, IA: Maharishi International University Press.

Orme-Johnson, D. W., & Haynes, C. T. (1981). EEG phase coherence, pure consciousness, and TM-Sidhi experiences. *International Journal of Neuroscience, 13,* 211–217.

Orme-Johnson, D. W., Wallace, R. K., Dillbeck, M. C., Alexander, C. N., & Ball, O. E. (1991). Improved functional organization of the brain through the Maharishi technology of the unified field as indicated by changes in EEG coherence and its cognitive correlates: A proposed model of higher states of consciousness. In R. A. Chalmers, G. Clements, H. Schenkluhn, & M. Weinless (Eds.), *Scientific research on Maharishi's Transcendental Meditation and TM-Sidhi programme: Collected papers* (Vol. 4, pp. 2245–2266). The Netherlands: Maharishi Vedic University Press.

Ormrod, J. E. (1990). *Human learning: Theories, principles, and educational applications.* Columbus, OH: Merrill.

Orne, M. T. (1951). The mechanisms of hypnotic age regression: An experimental study. *Journal of Abnormal and Social Psychology, 46,* 213–225.

Orne, M. T. (1970). Hypnosis, motivation and the ecological validity of the psychological experiment. In W. J. Arnold & M. M. Page (Eds.), *Nebraska Symposium on Motivation.* Lincoln, Neb.: University of Nebraska Press.

Orne, M. T. (1979). On the simulating subject as a quasi-control group in hypnosis research: What, why, and how. In E. Fromm & R. E. Shor (Eds.), *Hypnosis: Developments in research and new perspectives.* New York: Aldine.

Orne, M. T. (1979). The use and misuse of hypnosis in court. *International Journal of Clinical and Experimental Hypnosis, 27,* 311–341.

Orne, M. T., Soskis, D., Dinges, D., & Orne, E. (1984). Hypnotically induced testimony. In G. Wells, & E. Loftus, (Eds.), *Eyewitness testimony: Psychological perspectives* (pp. 171–213). New York: Cambridge University Press.

Ornstein, A. C. (1982). Curriculum contrasts: A historical overview. *Phi Delta Kappan, 63,* 404–408.

Ornstein, R. (1980/1972). *The psychology of consciousness.* Harmondsworth, England: Penguin Books.

Ornstein, R., & Swencionis, C. (Eds.). (1991). *The healing brain: A scientific reader.* New York: Guilford.

Ornstein, R. E. (1977). *The psychology of consciousness* (2nd ed.). New York: Harcourt Brace Jovanovich. (Original work published 1972)

Ornstein, R. E. (Ed.). (1973). *The nature of human consciousness: A book of readings.* San Francisco: Freeman.

Orr, L., & Ray, S. (1977). *Rebirthing in the new age.* Millbrae, Calif.: Celestial Arts.

Ortega, P., & Lopez, M. (1953). La medición psicologica en México. In Universidad Nacional Autonoma de México (Ed.), *Memoria del Congreso Científico Méxicano,* Ciencias de la Educación, Psicologia, Fifosofia, Vol. 15. Mexico, D. F.

Ortiz, D. (1990). *Gambling scams.* New York: Carol.

Ortner, S. S., & Whitehead, H. (Eds.). (1981). *Sexual meanings: The cultural construction of gender and sexuality.* Cambridge, UK: Cambridge University Press.

Orton, J. L. (1966). The Orton–Gillingham approach. In J. Money (Ed.), *The disabled reader.* Baltimore, Md.: Johns Hopkins Press.

Orton, S. T. (1925). "Word-blindness" in school children. *Archives of Neurology and Psychiatry, 14,* 582–615.

Orton, S. T. (1937). *Reading, writing, and speech problems in children.* New York: Norton.

Osborn, A. F. (1963/1953). *Applied imagination* (3rd ed.). New York: Scribners.

Osborn, R. N., & Hunt, J. G. (1975). An adaptive-reactive theory of leadership. *Organization and Administrative Sciences, 6,* 27–44.

Osborn, S. G., & West, D. J. (1980). Do young delinquents really reform? *Journal of adolescence, 3,* 99–114.

Osborne, H. (1970). *The art of appreciation.* London: Oxford University Press.

Osborne, R. T., Noble, C. E., & Weyl, N. (1978). *Human variation.* London: Academic Press.

Oscar-Berman, M. (1980). Neuropsychological consequences of long-term chronic alcoholism. *American Scientist, 68,* 410–419.

Oseretzky, N. (1930). *Psychomotorik,* Leipzig: Barth.

Osgood, C. E. (1962). *An alternative to war or surrender.* Urbana, Ill.: University of Illinois Press.

Osgood, C. E. (1971). Conservative words and radical sentences in the semantics of international politics. In G. Abcarian & J. W. Soule (Eds.), *Social psychology and political behavior.* Columbus, Ohio: Merrill.

Osgood, C. E. (1979). GRIT for MBFR: A proposal for unfreezing force-level postures in Europe. *Peace Research Reviews, 8*(2), 77–94.

Osgood, C. E. (1980). GRIT: A strategy for survival in mankind's nuclear age? Presented at the Pugwash Conference on New Directions in Disarmament, Johnson Foundation, Racine, Wis., June.

Osgood, C. E. (1953). *Method and theory in experimental psychology.* New York: Oxford University Press.

Osgood, C. E. (1952). The nature and measurement of meaning. *Psychological Bulletin, 49,* 197–237.

Osgood, C. E. (1959). The representation model and relevant research methods. In I. de Sola Pool (Ed.), *Trends in content analysis.* Urbana, Ill.: University of Illinois Press.

Osgood, C. E., May, W. H., & Miron, M. S. (1975). *Cross-cultural universals of affective meaning.* Urbana, Ill.: University of Illinois Press.

Osgood, C. E., & Richards, M. M. (1973). From Yang and Yin to *and* or *but. Language, 39,* 380–412.

Osgood, E. C. & Sebeok, T. A. (Eds.) (1954). *Psycholinguistics. A survey of theory and research problems.* Bloomington, Ind.: Indiana University Press.

Osgood, C. E., Suci, G. J., & Tannenbaum, P. H. (1957). *The measurement of meaning.* Urbana, Ill.: University of Illinois Press.

Osgood, C. E., & Tannenbaum, P. H. (1955). The principle of congruity in the prediction of attitude change. *Psychological Review, 62,* 42–55.

O'Shea, J. A., & Porter, S. F. (1981). Double-blind study of children with hyperkinetic syndrome treated with multi-allergen extract sublingually. *Journal Of Learning Disabilities, 14,* 189–191.

Oshman, H., & Manosevitz, M. (1976). Father-absence: Effects of stepfathers upon psychosocial development in males. *Developmental Psychology, 12,* 479—480.

Osipow, S. H. (1982). Counseling psychology: Applications in the world of work. *The Counseling Psychologist,* in press.

Osipow, S. H. (1980). *Manual for the Career Decision Scale* (2nd ed.). Columbus, Ohio: Marathon.

Osipow, S. H. (1979). Occupational mental health: Another role for counseling psychologists. *Counseling Psychologist, 8,* 65–70.

Osipow, S. H. (1983/1968). *Theories of career development.* Englewood Cliffs, N.J.: Prentice-Hall.

Osipow, S. H. (1980). Will the real counseling psychologist please stand up? In J. M. Whiteley & B. R. Fretz (Eds.), *The present and future of counseling psychology.* Monterey, Calif.: Brooks/Cole.

Osipow, S. H., Carney, G. G., Winer, J., Yanico, B., & Koschier, M. (1976). *The career decision scale.* Columbus, Ohio: Marathon.

Osler, W. (1910). The faith that heals. *British Medical Journal, 1.*

Osler, W. (1897). *Lectures on angina pectoris and allied states.* New York: Appleton.

Osmond, H. (1973). Come home psychiatry! The megavitamin treatment and the medical model. *Psychiatric Opinion, 10,* 14–23.

Osofsky, J. (Ed.). (1979). *Handbook of infant development.* New York: Wiley.

Osofsky, J., & Comers, K. (1979). Mother–infant interaction: An integrative view of a complex system. In J. Osofsky (Ed.), *Handbook of infant development.* New York: Wiley.

OSS Assessment Staff. (1948). *Assessment of men.* New York: Rinehart.

Ostapiuk, E., Morrison, N., & Porteous, M. A. (1974). A brief numerical summary of some family variables among boys in an assessment centre. *Community Schools Gazette* (Ostivestry, Salop, England), *67*(10), 571–580.

Oster, H., & Ekman, P. (1978). Facial behavior in child development. *Minnesota Symposium of Child Psychology, 11,* 231–276.

Ostheimer, J. M. (1969). Measuring achievement motivation among the Chagga of Tanzania. *Journal of Social Psychology, 78,* 17–30.

Ostrom, T. M. (1977). Between theory and within theory conflict in explaining context effects in impression formation. *Journal of Experimental Social Psychology, 13,* 492–503.

Ostrom, T. M. (1968). The emergence of attitude theory: 1930–1950. In A. Greenwald, T. Brock, & T. Ostrom (Eds.), *Psychological foundations of attitudes.* New York: Academic Press.

Ostrom, T. M. (1971). Item construction in attitude measurement. *Public Opinion Quarterly, 35,* 593–600.

Osuch, J. R. (1974). Psychomotor development and the postnatal fate of children from multiple pregnancy. *Acta Geneticae Medicae et Gemellologiae* (Bologna), *22*(suppl), 113–119.

O'Sullivan, M., & Guilford, J. P. (1975). Six factors of behavioral cognition. *Journal of Educational Measurement, 12,* 255–271.

Oswald, I. (1957). The EEG, visual imagery and attention. *Quarterly Journal of Experimental Psychology, 9,* 113–118.

Otis, A. S. (1918). An absolute point scale for the group measurement of intelligence. *Journal of Educational Psychology, 9,* 238–261, 333–348.

Otis, A. S. (1920). *Otis Group Intelligence Scale.* Yonkers, N.Y.: World.

Otis, A. S., & Lennon, R. T. (1978). *Otis–Lennon School Ability Test.* New York: Psychological Corp.

Otis, J. L., & Leukart, R. H. (1954/1948). *Job evaluation: A basis for sound wage administration.* Englewood Cliffs, N.J.: Prentice-Hall.

Otis, L. S. (1974). If well integrated but anxious try TM. *Psychology Today, 7,* 45–46.

Ottenberg, D. J. (1974). Addiction as metaphor. *Alcohol, Health and Research World,* Fall experimental issue, 18–20.

Otto, H. A. (Ed.). (1972). *Love today: A new exploration.* New York: Association Press.

Otto, H. J., & Sanders, D. C. (1964). *Elementary school organization and administration* (4th ed.). New York: Appleton.

Otto, L. B., Call, V. R. A., & Spenner, K. I. (1981). *Design for a study of entry into careers,* Vol. I. Boston: Lexington Books.

Otto, R. (1923). *The idea of the holy.* London: Oxford University Press.

Otto, T., Eichenbaum, H. Wiener, S. I., & Wible, C. G. (1991). Learning-related patterns of CA1 spike trains parallel stimulation parameters optimal for inducing hippocampal long-term potentiation. *Hippocampus, 1,* 181–192.

Ottoson, J. O. (1977). *Transcendental Medtation* (Report No. D:nr 3-9-1194n3). Sweden: National Health Board.

Ouchi, W. (1981). *Theory Z: How American business can meet the Japanese challenge.* Reading, Mass: Addison-Wesley.

Ounsted, C., Oppenheimer, R., & Lindsay, J. (1974). Aspects of bonding failure: The psychopathology and psychotherapeutic treatment of families of battered children. *Developmental Medicine and Child Neurology, 16,* 447–456.

Ourth, L., & Brown, K. B. (1961). Inadequate mothering and disturbance in the neonatal period. *Child Development, 32,* 287–295.

Over, R. (1981b). Employment prospects for psychology graduates in Australia. *Australian Psychologist, 16,* 335–345.

Over, R. (1981a). Impending crises for psychology departments in Australian universities. *Australian Psychologist, 16,* 221–233.

Overall, J. E., & Gorham, D. R. (1962). The brief psychiatric rating scale. *Psychological Reports, 10,* 799–812.

Overmier, J. B. (1968). Interference with avoidance behavior: Failure to avoid traumatic shock. *Journal of Experimental Psychology, 78,* 340–343.

Overmier, J. B. (1979). Punishment. In M. E. Bitterrnan, V. M. Lo-Lordo, J. B. Overmier, & M. E. Rashotte (Eds.), *Animal learning: Survey and analysis.* (pp. 279–312). New York: Plenum.

Overmier, J. B. (1985). Toward a reanalysis of the casual structure of the learned helplessness syndrome. In F. R. Brush & J. B. Overmier (Eds.), *Affect, conditioning, and cognition: Essays on the determinants of behavior* (pp. 211–227). Hillsdale, NJ: Erlbaum.

Overmier, J. B. (1988). Psychological determinants of when stressers stress. In D. H. Hallhammer, I. Florin, & I.-L. Weiner (Eds.), *Neurobiological approaches to the human disease* (pp. 235–259). Toronto: Hans Huber.

Overmier, J. B., & Brackbill, R. M. (1977). On the independence of stimulus evocation of fear and fear evocation of responses. *Behavior Research and Therapy, 15,* 51–56.

Overmier, J. B. & Bull, J. A. (1969). On the independence of stimulus control of avoidance, *Journal of Experimental Psychology, 12,* 464–467.

Overmier, J. B., Bull, J. A., & Trapold, M. A. (1971). Discriminative cue properties of different fears and their role in response selection. *Journal of Comparative and Physiological Psychology,* 478–482.

Overmier, J. B., & Burke, P. D. (Eds.). (1992). *Animal models of human pathology: A bibliography of a quarter century of behavioral research, 1967–1992* (Bibliographies in Psychology, No. 12). Washington, DC: American Psychological Association.

Overmier, J. B., Ehrman, R. N., & Vaughn, J. C. (1983). Pavlovian processes do mediate control of the "advance" response strategy. *Learning and Motivation, 14,* 182–203.

Overmier, J. B., & Hallhammer, D. (1988). The teamed helplessness psychological model of human depression. In P. Soubrie, P. Simon, & D. Widlocher (Eds.), *Animal models of psychiatric disorders: Vol. II. An inquiry into schizophrenia and depression* (pp. 177–202). Basel: Karger.

Overmier, J. B., & Lawry, J. A. (1979). Pavlovian conditioning and the mediation of avoidance behavior. In G. Bower (Ed.), *The psychology of learning and motivation* (Vol. 13, pp. 1–55). New York: Academic.

Overmier, J. B., & Papini, M. R. (1986). Factors modulating the effects of teleost telencephalon ablation upon retention, reteaming, and extinction of instrumental avoidance behavior. *Behavioral Neuroscience,* 190–199.

Overmier, J. B., & Patterson, J. (1988). Animal models of psychopathology. In P. Soubrie, P. Simon, & D. Widlocher (Eds.), *Animal models of psychiatric disorders, YDU selected models of agression and psychosis* (pp. 1–35). Basel: Karger.

Overmier, J. B., Payne, R. J., Brackbill, R. M., Linder, B., & Lawry, J. A. (1979). On the mechanism of the post-asymptotic decrement phenomenon. *Acta Neurobioloqiae Experimentalis, 39,* 603–620.

Overmier, J. B., & Seligman, M. E. P. (1967). Effects of inescapable shock upon subsequent escape and avoidance learning. *Journal of Comparative and Physiological Psychology, 63,* 23–33.

Overstreet, D. H., & Russell, R. W. (1984). Animal models of memory disorders. In N. W. Bond, (Ed.), *Animal models in psychopathology.* New York: Academic.

Overton, D. A. (1964). State dependent or "dissociated" learning produced with pentobarbitol. *Journal of Comparative and Physiological Psychology, 57,* 3–12.

Overton, W. F., & Reese, H. W. (1973). Models of development: Methodological implications. In J. R. Nesselroade & H. W. Reese (Eds.), *Life-span developmental psychology: Methodological issues.* New York: Academic Press.

Ovesey, L. (1965). *Homosexuality and pseudohomosexuality.* New York: Science House.

Owen, A. R. G. (1971). *Hysteria, hypnosis and the healing: The work of J-M Charcot.* New York: Gannett.

Owens, J. E., Cook, E. W., & Stevenson, I. (1990). Features of "near-death experience" in relation to whether or not patients were near death. *Lancet,* (336), 1175–1177.

Owens, W. A. (1966). Age and mental abilities: A second adult follow-up. *Journal of Educational Psychology, 57,* 311–325.

Owens, W. A. (1976). Background data. In M. D. Dunnette (Ed.), *Handbook of industrial and organizational psychology.* Chicago: Rand-McNally.

Pace, C. R., & Stern, G. G. (1958). An approach to the measurement of psychological characteristics of college environments. *Journal of Educational Psychology, 49,* 269–277.

Pacini, A., & Martinotti, A. (1975). Birth order and alcoholism: A controlled statistical investigation. *Lavora Neuropsichiatrico, 57,* 261–290.

Packard, V. (1957). *The hidden persuaders,* New York: McKay.

Packer, C. (1977). Reciprocal altruism in *Papio anubis. Nature, 265,* 441–443.

Padilla, A. M. (1980). Notes on the history of Hispanic psychology. *Hispanic Journal of the Behavioral Sciences, 2*(2), 109–128.

Pafford, M. K. (1970). Creative activities and "peak" experiences. *British Journal of Educational Psychology, 40,* 283–290.

Pagano, R. R., Rose, R. M., Stivers, R. M., & Warrenbtirg, S. (1976). Sleep during Transcendental Meditation. *Science, 191,* 308–310.

Page, R. C. (1978). The social learning process of severely disabled group counseling participants. *Psychosocial Rehabilitation Journal 2,* 28–36.

Page, R. C. (1979). Developmental stages of unstructured counseling groups with prisoners. *Small Group Behavior, 10,* 271–279.

Page, R. C. (1979). Major ethical issues in public offender counseling. *Counseling and Values, 24,* 33–41.

Page, R. C. (1979). Staff and resident involvement in a therapeutic community: For better or worse? *The Personnel and Guidance Journal 57,* 361–364.

Page, R. C. (1980). Marathon groups: Counseling the imprisoned drug abuser. *The International Journal of the Addictions, 15,* 765–770.

Page, R. C. (1981). Client rights and agency demands: The ethical tightrope of the offender counselor. *Counseling and Values, 26,* 55–62.

Page, R. C., King, M., Pass, R., & Glenn, D. (1980). A comparison of the parents of male inmates with and without drug abuse problems. *Journal of Offender Counseling, Services and Rehabilitation, 5,* 41–54.

Page, R. C., & Kubiak, L. (1978). Marathon groups: Facilitating the personal growth of imprisoned, black female heroin abusers. *Small Group Behavior, 9,* 409–417.

Page, R. C., & Mannion, J. (1980). Marathon group therapy with former drug users. *Journal of Employment Counseling, 17,* 307–314.

Page, R. C., Mannion, J., & Wattenbarger, W. (1980). Marathon group counseling: A study with imprisoned male former drug users. *Small Group Behavior, 11,* 399–410.

Page, R. C., & Miehl, H. (1982). Marathon groups: Facilitating the personal growth of male illicit drug users. *The International Journal of the Addictions, 17,* 393–397.

Page, R. C., & Myrick, R. D. (1977). Perceptions of imprisoned drug abusers: Implications for counseling. *Rehabilitation Counseling Bulletin, 20,* 304–308.

Page, R. C., & Powell, G. (1981). Family counseling with illicit drug users. *Journal of Offender Counseling, 1,* 48–57.

Page, R. C., & Sanders, J. (1979). Some characteristics of imprisoned, female drug abusers and implications for rehabilitation. *Rehabilitation Counseling Bulletin, 23,* 59–63.

Page, R. C., Smith, M., & Beamish, P. (1977). Establishing a drug rehabilitation center. *The Personnel and Guidance Journal, 56,* 180–184.

Page, R. C., & Wattenbarger, W. (1981). A comparison of the problems of the family members of male prison inmates with and without drug abuse problems. *The International Journal of the Addictions, 16,* 1241–1246.

Pagelow, M. D. (1984). *Family violence.* New York: Praeger.

Paholpak, S. (1990). Delusion of parasitosis: A report of ten cases at Srinagarind Hospital. *Journal of the Medical Association of Thailand, 73*(2), 111–114.

Paige, M. (Ed.). (1992). *Education for the intercultural experience.* Yarmouth, ME: Intercultural.

Paillard, J. (1955). Réflexes et régulations d'origine proprioceptive chez l'homme. Étude neurophysiologique et psychophysiologique. Doctor-of-science thesis, Paris.

Paillard, J. (1960). The patterning of skilled movements. *Handbook of Physiology. Section I, Neurophysiology, 3,* (67), 1679–1708.

Paillard, J. (1974). Nervous programmed activity. *Brain Research, 71,* 189–572.

Paillard, J. (1976). Tonus, posture et mouvement. In C. Kayser (Ed.), *Traité de physiologie,* Vol. III. Paris: Flammarion.

Paillard, J. (1978). Pyramidal micro-connexions and motor control. *Journal of Physiology* (Paris), *74,* 152–347.

Paine, W. S. (1981). The burnout syndrome in context. In J. W. Jones (Ed.), *The burnout syndrome: Current research, theory interventions.* Park Ridge, Ill.: London House Press.

Painter, G., & Vernon, S. (1981). Primary relationship therapy. In R. J. Corsini (Ed.), *Handbook of innovative psychotherapies.* New York: Wiley.

Pais, A. (1991). *Neils Bohr's times, in physics, philosophy and polity.* Oxford, UK: Clarendon Press.

Paivio, A. (1965). Personality and audience influence. In B. A. Maher (Ed.)., *Progress in experimental personality research,* Vol. 2. New York: Academic Press.

Paivio, A. (1969). Mental imagery in associative learning and memory. *Psychological Review, 76,* 241–263.

Paivio, A. (1971). *Imagery and verbal processes.* New York: Holt, Rinehart & Winston.

Paivio, A. (1973). Psychophysiological correlates of imagery. In F. J. McGuigan & R. A. Schoonover (Eds.), *The psychophysiology of thinking.* New York: Academic Press.

Paivio, A. (1975). Perceptual comparisons through the mind's eye. *Memory and Cognition, 3,* 635–647.

Paivio, A. (1976). Images, propositions, and knowledge. In J. M. Nicholas (Ed.), *Images, perception, and knowledge.* Dordrecht, Netherlands: Reidel.

Paivio, A. (1982). The empirical case for dual coding. In J. Yuille (Ed.), *Imagery, cognition and memory.* Hillsdale, N.J.: Erlbaum.

Paivio, A., & Begg, I. (1981). *The psychology of language.* Englewood Cliffs, N.J.: Prentice-Hall.

Paivio, A., & Lambert, W. (1981). Dual coding and bilingual memory. *Journal of Verbal Learning and Verbal Behavior, 20,* 532–539.

Paivio, A., & Linde, J. (1982). Imagery, memory, and the brain. *Canadian Journal of Psychology, 36,* 243–272.

Paivio, A., & Okovita, H. W. (1971). Word imagery modalities and associative learning in blind and sighted subjects. *Journal of Verbal Learning and Verbal Behavior, 10,* 506–510.

Pakes, E. H. (1975). Dependence and psychotherapy—Developmental considerations. *American Journal of Psychotherapy, 29,* 128–133.

Palazzoli, M. (1978). *Self-starvation.* New York: Aronson.

Palazzoli, M., Boscolo, L., & Cecchin, G. (1978). *Paradox and counterparadox.* New York: Aronson.

Palazzoli, M., Boscolo, L., Cecchin, G., & Prata, G. (1976). Hypothesizing-circularity-neutrality: Three guidelines for the conduction of the session. *Family Process, 19,* 3–12.

Palermo, D. S. (1971). Is a scientific revolution taking place in psychology? *Science Studies, 1,* 135–155.

Palermo, D. S. (1978). *Psychology of language.* Glenview, Ill.: Scott, Foresman.

Palinurus, C. C. (1945). *The unquiet grave.* New York: Harper.

Pallone, N. J. (1977). Counseling psychology: Toward an empirical definition. *The Counseling Psychologist, 1,* 29–32.

Palmblad, H., Cantell, K., Strander, H., Froberg, J., Karlson, C., Levi, L., Gronstrom, M., & Unger, P. (1976). Stressor exposure and immunological response in man: Interferon producing capacity and phagocytosis. *Journal of Psychosomatic Research, 20,* 193–199.

Palmblad, J. (1981). Stress and immunologic competence: Studies in man. In R. Ader (Ed.), *Psychoneuroimmunology.* New York: Academic Press.

Palmer, D. C., & Donahoe, J. W. (in press). Essentialism and selectionism in cognitive science and behavior analysis. *American Psychologist.*

Palmer, D. C., & Donahoe, J. W. (in press). Selectionism and essentialism in behaviorism and cognitive science. *American Psychologist.*

Palmer, D. J. (1980). Factors to be considered in placing handicapped children in regular classes. *Journal of School Psychology, 18,* 163–169.

Palmer, F. H., & Anderson, L. W. (1979). Long term gains from early intervention: Findings from longitudinal studies. In E. Zigler & J. Valentine (Eds.), *Project Head Start: A legacy of the war on poverty.* New York: Free Press.

Palmer, J. (1971). Scoring in ESP tests as a function of belief in ESP. Part I: The sheep–goat effect. *Journal of the American Society for Psychical Research, 65,* 373—408.

Palmer, J. (1978). Extrasensory perception: Research findings. In S. Krippner (Ed.), *Advances in parapsychological research II: Extrasensory perception.* New York: Plenum.

Palmer, S. (1980). *A primer of eclectic psychotherapy.* Monterey, Calif.: Brooks/Cole.

Palmer, T. (1975). Martinson revisited. *Journal of Research in Crime and Delinquency, 12,* 133–152.

Palmore, E. (1979). Predictors of successful aging. *The Gerontologist, 5,* 427–431.

Palmore, E. (Ed.). (1980). *International handbook on aging: Contemporary developments and research.* Westport, Conn.: Greenwood Press.

Palmore, E., Busse, E., Maddox, G., Nowlin, J., & Siegler, I. (1985). *Normal aging III.* Durham, NC: Duke University Press.

Pan, S. (1964). *Educational psychology.* Beijing: People's Educational Publishers.

Pan, S., & Jing, Q. (Eds.). (1992). *Chinese encyclopedia: Psychology.* Beijing, People's Republic of China: Chinese Encyclopedia.

Panagiotou, N., & Sheikh, A. A. (1977). The image and the unconscious. *International Journal of Social Psychiatry, 23,* 169–186.

Panda, I. C., & Bartel, N. C. (1972). Teacher perception of exceptional children. *Journal of Special Education, 6,* 261–265.

Pandey, J. (Ed.). (1988). *Psychology in India: The state-of-the-art.* New Delhi: Sage.

Pankratz, L. D. (1981). A review of the Munchausen syndrome. *Clinical Psychology Review, 1,* 65–78.

Pankratz, L. D., & Lipkin, J. (1978). The transient patient in a psychiatric ward: Summering in Oregon. *Journal of Operational Psychiatry, 9,* 42–47.

Pankratz, L. D., & Taplin, J. R. (1982). Issues in psychological assessment. In J. R. McNamara & A. G. Barclay (Eds.), *Critical issues, trends, and developments in professional psychology.* New York: Praeger.

Panzetta, A. F. (1971). *Community mental health: Myth and reality.* Philadelphia, Pa.: Lea & Febiger.

Paolino, T., & McCrady, B. S. (Eds.). (1978). *Marriage and marital therapy: Psychoanalytic, behavioral and systems therapy perspectives.* New York: Brunner/Mazel.

Paolino, T. J., Jr. (1981). *Psychoanalytic psychotherapy: Theory, technique, therapeutic relationship and treatability.* New York: Brunner/Mazel.

Papageorgis, D. (1963). Bartlett effect and the persistence of induced opinion change. *Journal of Abnormal and Social Psychology, 67,* 61–67.

Papagno, C., Valentine, T., & Baddeley, A. D. (1991). Phonological short-term memory and foreign-language vocabulary learning. *Journal of Memory and Language, 30,* 331–347.

Papalia, D. (1972). The status of several conservation abilities across the lifespan. *Human Development, 15,* 229–243.

Papalia, D., & Bielby, D. D. (1974). Cognitive functioning in middle aged and elderly adults: A review of research based on Piaget's theory. *Human Development, 17,* 424–443.

Papanek, H. (1961). Individual psychology today. *American Journal of Psychotherapy, 15,* 4–26.

Papez, J. W. (1937). A proposed mechanism of emotion. *Archives of Neurology and Psychiatry, 38,* 725–744.

Papez, J. W. (1964). A proposed mechanism of emotion. In R. L. Isaacson (Ed.), *Basic readings in neuropsychology.* New York; Evanston, Ill.; London: Harper & Row.

Parad, H. J. (1965). *Crisis intervention: Selected readings.* New York: Family Service Association of America.

Parameswaran, E. G. (1972). Developmental psychology. In S. K. Mitra (Ed.), *A survey of research in psychology.* Bombay: Popular Prakashan.

Parameswaran, E. G. (1978). Psychology in Indian universities. *Manas 25,* 69–79.

Parameswaran, E. G., & Ravichandra, K. (in press). *Experimental psychology—A laboratory manual.* New Delhi: Sema.

Parameswaran, E. G., & Shalini, B. (Eds.). (1979). *Developmental psychology.* New Delhi: Light & Life.

Parameswaran, E. G.,& Taramunohar, R. B. (1968). *Manual of experimental psychology.* Bombay: Lalvani.

Paraskevopuulos, J., & Hunt, J. McV. (1971). Object construction and imitation under differing conditions of rearing. *Journal of Genetic Psychology, 119,* 301–321.

Pareek, U. (Ed.). (1980). *A survey of research in psychology.* Bombay: Popular Prakashan.

Pareek, U. (Ed.). (1981). *A survey of research in psychology, 1971–76, Part II.* Bombay: Popular Prakashan.

Pareek, U., & Rao, T. (1980). Cross-cultural surveys and interviewing. In H. Triandis & J. Berry (Eds.), *Handbook of cross-cultural psychology,* Vol. 2. Boston: Allyn & Bacon.

Parens, H., & Saul, L. (1971). *Dependence in man.* New York: International Universities Press.

Paris, S. G., & Lindauer, B. K. (1976). The role of inference in children's comprehension and memory for sentences. *Cognitive Psychology, 8,* 217–227.

Parish, E. (1914). *Hallucinations and illusions.* London: Walter Scott.

Parisi, A., & Pizzamiglio, L. (1970). Syntactic comprehension in aphasia. *Cortex, 6,* 204–215.

Parisi, T. (1987). Why Freud failed. *American Psychologist, 42,* 235–245.

Parke, R. D. (1979). Perspective on father–infant interaction. In J. Osofsky (Ed.), *The handbook of infant development.* New York: Wiley.

Parke, R. D., & O'Leary, S. E. (1976). Father–mother–infant interaction in the newborn period: Some findings, some observations and some unresolved issues. In K. Riegel & J. Meacham (Eds.), *The developing individual in a changing world.* Vol. 2: *Social and environmental issues.* The Hague: Mouton.

Parke, R. D., & Sawin, D. B. (1980). The family in early infancy: Social interactional and attitudinal analyses. In F. Pederson (Ed.), *The father–infant relationship: Observational studies in a family context.* New York: Praeger.

Parke, R. D., & Suomi, S. (1981). Adult male–infant relationships: Human and nonhuman primate evidence. In K. Immelmann, G. Barlow, M. Main, & L. Petrinovitch (Eds.), *Behavioral development: The Bielefeld interdisciplinary project.* New York: Cambridge University Press.

Parker, G. A. (1970). Sperm competition and its evolutionary consequences in the insects. *Biological Reviews, 45,* 525–567.

Parker, I., & Shotter, J. (Eds.). (1990). *Deconstructing social psychology.* London: Routledge.

Parker, N. (1964). Homosexuality in twins: A report on three discordant pairs. *British Journal of Psychiatry, 110.*

Parkes, C. M. (1972). *Bereavement: Studies of grief in adult life.* New York: International Universities Press.

Parlee, M. B. (1973). The premenstrual syndrome. *Psychological Bulletin, 83,* 454–465.

Parloff, M. B. (1970). Group therapy and the small-group field: An encounter. *International Journal of Group Psychotherapy, 20,* 267–304.

Parloff, M. B., Waskow, I. E., & Wolfe, B. E. (1978). Research on therapist variables in relation to process and outcome. In S. L. Garfield & A. E. Bergin (Eds.), *Handbook of psychotherapy and behavior change: An empirical analysis.* New York: Wiley.

Parnes, H. S. (Ed.). (1981). *Work and retirement, a longitudinal study of men.* Cambridge, Mass.: M.I.T. Press.

Parnes, H. S., et al. (1970). *Career thresholds: A longitudinal study.* Washington, D.C.: U.S. Government Printing Office.

Parnes, H. S. & Nestel, G., (1981). The retirement experience. In H. Parnes (Ed.), *Work and retirement, a longitudinal study of men.* Cambridge, Mass.: M.I.T. Press.

Parnes, S. (1967). *Creative behavior guidebook.* New York: Scribner's.

Parnes, S. (1972). *Creativity: Unlocking human potential.* Buffalo, N.Y.: DOK.

Parnes' Survey Source: Ohio State University, Columbus: Center for Human Resource Research. (1970). *The pre-retirement years; a longitudinal study of the labor market experience of men* (Washington, D.C.: U.S. Department of Labor, Manpower Administration. Manpower Research Monograph, no. 15), Vol. 4, pp. 153–194.

Parron, D. L., Solomon, F., & Rodin, J. (Eds.). (1981). *Health, behavior and aging,* Interim Report no. 5. Washington, D.C.: National Academy Press.

Parrott, W. G., & Sabini, J. (1990). Mood and memory under natural conditions: Evidence for mood incongruent recall. *Journal of Personality and Social Psychology, 59,* 321–336.

Parson, T., & Clark, K. B. (Eds.). (1966). *Negro American.* Boston: Beacon Press.

Parsons, F. (1967/1909). *Choosing a vocation.* New York: Agathon.

Parsons, H. M. (1972). *Man–machine system experiments.* Baltimore, Md.: Johns Hopkins Press.

Parsons, H. M. (1974). What happened at Hawthorne? *Science, 183,* 922–932.

Parsons, H. M. (1976). Psychology for engineering and technology. In P. J. Woods (Ed.), *Career opportunities for psychologists. Expanding and emerging areas.* Washington, D.C.: American Psychological Association.

Parsons, H. M. (1976). What caused the Hawthorne effect? A scientific detective story. Presented at the annual meeting of the American Psychological Association, Washington, D.C.

Parsons, J. E. (Ed.). (1980). *The psychobiology of sex differences and sex roles.* New York: McGraw-Hill.

Parsons, T. (1949). *The structure of social action.* Glencoe, Ill.: Free Press.

Parsons, T. (1951). *The social system.* Glencoe, Ill.: Free Press.

Parsons, T., & Bales, R. E. (1955). *Family socialization and the interaction process.* Glencoe, Ill.: Free Press.

Parsons, T., & Shils, E. A. (Eds.). (1951). *Toward a general theory of action.* New York: Harper & Row.

Parten, M. B. (1932). Social participation among pre-school children. *Journal of Abnormal and Social Psychology, 27,* 243–269.

Partridge, D., & Wilks, Y. (Eds.). (1990). *The foundation of artificial intelligence.* Cambridge, UK: Cambridge University Press.

Partridge, G. E. (1930). Current conceptions of psychopathic personality. *American Journal of Psychiatry, 10,* 53–99.

Parvin, R., & Biaggio, M. (1991). Paradoxes in the practice of feminist therapy. *Women in Therapy, 11*(2), 3–12.

Pasamanick, B., Dinitz, S., & Lefton, M. (1959). Psychiatric orientation and its relation to diagnosis and treatment in the mental hospital. *American Journal of Psychiatry, 116,* 127–132.

Pascal, G. R., & Suttel, B. J. (1951). *The Bender Gestalt test: Quantification and validity for adults.* New York: Grune & Stratton.

Pase v. Hannon et al. U.S.D.C.N.D. of Illinois, Eastern Division, no. 74C 3586, July 1980, slip opinion.

Pask, G. (1976). Styles and strategies of learning. *British Journal of Educational Psychology, 46,* 128–148.

Pasquale, F. (Ed.). (1981). *Directory of self-help mutual aid groups—Chicago metropolitan area, 1981–82.* Evanston, Ill.: Self-Help Center.

Pass, R. F., Hutto, C., Stagno, S., Britt, W. J., & Alford, C. A. (1986). Congenital cytomegalovirus infection: Prospects for prevention. *Annals of the New York Academy of Sciences, 477,* 123–127.

Passantino, B., & Passantino, G. (1992). The hard facts about satanic ritualistic abuse. *Christian Research Journal, 14*(3), 20–27.

Pastore, N. (1949). *The nature-nurture controversy.* New York: Columbia University Press.

Paterson, D. G. (1930), *Physique and Temperament.* New York; Century.

Paterson, D. G. (n.d.) *Character reading at sight of Mr. X according to the system of Mr. P. T. Barnum.* Unpublished manuscript, University of Minnesota, Minneapolis.

Paterson, D. G., & Darley, J. G. (1936). *Men, women, and jobs.* Minneapolis, Minn.: University of Minnesota Press.

Paterson, D. G., Elliott, R. M., Anderson, L. D., Tooks, H. A., & Heidbreder, E. (1930). *the Minnesota Mechanical Ability Tests.* Minneapolis, Minn.: University of Minnesota Press.

Paterson, D. G., & Tinker, M. A. (1940). *How to make type readable.* New York: Harpers.

Patrick, G. T. W. (1895). The psychology of woman. *Popular Science Monthly, 47,* 209–255.

Patten, B. M. (1980). Diseases of muscle. In R. Rosenberg (Ed.), *Neurology.* New York: Grune & Stratton.

Patterson, C. H. (1978). Cross-cultural or intercultural psychotherapy. *International Journal for the Advancement of Counseling, 1,* 231–248.

Patterson, C. H. (1980/1966). *Theories of counseling and psychotherapy* (3rd ed.). New York: Harper & Row.

Patterson, C. H. (1986). Culture and counseling in Hong Kong, *Chinese University Education Journal, 14*(2), 77–81.

Patterson, C. H. (1989). Foundations for a systematic eclecticism in psychotherapy. *Psychotherapy, 26,* 427–435.

Patterson, F. (1977). The gestures of a gorilla: Language acquisition in another pongid species. In D. Hamburg, J. Goodall, & R. E. McCown (Eds.), *Perspectives on human evolution,* Vol. 5. Menlo Park, Calif.: Benjamin.

Patterson, F. (1980). Creative and innovative uses of language by a gorilla; a case study. In K. E. Nelson (Ed.), *Children's language,* Vol. 2. New York: Gardner Press.

Patterson, F. G. (1978). The gestures of a gorilla: Language acquisition in another pongid. *Brain and Language, 5,* 72–97.

Patterson, G. R. (1976). *Living with children (rev. ed.).* Champaign, Ill.: Research Press.

Patterson, G. R. (1976). Parents and teachers as change agents: A social learning approach. In D. Olson (Ed.), *Treating relationships,* Lake Mills, Iowa: Graphic.

Patterson, G. R. (1982). *Coercive family process.* Eugene, OR: Castalia.

Patterson, G. R. (1986). Performance models for antisocial boys. *American Psychologist, 41,* 432–444.

Patterson, G. R., Capaldi, D., & Bank, L. (1991). An early starter model for predicting delinquency. In D. J. Pepler & K. H. Rubin (Eds.), *The development and treatment of childhood aggression* (pp. 139–168). Hillsdale, NJ: Erlbaum.

Patterson, G. R., Chamberlain, P., & Reid, J. B. (1982). A comparative evaluation of a parent-training program. *Behavior Therapy, 13,* 638–650.

Patterson, G. R., & Gullion, M. E. (1971). *Living with children.* Champaign, Ill.: Research Press.

Patterson, G. R., Hops, H., & Weiss, R. L. (1975). Interpersonal skills training for couples in early stages of conflict. *Journal of Marriage and the Family, 1,* 295–303.

Patterson, M. L., & Sechrest, L. B. (1970). Interpersonal distance and impression formation. *Journal of Personality, 38,* 161–166.

Patterson, M. M., & Kesner, R. P. (1981). *Electrical stimulation research techniques.* New York: Academic Press.

Pattison, E. (1977). *The experience of dying.* Englewood Cliffs, NJ: Prentice-Hall.

Pattison, E. M. (1977). A theoretical-empirical base for social system therapy. In E. F. Foulks, R. M. Wintrob, J. Westermeyer, & A. R. Favazza (Eds.), *Current perspectives in cultural psychiatry* (pp. 217–253). New York: Spectrum.

Pattison, E. M. (1977). *The experience of dying.* Englewood Cliffs, N.J.: Prentice Hall.

Pattison, E. M. (1979). The selection of treatment modalities for the alcoholic patient. In J. H. Mendelson & N. K. Mello (Eds.), *The diagnosis and treatment of alcoholism.* New York: McGraw-Hill.

Pauk, W. (1974). *How to study in college* (2nd ed.). Boston: Houghton Mifflin.

Paul, G. L. (1966). *Insight vs desensitization in psychotherapy.* Stanford, Calif.: Stanford University Press.

Paul, G. L. (1968). Outcome of systematic desensitization. II: Controlled investigations of individual treatment, technique variations, and current status. In C. M. Franks (Ed.), *Assessment and status of the behavior therapies*. New York: McGraw-Hill.

Paul, G. L., & Lentz, R. J. (1977). *Psychosocial treatment of chronic mental patients*. Cambridge, Mass.: Harvard University Press.

Paul, I. H. (1981). Nondirective psychoanalysis. In R. J. Corsini (Ed.), *Handbook of innovative psychotherapies*. New York: Wiley.

Paul, N., Bloom, J., & Paul, B. (1981). Outpatient multiple family group therapy—Why not? In L. Wolberg & M. Aronson (Eds.), *Group and family therapy 1981*. New York: Brunner/Mazel.

Paul, N., & Paul, B. (1975). *A marital puzzle*. New York: Norton.

Paul, R. E. (1981). Legal requirements for assessing handicapped children. In C. S. Lidz (Ed.), *Improving assessment of schoolchildren*. San Francisco: Jossey-Bass.

Paul, S. M., Extein, I., Calil, H. M., Potter, W. Z., Chodoff, P., & Goodwin, F. K. (1981). Use of ECT with treatment-resistant depressed patients at the National Institute of Mental Health. *American Journal of Psychiatry, 138*, 486–489.

Paul, W. J., Robinson, K. B., & Herzberg, F. (1969). Job enrichment pays off. *Harvard Business Review, 47*, 61–78.

Paulhus, D. L. (1984). Two-component models of socially desirable responding. *Journal of Personality and Social Psychology, 46*, 598–609.

Pauli, R. (1933). *Der Arbeitsversuch als charakterologisches Prüfverfahren*. Leipzig: Barth.

Pauli, W. F. (1949). *The world of life*. New York: Houghton Mifflin.

Pauling, L. (1968). Orthomolecular psychiatry. *Science, 160*, 265–271.

Pauling, L. (1974). On the orthomolecular environment of the mind: Orthomolecular theory. *American Journal of Psychiatry, 131*, 1251–1257.

Paull, D. (1980). S.B. 133: The near resolution of a major problem: Fitness in the criminal law. *Chicago–Kent Law Review, 56*, 1107–1121.

Paulsen, S., & Hall, H. V. (1991). Common sense process factors in deception analysis. *Forensic Reports, 4*, 37–39.

Paulus, P. B., McCain, G., & Cox, V. C. (1978). Death rates, psychiatric commitments, blood pressure, and perceived crowding as a function of institutional crowding. *Environmental Psychology and Nonverbal Behavior, 3*, 107–116.

Pauly, I. (1968). The current status of the change of sex operations. *Journal of Nervous and Mental Diseases, 147*, 460–471.

Pavlov, I. (1983/1928). *Twenty-five years of objective study of the higher nervous activity (behavior) of animals*. Dover, N.H.: Pinter.

Pavlov, I. P. (1927). *Conditioned Reflexes: an investigation of the physiological activity of the cerebral cortex*. Oxford: Oxford University Press.

Pavlov, I. P. (1927). *Conditioned reflexes*. Oxford, UK: Oxford University Press.

Pavlov, I. P. (1928). *Lectures on conditioned reflexes*. New York: International Publishers.

Pavlov, I. P. (1934). An attempt at a physiological interpretation of obsessional neurosis and paranoia. *Journal of Mental Science, 80*, 187.

Pavlov, I. P. (1941). *Conditioned reflexes and psychiatry*. New York: International Publishers.

Pavlov, I. P. (1960/1927). *Conditioned reflexes*. New York: Dover.

Pavlov, I. P. (1982/1902). *The work of the digestive glands*. Birmingham, Ala.: Classics of Medicine Library.

Pawlik, K. (1976). *Dimensionen des Verhaltens (Dimensions of behavior)* (3rd ed.). Bern: Huber.

Pawlik, K. (Ed.). (1982). *Diagnose der Diagnostik (Diagnosis of psychodiagnostics)* (2nd ed.). Stuttgart: Klett-Cotta. Barcelona, Spain: Herder, 1979.

Pawlik, K. (Ed.). (1982). *Multivariate Persönlichkeitsforschung. (Multivariate personality research)*. Bern: Huber.

Paykel, E. (Ed.). (1992). *The handbook of affection disorders*. New York: Guilford.

Payne, A. F. (1928). *Sentence completions*. New York: New York Guidance Clinic.

Payne, R. (1989). Pain management in sickle cell disease: Rationale and techniques. *Annals of New York Academy of Sciences, 565*, 189–206.

Payne, R. S., & McVay, S. (1971). Songs of humpback whales. *Science, 173*, 587–597.

Peacock, K. (1985). Synesthetic perception: Alexander Scriabin's color hearing. *Music Perception, 2*, 483–506.

Peal, E., & Lambert, W. E. (1962). The relation of bilingualism to intelligence. *Psychological Monographs, 76*.

Peale, N. V. (1960). *The power of positive thinking*. Englewood Cliffs, N.J.: Prentice-Hall.

Pearce, J. M., & Hall, G. (1980). A model for Pavlovian learning: Variations in the effectiveness of conditioned but not of unconditioned stimuli. *Psychological Review, 87*, 532–552.

Pearce, M., & Walbridge, D. (1991). Myxoedema madness: A case report. *International Journal of Geriatric Psychiatry, 6*, 189–190.

Pearlin, L. I., Lieberman, M. A., Menaghan, E. G., & Mullan, J. T. (1981). The stress process. *Journal of Health and Social Behavior, 22*, 337–356.

Pearlin, L. I., & Schooler, C. (1978). The structure of coping. *Journal of Health and Social Behavior, 19*, 2–21.

Pearlman, K., Schmidt, F. L., & Hunter, J. L. (1980). Validity generalization results for tests used to predict job proficiency and training success in clerical occupations. *Journal of Applied Psychology, 65*, 373–406.

Pearson, E. S. (1938). *Karl Pearson: An appreciation of some aspects of his life and work*. Cambridge, England: Cambridge University Press.

Pearson, J. (1992). Managed mental health: The buyer's perspective. In S. Feldman (Ed.), *Managed mental health services* (pp. 27–43). Springfield, IL: Thomas.

Pearson, K. (1930). *The life, letters and labours of Francis Galton*. Cambridge, England: Cambridge University Press, Vol. I, 1914; Vol. II, 1924; Vols. IIIA, IIIB.

Pearson, K. (1901). On lines and planes of closest fit to systems of points in space. *Philosophical Magazine, 6*, 559–572.

Pearson, R. (1991). *Race, intelligence, and bias in academe*. Washington, DC: Scott–Townsend.

Peberdy, G. R. (1961). Moustaches. *Journal of Mental Science, 107*, 40–47.

Pečjak, V. (1970). Verbal synesthesia of colors, emotions, and days of the week. *Journal of Verbal Learning and Verbal Behavior, 9*, 623–626.

Pečjak, V. (1977). *Psihologija spoznavanja (Psychology of cognition)* (2nd ed.). Ljubljana, Yugoslavia: Državna Založba Slovenije.

Pečjak, V. (1980). Short history of Yugoslav psychology. *Primenjena psihologija (Applied Psychology), 1*, 205–216.

Pečjak, V. (1982). *Nastajanje psihologije (Psychology in making)*. Ljubljana, Yugoslavia: Univerzum.

Pečjak, V. (1982). *Veliki psihologi 0 psihologiji (Great psychologists about psychology). Ljubljana, Yugoslavia: Cankarjeva Založba*.

Peck, R. C. (1956). Psychological aspects of aging. In J. E. Anderson (Ed.), *Proceedings of a conference on planning research*. Bethesda, Md.: April 1955. Washington, D. C.: American Psychological Association.

Pedersen, D. M., Shinedling, M. M., & Johnson, D. L. (1968). Effects of sex of examiner and subject on children's quantitative test performance. *Journal of Personality and Social Psychology, 10,* 251–254.

Pedersen, P. (1988). *A handbook for developing multicultural awareness*. Alexandria, VA: American Association for Counseling and Development.

Pedersen, P. B. (1981). International conferences: Significant measures of success. *International Journal of Intercultural Relations, 5,* 51–69.

Pedersen, P. B. (1981). The cultural inclusiveness of counseling. In P. Pedersen, J. Draguns, W. Lonner, & J. Trimble (Eds.), *Counseling across cultures* (2nd ed.). Honolulu: University Press of Hawaii.

Pedersen, P. B. (1981). Triad counseling. In R. J. Corsini (Ed.), *Innovative psychotherapies*. New York: Wiley Interscience.

Pedersen, P. B. (1982). The intercultural context of counseling and therapy. In A. J. Marsella & G. M. White (Eds.), *Cultural conceptions of mental health and therapy*. Dordrecht, Netherlands: Reidel.

Pedersen, P. B. (1991). Multiculturalism as a generic approach to counseling, *Journal of counseling and development, 70,*(1), 6–12.

Pedersen, P. B., Draguns, J., Lonner, W., & Trimble, J. (1989). *Counseling across cultures:* (3rd ed.). Honolulu: University of Hawaii Press.

Pedersen, P. B., Lonner, W. J., & Draguns, J. G. (Eds.). (1976). *Counseling across cultures*. Honolulu: University of Hawaii.

Pederson, F. A., Anderson, B. J., & Cain, R. L. (1977). An approach to understanding linkages between the parent-infant and spouse relationships. Presented at the meeting of the Society for Research in Child Development, New Orleans, March.

Pedhazur, E. J. (1977). Coding subjects in repeated measures designs. *Psychological Bulletin, 84,* 298–305.

Pedhazur, E. J. (1982). *Multiple regression in behavioral research* (2nd ed.). New York: Holt, Rinehart, Winston.

Pedhazur, E. J., & Tetenbaum, T. J. (1979). Bem Sex Role Inventory: A theoretical and methodological critique. *Journal of Personality and Social Psychology, 37,* 996–1016.

Peel, E. A. (1971). *The nature of adolescent judgment*. London: Staples Press.

Peele, S. (1976). *Love and addiction*. New York: New American Library.

Pefley, D., & Smith, H. (1976). *It's Monday morning: A history of twenty-seven handicapped children's early education projects*. Chapel Hill, N.C.: Technical Assistance Developmental System.

Peirce, C. S. (1891). The architecture of theories, *The Monist,* 161–176.

Peirce, C. S. (1931–1958). *The collected works of Charles Sanders Peirce,* C. Hartshorne & P. Weiss (Eds.). Cambridge, Mass.: Harvard University Press.

Pelham, W. E., Bender, M. E., Caddell, J., Booth, S., & Moorer, S. H. (1985). Methylphenidate and children with attention deficit disorder. *Archives of General Psychiatry, 42,* 948–952.

Pelletier, K. (1977). *Mind as healer, mind as slayer: A holistic approach to preventing stress disorders*. New York: Dell.

Pelletier, K. (1979). *Holistic medicine: From stress to optimum health*. New York: Delacorte/Lawrence.

Pelletier, K., & Garfield, C. (1976). *Consciousness: East and west*. New York: Harper & Row.

Pelletier, K. R., & Herzing, D. L. (1988). Psychoneuroimmunology: Toward a mindbody model. *Advances, 5*(1), 27–56.

Pelto, J. P. (1970). *Anthropological research: The structure*. New York: Harper & Row.

Pelto, P. J., & Pelto, G. H. (1978). *Anthropological research: The structure of inquiry*. (2nd ed.). Cambridge, UK: Cambridge University Press.

Pelz, K., Pike, F., & Ames, L. B. (1962). A proposed battery of childhood tests for discriminating between different levels of intactness of function in geriatric patients. *Journal of Genetic Psychology, 100,* 23–40.

Pencavel, J. H. (1976). A note on the IQ of monozygotic twins raised apart and the order of their birth. *Behavior Genetics, 6*(4), 455–460.

Penck, W. E., Carpenter, J. C., & Rylee, K. E. (1979). MMPI correlates of social and physical anhedonia. *Journal of Counseling Psychology, 47,* 1046–1052.

Penfield, W. (1958). *The excitable cortex in conscious man*. Springfield, Ill.: Thomas.

Penfield, W. (1963). *The second career*. Boston: Little, Brown.

Penfield, W. (1975). *The mastery of the mind: A critical study of consciousness and the human brain*. Princeton, N.J.: Princeton University Press.

Penfield, W., & Jasper, H. H. (1954). *Epilepsy and the functional anatomy of the human brain*. Boston: Little, Brown.

Penfield, W., & Roberts, L. (1959). *Speech and brain mechanisms*. Princeton, N.J.: Princeton University Press.

Peng, R. X. (1980). Thirty years of industrial psychology in China, *Acta Psychologica Sinica, 12,* 16–21.

Penna, M., & Laddis, A. (1978). Chronic brain syndromes. In G. U. Balis, L. Wurmser, E. McDaniel, & R. G. Grenell (Eds.), *Clinical psychopathology*. Boston: Butterworth.

Pennebaker, J. W., Burnam, M. A., Schaeffer, M. A., & Harper, D. C. (1977). Lack of control as a determinant of perceived physical symptoms. *Journal of Personality and Social Psychology, 35,* 167–174.

Pennebaker, J. W., & Sanders, D. Y. (1976). American graffiti: Effects of authority and reactance arousal. *Personality and Social Psychology Bulletin, 2,* 264–267.

Pennington, J. S. (1973). *The musical peak experience* (doctoral dissertation, Ohio State University, 1972). *Dissertation Abstracts International, 34*(2-A), 601–602.

Penrose, L. S. (1949). *The biology of mental defect*. London: Sidgwick & Jackson.

Penrose, L. S., & Penrose, R. (1958). Impossible objects: A special type of visual illusion. *British Journal of Psychology, 49.* 31–33.

Penrose, L. S., & Raven, J. C. (1936). A new series of perceptual tasks: Preliminary communication. *British Journal of Medical Psychology, 16,* 97–104.

Penrose, R. (1989). *The emperor's new mind: Concerning computers, minds and the laws of physics*. Oxford, UK: Oxford University Press.

Pentony, P. (1978). Rogers' formative tendency: An epistemological perspective. Unpublished manuscript, University of Canberra, Australia.

Peoples, V. Y., & Dell, D. M. (1975). *Black and white student preferences for counselor roles. Journal of Counseling Psychology, 22,* 529–534.

Pepinsky, H. B., Hill-Frederick, K., & Epperson, D. L. (1978). The *Journal of Counseling Psychology* as a matter of policies. *Journal of Counseling Psychology, 25,* 483–498. Also in J. M. Whiteley (Ed.), *The history of counseling psychology.* Monterey, Calif.: Brooks/Cole, 1980.

Peplau, L. A., & Periman, D. (1982). *Loneliness: A source book of current theory, research and therapy.* New York: Wiley.

Peppers, L. G. (1976). Patterns of leisure and adjustment to retirement. *The Gerontologist, 16,*(5).

Percy, W. (1961). The symbolic structure of interpersonal processes. *Psychiatry, 24,* 39–52.

Percy, W. (1976). *The message in the bottle.* New York: Farrar, Straus & Giroux.

Peretti, P. O., & Wilson, L. (1975). Voluntary and involuntary retirement of aged males and their effect on emotional satisfaction, usefulness, self-image, emotional stability, and interpersonal relationships. *International Journal of Aging and Human Development, 6*(2), 131–138.

Peretz, D. (1970). Development, object-relationships, and loss. In B. Schoenberg, S. C. Carr, D. Pereta, & A. K. Kutscher (Eds.), *Loss and grief: Psychological management in medical practice.* New York: Columbia University Press.

Perez, J. F. (1979). *Family counseling: Theory and practice.* New York: Van Nostrand.

Perino, J., & Emhart, C. B. (1974). The relation of subclinical lead level to cognitive and perceptual performance in Black preschoolers. *Journal of Learning Disabilities, 7,* 616–620.

Perkins, D. V., Burns, T. F., Perry, J. C., & Nielson, K. P. (1988). Behavior setting theory and community psychology: An analysis and critique. *Journal of Community Psychology, 16,* 355–372.

Perkins, M. W. (1973). Homosexuality in female monozygtic twins. *Behavior Gentics, 3,* 387–388.

Perlin, M. L. (1977). The legal status of the psychologist in the courtroom. *Journal of Psychiatry and Law, 5,* 41–54.

Perlin, M. L. (1980). The legal status of the psychologist in the courtroom. *Mental Disability Law Reporter, 4,* 194–200.

Perlman, H. H. (1957). *Social casework: A problem-solving process.* Chicago: University of Chicago Press.

Perlman, S. (1928). *A theory of the labor movement.* New York: Macmillan.

Perloff, R. (1968). Consumer analysis. In P. R. Farnsworth (Ed.), *Annual Review of Psychology, 19,* 437–460.

Perloff, R. (1982). The case for life satisfaction as a critical role for the counseling psychologist in industry. *The Counseling Psychologist, 10,* 41–45.

Perloff, R. (1986). Toward congenial environments for knowledge utilization in today's university. *Knowledge, 8,* 282–293.

Perloff, R. (1987). Self-interest and personal responsibility redux. *American Psychologist, 42,* 3–11.

Perloff, R. (1992). The peregrinations of an applied generalist. *Professional Psychology.*

Perloff, R. (Ed.). (1979). *Evaluator intervention: Pros and cons.* Beverly Hills, CA: Sage.

Perloff, R., with Gatewood, R. (1990). Testing and industrial application. In Goldstein & Hersen (Eds.), *Handbook of psychological assessment* (2nd ed.). New York: Pergamon Press.

Perloff, R., with Rich, R. F. (1986). The teaching of evaluation in schools of management. In B. G. Davis (Ed.), *Teaching of evaluation across the disciplines* (pp. 29–37). San Francisco: Jossey-Bass.

Perls, F. S. (1947). *Ego, hunger, and aggression.* New York: Vintage Books.

Perls, F. S. (1969). *Gestalt therapy verbatim.* Layfayette, Calif.: Real People Press.

Perls, F. S. (1969). *In and out the garbage pail.* Lafayette, Calif.: Real People Press.

Perls, F. S. (1973). *The Gestalt approach.* Palo Alto, Calif.: Science & Behavior Books.

Perls, F. S., Hefferline, R. E., & Goodman, P. (1951). *Gestalt therapy.* New York: Dell.

Perls, L. (1973). Some aspects of Gestalt therapy. Presented at Annual Meeting of American Orthopsychiatric Association.

Perone, M., DeWaard, R. J., & Baron, A. (1979). Satisfaction with reas and simulated jobs in relation to personality variables and drug use. *Journal of Applied Psychology, 64,* 660–668.

Perri, M. G., & Richards, C. S. (1977). An investigation of naturally occurring episodes of self-controlled behaviors. *Journal of Counseling Psychology, 24,* 178–183.

Perry, C., & Chisholm, W. (1973). Hypnotic age regression and the Ponzo and Poggendorff illusions. *Journal of Clinical and Experimental Hypnosis, 21,* 192–204.

Perry, D. G., & Bussey, K. (1979). The social learning theory of sex differences: Imitation is alive and well. *Journal of Personality and Social Psychology, 37,* 1699–1712.

Perry, H. S. & Gawel, M. L. (Eds.). (1954). Editors' preface. In H. S. Sullivan, *The psychiatric interview.* New York: Norton.

Perry, R. B. (1904). Conceptions and misconceptions of consciousness. *Psychological review, 11,* 282–296.

Perry, W. G., Jr. (1970). *Forms (intellectual and ethical development in the college years.* New York: Holt, Rinehart & Winston.

Pert, A. (1981). The body's own tranquilizers. *Psychology Today, 15*(9), 100.

Pert, C. (1986). The wisdom of the receptors: Neuropeptides, the emotions, and bodymind. *Advances, 3*(3), 8–16.

Pert, C., Ruff, M. R., Weber, R. J., & Herkenham, M. (1985). Neuropeptides and their receptors: A psychosomatic network. *Journal of Immunology, 135,* 820s–826s.

Pervin, L. A. (1963). The need to predict and control under conditions of threat. *Journal of Personality, 31,* 570–587.

Pervin, L. A. (1978). *Controversial issues in personality.* New York: Wiley.

Pervin, L. A. (1980). *Personality: Theory, assessment, and research* (3rd ed.). New York: Wiley.

Peschel, E. R., & Peschel, R. E. (1987). Medical insights into the castrati in opera. *American Scientist, 75,* 578–583.

Peskin, H. (1967). Pubertal onset and ego functioning. *Journal of Abnormal Psychology, 72,* 1–15.

Peskin, H. (1973). Influence of the developmental schedule of puberty on learning and ego functioning. *Journal of Youth and Adolescence, 4,* 273–290.

Pesso, A. (1969). *Movement in psychotherapy: Psychomotor techniques and training.* New York: New York University Press.

Pesso, A. (1973). *Experience in action: A psychomotor psychology.* New York.: New York University Press.

Pestalozzi, J. H. (1827). *Letters on early education, addressed to J. P. Greaves, esq.* London: Sherwood, Gilbert & Piper.

Pestalozzi, J. H. (1894/1801). *How Gertrude teaches her children; an attempt to help mothers to teach their own children and an account of The Method.* London: Sonnenschein.

Pestalozzi, H. (1972). Über die Naturgemässheit in der Erziehung. In E. Dejung (Ed.), *Pestalozzi sämtliche Werke, 23.* Zürich: Füssli.

Pestalozzi, H. (1978/1781). *Lienhard und Gertrud.* Boston: Heath.

Peszke, M. A. (1975). *Involuntary treatment of the mentally ill: The problem of autonomy.* Springfield, Ill.: Thomas.

Peter, L. J. (1977). *Peter's quotations.* New York: Morrow.

Peters, G. A., & Merrifield, P. R. (1958). Graphic representation of emotional feeling. *Journal of Clinical Psychology, 14,* 375–378.

Peters, H. N. (1942). Experimental study of aesthetic judgments. *Psychological Bulletin, 39,* 273–305.

Peters, J. S., Romine, J. S., & Dykman, R. A. (1974). A special neurological examination of children with learning disabilities. *Developmental Medicine and Child Neurology, 17,* 63–78.

Peters, R. S. (1965/1953). *Brett's history of psychology.* Cambridge, Mass.: M.I.T. Press.

Peters, W. (1925). *Die Vererbung geistiger Eigenschaften und der psychischen Konstitution.* Jena, East Germany: Fischer.

Petersen, A. (1963). The philosophy of Neils Bohr. *Bulletin of the Atomic Scientists, 63,* 12.

Petersen, A. C. (1979). Can puberty come any faster? *Psychology Today,* February, 45–56.

Petersen, A. C. (1979). Hormones and cognitive functioning in normal development. In M. A. Wittig & A. C. Petersen (Eds.), *Sex-related differences in cognitive functioning: Developmental issues.* New York: Academic Press.

Petersen, A. C., & Taylor, B. (1980). The biological approach to adolescence. In J. Adelson (Ed.), *Handbook Of adolescent psychology.* New York: Wiley.

Petersen, A. C., & Wittig, M. A. (1979). Sex-related differences in cognitive functioning: An overview. In M. A. Wittig & A. C. Petersen (Eds.), *Sex-related differences in cognitive functioning: Developmental issues.* New York: Academic Press.

Petersen, A. C., & Wittig, M. A. (Eds.). (1979). *Sex-related differences in cognitive functioning: Developmental issues.* New York: Academic Press.

Petersen, C. R., & Al-Haik, A. R. (1976). The development of the Defense Language Aptitude Battery (DLAB). *Educational and Psychological Measurement, 36,* 369–380.

Petersilia, J., Greenwood, P., & Lavin, M. (1977). *Criminal careers of habitual felons.* Santa Monica, CA: Rand.

Peterson, C., Semmel, A., von Baeyer, C., Abramson, L. Y., Metalsky, G. I., & Seligman, M. E. P. (1982). The Attributional Style Questionaire. *Cognitive Therapy and Research, 6,* 287–300.

Peterson, C., & Stunkard, A. J. (1992) Cognates of personal control: Locus of control, self-efficacy, and explanatory style. *Applied and Preventive Psychology, 1,* 111–117.

Peterson, D. (1982). *Status of professional standards in school psychology.* Washington, D.C.: National Association of School Psychologists.

Peterson, D. I., Lonengan, L. H., Hardinger, M., & Ted, C. W. (1968). Results of a stop-smoking program. *Archives of Environmental Health, 16*(2), 211–214.

Peterson, D. R. (1992). The doctor of psychology degree. In D. K. Freedheim (Ed.), *History of Psychotherapy: A century of change.* Washington, DC: American Psychological Association.

Peterson, H. W., & Martin, M. J., (1973). Organic disease presenting as psychiatric syndrome. *Postgraduate Medicine, 54,* 78–82.

Peterson, J. (1926). *Early conceptions and tests of intelligence.* New York: World Book.

Peterson, J. (1926). *Early conceptions and tests of intelligence.* Yonkers, N.Y.: World.

Peterson, J. A. (1970). A developmental view of the aging family. In J. E. Birren (Ed.), *Contemporary gerontology: Concepts and issues.* Los Angeles: University of Southern California Gerontology Center.

Peterson, L. (1989). Coping by children undergoing stressful medical procedures: Some conceptual, methodological, and therapeutic issues. *Journal of Consulting and Clinical Psychology, 57,* 380–387.

Peterson, L. R., & Peterson, M. J. (1959). Short-term retention of individual verbal items. *Journal of Experimental Psychology, 58,* 193–198.

Peterson, P. L., & Walberg, H. J. (Eds.). (1979). *Research on teaching: Concepts, findings, and implications.* Berkeley, Calif.: McCutchan.

Peterson, R. C., & Thurstone, L. L. (1933). *Motion pictures and the social attitudes of children.* New York: MacMillan.

Petit, T. L. (1984). Lead-zinc interactions in the central nervous system, with particular reference to the hippocampus. In C. J. Frederickson, G. A. Howell, & E. J. Kasarskis (Eds.), *The neurobiology of zinc: Part B. Deficiency, toxicity, and pathology.* New York: Liss.

Petrauskas, R., & Rourke, B. P. (1979). Identification of subgroups of retarded readers: A neuropsychological multivariate approach. *Journal of Clinical Neuropsychology, 1,* 17–37.

Pettigrew, C. G., & Dawson, J. G. (1979). Death anxiety "state" or "trait"? *Journal of Clinical Psychology, 35,* 154–158.

Pettinati, H. M. (1982). Measuring hypnotizability in psychotic patients. *International Journal of Clinical and Experimental Hypnosis, 30,* 404–416.

Petty, R. E., & Cacioppo, J. T. (1981). *Attitudes and persuasion: Classic and contemporary approaches.* Dubuque, Iowa: Brown.

Petty, R. E., Ostrom, T. M., & Brock, T. C. (Eds.). (1981). *Cognitive responses in persuasion.* Hillsdale, N.J.: Erlbaum.

Pfaffman, C. (1951). Taste and smell. In S. S. Stevens (Ed.), *Handbook of experimental psychology.* New York: Wiley.

Pfaffman, C. (Ed.). (1969). *Olfaction and taste.* New York: Rockefeller University Press.

Pfaffmann, C. (1964). Taste, its sensory and motivating properties. *American Scientist, 52,* 187–206.

Pfahler, G. (1943/1929). *System der Typenlehren.* Leipzig: Barth.

Pfanzagl, J. (1959). *Die axiomatischen Grundlagen des Messens.* Würzburg: Physica-Verlag.

Pfeiffer, C. C., (1976). Psychiatric hospital versus brain biocenter. *Journal of Orthomolecular Psychiatry, 5,* 28–34.

Pfeiffer, E., Eisenstein, R. B., & Dabbs, E. G. (1967). Mental competency evaluation for the federal courts: I. Methods and results. *Journal of Nervous and Mental Diseases, 144,* 320–328.

Pfeiffer, J. W., & Jones, J. E. (1980). *Reference guide to handbooks and annuals* (rev. ed.). San Diego, Calif.: University Associates.

Pfeiffer, W. (1971). *Transculturelle Psychiatrie: Ergebnisse und Probleme.* Stuttgart: Thieme Verlad.

Pfister, O. (1913). *Die psychoanalytische Methode.* Leipzig, Berlin: Klinkhardt.

Pfungst, O. (1911). *Clever Hans.* New York: Holt.

Phares, E. J. (1957). Expectancy changes in skill and chance situations. *Journal of Abnormal and Social Psychology, 54,* 339–342.

Phares, E. J. (1976). *Locus of control in personality*. Morristown, N.J.: General Learning Press.

Phares, E. J. (1978). Locus of control. In H. London and J. Exner (Eds.), *Dimensions of personality*. New York: Wiley Interscience.

Phares, E. J. (1979). *Clinical psychology: Concepts, methods, and profession*. Homewood, Ill.: Dorsey.

Phares, E. J. (1979). Defensiveness and perceived control. In L. C. Perlmutter & R. A. Monty (Eds.), *Choice and perceived control*. Hillsdale, N.J.: Erlbaum.

Phares, E. J. (1980). Rotter's social learning theory. In G. M. Gazda & R. J. Corsini (Eds.), *Theories of learning: A comparative approach*. Itasca, Ill.: Peacock.

Phares, E. J., & Wilson, K. G. (1972). Responsibility attribution: Role of outcome severity, situational ambiguity and internal-external control. *Journal of Personality, 40,* 392–400.

Phelps, R. H. (1978). Expert livestock judgment: A descriptive analysis of the development of expertise. (Doctoral dissertation, Kansas State University, 1977). *Dissertation Abstracts International 38,* 9513B (University Microfilms No. 78–02413).

Phelps, R. H., & Shanteau, J. (1978). Livestock judges: How much information can an expert use? *Organizational Behavior and Human Performance, 21,* 209–219.

Philipp, T., Holzgreve, H., Vaitl, D., & Schrey, A. (Eds.). (1982). *Compliance*. Munich: Universitätsdruckerei & Verlag Dr. C. Wolf.

Phillips, B. N. (Ed.). (1973). Assessing minority group children, special issue of *Journal of School Psychology, 11.*

Phillips, E. L. (1956). *Psychotherapy: A modern theory and practice*. Englewood-Cliffs, N.J.: Prentice-Hall.

Phillips, E. L. (1977). *Counseling and psychotherapy: A behavioral approach*. New York: Wiley.

Phillips, E. L. (1978). *The social skills basis of psychopathology: alternatives to abnormal psychology and psychiatry*. New York: Grune & Stratton.

Phillips, E. L. (1978). *The social skills basis of psychopathology*. New York: Grune & Stratton.

Phillips, E. L. (1980). *Vicarious therapies (art. dance, poetry, music, writing) and behavioral principles*. Presented at World Conference on Behavior Therapy, Jerusalem.

Phillips, E. L. (1981a). Conflict resolution therapy. In R. J. Corsini (Ed.), *Handbook of innovative psychotherapies*. New York: Wiley.

Phillips, E. L. (1981b). Supportive therapies, In G. Brown, R. L. McDowell, & J. Smith (Eds.), *Educating adolescents with behavior disorders*. Columbus, Ohio: Merrill.

Phillips, E. L., & Fagan, P. (1982). *Long-term results from short-term psychotherapy*. Presented at International Conference on Applied Psychology, Edinburgh.

Phillips, E. L., & Hall, M. (1953). An experimental analogue of reaction formation. *Journal of General Psychology, 49,* 97–123.

Phillips, E. L., Phillips, E. A., Fixsen, D. L., & Wolf, M. M. (1971). Achievement place: Modification of the behaviors of predelinquent boys within a token economy. *Journal of Applied Behavior Analysis, 4,* 45–59.

Phillips, E. L. & Wiener, D. N. (1966). *Short-term psychotherapy and structured behavior change*. New York: McGraw-Hill.

Phillips, E. L., & Wolf, M. M. (1978). Mission-oriented behavior research: The teaching family model. In T. A. Brigham & A. C. Catania (Eds.). *Handbook of applied behavior analysis, social and instructional processes*. New York: Irvington.

Phillips, L. (1985). *Psychotherapy revised: New frontiers in research and practice*. Hillsdale, NJ: Erlbaum.

Phoenix, C. H., Goy, R. W., Gerall, A. A., & Young, W. C. (1959). Organizing action of prenatally administered testosterone propionate on the tissues mediating mating behavior in the female guinea pig. *Endocrinology, 65,* 369–382.

Piaget, J. (1929). *The child's conception of the world*. New York: Harcourt, Brace.

Piaget, J. (1954). *The construction of reality in the child*. New York; Basic Books.

Piaget, J. (1959). *Judgement and reasoning in the child*. Totowa, NJ: Littlefield Adams.

Piaget, J. (1962). The stages of the intellectual development of the child. *Bulletin of the Menninger Clinic, 26,* 120–145.

Piaget, J. (1963). *The origins of intelligence in children*. New York: Norton Library.

Piaget, J. (1963/1926). *The language and thought of the child*. New York: World.

Piaget, J. (1963/1929). *The child's conception of the world*. New York: Littlefield, Adams.

Piaget, J. (1963/1950). *The psychology of intelligence*. Paterson, N.J.: Littlefield, Adams.

Piaget, J. (1965/1932). *The moral judgment of the child*. New York: Free Press.

Piaget, J. (1966/1952/1936). *Origins of Intelligence*. New York: International Universities Press.

Piaget, J. (1967). *Biologie et connaissance*. Paris: Gallimard.

Piaget, J. (1968). *Six psychological studies*. New York: Vintage.

Piaget, J. (1969). *Psychologie et épistémologie*. Paris: Denoël.

Piaget, J. (1970a). Piaget's theory. In P. H. Mussen (Ed.), *Carmichael's manual of child psychology* (3rd ed.), New York: Wiley.

Piaget, J. (1970b). *Genetic epistemology*. New York: Columbia University Press.

Piaget, J. (1970b). *Structuralism*. New York: Harper & Row.

Piaget, J. (1973). *The child and reality: Problems of genetic psychology*. New York: Grossman.

Piaget, J. (1975). *L'équilibration des structures cognitives*. Paris: Presses Universitaires de France.

Piaget, J. (1981/1953). *Intelligence and affectivity: Their relationship during child development*. Palo Alto, Calif.: Annual Reviews.

Piaget, J., & Inhelder, B. (1941). *Le développement des quantités chez l'enfant*. Neuchâtel, Switzerland: Delachaux & Niestlé.

Piaget, J., & Inhelder, B. (1956). *The child's conception of space*. London: Routledge & Kegan Paul.

Piaget, J., & Inhelder, B. (1958). In M. Tanner & B. Inhelder (Eds.), *Discussions on child development*, Vol. III. London: Tavistock.

Piaget, J., & Inhelder, B. (1969). *The psychology of the child*. New York: Basic Books.

Piccione, C., Hilgard, E. R., & Zimbardo, P. G. (1989). On the degree of stability of measured hypnotizability over a 25-year period. *Journal of Personality and Social Psychology, 56,* 289–295.

Pichot, P. (1978). Psychopathic behavior: A historical overview. In R. Hare & D. Schalling (Eds.), *Psychopathic behavior: Approaches to research*. New York: Wiley.

Pick, A. D. (1979). Listening to melodies: Perceiving events. In A. D. Pick (Ed.), *Perception and its development: A tribute to Eleanor J. Gibson*. Hillsdale, N.J.: Erlbaum.

Pick, A. D. (Ed.). (1979). *Perception and its development*. Hillsdale, N.J.: Erlbaum.

Pickford, R. W. (1976). Gibson and the success of experimental aesthetics. *Leonardo, 9,* 56—57.

Piening, E., & Lyons, N. (Eds.). (1975). *Educating as an art: The Rudolf Steiner method.* New York: Rudolf Steiner School.

Piercy, M. (1964). *The effects of cerebral lesions on intellectual function: A review of current research trends. British Journal of Psychiatry, 110,* 310–352.

Piéron, H. (1913). *Le probléme physiologique du sommeil.* Paris: Masson.

Piéron, H. (1923). *Le cerveau et la pensée.* Paris: Alcan.

Piéron, H. (1927). *Psychologie expérimentale.* Paris: A Colin.

Piéron, H. (1949). *La psychologie différentielle.* Paris: Presses Universitaires de France.

Piéron, H. (1952). *The sensations: Their functions, processes, and mechanisms.* New Haven, Conn.: Yale University Press.

Piéron, H. (1955). *La sensation, guide de vie* (2nd ed.). Paris: Gallimard.

Piéron, H. (1959). *De l'actinie á l'homme.* Paris: Presses Universitaires de France, Vol I, 1958; Vol II.

Piéron, H. (1963). *Examens et docimologie.* Paris: Presses Universitaires de France.

Piéron, H. (1973). *Vocabulaire de la psychologie* (5th ed.). Paris: Presses Universitaires de France.

Pietzner, C. (Ed.). (1986). *Village life—The Camphill communities.* Boston: Neugebauer Press.

Pike, K. (1954). *Language in relation to a unified theory of the structure of human behavior.,* Vol. 1. Glendale, Calif.: Summer Institute of Linguistics.

Piker, E. (1971). Learning of motor skills on the basis of self-induced movements. In J. Hellmuth (Ed.), *Exceptional infant,* Vol. 2. New York: Brunner/Mazel.

Pikulski, J. (1974). A critical review: Informal reading inventories. *The Reading Teacher, 28,* 141–151.

Piliavin, J. A., Dovidio, J. F., Gaertner, S. L. & Clark, R. D., III. (1981). *Emergency intervention.* New York: Academic Press.

Piliavin, J. A., & Piliavin, I. M. (1973). *The good samaritan: Why does he help?* Unpublished manuscript.

Piliavin, J. A., Piliavin, I. M., Loewenton, E. P., McCauley, C., & Hammond, P. (1969). On observers' reproductions of dissonance effects: The right answers for the wrong reasons? *Journal of Personality and Social Psychology, 13,* 98–106.

Pillard, R., Poumadere, J., & Caretta, R. (1982). A family study of sexual orientation. *Archives of Sexual Behavior, 11*(6) 511–520.

Pillard, R., & Weinrich, J. (1986). Evidence of familial nature of male homosexuality. *Archives of General Psychiatry, 43,* 808–812.

Pillemer, D. (1992). Preschool children's memories of personal circumstances: The fire alarm study. In E. Winograd & U. Neisser (Eds.), *Affect and accuracy in recall: The problem of "flashbulb" memories.* NY: Cambridge University Press.

Pillsbury, W. B. (1911). *The essentials of psychology.* New York: Macmillan.

Pillsbury, W. B. (1916). *The fundamentals of psychology.* New York: Macmillan.

Pillsbury, W. B. (1925). *Education as the psychologist sees it.* New York: Macmillan.

Pillsbury, W. B. (1929). *The history of psychology.* New York: Norton.

Pillsbury, W. B. (1930). Autobiography. In C. Murchison (Ed.), *A history of psychology in autobiography,* Vol. 2. Worcester, Mass.: Clark University Press.

Pillsbury, W. B., & Pennington, L. A. (1942). *Handbook of general psychology, a summary of essentials and a dictionary of terms.* New York: Dryden Press.

Pilowsky, I. (1978). A general classification of abnormal illness behaviors. *British Journal of Medical Psychology, 51,* 131–137.

Pimsleur, P. (1966). *The Pimsleur Language Aptitude Battery.* New York: Harcourt Brace Jovanovich.

Pincus, A., & Minahan, A. (1973). *Social work practice: Model and method.* Itasca, Ill.: Peacock.

Pincus, J. (1976). Incentives for innovation in the public schools. *Review of Educational Research, 44,* 113–144.

Pincus, J. H., & Tucker, G. J. (1974). *Behavioral neurology.* New York: Oxford University Press.

Pinder, M., Hayslip, B., & Lumsden, D. (1981). The measurement of death anxiety in adulthood: Implications for counseling. In R. Pacholski & C. Carr (Eds.), *New directions in death education and counseling* (pp. 110–118). Arlington, VA: Forum for Death Education and Counseling.

Pine, V. R. (1977). A socio-historical portrait of death education. *Death Education, 1,* 57–84.

Pinel, J. P. J. (1990). *Biopsychology.* Boston: Allyn & Bacon.

Pinel, P. (1809). *Traité médico-philosophique sur l'aliénation mentale,* (2nd ed.). Paris: Brosson.

Pinel, P. (1962/1801). *Treatise on insanity,* New York: Hafner.

Pines, A. M., Aronson, E., & Kafry, D. (1981). *Burnout: From tedium to personal growth.* New York: Free Press.

Pines, M. (1973). *The brain changers.* New York: Harcourt Brace Jovanovich, 1973.

Pinillos, J. L. (1962). *Introducción a la psicología contemporánea.* Madrid: Consejo Superior de Investigaciones Científicas.

Pinillos, J. L. (1969). *La mente humana.* Madrid: Editorial Salvat.

Pinillos, J. L. (1976). El "examen de ingenios," cuatro siglos después. *Revista de Psicología General y Aplicada, 31, 4—15*

Pinillos, J. L. (1976). *Más allá de Freud.* Madrid: Universidad Internacional.

Pinillos, J. L. (1977). *Psicopatología de la vida urbana.* Madrid: Espasa-Calpe.

Pinillos, J. L. (1981). La segunda vida de José Germain, el patrón del buen ánimo. *Revista de Psicología General y Aplicada, 36,* 1115–1120.

Pinillos, J. L. (1982). *Principios de psicología* (8th ed.). Madrid: Alianza Editorial.

Pinillos, J. L., et al. (1966). *Constitución y personalidad. Historia y teoría de un problema.* Madrid: Consejo Superior de Investigaciones Científicas.

Pinillos, J. L. (in press). *Historia y método de la psicología.* Madrid: Alianza Editorial.

Pinker, S., & Kosslyn, S. (1983). Theories of mental imagery. In A. Sheikh (Ed.), *Imagery: current theory, research, and application.* New York: Wiley.

Pinkerton, S., Hughes, H., & Wenrich, W. (1982). *Behavioral medicine: Clinical applications.* New York: Wiley.

Pinkston, E. M., Reese, N. M., LeBlanc, J. M., & Baer, D. M. (1973). Independent control of a preschool child's aggression and peer interaction by contingent teacher attention. *Journal of Applied Behavior Analysis, 6,* 115–124.

Pinney, J. M. (1979). The largest preventable cause of death in the United States. *Public Health Reports, 94*(2), 107–108.

Piotrowski, C. (1989). Prescription privileges: A time for some serious thought. *Psychotherapy Bulletin, 24,* 16–18.

Piotrowski, Z. A. (1957). *Percept analysis.* New York: Macmillan.

Pirenne, M. H. (1970). *Optics, painting and photography.* Cambridge, England: Cambridge University Press.

Pirozzolo, F. J. (1979). *The neuropsychology of developmental reading disorders.* New York: Praeger.

Pirozzolo, F. J., & Lawson-Kerr, K. (1980). Neuropsychological assessment of dementia. In G. J. Maletta & F. J. Pirozzolo (Eds.), *The aging nervous system.* New York: Praeger.

Pitcher, E. G. (1966). An evaluation of the Montessori method in schools for young children. *Childhood Education, 42,* 92–96.

Pitt, B. (1980). Growing pains in the psychiatry of old age. Part 1: Specialty and body of clinical knowledge. Part II: Organization of services. *Canadian Journal of Psychiatry, 25,* 1–14, 15–25.

Pittman, N. L., & Pittman, T. S. (1979). Effects of amount of helplessness training and internal–external locus of control on mood and performance. *Journal of Personality and Social Psychology, 37,* 39–47.

Pitz, G. F., & Mckillip, J. (1984). *Decision analysis for program evaluators.* Beverly Hills: Sage.

Pizano Aguilar, J. (1965). Ezequiel A. Chavez y su contribucion a la psicologia del pueblo mexicano. Master's thesis, Facultad de Filosofia y Letras. U. N. A. M., Mexico, D.F.

Pizzamiglio, L. (1974). Handedness, ear preference and field dependence. *Perceptual and Motor Skills, 38,* 700–702.

Pizzamiglio, L., & Appicciafuoco, A. (1971). Semantic comprehension in aphasia. *Journal of Communication Disorders, 4,* 280–288.

Pizzamiglio,L., & Parisi, D. (1971). Studies in verbal comprehension in aphasia. In G. Flores d'Arcais & P. Levelt (Eds.), *Advances in psycholinguistics.* Amsterdam: North Holland.

Pizzamiglio, L., & Zoccolotti, P. (1981). Sex and cognitive influence on visual hemifield superiority for face and letter recognition. *Cortex, 17,* 215–226.

Pizzey, E. (1974). *Scream quietly or the neighbors will hear.* London: Penguin Books.

Plant, R. (1986). *The pink triangle: The Nazi war against homosexuals.* New York: Holt.

Plateau, J. A. F. (1872). Sur la mesure des sensations physiques, et sur la loi qui lie l'intensité de ces sensations à l'intensité de la cause excitante. *Bulletins de l'Academie Royale des Sciences, des Lettres, et des Beaux- Arts de Belgique, 33,* 376–388.

Plato. (1952). *Gorgias* (Socratic dialogue). In R. M. Hutchins (Ed.), *The great books of the Western world,* Vol. 7. Chicago: Encyclopedia Britannica.

Plato. (1953). *The dialogues of Plato* (4th ed.), (4 vols.). Oxford: Clarendon Press.

Plato. (1973). *The republic and other works.* Garden City, N.Y.: Anchor Books.

Platonov, K. (1959). *The word as a physiological and therapeutic factor.* Moscow: Foreign Languages Publishing House.

Platt, J. J., & Labate, C. (1976). *Heroin addiction: Theory, research and treatment.* New York: Wiley.

Platt, S. (1980). On establishing the validity of "objective" data: Can we rely on cross-interview agreement? *Psychological Medicine, 10,* 573–581.

Pleck, J. H. (1981). *The myth of masculinity.* Cambridge, Mass.: M.I.T. Press.

Plinius, G. S. (1469). *Historia naturalis.* Venice, Italy: De Spira.

Plionis, E. M. (1977). Family functioning and childhood accident occurrence. *American Journal of Orthopsychiatry, 47,* 250–263.

Plomin, R., & DeFries, J. C. (1980). Genetics and intelligence: Recent data. *Intelligence, 4,* 15–24.

Plomin, R., DeFries, J. C., & McClern, G. E. (1980). *Behavioral genetics: A primer.* San Francisco: Freeman.

Plomin, R., DeFries, J. C., & McClearn, G. E. (1990). *Behavioral genetics: A primer* (2nd ed.). New York: Freeman.

Plotinus. (1957). *Enneades.* New York: Pantheon.

Plum, F., Gjedde, A., & Samson, F. E. (1976). Neuroanatomical functional mapping by the radioactive 2-dioxy-d-glucose method. *Neurosciences Research Program Bulletin, 14,* 457–518.

Plumer, W. S. (1859–1860). Mary Reynolds: A case of double consciousness. *Harper's New Monthly Magazine,20,* 807–812.

Plutchik, R. (1962). *The emotions: Facts, theories and a new model.* New York: Random House.

Plutchik, R. (1980). *Emotion: A psychoevolutionary synthesis.* New York: Harper & Row.

Poe, W. D., & Holloway, D. A. (1980). *Drugs and the aged.* New York: McGraw-Hill.

Polansky, N. A., Borgman, R. D., & DeSaix, C. (1972). *Roots of futility.* San Francisco: Jossey-Bass.

Polansky, N. A., Chalmers, M. A., Buttenwieser, E., & Williams, D. P. (1981). *Damaged parents: An anatomy of child neglect.* Chicago: University of Chicago Press.

Polansky, N. A., Hally, C., & Polansky, N. F. (1976/1975). *Profile of neglect: A survey of the state of knowledge of child neglect.* Washington, D.C.: U.S. Department of Health, Education, and Welfare.

Polanyi, M. (1964). *Personal knowledge.* New York: Harper & Row.

Polatin, P., & Hoch, P. (1947). Diagnostic evaluation of early schizophrenia. *Journal of Nervous and Mental Diseases, 105,* 221–230.

Polhemus, T. (Ed.). (1978). *The body reader: Social aspects of the human body.* New York: Pantheon.

Politzer, G. (1968). *Critique des fondements de la psychologie.* Paris: Presses Universitaires de France.

Politzer, G. (1973). In J. Debouzz, (Ed.), *Ecrits 2. Les fondements de la psychologie.* Paris: Editions Sociales.

Polk, W. J., & Maclennan, B. W. (1975). Experiences in the training of mental health consultants. In F. V. Mannino, B. W. Maclennan, & M. F. Shore (Eds.), *The practice of mental health consultation.* New York: Gardner Press.

Pollack, C. (1976). Neuropsychological aspects of reading and writing. *Bulletin of the Orton Society, 26,* 19–33.

Pollack, R. H., & Atkeson, B. M. (1978). A life-span approach to perceptual development. In P. B. Baltes (Ed.). *Life-span development and behavior.* Vol. 1. New York: Academic Press.

Pollak, J. M. (1979). Obsessive-compulsive personality: A review. *Psychological Bulletin,* 225–239.

Pollatsek, A., Lima, S., & Well, A. D. (1981). Concept or computation: Students' understanding of the mean. *Educational Studies in Mathematics, 12,* 191–204.

Pollitt, E. (1980). *Poverty and malnutrition in Latin America: Early childhood intervention programs.* New York: Praeger.

Poloma, M. M., & Garland, T. N. (1971). The myth of the egalitarian family: Familial roles and the professionally employed wife. In A. Theodore (Ed.), The professional woman. Cambridge, Mass.: Schenkman.

Polster, E., & Polster, M. (1973). *Gestalt therapy integrated: Contours of theory and practice.* New York: Brunner/Mazel.

Polten, E. P. (1973). *Critique of the psycho-physical identity theory.* The Hague: Mouton.

Polya, G., (1957/1945). *How to solve it: A new aspect of mathematical method.* Princeton, N.J.: Princeton University Press.

Polygraph Control and Civil Liberties Protection Act (1978). (Senate hearings, Subcommittee on the Constitution, Committee on the Judiciary, Document 052–070–04772–1). Washington, D.C.: U.S. Government Printing Office.

Pomerleau, O. F. (1979). Behavioral medicine. *American Psychologist, 34,* 654–663.

Pomerleau, O. F., & Brady, J. P. (Eds.) (1979). *Behavioral medicine: Theory and practice.* Baltimore, Md.: Williams & Wilkins.

Pongratz, L. J. & Traxel, W. (Eds.) (1977–1982). *Psychologie in Selbstdarstellungen.* Bern: Huber.

Ponterotto, J. G. (1988). Racial consciousness development among White counselor trainees: A stage model. *Journal of multicultural counseling and development, 16,* 146–156.

Ponterotto, J. G., & Casas, I. M. (1991). *Handbook of racial/ethnic minority counseling research.* Springfield, IL: Thomas.

Poole, A., & Kuhn, A. (1973). Family size and ordinal position: Correlates of academic success. *Journal of Biosocial Science, 5*(1), 51–59.

Poon, L. W. (1985). Differences in human memory with aging: Nature, causes and clinical implications. In J. E. Birren & W. K. Schaie (Eds.), *Handbook of the psychology of aging* (2nd ed.). New York: Van Nostrand.

Poon, L. W. (Ed.) (1980). *Aging in the 1980s.* Washington, D.C.: American Psychological Association.

Pope, K., & Bouhoutsos, J. (1986). *Sexual intimacy between therapists and patients.* New York: Praeger.

Pope, K. S., et al. (1980). *On love and loving.* San Francisco: Jossey-Bass.

Pope, K. S., & Singer, J. L. (Eds.) (1978). *The stream of consciousness.* New York: Plenum.

Popham, W. J. (1960). The validity of the SSHA with scholastic overachievers and underachievers. *Educational Research Bulletin, 39,* 214–216.

Popham, W. J. (1981). *Modern educational measurement.* Englewood Cliffs, N.J.: Prentice-Hall.

Poppelreuther, W. (1934). *Hitler, der politische Psychologe.* Langensalza, Germany: Mann.

Popper, K. (1963). *Conjectures and refutations.* London: Routledge & Kegan Paul.

Popper, K. (1972). *Objective knowledge: An evolutionary approach.* Oxford, UK: Clarendon.

Popper, K. R. (1959/1935). *The logic of scientific discovery.* New York: Basic Books.

Popper, K. R., & Eccles, J. C. (1977). *The self and its brain: An argument for interactionism.* Berlin: Springer-Verlag.

Porac, C., Coren, S., & Searleman, A. (1986). Environmental factors in hand preference: Evidence from attempts to switch the preferred hand. *Behavior Genetics, 16,* 251–261.

Porter, E. H. (1943). The development and evaluation of a measure of counseling interview procedures. *Educational and Psychological Measurement, 3,* 105–126, 215–238.

Porter, R. H., & Moore, J. D. (1981). Human kin recognition by olfactory cues. *Physiology and Behavior, 27* 493–495.

Porteus, S. D. (1937). *Intelligence and environment.* New York: Macmillan.

Porteus, S. D. (1941). *The practice of clinical psychology.* New York: American Book.

Porteus, S. D. (1959). *The maze test and clinical psychology.* Palo Alto, Calif.: Pacific Books.

Porteus, S. D. (1965). *Porteus Maze Test: Fifty years' application.* Palo Alto, Calif.: Pacific Books.

Porteus, S. D. (1969). *A psychologist of sorts; The autobiography and publications of the inventor of the Porteus Maze Tests.* Palo Alto, Calif.: Pacific Books.

Portugues, S. (1981). Media ethics. *APA Monitor, 12,* 2.

Porwoll, P. J. (1977). *ERS report: School absenteeism.* Arlington, Va.: Educational Research Service.

Poser, E. (1966). The effect of therapist training on group therapeutic outcomes. *Journal of Consulting Psychology, 30,* 283–289.

Posey, T., & Losch, M. (1983). Auditory hallucinations of hearing voices in 375 normal subjects. *Imagination, Cognition and Personality, 3,* 99–113.

Posner, M. I. (1978). *Chronometric explorations of mind.* Hillsdale, N.J.: Erlbaum.

Post, E. L. (1943). Formal reductions of the general combinatorial decision problem. *American Journal of Mathematics, 65,* 197–268.

Post, F. (1965). *The clinical psychiatry of late life.* Oxford: Pergamon Press.

Post, R. M., Jimerson, D. C., Reus, V. I., Goodwin, F. K., Silberman, E., & Bunney, W. E. (1979). Dopaminergic agents in affective illness: Studies with prebidil, amphetamine, and pimozide. In E. Usdin, I. J. Kopin, & J. Barchas (Eds.), *Catecholamines: Basic and clinical frontiers. II.* New York: Pergamon Press.

Postman, L. (1971). Transfer, interference and forgetting. In J. Kling & L. Riggs (Eds.), *Woodworth and Schlosberg's experimental psychology* (3rd ed.). New York: Holt, Rinehart & Winston.

Postman, L., Bruner, J. S., & McGinnies, E. (1948). Personal values as selective factors in perception. *Journal of Abnormal and Social Psychology, 43,* 142–154.

Postman, L., & Underwood, B. J. (1973). Critical issues in interference theory. *Memory and Cognition, 1,* 19–40.

Postman, N. (1982). *The disappearance of childhood.* New York: Delacorte.

Postman, N., & Weingartner, C. (1969). *Teaching as a subversive activity.* New York: Delta/Dell.

Potkay, C. C. (1971). The Rorschach clinician. New York: Grune & Stratton.

Potter, D. M. (1954). *People of plenty: Economic abundance and the American character.* Chicago: University of Chicago Press.

Potter, G., Kappeler, V., & Blumberg, M. (1993). *The mythology of crime and criminal justice.* Prospect Heights, IL.: Waveland.

Potter, J., & Wetherell, M. (1987). *Discourse and social psychology.* London: Sage.

Poulton, E. C. (1968). The new psychophysics: Six models of magnitude estimation. *Psychological Bulletin, 69,* 1–9.

Poulton, E. C. (1970). *Environment and human efficiency.* Springfield, Ill.: Thomas.

Powdermaker, F. B., & Frank, J. D. (1953). *Group psychotherapy.* Cambridge, Mass.: Harvard University Press.

Powell, A. D., & Royce, J. R. (1981a). An overview of a multifactor-system theory of personality and individual differences: I. The factor and system models and the hierarchical factor structure of individuality. *Journal of Personality and Social Psychology, 41,* 818–829.

Powell, A. D., & Royce, J. R. (1981b). An overview of a multifactor-system theory of personality and individual differences: III. Life span development and the heredity-environment issue. *Journal of Personality and Social Psychology, 41,* 1161–1173.

Powell, A. G. (1971). Speculations on the early impact of schools of education on educational psychology. *History of Education Quarterly, 11,* 406–412.

Powell, C. V. (1973). Sound and meaning correlates of word preferences. *Journal of General Psychology, 88,* 45–53.

Powell, G. E. (1979). *Brain and personality.* Westmead, England: Saxon House/Teakfield.

Powers, R. B., Osborne, J. G., & Anderson, E. G. (1973). Positive reinforcement of litter removal in the natural environment. *Journal of Applied Behavior Analysis, 6,* 579–586.

Powers, W. T. (1971). A feedback model for behavior: Application to a rat experiment. *Behavioral Science, 16,* 558–563.

Powers, W. T. (1973). *Behavior: The control of perception.* Chicago: Aldine.

Powers, W. T. (1973). Behaviorism and feedback control (letters). *Science 181,* (4105).

Powers, W. T. (1973). Feedback beyond behaviorism. *Science, 179,* 351–356.

Powers, W. T. (1978). Qualitative analysis of purposive systems: Some spade-work at the foundations of scientific psychology. *Psychological Review, 85,* 417–435.

Powers, W. T. (1979). A cybernetic model for research in human development. In M. Ozer (Ed.), *A cybernetic approach to the assessment of children: Toward a more humane use of human beings.* Boulder, Colo.: Westview Press.

Powers, W. T. (June-September 1979). The nature of robots (parts I, II, III, IV) *BYTE.*

Powers, W. T. (March 1980). Control-theory psychology and social organizations: Background for a theory of the corruption of social indicators when used for social decision making. Unpublished working paper. Distributed by W. T. Powers, Northbrook, Ill., & D. T. Campbell, Syracuse University, Syracuse, N.Y.

Powers, W. T., Clark, R. K., & McFarland, R. L. (1960). A general feedback theory of human behavior. Part I. *Perceptual and Motor Skills Monograph, 11* (1, serial no. 7).

Poythress, N. G. (1978). Psychiatric expertise in civil commitment: Training attorneys to cope with expert testimony. *Law and Human Behavior, 2,* 1–23.

Poythress, N. G., Jr. (1979). A proposal for training in forensic psychology. *American Psychologist, 34,* 612–621.

Poythress, N. G., Jr. (1980). Coping on the witness stand: "Learned responses" to "learned treatises." *Professional Psychology, 11,* 139–149.

Poythress, N. G., & Stock, H. V. (1980). Competency to stand trial: A historical review and some new data. *Journal of Psychology and Law, 8,* 131–146.

Pratkanis, A. R. (1988). The attitude heuristic and selective fact identification. *British Journal of Social Psychology, 27,* 257–263.

Pratkanis, A. R. (1989). The cognitive representation of attitudes. In A. R. Pratkanis, S. J. Breckler, & A. G. Greenwald (Eds.), *Attitude structure and function* (pp. 71–98). Hillsdale, NJ: Erlbaum.

Pratkanis, A. R. (1992). The cargo-cult science of subliminal persuasion. *Skeptical Inquirer, 16,* 260–272.

Pratkanis, A. R., & Aronson, E. (1992). *Age of propaganda: The everyday use and abuse of persuasion.* New York: Freeman.

Pratkanis, A. R., Breckler, S. J., & Greenwald, A. G. (Eds.). (1989). *Attitude structure and function.* Hillsdale, NJ: Erlbaum.

Pratkanis, A. R., Eskenazi, J., & Greenwald, A. G. (1990, April). *What you expect is what you believe (but not necessarily what you get): On the effectiveness of subliminal self-help audiotapes.* Paper presented at the meetings of the Western Psychological Association, Los Angeles.

Pratkanis, A. R., & Farquhar, P. H. (1992). A brief history of research on phantom alternatives: Evidence for seven empirical generalizations about phantoms. *Basic and Applied Social Psychology, 13.*

Pratkanis, A. R., & Greenwald, A. G. (1985). A reliable sleeper effect in persuasion: Implications for opinion change theory and research. In L. Alwitt & A. A. Mitchell (Eds.), *Psychological processes and advertising effects* (pp.157–173). Hillsdale, NJ: Erlbaum.

Pratkanis, A. R., & Greenwald, A. G. (1985). How shall the self be conceived? *Journal for the Theory of Social Behavior, 15,* 311–330.

Pratkanis, A. R. & Greenwald, A. G. (1989). A socio-cognitive model of attitude structure and function. In L. Berkowitz (Ed.), *Advances in experimental social psychology* (Vol. 22, pp. 245–285). New York: Academic.

Pratkanis, A. R., Greenwald, A. G., Leippe, M. R., & Baumgardner, M. H. (1988). In search of reliable persuasion effects: III. The sleeper effect is dead. Long live the sleeper effect. *Journal of Personality and Social Psychology, 54,* 203–218.

Pratkanis, A. R., Greenwald, A. G., Ronis, D. L., Leippe, M. R., & Baumgardner, M. H. (1986). Consumer-product and sociopolitical messages for use in studies of persuasion. *Personality and Social Psychology Bulletin, 12,* 536–538.

Pratt, A. B., & Mastroianni, M. (1981). Summary of research on individual education. *Journal of Individual Psychology, 37*(2), 232–246.

Pratt, C. C. (1961). Aesthetics. *Annual Review of Psychology, 12,* 71–92.

Pratt, C. C. (1969). Introduction. In W. Köhler (Ed.), *The task of Gestalt psychology.* Princeton, N.J.: Princeton University Press.

Pratt, D. (1976). *Painful experiments on animals.* New York: Argus Archives.

Pratt, J. G. (1973). A decade of research with a selected ESP subject: An overview and reappraisal of the work with Pavel Stepanek. *Proceedings of the American Society for Psychical Research, 30,* 1–78.

Pratt, J. G., & Woodruff, J. L. (1939). Size of stimulus stymbols in extrasensory perception. *Journal of Parapsychology, 3,* 121–158.

Pratt, J. H. (1907). The class method of treating consumption in the homes of the poor. *Journal of the American Medical Association, 20,* 475–492.

Pratt, R., & Nideffer, R. (1981). *Taking care of business.* San Diego, Calif.: Enhanced Performance Associates.

Premack, A. J., & Premack, D. (1972). Teaching language to an ape. *Scientific American, 227*(4), 92–99.

Premack, D. (1965). Reinforcement theory. In D. Levine (Ed.), *Nebraska Symposium on Motivation.* Lincoln, Neb.: University of Nebraska Press.

Premack, D. (1970). The education of Sarah. *Psychology Today, 4,* 54–58.

Premack, D. (1976). *Intelligence in ape and man.* Hillsdale, N.J.: Erlbaum.

Presbrey, F. S. (1929). *The history and development of advertising.* Garden City, N.Y.: Doubleday Doran.

Prescott, E. (1965). *A pilot study of day care centers and their clientele.* Washington, D.C.: U.S. Department of Education and Welfare, Children's Bureau.

Prescott, F. C. (1959/1922). *The poetic mind.* Ithaca, N.Y.: Cornell University Press.

Present and future problems in conducting animal research. (August 29, 1978). Symposium at the 86th annual meeting of the American Psychological Association, Toronto, Ont., Canada.

President's Commission on Mental Health. (1978). *Report to the President from the President's Commission on Mental Health,* Vols. 1–4. Washington, D.C.: U.S. Government Printing Office.

Pressey, S. L. (1926). A simple apparatus which gives tests and scores—and teaches. *School and Society, 23,* 373–376.

Pressey, S. L., Janney, J. E., & Kuhlen, R. G. (1939). *Life: A psychological survey.* New York: Harper.

Pressly, M. M., & Tullar, W. L. (1977). A factor interactive investigation of mail survey response rates from a commercial population. *Journal of Marketing Research, 14,* 108–111.

Previn, L., & Leiblum, S. (Eds.) (1980). *Principles and practice of sex therapy.* New York: Guilford.

Preyer, W. (1888, 1882). *The mind of the child.* New York: Appleton-Century.

Pribram, K. H. (1970). *The biology of learning.* New York: Academic Press.

Pribram, K. H. (1971). *Languages of the brain: Experimental paradoxes and principles in neurology.* Englewood Cliffs, N.J.: Prentice-Hall.

Pribram, K. H. (1975). *Central processing of sensory input.* Cambridge, Mass.: M.I.T. Press.

Pribram, K. H. (1976). Self-consciousness and intentionality: A model based on an experimental analysis of the brain mechanisms involved in the Jamesian theory of motivation and evolution. In G. E. Schwartz & D. Shapiro (Eds.), *Consciousness and self-regulation* (Vol. 1, pp. 51–100). New York: Plenum.

Pribram, K. H. (1981). Emotions. In S. B. Filskov & T. J. Boll (Eds.), *Handbook of clinical neuropsychology,* New York: Wiley, pp. 102–134.

Pribram, K. H. (1984). What is iso and what is morphic in isomorphism? *Psychological Research, 48,* 329–332.

Pribram, K. H. (Ed.) (1969). *Brain and behaviour* I, II, III, IV. London: Penguin Books.

Pribram, K. H., & Broadbent, D. E. (Eds.) (1970). *Biology of memory.* New York: Academic Press.

Pribram, K. H., & Gill, M. (1976). *Freud's "project" reassessed.* New York: Basic Books.

Pribram, K. H., & Luria, A. R. (Eds.) (1973). *Psychophysiology of the frontal lobes.* New York: Academic Press.

Price, G. R. (1955). Science and the supernatural. *Science, 122,* 359–367.

Price, G. R. (1972). Apology for Rhine and Soal. *Science, 175,* 359.

Price, J. (1966). The genetics of depressive behavior. *British Journal of Psychiatry,* Special Publication No. 2, 37–54.

Price, R. H., Cowen, E. L., Lorion, R. P., & Ramos-McKay, J. (1988). *Fourteen ounces of prevention: A casebook for practitioners.* Washington, DC: American Psychological Association.

Price-Williams, D. R. (1961). A study concerning concepts of conservation of quantities among primitive children. *Acta Psychologica, 18,* 297–305.

Price-Williams, D. R. (1974). Psychological experiments and anthropology: The problem of categories. *Ethos, 2,* 95–114.

Price-Williams, D. R. (1980). Anthropological approaches to cognition and their relevance to psychology. In H. C. Triandis & W. Lonner (Eds.), *Handbook of cross-cultural psychology.* Vol. 3: *Basic processes.* Boston: Allyn & Bacon.

Prichard, J. C. (1835). *A treatise on insanity and other disorders affecting the mind.* London: Sherwood, Gilbert & Piper.

Prien, E. P. (1977). The function of job analysis in content validation. *Personnel Psychology, 30,* 167–174.

Priester, H. J. (1958). *Die Standardisierung des Hamburg-Wechsler-Intellgienztests für Kinder (HAWIK).* Bern: Huber.

Prigatano, G. P., & Parsons, O. A. (1976). Relationship of age and education to Halstead test performance in different patient populations. *Journal of Consulting and Clinical Psychology, 44,* 527–533.

Prigogine, I. (1979). *From being to becoming.* San Francisco: Freeman.

Prince, M. (1905). *The dissociation of a personality,* New York: Longman, Green.

Prince, V., & Bentler, P. (1972). Survey of 504 cases of transvestism. *Psychological Reports, 31,* 903–917.

Prince, W. F. (1916–1917). The Doris case of quintuple personality. *Journal of Abnormal Psychology, 11,* 73–122.

Prinzhorn, H. (1972). *Artistry of the mentally ill.* New York: Springer.

Pritchard, R., & Karasick, B. (1973). The effects of organizational climate on managerial job performance and job satisfaction. *Organizational Behavior and Human Performance, 9,* 110–119.

Pritchard, W. S. (1981). Psychophysiology of P300. *Psychological Bulletin, 89,* 506–540.

Privette, P. G. (1964). *Factors associated with functioning which transcends modal behavior.* Unpublished doctoral dissertation, University of Florida.

Privette, P. G. (1981). Dynamics of peak performance. *Journal of Humanistic Psychology, 21,* 57–67.

Prochaska, J. O. (1979). *Systems of psychotherapy.* Homewood, Ill.: Dorsey.

Progoff, I. (1977/1975). *At a Journal workshop.* New York: Dialogue House Library.

Program Abstracts. (1991). Special issues 1 and 2. *The Gerontologest, 31.*

Prokasy, W. F., Ebel, H. C., & Thompson, D. D. (1963). Response shaping at long interstimulus intervals in classical eyelid conditioning. *Journal of Experimental Psychology, 66,* 138–141.

Prokasy, W. F., & Hall, J. F. (1963). Primary stimulus generalization. *Psychological Review, 70,* 310–322.

Pronko, N. H. (1973). *Panorama of psychology* (2nd ed.). Monterey, Calif.: Brooks/Cole.

Pronko, N. H. (1980). *Psychology from the standpoint of an interbehaviorist.* Monterey, Calif.: Brooks/Cole.

Proshansky, H. M., Ittelson, W., & Rivlin, L. G. (1970). Freedom of choice and behavior in a physical setting. In H. M. Proshansky, W. H. Ittelson, & L. G. Rivlin (Eds.), *Environmental psychology.* New York: Holt, Rinehart & Winston.

Provine, R. R., & Hamernik, H. B. (1986). Yawning: Effects of stimulus interest. *Bulletin of the Psychonomic Society, 24,* 437–438.

Pruch, J. (1972). *Soviet psycholinguistics.* The Hague: Mouton.

Pruitt, D. G. (1972). Methods for resolving conflicts of interest: A theoretical analysis. *Journal of Social Issues, 28,* 133–154.

Pruitt, D. G., & Kimmel, M. J. (1977). Twenty years of experimental gaming: Critique, synthesis, and suggestions for the future. *Annual Review of Psychology, 28,* 363–392.

Pruitt, D. G. (1981). *Negotiation behavior.* New York: Academic Press.

Pruyser, P. W. (1968). *A dynamic psychology of religion.* New York: Harper & Row.

Pruyser, P. W. (1979). *The psychological examination: A guide for clinicians.* New York: International Universities Press.

Pruzansky, S. (1975). How to use SINDSCAL: A computer program for individual differences in multidimensional scaling. Unpublished manuscript, Bell Laboratories.

Przeworski, A., & Teune, H. (1966). Equivalence in cross-national research. *Public Opinion Quarterly, 30,* 33–43.

Przeworski, A., & Teune, H. (1970). *The logic of comparative social inquiry.* New York: Wiley.

Psychiatric aspects of sports. (1979). *Psychiatric Annals,* 9 (entire no. 3).

Psychokinetic fraud. (September 1974). *Scientific American, 231*(3), 68, 72.

Psychological Corporation. (1947–1981). *The Differential Aptitude Tests.* New York: Psychological Corp.

Psychologists for Social Responsibility. (1992). *The mission of psychologists for social responsibility.* Washington, DC: National Office PsySR.

Psychology as a profession. (1968). *American Psychologist, 23,* 195–200.

Puder, M. (1979). A professional employee counseling program: Credibility issues. In H. V. Schmitz (Chair), *Occupational clinical psychology: A new field for psychologists.* Symposium presented at the convention of the American Psychological Association, New York, September.

Puk, G. (1991). Treating traumatic memories: A case report on the eye movement desensitization procedure. *Journal of Behavior Therapy and Experimental Psychiatry, 22,* 149–151.

Pulling, P. (1989). *The devil's web.* Louisiana: Huntington House.

Pulver, U. (1959). *Spannungen und Störungen im Verhalten der Säuglinge.* Bern: Huber.

Punnett, R. C. (1928). *Collected papers of William Bateson.* Cambridge, England: Cambridge University Press.

Purcell, K. (1956). The Thematic Apperception Test and antisocial behavior. *Journal of Consulting Psychology, 20,* 449–456.

Purcell, K. (1965). Critical appraisal of psychosomatic studies of asthma. *New York State Journal of Medicine, 65,* 2103.

Purdy, W. C. (1958). The hypothesis of psychophysical correspondence in space perception. Unpublished Ph. D. dissertation, Cornell University, (university microfilms, no. 58–5594).

Purisch, A. D., Golden, C. J., & Hammeke, T. A. (1978). Discrimination of schizophrenic and brain-injured patients by a standardized version of Luria's neuropsychological tests. *Journal of Consulting and Clinical Psychology, 46,* 1266–1273.

Purkyně, J. E. (1819). *Beiträge zur Kenntniss des Sehens in subjectiver Hinsicht.* Prague: Calve.

Purkyně, J. E. (1823). *Commentatio de examine physiologic organi visus et systematis cutanei.* Bratislava, Czechoslovakia. Typ. Universitatis.

Purkyně, J. E. (1825). *Neue Beiträge zur Kenntniss des Sehens in subjectiver Hinsicht.* Berlin: Reimer.

Putnam, F. (1991). The satanic ritual abuse controversy. *Child Abuse and Neglect, 15,* 175–179.

Pütter, A. (1922). Die Unterschiedsschwellen des Temperatursinnes. *Zeitschrift für Biologie, 84.*

Puttick, W. H. (1964). *A factor analytic study of positive modes of experiencing and behaving in a teacher college population.* Unpublished doctoral dissertation, University of Florida.

Pyle, R., Mitchell, J., & Eckert, E. (1981). Bulimia: A report of 34 cases. *Journal of Clinical Psychiatry, 42*(2), 60–64.

Pyles, M. K., Stolz, H. R., & Macfarlane, J. W. (1935). The accuracy of mothers' reports on birth and developmental data. *Child Development, 6,* 165–176.

Pylyshyn, Z. W. (1973). What the mind's eye tells the mind's brain: A critique of mental imagery. *Psychological Bulletin, 80,* 1–24.

Quadagno, D. M., Briscoe, R., & Quadagno, J. S. (1977). Effect of perinatal gonadal hormones on selected nonsexual behavior patterns: A critical assessment of the nonhuman and human literature. *Psychological Bulletin 84,* 62–80.

Quagliano, A. (1977). Existential modes in the moviegoer. *Research Studies, 4,* 214–224.

Quarter, J., & Marcus, A. (1971). Drive level and the audience effect: A test of Zajonc's theory. *Journal of Social Psychology, 83,* 99–105.

Quay, (Ed.). *Handbook of juvenile delinquency.* (pp. 290–324). New York: Wiley.

Quay, H. (1977). The three faces of evaluation: What can be expected to work. *Criminal Justice and Behavior, 4,* 341–354.

Quay, H. C., & Werry, J. S. (Eds.). (1986). *Psychopathological disorders of childhood* (3rd ed.). New York: Wiley.

Quetelet, L. A. J. (1839). *Popular instructions on the calculation of probabilities.* London: Weale.

Quine, W. V. O. (1953). Two dogmas of empiricism. In W. V. O. Quine (Ed.), *From a logical point of view.* Cambridge, Mass.: Harvard University Press.

Quinn, W. G., & Gould, J. L. (1979). Nerves and genes. *Nature, 278,* 19–23.

Quinton, D., & Rutter, M. (1976). Early hospital admissions and later disturbances of behavior: An attempted replication of Douglas' findings. *Developmental Medicine and Child Neurology, 18,* 447–459.

Raasoch, J., & Laqueur, H. P. (1979). Learning multiple family therapy through simulated workshops. *Family Process, 18,* 95–98.

Rabbie, J. M., & de Brey, J. H. C. (1971). The anticipation of intergroup cooperation and competition under private and public conditions. *International Journal of Group Tensions, 1,* 230–251.

Rabbie, J. M., & Wilkens, G. (1971). Intergroup competition and its effects on intragroup and intergroup relations. *European Journal of Social Psychology, 1,* 215–234.

Rabin, A. I. (1945). The use of the Wechsler–Bellevue scales with normal and abnormal persons. *Psychological Bulletin, 42,* 410–422.

Rabin, A. I. (1961). Devising projective methods for personality research. *Journal of Projective Techniques, 25,* 6–10.

Rabin, A. I. (1963). Do we need another projective technique? *Merrill-Palmer Quarterly, 9,* 73–77.

Rabin, A. I. (1965). *Growing up in the kibbutz.* New York: Springer.

Rabin, A. I. (1972). Rorschach. In O. K. Buros, (Ed.), *Seventh mental measurements yearbook,* Vol. I. Highland Park, N.J.: Gryphon.

Rabin, A. I. (Ed.) (1968). *Projective techniques in personality assessment.* New York: Springer.

Rabin, A. I. (Ed.) (1981). *Assessment with projective techniques.* New York: Springer.

Rabin, A. I., & Guertin, W. H. (1951). Research with the Wechsler–Bellevue test: 1945–1950. *Psychological Bulletin, 48,* 211–248.

Rabin, A. I., & Haworth, M. R. (1960). *Projective techniques with children.* New York: Grune & Stratton.

Rabkin, J. (1974). Public attitudes toward mental illness. A review of the literature. *Schizophrenia Bulletin, 10,* 9–33.

Rachlin, H. (1980). *Behaviorism in everyday life.* Englewood Cliffs, N.J.: Prentice-Hall.

Rachlin, H., & Burkhard, R. (1978). The temporal triangle: Response substitution in instrumental conditioning. *Psychological Review, 85,* 22–48.

Rachman, S. (1971). *The effects of psychotherapy*. London: Pergamon Press.

Rachman, S., & Teasdale, J. (1969). *Aversion therapy and behavior disorders: An analysis*. Miami, Fla.: University of Miami Press.

Rachman, S. J. (1978). *Fear and courage*. San Francisco: Freeman.

Rada, R. T., & Kellner, R. (1979). Drug treatment in alcoholism. In J. Davis & D. J. Greenblatt (Eds.), *Psychopharmacology update: New and neglected areas*. New York: Grune & Stratton.

Radcliffe-Brown, A. R. (1922). *The Andaman islanders*. Glencoe, Ill.: Free Press.

Rader, C. M., & Tellegen, A. (1987). An investigation of synesthesia. *Journal of Personality and Social Psychology, 52*, 981–987.

Radhakrishan, S. (1947). *The idealistic view of life*. London: Allen & Unwin.

Radical constructivism, autopoesis and psychotherapy. [Special Issue] (1988). *Irish Journal of Psychology, 8*.

Radin, P. (1970/1968). *Primitive religion*. New York: Viking, 1937.

Radnitzky, G. *Contemporary schools of metascience*. Goteborg, Sweden: Akademi forlaget.

Rado, S. (1956). Schizotypal organization: Preliminary report on a clinical study of schizophrenia. In S. Rado & G. E. Daniels (Eds.), *Changing concepts of psychoanalytic medicine*. New York: Grune & Stratton.

Rado, S. (1957). *Psychoanalysis of behavior: Collected papers*. New York: Grune & Stratton.

Rado, S. (1969). *Adaptational psychodynamics*. New York: Science House.

Rahe, R. H. (1975). Epidemiological studies of life change and illness. *International Journal of Psychiatry and Medicine, 6*, 133–146.

Rahman, F. (1952). *Avicenna's psychology. An English translation of Kitab al-Najab, Book III, Chapter VI, with historical-philosophical notes and textual improvements on the Cairo edition*. London: Oxford University Press.

Rahmani, L. (1973). *Soviet psychology: Philosophical theoretical and experimental issues*. New York: International Universities Press.

Rahula. (1974). *What the Buddha taught* (2nd ed.). New York: Grove Press.

Rahula, W. (1978). *Zen and the training of the bull: Towards a definition of Buddhist thought*. London: Fraser.

Raikov, V. L. (1982). Hypnotic age regression to the neonatal period: Comparisons with role playing. *Journal of Clinical and Experimental Hypnosis, 30*, 108–116.

Raimy, V. (1971). *The self-concept as a factor in counseling and personality organization*. Columbus, Ohio: Ohio State University Libraries.

Raimy, V. (1975). *Misunderstandings of the self: Cognitive psychotherapy and the misconception hypothesis*. San Francisco: Jossey-Bass.

Raimy, V. C. (1948). Self-reference in counseling interviews. *Journal of Consulting Psychology, 12*, 153–163.

Raimy, V. C. (Ed.). (1970/1950). *Training in clinical psychology*. New York: Prentice-Hall.

Raina, M. K. (1980). *Serum urate concentrations, intellectual style and personality*. New Delhi: National Council of Educational Research & Training.

Raina, M. K. (1982). *Research and development in talent: The role of creativity tests*. New Delhi: National Council of Educational Research & Training.

Raina, M. K. (Ed.), (1980). *Creativity research: International perspective*. New Delhi: National Council of Educational Research & Training.

Raina, M. K., et al. (1981). *Studies on national talent search*. New Delhi: National Council Educational Research & Training.

Rainer, J. D., Mesnikoff, A., Kolb, L. C., & Carr, A. (1960). Homosexuality and heterosexuality in identical twins. *Psychosomatic Medicine, 22*, 251–259.

Raines, G. N., & Rohner, J. H. (1955). The operational matrix of psychiatric practice. I: Consistency and variability in interview impressions of different psychiatrists. *American Journal of Psychiatry, 111*, 721–733.

Rainey, R. G. (1965). Study of four school-ability tests. *Journal of Experimental Education, 33*, 305–319.

Rains, P. M., Kitsuse, J. I., Duster, T., & Freidson, E. (1976). In N. Hobbs *(Ed.), Issues in the classification of children*. Vol. 1. San Francisco: Jossey-Bass.

Raisman, G., & Field, P. M. (1971). Sexual dimorphism in the preoptic area of the rat. *Science, 173*, 731–733.

Raisman, G., & Field, P. M. (1973). Sexual dimorphism in the neuropil of the preoptic area of the rat and its dependence on neonatal androgen. *Brain Research, 54*, 1–29.

Rajala, D. W., & Sage, A. P. (1979). On information structuring in choice making: A case study of systems engineering decision making in beef cattle production. *IEEE Transactions on Systems, Man, and Cybernetics, SMC-9*, 525–533.

Rajecki, D. W. (Ed.). (1983). *Comparing behavior: Studying man studying animals*. Hillsdale, NJ: Erlbaum.

Rajneesh, S. B. (1982). Then you are it. In R. N. Walsh & D. H. Shapiro (Eds.), *Beyond health and normality: Toward a vision of exceptional psychological health*. New York: Van Nostrand.

Raju, P. T. (1953). Indian psychology. In H. Bhattacharya (Ed.), *The cultural heritage of India*. Calcutta: Ramakrishna Mission Institute of Culture.

Raknes, O. (1970). *Wilhelm Reich and orgonomy*. New York: St. Martin's Press.

Rakos, R. F. (1979). Content consideration in the distinction between assertive and aggressive behavior. *Psychological Reports, 44*, 767–773.

Rakos, R. F., & Schroeder, H. E. (1979). Development and empirical evaluation of a self-administered assertiveness training program. *Journal of Consulting and Clinical Psychology, 47*, 991–993.

Raloff, J. (1982). Occupational noise—The subtle pollutant. *Science News, 121*(21), 347–350.

Rama, S., Ballentine, R., & Ajaya, S. (1976). *Yoga and psychotherapy: The evolution of consciousness*. Glenview, Ill.: Himalayan Institute.

Ramage, J. C. (1979). National survey of school psychologists: Update. *School Psychology Digest, 8*, 153–161.

Ramalingaswami, P. (1978). Psychology in India: A challenge and an opportunity. *Indian Educational Review, 13*, 22–42.

Ram Dass. (1975). *The only dance there is*. New York: Doubleday.

Ram Dass. (1977). *Grist for the mill*. Santa Cruz, Calif.: Unity Press.

Ram Dass. (1978). *Journey of awakening: A meditator's guidebook*. New York: Doubleday.

Ramirez, E., Maidonado, A., & Martos, R. (1992). Attributions modulate immunization against learned helplessness in humans. *Applied and Preventive Psychology, 1*, 139–146.

Ramírez, M., & Castañeda, A. (1974). *Cultural democracy: Bicognitive development and education*. New York: Academic Press.

Ramón y Cajal, S. (1899–1904). *Textura del sistema nervioso del hombre y de los vertebrados* (3 vols.). Madrid: Moya.

Ramón y Cajal, S. (1909). *Histology* (2 vols.). Paris: Maloine.

Ramón y Cajal, S. (1928). *Degeneration and regeneration of the nervous system* (2 vols.). London: Oxford University Press.

Ramón y Cajal, S. (1937). Recollections of my life. *Memoirs of the American Philosophical Society, 8,* 1–2.

Ramón y Cajal, S. (1981). *Recuerdos de mi vida: Historia de mi labor científica.* Madrid: Alianza.

Ramsay, J. O. (1977). Maximum likelihood estimation in multidimensional scaling. *Psychometrika, 42,* 241–266.

Ramsden, P., & Entwistle, N. J. (1981). Effects of academic departments on students' approaches to learning. *British Journal of Educational Psychology, 51,* 368–383.

Ramsey, G. V. (1953). Studies of dreaming. *Psychological Bulletin, 50,* 432–455.

Ranan, W., & Blodgett, A. (1983). Using telephone therapy for "unreachable" clients. *Social Casework, 64.*

Rancurello, A. (1968). *A study of Franz Brentano.* New York: Academic Press.

Rand, C. S. W. (1978). Treatment of obese patients in psychoanalysis. *Psychiatric Clinics of North America, 1,* 661–672.

RAND Corporation. (1955). *A million digits with 100,000 normal deviates.* Santa Monica, Calif.: RAND.

Randi, J. (1980). *Flim-flam.* New York: Harper & Row.

Rank, O. (1929/1924). *The trauma of birth.* New York: Harcourt, Brace.

Rank, O. (1932). *Art and artist: Creative urge and personality development.* New York: Knopf.

Rank, O. (1945/1929). *Will therapy and truth and reality.* New York: Knopf.

Rank, O. (1950/1931). *Psychology and the soul.* Philadelphia, Pa.: University of Pennsylvania Press.

Rank, O. (1952). *The myth of the birth of the hero.* New York: Springer.

Rank, O. (1958/1941). *Beyond psychology.* New York: Dover.

Ransen, D. L. (1980). The mediation of reward-induced motivation decrements in early and middle childhood: A template matching approach. *Journal of Personality and Social Psychology, 39,* 1088–1100.

Rao, K. R. (1957). *Psi cognition.* Tenali, India: Tagore Publishing House.

Rao, K. R. (1962). The preferential effect in ESP. *Journal of Parapsychology, 26,* 252–259.

Rao, K. R. (1965). The bidirectionality of psi. *Journal of Parapsychology, 29,* 230–250.

Rao, K. R. (1966). *Experimental parapsychology: A review and interpretation.* Springfield, Ill.: Thomas.

Rao, K. R. (1968). *Gandhi and pragmatism.* Calcutta: Oxford/IBH.

Rao, K. R. (1972). *Mystic awareness: Four lectures on the paranormal.* Mysore, India: Mysore University Press.

Rao, K. R. (1977). On the nature of psi. *Journal of Parapsychology, 41,* 294–351.

Rao, K. R. (1979). Psi: Its place in nature. In W. G. Roll (Ed.), *Research in parapsychology, 1978.* Methchen, N. J.: Scarecrow Press.

Rao, K. R. (1989). Meditation: Secular and sacred: Review and assessment of some recent research. *Journal of the Indian Academy of Applied Psychology, 15,* 51–74.

Rao, K. R., Dukhan, H., & Rao, P. V. K. (1978). Yogic meditation and psi scoring in forced-choice and free-response tests. *Journal of Indian Psychology, 1,* 160–175.

Rao, K. R., & Feola, J. (1979). Electrical activity of the brain and ESP: An exploratory study of alpha rhythm and ESP scoring. *Journal of Indian Psychology, 2,* 118–133.

Rao, K. R., & Palmer, J. (1987). The anomaly called psi: Recent research and criticism. *Behavioral and Brain Sciences, 10,* 539–555.

Rapaport, D. (1953). On the psychoanalytic theory of affects. *International Journal of Psychoanalysis, 34,* 177–198.

Rapaport, D. (1960). The structure of psychoanalytic theory. *Psychological Issues, 2* (2, monograph 6).

Rapaport, D. (1961). On the psychoanalytic theory of motivation. In M. Jones (Ed.), Nebraska Symposium on Motivation, 1960. Lincoln, Neb.: University of Nebraska Press.

Rapaport, D. (1967). *Collected papers.* M. M. Gill (Ed.) New York: Basic Books.

Rapaport, D. (1974). *The history of the concept of association of ideas.* New York: International Universities Press.

Rapaport, D. (Ed.) (1951). *Organization and pathology of thought: Selected sources.* New York: Columbia University Press.

Rapaport, D., & Gill, M. M. (1959). The points of view and assumptions of metapsychology. *International Journal of Psychoanalysis, 40,* 153–162.

Rapaport, D., Gill, M., & Schafer, R. (1946). *Diagnostic psychological testing: The theory, statistical evaluation and diagnostic application of a battery of tests,* Vol. 2. Chicago: Year Book Publishers.

Rapaport, D., Gill, M., Schafer, R. (1968/1946). *Diagnostic psychological testing.* New York: International Universities Press.

Rapier, J., Adelson, R., Carey, R., & Croke, K. (1972). Changes in children's attitude toward physically handicapped. *Exceptional Children, 39,* 212–219.

Rapoport, A. (1962). Modern developments in behavioral science in Poland. *Behavioral Science, 7,* 379–389.

Rapoport, A. (1970). Modern systems theory—An outlook for coping with change. *General Systems Yearbook, 15.*

Rapoport, A. (Winter 1980). Verbal maps and global politics. *Et cetera,* 297–312.

Rapoport, A., & Chammah, A. M. (1965). *Prisoner's dilemma: A study in conflict and cooperation.* Ann Arbor, Mich.: University of Michigan Press.

Rapoport, A., & Wallsten, T. S. (1972). Individual decision behavior. *Annual Review of Psychology, 23,* 131–176.

Rapoport, J., & Zametkin, A. (1980). Attention deficit disorder. *Psychiatric Clinics of North America, 3*(3), 425–441.

Rapoport, J. I., Mikkelson, E. J., Zavadil, A., Nee, L., Gruenau, C., Mendelson, W., & Gillin, C. (1980). Childhood enuresis. *Archives of General Psychiatry, 37,* 1146–1152.

Rapoport, R., & Rapoport, R. N. (1972). The dual career family: A variant pattern and social change. In C. Safilios-Rothschild (Ed.), *Towards a sociology of women.* Lexington, Mass.: Xerox.

Rappaport, A., (1974). *Conflict in man-made environment.* Baltimore, Md.: Penguin Books.

Rappaport, J. (1977). *Community psychology: Values, research and action.* New York: Holt, Rinehart & Winston.

Rappaport, J. (1981). In praise of paradox: A social policy of empowerment over prevention. *American Journal of Community Psychology, 9,* 1–25.

Rappaport, S. R. (1975). Ego development in learning disabled children. In W. Cruickshank & D. Hallahan (Eds.), *Perceptual and learning disabilities in children,* Vol. I. Syracuse, N.Y.: Syracuse University Press.

Rapport, M. D. (in press). Attention deficit-hyperactivity disorder. In T. H. Ollendick, & M. Hersen (Eds.), *Handbook of child and adolescent assessment*. New York: Pergamon.

Rapport, M. D., & Kelly, K. L. (1991). Psychostimulant effects on learning and cognitive function: Findings and implications for children with attention deficit hyperactivity disorder. *Clinical Psychology Review, 11*, 61–92.

Rapport, M. D., Stoner, G., DuPaul, G. J., Kelly, K. L., Tucker, S. B., & Schoeler, T. (1988). Attention deficit disorder and methylphenidate: A multilevel analysis of dose-response effects on children's impulsivity across settings. *Journal of the American Academy of Child and Adolescent Psychiatry, 27*, 60–69.

Raskin, D., & Klein, Z. (1976). Losing a symptom through keeping it: A review of paradoxical treatment techniques and rationale. *Archives of General Psychiatry, 33*, 548–555.

Raskin, L. M., & Bloom, A. S. (1979). Kinetic family drawings of children with learning disabilities. *Journal of Pediatric Psychology, 4*, 247–251.

Raskin, N. J. (1974). *Studies of psychotherapeutic orientation: Ideology and practice*. Research Monograph No. 1. Orlando, Fla. (now Atlanta, Ga.): American Academy of Psychotherapists.

Raskin, N. J. (1979). Carl R. Rogers. *International encyclopedia of the social sciences. Biographical supplement*. New York: Free Press.

Rath, R. (1973). *Psychosocial problems of social change*. New Delhi: Allied Publishers.

Rath, R. (1979). *Cognitive abilities and school achievement of the socially disadvantaged in primary schools*. New Delhi: Allied Publishers.

Rath, R. N. (1972). *Social psychology*. In S. K. Mitra (Ed.), *A survey of research in psychology*. Bombay: Popular Prakashan.

Rath, R. N. (1979). *Reorientation of teaching and research in psychology in the Indian Universities*. New Delhi: University Grants Commission.

Rathod, P. (1981). Methods for the analysis of rep grid data. In H. Bonarius, R. Holland, & S. Rosenberg (Eds.), *Personal construct psychology: Recent advances in theory and practice*. London: Macmillan.

Raths, L. E., Harmin, M., & Simon, S. B. (1966). *Values and teaching: Working with values in the classroom*. Columbus, Ohio: Merrill.

Rathus, S. A. (1973). A 30-item schedule for assessing assertive behavior. *Behavior Therapy, 4*, 398–406.

Ratner, S. C. (1967). Comparative aspects of hypnosis. In J. E. Gordon (Ed.), *Handbook of clinical and experimental hypnosis*. New York: Macmillan.

Ratner, S. C., & Denny, M. R. (1964). *Comparative psychology*. Homewood, IL: Dorsey.

Rauner, I. M. (1962). Occupational information and occupational choice. *Personnel and Guidance Journal 41*, 311–317.

Raush, H. L., Barry, W. A., Hertel, R. K., & Swain, M. A. (1974). *Communication, conflict, and marriage*. San Francisco: Jossey-Bass.

Raush, H. L., & Raush, C. L. (1968). *The halfway house movement, a search for sanity*. New York: Appleton-Century-Crofts.

Raven, B. H., & Kruglanski, A. W. (1970). Conflict and power. In P. Swingle (Ed.), *The structure of conflict*. New York: Academic Press.

Raven, B. H., & Rubin, J. Z. (1976). *Social psychology*. New York: Wiley.

Raven, J. C. (1960). *Guide to the standard progressive matrices*. London: Lewis.

Raven, J. C., Court, J. H., & Raven, J. (1976). *Manual for Raven's progressive matrices and vocabulary scales*. London: Lewis.

Ravensborg, M. R. (1976). Relaxation as therapy for addictive smoking. *Psychological Reports, 39*, 894.

Raviv, A. (1979). Reflections on the role of the school psychologist in Israel. *Professional Psychology, 10*, 820–826.

Raviv, A., Wiesner, E., & Bar-Tal, D. (1981). *Survey of psychologists in school psychological services: Research report* (in Hebrew). Jerusalem: Ministry of Education and Culture.

Ravizza, K. (1977). Peak experiences in sport. *Journal of Humanistic Psychology, 17*, 35–40.

Rawlings, E. I., & Carter, D. K. (1977). *Psychotherapy for women: Treatment toward equality*. Springfield, Ill.: Thomas.

Rawlings, E. I., & Carter, D. K. (Eds.). (1977). *Psychotherapy for women: Treatment towards equality*. IL: Thomas.

Rawls, J. (1971). *A theory of justice*, Cambridge, MA: Harvard University Press.

Rawson, M. B. (1968). *Developmental language disabilities: Adult accomplishments of dyslexic boys*. Baltimore, Md.: Johns Hopkins Press.

Ray, W., & Ravizza, R. (1981). *Methods toward a science of behavior and experience*. Belmont, Calif.: Wadsworth.

Rayman, J. (1976). Sex and the single interest inventory: The empirical validation of sex-balanced interest inventory items. *Journal of Counseling Psychology, 23*, 239–246.

Raynor, J. O. (1968). The relationship between distant future goals and achievement motivation. Unpublished doctoral dissertation, University of Michigan, Ann Arbor.

Razran, G. (1942). Current psychological theory in the U.S.S.R. *Psychological Bulletin, 39*, 445–446.

Razran, G. (1957). Soviet psychology since 1950. *Science, 126*, 1100–1107.

Razran, G. (1958). Soviet psychology and psychophysiology. *Science, 128*, 1187–1194.

Razran, G. (1961). The observable unconsciousness and the inferable conscious in current Soviet psychophysiology: Interoceptive conditioning and the orienting reflex. *Psychological Review, 68*, 81–147.

Razran, G. (1965). Russian physiologist's psychology and American experimental psychology: A historical and a systematic collation and a look into the future. *Psychological Bulletin, 63*, 42–64.

Razran, G. (1971). *Mind in evolution: An east-west synthesis*. New York: Academic Press.

Razran, G., & Kornilov, K. N. (1958). Theoretical and experimental psychologist. *Science, 128*, 74–75.

Read, H. (1958/1943). *Education through art*. London: Faber.

Read, J. D., Tollestrup, P., Hammersley, R., & McFadzen, E. (1990). The unconscious transference effect: Are innocent bystanders ever misidentified? *Applied Cognitive Psychology, 4*, 3–31.

Rebec, G. V., & Zimmerman, K. S. (1980). Opposite effects of d-amphetamine on spontaneous neuronal activity in the neostriatum and nucleus accumbens. *Brain Research, 201*, 485–491.

Rebecca, M., Hefner, R., & Oleshansky, B. (1976). A model of sex-role transcendence. *Journal of Social Issues, 32*, 197–206.

Reber, A. S. (1967). Implicit learning of artificial grammars. *Journal of Verbal Learning and Verbal Behavior, 6*, 855–863.

Reck, A. (Ed.) (1964). *Selected writings: George Herbert Mead*. New York: Bobbs-Merrill, 1964.

Recommended graduate training program in clinical psychology. (1947). *American Psychologist, 2*, 539–558.

Rector, M. (1973). Who are the dangerous? *Bulletin of the American Academy of Psychiatry and the Law, 1,* 186–188.

Redd, W. H., Andresen, G. V., & Minagawa, R. Y. (1982). Hypnotic control of anticipatory emesis in patients receiving cancer chemotherapy. *Journal of Consulting and Clinical Psychology, 50,* 14–19.

Redford, E., & Redford, M. A. (1949). *Encyclopedia of superstition,* New York: Philosophical Library.

Redl, F. (1951). *Children who hate.* Glencoe, Ill.: Free Press.

Redl, F., & Wineman, D. (1957). *The aggressive child.* New York: Free Press.

Redlich, F. C., Hollingshead, A. B. & Bellis, E. (1955). Social class differences in attitudes toward psychiatry. *American Journal of Orthopsychiatry, 25,* 60–70.

Reed, G. (1984, August 28). *Superstitious beliefs and cognitive processes.* Paper presented at the Symposium on Anomalistic Psychology, annual meeting of the American Psychological Association. Toronto.

Reed, J. C., & Reitan, R. M. (1969). Verbal and performance differences among brain injured children with lateralized motor deficits. *Perceptual and Motor Skills, 29.* 747–752.

Reese, H. W. (1973). Behaviorism and feedback control (letter). *Science, 181,* (4105).

Reese, H. W., & Overton, W. F. (1977). Models of development and theories of development. In L. R. Goulet & P. B. Baltes (Eds.), *Life-span developmental psychology: Research and theory.* New York: Academic Press.

Reese, J., & Goldstein, H. (Eds.). (1986). *Psychological services for law enforcement.* Washington, DC: U.S. Government Printing Office.

Reever, K. E., Bach-Peterson, J. M., & Zarit, S. H., (1979). Relatives of the impaired elderly. In *32nd Annual Scientific Meeting Program, Part II.* Washington, D.C.: Gerontological Society.

Regan, T., & Singer, P. (Eds.) (1976). *Animal rights and human obligations.* Englewood Cliffs, N.J.: Prentice-Hall.

Rehabilitation Act, Public Law 93–516, 88 Stat. 1619 *United States Code Congressional and Administrative News.*

Reich, C. A. (1970). *The greening of America.* New York: Random House.

Reich, J., Noyes, R., & Yates, W. (1988). Anxiety symptoms distinguishing social phobia from panic and generalized anxiety disorders. *The Journal of Nervous and Mental Disease,* 510–513.

Reich, J., Noyes, R., & Yates, W. (1989). Alprazolam treatment of avoidant personality traits in social phobic patients. *Journal of Clinical Psychiatry, 50,* 91–95.

Reich, J. W., & Zautra, A. (1981). Life events and personal causation: Some relationships with satisfaction and distress. *Journal of Personality and Social Psychology, 41,* 1002–1012.

Reich, W. (1945). The masochistic character. In W. Reich (Ed.), *Character analysis.* New York: Orgone Institute Press.

Reich, W. (1949/1933). *Charakteranalyse.* Leipzig: Sexpol Verlag.

Reich, W. (1970/1942). *The function of the orgasm.* New York: Farrat, Straus.

Reich, W. (1972/1945). *Character analysis* (3rd ed.). New York: Orgone Institute Press.

Reid, J. E. (1980/1951). *The Reid report.* Chicago: Reid.

Reid, J. E., & Inbau, F. E. (1977). *Truth and deception* (2nd ed.). Baltimore, Md.: Williams & Wilkins.

Reid, J. F. (1966). Learning to think about reading. *Educational Research, 9,* 56–62.

Reid, T. (1849). Essays on the intellectual powers of the mind, W. Hamilton (Ed.). Edinburgh: Macachian, Stewart.

Reid, W. H. (Ed.) (1978). *The psychopath: A comprehensive study of antisocial disorders and behaviors.* New York: Brunner/Mazel.

Reid, W. J., & Crisafulli, A. (1990). Marital discord and child behavior problems: A meta-analysis. *Journal of Abnormal Child Psychology, 18,* 105–117.

Reid, W. J., & Epstein, L. (1972). *Task-centered casework.* New York: Columbia University Press.

Reidy, T. J. (1977). The aggressive characteristics of abused and neglected children. *Journal of Clinical Psychology, 33*(4), 1140–1145.

Reiff, R., & Scheerer, M. (1959). *Memory and hypnotic age regression.* New York: International Universities Press.

Reiff, R. R., & Reissman, F. (1965). The indigenous nonprofessional: A strategy of change in community action and community mental health programs. *Community Mental Health Journal,* Monograph no. 1.

Reik, T. (1938). *Rituals.* New York: International Universities Press.

Reik, T. (1941). *Masochism in modern man,* New York: Grove Press.

Reik, T. (1948). *Listening with the third ear,* New York: Farrar, Straus.

Reik, T. (1949). *The unknown murderer,* New York: International Universities Press.

Reilly, M. (1974). Defining a cobweb. In M. Reilly (Ed.), *Play as exploratory learning.* London: Sage Publications.

Reimanis, G. (1974). Psychosocial development, anomie, and mood. *Journal of Personality and Social Psychology, 29,* 355–357.

Reinisch, J. M., Gandelman, R., & Spiegel, F. S. (1979). Prenatal influences on cognitive abilities: Data from experimental animals and human and endocrine syndromes. In M. A. Wittig & A. C. Petersen (Eds.), *Sexrelated differences in cognitive functioning: Developmental issues.* New York: Academic Press.

Reinisch, J. M., & Karow, W. G. (1977). Prenatal exposure to synthetic progestins and estrogens: Effects on human development. *Archives of Sexual Behavior, 6,* 257–288.

Reis, I. L. (1960). *Premarital sexual standards in America.* New York: Free Press.

Reisberg, D., & Heuer, F. (1992). Remembering emotional events. In E. Winograd & U. Neisser (Ed.), *Affect and flashbulb memories.* New York: Cambridge University Press.

Reisberg, D., & Leak, S. (1987). Visual imagery and memory for appearance: Does Clark Gable or George C. Scott have bushier eyebrows? *Canadian Journal of Psychology, 41,* 521–526.

Reisberg, D., Rappaport, I., & O'Shaughnessy, M. (1984). The limits of working memory: The digit digit-span. *Journal of Experimental Psychology: Learning, Memory, and Cognition, 10,* 203–221.

Reiser, M. (1980). *Handbook of investigative hypnosis.* Los Angeles: Lehi.

Reisman, J. M. (1976). *A history of clinical psychology.* New York: Irvington.

Reiss, A., Duncan, 0., Hatt, P., & North, C. (1961). *Occupations and social status.* New York: Free Press.

Reiss, D., Plomin, R., & Hetherington, E. (1991). Genetics and psychiatry: An unheralded window on the environment. *American Journal of Psychiatry, 148,* 283–291.

Reiss, I. L. (1960). Toward a sociology of the heterosexual love relationship. *Marriage and Family Living, 22,* 139–145.

Reiss, I. L. (1971). *The family system in America.* New York: Holt, Rinehart & Winston.

Reiss, M. (1958). *Psychoendocrinology*. New York: Grune & Stratton.

Reiss, M. L., Piotrowski, W. D., & Bailey, J. S. (1976). Behavioral community psychology: Encouraging low-income parents to seek dental care for their children. *Journal of Applied Behavioral Analysis, 9*, 387–397.

Reissman, F. (1965). The helper therapy principle. *Social Work, 10*, 27–32.

Reit, S. (1978). *Masquerade: The amazing camouflage deceptions of World War II*. New York: Hawthorn.

Reitan, R. M. (1955). The distribution according to age of a psychologic measure dependent upon organic brain function. *Journal of Gerontology, 10*, 338–340.

Reitan, R. M. (1966). A research program on the psychological effect of brain lesions in human beings. In N. R. Ellis (Ed.), *International review of research in mental retardation*. New York: Academic Press.

Reitan, R. M. *Manual for administration of neuropsychological test battery for adults and children*. Seattle, Wash.: Neuropsychology Laboratory, n.d.

Reitan, R. M., & Heineman, C. E. (1968). Interactions of neurological deficits and emotional disturbances in children with learning disorders: Methods for differential assessment. In H. R. Myklebust (Ed.), *Learning disorders*. Seattle, Wash.: Special Child Publications.

Reitan, R. M., & Wolfson, D. (1985). *The Halstead-Reitan neuropsychological test battery: Theory and clinical interpretation*. Tucson, AZ: Neuropsychology.

Reith, J. (1976). Group methods: Conferences, meetings, workshops, seminars. In R. Craig (Ed.). *Training & development handbook*. New York: McGraw-Hill.

Reitz, E. (1981). *The phenomenology of cancer patients: A holistic/Adlerian interpretation*. Unpublished doctoral dissertation, California School of Professional Psychology, Los Angeles.

Remplein, H. (1954). *Psychologie der Persönlichkeit*. Munich: Reinhardt.

Renneberg, B., Goldstein, A. M., Phillips, D., & Chambless, D. L. (1990). Intensive behavioral group treatment of avoidant personality disorder. *Behavior Therapy, 21*.

Rennie v. Klein, 476 F. Supp 1294 (D. N.J. 1979), *modified*, Nos. 79–2576 and 79–2577 (3rd. Cir. July 9, 1981).

Reno, V. R. (March 1972). Compulsory retirement among newly entitled workers. Preliminary findings from the survey of new beneficiaries report no. 7, Social Security Administration, Office of Research and Statistics.

Renouvier, P. (1948). Group psychotherapy in the United States. *Sociatry, 2*, 75–83.

Rentos, P. G., & Shepard, R. D. (Eds.) (1976). *Shift work and health*. Washington, D.C.: U.S. Department of Health, Education, and Welfare.

Renzulli, J. S. (1978). What makes giftedness? Reexamining a definition. *Phi Delta Kappan, 60*, 180–184, 261.

Report of The President's Commission on Mental Health: Task Panel on the Elderly. (1979). *Mental health and the elderly: Recommendations for action*. Washington, D.C.: U.S. Department of Health, Education, and Welfare, Federal Council on the Aging.

Repucci, N. D., & Clingempeel, W. G. (1978). Methodological issues in research with correctional populations. *Journal of Consulting and Clinical Psychology, 46*, 727–746.

Reschly, D. J. (1981). Psychological testing in educational classification and placement. *American Psychologist, 36*, 1094–1102.

Rescorla, R. A. (1966). Predictability and number of pairings in Pavlovian fear conditioning. *Psychonomic Science, 4*, 383–384.

Rescorla, R. A. (1969). Pavlovian conditioned inhibition. *Psychological Bulletin, 72*, 77–94.

Rescorla, R. A., & Solomon, R. L. (1967). Two-process learning theory: Relationships between Pavlovian conditioning and instrumental learning. *Psychological Review, 74*, 151–182.

Rescorla, R. A., & Wagner, A. R. (1972). A theory of Pavlovian conditioning: Variations in the effectiveness of reinforcement and nonreinforcement. In A. Black & W. F. Prokasy (Eds.), *Classical conditioning. II: Current research and theory*. New York: Appleton-Centry-Crofts.

Rescorla, R. A. & Wagner, A. R. (1972). A theory of Pavlovian conditioning: Variations in the effectiveness of reinforcement and nonreinforcement. In A. H. Black & W. F. Prokasy (Eds.), *Classical conditioning II* (pp. 64–99). New York: Appleton-Century-Crofts.

Research Task Force of the National Institute of Mental Health. (1975). *Research in the service of mental health*. (DHEW Publication No. ADM 75-236). Rockville, MD: National Institute of Mental Health.

Resnick, L. B. (1981). Instructional psychology. *Annual Review of Psychology, 32*, 659–704.

Resnick, L. B., & Ford, W. (1981). *The psychology of mathematics for instruction*. Hillsdale, N.J.: Erlbaum.

Resnick, P. (1984). The detection of malingered mental illness. *Behavioral Sciences and the Law, 2*, 21–38.

Resnick, R. J. (1992). National health is coming. *The Psychotherapy Bulletin, 26*(4), 17–20.

Ressier, L. E. (1991). Improving elderly recall with bimodal presentation: A natural experiment of discharge planning. *The Gerontologist, 31*, 364–370.

Rest, J. R. (1979). *Development in judging moral issues*. Minneapolis, Minn.: University of Minnesota Press.

Restak, R. M. (1979). *The brain: the last frontier*. Garden City, N.Y.: Doubleday.

Restle, F. (1962). The selection of strategies in cue learning. *Psychological Reports, 69*.

Results of poll. (1989, June 6). *San Francisco Examiner*, p. A19.

Reuben, D. (1969). *Everything you always wanted to know about sex but were afraid to ask*. New York: McKay.

Reuchlin, M. (1964). *Méthodes d'analyse factorielle à l'usage des psychologues*. Paris: Presses Universitaires de France.

Reuchlin, M. (1975/1962). *Les méthodes quantitatives en psychologie* (2nd ed.). Paris: Presses Universitaires de France.

Reuchlin, M. (1979). *Précis de statistique* (2nd ed.). Paris: Presses Universitaires de France.

Reuchlin, M. (1980/1957). *Histoire de la psychologie* (11th ed.). Paris: Presses Universitaires de France.

Reuchlin, M. (1981/1969). *La psychologie différentielle* (3rd ed.). Paris: Presses Universitaires de France.

Reuchlin, M., & Bacher, F. (1968). *L'orientation à lafin du premier cycle secondaire*. Paris: Presses Universitaires de France.

Revers, W. J. (1979/1958). *Der thematische Apperzeptionstest (TAT)*. Bern: Huber.

Revusky, S. (1962). Mathematical analysis of the durations of reinforced interresponse times during variable interval reinforcement. *Psychometrika, 27*, 307–314.

Revusky, S. (1968). Aversion to sucrose produced by contingent X-irradiation: Temporal and dosage parameters. *Journal of Comparative and Physiological Psychology, 65*, 17–22.

Revusky, S. (1971). The role of interference in association over a delay. In W. K. Honig & P. H. R. James (Eds.), *Animal memory*. New York: Academic Press.

Revusky, S. (1977). Learning as a general process with an emphasis on data from feeding experiments. In N. W. Milgram, L. Krames, & T. M. Alloway (Eds.), *Food aversion learning*. New York: Plenum.

Revusky, S., & Coombes, S. (1982). Long-delay associations between drug states produced by injecting two drugs in sequence. *Journal of Comparative and Physiological Psychology, 96*, 549–556.

Rex v. Arnold, 16 Haw. St. tr. 695 (1724).

Rey, A. (1947). *Etude des insuffissances psychologiques*. Vol. I. *Méthodes et problèmes*. Vol. II: *Le diagnostic psychologique*. Neuchâtel, Switzerland: Delachaux & Niestlé.

Rey, A. (1969). *Psychologie clinique et neurologie*. Neuchâtel, Switzerland: Delachaux & Niestlé.

Reykowski, J. (1982). Motivation of prosocial behavior. In V. J. Derlega & J. Grzelak (Eds.), *Cooperation and helping behavior*. New York: Academic Press.

Reykowski, J. (1982). Social motivation. *Annual Review of Psychology, 33*, 123–154.

Reynolds, C. R. (1981). In support of bias in mental testing and scientific inquiry. *Behavioral and Brain Sciences, 3*, 352.

Reynolds, C. R. (1982). The problem of bias in psychological assessment. In C. R. Reynolds & T. B. Gutkin (Eds.), *The handbook of school psychology*. New York: Wiley.

Reynolds, C. R., & Brown, R. T. (1984). *Perspectives on bias in mental testing*. New York: Plenum.

Reynolds, D. K. (1976). *Morita psychotherapy*. Berkeley, Calif.: University of California Press.

Reynolds, D. K. (1977). Naikan therapy—An experiential view. *International Journal of Social Psychology, 23*, 252–264.

Reynolds, D. K. (1980). *The quiet therapies*. Honolulu: University Press of Hawaii.

Reynolds, D. K.(1981). Morita therapy. In R. J. Corsini (Ed.), *Handbook of innovative psychotherapies*. New York: Wiley.

Reynolds, D. K. (1983). *Naikan psychotherapy*. Chicago: University of Chicago Press.

Reynolds, D. K., & Yamamoto, J. (1973). Morita psychotherapy in Japan. *Current Psychiatric Therapies, 13*, 219–227.

Reynolds, G. S. (1961). Attention in the pigeon. *Journal of the Experimental Analysis of Behavior, 4*, 203–208.

Reynolds, G. S. (1968). *A primer of operant conditioning*, Glenview, Ill.: Scott, Foresman.

Reynolds, M., & Birch, J. (1977). *Teaching exceptional children in all America's schools: A first course for teachers and principals*. Reston, Va.: Council for Exceptional Children.

Reynolds, P. D. (1979). *Ethical dilemmas and social science research: An analysis of moral issues confronting investigators in research using human participants*. San Francisco: Jossey-Bass.

Rheingold, H. (1968). Infancy. *International encyclopedia of the social sciences*, Vol. 7. New York: Crowell-Collier/Macmillan.

Rheingold, H. L. (Ed.). (1963). *Maternal behavior in mammals*. New York: Wiley.

Rheingold, H. L. (1969). The social and socializing infant. In D. A. Goslin (Ed.), *Handbook of socialization theory and research*. Chicago: Rand-McNally.

Rheingold, H. L. (1982). Little children's participation in the work of adults, anascent prosocial behavior. *Child Development, 53*, 114–125.

Rheingold, H. L., & Adams, J. L. (1980). The significance of speech to newborns. *Developmental Psychology, 16*, 397–403.

Rheingold, H. L., & Cook, K. V. (1975). The contents of boys' and girls' rooms as an index of parents' behavior. *Child Development, 46*, 459–463.

Rheingold, H. L., & Eckerman, C. O. (1973). Fear of the stranger: A critical examination. In H. W. Reese (Ed.), *Advances in child development and behavior*, Vol. 8. New York: Academic Press.

Rheingold, H. L., Gewirtz, J. L., & Ross, H. W. (1959). Social conditioning of vocalizations in the infant. *Journal of Comparative and Physiological Psychology, 52*, 68–73.

Rheingold, H. L., Hay, D. F., & West, M. J. Sharing in the second year of life. *Child Development, 47*, 1148–1158.

Rhine, J. B. (1952). The problem of psi-missing. *Journal of Parapsychology, 16*, 90—129.

Rhine, J. B. (1969). Psi-missing reexamined. *Journal of Parapsychology, 33*, 1–38.

Rhine, J. B. (1971/1953). *New world of the mind*. New York: Morrow.

Rhine, J. B. (1972/1937). *New frontiers of the mind*. Westport, Conn.: Greenwood Press.

Rhine, J. B. (1972/1947). *The reach of the mind*. New York: Sloane.

Rhine, J. B. (1973/1934). *Extrasensory perception* (rev. ed.). Boston: Humphries.

Rhine, J. B. (1974). *Comments: A New Case of Experimenter Unreliability*. *Journal of Parapsychology, 38*, 2, 215–225.

Rhine, J. B., & Humphrey, B. M. (1944). The PK effect: Special evidence from hit patterns: I—Quarter distributions of the page. *Journal of Parapsychology, 8* 18–60.

Rhine, J. B., & Pratt, J. G. (1954). A review of the Pearce-Pratt distance series of ESP tests. *Journal of Parapsychology, 18*, 165–177.

Rhine, J. B., Pratt, J. G., Stuart, C. E., Smith, B. M., & Greenwood, J. A. (1966/1940). *Extrasensory perception after sixty years*. Boston: Humphries.

Rhine, L. E. (1961). *Hidden channels of the mind*. New York: Sloane.

Rhoades, G. (1992). *Comments. Understanding and treatment of satanic ritualistic abuse*. Inservice at Kahi Mohala Psychiatric Hospital, Honolulu.

Rhyne, J. L. (1973). *The gestalt art experience*. Monterey, Calif.: Brooks/Cole.

Rhys, W. T. (1972). Geography and the adolescent. *Educational Review, 24*, 183–196.

Ribble, M. (1943). *The rights of infants*. New York: Columbia University Press.

Ribes-Iñesta, E. *El conductismo: Reflexiones críticas*.

Ribes-Iñesta, E. (1968). Psychology in Mexico. *American Psychologist, 23*, 565–566.

Ribes-Iñesta, E. (1975). Some recent developments in psychology in Mexico. *American Psychologist, 30*, 774–776.

Ribes-Iñesta, E. (1976/1974). *Técnicas de modificación de conducta: Su aplicación al retardo en el desarrollo*. Mexico, D.F.: Trillas.

Ribes-Iñesta, E., & Bandura, A. (1976). *Analysis of delinquency and aggression*. New York: Halstead.

Ribes-Iñiesta, E., & Bijou, S. W. (1972). *Behavior modification: Issues and extensions*. New York: Academic Press.

Ribes-Iñesta, E., Lopez, F., et al. *Enseñanza, investigación y ejercicio de la psicología: Un modelo integral*.

Ribordy, S. C., Holmes, D. S., & Buchsbaum, H. K. (1980). Effects of affective and cognitive distractions on anxiety reduction. *Journal of Social Psychology, 112*, 121–127.

Ribot, T. (1870). *English psychology,* London: King.

Ribot, T. (1870). *La psychologie anglaise contemporaine.* Paris: Alcan.

Ribot, T. (1881). *Les maladies de la mémoire.* Paris: Alcan.

Ribot, T. (1883). *Les maladies de la volonté.* Paris: Alcan.

Ribot, T. (1885). *Les maladies de la personnalité.* Paris: Alcan.

Ribot, T. (1886). *German psychology of today,* New York: Scribner's.

Ribot, T. (1896). *La psychologie des sentiments.* Paris: Alcan.

Ribot, T. (1900). *L'imagination créative.* Paris: Alcan.

Ribot, T. (1907). *Essai sur les passions.* Paris: Alcan.

Ribot, T. (1914). *La vie inconsciente et les mouvements.* Paris: Alcan.

Rice, B. (1982). The Hawthorne defect: Persistence of a flawed theory. *Psychology Today, 16*(2), 70—74.

Rich, A. R., & Schroeder, H. E. (1976). Research issues in assertiveness training. *Psychological Bulletin, 83,* 1081–1096.

Rich, E., & Knight, K. (1991). *Artificial intelligence.* New York: McGraw-Hill.

Richards, C. (1987). *Human evolution.* London: Routledge & Kegan Paul.

Richards, G. L., & Inskeep, G. C. (Spring, 1974). The middle manager—his continuing education and the business school. *Collegiate News and Views,* 5–7.

Richards, I. A. (1977). *The republic of Plato, book 111.* New York: Norton.

Richards, I. A., Ogden, C. K., & Wood, J. (1974/1925). *The foundations of aesthetics.* New York: Haskill House.

Richards, J. (1974). *But deliver us from evil: An introduction to the demonic dimensions in pastoral care.* London: Darton, Longman & Todd.

Richards, M. C. (1980). *Toward wholeness: Rudolf Steiner education in America.* Middletown, Conn.: Wesleyan University Press.

Richards, M. P. M. (1974). First steps in becoming social. In M. P. M. Richards (Ed.), *The integration of a child into a social world.* London: Cambridge University Press.

Richards, W. A. (1975). Counseling, peak experiences and the human encounter with death: An empirical study of the efficacy of DPT-assisted counseling in enhancing the quality of life of persons with terminal cancer. Unpublished doctoral dissertation, Catholic University of America.

Richardson, A. (1969). *Mental imagery.* New York: Springer.

Richardson, A. (1977). Verbalizer-visualizer: A cognitive style dimension. *Journal of Mental Imagery, 1,* 109–126.

Richardson, A. (1983). Imagery: Definition and types. In A. A. Sheikh (Ed.), *Imagery: Current theory, research, and application.* New York: Wiley.

Richardson, C., & Meyer, R. C. (1972). Techniques in guided group interaction programs. *Child Welfare, 51,* 519–527.

Richardson, G. F. (1987). Munchausen syndrome by proxy. *American Family Physician, 16,* 119–123.

Richardson, J. (1980). *Mental imagery and human memory.* New York: St. Martin's.

Richardson, L. F., & Ross, J. S. (1930). Loudness and telephone current. *Journal of General Psychology, 3,* 288–306.

Richardson, M. W. (1938). Multidimensional psychophysics. *Psychological Bulletin, 35,* 659–660.

Richardson, S. A. (1976). The relation of severe malnutrition in infancy to intelligence of school children with different life histories. *Pediatric Research, 10,* 57–61.

Richet, C. (1975/1923). *Thirty years of psychical research.* New York: Arno Press.

Richman, N., Stevenson, J. S., & Graham, P. J. (1982). *Preschool to school. A behavioral study.* London: Academic.

Richman, S., & Schoon, C. G. (September 2, 1980). Candidates' characteristics: The examination for professional practice in psychology, 1979–80. Presented at the meeting of the American Psychological Association, Montreal.

Richmond, M. (1917). *Social diagnosis.* New York: Columbia University Press.

Richter, C. P. (1936). Increased salt appetite in adrenalectomized rats. *American Journal of Psychology, 115,* 155–161.

Richter, C. P. (1943). The self-selection of diets. In *Essays in biology in honor of Herbert M. Evans,* Berkeley, Calif.: University of California Press.

Richter, C. P. (1947). Biology of drives. *Journal of Comparative and Physiological Psychology,40,* 129–134.

Richter, C. P. (1956). Salt appetite of mammals: Its dependence on instinct and metabolism. In P. P. Grasse (Ed.), *L'instinct dans le comportement des animaux et de l'homme.* Paris: Masson.

Richter, C. P. (1959). The phenomenon of unexplained sudden death in animals and man. In H. Feifel (Ed.), *The meaning of death.* New York: McGraw Hill.

Richter, E. D., Gordon, M., Halamish, M., & Gribetz, B. (1981). Death and injury in aerial spraying: Pre-crash, crash, and post-crash prevention strategies. *Aviation, Space, and Environmental Medicine, 52,* 53–56.

Rickers-Ovsiankina, M. A., (Ed.). (1977/1960). *Rorschach psychology.* New York: Krieger.

Ricketson, D. S., Brown, W. R., & Graham, K. N. (1980). 3W approach to the investigation, analysis, and prevention of human-error aircraft accidents. *Aviation, Space, and Environmental Medicine, 51,* 1036–1104.

Rie, E. D., Rie, H. E., Stewart, S., & Rettenmier, S. C. (1978). An analysis of neurological soft signs in children with learning problems. *Brain and Language, 6,* 32–46.

Rie, H. E. (1975). Hyperactivity in children. *American Journal of Diseases of Children, 130,* 783–789.

Rieben, L. (1978). *Intélligence et pensée créative.* Neuchâtel, Switzerland: Delachaux & Niestlé.

Richer, R. W. (Ed.). (1980). *Wilhelm Wundt and the making of a scientific psychology.* New York: Plenum.

Ridley, C. R. (1989). Racism in counseling as an aversive behavioral process. In P. Pedersen, J. Draguns, W. Lonner, & J. Trimble (Eds.), *Counseling across cultures.* (3rd ed.). Honolulu: University of Hawaii Press.

Riebel, L. (1984). Paradoxical intention strategies: A review of rationales. *Psychotherapy, 21,* 260–272.

Rieber, R. W., & Salzinger, K. (Eds.). (1977). The roots of American psychology: Historical influences and implications for the future. *Annals of the New York Academy of Sciences, 291.*

Riecken, H. W., & Borueh, R. F. (Eds.). (1974). *Social experimentation: A method for planning and evaluating social intervention.* New York: Academic Press.

Riegel, K. F. (1976). The dialectics of human development. *American Psychologist, 31,* 689–700.

Riegel, K. F. (1979). *Foundations ofdialecticalpsychology.* New York: Academic Press.

Riegel, K. F. (Ed.). (1975). *The development of dialectical operations.* Basel: Karger.

Riegel, K. F., & Riegel, R. M. (1972). Development, drop, and death. *Developmental Psychology, 6,* 306–319.

Rieger, C. Beschriebung der Intelligenzstörnng in Folge einer Hirnverletzung nebst einem Entwurf zu einer allgemein anwendbaren Methode der Intelligenzprüfung. Würzburg: *Verhandlungen der physiologisch medizinischen Gesellschaft zu Würzburg,* Neue Folge 22.

Rieken, H. W. (1977, November). Principal components of the evaluation process. *Professional Psychology.*

Riesman, D., Glazer, N., & Denny, R. (1953). *The lonely crowd.* New York: Doubleday.

Riessman, F. (1965). The "helper" therapy principle. *Social Work, 10,* 27–32.

Riley, D., & Eckenrode, J. (1986). Social ties: Subgroup differences in costs and benefits. *Journal of Personality and Social Psychology, 51,* 770–778.

Riley, D. A. (1968). *Discrimination learning.* Boston: Allyn & Bacon.

Riley, D. A., & Lamb, M. R. (1979). Stimulus generalization. In A. D. Pick (Ed.), *Perception and its development: A tribute to E. J. Gibson.* Hillsdale, N.J.: Erlbaum.

Riley, E. P., & Barron, S. (1989). The behavioral and neuroanatomical effects of prenatal alcohol exposure in animals. *Annals of the New York Academy of Sciences, 592,* 173–177.

Riley, M. W. (1976). Age strata in social systems. In R. H. Bistock & E. Shanas (Eds.), *Handbook of aging and the social sciences.* New York: Van Nostrand Reinhold.

Riley, M. W. (Ed.). (1979). *Aging from birth to death: Interdisciplinary perspectives.* Boulder, Colo.: Westview Press.

Riley, S. (1982). Common drugs used by pregnant women and their effects on babies. Bay Area Addiction Research and Treatment Center, Unpublished report.

Riley, V. (1981). Psychoneuroendocrine influences on immunocompetence and neoplasia. *Science, 212,* 1100–1109.

Rimland, B. (1964). *Infantile autism: The syndrome and its implications for a neural theory of behavior.* Englewood Cliffs, N.J.: Prentice-Hall.

Rimland, B. (1974). Infantile autism: Status of research. *Canadian Psychiatric Association Journal 19,* 130–133.

Rimland, B. (August 1978). Inside the mind of the autistic savant. *Psychology Today,* 69–80.

Rimm, D. C., & Masters, J. C. (1979). *Behavior therapy: Techniques and empirical findings* (2nd ed.). New York: Academic Press.

Rin, H. (1965). A study of the etiology of *Koro* in respect to the Chinese concept of illness. *International Journal of Social Psychiatry, 11,* 7–13.

Rinehart, J. (1966). *The Australians.* Adelaide, Australia: Rigby.

Ring, K. (1980). *Life at death: A scientific investigation of the near-death experience.* New York: Coward, McCann & Geoghegan.

Ring, K. (1984). *Heading toward omega: In search of the meaning of the near-death experience.* New York: Morrow.

Ring, K., & Rosing, C. J. (1990). The Omega Project: An empirical study of the NDE-prone personality. *Journal of Near-Death Studies, 8,* 211–239.

Rioch, M. (1966). Changing concepts in the training of therapists. *Journal of Consulting Psychology, 30,* 290–292.

Rioch, M. J., Coulter, W. R., & Weinberger, D. M. (1976). *Dialogues for therapists.* San Francisco: Jossey-Bass.

Riopelle, A. J., & Hill, C. W. (1973). Complex processes. In D. A. Dewsbury & D. A. Rethlingshafer (Eds.), *Comparative psychology: A modern survey.* New York: McGraw-Hill.

Risman, B. J., Hill, C. T., Rubin, Z., & Peplau, L. A. (1981). Living together in college: Implications for courtship. *Journal of Marriage and the Family, 43,* 77–83.

Riso, O. (Ed.). (1980). *The Dartnell sales managers' handbook.* Chicago: Dartnell.

Ristau, C. A., & Robbins, D. (1982). Language in great apes: A critical review. In J. S. Rosenblatt (Ed.), *Advances in the study of behavior.* New York: Academic Press.

Ritchie, J. F. (1943). The African as suckling and as adult. A psychological study. Rhodes-Livingstone Institute paper no 9.

Ritchie, J. M. (1970). Central nervous system stimulants: The xanthines. In L. S. Goodman, & A. Gilman (Eds.). *The pharmacological basis of therapeutics.* Toronto: Collier/Macmillan.

Ritter, P., & Ritter, J. (1959). *The free family: A creative experiment in self-regulation for children.* New York: Doubleday.

Ritual Abuse Task Force. (1989, September 15). *Ritual abuse: Definitions, glossary, the use of mind control.* Los Angeles: Los Angeles County Commission for Women.

Ritzer, G. (1975). *Society: A multiple paradigm science.* Boston: Allyn & Bacon.

Riva, D., & Cazzaniga, L. (1986). Late effects of unilateral brain lesions sustained before and after age one. *Neuropsychologia, 24,* 423–428.

Rivera-Sierra, R., & Urbina-Soria J. (1989). Estadisticas basicas sobre la formacion de psicologos en Mexico. In J. Urbina-Soria (Ed.), *El psicologo, formacion, ejercicio professional, prospectiva.* Mexico City: UNAM.

Rivers, W. H. R. (1914). *History of Melanesian society* (2 vols.). London: Cambridge University Press.

Rivers, W. H. R. (1922). *Instinct and the unconscious,* Cambridge, England: Cambridge University Press.

Rivers, W. H. R. (1923). *Conflict and dreams,* London: Harcourt.

Rivers, W. H. R. (1924). *Medicine, magic and religion,* London: Harcourt.

Rizzo, M., & Eslinger, P. J. (1989). Colored hearing synesthesia: An investigation of neural factors. *Neurology, 39,* 781–784.

Roach, M. E., & Eicher, J. B. (Eds.). (1965). *Dress, adornment, and the social order.* New York: Wiley.

Roazen, P. (1976/1975). *Freud and his followers.* New York: Meridian, .

Roback, A. A. (1927). *The psychology of character.* New York: Harcourt, Brace.

Roback, A. A. (1952). *History of American psychology.* New York: Library Publishers.

Roback, H. B. (1971). The comparative influence of insight and noninsight psychotherapies (or) therapeutic outcome: A review of the experimental literature. *Psychotherapy: Theory, Research and Practice, 8,* 23–25.

Robaye, E., Robaye, F., & Falmagne, J. C. (1960). Le testing de l'éducabilité dans un groupe de noirs congolais. *Bulletin de l'Academie Royale des Sciences d'Outre-Mer, Nouvelle Série, 6,* 295–321.

Robbins, A. (1980). *Expressive therapy.* New York: Human Sciences Press.

Robbins, J., & Fisher, D. (1972). *Tranquility without pills.* New York: Wyden.

Robbins, P. R., Tanck, R. H., & Meyerberg, H. A. (1972). Psychological factors in smoking, drinking, and drug experimentation. *Journal of Clinical Psychology, 27*(4), 450–452.

Robbins, W. S. (1975). Termination: Problems and techniques, *Journal of the American Psychoanalytic Association, 23,* 166–176.

Roberts, J. A. P., & Pembrey, M. E. (1985). *An introduction to medical genetics* (8th ed.). Oxford, UK: Oxford University Press.

Roberts, K. (1977). The social conditions, consequences, and limitations of careers guidance. *British Journal of Guidance and Counselling, 5,* 1–9.

Roberts, K. H., & Glick, W. (1981). The job characteristics approach to task design: A critical review. *Journal of Applied Psychology, 66,* 193–217.

Roberts, M., LaGreca, A., & Harper, D. (1988). Another stage of development. *Journal of Pediatric Psychology, 13,* 1–5.

Roberts, M. C., & Walker, C. E. (Eds.). (1989). *Casebook of child and pediatric psychology.* New York: Guilford.

Roberts, M. C., & Wright, L. (1982). The role of the pediatric psychologist as consultant to pediatricians. In J. Tuma (Eds.), *Handbook for the practice of pediatric psychology.* (pp. 251–289).

Roberts, T. (1978). Beyond self-actualization, *Re-Vision, 1,* 42–46.

Robertson, G. J. (1970). Innovation in the assessment of individual differences: Development of the first group mental ability test. *Test service notebook 30.* New York: Harcourt Brace Jovanovich.

Robertson, J., & Bowlby, J. (1952). Responses of young children to separation from their mother. II. Observations of the sequences of response of children aged 16 to 24 months during the course of separation. *Courrier du Centre International de l'Enfance, 2,* 131–142.

Robertson, R. J. (1961). Some applications of feedback theory to clinical work with organic and aphasic patients. In *V.A. Research Hospital and Northwestern University Medical School, Psychiatric Research Papers.*

Robertson, R. J. (1966). Factory reject personalities and the human salvage operations, *Journal of Applied Behavioral Science, 2,* 331–335.

Robertson, R. J. (1971). A "naturalistic" approach to psychotherapy training. *Psychotherapy: Theory, Research and Practice, 8,* 246–250.

Robertson, R. J., Clark, R. K., & McFarland, R. L. (1964). A new approach to the study of complex learning. Unpublished, Veterans Administration Research Hospital and Northwestern University Medical School.

Robertson, T. S. (1970). *Consumer behavior.* Glenview, Ill.: Scott, Foresman.

Robie, W. F. (1963). *The art of love.* New York: Paperback Library.

Robin, E. D. (Ed.). (1979). *Claude Bernard and the internal environment: A memorial symposium.* New York: Dekker.

Robins, L. N. (1966). *Deviant children grown up.* Baltimore, Md.: Williams & Wilkins.

Robins, L. N. (1978). Sturdy childhood predictors of adult antisocial behavior: Replication from longitudinal studies. *Psychological Medicine, 8,* 611–622.

Robinson v. *California,* 370 U.S. 660.

Robins, L. N. (1981). Epidemiological approaches to natural history research: Antisocial disorders in children. *Journal of the American Academy of Child Psychiatry, 20,* 566–580.

Robins, L. N. (1986). Changes in conduct disorder over time. In D. C. Farran & J. D. McKinney (Eds.), *Risk in intellectual and psychosocial development.* Orlando: Academic.

Robins, L. N., Heizer, J. E., Croughan, J., & Ratcliff, K. S. (1981). National Institute of Mental Health diagnostic schedule. *Archives of General Psychiatry, 38,* 381–389.

Robins, L. N., & Price, R. (in press). Conduct problems and adult psychiatric disorder. *Psychiatry.*

Robins, L. N., Tipp, J., & McEvoy, L. (in press). Antisocial personality. In L. N. Robins & D. Regier (Eds.), *Psychiatric disorders in America.* New York: Free Press.

Robinson, D. K. (1974). Harm, offense, and nuisance: Some first steps in the establishment of an ethics of treatment. *American Psychologist, 29,* 233–238.

Robinson, D. N. (1973). Therapies: A clear and present danger. *American Psychologist, 28,* 129–133.

Robinson, D. N. (1976). *An intellectual history of psychology.* New York: Macmillan.

Robinson, E. S., & Bills, A. G. (1926). Two factors in the work decrement. *Journal of Experimental Psychology, 9,* 415–443.

Robinson, F. P. (1970). *Effective study* (4th ed.). New York: Harper & Row.

Robinson, F. P. (1980). Counseling psychology since the Northwestern Conference. In A. S. Thompson & D. E. Super (Eds.), *The professional preparation of counseling psychologists. Report of the 1964 Greyston Conference.* New York: Bureau of Publications, Teachers College, Columbia University, 1964. Also in J. M. Whiteley (Ed.), *The history of counseling psychology.* Monterey, Calif.: Brooks/ Cole.

Robinson, H., & Robinson, N. (1971). Longitudinal development of very young children in a comprehensive day care program: The first two years. *Child Development, 42,* 1673–1683.

Robinson, H. M. (1972). Perceptual training—Does it result in reading improvement? In R. C. Aukerman (Ed.), *Some persistent questions on beginning reading.* Newark, Dela.: International Reading Association.

Robinson, H. M., & Smith, H. K. (1962). Reading clinic clients—Ten years after. *Elementary School Journal, 63,* 22–27.

Robinson, J. P., & Shaver, P. R. (1973/1969). *Measures of social psychological attitudes* (rev. ed.). Ann Arbor, Mich.: Institute for Social Research.

Robinson, N. M., & Robinson, H. B. (1972). A cross-cultural view of early education. In I. J. Gordon (Ed.), *Early childhood education—Seventy-first yearbook of the National Society for the Study of Education.* Chicago: University of Chicago Press.

Robinson, N. M., Robinson, H. B., Darling, N., & Holm, G. (1979). *A world of children: Day care and preschool institutions.* Monterey, Calif.: Brooks/ Cole.

Robinson, P. W., & Foster, D. F. (1979). *Experimental psychology: A small-n approach.* New York: Harper & Row.

Robinson, V. P. (1930). A changing psychology in social case work. Philadelphia, Pa.: University of Pennsylvania Press.

Robinson, W. J. (1915). *Treatment of sexual impotence.* New York: Critic & Guide.

Robinson, W. J. (1939). *Woman: Her sex and love life.* New York: Eugenics.

Robinson, W. P. (1975). Boredom in school. *British Journal of Educational Psychology, 45,* 141–152.

Robitscher, J. (1978). The limits of psychiatric authority. *International Journal of Law and Psychiatry, 1,* 183–204.

Robles, O. (1952). Panorama de la psicología en México, pasado y presente. *Filosofiá y Letras, 23,* 239–263.

Rock, I. (1966). *The nature of perceptual adaptation.* New York: Basic Books.

Rock, I. (1977). In defense of unconscious inference. In W. Epstein (Ed.), *Stability and constancy in visual perception*. New York: Wiley.

Rock, I, & Ebenholtz, S. (1959). The relational determination of perceived size. *Psychological Review, 66*, 387–401.

Rock, P. (1979). *The making of symbolic interactionism*, Totowa, N.J.: Row & Littlefield.

Rockerfeller, J. D. (1992). *Congressional Record*, S.117.

Rockowitz, R. J., & Davidson, P. W. (1979). Discussing diagnostic findings with parents. *Journal of Learning Disabilities,12*, 2–7.

Rodin, J., & Langer, E. J. (1977). Long-term effects of control-relevant intervention with the institutionalized aged. *Journal of Personality and Social Psychology, 35*, 897–902.

Rodriguez de Arizmendi, G. (1971/1972). L'enseignement universitaire de la psychologie au Mexique. *Bulletin de Psychologie, 294, 25*, 38–44.

Roe, A. (1951). A psychological study of eminent biologists. *Psychological Monographs, 65*(14, entire no. 331).

Roe, A. (1951). A psychological study of eminent physical scientists. *Genetic Psychological Monographs, 43*, 121–239.

Roe, A. (1951). A study of imagery in research scientists. *Journal of Personality, 19*, 459–470.

Roe, A. (1953). A psychological study of eminent psychologists and anthropologists, and a comparison with biological and physical scientists. *Psychological Monographs, 67*(2, entire no. 352).

Roe, A. (1956). *Psychology of occupations*. New York: Wiley.

Roe, A. (1957). Early determinants of vocational choice. *Journal of Counseling Psychology, 4*, 212–217.

Roe, A., Gustad, J. W., Moore, B. V., Ross, S., & Skodak, M. (Eds.). (1959). *Graduate education in psychology*. Washington, D.C.: American Psychological Association.

Roebuck, J. A., Jr., Kroemer, K. H. E., & Thomson, W. G. (1975). *Engineering anthrometry methods*. New York: Wiley.

Roeder, K. D. (1963). *Nerve cells and insect behavior*. Cambridge, Mass.: Harvard University Press.

Roediger, H. L. (1985). Remembering Ebbinghaus. *Contemporary Psychology, 30*, 519–523.

Roediger, H. L. (1990). Implicit memory: Retention without remembering. *American Psychologist, 45*, 1043–1056.

Roesch, R., & Golding, S. (1980). *Competency to stand trial*. Urbana, Ill.: University of Illinois Press.

Roethlisberger, F. J. (1941). *Management and morale*. Cambridge, Mass.: Harvard University Press.

Roethlisberger, F. J., & Dickson, W. J. (1939). *Management and the worker*. Cambridge, Mass.: Harvard University Press.

Rofman, E. S., Aszinazi, C., & Fant, E. (1980). The prediction of dangerous behavior in emergency civil commitment. *American Journal of Psychiatry, 137*, 1061–1064.

Rogawski, A. S. (1979). *Mental health consultations in community settings: New directions for mental health services*. San Francisco: Jossey-Bass.

Rogers v. *Okin*, 478 F. Snpp. 1342 (D. Mass. 1979) *aff'd in part, rev'd in part*, 634 F.2d 650 (1st Cir. 1980), *cert. granted*, 49 U.S.L.W. 3779 (1981).

Rogers, C. (1957). Necessary and sufficient conditions for therapeutic personality change. *Journal of Consulting Psychology, 21*, 95–103.

Rogers, C. (1957). The necessary and sufficient conditions of therapeutic personality change. *Journal of Consulting Psychology, 21*, 95–103.

Rogers, C. R. (1939). *The clinical treatment of the problem child*. Boston: Houghton Mifflin.

Rogers, C. R. (1942). *Counseling and Psychotherapy*. Boston: Houghton Mifflin.

Rogers, C. R. (1942). *Counseling and psychotherapy*. New York: Houghton Mifflin.

Rogers, C. R. (1951). *Client-centered therapy*. Boston:Houghton Mifflin.

Rogers, C. R. (1958). A process conception of psychotherapy. *American Psychologist, 13*, 142–149.

Rogers, C. R. (1959). A theory of therapy, personality, and interpersonal relationships, as developed in the client-centered framework. In S. Koch (Ed.), *Psychology: A study of a science*. Vol. III: *Formulations of the person and the social context*. New York: McGraw-Hill.

Rogers, C. R. (1961). *On becoming a person*. Boston: Houghton Mifflin, 1961.

Rogers, C. R. (1962). Toward becoming a fully functioning person. *Perceiving, behaving, becoming, 1962 Yearbook, Association for Supervision and Curriculum Development* Washington, D.C.: National Education Association.

Rogers, C. R. (1963). Psychotherapy today: Or, where do we go from here? *American Journal of Psychotherapy, 17*, 5–16.

Rogers, C. R. (1963). The actualizing tendency in relation to "motives' and to consciousness. In M. Jones (Ed.), *Nebraska Symposium on Motivation*. Lincoln, Neb.: University of Nebraska Press.

Rogers, C. R. (1965/1951). *Client-centered therapy*. Cambridge, Mass.: Houghton Mifflin.

Rogers, C. R. (1970). *Carl Rogers on encounter groups*. New York: Harper & Row.

Rogers, C. R. (1972). *Becoming partners: Marriage and its alternatives*. New York: Delacorte.

Rogers, C. R. (1975). Empathic: An unappreciated way of being. *The Counseling Psychologist, 5*, 2–10.

Rogers, C. R. (1977). *Carl Rogers on personal power*. New York: Delacorte.

Rogers, C. R. (1978). The formative tendency. *Journal of Humanistic Psychology, 18*, 23–26.

Rogers, C. R. (1980). *A way of being*. Boston: Houghton Mifflin.

Rogers, C. R. (1980). Client-centered psychotherapy. In A. M. Freedman, H. I. Kaplan, & B. J. Sadock (Eds.), *Comprehensive textbook of psychiatry* (3rd ed.). Baltimore, Md.: Williams & Wilkins.

Rogers, C. R. (1980). Foundations of the person-centered approach. In *A way of being*. Boston: Houghton Mifflin.

Rogers, C. R. (1982/1969). *Freedom to learn*. Columbus, Ohio: Merrill.

Rogers, C. R., & Dymond R. (Eds.). (1954). *Psychotherapy and personality change*. Chicago: University of Chicago Press.

Rogers, C. R., Gendlin, E. T., Kiesler, D. J., & Truax, C. B. (1967). *The therapeutic relationship and its impact: A study of psychotherapy with schizophrenics*. Madison, Wis.: University of Wisconsin Press.

Rogers, C. R., Kell, B. I. & McNeil, H. (1948). The role of self-understanding in the prediction of behavior. *Journal of Consulting Psychology, 12*, 174–186.

Rogers, C. R., Raskin, N. J., et al. (1949). A coordinated research in psychotherapy. *Journal of Consulting Psychology, 1949, 13*, 149–220.

Rogers, C. R., & Skinner, B. F. (1956). Some issues concerning the control of human behavior: A symposium. *Science, 124*, 1057–1066.

Rogers, E. M., & Shoemaker, F. F. (1971). *Communication of innovations: A cross-cultural approach*. New York: Free Press.

Rogers, M. P., Dubey, D., & Reich, P. (1979). The influence of the psyche and brain on immunity and disease susceptibility: A critical review. *Psychosomatic Medicine, 41*, 147–165.

Rogers, S. M., & Turner, C. F. (1991). Male-male sexual contact in the U.S.A.: Findings from five sample surveys. *Journal of Sex Research, 28*, 491–519.

Rogers, R. (1984). Towards an empirical model of malingering and deception. *Behavioral Sciences and the Law, 2*, 93–111.

Rogers, R. (1990). Development of a new classification model of malingering. *Bulletin American Academy of Psychiatry and the Law, 18*(3), 323.

Rogers, R. (Ed.). (1988). *Clinical assessment of malingering and deception*. New York: Guilford.

Rogers, R., & Lynett, E. (1991). The role of Canadian Psychiatry in dangerous offender testimony. *Canadian Journal of Psychiatry, 36*, 79–84.

Rogoff, B. (1981). Schooling and the development of cognitive skills. In H. C. Triandis & A. Heron (Eds.), *Handbook of cross-cultural psychology*. Vol. 4: *Developmental psychology*. Boston: Allyn & Bacon.

Rohde, A. R. (1957). *The sentence completion method*. New York: Ronald Press.

Rohe, W., & Patterson, A. (1974). The effects of varied levels of resources and density on behavior in a day care center. In D. H. Arson (Ed.), *Man–environment interactions*. New York: Education Development, Research Association.

Roheim, G. (1943). The origin and function of culture. *Nervous and Mental Diseases Monograph number 69*.

Ronner, R. P. (1984). Towards a conception of culture for cross cultural psychology. *Journal of Cross-Cultural Psychology, 15*, 111–138.

Rohracher, H. (1970/1946). *Einführung in die Psychologie*. Vienna: Urban & Schwarzenberg.

Rohracher, H. (1971/1943). *Kleine Charakterkunde*. Vienna: Urban & Schwarzenberg.

Rohrbaugh, M., Tennen, H., & Eron, J. B. (1982). Paradoxical interventions. *Current Psychiatric Therapies, 21*, 67–74.

Rohrbaugh, M., Tennen, H., Press, S., & White, L. (1981). Compliance, defiance, and therapeutic paradox: Guidelines for strategic use of paradoxical interventions. *American Journal of Orthopsychiatry, 51*, 454–467.

Roitblatt, H. L., & Von Fersen, L. (1992), Comparative cognition: Representations and processes in learning and memory. In M. R. Rosenzweig & L. W. Porter (Eds.), *Annual Review of Psychology*.

Rokeach, M. (1960). *The open and closed mind*. New York: Basic Books.

Rokeach, M. (1964). *The three Christs of Ypsilanti: A psychological study*. New York: Knopf. (Also published in a French edition, *Les trois Christs*, Gallimard, 1967.)

Rokeach, M. (1968). *Beliefs, attitudes, and values*. San Francisco: Josey-Bass.

Rokeach, M. (1973). *The nature of human values*. New York: Free Press/Macmillan.

Rokeach, M., Ball-Rokeach, S. J., & Gruke, J. W. (in preparation). Influencing political beliefs and behavior through television.

Rokeach, M. (Ed.). (1979). *Understanding human values: individual and societal*. New York: Free Press/Macmillan.

Rokeach, M. J. (1973). *The nature of human values*. New York: Free Press.

Rolf, I. (1978). *Ida Rolf speaks*. New York: Harper & Row.

Rolf, I. (1977). *Rolfing: Integration of human structures*. Santa Monica, Calif.: Dennis-Landman.

Rolfwarg, H. P., Muzio, J. N., & Dement, W. D. (1966). Ontogenetic development of human sleep dream cycle. *Science, 152*, 604–619.

Roll, W. G., & Klein, J. (1972). Further forced choice ESP experiments with Lalsingle Harribance. *Journal of the American Society for Psychical Research, 66*, 103–112.

Rollin, B. (1981). *Animal rights and human morality*. Buffalo, N.Y.: Prometheus.

Rollin, B. E., & Kesel, M. L. (Eds.). (1990). *The experimental animal in biomedical research: Volume l. A survey of scientific and ethical issues for investigators*. Boca Raton: CRC Press.

Roman, P. M., (March 1978). *The current status of occupational alcoholism: Review and documentation*. Washington, D.C., National Institute on Alcohol Abuse, and Alcoholism.

Romanes, G. J. (1882). *Animal intelligence*. London: Kegan Paul, Trench.

Romanes, G. J. (1883). *Mental evolution in animals*. London: Kegan Paul, Trench.

Romanes, G. J. (1884). *Mental evolution in animals*. New York: Appleton.

Romanes, G. J. (1983). *Animal intelligence*. New York: Appleton.

Romanyshyn, R. (1981). Science and reality: Metaphors of experience and experience as metaphorical in R. Valle, & R. von Eckartsberg (Eds.), *The metaphors of consciousness*. New York: Plenum.

Romme, M., & Escher, A. (1989). Hearing voices. *Schizophrenia Bulletin, 5*, 209–216.

Ronan, W. W. (1970). Relative importance of job characteristics. *Journal of Applied Psychology, 54*, 192–200.

Rones, P. L. (1978, November). Older men—The choice between work and retirement. *Monthly Labor Review*.

Rones, P. L. (November, 1980). The retirement decision: A question of opportunity? *Monthly Labor Review*.

Ronjat, J. (1913). *Le developement du langage chez un enfant bilingue*. Paris: Champion.

Rony, P. R., Larsen, D. G., & Titus, J. A. (1977). *The 8080A bugbook microcomputer interfacing and programming*. Indianapolis, Ind.: Sams.

Rook, K. S. (1992). Detrimental aspects of social relationships: Taking stock of an emerging literature. In H. O. F. Veiel & U. Baumann (Eds.), *The meaning and measurement of social support* (pp. 157–169). New York: Hemisphere.

Rook, K. S., & Hammen, C. L. (1977). A cognitive perspective on the experience of sexual arousal. *Journal of Social Issues, 33*, 7–29.

Rorer, L. (1965). The great response-style myth. *Psychological Bulletin, 63*, 129–156.

Rorschach, H. (1949/1921). *Psychodiagnostics*. New York: Grune & Stratton.

Rosch, E. H., & Lloyd, B. (Eds.). (1978). *Cognition and categorization*. Hillsdale, N. J.: Erlbaum.

Rosch, E. H., Mervis, C. B., Gray, W. D., Johnson, D. M., & Boyes-Braem, P. (1976). Basic objects in natural categories. *Cognitive Psychology, 8*, 382–439.

Roscoe, S. N. (1980). *Aviation psychology*. Ames, Iowa: Iowa State University Press.

Rose, P. I. (Ed.). (1979). *Socialization and the life cycle.* New York: St. Martin's Press.

Rose, S. (1976). *Group therapy: A behavioral approach.* Englewood Cliffs, N. J.: Prentice-Hall.

Rose, T. L., Lessen, E. I., & Gottlieb, J. (1982). A discussion of transfer of training in mainstreaming programs. *Journal of Learning Disabilities, 15,* 162–165.

Rosebrock, P. (1981). Cognitive compatability as a factor in interpersonal attraction and mate selection. Unpublished doctoral dissertation, California School of Professional Psychology, Los Angeles.

Rosen, B., & Jetdee, T. H. (1974). Influence of sex role stereotypes on personnel decisions. *Journal of Applied Psychology, 59,* 9–14.

Rosen, E., Fox, R. E., & Gregory, I. (1972). *Abnormal psychology* (2nd ed.). Philadelphia, Pa.: Saunders.

Rosen, G. (1969/1968). *Madness in society: Chapters in the historical sociology of mental illness.* New York: Harper & Row.

Rosen, G. (1977). *The relaxation book: An illustrated self-help program.* Englewood Cliffs, N.J.: Prentice-Hall.

Rosen, J. (1953). *Direct Psychoanalysis.* NY: Grune & Stratton.

Rosen, J. N. (1945). The treatment of schizophrenic psychosis by direct analytic therapy. *Psychiatric Quarterly.*

Rosen, J. N. (1968). *Direct psychoanalytic psychiatry.* New York: Grune & Stratton.

Rosen, S. (1979). *Weathering.* New York: Evans.

Rosenbaum, M. (1977). Premature interruption of psychotherapy: Continuation of contact by telephone and correspondence. *American Journal of Psychiatry, 134*(2).

Rosenbaum, M., & Berger, M. (1963). *Group psychotherapy and group function.* New York: Basic Books.

Rosenbaum, M., & Snadowsky, A. (Eds.) (1976). *The intensive group experience.* New York: Free Press.

Rosenbaum, R. W. (1976). Predictability of employee theft using weighted application blanks. *Journal of Applied Psychology, 61,* 94–98.

Rosenberg, B. G., Goldman, R., & Sutton-Smith, B. (1969). Sibling age-spacing effects on cognitive activity in children. *Proceedings of the Seventy-Seventh Annual Convention of the American Psychological Association, 77,* 261–262.

Rosenberg, B. G., & Limger, J. (1969). Nonverbal learning. *American Journal of Psychology, 82,* 181–190.

Rosenberg, B. S., & Gaier, E. L. (1977). The self concept of the adolescent with learning disabilities. *Adolescence, 12,* 489–498.

Rosenberg, D. A. (1987). Web of deceit: A literature review of Munchausen syndrome by proxy. *Child Abuse and Neglect, 11,* 547–563.

Rosenberg, M., & Pearlin, L. I. (1978). Social class and self-esteem among children and adults. *American Journal of Sociology, 84,* 53–75.

Rosenberg, M., & Simmons, R. G. (1972). *Black and white self-esteem: The urban school child.* Washington, D.C.: American Sociological Association.

Rosenberg, M. B. (1979). *From now on.* St. Louis, Mo.: Community Psychological Consultants.

Rosenberg, M. J. (1969). The conditions and consequences of evaluation apprehension. In R. Rosenthal and R. L. Rosnow (Eds.), *Artifact in behavioral research.* New York: Academic Press.

Rosenblatt, A. D., & Thickstun, J. T. (1977). Modern psychoanalytic concepts in a general psychology. *Psychological Issues, 11,* Monograph 42/43, 42–47.

Rosenblatt, H. S., & Bartlett, I. (1976). Some phenomenological aspects of the peak experience. *Southern Journal of Educational Research, 10,* 29–42.

Rosenblatt, J. S. (1967). Nonhormonal basis of maternal behavior in the rat. *Science, 156,* 1512–1514.

Rosenblatt, J. S., & Lehrman, D. S. (1963). Maternal behavior of the laboratory rat. In H. L. Rheingold (Ed.), *Maternal behavior in mammals.* New York: Wiley.

Rosenbloom, P., Laird, J., Newell, A., & McCarl, R. (1991). A preliminary analysis of the Soar architecture as a basis for general intelligence. *Artificial Intelligence, 47,* 327–346.

Rosenblatt, P., & Skoogberg, G. (1974). Birth order in cross-cultural perspective. *Developmental Psychology, 10,* 48–54.

Rosenblatt, P. C., & Cunningham, M. R. (1976). Sex differences in cross-cultural perspective. In B. Lloyd & J. Archer (Eds.), *Exploring sex differences.* New York: Academic Press.

Rosenblueth, A., & Wiener, N. (1950). Purposeful and non-purposeful behavior. *Philosophy of Science, 17,* 318–326.

Rosenblueth, A., Wiener, N., & Bigelow, J. (1943). Behavior, purpose, and teleology. *Philosophy of Science, 10,* 18–24.

Rosenblueth, A., Wiener, N., & Bigelow, J. (1968). Behavior, purpose and teleology, *Philosophy of Science 13, 10,* 18–24. Reprinted in W. Buckley (Ed.), *Modern systems research for the behavioral scientist.* Chicago: Aldine.

Rosenbluh, E. S. (1974). *Techniques of crisis intervention.* New York: Behavioral Science Services.

Rosenblum, L. A., & Kaufman, I. C. (1968). Variations in infant development and response to maternal loss in monkeys. *American Journal of Orthopsychiatry, 38,* 418–426.

Rosencranz, M. L. (1965). Social and psychological approach to clothing research. *Journal of Home Economics, 57,* 26–29.

Rosenham, D. (1973). On being sane in insane places. *Science, 197,* 250–258.

Rosenman, R. H., Brand, R. J., Jenkins, C. D. (1975). Coronary heart disease in the Western Collaborative Group Study: Final follow-up experience of 8½ years. *Journal of the American Medical Association, 233,* 872–877.

Rosenman, R. H., & Friedman, M. (1961). Association of specific behavior pattern in women with blood and cardiovascular findings. *Circulation, 24,* 1173–1184.

Rosenstiel, A. K., & Keefe, F. J. (1983). The use of coping strategies in low back pain patients: Relationship to patient characteristics and current adjustment. *Pain, 17,* 33–40.

Rosenthal, D. (1970). *Genetic theory and abnormal behavior.* New York: McGraw-Hill.

Rosenthal, D. (1971). *Genetics of psychopathology.* New York: McGraw-Hill.

Rosenthal, R. (1965). A case study of scientific method. In O. Pfungst, *Clever Hans.* New York: Holt, Rinehart & Winston.

Rosenthal, R. (1969). Interpersonal expectations: Effects of the experimenters' hypothesis. In R. Rosenthal & R. Rosnow (Eds.), *Artifact in behavioral research.* New York: Academic Press.

Rosenthal, R. (1971). Clever Hans: A case study of scientific method. In M. S. Gazzaniga & E. P. Lovejoy (Eds.), *Good reading in psychology.* Englewood Cliffs, N.J.: Prentice-Hall.

Rosenthal, R. (1976). *Experimenter effects in behavioral research.* New York: Irvington.

Rosenthal, R. (1978). Combining results of independent studies. *Psychological Bulletin, 65,* 185–193.

Rosenthal, R. (1979). The file-drawer problem and tolerance for null results. *Psychological Bulletin, 86*, 638–641.

Rosenthal, R. (1981). Pavlov's mice, Pfungst's horse, and Pygmalion's PONS: Some models for the study of interpersonal expectancy effects. In T. A. Sebeok & R. Rosenthal (Eds.), *The Clever Hans phenomenon: Communication with horses, whales, apes, and people.* New York: New York Academy of Sciences.

Rosenthal, R. (1984). *Meta-analytic procedures for social research.* Beverly Hills, CA: Sage.

Rosenthal, R. (1987). *Judgment studies: Design, analysis, and meta-analysis.* Cambridge, UK: Cambridge University Press.

Rosenthal, R. (Ed.). (1979). *Skill in nonverbal communications: Individual differences.* Cambridge, Mass.: Oelgeschlager, Gunn & Hain.

Rosenthal, R., Hall, J. A., DiMatteo, M. R., Rogers, P. L., & Archer, D. (1979). *Sensitivity to nonverbal communication: The PONS test.* Baltimore: John Hopkins University Press.

Rosenthal, R., & Jacobson, L. (1968). Pygmalion in the classroom: *Teacher expectation and pupils' intellectual development.* New York: Holt, Rinehart & Winston.

Rosenthal, R., Persinger, G., & Fode, K. (1962). Experimental bias, anxiety, and social desirability. *Perceptual and Motor Skills, 15*(1), 73–74.

Rosenthal, R., & Rosnow, R. L. (1969). The volunteer subject. In R. Rosenthal & R. L. Rosnow, *Artifact in behavioral research.* New York: Academic Press.

Rosenthal, R., & Rubin, D. (1982). Comparing effect sizes of independent studies. *Psychological Bulletin, 92*, 500–504.

Rosenthal, R., & Rubin, D. B. (1978). Interpersonal expectancy effects: The first 345 studies. *The Behavioral and Brain Sciences, 3*, 377–386.

Rosenthal, R., & Rubin, D. B. (1980). Summarizing 345 studies of interpersonal expectancy effects. In R. Rosenthal (Ed.), *Quantitative assessment of research domains. New directions for methodology of social and behavioral science,* no. 5. San Francisco: Jossey-Bass.

Rosenzweig, M. (1982). Trends in development and status of psychology: An international perspective. *International Journal of Psychology, 17*, 117–140.

Rosenzweig, M. R., Kretch, D, Bennett, E. L, & Diamond, M. C. (1968). In G. Newton & S. Levine (Eds.), *Early experience and behavior.* Springfield, Ill.: Thomas.

Rosenzweig, S. (1933). The experimental situation as a psychological problem. *Psychological Review, 40*, 337–354.

Rosenzweig, S. (1936). Some implicit common factors in diverse methods of psychotherapy, *American Journal of Orthopsychiatry, 6*, 412–415.

Rosenzweig, S. (1937). Schools of Psychology: A complementary pattern. *Philosophy of Science, 41*, 96–106.

Rozensweig, S. (1937). Schools of psychology: a complementary pattern. *Philosophy of Science, 4*, 96–106.

Rosenzweig, S. (1944). An outline of frustration theory. In J. McV. Hunt (Ed.), *Personality and the behavior disorders,* New York: Ronald Press.

Rosenzweig, S. (1944). Converging approaches to personality: Murray, Allport, Lewin. *Psychological Review, 51*, 248–256.

Rosenzweig, S. (1950). Levels of behavior in psychodiagnosis with special reference to the Picture-Frustration Study. *American Journal of Orthopsychiatry, 20*, 63–72.

Rosenzweig, S. (1950). Norms and the individual in the Psychologist's perspective. In M. L. Reymert (Ed.), *Feelings and emotion: The Mooseheart symposium.* New York: McGraw-Hill.

Rosenzweig, S. (1951). Idiodynamics in personality theory with special reference to projective methods. *Psychological Review, 58*, 213–223.

Rosenzweig, S. (1952). The investigation of repression as an instance of experimental idiodynamics. *Psychological Review, 59*, 339–345.

Rosenzweig, S. (1958). The idiocultural dimension of psychotherapy: Pre- and posthistory of the relations between Sigmund Freud and Josef Popper-Lynkeus. In W. Muensterberger & Axelrad (Eds.). *Psychoanalysis and the social sciences* (Vol. 5, pp. 9–50). New York: International Universities Press.

Rosenzweig, S. (1959). The place of the individual and of idiodynamics in psychology: A dialogue. *Journal of Individual Psychology, 14*, 3–20.

Rosenzweig, S. (1960). The Rosenzweig picture-frustration study. In A. I. Rohm &A. M. Hayworth (Eds.), *Projectire techniques with children.* New York: Grune & Stratton.

Rosenzweig, S. (1973). Human sexual autonomy as an evolutionary attainment, anticipating proceptive sex choice and idiodynamic bisexuality. In J. Zubin & J. Money (Eds.), *Contemporary sexual behavior: Critical issues in the 1970s.* Baltimore: John Hopkins University Press.

Rosenzweig, S. (1976). Aggressive behavior and the Rosenzweig picture-frustration (P-F) study. *Journal of Clinical Psychology, 32*, 885–891.

Rosenzweig, S. (1978a). *The Rosenzweig Picture-Frustration (p-F) Study, basic manual.* St. Louis: Rana House.

Rosenzweig, S. (1985). *Freud and experimental psychology: The emergence of idiodynamics.* New York: McGraw-Hill.

Rosenzweig, S. (1986). Background to Idiodynamics. *The Clinical Psychologist, 39*, 83–89.

Rosenzweig, S. (1986). Idiodynamics vis-à-vis psychology. *American Psychologist, 41*, 241–245.

Rosenzweig, S. (1987). Sally Beauchamp's career: A psychoarchaeological key to Morton Prince's classic case of multiple personality. *Genetic, Social and General Psychology Monographs, 113*, 5–60.

Rosenzweig, Saul. (1978b). *Aggressive behavior and the Rosenzweig Picture-Frustration Study.* New York: Praeger.

Rosett, H. L. (1980). A clinical perspective of the fetal alcohol syndrome. *Alcoholism: Clinical and Experimental Research, 4*, 119–122.

Rosett, H. L., & Weiner, L. (1984). *Alcohol and the fetus.* New York: Oxford University Press.

Rosewater, L. B., & Walker, L. E. (Eds.). (1985). *Handbook of feminist therapy: Women's issues in psychotherapy.* New York: Springer.

Rosinsky, R. R. (1977). *The development of visual perception.* Santa Monica, Calif.: Goodyear.

Roskam, E. E., & Lingoes, J. C. (1970). MINISSA-I: A Fortran IV (G) program for the smallest space analysis of square symmetric matrices. *Behavioral Science, 15*, 204–205.

Roskind, W. (1980). DECo. V. NLRB and the consequences of open testing in industry. *Personnel Psychology, 33*, 3–10.

Rosnow, R. L. (1981). *Paradigms in transition.* New York, London: Oxford University Press.

Rosow, I. (1976). Status and role change through the life span. In R. H. Binstock & E. Shanas (Eds.), *Handbook of aging and the social sciences.* New York: Van Nostrand Reinhold.

Ross, A. O. (1959). The practice of clinical child psychology. New York: Grune & Stratton.

Ross, D., & Ross, S. (1976). *Hyperactivity: Research, theory, action.* New York: Wiley.

Ross, D. M., & Ross, S. A. (1984). Childhood pain: The school-aged child's viewpoint. *Pain, 20,* 179–191.

Ross, E. A. (1901). *Social control,* New York: Macmillan.

Ross, E. A. (1908). *Social psychology.* New York: Macmillan.

Ross, H. E. (1974). *Behaviour and perception in strange environments.* London: Allen & Unwin.

Ross, L. (1977). The intuitive psychologist and his shortcomings: Distortions in the attribution process. In L. Berkowitz (Ed.), *Advances in experimental social psychology.* (Vol. 10, pp. 174–221). New York: Academic.

Ross, L., Lepper, M. R., Strack, F., & Steinmetz, J. (1977). Social explanation and social expectation: Effects of real and hypothetical explanations on subjective likelihood. *Journal of Personality and Social Psychology, 35,* 817–829.

Ross, M. Salience of reward and intrinsic motivation. (1975). *Journal of Personality and Social Psychology, 32,* 245–254.

Ross, M., Karniol, R., & Rothstein, M. (1976). Reward contingency and intrinsic motivation in children: A test of the delay of gratification hypothesis. *Journal of Personality and Social Psychology, 33,* 442–447.

Ross, M., & Olson, J. M. (1981). An expectancy-attribution model of the effects of placebos. *Psychological Review, 88,* 408–437.

Ross, M. H. (1978). Nutritional regulation of longevity. In J. A. Behnke, C. E. Finch, & G. B. Moment (Eds.), *The biology of aging.* New York: Plenum.

Ross, R. R., & Gendreau, P. (Eds.). (1980). *Effective correctional treatment.* Toronto: Butterworth.

Rossen, B. (1989). Mass hysteria in Oude Pekela. *Issues in Child Abuse Accusations, 1,* 49–51.

Rossen, B. (1992). Response to the Oude Pekela incident and the accusations of Drs. F. Jonker and I. Jonker-Bakker. *Journal of Psychology and Theology, 20*(3), 263–266.

Rosser, J. B. (1936). Extensions of some theorems of Godel and Church. *Journal of Symbolic Logic, 1,* 87–91.

Rossi, A. M. (1962). Some pre-World War II antecedents of community mental health theory and practice. *Mental Hygiene, 46,* 78–94.

Rossi, A. S., & Calderwood, A. (Eds.). (1973). *Academic women on the move.* New York: Russell Sage Foundation.

Rossi, E. L. (1972). *Dreams and the growth of personality: Expanding awareness in psychotherapy.* New York: Pergamon Press.

Rossi, E. R. (1990). From mind to molecule: More than a metaphor. In J. K. Zeig & S. Gilligan (Eds.), *Brief therapy: Myths, methods* (pp. 456–472). New York: Brunner/Mazel.

Rossi, E. R., & Cheek, D. (1988). *Mind-body therapy.* New York: Norton.

Rossi, P. H. (1986). *The psychobiology of mind-body healing: New concepts of therapeutic hypnosis.* New York: Norton.

Rossi, P. H. (1989). *Down and out in America: The origins of homelessness.* Chicago: University of Chicago Press.

Rossi, P. H. (1990). The old homelessness and the new homelessness in historical perspective. *American Psychologist, 45,* 954–959.

Rossi, P. J. (1968). Adaptation and negative aftereffect to lateral optical displacement in newly hatched chicks. *Science, 160,* 430–432.

Rossi, R., Bartlett, W., Campbell, E., Wise, L., & McLaughlin, D. (1975). *Using the talent profiles in counseling.* Palo Alto, Calif.: American Institutes for Research.

Rossiter, C. (1968). Conservatism. In D. Sills (Ed.), *International encyclopedia of social science.* Vol. 3. New York: Macmillan.

Rossman, J. (1921). *The psychology of the inventor.* Washington, D.C.: Inventor's Press.

Rossman, P. (1973). The pederasts. *Society, 10,* 28–32, 34–35.

Rossman, P. (1979). *Hospice: Creating new models of care for the terminally ill.* New York: Fawcett Columbine.

Rossolimo, G. J. (1911,1912). Die psychologischen Profile. *Kleinepsychische und nervöse Krankheiten, 6,* 249–326; *7,* 22–26.

Roswell, F. G., & Natchez, G. (1977/1964). *Reading disability: A human approach to learning* (3rd ed.). New York: Basic Books.

Roszak, T. (1968). *The making of a counter culture.* Garden City, N.Y.: Doubleday Anchor.

Rot, N. (1970). *Influence of structure of judgements on the degree of confidence in judging.* Belgrade, Yugoslavia: Zavod za udžbenike.

Rot, N. (1980/1972). *Fundamentals of social psychology.* Belgrade, Yugoslavia: Zavod za udžbenike.

Rot, N. (1981/1963). *Psychology of personality.* Belgrade, Yugoslavia: Zavod za udžbenike.

Rot, N. (1981/1966). *General psychology.* Belgrade, Yugoslavia: Zavod za udžbenike.

Rot, N. (1982). *Verbal and non-verbal communication.* Belgrade, Yugoslavia: Nolit.

Rot, N., & Havelka, N. (1973). *National attachment values of high-school youth.* Belgrade, Yugoslavia: Institute for Psychology/Institute of Social Science.

Roth, R. (1971, December). Nude therapy group: A countermovement. *Modern Medicine.* 42–44.

Roth, R. M., & Meyersburg, H. A. (1963). The non-achievement syndrome. *Personnel and Guidance Journal 41,* 535–546.

Roth, S. (1980). Learned helplessness in humans: A review. *Journal of Personality, 48,* 103–133.

Roth, S., & Kubal, L. (1975). Effects of noncontingent reinforcement on tasks of differing importance: Facilitation and learned helplessness. *Journal of Personality and Social Psychology, 32,* 680–691.

Rothacker, E. (1952/1938). *Die Schichten der Persönlichkeit.* Leipzig: Barth.

Rothbart, M., Evans, M., & Fulero, S. (1979). Recall for confirming events: Memory processes and the maintenance of social stereotypes. *Journal of Experimental Social Psychology, 15,* 343–355.

Rothe, H. F. (1978). Output rates among industrial employees. *Journal of Applied Psychology, 63,* 40–46.

Rothen, W., & Tennyson, R. D. (1978). Application of Bayes' theory in designing computer-based adaptive instructional strategies. *Educational Psychologist, 12,* 317–323.

Rothenberg, A. (1972). Poetic process and psychotherapy. *Psychiatry, 35,* 238–254.

Rothenberg, A. (1979). *The emerging goddess: The creative process in art, science, and other fields.* Chicago: University of Chicago Press.

Rotheram-Borus, M. J., Koopman, C., & Ehrhardt, A. A. (1991). Homeless youths and HIV infection. *American Psychologist, 46,* 1188–1197.

Rothkopf, E. Z. (1957). A measure of stimulus similarity and errors in some paired-associate learning tasks. *Journal of Experimental Psychology, 53,* 94–101.

Rothman, D. (1978). Introduction. In W. Gaylin, I. Glasser, S. Marcus, & D. Rothman (Eds.), *Doing good: The limits of benevolence.* New York: Pantheon.

Rothman, D. J. (1975). *The discovery of the asylum: Social order in the new republic.* Boston: Little, Brown.

Rothman, J. (1974). Three models of community organization practice. In J. L. Cox, J. Rothman, & J. E. Tropman (Eds.), *Strategies of community organization* (pp. 22–39). Itasca, IL: Peacock.

Rothschuh, K. E. (1973). *History of physiology.* Huntington, N.Y.: Krieger.

Rothstein. A. (1980). *The narcissistic pursuit of perfection.* New York: International Universities Press.

Rothstein, A. (1981). Hallucinatory phenomena in childhood. *Journal of the American Academy of Child Psychiatry, 20,* 623–635.

Rothwell, N. D., & Doniger, J. M. (1966). *The psychiatric halfway house.* Springfield, Ill.: Thomas.

Rotter, J. B. (1942). Level of aspiration as a method of studying personality. II. Development and evaluation of a controlled method. *Journal of Experimental Psychology, 31,* 410–422.

Rotter, J. B. (1946). The Incomplete Sentence Test as a method for studying personality. *American Psychologist, 1,* 286.

Rotter, J. B. (1951). Word association and sentence completion methods. In H. H. Anderson & G. L. Anderson (Eds.), *An introduction to projective techniques.* Englewood Cliffs, N.J.: Prentice-Hall.

Rotter, J. B. (1966). Generalized expectancies for internal versus external control of reinforcement. *Psychological Monographs, 80* (1, entire no. 609), 1–28.

Rotter, J. B. (1967). Personality theory. In H. Helson & W. Bevan (Eds.), *Contemporary approaches to psychology.* New York: Van Nostrand.

Rotter, J. B. (1971). Generalized expectancies for interpersonal trust. *American Psychologist, 26,* 443–452.

Rotter, J. B. (1975). Some problems and misconceptions related to the construct of internal versus external control of reinforcement. *Journal of Consulting and Clinical Psychology, 43,* 56–67.

Rotter, J. B. (1978). Generalized expectancies for problem solving and psychotherapy. *Cognitive Therapy and Research, 2,* 1–10.

Rotter, J. B. (1980/1973/1954). *Social learning and clinical psychology.* New York: Johnson Reprint.

Rotter, J. B. (1982). *The development and applications of social learning theory: Selected papers.* New York: Praeger.

Rotter, J. B., Chance, J. E., & Phares, E. J. (Eds.). (1972). *Applications of a social learning theory of personality.* New York: Holt, Rinehart & Winston.

Rotter, J. B., Rafferty, E., & Schachtitz, E. (1949). Validation of the Rotter Incomplete Sentences Blank for college screening. *Journal of Consulting Psychology, 13,* 345–356.

Rotter, J. B., & Rafferty, J. E. (1950). *The Rotter Incomplete Sentences Blank manual: College form.* New York: Psychological Corp.

Rotter, J. B., Seeman, M., & Liverant, S. (1962). Internal verses external control of reinforcements: A major variable in behavior theory. In N. F. Washburne (Ed.), *Decisions, values and groups,* (Vol. 2). London: Pergamon.

Rotzoll, K., Haefner, J., & Sandage, C. (1976). *Advertising in contemporary society: Perspectives toward understanding.* Columbus, Ohio: Grid.

Roueche, J. E., & Snow, J. J. (1977). *Overcoming learning problems: A guide to developmental education in college.* San Francisco: Jossey-Bass.

Rouse v. Cameron, 387 F. 2d 241 (D.C. Cir. 1967).

Rousseau, J.-J. (1939). *Les confessions, Genève 1782.* Paris: Bibliothèque de la Pleiade, Nouvelle Revue Francaise.

Rousseau, J. J. (1962/1738). *Emile, or concerning education.* New York: Dutton.

Rousseau, J.-J. (1967/1781). *Essai sur l'origine du langage.* Paris: Larousse.

Routh, D. K. (1979). Activity, attention, and aggression in learning disabled children. *Journal of Clinical Child Psychology, 8,* 183–187.

Routh, D. K., (Ed.). (1988). *Handbook of pediatric psychology.* New York: Guilford.

Routtenberg, A. (1968). The two-arousal hypothesis: Reticular formation and limbic system. *Psychological Review, 75,* 51–80.

Rovee-Collier, C., Griesler, P. C., & Earley, L. A. (1985). Contextual determinants of retrieval in three-month-old infants. *Learning and Motivation, 16,* 139–157.

Roviaro, S., & Holmes, D. S. (1980). Arousal transfer: The influence of fear arousal on subsequent sexual arousal for subjects with high and low sex guilt. *Journal of Research in Personality, 14,* 307–320.

Rowan, A. (October 14, 1981). Statement before the Subcommittee on Science, Research, and Technology, U.S. House of Representatives. Hearings on "The use of animals in medical research and testing."

Rowan, J. (1975). Encounter group research: No joy? *Journal of Humanistic Psychology, 15,* 19–28.

Rowe, D. (1978). *The experience of depression.* New York: Wiley.

Rowe, J. W., Berkman, L. F., Seeman, T. E., Blazer, D., Hughes, D. C., Inouye, S. K., Chang, K. S., Guralnik, J. M., Tinetti, M., & Nevitt, M. (1991). MacArthur studies of successful aging: Initial results [Special issue, 2]. *The Gerontologist, 31,* 181–182.

Rowell, L. (1978). Human adjustments and adaptations to heat stress—where and how? In L. Folinsbee, J. Wagner, J. Borgia, B. Drinkwater, J. Gliner, & J. Bedi (Eds.), *Environmental stress: Individual human adaptation.* New York: Academic Press.

Roy, M. (1977). A current survey of 150 cases. In M. Roy (Ed.), *Battered women.* New York: Van Nostrand Reinhold.

Royce, J. (1892). *The spirit of modern philosophy.* New York: Houghton Mifflin.

Royce, J. (1904). *The world and the individual* (2 vols.). New York: Macmillan.

Royce, J. R. (1964). *The encapsulated man.* Princeton, N.J.: Van Nostrand.

Royce, J. R. (1973). The present situation in theoretical psychology. In J. R. Royce (Ed.), *Toward unification in psychology.* Toronto: University of Toronto Press, 1970b. Reprinted in B. B. Wolman (Ed.), *Handbook of general psychology.* Englewood Cliffs, N.J.: Prentice-Hall.

Royce, J. R. (1974). Cognition and knowledge: Psychological epistemology. In E. C. Carterette & M. F. Friedman (Eds.), *Handbook of perception: Historical and philosophical roots to perception,* Vol. I. New York: Academic Press.

Royce, J. R. (1976). Psychology is multi: Methodological, variate, epistemic, worldview, systemic, paradigmatic, theoretic, and disciplinary. In W. J. Arnold (Ed.), *Nebraska Symposium on the Conceptual Foundations of Theory and Methods in Psychology.* Lincoln, Neb.: University of Nebraska Press.

Royce, J. R. (1977a). Meaning, value, and personality. In *Proceedings of the Fifth International Conference on the Unity of the Sciences.* New York: International Cultural Foundation Press.

Royce, J. R. (1977b). Toward an indigenous philosophy for psychology. *The Ontario Psychologist, 9,* 16–32.

Royce, J. R. (1978). How we can best advance the construction of theory in psychology. *Canadian Psychological Review, 19,* 259–276.

Royce, J. R. (1978). Three ways of knowing and the scientific world view. *Methodology and Science, 11,* 146–164.

Royce, J. R. (1981). A personal portrayal of Ludwig von Bertalanffy (1901–1972): System theorist and interdisciplinary scholar at the University of Alberta. *Journal of the History of the Behavioral Sciences, 17*, 340–342.

Royce, J. R. (1982). Philosophic issues, Division 24, and the future. *American Psychologist, 37*, 258–266.

Royce, J. R., & Buss, A. R. (1976). The role of general systems and information theory in multifactor individuality theory. *Canadian Psychological Review, 17*, 1–21.

Royce, J. R., Coward, H., Egan, E., Kessel, F., & Mos, L. P. (1978). Psychological epistemology: A critical review of the empirical literature and the theoretical issues. *Genetic Psychology Monographs, 97*, 265–353.

Royce, J. R., & Diamond, S. R. (1980). A multifactor-system dynamics theory of emotion: Cognitive-affective interaction. *Motivation and Emotion, 4*, 263–298.

Royce, J. R. (Ed.). (1965). *Psychology and the symbol*. New York: Random House.

Royce, J. R. (Ed.). (1970a). *Toward unification in psychology*. Toronto: University of Toronto Press.

Royce, J. R., & Mos, L. P. (1980). *Psycho-epistemological profile test manual*. Edmonton, Alta., Canada: University of Alberta Press.

Royce, J. R., & Mos, L. P. (Eds.). (1981). *Humanistic psychology: Concepts and criticisms*. New York: Plenum.

Royce, J. R., & Mos, L. P. (Eds.). (1979). *Theoretical advances in behavior genetics*. Alphen aan den Rijn, Netherlands: Sitjhoff & Noordhof.

Royce, J. R., & Powell, A. (1978). Toward a theory of man: A multi-disciplinary, multi-systems, multi-dimensional approach. In *Proceedings of the Sixth International Conference on the Unity of the Sciences*. New York: International Cultural Foundation Press.

Royce, J. R., & Powell, A. D. (1981). An overview of a multifactor-system theory of personality and individual differences: II. System dynamics and person-situation interactions. *Journal of Personality and Social Psychology, 41*, 1019–1030.

Royce, J. R., & Powell, A. D. (1983). *A theory of personality and individual differences: Factors, systems, and processes*. Englewood Cliffs, N.J.: Prentice-Hall.

Royce, J. R., & Rozeboom, W. W. (1972). *The psychology of knowing*. London, New York: Gordon & Breach.

Rozin, P. (1967). Specific aversions as a component of specific hungers. *Journal of comparative and physiological psychology, 64*, 237–242.

Rozin, P., & Kalat, J. W. (1971). Specific hungers and poison avoidance as adaptive specializations of learning. *Psychological review, 78*, 459–486.

Rubel, A., (1964). The epidemiology of a folk illness: Susto in Hispanic America. *Ethnology, 3*, 268–283.

Ruben, B. D., & Kealey, D. J. (1979). Behavioral assessment of communication competency and the prediction of cross-cultural adaption. *International Journal of Intercultural Relations, 3*(1), 15–47.

Ruben, I., Plovnick, M., & Fry, R., (1975). *Improving the coordination of care: A program for health team development*. Cambridge, Mass.: Ballinger.

Rubin, B. (1972). Prediction of dangerousness in mentally ill criminals. *Archives of General Psychiatry, 72*, 397–407.

Rubin, D. C. (1976). Frequency of occurrence as a psychophysical continuum: Weber's fraction, Ekman's fraction, range effects, and the phi-gamma hypothesis. *Perception and Psychophysics, 20*, 327–330.

Rubin, D. C. (1980). Fifty-one properties of 125 words: A unit analysis of verbal behavior. *Journal of Verbal Learning and Verbal Behavior, 19*, 736–755.

Rubin, E. (1921). *Visuell wahrgenommene Figuren*. Copenhagen: Glydendalske.

Rubin, E. (1958/1915). Synsoplevede figurer. In D. C. Beardslee & M. Wertheimer (Eds.), *Readings in perception*. Princeton, N.J.: Van Nostrand.

Rubin, J. Z. (1980). Experimental research on third-party interventions in conflict: Toward some generalizations. *Psychological Bulletin 87*, 379–381.

Rubin, J. Z., & Brown, B. R. (1975). *The social psychology of bargaining and negotiation*. New York: Academic Press.

Rubin, K. H., & Maioni, T. L. (1975). Play preference and its relationship to egocentrism, popularity, and classification skills. *Merrill-Palmer Quarterly, 21*, 171–179.

Rubin, K. H., Maioni, T. L., & Hornung, M. (1976). Free play behaviors in middle- and lower-class preschoolers: Parten and Piaget revisited. *Child Development, 47*, 414–419.

Rubin, R. J. (1978). *Using bibliotherapy: A guide to theory and practice*. Phoenix, Ariz.: Oryx Press.

Rubin, R. J. (Ed.). (1978). *Bibliotherapy sourcebook Phoenix, Ariz.: Oryx Press*.

Rubin, Z. (1973). *Liking and loving*. New York: Holt, Rinehart & Winston.

Rubin, Z., Hill, C. T., Peplau, L. A., & Dunkel-Schetter, C. (1980). Self-disclosure in dating couples: Sex roles and the ethic of openness. *Journal of Marriage and the Family, 42*, 30.

Rubinstein, S. L. (1946). *Foundations of general psychology* (2nd ed.). Moscow: Uchpedgig.

Rubinstein, S. L. (1957). *Existence and consciousness*, Moscow: Akad Nauk, SSSR.

Rubinstein, S. L. (1957). Questions of psychological theory. In B. Simon (Ed.), *Psychology in the Soviet Union*. Stanford, Calif.: Stanford University Press.

Rubinstein S. L. (1976/1934). Problemy psikhologii v trudah K. Marxa (Problems of psychology in the works of K. Marx). In S. Rubinstein, (Ed.), *Problemy obschej psikhologii (Problems of general psychology)*. Moscow: Pedagogika.

Ruble, D. N., Balaban, T., & Cooper, J. (1981). Gender constancy and the effects of sex-typed televised toy commercials. *Child Development, 52*, 667–673.

Rucci, A. J., & Tweney, R. D. (1980). Analysis of variance and the "second discipline" of scientific psychology: A historical account. *Psychological Bulletin, 87*, 166–184.

Ruch, F. L. (1967). *Psychology and life* (7th ed.). Glenview, Ill.: Scott, Foresman.

Ruch, G. M., & Terman, L. M. (1925/1923). *Stanford Achievement Test, Manual of directions, revised*. Yonkers, N.Y.: World.

Ruch, W. A., & Hershauer, J. C. (1974). *Factors affecting worker productivity*. Tempe, Ariz.: Bureau of Business and Economic Research.

Rudd, B. T., Galal, O. M., & Casey, M. D. (1968). Testosterone excretion rates in normal males and males with an XYY complement. *Journal of Medical Genetics, 5*, 286.

Ruddy, M. G., & Bornstein, M. H. (1982). Cognitive correlates of infant attention and maternal stimulation over the first year of life. *Child Development, 53*, 183–188.

Rudel, J., & Rudel, S. (Eds.). (1976). *Education towards freedom.* East Grinstead, England: Lanthorn Press.

Rudel, R. G. (1980). Learning disability, diagnosis by exclusion and discrepancy. *Journal of the American Academy of Child Psychiatry, 19,* 547–569.

Rudestam, K. E. (1982). *Experiential groups in theory and practice.* Monterey, Calif.: Brooks/Cole.

Rudner, L. M., Getson, P. R., & Knight, D. L. (1980). Biased item detection techniques. *Journal of Educational Statistics, 2,* 213–233.

Rudolph, J. P, & Borland, B. L. (1976). Factors affecting the incidence and acceptance of cigarette smoking among high school students. *Adolescence, 11*(44), 519–525.

Rudy, T. E., Merluzzi, T. V., & Henahan, P. T. (1982). Construal of complex assertion situations: A multidimensional analysis. *Journal of Consulting and Clinical Psychology, 50,* 125–137.

Ruesch, J., & Bateson, G. (1968). *Communication: The social matrix of psychiatry.* New York: Norton.

Ruesch, J., & Kees, W. (1970). *Nonverbal communication: Notes on the visual perception of human relations.* Berkeley, Calif.: University of California Press.

Ruitenbeek, H. M. (1970). *The new group therapies.* New York: Avon Books.

Ruitenbeek, H. M. (Ed.). (1962). *Psychoanalysis and existential philosophy.* New York: Dutton.

Rumbaugh, D. M. (Ed.). (1977). *Language learning by a chimpanzee: The Lana project.* New York: Academic Press.

Rumbaugh, D. M., & Gill, T. V. (1976). Language and the acquisition of language-type skills by a chimpanzee (Pan). *Annals of the New York Academy of Sciences, 270,* 90–123.

Rumbaugh, D. M., Savage-Rumbaugh, E. S., & Scanlon, J. L. (1982). The relationship between language in apes and human beings. In J. L. Fobes & J. E. King (Eds.), *Primate behavior.* New York: Academic Press.

Rumbaugh, D. M., Von Glaserfeld, E., Warner, H., Pisani, P., & Gill, T. V. (1974). Lana (chimpanzee) learning language: A progress report. *Brain and Language, 1,* 205–212.

Rumelhart, D. E. (1977). *An introduction to human information processing.* New York: Wiley.

Rumelhart, D. E., Hinton, G. E., & Williams, R. J. (1986). Learning internal representations by error propagation. In D. E. Rumelhart (Ed.), *Parallel distributed: Explorations in the microstructures of cognition* (pp. 318–362). Cambridge: MIT Press.

Rumelhart, D. E., Hinton, G. E., & Williams, R. J. (1986). Learning internal representations by error propagation. In D. E. Rumelhart (Ed.), *Parallel distributed processing Explorations in the microstructure of cognition* (pp. 318–362). Cambridge: MIT Press.

Rumelhart, D. E., & McClelland, J. L. (Eds.). (1986). *Parallel distributed processing: Vol. 1. Foundations.* Cambridge: MIT Press.

Rumelhart, D. E., & Ortony, A. (1977). The representation of knowledge in memory. In R. C. Anderson, R. J. Spiro, & W. E. Montague (Eds.), *Schooling and the acquisition of knowledge.* Hillsdale, NJ: Erlbaum.

Rumenik, D. K., Capasso, D. R., & Hendrick, C. (1977). Experimenter sex effects in behavioral research. *Psychological Bulletin, 84,* 852–877.

Runyan, W. M. (1982). In defense of the case study method. *American Journal of Orthopsychiatry, 52,* 440–446.

Rupert, D. (Ed.). (1981). Loss. *Personnel and Guidance Journal,* Special issue, 59(6).

Ruppert, P. H. (1986). Postnatal exposure. In Z. Annau (Ed.), *Neurobehavioral toxicology* (pp. 170–189). Baltimore: The Johns Hopkins University Press.

Rusak, B., & Zucker, I. (1975). Biological rhythms and animal behavior. *Annual Review of Psychology, 26,* 137–171.

Rusak, B., & Zucker, I. (1979). Neural regulation of circadian rhythms. *Physiological Reviews, 59,* 449–526.

Ruse, M. (1979). *Sociobiology: Sense or nonsense.* Boston: Reidel.

Rush, A. J., Beck, A. T, Kovacs, M., & Hollon, S. (1977). Comparative efficacy of cognitive therapy and pharmacotherapy in the treatment of depressed outpatients. *Cognitive Therapy and Research, 1,* 17–37.

Rush, B. (1962/1812). *Medical inquiries and observations upon the diseases of the mind.* New York: Hafner.

Rush, J., & Altschuler, K. (Eds). (1992). *Depression.* New York: Guilford.

Rush, J. H. (1977). Problems and methods in psychokinesis research. In S. Krippner (Ed.), *Advances in parapsychological research: 1. Psychokinesis.* New York: Plenum.

Rushall, B. S., & Siedentop, D. (1972). *The development and control of behavior in sports and physical education.* Philadelphia, Pa.: Lea & Febiger.

Rushton, J. P. (1935). Differential K theory: The sociobiology of individual and group differences. *Personality and Individual Differences,* 441–452.

Rushton, J. P. (1980). *Altruism, socialization, and society.* Englewood Cliffs, N.J.: Prentice-Hall.

Rushton, J. P., & Sorrentino, R. M. (Eds.). (1981). *Altruism and helping behavior.* Hillsdale, N.J.: Erlbaum.

Rusling, L. A. (1905). Children's attitudes toward clothes. *Pedagogical Seminary, 12,* 525–526.

Russell, D., & Cutrona, C. (1984, August). *The provisions of social relationships and adaption to stress.* Paper presented at the American Psychological Association meeting, Toronto.

Russell, D., Peplau, L. A., & Fergusson, J. L. Developing a measure of loneliness. *Journal of Personality Assessment,* submitted.

Russell, G. (1979). Bulimia nervosa: An ominous variant of anorexia nervosa. *Psychological Medicine, 9*(3), 429–448.

Russell, M. A. H. (1971). Cigarette dependence: 1—Nature and classification. *British Medical Journal 2*(5757), 330–331.

Russell, M. N. (1984). *Skills in counseling women: The feminist approach.* IL: Thomas.

Russell, R. W. (1977). Australian psychologists in the world context. In M. Nixon, & R. Taft, (Eds.), *Psychology in Australia: Achievements and prospects.* Rushcutters Bay, Australia: Pergamon Press.

Russell, W., & Burch, R. (1959). *The principles of humane experimental technique.* London: Methuen.

Russell, W. R. (1961). *Traumatic aphasia.* London: Oxford University Press.

Russo, D., (1987). Personal communication.

Russo, M. F., Lakey, B. B., Christ, M. A. G., Frick, P. J., McBurnett, K., Walker, J. L., Loeber, R., Stouthhamer-Loeber, M., & Green, S. (1991). Preliminary development of a sensation seeking scale for children. *Personality and Individual Differences, 12,* 399–405.

Russo, S., & Dallenbach, K. M. (1939). Age and the effects of rotation. *American Journal of Psychology, 52,* 83–88.

Rutherford, W. (1886). The sense of hearing. *Journal of Anatomy and Physiology, 21,* 166–168.

Rutherford, W. (1880). *A text book of physiology*. Edinburgh: Black.

Rutledge, A. L. (1966). *Pre-marital counseling* Cambridge, Mass.: Schenkman.

Rutledge, A. L. (1968). An illustrative look at the history of pre-marital counseling. In J. A. Peterson (Ed.), *Marriage and family counseling: Perspective and prospect*. New York: Association Press.

Rutman, L. (1980). *Planning useful evaluations: Evaluability assessment*. Beverly Hills, Calif.: Sage Publications.

Rutter, M. Diagnosis and definition of childhood autism. *Journal of Autism and Childhood Schizophrenia, 8*(2), 137–156.

Rutter, M. (1972). *Maternal deprivation reassessed*. Baltimore, Md.: Penguin Education.

Rutter, M. (1979). Maternal deprivation, 1972–1978: New findings, new concepts, new approaches. *Child Development, 50*, 283–305.

Rutter, M. (1979). Protective factors in children's responses to stress and disadvantage. In M. W. Kent & J. E. Rolf(Eds.), *Primary prevention of pathology. Vol. III: Social competence in children*. Hanover, N.H.: University Press of New England.

Rutter, M., & Bartak, L. (1973). Special educational treatment of autistic children: A comparative study. II. Follow-up findings and implications for services. *Journal of Child Psychology and Psychiatry, 14,* 241–270.

Rutter, M., & Giller, H. (1983). *Juvenile delinquency: Trends and perspectives*. New York: Penguin Books.

Rutter, M., & Lockyet, L. (1967). A five to fifteen year follow-up of infantile psychosis. I. Description of sample. *British Journal of Psychiatry, 113*, 1169–1182.

Rutter, M., Yule, B., Quinton, D., Rowlands, O., Yule, W., & Berger, M. (1974). Attainment and adjustment in two geographical areas: III. Some factors accounting for area differences. *British Journal of Psychiatry, 125*, 520–533.

Ryan, B., & Gross, N. C. (1943). The diffusion of hybrid seed corn in two Iowa communities. *Rural Sociology, 8*, 15–24.

Ryan, F. (1981). *Sports and psychology*. Englewood Cliffs, N.J.: Prentice-Hall.

Ryan, F. J. (1973). Cold turkey in Greenfield, Iowa: A follow-up study. In W. L. Dunn (Ed.), *Smoking behavior: Motives and incentives*. Washington, D.C.: V. Winston.

Ryan, M. S. (1966). *Clothing: A study in human behavior*. New York: Holt, Rinehart & Winston.

Ryan, R. M. (1982). Control and information in the intrapersonal sphere: An extension of cognitive evaluation theory. *Journal of Personality and Social Psychology, 43*(3), 450–461.

Ryan, T. A. (1981). Intention and kinds of learning. In G. d'Ydewalle & W. Lens (Eds.), *Cognition in human motivation and learning*. Hillsdale, N.J.: Erlbaum. Louvain, Belguim: Leuven University Press.

Ryan, W. (1976). *Blaming the victim*. New York: Vintage Books.

Ryans, D. G. (1957). Notes on the criterion problem in research, with special reference to the study of teacher characteristics. *Journal of Genetic Psychology, 91*, 33–61.

Ryans, D. G. Problems in validating teacher selection policies and procedures. ERIC microfiche #ED014465.

Rybash, J. M., Hoyer, W. J., & Roadin, P. A. (1986). *Adult Cognition and aging*. New York: Pergamon.

Rychlak, J. (1977). *The psychology of rigorous humanism*. New York: Wiley Interscience.

Rychlak, J. (1980). Concepts of free will in modern psychological science. *The Journal of Mind and Behavior, 1*, 9–32.

Rychlak, J. E. (1979). *Discovering free will and moral responsibility*. New York: Oxford University Press.

Rychlak, J. F. (1973). *Introduction to personality and psychotherapy*. Boston: Houghton Mifflin.

Rychlak, J. F. (1973). *Personality and psychotherapy*. (2nd ed.). Boston: Houghton Mifflin.

Rychlak, J. F. (1981/1973). *Personality and psychotherapy* (2nd ed.). Boston: Houghton Mifflin.

Rychlak, J. F. (1981). *A philosophy of science for personality theory* (2nd ed.). Malabar, Fla.: Krieger.

Rychlak, J. F. (Ed.). (1976). *Dialectic: Humanistic rationale for behavior and development*. Basel: Karger.

Rychman, R. M., Rodda, W. C., & Sherman, M. F. (1972). Locus of control and expertise relevant as determinants of changes in opinion about student activism. *Journal of Social Psychology, 88*, 107–114.

Ryckman, D. B. (1981). Searching for a WISC-R profile for learning disabled children: An inappropriate task? *A journal of Learning Disabilities, 14*, 508–510.

Ryckman, R. M. (1978). *Theories of personality*. New York: Van Nostrand.

Ryckman, R. M., Gold, J. A., & Redda, W. C. (1971). Confidence rating shifts and performance as a function of locus of control, self-esteem, and initial task experience. *Journal of Personality and Social Psychology, 18*, 305–310.

Rydelius, P. A., (1988). The development of antisocial behaviour and sudden violent death. *Acta Psychiatrics Scandinavica, 77*, 398–403.

Ryder, D. (1992). *Breaking the circle of satanic ritual abuse*. Minneapolis: CompCare.

Ryder, R.(1975). *Victims Of science*. London: Davis-Poynter.

Ryder, R. D. (1973). Pets in man's search for sanity. *Journal of Small Animal Practice, 14*(11), 657–668.

Ryle, A. (1975). *Frames and cages: The repertory grid approach to human understanding*. London: University of Sussex Press.

Ryle, G. (1949). *The concept of mind*. London: Hutchinson.

Ryle, G. (1971). *Collected papers*, Vol. II. New York: Barnes & Noble.

Ryterband, E. E., & Bass, B. M. (1974). Management development. In J. W. McGuire (Ed.), *Contemporary management: Issues and viewpoints*, Englewood Cliffs, N.J.: Prentice-Hall.

Saal, F. E. (1979). Mixed Standard Rating Scale: A consistent system for numerically coding inconsistent response combinations. *Journal of Applied Psychology, 64*, 422–428.

Saal, F. E. & Landy, F. J. (1977). The Mixed Standard Rating Scale: An evaluation. *Organizational Behavior and Human Performance, 18*, 19–35.

Saario, T. N., Jacklin, C. N., & Tittle, C. K. (1973). Sex role stereotyping in the public schools. *Harvard Educational Review, 43*, 386–416.

Saavedra-Aguilar, J. C., & Gomez-Jeria, J. S. (1989). A neurobiological model for near-death experiences. *Journal of Near-Death Studies, 7*, 205–222.

Sabatino, D. A., & Miller, T. C. (1979). *Describing learner characteristics of handicapped children and youth*. New York: Grune & Stratton.

Sabini, J. P., & Silver, M. (Eds.). (1992). *Second edition of Milgram, S. Individual in a social world: Essays and experiments*. New York: McGraw-Hill.

Sabom, M. B. (1982). *Recollections of death: A medical investigation*. New York: Harper & Row.

Sachar, E. (1982). Endocrine abnormalities in depression. In E. Paykel (Ed.), *Handbook of affective disorders*. New York: Guilford Press.

Sachar, E., Hellman, L., Fukushima, D., & Gallagher, R. (1970). Cortisol production in depressive illness. *Archives of General Psychiatry, 23,* 189–298.

Sachar, E. J. (1975). *Topics in psychoendocrinology.* New York: Grune & Stratton.

Sackeim, H. A., Nordlie, J. S., & Gut, R. C. (1979). A model of hysterical and hypnotic blindness: Cognition, motivation, and awareness. *Journal of Abnormal Psychology, 88,* 474–489.

Sackett, G. P. (1967). Some persistent effects of different rearing conditions on preadult social behavior of monkeys. *Journal of Comparative and Physiological Psychology, 64,* 363–365.

Sackett, P. R., Burris, L. R., & Callahan, C. (1989). Integrity testing for personnel selection: An update. *Personnel Psychology, 44,* 491–529.

Sackett, P. R., & Harris, M. M. (1984). Honesty testing for personnel selection: Review and critique. *Personnel Psychology, 37,* 221–245.

Sacks, J. M. & Levy, S. (1950). The Sentence Completion Test. In L. E. Abt & L. Bellak (Eds.), *Projectire psychology.* New York: Knopf.

Sadd, S., Lenauee, M., Shaver, P., & Dunivant, N. (1978). Objective measurement of fear of success and fear of failure: A factor analytic approach. *Journal of Consulting and Clinical Psychology, 46,* 405–416.

Sadlet, W. S. (1936). *Theory and practice of psychiatry.* St. Louis, Mo.: Mosby.

Saers, D. J. (1923). The effects of bilingualism on intelligence. *British Journal of Psychology, 14.*

Safer, D. J. (1984). Subgrouping conduct disordered adolescents by early risk factors. *American Journal of Orthopsychiatry, 54,* 603–612.

Safer, D. J., & Allen, R. P. (1976). *Hyperactive children: Diagnosis and management.* Baltimore, Md.: University Park Press.

Safer, D. J., & Krager, M. D. (1988). A survey of medication treatment for hyperactive/inattentive students. *Journal of the American Medical Association, 260,* 2256–2258.

Safford, P. L. (1978). *Teaching young children with special needs.* St. Louis, Mo.: Mosby.

Safir, M. P., & Hoch, Z. (1980). Couple interactional classification of sexual dysfunction—A new theoretical conceptualization. *Journal of Sex and Marital Therapy, 6,* 129–134.

Safran, J. D., Alden, L. E., & Davidson, P. O. (1980). Client anxiety level as a moderator variable in assertion training. *Cognitive Therapy and Research, 4,* 189–200.

Sagara, M. (1950). *Kioku towa nanika (What is the memory?)* Tokyo: Iwanami.

Sagara, M. (1952). *Geshutaruto-shinrigaku (Gestalt psychology).* Tokyo: Iwanami.

Sager, C. J. (1976). *Marriage contracts and couple therapy.* New York: Brunner/Mazel.

Sager, C. J., & Kaplan, H. S. (Eds.), (1972). *The progress in group and family therapy.* New York: Brunner/Mazel.

Sagotsky, G., Wood-Schneider, M., & Konop, M. (1981). *Child Development, 52,* 1037–1042.

Sialdan, W. S. (1968). History of philosophy. New York: Harper & Row.

Sahakian, W. S. (1969). Stoic philosophical psychotherapy, *Journal of Individual Psychology, 25,* 32–35.

Sahakian, W. S. (1974). Philosophical psychotherapy. *Psychologia: An International Journal of Psychology in the Orient, 17,* 179–185.

Sahakian, W. S. (1976). Psychotherapy: An existential approach. *Journal of Individual Psychology, 32,* 62–68.

Sahakian, W. S. (1977). Personalism. In R. J. Corsini (Ed.), *Current personality theories.* Itasca, Ill.: Peacock.

Sahakian, W. S. (1977). Psychology of personality (3rd ed.). Boston: Houghton Mifflin.

Sahakian, W. S. (1978). *Psychopathology today: The current status of abnormal psychology* (2nd ed.). Itasca, Ill.: Peacock.

Sahakian, W. S. (1980). Philosophical psychotherapy. In R. Herink (Ed.), *The psychotherapy handbook* New York: New American Library.

Sahakian, W. S. (1980). Philosophical therapy: A variation on logotherapy. *International Forum for Logotherapy, 3,* 37–40.

Sahakian, W. S. (1980). The infection theory in social psychology. *Society for the Advancement of Social Psychology Newsletter, 6,* 3–4.

Sahakian, W. S. (1982). History and systems of social psychology. New York: McGraw-Hill Hemisphere.

Sahakian, W. S. (1982). *Introduction to psychology of learning.* (2nd ed.), Itasca, Ill.: Peacock.

Sahakian, W. S. (Ed.). (1968). History of psychology: A source book in systematic psychology. Itasca, Ill.: Peacock.

Sahakian, W. S. (Ed.). (1969). *Psychotherapy and counseling: Studies in technique.* Chicago: Rand-McNally.

Sahlins, M. (1976). *The use and abuse of biology: An anthropological critique of sociobiology.* Ann Arbor, Mich.: University of Michigan Press.

Sailaja, P., & Rao, K. R. (1973). *Experimental studies of the differential effect in life setting.* New York: Parapsychology Foundation.

Sainsbury, P. (1955). *Suicide in London: An ecological study.* London: Chapman & Hall.

Sakel, M. (1938). *The pharmacological shock treatment of schizophrenia.* New York: Nervous and Mental Disease.

Sakles, C. J., & Balis, G. U. (1978). Acute brain syndromes. In G. U. Balis, L. Wurmser, E. McDaniel, & R. G. Grenell (Eds.), *Clinical-psychopathology.* Boston: Butterworth.

Sakheim, D., & Devine, S. (1992). *Out of darkness.* New York: Lexington Books.

Saks, M. J. (1978). Some psychological contributions to a legislative subcommittee on organ and tissue transplants. *American Psychologist, 33,* 680–690.

Saks, M. J., & Hasfie, R. (1978). *Social psychology in court.* New York: Van Nostrand Reinhold.

Salafia, W. R., Lambert, R. W., Host, K. C, Chiaia, N. L., & Ramirez, J. J. (1980). Rabbit nictitating membrane conditioning: Lower limit of the effective interstimulus interval. *Animal Learning and Behavior, 8,* 85–91.

Salamone, F. A. (1969). Further notes on Hausa culture and personality. *International Journal of Social Psychiatry, 16,* 39–44.

Salancik, G. R., & Pfeffer, J. (1978). A social information processing approach to job attitudes and task design. *Administrative Science Quarterly, 23,* 224—253.

Saldanha, E., & Corso, J. F. (1964). Timbre cues and the identification of musical instruments. *Journal of the Acoustical Society of America, 36,* 2021–2026.

Säljö, R. (1975). *Qualitative differences in learning as a function of the learner's conception of the task.* Goteborg, Sweden: Acta Universitatis Gothoburgensis.

Säljö, R. (1981). Learning approach and outcome: Some empirical observations. *Instructional Science, 10,* 47–65.

Salk, J. (1961). Biological basis of disease and behavior. *Perspectives in Biology and Medicine, 5,* 198–206.

Salmela, J. H. (Ed.). (1981). *The world sport psychology sourcebook.* Ithaca, N.Y.: Mouvement Publications.

Salmon, R., & Salmon, S. (1977). The career of heroin addiction: A review of the literature: Part II. *The International Journal of the Addictions, 12,* 937–951.

Salokangas, R. K. R. (1979). First admissions for psychosis in Türkü (Finland): A time trend study. *Acta Psychiatrica Scandinavica, 60,* 249–262.

Salokangas, R. K. R. (1980). Hospital and outpatient care for psychotic patients during the last three decades. *Acta Psychiatrica Scandinavica, 62,* 47–62.

Salomone, R. R., & Slaney, R. B. (1978). The applicability of Holland's theory to non-professional workers. *Journal of Vocational Behavior, 13,* 63–74.

Salter, A. (1961/1949). Conditioned reflex therapy: The direct approach to the reconstruction of personality. New York: Farrar, Straus.

Salter, A. (1964). Theory and practice of conditioned reflex therapy. In J. Wolpe, A. Salter, & L. J. Reyna (Eds.) *The conditioning therapies: The challenge in psychotherapy.* New York: Holt, Rinehart & Winston.

Salter, A. (1972/1952). *The case against psychoanalysis.* New York: Harper & Row.

Salter, A. (1975/1944). *What is hypnosis: Studies in auto and hetero conditioning.* New York: Farrar, Straus.

Salter, A. (1981). Conditioned reflex therapy. In R. J. Corsini (Ed.), *Handbook of innovative psychotherapies.* New York: Wiley.

Salvia, J., & Ysseldyke, J. E. (1978). *Assessment in special and remedial education.* Boston: Houghton Mifflin.

Salzman, C., & Gutfreund, J. (1986). Clinical techniques and research strategies for studying depression and memory. In L. Poon (Ed.), *Handbook for clinical memory assessment of older adults.* Washington, DC: American Psychological Association.

Salzman, L. (1968). *The obsessive personality: Origins, dynamics and therapy.* New York: Aronson.

Salzman, L. (1969). Religious conversion. In E. Mansell Pattison (Ed.), *Clinical psychiatry and religion.* Boston: Little, Brown.

Samaan, M. (1972). The control of nocturnal enuresis by operant conditioning. *Journal of Behavior Therapy and Experimental Psychiatry, 3,* 103–105.

Samelson, F. (1981). Struggle for scientific authority: The reception of Watson's behaviorism, 1913–1920, *Journal of the History of the Behavioral Sciences, 17,* 399—425.

Samler, J. (1964). Where do counseling psychologists work? What do they do? What should they do? In A. S. Thompson & D. E. Super (Eds.), *The professional preparation of counseling psychologists. Report of the 1964 Greyston Conference.* New York: Bureau of Publications. Teachers College, Columbia University.

Samovar, L. A., & Rintye, E. D. (1970). Interpersonal communication: Some working principles. In R. S. Cathcart, & L. A. Samovar (Eds.), *Small group communication: A reader.* Dubuque, Iowa: Brown.

Samples, R. E. (1975). Learning with the whole brain. *Human Behavior, 4,* 16–23.

Sampson, E. E: (1965). The study of ordinal position: Antecedents and conditions. In B. A. Maher (Ed.), *Progress in experimental personality research,* New York: Academic Press.

Sampson, E. E. (1977). Psychology and the American ideal. *Journal of Personality and Social Psychology, 35,* 767–782.

Samuda, R. J. (1975). *Psychological testing of American minorities: Issues and consequences.* New York: Dodd, Mead.

Samuel, J. M. F. (1981). Individual differences in the interaction of vision and proprioception. In R. D. Walk & H. L. Pick, Jr. (Eds.), *Intersensory perception and sensory integration.* New York: Plenum.

Samuels, H. R. (1980). The effect of an older sibling on infant locomotor exploration of a new environment. *Child Development, 51,* 607–609.

Samuels, S. J. (1979). The method of repeated readings. *The Reading Teacher, 32,* 403–408.

Sanborn, P. F. (1968). *Existentialism.* New York: Pegasus.

Sánchez de Almeida, M. E., & Almeida, E. (1978). Experiencia Comunitaria en San Miguel Tzinacapan. *América Indígena, 38*(3).

Sánchez, G. I. (1934). Bilingualism and mental measures. *Journal of Applied Psychology, 18,* 765–772.

Sander, F. (1928). Experimentelle Ergebnisse der Gestalt Psychologie. In E. Becker (Ed.), *Bericht über den 10. Kongress der Deutschen Gesellschaft für Psychologie in Jena 1927.* Jena, East Germany: Fischer.

Sanders, G., & Simmons, W. L. (1983). Use of hypnosis to enhance eyewitness accuracy: Does it work? *Journal of Applied Psychology, 68,* 70–77.

Sanders, J. C., Sterns, H. L., Smith, M., & Sanders, R. E. (1975). Modification of concept identification performance in older adults. *Developmental Psychology, 11,* 824–829.

Sandifer, M. G., Hordern, A., & Green, L. M. (1970). The psychiatric interview: The impact of the first three minutes. *American Journal of Psychiatry, 126,* 968–973.

Sandiford, P. (1938). *Foundations of educational psychology.* New York: Longman, Green.

Sandler, P. C., & Sandler, E. H. (1975). Epilepsy and birth order. *Arquivos do Neuro-Psiquiatria* (Sao Paulo), *33*(3), 244–251.

Sanford, A. Semrau, B., & Wilson, D. (1974). *The Chapel Hill model for training Head Start personnel in mainstreaming handicapped children.* Winston Salem, N.C.: Kaplan Press.

Sanford, E. C. (1898). *A course in experimental psychology:* Part I, *Sensation and perception.* Boston: Heath.

Sanford, N. W. (1937). The effects of abstinence from food upon imaginal processes: A further experiment. *Journal of Psychology, 3,* 145–159.

Sanford, R. N. (1962). *The American College.* New York: Wiley.

Santostefano, S. (1985). *Cognitive control therapy with children and adolescents.* (pp. 1–83). New York: Pergaman.

Santostefano, S. A (1978). *biodevelopmental approach to clinical child psychology,* New York: Wiley.

Santrock, J. W. (1972). The relations of onset and type of father absence to cognitive development. *Child Development, 43,* 455–469.

Santrock, J. W., Warshak, R. A., & Eliot, G. L. (1982). Social development and parent–child interaction in father-custody and stepmother families. In M. Lamb (Ed.), *Nontraditional families.* Hillsdale, N.J.: Erlbaum.

Santrock, J. W., Warshak, R. A., Lindbergh, C., & Meadows, L. (in press). Children's and parents' observed social behavior in stepfather families. *Child Development.*

Sanua, V. D. (1966). Socio-cultural aspects of psychotherapy and treatment. A review of the literature. *Progress in Clinical Psychology, 7,* 151–190.

Sanua, V. D. (1971). Psychology in action. *American Psychologist, 26,* 602–605.

Sapir, E., (1921). *Language, an introduction to the study of speech.* New York: Harcourt, Brace.

Sapir, E. (1949). The unconscious patterning of behavior in society. In D. Mandlebaum (Ed.), *Selected writings of Edward Sapir in language, culture and personality.* Berkeley, Calif.: University of California Press.

Sapir, S. G. & Nitzburg, A. C. (1973). *Children with learning problems—Readings in a developmental-interaction approach.* New York: Brunner/Mazel.

Sapir, S. G. & Wilson. (1978). *A professional's guide to working with the learning disabled child.* New York: Brunner/Mazel.

Saposnek, D. (1972). An experimental study of rage-reduction treatment in autistic children. *Child Psychiatry and Human Development, 3,* 50–62.

Sappenfield, B. R. (1965). The Blacky pictures. In O. K. Buros (Ed.), *The sixth mental measurements yearbook,* Highland Park, N.J.: Gryphon Press.

Sarafino, E. P. (1982a). Intrinsic motivation and delay of gratification in preschoolers: The effects of reward salience and expected delay. Submitted for publication.

Sarafino, E. P. (1982b). Peer–peer interaction among infants and toddlers with extensive day-care experience. Submitted for publication.

Sarafino, E. P. (1982c). *The child's fears.* Submitted for publication.

Sarafino, E. P., & DiMattia, P. A. (1978). Does grading undermine intrinsic interest in a college course? *Journal of Educational Psychology, 70,* 916–921.

Sarafino, E. P., & Helmuth, H. (1981). Development of personal space in preschool children as a function of age and day-care experience. *Journal of Social Psychology, 115,* 59–63.

Sarason, I. G. (1980). Introduction to the study of test anxiety. In I. G. Sarason (Ed.), Test anxiety: Theory, research and applications. Hillsdale, N.J.: Erlbaum.

Sarason, I. G. (1980). Life stress, self-preoccupation, and social supports. In I. G. Sarason & C. D. Spielberger (Eds.), *Stress and anxiety.* Washington, D.C.: Hemisphere.

Sarason, I. G. (Ed.). (1980). *Test anxiety: Theory, research, and applications.* Hillsdale, N.J.: Erlbaum.

Sarason, I. G., Johnson, J. H., & Siegel, J. M. (1978). Assessing the impact of life changes: Development of the Life Experiences Survey. *Journal of Consulting and Clinical Psychology, 46,* 932–946.

Sarason, I. G., Levine, H. M., Basham, R. B., & Sarason, B. R. (1983). Assessing social support: The social support questionaire. *Journal of Personality and Social Psychology, 44,* 127–139.

Sarason, I. G., Sarason, B. R., & Pierce, G. R. (1992). Three contexts of social support. In H. O. F. Veiel & U. Baumann (Eds.), *The meaning and measurement of social support* (pp.143–154). New York: Hemisphere.

Sarason, I. G., Sarason, B. R., Potter, E. H., & Antoni, M. H. (1985). Life events, social support and illness. *Psychosomatic Medicine, 47,* 156–163.

Sarason, I. G., Smith, R. E., & Diener, E. (1975). Personality research: Components of variance attributable to the person and the situation. *Journal of Personality and Social Psychology, 82,* 199–204.

Sarason, S. B. (1974). *The psychological sense of community: Prospects for the community psychology.* San Francisco: Jossey-Bass.

Sarason, S. B. (1976). The unfortunate fate of Alfred Binet and school psychology. *Teachers College Record, 77,* 579–592.

Sarason, S. B. (1978). The nature of problem solving in social action. *American Psychologist, 33,* 370–380.

Sarason, S. B. (1981). *Psychology misdirected.* New York: Free Press.

Sarason, T. G. (1980). *Test anxiety: Theory research and applications.* Hillsdale, NJ: Erlbaum.

Sarbin, T., Taft, R., & Bailey, D. (1960). *Clinical inference and cognitive theory.* New York: Holt, Rinehart & Winston.

Sargant, W. (1957). *Battle for the mind.* New York: Doubleday.

Sargant, W. (1973). *The mind possessed.* London: Heinemann.

Sargeant, A. B., & Eberhardt, L. E. (1975). Death feigning by ducks in response to predation by red foxes (*Vulpesfulva*). *American Midland Naturalist, 94,* 108–119.

Sargent, C. L. (1980). *Exploring psi in the ganzfeld.* New York: Parapsychology Foundation.

Sargent, C. L. (1981). Extraversion and performance in "extra-sensory perception" tasks. *Personality and Individual Differences, 2,* 137–143.

Saris, W. E., & van Meurs A. (Eds.). (1990). *Evaluation of measurement instruments by meta-analysis of multitrait multimethod studies.* Amsterdam, The Netherlands: Royal Netherlands Academy of Arts and Sciences.

Sarnoff, I. (1960). Reaction formation and cynicism. *Journal of Personality, 28,* 129–143.

Sarris, V. (Ed.). (1983). *Perspectives in psychological experimentation towards the year 2000.* Hillsdale, N.J.: Erlbaum.

Sarris, V., & Lienert, G. A. (1974). Konstruktion und Bewähren von klinischpsychologischen Testverfahren. In W. J. Schraml & U. Baumann (Eds.), *Klinische Psychologie II: Methoden, Ergebnisse und Probleme der Forschung.* Bern, Stuttgart, Vienna: Huber.

Sartorius, N. (1974). Depressive illness as a worldwide problem. In P. Keilholz (Ed.), Depression in everyday practice. Bern: Huber.

Sartre, J. P. (1956). *Being and nothingness.* (H. E. Barnes, Trans.). New York: Philosophical Library.

Sartre, J.-P. (1956). *Being and nothingness.* New York: Philosophical Library.

Sartre, J.-P. (1957). *Existenialism and human emotion.* New York: Philosophical Library.

Sartre, J.-P. (1962/1939). *Sketch for a theory of the emotions.* London: Methuen.

Sartre, J.-P. (1963). *Search for a method.* New York: Knopf.

Sartre, J.-P. (1981). *The family idiot: Gustave Flaubert, 1821–1857.* Chicago: University of Chicago Press.

Sasano, E. M., Shepard, K. F., Bell, J. E., Daviers, N. H., Hansen, E. M., & Sanford, T. L. The family in physical therapy. *Physical Therapy, 57,* 153–159.

Sashkin, M. (1981). *Assessing performance appraisal.* San Diego, Calif.: University Associates.

Sastry, N. S. N. (1932). Growth of psychology in India, *Indian Journal of Psychology, 3,* 1–40.

Sataloff, J., Sataloff, R. T., & Vassall, L. A. (1980). *Hearing loss.* Philadelphia, Pa.: Lippincott.

Satir, V. (1967). *Conjoint family therapy.* Palo Alto, Calif.: Science and Behavior Books, 1967.

Sato, K. (1947). *Towards the integrated science of humankind—"Ki" and moral.* Tokyo: Kotoshoin.

Sato, K. (1948). *Fundamentals of psychology.* Nagoya, Japan: Reimcishobo.

Sato, K. (1951). *Psychology of personality.* Tokyo: Tokyo Sogensha.

Sato, K. (1961). *Psychological approach to Zen.* Tokyo: Tokyo Sogensha.

Sato, K. (1964). *Exhortation toward Zen*. Tokyo: Kodansha.

Sato, K. (1966). *Life of Zen*. Kyoto, Japan: Tankoshinsha.

Sato, K. (1967). *Invitation to Zen*. Tokyo: Shibundo.

Sato, K. (1968). *Conversation in death*. Tokyo: Shibundo.

Sato, K. (1968). *Record of life and death*. Tokyo: Kodansha.

Satterfield, J. H. (1990). BEAM studies in ADD boys. In K. Conners, & M. Kinsbourne (Eds.), *Attention deficit pyperactivity disorder: ADHD; clinical experimental and demographic issues* (pp. 127–136). Munich, Germany: MMV Medizin Verlag.

Sattin, B. (1980). Possible sources of error in the evaluation of psychopathology. *Journal of Clinical Psychology, 36*(1), 99–105.

Sattler, J. M. (1982/1974). *Assessment of children's intelligence and special abilities* (2nd ed.). Boston: Allyn & Bacon.

Satz, P., & Morris, R. (1980). Learning disability subtypes: A review. In R. E. Tarter (Ed.), *The child at risk*, New York: Oxford University Press.

Saunders, C. (1977). Dying they live: St. Christopher's Hospice. In H. Feifel (Ed.), *New meanings of death*. New York: McGraw-Hill.

Saussure, F. de. (1959). *Course in general linguistics*. New York: Philosophical Library.

Savage, I. R., Greenberg, B. G., Moore, P. G., & David, H. A. (1978). Nonparametric statistics. In W. H. Kruskal & J. M. Tanur (Eds.), *International encyclopedia of statistics*, Vol. 1. New York: Free Press.

Savage, L. J. (1954). *The foundations of statistics*. New York: Wiley.

Savage-Rumbaugh, E. S. (1981). Can apes use symbols to represent their world? In T. A. Sebeok & R. Rosenthal (Eds.), *The Clever Hans phenomenon: Communication with horses, whales, apes, and people*. New York: New York Academy of Sciences.

Savage-Rumbaugh, E. S., Rumbaugh, D. M., & Boysen, S. (1978). Linguistically mediated tool use and exchange by chimpanzees *(Pan troglodytes)*. *The Behavioral and Brain Sciences, 4*, 539–554.

Savage-Rumbaugh, E. S., Rumbaugh, D. M., & Boysen, S. (1980). Do apes use language? *American Scientist, 68*, 49–61.

Savitsky, J. C., Izard, C. E., Kotsch, W. E., & Christy, L. (1974). Aggressor's response to the victim's facial expression of emotion. *Journal of Research in Personality, 7*, 346–357.

Savitt, R. A. (1963). Psychoanalytic studies on addiction: Ego structure in narcotic addiction, *Psychoanalytic Quarterly, 32*, 43–57.

Savitt, R. A. (1965). Psychoanalytic studies on addiction II: Hypersexuality (love addiction). Presented at midwinter meeting of the American Psychoanalytic Association.

Savitt, R. A. (1968). The psychopathology of the addiction process. *Journal of Hillside Hospital, 17*, 277–286.

Savitt, R. A. (1971). Psychoanalytic studies on addiction, III: Food addiction (obesity). Presented at spring meeting of the American Psychoanalytic Association.

Sawrey, W. L., Conger, J. J., & Turrell, E. S. (1956). An experimental Investigation of the Role of Psychological Factors in the Production of Gastric Ulcers in Rats. *Journal of Comparative & Physiological Psychology, 49*, 445–461.

Sawyer, J. (1966). Measurement *and* prediction, clinical *and* statistical. *Psychological Bulletin, 66*, 178–200.

Sax, G. (1980). *Principles of educational and psychological measurement and evaluation* (2nd ed.). Belmont, Calif.: Wadsworth.

Saxe, L. (1991, April). Lying: Thoughts of an applied social psychologist. *American Psychologist, 46*(4), 409–415.

Sayers, J. (1982). *Biological politics*. New York: Tavistock Publications.

Scaife, M., & Bruner, J. S. (1975). The capacity for joint visual attention in the infant. *Nature, 253*, 265–266.

Scandura, J. M. (1964). An analysis of expository and discovery modes of problem solving instruction. *Journal of Experimental Education, 33*, 149–159.

Scandura, J. M. (1970). The role of rules in behavior: Toward an operational definition of what (rule) is learned. *Psychological Review, 77*, 516–533.

Scandura, J. M. (1971). Deterministic theorizing in structural learning: Three levels of empiricism. *Journal of Structural Learning, 3*, 21–53.

Scandura, J. M. (1973). *Structural learning I: Theory and research*. London, New York: Gordon & Breach.

Scandura, J. M. (1974, Spring). The structure of memory: Fixed or flexible? *Catalog of Selected Documents in Psychology*, 37–78.

Scandura, J. M. (1976). *Structural learning II: Issues and approaches*. London, New York: Gordon & Breach.

Scandura, J. M. (1977). A deterministic theory of teaching and learning. In H. Spada & W. F. Kempf (Eds.), *Structural models of thinking and learning*. Bern: Huber.

Scandura, J. M. (1977). *Problem solving: A structural process approach with instructional implications*. New York: Academic Press.

Scandura, J. M. (1978). Discussion of selected issues in structural learning. In J. M. Scandura & C. J. Brainerd (Eds.), *Structural/process models of complex human behavior*. Leyden, Netherlands: Sijthoff.

Scandura, J. M. (1980). Theoretical foundations of instruction: A systems alternative to cognitive psychology. *Journal of Structural Learning, 6*, 347–394.

Scandura, J. M. (1981). Problem solving in schools and beyond: Transitions from the naive to the neophyte to the master. *Journal of Structural Learning, .*

Scandura, J. M. (1981). Structural learning and instructional strategies. In C. Reigeluth (Ed.), *Prescriptive theories of instruction*. New York: Academic Press.

Scandura, J. M., & Scandura, A. B. (1980). *The acquisition of concrete operations. A rule based analysis of Piagetian conservation*. New York: Praeger.

Scarborough, H. E. (1943). A quantitative and qualitative analysis of the electroencephalograms of stutterers and nonstutterers. *Journal of Experimental Psychology, 32*, 156–167.

Scarf, M. (1981). *Unfinished business*. Garden City, N.Y.: Doubleday.

Scarr, S. (1965). The inheritance of sociability. Presented at the annual meeting of the American Psychological Association.

Scarr, S. (1969). Social introversion-extraversion as a heritable response. *Child Development, 40*, 823–832.

Scarr, S. (1981). *Race, social class, and individual differences in IQ*. Hillsdale, N.J.: Erlbaum.

Scarr, S., & Weinberg, R. A. (1976). I.Q. test performance of black children adopted by white families. *American Psychologist, 31*, 726–739.

Schacht, T., & Nathan, P. E. (1977). But is it good for psychologists? Appraisal and status of the DSM-III. *American Psychologist, 32*, 1017–1025.

Schachter, D. L. (1992). Understanding implicit memory: A cognitive neuroscience approach, *American Psychologist, 47*, 559–569.

Schachter, S. (1959). *The psychology of affiliation*. Stanford, Calif.: Stanford University Press.

Schachter, S. (1963). Birth order, eminence and higher education. *American Sociological Review, 28*(5), 757–768.

Schachter, S. (1966). The interaction of cognitive and physiological determinants in emotional state. In C. D. Spielberger (Ed.), *Anxiety and behavior*. New York: Academic Press.

Schachter, S. (1967). Cognitive effects on bodily functioning: Studies of obesity and eating. In D. C. Glass (Ed.), *Biology and behavior: Neurophysiology and emotion*. New York: Rockefeller University Press.

Schachter, S. (1968). Obesity and eating. *Science, 161,* 751–756.

Schachter, S. (1971). *Emotion, obesity and crime*. New York: Academic Press.

Schachter, S. (1982). Recidivism and self-cure of smoking and obesity. *American Psychologist, 37*(4), 436–444.

Schachter, S. & Gross, L. P. (1968). Manipulated Time and Eating Behavior. *Journal of Personality & Social Psychology 10,* 98–106.

Schachter, S., & Singer, J. E. (1962). Cognitive, social and physiological determinants of emotional state. *Psychological Review, 69,* 379–399.

Schactel, E. *Metamorphosis*. New York: Basic Books, 1959.

Schacter, D. L. (1987). Implicit memory: History and current status. *Journal of Experimental Psychology: Learning, Memory, and Cognition, 13,* 501–518.

Schaef, R. F. A., Kirkman, D. O., & Ungashick, B. (1981). Primal therapy. In R. J. Corsini (Ed.), *Handbook of innovative psychotherapies*. New York: Wiley.

Schaefer-Simmern, H. (1948). *The unfolding of artistic activity*. Berkeley, Los Angeles: University of California Press.

Schafer, R. (1948). *The clinical application of psychological tests*. New York: International Universities Press.

Schafer, R. (1954). *Psychoanalytic interpretation in Rorschach testing*. New York: Grune & Stratton.

Schafer, R. (1968). *Aspects of internalization*. New York: International Universities Press.

Schafer, R. (1976). *A new language for psychoanalysis*. New Haven, Conn.: Yale University Press.

Schafer, S. (1977). *Victimology: The victim and his criminal*. Reston, Va.: Reston.

Schaffer, C. B., & Pauli, M. W. (1980). Psychotic reaction caused by proprietary oral diet agents. *American Journal of Psychiatry, 137,* 1256–1257.

Schaffer, H. R. (1977). *Mothering*. Cambridge, Mass.: Harvard University Press.

Schaffer, H. R. (1979). Acquiring the concept of the dialogue. In M. H. Bornstein & W. Kessen (Eds.), *Psychological development from infancy: Image to intention*. Hillsdale, N.J.: Erlbaum.

Schaffer, H. R., & Emerson, P. E. (1964). The development of social attachments in infancy. *Monographs of the Society for Research in Child Development, 29*(3).

Schaffer, J., & Galinsky, M. (1974). *Models of group therapy and sensitivity training*. Englewood Cliffs, N.J. Prentice-Hall.

Schaie, K. W. (1965). A genetic model for the study of developmental problems. *Psychological Bulletin, 64,* 92–107.

Schaie, K. W. (1970). A reinterpretation of age-related changes in cognitive structure and functioning. In L. R. Goulet & P. B. Baites (Ed.), *Lifespan developmental psychology: Research and theory*. New York: Academic Press.

Schaie, K. W. (1973). Methodological problems in descriptive developmental research on adulthood and aging. In J. R. Nesselroad & H. W. Reese (Eds.), *Life-span developmental psychology: Methodological issues*. New York: Academic Press.

Schaie, K. W. (1977). Quasi-experimental designs in the psychology of aging. In J. E. Birren & K. W. Schaie (Eds.), *Handbook of the psychology of aging* (pp. 39–58). New York: Van Nostrand Reinhold.

Schaie, K. W. (1977–1978). Toward a stage theory of adult cognitive development. *International Journal of Aging and Human Development, 8,* 129–138.

Schaie, K. W. (1978). External validity in the assessment of intellectual development in adulthood. *Journal of Gerontology, 33,* 696–701.

Schaie, K. W. (1979). The primary mental abilities in adulthood: An exploration in the development of psychometric intelligence. In P. Baltes & O. Brim (Eds.), *Life-span development and behavior* (Vol. 2, pp. 68–115). New York: Academic.

Schaie, K. W. (1983). The Seattle Longitudinal Study: A twenty-one year exploration of psychometric intelligence in adulthood. In K. W. Schaie (Ed.), *Longitudinal studies of adult cognitive development.* (pp. 64–135). New York: Guilford.

Schaie, K. W. (1984). Midlife influences upon intellectual functioning in old age. *International Journal of Behavioral Development, 7,* 463–478.

Schaie, K. W. (1985). *Manual for the Schaie-Thurstone adult mental Abilities Test (STAMAT)*. Palo Alto, CA: Consulting Psychologists.

Schaie, K. W. (1986). Beyond calendar definitions of age, time and cohort: The general developmental model revisited. *Developmental Review, 6,* 252–277.

Schaie, K. W. (1988). Internal validity threats in studies of adult cognitive development. In M. L. Howe & C. J. Brainard (Eds.), *Cognitive development in adulthood: Progress in cognitive development research* (pp. 241–272). New York: Springer-Verlag.

Schaie, K. W. (1989a). The hazards of cognitive aging. *Gerontologist, 29,* 484–493.

Schaie, K. W. (1989b). Perceptual speed in adulthood. Cross-sectional and longitudinal studies. *Psychology and Aging, 4,* 443–453.

Schaie, K. W. (1990). Adult intellectual development. In J. E. Birren & K. W. Schaie (Ed.), *Handbook of the psychology of aging* (3rd ed. pp. 292–309). New York: Academic

Schaie, K. W. (1990a). Intellectual development in adulthood. In J. E. Birren & K. W. Schaie (Eds.), *Handbook of the psychology of aging* (3rd ed., pp. 292–310). New York: Academic.

Schaie, K. W. (1990b). The optimization of cognitive functioning in old age: Predictions based on cohort-sequential and longitudinal data. In P. B. Baltes & M. M. Baltes (Eds.), *Successful aging: Perspectives from the behavioral sciences* (pp. 94–117). Cambridge, UK: Cambridge University Press.

Schaie, K. W., & Baites, P. B. (1977). Some faith helps to see the forest: A final comment on the Horn and Donaldson myth of the Baltes and Schaie position on adult intelligence. *American Psychologist, 32,* 1118–1120.

Schaie, K. W., & Gribbin, K. (1975). Adult development and aging. *Annual Review of Psychology, 26,* 65–96.

Schaie, K. W., & Hertzog, C. (1982). Longitudinal methods. In B. B. Wolman (Ed.), *Handbook of developmental psychology*. Englewood Cliffs, NJ: Prentice-Hall.

Schaie, K. W., & Hertzog, C. (1986). Towards a comprehensive model of adult intellectual development: Contributions of the Seattle Longitudinal Study. In R. J. Sternberg (Ed.), *Advances in human intelligence* (Vol. 3, pp. 79–118). Hillsdale, NJ: Erlbaum.

Schaie, K. W., Labouvie, G. V., & Buech, B. U. (1973). Generational and cohort-specific differences in adult cognitive behavior: A fourteen-year study of independent samples. *Developmental Psychology, 9,* 151–166.

Schaie, K. W., & Labouvie-Vief, G. (1974). Generational versus ontogenetic components of change in cognitive behavior: A fourteen-year cross-sequential study. *Developmental Psychology, 10,* 305–320.

Schaie, K. W., & Parham, I. A. (1976). Stability of adult personality traits: Fact or fable? *Journal of Personality and Social Psychology, 34,* 146–158.

Schaie, K. W., & Strother, C. R. (1968). The cross-sequential study of age changes in cognitive behavior. *Psychological Bulletin, 70,* 671–680.

Schaie, K. W., & Willis, S. L. (1986). Can intellectual decline in the elderly be reversed? *Developmental Psychology, 22,* 223–232.

Schaie, K. W., & Willis, S. L. (1990). *Adult development and aging.* New York: HarperCollins. (Original work published 1986).

Schaie, K. W., Willis, S. L., Jay, G., & Chipuer, H. (1989). Structural invariance of cognitive abilities across the adult life span: A cross-sectional study. *Developmental Psychology, 25,* 652–662.

Schaie, K. W., & Willis, S. V. (1978). Life-span development: Implications for education. *Review of Research in Education, 6,* 120–156.

Schaller, J. (1978). A critical note on the conventional use of the birth order variable. *Journal of Genetic Psychology, 133*(1), 91–95.

Schalling, D., & Asberg, M. (1985). Biological and psychological correlates of impulsiveness and monotony avoidance. In J. Strelau, F. H. Farley, & A. Gale (Eds.), *The biological bases of personality and behavior: Theories, measurement techniques, and development* (Vol. 1). New York: Hemisphere.

Schank, R. C. (1985). *Dynamic memory.* Hillsdale, NJ: Erlbaum.

Schank, R. C., & Abelson, R. P. (1977). *Scripts, plans, goals and understanding: An inquiry into human knowledge structures.* Hillsdale, N.J.: Earlbaum.

Scharlach, A. E., Sobel, E. L., & Roberts, E. E. L. (1991). Employment and caregiver strain: An integrative model. *The Gerontologist, 31,* 778–787.

Scharrer, E., & Scharrer, B. (1963). *Neuroendocrinology.* New York: Columbia University Press.

Schechter M., Carlson P., Simmons, J. Q., III, & Work, H. (1964). Emotional problems in the adoptee. *Archives of General Psychiatry, 10,* 109–118.

Schedler, D. E. (1980). The impact of Ohlsen triad model of couples group counseling in treatment-training workshops for clergy and spouses. Unpublished Ph. D. dissertation, Indiana State University.

Scheff, T. J. (1974). The labeling theory of mental illness. *American Sociological Review, 39,* 444–452.

Scheff, T. J. (1979). *Catharsis in healing, ritual and drama.* Berkeley, Calif.: University of California Press.

Scheffe, H. (1959). *The analysis of variance.* New York: Wiley.

Scheflen, A. E. (1961). *A psychotherapy of schizophrenia: Direct analysis.* Springfield, Ill.: Thomas.

Scheflen, A. E. (1965). Quasi-courtship behavior in psychotherapy. *Psychiatry, 28,* 245–257.

Scheflen, A. E. (1965). *The stream and structure of communicational behavior: Context analysis of a psychotherapy session. Behavioral Studies Monograph no. 1,* Philadelphia, Pa.: Eastern Pennsylvania Psychiatric Institute.

Scheflen, A. E. (1974). *How behavior means.* New York: Aronson.

Scheiber, E., & Pirtle, R. (1979). The Z-process approach to psychotherapy: A formal analysis toward theory and integration. Master's thesis, Fresno State University, Fresno, Calif..

Scheidt, R. (1981). Ecologically valid inquiry: Fait accompli? *Human Development, 23,* 225–228.

Schein, E. H. (1969). *Process consultation.* Reading, Mass.: Addison-Wesley.

Schein, E. H. (1978). *Career dynamics: Matching individual and organizational needs.* Reading, Mass.: Addison-Wesley.

Schein, E. H. (1980). *Organizational Psychology* (3rd ed.). Englewood Cliffs, NJ: Prentice-Hall.

Schell, L. M. (Ed.). (1981). *Diagnostic and criterion-referenced reading tests: Review and evaluation.* Newark, Dela.: International Reading Association.

Schellenberg, J. A., & Bee, L. S. (1960). A re-examination of the theory of complementary needs in mate selection. *Marriage and Family Living, 22,* 227–232.

Scherer, G. A. C., & Wertheimer, M. (1964). *A psycholinguistic experiment in foreign-language teaching.* New York: McGraw-Hill.

Schermerhorn, R. A. (1970). *Comparative ethnic relations: A framework for theory and action.* New York: Random House.

Scheuer, A. D. (1991). A reconceptualization of paranoia: Applications for research, classification, and intervention. Doctoral dissertation, University of Hawaii.

Scheving, L. E., & Halberg, F. (Eds.). (1980). *Chronobiology: Principles and applications to shifts in schedules.* Rockville, Md.: Sijthoff & Noordhoff.

Schiamberg, L. H., & Smith, K. U. (1982). *Human development.* New York: Macmillan.

Schickedanz, J., Schickedanz, D. I., & Forsyth, P. D. (1982). *Toward understanding children.* Boston: Little, Brown.

Schiedenhoevel, W. (1990). Ritualized adult-male/adolescent-male sexual behavior in Melanesia: An anthropological and ethological perspective. In J. R. Feierman (Ed.), *Pedophilia-biosocial dimensions.* New York: Springer Verlag.

Schierberl, J. P. (1979). Physiological models of hyperactivity: An integrative review of the literature. *Journal of Child Clinical Psychology, 8,* 227–233.

Schiff, W., Caviness, J. A., & Gibson, J. J. (1962). Persistent fear responses in Rhesus monkeys to the optical stimulus of "looming." *Science, 136,* 982–983.

Schiffman, H. (1961/1962). *A mathematical model of interpersonal communication. Doctoral dissertation, Princeton University, 1960 (Dissertation Abstracts, 22,).* Also in A mathematical analysis of the impact of the source and content on the evaluation of a message. June 1963, *Educational Testing Service Research Bulletin,* RB 63–17.

Schiffman, H. R. (1982/1976). *Sensation and perception. An integrated approach* (2nd ed.). New York: Wiley.

Schiffman, S. S. Reynolds, M. L., & Young F. W. (1981). *Introduction to multidimensional scaling: Theory methods, and applications.* New York: Academic Press.

Schilder, P. (1950). *The image and appearance of the human body.* New York: International Universities Press.

Schildkraut, J. (1965). The catcholamine hypothesis of affective disorders: A review of supporting evidence. *American Journal of Psychiatry, 122,* 509–522.

Schildkraut, J. J. (1965). The catecholamine hypothesis of affective disorders; a review of supporting evidence. *American Journal of Psychiatry, 122,* 509–522.

Schildkraut, J. J. (1970). *Neuropsychopharmacology and the affective disorders.* Boston: Little, Brown.

Schildkraut, J. J. (1973). Norepinepherine metabolites as biochemical criteria for classifying depressive disorders and predicting responses to treatment: Preliminary findings. *American Journal of Psychiatry, 130,* 695–698.

Schildkraut, J. J. (1978). Current status of the catecholamine hypothesis of affective disorders. In M. A. Lipton, A. Di Mascio, & K. F. Killam (Eds.). *Psychopharmacology: A generation of progress.* New York: Raven Press.

Schildkraut, J., Orsvlak, P., Schatzberg, A. & Herzog, J. (1980). Platelet monoamine oxidase activity in subgroups of schizophrenic disorders. *Schizophrenia Bulletin, 6,* 220–225.

Schildkraut, J. J., Davis, J. M., & Klerman, G. L. (1968). *Biochemistry of depressions.* In D. H. Effon (Ed.), *Psychopharmacology: A review of progress, 1957–1967.* Washington, D.C.: U.S. Government Printing Office.

Schiller, P. (1981). *The sex profession: What sex therapy can do.* Washington, D.C.: Chilmark.

Schiller, P. H. (1952). Innate constituents of complex responses in primates. *Psychological Review, 59,* 177–191.

Schiller, P. H. (1957). Innate motor action as a basis of learning: Manipulative patterns in the chimpanzee. In C. H. Schiller (Ed.), *Instinctive behavior: The development of a modern concept.* (pp. 264–287). New York: International Universities.

Schilpp, P. A. (Ed.). (1949). *Albert Einstein: Philosopher-scientist.* Evanston, Ill.: Library of Living Philosophers.

Schlacter, M. (1989). Personal communication.

Schlei, B. L., & Grossman, P. (1979/1976). *Employment discrimination law, 1979 supplement.* Chapter 4: *Scored tests.* Washington, D.C.: Bureau of National Affairs.

Schlenker, B. R. (1980). *Impression management: The self concept, social identity, and interpersonal relations.* Monterey, Calif.: Brooks/Cole.

Schlesinger, H. J. (1974). Problems of doing research on the therapeutic process in psychoanalysis. *Journal of the American Psychoanalytic Association, 22,* 3–13.

Schlesinger, L. B. (1979). Physiognomic sensitivity: its development and modification. *Journal of Genetic Psychology, 134,* 107–123.

Schlesinger, L. B. (1980). Physiognomic perception: Empirical and theoretical perspectives. *Genetic Psychology Monographs, 101,* 71–97.

Schlesser, M. (1986). Neuroendocrine abnormalities in affective disorders. In J. Rush & K. Altschuler (Eds.), *Depression: Basic mechanisms, diagnosis, and treatment.* New York: Guilford.

Schlien, J. M., Mosak, H. H., & Dreikurs, R. (1962). Effects of time limits: A comparison of two psychotherapies. *Journal of Counseling Psychology, 9,* 31–34.

Schlosberg, H. (1937). The relationship between success and the laws of conditioning. *Psychological Review, 44,* 379–394.

Schlosberg, H. (1954). Three dimensions of emotion. *Psychological Review, 61,* 81–82.

Schloss, G. A. (1976). *Psychopoetry.* New York: Grosset & Dunlap.

Schlossberg, H. (1974). *Psychologist with a gun.* New York: Coward, McCann & Geoghegan.

Schmais, A. (1967). *Implementing nonprofessional programs in the human services.* New York: Center for the Study of Unemployed Youth.

Schmaus, M. (1967). *Die psychologische Trinitätslehre des hl. Augustinus* (2nd ed.). Münster, West Germany: Aschendorff.

Schmeidler, G. R. (1960). *ESP in relation to Rorschach test evaluation.* New York: Parapsychology Foundation.

Schmeidler, G. R. (1977). Research findings in psychokinesis. In S. Krippner (Ed.), *Advances in parapsychological research.* 1: *Psychokinesis.* New York: Plenum.

Schmeidler, G. R., & McConnell, R. A. (1958). *ESP and personality patterns.* New Haven, Conn.: Yale University Press.

Schmideberg, M. (1947). The treatment of psychopaths and borderline patients. *American Journal of Psychotherapy, 1,* 45–55.

Schmidt, F. L. (1977). Are employment tests appropriate for minority group members? *Civil Service Journal 18,* 10–11.

Schmidt, F. L., & Hunter, J. E. (1980). The future of criterion-related validity. *Personnel Psychology, 33,* 41–60.

Schmidt, F. L., & Hunter, J. E. (1981). Employment testing: Old theories and new research findings. *American Psychologist, 36,* 1128–1137.

Schmidt, F. L., Hunter, J. E., & Pearlman, K. (1981). Task differences as moderators of aptitude test validity in selection: A red herring. *Journal of Applied Psychology, 66,* 166–185.

Schmidt, H. (1969). Precognition of a quantum process. *Journal of Parapsychology, 33,* 99–108.

Schmidt, H. (1973). PK tests with a high-speed random number generator. *Journal of Parapsychology, 37,* 105–118.

Schmidt, H.-D. (1980). Psychology in the German Democratic Republic. *Annual Review of Psychology, 31,* 195–209.

Schmidt, L. J., Reinhardt, A. M., Kane, R. L., & Olsen, D. M. (1977). The mentally ill in nursing homes. *Archives of General Psychiatry, 39,* 687–691.

Schmitt, N. (1976). Social and situational determinants of interview decisions: Implications for the employment interview. *Personnel Psychology, 29,* 79–101.

Schmitt, N., & Coyle, B. W. (1976). Applicant decisions in the employment interview. *Journal of Applied Psychology, 61,* 184–192.

Schmitz, H. V. (Chair). (September 1979). *Occupational clinical psychology: A new field for psychologists.* Symposium presented at the Convention of the American Psychological Association, New York.

Schmitz, H. V. (1982). *Executive and employee counseling.* New York: New York Business Group on Health/New York Chamber of Commerce.

Schmuck, R. A., & Schmuck, P. A. (1979). *Group processes in the classroom* (3rd ed.). Dubuque, Iowa: Brown.

Schneck, J. M. (1963/1953). *Hypnosis in modern medicine.* Springfield, Ill.: Thomas.

Schneck, J. M. (1965). *Principles and practice of hypnoanalysis.* Springfield, Ill.: Thomas.

Schneider, B. (1976). *Staffing organizations.* Santa Monica, Calif.: Goodyear.

Schneider, D., Hastorf, A., & Ellsworth, P. (1979). *Person perception* (2nd ed.). Reading, Mass.: Addison-Wesley.

Schneider, K. (1950/1923). *Psychopathic personalities.* London: Cassell.

Schneider, K. (1959). *Clinical psychopathology.* New York: Grune & Stratton.

Schneider, R. & Crosby. (1980). Motion sickness: II. A clinical study based on surgery of cerebral hemisphere lesions. *Aviation, Space & Environmental Medicine, 51,* 65–73.

Schneider, R. H., Alexander, C. N., & Wallace, R. K. (1992). In search of an optimal behavioral treatment for hypertension: A review and focus on Transcendental Meditation. In E. H. Johnson, W. D. Gentry, & S. Julius (Eds.), *Personality, elevated blood pressure, and essential hypertension.* Washington DC: Hemisphere.

Schneider, W., & Shiffrin, R. M. (1977). Controlled and automatic human human information processing: I. Detection, search and attention. *Psychological Review, 84*, 1–66.

Schneirla, T. C. (1953). Basic problems in the nature of insect behavior. In K. D. Roeder (Ed.), *Insect physiology*. New York: Wiley.

Schneirla, T. C. (1972). In L. R. Aronson, E. Tobach, J. S. Rosenblatt, & D. S. Lehrman (Eds.), *Selected writings of T. C. Schneirla*. San Francisco: Freeman.

Schneirla, T. C., Rosenblatt, J. S., & Tobach, E. (1963). Maternal behavior in the cat. In H. L. Rheingold (Ed.), *Maternal behavior in mammals*. New York: Wiley.

Schoen, M. (1940). *The psychology of music*. New York: Ronald Press.

Schoenfeld, W. N. (Ed.). (1970). *The theory of reinforcement schedules*. New York: Appleton-Century-Crofts.

Schofield, W. (1964). *Psychotherapy: The purchase of friendship*. Englewood Cliffs, N.J.: Prentice-Hall.

Schofield, W. (1979). Clinical psychologists as health professionals. In G. Stone, F. Cohen, & N. Adler (Eds.), *Health psychology: A handbook*. San Francisco: Jossey-Bass.

Schonick, H. (1975). Premarital counseling: Three years' experience of a unique service. *Family Coordinator, 24*, 321–324.

Schooler, C. (1972). Birth order effects: Not here not now! *Psychological Bulletin, 78*(3), 161–175.

Schoop, T. (1974). *Won't you join the dance? A dancer's essay into the treatment of psychosis*. Palo Alto, Calif.: National Press.

Schopenhauer, A. (1896). *The world as will and idea*, London: Paul, Trenchen, Trubner.

Schopenhauer, A. (1928). *The philosophy of Schopenhauer*. I. Edman (Ed.), New York: Modern Library.

Schopler, E. (1974). Changes of direction with psychotic children. In A. Davids (Ed.), Child personality and psychopathology: Current topics, Vol. 1. New York: Wiley.

Schreiber, F. R. (1974). *Sybil*. New York: Warner Paperback Library.

Schreiber, J. (1979). Assessing competency to stand trial: A case study of technology diffusion in four states. *Bulletin of the American Academy of Science and the Law, 6*, 439–457.

Schreier, H., & Libow, J. (1986). Acute phobic hallucinations in very young children, *Journal of the American Academy of Child Psychiatry, 25*, 574–578.

Schroder, J., de la Chapelle, A., Hakola, P., & Virkkunen, M. (1981). The frequency of XYY and XXY men among criminal offenders. *Acta Psychiatrica Scandinavica, 63*, 272–276.

Schroeder, S. R., Breese, G. R., & Mueller, A. B. (1990). Dopaminergic mechanisms in self-injurious behavior. In M. Wolraich & D. K. Routh (Eds.), *Advances in developmental and behavioral pediatrics* (Vol. 9, pp. 181–198). London: Kingsley.

Schubert, D. S. P. (1977). Boredom as an antagonist of creativity. *Journal of Creative Behavior, 11*, 233–240.

Schubert, D. S., Wagner, M. E., & Schubert, J. (1977). Interest in creativity training by birth order and sex. *Journal of Creative Behavior, 11*(2), 144–145.

Schuck, J. R., Leventhal, D., Rothstein, H., & Izizarry, V. (1984). Physical anhedonia and schizophrenia. *Journal of Abnormal Psychology, 93*(3), 342–344.

Schucket, M. A. (1979). *Drug and alcohol abuse: A clinical guide to diagnosis and treatment*. New York: Plenum.

Schuessler, K. E., & Cressey, D. R. (1950). Personality characteristics of criminals. *American Journal of Sociology, 55*, 476–484.

Schulberg, C. (1981). *The music therapy sourcebook*. New York: Human Sciences Press.

Schull, W. J., & Neel, J. V. (1965). *The effects of inbreeding on Japanese children*. New York: Harper & Row.

Schulman, E. D. (1974). *Intervention in human services*. St. Louis, Mo.: Mosby.

Schulman, J., Shaver, P., Celman, R., Emrich, B., & Christie, R. (1973). Recipe for a jury. *Psychology Today, 6*(12), 37–44, 77–84.

Schultz, D. (1981/1975). *A history of modern psychology* (3rd ed.). New York: Academic Press.

Schultz, D. (1981). *Theories of personality* (2nd ed.). Monterey, Calif.: Brooks/ Cole.

Schultz, D. P. (1978/1973). *Psychology and industry today*. New York: Macmillan.

Schultz, J. & Luthe, W. (1959). *Autogenic training: A psychophysiologic approach in psychotherapy*. New York: Grune & Stratton.

Schultz, K. (1958). The psychologically healthy person: A study in identification and prediction, *Journal of Clinical Psychology, 14*, 112–117.

Schulz, J. H. (1974, Winter). The economics of retirement. *Industrial Gerontology*.

Schulz, J. H. (1976). *The economics of aging*. Belmont, Calif: Wadsworth.

Schulz, R. (1976). The effects of control and predictability on the psychological and physical well-being of the institutionalized aged. *Journal of Personality and Social Psychology, 33*, 563–573.

Schulz, R. (1978). *The psychology of death, dying and bereavement*. Reading, Mass.: Addison-Wesley.

Schulz, R., & Aderman, D. (1974). Clinical research and the stages of dying. *Omega, 5*, 137–143.

Schumacher, S., & Lloyd C. W. (1981). Physiological and psychological factors in impotence. *Journal of Sex Research, 17*, 40–53.

Schumacher, S. S., & Lloyd, C. W. (July 1974). Interdisciplinary treatment and study of sexual distress. Presented at the International Congress of Medical Sexology, Paris.

Schuster, R. (1979). Empathy and mindfulness. *Journal of Humanistic Psychology, 19*(1), 71–77.

Schutz, C. G. (1980). Discussion of neuroleptics and psychosocial treatment. *Schizophrenia Bulletin, 6*(1), 135–138.

Schutz, D. P. (1960). *A history of modern psychology*. New York: Academic Press.

Schutz, W. C. (1967). *Joy*. New York: Grove Press.

Schutz, W. C. (1973). Encounter. In R. J. Corsini (Ed.), *Current psychotherapies*. Itasca, Ill.: Peacock.

Schutz, W. C. (1975). Not encounter and certainly not fact. *Journal of Humanistic Psychology, 15*, 7–18.

Schwab, D., Heneman, H. A., III, & De Cotiis, T. A. (1975). In Behaviorally anchored rating scales: A review of the literature. *Personnel Psychology, 28*, 549–562.

Schwab, D. F., & Hoffman, M. A. (1990). An enlarged suprachiasmatic nucleus in homosexual men. *Brain Research, 537*.

Schwab, D. P. (1980). Job evaluation and pay setting: Concepts and practices. In E. R. Livernash (Ed.), *Comparable worth: Issues and alternatives*. Washington, D.C.: Equal Employment Advisory Council.

Schwab, J. J., & Schwab, M. E. (1978). *Sociocultural roots of mental illness: An epidemiologic survey*. New York: Plenum Medical.

Schwartz, A., & Goldiamond, L. (1975). *Social casework: A behavioral approach*. New York: Columbia University Press.

Schwartz, B., & Lacey, H. (1982). *Behaviorism, science, and human nature*. New York: Norton.

Schwartz, B., & Reisberg, D. (1991). *Learning and memory*. New York: Norton.

Schwartz, D., Flinn, D., & Slawson, P. (1974). Treatment of the suicidal character. *American Journal of Psychotherapy, 28,* 194—207.

Schwartz, G. E. (1973). Biofeedback as therapy: Some theoretical and practical issues. *American Psychologist, 28,* 666–673.

Schwartz, G. E. (1979). Disregulation and systems theory: A biobehavioral framework for biofeedback and behavioral medicine. In N. Birbauer & H. D. Kimmel (Eds.), *Biofeedback and self-regulation.* Hillsdale, N.J.: Erlbaum.

Schwartz, G. E., Davidson, R., & Coleman, D. (1978). Patterning of cognitive and somatic processes in the self-regulation of anxiety: Effects of meditation versus exercise. *Psychosomatic Medicine, 40,* 321–328.

Schwartz, G. E., & Shapiro, D. (1973). Social psychophysiology. In W. F. Prokasy & D. C. Raskin (Eds.), *Electrodermal activity in psychological research.* New York: Academic Press.

Schwartz, G. E., & Weiss, S. M. (1977). What is behavioral medicine? *Psychosomatic Medicine, 39,* 377–381.

Schwartz, G. E., & Weiss, S. M. (1978). Behavioral medicine revised: An amended definition. *Journal of Behavioral Medicine, 1,* 249–250.

Schwartz, J. L. (1977). The illogic of IQ tests. In P. L. Houts (Ed.), *The myth of measurability.* New York: Hart.

Schwartz, J. L., & Dubitzky, M. (1968). Smoking behavior and attempts to discontinue smoking. *Bulletin of the New York Academy of Medicine, 44*(12), 1536–1545.

Schwartz, S. H., & Howard, J. (1981). A normative decision-making model of altruism. In J. P. Rushton & R. M. Sorrentino (Eds.), *Altruism and helping behavior.* Hillsdale, N.J.: Erlbaum.

Schwartz, T. (1981). *The Hillside strangler.* Garden City, N.Y.: Doubleday.

Schwartz, W. B., Gorry, G. A., Kassirer, J. P., & Essig, A. (1973). Decision analysis and clinical judgment. *American Journal of Medicine, 55,* 459—472.

Schwarz, P. A. (1963). Adapting tests to the cultural setting. *Educational and Psychological Measurement, 23,* 673–686.

Schwarzer, R., & Leppin, A. (1991). Social support and health: A theoretical and empirical overview. *Journal of Social and Personal Relationships, 8,* 99–127.

Schweinhart, L. H., & Weikart, D. P. (1980). *Young children grow up: The effects of the Perry preschool program on youths through age 15. Monographs of the High/Scope Educational Research Foundation, no. 7.* Ypsilanti, Mich.: High/Scope Press.

Schwitzgebel, R. L., & Schwitzgebel, R. K. (1980). *Law and psychological practice.* New York: Wiley.

Sclafani, A. (1989). Dietary-induced overeating. In: *The psychobiology of human eating disorders* (pp. 281–291). New York: New York Academy of Sciences.

Scogin, F., & Bienias, J. L. (1988). A three year follow-up of older adult participants in a memory-skills training program. *Psychology and Aging, 3,* 334–337.

Scott, B. I. H. (1962). Electricity in plants. *Scientific American, 207,* 107–111, 113–114, 116–117.

Scott, C. W. (1980). The history of counseling psychology: 1945–1963. In J. M. Whiteley (Ed.), *The history of counseling psychology.* Monterey, Calif.: Brooks/Cole.

Scott, E. L., & Bolz, R. W. (Eds.). (1969). *Automation and society.* Athens, Ga.: Center for the Study of Automation and Society.

Scott, G. C. (1950). Measuring Sudanese intelligence. *British Journal of Educational Psychology, 20,* 43–54.

Scott, W. A. (1968). Attitude measurement. In G. Lindzey & E. Aronson (Eds.), *Handbook of social psychology,* Vol. 2 (2nd ed.). Reading, Mass.: Addison-Wesley.

Scott, W. A., & Wertheimer, M. (1959). *Introduction to psychological research.* New York: Wiley.

Scott, W. D. (1903). *The theory of advertising.* Boston: Small, Maynard.

Scott, W. D. (1978/1908). *The psychology of advertising.* New York: Arno Press.

Scottish Council for Research in Education. (1939). *The intelligence of Scottish children.* London: University of London Press.

Scottish Council for Research in Education. (1949). *The trend of Scottish intelligence.* London: University of London Press.

Scovern, A. W., & Kilmann, P. R. (1980). Status of electroconvulsive therapy: Review of the outcome literature. *Psychological Bulletin, 87,* 260–303.

Scripture, E. W. (1897). *The new psychology.* New York: Scribner's.

Scriver, C. R., Beaudet, A. L., Sly, W. S., & Valle, D. (Eds.). *The metabolic basis of inherited disease* (6th ed.). New York: McGraw-Hill.

Seabrook, M. F. (1972). A study of the influence of cowman's personality and job satisfaction on yield of dairy cows. *Journal of Agricultural Laboratory Science, 1.*

Seagoe, M. V. (1960). Educational psychology. In C. W. Hams (Ed.), *Encyclopedia of educational research.* New York: Macmillan.

Seagoe, M. V. (1974). Some characteristics of gifted children. In R. A. Martinson (Ed.), The identification of the gifted and talented. Ventura, Calif.: Office of the Ventura County Superintendent of Schools.

Seaman, J. M., & Koenig, F. (1974). A comparison of measures of cognitive complexity. *Sociometry, 37,* 375–390.

Searle, J. R. (1983). *Intentionality: An essay in the philosophy of mind.* New York: Cambridge University Press.

Searle, L. V. (1949). The organization of hereditary maze-brightness and maze-dullness. *Genetic Psychology Monographs, 39,* 279–325.

Searles, H. (1961). Schizophrenia and the inevitability of death. *Psychiatric Quarterly, 35,* 634–665.

Sears, P. S., & Barbee, A. H. (1977). Career and life satisfaction among Terman's gifted women: In J. C. Stanley, W. C. George, & C. H. Solano (Eds.), *The gifted and the creative: A fifty-year perspective.* Baltimore, Md.: Johns Hopkins University Press.

Sears, R. R. (1934). Effect of optic lobe ablation on the visuo-motor behavior of goldfish. *Journal of Comparative Psychology, 17,* 233–265.

Sears, R. R. (1936). Experimental studies of projection, 1. Attribution of traits. *Journal of Social Psychology, 7,* 151–163.

Sears, R. R. (1936). Functional abnormalities of memory with special reference to amnesia. *Psychological Bulletin, 33,* 229–274.

Sears, R. R. (1941). Success and failure: A study of motility. In Q. McNemar, & M. M. James (Eds.), *Studies of personality.* New York: McGraw-Hill.

Sears, R. R. (1943). *Survey of objective studies of psychoanalytic concepts.* New York: Social Science Research Council.

Sears, R. R. (1944). Experimental analysis of psychoanalytic phenomena. In J. McV. Hunt (Ed.), *Personality and the behavior disorders.* New York: Ronald Press.

Sears, R. R. (1951). A theoretical framework for personality and social behavior. *American Psychologist, 6,* 476–483.

Sears, R. R. (1975). Your ancients revisited: A history of child development. In E. M. Hetherington (Ed.), *Recent research in child development.* Chicago: University of Chicago Press.

Sears, R. R. (1977). Sources of life satisfaction of the Terman gifted men. *American Psychologist, 32,* 119–128.

Sears, R. R. (1981). The role of expectancy in adaptation to aging. In S. B. Kiesler, J. N. Morgan, & V. K. Oppenheimer (Eds.), *Aging: Social change.* New York: Academic Press.

Sears, R., Maccoby, E., & Levin, H. (1957). *Patterns of child rearing* Evanston, Ill.: Row, Peterson.

Sears, R. R., & Feldman, S. S. (Eds.). (1973). *The seven ages of man,* Los Altos, Calif.: Kaufmann.

Sears, R. R., Maccoby, E. E., & Levin, H. (1960). Patterns of child rearing. In M. Haimowitz & N. Haimowitz (Eds.), *Human development.* New York: Crowell.

Sears, R. R., Pintler, M. H., & Sears, P. S. (1946). Effect of father separation on preschool children's doll play aggression. *Child Development, 17,* 219–243.

Sears, R. R., Rau, L., & Alpert, R. (1965). *Identification and child rearing.* Stanford, Calif.: Stanford University Press.

Sears, R. R., Whiting, J. W. M., Nowlis, V., & Sears, P. S. (1953). Some childrearing antecedents of dependency and aggression in young children. *Genetic Psychology Monographs, 47,* 135–234.

Sears, R. R., & Wise, C. W. (1950). Relation of cup-feeding in infancy to thumbsucking and the oral drive. *American Journal of Orthopsychiatry, 20,* 123–138.

Seashore, C. E. (1919). *Seashore Measures of Musical Talent,* Chicago: Stoelting.

Seashore, C. E. (1930). Measures of musical talents. *Psychological Review, 37,* 178–183.

Seashore, C. E. (1938). *The psychology of music,* New York: McGraw-Hill.

Seashore, C. E. (1947). *In search of beauty in music,* New York: Ronald Press.

Seashore, S. E. (1954). Group cohesiveness as a factor in industrial morale and productivity *American Psychologist, 8,* 468.

Seavey, C. A., Katz, P. A., & Zalk, S. R. (1975). Baby X: The effect of gender labels on adult responses to infants. *Sex Roles, 1,* 103–110.

Sebba, R., & Churchman, A. (1983). Territories and territoriality in the home. *Environment and behavior, 15,* 191–210.

Sebeok, T. A. (Ed.). (1977). *How animals communicate.* Bloomington, Ind.: Indiana University Press.

Sebeok, T. A., & Umiker-Sebeok, J. (Eds.). (1980). *Speaking of apes; a critical anthology of two-way communication with man.* New York: Plenum.

Sechenov, I. (1935). *Selected works.* Moscow, Leningrad: State Publishing House for Biological & Medical Literature.

Sechenov, I., (1965). *Reflexes of the brain.* Cambridge, Mass.: M.I.T. Press.

Sechenov, I. M. (1965). *Reflexes of the brain.* Cambridge: MIT Press. (original work published 1866).

Sechrest, L. (1977). Personal constructs theory. In R. J. Corsini (Ed.), *Current personality theories.* Itasca, Ill.: Peacock.

Sechzer, J. (1981). Historical issues concerning animal experimentation in the United States. *Social Science and Medicine, 15,* 13–17.

Secord, P. (1958). Facial features and inference processes in interpersonal perception. In R. Tagiuri & L. Petrullo (Eds.), *Person perception and interpersonal behavior.* Palo Alto, Calif.: Stanford University.

Secord, P. F. (Ed.). (1982). *Explaining human behavior: Consciousness, human actions and social structure.* Beverly Hills, Calif.: Sage Publications.

Secord, P. F., & Backman, C. W. (1964). *Social psychology.* New York: McGraw-Hill.

Seeman, J. (1959). Toward a concept of personality integration. *American Psychologist, 14,* 633–637.

Seeman, J. (1982). *Personality integration: Studies and reflections.* New York: Human Sciences Press.

Seeman, M. (1963). Alienation and social learning in a reformatory. *American Journal of Sociology, 69,* 270–284.

Seeman, M. (1972). Alienation and engagement. In A. Campbell & P. Converse (Eds.), *The human meaning of social change.* New York: Russell Sage Foundation.

Seeman, M. (1975). Alienation studies. In A. Inkeles (Ed.), *Annual review of sociology.* Palo Alto, Calif.: Annual Reviews.

Seeman, W., Nidich, S., & Banta, T. (1972). Influence of transcendental meditation on a measure of self-actualization. *Journal of Counseling Psychology, 19,* 184–187.

Segal, J., & Yahraes, H. (1979). *A child's journey: Forces that shape the lives of our young.* New York: McGraw-Hill.

Segal, M. (1976). *Reflexology.* Hollywood, Calif.: Wilshire Books.

Segal, S. J. (1954). The role of personality factors in vocational choice: A study of accountants and creative writers (doctoral thesis, University of Michigan, 1954). *Microfilm Abstracts, 14*(4), 714.

Segal, S. J., & Fusella, V. (1970). Influence of imaged pictures and sounds in detection of visual and auditory signals. *Journal of Experimental Psychology, 83,* 458–474.

Segall, M. (1979). *Cross-cultural psychology: Human behavior in global perspective.* Monterey, Calif.: Brooks/Cole.

Segall, M. H. (1959). *A preliminary report on psychological research in Ankole.* Kempala: East African Institute for Social Research.

Segall, M. H., Campbell, D. T., & Herskovits, M. J. (1966). *The influence of culture on visual perception.* New York: Bobbs-Merrill.

Segall, M. H., Dasen, P. R., Berry, J. W., & Poortinga, Y. H. (1990). *Human behavior in global perspective: An introduction to cross-cultural psychology.* New York: Pergamon.

Seguin, E. (1907/1866). *Idiocy: Its treatment by the physiological method.* New York: Teachers College, Columbia University.

Sehnert, K. W., & Tillotson, J. K. (1978). *A national health care strategy: How business can promote good health for employees and their families.* Washington, D.C.: National Chamber Foundation.

Seiden, L. S., & Dykstra, L. A. (1977). *Psychopharmacology: A biochemical and behavioral approach.* New York: Van Nostrand Reinhold.

Seidman, E. (1978). Justice, values and social science: Unexamined premises. In J. R. Simon (Ed.). *Research in law and sociology,* Vol. 1. Greenwich, Conn.: JAI Press.

Seidman, E. (Ed.).(1983). *Handbook of social intervention.* Beverly Hills, CA: Sage.

Seidman, E., & Rappaport, J. (1986). *Redefining social problems.* New York: Plenum.

Seiter, R. P., Petersillia, J. R., & Allen, H. E. (1974). *Evaluation of adult halfway houses in Ohio,* (Vols. 1, 2). Columbus, Ohio: Program for the Study of Crime and Deliquency.

Sekuler, R. W., & Ganz, L. (1963). Aftereffect of seen motion with a stabilized retinal image. *Science, 139,* 419–420.

Seliger, M. (1976). *Ideology and politics.* New York: Free Press.

Seligman, K. (1971/1948). *Magic, supernaturalism and religion.* New York: Random House.

Seligman, M. (1975). *Helplessness: On depression, development, and death.* San Francisco: Freeman.

Seligman, M. E. P. (1970). On the generality of the laws of learning. *Psychological Review, 77,* 406–418.

Seligman, M. E. P. (1975). *Helplessness: On depression, development, and death.* San Francisco: Freeman.

Seligman, M. E. P. (1978). Comment and integration. *Journal of Abnormal Psychology, 87,* 165–179.

Seligman, M. E. P., & Hager, J. L. (Eds.). (1972). *Biological boundaries of learning.* New York: Appleton-Century-Crofts.

Seligman, M. E. P. & Maier, S. F. (1967). Failure to escape traumatic shock. *Journal of Experimental Psychology, 74,* 1–9.

Seligman, M. E. P., Maier, S. F., & Geer, J. (1968). The alleviation of learned helplessness in the dog. *Journal of Abnormal Psychology, 73,* 256–262.

Seligman, M. E. P., Maier, S. F., & Solomon, R. R. (1971/1969). Unpredictable and uncontrollable aversive events. In F. R. Brush (Ed.), *Aversive conditioning and learning.* New York: Academic Press.

Sellars, W. (1963). *Science, perception, and reality.* London, Routledge & Kegan Paul.

Sells, S. B. (1968). An approach to the nature of organizational climate. In R. Tagiuri, & G. H. Litwin (Eds.), *Organizational climate: Explorations of a concept.* Boston: Division of Research, Harvard Graduate School of Business Administration.

Sells, S. B. (1976). Organizational climate as a mediator for organizational performance. In E. I. Salkovitz, (Ed.), *Science, technology, and the modern navy.* Arlington, Va.: Office of Naval Research.

Sells, S. B. (Ed.). (1974a). *The effectiveness of drug treatment,* Vol. 1: *Evaluation of treatment.* Cambridge, Mass.: Ballinger.

Sells, S. B. (Ed.). (1974b). *The effectiveness of drug abuse treatment,* Vol. 2. *Patient profiles, treatment and outcomes.* Cambridge, Mass.: Ballinger.

Sells, S. B., Demaree, R. G., & Will, D. P. (1970). Dimensions of personality: 1. Conjoint factor structure of Guilford and Cattell trait markers. *Multivariate Behavioral Research, 5,* 391–422.

Sells, S. B., Demaree, R. G., & Will, D. P. (1971). Dimensions of personality: 2. Separate factor structures in Guilford and Cattell trait markers. *Multivariate Behavioral Research, 6,* 135–185.

Sells, S. B., & Murphy, D. L. (1983). Factor theories of personality. In N. Endler & J. McV. Hunt (Eds.), *Personality and the behavioral sciences,* Vol. 1. New York: Wiley.

Sells, S. B., & Simpson, D. D., (1980). The case for drug abuse treatment effectiveness, based on the DARP research programs. *British Journal of Addiction, 75,* 117–131.

Sells, S. B., & Simpson, D. D. (Eds.). (1976). *The effectiveness of drug abuse treatment,* Vols. 1–5. Cambridge, Mass.: Ballinger.

Selltiz, C., & Wormser, M. (1949). Community self-surveys: An approach to social change. *Journal of Social Issues, 5,* Special Issue.

Selltiz, C., Wrightsman, L. S., & Cook, S. W. (1976). *Research methods in social relations* (3rd ed.). New York: Holt, Rinehart & Winston.

Selman, R. L. (1980). *The growth of interpersonal understanding: Developmental and clinical analyses.* New York: Academic Press.

Seltzer, L. F. (1986). *Paradoxical strategies in psychotherapy: A comprehensive overview and guide book.* New York: Wiley.

Selvin, S., & Garfinkel, J. (1972). The relationship between parental age and birth order with the percentage of low birth-weight infants. *Human Biology, 44*(3), 501–510.

Selvini-Palazzoli, M., Cecchin, G., Prata, G., & Boscolo, E. L. (1978). *Paradox and counterparadox.* New York: Aronson.

Selye, H. (1936). A syndrome produced by diverse nocuous agents. *Nature, 138,* 32.

Selye, H. (1946). General adaptation syndrome and diseases of adaptation. *Journal of Clinical Endocrinology and Metabolism, 6,* 117.

Selye, H. (1950). *Stress.* Montreal: Acta.

Selye, H. (1950). *The physiology and psychology of exposure to stress.* Montreal: Acta.

Selye, H. (1956). *The stress of Life.* New York: McGraw-Hill.

Selye, H. (1967). *In vivo.* New York: Liveright.

Selye, H. (1974). *Stress without distress.* New York: New American Library.

Selye, H. (1975). *From dream to discovery.* New York: Arno Press.

Selye, H. (1976). *Stress in health and disease.* Toronto: Butterworth.

Selye, H. (1978/1956). *Stress of life.* New York: McGraw-Hill.

Selye, H. (Ed.). (1980). *Selye's guide to stress research.* New York: Van Nostrand Reinhold.

Selye, H. (Ed.). (1980–1983). *Selye's guide to stress research* (3 Vols.). New York: Van Nostrand Reinhold.

Semans, J. H. (1956). Premature ejaculation: A new approach. *Southern Medical Journal, 49,* 353–358.

Semel, V. G. (1980). Planned psychotherapy in the office and by telephone: An adolescent moves from crisis to consistency. *Dissertation Abstracts International 41,* 1.

Sen, I. (1951). The standpoint of Indian psychology. *Indian Journal of Psychology, 26,* 89–95.

Sen, I. (1953). The psychological system of Sri Aurobindu. *Indian Journal of Psychology, 28,* 79–89.

Sen, I. (1959). The Indian psychologist's research for his soul. *Journal of Education and Psychology, 17,* 68–73.

Senders, J. W., Fisher, D. F., & Monty, R. A. (Eds.). (1978). *Eye movements and the higher psychological functions.* Hillsdale, N.J.: Erlbaum.

Seng, R. (1977). *The skills of selling.* New York: AMACOM.

Sengtsan. (1975). *Verses on the faith mind.* Sharon Springs, N.Y.: Zen Center.

Sequin, E. (1907/1866). *Idiocy: Its treatment by the physiological method.* New York: Bureau of Publications, Teachers College, Columbia University.

Serafica, F. C., & Harway, N. J. (1979). Social relations and self-esteem of children with learning disabilities. *Journal of Clinical Child Psychology, 8,* 227–233.

Serpell, R. (1969). Cultural differences in attentional preference for colour over form. *International Journal of Psychology, 4,* 183–194.

Serpell, R. (1972). How perception differs among cultures. *New Society, 20,* 620–623.

Serpell, R. (1976). *Culture's influence on behaviour.* London: Methuen.

Serpell, R. (1977). Strategies for investigating intelligence in its cultural context. *Quarterly Newsletter of the Institute for Comparative Human Development, 1*(3), 11–15.

Serpell, R. (1979). How specific are perceptual skills? *British Journal of Psychology, 70,* 365–380.

Serra, A., Pizzamiglio, L., Boari, A., & Spera, R. (1978). A comparative study of cognitive traits in human sex chromosome euploids and sterile and fertile euploids. *Behavior Genetics, 8,* 143–154.

Settler, J. M. (1990). *Assessment of children.* (3rd ed.). San Diego: Settler.

Severin, F. (Ed.). (1965). *Humanistic viewpoints in psychology: A book of readings*. New York: McGraw-Hill.

Seward, J. P. (1952). Introduction to a theory of motivation in learning. *Psychological Review, 59,* 405–413.

Sewell, E., McCoy, J. F., & Sewell, W. R. (1973). Modification of an antagonistic social behavior using positive reinforcement for other behavior. *The Psychological Record, 23,* 499–504.

Sewell, W. H., & Hauser, R. M. (1975). *Education, occupation, and earnings.* New York: Academic Press.

Sexton, R. E., & Sexton, V. S. (1982). Intimacy: A historical perspective. In M. Fisher & G. Stricker (Eds.), *Intimacy.* New York, Plenum.

Sexton, V. S., & Misiak, H. (Eds.). (1971). *Historical perspectives in psychology: Readings.* Belmont, Calif.: Brooks/Cole.

Sexton, V. S., & Misiak, H. (Eds.). (1976). *Psychology around the world.* Monterey, Calif.: Brooks/Cole.

Seyfarth, R. M., & Cheney, D. L. (1992). Meaning and mind in monkeys, *Scientific American, 267,* 122–128.

Seyfried, B. A., & Hendrick, C. (1973). When do opposites attract? When they are opposite in sex and sex-role attitudes. *Journal of Personality and Social Psychology, 23,* 15–20.

Shader, R. I., & Greenblatt, D. J. (1971). Uses and toxicity of belladonna alkaloids and synthetic anticholinergics. *Seminars in Psychiatry, 3,* 449–476.

Shaffer, D., & Dunn, J. (Eds.). (1979). *The first year of life. Psychological and medical implications of early experience.* New York: Wiley.

Shaffer, D., & Greenhill, L. (1979). A critical note on the predictive validity of the hyperkinetic syndrome. *Journal of Child Psychology and Psychiatry, 20,* 61–72.

Shaffer, J. B. P., & Galinsky, M. D. (1974). *Models of group therapy and sensitivity training.* Englewood Cliffs, N.J.: Prentice-Hall.

Shaffer, L. F. (1947). Fear and courage in aerial combat. *Journal of Consulting Psychology, 11,* 137–143.

Shaffer, M. (1979). Primal terror: A perspective of vestibular dysfunction. *Journal of Learning Disabilities, 12,* 89–92.

Shaffer, R. (1950). *The clinical application of psychological tests.* New York: International Universities Press.

Shaffer, R., & Cozolino, L. (1992). Adults who report childhood ritualistic abuse. *Journal of Psychology and Theology, 20*(3), 188–193.

Shaffer, T., & Galensky, M. (1974). *Models of group therapy and sensitivity training.* Englewood Cliffs, N.J.: Prentice-Hall.

Shaffer, T. L. (1976). Legal views of suicide. In E. S. Shneidman (Ed.), *Suicidology: Contemporary developments.* New York: Grune & Stratton.

Shafii, M., Lavely, R., & Jaffe, R. (1975). Meditation and the prevention of alcohol abuse. *American Journal of Psychiatry, 132,* 942–945.

Shah, H. (1978). Dangerousness and mental illness: Some conceptual prediction and policy dilemmas. In C. Frederick (Ed.), *Dangerousness behavior: A problem in law and mental health* (NIMH DHEW Publication No. ADM 78–563, pp. 153–191). Washington, DC: U.S. Government Printing Office.

Shah, S. A. (1969). Privileged communications, confidentiality, and privacy. *Professional Psychology, 1,* 56–59.

Shah, S. A. (1978). Dangerousness: A paradigm for exploring some issues in law and psychology. *American Psychologist, 33,* 224–238.

Shah, S. A. (1978). Dangerousness in mental illness: Some conceptual, prediction and policy dilemmas. In C. P. Frederick (Ed.), *Dangerous behavior: A problem in law and mental health.* Washington, D.C.: DHEW, Publication no. 78–563. U.S. Government Printing Office.

Shakespeare, W. (1959). *Macbeth.* New York: Simon & Schuster.

Shakow, D. (1969). *Clinical psychology as science and profession.* Chicago: Aldine.

Shakow, D. (1976). Reflections on a do-it-yourself training program in clinical psychology. *Journal of the History of Behavioral Science, 12,* 14–30.

Shahow, D. (1978). The contributions of Worcester State Hospital and Post-Hall Clark University to psychoanalysis. In *Psychoanalysis, psychotherapy and the New England medical scene.* New York: Scientific & Historical Publications.

Shanan, J., & Weiss, A. A. (1963). Clinical psychology in Israel. *Israel Annals of Psychiatry and Related Disciplines, 1,* 107–111.

Shanas, E. (1967). Family help patterns and social class in three countries. *Journal of Marriage and the Family, 29,* 257–266.

Shanas, E. (1968). The family and social class. In E. Shanas, P. Townsend, D. Wedderbarn, H. Frus, P. Milkoj, & J. Stehouwer (Eds.), *Old people in three industrial societies.* New York: Atherton.

Shanas, E. (1973). Family-kin networks and aging in cross-cultural perspective. *Journal of Marriage and the Family, 35,* 505–511.

Shand, M. (1982). Sign-based short-term coding of American Sign Language signs and printed English words by congenitally deaf signers. *Cognitive Psychology, 14,* 1–12.

Shanmugam, T. W. (1972). Personality. In S. K. Mitra (Ed.), *A survey of research in psychology.* Bombay: Popular Prakashan.

Shannon, C., & Weaver, W. (1949). *The mathematical theory of communication.* Urbana, Ill.: University of Illinois Press.

Shannon, C. E. (1948). A mathematical theory of communication. *Bell System Technical Journal, 27,* 379–423, 623–656.

Shanteau, J. (1975). An information integration analysis of risky decision making. In M. Kaplan & S. Schwartz (Eds.), *Human judgment and decision processes.* New York: Academic Press.

Shanteau, J. (1978). *Psychological abilities of livestock judges.* Manhattan, Kans.: Agricultural Experiment Station Bulletin 620.

Shanteau, J., & Gaeth, G. J. (1983). Evaluation of the field method of soil texture classification: A psychometric analysis of performance. *Journal of Agronomic Education.*

Shanteau, J., & Phelps, R. H. (1977). Judgment and swine: Approaches and issues in applied judgment analysis. In M. F. Kaplan & S. Schwartz (Eds.), *Human judgment and decision processes in applied settings.* New York: Academic Press.

Shantz, C. U. (1975). The development of social cognition. In E. M. Hetherington (Ed.), Review of child development research, Vol. 5. Chicago: University of Chicago Press.

Shanxi Normal University. (1980). Thirty years of Chinese child and educational psychology. *Acta Psychologica Sinica, 12,* 127–134.

Shao, R. Z., Li, D., & Wu, J. Z. (1980). Characteristics of inference by analogy of children. Presented at the 1978 meeting of the Chinese Psychological Society. In *Selected papers in developmental and educational psychology.* Beijing: People's Educational Publishers.

Shapiro, A. (1977). The evaluation of clinical prediction: A method and initial application. *New England Journal of Medicine, 296,* 1509–1514.

Shapiro, A. K. (1960). A contribution to a history of the placebo effect. *Behavioral Sciences, 5,* 109–135.

Shapiro, A. K. (1968). Semantics of the placebo. *Psychiatric Quarterly, 42,* 653–695.

Shapiro, A. K. (1971). Placebo effects in medicine, psychotherapy, and psychoanalysis. In A. E. Bergin & S. L. Garfield, (Eds.), *Handbook of psychotherapy and behavior change.* New York: Wiley.

Shapiro, B. S. (1989). The management of pain in sickle cell disease. *Pediatric Clinics of North America, 36,* 1029–1045.

Shapiro, D. (1965). *Neurotic styles.* New York: Basic Books.

Shapiro, D. (1980). *Meditation: Self-regulation strategy and altered state of consciousness.* New York: Aldine.

Shapiro, D. (1981). *Autonomy and rigid character.* New York: Basic Books.

Shapiro, D. (1982). A content analysis of views of self-control: Relation to positive and negative valence. *Biofeedback and Self-Regulation.*

Shapiro, D., & Crider, A. (1969). Psychophysiological approaches to social psychology. In G. Lindzey & E. Aronson (Eds.), *The handbook of social psychology,* Vol. 3 (2nd ed.). Reading, Mass.: Addison-Wesley.

Shapiro, D., et al. (1981). *Biofeedback and behavioral medicine.* New York: Aldine.

Shapiro, D., & Schwartz, G. E. (1970). Psychophysiological contributions to social psychology. *Annual Review of Psychology, 21,* 87–112.

Shapiro, D. A. (1981). Comparative credibility of treatment rationales: Three tests of expectancy theory. *British Journal of Clinical Psychology, 21,* 111–122.

Shapiro, D. H. (1976). Zen meditation and behavioral self-control skills applied to a case of generalized anxiety. *Psychologia: An International Journal of Psychology in the Orient, 19,* 134–138.

Shapiro, D. H. (1978). *Precision nirvana.* Englewood Cliffs, N.J.: Prentice-Hall.

Shapiro, D. H. (1980). *Meditation: Self regulation strategy and altered state of consciousness.* New York: Aldine.

Shapiro, D. H. (1982). A clinical and physiological comparison of meditation with other self-control strategies—biofeedback, hypnosis, progressive relaxation. A review of the literature. *American Journal of Psychiatry, 139,* 276–284.

Shapiro, D. H. (1982). A content analysis of Eastern and Western, traditional and new-age, approaches to therapy, health, and healing. In R. Walsh & D. H. Shapiro (Eds.), *Beyond health and normality: Toward a vision of extreme psychological health.* New York: Van Nostrand.

Shapiro, D. H., & Giber, D. (1978). Meditation and psychotherapeutic effects. *Archives of General Psychiatry, 35,* 274–302.

Shapiro, D. H., & Shapiro, J. (1980). The clinical management of stress: Nonpharmacological approaches. *Family Practice Recertification,* 2(10), 55–63.

Shapiro, D. H., & Shapiro, J. (1982). Self-control concerns for men and women: Refinement and extension of a construct. *Journal of Clinical Psychology.*

Shapiro, D. H., & Zifferblatt, S. (1976). Zen meditation and behavioral self-control: Similarities, differences, clinical applications. *American Psychologist, 31,* 519–532.

Shapiro, F., & Weber, E. (Eds.). (1981). *Cognitive and affective growth: Developmental interaction.* Hillsdale, N.J.: Erlbaum.

Shapiro, F. (1989). Efficacy of the eye movement desensitization procedure in the treatment of traumatic memories. *Journal of Traumatic Stress Studies, 2,* 199–223.

Shapiro, F. (1989). Eye movement desensitization: A new treatment for post-traumatic stress disorder. *Journal of Behavior and Experimental Psychiatry, 20,* 211–217.

Shapiro, F. (1991). Eye movement desensitization and reprocessing procedure: From EMD to EMD/R—A new treatment model for anxiety and related traumata. *Behavior Therapist, 5,* 133–136.

Shapiro, F., et al. (1991). Eye desensitization. *The California Psychologist, 24.*

Shapiro, J., & Shapiro, D. H. (1979). The psychology of responsibility: Some second thoughts on holistic medicine. *New England Journal of Medicine, 301,* 311–212.

Shapiro, J. L. (1978). *Methods of group psychotherapy and encounter.* Itasca, Ill.: Peacock.

Shapiro, M. M., & Miller, T. M. (1965). On the relationship between conditioned and discriminative stimuli and between instrumental and consummatory responses. In W. K. Prokasy (Ed.), *Classical conditioning: A symposium.* New York: Appleton-Century-Crofts.

Shapiro, P. N., & Penrod, S. (1986). Meta-analysis of facial identification studies. *Psychological Bulletin, 100,* 139–156.

Shapiro, S. I., & Gordon, G. P. (1971). Contemporary norms of word and phonetic frequencies. *Journal of Verbal Learning and Verbal Behavior, 10,* 92–94.

Shapiro, S. K., & Garfinkel, B. D. (1986). The occurrence of behavior disorders in children: The interdependence of attention deficit disorder and conduct disorder. *Journal of the American Academy of Child Psychiatry, 25,* 809–819.

Sharit, J., & Salvendy, G. (1982). Occupational stress: Review and reappraisal. *Human Factors, 24,* 129–162.

Sharni, S., & Zemet, R. (1981). Clinical psychologists as part of the mental health services in the Ministry of Health in Israel. Their tasks, contributions, and prospectives. *The Israel Annals Of Psychiatry and Related Disciplines, 18,* 237–245.

Sharp, W. R. (1953). A check list of subjects for systematic study of international conferences. *International Social Science Bulletin, 5,* 311–339.

Sharpe, D., & Viney, L. (1973). Weltanschaung and the Purpose-in-life Test. *Journal of Clinical Psychology, 29,* 489–491.

Sharpe, E. F. (1937). *Dream analysis.* London: Hogarth.

Shaw, C. R., & McKay, H. D. (1942). *Juvenile delinquency and urban areas.* Chicago: University of Chicago Press.

Shaw, D., & Coppen, A. (1966). Potassium and water distribution in depression. *British Journal Of Psychiatry, 112,* 269–279.

Shaw, M. (1981/1971). *Group dynamics: The psychology of small group behavior.* New York: McGraw-Hill.

Shaw, M. E. (1954). Some effects of problem complexity upon problem solving efficiency in different communication nets. *Journal of Experimental Psychology, 48,* 211–217.

Shaw, M. E., & Ashton, N. (1967). Do assembly bonus effects occur on disjunctive tasks? A test of Steiner's theory. *Bulletin of the Psychonomic Society, 8,* 469–471.

Shaw, M. E., Blake, R. R., Corsini, R. J., & Mouton, J. S. (1980). *Role playing: A practical manual for group facilitators.* San Diego, Calif.: University Associates.

Shaw, M. E., & Breed, J. S. (1971). Some effects of attribution of responsibility upon the effectiveness of small problem-solving groups. *Psychonomic Science, 22,* 207–209.

Shaw, M. E., & Sulzer, J. L. (1964). An empirical test of Heider's levels in attribution of responsibility. *Journal of Abnormal and Social Psychology, 69,* 39–46.

Shaw, M. E. & Tremble, T. R. (1971). Effects of attribution of responsibility for a negative event to a group member upon group process as a function of the structure of the event. *Sociometry, 34,* 504—514.

Shaw, M. E., & Trumble, T. R., Jr. (1971). Effects of attribution of responsibility for a negative event to a group member upon group process as a function of the structure of the event. *Sociometry, 34,* 504–514.

Shaw, M. E., & Wright, J. M. (1967). *Scales for the measurement of attitudes.* New York: McGraw-Hill.

Shaw, M. L. G. (Ed.). (1981). *Recent advances in personal construct technology.* New York: Academic Press.

Shayer, M. (1976). Development in thinking of middle school and early secondary school pupils. *School Science Review, 57,* 568–571.

Shayer, M., Kuchemann, D. E., & Wylam, H. (1976). The distribution of Piagetian stages of thinking in British middle and secondary school children. *British Journal of Educational Psychology, 46,* 164–173.

Shealy, A. E. (undated). *Police integrity: The role of psychological screening of applicants.* Criminal Justice Center Monograph no. 4. New York: John Jay Press.

Sheanin, M. (1972). Adventures in developing a psychological services curriculum in a two-year community college. *American Psychologist, 27,* 584–587.

Shechet, A. (1990). Personal communications.

Sheehan, F. (1972). *The function and nature of imagery.* New York: Academic Press.

Sheehan, J. G. (1954). An integration of psychotherapy and speech therapy through a conflict theory of stuttering. *Journal of Speech and Hearing Disorders, 19,* 474–482.

Sheehan, J. G., (1970). *Stuttering: Research and therapy.* New York: Harper & Row.

Sheehan, P. (1982). *Hypnosis and experience.* Hillsdale, N. J.: Erlbaum.

Seehan, P. (1976). *Methodologies of hypnosis.* Hillsdale, N. J.: Erlbaum.

Sheehan, P., Ashton, R., & White, K. (1983). The assessment of mental imagery. In A. Sheikh (Ed.), *Imagery: Current theory, research, and application.* New York: Wiley.

Sheehan, P. W. (Ed.). (1972). *The function and nature of imagery.* New York: Academic Press.

Sheehan, P. W., McConkey, K. M., & Cross, D. G. (1978). The experiential analysis technique: Some new observations on hypnotic phenomena. *Journal of Abnormal Psychology, 87,* 570–573.

Sheehan, P. W., & Perry, C. W. (1976). *Methodologies of hypnosis: A critical appraisal of contemporary paradigms of hypnosis.* New York: Wiley.

Sheehy, G. (1976). *Passages: Predictable crises of adult life.* New York: Dutton.

Sheffield, F. D. (1965). Relation between classical conditioning and instrumental learning. In W. F. Prokasy (Ed.), *Classical conditioning: A symposium.* New York: Appleton-Century-Crofts.

Sheffield, F. D. (1966). A drive-induction theory of reinforcement. In R. N. Haber (Ed.), *Current research in motivation.* New York: Holt, Rinehart & Winston.

Sheffield, F. D., Roby, T. B., & Campbell, B. A. (1954). Drive reduction versus consummatory behavior as determinants of reinforcement. *Journal of Comparative and Physiological Psychology, 47,* 349–354.

Sheffield, F. D., Wulff, J. J., & Backer, R. (1951). Reward value of copulation without sex drive reduction. *Journal of Comparative and Physiological Psychology, 44,* 3–8.

Sheikh, A. A. (Ed.). (1983). *Imagery: Current theory research and application.* New York: Wiley.

Sheikh, A. A. (Ed.). (1983). *Imagination and healing.* New York: Baywood.

Sheikh, A. A., & Jordan, C. S. (1981). Eidetic psychotherapy. In R. J. Corsini (Ed.), *Handbook of innovative psychotherapies.* New York: Wiley.

Sheikh, A. A., & Jordan, C. S. (1983). Clinical uses of mental imagery. In A. Sheikh (Ed.), *Imagery: Current theory, research, and application.* New York: Wiley.

Sheikh, A. A., & Kunzendorf, (1983). Imagery, physiology and psychosomatic illness. *International Review & Mental Imagery, 1.*

Sheikh, A. A., & Panagiotou, N. C. (1975). Use of mental imagery in psychotherapy: A critical review. *Perceptual and Motor Skills, 41,* 555–585.

Sheikh, A. A., & Shaffer, J. T. (Eds.). (1979). *The potential of fantasy and imagination.* New York: Brandon House.

Shein, H., & Stone, A. (1969). Psychotherapy designed to detect and treat suicidal potential. *American Journal of Psychiatry, 125,* 141–153.

Sheldon, W. H. (1954). *Atlas of men; a guide for somatotyping the adult male at all ages.* New York: Harper.

Sheldon, W. H., & Stevens, S. S. (1942). *Varieties of human temperament: A psychology of constitutional differences.* New York: Harper.

Sheldon, W. H., Stevens, S. S., & Tucker, W. B. (1940). *The varieties of human physique.* New York: Harper.

Shell, J. (1977). Familial, situational, and cognitive determinants of sharing behavior in African-American children (doctoral dissertation, City University of New York, 1977). *Dissertation Abstracts International 38,* 2949B–3075B (University of Michigan Microfilms no. 77-27626).

Shelley, P. B. (1970/1905). The triumph of life. In T. Hutchinson (Ed.), *Shelley: Poetical works.* Oxford: Oxford University Press.

Shen, W. M. (1990). Functional transformations in AI discovery systems. *Artificial Intelligence, 41,* 257–272.

Shenep, J. L. (1990). Syphilis. In R. L. Summit (Ed.), *Comprehensive pediatrics* (pp. 851–855). St. Louis: Mosby.

Shepard, L. (1982). Definitions of test bias. In R. A. Berk (Ed.), *Handbook of methods for detecting test bias.* Baltimore, Md.: Johns Hopkins University Press.

Shepard, M. (1975). *Fritz: An intimate portrait of Fritz Perls and Gestalt therapy.* New York: Saturday Review Press.

Shepard, R. J. (1974). *Men at work.* Springfield, Ill.: Thomas.

Shepard, R. N. (1962). The analysis of proximities: Multidimensional scaling with an unknown distance function, part I. *Psychometrika, 27*(2), 125–140.

Shepard, R. N. (1962). The analysis of proximities: Multidimensional scaling with an unknown distance function, part II. *Psychometrika, 27*(3), 219–246.

Shepard, R. N. (1963). Analysis of proximities as a technique for the study of information processing in man. *Human Factors, 35,* 33–48.

Shepard, R. N. (1978). The mental image. *American Psychologist, 33,* 125–137.

Shepard, R. N. (1980). Multidimensional scaling, tree-fitting and clustering. *Science, 210,* 390–398.

Shepard, R. N., & Cooper, L. A. (1982). *Mental images and their transformations.* Cambridge, Mass.: M.I.T. Press.

Shepard, R. N., & Metzler, J. (1971). Mental rotation of three-dimensional objects. *Science, 171,* 701–703.

Shepard, R. N., Romney, A. K., & Nerlove, S. B. (Eds.). (1972). *Multidimensional scaling: Theory and applications in the behavioral sci-*

ences. Vol. I: *Theory.* Vol. II: *Applications.* New York: Seminar Press.

Shepard, W. O., & Hess, D. T. (1975). Attitudes in four age groups toward sex role division in adult occupations and activities. *Journal of Vocational Behavior, 6,* 27–39.

Shepherd, I. L. (1970). Limitations and cautions in the Gestalt approach. In J. Fagan & I. L. Shepherd (Eds.), *Gestalt therapy now: Theory, techniques, applications.* Palo Alto, Calif.: Science & Behavior Books.

Shepherd-Look, D. L. (1982). Sex differentiation and the development of sex roles. In B. B. Wolman (Ed.), *Handbook of developmental psychology.* Englewood Cliffs, N. J.: Prentice-Hall.

Sheppard, D. (1954). The adequacy of everyday quantitative expressions as measurements of qualities. *British Journal of Psychology, 45,* 40–50.

Sheppard, H. L., & Herrick, N. Q. (1972). *Where have all the robots gone? Worker dissatisfaction in the '70's.* New York: Free Press.

Sherif C. W. (1982). Needed concepts in the study of gender identity. *Psychology of Women Quarterly, 6.*

Sherif, M. (1935). A study of some social factors in perception. *Archives of Psychology, 27* (entire no. 187).

Sherif, M. (1937). An experimental approach to the study of attitudes. *Sociometry, 1,* 90–98.

Sherif, M. (1966/1936). *The psychology of social norms.* New York: Harper & Row.

Sherif, M., & Cantril, H. (1965/1947). *The psychology of ego-involvements.* New York: Wiley.

Sherif, M., Harvey, O. J., White, B. J., Hood, W. R., & Sherif, C. W. (1961). *Intergroup conflict and cooperation: The Robber's Cave experiment.* Norman, Okla.: University of Oklahoma Press.

Sherif, M., & Hovland, C. I. (1961). *Social judgment: Assimilation and contrast effects in communication and attitude change.* New Haven, Conn.: Yale University Press.

Sherif, M., & Sherif, C. W. (1964). *Reference groups: Explorations into conformity and deviation of adolescents.* New York: Harper & Row.

Sherif, M., & Sherif, C. W. (1966/1953). *Groups in harmony and tension. An integration of studies on intergroup relations.* New York: Octagon.

Sherif, M., & Sherif, C. W. (1969). *Social psychology.* New York: Harper & Row.

Sherman, J. A. (1978). *Sex-related cognitive differences: An essay on theory and evidence.* Springfield, Ill.: Thomas.

Sherman, J. A., & Denmark, F. L. (Eds.). (1979). *The psychology of women: Future directions in research.* New York: Psychological Dimensions.

Sherman, L. W., & Blumberg, M. (1981). Higher education and police use of deadly force. *Journal of Criminal Justice, 9,* 317–331.

Sherman, P. W. (1977). Nepotism and the evolution of alarm calls. *Science, 197,* 1246–1253.

Sherman, S. J. (1973). Internal-external control and its relationship to attitude change under different social influence techniques. *Journal of Personality and Social Psychology, 26,* 23–29.

Sherman, S. N. (1981). A social work frame for family therapy. In E. R. Tolson & W. J. Reid (Eds.), *Models of family treatment.* New York: Columbia University Press.

Sherrington, C. (1963). *Man on his nature.* Cambridge, England: Cambridge University Press.

Sherrington, C. S. (1906). *The integrative action of the nervous system.* New Haven, Conn.: Yale University Press.

Sherrod, D. (1987). The bonds of men: Problems and possibilities in close male relationships. In H. Brod (Ed.), *The making of masculinities: The new men's studies* (pp. 213–241). Boston: Unwin Hyman.

Sherrod, D. R., Hage, J. N., Halpern, P. L., & Moore, B. S. (1977). Effects of personal causation and perceived control on responses to an aversive environment: The more control, the better. *Journal of Experimental Social Psychology, 13,* 14—27.

Shertzer, B., & Stone, S. (1974). *Fundamentals of counseling.* Boston: Houghton Mifflin.

Shevrin, H., & Dickman, S. (1980). The psychological unconscious: A necessary assumption for all psychological theory? *American Psychologist, 35,* 421—434.

Shibutani, T. (1968). A cybernetic approach to motivation. In W. Buckley (Ed.), *Modern systems research for the behavioral scientist.* Chicago: Aldine.

Shields, J. (1962). *Monozygotic twins.* Oxford: Oxford University Press.

Shields, J. (1973). Heredity of psychological abnormality. In H. J. Eysenck (Ed.), *Handbook of abnormal psychology.* London: Pitman.

Shields, S. A. (1975). Functionalism, Darwinism, and the psychology of women: A study of social myth. *American Psychologist, 30,* 739–754.

Shiffrin, R. M. (1975). The locus and role of attention in memory systems. In P. M. A. Rabbitt & S. Dornic (Eds.), *Attention and performance,* Vol. V, London: Academic Press.

Shiffrin, R. M., & Schneider, W. (1977). Controlled and automatic human information processing; II. Perceptual learning, automatic attending, and a general theory. *Psychological Review, 84,* 127–190.

Shils, E. (1976). Center and periphery: Essays in macrosociology. Chicago: University of Chicago Press.

Shils, E., & Young, M. (1953). The meaning of the coronation. *Sociological Review, 1,* 63–81.

Shimamura, A. P. (1986). Priming effects in amnesia: Evidence for a dissociative memory function. *Quarterly Journal of Experimental Psychology, 38A,* 619–644.

Shimberg, E. (1979). *The handbook of private practice in psychology.* New York: Brunner/Mazel.

Shimizu, I. (1951). *Shakai-shinrigaku (Social psychology).* Tokyo: Iwanami.

Shimp, C. P. (1969). Optimal behavior in free-operant experiments. *Psychological Review, 76,* 97–112.

Shinn, M. (1978). Father absence and children's cognitive development. *Psychological Bulletin, 85,* 295–324.

Shinn, M. (1987). Expanding community psychology's domain. *American Journal of Community Psychology, 15,* 555–574.

Shinn, M., & Weitzman, B. C. (1990). Research of homelessness: An introduction. *Journal of Social Issues, 46,* 1–11.

Shinn, M., & Weitzman, B. C. (Eds.). (1990). Urban homelessness [Special issue]. *Journal of Social Issues, 46*(4).

Shioda, G. (1968). *Dynamic akido.* Tokyo, New York, San Francisco: Kodamsha.

Shipley, P. (1981). An ergonomics contribution to the International Year of Disabled Persons. *Ergonomics, 24,* 817–819.

Shipley, W. C. (1940). A self-administering scale for measuring intellectual impairment and deterioration. *Journal of Psychology, 9,* 371–377.

Shipley, W. C. (1946). *Institute of living scale*. Los Angeles: Western.

Shipton, E. J., Endler, N. S., & Kemper, F. D. (1971). *Maturing in a changing world*. Toronto: Prentice-Hall.

Shirai, T. (1957). *Hebb: Organization of Behavior*. Tokyo: Sanseido.

Shirai, T. (1976). Hebb: Organization of behavior, theoretical approach of physiological psychology. In H. Minami (Ed.), *Twelve outstanding books in psychology*. Tokyo: Gakuyodo.

Shirai, T. (1976). History of developmental psychology. In A. Yoda (Ed.), *Developmental psychology*. Tokyo: Nihon Tosho.

Shirai, T. (1977). *Home life of preschool children*. Tokyo: Nihon Kirisu-tokyodan.

Shirai, T. (1980). *Textbook of infant psychology*. Tokyo: Shufunotomo.

Shirai, T. (1980). What is child psychology? In T. Shirai (Ed.), *Child psychology*. Tokyo: Koseikan.

Shirai, T. (1981). The problem of television in childhood. In S. Takano & K. Fukaya (Eds.), *Psychology of infant and preschool child*. Tokyo: Yuhikaku.

Shirai, T. (1982). *Developmental achievement by three years of age*. Tokyo: Mikasa.

Shirley, M. M. (1931). *The first two years*. Minneapolis, Minn.: University of Minnesota Press.

Shlien, J. M., Mosak, H. H., & Dreikurs, R. (1962). Effects of time limits: A comparison of two psychotherapies. *Journal of Counseling Psychology, 9*, 31–34.

Shneiderman, B. (1980). *Software psychology. Human factors in computer and information systems*. Cambridge, Mass.: Winthrop.

Shneidman, E. S. (1948). Schizophrenia and the MAPS test. *Genetic Psychology Monographs, 38*, 145–223.

Shneidman, E. S. (1951). Manual for the MAPS test. *Projective Techniques Monographs, 1951, 1*(2), 1–92.

Shneidman, E. S. (1963). Orientations toward death: A vital aspect of the study of lives. In R. W. White (Ed.), *The study of lives*. New York: Atherton Press.

Shneidman, E. S. (1971). Prevention, intervention, and postvention of suicide. *Annals of Internal Medicine, 75*, 453–458.

Shneidman, E. S. (1973). Suicide. In *Encyclopaedia Britannica* (14th ed.). Chicago: Benton.

Shneidman, E. S. (1976). A psychological theory of suicide. *Psychiatric Annals, 6*, 51–66.

Shneidman, E. S. (1980). Psychotherapy with suicidal patients. In T. B. Karasu & L. Bellak (Eds.), *Specialized techniques in individual psychotherapy*. New York: Brunner/Mazel.

Shneidman, E. S. (1980). *Voices of death*. New York: Harper & Row.

Shneidman, E. S. (1981). *Suicide thoughts and reflections 1960–1980*. New York: Behavioral Science Press.

Shneidman, E. S. (1983/1973). *Deaths of man*. New York: Aronson.

Shneidman, E. S. (Ed.). (1951). *Thematic test analysis*. New York: Grune & Stratton.

Shneidman, E. S. (Ed.). (1967). *Essays in self destruction*. New York: Science House.

Shneidman, E. S. (Ed.). (1972). *Death and the college student*. New York: Behavioral Publications.

Shneidman, E. S. (Ed.). (1976). *Death: Current perspectives*. Palo Alto, Calif.: Mayfield.

Shneidman, E. S. (Ed.). (1981). *Endeavors in psychology: Selections from the personology of Henry A. Murray*. New York: Harper & Row.

Shneidman, E. S., & Farberow, N. (Eds.). (1957). *Clues to suicide*. New York: McGraw-Hill.

Shneidman, E. S., Farberow, N., & Litman, R. (1976/1970). *The psychology of suicide*. New York: Aronson.

Shneidman, E. S., & Ortega, M. (Eds.). (1969). *Aspects of depression*. Boston: Little, Brown.

Shoben, E., (1978). Differential pass—fail rates in employment testing: Statistical proof under Title VII. *Harvard Law Review, 91*, 793–811.

Shoben, E. J., Jr. (1957). Toward a concept of the normal personality. *American Psychologist, 12*, 183–189.

Shock, N., Greulich, R., Andres, R., Arenberg, D., Costa, P., Lukatta, E., & Tobin, J. (1984). *Normal human aging: The Baltimore longitudinal study of aging*. Washington, DC: U.S. Government Printing Office.

Shock, N. W. (1967). In K. Soddy & M. C. Kidson (Eds.), *Cross cultural studies in mental health*. London: Tavistock.

Shoham-Saloman, V., Awner, R., & Neeman, R. (in press). You're changed if you do and changed if you don't: Mechanisms underlying paradoxical interventions. *Journal of Consulting and Clinical Psychology*.

Shoham-Saloman, V., & Rosenthal, R. (1987). Paradoxical interventions: A meta-analysis. *Journal of Consulting and Clinical Psychology, 55*, 22–28.

Shontz, F. (1980). Theories about the adjustment to having a disability. In W. Cruickshank (Ed.), *Psychology of exceptional children and youth* (4th ed.). Englewood Cliffs, N. J.: Prentice-Hall.

Shook, E. V. (1989). *Ho'opononpo*. Honolulu: East-West Center.

Shooter, E., & Hall, H. V. (1989). Distortion analysis on the MMPI and MMPI-2. *Bulletin of the American Academy of Forensic Psychology, 10*, 9.

Shooter, E., & Hall, H. V. (1990). Explicit alternative testing for deliberate distortion: Towards an abbreviated format. *Forensic Reports, 4*, 45–49.

Shor, R. E. (1962). Three dimensions of hypnotic depth. *Internal Journal of Experimental Hypnosis, 10*, 23–38.

Shorr, J. E. (1972). *Psycho-imagination therapy: The integration of phenomenology and imagination*. New York: Intercontinental.

Shorr, J. E. (1974). *Psychotherapy through imagery*. New York: Intercontinental.

Shorr, J. E. (1980). Discoveries about the mind's ability to organize and find meaning in imagery. In J. E. Shorr et al. (Eds.), *Imagery: Its many dimensions and applications*. New York: Plenum.

Shostrom, E. (1964). An inventory for the measurement of self-actualization, *Educational and Psychological Measurement, 24*, 207–218.

Shostrom, E. L. (1962). *Manual for the Personal Orientation Inventory (POI). An inventory for the measurement of self-actualization*. San Diego, Calif.: Educational and Industrial Testing Service.

Shostrom, E. L. (1976). *Actualizing therapy: Foundations for a scientific ethic*. San Diego, Calif.: EDITS.

Shotel, J. R., Iano, R. P., & McGettigan, J. F. (1972). Teacher attitudes associated with integration of handicapped children. *Exceptional Children, 38*, 677–683.

Shotter, J., & Gergen, K. J. (Eds.). (1989). *Texts of identity*. London: Sage.

Showalter, C., & Thornton, W. E. (1977). Clinical pharmacology of phencyclidine toxicity. *American Journal of Psychiatry, 134*, 1234–1238.

Shrodes, C. (1949). Bibliotherapy: A theoretical and clinical experimental study. Unpublished doctoral dissertation, University of California.

Shuey, A. M. (1966). *The testing of Negro intelligence.* Lynchburg, Va.: Bell.

Shulgrin, A. T. (1978). Psychotomimetic drugs: Structure-activity relationships. In L. L. Iversen, S. D. Iversen, & S. H. Snyder (Eds.), *Handbook of psychopharmacology,* Vol. 11. New York: Plenum.

Shulman, B., & Mosak, H. (1967). Various purposes of symptoms. *Journal of Individual Psychology, 23,* 79–87.

Shulman, B. H. (1962). The family constellation in personality diagnosis. *Journal of Individual Psychology, 18,* 35–47.

Shulman, B. H. (1968). *Essays in schizophrenia.* Baltimore, Md.: Williams & Wilkins.

Shulman, B. H., & Forgus, R. (1979). *Personality: A cognitive view.* Englewood Cliffs, N. J.: Prentice-Hall.

Shulman, B. H., & Mosak, H. M. (1977). Birth order and ordinal position: Two Adlerian views. *Journal of Individual Psychology, 33,* 114–121.

Shulman, K. (1978). Suicide and parasuicide in old age: A review. *Age and Ageing, 7,* 201–209.

Shur, S., Beit-Hallahmi, B., Blasi, J. R., & Rapin, A. (Eds.). (1981). *The kibbutz: A bibliography of scientific and professional publications in English.* Darby, Pa.: Norewood Editions.

Shurtleff, D., & Ayres, J. J. B. (1981). One-trial backward excitatory fear conditioning in rats: Acquisition, retention, extinction, and spontaneous recovery. *Animal Learning and Behavior, 9,* 65–74.

Shusterman, G., & Saxe, L. (1990). *Deception in romantic relationships.* Unpublished manuscript, Brandeis University.

Shute, C. C. D., & Lewis, P. R. (1967). The ascending cholinergic reticular system: Neocortical, olfactory and subcortical projections. *Brain, 90,* 497–520.

Shweder, R. A. (1977). Likeness and likelihood in everyday thought: Magical thinking in judgments about personality. *Current Anthropology, 18,* 637–648.

Sicher, L. (1954). Education for freedom. *The American Journal of Individual Psychology, 11,* 97–103.

Sicher, L., & Mosak, H. H. (1967). Aggression as a secondary phenomenon. *Journal of Individual Psychology, 23,* 232–235.

Sid, A. K. W., & Lindgren, H. C. (August 1981). Achievement and affiliation motivation and their correlates. Presented at American Psychological Association convention, Los Angeles.

Sidel, R. (1972). *Woman and child care in China: A first hand report.* New York: Hill & Wang.

Sidgwick, E. M. (1975/1886). *Phantasms of the living: Cases of telepathy printed in the Journal of the Society for Psychical Research during thirty-five years.* Bound with *Phantasms of the living.* New York: Arno Press.

Sidgwick, S., Sidgwiek, E. M., & Smith, G. A. (1889). Experiments in thought transference. *Proceedings of the Society for Psychical Research, 6,* 128–170.

Sidman, M. (1953). Avoidance conditioning with brief shock and no exteroceptive warning signal. *Science, 118,* 157–158.

Sidman, M. (1960). *Tactics of scientific research: Evaluating experimental data in psychology.* New York: Basic Books.

Sieben, R. L. (1977). Controversial medical treatments of learning disabilities. *Academic Therapy, 13,* 133–147.

Sieber, J. E. (1980). Defining test anxiety: Problems and approaches. In I. G. Sarason (Ed.), *Test anxiety: Theory, research, and applications.* Hillsdale, N. J.: Erlbaum.

Sieber, J. E., O'Neil, H. F., & Tobias, S. (Eds.). (1977). *Anxiety, learning, and instruction.* New York: Wiley.

Siegel, B., Vukicevic, J., Elliott, G., Kraemer, H. (1989). The use of signal detection theory to assess DSM-III-R criteria for autistic disorder. *Journal of the American Academy of Child and Adolescent Psychiatry, 28,* 542–548.

Siegel, J. M. (1979). Behavioral functions of the reticular formation. *Brain Research Reviews, 1,* 69–105.

Siegel, L. J., & Smith, K. E. (1980). Children's strategies for coping with pain. *Pediatrician, 16,* 110–118.

Siegel, M. (1961). *The improvement of reading.* New York: Carnegie.

Siegel, M. (1972). Special problems in group psychotherapy practice. In G. D. Goldman & G. Stricker (Eds.), *Practical problems of a private psychotherapy practice.* Springfield, Ill.: Thomas.

Siegel, M. (1973). Individual and group psychotherapy: Fads and foolishness. *Psychotherapy: Theory, Research, and Practice, 10,* 261–264.

Siegel, M. (1976). Confidentiality. *The Clinical Psychologist, 30,* 1–2.

Siegel, M. (1979). Privacy, ethics and confidentiality. *Professional Psychology, 10,* 249–258.

Siegel, M. (Ed.). (1968). *The counseling of college students.* New York: Free Press.

Siegel, P. M. (1970). Occupational prestige in the Negro subculture. In E. O. Laumann (Ed.), *Social stratification: Research and theory for the 1970s.* Indianapolis, Ind.: Bobbs-Merrill.

Siegel, S. (1958). *Nonparametric statistics for the behavioral sciences.* New York: McGraw-Hill.

Siegel, S. (1975a). Conditioning insulin effects. *Journal of Comparative and Physiological Psychology, 89,* 189–199.

Siegel, S. (1975b). Evidence from rats that morphine tolerance is a learned response. *Journal of Comparative and Physiological Psychology, 89,* 498–506.

Siegel, S. (1977). Morphine tolerance acquisition as an associative process. *Journal of Experimental Psychology: Animal Behavior Processes, 3,* 1–13.

Siegel, S., & Fouraker, L. E. (1960). *Bargaining and group decision making: Experiments in bilateral monopoly.* New York: McGraw-Hill.

Sierles, F. (1984). Correlates of malingering. *Behavioral Sciences and the Law, 2,* 113–118.

Sierles, F. (Ed.). (1982). *Clinical behavioral science.* New York: Spectrum.

Sieveking, A. (1979). *The cave artists.* London: Thames.

Sifneos, P. E. (1979). *Short-term dynamic psychotherapy.* New York, Plenum.

Sigall, H., & Landy, D. (1973). Radiating beauty: The effects of having a physically attractive partner on person perception. *Journal of Personality and Social Psychology, 28,* 218–224.

Sigel, I. E. (1963). How intelligence tests limit understanding of intelligence. *Merrill-Palmer Quarterly, 9,* 39–56.

Sigel, I. E. (1972). Developmental theory and preschool education: Issues, problems and implications. In I. J. Gordon (Ed.), *Early childhood education. The seventy-first yearbook of the National Society for the Study of Education.* Chicago: University of Chicago Press.

Sigel, I. E. (1973). Where is preschool education going: Or are we en route without a road map? In *Proceedings of the 1972 International Conference on Testing Problems. Assessment in a pluralistic society.* Washington, D. C.: Educational Testing Service.

Sigerist, H. E. (Ed.). (1941). *Four treatises of Theophrastus von Hohenheim called Paracelsus.* Baltimore, Md.: Johns Hopkins Press.

Sighele, D. (1903). *L'intelligenza della folla,* Turin, Italy: Bocca.

Sighele, S. (1897). *La coppia criminale*. Turin, Italy: Bocca.

Signell, K. A., & Scott, P. A. (1972). Training in consultation: A crisis of role transition. *Community Mental Health Journal, 8*(2), 149–160.

Signorella, M. L., Vegega, M. E., & Mitchell, M. E. (1981). Subject selection and analysis for sex-related differences: 1968–1970 and 1975–1977. *American Psychologist, 36*, 988–990.

Siguán, M. (1958). *Problemas humanos del trabajo industrial (Human problems of industrial work)*. Madrid: Rial.

Siguan, M. (1959). *Del campo al suburbio (From the country to the industrial slum)*. Madrid: C.S.I.C.

Siguan, M. (1976). Bilinguismo y personalidad. *Anuario de Psicología, 15*.

Siguán, M. (1976). Spain. In V. S. Sexton & H. K. Misiak (Eds.), *Psychology around the world*. Monterey, Calif.: Brooks/Cole.

Siguan, M. (1977). Du geste au langage. In *Genese de la parole* Paris: Presses Universitaires de France.

Siguán, M. (1978). La enseñanza universitaria de la psicología en España. Notas para su historia. *Anuario de Psicología, 19*, 125–137.

Siguán, M. (1981). *La psicologia a Catalunya*. Barcelona, Spain: Ediciones 62.

Siipola, E., Walker, W. N., & Kolb, D. (1955). Task attitudes in word association, projective and nonprojective. *Journal of Personality, 23*, 441–459.

Siipola, E. M. (1968). Incongruence of sentence completions under time pressure and freedom. *Journal of Projective Techniques and Personality Assessment, 32*, 562–571.

Silber, D. E. (1974). Controversy concerning the criminal justice system and its implications for the role of mental health workers. *American Psychologist, 29*, 239–244.

Silbergeld, E. K. (1985). Neurotoxicology of lead. In K. Blum & L. Manzo (Eds.), *Neurotoxicology* (pp. 299–322). New York: Marcel Dekker.

Silberman, C. (1970). *Crisis in the classroom*. New York: Vintage Books/Random House.

Silberman, C. E. (1978). *Criminal violence, criminal justice*. New York: Random House.

Silberman, M. L., Allender, J. E. & Yanoff, J. M. (Eds.). (1972). *The psychology of open teaching and learning: An inquiry approach*. Boston: Little, Brown.

Silva, A. J., Paylro, R., Wehner, J. M., & Tonegawa, S. (1992). Impaired spatial learning in a-calcium calmodulin kinase II mutant mice. *Science, 257*, 206–211.

Silva, A. J., Stevens, C. F., Tonegawa, S., & Wang, Y. (1992). Deficient hippocampal long-term potentiation in a-calcium-colmodulin kinase II mutant mice. *Science, 257*, 201–206.

Silver, A. A. (1948, August). Behavioral syndromes associated with brain damage in children. *Pediatric Clinics of North America*, 687–698.

Silver, A. A. (1971). Familial patterns in children with neurologically-based learning disabilities. *Journal of Learning Disabilities, 4*, 349–358.

Silver, R. (1978). The parental behavior of ring doves. *American Scientist, 66*, 209–215.

Silverman, I. (September 1971). Physical attractiveness and courtship. *Sexual Behavior*, 22–25.

Silverman, J. (1964). The problem of attention in research and theory in schizophrenia. *Psychological Review, 71*, 352.

Silverman, L. H. (1974). Some psychoanalytic considerations of non-psychoanalytic therapies. *Psychotherapy, 11*, 298–305.

Silverman, L. H. (1976). Psychoanalytic theory: "The reports of my death are greatly exaggerated:" *American Psychologist, 31*, 621–637.

Silverman, L. H. (1983). The subliminal psychodynamic method: Overview and comprehensive listing of studies. In J. Masling (Ed.), *Empirical studies of psychoanalytic theory* (Vol. 1, pp. 69–103). Hillsdale, NJ: Erlbaum.

Silverman, L. H., & Fishel, A. (1982). The Oedipus complex: Studies in adult male behavior. In L. Wheeler (Ed.), *Review of Personality and Social Psychology* (Vol. 2). London: Sage.

Silverman, L. H., Klinger, H., Lustbader, L., Farrell, J., & Martin, A. D. (1972). The effects of subliminal drive stimulation on the speech of stutterers. *The Journal of Nervous and Mental Disease, 155*, 14–21.

Silverman, L. H., Kwawer, J. S., Wolitsky, C., & Coron, J. N. (1973). An experimental study of aspects of the pschoanalytic theory of male homosexuality. *Journal of Abnormal Psychology, 82*, 78–188.

Silverman, L. H., Lachmann, F. M., & Milichi, R. H. (1982). *The search for oneness*. New York: International Universities Press.

Silverman, L. H., & Silverman, D. K. (1964). A clinical-experimental approach to the study of subliminal stimulation: The effects of a drive-related stimulus upon Rorschach responses. *Journal of Abnormal and Social Psychology, 69*, 158–172.

Silverman, L. H., & Weinberger, J. (1985). Mommy and I are one: Implications for psychotherapy, *American Psychologist, 40*, 1296–1308.

Silverman, P. R. (1969). The widow-to-widow program: An experiment in preventive intervention. *Mental Hygiene, 53*, 333–337.

Silverman, P. R., et al. (1974). *Helping each other in widowhood*. New York: Health Sciences.

Silverman, R. E. (1982). *Psychology* (4th ed.). Englewood Cliffs, N.J.: Prentice-Hall.

Silverman, W. H. (1981). *Community mental health: A sourcebook for professionals and advisory board members*. New York: Praeger.

Silverstein, C. (Ed.). (1991). *Gays, lesbians, and their therapists: Studies in psychotherapy*. New York: Norton.

Silverstein, M. L., & Harrow, M. (1978). First-rank symptoms in the postacute schizophrenic: A follow-up study. *American Journal of Psychiatry, 135*, 1481–1486.

Silvey, J. (1963). Aptitude testing and educational selection in Africa. *Rhodes-Livingstone Journal, 34*, 9–22.

Silvey, J. (1963). Testing ability tests: The measurement of ability among African schoolboys. East African Institute for Social Research Conference, Dar es Salaam.

Silvey, J. (1969). The occupational attitudes of secondary school leavers in Uganda. In R. Jolly (Ed.), *Education in Africa*. Nairobi: East African Publishing House.

Silvey, J. (1972). A longitudinal study of ability and attainment from the end of primary to the end of secondary school in Uganda. In L. J. Cronbach & P. J. D. Drenth (Eds.), *Mental tests and cultural adaptations*. The Hague: Mouton.

Silving, H. (1957). Suicide and the law. In E. S. Shneidman & N. L. Farberow (Eds.), *Clues to suicide*. New York: McGraw-Hill.

Simandl, R. (1992). *Satanic worship and ritualistic criminal activity*. Paper delivered at preconference workshop on sadastic ritual abuse in the 1990s, at the Ninth International Conference on Multiple Personality and Dissociative States, Chicago.

Simek, T. C., & O'Brien, R. M. (1981). *Total golf.: A behavioral approach*. Garden City, N. Y.: Doubleday.

Simkin, J. S. (1974). *Mini-lectures in Gestalt therapy.* Albany, Calif.: Wordpress.

Simkin, J. S. (1976). *Gestalt therapy mini-lectures.* Millbrae, Calif.: Celestial Arts.

Simmel, E. C., Cheney, J. H., & Landy, E. E. (1965). Visual vs. locomotor response effects on satiation to novel stimuli: A sex difference in rats. *Psychological Reports, 16,* 893–896.

Simmel, G. (1896). Superiority and subordination as subject-matter of sociology. *American Journal of Sociology, 2,* 167–189, 392–415.

Simmel, G. (1902). The number of members as determining the sociological form of the group. *American Journal of Sociology, 8,* 1–46, 158–196.

Simmel, G. (1950). *The sociology of George Simmel.* New York: Glencoe Press.

Simon, H. A. (1955). On a class of skew distribution functions. *Biometrika, 42,* 425–440.

Simon, H. A. (1957). *Models of man.* New York: Wiley.

Simon, H. A. (1967). Motivational and emotional controls of cognition. *Psychological Review, 74,* 29–39.

Simon, H. A. (1974). How big is a chunk? *Science, 183,* 482–488.

Simon, H. A. (1976). *Administrative behavior.* New York: Macmillan.

Simon, H. A. (1976/1947). *Administrative behavior.* New York: Macmillan.

Simon, H. A. (1977). *Models of discovery.* Boston: Reidel.

Simon, H. A. (1979). *Models of thought.* New Haven, Conn.: Yale University Press.

Simon, H. A. (1981/1969). *The sciences of the artificial.* Cambridge, Mass.: M.I.T. Press.

Simon, H. A., & Barenfeld, M. (1969). Information processing analysis of perceptual processes in problem solving. *Psychological Review, 76,* 473–483.

Simon, H. A., & Lea, G. (1974). Problem solving and rule induction: A unified view. In L. Gregg (Ed.), *Knowledge and cognition.* Hillsdale, NJ: Erlbaum.

Simon, H. A., & Newell, A. (1964). Information processing in computer and man. *American Scientist, 52,* 281–300.

Simon, H. A., & Newell, A. (1972). *Human problem-solving.* Englewood Cliffs, N. J.: Prentice-Hall.

Simon, J. L. (1978). *Basic research methods in social science.* New York: Random House.

Simon, S. B., Howe, L. W. & Kirschenbaum, H. (1972). *Values clarification: A handbook of practical strategies for teachers and students.* New York: Hart.

Simon, W., & Gagnon, J. H. (1969). On psychosexual development. In D. Goslin (Ed.), *Handbook of socialization theory and research.* New York: Rand-McNally.

Simonton, O., & Mathews-Simonton, S. (1978). *Getting well again.* Los Angeles: Tarcher.

Simos, B. G. (1979). *A time to grieve: Loss as a universal human experience.* New York: Family Service Association of America.

Simpson, D. D., & Sells, S. B. (1982). Effectiveness of treatment for drug abuse: An overview of the DARP research program. *Advances in Alcohol and Substance Abuse, 2*(1), 7–29.

Simpson, D. D., & Sells, S. B. (1982). *Evaluation of drug abuse treatment effectiveness: Summary of the DARP research.* Washington, D.C.: National Institute on Drug Abuse, Treatment Research Monograph. [DHHS Publication no. (ADM) 82–1194].

Simpson, D. D., & Sells, S. B. (Eds.). (1990). *Opioid addiction and treatment: A 12-year follow-up.* Malabar, FL: Krieger.

Simpson, G. E., & Yinger, J. M. (1972). *Racial and cultural minorities: An analysis of prejudice and discrimination.* New York: Harper & Row.

Simpson, M. A. (1979). *Dying, death, and grief: A critically annotated bibliography and source book of thanatology and terminal care.* New York: Plenum.

Simpson, R. L. (1973). *Theories of social exchange.* Morristown, N.J.: General Learning Press.

Sinclair, H. (1967). *Langage et opérations.* Paris: Dunod.

Sines, J. O. (1970). Actuarial versus clinical prediction in psychopathology. *British Journal of Psychiatry, 116,* 129–144.

Sines, J. O. (1979). Non-pharmacological and non-surgical resistance to stress ulcers in temperamentally and physiologically susceptible rats. *Journal of Psychosomatic Research, 23,* 77–82.

Singer, C. (Ed.). (1921). *Studies in the history and method of science.* Vol. 11. Oxford: Clarendon Press.

Singer, E. (1965). *Key concepts in psychotherapy.* New York: Random House.

Singer, G. (1961). *Morale factors in industrial management.* New York: Exposition Press.

Singer, G. (1967). *Perception: A laboratory manual.* A. Bennett & R. H. Day (Eds.). Sydney, Australia: New South Wales University Press.

Singer, J. E., & Glass, D. C. (1975). Some reflections upon losing our social psychological purity. In M. Deutsch & H. A. Hornstein (Eds.), *Applying social psychology.* Hillsdale, N. J.: Erlbaum.

Singer, J. E., Lundberg, U., & Frankenhaeuser, M. (1978). Stress on the train: A study of urban commuting. In A. Baum, J. E. Singer, & S. Valins (Eds.), *Advances in environmental psychology,* Vol. 1. Hillsdale, N. J.: Erlbaum.

Singer, J. L. (1973). *The child's world of make-believe.* New York, London: Academic Press.

Singer, J. L. (1974). *Imagery and daydream methods in psychotherapy and behavior modification.* New York: Academic Press.

Singer, J. L. (1976). *Daydreaming and fantasy.* London: Allen & Unwin.

Singer, J. L. (1979). Imagery and affect in psychotherapy: Elaborating private scripts and generating contexts. In A. A. Sheikh & J. T. Shaffer (Eds.), *The potential of fantasy and imagination.* New York: Brandon House.

Singer, J. L., & Pope, K. S. (Eds.) (1978). *The power of human imagination,* New York: Plenum.

Singer, M. (1988). Inferences in reading comprehension. In M. Daneman, G. MacKinnon, & T. Waller (Eds.), *Reading research: Advances in theory and practice* (Vol. 6, pp. 177–219).

Singer, M. F., & Wynne, L. C. (1963). Differentiating characteristics of parents of childhood schizophrenics, childhood neurotics, and young adult schizophrenics. *American Journal of Psychiatry, 120,* 234–243.

Singer, P. (1975). *Animal liberation: A new ethics for our treatment of animals.* New York: Avon.

Singer, R. (1977). Consent of the unfree: Medical experimentation and behavior modification in the closed institution. *Law and Human Behavior, 1,* 1–43 (Pt. I), 101–162 (Pt. II).

Singh, M. V., Anand, N. K., Gupta, S., & Dhingra, D. C. (1976). Intelligence in relation to the degree of malnutrition. *Indian Journal of Clinical Psychology, 3,* 117.

Singleton, W. T., Spurgeon, P., & Stammers, R. B. (1980). *The analysis of social skill*. New York: Plenum.

Sinha, D. (1969). *Academic achievers and non-achievers: A psychological analysis of some factors associated with success and failure in university education*. Allahabad, India: United Publishers.

Sinha, D. (1969). *Motivation of rural population in a developing country*. Bombay: Allied Publishing House.

Sinha, D. (1969). *Villages in transition: A motivational analysis*. New Delhi: Associated Publishing House.

Sinha, D. (1972). *The Mughal syndrome: Psychological study of intergenerational differences*. New Delhi: Tara/McGraw-Hill.

Sinha, D. (1974). *Motivation and rural development: Two studies on Indian farmers*. Calcutta: Minerva Associates.

Sinha, D. (1975). Social psychologists' stance in a developing country. *Indian Journal of Psychology, 50*, 91–107.

Sinha, D. (1980, May 12–23). Socio-cultural deprivation and acquisition of perceptual and cognitive skills in Indian children. Presented at Indo-U.S. Seminar on Socio-cultural Effects of Deprivation on Learning, New Delhi.

Sinha, D. (Ed.). (1981). *Psychological study of deprivation*. New Delhi: Concept.

Sinha, D. (Ed.). (1981). *Socialization of the Indian child*. New Delhi: Concept.

Sinha, O. (1986). *Psychology in a third world country: The Indian experience*. New Delhi: Sage.

Siperstein, G. N., Bak, J. J., & Gottlieb, J. (1977). Effects of group discussion on children's attitudes toward handicapped peers. *Journal of Educational Research, 70*, 131–134.

Siperstein, G. N., & Gottlieb, J. (1978). Parents' and teachers' attitudes toward mildly and severely retarded children. *Mental Retardation, 16*, 321–322.

Siqueland, E. R., & DeLucia, C. A. (1969). Visual reinforcement of nonnutritive sucking in human infants. *Science, 165*, 1144–1146.

Sisson, E. D. (1948). Forced choice—The new army rating. *Personnel Psychology, 1*, 365–381.

Siverstein, S. M., Rawlin, M. L. Pristach, E. A., & Pomerantz, J. R. (1992). Perceptual organization and schizotype. *Journal of Abnormal Psychology, 101*(2), 265–270.

Sjoberg, G. (1960). *The preindustrial city: Past and present*. Glencoe, Ill.: Free Press.

Skeels, H. M. (1940). Some Iowa studies of the mental growth of children in relation to differentials of the environment: A summary. *Yearbook of the National Society for the Study of Education*, Pt. II, 281–308.

Skelton, R. W., Scarth, A. S., Wilkie, D. M., Miller, J. J., & Phillips, A. G. (1987). Long-term increases in dentate granule cell responsibility accompany operant conditioning. *Journal of Neuroscience, 7*(10), 3081–3087.

Skinner, B. F. (1932). Drives and reflex strength: II. *Journal of Genetic Psychology, 6*, 38–48.

Skinner, B. F. (1935). The generic nature of the concepts of stimulus and response. *Journal of General Psychology, 12*, 40–65.

Skinner, B. F. (1937). Two types of conditioned reflex: A reply to Konorski and Miller. *Journal of Genetic Psychology, 16*, 272–279.

Skinner, B. F. (1938). *Behavior of organisms*. New York: Appleton-Century-Crofts.

Skinner, B. F. (1938). *The behavior of organisms: An experimental analysis*. New York: Appleton-Century.

Skinner, B. F. (1948). "Superstition" in the pigeon. *Journal of Experimental Psychology, 38*, 168–172.

Skinner, B. F. (1948). *Walden two*. New York: Macmillan.

Skinner, B. F. (1950). Are theories of learning necessary? *Psychological Review. 57*, 193–216.

Skinner, B. F. (1953). *Science and human behavior*. New York: Macmillan.

Skinner, B. F. (1957). *Verbal behavior*. New York: Appleton-Century-Crofts.

Skinner, B. F. (1958). Teaching machines. *Science, 128*, 969–977.

Skinner, B. F. (1959). A case history in scientific method. In S. Koch (Ed.), *Psychology: A study of a science*, Vol. 2. New York: McGraw-Hill.

Skinner, B. F. (1963). Behaviorism at fifty. *Science, 140*, 951–958.

Skinner, B. F. (1964). Behaviorism at fifty. In T. W. Wann (Ed.), *Behaviorism and phenomenology*. Chicago: University of Chicago Press.

Skinner, B. F. (1966). Operant behavior. In W. Honig (Ed.), *Operant behavior: Areas of research and application*. New York: Appleton-Century-Crofts.

Skinner, B. F. (1966a). The phylogeny and ontogeny of behavior. *Science, 153*, 1205–1213.

Skinner, B. F. (1966b). What is the experimental analysis of behavior? *Journal of the Experimental Analysis of Behavior, 9*, 213–218.

Skinner, B. F. (1968). *The technology of teaching*. New York: Appleton-CenturyCrofts.

Skinner, B. F. (1972). *Cumulative record* (3rd ed.). New York: Appleton-Century-Crofts.

Skinner, B. F. (1972/1971). *Beyond freedom and dignity*. New York: Bantam Books.

Skinner, B. F. (1974). *About behaviorism*. New York: Knopf.

Skinner, B. F. (1976). *Particulars of my life*. New York: Knopf.

Skinner, B. F. (1979). *The shaping of a behaviorist: Part two of an autobiography*. New York: Knopf.

Skinner, B. F. (1981). Selection by consequences. *Science, 213*, 501–504.

Skinner, B. F. (1987). Whatever happened to psychology as the science of behavior? *American Psychologist, 42*, 780–786.

Skinner, B. F., & Morse, W. A. (1957). A second type of superstition in the pigeon. *American Journal of Psychology, 70*, 308–311.

Sklar, L. S., & Anisman, H. (1981). Stress and cancer. *Psychological Bulletin, 89*, 369–406.

Skodak, M. (1939). Children in foster homes. A study in mental development. University of Iowa study. *Child Welfare, 16*(1), 156.

Skodak, M. (1970). *A follow-up and comparison of graduates from two types of high school programs for the mentally handicapped*. Washington, D.C.: U.S. Department of Health, Education, and Welfare, Office of Education Bureau of Research.

Skodak, M., & Skeels, H. M. (1949). A final follow-up study of 100 adopted children. *Journal of Genetic Psychology, 75*, 85–125.

Skolnick, J. H. (1979). The social risks of casino gambling. *Psychology Today, 13*, 52–58, 63–64.

Skovholt, T. M. (1974). The client as helper: A means to promote psychological growth. *Counseling Psychologist, 4*, 58–64.

Skovholt, T. M., Resnick, J. L., & Dewey, C. R. (1979). Weight treatment: A group approach to weight control. *Psychotherapy: Theory, Research, and Practice, 16*, 121.

Slaby, A. E., Lieb, J., & Tancriedi, L. R. (1975). *Handbook of psychiatric emergencies*. Flushing, N. Y.: Medical Examination.

Slack, C. (1955). Feedback theory and the reflex arc concept. *Psychological Review, 62*, 263–267.

Slack, D., & Vaux, A. (1988). Undesirable life events and depression: The role of event appraisals and social support. *Journal of Social and Clinical Psychology, 7*, 290–296.

Slangen, J. L., Miller, N. E. (1969). Pharmacological tests for the function of hypothalamic norepinephrine in eating behavior. *Physiology and Behavior, 4,* 543–552.

Slater, P. (Ed.). (1976). *Explorations of intrapersonal space.* New York: Wiley.

Slater, P. (Ed.). (1977). *The measurement of intrapersonal space by grid technique.* New York: Wiley.

Slavson, S. R. (1951). *The practice of group psychotherapy.* New York: International Universities Press.

Slavson, S. R. (1959). Parallelisms in the development of group psychotherapy. *International Journal of Group Psychotherapy, 9,* 451.

Sleight, R. B. (1948). The effect of instrument dial shape on legibility. *Journal of Applied Psychology, 32,* 107–188.

Sleight, R. B., & Cook, K. G. (November, 1974). *Problems in occupational safety and health: A critical review of selected worker physical and psychological factors.* HEW Publication no. (NIOSH) 75-124, Cincinnati, Ohio.

Slife, B., & Rubenstein, J. (Eds.). (1992). *Taking sides.* Guilford, CT: Dushkin.

Sloan, R. B. (1975). *Psychotherapy versus behavior therapy.* Cambridge, Mass.: Harvard University Press.

Sloan, W., & Guertin, W. H. (1948). A comparison of H-T-P and Wechsler—Bellevue I.Q.'s in mental defectives. *Journal of Clinical Psychology, 4,* 424–426.

Sloane, R. B., Staples, F. R., Cristol, A. H., Yorkston, N. J., & Whipple, K. (1975). *Psychotherapy versus behavior therapy,* Cambridge, Mass.: Harvard University Press.

Slobin, D. I. (1971). *The ontogenesis of grammar.* New York: Academic Press.

Slotnick, B. M., & Katz, H. M. (1974). Olfactory learning-set formation in rats. *Science, 185,* 796–798.

Slovenko, R. (1971). Competency to stand trial: The reality behind fiction. *Wake Forest Law Review, 8,* 1–29.

Slovic, P., Fischhoff, B., & Lichtenstein, S. (1977). Behavioral decision theory. *Annual Review of Psychology, 28,* 1–39.

Slovic, P., & Lichtenstein, S. (1973). Comparison of Bayesian and regression approaches to the study of human judgment. In L. Rappoport & D. A. Summers (Eds.), *Human judgment and social interaction.* New York: Holt.

Slovic, P., Lichtenstein, S., & Fischhoff, S. (1988). Decision making. In R. C. Atkinson, R. J. Herrnstein, G. Lindzey, & R. D. Luce (Eds.), *Stevens' handbook of experimental psychology* (Vol. 2, chap. 10). New York: Wiley.

Sluckin, W. (1954). *Minds and machines.* London: Pelican Books.

Sluckin, W. (1965). *Imprinting and early learning.* Chicago: Aldine.

Sluzki C. E., & Ranson, D. C. (1976). *Double bind: The foundation of the communicational approach to the family.* New York: Grune & Stratton.

Small, J. G., Kellams, J. J., Milstein, V., & Small, I. F. (1980). Complications with electroconvulsive treatment combined with lithium. *Biological Psychiatry, 15,* 103–112.

Small, L. (1973). *Neuropsychodiagnosis in psychotherapy.* New York: Brunner/Mazel.

Smalley, R. E. (1967). *Theory for social work practice.* New York: Columbia University Press.

Smalley, W. (1963). Culture shock, language shock, and the shock of self discovery. *Practical anthropology, 10,* 49–56.

Smart, J. L. (1977). Early life malnutrition and later learning ability: A critical analysis. In A. Oliverio (Ed.), *Genetics, environment and intelligence.* Amsterdam: Elsevier/North Holland.

Smart, M. S., & Smart, R. C. (1973). *Infants: Development and relationships.* New York: Macmillan.

Smedslund, J. (1977). Piaget's psychology in practice. *British Journal of Educational Psychology, 47,* 1–6.

Smelsel, N. T. (1980). Themes of love and work in adulthood. Cambridge, Mass.: Harvard University Press.

Smelser, W. T. (1963). Adolescent and adult occupational choice as a function of family socioeconomic history. *Sociometry, 36,* 393–409.

Smetana, J., Bridgeman, D. L., & Bridgeman, B. (1978). A field study of interpersonal distance in early childhood. *Personality and Social Psychology Bulletin, 4,* 309–313.

Smith, A. (1975). Neuropsychological testing in neurological disorders. *Advances in Neurology, 7,* 49–110.

Smith, A. (1967). Self-approbation, self-disapprobation, and the man within the beast. In L. Schneider (Ed.), *The Scottish moralists on human nature and society.* Chicago: University of Chicago Press.

Smith, A. (1892). *The theory of moral sentiments.* London, New York: Bell.

Smith, A., & Reid, J. (1986). *Role sharing in marriage.* New York: Columbia University Press.

Smith, A. J., & Siegel, R. F. (1985). Feminist therapy: Redefining power for the powerless. In L. B. Rosewater & L. E. Walker (Eds.), *Handbook of feminist therapy: Women's issues in psychotherapy.* New York: Springer.

Smith, B. L., & Smith, C. M. (1956). *International communication and public opinion. A guide to the literature.* Princeton, N. J.: Princeton University Press.

Smith, C., & Lloyd, B. (1978). Maternal behavior and perceived sex of infant. *Child Development, 49,* 1263–1265.

Smith, C. U. M. (1970). *The brain: Towards an understanding.* New York: Putnam's.

Smith, D. (1968). Liberalism. In D. Sills (Ed.), *International encyclopedia of social science.* Vol. 9. New York: Macmillan.

Smith, D. (1982). Trends in counseling and psychotherapy. *American Psychologist, 37,* 802–809.

Smith, D. A., Galosy, R., & Weiss, S. M. (Eds.). (1982). *Circulation, neurobiology, and behavior.* New York: Elsevier/North Holland.

Smith, D. E. P., & Carrigan, P. M. (1959). *The nature of reading disability.* New York: Harcourt Brace Jovanovich.

Smith, D. S. (1973). The dating of the American Revolution. In M. Gordon (Ed.), *The American family in social-historical perspective.* New York: St. Martin's Press.

Smith, F., & Miller, G. A. (Eds.). (1966). *The genesis of language: a psycholinguistic approach.* Cambridge: MIT Press.

Smith, G. (1976). Institutional dependence is reversible. *Gerontology, 22,* 227–234.

Smith, G., Ivnik, R. F., Peterson, R. C., Malec, J. F., Kokmen, E., & Tangalos, E. (1991). Age associated memory impairment diagnoses: Problems of reliability and concerns for terminology. *Psychology and Aging, 6,* 551–558.

Smith, G. M., & Fogg, C. P. (1974). Teenage drug use: A search for causes and consequences. *Personality and Social Psychology Bulletin, 1*(1), 426–429.

Smith, H. (1976). *Forgotten truth: The primordial tradition.* New York: Harper & Row.

Smith, H. (1982). The sacred unconscious. In R. N. Walsh & D. H. Shapiro (Eds.), *Beyond health and normality: Toward a vision of exceptional psychological health.* New York: Van Nostrand.

Smith, H. (1988). *The power game: How Washington works.* New York: Random House.

Smith, J. (1975). Meditation as psychotherapy. *Psychological Bulletin*, *82*(4), 558–564.

Smith, J. H. (Ed.). (1976). *Psychiatry and the humanities*. Vol. 4: *The literary Freud: Mechanisms of defense and the poetic will*. New Haven, Conn.: Yale University Press.

Smith, J. K., & Katims, M. (1977). Reading in the city: The Chicago Mastery Learning Reading Program. *Phi Delta Kappan, 59*, 199–202.

Smith, J. M., Oswald, W. T., Kucharski, T., & Waterman, L. J. (1978). Tardive dyskinesia: Age and sex differences in hospitalized schizophrenics. *Psychopharmacology, 58*, 207–211.

Smith, J. M., & Smith, D. E. (1976). *Child management: A program for parents and teachers*. Champaign, Ill.: Research Press.

Smith, Jr., & Bennett, J. C. (Eds.). *Cecil textbook of medicine* (19th ed.). Philadelphia: Saunders.

Smith, K. U., & Smith, M. F. (1966). *Cybernetic principles of learning and educational design*. New York: Holt, Rinehart & Winston.

Smith, M. (1982). *Hypnotic memory enhancement of witnesses: Does it work?* Paper presented at the meetings of the Psychonomic Society, Minneapolis.

Smith, M., & Pazdar, L. (1980). *Michelle remembers*. New York: Congdon & Lattes.

Smith, M. B. (1955). Some features of foreign student adjustment. *Journal of Higher Education, 26*, 231–241.

Smith, M. B. (1959). Research strategies toward a conception of positive mental health. *American Psychologist, 14*, 673–681.

Smith, M. B. (1961). ''Mental health'' reconsidered: A special case of the problem of values in psychology. *American Psychologist, 16*, 299–306.

Smith, M. B. (1969). *Social psychology and human values: Selected essays*. Chicago: Aldine.

Smith, M. B. (1974). *Humanizing social psychology*. San Francisco: Jossey-Bass.

Smith, M. B. (1978). Encounter groups and humanistic psychology. In K. W. Back, (Ed.), *In search for community: Encounter groups and social change*. Boulder, Colo.: Westview Press.

Smith, M. B. (1978). Humanism and behaviorism in psychology: Theory and practice. *Journal of Humanistic Psychology, 18*(1), 27–36.

Smith, M. B. (1980). Attitudes, values, and selfhood. In H. E. Howe, Jr., & M. M. Page (Eds.), *Nebraska Symposium on Motivation 1979*. Lincoln, Neb.: University of Nebraska Press.

Smith, M. B., Bruner, J. S., & White, R. W. (1956). *Opinions and personality*. New York: Wiley.

Smith, M. B., & Frenkel-Brunswick, E. (1980). In B. Sicherman & C. H. Green (Eds.), *Notable American women*, Vol. 3. Cambridge, Mass.: Belknap/ Harvard.

Smith, M. C. (1968). CS-US interval and US intensity in classical conditioning of the rabbit's nictitating membrane response. *Journal of Comparative and Physiological Psychology, 66*, 679–687.

Smith, M. C. (1975). Children's use of the multiple sufficient cause schema in social perception. *Journal of Personality and Social Psychology, 32*, 737–747.

Smith, M. C., Coleman, S. R., & Gormezano, I. (1969). Classical conditioning of the rabbit's nictitating membrane response at backward, simultaneous, and forward CS-US intervals. *Journal of Comparative and Physiological Psychology, 69*, 226—231.

Smith, M. D. (1979). Prediction of self-concept among learning disabled children. *Journal of Learning Disabilities, 12*, 664–669.

Smith, M. J., Cohen, B. G. F., Stammerjohn, L. W., Jr., & Happ, A. (1981). An investigation of health complaints and job stress in video display operators. *Human Factors, 23*, 387–400.

Smith, M. L., & Glass, G. V. (1977). Meta-analysis of psychotherapy outcome studies. *American Psychologist, 32*, 752–760.

Smith, M. L., Glass, G. V., & Miller, T. I. (1980). *The benefits of psychotherapy*. Baltimore, Md.: Johns Hopkins University Press.

Smith, O. E. (1987). The everyday world as problematic: A feminist sociology. Boston: Northeastern University Press.

Smith, O. W., & Smith, P. C. (1957). Interaction of the effects of cues involved in judgments of curvature. *American Journal of Psychology, 70*, 361–375.

Smith, P. B. (1975). Are there adverse effects on sensitivity training? *Journal of Humanistic Psychology, 15*, 29–47.

Smith, P. C. (1976). Behaviors, results, and organizational effectiveness: The problem of criteria. In M. D. Dunnette (Ed.), *Handbook of industrial and organizational psychology*. Chicago: Rand-McNally.

Smith, P. C., & Kendall, L. M. (1963). Retranslation of expectations: An approach to the construction of unambigous anchors for rating scales. *Journal of Applied Psychology, 47*, 149–155.

Smith, R. (1981). Boredom: A review. *Human Factors, 23*, 329–340.

Smith, R. I. (1978). *The psychopath in society*. New York: Academic Press.

Smith, R. M. (1971). *An introduction to mental retardation*. New York: McGraw-Hill.

Smith, R. N. (1973). *Probabilistic performance models of language*. The Hague: Mouton.

Smith, R. P. (1981). Boredom: A review. *Human Factors, 23*, 329–340.

Smith, R. R. (1980). *Essentials of neurosurgery*. Philadelphia, Pa.: Lipincott.

Smith, R. T. (1965). A comparison of socio-environmental factors in monozygotic and dyzygotic twins. In S. G. Vandenberg (Ed.), *Methods and goals in human behavior genetics*. New York: Academic Press.

Smith, R. W., Preston, F., & Humphries, H. L. (1976). Alienation from work: A study of casino card dealers. In W. R. Eadington (Ed.), *Gambling and society*. Springfield, Ill.: Thomas.

Smith, S., & Guthrie, E. R. (1921). *General psychology in terms of behavior*. New York: Century.

Smith, S. M. (1979). Remembering in and out of context. *Journal of Experimental Psychology: Human Learning and Memory, 5*, 460–471.

Smith, S. M., Glenberg, A., & Bjork, R. A. (1978). Environmental context and human memory. *Memory and Cognition, 6*, 342–353.

Smith, T. E. (1971). Birth order, sibship size and social class as antecedents of adolescents' acceptance of parents' authority. *Social Forces, 50*(2), 223–232.

Smith, T. L. (1986). Biology as allegory: A review of Elliott Sober's *The nature of selection*. *Journal of the Experimental Analysis of Behavior, 46*, 105–112.

Smith, T. W. (1991). Adult sexual behavior in 1989: Number of partners, frequency of intercourse and risk of AIDS. *Family Planning Perspectives, 233*, 102–107.

Smith, W. J. (1977). *The behavior of communicating*. Cambridge, Mass.: Harvard University Press.

Smith, W. L., & Kinsbourne, M. (Eds.). (1977). *Aging and dementia*. New York: Spectrum.

Smith, W. R. (1889). *The religion of the Semites*. New York: Meridian.

Smith, W. R., & Monastersky, C. (1986). Assessing juvenile sexual offenders' risk for reoffending. *Criminal Justice and Behavior, 13,* 115–140.

Smolensky, P. (1988). On the proper treatment of connectionism, *Behavorial Brain Science, 11,* 1–23.

Smuts, J. C. (1961/1926). *Holism and evolution.* New York: Viking Press.

Smyer, M. (1992, April). *Psychopharmacology: An essential element in educating clinical psychologists for working with older adults.* Paper presented at the National Conference on Clincial Training in Psychology: Improving psychological services for older adults, Washington, DC.

Smythies, J. R., & Beloff, J. (Eds.). (1989). *The case for dualism.*Charlottesville, VA: University Press of Virginia.

Snarey, J. (1982). The moral and social development of kibbutz founders and sabras. Unpublished doctoral dissertation, Harvard University.

Sneath, P. H. A., & Sokal, R. R. (1973). *Numerical taxonomy: The principles and practice of numerical classification.* San Francisco: Freeman.

Snider, J. G., & Osgood, C. E. (1969). *Semantic differential technique: A sourcebook.* Chicago: Aldine.

Snow, B., & Sorenson, T. (1990). Ritualistic child abuse in a neighborhood setting. *Journal of Interpersonal Violence, 5*(4), 474–487.

Snow, C. E. (1972). Mothers' speech to children learning language. *Child Development, 43,* 549–565.

Snow, M. E. (1981, April). Birth and differences in young children's intentions with mother, father, and peer. Presented at the Society for Research in Child Development, Boston.

Snow, M. E., Jacklin, C. N., & Maccoby, E. E. (1981). Birth order differences in peer sociability at thirty-three months. *Child Development, 52,* 589–595.

Snow, S. S., Logan, T. P., & Hollander, M. H. (1980). Nasal spray "addiction" and psychosis: A case report. *British Journal of Psychiatry, 136,* 297–299.

Snyder, C. R., & Endelman, J. R. (1979). Effects of degree of interpersonal similarity on physical distance and self-reported attraction: A comparison of uniqueness and reinforcement theory predictions. *Journal of Personality, 47,* 492–505.

Snyder, J. J., & White, M. J. (1979). The use of cognitive self-instruction in the treatment of behaviorally disturbed adolescents. *Behavior Therapy, 10,* 227–235.

Snyder, M., & Gangestad, S. (1982). Choosing social situations: Two investigations of self-monitoring processes. *Journal of Personality and Social Psychology, 43,* 123–135.

Snyder, M., Tanke, E. D., & Berscheid, E. (1977). Social perception and interpersonal behavior: On the self-fulfilling nature of social stereotypes. *Journal of Personality and Social Psychology, 35,* 656–666.

Snyder, S. H. (1974). *Madness and the brain.* New York: McGraw-Hill.

Snyder, S. H., Banerjee, S. P., Yamamura, H. I., & Grienberg, D. (1974). Drugs, neurotransmitters, and schizophrenia. *Science, 184,* 1243–1253.

Snyder, W. O. (1963). *Dependency in psychotherapy: A casebook.* New York: Macmillan.

Snyder, W. U. (1945). An investigation of the nature of non-directive psychotherapy. *Journal of Genetic Psychology, 13,* 193–223.

Snygg, D. (1941). The need for a phenomenological system of psychology. *Psychological Review, 18,* 404–423.

Snygg, D., & Combs, A. W. (1959). *Individual behavior: A perceptual approach to behavior.* New York: Harper.

Sobell, L. C. (1978). Alcohol treatment outcome evaluation: Contributions from behavioral research. In P. E. Natham, G. A. Marlott, & T. Loberg (Eds.), *Alcoholism: New directions in behavioral research and treatment.* New York: Plenum.

Sobey, F. (1970). *The nonprofessional revolution in mental health.* New York: Columbia University Press.

Socarides, C. W. (1978). *Homosexuality.* New York: Aronson.

Social Policy, (1976). 7 (no. 2: Special double issue on self-help).

Social Welfare Commission. (1976). *Needs of lone parent families in Australia.* Canberra, Australia: Department of Social Security.

Soddy, K., & Kidson, M. C. (1967). *Men in middle life.* London: Tavistock.

Soderstrom, D., & Wright, E. W. (1977). Religious orientation and meaning in life. *Journal of Clinical Psychology, 33,* 65–68.

Soeffing, M. Y. (1977). New assessment techniques for the mentally retarded and culturally different—A conversation with Jane R. Mercer. In C. J. Drew, M. I. Hardman, & H. P. Bluhm (Eds.), *Mental retardation: Social and educational perspectives.* St. Louis, Mo.: Moshy.

Sokal, M. M. (1973). APA's first publication: *Proceedings of the American Psychological Association,* 1892–1893. *American Psychologist, 28,* 277–292.

Sokal, M. M. (1992). Origins and early years of the American Psychological Association, 1890–1906. *American Psychologist, 47,* 111–122.

Sokal, M. M., & Rafail, P. A. (1982). *A guide to manuscript collections in the history of psychology and related areas.* Millwood, N. Y.: Kraus International.

Sokal, R. R. (1974). Classification: Purposes, principles, progress, prospects. *Science, 185,* 1115–1123.

Sokol, R. J., Ager, J., Martier, S., Debanne, S., Ernhart, C., Kuzma, J., & Miller, S. I. (1986). Significant determinants of susceptibility to alcohol teratogenicity. *Annals of the New York Academy of Sciences, 477,* 87–100.

Sokolov, E. N. (1963). Higher neuron functions: The orienting reflex. *Annual Review of Physiology, 25,* 545–580.

Sokolov, E. N. (1963/1958). *Perception and the conditioned reflex.* New York: Macmillan

Sokolov, E. N. (1975/1970). The neuronal mechanism of the orienting reflex. In E. N. Sokolov & O. S. Vinogradona (Eds.), *Neutral mechanisms of the orienting reflex.* Hillsdale, N. J.: Erlbaum.

Solana, F., Cardiel Reyes, R., & Bolaños Martinez, R. (Eds.). (1981). *Historia de la educacion publica en Mexico.* Mexico, D.F.: Fondo de Cultura Economica.

Solem, A. R., Onachilla, V. J., & Heller, K. Z. (1961). The posting problems technique as a basis for training. *Personnel Administration, 24,* 22–31.

Solis Quiroga, R. (1953). Los anormales mentales educable y la necesidad de maestros especialistas. In Universidad Nacional Autonoma de Mexico (Ed.), *Memoria de Congreso Científico Mexicano, Ciencias de la Educacion, Psicologia-Filosofia, 15,* 332–341.

Solomon, D., Hirsch, J. G., Scheinfeld, R., & Jackson, C. (1972). Family characteristics and elementary school achievement in an urban ghetto. *Journal of Consulting and Clinical Psychology, 39*(3), 462–466.

Solomon, G. F. (1985). The emerging field of psychoneuroimmunology, with a special note on AIDS. *Advances, 2*(1), 6–19.

Solomon, G. F. (1987). Psychoneuroimmunology: Interactions between central nervous system and immune responses. *Journal of Neuroscience Research, 18,* 1–9.

Solomon, G. F. (1990). Emotions, stress, and immunity. In R. Ornstein & C. Swencionis (Eds.), *The healing brain: A scientific reader* (pp. 174–181). New York.

Solomon, G. F., & Amkraut, A. A. (1979). Neuroendocrine aspects of the immune response and their implications for stress effects on tumor immunity. *Cancer Detection and Prevention, 2,* 197–223.

Solomon, G. F., Amkraut, A. A., & Kasper, P. (1974). Immunity, emotions, and stress. *Psychotherapy and Psychosomatics, 23,* 209–217.

Solomon, G. F., & Moos, R. H. (1965). The relationship of personality to the presence of rheumatoid factor in asymptomatic relatives of patients with rheumatoid arthritis. *Psychosomatic Medicine, 27,* 350–360.

Solomon, K. M., Solomon, R. J., & Silien, J. S. (1968). Passenger psychological dynamics. *Journal of Urban Transportation.*

Solomon, L. (1975). Atopic dermatitis. In S. Moshella, D. Pillsbury, & H. Hurley (Eds.), *Dermatology.* Philadelphia, Pa.: Saunders.

Solomon, R. L. (1964). Punishment. *American Psychologist, 19*(4), 239–253.

Solomon, R. L. (1980). The opponent-process theory of acquired motivation. *American Psychologist, 35,* 691–712.

Solomon, R. L., Kamin, L., & Wynne, L. C. (1953). Traumatic avoidance learning: The outcome of several extinction procedures with dogs. *Journal of Abnormal and Social Psychology, 48,* 291–302.

Solomon, R. L., & Lessac, M. S. (1968). A control group design for experimental study of developmental processes. *Psychological Bulletin, 70,* 145–150.

Solomon, R. L., & Wynne, L. C. (1954). Traumatic avoidance learning: The principles of anxiety conservation and partial irreversibility. *Psychological Review, 61,* 129–139.

Solso, R. L. (1979). *Cognitive psychology.* New York: Harcourt Brace Jovanovich.

Solso, R. L. (1991). *Cognitive psychology* (3rd ed.). Boston: Allyn & Bacon.

Soltz, V. (1967). *Study group leader's manual for children: The challenge.* Chicago: Alfred Adler Institute.

Somerset, H. C. A. (1968). *Predicting success in school certificate.* Nairobi: East African Publishing House.

Sommer, R. (1898). Dreidimensionale Analyse von Ausdrucksbewegungen. *Zeitschrift für Psychologie, 16,* 275–297.

Sommer, R. (1969). *Personal space.* Englewood Cliffs, N. J.: Prentice-Hall.

Sommerhoff, G. (1974). *Logic of the living brain.* New York: Wiley.

Sommerschield, H., & Reyher, J. (1973). Posthypnotic conflict, repression, and psychopathology. *Journal of Abnormal Psychology, 82,* 278–290.

Sontag, L. W., & Richards, T. W. (1938). Studies in fetal behavior. *Monograph of the Society for Research in Child Development, 3.*

Soothill, K., Kupituksa, P., & MacMillan, F. (1990). Compulsory hospital admissions: Dangerous decisions? *Medicine, Science and the Law, 30,* 17–25.

Sorce, J. F., Emde, R. N., Campos, J. Klinnert, M. D. (1985). Maternal Emotional Signaling: Its Effect on the Visual Cliff Behavior of 1-Year-Olds. *Developmental Psychology 21,* 195–200.

Sorokin, P. A. (1975/1922). *Hunger as a factor in human affairs.* Gainesville, Fla.: University Presses of Florida.

Sorosky, A., Baran, A., & Pannor, R. (1978). The adoption triangle. Garden City, N. Y.: Anchor.

Sosis, R. H. (1974). Internal-external control and the perception of responsibility for another in an accident. *Journal of Personality and Social Psychology, 30,* 393–399.

Soter, N., & Fitzpatrick, T. (1979). Cutaneous changes in disorders of altered reactivity: Eczematous dermatitis. In T. Fitzpatrick, A. Eisen, W. Klaus, I. Freedberg, & F. Austen (Eds.), *Dermatology in general medicine* (2nd ed.). New York: McGraw-Hill.

Southerland, T. C., & McCleery, W. (1973). *The way to go: The coming revival of U. S. rail passenger service.* New York: Simon & Schuster.

Southwick, C. H. (1968). Effect of maternal environment on aggressive behavior of inbred mice. *Communications in Behavioral Biology, 1A,* 129–132.

Southwick, C. H. (Ed.). (1970). *Animal aggression: Selected readings.* New York: Van Nostrand Reinhold.

Soviet psychology (journal of reprints). (1962). New York: Sharpe.

Space, L. G., & Cromwell, R. L. (1980). Personal constructs among depressed patients. *Journal of Nervous and Mental Disease, 168,* 150–158.

Spache, G. D. (1976). *Investigating the issues of reading disabilities.* Boston: Allyn & Bacon.

Spanier, G. B. (1976). Measuring dyadic adjustment: New scales for assessing the quality of marriage and similar dyads. *Journal of Marriage and the Family, 38,* 15–28.

Spanier, G. B., & Cole, C. L. (1976). Toward clarification and investigation of marital adjustment. *International Journal of Sociology of the Family, 6,* 121–146.

Spann, O. (1923/1915). *Gesellschaftslehre.* Leipzig: Quelle & Meyer.

Spano, I. (1982). Counseling groups for the adult dyslexics at the New York Branch of the Orton Dyslexia Society. Personal communication.

Sparling, P. F. (1992). Sexually transmitted diseases. In J. B. Wyngaarden, L. H. Smith, Jr., & J. C. Bennett (Eds.), *Cecil textbook of medicine* (19th ed., pp. 1751–1770). Philadelphia: Saunders.

Spaulding, D. A. (1873). Instinct with original observation on young animals. *Macmillan Magazine, 27,* 282–283.

Spear, N. E., & Miller, R. R. (Eds.). (1981). *Information processing in animals, memory mechanisms.* Hillsdale, N. J.: Erlbaum.

Spearman, C. E. (1904). "General intelligence," objectively determined and measured. *American Journal of Psychology, 15,* 201–292.

Spearman, C. E. (1930). Autobiography. In C. Murchison (Ed.), *A history of psychology in autobiography,* Vol. 1. Worcester, Mass.: Clark University Press.

Spearman, C. E. (1934). The battle between "intuitionists" and "psychometrists." *British Journal of Psychology, 24,* 403–408.

Spearman, C. E. (1970/1927). *The abilities of man: Their nature and measurement.* New York: AMS Press.

Spearman, C. E. (1973/1923). *The nature of "intelligence" and the principles Of cognition.* New York: Arno Press.

Special Education Resource Center, National Learning Resource Center for Pennsylvania, National Regional Resource Center for Pennsylvania, in cooperation with the Pennsylvania Department of Education. *Mainstreaming conference II proceedings.* Harrisburg.

Special report on Satanism. (1989, March). *Mood Monthly, 89*(7).

Special Task Force, U.S. Department of Health, Education and Welfare. (1973). *Work in America.* Cambridge, Mass.: M.I.T. Press.

Speck, R. V., & Attneave, C. L., (1973). *Family network,* New York: Pantheon.

Spector, N. H., & Korneva, E. A. (1981). Neurophysiology, immunophysiology, and neuroimmunomodulation. In R. Ader (Ed.), *Psychoneuroimmunology.* New York: Academic Press.

Speer, D. (1970). Family systems morphostasis and morphogenesis, or is "homostasis" enough? *Family Process, 9*(1), 259–278.

Spence, D. (1982). *Narrative truth and historical truth.* New York: Norton.

Spence, J. (1987). Centrifugal versus centripetal tendencies in psychology. Will the center hold? *American Psychologist, 43,* 1052–1054.

Spence, J. T. (1963). Learning theory and personality. In J. M. Wepman & R. W. Heine (Eds.), *Concepts of personality.* Chicago: Aldine.

Spence, J. T. (1979). Traits, roles, and the concept of androgyny. In J. Gullahorn (Ed.), *Perspectives on the psychology of women.* New York: Wiley.

Spence, J. T., Deaux, K., & Helmreich, R. L. (in press). Sex roles in contemporary American society. In G. Lindzey & E. Aronson (Eds.), *Handbook of social psychology* (3rd ed.). Reading, Mass.: Addison-Wesley.

Spence, J. T., & Helmreich, R. L. (1972). The Attitudes toward Women Scale: An objective instrument to measure attitudes toward the rights and roles of women in contemporary society. *JSAS Catalog of Selected Documents in Psychology, 2,* 66.

Spence, J. T., & Helmreich, R. L. (1978). *Masculinity and femininity: Their psychological dimensions, correlates, and antecedents.* Austin, Tex.: University of Texas Press.

Spence, J. T., & Helmreich, R. L. (1980). Masculine instrumentality and feminine expressiveness: Their relationships with sex role attitudes and behaviors. *Psychology of Women Quarterly, 5,* 147–163.

Spence, J. T., & Helmreich, R. L. (in press). Achievement-related motives and behavior. In J. T. Spence (Ed.), *Perspectives on achievement and achievement motives.* San Francisco: Freeman.

Spence, J. T., Helmreich, R. L., & Stapp, J. (1974). The Personal Attributes Questionnaire: A measure of sex-role stereotypes and masculinity-femininity. *JSAS Catalog of Selected Documents in Psychology, 4,* 127.

Spence, J. T. Helmreich, R. L., & Stapp, J. (1975). Ratings of self and peers on sex-role attributes and their relation to self esteem and conceptions of masculinity and femininity. *Journal of Personality and Social Psychology, 32,* 29–39.

Spence, J. T., & Sawin, L. L. (in press). Images of masculinity and femininity: A reconceptualization. In V. E. O'Leary, R. K. Unger, & B. S. Wallston (Eds.), *Women, gender, and social psychology.* Hillsdale, N.J.: Erlbaum.

Spence, J. T., & Spence, K. W. (1966). The motivational components of manifest anxiety: Drive and drive stimuli. In C. Spielberger (Ed.), *Anxiety and behavior.* New York: Academic Press.

Spence, K. W. (1936). The nature of discrimination learning in animals. *Psychological Review, 43,* 427–449.

Spence, K. W. (1937). The differential response in animals to stimuli varying within a single dimension. *Psychological Review, 44,* 430–444.

Spence, K. W. (1940). Continuous vs. non-continuous interpretations of discrimination learning. *Psychological Review, 47,* 271–288.

Spence, K. W. (1942). The basis of solution by chimpanzees of the intermediate size problem. *Journal of Experimental Psychology, 31,* 257–271.

Spence, K. W. (1948). The postulates and methods of "behaviorism." *Psychological Review, 55,* 67–78.

Spence, K. W. (1951). Theoretical interpretations of learning. In S. S. Stevens (Ed.), *Handbook of experimental psychology.* New York: Wiley, 1951.

Spence, K. W. (1956). *Behavior theory and conditioning.* New Haven, Conn.: Yale University Press.

Spence, K. W. (1957). The empirical basis and theoretical structure of psychology. *Philosophy of Science, 24,* 97–108.

Spence, K. W. (1958). A theory of emotionally-based drive (D) and its relation to performance in simple learning situations. *American Psychologist, 13,* 131–141.

Spence, K. W. (1959). The relation of learning theory to the technology of education. *Harvard Educational Review, 29,* 84–95.

Spence, K. W. (1960). *Behavior theory and learning.* Englewood Cliffs, N.J.: Prentice-Hall.

Spence, K. W. (1964). Anxiety (drive) level and performance in eyelid conditioning. *Psychological Bulletin, 61,* 129–139.

Spence, K. W. (1966). Cognitive and drive factors in the extinction of the conditioned eyeblink in human subjects. *Psychological Review, 73,* 445–449.

Spence, S. H., & Marzillier, J. S. (1981). Social skills training with adolescent male offenders—II. Short term, long term and generalized effects. *Behavior Research and Therapy, 19,* 349–368.

Spencer F. M., & Deutsch, F. (1982). Parent/child interaction and intervention. In F. Deutsch, *Child services: On behalf of children.* Monterey, Calif.: Brooks/Cole.

Spencer, H. (1862). *First principles.* London: Williams & Norgate.

Spencer, H. (1870/1872/1855). *Principles of psychology,* (2nd ed.), London: Williams & Norgate.

Spencer, H. (1891). *The study of sociology.* New York: Appleton.

Spender, D. (1981). *Man made language.* London: Routledge & Kegan Paul.

Spender, D. (1982). *Women of ideas: And what men have done to them.* Boston: Rutledge & Kegan Paul.

Spengler, A. (1977). Manifest sadomasochism in males: results of an empirical study. *Archives of Sexual Behavior, 6,* 441–456.

Spenner, K. I., Otto, L. B., & Call, V. R. A. (1982). *Career lines and careers,* Vol. III. Boston: Lexington Books.

Sperber, M. (1974). *Masks of loneliness: Alfred Adler in perspective.* New York: Macmillan.

Sperry, R. (1964). The great cerebral commissure. *Scientific American, 210,* 42–52.

Sperry, R. (1965). Mind, brain, and humanist values. In J. R. Platl (Ed.), *New views of the nature of man.* Chicago: University of Chicago Press.

Sperry, R. W. (1968). Hemisphere deconnection and unity in conscious awareness. *American Psychologist, 23,* 723–733.

Sperry, R. (1969). A modified concept of consciousness. *Psychological Review, 76,* 532–536.

Sperry, R. W. (1976). Changing conceptions of consciousness and free will. *Perspectives in Biology and Medicine, 20,* 9–19.

Sperry, R. W. (1976). Mental phenomena as causal determinants in brain function. In G. G. Globus, G. Maxwell, & I. Savodnik (Eds.), *Consciousness and the brain* (pp. 163–177). New York: Plenum.

Sperry, R. W., & Miner, N. (1955). Pattern perception following insertion of mica plates into visual cortex. *Journal of Comparative and Physiological Psychology, 48,* 463–469.

Sperry, R. W., Miner, N., & Myers, R. E. (1955). Visual pattern perception following subpial slicing and tantalum wire implantations in the visual cortex. *Journal of Comparative and Physiological Psychology, 48,* 50–58.

Spetch, M. L., Wilkie, D. M., & Pinel, J. P. L. (1981). Backward conditioning: A reevaluation of the empirical evidence. *Psychological Bulletin, 89,* 163–175.

Spiegel, D. (1991). A psychosocial intervention and survival time of patients with metastatic breast cancer. *Advances, 2,* 11–19.

Spiegel, D., Bloom, J. R., Kraemer, H. C., & Gottheil, E. (1989, October 14). Effect of psychosocial treatment on survival of patients with metastatic breast cancer. *Lancet,* 888–891.

Spiegel, H. (1970). Termination of smoking by a single treatment. *Archives of Environmental Health, 20*(6), 736–742.

Spiegel, H., & Spiegel, D. (1978). *Trance and treatment: Clinical uses of hypnosis.* New York: Basic Books.

Spiegel, J., & Machotka, P. (1959). *Messages of the body.* London: Free Press, 1974.

Spiegel, J. P. Some cultural aspects of transference and countertransference. In J. H. Masserman (Ed.), *Individual and familial psychodynamics,* Vol. 11. New York: Grune & Stratton.

Spiegelberg, H. (1971/1960). *The phenomenological movement: A historical introduction,* Vols. 1, 11. (2nd ed.) The Hague: Nijhoff.

Spiegelberg, H. (1972). *Phenomenology in psychology and psychiatry: A historical introduction.* Evanston, Ill.: Northwestern University Press.

Spiegler, M. D., & Guevremont, D. (1992). *Contemporary behavior therapy* (2nd ed.). New York: Brooks/Cole.

Spiel, O. (1962). *Discipline without punishment.* London: Faber & Faber.

Spielberger, C. D. (1979). *Understanding stress and anxiety.* New York: Harper & Row.

Spielberger, C. D., Sarason, I. G., & Milgram, N. A. (1982). *Stress and anxiety,* Vol. 8. Washington, D. C.: Washington Hemisphere.

Spilerman, S. (1977). Careers, labor market structure, and socioeconomic achievement. *American Journal of Sociology, 83,* 551–593.

Spinoza, B. (1927). *Ethics.* London: Oxford University Press.

Spirito, A., Stark, L. J., & Williams, C. (1988). Development of a brief coping checklist for use with pediatric populations. *Journal of Pediatric Psychology, 13,* 555–574.

Spiro, M. E. (1958). *Children of the kibbutz.* Cambridge, Mass.: Harvard University Press.

Spitz, R. A, (1945). Hospitalism: An inquiry into the genesis of psychiatric conditions in early childhood. In *Psychoanalytic studies of the child,* Vol. I. New York: International Universities, Press.

Spitz, R. A. (1947). Anaclitic depression. In *Psychoanalytic Studies of the Child,* Vol. 2. New York: International Universities Press.

Spitz, R. A. (1947). Hospitalism: A follow-up report. In *Psychoanalytic studies of the child,* Vol. 2. New York: International Universities Press.

Spitz, R. A. (1949). Motherless infants. In *Child development.* Society for the Research in Child Development.

Spitz, R. A. (1950). Anxiety in infancy: A study of its manifestations in the first year of life. *International Journal of Psycho-Analysis, 31,* 138–143.

Spitz, R. A. (1957). *Die Entstehung der ersten Objektbeziehungen.* Stuttgart: Klett.

Spitz, R. A. (1957). *No and yes: On the genesis of human communication.* New York: International Universities Press.

Spitz, R. A. (1963). Life and the dialogue. In H. S. Gaskill (Ed.), *Counterpoint: Libidinal object and subject.* New York: International Universities Press.

Spitz, R. A., & Wolf, K. M. (1946). Anaclitic depression: An enquiry into the genesis of psychiatric conditions in early childhood, II. *Psychoanalytic study of the child, 2,* 313–342.

Spitzer, R. L. (1981). Letter. *Archives of General Psychiatry, 38,* 1299–1300.

Spitzer, R. L. (1987). *Diagnostic and statistical manual of mental disorders.* Washington, DC: American Psychiatric Association.

Spitzer, R. L, & Endicott, J. (1975). Computer applications in psychiatry. In S. Arieti (Ed.), *American handbook of psychiatry,* Vol. 6. New York: Basic Books.

Spitzer, R. L., & Endicott, J. (1969). DIAGNO II: Further developments in a computer program for psychiatric diagnosis. *American Journal of Psychiatry, 125,* (suppl.), 12–21.

Spitzer, R. L., Endicott, J., & Robins, E. (1978). Research diagnostic criteria. *Archives of General Psychiatry, 35,* 773–782.

Spitzer, R. L., & Williams, J. B. W. (1980). Classification in psychiatry. In A. Kaplan, A. Freedman, & B. Sadok (Eds.), *Comprehensive textbook of psychiatry 111.* Baltimore, Md.: Williams & Wilkins.

Spivack, G., Platt, J. J., & Shure, M. D. (1976). *The problem-solving approach to adjustment.* San Francisco: Jossey-Bass.

Spivack, G., & Shure, M. (1974). *Social adjustment of young children: A cognitive approach to solving real-life problems.* San Francisco: Jossey-Bass.

Spivack, G., & Shure, M. B. (1985). ICPS and beyond: Centripetal and centifugal forces. *American Journal of Community Pychology, 13,* 226–243.

Spoerl, H. D. (1935–1936). Faculties *vs.* traits: Gall's solution. *Character and Personality, 4,* 216–231.

Spokane, A. R. (1979). Occupational preference and the validity of the Strong–Campbell Interest Inventory for college women and men. *Journal of Counseling Psychology, 26,* 312–318.

Sporer, S. (1991). Deep-deeper-deepest? Encoding strategies and the recognition of human faces. *Journal of Experimental Psychology: Learning, Memory and Cognition, 17,* 323–333.

Sprague, C. (Ed.). (1979). *GROW comes of age: A celebration and a vision.* Sidney, Australia: GROW Publications.

Sprague, R. L., & Sleator, E. K. (1977). Methylphenidate in hyperkinetic children: Differences in dose effects on learning and social behavior. *Science, 198,* 1274–1276.

Spranger, E. (1928/1920). *Types of men,* Halle, East Germany: Niemeyer.

Spranger, E. (1949/1925). *Psychologie des Jugendalters.* Heidelberg, West Germany: Quelle & Meyer.

Spranger, E. (1969/1914). *Lebensformen.* Halle, East Germany: Niemeyer.

Spreen, O. (1977/1963). *MMPI Saarbrücken.* Bern: Huber.

Spreen, O., & Benton, A. L. (1977). *Neurosensory Center comprehensive examination for aphasia.* Victoria, B. C.: University of Victoria.

Spring, C., & Sandoval, J. (1976). Food additives and hyperkinesis: A critical evaluation of the evidence. *Journal of Learning Disabilities, 9,* 560–569.

Spring, D. (1992). *Comments.* Made at the Multiple personality workshop at Advanced Psychotherapeutic Techniques, California.

Springer, S. P., & Deutsch, G. (1981). *Left brain, right brain.* San Francisco: Freeman.

Sprinthall, R. C., & Sprinthall, N. A. (1974). *Educational psychology: a developmental approach.* Reading, Mass.: Addison-Wesley.

Sproull, L. S. (1986). Using electronic mail for data collection in organizational research. *Academy of Management Journal, 29,*1.

Spurzheim, J G. (1817). *Observations on the deranged manifestations of the mind, or insanity.* London: Baldwin, Cradock & Joy.

Spurzheim, J. G. (1825). *Phrenology, or the doctrine of the mind; and of the relations between its manifestations and the body.* London: Knight.

Spurzheim, J. G. (1827). *Outlines of phrenology; being also a manual of reference for the marked busts.* London: Treuttel, Wurtz & Richter.

Squire, L. R. (1992). Memory and the hippocampus: A synthesis from findings with rats, monkeys, and humans. *Psychological Review, 99*(2), 195–231.

Squire, L. R., Wetzel, C. D., & Slater, P. C. (1979). Memory complaint after electroconvulsive therapy: Assessment with a new self-rating instrument. *Biological Psychiatry, 14,* 791–801.

Squires, P. C. (1956). *The shape of the normal work area.* USN Bureau of Medicine and Surgery, Medical Research Laboratory, Report no. 275.

Srole, L. (1956). Social integration and certain corollaries: An exploratory study. *American Sociological Review, 21,* 709–716.

Srole, L., & Fischer, A. K. (1973). Smoking behavior 1953 and 1970: The Midtown Manhattan Study. In W. L. Dunn (Ed.), *Smoking behavior: Motives and incentives.* Washington, D. C.: Winston.

Srole, L., Langer, T. S., Michael, S. T., Opler, M. K., & Remic, T. A. C. (1962). *Mental health in the metropolis: The Midtown Manhattan Study.* New York: McGraw-Hill.

Sroufe, L. A. (1979). Emotional development. In J. Osofsky (Ed.), *Handbook of infant development.* New York: Wiley.

Staats, A. W. (1975). *Social behaviorism.* Homewood, Ill.: Dorsey.

Staats, A. W., & Butterfield, W. H. (1965). Treatment of non-reading in a culturally deprived juvenile delinquent: An application of reinforcement principles. *Child Development, 36,* 925–942.

Stachnik, T. J. (1980). Priorities for psychology in medical education and health care delivery. *American Psychologist, 35,* 8–15.

Stacy, C. (1987). Complex haptic hallucinations & palinaptia. *Cortex, 23,* 337–340.

Staddon, J. E. R. (1979). Operant behavior as adaptation to constraint. *Journal of Experimental Psychology: General, 108,* 48–67.

Staddon, J. E. R., & Ettinger, E. H. (1988). *Learning: Introduction to the principles of adaptive behavior.* New York: Harcourt Brace Jovanovich.

Staddon, J. E. R., Hinson, J. M., & Kram, R. (1981). Optimal choice. *Journal of the Experimental Analysis of Behavior, 35,* 397–412.

Staffieri, J. R. (1970). Birth order and creativity. *Journal of Clinical Psychology, 26*(1), 65–66.

Stafford, R. E. (1961). Sex differences in spatial visualization as evidence of sex-linked inheritance. *Perceptual and Motor Skills, 13,* 428.

Stager, S. F., & Young, R. D. (1981). Intergroup contact and social outcomes for mainstreamed EMR adolescents. *American Journal of Mental Deficiency, 85,* 497–503.

Stagner, R. (1951). Homeostasis as a unifying concept in personality theory. *Psychological Review, 58,* 5–17.

Stagner, R. (1958). The Gullibility of Personnel Managers. *Pesonnel Psychology, 11,* 347–352.

Stagner, R. (1976). Traits are relevant: Theoretical analysis and empirical evidence. In N. S. Endler & D. Magnusson (Eds.), *Interactional-psychology and personality.* Washington, D.C.: Hemisphere.

Stagner, R. (1979, Summer). Propensity to work: An important variable in retiree behavior. *Aging and Work, 2,* 161–171.

Stahmann, R. F. (1972). Treatment forms for marital counseling. In R. F. Stahmann & W. J. Hiebert, (Eds.), *Klemer's counseling in marital and sexual problems.* Baltimore, Md.: Williams & Wilkins.

Stahmann, R. F., & Barclay-Cope, A. (1977). Pre-marital counseling: An overview. In R. F. Stahmann & W. J. Hiebert (Eds.), *Klemer's counseling in marital and sexual problems: A clinician's handbook* (2nd ed.). Baltimore, Md.: Williams & Wilkens.

Stahmann, R. F., & Hiebert, W. J. (1980). *Premarital counseling.* Lexington, Mass.: Heath.

Stahmann, R. F., & Hiebert, W. J. (Eds.). (1972). *Klemer's counseling in marital and sexual problems.* Baltimore: Williams & Wilkins.

Staines, G. L., & Quinn, R. P. (1979). American workers evaluate the quality of their jobs. *Monthly Labor Review, 102,* 3–12.

Stake, R. E. (Ed.) (1975). *Evaluating the arts in education: A responsive approach.* Columbus, Ohio: Merrill.

Stampfl, T. G. & Levis, D. J. (1967). Essentials of implosive therapy: A learning theory-based psychodynamic behavioral therapy. *Journal of Abnormal Psychology, 72,* 496–503.

Standing, E. M. (1962). *Maria Montessori, her life and work.* New York: New American Library.

Standing, E. M. (1962). *The Montessori method: A revolution in education.* Fresno, Calif.: Academy Guild Press.

Stanford, R. G. (1974a). An experimentally testable model for spontaneous psi events. I. Extrasensory events. *Journal of the American Society for Psychical Research, 68,* 34–57.

Stanford, R. G. (1974b). An experimentally testable model for spontaneous psi events. II. Psychokinetic events. *Journal of the American Society for Psychical Research, 68,* 321–356.

Stanford, R. G. (1977). Are parapsychologists paradigmless in psiland? In B. Shapin & L. Coly (Eds.), *The philosophy of parapsychology 1976.* New York: Parapsychology Foundation.

Stanford, R. G. (1977). Experimental psychokinesis: A review from diverse perspectives. In B. B. Wolman (Ed.), *Handbook of parapsychology.* New York: Van Nostrand Reinhold.

Stanford Research Institute. (1976). *Occupational alcoholism programs in U.S. companies.* LRPS Report no. 572, Menlo Park, Calif.: Stanford Research Institute.

Stanovich, K. E. (1991). Damn! There goes that ghost again! *Behavioral and brain sciences, 14,* 696–698.

Stang, D. J., & Wrightsman, L. S. (1981). *Dictionary of social behavior and social research methods.* Monterey, Calif.: Brooks/Cole.

Stanley, J. C. (1967). Elementary experimental design—An expository treatment. *Psychology in the Schools, 4,* 195–203.

Stanley, J. C. (1971). Reliability. In R. L. Thorudike (Ed.), *Educational measurement* (2nd ed.) Washington, D.C.: American Council on Education.

Stanley, J. C. (1977). Rationale of the study of mathematically precocious youth (SMPY) during its first five years of promoting educational acceleration. In J. C. Stanley, W. C. George, & C. H. Solano (Eds.), *The gifted and the creative: A fifty-year perspective.* Baltimore, Md.: Johns Hopkins University Press.

Stanley, J. C., & Benbow, C. P. (Winter, 1981–82). Using the SAT to find intellectually talented seventh graders. *College Board Review,* no. 122, 2–7 & 26–27.

Stanley, J. C., George, W. C., & Solano, C. H. (Eds.). (1977). *The gifted and the creative: A fifty-year perspective.* Baltimore, Md.: Johns Hopkins University Press.

Stanley, J. C., Keating, D. P., & Fox, L. H. (Eds.). (1974). *Mathematical talent: Discovery, description and development.* Baltimore, Md.: Johns Hopkins University Press.

Stanley, S. M. (1981). *The new evolutionary timetable.* New York: Basic Books.

Stanton, H. F. (1976). Fee-paying and weight loss: Evidence for an interesting interaction. *American Journal of Clinical Hypnosis, 19,* 47–49.

Stanton, M. D. (1981). An integrated structural/strategic approach to family therapy. *Journal of Family Therapy, 7,* 427–440.

Stanton, M. D. (1984). Fusion, compression, diversion, and the workings of paradox: A theory of therapeutic/systematic change. *Family Process, 23,* 135–168.

Stanton, M. D.,& Todd, T. C. (1979). Structural family therapy with drug addicts. In E. Kaufmann, & P. Kaufman (Eds.), *Family therapy of drug and alcohol abuse.* New York: Gardner Press.

Stanton, W. R., Feehan, M., McGee, R., & Silva, P. A. (1990). The relative value of reading ability and IQ as predictors of teacher-reported behavior problems. *Journal of Learning Disabilities, 23,* 514–517.

Staples, R. (1971). Towards a sociology of the black family: A theoretical and methodological assessment. *Journal of Marriage and the Family, 33,* 119–138.

Staples, R, & Mirande, A. (1980). Racial and cultural variations among American families: A decennial review of the literature of minority families. *Journal of Marriage and the Family, 42,* 887–903.

Starch, D. (1923). *Principles of advertising.* Chicago: Shaw.

Starch, D. (1966). *Measuring advertising readership and results.* New York: McGraw-Hill.

Starkey, D. (1981). The origins of concept formation: Object sorting and object preference in early infancy. *Child Development, 52,* 489–497.

Starr, A. (1977). *Psychodrama: Rehearsal for living.* Chicago: Nelson-Hall.

Starr, P. (1986). *The social transformation of American medicine.* New York: Basic Books.

Stary, D. (1975). Published works of Yugoslav psychologists till 1972, *Revija za psihologiju, 5,* 129–135.

State of Maine v. *Waterhouse,* No. 4216, Lin-85-23.

State of Nebraska v. *Michael Ryan.* (1989). 444 N.W.d. 610, 233, Neb. 74.

State v. *Pike,* (1870). 49 N. H. 399.

Stattin, H., & Klackenberg-Larsson, I. (1990). The relationship between maternal attributes in the early life of the child and the child's future criminal behavior. *Development and Psychopathology, 2,* 99–111.

Stattin, H., & Magnussen, D. (1989). The role of early aggressive behavior in the frequency, seriousness, and types of later crime. *Journal of Consulting and Clinical Psychology, 57,* 710–718.

Staub, E. (1978). *Posiave social behavior and morality.* Vol. 1: *Social and personal influences.* New York: Academic Press.

Staub, E. (1979). *Positive social behavior and morality.* Vol. 2: *Socialization and development.* New York: Academic Press.

Staub, E., Bar-Tal, D., Karylowsld, J., & Reykowski, J. (Eds.). (in press). *Development and maintenance of prosocial behavior: International perspectives.* New York: Plenum.

Staudenmayer, H, Kinsman, R. A, Dirks, J. F., Spector, S. L., & Wangaard, C. (1979). Medical outcome in asthmatic patients: Effects of airways hyperactivity and symptom-focused anxiety. *Psychosomatic Medicine, 41,* 109–118.

Staw, B. M., Calder, B. J., Hess, R. K., & Sandelands, L. E. (1980). Intrinsic motivation and norms about payment. *Journal of Personality, 48,* 1–14.

Stayton, D. J, Hogan, R., & Ainsworth, M. D. S. (1971). Infant obedience and maternal behavior: The origins of socialization reconsidered. *Child Development, 42,* 1057–1069.

Steadman, H. (1981). A situational approach to violence. *International Journal of Law and Psychiatry, 5,* 171–186.

Steadman, H., & Cocozza, J. (1974). *Careers of the criminal insane.* Lexington, MA: Lexington Books.

Steadman, H. J. (1977). A new look at recidivism among Patuxent inmates. *Bulletin of the American Academy of Psychiatry and the Law, 5,* 200–209.

Steadman, H. J. (1979). *Beating a rap: Defendants found incompetent to stand trial.* Chicago: University of Chicago Press.

Steadman, H. J. (1979). The use of social science in forensic psychiatry. *International Journal of Law and Psychiatry, 2,* 519–531.

Steadman, H. J, & Cocozza, J. J. (1974). *Careers of the criminally insane.* Lexington, Mass.: Lexington Books.

Stebbins, W. C. (Ed.). (1970). *Animal psychophysics: The design and conduct of sensory experiments.* New York: Appleton-Century-Crofts.

Steele, F. I. (1973). *Physical setting and organization development.* Reading, Mass.: Addison-Wesley.

Steen, C., & Monnette, B. (1989). *Treating adolescent sex offenders in the community.* Springfield, IL: Thomas.

Steen, E. B, & Montagu, A. (1959). *Anatomy and physiology,* Vol 2. New York: Barnes & Noble.

Steers, R. M, & Braunstein, D. N. (1976). A behaviorally based measure of manifest need in work settings. *Journal of Vocational Behavior, 9,* 251–266.

Steffens, A. B., Morgenson, G. J., & Stevenson, J. (1972). Blood glucose, insulin and free fatty acids after stimulation and lesions of the hypothalamus. *American Journal of Physiology, 222,* 1446–1452.

Steger, C, & Kotler, T. (1979). Contrasting resources in disturbed and non-disturbed family systems. *British Journal of Medical Psychology, 52,* 243–251.

Stein, A. A. (1976). Conflict and cohesion: A review of the literature. *Journal of Conflict Resolution, 20,* 143–172.

Stein, H., Seidman, F., & Swift, C. R. (1967). Adjustment problems in juvenile diabetes. *Psychosomatic Medicine, 29*(6), 555–571.

Stein, L., Belluzzi, J. D., & Wise, C. D. (1977). Benzodiazepines: Behavioral and neurochemical meehanisms. *American Journal of Psychiatry, 134,* 665–669.

Stein, M., Schleifer, S. J., & Keller, S. E. (1981). Hypothalamic influences on immune responses. In R. Ader (Ed.), *Psychoneuroimmunology.* New York: Academic Press.

Stein, M. B., Tancer, M. E., Gelemter, C. S., Vittone, B. J., & Uhde, T. W. (1990). Major depression in patients with social phobia. *American Journal of Psychiatry, 147,* 637–639.

Stein, M. I. (1947). The use of a sentence completion test for the diagnosis of personality. *Journal of Clinical Psychology, 3,* 46–56.

Stein, M. L. (1975). *Physiognomic Cue Test—test and manual.* New York: Behavioral Publications.

Stein, N. L., & Glenn, C. G. (1979). An analysis of story comprehension in elementary school children. In R. O. Freedle, (Ed.), *New directions in discourse Processing: Vol. 2. Advances in discourse processes* (pp. 53–120). Norwood, NJ: Ablex.

Stein, T. S., & Cohen, C. J. (Eds.). (1986). *Contemporary perspectives on psychotherapy with lesbians and gay men.* New York: Plenum.

Stein, Z. (1975). Environmental predictors of IQ. *Science, 190,* 548–549.

Stein, Z., & Susser, M. (1976). Prenatal nutrition and mental competence. In J. D. Lloyd-Still (Ed.), *Malnutrition and intellectual development.* Littleton, Mass.: Publishing Science Group.

Stein, Z., Susser, M., Saenger, G., & Marolla, F. (1975). *Famine and human development: The Dutch hunger winter of 1944–45*. New York: Oxford University Press.

Steinbeck, J. (1933). *To a God unknown*. New York: Covici-Fried.

Steiner, C. (1970). *Games alcoholics play*. New York: Grove Press.

Steiner, C. (1975). *Readings in radical psychotherapy*. New York: Grove Press.

Steiner, C. (1981). Radical psychotherapy. In R. J. Corsini (Ed.), *Handbook of innovative psychotherapies*. New York: Wiley.

Steiner, G. (1980). *Visuelle Vorstellungen beim Lösen von elementaren Problemen*. Stuttgart: Klett-Cotta.

Steiner, G. A. (1981). The new class of chief executive officer. *Long-Range Planning, 14*, 10–20.

Steiner, G. A., & Berelson, B. (1969). *Human behavior*. New York: Harcourt, Brace & World.

Steiner, I. (1954). Ethnocentrism and tolerance of trait inconsistency. *Journal of Abnormal and Social Psychology, 49*, 349–354.

Steiner, I. (1970). Perceived freedom. In L. Berkowitz (Ed.), *Advances in experimental social psychology*. New York: Academic Press.

Steiner, I. (1972). *Group process and productivity*. New York: Academic Press.

Steiner, I. D. (1976). Task-performing groups. In J. Thibaut, J. Spence, & R. Carson (Eds.), *Contemporary trends in social psychology*. Morristown, N.J.: General Learning Press.

Steiner, R. (1947). *Knowledge of the higher worlds and its attainment* (3rd ed.). New York: Anthroposophic Press.

Steiner, R. (1965). *Theosophy*. London: R. Steiner.

Steiner, R. (1970). *The Philosophy of freedom: The basis for a modern world conception*. London: Steiner.

Steiner, R. (1990). *Theosophy*. Hudson, NY: Anthroposophic.

Steiner, S. S., & Dince, W. M. (1981). Biofeedback efficacy studies: A critique of critiques. *Biofeedback and Self-Regulation, 6*, 275–287.

Steinglass, P. (1977). Family therapy in alcoholism. In B. Kissin & H. Begleiter, (Eds.). *Treatment and rehabilitation of the chronic alcoholic. The biology of alcoholism*, Vol. 5. New York: Plenum.

Steinmetz, S. K., & Strans, M. A. (Eds.). (1974). *Violence in the family*. New York: Dodd, Mead.

Stekel, W. (1950). *The autobiography of Wilhelm Stekel*. New York: Liveright.

Stekel, W. (1956). *Patterns of psychosexual infantilism*. New York: Grove Press.

Stellar, E. (1954). The physiology of motivation. *Psychological Review, 61*, 5–22.

Stengel, E. (1974). *Suicide and attempted suicide*. Baltimore, Md.: Penguin Books, 1964, New York: Aronson (rev. ed.).

Stenger, J. E. (1975). *A study of the relationship of family constellation to work value, occupational choice and psychological factors among college students*. Ph.D. dissertation, University of Iowa.

Stensrud, R. L. (September 1979). *New initiatives for promoting health*. Presented at the tenth International Conference on Health Education, London, England.

Stensrud, R. L., & Stensrud, K. (1981). Counseling may be hazardous to your health: How we teach people to feel powerless. *Personnel and Guidance Journal, 59*, 300–304.

Stensrud, R. L., & Stensrud, K. (1982). Counseling for health empowerment. *Personnel and Guidance Journal. 60*, 377–381.

Stephan, F. F. (1948). History and uses of modern sampling procedures. *Journal of the American Statistical Association, 43*, 12–39.

Stephan, W., Berscheid, E., & Walster (Hatfield), E. (1971). Sexual arousal and heterosexual perception. *Journal of personality and Social Psychology, 20*, 93–101.

Stephenson, W. (1953). *The study of behavior: Q-technique and its methodology*. Chicago: University of Chicago Press.

Sterling, C. H., & Haight, T. R. (1978). *The mass media: Aspen Institute guide to communication industry trends*. New York: Praeger.

Sterman, M. B., MacDonald, L. R., & Stone, R. K. (1974). Biofeedback training of the sensorimotor EEG rhythm in man: Effects on epilepsy. *Epilepsia, 15*, 395–416.

Stern, (1938). A. Psychoanalytic investigation of and therapy in the borderline group of neuroses. *Psychoanalytic Quarterly, 7*, 467–489.

Stern, D. (1974). Mother and infant at play: The dyadic interaction involving facial, vocal, and gaze behaviors. In M. Lewis & L. A. Rosenbloom (Eds.), *The effect of the infant on its caregiver*. New York: Wiley.

Stern, D. (1977). *The first relationship*. Cambridge, Mass.: Harvard University Press.

Stern, E. (Ed.). (1954/1955). *Die Tests in der klinischen Psychologie*. Zurich: Rascher.

Stern, G. G. (1970). *People in context*. New York: Wiley.

Stern, G. M. (1976). *The Buffalo Creek disaster*. New York: Random House.

Stern, M. (Ed.). (1981). Humor and illumination. *Voices: The Art and Science of Psychotherapy, 16*(4).

Stern, R. M., Ray, W. J., & Davis, C. M. (1980). *Psychophysiological recording*. New York: Oxford University Press.

Stern, W. (1900). *Über Psychologie der individuellen Differenzen (Ideen zur einer "differentielle Psychologie")*. Leipzig: Barth.

Stern, W. (1903/1906). *Beiträge zur Psychologie der Aussage*. Leipzig: Barth.

Stern, W. (1906). *Person und Sache (Person and thing) (3 vols.)*. Leipzig: Barth.

Stern, W. (1914/1912). *The psychological methods of testing intelligence*. Baltimore, Md.: Warwick & York.

Stern, W. (1921/1911). *Die differentielle Psychologie in ihren methodischen Grundlagen*. Leipzig: Barth.

Stern, W. (1924/1923). *Psychology of early childhood up to the sixth year of age*. London: Allen & Unwin.

Stern, W. (1930). Autobiography. In C. Murchison (Ed.), *A history of psychology in autobiography*, Vol. 1. Worcester, Mass.: Clark University Press.

Stern, W. (1938/1935). *General psychology from the personalistic standpoint*. New York: Macmillan.

Sternberg, R. J. (1979). The nature of human abilities. American *Psychologist, 34*, 214–230.

Sternberg, R. J. (1980). Sketch of a compotential subtheory of human intelligence. *The Behavioral and Brain Sciences, 3*, 573—614.

Sternberg, R. J. (1981). Testing and cognitive psychology. *American Psychologist, 36*, 1181–1189.

Sternberg, R. J. (1990). *Metaphors of mind*. New York: Cambridge University Press.

Sternberg R. J. (Ed.). (1982). *Handbook of intelligence*. New York: Cambridge University Press.

Sternberg, R. J. (Ed.). (1988). *The nature of creativity*. Cambridge, UK: Cambridge University Press.

Sternberg, S. (1966). High-speed scanning in human memory. *Science 153*, 652–654.

Sternberg, S. (1969). Memory scanning: Mental processes revealed by reaction time experiments. *American Scientist, 57,* 421–457.

Sternberg, S. (1969). The discovery of processing stages: Extensions of Donders' method. (Attention and performance II.) *Acta Psychologica, 30,* 376–315.

Sternberg, S. (1975). Memory scanning: New findings and current controversies. *Quarterly Journal of Experimental Psychology, 27,* 1–32.

Sternglanz, S. H., & Serbia, L. A. (1974). Sex role stereotyping in children's television programs. *Developmental Psychology, 10,* 710–715.

Steury, S. & Blank, M. L. (Eds.). (1981). *Readings in psychotherapy with older people.* Rockville, Md.: National Institute of Mental Health, U.S. Department of Health and Human Services.

Stevens, C. M. (1966). Is arbitration compatible with collective bargaining? *Industrial Relations, 5,* 38–52.

Stevens, G. N. (1970). The human operator and quality inspection of horticultural produce. *Journal of the Institute of Agricultural Engineering, 25,* 1.

Stevens, J. O. (1971). Awareness: *Exploring, experimenting. experiencing.* Lafayette, Calif.: Real People Press.

Stevens, J. O. (1980). Neuro-linguistic programming. In R. Herink (Ed.), *The psychotherapy handbook.* New York: Meridian Books.

Stevens, S. S. (1935). The operational basis of psychology. *American Journal of Psychology, 47,* 323–330.

Stevens, S. S. (1935). The operational definition of psychological concepts. *Psychological Review, 42,* 517–527.

Stevens, S. S. (1939). Psychology and the science of science, *Psychological Bulletin, 36,* 221–263.

Stevens, S. S. (1946). On the theory of scales of measurement. *Science 103,* 677–680.

Stevens, S. S. (1951). Mathematics, measurement, and psychophysics. In S. S. Stevens (Ed.), *Handbook of experimental psychology.* New York: Wiley.

Stevens, S. S. (1956). The direct estimation of sensory magnitude—loudness. *American Journal of Psychology, 69,* 1–25.

Stevens, S. S. (1957). On the psychophysical law. *Psychological Review, 64,* 153–181.

Stevens, S. S. (1960). Ratio scales, partition scales, and confusion scales. In H. Gulliksen & S. Messick (Eds.), *Psychological scaling: Theory and applications.* New York: Wiley.

Stevens, S. S. (1961). The psychophysics of sensory function. In W. A. Rosenblith (Ed.), *Sensory communication.* New York: Wiley.

Stevens, S. S. (1970). Neural events and the psychophysical law. *Science, 1043–1050.*

Stevens, S. S. (1975). *Psychophysics: Introduction to its perceptual. neural and social aspects.* New York: Wiley.

Stevens, S. S. (Ed.). (1951). *Handbook of experimental psychology.* New York: Wiley.

Stevens, S. S., & Dafis, H. (1938). *Hearing: Its Psychology and Physiology.* New York: Wiley.

Stevens-Long, J. (1979). *Adult life: Developmental processes.* Palo Alto, Calif.: Mayfield.

Stevenson, A. (1972). Quoted in G. Hardin, *Exploring the new ethics for survival.* New York: Viking.

Stevenson, M. K., Busemeyer, J. R., & Naylor, J. C. (1991). Judgment and decision-making theory. In M. D. Dunnette & L. M. Hough (Eds.), *Handbook of industrial Psychology* (Vol. 1, pp. 283–374). Palo Alto, CA: Consulting Psychologists.

Stevenson, R. E. (1977). *The fetus and the newly born infant.* St. Louis, Mo.: Mosby.

Stevenson, R. L. (1961). *The strange case of Dr. Jekyll and Mr. Hyde.* New York: Putnam.

Stewart, A. J., & Rubin, Z. (1976). The power motive in the dating couple. *Journal of Personality and Social Psychology, 34,* 305–309.

Stewart, D. (1990, May). Interview with Arnold S. Relman. *Omni,* pp. 78, 80, 82, 84–87, 117.

Stewart, J. E. (1980). Defendants' attractiveness as a factor in the outcome of criminal trials: An observational study. *Journal of Applied Social Psychology, 10,* 348–361.

Stewart, P. L, & Cantor, M. G. (1974). *Varieties of work experience.* New York: Wiley.

Stewart, R. (Ed.) (1981). *East meets west: The transpersonal approach.* Wheaton, Ill.: Theosophical Publishing House.

Stewart, T. D. (1977). Spinal cord injury: A role for the psychiatrist. *American Journal of Psychiatry, 134,* 538–541.

Stewart, W. (1987). Irritable bowel syndrome. In E. M. Catalano (Ed.), *The chronic pain workbook.* Oakland, CA: New Harbinger.

Sticco, M. (1974). *Padre Gemelli: Appunti per la biografia di un uomo difficile.* Milan, Italy: Ed. O.R.

Stierlin, H. (1974). *Separating parents and adolescents.* New York: Quadrangle.

Štikar, J., & Hoskovec, J. (1981). *Technical simulators and development of man's activities* (in Czech). Prague: SNTL.

Štikar, J., Hoskovec, J., & Pour, J. (1981). *Psychology of safe driving* (in Czech) Prague: NADAS.

Štikar, J., Hoskovec, J., & Střizenec, M. (1982). *Engineering psychology. Handbook* (in Czech). Prague: SPN.

Stiles, W. B., Shapiro, D. A., & Elliot, R. (1986). Are all psychotherapies equivalent. *American Psychologist, 41*(2), 165–180.

Stimson, D. J., Smith, W. G., Amidjaya, I., & Kaplan, J. M. (1979). Systems of care and treatment outcomes for alcoholic patients. *Archives of General Psychiatry, 36,* 535–539.

Stockard, J. (1980). Sex inequities in the experiences of students. In J. Stockard, P. A. Schmuck, K. Kempnet, P. Williams, S. K. Edson, & M. A. Smith (Eds.), *Sex equity in education.* New York: Academic Press.

Stockford, L., & Bissell, H. W. (1949). Factors involved in establishing a merit rating scale. *Personnel, 26,* 94–116.

Stockhorst, U., Klosterhalfen, S., Klosterhalfen, W., Winkelmann, M., & SteingrUber, H. J. (1992). Anticipatory nausea in cancer patients receiving chemotherapy: Classical conditioning etiology and therapeutical implications. *Integrative Physiological and Behavioral Sciences*

Stocking, M., et al. (1972). Psychopathology in the pediatric hospital: Implications for community health. *American Journal of Public Health, 62,* 551–556.

Stoddard, S. (1978). *The hospice movement: A better way of caring for the dying.* New York: Stein & Day.

Stogdill, R. M. (1948). Personal factors associated with leadership: A survey of the literature. *Journal of Psychology, 25,* 35–71.

Stogdill, R. M. (1974). *Handbook of leadership,* New York: Free Press.

Stogdill, R. M., & Coons, A. E. (1957). *Leader behavior: Its description and measurement.* Columbus, Ohio: Ohio State University, Bureau of Business Research.

Stogdill, R. M., Goede, O. S., & Day, D. R. (1962). New leader behavior description subscales. *Journal of Psychology, 54,* 259–269.

Stokes, C. S., & Johnson, N. E. (1977). Birth order, size of family of orientation, and desired family size. *Journal of Individual Psychology, 33*(1), 42–46.

Stokes, P. (1987). The neuroendocrine measurement of depression. In A. J. Marsella, R. Hirshfeld, & M. Katz (Eds.), *The measurement of depression*. New York: Guilford.

Stokols, D. (1975). Toward a psychological theory of alienation. *Psychological Review, 82*, 26–44.

Stokols, D. (1978). A typology of crowding experiences. In A. Baum & Y. Epstein (Eds.), *Human response to crowding*. Hillsdale, N.J.: Erlbaum.

Stolberg, A. L., & Garrison, K. M. (1985). Evaluating a primary prevention program for children of divorce: The divorce adjustment project. *American Journal of Community Psychology, 13*, 111–124.

Stoline, M. R., Huitema, B. E., & Mitchell, B. T. (1980). Intervention time-series model with different pre- and postintervention first-order autoregressive parameters. *Psychological Bulletin, 88*, 46–53.

Stoll, F. (1972). *La construction des échelles d'intérèts professionnels.* Neuchâtel, Switzerland: La Baconnière.

Stoller, F. H. (1968). Marathon group therapy. In G. Gazda (Ed.), *Innovations to group psychotherapy*. Springfield, Ill.: Thomas.

Stoller, R. J. (1968). *Sex and gender*. New York: Science House.

Stoller, R. J. (1975). *Perversion: The erotic form of hatred*. New York: Pantheon.

Stoller, R. J. (1978). *Sexual excitement*. New York: Pantheon.

Stolorow, R. D., & Atwood, G. E. (1979). *Faces in a cloud: Subjectivity in personality theory*. New York: Aronson.

Stolov, W. C., & Clowers, M. R. (1981). *Handbook of severe disability*. Washington D.C.: U.S. Department of Education, Rehabilitation Services Administration.

Stolz, S. B., et al. (1978). *Ethical issues in behavior modification*. San Francisco: Jossey-Bass.

Stone, A. (1975). *Mental health and the law: A system in transition* (NIMH DHEW Publication No. ADM 76-176). Washington, DC: U.S. Government Printing Office.

Stone, A., & Lefine, L. (1956). *The pre-marital consultation, a manual for physicians*. New York: Grune & Stratton.

Stone, A. A. (1975). *Mental health and law: A system in transition*. Rockville, Md.: National Institute of Mental Health.

Stone, E. A. (1979). Subsensitivity to norepinephrine as a link between adaptation to stress and antidepressant therapy: An hypothesis. *Research Communications in Psychology and Psychiatric Behavior, 4*, 241–255.

Stone, G. (1979). Psychology and the health system. In G. Stone, F. Cohen, & N. Adler (Eds.), *Health psychology: A handbook*. San Francisco: Jossey-Bass.

Stone, G., Cohen, F., & Adler, N. (Eds.). (1979). *Health psychology: A handbook*. San Francsico: Jossey-Bass.

Stone, G. L. (1980). *A cognitive-behavioral approach to counseling psychology*. New York: Praeger.

Stone, G. P. (1981). Appearance and the self: A slightly revised version. In G. P. Stone & H. Farberman (Eds.), *Social psychology through symbolic interaction* (2nd ed.). New York: Wiley.

Stone, H. M, & Stone, A. (1952). *A marriage manual*. New York: Simon & Schuster.

Stone, L. (1960–1961). Marriage among the English nobility. *Comparative Studies in Society and History, 3*, 182–206.

Stone, L. J., Smith, H. T., & Murphy, L. B. (1973). *The competent infant*. New York: Basic Books.

Stoner, C., & Parke, J. (1977). *All God's children*. Radnor, Pa.: Chilton.

Stopes, M. (1950). *Married love*. Garden City, N.Y.: Permabooks.

Storms, M. (1980). Theories of sex-role identity. *Journal of Personality and Social Psychology, 38*, 783–792.

Story, M. & Brown, J. E. (1967). Do Young Children Instinctively Know What to Eat? The Studies of Clara Davis Revisited. *The New England Journal of Medicine, 316*, 103–105.

Stotland, E. (1969). *The psychology of hope*. San Francisco: Jossey-Bass.

Stotland, E., Katz, D., & Patchen, M. (1959). Reduction of prejudice through arousal of insight. *Journal of Personality, 27*, 507–531.

Stotland, E., Mathews, K., Sherman, S., Hansson, R. & Richardson, B. (1978). *Fantasy, empathy, and helping*. Beverly Hills, Calif.: Sage Publications.

Stotland, E., & Patchen, M. (1961). Identification and change in prejudice and authoritarianism. *Journal of Abnormal and Social Psychology, 62*, 265–274.

Stotland, E., Shaver, K., & Sherman, S. (1971). *Empathy and birth order*. Lincoln, Neb.: University of Nebraska Press.

Stott, L. H., & Ball, R. S. (1963). *Evaluation of infant and preschool tests*. Detroit, Mich.: Merrill Palmer.

Stouffer, S. A., Lumsdahe, A. A, Lumsdaine, M. H., Williams, R. M., Jr., Smith, M. B., Janis, I. L., Star, S. A., & Cottrell, L. S., Jr. (1949). *The American soldier: Combat and its aftermath*. Princeton, N.J.: Princeton University Press.

Stouffer, S. A., Suchman, E. A., DeVinney, L. C., Star, S. A., & Williams, R. M., Jr. (1949). *The American soldier: Adjustment during army life*. Princeton, N. J.: Princeton University Press.

Stout, G. F. (1896). *Analytic psychology* (2 vols.). London: Sonnenschein.

Stout, G. F. A (1898–1899). *A manual of psychology*. London: Clive.

Stout, J. T., & Caskey, C. T. (1989). Hypoxanthine phosphoribosyltransferase deficiency: The Lesch Nyhan syndrome and gouty arthritis. In C. R. Scriver, A. L. Beaudet, W. S. Sly, & D. Valle (Eds.), *The metabolic basis of inherited disease* (6th ed., Vol. 1, pp. 1007–1028). New York: McGraw-Hill.

Stouthamer-Loeber, M. (1986). Lying as a problem behavior in children: A review. *Clinical psychology Review, 6*, 267–289.

Stouthamer-Loeber, M., Loeber, R., & Green, S. M. (1989, February). *Dishonesty and covert problem behavior in adolescence and early adulthood*. Paper presented at the meeting of the Society for Research in Child and Adolescent Psychopathology, Miami.

Stoyva, J., & Budzynski, T. (1973). Cultivated low arousal—An anti-stress response? in L. DiCara, *Recent advances in limbic and autonomic nervous system research*. New York: Plenum.

Stoyva, J. M. (1979). Musculoskelatal and stress related disorders. In O. F. Pomerleau, & J. P. Brady (Eds.), *Behavioral medicine: Theory and practice*. Baltimore, Md.: Williams & Wilkins.

Stoyva, J. M., & Budzynski, T. H. (1975). Cultivated low arousal—an anti-stress response. In L. V. DiCara, T. X. Barber, J. Kamiya, N. E. Miller, D. Shapiro, & J. M. Stoyva (Eds.), *Biofeedback and self-control*. Chicago: Aldine.

Strain, P. S. (Ed.). (1981). *The utilization of classroom peers as behavior change agents*. New York: Plenum.

Strange, W., & Jenkins, J. J. (1978). Role of linguistic experience in the perception of speech. In R. D. Walk & H. L. Pick, Jr. (Eds.), *Perception and experience*. New York: Plenum.

Strathern, M. (1976). An anthropological perspective. In B. Lloyd & J. Archer (Eds.), *Exploring sex differences*. New York: Academic Press.

Stratton, G. M. (1897). Vision without inversion of the retinal image, *Pyschological Review, 4,* 341–360.

Straughan, J., & Dufort, W. (1969). Task difficulty, relaxation, and anxiety level during verbal learning and recall. *Journal of Abnormal Psychology, 74,* 621–624.

Straus, M., Gelles, R., & Steinmetz, S. (1980). *Behind closed doors: Violence in the American family.* Garden City, N.Y.: Anchor Press.

Straus, M. A. (1980). Wife-beating: How common and why? In M. A. Straus & G. T. Hotaling (Eds.), *The social causes of husband-wife violence.* Minneapolis, Minn.: University of Minnesota Press.

Straus, M. A., & Hotaling, G. T. (Eds.) (1980). *The social causes of husband–wife violence.* Minneapolis, Minn.: University of Minnesota Press.

Strauss, A. (1969/1958). *Mirrors and masks.* San Francisco: Sociology Press.

Strauss, A. (1947). Personality needs and marital choice. *Social Forces, 23,* 332–335.

Strauss, A. (1977). Sociological theories of personality. In R. J. Corsini (Ed.), *Current personality theories.* Itasca, Ill.: Peacock.

Strauss, A. (1978). *Negotiations.* San Francisco: Jossey-Bass.

Strauss, A. A., & Kephart, N. C. (1955). *Psychopathology and education of the brain injured child, 11.* New York: Grnne & Stratton.

Strauss, A. A., & Lehtinen, L. W. (1947). *Psychopathology and education of the brain injured child.* New York: Grune & Stratton.

Strauss, J. S., Bartko, J. J., & Carpenter, W. T. (1973). The use of clustering techniques for the classification of psychiatric patients. *British Journal of Psychiatry, 122,* 531–540.

Stravynski, A., Lesage, A., Marcouiller, M., & Elie, R. (1989). A test of the therapeutic mechanism in social skills training with avoidant personality disorder. *Journal of Nervous and Mental Disease, 177,* 739–744.

Strawbridge, W. J., & Wallhagen, M. I. (1991). Impact of family conflict on adult child caregivers. *The Gerontologist, 31,* 770–777.

Strean, H. S. (Ed.). (1970). *New approaches in child guidance.* Metuchen, N.J.: Scarecrow Press.

Streissguth, A. P. (1986). The behavioral teratology of alcohol: Performance, behavioral, and intellectual deficits in prenatally exposed children. In J. R. West (Ed.), *Alcohol and brain development* (pp. 3–44). New York: Oxford University Press.

Streissguth, A. P., Aase, J. M., Clarren, S. K., Randels, S. P., LaDue, R. A., & Smith, D. F. (1991). Fetal alcohol syndrome in adolescents and adults. *Journal of the American Medical Association, 265,* 1961–1967.

Streissguth, A. P., Clarren, S. K., & Jones, K. L. (1985). Natural history of fetal alcohol syndrome: A 10-year follow-up of eleven children. *Lancet, 2,* 85–91.

Streissguth, A. P., & LaDue, R. A. (1987). Fetal alcohol: teratogenic causes of developmental disabilities. In S. R. Schroeder (Ed.), *Toxic substances and mental retardation* (pp. 1–32). Washington, DC: American Association on Mental Deficiency.

Streissguth, A. P., Landesman-Dwyer, S., Martin, J. C., & Smith, D. W. (1980). Teratogenic effects of alcohol in humans and laboratory animals. *Science, 209,* 353–361.

Streissguth, A. P., Sampson, P. D., Barr, H. M., Clarren, S. K., & Martin, D. C. (1986). Studying alcohol teratogenesis from the perspective of the fetal alcohol syndrome: Methodological and statistical issues. *Annals of the New York Academy of Sciences, 477,* 63–86.

Stricker, E. (1990). Neurobiology of food and water intake. In *Handbook of Behavioral Neurobiology* (Vol. 10). New York: Plenum.

Stricker, G., & Cummings, N. A. (1992). The professional school movement. In D. K. Freedheim (Ed.), *History of psychotherapy: A century of change.* Washington, DC: American Psychological Association.

Stricker, L. J., & Ross, J. (1962). A description and evaluation of the Myers-Briggs type indicator. *Research Bulletin 62–6.* Princeton, N.J.: Educational Testing Service.

Strickland, B. R. (1965). The prediction of social action from a dimension of internal-external control. *Journal of Social Psychology, 66,* 353–358.

Strickland, B. R. (1977). Internal versus external control of reinforcement. In T. Blass (Ed.), *Personality variables in social behavior.* Hillsdale, N.J.: Erlbaum.

Strickland, B. R. (1978). Internal–external expectancies and health-related behaviors. *Journal of Consulting and Clinical Psychology, 46,* 1192–1211.

Strickland, B. R., & Jenkins, O. (1964). Simple motor performance under positive and negative approval motivations. *Perceptual and Motor Skills, 19,* 599–605.

Strickland, L. H. (1958). Surveillance and trust. *Journal of Personality, 26,* 200–215.

Stringer, P., & Bannister, D. (Eds.) (1979). *Constructs of sociality and individuality.* New York: Academic Press.

Stripling, T., & Ames, S. J. (1975). *Intermediate care facilities for the mentally retarded.* Washington, D.C.: U.S. Government Printing Office.

Strodtbeck, F. L., James, R. M., & Hawkins, C. (1957). Social status on jury deliberations. *American Sociological Review, 22,* 713–719.

Strodtbeck, F. L., & Mann, R. (1956). Sex role differentiation on jury deliberations. *Sociometry, 19,* 3–11.

Strom, R. D., & Bernard, H. W. (1982). *Educational psychology.* Monterey, Calif: Brooks/Cole.

Strong, E. K. (1925). *The psychology of selling and advertising.* New York: McGraw-Hill.

Strong, E. K. (1927). Differentiation of CPAs from other occupational groups. *Journal (Educational Psychology, 18,* 227–238.

Strong, E. K. (1931). *Change of interests with age, based on examination of more than two thousand men between the ages (twenty and sixty representing eight occupations.* Stanford, Calif.: Stanford University Press.

Strong, E. K. (1934). *Manual for Vocational Interest Blank.* Stanford, Calif.: Stanford University Press.

Strong, E. K. (1938). *Psychological aspects of business.* New York: McGraw-Hill.

Strong, E. K. (1943). *Vocational interests of men and women.* Stanford, Calif.: Stanford University Press.

Strong, E. K. (1955). *Vocational interests 18 years after college.* Minneapolis, Minn.: University of Minnesota Press.

Strong, S. R. (1968). Counseling: An interpersonal influence process. *Journal of Counseling Psychology, 15,* 215–224.

Strong, S. R., & Claiborn, C. D. (1982). *Change through interaction.* New York: Wiley.

Strongman, K. T., & Russel, P. N. (1986). Salience of emotion in recall. *Bulletin of the Psychonomic Society, 24,* 25–27.

Strosahl, K. D., & Linehan, M. M. (1986). Basic issues in behavioral assessment. In A. R. Ciminero, K. S. Calhoun, & H. E. Adams (Eds.), *Handbook of behavioral assessment* (2nd ed., pp. 12–46). New York: Wiley.

Strother, C. R. (Ed.). (1956). *Psychology and mental health.* Washington, D.C.: American Psychological Association.

Strub, R., & Black, F. (1981). *Organic brain syndromes.* Philadelphia: Davis.

Strube, M. J., & Garcia, J. E. (1981). A metatheoretical analysis of Fiedler's contingency model of leadership effectiveness. *Psychological Bulletin, 90,* 307–321.

Strumpfer, D. J. W. (1970). Fear and affiliation during a disaster. *Journal of Social Psychology, 82,* 263–268.

Strupp, H., & Bergin, A. E. (1969). Some empirical and conceptual bases for coordinated research in psychotherapy. *International Journal of Psychiatry, 7,* 20.

Strupp, H. H. (1960). *Psychotherapists in action: Explorations of the therapist's contribution to the treatment process.* New York: Grune & Stratton.

Strupp, H. H. (1973). *Psychotherapy: Clinical research, and theoretical issues.* New York: Aronson.

Strupp, H. H. (1975). On failing one's patient. *Psychotherapy: Theory, Research and Practice, 12,* 39–41.

Strupp, H. H. (1978/1971). Psychotherapy research and practice: An overview. In S. Garfield & A. Bergin (Eds.), *Handbook of psychotherapy and behavior change: An empirical analysis.* New York: Wiley.

Strupp, H. H., & Binder, J. L. (1984). *Psychotherapy in a new key: A guide to time-limited dynamic psychotherapy.* New York: Basic Books.

Strupp, H. H, Fox, R. E, & Lessler, K. (1969). *Patients view their psychotherapy.* Baltimore, Md.: Johns Hopkins Press.

Strupp, H. H., & Hadley, S. W. (1977). A tripartite model of mental health and therapeutic outcomes. *American Psychologist, 32,* 187–196.

Strupp, H. H., & Hadley, S. W. (1979). Specific versus non-specific factors in psychotherapy: A controlled study of outcome. *Archives of General Psychiatry, 36,* 1125–1136.

Strupp, H. H., Hadley, S. W., & Gomes-Schwartz, B. (1977). *Psychotherapy for better or worse: An analysis of the problem of negative effects.* New York: Aronson.

Strupp, H. H., & Luborsky, L. (Eds.). (1962). *Research in psychotherapy,* Vol. 2, Washington, D.C.: American Psychological Association.

Stuart, C. E. (1946). An interest inventory relation to ESP scores. *Journal of Parapsychology, 10,* 154–161.

Stuart, C. E., Humphrey, B. M., Smith, B. M, & McMahan, E. (1947). Personality measurements and ESP tests with cards and drawings. *Journal of Parapsychology, 11,* 118–146.

Stuart, R. B. (1971). Behavioral contracting within the families of delinquents. *Journal of Behavior, Therapy and Experimental Psychiatry, 2,* 1–11.

Stuart, R. B. (1967). Behavioral control of overeating. *Behavior Research and Therapy, 5,* 357–365.

Stuart, R. B. (1980). *Helping couples change.* New York: Guilford Press.

Stuart, R. B. (1976). An operant interpersonal program for couples. In D. Olson (Ed.), *Treating relationships,* Lake Mills, Iowa: Graphic.

Stuart, R. B. (1972). Situational versus self-control. In R. D. Rubin, H. Fensterheim, J. D. Henderson, & L. P. Ullmann (Eds.), *Advances in behavior therapy,* New York: Academic Press.

Student. (1908). The probable error of the mean. *Biometrika, 6,* 1–25.

Stumpf, C. (1983). *Tonpsychologie* (2 vols.). Leipzig: Hirzel.

Stunkard, A. (1979). Behavioral medicine and beyond: The example of obesity. In O. F. Pomerleau &J. P. Brady (Eds.), *Behavioral medicine.* Baltimore, Md.: Williams & Wilkins.

Stunkard, A. J, & Koch, C. (1964). The interpretation of gastric motility: Apparent bias in the report of hunger by obese persons. *Archives of General Psychology, 11,* 74–82.

Stunkard, A. J., & Mahoney, M. J. (1976). Behavioral treatment of eating disorders. In H. Leitenberg (Ed.), *The handbook of behavior modification and behavior therapy.* Englewood Cliffs, N.J.: Prentice-Hall.

Stunkurd, A. J, & McLaren-Hume, M. (1959). The results of treatment for obesity. *Archives of Internal Medicine, 103,* 79–85.

Sturdivant, S. (1980). *Therapy with women: A feminist philosophy of treatment.* New York: Springer.

Stutsman, R. (1931/1948). *Guide for administering the Merrill-Palmer scale of mental tests.* New York: Harcourt Brace Jovanovich.

Suarez, A. (1980). Connaissance et action, l'enjeu d' une position épistémologique contemporaine. *Revue Suisse de Psychologie, 39,* 177–199.

Suarez, S. D, & Gallup, G. G., Jr. (1981). Self-recognition in chimpanzees and orangutans, but not gorillas. *Journal of Human Evolution, 10,* 175–188.

Sub, J. M. (1972). A two-stage model for the appreciation of jokes and cartoons. In J. H. Goldstein & P. McGhee (Eds.), *The psychology of humor.* New York: Academic Press.

Subotnik, L. (1972). Spontaneous remission: Fact or artifact? *Psychological Bulletin, 77,* 32–48.

Suda, M., Hayaishi, O., & Nakagawa, H. (Eds.). (1979). *Biological rhythms and their central mechanism.* Amsterdam: Elsevier North Holland.

Sue, D. W. (1981). *Counseling the culturally different: Theory and practice.* New York: Wiley.

Sue, D. W., Bernier, J. E., Durran, A., Feinberg, L., Pedersen, P. B., Smith, E. J., & Vasquez-Nuttall, E. (1982). Position paper: Cross cultural counseling competencies. *The Counseling psychologist, 10*(2), 45–52.

Sue, D. W., & Sue, D. (1973). Understanding Asian Americans: The neglected minority. *Personnel and Guidance Journal, 51,* 386–389.

Sue, S., & Moore, T. (1982). *The pluralistic society: A community health perspective.* New York: Human Sciences Press.

Sue, S., Sue, D. W., & Sue, D. (1975). Asian Americans as a minority group. *American Psychologist, 31,* 905–910.

Sue, W. S., & Sue, D. (1990). *Counseling the culturally different: theory and practice* (2nd ed.). New York: Wiley.

Suedfeld, P., Tetlock, P. E., & Ramirez, C. (1977). War, peace and integrative complexity. *Journal of Conflict Resolution, 21,* 427–441.

Suellwold, F. (1980). Wissenschaftssprache und Originalität. *Psychologische Beiträge, 22,* 372–376.

Sugarman, S. (1981). The cognitive basis of classification in very young children: An analysis of object ordering trends. *Child Development, 52,* 1172–1178.

Suggs, D, & Sales, B. D. (1976). Using communication cues to evaluate prospective jurors during voir dire. *Arizona Law Review, 20,* 602–642.

Suinn, R., & Richardson, F. (1971). Anxiety management training: A nonspecific behavior therapy program for anxiety control. *Behavior Therapy, 2,* 498–510.

Suinn, R. M. (1976). Visual motor behavior rehearsal for adaptive behavior. In J. Krumboltz & C. Thoreson (Eds.), *Counseling methods.* New York: Holt.

Suinn, R. M., & Richardson, F. (1971). Anxiety management training: A nonspecific behavior therapy program for anxiety control. *Behavior Therapy, 2,* 498–510.

Suinn, R. M., & Weigel, R. G. (1975). *The innovative psychological therapies: Critical and creative contributions.* New York: Harper & Row.

Suits, D. B. (1979). Economic background for gambling policy. *Journal of Social Issues, 35,* 43–61.

Suleiman, S. R., & Crosman, I. (1980). *The reader in the text: Essays on audience and interpretation.* Princeton, N. J.: Princeton University Press.

Sullivan, C., Grant, M. Q., & Grant, J. D. (1957). The development of interpersonal maturity: Applications to delinquency. *Psychiatry, 20,* 373–385.

Sullivan, C. A., Francis, G. L., Bain, M. W., & Hartz, J. (1991). Munchausen syndrome by proxy: 1990 A portent for problems? *Clinical Pediatrics, 30,* 112–116.

Sullivan, H. S. (1938). Psychiatry: Introduction to the study of interpersonal relations. *Psychiatry, 1,* 121–134.

Sullivan, H. S. (1953/1940). *Conceptions of modern psychiatry.* New York: Norton.

Sullivan, H. S. (1954). *The psychiatric interview.* New York: Norton.

Sullivan, H. S. (1962). *Schizophrenia as a human process.* New York: Norton.

Sullivan, H. S. (1964). *The fusion of psychiatry and social science.* New York: Norton.

Sullivan, H. S. (1968/1953). *The interpersonal theory of psychiatry.* New York: Norton.

Sullivan, H. S. (1972). *Personal psychopathology: Early formulations.* New York: Norton.

Sullivan, H. S. (1973/1956). *Clinical studies in psychiatry.* New York: Norton.

Sullivan, H. S. (1980). *Concepts of personality development and psychiatric illness.* New York: Brunner-Mazel.

Sullivan, L. L. (1979). *Sullivan's guide to learning centers in higher education.* Portsmouth, N. H.: Entelek Ward-Widden House.

Sulloway, F. R. (1972). The role of cognitive flexibility in science. Unpublished paper, Harvard University.

Sully, J. (1884). *Outlines of psychology with special reference to the theory of education.* New York: Appleton.

Sulser, F. (1978). Functional aspects of the norepinephrine receptor coupled adenylate cyclase system in the limbic forebrain and its modification by drugs which precipitate or alleviate depression: Molecular approaches to an understanding of affective disorders. *Pharmakopsychiatrie Neuropsychopharmako, 11,* 43–52.

Sulzer-Azaroff, B., & Mayer, G. R. (1977). *Applying behavior-analysis procedures with children.* New York: Holt, Rinehart & Winston.

Summers, D. A., Taliaferro, D. J., & Fletcher, D. J. (1969). Subjective vs. objective description of judgment policy. *Psychonomic Science, 18,* 249–250.

Summers, G. F. (Ed.). (1970). *Attitude measurement.* Chicago: Rand-McNally.

Summit, R. (1989). Comments. In *Ritual child abuse: A professional overview* [Videotape]. Uria, CA: Cavalcade Productions.

Summitt, R. L. (Ed.). (1990). *Comprehensive pediatrics.* St. Louis: Mosby.

Sumner, W. G. (1940/1906). *Folkways* (3rd ed.) New York: Ginn.

Sumner, W. G., Keller, A. G., & Davie, M. R. (1927). *The science of society.* New Haven, Conn: Yale University Press.

Sundberg, N. D. (1966). A method for studying sensitivity to implied meanings. *Gawein, 15,* 1–8.

Sundberg, N. D. (1977). *Assessment of persons.* Englewood Cliffs, N.J.: Prentice-Hall.

Sundberg, N. D. (1980). Cross-cultural counseling and psychotherapy: A research overview. In A. J. Marsella & P. Pedersen (Eds.), *Cross-cultural counseling and psychotherapy.* Elmsford, N.Y.: Pergamon Press.

Sundberg, N. D. (1981). Historical and traditional approaches to cognitive assessment. In T. V. Merluzzi, C. R. Glass, & M. Genest (Eds.), *Cognitive assessment.* New York: Guilford Press.

Sundberg, N. D., Latkin, C. A., Farmer, R. F., & Saoud, J. (1991). Boredom in young adults: Gender and cultural comparisons. *Journal of Cross-Cultural Psychology, 22,* 209–223.

Sundberg, N. D., Snowden, L. R., & Reynolds, W. M. (1978). Toward assessment of personal competence and incompetence in life situations. *Annual Review of Psychology, 29,* 179–221.

Sundberg, N. D., & Thurber, C. E. (1980). World trends and future prospects for the development of human resources. *International Journal of Interculture Relations, 4,* 245–284.

Sundberg, N. D., Tyler, L. E., & Rohila, P. K. (1970). Values of Indian and American adolescents. *Journal of Personality and Social Psychology, 16,* 374–397.

Sundberg, N. D., Tyler, L. E., & Taplin, J. R. (1973). *Clinical psychology: Expanding horizons.* New York: Appleton-Century-Crofts.

Sundland, D. M. (1977). Theoretical orientations of psychotherapy. In A. S. Gurman & A. M. Razin (Eds.), *Effective psychotherapy, a handbook of research.* Oxford: Pergamon Press.

Suomi, S. J., Mineka, S., & Harlow, H. F. (1983). Social separation in monkeys as viewed by several motivational perspectives. In E. Satinoff & P. Teitelbaum (Eds.), *Handbook of behavioral neurobiology: Vol. 6. Motivation* (pp. 543–584). New York: Plenum.

Supe, M., Cotzin, M., & Dallenbach, K. (1944). Facial vision. The perception of obstacles by the blind. *American Journal of Psychology, 57,* 133–183.

Super, C. M. (1972). Cognitive changes in Zambian children during the late preschool years. Human Development Research Unit, Report no 22, University of Zambia.

Super, C. M., & Harkness, S. (1982). The infant's niche in rural Kenya and metropolitan America. In L. L. Adler (Ed.), *Issues in cross-cultural research.* New York: Academic Press.

Super, D. E. (1942). *Dynamics of vocational adjustment.* New York: Harper.

Super, D. E. (1949). Appraising *vocational fitness.* New York: Harper.

Super, D. E. (1951). Vocational adjustment: Implementing a self-concept. *Occupations, 30,* 88–92.

Super, D. E. (1953). A theory of vocational development. *American Psychologist, 8,* 185–190.

Super, D. E. (1957). *Psychology of careers.* New York: Harper.

Super, D. E. (1963). Vocational development in adolescence and early adulthood: Tasks and behaviors. In D. E. Super, R. Starishevsky, N. Matlin, & J. P. Jordaan (Eds.), *Career development: Self-concept theory.* New York: College Entrance Examination Board.

Super, D. E. (1969). Vocational development theory: Persons, positions, processes. *Counseling Psychologist, 1,* 2–9.

Super, D. E. (1976). *Career education and the meanings of work.* Washington, D.C.: U.S. Government Printing Office.

Super, D. E. (1980). A life-span, life-space approach to career development. *Journal of Vocational Behavior, 16,* 282–298.

Super, D. E. (1980). Transition: From vocational guidance to counseling psychology. *Journal of Counseling Psychology, 1955, 2,* 3–9. Also in J. M. Whiteley (Ed.), *The history of counseling psychology.* Monterey, Calif.: Brooks/Cole.

Super, D. E. (1981a). A developmental theory: Implementing a self-concept. In D. H. Montross & C. J. Shinkman *Career development in the 1980s.* Springfield, Ill.: Thomas.

Super, D. E. (1981b). Approaches to occupational choice and career development. In A. G. Watts, D. E. Super, & J. M. Kidd (Eds.), *Career development in Britain.* Cambridge, England: Hobsons Press.

Super, D. E. (1983). The history and development of vocational psychology: A personal perspective. In S. H. Osipow & W. B. Walsh (Eds.), *The handbook of vocational psychology.* Hillsdale, N.J.: Erlbaum.

Super, D. E. (Ed.). (1974). *Measuring vocational maturity for counseling and evaluation.* Washington, D.C.: National Vocational Guidance Association.

Super, D. E., & Crites, J. O. (1962). *Appraising vocational fitness* (rev. ed.). New York: Harper.

Super, D. E., & Hall, D. T. (1978). Career development: Exploration and planning. *Annual Review of Psychology, 29,* 333–372.

Super, D. E., & Hall, D. T. (1978). Career development: Exploration and planning. In M. R. Rosenzweig & L. W. Porter (Eds.), *Annual Review of Psychology* (Vol. 29). Palo Alto, CA: Annual Review.

Super, D. E., & Overstreet, P. L. (1960). *The vocational maturity of ninth-grade boys.* New York: Teachers College Press.

Super, D. E., Starishevsky, R., Matlin, N., & Jordaan, J. P. (1963). *Career development: Self-concept theory.* New York: College Entrance Examination Board.

Super, D. E., Thompeon, A. S., Lindeman, R. H., Jordaan, J. P., & Myers, R. A. (1981). *The career development inventory.* Palo Alto, Calif.: Consulting Psychologists Press.

Suppe, F. (1972). Theories, their formulations, and the operational imperative. *Synthese, 25,* 129–165.

Suppe, F. (1977). The search for philosophical understanding of scientific theories. In F. Suppe (Ed.), *The structure of scientific theories* (2nd ed.). Urbana, Ill.: University of Illinois Press.

Suppe, F. (Ed.). (1974). *The structure of scientific theories.* Urbana, Ill.: University of Illinois Press.

Suppes, P., & Groen, G. J. (1967). Some counting models for first-grade performance data on simple addition facts. In J. M. Scandura (Ed.), *Research in mathematics education.* Washington, D.C.: National Council of Teachers of Mathematics.

Suppes, P., & Zinnes, J. L. (1963). Basic measurement theory. In R. D. Luce, R. R. Bush, & E. Galanter (Eds.), *Handbook of mathematical psychology,* Vol. 1. New York: Wiley.

Surgeon General. (1979). *Healthy people.* Washington, D.C., U.S. Government Printing Office.

Sussman, M. (1953). Parental participation in mate selection and its effect upon family continuity. *Social Forces, 31,* 76–81.

Suter, J. (1922). *Intelligenz und Begabungsprüfungen.* Zürich: Rascher.

Suter, J. (1942). *Psychologie, Grund und Aufbau.* Bern: Huber.

Sutherland, G. R. (1977). Fragile sites on human chromosomes: demonstration of their dependence on the type of tissue culture medium. *Science, 197,* 265–266.

Sutherland, G. R., & Hecht, F. (1985). *Fragile sites on human chromosomes.* New York: Oxford University Press.

Sutherland, N. S., & Mackintosh, N. J. (1971). *Mechanisms of animal discrimination learning.* New York: Academic Press.

Sutherland, R. W., & Rudy, J. W. (1989). Configural association theory: The role of the hippocampal formation in learning, memory and amnesia. *Psychobiology, 17,* 129–144.

Sutich, A. J. (1969). Some considerations regarding transpersonal psychology. *Journal of Transpersonal Psychology, 1,* 11–20.

Sutor, B., & Hablitz, J. (1989). Long-term potentiation in frontal cortex: Role of NMDA-modulated polysynaptic excitatory pathways. *Neuroscience Letters, 97,* 111–117.

Sutton, R. S., & Barto, A. G. (1981). Toward a modern theory of adaptive networks: Expectation and prediction. Psychological Review, 88, 135–171.

Sutton, R. S., & Barto, A. G. (1990). Time-derivative models of Pavlovian reinforcement. In M. Gabriel & J. W. Moore (Eds.), *Learning and computational neuroscience* (pp. 497–537). Cambridge: MIT Press.

Sutton-Smith, B. (1980). Children's play: Some sources of play theorizing. In K. H. Rubin (Ed.), *New directions for child development—children's play.* San Francisco: Jossey-Bass.

Sutton-Smith, B., & Rosenberg, B. G. (1960). Manifest anxiety and games preferences in children. *Child Development, 31,* 307–311.

Sutton-Smith, B., & Rosenberg, B. G. (1968). Sibling consensus on power tactics. *Journal of Genetic Psychology, 112,* 63–72.

Suzuki, D. (1973/1959). *Zen and Japanese culture.* Princeton, N.J.: Princeton University Press.

Suzuki, D. T. (1962). *The essentials of Zen Buddhism* B. Phillips (Ed.). New York: Dutton.

Suzuki, D. T., Fromm, E., & De Martino, R. (1963/1960) *Zen Buddhism and psychoanalysis.* New York: Grove Press.

Suzuki, T., & Suzuki, R. (1977). A follow-up of neurotics treated by Morita therapy. Presented at Sixth World Congress of Psychiatry, Honolulu.

Svartdal, F., & Iversen, T. (1989). Consistency in synesthetic experience to vowels and consonants: Five case studies. *Scandinavian Journal of Psychology, 30,* 220–227.

Svenson, O. (1979). Process descriptions of decision making. *Organizational Behavior and Human Performance, 23,* 86–112.

Svensson, L. (1977). On qualitative differences in learning. III—Study skill and learning. *British Journal of Educational Psychology, 47,* 233–243.

Swados, E. (1979). *Runaways.* New York: Bantam Books.

Swan, G. E. (1979). On the structure of eclecticism: Cluster analysis of eclectic behavior therapists. *Professional Psychology, 10,* 732–734.

Swan, G. E., & MacDonald, M. L. (1978). Behavior therapy in practice: A national survey of behavior therapists. *Behavior Therapy, 9,* 799–807.

Swanson, D. W., Bohnert, P. J., & Smith, J. A. (1970). *The paranoid.* Boston: Little, Brown.

Swanson, J. M., Cantwell, D., Lerner, M., McBurnett, K., & Hanna, G. (1991). Effects of stimulant medication on learning in children with ADHD. *Journal of Learning Disabilities, 24,* 219–230.

Sward, K. (1980). Self-actualization and women: Rank and Freud contrasted. *Journal of Humanistic Psychology, 20,* 5–26.

Swartz, P. (1978). Marcel Proust and the problem of time and space. *Psychological Reports, 34,* 291–297.

Swartz, R., & Gottman, J. M. (1976). Toward a task analysis of assertive behavior. *Journal of Consulting and Clinical Psychology, 44*, 910–920.

Sweet, W. H., Obrador, S., & Martin-Rodriguez, J. G. (Eds.). (1977). *Neurosurgical treatment in psychiatry, pain, and epilepsy.* Baltimore, Md.: University Park Press.

Swenson, C. H. (1968). Empirical evaluations of human figure drawings: 1957–1966. *Psychological Bulletin, 70*(1), 20–44.

Swerts, A., & d'Ydewalle, G. (1982). Motivational variables in knowledge acquisition: Test expectancies. In R. Glaser & J. Lompscher (Eds.), *Cognitive and motivational aspects of instruction.* Amsterdam, New York: North Holland.

Swets, J., Tanner, W. P., & Birdsall, T. G. (1961). Decision processes in perception. *Psychological Review, 68*, 301–340.

Swiercinsky, D. P. (Ed.). (1985). *Testing adults.* Kansas City: Test Corporation of America.

Swisher, J. P. (1979). Prevention issues. In R. J. Dupont, A. Goldstein, J. O'Donnell, & B. Brown (Eds.), *Handbook on drug abuse.* Rockville, Md.: National Institute on Drug Abuse.

Swoboda, J. S., Elwork, A., Sales, B. D., & Levine, D. (1980). Knowledge of and compliance with privileged communication and child-abuse-reporting laws. *Professional Psychology, 11*, 714—721.

Sydenham, T. (1695). *Compleat method of curing almost all diseases* (7th ed.). London: Printed for Hugh Newman at the Grasshopper in the Poultry.

Sykes, G. M., & Matza, D. (1957). Techniques of neutralization: A theory of delinquency. *American Sociological Review, 22*, 664–670.

Syme, S. L., & Berkman, L. F. (1976). Social class, susceptibility and sickness. *American Journal of Epidemiology, 104*, 1–8.

Symonds, P. M. (1931). *Diagnosing personality and conduct.* New York: Century.

Symons, D. (1979). *The evolution of human sexuality.* New York: Oxford University Press.

Synodinos, N. E. (1988). Subliminal stimulation: What does the public think about it? *Current Issues and Research in Advertising, 11*, 157–187.

Syrotuik, J. M. (1978). The relationship between birth order and parole outcome. *Canadian Journal of Criminology* (Ottawa), *20*(4), 456–458.

Szasz, T. (1974). *Ceremonial chemistry.* Garden City, N.Y.: Doubleday.

Szasz, T. S. (1960). The myth of mental illness. *American Psychologist, 15*, 113–118.

Szasz, T. S. (1963). *Law, liberty, and psychiatry.* New York: Macmillan.

Szasz, T. S. (1966). The psychiatric classification of behavior: A strategy of personal constraint. In L. D. Eron (Ed.), *The classification of behavior disorders.* Chicago: Aldine.

Szasz, T. S. (1970). *Ideology and insanity: Essays on the psychiatric dehumanization of man.* Garden City, N.Y.: Anchor Books.

Szasz, T. S. (1970). *The manufacture of madness.* New York: Harper & Row.

Szasz, T. S. (1974/1961). *The myth of mental illness: Foundations of a theory of personal conduct.* New York: Harper & Row.

Szasz, T. S. (1977). *Psychiatric slavery.* New York: Free Press.

Szasz, T. S. (1978). *The myth of psychotherapy.* Garden City, N.Y.: Doubleday.

Szatmari, R., Boyle, M., & Offord, D. R. (1989). ADDH and conduct disorder: Degree of diagnostic overlap and differences among correlates. *Journal of American Academy of Child and Adolescent Psychiatry, 28*, 865–872.

Szent-Gyoergi, A. (1974). Drive in living matter to perfect itself. *Synthesis*, Spring 12–24.

Szewczuk, W. (1968). Experimental psychology in Poland during the past decade (1957–1966). *Studia Psychologica, 10*, 3–13.

Szewczuk, W. L. (1938). *Les illusions opticogeometriques.* Paris, Cracovie: Alcan.

Szewczuk, W. L. (1951). *Theory of Gestalt and psychology of Gestalt.* Crakow, Poland: Naukowe Towarzystwo Pedagogiczne.

Szewczuk, W. L. (1960). *Experimental investigations on the understanding of sentences.* Crakow, Poland: Jagellonian University.

Szewczuk, W. L. (1972). *Great dispute about psyche.* Warsaw: Państwowe Wydawnictwo Naukowe.

Szewczuk, W. L. (1972). *Psychological foundation of the principles of education.* Warsaw: Państwowe Zaklady Wydawnictw Szkolnych.

Szewczuk, W. L. (1976). *Psychological album.* Warsaw: Państwowe Wydawnictwo Naukowe.

Szewczuk, W. L. (1977). *Psychology of memorization* (5th ed.). Warsaw: Państwowe Wydawnictwo Naukowe.

Szondi, L. (1952/1947). *Experimental diagnostics of drives.* New York: Grune & Stratton.

Szondi, L. (1972). *Lehrbuch der experimentellen Triebdiagnostik*, Vol. I (3rd ed.). Bern: Huber.

Szondi, L., Moser, U., & Webb, M. W. (1959). *The Szondi test: In diagnosis, prognosis, and treatment.* Philadelphia, Pa.: Lippincott.

Szpiler, J., & Epstein, S. (1976). Availability of an avoidance response as related to autonomic arousal. *Journal of Abnormal Psychology, 85*, 73–82.

Taber, M. A., & Vattano, A. J. (1970). Clinical and social orientations in social work: An empirical study *Social Service Review, 44*, 34–43.

Taft, J. (1958). *Otto Rank: A biographical study based on notebooks, letters, collected writings, therapeutic achievements and personal associations.* New York: Julian Press.

Taft, R. (1955). The ability to judge people. *Psychological Bulletin, 52*, 1–28.

Taft, R. (1982). Psychology and its history in Australia. *Australian Psychologist, 17*, 31–39.

Tageson, C. (1982). *Humanistic psychology: A synthesis.* Homewood, Ill.: Dorsey.

Tagiuri, R., & Litwin, G. H. (1967). *Organizational climate.* Boston: Harvard Business School.

Tainter, Z. (1970). Birth order and psychiatric problems in boot camp. *American Journal of Psychiatry, 126*, 1604–1610.

Tajfel, H. (1982). Social psychology of intergroup relations. *Annual Review of Psychology, 33*, 1–39.

Tajfel, H. (1982). Social psychology of intergroup relations. In M. Rosenzweig & L. Porter (Eds.), *Annual review of psychology*, Vol. 33. Palo Alto, Calif.: Annual Reviews.

Tajfel, H. (Ed.). (1978). *Differentiation between social groups: Studies in the social psychology of intergroup relations.* London: Academic Press.

Tajfel, H., & Turner, J. C. (1979). An integrative theory of intergroup conflict. In W. Austin & S. Worchel (Eds.), *The social psychology of intergroup relations.* Monterey, Calif.: Brooks/Cole.

Takahashi, Y. (1989). Suicidal patients: recommendations for treatment. *Suicide Life Threatening Behavior, 19*(3), 305–313.

Takane, Y., Young, F. W., & deLeeuw, J. (1977). Nonmetric individual differences multidimensional scaling: An alternating least squares method with optimal scaling features. *Psychometrika, 42,* 7–67.

Takeuchi, K. (1965). On Naikan. *Psychologia, 8,* 2–8.

Takuma, T. (1967). *Seikaku wa ikani tsukurareruka? (How is personality developed?)* Tokyo: Iwanami Shoten.

Takuma, T. (1971). *Seikaku (Personality).* Tokyo: Kodansha.

Takuma, T. (1974). *Seikaku shinrigaku (Psychology of personality).* Tokyo: Dainihon Tosho.

Takuma, T. (1978). *Seinen no shinri (Psychology of adolescence.)* Tokyo: Baifukan.

Talamo, J. D. C., & Stayner, R. M. (1973). *Some aspects of environmental noise in farm buildings and plant.* Department Note DN/TE/199/1435, National Institute of Agricultural Engineering, England.

Talbot, L. (1972). Ecological consequences of rangeland development in Masailand, East Africa. In M. Farvar & J. Milton (Eds.), *The careless technology: Ecology and international development.* Garden City, N.Y.: Natural History Press.

Talbott, J. H. (1970). *A biographical history of medicine.* New York: Grune & Stratton.

Talland, G. A. (1965). *Deranged memory.* New York: Academic Press.

Talland, G. A., & Waugh, N. C. (Eds.). (1969). *The pathology of memory.* New York: Academic Press.

Tallent, N. (1976). *Psychological report writing.* Englewood Cliffs, N.J.: Prentice-Hall.

Tamerin, J. S., & Neuman, C. P. (1971). Prognostic factors in the evaluation of addicted individuals. *International Pharmacopsychology, 6,* 69–76.

Tan, L. T., Tan, M. Y.-C., & Veith, I. (1974/1973). *Acupuncture therapy: Current Chinese practice.* Philadelphia, Pa.: Temple University Press.

Tanabe, T., Iino, M., & Takagi, S. F. (1975). Discrimination of odors in olfactory bulb, pyriform-amygdaloid areas and orbito-frontal cortex of the monkey. *Journal of Neurophysiology, 38,* 1284—1296.

Tanaka, Y. (1967). The sign behavior. Tokyo: Kyōritsu Shuppan (in Japanese).

Tanaka, Y. (1969). *The behavioral sciences: The science of humans in an age of information.* Tokyo: Chikuma Shobō (in Japanese).

Tanaka; Y. (1971). Psychological factors in international persuasion. *Annals of the American Academy of Political and Social Sciences,* (November), *398,* 50–60.

Tanaka, Y. (1972). Toward multi-level, multi-stage model of modernization: A cross-cultural social psychology approach. *International Journal of Psychology, 8*(3), 205–214.

Tanaka, Y. (1979). Pacific-basin nations: A cross-national value-attitude study. *Peace research in Japan, 1978–79,* 35–60.

Tanaka, Y. (1982). *Sociology of nuclear power.* Tokyo: Denryoku Shinpōsha (in Japanese).

Tanaka, Y. (1982). Subjective culture of the contemporary Japanese. In *Kōza gendai no shinrigaku (Contemporary psychology series),* Vol. 8. Tokyo: Shōgakukan (in Japanese).

Tanaka, Y., & Osgood, C. E. (1965). Cross-culture, cross-concept, and cross-subject generality of affective meaning systems. *Journal of Personality and Social Psychology, 2,* 143.

Tanke, E. T., & Tanke, T. J. (1979). Getting off a slippery slope: Social science in the judicial process. *American Psychologist, 34,* 1130–1138.

Tanner, D., & Tanner, L. N. (1980). *Curriculum development.* New York: Macmillan.

Tanner, J. M. (1978). *Education and physical growth* (2nd. ed.). New York: International Universities Press.

Tanner, J. M. (1978). *Foetus into man.* Cambridge, MA: Harvard University Press.

Tanner, J. M. (1978). *Fetus into man. Physical growth from conception to maturity.* Cambridge, Mass.: Harvard University Press.

Tansey, M. J., Burke, W. F. (1969). *Understanding countertransference: From projective identification to empathy.* Hillsdale, NJ: Analytic.

Tape, G. (1977). Les activités de classifications et les opérations logiques chez l'enfant ivoirien. *Annales Université Abidjan* (série D lettres), *10,* 155–163.

Tape, G. (January 1980). Le profil du professéur de l'enseignement secondaire. *Seminaire des Ecoles Normales Supérieures d'Afrique* (Dakar) 13–20.

Tape, G., & Kihm, J.-M. (1977). La langue des Amulettes en pays M'batto. *Annales Université Abidjan* (série D lettres), *10,* 123–151.

Tape, G., & Sakoto, M. (1980). Mathématique et milieu en Afrique. *Colloque Inter-IREM,* January 30-February 4, 1978, University of Abidjan.

Taplin, J. R. (1976). Implications of general systems theory for assessment and intervention. *Professional Psychology, 11,* 722–727.

Tapp, J. L. (1976). Psychology and the law: An overture. *Annual Review of Psychology, 27,* 359–404.

Tarde, G. (1895). *Les lois de l'imitation.* Paris: Alcan.

Tarde, G. (1898). *Etudes de psychologie sociale.* Paris: Giard & Briere.

Tardiff, K., & Deane, K. (1980). The psychological and physical status of chronic psychiatric inpatients. *Comprehensive Psychiatry, 21,* 91–97.

Tardy, C. H. (1985). Social support measurement. *American Journal of Community Psychology, 13,* 187–202.

Tarnapol, L., & Tarnapol, M. (Eds.). (1976). *Reading disabilities: An international perspective.* Baltimore, Md.: University Park Press.

Tarsy, D., & Baldessarini, R. J. (1977). The pathophysiologic basis of tardive dyskinesia. *Biological Psychiatry, 12,* 431–450.

Tart, C. T. (1972). Scientific foundations for the study of altered states of consciousness. *Journal of Transpersonal Psychology, 3,* 93–124.

Tart, C. T. (1975). *States of consciousness.* New York: Dutton.

Tart, C. T. (1976). The basic nature of altered states of consciousness: A systems approach. *Journal of Transpersonal Psychology, 8,* 45–64.

Tart, C. T., (Ed.). (1969). *Altered states of consciousness: A book of readings.* New York: Wiley.

Tart, C. T. (Ed.) (1975). Transpersonal psychologies. New York: Harper & Row.

Tashkin, D. P., Calvarese, B. M., Simmons, M. S., & Shapiro, B. J. (1980). Respiratory status of seventy-four habitual marijuana smokers. *Chest, 78,* 699–706.

Task Force on Assessment Center Standards. (1979). Standards and ethical considerations for assessment center operations: December 1978. *Journal of Assessment Center Technology, 2*(2), 19–23.

Task Force on Nomenclature and Statistics. (1979). *Diagnostic and statistical manual III.* Washington, D.C.: American Psychiatric Association.

Task Force on the Role of Psychology in the Criminal Justice System. (1978). Report of the Task Force on the Role of Psychology in the Criminal Justice System. *American Psychologist, 33,* 1099–1113.

Tasto, D. L., Colligan, M. J., Skjei, E. W., & Polly, S. J. (1978). *Health consequences of shift work.* Washington, D.C.: U.S. Government Printing Office.

Tatara, M. (1974). Problems of separation and dependence. Psychotherapy in Japan and some technical considerations. *Journal of the American Academy of Psychoanalysis, 2,* 231–242.

Tatlock, P. E., McGuire, C. B., & Mitchell, G. (1991) Psychological perspectives on nuclear deterrence. *Annual Review of Psychology, 42,* 239–276.

Taube, C. A. (1974). *Staffing of mental health facilities U.S.* Washington, D.C.: U.S. Department of Health, Education, and Welfare, Public Health Service; Alcohol, Drug Abuse, and Mental Health Administration, National Institute of Mental Health, Series B (no. 8).

Taulbee, E. S., & Stenmark, D. E. (1968). The Blacky pictures test: A comprehensive annotated and indexed bibliography (1949–1967). *Journal of Projective Techniques and Personality Assessment, 32,* 105–137.

Tausch, R. (1960). *Das psychotherapeutische Gespräch.* Göttingen, West Germany: Hogrefe.

Tausch, R. (1978). Facilitative dimensions in interpersonal relations: Verifying the theoretical assumptions of Carl Rogers. *College Student Journal 12,* 2–11.

Tansky, C., & Parke, E. L. (1976). Job enrichment, need theory, and reinforcement theory. In R. Dubin (Ed.), *Handbook of work, organization and society.* Chicago: Rand-McNally.

Taylor, A., & Budshaw, G. D. (1965). Secondary school selection: The development of an intelligence test for use in Nigeria. *West African Journal of Education, 9,* 6–11.

Taylor, A. (Ed.) (1967). *Educational and occupational selection in West Africa,* London: Oxford University Press.

Taylor, C. B. (1983). DSM-III and behavioral assessment. *Behavioral Assessment, 5,* 5–14.

Taylor, D. A. (1976). Stage analysis of reaction time. *Psychological Bulletin, 83,* 161–191.

Taylor, D. A., & Aftman, I. (1966). Intimacy-scaled stimuli for use in studies of interpersonal relationships. Naval Medical Research Institute Report MF 022,01,03–1002 (9) Bethesda, Md., 1966. (Abridged version: *Psychological Reports, 19,* 729–730.)

Taylor, D. W., Berry, P. C., & Block, C. H. (1958). Does group participation when using brainstorming facilitate or inhibit creative thinking? *Administrative Science Quarterly, 3,* 23–47.

Taylor, E., Gibbs, G., & Morgan, A. R. (1980). The orientations of students studying the Social Science Foundation Course. *Study Methods Group report.* Institute of Educational Technology, Open University.

Taylor, E., Gibbs, G., & Morgan, A. R. (1981(a)). The outcomes of learning from the Social Science Foundation Course: Students' understanding of price control, power and oligopoly. *Study Methods Group report no 9.* Institute of Educational Technology, Open University.

Taylor, E., Morgan, A. R., & Gibbs, G. (1981(b)). Students' understandings of the concept of social class. *Study Methods Group report no 10.* Institute of Educational Technology, Open University.

Taylor, E. A. (1937). *Controlled reading* Chicago: University of Chicago Press.

Taylor, F. V. (1957). Psychology and the design of machines. *American Psychologist 12,* 249–258.

Taylor, F. V. (1963). Human engineering and psychology. In S. Koch (Ed.), *Psychology: A study of a science,* Vol. 5: *The process areas, the person, and some applied fields: Their place in psychology and in science.* New York: McGraw-Hill.

Taylor, F. W. (1903). *Shop management.* New York: Harper.

Taylor, F. W. (1903). Shop management. *Transactions of the American Society of Mechanical Engineers, 24,* 1337–1480.

Taylor, F. W. (1911). *The principles of scientific management.* New York: Harper.

Taylor, H. C., & Russell, J. T. (1930). The relationship of validity coefficients to the practical effectiveness of tests in selection: Discussion and tables. *Journal of Applied Psychology, 22,* 565–578.

Taylor, H. F. (1980). *The IQ game: A methodological inquiry into the heredity environment controversy.* New Brunswick, N.J.: Rutgers University Press.

Taylor, J. A. (1953). A personality scale of manifest anxiety. *Journal of Abnormal and Social Psychology, 48,* 285–290.

Taylor, J. A. (1956). Drive theory and manifest anxiety. *Psychological Bulletin, 53,* 303–320.

Taylor, J. A. (1975). Early recollections as a projective technique: A review of some recent validation studies, *Journal of Individual Psychology, 30,* 213–218.

Taylor, K. (1982). "Standing up" for this APS. *Bulletin of the Australian Psychological Society,* 8–10.

Taylor, K. F., & Taft, R. (1977). Psychology in the Australian Zeitgeist. In M. Nixon & R. Taft (Eds.), *Psychology in Australia: Achievement and prospects.* Rushcutters Bay, Australia: Pergamon Press (Australia).

Taylor, M. (1987). *The possibility of cooperation.* Cambridge, UK: University of Cambridge Press.

Taylor, P. D., & Turner, R. K. (1975). A clinical trial of continuous, intermittent and overlearning "bell-and-pad" treatments for nocturnal enuresis. *Behavior Research and Therapy, 13,* 281–293.

Taylor, R. (1950). Comments on a mechanistic conception of purposefulness. *Philosophy of Science, 17,* 310–317.

Taylor, R. (1950). Purposeful and non-purposeful behavior: A rejoinder. *Philosophy of Science, 17,* 327–332.

Taylor, S. J., & Bogdan, R. (1984). *Introduction to qualitative research methods. The search for meanings.* New York: Wiley.

Tecce, J. J. (1971). Contingent negative variation and individual differences: A new approach in brain research. *Archives of General Psychiatry, 24,* 1–16.

Teilhard de Chardin, P. (1965/1959). *The phenomenon of man.* New York: Harper & Row.

Tefford, C., & Sawrey, J. (1981). *The exceptional individual* (4th ed.). Englewood Cliffs, N.J.: Prentice-Hall.

Templer, D. I. (1975). The efficacy of electrosleep therapy. *Canadian Psychiatric Association Journal, 20*(8), 607–613.

Tennant-Clark, C., Fritz, J., & Beauvais, F. (1989). Occult participation: Its impact on adolescent development. *Adolescence, 24,* (96), 757–772.

Tennen, H., & Eller, S. J. (1977). Attributional components of learned helplessness and facilitation. *Journal of Personality and Social Psychology, 35.* 265–271.

Tennen, H., Eron, J. B., & Rohrbaugh, M. (1991). Paradox in context. In G. E. Weeks (Ed.), *Promoting change through paradoxical therapy* (pp. 187–215). New York: Brunner/Mazel.

Tennis, G. H., & Dabbs, J. M. (1975). Sex, setting, and personal space: First grade through college. *Sociometry, 38,* 385–394.

Tennov, D. (1979). *Love and limerence.* New York: Stein & Day.

Tennyson, C. L, Tennyson, R. D, & Rothen, W. (1980). Content structure and instructional control strategies as design variables in concept acquisition. *Journal of Educational Psychology, 72*, 499–505.

Tennyson, R. D. (1973). Effect of negative instances in concept acquisition using a verbal learning task. *Journal of Educational Psychology, 64*, 247–260.

Tennyson, R. D. (1980). Instructional control strategies and content structure as design variables in concept acquisition using computer-based instruction. *Journal of Educational Psychology, 72*, 525–532.

Tennyson, R. D., & Buttrey, T. (1980). Advisement and management strategies as design variables in computer-assisted instruction. *Educational Communication and Technology Journal, 28*, 169–176.

Tennyson, R. D., Woolley, F. R., & Merrill, M. D. (1972). Exemplar and nonexemplar variables which produce correct concept classification behavior and specified classification errors. *Journal of Educational Psychology, 63*, 144—152.

Tenopyr, M. L. (1981). The realities of employment testing. *American Psychologist, 36*, 1120–1127.

Tenopyr, M. L, & Oeltjen, P. D. (1982). Personnel selection and classification. In M. R. Rosenzweig & L. W. Porter (Eds.), *Annual Review of Psychology, 33*, 581–618.

Teplov, B. R. (1947). *Fifty years of Soviet psychological sciences.* Moscow: Pravda.

Teplov, B. R. (1961). *Problems of individual differences.* Moscow: Academy of Pedagogy Nauk, RSFSR.

Terasaki, M., & Imada, S. (1988). Sensation seeking and food preferences. *Personality and Individual Differences, 9*, 87–93.

Terkel, J., & Rosenblatt, J. S. (1972). Humoral factors underlying maternal behavior at parturition: Cross transfusion between freely moving rats. *Journal of Comparative and Physiological Psychology, 80*, 365–371.

Terkel, S. (1974/1972). *Working.* New York: Pantheon.

Terman, L. A., & Merrill, M. A. (1960). *Stanford-Binet Intelligence Scale: Manual for the third revision form L-M.* Boston: Houghton Mifflin/Riverside.

Terman, L. & Miles, C. (1936). *Sex and personality.* New York: McGraw-Hill.

Terman, L. M. (1904). A preliminary study of the psychology and pedagogy of leadership. *Pedagogical Seminary 11*, 413–451.

Terman, L. M. (1916). *The measurement of intelligence.* Boston: Houghton Mifflin.

Terman, L. M. (1919). *The intelligence of school children.* Boston: Houghton Mifflin.

Terman, L. M. (1931). Psychology and the law. *Los Angeles Bar Association Bulletin, 6*, 142–153.

Terman, L. M. (1935). Psychology and the law. *Commercial Law Journal 40*, 639–646.

Terman, L. M. (1950). The intelligence quotient of Francis Galton in childhood. *American Journal of Psychology, 14*, 210–214.

Terman, L. M. (1961). Mental and physical traits of a thousand gifted children. In J. J. Jenkins & D. G. Paterson (Eds.), *Studies in individual differences.* New York: Appleton-Century-Crofts.

Terman, L. M., & Merrill, M. A. (1937). *Measuring intelligence.* Boston: Houghton Mifflin.

Terman, L. M. & Merrill, M. A. (1960). *Stanford-Binet intelligence scale: Manual for the third revision, form LM.* Boston: Houghton Mifflin.

Terman, L. M., & Oden, M. H. (1959). *The gifted group at mid-life: Thirty-five years' follow-up of the superior child.* Stanford, Calif.: Stanford University Press.

Terner, J., & Pew, W. L. (1978). *The courage to be imperfect: The life and work of Rudolf Dreikurs.* New York: Hawthorn.

Terrace, H. S. (1963). Discrimination learning with and without "errors." *Journal of the Experimental Analysis of Behavior, 6*, 1–27.

Terrace, H. S. (1968). Discrimination learning, the peak shift, and behavioral contrast. *Journal of the Experimental Analysis of Behavior, 11*, 727–741.

Terrace, H. S. (1979). *Nim: A chimpanzee who learned sign language.* New York: Knopf.

Terry, L. C., & Martin, J. B. (1978). Hypothalamic hormones: Subcellular distribution and mechanisms of release. In R. George & R. Okun (Eds.), *Annual review of pharmacology and toxicology*, Vol. 18. Palo Alto, Calif.: Annual Reviews.

Terry, M. (1987). *The ultimate evil: An investigation of America's most dangerous satanic cult.* Garden City, NY: Doubleday.

Tetlock, P. E., & Kim, J. I. (1987). Accountability and judgment processes in a personality prediction task. *Journal of Personality and Social Psychology, 52*, 700–709.

Teuber, H.-L. (1975). Effects of focal brain injury on human behavior. In D. B. Tower (Ed.), *The nervous system.* Vol. 2: *The clinical neurosciences.* New York: Raven Press.

Teuber, H. L., & Rudel, R. G. (1962). Behavior after cerebral lesions in children and adults. *Developmental Medicine and Child Neurology, 4*, 3–20.

Teuber, M. L. (1974). Sources of ambiguity in the prints of Maurits C. Escher. *Scientific American, 231*(1), 90–104.

Thalen, M. A., Fry, R. A., Dollinger, S. J., & Paul, S. C. (1976). Use of videotaped models to improve the interpersonal adjustment of adolescents. *Journal of Consulting and Clinical Psychology, 44*, 492.

Tharp, R. G., & Gallimore, R. (1976). What a coach can teach a teacher. *Psychology Today, 9*, 75–78.

Thayer, P. W. (1977). Somethings old, somethings new. *Personnel Psychology, 30*, 513–524.

Thayer, R. E. (1978). Toward a psychological theory of multidimensional activation (arousal). *Motivation and Emotion, 2*, 1–34.

Thelen, M. H., Fry, R. A., Fehrenbach, P. A., & Frautschi, N. M. (1979). Therapeutic videotape and film modeling: A review. *Psychological Bulletin, 86*, 701–720.

Thibaut, J. W., & Kelley, H. H. (1959). *The social psychology of groups.* New York: Wiley.

Thibaut, J. W., & Riecken, H. W. (1955). Some determinants and consequences of the perception of social causality. *Journal of Personality, 24*, 113–133.

Thie, J. (1979). Touch for health. Marina del Rey, Calif.: DeVorss.

Thiessen, D. D. (1973). Footholds for survival. *American Scientist, 61*, 346–351.

Thiessen, D. D. (1976). *The evolution and chemistry of aggression.* Springfield, Ill.: Thomas.

Thigpen, C., & Cleckley, H. (1974/1957). *The three faces of Eve.* Los Angeles: Regent House.

Thoits, P. A. (1982). Conceptual, methodological, annd theoretical problems in studying social support as a buffer against life stress. *Journal of Health and Social Behavior, 23*, 145–159.

Thomas, A. (1979). Learned helplessness and expectancy factors: Implications for research in learning disabilities. *Review of Educational Research, 49*, 208–221.

Thomas, A., & Chess, S. (1977). *Temperament and development.* New York: Brunner/Mazel.

Thomas, A., & Chess, S. (1980). *The dynamics of psychological development*. New York: Brunner/Mazel.

Thomas, A., Chess, S., & Birch, H. (1968). *Temperament and behavior disorders in children*. New York: New York University Press.

Thomas, A., Chess, S., & Birch, H. G. (1970). The origin of personality. *Scientific American, 223*, 102–109.

Thomas, C. B. (1981). Stamina: The thread of human life. *Journal of Chronic Diseases, 34*, 41–44.

Thomas, D. A. (1979). Retention of conditioned inhibition in a bar-press suppression paradigm. *Learning and Motivation, 10*, 161–177.

Thomas, D. A., Nielsen, L. J., Kuypers, D. S., & Becker, W. C. (1968). Social reinforcement and remedial instruction in the elimination of a classroom behavior problem. *The Journal of Special Education, 2*, 291–305.

Thomas, E., & DeWald, L. (1977). Experimental neurosis: Neurpsychological analysis. In J. D. Maser & M. E. P. Seligman (Eds.), *Psychopathology: Experimental models*. San Francisco: Freeman.

Thomas, E. J. (1968). Selected sociobehavioral techniques and principles: An approach to interpersonal helping. *Social Work, 13*, 12–26.

Thomas, E. L., & Robinson, H. A. (1972). *Improving reading in every class: A sourcebook for teachers*. Boston: Allyn & Bacon.

Thomas, H. (1951). *Persönlichkeit. Eine dynamische Interpretation*. Bonn: Bouvier.

Thomas, K. (1973/1971). *Religion and the decline of magic*. Harmondsworth, England: Penguin Books.

Thomas, R. M., & Thomas, S. M., (1965). *Individual differences in the classroom*. New York: McKay.

Thomas, W. I., & Znaniecki, F. (1927.1). *The Polish peasant in Europe and America*. New York: Knopf.

Thomas Aquinas, St. (1265). *Summa Theologica*.

Thomas Aquinas, St. (1951). *Commentary*. In Aristotle's *De anima*, in the version of William of Moerbeke. New Haven, Conn.: Yale University Press.

Thomason, J., & Arkell, C. (1980). Educating the severely/profoundly handicapped in the public schools: A side by side approach. *Exceptional Children, 47*, 114–122.

Thome, F. C., & Pishkin, V. (1973). The existential study. *Journal of Clinical Psychology, 29*, 387–410.

Thompson, A. S., & Super, D. E. (Eds.) (1964). *The professional preparation of counseling psychologists. Report of the 1964 Greyston Conference*. New York: Bureau of Publications. Teachers College, Columbia University.

Thompson, C. (1950). *Psychoanalysis: Evolution and development*. New York: Hermitage.

Thompson, D. A., & Campbell, R. G. (1977). Hunger in humans induced by 2deoxy-*d*-glucose: Glucoprivic control of taste perference and food intake. *Science, 198*, 1065–1068.

Thompson, D. S., & Wilson, T. R. (1966). Discontinuance of cigarette smoking: Natural and with therapy. A ten week and ten month survey of 298 people in a five day stop smoking program. *Journal of the American Medical Association, 196*(12), 1048–1052.

Thompson, H. L. (1971). Malnutrition as a possible contributing factor to learning disabilities. *Journal of Learning Disabilities, 4*, 312–314.

Thompson, J. S., & Thompson, M. W. (1985). *Genetics in medicine*, (4th ed.). Philadelphia: Saunders.

Thompson, M. M. (1975). Congregate housing for older adults: Assisted residential living combining shelter and services. *Report for Committee on Aging, U.S. Senate*. Washington, D.C.: U.S. Government Printing Office.

Thompson, R., & McConnell, J. V. (1955). Classical conditioning in the planarian, *Dugesia dorotocephala*. *Journal of Comparative and Physiological Psychology, 48*, 65–68.

Thompson, R. F. (1967). *Foundations of physiological psychology*. New York: Harper & Row.

Thompson, R. F. (1990). Neural mechanisms of classical conditioning in mamals. *Philosophical Transactions of the Royal Society of London. Ser. B: Biological Sciences, 329*(12153), 161–170.

Thompson, R. F., Berger T. W., Cegavske, C. F., Patterson, M. M., Roemer, R. A., Teyler, T. J., & Young, R. A. (1976). The search for the engram. *American Psychologist, 31*, 209–227.

Thompson, R. F., McCormick, D. A., Lavond, D. G., Clark, G. A., Kettner, R. E., & Mauk, M. D. (1982). The engram found?—Initial localization of the memory trace for a basic form of associative learning. *Progress in Psychobiology and Physiological Psychology*.

Thompson, R. F., & Spencer, W. A. (1966). Habituation: A model phenomenon for the study of neuronal substrates of behavior. *Psychological Review, 173*, 16–43.

Thompson, R. J., Gil, K. M., Abrams, M. R., & Phillips, G. (1993). Stress, coping, and psychological adjustment of adults with sickle cell disease. *Journal of Consulting and Clinical Psychology*.

Thompson, R. J., Gil, K. M., Burbach, D. A., Keith, B. R., & Kinney, T. R. (1991). *Psychological adjustment of children with sickle cell disease: The role of maternal adjustment and child cognitive processes and pain coping strategies*. Unpublished manuscript.

Thompson, R. J., & O'Quinn, A. N. (1979). *Developmental disabilities*. New York: Oxford University Press.

Thompson, R. K. R., Foltin, R. W., Boylan, R. J., Sweet, A., Graves, C. A., & Lowitz, C. E. (1981). Tonic immobility in Japanese quail can reduce the probability of sustained attack by cats. *Animal Learning and Behavior, 9*, 145–149.

Thompson, S. K. (1975). Gender labels and early sex role development. *Child Development, 46*, 339–347.

Thompson, W. R. (1957). Influence of prenatal maternal anxiety on emotionality in young rats. *Science, 125*, 698–699.

Thompson, W. R., & Crusec, J. (1970). Studies in early experience. In P. H. Mussen (Ed.), *Carmichael's manual of child psychology*, Vol. 1 (3rd ed.). New York: Wiley.

Thomson, G. H. (1924). *Instinct, intelligence and character*. London: Allen & Unwin.

Thomson, G. H. (1929). *A modern philosophy of education*. London: Allen & Unwin.

Thomson, G. H. (1937). *The factorial analysis of human ability*. London: University of London Press.

Thoresen, C. E. (1980). Control and human ethology. In J. M. Whiteley & B. R. Fretz (Eds.), *The present and future of counseling psychology*. Monterey, Calif.: Brooks/Cole.

Thoreson, C. E., Coates, T. J., Kirmil-Gray, K., & Rosekind, M. (1981). Behavioral self-management in treating sleep maintenance insomnia. *Journal of Behavioral Medicine, 4*(1), 41–52.

Thoresen, C. E., Telch, M. A., & Eagleston, J. R. (1981). Approaches to altering the type A behavior pattern. *Psychosomatics, 22*, 472–482.

Thoresen, C. T., & Mahoney, M. J. (1974). *Behavioral self-management*. New York: Holt, Rinehart & Winston.

Thornberry, T., & Jacoby, J. (1979). *The criminally insane: A community followup of mentally ill offenders*. Chicago: University of Chicago Press.

Thorndike, E. L. (1898). Animal intelligence: An experimental study of the associative processes in animals. *Psychological Review Monograph Supplement, 2*(8), 1–109.

Thorndike, E. L. (1899). The instinctive reactions of young chicks. *Psychological Review, 6,* 282–291.

Thorndike, E. L. (1910). The contribution of psychology to education. *Journal of Educational Psychology, 1,* 5–12.

Thorndike, E. L. (1911/1898). *Animal intelligence.* New York: Macmillan.

Thorndike, E. L. (1913). *The psychology of learning.* New York: Teachers College, Columbia University.

Thorndike, E. L. (1913–1914/1903). *Educational psychology* (3 vols.). New York: Teachers College, Columbia University.

Thorndike, E. L. (1920). A constant error on psychological ratings. *Journal of Applied Psychology, 4,* 25–29.

Thorndike, E. L. (1924). Mental discipline in high school studies. *Journal of Educational Psychology, 15,* 1–22, 83–98.

Thorndike, E. L. (1931). *Human learning.* New York: Appleton.

Thorndike, E. L. (1932/1899). *The fundamentals of learning.* New York: Teachers College.

Thorndike, E. L. (1933). An experimental study of rewards. *Teachers College Contributions to Education,* No. 580.

Thorndike, E. L. (1949). *Selected writings from a connectionist's psychology.* New York: Appleton-Century-Crofts.

Thorndike, E. L, Bregman, E. O., Felton, J. W., & Woodward, E. (1957). Adult learning. In S. L. Pressey & R. G. Kuhlen (Eds.), *Psychological development through the life span.* New York: Harper.

Thorndike, E. L., & Lorge, I. (1944). *The teacher's word book of 30,000 words.* New York: Bureau of Publications, Teachers College, Columbia University.

Thorndike, E. L., & Woodworth, R. S. (1901). The influence of improvement in one mental function upon the efficiency of other functions. *Psychological Review, 8,* 247–261, 384–395, 553–564.

Thorndike, L. (1964). *A history of magic and experimental science,* Vols. 7, 8, New York: Columbia University Press.

Thorndike, R. L. (1949). *Personnel selection: Test and measurement techniques.* New York: Wiley.

Thorndike, R. L. (1963). *The concepts of over- and underachievement.* New York: Bureau of Publications, Teachers College, Columbia University.

Thorndike, R. L. (1982). *Applied psychometrics.* Boston: Houghton Mifflin.

Thorndike, R. L., & Hagen, E. P. (1959). *Ten thousand careers.* New York: Wiley.

Thorndike, R. L., & Hagen, E. P. (1977). *Measurement and evaluation in psychology and education* (4th ed.). New York: Wiley.

Thorndike, R. L., & Hagen, E. P. (1978). *Manual for the cognitive abilities test.* Iowa City, Iowa: Riverside Press.

Thorndyke, P. W. (1976). The role of inferences in discourse comprehension. *Journal of Verbal Learning and Verbal Behavior, 15,* 437–446.

Thorndyke, P. W. (1977). Cognitive structures in comprehension and memory of narrative discourse. Cognitive Psychology, 9, 77–110.

Thorne, B., & Henley, N. (Eds.) (1975). *Language and sex: Difference and dominance.* Rowley, Mass.: Newbury House.

Thorne, B. M., Donohoe, T., Lin, K-N, Lyon, S., Medeiros, D., & Weaver, M. L. (1986). Aluminum ingestion and behavior in the Long-Evans rat. *Physiology and Behavior, 36,* 63–67.

Thorne, F. C. (1950). *Principles of personality counseling.* Brandon, Vt.: Journal of Clinical Psychology Press.

Thorne, F. C. (1961). *Personality: A clinical eclectic viewpoint.* Brandon, Vt.: Journal of Clinical Psychology Press.

Thorne, F. C. (1965). Tutorial counseling: How to be psychologically healthy. *Clinical Psychology Monograph, 20,* 1–157.

Thorne, F. C. (1968). Psychological case handling: An eclectic system of counseling and psychotherapy. Brandon, Vt.: Clinical Psychology.

Thorne, F. C. (1975). The life style analysis. *Journal of Clinical Psychology, 31,* 236–240.

Thornquist, M. H., Zuckerman, M., & Exline, R. V. (1991). Loving, liking, looking and sensation seeking in unmarried couples. *Personality and Individual Differences, 12,* 1283–1292.

Thornton, E. E. (1970). *Professional education for ministry: A history of clinical pastoral education.* Nashville, Tenn.: Abingdon.

Thorpe, W. H. (1962). *Biology, psychology, and belief.* Cambridge, England: Cambridge University Press.

Thouless, R. H. (1935). Dr. Rhine's recent experiments on telepathy and clairvoyance and a reconsideration of J. E. Coover's conclusions on telepathy. *Proceedings of the Society for Psychical Research, 43,* 24–37.

Thouless, R. H. (1971). *An introduction to the psychology of religion* (3rd ed.). Cambridge, England: Cambridge University Press.

Thurman, C. W. Baron, A., Jr., & Klein, R. L. (1979). Self-help tapes in a telephone counseling service: A three-year analysis. *Journal of College Student Personnel 20,* 546–550.

Thurman, S. K., & Fiorelli, J. S. (1979). Perspectives on normalization. *Journal of Special Education, 13,* 339–346.

Thurstone, L. L. (1919). The learning curve equation. *Psychological Monographs, 26,* no. 3.

Thurstone L. L. (1926). The mental age concept. *Psychological Review, 33,* 268–278.

Thurstone, L. L. (1927). A law of comparative judgment. *Psychological Review, 38,* 273–286.

Thurstone, L. L. (1928). The absolute zero in intelligence measurement. *Psychological Review, 35,* 175–197.

Thurstone L. L. (1931). A multiple factor study of vocational interests. *Personnel Journal, 10,* 198–205.

Thurstone, L. L. (1931). The measurement of social attitudes. *Journal of Abnormal and Social Psychology, 26,* 249–269.

Thurstone, L. L. (1935). *The vectors of mind: Multiple-factor analysis for the isolation of primary traits.* Chicago: University of Chicago Press.

Thurstone, L. L. (1938). *Primary mental abilities.* Psychometric Monographs, no. 1. Chicago: University of Chicago Press.

Thurstone L. L. (1947). *Multiple-factor analysis: A development and expansion of the vectors of the mind.* Chicago: University of Chicago Press.

Thurstone, L. L. (1952). Autobiography. In C. Murchison (Ed.), *A history of psychology in autobiography,* Vol. 4. Worcester, Mass.: Clark University Press.

Thurstone, L. L. (1955). *Differential growth of mental abilities.* Chapel Hill, N.C.: Psychometric Laboratory.

Thurstone, L. L. (1959). *The measurement of values.* Chicago: University of Chicago Press.

Thurstone L. L., & Ackerson, L. (1929). The mental growth curve for the Binet tests, *Journal of Educational Psychology, 20,* 569–583.

Thurstone, L. L., & Chave, E. J. (1929). *The measurement of attitude.* Chicago: University of Chicago Press.

Thurstone, L. L., & Jones, L. V. (1957). The rational origin for measuring subjective values. *Journal of the American Statistical Association, 52,* 458–471.

Thurstone, L. L. & Thurstone, T. G. (1941). Factorial studies of intelligence. *Psychometric Monographs*, no. 2.

Thurstone, L. L., & Thurstone, T. G. (1962). *SRA primary mental abilities, 1962 edition*. Chicago: Science Research Associates.

Thurstone, T. G., & Strandskor, H. H. (1953). *A psychological study of twins. 1. Distributions of absolute twin differences for identical and fraternal twins*. Chapel Hill, N.C.: Psychometric Laboratory, Report no. 4.

Tiebout, N. M. (1943). The misnamed lazy student. *Educational Record, 24*, 113–129.

Tiedeman, D. V. and O'Hara, R. P. (1963). *Career development: Choice and adjustment*. New York: College Entrance Examination Board.

Tiedemann, D. (1787). *Beobachtungen über die Entwicklung der Seelenfähigkeiten bei Kindern*. Altenburg: Bonde.

Tiefer, L. (1991). A brief history of the Association for Women in Psychology: 1969–1991. *Psychology of Women quarterly, 15*, 635–649.

Tiffin, J. (1942). *Industrial psychology*. Englewood Cliffs, N.J.: Prentice-Hall.

Tiffin, J., & Roger, H. B. (1941). The selection and training of inspectors. *Personnel 1*, 14–31.

Tiffin, J. & Winick, D. M. (1954). A comparison of two methods of measuring the attention-drawing power of magazine advertisements. *Journal of Applied Psychology, 38*, 272–275.

Tighe, T. J., & Tighe, L. S. (1968). Differentiation theory and concept-shift behavior. *Psychological Bulletin, 70*, 756–761.

Tille, A. (Ed.) (1897). *The works of Friedrich Nietzche*. New York: Macmillan.

Tillich, P. (1952). *The courage to be*. New Haven, Conn.: Yale University Press.

Tillich, P. (1957). *The dynamics of faith*. New York: Harper.

Tillich, P. (1975/1951–1963). *Systematic theology*. Chicago: University of Chicago Press.

Tillyard, E. M. W. *The Elizabethan world picture*. New York: Vintage Press, n.d.

Timberlake, W. (1983). The finctional organization of appatitive behavior: Behavior systems & learning. In M. D. Zeiler & P. Harzem (Eds.), *Awareness in the analysis of behavior: Vol. 3. Biological factors in learning*. Chichester, UK: Wiley.

Timberlake, W., & Allison, J. (1974). Response deprivation: An empirical approach to instrumental performance. *Psychological Review, 81*, 146–164.

Time-CNN Poll. (1992, April 27). *USA Today*, p. 1B.

Tims, F. M., & Ludford, J. P. (Eds.). (1984). *Drug abuse treatment evaluation: Strategies, progress, and prospects*. (DHHS Publication No. 84-1329). Washington, DC: U.S. Government Printing Office.

Tinbergen, N. (1951). *The study of instinct*. New York: Oxford University Press.

Tinbergen, N. (1951). *The study of instinct*. Oxford, UK: Oxford University Press.

Tinbergen, N. (1952). The curious behavior of the stickleback. *Scientific American, 182*, 22–26.

Tinbergen, N. (1953). *Social behaviour of animals*. New York: Halsted.

Tinbergen, N. (1955). Some aspects of ethology, the biological study of animal behavior. *Advances in Science, 12*, 17–27.

Tinbergen, N. (1971/1960). *The herring gull's world. A study of the social behavior of birds*. San Francisco: Harper & Row.

Tinbergen, N. (1972). *Childhood autism: An ethological approach*. Berlin: Parry.

Tinbergen, N. (1973). *The animal in its world: Explorations of an ethologist*. Cambridge, Mass.: Harvard University Press, Vol. 1, 1972; Vol. 2.

Tinbergen, N. (1982). About *autistic children and how they might be cured*. London: Allen & Unwin.

Tinkelpaugh, D. L. (1928). An experimental study of representative factors in monkeys. *Journal of Comparative Psychology, 8*, 197–236.

Tinklepaugh, D. L. (1932). Multiple delayed reaction with chimpanzees and monkeys. *Journal of Comparative Psychology, 13*, 207–243.

Tinker, M. A. (1963). *Legibility of print*. Ames, Iowa: Iowa State University Press.

Tinklepaugh, O. L. (1928). An experimental study of representative factors in monkeys. *Journal of Comparative Psychology, 8*, 197–236.

Tinsley, H. E. A., & Tinsley, D. J. (1981). An analysis of leisure counseling models. In E. T. Dowd (Ed.), Leisure counseling. *The Counseling Psychologist, 9*, 45–54.

Titchener, E. B. (1897). *An outline of psychology*. New York: Macmillan.

Titchener, E. B. (1898). The postulates of a structural psychology. *Psychological Review, 7*, 449–465.

Titchener, E. B. (1899). Structural and functional psychology. *Psychological Review, 8*, 290–299.

Titchener, E. B. (1901). *Experimental psychology: I. Qualitative experiments; Part II, Instructor's manual*. New York: Macmillan.

Titchener, E. B. (1903). A Plea for Summaries and Indexes. *American Journal of Psychology, 14*, 84–87.

Titchener, E. B. (1908). *Lectures on the experimental psychology of feeling and attention*. New York: Macmillan.

Titchener, E. B. (1909). *Lectures on the experimental psychology of the thought process*. New York: Macmillan.

Titchener, E. B. (1923). *An outline of psychology*. New York: Macmillan.

Titchener, E. B. (1923/1916/1910). *A textbook of psychology*. New York: Macmillan.

Tittle, C. (1969). *Crime rates and legal sanctions. Social Problems, 16*, 409–423.

Tittle, C. K. (1978). *Sex bias in testing: A review with policy recommendations*. Princeton, N.J.: ERIC Clearinghouse on Tests, Measurement, and Evaluation.

Tittle, C. K. (1981). *Careers and family: Sex roles and adolescent life plans*. Beverly Hills, Calif.: Sage Publications.

Tittle, C. K., & Zytowski, D. G. (Eds.) (1978). *Sex-fair interest measurement: Research and implications*. Washington, D.C.: National Institute of Education.

Tizard, B. (1974). *Early childhood education—A review discussion of current research in Britain*. Windsor, England: NFER.

Toates, R. (1986). *Motivational systems*. Cambridge, UK: Cambridge University Press.

Tobias, J. V. (1970). *Foundations of modern auditory theory*, Vol. 1. New York: Academic Press.

Toch, H. (1969). *Violent men*. Chicago: Aldine.

Todd, T. C. (1984). Strategic approaches to marital stuckness. *Journal of Marital and Family Therapy, 10*, 373–379.

Toder, N. L., & Marcia, J. E. (1973). Ego identity status and response to conformity pressure in college women. *Journal of Personality and Social Psychology, 26*, 287–294.

Toge, T., Hirai, T., Takiyama, W., & Hatton, T. (1981). Effects of surgical stress on natural killer cell activity, proliferative response of spleen cells and cytostatic activity of lung macrophages in rats. *Gann, 72,* 790–794.

Toi, M., & Batson, D. (1981). More evidence that empathy is a source of altruistic motivation. Unpublished manuscript, University of Kansas.

Tolan, R. H. (1987). Implications of age on onset for delinquency risk. *Journal of Abnormal Child Psychology, 15,* 47–65.

Tollison, C. D., & Adams, H. E. (1979). *Sexual disorders.* New York: Gardner Press.

Tolman, E. (1958). *Behavior and psychological man.* Berkeley: University of California Press.

Tolman, E. C. (1920). Instinct and purpose. *Psychological Review, 27,* 217–233.

Tolman E. C. (1925). Purpose and cognition: The determiners of animal learning. *Psychological Review, 32,* 285–297.

Tolman, E. C. (1926). A behavioristic theory of ideas. *Psychological Review, 33,* 352–396.

Tolman, E. C. (1927). A behaviorist's definition of consciousness. *Psychological Review, 34,* 433–439.

Tolman E. C. (1928). Habit formation and higher mental processes in animals. *Psychological Bulletin, 25,* 24–53.

Tolman, E. C. (1928). Purposive behavior. *Psychological Review, 35,* 524–530.

Tolman, E. C. (1932). *Purposive behavior in animals and men.* New York: Appleton-Century Crofts.

Tolman E. C. (1932). *Purposive behavior.* New York: Appleton-Century.

Tolman E. C. (1938). The determiners of behavior at a choice point. *Psychological Review, 45,* 1–41.

Tolman E. C. (1941). Psychological man. *Journal of Social Psychology, 13,* 205–218.

Tolman E. C. (1942). *Drives toward war.* New York: Appleton-Century-Crofts.

Tolman, E. C. (1948). Cognitive maps in rats and men. *Psychological Review, 55,* 189–208.

Tolman; E. C. (1949). There is more than one kind of learning. *Psychological Review, 56,* 144–155.

Tolman, E. C. (1949/1932). *Purposive behavior in animals and men.* Berkeley, Calif.: University of California Press.

Tolman E. C. (1959). Principles of purposive behaviorism. In S. Koch (Ed.), *Psychology: A study of a science,* Vol. 2. New York: McGraw-Hill.

Tolman E. C. (1959). Principles of purposive behavior. In S. Koch (Ed.), *Psychology: The study of a science* (pp. 92–157). New York: McGraw-Hill.

Tolman, E. C., & Honzik, C. H. (1930). Introduction and removal of reward and maze performance in the rat. *University of California Publications in Psychology, 4,* 257–275.

Tolor, A., & Siegel, M. C. (1989). Boredom proneness and political activism. *Psychological Reports, 65,* 235–240.

Tolsdorf, C. C. (1976). Social networks, support, and coping: An exploratory study. *Family Process, 15,* 407–417.

Tolson, E. R. (1981). Conclusions: Toward a metamodel for eclectic family practice. In E. R. Tolson & W. J. Reid (Eds.), *Models of family treatment.* New York: Columbia University Press.

Toman, W. (1976). *Family constellation* (3rd ed.). New York: Springer.

Toman, W., & Gray, B. (1961). Family constellations of "normal" and "disturbed" marriages: An empirical study. *Journal of Individual Psychology, 17,* 93–95.

Tomeh, A. K. (1971). Birth order and familial influences in the Middle East. *Journal of Comparative Family Studies, 2,* 88–106.

Tomikawa, S. A., & Dodd, D. H. (1980). Early word meanings: Perceptually or functionally based. *Child Development, 51,* 1103–1109.

Tomkins, S. (1963). Left and right: A basic dimension of ideology and personality. In R. White (Ed.), *The study of lives: Essays on personality in honor of Henry A Murray.* New York: Atherton Press.

Tomkins, S. (1981). The rise, fall, and resurrection of the study of personality. *Journal of Mind and Behavior, 2,* 443–452.

Tomkins, S. S. (in press). *Affect, imagery, consciousness,* New York: Springer. Vol. *1. The positive affects,* 1962. Vol. 2. *The negative affects,* 1963. Vol., 3.

Tomlinson, B. E. (1972). Morphological brain changes in non-demental people. In A. M. Van Praag & S. F. Kalverboer (Eds.), *Aging of the central nervous system: Biological and psychological aspects.* Haarlem, Netherlands: De Erven F. Bohn N.V.

Tomlinson, R. W. (1970). The assessment of workload in agricultural tasks. *Journal of the Proceedings of the Institute of Agricultural Engineering, 25,* 18.

Toormer, J. E. (1982). Counseling psychologists in business and industry. *The Counseling Psychologist.*

Torgerson, S. (1983). Genetic factors in anxiety disorders. *Archives of General Psychiatry, 40,* 1085–1089.

Torgerson, W. S. (1958). *Theory and methods of scaling.* New York: Wiley.

Tornatzky, L. G., Fairweather, G. W., & O'Kelly, L. I. (1970). A Ph.D. program aimed at survival. *American Psychologist, 25,* 884–888.

Tornatzky, L. G., Fergus, E. O., Avellar, J. W., & Fairweather, G. W. (1980). Innovation and social process. New York: Pergamon Press.

Torrance, E. P. (1962). *Guiding creative talent.* Englewood Cliffs, N.J.: Prentice-Hall.

Torrance, E. P. (1966). *Torrance tests of creative thinking.* Bensenville, IL: Scholastic Testing Service.

Torrance, E. P. (1970). *Creative learning and teaching.* New York: Dodd, Mead.

Torrance, E. P. (1975). Sociodrama as a creative problem-solving approach to studying the future. *Journal of Creative Behavior, 9,* 182–195.

Torrance, E. P. (1977). Creatively gifted and disadvantaged gifted students. In J. C. Stanley, W. C. George, & C. H. Solano (Eds.), *The gifted and the creative: A fifty-year perspective.* Baltimore, Md.: Johns Hopkins University Press.

Torrance, E. P. (1977). *Discovery and nurturance of giftedness in the culturally different.* Reston, Va.: Council for Exceptional Children.

Torrance, E. P. (1982). Sociodrama: Teaching creative problem solving as a therapeutic technique. In C. R. Reynolds & T. B. Gutkin (Eds.), *The handbook of school psychology.* New York: Wiley.

Torrens, P. (1978). *American health care system: Issues and problems.* St. Louis, Mo.: Mosby.

Torrey, E. F. (1972). *The mind game: Witchdoctors and psychiatrists.* New York: Bantam Books.

Torrey, E. F. (1972). What Western psychotherapists can learn from witchdoctors. *American Journal of Orthopsychiatry, 42,* 69–76.

Torshen, K. P. (1977). *The mastery approach to competency-based education.* New York: Academic Press.

Tortor, D. F. (1983). Safety training: The elimination of avoidance-motivated aggression in dogs. *Journal of Experimental Psychology: General, 112,* 176–214.

Tosi, D., & Hoffman, S. (1972). A factor analysis of the personal orientation inventory. *Journal of Humanistic Psychology, 12,* 86–93.

Touhey, J. (1981). Replication failures in personality and social psychology. Negative findings or mistaken assumptions. *Personality and Social Psychology Bulletin, 7,* 593–595.

Toulmin, S. (1961). *Foresight and understanding: An enquiry into the aims of science.* New York: Harper & Row.

Toulmin, S. (1967). The evolutionary development of natural science. *American Scientist, 55,* 456–471.

Toulmin, S. (1982). The genealogy of "consciousness:" In P. F. Secord (Ed.), *Explaining human behavior: Consciousness, human action and social structure.* Beverly Hills, Calif.: Sage Publications.

Tower, R. B., & Singer, J. L. (1981). The measurement of imagery: How can it be clinically useful? In P. C. Kendall & S. Holland (Eds.), *Cognitive behavioral interventions: Assessment methods.* New York: Academic Press.

Towers, B. (1982). Changing concepts of death: Clinical care. *Death Education, 6,* 125–135.

Townsend, J. T. (1974). Issues and models concerning the processing of a finite number of inputs. In B. H. Kantowitz (Ed.), *Human information processing.* Hillsdale, N.J.: Erlbaum.

Toynbee, A. J. (1967/1946). *A study of history* (2 vol. abridgement). New York, London: Oxford University Press.

Tractman, G. (1981). On such a full sea. *School Psychology Review, 10*(2), 138–181.

Trainer, J. B. (1979). Premarital counseling and examination. *Journal of Marital and Family Therapy, 5*(2), 61–78.

Trapold, M. A. (1970). Are expectancies based upon different positive reinforcing events discriminably different? *Learning and Motivation, 1,* 129–140.

Trapold, M. A., & Overier, J. B. (1972). The second learning process in instrumental learning. In A. A. Black & W. F. Prokasy (Eds.), *Classical conditioning. II. Current research and theory,* New York: Appleton-Century-Crofts.

Traub, R. (Ed.) (1979). Methodological developments. *New Directions for Testing and Measurement, 4* (entire issue).

Traupmann, J., & Hatfield, E. (1981). *Love and its effect on mental and physical health.* In R. Fogel, E. Hatfield, S. Kiesler & E. Shanas (Eds.), *Aging: Stability and change in the family* (pp. 253–274). New York: Academic.

Travers, J., & Ruopp, R. (1978). *National day care study: Preliminary findings and their implications.* Cambridge, Mass.: Abt Associates.

Travis, C. B. (1988). *Women and health psychology: Mental health issues.* Hillsdale, NJ: Erlbaum.

Travis, F. T. (1991). Eyes open and TM EEG patterns after one and after eight years of TM practice. *Psychophysiology, 28*(3a), S58.

Travis, F. T. (1993). The junction point model: A theoretical foundation for understanding awareness during sleeping and dreaming. In J. Gackenbach, H. Hunt, & C. N. Alexander (Eds.), *Higher states of consciousness: Theoretical and experiential perspectives.* New York: Plenum.

Travis, L. E. (1931). *Speech pathology.* New York: Appleton-Century.

Travis, L. E. (1934). Dissociation of the homologous muscle function in stuttering. *Archives of Neurology and Psychiatry, 31,* 127–131.

Traxel, W. (1975). Internationalitat oder Provinzialität? Über die Bedeutung der deutschen Sprache für die deutschsprachige Psychologie. *Psychologische Beiträge, 17,* 584–594.

Traxel, W. (1975). "Publish or perish!"—auf Deutsch oder auf Englisch? *Psychologische Beitraege, 21,* 62–77.

Treegoob, M. & Walker, K. P. (1976). The use of stimulant drugs in the treatment of hyperactivity. *School Psychology Digest, 5,* 5–10.

Treichell, M., Clinch, N., & Cran, M. (1973). The metabolic effects of transcendental meditation. *Physiologist, 16,* 472.

Treiman, D. J. (1977). *Occupational prestige in comparative perspective.* New York: Academic Press.

Treiman, D. J., & Hartmann, H. I. (1981). *Women, work, and wages: Equal pay for jobs of equal value.* Washington, D.C.: National Academy Press.

Treiman, D. J., & Terrell, K. (1975). Sex and the process of status attainment: A comparison of working women and men. *American Sociological Review, 40,* 174–200.

Treisman, A. M. (1960). Contextual cues in selective listening. *Quarterly Journal of Experimental Psychology, 12,* 242–248.

Treisman, A. M. (1969). Strategies and models of selective attention. *Psychological Review, 76,* 242–299.

Treisman, A. M., & Gormican, S. (1988). Feature analysis in early vision: Evidence from search symmetries. *Psychological Review, 95,* 15–48.

Tremaine, L., Schau, C. G., & Busch, J. W. (1982). Children's occupational sextyping. *Sex Roles: A Journal of Research, 8,* 691–710.

Trembly, D. (1964). Age and sex differences in creative thinking. *American Psychologist, 516* (abstract).

Trentini, G. G. (1980). Investigacion e intervencion psicosocial en el "marketing." In L. Ancona (Ed.), *Enciclopedia ternatica de psicologia.* Barcelona, Spain: Herder.

Trentini, G. G., & Binda, W. (1982). La leadership. In E. Scabini (Ed.), *Psicologia sociale.* Turin, Italy: Boringhieri.

Trentini, G. G., & Bolla, M. C. (1982). Research in the field of marketing: a follow-up on its use. *European Research, 10,* 165–170.

Trentini, G. G. (Ed.) (1980). *Manuale del colloquio e dell'intervista.* Milan, Italy: Isedi-Mondadori.

Triandis, H. (1977). *Interpersonal behavior.* Monterey, Calif.: Brooks/Cole.

Triandis, H., & Berry, J. (Eds.) (1980). Methodology, *Handbook of cross-cultural psychology,* Vol. 2. Boston: Allyn & Bacon.

Triandis, H., Brislin, R., & Hui, C. H. (1988). Cross-cultural training across the individualism-collectivism divide. *International Journal of Intercultural Relations, 12,* 269–289.

Triandis, H, Lambert, W., Berry, J., Lonner, W., Heron, A., Brislin, R., & Draguns, J. (1981). *Handbook of cross-cultural psychology* (6 vols.). Boston: Allyn & Bacon, Vols. 1–3, 5–6, 1980; Vol. 4.

Triandis, H. C., & Lambert, W. W. (Eds.) (1980–1981). *Handbook of cross-cultural psychology.* Boston: Allyn & Bacon.

Triandis H. C., & Triandis, L. M. (1960). Race, social class, religion and nationality as determinants of social distance. *Journal of Abnormal and Social Psychology, 61,* 110–118.

Triandis, H. C., & Triandis, L. M. (1962). A cross-cultural study of social distance. *Psychological Monographs, 76,* no. 540.

Triandis, H. C., & Triandis, L. M. (1965). Some studies of social distance. In I. D. Steiner & M. Fishbein, (Eds.), *Current studies in social psychology.* New York: Holt, Rinehart & Winston.

Triandis, H. C., & Vassiliou, V. (1967). Frequency of contact and stereotyping. *Journal of Personality and Social Psychology, 7,* 316–328.

Tiandis, H. C., Vassiliou, V., Vassiliou, G., Tanaka, Y., & Shanmugam, A. V. (1972). *The analysis of subjective culture.* New York: Wiley.

Trickett, E. J. (1984). Toward a distinctive community psychology: An ecological metaphor for the conduct of community research and the nature of training. *American Journal of Community Psychology, 12,* 261–280.

Trickett, E. J., Kelly J. G., & Todd, D. M. (1972). The social environment of the high school: Guidelines for individual change and organizational redevelopment. In S. E. Golann & C. Eisdorfer (Eds.), *Handbook of community mental health.* New York: Appleton-Century-Crofts.

Trieschmann, R. B. (1980). *Spinal cord injuries.* New York: Pergamon Press.

Trifonovitch, G. (1977). On cross-cultural orientation techniques. In R. Brislin (Ed.), *Culture learning: Concepts, applications, and research* (pp. 213–222). Honolulu: University Press of Hawaii.

Trimble, M. D. (1985). Post-traumatic stress disorder: History of a concept. In C. R. Figley (Ed.), *Trauma and its wake: The study and treatment of post-traumatic stress disorder.* New York: Brunner/Mazel.

Triplett, N. (1900). The psychology of conjuring deceptions. *The American Journal of Psychology, 11*(4), 439–510.

Triseliotis, J. (1973). *In search of origins, the experiences of adopted people.* Toronto: Saunders.

Trivers, R. L. (1972). Parental investment and sexual selection. In B. Campbell (Ed.), *Sexual selection and the descent of man, 1871–1971.* Chicago: Aldine.

Trivers, R. L. (1974). Parent-offspring conflict. *American Zoologist, 14,* 249–264.

Troland, L. T. (1929). *The principles of psychophysiology,* Vol. 1. New York: Van Nostrand.

Troland, L. T. *A technique for the experimental study of telepathy and other alleged clairvoyant processes.* Albany, N.Y.: n.d.

Troll, L. E. (1982). *Continuations: Adult development and aging.* Monterey, Calif.: Brooks/Cole.

Trotman, F. K. (1977). Race, IQ, and the middle class. *Journal of Educational Psychology, 69,* 266–273.

Trotter, S., & Thoman, E. (1978). *Social responsiveness of infants, pediatric round table 2.* Johnson & Johnson.

Trow, D. B. (1957). Autonomy and job satisfaction in task oriented groups. *Journal of Abnormal and Social Psychology, 54,* 204–210.

Trow, W. C. (1977). Historical perspective. In D. J. Treffinger, J. K. Davis, & R. E. Ripple (Eds.), *Handbook on teaching educational psychology.* New York: Academic Press.

Troyer, P., Bryant, B., Argyle, M., & Marzillier, J. (1978). *Social skills and mental health.* Pittsburgh, Pa.: University of Pittsburgh Press.

Trstenjak, A. (1956). A critical study of the hypothesis of the affinity of instincts and sympathetic facial expression. *Archivio di Psicologia* (Milan) 17.

Trstenjak, A. (1956). The experience of time and the question of subjective boredom. In *Rivista di psicologia, fasciculo giubilare.* Florence, Italy.

Trstenjak, A. (1974). *Contemporary psychology* (2 vols.) (3rd ed.). Ljubljana, Yugoslavia: Obzorja.

Trstenjak, A. (1976). *Problems of modern psychology.* Ljubljana, Yugoslavia: Slovenska Matica.

Trstenjak, A. (1978). *Man and colors.* Ljubljana, Yugoslavia: Universum.

Trstenjak, A. (1979). *Psychology of work and organization* (2nd ed.). Ljubljana, Yugoslavia: Universum.

Trstenjak, A. (1981). *Psychology of creativity.* Ljubljana, Yugoslavia: Slovenska Matica.

Truax, C. (1961). A scale for the measurement of accurate empathy. *Psychiatric Institute Bulletin 1, 12.*

Truax, C., & Mitchell, K. (1971). Research on certain therapist interpersonal skills in relation to process and outcome. In S. Garfield & A. Bergin (Eds.), *Handbook of psychotherapy and behavior change: An empirical analysis.* New York: Wiley.

Truax, C. B., & Carkhuff, R. R. (1967). *Toward effective counseling and psychotherapy: Training and practice.* Chicago: Aldine.

True, R. M. (1949). Experimental control in hypnotic age regression states. *Science, 110,* 583–584.

True, R. M., & Stephenson, C. W. (1951). Controlled experiments correlating electroencephalogram, pulse, and plantar reflexes with hypnotic age regression and induced emotional states. *Personality, 1,* 252–263.

Trull, T. M., Widiger, T. A., & Frances, A. (1987). Covariation of criteria sets for avoidant, schizoid and dependent personality disorder. *American Journal of Psychiatry, 144,* 767–772.

Trumball, R., & Appley, M. H. (1986). A conceptuel model for the examination of stress dynamics. In M. H. Appley & R. Trumbull (Eds.), *Dynamics of stress: Physiological, psychological and social perspectives* (pp. 1–46). New York: Plenum.

Trumbo, D., Adams, C., Milner, M., & Schipper, L. (1962). Reliability and accuracy in the inspection of hard red winter wheat. *Cereal Science Today, 7,* 62–71.

Trungpa, C. (1973). *Cutting through spiritual materialism.* Berkeley, Calif.: Shambala.

Truzzi, M. (1971). Definition and dimensions of the occult: Towards a sociological perspective. *Journal of Popular Culture, 3,* 635–646.

Truzzi, M. J. B. (1980). Rhine and pseudo-science: Some Zetetic reflections on parapsychology. In K. Ramakrishna Rao (Ed.), *J. B. Rhine: On the frontiers of science.* Jefferson, N.C.: McFarland.

Tryon, G. S. (1980). The measurement and treatment of test anxiety. *Review of Educational Research, 50,* 343–372.

Tryon, R. C. (1940). Genetic differences in maze-learning ability in rats. *39th Yearbook, National Society for the Study of Education,* pt. I, 111–119.

Tryon, R. C., & Bailey, D. E. (1970). *Cluster analysis.* New York: McGraw-Hill.

Tsai, M., Feldman-Summers, S., & Edgar, M. (1979). Childhood molestation: Differential impacts on psychosexual functioning. *Journal of Abnormal Psychology, 88,* 407–417.

Tseng, W. S. (1973). The concept of personality in Confucian thought. *Psychiatry, 36,* 191–202.

Tseng, W. S., & McDermott, J. F., Jr. (1981). *Culture, mind and therapy. An introduction to cultural psychiatry.* New York: Brunner/Mazel.

Tsujioka, B. (1960). *Factors of personality.* Osaka: Kansai University Press.

Tsujioka, B. (1978). *New method of personality testing.* Osaka: Institute for Psychological Testing.

Tsujioka, B., & Yamamoto, Y. (1977). *Parent-child relation scales.* Osaka: Institute for Psychological Testing.

Tsujioka, B., Yatabe, T., & Sonohara, T. (1957). *Y-G personality inventory.* Tokyo: Takei Kiki.

Tsushima, W. T., & Wedding, D. (1979). A comparison of the Halstcad-Reitan psychological battery and computerized tomography in the identification of brain disorder. *Journal of Nervous and Mental Disease, 167,* 704–707.

Tubbs, S. L., & Baird, J. W. (1976). *The open person: Self-disclosure and personal growth.* Columbus, Ohio: Merrill.

Tucker, B., Megenity, D., & Vigil, L. (1975). Anatomy of a campus crisis center. In R. Suinn & R. Weigel (Eds.), *The innovative psychological therapies: Critical and creative contributions.* New York: Harper & Row.

Tucker, J. A., Vuchinich, R. E., & Harris, C. V. (1985). Determinants of substance abuse relapse. In M. Galizio & S. A. Maisto (Eds.), *Determinants of substance abuse* (pp. 383–421). New York: Plenum.

Tucker, L. R. (1960). Intra-individual, and interindividual multidimensionality. In H. Gulliksen & S. J. Messick (Eds.), *Psychological scaling, theory and applications.* New York, London: Wiley.

Tucker, L. R. (1963). Implications of factor analysis of three-way matrices for measurement of change. In C. W. Harris, (Ed.), *Problems in measuring change.* Madison, Wis.: University of Wisconsin Press.

Tucker, L. R. (1964). The extension of factor analysis to three-dimensional matrices. In N. Frederiksen & H. Gulliksen (Eds.), *Contributions to mathematical psychology.* New York: Holt, Rinehart & Winston.

Tucker, L. R. (1965). Experiments in multi-mode factor analysis. In *Proceedings of the 1964 Invitational Conference on Testing Problems.* Princeton, N.J.: Educational Testing Service.

Tucker, L. R. (1966). Some mathematical notes on three-mode factor analysis. *Psychometrika, 31,* 279–311.

Tucker, L. R. (1972). Relations between multidimensional scaling and three-mode factor analysis. *Psychometrika, 37,* 3–27.

Tucker, L. R., & Messick, S. J. (1963). Individual difference model for multidimensional scaling. *Psychometrika, 28,* 333–367.

Tuckman, J., & Reagan, R. A. (1966). Intactness of the home and behavioral problems in children. *Journal of Child Psychology and Psychiatry, 7,* 225–233.

Tuddenham, R. D. (1948). Soldier intelligence in World Wars I and II. *American Psychologist, 3,* 54–56.

Tuke, S. (1964). *Description of The Retreat: An institution near York for insane persons of the Society of Friends.* London: Dawsons of Pall Mall.

Tulku, T. (1977). *Time, space and knowledge.* Emeryville, Calif.: Dharma.

Tulving, E. (1962). Subjective organization in free recall of "unrelated" words. *Psychological Review, 69,* 344–354.

Tulving, E. (1968). Theoretical issues in free recall. In T. R. Dixon & D. L. Horton (Eds.), *Verbal behavior and general behavior theory.* Englewood Cliffs, NJ: Prentice-Hall.

Tulving, E. (1972). Episodic and semantic memory. In E. Tulving & W. Donaldson (Eds.), *Organization of memory.* New York: Academic Press.

Tulving, E. (1982). *Elements of episodic memory.* Oxford: Clarendon Press.

Tulving, E. (1982). Synergistic ecphory in recall and recognition. *Canadian Journal of Psychology, 36,* 130–147.

Tulving, E. (1985). How many memory systems are there? *American Psychologist, 40,* 385–398.

Tulving, E., & Donaldson, W. (1972). *Organization of memory.* New York: Academic Press.

Tulving, E., & Pearlstone, Z. (1966). Availability versus accessibility of information in memory for words. *Journal of Verbal Learning and Verbal Behavior, 5,* 381–391.

Tulving, E., & Thomson, D. M. (1973). Encoding specificity and retrieval processes in episodic memory. *Psychological Review, 80,* 352–373.

Tulving, E., & Watkins, M. J. (1975). Structure of memory traces. *Psychological Review, 82,* 261–275.

Tuma, J. M. (1989). Mental health servces for children: The state of the art. *American Psychologist, 44,* 188–199.

Tuma, J. M. (Ed.). (1987). *Handbook for the practice of pediatric psychology.* New York: Wiley. (Original work published 1982).

Tupes, E., & Shaycoft, M. (1964). *Normative distributions of AQE aptitude indexes for high school age boys.* (Tech. Doc. Rep. PRL-TDR-64-17) Lackland Air Force Base, Texas.

Turing, A. M. (1936). On computable numbers, with an application to the *Entscheidungsproblem. Proceedings of the London Mathematics Society* (Series 2) 42, 230–265.

Turing, A. M. (1950). Computing machinery and intelligence. *Mind, 59,* 433–460.

Turk, D., Meichenbaum, D., & Genest, M. (1983). *Pain and behavior medicine.* New York: Guilford Press.

Turk, D. C., Meichenbaum, D., & Genest, M. (1983). *Pain and behavioral medicine: A cognitive-behavioral perspective.* New York: Guilford.

Turk, D. C., & Salovey, P. *Reasoning, inference, and judgement in clinical psychology.*

Turnbull, C. M. (1961). Some observations regarding the experiences and behavior of Bambuti Pygmies. *American Journal of Psychology, 74,* 304–308.

Turner, A. N., & Lawrence, P. R. (1965). *Industrial jobs and the worker.* Cambridge, Mass.: Harvard University, Graduate School of Business Administration.

Turner, B. (1974). *Truancy.* London: Word Lock Educational.

Turner, J. A., & Clancy, S. (1986). Strategies for coping with chronic low back pain: Relationship to pain and disability, *Pain, 24,* 355–362.

Turner, J. S., & Helms, D. B. (1979). *Life span development.* Philadelphia, Pa.: Saunders.

Turner, M. E., & Pratkanis, A. R. (Eds.). (in press). The social psychology of affirmative action. [Special issue]. *Basic and Applied Social Psychology.*

Turner, M. E., Pratkanis, A. R., & Hardaway, T. J. (1991). Sex differences in reactions to preferential selection: Towards a model of preferential selection as help. *Journal of Social Behavior and Personality, 6,* 797–814.

Turner, R. H. (1956). Role-taking, role standpoint, and reference-group behavior. *American Journal of Sociology, 61,* 316–328.

Turner, R. H. (1962). Roletaking: Process versus conformity. In A. M. Rose (Ed.), *Human behavior and social processes: An interactionist approach.* Boston: Houghton Mifflin.

Turner, R. H. (1978). The role and the person. *American Journal of Sociology, 84,* 1–23.

Turner, R. J. (1981). Experienced social support as a contingency in emotional well-being. *Journal of Health and Social Behavior, 22,* 357–367.

Turner, R. R., & Resse, H. W. (1980). *Life-span development: Intervention.* New York: Academic Press.

Turner, S. (March 29, 1981). Why we shouldn't build the MX. *New York Times.*

Turner, S. M., & Beidel, D. C. (1989). Social phobia: Clinical syndrome, diagnosis, and comorbidity. *Clinical Psychology Review, 9,* 3–18.

Turner, S. M., Beidel, D. C., Borden, J. W., Stanley, M. A., & Jacob, R. G. (1991). Social phobia: Axis I and II correlates. *Journal of Abnormal Psychology, 100,* 102–106.

Turner, S. M., Beidel, D. C., Dancee, C. V., & Keys, D. J. (1986). Psychopathology of social phobia and comparison to avoidant personality disorder. *Journal of Abnormal Personality, 95,* 389–394.

Turner, V. (1969). *The ritual process: Structure and anti-structure.* Chicago: Aldine.

Turró, R. (1912). *Origens del coneixement: La fam.* Barcelona, Spain: Societat Catalana d'Edicions.

Tustin, F. (1972). *Autism and childhood psychosis.* Englewood Cliffs, N.J.: Prentice-Hall.

Tutko, T., & Tosi, U. (1976). *Sports psyching.* Los Angeles: Tarcher.

Tuttle, T. C., Duchler, H. P., & Schneider, B. (1975). Organizational psychology. In B. L. Margolis & W. H. Kroes (Eds.), *The human side of accident prevention.* Springfield, Ill.: Thomas.

Tutundjian, H. M. (1959). *The education of attention of junior school children during teaching process.* Erevan, Armenia: State.

Tutundjian, H. M. (1962). *Fundamental psychological features of junior school children.* Erevan, Armenia: State.

Tutundjian, H. M. (1966). *The psychological conception of Henri Wallon.* Erevan, Armenia: State.

Tutundjian, H. M. (1980). *Problems of child psychology.* Erevan, Armenia: State.

Tversky, A., & Kahneman, D. (1974). Judgments under uncertainty: Heuristics and biases. *Science, 185,* 1124–1131.

Tversky, A., & Kahneman, D. (1982). Judgment under uncertainty: Heuristics and biases. In D. Kahneman, P. Slavic, & A. Tversky, (Eds.), *Judgment under uncertainty: Heuristics and biases* (pp. 3–22). Cambridge, UK: Cambridge University Press.

Twemlow, S. W., Gabbard, G. O., & Coyne, L. (1982). A multivariate method for the classification of preexisting near-death conditions. *Anabiosis: The Journal of Near-Death Studies, 2,* 132–139.

Twentyman, C. T., & Zimering, R. T. (1979). Behavioral training of social skills: A critical review. In M. Hersen, R. M. Eisler, & P. M. Miller (Eds.), *Progress in behavior modification,* Vol. 7. New York: Academic Press.

Tyler, L., Tiedeman, D., & Wrenn, C. G. (1980). The current status of counseling psychology. In J. M. Whitely (Ed.), *The history of counseling psychology.* Monterey, Calif.: Brooks/Cole.

Tyler, L. E. (1959). Toward a workable science of individuality. *American Psychologist, 14,* 75–81.

Tyler, L. E. (1962). Research explorations in the realm of choice. *Journal of Counseling Psychology, 9,* 99–105.

Tyler, L. E. (1964). The antecedents of two varieties of interest pattern. *Genetic Psychology Monographs, 70,* 177–227.

Tyler, L. E. (1965/1947). *The psychology of human differences* (3rd ed.). New York: Appleton-Century-Crofts.

Tyler, L. E. (1969/1961/1953). *The work of the counselor.* New York: Appleton-Century-Crofts; Prentice-Hall.

Tyler, L. E. (1973). Design for a hopeful psychology. *American Psychologist, 28,* 1021–1029.

Tyler, L. E. (1974). *Individual differences: Abilities and motivational directions.* Englewood Cliffs, N.J.: Prentice-Hall.

Tyler, L. E. (1978). *Individuality: Human possibilities and personal choice in the psychosocial development of men and women.* San Francisco: Jossey-Bass.

Tyler, L. E. (1979/1971/1963). *Tests and measurements.* Englewood Cliffs, N.J.: Prentice-Hall. (Third edition with W. B. Walsh.)

Tyler, L. E. (1981). More stately mansions: Psychology extends its boundaries. *Annual Review of Psychology, 32,* 1–20.

Tyler, L. E. (1981/1978). *Individuality.* San Francisco: Jossey-Bass.

Tyler, R. W. (1980). Curriculum issues: Retrospect and prospect. *Illinois School Research and Development, 17,* 1–7.

Tymoczko, T. (1980). Computers, proofs, and mathematicians: A philosophical investigation of the four-color proof. *Mathematics Magazine, 3,* 131–138.

Tymoczko, T. (1979). The four-color problem and its philosophical significance. *Journal of Philosophy, 76,* 57–83.

Tzu, S. (1973). *The art of war* (S. B. Griffith, Trans.). New York: Oxford University Press.

Udry, J. R. (1974). *The social context of marriage* (3rd ed.), Philadelphia, Pa.: Lippincott.

Uehling, B., & Sprinkle, R. (1968). Recall of a serial list as a function of arousal and retention interval. *Journal of Experimental Psychology, 78,* 103–106.

Uexkuell, F. von. (1921/1906). *Umwelt und Innenwelt der Tiere.* Berlin: Springer.

Uhlaner, J. E. (1977, October). *The research psychologist in the Army—1917 to 1977.* ARI Research Report 1155 (rev.). Alexandria, Va.: U.S. Army Research Institute for the Behavioral and Social Sciences.

Uhlenberg, P. (1979). Demographic change and problems of the aged. In M. W. Riley (Ed.), *Aging from birth to death: Interdisciplinary perspectives.* Boulder, Colo.: Westview Press.

Uhr, L. (1973). *Pattern recognition, learning, and thought.* Englewood Cliffs, N.J.: Prentice-Hall.

Uhr, L. (Ed.). (1966). *Pattern recognition: theory, experiment, computer simulations, and dynamic models of form perception and discovery.* New York: Wiley.

Uhrbrand, L., & Faurhye, A. (1960). Reversible and irreversible dyskinesia after treatment with perphenazine, chlorpromazine, reserpine and electroconvulsive shock. *Psychopharmacologia, 1,* 408–418.

Uhrbrock, R. S. (1961). Music on the job: Its influence on worker morale and productivity. *Personnel Psychology, 14,* 9–38.

Ulich, E., Brnggemann, A., & Groskurth, P. (1973). *Neue Formen der Arbeitsgestaltung* Frankfurt: Europäische Verlagsanstalt.

Ullman, G., Barkley, R. A., & Brown, H. (1978). The behavioral symptoms of hyperkinetic children who successfully responded to stimulant drug treatment. *American Journal of Orthopsychiatry, 48,* 425–437.

Ullmam, L. P. (1969). Behavior therapy as a social movement. In C. M. Wagman (Ed.). (1991). *Cognitive science and concepts of mind: Toward a general theory of human and artificial intelligence.* New York: Praeger. M. Franks (Ed.), *Behavior therapy: Appraisal and status* (pp. 495–523). New York, McGraw-Hill.

Ullmann, L. P., (1967). *Institution and outcome.* Elmsford, N.Y.: Pergamon Press.

Ullmann, L. P., & Krasner, L. (1965). What is behavior modification? In, L. P. Ullmann & L. Krasner (Eds.), *Case studies in behavior modification.* New York: Holt, Rinehart & Winston.

Ullmann, L. P., & Krasner, L. (1965/1963). *Case studies in behavior modification.* New York: Holt, Rinehart & Winston.

Ullmann, L. P., & Krasner, L. A (1975/1969). *A psychological approach to abnormal behavior.* Englewood Cliffs, N.J.: Prentice-Hall.

Ulman, E. & Dachinger, P. (Eds.). (1975). *Art in theory and practice.* New York: Schocken Books.

Ulman, E., & Levy, C. A. (1980). Art therapy viewpoints. New York: Schocken.

Ulrich, R. (1967). Behavior control and public concern. *Psychological Record*, 229–234.

Ulrich, R. E., & Azrin, N. H. (1962). Reflexive fighting in response to aversive stimulation. *Journal of Experimental Analysis of Behavior, 5*, 511–520.

Umana, R. F., Gross, S. J., & McConville, N. T. (1980). *Crisis in the family,* New York: Gardner Press.

Umemoto, T., Hoshino, M. (1981, August). *Historical development of psychology in Japan.* Paper presented at Joint IACCP-ICP Asian Regional Meeting, Taipei, Tawain.

Umezu, H., Sagara, M., Miyagi, O., & Yoda, S. (Eds.). (1981/1958). *Shinpan shinrigaku jiten (Encyclopedia of psychology),* (rev. ed.). Tokyo: Heibonsha.

Umiker-Sebeok, J., & Sebeok, T. A. (1980). Questioning apes. In T. A. Sebeok & J. Umiker-Sebeok (Eds.), *Speaking of apes: A critical anthology of two-way communication with man.* New York: Plenum.

Underwood, B., & Underwood, B. (1979). *Hostage to heaven.* New York: Potter.

Underwood, B. J. (1948). Retroactive and proactive inhibitions after 5 and 48 hours. *Journal of Experimental Psychology, 38,* 29–35.

Underwood, B. J. (1957). Interference and forgetting. *Psychological Review, 64,* 49–60.

Underwood, B. J. (1966/1949). *Experimental psychology.* New York: Appleton-Century-Crofts.

Underwood, B. J. (1967). *Psychological research,* New York: Appleton-Century-Crofts.

Underwood, B. J., & Schulz, R. W. (1960). *Meaningfulness and verbal learning.* Philadelphia, Pa.: Lippincott.

UNESCO. (1952). *Statement on race.* New York: United Nations.

Unger, R. K. (1976). Male is greater than female: The socialization of status inequality. *The Counseling Psychologist, 6,* 2–9.

Unger, R. K. (1978). The politics of gender: A review of relevant literature. In J. Sherman & F. Denmark (Eds.)., *Psychology of women: Future directions of research.* New York: Psychological Dimensions.

Unger, R. K. (1979). *Female and male: Psychological perspectives.* New York: Harper & Row.

Unger, R. K. (1979). Toward a redefinition of sex and gender. *American Psychologist, 34,* 1085–1094.

Unger, R. K. (1981). Sex as a social reality: Field and laboratory research. *Psychology of Women Quarterly, 5,* 645–653.

Unger, R. K. (1982). Through the looking glass: No Wonderland yet! *Psychology of Women Quarterly, 7.*

Ungerstedt, U. (1971). Stereotaxic mapping of the monoamine pathways in the rat brain. *Acta Physiologica Scandinavica* (suppl. 10), *367,* 1–48.

Uniform Guidelines on Employee Selection Procedures. (1978, August 25). *Federal Register,* Part IV, Vol. 43, no. 166, Pp. 38295–38309.

United Nations. (1956). Day care services for children. *International Social Service Review, 1.*

United States Army Technical Bulletin no. 203. (1945, October 19). Washington, D.C.: U.S. Government Printing Office, section 18.

U.S. Bureau of the Census. (1973, February). *Current population reports,* Series P-23, Washington, D.C.: U.S. Government Printing office.

U.S. Congress, Office of Technology Assessment. (1986). *Children's mental health: Problems and services—A background paper* (OTA BP H 33). Washington, DC: U.S. Government Printing Office.

U.S. Congress, Office of Technology Assessment. (1990). *The use of integrity tests for pre-employment screening* (OTA-Set-442). Washington, DC: U.S. Government Printing Office.

U.S. Congress, Office of Technology Assessment. (1991). *Adolescent health: Vol. 1. Summary and policy options.* (OTA H 468). Washington, DC: U.S. Government Printing Office.

U.S. Department of Health, Education, and Welfare. (1970). *Toward a social report.* Ann Arbor, Mich.: University of Michigan Press.

U.S. Department of Health, Education, and Welfare. (1976). *The condition of education: A statistical report on the condition of education in the United States.* Washington, D.C.: U.S. Government Printing Office.

U. S. Department of Health, Education and Welfare. (1979). *Healthy people: The surgeon general's report on health promotion and disease prevention* (DHEW Publication No. PHS 79–55071). Washington, DC: U.S. Government Printing Office.

U.S. Department of Health, Education and Welfare. (1979a). *1978 directory of ongoing research in smoking and health.* Washington, D.C.: Superintendent of Documents, U.S. Government Printing Office.

U.S. Department of Health, Education, and Welfare. (1979b). *Smoking and health: A report of the Surgeon General.* Washington, D.C.: Superintendent of Documents, U.S. Government Printing Office.

U.S. Department of Health, Education and Welfare. (1991). *Healthy people 2000: national health promotion and disease preventnion objectives* (DHHS Publication No. PHS 91-50212 3). Washington DC: U.S. Government Printing Office.

U.S. Department of Justice. (1981). *Bureau of Justice statistics* (2nd ed., NCJ-76939). Washington, DC: U.S. Government Printing Office.

U.S. Department of Justice. (1983). *Report to the nation on crime and justice* (NCJ-87068). Washington, DC: U.S. Government Printing Office.

U.S. Department of Labor. (1946–1977). *General aptitude test battery.* Washington, D.C.: U.S. Department of Labor.

U.S. Department of Labor. (1977/1965). *Dictionary of occupational titles* (3rd ed.). Washington, D.C.: U.S. Government Printing Office.

U.S. Department of Labor. (1980). *Occupational outlook handbook* Washington, D.C.: U.S. Government Printing Office.

U.S. Department of Labor, Employment and Training Administration. (1977). *Dictionary of occupational titles* (4th ed.). Washington, D.C.: U.S. Government Printing Office.

U.S. Equal Employment Opportunity Commission (USEEOC), (1978, August 25). U.S. Civil Service Commission, U.S. Department of Labor, and U.S. Department of Justice. Uniform guidelines on employee selection procedures. *Federal Register, 43*(166), 38290–38315.

U.S. General Accounting Office. (1989). *Medicare: Indirect medical education payments are too high.* (GAO/HRD-89-33). Washington, DC: U.S. Government Printing Office.

U.S. General Accounting Office. (1993). *Emergency departments: Unevenly affected by growth and change in patient use.* (GAO/HRD-93-4). Washington, DC: U.S. Government Printing Office.

U.S. National Institute of Mental Health. (1971). *Halfway houses serving the mentally ill and alcoholics, 1969–1970* (DHEW Publ. no. HSM-72-9049). Rockville, Md.: U.S. National Institute of Mental Health.

U.S. v. Brawner, (1972). *471 F. 21.969 D.C Cir.*

U.S. v. Hazelwood, (1977). 15 Fair Employment Practices 1, Bureau of National Affairs, Washington, D.C..

University Grants Commission. (1981). *University development in India: Basic facts and figures, 1972–1973 to 1976–1977* Part I: *Postgradu-*

ate and research enrolment, New Delhi- University Grants Commission.

University of Michigan. (1970). *Survey of working conditions. Final report on univariate and bivariate tables* (contractor's report). Washington, D.C.: Employment Standards Administration, U.S. Department of Labor.

Unruh, D. R. (1980). The social organization of older people: A social world perspective. In N. K. Denzin (Ed.), *Studies in symbolic interaction*, Vol. 3. Greenwich, Conn.: JAI Press.

Upper, D., & Cantela, J. R. (1977). *Covert conditioning*. New York: Pergamon Press.

Urban, H., & Ford, D. (1971). Some historical and conceptual perspectives on psychotherapy and behavior change. In S. Garfield & A. Bergin (Eds.), *Handbook of psychotherapy and behavior change: An empirical analysis*. New York: Wiley.

Urberg, K. A. (1979). Sex role conceptualization in adolescents and adults. *Developmental Psychology, 15*, 90–92.

Urbina-Sorbia, J. (1989). *El Psicologo, formacion, ejercicio profesional, prospective*. Mexico City: Universidad Nacional Autonoma de Mexico.

Usdin, E., Kvetnansky, R., & Kopin, I. J. (1976). *Stress and catecholamines*. Oxford: Pergamon Press.

Usdin, E., Kvetnansky, R., & Kopin, I. J. (1980). *Catecholamines and stress: Recent advances*. New York: Elsevier North Holland.

Usdin, G. (Ed.). (1973). *Sleep research and clinical practice*. New York: Brunner/Mazel.

Uttal, W. R. (1973). *The psychology of sensory coding*. New York: Harper & Row.

Uttal, W. R. (1978). Solutions to the mind—body problem. In *The psychobiology of mind*. Hillsdale, N.J.: Erlbaum.

Uttal, W. R., Pasich, T., Rogers, M., & Hieronymus, R. (1973). Generative computer assisted instruction. In B. Weiss (Ed.), *Digital computers in the behavioral laboratory*. New York: Appleton-Century-Crofts.

Užgiris, I. C., & Hunt, J. McV. (1975). *Assessment in infancy: Ordinal scale of psychological development*. Chicago,: University of Chicago Press.

Uznadze, D. N. (1966/1961). *The psychology of set*. New York: Plenum.

Vaca, N. C. (1970). The Mexican-American in the social sciences, 1912–1970. Part I: 1912–1935. *El Grito, 3*(3), 3–24.

Vaca, N. C. (1970b). The Mexican-American in the social sciences, 1912–1970. Part II: 1936–1970. *El Grito, 4*, 17–51.

Vahia, N., Doongaji, D., Kapoor, S., Ardhapurkar, I., & Ravindra Nath, S. (1973). Further experience with the therapy based upon concepts of pantanjali in the treatment of psychiatric disorders. *Indian Journal of Psychiatry, 15*, 32–37.

Vaihinger, H. (1924/1920). *The philosophy of "as if," a system of the theoretical, practical and religious fictions of mankind*. London: Paul, Trench, Trubner.

Vailetutti, P. J, & Christoplos, F. (Eds.). (1977). *Interdisciplinary approaches to human services*, Baltimore, Md.: University Park Press.

Vaillant, G. D. (1977). *Adaptation to life*. Boston: Little, Brown.

Vaillant, G. E. (1978). Natural history of male psychological health: Correlates of successful marriage and fatherhood. *American Journal of Psychiatry, 135*, 653–659.

Vaillant, G. E. (1978). Natural history of male psychological health. IV: What kinds of men do not get psychosomatic illness? *Psychosomatic Medicine, 40*, 420–431.

Vaillant, G. E., & McArthur, C. C. (1972). Natural history of male psychological health. I. The adult life cycle from 18–50. *Seminars in Psychiatry, 4*, 4.

Vaillant, G. E., & Milofsky, E. (1980). Natural history of male psychological health: Empirical evidence for Erickson's model of the life-cycle. *American Journal of Psychiatry, 137*, 1348–1359.

Vaillant, G. E, & Vaillant, C. O. (1981). Natural history of male psychological health, X: Work as a predictor of positive mental health. *American Journal of Psychiatry, 138*, 1433–1440.

Vaitl, D. (1982). Psychological management of essential hypertension. *Contributions to Nephrology, 30*, 87–91.

Vaitl, D. (Ed.). (1982). *Essentielle Hypertonie. Psychologischmedizinische Aspekte (Essential hypertension: Psychological and medical aspects)*. Berlin: Springer-Verlag.

Vaitl, D., Hülter, K., & Borlinghaus, K. (1974). Der Einfluss komplexer Reize auf die phasischen Komponenten der Herzfrequenz. *Psychologische Beitrage, 16*, 496–525.

Vaitl, D., & Kenkmann, H.-J. (1972). Stabilisation der Pulsfrequenz durch visuelle Ruckmeldung. *Zeitschrift für Klinische Psychologie, 1*, 251–271.

Vaitl, D., Kenkmann, H.-J., & Kuhmann, W. (1979). Heart rate stabilization feedback and concomitant physiological changes. In N. Birbaumer & H. D. Kimmel (Eds.), *Biofeedback and self-regulation*. Hillsdale, N.J.: Erlbaum.

Valenstein, E. S. (1973). *Brain control: A critical examination of brain stimulation and psychosurgery*. New York: Wiley.

Valenstein, E. S. (Ed.). (1980). *The psychosurgery debate: Scientific, legal and ethical perspectives*. San Francisco: Freeman.

Valentine, C. W. (1930). The innate basis of fear. *Journal of Genetic Psychology, 37*, 354–419.

Valentine, C. W. (1950/1942). *The psychology of early childhood*. London: Methuen.

Valentine, C. W. (1962). *The experimental psychology of beauty*. London: Methuen.

Valins, S. (1966). Cognitive effects of false heart rate feedback. *Journal of Personality and Social Psychology, 4*, 400–408.

Vallance, T. R. (1972). Social science and social policy: Amoral methodology in a matrix of values. *American Psychologist, 27*, 103–113.

Vallar, G., & Shallice, T. (Eds.). (1990). *Neuropsychological impairments of short-term memory*. Cambridge, UK: Cambridge University Press.

Valle, R. S., & King, M. (Eds.). (1978). *Existential-phenomenological alternatives for psychology*. New York: Oxford University Press.

Valtin, R. (1978–1979). Dyslexia: Deficit in reading or deficit in research? *Reading Research Quarterly, 14*, 201–221.

Van Bertalanffy, L. (1981). *A systems view of man*. Bouler CO: Westview Press.

Vance and Belknap v. Judas Priest and CBS Records. (1990, August 24). 86-5844/86-3939, 2d Dist. Court Nev.

Van Cott, H. P., & Kinkade, R. G. (Eds.). (1972). *Human engineering guide to equipment design* (rev. ed.). Washington, D.C.: U.S. Government Printing Office.

Vandell, D. L., Wilson, K. S., & Buchanan, N. R. (1980). Peer interaction in the first year of life: An examination of its structure, content, and sensitivity to toys. *Child Development, 51*, 481–488.

Vandell, R., Davis, R. A., & Clugston, N. A. (1943). Function of mental practice in the acquisition of motor skills. *Journal of General Psychology, 29*, 243–250.

Vandenberg, S. G. (1972). Assortative mating, or who marries whom? *Behavior Genetics, 2,* 127–157.

Vandenberg, S. G. (Ed.). (1965). *Progress in human behavior genetics.* Baltimore, Md.: Johns Hopkins.

Vandenberg, S. G., & Kuse, A. R. (1979). Spatial ability: A critical review of the sex-linked major gene hypothesis. In M. A. Wittig & A. C. Petersen (Eds.), *Sex-related differences in cognitive functioning: Developmental issues.* New York: Academic Press.

Vandenbos, G. R. (1992). The APA knowledge dissemination program: An overview of 100 years. In R. B. Evans, V. S. Sexton, & T. C. Cadwallader (Eds.), *100 years of the American Psychological Association: A historical perspective* (pp. 347–381). Washington, DC: American Psychological Association.

Van de Velde, F. H. (1965). *Ideal marriage: Its physiology and technique.* New York: Random House.

Van Dusen, W. (1958). Wu-wei, no-mind, and the fertile void in psychotherapy. *Psychologia, 1.*

Van Fleet, A. A. (1976). Charles Judd's psychology of schooling. *Elementary School Journal 76,* 455–463.

Van Gennep, A. (1960/1908). *Rites de passage.* Chicago: University of Chicago Press.

Van Hattum, R. (Ed.). (1980). *Communication disorders: An introduction.* Toronto: Macmillan.

Van Kaam; A. (1966). *Existential foundations of psychology.* Pittsburgh, Pa: Duquesne University Press.

Van Kaam, A. (1975). *In search of spiritual identity.* Denville, N.J.: Dimension Books.

Van Kaam, A. (1979). *The transcendent self.* Denville, N.J.: Dimension Books.

Van Kaam, A. (1980). Provisional glossary of the terminology of the science of foundational formative spirituality. *Studies in Formative Spirituality, 1,* 137–155.

Van Kaam, A. (1980/1964). *Religion and personality* (rev. ed.). Denville, N.J.: Dimension Books.

Van Kaam, A. (1981). Explanatory charts of the science of foundational formation. *Studies in Formative Spirituality, 1,* 127–143.

Van Kaam, A. (1981). Provisional glossary of the terminology of the science of foundational formation. *Studies in Formative Spirituality, 2,* 287–304.

Van Kaam, A. (1982). Editor's note: The science of foundational human formation. *Studies in Formative Spirituality, 2,* 179–181.

Van Kaam, A. (1982). Provisional glossary of the terminology of the science of foundational formation. *Studies in Formative Spirituality, 3,* 123–154.

Van Lawick-Goodall, J. (1968). *My friends the wild chimpanzees.* Washington, D.C.: National Geographic Society.

Van Lawick-Goodall, J. (1968). Tool using bird: The Egyptian vulture. *National Geographic Magazine, 133,* 630–641.

Van Olst, E. H. (1971). *The orienting reflex.* The Hague: Mouton.

Van Rensburg, J. A. (1938). The learning ability of the South African native compared with that of the European. *Research series no 5.* Pretoria: South African Council for Educational and Sociological Research.

Van Riper, C. (1947). *Speech correction.* New York: Prentice-Hall.

Van Wagenen, R. K., Meyerson, L., Kerr, N. J., & Mahoney, K. (1966). Field trials of a new procedure for toilet training. *Journal of Experimental Child Psychiatry, 3,* 312–314.

Van Zelst, R. H., (1952). Sociometrically selected work teams increase production. *Personnel Psychology, 5,* 175–185.

Varah, C. (1966). *The samaritans.* New York: Macmillan.

Varble, D. L. (1971). Current status of the Thematic Apperception Test. In P. McReynolds (Ed.), *Advances in psychological assessment,* Vol. 2. Palo Alto, Calif: Science and Behavior Books.

Varendonck, J. (1921). *The psychology of daydreams.* New York: Macmillan.

Vasiliev, L. L. (1963). *Experiments in mental suggestion.* Church Crookham, England: Institute for the Study of Mental Images.

Vattano, A. J. (1981). Integrity groups. In R. J. Corsini (Ed.), *Handbook of innovative psychotherapies.* New York: Wiley.

Vaughan, F. E. (1982). The transpersonal perspective: A personal overview. *Journal of Transpersonal Psychology, 14,* 37–45.

Vaughan, G. M. (1964). The trans-situational aspect of conformity behavior. *Journal of Personality, 32,* 335–354.

Vaughan, K. B., & Lanzetta, J. T. (1979). The observer's facial expressive response in vicarious emotional conditioning. Presented at the annual meeting of the Eastern Psychological Association. Philadelphia, Pa.

Vaughn, B. E., & Sroufe, L. A. (1979). The face of surprise in infants. Presented at the Animal Behavior Society meeting, Boulder, Colo., 1976. Cited in P. Ekman, & H. Oster, Facial expressions of emotion. *Annual Review of Psychology, 30,* 527–554.

Vaughn, F., & Walsh, R. (Eds.). (1983). *Accept this gift.* Los Angeles: Tarcher.

Vaughter, R. M. (1976). Review essay: Psychology. *Signs, 2,* 120–146.

Vaux, A. (1988). *Social support: Theory, research, and intervention.* New York: Praeger.

Vaux, A. (1992). Assessment of social support. In H. O. F. Veiel & U. Baumann (Eds.), *The meaning and measurement of social support* (pp. 193–216). New York: Hemisphere.

Vaux, A., & Harrison, D. (1985). Support network characteristics associated with support satisfaction and perceived support. *American Journal of Community Psychology, 13,* 245–268.

Vaux, A., Phillips, J., Holly, L., Thomson, B., Williams, D., & Stewart, D. (1986). The Social Support Appraisals (SSA) Scale: Studies of reliability and validity. *American Journal of Community Psychology, 14,* 195–220.

Vaux, A., Riedel, S., & Stewart, D. (1987). Modes of social support: The Social Support Behaviors (SS-B) Scale. *American Journal of Community Psychology, 15,* 209–237.

Veatch, R. M. (1976). *Death, dying and the biological revolution: Our last quest for responsibility.* New Haven, Conn.: Yale University Press.

Vega, A., & Parsons, O. A. (1967). Cross validation of the Halstead-Reitan tests for brain damage. *Journal of Consulting Psychology, 31,* 619–625.

Veiel, H. O. F., & Baumann, U. (Eds.). (1992). *The meaning and measurement of social support.* New York: Hemisphere.

Veith, I. (1965). *Hysteria. The history of a disease.* Chicago: The University of Chicago Press.

Velasco Hernandez, R. (1978). La enseñanza de la psicologia en Mexico. *Enseñanza e Investigacion en Psicologia, 4,* 10–24.

Vellutino, F. R. (1979). *Dyslexia: Theory and research.* Cambridge, Mass.: M.I.T. Press.

Velmans, M. (1991). Is human information processing conscious? *Behavioral and Brain Sciences, 14,* 651–726.

Veno, A., & Davidson, M. (1978). A relational model of stress and adaptation. *Man-Environment Systems, 8,* 75–89.

Verhaegen, P. (1962). Possibilité d'une orientation scolaire basée sur les épreuves psychologiques chez des enfants africains. *Revue de Psychologie Appliquée, 12,* 123–133.

Verhave, T. (1959). Techniques for differential reinforcement of rate of avoidance responding. *Science, 129,* 959–960.

Vernon, P. (1933). Some characteristics of the good judge of personality. *Journal of Social Psychology, 4,* 42–57.

Vernon, P. A. (Ed.). (1987). *Speed of information-processing and intelligence.* Norwood, NJ: Ablex.

Vernon, P. E. (1961/1950). *The structure of human abilities.* London: Methuen.

Vernon, P. E. (1964). *Intelligence and cultural environment.* London: Methuen.

Vernon, P. E. (1964). *Personality assessement: A critical survey.* London: Methuen.

Vernon, P. E. (1982/1979). *Intelligence, heredity, and environment.* San Francisco: Freeman.

Vernon, P. E., Adamson, G., & Vernon, D. F. (1977). *The psychology and education of gifted children.* London: Methuen.

Vernon, P. E., & Parry, J. B. (1949). *Personnel selection in the British forces.* London: University of London Press.

Verplanck, W. S. (1955). The control of the content of conversation: Reinforcement of statements of opinion. *Journal of Abnormal and Social Psychology, 51,* 558–576.

Verplanck, W. S., Burrhus, S., & Skinner, B. F. W. K. Estes, S. Koch, K. McCorquodale, W. N. Schoenfeld, & W. S. Verplanck (Eds.). (1954). *Modern learning theory.* New York: Appleton-Century-Crofts.

Very, P. S., & Prull, R. W. (1970). Birth order, personality development, and the choice of law as a profession. *Journal of Genetic Psychology, 116,* 219–221.

Veterans Administration. (1981, April). Veterans benefits under current educational programs: (IB 04—81–12). Washington, D.C.: U.S. Veterans Administration.

Vichinsky, E. P., Johnson, R., & Lubin, B. H. (1982). Multidisciplinary approach to pain management in sickle cell disease. *The American Journal of Pediatric Hematology/Oncology, 4,* 328–333.

Vicino, F., & Miller, J. A. (1972). *Prospects.* Scottsville, N.Y.: Transnational Programs.

Victor, G. (1975). Letter: Sybil: Grande hysterie or folie à deux? *American Journal of Psychiatry, 132,* 202.

Victor, J. (1990). The spread of satanic cult rumors. *Skeptical Inquirer, 15,* 287–291.

Victor, R. G. (1981). Gambling. In S. J. Mulé (Ed.), *Behavior in excess.* New York: Macmillan.

Victor, R. G., & Krug, C. M. (1967). Paradoxical intention in the treatment of compulsive gambling. *American Journal of Psychotherapy, 21,* 808–814.

Vidmar, N. (1979). The other issues in jury simulation research: A commentary with particular reference to defendant character studies. *Law and Human Behavior, 3,* 95–106.

Vidoni, D., Fleming, N., & Mintz, S. (1983). Behavior problems of children as perceived by teachers, mental health professionals, and children. *Psychology in the Schools, 20,* 93–98.

Villalpando Nava, J. M. (1953). La orientacion profesional en la vida de los pueblos cultos. In Universidad Nacional Autonoma de Mexico (Ed.), *Memoria del Congreso Cientifico Mexicano, Ciencias de la Educacion, Psicologia-Filosofia,* Vol. 15. Mexico, D.F.: UNAM.

Villenueve, J. J. (1972). Challenging the juror selection system in New York. *Albany Law Review, 36,* 305–329.

Vinacke, W. E., & Arkoff, A. (1957). An experimental study of coalitions in the triad. *American Sociological Review, 22,* 406–414.

Vincent, S. B. (1912). The function of vibrissae in the behavior of the white rat. *Behavior Monographs,* 1, no. 5.

Vincent, T. A. (1990). A view from the Hill: The human element in policy making on Captiol Hill. *American Psychologist, 45,* 61–64.

Viney, L. (1969). Self: The history of a concept. *Journal of the History of the Behavioral Sciences, 4,* 349–359.

Viney, L. L. (1974). Multidimensionality of perceived locus of control: Two replications. *Journal of Consulting and Clinical Psychology, 42*(3), 463–464.

Viney, W., Wertheimer, M., & Wertheimer, M. L. (1979). *History of psychology: A guide to information sources.* Detroit, Mich.: Gale Research.

Vinson, D. E. (1982). Juries: Perception and the decision making process. *Trial, 18,* 52–55.

Vioebergh, A. (1976). Family and intellectual development. *Famille et Developpement Intellectuel, 7*(71), 890–891.

Viola, G. (1933). *La costituzione individuale.* Bologna, Italy: Cappeli.

Vishnudevananda. (1960). *The complete illustrated book of yoga.* New York: Pocket Books.

Viteles, M. (1932). *Industrial psychology.* New York: Norton.

Vivas, E., & Krieger, M. (Eds.). (1960/1963). *The problems of aesthetics: A book of readings.* New York: Holt, Rinehart & Winston.

Vives, J. L. (1526). *De subventione pauperum.* Cambridge, England: University Press.

Vives, J. L. (1531). De tradendis disciplinis. Cambridge, England: University Press.

Vives, J. L. (1923/1538). *De anima et vita libri tres.* Madrid: Ediciones de Lectura.

Vlietstra, A. G. (1981). Full versus half-day preschool attendance: Effects in young children as assessed by teacher ratings and behavioral observations. *Child Development, 52,* 603–610.

Vockell, E. L., Felker, D. W., & Miley, C. H. (1973). Birth order literature 1967–1971: Bibliography and index. *Journal of Individual Psychology, 29,* 39–53.

Vodanovich, S. J., & Kass, S. J. (1990a). A factor analytic study of the Boredom Proneness Scale. *Journal of Personality Assessment, 55,* 115–123.

Vodanovich, S. J., & Kass, S. J. (1990b). Age and gender differences in boredom proneness. *Journal of Social Behavior and Personality, 5,* 297–307.

Voeller, K. (1981). A proposed extended behavioral, cognitive and sensorimotor pediatric neurological examination. In R. Ochroch (Ed.), *The diagnosis and treatment of minimal brain dysfunction in children: A clinical approach.* New York: Human Sciences Press.

Voeltz, L. M. (1980). Children's attitudes toward handicapped peers. *American Journal of Mental Deficiency, 84,* 455–464.

Vogel, J. M., & Teghtsoonian, M. (1972). The effects of perspective alterations on apparent size and distance scales. *Perception and Psychophysics, 11,* 294–298.

Vogel, W., & Broverman, D. M. (1964). Relationship between EEG and test intelligence. *Psychological Bulletin, 62,* 132–144.

Vokey, J. R., & Read, J. D. (1985). Subliminal messages: Between the devil and the media. *American Psychologist, 40,* 1231–1239.

Völgyesi, F. A. (1966). *Hypnosis of man and animals.* Baltimore, Md.: Williams & Wilkins.

Volkelt, H. (1963). *Grundfragen der Psychologie*. Munich: Beck.

Volle, R. L., & Kolle, G. B. (1970). Ganglionic stimulating and blocking agents. In L. S. Goodman & A. Gilman (Eds.), *The pharmacological basis of therapeutics*. Toronto: Collier-Macmillan.

Vollhardt, L. T. (1991). Psychoneuroimmunology: A literature review. *American Journal of Orthopsychiatry, 61*, 35–47.

Von Baeyer, C. L., Sherk, D. L., & Zanna, M. P. (1981). Impression management in the job interview: When the female applicant meets the male (chauvinist) interviewer. *Personality and Social Psychology Bulletin, 7*, 45–51.

von Clausewitz, C. (1976). *On war* (M. Howard & P. Paret, Eds. & Trans.). Princeton, NJ: Princeton University Press.

Von Foerster H., White, J., Peterson, L., & Russell, J. (Eds.). (1968). *Purposive systems*. London: Macmillan.

Von Haller Gilmer, B. (1966). *Industrial psychology*. New York: McGraw-Hill.

Von Hentig, H. (1948). *The criminal and his victim*. New Haven, Conn.: Yale University Press.

von Neumann, J., & Morgenstern, O. (1947). *Theory of games and economic behavior*. Princeton, NJ: Princeton University Press.

Von Pragg, H. M., Lader, M. H., Rafaelsen, O. J., & Sachar, E. J. (Eds.). (1980). *Handbook of biological psychiatry: Brain mechanisms and abnormal behavior*, Vol. 3. New York: Dekker.

Von Richthofen, C. L., & Mellor, C. S. (1979). Cerebral electrotherapy: Methodological problems in assessing its therapeutic effectiveness. *Psychological Bulletin, 86*(6), 1264–1271.

von Winterfeldt, D., & Edwards, W. (1986). *Decision analysis and behavioral research*. Cambridge, UK: Cambridge University Press.

Voorhies, D., & Scandura, J. M. (1967). Determination of memory load in information processing. In J. M. Scandura (Ed.), *Problem solving*. New York: Academic Press.

Vorrath, H. H., & Bendtro, L. K. (1974). *Positive peer culture*. Chicago: Aldine.

Vough, C. F., & Asbell, B. (1975). *Human resource: A strategy for productivity*. New York: AMACON.

Voyce, C. D., & Jackson, D. N. (1977). An evaluation of a threshold theory for personality assessment. *Educational and Psychological Measurement, 37*, 383–408.

Vreeland, R. S. (1972). Is it true what they say about Harvard boys? *Psychology Today, 5*, 65–68.

Vreven, R., & Nuttin, J. R. (1976). Frequency perception of successes. *Journal of personality and Social Psychology, 34*, 734–745.

Vroom, V. H. (1964). *Work and motivation*. New York: Wiley.

Vroom, V. H. (1976). Leadership. In M. D. Dunnette (Ed.), *Handbook of industrial and organizational psychology*. Chicago: Rand-McNally.

Vroom, V. H., & Yetton, P. W. (1973). *Leadership and decision making*. Pittsburgh, Pa.: University of Pittsburgh Press.

Vuyk, R. (1981). Overview and critique of *Piaget's genetic epistemology 1965–1980*. New York: Academic Press.

Vygotsky, L. S. (1962). *Thought and language*. W. E. Hanfmann & G. Vakar (Eds.). Cambridge, Mass.: M.I.T. Press.

Vygotsky, L. S. (1971). Art as a catharsis. In L. S. Vygotsky (Ed.), *The psychology of art*. Cambridge, Mass.: M.I.T. Press.

Vygotsky, L. S. (1982/1927). Istoricheskij smysl psikhologicheskogo crizisa (Historical meaning of the crisis in psychology). In L. Vygotsky, *Sobrahie sochinenij (Collected papers)*, (Vol 1). Moscow: Pedagogika.

Waber, D. P. (1976). Sex differences in cognition: A function of maturation rate? *Science, 192*, 572–574.

Waber, D. P. (1979). Cognitive abilities and sex-related variations in the maturation of cerebral cortical functions. In M. A. Wittig & A. C. Petersen (Eds.), *Sex-related differences in cognitive functioning: Developmental issues*. New York: Academic Press.

Wachtel, P. L. (1973). Psychodynamics, behavior therapy, and the implacable experimenter: An inquiry into the consistency of personality. *Journal of Abnormal Psychology, 82*, 324–334.

Wachtel, P. L. (1975). Behavior therapy and the facilitation of psychoanalytic exploration. *Psychotherapy, 12*, 68–72.

Wachtel, P. L. (1977). *Psychoanalysis and behavior therapy: Toward an integration*. New York: Basic Books.

Wachtel, P. L. (1984). Forward, In K. S. Bowers & D. Meichenbaum (Eds.), *The unconscious reconsidered*. New York: Wiley.

Wachter, K. W., & Straf, M. L. (Eds.). (1990). *The effect of school desegregation on the academic achievement of black children*. New York: Russell Sage Foundation.

Wachter, K. W., & Straf, M. L. (Eds.). (1990). *The future of meta-analysis*. New York: Russell Sage Foundation.

Wada, J. A. (1977). Fundamental asymmetry of the infant brain. In S. J. Dimond & D. A. Blizard (Eds.), *Annals of New York Academy of Sciences, 299*, 370–379.

Wada, J. A., Clarke, R., & Harem, G. (1975). Cerebral hemispheric asymmetry in humans. *Archives of Neurology, 32*, 239–246.

Wada, J. A., & Rasmussen, T. (1960). Intracarotid injection of sodium-amytal for the lateralization of cerebral speech dominance: Experimental and clinical observations. *Journal of Neurosurgery, 17*, 266–282.

Wade, T. C., & Baker, T. B. (1977). Opinions and use of psychological tests: A survey of clinical psychologists, *American Psychologist, 32*, 874–882.

Wadeson, H. (1980). *Art psychotherapy*. New York: Wiley.

Wadham, R. A. (1979). *Microcomputer application in interaction analysis (TICOR), (ERIC #ED175433)*. Provo, Utah: Brigham Young University.

Wadsworth, B. J. (1971). *Piaget's theory of cognitive development*. New York: McKay.

Wadsworth, B. J. (1978). *Piaget for the classroom teacher*. New York: Longman.

Wagenaar, W. A., & Groenweg, J. (1990). The memory of concentration camp survivors. *Applied Cognitive Psychology, 4*, 77–87.

Wagley, C., & Harris, M. (1958). *Minorities in the new world*. New York: Columbia University Press.

Wagman, M. (1983). A factor analytic study of the psychological implications of the computer for the individual and society. *Behavior Research Methods and Instrumentation, 15*, 413–419.

Wagman, M. (1988). *Computer psychotherapy systems: Theory and research foundations*. New York: Gordon and Breach Science.

Wagman, M. (1991a). *Artificial intelligence and human cognition: A theoretical intercomparison of two realms of intellect*. New York: Praeger.

Wagman, M. (1991b). *Cognitive science and concepts of mind: Toward a general theory of human and artificial intelligence*. New York: Praeger.

Wagman, M. (in press). *Cognitive psychology and artificial intelligence: Theory and research in cognitive science*. New York: Praeger.

Wagner, A. R. (1976). Priming in STM: An information processing mechanism for self-generated or retrieval-generated depression in performance. In T. J. Tighe & R. N. Leaton (Eds.), *Habituation:*

Perspectives from child development, animal behavior, and neurophysiology. Hillsdale, N.J.: Erlbaum.

Wagner, A. R. (1978). Expectancies and the priming of STM. In S. H. Hulse, H. Fowler, & W. K. Honig (Eds.), *Cognitive processes in animal behavior.* Hillsdale, N.J.: L. Erlbaum.

Wagner, A. R., & Rescorla, R. A. (1972). Inhibition in Pavlovian conditioning: Application of a theory. In R. A. Boakes & M. S. Halliday (Eds.), *Inhibition and learning.* London: Academic.

Wagner, A. R. & Rescorla, R. A. (1972). Inhibition in Pavlovian conditioning: Applications of a theory. In R. A. Bokes & M. S. Halliday (Eds.), *Inhibition and learning.* New York: Academic Press.

Wagner, B. R., & Paul, G. L. (1970). Reduction of incontinence in chronic mental patients: A pilot project. *Journal of Behavior Therapy and Experimental Psychiatry, 1,* 29–38.

Wagner, D. A., & Stevenson, H. W. (Eds.). (1982). *Cultural perspectives on child development.* San Francisco: Freeman.

Wagner, E. E. (1983). *The Hand Test manual (rev. ed.).* Los Angeles: Western Psychological.

Wagner, E. E., Rasch, M., & Marsico, D. S. (1991). *Hand Test manual supplement: interpreting child and adolescent responses.* Los Angeles: Western Psychological.

Wagner, E. E., & Wagner, C. F. (1981). *The interpretation of projective test data: Theoretical and practical guidelines.* Springfield, IL: Thomas.

Wagner-Jauregg, J. (1968). The effect of malaria on progressive paralysis. In W. S. Sahakian (Ed.), *History of psychology: A source book* Itasca, Ill.: Peacock.

Wahl, C. W. (1958). The fear of death. *Bulletin of the Menninger Clinic, 22,* 214–223.

Wahl, J. (1949). *A short history of existentialism.* New York: Philosophical Library.

Wahler, R. G., & Dumas, J. E. (1986). "A chip off the old block": Some interpersonal characteristics for coercive children across generations. In P. S. Strain, M. J. Guralnick, & H. M. Walker (Eds.), *Children's social behavior: Development, assessment, and modification* (pp. 49–91). New York: Academic.

Wahler, R. G., & Dumas, J. E. (1987). Family factors in childhood psychopathology: A coercion-neglect model. In T. Jacob (Ed.), *Family interaction and psychopathology: Theories, methods, and findings* (pp. 581–627). New York: Plenum.

Wahler, R. G., House, A. E., & Stambaugh, E. F., II, (1976). *Ecological assessment of child problem behavior.* New York: Pergamon Press.

Waid, W. *Sociophysiology.* New York: Springer-Verlag, in press.

Wainer, H., Dorans, N. J., Flaugher, R., Green, B. F., Mislevy, R. J., Steinberg, L., & Thissen, D. *Computerized adaptive testing: A primer.* Hillsdale, NJ: Erlbaum.

Waite, A. E. (1894). *The hermetic and alchemical writings of Aureolus Philippus Theophrastus Bombast, of Hohenheim called Paracelsus the Great. Vol. I: Hermetic chemist. Vol. II: Hermetic medicine and hermetic philosophy.* London: Elliot.

Walberg, H. J. (1981). A psychological theory of educational productivity. In F. H. Farley & N. J. Gordon (Eds.), *Psychology and education: The state of the union.* Berkeley, Calif.: McCutchan.

Walco, G. A., & Dampier, C. D. (1987). Chronic pain in adolescent patients. *Journal of Pediatric Psychology, 12,* 215–225.

Wald, A. (1947). *Sequential analysis.* New York: Wiley.

Wald, P. M. (1982). Become a real "friend of the court." *APA Monitor, 13*(2), 5.

Wald, P. M., & Friedman, P. R. (1978). The politics of mental health advocacy in the United States. *International Journal of Law and Psychiatry, 1,* 137–152.

Waldo, G. P., & Dinitz, S. (1967). Personality attributes of the criminal: An analysis of research studies: 1950–1965. *Journal of Research on Crime and Delinquency, 4,* 185–202.

Waldron, I, Zyzanski, S., Shekelle, R. B., Jenkins, C. D., & Tannenbaum, S. (1977). The coronary-prone behavior pattern in employed men and women. *Journal of Human Stress, 3,* 2–18.

Waldrop, M. F., Bell, R. Q., McLaughlin, B., & Halverson, C. F. (1978). Newborn minor physical anomalies predict short attention span, peer aggression, and impulsivity at age 3. *Science, 199,* 563–565.

Walk, R. D. (1981). Perceptual development. Monterey, Calif.: Brooks/Cole.

Walk, R. D., & Gibson, E. J. (1961). A comparative and analytic study of visual depth perception. *Psychological Monographs, 75* (entire no. 519).

Walker-Andrews, A. S. (1986). Intermodal perception of expressive behaviors: Relation of eye and voice? *Developmental Psychology, 22,* 373–377.

Walker, C. (1980). The learning assistance center in a selective institution. In *New directions for college learning assistance.* San Francisco: Jossey-Bass.

Walker, D. F., & Schaffarzick, J. (1974). Comparing curricula. *Review of Educational Research, 44,* 83–111.

Walker, E. H. (1975). Foundations of paraphysical and parapsychological phenomena. In L. Oteri (Ed.), *Quantum physics and parapsychology.* New York: Parapsychology Foundation.

Walker, E. L. (1958). Action decrement and its relation to learning. *Psychological Review, 65,* 129–142.

Walker, E. L. (1969). Experimental psychology and social responsibility *American Psychologist, 24,* 862–868.

Walker, J. L., Lahey, B. B., Hynd, G. W., & Frame, C. L. (1987). Comparison of specific patterns of antisocial behavior in children with conduct disorder with or without coexisting hyperactivity. *Journal of Consulting and Clinical Psychology, 55,* 910–913.

Walker, J. M. (1979). Energy demand in a master-metered apartment complex: An experimental analysis. *Journal of Applied Psychology, 64,* 190–196.

Walker, J. W., Kimmel, D. C., Price, K. F. (1980–1981). Retirement style and retirement satisfaction: Retirees aren't all alike. *International Journal of Aging and Human Development, 12*(4).

Walker, L. E. A. (1990). A feminist therapist views the case. In D. W. Cantor (Ed.), *Women as therapists: A multithereotical casebook.* New York: Springer.

Walker, P., & Smith, S. (1984). Stroop interference based on the synaesthetic qualities of auditory pitch. *Perception, 13,* 75–81.

Wallace, H. A. (1923). What is in the corn judge's mind? *Journal of the American Society of Agronomy, 15,* 300–304.

Wallace, M., & Rabin, A. I. (1960). Temporal experience. *Psychological Bulletin, 57,* 213–236.

Wallace, R. K. (1970). Physiological effects of transcendental meditation. *Science, 167,* 1751–1754.

Wallace, R. K. (1986). *The Maharishi technology of the unified field: The neurophysiology of enlightenment.* Fairfield, IA: Maharishi International University Neuroscience.

Wallace, R. K. (1993). The neurophysiology of enlightenment. In J. Gackenbach, H. Hunt, & C. N. Alexander (Eds.), *Higher states* *of consciousness: Theoretical and experiential perspectives*. New York: Plentim.

Wallace, R. K., & Benson, H. (1972). The physiology of meditation. *Scientific American, 226*, 84–90.

Wallace, R. K., Benson, H., & Wilson, A. F. (1971). A wakeful hypometabolic physiologic state. *American Journal of Physiology 221*, 795–799.

Wallace, T., & Weeks, S. G. (1972). Youth in Uganda: Some theoretical perspectives. *International Social Science Journal, 24*, 354–361.

Wallach, H. (1948). Brightness constancy and the nature of achromatic colors. *Journal of Experimental Psychology, 38*, 310–324.

Wallach, M., & Kogan, N. (1965). *Modes of thinking in young children.* New York: Holt, Rinehart & Winston.

Waller, N. G., Kojetin, B. A., Bouchard, T. J., Lykken, D. T., & Tellegen, A. (1990). Genetic and environmental influence on religious interests, attitudes, and values: A study of twins reared apart and together. *Psychological Science, 1*, 138–142.

Waller, W. (1937). The rating and dating complex. *American Sociological Review, 2*, 727–734.

Wallerstein, J. S., & Kelly, J. B. (1974). The effects of parental divorce: The adolescent experience. In J. Anthony & C. Koupernic (Eds.), *The child in his family: Children at psychiatric risk*. New York: Wiley.

Wallerstein, J. S., & Kelly, J. B. (1975). The effects of parental divorce: Experiences of the preschool child. *Journal of American Academy of Child Psychiatry, 14*, 600–616.

Wallerstein, J. S., & Kelly, J. B. (1976). The effects of parental divorce: Experiences of the child in later latency. *American Journal of Orthopsychiatry, 46*, 256–269.

Wallerstein, R. S., & Nemetz, S. J. (1979). Conceptualizing the nature of the therapeutic action of psychoanalytic psychotherapy. *Journal of the American Psychoanalytic Association, 27*, 127–144.

Wallin, J. E. W. (1909). Medical and psychological inspection of school children. *Western Journal of Education, 2*, 434–436.

Wallin, J. E. W. (1960). History of the struggles within the American Psychological Association to attain membership requirements, test standardization, certification of practitioners, and professionalization. *Journal of General Psychology, 63*, 287–308.

Wallock, S. (1981). Reflections on Mary Whitehouse. *American Journal of Dance Therapy, 4*(2), 45–56.

Wallock, S., & Eckstein, D. (1983). Dance/movement therapy: A primer for group facilitators. In *1983 annual handbook*, San Diego, Calif.: University Associates.

Wallon, H. (1925). *L'enfant turboulent*. Paris: Alcan.

Wallsten, T. S. (Ed.). (1980). *Cognitive processes in choice and decision behavior*. Hillsdale, N.J.: Erlbaum.

Wallston, B. S., & O'Leary, V. E. (1981). Sex and gender make a difference: The differential perceptions of women and men. In L. Wheeler (Ed.), *Review of personality and social psychology*, Vol. 2. Beverly Hills, Calif.: Sage Publications.

Walrath, L., & Hamilton, D. (1975). Autonomic correlates of meditation and hypnosis. *American Journal of Clinical Hypnosis, 17*, 190–197.

Walsh, B. M. (1973). Marital status and birth order in a sample of Dublin males. *Journal of Biosocial Science* (Oxford), 5(2), 187–193.

Walsh, D. A. (1975). Age differences in learning and memory. In D. S. Woodruff & J. E. Birren (Eds.), *Aging: Scientific perpectives and social issues*. New York: Van Nostrand.

Walsh, K. W. (1978). *Neuropsychology*. New York: Churchill Livingstone.

Walsh, R. (1980). The consciousness disciplines and the behavioral sciences: Questions of comparison and assessment. *American Journal of Psychiatry, 137*, 663–673.

Walsh, R. (1981). *Towards an ecology of brain*. Jamaica, NY: Spectrum.

Walsh, R. (1984). *Staying alive: The psychology of human survival*. Boston: Shambhala.

Walsh, R. (1988). Two Asian psychologies and their implications for Western psychotherapists. *American Journal of Psychotherapy, 42*, 543–560.

Walsh, R. (1989). Toward a psychology of human survival. *American Journal of Psychotherapy, 43*, 158–180.

Walsh, R. (1990). *The spirit of shamanism*. Los Angeles: Tarcher.

Walsh, R., & Greenough, W. T. (Eds.). (1976). *Environments as therapy for brain dysfunction*. New York: Plemum.

Walsh, R. N. (1977). Initial meditative experiences: Part I. *Journal of Transpersonal Psychology, 9*, 151–192.

Walsh, R. N. (1978). Initial meditative experiences: Part II. *Journal of Transpersonal Psychology, 10*, 1–28.

Walsh, R. N. (1980). The consciousness disciplines and the behavioral sciences: Questions of comparison and assessment. *American Journal of Psychiatry, 137*(6), 663–673.

Walsh, R. N. (1981). Meditation. In R. J. Corsini (Ed.), *Handbook of innovative psychotherapies*. New York: Wiley.

Walsh, R. N. (1982). A model for viewing meditation research. *Journal of Transpersonal Psychology 14*, 69–84.

Walsh, R. N. (1982). The ten paramis (perfections) of Buddhism. In R. N. Walsh & D. H. Shapiro (Eds.), *Beyond health and normality: Toward a vision of exceptional psychological health*. New York: Van Nostrand.

Walsh, R. N. (1983). *The universe within us: Contemporary perspectives on Buddhist psychology*. New York: Morrow.

Walsh, R. N., et al. (1980). Paradigms in collision. In R. Walsh & F. Vaughan (Eds.), *Beyond ego*. Los Angeles: Tarcher.

Walsh, R. N., & Shapiro, D. H. (Eds.). (1983). *Beyond health and normality: Explorations of exceptional psychological wellbeing*. New York: Van Nostrand Reinhold.

Walsh, R. N., & Vaughan, F. E. (Eds.). (1980). *Beyond ego: Transpersonal dimensions in psychology*. Los Angeles: Tarcher.

Walsh, W. B. (1973). *Theories of person-environment interaction: Implications for the college student*. Iowa City, Iowa: American College Testing.

Walsh, W. B., & Osipow, S. H. (1983). *Handbook of vocational psychology*. Hillsdale, N.J. Erlbaum.

Walster, E., Aronson, V., Abrahams, D., & Rottmann, L. (1966). Importance of physical attractiveness in dating behavior. *Journal of Personality and Social Psychology, 4*, 508–516.

Walster, E., Berscheid, E., & Walster, G. W. (1970). The exploited: Justice or justification? In J. Macaulay & L. Berkowitz (Eds.), *Altruistn and helping behavior*. New York: Academic Press.

Walster, E., Berscheid, E., & Walster, G. W. (1973). New directions in equity research. *Journal of Personality and Social Psychology, 25*, 151–176.

Walster, E., & Prestholdt, P. (1966). The effect of misjudging another: Overcompensation or dissonance reduction? *Journal of Experimental Social Psychology, 2*, 85–97.

Walster, E, Walster, G. W., & Berseheid, E. (1978). *Equity: Theory and research*. Boston: Allyn & Bacon.

Walters, E. T., & Byrne, J. H. (1983). Associative conditioning of single sensory neurons suggests a cellular mechanism for learning. *Science, 219*, 405–408.

Walters, G. C., & Grusec, J. E. (1977). *Punishment*. San Francisco: Freeman.

Walther, L. (1926). *La technopsychologie du travail industriel*. Neuchâtel, Switzerland: Delachaux & Niestlé.

Walther, L. (1936). *Orientation professionnelle et carrières libérales. Etude psychologique*. Paris: Delachaux & Niestlé.

Walton, R. E., Hutt, M. L., Andrew, G., & Hartwell, H. W. (1951). A tension index of adjustment based on picture stories elicited by the Michigan picture test. *Journal of Abnormal and Social Psychology, 46*, 438–441.

Wandersman, A., Poppen, P., & Ricks, D. (1976). *Humanism and behaviorism: Dialogue and growth*. New York: Pergamon Press.

Wandhofer, A., Kobal, G., & Plattig, K.-H. (1976). I-atenzverkiirzung menschlicher auditorisch evozierter Himpotenfiale bei transzendentaler meditation [Decrease of latency of human auditory evoked potentials during the Transcendental Meditation technique]. *Zeitschrift feur Elektroenzephalographie lind Elektromyographie, 7*, 99–103.

Wang, H. S. (1981). Neuropsychiatric procedures for the assessment of Alzheimer's disease, senile dementia, and related disorders. In N. E. Miller & G. D. Cohen (Eds.), *Clinical aspects of Alzheimer's disease and senile dementia*. New York: Raven Press.

Wang, Z. M. (1986). Worker's attribution and its effects on performance under different work responsibility systems. *Chinese Journal of Applied Psychology, 1*(2), 6–10.

Wang, Z. M. (1988). *Work and personnel psychology*. Hangzhou, People's Republic of China: Zhejiang Educational Press.

Wang, Z. M. (1989). Participation and skill utilization in organizational decision making in Chinese enterprises. In B. J. Fallon, H. P. Pfister, & J. Brebner (Eds.), *Advances in industrial organizational psychology*. North-Holland: Elsevier.

Wang, Z. M. (1989). The human-computer interface hierarchy model and strategies in system development. *Ergonomics, 32*(11), 1391–1400.

Wang, Z. M. (1990). Information structures and cognitive strategies in decision-making on systems development. *Ergonomics, 33*(7), 907–916.

Wang, Z. M. (1990). *Research methods in psychology*. Beijing, People's Republic of China: People's Educational Press.

Wang, Z. M. (in press). *Culture, economic reform and role of industrial and organizational psychology in China*. In M. D. Dunnette & L. K. Hough (Eds.).

Wang, Z. M. (in press). Psychology in China. *Annual Review of Psychology, 44*.

Wang, Z. M., & Zhong, J. A. (in press). The effects of decision support information on decision making patterns in systems development. *Ergonomics, 35*.

Wangensteen, O. H., & Carlson, A. J. (1931). Hunger sensations in a patient after total gastrectomy. *Proceedings of the Society for Experimental Biology and Medicine, 28*, 545–547.

Wann, T. W. (1964). *Behaviorism and phenomenology*. Chicago: University of Chicago Press.

Wanous, J. P. (1977). Organizational entry: Newcomers moving from outside to inside. *Psychological Bulletin, 84*, 601–618.

Wanous, J. P. (1980). *Organizational entry: Recruitment, selection, and socialization of newcomers*. Reading, Mass.: Addison-Wesley.

Wanous, S. (1976). Commentary: Process and context in the conception of cognitive style. In S. Messick et al. (Eds.), *Individuality in learning: Implications of cognitive styles and creativity for human development*. San Francisco: Jossey-Bass.

Warburton, F. E. (1960). The lab coat as a status symbol. *Science, 131*, 895.

Ward, D. (1979). *Sing a rainbow: musical activities with mentally handicapped children*. London: Oxford University Press.

Ward, J. (1886). Psychology. In *Encyclopaedia Britannica* (9th ed.). New York: Encyclopaedia Britannica.

Ward, J. C. (1990). Inborn errors of metabolism. In R. L. Summitt (Ed.), *Comprehensive pediatrics* (pp. 738–772). St. Louis: Mosby.

Wardell, D., & Royce, J. R. (1978). Toward a multifactor theory of styles and their relationships to cognition and affect. *Journal of Personality, 46*, 474–505.

Warden, C. J. (1931). *Animal motivation studies: The albino rat*. New York: Columbia University Press.

Warfwl, J. H., & Schlagenhauff, R. E. (1980). *Understanding neurologic disease*. Baltimore, Md.: Urban & Schwarzenberg.

Warheit, G. J., Bell, R. A., & Schwab, J. J. (1974). *Planning for change: Needs assessment approaches*. Rockville, Md.: National Institute of Mental Health.

Warheit, G. J., Bell, R. A., & Schwab, J. J. (1979). *Needs assessment approaches: Concepts and methods*. Washington DC: U.S. Department of Health, Education, and Welfare.

Warkentin, J. (Ed.). (1969). Humor in therapy. *Voices: The Art and Science of Psychotherapy. Journal of the American Academy of Psychotherapists, 5*(2).

Warner, R. (1990). *Interaction tempo and evaluation of affect in social interaction: Rhythmic systems versus causal modeling approaches*. Unpublished manuscript.

Warner, W. L. (1962). *American life: Dream and reality* (rev. ed.). Chicago: University of Chicago Press.

Warner, W. L, et al. (1949). *Social class in America*. Chicago: Science Research Associates.

Warner, W. L. (Ed.). (1941–1959). *Yankee city series* (5 vols.). New Haven, Conn.: Yale University Press.

Warnick, D. H., & Sanders, G. S. (1980). Why do eyewitnesses make so many mistakes? *Journal of Applied Psychology, 10*, 362–366.

Warnke, M. (1972). *The satan seller*. Plainfield, NJ: Logos International.

Wart, P., & Wall, T. (1975). *Work and well-being*. Baltimore, Md.: Penguin Books.

Warren, H. C. (1921). *A history of the association psychology*. New York: Scribners.

Warren, H. C. (Ed.). (1934). *Dictionary of psychology*. Cambridge, Mass.: Houghton Mifflin.

Warren, J. M. (1973). Learning in vertebrates. In D. A. Dewsbury & D. A. Rethlingsharer (Eds.), *Comparative psychology: A modern survey*. New York: McGraw-Hill.

Warren, J. M., Abplanalp, J. M., & Warren, H. B. (1967). The development of handedness in cats and rhesus monkeys. In H. W. Stevenson, E. H. Hess, & H. L. Reingold (Eds.), *Early behavior: Comparative and developmental approaches*. New York: Wiley.

Warren, J. M., & Akert, K. (Eds.). (1964). *The frontal granular cortex and behavior*. New York: McGraw-Hill.

Warren, N. (1972). African infant precocity. *Psychological Bulletin, 78*, 353–367.

Warren, N. (1980). *Studies in cross-cultural psychology*. New York: Academic Press, Vol. 1, 1977; Vol. 2.

Warren, R. L. (1973). Perspectives on the American community. Chicago: Rand McNally.

Warren, S. A., & Turner, D. R. (1966). Attitudes of professionals and students toward exceptional children. *Training School Bulletin, 62*, 136–144.

Warrington, E. K., & Weiskrantz, L. (1970). Amnesic syndrome: Consolidation or retrieval? *Nature, 228*, 629–630.

Wartegg, E. (1939). *Gestalt und Charakter*. Leipzig: Barth.

Warwick, D. P., & Kelman, H. C. (1976). Ethical issues in social interventions. In W. G. Bennis, K. D. Benne, R. Chin, & K. E. Corey (Eds.), *The planning of change* (pp. 470–496). New York: Holt, Rinehart & Winston.

Warwick, R., & Williams, P. L. (1973/1858). *Gray's anatomy* (35th British ed.). Philadelphia, Pa.: Saunders.

Washburn, M. F. (1917). *The animal mind*. New York: Macmillan.

Washington v. Davis (April 21, 1978). 426 U.S. 229, 12FEP1415 (1976). *Washington Post*. Cries of a woman possessed: German court hears tapes in exorcism death trial. Friday, p. A15.

Wasserman, E. A., Dorner, W. W., & Kao, S. F. (1990). Contributions of specific cell information to judgments of interevent contingency. *Journal of Experimental Psychology: Learning, Memory, and Cognition, 16*, 509–521.

Wasserman, H., Solomon, H., Alvarez, R., & Walters, E. (1982). *Killing our own*. New York: Delacorte Press.

Watanabe, F., & Ōtsuka, K. (1979). Nihon ni okeru Ibunkakan Shinri-gaku no Kenkyū Dōkō 1960–1979. (The trends in cross-cultural psychological research in Japan, 1960–1979). *Shinrigaku Hyōron, 22*(3), 247–277.

Waterman; J. (1963). *Perspectives in linguistics*. Chicago Press.

Waterton, J., & Duffy, J. (1984). A comparison of computer interviewing techniques and traditional methods in the collection of self-report alcohol comsuption data in a field survey. *International Statistical Review, S2*, 2.

Watkins, H. H. (1978). Ego-state therapy. In J. G. Watkins (Ed.), *The therapeutic self*. New York: Human Sciences Press.

Watkins, J. G. (1949). *Hypnotherapy of war neuroses*. New York: Ronald Press.

Watkins, J. G. (1976, Winter). Ego states and the problem of responsibility: A psychological analysis of the Patty Hearst case. *Journal of Psychiatry and Law*, 471–489.

Watkins, J. G. (1977). The psychodynamic manipulation of ego states in hypnotherapy. In F. Antorelli (Ed.), *Therapy in psychosomatic medicine*. Vol. II: *Symposia. Proceedings of the Fourth International Congress of Psychosomatic Medicine*, Rome, Italy.

Watkins, J. G. (1978, Winter). Ego states and the problem of responsibility II. The case of Patricia W. *Journal of Psychiatry and Law*, 519–535.

Watkins, J. G. (1982). *Clinical hypnosis*. Vol. I: *Hypnotherapeutic technique*. Vol. II: *Hypnoanalytic technique*. New York: Irvington.

Watkins, J. G., & Johnson, R. J. (1982). *We, the divided self*. New York: Irvington.

Watkins, J. G., & Watkins, H. H. (1978). *Abreactive technique* (audio tape). New York: Psychotherapy Tape Library.

Watkins, J. G., & Watkins, H. H. (1979). The theory and practice of ego-state therapy. In H. Grayson (Ed.), *Short term approaches to psychotherapy*. New York: National Institute for the Psychotherapies/Human Sciences Press.

Watkins, J. G., & Watkins, H. H. (1979–1980). Ego states and hidden observers. *Journal of Altered States of Consciousness, 5*, 3–18.

Watkins, J. G., & Watkins, H. H. (1980). *I. Ego states and hidden observers. II. Ego-state therapy: The woman in black and the lady in white* (audio tape and transcript), New York: Norton.

Watkins, J. G., & Watkins, H. H. (1981). Ego-state therapy. In R. J. Corsini (Ed.), *Handbook of innovative psychotherapies*. New York: Wiley.

Watkins, M. M. (1976). *Waking dreams*. New York: Harper & Row.

Watson, C. G., Thomas, R. W., Felling, J. & Andersen, D. (1968). Differentiation of organics from schizophrenics at two chronicity levels by use of the Reitan-Halstead organic test battery. *Journal of Consulting and Clinical Psychology, 32*, 675–685.

Watson, D., & Friend, R. (1969). Measurement of social-evaluative anxiety. *Journal of Consulting and Clinical Psychology, 33*, 448–457.

Watson, D., & Pennebaker, J. W. (1989). Health complaints, stress and distress: Exploring the central role of negative affectivity. *Psychological Review, 96*, 234–255.

Watson, F. (1915). The father of modern psychology. *Psychological Review, 22*, 333–353.

Watson, G, & Johnson, D. W. (1972). *Social psychology: Issues and insights* (2nd ed.). Philadelphia, Pa.: Lippincott.

Watson, J. B. (1903). *Animal education*. Chicago: University of Chicago Press.

Watson, J. B. (1912). Content of a course in psychology for medical students. *Journal of the American Medical Association, 58*, 916–918.

Watson, J. B. (1913). Psychology as the behaviorist views it. *Psychological Review, 20*, 158–177.

Watson, J. B. (1914). *Behavior: An introduction to comparative psychology*. New York: Holt.

Watson, J. B. (1928). The unconscious of the behaviorist. In C. M. Child, K. Koffka, & J. E. Anderson (Eds.), *The unconscious: A symposium* (pp. 91–113). New York: Knopf.

Watson, J. B. (1928). *The ways of behaviorism*. New York: Norton.

Watson, J. B. (1929/1919). *Psychology from the standpoint of a behaviorist*. Philadelphia, Pa.: Lippincott.

Watson, J. B. (1958/1925). *Behaviorism*. New York: Norton.

Watson, J. B., & McDougall, W. (1929). *The battle of behaviorism*. New York: Norton.

Watson, J. B., & Rayner, R. (1920). Conditioned emotional reactions. *Journal of Experimental Psychology, 3*, 1–14.

Watson, J. B., & Rayner, R. (1921). Studies in infant behavior. *Scientific Monthly, 13*, 493–515.

Watson, P. (1978). *War on the mind: The military uses and abuses of psychology*. New York: Basic Books.

Watson, R. I. (1974–1976). *Eminent contributors to psychology*. New York: Springer.

Watson, R. I. (1978/1968). *The great psychologists: From Aristotle to Freud*. Philadelphia, Pa.: Lippincott.

Watson, R. I. (1979). *Basic writings in the history of psychology*. New York: Oxford University Press.

Watson, R. I., & Hall, G. S. (1928). *International encyclopedia of the social sciences*, Vol. 6. New York: Macmillan/Free Press.

Watson, W. C. (1981). *Physiological psychology, an introduction*. Boston: Houghton Mifflin.

Watt, H. J. (1905). Experimentelle Beitrage zu Einer Theorie des Denkens, *Archiv für die gesamte Psychologie, 4*, 289–436.

Wattie, B. (1973). Evaluating short term casework in a family agency. *Social casework,54*, 609–616.

Watts, A. G., Super, D. E., & Kidd, J. M. (Eds.). (1981). *Career development in Britain*. Cambridge, England: Hobson's Press.

Watts, A. W. (1975/1961). *Psychotherapy east and west*. New York: Random House.

Watts, G. O. (1975). *Dynamic neuroscience: Its application to brain disorders*. New York: Harper & Row.

Watts, W. A., & Holt, L. E. (1979). Persistence of opinion change induced under conditions of forewarning and distraction. *Journal of Personality and Social Psychology, 37,* 778–789.

Watzlawick, P., Bevan, J. H., & Jackson, D. D. (1967). *Pragmatics of human communication.* New York: Norton.

Watzlawick, P, Weakland, J, & Fisch, R. (1974). *Change: Principles of problem formation and problem resolution.* New York: Norton.

Watzlawick, P., Weakland, J. H., & Fisch, R. (1974). *Change.* New York: Norton.

Wax, R. H. (1971). *Doing fieldwork: Warnings and advice.* Chicago: University of Chicago Press.

Waxman, H. (1992). *Congressional Record,* H.R. 2535.

Way, L. (1962). *Adler's place in psychology.* New York: Collier Books.

Weakland, J., Fisch, R, Watzlawick, P., & Bodin, A. (1974). Brief therapy: Focused problem resolution. *Family Process, 13,* 141–168.

Weakland, J. H., Fisch, R., Watzlawick, P., & Bodin, A. (1974). Brief therapy: Focused problems resolution. *Family Process, 13,* 141–168.

Weary, G., Stanley, M. A., & Harvey, J. H. (1989). *Attribution.* New York: Springer-Verlag.

Weatherly, D. (1965). Some personality correlates of the ability to stop smoking cigarettes. *Journal of Consulting Psychology, 29*(5), 483–485.

Weaver, C. N. (1980). Job satisfaction in the United States in the 1970s. *Journal of Applied Psychology, 65,* 364—367.

Weaver, P. A. (1976). Sentence anagram organizational training and its effect on reading comprehension. (doctoral dissertation, University of Pittsburgh, 1976) *Dissertation Abstracts International, 37,* 1312A.

Weaver, S. J. (Ed.). (1984). *Testing children: A reference guide for effective clinical and psyhoeducational assessment.* Kansas City, MO: Test Corporation.

Weaver, W. (1948). Probability, rarity, interest and surprise. *Scientific Monthly, 67,* 390–392.

Weaver, W. (1963). *Lady Luck: The theory of probability.* Garden City, N.Y.: Doubleday (Anchor).

Webb, E. J., Campbell, D. T., Schwartz, P. D., & Sechrest, L. (1966). *Unobtrusive measures: Nonreactive research in the social sciences.* Chicago: Rand McNally.

Webb, E. J., Campbell, D. T., Schwartz, R. C., & Sechrest, L. (1966). *Unobtrusive measures: Nonreactive research in the social sciences.* Chicago: Rand-McNally.

Webb, W. B. (1974). Sleep as an adaptive response. *Perceptual and Motor Skills, 38,* 1023–1027.

Webb, W. B. (1975). *Sleep, the gentle tyrant.* New York: Prentice-Hall.

Webb, W. B. (1983). In A. Mayes (Ed.), *Theories in modern sleep research* (pp. 1–15). Berkshire, UR: Van Nostrand Reinhold.

Webb, W. B. (1988). An objective behavioral model of sleep. *Sleep, 11,* 488–496.

Webb, W. B. (1990). In S. Krippner (Ed.), *Dreamtime and dreamwork* (pp. 175–184). Los Angeles: Tarcher.

Webb, W. B. (Ed.). (1973). *Sleep: An active process.* Glenview, Ill.: Scott, Foresman.

Webb, W. B., & Cartwright, R. D. (1978). Sleep and dreams. In M. R. Rosenzweig & L. W. Porter (Eds.), *Annual review of psychology,* Vol. 29. Palo Alto, Calif.: Annual Reviews.

Weber, E. (1970). *Early childhood education: Perspectives on change.* Belmont, Calif.: Wadsworth.

Weber, E. H. (1834). De pulsu, resorptione, auditu et tactu. In *Annotationes anatomicae et physiologicae.* Leipzig: Koehler.

Weber, L. (1971). *The English infant school and informal education.* Englewood Cliffs, N.J.: Prentice-Hall.

Weber, M. (1930). *The Protestant ethic and the spirit of capitalism.* London: Allen & Unwin.

Webster, A. M. (1975/1973). *Webster's new collegiate dictionary.* Springfield, Mass.: Merriam.

Webster, C., Slomen, D., Sepejak, D., Butler, B., Jensen, F., & Turral, G. (1979). *Dangerous behavior rating scheme (DBRS) construction and inter-rater reliability.* Unpublished manuscript, Toronto, Ontario.

Webster, E. C. (Ed.). (1967). *The Couchiching Conference on Professional Psychology.* Montreal: Eagle.

Webster, M. Divorce: The new American rite of passage. Unpublished doctoral dissertation.

Webster-Stratton, C. Hollinsworth, T., & Kolpacoff, M. (1989). The long-term effectiveness and clinical significance of three cost-effective training programs for families with conduct-problem children. *Journal of Consulting and Clinical Psychology, 57,* 550–553.

Webster-Stratton, C., Kolpacoff, M., & Hollinsworth, T. (1988). Self-administered videotape therapy for families with conduct problem children: Comparison with two cost-effective treatments and a control group. *Journal of Consulting and Clinical Psychology, 56,* 558–566.

Webster's encyclopedia unabridged dictionary of the English language. (1989). New York: Grammercy Books.

Webster's ninth new collegiate dictionary. (1989). MA: Merriam-Webster.

Webster's seventh new collegiate dictionary. (1963). Springfield, Mass.: Merriam.

Webster's sports dictionary. (1976). Springfield, Mass.: Merriam.

Wechsler, D. (1940). Nonintellective factors in general intelligence. *Psychological Bulletin, 37,* 444–445.

Wechsler, D. (1949). *WISC manual.* New York: Psychological Corp.

Wechsler, D. (1950). Cognitive, conative, and nonintellective intelligence. *American Psychologist, 5,* 78–83.

Wechsler, D. (1954). The measurement and evaluation of intelligence of older persons. The Third Congress of International Assessment of Gerontology. In *Old age in the modern world.* London: *International Association of Gerontology.*

Wechsler, D. (1958/1939). The measurement and appraisal of adult intelligence (4th ed.). Baltimore, Md.: Williams & Wilkins.

Wechsler, D. (1967). *Wechsler Preschool and Primary Scale of Intelligence.* New York: Psychological Corp.

Wechsler, D. (1974). *Manual for the Wechsler Intelligence Scale for Children* (rev. ed.). New York: Psychological Corp.

Wechsler, D. (1974). *Selected papers of David Wechsler with introductory material by Allen J. Edwards.* New York: Academic Press.

Wechsler, D. (1974/1949). *Wechsler Intelligence Scale for Children, revised.* New York: Psychological Corp.

Wechsler, D. (1981/1955). *The Wechsler Adult Intelligence Scale, revised.* New York: Psychological Corp.

Wechsler, D. (1981/1974). *Manual for the Wechsler Adult Intelligence scale—revised.* New York: Psychological Corp.

Weckowicz, T. (In preparation). Models of mental illness.

Wedding, D., & Corsini, R. J. (Eds.) (1979). *Great cases in psychotherapy.* Itasca, Ill.: Peacock.

Wedding, D., & Gudeman, H. (1980). Implications of computerized axial tomography for clinical neuropsychology. *Professional Psychology, 11,* 31–35.

Weed, L. L. (1969). Medical records, medical education, and patient care. Chicago: Press of Case Western Reserve University.

Weeks, G. R. (1991). A metatheory of paradox. In G. E. Weeks (Ed.), *Promoting change through paradoxical therapy* (pp. 302–316). New York: Brunner/Mazel.

Weeks, G. R., & L'Abate, L. (1982). *Paradoxical pyschotherapy: Theory and practice with individuals, couples, and families.* New York: Brunner/Mazel.

Wegner, D. M., & Vallacher, R. R. (1977). *Implicit psychology: An introduction to social cognition.* New York: Oxford University Press.

Weick, K. (1984). Small wins: Redefining the scale of social problems. *American Psychologist, 39,* 40–49.

Weick, K. E. (1985). Systematic observational methods. In E. Aronson & G. Lindzay (Eds.), *Handbook of social psychology* (3rd ed., pp. 567–634). New York: Random House.

Weihs, T. (1977). *Children in need of special care.* London: Souvenir Press.

Weil, A. T., Zinberg, N. E., & Nelsen, J. M. Clinical and psychological effects of marijuana in man. *Science, 162,* 1234—1242.

Weimer, W. B. (1979). *Notes on the methodology of scientific research.* Hillsdale, N.J.: Erlbaum.

Weimer, W. B., & Palermo D. S. (Eds.). (1974). *Cognition and the symbolic processes.* Hillsdale, N.J.: Erlbaum.

Weinberg, M., & Clark, K. B. (Eds.). (1970). *W. E. B. DuBois: A reader.* New York: Harper & Row.

Weinberg, M. S., & Bell, A. P. (1972). *Homosexuality: An annotated bibliography.* New York: Harper & Row.

Weinberg, N. (1978). Modifying social steretypes of the physically disabled. *Rehabilitation Counseling Bulletin, 22*(2), 114–124.

Weinberger, D. R., Torrey, E. F., Neophytides, A. N., & Wyatt, R. J. (1979). Lateral cerebral ventricular enlargement in chronic schizophrenia. *Archives of General Psychiatry, 36,* 735–739.

Weinberger, J. (1990a). *Application of the REMA model to psychodynamic psychotherapy.* Paper presented at the Society for the Exploration for Psychotherapy Inteqration, Philadelphia.

Weinberger, J. (1991). *The REMA (relationship, exposure, mastery, attribution) common factor model of psychhotherapy.* Unpublished manuscript, Derner Insititute, Adelphi University.

Weinberger, J. (in press). Factors in psychotherapy. In G. Strickler (Ed.), *Comprehensive handbook of psychotherapy integration.* New York: Plenum.

Weinberger, J., & Hardaway, R. (1990). Separating science from myth in subliminal psychodynamic activation. *Clinical Psychology Review, 10,* 727–756.

Weinberger, J. L., & Silverman, L. H. (1987). Subliminal psychodynamic activation: A method for studying psychoanalytic dynamic propositions. In R. Hogan & W. H. Jones (Ed.), *Perspectives in personality* (Vol. 2, pp. 251–287). Greenwich, CT: JAI.

Weinberger, N. M., Ashe, J. H., Metherate, R., McKenna, T. M., Diamond, D. M., Bakin, J. S., Lennartz, R. C., & Cassady, J. M. (1990). Neural adaptive information processing: A preliminary model of receptive-field plasticity in auditory cortex during Pavlovian conditioning. In M. Gabriel & J. W. Moore (Eds.), *Learning and computational neuroscience: Foundations of adaptive networks* (pp. 91–138). Cambridge: MIT Press.

Weinberqer, J. (1990b). *The REMA common factor model of psychotherapy.* Paper presented at the Society for the Exploration for Psychotherapy Integration, Philadelphia.

Weiner, B. (1966). Effects of motivation on the avialability and retrieval or memory traces. *Psychological Bulletin, 65,* 24–37.

Weiner, B. (1980). *Human motivation.* New York: Holt, Rinehart & Winston.

Weiner, B. (1986). *An attributional theory of achievement, motivation, and emotion.* New York: Springer-Verlag.

Weiner, B., (Ed.). (1974). *Achievement motivation and attribution theory.* Morristown, N.J.: General Learning Press.

Weiner, B., Frieze, I., Kukla, A., Reed, L., Rest, S., & Rosenblum, R. M. (1971). Perceiving the causes of success and failure. In E. E. Jones, D. E. Kanouse, H. H. Kelley, R. E. Nisbett, S. Valins, & B. Weiner (Eds.), *Attribution: Perceiving the causes of behavior.* Morristown, N.J.: General Learning Press.

Weiner, B., Johnson, P. B., & Mehrabian, A. (1968). Achievement motivation and the recall of incompleted and completed exam questions. *Journal of Educational Psychology, 59,* 181–185.

Weiner, B., & Peters, N. (1973). A cognitive-developmental analysis of achievement and moral judgment. *Developmental Psychology, 9,* 290–309.

Weiner, B., & Walker, E. L. (1966). Motivational factors in short-term retention. *Journal of Experimental Psychology, 71,* 190–193.

Weiner, E. (1980). *Discipline in the classroom* (2nd ed.). Washington, D.C.: National Education Association.

Weiner, H. (1991). From simplicity to complexity (1950–1990): The case of peptic ulceration—I. Human Studies. *Psychosomatic Medicine, 53,* 467–490.

Weiner, I. B. (1975). *Principles of psychotherapy.* New York: Wiley.

Weiner, N. (1948). *Cybernetics: Control and communication of the animal and machine.* Cambridge, Mass.: M.I.T. Press.

Weiner, R. D. (1979). The psychiatric use of electrically induced seizures. *American Journal of Psychiatry, 136,* 1507–1517.

Weiner, S., Sutherland, G., Bartholomew, A. A., & Hudson, B. (1968). XYY males in a Melbourne prison. *Lancet, 1,* 150.

Weinert, F. E. (1967). *Persönlichkeit und Lernen. Untersuchungen zur differentiellen Psychologie des kindlichen Lernens.* Bonn: University Press.

Weinert, F. E. (1970). *Schreiblehrmethode und Schreibentwicklung* (2nd ed.), Weinheim: Beltz.

Weinert, F. E. (1972). Schule und Beruf als institutionelle Sozialisationsbedingungen. In C. F. Graumann (Ed.), *Sozialpsychologie. Handbuch der Psychologie.* Göttingen, West Germany: Hogrefe.

Weinert, F. E. (1974/1967). *Pädagogische Psychologie* (8th ed.), Cologne, West Germany: Kiepenheuer & Witsch.

Weinert, F. E. (1976). *Lernen im System der Schule.* Tübingen, West Germany: Deutsches Institut für Fernstudien.

Weinert, F. E., & Kluwe, R. (1983). *Metakognition, Motivation und Lernen.* Stuttgart: Kohlhammer.

Weinert, F. E., & Trieber, B. (1982). School socialization and cognitive development. In W. W. Hartup (Ed.), *Review of child development research,* Vol. 6. Chicago: University of Chicago Press.

Weingarten, R., & Almond, R. (1972). A contribution to the psychology of romantic love: Overview and phenomenology. Mimeo.

Weininger, O. (1903). *Geschlecht und Charakter.* Vienna: Braumueller.

Weinstein, G., & Fantini, M. (1970). *Toward humanistic education: A curriculum of affect.* New York: Praeger.

Weinstein, H. C. (1980). Psychiatry on trial: Clinical and ethical problems in the psychiatric assessment of competency to stand trial. In F. Wright, C. Bahn, & R. W. Rieber (Eds.), *Forensic psychology and psychiatry*. New York: New York Academy of Sciences.

Weinstein, M. S. (1969). Achievement motivation and risk preference. *Journal of Personality and Social Psychology, 13*, 153–172.

Weinstock, S. (1970). Contiguity theory: An appraisal. In M. H. Marx (Ed.) *Learning: Theories*. New York: Macmillan.

Weir, W. (1984, October 15). Another look at subliminal "facts." *Advertising Age*, p. 46.

Weis, J. P., & Henney, J. S. (1980). Crime and criminals in the United States. In E. Bittner & S. L. Messinger (Eds.), *Criminology review yearbook*, Vol. II. Beverly Hills, Calif.: Sage Publications.

Weisbord, M. W. (1978). *Organizational diagnosis*. Reading, Mass.: Addison-Wesley.

Weisfeld, G. E. (1982). The nature-nurture issue and the integrating concept of function. In B. B. Wolman (Ed.), *Handbook of developmental psychology*. Englewood Cliffs, N.J.: Prentice-Hall.

Weiskrantz, L. (1986). *Blindsight: A case study and implications*. Oxford, UK: Oxford University Press.

Weisman, A. D. (1975). Thanatology. In A. M. Friedman, H. J. Kaplan, & B. J. Sadock (Eds.), *Comprehensive textbook of psychiatry/II* (2nd Ed.). Baltimore, Md.: Williams & Wilkins.

Weisman, A. D., & Hackett, T. P. (1961). Predilection to death: Death and dying as a psychiatric problem. *Psychosomatic Medicine, 23*, 232–256.

Weisner, T. S., & Gallimore, R. (1977). My brother's keeper: Child and sibling caretaking. *Current Anthropology, 18*, 169–190.

Weiss, B. (1982). Food additives and environmental chemicals as sources of childhood behavior disorders. *Journal of the American Academy of Child Psychiatry, 21*, 144–152.

Weiss, B., & Laties, V. G. (Eds.). (1975). *Behavioral toxicology*. New York: Plenum.

Weiss, D. J. (1976). Adaptive testing research at Minnesota: Overview, recent results, and future directions. In C. L. Clark (Ed.), *Proceedings of the First Conference on Computerized Adaptive Testing* (pp. 24–35). Washington, DC: U.S. Civil Service Commission.

Weiss, E., & English, O. S. (1949). *Psychosomatic medicine*. New York: Saunders.

Weiss, G. (1981). Controversial issues of the psychopharmacology of the hyperactive child. *Canadian Journal of Psychiatry, 26*, 385–392.

Weiss, G., & Hechtman, L. (1979). The hyperactive child syndrome. *Science, 205*, 1348–1354.

Weiss, G., & Hechtman, L. (1986). *Hyperactive children grown up*. New York: Guilford.

Weiss, G., Hechtman, L., & Perlman, T. (1978). Hyperactives as young adults: School, employer, and self-ratings obtained during 10-year follow-up evaluations. *American Journal of Orthopsychiatry, 48*, 438–445.

Weiss, G., Minde, K., Werry, J. S., Douglas, V., & Nemeth, E. (1972). Studies on the hyperactive child: Five year follow-up. In S. Chess, & A. Thomas (Eds.), *Annual progress in child psychiatry and child development*. New York: Brunner/Mazel, 1972.

Weiss, J. H. (1968). Birth order and asthma in children. *Journal of Psychosomatic Research* (London), *12*(2), 137–140.

Weiss, J. M. (1970). Somatic effects of predictable and unpredictable shock. *Psychosomatic Medicine, 32*, 397–408.

Weiss, J. M. (1991). Stress-induced depression: Critical neurochemical and electrophysiological changes. In J. Madden IV (Ed.), *Neurobiology of learning, emotion and affect* (pp. 123–154). New York: Raven.

Weiss, J. M., Glazer, H. I., & Pohorecky, L. A. (1976). Coping behavior and neurochemical changes in rats: An alternative explanation for the original "learned helplessness" experiments. In G. Serban & A. Kling (Eds.), *Animal models in human psychobiology*. New York: Plenum.

Weiss, J. M., Glazer, H. I., Pohorecky, L. A., Brick, J., & Miller, N. E. (1975). Effects of chronic exposure to stressors on avoidance-escape behavior and on brain norepinephrine. *Psychosomatic Medicine, 37*, 522–534.

Weiss, J. M., Goodman, P. A., Losito, B. G., Corrigan, S., Charry, J. M., & Bailey, W. H. (1981). Behavioral depression produced by an uncontrollable stressor: Relationship to norepinephrine, dopamine and serotonin levels in various regions of rat brain. *Brain Research Reviews, 3*, 167–205.

Weiss, J. M., Pohorecky, L. A., Salman, S., & Gruenthal, M. (1976). Attenuation of gastric lesions by psychological aspects of aggression in rats. *Journal of Comparative and Physiological Psychology, 90*, 252–259.

Weiss, P. A. (1969). The living system: Determinism stratified. *Studium Generale, 22*, 361–400.

Weiss, R. L. (1968). Operant conditioning techniques in psychological assessment. In P. McReynolds (Ed.), *Advances in psychological assessment*, Vol. I. Palo Alto, Calif.: Science & Behavior Books.

Weiss, R. L. (1975). Contracts, cognition, and change: A behavioral approach to marriage therapy. *The Counseling Psychologist, 5*, 15–26.

Weiss, R. L. (1978). The conceptualization of marriage from a behavioral perspective. In T. J. Paolino & B. S. McCrady (Eds.), *Marriage and marital therapy: Psychoanalytic, behavioral and systems theory perspectives*. New York: Brunner/Mazel.

Weiss, R. L., Birchler, G. R., & Vincent, J. P. (May, 1974). Contractual models for negotiation training in marital dyads. *Journal of Marriage and the Family*, 321–330.

Weiss, R. L., & Margolin, G. (1977). Assessment of marital conflict and accord. In A. R. Ciminero, K. D. Calhoun, & H. E. Adams (Eds.), *Handbook of behavioral assessment*. New York: Wiley.

Weiss, R. S. (1974). The provisions of social relationships. In Z. Rubin (Ed.), *Doing unto others* (pp. 17–26). Englewood Cliffs, NJ: Prentice-Hall.

Weiss, R. W. (1980). *Dealing with alcoholism in the workplace*. New York: Conference Board, Report no. 784.

Weiss, S. M., Herd, J. A., & Fox, B. H. (1981). *Perspectives on behavioral medicine*. New York: Academic Press.

Weiss, V. (1972). Empirische Untersuchung zu einer Hypothese über den Autosomalrezessiven der mathematisch-technischen Begabung. *Biologisches Zentralblatt, 91*, 429–435.

Weiss, V., & Mehlhorn, M. G. (1980). Der Hauptgenlocus der allgemeinen Intelligenz: Diskrete und ganzzahlige Unterschiede in der Zentralen Informationsverarbeitungsgeschwindigkeit. *Biologisches Zentralblatt, 99*, 297–310.

Weissberg, R. (1975). Political efficacy and political illusion. *Journal of Politics, 37*, 469–487.

Weissbourd, R., & Sears, R. R. (1982). Mark Twain's exhibitionism. *Biography, 5*, 95–117.

Weissman, M., & Smith, R. (1992). Epidemiology. In E. Paykel (Ed.), *Handbook of affective disorders*. New York: Guilford.

Weissman, M. M., & Merikangas, K. R. (1986). The epidemiology of anxiety and panic disorders: An update. *Journal of Clinical Psychiatry, 47*, 11–17.

Weisstein, N. (1971). Psychology constructs the female. In V. Gornick & B. Moran (Eds.), *Woman in sexist society*. New York: Basic Books.

Weiten, W., & Diamond, S. S. (1979). A critical review of the jury simulation paradigm: The case of defendant characteristics. *Law and Human Behavior, 3*, 71–93.

Weitz, S. (1976). Sex differences in nonverbal communication. *Sex Roles, 2*, 175–184.

Weitz, S. (1977). *Sex roles: Biological, psychological, and social foundations*. New York: Oxford University Press.

Weitzenhoffer, A. M., & Hilgard, E. R. (1959). *Stanford Hypnotic Susceptibility Scale, Forms A & B*. Palo Alto, Calif.: Consulting Psychologists Press.

Weitzenhoffer, A. M. Mesmer, Franz Anton. (1968). *International encyclopedia of the social sciences*, Vol. 10. New York: Macmillan/Free Press.

Weitzman, E. D. (1981). Sleep and its disorders. *Annual Review of Neuroscience, 4*, 381–417.

Weitzman, E. D. (Ed.). (1974). *Advances in sleep research*, Vol. 1. New York: Spectrum.

Weizsaecker, V. von. (1947). *Der Gestaltkreis*. Stuttgart: Klett.

Wekstein, L. (1979). *Handbook of suicidology*. New York: Brunner/Mazel.

Welch, B. L. (1977). A psychological study of only children. Ph.D. dissertation, University of North Carolina.

Welch, J. P., Borgaonkar, D. S., & Herr, H. M. (1967). Psychopathy, mental deficiency, aggressiveness and the XYY syndrome. *Nature, 214*, 500.

Welch, R. B. (1978). *Perceptual modification: Adapting to altered sensory environments*. New York: Academic Press.

Welford, A. T. (1958). *Ageing and human skill*. London: Oxford University Press.

Welford, A. T. (1976). *Skilled performance: Perceptual and motor skills*. Glenview, Ill.: Scott, Foresman.

Welford, A. T. (Ed.). (1980). *Reaction times*. New York: Academic.

Welkowitz, J., Ewen, R. B., & Cohen, J. (1971). *Introductory statistics for the behavioral sciences*. New York: Academic Press.

Wellek, A. (1939). *Psychologie der Musikbegabung im deutschen Volke*. Munich: Barth.

Wellek, A. (1950). *Die Polarität im Aufbau des Charakters*. Bern: Franke.

Wellek, A. (1953). *Bericht über den 17. und 18. Kongress der Deutschen Gesellschaft für Psychologie in Göttingen 1948 und in Marburg 1951*. Göttingen, West Germany: Hogrefe.

Wellek, A. (1964). Der Einfluss der deutschen Emigration auf die amerikanische Psychologie. (1964). *Psychologische Rundschau, 15*, 1–4.

Wellek, A. (1966). Deutsche Psychologie und Nationalsozialismus. *Psychologie und Praxis, 4*, 177–182.

Wellek, A. (Ed.). (1965). *Gesamtverzeichnis der deutschsprachigen psychologischen Literatur der Jahre 1942 bis 1960*. Göttingen, West Germany: Hogrefe.

Weller, L. Natan, O., & Haft, O. (1974). Birth order and marital bliss in Israel. *Journal Of Marriage and the Family, 36*(4), 794–797.

Wellings, K., Field, J., Wadsworth, A. M., Johnson, A. M., Anderson, R. M., & Bradshaw, S. A. (1990). Sexual lifestyles under scrutiny. *Nature, 348*.

Wells, C. E. (1979). Pseudodementia. *American Journal of Psychiatry, 136*, 895–900.

Wells, C. E. (Ed.). (1977). *Dementia*. Philadelphia, Pa.: Davis.

Wells, G. L. (1978). Applied eyewitness-testimony research: System variables and estimator variables. *Journal of Personality and Social Psychology, 36*, 1546–1557.

Wells, G. L., Lindsay, R. C. L., & Ferguson, T. J. (1979). Accuracy, confidence, and juror perceptions in eyewitness identification. *Journal of Applied Psychology, 64*, 440–448.

Wells, G. L., & Loftus, E. F. (Eds.), *Eyewitness testimony: Psychological perspectives*. New York: Cambridge University Press.

Wells, H. G., Huxley, J. S., & Wells, G. P. (1934). *The science of life*. Garden City, N.Y.: Literary Guild, Country Life Press.

Wells, S. P., & Brown, R. T. (1986). Fragile-X syndrome. In C. R. Raynolds & L. Mann (Eds.), *Encyclopedia of special education* (vol. 2, pp. 676–677). New York: Wiley.

Wells, W. D., & Gubar, G. (1966). The life cycle concept in marketing research. *Journal of Marketing Research, 3*, 355–363.

Welwood, J. (1980, Spring). Working with emotion: Western and eastern. *American Theosophist*.

Welwood, J. (Ed.). (1979). *The meeting of the ways: Explorations in east/west psychology*. New York: Shocken.

Wenar, C. (1971). *Personality development from infancy to adulthood*. Boston: Houghton Mifflin.

Wender, P., Kety, S., Rosenthal, D., Schulsinger, F., Ortmann, J., & Lunde, I. (1986). Psychiatric disorders in the biological and adoptive families of adopted individuals with affective disorders. *Archives of General Psychiatry, 43*, 923–929.

Wender, P. H. (1971). *Minimal brain dysfunction in children*. New York: Wiley.

Wendorf, D. J., & Wendorf, R. J. (1985). A systemic view of family therapy ethics. *Family Process, 24*, 443–453.

Wendt, R. N. (1979). Prekindergarten screening: Point-counterpoint. *Viewpoints in Teaching and Learning, 55*, 18–24.

Wenger, M., & Bagchi, B. (1961). Studies of autonomic functions in practitioners of Yoga in India. *Behavioral Science, 6*, 312–323.

Wenner, A. M. (1971). *The bee language controversy*. Boulder, Colo.: Educational Programs Improvement Corp.

Werner, A. (1972). Rape: Interruption of the therapeutic process. *Psychotherapy: Theory, Research and Practice, 9*, 349–351.

Werner, H. (1926). *Einführung in die Entwicklungspsychologie*. Leipzig: Barth.

Werner, H. (1961/1948/1940). *Comparative psychology of mental development*. New York: Science Editions.

Werner, H. (Ed.). (1955). *On expressive language*. Worcester, Mass.: Clark University Press.

Werner, H., & Kaplan B. (1963). *Symbol formation*. New York: Wiley.

Werner, H., & Wapner, S. (1952). Toward a general theory of perception. *Psychological Review, 59*, 324–338.

Wernimont, P. F., & Fitzpatrick, S. (1972). The meaning of money. *Journal of Applied Psychology, 56*, 218–226.

Werry, J. S. (1979). The childhood psychoses. In H. C. Quay & J. S. Werry (Eds.), *Psychopathological disorders of childhood*. New York: Wiley.

Wertheimer, M. (1905). Experimentelle Untersuchungen zur Tatbestandsdiagnostik. *Archiv für die Gesamte Psychologie, 6*, 59–131.

Wertheimer, M. (1912). Experimental studies of the perception of movement. *Zeitschrift für Psychologie, 61*, 161–265.

Wertheimer, M. (1912). Experimentelle Studien ueber das Sehen von Bewegung. *Zeitschrift fuer Psychologie, 60*, 321–378.

Wertheimer, M. (1923). Studies in the theory of Gestalt. *Psychologische Forschung, 4*, 301–350.

Wertheimer, M. (1923). Untersuchungen zur Lehre von der Gestalt: II. *Psychologische Forschung, 4*, 301–350.

Wertheimer, M. (1934). On truth. *Social Research, 1*, 135–146.

Wertheimer, M. (1937). On the concept of democracy. In M. Ascoli & F. Lehmann (Eds.), *Political and economic democracy*. New York: Norton.

Wertheimer, M. (1938). Laws of organization in perceptual forms. In W. D. Ellis (Ed.), *A sourcebook of Gestalt psychology*. London: Paul, Trench, Trubner.

Wertheimer, M. (1940). A story of three days. In R. N. Anshen, (Ed.), *Freedom: Its meaning*. New York: Harcourt, Brace.

Wertheimer, M. (1958/1923). Principles of perceptual organization. In D. C. Beardslee & M. Wertheimer (Eds.), *Readings in perception*. Princeton, N.J.: Van Nostrand Reinhold.

Wertheimer, M. (1972). *Fundamental issues in psychology*. New York: Holt, Rinehart & Winston.

Wertheimer, M. (1979/1970). *A brief history of psychology*. New York: Holt, Rinehart & Winston.

Wertheimer, M. (1980). Max Wertheimer, Gestalt prophet. *Gestalt theory*. Darmstadt, West Germany: Steinkopff.

Wertheimer, M. (1982). Gestalt theory, holistic psychologies, and Max Wertheimer. *Zeitschrift für Psychologie, 190*, 125–140.

Wertheimer, M. (1982/1959/1945). *Productive thinking*. Chicago: University of Chicago Press.

Wertheimer, M. (Ed.). (1970). *Confrontation: Psychology and the problems of today*. Glenview, Ill.: Scott, Foresman.

Wertheimer, M., Barclay, A. G., Cook, S. W., Kiesler, C. A., Koch, S, Riegel, K. F., Rorer, L. G, Senders, V. L., Smith, M. B., & Sperling, S. E. (1978). Psychology and the future. *American Psychologist, 33*, 631–647.

Wertheimer, M., Björkman, M., Lundberg, I., & Magnusson, D. (1971). *Psychology: A brief introduction*. Glenview, Ill.: Scott, Foresman.

Wertheimer, M., & Rappoport, L. (Eds.). (1978). *Psychology and the problems of today*. Glenview, Ill.: Scott, Foresman.

Wertlieb, D. (1979). A preventive health paradigm for health care psychologists. *Professional Psychology,10*, 548–557.

Wertlieb, D., & Budman, S. (1982). The health-mental health linkage: Mandates and challenges for program evaluation research. In G. Stahler & W. Tash (Eds.), *Innovative approaches to mental health evaluation*. New York: Academic Press.

Wertsch, J. V. (1981). *The concept of activity in Soviet psychology*. Armonk, N.Y.: Sharpe.

Wesche, M. B. (1981). Language aptitude measures in streaming, matching students with methods, and diagnosis of learning problems. In K. C. Diller (Ed.), *Individual differences and universals in language learning aptitude*. Rowley, Mass.: Newbury House.

Weschler, D. (1958). *The measurement and appraisal of adult intelligence*. Baltimore: Williams & Wilkins.

Wesman, A. G. (1968). Intelligent testing. *American Psychologist, 23*, 267–274.

Wessler, R. A., & Wessler, R. L. (1980). *The principles and practice of rational-emotive therapy*. San Francisco: Jossey-Bass.

Wessman, A. E. (1979). Moods: Their personal dynamics and significance. In C. E. Izard (Ed.), *Emotions in personality and psychopathology*. New York: Plenum.

Wessman, A. E., & Ricks, D. F. (1966). *Mood and personality*. New York: Holt, Rinehart & Winston.

West, J. R. (1986b). Preface. In J. R. West (Ed.), *Alcohol and brain development*. New York: Oxford University Press.

West, J. R. (Ed.). (1986a). *Alcohol and brain development*. New York: Oxford University Press.

West, M. (1953). *A general service list of English words, with semantic frequencies and a supplementary word-list for the writing of popular science and technology*. New York: Longman, Green.

West, M. (1979). Meditation (review article). *British Journal of Psychiatry, 135*, 457–467.

West, M. (1980). Meditation and the EEG. *Psychological Medicine, 10*, 369–375.

West, R. (1989). Planning practical memory training for the aged. In L. Poon, D. Rubin, & A. Wilson (Eds.), *Everyday cognition in adulthood and old age* (pp. 573–597). New York: Cambridge University Press.

Westcott, M. R. (1968). *Toward a contemporary psychology of intuition*. New York: Holt, Rinehart & Winston.

Westcott, M. R. (1978). Toward psychological studies of human freedom. *Canadian Psychological Review, 19*, 277–290.

Westcott, M. R. (1982). Quantitative and qualitative aspects of experienced freedom. *The Journal of Mind and Behavior, 3*, 99–126.

Westermeyer, J., Lyfoung, T., Wahmenholm, K., & Westermeyer, M., (1989). Delusions of fatal contagion among refugee patients. *Psychosomatics, 30*(4), 374–382.

Westin, M. T., & Reiss, D. (1979). The family's role in rehabilitation: Early warning system, *Journal of Rehabilitation, 45*, 26–29.

Westinghouse and Ohio University. (1973). The impact of Head Start: An evaluation of the effects of Head Start on children's cognitive and affective development. In J. L. Frost (Ed.), *Revisiting early childhood education—Readings*. New York: Holt, Rinehart & Winston.

Wettendorf, H. (1901). Modifications du sang sous l'influence de la privation d'eau: Contribution à l'étude de la soif. *Travaux du Laboratoire de Physiologie, Institute Solvay, 4*, 353–484.

Wettler, M. (1980). *Sprache, Gedächtnis, Verstehen*. Berlin: De Gruyter.

Wetzel, L., & Ross, N. (1983). Psychological and social ramifications of battering: Observations leading to a counseling methodology for victims of domestic violence. *Personnel and Guidance Journal, 61*, 423–428.

Wever, R. A. (1979). *The circadian system of man: Results of experiments under temporal isolation*. New York: Springer-Verlag.

Wexler, D. A., & Rice, L. N. (Eds.) (1974). *Innovations in client-centered therapy*. New York: Wiley.

Wexler, M. (1976). The behavioral sciences in medical education. *American Psychologist, 31*, 275–283.

Wexley, K. N., & Yukl, G. A. (1977). *Organizational behavior and personnel psychology*. Homewood, Ill.: Irwin.

Whalen, C. K., & Henker, B. (1976). Psychostimulants and children: A review and analysis. *Psychological Bulletin 83*, 1113–1130.

Whalen, C. K., & Henker, B. (1991). Therapies for hyperactive children: Comparisons, combinations, and compromises. *Journal of Consulting and Clinical Psychology, 59*, 126–137.

Whalen, R. E. (Ed.). (1967). *Hormones and behavior.* Princeton, N.J.: Van Nostrand.

Whalen, R. E., & Edwards, D. A. (1967). Hormonal determinants of masculine and feminine behavior in male and female rats. *Anatomical Record, 157,* 173–180.

Whaley, B. (1969). *Stratagem: Deception and surprise in war.* Cambridge: Center for International Studies, MIT.

Whaley, B. (1981). *The special theory of magic: Conjurers are deception planners.* Unpublished manuscript.

Whaley, B. (1982). Toward a general theory of deception. *The Journal of Strategic Studies, 5,* 178–192.

Wheatley, P. M. (1974). Effects of nude marathon regression therapy on interpersonal and intrapersonal change in self-selected subjects: Psychological nudism or psychic strip-tease? Doctoral dissertation, California School of Professional Psychology, Los Angeles.

Wheaton, B. (1985). Models for the stress-buffering functions of coping resources. *Journal of Health and Social Behavior, 26,* 352–364.

Wheeler, L. (1966). Toward a theory of behavioral contagion. *Psychological Review, 73,* 179–192.

Wheeler, L. R. (1932). The intelligence of east Tennessee children. *Journal of Educational Psychology, 23,* 351–370.

Wheeler, M., Kern, R. M., & Curlette, W. *Life style personality inventory.* Test construction underway in Department of Counseling and Psychological Services, Georgia State University.

Wheeler, R. H. (1932). *The laws of human nature.* New York: Century.

Whipple, G. M. (1910). *Manual of mental and physical tests,* Baltimore, Md.: Warwick & York.

Whishaw, I. Q., & Vanderwolf, C. H. (1973). Hippocampal EEG and behavior: Changes in amplitude and frequency of RSA (theta rhythm) associated with spontaneous and learned movement patterns in rats and cats. *Behavioral Biology, 8,* 461–484.

Whitaker, D. S., & Lieberman, M. A. (1964). *Psychotherapy through the group process.* New York: Atherton Press.

Whitaker, H. A. Dementia: Clinical issues. *Neuropsychological studies of nonfocal brain damage: Dementia and trauma.* New York: Springer-Verlag.

White, B. L. (1971). *Human infants: Experience and psychological development.* Englewood Cliffs, N.J.: Prentice-Hall.

White, B. L. (1975). *The first three years of life.* Englewood Cliffs, N.J.: Prentice-Hall.

White, B. L., Kaban, B. T., & Attannucci, J. S. (1979). *The origins of human competence.* Lexington, Mass.: Heath.

White, B. W., Saunders, F. A., Scadeen, L., Bach-y-Rita, P., & Collins, C. C. (1970). Seeing with the skin. *Perception and Psychophysics, 7,* 23–27.

White, G., Fishbein, S., & Rutstein, J. (1981). Passionate love and the misattribution of arousal. *Journal of Personality and Social Psychology, 41,* 56–62.

White, J., & Fadiman, J. (1976). *Relax.* New York: Confucian Press.

White, J. L., Moffitt, T. E., Earls, F., Robins, L., & Silva, P. A. (1990). How early can we tell?: Predictors of childhood conduct disorder and adolescent delinquency. *Criminology, 28,* 507–533.

White, K. D., Sheehan, P. W., & Ashton, R. (1977). Imagery assessment. A survey of self-report measures. *Journal of Mental Imagery, 1,* 145–170.

White, L. A. (1949). *The science of culture.* New York: Grove Press.

White, M. D., & White, C. A. (1981). Involuntarily committed patients' constitutional right to refuse treatment: A challenge to psychology. *American Psychologist, 36*(9), 953–962.

White, M. J. (1975). Interpersonal distance as affected by room size, status, and sex. *Journal of Social Psychology, 95,* 241–249.

White, R. W. (1959). Motivation reconsidered: The concept of competence. *Psychological Review, 66,* 297–333.

White, R. W. (1972). *The enterprise of living: Growth and organization in personality.* New York: Holt, Rinehart & Winston.

White, R. W. (1973). The concept of healthy personality: What do we really mean? *Counseling Psychologist, 4,* 3–12.

White, R. W. (1975/1966). *Lives in progress.* New York: Holt.

White, R. W. (Ed.). (1963). *The study of lives.* New York: Atherton.

White, R. W. (Ed.). (1964). *The study of lives.* New York: Atherton.

White, R. K., & Lippitt, R. (1960). *Autocracy and democracy.* New York: Harper.

White, R. W., & Watt, N. F. (1981). *The abnormal personality* (5th ed.). New York: Wiley.

White, S. (1970). Some general outlines of the matrix of developmental changes between five and seven years. *Bulletin of the Orton Society, 20,* 41–57.

White, S. H. (1965). Evidence for a hierarchical arrangement of learning processes. In L. L. Lipsitt & C. C. Spiker (Eds.), *Advances in child development and behavior,* Vol. 2. New York: Academic Press.

White, S. H. (1970). The national impact study of Head Start. In J. Hellmuth (Ed.), *Disadvantaged child,* Vol. 3. New York: Brunner/Mazel.

White, W. A. (1915). *Outlines of psychiatry.* New York: Nervous & Mental Disease.

White, W. A. (1933). *Crime and criminals.* New York: Farrar & Rinehart.

Whitehead, A. N. (1948). *Science and the modern world.* New York: New American Library.

Whitehead, A. N., & Russell, B. (1910). *Principia mathematica.* Cambridge, England: Cambridge University Press.

Whitehead, W. E. & Shuster, M. M. (Eds.). (1985). *Gastrointestinal disorders: Behavioral and physiological basis for treatment.* Orlando: Academic.

Whitam, F., Diamond, M., & Martin, J. (1993). Homosexual orientation in twins: A report on 61 pairs and three triplet sets. *Archives of Sexual Behavior, 22*(3).

Whitehouse, M. (1958). The tao of the body. Presented to the Analytical Psychology Club of Los Angeles.

Whitehouse, M. (1963). Physical movement and personality. Presented to the Analytical Psychology Club, Los Angeles.

Whitehouse, M. (1969–1970). Reflections on a metamorphosis. *Impulse* 62–65.

Whitehouse, M. (1977). The transference and dance therapy. *American Journal of Dance Therapy, 1*(1), 4.

Whiteley, J. M. (1977). Professional identity. *The Counseling Psychologist, 7.*

Whiteley, J. M. (1979). Research in counseling psychology. *The Counseling Psychologist, 8.*

Whiteley, J. M. (1980). Counseling psychology in the year 2000 A. D. *The Counseling Psychologist, 4,* 2–60.

Whiteley, J. M. (1980). The historical development of counseling psychology. In J. M. Whiteley (Ed.), *The history of counseling psychology.* Monterey, Calif.: Brooks/Cole.

Whiteley, J. M. (Ed.). (1980). *The history of counseling psychology.* Monterey, Calif.: Brooks/Cole.

Whiteley, J. M., & Fretz, B. R. (Eds.). (1980). *The present and future of counseling psychology.* Monterey, Calif.: Brooks/Cole.

Whiting, B., & Edwards, C. P. (1973). A cross-cultural analysis of sex differences in the behavior of children aged three through 11. *Journal of Social Psychology, 91,* 171–188.

Whiting, B. B. (Ed.). (1963). *Six cultures: Studies in child rearing.* New York: Wiley.

Whiting, J. (1954). The cross-cultural method. In G. Lindzey (Ed.), *Handbook of social psychology,* Vol. 1. Reading, Mass.: Addison-Wesley.

Whiting, J. (1968). Methods and problems in cross-cultural research. In G. Lindzey & E. Aronson (Eds.), *Handbook of social psychology,* Vol. 2 (2nd ed.). Reading, Mass.: Addison-Wesley.

Whiting, J. W. M., & Child, I. L. (1953). *Child training and personality: A cross- cultural study.* New Haven, Conn.: Yale University Press.

Whitlock, F. A., Stoll, J. R., & Rekhdahl, R. J. (1977). Crisis, life events and accidents. *Australian and New Zealand Journal of Psychiatry, 11,* 127–132.

Whitmont, E. C. (1969). *The symbolic quest.* New York: Putnam's.

Whittaker, J. O., & Meade, R. D. (1968). Retention of opinion change as a function of differential source credibility: A cross-cultural study. *International Journal of Psychology, 3,* 103–108.

Whitten, C. P., & Fischhoff, J. (1974). Psychosocial effects of sickle cell disease. *Archives of Internal Medicine, 133,* 681–689.

Whyte, L. (1962/1951). *Aspects of form: A symposium on form in nature and art.* Bloomington, Ind.: Indiana University Press.

Whyte, L. (1974). *The universe of experience.* New York: Harper & Row.

Whyte, W. F. (1943). *Street corner society: The social structure of an Italian slum.* Chicago: University of Chicago Press.

Whyte, W. F., & Hamilton, E. L. (1964). *Action research for management.* Homewood, Ill.: Irwin-Dorsey.

Wickelgren, W. A. (1977). *Learning and memory.* Englewood Cliffs, N.J.: Prentice-Hall.

Wickelgren, W. A. (1979). *Cognitive psychology.* Englewood Cliffs, N.J.: Prentice-Hall.

Wickens, D. D. (1938). The transference of conditioned excitation and conditioned inhibition from one muscle group to the antagonistic muscle group. *Journal of Experimental Psychology, 22,* 101–123.

Wickens, D. D. (1970). Encoding categories of words; an empirical approach to meaning. *Psychological Review, 77,* 1–15.

Wickens, D. D., Nield, A. F., Tuber, D. S., & Wickens, C. D. (1969). Strength, latency and form of conditioned skeletal and antonomic responses as functions of CS-UCS intervals. *Journal of Comparative and Physiological Psychology, 80,* 165–170.

Wickens, D. D., Nield, A. F., Tuber, D. S., & Wickens, C. D. (1977). Memory for the conditioned response: The effects of potential interference introduced before and after original conditioning. *Journal of Experimental Psychology: General, 106,* 47–70.

Wicker, A. W. (1979). *An introduction to ecological psychology.* Monterey, Calif.: Brooks/Cole.

Wicker, A. W. (1979). Ecological psychology: Some recent and prospective developments. *American Psychologist, 34,* 755–765.

Wicker, A. W. (1981). Nature and assessment of behavior settings: Recent contributions from the ecological perspective. In P. McReynolds (Ed.), *Advances in psychological assessment,* Vol. 5. San Francisco: Jossey-Bass.

Wickert, F. R. (1967). *Readings in African psychology from French language sources.* East Lansing, Mich.: African Studies Center, Michigan State University.

Wickes, F. G. (1927). *The inner world of childhood.* New York: Appleton-Century-Croft.

Wicklund, R. A. (1974). *Freedom and reactance.* Hillsdale, N.J.: Erlbaum.

Wicklund, R. A. (1979). The influence of self-awareness on human behavior. *American Scientist, 67,* 187–193.

Wicklund, R. A., & Brehm, J. W. (1968). Attitude change as a function of felt competence and threat to attitudinal freedom. *Journal of Experimental Social Psychology, 4,* 64–75.

Wicklund, R. A., & Brehm, J. W. (1976). *Perspectives on cognitive dissonance.* Hillsdale, N.J.: Erlbaum.

Wickramasekera, I. E. (1988). *Clinical behavioral medicine: Some concepts and procedures.* New York: Plenum.

Wicks, R. J. (1977). *Counseling strategies and intervention techniques for the human services.* Philadelphia, Pa.: Lippincott.

Wicks, R. J. (1978). *Human services: New careers and roles in the helping professions.* Springfield, Ill.: Thomas.

Widiger, T. A., & Trull, T. J. (1991). Diagnosis and clinical assessment. *Annual Review of Psychology, 42,* 109–134.

Widmer, E. L. (1970). *The critical years: Early childhood education at the crossroads.* Scranton, Pa.: International Textbook.

Widom, C. S. (1991). A tail on an untold tale: Response to Biological and genetic contributors to violence—Widom's untold tale. *Psychological Bulletin, 109,* 130–132.

Widrow, G., & Hoff, M. E. (1960). Adaptive switching circuits. In *Institute of Radio Engineers, western electornic show and convention, convention record* (part 4, pp. 96–104).

Wiener, N. (1948). *Cybernetics: Control and communication in the animal and the machine.* Cambridge, Mass.: M.I.T. Press.

Wiener, N. (1954/1950). *The human use of human beings: Cybernetics and society.* New York: Doubleday/Anchor.

Wiens, A. N. (1980). The examination for professional practice in psychology. *Journal of Professional Practice in Psychology, 1,* 11–21.

Wiens, A. N., & Menne, J. W. (1981). On disposing of "straw people" or an attempt to clarify statutory recognition and educational requirements for psychologists. *American Psychologist, 36,* 390–395.

Wigdor, A. K., & Garner, W. R. (Eds.). (1982). Ability testing: Uses, consequences, and controversies, Part I:Report of the Committee. Washington, D.C.: National Academy Press.

Wiggins, J. (1974). In defense of traits. Unpublished manuscript, University of British Columbia.

Wiggins, J. G. (1992, April). The field must contribute wisdom, help society *The A.P.A. Monitor,* 3.

Wiggins, J. S. (1973). *Personality and prediction: Principles of personality assessment.* Reading, Mass.: Addison-Wesley.

Wiggins, J. S. (1979). A psychological taxonomy of trait-descriptive terms: The interpersonal domain. *Journal of Personality and Social Psychology, 37,* 395–412.

Wiggins, J. S. (1981). Clinical and statistical prediction: Where are we and where do we go from here? *Clinical Psychology Review, 1,* 3–18.

Wiggins, J. S. (1982). Circumplex models of interpersonal behavior in clinical psychology. In P. C. Kendall & J. N. Butcher (Eds.), *Handbook of research methods in clinical psychology.* New York: Wiley/Interscience.

Wiggins, N., & Wiggins, J. S. (1969). A typological analysis of male preferences for female body types. *Multivariate Behavioral Research, 4,* 89–102.

Wigmore, J. H. *On evidence.* Wigmore, *Evidence,* 367-368.

Wigmore, J. H. (1909). Professor Münsterberg and the psychology of testimony. *Illinois Law Review, 3*(7), 399–445.

Wiig, E. H., & Semel, E. M. (1976). *Language disabilities in children and adolescents.* Columbus, Ohio: Merrill.

Wilber, K. (1977). *The spectrum of consciousness.* Wheaton, Ill.: Theosophical.

Wilber, K. (1980). *The Atman project.* Wheaton, Ill.: Quest.

Wilber, K. (1981/1979). *No boundary.* Boulder, Colo.: Shambala.

Wilber, K. (1982). Odyssey: A personal inquiry into humanistic and transpersonal psychology. *Journal of Humanistic Psychology, 22,* 57–90.

Wilber, K. (1982). The problem of proof. *Revision, 5*(1), 80–100.

Wilbur, R. H. (1976). Pets, pet ownership, and animal control: Social and psychological attitudes. Presented at the National Conference on Dog and Cat Control, American Humane Association, Denver, Colo.

Wilcox, M. R. (1980). Variables affecting group mental health consultation for teachers. *Professional Psychology, 11*(5), 728–732.

Wilcox, P., & Dawson, J. G. (1977). Role-played and hypnotically induced simulation of psychopathology on the MMPI. *Journal of Clinical Psychology, 33,* 743–745.

Wilcoxon, H. C., Dargoin, W. B., & Kral, P. A. (1969). Differential conditioning to visual and gustatory cues in quail and rat: Illness induced aversion. *Psychonomic Science, 17,* 52.

Wild, K. (1938). *Intuition.* London: Cambridge University Press.

Wiley, D. E., & Harnischfeger, A. (1974). Explosion of a myth: Quantity of schooling and exposure to instruction, major educational vehicles. *Educational Researcher, 3*(4), 7–12.

Wilgenbusch, N. (1980). *Maslow's concept of peak experience education: Impossible myth or possible mission?* Flat River, Mo.: Mineral Area College (ERIC Document Reproduction Service no. ED 199 250).

Wilhite, R. G. (1981). "The Wilhite": A creative extension of the early recollection process. In L. Baruth & D. Eckstein (Eds.), *Life style: Theory and practice and research* (2nd ed.). Dubuque, Iowa: Kendall/Hunt.

Wilierman, L. (1979). *The psychology of individual and group differences.* San Francisco: Freeman.

Wilkins, L., & Richter, C. P. (1940). A great craving for salt by a child with cortico-adrenal insufficiency. *Journal of the American Medical Association, 114,* 866–868.

Will, G. (1917). *Corn among the Indians of the Upper Missouri.* St. Louis, Mo.: Harvery, Miner.

Will, G. A., & Spinden, J. J. (1906). *The Mandans.* Papers of the Peabody Museum of Archaeology and Ethnology, Vol. 3.

Willems, E. P., & Raush, H. L. (Eds.). (1969). *Naturalistic viewpoints in psychological research.* New York: Holt, Rinehart, and Winston.

Williams, A. F. (1973). Personality and other characteristics associated with cigarette smoking among young teenagers. *Journal of Health and Social Behavior, 14,* 374–379.

Williams, B. A. (1991). Choice as a function of local versus molar reinforcement contingencies. *Journal of the Experimental Analysis of Behavior, 56,* 445–473.

Williams, B. W. (1980). Reinforcement, behavior constraint, and the overjustification effect. *Journal of Personality and Social Psychology, 39,* 599–614.

Williams, C. D. (1959). The elimination of tantrum behavior by extinction procedures. *Journal of Abnormal and Social Psychology, 59,* 269.

Williams, D. A., Overmier, J. B., & Lolordo, V. M. (1992). *Psychological Bulletin, Ill.* 275–290.

Williams, E. F. (1976). *Notes of a feminist therapist.* New York: Praeger.

Williams, G. (1957). *The sanctity of life and the criminal law,* New York: Knopf.

Williams, G. (1980). Child abuse and neglect: Problems of definition and incidence. In G. Williams & J. Money (Eds.), *Traumatic abuse and neglect of children at home.* Baltimore, Md.: John Hopkins University Press.

Williams, G. C. (1966). *Adaptation and natural selection: A critique of some current evolutionary thought.* Princeton, NJ: Princeton University Press.

Williams, G. H., & Wood, M. W. (1977). *Developmental art therapy.* Baltimore, Md.: University Park Press.

Williams, J. P. (1980). Teaching decoding with an emphasis on phoneme analysis and phoneme blending. *Journal of Educational Psychology, 72,* 1–15.

Williams, K. D., Loftus, E. F., & Deffenbacher, K. (1992). Eyewitness evidence and testimony. In D. K. Kagehiro & W. S. Laufer (Ed.), *Handbook of psychology and law* (pp. 141–166). New York: Springer-Verlag.

Williams, M. (1979). *Brain damage, behavior, and the mind.* New York: Wiley.

Williams, M. B., & Sommers, J. F. (Eds.) (in press). *Handbook of post-traumatic therapy.* Westport, CT: Greenwood.

Williams, S., & Torrens, P. (1980). *Introduction to health services.* New York: Wiley.

Williams, T., & Douds, J. (1973). The unique contribution of telephone therapy. In D. Lester & G. Brockopp (Eds.), *Telephone therapy and crisis intervention.* Springfield, Ill.: Thomas.

Williams, W. (1971). *Social policy research and analysis: The experience in the federal social agencies.* New York: American Elsevier.

Williams, W. M. (Ed.). (1974). *Occupational choice.* London: Allen & Unwin.

Williams, W. S., & Jaco, E. G. (1958). An evaluation of functional psychoses in old age. *American Journal of Psychiatry, 114,* 910–916.

Willamson, E. G. (1939). *How to counsel students.* New York: McGraw-Hill.

Williamson, E. G. (1965). *Vocational counseling.* New York: McGraw-Hill.

Williamson, E. G., & Darley, J. G. (1937). *Student personnel work.* New York: McGraw-Hill.

Willie, C. V., Kramer, B. M., & Brown, B. S. (1973). *Racism and mental health: Essays.* Pittsburgh, Pa.: University of Pittsburgh Press.

Williges, R. C. (1981). Development and use of research methodologies for complex system/simulation experimentation. In M. J. Moraal & K. F. Kraiss (Eds.), *Manned system design.* New York: Plenum.

Willington, A. M., & Strickland, B. R. (1965). Need for approval and simple motor performance. *Perceptual and Motor Skills, 21,* 879–884.

Willis, R. H. (1965). The phenomenology of shifting agreement and disagreement in dyads. *Journal of personality, 33,* 188–199.

Willis, S. L. (1991). Cognitive and everyday competence. In K. W. Schaie & M. P. Lawton (Eds.), *Annual review of geriatrics and gerontology* (Vol. 11, pp. 80–109). New York: Springer.

Willis, S. L., & Nesselroade, C. S. (1990). Long-term effects of fluid ability training in old-old age. *Developmental Psychology, 26,* 905–910.

Willis, S. L., & Schaie, K. W. (1988). Gender differences in spatial ability in old age: Longitudinal and intervention findings. *Sex Roles, 18*, 189–203.

Willis, T. (1664). *Cerebri anatome: cui accessit nervorum descriptio et usus.* London: Martyn & Allestry.

Willson, V., & Putnam, R. (1982). A meta-analysis of pretest sensitization effects in experimental design. *American Educational Research Journal, 19*, 249–258.

Wilson, A. B. (1981). Longitudinal analysis of diet, physical growth, verbal development, and school performance. In J. B. Balderston, A. B. Wilson, M. E. Freire, & M. Simonen, *Malnourished children of the rural poor.* Boston: Auburn House.

Wilson, E. O. (1963). Pheromones. *Scientific American, 208* (5), 100–115.

Wilson, E. O. (1971). *The insect societies.* Cambridge, Mass.: Harvard University Press.

Wilson, E. O. (1975). *Sociobiology: The new synthesis.* Cambridge, Mass.: Harvard University Press.

Wilson, E. O. (1978). *On human nature.* Cambridge, Mass.: Harvard University Press.

Wilson, G. (1973). A dynamic theory of conservatism. In G. Wilson (Ed.), *The psychology of conservatism.* New York: Academic Press.

Wilson, G. (1976). From practice to theory: A personalized history. In R. W. Roberts & H. Northen (Eds.), *Theories of social work with groups.* New York: Columbia University Press.

Wilson, G. T. (1978). On the much discussed nature of the term "behavior therapy." *Behavior Therapy, 9*, 89–98.

Wilson, G. T., & Brownell, K. D. (1980). Behavior therapy for obesity: An evaluation of treatment outcome. *Advances in Behavior Research and Therapy, 3*, 49–86.

Wilson, G. T., & Davidson, G. C., (1971). Processes of fear reduction in systematic desensitization: Animal studies. *Psychological Bulletin, 76*, 1–14.

Wilson, G. T., O'Leary, K. D., & Nathan, P. E. (1992). *Abnormal pschology.* New York: Prentice-Hall.

Wilson, I., Prange, A., & Lynn, C. (1974). L-tryptophan mania; Contribution to a permissive amine hypothesis of affective disorder. *Archives of General Psychiatry, 30*, 56–42.

Wilson, J. (1971). *Practical methods of moral education.* London: Heinemann.

Wilson, J. (1977). The political feasibility of punishment. Cederblom, & Blizek W. (Eds.). *Justice and punishment.* Cambridge, MA: Ballinger.

Wilson, J. D. (1981). *Student learning in higher education.* London: Croom Helm.

Wilson, M. S., & Meyer, E. (1962). Diagnostic consistency in a psychiatric liaison service. *American Journal Psychiatry, 119*, 207–209.

Wilson, R. C., Guilford, J. P., Christensen, P. R., & Lewis, D. J. (1954). A factoranalytic study of creative-thinking abilities. *Psychometrika, 10*, 297–311.

Wilson, W. R., Welch, C. G., & Gulliksen, H. (1924). An evaluation of some information questions. *Journal of Applied Psychology, 8*, 206–214.

Winch, R. F. (1955). The theory of complementary needs in mate selection: Final results on the test of the general hypothesis. *American Sociological Review, 20*, 552–555.

Winch, R. F. (1958). *Mate selection: A study of complementary needs.* New York: Harper & Row.

Winch, W. H. (1923). The transfer of improvement in reasoning in school children. *British Journal of Psychology, 13*, 381.

Windmiller, M., Lambert, N., & Turiel, E. (1980). *Moral development and socialization,* Boston: Allyn & Bacon.

Wine, J. D. (1971). Test anxiety and direction of attention. *Psychological Bulletin, 76*, 92–104.

Wine, J. D. (1980). Cognitive-attentional theory of test anxiety. In I. G. Sarason *(Ed.), Test anxiety: Theory, research, and applications.* Hillsdale, N.J.: Erlbaum.

Winer, B. J. (1971). *Statistical principles in experimental design.* New York: McGraw-Hill.

Winer, B. J. (1971). *Statistical principles in experimental design* (2nd ed.). New York: McGraw-Hill.

Wing, H. (1953). *Standardized tests of musical intelligence.* Shefford, England: Shefford Training Center.

Wing, H. (1980). Profiles of cognitive ability of different racial/ethnic and sex groups on a multiple abilities test battery. *Journal of Applied Psychology, 65*, 289–298.

Wing, R. R., & Jeffery, R. W. (1979). Outpatient treatments of obesity: A comparison of methodology and clinical results. *International Journal of Obesity, 3*, 261–279.

Wingate, M. E. (1964). A standard definition of stuttering. *Journal of Speech and Hearing Disorders, 29*, 484–489.

Winget, C., & Kramer, M. (1979). *Dimensions of dreaming.* Gainesville, Fla.: University Presses of Florida.

Winick, B. J. (1977). Psychotropic medication and competence to stand trial. *American Bar Association Research Journal,* 769–816.

Winick, C. (1960). How to find out what kind of image you have. In L. H. Bristol (Ed.), *Developing the corporate image.* New York: Scribner's.

Winick, C. (1963). Dear sir or madam, as the case may be. *Antioch Review, 23*, 35–49.

Winick, C. (1968). *The new people: Desexualization in American life.* New York: Pegasus.

Winick, C. (1977). The behavioral sciences and advertising. In S. Ulanoff (Ed.), *Advertising in America.* New York: Hastings House.

Winick, M. (1976). *Malnutrition and brain development.* New York: Oxford University Press.

Winkler, J. K., & Bromberg, W. (1939). *Mind explorers.* New York: World.

Winkless, N., & Browning, I. (1975). *Climate and the affairs of men.* New York: Harper & Row.

Winnik, H. Z. (1977). Milestones in the development of psychoanalysis in Israel. *Israel Annals of Psychiatry and Related Disciplines, 15*, 85–91.

Winograd, E., & Neisser U. (Eds.). (1992). *Affect and accuracy in recall: The problem of "flashbulb" memories.* New York: Cambridge University Press.

Winokur, G. (1972). Depression spectrum disease: Description and family study. *Comprehensive Psychiatry, 13*, 3–8.

Winokur, G. (1979). Unipolar depression: Is it divisible into autonomous subtypes? *Archives of General Psychiatry, 36*, 47–52.

Winokur, G. (1977). Delusional disorder (paranoia). *Comprehensive Psychiatry, 18*(6), 511–621.

Winokur, G. (1981). *Depression: The facts.* Oxford: Oxford University Press.

Winter, A. (April, 1978). Clinical highlights: Some important clinical features of the tremors of Parkinsonism. *Hospital Medicine,* 98–99.

Winter, D. (1973). *The power motive.* New York: Macmillan.

Winter, D. G. (1973). *The power motive*. New York: Free Press.

Winterbottom, M. R. (1958). The relation of need for achievement to learning experiences in independence and mastery. In J. W. Atkinson (Ed.), *Motives in fantasy, action, and society*. Princeton, N.J.: Van Nostrand.

Winters, L., & Reisberg, D. (1988). Mental practice or mental preparation: Why does imagined practice help? *Journal of Human Movement Studies, 15*, 279–290.

Wintrob, R. M., & Harvey, Y. K. (1981). The self-awareness factor in intercultural psychotherapy: Some personal reflections. In P. Pedersen, J. Draguns, W. Lenner, & J. Trimble (Eds.), *Counseling across cultures* (2nd ed.). Honolulu: University Press of Hawaii.

Wirtenberg, J., Klein, S., Richardson, B., & Thomas, V. (1981, January). Sex equity in American education. *Educational Leadership*, 311–319.

Wirth, L. (1945). The problem of minority groups. In R. Linton (Ed.), *The science of man in the world crisis*. New York: Columbia University Press.

Wisconsin Department of Health and Social Services. (1975). *Guidelines to community living systems for the developmentally disabled*. Madison, Wis.: State Printing Office.

Wish, M., Deutsch, M., & Biener, L. (1970). Differences in conceptual structures of nations: An exploratory study. *Journal of Personality and Social Psychology, 16*, 361–373.

Wish, P. A., Cautela, J. R., & Steffan, J. J. (1970). Covert reinforcement: An experimental test. *Proceedings of the Annual Convention of the American Psychological Association, 5*, 513–514.

Wishaw, I. Q. (1991). Latent learning in a swimming pool place test by rats: Evidence for the associative and not cognitive mapping processes. *Quarterly Journal of Experimental Psychology, 43*, 83–103.

Wishnie, H. (1977). *The impulsive personality*. New York: Plenum.

Wisniewski, H. M., Coblentz, J. M., & Terry, R. D. (1972). Pick's disease: A clinical and ultrastructural study. *Archives of Neurology, 26*, 97–108.

Wisocki, P. A. (1973). The successful treatment of heroin addiction by covert conditioning techniques. *Journal of Behavior Therapy and Experimental Psychiatry, 4*, 55–61.

Wispé, L. (Ed.). (1972). Positive forms of social behavior: An overview. *The Journal of Social Issues, 28*, 1–19.

Wispé, L. (Ed.). (1978). *Altruism, sympathy and helping*. New York: Academic Press.

Wissler, C. (1901). The correlation of mental and physical tests. *Psychological Monograph Supplements, 3* (16).

Witelson, S. F., & Pallie, W. (1973). Left hemisphere specialization for language in newborn: Neuroanatomical evidence of asymmetry. *Brain, 96*, 641–646.

Witkin, H. A. (1950). Individual differences in ease of perception of embedded figures. *Journal of Personality, 19*, 1–15.

Witkin, H. A. (1965). Psychological differentiation and forms of pathology. *Journal of Abnormal Psychology, 70*, 317–336.

Witkin, H. A. (1967). A cognitive style approach to cross cultural research. *International Journal of Psychology, 2*, 233–250.

Witkin, H. A. (1978). *Cognitive styles in personal and cultural adaptation. The 1977 Heinz Werner lectures*. Worcester, Mass.: Clark University Press.

Witkin, H. A., Dyk, R. B., Faterson, H. F., Goodenough, D. R., & Karp, S. A. (1974/1962). *Psychological differentiation*. Potomac, Md.: Erlbaum.

Witkin, H. A., & Goodenough, D. R. (1981). *Cognitive styles: Essence and origins—Field dependence and independence*. New York: International Universities Press.

Witkin, H. A., & Goodenough, D. R. Field dependence and interpersonal behavior. (1977). *Psychological Bulletin, 84*, 661–689.

Witkin, H. A., Goodenough, D. R., & Hirschhorn, K. (1978). XYY men: Are they criminally aggressive? *The Sciences, 17*, 10–13.

Witkin, H. A., Goodenough, D. R., & Karp, S. A. (1967). Stability of cognitive style from childhood to young adulthood. *Journal of Personality and Social Psychology, 7*, 291–300.

Witkin, H. A., Goodenough, D. R., & Oltman, P. K. (1979). Psychological differentiation: Current status. *Journal of Personality and Social Psychology, 37*, 1127–1145.

Witkin, H. A., Lewis, H. B., Hartzman, M., Machover, K., Meissner, P. B., & Wapner, S. (1972/1954). *Personality through perception: An experimental and clinical study*. Westport, Conn.: Greenwood Press.

Witmer, L. (1902). *Analytical psychology: practical manual for colleges and normal schools, presenting the facts and principles of mental analysis in the form of simple illustrations and experiments*. Boston: Ginn.

Witmer, L. (1907). Clinical psychology. *Psychological Clinic, 1*, 4–5.

Witmer, L. (1935). The association value of three-place consonant syllables. *Journal of Genetic Psychology, 47*, 337–360.

Wittenberger, J. F. (1981). *Animal social behavior*. Boston: Duxbury.

Wittgenstein, L. (1922). *Tractatus logico-philosophicus*. London: Kegan Paul.

Wittig, M. A. (1976). Sex differences in intellectual functioning: How much of a difference do genes make? *Sex Roles, 2*, 63–74.

Wittig, M. A., & Petersen, A. C. (Eds.). (1979). *Sex-related differences in cognitive functioning*. New York: Academic Press.

Wittkower, E. D., & Warnes, H. (1977). *Psychosomatic medicine: Its clinical applications*. New York: Harper & Row.

Wittreich, W. J. (1959). Visual perception and personality. *Scientific American, 200*(4), 56–60.

Wittreich, W. J., Grace, M., & Radcliffe, K. B., Jr. (1961). Three experiments in selective perceptual distortion. In F. P. Kilpatrick (Ed.), *Explorations in transactional psychology*. New York: New York University Press.

Wittrock, M. C. (1977). *The human brain*. Englewood Cliffs, N.J.: Prentice-Hall.

Wittrock, M. C., & Lumsdaine, A. A. (1977). Instructional psychology. *Annual Review of Psychology, 28*, 417–459.

Wlazlo, Z., Schroeder-Hartwig, K., Hand, I., Kaiser, G., & Munchau, N. (1990). Exposure *in vivo* vs social skills training for social phobia: Long-term outcome and differential effects. *Behaviour Research and Therapy, 28*, 181–193.

Wlodarski, Z. (1978). Psychology in the service of education. *Psychologia Wychowawcza, 21*, 1–12.

Wober, M. (1975). *Psychology in Africa*. London: International African Institute.

Wohl, J. (1981). Intercultural psychotherapy: Issues, operations and reflections. In P. Pedersen, J. Draguns, W. Lonner, & J. Trimble (Eds.), *Counseling across cultures*. Honolulu: University Press of Hawaii.

Wohlgemuth, A. (1911). On the aftereffect of seen movement. *British Journal of Psychology Monograph Supplement, 1*.

Wohlwill, J. F. (1976). Environmental aesthetics: The environment as a source of affect. In I. Altman & J. F. Wohlwill (Eds.), *Human behavior and environment: Idioms in theory and research,* Vol. 1. New York: Plenum.

Wohlwill, J. F., et al. (1980). A memorial tribute to Daniel E. Berlyne. *Motivation and Emotion, 4,* 103–148.

Wolberg, A. (1952). The "borderline patient." *American Journal of Psychotherapy, 6,* 694–701.

Wolberg, L. R. (1945). *Hypnoanalysis.* New York: Grune & Stratton.

Wold, R. M. (Ed.). (1969). *Visual and perceptual aspects for the achieving and underachieving child.* Seattle, Wash.: Special Child Publications.

Wolf, A. (1968). Psychoanalysis in groups. In G. M. Gazda (Ed.), *Basic approaches to group psychotherapy and group counseling.* Springfield, Ill.: Thomas.

Wolf, S. (1977). Presidential address: Social anthropology in medicine. The climate you and I create. *Trans-American Clinical and Climatological Association, 88,* 1–17.

Wolf, T. (1980). *The right stuff.* New York: Bantam Press.

Wolf, T. H. (1973). *Alfred Binet.* Chicago: University of Chicago Press.

Wolfe, J. B. (1936). Effectiveness of token-rewards for chimpanzees. *Comparative Psychology Monographs, 12*(60).

Wolfe, J. L. (1974). *Rational-emotive therapy and women's problems* (cassette recording). New York: Institute for Rational Living.

Wolfe, J. L. (1977). *Assertiveness training for women* (cassette recording). New York: BMA Audio Cassettes.

Wolfenstein, M., & Mead, M. (Eds.). (1955). *Childhood in contemporary cultures.* Chicago: University of Chicago Press.

Wolff, C. (1945). *A psychology of gesture.* London: Methuen.

Wolff, C. von. (1732). *Psychologie empirica,* Frankfurt: Rengeriana.

Wolff, C. von. (1734). *Psychologie rationalia,* Frankfurt: Rengeriana.

Wolff, H. (1947). Protective reaction patterns and disease, *Annals of Internal Medicine, 22.*

Wolff, P. H. (1963). Observations on the early development of smiling. In B. M. Foss (Ed.), *Determinants of infant behavior II.* New York: Wiley.

Wolff, P. H. (1966). The causes, controls and organization of behavior in the neonate. New York: International Universities Press.

Wolff, P. H. (1966). The causes, controls, and organizations of behavior in the newborn. *Psychological Issues, 17,* 1–105.

Wolfgang, A. (1979). *Nonverbal behavior: Applications and cultural implications.* New York: Academic Press.

Wolfgang, C. H., & Sanders, T. S. (1981). Defending young children's play as the ladder to literacy. *Theory Into Practice, 20,* 116–120.

Wolfgang, M. (1970). *The sociology (crime and delinquency.* New York: Wiley.

Wolfgang, M. (1977). *From boy to man—From delinquency to crime.* Paper presented at the National Symposium on the Serious Juvenile Offender. Minneapolis.

Wolfgang, M., Figlio, R., & Sellin, T. (1972). *Delinquency in a birth cohort.* Chicago: University of Chicago Press.

Wolfgang, M., Figlio, R., Tracy, P., & Singer, S. (1985). The *National survey of crime severity* (Bureau of Justice NCJ-99643). Rockville, MD: U.S. Department of Justice.

Wolfgang, M. E., & Ferracuti, F. (1967). *The subculture of violence: Towards an integrated theory in criminology.* London: Social Science Paperbacks.

Wolfgang, M. E., Figlio, R. M., & Sellin, T. (1972). *Delinquency in a birth cohort.* Chicago: University of Chicago Press.

Wolfgang, M. E. Thornberry, T. R., & Figlio, R. M. (1987). *From boy to man, from delinquency to crime.* Chicago: University of Chicago Press.

Wolfle, D. (1946). The reorganized American Psychological Association. *American Psychologist, 1,* 3–6.

Wolfle, D. (1947). The sensible organization of courses in psychology. *American Psychologist, 2*(10), 437–445.

Wolfle, D., Buxton, C. E., Cofer, C. N., Gustad, J. W., MacLeod, R. B., & McKeachie, W. J. (1952). *Improving undergraduate instruction in psychology.* New York: Macmillan.

Wolins, L. (1978). Interval measurement: physics, psychophysics, and metaphysics. *Educational and Psychological Measurement, 38,* 1–9.

Wolinski, J. (1982). Programs join "distrustful" disciplines. *APA Monitor, 3*(2), 15.

Wolinsky, J. (1982, April). Polish research curtailed, jobs in peril. *APA Monitor, 13,* 20.

Wolk, S., & Brandon, J. (1977). Runaway adolescents' perceptions of parents and self. *Adolescence, 12,* 175–188.

Wolk, S., & DuCette, J. (1973). The moderating effect of locus of control in relation to achievement-motivation variables. *Journal of Personality, 41,* 59–70.

Wolk, S., & Du Cette, J. (1974). Intentional performance and incidental learning as a function of personality and talk dimensions. *Journal of Personality and Social Psychology, 29,* 91–101.

Wollen, K. A., & Ruggiero, F. T. (1983). Colored-letter synesthesia. *Journal of Mental Imagery, 7,* 83–86.

Wolman, B. B. (1971). Does psychology need its own philosophy of science? *American Psychologist, 26,* 877–886.

Wolman, B. B. (1976). *The therapist's handbook.* New York: Van Nostrand Reinhold.

Wolman, B. B. (Ed.). (1973). *Handbook of general psychology.* Englewood Cliffs, N.J.: Prentice-Hall.

Wolman, B. B. (Ed.). (1979). *Handbook of dreams: Research, theories, and applications.* New York: Van Nostrand Reinhold.

Wolman, B. B. (Ed.). (1979). *International directory of psychology.* New York: Plenum.

Wolman, W. J. (1960). *Contemporary theories and systems in psychology.* New York: Harper.

Wolpe, J. (1952). Experimental neurosis as learned behavior. *British Journal of Psychology, 43,* 243–268.

Wolpe, J. (1954). Reciprocal inhibition as the main basis of psychotherapeutic effects. *Archives of neurology and psychiatry, 72,* 205–226.

Wolpe, J. (1958). *Psychotherapy by reciprocal inhibition.* Stanford, Calif.: Stanford University Press.

Wolpe, J. (1976). *Theme and variations: A behavior therapy casebook.* New York: Pergamon Press.

Wolpe, J. (1978). Cognition and causation in human behavior and its therapy. *American Psychologist, 33,* 437–446.

Wolpe, J. (1982/1969). *The practice of behavior therapy.* New York: Pergamon Press.

Wolpe, J. (1986). Misrepresentation and underemployment of behavior therapy. *Comprehensive Psychiatry, 27,* 192–200.

Wolpe, J. (1990). *The practice of behavior therapy* (4th ed.). Elmsford, NY: Pergamon.

Wolpe, J., & Abrams, J. (1991). Post-traumatic stress disorder overcome by eye-movement desensitization: A case report. *Journal of Behavior Therapy and Experimental Psychiatry, 22,* 39–43.

Wolpe, J., Knopp, W., & Garfield, Z. (1966). Postgraduate training in behavior therapy. *Exerta Medica International Congress Series, No. 150, Proceedings of the IV World Congress of Psychiatry,* Madrid, Spain.

Wolpe, J., & Lazarus, A. A. (1966). *Behavior therapy techniques.* London: Pergamon Press.

Wolpe, J., & Reyna, L. J. (1967). *Behavior therapy for psychiatrists.* New York: Pergamon Press.

Wolpe, J., Salter, A., & Reyna, L. J. (Eds.). (1964/1964). *The conditioning therapies: The challenge in psychotherapy.* New York: Holt, Rinehart & Winston.

Wolpe, J., & Wolpe, D. (1981). *Our useless fears.* Boston: Houghton Mifflin.

Wolpert, E. A. (Ed.). (1977). *Manic-depressive illness: History of a syndrome.* New York: International Universities Press.

Wolpin, M., & Raines, J. (1966). Visual imagery, expected roles and extinction as possible factors in reducing fear, and avoidance behavior. *Behavior Research and Therapy, 4,* 25–37.

Woltmann, A. G. (1950). The Bender visual-motor Gestalt test. In L. E. Abt & L. Bellak (Eds.), *Projective psychology.* New York: Knopf.

Wong, E. (1975). Visual and tactile perception reconsidered from an empirical-phenomenological perspective. *Journal of Phenomenological Psychology, 6,* 75–87.

Wong, P., & Wiener, B. (1981). When people ask "why" questions and the heuristics of attributional search. *Journal of Personality and Social Psychology, 40,* 650–663.

Wood, B. S. (1976). Children and communication. Englewood Cliffs, N.J.: Prentice-Hall.

Wood, C. C., Goff, W. R., & Day, R. S. (1971). Auditory evoked potentials during speech perception. *Science, 173,* 1248–1251.

Wood, G. (1974). Fundamentals of psychological research. Boston: Little, Brown.

Wood, R. E., & Bandura, A. (1989a). Social cognitive theory of organizational management. *Academy of Management Review, 14,* 361–384.

Woodbridge, F. J. E. (1965). *Nature and mind: Selected essays.* New York: Russell & Russell.

Woodger, J. H. (1929). *Biological principles.* London: Kegan Paul.

Woodger, J. H. (1956). *Physics, psychology and medicine.* Cambridge, England: Cambridge University Press.

Woodman, N. J., & Lenna, H. R. (1980). *Counseling gay men and women: A guide for facilitating positive life styles.* San Francisco: Jossey-Bass.

Woodrow, H. (1927). The effect of type of training upon transference. *Journal of Educational Psychology, 18,* 159–172.

Woodruff, G., & Premack, D. (1979). Intentional communication in the chimpanzee: The development of deception. *Cognition, 7,* 333–362.

Woodruff, G., Premack, D., & Kennel, K. (1978). Conservation of liquid and solid quantity by the chimpanzee. *Science, 202,* 991–994.

Woodruff, M. L., Baisden, R. H., & Douglas, J. R. (1981). The effect of cingulate and fornix lesions on emotional behavior in rabbits. *Experimental Neurology, 74,* 379–395.

Woodruff, M. L., & Lippincott, W. I. (1976). Hyperemotionality and enhanced tonic immobility after septal lesions in the rabbit. *Brain Behavior and Evolution, 13,* 22–33.

Woodruff, R. A., Jr., Goodwin, D. W., & Guze, S. B. (1974). *Psychiatric diagnosis.* New York: Oxford University Press.

Woodson, W. E. (1981). *Human factors design handbook.* New York: McGraw-Hill.

Woodson, W. E., & Conover, D. W. (1964). *Human engineering guide for equipment designers.* Berkeley, Calif.: University of California Press.

Woodward, W. R., & Ash, M. G. (Eds.). (1982). *The problematic science: Psychology in the nineteenth century.* New York: Praeger.

Woodworth, R. S. (1918). *Dynamic psychology.* New York: Columbia University Press.

Woodworth, R. S. (1921). *Psychology.* New York: Holt.

Woodworth, R. S. (1937). The future of clinical psychology. *Journal of Consulting Psychology, 1,* 4–5.

Woodworth, R. S. (1938). *Experimental psychology.* New York: Holt.

Woodworth, R. S. (1943). The adolescence of American psychology. *Psychological Review, 50,* 10–32.

Woodworth, R. S. (1958). *Dynamics of behavior.* New York: Holt, Rinehart & Winston.

Woodworth, R. S., & Ladd, G. T. (1911). *Elements of physiological psychology* (rev. ed.). New York: Scribner.

Woodworth, R. S., & Schlosberg, H. (1954). *Experimental psychology* (rev. ed.). New York: Holt, Rinehart, and Winston.

Woodworth, R. S., & Sheehan, M. R. (1964). *Contemporary schools of psychology* (3rd ed.). New York: Ronald Press.

Woody, R. H., & Woody, J. D. (1972). *Clinical assessment in counseling and psychotherapy.* New York: Meredith.

Wool, H. (1975). What's wrong with work in America?—A review essay. *Vocational Guidance Quarterly, 24,* 155–164.

Wooley, S. C., Wooley, O. W., & Dyrenforth, S. R. (1979). Theoretical, practical, and social issues in behavioral treatments of obesity. *Journal of Applied Behavioral Analysts, 12,* 3–25.

Woolf, V. (1957/1929). *A room of one's own.* New York: Harcourt, Brace & World.

Woolfolk, A. E. (1993). *Education psychology.* Boston: Allyn & Bacon.

Woolley, H. T. (1910). Psychological literature: A review of the recent literature on the psychology of sex. *Psychological Bulletin, 7,* 335–342.

Worcester, D. A. (1927). The wide diversities of practice in first courses in educational psychology. *Journal of Educational Psychology, 18,* 11–17.

Worchel, S. (1974). The effect of three types of arbitrary thwarting on the instigation to aggression. *Journal of Personality, 42,* 300–318.

Worchel, S., & Cooper, J. (1979). *Understanding social psychology.* Homewood, Ill.: Dorsey.

Wordsworth, W. (1971/1850). *The prelude: A parallel text.* J. C. Maxwell (Ed.). Baltimore, Md.: Penguin Books.

World Health Organization, (1946, 1979). In G. C. Stone, F. Cohen, & N. E. Adler (Eds.), *Health psychology.* San Francisco: Jossey-Bass.

World Health Organization. (1960). Expert Committee on Mental Health, 8th Report: Geneva: World Health Organization.

World Health Organization. (1968). *Prevention of suicide.* Geneva: World Health Organization.

World Health Organization. (1973). *Twentieth report of the expert committee on drug dependence.* Technical report No. 550. Geneva: World Health Organization.

World Health Organization. (1977). *Alcohol-related disabilities.* G. Edwards, M. M. Gross, M. Keller, J. Moser, & R. Room, (Eds.). WHO Offset Publication no. 32. Geneva: World Health Organization.

World Health Organization. (1977/1948). *Manual of the international statistical classification of diseases, injuries and causes of death.* (ninth revision). Geneva: World Health Organization.

Worringer, W. (1916). *Abstraktion und Einfühlung.* Munich: Piper.

Worthen, B. R. (1968). Discovery and expository task presentation in elementary mathematics. *Journal of Educational Psychology, 59*(1) (pt. II), monograph supplement.

Worthy, M. M., Wright, J. M., & Shaw, M. E. (1964). Effects of varying degrees of legitimacy in the attribution of responsibility for negative events. *Psychonomic Science, 1,* 169–170.

Wortman, C. B. (1975). Some determinants of perceived control. *Journal of Personality and Social Psychology, 31,* 282–294.

Wortman, C. B., & Brehm, J. W. (1975). Responses to uncontrollable outcomes: An integration of reactance theory and the learned helplessness model. In L. Berkowitz (Ed.), *Advances in experimental social psychology.* Vol. 8. New York: Academic Press.

Wortman, C. B., & Dintzer, L. (1978). Is an attributional analysis of the learned helplessness phenomenon viable?: A critique of the Abramson–Seligman–Teasdale reformulation. *Journal of Abnormal Psychology, 87,* 75–90.

Wortman, C. B., Panciera, L., Shusterman, L., & Hibscher, J. (1976). Atributions of causality and reactions to uncontrollable outcomes. *Journal of Experimental Social Psychology, 12,* 301–306.

Wrenn, C. G. (1938). Counseling with students. In G. M. Whipple (Ed.), *Guidance in educational institutions, Part I. National Society for the Study of Education.* Bloomington, Ind.: Public School Publishing.

Wrenn, C. G. (1962). The culturally encapsulated counselor. *Harvard Educational Review, 32*(4), 444–449.

Wrenn, C. G. (1980). Birth and early childhood of a journal. *Journal of Counseling Psychology, 13,* 485–488. Also in J. M. Whiteley (Ed.), *The history of counseling psychology.* Monterey, Calif.: Brooks/Cole.

Wrenn, C. G. (1980). Landmark years and the growing edge. In J. M. Whiteley & B. R. Fretz (Eds.), *The present and future of counseling psychology.* Monterey, Calif.: Brooks/Cole.

Wrenn, C. G. (1985). Afterward: The culturally encapsulated counselor revisited. In P. B. Pedersen (Ed.), *Handbook of cross-cultural counseling and therapy* (pp. 323–329). Westport, CT: Greenwood.

Wrenn, G. C. (1962). The culturally encapsulated counselor. *Harvard Educational Review, 32*(4), 444–449.

Wright, B. (1960). *Physical disability: psychological approach.* New York: Harper & Row.

Wright, B. D., & Stone, M. H. (1979). *Best test design.* Chicago: MESA Press.

Wright, J. (1976). *The dissent of the governed: Alienation and democracy in America.* New York: Academic Press.

Wright, J. Political disaffection. (1981). In S. Long (Ed.), *The handbook of political behavior,* Vol. 4. New York: Plenum.

Wright, L., (1967). The pediatric psychologist: A role model. *American Psychologist, 22,* 323–325.

Wright, L. (1979). Health care psychology: Prospects for the well-being of children. *American Psychologist, 34,* 1001–1006.

Wright, L., Schaefer, A. B., & Solomons, G. (1979). *The encyclopedia of pediatric psychology.* Baltimore: University Park Press.

Wright, M. J. (1969). Canadian psychology comes of age. *The Canadian Psychologist, 10*(3), 229–253.

Wright, M. J., & Myers, C. R. (Eds.). (1982). *A history of academic psychology in Canada.* Toronto: Hogrefe.

Wright, R. A., & Brehm, S. S. (in press). Reactance as impression management: A critical review. *Journal of personality and Social Psychology.*

Wright, R. H. (1979). Odor and molecular vibration: Neural coding of olfactory information. *Journal of Theoretical Biology, 64,* 473–502.

Wrightsman, L. S., O'Connor, J., & Baker, N. J. (1972). *Cooperation and competition: Readings on mixed-motive games.* Belmont, Calif.: Wadsworth.

Wu,T. M., & Xu, Z. Y. (1979). A preliminary analysis of language of children during the first three years. *Acta Psychologica Sinica, 11,* 153–165.

Wundt, W. (1862). *Beiträge zur Theorie der Sinneswahrnehmung (Contributions to the theory of sensory perception).* Leipzig, Heidelberg: Wunter'sck Verlaghandlung.

Wundt, W. (1873). *Grundzuege der physiologischen Psychologie.* Leipzig: Engelmann.

Wundt, W. (1897). *Outline of psychology.* Leipzig: Englemann.

Wundt, W. (1897). *Principles of psychology,* Leipzig: Englemann.

Wundt, W. (1900–1920). *Folk psychology,* (10 vols.). Leipzig: Engelmann.

Wundt, W. (1904/1873–1874). *Principles of physiological psychology.* New York: Macmillan.

Wundt, W. Kritische Nachlese zur Ausfragemethode. (1908). *Archiv für die gesamte Psychologie, 11,* 444–459.

Wundt, W. (1911/1902–1903/1874). *Grundzüge der physiologischen Psychologie,* Vol. 3. Leipzig: Engelmann.

Wundt, W. (1916). *Volkerpsychologie.* Leipzig: Engelmann. 1910. Translated as *Elements of folk psychology.* New York: Macmillan.

Wundt, W. (1973). *The language of gestures.* The Hague: Mouton.

Wundt, W. (1981/1883). *Philosophische Studien.* Leipzig: Engelmann.

Wurtz, R. H., Castelucci, V. F., & Nusrala, J. M. (1967). Synaptic placticity: The effect of the action potential in postsynaptic neuron. *Experimental Neurology, 18,* 350–368.

Wuthmow, R. (1978). Peak experiences: Some empirical tests. *Journal of Humanistic Psychology, 18,* 59–76.

Wyatt v. Stickney, 325 F. Supp. 781, 784 (M. D. Ala. 1971), 334 F. Supp. 1341 (M.D. Ala. 1971), 344 F. Supp. 373 and 387 (M.D. Ala. 1972), aff'd sub nom *Wyatt v. Aderholt,* 503 F. 2d 1305 (5th Cir. 1974).

Wyer, R. S. (1981). An information-processing perspective on social attribution. In J. Harvey, W. Ickes, & R. Kidd (Eds.), *New directions in attribution research,* Vol. 3. Hillsdale, N.J.: Erlbaum.

Wyers, F. J. (1980). The sociobiological challenge to psychology: On the proposal to "cannibalize" comparative psychology. *American Psychologist, 35,* 955–979.

Wylie, R. C. (1974). *The self-concept,* (rev. ed.). Vol. 1: *review of methodological considerations and measuring instruments.* Lincoln, Neb.: University of Nebrasia Press.

Wylie, R. C. (1979). *The self-concept,* Vol. 2 (rev. ed.). *Theory and research on selected topics.* Lincoln, Neb.: University of Nebraska Press.

Wynar, B. S. (1986). *ARBA guide to subject encyclopedias and dictionaries.* Littleton, CO: Libraries Unlimited.

Wyngaarden, J. B. (1992). *Inborn errors of metabolism.* In J. B. Wyngaarden, L. H.

Wyngaarden, J. B., Smith, L. H., Jr., & Bennett, J. C. (Eds.). (1992). *Cecil textbook of medicine* (19th ed.). Philadelphia: Saunders.

Wynne, L. (1961). The study of intrafamilial alignments and splits in exploratory family therapy. In N. Ackerman, F. Beatman, & S.

Sherman (Eds.), *Exploring the base for family therapy*. New York: Family Service Association.

Wynne, L., Ryckoff, I., Day, J., & Hirsch, S. (1958). Pseudomutuality in the family relations of schizophrenics. *Psychiatry, 21,* 205–220.

Wynne, L., & Singer, M. (1963). Thought disorder and family relations of schizophrenics, I. *Archives of General Psychiatry, 9,* 191–198.

Wynne, S., Ulfelder, L. S., & Dakof, G. (1975). *Mainstreaming and early childhood education for handicapped children: Review and implications of research*. Washington, D.C.: Division of Innovation and Development, Bureau of Education of the Handicapped., U.S. Office of Education, U.S. Department of Health, Education, and Welfare.

Wynne-Edwards, V. C. (1962). *Animal dispersion in relation to social behavior*. Edinburgh: Oliver & Boyd.

Wyszecki, G., & Stiles, W. S. (1967). *Color science: Concepts and methods, quantitative data and formulas*. New York: Wiley.

Yablonsky, L. (1965). *Synanon: The tunnel back,* Baltimore, Md.: Penguin Books.

Yablonsky, L. (1976). *Psychodrama*. New York: Basic Books.

Yalom, I. (1975). The curative factors in group psychotherapy. In *The theory and practice of gioup pgythotherapy* (2nd ed., p. 3018). New York: Basic Books.

Yalom, I. D. (1975/1970). *The theory and practice of group psychotherapy* (2nd ed.). New York: Basic Books.

Yamamoto, J. (1968). Cultural problems in psychiatric therapy. *Archives of General Psychiatry, 19,* 45–49.

Yandell, D. W. (1982). Epidemic convulsions. *Popular Science Monthly,* 1882, *20,* 498–507. Reprinted in W. R. Corliss (Ed.), *The unfathomed mind*. Glen Arm, Md.: Sourcebook Project.

Yankelovich, D. (1974). *The new morality: A profile of American youth in the 70's*. New York: McGraw-Hill.

Yankelovich, D. (1981). *New rules*. New York: Random House.

Yap, P. M. (1951). Mental diseases peculiar to certain cultures. *Journal Of Mental Science, 97,* 313–327.

Yap, P. M. (1969). The culture-bound reactive syndromes. In W. Caudill & T. Lin (Eds.), *Mental health research in Asia and the Pacific*. Honolulu: University Press of Hawaii.

Yap, P. M. Koro. (1965). A culture-bound depersonalization syndrome. *British Journal of Psychiatry, 111,* 43–50.

Yapko, M. D. (1984). *Trancework: An introduction to clinical hypnosis*. New York: Irvington.

Yapko, M. D. (1986). What is Ericksonian hypnosis? In B. Zilbergeld, M. G. Edestin, & D. L. Araoz (Eds.), *Hypnosis: Questions and Answers*. New York: Norton.

Yarmey, A. D. (1979). *The psychology of eyewitness testimony*. New York: Free Press.

Yarrow, L. J. (1963). Research in the dimensions of early child care. *Merrill-Palmer Quarterly, 8,* 101–114.

Yarrow, L. J. (1979). Emotional development. *American Psychologist, 34,* 951–957.

Yarrow, L. J., Rubenstein, J. L., & Pederson, F. A. (1975). *Infant and environment: Early cognitive and motivotional development*. Washington, D.C.: Hemisphere.

Yates, A. J. (1954). The validity of some psychological tests of brain damage. *Psychological Bulletin, 51,* 359–379.

Yates, A. J. (1958). Symptoms and symptom substitution. *Psychological Review, 65,* 371–374.

Yates, A. J. (1958b). The application of learning theory to the treatment of tics. *Journal of Abnormal and Social Psychology, 56,* 175–182.

Yates, A. J. (1962). *Frustration and conflict,* London: Methuen.

Yates, A. J. (1970). *Behavior therapy,* New York: Wiley.

Yates, A. J. (1975). *Theory and practice in behavior therapy*. New York: Wiley.

Yates, A. J. (1980). *Biofeedback and the modification of behavior*. New York: Plenum.

Yates, F. (1966). *The art of memory*. Chicago: University of Chicago Press.

Yates, F. (1981). *Sample methods for censuses and surveys* (4th ed.). New York: Macmillan.

Yates, F. E., Marsh, D. J., & Maran, J. W. (1980/1918). The adrenal cortex. In V. B. Mountcastle (Ed.), *Medical physiology*. St. Louis, Mo.: Mosby.

Yee, A. H. (1970). Educational psychology as seen through its textbooks. *Educational Psychologist, 8,* 4–6.

Yela, M. (1956). *Psicología de las aptitudes*. Madrid: Gredos.

Yela, M. (1957). *La técnica del análisis factorial*. Madrid: Biblioteca Nueva.

Yela, M. (1957). *Los tests*. Madrid: Biblioteca de la Revista de Educaci6n, Ministerio de Educación.

Yela, M. (1967). *Educación y Libertad*. Bilbao, Spain: Banco de Vizcaya.

Yela, M. (1972/1956). *Psicometría y estadística*. Madrid: Escuela de Psicología y Psicotecnia. Universidad de Madrid.

Yela, M. (1974). *La estructura de la conducta*. Madrid: Real Academia de Ciencias Morales y Políticas.

Yela, M. (1974). *Personalidad y eficacia. La dinámica de las actitudes en la empresa*. Barcelona, Spain: Cros.

Yela, M. (1976). La psicología española: Ayer, hoy, mañana. *Revista de Psicología General y Aplicada, 31,* 585–590.

Yela, M. (1981). Germain y la metáfora del pedestal. *Revista de Psicología General y Aplicada, 36,* 1161–1166.

Yela, M. (1981). *Introducción a la teoría de los tests*. Madrid: Facultad de Psicologia. Universidad de Madrid.

Yellin, A. M. (1978). Recent advances in psychophysiology: Psychophysiological studies in hyperkinesis. *Research Communications in Psychology, Psychiatry and Behavior, 3,* 237–255.

Yerkes, R. M. (1927). *Almost human*. New York: Century.

Yerkes, R. M., & Dodson, J. D. (1908). The relation of strength of stimulus to rapidity of habit-formation. *Journal of Comparative Neurology, 18,* 459–482.

Yerkes, R. M. (Ed.). (1921). Psychological examining in the United States Army, *Memoirs of the National Academy of Sciences, 15.*

Yerkes, R. M., & Morgulis, S. (1909). The method of Pavlov in animal psychology. *Psychological Bulletin, 6,* 257–273.

Yesavage, J. A. (1979). Vasodilators in senile dementia. *Archives of General Psychiatry, 36,* 220–223.

Yesavage, J. A., & Freman, A. M. (1978). Acute phencyclidine (PCP) intoxication: Psychopathology and prognosis. *Journal of Clinical Psychiatry, 39,* 664–666.

Yin, R. K. (1978). *Changing urban bureaucracies: How new practices become routinized*. Washington, D.C.: Rand.

Yogev, S. (1982). An eclectic model of supervision. A developmental sequence for beginning psychotherapy students. *Professional Psychology, 13,* 236–243.

Yost, W. A., & Nielsen, D. W. (1977). *Fundamentals of hearing: An introduction*. New York: Holt, Rinehart & Winston.

Young, D. (1970). *Mind, brain and adaptation in the nineteenth century*. Oxford: Clarendon Press.

Young, D. M., & Beier, E. G. (1982). Being asocial in social places: Giving the client a new experience. In J. Anchin & D. Kiesler (Eds.), *Handbook of interpersonal psychotherapy*. New York: Pergamon Press.

Young, G., & Householder, A. S. (1938). Discussion of a set of points in terms of their mutual distances. *Psychometrika, 3,* 19–22.

Young, J. Z. (1974). *An introduction to the study of man*. London: Oxford University Press.

Young, L. (1964). *Wednesday's children: A study of neglect-abuse*. New York: McGraw-Hill.

Young, L. R., & Sheena, D. (1975). Survey of eye movement recording methods. *Behavioral Research Methods and Instrumentation, 1,* 397–429.

Young, P. C. (1940). Hypnotic regression—Fact or artifact? *Journal of Abnormal and Social Psychology, 35,* 273–278.

Young, P. T. (1961). *Motivation and emotion*. New York: Wiley.

Young, P. T. (1973). *Emotion in man and animal* Huntington, N.Y.: Krieger.

Young, S., & Concar, D. (1992, November). These cells were made for learning. *New Scientist* (Suppl. 21), 2–8.

Young, S. J., Alpers, D. H., Norland, C. C., & Woodruff, R. A. (1976). Psychiatric illness and the irritable bowel syndrome. *Gastroenterology, 70,* 162–166.

Young, T. (1802). On the theory of light and colours. *Philosophical Transactions, 92,* 20 ff.

Young, T. (1807). *A course of lectures on natural philosophy and the mechanical arts*. London: Johnson.

Young, W. (1992). Recognition and treatment of survivors reporting ritual abuse. In *Out of darkness*. New York: Lexington Books.

Young, W., Sachs, R., Brain, B., & Watkins, R. (1991). Patients reporting ritual abuse in childhood: A clinical syndrome. *International Journal of Child Abuse and Neglect* (2nd quarter).

Young, W. C., Coy, R. W., & Phoenix, C. H. (1964). Hormones and sexual behavior. *Science, 143,* 212–218.

Yovits, M. C., Jacobi, G., & Goldstein, G. (Eds.). (1962). *Self-organizing systems*. Washington, D.C.: Spartan Books.

Ysseldyke, J. E. & Regan, R. R. (1980). Nondiscriminatory assessment: A formative model. *Exceptional Children, 46,* 465–466.

Yudofsky, S. (1991). *Biopsychiatry & psychopharmacology of organic aggression*. Paper presented at the Fourth Annual New York State Office of Mental Health, New York.

Yuille, J. C. (1980). A critical examination of the psychological and practical implications of eyewitness research. *Law and Human Behavior, 4,* 335–345.

Yuille, J. C. (1983). *Imagery, memory, and cognition*. Hillsdale, NJ: Erlbaum.

Yuille, J. C. (1984). Research and teaching with police: A Canadian example. *International Review of Applied Psychology, 33,* 5–23.

Yuille, J. C., & Cutshall, J. L. (1986). A case study of eyewitness memory of a crime. *Journal of Applied Psychology, 71,* 291–301.

Yuille, J. C., & Marschark, M. (1983). Imagery effects on memory: Theoretical intepretations. In A. Sheikh (Ed.), *Imagery: Current theory research and application*. New York: Wiley.

Yukl, G. A. (1981). *Leadership in organizations*. Englewood Cliffs, N.J.: Prentice Hall.

Yule, W. (1981). The epidemiology of child psychopathology. In B. Lahey & A. Kazdin, (Eds.), *Advances in clinical child psychology*, Vol. 4. New York: Plenum.

Zagona, S. V., & Zurcher, L. A., Jr. (1965). An analysis of some psychosocial variables associated with smoking behavior in a college sample. *Psychological Reports, 17,* 967–978.

Zahn-Waxler, C., Radke-Yarrow, M., & King, R. A. (1979). Child rearing and children's prosocial initiations toward victims of distress. *Child Development, 50,* 319–330.

Zahorik, D. M. (1977). Associative and non-associative factors in learned food preferences. In L. M. Barker, M. Best, & M. Dom jan (Eds.), *Learning mechanisms in food selection*. Waco, Tex.: Baylor University Press.

Zajonc, R. B. (1957). Psychology in Poland. From M. Choynowski, On the awakening of Polish psychology. *American Psychologist, 12,* 730–733.

Zajonc, R. B. (1960). Balance, congruity, and dissonance. *Public Opinion Quarterly, 24,* 280–296.

Zajonc, R. B. (1976). Family configuration and intelligence: Variations in scholastic aptitude scores parallel trends in family size and the spacing of children. *Science, 192,* 227–236.

Zajonc, R. B. (1980). Feeling and thinking: Preferences need no inferences. *American Psychologist, 35,* 151–175.

Zajonc, R. B., & Markus, G. B. (1975). Birth order and intellectual development. *Psychological Review, 82,* 74–88.

Zalba, S. R. (1966). The abused child: A survey of the problem. *Social Work, 11,* 3–16.

Zaleznik, A. (1977). Managers and leaders: Are they different? *Harvard Business Review, 55,* 67–78.

Zaleznik, A., & Kets de Vries, M. R. F. (1975). *Power and the corporate mind*. Boston: Houghton Mifflin.

Zametkin, A. J., Nordahl, T. E., Gross, M., King, A. C., Semple, W. E., Rumsey, J., Hamburger, S., & Cohen, R. M. (1990). Cerebral glucose metabolism in adults with hyperactivity of childhood onset. *New England Journal of Medicine, 323,* 1361–1366.

Zangwill, O. L. (1966). The amnesic syndrome. In C. W. Whitty & O. L. Zangwill (Eds.), *Amnesia*. London: Butterworth.

Zangwill, O. L. (1972). 'Remembering' revisited. *Quarterly Journal of Experimental Psychology, 24,* 124–138.

Zangwill, O. L. (1980). Kenneth Craik: The man and his work. *British Journal of Psychology, 71,* 1–16.

Zanna, M. P., & Cooper, J. (1974). Dissonance and the pill: An attribution approach to studying the arousal properties of dissonance. *Journal of Personality and Social Psychology, 29,* 703–709.

Zanna, M. P., & Pack, S. J. (1975). On the self-fulfilling nature of apparent sex differences in behavior. *Journal of Experimental Social Psychology, 11,* 583–591.

Zanot, E. J., Pincus, J. D., & Lamp, E. J. (1983). Public perceptions of subliminal advertising. *Journal of Advertising, 12,* 37–45.

Zaporozhets, A. (1960). *Razvitie proizvol'nykh dvizhenii*. Moscow: Uzdatel'stvo APN.

Zaporozhets, A. (1969). Some of the psychological problems of sensory training in early childhood and the preschool period. In M. Cole & I. Maltzman (Eds.), *A handbook of contemporary Soviet psychology*. New York: Basic Books.

Zaporozhets, A. (1979–1980). Thought and activity in children, *Soviet Psychology, 18*, 9–22.

Zaporozhets, A., & Elkonin, D. (Eds.). (1971). *The psychology of preschool children*. Cambridge, Mass.: M.I.T. Press.

Zaporozhets, A., & Lukov, U. (1979–1980). The development of reasoning in young children. *Soviet Psychology, 18*, 47–66.

Zaragoza, M. S., & McCloskey, M. (1989). Misleading postevent information and the memory impairment hypothesis: Comment on Belli and reply to Tversky and Tuchin. 118, 92–99.

Zaslow, M. J. (1989). Sex differences in children's response to parental divorce: 2. Samples, variables, ages, and sources. *American Journal of Orthopsychiatry, 59*, 118–140.

Zaslow, R. W. (1970). *Resistance to attachment and growth*. San Jose, Calif.: San Jose State University Press.

Zaslow, R. W. (1981). Z-process attachment therapy. In R. J. Corsini (Ed.), *Handbook of innovative psychotherapies*. New York: Wiley.

Zaslow, R. W. (1982). Der Medusa-Komplex. Die Psychopathologie der menschlichen Aggression im Rahmen der Attachment-Theorie, widergespiegelt im Medusa-Mythos, dem Autismus und der Schizophrenie. *Zeitschrift für Klinische Psychologie und Psychotherapie, 30*(2), 66–84.

Zaslow, R. W., & Breger, L. A. (1969). Theory and treatment of autism. In L. Breger (Ed.), *Clinical cognitive psychology: Models and integration*. Englewood Cliffs, N.J.: Prentice-Hall.

Zaslow, R. W., & Menta, M. (1975). *The psychology of the Z-process*. San Jose, Calif.: San Jose State University Press.

Zastrow, C. H. (1977). Outcome of black children–white parents. San Francisco: R.&E. Research.

Zautra, A., & Goodhart, D. (1979). Quality of life indicators: A review of the literature. *Community Mental Health Review, 4*, 3–10.

Zavalloni, R. (1962). *Self-determination: The psychology of personal freedom*. Chicago: Forum Books.

Zawitz, M. (1988). *Report to the nation on crime and justice* (2nd ed. NCJ-105506). Rockville, MD: U.S. Department of Justice.

Zeaman, D. (1949). Response latency as a function of the amount of reinforcement. *Journal of Experimental Psychology, 39*, 466–483.

Zeïgarnik, B. (1927). Untersuchungen zur Handlungsund Affektpsychologie, Herausgegeben von K. Lewin. 3. Das Behalten erledigter und underledigter Handlungen. *Psychologisches Forschung, 9*, 1–85.

Zeïgarnik, B. V. (1965/1958). *The pathology of thinking*. New York: Consultants Bureau.

Zeïgarnik, B. V. (1972/1969). *Experimental abnormal psychology*. New York: Plenum.

Zeiler, M. (1977). Schedules of reinforcement: The controlling variables. In W. K. Honig & J. E. R. Staddon (Eds.), *Handbook of operant behavior*. Englewood Cliffs, N.J.: Prentice-Hall.

Zeiler, M. D. (1963). The ratio theory of intermediate size discrimination. *Psychological Review, 70*, 516–533.

Zelnik, M., & Kanter, J. F. (1977). Sexual and contraceptive experience of young unmarried women in the United States, 1976 and 1971. *Family Planning Perspectives, 9*, 55–71.

Zepelin, H., Wolfe, C. S., & Kleinplatz, F. (1981). Evaluation of a yearlong reality orientation program. *Journal of Gerontology, 36*, 70–77.

Zessen, G. van, & Sandfort, T. (1991). *Sex and AIDS in the Netherlands*. Amsterdam: Swets & Zeitlinger.

Zetzel, E., & Meissner, W. (1973). *Basic concepts of psychoanalytic psychiatry*. New York: Basic Books.

Zeydel, E. H. (1944). *The ship of fools by Sebastian Brant*. New York: Columbia University Press.

Zhang, G. & Simon, H. A. (1985). STM capacity for Chinese words and idioms: Chunking and acoustical loop hypotheses. *Memory and Cognition, 13*, 193–201.

Zhu, M. S., Wu, J. Z., & Miao, X. C. (1979). An investigation of the development of oral speech in preschool children (I). *Acta Psychologica Sinica, 11*, 281–286.

Zhu, Z. X. (1962). *Child psychology*. Beijing: People's Educational Publishers.

Ziehen, T. (1911/1891). *Leitfaden der physiologischen Psychologie*. Leipzig: Jena.

Zieman, G. L., & Benson, G. P. (1980). School perceptions of truant adolescent boys. *Behavioral Disorders, 5*, 212–222.

Zieman, G. L., & Benson, G. P. (1981). School perceptions of truant adolescent girls. *Behavioral Disorders, 6*, 197–205.

Ziesat, H. A., Jr. (1978). Are family patterns related to the development of chronic back pain. *Perceptual and Motor Skills, 46*(3. Pt. 2), 1062.

Ziferstein, I. (1977). Soviet personality theory. In R. J. Corsini (Ed.), *Current personality theories*. Itasca, Ill.: Peacock.

Zigler, B., & Hodapp, R. M. (1991). Behavioral functioning in individuals with mental retardation. *Annual Review of Psychology, 42*, 29–50.

Zigler, E. (1990). Shaping child care policies in America. *American Journal of Community Psychology, 18*, 183–216.

Zigler, E., & Muenchow, S. (1979). Mainstreaming: The proof is in the implementation. *American Psychologist, 34*, 993–996.

Zigler, E., & Phillips, L. (1960). Social effectiveness and symptomatic behaviors. *Journal of Abnormal and Social Psychology, 61*, 231–238.

Zigler, E., & Phillips, L. (1961). Social competence and outcome in psychiatric disorder. *Journal of Abnormal and Social Psychology, 63*, 264–271.

Zigler, E., & Seitz, V. (1980). Early childhood intervention programs: A reanalysis. *School Psychology Review, 9*, 354–367.

Zigler, E., & Trikett, P. K. (1978). IQ, social competence, and evaluation of early childhood intervention programs. *American Psychologist, 37*, 789–798.

Zigler, E., & Valentine, J. (Eds.). (1979). *Project Head Start: A legacy of the war on poverty*. New York: Free Press.

Zilbergeld, B. (1978). *Male sexuality: A guide to sexual fulfillment*. Boston: Little, Brown.

Zilbergeld, B., & Evans, M. (August 1980). The inadequacy of Masters and Johnson. *Psychology Today*, 29–43.

Zilboorg, G. (1937). Considerations on suicide. *American Journal of Orthopsychiatry, 7*, 15–31.

Zilboorg, G. (1941). Ambulatory schizophrenia. *Psychiatry, 4*, 149–155.

Zilboorg, G. (1941). The diseases that deprive man of his reason, such as St. Vitus' dance, falling sickness, melancholy, and insanity, and their correct treatment by Theophrastus von Hohenheim called Paracelsus. In H. E. Sigerist (Ed.), *Four treatises of Theophrastus von Hohenheim called Paracelsus*. Baltimore, Md.: Johns Hopkins Press.

Zilboorg, G. (1943). Fear of death. *Psychoanalytic Quarterly, 12*, 465–475.

Zilboorg, G., & Henry, G. W. (1941). *A history of medical psychology*. New York: Norton.

Ziller, R. C. (1964). Individuation and socialization. *Human Relations, 17*, 341–360.

Zillmann, D. (1971). Excitation transfer in communication-mediated aggressive behavior. *Journal of Experimental Social Psychology, 7*, 419–434.

Zillmann, D. (1978). Attribution and the misattribution of excitatory reaction. In J. H. Harvey, W. J. Ickes, & R. F. Kidd (Eds.), *New directions in attribution research*, Vol. 2. Hillsdale, N.J.: Erlbaum.

Zillmann, D. (1979). *Hostility and aggression*. Hillsdale, N.J.: Erlbaum.

Zimbardo, P. G. (1969). The human choice: Individuation, reason, and order versus deindividuation, impulse, and chaos. In W. J. Arnold & D. Levine (Eds.), *Nebraska Symposium on Motivation*. Lincoln, Neb.: University of Nebraska Press.

Zimbardo, P. G. (1973). A Pirandellian Prison. *New York Times Magazine*, April 8, p. 38 passim.

Zimbardo, P. G. (1973, April 8). The mind is a formidable jailer: A Pirandellian prison. *The New York Times*, 38.

Zimbardo, P. G. (1977). *Shyness: What it is, what to do about it*. Reading, Mass.: Addison-Wesley.

Zimbardo, P. G. (1992). *Psychology and life* (13th ed.). New York: HarperCollins.

Zimbardo, P. G. (Ed.). (1969). *The cognitive control of motivation*. Glenview, Ill.: Scott, Foresman.

Zimbardo, P. G., Maslach, L., & Marshall, G. (1972). Hypnosis and the psychology of cognitive and behavioral control. In E. Fromm & R. E. Shor (Eds.), *Hypnosis: Research and developments*. Chicago: Aldine.

Zimbardo, P. G., & Radl, S. (1981). *The shy child: Overcoming, a parent's guide to and preventing shyness from infancy to adulthood*. New York: McGraw-Hill.

Zimberg, S., Wallace, J., & Blume, S. B. (Eds.). (1978). *Practical approaches to alcoholism psychotherapy*. New York: Plenum.

Zimler, J., & Keenan, J. M. (1983). Imagery in the congenitally blind: How visual are visual images? *Journal of Experimental Psychology: Learning, Memory, and Cognition, 9*, 269–282.

Zimmer, H. (1978). *The king and the corpse: Tales of the soul's conquest of evil* (Bollingen Series XL). New York: Pantheon.

Zimmer-Hart, C. L., & Rescorla, R. A. (1974). Extinction of Pavlovian conditioned inhibition. *Journal of Comparative and Physiological Psychology, 86*, 837–845.

Zimmerman, J. M. (1981). *Hospice: Complete care for the terminally ill*. Baltimore, Md.: Urban & Schwartzenburg.

Zinchenko, P. (1939). Problema neproizvolnogo zapominanija *(The problem of spontaneous memory)*. In *Nauchnye Zapiski Kharkovskogo Instituta Inostrannyh Jazykov (Transactions of the Kharkov Institute of Foreign Languages)*. Kharkov: KIIJ.

Zinker, J. C. (1977). *Creative process in Gestalt therapy*. New York: Brunner/ Mazel.

Zinner, E. (1931). Über die Darstellung der Reizemfindungskurve. *Zeitschrift für Sinnesphysiologie, 64*, 175–176.

Zipf, G. K. (1945). The meaning-frequency relationship of words. *Journal of General Psychology, 33*, 251–256.

Zipf, G. K. (1965/1935). *The psychobiology of language*. Cambridge, Mass.: M.I.T. Press.

Ziskin, J. (1975). *Coping with psychiatric and psychological testimony*. Beverly Hills, Calif.: Law and Psychology Press.

Ziskin, J. (1981). *Coping with psychiatric and psychological Testimony* (2nd ed., 2 vols.). Beverly Hills, CA: Law and Psychology.

Zisook, S., & Gammon, E. (1980–1981). Medical noncompliance. *International Journal of Psychiatry in Medicine, 10*, 291–303.

Zitelli, B. J., Seltman, M. F., & Shannon, M. R. (1987). Munchausen's syndrome by proxy and its professional participants. *American Journal of Diseases of Children, 141*, 1099–1102.

Zola-Morgan, S. M., & Squire, L. R. (1990). The primate hippocampal formation: Evidence for a time-limited role in memory storage. *Science, 250*, 288–290.

Zuane, L. (1975). *Names in the history of psychology: A biographical sketchbook*. New York: Wiley.

Zubin, J. (1967). Classification of behavior disorders. In P. R. Farnsworth, O. McNemar, & Q. McNemar (Eds.), *Annual review of psychology*, Vol. 18. Palo Alto, Calif.: Annual Review, 373–406.

Zubin, J. (1972). Discussion of symposium on newer approaches to personality assessment. *Journal of Personality Assessment, 36*, 427–434.

Zubin, J., Eton, L., & Schumer, F. (1965). *An experimental approach to projective techniques*. New York: Wiley.

Zuckerman, M. (1969). Theoretical formulations I. In J. P. Zubeck (Ed.), *Sensory deprivation: Fifteen years of research* (pp. 407–432). New York: Appleton-Century.

Zuckerman, M. (1974). The sensation-seeking motive. In B. Maher (Ed.), *Progress in experimental personality research*, Vol. 7. New York: Academic Press.

Zuckerman, M. (1979a). *Sensation seeking: Beyond the optimal level of arousal*. Hillsdale, NJ: Erlbaum.

Zuckerman, M. (1979b). Sensation seeking and risk taking. In C. E. Izard (Ed.), *Emotions in personality and psychopathology* (pp. 163–197). New York: Plenum.

Zuckerman, M. (1983a). A biological theory of sensation seeking. In N. Zuckerman (Ed.), *Biological bases of sensation seeking, impulsivity and anxiety* (pp. 37–76). Hillsdale, NJ: Erlbaum.

Zuckerman, M. (1983b). Sensation seeking: The initial motive for drug abuse. In E. H. Gottheil, K. A. Druley, T. E. Skoloda, & H. M. Waxman (Eds.), *Etiological aspects of alcohol and drug abuse* (pp. 202–220). Springfield, IL: Thomas.

Zuckerman, M. (1984a). Experience and desire: A new format for sensation seeking scales. *Journal of Behavioral Assessment, 6*, 101–114.

Zuckerman, M. (1984b). Sensation seeking: A comparative approach to a human trait. *Behavioral and Brain Sciences, 7*, 413–471.

Zuckerman, M. (1985). Sensation seeking, mania, and monoamienes. *Neuropsychobioogy, 13*, 121–128.

Zuckerman, M. (1986). Sensation seeking and the endogenous deficit theory of drug abuse. *National Institute of Drug Abuse Research Monograph Series, 74*, 49–70.

Zuckerman, M. (1987). Is sensation seeking a predisposing trait for alcoholism? In E. Gottheil, K. A. Druley, S. Pashkey, & S. P. Weinstein (Eds.), *Stress and addiction* (pp. 283–301). New York: Bruner/Mazel.

Zuckerman, M. (1988). Behavior and biology: Research on sensation seeking and reactions to the media. In L. Donohew, H. E. Sypher, & E. T. Higgins (Eds.), *Communication, social cognition and affect* (pp. 173–194). Hillsdale, NJ: Erlbaum.

Zuckerman, M. (1990). The psychophysiology of sensation seeking. *Journal of Personality, 58*, 313–345.

Zuckerman, M. (1991). *Psychobiology or personality*. New York: Cambridge University Press.

Zuckerman, M. (1993). *Behavioral expressions and psychological bases of sensation seeking*. New York: Cambridge University Press.

Zuckerman, M., Amidon, M. D., Bishop, S. E., & Pomerantz, S. D. (1982). Face and tone of voice in the communication of deception. *Journal of Personality and Social Psychology, 43*, 347–357.

Zuckerman, M., Ball, S., & Black, J. (1990). Influences of sensation seeking, gender, risk appraisal, and situational motivation on smoking. *Addictive Behaviors, 15,* 209–220.

Zuckerman, M., Buchsbaum, M. S., & Murphy, D. L. (1980). Sensation seeking and its biological correlates. *Psychological Bulletin, 88,* 187–214.

Zuckerman, M., Eysenck, S. B. G., & Eysenck, H. J. (1978). Sensation seeking in England and American: Cross-cultural, age, sex comparisons. *Journal of Consulting and Clinical Psychology, 46,* 139–149.

Zuckerman, M., & Little, P. (1986). Personality and curiosity about morbid and sexual events. *Personality and Individual Differences, 7,* 49–56.

Zuckerman, M., & Myers, P. L. (1983). Sensation seeking in homosexual and heterosexual males. *Archives of Sexual Behavior, 12.* 347–356.

Zuckerman, M., & Neeb, M. (1980). Demographic influences in sensation seeking and expressions of sensation seeking in religion, smoking, and driving habits. *Personality and Individual Differences, 1,* 197–206.

Zuckerman, M., Tushup, R., & Finner, S. (1976). Sexual attitudes and experience: Attitude and personality correlations and changes produces by a course in sexuality. *Journal of Consulting and Clinical Psychology, 44,* 7–19.

Zuckerman, M., Ulrich, R. S., & McLaughlin, J. (in press). Sensation seeking and reactions to nature paintings. *Personality and Individual Differences.*

Zuger, B. (1973). Effeminate behavior in boys: Parental age and other facts. *Archives of General Psychiatry, 30*(2), 173–177.

Zuger, B. (1976). Monozygotic twins discordant for homosexuality: Report on a pair and significance of the phenomenon. *Comprehensive Psychiatry, 17,* 661–669.

Zukav, G. (1980/1979). *The dancing wu li masters: An overview of the new physics.* New York: Bantam Books.

Zuniga, R. B. (1975). The experimenting society and radical social reform. *American Psychologist, 30,* 99–115.

Zuriff, G. E. (1985). *Behaviorism: A conceptual reconstruction.* New York: Columbia University Press.

Zuroff, D. C. (1980). Learned helplessness in humans: An analysis of learning processes and the roles of individual and situational differences. *Journal of Personality and Social Psychology, 39,* 130–146.

Zuroff, D. C., & Schwarz, J. C. (1980). Transcendental meditation versus muscle relaxation: A two year follow-up of a controlled experiment. *American Journal of Psychiatry, 137,* 1229–1231.

Zusne, L. (1970). *Visual perception of form.* New York: Academic Press.

Zusne, L., & Jones, W. H. (1982). *Anomalistic psychology.* Hillsdale, N.J.: Erlbaum.

Zwaardemaker, H. (1975). *Die physiologie des Geruchs.* Leipzig: Englemann.

Zwaardemaker, H. (1925). *L'odorat.* Paris: Doin.

Zwibelman, B. B. (1977). Differences in the utilization of professional and paraprofessional counseling services. *Journal of College Student Personnel, 18,* 358–361.

Zyzanski, S. J., & Jenkins, C. D. (1967). Basic dimensions within the coronary-prone behavior pattern. *Journal of Chronic Diseases, 22,* 781–795.

APPENDIX

Ethical Principles of Psychologists and Code of Conduct

Reprinted with permission from *American Psychologist*, Dec. 1992.

CONTENTS

INTRODUCTION

The American Psychological Association's (APA's) Ethical Principles of Psychologists and Code of Conduct (hereinafter referred to as the Ethics Code) consists of an Introduction, a Preamble, six General Principles (A–F), and specific Ethical Standards. The Introduction discusses the intent, organization, procedural considerations, and scope of application of the Ethics Code. The Preamble and General Principles are *aspirational* goals to guide psychologists toward the highest ideals of psychology. Although the Preamble and General Principles are not themselves enforceable rules, they should be considered by psychologists in arriving at an ethical course of action and may be considered by ethics bodies in interpreting the Ethical Standards. The Ethical Standards set forth *enforceable* rules for conduct as psychologists. Most of the Ethical Standards are written broadly, in order to apply to psychologists in varied roles, although the application of an Ethical Standard may vary depending on the context. The Ethical Standards are not exhaustive. The fact that a given conduct is not specifically addressed by the Ethics Code does not mean that it is necessarily either ethical or unethical.

Membership in the APA commits members to adhere to the APA Ethics Code and to the rules and procedures used to implement it. Psychologists and students, whether or not they are APA members, should be aware that the Ethics Code may be applied to them by state psychology boards, courts, or other public bodies.

This Ethics Code applies only to psychologists' work-related activities, that is, activities that are part of the psychologists' scientific and professional functions or that are psychological in nature. It includes the clinical or counseling practice of psychology, research, teaching, supervision of trainees, development of assessment instruments, conducting assessments, educational counseling, organizational consulting, social intervention, administration, and other activities as well. These work-related activities can be distinguished from the purely private

This version of the APA Ethics Code was adopted by the American Psychological Association's Council of Representatives during its meeting, August 13 and 16, 1992, and is effective beginning December 1, 1992. Inquiries concerning the substance or interpretation of the APA Ethics Code should be addressed to the Director, Office of Ethics, American Psychological Association, 750 First Street, NE, Washington, DC 20002-4242.

This Code will be used to adjudicate complaints brought concerning alleged conduct occurring on or after the effective date. Complaints regarding conduct occurring prior to the effective date will be adjudicated on the basis of the version of the Code that was in effect at the time the conduct occurred, except that no provisions repealed in June 1989, will be enforced even if an earlier version contains the provision. The Ethics Code will undergo continuing review and study for future revisions; comments on the Code may be sent to the above address.

The APA has previously published its Ethical Standards as follows:

American Psychological Association. (1953). *Ethical standards of psychologists.* Washington, DC: Author.

American Psychological Association. (1958). Standards of ethical behavior for psychologists. *American Psychologist, 13,* 268–271.

American Psychological Association. (1963). Ethical standards of psychologists. *American Psychologist, 18.* 56–60.

American Psychological Association. (1968). Ethical standards of psychologists. *American Psychologist, 23,* 357–361.

American Psychological Association. (1977, March). Ethical standards of psychologists. *APA Monitor,* pp. 22–23.

American Psychological Association. (1979). *Ethical standards of psychologists.* Washington, DC: Author.

American Psychological Association. (1981). Ethical principles of psychologists. *American Psychologist, 36,* 633–638.

American Psychological Association. (1990). Ethical principles of psychologists (Amended June 2, 1989). *American Psychologist, 45,* 390–395.

Request copies of the APA's Ethical Principles of Psychologists and Code of Conduct from the APA Order Department, 750 First Street, NE, Washington, DC 20002-4242, or phone (202) 336-5510.

conduct of a psychologist, which ordinarily is not within the purview of the Ethics Code.

The Ethics Code is intended to provide standards of professional conduct that can be applied by the APA and by other bodies that choose to adopt them. Whether or not a psychologist has violated the Ethics Code does not by itself determine whether he or she is legally liable in a court action, whether a contract is enforceable, or whether other legal consequences occur. These results are based on legal rather than ethical rules. However, compliance with or violation of the Ethics Code may be admissible as evidence in some legal proceedings, depending on the circumstances.

In the process of making decisions regarding their professional behavior, psychologists must consider this Ethics Code, in addition to applicable laws and psychology board regulations. If the Ethics Code establishes a higher standard of conduct than is required by law, psychologists must meet the higher ethical standard. If the Ethics Code standard appears to conflict with the requirements of law, then psychologists make known their commitment to the Ethics Code and take steps to resolve the conflict in a responsible manner. If neither law nor the Ethics Code resolves an issue, psychologists should consider other professional materials[1] and the dictates of their own conscience, as well as seek consultation with others within the field when this is practical.

The procedures for filing, investigating, and resolving complaints of unethical conduct are described in the current Rules and Procedures of the APA Ethics Committee. The actions that APA may take for violations of the Ethics Code include actions such as reprimand, censure, termination of APA membership, and referral of the matter to other bodies. Complainants who seek remedies such as monetary damages in alleging ethical violations by a psychologist must resort to private negotiation, administrative bodies, or the courts. Actions that violate the Ethics Code may lead to the imposition of sanctions on a psychologist by bodies other than APA, including state psychological associations, other professional groups, psychology boards, other state or federal agencies, and payors for health services. In addition to actions for violation of the Ethics Code, the APA Bylaws provide that APA may take action against a member after his or her conviction of a felony, expulsion or suspension from an affiliated state psychological association, or suspension or loss of licensure.

PREAMBLE

Psychologists work to develop a valid and reliable body of scientific knowledge based on research. They may apply that knowledge to human behavior in a variety of contexts. In doing so, they perform many roles, such as researcher, educator, diagnostician, therapist, supervisor, con-

---

[1]Professional materials that are most helpful in this regard are guidelines and standards that have been adopted or endorsed by professional psychological organizations. Such guidelines and standards, whether adopted by the American Psychological Association (APA) or its Divisions, are not enforceable as such by this Ethics Code, but are of educative value to psychologists, courts, and professional bodies. Such materials include, but are not limited to, the APA's *General Guidelines for Providers of Psychological Services* (1987), *Specialty Guidelines for the Delivery of Services by Clinical Psychologists, Counseling Psychologists, Industrial/Organizational Psychologists, and School Psychologists* (1981), *Guidelines for Computer Based Tests and Interpretations* (1987), *Standards for Educational and Psychological Testing* (1985), *Ethical Principles in the Conduct of Research With Human Participants* (1982), *Guidelines for Ethical Conduct in the Care and Use of Animals* (1986), *Guidelines for Providers of Psychological Services to Ethnic, Linguistic, and Culturally Diverse Populations* (1990), and *Publication Manual of the American Psychological Association* (3rd ed., 1983). Materials not adopted by APA as a whole include the APA Division 41 (Forensic Psychology)/American Psychology–Law Society's *Specialty Guidelines for Forensic Psychologists* (1991).

sultant, administrator, social interventionist, and expert witness. Their goal is to broaden knowledge of behavior and, where appropriate, to apply it pragmatically to improve the condition of both the individual and society. Psychologists respect the central importance of freedom of inquiry and expression in research, teaching, and publication. They also strive to help the public in developing informed judgments and choices concerning human behavior. This Ethics Code provides a common set of values upon which psychologists build their professional and scientific work.

This Code is intended to provide both the general principles and the decision rules to cover most situations encountered by psychologists. It has as its primary goal the welfare and protection of the individuals and groups with whom psychologists work. It is the individual responsibility of each psychologist to aspire to the highest possible standards of conduct. Psychologists respect and protect human and civil rights, and do not knowingly participate in or condone unfair discriminatory practices.

The development of a dynamic set of ethical standards for a psychologist's work-related conduct requires a personal commitment to a lifelong effort to act ethically; to encourage ethical behavior by students, supervisees, employees, and colleagues, as appropriate; and to consult with others, as needed, concerning ethical problems. Each psychologist supplements, but does not violate, the Ethics Code's values and rules on the basis of guidance drawn from personal values, culture, and experience.

GENERAL PRINCIPLES

Principle A: Competence

Psychologists strive to maintain high standards of competence in their work. They recognize the boundaries of their particular competencies and the limitations of their expertise. They provide only those services and use only those techniques for which they are qualified by education, training, or experience. Psychologists are cognizant of the fact that the competencies required in serving, teaching, and/or studying groups of people vary with the distinctive characteristics of those groups. In those areas in which recognized professional standards do not yet exist, psychologists exercise careful judgment and take appropriate precautions to protect the welfare of those with whom they work. They maintain knowledge of relevant scientific and professional information related to the services they render, and they recognize the need for ongoing education. Psychologists make appropriate use of scientific, professional, technical, and administrative resources.

Principle B: Integrity

Psychologists seek to promote integrity in the science, teaching, and practice of psychology. In these activities psychologists are honest, fair, and respectful of others. In describing or reporting their qualifications, services, products, fees, research, or teaching, they do not make statements that are false, misleading, or deceptive. Psychologists strive to be aware of their own belief systems, values, needs, and limitations and the effect of these on their work. To the extent feasible, they attempt to clarify for relevant parties the roles they are performing and to function appropriately in accordance with those roles. Psychologists avoid improper and potentially harmful dual relationships.

Principle C: Professional and Scientific Responsibility

Psychologists uphold professional standards of conduct, clarify their professional roles and obligations, accept appropriate responsibility for their behavior, and adapt their methods to the needs of different populations. Psychologists consult with, refer to, or cooperate with other professionals and institutions to the extent needed to serve the best interests of their patients, clients, or other recipients of their services.

Psychologists' moral standards and conduct are personal matters to the same degree as is true for any other person, except as psychologists' conduct may compromise their professional responsibilities or reduce the public's trust in psychology and psychologists. Psychologists are concerned about the ethical compliance of their colleagues' scientific and professional conduct. When appropriate, they consult with colleagues in order to prevent or avoid unethical conduct.

Principle D: Respect for People's Rights and Dignity

Psychologists accord appropriate respect to the fundamental rights, dignity, and worth of all people. They respect the rights of individuals to privacy, confidentiality, self-determination, and autonomy, mindful that legal and other obligations may lead to inconsistency and conflict with the exercise of these rights. Psychologists are aware of cultural, individual, and role differences, including those due to age, gender, race, ethnicity, national origin, religion, sexual orientation, disability, language, and socioeconomic status. Psychologists try to eliminate the effect on their work of biases based on those factors, and they do not knowingly participate in or condone unfair discriminatory practices.

Principle E: Concern for Others' Welfare

Psychologists seek to contribute to the welfare of those with whom they interact professionally. In their professional actions, psychologists weigh the welfare and rights of their patients or clients, students, supervisees, human research participants, and other affected persons, and the welfare of animal subjects of research. When conflicts occur among psychologists' obligations or concerns, they attempt to resolve these conflicts and to perform their roles in a responsible fashion that avoids or minimizes harm. Psychologists are sensitive to real and ascribed differences in power between themselves and others, and they do not exploit or mislead other people during or after professional relationships.

Principle F: Social Responsibility

Psychologists are aware of their professional and scientific responsibilities to the community and the society in which they work and live. They apply and make public their knowledge of psychology in order to contribute to human welfare. Psychologists are concerned about and work to mitigate the causes of human suffering. When undertaking research, they strive to advance human welfare and the science of psychology. Psychologists try to avoid misuse of their work. Psychologists comply with the law and encourage the development of law and social policy that serve the interests of their patients and clients and the public. They are encouraged to contribute a portion of their professional time for little or no personal advantage.

ETHICAL STANDARDS

1. General Standards

These General Standards are potentially applicable to the professional and scientific activities of all psychologists.

1.01 Applicability of the Ethics Code

The activity of a psychologist subject to the Ethics Code may be reviewed under these Ethical Standards only if the activity is part of his or her work-related functions or the activity is psychological in nature. Personal activities having no connection to or effect on psychological roles are not subject to the Ethics Code.

1.02 Relationship of Ethics and Law

If psychologists' ethical responsibilities conflict with law, psychologists make known their commitment to the Ethics Code and take steps to resolve the conflict in a responsible manner.

1.03 Professional and Scientific Relationship

Psychologists provide diagnostic, therapeutic, teaching, research, supervisory, consultative, or other psychological services only in the context of a defined professional or scientific relationship or role. (See also Standards 2.01, Evaluation, Diagnosis, and Interventions in Professional Context, and 7.02, Forensic Assessments.)

1.04 Boundaries of Competence

(a) Psychologists provide services, teach, and conduct research only within the boundaries of their competence, based on their education, training, supervised experience, or appropriate professional experience.

(b) Psychologists provide services, teach, or conduct research in new areas or involving new techniques only after first undertaking appropriate study, training, supervision, and/or consultation from persons who are competent in those areas or techniques.

(c) In those emerging areas in which generally recognized standards for preparatory training do not yet exist, psychologists nevertheless take reasonable steps to ensure the competence of their work and to protect patients, clients, students, research participants, and others from harm.

1.05 Maintaining Expertise

Psychologists who engage in assessment, therapy, teaching, research, organizational consulting, or other professional activities maintain a reasonable level of awareness of current scientific and professional information in their fields of activity, and undertake ongoing efforts to maintain competence in the skills they use.

1.06 Basis for Scientific and Professional Judgments

Psychologists rely on scientifically and professionally derived knowledge when making scientific or professional judgments or when engaging in scholarly or professional endeavors.

1.07 Describing the Nature and Results of Psychological Services

(a) When psychologists provide assessment, evaluation, treatment, counseling, supervision, teaching, consultation, research, or other psychological services to an individual, a group, or an organization, they provide, using language that is reasonably understandable to the recipient of those services, appropriate information beforehand about the nature of such services and appropriate information later about results and conclusions. (See also Standard 2.09, Explaining Assessment Results.)

(b) If psychologists will be precluded by law or by organizational roles from providing such information to particular individuals or groups, they so inform those individuals or groups at the outset of the service.

1.08 Human Differences

Where differences of age, gender, race, ethnicity, national origin, religion, sexual orientation, disability, language, or socioeconomic status significantly affect psychologists' work concerning particular individuals or groups, psychologists obtain the training, experience, consultation, or supervision necessary to ensure the competence of their services, or they make appropriate referrals.

1.09 Respecting Others

In their work-related activities, psychologists respect the rights of others to hold values, attitudes, and opinions that differ from their own.

1.10 Nondiscrimination

In their work-related activities, psychologists do not engage in unfair discrimination based on age, gender, race, ethnicity, national origin, religion, sexual orientation, disability, socioeconomic status, or any basis proscribed by law.

1.11 Sexual Harassment

(a) Psychologists do not engage in sexual harassment. Sexual harassment is sexual solicitation, physical advances, or verbal or nonverbal conduct that is sexual in nature, that occurs in connection with the psychologist's activities or roles as a psychologist, and that either: (1) is unwelcome, is offensive, or creates a hostile workplace environment, and the psychologist knows or is told this; or (2) is sufficiently severe or intense to be abusive to a reasonable person in the context. Sexual harassment can consist of a single intense or severe act or of multiple persistent or pervasive acts.

(b) Psychologists accord sexual-harassment complainants and respondents dignity and respect. Psychologists do not participate in denying a person academic admittance or advancement, employment, tenure, or promotion, based solely upon their having made, or their being the subject of, sexual-harassment charges. This does not preclude taking action based upon the outcome of such proceedings or consideration of other appropriate information.

1.12 Other Harassment

Psychologists do not knowingly engage in behavior that is harassing or demeaning to persons with whom they interact in their work based on factors such as those persons' age, gender, race, ethnicity, national origin, religion, sexual orientation, disability, language, or socioeconomic status.

1.13 Personal Problems and Conflicts

(a) Psychologists recognize that their personal problems and conflicts may interfere with their effectiveness. Accordingly, they refrain from undertaking an activity when they know or should know that their personal problems are likely to lead to harm to a patient, client, colleague, student, research participant, or other person to whom they may owe a professional or scientific obligation.

(b) In addition, psychologists have an obligation to be alert to signs of, and to obtain assistance for, their personal problems at an early stage, in order to prevent significantly impaired performance.

(c) When psychologists become aware of personal problems that may interfere with their performing workrelated duties adequately, they take appropriate measures, such as obtaining professional consultation or assistance, and determine whether they should limit, suspend, or terminate their work-related duties.

1.14 Avoiding Harm

Psychologists take reasonable steps to avoid harming their patients or clients, research participants, students, and others with whom they work, and to minimize harm where it is foreseeable and unavoidable.

1.15 Misuse of Psychologists' Influence

Because psychologists' scientific and professional judgments and actions may affect the lives of others, they are alert to and guard against personal, financial, social, organizational, or political factors that might lead to misuse of their influence.

1.16 Misuse of Psychologists' Work

(a) Psychologists do not participate in activities in which it appears likely that their skills or data will be misused by others, unless corrective mechanisms are available. (See also Standard 7.04, Truthfulness and Candor.)

(b) If psychologists learn of misuse or misrepresentation of their work, they take reasonable steps to correct or minimize the misuse or misrepresentation.

1.17 Multiple Relationships

(a) In many communities and situations, it may not be feasible or reasonable for psychologists to avoid social or other nonprofessional contacts with persons such as patients, clients, students, supervisees, or research participants. Psychologists must always be sensitive to the potential harmful effects of other contacts on their work and on those persons with whom they deal. A psychologist refrains from entering into or promising another personal, scientific, professional, financial, or other relationship with such persons if it appears likely that such a relationship reasonably might impair the psychologist's objectivity or otherwise interfere with the psychologist's effectively performing his or her functions as a psychologist, or might harm or exploit the other party.

(b) Likewise, whenever feasible, a psychologist refrains from taking on professional or scientific obligations when preexisting relationships would create a risk of such harm.

(c) If a psychologist finds that, due to unforeseen factors, a potentially harmful multiple relationship has arisen, the psychologist attempts to resolve it with due regard for the best interests of the affected person and maximal compliance with the Ethics Code.

1.18 Barter (With Patients or Clients)

Psychologists ordinarily refrain from accepting goods, services, or other nonmonetary remuneration from patients or clients in return for psychological services because such arrangements create inherent potential for conflicts, exploitation, and distortion of the professional relationship. A psychologist may participate in bartering only if (1) it is not clinically contraindicated, and (2) the relationship is not exploitative. (See also Standards 1.17, Multiple Relationships, and 1.25, Fees and Financial Arrangements.)

1.19 Exploitative Relationships

(a) Psychologists do not exploit persons over whom they have supervisory, evaluative, or other authority such as students, supervisees, employees, research participants, and clients or patients. (See also Standards 4.05–4.07 regarding sexual involvement with clients or patients.)

(b) Psychologists do not engage in sexual relationships with students or supervisees in training over whom the psychologist has evaluative or direct authority, because such relationships are so likely to impair judgment or be exploitative.

1.20 Consultations and Referrals

(a) Psychologists arrange for appropriate consultations and referrals based principally on the best interests of their patients or clients, with appropriate consent, and subject to other relevant considerations, including applicable law and contractual obligations. (See also Standards 5.01, Discussing the Limits of Confidentiality, and 5.06, Consultations.)

(b) When indicated and professionally appropriate, psychologists cooperate with other professionals in order to serve their patients or clients effectively and appropriately.

(c) Psychologists' referral practices are consistent with law.

1.21 Third-Party Requests for Services

(a) When a psychologist agrees to provide services to a person or entity at the request of a third party, the psychologist clarifies to the extent feasible, at the outset of the service, the nature of the relationship with each party. This clarification includes the role of the psychologist (such as therapist, organizational consultant, diagnostician, or expert witness), the probable uses of the services provided or the information obtained, and the fact that there may be limits to confidentiality.

(b) If there is a foreseeable risk of the psychologist's being called upon to perform conflicting roles because of the involvement of a third party, the psychologist clarifies the nature and direction of his or her

responsibilities, keeps all parties appropriately informed as matters develop, and resolves the situation in accordance with this Ethics Code.

1.22 Delegation to and Supervision of Subordinates

(a) Psychologists delegate to their employees, supervisees, and research assistants only those responsibilities that such persons can reasonably be expected to perform competently, on the basis of their education, training, or experience, either independently or with the level of supervision being provided.

(b) Psychologists provide proper training and supervision to their employees or supervisees and take reasonable steps to see that such persons perform services responsibly, competently, and ethically.

(c) If institutional policies, procedures, or practices prevent fulfillment of this obligation, psychologists attempt to modify their role or to correct the situation to the extent feasible.

1.23 Documentation of Professional and Scientific Work

(a) Psychologists appropriately document their professional and scientific work in order to facilitate provision of services later by them or by other professionals, to ensure accountability, and to meet other requirements of institutions or the law.

(b) When psychologists have reason to believe that records of their professional services will be used in legal proceedings involving recipients of or participants in their work, they have a responsibility to create and maintain documentation in the kind of detail and quality that would be consistent with reasonable scrutiny in an adjudicative forum. (See also Standard 7.01, Professionalism, under Forensic Activities.)

1.24 Records and Data

Psychologists create, maintain, disseminate, store, retain, and dispose of records and data relating to their research, practice, and other work in accordance with law and in a manner that permits compliance with the requirements of this Ethics Code. (See also Standard 5.04, Maintenance of Records.)

1.25 Fees and Financial Arrangements

(a) As early as is feasible in a professional or scientific relationship, the psychologist and the patient, client, or other appropriate recipient of psychological services reach an agreement specifying the compensation and the billing arrangements.

(b) Psychologists do not exploit recipients of services or payors with respect to fees.

(c) Psychologists' fee practices are consistent with law.

(d) Psychologists do not misrepresent their fees.

(e) If limitations to services can be anticipated because of limitations in financing, this is discussed with the patient, client, or other appropriate recipient of services as early as is feasible. (See also Standard 4.08, Interruption of Services.)

(f) If the patient, client, or other recipient of services does not pay for services as agreed, and if the psychologist wishes to use collection agencies or legal measures to collect the fees, the psychologist first informs the person that such measures will be taken and provides that person an opportunity to make prompt payment. (See also Standard 5.11, Withholding Records for Nonpayment.)

1.26 Accuracy in Reports to Payors and Funding Sources

In their reports to payors for services or sources of research funding, psychologists accurately state the nature of the research or service provided, the fees or charges, and where applicable, the identity of the provider, the findings, and the diagnosis. (See also Standard 5.05, Disclosures.)

1.27 Referrals and Fees

When a psychologist pays, receives payment from, or divides fees with another professional other than in an employer–employee relationship, the payment to each is based on the services (clinical, consultative, administrative, or other) provided and is not based on the referral itself.

2. Evaluation, Assessment, or Intervention

2.01 Evaluation, Diagnosis, and Interventions in Professional Context

(a) Psychologists perform evaluations, diagnostic services, or interventions only within the context of a defined professional relationship. (See also Standard 1.03, Professional and Scientific Relationship.)

(b) Psychologists' assessments, recommendations, reports, and psychological diagnostic or evaluative statements are based on information and techniques (including personal interviews of the individual when appropriate) sufficient to provide appropriate substantiation for their findings. (See also Standard 7.02, Forensic Assessments.)

2.02 Competence and Appropriate Use of Assessments and Interventions

(a) Psychologists who develop, administer, score, interpret, or use psychological assessment techniques, interviews, tests, or instruments do so in a manner and for purposes that are appropriate in light of the research on or evidence of the usefulness and proper application of the techniques.

(b) Psychologists refrain from misuse of assessment techniques, interventions, results, and interpretations and take reasonable steps to prevent others from misusing the information these techniques provide. This includes refraining from releasing raw test results or raw data to persons, other than to patients or clients as appropriate, who are not qualified to use such information. (See also Standards 1.02, Relationship of Ethics and Law, and 1.04, Boundaries of Competence.)

2.03 Test Construction

Psychologists who develop and conduct research with tests and other assessment techniques use scientific procedures and current professional knowledge for test design, standardization, validation, reduction or elimination of bias, and recommendations for use.

2.04 Use of Assessment in General and With Special Populations

(a) Psychologists who perform interventions or administer, score, interpret, or use assessment techniques are familiar with the reliability, validation, and related standardization or outcome studies of, and proper applications and uses of, the techniques they use.

(b) Psychologists recognize limits to the certainty with which diagnoses, judgments, or predictions can be made about individuals.

(c) Psychologists attempt to identify situations in which particular interventions or assessment techniques or norms may not be applicable or may require adjustment in administration or interpretation because of factors such as individuals' gender, age, race, ethnicity, national origin, religion, sexual orientation, disability, language, or socioeconomic status.

2.05 Interpreting Assessment Results

When interpreting assessment results, including automated interpretations, psychologists take into account the various test factors and characteristics of the person being assessed that might affect psychologists' judgments or reduce the accuracy of their interpretations. They indicate any significant reservations they have about the accuracy or limitations of their interpretations.

2.06 Unqualified Persons

Psychologists do not promote the use of psychological assessment techniques by unqualified persons. (See also Standard 1.22, Delegation to and Supervision of Subordinates.)

2.07 Obsolete Tests and Outdated Test Results

(a) Psychologists do not base their assessment or intervention decisions or recommendations on data or test results that are outdated for the current purpose.

(b) Similarly, psychologists do not base such decisions or recommendations on tests and measures that are obsolete and not useful for the current purpose.

2.08 Test Scoring and Interpretation Services

(a) Psychologists who offer assessment or scoring procedures to other professionals accurately describe the purpose, norms, validity, reliability, and applications of the procedures and any special qualifications applicable to their use.

(b) Psychologists select scoring and interpretation services (including automated services) on the basis of evidence of the validity of the program and procedures as well as on other appropriate considerations.

(c) Psychologists retain appropriate responsibility for the appropriate application, interpretation, and use of assessment instruments, whether they score and interpret such tests themselves or use automated or other services.

2.09 Explaining Assessment Results

Unless the nature of the relationship is clearly explained to the person being assessed in advance and precludes provision of an explanation of results (such as in some organizational consulting, preemployment or security screenings, and forensic evaluations), psychologists ensure that an explanation of the results is provided using language that is reasonably understandable to the person assessed or to another legally authorized person on behalf of the client. Regardless of whether the scoring and interpretation are done by the psychologist, by assistants, or by automated or other outside services, psychologists take reasonable steps to ensure that appropriate explanations of results are given.

2.10 Maintaining Test Security

Psychologists make reasonable efforts to maintain the integrity and security of tests and other assessment techniques consistent with law, contractual obligations, and in a manner that permits compliance with the requirements of this Ethics Code. (See also Standard 1.02, Relationship of Ethics and Law.)

3. Advertising and Other Public Statements

3.01 Definition of Public Statements

Psychologists comply with this Ethics Code in public statements relating to their professional services, products, or publications or to the field of psychology. Public statements include but are not limited to paid or unpaid advertising, brochures, printed matter, directory listings, personal resumes or curricula vitae, interviews or comments for use in media, statements in legal proceedings, lectures and public oral presentations, and published materials.

3.02 Statements by Others

(a) Psychologists who engage others to create or place public statements that promote their professional practice, products, or activities retain professional responsibility for such statements.

(b) In addition, psychologists make reasonable efforts to prevent others whom they do not control (such as employers, publishers, sponsors, organizational clients, and representatives of the print or broadcast media) from making deceptive statements concerning psychologists' practice or professional or scientific activities.

(c) If psychologists learn of deceptive statements about their work made by others, psychologists make reasonable efforts to correct such statements.

(d) Psychologists do not compensate employees of press, radio, television, or other communication media in return for publicity in a news item.

(e) A paid advertisement relating to the psychologist's activities must be identified as such, unless it is already apparent from the context.

3.03 Avoidance of False or Deceptive Statements

(a) Psychologists do not make public statements that are false, deceptive, misleading, or fraudulent, either because of what they state, convey, or suggest or because of what they omit, concerning their research, practice, or other work activities or those of persons or organizations with which they are affiliated. As examples (and not in limitation) of this standard, psychologists do not make false or deceptive statements concerning (1) their training, experience, or competence; (2) their academic degrees; (3) their credentials; (4) their institutional or association affiliations; (5) their services; (6) the scientific or clinical basis for, or results or degree of success of, their services; (7) their fees; or (8) their publications or research findings. (See also Standards 6.15, Deception in Research, and 6.18, Providing Participants With Information About the Study.)

(b) Psychologists claim as credentials for their psychological work, only degrees that (1) were earned from a regionally accredited educational institution or (2) were the basis for psychology licensure by the state in which they practice.

3.04 Media Presentations

When psychologists provide advice or comment by means of public lectures, demonstrations, radio or television programs, prerecorded tapes, printed articles, mailed material, or other media, they take reasonable precautions to ensure that (1) the statements are based on appropriate psychological literature and practice, (2) the statements are otherwise consistent with this Ethics Code, and (3) the recipients of the information are not encouraged to infer that a relationship has been established with them personally.

3.05 Testimonials

Psychologists do not solicit testimonials from current psychotherapy clients or patients or other persons who because of their particular circumstances are vulnerable to undue influence.

3.06 In-Person Solicitation

Psychologists do not engage, directly or through agents, in uninvited in-person solicitation of business from actual or potential psychotherapy patients or clients or other persons who because of their particular circumstances are vulnerable to undue influence. However, this does not preclude attempting to implement appropriate collateral contacts with significant others for the purpose of benefiting an already engaged therapy patient.

4. Therapy

4.01 Structuring the Relationship

(a) Psychologists discuss with clients or patients as early as is feasible in the therapeutic relationship appropriate issues, such as the nature and anticipated course of therapy, fees, and confidentiality. (See also Standards 1.25, Fees and Financial Arrangements, and 5.01, Discussing the Limits of Confidentiality.)

(b) When the psychologist's work with clients or patients will be supervised, the above discussion includes that fact, and the name of the supervisor, when the supervisor has legal responsibility for the case.

(c) When the therapist is a student intern, the client or patient is informed of that fact.

(d) Psychologists make reasonable efforts to answer patients' questions and to avoid apparent misunderstandings about therapy. Whenever possible, psychologists provide oral and/or written information, using language that is reasonably understandable to the patient or client.

4.02 Informed Consent to Therapy

(a) Psychologists obtain appropriate informed consent to therapy or related procedures, using language that is reasonably understandable to participants. The content of informed consent will vary depending on many circumstances; however, informed consent generally implies that the person (1) has the capacity to consent, (2) has been informed of significant information concerning the procedure, (3) has freely and without undue influence expressed consent, and (4) consent has been appropriately documented.

(b) When persons are legally incapable of giving informed consent, psychologists obtain informed permission from a legally authorized person, if such substitute consent is permitted by law.

(c) In addition, psychologists (1) inform those persons who are legally incapable of giving informed consent about the proposed interventions in a manner commensurate with the persons' psychological capacities, (2) seek their assent to those interventions, and (3) consider such persons' preferences and best interests.

4.03 Couple and Family Relationships

(a) When a psychologist agrees to provide services to several persons who have a relationship (such as husband and wife or parents and children), the psychologist attempts to clarify at the outset (1) which of the individuals are patients or clients and (2) the relationship the psychologist will have with each person. This clarification includes the role of the psychologist and the probable uses of the services provided or the information obtained. (See also Standard 5.01, Discussing the Limits of Confidentiality.)

(b) As soon as it becomes apparent that the psychologist may be called on to perform potentially conflicting roles (such as marital counselor to husband and wife, and then witness for one party in a divorce proceeding), the psychologist attempts to clarify and adjust, or withdraw from, roles appropriately. (See also Standard 7.03, Clarification of Role, under Forensic Activities.)

4.04 Providing Mental Health Services to Those Served by Others

In deciding whether to offer or provide services to those already receiving mental health services elsewhere, psychologists carefully consider the treatment issues and the potential patient's or client's welfare. The psychologist discusses these issues with the patient or client, or another legally authorized person on behalf of the client, in order to minimize the risk of confusion and conflict, consults with the other service providers when appropriate, and proceeds with caution and sensitivity to the therapeutic issues.

4.05 Sexual Intimacies With Current Patients or Clients

Psychologists do not engage in sexual intimacies with current patients or clients.

4.06 Therapy With Former Sexual Partners

Psychologists do not accept as therapy patients or clients persons with whom they have engaged in sexual intimacies.

4.07 Sexual Intimacies With Former Therapy Patients

(a) Psychologists do not engage in sexual intimacies with a former therapy patient or client for at least two years after cessation or termination of professional services.

(b) Because sexual intimacies with a former therapy patient or client are so frequently harmful to the patient or client, and because such intimacies undermine public confidence in the psychology profession and thereby deter the public's use of needed services, psychologists do not engage in sexual intimacies with former therapy patients and clients even after a two-year interval except in the most unusual circumstances. The psychologist who engages in such activity after the two years following cessation or termination of treatment bears the burden of demonstrating that there has been no exploitation, in light of all relevant factors, including (1) the amount of time that has passed since therapy terminated, (2) the nature and duration of the therapy, (3) the circumstances of termination, (4) the patient's or client's personal history, (5) the patient's or client's current mental status, (6) the likelihood of adverse impact on the patient or client and others, and (7) any statements or actions made by the therapist during the course of therapy suggesting or inviting the possibility of a posttermination sexual or romantic relationship with the patient or client. (See also Standard 1.17, Multiple Relationships.)

4.08 Interruption of Services

(a) Psychologists make reasonable efforts to plan for facilitating care in the event that psychological services are interrupted by factors such as the psychologist's illness, death, unavailability, or relocation or by the client's relocation or financial limitations. (See also Standard 5.09, Preserving Records and Data.)

(b) When entering into employment or contractual relationships, psychologists provide for orderly and appropriate resolution of responsibility for patient or client care in the event that the employment or contractual relationship ends, with paramount consideration given to the welfare of the patient or client.

4.09 Terminating the Professional Relationship

(a) Psychologists do not abandon patients or clients. (See also Standard 1.25e, under Fees and Financial Arrangements.)

(b) Psychologists terminate a professional relationship when it becomes reasonably clear that the patient or client no longer needs the service, is not benefiting, or is being harmed by continued service.

(c) Prior to termination for whatever reason, except where precluded by the patient's or client's conduct, the psychologist discusses the patient's or client's views and needs, provides appropriate pretermination counseling, suggests alternative service providers as appropriate, and takes other reasonable steps to facilitate transfer of responsibility to another provider if the patient or client needs one immediately.

5. Privacy and Confidentiality

These Standards are potentially applicable to the professional and scientific activities of all psychologists.

5.01 Discussing the Limits of Confidentiality

(a) Psychologists discuss with persons and organizations with whom they establish a scientific or professional relationship (including, to the extent feasible, minors and their legal representatives) (1) the relevant limitations on confidentiality, including limitations where applicable in group, marital, and family therapy or in organizational consulting, and (2) the foreseeable uses of the information generated through their services.

(b) Unless it is not feasible or is contraindicated, the discussion of confidentiality occurs at the outset of the relationship and thereafter as new circumstances may warrant.

(c) Permission for electronic recording of interviews is secured from clients and patients.

5.02 Maintaining Confidentiality

Psychologists have a primary obligation and take reasonable precautions to respect the confidentiality rights of those with whom they work or consult, recognizing that confidentiality may be established by law, institutional rules, or professional or scientific relationships. (See also Standard 6.26, Professional Reviewers.)

5.03 Minimizing Intrusions on Privacy

(a) In order to minimize intrusions on privacy, psychologists include in written and oral reports, consultations, and the like, only information germane to the purpose for which the communication is made.

(b) Psychologists discuss confidential information obtained in clinical or consulting relationships, or evaluative data concerning patients, individual or organizational clients, students, research participants, supervisees, and employees, only for appropriate scientific or professional purposes and only with persons clearly concerned with such matters.

5.04 Maintenance of Records

Psychologists maintain appropriate confidentiality in creating, storing, accessing, transferring, and disposing of records under their control, whether these are written, automated, or in any other medium. Psychologists maintain and dispose of records in accordance with law and in a manner that permits compliance with the requirements of this Ethics Code.

5.05 Disclosures

(a) Psychologists disclose confidential information without the consent of the individual only as mandated by law, or where permitted by law for a valid purpose, such as (1) to provide needed professional services to the patient or the individual or organizational client, (2) to obtain appropriate professional consultations, (3) to protect the patient or client or others from harm, or (4) to obtain payment for services, in which instance disclosure is limited to the minimum that is necessary to achieve the purpose.

(b) Psychologists also may disclose confidential information with the appropriate consent of the patient or the individual or organizational client (or of another legally authorized person on behalf of the patient or client), unless prohibited by law.

5.06 Consultations

When consulting with colleagues, (1) psychologists do not share confidential information that reasonably could lead to the identification of a patient, client, research participant, or other person or organization with whom they have a confidential relationship unless they have obtained the prior consent of the person or organization or the disclosure cannot be avoided, and (2) they share information only to the extent necessary to achieve the purposes of the consultation. (See also Standard 5.02, Maintaining Confidentiality.)

5.07 Confidential Information in Databases

(a) If confidential information concerning recipients of psychological services is to be entered into databases or systems of records available to persons whose access has not been consented to by the recipient, then psychologists use coding or other techniques to avoid the inclusion of personal identifiers.

(b) If a research protocol approved by an institutional review board or similar body requires the inclusion of personal identifiers, such identifiers are deleted before the information is made accessible to persons other than those of whom the subject was advised.

(c) If such deletion is not feasible, then before psychologists transfer such data to others or review such data collected by others, they take reasonable steps to determine that appropriate consent of personally identifiable individuals has been obtained.

5.08 Use of Confidential Information for Didactic or Other Purposes

(a) Psychologists do not disclose in their writings, lectures, or other public media, confidential, personally identifiable information concerning their patients, individual or organizational clients, students, research participants, or other recipients of their services that they obtained during the course of their work, unless the person or organization has consented in writing or unless there is other ethical or legal authorization for doing so.

(b) Ordinarily, in such scientific and professional presentations, psychologists disguise confidential information concerning such persons or organizations so that they are not individually identifiable to others and so that discussions do not cause harm to subjects who might identify themselves.

5.09 Preserving Records and Data

A psychologist makes plans in advance so that confidentiality of records and data is protected in the event of the psychologist's death, incapacity, or withdrawal from the position or practice.

5.10 Ownership of Records and Data

Recognizing that ownership of records and data is governed by legal principles, psychologists take reasonable and lawful steps so that records and data remain available to the extent needed to serve the best interests of patients, individual or organizational clients, research participants, or appropriate others.

5.11 Withholding Records for Nonpayment

Psychologists may not withhold records under their control that are requested and imminently needed for a patient's or client's treatment solely because payment has not been received, except as otherwise provided by law.

6. Teaching, Training Supervision, Research, and Publishing

6.01 Design of Education and Training Programs

Psychologists who are responsible for education and training programs seek to ensure that the programs are competently designed, provide the proper experiences, and meet the requirements for licensure, certification, or other goals for which claims are made by the program.

6.02 Descriptions of Education and Training Programs

(a) Psychologists responsible for education and training programs seek to ensure that there is a current and accurate description of the program content, training goals and objectives, and requirements that must be met for satisfactory completion of the program. This information must be made readily available to all interested parties.

(b) Psychologists seek to ensure that statements concerning their course outlines are accurate and not misleading, particularly regarding the subject matter to be covered, bases for evaluating progress, and the nature of course experiences. (See also Standard 3.03, Avoidance of False or Deceptive Statements.)

(c) To the degree to which they exercise control, psychologists responsible for announcements, catalogs, brochures, or advertisements describing workshops, seminars, or other non-degree-granting educational programs ensure that they accurately describe the audience for which the program is intended, the educational objectives, the presenters, and the fees involved.

6.03 Accuracy and Objectivity in Teaching

(a) When engaged in teaching or training, psychologists present psychological information accurately and with a reasonable degree of objectivity.

(b) When engaged in teaching or training, psychologists recognize the power they hold over students or supervisees and therefore make reasonable efforts to avoid engaging in conduct that is personally demeaning to students or supervisees. (See also Standards 1.09, Respecting Others, and 1.12, Other Harassment.)

6.04 Limitation on Teaching

Psychologists do not teach the use of techniques or procedures that require specialized training, licensure, or expertise, including but not limited to hypnosis, biofeedback, and projective techniques, to individuals who lack the prerequisite training, legal scope of practice, or expertise.

6.05 Assessing Student and Supervisee Performance

(a) In academic and supervisory relationships, psychologists establish an appropriate process for providing feedback to students and supervisees.

(b) Psychologists evaluate students and supervisees on the basis of their actual performance on relevant and established program requirements.

6.06 Planning Research

(a) Psychologists design, conduct, and report research in accordance with recognized standards of scientific competence and ethical research.

(b) Psychologists plan their research so as to minimize the possibility that results will be misleading.

(c) In planning research, psychologists consider its ethical acceptability under the Ethics Code. If an ethical issue is unclear, psychologists seek to resolve the issue through consultation with institutional review boards, animal care and use committees, peer consultations, or other proper mechanisms.

(d) Psychologists take reasonable steps to implement appropriate protections for the rights and welfare of human participants, other persons affected by the research, and the welfare of animal subjects.

6.07 Responsibility

(a) Psychologists conduct research competently and with due concern for the dignity and welfare of the participants.

(b) Psychologists are responsible for the ethical conduct of research conducted by them or by others under their supervision or control.

(c) Researchers and assistants are permitted to perform only those tasks for which they are appropriately trained and prepared.

(d) As part of the process of development and implementation of research projects, psychologists consult those with expertise concerning any special population under investigation or most likely to be affected.

6.08 Compliance With Law and Standards

Psychologists plan and conduct research in a manner consistent with federal and state law and regulations, as well as professional standards governing the conduct of research, and particularly those standards governing research with human participants and animal subjects.

6.09 Institutional Approval

Psychologists obtain from host institutions or organizations appropriate approval prior to conducting research, and they provide accurate information about their research proposals. They conduct the research in accordance with the approved research protocol.

6.10 Research Responsibilities

Prior to conducting research (except research involving only anonymous surveys, naturalistic observations, or similar research), psychologists enter into an agreement with participants that clarifies the nature of the research and the responsibilities of each party.

6.11 Informed Consent to Research

(a) Psychologists use language that is reasonably understandable to research participants in obtaining their appropriate informed consent (except as provided in Standard 6.12, Dispensing With Informed Consent). Such informed consent is appropriately documented.

(b) Using language that is reasonably understandable to participants, psychologists inform participants of the nature of the research; they inform participants that they are free to participate or to decline to participate or to withdraw from the research; they explain the foreseeable consequences of declining or withdrawing; they inform participants of significant factors that may be expected to influence their willingness to participate (such as risks, discomfort, adverse effects, or limitations on confidentiality, except as provided in Standard 6.15, Deception in Research); and they explain other aspects about which the prospective participants inquire.

(c) When psychologists conduct research with individuals such as students or subordinates, psychologists take special care to protect the prospective participants from adverse consequences of declining or withdrawing from participation.

(d) When research participation is a course requirement or opportunity for extra credit, the prospective participant is given the choice of equitable alternative activities.

(e) For persons who are legally incapable of giving informed consent, psychologists nevertheless (1) provide an appropriate explanation, (2) obtain the participant's assent, and (3) obtain appropriate permission from a legally authorized person, if such substitute consent is permitted by law.

6.12 Dispensing With Informed Consent

Before determining that planned research (such as research involving only anonymous questionnaires, naturalistic observations, or certain kinds of archival research) does not require the informed consent of research participants, psychologists consider applicable regulations and institutional review board requirements, and they consult with colleagues as appropriate.

6.13 Informed Consent in Research Filming or Recording

Psychologists obtain informed consent from research participants prior to filming or recording them in any form, unless the research involves simply naturalistic observations in public places and it is not anticipated that the recording will be used in a manner that could cause personal identification or harm.

6.14 Offering Inducements for Research Participants

(a) In offering professional services as an inducement to obtain research participants, psychologists make clear the nature of the services, as well as the risks, obligations, and limitations. (See also Standard 1.18, Barter [With Patients or Clients].)

(b) Psychologists do not offer excessive or inappropriate financial or other inducements to obtain research participants, particularly when it might tend to coerce participation.

6.15 Deception in Research

(a) Psychologists do not conduct a study involving deception unless they have determined that the use of deceptive techniques is justified by the study's prospective scientific, educational, or applied value and that equally effective alternative procedures that do not use deception are not feasible.

(b) Psychologists never deceive research participants about significant aspects that would affect their willingness to participate, such as physical risks, discomfort, or unpleasant emotional experiences.

(c) Any other deception that is an integral feature of the design and conduct of an experiment must be explained to participants as early as is feasible, preferably at the conclusion of their participation, but no later than at the conclusion of the research. (See also Standard 6.18, Providing Participants With Information About the Study.)

6.16 Sharing and Utilizing Data

Psychologists inform research participants of their anticipated sharing or further use of personally identifiable research data and of the possibility of unanticipated future uses.

6.17 Minimizing Invasiveness

In conducting research, psychologists interfere with the participants or milieu from which data are collected only in a manner that is warranted by an appropriate research design and that is consistent with psychologists' roles as scientific investigators.

6.18 Providing Participants With Information About the Study

(a) Psychologists provide a prompt opportunity for participants to obtain appropriate information about the nature, results, and conclusions of the research, and psychologists attempt to correct any misconceptions that participants may have.

(b) If scientific or humane values justify delaying or withholding this information, psychologists take reasonable measures to reduce the risk of harm.

6.19 Honoring Commitments

Psychologists take reasonable measures to honor all commitments they have made to research participants.

6.20 Care and Use of Animals in Research

(a) Psychologists who conduct research involving animals treat them humanely.

(b) Psychologists acquire, care for, use, and dispose of animals in compliance with current federal, state, and local laws and regulations, and with professional standards.

(c) Psychologists trained in research methods and experienced in the care of laboratory animals supervise all procedures involving animals and are responsible for ensuring appropriate consideration of their comfort, health, and humane treatment.

(d) Psychologists ensure that all individuals using animals under their supervision have received instruction in research methods and in the care, maintenance, and handling of the species being used, to the extent appropriate to their role.

(e) Responsibilities and activities of individuals assisting in a research project are consistent with their respective competencies.

(f) Psychologists make reasonable efforts to minimize the discomfort, infection, illness, and pain of animal subjects.

(g) A procedure subjecting animals to pain, stress, or privation is used only when an alternative procedure is unavailable and the goal is justified by its prospective scientific, educational, or applied value.

(h) Surgical procedures are performed under appropriate anesthesia; techniques to avoid infection and minimize pain are followed during and after surgery.

(i) When it is appropriate that the animal's life be terminated, it is done rapidly, with an effort to minimize pain, and in accordance with accepted procedures.

6.21 Reporting of Results

(a) Psychologists do not fabricate data or falsify results in their publications.

(b) If psychologists discover significant errors in their published data, they take reasonable steps to correct such errors in a correction, retraction, erratum, or other appropriate publication means.

6.22 Plagiarism

Psychologists do not present substantial portions or elements of another's work or data as their own, even if the other work or data source is cited occasionally.

6.23 Publication Credit

(a) Psychologists take responsibility and credit, including authorship credit, only for work they have actually performed or to which they have contributed.

(b) Principal authorship and other publication credits accurately reflect the relative scientific or professional contributions of the individuals involved, regardless of their relative status. Mere possession of an institutional position, such as Department Chair, does not justify authorship credit. Minor contributions to the research or to the writing for publications are appropriately acknowledged, such as in footnotes or in an introductory statement.

(c) A student is usually listed as principal author on any multiple-authored article that is substantially based on the student's dissertation or thesis.

6.24 Duplicate Publication of Data

Psychologists do not publish, as original data, data that have been previously published. This does not preclude republishing data when they are accompanied by proper acknowledgment.

6.25 Sharing Data

After research results are published, psychologists do not withhold the data on which their conclusions are based from other competent professionals who seek to verify the substantive claims through reanalysis and who intend to use such data only for that purpose, provided that the confidentiality of the participants can be protected and unless legal rights concerning proprietary data preclude their release.

6.26 Professional Reviewers

Psychologists who review material submitted for publication, grant, or other research proposal review respect the confidentiality of and the proprietary rights in such information of those who submitted it.

7. Forensic Activities

7.01 Professionalism

Psychologists who perform forensic functions, such as assessments, interviews, consultations, reports, or expert testimony, must comply with all other provisions of this Ethics Code to the extent that they apply to such activities. In addition, psychologists base their forensic work on appropriate knowledge of and competence in the areas underlying such work, including specialized knowledge concerning special populations. (See also Standards 1.06, Basis for Scientific and Professional Judgments; 1.08, Human Differences; 1.15, Misuse of Psychologists'

Influence; and 1.23, Documentation of Professional and Scientific Work.)

7.02 Forensic Assessments

(a) Psychologists' forensic assessments, recommendations, and reports are based on information and techniques (including personal interviews of the individual, when appropriate) sufficient to provide appropriate substantiation for their findings. (See also Standards 1.03, Professional and Scientific Relationship; 1.23, Documentation of Professional and Scientific Work; 2.01, Evaluation, Diagnosis, and Interventions in Professional Context; and 2.05, Interpreting Assessment Results.)

(b) Except as noted in (c), below, psychologists provide written or oral forensic reports or testimony of the psychological characteristics of an individual only after they have conducted an examination of the individual adequate to support their statements or conclusions.

(c) When, despite reasonable efforts, such an examination is not feasible, psychologists clarify the impact of their limited information on the reliability and validity of their reports and testimony, and they appropriately limit the nature and extent of their conclusions or recommendations.

7.03 Clarification of Role

In most circumstances, psychologists avoid performing multiple and potentially conflicting roles in forensic matters. When psychologists may be called on to serve in more than one role in a legal proceeding—for example, as consultant or expert for one party, or for the court and as a fact witness—they clarify role expectations and the extent of confidentiality in advance to the extent feasible, and thereafter as changes occur, in order to avoid compromising their professional judgment and objectivity and in order to avoid misleading others regarding their role.

7.04 Truthfulness and Candor

(a) In forensic testimony and reports, psychologists testify truthfully, honestly, and candidly and, consistent with applicable legal procedures, describe fairly the bases for their testimony and conclusions.

(b) Whenever necessary to avoid misleading, psychologists acknowledge the limits of their data or conclusions.

7.05 Prior Relationships

A prior professional relationship with a party does not preclude psychologists from testifying as fact witnesses or from testifying to their services to the extent permitted by applicable law. Psychologists appropriately take into account ways in which the prior relationship might affect their professional objectivity or opinions and disclose the potential conflict to the relevant parties.

7.06 Compliance With Law and Rules

In performing forensic roles, psychologists are reasonably familiar with the rules governing their roles. Psychologists are aware of the occasionally competing demands placed upon them by these principles and the requirements of the court system, and attempt to resolve these conflicts by making known their commitment to this Ethics Code and taking steps to resolve the conflict in a responsible manner. (See also Standard 1.02, Relationship of Ethics and Law.)

8. Resolving Ethical Issues

8.01 Familiarity With Ethics Code

PsycholoGists have an obligation to be familiar with this Ethics Code, other applicable ethics codes, and their application to psychologists' work. Lack of awareness or misunderstanding of an ethical standard is not itself a defense to a charge of unethical conduct.

8.02 Confronting Ethical Issues

When a psychologist is uncertain whether a particular situation or course of action would violate this Ethics Code, the psychologist ordinarily consults with other psychologists knowledgeable about ethical issues, with state or national psychology ethics committees, or with other appropriate authorities in order to choose a proper response.

8.03 Conflicts Between Ethics and Organizational Demands

If the demands of an organization with which psychologists are affiliated conflict with this Ethics Code, psychologists clarify the nature of the conflict, make known their commitment to the Ethics Code, and to the extent feasible, seek to resolve the conflict in a way that permits the fullest adherence to the Ethics Code.

8.04 Informal Resolution of Ethical Violations

When psychologists believe that there may have been an ethical violation by another psychologist, they attempt to resolve the issue by bringing it to the attention of that individual if an informal resolution appears appropriate and the intervention does not violate any confidentiality rights that may be involved.

8.05 Reporting Ethical Violations

If an apparent ethical violation is not appropriate for informal resolution under Standard 8.04 or is not resolved properly in that fashion, psychologists take further action appropriate to the situation, unless such action conflicts with confidentiality rights in ways that cannot be resolved. Such action might include referral to state or national committees on professional ethics or to state licensing boards.

8.06 Cooperating With Ethics Committees

Psychologists cooperate in ethics investigations, proceedings, and resulting requirements of the APA or any affiliated state psychological association to which they belong. In doing so, they make reasonable efforts to resolve any issues as to confidentiality. Failure to cooperate is itself an ethics violation.

8.07 Improper Complaints

Psychologists do not file or encourage the filing of ethics complaints that are frivolous and are intended to harm the respondent rather than to protect the public.

EDITOR'S NOTE

The United States Federal Trade Commission issued on December 16, 1992 a "draft of complaint" reprinted below (Docket C-3406) directed to the American Psychological Association claiming that the APA had violated the Federal Trade Commission Act (probably referring to the APA's *Ethical Principles for Psychologists and Code of Conduct*. The reader should examine the Ethical Principles and the Federal Trade Commissions statement, paying special attention to sections 3—*Advertising and other public statements* and 4–*Therapy*.

A careful reading of both items should be read by psychologists who offer their services via private practice to the general community.

Other related entries in the *American Psychologist* have been published on this topic that have appeared after the February 1993 issue.

R J C

In the Matter of: American Psychological Association, a corporation.
Docket No. C-3406
Decision and Order

The Federal Trade Commission having initiated an investigation of certain acts and practices of the respondent named in the caption hereof, and the respondent having been furnished thereafter with a copy of a draft of complaint that the Bureau of Competition proposed to present to the Commission for its consideration and that, if issued by the Commission, would charge respondent with violation of the Federal Trade Commission Act; and

The respondent, its attorney, and counsel for the Commission having thereafter executed an agreement containing a consent order, an admission by the respondent of all the jurisdictional facts set forth in the aforesaid draft of complaint, a statement that the signing of said agreement is for settlement purposes only and does not constitute an admission by respondents that the law has been violated as alleged in such complaint, and waivers and other provisions as required by the Commission's Rules; and

The Commission having thereafter considered the matter and having determined that it had reason to believe that the respondent has violated the said Act, and that a complaint should issue stating its charges in that respect, and having thereupon accepted the executed consent agreement and placed such agreement on the public record for a period of sixty (60) days, now in further conformity with the procedure prescribed in §2.34 of its Rules, the Commission hereby issues its complaint, makes the following jurisdictional findings and enters the following order:

1. Respondent American Psychological Association is a corporation organized, existing and doing business under and by virtue of the laws of the District of Columbia, with its office and principal place of business located at 1200 17th Street, N.W., Washington, D.C. 20036.

2. The Federal Trade Commission has jurisdiction of the subject matter of this proceeding and of the respondent, and the proceeding is in the public interest.

Order

I.

For the purpose of this order:

"Respondent" means the American Psychological Association, its directors, trustees, councils, committees, boards, divisions, officers, representatives, delegates, agents, employees, successors, or assigns.

"Members" means the Fellows, Members, and Associates classes of members of the American Psychological Association, and persons that hold Affiliate status with the American Psychological Association.

"Psychotherapy" means the therapeutic treatment of mental, emotional, or behavioral disorders by psychological means, and excludes programs, seminars, workshops, or consultations that address specific limited goals, such as career planning; improving employment skills or performance; increasing assertiveness; losing weight, giving up smoking; or obtaining non-individualized information about methods of coping with concerns common in everyday life.

"Current psychotherapy patient" means a patient who has commenced an evaluation for or a planned course of individual, family, or group psychotherapy, where the patient and the therapist have not agreed to terminate the treatment. However, a person who has not participated in psychotherapy with the psychologist for one year shall not be deemed a current psychotherapy patient.

II.

It is ordered that respondent, directly, indirectly, or through any corporate or other device, in or in connection with respondent's activities as a professional association, in or affecting commerce, as "commerce" is defined in Section 4 of the Federal Trade Commission Act, 15 U.S.C. §44, do forthwith cease and desist from:

A. Restricting, regulating, impeding, declaring unethical, interfering with, or restraining the advertising, publishing, stating, or disseminating by any person of the prices, terms, availability, characteristics, or conditions of sale of services, products, or publications offered for sale or made available by any psychologist, or by any organization or institution with which a psychologist is affiliated, through any means, including but not limited to the adoption or maintenance of any principle, rule, guideline, or policy that restricts any psychologist from:

1. Making public statements about the comparative desirability of offered services, products, or publications;

2. Making public statements claiming or implying unusual, unique, or one-of-a-kind abilities;

3. Making public statements likely to appeal to a client, patient or other consumer's emotions, fears, or anxieties concerning the possible results of obtaining or failing to obtain offered services, products, or publications;

4. Presenting testimonials from clients, patients, or other consumers;

5. Engaging in any direct solicitation of business from actual or prospective clients, patients, or other consumers or offering of services directly to a client, patient, or other consumer receiving similar services from another professional.

Provided that nothing contained in this order shall prohibit respondent from adopting and enforcing reasonable principles, rules, guidelines, or policies governing the conduct of its members with respect to:

1. Representations that respondent reasonably believes would be false or

541

deceptive within the meaning of Section 5 of the Federal Trade Commission Act;

2. Uninvited, in-person solicitation of business from persons who, because of their particular circumstances, are vulnerable to undue influence; or

3. Solicitation of testimonial endorsements (including solicitation of consent to use the person's prior statement as a testimonial endorsement) from current psychotherapy patients, or from other persons who, because of their particular circumstances, are vulnerable to undue influence.

Provided further that nothing in this order shall prohibit respondent from adopting and enforcing editorial, scientific, peer review, or display standards for its publications and conferences.

B. Prohibiting, restricting, regulating, impeding, declaring unethical, interfering with, or restraining any of its members, or any organization or institution with which any of its members is associated, from giving or paying any remuneration to any patient referral service or other similar institution for referral of clients, patients, or other consumers for professional services.

Provided that nothing contained in this order shall prohibit respondent from formulating, adopting, disseminating, and enforcing reasonable principles, rules, guidelines, or policies requiring that disclosures be made to clients, patients, or other consumers that the psychologist, or organization or institution with which he or she is associated, will pay or give, or has paid or given, remuneration for the referral of the clients, patients, or other consumers for professional services.

III.

It is further ordered that respondent shall:

A. Cease and desist for ten (10) years from the date at which this order becomes final, from taking any action against a person alleged to have violated any ethical principle, rule, policy, guideline, or standard, or taking disciplinary action on any other basis against a person, so as to restrain or otherwise restrict advertising, solicitation of business, or the payment of fees for the referral of clients, patients, or other consumers for services without first providing such person, at a minimum, with written notice of any such allegation and without providing such person a reasonable opportunity to respond. The notice required by this part shall, at a minimum, clearly specify the ethical principle, rule, policy, guideline, or other basis of the allegation and the reasons the conduct is alleged to have violated the ethical principle, rule, policy, guideline, or standard or other applicable criterion.

B. Maintain for five (5) years following the taking of any action referred to in Part II.A. of this order, in one separate file, segregated by the names of any person against whom such action was taken, and make available to Commission staff for inspection and copying, upon reasonable notice, all documents and correspondence that embody, discuss, mention, refer, or relate to the action taken and all bases for or allegations relating to it.

IV.

It is further ordered that respondent shall:

A. Within thirty (30) days after the date this order becomes final, remove or amend to eliminate from the respondent's *Ethical Principles,* Bylaws, and any officially promulgated or authorized guidelines or interpretations of respondent's official policies any statement of policy that is inconsistent with Parts II and III of this order.

B. Within sixty (60) days after the date this order becomes final, publish in *The APA Monitor,* or any successor publication that serves as an official journal of respondent, a copy of this order with such prominence as is therein given to regularly published feature articles.

C. Within sixty (60) days after the date this order becomes final, publish in *The APA Monitor,* or any successor publication that serves as an official journal of respondent:

1. Notice of the removal of amendment, pursuant to this order, of any Principle, Bylaw, guideline, interpretation, provision, or statement, together with;

2. A copy of any such Principle, Bylaw, guideline interpretation, provision, or statement, as worded after any such amendment.

D. Within sixty (60) days after the date this order becomes final, distribute by mail a copy of Appendix A (cover letter) to this order, along with a copy of the order itself, to each of respondent's members and to each state psychological association affiliate.

E. Cease and desist for a period of one (1) year from maintaining or continuing respondent's affiliation with any state, regional, or other psychological association affiliate within one hundred twenty (120) days after respondent learns or obtains information that would lead a reasonable person to conclude that said association has, following the effective date of this order, maintained or enforced any prohibition against:

1. advertising or making public statements concerning the comparative desirability of offered services;

2. advertising or making any public statement representing or implying unusual, unique, or one-of-a-kind abilities;

3. advertising or making any public statement intended or likely to appeal to a client's fears, anxieties, or emotions;

4. using a testimonial regarding the quality of a psychologist's services or products;

5. directly soliciting individual clients;

6. offering services directly to persons receiving similar services from another professional; or

7. making payments to patient referral services; where maintenance or enforcement of such prohibition by respondent would be prohibited by Part II of this order; unless, prior to the expiration of the one hundred twenty (120) day period, said association informs respondent by a verified written statement of an officer that the association has eliminated and will not reimpose such prohibitions(s), and respondent has no grounds to believe otherwise.

V.

It is further ordered that respondent

A. Within 90 days after the date of this order becomes final, and at such other times as the Commission may require by written notice to the respondent, file with the Commission a written report setting forth in detail the manner and form in which respondent has complied and is complying with the order;

B. For a period of five (5) years after the date this order becomes final, maintain and make available to Commission staff for inspection and copying, upon reasonable notice, records adequate to describe in detail any action taken in connection with the activities covered by Parts II, III, and IV of this order, including but not limited to all documents generated by the respondent or that come into the possession, custody, or control of respondent, regardless of the source, that discuss, refer to, or relate to any advice or interpretation rendered with respect to advertising, solicitation, or giving or receiving any remuneration for referring clients for professional services, involving any of its members.

VI.

It is further ordered that respondent shall notify the Commission at least thirty (30) days prior to any proposed change in respondent, such as dissolution, assignment, sale resulting in the emergence of a successor corporation or association, or any other change which may affect compliance obligations arising out of this order.

By the Commission.

Issued: December 16, 1992

CONTRACTS FOR PRACTICING PSYCHOLOGISTS

Whether a psychologist provider should offer clients a written contract, explicitly listing conditions and limitations, has been a matter of debate whether it should be required, recommended or ignored. The California licensure board at one point proposed a contract requirement, with a copy to be filed with the state, but energetic lobbying defeated the measure.

The author of this entry, Neal Pinckney, who served as a consultant to the licensing board in California and who was qualified as an expert witness in malpractice suits, studied more than 2,000 lawsuits and disciplinary hearing transcripts, and he came to the opinion that the single factor most likely to have prevented actions against therapists would have been a comprehensive contract. He wrote Law and Ethics in Counseling and Psychotherapy, Case Problems from which this section was adapted by Pinckney for this encyclopedia.

The sample contract here shown is a fictitious example of a contract based on Pinckney's recommendations.

CONTRACTS FOR PRACTICING PSYCHOLOGISTS

Although a comprehensive knowledge of and strict adherence to all applicable laws and ethical standards is the surest way to avoid problems of all kinds for psychologists in private practice, including lawsuits and licensing board actions; misunderstandings and imperfections of human memory frequently lead to adversarial actions which most often could have been prevented through a written agreement. A contract should be personalized to suit the needs and styles of each therapist, but should include, at a minimum, the following factors:

1. *Qualifications, training and experience of the provider.* Patients/clients may later assert you represented yourself to them as being other than what you are.

2. *A statement of your personal philosophy with an explanation of your procedures used and their purposes.* Answers the questions "Where are you coming from and how do you help people?"

3. *Discomforts and risks to be reasonably expected.* This should include a statement about risks to personal relationships as a result of changes in behavior, values, understandings. The patient/client may hold the change or loss of a relationship against you, and other persons may feel aggrieved by the changes effected.

4. *Benefits to be reasonably expected.* Promises are poison! They are the cause of many misunderstandings leading to malpractice suits and disciplinary hearings.

5. *Conditions and limits of confidentiality.* It does little good to inform a person that you must notify authorities *after* a disclosure is made. All states require reporting of abuse to minors, some also require notification of elder abuse. Following the *Tarasoff* decision, you are expected to notify any person who is the object of threatened harm (or family members and law enforcement authorities if the person cannot be reached).

6. *Alternatives to treatment of possible similar benefit.* This is to negate the "capture" effect. Alleged exploitation of a disoriented person can be defused.

7. *Freedom to withdraw from treatment, testing and activities at any time.* Allegations of coercive pressure are frequently claimed.

8. *Termination (both early and normal).* The bases for ending sessions and the responsibilities you assume following this.

9. *Policy regarding fees.* The statement should clarify how much is to be charged, how and when the practitioner–psychologist is to be paid, and how any differences in opinions about charges are to be handled.

10. *Recording of sessions: conditions, limits, uses, content, and storage.* Typically unclear, this issue is a common cause for lawsuits.

11. *Testimony in civil suits.* Having a clear-cut policy (to which you may make individual exceptions) can prevent you from wasting days in court, being involved in domestic disputes, or other lawsuits.

12. *Physical contact policy.* This is a major cause of malpractice and disciplinary actions. The safest practice is to refrain from all physical contact with clients. Disclosure of your position (and adherence to it) can prevent trouble.

13. *Availability: routine and emergency.* An understanding when and how clients are to contact you, especially during hours when your office is closed is essential, including how these calls will be handled and who else may respond. This is especially a problem presented by alcoholics.

14. *Statement of fees, charges, notice and cancellation of sessions, insurance, billing, telephone contact.* Absence of or vague statements may result in inability to collect for services and later anger leading to harassment allegations.

15. *Records release.* Release of records or notes, including to the patient/client.

16. *Drug or alcohol use during sessions.* Policy for first and subsequent attempts to services in an altered state.

17. *Concurrent therapy or treatment.* Disclosure requirements, communications with other practitioners.

18. *Other conditions.* All other special considerations, conditions and requirements which could become an issue of dispute or differing interpretation at a later time.

19. *Informed Consent.* Following an opportunity to discuss all points of concern in the contract, there should be an acknowledgement that the patient/client had read, understood and been able to clarify all the terms in the document, including the date and signature(s).

NEAL PINCKNEY

This contract, shown here with a fictional name and biography, is the author's personal therapy agreement. It reflects his professional philosophy and therapeutic style. Other psychologists may wish to create a personal contract which most closely reflects their own style and needs.

(LETTERHEAD HERE)
SAMPLE COUNSELING/THERAPY AGREEMENT

This clinical practice, as in any other professional office, best serves you when all communications and undertakings are clearly understood. We would like you to read this agreement carefully and make notes where you would like, so you can question or discuss any points which concern you or that are unclear. This agreement explains your rights as well as your obligations. When we have had an opportunity to discuss and clarify all the points, you will be asked to sign it. You will not be accepted as a patient (and no one at this clinic is considered to be your therapist) until we have both signed this agreement.

YOUR THERAPIST

Jane Doe, Ph.D., received her Bachelor of Science degree from the University of California, Berkeley in 1971. She was awarded a Masters of Science in Parapsychology from Duke University in 1972 and her Doctorate in Clinical Psychology from the University of Chicago in 1975. She was a member of the Simpkins Institute in Chicago from 1975 to 1979, did post-doctoral studies at the *Psychologishes Institut,* Vienna from 1979 to 1980, and was a member of the Client-Directed Therapy Group, Santa Barbara from 1981 to 1985. She has been in independent private practice since 1985. Dr. Rigney is licensed to practice psychology in Illinois and California. She is a fellow of the American Psychological Association and was chair of the Clinical Division in 1978 and 1979, and is a member of the California and Western Psychological Association and the National Association of Sexual Abuse Therapists. She has taught a number of courses at various universities in the area of clinical psychology and is the author of several published articles in professional journals, as well as the author of a chapter on Client-centered therapy in an edited book.

HOW YOUR THERAPIST WORKS

Therapy is a means of helping people. It can be through counseling or advising; in teaching you about yourself, your feelings, or of things you may not be aware; in examining your past; looking to your future; helping to deal with difficult situations and much more.

Just as there is no single prescription your physician can give you for all possible medical problems, there are as many different approaches to solving problems of personal growth, adjustment and behavior as there are therapists. What may be appropriate for others may not be best for you. Your therapist believes in setting goals which can be mutually agreed upon and holding you accountable for achieving them within a specified time. You will find that your therapist will not necessarily react to or judge you in many of the things you talk about, and that he or she may not always tell you how they feel about things you may wish some reaction to, but they will listen carefully to you. Their training and experience lead them to believe that some concerns of adulthood can be related to events of childhood but the focus may be on dealing with the present. We have found that what some people think is a major concern may, in reality, be keeping them from seeing the real problem. Understanding why we do things which cause us concern often aids us in changing problem behavior.

BENEFITS AND RISKS OF THERAPY

The ultimate goal of therapy is to render itself no longer necessary. How soon or completely this happens depends primarily on your willingness to cooperate, to be open and candid, and to take the steps (which can be risky) recommended. Relatively small steps in therapy may be the foundation to great leaps in future endeavors, but no promise of benefits or results can be guaranteed; the results may be influenced by factors often out of the control of the patient or the therapist.

There are some potential risks in the process. You may find your feelings about yourself and your relationships with others changed, and this can be the source of pain. Those close to you may resist your changes and react negatively to you. Some persons do not respond to the therapeutic process, and others may feel worse for the experience. As you begin to sense achievement of your goals and understandings of concerns which brought you here, you may feel you see some light at the end of the tunnel.

YOUR ALTERNATIVES TO THIS CLINIC

There are often other ways to meet your needs besides using this clinic. Some public agencies and hospitals offer free or low-cost counseling, individually and in group settings; services are provided by some religious organizations; and universities which train counselors and psychologists sometimes offer therapy at reduced cost. Other private practitioners use radically differing ways of achieving often similar results. Referral information is available on request.

YOUR RIGHTS

Whatever you may be asked to participate in is voluntary—you can choose not to take part in any activity, test, game, "homework" or response without upsetting our relationship, though you may be asked about your reasons. If at any time you do not want to continue, you have that right. You will be offered help in finding another person to help if you wish. But you may be asked to explain why you do not wish to continue, with no charge for that session.

You should feel free to ask questions at any time about treatment, fees, records, or any other matters that concern you. Time to clarify fees will not be billed to you.

What you disclose to your therapist is confidential; he or she cannot and will not reveal *anything*—even that you are a patient—unless required by law. We must notify appropriate authorities of information concerning abuse, neglect, or molestation of a minor (and in some places of an elderly person) and of threatened harm to a specific person (as well as notifying that person), and to testify and surrender records when ordered by a court of law.

When a patient is under 12 years of age, his or her parents or guardians have the right to be informed of the essence of therapy, but often it is in the best interests of the entire family to trust in the judgment of your therapist when patience is recommended. A minor 12 or older may request and be given confidential status to information as permitted by law. Parents paying for treatment should understand they may not have the right to know what is said in sessions.

Your personal records and files are kept in a secure place and will not be released to anyone without your written request or by court order.

In some situations you may be asked for permission to audio or video record sessions. You are free to refuse; but if you consent, a written agreement will be undertaken before any recording is made. You will never be recorded without your knowledge and consent.

Since the goal of therapy is to no longer need it, a time will come when you or your therapist feels this is the case. It might be that you do not agree—but it would be unethical for therapists to continue if they felt they could no longer be of benefit to you. You will be given at least a month to consider this, and following termination of therapy a follow-up contact will be requested.

Sometimes a patient does not participate fully or refuses suggestions or goals. In that case the patient is given notice that the sessions are terminated and he or she may only expect help in emergencies until time permits another source of help to be found, usually for a maximum of two weeks.

Therapists do not testify in divorce proceedings or civil cases unless action is brought against them or as ordered by a court.

While physical contact is not a policy of this clinic, an occasional clasp of support or hug may spontaneously occur. If this may concern you, please discuss it now and every effort will be taken not to offend you.

YOUR OBLIGATIONS

Fees are $— for a — minute therapy session, — minutes in direct contact plus — minutes reserved for review and notations to your records. You will be expected to pay for services at the time you make an appointment. While you may be eligible for insurance benefits, fees are your responsibility. Customary forms will be completed at no charge, but lengthy reports or forms will incur additional charges. When an insurance company authorizes direct billing, we will extend that courtesy. If you are forced to cancel an appointment, you must give three-working days notice.

If less notice is given but the hour can be scheduled for another patient, no fees will be lost. Otherwise, the hour will be charged to you. Telephone consultations are charged at $— for every interval of five minutes or less. Occasionally it becomes necessary to alter fees, but no fees will be increased until after three-months notice. The fee in this agreement is guaranteed for at least six months from the date you begin.

Patients who arrive in a state influenced by alcohol or drugs cannot participate in any type of sessions. After an initial refusal, subsequent appearance under the influence will result in termination of services.

If you are presently under the care of any other therapist, counselor or physician for a matter related in any way to your reason for being here, you cannot begin therapy here until you have disclosed that information and given consent for release of information to this clinic.

Office hours vary with demand and obligations elsewhere; usually the clinic is open on weekdays from (9 to 1) and (2 to 6,) but additional hours may be arranged. The telephone number, (555-5555) is answered (24) hours a day. If your therapist is not available to respond with the urgency your situation requires, another licensed therapist will contact you or you will be given assistance in meeting your needs.

The terms of this agreement are subject to change by mutual agreement, but nothing can be considered changed unless it is in writing and amended to this agreement.

YOUR ACKNOWLEDGEMENT

I have read this agreement carefully and have discussed all aspects which I felt concerned about or did not fully understand. I freely agree with the conditions.

I ☐ am / ☐ am not under the care of another therapist, counselor or physician or practitioner, or currently taking any medication which may effect my behavior. If you are, list names, addresses and medications on the attached form.

(Lines for Patients' and Therapists' signatures and dates here)

Adapted and reprinted from *Law & Ethics in Counseling & Psychotherapy; Case Problems*. California State University Press, Sacramento ©1986 Neal T. Pinckney, Ph.D.

NAME INDEX

This index is designed to locate names discussed in a substantive way in the encyclopedia. It is not meant to include every name cited in passing or as the author of a reference citation.

Entries are indicated by volume and page numbers: boldface numbers indicate volumes; numbers that follow indicate pages.

Tillich, P., **1**, 522; **2**, 177; **4**, 163–164

Tinbergen, N., **1**, 516, 517; **2**, 259, 260, 456; **3**, 191; **4**, 164

Tinker, M. A., **1**, 490, 545

Titchener, E. B., **1**, 150, 228, 316, 537; **2**, 45, 138, 139, 209, 210, 287; **3**, 177, 190, 280, 476, 477, 501, 509; **4**, 164

Toch, H., **2**, 421; **3**, 333

Tocqueville, A. de, **2**, 450

Tokarsky, A., **3**, 154

Tollison, C. D., **2**, 16

Tolman, E. C., **1**, 11, 151, 152, 154, 157, 253, 368, 444, 525; **2**, 252, 331, 332, 423, 503, 528; **3**, 99, 266, 270, 290, 316, 367, 513, 524; **4**, 164–165

Tolman, R. A., **2**, 465

Tolson, E. R., **3**, 134–136

Toman, W., **3**, 174

Tomkins, S., **1**, 306, 444, 180; **2**, 394

Tomlinson, R. W., **1**, 48

Tornatzky, L. G., **1**, 456–457; **2**, 24–25, 254–255

Torrance, E. P., **2**, 64, 94; **3**, 447

Tosti, D., **3**, 109

Toulmin, S., **3**, 71, 84

Tower, J., **3**, 517

Toynbee, A., **3**, 71

Trainer, J. B., **3**, 112

Traux, C., **1**, 333; **3**, 259, 531

Treiman, D. J., **2**, 300, 301

Treisman, A., **3**, 193

Trentini, G. G., **4**, 165

Triandis, H. C., **1**, 353; **2**, 167, 277; **3**, 469; **4**, 165

Trieschmann, R. B., **3**, 269

Trist, E. L., **1**, 125

Troland, L., **3**, 145

Troll, L. E., **2**, 167

Trotman, F. K., **1**, 423

Trower, P., **1**, 456

Trstenjak, A., **4**, 165

Truax, C. B., **1**, 479; **2**, 284

Truman, H. S., **2**, 523

Truzzi, M., **2**, 505

Tryon, R. C., **1**, 420

Tsujoika, B., **4**, 165

Tsushima, W. T., **2**, 355–356, 418–419; **3**, 247–248

Tucker, L., **3**, 340

Tuddenham, R. D., **2**, 117

Tuke, H., **2**, 183

Tuke, S., **2**, 183

Tuke, W., **2**, 183

Tulkin, S. R., **2**, 233

Tulving, E., **2**, 39, 383, 386; **4**, 165–166

Turek, J., **2**, 188

Turing, A. M., **1**, 101, 304; **2**, 248

Turner, A. N., **3**, 506

Turner, J., **2**, 251

Turner, K., **1**, 493

Turner, R. H., **3**, 328

Turner, R. R., **2**, 168

Turner, V., **3**, 324

Turoff, M., **2**, 94

Turró, R., **3**, 212; **4**, 166

Tutundjian, H. M., **4**, 166

Tversky, A., **2**, 362

Twain, M., **3**, 95

Twardowski, K., **3**, 209, 210

Tyler, L. E., **2**, 64, 404; **4**, 166

Tyler, R. W., **1**, 381

Uhlaner, J. E., **2**, 407

Ullmann, L. P., **1**, 154–157; **2**, 500; **3**, 212, 540; **4**, 166

Umana, R., **2**, 9

Umezu, H., **3**, 200

Underwood, B. J., **2**, 34, 384; **3**, 584; **4**, 166–167

Unger, R. K., **1**, 69–70; **3**, 384–385, 387–388, 391–392, 498

Ungerer, G. A., **3**, 153

Urbina, S. P., **1**, 64–65, 111–112, 162–163, 463, 502–503; **3**, 89–90

Uttal, W. R., **2**, 412

Uznadze, D. N., **3**, 219; **4**, 167

Vaca, N. C., **1**, 514

Vaihinger, H., **4**, 167

Vaillant, G. E., **2**, 147, 340

Vaitl, D., **4**, 167

Valenstein, E. S., **2**, 346; **3**, 250; **4**, 167–168

Valentine, C. W., **1**, 408, 410, 411, 527

Valentine, J., **2**, 233

Valins, S., **3**, 452

Van Biervliet, J. J., **3**, 176

Van den Berg, J. H., **1**, 521

Vandenberg, S. G., **1**, 245

Vanderploeg, R. D., **2**, 474–476

Van Fleet, A. A., **1**, 461

Van Gennep, A., **3**, 323, 324

Van Gogh, V., **3**, 45

Van Hattum, R., **3**, 459

Van Kaam, A., **2**, 34–35, 341

Varendonck, T., **2**, 11

Vasiliev, L. L., **3**, 11

Vassiliou, V., **3**, 469

Vatiano, A. J., **2**, 96, 264; **3**, 421–423

Vaughan, F., **3**, 548–550

Vaughan, G. M., **1**, 297

Vaux, A., **2**, 462–463; **3**, 434–436, 444–446

Velmans, M., **1**, 302

Vernon, P. E., **1**, 55–56, 243; **2**, 173; **3**, 117, 192; **4**, 168

Vernon, S., **2**, 257

Verplanck, W. S., **4**, 168

Viano, E., **3**, 564

Vicary, J., **3**, 484, 485

Vico; **2**, 345

Victor, R. G., **2**, 52

Vinacke, W. E., **2**, 111–114, 222–223, 252–254, 464

Vinson, D. E., **2**, 302

Viola, G., **3**, 59

Viteles, M. S., **4**, 168

Vives, J. L., **3**, 212; **4**, 168

Vogt, O., **1**, 124

Voltaire; **2**, 458

Von Frisch, K., **1**, 72

Vroom, V. H., **2**, 94, 333, 428, 531

Vygotsky, L. S., **1**, 198, 304, 410; **2**, 355; **3**, 5, 219, 220; **4**, 168–169

Wachtel, P., **1**, 161

Wadham, R. A., **2**, 368–369; **3**, 77–79

Wadsworth, B. J., **1**, 221

Wagley, C., **1**, 513

Wagman, M., **1**, 102–105

Wagner, A. R., **1**, 92, 174, 316; **2**, 252; 332

SUBJECT INDEX

Entries are indicated by volume and page numbers: boldface numbers indicate volumes; numbers that follow indicate pages. For organization, see also Name Index.